ZHONGDA
Chinese-English Dictionary
中大汉英词典

Liang Derun • Zheng Jiande

梁德润 • 郑建

主编

中文大學出版社

《中大汉英词典》
梁德润、郑建德 主编

本书由北京外文出版社授权，其中经过修订及
重新制版，在中国大陆以外地区出版发行。

国际统一书号 (ISBN)：962–996–093–1 (精装)
962–996–172–5 (平装)

2003年第一版

出版：中文大学出版社
香港 新界 沙田 • 香港中文大学
图文传真：+852 2603 6692
+852 2603 7355
电子邮递：cup@cuhk.edu.hk
网　　址：www.chineseupress.com

Zhongda Chinese-English Dictionary
Edited by Liang Derun and Zheng Jiande

Published with revision by permission
of the Foreign Language Press.

ISBN: 962–996–093–1 (Hardcover)
962–996–172–5 (Paperback)

First edition 2003

Published by The Chinese University Press,
The Chinese University of Hong Kong,
Sha Tin, N.T., Hong Kong.
Fax: +852 2603 6692
+852 2603 7355
E-mail: cup@cuhk.edu.hk
Web-site: www.chineseupress.com

Printed in Hong Kong

Contents
目　录

Preface

China saw rapid social and economic changes in the later part of the twentieth century. Most of the Chinese-English dictionaries available at present were compiled in the People's Republic of China, and they suffer the following drawbacks: Firstly, entries in dictionaries published prior to the mid-nineties were affected by the socio-political needs of the time. For instance, a dictionary compiled in 1995 carries twice the number of entries for the word "*shi*" (market) than that compiled in the seventies, obviously owing to the government's emphasis on the market economy two decades later. * Secondly, for dictionaries published after the mid-nineties, although more in line with lexicographical considerations, their texts have become bulkier and bulkier as new terms are coined daily in view of China's increasing role in the international community. As such, there is still no medium-sized dictionary that can be consulted with convenience. *The Zhongda Chinese-English Dictionary* is meant to fill such a need. Compiled only in 1999, the choice of entries better reflects the current usage of the Chinese language.

This dictionary has been compiled with the following purposes in mind:

- Addition of new entries: There are over 20,000 new entries/new interpretations among the 4,500 single characters and over 70,000 linguistic entries in this dictionary. Examples include: *guāngbiāo* (cursor), *nèicún* (memory), *yìngpán* (hard disk), *táoshuì* (tax evasion), *tuìshuì* (tax refund), *bìshuì* (tax avoidance), *xīuxián* (leisure), *chūtái* (to appear on the stage), *jiājiào* (private teacher), *kāngfù* (rehabilitate), *páihángbǎng* (charts), *gōngzuò wǔcān* (working lunch), etc. All these terms have arrived only over the last decade during China's interaction with the West. The advent of the computer also brings new terms in Chinese: CD-ROM (*guāngpán*), configuration (*guīgé*), memory (*nèicún*) and Windows (*shìchuāng*).
- Reinterpretation or adding new meanings to existing terms: The frequent use of

---

* There are fifty entries for this word in *A Chinese-English Dictionary* (Revised Edition) (Beijing: Foreign Language Teaching & Research Press, 1995) compared to twenty-three entries in the *Pinyin Chinese-English Dictionary* (Hong Kong: The Commercial Press, 1978).

these linguistic terms in the mass media indicates that they are being accepted as part of daily usage in the society. A case in mind is *kāngfù*, which was previously interpreted as "to restore to health; to recover". This obviously is not adequate. Therefore, the extended meaning "rehabilitate; rehabilitation" has been added.

To enrich this dictionary, we have consulted many dictionaries and references both in the English and the Chinese languages. We have also adopted the following formats:

(1) All entries including single-word entries, multiple-word entries and phrasal expressions are arranged according to the *pinyin* system, and the corresponding *pinyin* pronunciation is attached to each entry.

(2) We use "～" to denote the location of the original entry. For instance:

决 (jué) **1.**(决定) decide; determine: 悬而未～ be undecided; be awaiting decision / 犹豫不～ be in a state of indecision **2.**(一定,用在否定词前面) definitely; certainly; under any circumstances: ～无此事 no such things ever happened **3.**(执行死刑) execute a person by shooting **4.**(决口) be breached; burst: 全堤溃～。The bank burst and totally collapsed.

(3) Related information is also stated for more detailed reference. For example:

【风级】fēngjí 〈*Meteorol.*〉 Beaufort scale ‖ 蒲福风级分 13 个等级:0 级风 calm; 1 级风 light air; 2 级风 light breeze; 3 级风 gentle breeze; 4 级风 moderate breeze; 5 级风 fresh breeze; 6 级风 strong breeze; 7 级风 moderate gale; 8 级风 fresh gale; 9 级风 strong gale; 10 级风 whole gale; 11 级风 storm; 12 级风 hurricane

(4) Within the text, "AmE." denotes American English while "BrE." denotes British English. Likewise, "m." refers to the masculine gender and "f." to the feminine gender.

(5) We have also included a substantial amount of data which might be of use to students of Chinese, in particular data relating to China and its culture which may be hard to find elsewhere. For the sake of convenience, they are placed in the Appendix Section.

Abbreviations
略 语 表

* Arranged alphabetically by category
(类别内按英文字母序)

abbr.	abbreviation	缩略词
adj.	adjective	形容词
adv.	adverb	副词
art.	article	冠词
comb.	combination	组合词素
conj.	conjunctive	连接词
contr.	contraction	缩约词
f.	female	女性
inf.	infinitive	原形动词
int.	interjection	感叹词
m.	male	男性
n.	noun	名词
pl.	plural	复数
pref.	prefix	前缀
prep.	preposition	介词
pron.	pronoun	代词
sing.	single	单数
suf.	suffix	后缀
symb.	symbol	符号
v.	verb	动词
var.	variant	变体
vi.	verb intransitive	不及物动词
vt.	verb transitive	及物动物
AmE.	American English	美式英语
BrE.	British English	英式英语
Chi.	Chinese	汉语
Fr.	French	法语
Ger.	German	德语
Ital.	Italy	意大利语
Jap.	Japanese	日语
Lat.	Latin	拉丁文
Rus.	Russian	俄语
Sp.	Spanish	西班牙语
Agric.	*Agriculture*	农业
Anat.	*Anatomy*	解剖学
Archit.	*Architecture*	建筑
Astron.	*Astronomy*	天文学
Biochem.	*Biochemistry*	生物化学
Biol.	*Biology*	生物

Bot.	*Botany*	植物;植物学
Cartog.	*Cartography*	测绘
Chem.	*Chemistry*	化学;化工
Computer		计算机
Econ.	*Economy*	经济
Education		教育
Electr.	*Electricity*	电学;电工
Fishery		渔业
Forestry		林业
Geol.	*Geology*	地质学;地理学
Hist.	*History*	历史
Husbandry		畜牧业
Law		法律
Logics		逻辑学
Math.	*Mathematics*	数学
Mech.	*Mechanics*	机械
Med.	*Medical*	医学
Metall.	*Metallurgy*	冶金
Meteorol.	*Meteorology*	气象学
Microbiol.	*Microbiology*	微生物
Mil.	*Military*	军事
Mineral.	*Mineralogy*	矿物;矿业
Music		音乐
Pharm.	*Pharmacy*	药物;药物学
Philos.	*Philosophy*	哲学
Photog.	*Photography*	摄影
Physics		物理学
Physiol.	*Physiology*	生理学
Postal Service		邮政
Printing		印刷
Radio		无线电
Religion		宗教
Sports		体育
Textiles		纺织印染
Theatre		戏剧
Trade		商业
Transport		交通运输
Water Conservancy		水利
Zool.	*Zoology*	动物;动物学

Index Based on *Hanyu Pinyin*

汉语拼音索引

Q (596－645)

R (646－670)

S (671－781)

T (782—830)

W (831—871)

X (872—936)

Y (937—1018)

Z (1019－1121)

Index of Radicals
汉字部首检字表

Index Based on Radicals
汉字部首索引表

Guide to the Use of the Dictionary

1. All entries are arranged according to the alphabetical order of their Pinyin romanization.
2. Single-character entries are set in large, boldface type, and compound-character entries are set in smaller typeface and placed in boldface square brackets "【 】".
3. If an entry has two or more definitions, the respective definitions are listed numerically 1, 2, 3, 4 and so forth, with brief explanation in Chinese in brackets, or annotations for specialized terms in angle brackets "〈 〉". A wave line "~" is used to represent the entry when it is used in an example.
4. Under an entry, synonyms are separated by a semicolon ";", examples by a slash "/", and derivatives and related words by double vertical lines " ‖ ".
5. The Pinyin romanization of the entries in this dictionary is based on *Table of Censured Sounds of Chinese Characters with Variant Pronunciations in Common Speech (Putonghua).*

体例说明

1. 本词典所收条目，一律按汉语拼音顺序排列。
2. 单字条目以粗体大字排印，多字条目则以小字排印并置于粗体方括号"【 】"内。
3. 多释义条目中，每个义项分别用数字1、2、3、4等排序，并有简明汉语标注或学科术语；汉语标注括在圆括号中，学科术语括在单书名号"〈 〉"中；条目词在例句或例证中出现时，以代字号"～"表示。
4. 释义中的多个同义词用分号"；"隔开，例句用斜线"/"分隔，派生词、相关词则以双竖线"‖"分开。
5. 本词典读音以《普通话异读词审音表》为准。

A

a

阿 (ā)
(另见"阿"ē)

【阿坝】 Ābā 〈place〉 Ngawa; Aba

【阿昌族】 Āchāngzú Achang (中国少数民族,主要分布在云南)

【阿斗】 Ā Dǒu a weak-minded person; fool

【阿尔法粒子】 ā'ěrfǎ lìzǐ alpha particle

【阿尔法射线】 ā'ěrfǎ shèxiàn alpha ray

【阿尔金山】 Ā'ěrjīnshān 〈place〉 Altun

【阿尔泰】 Ā'ěrtài 〈place〉 Altay

【阿飞】 āfēi hooligan; young rowdy

【阿訇】 āhōng ahung; imam

【阿克赛钦】 Ākèsàiqīn 〈place〉 Aksayqin

【阿克苏】 Ākèsū 〈place〉 Aksu

【阿拉伯】 Ālābó Arabian; Arabic; Arab

【阿拉伯国家】 Ālābó guójiā Arab countries; Arab states

【阿拉伯胶树】 Ālābó jiāoshù 〈*Bot.*〉 acacia

【阿拉伯人】 Ālābórén Arab

【阿拉伯数字】 Ālābó shùzì Arabic numerals

【阿拉伯树胶】 Ālābó shùjiāo gum arabic

【阿拉伯语】 Ālábóyǔ Arabic

【阿拉善】 Ālāshàn 〈place〉 Alxa

【阿勒泰】 Ālètài 〈place〉 Altay

【阿里】 Ālǐ 〈place〉 Ngari

【阿盟】 Āméng (阿拉伯国家联盟) the Arab League; the League of the Arab States

【阿摩尼亚】 āmóníyà ammonia

【阿片】 āpiàn 〈*Pharm.*〉 opium

【阿司匹林】 āsīpīlín 〈*Pharm.*〉 aspirin: 吃两片～ take two aspirins

【阿嚏】 ātì atishoo

【阿托品】 ātuōpǐn 〈*Pharm.*〉 atropine

【阿姨】 āyí **1.**(姨母) aunt; auntie **2.**(称母辈妇女) aunt **3.**(称保育员或保姆) nurse

啊[呵] (ā) 〈*int.*〉 eh; oh; o; ah

锕 (ā) 〈*Chem.*〉 actinium (元素符号 Ac)

ai

哎[嗳] (āi) 〈*int.*〉 hey; ah

【哎呀】 āiyā (表示惊奇等) my God

【哎哟】 āiyō 〈*int.*〉 ouch; ow

哀 (āi) **1.**(悲哀) grief; sorrow **2.**(哀悼) mourn over sb.'s death **3.**(怜悯) pity

【哀愁】 āichóu sad; depressed; grieved

【哀悼】 āidào grieve over sb.'s death; mourn over sb.'s death; lament sb.'s death: 深切～ profound condolence / 他～朋友的死。He lamented the death of his friend.

【哀号】 āiháo cry piteously; wail

【哀鸣】 āimíng **1.**(悲哀地叫) wail **2.**(悲哀的叫声) a plaintive whine; a cry of lament

【哀求】 āiqiú entreat; implore

【哀伤】 āishāng distressed; grieved; agonized

【哀思】 āisī grief; deep sorrow; sad memories of the deceased

【哀叹】 āitàn lament; bemoan; bewail

【哀痛】 āitòng deep sorrow; grief

【哀怨】 āiyuàn sad; plaintive

【哀乐】 āiyuè funeral music; dirge: 奏～ play funeral music

锿 (āi) 〈*Chem.*〉 einsteinium (人造元素,符号 Es)

埃 (āi) **1.**(尘埃) dust **2.**〈*Physics*〉 angstrom

【埃尔特克斯网眼织物】 Āiěrtèkèsī wǎngyǎn zhīwù Aertex (商标名称)

【埃及金字塔】 Āijí jīnzìtǎ Pyramids

【埃及狮身人面像】 Āijí shīshēnrénmiànxiàng Egyptian sphinx

【埃及学】 āijíxué Egyptology

【埃居】 āijū ECU; European Currency Unit (欧洲货币单位)

【埃米尔】 āimǐ'ěr amir; emir

挨 (āi) 1.(挨近) be next to; get close to: ～着门口坐 sit by the door 2.(依次) by turns; in sequence
(另见"挨"ái)

【挨边】 āibiān 1.(靠着边) keep close to the edge 2.(相近) be near; be close to 3.(接近) be relevant

【挨次】 āicì in turn; in order; one after another; one by one

【挨个儿】 āigèr 〈*colloq.*〉 in turn; one by one

【挨家挨户】 āijiā-āihù door-to-door

【挨近】 āijìn be near to; get close to

【挨门挨户】 āimén-āihù go from door to door; house-to-house (adj.)

唉 (āi) 1.(答应) right; yes 2.(感叹声) alas

【唉声叹气】 āi shēng tàn qì heave deep sighs; moan and groan; sigh in despair

挨[捱] (ái) 1.(遭受) suffer; endure: ～冻 suffer from cold / ～雨淋 be caught in the rain 2.(困难地度过) drag out 3.(拖延) delay; play for time; stall
(另见"挨"āi)

【挨打】 áidǎ take a beating; get a thrashing; come under attack

【挨饿】 ái'è suffer from hunger

【挨骂】 áimà get a scolding; get a dressing down

【挨批评】 áipīpíng be criticized

皑[皚] (ái) pure white; snow white

【皑皑】 ái'ái pure white; brightly white

癌 (ái) 〈*Med.*〉 cancer: 肠～ cancer of the bowels / 肺～ cancer of the lungs / 肝～ cancer of the liver / 乳腺～ mammary cancer / 食道～ cancer of the esophagus / 胃～ cancer of the stomach

【癌扩散】 áikuòsàn 〈*Med.*〉 metastasis of cancer; spread of the cancer

【癌细胞】 áixìbāo 〈*Med.*〉 cancer cell

【癌症】 áizhèng 〈*Med.*〉 cancer

矮 (ǎi) 1.(指人) short 2.(指事物) low: ～墙 a low wall

【矮个儿】 ǎigèr a person of short stature; a short person

【矮胖】 ǎipàng short and stout; pudgy; roly-poly: 一个～的男孩 a chunky boy

【矮小】 ǎixiǎo short and small; low and small: ～的棚子 a small, low shed / 身材～ short and slight in figure

【矮星】 ǎixīng 〈*Astron.*〉 dwarf (star)

【矮子】 ǎi·zi a short person; dwarf; shorty; shortie

【矮子里拔将军】 ǎi·zi lǐ bá jiāngjūn pick a general from among the dwarfs; choose the best person available

蔼 (ǎi) friendly; amiable

【蔼然可亲】 ǎirán-kěqīn kindly; amiable; affable

艾 (ài) 1.〈*Bot.*〉 argy wormwood 2.(停止) end; stop

【艾丁湖】 Àidīnghú 〈place〉 Aydingkol

【艾蒿】 àihāo 〈*Bot.*〉 argy wormwood

【艾灸术】 àijiǔshù 〈*Chin. Med.*〉 moxibustion

【艾伦内六角扳手】 àilún nèiliùjiǎo bānshǒu Allen key

【艾伦内六角螺栓】 àilún nèiliùjiǎo luóshuān Allen screw

【艾绒】 àiróng moxa

【艾滋病】 àizībìng Aids, AIDS (Acquired Immune Deficiency Syndrome)

【艾滋病病毒】 àizībìng bìngdú human immunodeficiency virus; HIV

砹 (ài) 〈*Chem.*〉 astatine (元素符号 At)

爱[愛] (ài) 1.(热爱) love; affection: 相～ fall in love / ～父母 love one's parents / 我们～祖国。We love our country. 2.(喜欢) like; be fond of; be keen on: ～花 be fond of flowers / ～滑冰 like skating 3.(爱惜;爱护) cherish; hold dear; take good care of; treasure 4.(常发生,容易发生) be apt to; be in the habit of: ～生气 have the habit of getting angry / 生铁～长锈。Cast iron is apt to rust.

【爱不释手】 àibù-shìshǒu unputdownable; fondle admiringly

【爱称】 àichēng pet name

【爱戴】 àidài love and esteem：受到…～ enjoy the love and esteem of
【爱尔兰】 Ài'ěrlán Ireland；Irish（adj.）
【爱尔兰热咖啡】 Àiěrlán rèkāfēi Irish coffee
【爱抚】 àifǔ show tender care for
【爱国】 àiguó love one's country；be patriotic
【爱国人士】 àiguó rénshì patriotic personage
【爱国统一战线】 àiguó tǒngyī zhànxiàn patriotic united front
【爱国卫生运动】 àiguó wèishēng yùndòng patriotic health campaign
【爱国心】 àiguóxīn patriotism；patriotic feeling
【爱国者】 àiguózhě patriot
【爱国主义】 àiguó zhǔyì patriotism：发扬～精神 give full play to one's patriotism
【爱好】 àihào 1.（有兴趣）like；love；be fond of；be keen on：～集邮 be keen on stamp collecting／对音乐的～ love of music 2.（喜爱）interest；hobby
【爱好者】 àihàozhě amateur；enthusiast；fan；lover（of art，sports，etc.）
【爱恨交加】 àihèn-jiāojiā love-hate relationship
【爱护】 àihù cherish；take good care of；treasure：～公物 take good care of the public property
【爱克斯射线】 àikèsī shèxiàn X ray；Roentgen ray
【爱怜】 àilián show tender affection for
【爱恋】 àiliàn be in love with
【爱面子】 ài miàn·zi be concerned about face-saving；be sensitive about one's reputation
【爱莫能助】 àimònéngzhù willing to help but unable to do so
【爱慕】 àimù admire；adore
【爱情】 àiqíng love；love affair
【爱情歌曲】 àiqíng gēqǔ love song
【爱情鸟】 àiqíngniǎo （情侣鹦鹉）love-bird
【爱人】 ài·ren 1.（夫或妻）husband；wife 2.（恋爱的一方）sweetheart
【爱上】 àishàng be in love；fall in love：小伙子～了那姑娘。The boy fell in love with the girl.
【爱委会】 àiwěihuì the Committee of the Patriotic Health Movement
【爱卫会】 àiwèihuì 见“爱委会”
【爱屋及乌】 àiwū-jíwū love me，love my dog
【爱惜】 àixī cherish；treasure；use sparingly
【爱乐】 àiyuè philharmonic
【爱乐乐团】 àiyuè yuètuán philharmonic orchestra
【爱憎】 ài-zèng love and hate

暧［曖］（ài） 〈*written*〉（of daylight） dim
【暧昧】 àimèi 1.（指态度、用意）ambiguous；equivocal 2.（指行为）dubious；shady：关系～ dubious relationship

隘（ài） 1.（窄）narrow 2.（险要地方）pass
【隘口】 àikǒu （mountain）pass

碍［礙］（ài） be in the way of；hinder；obstruct：～于健康 be harmful to one's health
【碍面子】 ài miàn·zi for fear of hurting sb.'s feelings
【碍事】 àishì 1.（有妨碍）be in the way；be a hindrance 2.（严重）be of consequence；matter：不～ nothing serious；It doesn't matter.
【碍手碍脚】 àishǒu-àijiǎo be in the way；be a hindrance

an

安（ān） 1.（安定）peaceful；calm；quiet；tranquil 2.（使安定）set（sb.'s mind）at ease；calm 3.（满足）be satisfied；rest content 4.（平安；安全；安好）safe；secure；in good health：晚～。Good night. 5.（安置）place in a suitable position；find a place for 6.（安装）install；fit；fix：～电话 install a telephone／给车上～新座套 fit new seat covers on the car／给窗户～玻璃 glaze a window 7.（加上）bring（a charge against sb.）；give（sb. a nickname） 8.（安有）harbor：～坏心眼 harbor evil intentions 9.〈*Electr.*〉ampere
【安插】 ānchā place in a certain position；assign to a job；plant in key positions
【安抵】 āndǐ arrive safely；arrive safe and sound
【安定】 āndìng 1.（稳定正常）stable；quiet；settled 2.（使安定）stabilize；maintain 3.

〈*Pharm*.〉 diazepam; Valium（商标名称）

【安定团结】 ān dìng tuán jié stability and unity：～的政治局面 the political situation of stability and unity

【安顿】 āndùn **1.**（安排好）arrange for; find a place for;（help）settle down：等我～下来后，我将请你们到我家来。When I settle down, I shall invite you to our house. **2.**（安稳）peaceful; undisturbed

【安放】 ānfàng lay; place; put in a certain place

【安非他明】 ānfēitāmíng amphetamine

【安分】 ānfèn be law-abiding; not go beyond one's bounds; know one's place

【安分守己】 ānfèn-shǒujǐ observe disciplines; comply with the law and behave oneself

【安抚】 ānfǔ appease

【安好】 ānhǎo well; safe and sound

【安家】 ānjiā set up a home; settle down

【安家费】 ānjiāfèi settling-in allowance

【安家落户】 ānjiā-luòhù settle in：在陕西～have settled in Shaanxi

【安检】 ānjiǎn safety inspection; security clearance：对某人进行～ give sb. security clearance

【安静】 ānjìng quiet; peaceful

【安居乐业】 ānjū-lèyè live and work in peace and contentment

【安康】 ānkāng well-being

【安拉】 ānlā 〈*Islam*〉Allah

【安乐】 ānlè peace and happiness

【安乐富足】 ānlè-fùzú Easy Street

【安乐死】 ānlèsǐ 〈*Med*.〉euthanasia

【安乐窝】 ānlèwō cosy nest

【安乐椅】 ānlèyǐ easy chair

【安理会】 Ānlǐhuì the（U.N.）Security Council

【安眠】 ānmián sleep peacefully

【安眠药】 ānmiányào sleeping pill; sleeping tablet

【安乃近】 ānnǎijìn 〈*Pharm*.〉analgin

【安宁】 ānníng **1.**（指秩序）peaceful; tranquil **2.**（指心情）calm; composed; free from worry

【安排】 ānpái **1.**（处理）arrange; fix up; plan：～时间 arrange the time / ～参观日程 arrange itineraries of visit / 旅行社～了中途在摩纳哥停留的旅程。The travel agent arranged the trip with a stopover in Monaco. / 你去巴黎的旅行～好了吗？Have you made arrangements for your trip to Paris? **2.**（安置）ensconce：约翰幸运地～在西点军校。John was happily ensconced at West Point.

【安培】 ānpéi 〈*Electr*.〉ampere

【安培定律】 ānpéi dìnglǜ Ampere's law

【安培计】 ānpéijì ammeter; amperemeter

【安培数】 ānpéishù amperage

【安培小时】 ānpéi xiǎoshí ampere-hour

【安全】 ānquán safe; secure：交通～ traffic safety / ～抵达 arrive all right

【安全保护】 ānquán bǎohù safe keeping

【安全别针】 ānquán biézhēn safety pin

【安全藏身处】 ānquán cángshēnchù safe house

【安全车距】 ānquán chējù slipstream

【安全带】 ānquándài 〈*Auto*〉 safety belt; seat belt; inertia reel

【安全岛】 ānquándǎo pedestrian island; traffic island

【安全灯】 ānquándēng 〈*Mineral*.〉 Davy; Davy lamp; safety lamp

【安全第一】 ānquán dìyī safety first

【安全阀】 ānquánfá safety valve

【安全阀门】 ānquán fámén（用发泄的办法平息怒气）safety-valve

【安全感】 ānquángǎn sense of security

【安全港】 ānquángǎng safe port

【安全火柴】 ānquán huǒchái safety match

【安全检查】 ānquán jiǎnchá safety inspection; security clearance

【安全理事会】 Ānquán Lǐshìhuì Security Council

【安全帽】 ānquánmào （safety）helmet

【安全门】 ānquánmén emergency exit

【安全门镜】 ānquán ménjìng security peephole

【安全期】 ānquánqī 〈*Contraception*〉safe period

【安全期避孕法】 ānquánqī bìyùnfǎ rhythm method; safe period

【安全区】 ānquánqū safety zone

【安全设施】 ānquán shèshī safety devices （installations）

【安全生产】 ānquán shēngchǎn safety in production

【安全剃刀】 ānquán tìdāo safety razor
【安全通行证】 ānquán tōngxíngzhèng safe conduct
【安全网】 ānquánwǎng safety net
【安全系数】 ānquán xìshù safety coefficient; safety factor
【安全行车】 ānquán xíngchē safe driving
【安全性交】 ānquán xìngjiāo safe sex
【安全着陆】 ānquán zhuólù safe landing
【安然】 ānrán **1.**（平安）safely: ～脱险 be out of danger **2.**（放心）peacefully; at rest
【安然无恙】 ānrán-wúyàng safe and sound
【安如磐石】 ānrú-pánshí as solid as a rock
【安如泰山】 ānrú Tàishān as secure as Mount Taishan; as solid as a rock
【安身】 ānshēn make one's home
【安神】 ānshén calm the nerves; quiet down the mind
【安生】 ānshēng **1.**（安定）peaceful; restful **2.**（安静）quiet; still
【安适】 ānshì quiet and comfortable
【安妥】 āntuǒ safe and reliable
【安危】 ānwēi safety; safety and danger
【安慰】 ānwèi comfort; console: 在…中寻找～ find consolation in / 因他的不幸而～他 comfort him for his misfortunes
【安慰剂】 ānwèijì placebo
【安慰奖】 ānwèijiǎng consolation prize
【安慰赛】 ānwèisài consolation event; consolation match
【安稳】 ānwěn smooth and steady
【安息】 ānxī **1.**（入睡）rest; go to sleep **2.**（悼念用语）rest in peace
【安闲】 ānxián leisurely; peaceful and carefree
【安详】 ānxiáng composed; serene; unruffled
【安心】 ānxīn **1.**（放心）feel at ease; be relieved; set one's mind at rest **2.**（心情安定）keep one's mind on sth. **3.**（居心）harbor an evil intention: 没安好心 have an evil intention
【安逸】 ānyì easy; easy and comfortable: 生活～ be in easy circumstances / 他过着～的生活。He lives a comfortable life.
【安营】 ānyíng camp; pitch a camp
【安营扎寨】 ān yíng zhā zhài camp; pitch a camp
【安于】 ānyú be satisfied with; be content with
【安于现状】 ānyú-xiànzhuàng be satisfied with things as they are
【安葬】 ānzàng bury (the dead)
【安枕无忧】 ānzhěn-wúyōu sleep without anxiety
【安置】 ānzhì arrange for; find a place for: 把客人～好 help guests to settle in
【安装】 ānzhuāng install; erect; fix; mount: 在硬盘上～MS-DOS install MS-DOS on hard disk / ～机器 erect the machine
【安装费】 ānzhuāngfèi installation fee

桉（ān） eucalyptus
【桉树】 ānshù eucalyptus

氨（ān） 〈*Chem.*〉 ammonia: 合成～ synthetic ammonia
【氨茶硷】 ānchájiǎn 〈*Pharm.*〉 aminophylline
【氨基】 ānjī 〈*Chem.*〉 amino; amino-group
【氨基酸】 ānjīsuān 〈*Chem.*〉 amino acid
【氨水】 ānshuǐ 〈*Chem.*〉 ammonia water

鞍（ān） saddle
【鞍部】 ānbù saddle (of a hill or mountain)
【鞍马】 ānmǎ **1.**〈*Sports*〉 pommel horse; side horse; vaulting horse **2.**（指器材）horse **3.**（鞍与马）saddle and horse
【鞍马劳顿】 ānmǎ-láodùn be travel-worn
【鞍子】 ān·zi saddle

鹌（ān）
【鹌鹑】 ān·chún quail

谙（ān） know well
【谙练】 ānliàn conversant; proficient; skilled

岸（àn） bank; coast; shore: 海～ coast; seashore / 河～ the bank of a river; a river bank / 靠～ pull into shore / 上～ go ashore
【岸边】 ànbiān alongshore
【岸然】 ànrán in a solemn manner
【岸线】 ànxiàn water front

按（àn） **1.**（摁）press; push down **2.**（压住）leave aside; shelve **3.**（抑制）control; restrain 4.(压住不动) keep a tight grip on; keep one's hand on 5.(按照) according to; in accordance with; in the light of; on the basis of: ～规章办事 do sth. according to the rules and regulations 6.(核对) check; refer to 7.(按语) note

【按比例】 ànbǐlì pro rata; in proportion: ～发展 develop in proportion; proportional development / ～均摊 pro rata average

【按部就班】 ànbù-jiùbān follow the prescribed order; keep to conventional ways of doing things

【按成本】 ànchéngběn at cost

【按股分红】 àngǔ fēnhóng to share profits according to contributions

【按键】 ànjiàn 1.(键) button; key 2.(按一下键) keystroke

【按键电话】 ànjiàn diànhuà push-button phone

【按揭】 ànjiē 〈*Econ.*〉mortgage

【按扣】 ànkòu snap-fastener

【按劳分配】 àn láo fēn pèi distribution according to work

【按理】 ànlǐ according to reason

【按脉】 ànmài feel the pulse; take the pulse

【按摩】 ànmó massage

【按摩器】 ànmóqì massager

【按摩师】 ànmóshī masseur; masseuse (f.)

【按摩院】 ànmóyuàn massage parlor

【按捺】 ànnà control; restrain

【按年代顺序】 àn niándài shùnxù in chronological order; chronological

【按年计算】 àn nián jì suàn annualized

【按钮】 ànniǔ push button

【按期】 ànqī on time; on schedule

【按期付息】 ànqī fùxī pay an interest at regular internals; pay an interest on schedule

【按人分配】 àn rén fēn pèi personal distribution

【按人口平均】 àn rénkǒu píngjūn per capita; per head; average per capita

【按人口平均收入】 àn rénkǒu píngjūn shōurù per capita income

【按时】 ànshí on time; on schedule

【按市价】 ànshìjià at market price

【按说】 ànshuō ordinarily; normally; in the ordinary course of events

【按四舍五入去尾】 àn sìshě wǔrù qùwěi round off

【按现在的样子】 àn xiànzài de yàng·zi (用在句末) as it is/was: 桌子就～别动。Leave the table as it is.

【按姓氏笔画为序】 àn xìngshì bǐhuà wéi xù in the order of the number of strokes in the surnames

【按需分配】 ànxū-fēnpèi distribution according to need

【按业务需要】 àn yèwù xūyào according to requirements of service

【按优惠条件】 àn yōuhuì tiáojiàn give on favorable terms; give on liberal terms

【按语】 ànyǔ note; comment

【按原价计算】 àn yuánjià jìsuàn calculate on the basis of their original price

【按月】 ànyuè monthly; by the month

【按月分期付款】 àn yuè fēnqī fùkuǎn monthly installment

【按照】 ànzhào according to; in accordance with; in the light of; on the basis of: ～你的命令 in accordance with your orders / 书是～学科排在书架上的。The books are arranged on the shelves according to subject.

【按照惯例】 ànzhào guànlì according to the custom; according to the practice

【按照规定】 ànzhào guīdìng according to the rules

【按照实际情况】 ànzhào shíjì qíngkuàng in the light of actual conditions

【按照要求】 ànzhào yāoqiú as requested

【按照预定计划】 ànzhào yùdìng jìhuà according to schedule

【按质论价】 ànzhì-lùnjià fix the price according to the quality

【按重量分级】 àn zhòngliàng fēnjí grade by weight

【按重量计算】 àn zhòngliàng jìsuàn calculate by weight

案 (àn) 1.(长桌) table; desk 2.(案件) case; law case: 办～ handle a case / 破～ clear up a criminal case; solve a criminal case 3.(案卷) file; record 4.(提案) proposal; a plan submitted for consideration

【案板】 ànbǎn cutting board (AmE.); chopping board (BrE.)

【案犯】 ànfàn criminal; person having committed a crime

【案犯照片栏】 ànfàn zhàopiānlán rogues' gallery

【案件】 ànjiàn law case; case; legal case: 恶性～ pernicious case / 民事～ civil case / 刑事～ criminal case

【案卷】 ànjuàn files; records; archives

【案例】 ànlì case; example of case

【案例记录】 ànlì jìlù case history

【案情】 ànqíng case; details of a case: 了解～ investigate the details of a case

【案情大白】 ànqíng-dàbái The riddle of a puzzling case has been completely unraveled.

【案头工作】 àntóu gōngzuò desktop

【案由】 ànyóu cause of action; main points of a case

【案子】 àn·zi **1.**(长桌) long table; counter **2.**(案件) case; law case: 一个很难办的～ a difficult case to prove

胺(àn) 〈*Chem.*〉 amine

暗[闇[1,3]] (àn) **1.**(黑暗) dark; dim; dull **2.**(不公开的) hidden; secret **3.**(糊涂) unclear; hazy

【暗暗】 àn'àn secretly; inwardly; to oneself

【暗堡】 ànbǎo bunker

【暗补】 ànbǔ invisible subsidy

【暗藏】 àncáng hide; conceal

【暗娼】 ànchāng demi-monde; unlicensed prostitute

【暗淡】 àndàn dim; dismal; faint; gloomy

【暗地里】 àndì·li secretly; inwardly; on the sly

【暗房】 ànfáng 〈*Photog.*〉 darkroom

【暗光】 ànguāng half-light

【暗害】 ànhài **1.**(暗杀) kill secretly **2.**(陷害) stab in the back

【暗号】 ànhào secret signal; countersign; keyword; cipher

【暗盒】 ànhé 〈*Photog.*〉 magazine; cassette

【暗箭伤人】 ànjiàn-shāngrén stab sb. in the back; injure sb. by underhand means

【暗箭难防】 ànjiàn-nánfáng Hidden arrows are difficult to guard.

【暗礁】 ànjiāo submerged reef; submerged rock

【暗扣】 ànkòu hidden discount

【暗码锁】 ànmǎsuǒ combination lock

【暗流】 ànliú undercurrent

【暗杀】 ànshā assassinate

【暗杀名单】 ànshā míngdān hit list

【暗射地图】 ànshè dìtú blank map

【暗示】 ànshì drop a hint; hint; suggest

【暗示疗法】 ànshì liáofǎ suggestion therapy

【暗室】 ànshì 〈*Photog.*〉 darkroom

【暗算】 ànsuàn plot against: 遭人～ fall a prey to a plot

【暗锁】 ànsuǒ built-in lock

【暗滩】 àntān hidden shoal

【暗探】 àntàn detective; secret agent

【暗无天日】 ànwú-tiānrì complete darkness; total absence of justice

【暗笑】 ànxiào snigger; laugh in one's sleeve

【暗影】 ànyǐng **1.**(阴影) shadow **2.**〈*Astron.*〉 umbra

【暗语】 ànyǔ code word

【暗账】 ànzhàng secret ledger

【暗指】 ànzhǐ allude

【暗中】 ànzhōng **1.**(在黑暗中) in the dark **2.**(在背地里) in secret; on the sly; surreptitiously: ～破坏 disrupt furtively / ～支持 give secret support to

【暗中操纵】 ànzhōng cāozòng stage-manage

【暗中进行】 ànzhōng jìnxíng undercover

【暗自】 ànzì inwardly; secretly; to oneself

【暗自庆幸】 ànzì qìngxìng congratulate oneself; consider oneself lucky

黯(àn) dim; gloomy

【黯然】 ànrán **1.**(指阴暗) dim; faint **2.**(指情绪) dejected; downcast; low-spirited

【黯然失色】 ànrán-shīsè be overshadowed; be eclipsed

ang

肮[骯] (āng)

【肮脏】 āng·zāng dirty; filthy: 一条～的牛仔裤 a grubby jeans

昂(áng) **1.**(抬起头) hold (one's head) high **2.**(高昂) high; soaring

【昂昂】 áng'áng high-spirited; brave-looking

【昂贵】 ángguì expensive; costly; pricey;

pricy

【昂然】 ángrán upright and unafraid

【昂首】 ángshǒu hold one's head high

【昂首阔步】 ángshǒu-kuòbù stride forward with one's chin up; stride proudly ahead

【昂扬】 ángyáng high-spirited

盎 (àng)

【盎然】 àngrán abundant; exuberant; full; overflowing

【盎司】 àngsī ounce：液量～ fluid ounce

ao

凹 (āo) concave; hollow; sunken; dented

【凹背单人坐椅】 āobèi dānrén zuòyǐ 〈*Auto*〉 bucket seat

【凹面镜】 āomiànjìng concave mirror

【凹透镜】 āotòujìng concave lens

【凹凸不平】 āo tū bù píng uneven; full of bumps and holes

【凹凸镜】 āotūjìng concave and convex lenses

【凹陷】 āoxiàn hollow; sunken; depressed

熬 (āo) boil; decoct; stew
(另见"熬"áo)

遨 (áo) stroll; saunter

【遨游】 áoyóu roam; travel：～太空 roam in the heavens; travel in space

熬 (áo) **1.**（煮）boil; decoct; stew **2.**（忍受）endure; hold out
(另见"熬"āo)

【熬药】 áoyào decoct medicinal herbs

【熬夜】 áoyè stay up late; stay up all night

【熬粥】 áozhōu cook gruel

翱［翶］(áo) 〈*written*〉 take wing

【翱翔】 áoxiáng hover; soar

鏖 (áo) engage in fierce battle

【鏖战】 áozhàn fight hard; engage in fierce battle

拗［抝］(ǎo)
(另见"拗"ào, niù)

【拗断】 ǎoduàn break sth.

袄［襖］(ǎo) coat; jacket：棉～ a cotton-padded jacket

拗［抝］(ào)
(另见"拗"ǎo, niù)

【拗口】 àokǒu hard to pronounce

【拗口令】 àokǒulìng tongue twister

傲 (ào) **1.**（指人）proud; haughty **2.**（指性格）refuse to yield to; brave; defy

【傲岸】 ào'àn 〈*written*〉 proud; haughty

【傲慢】 àomàn arrogant; haughty：～的态度 high horse / 用～的口气讲话 speak in an arrogant tone

【傲气】 àoqì air of arrogance; haughtiness

【傲然】 àorán loftily; proudly; unyieldingly

【傲视】 àoshì despise; look down upon

奥 (ào) profound; abstruse; difficult to understand

【奥博】 àobó profound; erudite

【奥纶】 àolún Orlon（聚丙烯腈短纤维）

【奥秘】 àomì profound mystery

【奥妙】 àomiào profound; secret; subtle

【奥斯卡金像奖】 Àosīkǎ jīnxiàngjiǎng Oscar

【奥委会】 Àowěihuì the Olympic Committee

【奥运】 Àoyùn the Olympic Games; Olympiad

【奥运会】 Àoyùnhuì the Olympic Games; Olympiad

懊 (ào) **1.**（懊恨）regretful; remorseful **2.**（烦恼）annoyed; vexed

【懊恨】 àohèn regretful; remorseful

【懊悔】 àohuǐ feel remorse; regret; repent

【懊恼】 àonǎo annoyed; upset; vexed

【懊丧】 àosàng dejected; depressed; despondent

澳 (Ào) **1.**（澳大利亚）Australia; Australian (adj.) **2.**（澳门）Macao

【澳大利亚】 Àodàlìyà Australia; Australian (adj.)

【澳抗】 àokàng 〈*Bacteriol.*〉 Au antigen; Australia antigen

【澳门】 Àomén Macao

【澳门元】 Àoményuán Macao Dollar

【澳式橄榄球】 àoshì gǎnlǎnqiú Australian Rules football

【澳元】 Àoyuán Australian Dollar

【澳洲】 Àozhōu Australia; Australian (adj.)

【澳洲鸵鸟】 Àozhōu tuóniǎo emu

B

ba

八（bā） eight; eighth
（在本词典中"八"统注 bā）

【八百】 bābǎi eight hundred; eight-hundredth

【八宝粥】 bābǎozhōu mixed congee

【八倍体】 bābèitǐ 〈*Biol.*〉 octoploid

【八边形】 bābiānxíng octagon

【八成】 bāchén 1.（十分之八） eighty per cent 2.（大概） most probably; very likely

【八度】 bādù 〈*Music*〉 octave

【八分音符】 bāfēnyīnfú eighth note

【八分之一】 bā fēn zhī yī an eighth; one eighth

【八哥】 bā·ge 〈*Zool.*〉 myna

【八股】 bāgǔ eight-legged essay; stereotyped writing

【八卦】 bāguà the Eight Diagrams

【八角】 bājiǎo 1.〈*Bot.*〉 anistree; truestar anistree 2.（大料） aniseed

【八角枫】 bājiǎofēng 〈*Bot.*〉 alangium

【八进制】 bājìnzhì octal system

【八路】 Bālù 见"八路军"

【八路军】 Bā Lù Jūn the Eighth Route Army

【八面玲珑】 bāmiàn línglóng be a perfect mixer in any company

【八千】 bāqiān eight thousand; eight thousandth

【八十】 bāshí eighty; eightieth

【八万】 bāwàn eighty thousand; eighty thousandth

【八小时工作制】 bāxiǎoshí gōngzhuòzhì eight-hour day

【八一建军节】 Bā-Yī JiànJūn Jié Army Day (August 1)

【八月】 Bāyuè August

【八月节】 Bāyuè Jié the Mid-Autumn Festival

【八字形】 bāzìxíng splayed

【八折】 bāzhé twenty per cent discount：打～ give twenty per cent discount

扒（bā） 1.（抓住） cling to; hold to：～在墙上 catch hold of the top of the wall 2.（刨；挖；拆） dig up; pull down; rake：～房子 pull down a house 3.（扒开） push aside 4.（扒掉；扒下） strip off; take off：～动物的皮 skin an animal

（另见"扒"pá）

巴（bā） 1.（盼望） hope for; expect 2.（紧贴；粘住） cling to; stick to 3.（压强单位） bar：毫～ millibar

【巴不得】 bā·bu·de eagerly look forward to; earnestly wish

【巴结】 bā·jie curry favor with; fawn on; make up to; underlings fawn on their bosses

【巴拉莱卡琴】 bālāláikǎ qíng balalaika

【巴纳德星】 bānàdé xīng Barnard's Star（距地球第二近，约六光年）

【巴士】 bāshì bus

【巴松管】 bāsōngguǎn 〈*Music*〉 bassoon

【巴望】 bāwàng look forward to

【巴西木】 bāxīmù Brazil

【巴颜高勒】 Bāyángāolè 〈place〉 Bayan Gol

【巴颜喀拉山】 Bāyánkālā shān 〈place〉 Bayan Har

【巴掌】 bā·zhang palm; hand：给他一～ give him a slap

芭（bā）

【芭蕉】 bājiāo 〈*Bot.*〉 banana; plantain banana

【芭蕾舞】 bālěiwǔ ballet：古典～ classical ballet

【芭蕾舞演员】 bālěiwǔ yǎnyuán ballet dancer; ballerina (f.)

吧（bā）

【吧嗒】 bādā 〈*onomat*.〉 click：门～一声关上了。The door clicked shut.

【吧嗒】 bā·da **1**.（吧嗒嘴）smack one's lips **2**.（用烟袋抽旱烟）pull at a pipe

【吧女】 bānǚ bar girl；B-girl；barmaid

疤（bā） scar

【疤痕】 bāhén scar

捌（bā） eight；eighth

八（bá） eight；eighth（请见"八"bā）

拔（bá） **1**.（拉出；抽出）pull out；pull up：～花园的杂草 weed a garden / ～手枪 take out one's revolver **2**.（吸出）draw；suck out **3**.（选拔）choose；pick；select **4**.（向高提）lift；raise **5**.（超出）stand out among；surpass **6**.（夺取）capture；seize

【拔除】 báchú pull out；remove：～杂草 weed out the rank grass

【拔高】 bágāo **1**.（提高）lift；raise：～嗓子 raise one's voice **2**.（有意抬高）bring to a higher position intentionally；inflate sb's image

【拔罐子】 bá guàn·zi cup（v.）；cupping（n.）

【拔河】 báhé tug-of-war

【拔尖儿】 bájiānr **1**.（出众）tiptop；top-notch：工作～ a top-notch work / 学习成绩～ be a top-notch student **2**.（突出个人）push oneself to the front

【拔苗助长】 bámiáo-zhùzhǎng Haste makes waste.

【拔腿就跑】 bátuǐ-jiùpǎo start running away at once

【拔牙】 báyá draw one's teeth

跋（bá） **1**.（翻山越岭）cross mountains **2**.（书后或文后的短文）postscript

【跋山涉水】 bá shān shè shuǐ travel over land and water

【跋涉】 báshè trek a long way

把（bǎ） **1**.（抓住）grasp；hold：～住楼梯栏杆 hold the banisters **2**.（掌握）control；dominate；monopolize **3**.（把守）guard；watch **4**.（车把）handle **5**.〈*classifier*〉一～花生 a handful of groundnuts / 一～剑 a sword / 一～扇子 a fan / 一～雨伞 an umbrella **6**.（大约）about；or so **7**.〈*prep*.〉～房间收拾一下 tidy up the room（另见"把"bà）

【把柄】 bǎbǐng handle

【把持】 bǎchí control；dominate；monopolize：～公司的一切 monopolize everything of the company

【把舵】 bǎduò steer

【把关】 bǎguān check on；guard a pass：把好产品的质量关 guarantee the quality of products

【把角儿】 bǎjiǎor corner

【把门】 bǎmén guard a gate

【把守】 bǎshǒu guard：～营房大门 guard a camp gate

【把手】 bǎ·shou grip；handle；knob：装上～ fit a handle on

【把握】 bǎwò **1**.（掌握）grasp；hold：～方向盘 hold the steering wheel **2**.（抓住）hold；get hold：～有利时机 get hold the favorable opportunity **3**.（可靠性）assurance；certainty：对选举的结果没有～ have no certainty of the election

【把戏】 bǎxì **1**.（杂耍）acrobatics；jugglery **2**.（花招儿）cheap trick；game

钯（bǎ） 〈*Chem*.〉 palladium（元素符号 Pd）

靶（bǎ） target：打～ shoot at the target/ 我的头两枪未中～。My first two shoots missed the target.

【靶场】 bǎchǎng shooting range；range

【靶心】 bǎxīn bull's eye

【靶子】 bǎ·zi target

坝［壩］（bà） **1**.（水坝）dam **2**.（防洪堤坝）dike；embankment

【坝子】 bà·zi flatland；plain

把［欛］（bà） **1**.（器具上的）grip；handle：金属～ metal handle / 平锅～儿 handle of a pan / 扫帚～儿 broom handle **2**.（花、叶、果实等的柄）stem（of leaf, flower or fruit）（另见"把"bǎ）

爸（bà） pa；dad；father

【爸爸】 bà·ba papa；dad；father

耙［耚］（bà） **1**.（农具）harrow **2**.（耙地）harrow a field：～地 draw a harrow over a field; harrow a field (另见"耙"pá)

罢[罷](bà) 1.(停止) cease; stop 2.(罢免) dismiss 3.(完了) finish

【罢黜】 bàchù 1.(免职) dismiss from one's office 2.(排斥) ban; reject

【罢工】 bàgōng strike; go on strike; be on strike: 静坐～ sit-down strike

【罢官】 bàguān 1.(免职) dismiss from one's office 2.(被免职) be dismissed from office

【罢课】 bàkè students' strike; school boycott

【罢免】 bàmiǎn recall (officials by the people)

【罢市】 bàshì shopkeepers' strike

【罢手】 bàshǒu give up; abandon

【罢休】 bàxiū give up; let the matter drop

霸[覇](bà) 1.(暴君;恶霸) despot; tyrant 2.(霸权) hegemonist power; hegemony; hegemonism 3.(依仗权势统治) dominate; lord it over; tyrannize over

【霸道】 bàdào high-handed; overbearing; tyrannical: 横行～ act tyrannically

【霸权】 bàquán hegemony; supremacy

【霸王】 bàwáng overlord; tyrant

【霸占】 bàzhàn forcibly occupy; seize; occupy illegally

bai

掰[擘](bāi) break off; break

白(bái) 1.(白色) white 2.(明白) clear 3.(没加其他东西) pure; plain 4.(白白) in vain; for nothing 5.(无代价) free of charge; gratis 6.(空白) blank: 一页～纸 a blank sheet of paper

【白白】 báibái in vain; for nothing

【白班儿】 báibānr 〈*colloq.*〉 day shift

【白报纸】 báibàozhǐ newsprint

【白璧无瑕】 báibì-wúxiá flawless white jade; impeccable moral integrity

【白菜】 báicài Chinese cabbage; Chinese cabbage

【白吃】 báichī eat without payment

【白痴】 báichī 1.(指病) idiocy 2.(指病人) idiot

【白炽】 báichì white heat; incandescence

【白炽灯】 báichìdēng incandescent lamp

【白搭】 báidā 〈*colloq.*〉 no use; no good

【白大褂】 báidàguà 〈*colloq.*〉 gown of a doctor

【白带】 báidài 〈*Med.*〉 leucorrhea

【白发】 báifà white hairs

【白费】 báifèi waste: ～钱 waste money / 他的努力全～了。His efforts were wasted.

【白费蜡】 báifèilà waste one's efforts

【白格】 báigé 〈*Chess*〉 white square

【白宫】 báigōng the White House (指美国政府)

【白果】 báiguǒ gingko; ginkgo

【白鹤】 báihè white crane

【白喉】 báihóu 〈*Med.*〉 diphtheria

【白话】 báihuà promise that cannot be realized: 空口说～ give empty promises

【白桦】 báihuà 〈*Bot.*〉 white birch

【白暨豚】 báijìtún 〈*Zool.*〉 white flag dolphin

【白金】 báijīn platinum

【白净】 bái·jing (of skin) fair and clear

【白酒】 báijiǔ spirit; white spirit

【白卷】 báijuàn blank test paper: 交～ hand in an unanswered test paper

【白开水】 báikāishuǐ plain boiled water

【白口铁】 báikǒutiě white iron

【白兰地】 báilándì brandy

【白磷】 báilín 〈*Chem.*〉 white phosphorus

【白领】 báilǐng white-collar

【白鹭】 báilù egret

【白露】 Báilù the White Dew (9月7-9日交节)

【白茫茫】 báimángmáng a vast expanse of whiteness

【白米】 báimǐ rice; husked rice

【白面】 báimiàn flour; wheat flour

【白面儿】 báimiànr heroin

【白木耳】 báimù'ěr tremella; white fungus

【白内障】 báinèizhàng 〈*Med.*〉 cataract

【白牌儿】 báipáir blank label

【白皮书】 báipíshū white paper; white book

【白鳍豚】 báiqítún 〈*Zool.*〉 white flag dolphin

【白热】 báirè white heat; incandescence

【白人】 báirén white; white man; white

woman
【白刃战】 báirènzhàn bayonet assault; hand-to-hand combat
【白日】 báirì 1.(白天) day; daytime 2.(指太阳) the sun
【白日做梦】 báirì-zuòmèng daydream; indulge in wishful thinking
【白色】 báisè white
【白色恐怖】 báisè kǒngbù white terror
【白薯】 báishǔ 〈*Bot*.〉 sweet potato
【白糖】 báitáng refined sugar
【白天】 bái·tiān daytime; day: ～黑夜 day and night
【白条】 báitiáo informal IOU; informal vouchers; informal financial documents
【白铁】 báitiě galvanized iron
【白厅】 Bái Tīng Whitehall (指英国政府)
【白皙】 báixī white-skinned
【白细胞】 báixìbāo 〈*Physiol*.〉 leukocyte; leukocytic (adj.); white blood cell
【白线】 báixiàn 〈*Transport*〉 white line
【白熊】 báixióng 〈*Zool*.〉 polar bear; white bear; ice bear
【白血病】 báixuèbìng 〈*Med*.〉 leukemia; leukemic (adj.)
【白血球】 báixuèqiú 〈*Physiol*.〉 leukocyte; leukocytic (adj.); white blood cell
【白眼】 báiyǎn supercilious look: 给人～ contempt for
【白眼珠】 báiyǎnzhū white eyeball
【白羊宫】 Báiyánggōng 〈*Astron*.〉 Aries (3月21日至4月20日): 生于～ be born under Aries
【白羊座】 Báiyángzuò 〈*Astron*.〉 Aries
【白杨】 báiyáng 〈*Bot*.〉 white poplar
【白页】 báiyè a blank page on a book
【白衣天使】 báiyī tiānshǐ nurse
【白蚁】 báiyǐ termite; white ant
【白银】 báiyín silver; silvery (adj.)
【白鼬】 báiyòu 〈*Zool*.〉 stoat; ermine
【白云】 báiyún white clouds
【白云鄂博】 Báiyún'èbó 〈place〉 Bayan Obo
【白纸黑字】 báizhǐ-hēizì in black and white
【白种】 Báizhǒng the white race
【白种人】 báizhǒngrén white people
【白昼】 báizhòu daytime
【白煮】 báizhǔ boil in plain water
【白字】 báizì wrongly written or pronounced character
【白族】 Báizú Baizu (中国少数民族, 主要分布在云南)

百 (bǎi) 1.(数字) hundred; hundredth: 数以～计 by hundreds 2.(很多) numerous; all kinds of
【百般】 bǎibān in every possible way; by every means: ～劝说 try to persuade in every possible way / ～阻挠 set up obstacles in every possible way
【百倍】 bǎibèi a hundred times; a hundredfold: 信心～ with full confidence
【百搭】 bǎidā 〈*Cards*〉 Joker
【百分】 bǎifēn 1.(一百分) a hundred points 2.(百分之几) per cent; percent: ～之六 6 per cent / 获～之九的利息 get 9 per cent interest
【百分比】 bǎifēnbǐ percentage
【百分点】 bǎifēndiǎn per cent; percent: 六个～ 6 per cent / 下降 7.8 个～ drop by 7.8 per cent
【百分号】 bǎifēnhào percentage sign (%)
【百分数】 bǎifēnshù figure in percentage
【百分之…】 bǎi fēn zhī … per cent (符号为%)
【百分之百】 bǎifēnzhībǎi a hundred per cent; out and out; absolutely
【百分制】 bǎifēnzhì hundred mark system; hundred point system
【百合】 bǎihé 〈*Bot*.〉 lily
【百花奖】 bǎihuājiǎng the Hundred Flowers Award
【百花齐放, 百家争鸣】 bǎihuā-qífàng, bǎijiā-zhēngmíng let a hundred flowers blossom and a hundred schools of thought contend
【百货】 bǎihuò general merchandise
【百货公司】 bǎihuò gōngsī department store
【百货商店】 bǎihuò shāngdiàn department store
【百科全书】 bǎikē quánshū encyclopedia
【百灵】 bǎilíng 〈*Zool*.〉 lark
【百忙中】 bǎimángzhōng while fully engaged; in the thick of things
【百年】 bǎinián 1.(指很长时间) a hundred years; a century 2.(指死亡) lifetime: ～之后 after one's death

【百日咳】　bǎirìké　〈*Med*.〉 whooping cough; pertussis
【百事可乐】　Bǎishì Kělè　Pepsi Cola
【百万】　bǎiwàn　million; millionth
【百万富翁】　bǎiwàn fùwēng　millionaire
【百闻不如一见】　bǎiwén-bùrú-yījiàn　it is better to see once than hear a hundred times; seeing for oneself is a hundred times better than hearing from others
【百姓】　bǎixìng　common people
【百叶窗】　bǎiyèchuāng　shutter; blind
【百叶箱】　bǎiyèxiāng　〈*Meteorol*.〉 thermometer screen
【百折不挠】　bǎizhé-bùnáo　keep on doing sth. despite all setbacks
【百周年纪念】　bǎi zhōunián jìniàn　centenary; centenary celebration; centennial

佰 (bǎi)　hundred; hundredth

柏[栢] (bǎi)　cypress
【柏树】　bǎishù　〈*Bot*.〉 cypress (tree)
【柏油】　bǎiyóu　pitch; tar; asphalt
【柏油路】　bǎiyóulù　asphalt road

摆[擺] (bǎi)　1.(摆放) put; place; arrange: 把…～在首位 give priority to / 把瓶子～在架子上 put the bottle on the shelf 2.(陈述) lay bare; state clearly 3.(炫耀) put on; assume 4.〈*Mech*.〉 pendulum
【摆布】　bǎi·bu　order about; manipulate
【摆动】　bǎidòng　swing; sway
【摆渡】　bǎidù　ferry
【摆架子】　bǎi jià·zi　put on airs; put on side
【摆阔气】　bǎi kuò·qi　parade one's wealth; be ostentatious and extravagant
【摆来摆去】　bǎilái-bǎiqù　swing to and fro
【摆弄】　bǎinòng　1.(反复拨弄) move back and forth; fiddle with 2.(摆布) order about; manipulate
【摆设】　bǎishè　1.(布置) furnish and decorate (a room) 2.(摆设的东西) ornaments; adornment
【摆事实,讲道理】　bǎi shìshí, jiǎng dàolǐ　present the facts and reason things out
【摆摊子】　bǎi tān·zi　1.(摆摊卖东西) set up a stall 2.(铺张) maintain a large staff or organization
【摆脱】　bǎituō　cast off; shake off; break away from; free oneself from; extricate oneself from: ～贫穷落后 be lifted oneself out of poverty and backwardness
【摆样子】　bǎi yàng·zi　do sth. for show
【摆钟】　bǎizhōng　pendulum clock

败 (bài)　1.(失败,跟"胜利"相对) fail; lost: 主队以一比三～于客队。The home team lost to the visitors 1 to 3. 2.(打败) defeat; beat 3.(失败,跟"成功"相对) fail 4.(搞坏) spoil 5.(解除;消除) counteract 6.(衰败;凋谢) decay; wither
【败北】　bàiběi　lose a battle; be defeated in a battle
【败坏】　bàihuài　1.(指名誉、风气等) ruin; corrupt; undermine: ～社会风气 corrupt social values / 他说该文～了他的名誉,说他是骗子。He said that the article had defamed him as a swindler. 2.(指道德、纪律等) degenerate: 道德～ morally degenerate
【败家子】　bàijiāzǐ　spendthrift; wastrel; prodigal
【败局】　bàijú　1.(指比赛等) lost game: 我们队挽回了～。Our team retrieved a defeat. 2.(指战斗) losing battle
【败类】　bàilèi　scum of a community; degenerate
【败露】　bàilù　(a plot) be revealed; be disclosed
【败诉】　bàisù　〈*Law*〉 lose a law suit
【败退】　bàituì　retreat in defeat
【败兴】　bàixìng　disappointed; disillusioned
【败血病】　bàixuèbìng　〈*Med*.〉 septicemia
【败仗】　bàizhàng　lost battle; defeat

拜 (bài)　1.(崇拜) do obeisance 2.(拜访) make a courtesy call 3.(确立某种关系) acknowledge sb. as one's master, godfather, etc.: ～他为老师 take him as one's teacher
【拜拜】　bài·bai　1.(再见) good-by; bye-bye 2.(断绝来往) break off with sb.; cut off relations
【拜倒】　bàidǎo　prostrate oneself; fall on one's knees: ～在某人的脚下 prostrate oneself before sb.
【拜读】　bàidú　have the honor to read

【拜访】 bàifǎng pay a visit; call on: ～亲友 visit relatives and friends
【拜会】 bàihuì pay an official visit
【拜见】 bàijiàn pay a formal visit; call to pay respects
【拜金主义】 bàijīn zhǔyì money worship
【拜客】 bàikè pay a visit to one's friend; call on one's friend
【拜年】 bàinián pay a New Year call; wish sb. a Happy New Year
【拜师】 bàishī take sb. as one's teacher
【拜寿】 bàishòu congratulate sb. on his birthday
【拜托】 bàituō 〈*politeness*〉 request sb. to do sth.
【拜物教】 bàiwùjiào fetishism
【拜谒】 bàiyè 1.(拜见) pay a formal visit 2.(瞻仰陵墓等) pay tribute; pay homage: ～黄帝陵 pay tribute to the Mausoleum of Yellow Emperor

ban

扳(bān) pull; turn
【扳道】 bāndào 〈*Railway*〉 pull railway switches
【扳道员】 bāndàoyuán 〈*Railway*〉 pointsman; switchman
【扳机】 bānjī trigger
【扳手】 bān·shou 1.(工具) spanner; wrench 2.(器具上用手扳动的部分) lever (on a machine)
【扳子】 bān·zi spanner; wrench
颁(bān) promulgate; issue
【颁布】 bānbù promulgate; issue; publish: ～法令 promulgate a decree; issue a decree
【颁发】 bānfā 1.(发布) issue; promulgate 2.(授与) award: 向某人～奖章 award a medal to sb.
【颁奖】 bānjiǎng present awards; hand out awards to
【颁奖仪式】 bānjiǎng yíshì prize-giving ceremony
【颁行】 bānxíng issue for enforcement
【颁证】 bānzhèng 1.(发证件) present cards 2.(发证书) award a certificate
班(bān) 1.(班组) class; team 2.(班次) shift; duty: 上～ go to work / 上夜～ be on night shift 3.〈*Mil.*〉 squad
【班车】 bānchē regular bus
【班次】 bāncì 1.(学校的) classes 2.(公共交通的) number of runs or flight: 增加公共汽车～ increase the number of runs of bus
【班房】 bānfáng jail; gaol; prison
【班公错】 Bāngōngcuò 〈place〉 Bangong Co
【班机】 bānjī airliner; regular air service
【班级】 bānjí classes and grades in school
【班门弄斧】 Bānmén-nòngfǔ show off one's skill or knowledge before an expert
【班师】 bānshī 1.(调回军队) withdraw troops from the front 2.(胜利归来) return home in triumph
【班长】 bānzhǎng 1.(班级的) class monitor 2.〈*Mil.*〉 squad leader
【班主任】 bānzhǔrèn a teacher in charge of a class
【班卓琴】 bānzhuóqín banjo
【班子】 bān·zi 1.(戏班) theatrical troupe 2.(组织) body; collective: 领导～ leading body / 业务～ vocational collective
【班组】 bānzǔ teams and groups
斑(bān) 1.(斑点;斑纹) spot; speck; speckle; stripe: 霉～ speck of mold 2.(有斑点的;有斑纹的) spotted; striped
【斑白】 bānbái grizzled; greying: 头发～ with streaks of white hair
【斑斑】 bānbān full of stains or spots: 血迹～ covered with blood stains
【斑驳陆离】 bānbó-lùlí variegated
【斑点】 bāndiǎn spot; stain; speckle
【斑鸠】 bānjiū turtledove; turtle dove
【斑斓】 bānlán bright-colored; gorgeous; multi-colored
【斑马】 bānmǎ zebra
【斑马线】 bānmǎxiàn 〈*Transport*〉 zebra crossing; crosswalk
【斑纹】 bānwén stripe; streak
【斑疹伤寒】 bānzhěn shānghán typhus
般(bān) sort; kind; way
【般配】 bānpèi be well matched
搬[般](bān) 1.(搬动) take away; move; remove: 把桌子～走

take the table away 2.（迁移）move（house）3.（搬用；照抄）apply indiscriminately; copy mechanically

【搬家】 bānjiā move（house）

【搬家公司】 bānjiā gōngsī removal company

【搬弄是非】 bānnòng shìfēi sow discord; tell tales; make mischief

【搬迁】 bānqiān move（house）from one place to another

【搬迁户】 bānqiānhù household having to move（house）

【搬运】 bānyùn carry; transport: ～行李 carry luggage

【搬运工】 bānyùngōng 1.（车站等的）porter 2.（码头的）docker

板（bǎn） 1.（各种板）board; plank; plate 2.（店铺门板）shutter 3.（音乐节拍）an accented beat; time; measure 4.（硬结）hard 5.（呆板）stiff; unnatural 6.（表情严肃）stop smiling; look serious

【板壁】 bǎnbì wooden partition

【板擦儿】 bǎncār eraser; board rubber

【板材】 bǎncái 〈*Forestry*〉board; plates

【板凳】 bǎndèng wooden bench; wooden stool

【板结】 bǎnjié harden: 地面在太阳下晒～了。The ground was hardened in the sun.

【板块】 bǎnkuài 〈*Geol.*〉plate

【板块构造】 bǎnkuài gòuzào 〈*Geol.*〉plate tectonics

【板栗】 bǎnlì Chinese chestnut

【板刷】 bǎnshuā brush; scrubbing brush

【板条箱】 bǎntiáoxiāng crate

【板鸭】 bǎnyā pressed salted duck; dried salted duck

【板眼】 bǎnyǎn 1.（民乐节拍）measure in traditional Chinese music 2.（条理；层次）orderliness

【板子】 bǎn·zi board; plank

版（bǎn） 1.（印版）printing plate; printing block 2.（版本）edition: 初～ first edition / 新～ new edition / 修订～ revised edition / 再～ second edition 3.（报纸的页）page（of a newspaper）

【版本】 bǎnběn edition

【版画】 bǎnhuà woodcut; woodblock; engraving

【版面】 bǎnmiàn 1.（一整页）space of a whole page 2.（版面编排）layout of a printed sheet; make-up of a printed sheet

【版权】 bǎnquán copyright

【版权法】 bǎnquánfǎ copyright law

【版权所有】 bǎnquán suǒyǒu all rights reserved

【版税】 bǎnshuì royalty（on books）

【版图】 bǎntú domain; territory

办［辦］（bàn） 1.（办理）do; handle; manage; attend to: 齐心协力～好几件大事 make concerted efforts to accomplish a few major tasks / 怎么～? What's to be done? 2.（创办）set up; run: ～工厂 start a factory / 离开学校后他一直在自己～公司。He's been running his own company since he left school. 3.（置办）buy a fair amount of; get sth. ready: ～货 purchase goods 4.（惩治）punish（by law）; bring to justice

【办案】 bàn'àn handle a case

【办报】 bànbào run a newspaper

【办法】 bànfǎ way; means; measure: 采取有效的～ adopt effective measures / 没～ have no way to do sth.

【办公】 bàngōng handle official business; work（in an office）

【办公会议】 bàngōng huìyì working conference

【办公时间】 bàngōng shíjiān office hours

【办公室】 bàngōngshì office

【办公室自动化】 bàngōngshì zìdònghuà office automation; OA

【办公厅】 bàngōngtīng general office

【办公椅】 bàngōngyǐ office chair

【办公桌】 bàngōngzhuō desk; bureau

【办结】 bànjié take up and complete; deal with and finish

【办理】 bànlǐ handle; conduct; transact

【办事】 bànshì handle affairs; work: ～认真 be conscientious in one's work

【办事处】 bànshìchù office; agency

【办事员】 bànshìyuán office worker; clerk

【办手续】 bànshǒuxù go through the formalities

【办学】 bànxué run a school

【办学方式】 bànxué fāngshì way of running

school

【办学方针】 bànxué fāngzhēn guidelines for running school

半 (bàn) 1.(一半) half; semi-: ～年 half a year; six months / 一年～ one year and a half 2.(在…中间) in the middle; halfway: ～山腰 half way up a hill 3.(比喻很少) very little; the least bit 4.(不完全) partly; about half: ～熟练的 semiskilled

【半百】 bànbǎi fifty (years of age): 年过～ over fifty; above fifty

【半辈子】 bànbèi·zi half a lifetime; half part of one's life

【半边天】 bànbiāntiān half the sky

【半场】 bànchǎng 〈*Sports*〉 1.(指时间) half time 2.(指场地) half-court

【半沉头螺帽】 bànchéntóu luómào oval head

【半成品】 bànchéngpǐn semi-manufactured goods

【半导体】 bàndǎotǐ semiconductor

【半导体集成电路】 bàndǎotǐ jíchéng diànlù semiconductor integrated circuit

【半导体器件】 bàndǎotǐ qìjiàn semiconductor devices

【半导体收音机】 bàndǎotǐ shōuyīnjī transistor radio; transistor receiver

【半导体元件】 bàndǎotǐ yuánjiàn semiconductor element

【半岛】 bàndǎo peninsula: 朝鲜～ the Korean Peninsula

【半点儿】 bàndiǎnr the least bit

【半费】 bànfèi half the fee; fifty per cent reduction in fees

【半封建】 bànfēngjiàn semi-feudal

【半工半读】 bàngōng-bàndú work-study program; part work, part study

【半官方】 bànguānfāng semi-official

【半机械化】 bànjīxièhuà semi-mechanization

【半价】 bànjià half price: ～出售 sell at half price

【半截】 bànjié half (a section)

【半斤八两】 bànjīn-bāliǎng the blind leading the blind

【半径】 bànjìng radius

【半决赛】 bànjuésài 〈*Sports*〉 semifinal

【半空中】 bànkōngzhōng in mind air; in the air

【半劳动力】 bànláodònglì part-time laborer; one who is able to do light manual labor only

【半路】 bànlù halfway; midway; on the way

【半路出家】 bànlù-chūjiā switch to a job one was not trained for

【半票】 bànpiào half-price ticket; half fare

【半旗】 bànqí half-mast: 下～ fly a flag at half-mast

【半球】 bànqiú hemisphere: 北～ the Northern Hemisphere / 南～ the Southern Hemisphere / 东～ the Eastern Hemisphere / 西～ the Western Hemisphere

【半人马座】 Bànrénmǎzuò 〈*Astron.*〉 Centaurus

【半人马座 α】 bànrénmǎzuò α 〈*Astron.*〉 Alpha Centauri (距太阳最近, 约 4.3 光年)

【半日制学校】 bànrìzhì xuéxiào half-day school; double- shift school

【半身】 bànshēn half of one's body: 上～ the upper half of one's body / 下～ the lower half of one's body

【半身不遂】 bànshēn-bùsuí 〈*Med.*〉 hemiplegia

【半生】 bànshēng half a lifetime: 前～ the first half of one's life / 后～ the later half of one's life

【半生不熟】 bànshēng-bùshú half cooked

【半数】 bànshù half the number; half: ～以上 more than half

【半衰期】 bànshuāiqī 〈*Physics*〉 half-life

【半死不活】 bàn sǐ bù huó half-dead; more dead than alive

【半天】 bàntiān 1.(半日) half of the day 2.(长时间) a long time; quite a while

【半透明】 bàntòumíng translucent; semi-transparent

【半途而废】 bàntú-érfèi leave sth. unfinished; give up halfway

【半脱产】 bàntuōchǎn partly released form one's regular work

【半文盲】 bànwénmáng semiliterate

【半信半疑】 bànxìn-bànyí not quite believe

【半夜】 bànyè midnight; in the middle of the night

【半夜三更】 bànyè-sāngēng in the depth of night; late at night

【半影】 bànyǐng 〈*Astron.*〉 penumbra

【半圆】 bànyuán semicircle

【半圆头螺帽】 bànyuántóu luómào round

head

【半圆形】 bànyuánxíng semicircular

【半月刊】 bànyuèkān semimonthly; fortnightly

【半真半假】 bànzhēn-bànjiǎ partly true, partly false

【半殖民地】 bànzhímíndì semi-colony

【半殖民地半封建社会】 bànzhímíndì bànfēngjiàn shèhuì semi-colonial, semi-feudal society

【半自动】 bànzìdòng semiautomatic

【半自动化】 bànzìdònghuà semi-automatization

【半自动控制】 bànzìdòng kòngzhì semiauto matic control

【半自动装置】 bànzìdòng zhuāngzhì semiautomatic plant

伴 (bàn) 1.(同伴) companion; partner 2.(伴随) accompany

【伴唱】 bànchàng 1.(指歌唱) vocal accompaniment 2.(配合表演) accompany (a singer)

【伴酒】 bànjiǔ drink in company of (with) sb.

【伴侣】 bànlǚ companion; mate; partner

【伴儿】 bànr companion; partner

【伴随】 bànsuí accompany; follow: 姑娘们～着欢乐的乐曲,跳起舞来。Accompanied by cheerful music, the girls began to dance.

【伴同】 bàntóng accompany

【伴舞】 bànwǔ be a dancing partner

【伴音】 bànyīn 〈*TV*〉 audio

【伴音信号】 bànyīn xìnhào 〈*TV*〉 audio signal

【伴奏】 bànzòu accompany (v.); accompaniment (n.): 由管弦乐队～ with orchestral accompaniment / 我弹钢琴给她～。I accompanied her on the piano.

拌 (bàn) mix; toss: ～色拉 toss the salad

【拌和】 bàn·huò mix and stir; blend

【拌匀】 bànyún mix thoroughly

【拌嘴】 bànzuǐ bicker; squabble; quarrel

绊 (bàn) (cause to) stumble; trip: 给石头～了一跤摔倒了 stumble over a stone and fall down

【绊脚石】 bànjiǎoshí stumbling block; obstacle

扮 (bàn) 1.(指化装) be dressed up as; play the part of; disguise oneself as 2.(指表情) put on (an expression)

【扮相】 bànxiàng the appearance of an actor or actress in costume and makeup

【扮演】 bànyǎn play the part of; act: 他～一个商人。He plays the part of a merchant.

瓣 (bàn) 1.(花瓣) petal 2.(种子或果实的瓣) segment; section 3.(器官的瓣膜) valve; lamella 4.(小块;碎块) fragment; piece: 碎成几～ be broken into pieces

bang

邦[邦] (bāng) nation; state; country: 友～ friendly country; fraternal country

【邦交】 bāngjiāo relations between two countries; diplomatic relations: ～正常化 normalization of diplomatic relations

【邦联】 bānglián confederation

帮[幫] (bāng) 1.(帮助) help; assist: 我～你拿行李好吗? May I help you with your luggage? 2.(船帮;车帮) side (of a boat, truck, etc.) 3.(菜帮子) outer leaf (of cabbage, etc.) 4.(集团;群伙) gang; band; clique

【帮倒忙】 bāng dàománg be more of a hindrance than a help

【帮工】 bānggōng 1.(帮助干活) help with farm work 2.(帮工的人) helper

【帮会】 bānghuì secret society

【帮教】 bāngjiào help and educate

【帮忙】 bāngmáng help; give a hand; lend a hand: 给某人～ lend one's help to sb. / 她听到这事后,马上过来帮我的忙。When she heard of it, she immediately came to my help.

【帮派】 bāngpài faction

【帮腔】 bāngqiāng speak in support of sb.; echo sb.; chime in with sb.

【帮手】 bāng·shou helper; assistant

【帮凶】 bāngxiōng accomplice; accessory

【帮佣】 bāngyōng 1.(做佣工) work as a help 2.(佣工) (hired) help; lady help (f.)

【帮主】 bāngzhǔ head of a secret society

【帮助】 bāngzhù help; assist; aid: 在…的～下 with the help of sb. / ～他克服困难 help him over his difficulties

【帮助菜单】 bāngzhù càidān 〈*Computer*〉 help menu

【帮子】 bāng·zi 1.(菜帮子) outer leaf (of

cabbage, etc.) **2.**(鞋帮) upper of a shoe

绑(bǎng) bind; tie

【绑架】 bǎngjià **1.**(劫持) kidnap **2.**〈*Agric.*〉 staking

【绑架者】 bǎngjiàzhě kidnapper; kidnaper

【绑腿】 bǎngtuǐ leg wrappings; puttee

榜(bǎng) **1.**(名单) a list of names posted up **2.**(文告) announcement; notice

【榜样】 bǎngyàng example; model: 给我们树立了～ set an example to us

膀(bǎng) **1.**(胳膊) upper arm; arm **2.**(肩膀) shoulder **3.**(翅膀) wing (of a bird)

(另见"膀"pāng, páng)

【膀臂】 bǎngbì **1.**(胳膊) upper arm; arm **2.**(得力助手) reliable helper; right-hand man

【膀子】 bǎng·zi **1.**(胳膊) upper arm; arm: 光着～ stripped to the waist **2.**(翅膀) wing

蚌(bàng) freshwater mussel; clam

棒(bàng) **1.**(棍) stick; club; cudgel **2.**(好;强) good; fine; excellent; strong: 画儿画得～ paint a good hand

【棒球】 bàngqiú baseball

【棒球场】 bàngqiúchǎng baseball field

【棒球帽】 bàngqiúmào baseball cap

【棒子】 bàng·zi **1.**(棍子) stick; club; cudgel **2.**(玉米) maize; corn

傍(bàng) draw near; be close to: ～水 be close to a river

【傍晚】 bàngwǎn toward evening; at nightfall; at dusk

磅(bàng) **1.**(重量单位) pound **2.**(磅秤) scale; scales: 浴室～ bathroom scale **3.**(称重量) weigh: ～体重 weigh oneself or sb. on the scales **4.**〈*Printing*〉 point (type): 8～字 8-point type

(另见"磅"páng)

【磅秤】 bàngchèng platform scale; platform balance

镑(bàng) pound (符号为: £): 英～ pound sterling

bao

包(bāo) **1.**(包起来) wrap: 他把礼物～好,并扎上丝带。He wrapped (up) the present and tied with ribbon. **2.**(包好的包) bundle; package; pack; packet; parcel **3.**(袋子) bag; sack **4.**(承包) farm out: 我们必须把许多活儿～出去。We have to farm out a lot of work. **5.**(肿起的包) protuberance; swelling; lump **6.**(包围) surround; encircle; envelop **7.**(包括) include; contain **8.**(承担) undertake the whole thing **9.**(担保) assure; guarantee **10.**(包租) hire; charter: ～一架专机 charter a plane / ～一桌酒席 order a feast

【包办】 bāobàn take care of everything concerning a job; run the whole show; monopolize everything

【包庇】 bāobì shield; harbor; cover up: 互相～ shield each other / 在…的～下 under the cover up of ...

【包产】 bāochǎn make a production contract; take full responsibility for output quotas

【包产到户】 bāochǎn dàohù fixing of farm output quotas to the household

【包产田】 bāochǎntián contracted field

【包抄】 bāochāo outflank; envelop: ～敌军 outflank the enemy armies

【包抄运动】 bāochāo yùndòng 〈*Mil.*〉 outflanking movement

【包车】 bāochē a charter car

【包乘组】 bāochéngzǔ 〈*Railway*〉(responsible) crew

【包饭】 bāofàn board at; get or supply meals at a fixed rate

【包袱】 bāofu **1.**(包袱皮儿) cloth-wrappers **2.**(布包) a bundle wrapped in cloth **3.**(负担) load; weight; burden; millstone round one's neck

【包袱皮儿】 bāo·fupír cloth-wrappers

【包干】 bāogān be responsible for a task until it is completed: 分片～ divide up the work and assign a part to each individual or group / 经费～ take responsibility for one's funding needs after receiving fixed allocations

【包干制】 bāogānzhì a system of fixed amount of tax and profit according to the contract

【包工】 bāogōng **1.**(承包任务) contract for a job **2.**(包工头) labor contractor

【包工包料】 bāogōng bāoliào contract for labor and material
【包工头】 bāogōngtóu labor contractor
【包裹】 bāoguǒ 1.(包;包扎) wrap up; bind up 2.(包好的包) bundle; package; parcel: 包好～ wrap a parcel / 解开～ undo a parcel
【包含】 bāohán contain; embody; include: 他的发言～了他的全部论点。His statement embraces all his arguments.
【包涵】 bāo·han 〈*politeness*〉 excuse; forgive; bear with
【包机】 bāojī a chartered plane
【包括】 bāokuò include; consist of; comprise; incorporate: 这发票～了税款和服务费用。The bill includes tax and service.
【包揽】 bāolǎn undertake the whole thing; take on everything
【包罗】 bāoluó include; cover; embrace
【包罗万象】 bāoluó-wànxiàng all-inclusive; all-embracing
【包赔】 bāopéi guarantee to pay compensations
【包皮】 bāopí 1.〈*Anat.*〉 prepuce 2.(包袱皮) wrapper
【包围】 bāowéi 1.(四面围住) surround; encircle: 今天清早,全副武装的警察～了大楼。Early this morning, armed police were surrounding the building. 2.(包围圈) ring of encirclement: 冲出～ break through a ring of encirclement
【包围圈】 bāowéiquān ring of encirclement
【包席】 bāoxí order a feast
【包厢】 bāoxiāng box
【包销】 bāoxiāo have exclusive selling rights; be the sole agent for a production unit or a firm
【包销协议】 bāoxiāo xiéyì exclusive sales agreement
【包圆儿】 bāoyuánr 1.(全部买下) buy the whole lot 2.(全部承担) finish up; finish off
【包扎】 bāozā wrap up; bind up; pack: ～伤口 bind up a wound
【包装】 bāozhuāng pack; package
【包装箱】 bāozhuāngxiāng packing box; packing case
【包装纸】 bāozhuāngzhǐ packing paper
【包子】 bāo·zi baozi; steamed stuffed bun: 肉～ steamed bun with meat stuffing
【包租】 bāozū charter: ～一条船 charter a boat

胞(bāo) 1.(胞衣) afterbirth 2.(同胞) born of the same parents
【胞兄弟】 bāoxiōngdì blood brothers
【胞衣】 bāoyī afterbirth

剥(bāo) shell; peel; skin: ～豆 shell the peas
(另见“剥”bō)
【剥皮】 bāopí skin; peel off the skin

褒[**襃**](bāo) praise; honor; commend
【褒贬】 bāobiǎn 1.(评论) pass judgment on; appraise; make comment 2.(批评;指责) speak ill of; cry down
【褒奖】 bāojiǎng praise and honor; commend and award
【褒扬】 bāoyáng praise; commend
【褒义】 bāoyì commendation; commendatory (adj.): ～和贬义 commendation and derogation
【褒义词】 bāoyìcí commendatory term

雹(báo) hail
【雹灾】 báozāi disaster caused by hail
【雹子】 báo·zi hail; hailstone

薄(báo) 1.(与“厚”相对) thin; flimsy: 一本～书 a thin book / 一件～上衣 a thin jacket 2.(淡) weak; light 3.(冷淡) lacking in warmth; cold 4.(不肥沃) infertile; poor
(另见“薄”bó, bò)
【薄钢板】 báogāngbǎn steel sheet
【薄壳】 báoké 〈*Archit.*〉 shell
【薄壳建筑】 báoké jiànzhù shell construction
【薄壳屋顶】 báoké wūdǐng shell roof
【薄膜】 báomó membrane; film: 透明～ transparent membrane / 塑料～ plastic film
【薄片】 báopiàn slice; flake
【薄田】 báotián infertile soil

饱(bǎo) 1.(吃饱) have eaten one's fill; be full; have enough 2.(饱满) full; plump 3.(充分地) fully; to the full 4.(满足) satisfy
【饱和】 bǎohé 1.(指溶液) saturation (n.); saturate (v.) 2.(指达到最高限度) saturate:

在美国市场～后，他们开始注意欧洲。Since the US market has now been saturated, they are looking to Europe.

【饱和溶液】 bǎohé róngyè saturated solution

【饱经沧桑】 bǎojīng-cāngsāng have seen much of the changes in human life; have been through the vicissitudes of life

【饱经风霜】 bǎojīng-fēngshuāng weather-beaten; having experienced the hardships of life

【饱满】 bǎomǎn full; plump

宝［寳、寶］(bǎo) 1.(珍宝) treasure: 无价之～ priceless treasure 2.(珍贵的) precious; treasured

【宝贝】 bǎobèi 1.(珍贵之物) treasured object; treasure 2.(爱称) darling; baby

【宝塔】 bǎotǎ 1.(佛塔) pagoda 2.(指对方寺庙) your temple; your monastery

【宝刀】 bǎodāo precious sword; treasured sword

【宝贵】 bǎoguì valuable; precious

【宝号】 bǎohào 1.(指对方店铺) your shop 2.(指对方名字) your name

【宝剑】 bǎojiàn a double-edged sword

【宝眷】 bǎojuàn 1.(指对方妻子) your wife 2.(指对方妻子儿女) your family

【宝库】 bǎokù treasure-house: 知识～ treasure-house of ideas

【宝瓶宫】 Bǎopínggōng 〈*Astron*.〉 Aquarius (1月21日至2月19日): 生于～ be born under Aquarius

【宝瓶座】 Bǎopíngzuò 〈*Astron*.〉 Aquarius

【宝石】 bǎoshí precious stone; gem

【宝塔】 bǎotǎ pagoda

【宝藏】 bǎozàng precious (mineral) deposits

【宝座】 bǎozuò throne

保(bǎo) 1.(保护;保卫) protect; defend 2.(保持) keep; maintain; preserve 3.(保证) guarantee; ensure 4.(担保) stand guarantor for sb.; stand surety for sb. 5.(保人) guarantor

【保安】 bǎo'ān ensure public security; ensure safety

【保安措施】 bǎo'ān cuòshī security measures

【保安公司】 bǎo'ān gōngsī safety ensuring service company

【保安人员】 bǎo'ān rényuán security personnel

【保安族】 Bǎo'ānzú Bonan (中国少数民族，主要分布在甘肃)

【保本】 bǎoběn ensure not to lose capital investment

【保镖】 bǎobiāo bodyguard; escort

【保不住】 bǎo·bu zhù most likely; more likely than not; may well: ～会下雪。Most likely it's going to snow.

【保藏】 bǎocáng keep in store; preserve

【保持】 bǎochí keep; maintain; preserve: ～廉洁 maintain the cleanness / ～长期稳定 maintain a long-term stability

【保存】 bǎocún preserve; conserve; keep: ～精力 conserve one's vitality

【保单】 bǎodān 1.(保证凭证) guarantee slip; guarantee form 2.(保险单据) insurance policy

【保底】 bǎodǐ guarantee the minimum: 下不～ no guarantee for the minimum

【保管】 bǎoguǎn 1.(保藏) take care of: 我外出期间，请你～好我的书。Please take care of my books for me while I am away. 2.(担保) certainly; surely

【保管员】 bǎoguǎnyuán storeman; stockman; storekeeper

【保护】 bǎohù protect; safeguard; protection (n.): 劳动～ labor safety protection

【保护措施】 bǎohù cuòshī safeguarding (protective)

【保护国】 bǎohùguó protectorate

【保护人】 bǎohùrén guardian

【保护伞】 bǎohùsǎn umbrella; protective umbrella

【保护色】 bǎohùsè protective coloration

【保护主义】 bǎohù zhǔyì protectionism

【保皇党】 bǎohuángdǎng royalists

【保价】 bǎojià support value

【保驾】 bǎojià escort the Emperor

【保健】 bǎojiàn health protection; health care: 妇幼～ maternal and child hygiene; mother and child care

【保健护士】 bǎojiàn hù·shi health nurse

【保健食品】 bǎojiàn shípǐn health food

【保健站】 bǎojiànzhàn health station; health center

【保教】 bǎojiào nursing and teaching

【保教人员】 bǎojiào rényuán child care worker

【保龄球】 bǎolíngqiú 1.(指运动) bowling; tenpin bowling: 我兄弟最近打起～来了。My brother has recently taken up bowling. 2.(指球) bowl; bowling bowl

【保龄球球道】 bǎolíngqiú qiúdào bowling alley

【保留】 bǎoliú 1.(保存) continue to have; retain: ～军队 retain armed forces 2.(不赞同) hold back; keep back; reserve: 持～意见 have reservations / 毫无～地同意 agree without reservation

【保留剧目】 bǎoliú jùmù repertory; repertoire

【保留内存】 bǎoliú nèicún 〈*Computer*〉 reserved memory

【保留条款】 bǎoliú tiáokuǎn reservation clause

【保密】 bǎomì maintain secrecy; keep sth. secret

【保密文件】 bǎomì wénjiàn classified document

【保姆】 bǎomǔ 1.(照顾小孩的) (children's) nurse 2.(做家务的) housekeeper; lady help

【保暖】 bǎonuǎn keep warm

【保全】 bǎoquán 1.(使不受损失) save from damage; preserve: ～名誉 preserve one's reputation 2.(保养;维修) maintain; keep in good repair

【保全工】 bǎoquángōng maintenance worker

【保人】 bǎorén 1.(保释担保人) bail; bailman 2.(保证人) sponsor

【保释】 bǎoshì 〈*Law*〉 release on bail; bail out; bail (n.): 请求朋友把他～出来 ask friends to bail him out / 他获准～。He was granted bail.

【保释金】 bǎoshìjīn 〈*Law*〉 bail

【保守】 bǎoshǒu 1.(保持) guard; keep 2.(守旧的) conservative

【保守疗法】 bǎoshǒu liáofǎ conservative treatment

【保税区】 bǎoshuìqū bonded area; free-trade zone; tariff-free zone

【保送】 bǎosòng recommend sb. for admission to school, etc.

【保外就医】 bǎowài jiùyī be released on bail for medical treatment

【保外执行】 bǎowài zhíxíng serve a sentence on bail

【保卫】 bǎowèi defend; safeguard

【保卫科】 bǎowèikē security section

【保温杯】 bǎowēnbēi vacuum cup

【保温瓶】 bǎowēnpíng vacuum flask; vacuum bottle; thermos

【保温桶】 bǎowēntǒng heat-preserving container

【保鲜】 bǎoxiān keep fresh

【保鲜膜】 bǎoxiānmó wrap; wrapper

【保险】 bǎoxiǎn 1.(保险业务) insurance; assurance; insure (v.): 人身～ life insurance / 航空运输～ air transportation insurance / 保全险 insurance against all risks / 给房子保了火险 insure one's house against fire / 所有家产都保了意外损失险。All household goods are insured against accidental damage. 2.(稳妥) safe (adj.); safety (n.): 为了～起见,把钱存入银行 deposit money in a bank for safety / 把它放到～的地方。Keep it in a safe place. 3.(保证;担保) be sure; be bound to

【保险单】 bǎoxiǎndān insurance policy

【保险刀】 bǎoxiǎndāo safety razor

【保险法】 bǎoxiǎnfǎ insurance law

【保险范围】 bǎoxiǎn fànwéi insurance coverage

【保险费】 bǎoxiǎnfèi (insurance) premium

【保险杠】 bǎoxiǎngàng bumper

【保险公司】 bǎoxiǎn gōngsī insurance company

【保险柜】 bǎoxiǎnguì safe: 撬开～ break a safe / 把首饰放在～里。Put the jewelry in the safe.

【保险金】 bǎoxiǎnjīn insurance: 他得到了3万元的～。He received 30,000 yuan insurance.

【保险金额】 bǎoxiǎn jīn'é sum insured; insurance amount; insured amount

【保险期】 bǎoxiǎnqī insurance period

【保险丝】 bǎoxiǎnsī 〈*Electr.*〉 fuse; fuse-wire

【保险丝盒】 bǎoxiǎnsīhé fuse box

【保险箱】 bǎoxiǎnxiāng safe; strong-box; safe-deposit box

【保险业】 bǎoxiǎnyè insurance business
【保险业务】 bǎoxiǎn yèwù insurance services
【保险责任】 bǎoxiǎn zérèn insured liability
【保修】 bǎoxiū guarantee to keep sth. in good repair; guarantee (n.)：这台计算机～三年。This computer is guaranteed for three year. / 这台录像机有两年的～。The video recorder has (或 comes with) a two-year guarantee.
【保修单】 bǎoxiūdān guarantee statement
【保修期】 bǎoxiūqī guarantee period：尚在～内 be still under guarantee
【保养】 bǎoyǎng 1.(指人) take good care of (one's health)：～身体 take good care of one's health 2.(指机械) maintain; keep in good repair; maintenance (n.)：设备的～ maintenance of equipment / 这车～得很糟糕。The car have been very poorly maintained.
【保佑】 bǎoyòu bless and protect
【保育】 bǎoyù child care; child welfare
【保育员】 bǎoyùyuán nurse; child-care worker
【保育院】 bǎoyùyuàn nursery school
【保障】 bǎozhàng ensure; guarantee; safeguard：提供充分的法律～ give full legal protection
【保真度】 bǎozhēndù 〈*Electron.*〉 fidelity：高～ high fidelity
【保证】 bǎozhèng 1.(担保) guarantee; assure; ensure：～顾客满意 guarantee satisfaction to customers / ～货币正常流通 ensure normal money circulation / 我向你～没危险。I assure you there's no danger. / 证人向法官～他说的是真话。The witness assured the judge that he was telling the truth. 2.(确保应有标准) guarantee：～质量 guarantee the quality 3.(起保证作用) guarantee; guaranty：拒绝作出～ refuse to give guarantee / 提供银行～ give a banker's guarantee / 产品质量是商业成功的～。The quality of products is a guarantee of commercial success.
【保证金】 bǎozhèngjīn guaranty money
【保证人】 bǎozhèngrén 1.(担保人) guarantor 2.(保释人) bail; recognizance
【保证书】 bǎozhèngshū letter of guarantee; guarantee; guaranty; written pledge
【保值】 bǎozhí inflation proof
【保值储蓄】 bǎozhí chǔxù inflation proof savings deposit
【保重】 bǎozhòng take care of oneself

堡 (bǎo) fort; fortress

【堡垒】 bǎolěi fort; fortress; stronghold; block- house

报[報] (bào) 1.(报告) report; announce; declare 2.(回答) reply; respond; reciprocate 3.(报答) recompense; requite 4.(报纸) newspaper：日～ daily paper / 晚～ evening paper 5.(刊物) periodical; journal：学～ college journal 6.(报道;墙报) bulletin; report 7.(电报) telegram; cable

【报案】 bào'àn report a case to the security authorities
【报表】 bàobiǎo report forms
【报偿】 bàocháng repay; recompense; refund：没有得到任何～ get no recompense at all
【报呈】 bàochéng present; send in
【报仇】 bàochóu revenge; avenge：为兄弟～ avenge one's brother
【报酬】 bào·chou reward; pay; remuneration：不计～ not concerned about pay / 索要～ claim pay / 他的～丰厚。He was amply paid.
【报答】 bàodá repay; requite：～某人的好意 repay sb. for his kindness
【报导】 bàodǎo 见"报道"
【报到】 bàodào report for duty; check in at; register
【报道】 bàodào 1.(发布新闻) report (news); cover：～会议情况 cover the conference / 据～ it is reported that / 中国报纸广泛地～了这一事件。The press in China widely reported the event. 2.(新闻稿) news report; story：据～ The report goes that / 根据后来的～ according to later reports / 根据来自上海的～ according to a report from Shanghai
【报端】 bàoduān in a newspaper
【报废】 bàofèi report sth. as worthless; scrap; discard as useless：～一辆汽车 scrap a

car

【报复】 bào·fù make reprisals; retaliate

【报复行为】 bào·fù xíngwéi vindictive act

【报复性措施】 bào·fùxìng cuòshī retaliatory measures

【报复性关税】 bào·fùxìng guānshuì retaliatory tariffs

【报告】 bàogào 1.(告诉) report; make known: 向上级～ report to the higher authorities 2.(讲演) report; speech; talk; lecture: 做～ make a speech; give a talk 3.(书面申请或总结) report: 调查～ investigation report / 打～ give a report

【报告会】 bàogàohuì public lecture

【报告人】 bàogàorén speaker; lecturer

【报告文学】 bàogào wénxué reportage

【报关】 bàoguān declare sth. at customs; apply to customs; customs declaration (n.): ～物品 goods to declare / 您有什么要～吗? Anything to declare? / 没有要～的东西。Nothing to declare.

【报关单】 bàoguāndān customs declaration

【报关费】 bàoguānfèi customs fees

【报国】 bàoguó dedicate oneself to the service of one's country: 以身～ devote one's life to one's country

【报户口】 bàohùkǒu apply for a residence permit

【报话】 bàohuà speak on one's walkie-talkie: 警察用报话机向总部～。The policeman was speaking to HQ on his walkie-talkie.

【报话机】 bàohuàjī walkie-talkie

【报价】 bàojià 1.(指行为) offer; quote; quotation (n.): 报优惠价 quote favorable terms / 建筑师～8,000万元建这个大楼。The architect has quoted 80,000,000 yuan to build the building. 2.(指价目) offer; offering: "你能把那幅画卖给我吗?" "你～是多少?" "Would you sell me that painting?" "What are you offering for it?" / 这是非常优惠的～。This is a very kind offer.

【报界】 bàojiè the press; journalistic circles: 向～发表谈话 make a statement to the press

【报警】 bàojǐng report (an incident) to the police; give an alarm: 报火警 raise an alarm for a fire

【报警装置】 bàojǐng zhuāngzhì warning device; alarm device

【报刊】 bàokān newspapers and periodicals; the press

【报刊订阅单】 bàokān dìngyuèdān subscription order form (for newspapers and periodicals)

【报刊广告】 bàokān guǎnggào press advertising

【报刊亭】 bàokāntíng news-stand

【报考】 bàokǎo enter oneself for an examination: ～清华 apply for entrance to Tsinghua University

【报名】 bàomíng enter one's name; sign up

【报名单】 bàomíngdān entry form; application form

【报幕】 bàomù announce the items on a (theatrical) program

【报幕员】 bàomùyuán announcer

【报批】 bàopī submit sth. for approval

【报社】 bàoshè general office of a newspaper; newspaper office

【报失】 bàoshī report the loss of sth. to the authorities concerned

【报时】 bàoshí give the correct time

【报时信号】 bàoshí xìnhào time signal

【报数】 bàoshù 1.(报告数目) number off 2.(口令) Count off!

【报税】 bàoshuì declare dutiable goods; make a statement of dutiable goods

【报摊】 bàotān news-stand; news stall

【报务员】 bàowùyuán telegraph operator; radio operator

【报喜】 bàoxǐ announce good news; report success

【报喜不报忧】 bàoxǐ bù bàoyōu report only the good news concealing what is unpleasant

【报销】 bàoxiāo 1.(报销账目) submit an expense account; apply for reimbursement 2.(报废销账) hand in a list of expended articles 3.(消灭) write off; wipe out

【报效】 bàoxiào render service to repay sb.'s kindness

【报信】 bàoxìn notify; inform: 通风～ tip off information

【报应】 bàoyìng 〈*Relig.*〉 retribution; judgment

【报章】 bàozhāng newspapers

【报章杂志】 bàozhāng zázhì newspapers and magazines

【报账】 bàozhàng render an account; submit an expense account; apply for reimbursement

【报纸】 bàozhǐ 1.(报) newspaper 2.(白报纸) newsprint

刨[鉋、鑤] (bào) 1.(刨光;刨平) plane sth. down; plane: 把镜框的边儿～光。Plane the edge of the frame smooth. 2.(刨子或刨床) plane; planer; planing machine

(另见"刨"páo)

【刨床】 bàochuáng planer; planing machine

【刨刀】 bàodāo planer tool

【刨工】 bàogōng 1.(指活计) planing 2.(指工人) planing machine operator

【刨花】 bàohuā wood shavings

【刨子】 bào·zi plane

抱 (bào) 1.(用手抱) hold or carry in the arms; embrace; hug: ～小孩 take a child in one's arms 2.(初次得到) have one's first child or grandchild 3.(领养) adopt (a child) 4.(结合在一起) hang together 5.(抱有) cherish; harbor: ～必胜的信心 hold a firm belief in victory

【抱病】 bàobìng be ill; be in bad health

【抱不平】 bào bùpíng indignant at injustice: 打～ defend sb. against an injustice

【抱单腿拦腿摔】 bào dāntuǐ lán tuǐ shuāi 〈*Wrestling*〉 double leg lock

【抱负】 bàofù aspiration; ambition

【抱恨】 bàohèn have a regret; regret

【抱歉】 bàoqiàn be sorry; feel apologetic; regret: 对此我感到～。I'm sorry for it.

【抱屈】 bàoqū feel wronged; feel being treated unfairly

【抱头痛哭】 bàotóu-tòngkū weep in each other's arms; cry on each other's shoulder

【抱养】 bàoyǎng adopt (a child)

【抱怨】 bào·yuàn complain; grumble: ～某人 complain about sb. / 我没有什么可～的。I have nothing to complain of (或 about).

鲍 (bào)

【鲍鱼】 bàoyú 1.(咸鱼) salted fish 2.(软体动物) abalone

豹 (bào) leopard; panther ‖ 金钱豹 leopard / 美洲豹 jaguar / 黑豹 black panther

暴 (bào) 1.(突然、猛烈) sudden and violent 2.(凶暴) cruel; savage; fierce 3.(急躁) short-tempered; hot-tempered 4.(鼓起来) stick out; stand out; bulge: 青筋～出。Veins stick out.

【暴病】 bàobìng sudden attack of a serious illness: 得～ be suddenly seized with a severe illness

【暴跌】 bàodiē steep fall (in price); slump: 股票价格～ a slump in the prices of stocks

【暴动】 bàodòng insurrection; rebellion: 武装～ armed insurrection

【暴发】 bàofā 1.(突然发作) break out 2.(突然发财) suddenly become rich or important; get rich quick

【暴发户】 bàofāhù upstart

【暴风】 bàofēng storm wind; storm (force 11 wind)

【暴风雪】 bàofēngxuě snowstorm; blizzard

【暴风雨】 bàofēngyǔ rainstorm; storm; tempest

【暴风骤雨】 bàofēng-zhòuyǔ fierce storm; tempest

【暴君】 bàojūn tyrant; despot

【暴力】 bàolì violence; force: 采用～ resort to violence

【暴利】 bàolì sudden huge profits: 牟取～ reap staggering profits; reap colossal profits

【暴露】 bàolù expose; reveal; lay bare

【暴露无遗】 bàolù-wúyí be thoroughly exposed; be fully revealed

【暴乱】 bàoluàn riot; rebellion; revolt: 平息～ put down a riot; suppress a riot; put down a revolt

【暴民】 bàomín rioter; rebel

【暴怒】 bàonù violent rage; fury

【暴跳如雷】 bàotiào-rúléi stamp with fury; fly into a rage: 他很容易～。He is liable to break out into furious passions.

【暴徒】 bàotú rioter; ruffian; thug

【暴行】 bàoxíng savage act; atrocity; outrage: 战争～ war atrocity / 犯下了一桩桩～ commit one atrocity after another

【暴雨】 bàoyǔ torrential rain; rainstorm

【暴躁】 bàozào irascible; irritable

【暴涨】 bàozhǎng rise suddenly and sharply

【暴政】 bàozhèng tyranny; despotic rule

【暴卒】 bàozú die of a sudden illness; die suddenly

曝(bào) expose to the sun
(另见"曝"pù)

【曝光】 bàoguāng 1.〈*Photog*.〉 expose; exposure (n.): 已～的胶片 exposed film 2.(揭露) expose; reveal to the public: 丑闻被报纸曝了光。The scandal was exposed by the press.

【曝光表】 bàoguāngbiǎo 〈*Photog*.〉 exposure meter; light meter

【曝光不足】 bàoguāng bùzú 〈*Photog*.〉 underexposure; underexposed

【曝光过度】 bàoguāng guòdù 〈*Photog*.〉 overexposure; over-exposed

【曝光宽容度】 bàoguāng kuānróngdù 〈*Photog*.〉 exposure latitude

【曝露】 bàolù exposed to the open air

爆(bào) 1.(猛然破裂) explode; burst; blew: 车胎～了。The tire blew out. 2.(用猛火炒菜) quick-fry; quick-boil

【爆发】 bàofā erupt; burst out; break out; eruption (n.): 火山～ volcanic eruption / 火山突然～了。The volcano burst out. / 全场～出雷鸣般的掌声。The entire hall burst into thunderous applauses. / 第二次世界大战是什么时候～的? When did the Second World War break out?

【爆发变星】 bàofā biànxīng 〈*Astron*.〉 cataclysmic variable; explosive variable

【爆冷门】 bàolěngmén be a surprise; be an unexpected results

【爆满】 bàomǎn overflowing audience

【爆棚】 bàopéng 见"爆满"

【爆破】 bàopò blow up; demolish; dynamite; blast

【爆玉米花】 bào yùmǐhuā popcorn

【爆炸】 bàozhà 1.(弹药等爆炸) explode; blow up; detonate; explosion (n.): 核～ nuclear explosion / 炸弹～了。The bomb exploded. / 汽车～了。The car blew up. 2.(指数量剧增) explode; explosion: 人口～ a population explosion

【爆炸物】 bàozhàwù explosives; explosive article

【爆炸性】 bàozhàxìng explosive: 大学生数量的～增长 explosive increase in the number of students

【爆炸性新闻】 bàozhàxìng xīnwén explosive news; startling news

【爆竹】 bàozhú firecracker: 放～ let off firecrackers

bei

杯[盃](bēi) 1.(杯子;杯) cup: 茶～ tea cup / 啤酒～ beer mug / 咖啡～ coffee cup / 塑料～ plastic cup / 纸～ paper cup / 一～茶 a cup of tea / 一份～碟 a cup and saucer 2.(一杯之量) cupful: 两满～牛奶 two cupfuls of milk 3.(锦杯) (prize) cup; trophy: 金～ golden cup / 1996年世界～赛谁赢了? Who won the 1996 World Cup?

【杯赛】 bēisài Cup: 世界～ World Cup

【杯水车薪】 bēishuǐ-chēxīn an utterly inadequate measure

【杯中物】 bēizhōngwù alcoholic drink

【杯子】 bēi·zi cup; glass

卑(bēi) 1.(低下) low 2.(低劣) inferior

【卑鄙】 bēibǐ base; mean; despicable; crooked: ～诽谤 mean slander / ～手段 crooked ways / ～行为 despicable action

【卑鄙无耻】 bēibǐ-wúchǐ mean and shameless

【卑躬屈节】 bēigōng-qūjié bow and scrape; act servilely; cringe; act obsequiously

【卑贱】 bēijiàn 1.(地位低下) lowly 2.(卑鄙下贱) mean and low

【卑劣】 bēiliè base; mean; despicable: ～的手法 a mean trick; a despicable trick

碑(bēi) monument; tablet; stele: 人民英雄纪念～ the Monument to the People's Heroes

【碑帖】 bēitiè a rubbing from a stone inscription

【碑文】 bēiwén an inscription on a tablet

背[揹](bēi) 1.(背负) carry on the back 2.(负担) bear; shoulder (responsibility; burden; etc.)
(另见"背"bèi)

【背包袱】 bēi bāo·fu have a weight on one's

mind; have a load on one's mind

【背带】 bēidài 1.（裙、裤的）braces; suspenders 2.（枪的）sling 3.（背包的）straps

【背带扣】 bēidàikòu suspender clip

【背负】 bēifù bear; carry on the back; have on one's shoulder

【背黑锅】 bēi hēiguō be unjustly blamed; take the blame for sb.

【背债】 bēizhài be in debt; be saddled with debts

悲（bēi） 1.（悲伤）sad; sorrowful; melancholy 2.（怜悯）compassion

【悲哀】 bēi'āi grieved; sorrowful

【悲惨】 bēicǎn miserable; tragic：～的结局 tragic ending

【悲愤】 bēifèn grief and indignation

【悲歌】 bēigē 1.（指歌曲）elegy; dirge; threnody 2.（指歌唱）sing with solemn fervor

【悲观】 bēiguān pessimistic：～失望 feel disheartened / 医生们对他康复的可能很～。The doctors are pessimistic about his chances of recovery.

【悲观主义】 bēiguān zhǔyì pessimism; pessimistic (adj.)

【悲欢离合】 bēihuān-líhé joys and sorrows, partings and reunions; vicissitudes of life

【悲剧】 bēijù 1.〈*Theatre*〉tragedy：莎士比亚的三大～包括《哈姆雷特》、《李尔王》和《奥塞罗》。Shakespeare's tragedies include "Hamlet", "King Lear" and "Othello". 2.（不幸遭遇）tragedy; a very sad event：个人～ personal tragedy 3.（不幸的）tragic

【悲伤】 bēishāng sad; sorrowful

【悲叹】 bēitàn sign mournfully; lament

【悲痛】 bēitòng grieved; sorrowful：如果一个人很～，他（她）应该设法把它说出来。If someone is grieved, he or she needs to find ways of talking about it.

【悲喜交集】 bēixǐ-jiāojí mixed feelings of grief and joy; grief and joy intermingled

【悲喜剧】 bēixǐjù 〈*Theatre*〉tragicomedy; tragicomic (adj.)

【悲壮】 bēizhuàng solemn and stirring; moving and tragic

北（běi） north; northern

【北半球】 běibànqiú the Northern Hemisphere

【北冰洋】 Běibīngyáng Arctic Ocean; Arctic (adj.)

【北大西洋】 Běidàxīyáng North Atlantic

【北大西洋公约组织】 Běidàxīyáng Gōngyuē Zǔzhī North Atlantic Treaty Organization (NATO)

【北斗星】 běidǒuxīng the Big Dipper; the Plough

【北伐战争】 Běifá Zhànzhēng the Northern Expedition

【北方】 běifāng 1.（北）north 2.（北部地区）the northern part of the country; the North：～的风俗习惯 northern habits and customs

【北房】 běifáng a room with a southern exposure

【北非】 Běi Fēi North Africa; North African (adj.)

【北海】 Běihǎi North Sea

【北回归线】 běihuíguīxiàn 〈*Geog.*〉the Tropic of Cancer

【北极】 běijí 1.（北极地区）the Arctic 2.（地极）the North Pole; the Arctic Pole 3.（北磁极）the north magnetic pole

【北极地区】 běijí dìqū the Arctic regions

【北极狐】 běijíhú Arctic fox; white fox

【北极圈】 běijíquān the Arctic Circle

【北极星】 běijíxīng Polaris; the polestar

【北极熊】 běijíxióng polar bear

【北京时间】 Běijīng shíjiān Beijing time

【北美洲】 Běi Měizhōu North America; North American (adj.)

【北南对话】 Běi-Nán duìhuà North-South dialog

【北上】 běishàng northwards; northward：外出的短工随着收获的季节～。Migrant worker follow the harvest northwards.

【北纬】 běiwěi 〈*Geog.*〉north latitude：～41度10分 latitude 41 degrees 10 minutes north / 我们的位置在～39.9度，东经116.4度。Our position is latitude 39.9 degrees north; longitude 116.4 degrees east

【北温带】 běiwēndài the North Temperate Zone

【北洋军阀】 Běi Yáng Jūnfá 〈*Hist.*〉the Northern Warlords

【北约】 Běi Yuē 〈*abbr*.〉 NATO（北大西洋公约组织）

贝［貝］（bèi） 1.（软体动物）shellfish 2.（古代贝壳货币）cowrie

【贝雕】 bèidiāo 〈*Art*〉 shell carving

【贝尔湖】 Bèi'ěrhú 〈place〉 Buir Nur

【贝壳】 bèiké shell

【贝塔节律】 bèitǎ jiélǜ 〈*Physiol*.〉 beta rhythm; beta waves

【贝塔粒子】 bèitǎ lìzǐ beta particle

【贝塔射线】 bèitǎ shèxiàn beta ray

钡（bèi） 〈*Chem*.〉 barium（元素符号 Ba）

【钡餐】 bèicān 〈*Med*.〉 barium meal

背（bèi） 1.（脊背）the back of the body 2.（背面）the back of an object 3.（背对着）with the back towards 4.（转过去）turn away 5.（躲避；瞒）hide sth. from; do sth. behind sb's back 6.（背诵）recite from memory; learn by heart; learn by rote: ～课文 learn a lesson by heart 7.（违背；违反）act contrary to; violate; break 8.（听觉不灵）hard of hearing 9.（倒霉）unlucky

（另见"背"bēi）

【背包】 bèibāo backpack; packsack; knapsack

【背道而驰】 bèidào-érchí run in the opposite direction; run counter to

【背地里】 bèidì·lǐ behind sb.'s back; privately; on the sly

【背对背】 bèiduìbèi 1.（背靠背）back to back 2.（不当面）behind sb.'s back

【背风】 bèifēng out of the wind; on the lee side; leeward

【背光】 bèiguāng be in a poor light; do sth. with one's back to the light

【背后】 bèihòu 1.（后面）behind; at the back; in the rear 2.（不当面）behind sb.'s back: ～说坏话 backbite; speak ill of sb. behind his back

【背脊】 bèijǐ the back of the body

【背井离乡】 bèijǐng-líxiāng leave one's native place

【背景】 bèijǐng 1.（指布景）background: 舞台～ stage background 2.（指所处环境）background; backdrop: 时代～ background characteristic of times / 历史～ historical background 3.（指背后依仗的力量）background: 家庭～ one's family background / 政治～ political background / 社会～复杂的人 a person with a complex social background

【背景情况】 bèijǐng qíngkuàng background: 提供～ background (v.); supply a background for

【背景音乐】 bèijǐng yīnyuè background music

【背景噪音】 bèijǐng zàoyīn background noise

【背景知识】 bèijǐng zhī·shi cultural background; background information

【背静】 bèi·jing quiet and secluded

【背靠背】 bèikàobèi back to back; back-to-back (adj.)

【背靠垫】 bèikàodiàn back cushion

【背离】 bèilí deviate from; depart from: ～原则 deviate from the principle

【背面】 bèimiàn the back; the reverse side; the wrong side

【背叛】 bèipàn betray; forsake

【背鳍】 bèiqí 〈*Zool*.〉 dorsal fin

【背弃】 bèiqì abandon; desert; renounce: ～诺言 go back on one's word

【背时】 bèishí 1.（不合时宜）behind the times 2.（倒霉）unlucky

【背书】 bèishū 1.（背诵）recite a lesson from memory; repeat a lesson 2.（票据背面的签字）endorsement (on a check)

【背诵】 bèisòng recite; repeat from memory

【背心】 bèixīn a sleeveless garment: 西服～ waistcoat / 汗～ singlet

【背信弃义】 bèixìn-qìyì break faith with sb.; be perfidious

【背阴】 bèiyīn in the shade; shady

【背影】 bèiyǐng a view of sb.'s back; a figure viewed from behind

【背越式跳高】 bèiyuèshì tiàogāo 〈*Sports*〉 back style; Fosbury flop; flop

【背运】 bèiyùn have bad luck; be unlucky

【背着手】 bèi·zhe shǒu with one's hands crossed behind one's back

【背字儿】 bèizìr bad luck; unluck: 我们队这次联赛走～。Our team have had bad luck throughout this series.

备［備、俻］（bèi） 1.（具备）be equipped with; have: 德

才兼～ have both ability and political integrity 2.（备有）prepare; get ready 3.（防备）provide against; prepare against; take precautions against 4.（设备；装备）equipment 5.（完全；尽）fully; in every possible way
【备案】 bèi'àn put on record; put on file; enter (a case) in the records
【备查】 bèichá for future reference
【备而不用】 bèi'érbùyòng have sth. ready just in case; keep sth. for possible future use
【备份】 bèifèn backup
【备耕】 bèigēng make preparations for cultivation
【备荒】 bèihuāng prepare against natural calamities
【备货】 bèihuò get ready the goods
【备件】 bèijiàn spare parts
【备课】 bèikè prepare lessons
【备受欢迎】 bèi shòu huānyíng enjoy great popularity; be very popular
【备胎】 bèitāi 〈*Auto*〉 spare tire
【备忘录】 bèiwànglù 1.（外交文书）memorandum; aide-mémoire 2.（记事本）memorandum book
【备用】 bèiyòng reserve; spare; alternate
【备用轮】 bèiyònglún 〈*Auto*〉 spare wheel
【备用胎】 bèiyòngtāi 〈*Auto*〉 spare tire
【备战】 bèizhàn 1.（准备发动战争）prepare for war 2.（进行抵抗战争的准备）be prepared against war
【备至】 bèizhì to the utmost; in every possible way
【备注】 bèizhù remarks
【备注栏】 bèizhùlán remarks column

倍 (bèi) 1.（倍数）times; -fold 2.（加倍）double; twice as much
【倍低音管】 bèidīyīnguǎn 〈*Music*〉 contrabassoon
【倍加】 bèijiā extraordinarily; extremely; especially: ～爱护 take extra care of / ～小心 be especially careful
【倍率】 bèilǜ multiplying power
【倍数】 bèishù 〈*Math.*〉 multiple
【倍增】 bèizēng multiply; increase greatly in number; multiplication (n.)

被 (bèi) 1.（被子）quilt: 棉～ cotton-wadded quilt 2.〈*prep.*〉〈v. aux.〉（与过去分词连用）be
【被乘数】 bèichéngshù multiplicand
【被除数】 bèichúshù dividend
【被单】 bèidān (bed) sheet
【被动】 bèidòng passive; passivity: 摆脱～ emerge from passivity / 处于～ remain passive / 陷于～ be thrown into passivity
【被服】 bèifú bedding and clothing
【被服厂】 bèifúchǎng clothing factory
【被俘】 bèifú be captured; be taken prisoner
【被告】 bèigào 〈*Law*〉 defendant; the accused
【被告席】 bèigàoxí defendant's seat; dock
【被害人】 bèihàirén the injured party; the victim
【被加数】 bèijiāshù summand
【被减数】 bèijiǎnshù minuend
【被里】 bèilǐ the underneath side of a quilt
【被面】 bèimiàn the facing of a quilt
【被迫】 bèipò be compelled; be forced; be constrained
【被褥】 bèirù bedding; bedclothes
【被套】 bèitào 1.（装被褥的袋子）bedding bag 2.（被罩）quilt cover 3.（被子的棉胎）cotton wadding for a quilt
【被窝儿】 bèiwōr a quilt folded to form a sleeping bag
【被选举权】 bèixuǎnjǔquán the right to be elected
【被罩】 bèizhào quilt cover
【被子】 bèi·zi quilt

辈 (bèi) 1.（某类人）people of a certain kind; the like 2.（辈分）generation: 老一～ the older generation / 下一～ the coming generation; the younger generation 3.（一生）lifetime
【辈出】 bèichū appear one after another; come out in succession: 人才～ people of talent appear successively
【辈分】 bèi·fen seniority in the family or clan; position in the family hierarchy
【辈子】 bèi·zi lifetime: 半～ half a lifetime

ben

奔 (bēn) 1.（急跑）run quickly horse 2.（紧赶）hurry; hasten; rush 3.（逃跑）flee

（另见"奔"bèn）

【奔波】 bēnbō rush about; be busy running about

【奔驰】 bēnchí run quickly; speed

【奔窜】 bēncuàn flee about; scuttle of

【奔放】 bēnfàng bold and unrestrained; untrammelled：热情～ full of enthusiasm

【奔赴】 bēnfù go to; hurry to; rush to：～抗日前线 hurry to the front of the War of Resistance Against Japan

【奔流】 bēnliú 1.（流得很快）flow at great speed; pour 2.（急流的水）racing current

【奔忙】 bēnmáng be busy rushing about; bustle about

【奔命】 bēnmìng rush about on errands; be kept on the run：疲于～ be tired from rushing around (on business)

【奔跑】 bēnpǎo run

【奔逃】 bēntáo flee; run away

【奔腾】 bēnténg 1.（跳跃奔跑）gallop 2.（比喻汹涌）surge forward; roll on in waves：洪水～而下 the floodwater rolled downwards 3.〈*Computer*〉Pentium

【奔泻】 bēnxiè rush down; pour down

【奔逐】 bēnzhú chase; run after

【奔走】 bēnzǒu 1.（急走）run 2.（到处活动）rush about; be busy running about

【奔走呼号】 bēnzǒu-hūháo go around crying for help

【奔走相告】 bēnzǒu-xiānggào spread the news in a hurry; go round telling everyone that ...

锛（bēn） 1.（锛子）adz; adze 2.（用锛子砍）cut with an adz

【锛子】 bēn·zi adz; adze

贲（bēn）

【贲门】 bēnmén 〈*Anat.*〉cardia

本（běn） 1.（根、茎）the root or stem of a plant 2.（根本）foundation; basis; origin 3.（本钱）capital; principal：赔～ lose one's capital 4.（本来）original 5.（自己方面）one's own; native 6.（现今）this; current; present：～月 this month 7.（按照）according to; based on 8.（本子）book; notebook 9.（版本）edition; version：精装～ de luxe edition / 平装～ paperback / 普及～ popular edition / 袖珍～ pocket edition 10.〈*Cinematog.*〉reel; film reel

【本本主义】 běn·běn zhǔyì book worship; bookishness

【本埠】 běnbù local

【本初子午线】 běnchū-zǐwǔxiàn the first meridian; the prime meridian

【本岛】 běndǎo main island

【本地】 běndì 1.（此地）this locality 2.（当地的）local：～风俗 local customs / ～新闻 local items; local news

【本地货】 běndìhuò local goods; native goods

【本分】 běnfèn one's duty：尽～ do one's duty; do one's bit

【本国】 běnguó one's own country

【本国产品】 běnguó chǎnpǐn home products

【本行】 běnháng one's line; one's own profession

【本家】 běnjiā a member of the same clan; a distant relative with the same family name

【本届】 běnjiè current; this year's

【本届毕业生】 běnjiè bìyèshēng this year's graduates

【本金】 běnjīn capital; principal

【本科】 běnkē undergraduate course; regular college course

【本科生】 běnkēshēng undergraduate

【本来】 běnlái 1.（原有的）original 2.（原先）originally; at first 3.（理所当然）it goes without saying; of course

【本垒】 běnlěi 〈*Baseball*〉home base

【本垒板】 běnlěibǎn 〈*Baseball*〉home plate

【本利】 běnlì 1.（资本和利润）investment and profit; capital and profit 2.（本金和利息）principal and interest

【本领】 běnlǐng skill; ability; capability：掌握…的～ master the skills needed in ...

【本名】 běnmíng name

【本命年】 běnmìngnián year of one's symbolic animal

【本末倒置】 běnmò-dàozhì take the branch for the root; put the incidental before the fundamental; put the cart before the horse

【本能】 běnnéng instinct; innate ability; intuition：好奇～ instinct of curiosity

【本年度】 běnniándù this year; the current year

【本钱】 bĕn·qián capital
【本人】 bĕnrén I; me; myself; oneself; in person
【本色】 bĕnsè 1.（本来面貌）true qualities; inherent qualities; distinctive character 2.（原来的颜色）natural color
【本身】 bĕnshēn itself; in itself
【本事】 bĕnshì 1.（故事情节）source material; original story 2.（本领）skill; ability; capability
【本题】 bĕntí the subject under discussion; the point at issue
【本土】 bĕntŭ 1.（乡土）one's native country 2.（指殖民国家本土）metropolitan territory
【本位】 bĕnwèi 1.（货币本位）standard：金～ gold standard 2.（本单位）one's own department or unit
【本位主义】 bĕnwèi zhŭyì selfish departmentalism
【本文】 bĕnwén 1.（这篇文章）this text, article, etc. 2.（原文）the main body of a book
【本小利微】 bĕnxiăo-lìwēi have tiny funds and small earnings
【本性】 bĕnxìng natural instincts; natural character; nature; inherent quality
【本意】 bĕnyì original idea; real intention
【本影】 bĕnyĭng 〈*Astron.*〉 umbra
【本月】 bĕnyuè this month; the current month
【本着】 bĕn·zhe in line with; in conformity with; in the light of
【本职】 bĕnzhí one's job; one's duty
【本质】 bĕnzhì essence; nature; innate character; intrinsic quality
【本周】 bĕnzhōu this week; the current week
【本子】 bĕn·zi 1.（本册）book; notebook 2.（指练习或作业）exercises 3.（指证件）pass; license：驾驶～ driving license

苯（bĕn） benzol; benzene
【苯胺】 bĕn'ān aniline
【苯巴比妥】 bĕnbābĭtuŏ phenobarbital
【苯海拉明】 bĕnhăilāmíng benadryl
【苯乙烯】 bĕnyĭxī styrene
【苯中毒】 bĕnzhòngdú benzolism

畚（bĕn） 1.（簸箕）dustpan 2.（用簸箕撮）scoop up with a dustpan
【畚箕】 bĕnjī dustpan

奔［逩］（bèn） 1.（走向目的地）go straight towards; head for：直～办公室 head straight for the office 2.（年龄接近）approach; be getting on for
（另见"奔"bēn）
【奔头儿】 bèn·tour sth. to strive for; prospect

笨（bèn） 1.（智力差）stupid; dull; foolish 2.（不灵巧）clumsy; awkward 3.（笨重）cumbersome; awkward; unwieldy
【笨蛋】 bèndàn 〈*Offens.*〉 fool; idiot
【笨人】 bènrén a stupid person; fool
【笨手笨脚】 bènshŏu-bènjiăo clumsy; inept; ham-fisted
【笨重】 bènzhòng heavy; cumbersome; unwieldy
【笨拙】 bènzhuō clumsy; awkward; stupid

beng

崩（bēng） 1.（倒塌）collapse 2.（破裂）burst 3.（击中）be hit by sth. bursting 4.（枪毙）shoot
【崩溃】 bēngkuì collapse; crumble; fall apart
【崩裂】 bēngliè burst apart; break apart; crack
【崩塌】 bēngtā collapse; crumble

绷［繃］（bēng） 1.（拉紧）stretch tight; draw tight 2.（弹起）spring; bounce 3.（长针疏缝）baste; tack; pin
（另见"绷"bĕng）
【绷床】 bēngchuáng 〈*Circus*〉 trampoline
【绷带】 bēngdài bandage
【绷索】 bēngsuŏ 〈*Circus*〉 tightrope
【绷子】 bēng·zi embroidery frame; tambour; hoop

甭（béng） don't; needn't：～客气。Don't stand on ceremony.

绷［繃］（bĕng） 1.（板着）look serious：～着脸 pull a long face; look displeased 2.（勉强支撑）strain oneself
（另见"绷"bēng）

泵（bèng） pump：水～ water pump; pump

【泵舱】 bèngcāng pump-room
【泵房】 bèngfáng pump house
迸 (bèng) spout; spurt; burst forth
【迸发】 bèngfā burst forth; burst out
【迸裂】 bèngliè split; burst (open)
蹦 (bèng) leap; jump; spring

bi

逼［偪］(bī) 1.(逼迫) force; compel 2.(强迫索取) press for; extort 3.(逼近) press on towards; press up to; close in on
【逼供】 bīgòng extort a confession
【逼供信】 bīgòngxìn obtain confessions by compulsion and give them credence
【逼近】 bījìn press on towards; close in on; approach; draw near
【逼迫】 bīpò force; compel; coerce
【逼人】 bīrén pressing; threatening: ～太甚 drive sb. too hard; put too much pressure on sb.
【逼死】 bīsǐ hound sb. to death
【逼债】 bīzhài press for payment of debts; dun sb. for the payment of a debt
【逼真】 bīzhēn 1.(非常像真的) lifelike; true to life: 十分～ be really true to life 2.(真切) distinctly; clearly
荸 (bí)
【荸荠】 bí·qí water chestnut
鼻 (bí) nose
【鼻出血】 bíchūxuè nosebleed
【鼻窦炎】 bídòuyán 〈*Med.*〉 nasosinusitis
【鼻骨】 bígǔ 〈*Anat.*〉 nasal bone
【鼻孔】 bíkǒng nostril
【鼻梁】 bíliáng bridge of the nose
【鼻黏膜】 bíniánmó schneiderian membrane; tunica mucosa nasi
【鼻腔】 bíqiāng 〈*Anat.*〉 nasal cavity
【鼻青脸肿】 bíqīng-liǎnzhǒng a bloody nose and a swollen face; badly battered
【鼻儿】 bír 1.(小孔) a hole in an implement, utensil, etc., for sth. to be inserted into; eye 2.(笛声) whistle
【鼻塞】 bísāi have a stuffy nose
【鼻涕】 bítì nasal mucus; snivel: 流～ have a running nose
【鼻息】 bíxī breath: 仰人～ be slavishly dependent on others
【鼻烟】 bíyān snuff
【鼻烟壶】 bíyānhú snuff bottle
【鼻咽癌】 bíyān'ái 〈*Med.*〉 nasopharyngeal darcinoma
【鼻炎】 bíyán 〈*Med.*〉 rhinitis
【鼻中隔】 bízhōnggé 〈*Anat.*〉 nasal septum
【鼻子】 bí·zi nose: 抠～ pick one's nose
【鼻祖】 bízǔ the earliest ancestor; originator
匕 (bǐ)
【匕首】 bǐshǒu dagger
比 (bǐ) 1.(比较) compare; contrast 2.(较量) emulate; compete; match: ～力气 compare strength 3.(比拟) draw an analogy; liken to; compare to 4.(比画) gesture; gesticulate 5.(比率) ratio; proportion: 约为一与三之～ a ratio of about one to three 6.(得分对比) to (in a score): 三～五 three to five
【比比皆是】 bǐbǐ-jiēshì can be found everywhere
【比方】 bǐ·fang analogy; instance: 打～ draw an analogy
【比分】 bǐfēn 〈*Sports*〉 score: 拉开～ widen the lead
【比高低】 bǐgāodī compare so as to see who is superior
【比画】 bǐ·hua gesture; gesticulate
【比基尼】 bǐjīní bikini
【比基尼乳罩】 bǐjīní rǔzhào bikini top
【比基尼式泳裤】 bǐjīníshì yǒngkù bikini bottom; bikini briefs
【比基尼泳衣】 bǐjīní yǒngyī bikini
【比价】 bǐjià rate of exchange: 人民币和美元的～ the rate of exchange between the RMB yuan and U.S. dollar
【比较】 bǐjiào 1.(对比) compare; contrast 2.〈*adv.*〉 fairly; comparatively; relatively; quite; rather: ～简单 fairly simple
【比例】 bǐlì 1.(倍数关系) proportion: 反～ inverse proportion / 正～ direct proportion

2.(比例尺) scale

【比例尺】 bǐlìchǐ 1.(地图的) scale 2.(绘图工具) architect's scale; engineer's scale

【比邻】 bǐlín 1.(近邻) neighbor; next-door neighbor 2.(接近) near; next to

【比率】 bǐlǜ ratio; rate

【比拟】 bǐnǐ 1.(比较) compare; draw a parallel; match: 无可～ beyond compare; incomparable 2.(修辞手法) analogy; metaphor; comparison

【比如】 bǐrú for example; for instance; such as

【比赛】 bǐsài match; competition: 参加～ take part in the competition

【比赛规则】 bǐsài guīzé rules of the game; rules of a contest

【比赛项目】 bǐsài xiàngmù event

【比上不足,比下有余】 bǐshàng-bùzú, bǐxià-yǒuyú fall short of the best but be better than the worst; can pass muster

【比试】 bǐ·shi 1.(较量) have a competition 2.(试做某种动作) measure with one's hand or arm; make a gesture of measuring

【比特】 bǐtè 〈*Computer*〉 bit: 每秒传输～数 bits per second

【比喻】 bǐyù figure of speech; metaphor; analogy

【比照】 bǐzhào 1.(按照) according to; in the light of 2.(对比) contrast

【比值】 bǐzhí specific value; ratio

【比重】 bǐzhòng 1.(所占比例) proportion: 第三产业在整个国民经济中的～ the proportion of tertiary industry in the national economy as a whole 2.〈*Physics*〉 specific gravity

【比重计】 bǐzhòngjì 〈*Physics*〉 hydrometer

【比作】 bǐzuò compare to; liken to

吡(bǐ)

【吡啶】 bǐdìng 〈*Chem.*〉 pyridine

【吡咯】 bǐluò 〈*Chem.*〉 pyrrole

妣(bǐ) mother: 先～ my decease mother; my late mother

秕[粃](bǐ) blighted

【秕糠】 bǐkāng chaff; husk

【秕粒】 bǐlì blighted grain

彼(bǐ) 1.(那,那个) that; those; the other; another 2.(对方) the other party

【彼此】 bǐcǐ each other; one another

笔[筆](bǐ) 1.(写、画用具) pen: 钢～ fountain pen / 毛～ (Chinese) writing brush / 圆珠～ ball-point pen / 自来水～ fountain pen 2.(笔法) technique of writing, calligraphy or drawing 3.(用笔写出) write 4.(笔画) stroke; touch

【笔调】 bǐdiào (of writing) tone; style: 轻松的～ a light touch / 优美的～ an elegant style

【笔锋】 bǐfēng 1.(毛笔尖) the tip of a writing brush 2.(文章锋芒) vigor of style in writing; stroke; touch

【笔杆】 bǐgǎn 1.(笔的杆) the shaft of a pen or writing brush; pen-holder 2.(笔) pen

【笔杆子】 bǐgǎn·zi an effective writer

【笔画】 bǐhuà strokes of a Chinese character

【笔会】 bǐhuì P.E.N. 国际～ International Association of Poets, Playwrights, Editors, Essayists, and Novelists

【笔迹】 bǐjì a person's handwriting; hand: 对～ identify sb.'s handwriting

【笔记】 bǐjì 1.(做记录) take down sth. (in writing) 2.(做的记录) notes

【笔记本】 bǐjìběn notebook

【笔记本式电脑】 bǐjìběnshì diànnǎo notebook computer

【笔尖】 bǐjiān nib; pen point

【笔力】 bǐlì vigor of strokes in calligraphy or drawing; vigor of style in literary composition

【笔录】 bǐlù 〈*Law*〉 1.(用笔记录) put down (in writing); write down 2.(笔头记录) notes; record

【笔名】 bǐmíng pen name; pseudonym: 用～写作 write under a pen name

【笔墨】 bǐmò pen and ink; words; writing

【笔试】 bǐshì written examination; written test

【笔算】 bǐsuàn do a sum in writing; written calculation

【笔挺】 bǐtǐng 1.(很直) (standing) very straight; straight as a ramrod; bolt upright 2.(烫得很平) well-ironed; trim

【笔筒】 bǐtǒng pen container; brush pot

【笔头】 bǐtóu 1.(笔尖) nib; pen point 2.(写作能力) ability to write; writing skill 3.(书

面的）written; in written form
【笔误】 bǐwù a slip of the pen
【笔下】 bǐxià the wording and purport of what one writes
【笔心】 bǐxīn 1.（铅笔心）pencil lead 2.（圆珠笔心）refill (for a ball-point pen)
【笔译】 bǐyì 1.（笔头翻译）written translation 2.（笔译者）translator
【笔者】 bǐzhě this author; this writer
【笔直】 bǐzhí perfectly straight; straight as a ramrod; bolt upright: ～的树 upright tree

鄙（bǐ） 1.（粗俗）low; mean; vulgar 2.（看不起）despise; disdain; scorn
【鄙薄】 bǐbó despise; scorn
【鄙弃】 bǐqì disdain; loathe
【鄙视】 bǐshì despise; disdain; look down upon: ～某人 despise sb.; hold sb. in contempt
【鄙俗】 bǐsú vulgar; philistine

币［幣］（bì） money; currency
【币值】 bìzhí currency value
【币制】 bìzhì currency system; monetary system

必（bì） 1.（必定;必然）certainly; necessarily; surely 2.（必须）must; have to
【必不得已】 bì bù dé yǐ have no choice but to; be under the necessity of
【必不可少】 bìbù-kěshǎo indispensable; absolutely necessary; essential
【必得】 bìděi must; have to
【必定】 bìdìng be bound to; be sure to
【必恭必敬】 bì gōng bì jìng extremely deferential; reverent and respectful
【必然】 bìrán 1.（指事理）inevitable; certain: ～联系 positive connection 2.〈*Philos.*〉necessity
【必然规律】 bìrán guīlǜ inexorable law
【必然性】 bìránxìng necessity; inevitability; certainty
【必修课】 bìxiūkè a obligatory course; a compulsory course
【必须】 bìxū must; have to: 我们～遵守纪律。We must abide by discipline.
【必需】 bìxū essential; indispensable
【必需品】 bìxūpǐn necessities; necessaries: 生活～ daily necessities
【必要】 bìyào necessary; essential; indispensable
【必由之路】 bìyóu-zhīlù the road one must follow; the only way: 中国现代化的～ the only way to modernize China

铋（bì）〈*Chem.*〉bismuth（元素符号 Bi）

闭（bì） 1.（关;合）shut; close 2.（堵塞不通）stop up; obstruct
【闭关自守】 bì guān zì shǒu close the country to international intercourse
【闭合】 bìhé close
【闭合电路】 bìhé diànlù closed circuit
【闭会】 bìhuì close a meeting; end a meeting; adjourn a meeting
【闭经】 bìjīng 〈*Med.*〉amenorrhea; menostasis
【闭口】 bìkǒu shut up
【闭口不谈】 bìkǒu-bùtán refuse to say anything about
【闭路电视】 bìlù diànshì closed-circuit television
【闭门羹】 bìméngēng refusal of entrance: 吃～ be denied entrance
【闭门思过】 bìmén-sīguò shut oneself up and ponder over one's mistakes
【闭门造车】 bìmén-zàochē make a cart behind closed doors; work behind closed doors
【闭幕】 bìmù 1.（指演出）the curtain falls; lower the curtain 2.（指会议等）close; conclude
【闭幕式】 bìmùshì closing ceremony
【闭塞】 bìsè 1.（堵塞）stop up; close up 2.（偏僻）hard to get to; out-of-the-way; inaccessible 3.（消息不灵通）unenlightened 4.〈铁路〉block
【闭塞区间】 bìsè qūjiān 〈*Railway*〉block section
【闭塞信号】 bìsè xìnhào 〈*Railway*〉block signal
【闭塞站】 bìsèzhàn 〈*Railway*〉block station

毕［畢］（bì） 1.（完毕）finish; accomplish; conclude 2.（完全）fully; altogether; completely
【毕恭毕敬】 bìgōng-bìjìng extremely deferential; reverent and respectful
【毕竟】 bìjìng after all; all in all; when all is said and done; in the final analysis

【毕生】 bìshēng all one's life; lifetime: ～精力 energy throughout one's life
【毕业】 bìyè graduate; finish school
【毕业班】 bìyèbān graduating class
【毕业鉴定】 bìyè jiàndìng graduation appraisal
【毕业论文】 bìyè lùnwén graduation thesis; graduation dissertation
【毕业设计】 bìyè shèjì graduation project
【毕业生】 bìyèshēng graduate
【毕业证书】 bìyè zhèngshū diploma; graduation certificate

哔[嗶](bì)
【哔叽】 bìjī serge

庇(bì) shelter; protect; shield
【庇护】 bìhù shelter; shield; put under one's protection; take under one's wing
【庇护权】 bìhùquán right of asylum

陛(bì)
【陛下】 bìxià 1.(直接称呼) Your Majesty 2.(间接称呼) His Majesty; Her Majesty

毙[斃](bì) 1.(死) die; get killed 2.(枪毙) kill or execute by shooting; shoot
【毙命】 bìmìng meet violent death; get killed

蓖(bì)
【蓖麻】 bìmá 〈*Bot.*〉 castor-oil plant
【蓖麻油】 bìmáyóu castor oil
【蓖麻籽】 bìmázǐ castor bean

篦(bì) comb
【篦子】 bì·zi a double-edged fine-toothed comb

箅(bì)
【箅子】 bì·zi grate; grid

敝(bì) 1.(破的，坏的) shabby; worn-out; ragged 2.(谦辞) my; this

蔽(bì) cover; shelter; hide: 乌云～日。The sun is hidden by clouds.

弊(bì) 1.(指行为) fraud; abuse; malpractice: 作～ cheat; be dishonest 2.(害处;毛病) disadvantage; harm
【弊病】 bìbìng 1.(弊端) malady; evil; malpractice 2.(毛病) drawback; disadvantage
【弊端】 bìduān malpractice; abuse; corrupt practice
【弊多利少】 bìduō-lìshǎo the disadvantages outweigh the advantages

婢(bì) slave girl; servant-girl
【婢女】 bìnǚ slave girl; servant-girl

裨(bì) benefit; advantage
【裨益】 bìyì benefit; advantage; profit: 不无～ not without benefits / 大有～ be of great benefit

滗[潷](bì) decant; strain; drain

壁(bì) 1.(墙) wall 2.(物体的壁) sth. resembling a wall 3.(峭壁) cliff 4.(壁垒) rampart; breastwork
【壁橱】 bìchú a built-in wardrobe or cupboard; closet
【壁灯】 bìdēng wall lamp; bracket light
【壁虎】 bìhǔ 〈*Zool.*〉 wall gecko; house lizard; wala lizard
【壁画】 bìhuà mural (painting); fresco
【壁垒】 bìlěi rampart; barrier
【壁垒森严】 bìlěi sēnyán closely guarded; strongly fortified
【壁炉】 bìlú fireplace
【壁毯】 bìtǎn tapestry (used as a wall hanging)
【壁纸】 bìzhǐ 〈*Archit.*〉 wallpaper
【壁钟】 bìzhōng wall clock

薜(bì)
【薜荔】 bìlì climbing fig

避(bì) 1.(回避) avoid; evade; shun: ～而不见 avoid meeting sb.; evade a meeting with sb. 2.(防止) prevent; keep away; repel
【避弹衣】 bìdànyī bulletproof jacket
【避风】 bìfēng 1.(躲避大风) take shelter from the wind 2.(避开风头) lie low; stay away from trouble
【避风港】 bìfēnggǎng haven; harbor
【避讳】 bì·hui 1.(忌讳) a word or phrase to be avoided as taboo; taboo 2. bìhuì (回避) e-

vade; dodge

【避开】 bìkāi avoid; evade; keep away from: ～危险地带 avoid a dangerous zone

【避雷针】 bìléizhēn lightning rod

【避免】 bìmiǎn avoid; refrain from; avert: ～不必要的牺牲 avoid unnecessary sacrifice

【避难】 bìnàn take refuge; seek asylum

【避人耳目】 bìrén-ěrmù avoid being noticed; elude observation

【避实就虚】 bìshí-jiùxū stay clear of the enemy's main force and strike at his weak point

【避暑】 bìshǔ be away for the summer holidays; spend a holiday at a summer resort

【避暑胜地】 bìshǔ shèngdì summer resort

【避税】 bìshuì tax avoidance

【避蚊剂】 bìwénjì mosquito repellent

【避嫌】 bìxián avoid doing anything that may arouse suspicion; avoid arousing suspicion

【避雨】 bìyǔ take shelter from rain

【避孕】 bìyùn contraception

【避孕措施】 bìyùn cuòshī contraceptives; contraception measures

【避孕环】 bìyùnhuán intrauterine device (IUD)

【避孕套】 bìyùntào condom

【避重就轻】 bìzhòng-jiùqīng avoid the important and dwell on the trivial; keep silent about major charges while admitting minor ones

臂 (bì) 1.(胳膊) arm: 右～ the right arm 2.(指上臂) upper arm

【臂膀】 bìbǎng arm

【臂章】 bìzhāng armband; armlet

璧 (bì) a round flat piece of jade with a hole in its center

【璧还】 bìhuán 1.(原样归还) return (a borrowed object) with thanks 2.(辞谢赠品) decline (a gift) with thanks

碧 (bì) 1.(青玉) green jade 2.(青绿色) bluish green; blue

【碧波】 bìbō blue waves

【碧蓝】 bìlán dark blue

【碧绿】 bìlǜ dark green

【碧玉】 bìyù jasper

bian

边[邊] (biān) 1.〈*Math.*〉 side 2.(边缘) margin; edge; brim; rim 3.(边界) border; frontier; boundary 4.(界线) limit; bound 5.(身旁) by the side of; close by 6.(方位词后缀) 东～ in the east / 后～ at the back / 左～ on the left

【边车】 biānchē sidecar (摩托车挎斗)

【边城】 biānchéng border town; frontier town

【边陲】 biānchuí border area; frontier

【边防】 biānfáng frontier defense; border defense

【边防部队】 biānfáng bùduì frontier guards

【边防检查站】 biānfáng jiǎncházhàn frontier inspection station

【边防军】 biānfángjūn frontier force

【边防战士】 biānfáng zhànshì frontier guard

【边锋】 biānfēng 〈*Football*〉 wing; wing forward: 左～ left wing / 右～ right wing

【边际】 biānjì limit; bound; boundary

【边际效用论】 biānjì xiàoyònglùn 〈*Econ.*〉 the theory of marginal utility

【边疆】 biānjiāng border area; frontier region; border region

【边界】 biānjiè boundary; border

【边界谈判】 biānjiè tánpàn boundary negotiation

【边界现状】 biānjiè xiànzhuàng status quo on the border; status quo of the boundary

【边境】 biānjìng border; frontier

【边境冲突】 biānjìng chōngtū border clash; clash conflict

【边境检查站】 biānjìng jiǎncházhàn border check point; frontier inspection station

【边境贸易】 biānjìng màoyì frontier trade; frontier traffic

【边贸】 biānmào frontier trade

【边门】 biānmén side door

【边民】 biānmín borderer; people living on the frontiers; inhabitants of a border area

【边区】 biānqū border area

【边线】 biānxiàn 1.〈*Baseball*〉 foul line 2.〈*Basketball, volleyball*〉 sideline 3.〈*Football*〉 touch-line

【边沿】 biānyán edge; fringe

【边缘】 biānyuán 1.(边沿) edge; fringe; verge; brink; periphery 2.(靠近界线的)

marginal; borderline
【边缘地带】 biānyuán dìdài border region; border districts
【边缘科学】 biānyuán kēxué borderline science
【边缘学科】 biānyuán xuékē borderline subject
【边远】 biānyuǎn far from the center; remote: ～地区 an outlying district

编 (biān) 1.(编织) weave; plait 2.(编排) organize; group; arrange 3.(编辑) edit; compile: ～词典 compile a dictionary 4.(创作) write; compose 5.(编造) fabricate; invent; make up; cook up
【编创】 biānchuàng edit and write
【编创人员】 biānchuàng rényuán editors and writers
【编导】 biāndǎo 1.(编写剧本和进行导演) write and direct; write a play and direct a film 2.(编导人员) scenarist-director; playwriter-director
【编队】 biānduì 1.(编成队) form into columns; organize into teams 2.(战斗单位) formation
【编发】 biānfā edit and sent to the press
【编号】 biānhào 1.(编号数) number: 给运动员～ give numbers to the athletes 2.(编定的号数) serial number
【编辑】 biānjí 1.(加工) edit; compile 2.(编辑人员) editor; compiler: 总～ editor-in-chief
【编辑部】 biānjíbù editorial department
【编校】 biānjiào edit and proof
【编剧】 biānjù 1.(写剧本) write a play; write a scenario 2.(剧本编者) playwriter; screenwriter
【编码】 biānmǎ encode; put into code
【编目】 biānmù 1.(编制目录) catalogue; catalog; make a catalogue 2.(编目的人) cataloguer; catalogist
【编年史】 biānniánshǐ annals; chronicle
【编排】 biānpái arrange; lay out: 杂志的～ the layout of a magazine
【编审】 biānshěn 1.(编辑和审阅) edit and revise 2.(指人员) senior editor
【编外人员】 biānwài rényuán non-permanent staff; extra-organizational personnel
【编委】 biānwěi members of an editorial board
【编写】 biānxiě 1.(整理写成) compile 2.(创作) write; compose
【编选】 biānxuǎn collect and edit
【编译】 biānyì translate and edit; translate and compile
【编译人员】 biānyì rényuán translator and compiler
【编印】 biānyìn compile and print; publish
【编余人员】 biānyú rényuán personnel left over after reorganization
【编造】 biānzào 1.(编制) compile; draw up; work out: ～预算 compile statistical tables 2.(捏造) fabricate; invent; concoct; make up; cook up 3.(凭想像创造) create out of the imagination
【编者】 biānzhě editor; compiler
【编者按】 biānzhě'àn editor's note; editorial note
【编织】 biānzhī weave; knit; plait; braid: ～地毯 weave a rug
【编织物】 biānzhīwù knitting; knitwear
【编制】 biānzhì 1.(指手工艺) weave; plait; braid 2.(根据资料做出) work out; draw up 3.(指人员、机构等) authorized strength; establishment: 紧缩～ reduce the staff
【编钟】 biānzhōng 〈*Music*〉 bells
【编著】 biānzhù compile; write
【编组】 biānzǔ 1.(编成组) organize into groups 2.〈*Railway*〉 marshalling
【编组场】 biānzǔchǎng marshalling yard; classification yard
【编纂】 biānzuǎn compile: ～词典 compile a dictionary

煸 (biān) stir-fry before stewing

蝙 (biān)
【蝙蝠】 biānfú bat

鳊[鯿] (biān) bream

鞭 (biān) whip; lash
【鞭策】 biāncè spur on; urge on
【鞭长莫及】 biāncháng-mòjí beyond the reach of one's power; too far away for one to be

able to help
【鞭打】 biāndǎ whip; lash; flog; thrash
【鞭打快牛】 biāndǎ kuàiniú whip the fast ox
【鞭炮】 biānpào firecrackers
【鞭挞】 biāntà lash; castigate
【鞭子】 biān·zi whip

贬（biǎn） 1.（降低官职）demote; relegate 2.（降价）reduce; devalue 3.（评价低）censure; depreciate：～得一钱不值 condemn as worthless
【贬斥】 biǎnchì 1.（降低官职）demote 2.（贬低）denounce
【贬低】 biǎndī belittle; depreciate; play down
【贬义】 biǎnyì derogatory sense
【贬谪】 biǎnzhé banish from the court; relegate
【贬值】 biǎnzhí 1.（指货币）devalue; devaluate; devaluation（n.）：美元～ devalue the dollar 2.（指兑换率）depreciate：该公司的股票～了。Shares in this company have depreciated. 3.（泛指）devalue
【贬职】 biǎnzhí demote

扁（biǎn） flat
【扁铲】 biǎnchǎn chisel
【扁担】 biǎndan carrying pole; shoulder pole
【扁豆】 biǎndòu hyacinth bean
【扁平足】 biǎnpíngzú flat foot; pes planus
【扁桃】 biǎntáo sweet peach
【扁桃体】 biǎntáotǐ 〈*Anat.*〉 tonsil
【扁桃体切除术】 biǎntáotǐ qiēchúshù 〈*Med.*〉 tonsillectomy
【扁桃体炎】 biǎntáotǐyán 〈*Med.*〉 tonsillitis

匾（biǎn） 1.（木制横匾）a horizontal inscribed board 2.（绣匾）a silk banner embroidered with words of praise
【匾额】 biǎn'é a horizontal inscribed board
【匾文】 biǎnwén inscription in the board

变［變］（biàn） 1.（变化；改变）change; become different; vary：情况～了。The situation has changed. 2.（变成）change into; become 3.（改变）transform; change; alter; turn into 4.（突变）an unexpected turn of events
【变本加厉】 biànběn-jiālì become aggravated; be further intensified
【变成】 biànchéng change into; turn into; become
【变电站】 biàndiànzhàn （transformer）substation
【变动】 biàndòng change; alteration：人事～ personnel changes
【变法】 biànfǎ 〈*Hist.*〉 political reform
【变法维新】 biànfǎ-wéixīn Constitutional Reform and Modernization（1898）
【变革】 biàngé transform; change：社会～ social change
【变更】 biàngēng change; alter; modify
【变故】 biàngù an unforeseen event; accident; misfortune
【变卦】 biànguà go back on one's word; break an agreement
【变化】 biànhuà change; vary; variation（n.）：适应市场需求的～ satisfy the changing need of markets/ 随着条件的～ with changing conditions
【变化多端】 biànhuà-duōduān changing all the time
【变化无常】 biànhuà-wúcháng constantly changing; changing all the time
【变幻】 biànhuàn change irregularly; fluctuate
【变换】 biànhuàn 1.（交替）vary; alternate 2.（变化）transformation
【变焦距镜头】 biànjiāojù jìngtóu 〈*Photog.*〉 zoom lens
【变节】 biànjié switch political loyalty; turn one's coat
【变脸】 biànliǎn suddenly turn hostile
【变量】 biànliàng variable
【变卖】 biànmài sell off; sell up; sell out：～家产 sell off one's properties
【变迁】 biànqiān changes; vicissitudes
【变色】 biànsè 1.（指颜色）change color; discolor 2.（指脸色）change countenance; become angry
【变色镜】 biànsèjìng color-changing sunglass
【变色龙】 biànsèlóng 〈*Zool.*〉 chameleon
【变速杆】 biànsùgǎn 1.〈*Auto*〉 gear shift; gear stick 2.〈*Bicycle*〉 stick shift; gear lever
【变速器】 biànsùqì 〈*Auto*〉 gearbox; transmission
【变速箱】 biànsùxiāng 〈*Auto*〉 gearbox

【变速运动】 biànsù yùndòng variable motion
【变速装置】 biànsù zhuāngzhì 〈*Bicycle*〉 gear change mechanism
【变态】 biàntài **1**.〈*Biol*.〉 metamorphosis **2**.〈*Psycho*.〉 abnormal; aberrant; anomalous
【变态心理】 biàntài xīnlǐ aberration; aberrant personality
【变天】 biàntiān **1**.（指天气）change of weather **2**.（指复辟）restoration of reactionary rule
【变通】 biàn·tōng be flexible; adapt sth. to circumstances
【变温层】 biànwēncéng 〈*Meteorol*.〉 troposphere
【变相】 biànxiàng in disguised form; covert: ～贪污 embezzlement in disguised form
【变相涨价】 biànxiàng zhǎngjià disguised inflation
【变心】 biànxīn cease to be faithful
【变星】 biànxīng 〈*Astron*.〉 variable
【变形】 biànxíng **1**.（形状变化）be out of shape; become deformed **2**.（指童话、神话中人或动物的变形）metamorphosis
【变性】 biànxìng **1**.〈*Physics*〉 denature; denaturation (n.) **2**.〈*Biochem*.〉 denaturation; denaturalization
【变性酒精】 biànxìng jiǔjīng denatured alcohol
【变性手术】 biànxìng shǒushù transsexual operation
【变压器】 biànyāqì 〈*Electr*.〉 transformer: 电源～ mains transformer
【变样】 biànyàng become different; change
【变质】 biànzhì go bad; deteriorate; become degenerate: 牛奶～了。The milk has turned sour.
【变种】 biànzhǒng variety; variant
【变奏】 biànzòu 〈*Music*〉 variation
【变奏曲】 biànzòuqǔ 〈*Music*〉 variation
【变阻器】 biànzǔqì 〈*Electr*.〉 rheostat

便 (biàn) **1**.（方便）convenient; handy **2**.（方便的时候）when an opportunity arises; when it is convenient: 得～ be convenient **3**.（非正式的）informal; plain; ordinary **4**.（排泄屎尿）relieve oneself: 大～ shit; defecate / 小～ piss; urinate **5**.（屎尿）piss or shit; urine or excrement **6**.（就）then; just: 这座建筑今年～可完工。The building can be finished this year.
（另见"便"pián）
【便餐】 biàncān a simple meal; an informal dinner
【便池】 biànchí urinal
【便当】 biàn·dang convenient; handy; easy
【便道】 biàndào **1**.（近路）shortcut **2**.（人行道）pavement; sidewalk **3**.（临时的道）makeshift road
【便饭】 biànfàn a simple meal; potluck
【便服】 biànfú **1**.（日常穿的）everyday clothes; informal dress **2**.（中式服装）civilian clothes
【便函】 biànhán an informal letter sent by an organization
【便笺】 biànjiān **1**.（便条）short note **2**.（便条纸）notepad; memo pad
【便览】 biànlǎn brief guide: 交通～ roadbook / 旅游～ guidebook
【便利】 biànlì **1**.（方便）convenient; easy: 交通～ have good transport facilities **2**.（使方便）facilitate
【便秘】 biànmì 〈*Med*.〉 constipation
【便民】 biànmín handy service for the people; make things convenient for the people
【便民措施】 biànmín cuòshī convenience-for-people measures
【便盆】 biànpén bed pan
【便桥】 biànqiáo temporary bridge; makeshift bridge
【便士】 biànshì penny: 100～ = 1英镑 100 pence = £1
【便条】 biàntiáo (informal) note
【便条纸】 biàntiáozhǐ notepad; memo pad
【便鞋】 biànxié cloth shoes; slippers
【便携式】 biànxiéshì portable: ～打字机 portable typewriter / ～计算机 portable computer
【便宴】 biànyàn an informal dinner
【便衣】 biànyī **1**.（平常的服装）civilian clothes; plain clothes **2**.（指便衣警察）plain-clothes man
【便于】 biànyú easy to; convenient for: ～携带 easy to carry; portable
【便中】 biànzhōng at one's convenience; when it's convenient

遍［徧］（biàn） 1.（普遍）all over；everywhere 2.〈*classifier*〉time：这本书我看过两～。I've read the book twice. / 这部电影他看了三～。He have seen the film three times.

【遍布】 biànbù be found everywhere；spread all over：～全国 can be found all over the country

【遍地】 biàndì everywhere；all around

【遍及】 biànjí extend all over；spread all over

【遍体鳞伤】 biàntǐ-línshāng beaten black and blue；be a mass of bruises

辨（biàn） differentiate；distinguish；discriminate

【辨别】 biànbié differentiate；distinguish；discriminate：～是非 differentiate between right and wrong

【辨别方向】 biànbié fāngxiàng take one's bearings

【辨别力】 biànbiélì ability to see things in their true light；discerning power

【辨认】 biànrèn identify；recognize

【辨析】 biànxī differentiate and analyse；distinguish

辩［辯］（biàn） argue；dispute；debate

【辩白】 biànbái give an explanation；offer an explanation；justify

【辩驳】 biànbó dispute；refute

【辩护】 biànhù 1.（说明见解或行为正确）speak in defense of；argue in favor of；defend 2.（法律辩护）plead；defend

【辩护律师】 biànhù lǜshī counsel for the defense；defense counsel

【辩护权】 biànhùquán right to defense

【辩护人】 biànhùrén defender；counsel；advocate

【辩解】 biànjiě provide an explanation；try to defend oneself：不要～。Don't try to explain it away.

【辩论】 biànlùn argue；debate：～这件事 argue about this matter

【辩论会】 biànlùnhuì a debate

【辩证】 biànzhèng dialectical（adj.）

【辩证法】 biànzhèngfǎ dialectics

【辩证唯物主义】 biànzhèng wéiwù zhǔyì dialectical materialism

辫［辮］（biàn） plait；braid；pigtail：发～ braid；plait

【辫子】 biàn·zi 1.（发辫）braid；plait：梳～ wear plaits；wear one's hair into braid 2.（像辫子的东西）sth. like braid：一～蒜 a braid of garlic 3.（把柄）a mistake or shortcoming that may be exploited by an opponent；handle：抓～ seize on sb.'s mistake or shortcoming 4.（比喻）把问题梳梳～ sort out and classify the problems

biao

标［標］（biāo） 1.（标志）mark；sign：路～ road sign 2.（标明）put a mark；label 3.（奖品）prize；award 4.（标的）bid；tender：投～ make a tender / 招～ invite tenders 5.（枝节或表面）triviality；superficiality；outward sign：治～不治本 tackle a problem on the surface，not at the root

【标榜】 biāobǎng 1.（宣扬）flaunt；advertise；parade 2.（吹嘘）boost；praise excessively：互相～ laud each other to the skies

【标本】 biāoběn specimen；sample：恐龙化石～ dinosaur fossil specimen / 采集血液～ take a blood sample / 从患者胳膊上采集血液～ take a specimen of blood from patient's arm

【标兵】 biāobīng 1.（榜样）example；model；pacesetter：被树为～ be cited as a pacesetter 2.（标志界线的人）marker

【标尺】 biāochǐ 1.〈*Surveying*〉surveyor's rod 2.〈*Hydro.*〉staff gauge 3.（枪炮的）rear sight

【标底】 biāodǐ the minimum bid

【标的】 biāodì bid；tender

【标点】 biāodiǎn 1.（标点符号）punctuation 2.（加上标点）punctuate

【标点符号】 biāodiǎn fúhào punctuation mark

【标定】 biāodìng 1.（规定标准）standardize；standardization（n.） 2.（测定）demarcate：～两国分界线 demarcate a line between two countries 3.（符合标准的）standard：～自行车 standard bicycle

【标杆】 biāogān 1.〈*Surveying*〉surveyor's pole；gage stuff 2.（榜样）example；model

【标高】 biāogāo 〈*Geog.*〉elevation；level

【标号】 biāohào 1.(产品的) grade：水泥～ grade of cement / 高～水泥 high-grade cement 2.(泛指) marks and symbols
【标记】 biāojì sign；mark；symbol：作为～ serve as a mark
【标记原子】 biāojì yuánzǐ labelled atom；tagged atom；tracer
【标价】 biāojià 1.(标出价格) mark the price 2.(所标价格) marked price
【标价签】 biāojiàqiān price tag
【标明】 biāomíng mark；indicate
【标签】 biāoqiān label；tag：价格～ price tag / 给行李上贴～ put label on one's luggage
【标枪】 biāoqiāng javelin：投掷～ throw the javelin
【标枪运动员】 biāoqiāng yùndòngyuán javelin thrower
【标售】 biāoshòu sell by tender
【标题】 biāotí title；heading；headline；caption：通栏～ banner headline / 大～ headline / 小～ subheading
【标题音乐】 biāotí yīnyuè program music
【标新立异】 biāoxīn-lìyì do sth. unconventional or unorthodox
【标语】 biāoyǔ slogan；poster：贴～ put up posters
【标志】 biāozhì 1.(记号) sign；mark；symbol；hallmark：交通～ traffic signs 2.(表明) indicate；mark；symbolize
【标志带】 biāozhìdài 〈*Judo*〉 colored belt
【标识】 biāozhì 同"标志"
【标准】 biāozhǔn standard；criterion：达到～ be up to the standard
【标准大气压】 biāozhǔn dàqìyā standard atmosphere pressure
【标准粉】 biāozhǔnfěn standard flour
【标准轨距】 biāozhǔn guǐjù 〈*Railway*〉 standard railway gage
【标准化】 biāozhǔnhuà standardize；standardization (n.)
【标准件】 biāozhǔnjiàn standard component；standard unit
【标准时】 biāozhǔnshí 〈*Astron*.〉 standard time
【标准像】 biāozhǔnxiàng official portrait
【标准信封】 biāozhǔn xìnfēng standardized envelope
【标准型】 biāozhǔnxíng standard form；canonical form
【标准语】 biāozhǔnyǔ standard language；standard speech

彪 (biāo)

【彪炳】 biāobǐng 〈*written*〉 brilliant and shining；splendid
【彪形大汉】 biāoxíng-dàhàn burly chap；husky fellow

膘[**膔**] (biāo) fat；flesh：长～ get fat；put on flesh；flesh out / 掉～ lose flesh

表[**錶**[6]] (biǎo) 1.(外表) surface；external；outside 2.(表示) show；express；demonstrate 3.(榜样) model；example 4.(表格) table；form；list：填～ fill in a form 5.(器具) meter；gauge：电～ electric meter / 煤气～ gas meter / 水～ water meter 6.(钟表) watch：怀～ pocket watch 7.(中表) cousinship

【表白】 biǎobái vindicate：～心迹 bare one's heart；bare true intentions
【表层】 biǎocéng surface layer
【表尺】 biǎochǐ rear sight
【表达】 biǎodá express；show；voice；convey：非语言所能～ can't be conveyed by words / 无法～ beyond expression
【表达能力】 biǎodá nénglì expressiveness；power of expression
【表带】 biǎodài watchband；watch strap
【表格】 biǎogé form；table：填一份～ fill in a form；fill up a form
【表功】 biǎogōng boast of one's bit of contribution；claim merit for oneself
【表姐妹】 biǎojiěmèi (female) cousin
【表决】 biǎojué decide by vote；vote：交付～ put to the vote；bring to a vote
【表决权】 biǎojuéquán right to vote；vote：行使～ exercise the right to vote
【表决通过】 biǎojué tōngguò vote sth. through
【表决指示牌】 biǎojué zhǐshìpái vote indicator
【表里】 biǎolǐ the outside and the inside；one's outward show and inner thoughts：～如一 the outside is the same as the inside
【表链】 biǎoliàn watch chain

【表露】 biǎolù show; reveal; express: ～真情 **reveal one's true feeling**

【表蒙子】 biǎoméng·zi watch glass; crystal

【表面】 biǎomiàn 1.（外表）surface; face; outside appearance: ～现象 superficial appearance / ～之词 a superficial statement 2.（表蒙子）watch glass; crystal 3.（表盘）dial plate; dial

【表面化】 biǎomiànhuà become apparent; come to the surface

【表面上】 biǎomiàn·shang superficial; ostensible; seeming; apparent: 从～看来 outwardly; seemingly

【表面文章】 biǎomiàn wénzhāng 1.（华而不实的言论）specious writing 2.（掩饰）pretense; cover-up

【表面现象】 biǎomiàn xiànxiàng superficial phenomenon

【表明】 biǎomíng make known; make clear; state clearly; indicate: ～态度 make clear one's attitude / 有迹象～… there are indications that ...

【表盘】 biǎopán dial plate; dial

【表皮】 biǎopí 〈*Anat.*〉 epidermis; cuticle

【表亲】 biǎoqīn 1.（中表）cousinship 2.（中表亲戚）cousin

【表情】 biǎoqíng expression; countenance; look: 显出高兴的～ wear a cheerful look / 愉快的～ cheerful countenance

【表示】 biǎoshì show; express; indicate: ～感谢 express one's thanks / ～决心 show one's determination / ～同情 show sympathy / ～同意 give one's adhesion to / ～对…的关切 show concern over ...

【表述】 biǎoshù explain; state

【表率】 biǎoshuài model; example: 起～作用 play an exemplary role / 做…的～ set a good example to

【表态】 biǎotài make known one's position; declare where one stands: 明确～ take a clearcut stand

【表现】 biǎoxiàn 1.（表示）show; express; display; manifest 2.（行为或作风）show; behavior; conduct: ～好 behave oneself well 3.（故意显示自己）show off: 好～ be fond of showing off

【表现力】 biǎoxiànlì power of expression

【表现手法】 biǎoxiàn shǒufǎ technique of expression

【表现形式】 biǎoxiàn xíngshì form of expression; manifestation

【表现主义】 biǎoxiàn zhǔyì expressionism; expressionist

【表兄弟】 biǎoxiōngdì cousin

【表演】 biǎoyǎn 1.（演出）perform; act; play: 精彩的～ excellent performance 2.（示范）demonstrate

【表演赛】 biǎoyǎnsài exhibition match

【表扬】 biǎoyáng praise; commend

【表扬信】 biǎoyángxìn commendatory letter

【表彰】 biǎozhāng commend; cite; honor: ～先进集体 give commendation to the advanced units

婊 (biǎo)

【婊子】 biǎo·zi prostitute; whore

裱 (biǎo) mount; paste up: ～一幅国画 mount a traditional Chinese painting

【裱糊】 biǎohú paper; paste paper on: ～房间 paper the room

鳔 (biào) 1.（鱼泡）air bladder 2.（鳔胶）fish glue

【鳔胶】 biàojiāo fish glue

bie

憋 (biē) 1.（抑制）keep down; hold back: ～着一肚子气 keep down one's smoldering anger 2.（闷）suffocate; feel oppressed: 心里～得慌 feel very much oppressed

【憋劲儿】 biējìnr be bursting with a spurt of energy

【憋闷】 biē·men feel oppressed; be depressed; be dejected

【憋气】 biēqì 1.（窒息的感觉）feel suffocated 2.（不能发泄）choke with resentment; feel injured and resentful

鳖［**鼈**］(biē) Chinese soft-shelled turtle

【鳖精】 biējīng 1.（用鳖制成的滋补品）essence of turtle 2.（神话中鳖变成的精灵）turtle spirit

【鳖裙】 biēqún calipash

别 (bié) 1.（离别）leave; part: 久～重逢 meet after a long separation 2.（另外）

other; another 3.（类别）distinction 4.（差别）difference; distinction 5.（区别）differentiate; distinguish 6.（用别针别上）fasten with a pin or clip：用针把文件～起来 pin papers together 7.（插住）stick in 8.（不要）don't：～见怪 don't be offended

（另见"别"biè）

【别出心裁】 biéchū-xīncái adopt an original approach; try to be different

【别处】 biéchù else where; another place

【别动队】 biédòngduì special detachment; commando

【别管】 biéguǎn 1.（不管）no matter 2.（不要过问）never mind; leave sb.（sth.）alone：～闲事。Don't put your finger in the pie.

【别家】 biéjiā other; others

【别具一格】 biéjù-yīgé have a distinctive style

【别开生面】 biékāi-shēngmiàn start something new; break a new path; break fresh ground

【别离】 biélí take leave of; leave

【别人】 biérén other people; others; people

【别树一帜】 bié shù yī zhì have a style of one's own; found a new school of thought

【别墅】 biéshù villa; country house

【别提】 biétí indescribably

【别有风味】 biéyǒu-fēngwèi have a distinctive flavor

【别有用心】 biéyǒu-yòngxīn have ulterior motives; have an axe to grind

【别针】 biézhēn 1.（妇女装饰用）brooch 2.（普通的别针）safety pin; pin

【别致】 biézhì unique; unconventional; interesting and novel

【别字】 biézì 1.（写错的字）wrongly written character; misspelt word 2.（读错的字）mispronounced character; misspelt word

蹩（bié）

【蹩脚】 biéjiǎo inferior; shoddy; poor; cheap：～的英语 poor English

瘪［癟］（biě）

shrivelled; shrunken：～谷粒 blighted grains

别［彆］（biè）

try to make sb. change one's opinion

【别扭】 biè·niu 1.（不顺心）difficult to deal with; troublesome 2.（意见不合）cannot see eye to eye; not get along well：闹～ be in disagreement; not get on well 3.（不流畅）not smooth; awkward

bin

宾［賓、賔］（bīn）

guest：贵～ distinguished guest

【宾馆】 bīnguǎn guesthouse

【宾客】 bīnkè guests; visitors

【宾朋】 bīnpéng guests

【宾朋满座】 bīnpéng-mǎnzuò the house is full of guests

【宾至如归】 bīnzhì-rúguī where guests feel at home; a home from home

滨［濱］（bīn）

1.（水边）bank; brink; shore 2.（靠近水边）by; be close to：东～大海 bordering the sea on the east

【滨临】 bīnlín be close to; border on

缤［繽］（bīn）

【缤纷】 bīnfēn 〈*written*〉in riotous profusion

彬（bīn）

【彬彬有礼】 bīnbīn-yǒulǐ refined and courteous urbane

濒（bīn）

1.（紧靠）be close to; border on 2.（临近）be on the brink of; be on the point of

【濒临】 bīnlín be close to; border on; be on the verge of：～太平洋 border on the Pacific Ocean

【濒危】 bīnwēi 1.（危险临近）be in imminent danger 2.（病危）be critically ill

【濒于】 bīnyú on the verge of：～破产 on the verge of bankruptcy / ～死亡 on the verge of one's grave

摈［擯］（bìn）

【摈斥】 bìnchì reject; dismiss

【摈除】 bìnchú discard; get rid of; dispense with：～障碍 remove obstacles

【摈弃】 bìnqì abandon; discard; cast away

殡［殯］（bìn）

1.（停放灵柩）lay a coffin in a memorial hall 2.（出殡）

carry a coffin to the burial place
【殡仪车】 bìnyíchē hearse
【殡仪馆】 bìnyíguǎn the undertaker's; funeral parlor
【殡葬】 bìnzàng funeral and interment

髌［髕］(bìn) kneecap
【髌骨】 bìngǔ 〈*Anat.*〉kneecap; patella

鬓［鬢、髩］(bìn) temples; hair on the temples
【鬓发】 bìnfà hair on the temples：～皆白 with greying temples; hoary-haired
【鬓脚】 bìnjiǎo temples; hair on the temples
【鬓角】 bìnjiǎo 同"鬓脚" temples; hair on the temples

bing

冰［氷］(bīng) **1.**（冰）ice **2.**（把东西冰凉）ice; put on the ice：～一瓶啤酒 ice a bottle of beer **3.**（感到寒冷）feel cold
【冰雹】 bīngbáo hail; hailstone
【冰场】 bīngchǎng skating rink; ice stadium
【冰川】 bīngchuān glacier; glacial (adj.)
【冰川湖】 bīngchuānhú glacial lake
【冰川学】 bīngchuānxué glaciology
【冰川作用】 bīngchuān zuòyòng glaciation
【冰袋】 bīngdài 〈*Med.*〉ice bag
【冰刀】 bīngdāo 〈*Sports*〉(ice) skates
【冰灯】 bīngdēng ice lamp; ice lantern
【冰点】 bīngdiǎn 〈*Physics*〉freezing point
【冰雕】 bīngdiāo ice carvings; ice sculpture
【冰冻】 bīngdòng freeze
【冰毒】 bīngdú ice; smokable methamphetamine
【冰帆运动】 bīngfān yùndòng ice boating; ice yachting
【冰糕】 bīnggāo **1.**（冰激凌）ice cream **2.**（冰棍儿）ice-lolly; popsicle
【冰镐】 bīnggǎo ice ax; ice axe
【冰壶】 bīnghú curling stone（又名：溜石）
【冰壶运动】 bīnghú yùndòng curling（又名：溜石运动）
【冰壶帚】 bīnghúzhǒu 〈*Curling*〉curling brush
【冰柜】 bīngguì refrigerator-freezer; fridge-freezer
【冰棍儿】 bīnggùnr ice-lolly; popsicle
【冰激凌】 bīng·jilíng ice cream：水果～ sundae
【冰晶】 bīngjīng ice crystal
【冰块】 bīngkuài lump of ice; ice cube
【冰冷】 bīnglěng ice-cold：～的态度 icy manner
【冰凉】 bīngliáng ice-cold
【冰球】 bīngqiú **1.**（指项目）ice hockey **2.**（指用的球）puck
【冰球杆】 bīngqiúgān ice stick
【冰球鞋】 bīngqiúxié hockey skate
【冰球运动】 bīngqiú yùndòng ice hockey
【冰球运动员】 bīngqiú yùndòngyuán ice hockey player
【冰山】 bīngshān iceberg
【冰上芭蕾舞】 bīngshàng bālěiwǔ ice ballet
【冰上表演】 bīngshàng biǎoyǎn ice show
【冰上舞蹈】 bīngshàng wǔdǎo ice dancing
【冰上运动】 bīngshàng yùndòng ice sport
【冰上运动会】 bīngshàng yùndònghuì ice-sports meet
【冰释】 bīngshì disappear; vanish; be dispelled
【冰霜】 bīngshuāng **1.**（有节操）moral integrity **2.**（神情严肃）austerity：凛若～ severe-looking; have a stern look
【冰糖】 bīngtáng crystal sugar; rock candy
【冰糖葫芦】 bīngtáng hú·lu candied haws on a stick
【冰天雪地】 bīng tiān xuě dì a world of ice and snow
【冰箱】 bīngxiāng refrigerator-freezer; fridge-freezer
【冰消瓦解】 bīngxiāo-wǎjiě melt like ice and break like tiles; disintegrate; dissolve
【冰鞋】 bīngxié **1.**（冰刀鞋）skating shoes **2.**（四轮旱冰鞋）roller skates **3.**（单排四轮旱冰鞋）rollerblade
【冰雪运动】 bīngxuě yùndòng ice skating and skiing
【冰镇】 bīngzhèn ice; iced：～可乐 iced Coke / ～啤酒 ice beer / ～饮料 iced drinks
【冰砖】 bīngzhuān ice-cream brick

兵(bīng) **1.**（兵器）weapons; arms **2.**（军人）soldier; fighter **3.**（部队）troops;

army：装甲～ armored corps **4**.（军事）military affairs：用～如神 marvellous in generalship；superb in strategy **5**.〈*Chess*〉pawn
【兵变】 bīngbiàn mutiny
【兵不厌诈】 bīngbù-yànzhà there can never be too much deception in war
【兵多将广】 bīngduō-jiàngguǎng enjoy numerical superiority
【兵法】 bīngfǎ art of war；military strategy and tactics
【兵工厂】 bīnggōngchǎng munitions factory；arsenal
【兵工企业】 bīnggōng qǐyè arms enterprise
【兵贵神速】 bīngguì-shénsù speed is precious in war
【兵荒马乱】 bīnghuāng-mǎluàn turmoil and chaos of war
【兵舰】 bīngjiàn warship
【兵力】 bīnglì military strength；armed forces：集中优势～ concentrate a superior force
【兵临城下】 bīnglín-chéngxià the attacking army has reached the city gates；the city is under siege
【兵马俑】 bīngmǎyǒng 〈*Archaeol*.〉clay figures of warriors and horses；terra-cotta soldiers and horses
【兵器】 bīngqì weaponry；weapons；arms
【兵权】 bīngquán military leadership；military power
【兵戎】 bīngróng arms；weapons：～相见 resort to arms；appeal to arms
【兵士】 bīngshì ordinary soldier
【兵团】 bīngtuán **1**.（泛指大部队）large unit；corps；formation：生产建设～ production and construction corps **2**.〈*Mil*.〉army
【兵役】 bīngyì military service：服～ serve in the army；perform military service
【兵役法】 bīngyìfǎ military service law
【兵营】 bīngyíng military camp；barracks
【兵源】 bīngyuán manpower resources；sources of troops
【兵站】 bīngzhàn army service station；military depot
【兵种】 bīngzhǒng arm of the services

槟［檳、梹］（bīng）
【槟榔】 bīng·lang **1**.〈*Bot*.〉betel palm；areca **2**.（果实）betel nut；areca

丙（bǐng） third
【丙纶】 bǐnglún 〈*Textiles*〉polypropylene fiber
【丙酮】 bǐngtóng 〈*Chem*.〉acetone
【丙酮树脂】 bǐngtóng shùzhǐ acetone resin
【丙烯腈】 bǐngxījīng 〈*Chem*.〉acrylonitrile；vinylcyanide

柄（bǐng） **1**.（把儿）handle **2**.〈*Bot*.〉stem：果～ stem of fruit / 花～ stem of flower / 叶～ stem of leaf **3**.（权柄）power；authority
【柄不可授】 bǐngbù-kěshòu do not offer the handle to another

秉（bǐng） **1**.（拿着）grasp；hold **2**.（掌握）control；preside over
【秉承】 bǐngchéng in accordance with；obedience to：～某人旨意 subservient to the will of sb.
【秉公】 bǐnggōng justly；impartially：～办理 decide case according to law
【秉性】 bǐngxìng nature；disposition

饼（bǐng） **1**.（面食）a round flat cake **2**.（像饼的东西）sth. shaped like a cake
【饼铛】 bǐngchēng baking pan
【饼肥】 bǐngféi cake fertilizer
【饼干】 bǐnggān biscuit；cracker
【饼子】 bǐng·zi pancake

屏（bǐng） **1**.（抑止）hold：～着呼吸 hold one's breath **2**.（除去）reject；get rid of；abandon

（另见"屏"píng）
【屏除】 bǐngchú remove；get rid of；do away with：～成见 remove prejudices
【屏气】 bǐngqì hold one's breath：～凝神 deep concentration
【屏弃】 bǐngqì discard；abandon；reject：～不用 casting aside and not using it
【屏息】 bǐngxī hold one's breath：～不动 hardly daring to breathe

禀［稟］（bǐng） **1**.（禀报）report；petition **2**.（承受）receive；be endowed with
【禀报】 bǐngbào report to a superior
【禀赋】 bǐngfù natural ability；born gift；tal-

ent

【禀告】 bǐnggào report

【禀性】 bǐngxìng natural disposition：～难移 human nature is hardly changed

并[併[1]、並、竝]（bìng） 1.（合并）combine；merge；incorporate 2.（并存，并行）simultaneously；side by side 3.〈*Math.*〉intersection of（符号为 ∪ ）4.〈*conj.*〉and；moreover

【并不】 bìngbù not；not at all；by no means；in no sense

【并存】 bìngcún exist side by side；coexist

【并发症】 bìngfāzhèng 〈*Med.*〉complication：引起～ lead to complications

【并非如此】 bìngfēi-rúcǐ That's not the case.

【并驾齐驱】 bìngjià-qíqū run neck and neck；keep abreast of one another

【并肩】 bìngjiān shoulder to shoulder；side by side：～前进 advance shoulder to shoulder

【并举】 bìngjǔ develop simultaneously

【并口】 bìngkǒu 〈*Computer*〉parallel port

【并联】 bìnglián 1.（并排相联）connect side by side 2.〈*Electr.*〉parallel connection；parallel

【并联电路】 bìnglián diànlù parallel circuit

【并列】 bìngliè stand side by side；be juxtaposed：与某人～第二名 be tied with sb. for second place

【并排】 bìngpái side by side；abreast：～坐着 sit in a line

【并且】 bìngqiě 1.（表示同时或先后进行）and；also；and ... as well；in addition 2.（表示更进一层）besides；moreover；furthermore：她这么说了，～也这么做了。This is what she said and, moreover, what she did.

【并吞】 bìngtūn swallow up；annex；merge：～小企业 swallow up small enterprises

【并无】 bìngwú not at all；by no means：～此意。That's not my intention at all.

【并行】 bìngxíng act simultaneously

【并行不悖】 bìngxíng bù bèi not interfere one another；not be mutually exclusive；run parallel

【并重】 bìngzhòng lay equal stress on；pay equal attention to

摒（bìng） get rid of；dismiss；brush aside

【摒除】 bìngchú remove；get rid of；do away with：～成见 remove prejudices

【摒弃】 bìngqì abandon；get rid of：～前嫌 disregard previous enmity

病（bìng） 1.（疾病）illness；sickness；disease：常见～ common disease；common illnesses /（通过空气的）传染～ infectious disease /（通过接触的）传染～ contagious disease / 地方～ endemic disease / 多发～ frequently occurring illnesses / 急性～ acute disease / 流行～ epidemics；epidemic disease / 慢性～ chronic disease / 小～ minor ailment；slight disease / 心脏～ heart trouble / 职业～ occupational disease / 重～ serious disease 2.（生病）be ill；be taken ill；fell unwell：卧～在床 lie stick in bed 3.（有病的）sick；sickly：～树 sickly tree 4.（缺点）fault；defect

【病变】 bìngbiàn pathological changes

【病残】 bìngcán sick and disabled；sick and handicapped

【病虫害】 bìngchónghài plant diseases and insect pests

【病床】 bìngchuáng 1.（医院的病床）hospital bed 2.（病人睡的床）sickbed

【病从口入】 bìngcóng-kǒurù illness finds its way in by the mouth

【病倒】 bìngdǎo be down with an illness；be laid up

【病毒】 bìngdú 1.〈*Med.*〉virus：滤过性～ filterable virus 2.〈*Computer*〉computer virus

【病毒性】 bìngdúxìng 〈*Med.*〉virus：～肝炎 virus hepatitis

【病房】 bìngfáng 1.（医院的病房）ward：产科～ maternity ward / 查～ make ward rounds；go on rounds in the wards 2.（病人住的房间）sickroom

【病根】 bìnggēn 1.（指病源）the lingering effect of a chronic disease；an old complaint 2.（比喻失败原因）the root cause of trouble

【病故】 bìnggù die of an illness

【病号】 bìnghào sick personnel；person on the sick list；patient

【病号饭】 bìnghàofàn patient's diet

【病假】 bìngjià sick leave：请～ ask for sick leave

【病假证明】 bìngjià zhèngmíng certificate for

sick leave
【病菌】 bìngjūn pathogenic bacteria; germs
【病理】 bìnglǐ pathology
【病理诊断】 bìnglǐ zhěnduàn pathological diagnosis
【病理学】 bìnglǐxué pathology; pathological (adj.)
【病历】 bìnglì medical record; case history
【病历卡】 bìnglìkǎ case record card
【病例】 bìnglì case
【病例报告】 bìnglì bàogào case report
【病魔】 bìngmó serious illness: ～缠身 be afflicted with a lingering disease
【病情】 bìngqíng state of an illness; patient's condition
【病情公报】 bìngqíng gōngbào medical bulletin
【病人】 bìngrén patient; invalid
【病入膏肓】 bìngrù-gāohuāng the disease has attacked the vitals; beyond cure
【病史】 bìngshǐ medical history
【病逝】 bìngshì die of illness
【病态】 bìngtài morbid state
【病态心理】 bìngtài xīnlǐ morbid psychology
【病痛】 bìngtòng indisposition; ailment
【病退】 bìngtuì withdraw (from the countryside) because of illness
【病危】 bìngwēi be critically ill; be terminally ill
【病休】 bìngxiū sick rest; lie up
【病愈】 bìngyù recover
【病院】 bìngyuàn a specialized hospital
【病灶】 bìngzào 〈*Med.*〉 focus
【病征】 bìngzhēng 〈*Med.*〉 symptoms
【病症】 bìngzhèng disease; illness
【病株】 bìngzhū 〈*Agric.*〉 diseased plant; infected plant

bo

拨[撥] (bō) 1. (拨动) stir; poke; turn: ～一下炉火 poke the fire 2. (拨发) allocate; appropriate; set aside: ～款建一座新医院 alocate funds for a new hospital 3. 〈*classifier*〉 group; batch: 新到的一～来访者 a fresh batch of visitors
【拨出】 bōchū transfer to
【拨电话】 bōdiànhuà dial; dial a telephone
【拨动】 bōdòng stir; poke
【拨动开关】 bōdòng kāiguān toggle-switch
【拨付】 bōfù appropriate (a sum of money); make payment as earmarked
【拨付凭单】 bōfù píngdān invoice of transfer
【拨号】 bōhào 〈*Telephone*〉 dial; dial a number; dial a telephone
【拨号盘】 bōhàopán 〈*Telephone*〉 dial
【拨号音】 bōhàoyīn 〈*Telephone*〉 dialling tone
【拨开】 bōkāi push aside
【拨款】 bōgkuǎn 1. (拨给款项) appropriate funds; allocate funds 2. (拨款给) to obligate funds to 3. (指款项) appropriation; allocate funds; the amount allotted to sb.: 财政～ financial allocation / 过期～ expired appropriation
【拨浪鼓】 bō·langgǔ rattle-drum
【拨乱反正】 bōluàn-fǎnzhèng rectification; bring order out of chaos; set wrong things right
【拨弄】 bō·nong 1. (来回拨动) fiddle with; move to and fro: 用手不停地～铅笔 fiddle about with a pencil 2. (挑拨) stir up; incite; rouse
【拨片】 bōpiàn 〈*Music*〉 plectrum
【拨入】 bōrù transfer from others
【拨正】 bōzhèng set right; correct: ～航向 correct the course
【拨奏】 bōzòu 〈*Music*〉 pizzicato

波 (bō) 1. (波浪) wave 2. 〈*Physics*〉 wave: 短～ short wave / 中～ medium wave / 声～ sound wave 3. (风波) an unexpected turn of events: 一～未平, 一～又起 before one upheaval quiets down, there comes another
【波表】 bōbiǎo 〈*Physics*〉 wave table
【波长】 bōcháng wavelength
【波导管】 bōdǎoguǎn 〈*Electr.*〉 wave guide
【波动】 bōdòng 1. (起伏不定) undulate; fluctuate; rise and fall; fluctuation (n.): 情绪～ be in a changing mood / 价格在 900 到 1,000元之间～。The price fluctuates between $900 and $1,000. 2. 〈*Physics*〉 wave (motion)
【波动幅度】 bōdòng fúdù fluctuation range;

fluctuation spread
【波动汇率】 bōdòng huìlǜ fluctuating exchange rate; fluctuating rate
【波段】 bōduàn 〈*Radio*〉 wave band
【波及】 bōjí spread to; involve; affect: ～他人 be involved in
【波澜】 bōlán great waves; billow
【波澜壮阔】 bōlán-zhuàngkuò unfolding on a magnificent scale; surging forward with great momentum
【波浪】 bōlàng wave
【波浪式】 bōlàngshì in a wave-like manner
【波普文化】 bōpǔ wénhuà pop culture
【波普艺术】 bōpǔ yìshù pop art
【波谱】 bōpǔ 〈*Physics*〉 spectrum
【波涛】 bōtāo great waves; billows: ～起伏 swellings, heaving and subsiding
【波纹】 bōwén **1.**（水纹）ripple **2.**（褶皱）corrugation
【波纹铁】 bōwéntiě corrugated iron
【波纹纸板】 bōwén zhǐbǎn corrugated cardboard: ～盒 corrugated cardboard box
【波形号】 bōxínghào swung dash; tilde（符号为: ～）
【波折】 bōzhé twists and turns

玻 (bō)

【玻璃】 bō·lí **1.**（玻璃）glass: 钢化～ tempered glass / 毛～ ground glass / 磨沙～ frosted glass / 一块～ a piece of glass / 给窗子装～ glaze a window **2.**（像玻璃的塑料）nylon; plastic
【玻璃板】 bō·libǎn glass plate; plate glass; glass top (of a desk)
【玻璃杯】 bō·libēi **1.**（杯子）glass; tumbler: 一～牛奶 a glass of milk **2.**（一玻璃杯的量）glassful
【玻璃厂】 bō·lichǎng glass-works
【玻璃橱窗】 bō·li chúchuāng showcase: 在～中陈列 showcase
【玻璃刀】 bō·lidāo razor knife; Stanley knife
【玻璃钢】 bō·ligāng glass fiber reinforced plastic
【玻璃瓶】 bō·lipíng glass bottle
【玻璃器皿】 bō·li qìmǐn glassware
【玻璃绒】 bō·liróng glass wool
【玻璃体】 bō·litǐ 〈*Anat.*〉 vitreous body
【玻璃纤维】 bō·li xiānwéi glass fiber
【玻璃纤维杆】 bō·li xiānwéigān 〈*Sports*〉 fiberglass pole
【玻璃纸】 bō·lizhǐ cellophane; glassine
【玻璃制品】 bō·li zhìpǐn glassware
【玻璃装配业】 bō·li zhuāngpèiyè glazing

菠 (bō)

【菠菜】 bōcài spinach
【菠萝】 bōluó pineapple

钵[缽] (bō)

1.（陶碗）earthen bowl **2.**〈*Buddhism*〉 alms-bowl

剥 (bō)

（另见"剥"bāo）
【剥夺】 bōduó deprive; expropriate; strip; deprivation (n.): ～权利 deprive sb. of his rights / ～某人一切政治权利 deprive sb. of all political rights
【剥落】 bōluò peel off; come off
【剥蚀】 bōshí erode; wear away: 风雨的～ eroded by weather
【剥削】 bōxuē exploit; exploitation (n.)
【剥削阶级】 bōxuē jiējí exploiting classes
【剥削者】 bōxuēzhě exploiter

播 (bō)

1.（播种）sow; seed: 在地里～小麦 seed a field with wheat **2.**（传播）spread; carry
【播放】 bōfàng broadcast; telecast
【播弄】 bō·nong **1.**（摆布）order sb. about **2.**（挑拨）stir up: ～是非 sow discord
【播送】 bōsòng broadcast; transmit: ～国际新闻 broadcast world news / ～音乐 broadcast music / 现在～新闻。Here is the news.
【播音】 bōyīn transmit; broadcast: 开始～ go on the air
【播音室】 bōyīnshì broadcasting studio
【播音员】 bōyīnyuán announcer; broadcaster
【播映】 bōyìng telecast a film or a telefilm; show on television
【播种】 bōzhǒng sow seeds; sow; seed
【播种机】 bōzhǒngjī seeder; planter; grain drill
【播种】 bōzhòng sowing; seeding
【播种面积】 bōzhòng miànjī sown area; seeded area

伯 (bó)

1.（伯父）father's elder brother; uncle **2.**（兄弟排行老大）the eldest of brothers

【伯伯】 bó·bo father's elder brother; uncle

【伯父】 bófù father's elder brother; uncle

【伯爵】 bójué count; earl; countess (f.)

【伯劳】 bóláo 〈*Birds*〉 shrike

【伯母】 bómǔ wife of father's elder brother; aunt

【伯仲之间】 bózhòng zhījiān almost on a par

泊 (bó) be at anchor; moor; berth: ～船 anchor a vessel / (船)～岸 moor alongside the shore

【泊位】 bówèi berth: 深水～ deepwater berth

【泊位费】 bówèifèi berthage; quayage; a charge for the use of a quay

【泊位通知】 bówèi tōngzhī berth note

铂 (bó) 〈*Chem.*〉 platinum (元素符号 Pt)

舶 (bó) oceangoing ship

【舶来品】 bóláipǐn imported goods; foreign goods

箔 (bó) 1.(金属薄片) foil; tinsel: 金～ gold foil 2.(苇帘子) screen (of reeds, etc.) 3.(蚕箔) bamboo tray for rearing silkworms

【箔材】 bócái foil

驳[駁[1]] (bó) 1.(反駁) refute; argue; contradict: 不值一～ not worth arguing 2.(駁船) barge; lighter 3.(駁運) transport by lighter

【駁岸】 bó'àn revet; revetment (n.)

【駁斥】 bóchì refute; denounce; refutation (n.): ～謬論 refute a fallacy

【駁船】 bóchuán barge; lighter; craft: 用～轉運 transfer by lighter

【駁船船夫】 bóchuán chuánfū bargeman

【駁倒】 bódǎo demolish sb.'s argument; outargue; refute; refutation (n.)

【駁回】 bóhuí reject; turn down; overrule: ～某人的請求 overrule sb.'s claim

【駁回上訴】 bóhuí shàngsù 〈*Law*〉 reject an appeal

【駁價】 bójià cavil at the price

【駁殼槍】 bókéqiāng Mauser pistol

【駁運】 bóyùn transport by lighter

【駁雜】 bózá heterogeneous

勃[敎] (bó) vigorous, thriving

【勃勃】 bóbó thriving; vigorous; exuberant: 生气～ full of vitality; alive with activity / 兴致～ full of enthusiasm; in high spirits / 野心～ overweeningly ambitious; driven by wild ambition

【勃发】 bófā 1.(焕发) thrive; prosper 2.(突然发生) break out: 战争～。A war broke out.

【勃起】 bóqǐ 〈*Physiol.*〉 erect; erection; get (或 have) an erection: 不能～ unable to achieve erection / 能～ be erectile

【勃起组织】 bóqǐ zǔzhī 〈*Anat.*〉 erectile tissue

【勃然】 bórán agitatedly; excitedly: ～大怒 fly into a rage

【勃兴】 bóxīng rise suddenly; grow vigorously: 一个新工业区的～ the vigorous growth of a new industrial park

脖 (bó) neck

【脖梗儿】 bógěngr back of the neck

【脖子】 bó·zi neck: 卡～ wring sb.'s neck / 抓住动物的～ seize the animal by the neck

博 (bó) 1.(多) rich; abundant; plentiful 2.(取得) win; gain

【博爱】 bó'ài universal fraternity; universal love

【博大精深】 bódà-jīngshēn broad and profound

【博得】 bódé win; gain; command: ～畅销 command a ready sale / ～观众热烈的掌声 to draw warm applause from the spectators ～好评 command a fine reputation / ～同情 win sympathy / ～信任 win the confidence

【博格达峰】 Bógédáfēng 〈place〉 Bogda (5445m.)

【博览】 bólǎn read extensively: ～群书 well-read

【博览群书】 bólǎn-qúnshū well-read

【博览会】 bólǎnhuì fair: 国际～ international fair

【博取】 bóqǔ try to gain; court: ～信任 try to win sb.'s confidence

【博士】 bóshì 1.(具有博士学位的人) doctor; doctoral (adj.): 理科～ Doctor of Science；（D. Sc.；Sc. D.）/ 文学～ Doctor of Letters；Doctor of Literature；（D. Litt；Litt. D）/ 医学～ Doctor of Medicine（MD）/ 音乐～ Doctor of Music（D. Mus；Mus. D.）/ 哲学～ Doctor of Philosophy（Ph. D.）**2.**（指博士学位）doctorate：读～ study/read for a doctorate **3.**（有学问的人）learned scholar

【博士后】 bóshìhòu postdoc；postdoctoral；post doctorate：读～ study/read for a post-doc

【博士学位】 bóshì xuéwèi doctor's degree；doctorate：读～ study/read for a doctorate / 授与～ confer a doctor's degree on sb.

【博斯腾湖】 Bósīténghú 〈place〉 Bosten；Bagrax

【博物】 bówù natural science

【博物馆】 bówùguǎn museum：历史～ the museum of history

【博物院】 bówùyuàn museum：故宫～ Palace Museum

【博学】 bóxué learned；erudite：～多才 be of great learning and great ability

【博奕论】 bóyìlùn game theory

搏（bó） **1.**（搏斗）wrestle；struggle；fight；combat **2.**（扑上去抓）pounce on **3.**（跳动）beat；throb

【搏斗】 bódòu **1.**（对打）wrestle；fight；struggle：近距离～ fight at close quarters **2.**（斗争）battle；fight；struggle：与风浪～ battle with the wind and waves

【搏击】 bójī strike；fight with hands

薄（bó） **1.**（轻微）slight；meager；small **2.**（不厚道）unkind；ungenerous；mean **3.**（看不起）despise；belittle：鄙～某人 despise sb.
（另见"薄"báo，bò）

【薄酒】 bójiǔ diluted wine

【薄礼】 bólǐ a meager present；my humble gift

【薄利】 bólì small profits：～多销 small profits but quick turnover；small profit and quick return

【薄弱】 bóruò weak；frail

【薄弱环节】 bóruò huánjié weak link；vulnerable spot

跛（bǒ） lame

【跛行】 bǒxíng walk lamely；have a limp

【跛子】 bǒ·zi lame person；cripple

簸（bǒ） **1.**（簸粮食等）winnow **2.**（颠簸）roll；rock
（另见"簸"bò）

薄（bò）
（另见"薄"báo，bó）

【薄荷】 bò·he 〈*Bot.*〉 field mint；peppermint

【薄荷糖】 bò·hetáng peppermint drops

【薄荷油】 bò·heyóu peppermint oil

簸（bò）
（另见"簸"bǒ）

【簸箕】 bò·ji **1.**（簸粮食用）winnowing pan **2.**（清除垃圾用）dustpan

bu

卜（bǔ） **1.**（占卜）divine；divination（n.）；fortune-telling **2.**（预料）foretell；predict：胜负难～ difficult to tell who will win / 生死未～ hard to tell whether the person is alive of not **3.**（选择）select；choose：行期未～。The date of departure remains undecided.

【卜卦】 bǔguà divine by the Eight Diagrams

卟（bǔ）

【卟吩】 bǔfēn 〈*Chem.*〉 porphine

补［補］（bǔ） **1.**（修补）mend；patch；repair：～车胎 mend a puncture / 把鞋～一～ have the shoes repaired **2.**（补充；填补）fill；supply；make up for：～空缺 fill up a vacancy **3.**（补养）nourish **4.**（利益；用处）help；benefit；use：于大局无～ be of no help to the overall situation

【补白】 bǔbái filler

【补差】 bǔchā make up the difference；make up the difference between the pension and one's original salary before retirement

【补偿】 bǔcháng compensate；make up：～损失 indemnify；recover damage

【补偿贸易】 bǔcháng màoyì compensation trade

【补充】 bǔchōng **1.**（增加）replenish；supplement；complement；add：～库存 replenish the stock **2.**（追加）additional；complementary; supplementary

【补充读物】 bǔchōng dúwù supplementary reading material

【补充规定】 bǔchōng guīdìng additional regulations

【补充条款】 bǔchōng tiáokuǎn subsidiary; supplementary terms

【补丁】 bǔ·ding patch：打～ put a patch on; patch up

【补给】 bǔjǐ 〈*Mil.*〉 supply; provision：缺乏～ go short of supply; supplies running short

【补给线】 bǔjǐxiàn 〈*Mil.*〉 supply line; supply route

【补假】 bǔjià take a deferred holiday; get compensatory leave

【补角】 bǔjiǎo 〈*Math.*〉 supplementary angle

【补救】 bǔjiù remedy; corrective

【补救办法】 bǔjiù bànfǎ remedy; remedial measure

【补救措施】 bǔjiù cuòshī remedial measure

【补考】 bǔkǎo make-up examination; re-examination

【补课】 bǔkè **1.**（老师给学生补课）make up a missed lesson **2.**（重做）do remedial work

【补票】 bǔpiào buy one's ticket after the normal time

【补品】 bǔpǐn tonic

【补缺】 bǔquē **1.**（填补缺额）fill a vacancy **2.**（弥补缺漏的部分）supply a deficiency

【补色】 bǔsè complementary color

【补税】 bǔshuì **1.**（补交逃税）pay a tax one has evaded **2.**（交过期的税）pay an overdue tax

【补贴】 bǔtiē subsidy; allowance：价格～ price subsidy / 旅费～ travelling allowances / 由国家给予～ be subsidized by the state

【补习】 bǔxí take lessons after school or work

【补习班】 bǔxíbān a class for supplementary schooling

【补休】 bǔxiū compensatory leave; compensatory time off

【补选】 bǔxuǎn by-election：～代表 hold a by-election for a deputy

【补血】 bǔxuè enrich the blood

【补血药】 bǔxuèyào blood tonic

【补牙】 bǔyá 〈*Med.*〉 fill a tooth; have a tooth stopped

【补养】 bǔyǎng take a tonic or nourishing food to build up one's health

【补药】 bǔyào tonic

【补液】 bǔyè 〈*Med.*〉 fluid infusion

【补遗】 bǔyí addendum

【补益】 bǔyì 〈*written*〉 benefit; help

【补语】 bǔyǔ 〈*Gram.*〉 complement：直接～ direct complement / 间接～ indirect complement

【补助】 bǔzhù subsidy; allowance：生活～ extra expenses; cost of living

【补助金】 bǔzhùjīn grant-in-aid; subsidy; allowance

【补足】 bǔzú fill; make up a deficiency：～金额 fill vacancies

捕 (bǔ) catch; seize; arrest：被～ be arrested

【捕风捉影】 bǔfēng-zhuōyǐng chase the wind and clutch at shadows; make groundless accusations; speak or act on hearsay evidence

【捕获】 bǔhuò catch; capture; seize：当场～ catch sb. red-handed

【捕鲸船】 bǔjīngchuán whaler; whale catcher

【捕捞】 bǔlāo fish for; catch

【捕捞过度】 bǔlāo guòdù excessive amount of fishing

【捕捞量】 bǔlāoliàng amount of fishing

【捕食】 bǔshí catch and feed on; prey on

【捕鱼】 bǔyú catch fish; fish

【捕鱼船】 bǔyúchuán fisher; fisherman

【捕鱼区】 bǔyúqū area of fishing

【捕捉】 bǔzhuō catch; seize：～镜头 seize the right moment to get a good shot / ～战机 seize the opportunity for battle

哺 (bǔ) **1.**（喂食）feed; nurse **2.**（咀嚼着的食物）the food in one's mouth

【哺乳】 bǔrǔ breast-feed; nurse

【哺乳动物】 bǔrǔ dòngwù mammal

【哺育】 bǔyù **1.**（喂养）feed **2.**（培养）nurture; foster：在…的～下 be nurtured by ...

不 (bù) 〈*adv.*〉 **1.**（表示否定）not; no：～完全 not complete; incomplete / ～严重 not serious / ～愿意 not willing; reluctant **2.**（做否定回答）no：他是在图书馆工作吗？～，他不在图书馆工作。Does he work in a library? No, he doesn't. **3.**（不能）can't; be not able to：举～起来这个 be unable to lift it

【不安】 bù'ān 1.（不安宁）intranquil；unpeaceful；unstable：动荡～ turbulence and intranquillity / 坐立～ like sitting on pins and needles 2.（过意不去）sorry：这样麻烦您，真是～。Sorry to have caused you so much trouble.

【不安定】 bù'āndìng unsettled；unstable；insecure；precarious：～的局面 unstable situation / ～的生活 unsettled life

【不安分】 bù'ānfèn discontented with one's lot

【不谙世故】 bù'ān-shìgù know the world as little

【不安心】 bù'ānxīn not settle down to：～工作 not settle down to one's work

【不按时】 bù'ànshí be late for

【不白之冤】 bùbái-zhīyuān unrighted wrong；unredressed injustice：蒙受～ suffer an unredressed injustice

【不败】 bùbài unbeaten；undefeated；invincible：保持～纪录 hold an unbeaten record / 立于～之地 put oneself in an invincible position

【不卑不亢】 bùbēi-bùkàng neither haughty nor humble；neither overbearing nor servile；neither supercilious nor obsequious

【不备】 bùbèi unprepared；off one's guard

【不比】 bùbǐ unlike：～任何人差 second to none；not inferior to anyone

【不必】 bùbì 〈*adv.*〉 need not；not have to：～说 needless to say；it goes without saying

【不必要】 bùbìyào unnecessary；dispensable；uncalled-for：～的忧虑 uncalled-for worries / 避免～的牺牲 avoid unnecessary sacrifice

【不避艰险】 bùbì-jiānxiǎn shrink from no difficulty or danger；make light of difficulties and dangers

【不变】 bùbiàn unchanging；fixed；constant

【不变价格】 bùbiàn jiàgé 〈*Econ.*〉 fixed price；constant price

【不变资本】 bùbiàn zīběn 〈*Econ.*〉 constant capital

【不便】 bùbiàn 1.（不方便）inconvenient：交通～ have poor transport facilities；not be conveniently located / 如果对你没有什么～的话 if it is not inconvenient to you 2.（不适当）not suitable；inappropriate 3.（手边无钱）have no money at hand；be short of cash：手头～ have no cash at hand

【不辨是非】 bùbiàn-shìfēi fail to make a distinction between right and wrong

【不…不…】 bù…bù… 1.（表示否定）～慌～忙 unhurried；calm；leisurely / ～声～响 quiet；silent 2.（表示"既不…又不…"）～大～小 neither too big nor too small；just right 3.（表示条件）no ... without ...

【不才】 bùcái without capability

【不测】 bùcè accident；mishap；contingency：以防～ be prepared for any contingency

【不曾】 bùcéng never

【不称职】 bùchènzhí incompetent；unfit for the job

【不称霸】 bùchēngbà not seek hegemony

【不成】 bùchéng 1.（不行）won't do 2.（表示反问）难道这就算了～？Is this to be the end，then？

【不承担义务】 bùchéngdān yìwù not commit oneself（to）；make no commitment（to）

【不承担责任】 bùchéngdān zérèn irresponsibility

【不成敬意】 bùchéng-jìngyì just a little token to show my respect to you

【不承认】 bùchéngrèn derecognition；nonrecognition

【不承认主义】 bùchéngrèn zhǔyì policy of nonrecognition

【不诚实】 bùchéng·shí dishonesty

【不成体统】 bùchéng-tǐtǒng behave very badly；wildly

【不成文】 bùchéngwén unwritten

【不成文法】 bùchéng wénfǎ 〈*Law*〉 unwritten law

【不耻下问】 bùchǐ-xiàwèn not feel ashamed to ask and learn from one's subordinates

【不充分】 bùchōngfèn insufficient；insufficiency（n.）：～证据 insufficient evidence

【不出所料】 bùchū-suǒliào as expected；not beyond expectation：不出我所料 not beyond my expectation

【不出庭】 bùchūtíng default of appearance；non-appearance

【不出庭证书】 bùchūtíng zhèngshū nonappearance certificate

【不辞而别】 bùcí-érbié leave without saying good-bye

【不辞而行】 bùcí-érxíng take French leave; go away without saying good-bye

【不辞辛苦】 bùcí-xīnkǔ make nothing of hardships

【不错】 bùcuò 1.(正确) correct; right: 假如我理解得～的话 ... if I understand right 2.(好) not bad; pretty good: 这部电影真～。This film is not bad at all.

【不打不相识】 bùdǎbùxiāngshí from an exchange of blows friendship grows; no discord, no concord

【不打自招】 bùdǎ-zìzhāo reveal unintentionally

【不大】 bùdà 1.(不经常) not often; seldom; rarely; hardly; scarcely: 他～看电影。He seldom goes to cinema. 2.(程度不深) not very; not quite: ～可能的事 something improbable / ～清楚 not too clear

【不大于】 bùdàyú is not more than (符号为 ≯)

【不单】 bùdān 1.(不止) not the only 2.(不但) not merely; not simply

【不但】 bùdàn 〈*conj.*〉 not only

【不当】 bùdàng inappropriate; improper; undue; unsuitable: 处理～ not be handled properly / 措词～ wrong choice of words

【不当裁决】 bùdàng cáijué unfair verdict

【不当判决】 bùdàng pànjué unjust judgement

【不当行为】 bùdàng xíngwéi improper act; undue behavior

【不倒翁】 bùdǎowēng tumbler; roly-poly

【不到】 bùdào 1.(不足) less than: ～两小时 less than two hours 2.(没考虑到) inconsiderate; inattentive; unthoughtful: ～之处 anything that is wanting in one's arrangements

【不到黄河心不死】 bù dào Huáng Hé xīn bù sǐ 〈*Proverb*〉 not stop until one reaches the Huanghe River; not stop until one reaches one's goal; refuse to give up until all hope is gone

【不到庭】 bùdàotíng 〈*Law*〉 absence

【不道德】 bùdàodé immoral

【不得】 ·bù·de 1.(表示不可能、不能够) cannot; not to: 吃～ not to be eaten / 记～ can't remember / 提～ not to be mentioned 2.(表示不应该、不可以) should not; must not; be not supposed to; not be allowed: 马虎～ mustn't be careless

【不得不】 bùdébù have no choice but to; cannot but; have to

【不得而知】 bùdé-érzhī unknown; unable to find out

【不得劲】 bù déjìn 1.(不顺手) awkward; unhandy 2.(不舒服) be indisposed; not feel well

【不得了】 bù déliǎo 1.(指情况) terrible; horrible; desperately serious 2.(指程度) very; extremely; terribly: 热得～ be awfully hot

【不得其法】 bùdé-qífǎ do not know the right way

【不得人心】 bùdé-rénxīn not enjoy popular support; be unpopular

【不得要领】 bùdé-yàolǐng fail to grasp the main points

【不得已】 bùdéyǐ act against one's will; have no alternative but to; have to: ～而为之 feel constrained to act against one's will

【不等】 bùděng vary; differ: 长短～ differ in length / 大小～ differ in size

【不等号】 bùděnghào sign of inequality (符号为 ≠)

【不等价交换】 bùděngjià jiāohuàn 〈*Econ.*〉 exchange of unequal values

【不等式】 bùděngshì inequality

【不等于】 bùděngyú is not equal to (符号为 ≠)

【不提防】 bùdīfáng off one's guard

【不抵抗主义】 bùdǐkàng zhǔyì policy of non-resistance

【不迭】 bùdié 1.(急忙) cannot cope; find it too much 2.(不停止) incessantly

【不定】 bùdìng 1.(表示不肯定) indefinite; indeterminate 2.(不稳定) unsteady; drifting; fitful: 心神～ unsteady in mind

【不定期】 bùdìngqī nonscheduled; irregularly scheduled: ～航班 nonregular service / ～航线 tramp route / ～刊物 publication issued at irregular intervals

【不定式】 bùdìngshì infinitive

【不动产】 bùdòngchǎn real estate; immovable property; immovables

【不冻港】 bùdònggǎng ice-free port; open port

【不动脑筋】 bù dòng nǎojīn don't use one's brain; don't take the trouble to think

【不动声色】 bù dòng shēngsè maintain one's composure; stay calm and collected; not turn a hair

【不动摇】 bùdòngyáo firm; stand firm; steadfast

【不端】 bùduān improper; dishonorable: 行为～ bad conduct; dishonorable behavior

【不断】 bùduàn unceasing; uninterrupted; continuous; constant: 促进…的～发展 promote the uninterrupted growth of ...

【不对】 bùduì 1.（错误）incorrect; wrong 2.（不正常）amiss; abnormal; queer

【不对劲】 bùduìjìn not in harmony; feeling not at par

【不多】 bùduō not much

【不多不少】 bùduō bùshǎo not too much and not too little; just the right number（或：amount）

【不二价】 bù èr jià uniform price

【不发达】 bùfādá underdeveloped

【不发达国家】 bùfādá guójiā underdeveloped country

【不乏】 bùfá 〈*written*〉 there is no lack of: ～其人 there is no lack of such people; such people are not rare / ～先例 there is no lack of precedents

【不法】 bùfǎ lawless; illegal; unlawful: ～活动 illegal activity / ～行为 unlawful practice; an illegal act

【不法之徒】 bùfǎ-zhītú a lawless person

【不凡】 bùfán out of the ordinary; out of the common run: 自命～ fancy oneself an extraordinary man

【不妨】 bùfáng there is no harm in; might as well: ～一试 there is no harm in try

【不放心】 bùfàngxīn be anxious for; feel worried about

【不费吹灰之力】 bùfèi-chuīhuī-zhīlì as easy as blowing off dust; not needing the slightest effort

【不分彼此】 bùfēn-bǐcǐ make no distinction between what's one's own and what's another's; share everything; be on very intimate terms

【不分敌我】 bùfēn-dí-wǒ not to distinguish between the enemy and ourselves

【不分高低】 bùfēn-gāodī be equally matched

【不分巨细】 bùfēn-jùxì regardless of size

【不分青红皂白】 bùfēn qīnghóng-zàobái indiscriminately

【不分轻重缓急】 bùfēn qīngzhòng-huǎnjí without regard to the relative importance or urgency

【不分胜负】 bùfēn-shèngfù tie; draw; come out even

【不分是非】 bùfēn-shìfēi fail to distinguish right from wrong

【不分昼夜】 bùfēn-zhòuyè day and night

【不孚众望】 bùfù-zhòngwàng not inspire popular confidence; not popular with the masses

【不符】 bùfǔ not agree with; not conform to: 名实～ hold an undeserved reputation; fame not in line with reality

【不服】 bùfú refuse to obey; refuse to accept as final; remain unconvinced by; not give in to

【不服从】 bùfúcóng disobey

【不服气】 bùfúqì recalcitrant; unwilling to submit

【不服输】 bùfúshū refuse to take defeat lying down

【不服水土】 bùfú-shuǐtǔ not accustomed to the climate of a new place; not acclimatized

【不负责任】 bùfù zérèn breach of duty

【不甘】 bùgān unreconciled to; not resigned to; unwilling: ～人后 not willing to be outdone

【不甘寂寞】 bùgān-jìmò unwilling to remain out of the limelight; eager to seek publicity

【不干涉】 bù gānshè noninterference; nonintervention: 互～内政 noninterference in each other's internal affairs

【不甘心】 bùgānxīn not reconciled to; not resigned to: ～于失败 not take one's defeat lying down

【不干预】 bù gānyù non-intervention

【不敢】 bùgǎn dare not; not dare

【不感兴趣】 bù gǎn xìngqù lose interest in

【不敢越雷池一步】 bùgǎn yuè Léichí yībù

dare not go one step beyond the prescribed limit

【不公】 bùgōng unjust; unfair

【不公开】 bù gōngkāi not public; not published; private

【不公平】 bù gōngpíng unfair; unjust: ～交易 wrongful dealing

【不公正】 bù gōngzhèng injustice: ～行为 injustice

【不攻自破】 bùgōng-zìpò collapse of itself

【不共戴天】 bùgòng-dàitiān will not live under the same sky; absolutely irreconcilable

【不苟】 bùgǒu not lax; not casual; careful; conscientious

【不够】 bùgòu not enough; insufficient; short of; lack: ～朋友 hardly a friend in need / ～条件 fail to meet the requirements

【不辜负】 bù gūfù be worthy of; live up to: ～…的信任 be worthy of the trust of ... / ～…的希望 justify the hope of; not to disappoint

【不顾】 bùgù disregard; ignore; in spite of; without giving any thought to: ～大局 ignore the larger issues / ～后果 regardless of the consequences / ～情面 without any consideration of personal feelings / ～事实 ignore the facts; have no regard for the truth / ～死活 take no notice of dead or alive / ～一切 up hill and down dale

【不关痛痒】 bùguān-tòngyǎng irrelevant; insignificant

【不关心】 bù guānxīn be indifferent to; not concern oneself with

【不管】 bùguǎn no matter; whether ... or; regardless of: ～结果如何 whatever the consequences / ～什么地方 wherever; no matter where / ～什么时候 no matter when; whenever / ～是谁 whoever; whosever; no matter who / ～怎样 whatever happens; come what may; in any case

【不管部长】 bùguǎn bùzhǎng minister without portfolio

【不管三七二十一】 bùguǎn sān qī èrshí yī casting all caution to the winds; regardless of the consequences; recklessly

【不光】 bùguāng 1.(不止) not the only one 2.(不但) not only

【不光彩】 bù guāngcǎi disgraceful; dishonorable; ignominious: ～的行为 a disgraceful act / 充当～的角色 play a dishonorable role

【不规则】 bù guīzé irregular: ～曲线 irregular curve

【不轨】 bùguǐ against the law or discipline

【不过】 bùguò 1.(只;仅仅) only; just; merely; nothing but; no more than: ～是个烟幕 no more than a smoke screen 2.(转折) but; nevertheless; however; only

【不过如此】 bùguò-rúcǐ so-so; tolerably passable; barely acceptable

【不过问】 bù guòwèn keep aloof from; not inquire into; not look into

【不过意】 bù guòyì sorry; regretful; apologetic

【不寒而栗】 bùhán-érlì shiver all over though not cold; tremble with fear: 使人～ make sb.'s flesh creep; give sb. the creeps; make sb.'s hair stand on end

【不含糊】 bù hán·hu 1.(不模棱两可) unambiguous; unequivocal; explicit 2.(不平凡) not ordinary; really good; uncommonly

【不好过】 bù hǎoguò 1.(指生病) unwell; not well; indisposed; out of sorts; under the weather 2.(日子不好过) have a very hard time; things are tough

【不好惹】 bù hǎorě not to be trifled with; stand no nonsense

【不好意思】 bù hǎoyì·si 1.(害羞) embarrassed; shy; coy; diffident 2.(碍于情面而不便或不肯) would be rude; find it embarrassing (to do sth.) 3.(对不起) sorry

【不合】 bù hé 1.(不符合) not conform to; be unsuited to; be out of keeping with: ～标准 not up to the standard / ～规格 fall short of the specifications / 与事实～ at variance with the facts 2.(不适合) not fit; not suited to: ～他的胃口 be not to his taste

【不合法】 bù héfǎ wrongful; wrongfulness

【不合格】 bù hégé unqualified; substandard: ～的医务人员 unqualified medical worker

【不合格产品】 bù hégé chǎnpǐn substandard products

【不合理】 bù hélǐ unreasonable; irrational: 一个～的要求 an unreasonable demand / 各种～的现象 all sorts of irrational practices

【不合逻辑】 bùhé luójì not logical; illogical
【不合时宜】 bùhé-shíyí untimely; ill-timed; be out of keeping with the times: ～的话 untimely remark
【不合适】 bù héshì improper; inappropriate; out of place
【不和】 bùhé discord; dissension; be on bad terms; be at loggerheads (with)
【不怀好意】 bùhuái-hǎoyì harbor evil designs; harbor malicious intentions; have evil intentions
【不欢而散】 bùhuānérsàn part on bad terms; break up in discord
【不慌不忙】 bùhuāng-bùmáng unhurriedly; leisurely: ～地走来 come over in an unhurried manner
【不讳】 bùhuì without concealing anything
【不会】 bùhuì 1.(不可能) will not; not likely: 人～多 there won't be too many people 2.(不能做) can't; be unable to; be incapable of: ～抽烟 do not smoke
【不惑】 bùhuò without doubt; with full self-confidence
【不及】 bùjí 1.(比不上) not as good as; inferior to 2.(来不及) too late 3.(够不上) fall short of; fail to reach: 力所～ beyond one's power
【不及格】 bù jígé fail; flunk: 她英语～。She failed in English.
【不计】 bùjì disregard; not take into account; irrespective of: ～报酬 regardless of pay / ～个人得失 disregard one's personal gain or loss / ～名利 not mindful of fame and gain
【不计其数】 bùjì-qíshù countless; innumerable; more than one can count
【不记名投票】 bùjìmíng tóupiào secret ballot
【不加可否】 bùjiā-kěfǒu refuse to comment
【不假思索】 bùjiǎ-sīsuǒ without thinking; without hesitation; readily; offhand
【不间断电源】 bùjiànduàn diànyuán UPS; uninterruptible power supply
【不坚定】 bù jiāndìng lack resolution; not to be firm enough
【不坚定分子】 bùjiāndìng fènzǐ waverer; wavering element
【不简单】 bù jiǎndān 1.(复杂) not simple; fairly complicated 2.(不平凡) unusual; remarkable
【不见】 bùjiàn 1.(未见面) haven't seen; haven't met 2.(失踪) disappear; be lost; be missing
【不见得】 bù jiàn·dé not likely; not necessarily
【不见经传】 bùjiàn-jīngzhuàn not to be found in the classics; not authoritative; unknown
【不健全】 bù jiànquán unsound; imperfect; defective: 机构～ organizationally imperfect / 精神～ unsound in mind; mentally defective / 心脏～ have an unsound heart
【不讲道理】 bù jiǎng dào·li be unreasonable; refuse to see reason; be impervious to reason: 一个～的人 an unreasonable person
【不讲情面】 bù jiǎng qíngmiàn without sparing sensibilities; not care to save sb.'s face
【不骄不躁】 bùjiāo-bùzào not conceited or rash; free from arrogance and rashness
【不结盟】 bùjiéméng nonalignment; nonaligned (adj.)
【不结盟国家】 bùjiéméng guójiā nonaligned countries
【不结盟运动】 bùjiéméng yùndòng nonaligned movement
【不解】 bùjiě 1.(不理解) not understand: ～其意 not understand what he means 2.(解不开) indissoluble: ～之仇 irreconcilable enmity
【不介入】 bù jièrù nonintervention; refusal to intervene: ～政策 policy of nonintervention
【不介意】 bù jièyì not mind; not care
【不禁】 bùjīn can't help (doing sth.); can't refrain from: ～大笑 can't help bursting into laughter
【不仅】 bùjǐn 1.(不止) not the only one 2.(不但) not only: ～如此 not only that; what's more
【不尽然】 bùjìnrán not exactly so; not necessarily so
【不近人情】 bùjìn-rénqíng not amenable to reason
【不进则退】 bùjìn-zétuì not to advance is to go back
【不经一事,不长一智】 bù jīng yī shì, bù zhǎng

yī zhì you can't gain knowledge without practice; wisdom comes from experience

【不景气】 bù jǐngqì 1.(不繁荣) depression; recession; slump 2.(不兴旺) depressing state

【不久】 bùjiǔ soon; before long

【不咎既往】 bùjiū-jìwǎng not censure sb. for his past misdeeds; overlook sb's past mistakes; let bygones be bygones

【不拘】 bùjū 1.(不计较) regardless of; not stick to; not confine oneself to: ～形式 not particular about form 2.(不论) whatever

【不拘小节】 bùjū-xiǎojié regardless of trivial matters; not bother about small matters

【不拘一格】 bùjū-yīgé not stick to one pattern

【不倦】 bùjuàn tireless; untiring; indefatigable

【不绝】 bùjué without cease

【不堪】 bùkān 1.(经不得) can't bear; can't stand; be too deplorable to: ～一击 can't stand a single blow 2.(程度深) utterly; extremely: 狼狈～ be in a sorry plight

【不堪入目】 bùkān-rùmù disgusting

【不堪设想】 bùkān-shèxiǎng worse than anything imaginable; worse than one can imagine

【不可】 bùkě 1.(不可以) cannot; should not; must not 2.(非…不可) must: 非去～ simply must go

【不可避免】 bùkě-bìmiǎn be inevitable: ～的错误 inevitable mistake / ～的事故 inevitable accident

【不可多得】 bùkě-duōdé rare; exceptional; hard to come by; hard to get: ～的机会 rare opportunity / ～的人才 exceptional talent

【不可分割】 bùkě-fēngē indivisible; inseparable: ～的领土 inseparable territory / ～的权利 undivided right / ～的整体 indivisible whole

【不可告人】 bùkě-gàorén not to be divulged; hidden

【不可割让性】 bùkě gēràngxìng inalienability: 领土的～ inalienability of territory

【不可救药】 bùkě-jiùyào 1.(指疾病) incurable; beyond cure 2.(指人或事) incorrigible; hopeless

【不可开交】 bùkě-kāijiāo be locked; be tied up: 争得～ be engaged in a heated argument

【不可抗拒】 bùkě-kàngjù irresistible; inexorable: ～的原因 irresistible cause

【不可抗力】 bùkě-kànglì act of god

【不可弥补】 bùkě-míbǔ irretrievable; irrecoverable; irredeemable: ～的损失 irretrievable loss

【不可磨灭】 bùkě-mómiè indelible: ～的功绩 everlasting merit

【不可偏废】 bùkě-piānfèi not to stress one to the neglect of the other

【不可缺少】 bùkě-quēshǎo indispensable; requisite; essential; absolutely necessary

【不可胜数】 bùkě-shèngshǔ countless; innumerable

【不可收拾】 bùkě-shōu·shi irremediable; unmanageable; out of hand; hopeless

【不可思议】 bùkě-sīyì inconceivable; unimaginable: ～的逻辑 inconceivable logic / ～的神态 a mysterious look

【不可同日而语】 bùkě tóngrì ér yǔ cannot be mentioned in the same breath

【不可推卸】 bùkě-tuīxiè bounden; inescapable: ～的责任 inescapable responsibility

【不可一世】 bùkě-yīshì consider oneself unexcelled in the world; be insufferably arrogant

【不可逾越】 bùkě-yúyuè impassable; insurmountable; insuperable

【不可终日】 bùkě-zhōngrì be unable to carry on even for a single day; be in a desperate situation

【不可转让】 bùkě-zhuǎnràng non-assignable; non-negotiable; non-transferable; unalienable

【不可捉摸】 bùkě-zhuōmō subtle; elusive; intangible; hard to grasp or trace: ～的性格 subtle temperament; elusive character

【不客气】 bù kè·qi 1.(使人难堪) be rude to; be hard on: 对某人太～ be too rude to sb. 2.(直率) frank; candid; straight forward: ～地告诉你 tell you frankly 3.(客套) don't mention it; you're welcome; not at all

【不快】 bùkuài 1.(指心情) be unhappy; be displeased 2.(指身体) be indisposed; feel under the weather; be out of sorts 3.(慢)

slow; not fast
【不愧】 bùkuì be worthy of; deserve to be called; prove oneself to be
【不劳而获】 bùláo-érhuò reap without sowing; gain without any work
【不冷不热】 bùlěng-bùrè neither very warm nor cold; lukewarm: ～的态度 lukewarm attitude
【不理睬】 bù lǐcǎi ignore; neglect; take not heed; turn a deaf ear to: ～那些流言蜚语 ignore those gossips
【不力】 bùlì not do one's best; not exert oneself
【不利】 bùlì 1.(没有好处的) unfavorable; disadvantageous; harmful 2.(不顺利的) unsuccessful
【不良】 bùliáng bad; harmful; unhealthy: 存心～ harbor evil intentions; have ulterior motives / 消化～ poor digestion
【不良贷款】 bùliáng dàikuǎn non-performing loan
【不良导体】 bùliáng dǎotǐ non-conductor
【不良倾向】 bùliáng qīngxiàng unhealthy tendencies; harmful trends
【不量力】 bù liànglì lack of proper estimation of one's strength; not reckon oneself fairly
【不了解】 bù liǎojiě do not understand; not familiar with
【不了了之】 bùliǎo-liǎozhī settle a matter by leaving it unsettled; end up with nothing definite
【不料】 bùliào unexpectedly; to one's surprise
【不列颠百科全书】 bùlièdiān bǎikē quánshū Encyclopedia Britannica
【不灵】 bùlíng not work; be ineffective: 这机器～了。The machine doesn't work.
【不留情面】 bùliú-qíngmiàn be very strict; disregard other's "face" or feelings
【不留余地】 bùliú-yúdì leave no room; make no allowance (for)
【不露声色】 bùlù-shēngsè not show one's feelings, intentions, etc.
【不伦不类】 bùlún-bùlèi neither fish nor fowl; nondescript
【不论】 bùlùn no matter; irrespective of; regardless of; whether ... or ...: ～什么时候 no matter when; whenever / ～是谁 whoever; whosever; no matter who / ～性别年龄 regardless of sex and age
【不满】 bùmǎn resentful; discontented; dissatisfied: 对工作～ be discontented with one's work
【不忙】 bùmáng there's no hurry; take one's time
【不免】 bùmiǎn would naturally; unavoidable: ～失望 would naturally be disappointed
【不妙】 bùmiào not going well; anything but reassuring
【不明】 bùmíng 1.(不知道) not clear; unknown: 下落～。The whereabouts is still unknown. 2.(不懂, 不明白) fail to understand: ～事理 lack common sense
【不明不白】 bùmíng-bùbái of unknown causes; without any known reason
【不明飞行物】 bùmíng fēixíngwù unidentified flying objects; UFO
【不明确】 bù míngquè indeterminate; undefined
【不明智】 bù míngzhì unwise; ill-advised: ～的行动 unwise action
【不名数】 bùmíngshù 〈*Math.*〉 abstract number
【不名一文】 bùmíng-yīwén without a penny to one's name; penniless; stony-broke
【不谋而合】 bùmóu-érhé have the same idea by coincidence; happen to hold the same view
【不耐烦】 bù nàifán impatient; out of patience
【不男不女】 bùnán-bùnǚ neither a male nor a female
【不能】 bùnéng cannot; must not; should not
【不能不】 bùnéngbù have to; cannot but
【不能自圆其说】 bùnéng zì yuán qí shuō unable to make out one's case; unable to justify one's own assertion
【不怕】 bùpà be not afraid of; not fear: ～艰难困苦 defy difficulties and hardships / ～牺牲 be not afraid of sacrifice
【不配】 bùpèi be unworthy of; be not qualified to
【不偏不倚】 bùpiān-bùyǐ evenhanded; impartial; unbiased: ～的评价 unbiased appraisal

【不平】 bùpíng 1.(不平坦) uneven; not level; not smooth 2.(不公平) injustice; unfairness 3.(因不公平而气愤) indignant; resentful

【不平等待遇】 bùpíngděng dàiyù unequal treatment

【不平等条约】 bùpíngděng tiáoyuē unequal treaty

【不恰当】 bù qiàdàng inappropriate: ～的比喻 an inappropriate metaphor; a far-fetched analogy

【不巧】 bùqiǎo unfortunately; as luck would have it

【不切实际】 bùqiè-shíjì unrealistic; unpractical; impracticable

【不切题】 bù qiètí irrelevant to the subject; off the point; beside the mark

【不求上进】 bùqiú-shàngjìn have no desire for progress; not seek to make progress

【不求甚解】 bùqiú-shènjiě not seek to understand things thoroughly; be content with superficial understanding

【不屈】 bùqū unyielding; unbending; indomitable

【不屈不挠】 bùqū-bùnáo inflexible; unyielding; indomitable

【不然】 bùrán 1.(不是这样) not so; not the case; no 2.(否则) if not so; otherwise; or else

【不仁】 bùrén 1.(不仁慈) not benevolent; heartless 2.(失去知觉) numb

【不忍】 bùrěn cannot bear to

【不认账】 bù rènzhàng go back on one's word; refuse to acknowledge

【不日】 bùrì within the next few days

【不容】 bùróng not tolerate; not allow; not brook: ～辩解 allow of no excuse / ～耽搁 allow of no delay / ～讳言 there is no denying that / ～申辩 immune to all pleas

【不容置疑】 bùróng-zhìyí undoubtedly; beyond doubt

【不如】 bùrú 1.(比不上) not equal to; not as good as 2.(还是) had better; would rather

【不三不四】 bùsān-bùsì 1.(指人) dubious; shady; indecent 2.(指事) nondescript; neither fish nor fowl

【不善】 bùshàn 1.(不擅长) not good at; a bad hand at 2.(不好) bad; ill; evil

【不上不下】 bùshàng-bùxià suspended in mid air; in a fix

【不设防城市】 bù shèfáng chéngshì open city; undefended city; unfortified city

【不声不响】 bùshēng-bùxiǎng stealthily; furtively

【不生育】 bù shēngyù infertility; infertile (adj.)

【不胜】 bùshèng 1.(经不起) cannot bear; be unequal to 2.(非常) tremendously; very deeply 3.(表示无法做或永远做不完) too ... to: 防～防 be impossible to prevent / 数～数 too numerous to count

【不胜枚举】 bùshèng-méijǔ too numerous to mention individually

【不胜任】 bù shèngrèn incompetent; unfit for the post

【不失时机】 bùshī-shíjī seize the opportune moment; lose no time

【不识】 bùshí fail to see; be ignorant of; not know; not appreciate: ～大体 fail to see the general interest / ～时务 be ignorant of the times

【不时】 bùshí 1.(时时) frequently; often 2.(随时) at any time

【不识抬举】 bùshí-tái·ju not know how to appreciate favors

【不时之需】 bùshí-zhīxū a possible period of want or need

【不是】 bù·shi 1.(否) no; not 2.(错处, 过失) fault; blame: 落～ get blamed / 是…的～ be sb.'s fault

【不是味儿】 bù shì wèir 1.(味道不正) not the right flavor; not quite right; a bit off 2.(不对头) fishy; queer; amiss 3.(不好受) feel bad; be upset

【不适】 bùshì unwell; indisposed; out of sorts: 略感～ feel a bit unwell / 全身～ general malaise / 胃部～ have a stomach upset

【不适应】 bù shìyìng not adapted to; not fit to; not suited to: 对气候～ not accustomed to the climate; not acclimatized

【不守信用】 bùshǒu-xìnyòng break one's word; not keep one's word; go back on one's word

【不受法律保护】 bù shòu fǎlǜ bǎohù outlawry

【不受欢迎的人】 bù shòu huānyíng de rén 〈*Foreigh Affairs*〉 persona non grata

【不熟】 bùshú **1.**（未烧熟）not yet done; still raw **2.**（生疏）unacquainted with; unfamiliar with

【不爽快】 bù shuǎngkuài not frank

【不顺眼】 bù shùnyǎn incurring dislike; disagreeable to the eye; look odd：～的事 something offending the eye

【不死不活】 bùsǐ-bùhuó neither dead nor alive; lifeless; lethargic

【不死心】 bù sǐxīn unwilling to give up; unresigned; not give up hope

【不俗】 bùsú original; uncommon; not hackneyed

【不速之客】 bùsù-zhīkè uninvited guest; unexpected guest; chance comer; casual visitor

【不通】 bùtōng **1.**（阻隔）be obstructed; be blocked up; be impassable：鼻子～ have a stuffed up nose / 电话～。The line's dead. **2.**（文理错误）not make sense; be illogical; be ungrammatical

【不通情理】 bùtōng-qínglǐ unreasonable; impervious to reason

【不同】 bùtóng not alike; different; distinct：～情节 distinctive circumstances / 在～的程度上 to varying degrees

【不同步】 bù tóngbù outer-sync; out of step

【不同凡响】 bùtóng-fánxiǎng outstanding; out of the ordinary; out of the common run

【不痛不痒】 bùtòng-bùyǎng scratching the surface; superficial; perfunctory

【不透风】 bù tòufēng stuffy

【不透气】 bù tòuqì **1.**（密封）airtight; air proof **2.**（通风不良）stuffy; badly ventilated

【不妥】 bùtuǒ not proper; inappropriate

【不外】 bùwài not beyond the scope of; nothing more than

【不完全】 bù wánquán incomplete; imperfect

【不为所动】 bùwéi-suǒdòng remain unmoved

【不畏】 bùwèi defy：～艰险 defy hardship and danger; take the bull by the horns / ～强暴 defy brutal force

【不闻不问】 bùwén-bùwèn not bother to ask questions or listen to what's said; show no interest in sth.; be indifferent to sth.

【不稳】 bùwěn unstable; unsteady; insecure; not firm：站～ be not steady on one's legs; can't keep one's balance

【不稳定因素】 bù wěndìng yīnsù instability

【不问】 bùwèng **1.**（不过问）pay no attention to; ignore; disregard; not consider：～前因后果 not consider the cause and effect / ～是非曲直 make no distinction between right and wrong **2.**（不审讯；不追究）let go unpunished; let off

【不问青红皂白】 bùwèn qīnghóng-zàobái without forethought

【不无】 bùwú not without：～可取之处 not without merit; not altogether unacceptable

【不务正业】 bùwù-zhèngyè **1.**（不专心本职工作）be unmindful of one's own work; not attend to one's duties **2.**（不从事正当行业）not engage in honest work

【不惜】 bùxī **1.**（不顾惜）not stint; not spare：～一切代价 at all costs; at any cost **2.**（舍得）not scruple; not hesitate：～牺牲个人的一切 never balk at any personal sacrifice

【不下】 bùxià as many as; no less than

【不下于】 bùxiàyú **1.**（不少于）as many as; no less than **2.**（不低于）not inferior to; as good as; on a par with

【不现实】 bù xiànshí unrealistic; impractical; fanciful：～的态度 unrealistic attitude

【不相称】 bù xiāngchèn unbecoming; unsuited; out of proportion：同某人地位～ be unsuited to sb.'s position

【不相干】 bù xiānggān be irrelevant; have nothing to do with：完全～ altogether irrelevant

【不相容】 bù xiāngróng be incompatible as

【不相上下】 bùxiāng-shàngxià equally matched; about the same

【不相往来】 bùxiāng-wǎnglái have no dealings with each other; be not on speaking terms

【不祥】 bùxiáng ominous; inauspicious

【不祥之兆】 bùxiáng-zhīzhào an ill omen

【不详】 bùxiáng **1.**（不清楚）not quite clear：内容～ contents are not clear **2.**（不详细）not in detail; unspecified

【不像话】 bù xiànghuà **1.**（形容言语、行动）unreasonable; nonsensical; absurd **2.**（非常

坏）outrageous; monstrous; scandalous; shocking

【不像样】 bù xiàngyàng in poor shape; unpresentable; shapeless

【不小于】 bùxiǎoyú is not less than（符号为 ≮）

【不肖】 bùxiào 〈*written*〉 unworthy：～子孙 unworthy descendants

【不孝】 bùxiào not in accordance with filial

【不协调】 bùxiétiáo inharmonious; discordant; out of tune

【不屑】 bùxiè disdain to do sth.; think sth. not worth doing; feel it beneath one's dignity to do sth.：～一顾 not worth a single glance; cock a snoot at

【不懈】 bùxiè untiring; unremitting; indefatigable：作～的努力 make unremitting efforts to; make a sustained effort / 对…的～努力表示感谢 thank sb. for its tireless efforts in sth.

【不信任】 bù xìnrèn distrust; not believe in; have no confidence in

【不信任案】 bùxìnrèn'àn no-confidence motion

【不信任投票】 bùxìnrèn tóupiào vote of no-confidence

【不信邪】 bù xìnxié not believe in heresy; refuse to be misled by fallacies

【不兴】 bùxīng 1.（不流行）out of fashion; outmoded 2.（不许）impermissible; not allowed 3.（不能）can't

【不行】 bùxíng 1.（不可以）will not do; be not allowed 2.（不中用）be no good; not work：这个计划～。This plan just doesn't work. 3.（不好）not good; poor：她画画儿～。She is a poor painter. 4.（表示程度很深）awfully; extremely; deeply：累得～ extremely tired

【不行了】 bùxíng·le on the point of death; dying

【不省人事】 bùxǐng-rénshì be unconscious; be in a coma

【不幸】 bùxìng 1.（灾祸）misfortune; adversity：～中之大幸 a lucky break out of misfortune / 遭遇～ suffer a misfortune; have bad luck 2.（不希望而发生的）unfortunately 3.（不幸运）unfortunate; sad：～的消息 sad news

【不休】 bùxiū endlessly; ceaselessly：争论～ argue endlessly

【不修边幅】 bùxiū-biānfú not care about one's appearance; be slovenly：～的人 a sloven

【不朽】 bùxiǔ immortal; eternal：～的功勋 immortal deeds

【不锈钢】 bùxiùgāng stainless steel

【不虚此行】 bùxū-cǐxíng the trip has not been made in vain; the trip has been well worthwhile

【不许】 bùxǔ 1.（不允许）not allow; not permit; must not：～停车！No Parking! 2.（不能）can't

【不学无术】 bùxué-wúshù have neither learning nor skill; be ignorant and incompetent

【不寻常】 bù xúncháng unusual; uncommon; extraordinary：～的记忆力 phenomenal memory

【不逊】 bùxùn 〈*written*〉 rude; impertinent

【不雅观】 bù yǎguān offensive to the eye; unbecoming

【不亚于】 bùyàyú not second to; as good as

【不言不语】 bùyán-bùyǔ keep silent

【不言而喻】 bùyán-éryù it goes without saying; it is self-evident

【不厌】 bùyàn not mind doing sth.; not tire of; not object to：～其烦 not mind taking all the trouble; take great pains; be very patient

【不扬】 bùyáng bad-looking：其貌～ have a ugly face

【不要】 bùyào don't

【不要紧】 bù yàojǐn 1.（没有妨碍）not serious; unimportant 2.（不碍事）it doesn't matter; never mind 3.（表示转折）it looks all right, but

【不要脸】 bù yàoliǎn shameless; brazen; have no sense of shame

【不一】 bùyī vary; differ：大小～ differ in size

【不一定】 bù yīdìng uncertain; not sure; not necessarily so

【不一而足】 bùyī-érzú by no means an isolated case; numerous：如此等等，～ and so on and so forth

【不一会儿】 bù yīhuìr in a moment; in a little

while; after a while; a few moments later

【不依】 bùyī 1.(不听从) not comply; not go along with 2.(不放过) not let off easily; not let sb. get away with it

【不宜】 bùyí not suitable; inadvisable: 儿童～ unsuitable for children / ～操之过急。It's no good being overhasty.

【不遗余力】 bùyí-yúlì spare no pains; spare no efforts; do one's utmost

【不已】 bùyǐ endlessly; unceasingly: 赞叹～ praise all the time

【不以为然】 bùyǐ-wéirán object to; take exception to; not approve

【不义之财】 bùyì-zhīcái ill-gotten wealth

【不亦乐乎】 bùyì-lèhū awfully; terribly; exceedingly; extremely: 忙得～ awfully busy

【不意】 bùyì 1.(不料) unexpectedly 2.(没想到) unawareness; unpreparedness

【不翼而飞】 bùyì-érfēi 1.(突然不见了) take to itself wings; disappear without trace 2.(流传迅速) spread fast; spread like wildfire

【不用】 bùyòng need not: ～客气 don't mention it; don't stand on ceremony / ～说 it goes without saying; needless to say

【不由得】 bùyóu·de can't help; cannot but

【不由分说】 bùyóu-fēnshuō allowing no explanation; leaving no chance to explain

【不由自主】 bùyóu-zìzhǔ can't help; can't hold back; involuntarily

【不予】 bùyǔ not give; deny; refuse; not grant: ～承认 deny recognition / ～答复 give no reply / ～理睬 ignore; pay no attention to / ～追究 not inquire into the responsibility

【不育】 bùyù infertile; infertility: 男性～ male sterility

【不约而同】 bù yuē ér tóng take the same action or view without prior consultation; happen to coincide

【不悦】 bùyuè unhappy; displeased

【不孕】 bùyùn 1.(不能怀孕) sterile 2.(不孕性) sterility 3.(不孕症) sterility; barrenness

【不再】 bùzài no longer; not any more

【不在】 bùzài 1.(指外出) be out; be not in: 他～。He is out. 2.(指已死) died; be dead

【不在此例】 bùzài-cǐlì not within the rule

【不在此限】 bùzài-cǐxiàn not subject to the limits or restrictions; do not apply

【不在犯罪现场】 bù zài fànzuì xiànchǎng 〈*Law*〉 alibi

【不在乎】 bùzài·hu dot not mind; do not care

【不在话下】 bùzài-huàxià be nothing difficult; be a cinch: 再大的困难也～。No difficulty amounts to much.

【不在其位】 bùzài-qíwèi not in the position to

【不在其位,不谋其政】 bùzài-qíwèi, bùmóu-qízhèng unwilling to comment on sth. which is not one's own concern

【不在意】 bùzàiyì 1.(不在乎) pay no attention to; take no notice of; not mind 2.(疏忽) negligent; careless

【不择手段】 bùzé-shǒuduàn by fair means or foul; by hook or by crook; unscrupulously: ～地达到目的 attain one's end by hook or by crook / 一个～的人 a man of no scruples

【不怎么样】 bù zěn·meyàng so-so; not up to much; very indifferent

【不粘锅】 bùzhānguō non-stick pan

【不战而胜】 bùzhàn-érshèng win without fighting a battle; win hands down

【不折不扣】 bùzhé-bùkòu to the full; one hundred percent: ～地执行指示 carry out the instructions to the full

【不争气】 bù zhēngqì be disappointing; fail to live up to expectations

【不正常】 bù zhèngcháng abnormal; irregular: ～的行为 irregular by behavior / ～状态 abnormal state of affairs

【不正当】 bù zhèngdàng improper; illegitimate; dishonest; devious: ～的理由 improper reason / ～的手段 dishonest methods; devious means / ～的收益 unlawful profits / ～的职业 illegitimate occupation

【不正当竞争】 bù zhèngdāng jìngzhēng unfair competition

【不正之风】 bùzhèng-zhīfēng unhealthy tendency: 纠正～ overcome unhealthy tendencies; check unhealthy tendencies

【不知】 bùzhī 1.(不知道) not know; have no idea of; be ignorant of 2.(表示疑问或请求) wonder if: ～你是否可以告诉我… I wonder if you can tell me ...

【不知不觉】 bùzhī-bùjué unconsciously; unwittingly

【不知分寸】 bùzhī-fēncùn indiscreet; lacking a sense of propriety; not knowing how far one can go

【不知好歹】 bùzhī-hǎodǎi not know good from bad; not know what's good for oneself

【不知所措】 bùzhī-suǒcuò be at a loss; be at one's wits' end

【不知所云】 bùzhī-suǒyún not know what sb. is driving at; be unintelligible

【不知天高地厚】 bùzhī tiāngāo-dìhòu not know the immensity of heaven and earth; have an exaggerated opinion of one's abilities

【不知羞耻】 bùzhī-xiūchǐ shameless; unblushing; barefaced; brazenfaced

【不知自爱】 bùzhī-zìài act without self-respect

【不织布】 bùzhībù 〈*Textiles*〉 adhesive-bonded fabric

【不值】 bùzhí not worth：～一提 unworthy of mentioning

【不止】 bùzhǐ **1.**（超出某个范围）more than; not limited to **2.**（继续）incessantly; without end

【不只】 bùzhǐ not only; not merely

【不至于】 bùzhìyú **1.**（不会到某种程度）can't go so far as to; not to such an extent as to **2.**（未必）be unlikely to

【不治之症】 bùzhì-zhīzhèng incurable disease; fatal disease

【不置可否】 bùzhì-kěfǒu decline to comment; not express an opinion; be noncommittal; hedge

【不中听】 bù zhōngtīng not worth listening

【不中用】 bù zhōngyòng useless; not good for use; good for nothing

【不中意】 bù zhōngyì not to one's liking

【不周】 bùzhōu inconsiderate; thoughtless

【不准】 bùzhǔn not allow; forbid; prohibit：～入内。No admittance. / ～吸烟！No Smoking!

【不着边际】 bùzhuó-biānjì not to the point; wide of the mark; neither here nor there：～的话 irrelevant remarks

【不着陆飞行】 bùzhuólù fēixíng nonstop flight

【不自爱】 bùzìài do not have self-respect

【不自量】 bù zìliàng not take a proper measure of oneself; overrate one's own abilities

【不自量力】 bùzì-liànglì overrate one's own abilities; put a quart into a pint pot

【不自在】 bù zì·zai uneasy; ill at ease; feel uncomfortable

【不足】 bùzú **1.**（不充足）not enough; insufficient; inadequate：光线～ insufficient light / 信心～ lack confidence **2.**（不满某个数目）less than：～一年 in less than a year **3.**（不值得）not worth; be beneath：～道 of no consequence / ～为训 not fit to be regarded as an example **4.**（不能）can't; should not：～为凭 can't be taken as evidence

【不足法定人数】 bùzú fǎdìng rénshù insufficient quorum

【不足挂齿】 bùzú-guàchǐ be hardly worth mentioning; don't mention it; that's nothing

【不足为奇】 bùzú-wéiqí nothing surprising; no wonder

【不作为】 bù zuòwéi omission

【不做声】 bù zuòshēng say nothing; keep silent

钚（bù） 〈*Chem.*〉 plutonium（元素符号 Pu）

布［佈$^{2-4}$］（bù） **1.**（棉、麻等织物）cloth; fabric; textiles：绸～ silk textile / 棉～ cotton cloth; cotton **2.**（宣布）declare; announce; publish; proclaim **3.**（散布）spread; disseminate **4.**（布置）dispose; arrange; deploy

【布道】 bùdào 〈*Relig.*〉 preach; evangelize

【布点】 bùdiǎn distribution of

【布店】 bùdiàn cloth store; drapery

【布丁】 bùdīng 〈*Food*〉 pudding

【布尔津】 Bù'ěrjīn 〈place〉 Burqin

【布尔什维克】 Bù'ěrshíwéikè Bolshevik（Rus.）

【布告】 bùgào notice; bulletin; proclamation：张贴～ put up a notice

【布告栏】 bùgàolán notice board; bulletin board

【布谷鸟】 bùgǔniǎo cuckoo

【布景】 bùjǐng **1.**〈*Theatre*〉 setting; scenery **2.**（国画用语）composition

【布局】 bùjú **1.**（全面安排）overall arrangement; layout; distribution：促进地区经济合

理～和协调发展 promote a rational distribution and coordinated development of regional economies 2.（指绘画、作文等）composition 3.〈*Chess*〉position

【布朗族】 Bùlǎngzú Blang（中国少数民族，主要分布在云南）

【布雷】 bùléi 〈*Mil.*〉 lay a mine; mine; place a mine

【布雷舰】 bùléijiàn minelayer

【布料】 bùliào cotton material

【布满尘埃】 bù mǎn chén āi covered with dust all over

【布匹】 bùpǐ cloth; piece goods

【布头】 bùtóu leftover of bolt of cloth; odd bits of cloth

【布鞋】 bùxié cloth shoes

【布依族】 Bùyīzú Bouyei（中国少数民族，主要分布在贵州）

【布置】 bùzhì 1.（陈设）fix up; arrange; decorate：我们的房间已经～好了。We have our room fixed up. 2.（安排）arrange; make arrangements for; give instructions about：～任务 assign a task / ～工作 assign a work / 向某人～工作 give sb. the job of doing sth.

步（bù） 1.（步子）step; pace：没几～路 only a few steps away; within a stone's throw 2.（阶段）stage; step 3.（地步）situation; condition; state 4.（用脚走）walk; go on foot 5.（一步棋）move：一～好棋 an excellent move / 五～棋 five moves

【步兵】 bùbīng 1.（兵种）infantry 2.（士兵）foot soldier; infantryman; rifleman

【步步】 bùbù step by step; at every step：～高升 get promotion continuously; attain eminence step by step

【步步为营】 bùbù-wéiyíng advance gradually and entrench oneself at every step; consolidate at every step

【步调】 bùdiào pace; step：～一致 keep step with

【步伐】 bùfá 1.（操练时的步子）step：战士们～整齐。The soldiers marched in step. 2.（行走的步子）pace：跟上时代的～ keep pace with the times

【步话机】 bùhuàjī walkie-talkie

【步履】 bùlǚ walking

【步履维艰】 bùlǚ-wéijiān 〈*written*〉 have difficulty walking; walk with difficulty

【步枪】 bùqiāng rifle：半自动～ semi-automatic rifle

【步桥】 bùqiáo 〈*Ship*〉 fore-and-aft gangway

【步人后尘】 bùrén-hòuchén follow in other people's footsteps; trail along behind others

【步入歧途】 bùrù-qítú take the wrong turning

【步行】 bùxíng go on foot; walk

【步行街】 bùxíngjiē pedestrian precinct

【步骤】 bùzhòu step; move; procedure：采取适当的～ take proper steps / 在…上的重大～ an important step in ...

【步子】 bù·zi step; pace：～轻快 walk with brisk steps

部（bù） 1.（部分）part; section：上～ upper part / 下～ lower part 2.（单位）unit; department：编辑～ editorial department 3.（军队机构）headquarters; department：总参谋～ Headquarters of the General Staff 4.（政府部门）ministry：外交～ the Ministry of Foreign Affairs 5.（部队）troops; forces

【部队】 bùduì 1.（军队）army; armed forces 2.（军、兵种）troops; unit; force：边防～ frontier forces / 地面～ ground forces / 空降～ airborne troops / 野战～ field forces

【部分】 bù·fen part; section; portion：～自给 partly self-supporting

【部件】 bùjiàn parts; components; assembly

【部落】 bùluò tribe; tribal (adj.)

【部落社会】 bùluò shèhuì tribal society

【部门】 bùmén department; branch：交通～ communications department

【部门垄断】 bùmén lǒngduàn sectoral monopoly：打破地区封锁和～ break regional blockade and sectoral monopoly

【部属】 bùshǔ 1.（下级）subordinate 2.（部的附属单位）affiliated to a ministry

【部属学校】 bùshǔ xuéxiào colleges subordinated to a ministry

【部署】 bùshǔ 1.（安排）arrange; map out; lay out 2.〈*Mil.*〉 disposition; deployment：作战～ battle disposition

【部头】 bùtóu volume：大～的书 a voluminous book

【部委】 bùwěi ministries and commissions

【部位】 bùwèi position; place

【部下】 bùxià 1.（被统率的部队）troops under one's command **2**.（下级）subordinate

【部优产品】 bùyōu chǎnpǐn products of quality on a ministry scale

【部长】 bùzhǎng minister; head of a department：外交～ foreign minister; Minister of Foreign Affairs / 国防～ Minister of National Defense

【部长会议】 bùzhǎng huìyì Council of Ministers

【部长助理】 bùzhǎng zhùlǐ assistant minister

埠（bù） **1**.（码头）wharf; pier **2**.（商埠）port **3**.（邮政用语，指所在地）port：本～ this port / 外～ other port

簿（bù） book：练习～ exercise book

【簿记】 bùjì bookkeeping

【簿子】 bù·zi notebook; book

C

ca

擦(cā) 1.(摩擦) rub：在手上～肥皂 rub one's hands with soap 2.(擦干净) wipe：～盘子 wipe the dishes/ ～眼睛 wipe one's eyes / ～眼泪 wipe one's tears away 3.(涂抹) spread on; put on：～胭抹粉 paint rouge and powder 4.(擦近，贴近) brush; shave：～身而过 pass each other so close that they almost rubbed each other

【擦干】 cāgān wipe sth. dry

【擦亮眼睛】 cāliàng yǎnjīng remove the scales from one's eyes; sharpen one's vigilance

【擦屁股】 cā pì·gu clean the bottom; clear up a messy situation to settle an impasse

【擦伤】 cāshāng abrasion; gall; scratch

【擦拭】 cāshì clean; cleanse

【擦鞋机】 cāxiéjī shoe-cleaning machine

【擦澡】 cāzǎo rub oneself down with a wet towel; take a sponge bath

【擦子】 cā·zi eraser：橡皮～ rubber

cai

猜(cāi) 1.(猜测) guess; conjecture; speculate：～一～ make a guess; have a guess / ～中 guess right 2.(起疑心) suspect

【猜不透】 cāibùtòu unable to guess; unable to make out

【猜测】 cāicè guess; conjecture; surmise

【猜度】 cāiduó surmise; conjecture

【猜忌】 cāijì have a suspicion; be jealous

【猜谜】 cāimí 1.(猜谜底) guess a riddle; solve riddles 2.(猜测) guess

【猜拳】 cāiquán a finger-guessing game

【猜想】 cāixiǎng suppose; guess; suspect

【猜疑】 cāiyí be suspicious; have misgivings; harbor suspicions：互相～ be suspicious of each other; have misgivings about each other

才[纔[3]](cái) 1.(才能) ability; talent; gift 2.(指有才能者) capable person; person of talent 3.(仅，只) just; only：她～卖掉了三个。She sold only three.

【才干】 cáigàn ability; competence; talent：这人很有～。He is a man of great ability.

【才华】 cáihuá literary of artistic talent：～出众 of uncommon brilliance; possess exceptional talent

【才路】 cáilù ways to train men of profession：广开～ be open for people of talent

【才貌双全】 cái mào shuāng quán have both looks and real talent

【才能】 cáinéng ability; talent

【才气】 cáiqì literary talent：有～ have superb talent

【才疏学浅】 cáishū-xuéqiǎn have little talent and less learning

【才思】 cáisī imaginative power; creativeness

【才学】 cáixué talent and learning; scholarship：～超群 one's ability and learning surpass the average

【才智】 cáizhì ability and wisdom

【才子】 cáizǐ gifted scholar; erudite person

材(cái) 1.(木料) timber 2.(材料) material 3.(才能) ability; talent; aptitude 4.(人才) capable person：培养成～ bring sb. up to be a useful person

【材料】 cáiliào 1.(原料) material：建筑～ building material 2.(资料) data; material：参考～ reference material / 第一手～ first-hand information 3.(人才) makings; stuff

【材料加工】 cáiliào jiāgōng materials processing

财(cái) wealth; money：发～ get rich

【财宝】 cáibǎo money and valuables

【财产】 cáichǎn property：公共～ public

property / 私人～ privately owned property
【财产权】 cáichǎnquán property right
【财大气粗】 cáidà-qìcū he who has wealth speaks louder than others
【财阀】 cáifá zaibatsu (Jap.)
【财富】 cáifù wealth; riches: 精神～ spiritual wealth / 社会～ wealth of the society / 物质～ material wealth
【财经】 cáijīng finance and economics
【财会人员】 cái kuài rényuán financial and accountancy personnel
【财力】 cáilì financial resources; financial capacity
【财路】 cáilù ways to obtain money: 开辟～ open ways to get better
【财贸】 cáimào finance and commerce; finance and trade
【财迷】 cáimí moneygrubber; miser
【财权】 cáiquán 1.(指所有权) right of property 2.(经济权) economic rights
【财神】 cáishén deity that brings wealth to people; able persons
【财神爷】 cáishényé deity of wealth
【财团】 cáituán financial group
【财务】 cáiwù financial affairs
【财物】 cáiwù property; belongings
【财务代理人】 cáiwù dàilǐrén fiscal agent
【财物管理】 cáiwù guǎnlǐ financial administration
【财务科】 cáiwùkē finance section
【财务年度】 cáiwù niándù fiscal year
【财源】 cáiyuán financial resources; source of revenue: 开辟～ explore more source of revenue
【财政】 cáizhèng (public) finance; financial (adj.)
【财政包干】 cáizhèng bāogān be responsible for one's finance
【财政补贴】 cáizhèng bǔtiē financial subside
【财政部】 cáizhèngbù the Ministry of Finance
【财政赤字】 cáizhèng chìzì financial deficits
【财政纪律】 cáizhèng jìlǜ financial discipline: ～松弛 financial discipline is lax
【财政局】 cáizhèngjú the Bureau of Finance
【财政年度】 cáizhèng niándù financial year; fiscal year
【财政收支平衡】 cáizhèng shōuzhī pínghéng balance of revenue and expenditure
【财政危机】 cáizhèng wēijī financial crisis
【财主】 cái·zhu moneybags; rich person

裁 (cái) 1.(剪裁) cut into parts 2.(裁减) reduce; cut down; dismiss 3.(衡量) judge; decide 4.(制裁) check; sanction 5.(安排取舍) mental planning
【裁处】 cáichǔ make arrangement after due consideration
【裁定】 cáidìng 〈*Law*〉 ruling; holding; judge
【裁夺】 cáiduó consider and decide
【裁缝】 cái·feng tailor; dressmaker
【裁缝店】 cái·fengdiàn the tailor's (shop)
【裁减】 cáijiǎn reduce; cut down: ～军备 reduce military preparations
【裁剪】 cáijiǎn cut out
【裁决】 cáijué ruling; adjudication: 接受～ accept the ruling
【裁军】 cáijūn disarmament: ～会议 a disarmament conference
【裁判】 cáipàn 1.(评判) act as referee; referee 2.(裁判员) judge; umpire; referee
【裁判权】 cáipànquán jurisdiction: 领事～ consular jurisdiction
【裁判员】 cáipànyuán 1.(运动会或竞赛的) judge 2.(排球、乒乓球、羽毛球、网球、棒球的) umpire 3.(篮球、足球、拳击、柔道的) referee
【裁员】 cáiyuán reduce the staff; cut down the number of persons employed

采[採$^{1-3}$] (cǎi) 1.(采摘) pick; pluck; gather: ～花 pick flowers 2.(开采) mine; extract: ～金 mine for gold 3.(采取) adopt; select 4.(精神) complexion; spirit
【采茶】 cǎichá pick tea
【采伐】 cǎifá fell; cut; cut over: ～森林 open up a forest
【采访】 cǎifǎng report; cover; gather material: 向某人～ interview sb.
【采访记者】 cǎifǎng jìzhě reporter
【采购】 cǎigòu make purchases for an organization or enterprise; purchase
【采购团】 cǎigòutuán purchasing group; purchasing mission

【采购员】 cǎigòuyuán purchasing agent
【采光】 cǎiguāng 〈*Archit.*〉(natural) lighting; daylighting
【采集】 cǎijí gather; collect: ～民歌 collect folks songs
【采掘】 cǎijué excavate; dig
【采矿】 cǎikuàng mine; mining
【采买】 cǎimǎi purchase; buy
【采煤】 cǎiméi excavate coal; mine coal
【采煤工人】 cǎiméi gōngrén coal miner
【采纳】 cǎinà accept; adopt: ～合理的建议 accept rational suggestions
【采暖】 cǎinuǎn 〈*Archit.*〉 heating
【采暖设备】 cǎinuǎn shèbèi heating equipment
【采取】 cǎiqǔ adopt; take: ～步骤 take steps / ～积极措施 adopt vigorous measures / ～坚决的手段 take a firm hand / ～一系列措施 adopt a series of measures / ～主动 take the initiative
【采写】 cǎixiě collect materials through interviews and write articles or reports about them
【采血】 cǎixiě 〈*Med.*〉 take a blood sample
【采样】 cǎiyàng take a sample; sample (v.)
【采药】 cǎiyào gather medicinal herbs
【采用】 cǎiyòng put to use; adopt; use; employ: ～新工艺 adopt new technology
【采油】 cǎiyóu 〈*Petroleum*〉 extract oil; oil recovery
【采摘】 cǎizhāi pluck; pick: ～果子 pick fruit
【采制】 cǎizhì **1.**(采集加工) gather and process **2.**(采访录制) interview sb. and record; collect and process sound and pictures

彩[綵²] (cǎi) **1.**(彩色) color **2.**(彩绸) colored silk **3.**(喝彩的欢呼声) applause; cheer **4.**(精彩) variety; splendor **5.**(中彩; 奖品) prize **6.**(挂彩) blood from a wound
【彩绸】 cǎichóu colored silk; silk of various colors
【彩电】 cǎidiàn color receiver; color television
【彩虹】 cǎihóng rainbow
【彩绘】 cǎihuì **1.**(彩色图案) colored drawing; colored pattern **2.**(用彩色绘画) paint with color
【彩卷】 cǎijuǎn color film
【彩扩】 cǎikuò enlarge color photos; enlargement of color photos
【彩礼】 cǎilǐ betrothal gifts; bride-price
【彩排】 cǎipái dress rehearsal
【彩牌楼】 cǎipái·lou decorative pailou; decorative gateway
【彩票】 cǎipiào lottery ticket
【彩旗】 cǎiqí colored flag; bunting
【彩色】 cǎisè multicolor; color (AmE.); colour (BrE.)
【彩色电视】 cǎisè diànshì color television
【彩色电视接收机】 cǎisè diànshì jiēshōujī color receiver
【彩色放大机】 cǎisè fàngdàjī color enlarger
【彩色胶片】 cǎisè jiāopiàn color film
【彩色影片】 cǎisè yǐngpiàn color film
【彩霞】 cǎixiá rosy clouds; pink clouds
【彩印】 cǎiyìn color printing

踩[跴] (cǎi) step on; trample: ～油门 step on the gas (accelerator)
【踩坏】 cǎihuài tread on; stamp down
【踩水】 cǎishuǐ 〈*Swimming*〉 treading water

菜 (cài) **1.**(蔬菜) vegetable; greens **2.**(泛指副食) food **3.**(菜肴) dish; course
【菜场】 càichǎng market; food market
【菜单】 càidān menu; bill of fare
【菜刀】 càidāo kitchen knife
【菜地】 càidì vegetable plot
【菜豆】 càidòu kidney bean
【菜瓜】 càiguā snake melon
【菜馆】 càiguǎn 〈*dial.*〉 restaurant
【菜花】 càihuā **1.**(花椰菜) cauliflower **2.**(油菜花) rape flower
【菜窖】 càijiào vegetable cellar; clamp
【菜篮子】 càilán·zi **1.**(买菜用的) vegetable basket; basket for carrying vegetables and food items **2.**(指副食品) non-staple food
【菜篮子工程】 càilán·zi gōngchéng vegetable basket project
【菜牛】 càiniú beef cattle
【菜农】 càinóng vegetable grower
【菜谱】 càipǔ cookery-book; cookbook
【菜青】 càiqīng dark greyish green
【菜色】 càisè famished complexion; starved complexion

【菜蔬】 càishū 1.（蔬菜）vegetables; greens 2.（菜肴）dishes at a meal
【菜摊】 càitān vegetable stall
【菜心】 càixīn heart of cabbage plants
【菜蚜】 càiyá 〈*Agric.*〉 vegetable aphid
【菜肴】 càiyáo cooked food; meat dishes
【菜油】 càiyóu rapeseed oil; rape oil; colza oil
【菜园子】 càiyuán·zi vegetable garden; vegetable farm
【菜子】 càizǐ 1.（蔬菜种子）vegetable seeds 2.（油菜子）rapeseed
【菜子油】 càizǐyóu rape oil; rapeseed oil; colza oil

参［參］（cān） 1.（参加）join; enter; take part in 2.（参考）refer; consult 3.（参见，谒见）call to pay one's respects to
（另见“参”cēn, shēn）
【参拜】 cānbài pay respects to; make a formal visit to
【参半】 cānbàn half; half-and-half
【参观】 cānguān visit; look around: ～博物馆 visit a museum
【参加】 cānjiā 1.（加入）join; attend; take part in: ～比赛 take part in game / ～婚礼 attend a wedding / ～讨论 take part in discussion 2.（提出意见）give (advice, suggestion, etc.)
【参加国】 cānjiāguó acceding state
【参见】 cānjiàn 1.（参看）see also; cf.: ～第二章 see also Chapter 2 2.（进见，谒见）pay one's respects to (a superior, etc.)
【参见号】 cānjiànhào arrow（符号为 → ）
【参军】 cānjūn join the army; join up; enlist
【参看】 cānkàn 1.（参见）see (also): ～第123页 see page 123 2.（查阅）consult 3.（参考）read sth. for reference
【参考】 cānkǎo 1.（查阅）consult; refer to 2.（参考）reference: 仅供～ for reference only
【参考书】 cānkǎoshū reference book
【参考书目】 cānkǎo shūmù bibliography; a list of reference books
【参考资料】 cānkǎo zīliào reference material
【参谋】 cānmóu 1.〈*Mil.*〉 staff officer 2.（出主意）give advice 3.（指人）adviser; advisor
【参谋部】 cānmóubù 〈*Mil.*〉 the general staff
【参谋长】 cānmóuzhǎng chief of staff: 总～ chief of the general staff
【参评】 cānpíng participate in evaluation and electing
【参赛】 cānsài participate in competition and contest
【参事】 cānshì adviser; counsellor
【参试】 cānshì participate in the experiment
【参事室】 cānshìshì advisory office: 国务院～ advisory office of the State Council
【参数】 cānshù 〈*Math.*〉 parameter
【参天】 cāntiān reaching to the sky; towering; very tall: ～古树 old trees that reach into the skies
【参选】 cānxuǎn participate in evaluation and election
【参演】 cānyǎn take part in a performance
【参谒】 cānyè have an audience with sb.; pay one's respects to sb.
【参议员】 cānyìyuán senator
【参议院】 cānyìyuàn senate
【参与】 cānyù participate in; have a hand in: ～国际竞争 take part in international competition / ～其事 have a hand in the matter
【参预】 cānyù 同“参与”
【参与意识】 cānyù yì·shí sense of participation
【参阅】 cānyuè see also; cf.; see
【参赞】 cānzàn counsellor; councillor: 商务～ commercial counsellor / 文化～ cultural attaché
【参展】 cānzhǎn participate in an exhibition
【参战】 cānzhàn enter a war; participate in a war; take part in a war
【参战国】 cānzhànguó belligerent state; belligerent
【参照】 cānzhào consult; refer to
【参照前例】 cānzhào qiánlì with reference to the previous case
【参照系】 cānzhàoxì reference frame
【参政】 cānzhèng participate in government and political affairs
【参政党】 cānzhèngdǎng party participant in

government and political affairs

【参政议政】 cānzhèng yìzhèng participate in and discuss government and political affairs

餐［飡、湌］(cān) 1.（吃饭）eat 2.（饭食）food; meal: 便～ light meal / 快～ fast food / 冷～ buffet / 西～ Western food / 中～ Chinese food 3.（每顿饭）regular meal

【餐车】 cānchē restaurant car; dining car; diner

【餐馆】 cānguǎn restaurant

【餐巾】 cānjīn table napkin

【餐巾纸】 cānjīnzhǐ napkin paper; paper napkin

【餐具】 cānjù tableware; dinner service; dinner set

【餐券】 cānquàn meal coupon; meal ticket

【餐厅】 cāntīng 1.（饭厅）dining room; dining hall 2.（餐馆）restaurant

【餐桌】 cānzhuō dinner table; dining table

【餐桌转盘】 cānzhuō zhuànpán lazy Susan

残［殘］(cán) 1.（残缺）incomplete; deficient 2.（残余的）remnant; remaining 3.（伤害；毁坏）injure; damage 4.（残忍）savage; barbarous; ferocious

【残暴】 cánbào cruel and ferocious; ruthless; brutal; savage

【残存】 cáncún remnant; remaining; surviving

【残冬】 cándōng the last days of winter

【残废】 cánfèi 1.（丧失机能）maimed; crippled; disabled 2.（残废的人）a maimed person; cripple

【残废军人】 cánfèi jūnrén disabled serviceman

【残羹剩饭】 cángēng-shèngfàn remains of a meal

【残骸】 cánhái wreckage; remains; fragments: 飞机～ the wreckage of an plane

【残害】 cánhài cruelly injure or kill

【残疾】 cán·ji deformity; deformed (adj.)

【残疾人】 cán·jirén deformed man; deformed person

【残迹】 cánjì a remaining trace, sign, etc.; vestiges

【残局】 cánjú 1.（指棋局）the final phase of a game of chess 2.（指局面）the situation after the failure of an undertaking or after social unrest: 收拾～ pick up the pieces

【残酷】 cánkù cruel; brutal; ruthless

【残留】 cánliú remain; be left over

【残留气排气管】 cánliúqì páiqìguǎn 〈*Ship*〉 gas vent for burning gas residues

【残品】 cánpǐn damaged article; defective goods

【残破】 cánpò broken; dilapidated

【残缺】 cánquē incomplete; fragmentary

【残缺不全】 cánquē-bùquán incomplete; fragmentary

【残忍】 cánrěn cruel; ruthless

【残杀】 cánshā murder; massacre; slaughter: 自相～ mutual slaughter; kill each other

【残余】 cányú remnants; remains; survivals

【残渣】 cánzhā residue; less; caput mortuum

【残渣余孽】 cánzhā-yúniè evil elements from the old society; dregs of the old society

【残照】 cánzhào the setting sun

蚕［蠶］(cán) silkworm

【蚕豆】 cándòu broad bean

【蚕蛾】 cán'é silk moth

【蚕茧】 cánjiǎn cocoon; silkworm cocoon

【蚕农】 cánnóng silkworm raiser; sericulturist

【蚕沙】 cánshā silkworm excrement

【蚕食】 cánshí nibble; nibble up

【蚕丝】 cánsī tural silk; silk

【蚕蛹】 cányǒng silkworm chrysalis

【蚕子】 cánzǐ silkworm seed; silkworm egg

惭［慚］(cán) feel ashamed

【惭愧】 cánkuì be ashamed: ～万分 be extremely ashamed

惨［慘］(cǎn) 1.（悲惨）miserable; pitiful; tragic 2.（凶狠）cruel; savage 3.（程度严重）to a serious degree; disastrously

【惨案】 cǎn'àn 1.（政治性的）massacre 2.（凶杀案）murder case; tragic case; tragedy

【惨白】 cǎnbái pale: 脸色～ look deathly pale

【惨不忍睹】 cǎnbù-rěndǔ so tragic that one cannot bear to look at it; too horrible to look at

【惨淡经营】 cǎndàn-jīngyíng keep (an enterprise, etc.) going by painstaking effort; take great pains to carry on one's work under difficult circumstances

【惨祸】 cǎnhuò catastrophe; a catastrophic disaster

【惨杀】 cǎnshā massacre; murder

【惨死】 cǎnsǐ die a tragic death

【惨痛】 cǎntòng deeply grieved; painful; bitter: ～的经验 a bitter experience

【惨无人道】 cǎnwú-réndào very cruel and inhuman

【惨重】 cǎnzhòng heavy; grievous; disastrous: 损失～ suffer heavy losses

灿[燦] (càn)

【灿烂】 cànlàn magnificent; splendid; resplendent; bright: ～的前景 magnificent prospects

粲 (càn)

【粲然】 cànrán bright; brilliant

【粲然一笑】 cànrán-yīxiào give a beaming smile

cang

仓[倉] (cāng) storehouse; warehouse

【仓储】 cāngchǔ keep sth. in a storehouse

【仓储制度】 cāngchǔ zhìdù warehousing system

【仓促】 cāngcù hurriedly; hastily; all of a sudden: ～做出结论 rush to a conclusion; jump to a conclusion

【仓皇】 cānghuáng in a flurry; in panic: ～出逃 run away in panic

【仓皇失措】 cānghuáng-shīcuò be at a loss; be panic-stricken

【仓库】 cāngkù warehouse; storehouse; depository

【仓库保管员】 cāngkù bǎoguǎnyuán warehouseman

【仓租】 cāngzū warehouse storage charges

苍[蒼] (cāng) 1.(绿色的) dark green 2.(蓝色的) blue

【苍白】 cāngbái pale; pallid; wan: ～的面孔 a pallid complexion

【苍苍】 cāngcāng 1.(灰白) grey 2.(苍茫) vast and hazy 3.(深绿色) dark green

【苍翠】 cāngcuì dark green; verdant

【苍劲】 cāngjìng 1.(用于树木) old and strong 2.(用于书画) vigorous; bold

【苍老】 cānglǎo 1.(老态) old; aged 2.(指笔力) vigorous; forceful

【苍茫】 cāngmáng 1.(辽远) vast; boundless 2.(没有边际) indistinct: 暮色～ deepening shades of dusk

【苍穹】 cāngqióng the vault of heaven; the firmament

【苍松翠柏】 cāngsōng-cuìbǎi pines and cypresses of verdant green

【苍天】 cāngtiān 1.(天空) the blue sky 2.(天;天神) Heaven

【苍蝇】 cāng·ying fly

【苍蝇拍】 cāng·yingpāi swatter; fly swatter

沧[滄] (cāng)

【沧海】 cānghǎi the blue sea; the sea

【沧海桑田】 cānghǎi-sāngtián the swift changes of the world; vicissitudes of human affairs

【沧海一粟】 cānghǎi-yīsù a drop in the ocean

【沧桑】 cāngsāng 饱经～ have experienced many vicissitudes of life

舱[艙] (cāng) 1.(舱房) cabin: 船～ cabin; ship's hold / 装～ stow the hold 2.〈*Aeron.*〉 module: 指令～ command module

【舱口】 cāngkǒu 〈*Aeron.*〉 hatch

【舱门】 cāngmén 〈*Aeron.*〉 door

【舱位】 cāngwèi 1.(铺位或座位) cabin seat; cabin berth 2.(船仓) shipping space

藏 (cáng) 1.(躲藏;隐藏) hide; conceal: 你把它～在哪儿啦? Where did you hide it? 2.(收藏;储藏) store; lay by (另见"藏"zàng)

【藏垢纳污】 cánggòu-nàwū shelter evil people and countenance evil practices

【藏龙卧虎】 cánglóng-wòhǔ "hidden dragons and crouching tigers"; talented men still remained in concealment

【藏匿】 cángnì conceal; hide; go into hiding

【藏身】 cángshēn hide oneself; go into hiding: 无处～ no place to hide

【藏身之处】 cángshēn-zhīchù hiding-place;

shelter
【藏书】 cángshū 1.(收藏书籍) collect books 2.(所藏的书籍) a collection of books; library
【藏书票】 cángshūpiào bookplate

cao

操(cāo) 1.(拿) grasp; hold: 稳～胜券 have full assurance of success; be sure to win 2.(做;从事) act; do; operate 3.(说) speak: ～法语 speak French 4.(操练) drill; exercise: 出～ go out to do exercises 5.(品行;行为) conduct; behavior
【操场】 cāochǎng playground; sports ground
【操持】 cāochí manage; handle
【操劳】 cāoláo 1.(辛苦劳动) work hard 2.(费心料理) take care; look after
【操练】 cāoliàn 1.(指队列) drill; practice 2.(泛指训练或锻炼) exercise
【操琴】 cāoqín play the erhu
【操心】 cāoxīn 1.(费心) worry about; trouble about; take pains 2.(费心考虑或料理) rack one's brains
【操行】 cāoxíng behavior or conduct of a student
【操之过急】 cāozhī-guòjí act with undue haste; act too hastily
【操纵】 cāozòng 1.(开动) operate; control: ～机器 operate machines 2.(支配) rig; manipulate: 幕后～ manipulate from behind the scenes; pull strings
【操纵台】 cāozòngtái control panel; control board
【操纵自如】 cāozòng-zìrú restraint or lenient as it pleases one
【操作】 cāozuò 1.(指进行活动) operate; manipulate 2.(劳动;干活) work
【操作规程】 cāozuò guīchéng operating rules; operating instructions; working order
【操作环境】 cāozuò huánjìng operation environment
【操作人员】 cāozuò rényuán attending personnel; operating staff
【操作手册】 cāozuò shǒucè operation manual
【操作系统】 cāozuò xìtǒng operation system: 磁盘～ DOS; Disk Operation System

糙(cāo) rough; coarse: ～布 coarse cloth
【糙米】 cāomǐ brown rice; half-polished rice

嘈(cáo) noise; din
【嘈杂】 cáozá noisy: 多么～! What a noise!

槽(cáo) 1.(器具) trough: 水～ water trough 2.(槽儿) groove; slot
【槽车】 cáochē tank wagon
【槽钢】 cáogāng channel; box iron; channel steel

草[艸](cǎo) 1.(植物) grass; straw 2.(草率) careless; hasty; rough 3.(草稿) draft
【草案】 cǎo'àn draft: 决议～ a draft resolution
【草包】 cǎobāo 1.(草袋) straw bag; straw sack 2.(无能的人) good-for-nothing; idiot; blockhead
【草本】 cǎoběn 〈*Bot.*〉 herbaceous
【草本植物】 cǎoběn zhíwù herb
【草草】 cǎocǎo carelessly; hastily: ～了事 dispose of a thing carelessly or hastily / ～收场 declare the matter closed before it is thoroughly settled
【草场】 cǎochǎng grassland
【草创】 cǎochuàng start (an enterprise, etc.)
【草丛】 cǎocóng a thick growth of grass
【草地】 cǎodì 1.(长草的地方) grassland; meadow 2.(草坪) lawn
【草地网球】 cǎodì wǎngqiú lawn tennis
【草垫子】 cǎodiàn·zi straw mattress
【草垛】 cǎoduò haystack; hayrick
【草稿】 cǎogǎo rough draft; draft
【草菅人命】 cǎojiān-rénmìng treat human life as if it were not worth a straw; act with utter disregard for human life
【草料】 cǎoliào forage; fodder
【草绿色】 cǎolǜsè grass green
【草帽】 cǎomào straw hat
【草莓】 cǎoméi strawberry
【草木皆兵】 cǎomù-jiēbīng every bush and tree looks like an enemy
【草拟】 cǎonǐ draw up; draft: ～一个议案 draft a parliamentary bill
【草皮】 cǎopí sod; turf

【草坪】 cǎopíng lawn
【草签】 cǎoqiān initial：～一份文件 initial a document / ～合同 initial a contract / ～协定 initial an agreement
【草签文本】 cǎoqiān wénběn initialed text
【草食】 cǎoshí 〈*Zool*.〉 herbivore
【草率】 cǎoshuài careless; perfunctory：～从事 take any hasty action; do a job carelessly or perfunctorily
【草酸】 cǎosuān oxalic acid
【草图】 cǎotú sketch (map); draft
【草席】 cǎoxí straw mat
【草鞋】 cǎoxié straw sandals
【草药】 cǎoyào medicinal herbs; herb medicine
【草鱼】 cǎoyú grass carp
【草原】 cǎoyuán grasslands; prairie
【草纸】 cǎozhǐ **1**.(粗制包装纸) rough straw paper **2**.(卫生纸) toilet paper

ce

册[冊] (cè) volume; book：第二～ Volume II
【册封】 cèfēng confer titles of nobility on
【册子】 cè·zi book; volume：小～ booklet
厕[廁] (cè) lavatory; toilet; washroom; W.C.：公～ public lavatory / 男～ men's; men's room / 女～ women's; women's room; women's toilet / 如～ go to the toilet
【厕所】 cèsuǒ lavatory; toilet; W.C.
侧 (cè) **1**.(旁边) side：右～ the right side / 左～ the left side **2**.(向旁边歪斜) incline; lean
(另见"侧"zhāi)
【侧板】 cèbǎn 〈*Guitar*〉 waist
【侧耳细听】 cè ěr xì tīng incline the head and listen attentively; prick up one's ears
【侧滑】 cèhuá 〈*Auto*〉 skid：汽车～，撞上了一棵树。The car skidded and hit a tree.
【侧门】 cèmén side door; side entrance
【侧面】 cèmiàn side; aspect; flank; profile; side face：问题的一个～ one side of the problem
【侧目】 cèmù sidelong glance; look askance at sb.
【侧身】 cèshēn on one's side; sideways：～而卧 lie on one's side
【侧视镜】 cèshìjìng 〈*Auto*〉 side-view mirror
【侧视图】 cèshìtú lateral view
【侧线】 cèxiàn 〈*Fish*〉 lateral line
【侧卸汽车】 cè xiè qìchē side dump truck
【侧翼】 cèyì flank; wing
【侧影】 cèyǐng silhouette; profile
【侧泳】 cèyǒng sidestroke
【侧重】 cèzhòng lay particular emphasis on; pay special attention to
恻 (cè)
【恻隐】 cèyǐn compassion; pity：～之心 sense of pity; natural compassion
测 (cè) **1**.(测量) survey; fathom; measure：～海洋深度 fathom a sea **2**.(测度) conjecture; infer：变化莫～ constantly changing
【测电笔】 cèdiànbǐ test pencil
【测定】 cèdìng determine; identify
【测高计】 cègāojì altimeter; height indicator
【测绘】 cèhuì survey and drawing; mapping
【测绘员】 cèhuìyuán surveyor; cartographer
【测距器】 cèjùqì 〈*Photog*.〉 range finder
【测控】 cèkòng observe and control; survey and control
【测量】 cèliáng survey; measure; gauge：～地形 survey the topography / 大地～ geodetic survey
【测量学】 cèliángxué surveying
【测量仪器】 cèliáng yíqì surveying instrument
【测试】 cèshì test
【测算】 cèsuàn **1**.(调查计算) survey and calculate **2**.(推算) infer and estimate
【测验】 cèyàn test：老师给我们～算术。The teacher gave us an arithmetic test.
策[筴] (cè) plan; scheme; strategy：失～ take a false step / 献～ submit a scheme
【策动】 cèdòng instigate; engineer; stir up
【策反】 cèfǎn instigate rebellion within the enemy camp; incite defection
【策划】 cèhuà plan; plot; scheme; engineer：～夺权 scheme for power / ～反叛 plot rebellion
【策划者】 cèhuàzhě sponsor; plotter;

schemer

【策略】 cèlüè 1.(方针和方式) tactics 2.(讲究斗争艺术) tactful：做事要～一些 do things more tactfully

【策应】 cèyìng support according to the coordinated plan

【策源地】 cèyuándì source; place of origin; hotbed：战争～ a source of war; a hotbed of war

参[参] (cēn) (另见"参"cān, shēn)

【参差】 cēncī irregular; uneven; not uniform：～错落 confused with errors and omission

ceng

层[層] (céng) 1.〈*classifier*〉layer; tier; stratum：一～泥 a layer of clay 2.(楼层) story; floor：第一～ the ground floor (BrE.); the first floor (AmE.) / 第二～ the first floor (BrE.); the second floor (AmE.) / 第三～ the second floor (BrE.); the third floor (AmE.) / 第四～ the third floor (BrE.); the forth floor (AmE.) / 20～的大楼 a building of twenty stories 3.(可分项分步的事物) a component part in a sequence

【层层】 céngcéng layer upon layer; ring upon ring; tier upon tier：～把关 check at each level / ～发动 mobilize level by level

【层层叠叠】 céngcéng-diédié tier upon tier

【层层加码】 céngcéng-jiāmǎ raise the quota at each level

【层出不穷】 céngchū-bùqióng emerge in an endless stream; layer upon layer without an end

【层次】 céngcì 1.(指机构) administrative levels：～重叠 overlapping 2.(内容次序) arrangement of ideas (in writing or speech)：～不清 lack unity and coherence 3.(分层) gradation：～分明 gradation is distinct

【层积云】 céngjīyún 〈*Meteorol.*〉stratocumulus

【层云】 céngyún 〈*Meteorol.*〉stratus; stratus cloud

曾 (céng) (另见"曾"zēng)

【曾几何时】 céng jǐ hé shí before long; not long after; not long since

【曾经】 céngjīng 几年前我～见过她一面。I met her once several years ago.

蹭 (cèng) 1.(摩擦) rub：鞋子～脚。The shoe rubs my foot. 2.(沾上) be smeared with：小心～油漆。Mind the fresh paint. 3.(慢吞吞地) dillydally; loiter

cha

叉 (chā) 1.(叉子) fork 2.(叉取) work with a fork; fork 3.(叉形符号, "×") cross (另见"叉"chá, chǎ)

【叉车】 chāchē forklift; fork truck; forklift truck

【叉烧】 chāshāo grilled pork

【叉腰】 chāyāo akimbo：双手～ with arms akimbo

【叉子】 chā·zi fork

差 (chā) 1.(差别) difference; dissimilarity：时～ time difference 2.(差错) mistake：偏～ deviation 3.〈*Math.*〉difference (另见"差"chà, chāi)

【差别】 chābié difference; disparity：年龄～ disparity of age

【差别汇率】 chābié huìlǜ discriminatory cross-rates

【差错】 chācuò 1.(错误) mistake; error; slip 2.(意外变化) mishap; accident

【差动齿轮】 chādòng chǐlún differential gear

【差额】 chā'é difference; balance; margin：补足～ make up the balance

【差额选举】 chā'é xuǎnjǔ contested election

【差价】 chājià price difference; variation in price：季节～ seasonal price differences / 地区～ regional price differences

【差距】 chājù 1.(差别) gap; disparity：合理拉开收入～ widen differences in personal income to a reasonable degree 2.〈*Mech.*〉difference

【差异】 chāyì difference; divergence; discrepancy; diversity

插 (chā) 1.(放进、刺进或穿入) stick in; insert 2.(加进去) interpose; insert

【插班】 chābān join a class in the middle of

the course

【插播】 chābō interpose some other temporary items into the radio or TV station regular program during the broadcast

【插队】 chāduì stay and labor in a country production team

【插队落户】 chāduì luòhù move to and settle down in a country production team

【插花】 chāhuā floral arrangements; ikebana (Jap.)

【插话】 chāhuà 1.(插嘴) interpose (a remark, etc.); chip in 2.(小插曲) digression; episode

【插肩袖】 chājiānxiù raglan sleeve

【插口】 chākǒu 〈*Electr*.〉 socket; jack; outlet

【插曲】 chāqǔ 1.〈*Music*〉 interlude 2.(电影插曲) songs in a film or play 3.(作品中的一段) episode; interlude

【插手】 chāshǒu 1.(参加) take part; lend a hand 2.(参与) have a hand in; poke one's nose into; meddle in; take a hand in

【插条】 chātiáo 〈*Bot*.〉 transplant a cutting; cutting

【插头】 chātóu 〈*Electr*.〉 plug

【插图】 chātú illustration; plate

【插销】 chāxiāo 1.(门窗等用) bolt 2.〈*Electr*.〉 plug

【插秧】 chāyāng transplant rice seedlings

【插秧机】 chāyāngjī 〈*Agric*.〉 rice transplanter

【插页】 chāyè inset; insert

【插足】 chāzú 1.(放脚) put one's foot in 2.(参与) participate (in some activity)

【插嘴】 chāzuǐ interrupt; get a word in edgewise

【插座】 chāzuò 〈*Electr*.〉 socket; outlet

叉 (chá) block up; jam: 出租汽车把市中心给～住了。The cabs block up the center.
(另见"叉"chā, chǎ)

茬 (chá) 1.(庄稼的) stubble 2.(种植、生长次数) crop; batch

【茬口】 chákǒu 1.(轮作种类和次序) crops for rotation 2.(指土壤) soil on which a crop has been planted and harvested

茶 (chá) 1.(茶叶) tea: 红～ black tea / 绿～ green tea / 茉莉花～ jasmine tea / 沏～ make tea / 喝～ have tea 2.(某些饮料) certain kinds of drink or liquid food

【茶杯】 chábēi teacup

【茶场】 cháchǎng tea plantation; tea farm

【茶匙】 cháchí teaspoon

【茶炊】 cháchuī samovar (Rus.)

【茶点】 chádiǎn tea and pastries; refreshments

【茶碟儿】 chádiér saucer

【茶馆】 cháguǎn teahouse

【茶褐色】 cháhèsè dark brown

【茶壶】 cháhú teapot

【茶话会】 cháhuàhuì tea party

【茶几】 chájī tea table; teapoy; side table

【茶具】 chájù tea set; tea-things; tea service

【茶卡】 chákǎ 〈place〉 Caka

【茶林场】 chálínchǎng tea plantation

【茶农】 chánóng tea grower

【茶盘】 chápán tea tray; teaboard

【茶钱】 chá·qián 1.(喝茶的钱) payment for tea (in a teahouse) 2.(小费) tip

【茶色】 chásè dark brown

【茶室】 cháshì tearoom; teahouse

【茶树】 cháshù tea tree

【茶水】 cháshuǐ tea or boiled water

【茶碗】 cháwǎn teacup

【茶叶】 cháyè tea; tea-leaves

【茶园】 cháyuán tea plantation

【茶资】 cházī payment for tea (in a teahouse)

【茶座】 cházuò 1.(茶馆) teahouse 2.(指座位) seats in a teahouse or tea garden

搽 (chá) put on the skin; apply

【搽粉】 cháfěn powder the face

【搽药】 cháyào apply ointment

查 (chá) 1.(检查) check; examine 2.(调查) look into; investigate: 我要～一下这件事情。I will check up on the matter. 3.(翻检着看) look up; consult: ～字典 consult a dictionary

【查办】 chábàn investigate and deal with sb. accordingly: 撤职～ dismiss a person and have him prosecuted

【查处】 cháchǔ find out errors or criminal facts and give punishment

【查点】 chádiǎn check the number or amount

of; make an inventory of

【查对】 cháduì check; verify: ～答案 check answers / ～数字 check the figures / ～一个词的拼法 verify the spelling of a word

【查房】 cháfáng (查病房) make the rounds of the wards; go the rounds of the wards

【查封】 cháfēng seal up; close down: ～黄色书刊 seal up pornographic literature

【查户口】 cháhùkǒu check residence cards

【查获】 cháhuò hunt down and seize; uncover; track down: ～赃物 seize the spoils

【查禁】 chájìn ban; prohibit; forbid: ～赌博 ban gambling

【查究】 chájiū investigate and ascertain: ～事故原因 find out the cause of an accident

【查勘】 chákān survey; prospect

【查看】 chákàn look over; examine: ～账目 examine the accounts

【查明】 chámíng prove through investigation; find out; ascertain: ～事实真相 find out truth; ascertain the facts

【查票】 chápiào examine tickets; check tickets

【查票员】 chápiàoyuán ticket-checker

【查讫】 cháqì checked

【查清】 cháqīng make a thorough investigation of; check up on

【查哨】 cháshào inspect the sentries

【查收】 cháshōu 1.(用于书信) please find (sth. enclosed) 2.(检查后收下) check and accept: ～货物 check and accept the cargo

【查税】 cháshuì tax inspection

【查卫生】 cháwèishēng make a public health and sanitation check

【查问】 cháwèn inquire; question; interrogate

【查无实据】 chá wú shí jù investigations show no evidence (for it); investigation reveals no evidence

【查血】 cháxuè have a blood test

【查询】 cháxún inquire about: ～电话号码 enquire sb's telephone number

【查验】 cháyàn check; examine: ～护照 examine the passport / ～行李 inspect the baggage

【查夜】 cháyè 1.(夜间巡视) go the rounds at night 2.(夜间巡逻) night patrol

【查阅】 cháyuè consult; look up: ～百科全书 consult a encyclopedia / ～记录 look up the records

【查账】 cházhàng check accounts; audit accounts; examine accounts

【查找】 cházhǎo look for

【查证】 cházhèng investigate and verify; check

碴 (chá) prick; stab

【碴口】 chákǒu sharp edge of broken glass

【碴儿】 chár 1.(小碎块) broken pieces; fragments; shreds 2.(破口儿) sharp edge of broken glass 3.(争吵的原由) the cause of a quarrel 4.(刚说完的话) sth. just said or mentioned

察 (chá) examine; look into; scrutinize

【察访】 cháfǎng make calls and investigate; go about to find out

【察哈尔】 Cháhā'ěr 〈place〉 Qahar

【察觉】 chájué be conscious of; become aware of; perceive: ～到危险 sense the danger

【察看】 chákàn watch; look carefully at; observe: ～某人脸色 examine sb's face

【察其言,观其行】 chá qí yán, guān qí xíng check what he says against what he does

【察言观色】 chá yán guān sè carefully weigh up a person's words and closely watch his expression; examine a person's language and observe his countenance

【察隅】 cháyú 〈place〉 Zayu

叉 (chǎ) fork: ～着腿 cross one's legs; stand with one's legs apart

(另见"叉"chā, chá)

汊 (chà) branch of a river

杈 (chà) branch: 树～ a branch of a tree

岔 (chà) 1.(分岔) branch: 三～路口 a forked road; a junction of three roads 2.(拐弯) turn off 3.(岔子) accident; trouble

【岔道】 chàdào turnout

【岔开】 chàkāi 1.(分岔) branch off; diverge 2.(离题) diverge to (another topic): 把话～ change the subject of conversation 3.(使分开) stagger; space out

【岔口】 chàkǒu fork (in a road)
【岔路】 chàlù branch road; byroad; side road
【岔气】 chàqì feel a pain in the chest when breathing
【岔子】 chà·zi 1.(事故) accident; trouble; something wrong 2.(错误) fault 3.(岔路) branch road; byroad; side road

诧 (chà) be surprised
【诧异】 chàyì be surprised; be amazed; be astonished

刹 (chà) Buddhist temple; Buddhist monastery: 古～ a ancient Buddhist temple
(另见“刹”shā)
【刹那】 chànà instant; split second: 一～ in an instant; in a moment

差 (chà) 1.(不同) differ from; fall short of; difference 2.(错误) wrong; mistake 3.(缺欠) wanting; short of; missing: ～一个人 short of one person 4.(不好) not up to standard; poor; bad; inferior
(另见“差”chā, chāi)
【差不多】 chà·bu duō 1.(指时间、距离) almost; nearly; just about 2.(指程度) about the same; similar 3.(过得去) just about right; just about enough; not far off; not bad
【差不多的】 chà·bu duō·de the average person; ordinary people; common people
【差得多】 chà·de duō 1.(不相同) very different; entirely different 2.(相差) way below
【差点儿】 chàdiǎnr 1.(质量稍次) not quite up to the mark; not good enough; slightly inferior to 2.(几乎) almost; nearly; on the verge of
【差劲】 chàjìn no good; disappointing; not up to the mark
【差生】 chàshēng students who have a bad academic record: 淘汰～ clean out those students who have a bad academic record

chai

拆 (chāi) 1.(拆开) tear open; take apart: ～发动机 take apart the engine / ～信 open a letter 2.(拆卸;拆除) pull down; dismantle: ～船 dismantle a ship / ～一座建筑 pull down a building
【拆除】 chāichú demolish; dismantle; remove
【拆穿】 chāichuān expose; unmask: ～骗局 expose a fraud
【拆封】 chāifēng seal off
【拆毁】 chāihuǐ demolish; pull down
【拆开】 chāikāi take apart; open; separate: ～包裹 open a parcel / ～汽车 disassemble a car; take a car apart
【拆迁】 chāiqiān pull down and remove: 对破旧房屋进行～改造 pull down or reconstruct dilapidated houses
【拆迁户】 chāiqiānhù residents that have to remove from their original living area where new buildings will be constructed
【拆散】 chāisǎn break (a set)
【拆散】 chāisàn break up (a marriage, family, etc.)
【拆台】 chāitái cut the ground from under sb's feet; pull the rug from under sb's feet; pull away a prop; undercut
【拆洗】 chāixǐ 1.(拆洗衣服) wash after removing the padding or lining; unpick and wash 2.(拆洗机器) strip and clean
【拆线】 chāixiàn 〈*Med*.〉 take out stitches
【拆卸】 chāixiè dismantle; disassemble; dismount
【拆阅】 chāiyuè open and read: ～信件 open a letter and read it

差 (chāi) 1.(派遣) send on an errand; dispatch: 出～ be away on business 2.(公务;职务) errand; job
(另见“差”chā, chà)
【差遣】 chāiqiǎn send sb. on an errand or mission; dispatch; assign
【差使】 chāishǐ 1.(差遣) send; assign; appoint 2.(职务) official post; commission
【差事】 chāi·shi 1.(指事情) assignment 2.(指职位) official post

柴 (chái) firewood
【柴草】 cháicǎo firewood; faggot
【柴达木】 Cháidámù 〈place〉 Qaidam
【柴火】 chái·huo firewood; faggot
【柴米油盐】 cháimǐ-yóuyán fuel, rice, oil and

salt
【柴油】 cháiyóu diesel oil
【柴油机】 cháiyóujī diesel engine; diesel
豺(chái) jackal
【豺狼】 cháiláng jackals and wolves
【豺狼成性】 cháiláng-chéngxìng wolfish; rapacious and ruthless
【豺狼当道】 cháiláng-dāngdào bad guy in power

chan

觇(chān) observe; survey
【觇标】 chānbiāo 〈*Surveying*〉 surveyor's beacon
掺[摻](chān) mix; mingle
【掺兑】 chānduì mix; mingle
【掺杂】 chānzá mix; mingle
搀[攙](chān) **1**.(搀扶) help by the arm; support sb. with one's hand **2**.(混合) mix; mingle
【搀兑】 chānduì mix; mingle
【搀扶】 chānfú support sb. with one's hand
【搀和】 chān·huo mix; mingle: 把水和酒精～起来 mingle water with alcohol
【搀假】 chānjiǎ adulterate: ～的酒 adulterated wine
【搀杂】 chānzá mix; mingle
禅[禪](chán) 〈*Buddhism*〉 Dhyana; Zen
(另见"禅"shàn)
【禅房】 chánfáng meditation abode
【禅林】 chánlín Buddhist temple
【禅那】 chánnà 〈*Buddhism*〉 Dhyana
【禅师】 chánshī Zen master
【禅心】 chánxīn meditative mind
【禅杖】 chánzhàng Buddhist monk's staff
【禅宗】 chánzōng 〈*Buddhism*〉 Zen
蝉[蟬](chán) cicada
【蝉联】 chánlián continue to hold a post or title: ～冠军 continue to hold the championship
【蝉翼】 chányì cicada's wings

谗[讒](chán) slander; backbite
【谗害】 chánhài calumniate or slander sb. in order to have him persecuted; frame sb. up
【谗言】 chányán slanderous talk; calumny
馋[饞](chán) greedy; gluttonous
【馋涎欲滴】 chánxián-yùdī mouth drooling with greed
潺(chán)
【潺潺】 chánchán 〈*onomat*.〉 murmur; babble; purl: ～流水 a murmuring stream
缠[纏](chán) **1**.(缠绕) twine; wind **2**.(纠缠) tangle; tie up; pester **3**.(应付) deal with: 难～ be hard to deal with
【缠绕】 chánrào **1**.(缠绕) twine; bind; wind **2**.(纠缠) worry; harass
【缠手】 chánshǒu be hard to deal with
蟾(chán) toad
【蟾蜍】 chánchú toad
【蟾宫】 chángōng the moon
【蟾酥】 chánsū 〈*Chin*. *Med*.〉 toad-cake
产[產](chǎn) **1**.(生育) give birth to; be delivered of: 流～ miscarriage / 人工流～ abortion / 难～ a difficult delivery / 早～ premature birth **2**.(下崽) breed **3**.(生产;出产) produce; yield **4**.(物产) product; produce **5**.(产业) property; estate
【产床】 chǎnchuáng obstetric table
【产蛋率】 chǎndànlǜ laying rate
【产地】 chǎndì place of production; place of origin; producing area
【产房】 chǎnfáng delivery room
【产妇】 chǎnfù lying-in woman; puerpera
【产供销】 chǎngōngxiāo production, supply and sale
【产后】 chǎnhòu **1**.(分娩后) postpartum **2**.(收获之后) after agricultural harvest
【产假】 chǎnjià maternity leave
【产科】 chǎnkē obstetrical department; maternity department
【产科学】 chǎnkēxué obstetrics
【产科医生】 chǎnkē yīshēng obstetrician

【产科医院】 chǎnkē yīyuàn maternity hospital

【产量】 chǎnliàng output; yield: 煤～ output of coal

【产卵】 chǎnluǎn 1.(鸟、家禽) lay eggs 2.(鱼、蛙) spawn 3.(昆虫) oviposit

【产品】 chǎnpǐn product; produce: 农～ farm produce / 长线～ product in excess supply

【产品结构】 chǎnpǐn jiégòu product mix: 调整～ readjust the product mix

【产品性能】 chǎnpǐn xìngnéng properties of product

【产前】 chǎnqián 1.(分娩前) antenatal: ～检查 antenatal examination 2.(指收获或播种之前) before agricultural harvest; in the preparation of seeding

【产钳】 chǎnqián 〈*Med.*〉 obstetrical forceps

【产权】 chǎnquán property right

【产权关系】 chǎnquán guān·xì relation between ownership and management: 理顺～ straighten out relation between ownership and management

【产权所有人】 chǎnquán suǒyǒurén owner of title

【产褥热】 chǎnrùrè 〈*Med.*〉 puerperal fever; childbed fever

【产生】 chǎnshēng 1.(出现) produce; engender: ～影响 exert an influence; exercise influence over; have bearing on 2.(产生于) emerge; come into being

【产物】 chǎnwù outcome; result; product: 必然～ inevitable outcome / 集体智慧的～ result of collective wisdom

【产销】 chǎnxiāo production and marketing: ～合一 integration of production and marketing operation

【产销一体化】 chǎnxiāo yītǐhuà integration of production and marketing operations

【产销直接挂钩】 chǎnxiāo zhíjiē guàgōu direct contact between the producer and the marketing

【产业】 chǎnyè 1.(财产) estate; property 2.(工业生产的) industrial

【产业工人】 chǎnyè gōngrén industrial worker

【产业结构】 chǎnyè jiégòu structure of production: 调整～ readjust the industrial set-up / 优化～ optimize the structure of production

【产院】 chǎnyuàn maternity hospital

【产值】 chǎnzhí value of output; output value

铲[鏟、剷] (chǎn) 1.(铲子) shovel 2.(铲除) lift or move with a shovel; shovel: 在雪中～出一条路来 shovel through the snow

【铲草除根】 chǎncǎo-chúgēn destroy the weeds and dig up the roots

【铲车】 chǎnchē 〈*Mech.*〉 forklift (truck)

【铲除】 chǎnchú root out; uproot; eradicate

【铲球】 chǎnqiú 〈*Football*〉 slide tackle

【铲土机】 chǎntǔjī earth scraper

【铲运机】 chǎnyùnjī scraper; carry-scraper

【铲子】 chǎn·zi shovel

谄 (chǎn) flatter; fawn on

【谄媚】 chǎnmèi flatter; fawn on; toady

【谄上欺下】 chǎnshàng-qīxià be servile to one's superiors and tyrannical to one's subordinates; fawn on those above and bully those below

阐[闡] (chǎn) explain

【阐明】 chǎnmíng expound; clarify: ～形势 clarify the situation

【阐释】 chǎnshì explain; expound; interpret

【阐述】 chǎnshù expound; elaborate; set forth: 各自～了在这个问题上的立场。Each side set forth its position on this question.

忏[懺] (chàn) repent

【忏悔】 chànhuǐ 1.(后悔) repent; be penitent 2.〈*Relig.*〉 confess (one's sins)

颤 (chàn) quiver; tremble; vibrate (另见"颤"zhàn)

【颤动】 chàndòng vibrate; quiver: 树叶在～。The leaves are quivering.

【颤抖】 chàndǒu shake; tremble; quiver; shiver: 冻得～ shiver with cold / 全身～ be all of a tremble

【颤音】 chànyīn 1.〈*Phonet.*〉 trill 2.〈*Music*〉 trill; shake

【颤悠】 chàn·you shake; quiver; flicker

昌 (chāng) prosperous; flourishing

【昌都】 Chāngdū 〈place〉 Qamdo

【昌盛】 chāngshèng prosperous：繁荣～的国家 a prosperous country

猖 (chāng)

【猖獗】 chāngjué be rampant; run wild：～一时 run wild for a while / 疾病～ infested with various diseases

【猖狂】 chāngkuáng savage; furious：～进攻 savage onslaught

娼 (chāng) prostitute

【娼妓】 chāngjì prostitute; streetwalker; street girl; woman of the town

【娼门】 chāngmén brothel

长[長] (cháng) 1.（长度大）long 2.（长度）length 3.（时间久）of long duration; lasting 4.（长处）strong point; forte 5.（长于）be good at; be strong in：～于绘画 be good at painting
（另见"长"zhǎng）

【长臂猿】 chángbìyuán 〈*Zool.*〉 gibbon

【长波】 chángbō long wave

【长城】 Chángchéng 1.（中国长城）the Great Wall 2.（比喻坚不可摧的堡垒）impregnable bulwark

【长程】 chángchéng long-range

【长处】 cháng·chu good qualities; strong points; good points：每个人都有自已的～。Everyone has his own strong points.

【长此以往】 cháng cǐ yǐ wǎng if things go on like this; if things continue this way

【长凳】 chángdèng bench

【长笛】 chángdí flute

【长度】 chángdù length

【长短】 chángduǎn 1.（长度）length 2.（意外）accident; mishap：免得有个～ lest there should be any mishap 3.（是非）right and wrong; strong and weak points

【长方体】 chángfāngtǐ parallelepiped

【长方形】 chángfāngxíng rectangle; rectangular (adj.)

【长工】 chánggōng farm laborer (hired on yearly basis)

【长号】 chánghào 〈*Music*〉 trombone

【长河】 chánghé 1.（长的河流）long river; endless flow 2.（比喻历史进程）long process

【长假】 chángjià 1.（时间长的假期）a long leave of absence 2.（辞职）retire from office

【长江三峡水利枢纽】 Chángjiāng Sānxiá shuǐlì shūniǔ the key Yangtze Gorges water conservancy

【长焦距镜头】 chángjiāojù jìngtóu 〈*Photog.*〉 telelens; telephoto lens

【长颈鹿】 chángjǐnglù 〈*Zool.*〉 giraffe

【长久】 chángjiǔ for a long time; permanently

【长距离】 chángjùlí long distance

【长距离赛跑】 chángjùlí sàipǎo a long-distance race

【长空】 chángkōng vast sky

【长裤】 chángkù trousers; slacks; pants

【长廊】 chángláng long corridor

【长菱形】 chánglíngxíng rhomboid

【长毛绒】 chángmáoróng 〈*Textiles*〉 plush

【长眠】 chángmián 〈*euphem.*〉 eternal sleep; death

【长年】 chángnián all the year round

【长年累月】 cháng nián lěi yuè year in year out; over the years

【长跑】 chángpǎo long-distance race; long-distance running

【长篇】 chángpiān 1.（篇幅长的）full-length 2.（长篇小说）novel; full-length novel

【长篇大论】 chángpiān-dàlùn a lengthy speech or article

【长篇小说】 chángpiān xiǎoshuō novel; full-length novel

【长期】 chángqī long-term; over a long period of time：摆脱～停滞的困境 break out of long-term stagnation

【长期贷款】 chángqī dàikuǎn long-term loan

【长期共存，互相监督】 chángqī-gòngcún, hùxiāng-jiāndū long-term co-existence and mutual supervision

【长期计划】 chángqī jìhuà a long-term plan

【长期投资】 chángqī tóuzī long-term investment

【长期以来】 chángqī yǐ lái for a long time; for quite some time

【长枪】 chángqiāng 1.（长矛）spear 2.（长筒的枪）long-barrelled gun

【长驱】 chángqū make a long drive; push deep

【长驱直入】 chángqū-zhírù drive straight in; drive deep in

【长绒棉】 chángróngmián long-staple cotton
【长衫】 chángshān cheongsam; long gown
【长逝】 chángshì pass away; be gone forever
【长寿】 chángshòu long life; longevity: 良好的习惯使人～。Good habits promote longevity.
【长寿面】 chángshòumiàn noodle eaten on one's birthday
【长叹】 chángtàn deep sigh
【长天】 chángtiān vast sky
【长条校样】 chángtiáo xiàoyàng 〈*Printing*〉 galley proof
【长统袜】 chángtǒngwà stockings
【长统靴】 chángtǒngxuē boots
【长途】 chángtú a long distance: ～跋涉 travel a long distance
【长途电话】 chángtú diànhuà long-distance call
【长途汽车】 chángtú qìchē long-distance bus; coach
【长途直拨电话】 chángtú zhíbō diànhuà direct dialing; direct long distance dialing: 国际～ IDD; international direct dialing / 国内～ DDD; domestic direct dialing
【长袜】 chángwà stockings
【长物】 chángwù anything that may be spared; surplus: 别无～ have no valuable personal possessions
【长线】 chángxiàn in excess supply
【长线产品】 chángxiàn chǎnpǐn product in excess supply
【长效磺胺】 chángxiào huáng'ān sulphamethoxypyridazine (SMP)
【长吁短叹】 chángxū-duǎntàn sighs and groans; moan and groan
【长夜】 chángyè long night; eternal night
【长远】 chángyuǎn a long time; long-term; long-range: ～利益 long-term interest / ～目标 long-term objective / 从～的观点来看 from a long-term point of view
【长征】 chángzhēng **1.** (长途旅行) expedition; long march **2.** (红军二万五千里长征) the Long March
【长治久安】 chángzhì-jiǔān maintain long-term social stability
【长轴】 chángzhóu 〈*Math.*〉 major axis
【长足】 chángzú 〈*written*〉 by leaps and bounds: 取得～的进步 make marked progress

场[場、塲] (cháng) a level open space; threshing ground (另见"场"chǎng)
【场院】 chángyuàn threshing ground

肠[腸] (cháng) **1.** 〈*Anat.*〉 intestines: 十二指～ duodenum / 小～ small intestine / 回～ ilenum / 空～ jejunum / 盲～ caecum / 结～ colon / 升结～ ascending colon / 横结～ transverse colon / 降结～ descending colon / 乙状结～ sigmoid colon / 直～ rectum **2.** (食品) sausage
【肠癌】 cháng'ái 〈*Med.*〉 intestinal cancer
【肠穿孔】 chángchuānkǒng 〈*Med.*〉 enterobrosis; intestinal perforation
【肠儿】 chángr 〈*Food*〉 sausage
【肠梗阻】 chánggěngzǔ 〈*Med.*〉 ileus; intestinal obstruction
【肠绞痛】 chángjiǎotòng 〈*Med.*〉 gripe; cilic pains
【肠胃】 chángwèi **1.** (肠和胃) intestines and stomach **2.** (胃) stomach **3.** (消化) indigestion: ～不好 suffer from indigestion
【肠胃病】 chángwèibìng indigestion; enterogastritis
【肠炎】 chángyán 〈*Med.*〉 enteritis
【肠衣】 chángyī casing (for sausages)
【肠粘连】 chángzhānlián 〈*Med.*〉 intestinal adhesion
【肠子】 cháng·zi **1.** (肠) intestines **2.** 〈*Food*〉 sausage

尝[嘗、嚐[1,2]] (cháng) **1.** (品尝) taste; try the flavor of **2.** (感受) taste; experience; come to know **3.** (曾经) ever; once
【尝到甜头】 chángdào-tiántóu come to realize the good of
【尝试】 chángshì attempt; try: 大胆～ feel free to try
【尝鲜】 chángxiān have a taste of what is just in season

偿[償] (cháng) **1.** (偿还) repay; compensate for **2.** (满足) meet; fulfill
【偿付】 chángfù pay back; pay
【偿付能力】 chángfù nénglì solvency
【偿还】 chánghuán repay; pay back: ～债务

pay a debt; meet one's engagements

【偿还能力】 chánghuán nénglì repaying abilities; repaying capabilities

【偿还期】 chánghuánqī maturity

【偿还期限】 chánghuán qīxiàn term of redemption

【偿命】 chángmìng pay with one's life (for a murder); a life for a life

【偿清】 chángqīng clear off: ～债务 clear off one's debts

常 (cháng) **1.** (平常) ordinary; common; normal **2.** (经常) constant; invariable **3.** (时常) frequently; often; usually

【常备】 chángbèi be always ready; be ever prepared

【常备不懈】 chángbèi-bùxiè always be on the alert; be ever prepared (against war)

【常备军】 chángbèijūn standing army

【常常】 chángcháng frequently; often; usually; generally

【常服】 chángfú ordinary uniform

【常规】 chángguī **1.** (通常作法) convention; rule; common practice; routine **2.** 〈*Med.*〉 routine: ～检查 routine examination; routine inspection

【常规内存】 chángguī nèicún 〈*Computer*〉 conventional memory

【常规武器】 chángguī wǔqì conventional weapons

【常规战争】 chángguī zhànzhēng conventional war

【常见】 chángjiàn common

【常见病】 chángjiànbìng common disease; common ailment

【常客】 chángkè **1.** (指顾客) regular customer **2.** (指客人) regular visitor

【常来常往】 chánglái-chángwǎng exchange frequent visits; pay frequent calls; frequently see each other

【常量】 chángliàng constant

【常绿植物】 chánglǜ zhíwù evergreen plant

【常年】 chángnián **1.** (终年) throughout the year; perennial **2.** (长期) year in year out **3.** (平常年份) average year

【常情】 chángqíng reason; sense

【常任】 chángrèn permanent; standing

【常任代表】 chángrèn dàibiǎo permanent delegate; permanent representative

【常任理事国】 chángrèn lǐshìguó permanent member (of the Security Council)

【常设】 chángshè standing; permanent

【常设机构】 chángshè jīgòu standing body; permanent organization

【常识】 chángshí **1.** (指知识) general knowledge; elementary knowledge **2.** (指见识) common sense

【常数】 chángshù 〈*Math.*〉 constant

【常态】 chángtài normality; normal behavior or conditions: 恢复～ come to the normal state / 一反～ contrary to one's normal behavior; contrary to the way sb. usually behaves

【常委】 chángwěi member of the standing committee

【常委会】 chángwěihuì standing committee

【常温】 chángwēn normal atmospheric temperature

【常温动物】 chángwēn dòngwù warm-blooded animal; homoiothermal animal

【常务】 chángwù day-to-day business; standing

【常务董事】 chángwù dǒngshì managing director

【常务委员】 chángwù wěiyuán member of the standing committee

【常务委员会】 chángwù wěiyuánhuì standing committee

【常言】 chángyán saying: ～说 as the saying goes; as the saying is

【常用】 chángyòng in common use

【常住居民】 chángzhù jūmín inhabitant

【常驻】 chángzhù resident; permanent

【常驻代表】 chángzhù dàibiǎo permanent delegate; permanent representative; resident representative

【常驻代表机构】 chángzhù dàibiǎo jīgòu resident representative office

【常驻记者】 chángzhù jìzhě resident correspondent

厂 [廠、厰] (chǎng) **1.** (工厂) factory; mill; plant; works: 电机～ electrical machinery plant / 服装～ clothing factory / 钢铁～ iron and steel works / 化工～ chemical works / 水泥～ cement works / 针织～ knitwear mill 2.（厂子）yard; depot：煤～ coal yard / 木～ timberyard

【厂房】 chǎngfáng 1.（指建筑）factory building 2.（车间）workshop

【厂家】 chǎngjiā commodity manufacturing units

【厂矿】 chǎngkuàng factories and mines

【厂礼拜】 chǎnglǐbài factory rest day

【厂商】 chǎngshāng firm; factory and shop

【厂休】 chǎngxiū workers' day off; day of rest for factory workers

【厂长】 chǎngzhǎng factory director; factory manager

【厂长负责制】 chǎngzhǎng fùzézhì factory director responsibility system

【厂址】 chǎngzhǐ the site of a factory; the location of a factory

【厂主】 chǎngzhǔ factory owner; millowner

场［場、塲］（chǎng） 1.（场地）ground; field; a place where people gather 2.（农场；养殖场）farm：牛奶～ dairy（farm）/ 畜牧～ stock farm / 茶～ tea plantation 3.（场合）stage; spot; scene：不在～ be absent from the scene / 出～ come on the stage; appear on the scene / 当～ on the spot / 在～ be present at the scene 4.（舞台）stage 5.〈*Theatre*〉scene（另见“场”cháng）

【场次】 chǎngcì the number of showings of a film, play, etc.

【场地】 chǎngdì space; place; site：比赛～ competition arena; ground; court / 对方～ away ground; away court / 交换～ change sides

【场馆】 chǎngguǎn stadium and gymnasium

【场合】 chǎnghé occasion; situation：外交～ a diplomatic occasion

【场记】 chǎngjì 〈*Theatre*〉〈*Cinematog.*〉 1.（记录）log 2.（记录员）log keeper; script holder（m.）; script girl（f.）

【场面】 chǎngmiàn 1.（戏剧、电影中的场景）scene; spectacle 2.（情景）occasion; scene warm friendship 3.（排场）appearance; front; facade：撑～ keep up an appearance of

【场能】 chǎngnéng 〈*Physics*〉 field energy

【场频】 chǎngpín 〈*Physics*〉 field frequency

【场强】 chǎngqiáng 〈*Physics*〉 field intensity; field strength

【场上队长】 chǎngshàng duìzhǎng 〈*Sports*〉 field captain

【场所】 chǎngsuò place; arena：公共～ a public place

【场效应】 chǎngxiàoyìng 〈*Physics*〉 field effect

【场致发射】 chǎng zhì fāshè 〈*Physics*〉 field emission

【场子】 chǎng·zi 1.（剧场）theater; theatre 2.（大厅）hall 3.（体育场）sports ground

敞（chǎng） 1.（宽敞）spacious 2.（敞开）open; uncovered：～着大门 leave the gate open; with the gate open

【敞车】 chǎngchē 1.〈*Railway*〉 stockcar; open wagon; open freight car 2.（没有车篷的车）flatcar

【敞怀】 chǎnghuái with one's coat or shirt unbuttoned：～畅饮 being cheerful and happy, one drinks to capacity

【敞开】 chǎngkā 1.（打开；大开）open wide：～大门 open the gate wide 2.（无限制）unlimited; unrestricted

【敞亮】 chǎngliàng 1.（宽敞明亮）light and spacious 2.（心里豁亮）clear（in one's thinking）

【敞篷车】 chǎngpéngchē open car

【敞胸露怀】 chǎngxiōng-lùhuái bare the breast

怅［悵］（chàng） disappointed; sorry

【怅怅不乐】 chàngchàng-bùlè disconsolate; feeling gloomy

【怅然】 chàngrán disappointed; upset

【怅惘】 chàngwǎng distracted; listless

畅［暢］（chàng） 1.（通畅）smooth; unimpeded 2.（畅快）free; uninhibited

【畅达】 zhàngdá fluent; smooth：文章～。The article reads smoothly.

【畅快】 zhàngkuài free from inhibitions; carefree

【畅所欲言】 zhàngsuǒ-yùyán speak without any inhibitions; speak one's mind freely; speak out freely

【畅谈】 chàngtán talk freely and to one's

heart's content; speak glowingly of
【畅通】 chàngtōng unimpeded; unblocked: 前面道路～无阻 open road ahead
【畅销】 chàngxiāo be in great demand; sell well; have a ready market
【畅销书】 chàngxiāoshū best seller
【畅行无阻】 chàngxíng-wúzǔ pass unimpeded
【畅叙】 chàngxù chat cheerfully: ～友情 recall old friendship heartily
【畅饮】 chàngyǐn drink one's fill
【畅游】 chàngyóu 1.(指游泳) have a good swim 2.(指游览) enjoy a sightseeing tour

倡 (chàng) initiate; advocate
【倡办】 chàngbàn establish; found
【倡导】 chàngdǎo initiate; propose: 在某人的～下 on the initiative of sb.
【倡言】 chàngyán propose; initiate
【倡议】 chàngyì propose; sponsor: ～召开会议 propose the calling of a conference
【倡议书】 chàngyìshū written proposal; proposal
【倡议者】 chàngyìzhě initiator

唱 (chàng) 1.(唱歌) sing: 独～ solo / 二重～ duet 2.(大声叫) call; cry
【唱本】 chàngběn the libretto or script of a ballad-singer
【唱词】 chàngcí libretto; words of a ballad
【唱碟】 chàngdié disc; disk
【唱段】 chàngduàn aria: 越剧～ an aria from a Shaoxing opera
【唱对台戏】 chàng duìtáixì put on a rival show; enter into rivalry with; put up a rival show
【唱反调】 chàng fǎndiào sing a different tune; deliberately speak or act contrary to; strike up a discordant tune
【唱高调】 chàng gāodiào use high-flown words; affect a high moral tone; chant bombastic words
【唱歌】 chànggē sing (a song)
【唱机】 chàngjī gramophone; phonograph
【唱名】 chàngmíng 1.(逐一高声念姓名) roll call: ～表决 vote by roll call 2.〈*Music*〉 sol-fa syllables
【唱盘】 chàngpán disc; disk: 激光～ compact disc; CD
【唱片】 chàngpiàn gramophone record; phonograph record; disc: 密纹～ long-playing record / 放～ play a gramophone record
【唱票】 chàngpiào call out the names of those voted for while counting ballot-slips
【唱票人】 chàngpiàorén teller
【唱腔】 chàngqiāng vocal music in a Chinese opera
【唱头】 chàngtóu pickup
【唱戏】 chàngxì act in an opera
【唱针】 chàngzhēn stylus; gramophone needle

chao

抄[钞[1]] (chāo) 1.(抄写) copy; transcribe: ～写稿件 make a fair copy of the manuscript 2.(抄袭) plagiarize; lift 3.(搜查没收) search and confiscate; make a raid upon 4.(抓取) go off with; walk off with 5.(抄近路) take a shortcut 6.(袖手) fold: ～着手 with folded arms 7.(拿起) grab; take up
【抄道】 chāodào 1.(抄近路) take a shortcut 2.(近路) shortcut
【抄后路】 chāo hòulù outflank the enemy and attack him in the rear; turn the enemy's rear
【抄家】 chāojiā search sb's house and confiscate his property
【抄件】 chāojiàn duplicate; copy
【抄送】 chāosòng make a copy for; send a duplicate to
【抄袭】 chāoxí 1.(抄袭他人作品) plagiarize; lift; plagiarism (n.) 2.(照搬他人经验) borrow indiscriminately from other people's experience 3.(绕道袭击) launch a surprise attack on the enemy by making a detour
【抄写】 chāoxiě copy; transcribe

钞 (chāo) bank note; paper money
【钞票】 chāopiào bank note; paper money; bill

超 (chāo) 1.(超过) exceed; surpass; overtake 2.(超…) super-; extra- 3.(超出) transcend; go beyond
【超编】 chāobiān exceed the number of the authorized staff

【超编单位】 chāobiān dānwèi over-staffed unit

【超标】 chāobiāo exceed the provided standard

【超产】 chāochǎn overfulfill a production quota

【超常】 chāocháng go beyond the normal condition

【超车】 chāochē pass; overtake other cars on the road: 不准～! No passing! (AmE.); No overtaking! (BrE.)

【超车道】 chāochēdào fast; passing (AmE.); overtaking (BrE.)

【超尘拔俗】 chāochēn-bású transcend the worldly

【超出】 chāochū overstep; go beyond; exceed: ～范围 go beyond the scope

【超导】 chāodǎo superconduction

【超导技术】 chāodǎo jìshù superconductor technology

【超导体】 chāodǎotǐ superconductor

【超低频】 chāodīpín ultra-low frequency (ULF)

【超低碳钢】 chāodītàngāng ultra-low-carbon steel

【超低温】 chāodīwēn ultra-low temperature

【超短波】 chāoduǎnbō ultrashort wave

【超短裙】 chāoduǎnqún miniskirt

【超额】 chāo'é above quota; overfulfill: 钢厂可能～完成计划。The steel mill may overfulfill the plan.

【超额利润】 chāo'é lìrùn superprofit; excess profits

【超负荷】 chāofùhè excess load; overload: 不要让洗衣机～, 不然的话它会不工作的。Don't overload the washing machine, or it won't work properly.

【超高频】 chāogāopín 〈*Electr*.〉 ultrahigh frequency (UHF)

【超高压】 chāogāoyā 1. (指气压) superhigh pressure 2. (指电压) extrahigh voltage; extrahigh tension

【超购】 chāogòu purchase exceeding the amount stipulated

【超过】 chāoguò outstrip; surpass; exceed

【超级】 chāojí super

【超级大国】 chāojí dàguó superpower

【超级明星】 chāojí míngxīng superstar

【超级市场】 chāojí shìchǎng supermarket

【超级油轮】 chāojí yóulún supertanker

【超假】 chāojià overstay one's leave

【超巨星】 chāojùxīng 〈*Astron*.〉 supergiant (star)

【超绝】 chāojué unique; superb; extraordinary

【超龄】 chāolíng overaged: ～团员 overaged League member

【超期】 chāoqī exceed the time limit

【超前】 chāoqián move up; shift the scheduled time to an earlier date

【超前消费】 chāoqián xiāofèi excessive consumption; premature consumption

【超群】 chāoqún head and shoulders above all others; preeminent

【超然】 chāorán aloof; detached

【超人】 chāorén 1. (超过常人) be out of the common run; exceptional 2. 〈*Philos*.〉 superman

【超生】 chāoshēng babies born exceed the stipulated limit of the birth control

【超声波】 chāoshēngbō ultrasonic wave; supersonic wave

【超声波探伤】 chāoshēngbō tànshāng ultrasonic examination; supersonic flaw detecting

【超声速】 chāoshēngsù supersonic speed; supersonic (adj.)

【超速】 chāosù 1. (超出速度限制) exceed the speed limit 2. 〈*Mech*.〉 hypervelocity

【超速驾驶】 chāosù jiàshǐ furious driving

【超脱】 chāotuō 1. (不拘泥成规等) unconventional; original 2. (超出) be detached; stand aloof; hold aloof; keep aloof

【超现实主义】 chāoxiànshí zhǔyì surrealism; super-realism

【超新星】 chāoxīnxīng 〈*Astron*.〉 supernova (star)

【超音速】 chāoyīnsù supersonic speed; supersonic (adj.)

【超越】 chāoyuè surmount; overstep; transcend; surpass: 不能～阶段 not try to skip the stage / ～职权范围 go beyond one's terms of reference; overstep one's authority

【超载】 chāozài 〈*Transport*〉 overload

【超支】 chāozhī overspend

【超支户】 chāozhīhù overdrawn families
【超重】 chāozhòng 1.（指载重量）overload 2.（指规定重量）overweight
【超重费】 chāozhòngfèi heavy lift charge
【超重信件】 chāozhòng xìnjiàn overweight letter
【超轴】 chāozhóu 〈*Railway*〉 over haulage
【超轴牵引】 chāozhóu qiānyǐn 〈*Railway*〉 trains hauling above-normal tonnage
【超子】 chāozǐ 〈*Physics*〉 hyperon
【超自然】 chāozìrán supernatural

巢（cháo） nest
【巢穴】 cháoxué lair; den; nest; hideout

朝（cháo） 1.（朝廷）court; government 2.（朝代）dynasty 3.（向）facing; towards: ～前走 march ahead / 坐东～西 with a western exposure; facing west
（另见"朝"zhāo）
【朝拜】 cháobài pay respects to（a sovereign）; pay religious homage to; worship
【朝代】 cháodài dynasty
【朝觐】 cháojìn 1.〈*written*〉 have an audience with 2.〈*Relig.*〉 go on a pilgrimage（to a shrine or a sacred place）
【朝圣】 cháoshèng pilgrimage
【朝廷】 cháotíng 1.（宫廷）royal or imperial court 2.（君主政府）royal government; imperial government
【朝鲜】 Cháoxiǎn Korea; Korean（adj.）‖ 朝鲜人 Korean ‖ 朝鲜语 Korean（language）
【朝鲜族】 Cháoxiǎnzú Chaoxian（中国少数民族，主要分布在吉林、黑龙江、辽宁等地）
【朝向】 cháoxiàng 〈*Archit.*〉 orientation
【朝阳】 cháoyáng 1.（向阳）exposed to the sun; sunny 2.（向南）with a sunny aspect; with a southern aspect
【朝野】 cháoyě 1.（朝廷和民间）the court and the commonalty 2.（资本主义国家的政府与非政府方面）the government and the public

嘲［謿］（cháo） ridicule; deride: 冷～热讽 freezing irony and burning satire
【嘲讽】 cháofěng sneer at; taunt
【嘲弄】 cháonòng mock; poke fun at
【嘲笑】 cháoxiào ridicule; deride; jeer at; laugh at

潮（cháo） 1.（潮汐）tide; tidal（adj.）: 大～ spring tide / 低～ low tide; low water / 高～ high tide; high water / 平～ slack water / 小～ neap tide / 正在涨～。The tide is flowing. / 正在落～。The tide is ebbing. 2.（社会变动）（social）upsurge; current; tide 3.（潮湿）damp; moist
【潮流】 cháoliú 1.（潮汐）tide; tidal current 2.（社会发展趋势）trend: 历史～ historical trend
【潮气】 cháoqì moisture in the air; damp; humidity
【潮湿】 cháoshī moist; damp
【潮水】 cháoshuǐ tide; tidewater; tidal water: 我们能在沙滩上玩了，因为～落下去了。We can play on the sand because the tide is out. / 我们不能在沙滩上玩了，因为～涨上来了。We can't play on the sand because the tide is in.
【潮汐】 cháoxī tide; morning and evening tides
【潮汐电站】 cháoxī diànzhàn tidal power station
【潮汐时刻表】 cháoxī shíkèbiǎo tide-table
【潮汛】 cháoxùn spring tide

吵（chǎo） 1.（声音杂乱）make a noise 2.（争吵）quarrel; wrangle; squabble: 同某人～架 have a quarrel with sb.
【吵架】 chǎojià quarrel; wrangle; have a row
【吵闹】 chǎonào 1.（争吵）wrangle; kick up a row 2.（骚扰声）din; hubbub
【吵嚷】 chǎorǎng make a racket; shout in confusion; clamor
【吵人】 chǎorén disturb others（by noise）
【吵嘴】 chǎozuǐ quarrel; bicker

炒（chǎo） stir-fry; fry; sauté
【炒菜】 chǎocài 1.（炒菜）stir-fry; sauté 2.（炒的菜）a fried dish
【炒饭】 chǎofàn 1.（炒饭）fry rice 2.（炒的饭）fried rice
【炒更】 chǎogēng be engaged in a second occupation in sparetime
【炒股】 chǎogǔ play the stock market; play with the stocks
【炒汇】 chǎohuì 1.（指行动）play with the

foreign exchange 2.（指炒汇行为）illegal wheeling and dealings in foreign exchange
【炒货】 chǎohuò roasted seeds and nuts
【炒家】 chǎojiā speculator
【炒冷饭】 chǎo lěngfàn heat leftover rice; rehash; repeat without any new content
【炒买炒卖】 chǎomǎi-chǎomài speculate; quick buy and quick sell; speculation（n.）; speculative（adj.）：～股票 speculate in stocks
【炒米】 chǎomǐ 1.（干炒过的米）parched rice 2.（蒙古族食品）milletstir-fried in butter
【炒面】 chǎomiàn 1.（油炒面条）chow mein; fried noodles 2.（炒熟的面粉）parched flour
【炒勺】 chǎosháo wok
【炒鱿鱼】 chǎo yóuyú 1.（做菜肴）fry squid 2.（解雇）dismiss; fire：我炒了他的鱿鱼。I fired him.

che

车［車］（chē） 1.（汽车）car; vehicle：开～ drive / 超～ pass; overtake / 靠路边停～ pull over / 停～ park / 倒～ back up; reverse 2.（自行车）bike; bicycle：骑～ ride a bike 3.（有轮轴的工具）wheeled machine; wheeled instrument 4.（机器）machine：停～ stop the machine / 试～ trial run; test run 5.（用车床切削）lathe; turn：～零件 lathe a part 6.（用水车取水）lift water by waterwheel
（另见"车"jū）
【车把】 chēbǎ 1.（自行车、摩托车的）handlebar 2.（手推车等的）shaft
【车把势】 chēbǎ·shi carter; cart-driver
【车把套】 chēbǎtào 〈*Bicycle*〉 handlebar grips
【车帮】 chēbāng side board
【车场】 chēchǎng 1.（停车场）parking lot; car park 2.（保养场）garage
【车窗】 chēchuāng 〈*Auto*〉 door window：把～摇上 wind the window up / 一上车她就把～摇下去了。Once she'd got into the car, she wound the window down.
【车床】 chēchuáng lathe：万能～ universal lathe
【车次】 chēcì 1.（列车的）train number 2.（汽车的）motorcoach number
【车刀】 chēdāo lathe tool; turning tool
【车到山前必有路】 chē dào shānqián bì yǒu lù the cart will find its way round the hill when it gets there; things will eventually sort themselves out
【车道】 chēdào （traffic）lane
【车灯】 chēdēng headlight; front light
【车灯架】 chēdēngjià 〈*Bicycle*〉 lamp bracket
【车队】 chēduì autocade; motorcade：总统及其～ the President and his autocade
【车费】 chēfèi fare
【车工】 chēgōng 1.（工种）lathe work 2.（技工）turner; lather operator
【车祸】 chēhuò traffic accident; road accident; automobile accident
【车架】 chējià 〈*Bicycle*〉 frame
【车间】 chējiān workshop; shop：木工～ carpentry work-shop / 装配～ assembly shop; fitting shop
【车库】 chēkù garage
【车筐】 chēkuāng 〈*Bicycle*〉 basket
【车辆】 chēliàng vehicle; car
【车辆废气】 chēliàng fèiqì vehicle exhaust gas
【车铃】 chēlíng 〈*Bicycle*〉 bell
【车轮】 chēlún wheel（of a vehicle）
【车马费】 chēmǎfèi travel allowance
【车门】 chēmén 〈*Auto*〉 car door
【车门把】 chēménbà 〈*Auto*〉 door handle
【车牌】 chēpái license plate（AmE.）; number plate（BrE.）
【车棚】 chēpéng bicycle shed
【车篷】 chēpéng top; convertible
【车皮】 chēpí railway wagon; railway carriage
【车票】 chēpiào train or bus ticket; ticket
【车圈】 chēquān 〈*Bicycle*〉 rim
【车身】 chēshēn 1.（汽车的）automobile body 2.（摩托车挎斗的）sidecar body
【车手】 chēshǒu racing driver
【车水马龙】 chēshuǐ-mǎlóng heavy traffic; incessant stream of horses and carriages
【车速】 chēsù speed of a motor vehicle
【车速表】 chēsùbiǎo speedometer
【车胎】 chētāi tire; tyre
【车条】 chētiáo spoke
【车贴】 chētiē transportation allowance

【车头】 chētóu 1.(车的头部) headstock 2.(铁路机车) locomotive; engine

【车厢】 chēxiāng 1.〈*Railway*〉 railway carriage; railroad car 2.(车辆载人、装物的部分) carriage; car

【车箱】 chēxiāng railway carriage; railroad car

【车闸】 chēzhá brake

【车站】 chēzhàn station; depot; stop

【车照】 chēzhào license of car

【车辙】 chēzhé rut

【车轴】 chēzhóu axle; axletree

【车子】 chē·zi small vehicle; car; bike

【车座】 chēzuò 1.〈*Auto*〉 seat 2.〈*Bicycle*〉 saddle

【车座弹簧】 chēzuò tánhuáng 〈*Bicycle*〉 saddle springs

砗 (chē)

【砗磲】 chēqú 〈*Zool.*〉 giant clam; tridacna

扯[撦] (chě) 1.(拉) pull 2.(撕) tear 3.(买布等) buy (cloth, thread, etc.) 4.(闲扯) chat; gossip

【扯淡】 chědàn chat; gossip

【扯后腿】 chě hòutuǐ hold sb. back (from action); be a drag on sb.; be a hindrance to sb.

【扯谎】 chěhuǎng tell a lie; lie

【扯皮】 chěpí dispute over trifles; argue back and forth; wrangle

彻[徹] (chè) thorough; penetrating

【彻查】 chèchá thorough investigation and just handling

【彻底】 chèdǐ thorough; thoroughgoing: ～改变 radical change / ～改正 be changed thoroughly; correct thoroughly / ～消灭 utterly destroy

【彻骨】 chègǔ to the bone: ～之寒 biting cold

【彻头彻尾】 chètóu-chèwěi through and through; out and out; downright

【彻夜】 chèyè all night; all through the night: ～灯火通明。The lights were ablaze all through the night.

掣 (chè) 1.(拽,拉) pull; hold 2.(抽取) draw

【掣电】 chèdiàn lightning

【掣肘】 chèzhǒu tug at the elbow to prevent action; obstruct

撤 (chè) 1.(撤去) remove; take away: 孩子们负责把盘碗～了。The children had the task of taking away. 2.(撤退) pull out; withdraw; evacuate

【撤编】 chèbiān withdraw establishment

【撤兵】 chèbīng withdraw troops

【撤除】 chèchú remove; dismantle: ～军事基地 dismantle a military base

【撤防】 chèfáng withdraw a garrison; retreat from a defended position

【撤换】 chèhuàn dismiss and replace; recall; replace

【撤回】 chèhuí 1.(招回) recall; withdraw: ～代表 recall a representative 2.(收回) revoke; retract; withdraw: ～诉讼 withdraw a claim; revoke a court action / ～指控 withdraw a charge

【撤军】 chèjūn withdraw troops: 从该国～ withdraw its troops from the country

【撤离】 chèlí withdraw from; leave; evacuate: ～城市 evacuate a city

【撤退】 chètuì withdraw; pull out: 安全～ make good one's retreat

【撤销】 chèxiāo cancel; rescind; revoke: ～订单 recall an order / ～决议 annul a decision / ～命令 countermand an order / ～起诉 quash an indictment

【撤职】 chèzhí dismiss sb. from his post; remove sb. from office

【撤走】 chèzǒu withdraw

澈 (chè) clear; limpid: 清～的泉水 clear spring

chen

抻[捵] (chēn) pull out; stretch: ～一～衣服 stretch the clothes

【抻面】 chēnmiàn 1.(抻面条) make noodles by drawing out the dough by hand 2.(抻好的面条) hand-pulled noodles

嗔 (chēn) 1.(生气) be angry; be unhappy 2.(不满) be annoyed with sb.: 她～我说错了话。She was annoyed with me for having said the wrong thing.

【嗔怪】 chēnguài blame; upbraid; scold

臣 (chén) official under a feudal ruler; subject

【臣服】 chénfú submit oneself to the rule of

尘[塵] (chén) 1.(尘土) dust; dirt 2.(尘世) this world

【尘埃】 chén'āi dust

【尘暴】 chénbào 〈*Meteorol.*〉 dust devil; dust storm

【尘肺】 chénfèi 〈*Med.*〉 pneumokoniosis; pneumoconiosis

【尘封】 chénfēng covered with dust; dust-laden

【尘世】 chénshì 〈*Relig.*〉 this world; this mortal life

【尘土】 chéntǔ dust

晨 (chén) morning

【晨风】 chénfēng matinal; morning breeze

【晨光】 chénguāng the light of the early morning sun; dawn

【晨曦】 chénxī first rays of the morning sun; early dawn

【晨星】 chénxīng 1.(清晨的星) stars at dawn 2.〈*Astron.*〉 morning star; Venus

【晨衣】 chényī dressing gown

沉[沈] (chén) 1.(沉没水里) sink: 船～了。The ship has sunk. 2.(向下沉) keep down; lower 3.(程度深) deep; profound 4.(分量重) heavy

【沉底儿】 chéndǐr sink to the bottom

【沉甸甸】 chéndiāndiān heavy and not easy to wield; heavy

【沉淀】 chéndiàn 1.(指沉淀过程) precipitate; precipitation (n.): 冷却烧杯有助于～化合物。Cooling the beaker helps precipitate the compound. 2.(沉淀物) precipitate; sediment 3.(凝聚;积累) accumulate; accumulation (n.)

【沉积】 chénjī 1.〈*Geol.*〉 deposit: 陆相～ continental deposit / 海相～ marine deposit 2.(沉淀并聚积) sediment; sedimentation (n.) 3.(沉积物) deposit; sediment; sedimentary (adj.) 4.(比喻沉淀,积聚) accumulate; accumulation (n.): 文化～ cultural accumulation / 历史～ historical accumulation

【沉积层】 chénjīcéng 〈*Geol.*〉 sedimentary deposit

【沉寂】 chénjì 1.(寂静) quiet; still 2.(无消息) no news

【沉降】 chénjiàng subside; subsidence (n.): 地面～ earth subsidence

【沉浸】 chénjìn immerse; steep

【沉井】 chénjǐng 〈*Archit.*〉 open caisson

【沉静】 chénjìng quiet; calm; serene; placid

【沉沦】 chénlún sink into (vice, degradation, depravity, etc.)

【沉闷】 chémèn 1.(指天气、气氛等) oppressive; depressing: ～的天气 dull weather; depressing weather 2.(指心情) depressed; in low spirits: 心情～ feel depressed 3.(指性格) not outgoing; withdrawn

【沉没】 chénmò sink: 船～了。The boat has sunk.

【沉默】 chénmò 1.(不爱说笑) reticent; taciturn 2.(不说话) silent: 保持～ remain silent

【沉溺】 chénnì indulge; wallow

【沉睡】 chénshuì be sunk in sleep; be fast asleep

【沉思】 chénsī ponder; meditate; be lost in thought

【沉痛】 chéntòng 1.(很深的悲痛) deep feeling of grief or remorse: ～的哀悼 profound condolences 2.(深刻) deeply felt; bitter: ～的教训 bitter experience

【沉陷】 chénxiàn sink; cave in

【沉吟】 chényín 1.(低声吟) mutter to oneself; murmur to oneself 2.(迟疑) meditate; hesitate

【沉渣】 chénzhā sediment; dregs

【沉重】 chénzhòng 1.(分量大;程度深) heavy: 心情～ with a heavy heart; with heavy feelings 2.(严重) serious; critical

【沉住气】 chén zhù qì keep calm; keep cool; be steady: 沉不住气 unable to keep calm

【沉着】 chénzhuó cool-headed; composed; steady; calm: ～镇静 be steady and calm

【沉醉】 chénzuì get drunk; become intoxicated: ～在成功的喜悦中 be intoxicated with success

陈[陳] (chén) 1.(陈设) lay out; put on display 2.(陈说) state; explain 3.(旧的) old; stale

【陈词滥调】 chéncí-làndiào hackneyed and

stereotyped expressions; clichés
【陈腐】 chénfǔ old and decayed; stale; outworn: ～的词语 stale words
【陈规】 chénguī outmoded conventions: ～陋习 bad customs and habits / 打破～ break with outmoded conventions
【陈货】 chénhuò old stock; shopworn goods
【陈酒】 chénjiǔ old wine; mellow wine
【陈旧】 chénjiù outmoded; obsolete; old-fashioned; out-of-date
【陈列】 chénliè display; set out; exhibit
【陈列馆】 chénlièguǎn exhibition hall
【陈列柜】 chénlièguì display cabinet unit
【陈列室】 chénlèishì exhibition room; showroom
【陈酿】 chénniàng old wine; mellow wine
【陈皮】 chénpí 〈*Chin. Med.*〉 dried tangerine or orange peel
【陈设】 chénshè **1.**(摆设) display; set out **2.**(摆设的东西) furnishings
【陈述】 chénshù state; declare: ～自已的见解 state one's views
【陈述句】 chénshùjù declarative sentence

衬[襯] (chèn) **1.**(在里面衬一层) line; place sth. underneath: ～一层布 put a piece of clothe underneath **2.**(里面的衬) lining; liner **3.**(陪衬;衬托) set off
【衬布】 chènbù lining cloth
【衬垫料】 chèndiànliào wadding
【衬裤】 chènkù underpants; pants
【衬里】 chènlǐ lining
【衬裙】 chènqún underskirt; petticoat
【衬衫】 chènshān shirt
【衬托】 chèntuō set off; serve as a foil to
【衬衣】 chènyī underclothes; shirt

称[稱] (chèn) fit; match; suit (另见"称"chēng)
【称心】 chènxīn find sth. satisfactory; be gratified: ～如意 to one's satisfaction; in accord with one's wishes
【称愿】 chènyuàn be gratified at the misfortune of a rival
【称职】 chènzhí fill a post with credit; be competent

趁[趂] (chèn) **1.**(利用机会) take advantage of; avail oneself of **2.**(利用时间) while: ～你在这儿,咱们谈谈。Let's have a talk while you are here. **3.**(富有) be rich in
【趁火打劫】 chènhuǒ-dǎjié take advantage of sb's misfortune to do him harm
【趁机】 chènjī take advantage of the occasion; seize the chance: ～捣乱 seize the opportunity to make trouble
【趁钱】 chènqián have pots of money
【趁热打铁】 chènrè-dǎtiě Strike while the iron is hot.
【趁人之危】 chènrén-zhīwēi take advantage of another's perilous state
【趁势】 chènshì take advantage of a favorable situation
【趁早】 chènzǎo as early as possible; before it is too late; at the first opportunity

谶 (chèn) augury; foreboding
【谶语】 chènyǔ a saying which turns out to be a prophecy

cheng

柽[檉] (chēng)
【柽柳】 chēngliǔ 〈*Bot.*〉 Chinese tamarisk

蛏[蟶] (chēng) razor clam
【蛏子】 chēng·zi 〈*Zool.*〉 razor clam

称[稱] (chēng) **1.**(叫;叫做) call **2.**(名称) name **3.**(说) say; state: 据外交部发言人～ according to the Foreign Ministry spokesman **4.**(称赞) commend; praise **5.**(测定重量) measure weigh (另见"称"chèn)
【称霸】 chēngbà seek hegemony; assume hegemony; dominate
【称病】 chēngbìng plead illness
【称臣】 chēngchén regard oneself as the subject of sb.
【称道】 chēngdào speak approvingly of; commend: 无足～ nothing commendable; nothing praiseworthy
【称号】 chēnghào title; name; designation
【称呼】 chēng·hu **1.**(叫) call; address **2.**(招呼用的名称) form of address

【称快】 chēngkuài express one's gratification：拍手～ clap one's hands with satisfaction

【称颂】 chēngsòng praise；extol；eulogize；pay tribute to

【称王称霸】 chēngwáng-chēngbà act like an overlord；lord it over

【称谓】 chēngwèi appellation；title

【称谢】 chēngxiè express one's thanks；thank

【称兄道弟】 chēngxiōng-dàodì call each other brothers；be on intimate terms

【称誉】 chēngyù sing the praises of；praise；acclaim

【称赞】 chēngzàn praise；acclaim；commend

铛［鐺］（chēng） pan（另见"铛"dāng）

撑［撐］（chēng） 1.（抵住）prop up；support 2.（撑船）push or move with a pole 3.（支持）maintain；keep up 4.（张开）open；unfurl：～开雨伞 open an umbrella 5.（充满）fill to the point of bursting

【撑场面】 chēng chǎngmiàn keep up an appearance of

【撑船】 chēngchuán pole a boat

【撑杆】 chēnggān 〈*Sports*〉 vaulting pole

【撑杆跳高】 chēnggān tiàogāo 〈*Sports*〉 pole vault；pole jump

【撑杆跳高运动员】 chēnggān tiàogāo yùndòngyuán pole-vaulter

【撑脚】 chēngjiǎo 〈*Music*〉 spike

【撑腰】 chēngyāo support；back up；bolster up：给某人～ back sb. up

瞠（chēng） stare

【瞠目结舌】 chēngmù-jiéshé stare tongue-tied；gaze at sb. dumbfounded

成（chéng） 1.（完成；成功）accomplish；succeed 2.（成为）become；turn into：他～了队长。He has become a team leader. 3.（成果；成就）achievement；result 4.（成年）fully developed；fully grown 5.（现成的）established；ready-made 6.（数量多）in considerable numbers or amounts：～千上万 tens of thousands of 7.（答应；许可）all right；O.K. 8.（有能力）able；capable 9.（十分之一）one tenth：增产一～ a 10 % increase in output；output increased by 10 per cent

【成败】 chéngbài success or failure：～未卜 between cup and lip

【成本】 chéngběn cost：间接～ indirect cost／直接～ direct cost

【成本核算】 chéngběn hésuàn cost accounting

【成本价】 chéngběnjià cost price

【成本效益】 chéngběn xiàoyì cost benefit

【成比例】 chéngbǐlì 1.（成比例）varies as；proportional to（符号为 ∝ ）2.（等于）equals；as（proportion）（符号为 ∷ ）

【成才】 chéngcái become a useful person

【成材】 chéngcái 1.（可用做木料）grow into useful timber；grow to full size 2.（人才）become a useful person

【成虫】 chéngchóng 〈*Zool.*〉 imago；adult

【成堆】 chéngduī form a pile；be in heaps

【成法】 chéngfǎ established law

【成分】 chéng·fèn 1.（组成部分）composition；component part；ingredient：化学～ chemical composition 2.（个人成分）one's profession or economic status

【成份】 chéng·fen 同"成分"

【成风】 chéngfēng become a common practice；become the order of the day

【成功】 chénggōng succeed；success：试验～。The experiment has succeeded.

【成规】 chéngguī established practice；set rules；rut：打破～ break down the conventions／墨守～ stick to conventions；get into a rut

【成果】 chéngguǒ achievement；fruit；gain；positive result：科研～ achievements in scientific research

【成婚】 chénghūn get married

【成活】 chénghuó survive

【成活率】 chénghuólǜ survival rate

【成绩】 chéngjì result；achievement；success：～斐然 the achievement is elegant／～显著 make a remarkable achievement

【成绩报告单】 chéngjì bàogàodān score report

【成绩册】 chéngjìcè 〈*Sports*〉 results

【成绩单】 chéngjìdān school report card

【成家】 chéngjiā 1.（结婚）get married 2.（成为专家）become an expert

【成家立业】 chéngjiā-lìyè get married and

start one's career

【成见】 chéngjiàn 1.(指看法) preconceived idea; prejudice: 消除～ dispel prejudices 2.(指见解) concept; opinion; idea

【成交】 chéngjiāo strike a bargain; conclude a transaction; clinch a deal

【成交额】 chéngjiāo'é volume of business

【成就】 chéngjiù 1.(成绩) achievement; attainment success; accomplishment 2.(完成) achieve; accomplish

【成就感】 chéngjiùgǎn sense of accomplishment

【成立】 chénglì 1.(建立) found; establish; set up 2.(有根据) be tenable; hold water: 这个理论不能～。This theory is untenable.

【成龙配套】 chénglóng-pèitào fill in the gaps to complete a chain (of equipment, construction projects, etc.)

【成名】 chéngmíng become famous; make a name for oneself

【成名成家】 chéngmíng-chéngjiā establish one's reputation as an authority

【成命】 chéngmìng order already issued: 收回～ revoke a command

【成年】 chéngnián 1.(长大成人) grow up; come of age: 未～ be under age 2.(成年人) adult; grown-up 3.(整年) year after year; year in year out

【成年累月】 chéngnián-lěiyuè year in year out; for years on end

【成批】 chnégpī group by group; in batches; in large amount

【成品】 chéngpǐn end product; finished product

【成品尺寸】 chéngpǐn chǐcùn finished size

【成品服装】 chéngpǐn fúzhuāng ready-made clothes

【成品粮】 chéngpǐnliáng processed grain

【成气候】 chéng qìhòu (多用于否定) make good: 成不了什么气候 will not get anywhere

【成千成万】 chéngqiān-chéngwàn thousands of

【成亲】 chéngqīn get married

【成全】 chéngquán help (sb. to achieve his aim)

【成群】 chéngqún in groups; in large numbers

【成人】 chéngrén 1.(长大) grow up: 长大～ be grown to manhood 2.(成年人) adult; grown-up

【成人教育】 chéngrén jiàoyù adult education

【成人学校】 chéngrén xuéxiào adult school

【成仁】 chéngrén 〈*written*〉 die for a righteous cause: 取义～ die to preserve one's virtue intact

【成色】 chéngsè 1.(纯金、银含量) the percentage of gold or silver in a coin, etc.; the relative purity of gold or silver 2.(质量) quality

【成事】 chéngshì accomplish sth.; succeed

【成事不足,败事有余】 chéngshì-bùzú, bàishì-yǒuyú unable to accomplish anything but liable to spoil everything

【成熟】 chéngshú ripe; mature: 政治上～ politically mature

【成双成对】 chéngshuāng-chéngduì in pairs, female and male

【成诵】 chéngsòng able to recite; able to repeat from memory: 过目～ able to recite what one has casually read only once

【成套】 chéngtào form a complete set; whole set; complete set: ～设备 complete sets of equipment

【成天】 chéngtiān all day long; all the time

【成为】 chéngwéi become; turn into: ～事实 come true

【成文】 chéngwén 1.(现成文章) existing writings 2.(书面的) written

【成问题】 chéngwèntí be a problem; be open to question

【成效】 chéngxiào effect; result: 获得好的～ obtain good results

【成心】 chéngxīn intentionally; on purpose; deliberately

【成形】 chéngxíng take shape

【成型】 chéngxíng 〈*Mech.*〉 shaping; forming: 爆炸～ explosive forming

【成性】 chéngxìng by nature; become sb's second nature

【成宿】 chéngxiǔ all night

【成药】 chéngyào patent medicine

【成夜】 chéngyè all night

【成衣】 chéngyī 1.(指职业) tailoring 2.(指服装) ready-made clothes

【成因】 chéngyīn cause of formation; contributing factor

【成阴】 chéngyīn be shaded by (splendid trees)

【成语】 chéngyǔ set phrase; idiom

【成员】 chéngyuán member

【成员国】 chéngyuánguó member state; member country: 非～ non-member state

【成灾】 chéngzāi cause disaster

【成长】 chéngzhǎng 1.(长成) grow up; grow to maturity 2.(发展) grow up; develop; increase

诚 (chéng) 1.(真诚) sincere; honest 2.(的确) really; actually; indeed: ～非易事 be by no means easy / ～然不错 good indeed / ～如所言。It is exactly as you said. / ～有此事。There actually was such a thing.

【诚惶诚恐】 chénghuáng-chéngkǒng with reverence and awe; if fear and trepidation

【诚恳】 chéngkěn sincere: ～待人 treat others with earnestness

【诚然】 chéngrán true; indeed; to be sure

【诚实】 chéng·shí honest: ～可靠 honest and reliable

【诚心】 chéngxīn sincere desire; wholeheartedness

【诚意】 chéngyì good faith; sincerity: 表明～ show one's good faith / 毫无～ be not sincere in the least

【诚挚】 chéngzhì sincere; cordial: ～友好的气氛 a sincere and friendly atmosphere

城 (chéng) 1.(城墙) city wall; wall: 长～ the Great Wall 2.(城区) city: 内～ inner city / 外～ outer city 3.(城市) town

【城垛】 chéngduǒ battlements

【城防】 chéngfáng the defense of a city

【城府】 chéngfǔ shrewdness; subtlety: ～很深 shrewd and deep; subtle

【城关】 chéngguān the area just outside a city gate

【城建】 chéngjiàn urban construction

【城郊】 chéngjiāo outskirts of a town: 在北京～ in the suburbs of Beijing

【城里】 chénglǐ inside the city; in town

【城里人】 chénglǐrén city dwellers; townspeople

【城楼】 chénglóu a tower over a city gate; gate tower: 天安门～ Tian'anmen Gate Tower; the Tower over Tian'anmen

【城门】 chéngmén city gate

【城墙】 chéngqiáng city wall

【城区】 chéngqū the city proper: ～和郊区 the city proper and the suburbs

【城市】 chéngshì town; city

【城市干道】 chéngshì gàndào 〈*Transport*〉 arterial street

【城市公用设施】 chéngshì gōngyòng shèshī urban public utilities

【城市规划】 chéngshì guīhuà city planning

【城市集中供热】 chéngshì jízhōng gòngrè city's concentrated heating supply

【城市居民】 chéngshì jūmín city dwellers; urban population

【城市垃圾】 chéngshì lājī municipal refuse

【城市贫民】 chéngshì pínmín urban poor; city poor

【城市热岛】 chéngshì rèdǎo urban heat island

【城头】 chéngtóu on top of the city wall

【城乡】 chéngxiāng town and country; urban and rural; city and countryside

【城乡差别】 chéngxiāng chābié difference between town and country

【城乡接合部】 chéngxiāng jiēhébù rurbania; rurban (adj.)

【城运会】 chéngyùnhuì urban games

【城镇】 chéngzhèn cities and towns

盛 (chéng) 1.(装;舀) fill; ladle 2.(容纳) hold; contain: ～100公斤粮食 hold 100 kilos of grain
(另见"盛"shèng)

呈 (chéng) 1.(呈现) assume 2.(呈上) submit; present 3.(呈文) petition; memorial

【呈报】 chéngbào submit a report; report a matter: ～备案 report the matter for the record

【呈递】 chéngdì present; submit: ～国书 present letter of credence

【呈露】 chénglù appear; appearance (n.)

【呈请】 chéngqǐng apply (to the higher authorities for consideration or approval)

【呈送】 chéngsòng present; submit

【呈文】 chéngwén document submitted to a superior

【呈现】 chéngxiàn present (a certain appearance); appear; emerge: ～新的面貌 assume a new aspect

【呈阅】 chéngyuè apply to the higher authorities for consideration

程 (chéng) 1.(规矩) rule; regulation 2.(程序) order; procedure 3.(旅程) journey; stage of a journey: 归～ a homeward journey 4.(路程) distance 5.〈*Computer*〉 program: 编～ program

【程度】 chéngdù 1.(指水平) level; degree: 文化～ level of education; degree of literacy 2.(指状况) extent; degree: 在不同～上 in varying degrees / 在很大～上 to a great extent / 在一定～上 to a certain extent

【程控】 chéngkòng program control; program-controlled (adj.)

【程控数字电话交换机】 chéngkòng shùzì diànhuà jiāohuànjī program-controlled digital telephone switchboard

【程式】 chéngshì form; pattern; formula

【程序】 chéngxù 1.(次序) order; procedure; course; sequence: 符合～ be in order 2.〈*Computer*〉 program: ～设计 program design / 写～ write a program; program (v.)

【程序错误】 chéngxù cuòwù 〈*Computer*〉 program error

【程序对话框】 chéngxù duìhuàkuāng 〈*Computer*〉 program dialog box

【程序管理】 chéngxù guǎnlǐ 〈*Computer*〉 program management

【程序库】 chéngxùkù 〈*Computer*〉 program library

【程序盘】 chéngxùpán 〈*Computer*〉 program disks

【程序设计】 chéngxù shèjì 〈*Computer*〉 programming; program (v.)

【程序文件】 chéngxù wénjiàn 〈*Computer*〉 program file

【程序项】 chéngxùxiàng 〈*Computer*〉 program items

【程序员】 chéngxùyuán 〈*Computer*〉 programmer

【程序中断】 chéngxù zhōngduàn 〈*Computer*〉 program interruption

【程序组】 chéngxùzǔ 〈*Computer*〉 program groups

承 (chéng) 1.(托着;接着) bear; hold; carry 2.(承担) undertake; contract (to do a job) 3.(承蒙) be indebted (to sb. for a kindness); be granted a favor 4.(继续;接续) continue; carry on

【承办】 chéngbàn undertake

【承包】 chéngbāo contract (with); farm out: 家庭联产～ the household contract responsibility system with remuneration linked to output / ～建桥工程 contract to build a bridge / 把活～给某人 farm sth. out to sb.

【承包单位】 chéngbāo dānwèi contractor unit

【承包工程】 chéngbāo gōngchéng 1.(承包一项工程) contract for construction 2.(承包的工程) a contract works

【承包合同】 chéngbāo hé·tong contract

【承包商】 chéngbāoshāng contractor

【承包制】 chéngbāozhì contracting out system

【承担】 chéngdān bear; undertake; assume: ～风险 acceptance of risk / ～艰巨的使命 take up a difficult mission / ～经济责任 bear financial responsibility / ～一切费用 bear all the costs / ～义务 commit oneself; be committed to; accept the responsibility for / ～责任 undertake the responsibility; bear the responsibility / ～重任 take on heavy responsibilities; take a heavy task upon oneself

【承兑】 chéngduì 〈*Trade*〉 honor; accept: ～汇票 accept a draft; accept a bill

【承继】 chéngjì 1.(过继儿子给伯父或叔父) be adopted as heir to one's uncle 2.(把侄子过继来) adopt one's brother's son (as one's heir) 3.(继承) inherit; inheritance (n.)

【承建】 chéngjiàn be responsible for the construction and completion of a project

【承接】 chéngjiē 1.(接住流下的液体) hold out a vessel to have liquid poured into it 2.(接续) continue; carry on 3.(承担) undertake; accept: ～来料加工 accept processing on given materials / ～书刊印刷 undertake the printing of books

【承揽】 chénglǎn contract to do a job; hire of work

【承揽合同】 chénglǎn hé·tong contract of work; contractor's agreement

【承蒙】 chéngméng be indebted to; be granted a favor

【承蒙不弃】 chéngméng-bùqì meet with your

gracious consent

【承蒙错爱】 chéngméng-cuòài have received undeserved kindness from you

【承诺】 chéngnuò promise to undertake; undertake to do sth.; acceptance of offer

【承诺人】 chéngnuòrén accepter; acceptor

【承请】 chéngqǐng be much obliged to; owe a debt of gratitude to

【承认】 chéngrèn 1.(认可) admit; acknowledge; recognize: ～错误 admit one's mistake 2.(肯定法律地位) give diplomatic recognition; recognize

【承上启下】 chéngshàng-qǐxià form a connecting link between the preceding and the following

【承受】 chéngshòu 1.(承担;经受) bear; support; endure 2.(继承) inherit (a legacy, etc.)

【承袭海】 chéngxíhǎi patrimonial sea

【承先启后】 chéngxiān-qǐhòu inherit the past and usher in the future; serve as a link between past and future

【承印】 chéngyìn undertake the printing of

【承运】 chéngyùn carry; acknowledgement of consignment

【承运人】 chéngyùnrén carrier

【承载】 chéngzài bear the weight of

【承重墙】 chéngzhòngqiáng 〈*Archit*.〉 bearing wall

【承租人】 chéngzūrén lessee; tenant

乘 (chéng) 1.(搭乘) ride: ～出租汽车 take a taxi / ～无轨电车 ride in a trolleybus 2.(利用) take advantage of; avail oneself of 3.〈*Math*.〉 multiply; is multiplied by: 二～三等于六 two times three is six; 2 multiplied 3 is 6 (符号为 ×)

【乘法】 chéngfǎ 〈*Math*.〉 multiplication

【乘法表】 chéngfǎbiǎo 〈*Math*.〉 multiplication table

【乘方】 chéngfāng 〈*Math*.〉 involution; power

【乘风破浪】 chéngfēng-pòlàng ride the wind and cleave the waves; brave the wind and the waves

【乘号】 chénghào 〈*Math*.〉 multiplication sign (符号为×)

【乘机】 chéngjī 1.(利用机会) seize the opportunity 2.(乘坐飞机) travel by plane; board a plane: ～去广州 board a plane to Guangzhou

【乘警】 chéngjǐng railway policeman; passengers' police

【乘客】 chéngkè passenger

【乘凉】 chéngliáng enjoy the cool; relax in a cool place

【乘其不备】 chéngqí-bùbèi at unawares; take sb. unawares

【乘人之危】 chéngrén-zhīwēi take advantage of sb's precarious position

【乘胜】 chéngshèng exploit a victory; follow up a victory: ～前进 advance on the crest of a victory; push on in the flush of victory

【乘数】 chéngshù 〈*Math*.〉 multiplier: ～和被乘数 multiplier and multiplicand

【乘务员】 chéngwùyuán attendant on a train

【乘隙】 chéngxì take advantage of a loophole; turn sb's mistake to one's own account: ～而入 take advantage of the crack and enter

【乘兴】 chéngxìng while one is in high spirits: ～而来 be present taking advantage of one's good mood

【乘虚而入】 chéngxū-érrù attack where the enemy is unguarded; get a chance to step in

【乘坐】 chéngzuò ride: ～公共汽车 ride in a bus.

惩[懲] (chéng) punish; penalize

【惩办】 chéngbàn punish; chastise; punishment; chastisement

【惩处】 chéngchǔ penalize; punish; punishment: ～罪犯 inflict a punishment on a criminal / 依法～ punish in accordance with the law

【惩罚】 chéngfá punish; penalize

【惩罚措施】 chéngfá cuòshī punitive measures

【惩戒】 chéngjiè punish sb. to teach him a lesson; discipline sb. as a warning; take disciplinary action against

【惩前毖后，治病救人】 chéngqián-bìhòu, zhìbìng-jiùrén learn from past mistakes to avoid future ones, and cure the sickness to save the patient

【惩治】 chéngzhì punish; mete out punishment to

澄[澂](chéng) clear; transparent

【澄澈】 chéngchè clear; transparent

【澄清】 chéngqīng 1.（清亮）clear; transparent 2.（弄清楚）clear up; clarify: 发表声明～形势 issue a statement to clarify the situation / ～误会 clear up a misunderstanding 3. 〈*Chem.*〉 defecate; defecation (n.)

（另见"澄"dèng）

橙(chéng) 1.（橙子）orange 2.（橙色）orange color

【橙红】 chénghóng orange-red (color)

【橙黄】 chénghuáng orange (color)

【橙汁】 chéngzhī orangeade

【橙子】 chéng·zhi orange

逞(chěng) 1.（炫耀）show off; flaunt 2.（得逞）carry out (an evil design); succeed (in a scheme): 得～ succeed in one's schemes 3.（纵容；放任）indulge; give free rein to

【逞能】 chěngnéng show off one's ability; parade one's ability: 好～ like to show off

【逞强】 chěngqiáng flaunt one's superiority

【逞威风】 chěng wēifēng show off one's power

【逞凶】 chěngxiōng act violently; act ferociously

骋(chěng) 1.（奔跑）gallop 2.（放任）give free rein to

秤[称](chèng) balance; steelyard: 电子～ electronic weighing system / 台～ platform scale/弹簧～ spring balance

【秤锤】 chèngchuí the sliding weight of a steelyard

【秤钩】 chènggōu steelyard hook

【秤盘】 chèngpán the pan of a steelyard

【秤砣】 chèngtuó sliding weight of a steelyard

chi

吃(chī) 1.（吃东西）eat; take: ～晚餐 eat a supper / ～早餐 take breakfast 2.（在外边吃）eat; dine out 3.（以…为生）live on; live off 4.（消灭）annihilate; wipe out 5.（耗费）exhaust; be a strain 6.（吸收）absorb; soak up: ～墨 absorb ink 7.（挨）suffer; incur: ～批评 be criticized

【吃饱】 chībǎo eat one's fill; be full

【吃不开】 chī·bu kāi be unpopular; won't work

【吃不了，兜着走】 chī·bu liǎo, dōu·zhe zǒu get more than one bargained for; land oneself in serious trouble

【吃不下】 chī·bu xià not feel like eating; be unable to eat any more

【吃不消】 chī·bu xiāo be unable to stand: 痛得我～。The pain is more than I can stand.

【吃不住】 chī·bu zhù be unable to bear or support

【吃穿】 chīchuān food and clothing

【吃床板】 chī chuángbǎn improper profit made from hotel business

【吃醋】 chīcù be jealous: ～的妻子 a jealous wife

【吃大锅饭】 chī dàguōfàn mess together; eat in the canteen the same as everyone else

【吃大户】 chī dàhù improper profit made from mass project construction

【吃得开】 chī·de kāi be popular; be much sought after

【吃得下】 chī·de xià be able to eat

【吃得消】 chī·de xiāo be able to stand (exertion, fatigue, etc.)

【吃得住】 chī·de zhù be able to bear or support

【吃饭】 chīfàn 1.（进餐）eat; have a meal: 请客～ invite sb. to dinner 2.（指生活或生存）keep alive; make a living: 靠工资～ live on one's wages

【吃喝玩乐】 chīhē-wánlè eat, drink and be merry

【吃皇粮】 chī huángliáng live on the wages paid by the government

【吃荤】 chīhūn have a meat diet; eat meat

【吃角子老虎】 chī jiǎo·zi lǎohǔ fruit machine

【吃紧】 chījǐn be critical; be hard pressed

【吃惊】 chījīng be startled; be shocked; be amazed; be taken aback

【吃苦】 chīkǔ bear hardships: ～耐劳 bear hardships and stand hard work

【吃苦头】 chī kǔ·tou suffer

【吃苦在先，享乐在后】 chīkǔ-zàixiān, xiǎnglè-zàihòu be the first to bear hardships and the last to enjoy comforts

【吃亏】 chīkuī 1.(受损失) come to grief; suffer losses; get the worst of it: 吃眼前亏 immediately get the worst of it 2.(在某方面不利) at a disadvantage; in an unfavorable situation

【吃劳保】 chī láobǎo live on labor insurance

【吃老本】 chī lǎoběn live off one's past gains; rest on one's laurels

【吃里爬外】 chīlǐ-páwài live off one person while secretly helping another

【吃力】 chīlì entail strenuous effort; be a strain

【吃力不讨好】 chīlì bù tǎohǎo work laboriously only to earn criticisms

【吃零嘴】 chī língzuǐ take snacks between meals; nibble between meals

【吃奶】 chīnǎi suck the breast: ～的孩子 sucking child

【吃批评】 chī pīpíng be criticized; suffer criticism

【吃偏饭】 chī piānfàn give special care and partiality

【吃请】 chīqǐng accept an invitation to dinner

【吃水】 chīshuǐ 1.(饮用水) drinking water 2.(吸取水分) absorb water 3.〈*Naut*.〉 draught; draft

【吃水线】 chīshuǐxiàn waterline; line of floatation

【吃素】 chīsù be a vegetarian

【吃透】 chītòu have a thorough grasp

【吃闲饭】 chī xiánfàn eat the bread of idleness

【吃香】 chīxiāng be very popular; be much sought after; be well-liked

【吃一堑，长一智】 chī yī qiàn, zhǎng yī zhì a fall into the pit, a gain in your wit

【吃重】 chīzhòng 1.(艰巨) arduous; strenuous 2.(载重) carrying capacity; loading capacity

嗤 (chī) sneer

【嗤笑】 chīxiào laugh at; sneer at: 为人～ be laughed at; be sneered at

【嗤之以鼻】 chīzhī-yǐbí give a snort of contempt; despise

眵 (chī) 〈*Physiol*.〉 eye secretion; gum in the eyes

【眵目糊】 chī·mùhú 〈*Physiol*.〉 eye secretion; gum in the eyes

痴[**癡**] (chī) 1.(愚笨) silly; idiotic 2.(迷恋) crazy about

【痴呆】 chīdāi 1.(愚笨) dull-witted; stupid 2.〈*Med*.〉 dementia: 老年性～ senile dementia

【痴情】 chīqíng unreasoning passion; infatuation

【痴笑】 chīxiào silly smiles; foolish smiles

【痴心】 chīxīn infatuate; infatuation (n.)

【痴心妄想】 chīxīn-wàngxiǎng wishful thinking; fond dream; hope madly

【痴愚】 chīyú imbecility; moronity

池 (chí) 1.(池塘) pool; pond 2.(剧场池座) stalls

【池塘】 chítáng 1.(蓄水池) pond; pool 2.(浴池) a big pool in a bathhouse

【池盐】 chíyán lake salt

【池沼】 chízhǎo pond; pool

【池子】 chí·zi 1.(蓄水池) pond 2.(浴池) a big pool in a bathhouse

弛 (chí) relax; slacken; ease: 一张一～ tension alternating with relaxation

【弛缓】 zhíhuǎn relax; calm down; ease off

【弛张热】 zhízhāngrè 〈*Med*.〉 remittent fever

驰 (chí) 1.(跑得快) speed; gallop 2.(传播) spread 3.(向往) turn eagerly towards: 心～神往 let one's thoughts fly to (a place or person); long for

【驰骋】 chíchěng 〈*written*〉 gallop: ～疆场 gallop across the battlefield

【驰名】 chímíng known far and wide; well-known; famous; renowned: ～中外 well-known both at home and abroad

迟[**遲**] (chí) 1.(慢) slow; tardy 2.(晚) late

【迟迟】 chíchí slow; tardy

【迟到】 chídào be late; come late; arrive late

【迟钝】 chídùn slow (in thought or action); obtuse: 脑子～ slow of understanding

【迟缓】 chíhuǎn slow; tardy; sluggish: 进展～ make slow progress

【迟延】 chíyán delay; retard

【迟延交付】 chíyán jiāofù delay deliverance

【迟疑】 chíyí hesitate: ～不决 hesitate to make a decision / 毫不～ without a moment's hesita-

tion
【迟早】 chízǎo sooner or later
持(chí) 1.(拿着;握着) hold; grasp:～相同意见 hold a similar opinion 2.(支持;保持) support; maintain 3.(主持) manage; run 4.(相持) oppose
【持不同政见者】 chí bùtóng zhèngjiànzhě dissident; political dissident
【持家】 chíjiā run one's home; keep house: ～有方 manage the affairs of the family methodically
【持久】 chíjiǔ lasting; enduring; protracted: ～和平 lasting peace; enduring peace
【持久战】 chíjiǔzhàn protracted war
【持论】 chílùn present an argument; express a view
【持平】 chípíng 1.(数量上相等) maintain an equal level 2.(公正) just; fair
【持枪抢劫】 chíqiāng qiǎngjié gun robbery
【持续】 chíxù continued; sustained
【持有】 chíyǒu hold: ～相反意见 hold contrary views
【持之以恒】 chí zhī yǐ héng persevere: 刻苦学习,～ study assiduously and perseveringly
【持重】 chízhòng prudent; cautious; discreet: 老成～ experienced and prudent; dignified and experienced
匙(chí) spoon: 茶～ teaspoon / 点心～ dessert spoon / 汤～ table spoon
【匙子】 chí·zi spoon
踟(chí)
【踟蹰】 chíchú hesitate; waver; linger
【踟蹰不前】 chí chú bù qián hesitate to move forward
尺(chǐ) 1.(器具) rule; ruler 2.(像尺的东西) an instrument in the shape of a ruler: 计算～ slide rule
【尺寸】 chǐ·cun measurement; dimensions; size: 量～ take the size of
【尺寸板】 chǐcùnbǎn 〈*Photog*.〉 baseboard
【尺寸地方】 chǐcùn dìfāng a foot of land
【尺动脉】 chǐdòngmài 〈*Anat*.〉 ulnar artery
【尺牍】 chǐdú 1.(书信范本) a model of epistolary art 2.(书信) correspondence (of an eminent writer)
【尺度】 chǐdù yardstick; measure; scale
【尺骨】 chǐgǔ 〈*Anat*.〉 ulna
【尺码】 chǐmǎ size; measures
【尺子】 chǐ·zi rule; ruler
齿[**齒**](chǐ) 1.(牙齿) tooth 2.(齿状部分) a tooth-like part of anything: 锯～儿 the teeth of a saw 3.(说到) mention
【齿轮】 chǐlún gear wheel; gear
【齿轮传动】 chǐlún chuándòng gear drive
【齿轮箱】 chǐlúnxiāng gear box
【齿龈】 chǐyín 〈*Anat*.〉 gum
侈(chǐ) wasteful; extravagant
【侈谈】 chǐtán prate about; prattle about
耻[**恥**](chǐ) shame; disgrace; humiliation: 引以为～ regard as a disgrace
【耻骨】 chǐgǔ 〈*Anat*.〉 pubic bone; pubis bone
【耻骨联合】 chǐgǔ liánhé 〈*Anat*.〉 symphysis pubic
【耻辱】 chǐrǔ shame; disgrace; humiliation
【耻笑】 chǐxiào hold sb. to ridicule; sneer at; mock
【耻与为伍】 chǐyǔ-wéiwǔ feel ashamed to associate with him
褫(chǐ) strip off; deprive
【褫夺】 chǐduó strip off; deprive; take away
斥(chì) 1.(责备) upbraid; scold; denounce; reprimand 2.(使离开) repel; exclude; oust: 排～异己 exclude outsiders
【斥骂】 chìmà reproach; upbraid; scold: ～某人 give sb. a scolding
【斥退】 chìtuì 1.(罢免) dismiss sb. from his post 2.(开除) expel from a school 3.(喝令退出) shout at sb. to go away
【斥责】 chìzé reprimand; rebuke; denounce
【斥资】 chìzī pay
赤(chì) 1.(红色) red 2.(忠诚) loyal; sincere; single-hearted 3.(光着;露着) bare
【赤膊】 chìbó barebacked; be stripped to the waist
【赤膊上阵】 chìbó-shàngzhèn go into battle stripped to the waist; throw away all disguise; come out into the open
【赤诚】 chìchéng absolute sincerity: 待人～

treat people with absolute sincerity
【赤胆忠心】 chìdǎn-zhōngxīn utter devotion; loyalty
【赤道】 chìdào 1.〈*Geog*.〉 the equator; equatorial (adj.) 2.〈*Astron*.〉 the celestial equator
【赤道无风带】 chìdào wúfēngdài 〈*Geog*.〉 the equatorial clam belt
【赤脚】 chìjiǎo barefoot; barefooted
【赤经】 chìjīng 〈*Astron*.〉 right ascension
【赤裸】 chìluǒ bare; nude; naked
【赤裸裸】 chìluǒluǒ 1.(裸体) bare; nude; naked; without a stitch of clothing 2.(毫无掩饰) undisguised; naked; out-and-out
【赤贫】 chìpín in abject poverty; utterly destitute; in extreme poverty
【赤身】 chìshēn bare; nude; naked
【赤身裸体】 chìshēn-luǒtǐ bare; nude; naked
【赤手空拳】 chìshǒu-kōngquán bare-handed; unarmed
【赤纬】 chìwěi 〈*Astron*.〉 declination circle
【赤子】 chìzǐ a newborn baby: ～之心 the innocent heart of a child; utter innocence
【赤字】 chìzì deficit: 财政～ financial deficit / 贸易～ trade deficit / 预算～ budgetary deficit
【赤足】 chìzú barefoot; barefooted

饬 (chì) put in order; strengthen discipline
【饬令】 chìlìng order; instruct; direct

炽[熾] (chì) flaming; ablaze
【炽烈】 chìliè burning fiercely; flaming; blazing
【炽热】 chìrè 1.(热) red-hot; blazing: ～的阳光 blazing sun 2.(极热烈) passionate: ～的情感 passionate feelings

翅[翄] (chì) 1.(翅膀) wing 2.(鱼翅) shark's fin
【翅膀】 chìbǎng wing
【翅席】 chìxí banquet with shark's fin

敕[勅、勑] (chì) imperial order; edict
【敕赐】 chìcì grant by imperial order
【敕令】 chìlìng 1.(皇帝下命令) give the imperial order 2.(皇帝的命令) imperial order

chong

充 (chōng) 1.(充足) sufficient; full 2.(充满) fill; charge 3.(担任;充当) serve as; act as 4.(冒充) pretend to be; pose as; pass sth. off as: ～内行 pretend to be an expert
【充斥】 chōngchì flood; congest; be full of
【充当】 chōngdāng serve as; act as; play the part of: ～导游 act as guide
【充电】 chōngdiàn charge (a battery)
【充电器】 chōngdiànqì charger; battery charger
【充耳不闻】 chōng'ěr-bùwén stuff one's ears and refuse to listen; turn a deaf ear to
【充分】 chōngfèn full; ample; abundant: ～动员 mobilize to the fullest extent / ～发挥 bring ... into full play / ～利用 fully utilize; make full use of / ～体现 demonstrate fully / ～证明 full proof
【充分就业】 chōngfèn jiùyè full employment
【充公】 chōnggōng confiscate
【充饥】 chōngjī allay one's hunger; appease one's hunger
【充满】 chōngmǎn 1.(填满,装满) fill; be full of; be filled with 2.(充分具有) be full of; be filled with; brimming with; permeated with: ～信心 filled with unbounded confidence
【充沛】 chōngpèi plentiful; abundant; full of: 精力～ full of energy; full of vigor; full of vitality
【充其量】 chōngqíliàng at most; at best; at the maximum
【充任】 chōngrèn fill the post of; hold the position of: 挑选某人～经理 select sb. to fill the post of manager
【充实】 chōngshí 1.(丰富) substantial; rich: 内容～ substantial in content 2.(使充足) substantiate; enrich; replenish
【充数】 chōngshù make up the number; serve as a stopgap
【充血】 chōngxuè 〈*Med*.〉 hyperemia; congestion
【充裕】 chōngyù abundant; ample; plentiful
【充足】 chōngzú adequate; sufficient; abundant; full of

冲[沖[4,5,6]、衝[1,2,3]] (chōng) 1.(要冲) thoroughfare; important place 2.(冲破障碍) charge; rush; dash 3.(冲击) clash; collide 4.(用开水等冲) pour boiling water on 5.(冲洗) rinse; flush 6.〈*Photog.*〉develop; development (n.)
(另见"冲"chòng)

【冲程】 chōngchéng 〈*Mech.*〉stroke

【冲冲】 chōngchōng in a state of excitement

【冲刺】 chōngcì 〈*Sports*〉spurt; sprint; make a spurt

【冲淡】 chōngdàn 1.(稀释) dilute 2.(使减弱) water down; weaken; play down

【冲动】 chōngdòng 1.(神经兴奋) impulse: 出于一时～ act on impulse 2.(情感强烈) get excited; be impetuous: 他很容易～。He easily gets excited.

【冲锋】 chōngfēng charge; assault

【冲锋枪】 chōngfēngqiāng submachine gun; tommy gun

【冲锋陷阵】 chōngfēng-xiànzhèn charge the enemy lines; charge forward

【冲毁】 chōnghuǐ destroy by rush of water: ～堤岸 embarkment was destroyed by rush of waters

【冲昏头脑】 chōnghūn-tóunǎo turn sb's head; be giddy with; have one's head turned: 胜利～ overwhelmed by one's success

【冲击】 chōngjī 1.(水流撞击) lash; pound 2.〈*Physics*〉charge; assault 3.(干扰或打击) shock; attack: 受到各方面的～ be under attack from all sides

【冲击波】 chōngjībō 〈*Physics*〉shock wave; blast wave

【冲积】 chōngjī 〈*Geol.*〉alluviation

【冲积平原】 chōngjī píngyuán 〈*Geol.*〉alluvial plain

【冲积扇】 chōngjīshàn 〈*Geol.*〉alluvial fan

【冲剂】 chōngjì 〈*Chin. Med.*〉medicine to be taken after being mixed with boiling water

【冲减】 chōngjiǎn eat up part of: ～财政收入 eat up part of state's revenue

【冲决】 chōngjué burst; smash: 河水～堤岸。The river burst its banks.

【冲扩】 chōngkuò develop and enlarge

【冲浪】 chōnglàng 〈*Sports*〉surfing; surfing riding; surf (v.): 他们每周末都去～。They go surfing every weekend.

【冲浪板】 chōnglàngbǎn 〈*Sports*〉surfboard

【冲浪者】 chōnglàngzhě surfer

【冲破】 chōngpò break through; breach: ～重重障碍 surmount all obstacles

【冲散】 chōngsàn break up; scatter; disperse: ～人群 disperse a crowd

【冲杀】 chōngshā charge; rush ahead

【冲刷】 chōngshuā erode; scour; wash out; wash away

【冲水】 chōngshuǐ 〈*Photog.*〉bath

【冲塌】 chōngtā cause to collapse; burst: ～房屋 dash against the houses and wash them away

【冲天】 chōngtiān towering; soaring

【冲突】 chōngtū conflict; clash: 边境～ a border clash / 利害～ conflict of interests / 武装～ an armed conflict / 防止～ avoid a conflict (with)

【冲洗】 chōngxǐ 1.(用水冲) rinse; wash 2.〈*Photog.*〉develop: ～胶卷 develop a roll of film

【冲销】 chōngxiāo reverse an entry

【冲账】 chōngzhàng 1.(结账) strike a balance 2.(收支抵销) reverse an entry

【冲撞】 chōngzhuàng 1.(撞击) collide; bump; ram 2.(冲犯) give offense; offend: 我的话～了她。My words offended her.

忡[㤝] (chōng)

【忡忡】 chōngchōng laden with anxiety; careworn: 忧心～ in a disturbed state of mind

舂 (chōng) pound; pestle

【舂米】 chōngmǐ husk rice with a pestle

憧 (chōng)

【憧憧】 chōngchōng flickering; moving: 树影～ flickering shadows of trees

【憧憬】 chōngjǐng long for; look forward to: ～着幸福的明天 long for the happy days to come / 充满着对未来的～ have a great longing for a bright future

虫[蟲] (chóng) insect; worm: 害～ destructive insect; harmful insect / 益～ useful insect; beneficial insect

【虫害】 chónghài insect pest

【虫牙】 chóngyá carious tooth; decayed tooth

【虫灾】 chóngzāi plague of insects

【虫子】 chóng·zi insect; worm: 拉～ pass worms

重 (chóng) 1.(重复) repeat; duplicate 2.(再) again; once more: 旧地～游 revisit a once familiar place
(另见"重"zhòng)

【重版】 chóngbǎn 〈*Printing*〉 republish; republication (n.)

【重版书】 chóngbǎnshū 〈*Printing*〉 reprint

【重播】 chóngbō 1.(指播种) resow the seeds; reseed 2.(指播送) rebroadcast (a program)

【重操旧业】 chóngcāo-jiùyè return to one's old trade

【重重】 chóngchóng layer upon layer; ring upon ring: 顾虑～ full of misgivings / 克服～困难 overcome one difficulty after another; surmount numerous difficulties / 陷入～包围 be encircled ring upon ring

【重蹈覆辙】 chóngdǎo-fùzhé follow the same old disastrous road; recommit the same error

【重叠】 chóngdié one on top of another; overlapping

【重读】 chóngdú repeat the course; repetition (n.)

【重读生】 chóngdúshēng repeater

【重返】 chóngfǎn return: ～家园 return to one's homeland / ～前线 go back to the front

【重返大气层】 chóngfǎn dàqìcéng reentry

【重返大气层运载工具】 chóngfǎn dàqìcéng yùnzǎi gōngjù reentry vehicle

【重犯】 chóngfàn repeat (an error or offense)

【重逢】 chóngféng meet again; have a reunion: 久别～ meet again after a long separation

【重复】 chóngfù repeat; duplicate

【重婚】 chónghūn 〈*Law*〉 bigamy; a bigamous marriage

【重见光明】 chóng jiàn guāngmíng see light again

【重建】 chóngjiàn rebuild; reconstruct; reestablish; rehabilitate

【重申】 chóngshēn reaffirm; reiterate; restate: ～观点 reassert one's views / ～立场 reaffirm one's stand

【重施故技】 chóngshī-gùjì play the same old trick; repeat a stock trick

【重孙】 chóngsūn great-grandson

【重孙女】 chóngsūn·nü great-granddaughter

【重弹老调】 chóngtán-lǎodiào harp on the same string; sing the same old tune

【重提】 chóngtí bring up again: 往事～ bring up an old case

【重围】 chóngwéi tight encirclement: 杀出～ break through a tight encirclement

【重温旧梦】 chóngwēn-jiùmèng revive an old dream; relive an old experience

【重现】 chóngxiàn reappear; reappearance (n.)

【重新】 chóngxīn again; anew; afresh: ～分配 redistribute / ～开放 reopen / ～开始 make a fresh start / ～考虑 reconsider / ～使用 reactivate / ～做人 begin one's life anew; turn over a new leaf

【重修】 chóngxiū 1.(指翻修) rebuild 2.(指修订) revise; revision (n.)

【重修旧好】 chóngxiū-jiùhǎo renew cordial relations; become reconciled; bury the hatchet; pass the sponge over

【重演】 chóngyǎn 1.(重新上演) put on an old play, etc. 2.(再次出现) recur; reenact; repeat

【重洋】 chóngyáng the seas and oceans: 远隔～ be separated by seas and oceans

【重印】 chóngyìn reprint

【重印本】 chóngyìnběn reprint

【重整旗鼓】 chóngzhěng-qígǔ regroup for battle; rally one's forces (after a defeat)

【重奏】 chóngzòu 〈*Music*〉 ensemble: 准确而协调的～ good ensemble

崇 (chóng) 1.(高) high; lofty; sublime 2.(崇敬) esteem; worship

【崇拜】 chóngbài worship; adore: 盲目～ worship blindly

【崇高】 chónggāo lofty; sublime; high: ～的理想 a lofty ideal / ～的威望 high prestige / 顺致最～的敬意。I avail myself of this opportunity to renew to you the assurances of

my highest consideration.
【崇敬】 chóngjìng esteem; respect; revere
【崇山峻岭】 chóngshān-jùnlǐng high mountain ridges
【崇尚】 chóngshàng uphold; advocate
【崇洋】 chóngyáng worship everything foreign
【崇洋媚外】 chóngyáng-mèiwài worship and have blind faith in foreign things; have a servile attitude to foreign things

宠［寵］(chǒng) dote on; bestow favor on: 得～ find favor with sb.; be in sb's good graces / 失～ fall out of favor
【宠爱】 chǒng'ài make a pet of sb.; dote on: 受某人～ win sb's favor
【宠坏】 chǒnghuài spoil: ～孩子 spoil the child
【宠物】 chǒngwù pet; pet animal
【宠信】 chǒngxìn be specially fond of and trust unduly (a subordinate)

冲［衝］(chòng) 1.(劲头儿足) with vim and vigor; with plenty of dash; vigorously 2.(气味刺鼻) strong 3.(朝; 向; 对) facing; towards: 她～我笑了笑。She gave me a smile. 4.(根据) on the strength of; on the basis of; because 5.〈*Mech*.〉 punching
(另见"冲"chōng)
【冲床】 chòngchuáng 〈*Mech*.〉 punching machine; punch (press)
【冲压】 chòngyā 〈*Mech*.〉 stamping; punching
【冲子】 chòng·zi punching pin

chou

抽(chōu) 1.(取出) take out (from in between) 2.(取出一部分) take (a part from a whole) 3.(生长出) put forth 4.(吸) obtain by drawing 5.(收缩) shrink 6.(抽打) lash; whip; thrash
【抽不开身】 chōu bù kāi shēn cannot leave to do sth. else
【抽测】 chōucè test the samples from different parts
【抽查】 chōuchá conduct a selective examination; have a spot check; have a spot test
【抽搐】 chōuchù twitch; jerk
【抽打】 chōudǎ lash; whip; thrash
【抽调】 chōudiào transfer: ～技术骨干 transfer key scientists
【抽动】 chōudòng twitch; spasm; spasmodic jerk
【抽肥补瘦】 chōuféi-bǔshòu take from the fat to pad the lean; take from those have too much and give to those who have too little
【抽检】 chōujiǎn take a sample for examination; inspect by random samples
【抽奖】 chōujiǎng draw a lottery
【抽筋】 chōujīn 1.(抽掉筋) pull out a tendon 2.(痉挛) cramp; have a cramp in: 腿～了 have the cramp in the leg
【抽考】 chōukǎo select and examine
【抽空】 chōukòng manage to find time; find time to do sth.
【抽泣】 chōuqì sob
【抽签】 chōuqiān draw lots; cast lots
【抽取】 chōuqǔ extract; extraction (n.)
【抽纱】 chōushā 〈*Art*〉 drawnwork
【抽身】 chōushēn leave (one's work); get away
【抽水】 chōushuǐ draw water; pump water
【抽水机】 chōushuǐjī water pump; pumper
【抽水马桶】 chōushuǐ mǎtǒng flush toilet; water closet
【抽水蓄能电站】 chōushuǐ xùnéng diànzhàn storage plant
【抽税】 chōushuì levy a tax
【抽丝】 chōusī reel off raw silk from cocoons
【抽穗】 chōusuì 〈*Agric*.〉 heading; earing
【抽屉】 chōu·ti drawer
【抽头】 chōutóu 1.(提成) take a percentage of the winnings in gambling 2.〈*Electr*.〉 tap
【抽象】 chōuxiàng abstract
【抽象派】 chōuxiàngpài abstractionism
【抽象派艺术】 chōuxiàngpài yìshù abstract art
【抽象思维】 chōuxiàng sīwéi abstract thinking
【抽血】 chōuxuè draw blood
【抽芽】 chōuyá 〈*Bot*.〉 sprout; put forth buds
【抽烟】 chōuyān smoke (a cigarette or a pipe); smoking

【抽样】 chōuyàng 〈*Statistics*〉 sample; sampling: 随机～ random sampling

【抽样调查】 chōuyàng diàochá sampling survey

仇[讎](chóu) 1.(仇敌) enemy; foe 2.(仇恨) hatred; enmity

【仇敌】 chóudí foe; enemy

【仇恨】 chóuhèn hatred; enmity; hostility: ～某人 be in hatred of sb.

【仇人】 chóurén personal enemy

【仇视】 chóushì regard as an enemy; look upon with hatred; be hostile to

俦[儔](chóu) companion

【俦类】 chóulèi 〈*written*〉 people of the same class

【俦侣】 chóulǚ 〈*written*〉 companion

筹[籌](chóu) 1.(小棍儿;小片儿) chip; counter 2.(筹划;筹措) prepare; plan

【筹办】 chóubàn make preparations; make arrangements

【筹备】 chóubèi prepare; arrange

【筹备委员会】 chóubèi wěiyuánhuì preparatory committee

【筹措】 chóucuò raise (money): ～资金 raise funds

【筹措维艰】 chóucuò-wéijiān it is not easy to devise means

【筹划】 chóuhuà 1.(策划) plan and prepare; project; design 2.(筹措) raise (money)

【筹划不周】 chóuhuà-bùzhōu ill-designed

【筹集】 chóují raise (money)

【筹建】 chóujiàn prepare to construct or establish sth.

【筹款】 chóukuǎn raise funds; raise money

【筹码】 chóumǎ chip; counter

【筹拍】 chóupāi prepare to make a film or a TV play

【筹算】 chóusuàn 1.(计算) count 2.(谋划) plan and contrive; plot

【筹资】 chóuzī raise funds to

踌[躊](chóu)

【踌躇】 chóuchú hesitate; shilly-shally to

【踌躇满志】 chóuchú-mǎnzhì enormously proud of one's success; self-assured; puffed up with pride

惆(chóu)

【惆怅】 chóuchàng disconsolate; melancholy; down-hearted

绸[紬](chóu) silk fabric; silk: ～伞 silk parasol

【绸缎】 chóuduàn silks and satins

【绸缪】 chóumóu sentimentally attached

【绸缪缱绻】 chóumóu-qiǎnquàn bind closely and attach to

【绸子】 chóu·zi silk fabric

稠(chóu) 1.(浓) thick 2.(稠密) dense

【稠度】 chóudù density

【稠密】 chóumì dense: 人烟～ densely populated; populous

酬[酧、醻](chóu) 1.(敬酒) propose a toast; toast 2.(报酬) reward; payment 3.(交往) friendly exchange 4.(实现) fulfill; realize

【酬报】 chóubào 1.(报答) requite; reward; repay 2.(报酬) reward; repayment; recompense: 他常给我巧克力作为～。He used to give me chocolate as a reward.

【酬宾】 chóubīn supplied to customers at preferential prices: 九折～ with 10% discount (from the original price)

【酬金】 chóujīn monetary reward; remuneration

【酬劳】 chóuláo recompense; reward

【酬谢】 chóuxiè thank sb. with a gift; repay with thanks

愁(chóu) worry; be anxious: 别发～ don't worry

【愁苦】 chóukǔ anxiety; distress; sadness; anxious (adj.)

【愁眉】 chóuméi knitted brows; worried look: ～不展 with a worried frown; showing signs of worry

【愁眉苦脸】 chóuméi-kǔliǎn a distressed expression

【愁容】 chóuróng worried look; anxious expression: ～满面 look extremely worried

丑[醜[1,2]](chǒu) 1.(不好看) ugly; unsightly; hideous: 长得不～ not bad-looking 2.(不光彩) disgraceful;

shameful; scandalous 3.(丑角) clown

【丑恶】 chǒu'è ugly; repulsive; hideous: ～表演 a disgusting performance / ～面目 ugly features / 社会～现象 social evils; vile practices / ～嘴脸 hideous features

【丑化】 chǒuhuà smear; uglify; defame; vilify: ～某人的形象 smear the images of sb.

【丑剧】 chǒujù farce

【丑角】 chǒujiǎo clown; buffoon

【丑陋】 chǒulòu ugly; ill-looking

【丑事】 chǒushì scandal

【丑态】 chǒutài ugly performance; ludicrous performance; buffoonery

【丑态百出】 chǒutài-bǎichū show all sorts of disgraceful behaviors

【丑闻】 chǒuwén scandal

【丑闻曝光】 chǒuwén bàoguāng scandal exposure

瞅[瞅] (chǒu) look; see: 我来～～。Let me have a look. / 我没～见他。I don't see him.

臭 (chòu) 1.(气味难闻) smelly; foul; stinking 2.(惹人讨厌) disgusting; disgraceful

(另见"臭"xiù)

【臭不可闻】 chòubù-kěwén give off an unbearable stink

【臭虫】 chòuchóng bug; bedbug

【臭椿】 chòuchūn 〈*Bot.*〉 tree of heaven; ailanthus

【臭豆腐】 chòudòu·fu strong-smelling preserved bean curd

【臭骂】 chòumà curse roundly; scold angrily and abusively: 挨了一顿～ get a tongue-lashing; get a dressing down

【臭名】 chòumíng ill reputation

【臭名远扬】 chòumíng-yuǎnyáng notorious; infamous

【臭名昭著】 chòumíng-zhāozhù of ill repute; notorious

【臭气】 chòuqì bad smell; offensive smell; stink: ～冲天 stinking smell assaulting one's nostrils

【臭味】 chòuwèi stink; offensive odor; foul smell

【臭味相投】 chòuwèi-xiāngtóu People of the same ilk like each other.

【臭氧】 chòuyǎng 〈*Chem.*〉 ozone

【臭氧层】 chòuyǎngcéng ozonosphere

chu

出[齣[10]] (chū) 1.(从里到外) go or come out: ～国 go abroad 2.(来到) come: ～席 attend; be present 3.(超出) exceed; go beyond 4.(拿出) issue; put up; give; offer: ～钱 offer money / ～主意 offer advice; supply ideas; make suggestions 5.(生产;产生) produce; turn out: ～成果 produce result / ～煤 produce coal / ～人才 turn out talents 6.(发生) arise; happen; take place; occur: 这事故～在三年前。The accident happened three years ago. / 这事～在1952年。It took place in the year of 1952. 7.(发出;发泄) put forth; vent 8.(显得量多) rise well (with cooking) 9.(支出) pay out; expend 10.〈*Theatre*〉 两～戏 two dramatic pieces; two plays; two operas

【出版】 chūbǎn come off the press; publish; come out

【出版法】 chūbǎnfǎ law of publication; press law

【出版合同】 chūbǎn hé·tong contract for publication

【出版社】 chūbǎnshè publishing house; press

【出版物】 chūbǎnwù publication

【出版者】 chūbǎnzhě publisher

【出殡】 chūbìn carry a coffin to the cemetery; hold a funeral procession

【出兵】 chūbīng dispatch troops

【出操】 chūcāo (go out to) drill; go out to do exercises

【出差】 chūchāi be away on official business; be on a business trip

【出差补贴】 chūchāi bǔtiē travelling allowance

【出差费】 chūchāifèi allowances for a business trip

【出产】 chūchǎn 1.(生产,生长) produce; manufacture 2.(生产物) product

【出厂】 chūchǎng (of products) leave the factory

【出厂价】 chūchǎngjià producer's price; producer price; factory price

【出厂日期】 chūchǎng rìqī date of production; date of manufacture

【出场】 chūchǎng 1.(指演员) come on the stage; appear on the scene 2.(剧本用语) enter 3.(指运动员) enter the playing ground; enter the arena

【出超】 chūchāo 〈*Econ.*〉 favorable balance of trade

【出车】 chūchē 1.(开出车辆) dispatch a vehicle 2.(开车出去) be out driving a vehicle

【出丑】 chūchǒu 1.(出洋相) make a show of oneself; make a fool of oneself; become a laughing stock 2.(丢脸) bring shame on oneself: 当众～ be disgraced in public

【出处】 chūchù source (of a quotation or allusion): 注明～ give references

【出处同上】 chūchù tóngshàng ibid.; ib. (ibidem)

【出错】 chūcuò make mistakes

【出点子】 chūdiǎn·zi make suggestion; give references

【出动】 chūdòng 1.(队伍外出行动) set out; start off 2.(派出军事力量) call out; send out; dispatch: ～伞兵参战 call out paratroops to join the battle 3.(行动起来) go into action; turn out

【出尔反尔】 chūěr-fǎněr go back on one's word; contradict oneself; now yes, now no

【出发】 chūfā 1.(离开原地) set out; start off; leave: 准备～ get ready to start off 2.(指着眼点) start from; proceed from: 从客观实际～ proceed from objective realities / 从全局利益～ view the situation as a whole

【出发点】 chūfādiǎn starting point; point of departure; jumping-off point

【出发港】 chūfāgǎng port of department

【出发起跳】 chūfā qǐtiào 〈*Swimming*〉 starting dive

【出发台】 chūfātái 〈*Swimming*〉 starting block

【出访】 chūfǎng go abroad for visit: ～俄罗斯 go to visit Russia

【出风头】 chū fēng·tou seek or be in the limelight; cut a smart figure: 爱～ be fond of the limelight

【出格】 chūgé exceed what is proper

【出工】 chūgōng go to work; show up for work

【出轨】 chūguǐ 1.(车辆脱轨) be derailed; go off the rails: 列车～了。The train was derailed. 2.(出乎常规之外) overstep the bounds

【出国】 chūguó go abroad; leave one's native land

【出国考察】 chūguó kǎochá go abroad for observation

【出国热】 chūguórè crazy for going abroad

【出海】 chūhǎi go to sea; put out to sea; go fishing on the sea

【出汗】 chūhàn perspire; sweat

【出航】 chūháng 1.(指船舶) set out on a voyage; set sail 2.(指飞机) set out on a flight; take off

【出乎意料】 chūhū-yìliào exceeding one's expectations; contrary to one's expectations; to sb's surprise; unexpectedly

【出活】 chūhuó yield results in work; be efficient

【出击】 chūjī 1.(向敌攻击) launch an attack; hit out; make a sally: 四面～ hit out in all directions 2.(泛指斗争) fight against

【出家】 chūjiā become a monk or nun

【出家人】 chūjiārén monk; nun (f.)

【出价】 chūjià offer a price; bid

【出嫁】 chūjià get married; marry

【出界】 chūjiè 〈*Sports*〉 outside

【出借】 chūjiè lend; loan

【出境】 chūjìng leave the country: 办理～手续 go through exit formalities

【出局】 chūjú 〈*Baseball, Softball*〉 out

【出口】 chūkǒu 1.(说出) speak; utter 2.(出口处) exit; way out 3.〈*Econ.*〉 export; exportation (n.)

【出口产品基地】 chūkǒu chǎnpǐn jīdì base of export product

【出口成章】 chū kǒu chéng zhāng words flow from the mouth as from the pen of a master

【出口创汇基地】 chūkǒu chuànghuì jīdì base for export and foreign earning

【出口加工业】 chūkǒu jiākōngyè export processing industry

【出口检疫】 chūkǒu jiǎnyì export quarantine

【出口贸易】 chūkǒu màoyì export trade: 扩大～ expand export trade

【出口商品】 chūkǒu shāngpǐn export commodities: 改善～结构 change the export product mix

【出口商品交易会】 chūkǒu shāngpǐn jiāoyìhuì export commodities fair

【出口伤人】 chūkǒu-shāngrén speak bitingly

【出口税】 chūkǒushuì export duties

【出口信贷】 chūkǒu xìndài export credit

【出口许可证】 chūkǒu xǔkězhèng export licence

【出口转内销】 chūkǒu zhuǎn nèixiāo 1.(内销出口商品) export sold inside; export-oriented commodities 2.(指消息先传到国外再传回国内) give information to foreigners first, then it comes back to China

【出来】 chū·lái come out; emerge: 从房间里～ come out of the room

【出栏】 chūlán leave the feed lot

【出栏数】 chūlánshù the total amount of livestock for sale

【出类拔萃】 chūlèi-bácuì stand out from one's fellows; be out of the common run; be preeminent; prominent; outstanding

【出力】 chūlì 1.(用力) put forth one's strength; exert oneself; exert one's efforts; make great efforts 2.(输出功率) output power

【出列】 chūliè 〈*Mil.*〉 1.(离开队列) leave one's place in the ranks 2.(口令) Fall out!

【出笼】 chūlóng 1.(从蒸笼中取出) come out of the steamer 2.(出现) come out into the open; come forth; appear 3.(大量抛出) put forth in large quantities; dump; inflate (the paper currency)

【出路】 chūlù 1.(指道路) way out: 找～ find a way out 2.(销货去处) outlet 3.(途径) way; outlet

【出乱子】 chū luàn·zi go wrong; get into trouble

【出马】 chūmǎ go into action; take the field; take up a matter

【出卖】 chūmài 1.(卖) offer for sale; sell 2.(背叛) sell out; betray; barter away: ～朋友 betray one's friend / ～原则 barter away principles

【出毛病】 chū máo·bìng be out of order; go wrong; break down: 收音机～了。Something has gone wrong with the radio.

【出门】 chūmén 1.(外出) go out 2.(离家远行) leave home; be away from home; go on a journey

【出面】 chūmiàn act in one's own capacity or on behalf of an organization; appear personally; come forward: ～调解 act as a mediator / 自己不～ keep oneself in the background

【出苗】 chūmiáo 〈*Agric.*〉 come out; emerge; germinate

【出名】 chūmíng 1.(著名) well-known; famous 2.(出面) lend one's name (to an occasion or enterprise); use the name of

【出没】 chūmò appear and disappear; come and go; haunt

【出谋划策】 chūmóu-huàcè give counsel; offer advice; mastermind a scheme

【出纳】 chūnà 1.(现金、票据的出纳) receive and pay out money or bills 2.(出纳员) cashier; teller 3.(图书馆借还图书) receive and lend books, etc.

【出难题】 chū nántí set difficult questions; pose a difficult problem

【出偏差】 chū piānchā deviate; err on one side or the other

【出品】 chūpǐn 1.(制造) make; produce; manufacture 2.(产品) product

【出品人】 chūpǐnrén producer

【出其不意】 chūqí-bùyì take sb. by surprise; catch sb. unawares

【出奇】 chūqí unusually; extraordinarily: 冷得～ be unusually cold

【出奇制胜】 chūqí-zhìshèng defeat one's opponent by a surprise move; make a successful surprise raid

【出气】 chūqì 1.(发泄) give vent to one's anger; vent one's spleen: 在某人身上～ give vent to one's anger on sb. 2.(排气) air out

【出勤】 chūqín 1.(按时上班) turn out for work 2.(外出办理公务) be out on duty

【出勤率】 chūqínlǜ attendance

【出去】 chū·qù go out; get out

【出圈儿】 chūquānr overstep the bounds; go too far

【出让】 chūràng sell (one's own things)

【出人意料】 chūrén-yìliào contrary to one's expectations; come as a surprise

【出任】 chūrèn take up the post of

【出入】 chūrù 1.(出去和进来) come in and go out; go out and come in 2.(不相符) discrepancy; divergence; inconsistency

【出入证】 chūrùzhèng pass (identifying a staff member, etc.)

【出入自由,来去方便】 chūrù zìyóu, láiqù fāngbiàn come and go freely and easily

【出色】 chūsè outstanding; remarkable; splendid

【出山】 chūshān become an official; come back and take up the post of

【出身】 chūshēn 1.(家庭出身) class origin; family background 2.(个人经历) one's previous experience or occupation

【出身微寒】 chūshēn-wēihán be born of low extraction

【出神】 chūshén be spellbound; be in a trance; be lost in thought: 听得～ listen with rapt attention

【出生】 chūshēng be born

【出生地】 chūshēngdì birthplace

【出生率】 chūshēnglǜ birthrate

【出生日期】 chūshēng rìqī date of birth

【出生入死】 chūshēng-rùsǐ risk one's life; go through fire and water

【出生证】 chūshēngzhèng birth certificate

【出师】 chūshī 1.(学徒期满) finish one's apprenticeship 2.(出兵) dispatch troops to fight; send out an army

【出使】 chūshǐ serve as an envoy abroad; be sent on a diplomatic mission

【出示】 chūshì show; produce: ～证件 produce one's papers / ～证据 lodge a proof; presentation of evidence; tender evidence

【出世】 chūshì 1.(出生) come into the world; be born 2.(产生) renounce the world; stand aloof from worldly affairs

【出事】 chūshì meet with a mishap; have an accident

【出手】 chūshǒu 1.(卖出) get off one's hands; dispose of; sell 2.(指显出的本领) skill displayed in making opening moves

【出售】 chūshòu offer for sale; sell: ～一空 be sold out / 廉价～ sell sth. at a bargain price / 搭标～ combination sale / 按八五折～ sell at a discount of fifteen per cent / 按打～ sell by the dozen / 亏本～ sell at a loss / ～公房 sell publicly-owned houses

【出数儿】 chūshùr (of rice) rise well with cooking

【出台】 chūtái 1.(上场) appear on the stage; enter 2.(出面活动) appear personally 3.(公布并付诸实施) put into effect; be carried out

【出逃】 chūtáo run away

【出庭】 chūtíng appear in court; before the court; enter an appearance ～辩护 defend a case in court / ～作证 appear in court as a witness; serve as a witness at court

【出头】 chūtóu 1.(摆脱困苦) lift one's head; free oneself from 2.(出面;带头) appear in public; come forward 3.(整数后零头) a little over; odd: 一百～ one hundred odd

【出头露面】 chūtóu-lòumiàn appear in public; be in the limelight: 喜欢～ fond of being in the limelight

【出徒】 chūtú complete one's apprenticeship

【出土】 chūtǔ 1.(挖掘出来) be unearthed; be excavated 2.(幼苗出土) come up; come up out of the ground

【出土文物】 chūtǔ wénwù unearthed relics; unearthed artifacts

【出席】 chūxí attend; be present: ～会议 attend a meeting / ～宴会 be present at a banquet

【出息】 chū·xi promise; prospects; future: 有～的青年 a promising youth

【出险】 chūxiǎn 1.(脱险) be or get out of danger 2.(发生危险) be in danger; be threatened

【出现】 chūxiàn appear; arise; emerge; turn up: ～了新问题。A new problem has arisen.

【出线】 chūxiàn pass the line; go to higher competition: 中国队～世界杯足球赛尚有一线希望。There's still an outside possibility that China will get through into the World Cup.

【出血】 chūxiě 1.〈*Med.*〉 hemorrhage; bleeding: 大～ massive hemorrhage / 内～ internal hemorrhage / 脑～ brain hemorrhage / 伤口大量～。The wound bleeds profusely. 2.(不情愿的请客送礼) give dinners; send gifts 3.(给好处费) reward; pay middle-

man's fee **4.** 〈*Printing*〉 bleed
【出芽】 chūyá sprout; germinate; be budding
【出言不逊】 chūyán-bùxùn make impertinent remarks; use rude language; speak insolently
【出演】 chūyǎn play the part of
【出洋相】 chū yángxiàng make an exhibition of oneself
【出以公心】 chūyǐ-gōngxīn keep the public interest in mind; act without any selfish considerations; have the public interest at heart
【出游】 chūyóu go on a (sightseeing) tour
【出于】 chūyú start from; proceed from; stem from; out of: ～本意 of one's own accord / ～不可告人的目的 actuated by ulterior motives / ～同情 out of sympathy / ～无奈 as it cannot be helped; there being no alternative / ～无意 be not intentional; act unintentionally / ～无知 from ignorance / ～自愿 on a voluntary basis; of one's own accord
【出狱】 chūyù be discharged from prison; be released from prison
【出院】 chūyuàn leave hospital: 病愈～ be discharged from hospital after recovery
【出院处】 chūyuànchù discharge office
【出账】 chūzhàng **1.** (登上账) enter an item of expenditure in the accounts **2.** (开支;支出) items of expenditure
【出诊】 chūzhěn visit a patient at home; pay a home visit; make a house call
【出征】 chūzhēng go on an expedition; go out to battle
【出众】 chūzhòng be out of the ordinary; be outstanding: 人才～ a person of exceptional ability / 智力～ with exceptional intelligence
【出资】 chūzī finance; pay for
【出走】 chūzǒu leave; run away; flee
【出租】 chūzū hire; let; rent out: ～某物 let out sth.
【出租汽车】 chūzū qìchē taxi; taxicab; cab: 招呼～ hail a taxi / 打电话叫～ call a taxi / 乘～ go by taxi / 我从机场乘～去旅馆。I took a taxi from the airport to the hotel.
【出租汽车顶灯】 chūzū qìchē dǐngdēng taxi sign
【出租汽车司机】 chūzū qìchē sījī taxi-driver
【出租汽车停车站】 chūzū qìchē tíngchēzhàn taxi rank; taxistand
【出租汽车业】 chūzū qìchēyè taxi service

初 (chū) **1.** (开始) at the beginning of; in the early part of: ～冬 early winter / 十月～ early in October; in early October **2.** (第一个) first (in order): ～一 the first day (of a lunar month) **3.** (刚开始) just; for the first time **4.** (等级最低的) elementary; rudimentary **5.** (原来的) original

【初版】 chūbǎn first edition
【初步】 chūbù initial; preliminary; tentative: ～方案 a tentative program / ～分析 preliminary analysis / ～估计 preliminary estimates / ～加工 initial processing / ～交换意见 have a preliminary exchange of views / 根据～测算 according to an initial estimate / 获得～成果 reap first fruits; get initial results
【初产】 chūchǎn 〈*Med.*〉 primipararity
【初产妇】 chūchǎnfù 〈*Med.*〉 primipara
【初创】 chūchuàng newly established: ～阶段 initial stage / ～企业 a newly established enterprise
【初次】 chūcì the first time
【初等】 chūděng elementary; primary
【初等教育】 chūděng jiàoyù primary education
【初犯】 chūfàn **1.** (初犯者) first offender **2.** (第一次犯罪) first offense; first crime
【初稿】 chūgǎo first draft
【初级】 chūjí elementary; primary; junior: ～词典 elementary dictionary
【初级班】 chūjíbān junior class; elementary course
【初级产品】 chūjí chǎnpǐn primary products
【初级阶段】 chūjí jiēduàn primary stage: 社会主义～ primary stage of socialism
【初交】 chūjiāo new acquaintance; new friend
【初具规模】 chūjù guīmó begin to take shape
【初亏】 chūkuī 〈*Astron.*〉 first contact
【初恋】 chūliàn first love
【初露锋芒】 chūlù-fēngmáng display one's talent for the first time
【初露头角】 chūlù-tóujiǎo make first appearance
【初期】 chū qī initial stage; early days: 20世纪～ early in the twentieth century / 抗战～

in the early days of the Anti-Japanese War
【初审】 chūshěn 〈*Law*〉 trial of first instance; first trial
【初审判决】 chūshěn pànjué judgement of first instance
【初始】 chūshǐ initialize
【初始化】 chūshǐhuà 〈*Computer*〉 initialize; initialization (n.)
【初试】 chūshì **1.**(第一次试验) first try **2.**(分两次考试的第一次) preliminary examination
【初小】 chūxiǎo (初级小学) lower primary school
【初学】 chūxué begin to learn
【初愿】 chūyuàn one's original intention
【初诊】 chūzhěn first visit (to a doctor or hospital)
【初中】 chūzhōng junior middle school
【初衷】 chūzhōng original intention

樗 (chū) 〈*Bot.*〉 tree of heaven; ailanthus

刍[芻] (chú) **1.**(饲草) hay; fodder **2.**(割草) cut grass
【刍议】 chúyì my humble opinion

雏[雛] (chú) young (bird): ～鸡 chicken / ～鸭 duckling
【雏鸡】 chújī chick; chicken
【雏菊】 chújú daisy
【雏鸟】 chúniǎo nestling; fledgling
【雏形】 chúxíng **1.**(未定型之前的最初形式) embryonic form; embryo **2.**(缩小的模型) model; miniature

除 (chú) **1.**(除掉) get rid of; eliminate; remove: 为民～害 rid the people of a scourge **2.**(除去) except; except (for); but **3.**(除外) besides; in addition to **4.**〈*Math.*〉 divide; is divided by: 四～八得二。Eight divided by four is two. (符号为 ÷)
【除尘】 chúchén dust removal; dusting
【除尘器】 chúchénqì dust remover
【除臭剂】 chúchòujì deodorant
【除此之外】 chú cǐ zhī wài in addition
【除法】 chúfǎ 〈*Math.*〉 division
【除非】 chúfēi **1.**(只有…才) only if; only when **2.**(如果不) unless
【除号】 chúhào 〈*Math.*〉 division sign (符号为÷)
【除了】 chú·le **1.**(除去) except (for) **2.**(此外) besides; in addition to
【除名】 chúmíng remove sb's name from the rolls; take sb's name off the books; expunge sb's name from a list
【除湿】 chúshī dehumidify; dehumidification (f.)
【除数】 chúshù 〈*Math.*〉 divisor ‖ 被除数 dividend
【除霜】 chúshuāng defrost; defrosting (n.): 给冰箱～ defrost a freezer
【除外】 chúwài except; not counting; not including
【除夕】 chúxī New Year's Eve
【除锈剂】 chúxiùjì rust remover
【除莠剂】 chúxiùjì herbicide

锄[耡] (chú) **1.**(农具) hoe **2.**(松土除草) work with a hoe; hoe: ～地 hoe the fields **3.**(铲除) uproot; eliminate; wipe out
【锄草】 chúcǎo hoe up weeds; weed with a hoe
【锄头】 chú·tou hoe

厨[廚、厨] (chú) kitchen
【厨房】 chúfáng kitchen
【厨房用具】 chúfáng yòngjù kitchen utensils; cooking utensils
【厨师】 chúshī cook; chef

橱[櫥] (chú) cabinet; closet: 壁～ built-in cabinet
【橱窗】 chúchuāng **1.**(商店橱窗) show window; display window; showcase; shopwindow **2.**(宣传橱窗) glass-fronted billboard
【橱柜】 chúguì **1.**(食具柜) cupboard **2.**(矮立柜) a cupboard that also serves as a table; sideboard

处[處、處、処] (chǔ) **1.**(相处) get along (with sb.) **2.**(处于) be situated in; be in a certain condition **3.**(处理) manage; handle; deal with **4.**(处罚) punish; sentence
(另见"处"chù)
【处罚】 chǔfá punish; penalize
【处方】 chǔfāng **1.**(开药方) write out a prescription; prescribe **2.**(药方) prescription; recipe

【处分】 chǔfèn take disciplinary action against; punish

【处境】 chǔjìng unfavorable situation; plight：～尴尬 be in an awkward situation / ～困难 live in difficult circumstances / ～狼狈 in poor case / ～危险 be in a dangerous situation; be in peril

【处决】 chǔjué put to death; execute

【处理】 chǔlǐ 1.（安排；解决）handle; deal with; dispose of; manage; settle：～垃圾 dispose of rubbish / ～污水 dispose of sewage / ～遗留问题 settle the remaining problems 2.（变价、减价出售）sell at reduced prices：～积压商品 sell old stock at reduced prices 3.（用特定方法加工）treatment; treat by a special process 4.（惩办）put to death; execute

【处理品】 chǔlǐpǐn goods sold at reduced prices; shopworn or substandard goods

【处女】 chǔnǚ 1.（未出嫁的女子）virgin; maiden：老～ old maiden; spinster 2.（初次）maiden

【处女地】 chǔnǚdì virgin land; virgin soil; uncultivated land

【处女航】 chǔnǚháng maiden voyage; maiden flight

【处女作】 chǔnǚzuò maiden work; first effort

【处世】 chǔshì conduct oneself in society

【处世哲学】 chǔshì-zhéxué philosophy of life

【处世之道】 chǔshì-zhīdào ways of life; ways of the world

【处事精明】 chǔshì-jīngmíng be clever and smart in attending to business

【处暑】 chǔshǔ the Limit of Heat（8 月 22－24 日交节）

【处死】 chǔsǐ put to death; execute; put to execution

【处心积虑】 chǔxīn-jīlǜ deliberately plan（to achieve evil ends）; incessantly scheme; seek by all means

【处于】 chǔyú be（in a certain condition）：～窘境 in a tight box / ～困境 be in a hobble / ～逆境 be in adverse circumstances / ～平等地位 be on an equal footing / ～优势 have the advantage

【处之泰然】 chǔ zhī-tàirán take things calmly; remain unruffled; keep one's head

【处置】 chǔzhì 1.（处理）handle; deal with; manage; dispose of 2.（惩治）punish

杵（chǔ） 1.（木杵）pestle; stick 2.（捅）poke; nudge：她～了我一下。She give me a poke（或 nudge）.

础［礎］（chǔ） 〈*Archit*.〉 plinth

楮（chǔ） 1.〈*Bot*.〉 paper mulberry 2.（纸）paper

【楮墨】 chǔmò 1.（纸和墨）paper and ink 2.（诗和画）poetry and paintings

储［儲］（chǔ） store up; keep in reserve; have in reserve

【储备】 chǔbèi 1.（储存备用）store for future use; lay in; lay up：～粮食 store up grain; build up supplies of grain 2.（储藏品）reserve; store：黄金～ gold reserve / 外汇～ foreign exchange reserve

【储藏】 chǔcáng 1.（保藏）save and preserve; store; keep 2.（蕴藏）deposit

【储藏室】 chǔcángshì storeroom

【储存】 chǔcún lay in; lay up; store up; keep in reserve

【储户】 chǔhù depositor

【储量】 chǔliàng 〈*Mineral*.〉 reserves：可采～ recoverable reserves; workable reserves / 探明～ proved reserves

【储气】 chǔqì gas storage

【储气罐】 chǔqìguàn gas tank; gas receiver

【储蓄】 chǔxù save; deposit：定期～ fixed deposit / 活期～ current deposit

【储蓄存款】 chǔxù cúnkuǎn savings deposit

【储蓄存折】 chǔxù cúnzhé savings account book

【储蓄所】 chǔxùsuǒ savings department of a bank; savings bank

【储油罐】 chǔyóuguàn oil tank; oil storage tank：浮顶～ floating roof tank

楚（chǔ） 1.（清楚）clear; neat 2.（痛苦）pang; suffering

【楚楚】 chǔchǔ clear; tidy; neat

【楚楚动人】 chǔchǔ-dòngrén lovingly pathetic

处［處、處、処］（chù） 1.（地方）place 2.（点；部分）point; part 3.（机关；部门）department; office：登记～ registration office / 联络～ liaison office / 售票～ booking office / 问讯～

inquiry office
(另见"处"chǔ)
【处处】 chùchù everywhere; in all respects: ～掣肘 meet hindrance everywhere / ～碰壁 hit against a wall everywhere
【处所】 chùsuǒ place; location
【处长】 chùzhǎng the head of a department; section chief

黜 (chù) dismiss; remove from office
【黜免】 chùmiǎn dismiss; discharge; remove from office

畜 (chù) domestic animal; livestock: 耕～ farm animal / 家～ livestock / 母～ female animals / 驮～ beast of draught / 幼～ young animals
(另见"畜"xù)
【畜类】 chù·lei 1.(家畜) domestic animal 2.(骂人话) beast; dirty swine
【畜力】 chùlì animal power
【畜群】 chùqún drove
【畜生】 chù·sheng 1.(家畜) domestic animal 2.(骂人话) beast; dirty swine
【畜疫】 chùyì epidemic disease of domestic animals

搐 (chù) twitch
【搐动】 chùdòng twitch
【搐搦】 chùnuò twitch; jerk
【搐缩】 chùsuō shrink; contract

触［觸］(chù) 1.(接触) touch; contact 2.(碰) strike; hit 3.(触动) touch 4.(感触) move sb.; stir up sb's feelings
【触电】 chùdiàn 1.(接触电流) get an electric shock: 小心～! Danger! Electricity! 2.(涉足电影) set foot in the movie
【触电保护器】 chùdiàn bǎohùqì electric protective device
【触动】 chùdòng 1.(碰;撞) touch sth.; moving it slightly: ～某人的利益 affect sb's interests 2.(感触) move sb.; stir up sb's feeling: 对他～很大 shook him up a lot
【触发】 chùfā detonate by contact; touch off; spark; trigger
【触发地震】 chùfā dìzhèn initiating earthquake
【触犯】 chùfàn offend; violate; go against: ～法律 violate the law; break the law / ～某人 offend sb.
【触礁】 chùjiāo 1.(船只碰上暗礁) run (up) on rocks; strike a reef: 油轮～, 2,000 万加仑石油泄漏。Twenty million gallons of oil were dumped when the oil tanker ran into an underwater reef. 2.(遇到障碍) come to a deadlock; encounter obstacles: 谈判～搁浅。The talks came to a deadlock.
【触角】 chùjiǎo 〈*Zool.*〉 antenna; feeler; tentacle
【触景生情】 chùjǐng-shēngqíng the sight strikes a chord in one's heart; the scene brings back memories
【触觉】 chùjué 1.〈*Physiol.*〉 tactile sensation; sense of touch; tactual sensation 2.〈*Zool.*〉 touch reception
【触类旁通】 chùlèi-pángtōng grasp a typical example and you will grasp the whole category; comprehend by analogy
【触摸】 chùmō touch: 请勿～展品。Please don't touch the exhibits.
【触目】 chùmù 1.(看到) catch the eye; meet at eye 2.(显眼) attractive; conspicuous
【触目惊心】 chùmù-jīngxīn startling; shocking; horrifying; a ghastly sight
【触怒】 chùnù make angry; infuriate; enrage
【触杀】 chùshā 〈*Baseball, Softball*〉 touch-out; tag-out
【触杀剂】 chùshājì 〈*Agric.*〉 contact insecticide

憷 (chù) fear; feel timid; shrink from
【憷场】 chùchǎng feel nervous; get nervous at
【憷头】 chùtóu feel timid; shrink from difficulties

矗 (chù) stand tall and upright
【矗立】 chùlì stand tall and upright; tower over sth.

chuai

揣 (chuāi) hide or carry in one's clothes; tuck: ～进口袋 tuck sth. into one's

pocket / ～在兜儿里 hide in one's pocket
(另见"揣"chuǎi)

【揣手儿】 chuāishǒur tuck each hand in the opposite sleeve

搋 (chuāi) rub; knead: ～面 knead dough

【搋子】 chuāi·zi plunger; plumber's helper

揣 (chuǎi) 〈*written*〉 estimate; surmise; conjecture
(另见"揣"chuāi)

【揣测】 chuǎicè guess; conjecture; surmise; surmise; reckon: 纯属～ be mere conjecture

【揣度】 chuǎiduó estimate; appraise; conjecture

【揣摩】 chuǎimó try to fathom; try to figure out; elicit sth. by careful study

【揣摸】 chuǎi·mo try to fathom; try to figure out; elicit sth. by careful study

【揣想】 chuǎixiǎng guess; suppose; assume

踹 (chuài) **1.** (向外踢) kick **2.** (踩) tread; stamp; step in

chuan

川 (chuān) **1.** (河流) river **2.** (平;平地) plain

【川流不息】 chuānliú-bùxī never-ending; a continuous flow; flowing past in an endless stream

氚 (chuān) 〈*Chem.*〉 tritium (符号为 T)

穿 (chuān) **1.** (穿透) pierce through; penetrate: ～云破雾 pierce through fogs and clouds / 看～ see through **2.** (穿过) pass through; cross; go through: ～过马路 cross a street / ～过隧道 pass through a tunnel / 从人群中～过去 thread one's way through the crowd **3.** (穿着) wear; put on; be dressed in; have ... on: ～得很朴素 simply dressed

【穿插】 chuānchā **1.** (交替) alternate; do in turn; take turns **2.** (交叉) interweave; interlace; crisscross **3.** (次要情节) interlude; episode **4.** 〈*Mil.*〉 thrust deep: 打～ fight a deep-thrust

【穿刺】 chuāncì 〈*Med.*〉 puncture

【穿戴】 chuāndài **1.** (打扮) apparel; dress: ～整齐 be neatly dressed; dress neatly **2.** (衣帽、首饰等) dress and decorations

【穿孔】 chuānkǒng **1.** (打孔) bore a hole; punch a hole; perforate **2.** 〈*Med.*〉 perforate; perforation (n.)

【穿孔卡片】 chuānkǒng kǎpiàn 〈*Computer*〉 punched card

【穿孔纸带】 chuānkǒng zhǐdài 〈*Computer*〉 punched tape

【穿连裆裤】 chuān liándāngkù band together; gang up

【穿梭】 chuānsuō shuttle back and forth

【穿梭外交】 chuānsuō wàijiāo shuttle diplomacy

【穿堂风】 chuāntángfēng draught

【穿堂门】 chuāntángmén a passageway

【穿堂入室】 chuāntáng-rùshì get everywhere as one pleases

【穿小鞋】 chuān xiǎoxié wear tight shoes: 穿玻璃小鞋 wear glass shoes / 给某人～ give sb. tight shoes to wear; make things hard for sb. by abusing one's power; deliberately put sb. to trouble

【穿孝】 chuānxiào wear mourning; be in mourning

【穿心莲】 chuānxīnlián 〈*Bot.*〉 andrographis

【穿行】 chuānxíng pass through

【穿衣镜】 chuānyījìng full-length mirror

【穿越】 chuānyuè pass through; cut across

【穿凿附会】 chuānzáo-fùhuì give strained interpretations and draw farfetched analogies

【穿针引线】 chuānzhēn-yǐnxiàn act as a go-between; try to make a match

【穿着】 chuānzhuó dress; apparel: ～朴素整洁 be plainly but neatly dressed

传[傳] (chuán) **1.** (转给;传递) pass; pass on **2.** (交给另一代) hand down: 家～ be handed down in the family **3.** (传授) pass on; impart; teach **4.** (传播) spread: ～为佳话 become a favorite tale **5.** (传导) transmit; conduct: ～电 conduct electricity **6.** (表达) convey; express **7.** (传讯) summon: ～某人出庭 summon sb. to court **8.** (传染) infect; be contagious
(另见"传"zhuàn)

【传帮带】 chuánbāngdài pass on, help, guide; cultivation, support and help: 对新干部搞好～ do a good job in cultivating, supporting and helping juniors cadres

【传播】 chuánbō 1.(广泛散布) propagate; spread; disseminate 2.〈*Physics*〉propagation

【传布】 chuánbù disseminate; spread

【传抄】 chuánchāo make private copies

【传达】 chuándá 1.(转达) pass on (information, etc.); transmit; relay; communicate: ~命令 transmit an order / ~上级指示 communicate the instructions of the higher level 2.(传达室工作) reception and registration of callers at a public establishment 3.(传达室人员) janitor

【传达室】 chuándáshì reception office; janitor's room

【传单】 chuándān leaflet; handbill; propaganda sheet

【传导】 chuándǎo 〈*Physics*〉conduct; conduction (n.): 铜能够~电, 而木头不能。Copper can conduct electricity but wood does not.

【传导率】 chuándǎolǜ 〈*Physics*〉conductance; conductivity

【传道】 chuándào 〈*Religion*〉preach; deliver a sermon

【传道士】 chuándàoshì 〈*Religion*〉preacher

【传递】 chuándì transmit; deliver; transfer: ~信息 transmit messages

【传动】 chuándòng 〈*Mech.*〉transmission; drive: 液压~ hydraulic drive

【传动轴】 chuándòngzhóu 1.〈*Mech.*〉transmission shaft 2.〈*Mech.*〉driveshaft

【传粉】 chuánfěn 〈*Bot.*〉pollinate; pollination (n.)

【传呼】 chuánhū notify sb. of a phone call; pass on a message left by phone

【传呼电话】 chuánhū diànhuà neighborhood telephone service

【传话】 chuánhuà pass on a message: ~给某人 send word to sb.

【传唤】 chuánhuàn 〈*Law*〉summon to court

【传家宝】 chuánjiābǎo 1.(祖传宝物) family heirloom; hereditary treasure: 传家之宝 a treasure that has been handed down in the family 2.(作风, 传统) cherished tradition; cherished heritage

【传教】 chuánjiào 〈*Religion*〉do missionary work

【传教士】 chuánjiàoshì missionary

【传令】 chuánlìng transmit orders; dispatch orders: ~嘉奖 cite sb. in a dispatch

【传媒】 chuánméi medium; media: 这本杂志成了两国人民文化交流的~。This magazine become a cultural medium of intercourse between the two peoples.

【传奇】 chuánqí 1.(唐宋短篇小说) tales of marvels 2.(传奇故事) legend; romance

【传球】 chuánqiú 〈*Football*〉pass; pass the ball

【传染】 chuánrǎn infect; be contagious; infection (n.): 接触~ contagion; contagious infection / 空气~ infection through air

【传染病】 chuánrǎnbìng 1.(通过空气传染的) infectious disease 2.(通过接触传染的) contagious disease

【传染病院】 chuánrǎnbìng yuàn hospital for infectious diseases

【传神】 chuánshén vivid; lifelike

【传声筒】 chuánshēngtǒng 1.(喊话筒) megaphone; loud hailer 2.(鹦鹉学舌的) one who parrots another; sb's mouthpiece

【传世】 chánshì be handed down from ancient times: ~之作 work that will be handed on from age to age

【传授】 chuánshòu pass on; impart; teach: ~技术 pass on one's technical skill

【传输】 chuánshū 〈*Electr.*〉transmit; transmission (n.): 光纤电缆~电信号。Fiberoptic cables will transmit the electrical signals.

【传说】 chuánshuō 1.(据别人说) it is said; they say 2.(故事) legend; tradition: 民间~ popular legend

【传送】 chuánsòng convey; deliver

【传送带】 chuánsòngdài conveyer belt; band carrier; line belt

【传统】 chuántǒng 1.(指社会因素) tradition 2.(习惯的, 世代相传的) conventional; traditional: ~产业 conventional industries; traditional industries / ~观念 conventional thinking / ~习惯 traditional customs / ~友谊 traditional friendship

【传闻】 chuánwén 1.(听到流传) it is said; they say 2.(流传的事情) hearsay; rumor; talk

【传讯】 chuánxùn 〈*Law*〉cite; summon for

interrogation of trial; subpoena

【传言】 chuányán 1.(流传的话) hearsay; rumor 2.(传话) pass on a message

【传阅】 chuányuè pass round for perusal; circulate for perusal: ～有关文件 pass around the relevant documents

【传真】 chuánzhēn 1.(写真) portraiture 2.〈*Telecom.*〉 facsimile: 无线电～ radio facsimile

【传真电报】 chuánzhēn diànbào phototelegraph

【传真机】 chuánzhēnjī fax; facsimile machine

【传真照片】 chuánzhēn zhàopiàn radiophoto

【传种】 chuánzhǒng propagate; reproduce; reproduction (n.)

【传宗接代】 chuánzōng-jiēdài have a son to carry on his family name

船[**舩**] (chuán) boat; ship: 帆～ a sailing boat / 渔～ a fishing boat/ 划～ row a boat / 乘～去 go to boat; go by ship; embark (on a ship) for / 在～上 on board a ship

【船舶】 chuánbó shipping; boats and ships

【船舶国籍证书】 chuánbó guójí zhèngshū certificate of ship's nationality

【船舶证书】 chuánbó zhèngshū ship's papers

【船舱】 chuáncāng 1.(货舱) ship's hold 2.(客舱) cabin

【船厂】 chuánchǎng shipyard; dockyard; boatyard

【船队】 chuánduì fleet; flotilla

【船夫】 chuánfū boatman

【船工】 chuángōng boatman; junkman

【船级】 chuánjí ship's classification; ship's class

【船民】 chuánmín boat people

【船票】 chuánpiào steamer ticket

【船期】 chuánqī sailing date

【船期表】 chuánqībiǎo sailing schedule

【船蛆】 chuánqū 〈*Zool.*〉 shipworm; pileworm

【船艄】 chuánshāo stern; poop

【船身】 chuánshēn hull (of a ship)

【船首】 chuánshǒu stem; bow; prow

【船台】 chuántái berth; shipway; slipway; slip

【船体】 chuántǐ the body of a ship; hull

【船桅】 chuánwéi mast

【船尾】 chuánwěi stern

【船尾门】 chuánwěimén stern port

【船坞】 chuánwù dock; shipyard: 浮～ floating dock / 干～ dry dock; graving dock

【船舷】 chuánxián side (of a ship or boat)

【船用柴油机】 chuányòng cháiyóujī marine diesel

【船用钢板】 chuányòng gāngbǎn ship plate

【船员】 chuányuán (ship's) crew; seaman; sailor

【船载艇】 chuánzǎitǐng ship's boat

【船闸】 chuánzhá (ship) lock

【船长】 chuánzhǎng captain; skipper

【船只】 chuánzhī shipping; vessels

【船钟】 chuánzhōng ship's bell

【船主】 chuánzhǔ shipowner; shipmaster

椽 (chuán) rafter

【椽子】 chuán·zi rafter

舛 (chuǎn) 1.(差错) error; mistake 2.(违背) run counter

【舛错】 chuǎncuò 1.(错误) error; mistake 2.(意外) accident 3.(参差不齐) uneven; not uniform

【舛误】 chuǎnwù error; mistake

喘 (chuǎn) 1.(呼吸困难) breathe heavily; gasp for breath; pant 2.〈*Med.*〉 asthma

【喘气】 chuǎnqì 1.(呼吸) breathe (deeply); pant; gasp 2.(指休息) take a breather

【喘息】 chuǎnxī 1.(喘气) pant; gasp or breath 2.(指短暂的休息) breather; breathing spell; respite

串 (chuàn) 1.(连贯) string together: 把小珠子～起来 string the beads together 2.〈*classifier*〉 string; bunch; cluster: 一～葡萄 a cluster of grapes 3.(错误地连接) get things mixed up: ～行 skip a line; miss a line 4.(勾结) conspire; gang up 5.(走动) go here and there; go from place to place; run about; rove 6.(担任角色) play a part (in a play); act

【串岗】 chuàngǎng arbitrarily leave one's post and visit other's at work hours

【串换】 chuànhuàn exchange; change; swap

【串口】 chuànkǒu 〈*Computer*〉 serial ports: 设定～ set up serial ports

【串口打印机】 chuànkǒu dǎyìnjī serial printer

【串联】 chuànlián 1.（一个一个地联系）establish ties; contact 2.〈*Electr.*〉series connection

【串门】 chuànmén call on sb's home

【串骗】 chuànpiàn collaborate to swindle

【串通】 chuàntōng collaborate; gang up; collude with; be in collusion with

【串通一气】 chuàntōng-yīqì collaborate; gang up; take part in the conspiracy

【串戏】 chuànxì take part in play; be a guest performer

【串线】 chuànxiàn get the lines crossed

【串音】 chuànyīn crosstalk; overhear; overhearing (n.)

chuang

创［創］（chuāng） wound：重～敌人 cause the enemy heavy losses （另见"创"chuàng）

【创口】 chuāngkǒu wound; cut

【创伤】 chuāngshāng wound; trauma：精神上的～ a mental scar / 战争的～ wounds of war

疮［瘡］（chuāng） 1.（溃烂）sore; skin ulcer：生～ grow a boil 2.（外伤）wound

【疮疤】 chuāngbā 1.（疤）scar 2.（痛处）sore：揭人～ pull the scab right off sb's sore; touch sb's sore spot; tread on sb's corns

【疮口】 chuāngkǒu the open part of a sore

窗［窓、窻、牕］（chuāng） window：关～ close the window/开～open the window

【窗玻璃】 chuāngbō·li windowpane

【窗户】 chuāng·hu window; casement：关上～ shut the window/ 打开～ open the window

【窗口】 chuāngkǒu 1.（窗户前）window：坐在～ sit at the window; sit by the window 2.（售票、挂号等窗口）wicket; window 3.（窗户）window：在墙上开一个～ make a window in the wall 4.（比喻）window; model：经济改革的～ a showpiece for our economic reform 5.（渠道;途径）window; medium; intermediary：了解世界的～ a window on the world

【窗口行业】 chuāngkǒu hángyè "window" industry; service industry

【窗口环境】 chuāngkǒu huánjìng 〈*Computer*〉 Windows

【窗框】 chuāngkuàng window frame

【窗帘】 chuānglián （window）curtain：拉开～ draw the curtain apart; pull the curtain aside / 拉上～ draw the curtain together; pull the curtain across

【窗帘钩】 chuāngliángōu curtain hook

【窗帘棍】 chuāngliángùn pelmet

【窗帘匣】 chuāngliánxiá curtain box

【窗明几净】 chuāngmíng-jījìng with bright windows and clean tables; bright and clean

【窗台】 chuāngtái windowsill

【窗子】 chuāng·zi window

床［牀］（chuáng） 1.（卧具）bed：单人～ single bed / 双人～ double bed / 沙发～ sofa bed / 行军～ cot; camp bed / 双层～ bunk bed / 折叠～ folding bed / 对～ twin beds / 铺～ make the bed / 上～睡觉 go to bed / 卧病在～ be laid up in bed / 与某人上～ go to bed with sb. 2.（像床的器具、地面）sth. shaped like a bed：河～ riverbed / 海～ sea bed / 铣～ milling machine

【床单】 chuángdān sheet

【床垫】 chuángdiàn mattress：弹簧～ spring mattress

【床铺】 chuángpù bed

【床上用品】 chuángshàng yòngpǐn bedclothes

【床头】 chuángtóu the head of a bed; bedside

【床头灯】 chuángtóudēng bedside lamp

【床头柜】 chuángtóuguì bedside cupboard; bedside table

【床头小地毯】 chuángtóu xiǎo dìtǎn bedside rug

【床位】 chuángwèi berth; bunk; bed

【床罩】 chuángzhào bedspread; counterpane

【床柱】 chuángzhù bedpost

闯（chuǎng） 1.（猛冲）rush; dash; charge：～进来 rush in; break in; force one's way in 2.（闯练;突破）break through; temper oneself (by battling through difficulties and dangers)：敢～ dare to break through / ～出一条新路来 break a new path

【闯祸】 chuǎnghuò get into trouble; bring disaster

【闯将】 chuǎngjiàng daring general; pathbreaker

【闯劲】 chuǎngjìn dash; the spirit of a pathbreaker; pioneering spirit; daring spirit

【闯入】 chuǎngrù burst into; intrude: ～会场 intrude oneself into a meeting

创［創、刱、剏］(chuàng) achieve (sth. for the first time); start (doing sth.); initiate; establish; create: ～奇迹 create miracles; work miracles

(另见“创”chuāng)

【创办】 chuàngbàn establish; set up; found: ～一所学校 establish a school; set up a school / ～一所医院 found a hospital

【创汇】 chuànghuì earn foreign exchange income

【创汇农业】 chuànghuì nóngyè agriculture oriented for export and foreign exchange earning

【创见】 chuàngjiàn fresh idea; novel idea; original idea

【创建】 chuàngjiàn found; establish; set up

【创举】 chuàngjǔ pioneering work; pioneering undertaking

【创刊】 chuàngkān start publication

【创刊号】 chuàngkānhào first number; initial issue; first issue

【创立】 chuànglì found; originate

【创利】 chuànglì make profits

【创始】 chuàngshǐ originate; initiate

【创始人】 chuàngshǐrén founder; originator

【创收】 chuàngshōu 1.(创造收入) make extra earning; make economic income earning 2.(创造的收入) extra earning

【创新】 chuàngxīn 1.(创造新的) bring forth new ideas; make innovations 2.(新意) new ideas; innovation

【创演】 chuàngyǎn write and perform: ～不少优秀节目 write and perform quite a few good programs

【创业】 chuàngyè start an undertaking; do pioneering work; found an undertaking: ～容易守业难。It's easy to open a shop but hard to keep it open.

【创业精神】 chuàngyè jīngshén the enterprising spirit

【创优】 chuàngyōu create excellence

【创造】 chuàngzào create; produce; bring about: ～社会财富 create the wealth of society / ～优异成绩 produce excellent results

【创造性】 chuàngzàoxìng creativity; creativeness

【创作】 chuàngzuò 1.(创造作品) create; produce; write: ～美术作品 produce works of art 2.(作品) creative work; creation

怆［愴］(chuàng) 〈*written*〉 sorrowful

【怆然】 chuàngrán in a sorrowful way

【怆然泪下】 chuàng rán lèi xià burst into sorrowful tears

chui

吹 (chuī) 1.(吹气) blow; puff: ～哨子 blow a whistle 2.(吹奏) play (wind instruments): ～笛子 play the flute / 他在一支爵士乐队里～萨克斯。He plays the saxophone in a jazz band. 3.(夸口) boast; brag 4.(破裂;不成功) break off; break up; fall through: 我和她～了。I've fallen through with her.

【吹吹拍拍】 chuīchuī-pāipāi boasting and toadying; flattery and touting

【吹风】 chuīfēng 1.(被风吹) be in a draught; catch a chill 2.(理发吹风) dry one's hair; dry hair with a blower 3.(透露消息) let sb. in on sth. in advance; give a cue

【吹风会】 chuīfēnghuì information leaking meeting

【吹风机】 chuīfēngjī blower (for drying hair); hair drier

【吹拂】 chuīfú sway; stir

【吹鼓手】 chuīgǔshǒu 1.(吹奏乐器者) trumpeter trumpet player 2.(吹捧者) eulogist; lauder; laudator

【吹号】 chuīhào blow a bugler; blare the call

【吹喇叭】 chuī lǎba 1.(指吹奏乐器) blow trumpet 2.(指吹捧他人) lavish praise on others

【吹毛求疵】 chuīmáo-qiúcī find fault; pick holes; nitpick; cavil at

【吹牛】 chuīniú boast; brag; talk big ‖ 吹牛的人 boaster; braggart

【吹捧】 chuīpěng flatter; laud to the skies; lavish praise on; extol: 互相～ flatter each other

【吹嘘】 chuīxū lavish praise on oneself or others; boast of; boast about

【吹奏】 chuīzòu play (wind instruments)

【吹奏乐】 chuīzòuyuè band music; wind music

炊 (chuī) cook a meal

【炊具】 chuījù cooking utensils

【炊事】 chuīshì cooking; kitchen work

【炊事用具】 chuīshì yòngjù cooking utensils; appliances for food preparation

【炊事员】 chuīshìyuán a cook or the kitchen staff

【炊烟】 chuīyān smoke from kitchen chimneys: ～袅袅 smoke spiraling from kitchens

垂 (chuí) 1.(下垂) hang down; droop; let fall: ～发 have one's hair hang down 2.(流传) go down; hand down; bequeath to posterity: 名～青史 one's name will go down in history; leave a name in history 3.(将近) be on the verge of; nearing; approaching: ～老 approaching old age; getting on in years

【垂钓】 chuídiào angle; fish with a hook and line

【垂泪】 chuílèi shed tears; weep

【垂柳】 chuíliǔ weeping willow

【垂青】 chuíqīng 〈*written*〉 show appreciation for sb.; look upon sb. with favor

【垂死】 chuísǐ moribund; dying: ～挣扎 be in one's death throes; put up a last-ditch struggle

【垂体】 chuítǐ 〈*Anat.*〉 hypophysis; pituitary body

【垂头丧气】 chuítóu-sàngqì crestfallen; dejected; downcast; in low spirits

【垂危】 chuíwēi critically ill; at one's last gasp

【垂涎】 chuíxián drool; slaver; covet: ～三尺 drool with envy

【垂涎欲滴】 chuíxiǎn-yùdī make one's mouth watery

【垂线】 chuíxiàn 〈*Math.*〉 vertical line; perpendicular line

【垂直】 chuízhí perpendicular; vertical

【垂直起降】 chuízhí qǐjiàng 〈*Aeron.*〉 vertical takeoff and landing

【垂直起降飞机】 chuízhí qǐjiàng fēijī VTOL aircraft; vertical takeoff and landing aircraft

【垂直尾翼】 chuízhí wěiyì 〈*Aircraft*〉 vertical tail

【垂直于】 chuízhíyú perpendicular to (符号为⊥)

陲 (chuí) frontiers; borders: 边～ frontier; border area

捶[搥] (chuí) beat (with a stick or fist); thump; pound

【捶背】 chuíbèi pound sb's back (as in message)

【捶打】 chuídǎ beat

【捶胸顿足】 chuíxiōng-dùnzú thump one's chest and stamp one's feet; beat one's breast and stamp one's feet (in deep sorrow, etc.)

锤[鎚] (chuí) 1.(锤子) hammer 2.(锤打) hammer into shape; knock with a hammer 3.(秤锤等) weight

【锤炼】 chuíliàn 1.(磨炼) temper; steel and temper 2.(刻苦钻研) refine; polish; perfect

【锤子】 chuí·zi hammer

槌 (chuí) mallet

【槌子】 chuí·zi mallet

chun

春 (chūn) 1.(春季) spring: 大地回～。Spring has come. 2.(男女情欲) love; lust 3.(生机) life; vitality

【春分】 chūnfēn the Spring Equinox (3 月 20－22 日交节)

【春分点】 chūnfēndiǎn 〈*Astron.*〉 vernal equinoctial point

【春风】 chūnfēng 1.(春天的风) spring breeze 2.(比喻恩惠) a kindly and pleasant countenance

【春风得意】 chūnfēng-déyì ride on the crest to success

【春耕】 chūngēng spring ploughing

【春光】 chūnguāng sights and sounds of spring; spring scenery: ～明媚 a sunlit and

enchanting scene of spring
【春华秋实】 chūnhuá-qiūshí glorious flowers in spring and solid fruits in autumn
【春回大地】 chūnhuí-dàdì spring returns to the good earth
【春季】 chūnjì spring; springtime
【春季大扫除】 chūnjì dàsǎochú spring cleaning
【春假】 chūnjià spring vacation; spring holidays
【春节】 Chūn Jié the Spring Festival
【春卷】 chūnjuǎn spring roll; egg roll (AmE.); pancake roll (BrE.)
【春雷】 chūnléi spring thunder
【春联】 chūnlián Spring Festival couplets
【春秋】 chūnqiū **1**.(春秋两季) spring and autumn **2**.(指一年) year **3**.(指年岁) age **4**.(编年体史书) annals; history
【春色】 chūnsè spring scenery; the beauty of spring
【春笋】 chūnsǔn bamboo shoots in spring
【春天】 chūntiān spring; springtime
【春小麦】 chūnxiǎomài spring wheat
【春心】 chūnxīn desire for love; longing for love
【春汛】 chūnxùn **1**.〈*Hydrau*.〉 spring flood **2**.〈*Fishing*〉 spring season
【春药】 chūnyào aphrodisiac
【春意】 chūnyì spring in the air; the beginning of spring; the awakening of spring: ～盎然。Spring is very much in the air.
【春游】 chūnyóu spring outing
【春雨】 chūnyǔ spring rains
【春运】 chūnyùn spring transportation
【春装】 chūnzhuāng spring outing

椿(chūn) **1**.(香椿) Chinese toona; toon **2**.(臭椿) tree of heaven; alianthus
【椿象】 chūnxiàng 〈*Zool*.〉 stinkbug; shieldbug

纯(chún) **1**.(纯净) pure; unmixed: ～金 pure gold **2**.(纯粹; 单纯) simple; pure and simple **3**.(纯熟) skillful; practiced; well versed
【纯粹】 chúncuì **1**.(成分纯) pure; unadulterated **2**.(单纯地) solely; purely; only
【纯度】 chúndù purity; pureness
【纯碱】 chúnjiǎn 〈*Chem*.〉 sodium carbonate
【纯洁】 chúnjié **1**.(清白) pure; clean and honest; chaste **2**.(使纯洁) purify
【纯净】 chúnjìng pure; clean
【纯利】 chúnlì net income; net profit
【纯朴】 chúnpǔ honest; simple; unsophisticated
【纯收入】 chúnshōurù net income
【纯熟】 chúnshú skillful; practiced; well versed: 技术～ highly skilled
【纯真】 chúnzhēn pure; sincere
【纯正】 chúnzhèng pure; unadulterated
【纯种】 chúnzhǒng purebred: ～家禽 purebred poultry
【纯种马】 chúnzhǒngmǎ blood horse

唇[脣](chún) lip: 上～ upper lip / 下～ lower lip
【唇齿相依】 chúnchǐ-xiāngyī be as close as lips and teeth; be closely related and mutually dependent; close interdependence
【唇膏】 chúngāo lipstick
【唇裂】 chúnliè 〈*Med*.〉 cleft-lip; harelip
【唇舌】 chúnshé words; argument; talking round: 费一番～ take a lot of explaining or arguing
【唇亡齿寒】 chúnwáng-chǐhán if the lips are gone, the teeth will be cold; if one falls, the other is in danger

淳(chún) 〈*written*〉 pure; honest
【淳厚】 chúnhòu pure and honest; simple and kind
【淳朴】 chúnpǔ honest; simple; unsophisticated

醇(chún) **1**.(纯厚) pure; unmixed **2**.〈*Chem*.〉 alcohol **3**.(优质烧酒) mellow wine; good wine
【醇和】 chúnhé pure and mild
【醇美】 chúnměi pure and sweet
【醇香】 chúnxiāng aromatic

蠢[惷](chǔn) **1**.(愚蠢) stupid; foolish; dull **2**.(蠢笨) clumsy
【蠢笨】 chǔnbèn clumsy; awkward; stupid
【蠢材】 chǔncái idiot; fool; dumbbell; blockhead
【蠢蠢欲动】 chǔnchǔn-yùdòng ready to start wriggling; ready to make trouble; be restless and about to make trouble

【蠢货】 chǔnhuò blockhead; dunce; idiot
【蠢驴】 chǔnlǘ idiot; donkey; ass
【蠢人】 chǔnrén fool; block head
【蠢事】 chǔnshì folly: 干～ commit a folly; play the fool
【蠢猪】 chǔnzhū idiot; stupid swine; ass

chuo

戳 (chuō) 1.(戳破) jab; poke; stab 2.(戳坏,戳伤) sprain; blunt 3.(图章) stamp; seal; chop
【戳穿】 chuōchuān 1.(刺穿) pierce through; puncture 2.(揭穿) lay bare; expose; explode
【戳子】 chuō·zi stamp; seal
啜 (chuò) 1.(喝) sip; suck 2.(抽噎) sob
【啜泣】 chuòqì sob
辍 (chuò) 〈*written*〉 stop; cease
【辍工】 chuògōng stop work
【辍学】 chuòxué discontinue one's studies; leave off one's study
绰 (chuò) 〈*written*〉 ample; spacious
【绰绰有余】 chuòchuò-yǒuyú more than sufficient; enough and to spare; more than enough
【绰号】 chuòhào nickname

ci

疵 (cī) flaw; defect; blemish
【疵点】 cīdiǎn flaw; fault; defect; blemish
词 (cí) 1.〈*Linguis*.〉 word; term 2.(讲话) speech; statement: 欢迎～ speech of welcome / 各执一～ each holds to his own statement
【词不达意】 cíbùdáyì the words fail to convey the idea; the language fails to express the meaning
【词典】 cídiǎn dictionary: 简明～ concise dictionary / 双语～ bilingual dictionary / 袖珍～ pocket dictionary / 查～ consult the dictionary; look up a word in the dictionary / 编～ compile a dictionary / 修订～ revise a dictionary
【词典学】 cídiǎnxué lexicography
【词法】 cífǎ morphology
【词根】 cígēn root of a word
【词汇】 cíhuì 〈*Linguis*.〉 vocabulary; words and phrases: 常用～ common words / 科技～ scientific and technical terms
【词汇表】 cíhuìbiǎo word list; vocabulary; glossary
【词句】 cíjù words and phrases; expressions
【词类】 cílèi part of speech
【词首】 císhǒu prefix
【词素】 císù morpheme
【词条】 cítiáo entry (in a dictionary): 这部词典收有 8 万个～。This dictionary contains 80,000 entries.
【词头词】 cítóucí headword: 7 万个词语按字母顺序排列在 5 万个～之下。70,000 words and expressions arranged alphabetically under 50,000 headwords.
【词尾】 cíwěi suffix
【词义】 cíyì definition: 8 万多个词条和 12 万个～ over 80,000 entries and 120,000 definitions
【词语】 cíyǔ words and expressions; terms
【词藻】 cízǎo flowery language; ornate diction: 堆砌～ string together ornate phrases
【词缀】 cízhuì affix
【词组】 cízǔ word group; phrase
祠 (cí) ancestral temple; memorial temple
【祠堂】 cítáng ancestral temple; ancestral hall; memorial temple
雌 (cí) female
【雌黄】 cíhuáng 1.〈*Mineral*.〉 orpiment 2.(胡说八道) 信口～ make irresponsible remarks; wag one's tongue too freely
【雌激素】 cíjīsù estrogen; estrogenic hormone
【雌性】 cíxìng female
【雌雄】 cíxióng 1.(雌性和雄性) male and female 2.(胜和负) victory and defeat: 决一～ come to a showdown
瓷 [甆] (cí) porcelain; china: 青花～ blue and white porcelain
【瓷器】 cíqì porcelain; chinaware: 薄～

eggshell china / 细～ fine china
【瓷实】 cí·shi solid; firm; substantial
【瓷碗】 cíwǎn china bowl
【瓷砖】 cízhuān tiles; ceramic tile; glazed tile

慈 (cí) 1.(慈善) kind; loving 2.(母亲) mother
【慈爱】 cí'ài love; affection; kindness
【慈悲】 cíbēi mercy; benevolence; pity: ～好善 merciful and benevolent / 发～ have pity; be merciful
【慈姑】 cígū 〈*Bot.*〉 arrowhead
【慈眉善目】 cí méi shàn mù a benignant look
【慈母】 címǔ loving mother; mother
【慈善】 císhàn charitable; benevolent; philanthropic
【慈善为怀】 císhàn wéi huái cherish charity
【慈善机关】 císhàn jīguān charitable institution; charitable organization
【慈善家】 císhànjiā philanthropist
【慈善事业】 císhàn shìyè charities; good works; philanthropy
【慈祥】 cíxiáng kindly: ～的微笑 kindly smile; loving smile

磁 (cí) 1.〈*Physics*〉 magnetism 2.(瓷) porcelain; china
【磁场】 cíchǎng 〈*Physics*〉 magnetic field
【磁场强度】 cíchǎng qiángdù magnetic field intensity
【磁带】 cídài (magnetic) tape: 盒式～ cassette / 把～翻到背面/正面 wind the cassette back/forward
【磁带录像机】 cídài lùxiàngjī video tape recorder
【磁带录音机】 cídài lùyīnjī tape recorder
【磁导】 cídǎo 〈*Physics*〉 permeance
【磁道】 cídào 〈*Computer*〉 track
【磁鼓】 cígǔ drum; magnetic drum
【磁化】 cíhuà 〈*Physics*〉 magnetize; magnetization (n.)
【磁极】 cíjí 〈*Physics*〉 magnetic pole
【磁记录】 cíjìlù magnetic recording
【磁卡电话】 cíkǎ diànhuà cardphone
【磁力】 cílì 〈*Physics*〉 magnetic force
【磁力线】 cílìxiàn magnetic line of force
【磁力选矿】 cílì xuǎnkuàng magnetic dressing
【磁盘】 cípán disk; magnetic disc
【磁盘操作系统】 cípán cāozuò xìtǒng 〈*Computer*〉 DOS; disk operation system
【磁盘驱动器】 cípán qūdòngqì disk drive
【磁偏角】 cípiānjiǎo 〈*Geol.*〉 magnetic declination
【磁石】 císhí 1.〈*Mineral.*〉 magnetite 2.〈*Electr.*〉 magnet
【磁体】 cítǐ 〈*Physics*〉 magnetic body; magnet
【磁条】 cítiáo magnetic strip
【磁铁】 cítiě 〈*Physics*〉 magnet; ferromagnet
【磁铁矿】 cítiěkuàng magnetite
【磁通量】 cítōngliàng 〈*Physics*〉 magnetic flux; magnetic current
【磁头】 cítóu magnetic head
【磁性】 cíxìng 〈*Physics*〉 magnetism; magnetic
【磁悬浮】 cíxuánfú maglev; magnetic levitation
【磁悬浮列车】 cíxuánfú lièchē maglev train; magnetic levitation train
【磁针】 cízhēn magnetic needle
【磁转胶】 cízhuǎnjiāo 〈*Telev.*〉 videotape-to-film transfer process

辞[辭、辤] (cí) 1.(语言) diction; phraseology 2.(告别) take leave: 不～而别 leave without saying good-bye 3.(辞退) dismiss; discharge 4.(辞职) resign 5.(躲避;推托) decline; shirk; evade: 不～艰辛 no shirk any hardships
【辞呈】 cíchéng (written) resignation: 提出～ submit one's resignation; hand in one's resignation
【辞典】 cídiǎn dictionary
【辞工】 cígōng leave work
【辞工跳槽】 cígōng tiàocáo leave work and go to another
【辞令】 cílìng language appropriate to the occasion: 外交～ diplomatic language
【辞书】 císhū dictionary; lexicographical work
【辞退】 cítuì dismiss; discharge
【辞行】 cíxíng say good-bye (to one's friends, etc.) before setting out on a journey
【辞职】 cízhí resign; hand in one's resignation: 向…提出～ tender one's resignation to sb.

此 (cǐ) 1.(这个) this 2.(此时;此地) now; here: 从～以后 from now on; henceforward

【此地】 cǐdì this place; here

【此地人】 cǐdìrén local people

【此后】 cǐhòu after this hereafter; henceforth

【此间】 cǐjiān around here; here

【此刻】 cǐkè this moment; now; at present

【此路不通】 cǐlù bùtōng 1.（死胡同）dead end; blind alley 2.（路牌）No thoroughfare.

【此起彼伏】 cǐqǐ-bǐfú as one falls, another rises; rise one after another

【此时】 cǐshí this moment; right now

【此外】 cǐwài besides; in addition; moreover

【此一时，彼一时】 cǐ yīshí, bǐ yīshí this is one situation and that was another

次（cì） 1.（次序）order; sequence: 下～ next time 2.（第二）second; next: ～日 next day 3.（质量较差）second-rate

【次大陆】 cìdàlù subcontinent

【次第】 cìdì 1.（次序）order; sequence 2.（一个挨一个地）one after another

【次货】 cìhuò poor quality goods; defective goods

【次级】 cìjí secondary

【次级线圈】 cìjí xiànquān 〈*Electr.*〉 secondary coil

【次品】 cìpǐn substandard products; defective goods

【次生林】 cìshēnglín secondary forest

【次声波】 cìshēngbō infrasound; infrasonic sound; subsonic sound

【次数】 cìshù number of times; frequency

【次序】 cìxù order; sequence: 按字母～排列 be arranged in alphabetical order

【次要】 cìyào less important; secondary; subordinate; minor

【次于】 cìyú inferior to; worse than; poorer than

【次之】 cìzhī take second place

【次中音号】 cìzhōngyīnhào 〈*Music*〉 tenor horn

伺（cì）
（另见"伺"sì）

【伺候】 cì·hou wait upon; serve

刺（cì） 1.（刺儿）thorn; splinter 2.（扎）sting; stab; prick 3.（行刺）assassinate 4.（刺激）irritate; stimulate 5.（刺探）detect; spy 6.（讽刺）criticize

【刺鼻】 cìbí pungent; irritate the nose

【刺刀】 cìdāo bayonet

【刺耳】 cì'ěr grating on the ear; jarring; ear-piercing; harsh

【刺钢丝】 cìgāngsī （铁丝网）barbed wire

【刺骨】 cìgǔ piercing to the bones; piercing; biting: 寒风～。The cold wind chills one to the bone.

【刺激】 cìjī 1.（起刺激作用）stimulate; excite 2.（使激动）provoke; irritate; upset

【刺客】 cìkè assassin

【刺杀】 cìshā 1.（暗杀）assassinate; murder 2.〈*Mil.*〉 bayonet charge

【刺伤】 cìshāng stab and wound: 被～ be wounded by stabbing

【刺探】 cìtàn spy; pry; collect secret intelligence

【刺猬】 cì·wei hedgehog

【刺绣】 cìxiù 1.（指工艺）embroider 2.（指产品）embroidery

【刺眼】 cìyǎn 1.（晃眼）dazzling 2.（不顺眼）offending to the eye; unpleasantly colorful

赐（cì） grant; favor; gift

【赐复】 cìfù 〈*politeness*〉 kindly favor us with a reply

【赐教】 cìjiào 〈*politeness*〉 condescend to teach; grant instruction

【赐予】 cìyǔ 〈*politeness*〉 grant; bestow

cong

枞［樅］（cōng） 〈*Bot.*〉 fir

【枞树】 cōngshù （冷杉）fir

匆［怱、悤］（cōng） hastily; hurriedly

【匆匆】 cōngcōng hurriedly; in a rush; in haste: 来去～ come and go in haste

【匆促】 cōngcù hastily; in a hurry

【匆忙】 cōngmáng hastily; in a hurry; in haste

葱（cōng） 1.〈*Bot.*〉 onion; scallion 2.（青色）green

【葱翠】 cōngcuì fresh green; luxuriantly

green

【葱茏】 cōnglóng verdant; luxuriantly green: ～茂盛 luxuriant growth of vegetation

【葱绿】 cōnglǜ 1.(浅绿微黄) pale yellowish green 2.(青翠) verdant; fresh green

【葱头】 cōngtóu onion

【葱郁】 cōngyù verdant; luxuriantly green

聪[聰](cōng) 1.(听觉) faculty of hearing 2.(听觉灵敏) acute hearing

【聪明】 cōngmíng intelligent; bright; clever: ～活泼 wise and active / ～能干 bright and capable

【聪颖】 cōngyǐng intelligent; bright; clever

从[從](cóng) 1.(跟随) follow: 师～ be an apprentice of sb. 2.(顺从;听从)comply with; obey 3.(从事;参加) join; be engaged in 4.(随从的人) follower; attendant 5.(从属的;次要的) secondary; accessory 6.(表示起于或经过) from; through: ～长远看 from a long-term point of view; in the long run / ～根本上说 essentially; in essence / ～现在起 from now on / ～这儿往西 go west from here; west of here 7.(用在否定词前面) ever: ～未听说过 have never heard of

【从此】 cóngcǐ from this time on; from now on; from then on; henceforth; thereupon

【从…到…】 cóng…dào… from . . . to . . . : 从上到下 from top to bottom; from the higher levels to the grass roots / 从头到尾 from beginning to end; from first to last / 从左到右 from left to right

【从而】 cóng'ér thus; thereby

【从犯】 cóngfàn 〈*Law*〉 accessory; accessory criminal

【从简】 cóngjiǎn conform to the principle of simplicity

【从句】 cóngjù 〈*Gram.*〉 clause; collateral clause

【从军】 cóngjūn enlist; join the army

【从来】 cónglái always; at all times; all along

【从略】 cónglüè be omitted

【从前】 cóngqián before; formerly; in the past

【从容】 cóngróng 1.(不慌不忙) calm; unhurried; leisurely: ～地考虑 consider in an unhurried manner 2.(宽裕) plentiful; sufficient; enough: 手头不～ be hard for money; be out of cash / 时间很～。There is plenty of time.

【从容不迫】 cóngróng-bùpò calm and unhurried; steadily

【从事】 cóngshì 1.(投身于) go in for; be engaged in: ～各种活动 be engaged in various activities / ～科研工作 be engaged in scientific research 2.(处理) deal with

【从属】 cóngshǔ subordinate

【从属地位】 cóngshǔ dìwèi subordinate position; subordinate status

【从属关系】 cóngshǔ guān·xì 1.(指双方的关系) subordinate relation 2.(指被从属者的地位) a subordinate position

【从速】 cóngsù as soon as possible; as quickly as possible; without delay

【从头】 cóngtóu 1.(从最初) from the beginning 2.(重新) anew; once again

【从小】 cóngxiǎo from childhood; as a child

【从严】 cóngyán be as strict as possible

【从中】 cóngzhōng out of; from among; therefrom: ～吸取教训 draw lesson from it / ～渔利 profit from; cash in on

丛[叢、樷](cóng) 1.(聚集) crowd together 2.(指草木) clump; thicket; grove 3.(指人或物) crowd; collection

【丛刊】 cóngkān a series of books; collection

【丛林】 cónglín jungle; forest

【丛生】 cóngshēng 1.(指草木) grow thickly: 荆棘～ be overgrown with brambles 2.(指疾病等) break out

【丛书】 cóngshū a series of books; collection: 自学～ self-study series

【丛杂】 cóngzá motley

淙(cóng)

【淙淙】 cóngcóng murmuring; gurgling: 流水～ a gurgling stream

cou

凑[湊](còu) 1.(凑集) gather together; pool; collect: ～整数 make up a round number; make up an even amount 2.（碰；赶；趁）happen by chance; take advantage of：正～上雨天。It happened to be a rainy day. 3.（接近）move close to; come close to; press near：～近点儿。Come closer, please.

【凑份子】 còu fèn·zi club together (to present a gift to sb.)

【凑合】 còu·he 1.（聚集）gather together; collect; assemble 2.（拼凑）improvise 3.（将就）make do (with) 4.（还可以的）passable; not too bad

【凑钱】 còuqián pool money

【凑巧】 còuqiǎo luckily; fortunately; as luck would have it：我～在家。I happened to be at home.

【凑热闹儿】 còu rè·naor 1.（和大家一起玩儿）join in the fun 2.（添麻烦）add trouble to

【凑手】 còushǒu at hand; within easy reach：钱不～ have no money at hand

【凑数】 còushù make up the number or amount; serve as a stopgap

【凑整儿】 còuzhěngr make up a round number

cu

粗［觕、麤、麁］（cū） 1.（粗大）wide (in diameter); thick：～树干 thick trunk 2.（粗糙）coarse; crude; rough：～布 coarse cloth 3.（指声音）gruff; husky 4.（疏忽；不周密）careless; negligent 5.（粗野）rude; unrefined; vulgar 6.（略微）roughly; slightly：～通文字 can read and write a little

【粗暴】 cūbào rude; rough; crude; brutal

【粗笨】 cūbèn 1.（笨拙）clumsy; awkward：手脚～ clumsy in doing things 2.（笨重）unwieldy; heavy; bulky; cumbersome

【粗糙】 cūcāo coarse; rough; crude：～的译文 rough translation / ～的皮肤 rough skin

【粗大】 cūdà 1.（又粗又大）thick; bulky 2.（声音大而粗）loud; husky

【粗纺】 cūfǎng 〈*Textiles*〉 spin

【粗纺毛织物】 cūfǎng máozhīwù 〈*Textiles*〉 stamin

【粗放】 cūfàng 1.〈*Agric.*〉 extensive 2.（不细致）careless; thoughtless 3.（粗犷）straightforward and uninhibited

【粗放经营】 cūfàng jīngyíng extensive management

【粗放农业】 cūfàng nóngyè extensive agriculture

【粗犷】 cūguǎng 1.（粗野）rough; rude; boorish 2.（豪放）straightforward and uninhibited; bold and unconstrained; rugged

【粗花呢】 cūhuāní 〈*Textiles*〉 tweed

【粗话】 cūhuà vulgar language

【粗活】 cūhuó heavy manual labor; unskilled work

【粗加工】 cūjiāgōng 〈*Mech.*〉 rough finish; rough machining

【粗粮】 cūliáng coarse food grain (e. g. sorghum, maize, millet, etc.)

【粗劣】 cūliè of poor quality; cheap; shoddy

【粗陋】 cūlòu 1.（粗糙）coarse and crude 2.（粗俗丑陋）coarse and ugly 3.（粗俗浅陋）vulgar and meager

【粗鲁】 cū·lǔ rough; rude; boorish：说话～ have a rough tongue; say rude things

【粗略】 cūlüè rough; sketchy：～估计 a rough estimate

【粗毛呢】 cūmáoní 〈*Textiles*〉 corillas

【粗浅】 cūqiǎn superficial; shallow; simple：～的道理 a simple truth / ～的知识 elementary knowledge

【粗人】 cūrén rough fellow; boor; unrefined person

【粗率】 cūshuài rough and careless; ill-considered

【粗饲料】 cūsìliào fodder; coarse fodder

【粗俗】 cūsú vulgar; coarse：举止～ uncouth behavior

【粗细】 cūxì 1.（粗细程度）(degree of) thickness 2.（粗糙和细致的程度）crudeness or fineness; degree of finish; quality of work

【粗心】 cūxīn careless; thoughtless

【粗野】 cūyě rough; boorish; uncouth

【粗轧】 cūzhá 〈*Metall.*〉 rough down

【粗枝大叶】 cū zhī dà yè crude and careless; sloppy; slapdash; done in broad strokes or rough outline

【粗制滥造】 cūzhì-lànzào manufacture in a rough and slipshod way; turn out rough and slipshod work

【粗制品】 cūzhìpǐn semifinished product

【粗中有细】 cūzhōng-yǒuxì usually careless, but quite sharp at times; crude in most matters, but subtle in some

【粗壮】 cūzhuàng **1.** (粗而健壮) sturdy; thickset; brawny; robust **2.** (粗大结实) thick and strong **3.** (声音大) deep and resonant

猝 (cù) 〈*written*〉 sudden; abrupt; unexpected

【猝不及防】 cùbù-jífáng be taken by surprise; be caught off guard

【猝发】 cùfā 〈*Physics*〉 burst

【猝然】 cùrán suddenly; abruptly; unexpectedly: ～决定 make a sudden decision

【猝死】 cùsǐ sudden death

促 (cù) **1.** (短促) short; hurried; urgent **2.** (催促) urge; promote: 催～ urge; hurry **3.** (靠近) close to; near

【促成】 cùchéng help to bring about; facilitate

【促进】 cùjìn promote; advance; accelerate: 大力～ make greater efforts to promote / ～社会全面进步 ensure all-round social progress / ～团结 promote unity / ～效率 help raise efficiency / ～相互了解 further mutual understanding

【促使】 cùshǐ impel; urge; spur

【促膝谈心】 cùxī-tánxīn sit side by side and talk intimately; have a heart-to-heart talk; have intimate chat together

【促销】 cùxiāo promote sales; sales promotion (n.)

醋 (cù) **1.** (调味品) vinegar **2.** (嫉妒) jealousy (as in love affair): 吃～ feel jealous

【醋精】 cùjīng vinegar concentrate

【醋酸】 cùsuān 〈*Chem.*〉 acetic acid

【醋意】 cùyì jealousy

簇 (cù) **1.** (团;堆) form a cluster; pile up **2.** 〈*classifier*〉 cluster; bunch: 一～鲜花 a bunch of flowers **3.** 〈*Computer*〉 cluster

【簇新】 cùxīn brand new

【簇拥】 cùyōng cluster round

蹙 (cù) **1.** (紧迫) pressed; cramped **2.** (皱) knit (one's brows)

【蹙额】 cù'é knit one's brows; frown; scowl

cuan

汆 (cuān) quick-boil: ～丸子 quick-boiled meat balls with soup

撺[**攛**] (cuān)

【撺掇】 cuān·duo urge; egg sb. on

蹿[**躥**] (cuān) **1.** (向上或向前跳) leap up **2.** (喷射) spurt; spout

攒[**欑**] (cuán) collect together; assemble: ～一台计算机 assemble a computer

(另见"攒"zǎn)

【攒聚】 cuánjù gather closely together

窜[**竄**] (cuàn) **1.** (乱窜) run about; flee; scurry: 流～ flee hither and thither **2.** (窜改) change; alter

【窜犯】 cuànfàn raid; make an inroad; make incursions

【窜改】 cuàngǎi alter; tamper with; falsify: ～记录 tamper with the minutes / ～原文 alter the original text / ～账目 falsify accounts

【窜扰】 cuànrǎo harass: ～边境 harass the border area

【窜逃】 cuàntáo flee in disorder; scurry off

篡 (cuàn) usurp; seize

【篡夺】 cuànduó usurp; seize: 妄图～领导权 vainly attempt to usurp the leadership

【篡改】 cuàngǎi distort; misrepresent; tamper with; falsify: ～历史 distort history

【篡权】 cuànquán usurp power

【篡位】 cuànwèi usurp the throne; usurp the leadership

cui

催 (cuī) **1.** (催促) urge; hurry; press: ～办 press sb. to do sth. / ～人答复 press for an answer **2.** (使加快) hasten; expedite; speed up

【催办】 cuībàn hasten sb. to do sth.

【催促】 cuīcù urge; hasten; press

【催化】 cuīhuà 〈*Chem.*〉 catalysis

【催化剂】 cuīhuàjì catalyst; catalytic agent

【催泪弹】 cuīlèidàn tear bomb; tear-gas

grenade

【催眠】 cuīmián lull (to sleep); hypnotize; mesmerize

【催眠曲】 cuīmiánqǔ lullaby; cradlesong

【催眠术】 cuīmiánshù hypnotism; mesmerism

【催眠药】 cuīmiányào hypnotic; somnificant; soporfic

摧 (cuī) break; destroy; ruin

【摧残】 cuīcán wreck; destroy; devastate

【摧毁】 cuīhuǐ destroy; smash; wreck

璀 (cuǐ)

【璀璨】 cuǐcàn 〈*written*〉 bright; resplendent

【璀璨夺目】 cuǐcàn-duómù dazzling

脆［脃］(cuì) 1.(易折;易碎) fragile; brittle 2.(一咬就碎裂) crisp: 香～可口 crisp, fragrant and pleasant to taste 3.(声音清脆) clear; ringing; clear and sharp

【脆弱】 cuìruò fragile; frail; weak: 感情～ be easily upset

萃 (cuì) 1.(聚集) gather together; assemble 2.(聚集在一起的人) a gathering of people 3.(聚在一起的物) a collection of things

【萃取】 cuìqǔ 〈*Chem.*〉 extract; extraction (n.)

啐 (cuì) spit; expectorate: ～他一口 spit at him / ～在某人脸上 spit in sb's face

淬［焠］(cuì) temper by dipping in water, oil, etc.; quench

【淬火】 cuìhuǒ quench; temper by rapid cooling

粹 (cuì) 1.(纯粹) pure 2.(精粹) essence

【粹白】 cuìbái pure white

翠 (cuì) 1.(翠绿色) emerald green; green 2.(翡翠石) jadeite

【翠柏】 cuìbǎi 〈*Bot.*〉 incense cedar

【翠绿】 cuìlǜ emerald green; jade green

【翠鸟】 cuìniǎo kingfisher; halcyon

【翠竹】 cuìzhú green bamboos

cun

村［邨[1]］(cūn) 1.(村庄) village; hamlet 2.(粗俗) rustic; boorish

【村落】 cūnluò village hamlet

【村民】 cūnmín villager

【村民委员会】 cūnmín wěiyuánhuì villagers' committee

【村野】 cūnyě boorish

【村寨】 cūnzhài stockaded village

【村长】 cūnzhǎng village head

【村镇】 cūnzhèn villages and small towns

【村庄】 cūnzhuāng village; hamlet

皴 (cūn) 1.(裂口) wrinkle 2.(皴裂) chapped; wrinkled

【皴裂】 cūnliè chapped; wrinkled: 她在室外工作了一冬,双手都～了。She'd been working outside all winter and her hands were chapped.

存 (cún) 1.(存在;生存) exist; live; survive 2.(储存;保存) store; keep 3.(蓄积;聚集) accumulate; collect 4.(储蓄) deposit: 在银行里～钱 deposit money in a bank 5.(寄存) leave with; check: ～行李 deposit one's luggage 6.(保存) reserve; retain 7.(结存) remain on balance; be in stock 8.(心里存有) cherish; harbor: ～有希望 cherish the hopes

【存车处】 cúnchēchù parking lot (for bicycles)

【存储】 cúnchǔ 〈*Computer*〉 memory; storage

【存储错误】 cúnchǔ cuòwù 〈*Computer*〉 storage errors

【存储器】 cúnchǔqì 〈*Computer*〉 memory; storage

【存单】 cúndān deposit receipt

【存档】 cúndàng file; keep in the archives; place on file: 把文件～ place a document on file

【存底儿】 cúndǐr keep the original draft; keep a file copy

【存放】 cúnfàng leave with; leave in sb's care

【存根】 cúngēn counterfoil; stub: 支票～ check stub

【存户】 cúnhù depositor

【存活】 cúnhuó survive; survival (n.); surviving (adj.)

【存货】 cúnhuò goods in stock; existing stock

【存款】 cúnkuǎn deposit; bank savings: 储蓄

～ savings deposits / 定期～ fixed deposit; time deposit / 个人～ personal savings account / 活期～ current deposit; demand deposit

【存款利息】 cúnkuǎn lìxī interest on deposit

【存款人】 cúnkuǎnrén depositor

【存栏】 cúnlán 〈*Husbandry*〉 livestock on hand

【存栏总头数】 cúnlán zǒngtóushù 〈*Husbandry*〉(total) amount of livestock on hand

【存利除弊】 cúnlì-chúbì keep the good and eliminate the evil

【存粮】 cúnliáng **1.**(储存粮食) store (up) grain **2.**(储存的粮食) grain in storage

【存取】 cúnqǔ 〈*Computer*〉 access: 快速～ immediate access; short access

【存取时间】 cúnqǔ shíjiān 〈*Computer*〉 access time

【存身】 cúnshēn take shelter; make one's home: 无处～ find no shelter; have no place to call one's home

【存水弯】 cúnshuǐwān trap

【存亡】 cúnwáng live or die; survive or perish: 危急～之秋 at the critical juncture of life and death / ～未卜 to preserve or to ruin cannot be foretold

【存现】 cúnxiàn deposit cash

【存心】 cúnxīn **1.**(念头) cherish certain intentions **2.**(故意) intentionally; deliberately; on purpose

【存衣处】 cúnyīchù cloakroom

【存疑】 cúnyí leave a question open; leave a matter for future consideration

【存在】 cúnzài exist; be

【存折】 cúnzhé deposit book; bankbook

忖(cǔn) think over; speculate

【忖度】 cǔnduó speculate; meditate; contemplate

寸(cùn) **1.**(极短;极小) very little; very short; small **2.**(英寸) inch (1 英寸合 2.54厘米)

【寸步不离】 cùnbù-bùlí follow sb. closely; keep close to; not to move a step from

【寸步不让】 cùnbù-bùràng refuse to yield an inch; fight every inch of the way; not to yield a single step

【寸步难行】 cùnbù-nánxíng difficult to move even one step; cannot move a single step

【寸草不生】 cùncǎo-bùshēng not even a blade of grass grows

【寸土必争】 cùntǔ-bìzhēng fight for every inch of land

【寸心】 cùnxīn feelings: 聊表～ as a small token of my feelings; just to show my appreciation

【寸有所长】 cùnyǒu-suǒcháng an inch has length

cuo

搓(cuō) **1.**(捻) twist: ～线 twist thread **2.**(摩擦) rub; scrub; rub with the hands: ～衣服 give the clothes a scrubbing

【搓板】 cuōbǎn washboard

【搓麻将】 cuō májiàng play mah-jong

【搓麻绳】 cuō máshéng make cord

【搓澡】 cuōzǎo give sb. a rubdown with a damp towel

磋(cuō) consult

【磋商】 cuōshāng consult; exchange views: 与某人～某事 consult with sb. about sth.

蹉(cuō)

【蹉跎】 cuōtuó waste time; idle away

【蹉跎岁月】 cuōtuó-suìyuè waste time doing nothing; spend one's life in fruitless efforts

撮(cuō) **1.**(撮合;聚拢) gather; bring together **2.**(用簸箕撮) gather up; scoop up **3.**(摘取要点) extract; summarize **4.**〈*classifier*〉 pinch

(另见"撮"zuǒ)

【撮合】 cuō·he make a match; act as go-between

痤(cuó)

【痤疮】 cuózhuāng 〈*Med.*〉 acne

挫(cuò) **1.**(挫折) defeat; frustrate: 受～ suffer a setback **2.**(挫败) subdue; lower

【挫败】 cuòbài frustrate; foil; defeat; thwart

【挫其锋芒】 cuòqí-fēngmáng blunt the edge of one's advance

【挫伤】 cuòshāng 1.〈*Med*.〉contusion; bruise 2.(损伤积极性等) dampen; deflate; blunt; discourage: ～积极性 dampen one's enthusiasm

【挫折】 cuòzhé setback; reverse: 遇到～ meet with setbacks / 遭受～ suffer setbacks

锉 (cuò) 1.(工具) file: 圆～ round file / 方～ square file / 三角～ triangular file / 指甲～ nail file 2.(用锉加工) file; make smooth with a file: 这表面已经～平了。The surface had been filed smooth.

【锉刀】 cuòdāo file: 粗～ bastard file / 细～ smooth file

【锉屑】 cuòxiè filings

措 (cuò) 1.(措置) arrange; manage; handle: 不知所～ be at a loss what to do; be at one's wit's end 2.(筹划) make plans

【措辞】 cuòcí wording; diction: ～含糊 ambiguously worded

【措施】 cuòshī measure; step: 安全～ safety measure / 采取有效～ adopt an effective measure

【措手不及】 cuòshǒu-bùjí be caught unawares; be caught unprepared: 使人～ throw sb. off his guard; take sb. by surprise

【措置】 cuòzhì handle; manage; arrange: ～失当 mismanaged; improperly managed

错 (cuò) 1.(错杂) interlocked and jagged; intricate; complex 2.(相对摩擦) grind; rub 3.(措开;不碰上) alternate; stagger 4.(错误) wrong; mistaken; erroneous: 认～ admit one's mistake 5.(过错;错处) fault; demerit: 挑～ find fault 6.(用于否定式;坏,差) bad; poor: 这幅画不～。This picture is not bad.

【错案】 cuò'àn 〈*Law*〉misjudged case

【错别字】 cuòbiézì 1.(写错的字) wrongly written 2.(读错的字) mispronounced characters

【错车】 cuòchē one vehicle gives another the right of way

【错怪】 cuòguài blame sb. wrongly

【错过】 cuòguò miss; let slip: ～机会 miss an opportunity / ～这班汽车 miss this bus

【错角】 cuòjiǎo 〈*Math*.〉alternate angle

【错觉】 cuòjué illusion; wrong impression

【错开】 cuòkāi stagger: 把休假日～ stagger the holidays

【错乱】 cuòluàn in disorder; in confusion; deranged: 精神～ mentally deranged; insane

【错落】 cuòluò strewn at random: ～不齐 scattered here and there

【错判】 cuòpàn 〈*Sports*〉misjudge

【错位】 cuòwèi misplacement; dislocation

【错误】 cuòwù 1.(不正确) wrong; mistaken; erroneous: ～估计形势 make a wrong estimate of the situation 2.(不正确的事物、行为等) mistake; error; blunder; fault: 犯～ make a mistake; commit an error

【错字】 cuòzì 1.(写错的字) wrongly written character 2.(印错的字) misprint

【错综复杂】 cuòzōng-fùzá very complicated; complex; intricate: 这个问题～。It is a complicated problem.

D

da

耷(dā)

【耷拉】dā·la droop; hang down: ～着脑袋 hang one's head

答[荅](dā)
(另见"答"dá)

【答理】 dā·li acknowledge (sb's greeting, etc.); respond; answer

【答应】 dā·ying **1**.(回答) answer; reply; respond **2**.(许诺) promise; comply with: 他～尽力而为。He promised to do his best. **3**.(同意) agree; consent: ～她的请求 consent to her request

搭(dā) **1**.(架设) put up; build: ～一座桥 build a bridge **2**.(挂) hang over; put over **3**.(连接) come into contact; join: 与…～上关系 come into contact with sb. **4**.(加上;凑上) throw in more (people, money, etc.); add: 这笔钱～上还不够。It won't be enough even with this sum thrown in. **5**.(共同抬起) lift sth. together **6**.(搭乘) take (a ship, plane, etc.); travel by; go by: 没～上长途汽车 fail to catch the coach

【搭伴】 dābàn join sb. on a trip; travel together: ～旅行 travel in company

【搭便车】 dā biànchē thumb a ride; thumb a lift: 我们～去天津。We thumbed a lift to Tianjin.

【搭乘】 dāchéng travel by (plane, car, ship, etc.)

【搭档】 dádàng **1**.(协作) cooperate; work together **2**.(协作者) partner: 老～ old partner; old work-mate

【搭伙】 dāhuǒ **1**.(结伴) join as partner: 同他们～去郊游 join them in an outing **2**.(加入伙食团) eat regularly in (a mess, etc.): 在食堂～ take meals regularly at the canteen

【搭救】 dājiù rescue; go to the rescue of: 从危险中～某人 rescue sb. from danger; save sb. from danger

【搭扣】 dākòu hasp; clasp for a door

【搭卖】 dāmài sell by arranging goods

【搭配】 dāpèi **1**.(指分配) arrange in pairs or groups **2**.(词语配合) collocation **3**.(相称) match; suit: 你觉得这两种颜色～吗? Does you think these two colors match?

【搭腔】 dāqiāng **1**.(接话) answer; respond **2**.(交谈) talk to each other

【搭桥】 dāqiáo **1**.(架桥) bridge; set up bridges **2**.(作介绍人) bridge: 在失业者和需要工人的雇主之间～ bridge the gap between the unemployed and employer who need workers **3**.(作媒人) act as a matchmaker **4**.〈*Med*.〉 have a bridge

【搭讪】 dā·shàn strike up a conversation with sb.; say something to smooth over an embarrassing situation

【搭载】 dāzài carry sth. incidental to the main mission: 中国卫星～的试验装置 a experimental device carried by a Chinese satellite

打(dá) 〈*classifier*〉 dozen: 半～ half a dozen / 一～铅笔 a dozen pencils / 两～铅笔 two dozen pencils
(另见"打"dǎ)

达[達](dá) **1**.(通) extend: 四通八～ extend in all directions **2**.(达到) reach; attain; amount to: 面积～2万公顷。The area amount to 20,000 ha. **3**.(通达) understand thoroughly **4**.(表达) express; communicate

【达标】 dábiāo come up to the standards; reach the mark

【达成】 dáchéng reach; conclude; enter into: ～谅解 come to an understanding / ～协议 reach an agreement; conclude an agreement

【达旦】 dádàn until dawn：通宵～ all through the night
【达到】 dádào achieve；attain；reach：～国际先进水平 reach advanced world standards / ～目的 achieve the goal；attain the goal / 最终～共同富裕 ultimately to achieve common prosperity
【达尔文主义】 Dá'ěrwén zhǔyì Darwinism；Darwinist（adj.）‖ 达尔文主义者 Darwinist
【达日】 Dárì 〈place〉 Dagri
【达旺】 Dáwàng 〈place〉 Moindawang
【达斡尔族】 Dáwò'ěrzú Daur（中国少数民族，主要分布在内蒙古、黑龙江等地）
【达意】 dáyì express one's idea；convey one's ideas：词不～ the words fail to convey the idea
【达因】 dáyīn dyne

沓（dá） 〈*classifier*〉 pile；pad：一～钞票 a wad of dollar bills / 一～信封 a pad of envelope

答［荅］（dá） 1.（回答）answer；reply；respond：笑而不～ smile without replying 2.（还报）return（a visit，etc.）；reciprocate
（另见"答"dā）
【答案】 dá'àn answer；solution；key
【答辩】 dábiàn reply（to a charge，query or an argument）
【答词】 dácí answering speech；reply：致～ make a speech in reply
【答对】 dáduì answer sb's question；reply
【答非所问】 dáfēi-suǒwèn give an irrelevant answer
【答复】 dá·fù answer；reply：请尽早～。Please reply at your earliest convenience.
【答话】 dáhuà answer；reply
【答卷】 dájuàn 1.（答好的考卷）answered examination paper 2.（指对考验等的态度）position or attitude one takes when being tested
【答数】 dáshù answer
【答谢】 dáxiè express appreciation（for sb's kindness or hospitality）；acknowledge
【答谢宴会】 dáxiè yànhuì a return banquet

打（dǎ） 1.（击打）strike；hit；knock 2.（攻打）fight；attack 3.（破碎）break；smash：花瓶～得粉碎。The vase was smashed to pieces. 4.（建，造，做）construct；build 5.（锻造）make（in a smithy）；forge 6.（搅拌）mix；stir；beat：～鸡蛋 beat the eggs 7.（打捆）tie up；pack：～包裹 wrap up a parcel 8.（画）draw；paint；make a mark on：～格儿 draw squares 9.（喷撒）spray；spread：～农药 spray insecticide 10.（举着；提起）hold；raise；hoist：～伞 put up an umbrella / ～起精神来 raise one's spirits 11.（付给或领取）issue or receive（a certificate，etc.）12.（除去）remove；get rid of：～蛔虫 take worm medicine 13.（舀取）ladle；draw：～一盆水 fetch a basin of water 14.（用割、砍等动作来收集）gather in；collect：～柴 gather firewood 15.（买）buy：～酒 buy some liquor / ～票 buy a bus ticket 16.（计算；定出）estimate；calculate；reckon：成本～2,000美元 estimate the cost at 2,000 dollars 17.（玩要）play：～桥牌 play bridge 18.（表示某些动作）～哈欠 yawn / ～手势 make a gesture 19.（采用）adopt；use：～比喻 make an analogy 20.（从）from；since：～那以后 since then / ～今儿个起 from now on
（另见"打"dá）
【打靶】 dǎbǎ target practice；shooting practice
【打靶场】 dǎbǎchǎng target range
【打白条】 dǎ báitiáo write out an informal IOU
【打败】 dǎbài 1.（战胜）defeat；beat；worst 2.（失败）suffer a defeat；be defeated
【打扮】 dǎ·ban 1.（梳妆打扮）dress up；make up；deck out：～得整整齐齐 all dressed up / ～得入时 be dressed up according to the latest fashion 2.（装扮）pose as；disguise as：把自己～成英雄 pose as a hero
【打包】 dǎbāo 1.（包装）bale；pack 2.（打开）unpack
【打包机】 dǎbāojī baling machine
【打包票】 dǎbāopiào guarantee；vouch for
【打抱不平】 dǎ bàobùpíng take up the cudgels for the injured party；defend sb. against an injustice
【打比方】 dǎ bǐ·fāng draw an analogy
【打补丁】 dǎ bǔ·ding put a patch（on a garment，etc.）
【打草稿】 dǎ chǎogǎo prepare a draft；work

out a draft

【打草惊蛇】 dǎ cǎo jīng shé beat the grass and frighten away the snake; act rashly and alert the enemy

【打岔】 dǎchà interrupt; cut in

【打成一片】 dǎ chéng yī piàn become one with; identify oneself with; merge with

【打从】 dǎcóng since

【打倒】 dǎdǎo **1.**（推翻）overthrow **2.**（口号）Down with

【打的】 dǎdí take a taxi

【打底子】 dǎ dǐ·zi **1.**（起草）sketch (a plan, picture, etc.) **2.**（奠定基础）lay a foundation

【打点】 dǎ·dian **1.**（收拾；准备）get (luggage, etc.) ready **2.**（送礼请求照顾）bribe

【打点滴】 dǎ diǎndī 〈*Med.*〉 have an intravenous drip

【打电报】 dǎ diànbào send a telegram; telegraph

【打掉】 dǎdiào **1.**（打下去）destroy; knock out **2.**（指堕胎）have an abortion

【打动】 dǎdòng move; touch：我们被那故事深深地～了。We were greatly moved by the story.

【打赌】 dǎdǔ bet; wager; make a bet：咱们打个赌，看比赛的结果到底如何。Let's make a bet on the result of the games.

【打短工】 dǎ duǎngōng work as a casual laborer

【打断】 dǎduàn **1.**（折断）break **2.**（使中断）interrupt; cut short：～思路 interrupt sb's train of thought / 别～他的话。Don't interrupt him.

【打盹儿】 dǎdǔnr doze off; take a nap：午饭后打个盹儿 have a little nap after lunch

【打哆嗦】 dǎ duōsuō tremble; shiver：他冷得直～。He's trembling with cold.

【打发】 dǎ·fa **1.**（派出）send; dispatch：～人请医生 sent for a doctor **2.**（使离开）dismiss; send away：把孩子们～出去 sent the children away **3.**（消磨）while away (one's time)：～时间 while away one's time; idle away the hours

【打嗝儿】 dǎgér **1.**（呃逆）hiccup; hiccough **2.**（嗳气）belch; burp

【打工】 dǎgōng do manual work

【打工族】 dǎgōngzú young migrants

【打鼓】 dǎgǔ **1.**（敲鼓）beat a drum **2.**（心神不定）feel uncertain; feel nervous

【打官司】 dǎ guān·si **1.**（进行诉讼）go to court; go to law; engage in a lawsuit **2.**（争吵；口角）squabble

【打光棍】 dǎ guānggùn remain a bachelor; stay single

【打滚】 dǎgǔn roll about：疼得直～ writhe with pain

【打棍子】 dǎ gùn·zi come down with the big stick; use the big stick; criticize arbitrarily and unfoundedly

【打哈哈】 dǎ hā·ha make fun; crack a joke：别拿我们～。Don't make fun of us.

【打哈欠】 dǎ hā·qian yawn：我直～。I can't stop yawning.

【打鼾】 dǎhān snore：他～声音太大，弄得我夜里睡不着。He snores so loudly, it keeps me awake at night.

【打呼噜】 dǎ hū·lu snore：他是个特能打～的人。He is a terrible snorer.

【打火机】 dǎhuǒjī lighter; cigarette lighter

【打击】 dǎjī **1.**（攻击）hit; strike; attack：狠狠～敌人 strike the enemy a heavy blow **2.**（使受挫折）attack; crack down on：～走私活动 crack down on smuggling

【打击报复】 dǎjī bào·fù retaliate; retaliation (*n.*)

【打击乐器】 dǎjī yuèqì percussion instrument

【打基础】 dǎ jīchǔ do spade work; prepare oneself for bigger tasks ahead：为今后国民经济的持续发展～ lay the foundation for sustained economic growth in the future

【打架】 dǎjià come to blows; fight; scuffle

【打交道】 dǎ jiāo·dao come into contact with; make contact with; have dealings with

【打搅】 dǎjiǎo disturb; trouble：别～他。Don't disturb him.

【打结】 dǎjié tie a knot; tighten a knot

【打井】 dǎjǐng dig a well; sink a well

【打开】 dǎkāi **1.**（开）open; unfold **2.**（开收音机等）turn on; switch on：谁把电视～了？Who turned the television on? **3.**（攻开）break through：～缺口 make a breach / ～一条出路 break through an encirclement or fight a way out **4.**（开展）open up; spread：～地图 spread out the map / ～思路 broaden one's scope of mind

【打瞌睡】 dǎ kēshuì doze off; nod: 他坐在电视机前～。He sat and nodded in front of the television.

【打孔】 dǎkǒng drill a hole; punch a hole

【打孔机】 dǎkǒngjī hole punch

【打垮】 dǎkuǎ strike down; defeat; to beat

【打捞】 dǎlāo 1.(寻找并捞出沉在水里的东西) get out of water; salvage: ～沉船 salvage a sunken ship 2.(捞取) fishing

【打捞公司】 dǎlāo gōngsī salvage company

【打篮球】 dǎ lánqiú play basketball

【打雷】 dǎléi thunder: 天阴下来了, 并开始～。The sky grew dark and it started to thunder.

【打冷枪】 dǎ lěngqiāng snipe; fire a sniper's shot; stab in the back: 向某人～ snipe at sb.

【打冷战】 dǎ lěng·zhan 1.(身体抖动) shudder 2.(指非武力斗争) fight a cold war

【打冷颤】 dǎ lěng.zhan shudder

【打量】 dǎ·liang 1.(观察) measure with the eye; look sb. up and down; size up 2.(估计) think; suppose; reckon

【打猎】 dǎliè go hunting: 爱好～ be found of hunting; be found of shooting

【打乱】 dǎluàn throw into confusion; upset

【打麻将】 dǎ májiàng play mah-jong

【打马虎眼】 dǎ mǎ·huyǎn 〈*dial.*〉 pretend to be ignorant of sth. in order to gloss it over; act dumb

【打毛衣】 dǎ máoyī knit a sweater

【打埋伏】 dǎ mái·fu 1.(伏击) lie in ambush; set an ambush; ambush 2.(隐瞒) hold sth. back for one's own use

【打牌】 dǎpái 1.(打纸牌) play cards 2.(打麻将牌) play mah-jong

【打票】 dǎpiào buy a (train, bus, etc.) ticket

【打平手】 dǎ píngshǒu draw even; equalize

【打破】 dǎpò break; smash: ～常规, 尽量采用先进技术 break free from conventions and use advanced techniques as much as possible / ～僵局 break a deadlock; find a way out of a stalemate

【打扑克】 dǎ pūkè play cards

【打起精神】 dǎ qǐ jīng·shen cheer up; pluck up courage; with chin up

【打气】 dǎqì 1.(充气) inflate; pump up 2.(鼓动) bolster up the morale; boost the morale; encourage; cheer up

【打气筒】 dǎqìtǒng bicycle pump; inflator

【打桥牌】 dǎ qiáopái play a bridge game

【打秋千】 dǎ qiūqiān have a swing; get on a swing; play on the swing

【打球】 dǎqiú play ball games

【打趣】 dǎqù banter; tease; make fun of

【打拳】 dǎquán box; practice boxing: 打太极拳 practice t'ai chi chu'an; practice shadow boxing

【打群架】 dǎ qúnjià gang war

【打扰】 dǎrǎo disturb; trouble: 请勿～。Do not disturb. / (在门把手上)挂着"请勿～" have the "Do Not Disturb"

【打入】 dǎrù 1.(置于) throw into; banish to: ～冷宫 consign to the back shelf; throw into limbo 2.(渗透) infiltrate: ～敌方军事部门 infiltrate enemy military units / 派人～证券公司 infiltrate their own people into the security firm

【打伞】 dǎsǎn hold up an umbrella

【打扫】 dǎsǎo sweep; clean: ～房间 clean the room

【打闪】 dǎshǎn lightning: 先～, 然后是隆隆的雷声。There was a flash of lightning and then a loud peal of thunder.

【打伤】 dǎshāng wound; injure: 在枪战中, 他被～了胳膊。During the shoot-out, he was wounded in the arm.

【打胜仗】 dǎ shèngzhàng be victorious; win a war

【打手势】 dǎ shǒushì gesticulate; make a gesture; gesticulation (n.)

【打算】 dǎ·suan 1.(考虑) intend; plan; think; mean: 不～放弃 have no intention to give up 2.(想法) consideration; calculation: 另有个人～ have an ax to grind; have a purpose of one's own/ 没有个人～ with no consideration of personal interests

【打算盘】 dǎ suàn·pan calculate on an abacus; calculate: 打小算盘 be calculating; be petty and scheming

【打碎】 dǎsuì break into pieces; smash; destroy

【打胎】 dǎtāi have an (induced) abortion

【打天下】 dǎ tiānxià 1.（夺取政权）struggle to seize state power 2.（创立事业）establish an enterprise；start an enterprise；set up an enterprise

【打铁】 dǎtiě forge iron

【打听】 dǎ·ting ask about；inquire about：～某人的地址 try to find out sb's address / ～消息 ask for information

【打通】 dǎtōng get through；open up：电话打不通 be unable to get through（on the telephone）

【打通思想】 dǎtōng sīxiǎng talk sb. round

【打退】 dǎtuì beat back；beat off；repulse

【打退堂鼓】 dǎ tuìtánggǔ back out

【打下手】 dǎ xiàshǒu act as an assistant

【打先锋】 dǎ xiānfēng fight in the van；be a pioneer

【打响】 dǎxiǎng 1.（开火）start shooting；begin to exchange fire 2.（初步成功）win initial success；make a good start；come off well as a start

【打消】 dǎxiāo give up；dispel：～顾虑 dispel misgivings / ～念头 dismiss the idea；drop the idea / ～原计划 drop the original plan；cancel the original plan

【打雪仗】 dǎ xuězhàng have a snowball fight

【打眼】 dǎyǎn 1.（钻孔）punch（bore）a hole；drill 2.（惹人注意）catch the eye；attract attention

【打样】 dǎyàng 〈*Printing*〉proof

【打样机】 dǎyàngjī 〈*Printing*〉proof press

【打夜班】 dǎ yèbān go on night shift

【打印】 dǎyìn print；type

【打印机】 dǎyìnjī printer：24 针点阵～ 24-pin dot matrix printer

【打游击】 dǎ yóujī 1.〈*Mil.*〉fight as a guerrilla 2.（没有固定地点）work（eat，sleep，etc.）at no fixed place

【打鱼】 dǎyú catch fish

【打圆场】 dǎ yuánchǎng mediate a dispute；smooth things over

【打杂儿】 dǎzár do odds and ends

【打战】 dǎzhàn shiver；tremble；shudder

【打仗】 dǎzhàng fight；go to war；make war

【打招呼】 dǎ zhāo·hu 1.（问候）greet sb.；say hello；tip one's hat 2.（事先提醒）give a previous notice；warn

【打折扣】 dǎ zhékòu 1.（降低价格）sell at a discount；give a discount：打八折出售 sell at twenty per cent discount 2.（不完全按规定去做）fall short of a requirement or promise

【打针】 dǎzhēn 1.（让人给打针）have an injection 2.（给人打针）give an injection

【打钟】 dǎzhōng ring the bell

【打肿脸充胖子】 dǎ zhǒng liǎn chōng pàng·zi puff oneself up to one's own cost

【打中】 dǎzhòng hit the mark；hit the target；hit

【打主意】 dǎ zhǔ·yi 1.（想办法）think of a plan；evolve an idea 2.（设法谋取）try to obtain；seek

【打住】 dǎzhù come to a halt；（in speech or writing）stop

【打转】 dǎzhuàn spin；rotate；revolve

【打桩】 dǎzhuāng pile；drive piles

【打桩船】 dǎzhuāngchuán floating pile driver

【打桩机】 dǎzhuāngjī pile driver；pile engine

【打字】 dǎzì typewrite；type

【打字机】 dǎzìjī typewriter

【打字色带】 dǎzì sèdài typewriter ribbon

【打字员】 dǎzìyuán typist

【打字纸】 dǎzìzhǐ typing-paper

大（dà） 1.（不小）big；large；great：一所～房子 a big house / 世界～战 the Great War / 哪家公司是中国最～的计算机生产者？Which company is the largest computer manufacturer in China？ 2.（超过一般）heavy（rain，etc.）；strong（wind，etc.）；loud 3.（规模大）general；main；major：～路 main road；highway 4.（大小）size 5.（年龄）age；old：你多～了？How old are you？ 6.（程度深）greatly；fully 7.（排行第一）eldest：我～哥 my eldest brother
（另见“大”dài）

【大案】 dà'àn major case；legal cases of grave nature

【大白】 dàbái 1.（完全清楚）come out；become known：真相～ the truth has become known 2.（白垩）whiting

【大白菜】 dàbáicài Chinese cabbage

【大百科全书】 Dàbǎikē Quánshū encyclopedia；encyclopedic（adj.）

【大败】 dàbài 1.（打败）defeat utterly；put to rout 2.（被打败）suffer a crushing defeat

【大班】 dàbān 1.(幼儿园的) the top class in a kindergarten 2.(洋行经理) manager of a foreign firm 3.(舞厅领班) captain (of taxi dancers)

【大办】 dàbàn go in for sth. in a big way

【大半】 dàbàn 1.(过半数) more than half; greater part; most of: 他们～是青年人。Most of them are young. 2.(非常可能) very likely; most probably: 她～不来了。Most probably she isn't coming.

【大包干】 dàbāogān the all-round contract (system)

【大本营】 dàběnyíng 1.(最高统帅部) supreme headquarters 2.(登山营地) base camp

【大比例】 dàbǐlì high range

【大比武】 dàbǐwǔ demonstration and competition in military skill

【大便】 dàbiàn 1.(解大便) defecate; have a bowel movement; shit: ～干燥 (motions) be hard and dry 2.(屎) stool; human excrement; shit; feces

【大病】 dàbìng a serious illness: 患～ suffer from a serious illness

【大伯】 dàbó 1.(伯父) father's elder brother; uncle 2.(尊称) uncle

【大不了】 dà·buliǎo 1.(至多) at the worst; if the worst comes to the worst: ～再从头开始。If the worst comes to the worst, we'll start all over again. 2.(了不得) alarming; serious: 这不是什么～的成就。It's not so remarkable a success.

【大部分】 dàbù·fen greater part

【大材小用】 dàcái-xiǎoyòng put fine timber to petty use; use talented people for trivial tasks; waste one's talent on a petty job

【大菜】 dàcài 1.(主菜) main course 2.(西餐) Western meal; meal in Western style

【大长筒鼓】 dàchángtǒnggǔ 〈*Music*〉 large tom-tom

【大肠】 dàcháng 〈*Anat.*〉 large intestine

【大肠杆菌】 dàcháng gǎnjūn 〈*Med.*〉 colon bacillus

【大潮】 dàcháo spring tide

【大车】 dàchē 1.(畜力车) cart; dray: 赶～ drive a cart 2.(火车司机) engine driver 3.(轮机长) chief engineer (of a ship)

【大臣】 dàchén minister

【大成问题】 dà chéng wèntí very questionable; very doubtful; in doubt

【大乘】 dàchéng 〈*Buddhism*〉 Mahayana; Great Vehicle

【大吃大喝】 dàchī-dàhē eat and drink extravagantly; be spendthrift in feasting

【大吃一惊】 dàchī-yījīng be startled at; be taken aback; be astounded at

【大出血】 dàchūxuè 〈*Med.*〉 massive hemorrhage

【大处不算小处算】 dàchù bù suàn xiǎochù suàn penny-wise and pound-foolish

【大处着眼,小处着手】 dàchù-zhúoyǎn, xiǎochù-zhúoshǒu keep the general goal in sight and take the daily tasks in hand

【大串联】 dàchuànlián exchange experience widely: 世界～ exchange experience on the worldscale

【大吹大擂】 dàchuī-dàléi make a great fanfare; make a big noise

【大慈大悲】 dàcí-dàbēi infinitely compassionate; infinitely merciful

【大葱】 dàcōng green Chinese onion; fistular onion

【大打出手】 dàdǎ-chūshǒu strike violently; attack brutally

【大大】 dàdà greatly; enormously

【大…大…】 dà…dà… (表示规模大、程度深) ～吵～闹 kick up a row; make a scene / ～鱼～肉 plenty of meat and fish; rich food

【大大咧咧】 dà·da-liēliē (of a person) careless; casual

【大袋鼠】 dàdàishǔ kangaroo

【大胆】 dàdǎn bold; daring; audacious: ～的行动 a daring act / ～革新 bold innovation / ～探索 be bold in exploring new ways / ～吸收先进的经营方式和管理方法 not hesitate to adopt advanced methods of operation or management techniques

【大刀】 dàdāo broad sword

【大刀阔斧】 dàdāo-kuòfǔ bold and resolute; drastic

【大倒】 dàdǎo big profiteer; hardened speculator

【大道理】 dàdào·li general principle: 讲～ speak on the general principle

【大灯】 dàdēng 〈*Auto*〉 headlight
【大敌】 dàdí formidable enemy; archenemy
【大抵】 dàdǐ generally speaking; in the main; on the whole: ～相同 more or less the same
【大地】 dàdì the earth; mother earth; the world: 春回～。Spring returns to the earth.
【大典】 dàdiǎn **1.** (隆重典礼) grand ceremony **2.** (经典) a body of classical writings; canon
【大调】 dàdiào 〈*Music*〉 major: A～ A major / C～ C major
【大动脉】 dàdòngmài **1.** 〈*Anat.*〉 main artery; aorta **2.** (比喻) artery: 交通～ main artery of communications
【大豆】 dàdòu soybean; soya bean
【大都】 dàdōu for the most part; mostly
【大都市】 dàdūshì metropolis; a large city
【大度】 dàdù 〈*written*〉 magnanimous; generous
【大队】 dàduì **1.** 〈*Mil.*〉 a military unit corresponding to the battalion or regiment; group **2.** (人数多) a large body of; a large contingent of
【大多】 dàduō for the most part; mostly
【大多数】 dàduōshù great majority; the bulk; vast majority: 绝～ the overwhelming majority / 在～情况下 in most of the cases
【大而全】 dà'érquán large and complete; self-sufficient
【大发雷霆】 dàfā-léitíng be furious; fly into a rage; bawl at sb. angrily
【大方】 dàfāng 〈*wirtten*〉 expert; scholar: 贻笑～ incur the ridicule of experts
【大方】 dà·fang **1.** (不吝啬) generous; liberal: 用钱～ be openhanded **2.** (不拘束) natural and poised; easy; unaffected: 举止～ have an easy manner; have poise **3.** (不俗气) in good taste; tasteful: 式样～ style in good taste; graceful in style
【大方向】 dàfāngxiàng general orientation
【大放厥词】 dàfàng-juécí talk a lot of nonsense; spout a stream of empty rhetoric
【大放异彩】 dàfàng-yìcǎi yield unusually brilliant results
【大粪】 dàfèn human excrement; night soil
【大风】 dàfēng **1.** (八级风) fresh gale **2.** (强风) gale; strong wind
【大风大浪】 dàfēng-dàlàng wind and waves; great storms
【大风警报】 dàfēng jǐngbào gale warning
【大幅度】 dàfúdù by a wide margin; by a big margin; substantially: ～提高 be increased by a big margin / ～增长 increase by a wide margin; rise by a big margin
【大副】 dàfù first mate; chief mate; mate; chief officer
【大腹便便】 dàfù-piánpián potbellied; big-bellied
【大概】 dàgài **1.** (大致内容, 大致情况) general idea; broad outline: 只知道个～ have only a general idea **2.** (大约) general; rough; approximate **3.** (可能) probably; most likely; presumably
【大干】 dàgàn work energetically; go all out; make an all-out effort
【大纲】 dàgāng outline: 教学～ teaching program
【大钢琴】 dàgāngqín grand piano
【大搞】 dàgǎo do sth. vigorously; get sth. into full swing
【大哥】 dàgē **1.** (排行最大的哥哥) eldest brother **2.** (尊称) elder brother
【大哥大】 dàgēdà mobile phone
【大歌剧】 dàgējù 〈*Music*〉 grand opera
【大革命】 dàgémìng great revolution
【大公无私】 dàgōng-wúsī **1.** (没有私心) selfless; unselfish **2.** (公正) perfectly impartial
【大功】 dàgōng great merit; extraordinary service
【大功告成】 dàgōng-gàochéng (of a project, work, etc.) be accomplished; be crowned with success
【大股东】 dàgǔdōng senior partner
【大鼓】 dàgǔ bass drum
【大观】 dàguān grand sight; magnificent spectacle: 蔚为～ present a magnificent spectacle
【大管】 dàguǎn 〈*Music*〉 bassoon
【大规模】 dàguīmó large-scale; extensive; massive; mass
【大规模集成电路】 dàguīmó jíchéng diànlù large-scale integrated circuit (LSIC)
【大规模生产】 dàguīmó shēngchǎn mass pro-

duction; commercial production

【大锅饭】 dàguōfàn food prepared in a large canteen caldron; mess: 吃～ eat in the canteen the same as everyone else; "eating from the big public pot"

【大国】 dàguó power; leading powers; great power

【大国沙文主义】 dàguó shāwén zhǔyì great-nation chauvinism

【大过】 dàguò serious offense: 记～ record a serious mistake

【大海】 dàhǎi sea; ocean

【大海捞针】 dàhǎi-lāozhēn fish for a needle in the ocean; look for a needle in a haystack

【大寒】 dàhán the Great Cold (1月 20-21 日交节)

【大喊大叫】 dàhǎn-dàjiào 1.(大声喊叫) shout at the top of one's voice 2.(大力宣传) conduct vigorous propaganda

【大好】 dàhǎo very good; excellent: ～风光 a superb view / ～时机 opportune moment; golden opportunity; finest hour

【大号】 dàhào 1.(大的) large size: ～的衬衫 large-size shirt 2.(名字) your name 3. 〈*Music*〉 tuba; bass horn

【大合唱】 dàhéchàng cantata; chorus

【大亨】 dàhēng tycoon; big shot; bigwig; magnate: 海运～ shipping tycoon

【大轰大嗡】 dàhōng-dàwēng make a terrific din; raise a hue and cry

【大红】 dàhóng bright red; scarlet

【大后方】 dàhòufāng rear area

【大后年】 dàhòunián three years from now

【大后天】 dàhòutiān three days from now

【大户】 dàhù 1.(有钱人家) rich family; big family 2.(人口多) big family: ～人家 a wealthy and influential family; a family of long standing 3.(指单位或个人) 买…～ big buyer / 生产～ big producer / 用…～ large user; big consumer / 用电～ a big power-consumer

【大话】 dàhuà big talk; tall talk; boast; bragging: 说～ talk big; boast

【大黄鱼】 dàhuángyú yellow croacker

【大茴香】 dàhuíxiāng anise; star anise

【大会】 dàhuì 1.(全体会议) plenary session; general membership meeting 2.(群众大会) mass meeting; mass rally

【大会战】 dàhuìzhàn a decisive battle

【大火】 dàhuǒ a big fire; a conflagration

【大伙儿】 dàhuǒr we all; you all; everybody

【大祸】 dàhuò great misfortune; calamity; disaster: ～临头。A great misfortune has come.

【大计】 dàjì a major program of lasting importance; a matter of fundamental importance; matters of vital importance

【大家】 dàjiā 1.(专家) great master; authority 2.(大伙) all; everybody: ～的事 everybody's business

【大家庭】 dàjiātíng big family; community

【大奖】 dàjiǎng grand prix; grand prize

【大奖赛】 dàjiǎngsài grand prix; grand prize

【大教堂】 dàjiàotáng cathedral

【大街】 dàjiē main street; street; avenue: ～小巷 streets and lanes / 逛～ go for a walk in the street

【大节】 dàjié political integrity

【大捷】 dàjié great victory

【大姐】 dàjiě 1.(最大的姐姐) eldest sister 2.(尊称) elder sister

【大惊小怪】 dàjīng-xiǎoguài be surprised at sth. perfectly normal; be alarmed at sth. perfectly normal; make a fuss

【大局】 dàjú overall situation; general situation; whole situation: 顾全～ take the overall situation into account

【大举】 dàjǔ carry out (a military operation) on a large scale: ～进攻 attack in force; mount a large-scale offensive

【大军】 dàjūn 1.(主力部队) main forces; army 2.(人数众多) large contingent

【大卡】 dàkǎ 〈*Physics*〉 Calorie; kilocalorie

【大开眼界】 dàkāi-yǎnjiè eye-opening; widen one's horizon; an eye-opener

【大考】 dàkǎo end-of-term examination; final examination

【大课】 dàkè a lecture given to a large number of students; enlarged class

【大跨度】 dàkuàdù 〈*Archit.*〉 large-span

【大快人心】 dàkuài-rénxīn affording general satisfaction; most gratifying to the people; to the immense satisfaction of the people

【大款】 dàkuǎn rich people; moneybags

【大老粗】 dàlǎocū uncouth fellow; uneducated person; rough and ready fellow

【大礼堂】 dàlǐtáng hall; auditorium

【大理石】 dàlǐshí marble

【大力】 dàlì 1.(大的力量) great strength 2.(花大力气) devote major efforts to: ~支持 give energetic support

【大力士】 dàlìshì a man of unusual strength

【大丽花】 dàlìhuā 〈*Bot.*〉 dahlia

【大梁】 dàliáng 1.〈*Archit.*〉 girder 2.〈*Auto*〉 frame 3.〈*Bicycle*〉 cross bar

【大量】 dàliàng 1.(指数量) a large number; a great quantity: ~财富 enormous wealth; large fortune / ~生产轿车 mass-produce cars 2.(指气量) generous; magnanimous: 宽宏~ magnanimous; large-minded

【大龄青年】 dàlíng qīngnián unmarried youth exceeding the normal matrimonial age

【大楼】 dàlóu multi-storied building: 办公~ office building / 教学~ classroom building / 居民~ apartment house; block of flats

【大陆】 dàlù continent; mainland; continental (adj.)

【大陆架】 dàlùjià 〈*Geol.*〉 continental shelf

【大陆棚】 dàlùpéng 〈*Geol.*〉 continental shelf

【大陆漂移】 dàlù piāoyí 〈*Geol.*〉 continental drift; continental displacement

【大陆坡】 dàlùpō 〈*Geol.*〉 continental slope

【大陆性气候】 dàlùxìng qìhòu continental climate

【大路】 dàlù main road; highroad

【大路菜】 dàlùcài common vegetable; popular vegetable

【大路货】 dàlùhuò popular goods of dependable quality; popular commodities

【大略】 dàlüè 1.(大概) general idea; broad outline 2.(大约) generally; roughly; approximately

【大妈】 dàmā 1.(伯母) father's elder brother's wife; aunt 2.(尊称年长的妇人) aunt

【大麻】 dàmá 1.(线麻) hemp 2.(毒品) marijuana

【大麻哈鱼】 dàmáhǎyú chum salmon

【大麦】 dàmài barley

【大忙】 dàmáng very busy: ~季节 rush season; busy season

【大帽子】 dàmào·zi political label: 拿~吓唬人 try to intimidate people by pinning political labels

【大门】 dàmén entrance door; front door; gate

【大梦初醒】 dàmèng-chūxǐng wake up from a dream; wake up to; dawn on

【大米】 dàmǐ (husked) rice

【大面儿】 dàmiànr 〈*dial.*〉 general appearance; surface

【大面积】 dàmiànjī large tracts of land; large area

【大名】 dàmíng 1.(正式名字) one's formal personal name 2.〈*politeness*〉 your (given) name

【大名鼎鼎】 dàmíng-dǐngdǐng famous; celebrated; well-known

【大模大样】 dàmú-dàyàng in an ostentatious manner; with a swagger

【大拇指】 dà·mǔzhǐ thumb: 翘起~ give the thumb-up to

【大男大女】 dànán-dànǚ unmarried boys and girls over the normal matrimonial age

【大难】 dànàn catastrophe; disaster: ~不死 escape from death in a great catastrophe

【大脑】 dànǎo 〈*Anat.*〉 cerebrum; brain

【大脑皮层】 dànǎo-pícéng 〈*Anat.*〉 cerebral cortex

【大逆不道】 dànì-bùdào treason and heresy; worst offense; greatest outrage

【大年初一】 dànián chūyī first day of the lunar year; lunar New Year's Day

【大年夜】 dàniányè lunar New Year's Eve

【大娘】 dàniáng 1.(伯母) wife of father's elder brother; aunt 2.(尊称) aunt

【大农业】 dànóngyè big agriculture; agriculture in a broad sense

【大拍卖】 dàpāimài sell at a bargain

【大炮】 dàpào 1.〈*Mil.*〉 artillery; big gun; cannon 2.(好发表激烈意见的人) one who speaks boastfully or forcefully; one who noisily overstates things

【大批】 dàpī large quantities of; amounts of; numbers of: ~定货 large order / ~现钞 large sum in ready money

【大屏幕电视机】 dàpíngmù diànshìjī large-screen receiver

【大谱表】 dàpǔbiǎo 〈*Music*〉 great stave
【大瀑布】 dàpùbù cataract
【大起大落】 dà qǐ dà luò rise and fall sharply and quickly; sharp and quick change
【大气】 dàqì **1.** (空气) atmosphere; air; atmospheric (adj.) **2.** (沉重的呼吸) heavy breathing
【大气层】 dàqìcéng atmospheric layer; atmosphere
【大气尘埃】 dàqì chén'āi air-borne dust
【大气臭氧层】 dàqì chòuyǎngcéng atmospheric ozone layer
【大气候】 dàqìhòu **1.** 〈*Meteorol.*〉 macroclimate **2.** (指形势或思潮) general tendency; general political climate: 国际～ international general tendency
【大气压】 dàqìyā atmospheric pressure; atmosphere
【大钱】 dàqián **1.** (大面值的钱) bank note with big face value **2.** (大量的钱) a lot of money: 挣～ make a lot of money
【大前年】 dàqiánnián three years ago
【大前天】 dàqiántiān three days ago
【大庆】 dàqìng **1.** (大规模庆祝) grand celebration of an important event; great occasion: 50年～ the festive occasion of the 50th anniversary **2.** (老人寿辰) birthday: 80～ eightieth birthday
【大秋】 dàqiū **1.** (秋收季节) harvest season in autumn **2.** (秋收) crops harvested in autumn; autumn harvest
【大秋作物】 dàqiū zuòwù autumn-harvested crops
【大曲】 dàqū **1.** (指酒曲) yeast for making hard liquor **2.** (指曲酒) liquor made with yeast
【大全】 dàquán complete works of; a complete collection of
【大权】 dàquán power over major issues; authority: ～独揽 arrogate all authority to oneself / ～旁落。Power has fallen into the hands of others.
【大人】 dà·ren adult; grown-up
【大人物】 dàrénwù VIP; great personage; important person; big shot
【大容量】 dàróngliàng large capacity; high capacity
【大三弦】 dàsānxián 〈*Music*〉 *dasanxian*; 3-stringed Chinese violin
【大扫除】 dàsǎochú great cleaning; general cleaning; thorough cleanup
【大嫂】 dàsǎo **1.** (大哥的妻子) eldest brother's wife; sister-in-law **2.** (称呼) elder sister
【大厦】 dàshà large building; mansion
【大少爷】 dàshào·ye **1.** (主人的大儿子) eldest son (of a rich family) **2.** (挥霍的人) a spoilt son of a rich family; spendthrift: ～作风 behavior typical of the spoilt son of a rich family; extravagant ways
【大赦】 dàshè amnesty; general pardon
【大赦令】 dàshèlìng order of general pardon
【大婶儿】 dàshěnr aunt
【大声疾呼】 dàshēng-jíhū raise a cry of warning; loudly appeal to the public
【大牲口】 dàshēng·kou draught animal
【大失所望】 dàshī-suǒwàng greatly disappointed; to one's great disappointment
【大师】 dàshī **1.** (指造诣深的人) great master; master: 语言～ a great master of linguistics / 艺术～ master of arts **2.** (对和尚的尊称) Great Master
【大师傅】 dà·shi·fu (指厨师) cook
【大使】 dàshǐ ambassador (m.); ambassadress (f.): 特命全权～ ambassador extraordinary and plenipotentiary / 中国驻俄罗斯～ Chinese ambassador in Russia / 被任命为驻…～ be appointed ambassador to ... / 互派～ exchange ambassadors
【大使馆】 dàshǐguǎn embassy: 中国驻法国～ Chinese embassy in France
【大使级】 dàshǐjí ambassadorial: ～会谈 ambassadorial talks
【大使衔】 dàshǐxián ambassadorial rank: 获得～ achieve ambassadorial rank
【大事】 dàshì **1.** (重大的事) great event; major important matter; major issue **2.** (总形势) overall situation: ～不好。A disaster is imminent. **3.** (大搞) in a big way: ～宣传 play up; ballyhoo
【大势】 dàshì general trend of events: ～所趋 the trend of the times
【大是大非】 dàshì-dàfēi major issues of principle; cardinal questions of right and wrong
【大事化小，小事化了】 dàshì huà xiǎo, xiǎoshì

huà liǎo turn big problems into small problems and small problems into no problems at all

【大事记】 dàshìjì chronicle of events

【大手大脚】 dàshǒu-dàjiǎo wasteful; extravagant

【大叔】 dàshū 1.（父亲的弟弟）younger brother of one's father; uncle 2.（尊称）uncle

【大暑】 dàshǔ the Great heat（7月22-24日交节）

【大水】 dàshuǐ flood; inundation：发～ flood; inundate / 河水冲决堤岸时，全城发了～。The whole town flooded when the river burst its banks.

【大肆】 dàsì without restraint; wantonly：～叫嚣 set up a great clamor about; allege vociferously / ～污蔑 slander violently / ～宣扬 indulge in unbridled propaganda for; give enormous publicity to

【大蒜】 dàsuàn garlic

【大踏步】 dàtàbù in big strides

【大台阶】 dàtáijiē major progress：经济建设上了一个～ have made major progress in developing the economy

【大…特…】 dà…tè… 大错特错 make a gross error / 大谈特谈 talk at length

【大提琴】 dàtíqín violoncello; cello

【大体】 dàtǐ 1.（指道理）cardinal principle; general interest：识～ have the cardinal principles in mind 2.（大致）roughly; more or less; on the whole; by and large; for the most part：～上正确 generally correct

【大田】 dàtián land for growing field crops

【大田作物】 dàtián zuòwù field crop

【大厅】 dàtīng hall; lounge

【大庭广众】 dà tíng guǎng zhòng（before）a big crowd;（on）a public occasion

【大同小异】 dà tóng xiǎo yì largely identical but with minor differences; alike except for slight differences; very much the same

【大头菜】 dàtóucài 1.〈*Bot*.〉rutabaga 2.（结球甘蓝）cabbage

【大头钉】 dàtóudīng tack

【大头针】 dàtóuzhēn pin

【大团圆】 dàtuányuán 1.（指团聚）happy reunion 2.（美好结局）happy ending

【大腿】 dàtuǐ thigh

【大腿骨】 dàtuǐgǔ femur

【大王】 dàwáng king; magnate：石油～ oil king / 船舶～ shipping magnate

【大无畏】 dàwúwèi dauntless; utterly fearless; indomitable

【大西洋】 Dàxīyáng the Atlantic（Ocean）

【大喜】 dàxǐ great rejoicing

【大虾】 dàxiā prawn

【大显身手】 dàxiǎn-shēnshǒu display one's skill to the full

【大显神通】 dàxiǎn-shéntōng give full play to one's remarkable skill; give full play to one's remarkable abilities

【大相径庭】 dàxiāng-jìngtíng 〈*written*〉be widely divergent

【大象】 dàxiàng elephant

【大小】 dàxiǎo 1.（程度大小）big or small：～工厂10座 ten factories of varying sizes 2.（辈份高低）degree of seniority 3.（大人和孩子）adults and children

【大校】 dàxiào 1.（陆军）Senior Colonel 2.（空军）Air Senior Colonel 3.（海军）Senior Captain

【大协作】 dàxiézuò large-scale cooperation; a major pooling of efforts

【大写】 dàxiě 1.（指壹贰叁肆伍陆柒捌玖拾）the capital form of a Chinese numeral：～金额 amount in words 2.（指ABCD）capitalization

【大写字母】 dàxiě zìmǔ capital letter; majuscule

【大兴】 dàxīng go in for sth. in a big way：～水利 large-scale building of water conservancy projects / ～土木 go in for large-scale construction

【大兴安岭】 dàxīng'ānlǐng 〈place〉Da Hinggan Ling

【大猩猩】 dàxīng·xing gorilla

【大型】 dàxíng large-scale; large：～企业 large enterprise

【大型团体操】 dàxíng tuántǐcāo mass calisthenics

【大熊猫】 dàxióngmāo panda; giant panda

【大熊座】 dàxióngzuò 〈*Astron*.〉Ursa Major

【大修】 dàxiū 〈*Mech*.〉overhaul; heavy repair

【大选】 dàxuǎn general election
【大学】 dàxué university; college: 北京～ Peking University / 清华～ Tsinghua University / 师范～ normal university
【大学生】 dàxuéshēng student; university student; college student: 低年级～ lower grade students / 高年级～ upper grade students; higher grade students
【大学预科】 dàxué yùkē preparatory course
【大雪】 dàxuě the Great Snow (12 月 6-8 日交节)
【大牙】 dàyá 1.(槽牙) molar 2.(门牙) front tooth: 叫人笑掉～ make a laughingstock of oneself
【大雅】 dàyǎ 〈*written*〉 elegance; refinement; good taste
【大言不惭】 dà yán bù cán brag unblushingly; talk big
【大雁】 dàyàn wild goose
【大羊驼】 dàyángtuó llama
【大洋】 dàyáng 1.(海洋) ocean 2.(银元) silver dollar
【大洋洲】 Dàyángzhōu Oceania; Oceanic (adj.)
【大爷】 dà·ye 1.(伯父) father's elder brother; uncle 2.(尊称) uncle
【大业】 dàyè great cause; great undertaking: 创～ become pioneers in a great undertaking
【大衣】 dàyī overcoat; topcoat: 夹～ light overcoat / 棉～ cotton-padded overcoat
【大衣钩】 dàyīgōu coat hook
【大衣架】 dàyījià coat hanger
【大姨】 dàyí mother's eldest sister; aunt
【大义】 dàyì cardinal principles of righteousness; righteous cause: 深明～ be deeply conscious of the righteousness of a cause
【大义凛然】 dà yì lǐnrán inspiring awe by upholding justice
【大意】 dàyì (主要的意思) general idea; main points; gist; tenor: 一本书的～ the gist of a book
【大意】 dà·yi (疏忽) careless; negligent; inattentive
【大音阶】 dàyīnjiē 〈*Music*〉 major scale
【大印】 dàyìn the seal of power or authority
【大有好处】 dàyǒu-hǎochù be of great benefit to; be of much good
【大有可为】 dàyǒu-kěwéi have bright prospects; be well worth doing
【大有文章】 dàyǒu-wénzhāng there's sth. behind all this; there's more to it than meets the eye
【大有作为】 dàyǒu-zuòwéi there is plenty of scope for one's talents; be able to develop one's ability to the full
【大于】 dàyú is more than (符号为 >)
【大于或等于】 dàyú huò děngyú is more than or equal to (符号为 ≥)
【大雨】 dàyǔ heavy rain: ～倾盆 rain cats and dogs; a pouring rain
【大圆】 dàyuán great circle
【大圆航线】 dàyuán hángxiàn great-circle line
【大约】 dàyuē 1.(大概) approximately; about 2.(很可能) probably
【大展宏图】 dàzhǎn-hóngtú realize one's ambition; ride on the crest of success
【大战】 dàzhàn great war
【大张旗鼓】 dàzhāng-qígǔ on a grand scale; in a big way
【大丈夫】 dàzhàng·fu real man; a man (of real worth)
【大指】 dàzhǐ thumb
【大治】 dàzhì great order: 天下～ run the country well
【大志】 dàzhì high aim; lofty aim; exalted ambition; high aspirations: 有～ aim high
【大致】 dàzhì roughly; approximately; more or less: ～相同 roughly the same
【大中型企业】 dàzhōngxíng qǐyè big and medium-sized enterprises
【大众】 dàzhòng the masses; the people; the public; the broad masses of the people
【大众传媒】 dàzhòng chuánméi mass media
【大众化】 dàzhònghuà popular; in a popular style
【大众科学】 dàzhòng kēxué popular science
【大洲】 dàzhōu continent; continental (adj.)
【大专】 dàzhuān 1.(高等专科学校) junior colleges 2.(指学生) students of junior colleges; graduates of junior colleges
【大专生】 dàzhuānshēng students of junior colleges; graduates of junior colleges
【大专院校】 dàzhuān yuànxiào universities

and colleges; institutions of higher education

【大资本家】 dàzīběnjiā big capitalist; monopolist

【大字报】 dàzìbào *dazibao*; big character poster

【大字标题】 dàzì biāotí banner headline; banner-line; streamer

【大自然】 dàzìrán nature：保护～ protect nature

【大宗】 dàzōng 1.（大批）a large amount; a large quantity 2.（数量最大的产品）staple：本地产品以茶叶为～。Tea is the staple crop here.

【大作】 dàzuò your article; your work

【大做文章】 dàzuò wénzhāng make a fuss; make a big issue; turn out much propaganda (about)

dai

呆［獃］（dāi） 1.（呆笨）slow-witted; dull 2.（发呆）blank; wooden 3.（在）stay：他只在那里～了几个星期。He stayed there only a few weeks.

【呆板】 dāibǎn stiff; inflexible; rigid; stereotyped

【呆滞】 dāizhì 1.（不灵活）dull; inert; lifeless：目光～ with a dull look in one's eyes 2.（不景气）dull; sluggish; stagnant; slack; idle：市场～ dull market

【呆子】 dāi·zi idiot; simpleton; blockhead

待（dāi） stay

【待会儿】 dāihuìr in a moment

（另见“待”dài）

歹（dǎi） bad; evil; vicious：好～不分 cannot distinguish the good from the bad

【歹徒】 dǎitú scoundrel; ruffian; hoodlums

逮（dǎi） capture; catch：猫～老鼠 cats catch mice / 那小偷被警察～住了。The thief has been seized by the policeman.

（另见“逮”dài）

傣（dǎi）

【傣族】 Dǎizú Dai（中国少数民族，主要分布在云南）

大（dài）

（另见“大”dà）

【大夫】 dài·fu doctor; physician

代（dài） 1.（代替）take the place of; be in place of 2.（代理）acting：～主席 acting president 3.（历史年代）historical period 4.（地质年代）era 5.（辈）generation：～～相传 pass on from generation to generation

【代办】 dàibàn 1.（替人）do sth. for sb.; act on sb's behalf 2.〈*Foreign Affairs*〉chargé d'affaires：临时～ chargé d'affaires ad interim

【代办处】 dàibànchù office of the chargé d'affaires

【代办所】 dàibànsuǒ agency：储蓄～ savings agency / 邮政～ postal agency

【代笔】 dàibǐ write on sb's behalf

【代表】 dàibiǎo 1.（指人）deputy; delegate; representative：常驻～ permanent representative; permanent delegate / 全国人大～ deputy to the National People's Congress / 首席～ chief delegate 2.（体现）represent; stand for：～时代精神 embody the spirit of the era 3.（替人办事或讲话）on behalf of; in the name of

【代表大会】 dàibiǎo dàhuì congress; representative assembly; representative conference：中国共产党全国～ the National Congress of the Communist Party of China

【代表权】 dàibiǎoquán representation

【代表人物】 dàibiǎo rénwù representative figure; representative personage; typical representative; leading exponent

【代表团】 dàibiǎotuán delegation; mission; deputation：专家～ expert attached to a delegation

【代表作】 dàibiǎozuò representative work

【代词】 dàicí pronoun

【代沟】 dàigōu generation gap; difference between two generations

【代购】 dàigòu buy on sb's behalf; act as a purchasing agent

【代管】 dàiguǎn manage, govern or administer on behalf of another

【代号】 dàihào code name

【代换】 dàihuàn 〈*Math*.〉substitute; substitution (n.)

【代价】 dàijià price; cost：不惜任何～ prepared to pay any price; at any cost; at all

costs / 付出很高～ pay a high price (for)
【代课】 dàikè take over a class for an absent teacher
【代课老师】 dàikè lǎoshī supply teacher
【代劳】 dàiláo do sth. for sb.; take trouble on sb's behalf
【代理】 dàilǐ 1.(代人负责) act on behalf of someone in a responsible position: ～部长 acting minister 2.(代表别人工作) act as agent; act as procurator
【代理人】 dàilǐrén agent; deputy; proxy; procurator; attorney
【代理商】 dàilǐshāng agent
【代理制】 dàilǐzhì agent system
【代码】 dàimǎ code
【代名词】 dàimíngcí 1.(替代说法) synonym 2.(代词) pronoun
【代培】 dàipéi directional training; commissioned to train personnel for other units
【代培生】 dàipéishēng trainee on contract
【代人受过】 dàirén shòuguò suffer for the faults of another; bear the blame for sb. else
【代售】 dàishòu be commissioned to sell sth.
【代数】 dàishù algebra; algebraic (adj.)
【代数项】 dàishùxiàng 〈*Math*.〉 algebraic term
【代替】 dàitì replace; substitute for; take the place of
【代位】 dàiwèi 〈*Law*〉 subrogate; subrogation (n.)
【代位继承】 dàiwèi jìchéng 〈*Law*〉 subrogation representation
【代销】 dàixiāo be commissioned to sell sth. (usu. as a sideline); act as a commission agent
【代销店】 dàixiāodiàn commission agent
【代谢】 dàixiè 1.(更替;取代) supersede; supersession (n.): 新旧事物的～ the supersession of the old by the new 2.〈*Biol*.〉 metabolize; metabolism (n.): 分解～ catabolism / 合成～ anabolism
【代谢物】 dàixièwù metabolite
【代行】 dàixíng act on sb's behalf: ～职权 function in an acting capacity
【代序】 dàixù an article used in lieu of a preface
【代言人】 dàiyánrén spokesman; mouthpiece
【代用】 dàiyòng substitute: ～材料 substitute materials; ersatz materials
【代用品】 dàiyòngpǐn substitute; ersatz
【代职】 dàizhí hold a position in an acting capacity
【代字号】 dàizìhào swung dash (符号为 ～)

玳[瑇] (dài)

【玳瑁】 dàimào hawksbill turtle

贷 (dài) 1.(贷款) loan 2.(借入) borrow 3.(借出) lend 4.(推卸) shift (responsibility); shirk: 责无旁～ be one's unshirkable responsibility; be duty-bound 5.(饶恕) pardon; forgive: 严惩不～ punish without mercy
【贷方】 dàifāng credit side; credit
【贷款】 dàikuǎn provide a loan; extend credit to; make an advance to; loan; credit: 无息和低息～ loans with no or low interest / 向银行～ get a bank loan

袋 (dài) 1.(口袋) bag; sack; pocket; pouch: 睡～ slipping bag / 衣～ pocket / 旅行～ travelling bag 2.〈*classifier*〉 两～水泥 two sacks of cement
【袋鼠】 dàishǔ kangaroo
【袋装】 dàizhuāng in bags: ～奶粉 milk powder in bags / ～水泥 sacked cement
【袋子】 dài·zi sack; bag

怠 (dài) idle; remiss; slack
【怠工】 dàigōng slow down; go slow: 消极～ be slack in work
【怠工者】 dàigōngzhě saboteur; slow-down striker
【怠慢】 dàimàn cold-shoulder; slight
【怠速】 dàisù 〈*Mech*.〉 idling speed
【怠速运行】 dàisù yùnxíng 〈*Mech*.〉 idle: 让发动机～一会儿。Let the engine idle for a minute.

带[帶] (dài) 1.(带子) belt; girdle; ribbon; band; tape: 录像～ video tape 2.(轮胎) tire: 自行车～ bicycle tire 3.(地带) zone; area; belt 4.(携带) take; bring; carry 5.(捎带) do sth. incidentally 6.(带有) bear; have: ～有时代的特点 bear the imprint of the times 7.(附带) having sth. attached; simultaneous 8.(带领)

lead; head **9.**（照顾）look after; bring up; raise

【带病】 dàibìng in spite of illness

【带到】 dàidào take to

【带电】 dàidiàn electrified; live; charged

【带电操作】 dàidiàn cāozuò 〈*Electr.*〉 hot line job; hot line work

【带动】 dàidòng drive; spur on; bring along

【带队】 dàiduì **1.**（带领队伍）lead a group of people **2.**（带队的人）the leader of a group of people

【带分数】 dàifēnshù mixed fraction

【带钢】 dàigāng 〈*Metall.*〉 strip steel; band steel

【带坏】 dàihuài lead astray; rub bad habits on an innocent companion

【带回】 dàihuí bring back

【带劲】 dàijìn **1.**（有劲头）energetic; forceful：走的更～ walk in more vigorous steps **2.**（来劲）interesting; exciting; wonderful：听起来非常～ simply wonderful to listen to it

【带菌】 dàijūn carry disease germs

【带菌者】 dàijūnzhě 〈*Med.*〉 carrier

【带来】 dàilái bring：改革～的深刻变化 the most profound change brought about by the reform

【带领】 dàilǐng lead; guide

【带路】 dàilù show the way; lead the way; act as a guide

【带路人】 dàilùrén guide

【带去】 dàiqù bring away; take along

【带伤】 dàishāng be wounded; be injured：腿部～ be wounded in the leg

【带头】 dàitóu take the lead; be the first; take the initiative; set an example：～发言 be the first to speak; break the ice / 起～作用 play a leading role

【带头人】 dàitóurén lead; initiator

【带徒弟】 dài tú·di take on an apprentice

【带土栽培】 dàitǔ zhāipéi 〈*Agric.*〉 ball-and-burlap planting

【带笑】 dàixiào smilingly; carrying a smile

【带孝】 dàixiào be in mourning; wear mourning for sb.

【带信儿】 dàixìnr bring a massage; bear a massage

【带鱼】 dàiyú cutlass fish; hairtail; ribbon-fish

【带状分布】 dàizhuàng fēnbù zonal distribution

【带状疱疹】 dàizhuàng pàozhěn 〈*Med.*〉 herpes zoster; shingles zoster

【带子】 dài·zi **1.**（条状物）belt; girdle; ribbon; band **2.**（录音带、录像带）tape

待（dài） **1.**（对待）treat; deal with **2.**（招待）entertain **3.**（等待；留待）wait for; await：尚～证实 yet to be confirmed / 有～改进 have yet to be improved **4.**（需要）need **5.**（打算）going to; about to

（另见"待"dāi）

【待毙】 dàibì await death; be a sitting duck

【待产室】 dàichǎnshì 〈*Med.*〉 labor room; pre-delivery room

【待机而动】 dàijī-érdòng wait for one's opportunity; bide one's time

【待建】 dàijiàn yet to be built

【待客】 dàikè entertain a guest

【待理不理】 dàilǐ-bùlǐ lukewarm reception; give the cold shoulder to sb.

【待领】 dàilǐng wait for claimant

【待命】 dàimìng await orders：原地～ stay where one is, pending further orders

【待人接物】 dàirén-jiēwù the way one gets along with people

【待续】 dàixù to be continued

【待业】 dàiyè unemployment; waiting for employment

【待业青年】 dàiyè qīngnián young people waiting for employment

【待业人员】 dàiyè rényuán people waiting for employment

【待用】 dàiyòng inactive; stand-by

【待遇】 dàiyù **1.**（对待；权利）treatment：优惠的～ preferential treatment / 最惠国～ most-favored-nation treatment **2.**（物质报酬）remuneration; pay; wages; salary：～菲薄 treatment shabby

逮（dài）

（另见"逮"dǎi）

【逮捕】 dàibǔ arrest; take into custody

【逮捕证】 dàibǔzhèng arrest warrant

戴（dài） **1.**（戴上）put on; wear：～上眼镜 put on glasses **2.**（戴着）wear; have on：～着头盔 helmeted **3.**（拥戴）respect;

honor

【戴绿帽】 dài lǜmào be a cuckold; be cuckolded

【戴帽子】 dài mào·zi 1.(戴上或戴着帽子) wear one's hat; put on one's hat 2.(加罪名) pin the label on sb.; stigmatize; falsely accuse sb. of a crime

【戴孝】 dàixiào wear mourning for sb.; be in mourning

【戴罪立功】 dàizuì-lìgōng atone for one's crimes by doing good deeds

dan

丹(dān) red

【丹顶鹤】 dāndǐnghè red-crowned crane

【丹毒】 dāndú 〈*Chin. Med.*〉 erysipelas

【丹方】 dānfāng 〈*written*〉 folk prescription

【丹青】 dānqīng 〈*written*〉 painting

【丹心】 dānxīn a loyal heart; loyalty: 一片～ complete devotion; deep-seated loyalty

【丹田】 dāntián the pubic region

担[擔](dān) 1.(挑) carry on a shoulder pole 2.(担负; 承当) take on; undertake: ～重担 bear a heavy burden

(另见"担"dàn)

【担保】 dānbǎo assure; guarantee; vouch for

【担保书】 dānbǎoshū letter of guarantee

【担不是】 dān bù·shi take the blame

【担待】 dāndài 1.(担负) take the responsibility 2.(原谅) excuse: 请您～一下。Please excuse me.

【担当】 dāndāng take on; undertake; assume: ～重任 take on heavy responsibilities

【担风险】 dān fēngxiǎn take risks; face the risk (of doing sth.); assume the risk (of doing sth.)

【担负】 dānfù bear; shoulder; take on; be charged with: ～费用 bear an expense / ～责任 shoulder responsibility

【担架】 dānjià stretcher; litter: 抬在～上 be carried on a stretcher

【担惊受怕】 dānjīng-shòupà feel alarmed; be in a state of anxiety

【担任】 dānrèn assume the office of; hold the post of: ～裁判 serve as referee; act as referee / ～会议主席 take the chair

【担心】 dānxīn worry; feel anxious: ～她的健康 worry about her health

【担忧】 dānyōu worry; be anxious

单[單](dān) 1.(一个) one; single 2.(奇数) odd: ～号 odd number / ～日 odd-numbered days 3.(单独) singly; alone 4.(只;光) only; alone 5.(简单) simple 6.(单薄) thin; weak 7.(只有一层) unlined: ～衣 unlined jacket 8.(单子) sheet 9.(清单) bill; list: 工资～ pay sheet

【单板机】 dānbǎnjī 〈*Computer*〉 single board computer

【单薄】 dānbó 1.(衣服薄而且少) thin: 穿得～ be too thinly clad 2.(弱) thin and weak; frail: 力量～ weak in strength / 身体～ have a poor physique 3.(内容不充实) insubstantial; flimsy; thin

【单倍体】 dānbèitǐ 〈*Biol.*〉 monoploid

【单边】 dānbiān unilateral

【单边带】 dānbiāndài 〈*Communication*〉 single sideband

【单钹】 dānbó 〈*Music*〉 cymbal

【单车】 dānchē 1.(指单独一辆铁路机车) a engine 2.(指单独一辆汽车) truck; bus; car

【单程】 dānchéng one way

【单程车票】 dānchéng chēpiào one-way ticket; single ticket

【单纯】 dānchún 1.(简单纯一) simple; pure: 像孩子一样～ as simple as child 2.(仅仅) alone; purely; merely

【单词】 dāncí 1.〈*Linguis.*〉 individual word; word 2.(一个词素的词) single-morpheme word

【单词表】 dāncíbiǎo word list

【单打】 dāndǎ 〈*Sports*〉 singles: 男子～ men's singles / 女子～ women's singles

【单打边线】 dāndǎ biānxiàn 〈*Tennis*〉 singles sideline

【单单】 dāndān only; alone

【单调】 dāndiào monotonous; dull; drab: 色彩～ dull coloring

【单独】 dāndú alone; by oneself; on one's own; single-handed; independent

【单独行动】 dāndú xíngdòng take independent action; act by oneself

【单方面】 dānfāngmiàn one-sided; unilateral: ～停火 cease-fire carried out by one side only

【单放机】 dānfàngjī walkman

【单飞】 dānfēi 〈*Aeron.*〉 solo flight

【单峰驼】 dānfēngtuó dromedary camel

【单干】 dāngàn **1.**(单独干活) work on one's own; go it alone; work by oneself; do sth. single-handed **2.**(个体农户) individual farming

【单缸】 dāngāng 〈*Mech.*〉 one-cylinder; single-cylinder

【单杠】 dāngàng **1.**(体操器械) horizontal bar **2.**(体操项目) horizontal bar gymnastics

【单个儿】 dāngèr **1.**(独自一个) individually; alone **2.**(成套或成对中的一个) an odd one

【单工】 dāngōng 〈*Electr.*〉 simplex

【单轨】 dānguǐ single track

【单轨铁路】 dānguǐ tiělù single track railway

【单果】 dānguǒ 〈*Bot.*〉 single fruit

【单号】 dānhào odd numbers (of tickets, seats, etc.)

【单簧管】 dānhuángguǎn 〈*Music*〉 clarinet

【单机】 dānjī **1.**(指单独一辆铁路机车) an engine **2.**(指单独一辆汽车) truck; bus; car

【单价】 dānjià **1.**〈*Econ.*〉 unit price **2.**〈*Chem.*〉〈*Biol.*〉 univalent **3.**(价格) at (符号为 @)

【单间儿】 dānjiānr separate room

【单脚旋转】 dānjiǎo xuánzhuǎn 〈*Skating*〉 pivot

【单镜头反光照相机】 dānjìngtóu fǎnguāng zhàoxiàngjī single-lens reflex camera

【单据】 dānjù receipts; bills; vouchers; invoices

【单恋】 dānliàn one-sided love; unrequited love

【单轮自行车】 dānlún zìxíngchē unicycle

【单门独户】 dān mén dú hù a single isolated house

【单片机】 dānpiànjī 〈*Computer*〉 microcontroller

【单亲】 dānqīn single parent

【单亲家庭】 dānqīn jiātíng single parent family

【单人床】 dānrénchuáng single bed

【单人独马】 dān rén dú mǎ single-handed

【单人房间】 dānrén fángjiān a single-bed room; single room

【单人舞】 dānrénwǔ solo dance: 跳～ dance a solo

【单日】 dānrì odd-numbered days (of the month)

【单色光】 dānsèguāng 〈*Physics*〉 monochromatic light

【单身】 dānshēn **1.**(没结婚的) unmarried; single **2.**(不跟家属住在一起) not be with one's family; live alone

【单身汉】 dānshēnhàn bachelor

【单身宿舍】 dānshēn sùshè quarters for single men or women; bachelor quarters

【单声道录音机】 dānshēngdào lùyīnjī monophonic recorder

【单数】 dānshù **1.**(指 1, 3, 5, 7, 9 等) odd number **2.**〈*Linguis.*〉 singular number; singular (adj.)

【单位】 dānwèi **1.**(计量单位) unit: 货币～ monetary unit **2.**(部门) unit: 超编～ overstaffed units / 满编～ full-staffed units / 缺编～ under-staffed units / 基层～ basic unit; grass-roots unit / 行政～ administrative unit

【单线】 dānxiàn **1.**(单一的线) single line **2.**(单独联系) one and only one line (link): 与…保持～联系 keep the single-line link with sb. **3.**(单向) single track

【单线铁路】 dānxiàn tiělù single-track railway

【单相思】 dānxiāngsī unrequited love

【单项】 dānxiàng 〈*Sports*〉 individual event

【单项比赛】 dānxiàng bǐsài 〈*Sports*〉 individual competition

【单向】 dānxiàng one-way; unidirectional

【单相】 dānxiàng single-phase; monophase

【单行本】 dānxíngběn separate edition; offprint

【单行路】 dānxínglù one-way road; one-way street

【单行线】 dānxíngxiàn one-way; one-way traffic

【单一】 dānyī single; unitary: ～汇率 unified foreign exchange rate / ～经济 single-product economy

【单衣】 dānyī unlined garment

【单翼机】 dānyìjī 〈*Aeron.*〉 monoplane

【单引号】 dānyǐnhào single quotation marks (符号为‘ ’)

【单元】 dānyuán unit：28号楼12～302号 No. 302, Entrance 12, Building 28

【单子】 dān·zi 1.(纸) list; bill form 2.(床单) bed sheet

【单作】 dānzuò 〈*Agric.*〉 monoculture; single seeding

【单座】 dānzuò 〈*Motorcycle*〉 solo seat

眈 (dān)

【眈眈】 dāndān glaring covetously; eying greedily：虎视～～ glare like a tiger eying its prey

耽[躭[1]] (dān) 1.(拖延) delay 2.(入迷；沉溺) abandon oneself to; indulge in

【耽搁】 dān·ge 1.(停留) stop over; stay 2.(拖延) delay

【耽误】 dān·wu delay; hold up：～功夫 waste time / ～了火车 missed the train

【耽于】 dānyú addict; indulge in：～幻想 indulge in illusion

胆[膽] (dǎn) 1.〈*Anat.*〉 gall bladder 2.(胆量) courage; guts; bravery：丧～ be overwhelmed with fear; be terror-stricken / 壮～ boost sb's courage 3.(内胆) a bladder-like inner container

【胆大】 dǎndà bold; audacious

【胆道】 dǎndào 〈*Anat.*〉 biliary passage

【胆道蛔虫病】 dǎndào huíchóngbìng 〈*Med.*〉 biliary ascariasis

【胆敢】 dǎngǎn dare; have the audacity to

【胆固醇】 dǎngùchún 〈*Biochem.*〉 cholesterol

【胆寒】 dǎnhán terrified; frightened; struck with terror

【胆量】 dǎnliàng courage; guts; pluck; spunk

【胆略】 dǎnlüè courage and resourcefulness

【胆囊】 dǎnnáng 〈*Anat.*〉 gall bladder

【胆怯】 dǎnqiè timid; cowardly

【胆石】 dǎnshí 〈*Med.*〉 cholelith; gallstone

【胆识】 dǎnshí courage and insight

【胆小】 dǎnxiǎo timid; cowardly

【胆小鬼】 dǎnxiǎoguǐ coward

【胆战心惊】 dǎnzhàn-xīnjīng tremble with fear; be terror-stricken：使人～ strike terror into sb.

【胆汁】 dǎnzhī 〈*Anat.*〉 bile

【胆子】 dǎn·zi courage; nerve

【胆总管】 dǎnzǒngguǎn 〈*Anat.*〉 common bile duct

掸[撣、撢、担] (dǎn) brush lightly; whisk：她～去桌子上的灰尘。She whisked the dusts from the table.

【掸子】 dǎn·zi duster：鸡毛～ feather duster

旦 (dàn) 1.(天亮) dawn, daybreak 2.(天) day：元～ New Years Day

【旦夕】 dànxī 〈*written*〉 this morning or evening; in a short while

【旦夕祸福】 dànxī-huòfú unexpected good or bad fortune

但 (dàn) 1.(但是) but; yet; still; nevertheless 2.(只) only; merely

【但凡】 dànfán in every case; without exception; as long as

【但求无过】 dàn qiú wú guò seek only to avoid blame

【但是】 dànshì but; yet; still; nevertheless

【但愿】 dànyuàn if only; I wish

【但愿如此】 dànyuàn-rúcǐ I hope so.

担[擔] (dàn) 1.(挑子) a carrying pole and the loads on it; load; burden 2.〈*classifier*〉一～菜 a load of vegetables
(另见"担"dān)

【担子】 dàn·zi a carrying pole and the loads on it; load; burden

诞 (dàn) 1.(诞生) birth 2.(诞辰) birthday 3.(荒诞) absurd; fantastic

【诞辰】 dànchén birthday

【诞生】 dànshēng be born; come into being; emerge

淡 (dàn) 1.(稀薄) thin; light：烟味很～。The tobacco is very mild. 2.(不浓) tasteless; weak：～茶 weak tea 3.(指颜色) light; pale：～黄 light yellow 4.(冷淡) indifferent 5.(营业不旺盛) slack; dull 6.(无关紧要的) meaningless; trivial：扯～ talk nonsense

【淡泊】 dànbó not interested：～名利 not interested in fame or wealth

【淡薄】 dànbó 1.(不浓) thin; light 2.(不浓厚) become indifferent; flag 3.(渐渐消失) faint; dim; hazy：印象～了 leave a dim impression

【淡菜】 dàncài （贻贝）mussel

【淡出】 dànchū 〈*Cinematog.*〉fade out

【淡淡】 dàndàn light; slight

【淡化】 dànhuà 1.（除去盐分）desalinate; desalination (n.): 海水～ desalination of sea water 2.（使淡漠）abate; diminish lessen

【淡化厂】 dànhuàchǎng desalination plant

【淡季】 dànjì slack season; dull season; off season

【淡漠】 dànmò 1.（冷淡）indifferent; apathetic; nonchalant 2.（记忆不清）faint; dim; hazy

【淡然处之】 dànrán-chǔzhī treat with indifference; regard coolly

【淡入】 dànrù 〈*Cinematog.*〉fade in

【淡色】 dànsè pale color; light color

【淡水】 dànshuǐ fresh water

【淡水湖】 dànshuǐhú freshwater lake

【淡水养鱼】 dànshuǐ yǎngyú freshwater pisciculture

【淡水养殖】 dànshuǐ yǎngzhí freshwater aquiculture

【淡水鱼】 dànshuǐyú freshwater fish

【淡忘】 dànwàng fade from one's memory

【淡雅】 dànyǎ simple and elegant; quietly elegant

【淡月】 dànyuè a slack month

【淡妆】 dánzhuāng be lightly made up

弹［彈］(dàn) 1.（弹子）ball; pellet 2.（枪弹；炮弹）bullet; bomb: 穿甲～ armor-piercing bullet / 曳光～ tracer bullet / 原子～ atom-bomb; A-bomb / 照明～ flare bomb

（另见"弹"tán）

【弹道】 dàndào ballistic curve; trajectory

【弹道导弹】 dàndào dǎodàn ballistic missile

【弹道火箭】 dàndào huǒjiàn ballistic rocket

【弹弓】 dàngōng catapult; slingshot

【弹痕】 dànhén shot mark; shell hole

【弹尽粮绝】 dàn jìn liáng jué run out of ammunition and food supplies

【弹壳】 dànké shell case; cartridge case

【弹坑】 dànkēng (shell) crater

【弹片】 dànpiàn shell fragment; shell splinter; shrapnel

【弹头】 dàntóu bullet; projectile nose; warhead: 热核～ thermonuclear warhead

【弹无虚发】 dànwú-xūfā every shot told

【弹匣】 dànxiá 〈*Mil.*〉magazine

【弹药】 dànyào ammunition

【弹药库】 dànyàokù ammunition depot; ammunition storehouse

【弹着点】 dànzhuódiǎn point of impact; hitting point

【弹子】 dàn·zǐ 1.（弹丸）a pellet shot from a slingshot 2.（玩具）marble: 打～ play marbles 3.（台球）billiards

【弹子房】 dàn·zǐfáng billiard room

蛋 (dàn) 1.（带壳的卵）egg: 鸡～ hen's egg / 鲜～ fresh eggs / 下～ lay eggs 2.（蛋形的）an egg-shaped thing

【蛋白】 dànbái 1.（蛋清）egg white; albumen 2.（蛋白质）protein

【蛋白尿】 dànbáiniào 〈*Med.*〉albuminuria; proteinuria

【蛋白质】 dànbáizhì protein

【蛋糕】 dàngāo cake

【蛋羹】 dàngēng egg custard

【蛋黄】 dànhuáng yolk

【蛋卷】 dànjuǎn egg roll

【蛋壳】 dànké eggshell

【蛋品】 dànpǐn egg products

【蛋清】 dànqīng egg white

【蛋用鸡】 dànyòngjī layer

氮 (dàn) 〈*Chem.*〉nitrogen（元素符号 N）‖ 含氮的 nitric ‖ 含三价氮的 nitrous

【氮肥】 dànféi nitrogenous fertilizer

【氮气】 dànqì nitrogen

dang

当［當］(dāng) 1.（相当）equal 2.（应当）ought; should; must 3.（当面）in sb's presence; to sb's face 4.（正当…）just at (a time or place) 5.（担当；充当）work as; serve as; be: ～翻译 serve as interpreter; act as interpreter 6.（承当；承受）bear; accept; deserve: 一人做事一人～。One should answer for what he does. 7.（掌管；主持）direct; manage; be in charge of

（另见"当"dàng）

【当班】 dāngbān be on a shift; be on duty by turn

【当兵】 dāngbīng be a soldier; serve in the army

【当场】 dāngchǎng on the spot; then and there; in the act: ～被杀 be killed on the spot / 被～抓住 be caught in the act

【当初】 dāngchū originally; at the outset; in the first place; at that time

【当代】 dāngdài the present age; the contemporary era: ～文学 contemporary literature / ～英语 present-day English

【当地】 dāngdì at the place in question; in the locality; local: ～风俗 local customs / ～人民 local people / ～时间 local time

【当归】 dāngguī 〈*Chin. Med.*〉 Chinese angelica

【当机立断】 dāngjī-lìduàn make a prompt decision; decide promptly and opportunely

【当即】 dāngjí at once; right away

【当家】 dāngjiā manage (household) affairs

【当家作主】 dāngjiā-zuòzhǔ be master in one's own house; be the master of one's own affairs

【当今】 dāngjīn now; at present; nowadays

【当局】 dāngjú the authorities: 地方～ the local authorities / 有关～ the authorities concerned / 政府～ the government authorities

【当空】 dāngkōng high above in the sky

【当量】 dāngliàng 〈*Chem.*〉 equivalent (weight)

【当面】 dāngmiàn to sb's face; in sb's presence

【当年】 dāngnián 1.(过去某一时间) in those years; in those days 2.(身强力壮时) the prime of life: 她正～。She is in her prime.

【当前】 dāngqián 1.(在面前) before one; facing one 2.(目前) present; current: ～的中心任务 the central task at present / ～利益 immediate interests

【当权】 dāngquán be in power; hold power

【当权者】 dāngquánzhě person in power; people in authority

【当然】 dāngrán 1.(应当这样) as it should be; only natural 2.(合情合理) without doubt; certainly; of course; to be sure 3.(理所应当的) natural

【当仁不让】 dāng rén bù ràng not pass on to others what one is called upon to do; not decline to shoulder a responsibility

【当时】 dāngshí then; at that time

【当事人】 dāngshìrén 1.(诉讼的一方) party (to a lawsuit); litigant 2.(有关的人) person concerned; party concerned; interested parties

【当事人能力】 dāngshìrén nénglì 〈*Law*〉 capacity of party; capacity to be a party

【当事人行为】 dāngshìrén xíngwéi 〈*Law*〉 act of party

【当头】 dāngtóu 1.(迎头) right overhead; right on sb's head; head on 2.(临头) facing one; confronting one; imminent: 大难～ confronted with a disaster

【当头一棒】 dāngtóu-yībàng a head-on blow

【当务之急】 dāngwù-zhījí a pressing matter of the moment; a task of top priority; urgent matter

【当先】 dāngxiān 1.(赶在最前面) in the van; in the front ranks; at the head 2.(当初) originally; in the first place; at that time

【当心】 dāngxīn take care; be careful; look out: ～有车! Look out! Mind the car!

【当雄】 dāngxióng 〈place〉 Damxung

【当选】 dāngxuǎn be elected (to)

【当之无愧】 dāngzhī-wúkuì fully deserve (a title, an honor, etc.); be worthy of

【当中】 dāngzhōng 1.(正中) in the middle; in the center 2.(之中) among

【当众】 dāngzhòng in the presence of all; in public: ～出丑 make an exhibition of oneself / ～宣布 announce publicly

铛[鐺] (dāng) 〈*onom.*〉 clank; clang: 我听到了庙里大钟的～～声。I heard the clang of the temple bell. (另见"铛"chēng)

裆[襠] (dāng) crotch: 裤～ crotch of trousers

挡[擋、攩] (dǎng) 1.(拦挡) keep off; ward off; block 2.(遮挡) block; get in the way of 3.(挡子) fender; blind 4.(汽车的排挡) gear: 倒车～ reverse gear / 前进～ forward gear / 低速～ low gear / 高速～ top gear / 踩下离合器, 挂上～ press the clutch down and put the car in gear / 换～ change gear / 从一～换到二～ change from first gear into second gear / 你

的车是有四～，还是有五～? Does your car have four or five gears?
【挡板】 dǎngbǎn 〈*Auto*〉 fender; mudguard
【挡风】 dǎngfēng shelter sth. from the wind; keep out the wind
【挡风玻璃】 dǎngfēng bō·lí a windshield
【挡光】 dǎngguāng be in the light; get in the light
【挡箭牌】 dǎngjiànpái **1.**（盾牌）shield **2.**（借口）excuse; pretext
【挡路】 dǎnglù be in the way; obstruct traffic
【挡泥板】 dǎngníbǎn 〈*Auto*〉 fender; mudguard
【挡雨】 dǎngyǔ keep off the rain; shelter one from the rain
【挡住】 dǎngzhù block; hamper: ～风沙 shield off the sandstorm / ～去路 block the way

党［黨］(dǎng) **1.**（政党）political party; party **2.**（指中国共产党）the Party (the Communist Party of China): 入～ join the Party / 整～ Party consolidation **3.**（集团）clique; faction; gang: 死～ sworn follower **4.**（偏袒）be partial to; take sides with **5.**（亲族）kinsfolk; relatives: 父～ father's kinsfolk
【党八股】 dǎngbāgǔ stereotyped Party writing; Party jargon
【党办】 dǎngbàn the office of a Party committee
【党报】 dǎngbào party newspaper; organ of the party
【党代表】 dǎngdàibiǎo Party representative
【党费】 dǎngfèi party membership dues
【党风】 dǎngfēng party conduct
【党籍】 dǎngjí party membership: 开除～ expel from the party
【党纪】 dǎngjì party discipline: ～国法 party discipline and the law of the state
【党纪处分】 dǎngjì chǔfèn punishment according to the party discipline
【党建】 dǎngjiàn party building
【党课】 dǎngkè Party class; Party lecture: 讲～ give a Party lecture
【党龄】 dǎnglíng party years' standing
【党内】 dǎngnèi within the party; inside the party; inner-party
【党派】 dǎngpài political parties and groups; party groupings
【党票】 dǎngpiào membership of the Party: 要～ obtain the membership
【党旗】 dǎngqí party flag
【党同伐异】 dǎngtóng-fáyì defend those who belong to one's own faction and attack those who don't; be narrowly partisan
【党团】 dǎngtuán **1.**（政党和团体）political parties and other organization **2.**（共产党和共青团）the Party and the League **3.**（多用于外国议会）议会～ parliamentary group of a political party
【党团员】 dǎngtuányuán Party and League members
【党外】 dǎngwài outside the party
【党外人士】 dǎngwài rénshì non-Party personages
【党委】 dǎngwěi Party committee
【党委书记】 dǎngwěi shū·ji secretary of the Party committee
【党委委员】 dǎngwěi wěiyuán member of the Party committee
【党务】 dǎngwù party work; party affairs
【党小组】 dǎngxiǎozhǔ Party group
【党校】 dǎngxiào Party school
【党性】 dǎngxìng party spirit; party character
【党员】 dǎngyuán party member: 预备～ probationary member of the Party
【党章】 dǎngzhāng party constitution
【党政分开】 dǎng zhèng fēnkāi separation of the Party and government; separation of the Party from the administration; separation of Party function from that of government
【党政机关】 dǎng zhèng jīguān Party and government offices
【党支部】 dǎngzhībù Party branch
【党支部书记】 dǎngzhībù shū·ji Party branch secretary
【党中央】 dǎngzhōngyāng the Party Central Committee
【党总支】 dǎngzǒngzhī general Party branch
【党组】 dǎngzǔ leading Party group
【党组织】 dǎngzǔzhī Party organization: 基层～ Party organizations at the primary level

当[**當**] (dàng) 1.(恰当) proper; right 2.(抵得上) match; equal to 3.(当作) treat as; regard as; take for 4.(认为) think 5.(事情发生的时间) that very day etc. 6.(典当) pawn 7.(典当物) sth. pawned; pawn; pledge: 赎～ take sth. out of pledge; redeem sth. pawned 8.(上当) be duped: 他上了毒品犯子的～,给他们带了海洛因。He was duped by drug smugglers into carrying heroin for them.
(另见"当"dāng)

【当成】 dàngchéng treat as; regard as; look upon as

【当当】 dàngdàng pawn

【当年】 dàngnián the same year; that very year: ～有效 good for the year of issue only

【当票】 dàngpiào pawn ticket

【当铺】 dàng·pu pawnshop; pawnbroker's ‖当铺业主 pawnbroker

【当日】 dàngrì the same day; that very day: 车票～有效。The train ticket is good for the date of issue only.

【当时】 dàngshí right away; at once; immediately

【当天】 dàngtiān the same day; that very day

【当晚】 dàngwǎn the same night

【当夜】 dàngyè the same night

【当真】 dàngzhēn 1.(信以为真) take seriously 2.(果然) really true; really

【当做】 dàngzuò look on as; treat as; regard as

【当作】 dàngzuò look on as; take as; treat as; regard as: 不把书本～教条 not regard books as dogma

档[**檔**] (dàng) 1.(有格子的架或橱) shelves (for files); pigeonholes 2.(档案) files; archives: 查～ consult the files 3.(撑儿) crosspiece 4.(等级) grade: 高～商品 high grade goods

【档案】 dàng'àn files; archives; record; dossier

【档案馆】 dàng'ànguǎn archives

【档次】 dàngcì grade; class; differential: 高～商品 high grade commodities / 拉开职工收入的～ enlarge the differential between both staff members and workers

荡[**蕩**、**盪**[1－4]] (dàng) 1.(摇动) swing; sway; wave: ～秋千 play on a swing 2.(游荡) loaf 3.(冲洗) rinse 4.(清除) clear away; sweep off 5.(放荡) loose in morals; dissolute 6.(洼地) shallow lake; marsh: 芦～ a reed marsh

【荡荡悠悠】 dàngdàng-yōuyōu swing; moving to and fro

【荡涤】 dàngdí cleanse; clean up; wash away

【荡然无存】 dàngrán-wúcún 〈*written*〉 all gone; nothing left

【荡漾】 dàngyàng ripple; undulate; rise and fall: 湖水在微风中～。The lake rippled in the breeze.

dao

刀 (dāo) 1.(刀子) knife; sword 2.(形状像刀的东西) sth. shaped like a knife

【刀把子】 dāobà·zi 1.(刀柄) (sword) hilt 2.(权柄) military power; power 3.(把柄) sth. that may be used against one; a handle

【刀背】 dāobèi the back of a knife blade

【刀柄】 dāobǐng hilt; knife handle

【刀叉】 dāochā knife and fork

【刀豆】 dāodòu sword bean

【刀尖】 dāojiān 1.〈*Mech.*〉 end land; nose of tool 2.(刀的尖儿) point of a knife; point of a sword

【刀具】 dāojù 〈*Mech.*〉 tool; cutting tool

【刀口】 dāokǒu 1.(刀刃) the edge of a knife 2.(比喻) where a thing can be put to best use; the crucial point; the right spot 3.(刀伤) cut; incision

【刀口支承】 dāokǒu zhīchéng knife-edge support

【刀片】 dāopiàn 1.(刮胡刀片) razor blade 2.(片状机件) (tool) bit; blade

【刀枪】 dāoqiāng sword and spear; weapons

【刀鞘】 dāoqiào sheath; scabbard

【刀刃】 dāorèn 1.(刀口) the edge of a knife 2.(比喻) where a thing can be put to best use; the crucial point

【刀山火海】 dāo shān huǒ hǎi a mountain of swords and a sea of flames; most dangerous places; most severe trials

【刀子】 dāo·zi 〈*colloq.*〉 small knife; pocketknife

【刀子嘴】 dāo·zizuǐ 1.(说话尖刻) a sharp

tongue 2.（指人）a sharp-tongued person

叨（dāo）（另见“叨”tāo）

【叨登】 dāo·deng 1.（翻腾）turn things over 2.（重提旧事）harp on things past

【叨唠】 dāo·lao talk on and on; chatter away：别总～那小事。Don't rattle over that trifle.

氘（dāo） 〈*Chem.*〉 deuterium（符号为：D）

导［導］（dǎo） 1.（引导）lead; guide 2.（传导）transmit; conduct 3.（开导）instruct; teach; give guidance to：教～ teach; instruct

【导出单位】 dǎochū dānwèi derived unit

【导弹】 dǎodàn guided missile：弹道～ ballistic missile / 地对地～ surface-to-surface missile / 地对空～ ground-to-air missile; surface-to-air missile / 空对地～ air-to-ground missile / 空对空～ air-to-air missile / 中程弹道～ intermediate range ballistic missile / 洲际弹道～ international ballistic missile

【导弹发射井】 dǎodàn fāshèjǐng launching silo

【导弹核潜艇】 dǎodàn héqiántǐng nuclear submarine armed with guided missiles

【导弹驱逐舰】 dǎodàn qūzhújiàn guided missile destroyer

【导弹巡洋舰】 dǎodàn xúnyángjiàn guided missile cruiser

【导电】 dǎodiàn electric conduction

【导电体】 dǎodiàntǐ electric conductor

【导购】 dǎogòu shopping guide

【导购小姐】 dǎogòu xiǎojiě shopping guide lady

【导管】 dǎoguǎn 1.（管道）conduct; pipe 2.〈*Anat.*〉 vessel; duct

【导轨】 dǎoguǐ slideway; guide

【导航】 dǎoháng navigate; navigation (n.)：无线电信号常用于给飞机或船舶～。Radio signals are used for navigating both aircraft and ships.

【导航台】 dǎohángtái guidance station; non-direction radio beacon (NDB)

【导航卫星】 dǎoháng wèixīng navigational satellite

【导火线】 dǎohuǒxiàn 1.（引信）(blasting) fuse 2.（比喻）a small incident that touches off a big one

【导论】 dǎolùn an introduction

【导纳】 dǎonà 〈*Physics*〉 admittance

【导尿】 dǎoniào 〈*Med.*〉 catheterization

【导尿管】 dǎoniàoguǎn 〈*Med.*〉 catheter：插～排空患者膀胱 insert a catheter to empty the patient's bladder

【导热】 dǎorè heat conduction; heat transmission; thermal conductivity

【导师】 dǎoshī 1.（指导老师）tutor; teacher 2.（指导大事业的人）guide of a great cause; teacher

【导体】 dǎotǐ 〈*Physics*〉 conductor：半～ semiconductor / 超～ superconductor / 非～ nonconductor

【导线】 dǎoxiàn 〈*Electr.*〉 lead; (conducting) wire

【导向】 dǎoxiàng leading coverage：舆论～ leading coverage by the mass media

【导向架】 dǎoxiàngjià 〈*Railway*〉 leading truck

【导向性】 dǎoxiàngxìng directivity

【导言】 dǎoyán introduction (to a piece of writing); introductory remarks

【导演】 dǎoyǎn 1.（指工作）direct (a film, play, etc.) 2.（导演者）director

【导游】 dǎoyóu 1.（引导）conduct a sightseeing tour 2.（导游员）guide; tourist guide 3.（旅游指南）guidebook

【导游图】 dǎoyóutú tourist map

【导致】 dǎozhì lead to; bring about; result in; cause：～分裂 cause a split; bring about a split

岛［島］（dǎo） island：安全～ safety island / 海南～ Hainan Island / 小～ islet

【岛国】 dǎoguó island country

【岛弧】 dǎohú island arc

【岛屿】 dǎoyǔ islands and islets; islands

【岛宇宙】 dǎoyǔzhòu 〈*Astron.*〉 island universe

捣［搗、擣］（dǎo） 1.（捣碎）mash：～土豆 mash the potatoes 2.（捶打）pound with a pestle, etc.; beat; smash 3.（捣乱）harass; disturb

【捣蛋】 dǎodàn make trouble

【捣鬼】 dǎoguǐ play tricks; do mischief
【捣毁】 dǎohuǐ smash up; demolish; destroy
【捣乱】 dǎoluàn make trouble; create a disturbance: 别跟我～! Don't make trouble with me!
【捣麻烦】 dǎo má·fan make trouble
【捣碎】 dǎosuì pound to pieces

倒 (dǎo) 1.(摔倒) fall; topple: 摔～ fall over 2.(失败;倒台) collapse; fail 3.(倒闭) close down; go bankrupt; go out of business 4.(嗓子变低或变哑) become hoarse 5.(转换车船等) change; make connection 6.(作投机生意) speculate
(另见"倒"dào)

【倒把】 dǎobǎ engage in profiteering; speculate: 投机～ engage in speculation and profiteering
【倒班】 dǎobān change shifts; work in shifts; work by turns
【倒闭】 dǎobì close down; go bankrupt; go into liquidation: 企业～ bankruptcy of an enterprise
【倒毙】 dǎobì drop dead
【倒车】 dǎochē change trains; change buses: 在北京～去乌鲁木齐 change at Beijing for Urumqi / 我到这儿得倒两次汽车。I had to change buses twice to get there.
【倒伏】 dǎofú 〈*Agric.*〉(of crops) lodging
【倒戈】 dǎogē change sides in a war; turn one's coat
【倒戈投敌】 dǎogē-tóudí turn renegade; be a turncoat
【倒换】 dǎohuàn 1.(轮流替换) rotate; take turns 2.(换掉) rearrange (sequence, order, etc.); replace
【倒嚼】 dǎojiào ruminate; chew the cud
【倒买倒卖】 dǎomǎi-dǎomài fraudulent buying and selling
【倒卖】 dǎomài resell at a profit
【倒霉】 dǎoméi have bad luck; be out of luck; be down on one's luck: 真～! What lousy luck!
【倒手】 dǎoshǒu (of merchandise, etc.) change hands
【倒塌】 dǎotā collapse; topple down: 房子～了。The house collapsed.
【倒台】 dǎotái fall from power; downfall; collapse
【倒腾】 dǎo·teng 1.(翻腾) turn; move 2.(买进卖出) buy and sell; deal in
【倒胃口】 dǎo wèi·kou curb one's appetite; make one fed up
【倒休】 dǎoxiū change one's shift to get leave later
【倒牙】 dǎoyá set one's teeth on edge
【倒爷】 dǎoyé profiteer; speculator
【倒运】 dǎoyùn 1.(甲地买运到乙地卖) profiteer by buying cheap and selling dear 2.(倒霉) be unlucky; be out of luck
【倒账】 dǎozhàng a bad debt

祷[禱] (dǎo) 1.(祷告) pray 2.(盼望) ask earnestly; beg

【祷告】 dǎogào pray; say one's prayers
【祷念】 dǎoniàn say a prayer

蹈 (dǎo) 1.(踩,踏) pray 2.(遵循) tread; step: 循规～矩 not step out of bounds; stick to convention

到 (dào) 1.(到达) arrive; reach 2.(往) go to; leave for: ～西安去 go to Xi'an 3.(止) up until; up to: 从星期日～星期三 from Sunday to Wednesday 4.(用作动词补语,表示动作有结果)说～做～ be as good as one's word 5.(周到) thoughtful; considerate

【到场】 dàochǎng be present; show up; turn up
【到处】 dàochù at all places; everywhere: ～碰壁 run against the wall everywhere
【到达】 dàodá arrive; get to; reach
【到底】 dàodǐ 1.(到头) to the end; to the finish 2.(最后) at last; in the end; finally 3.(究竟) ever; indeed 4.(终究) after all; in the final analysis
【到点】 dàodiǎn it's time to do sth.
【到顶】 dàodǐng reach the summit; reach the peak; reach the limit; cannot be improved
【到会】 dàohuì be present at a meeting; attend a meeting
【到家】 dàojiā 1.(回到家) be home; get home: 他已～。He is home. 2.(达到很高水准) reach a very high level; be perfect; be excellent
【到来】 dàolái arrival; advent
【到目前为止】 dào mùqián wéizhǐ so far; by now; up to now

【到期】 dàoqī become due; mature; expire; terminate: 我们的合同～了。Our contract terminated.

【到任】 dàorèn assume a post; assume office

【到手】 dàoshǒu in one's hands; in one's possession

【到头】 dàotóu to the end; at an end; throughout: 一年～ throughout the year

【到头来】 dàotóulái in the end; finally

【到职】 dàozhí take office; arrive at one's post; assume office

倒 (dào) 1.(颠倒) upside down; inverted; inverse; reverse 2.(倒退) move backward; turn upside down: 把车～回车库 back a car into the garage 3.(倾倒) pour; tip: ～垃圾 tip rubbish; dump rubbish / ～一杯咖啡 pour a cup of coffee 4.(表示跟意料相反) on the contrary: 病人情况不但没有好转，～恶化了。The patient was no better but rather grew worse.
(另见"倒"dǎo)

【倒不如】 dàobùrú it's better to; no better than

【倒彩】 dàocǎi booing; hooting; catcall: 喝～ make catcalls; boo and hoot

【倒车】 dàochē 1.(把车向后退) back a car: 开～ turn the clock back 2.(使船向后退) astern

【倒车灯】 dàochēdēng 〈*Auto*〉 reverse light

【倒挡】 dàodǎng 〈*Auto*〉 reverse gear

【倒钩球】 dàogōuqiú 〈*Football*〉 overhead kick

【倒挂金钟】 dàoguà jīnzhōng fuchsia

【倒灌】 dàoguàn flow backward

【倒好儿】 dàohǎor booing; hooting; catcall: 叫～ make catcalls; boo and hoot

【倒计时】 dàojìshí count down

【倒睫】 dàojié 〈*Med.*〉 trichiasis

【倒立】 dàolì 1.(头朝下) stand upside down 2.〈*Sports*〉 handstand

【倒流】 dàoliú 1.(向上游流) flow backward(s) 2.(比喻反向运动) backward(s)

【倒轮闸】 dàolúnzhá 〈*Bicycle*〉 back-pedal brake; coaster brake

【倒片】 dàopiān 〈*Photog.*〉 rewind

【倒片手柄】 dàopiān shǒubǐng 〈*photog.*〉 rewind crank

【倒数】 dàoshǔ count backwards: ～第 3 行 the third line from the bottom

【倒数计时】 dàoshǔ jìshí 〈*Aeron.*〉 count down

【倒算】 dàosuàn seize back confiscated property

【倒贴】 dàotiē pay for the upkeep of a lover

【倒退】 dàotuì go backwards; fall back

【倒行逆施】 dào xíng nì shī 1.(违背时代潮流) go against the historical trend; try to put the clock back; push a reactionary policy 2.(违背社会正义) perverse acts

【倒因为果】 dàoyīn-wéiguǒ reverse cause and effect; take cause for effect

【倒影】 dàoyǐng inverted image; inverted reflection in water

【倒栽葱】 dàozāicōng fall head over heels; fall headlong

【倒置】 dàozhì place upside down; invert: 本末～ attend to the superficial and neglect the essentials

【倒转】 dàozhuǎn turn the other way round; reverse

悼 (dào) mourn; grieve

【悼词】 dàocí memorial speech: 致～ make a memorial speech

【悼辞】 dàocí memorial speech

【悼念】 dàoniàn mourn; grieve over: ～亡友 mourn for a dead friend

盗 (dào) 1.(偷盗) steal; rob 2.(强盗) thief; robber

【盗版】 dàobǎn piracy (n.); pirate (v.); pirated (adj.): 软件～ software piracy / 在中国，对他人的著作进行～是非法的。In China it's illegal to pirate someone's work.

【盗版软件】 dàobǎn ruǎnjiàn pirated software

【盗伐】 dàofá 〈*Forestry*〉 fell trees unlawfully

【盗汗】 dàohàn night sweat

【盗卖】 dàomài steal and sell: ～公物 steal and sell public property

【盗名】 dàomíng steal glory one does not deserve; seek undeserved publicity: 欺世～ steal fame by deceiving the public

【盗墓】 dàomù rob a thumb; rob a grave

【盗墓人】 dàomùrén grave robber

【盗窃】 dàoqiè steal; embezzle

【盗窃集团】 dàoqiè jítuán embezzling group
【盗取】 dàoqǔ steal; embezzle
【盗用】 dàoyòng embezzle; usurp: ～公款 embezzle public funds
【盗贼】 dàozéi robbers; bandits

道(dào) 1.(道路) road; way; path 2.(水道) channel; course 3.(方法) way; method 4.(学术或宗教体系) doctrine; principle: 孔孟之～ doctrines of Confucius and Mencius 5.(道教) Taoism; Taoist 6.(迷信组织) superstitious sect 7.(线条) line 8.(说) say; talk; speak 9.(以为) think; suppose
【道班】 dàobān 1.〈*Railway*〉railway maintenance squad 2.(公路道班) highway maintenance squad
【道岔】 dàochà 〈*Railway*〉switches; points
【道德】 dàodé morals; morality; ethics: 公共～ public morals / 商业～ commercial morality; business ethics
【道德败坏】 dàodé bàihuài degenerate
【道德规范】 dàodé guīfàn code of ethics
【道德品质】 dàodé pǐnzhì moral character
【道钉】 dàodīng 〈*Railway*〉spike
【道高一尺,魔高一丈】 dào gāo yī chǐ, mó gāo yī zhàng as virtue rises one foot, vice rises ten
【道贺】 dàohè congratulate
【道教】 Dàojiào 〈*Relig.*〉Taoism
【道具】 dàojù 〈*Theatre*〉stage property; prop
【道理】 dào·li 1.(规律) principle; truth; hows and whys 2.(情理;理由) reason; argument; sense: 摆事实, 讲～ bring out facts and reason things out
【道路】 dàolù road; way; path: ～阻塞 a passage is blocked up; a road is blocked / 为…铺平～ pave the way for
【道貌岸然】 dàomào-ànrán pose as a person of high morals; be sanctimonious
【道破】 dàopò point out frankly; lay bare; reveal: 一语～ lay bare sth. with one remark
【道歉】 dàoqiàn apologize; make an apology
【道-琼斯平均指数】 Dào Qióngsī píngjūn zhǐshù 〈*Econ.*〉Dow-Jones Averages
【道士】 dào·shi 〈*Religion*〉Taoist priest
【道听途说】 dàotīng-túshuō hearsay; rumor; hear on the grapevine
【道喜】 dàoxǐ congratulate sb. on a happy occasion
【道谢】 dàoxiè express one's thanks; thank
【道义】 dàoyì morality and justice: ～上说不过去 not justified on moral principles
【道院】 dàoyuàn Taoist temple

稻(dào) rice; paddy: 旱～ upland rice / 水～ paddy rice
【稻草】 dàocǎo rice straw
【稻草人】 dàocǎorén scarecrow
【稻谷】 dàogǔ paddy
【稻壳】 dàoké rice husk; rice hull
【稻米】 dàomǐ rice
【稻穗】 dàosuì ear of rice; spike of rice
【稻田】 dàotián (rice) paddy; rice field; paddy field
【稻秧】 dàoyāng rice seedlings; rice shoots
【稻种】 dàozhǒng seed rice
【稻子】 dào·zi rice; paddy

de

得(dé) 1.(得到) get; obtain; gain 2.(演算结果)(of a calculation) result in: 四二～八。Four times two makes eight. 3.(适合) fit; proper 4.(得意) satisfied; complacent 5.(完成) be finished; be ready
(另见"得"děi)
【得便】 débiàn when it's convenient
【得病】 débìng fall ill; become sick; contract a disease
【得不偿失】 débù-chángshī the loss outweighs the gain; the game is not worth the candle
【得逞】 déchěng have one's way; prevail; succeed
【得出】 déchū reach; obtain: ～结论 reach a conclusion / ～结果 obtain a result / 从中～教训 draw a lesson (from)
【得寸进尺】 décùn-jìnchǐ reach out for a yard after taking an inch; give him an inch and he'll take an ell
【得当】 dédàng apt; appropriate; proper; suitable: 举止～ behave properly; have good manners
【得到】 dédào get; obtain; gain; receive: ～成功 achieve success / ～广泛运用 find broad

application / ～及时治疗 get timely medical treatment / ～最充分发挥 be brought into fullest play
【得法】 défǎ do sth. in the proper way; get the knack
【得分】 défēn score; point: 你能在今天下午的比赛中～吗? Could you keep score (或 score) at this afternoon's match?
【得分者】 défēnzhě scorekeeper; scorer
【得过且过】 déguò-qiěguò muddle along; drift along
【得计】 déjì succeed in one's scheme: 自以为～ think oneself clever
【得奖】 déjiǎng win a prize; be awarded a prize; prizewinning: ～影片 prizewinning film / 在戏剧节上～ win a prize in the festival
【得奖人】 déjiǎngrén prizewinner
【得劲】 déjìn 1.(舒服) feel well 2.(好用) fit for use; handy
【得空】 dékòng have leisure; be free
【得了】 dé·le stop it; hold it
【得力】 délì 1.(得益) benefit from; get help from 2.(有能力的) capable; competent
【得力助手】 délì zhùshǒu a capable assistant; an able assistant
【得零分】 dé língfēn 〈*Sports*〉 draw a blank
【得人心】 dé rénxīn popular; beloved and supported by the people
【得胜】 déshèng win a victory; triumph
【得失】 déshī 1.(所得和所失) gain and loss; success and failure 2.(利弊) advantages and disadvantages; merits and demerits: ～各半 have both merits and demerits
【得势】 déshì 1.(掌权) be in power 2.(有影响) get the upper hand; be in the ascendant
【得手】 déshǒu go smoothly; come off; do fine; succeed
【得体】 détǐ befitting one's position or suited to the occasion; appropriate
【得天独厚】 détiān-dúhòu be richly endowed by nature; abound in gifts of nature; enjoy exceptional advantages
【得悉】 déxī hear of; learn about
【得闲】 déxián have leisure; be at leisure
【得心应手】 dé xīn yìng shǒu 1.(运用自如) with facility; with high proficiency 2.(好用) serviceable; handy
【得以】 déyǐ so that ... can ...; so that ... may ...
【得意】 déyì proud of oneself; pleased with oneself; complacent
【得意门生】 déyì-méngshēng favorite pupil
【得意忘形】 déyì-wàngxíng get dizzy with success; have one's head turned by success
【得意扬扬】 déyì-yángyáng be immensely proud; look triumphant
【得志】 dézhì achieve one's ambition; have a successful career: 小人～ villains holding sway
【得主】 dézhǔ prizewinner; medalist: 金牌～ gold medalist / 银牌～ silver medalist / 铜牌～ bronze medalist
【得罪】 dé·zuì offend; displease: ～人 offend sb. / 不怕～人 not be afraid of giving offense

锝 (dé) 〈*Chem.*〉 technetium (元素符号 Tc)

德[悳] (dé) 1.(道德) virtue; morals; moral character 2.(心意) heart; mind 3.(恩惠) kindness; favor: 感恩戴～ bear a debt of gratitude (for sb's kindness)
【德昂族】 Dé'ángzú De'ang (中国少数民族, 主要分布在云南)
【德才兼备】 décái-jiānbèi have both ability and political integrity
【德高望重】 dégāo-wàngzhòng be of noble character and high prestige; enjoy high prestige and command universal respect
【德国】 Déguó Germany; Germanic (adj.) ‖ 德国人 German
【德国马克】 Déguó Mǎkè Deutsche Mark
【德国牧羊犬】 Déguǒ mùyángquǎn German shepherd
【德让宗】 Déràngzōng 〈place〉 Dirangzong
【德行】 déxíng moral integrity; moral conduct
【德行】 dé·xing disgusting; shameful
【德性】 dé·xing disgusting; shameful
【德银】 déyín German silver
【德语】 Déyǔ German (language)
【德育】 déyù moral education
【德智体全面发展】 dézhìtǐ quánmiàn fāzhǎn all round development of morality, intelli-

gence, and physique

的 (de) 1.(表示所属)我～母亲 my mother 2.(代替前面提到的人或物)你的鞋是棕色的，我～是黑颜色的。Your shoes are brown; mine are black. 3.(表示某一种人或物)吃～ food; eatables; edibles / 开汽车～ a driver
(另见"的"dí, dì)

【…的话】 ·dehuà if ...: 如有人给我打电话～,请告诉他我 10 点钟回来。If anyone should ring for me, please tell them I'll be back at 10 o'clock.

dei

得 (děi) 1.(需要) need: 这一段～重写。This paragraph needs rewriting. 2.(必须;必要) must; have to: 你～认真考虑一下。You must think it over seriously. / 我～遵守诺言。I must keep my word. 3.(表示必然) will; ought: 你不快走,就～挨淋。You will get wet if you don't start right off. / 如果他在 7 点钟出发,现在～到了。If he started at seven, he ought to be there by now.
(另见"得"dé)

deng

灯[燈] (dēng) 1.(灯具) lamp; lantern; light: 壁～ wall lamp / 电～ electric light / 落地～ floor lamp / 日光～ fluorescent lamp / 台～ desk lamp 2.(电子管) valve; tube 3.(燃烧液体的加热器) burner: 酒精～ alcohol burner; spirit lamp

【灯标】 dēngbiāo beacon; light buoy

【灯彩】 dēngcǎi colored lanterns

【灯管】 dēngguǎn (fluorescent) tube

【灯光】 dēngguāng 1.(灯光亮度) the light of a lamp; lamplight 2.(照明设备) lighting; stage lighting; studio lighting

【灯红酒绿】 dēnghóng-jiǔlǜ red lanterns and green wine; scene of debauchery

【灯会】 dēnghuì lantern festival

【灯火】 dēnghuǒ lights

【灯火管制】 dēnghuǒ guǎnzhì blackout

【灯具】 dēngjù lamps and lanterns

【灯口】 dēngkǒu light socket ‖ 螺口 screw socket ‖ 卡口 bayonet socket

【灯笼】 dēng·long lantern

【灯笼花】 dēng·longhuā Chinese enkianthus

【灯笼裤】 dēng·longkù knee-length sports trousers

【灯谜】 dēngmí riddles written on lanterns; lantern riddles: 猜～ guess lantern riddles

【灯捻】 dēngniǎn lampwick; wick

【灯泡】 dēngpào (electric) bulb; light bulb: 乳白～ opal bulb

【灯绳】 dēngshéng lamp cord

【灯丝】 dēngsī filament (in a light bulb or valve)

【灯塔】 dēngtǎ lighthouse; beacon

【灯头】 dēngtóu 1.(灯口) electric light socket 2.(灯的数目) light: 这儿有三个～。There are three lights. 3.(煤油灯灯头) kerosene lamp holder

【灯箱】 dēngxiāng lamphouse

【灯心】 dēngxīn lampwick; wick

【灯心绒】 dēngxīnróng 〈*Textiles*〉 corduroy

【灯芯】 dēngxīn lampwick; wick

【灯烟子】 dēngyān·zi lamp-black

【灯罩】 dēngzhào lampshade; lamp-chimney

登 (dēng) 1.(攀登) ascend; mount; scale (a height) 2.(刊登) publish; record; enter 3.(谷物登场) be gathered and taken to the threshing ground: 五谷丰～ reap a bumper grain harvest 4.(用力踏) press down with the foot; pedal; treadle 5.(踩;踏) step on; tread

【登岸】 dēngàn go ashore

【登报】 dēngbào publish in the newspaper: ～声明 make an announcement in the press

【登簿】 dēngbù register; registry

【登场】 dēngchǎng come on stage

【登高】 dēnggāo ascend a height

【登广告】 dēng guǎnggào advertise: ～求售 advertise goods for sale / ～求职 advertise for a job

【登机】 dēngjī 〈*Aeron.*〉 board a plane

【登机牌】 dēngjīpái 〈*Aeron.*〉 boarding pass

【登机舷梯】 dēngjī xiántī 〈*Aeron.*〉 boarding ramp

【登机走廊停机坪】 dēngjī zǒuláng tíngjīpíng 〈*Aeron.*〉 pier apron

【登机走廊终端】 dēngjī zǒuláng zhōngduān 〈*Aeron.*〉 pier head

【登记】 dēngjì register; check in; enter one's name：在旅馆～住宿 check in at a hotel
【登陆】 dēnglù land; disembark：
【登陆部队】 dēnglù bùduì landing force
【登陆艇】 dēnglùtǐng landing boat
【登陆作战】 dēnglù zuòzhàn landing operations
【登录】 dēnglù record
【登门】 dēngmén call at sb's house：～拜访 pay sb. a visit / ～答谢 call on sb. to express gratitude
【登山】 dēngshān 〈*Sports*〉 mountain-climbing; mountaineering
【登山运动员】 dēngshān yùndòngyuán mountaineer; alpinist; climber
【登时】 dēngshí immediately; at once; then and there
【登台】 dēngtái mount a platform; go up on the stage：～演说 deliver a speech from a platform
【登堂入室】 dēngtáng-rùshì pass through the hall into the inner chamber; reach a higher level in one's studies or become more proficient in one's profession
【登月舱】 dēngyuècāng lunar module
【登月舱机动火箭】 dēngyuècāng jīdòng huǒjiàn LM-maneuvering rockets
【登载】 dēngzǎi publish; carry：比赛得胜者的名单将～在《北京晚报》上。The names of the winners of the competition will be published in *Beijing Evening News*.
【登账】 dēngzhàng enter an item in an account book

等(děng) 1.(等级) class; grade; rank 2.(相等) equal：～距离 equal distance / 大小不～ unequal in size / 长短相～ be equal in length 3.(等候) wait; await 4.(等到) when; till 5.(等等) and so on; and so forth; etc.
【等边三角形】 děngbiān sānjiǎoxíng equilateral triangle
【等次】 děngcì place in a series; grade
【等待】 děngdài wait; await：～有利时机 await a favorable opportunity
【等到】 děngdào by the time; when：～他来，我便告诉他。I'll tell him when he comes.
【等等】 děngděng 1.(表示列举未尽) and so on; and so on and so forth; etc. 2.(等一下) wait a minute
【等额选举】 děng'é xuǎnjǔ single-candidate election
【等候】 děnghòu wait; await; expect
【等级】 děngjí 1.(级别) grade; rank 2.(社会地位) order and degree; social estate
【等级观念】 děngjí guānniàn sense of hierarchy
【等级制度】 děngjí zhìdù hierarchy; social estate system
【等价】 děngjià of equal value; equal in value
【等价交换】 děngjià-jiāohuàn exchange of equal values; exchange at equal value
【等距离】 děngjùlí equidistance; equidistant (adj.)
【等距离外交】 děngjùlí wàijiāo equidistant diplomacy
【等式】 děngshì equality; equation
【等同】 děngtóng equate; be equal
【等外】 děngwài substandard; off-grade
【等外品】 děngwàipǐn substandard product
【等闲】 děngxián 1.(平常) ordinary; unimportant：～视之 regard as unimportant; treat lightly; treat casually 2.(随便；轻易) aimlessly; thoughtlessly
【等腰三角形】 děngyāo sānjiǎoxíng isosceles triangle
【等于】 děngyú 1.(相等) equal to; equivalent to：四加二～六。Four plus two equals (is) six. (符号为 =) 2.(几乎就是) amount to; be tantamount to：他的回答～拒绝。His answer amounts to a refusal.

邓[鄧](dèng)
【邓小平理论】 Dèng Xiǎopíng lǐlùn Deng Xiaoping theory

凳[櫈](dèng)
【凳子】 dèng·zi stool：方～ square stool / 竹～ bamboo stool

澄(dèng) (of a liquid) settle (另见"澄"chéng)
【澄清】 dèngqīng (of a liquid) settle; become clear：明矾可以～浊水。Alum will settle turbid water.

磴(dèng) step; stone step：这段楼梯有18～儿。The flight of stairs has 18 steps.

瞪(dèng) open (one's eyes) wide; stare; glare

【瞪眼】 dèngyǎn **1**.(睁大眼睛) open one's eyes wide; stare; glare **2**.(怒目而视) glower and glare at sb.; get angry with sb.

镫(dèng) stirrup

【镫骨】 dènggǔ 〈*Anat*.〉 stapes; stirrup bone

【镫子】 dèng·zi stirrup

di

低(dī) **1**.(不高) low: ～声 in a low voice / 代价很～ at a very low price **2**.(向下垂) let droop; hang down: ～下头 hang one's head

【低产】 dīchǎn low yield

【低产田】 dīchǎntián low-yield land; low-yielding land

【低产作物】 dīchǎn zuòwù low-yielding crop

【低潮】 dīcháo low tide; low ebb

【低沉】 dīchén **1**.(阴暗) overcast; lowering **2**.(指声音) low and deep **3**.(指情绪) low-spirited; downcast: 看来他今天情绪～。He seems in low spirits today.

【低垂】 dīchuí hang low

【低等植物】 dīděng zhíwù lower plant

【低地】 dīdì lowland

【低调】 dīdiào low key; low-key (adj.): ～讲话 low-key speech

【低飞】 dīfēi low flight; fly at a low altitude

【低估】 dīgū underestimate; underrate

【低谷】 dīgǔ **1**.〈*Geol*.〉 low ebb **2**.(最低点) bathos; low point; nadir

【低级】 dījí **1**.(初步) elementary; rudimentary; lower: ～阶段 lower stage **2**.(庸俗) vulgar; low

【低级趣味】 dījí qùwèi vulgar taste; vulgar interests: 迎合～ cater for vulgar interests

【低贱】 dījiàn low and degrading; humble

【低空】 dīkōng low altitude; low level

【低空飞行】 dīkōng fēixíng low-altitude flying; low-level flying

【低空轰炸】 dīkōng hōngzhà low-level bombing

【低空侦察】 dīkōng zhēnchá low-altitude reconnaissance

【低廉】 dīlián cheap; low; low-priced: 价格～。Prices are low.

【低劣】 dīliè inferior; low-grade: 质量～ of inferior quality

【低落】 dīluò low; downcast: 情绪～ be low-spirited; be downcast

【低能】 dīnéng **1**.〈*Physics*〉 low energy **2**.〈*Med*.〉 mental deficiency; feeble-mindedness

【低能儿】 dīnéng'ér imbecile; retarded child

【低年级】 dīniánjí primary grades

【低频】 dīpín 〈*Physics*〉 low frequence

【低气压】 dīqìyā 〈*Meteorol*.〉 low pressure; depression

【低热】 dīrè 〈*Med*.〉 low-grade fever; low fever; slight fever

【低人一等】 dī rén yī děng inferior to others

【低三下四】 dī sān xià sì **1**.(卑贱) lowly; mean; humble **2**.(奴态) servile; obsequious; cringing

【低烧】 dīshāo 〈*Med*.〉 low fever; slight fever

【低声】 dīshēng in a low voice; under one's breath; with bated breath

【低声下气】 dī shēng xià qì soft-spoken and submissive; meek and subservient

【低水箱】 dīshuǐxiāng low flush tank

【低水箱扳手】 dīshuǐxiāng bān·shou flush; handle

【低俗】 dīsú vulgar; low

【低速】 dīsù low speed: ～驾驶 drive at low speed

【低碳钢】 dītàngāng low carbon steel

【低糖】 dītáng light syrup

【低头】 dītóu **1**.(垂下头) lower one's head; bow one's head; hang one's head **2**.(屈服) yield; submit: ～认罪 plead guilty; admit one's guilt

【低洼】 dīwā low-lying

【低洼地】 dīwādì low-lying land

【低微】 dīwēi **1**.(指声音) low **2**.(少,微薄) meager (AmE.); meagre (BrE.); scanty **3**.(指地位) lowly; humble

【低温】 dīwēn **1**.(低的温度) low temperature **2**.(低气温) microtherm **3**.(低体温) hypothermia

【低息】 dīxī 〈*Econ*.〉 low interest

【低下】 dīxià **1**.(在标准之下) low; lowly:

地位～ be of low status 2.（指品质、格调等）vulgar; low
【低限】 dīxiàn lower bound
【低消耗】 dīxiāohào low consumption (of raw materials, fuel, etc.)
【低血糖】 dīxuètáng 〈*Med.*〉 hypoglycemia
【低压】 dīyā 1.（低的压力）low pressure 2.（低电压）low tension; low voltage 3.（低气压）low pressure; depression 4.（低血压）minimum pressure
【低压槽】 dīyācáo 〈*Meteorol.*〉 trough
【低音大号】 dīyīn dàhào 〈*Music*〉 tuba
【低音鼓】 dīyīngǔ 〈*Music*〉 bass drum
【低音管】 dīyīnguǎn 〈*Music*〉 bassoon
【低音键】 dīyīnjiàn 〈*Music*〉 bass buttons
【低音拾音器】 dīyīn shíyīnqì 〈*Music*〉 bass pick-up; rhythm pick-up
【低音提琴】 dīyīn tíqín 〈*Music*〉 contrabass; double bass
【低座摩托车】 dīzuò mótuōchē scooter

堤［隄］(dī) dike; dyke; embankment
【堤岸】 dī'àn embankment
【堤坝】 dībà dikes and dams
【堤防】 dīfáng dike; embankment：加固～ strengthen the dikes

提(dī)
（另见"提"tí）
【提防】 dī·fang take precautions against; be on guard against; beware of：～感染 take precautions against infections

嘀(dī)
（另见"嘀"dí）
【嘀嗒】 dīdā 〈*onom.*〉 tick; ticktack; tick-tock：台钟～响。The clock is ticking.
【嘀嗒】 dī·da drip

滴(dī) 1.（滴落，滴注）drip 2.〈*classifier*〉 drop
【滴答】 dīdā 〈*onom.*〉 tick; ticktack; tick-tock：台钟在～响。The clock is ticking.
【滴答】 dī·da drip
【滴滴答答】 dīdī-dādā ticktack; pitapat
【滴滴涕】 dīdītì 〈*Chem.*〉 DDT; dichloro-diphenyl- trichoroethane
【滴定】 dīdìng 〈*Chem.*〉 titration
【滴管】 dīguǎn 〈*Chem.*〉 dropper
【滴灌】 dīguàn 〈*Agric.*〉 drip irrigation; trickle irrigation
【滴剂】 dījì 〈*Med.*〉 drip
【滴水不漏】 dīshuǐ-bùlòu 1.（不漏水）water-tight; leakproof 2.（没有漏洞）flawless; without any omission
【滴水成冰】 dīshuǐ-chéngbīng (so cold that) dripping water freezes; freezing cold

镝(dī) 〈*Chem.*〉 dysprosium（元素符号 Dy）

迪［廸］(dí) enlighten; guide
【迪斯科】 dí·sikē disco; discotheque：跳～ disco (v.)
【迪斯科舞厅】 dí·sikē wǔtīng discotheque
【迪斯科音乐】 dí·sikē yīnyuè disco music
【迪厅】 dítīng discotheque

笛(dí) 1.（竹笛）bamboo flute 2.（发音器）whistle：汽～ steam whistle
【笛子】 dí·zi bamboo flute：吹～ flute; play the flute

的(dí) 1.（真实）true; really 2.（出租汽车）taxi：打～ take a taxi; go by taxi
（另见"的"de, dì）
【的确】 díquè indeed; really：影片～相当好。The film was quite good really.
【的确良】 díquèliáng 〈*Textiles*〉 dacron; polyester

涤［滌］(dí)
【涤除】 díchú wash away; do away with; eliminate：～旧习 do away with old customs
【涤荡】 dídàng wash away; cleanse
【涤卡】 díkǎ polyester-cotton khaki
【涤纶】 dílún 〈*Textiles*〉 polyester fiber
【涤棉布】 dímiánbù polyester-cotton blend

敌［敵］(dí) 1.（敌人）enemy; foe 2.（敌对）oppose; resist; fight 3.（相敌）match; equal
【敌百虫】 díbǎichóng 〈*Agric. Chem.*〉 dipterex
【敌不住】 díbùzhù be no match for
【敌敌畏】 dídíwèi 〈*Chem.*〉 DDVP; dichlovos
【敌对】 díduì hostile; antagonistic：～态度 hostile attitude
【敌对情绪】 díduì qíngxù hostilities; enmity：由来已久的～ historical enmity

【敌对行动】 díduì xíngdòng hostilities; hostile act
【敌国】 díguó enemy state
【敌后】 díhòu enemy's rear area
【敌机】 díjī an enemy plane; a hostile plane
【敌舰】 díjiàn an enemy war ship
【敌军】 díjūn enemy troops; the enemy
【敌情】 díqíng the enemy's situation
【敌情观念】 díqíng guānniàn alertness to the presence of the enemy; vigilance against the enemy
【敌人】 dírén enemy; foe
【敌视】 díshì be hostile to; be antagonistic to; adopt a hostile attitude towards
【敌手】 díshǒu 1.(对手) match; opponent; adversary 2.(敌人的掌握) enemy hands
【敌台】 dítái enemy broadcasting station
【敌特】 dítè enemy spy; enemy agent
【敌伪】 díwěi the enemy and the puppet regime
【敌伪人员】 díwěi rényuán enemy and puppet personnel
【敌伪时期】 díwěi shíqī the period of Japanese occupation; during the Japanese occupation
【敌我不分】 dí-wǒ-bùfēn fail to differentiate between the enemy and ourselves
【敌意】 díyì hostility; enmity; animosity
【敌营】 díyíng enemy camp
【敌占区】 dízhànqū enemy-occupied area; enemy-occupied territory

嘀［啾］(dí) whisper; murmur (另见"嘀"dī)

【嘀咕】 dí·gu 1.(小声说) whisper; talk in whispers 2.(猜疑) have sth. on one's mind; have misgivings about sth.

嫡(dí) 1.(妻子所生) of or by the wife 2.(血统近的) of lineal descent; closely related

【嫡传】 díchuán handed down in a direct line from the master
【嫡亲】 díqīn of lineal descent; blood relations; close parental relations
【嫡系】 díxì 1.(一线相传) direct line of descent 2.(正支) one's own clique
【嫡系部队】 díxì bùduì troops under one's direct control
【嫡子】 dízǐ son born of one's legal wife

诋(dǐ) slander; defame

【诋毁】 dǐhuǐ slander; defame; defamation (n.); vilify; vilification (n.); calumniate; calumny (n.): ～对手的好名声 slander his opponent's good name

邸(dǐ) residence: 官～ official residence

抵(dǐ) 1.(支撑) support; sustain; prop 2.(抵挡) resist; withstand 3.(抵偿) compensate for; make good 4.(抵押) mortgage 5.(抵消) balance; set off 6.(相当) be equal to: 他一个人～两个用。He can do the work of two. 7.(抵达) reach; arrive at

【抵偿】 dǐcháng compensate for; make good; make up for
【抵触】 dǐchù conflict; contradict
【抵触情绪】 dǐchù qíngxù resentment; resistance
【抵达】 dǐdá arrive at; arrive in; reach
【抵挡】 dǐdǎng keep out; ward off; check; withstand
【抵抗】 dǐkàng resist; stand up to: ～侵略 resist aggression; stand up against aggression
【抵抗力】 dǐkànglì resistance: ～低 have a low resistance
【抵赖】 dǐlài deny; disavow: 不容～ brook no denial / ～罪行 deny one's guilt; refuse to admit one's crime
【抵命】 dǐmìng pay for life with life; atone by life
【抵消】 dǐxiāo offset; cancel out; counteract: ～影响 offset an influence / 相互～ cancel out each other
【抵押】 dǐyā mortgage: 以某物作～ raise a mortgage on sth.
【抵押品】 dǐyāpǐn security; pledge
【抵御】 dǐyù resist; withstand: ～进攻 resist an attack
【抵债】 dǐzhài pay a debt in kind or by labor
【抵制】 dǐzhì resist; boycott

底(dǐ) 1.(底部) bottom; base 2.(底细) the heart of a matter; ins and outs 3.(底稿) rough draft 4.(底子) a copy kept as a record: 留个～儿 keep a copy on file 5.(末尾) end 6.(衬托面) ground; background; foundation

【底板】 dǐbǎn base plate
【底版】 dǐbǎn negative; photographic plate
【底边】 dǐbiān base
【底层】 dǐcéng 1.（一楼）first floor (AmE.); ground floor (BrE.) 2.（社会最低一层）bottom; the lowest rung
【底肥】 dǐféi 〈*Agric*.〉 base fertilizer
【底稿】 dǐgǎo draft; manuscript
【底火】 dǐhuǒ 1.（炉中的）the fire in a stove before fuel is added 2.（子弹底部的）primer; ignition cartridge
【底价】 dǐjià minimum price; base price
【底牌】 dǐpái hand; cards in one's hand: 摊出～ tip one's hand / 亮出～ show one's hand
【底盘】 dǐpán 1.〈*Auto*〉 chassis 2.（仪器主板）main board 3.（底座）base; pedestal
【底片】 dǐpiàn negative; photographic plate
【底片夹】 dǐpiànjiā film holder
【底片架】 dǐpiànjià negative rack
【底漆】 dǐqī priming paint; primer
【底色】 dǐsè bottom; ground color
【底数】 dǐshù 1.（事情原委）the truth or root of a matter; how a matter actually stands 2.〈*Math*.〉 base number
【底细】 dǐ·xì ins and outs; exact details
【底下】 dǐ·xia 1.（下面）under; below; beneath 2.（以后）next; later; afterwards
【底线】 dǐxiàn 1.〈*Math*.〉 base line 2.〈*Football*〉 goal line 3.〈*Basketball*〉 end line 4.〈*Volleyball*〉 back line 5.〈*Textiles*〉 bobbin thread 6.（卧底的人）a planted agent
【底薪】 dǐxīn base pay
【底子】 dǐ·zi 1.（底）bottom; base 2.（基础）foundation 3.（草稿）rough draft or sketch 4.（留底）a copy kept as a record 5.（剩下的残余）remnant
【底座】 dǐzuò base; pedestal; foundation

砥 (dǐ) whetstone

【砥砺】 dǐlì temper; fortify; toughen
【砥柱中流】 Dǐzhù-zhōngliú pillar standing in midstream; a giant rock obstructing the perilous current

地 (dì) 1.（地球）the earth 2.（陆地）land; soil: 山～ hilly land 3.（田地）fields 4.（地面）ground; floor 5.（地区）place; locality: 全国各～ all parts of the country; throughout the country 6.（形势；状况）position; situation 7.（衬托面）background; ground 8.（路程）distance

【地板】 dìbǎn 1.（木楼板）floor board 2.（室内地面）floor
【地磅】 dìbàng weighbridge
【地堡】 dìbǎo 〈*Mil*.〉 bunker; blockhouse; pillbox
【地表】 dìbiǎo the earth's surface
【地表水】 dìbiǎoshuǐ surface water
【地步】 dìbù 1.（处境）condition; plight 2.（程度）extent; degree 3.（余地）room for action
【地层】 dìcéng stratum; layer
【地产】 dìchǎn landed estate; landed property
【地磁】 dìcí 〈*Physics*〉 geomagnetism; terrestrial magnetism
【地大物博】 dìdà-wùbó vast territory and abundant resources; a big country abounding in natural wealth
【地带】 dìdài district; region; zone; belt: 森林～ a forest region / 沙漠～ a desert region / 危险～ a danger zone / 无人～ no man's land
【地道】 dìdào 1.（地下坑道）tunnel 2.（真名产）from the place noted for the product; genuine 3.（纯正的）pure; typical 4.（够标准；实在）well-done; thorough
【地点】 dìdiǎn place; site; locale: 事故发生的～ the locale of an accident
【地洞】 dìdòng a hole in the ground; burrow
【地段】 dìduàn a sector of an area; a section of an area: 划分～ divide into sections
【地对地导弹】 dìduìdì dǎodàn ground-to-ground missile
【地对舰导弹】 dìduìjiàn dǎodàn ground-to-ship missile
【地对空导弹】 dìduìkōng dǎodàn ground-to-air missile
【地对水下导弹】 dìduìshuǐxià dǎodàn ground-to-under-water missile
【地方】 dìfāng 1.（各行政区的）locality 2.（当地的）local 3.（某一地区）place; space; room: 你是什么～人？Where are you from? 4.（部分）part; respect: 剧中最动人的～ the most touching part of the play

【地方保护主义】 dìfāng bǎohù zhǔyì local protectionism; regional protectionism
【地方病】 dìfāngbìng endemic disease
【地方工业】 dìfāng gōngyè local industry
【地方税】 dìfāngshuì local tax
【地方戏】 dìfāngxì local opera; local drama
【地方志】 dìfāngzhì local chronicles; annals of local history
【地广人稀】 dìguǎng-rénxī a scarcely populated area
【地基】 dìjī 1.(土层) ground 2.(基础) foundation 3.(地皮) land for building
【地窖】 dìjiào cellar
【地界】 dìjiè the boundary of a piece of land
【地雷】 dìléi mine; land mine: 埋～ plant mines; lay mines
【地理】 dìlǐ 1.(总情况) geographical features of a place 2.(地理学) geography; geographical (adj.): 经济～ economic geography / 自然～ physical geography / ～位置 geographical position ‖ 地理学家 geographer
【地利】 dìlì 1.(地理优势) favorable geographical position; topographical advantages 2.(利于种植的土地条件) land productivity
【地漏】 dìlòu 〈*Archit.*〉 floor drain
【地幔】 dìmàn 〈*Geol.*〉 the earth's mantle
【地貌】 dìmào the general configuration of the earth's surface; landforms
【地面】 dìmiàn 1.(地的表面) the earth's surface; ground: 高出～ above ground level 2.(建筑物的地面) ground; floor 3.(地区) region; area; territory
【地面沉降】 dìmiàn chénjiàng 〈*Geol.*〉 surface subsidence
【地面接收站】 dìmiàn jiēshōuzhàn satellite earth station
【地面能见度】 dìmiàn néngjiàndù 〈*Aeron.*〉 control-tower visibility; ground visibility
【地名】 dìmíng place name; geographic name
【地膜】 dìmó film for covering earth
【地盘】 dìpán territory under one's control; domain: 争夺～ compete for spheres of influence
【地皮】 dìpí 1.(建筑用地) land for building 2.(地表面) ground
【地平线】 dìpíngxiàn horizon
【地铺】 dìpù shakedown on the floor
【地壳】 dìqiào 〈*Geol.*〉 the earth's crust
【地球】 dìqiú the earth; the globe
【地球同步通信卫星】 dìqiú tóngbù tōngxìn wèixīng Syncom satellite
【地球仪】 dìqiúyí (terrestrial) globe
【地区】 dìqū 1.(较大的地方) area; district; region: 上海～ the Shanghai area / 沿边～ border area 2.(行政划分单位) prefecture
【地区差价】 dìqū chājià regional price differences
【地区经济布局】 dìqū jīngjì bùjú the regional distribution of the economy
【地热】 dìrè 〈*Geol.*〉 the heat of the earth's interior; terrestrial heat
【地热发电】 dìrè fādiàn geothermal power generation
【地势】 dìshì physical features of a place; relief; terrain; topography
【地毯】 dìtǎn carpet; rug: 满铺～ wall-to-wall carpet / 铺～ carpet (v.)
【地铁】 dìtiě 1.(地下铁道) underground railway; metro; subway; tube: 乘坐～ take the subway 2.(地铁列车) railcar
【地铁车辆】 dìtiě chēliàng railcar
【地铁站】 dìtiězhàn subway station; tube station
【地铁站台】 dìtiě zhàntái subway platform
【地头】 dìtóu 1.(地边儿) edge of a field 2.(目的地) the destination
【地图】 dìtú map: 一张世界～ a map of the world / 大比例尺～ a large-scale map
【地图集】 dìtújí atlas: 世界～ an atlas of the world
【地委】 dìwěi prefectural Party committee
【地位】 dìwèi 1.(社会关系中的位置) position; standing; place; status: 经济～ economic status / 社会～ social position; social status / 国际～ international status; international standing 2.(所占的地方) place; space: ～不够 not enough space
【地峡】 dìxiá isthmus: 巴拿马～ the Isthmus of Panama / 苏伊士～ the Isthmus of Suez
【地下】 dìxià 1.(地面之下) underground; subterranean 2.(秘密活动) secret (activity); underground 3.(地面上) on the ground: 从～拣起 pick up from the ground / 掉在～ fall on the ground

【地下电缆】 dìxià diànlǎn buried cable; underground cable
【地下宫殿】 dìxià gōngdiàn underground palace
【地下河流】 dìxià héliú subterranean river
【地下核试验】 dìxià héshìyàn underground nuclear test
【地下室】 dìxiàshì basement; cellar
【地下水】 dìxiàshuǐ groundwater; subterranean water
【地下水位】 dìxià shuǐwèi groundwater level; water table
【地下铁道】 dìxià tiědào underground railway; metro; subway; tube
【地下通道】 dìxià tōngdào underpass
【地下资源】 dìxià zīyuán hidden resources
【地线】 dìxiàn 〈*Electr.*〉 ground wire; earth wire
【地心】 dìxīn the earth's core
【地心引力】 dìxīn yǐnlì gravity; terrestrial gravity
【地形】 dìxíng **1.**（地貌）terrain: ～地物 the terrain and its features **2.**（测绘学）topography; topographical (adj.)
【地形图】 dìxíngtú topographic map; relief map
【地形雨】 dìxíngyǔ orographic rain
【地狱】 dìyù hell; inferno; infernal (adj.)
【地域】 dìyù region; district
【地缘】 dìyuán geographical
【地震】 dìzhèn earthquake; seism; seismic (adj.): 里氏 4.3 级～ a shock of 4.3 magnitude on the Richter scale
【地震烈度】 dìzhèn lièdù earthquake intensity
【地震区】 dìzhènqū seismic area
【地震学】 dìzhènxué seismology; seismologic (adj.) ‖ 地震学家 seismologist
【地震仪】 dìzhènyí seismograph
【地震震级】 dìzhèn zhènjí (earthquake) magnitude
【地址】 dìzhǐ address: 能把您的地址给我吗? Could you give me your address, please? ‖ 写姓名地址 address (v.): 他在信上写好姓名地址,然后贴上邮票。He addressed the letter and stuck a stamp on it.
【地质】 dìzhì geology; geological (adj.) ‖ 地质学家 geologist
【地质博物馆】 dìzhì bówùguǎn geological museum
【地质地图】 dìzhì dìtú geological map
【地质勘探】 dìzhì kāntàn geological prospecting
【地质勘探队】 dìzhì kāntànduì geological prospecting party
【地质年代】 dìzhì niándài geological ages
【地质水文情况】 dìzhì shuǐwén qíngkuàng geological and hydrological condition
【地中海】 dìzhōnghǎi the Mediterranean (Sea)
【地主】 dìzhǔ **1.**（土地占有者）landlord **2.**（主人）host: 尽～之谊 perform the duties of the host
【地租】 dìzū land rent; ground rent; rent

弟 (dì) younger brother

【弟弟】 dì·di younger brother; brother
【弟妹】 dìmèi **1.**（弟弟和妹妹）younger brother and sister **2.**（弟媳）sister-in-law
【弟兄】 dì·xiong brothers
【弟子】 dìzǐ disciple; pupil; follower

递［遞］(dì) **1.**（传递）hand over; pass; give **2.**（顺次）successively; in the proper order

【递补】 dìbǔ fill vacancies in the proper order
【递给】 dìgěi hand over; pass on
【递归】 dìguī 〈*Math.*〉 recursion; recurrence
【递加】 dìjiā progressively increase; successively increase; increase by degrees
【递减】 dìjiǎn decrease progressively; decrease successively; decrease by degrees
【递降】 dìjiàng descend; descent (n.)
【递交】 dìjiāo hand over; present; submit: ～国书 present one's credentials
【递解】 dìjiè escort (a criminal) from one place to another: ～出境 send sb. across the border
【递升】 dìshēng promote to the next rank
【递送】 dìsòng send; deliver: ～公文 deliver a document / ～信件 deliver letters
【递眼色】 dìyǎnsè wink at sb.
【递增】 dìzēng increase progressively; increase by degrees

第 (dì) **1.**（表示次序）～一 first / ～二 second / ～三 third / ～四 fourth / ～五 fifth / ～六 sixth / ～七 seventh / ～八

eighth / ～九 ninth 2.（宅第）the residence of a high official
【第二把手】 dì èr bǎ shǒu number two man; second in command
【第二版】 dì'èrbǎn the second edition
【第二产业】 dì èr chǎnyè secondary industry
【第二次世界大战】 Dì Èr Cì Shìjiè Dàzhàn the Second World War; World War II
【第二审】 dì'èrshěn 〈*Law*〉 second instance
【第二小提琴】 dì èr xiǎotíqín 〈*Music*〉 second violin
【第二职业】 dì èr zhíyè second job; second occupation (in spare time)
【第六感觉】 dì liù gǎnjué the sixth sense
【第三产业】 dì sān chǎnyè tertiary industry
【第三度烧伤】 dì sān dù shāoshāng 〈*Med.*〉 third-degree burn
【第三轨】 dìsānguǐ 〈*Railway*〉 third rail
【第三人】 dìsānrén 〈*Law*〉 a third party
【第三人称】 dì sān rénchēng 〈*Gram.*〉 third person
【第三世界】 dì sān shìjiè the third world; third-world (adj.): 一个～国家 a third-world country
【第三梯队】 dì sān tīduì third echelon
【第三者】 dìsānzhě 1.（第三方）a third party (to a dispute, etc.) 2.（指插足者）a third person
【第三者责任保险】 dìsānzhě zérèn bǎoxiǎn 〈*Insurance*〉 third-party insurance
【第四媒体】 dì sì méitǐ fourth media
【第五纵队】 dì wǔ zòngduì fifth column
【第一】 dì yī first; primary; foremost: 获得～名 win first place; get a first; win a championship
【第一把手】 dì yī bǎ shǒu first in command; number one man; a person holding primary responsibility
【第一产业】 dì yī chǎnyè primary industry
【第一次世界大战】 Dì Yī Cì Shìjiè Dàzhàn the First World War; World War I
【第一夫人】 dì yī fū·rén the first lady
【第一副本】 dì yī fùběn first authentic copy
【第一轮投票】 dì yī lún tóupiào first round of voting
【第一审】 dìyīshěn 〈*Law*〉 first instance
【第一时间】 dì yī shíjiān to be the first
【第一手】 dìyīshǒu firsthand: ～材料 firsthand material
【第一线】 dìyīxiàn forefront; front line; first line: 在～工作 work in the forefront
【第一现场】 dì yī xiànchǎng 〈*Law*〉 primary scene
【第一小提琴】 dì yī xiǎotíqín 〈*Music*〉 first violin

的 (dì) target; bull's-eye: 有～放矢 shoot the arrow at the target; have a definite object in view
（另见“的”de, dí）

帝 (dì) 1.（上帝）God 2.（皇帝）emperor 3.（帝国主义）imperialism
【帝国】 dìguó empire; imperial (adj.)
【帝国主义】 dìguó zhǔyì 1.（指主义）imperialism; imperialist (adj.): ～战争 imperialist war / 反对～的斗争 the struggle against imperialism 2.（指国家）imperialist country ‖ 帝国主义者 imperialist
【帝王】 dìwáng emperor; monarch; empress (f.)
【帝制】 dìzhì monarchy; monarchic system

谛 (dì) 1.（仔细）carefully; attentively 2.（道理）meaning; significance: 真～ true significance; truth
【谛听】 dìtīng listen attentively

缔 (dì) from a friendship; conclude a treaty
【缔结】 dìjié conclude; establish
【缔约】 dìyuē conclude a treaty; sign a treaty: ～双方 both contracting parties
【缔约国】 dìyuēguó signatory (state) to a treaty; party to a treaty
【缔造】 dìzào found; create
【缔造者】 dìzàozhě founder

碲 (dì) 〈*Chem.*〉 tellurium (元素符号 Te)

dia

嗲 (diǎ) 〈*dial.*〉 playful tone or manner

dian

掂［敁］(diān) weigh in the hand

【掂量】 diān·liáng 1.（掂）weigh in the hand 2.（斟酌）think over; weigh up

颠 (diān) 1.（头顶）crown (of the head) 2.（山顶）top; summit 3.（颠簸）jolt; bump 4.（跌落）fall; turn over; topple down 5.（跑）run; go away

【颠簸】 diānbǒ jolt; bump; toss: 在山路上～行驶 bump along the mountain road; jolt along the mountain road

【颠倒】 diāndǎo 1.（倒置）put upside down; turn upside down; transpose; reverse; invert 2.（错乱）confused; disordered

【颠倒黑白】 diāndǎo-hēibái confound black and white; confuse right and wrong; stand facts on their heads

【颠覆】 diānfù overturn; subvert; subversion (n.); subversive (adj.): 企图～该国合法政府 attempt to subvert the legal government

【颠覆活动】 diānfù huódòng subversive activities: 进行～ conduct subversive activities

【颠沛流离】 diānpèi-liúlí drift from place to place, homeless and miserable; wander about in a desperate plight; lead a vagrant life

【颠扑不破】 diānpū-bùpò irrefutable; indisputable: ～的真理 irrefutable truth

【颠茄】 diānqié 〈*Pharm.*〉 belladonna

【颠三倒四】 diānsān-dǎosì incoherent; disorderly; confuse

巅 (diān) mountain peak; summit: 喜马拉雅山之～ the summit of the Himalayas

癫 (diān) mentally deranged; insane

【癫狂】 diānkuáng 1.（病）demented; mad; insane 2.（轻佻）frivolous

【癫痫】 diānxián 〈*Med.*〉 epilepsy; epileptic (adj.): 患有～ suffer from epilepsy; have epilepsy

【癫痫发作】 diānxián fāzuò 〈*Med.*〉 epileptic attack; epileptic fit

【癫痫病患者】 diānxiánbìng huànzhě epileptic

典 (diǎn) 1.（标准）standard; law; canon 2.（典范性书籍）standard work of scholarship 3.（典故）allusion; literary quotation 4.（典礼）ceremony: 盛～ a grand ceremony; a grand occasion 5.（主持）be in charge of 6.（抵典）mortgage

【典当】 diǎndàng 1.（典和当）pawn; mortgage 2.（当铺）pawn shop; pawnbroker's

【典当业】 diǎndàngyè pawnbroking

【典范】 diǎnfàn model; example; paragon

【典故】 diǎngù allusion; literary quotation

【典礼】 diǎnlǐ ceremony; celebration: 奠基～ corner-stone-lying ceremony / 开幕～ opening ceremony / 下水～ launching ceremony

【典型】 diǎnxíng 1.（有代表性的人或事）typical case; typical example; model; type: 用～进行示范 demonstrate with typical example 2.（个性特征）typical; representative

【典押】 diǎnyā pawn; mortgage

【典雅】 diǎnyǎ refined; elegant

碘 (diǎn) 〈*Chem.*〉 iodine（元素符号 I）

【碘甘油】 diǎngānyóu 〈*Pharm.*〉 iodine glycerin

【碘酒】 diǎnjiǔ 〈*Pharm.*〉 tincture of iodine

【碘钨灯】 diǎnwūdēng iodine-tungsten lamp

【碘中毒】 diǎnzhòngdú 〈*Med.*〉 iodism

点［點］ (diǎn) 1.（小滴）drop 2.（小痕迹）spot; dot; speck 3.〈*Meth.*〉 point 4.（小数点）point; decimal point: 八～三 eight point three 5.（少量）a little; a bit; some: 吃～东西 take some food 6.（地点或起步的标志）place; point 7.（事物的方面或部分）aspect; feature: 特～ characteristic feature 8.（加上点）put a dot: ～三个点表示省略 put three dots to show that sth. has been omitted 9.（触）touch on very briefly; skim 10.（钟点）o'clock: 上午9～ nine o'clock in the morning 11.（牌或色子等上的点）dot

【点播】 diǎnbō 1.〈*Agric.*〉 sow in holes; dibble 2.（点播广播节目）request: 下面一首歌是北京的赵先生～的。The next song is a request from Mr. Zhao in Beijing. / 下面一首歌是为李芳～的。The next song is a request for Li Fang.

【点播节目】 diǎnbō jiémù request program; request item: 听众～ a request program for the listeners

【点菜】 diǎncài order dishes; choose dishes from a menu (in a restaurant)

【点灯】 diǎndēng light a lamp

【点滴】 diǎndī 1.（零星）a bit: ～经验 bits of experience 2.〈*Med.*〉 (have an) intravenous

drip
【点焊】 diǎnhàn spot welding; point welding
【点焊机】 diǎnhànjī spot-welder
【点火】 diǎnhuǒ 1.（把火点着）light a fire 2.（使机器起动）ignition 3.（制造事端）stir up trouble
【点火系统】 diǎnhuǒ xìtǒng 〈*Mech.*〉 ignition system
【点货】 diǎnhuò check over goods; take stock
【点名】 diǎnmíng 1.（查点人数）call the roll 2.（指名）mention sb. by name：～批评 criticize sb. by name
【点名册】 diǎnmíngcè roll book; roll
【点明】 diǎnmíng point out; put one's finger on
【点破】 diǎnpò reveal; bring sth. out into the open：～某人的意图 reveal sb's intention
【点球】 diǎnqiú 〈*Football*〉 penalty kick
【点燃】 diǎnrán light; kindle; ignite：～导火线 light a fuse; ignite a fuse
【点收】 diǎnshōu check and accept
【点数】 diǎnshù check the number; check one by one; count
【点题】 diǎntí bring out the theme
【点头】 diǎntóu nod one's head; nod：向某人～ nod to sb.（as a greeting）
【点头之交】 diǎntóu-zhījiāo nodding acquaintance
【点心】 diǎn·xin light refreshments; pastry
【点眼药】 diǎn yǎnyào put drops in the eyes
【点阵】 diǎnzhèn dot matrix
【点阵式打印机】 diǎnzhènshì dǎyìnjī matrix printer; stylus printer
【点缀】 diǎn·zhuì 1.（衬托;装饰）embellish; ornament; adorn 2.（应景）use sth. merely for show
【点子】 diǎn·zi 1.（小滴）drop（of liquid）2.（小痕迹）spot; dot; speck 3.（节拍）beat（of percussion instruments）4.（要点）key point 5.（主意）idea; pointer：出～ give advice; offer advice

踮［跕］（diǎn） stand on tiptoe：他～起脚尖。He stood on tiptoe.

电［電］（diàn） 1.（电力）electricity：断～ cut off the power supply 2.（触电）give or get an electric shock 3.（电报）telegram; cable：～悉 acknowledge the receipt of a telegram 4.（打电报）send a telegram
【电霸】 diànbà overlord of electricity
【电报】 diànbào telegram; cable：打～ send a telegram / 传真～ facsimile telegraph / 加急～ urgent telegram; express telegram / 礼仪～ greeting telegram
【电报局】 diànbàojú telegraph office
【电报纸】 diànbàozhǐ telegram form; telegram blank
【电表】 diànbiǎo 1.（泛指电气仪表）electric meter 2.（计用电度数的）kilowatt-hour meter
【电冰箱】 diànbīngxiāng （electric）refrigerator; freezer; fridge
【电波】 diànbō electric wave
【电厂】 diànchǎng power plant; generating plant
【电唱机】 diànchàngjī electric gramophone; electric phonograph
【电炒勺】 diànchǎosháo electric wok
【电车】 diànchē 1.（有轨电车）tram; tramcar; streetcar 2.（无轨电车）trolleybus; trolley
【电池】 diànchí （electric）cell; battery
【电池仓】 diànchícāng battery compartment
【电池充电器】 diànchí chōngdiànqì battery charger
【电传】 diànchuán fax
【电传机】 diànchuánjī fax machine
【电磁波】 diàncíbō electromagnetic wave
【电磁铁】 diàncítiě electromagnet
【电大】 diàndà TV university
【电导】 diàndǎo 〈*Physics*〉 electrical conduction
【电灯】 diàndēng electric lamp; electric light
【电灯泡】 diàndēngpào electric（light）bulb
【电动】 diàndòng electic; power-driven; power-operated
【电动机】 diàndòngjī （electric）motor
【电动楼梯】 diàndòng lóutī （electric）escalator
【电动汽车】 diàndòng qìchē electromobile; electric car
【电动势】 diàndòngshì 〈*Physics*〉 eletrodynamical potential
【电动剃须刀】 diàndòng tìxūdāo electric

shaver; electric razor
【电度表】 diàndùbiǎo watt-hour meter; electric meter
【电镀】 diàndù electroplate
【电饭煲】 diànfànbāo electric rice cooker
【电费】 diànfèi charges for electricity
【电风扇】 diànfēngshàn electric fan
【电杆】 diàngān pole; mast
【电感】 diàngǎn 〈*Physics*〉 inductance
【电告】 diàngào inform by telegram
【电工】 diàngōng **1.**(电工学) electrical engineering **2.**(电气工人) electrician
【电功率】 diàngōnglǜ electric power
【电管局】 diànguǎnjú bureau in charge of electricity
【电焊】 diànhàn electric welding
【电焊工】 diànhàngōng electric welder
【电焊机】 diànhànjī electric welding machine; electric welder
【电焊条】 diànhàntiáo welding electrode; welding rod
【电荷】 diànhè electric charge; charge
【电弧】 diànhú electric arc
【电弧焊】 diànhúhàn arc welding
【电弧炉】 diànhúlú arc furnace
【电化教学】 diànhuà jiàoxué audiovisual education program
【电化教育】 diànhuà jiàoyù education with electrical audiovisual aids
【电话】 diànhuà **1.**(电话设备) telephone; phone: 无绳～ wireless telephone / 无线～ radio telephone / 公用～ public telephone; pay telephone **2.**(打电话) call; phone call: 长途～ trunk-call; long distance call / 市内～ local call / 长途直拨～ direct dialing; direct long distance dialing / 国内长途直拨～ DDD; domestic direct dialing / 国际长途直拨～ IDD; international direct dialing / 接话人付费～ collect call / 打～ make a phone call; phone sb.; call sb. up; ring sb. up; give sb. a ring / ～占线 number engaged
【电话簿】 diànhuàbù telephone directory; phone book
【电话分机】 diànhuà fēnjī extension (telephone)
【电话号码】 diànhuà hàomǎ telephone number
【电话会议】 diànhuà huìyì telephone conference
【电话机】 diànhuàjī telephone (set)
【电话间】 diànhuàjiān telephone box; telephone kiosk: 公用～ public telephone box; public telephone kiosk
【电话局】 diànhuàjú telephone office; telephone exchange: 长途～ long distance office
【电话门铃】 diànhuà ménlíng entryphone
【电话亭】 diànhuàtíng telephone box; telephone kiosk
【电话投币口】 diànhuà tóubìkǒu coin slot
【电话用户】 diànhuà yònghù telephone subscriber
【电话中继线】 diànhuà zhōngjìxiàn main line; trunk line
【电话总机】 diànhuà zǒngjī central exchange
【电汇】 diànhuì **1.**(通过电报汇兑) remit money by telegram **2.**(电汇款项) telegraphic money
【电机】 diànjī electrical machinery
【电机车】 diànjīchē electric locomotive
【电吉他】 diànjítā electric guitar
【电极】 diànjí electrode
【电键】 diànjiàn telegraph key; key button
【电教】 diànjiào electrified education; education with electrical audiovisual aids
【电教片】 diànjiàopiàn films or telefilms of audiovisual education
【电解】 diànjiě electrolysis
【电解质】 diànjiězhì electrolyte
【电介质】 diànjièzhì dielectric
【电锯】 diànjù electric saw
【电烤箱】 diànkǎoxiāng electric oven
【电缆】 diànlǎn electric cable; cable: 同轴～ coaxial cable
【电老虎】 diànlǎohǔ **1.**(指耗电大户) electric tiger; a big power-consumer **2.**(同"电霸") overlord of electricity
【电烙铁】 diànlào·tie **1.**(电熨斗) electric iron **2.**(电焊铁) electric soldering iron
【电离】 diànlí ionization
【电离层】 diànlícéng 〈*Meteorol.*〉 ionosphere
【电力】 diànlì electric power; power
【电力电缆】 diànlì diànlǎn electricity cables
【电力供应】 diànlì gòngyìng supply of electricity

【电力机车】 diànlì jīchē electric locomotive
【电力网】 diànlìwǎng power network
【电疗】 diànliáo 〈*Med.*〉 electrotherapy
【电料】 diànliào electric materials and appliances
【电铃】 diànlíng electric bell
【电流】 diànliú electric current
【电流表】 diànliúbiǎo galvanometer
【电炉】 diànlú **1.**(取暖电炉) electric stove; hot plate **2.**〈*Metall.*〉 electric furnace
【电路】 diànlù (electric) circuit: 集成～ integrated circuit / 印刷～ printed circuit
【电路图】 diànlùtú circuit diagram
【电码】 diànmǎ (telegraphic) code
【电码本】 diànmǎběn code book
【电门】 diànmén (electric) switch
【电木】 diànmù 〈*Plastic*〉 bakelite
【电木琴】 diànmùqín 〈*Music*〉 vibraphone
【电脑】 diànnǎo computer: 个人～ personal computer
【电脑病毒】 diànnǎo bìngdú computer virus
【电钮】 diànniǔ button; push button: 按～ press a button; push a button
【电平】 diànpíng electric level
【电瓶】 diànpíng storage battery; accumulator
【电瓶车】 diànpíngchē storage battery car
【电气】 diànqì electric
【电气化】 diànqìhuà electrify; electrification (n.)
【电气化铁路】 diànqìhuà tiělù electric railway
【电器】 diànqì **1.**(电器设备) electrical equipment; electrical appliance **2.**(家用电器) electrical home appliance
【电热】 diànrè electric heat; electrothermal
【电热器】 diànrèqì electric heater
【电热丝】 diànrèsī heating wire
【电热毯】 diànrètǎn electric bedding; electric blanket
【电容】 diànróng electric capacity; capacitance
【电容器】 diànróngqì condenser; capacitor: 可变～ variable capacitor
【电扇】 diànshàn electric fan
【电石】 diànshí 〈*Chem.*〉 calcium carbide
【电石灯】 diànshídēng acetylene lamp
【电视】 diànshì television; TV: 彩色～ color television / 高清晰度～ HDTV; high definition TV / 看～ watch television ‖ 用～播送 televise (v.)
【电视采访】 diànshì cǎifǎng television interview
【电视大奖赛】 diànshì dàjiǎngsài grand TV prize
【电视点歌】 diànshì diǎngē TV song request
【电视机】 diànshìjī TV set
【电视讲座】 diànshì jiǎngzuò telecourse
【电视接收机】 diànshì jiēshōujī television receiver; television set
【电视剧】 diànshìjù TV play
【电视连续剧】 diànshì liánxùjù TV serial
【电视片】 diànshìpiàn telefilm
【电视实况转播】 diànshì shíkuàng zhuǎnbō live television coverage; live telecast
【电视塔】 diànshìtǎ television tower
【电视台】 diànshìtái television station
【电视天线】 diànshì tiānxiàn television antenna
【电视系列片】 diànshì xìlièpiàn TV series
【电视信道】 diànshì xìndào television channel
【电势】 diànshì electrical potential
【电势差】 diànshìchā electrical potential difference
【电台】 diàntái **1.**(无线电台) transmitter-receiver; transceiver **2.**(广播电台) broadcasting station; radio station
【电梯】 diàntī lift; elevator
【电筒】 diàntǒng (electric) torch; flashlight
【电头】 diàntóu dateline
【电网】 diànwǎng **1.**(通电的铁丝网) electrified wire netting; live wire entanglement **2.**(电力网) power network
【电位】 diànwèi electrical potential
【电位差】 diànwèichā electrical potential difference
【电文】 diànwén text (of a telegram)
【电线】 diànxiàn (electric) wire
【电线杆子】 diànxiàn gān·zi (wire) pole
【电信】 diànxìn telecommunication
【电信局】 diànxìnjú telecommunication bureau
【电刑】 diànxíng electrucution
【电靴】 diànxuē 〈*Trolley*〉 trolley; trolley shoe

【电学】 diànxué electricity (as a science)
【电讯】 diànxùn 1.(电报发出的消息)(telegraphic) dispatch 2.(无线电讯号) telecommunications
【电讯稿】 diànxùngǎo news bulletin
【电压】 diànyā voltage
【电压表】 diànyābiǎo voltmeter
【电影】 diànyǐng film; movie; motion picture: 去看～ go to the cinema / 放映～ show a film / 拍摄～ shoot a film / 彩色～ color film / 宽银幕～ wide-screen film
【电影回顾展】 diànyǐng huígùzhǎn film retrospective show
【电影节】 diànyǐngjié film festival
【电影界】 diànyǐngjiè filmdom
【电影摄影机】 diànyǐng shèyǐngjī film camera
【电影演员】 diànyǐng yǎnyuán film actor (n.); film actress (f.)
【电影院】 diànyǐngyuàn cinema; movie (house)
【电影制片厂】 diànyǐng zhìpiànchǎng (film) studio
【电影周】 diànyǐngzhōu film week
【电泳】 diànyǒng 〈*Physics*〉 electrophoresis; phoresis
【电源】 diànyuán power supply; power source; mains: 接上～ connect with the mains / 切断～ cut off the electricity supply
【电源线】 diànyuánxiàn power cord
【电熨斗】 diànyùndǒu electric iron
【电灶】 diànzào electric cooking stove
【电闸】 diànzhá electric brake
【电站】 diànzhàn power station
【电钟】 diànzhōng electric clock; electroclock
【电子】 diànzǐ electron; electronic (adj.): 负～ negatron / 正～ positron
【电子秤】 diànzǐchèng electronic-weighing system
【电子管】 diànzǐguǎn electron tube; valve
【电子计算机】 diànzǐ jìsuànjī electronic computer
【电子商务】 diànzǐ shāngwù e-business
【电子显微镜】 diànzǐ xiǎnwēijìng electron microscope
【电子学】 diànzǐxué electronics; electronic
【电子音乐】 diànzǐ yīnyuè electronic music
【电子邮件】 diànzǐ yóujiàn e-mail
【电子游戏】 diànzǐ yóuxì video game; computer game; electronic game
【电子游戏机】 diànzǐ yóuxìjī video game machine
【电子战】 diànzǐzhàn electronic warfare
【电子政务】 diànzǐ zhèngwù e-government
【电阻】 diànzǔ 1.〈*Electr*.〉 resistance 2.(电阻器) resistor
【电阻器】 diànzǔqì resistor
【电钻】 diànzuàn electric drill

佃 (diàn) rent land (from a landlord)

【佃东】 diàndōng landlord
【佃户】 diànhù tenant (farmer)
【佃农】 diànnóng tenant-peasant; tenant farmer
【佃租】 diànzū 1.(指租赁行为) tenancy 2.(指租金) land rent

店 (diàn) 1.(店铺) shop; store 2.(客店) inn

【店面】 diànmiàn shop front
【店铺】 diànpù shop; store
【店员】 diànyuán shop assistant; salesclerk; clerk; salesman (m.); saleswoman (f.)
【店主】 diànzhǔ shopkeeper; storekeeper

惦 (diàn) remember with concern; be concerned about; keep thinking about

【惦记】 diànjì remember with concern; be concerned about; keep thinking about: ～朋友们的安全 be concerned about the safety of one's friends
【惦念】 diànniàn keep thinking about; be anxious about; worry about

玷 (diàn) 1.(白玉的斑点) a flaw in a piece of jade 2.(使有污点) blemish; disgrace

【玷辱】 diànrǔ bring disgrace on; be a disgrace to
【玷污】 diànwū 1.(弄脏,比喻辱没) stain; sully; tarnish: ～某人名誉 smear sb's reputation; sully sb. s reputation 2.(奸污) rape; debauch

垫 [墊] (diàn) 1.(垫平;垫高) put sth. under sth. else to raise it or make it level; fill up; pad 2.(垫子) pad; cushion; mat: 床～ mattress 3.(垫付) pay for sb. and expect to be repaid later

【垫板】 diànbǎn 〈*Railway*〉 tie plate; baseplate
【垫付】 diànfù pay for sb. and expect to be repaid later
【垫肩】 diànjiān shoulder pad
【垫款】 diànkuǎn money advanced for sb. to be paid back later
【垫平】 diànpíng level up: 把球场～ level a field
【垫圈】 diànquān 〈*Mech.*〉 washer
【垫上运动】 diànshàng yùndòng mat tumbling; mat work
【垫子】 diàn·zi mat; pad; cushion

淀[澱[1]](diàn) 1.(沉淀) form sediment; settle; precipitate 2.(浅湖) shallow lake: 白洋～ Baiyang Dian Lake
【淀粉】 diànfěn starch; amylum

靛(diàn) 1.(靛蓝) indigo 2.(深蓝) indigo-blue
【靛白】 diànbái indigo white
【靛红】 diànhóng 〈*Textiles*〉 isatin
【靛蓝】 diànlán indigo
【靛青】 diànqīng indigo-blue

奠(diàn) 1.(建立) establish; settle 2.(祭奠) make offerings to the spirits of the dead
【奠定】 diàndìng establish; settle
【奠基】 diànjī lay a foundation
【奠基礼】 diànjīlǐ foundation stone laying ceremony
【奠基人】 diànjīrén founder
【奠基石】 diànjīshí foundation stone; cornerstone

殿(diàn) 1.(宫殿) hall; palace; temple 2.(在最后) at the rear
【殿后】 diànhòu bring up the rear
【殿堂】 diàntáng hall; palace
【殿下】 diànxià 1.(直接称呼) Your Highness 2.(间接称呼) His Highness; Her Highness

diao

刁(diāo) tricky; artful; sly
【刁滑】 diāohuá cunning; crafty; sly
【刁难】 diāonàn create difficulties; make things difficult: 故意～ deliberately make things difficult for others
【刁钻】 diāozuān cunning; artful; wily: ～古怪 sly and capricious

叼(diāo) hold in the mouth: 嘴里～着枝香烟 with a cigarette dangling from one's lips

凋[彫](diāo) wither
【凋败】 diāobài wither and fall
【凋零】 diāolíng withered, fallen and scattered about
【凋落】 diāoluò wither and fall
【凋谢】 diāoxiè 1.(脱落) wither and fall 2.(老死) die of old age

碉(diāo)
【碉堡】 diāobǎo pillbox; blockhouse

雕[彫、琱、鵰[2]](diāo) 1.(刻画) carve; engrave: 石～ stone carving 2.(鹫) eagle; vulture
【雕花】 diāohuā 1.(刻花纹) carve patterns; carve designs (on woodwork): ～烟盒 engraved cigarette 2.(刻的花纹) carving
【雕刻】 diāokè 1.(指动作) carve; engrave: 这个雕像是用一根树干～出来的。The figure is carved from a single tree trunk. 2.(雕刻品) carving; engraving: 玉石～ jade carving
【雕刻师】 diāokèshī engraver
【雕塑】 diāosù 1.(指动作) sculpture: 用石块～一尊胸像 sculpture a bust out of the stone 2.(雕塑品) sculpture: 动物～ sculpture of animals
【雕塑家】 diāosùjiā sculptor
【雕像】 diāoxiàng statue: 半身～ bust / 大理石～ marble statue/ 给…立～ put up a statue to sb.; erect a statue to sb
【雕琢】 diāozhuó 1.(雕刻) cut and polish; carve 2.(过分修饰) write in an ornate style

貂[鼦](diāo) marten
【貂皮】 diāopí fur of marten; marten fur
【貂皮大衣】 diāopí dàyī marten coat

吊[弔](diào) 1.(悬挂) hang; suspend 2.(用绳子往上提或向下放) lift up or let down with a rope, etc. 3.(祭奠) condole; mourn 4.(吊车) crane

【吊车】 diàochē crane; hoist
【吊床】 diàochuáng hammock
【吊灯】 diàodēng pendent lamp
【吊儿郎当】 diào·er-lángdāng careless and casual; slovenly
【吊环】 diàohuán 〈*Sports*〉 rings
【吊货桅杆】 diàohuò wéigān 〈*Ship*〉 cargo boom
【吊桥】 diàoqiáo **1.**(用钢索悬吊的桥) suspension bridge **2.**(可吊起、放下的桥) drawbridge
【吊丧】 diàosāng pay a condolence call
【吊嗓子】 diào sǎng·zi train one's voice; exercise one's voice
【吊扇】 diàoshàn ceiling fan
【吊死】 diàosǐ hang by the neck; hang oneself
【吊袜带】 diàowàdài garters; suspenders
【吊胃口】 diào wèikǒu tantalize
【吊销】 diàoxiāo revoke; withdraw: ~驾驶执照 revoke a driving licence
【吊唁】 diàoyàn condole; offer one's condolences

钓 (diào) angle; fish with a hook and line

【钓饵】 diào'ěr bait
【钓竿】 diàogān fishing rod
【钓钩】 diàogōu fishhook
【钓具】 diàojù fishing tackle
【钓鱼】 diàoyú angle; go fishing

调 (diào) **1.**(调动) transfer; shift; move: 借~ transfer temporarily **2.**(腔调) accent **3.**〈*Music*〉 key **4.**(音调) air; tune; melody: 定~ call the tune **5.**(声调) tone; tune
(另见"调"tiáo)

【调兵遣将】 diàobīng-qiǎnjiàng move troops; deploy forces
【调拨】 diàobō allocate and transfer; allot: ~物资 allocate supplies / ~资金 allocate and transfer funds
【调查】 diàochá investigate; inquire into; look into; survey
【调查报告】 diàochá bàogào findings report
【调查提纲】 diàochá tígāng outline for investigation; questionnaire
【调查委员会】 diàochá wěiyuánhuì board of inquiry
【调车场】 diàochēchǎng 〈*Railway*〉 switchyard
【调动】 diàodòng **1.**(调换) transfer; shift: ~工作 transfer sb. to another post **2.**(调动军队) move (troops); maneuver; muster **3.**(动员) bring into play; arouse; mobilize: ~起群众的积极性 release the initiative of the masses
【调度】 diàodù **1.**(调遣) dispatch: ~车辆 dispatch buses **2.**(调度员) dispatcher **3.**(安排) manage; control
【调度室】 diàodùshì dispatcher's office; control room
【调防】 diàofáng 〈*Mil.*〉 relieve a garrison
【调干学员】 diàogàn xuéyuán a college student enrolled from among cadres; cadre student
【调函】 diàohán transfer letter
【调号】 diàohào **1.**(声调符号) tone mark **2.**〈*Music*〉 key signature
【调换】 diàohuàn exchange; change; swap
【调集】 diàojí assemble; muster
【调令】 diàolìng transfer order
【调门儿】 diàoménr pitch
【调派】 diàopài send; assign
【调配】 diàopèi allocate; deploy
【调遣】 diàoqiǎn dispatch; assign: 接受~ accept an assignment
【调任】 diàorèn be transferred to another post
【调研】 diàoyán investigate and study
【调演】 diàoyǎn assemble theater troupes to give performances
【调用】 diàoyòng transfer sb.; reallocate sth.
【调运】 diàoyùn allocate and transport
【调职】 diàozhí be transferred to another post
【调转】 diàozhuǎn **1.**(调动工作) transfer sb. to another post **2.**(掉转) turn round
【调子】 diào·zi **1.**〈*Music*〉 tune; melody: 降低~ play down one's tune **2.**(论调) tone (of speech); note: ~低沉的演说 low-keyed speech

掉 (diào) **1.**(掉落) fall; drop; shed; come off: ~进圈套 fall into a trap **2.**(失掉) lose; be missing **3.**(落在后边) fall behind 4.(掉转) turn 5.(降低;减少) drop; reduce: ～分量 reduce in weight / ～价 a drop in price 6.(掉换) change; exchange

【掉包】 diàobāo stealthily substitute one thing for another

【掉队】 diàoduì drop out; drop off; fall behind

【掉换】 diàohuàn exchange; change; swap: ～工作 be assigned a new job; be transferred to another / ～座位 exchange seats

【掉价】 diàojià 1.(价格降低) drop in price 2.(丢面子) lose one's face

【掉泪】 diàolèi come to tears; tears falling

【掉色】 diàoshǎi lose color; fade

【掉头】 diàotóu turn round; turn about: 公共汽车～ turn bus right round

【掉以轻心】 diàoyǐ-qīngxīn lower one's guard; treat sth. lightly

【掉转】 diàozhuǎn turn round

die

爹(diē) father; dad; daddy; pa: ～娘 mum and dad; ma and pa; parents

跌(diē) 1.(摔) fall; tumble: ～入小河 tumble into a stream 2.(物体落下) fall 3.(价格下落) drop; fall: 物价下～。Prices have dropped.

【跌倒】 diēdǎo fall; tumble: ～在地 fall to the ground

【跌跌撞撞】 diē·die-zhuàngzhuàng dodder along; stagger along

【跌价】 diējià go down in price; fall in price; drop in price

【跌跤】 diējiāo 1.(摔跟头) trip and fall; stumble and fall; have a fall 2.(犯错误;受挫折) make a mistake; meet with a setback

【跌落】 diēluò 1.(物体落下) fall 2.(价格下落) drop

【跌伤】 diēshāng get injured by a fall; fall and get hurt

迭(dié) 1.(轮流) alternate; change 2.(屡次) repeatedly; again and again

【迭次】 diécì repeatedly; again and again

【迭起】 diéqǐ occur repeatedly; happen frequently

【迭用】 diéyòng use alternately

谍(dié) 1.(谍报活动) espionage 2.(谍报人员) intelligence agent; spy

【谍报】 diébào information obtained through espionage; intelligence report; intelligence

【谍报员】 diébàoyuán intelligence agent; spy

喋(dié)

【喋喋不休】 diédié-bùxiū chatter away; talk endlessly; rattle on

碟(dié) small plate; small dish

【碟子】 dié·zi small plate; small dish

蝶[蜨](dié) butterfly

【蝶骨】 diégǔ 〈*Anat.*〉 sphenoid bone

【蝶兰】 diélán 〈*Bot.*〉 phalaenopsis

【蝶形螺母】 diéxíng luómǔ wing nut; butterfly nut

【蝶泳】 diéyǒng 〈*Sports*〉 butterfly stroke

叠[疊、疉](dié) 1.(重叠) pile up; repeat 2.(折叠) fold: 把床单～好 fold the sheet

【叠罗汉】 diéluóhàn 〈*Sports*〉 pyramid

【叠印】 diéyìn 〈*Printing*〉 trapping

ding

丁(dīng) 1.(成年男子) man 2.(人口) members of a family: population 3.(第四) fourth 4.(小块) cubes; small cubes (of meat or vegetable)

【丁醇】 dīngchún 〈*Chem.*〉 butanol; butyl alcohol

【丁当】 dīngdāng 〈*onomat.*〉 ding-dong; jingle; clatter

【丁点儿】 dīngdiǎnr a tiny bit: 这～事不必放在心上。Don't bother about such trifles.

【丁冬】 dīngdōng 〈*onomat.*〉 tinkle

【丁零】 dīnglíng 〈*onomat.*〉 tinkle; jingle

【丁宁】 dīngníng urge again and again; warn; exhort: ～周至 give thoughtful advice

【丁香】 dīngxiāng 1.〈*Bot.*〉 lilac 2.(香料) clove

【丁字】 dīngzì T-shaped

【丁字尺】 dīngzìchǐ T-square

【丁字钢】 dīngzìgāng T-steel

【丁字镐】 dīngzìgǎo pickax

【丁字街】 dīngzìjiē T-shaped road junction
【丁字路口】 dīngzì lùkǒu intersection (AmE.); T-junction (BrE.)
【丁字形】 dīngzìxíng T-shaped

叮 (dīng) 1.(叮咬) sting; bite 2.(追问) say or ask again to make sure
【叮咛】 dīngníng remind sb. of sth. repeatedly
【叮咬】 dīngyǎo sting; bite
【叮嘱】 dīngzhǔ urge again and again; warn; exhort

盯 (dīng) fix one's eyes on; gaze at; stare
【盯梢】 dīngshāo shadow sb.; tail sb.
【盯住】 dīng·zhù keep a close watch (on)

钉 (dīng) 1.(铁钉) nail; tack 2.(钉鞋上的钉) spike: 跑鞋上有～。The running shoes have spikes. 3.(紧钉不放) follow closely; tail 4.(督促) urge; press: ～着孩子做作业 urge the children to do their homework
(另见"钉"dìng)
【钉锤】 dīngchuí nail hammer; claw hammer
【钉帽】 dīngmào the head of a nail
【钉人】 dīngrén 〈*Sports*〉 watch an opponent in a game
【钉梢】 dīngshāo shadow sb.; tail sb.
【钉鞋】 dīngxié 〈*Sports*〉 spikes
【钉子】 dīng·zi 1.(铁钉) nail 2.(意外障碍) snag: 碰～ hit a snag; strike a snag; run against a snag 3.(埋伏的人) saboteur: 安插个～ plant a saboteur
【钉子户】 dīng·zihù nail household; nail unit

疔 (dīng) malignant boil
【疔毒】 dīngdú 〈*Chin. Med.*〉 serious case of furuncle

耵 (dīng)
【耵聍】 dīngníng earwax

酊 (dīng) tincture
【酊剂】 dīngjì tincture

顶 (dǐng) 1.(最高部分) crown; peak; top 2.(用头支撑) carry on the head 3.(用头撞击) gore; butt 4.(迎着) go against 5.(支撑) push from below or behind; push up; prop up: 把门～上 prop up the door 6.(顶撞) retort; turn down 7.(担当) cope with; stand up to 8.(顶替) take the place of; substitute; replace 9.(相当) equal; be equivalent to 10.(最) the most; exceedingly; best
【顶班】 dǐngbān work on regular shifts; work full time
【顶板】 dǐngbǎn 〈*Mineral.*〉 roof; apical plate
【顶灯】 dǐngdēng 〈*Auto*〉 dome light
【顶点】 dǐngdiǎn 1.(极点) apex; zenith; acme; pinnacle 2.〈*Math.*〉 vertex; apex
【顶端】 dǐngduān top; peak; apex
【顶多】 dǐngduō at (the) most; at best
【顶风】 dǐngfēng 1.(迎着风) against the wind 2.(迎面的风) head wind
【顶峰】 dǐngfēng 1.(指山) peak: 最难攀登的～ the most difficult peaks to climb 2.(指最高点) summit; pinnacle: 科学的～ summit of science
【顶骨】 dǐnggǔ 〈*Anat.*〉 parietal bone
【顶回去】 dǐng huíqù reject; turn down
【顶级】 dǐngjí top: 最新～小说 the latest top fiction
【顶尖】 dǐngjiān 1.(顶心) tip 2.(顶级) top: ～大学 top university
【顶角】 dǐngjiǎo 〈*Math.*〉 vertex angle
【顶楼】 dǐnglóu attic; garret
【顶名】 dǐngmíng assume sb's name
【顶牛儿】 dǐngniúr lock horns like bulls; clash
【顶棚】 dǐngpéng ceiling
【顶球】 dǐngqiú 〈*Football*〉 head (a ball); header (n.)
【顶事】 dǐngshì be useful; serve the purpose
【顶替】 dǐngtì take sb's place; replace
【顶天立地】 dǐngtiān-lìdì of gigantic stature; of indomitable spirit
【顶头上司】 dǐngtóu shàng·si one's immediate superior; one's direct superior
【顶推拖船】 dǐng tuī tuōchuán pusher tug
【顶用】 dǐngyòng be of use; be of help; serve the purpose
【顶针】 dǐngzhēn thimble
【顶住】 dǐngzhù withstand; hold out against; stand up to
【顶撞】 dǐngzhuàng talk back; contradict

(one's elder or superior)

【顶嘴】 dǐngzuǐ reply defiantly; answer back; talk back：不许你～! None of your lip!

鼎 (dǐng)

【鼎鼎大名】 dǐngdǐng-dàmíng a great reputation

【鼎力】 dǐnglì your kind effort

【鼎立】 dǐnglì tripartite confrontation of forces

【鼎盛】 dǐngshèng in a period of great prosperity; at the height of power and splendors

订 (dìng) 1.(制订) conclude; draw up; agree on：～计划 draw up a plan; work out a plan / ～条约 conclude a treaty 2.(预订) subscribe to; book; order：～杂志 subscribe to a magazine / ～货 order merchandise / ～票 book tickets 3.(订正) make corrections; revise 4.(装订) staple together

【订单】 dìngdān order for goods; order form

【订费】 dìngfèi subscription (rate)

【订购】 dìnggòu order (goods); place an order for sth.

【订户】 dìnghù subscriber：杂志～ magazine subscriber

【订婚】 dìnghūn be engaged to; be betrothed to

【订婚戒指】 dìnghūn jiè·zhi engagement-ring

【订货】 dìnghuò order goods; place an order for goods：接受～ accept an order for goods

【订金】 dìngjīn bargain money; earnest money; down payment

【订立】 dìnglì conclude; make：～合同 conclude a contract

【订书钉】 dìngshūdīng staples

【订书机】 dìngshūjī stapler; stapling-machine

【订阅】 dìngyuè subscribe to：～报纸 subscribe to a newspaper

【订正】 dìngzhèng make corrections; emend：～印刷上的错误 correct errors of printing

钉 (dìng) 1.(用钉子) nail：～钉子 drive in a nail 2.(用针线) sew on：～扣子 sew a button on

(另见"钉"dīng)

定 (dìng) 1.(稳定) calm; stable 2.(决定) decide; fix; set 3.(已确定的) fixed; settled; established 4.(预定) subscribe to; book; order：～杂志 subscribe to a magazine / ～货 order merchandise / ～票 book tickets 5.(必定) surely; certainly; definitely

【定案】 dìng'àn 1.(做最后决定) decide on a verdict; reach a conclusion on a case 2.(最后的决定) verdict; final decision

【定本】 dìngběn final version

【定单】 dìngdān order for goods; order form

【定点】 dìngdiǎn 1.(选定，指定) specially designated 2.(规定时间) scheduled; regular：～航班 regular flight; scheduled flight

【定点厂家】 dìngdiǎn chǎngjiā specially-designated factory

【定夺】 dìngduó make a final decision; decide

【定额】 dìng'é quota; norm; allotment

【定岗】 dìnggǎng fix post

【定岗定责】 dìnggǎng dìngzhé fix post and responsibility

【定稿】 dìnggǎo 1.(最后审稿) finalize a manuscript, text, etc. 2.(审定的稿件) final version or text

【定规】 dìngguī established rule or practice; set pattern

【定婚】 dìnghūn be engaged (to be married); be betrothed

【定货】 dìnghuò order goods; place an order for goods：看样～ sample order

【定计】 dìngjì devise a stratagem; work out a scheme

【定价】 dìngjià 1.(规定价格) fix a price 2.(规定的价格) fixed price

【定见】 dìngjiàn definite opinion; set view

【定金】 dìngjīn bargain money; earnest money; down payment

【定睛】 dìngjīng fix one's eyes upon

【定居】 dìngjū settle down：回大陆～ come and settle on the mainland

【定局】 dìngjú 1.(指形势) foregone conclusion; inevitable outcome 2.(指最后决定) settle finally

【定理】 dìnglǐ theorem

【定量】 dìngliàng 1.(规定数量) fixed quantity; ration 2.(测定物质成分的数量) determine the amounts of the components of a substance

【定量分析】 dìngliàng fēnxī quantitative analysis

【定律】 dìnglǜ law：物质不灭～ law of conservation of matter

【定论】 dìnglùn final conclusion

【定名】 dìngmíng name；denominate

【定期】 dìngqī 1.（定下日期）fix a date 2.（有期限的）regular；at regular intervals；periodical：～轮换 rotate at regular intervals

【定期存款】 dìngqī chúnkuǎn fixed deposit；time deposit

【定期航班】 dìngqī hángbān on-line carrier

【定钱】 dìng·qián deposit：付～ put down a deposit

【定亲】 dìngqīn engagement（arranged by parents）；betrothal

【定然】 dìngrán certainly；definitely：～如此。It most necessarily be so.

【定神】 dìngshén 1.（使心神安定）collect oneself；compose oneself；pull oneself together 2.（集中注意力）concentrate one's attention

【定时】 dìngshí definite time

【定时器】 dìngshíqì timer

【定时炸弹】 dìngshí zhàdàn time bomb

【定息】 dìngxī fixed interest

【定向】 dìngxiàng directional

【定向爆破】 dìngxiàng bàopò directional blasting

【定向天线】 dìngxiàng tiānxiàn directional antenna

【定向研究】 dìngxiàng yánjiū decision-orientated study

【定向招生】 dìngxiàng zhāoshēng directional enrollment

【定心丸】 dìngxīnwán sth. capable of setting sb's mind at ease

【定型】 dìngxíng finalize the design；fall into a pattern

【定型产品】 dìngxíng chǎnpǐn approved product

【定性】 dìngxìng 1.（确定性质）determine the nature 2.（测定成分及性质）determine the chemical composition of a substance

【定义】 dìngyì definition：下～ give a definition

【定音鼓】 dìngyīngǔ 〈*Music*〉 kettle drum；timpano

【定影】 dìngyǐng 〈*Photog.*〉 fixing；fixation

【定影剂】 dìngyǐngjì 〈*Photog.*〉 fixer

【定影液】 dìngyǐngyè 〈*Photog.*〉 fixing bath

【定于】 dìngyú due to；scheduled to

【定语】 dìngyǔ 〈*Gram.*〉 attribute；attributive（adj.）

【定员】 dìngyuán fixed number of staff members or passengers

【定则】 dìngzé 〈*Physics*〉 rule：右手～ right-hand rule

【定值】 dìngzhí value

【定制】 dìngzhì have sth. made to order；have sth. custom-made：～家具 have furniture made to order

【定子】 dìngzǐ 〈*Electr.*〉 stator

【定罪】 dìngzuì declare sb. guilty；convict sb.

【定座】 dìngzuò reservation

【定做】 dìngzuò have sth. made to order；have sth. made to measure：～的衣服 tailor-made clothes

碇［矴、椗］（dìng） stone anchor；killick

【碇泊】 dìngbó anchor；berth：船～在上海。The ship berthed at Shanghai.

锭（dìng） 1.（块状物）ingot-shaped tablet：一～墨 a cake of Chinese ink 2.（纱锭）spindle

【锭剂】 dìngjì 〈*Pharm.*〉 lozenge；pastille；troche

【锭子】 dìng·zi 〈*Textiles*〉 spindle

diu

丢［丟］（diū） 1.（丢失）lose；mislay：我的笔～了。I've lost my pen. 2.（丢掉）throw；cast；toss 3.（搁置；放）put aside；lay aside

【丢丑】 diūchǒu lose face；be disgraced

【丢掉】 diūdiào 1.（遗失）lose 2.（抛弃）throw away；cast away；discard

【丢饭碗】 diū fànwǎn lose one's job

【丢份】 diūfèn lose face；be disgraced

【丢开】 diūkāi leave it off；forget for a while

【丢脸】 diūliǎn lose face；be disgraced

【丢面子】 diū miàn·zi lose face
【丢弃】 diūqì abandon; discard; give up
【丢人】 diūrén lose face; be disgraced
【丢三落四】 diūsān-làsì forgetful; scatter-brained
【丢失】 diūshī lose
【丢下】 diūxià throw down; lay aside
【丢卒保车】 diūzú-bǎojū sacrifice minor things to save major
铥（diū） 〈*Chem.*〉 thulium（元素符号 Tm）

dong

东［東］（dōng） **1.**（东方）east; easterly（adj.）：远～ Far East / 中～ Middle East **2.**（主人）master; owner **3.**（东道）host
【东半球】 dōngbànqiú 〈*Geog.*〉 the Eastern Hemisphere
【东北】 dōngběi **1.**（东北方向）northeast **2.**（中国东北）northeast of China; the Northeast：～平原 Northeast Plain
【东奔西跑】 dōngbēn-xīpǎo run around here and there; bustle about; rush about; rush around
【东部】 dōngbù east; eastern（adj.）：该国的～ the eastern part of the country / 中国～ Eastern China
【东道】 dōngdào one who treats sb. to a meal; host：做～ play the host; stand treat
【东道国】 dōngdàoguó host country
【东道主】 dōngdàozhǔ host
【东东北】 dōngdōngběi east-north-east
【东东南】 dōngdōngnán east-south-east
【东方】 dōngfāng **1.**（东） east; eastern（adj.）**2.**（指亚洲）the East; eastern（adj.）; the Orient; oriental（adj.）：～文明 the eastern civilization **3.**（与西方相对）the East; eastern（adj.）
【东方人】 dōngfāngrén **1.**（指亚洲东部的）oriental **2.**（指一个国家东部的）easterner
【东非】 Dōng Fēi East Africa; East African（adj.）
【东非大裂谷】 Dōng Fēi Dàliègǔ East African Rift Valley
【东风】 dōngfēng **1.**（指春风）east wind **2.**（比喻革命力量）driving force of revolution; the East Wind
【东海】 Dōnghǎi East China Sea
【东家】 dōng·jia master; boss
【东经】 dōngjīng 〈*Geog.*〉 east longitude：我们的位置在～ 116.4 度，北纬 39.9 度。Our position is longitude 116.4 degrees east, latitude 39.9 degrees north.
【东拉西扯】 dōnglā-xīchě drag in all sorts of irrelevant matters; talk at random
【东盟】 Dōngméng ASEAN; Association of South East Asian Nations
【东南】 dōngnán **1.**（东南方向）southeast; southeastern（adj.）**2.**（中国东南沿海地区）southeast China; the Southeast
【东南风】 dōngnánfēng southeast wind：今天刮～。There's a southeast wind today.
【东南西北】 dōngnán-xīběi all directions; north, south, east and west
【东南亚】 Dōngnán Yà Southeast Asia; South East Asia
【东挪西借】 dōngnuó-xījiè scrape money; borrow all around
【东欧】 Dōng Ōu Eastern Europe
【东跑西颠】 dōngpǎo-xīdiān run about busily
【东拼西凑】 dōngpīn-xīcòu scrape together; knock together
【东山再起】 Dōng Shān zàiqǐ stage a comeback
【东西】 dōngxī **1.**（东边和西边）east and west **2.**（从东到西）from east to west **3.**（事物；物体）thing **4.**（指人或动物）thing; creature
【东西方文化】 dōngxīfāng wénhuà oriental and occidental cultures
【东…西…】 dōng…xī… here ... there：东一个，西一个（of things）be scattered here and there
【东乡族】 Dōngxiāngzú Dongxiang（中国少数民族，主要分布在甘肃）
【东瀛】 Dōngyíng **1.**（东海）East China Sea **2.**（日本）Japan
【东张西望】 dōngzhāng-xīwàng gaze around; peer around
【东正教】 Dōngzhèngjiào 〈*Religion*〉 the Orthodox Eastern Church

冬［鼕²］(dōng) 1.(冬季) winter; wintry (adj.) 2.〈*onomat.*〉rat-tat; rat-a-tat; rub-a-dub

【冬瓜】 dōngguā wax gourd; Chinese wax-gourd

【冬季】 dōngjì winter; wintertime; wintry (adj.)

【冬季奥运会】 dōngjì Àoyùnhuì the Olympic Winter Games

【冬季体育运动】 dōngjì tǐyù yùndòng winter sports

【冬眠】 dōngmián 〈*Biol.*〉 winter sleep; hibernation

【冬暖夏凉】 dōngnuǎn-xiàliáng cool in summer and warm in winter

【冬青】 dōngqīng 〈*Bot.*〉 Chinese ilex

【冬笋】 dōngsǔn winter bamboo shoots

【冬天】 dōntiān winter; wintry (adj.): ～的天气 wintry weather

【冬小麦】 dōngxiǎomài winter wheat

【冬训】 dōngxùn winter training

【冬泳】 dōngyǒng winter swimming; swimming in outdoor waters in winter

【冬泳爱好者】 dōngyǒng àihàozhě winter swimmer

【冬运】 dōngyùn winter transportation

【冬至】 dōngzhì the Winter Solstice (12月21-23日交节)

【冬装】 dōngzhuāng winter dress; winter clothes

氡(dōng) 〈*Chem.*〉 radon (元素符号 Rn)

董(dǒng)

【董事】 dǒngshì director; trustee

【董事会】 dǒngshìhuì 1.(企业的) board of directors 2.(学校等的) board of trustees

【董事长】 dǒngshìzhǎng chairman of the board

懂(dǒng) understand; know: ～规矩 have good manners / ～德语 know German

【懂得】 dǒng·de understand; know; grasp

【懂行】 dǒngháng know the business; know the ropes

【懂事】 dǒngshì sensible; intelligent: ～的孩子 a sensible child

动［動］(dòng) 1.(移动) move; stir 2.(行动) act; get moving: 一举一～ every movement; every action 3.(改动) change; alter 4.(动用) use 5.(触动;感动) touch; arouse

【动笔】 dòngbǐ take up the pen; start writing

【动不动】 dòng·budòng easily; frequently; at every turn

【动产】 dòngchǎn movable property; movables; personal property

【动词】 dòngcí 〈*Linguis.*〉 verb: 及物～ transitive verb

【动荡】 dòngdàng 1.(指波浪) wavy; turbulent: 湖水～。The lake was turbulent. 2.(指局势、情况) turbulent; turbulence (n.); upheaval; unrest: ～的一个月 a turbulent month / ～的年代 in times of turbulence

【动荡不安】 dòngdàng-bù'ān turbulent; in turmoil

【动电】 dòngdiàn 〈*Electr.*〉 dynamic electricity

【动工】 dònggōng begin construction; start building

【动画片】 dònghuàpiàn animated cartoon; cartoon

【动火】 dònghuǒ 〈*colloq.*〉 get angry; flare up

【动机】 dòngjī motive; intention: ～不纯 have impure motives

【动静】 dòng·jing 1.(动作或说话的声音) the sound of sth. astir: 没有一点～ not a single sound; not the slightest stir 2.(情况) movement; activity: 发现可疑～ spot sth. suspicious

【动力】 dònglì 1.(各种作用力) motive power; power 2.(推动力量) motive force; driving force; impetus: 社会发展的～ the motive force of the development of society

【动力车间】 dònglì chējiān power houses

【动力工程】 dònglì gōngchéng power engineering

【动力工业】 dònglì gōngyè power industry

【动力学】 dònglìxué dynamics; kinetics

【动乱】 dòngluàn turmoil; disturbance; upheaval; turbulence

【动脉】 dòngmài artery

【动脉硬化】 dòngmài yìnghuà 〈*Med.*〉 arte-

riosclerosis
【动脑筋】 dòngnǎojīn consider; think hard; rack one's brains
【动怒】 dòngnù lose one's temper; flare up
【动气】 dòngqì 〈*colloq.*〉 take offense; get angry
【动迁户】 dòngqiānhù relocated households
【动情】 dòngqíng **1.**(情绪激动) get worked up; become excited **2.**(产生感情) become enamored; have one's (sexual) passions aroused
【动人】 dòngrén moving; touching: ～的情景 a moving scene
【动人心弦】 dòngrén-xīnxián be deeply moving; tug at one's heartstring
【动身】 dòngshēn leave to; go on a journey; set out on a journey
【动手】 dòngshǒu **1.**(开始做) start work; get to work **2.**(用手接触) touch; handle: 请勿～! No touching! **3.**(打人) raise a hand
【动手动脚】 dòngshǒu-dòngjiǎo get fresh with sb.
【动手术】 dòngshǒushù **1.**(医生做手术) perform an operation; operate on sb. **2.**(患者接受手术) have an operation; be operated on
【动态】 dòngtài **1.**(发展情况) developments; trends: 科技新～ recent developments in science and technology **2.**(变化状态) dynamic state
【动态平衡】 dòngtài pínghéng shifting balance
【动弹】 dòng·tan move; stir: ～不得 cannot move
【动听】 dòngtīng interesting to listen to; pleasant to listen to: ～的故事 attractive story / 娓娓～ be very pleasant to the ear
【动窝儿】 dòngwōr 〈*dial.*〉 start moving; make a move
【动武】 dòngwǔ use force; start a fight; come to blows
【动物】 dòngwù animal: 反刍～ ruminant / 脊椎～ vertebrate / 两栖～ amphibian / 爬行～ reptile / 哺乳～ mammal / 软体～ mollusk
【动物学】 dòngwùxué zoology; zoological (adj.) ‖ 动物学家 zoologist
【动物园】 dòngwùyuán zoo; zoological garden
【动物园饲养员】 dòngwùyuán sìyǎngyuán zookeeper: 我们看～喂老虎。We watched the zookeeper feeding the tigers.
【动向】 dòngxiàng trend; tendency: 时局～ trends of current affairs
【动心】 dòngxīn one's mind is perturbed; one's desire, enthusiasm or interest is aroused
【动刑】 dòngxíng torture; subject sb. to torture
【动摇】 dòngyáo **1.**(不稳定) vacillate; waver **2.**(使不稳定) shake; make sb's mind waver: ～军心 shake the morale
【动议】 dòngyì motion: 提出一项～ put forward a motion
【动用】 dòngyòng put to use; employ; draw on: ～大量人力 employ a tremendous amount of manpower / ～公款 draw upon public funds
【动员】 dòngyuán mobilize; arouse
【动员令】 dòngyuánlìng order of mobilization
【动辄】 dòngzhé 〈*written*〉 easily; frequently; at every turn
【动植物检疫】 dòngzhíwù jiǎnyì quarantine of animals and plants
【动作】 dòngzuò movement; motion; action; move (v.): ～缓慢 slow in one's movements / ～敏捷 quick in one's movements/ ～优美 graceful movements
【动作片】 dòngzuòpiàn 〈*Cinematog.*〉 actioner

冻[凍] (dòng) **1.**(遇冷凝固) freeze: ～肉 frozen meat **2.**(汤、汁等凝结的) jelly: 肉～儿 jellied meat **3.**(受冷或感到冷) feel very cold; freeze; be frost-bitten: 我～得慌。I am freezing.
【冻冰】 dòngbīng freeze: 湖上～了。The lake is frozen.
【冻疮】 dòngchuāng chilblain: 生～ have chilblains
【冻害】 dònghài 〈*Agric.*〉 freeze injury
【冻僵】 dòngjiāng frozen stiff; numb with cold
【冻结】 dòngjié **1.**(液体遇冷凝固) freeze; congeal **2.**(阻止流动或变动) freeze: ～资产 freeze assets / ～工资 freeze wages / ～新建设项目 put a freeze on new construction
【冻伤】 dòngshāng frostbite

【冻死】 dòng·sǐ freeze to death; freeze and perish; die of frost

【冻土带】 dòngtǔdài 〈*Geol.*〉 permafrost zone

【冻雨】 dòngyǔ 〈*Meteorol.*〉 sleet

栋[棟] (dòng) 1.(正梁) ridgepole 2.〈*classifier*〉一～公寓楼 an apartment house

【栋梁】 dòngliáng ridgepole and beam: 国家的～ pillar of the state

胨[腖] (dòng) peptone

侗 (dòng)

【侗族】 Dòngzú Dong (中国少数民族，主要分布在贵州、湖南、广西等地)

洞 (dòng) 1.(洞穴) hole; cavity 2.(透彻) penetratingly; thoroughly

【洞察】 dòngchá see clearly; have an insight into: ～下情 fully perceive the feelings of the masses

【洞彻】 dòngchè understand thoroughly

【洞达】 dòngdá understand thoroughly

【洞房】 dòngfáng bridal chamber; nuptial chamber

【洞若观火】 dòngruò-guānhuǒ see sth. as clearly as a blazing fire

【洞悉】 dòngxī know clearly; understand thoroughly

【洞穴】 dòngxué 1.(山洞) cave; cavern 2.〈*Golf*〉 hole

恫 (dòng) fear

【恫吓】 dònghè threaten; intimidate: 不怕～ defy any intimidation; defy any threat

胴 (dòng) body

【胴体】 dòngtǐ body

dou

都 (dōu) 1.(总括) all 2.(跟"是"字合用，说明理由) just because of: ～是下雨，运动会才延期的。Just because of the rain, the sports meet was put off. 3.(甚至) even: 这个我连想～没想过。I haven't even thought of it. 4.(已经) already: 她～90岁了。She's already ninety.
(另见"都"dū)

兜 (dōu) 1.(口袋) pocket; bag 2.(兜住) wrap up in a piece of cloth, etc.: ～着几个苹果 carry a few apples wrapped up 3.(绕) move round 4.(招揽) canvass; solicit 5.(承担) take upon oneself; take responsibility for sth.: 出了问题我～着。If anything goes wrong, I'll take responsibility for it.

【兜风】 dōufēng 1.(船帆等挡住风) catch the wind 2.(坐车游逛) go for a drive; go for a spin (in a car)

【兜揽】 dōulǎn 1.(招揽) canvass; solicit: ～生意 solicit custom; drum up trade 2.(往自己身上拉) take upon oneself (sb. else's work)

【兜圈子】 dōu quān·zi 1.(绕圈儿) go around in circles; circle 2.(说话不直截了当) beat about the bush

【兜售】 dōushòu peddle; hawk: 在每个街角都有人在～他的货。On every street corner there were trader peddling his wares.

【兜子】 dōu·zi pocket; bag

斗 (dǒu)
(另见"斗"dòu)

【斗胆】 dǒudǎn 〈*politeness*〉 make bold; venture: ～建议 venture to suggest

【斗笠】 dǒulì bamboo hat

【斗篷】 dǒu·peng cape; cloak

【斗室】 dǒushì small room

抖 (dǒu) 1.(哆嗦) tremble; shiver; quiver: 冷得发～ shiver with cold 2.(抖动) shake; jerk: 把床单上的灰～掉 shake the dust off a sheet 3.(鼓起精神) rouse; stir up 4.(得意) get on in the world

【抖动】 dǒudòng shake; tremble; vibrate

【抖搂】 dǒu·lou 1.(振动) shake off; shake out of sth. 2.(揭露) expose; bring to light 3.(浪费) waste; squander: 把钱～光 waste all the money

【抖擞】 dǒusǒu enliven; rouse: 精神～ full of energy and vitality

【抖威风】 dǒu wēifēng throw one's weight about

陡 (dǒu) 1.(坡度大) steep; steeply; precipitous: 重庆的有些街道相当～。Some of the streets in Chongqing are rather steep.

2.（陡然）suddenly; abruptly：价格～涨。There has been a steep increase in price.

【陡岸】 dǒu'àn bold shore; steep coast

【陡坡】 dǒupō steep slope

【陡峭】 dǒuqiào cliffy; precipitous：～的山峰 cliffy summit

【陡然】 dǒurán suddenly; unexpectedly

斗［鬥、鬦、鬭］（dòu） 1.（对打）fight; tussle 2.（斗争）struggle against; denounce 3.（争斗）contest with; contend with 4.（使动物相斗）make animals fight（as a game）5.（往一块凑）fit together

（另见"斗"dǒu）

【斗法】 dòufǎ 1.（用法术）match magic powers 2.（用计谋）play tricks

【斗鸡】 dòujī 1.（公鸡相斗）cock fight; cockfighting 2.（指鸡）gamecock

【斗气】 dòuqì quarrel just to vent one's spleen

【斗心眼】 dòu xīnyǎn rival in trickery

【斗争】 dòuzhēng 1.（双方的冲突、争斗）struggle; fight; combat：作不疲倦的～ wage a tireless struggle（against）2.（说理；控诉）accuse and denounce at a meeting 3.（努力奋斗）strive for; fight for：为争取独立和自由而～ fight for the independence and liberty

【斗志】 dòuzhì will to fight; fighting will：～昂扬 have high morale

【斗智】 dòuzhì battle of wits

【斗嘴】 dòuzuǐ squabble; bicker; tiff：别再～了。Stop bickering!

豆［荳］（dòu） legumes; pulses; beans; peas

【豆瓣酱】 dòubànjiàng thick broad-bean sauce

【豆饼】 dòubǐng 〈*Agric.*〉 cake of soya-bean husks

【豆腐】 dòu·fu bean curd; tofu：冻～ frozen bean curd

【豆腐干】 dòu·fugān dried bean curd; dehydrated bean curd

【豆腐脑儿】 dòu·funǎor jellied bean curd

【豆腐皮】 dòu·fupí skin of soybean milk

【豆腐乳】 dòu·furǔ fermented bean curd

【豆荚】 dòujiá pod

【豆浆】 dòujiāng soybean milk; soya milk

【豆角儿】 dòujiǎor 〈*colloq.*〉 fresh kidney beans

【豆秸】 dòujiē beanstalk

【豆蔻年华】 dòukòu-niánhuá marriageable age

【豆沙】 dòushā sweetened bean paste

【豆芽儿】 dòuyár bean sprouts

【豆油】 dòuyóu soybean oil

【豆汁】 dòuzhī soybean milk

【豆制品】 dòuzhìpǐn bean products

【豆子】 dòu·zi beans; peas

逗［鬥1–3、鬦1–3、鬭1–3］（dòu） 1.（引逗）tease; play with 2.（逗人笑）provoke（laughter, etc.）; amuse 3.（有趣）funny：你真～！How funny you are! 4.（逗留）stay; stop

【逗号】 dòuhào comma（符号为，）

【逗留】 dòuliú stay; stop：～一夜 make an overnight stop

【逗遛】 dòuliú stay; stop

【逗弄】 dòu·nong tease; kid; make fun of

【逗引】 dòuyǐn tease

痘（dòu） 1.（天花）smallpox：出～ suffer from smallpox 2.（痘苗）（bovine）vaccine：种～ be vaccinated 3.（疱疹）pox

【痘苗】 dòumiáo （bovine）vaccine

窦［竇］（dòu） 1.（孔洞）hole 2.〈*Anat.*〉 sinus; antrum：鼻～ paranasal sinus

du

都（dū） 1.（首都）capital 2.（大城市）big city; metropolis

（另见"都"dōu）

【都城】 dūchéng capital

【都会】 dūhuì city; metropolis

【都市】 dūshì city; metropolis

【都市化】 dūshìhuà urbanization

【都市人口】 dūshìrénkǒu urban population

嘟（dū） 1.〈*onomat.*〉 toot; honk 2.（撅嘴）pout

【嘟噜】 dū·lu 1.〈*classifier*〉 bunch; cluster：一～葡萄 a bunch of grapes 2.（向下垂）hang down in a bunch

【嘟囔】 dū·nang mutter to oneself; mumble

督（dū） superintend and direct
【督察】 dūchá superintend；supervise
【督促】 dūcù supervise and urge；remind sb. to do sth.
【督学】 dūxué educational inspector
【督战】 dūzhàn supervise military operations

毒（dú） 1.（毒物）poison；toxin：服～ take poison 2.（毒品）narcotics：贩～ traffic in drugs；drug trafficking / 吸～ take drugs 3.（有毒的）poisonous；noxious；poisoned：有～气体 noxious gas 4.（毒辣；厉害）malicious；cruel；fierce：～打某人 beat sb. mercilessly 5.（用毒物害死）kill with poison
【毒草】 dúcǎo poisonous weeds
【毒打】 dúdǎ beat cruelly；beat sb. up
【毒饵】 dú'ěr poison bait
【毒害】 dúhài 1.（下毒杀死）kill with poison 2.（使人受毒害）poison（sb's mind）：～人们的身心健康 damage people physically and mentally
【毒化】 dúhuà 1.（用毒品）poison 2.（使变得恶劣）poison；spoil：～会谈的气氛 poison the atmosphere of the talks
【毒剂】 dújì toxical；toxic
【毒辣】 dúlà sinister；diabolic：心肠～ harbor a murderous heart
【毒瘤】 dúliú malignant tumor；cancer
【毒品】 dúpǐn narcotic drugs；narcotics：滥用～ drug abuse
【毒品贩子】 dúpǐn fàn·zi drug trafficker；drug dealer
【毒品管制】 dúpǐn guǎnzhì drug control
【毒品买卖】 dúpǐn mǎimài sale of drugs
【毒品走私】 dúpǐn zhǒusī drug trafficking
【毒气】 dúqì poison gas；toxic smoke
【毒气弹】 dúqìdàn gas bomb
【毒蛇】 dúshé poisonous snake；venomous snake；viper
【毒手】 dúshǒu violent treachery：下～ resort to violent treachery；lay murderous hands on sb.
【毒死】 dú·sǐ kill with poison；poison
【毒素】 dúsù 1.（有毒物质）toxin 2.（有毒影响）poisonous influence
【毒瓦斯】 dúwǎsī gas；poison gas
【毒物】 dúwù poisonous substance；poison
【毒腺】 dúxiàn 〈*Zool*.〉poison gland
【毒刑】 dúxíng cruel corporal punishment；horrible torture
【毒性】 dúxìng toxicity；poisonousness：～猛烈 with drastic toxicity
【毒药】 dúyào poison；toxicant
【毒瘾】 dúyǐn drug addiction

独[獨]（dú） 1.（一个）only；single 2.（独自）alone；by oneself；in solitude 3.（年老无子女者）old people without offspring；the childless
【独霸】 dúbà dominate exclusively；monopolize
【独白】 dúbái soliloquy；monologue
【独裁】 dúcái dictatorship；autocratic rule
【独裁者】 dúcáizhě autocrat；dictator
【独唱】 dúchàng （vocal）solo
【独唱音乐会】 dúchàng yīnyuèhuì recital of a vocalist
【独出心裁】 dúchū-xīncái show originality；be original
【独创】 dúchuàng original creation：～一格 create a style of one's own
【独创性】 dúchuàngxìng originality
【独当一面】 dúdāng-yīmiàn take charge of a department；take charge of a locality
【独到】 dúdào original；special：～之处 originality of ideas；special merits
【独断专行】 dúduàn-zhuānxíng make arbitrary decisions and take peremptory actions；act arbitrarily
【独家】 dújiā exclusive；exclusively（adv.）
【独家代理】 dújiā dàilǐ sole agency；exclusive agent；exclusive agency
【独家经营】 dújiā jīngyíng engage in a line of business without competition
【独家新闻】 dújiā xīnwén an exclusive news report
【独具匠心】 dújù-jiàngxīn show ingenuity；have originality
【独揽】 dúlǎn arrogate；monopolize：～经济大权 assume arbitrary power in finance
【独立】 dúlì 1.（单独站立）stand alone 2.（自主存亡）independence：宣布～ proclaim independence 3.（不依靠他人）independent；on one's own：～思考 independent thinking；have one's own views

【独立法人】 dúlì fǎrén independent legal person
【独立核算单位】 dúlì hésuàn dānwèi independent accounting unit; unit with independent accountability
【独立实体】 dúlì shítǐ independent entity
【独立王国】 dúlì wángguó independent kingdom
【独立性】 dúlìxìng independent character; independence
【独立自主】 dúlì-zìzhǔ maintain independence and keep the initiative in one's own hands; act independently and with the initiative in one's own hands
【独龙族】 Dúlóngzú Derung（中国少数民族，主要分布在云南）
【独门独院】 dúmén-dúyuàn a single house which has its own entrance and courtyard
【独木桥】 dúmùqiáo 1.（一根木头的便桥）single-plank bridge; single-log bridge 2.（艰难的途径）difficult path
【独木舟】 dúmùzhōu dugout canoe
【独幕剧】 dúmùjù one-act play
【独身】 dúshēn 1.（单身）separated from one's family 2.（不结婚的）unmarried; single
【独生女】 dúshēngnǚ only daughter
【独生子】 dúshēngzǐ only son
【独生子女】 dúshēng zǐnǚ only child; only child of one couple
【独生子女证书】 dúshēng zǐnǚ zhèngshū certificate of the only child
【独树一帜】 dúshù-yīzhì fly one's own colors; develop a school of one's own
【独特】 dútè unique; distinctive：～的性格 peculiar trait
【独吞】 dútūn pocket profit without sharing with anyone else
【独往独来】 dúwǎng-dúlái act independently without seeking company
【独舞】 dúwǔ solo dance
【独一无二】 dúyī-wúèr unique; unparalleled; unmatched
【独占】 dúzhàn have sth. all to oneself; monopolize：～市场 monopolize the market
【独占鳌头】 dúzhàn-áotóu come out first; head the list of successful candidates; be the champion
【独资】 dúzī ventures exclusively with one's own investment
【独资企业】 dúzī qǐyè enterprise exclusively with one's own investment; enterprise with exclusive investment
【独自】 dúzì alone; by oneself
【独奏】 dúzòu （instrumental）solo：钢琴～ piano solo

读［讀］（dú） 1.（阅读）read; read aloud 2.（上学）attend school：～完大学 finish college
【读本】 dúběn reader; textbook
【读出】 dúchū read; read-out
【读入】 dúrù read in
【读书】 dúshū 1.（看书）read; study：认真～ study in earnest 2.（上学）attend school
【读书人】 dúshūrén a scholar; an intellectual
【读物】 dúwù reading matter; reading material：儿童～ children's books / 科普～ popular science readings
【读者】 dúzhě reader
【读者来信】 dúzhě láixìn readers' letters; letters to the editor

渎［瀆、凟］（dú） show disrespect; contempt
【渎职】 dúzhí malfeasance; dereliction of duty; neglect of one's duty

犊［犢］（dú） calf：初生牛～不怕虎。Young people are fearless.（Newborn calves are not afraid of tigers.）

黩［黷］（dú） act wantonly
【黩武】 dúwǔ militaristic; warlike; bellicose

髑（dú） skull
【髑髅】 dúlóu skull

肚（dǔ） tripe（另见"肚"dù）
【肚儿】 dǔr tripe
【肚丝】 dǔsī slices of pork tripe

笃（dǔ） 1.（忠实）sincere; earnest：友谊甚～ in devoted friendship 2.（沉重）serious; critical
【笃厚】 dǔhòu sincere and magnanimous
【笃实】 dǔshí 1.（忠诚老实）honest and sincere：～可靠 honest and reliable 2.（实在）solid; sound

【笃信】 dǔxìn earnestly believe in：～不疑 believe undoubtedly in sb.(sth.)

堵(dǔ) 1.(堵塞) stop up; block up：2.(闷) stifled; suffocated; oppressed：～得慌 feel very much stifled

【堵车】 dǔchē jam; traffic jam (n.)：路上～了。The motorway was jammed. / 我们因～在路上卡了3个小时。We were stuck in a traffic jam for three hours.

【堵击】 dǔjī intercept and attack

【堵截】 dǔjié cut off

【堵塞】 dǔsè stop up; block up

赌(dǔ) 1.(赌博) gamble 2.(争输赢) bet：打～ make a bet

【赌本】 dǔběn money to gamble with

【赌博】 dǔbó gamble; gambling：一场政治上的～ a political gamble

【赌场】 dǔchǎng gambling house; casino

【赌棍】 dǔgùn hardened gambler; professional gambler

【赌具】 dǔjù gambling paraphernalia; gambling device

【赌气】 dǔqì feel wronged and act rashly

【赌钱】 dǔqián gamble：喜欢～ fond of gamble

【赌徒】 dǔtú gambler

【赌债】 dǔzhài a gambling debt

【赌咒】 dǔzhòu take an oath; swear

【赌注】 dǔzhù wager; stake：下～ make a wager; stake money

【赌桌】 dǔzhuō gambling table

【赌资】 dǔzī money to gamble

睹［覩］(dǔ) see; observe; notice：亲眼目～ see with one's own eyes

杜［敼[2]］(dù) 1.(杜梨) birch-leaf pear 2.(阻塞) shut out; stop; prevent

【杜鹃】 dùjuān 1.(布谷鸟) cuckoo 2.(杜鹃花) azalea

【杜绝】 dùjué stop; put an end to：～浪费 put an end to waste

【杜梨】 dùlí birch-leaf pear

【杜门】 dùmén close one's door

【杜门谢客】 dùmén-xièkè close one's door to visitors

【杜仲】 dùzhòng 〈*Chin. Med.*〉 the bark of eucommia

【杜撰】 dùzhuàn fabricate; make up

肚(dù) belly; abdomen; stomach (另见"肚"dǔ)

【肚量】 dùliàng 1.(度量) tolerance; magnanimity 2.(饭量) appetite

【肚皮】 dùpí belly：听到所发生的事,她笑破了～。She let out a real belly laugh when she heard what had happened.

【肚皮舞】 dùpíwǔ belly dance

【肚脐】 dùqí navel; belly button

【肚子】 dù·zi 1.(腹部) belly; abdomen 2.(像肚子的) 腿～ calf of a leg

【肚子痛】 dù·zitòng have a stomachache; suffer from abdominal pain

妒［妬］(dù) be jealous of; be envious of; envy

【妒忌】 dùjì be jealous of; be envious of; envy：出于～ out of envy; out of jealousy

【妒贤忌能】 dùxián-jìnéng be jealous of the worthy and able

度(dù) 1.(计量长短) linear measure 2.(程度) degree of intensity 3.(计量单位) degree (符号为 °) 4.(千瓦小时) kilowatt-hour (kwh) 5.(限度) limit; extent; degree：劳累过～ be overworked 6.(宽容程度) tolerance; magnanimity 7.(考虑) consideration：把生死置之～外 give no thought to personal safety 8.(次) occasion; time 9.(过度) spend; pass

【度假】 dùjià spend one's holidays; go vacationing

【度冷丁】 dùlěngdīng 〈*Pharm.*〉 dolantin

【度量】 dùliàng tolerance; magnanimity：～大 be magnanimous; be tolerant; be broad-minded

【度量衡】 dùliànghéng weights and measures; length, capacity and weight

【度蜜月】 dùmìyuè honeymoon

【度日】 dùrì subsist (in hardship); eke out an existence：靠救济～ live on relief

【度日如年】 dùrì-rúnián one day seems like a year; days wear on like years

【度数】 dù·shu number of degrees; reading

渡(dù) 1.(通过) cross：～河 cross a river / 飞～大西洋 fly (across) the Atlantic 2.(渡过) tide over; pull through 3.(运载过河) ferry (people, goods, etc.) across

【渡槽】 dùcáo aqueduct
【渡船】 dùchuán ferry; ferry boat
【渡过】 dùguò tide over: ～难关 tide over a difficulty; pull through / ～危机 tide over a crisis
【渡海】 dùhǎi sail across a sea
【渡口】 dùkǒu ferry; ferry crossing
【渡轮】 dùlún ferry; ferry boat: 乘～过海去海南 go across to Hainan by/on the ferry.
【渡轮甲板】 dùlún jiǎbǎn ferry duck

镀 (dù) plating

【镀层】 dùcéng cladding material; film
【镀金】 dùjīn 1.(镀上黄金) gold-plating; gilding 2.(为图虚名而学习) get gilded
【镀金属塑料】 dùjīnshǔ sùliào metalized plastics
【镀锡铁皮】 dùxī tiěpí tin plate; tinned plate
【镀锌】 dùxīn zinc-plating; galvanizing
【镀锌铁皮】 dùxīn tiěpí galvanized iron sheet

蠹[杢、蠧、蠹] (dù) 1.(虫子) insect; moth; silverfish 2.(蛀蚀) moth-eaten; worm-eaten

【蠹虫】 dùchóng 1.(虫子) insect; moth 2.(指坏人) vermin; scoundrel

duan

端 (duān) 1.(东西的头) end; extremity 2.(开头) beginning 3.(项目) point; item 4.(缘故) reason; cause 5.(端正) upright; proper 6.(平举着拿) hold sth. level with both hands; carry

【端口】 duānkǒu 〈*Computer*〉 port
【端线】 duānxiàn 〈*Tennis*〉 base line
【端线司线员】 duānxiàn sīxiànyuán 〈*Tennis*〉 base line judge
【端详】 duānxiáng 1.(详情) details: 听～ listen to a detailed accounts 2.(端庄安详) dignified and serene 3.(仔细看) look sb. up and down
【端正】 duānzhèng 1.(不歪斜) upright; regular: 五官～ have regular features 2.(正派) proper; correct 3.(使端正) rectify; correct: ～态度 correct one's attitude towards ...
【端庄】 duānzhuāng dignified; sedate: 举止～ conduct oneself sedately / 容貌～ decorous in appearance
【端子】 duān·zi 〈*Electr.*〉 terminal

短 (duǎn) 1.(跟"长"相对) short; brief 2.(缺少) lack; owe 3.(缺点) weak point; fault

【短兵相接】 duǎnbīng-xiāngjiē fight at close quarters
【短波】 duǎnbō shortwave
【短不了】 duǎn·buliǎo 1.(不能缺) cannot do without 2.(免不了) cannot avoid; have to
【短程】 duǎnchéng short distance; short range
【短处】 duǎn · chu shortcoming; failing; fault; weakness
【短促】 duǎncù of very short duration; very brief: 时间～ time is short and pressing
【短大衣】 duǎndàyī short overcoat
【短笛】 duǎndí 〈*Music*〉 piccolo
【短发】 duǎnfà bob; shingle: 一个～姑娘 a girl wearing her hair in a bob; a bobbed hair girl
【短工】 duǎngōng casual laborer; seasonal laborer
【短号】 duǎnhào 〈*Music*〉 cornet
【短见】 duǎnjiàn 1.(见解短) shortsighted view 2.(自杀) suicide: 寻～ commit suicide
【短距离赛跑】 duǎnjùlí sàipǎo sprint; dash
【短距起落飞机】 duǎnjù qǐluò fēijī short take-off and landing airplane; STOL airplane
【短裤】 duǎnkù shorts
【短路】 duǎnlù 〈*Electr.*〉 short circuit
【短跑】 duǎnpǎo sprint; dash
【短跑运动员】 duǎnpǎo yùndòngyuán sprinter
【短篇小说】 duǎnpiān xiǎoshuō short story
【短片】 duǎnpiàn 〈*Cinematog.*〉 short; short film
【短平快】 duǎn-píng-kuài spike with short low set
【短评】 duǎnpíng short commentary; brief comment
【短期】 duǎnqī short-term: 在～内 in a short time; in a brief space of time
【短期行为】 duǎnqī xíngwéi short-time planning
【短浅】 duǎnqiǎn narrow and shallow: 目光～ short-sighted / 见识～ lacking knowledge and experience; shallow

【短欠】 duǎnqiàn 1.（欠）owe; be in arrears 2.（缺少）be short of
【短枪】 duǎnqiāng pistol; revolver
【短缺】 duǎnquē shortage; deficiency; insufficiency
【短日照植物】 duǎnrìzhào zhíwù short-day plant
【短少】 duǎnshǎo deficient; short
【短视】 duǎnshì 1.（近视）nearsightedness; myopia 2.（眼光短浅）lack foresight; be short-sighted
【短途】 duǎntú short distance
【短途运输】 duǎntú yùnshū short-distance transport
【短袜】 duǎnwà socks
【短文】 duǎnwén short essay
【短吻鳄】 duǎnwěn'è 〈*Zool.*〉 alligator
【短纤维】 duǎnxiānwéi 1.（短绒）short-staple 2.（短化纤）staple (fiber)
【短线】 duǎnxiàn short line; in short supply
【短线产品】 duǎnxiàn chǎnpǐn short line products; products in short supply
【短线专业】 duǎnxiàn zhuānyè short line specialty; specialty in bad need
【短小】 duǎnxiǎo short and small; short; small
【短小精悍】 duǎnxiǎo jīnghàn 1.（指人）not of imposing stature but strong and capable 2.（指文章）short and pithy; terse and forceful
【短训班】 duǎnxùnbān short-term training course
【短暂】 duǎnzàn of short duration; transient; brief: ～的停留 brief stay; short stay

段(duàn) 1.（部分）section; segment; part: 边界西～ the western sector of the boundary 2.（文章的段落）paragraph; passage
【段落】 duànluò 1.（文章的一段）paragraph 2.（阶段）phase; stage: 此事现告一～。At this stage we can put a period to this issue.

缎(duàn) satin: 织锦～ brocade
【缎子】 duàn·zi satin

椴(duàn) 〈*Bot.*〉 Chinese linden; lime tree
【椴木】 duànmù linden

煅(duàn) 1.（锻）forge 2.（煅烧）calcine
【煅烧】 duànshāo calcine

锻(duàn) forge
【锻工】 duàngōng 1.（指工种）forging 2.（指技术工人）forger; blacksmith
【锻件】 duànjiàn forging
【锻炼】 duànliàn 1.（体育锻炼）take exercise; have physical training: 坚持～ take regular exercise 2.（磨炼）temper; steel; toughen
【锻造】 duànzào forging; smithing

断［**斷**］(duàn) 1.（分成段）break; snap 2.（断绝）break off; cut off; stop: ～水 cut off the water supply 3.（戒除）give up; abstain from 4.（决定）judge; decide 5.（绝对）absolutely; decidedly
【断案】 duàn'àn 〈*Law*〉 settle a case
【断层】 duàncéng 〈*Geol.*〉 fault
【断肠】 duàncháng heartbroken; profoundly distressed
【断代】 duàndài division of history into periods
【断代史】 duàndàishǐ dynastic history
【断档】 duàndàng discontinuity of supply or production of sth.; be out of stock
【断定】 duàndìng conclude; form a judgment; decide; determine
【断断续续】 duànduàn-xùxù off and on; intermittently
【断根】 duàngēn be completely cured
【断后】 duànhòu 1.（走在最后）bring up the rear; cover a retreat 2.（断绝子孙）have no progeny
【断乎】 duànhū （只用于否定式）absolutely: ～不可 absolutely impermissible
【断交】 duànjiāo 1.（结束友谊）break off a friendship 2.（断绝外交关系）sever diplomatic relations; break off diplomatic relations
【断绝】 duànjué break off; cut off; sever: ～交通 stop traffic / ～外交关系 sever diplomatic relations
【断裂】 duànliè 1.〈*Geol.*〉 break; rift 2.〈*Mech.*〉 failure
【断流器】 duànliúqì 〈*Electr.*〉 cutout
【断路】 duànlù 〈*Electr.*〉 open circuit; broken circuit
【断面】 duànmiàn 〈*Surveying*〉 section
【断奶】 duànnǎi weaning

【断气】 duànqì 1.(停止呼吸) breathe one's last; die 2.(切断燃气) cut off the gas

【断然】 duànrán 1.(果断) absolutely; flatly; categorically: ～否认 categorically deny / ～拒绝 flatly refuse 2.(断乎;严厉) resolute; drastic: 采取～措施 take drastic measures

【断送】 duànsòng forfeit (one's life, future, etc.); ruin

【断言】 duànyán say with certainty; assert categorically; affirm; state with certainty

【断语】 duànyǔ conclusion; judgment

【断章取义】 duànzhāng-qǔyì quote out of context; garble a statement, etc.

【断肢再植】 duànzhī zàizhí 〈*Med.*〉 replantation of a severed limb

dui

堆 (duī) 1.(堆积) pile up; heap up; stack 2.(堆积物) heap; pile; stack 3.(成堆的物或人) pile; heap; crowd

【堆放】 duīfàng pile up; stack

【堆肥】 duīféi 〈*Agric.*〉 compost

【堆积】 duījī 1.(聚集成堆) pile up; heap up: ～如山 pile up like a mountain 2.(堆积物) accumulation

【堆集】 duījí conglomerate; conglomeration (n.)

【堆砌】 duīqì 1.(使用大量华丽词汇) load one's writing with fancy phrases 2.(垒砌砖石) pile up

【堆栈】 duīzhàn 1.(仓库) storehouse; warehouse 2.〈*Computer*〉 stack

队[隊] (duì) 1.(行列) a row of people; line 2.(集体) team; group: 国家～ national team / 客～ visiting team / 种子～ seeded team / 主～ home team / 足球～ football team

【队部】 duìbù the office or headquarters of a team, etc.

【队旗】 duìqí team pennant: 互换～ exchange team pennants

【队伍】 duì·wu 1.(军队) troops 2.(有组织的行列或集体) ranks; contingent: 游行～ contingents of marchers

【队形】 duìxíng formation

【队员】 duìyuán team member: 上场～ players in uniform / 替补～ substitute

【队长】 duìzhǎng 〈*Sports*〉 captain: 不参加比赛的～ non-playing captain / 场上～ playing captain

对[對] (duì) 1.(回答) answer; reply 2.(对付;对待) treat; cope with; counter 3.(朝着) be trained on; be directed at 4.(两者相对) mutual; face to face 5.(对面的;敌对的) opposite; opposing 6.(相合) bring (two things) into contact; fit one into the other 7.(投合;适合) suit; agree; get along 8.(核对) compare; check; identify 9.(正确) right; correct: 猜～了 guess right 10.(掺和) mix; add: ～些水 dilute it with some water 11.〈*classifier*〉 pair; couple: 一～夫妇 a married couple

【对岸】 duì'àn the opposite bank; the other side of the river

【对白】 duìbái dialogue

【对半】 duìbàn 1.(各半) half-and-half; fifty-fifty: ～儿分 divide half-and-half; go halves 2.(一倍) double: ～儿利 a double profit

【对比】 duìbǐ 1.(比较) contrast; balance 2.(比例) ratio

【对比度】 duìbǐdù contrast

【对表】 duìbiǎo 1.(指个人) set one's watch 2.(指多人) synchronize watches

【对不起】 duì·buqǐ 1.(套语) pardon me; I beg your pardon 2.(辜负) let sb. down; do a disservice to; be unfair to

【对策】 duìcè the way to deal with a situation; countermeasure

【对策论】 duìcèlùn game theory

【对称】 duìchèn symmetry; symmetrical (adj.)

【对冲基金】 duìchōng jījīn hedge fund

【对床】 duìchuáng twin beds

【对答】 duìdá answer; reply

【对答如流】 duìdá-rúliú answer fluently

【对打】 duìdǎ fight each other

【对待】 duìdài treat; approach; handle: 区别～ treat different cases in different ways

【对得起】 duì·deqǐ not let sb. down; treat sb. fairly; be worthy of

【对等】 duìděng reciprocity; equity

【对调】 duìdiào exchange; swap: ～工作 ex-

change jobs
【对顶角】 duìdǐngjiǎo 〈*Math.*〉 vertical angles
【对方】 duìfāng the other side; the other party; the opposite side
【对方付费电话】 duìfāng fùfèi diànhuà a collect call
【对付】 duì·fu **1.**（应付）deal with; cope with; counter; tackle: ～各种复杂局面 deal with all kinds of complicate situations **2.**（将就）make do: 能～着看英文信 can manage to read English letters
【对过】 duìguò opposite; across the way
【对号】 duìhào **1.**（对号数）check the number **2.**（相符合）fit; tally **3.**（表示正确的符号）check mark; tick（符号为 √）
【对号入座】 duìhào rùzuò take one's seat according to the number on the ticket; sit in the right seat
【对话】 duìhuà dialogue; talk: 建设性～ constructive dialogue / 与政府进行～ enter into dialogue with the government
【对讲机】 duìjiǎngjī intercom
【对讲门铃】 duìjiǎng ménlíng entryphone
【对角线】 duìjiǎoxiàn 〈*Math.*〉 diagonal; diagonal line
【对接】 duìjiē **1.** 〈*Mech.*〉 butt joint **2.** 〈*Aeron.*〉 link up
【对劲儿】 duìjìnr **1.**（称心合意）be to one's liking; suit one **2.**（合适）normal; right **3.**（合得来）get along (well)
【对局】 duìjú play a game of chess, etc.
【对开】 duìkāi **1.**（相向开行）(of trains, buses or ships) run from opposite directions **2.**（对半分配）divide into two halves; go fifty-fifty
【对抗】 duìkàng **1.**（对立）antagonism; confrontation **2.**（抵抗）resist; oppose
【对抗赛】 duìkàngsài 〈*Sports*〉 dual meet
【对口】 duìkǒu **1.**（两人交替说唱）speak alternately; sing alternately **2.**（相一致）be geared to the needs of the job; fit in with one's vocational training or specialty: 专业～ a job suited to one's special training **3.**（味道合口）good to eat; tasty
【对垒】 duìlěi stand facing each other, ready for battle; be pitted against each other: 两军～ two armies pitted against each other
【对立】 duìlì **1.**（相互排斥、矛盾）oppose; set sth. against **2.**（抵触、敌对）antagonize sb.; be antagonistic to: 我不想和他～。I've no wish to antagonize him.
【对立关系】 duìlì guān·xì antagonistic relations
【对立情绪】 duìlì qíngxù antagonism; antagonistic (adj.): 逐渐消除两国间历史上形成的～ reduce the historic antagonism between two countries
【对立统一】 duìlì tǒngyī 〈*Philos.*〉 unity of opposites
【对联】 duìlián antithetical couplet
【对流层】 duìliúcéng 〈*Meteorol.*〉 troposphere
【对路】 duìlù **1.**（合乎要求）satisfy the need **2.**（对劲）be to one's liking; suit one
【对门】 duìmén **1.**（大门相对）face each other **2.**（大门相对的房子）the building opposite; the room opposite
【对面】 duìmiàn **1.**（对过）opposite **2.**（正前方）right in front **3.**（面对面）face to face
【对内】 duìnèi internal; domestic; at home: ～搞活经济 revitalization of the domestic economy
【对牛弹琴】 duìniú-tánqín cast pearls before swine; have the wrong audience
【对手】 duìshǒu **1.**（竞赛的对方）opponent; adversary **2.**（劲敌）match; equal: 他不是你的～。He is no match for you.
【对数】 duìshù 〈*Math.*〉 logarithm; logarithmic (adj.)
【对数表】 duìshùbiǎo 〈*Math.*〉 logarithmic table
【对台戏】 duìtáixì rival show: 唱～ put on a rival show
【对头】 duìtóu **1.**（正确）correct; on the right track **2.**（正常）normal **3.**（对劲）get on well; hit it off **4.**（仇敌）enemy: 死～ sworn enemy **5.**（对手）opponent; adversary
【对外】 duìwài external; foreign: 扩大～投资 expand one's investments abroad
【对外关系】 duìwài guān·xì external relations; foreign relations
【对外开放】 duìwài kāifàng opening to the outside world

【对外贸易】 duìwài màoyì foreign trade：～逆差 **foreign trade deficit；unfavorable balance of trade** / ～顺差 foreign trade surplus；favorable balance of trade

【对味儿】 duìwèir 1.（合口味）to one's taste；tasty 2.（符合某人思想感情）seem all right

【对虾】 duìxiā prawn

【对象】 duìxiàng 1.（目标）target；object 2.（恋爱对方）boy or girl friend：找～ look for a partner in marriage

【对应】 duìyìng 1.（相当）correspond 2.（针对）corresponding

【对照】 duìzhào 1.（参照）compare：～原文 compare to/with the original 2.（对比）compare；contrast：鲜明的～ sharp contrast / 这个看来贵了，你～其他商店的价格了吗？That seems expensive — have you compared prices in other shops?

【对折】 duìzhé 50% discount：照货价～ allow a fifty per cent discount off the price；reduce the price by one half

【对症下药】 duìzhèng-xiàyào suit the medicine to the illness；suit the remedy to the case

【对质】 duìzhì confront sb. with（in court）

【对峙】 duìzhì stand facing each other；confront each other；confrontation（n.）：军事～ military confrontation

【对准】 duìzhǔn aim at

兑（duì） 1.（兑换）exchange；convert 2.（添加）add

【兑付】 duìfù cash（a check，etc.）

【兑换】 duìhuàn exchange；convert：把港币～美元 exchange H.K dollar for US dollar

【兑换率】 duìhuànlǜ rate of exchange

【兑换券】 duìhuànquàn foreign exchange certificate

【兑现】 duìxiàn 1.（用票据换现款）cash（a check，etc.）2.（诺言的实现）honor（a commitment，etc.）；keep a promise：政策～ materialize a policy

dun

吨［噸］（dūn） ton（t.）

【吨公里】 dūngōnglǐ ton kilometer

【吨位】 dūnwèi tonnage；shipping ton：总～ total ton；gross ton

敦（dūn） honest；sincere

【敦促】 dūncù urge；press：～某人做某事 urge sb. to do sth.

【敦厚】 dūnhòu honest and sincere

【敦请】 dūnqǐng earnestly invite；earnestly request

墩（dūn） 1.（土墩）mound 2.（墩子）a block of stone or wood：桥～ pier（of a bridge）3.（丛生或合在一起的植物）cluster

【墩布】 dūnbù mop；swab

【墩子】 dūn·zi a block of wood；a block of stone

蹲（dūn） 1.（蹲着）squat on the heels：～下来 squat down 2.（呆着）stay：～在家里 stay at home

【蹲班】 dūnbān have to repeat courses；have to stay in the same grade

【蹲点】 dūndiǎn work at a selected spot（for investigation and study）

【蹲监狱】 dūn jiānyù lie in prison

盹（dǔn） doze；nap：打～儿 doze off；take a nap / 在长沙发上打个小～儿 take a little nap on the settee

趸［躉］（dǔn） 1.（整批）wholesale 2.（整批买进）buy wholesale：～货 buy goods wholesale

【趸批】 dǔnpī wholesale：～买进 buy wholesale / ～卖出 sell wholesale

盾（dùn） shield

【盾牌】 dùnpái 1.（防护武器）shield 2.（借口）pretext；excuse

遁［遯］（dùn） escape；flee

【遁词】 dùncí pretext；excuse

炖［燉］（dùn） 1.（用文火煮）stew：～排骨 stew spareribs 2.（加热）warm sth. by putting the container in hot water

钝（dùn） 1.（不锋利）blunt；dull：刀～了。The knife has become blunt. 2.（笨拙）stupid；dull-witted

【钝角】 dùnjiǎo 〈*Math.*〉 obtuse angle

【钝角三角形】 dùnjiǎo sānjiǎoxíng obtuse-angled triangle

顿 (dùn) 1.(稍停) pause 2.(顿笔) pause in writing in order to reinforce the beginning or ending of a stroke 3.(安顿) arrange; settle 4.(跺地) stamp 5.(顿时) suddenly; immediately 6.(困顿) fatigued; tired 7. 〈*classifier*〉一天吃三～饭 have three meals a day

【顿挫】 dùncuò pause and transition in rhythm or melody

【顿开茅塞】 dùnkāi-máosè suddenly see the light

【顿时】 dùnshí immediately; at once; forthwith

duo

咄 (duō) tut-tut

【咄咄逼人】 duōduō-bīrén overbearing; aggressive

【咄咄怪事】 duōduō-guàishì monstrous absurdity

多 (duō) 1.(数量大) many; much; more 2.(过多) more than the correct or required number; too many 3.(过分的;不必要的) excessive; too much 4.(放在数量词后,表示有零头) more; over; odd: 六十～岁 over sixty years old 5.(相差程度大) much more; far more: 难得～ much more difficult 6.(表示程度) how: 看他～精神! Look how energetic he is!

【多半】 duōbàn 1.(大半) the greater part; most 2.(大概) probably; most likely

【多倍体】 duōbèitǐ 〈*Biol.*〉 polyploid

【多边】 duōbiān multilateral

【多边贸易】 duōbiān màoyì multilateral trade

【多边协议】 duōbiān xiéyì multilateral agreement

【多边形】 duōbiānxíng 〈*Math.*〉 polygon; polygonous (adj.)

【多变】 duōbiàn changeable; changeful; varied

【多病】 duōbìng susceptible to diseases; constantly ill

【多才多艺】 duōcái-duōyì versatile; gifted in many ways

【多层次】 duōcéngcì at different levels

【多重】 duōchóng multiple

【多愁善感】 duōchóu-shàngǎn sentimental

【多此一举】 duōcǐ-yījǔ make an unnecessary move

【多次】 duōcì many times; time and again; repeatedly; on many occasions

【多弹头分导重返大气层运载工具】 duōdàntóu fēndǎo chóngfǎn dàqìcéng yùnzǎi gōngjù MIRV (multiple independently targeted reentry vehicle)

【多党合作】 duōdǎng hézuò multiparty cooperation; multiparty cooperative (adj.)

【多多少少】 duōduō-shǎoshǎo more or less

【多多益善】 duōduō-yìshàn the more the better

【多发病】 duōfābìng frequently-occurring disease

【多方】 duōfāng in many ways; in every way: ～设法 try all possible means; make every effort

【多方面】 duōfāngmiàn many-sided; in many ways

【多功能】 duōgōngnéng multipurpose; multifuntion; multifuntional (adj.)

【多管闲事】 duōguǎn xiánshì poke one's nose into others' business; be a busybody

【多管自行火炮】 duōguǎn zìxíng huǒpào carriage motor multiple gun

【多国公司】 duōguó gōngsī multinational corporation

【多会儿】 duōhuìr 1.(什么时候) when 2.(任一时间) ever; at any time

【多极】 duōjí multipolar

【多极化】 duōjíhuà multipolarization

【多级火箭】 duōjí huǒjiàn multistage rocket

【多久】 duōjiǔ how long: 你来了～了? How long have you been here?

【多亏】 duōkuī thanks to; luckily: ～你的帮助 thanks to your help

【多劳多得】 duōláo-duōdé more pay for more work

【多路】 duōlù 〈*Electr.*〉 multichannel

【多么】 duō·me (表示程度) how; what: ～大的变化啊! What a great change!

【多媒体】 duōméitǐ multimedia

【多米诺骨牌】 duōmǐnuò gǔpái domino

【多米诺骨牌理论】 duōmǐnuò gǔpái lǐlùn dominos theory

【多面手】 duōmiànshǒu a many-sided person; a versatile person; an all-rounder

【多面体】 duōmiàntǐ 〈*Math*.〉 polyhedron

【多民族国家】 duōmínzú guójiā multinational country

【多年生植物】 duōniánshēng zhíwù parennial; parennial plant

【多情】 duōqíng full of tenderness or affection (for a person of the opposite sex): 自作～ imagine oneself as a favorite of others

【多渠道】 duōqúdào through many channels

【多如牛毛】 duōrú-niúmáo countless; innumerable

【多少】 duō·shao **1**.(数量大小) number; amount **2**.(或多或少) somewhat; more or less; to some extent **3**.(问数量) how many; how much **4**.(不定数量) so much; as much as: 有～力,出～力 do as much as one can

【多时】 duōshí a long time

【多事】 duōshì **1**.(管闲事) meddlesome: 你不必～。Don't be meddling. **2**.(事故多) eventful

【多事之秋】 duōshì-zhīqiū an eventful year; an eventful period; a year fraught with happenings

【多数】 duōshù majority; most: 简单～ simple majority / 绝大～ an overwhelming majority / 三分之二的～ a two-thirds majority / 微弱的～ a small majority

【多头】 duōtóu **1**.〈*Econ*.〉 bull; long **2**.(不只一个方面的) multilateral

【多头市场】 duōtóu shìchǎng 〈*Econ*.〉 bull market

【多头政治】 duōtóu zhèngzhì polyarchy

【多退少补】 duōtuì-shǎobǔ refund for any overpayment or a supplemental payment for any deficiency

【多谢】 duōxiè many thanks; thanks a lot

【多心】 duōxīn oversensitive; suspicious

【多形式】 duōxíngshì in different forms

【多样化】 duōyànghuà diversify; make varied

【多一事不如少一事】 duō yī shì bùrú shǎo yī shì the less trouble the better; avoid trouble whenever possible

【多疑】 duōyí suspicious; oversensitive; given to suspicion: 你何必～? Why should you be so suspicious?

【多用途】 duōyòngtú multipurpose

【多余】 duōyú unnecessary; surplus; superfluous; uncalled for

【多元化】 duōyuánhuà pluralism

【多元文化】 duōyuán wénhuà multiculture

【多云】 duōyún 〈*Meteorol*.〉 cloudy; broken sky

【多灾多难】 duōzāi-duōnàn be dogged by bad luck; be plagued by frequent ills

【多种经营】 duōzhǒng jīngyíng diversified economy

【多嘴】 duōzuǐ speak out of turn; shoot off one's mouth: ～多舌 gossipy and meddlesome; long-tongued

哆 (duō)

【哆嗦】 duō·suō tremble; shiver: 冷得打～ shiver with cold / 气得直～ tremble with rage

夺[奪] (duó) **1**.(强夺) take by force; seize; wrest **2**.(争先取到) force one's way: ～路 force one's way **3**.(争取) contend for; compete for; strive for **4**.(剥夺) deprive: 剥～ deprive

【夺杯】 duóbēi win the cup

【夺标】 duóbiāo win the first prize

【夺冠】 duóguàn win the championship

【夺回】 duóhuí recapture; retake; seize back

【夺魁】 duókuí win the championship

【夺目】 duómù dazzle the eyes: 光彩～ with dazzling brightness

【夺取】 duóqǔ **1**.(用武力强取) capture; seize; wrest: ～主动权 seize the initiative **2**.(努力争取) strive for: ～…的伟大胜利 achieve greater successes in ...

【夺去】 duóqù take away from

【夺权】 duóquán seize power

踱 (duó) pace; stroll: ～来～去 pace to and fro; pace up and down

朵[朶] (duǒ) **1**.(花朵) flower **2**.〈*classifier*〉 一～花 a flower

【朵儿】 duǒr **1**.(花朵) flower **2**.〈*classifier*〉 一～花 a flower

垛[垜] (duǒ) **1**.(扶垛) buttress **2**.(城垛) battlements

（另见“垛”duò）

【垛口】 duǒkǒu crenel; crenelle

【垛子】 duǒ·zi **1.**（扶垛）buttress **2.**（城垛）battlements

躲［躱］（duǒ） **1.**（躲藏）hide（oneself）：～进山林 hide in a mountain forest **2.**（避）avoid; dodge：～雨 take shelter from the rain

【躲避】 duǒbì **1.**（回避）dodge; avoid; elude：～困难 dodge difficulties **2.**（藏）hide

【躲藏】 duǒcáng hide oneself; conceal oneself; go into hiding

【躲躲闪闪】 duǒ·duo-shǎnshǎn be evasive; equivocate; hedge

【躲闪】 duǒshǎn dodge; evade：～不及 be too late to dodge

【躲债】 duǒzhài avoid a creditor

驮（duò）
（另见“驮”tuó）

【驮子】 duò·zi pack; a load carried by a pack-animal：给骡子装上～。Load the pack onto the mule back.

剁［剁］（duò） chop; cut：～成两半 chop sth. in half

垛［垜、稞］（duò） **1.**（整齐地堆）pile up neatly; stack：～干草 stack hay **2.**（整齐地堆成的堆儿）pile; stack：干草～ a pile of hay / 纸～ a stack of papers

（另见“垛”duǒ）

跺［跥、跢］（duò） stamp（one's foot）

【跺脚】 duòjiǎo stamp one's foot

舵［柁］（duò） rudder; helm：掌～ take the helm; be at the helm

【舵杆】 duògǎn rudder stock

【舵机】 duòjī steering gear

【舵轮】 duòlún steering wheel

【舵手】 duòshǒu steersman; helmsman

惰（duò） lazy; indolent

【惰轮】 duòlún 〈*Mech.*〉 idle wheel; idle gear

【惰性】 duòxìng inertia

【惰性气体】 duòxìng qìtǐ inert gas：氦和氖是～。Helium and neon are inert gases.

【惰性元素】 duòxìng yuánsù 〈*Chem.*〉 inert element

堕［墮］（duò） fall; sink

【堕落】 duòluò **1.**（变坏）degenerate; sink low **2.**（沦落）sink into poverty

【堕入】 duòrù sink into; lapse into

【堕胎】 duòtāi **1.**（人工流产）induced abortion **2.**（做人工流产）have an（induced）abortion

【堕胎药】 duòtāiyào aborticide

E

e

阿 (ē) play up to; pander to (另见"阿"ā)

【阿胶】 ējiāo donkey-hide gelatin

【阿弥陀佛】 Ēmítuófó 1.（佛）Amitabha; Amitayus: 南无～Namas Amitabha 2.(佛教祈祷用语) Buddha preserve us; merciful Buddha

【阿其所好】 ē-qí-suǒhào pander to sb's whims

【阿谀】 ēyú fawn on; flatter

【阿谀奉承】 ēyú-fèng·cheng flatter and toady to; fawn upon

讹[譌[1]] (é) 1.（错误）erroneous; mistaken: 以～传～ spread an error or a falsehood 2.(讹诈) extort; blackmail sb.; bluff sb.

【讹传】 échuán false rumor; unfounded rumor

【讹误】 éwù error (in a text)

【讹诈】 ézhà extort under false pretenses; blackmail: ～钱财 extort money under false pretenses

俄 (é) very soon; presently; suddenly

【俄而】 é'ér 〈*written*〉 very soon; presently; suddenly: ～日出。Presently the sun emerged.

【俄尔】 é'ěr 〈*written*〉 very soon; presently; suddenly

【俄罗斯】 Éluósī Russia; Russian (adj.) ‖ 俄罗斯人 Russian

【俄罗斯族】 Éluósīzú Russ (中国少数民族，主要分布在新疆)

【俄顷】 éqǐng in a moment; presently

【俄语】 Éyǔ Russian (language)

娥 (é) pretty young woman

【娥眉】 éméi 1.(细弯的眉) delicate eyebrows 2.(美人) beautiful woman

【娥眉月】 éméiyuè 〈*Astron.*〉 crescent moon

锇 (é) 〈*Chem.*〉 osmium (元素符号 Os)

鹅[鵞、鵝] (é) goose (pl. geese) ‖ 雄鹅 gander / 雌鹅 goose / 幼鹅 gosling / 统称 gaggle

【鹅黄】 éhuáng light yellow

【鹅颈管】 éjǐngguǎn gooseneck

【鹅口疮】 ékǒuchuāng 〈*Med.*〉 mycotic stomatitis

【鹅卵石】 éluǎnshí cobblestone; cobble

【鹅毛】 émáo 1.(鹅的羽毛) goose feather 2.(比喻轻微的东西)千里送～，礼轻情义重。Send a trifling from afar with sincere wishes.

【鹅毛大雪】 émáo dàxuě large snow flakes

【鹅绒】 éróng goose down

蛾 (é) moth

【蛾子】 é·zi moth

额 (é) 1.(额头) forehead 2.(牌匾) a horizontal tablet 3.(数额) a specified number or amount

【额定】 édìng rated; specified (number or amount)

【额定吨位】 édìng dūnwèi specified tonnage

【额定功率】 édìng gōnglǜ rated power

【额定马力】 édìng mǎlì rated horsepower

【额定寿命】 édìng shòumìng rated life time

【额动脉】 édòngmài 〈*Anat.*〉 frontal artery

【额窦】 édòu 〈*Anat.*〉 frontal sinus

【额尔古纳】 É'ěrgǔnà 〈place〉 Ergun

【额尔齐斯河】 É'ěrqísīhé 〈place〉 Ertix

【额骨】 égǔ 〈*Anat.*〉 frontal bone

【额静脉】 éjìngmài 〈*Anat.*〉 frontal vein

【额头】 étóu forehead

【额外】 éwài extra; additional; added

【额外报酬】 éwài bàochóu extra pay

【额外负担】 éwài fùdān added burden

【额外开支】 éwài kāizhī extra expenses
【额外收入】 éwài shōurù additional income
【额外损失】 éwài sǔnshī extraneous loss

恶[噁、嗯] (ě) (另见"恶"è, wù)

【恶心】 ě·xin 1.(要呕吐) feel like vomiting; feel nauseated; feel sick 2.(使人厌恶) nauseating; disgusting

厄[戹] (è)

【厄尔尼诺】 Èěrnínuò 〈*Meteorol.*〉 El Nino
【厄运】 èyùn adversity; misfortune

苊 (è) 〈*Chem.*〉 acenaphthene

扼 (è)

【扼流圈】 èliúquān 〈*Electr.*〉 impedance coil; choke coil; choke
【扼杀】 èshā 1.(掐死) strangle; smother 2.(比喻压制) strangle: 把…～在摇篮里 strangle sth. in the cradle
【扼守】 èshǒu hold (a strategic point); guard
【扼要】 èyào to the point: 简明～ brief and to the point
【扼制】 èzhì control; restrain

呃 (è)

【呃逆】 ènì 〈*Med.*〉 hiccup

轭 (è) yoke

垩[堊] (è) chalk

恶[惡] (è) 1.(跟"善"相对) wickedness; evil; vice: 作～多端 commit all sorts of wickedness 2.(凶恶) fierce; ferocious 3.(恶劣) bad; evil; wicked
(另见"恶"ě, wù)

【恶霸】 èbà local tyrant
【恶变】 èbiàn 〈*Med.*〉 cancerate
【恶臭】 èchòu foul smell; stench
【恶毒】 èdú vicious; malicious; venomous: ～攻击 maliciously attack
【恶感】 ègǎn ill feeling; malice: 对某人并无～ bear sb. no malice / 对某人有～ entertain ill feelings against sb.
【恶贯满盈】 èguàn-mǎnyíng face retribution for a life of crime
【恶棍】 ègùn ruffian; scoundrel; bully
【恶果】 èguǒ evil consequence; disastrous effect
【恶狠狠】 èhěnhěn fierce; ferocious
【恶化】 èhuà 1.(变坏) worsen; deteriorate: 他的病情～了。His condition has worsened. 2.(使变坏) worsen; take a turn for the worse: ～国际形势 worsen the international situation / ～两国关系 worsen the relations between the two countries
【恶劣】 èliè odious; abominable; disgusting: ～行径 disgusting conduct / 影响～ make a very bad impression
【恶露】 èlù 〈*Med.*〉 lochia
【恶骂】 èmà vicious abuse
【恶梦】 èmèng nightmare
【恶名】 èmíng a bad reputation; infamy
【恶魔】 èmó demon; devil; evil spirit
【恶念】 èniàn evil intentions
【恶人】 èrén evil person; vile creature; villain
【恶势力】 èshìlì vicious power; pressure groups; evil force
【恶习】 èxí bad habit; pernicious habit
【恶行】 èxíng evil conduct; wicked conduct
【恶性】 èxìng malignant; pernicious; vicious
【恶性循环】 èxìng xúnhuán vicious circle
【恶性肿瘤】 èxìng zhǒngliú malignant tumor; cancer
【恶意】 èyì evil intentions; ill intentions; ill will; malice: ～中伤 malicious calumniation
【恶有恶报】 èyǒu-èbào evil will be recompensed with evil
【恶语中伤】 èyǔ-zhòngshāng viciously slander; calumniate
【恶战】 èzhàn hard fighting; a desperate fight
【恶作剧】 èzuòjù practical joke; prank; mischief

饿 (è) 1.(饥饿) hungry: 挨～ go hungry 2.(使受饿) starve: ～死 be starved to death

鄂 (è)

【鄂尔多斯】 È'ěrduōsī 〈place〉 Ordos
【鄂陵湖】 Èlínghú 〈place〉 Ngoring Hu
【鄂伦春族】 Èlúnchūnzú Oroqen (中国少数民

族,主要分布在内蒙古和黑龙江)

【鄂温克族】 Èwēnkèzú Ewenki(中国少数民族,主要分布在内蒙古和黑龙江)

萼(è) 〈*Bot*.〉calyx

【萼片】 èpiàn 〈*Bot*.〉sepal

愕(è) stunned; astounded

【愕然】 èrán stunned; astounded

腭(è) 〈*Anat*.〉palate: 软～ soft palate / 硬～ hard palate

【腭裂】 èliè 〈*Med*.〉cleft palate

颚(è) 1.(节肢动物器官) mandible 2.(腭) palate

鳄[鱷](è) crocodile; alligator

【鳄鱼】 èyú crocodile; alligator

【鳄鱼夹】 èyújiā crocodile clip

【鳄鱼眼泪】 èyú-yǎnlèi crocodile tears

遏(è) check; hold back

【遏制】 èzhì keep within limits; contain

【遏制政策】 èzhì zhèngcè policy of containment

噩(è) shocking; upsetting

【噩耗】 èhào sad news of the death of one's beloved

en

恩(ēn) kindness; favor; grace

【恩爱】 ēn'ài conjugal love

【恩爱夫妻】 ēn'ài fūqī an affectionate couple

【恩赐】 ēncì 1.(赏赐) bestow (favors, charity, etc.) 2.(施舍) favor; charity

【恩典】 ēndiǎn benevolence; kindness

【恩惠】 ēnhuì favor; kindness; grace; bounty

【恩将仇报】 ēnjiāng-chóubào requite kindness with enmity

【恩情】 ēnqíng loving-kindness

【恩人】 ēnrén benefactor

【恩义】 ēnyì spiritual debt; gratitude

【恩怨】 ēnyuàn 1.(恩惠和仇恨) feeling of gratitude or resentment 2.(怨恨) resentment; grievance; old scores

蒽(ēn) 〈*Chem*.〉anthracene

摁(èn) press: ～电铃 ring an electric bell / ～电钮 press a button; push a button

【摁钉儿】 èndīngr drawing pin; thumbtack

【摁扣儿】 ènkòur snap fastener

er

儿[兒](ér) 1.(小孩) child 2.(年轻的人) youngster; youth 3.(儿子) son

【儿歌】 érgē children's song; nursery rhymes

【儿科】 érkē (department of) pediatrics

【儿科医生】 érkē yīshēng pediatrician

【儿女】 érnǚ 1.(儿子和女儿) sons and daughters; children 2.(青年男女) young man and woman (in love)

【儿女情长】 érnǚ-qíngcháng be immersed in love

【儿孙】 érsūn children and grandchildren; descendants; posterity

【儿童】 értóng children

【儿童车】 értóngchē child's bike

【儿童节】 Értóngjié (International) Children's Day

【儿童医院】 értóng yīyuàn children's hospital

【儿媳妇儿】 érxí·fur daughter-in-law

【儿戏】 érxì trifling matter; trivial matter: 视同～ regard sth. as trivial

【儿子】 ér·zi son

而(ér) 1.〈*conj*.〉but; yet; while 2.(到) to: 由东～西 from east to west

【而后】 érhòu after that; then

【而今】 érjīn now; at the present time

【而且】 érqiě 1.(表示平列) and 2.(表示进一层) but also

【而已】 éryǐ that is all; nothing more

鸸(ér)

【鸸鹋】 érmiáo 〈*Zool*.〉emu

尔[爾](ěr)

【尔后】 ěrhòu thereafter; subsequently

【尔虞我诈】 ěryú-wǒzhà each trying to cheat or outwit the other

耳(ěr) 1.(耳朵) ear 2.(像耳朵的) ear of a utensil 3.(两边的) on both sides;

flanking; side
【耳背】 ěrbèi hard of hearing
【耳鼻喉科】 ěrbíhóukē 1.（医院部门）E. N. T. department; otorhinolaryngological department 2.（耳鼻喉科学）otorhinolaryngology; otorhinolaryngological (adj.)
【耳鼻喉科医生】 ěrbíhóukē yīshēng otorhinolaryngologist; E. N. T. specialist
【耳边风】 ěrbiānfēng unheeded advice; a puff of wind passing the ear
【耳垂】 ěrchuí 〈*Anat*.〉 earlobe
【耳聪目明】 ěrcōng-mùmíng 1.（听得清，看得清）(of old people) have good ears and eyes; can hear and see well 2.（头脑清楚）have a thorough grasp of the situation
【耳朵】 ěr·duo ear: ～尖 have sharp ears / ～软 credulous; easily influenced
【耳房】 ěrfáng 〈*Archit*.〉 aisle; side room
【耳垢】 ěrgòu earwax
【耳骨】 ěrgǔ 〈*Anat*.〉 otica
【耳鼓】 ěrgǔ 〈*Anat*.〉 ear drum; tympanum
【耳鼓膜】 ěrgǔmó 〈*Anat*.〉 ear drum membrane
【耳光】 ěrguāng a slap on the face; a box on the ear: 一记响亮的～ a ringing slap on the face
【耳环】 ěrhuán earrings: 金～ gold earrings / 戴～ wear earrings
【耳机】 ěrjī earphone; earphones: 一副～ a pair/set of earphones / 立体声头戴～ stereo headphones
【耳机插座】 ěrjī chāzuò earphone socket
【耳尖】 ěrjiān have sharp ears
【耳科】 ěrkē otology
【耳科医生】 ěrkē yīshēng otologist; ear specialist
【耳聋】 ěrlóng deaf; deafness
【耳鸣】 ěrmíng 〈*Med*.〉 tinnitus
【耳膜】 ěrmó 〈*Anat*.〉 ear drum membrane
【耳目】 ěrmù 1.（耳朵和眼睛）ears and eyes: 掩人～ not let others know what has really happened 2.（见闻）what one sees and hears; knowledge; information: ～闭塞 be ill-informed; be isolated 3.（刺探消息的人）informer; spay; one who spies for sb. else: ～众多 eyes and ears everywhere; too many people around
【耳目一新】 ěrmù-yīxīn find everything fresh and new
【耳濡目染】 ěrrú-mùrǎn be imperceptibly influenced by what one constantly sees and hears
【耳塞】 ěrsāi 〈*Electr*.〉 earplug
【耳熟】 ěrshú familiar to the ear
【耳听八方】 ěrtīng-bāfāng very alert; extremely vigilant
【耳闻】 ěrwén hear of; hear about
【耳闻目睹】 ěrwén-mùdǔ what one sees and hears
【耳蜗】 ěrwō 〈*Anat*.〉 cochlea
【耳炎】 ěryán 〈*Med*.〉 otitis

饵 (ěr) 1.（鱼饵）bait; fish bait 2.（引诱）trap; entice
【饵料】 ěrliào bait; feedstuff

铒 (ěr) 〈*Chem*.〉 erbium（元素符号 Er）

二 (èr) 1.（一加一）two; second 2.（两样）different
【二把刀】 èrbǎdāo 1.（技术不高）have a smattering of a subject 2.（技术不高的人）smatterer
【二把手】 èrbǎshǒu number two man; the second in command
【二百】 èrbǎi two hundred; two-hundredth
【二百海里海洋权】 èrbǎi hǎilǐ hǎiyángquán 200 nautical-mile maritime rights
【二百五】 èrbǎiwǔ 1.（做事莽撞的人）a stupid person 2.（半瓶醋）dabbler; smatterer
【二冲程】 èrchōngchéng 〈*Mech*.〉 two cycle; two stroke
【二冲程发动机】 èrchōngchéng fādòngjī 〈*Mech*.〉 two stroke engine
【二重唱】 èrchóngchàng 〈*Music*〉 (vocal) duet
【二重性】 èrchóngxìng dual character; duality
【二重奏】 èrchóngzòu 〈*Music*〉 (instrumental) duet
【二传手】 èrchuánshǒu 1.〈*Volleyball*〉 setter 2.（指媒介）medium; vehicle
【二次方程】 èrcìfāngchéng 〈*Math*.〉 quadratic equation
【二等】 èrděng second-class; second-rate
【二等舱】 èrděngcāng second cabin; state-

room
【二等奖】 èrděngjiǎng second prize
【二恶英】 èr'èyīng 〈*Chem.*〉 dioxin
【二分点】 èrfēndiǎn 〈*Astron.*〉 equinoctial points
【二分音符】 èrfēn yīnfú 〈*Music*〉 half note
【二分之一】 èrfēnzhīyī a half; one half
【二胡】 èrhú 〈*Music*〉 *erhu*; 2-stringed Chinese violin
【二话】 èrhuà demur; objection: ～不说 without demur
【二婚】 èrhūn remarry
【二级批发】 èrjí pīfā secondary wholesale
【二极管】 èrjíguǎn 〈*Electronics*〉 diode
【二尖瓣】 èrjiānbàn 〈*Anat.*〉 bicuspid valve
【二进制】 èrjìnzhì 〈*Math.*〉 binary system
【二进制代码】 èrjìnzhì dàimǎ 〈*Computer*〉 binary code; binary block code
【二进制数字】 èrjìnzhì shùzì 〈*Computer*〉 binary digits
【二老】 èrlǎo father and mother; parents
【二垒】 èrlěi 〈*Baseball*〉 second base
【二垒手】 èrlěishǒu 〈*Baseball*〉 second baseman
【二连浩特】 Èrliánhàotè 〈place〉 Erenhot
【二审】 èrshěn 〈*Law*〉 second instance
【二十】 èrshí twenty; twentieth
【二十四节气】 èrshísì jiéqì the 24 solar terms (参见"立春、雨水、惊蛰、春分、清明、谷雨、立夏、小满、芒种、夏至、小暑、大暑、立秋、处暑、白露、秋分、寒露、霜降、立冬、小雪、大雪、冬至、小寒、大寒"各条)
【二手】 èrshǒu second hand; second-hand (adj.)
【二手商品】 èrshǒu shāngpǐn second-hand goods
【二五眼】 èr·wuyǎn **1.** (能力差) of inferior ability or quality **2.** (能力差的人) an incompetent person
【二线】 èrxiàn **1.** (战略上的第二线) second line; regions between front line and strategic rear **2.** (指不主持工作) second line: 退居～ withdraw to the second line
【二项式】 èrxiàngshì 〈*Math.*〉 binomial
【二心】 èrxīn disloyalty; halfheartedness
【二氧化碳】 èryǎnghuàtàn 〈*Chem.*〉 carbon dioxide
【二一添做五】 èr yī tiān zuò wǔ go halves; go fifty-fifty
【二元论】 èryuánlùn dualism
【二月】 èryuè February
【二战】 Èrzhàn Second World War
【二者】 èrzhě the two; both: ～必居其一。It must be one or the other. / ～缺一不可。Neither of the two can be dispensed.
【二至点】 èrzhìdiǎn 〈*Astron.*〉 solstices

贰 (èr) two; second

F

fa

发[發](fā) 1.(发出;送出)send out; deliver; distribute; issue:~工资 pay out wages/~通知 issue a notice 2.(发言)utter; express 3.(发射)discharge; shoot; emit 4.(扩大;开发)develop; expand 5.(发生;产生)come or bring into existence 6.(打开;揭露)open up; discover; expose 7.(变为;散发)get into a certain state; become 8.(显出)show one's feeling 9.(觉得)feel; have a feeling 10.(出发)start; set out; begin an undertaking
(另见"发"fà)

【发案】 fāàn incidence of criminal offenses

【发白】 fābái turn white; become white: 气得脸~ turn pale with anger

【发包方】 fābāofāng the party awarding the contract

【发报】 fābào send a telegram

【发报机】 fābàojī transmitter

【发表】 fābiǎo publish; issue: ~文章 publish an article / ~消息 publish the news / ~意见 express one's opinion

【发病】 fābìng fall ill; suffer from an illness

【发病率】 fābìnglǜ incidence of a disease

【发布】 fābù issue; release: ~命令 issue orders

【发财】 fācái 1.(赚得大钱) get rich; make a fortune; make a pile: 发国难财 exploit the national crisis for profiteering purposes 2.(客套话) Wishing you property!

【发车】 fāchē 1.(派车) dispatch (send off) a car (truck, bus) 2.(开车) depart; pull out: 早7点半~。The train will depart at 7:30 a.m.

【发愁】 fāchóu worry; be anxious

【发出】 fāchū issue; send out; give out: ~紧急呼吁 send out an urgent appeal / ~警报 sound the alarm

【发达】 fādá developed; flourishing: 经济~ well-developed economically

【发达国家】 fādá guójiā developed country

【发呆】 fādāi stare blankly; be in a trance

【发嗲】 fādiǎ 〈*dial.*〉 playful tone or manner

【发电】 fādiàn 1.(生产电力) generate electricity 2.(发电报) send a telegram

【发电厂】 fādiànchǎng power plant; power station: 火力~ thermal power plant

【发电机】 fādiànjī generator; dynamo: 汽轮~ turbo generator

【发电机组】 fādiàn jīzǔ generating set: 柴油~ diesel generating set

【发动】 fādòng 1.(使开始) start; launch: ~侵略战争 launch an aggressive war 2.(使行动) call into action; mobilize; arouse: ~群众 mobilize the masses 3.(使运转) start; set ... going: ~机器 start a machine; set a machine going

【发动机】 fādòngjī engine; motor: 柴油~ diesel engine; diesel motor

【发动机吊舱】 fādòngjī diàocāng 〈*Aeron.*〉 engine pod

【发动机盖】 fādòngjī gài 〈*Auto*〉 hood

【发动机罩】 fādòngjī zhào 〈*Auto*〉 hood

【发抖】 fādǒu shiver; shake; tremble

【发放】 fāfàng provide; grant; extend: ~救济金 deal out relief fund; dispense relief fund

【发愤】 fāfèn make a firm resolution; do sth. with a determined mind

【发愤图强】 fāfèn-túqiáng work with a will to make the country strong

【发疯】 fāfēng 1.(发生精神病) go mad; go crazy; become insane; be out of one's mind 2.(做事超出常情) do sth. in an abnormal way

【发稿】 fāgǎo 1.(发新闻专稿) distribute news dispatches 2.(批准稿件付印) send manuscripts to the press：到～时为止 at press time

【发给】 fāgěi issue; distribute; grant：～护照 issue a passport

【发光】 fāguāng shine; give out light

【发号施令】 fāhào-shīlìng issue orders; order people about

【发黑】 fāhēi 1.（变黑）turn black; grow black; become black; blacken; darken 2.（一时眩晕）blackout：眼睛突然～ have a sudden blackout

【发还】 fāhuán give back; return sth.

【发慌】 fāhuāng feel nervous; get flustered; get flurried：别～。Don't get flurried.

【发挥】 fāhuī 1.（表现出内在能力）bring into play; give play to; give free rein to：充分～…的积极性 give full play to the initiative of ... / ～投资的效用 make the investment yield well / ～余热 bring extra power into play 2.（详尽论述）develop (an idea, a theme, etc.); elaborate：～自己的论点 elaborate one's own ideas

【发火】 fāhuǒ 1.（开始燃烧）catch fire; ignite 2.（使爆发）detonate; go off 3.（发脾气）get angry; flare up; lose one's temper：别惹我～。Don't make me lose my temper.

【发货】 fāhuò send out goods; deliver goods

【发迹】 fājì gain fame and fortune

【发家】 fājiā build up a family fortune

【发奖】 fājiǎng award prizes

【发酵】 fājiào ferment; fermentation (n.)

【发酵粉】 fājiàofěn yeast powder; baking powder

【发窘】 fājiǒng feel embarrassed; be ill at ease

【发觉】 fājué find; detect; discover

【发掘】 fājué 1.（挖掘）excavate; unearth：～人才 seek gifted people 2.（开发）explore：～潜力 explore potential ability

【发牢骚】 fā láo·sao grumble; complain; grouse

【发愣】 fālèng stare blankly; be in a daze; be in a trance

【发亮】 fāliàng shine

【发令员】 fālìngyuán 〈*Sports*〉 starter

【发霉】 fāméi go moldy; become mildewed

【发面】 fāmiàn 1.（发酵面粉）leaven dough 2.（已发酵的面）leavened dough

【发明】 fāmíng 1.（创造）invent：中国的四大～ four invents by China / 火药最早是中国人～的。The gunpowder was first invented by the Chinese. 2.（新创造）invention 3.（创造性阐发）expound

【发明权】 fāmíngquán inventor's patent right

【发明人】 fāmíngrén inventor

【发难】 fānàn rise in revolt; launch an attack

【发蔫】 fāniān 1.（指花木、水果等）withered 2.（指人）spiritless; listless

【发怒】 fānù be angry; become furious

【发脾气】 fā pí·qi lose one's temper; get angry：别惹我～。Don't make me lose my temper.

【发票】 fāpiào bill; receipt：开～ write up a bill

【发起】 fāqǐ 1.（倡议）initiate; sponsor 2.（发动）start; launch：～冲锋 sound the charge; start to charge

【发起人】 fāqǐrén initiator; sponsor

【发情】 fāqíng 1.（要求交配）estrus 2.（交尾期）be in heat

【发球】 fāqiú serve a ball; service (n.)

【发球区】 fāqiúqū 1.〈*Volleyball*〉 service area 2.〈*Table Tennis*〉 service court

【发球线】 fāqiúxiàn service line

【发球线司线员】 fāqiúxiàn sīxiànyuán service line judge

【发球员】 fāqiúyuǎn server

【发热】 fārè 1.（发出热量）give out heat; generate heat 2.（发烧）have a fever 3.（不冷静）be hotheaded

【发人深省】 fārén-shēnxǐng set people thinking; call for deep thought; provide food for thought

【发善心】 fā shànxīn show mercy; show philanthropy

【发烧】 fāshāo have a fever; have a temperature

【发射】 fāshè 1.（射出）launch; project; discharge; shoot; fire：～火箭 launch a rocket / ～卫星 launch a satellite 2.〈*Physics*〉 transmit; emit

【发射场】 fāshèchǎng launching site

【发射窗口】 fāshè chuāngkǒu launch window

【发射器】 fāshèqì 〈*Aeron.*〉 transmitter

【发射台】 fāshètái 〈*Aeron*.〉 launch pad; launching pad

【发生】 fāshēng happen; occur; take place: 这里～了巨大变化。Tremendous changes have taken place here.

【发誓】 fāshì vow; pledge; swear

【发售】 fāshòu sell; put on sale

【发水】 fāshuǐ flood

【发送】 fāsòng 1.(发出无线电信号) transmit by radio: ～电传 transmit a FAX 2.(送出) dispatch (letters, etc.)

【发条】 fātiáo spiral power spring; clockwork spring: 我忘了给钟上～。I've forgotten to wind the clock up again.

【发文】 fāwén dispatch documents: 联合～ dispatch a joint document

【发现】 fāxiàn 1.(找到,看到) find; discover; discovery (n.): 许多科学～ many scientific discovery / 牛顿～了万有引力。Issac Newton discovered the gravity. / 经过常规检查,～他有心脏病。Following a routine checkup, he was discovered to have heart disease. 2.(发觉) find; notice; be aware of: 善于～别人的长处 be good at finding other people's strong points

【发笑】 fāxiào laugh: 令人～ make one laugh

【发泄】 fāxiè give vent to; let off: ～不满 let off one's grievances

【发信】 fāxìn post a letter; send a letter

【发信人】 fāxìnrén addresser

【发行】 fāxíng (of currency, bonds, books, etc.) issue; publish; distribute; put on sale: ～报刊 publish newspapers and magazines / ～新邮票 issue new stamps / ～一批股票 float an issue of stock

【发芽】 fāyá germinate; sprout: 种子在温室里～了。The seeds were germinated in the greenhouse.

【发言】 fāyán speak; make a speech; take the floor: 要求～ request to make a speech

【发言稿】 fāyángǎo the text of a statement or speech

【发言权】 fāyánquán right to speak: 对…有～ have a say in

【发言人】 fāyánrén spokesman: 政府～ government spokesman

【发炎】 fāyán 〈*Med*.〉 inflammation

【发扬】 fāyáng 1.(提倡) develop; carry on: ～民主 develop a democratic style of work 2.(发挥) make the most of; make full use of

【发扬光大】 fāyáng-guāngdà carry forward; enhance; develop

【发痒】 fāyǎng itch; tickle: 我浑身～。I itch all over.

【发音】 fāyīn pronunciation; enunciation; articulation

【发育】 fāyù growth; development: ～健全 physically well developed

【发源】 fāyuán rise; originate

【发源地】 fāyuándì place of origin; source; birthplace

【发晕】 fāyūn feel dizzy

【发展】 fāzhǎn 1.(变化) develop; expand; grow; development (n.): ～生产力 development of production force / 加快经济～ accelerate economic development / ～友好合作关系 develop the relations of friendship and cooperation 2.(扩大) recruit; admit

【发展动力】 fāzhǎn dònglì motive force of development

【发展模式】 fāzhǎn móshì developmental model

【发展商】 fāzhǎnshāng developer

【发展中国家】 fāzhǎnzhōng guójiā developing country

【发肿】 fāzhǒng swell; become swollen: 他的腿～。His legs are swelling out.

【发作】 fāzuò 1.(突发) break out; show effect: 心脏病～ have a heart attack 2.(发脾气) have a fit of anger; flare up

乏 (fá) 1.(缺少) lack: 不～其人。There is no lack of such people. 2.(疲倦) tired; weary

【乏味】 fáwèi dull; insipid; drab; tasteless

伐 (fá) 1.(砍) fell; cut down 2.(攻打) send an expedition against; attack

【伐木】 fámù lumbering; felling; cutting

【伐木工】 fámùgōng lumberman

【伐树】 fáshù cut down trees; fell trees

阀 (fá) 1.(有势力的人或家族) a powerful person; a powerful family: 财～ plutocrat; financial magnate 2.(阀门) valve

【阀门】 fámén 〈*Mech*.〉 valve

筏[栰] (fá) raft: 橡皮～ rubber raft

【筏子】 fá·zi raft

罚［罸］(fá) punish; penalize: 挨～ be punished

【罚点球】 fádiǎnqiú 〈*Football*〉 spot kick

【罚金】 fájīn 1.(处以罚金) fine 2.(被罚缴纳的钱) fine; forfeit

【罚款】 fákuǎn 1.(处以罚金) fine sb.; impose a fine on sb.: 他因超速被～50元。He was fined fifty yuan for exceeding the speed limit. 2.(被罚缴纳的钱) fine; forfeit; penalty: 100元～ 100 yuan fine / 缴纳10元违章停车～ pay out 10 yuan in parking fine

【罚球】 fáqiú 1.(篮球) penalty shot 2.(足球) penalty kick

【罚球区】 fáqiúqū 1.〈*Football*〉 penalty area 2.〈*Basketball*〉 free-throw zone

【罚球线】 fáqiúxiàn 1.〈*Basketball*〉 free-throw line 2.〈*Handball*〉 penalty line

【罚任意球】 fá rènyìqiú 〈*Football*〉 free kick

法(fǎ) 1.(法律) law: 依～惩办 be punished by law 2.(方法) method; way; mode 3.(效法) follow; take as model 4.(标准) standard; model 5.(魔法) magic arts

【法办】 fǎbàn deal with according to law; punish by law; bring to justice

【法宝】 fǎbǎo 1.〈*Baddhism*〉 Buddhist doctrines 2.〈*Mythol.*〉 a magic weapon 3.(有效办法) an effective method; a powerful tool

【法典】 fǎdiǎn code; statute book: 民法～ civil code

【法定】 fǎdìng legal; statutory

【法定多数】 fǎdìng duōshù a required majority: 达到～ have a required majority

【法定继承权】 fǎdìng jìchéngquán forced heirship

【法定假日】 fǎdìng jiàrì legal holidays

【法定年龄】 fǎdìng niánlíng lawful age; legal age

【法定人数】 fǎdìng rénshù quorum: 达到～ have a quorum

【法官】 fǎguān judge; justice

【法规】 fǎguī laws and regulations: 经济～ economic regulations

【法国】 fǎguó France; French (adj.) ‖ 法国人 Frenchman; Frenchwoman

【法国号】 fǎguóhào 〈*Music*〉 French horn

【法纪】 fǎjì law and discipline: 目无～ act in utter disregard of law and discipline

【法兰绒】 fǎlánróng 〈*Textiles*〉 flannel

【法郎】 fǎláng franc

【法老】 fǎlǎo 〈*Hist.*〉 Pharaoh: 图坦阿蒙当～时，他还很年轻。Tutankhamun became Pharaoh when still very young.

【法令】 fǎlìng laws and decrees; decree: 政府～ government decree

【法律】 fǎlǜ law; statute: 制定～ make laws; enact laws / 提供充分的～保障 give full legal protection

【法律顾问】 fǎlǜ gùwèn legal adviser

【法律面前，人人平等】 fǎlǜ-miànqián, rénrén-píngděng All men are equal before the law.

【法律事务所】 fǎlǜ shìwùsuǒ law office

【法律手续】 fǎlǜ shǒuxù legal procedure

【法律制裁】 fǎlǜ zhìcái legal sanction

【法盲】 fǎmáng legally illiterate; illiteracy of law

【法权】 fǎquán right

【法人】 fǎrén 〈*Law*〉 legal person; juridical person

【法人团体】 fǎrén tuántǐ body corporate; corporation

【法术】 fǎshù magic arts

【法庭】 fǎtíng court; tribunal: 民事～ civil court / 军事～ military tribunal

【法网】 fǎwǎng the net of justice; the arm of the law: 落入～ be caught in the meshes of law

【法西斯】 fǎxīsī fascist

【法学】 fǎxué the science of law; law

【法医】 fǎyī legal medical expert

【法语】 fǎyǔ French (language)

【法院】 fǎyuàn court of justice; law court; court: 地方人民～ local people's court / 中级人民～ intermediate people's court

【法则】 fǎzé rule; law: 自然～ law of nature

【法治】 fǎzhì rule by law; be ruled by law

【法制】 fǎzhì legal system; legal institutions; legality: 加强～ strengthen the legal system

【法制委员会】 fǎzhì wěiyuánhuì commission for legal affairs

【法子】 fǎ·zi way; method: 想个～ have to think of a way to

砝(fǎ)

【砝码】 fǎmǎ weight (used on a balance)

发［髮］(fà) hair：理～ haircut / 烫～ have a permanent wave / 洗～ have one's hair washed; have one's hair shampooed
(另见"发"fā)

【发辫】 fàbiàn braid; plait
【发夹】 fàjiā hairpin; bobby pin; hairgrip
【发胶】 fàjiāo hairspray
【发卡】 fàqiǎ hairpin
【发蜡】 fàlà pomade
【发廊】 fàláng hairdresser's
【发乳】 fàrǔ hair cream
【发式】 fàshì hair style
【发刷】 fàshuā hairbrush
【发网】 fàwǎng hairnet
【发油】 fàyóu hair oil
【发型】 fàxíng hair style; hairdo; coiffure
【发指】 fàzhǐ bristle with anger; boil with anger

珐［琺］(fà)

【珐琅】 fàláng enamel
【珐琅质】 fàlángzhì enamel (of the teeth)

fan

帆(fān) sail：扬～ unfurl a sail

【帆板】 fānbǎn 〈*Sports*〉 **1.**（指运动） windsurfing; windsurf (v.) **2.**（指器材） sailboard; windsurfer
【帆板运动】 fānbǎn yùndòng 〈*Sports*〉 windsurfing; windsurf (v.)
【帆布】 fānbù canvas; duck
【帆布包】 fānbùbāo canvas bag; kit bag
【帆布床】 fānbùchuáng cot; camp bed
【帆船】 fānchuán sailing boat; sailing ship; sailboat; yacht
【帆船俱乐部】 fānchuán jùlèbù yacht club
【帆船运动】 fānchán yùndòng yachting; sailing; yacht racing

番(fān) 〈*classifier*〉听了这一～话 having heard this talk / 大豆产量翻了一～。Soybean output has doubled.

【番号】 fānhào designation (of a military unit)
【番茄】 fānqié tomato
【番茄酱】 fānqiéjiàng tomato ketchup
【番茄汁】 fānqiézhī tomato juice
【番薯】 fānshǔ sweet potato

翻(fān) **1.**（翻倒，翻转） turn over：把磁带～到背面 wind the cassette back / 车～了。The car turned over. / 风把我的伞里儿朝外～了过来。The wind turned my umbrella inside out. **2.**（翻越） cross; get over **3.**（翻找） rummage; search **4.**（翻译） translate **5.**（推翻） reverse **6.**（翻番） multiply **7.**（翻脸） fall out; break up

【翻案】 fān'àn reverse a (correct) verdict
【翻版】 fānbǎn reproduction; refurbished version
【翻车】 fānchē turn over
【翻船】 fānchuán **1.**（船倾覆） capsize：～了。The ship capsized. **2.**（指比赛失败） defeat; setback
【翻地】 fāndì turn up the soil
【翻动】 fāndòng turn; turn over; renovate
【翻斗】 fāndǒu tipping bucket; skip bucket
【翻斗车】 fāndǒuchē skip car; tipcart
【翻番】 fānfān be doubled
【翻改】 fāngǎi turn; renovate：～一件短上衣 have a jacket turned
【翻盖】 fāngài renovate (a house)
【翻跟头】 fān gēn·tou **1.**（体操动作） turn a somersault; loop the loop **2.**（受挫） suffer a defeat
【翻个儿】 fān'gèér turn over
【翻滚】 fāngǔn **1.**（上下滚动） roll; toss **2.**（打滚） tumble
【翻悔】 fānhuǐ back out; disavow
【翻建】 fānjiàn rebuild
【翻看】 fānkàn leaf through：～日历 leaf through the calendar
【翻来覆去】 fānlái-fùqù **1.**（来回翻动身体） toss and turn; toss from side to side **2.**（重复） again and again; repeatedly
【翻脸】 fānliǎn fall out; suddenly turn hostile
【翻两番】 fān liǎngfān quadruple
【翻领】 fānlǐng **1.**（西服的） lapel **2.**（其他的） revers
【翻然】 fānrán (change) quickly and completely：～悔悟 quickly wake up to one's error
【翻砂】 fānshā 〈*Metall.*〉 founding; mold-

ing; casting

【翻砂工】 fānshāgōng 〈*Metall.*〉 foundry worker; caster

【翻山越岭】 fānshān-yuèlǐng cross over mountain after mountain; tramp over hill and dale

【翻身】 fānshēn **1.**（躺着翻转身体）turn over **2.**（解放出来）free oneself; stand up **3.**（转身）turn round

【翻腾】 fān·téng **1.**（上下滚动）seethe; rise; churn **2.**（翻动）turn sth. over and over

【翻天覆地】 fāntiān-fùdì earth-shaking; world-shaking: ～的变化 an earth-shaking change

【翻下】 fānxià turn down: ～大衣领 turn down the coat collar

【翻箱倒柜】 fānxiāng-dǎoguì rummage through chests and cupboards; ransack boxes and chests

【翻新】 fānxīn **1.**（从旧变新）renovate; recondition; make over **2.**（衣服翻新）make new out of the old

【翻修】 fānxiū rebuild: ～房屋 rebuild a house

【翻译】 fānyì **1.**（语言翻译）translate; interpret: 机器～ machine translation / 把英语～成汉语 translate the English into Chinese / 你能给我～一下吗? Would you mind translating for me? **2.**（译员）translator; interpreter

【翻印】 fānyìn reprint; reproduce

【翻阅】 fānyuè browse; look over; glance over; leaf through

【翻云覆雨】 fānyún-fùyǔ produce clouds with one turn of the hand and rain with another; given to playing tricks

凡［凢］(fán) **1.**（平凡）commonplace; ordinary **2.**（凡是）every; any; all

【凡例】 fánlì notes on the use of a book, etc.; guide to the use of a book, etc.

【凡人】 fánrén **1.**（平常人）ordinary person **2.**（俗人）mortal

【凡士林】 fánshìlín vaseline; petrolatum

【凡事】 fánshì everything: ～开头难。It's the first step that costs.

【凡是】 fánshì every; any; all

矾［礬］(fán) 〈*Chem.*〉 vitriol

【矾土】 fántǔ alumina

钒(fán) 〈*Chem.*〉 vanadium（元素符号V）

烦(fán) **1.**（烦闷）be vexed; be irritated; be annoyed **2.**（厌烦）be tired of; be fed up with: 添～ make sb. feel more vexed **3.**（杂乱）superfluous and confusing **4.**（烦劳）trouble

【烦闷】 fánmèn be unhappy; be worried

【烦恼】 fánnǎo be vexed; be worried

【烦扰】 fánrǎo **1.**（搅扰）bother; disturb **2.**（心烦）feel disturbed

【烦人】 fánrén annoying; vexing; troubling: 多么～呀! How vexing!

【烦琐】 fánsuǒ loaded down with trivial details

【烦琐哲学】 fánsuǒ zhéxué **1.**（经院哲学）scholasticism **2.**（烦琐）overelaboration; hairsplitting

【烦躁】 fánzào be fidgety; be agitated: 令人～不安 make one feel uneasy and worried

蕃(fán) **1.**（茂盛）luxuriant **2.**（繁殖）multiply

繁［緐］(fán) **1.**（繁多）in great numbers; numerous; manifold **2.**（繁殖）propagate; multiply

【繁多】 fánduō numerous; a great number of; various: 品种～ many kinds; great in variety

【繁花似锦】 fánhuā-sìjǐn flowers blooming like a piece of brocade; a flourishing scene of prosperity

【繁华】 fánhuá flourishing; bustling; busy: ～地区 busy section of town

【繁忙】 fánmáng busy: ～的生活 a busy life

【繁茂】 fánmào lush; luxuriant: 枝叶～ with luxuriant foliage

【繁难】 fánnán hard to tackle; troublesome

【繁荣】 fánróng **1.**（昌盛）flourishing; prosperous; booming: ～富强 rich, strong and prosperous **2.**（使昌盛）make sth. prosper: ～经济 bring about a prosperous economy; promote economic prosperity

【繁荣昌盛】 fánróng-chāngshèng thriving and prosperous: 祝贵国～，人民幸福。We wish your country prosperity and her people happiness.

【繁荣富强】 fánróng-fùqiáng prosperity and strength

【繁体字】 fántǐzhì the original complex form of a simplified Chinese character

【繁育】 fányù breed: ～家畜 breed stock

【繁殖】 fánzhí 〈*Biol.*〉 breed; reproduce; propagate

【繁重】 fánzhòng heavy; strenuous; onerous: ～的体力劳动 strenuous manual labor

反 (fǎn) 1.(翻转) turn over 2.(方向向背) in an opposite direction; in reverse; inside out 3.(反之) on the contrary; instead 4.(回;还) return; counter 5.(背叛) revolt; rebel 6.(反对) oppose; combat 7.(指反动派;反革命) counterrevolutionaries; reactionaries

【反败为胜】 fǎnbài-wéishèng come from behind to win the game

【反比】 fǎnbǐ 〈*Math.*〉 inverse ratio: 成～ be in inverse proportion to

【反比例】 fǎnbǐlì 〈*Math.*〉 inverse ratio; inverse proportion

【反驳】 fǎnbó retort; rebut; counterplea

【反不正当竞争法】 fǎn bùzhèngdāng jìngzhēngfǎ 〈*Law*〉 the Anti-Unethical Competition Law

【反差】 fǎnchā contrast

【反常】 fǎncháng unusual; abnormal; perverse: 最近几年天气有点儿～。The weather is a bit unusual these years.

【反刍】 fǎnchú ruminate

【反刍动物】 fǎnchú dòngwù ruminant; ruminant animal: 牛、羊和鹿都是～。Cows, sheep, and deer are ruminants (或 ruminant animals).

【反党】 fǎndǎng anti-Party

【反党集团】 fǎndǎng jítuán an anti-Party gang

【反倒】 fǎndào on the contrary; instead

【反帝】 fǎndì anti-imperialist; against imperialism: ～斗争 anti-imperialist struggle

【反动】 fǎndòng 1.(逆革命潮流) reactionary 2.(相反作用) reaction

【反动派】 fǎndòngpài reactionaries

【反对】 fǎnduì oppose; be against; fight; combat

【反对票】 fǎnduìpiào dissenting vote; negative vote

【反而】 fǎn'ér 〈*conj.*〉 on the contrary; instead

【反方】 fǎnfāng negative side

【反腐】 fǎnfǔ anti-corruption

【反复】 fǎnfù 1.(多次重复) repeatedly; again and again; over and over again: ～较量 repeated trials of strength 2.(翻来复去) reversal; relapse

【反复无常】 fǎnfù-wúcháng changeable; tickle; capricious

【反感】 fǎngǎn be disgusted with; be averse to; dislike; take unkindly to

【反戈一击】 fǎngē-yījī turn one's weapon round and strike

【反革命暴乱】 fǎngémìng bàoluàn counterrevolutionary violence

【反革命分子】 fǎngémìng fènzǐ a counterrevolutionary

【反革命两面派】 fǎngémìng liǎngmiànpài counterrevolutionary double-dealer

【反革命政变】 fǎngémìng zhèngbiàn counterrevolutionary coup d'etat

【反攻】 fǎngōng counteroffensive; counterattack

【反光】 fǎnguāng 1.(反射光) reflect light 2.(光的反射) reflection of light

【反光道钉】 fǎnguāng dàodīng reflector (AmE.); cat's eye (BrE.)

【反光灯】 fǎnguāngdēng 〈*Auto*〉 reflector

【反话】 fǎnhuà irony

【反悔】 fǎnhuǐ go back on one's word; go back on one's promise

【反击】 fǎnjī counterattack; strike back; beat back: 自卫～ counterattack in self-defense

【反诘】 fǎnjié ask in retort; counter with a question

【反抗】 fǎnkàng revolt; resist

【反馈】 fǎnkuì 1.〈*Electr.*〉 feedback 2.(返回信息) feedback: 信息～ information feedback

【反馈电路】 fǎnkuì diànlù feedback circuit

【反面】 fǎnmiàn 1.(背面) reverse side; wrong side; back: 钱币的～ the reverse side of a coin 2.（消极的一面）opposite; negative side

【反拍击球】 fǎnpāi jīqiú 〈*Badminton*〉 backhand stroke

【反叛】 fǎnpàn revolt; rebel; rebellion

【反扑】 fǎnpū pounce on sb. again after being beaten off

【反其道而行之】 fǎn qí dào ér xíng zhī do exactly the opposite; act in a diametrically opposite way

【反射】 fǎnshè 1.〈*Biol.*〉 reflex：条件～ conditioned reflex 2.〈*Physics*〉 reflection

【反思】 fǎnsī review; turn over to think; reconsider past events to distinguish right and wrong

【反弹】 fǎntán 〈*Econ.*〉 bounce-back

【反坦克炮】 fǎn tǎnkèpào antitank gun

【反胃】 fǎnwèi 1.（胃不舒服）gastric disorder causing nausea 2.（令人厌恶）make sb's gorge rise：这事使她～。It made his gorge rise.

【反问】 fǎnwèn 1.（以问代答）ask (a question) in reply 2.（含反意的发问）rhetorical question

【反响】 fǎnxiǎng repercussion; echo; reverberation

【反向】 fǎnxiàng opposite direction; reverse

【反省】 fǎnxǐng introspection; self-questioning; self-examination

【反咬一口】 fǎnyǎo-yīkǒu trump up a countercharge against one's accuser; make a false countercharge

【反义词】 fǎnyìcí antonym

【反应】 fǎnyìng 1.（化学变化）reaction：化学～ chemical reaction / 热核～ thermo-nuclear reaction 2.（反响）response; repercussion; reaction：～不一。Reactions vary.

【反应堆】 fǎnyìngduī 〈*Physics*〉 reactor：核～ nuclear reactor; nuclear reaction pile / 原子～ reactor; atomic pile

【反映】 fǎnyìng 1.（反照）reflect; mirror：时代的～ mirror of the times 2.（报告上级）report; make known：向上级～ report to the higher level 3.〈*Biol.*〉 reflect; reflection

【反映冷淡】 fǎnyìng lěngdàn cold response

【反正】 fǎnzhèng 1.（敌方投诚）come over from the enemy's side 2.〈*adv.*〉 anyway; anyhow; in any case

【反之】 fǎnzhī conversely; on the contrary; otherwise

【反作用】 fǎnzuòyòng 1.（指作用）counteraction; reaction 2.（指作用力）reacting force

返 (fǎn) return

【返潮】 fǎncháo get damp

【返工】 fǎngōng do poorly done work over again

【返航】 fǎnháng return to base; return to port

【返回】 fǎnhuí return; come or go back

【返校】 fǎnxiào return to school after the vacation

犯 (fàn) 1.（违反）violate; offend (against law, etc.) 2.（侵犯）attack; assail; work against 3.（罪犯）criminal 4.（发作）have a recurrence of (an old illness) 5.（发生）commit (a mistake, crime, etc.)

【犯病】 fànbìng have an attack of one's old illness

【犯不着】 fàn·buzháo not worthwhile; not worth the effort; not worth the candle

【犯愁】 fànchóu worry; be anxious

【犯错误】 fàncuòwù make a mistake; commit an error

【犯得着】 fàn·dezháo it pays to; it is worthwhile

【犯法】 fànfǎ violate the law

【犯规】 fànguī 1.（违犯）break the rules 2.〈*Sports*〉 foul

【犯禁】 fànjìn violate a ban; break prohibition

【犯人】 fànrén prisoner; convict

【犯疑】 fànyí suspect; be suspicious

【犯罪】 fànzuì commit a crime：刑事～ criminal offender / 打击～ fight crime

【犯罪分子】 fànzuì fènzǐ offender; criminal

【犯罪集团】 fànzuì jítuán criminal gang

【犯罪率】 fànzuìlǜ crime rate

范［範］ (fàn) 1.（模子）pattern 2.（模范）model; example; pattern 3.（范围）limits

【范本】 fànběn model for calligraphy or painting

【范畴】 fànchóu 1.（基本范畴）category 2.

(类型) type; scope
【范例】 fànlì example; model
【范围】 fànwéi scope; limits; range: 活动～ scope of activities / 势力～ sphere of influence / 在法律许可～内 within the limits permitted by law
【范文】 fànwén model essay

饭 (fàn) 1. (米饭) cooked rice 2. (每餐吃的食物) meal: 早～ breakfast / 午～ lunch / 晚～ dinner
【饭菜】 fàncài 1. (饭和菜) meal; repast 2. (就饭的菜) dishes to go with rice, steamed buns, etc.
【饭店】 fàndiàn 1. (大旅馆) hotel 2. (饭馆) restaurant
【饭馆】 fànguǎn restaurant; luncheonette
【饭盒】 fànhé lunch-box; mess tin; dinner pail
【饭量】 fàn·liàng appetite: ～大 have a good appetite; have a good stomach / ～小 have a poor appetite; have a poor stomach
【饭票】 fànpiào meal ticket; mess card
【饭厅】 fàntīng dining hall; dining room; mess hall
【饭桶】 fàntǒng 1. (盛饭的桶) rice bucket 2. (饭量大) big eater 3. (无用之人) fathead; good-for-nothing
【饭碗】 fànwǎn 1. (盛饭的碗) rice bowl 2. (指职业) job: 丢了～ lose one's job
【饭桌】 fànzhuō dining table

贩 (fàn) 1. (贩卖) buy to resell 2. (贩子) dealer; monger; pedlar
【贩毒】 fàndú traffic in narcotics; drug trafficking (n.)
【贩卖】 fànmài traffic; peddle; sell: ～人口 traffic in person
【贩运】 fànyùn transport goods for sale; traffic
【贩子】 fàn·zi dealer; monger: 鱼～ fishmonger / 战争～ warmonger

泛[氾、汎³] (fàn) 1. (漂浮) float 2. (透出) be suffused with 3. (泛滥) flood; inundate 4. (广泛) extensive; general; nonspecific
【泛泛】 fànfàn generally; in generalities
【泛泛而谈】 fànfàn-értán talk in generalities
【泛泛之交】 fànfàn-zhījiāo nodding acquaintance
【泛滥】 fànlàn 1. (溢出) be in flood; overflow: 河水～。The river overflowed. 2. (扩展) spread unchecked: ～成灾 run rampant; run wild
【泛指】 fànzhǐ make a general reference
【泛舟】 fànzhōu ride in a boat for sightseeing

梵 (fàn) Buddhist
【梵文】 fànwén Sanskrit

fang

方 (fāng) 1. (方形) square: 四英尺见～ four feet square 2. (乘方) involution; power: 二的三次～ the third power of 2 3. (平方米) square meter 4. (立方米) cubic meter 5. (正直) upright; honest 6. (方向) direction 7. (方面) side; party: 罢工的双～ the two sides in the strike 8. (地方) place; region; locality: 远～ a faraway place 9. (方法) method; way: 千～百计 in a hundred and one ways; by every conceivable means 10. (药方) prescription: 处～ make out a prescription
【方案】 fāng'àn scheme; plan; program: 制定～ draw up a plan for
【方便】 fāngbiàn 1. (便利) convenient: ～群众 make things convenient for the people 2. (上厕所) go to the lavatory 3. (有富余钱) have money to spare or lend: 手头不～ have no money to spare
【方便面】 fāngbiànmiàn instant noodles
【方便食品】 fāngbiàn-shípǐn convenience food
【方便之门】 fāngbiàn zhīmén the door is thrown wide open for: 大开～ do everything to suit sb's convenience
【方才】 fāngcái just; just now; at the time when: 他～回来。He has just come back.
【方程】 fāngchéng 〈*Math.*〉 equation: 解～ solve an equation
【方程式】 fāngchéngshì 1. 〈*Math.*〉 equation; formula 2. 〈*Chem.*〉 equation: 化学～ chemical equation
【方城之战】 fāngchéng zhīzhàn battle of 'the quadrilateral city'; playing mah-jong

【方法】 fāngfǎ method; way; means: 改进～ improve one's methods / 科学～ scientific method / 学习～ method of study
【方法论】 fāngfǎlùn methodology
【方块】 fāngkuài 〈*Cards*〉 diamond
【方块字】 fāngkuàizì Chinese characters
【方框图】 fāngkuāngtú block plan; block diagram
【方括号】 fāngkuòhào square brackets (符号为 [ ])
【方螺母】 fāngluómǔ square nut
【方面】 fāngmiàn respect; aspect; side; field: 有关～ the parties concerned / 在这～ in this respect
【方式】 fāngshì way; fashion; pattern: 生产～ mode of production / 生活～ way of life; life-style
【方糖】 fāngtáng cube sugar; lump sugar
【方位】 fāngwèi points of the compass; position; direction; placement: 全～ in all domains
【方向】 fāngxiàng **1**.(方位) direction; orientation: 迷失～ lose one's way; get lost **2**.(前进目标) orientation: 发展～ new orientation in development
【方向灯】 fāngxiàngdēng 〈*Auto*〉 blinker; turning signal; indicator
【方向舵】 fāngxiàngduò 〈*Aeron*.〉 rudder
【方向盘】 fāngxiàngpán 〈*Auto*〉 steering wheel
【方兴未艾】 fāngxīng-wèiài be just unfolding; be in the ascendant
【方形】 fāngxíng square
【方言】 fāngyán 〈*Linguis*.〉 dialect
【方以类聚,物以群分】 fāngyǐ-lèijù, wùyǐ-qúnfēn like attracts like and birds of a feather flock together
【方圆】 fāngyuán **1**.(周长) circumference **2**.(周围) neighborhood **3**.(方形和圆形) square and circle
【方针】 fāngzhēn policy; guiding principle: 教育～ educational policy / 战略～ strategic principle
【方舟】 fāngzhōu 〈*Bible*〉 Noah's Ark
【方子】 fāng·zi **1**.(药方) prescription: 开～ write out a prescription **2**.(配方) directions for mixing chemicals; formula

芳 (fāng) **1**.(香) sweet-smelling; fragrant **2**.(好名声) good (name or reputation); virtuous
【芳香】 fāngxiāng fragrant; aromatic
【芳香剂】 fāngxiāngjì aromatic
【芳香植物】 fāngxiāng zhíwù scent plant

钫 (fāng) 〈*Chem*.〉 francium (元素符号 Fr)

防 (fáng) **1**.(防备) guard against; provide against **2**.(防守) defend **3**.(堤防) dike; embankment
【防暴】 fángbào anti-riot
【防暴警察】 fángbào jǐngchá riot police
【防备】 fángbèi guard against; take precautions against: ～天灾 make preparations against natural disasters
【防病】 fángbìng prevent disease: ～治病 prevent and cure
【防病毒卡】 fáng bìngdúkǎ anti-virus card
【防波堤】 fángbōdī breakwater; mole
【防不胜防】 fángbù-shèngfáng impossible to defend effectively; very hard to guard against
【防潮】 fángcháo **1**.(防潮湿) moistureproof; damp-proof **2**.(防潮水) protection against the tide
【防尘】 fángchén dust-proof
【防弹】 fángdàn bullet proof; shell proof
【防弹背心】 fángdàn bèixīn flak vest
【防弹玻璃】 fángdàn bōlí bullet proof glass
【防弹衣】 fángdànyī flak jacket
【防盗】 fángdào guard against theft; take precautions against burglars
【防盗警报器】 fángdào jǐngbàoqì burglar-alarm
【防盗门】 fángdàomén burglar-proof door; anti-theft door
【防冻】 fángdòng prevent frostbite
【防冻液】 fángdòngyiè anti-icing fluid
【防毒】 fángdú gas defense; gas protection
【防毒面具】 fángdú miànjù gas mask
【防范】 fángfàn be on guard; keep a lookout
【防风林】 fángfēnglín windbreak (forest)
【防腐】 fángfǔ antiseptic; anticorrosive
【防腐剂】 fángfǔjì preservative; antiseptic
【防洪】 fánghóng prevent or control flood: ～措施 flood control measures

【防洪工程】 fánghóng gōngchéng flood control works
【防护】 fánghù protect; shelter
【防护林】 fánghùlín shelter-forest
【防护装置】 fánghù zhuāngzhì protective device
【防火】 fánghuǒ fire prevention; fireproof
【防火墙】 fánghuǒqiáng fire wall
【防火涂料】 fánghuǒ túliào flame-proof paint
【防空】 fángkōng air defense; antiaircraft
【防空洞】 fángkōngdòng air raid shelter
【防空雷达】 fángkōng léidá air defense radar
【防区】 fángqū defense area; garrison area
【防身】 fángshēn defend oneself
【防湿层】 fángshīcéng 〈*Archit.*〉 damp course
【防守】 fángshǒu 1.（警戒）guard; defend 2.（防备对方进攻）safeguard
【防守队员】 fángshǒu duìyuán 〈*Sports*〉 defender
【防守区】 fángshǒuqū 〈*Sports*〉 defense area
【防暑】 fángshǔ heatstroke prevention; sunstroke prevention
【防水】 fángshuǐ waterproof
【防水表】 fángshuǐbiǎo waterproof watch
【防水涂料】 fángshuǐ túliào water-repellent paint
【防水信封】 fángshuǐ xìnfēng waterproof envelope
【防务】 fángwù defense; matters pertaining to defense
【防线】 fángxiàn line of defense
【防汛】 fángxùn flood prevention or control
【防疫】 fángyì epidemic prevention
【防疫站】 fángyìzhàn epidemic prevention station
【防疫针】 fángyìzhēn inoculation
【防雨布】 fángyǔbù tarpaulin; waterproof
【防御】 fángyù defense
【防御部队】 fángyù bùduì defending force
【防御地带】 fángyù dìdài zone of defense; defense of zone
【防灾】 fángzāi take precautions against natural calamities
【防震】 fángzhèn 1.（防备地震）take precautions against earthquakes: ～措施 precautions against earthquakes 2.（防震动）shockproof; quakeproof
【防止】 fángzhǐ prevent; guard against; forestall; avoid: ～感染 protect from infection / ～浪费人力 avoid waste of manpower / ～两极分化 prevent polarization
【防治】 fángzhì prevention and cure; prophylaxis and treatment

妨（fáng） hinder; obstruct

【妨碍】 fáng'ài hinder; hamper; impede; obstruct: ～视线 obstruct the view
【妨害】 fánghài impair; jeopardize; be harmful to: ～集体利益 be injurious to collective interests / ～健康 be harmful to one's health

房（fáng） 1.（房子）house 2.（房间）room

【房产】 fángchǎn house property
【房地产】 fángdìchǎn real estate
【房地产公司】 fángdìchǎn gōngsī real estate company
【房地产交易】 fángdìchǎn jiāoyì real estate transaction
【房地产开发】 fángdìchǎn kāifā real estate development
【房顶】 fángdǐng roof
【房东】 fángdōng landlord; landlady
【房改】 fánggǎi dwelling house reform
【房管】 fángguǎn housing administration
【房管处】 fángguǎnchù housing administrative office
【房间】 fángjiān room: 单人～ single room / 双人～ double room
【房间号码】 fángjiān hàomǎ room number
【房客】 fángkè tenant (of a room or house); lodger
【房钱】 fángqián rent
【房事】 fángshì sexual intercourse
【房屋】 fángwū houses; buildings
【房屋装饰】 fángwū zhuāngshì house decoration
【房檐】 fángyán eaves
【房主】 fángzhǔ house-owner
【房子】 fángzi 1.（房屋）house; building 2.（房间）room
【房租】 fángzhū rent (for a house, flat, etc.)

仿［倣］（fǎng） 1.（仿效）imitate；copy 2.（类似）resemble；be like；be similar

【仿佛】 fǎngfú 1.（好像）seem；as if 2.（类似）be more or less the same；be alike

【仿生学】 fǎngshēngxué bionics

【仿效】 fǎngxiào imitate；follow the example of

【仿造】 fǎngzào copy；be modelled on；counterfeit

【仿照】 fǎngzhào imitate；follow：～办理 act in imitation of

【仿真】 fǎngzhēn simulate；simulation

【仿制】 fǎngzhì copy；be modelled on

【仿制品】 fǎngzhìpǐn imitation；replica；copy

访（fǎng） 1.（访问）visit；call on 2.（调查；寻求）seek by inquiry or search；try to get

【访谈】 fǎngtán 1.（访问并交谈）visit and talk with 2.（电视访谈节目）talk show

【访问】 fǎngwèn visit；call on：非正式～ an unofficial visit / 私人～ private visit / 友好～ friendly visit；goodwill visit

【访问演出】 fǎngwèn yǎnchū visit and perform；visiting performance

【访问学者】 fǎngwèn xuézhě visiting scholar

纺（fǎng） 1.（纺纱）spin 2.（丝织品）a thin silk cloth

【纺车】 fǎngchē spinning wheel

【纺绸】 fǎngchóu a soft plain-weave silk fabric

【纺织】 fǎngzhī spinning and weaving

【纺织厂】 fǎngzhīchǎng textile mill

【纺织品】 fǎngzhīpǐn textile

放（fàng） 1.（放开）let go；set free；release 2.（燃放）let off；give out 3.（放牧）put out to pasture 4.（放纵）let oneself go；give way to 5.（扩展）let out；expand；make larger，longer，etc. 6.（加进）put in；add：～点糖 put in some sugar 7.（使处一定位置）put；place 8.（搁置）leave alone；lay aside 9.（放映）show：～电影 show a film

【放出】 fàngchū give out；let out；emit：～蒸汽 let off steam

【放大】 fàngdà enlarge；magnify；amplify：把照片～ have a photograph enlarged

【放大机】 fàngdàjī 〈*Photog.*〉 enlarger

【放大机头】 fàngdàjī tóu 〈*Photog.*〉 enlarger head

【放大镜】 fàngdàjìng magnifying glass；magnifier

【放大纸】 fàngdàzhǐ 〈*Photog.*〉 enlarging paper

【放荡】 fàngdàng 1.（淫乐）dissolute；dissipated 2.（不检点）unconventional：～不羁 unconventional and unrestrained

【放毒】 fàngdú 1.（放毒药）put poison；poison 2.（散布反动言论）spread erroneous ideas；spread slanderous rumors

【放风】 fàngfēng 1.（使空气流通）let in fresh air 2.（给囚犯放风）let prisoners out for exercise or to relieve themselves 3.（透露消息，散布消息）leak certain information；spread news or rumors

【放风筝】 fàngfēngzhēn fly a kite；kiteflying (n.)：在公园里～ fly kites in the park

【放工】 fànggōng （of workers）knock off

【放过】 fàngguò let off；let slip：～了一个机会 let slip an opportunity

【放活】 fànghuó relax control；relax restrictions

【放火】 fànghuǒ 1.（纵火）set fire to sth.；set sth. on fire 2.（煽动）incite；instigate；create disturbances

【放假】 fàngjià have a holiday or vacation；have a day off：～半天 have a half-day holiday / 放暑假 have summer holidays；have a summer vacation

【放开】 fàngkāi free from rein；relieve from restrictions；remove restrictions

【放开价格】 fàngkāi jiàgé relax control over the prices；lift price control

【放宽】 fàngkuān 1.（指尺寸）extend 2.（指要求、限制）relax restrictions；relax；less restricted：～期限 extend a time limit

【放疗】 fàngliáo 〈*Med.*〉 radiotherapy

【放慢】 fàngmàn slow down；slow up：～点儿(脚步)，你们俩走得太快了。Slow down，you two，you're walking too fast!

【放牧】 fàngmù put out to pasture；herd

【放炮】 fàngpào 1.（打炮）fire a gun 2.（车胎爆裂）blowout：轮胎～了。The tire's had a blowout. 3.（炸开）blasting 4.（攻击）shoot off one's mouth

【放屁】 fàngpì 1.（排气）break wind；fart 2.（骂人话）What crap!（或：Shit!）
【放弃】 fàngqì abandon；give up：～自己的权利 abdicate one's right；renounce one's privilege
【放晴】 fàngqíng clear up（after rain）
【放权】 fàngquán delegate power to lower levels
【放任】 fàngrèn 1.（听其自然）not interfere；let alone：～自流 let sb. drift along；let sth. drift；let sth. take their own course 2.（不干涉）noninterference
【放哨】 fàngshào 1.（站岗）stand sentry；be on sentry 2.（巡逻）patrol；go on patrol
【放射】 fàngshè radiate；radiation（n.）
【放射线】 fàngshèxiàn radioactive rays
【放射性】 fàngshèxìng radioactivity
【放射性同位素】 fàngshèxìng tóngwèisù radio isotope
【放手】 fàngshǒu 1.（松手）let go；let go one's hold 2.（解除）have a free hand；go all out：～发动群众 go all out to mobilize the masses
【放水】 fàngshuì 1.（打开水龙头）turn on the water 2.（打开水闸）（of a reservoir）draw off
【放私】 fàngsī let smuggled articles pass（the customs）
【放肆】 fàngsì unbridled；wanton
【放肆无礼】 fàngsì-wúlǐ unruly and impudent
【放松】 fàngsōng relax；slacken；loosen：～警惕 relax one's vigilance
【放下】 fàngxià lay down；put down：～架子 discard one's haughty airs；come off the high horse
【放像机】 fàngxiàngjī video player
【放心】 fàngxīn set one's mind at rest；be at ease；rest assured；feel relieved
【放学】 fàngxué classes are over；after school
【放养】 fàngyǎng put（fish，etc.）to breed
【放映】 fàngyìng show；project：～一部故事片 show a feature film
【放债】 fàngzhài lend（money）for interest
【放置】 fàngzhì lay up；lay aside
【放纵】 fàngzòng 1.（纵容）let sb. have his own way；connive at；indulge 2.（不守规矩）self-indulgent；undisciplined
【放走】 fàngzǒu release；set free；let go

fei

飞［飛］（fēi） 1.（指鸟等）fly；flit 2.（飘浮）hover or flutter in the air 3.（极快）swiftly 4.（意外的）unexpected；accidental 5.（无根据的）unfounded；groundless：流言～语 rumors and slanders 6.（挥发）disappear through volatilization
【飞奔】 fēibēn dash；tear along
【飞播】 fēibō plant seeds by airplane：～造林 scattered seeds by airplane for afforestation
【飞驰】 fēichí speed along
【飞虫】 fēichóng winged insect
【飞船】 fēichuán airship；dirigible：太空～ spaceship；spacecraft
【飞弹】 fēidàn 1.（导弹）missile 2.（流弹）stray bullet
【飞地】 fēidì 1.（在其他省、县内的）land of one province or county enclosed by that of another 2.（在别国境内的）enclave；exclave
【飞碟】 fēidié UFO；unidentified flying object
【飞短流长】 fēiduǎn-liúcháng spread embroidered stories and malicious gossip
【飞黄腾达】 fēihuáng-téngdá make rapid advances in one's career；have a meteoric rise
【飞机】 fēijī aircraft；airplane；plane
【飞机场】 fēijīchǎng airport；airfield；aerodrome
【飞机票】 fēijīpiào plane ticket
【飞溅】 fēijiàn splash
【飞快】 fēikuài 1.（非常快）very fast 2.（锋利）extremely sharp
【飞来横祸】 fēilái-hénghuò unexpected disaster
【飞轮】 fēilún 1.〈*Mech.*〉flywheel 2.〈*Bicycle*〉free wheel
【飞跑】 fēipǎo run quickly
【飞禽】 fēiqín birds
【飞速】 fēisù at full speed；at top speed
【飞速发展】 fēisù fāzhǎn develop rapidly
【飞腾】 fēiténg fly swiftly upward；soar
【飞艇】 fēitǐng dirigible；airship：齐伯林式～ Zeppelin
【飞吻】 fēiwěn throw a kiss；blow a kiss

【飞舞】 fēiwǔ dance in the air; flutter
【飞翔】 fēixiáng circle in the air; hover
【飞行】 fēixíng flight; flying
【飞行器】 fēixíngqì aircraft
【飞行员】 fēixíngyuán pilot; aviator; flyer
【飞扬】 fēiyáng fly upward; rise
【飞扬跋扈】 fēiyáng-báhù arrogant and domineering
【飞跃】 fēiyuè **1.**(突飞猛进) leap; great development: ～发展 a great leap forward; a rapid and great development **2.**〈*Philos.*〉leap
【飞涨】 fēizhǎng (of prices, etc.) soar; skyrocket

妃 (fēi) **1.**(皇帝的妾) imperial concubine **2.**(王室女成员) princess **3.**(王、侯的妻) the wife of a prince
【妃子】 fēi·zi imperial concubine

非 (fēi) **1.**(错) wrong; evildoing: 痛改前～ thoroughly redress a wrong; be determined to correct one's error **2.**(不合于) not conform to; run counter to **3.**(不以为然) censure; blame **4.**(不是) not; no **5.**(必须) have got to
【非常】 fēicháng **1.**(特殊) extraordinary; unusual; special: ～措施 emergency measures / ～事件 uncommon incident **2.**(十分) very; extremely; highly: ～感兴趣 be very much interested in sth. / ～有趣的影片 a very interesting film / ～重要 extremely important
【非但】 fēidàn not only
【非得】 fēiděi have got to; must
【非法】 fēifǎ illegal; unlawful; illicit: ～交易 illegal transaction / ～收入 illicit income / ～所得 illicit gain / ～同居 illicit cohabitation
【非法移民】 fēifǎ yímín **1.**(非法移居国外) illegal emigration **2.**(非法移居国外者) illegal emigrant **3.**(非法移入) illegal immigration **4.**(非法移入者) illegal immigrant
【非凡】 fēifán outstanding; uncommon; extraordinary: ～的成就 outstanding achievements
【非分】 fēifèn overstepping one's bounds; assuming
【非高峰时间】 fēigāofēng shíjiān off peak hours
【非公莫入】 fēigōng-mòrù no admittance except on business
【非官方】 fēiguānfāng unofficial: ～消息 news from unofficial sources
【非卖品】 fēimàipǐn (articles) not for sale
【非难】 fēinàn blame; censure; reproach: 百般～ try by every means to blame
【非请莫入】 fēiqǐng-mòrù no admittance except on invitation
【非同小可】 fēitóng-xiǎokě not insignificant; no small matter
【非文本文件】 fēiwénběn wénjiàn 〈*Computer*〉non-document file
【非议】 fēiyì (多用于否定式) reproach; censure: 无可～ beyond reproach; irreproachable
【非正式】 fēizhèngshì unofficial; informal: ～访问 an unofficial visit
【非洲】 Fēizhōu Africa; African (adj.) ‖ 非洲人 African
【非洲鼓】 fēizhōugǔ 〈*Music*〉conga drum

菲 (fēi) **1.**(美丽、芳香) luxuriant and fragrant **2.**〈*Chem.*〉phenanthrene (另见"菲"fěi)
【菲菲】 fēifēi **1.**(茂盛、美丽) luxuriant and beautiful **2.**(香) fragrant
【菲林】 fēilín film

绯 (fēi) red
【绯红】 fēihóng bright red; crimson

扉 (fēi) door leaf
【扉页】 fēiyè 〈*Printing*〉title page

蜚 (fēi) (另见"蜚"fěi)
【蜚声】 fēishēng 〈*written*〉make a name; become famous: ～文坛 win renown in literary circles
【蜚语】 fēiyǔ rumors; gossip: 散布流言～ spread rumors

霏 (fēi)
【霏霏】 fēifēi fall thick and fast: 雨雪～。It is sleeting hard.

鲱 (fēi)
【鲱鱼】 fēiyú Pacific herring

肥 (féi) **1.**(含脂肪多) fat **2.**(肥沃) fertile; rich **3.**(使肥沃) fertilize **4.**(肥料)

fertilizer; manure: 化～ chemical fertilizer / 施～ apply fertilizer / 追～ apply additional fertilizer **5**.(肥大的) loose; large; loose-fitting

【肥差】 féichāi lucrative task

【肥大】 féidà **1**.(又宽又大) loose; large **2**.(粗大) fat; plump; corpulent **3**.〈*Med*.〉 hypertrophy

【肥厚】 féihòu plump; fleshy

【肥料】 féiliào fertilizer; manure: 化学～ chemical fertilizer / 无机～ inorganic fertilizer

【肥美】 féiměi **1**.(肥沃) fertile; rich **2**.(丰美) luxuriant; plump; fat **3**.(肥而味美) fat and tasty

【肥胖】 féipàng fat; corpulent

【肥胖症】 féipàngzhèng 〈*Med*.〉 obesity

【肥缺】 féiquē lucrative post

【肥实】 féi·shi **1**.(肥胖) fat; corpulent **2**.(富足;有钱) rich

【肥田】 féitián **1**.(使土地肥沃) fertilize the soil **2**.(肥沃的土地) fertile land

【肥沃】 féiwò fertile; rich

【肥皂】 féizào soap: 一块～ a cake of soap; a bar of soap / 液体～ liquid soap

【肥皂粉】 féizàofěn soap powder; detergent

【肥皂剧】 féizàojù soap opera; soap

【肥壮】 féizhuàng stout; burly

腓 (fěi)

【腓肠肌】 fěichángjī 〈*Anat*.〉 gastrocnemius

【腓骨】 fěigǔ 〈*Anat*.〉 fibula

匪 (fěi) **1**.(强盗) bandit; brigand; robber **2**.(非) not

【匪帮】 fěibāng bandit gang

【匪军】 fěijūn bandit troops

【匪特】 fěitè enemy agent

【匪徒】 fěitú gangster; bandit

【匪夷所思】 fěiyí-suǒsī unimaginably queer; fantastic

诽 (fěi) slander

【诽谤】 fěibàng slander; calumniate; libel; defame; evil speaking

菲 (fěi) 〈*written*〉 poor; humble; unworthy

(另见"菲"fēi)

【菲薄】 fěibó **1**.(微薄) humble; poor **2**.(瞧不起) belittle; despise: 不要妄自～。Don't belittle yourself unduly.

悱 (fěi)

【悱恻】 fěicè depressed; moody

斐 (fěi)

【斐然】 fěirán brilliant; remarkable: 成绩～ brilliant achievements

榧 (fěi) 〈*Bot*.〉 Chinese torreya

【榧子】 fěi·zi **1**.〈*Bot*.〉 Chinese torreya **2**.(果实) Chinese torreya nut

蜚 (fěi) (另见"蜚"fēi)

【蜚蠊】 fěilián 〈*Zool*.〉 cockroach; roach

翡 (fěi)

【翡翠】 fěicuì jadeite

肺 (fèi) lungs

【肺动脉】 fèidòngmài 〈*Anat*.〉 pulmonary artery

【肺腑】 fèifǔ **1**.(肺脏) lung **2**.(内心) the bottom of one's heart

【肺腑之言】 fèifǔ-zhīyán words from the bottom of one's heart

【肺活量】 fèihuóliàng vital capacity

【肺结核】 fèijiéhé pulmonary tuberculosis

【肺静脉】 fèijìngmài 〈*Anat*.〉 pulmonary vein

【肺炎】 fèiyán pneumonia

狒 (fèi)

【狒狒】 fèifèi 〈*Zool*.〉 baboon

沸 (fèi) boil

【沸点】 fèidiǎn 〈*Physics*〉 boiling point

【沸水】 fèishuǐ boiling water

【沸腾】 fèiténg **1**.(指液体) boiling; ebullition **2**.(指情绪) seethe with excitement; boil over

费 (fèi) **1**.(费用) fee; dues; expenses; charge: 免～ free of charge / 军～ military expenditure / 医药～ medical free **2**.(花费) cost; spend; expend **3**.(浪费) wasteful; consuming too much; expending sth. too

quickly

【费工】 fèigōng take a lot of work; require a lot of labor

【费工夫】 fèigōngfū take time and energy; be time-consuming

【费解】 fèijiě difficult to understand; incomprehensible

【费尽心机】 fèijìn-xīnjī rack one's brains in scheming

【费劲】 fèijìn need or use great effort; be strenuous

【费力】 fèilì be strenuous; need or use great effort

【费钱】 fèiqián cost a lot; be costly

【费时】 fèishí take time; be time-consuming

【费事】 fèishì give or take a lot of trouble

【费心】 fèixīn 1.(费心思) give a lot of care; take a lot of trouble 2.〈*politeness*〉 may I trouble you (to do sth.); would you mind (doing sth.)

【费用】 fèi·yong cost; expenses: 生产～ production cost / 生活 ～ cost of living; living expenses

镄 (fèi) 〈*Med.*〉 Fermium (人造元素,符号 Fm)

废[廢] (fèi) 1.(作废) give up; abandon; abolish; abrogate 2.(无用) waste; useless; disused 3.(残废) disabled; maimed

【废除】 fèichú abolish; abrogate; annul; repeal: ～干部领导职务实际上的终身制 do away with de facto life tenure for leading cadres/ ～债务 abatement of debts

【废黜】 fèichù 1.(罢免) depose; deposition (n.) 2.(取消王位) dethrone

【废话】 fèihuà nonsense; rubbish; superfluous words: 说～ talk nonsense / 少说～! Don't talk nonsense!

【废料】 fèiliào waste material; waste; scrap

【废票】 fèipiào 1.(指车船票、戏票等) invalidated ticket 2.(指选票) invalidated ballot

【废品】 fèipǐn 1.(不合格产品) waste product; reject 2.(废旧物品) scrap; waste

【废品回收】 fèipǐn huíshōu waste recovery; salvage of waste material

【废品收购站】 fèipǐn shōugòuzhàn salvage station

【废气】 fèiqì waste gas or steam

【废弃】 fèiqì discard; abandon; cast aside

【废寝忘食】 fèiqǐn-wàngshí (so absorbed or occupied as to) forget food and sleep

【废水】 fèishuǐ waste water; liquid waste

【废水处理池】 fèishuǐ chǔlǐchí purification tank for liquid waste

【废铁】 fèitiě scrap iron

【废物】 fèi·wu 1.(指物) waste material; trash 2.(指人) good-for-nothing

【废物利用】 fèiwù-lìyòng make use of waste material

【废墟】 fèixū ruins; debris

【废止】 fèizhǐ abolish; annul; put an end to

【废纸】 fèizhǐ waste paper

痱[疿] (fèi)

【痱子】 fèizi 〈*Med.*〉 prickly heat

【痱子粉】 fèi·zifěn prickly-heat powder

fen

分 (fēn) 1.(分开) divide; separate; part 2.(分配) distribute; assign; allot 3.(分辨) distinguish; differentiate 4.(分支;部分) branch (of an organization) 5.(十分之一) one tenth 6.(时间、弧或角的单位) minute (符号为 ′) 7.(记分,分数) point; mark (另见"分"fèn)

【分贝】 fēnbèi 〈*Physics*〉 decibel (db): 发出大约90～的噪声 make about 90 decibels of noise

【分崩离析】 fēnbēng-líxī disintegrate; fall to pieces; come apart

【分辩】 fēnbiàn defend oneself (against a charge); offer an explanation

【分辨】 fēnbiàn 1.(辨别) distinguish; differentiate: ～是非 distinguish between right and wrong 2.〈*Physics*〉 resolution

【分辨率】 fēnbiànlǜ resolving power; resolution

【分别】 fēnbié 1.(离别) part; leave each other 2.(辨别) distinguish; differentiate 3.(不同) difference: 毫无～ without any difference 4.(各自) respectively; separately: ～和他们谈话 have a talk with them separately

【分布】 fēnbù be distributed (over an area); be dispersed; be scattered

【分册】 fēncè fascicle; a separately published part of a book

【分寸】 fēn·cun proper limits for speech or action; sense of propriety: 有～ have a sense of propriety

【分担】 fēndān share responsibility for: ～责任 share the responsibility

【分道线】 fēndàoxiàn 〈*Transport*〉 lines (AmE.); road markings (BrE.)

【分道扬镳】 fēndào-yángbiāo separate and go different ways; part company, each going his own way

【分等】 fēnděng grade; classify

【分店】 fēndiàn branch (of a shop)

【分队】 fēnduì platoon; squad; element

【分而治之】 fēnér-zhìzhī divide and rule

【分发】 fēnfā distribute; hand out; issue: 给…～奖品 distribute prizes to

【分割】 fēngē cut apart; break up; carve up

【分隔】 fēngé separate; divide; partition

【分工】 fēngōng divide the work; division of labor: 合理～ with a rational division of labor / ～负责 division of labor with individual responsibility

【分管】 fēnguǎn be assigned personal responsibility for; be put in charge of

【分行】 fēnháng branch (of a bank)

【分毫】 fēnháo fraction; iota

【分号】 fēnhào **1.** (标点符号) semicolon (符号为;) **2.** (分店) branch (of a shop or firm)

【分红】 fēnhóng share out bonus; draw extra dividends

【分化】 fēnhuà **1.** (分裂) split up; become divided; break up **2.** (使分化) disintegrate; make divided **3.** 〈*Biol.*〉 differentiation

【分化瓦解】 fēnhuà-wǎjiě divide and disintegrate; split and disintegrate

【分机】 fēnjī extension (telephone)

【分级】 fēnjí grade; classify: ～管理 manage by different levels

【分级目录结构】 fēnjí mùlù jiégòu 〈*Computer*〉 hierarchical directory structure

【分家】 fēnjiā divide up family property and live apart

【分节号】 fēnjiéhào section; division (符号为§)

【分解】 fēnjiě resolve; decompose; break down; decomposition (n.)

【分界】 fēnjiè **1.** (划界) have as the boundary; be demarcated by **2.** (划分的界线) dividing line; line of demarcation

【分界线】 fēnjièxiàn line of demarcation; boundary

【分镜头剧本】 fēnjìngtóu jùběn 〈*Cinematog.*〉 shooting script

【分居】 fēnjū (of members of a family) live apart

【分开】 fēnkāi **1.** (不在一起) separate **2.** (使分开) separate; part: 政企～ separate the functions of the government from those of enterprises

【分类】 fēnlèi classify; classification (n.)

【分类广告】 fēnlèi guǎnggào classified advertisement

【分离】 fēnlí separate; sever; separation (n.)

【分两步走】 fēn liǎngbùzǒu in two stages

【分裂】 fēnliè **1.** (分开) split; divide; break up: 制造～ create dissensions **2.** 〈*Biol.* & *Physics*〉 fission; division

【分流】 fēnliú **1.** (从干流中分出) split-flow **2.** (人财物分开流向) distributaries

【分路】 fēnlù **1.** (分若干路线) along separate routes; from several directions **2.** 〈*Electr.*〉 shunt

【分门别类】 fēnmén-biélèi put into different categories; classify

【分泌】 fēnmì 〈*Biol.*〉 secrete; secretion (n.)

【分泌物】 fēnmìwù secretion

【分娩】 fēnmiǎn childbirth; parturition

【分明】 fēnmíng **1.** (清楚) clearly demarcated; sharply contoured; distinct **2.** (明显) clearly; plainly; evidently: ～是你的错。Evidently you are in the wrong.

【分母】 fēnmǔ 〈*Math.*〉 denominator

【分派】 fēnpài assign (to different persons); apportion

【分配】 fēnpèi distribute; allot; assign

【分配不公】 fēnpèi bùgōng unfair income distribution

【分配单元】 fēnpèi dānyuán 〈*Computer*〉 allocation units

【分配制度】 fēnpèi zhìdù the system of distribution

【分批】 fēnpī in batches; in turn: ～交货 deliver the goods in batches

【分片包干】 fēnpiàn bāogān divide up the work and assign a part to each

【分期】 fēnqī by stages: ～交货 instalment delivery

【分期付款】 fēnqī fùkuǎn payment by instalments; hire purchase; instalment plan: 按月～购买汽车 pay for the car by monthly instalment

【分期付款商店】 fēnqī fùkuǎn shāngdiàn instalment house

【分歧】 fēnqí difference; divergence

【分清】 fēnqīng distinguish; draw a clear distinction between; draw a clear line of demarcation between

【分清是非】 fēnqīng-shìfēi discern between right and wrong

【分区表】 fēnqūbiǎo 〈*Computer*〉 partition table: 重建～ rebuild the partition table

【分散】 fēnsàn **1.** (不在一起的) dispersed; scattered **2.** (使分散) disperse; scatter; decentralize: ～注意力 take sb's mind off sth. **3.** (分发) distribute; give out

【分手】 fēnshǒu part company; say good-bye

【分数】 fēnshù **1.** 〈*Math.*〉 fraction **2.** (成绩) mark; grade; point

【分数线】 fēnshùxiàn point line

【分水岭】 fēnshuǐlǐng **1.** (分水线) watershed; divide **2.** (分界) line of demarcation; watershed

【分税制】 fēnshuìzhì revenue-sharing scheme

【分摊】 fēntān share: ～费用 share the expenses

【分庭抗礼】 fēntíng-kànglǐ stand up to sb. as an equal; make rival claims as an equal

【分头】 fēntóu **1.** (分别进行) separately; severally **2.** (指头发式样) parted hair

【分文】 fēnwén a single cent; a single penny: ～不值 not worth a farthing; be not worth straw

【分析】 fēnxī analyse: ～当前形势 analyse the present situation / 对…做了精辟的～ made a penetrating analysis of

【分享】 fēnxiǎng share; partake: ～我们的胜利 partake our triumph

【分销店】 fēnxiāodiàn retail shop

【分晓】 fēnxiǎo **1.** (底细;结果) outcome; solution **2.** (明白; 清楚) see or understand clearly: 问个～ inquire about and get to the bottom of a matter

【分校】 fēnxiào branch campus

【分心】 fēnxīn distract one's attention; divert one's attention

【分忧】 fēnyōu share sb's cares and burdens; help sb. to get over a difficulty

【分赃】 fēnzāng divide the spoils; share the booty

【分针】 fēnzhēn minute hand; big hand

【分支】 fēnzhī branch: 公司的～机构 branches of a corporation

【分子】 fēnzǐ **1.** 〈*Math.*〉 numerator (in a fraction) **2.** 〈*Chem.*〉 molecule

【分子式】 fēnzǐshì 〈*Chem.*〉 molecule formula

【分组】 fēnzǔ divide into groups

芬 (fēn) sweet smell; fragrance

【芬芳】 fēnfāng **1.** (香的) sweet-smelling; fragrant **2.** (香气) fragrance

吩 (fēn)

【吩咐】 fēn·fù tell; instruct: 照你的～去办吧。Do as you are told.

纷 (fēn) **1.** (杂乱) confused; tangled; disorderly **2.** (多) many and various; profuse; numerous

【纷繁】 fēnfán numerous and complicated; too many and too complicated

【纷纷】 fēnfēn **1.** (接二连三) one after another; in succession: ～提问 ask questions one after another **2.** (多而杂乱) numerous and confused: 议论～ talk about sth. endlessly

【纷乱】 fēnluàn numerous and disorderly; chaotic; helter-skelter

【纷纭】 fēnyún diverse and confused

【纷争】 fēnzhēng dispute; wrangle: ～不已 endless dispute

【纷至沓来】 fēnzhì-tàlái come thick and fast; come one after another

氛 (fēn) atmosphere

【氛围】 fēnwéi atmosphere：非常友好的～ a very friendly atmosphere / 很有～ have a lot of atmosphere

酚 (fēn) 〈*Chem*.〉 phenol

【酚醛】 fēnquán 〈*Chem*.〉 phenolic aldehyde

【酚醛塑料】 fēnquán sùliào phenolic plastics

坟［墳］(fén) grave; tomb：祖～ the grave of one's ancestors

【坟地】 féndì graveyard; cemetery

【坟墓】 fénmù grave; tomb

鼢 (fén)

【鼢鼠】 fénshǔ 〈*Zool*.〉 zokor

焚 (fén) burn

【焚化】 fénhuà incinerate; cremate

【焚毁】 fénhuǐ destroy by fire; burn down

【焚烧】 fénshāo burn; set on fire：～垃圾 burn away the refuse

粉 (fěn) 1.（粉末）powder：合成洗衣～ synthetic detergent / 去污～ cleanser / 爽身～ talcum powder 2.（淀粉制食品）noodles; vermicelli 3.（粉刷）white 4.（粉红）pink

【粉笔】 fěnbǐ chalk：彩色～ colored chalk

【粉彩】 fěncǎi 〈*Arts*〉 mixed glaze

【粉刺】 fěncì 〈*Med*.〉 acne

【粉盒】 fěnhé powder box; compact

【粉红】 fěnhóng pink

【粉剂】 fěnjì powder

【粉末】 fěnmò powder

【粉身碎骨】 fěnshēn-suìgǔ have one's body smashed to pieces; die the most cruel death

【粉饰】 fěnshì gloss over; whitewash：～错误 whitewash mistakes

【粉刷】 fěnshuā whitewash

【粉丝】 fěnsī vermicelli made from bean starch, etc.

【粉碎】 fěnsuì 1.（使失败、毁灭）smash; shatter; crush：～经济封锁 smash an economic blockade 2.（破碎）broken to pieces：轧得～ be ground to pieces

【粉条】 fěntiáo noodles made from bean or sweet potato starch

分 (fèn) 1.（成分）component 2.（限度）what is within one's rights or duty（另见"分"fēn）

【分量】 fèn·liàng weight：～不足 give short measure

【分内】 fènnèi one's job; one's duty：这是我～的事。It's something within my duty.

【分外】 fènwài 1.（特别）particularly; especially：～高兴 particularly happy 2.（本分以外）not one's job; not one's duty

【分子】 fènzǐ member; element：积极～ activist; active member / 先进～ advanced member

份 (fèn) share; portion：分成四～ divide into four parts

【份额】 fèn'é share; portion

【份子】 fèn·zi one's share of expenses for a joint undertaking, as in buying a gift for a mutual friend：凑～ club together to present a gift to sb.

奋［奮］(fèn) 1.（振作）exert oneself; act vigorously 2.（举起）raise; lift

【奋不顾身】 fènbù-gùshēn dash ahead regardless of one's safety

【奋斗】 fèndòu struggle; fight; strive：～目标 the objective of a struggle

【奋发】 fènfā rouse oneself; exert oneself

【奋发图强】 fènfā-túqiáng go all out to make the country strong

【奋发有为】 fènfā-yǒuwéi be promising and diligent in one's work

【奋力】 fènlì do all one can; spare no effort

【奋起】 fènqǐ rise with force and spirit; rise：～直追 do all one can to catch up

【奋勇】 fènyǒng summon up all one's courage and energy：～前进 forge ahead courageously / ～作战 fight bravely

【奋战】 fènzhàn fight bravely：日夜～ struggle hard day and night

愤 (fèn) indignation; anger; resentment

【愤愤不平】 fènfèn-bùpíng be indignant; feel aggrieved; be resentful

【愤恨】 fènhèn indignantly resent; detest

【愤慨】 fènkǎi (righteous) indignation：感到无比～ be overwhelmed with indignation

【愤懑】 fènmèn depressed and discontented; resentful

【愤怒】 fènnù indignation; anger; wrath: ～声讨 angrily denounce

粪［糞］(fèn) 1.(粪便) excrement; feces; dung; droppings 2.(施肥) apply manure

【粪便】 fènbiàn excrement and urine; night soil

【粪车】 fènchē dung-cart; night-soil cart

【粪肥】 fènféi muck; manure; dung

【粪坑】 fènkēng manure pit

【粪筐】 fènkuāng manure basket

【粪桶】 fèntǒng night-soil bucket; manure bucket

【粪土】 fèntǔ dung and dirt; muck

feng

丰［豐[1,2]］(fēng) 1.(丰富) abundant; plentiful 2.(大) great 3.(指容貌、姿态) fine-looking; handsome

【丰碑】 fēngbēi 1.(高大石碑) monument 2.(功绩) monumental work

【丰产】 fēngchǎn high yield; bumper crop; abundant harvest

【丰富】 fēngfù 1.(种类多、数量大) rich; abundant; plentiful: ～的经验 rich experience 2.(使丰富) enrich: ～知识 enrich one's knowledge

【丰富多彩】 fēngfù-duōcǎi rich and colorful; rich and varied

【丰功伟绩】 fēnggōng-wěijì great achievements; signal contributions

【丰厚】 fēnghòu 1.(多而厚实) thick 2.(丰富) rich and generous

【丰满】 fēngmǎn 1.(充足) plentiful 2.(匀称) full and round; well-developed; full-grown

【丰盛】 fēngshèng rich; sumptuous

【丰收】 fēngshōu bumper harvest: 连年～ score consecutive bumper harvests; have good harvests for many years in succession

【丰收计划】 fēngshōu jìhuà plan for a bumper harvest

【丰硕】 fēngshuò plentiful and substantial; rich: ～的成果 great successes

【丰衣足食】 fēngyī-zúshí have ample food and clothing; be well-fed and well-clothed

【丰盈】 fēngyíng 1.(丰满) have a full figure 2.(富裕) plentiful

风［風］(fēng) 1.〈*Meteorol.*〉wind 2.(借风力吹干) put out to dry or air 3.(借风力使纯净) winnow 4.(态度) style; practice; custom 5.(景象) scene; view 6.(消息) news; information: 闻～而动 act without delay upon hearing the news

【风暴】 fēngbào windstorm; storm; tempest

【风波】 fēngbō disturbance; upheaval: 政治～ political disturbance / 引起一场～ bring about an upheaval

【风采】 fēngcǎi 1.(人的仪表) elegant demeanor; graceful bearing 2.(文采) literary grace; literary talent

【风潮】 fēngcháo agitation; unrest: 闹～ create agitation

【风车】 fēngchē 1.(风动机械) windmill 2.(扇车) winnower 3.(玩具) pinwheel

【风尘】 fēngchén 1.(旅途劳累) travel fatigue 2.(指社会) hardships or uncertainties in an unstable society

【风驰电掣】 fēngchí-diànchè swift as the wind and quick as lightning

【风吹草动】 fēngchuī-cǎodòng the rustle of leaves in the wind; a sign of disturbance or trouble

【风吹浪打】 fēngchuī-làngdǎ be beaten by wind and waves; be battered by a storm

【风挡】 fēngdǎng 〈*Auto*〉 windshield (AmE.); windscreen (BrE.)

【风挡玻璃】 fēngdǎng bōlí 〈*Auto*〉 windshield; windscreen

【风挡刮水器】 fēngdǎng guāshuǐqì 〈*Auto*〉 windshield wiper; windscreen wiper

【风笛】 fēngdí 〈*Music*〉 bagpipe

【风洞】 fēngdòng 〈*Aeron.*〉 wind tunnel

【风洞试验】 fēngdòng shìyàn 〈*Aeron.*〉 wind tunnel test

【风度】 fēngdù manner; demeanor; bearing: ～翩翩 graceful bearing / 有～ have a charming manner

【风发】 fēngfā 1.(迅速) swift as the wind 2.(奋发) energetic

【风帆】 fēngfān sailboat

【风格】 fēnggé 1.(作风) way; style: 共产主义～ communist style of work / 发扬～ go out of one's way to help others 2.(特点) style: 独特的～ the characteristic style / 艺术～ artistic style

【风光】 fēngguāng scene; view; sight: 美好～ a beautiful sight

【风害】 fēnghài damage caused by a windstorm; windburn

【风寒】 fēnghán chill; cold: 受～ have a cold; catch cold

【风华】 fēnghuá elegance and talent: ～正茂 at life's full flowering; in one's prime

【风化】 fēnghuà 1.(风俗教化) morals and manners; decency: 有伤～ an offense against decency 2.〈*Chem.*〉 efflorescence 3.〈*Geol.*〉 weathering

【风机】 fēngjī fan

【风鸡】 fēngjī 〈*Meteorol.*〉 weathercock; weather vane

【风级】 fēngjí 〈*Meteorol.*〉 Beaufort scale ‖ 蒲福风级分 13 个等级: 0 级风 calm; 1 级风 light air; 2 级风 light breeze; 3 级风 gentle breeze; 4 级风 moderate breeze; 5 级风 fresh breeze; 6 级风 strong breeze; 7 级风 moderate gale; 8 级风 fresh gale; 9 级风 strong gale; 10 级风 whole gale; 11 级风 storm; 12 级风 hurricane

【风纪】 fēngjì 1.(作风和纪律) conduct and discipline 2.(风气) morale

【风纪扣】 fēngjìkòu hook and eye

【风景】 fēngjǐng scenery; landscape

【风景区】 fēngjǐngqū scenic spot

【风卷残云】 fēngjuǎn-cányún a strong wind scattering the last clouds; make a clean sweep of sth.

【风浪】 fēnglàng 1.(风和浪) stormy waves; storm 2.(艰险) risk

【风力】 fēnglì 1.(风的力量) wind-force 2.(以风为动力) wind power

【风力发电机】 fēnglì fādiànjī wind-driven generator; windmill generator

【风凉话】 fēngliánghuà irresponsible and sarcastic remarks

【风流】 fēngliú 1.(英俊杰出的) distinguished and admirable: ～人物 truly great men 2.(有才学但不拘礼法的) talented and romantic: ～才子 talented and romantic scholar 3.(行为放荡的) dissolute; loose: ～韵事 an affair; a love affair

【风流倜傥】 fēngliú-tìtǎng talented and gallant

【风貌】 fēngmào 1.(风格和面貌) style and features: 保持古城～ keep the original style of ancient city 2.(景象) view; scene

【风靡】 fēngmǐ fashionable: ～一时 become fashionable for a time; become a fad of the time

【风平浪静】 fēngpíng-làngjìng the wind has subsided and the waves have calmed down; calm and tranquil

【风气】 fēngqì general mood; atmosphere; common practice: 社会～ current tendencies in society; social mode

【风琴】 fēngqín organ

【风趣】 fēngqù humor; wit: 很有～ full of humor; feel of wit

【风骚】 fēngsāo 1.(泛称文学) literary excellence 2.(轻佻) coquettish

【风沙】 fēngshā sand blown by the wind: 这里冬天～很大。It's very windy and dusty here in winter.

【风扇】 fēngshàn 1.(电扇) electric fan 2.〈*Mech.*〉 fan

【风扇皮带】 fēngshàn pídài 〈*Auto*〉 fan belt

【风尚】 fēngshàng prevailing custom: 社会新～ new social tendency

【风声】 fēngshēng 1.(刮风声) sound of wind 2.(传出来的消息) rumor; news: 走漏～ reveal a secret

【风湿】 fēngshī 〈*Med.*〉 rheumatism

【风湿性关节炎】 fēngshīxìng guānjiéyán 〈*Med.*〉 rheumarthritis

【风霜】 fēngshuāng wind and frost; hardships of a journey or of one's life: 饱经～ weather-beaten; having had one's fill of hardships

【风俗】 fēngsú custom

【风俗画】 fēngsúhuà genre

【风速】 fēngsù wind speed; wind velocity

【风速表】 fēngsùbiǎo anemometer

【风调雨顺】 fēngtiáo-yǔshùn favorable weather; good weather for the crops

【风头】 fēngtóu 1.(情势) the trend of events

(as affecting a person)：避避～ lie low until sth. blow over 2.（出头露面）the publicity one receives：爱出～ be fond of the limelight

【风土】 fēngtǔ natural conditions and social customs of a place：～人情 local conditions and customs

【风味】 fēngwèi special flavor；local color：地方～ local cuisine / 家乡～ local flavor

【风闻】 fēngwén learn through hearsay；get wind of

【风险】 fēngxiǎn risk；hazard：经营～ business venture / ～很大 full of hazard / 冒～ take risks / 分散～ diversify risks / 共担～ joint adventure

【风险补偿】 fēngxiǎn bǔcháng compensate for a risk

【风险工资】 fēngxiǎn gōngzī subsidy for taking risk

【风险机制】 fēngxiǎn jīzhì risk mechanism

【风险金】 fēngxiǎnjīn risk fund

【风险赔偿】 fēngxiǎn péicháng indemnity for risk

【风险投资】 fēngxiǎn tóuzī risky investment

【风险意识】 fēngxiǎn yì·shí sense of risk

【风险资本】 fēngxiǎn zīběn venture capital

【风箱】 fēngxiāng bellows

【风向】 fēngxiàng wind direction

【风向标】 fēngxiàngbiāo weather vane；weathercock

【风行】 fēngxíng 1.（流行）be in fashion；be popular：～一时 be popular for a time 2.（迅速）rapidly

【风言风语】 fēngyán-fēngyǔ groundless talk；slanderous gossip

【风衣】 fēngyī dust coat

【风雨】 fēngyǔ 1.（风和雨）wind and rain 2.（艰难困苦）the elements；trials and hardships

【风雨交加】 fēngyǔ-jiāojiā it's raining and blowing hard；it's wet and windy

【风雨同舟】 fēngyǔ-tóngzhōu in the same storm-tossed boat；stand together through thick and thin

【风雨无阻】 fēngyǔ-wúzǔ stopped by neither wind nor rain；regardless of the weather；rain or shine

【风云】 fēngyún 1.（风和云）wind and cloud 2.（动荡的局势）a unstable situation：～不测 unexpected misfortune

【风云人物】 fēngyún-rénwù a personage of historic significance

【风韵】 fēngyùn gracefulness；attraction：～犹存 still look attractive

【风疹】 fēngzhěn 〈*Med.*〉 nettle rash；urticaria

【风筝】 fēng·zheng kite：放～ fly a kite

枫（fēng） 1.（枫香树）Chinese sweet gum 2.（枫树）maple

【枫叶】 fēngyè maple leaf：加拿大国旗上有一枚～。The Canadian flag has a maple leaf on it.

砜（fēng） 〈*Chem.*〉 sulfone

疯（fēng） 1.（神经错乱）mad；insane；crazy 2.（疯长）(of a plant, grain crop, etc.) spindle

【疯疯癫癫】 fēng·feng-diāndiān be mentally deranged；act like a lunatic；be flighty

【疯狂】 fēngkuáng 1.（发疯）insane 2.（猖狂）frenzied；unbridled

【疯牛病】 fēngniúbìng mad cow disease

【疯人院】 fēngrényuàn lunatic；madman；maniac

【疯长】 fēngzhǎng 〈*Agric.*〉 grow spindly

【疯子】 fēng·zi lunatic；madman

封（fēng） 1.（封闭）seal：～门 seal up a door 2.（信封）envelope

【封闭】 fēngbì 1.（关住）seal 2.（闭关锁国）closed-door policy：～只能导致落后。A closed-door policy can only perpetuate backwardness. 3.（查封）seal off；close

【封存】 fēngcún seal up for safekeeping

【封底】 fēngdǐ 〈*Printing*〉 back cover

【封顶】 fēngdǐng 1.（建筑完工）complete a building；finish work on the top of a building 2.（最高限）upper limit：奖金上不～ be no ceiling on bonus

【封二】 fēng'èr 〈*Printing*〉 inside front cover

【封官许愿】 fēngguān-xǔyuàn offer official posts and make lavish promises

【封火】 fēnghuǒ bank up a fire

【封建】 fēngjiàn 1.（指政治制度）the system of enfeoffment 2.（指社会形态）feudalism

【封建割据】 fēngjiàn gējù feudal separationist

rule
【封建社会】 fēngjiàn shèhuì feudal society
【封面】 fēngmiàn 1.（书皮）the front and back cover of a book 2.（封一）front cover
【封面女郎】 fēngmiàn nǚláng cover girl
【封皮】 fēngpí 1.（封面）paper wrapping 2.（信封）envelope
【封妻荫子】 fēngqī-yìnzǐ get one's wife and children rewarded by heritage
【封锁】 fēngsuǒ 1.（使断绝联系）blockade; block; seal off：经济～ economic blockade / 解除～ lift a blockade; raise a blockade 2.（禁止通行）close; blockade：～边境 close the border / ～港口 blockade a harbor; close a port with blockade
【封锁线】 fēngsuǒxiàn blockade; blockade line
【封条】 fēngtiáo paper strip seal; a strip of paper used for sealing
【封印】 fēngyìn 〈*Stamp*〉 seal; sealing stamp

峰［峯］(fēng) 1.（尖顶）peak; summit 2.（峰状物）hump
【峰峦】 fēngluán ridges and peaks
【峰年】 fēngnián peak year
【峰值】 fēngzhí 〈*Electr*.〉 peak value; crest value

烽(fēng) beacon
【烽火】 fēnghuǒ 1.（报警烟火）beacon-fire; beacon 2.（战火）flames of war：～连天 flames of battle raging everywhere
【烽火台】 fēnghuǒtái ramparts; alarm tower
【烽烟】 fēngyān beacon-fire; beacon

锋(fēng) 1.（刀、剑锋利部分）the sharp point or cutting edge of a sword, etc. 2.（带头的）van 3.〈*Meteorol*.〉 front
【锋利】 fēnglì 1.（刀的头尖、刃薄）sharp; keen 2.（指文笔）incisive; sharp; poignant
【锋芒】 fēngmáng 1.（刀剑的尖利部分）cutting edge; spearhead 2.（比喻才干）talent displayed; abilities
【锋芒毕露】 fēngmáng-bìlù make a showy display of one's abilities
【锋面】 fēngmiàn 〈*Meteorol*.〉 frontal surface

蜂［蠭］(fēng) 1.（黄蜂）wasp 2.（蜜蜂）bee：养～ keep bees; apiculture 3.（成群地）in swarms
【蜂巢】 fēngcháo honeycomb; beehive
【蜂房】 fēngfáng any of the six-sided wax cells in a honeycomb
【蜂蜡】 fēnglà beeswax
【蜂蜜】 fēngmì honey
【蜂鸣器】 fēngmíngqì buzzer
【蜂鸟】 fēngniǎo 〈*Birds*〉 hummingbird
【蜂乳】 fēngrǔ royal jelly
【蜂王】 fēngwáng 1.（母蜂）queen bee 2.（母的黄蜂）queen wasp
【蜂王浆】 fēngwángjiāng royal jelly
【蜂窝】 fēngwō 1.（蜂巢）honeycomb 2.（蜂巢状物）a honeycomb-like thing
【蜂窝煤】 fēngwōméi honeycomb briquette
【蜂箱】 fēngxiāng beehive; hive
【蜂拥】 fēngyōng swarm; flock
【蜂拥而至】 fēngyōng-érzhì come in great numbers

逢(féng) meet; come upon：久别重～ meet again after a long separation
【逢场作戏】 féngchǎng-zuòxì join in the fun on occasion
【逢年过节】 féngnián-guòjié on New Year's Day or other festivals
【逢凶化吉】 féngxiōng-huàjí turn ill luck into good
【逢迎】 féngyíng make up to; fawn on; curry favor with：阿谀～ insinuate oneself into another's favor

缝(féng) stitch; sew
【缝补】 féngbǔ sew and mend
【缝缝补补】 féngféng-bǔbǔ sew up
【缝合】 fénghé 〈*Med*.〉 suture; sew up：～切口 sew up the incision
【缝纫】 féngrèn sewing; tailoring
【缝纫机】 féngrènjī sewing machine

讽(fěng)
【讽刺】 fěngcì satirize; mock

凤［鳳］(fèng) phoenix
【凤凰】 fènghuáng phoenix
【凤梨】 fènglí pineapple
【凤毛麟角】 fèngmáo-línjiǎo (precious and rare as) phoenix feathers and unicorn horns;

rarity of rarities

【风尾鱼】 fèngwěiyú tapertail anchovy；long-tailed anchovy

【风仙花】 fèngxiānhuā garden balsam；touch-me-not（balsam）

【风眼兰】 fèngyǎnlán water hyacinth

奉（fèng） 1.（给）give or present with respect 2.（接受）receive（orders，etc.）：～上级指示 on orders from above 3.（信奉）believe in 4.（尊崇）esteem；revere 5.（奉养）wait upon；attend to

【奉承】 fèng·cheng flatter；fawn upon；toady

【奉告】 fènggào let sb. know；inform：无可～。No comment.

【奉公】 fènggōng be law-abiding

【奉公守法】 fènggōng-shǒufǎ be law-abiding

【奉命】 fèngmìng receive orders；act under orders：～出发 be under orders to start / ～来到 arrive under orders / ～发表声明 issue a statement under orders

【奉陪】 fèngpéi keep sb. company：恕不～。Sorry，I won't be able to keep you company.

【奉陪到底】 fèngpéi-dàodǐ have the honor of keep sb. company until the end

【奉劝】 fèngquàn may I offer a piece of advice

【奉若神明】 fèngruò-shénmíng make a fetish of；look upon as sacred

【奉送】 fèngsòng offer as a gift；give away free；throw sth. in；with sth. thrown in：个人计算机一台，～多媒体音箱 a personal computer with multimedia speakers thrown in

【奉献】 fèngxiàn offer as a tribute；present with all respect：无私～ devote oneself to；dedicate oneself to

【奉献精神】 fèngxiàn jīngshén spirit of utter devotion

【奉行】 fèngxíng pursue（a policy，etc.）：～和平的外交政策 follow a peaceful foreign policy

俸（fèng） pay；salary；reward

【俸禄】 fènglù salary；income

缝（fèng） 1.（接合处）seam：无～钢管 seamless steel tube 2.（缝隙）crack；crevice；fissure：石～ crevice in the rock

【缝隙】 fèngxì chink；crack；crevice

fo

佛（fó） 1.（佛；佛陀）Buddha：拜～ worship Buddha 2.（佛教）Buddhism 3.（佛像）image of Buddha：铜～ a bronze statue of Buddha

【佛教】 fójiào Buddhism；Buddhist（adj.）

【佛教徒】 fójiàotú Buddhist

【佛经】 fójīng Buddhist Scripture；Buddhist sutra

【佛境】 fójìng Buddhahood

【佛寺】 fósì temple

【佛塔】 fótǎ pagoda

【佛像】 fóxiàng figure of Buddha；image of Buddha

fou

否（fǒu） 1.（否定）negate；deny 2.（不同意）nay；no 3.（表示询问）先生知其事～？Do you know about that matter，Sir.？4.（表示不肯定）whether；if：我不知道他是～能来。I don't know if he'll be able to come.

【否定】 fǒudìng 1.（否认）negate；deny 2.（表示否认的）negative：他的答复是～的。His answer was negative

【否决】 fǒujué vote down；veto；overrule：这一提案已被～。This proposal has been voted down.

【否决权】 fǒujuéquán veto power；veto：行使～ exercise the power of veto

【否认】 fǒurèn deny；repudiate：～自己的声明 deny one's statement

【否则】 fǒuzé 〈*conj.*〉otherwise；if not；or else

fu

夫（fū） 1.（丈夫）husband 2.（成年男子）man 3.（体力劳动者）a person engaged in manual labor

【夫妇】 fūfù husband and wife：新婚～ a newlywed couple

【夫妻】 fūqī man and wife

【夫妻店】 fūqīdiàn mom-and-pop store

【夫人】 fū·rén lady; Madame; Mrs.: 第一～ the First Lady
【夫子】 fūzǐ 1.(旧指学者) a Confucian scholar 2.(旧指老师) master 3.(迂腐之人) pedant: 迂～ a pedantic old fogey

呋 (fū)

【呋喃】 fūnán 〈*Chem.*〉 furan
【呋喃西林】 fūnánxīlín 〈*Chem.*〉 furacilin; furancin

肤[膚] (fū) skin: 切～之痛 keenly felt pain

【肤浅】 fūqiǎn superficial; shallow: ～的认识 a superficial understanding of; a superficial knowledge of
【肤色】 fūsè color of skin

麸[麩] (fū) bran

【麸子】 fū·zi (wheat) bran

跗 (fū) 〈*Anat.*〉 tarsus

【跗骨】 fūgǔ 〈*Anat.*〉 tarsus; tarsal bones

孵 (fū) hatch; brood; incubate: 母鸡～蛋。The hen broods eggs.

【孵化】 fūhuà hatching; incubation: 人工～ artificial incubation

敷 (fū) 1.(擦;涂) apply: 外～ for external application 2.(铺开) spread; lay out 3.(足;够) be sufficient for: 入不～出 cannot make both ends meet

【敷料】 fūliào 〈*Med.*〉 dressing
【敷设】 fūshè lay: ～铁轨 lay a railway track
【敷衍】 fūyǎn 1.(表面应付) be perfunctory; go through the motions 2.(维持) manage
【敷衍】 fūyǎn (敷演) elaborate; expound
【敷衍了事】 fūyǎn-liǎoshì muddle through one's work
【敷衍搪塞】 fūyǎn-tángsāi explain away; give a lame excuse
【敷演】 fūyǎn elaborate; expound

芙 (fú)

【芙蓉】 fúróng 1.(木芙蓉) cottonrose; hibiscus 2.(荷花) lotus

扶 (fú) 1.(搀扶) support with the hand; place a hand on sb. or sth. for support 2.(扶起) help sb. up; straighten sth. up 3.(扶助) help; relieve

【扶持】 fúchí help sustain; give aid to; help sb. to stand or walk; support
【扶老携幼】 fúlǎo-xiéyòu holding the old by the arm and the young by the hand; bringing along the old and the young
【扶贫】 fúpín aid the poor; help the poor households or regions
【扶贫政策】 fúpín zhèngcè aid-to-the-poor policy
【扶手】 fú·shou 1.(栏杆扶手) handrail; rail; banisters 2.(椅子扶手) armrest
【扶手椅】 fúshǒuyǐ armchair
【扶梯】 fútī staircase; ladder: 自动～ escalator; moving staircase
【扶养】 fúyǎng provide for; foster; bring up: (把孩子)～成人 bring up (a child)
【扶摇直上】 fúyáo-zhíshàng soar on the wings of a cyclone; rise steeply; skyrocket
【扶优汰劣】 fúyōu-tàiliè favor producing goods of high quality and eliminate production of low quality goods
【扶植】 fúzhí foster; prop up
【扶助】 fúzhù help; assist; support

拂 (fú) 1.(轻轻擦过) stroke 2.(拂去) whisk; flick 3.(违背) go against (sb's wishes)

【拂晓】 fúxiǎo before dawn
【拂袖而去】 fúxiù'érqù leave with a flick of one's sleeve; go off in a huff

氟 (fú) 〈*Chem.*〉 fluorine (元素符号 F)

【氟利昂】 fúlìáng 〈*Chem.*〉 freon

伏 (fú) 1.(趴) bend over 2.(卧) lie prostrate 3.(低下去) subside; go down 4.(隐藏) hide 5.(伏天) hot season; dog days 6.(低头承认) admit (defeat or guilt) 7.(伏特) volt

【伏安】 fú'ān 〈*Electr.*〉 volt-ampere
【伏笔】 fúbǐ foreshadow (v.)
【伏兵】 fúbīng troops waiting in ambush; the ambushed: ～四起 the ambushed soldiers leapt out all round
【伏法】 fúfǎ 〈*Law*〉 be executed
【伏击】 fújī ambush: 遭到～ fall into an ambush
【伏特】 fútè 〈*Electr.*〉 volt

【伏特计】 fútèjì 〈*Electr.*〉 voltmeter
【伏特加】 fútèjiā vodka
【伏天】 fútiān hot summer days; dog days
【伏贴】 fútiē fit perfectly
【伏罪】 fúzuì plead guilty (to a crime); admit one's guilt

凫[鳧] (fú) 1.(野鸭) wild duck 2.(浮) swim
【凫水】 fúshuǐ swim

俘 (fú) 1.(俘获) capture; take prisoner 2.(战俘) prisoner of war; captive
【俘获】 fúhuò capture
【俘虏】 fúlǔ 1.(俘获) capture; take prisoner 2.(被俘的军人) P.O.W.; prisoner of war

浮 (fú) 1.(漂浮) float: 木头～在水上。Wood floats on water. 2.(游) swim 3.(浮在表面) on the surface; superficial 4.(暂时的) temporary; provisional 5.(轻浮) flighty; unstable; superficial 6.(空虚) hollow; inflated 7.(多余) excessive; surplus
【浮标】 fúbiāo buoy
【浮冰】 fúbīng floating ice; (ice) floe
【浮尘】 fúchén floating dust; surface dust
【浮雕】 fúdiāo relief (sculpture): 浅～ in low relief / 深～ in high relief
【浮吊】 fúdiào floating crane
【浮动】 fúdòng 1.(漂动) float; drift 2.(不稳定) be unsteady; fluctuate: 价格～。Prices fluctuates. 3.〈*Econ.*〉 float
【浮动工资】 fúdòng gōngzī floating wage
【浮动汇率】 fúdòng huìlǜ floating (exchange) rate
【浮泛】 fúfàn 1.(漂浮) float about 2.(流露) reveal; display 3.(空泛) superficial; too abstract: 她的发言内容～。Her speech was superficial and full of generalities.
【浮华】 fúhuá ostentatious; pompous
【浮夸】 fúkuā be boastful; exaggerate
【浮夸作风】 fúkuā zuòfēng proneness to boasting and exaggeration
【浮萍】 fúpíng duckweed
【浮桥】 fúqiáo pontoon bridge; floating bridge
【浮球】 fúqiú float ball
【浮球阀】 fúqiúfá ball-cock assembly
【浮球阀式恭桶】 fúqiúfáshì gōngtǒng ball-float toilet
【浮筒】 fútǒng float; pontoon; buoy
【浮腿】 fútuǐ 〈*Skating*〉 free leg
【浮现】 fúxiàn appear before one's eyes
【浮想联翩】 fúxiǎng-liánpiān thoughts thronging one's mind
【浮云】 fúyún floating clouds
【浮躁】 fúzào impetuous; impulsive
【浮肿】 fúzhǒng 〈*Med.*〉 dropsy; edema
【浮子】 fú·zi 1.〈*Fishery*〉 float 2.〈*Auto*〉 carburetor float

蜉 (fú)
【蜉游】 fúyóu 〈*Zool.*〉 mayfly

符 (fú) 1.(标记) symbol 2.(符合) tally with; accord with: 数字不～ the figures do not tally / 与事实不～ not tally with the facts 3.(符咒) magic figures to invoke or expel spirits and bring good or ill fortune: 护身～ amulet
【符号】 fúhào 1.(记号) symbol; mark; sign: 化学～ chemical symbol 2.(标志) insignia
【符号逻辑】 fúhào luójí 〈*Computer*〉 symbolic logic
【符合】 fúhé accord with; tally with; conform to; be in keeping with: ～标准 be up to the standard / ～要求 accord with the demands / ～人民的利益和要求 correspond to the interests and needs of the people
【符咒】 fúzhòu incantation; charm

服 (fú) 1.(衣服) clothes; dress 2.(服用) take (medicine): 必要时～ taken when necessary / 临睡时～ taken at bedtime / 日～两次 to be taken two times a day 3.(承当) serve 4.(信服) be convinced; obey 5.(适应) be accustomed to: ～水土 be accustomed to the climate
(另见"服"fù)
【服从】 fúcóng obey; submit (oneself) to; be subordinated to: ～全局利益 be subordinated to overall interest / ～真理 submit to the truth
【服毒】 fúdú take poison: ～自杀 poison oneself
【服气】 fúqì be convinced
【服饰】 fúshì dress and personal adornment
【服侍】 fú·shi wait upon; attend: ～病人 attend a patient

【服输】 fúshū admit defeat; acknowledge defeat

【服帖】 fútiē 1.（顺从）docile; obedient; submissive 2.（信服）be convinced 3.（妥当）fitting; well arranged

【服务】 fúwù give service to; be in the service of; serve: 居民～ neighborhood services / 提供～ provide services / ～周到 provide good service

【服务舱】 fúwùcāng 〈*Aeron*.〉 service module

【服务行业】 fúwù hángyè service trades; service industries

【服务台】 fúwùtái service desk

【服务态度】 fúwù tàidù attitude in attending to customers; attitude in waiting on guests

【服务员】 fúwùyuán attendant; waiter

【服刑】 fúxíng serve a sentence

【服药】 fúyào take medicine: 服中药 take traditional Chinese medicine

【服役】 fúyì 1.（服兵役）be on active service; enlist in the army 2.（服苦役）do corvée labor

【服用】 fúyòng take (medicine)

【服装】 fúzhuāng dress; clothing; costume: 现成的～ ready-made clothes

【服装表演】 fúzhuāng biǎoyǎn fashion show

【服装厂】 fúzhuāngchǎng clothing factory

幅 (fú) 1.（布匹宽度）width of cloth 2.（泛指宽度）size: 大～画像 a large-sized portrait

【幅度】 fúdù range; scope; extent: 大～调整物价 readjust the prices by a big margin

【幅员】 fúyuán the area of a country's territory; the size of a country

【幅员辽阔】 fúyuán liáokuò (a country) with a vast expanse; (a country) with a vast territory

辐 (fú) spoke

【辐射】 fúshè 〈*Physics*〉 radiation: 热～ heat radiation

【辐条】 fútiáo spoke

福 (fú) good fortune; blessing; happiness

【福分】 fú·fen share of happiness allotted by destiny

【福利】 fúlì material benefits; well-being; welfare: 社会～ social welfare; public welfare

【福利院】 fúlìyuàn welfare house

【福气】 fú·qi happy lot; good fortune

斧 (fǔ) axe; ax; hatchet

【斧头】 fǔ·tóu axe; ax; hatchet: 用～把一棵老苹果树砍倒 use an axe to chop the old apple tree down

【斧正】 fǔzhèng (please) make corrections

【斧子】 fǔ·zi axe; ax; hatchet

釜 (fǔ) caldron; cauldron

【釜底抽薪】 fǔdǐ-chōuxīn take drastic measures to deal with a situation

辅 (fǔ) assist; complement; supplement

【辅币】 fǔbì fractional currency; fractional money: 硬～ subsidiary coin; minor coin

【辅导】 fǔdǎo give guidance in study or training; coach

【辅导材料】 fǔdǎo cáiliào guidance material

【辅导员】 fǔdǎoyuán (political and ideological) assistant; instructor: 少先队～ Young Pioneers counsellor

【辅料】 fǔliào supplemental material

【辅助】 fǔzhù 1.（从旁帮助）assist 2.（非主要的）supplementary; auxiliary; subsidiary

【辅助机舱】 fǔzhù jīcāng auxiliary engine room

抚［撫］(fǔ) 1.（安慰；慰问）comfort; console 2.（保养）nurture; foster 3.（轻轻按着）stroke

【抚爱】 fǔ'ài caress; fondle

【抚摸】 fǔmō stroke

【抚摩】 fǔmó stroke: ～她的头发 stroke her hair

【抚慰】 fǔwèi comfort; console; soothe

【抚恤】 fǔxù comfort and compensate a bereaved family

【抚恤金】 fǔxùjīn pension for the disabled or for the family of the deceased

【抚养】 fǔyǎng foster; raise; bring up

【抚养费】 fǔyǎngfèi cost of maintenance; cost of upbringing

【抚育】 fǔyù 1.（照料、教育儿童）foster;

nurture 2.（照管动植物）tend

府（fǔ） 1.（政府；行政区域）prefecture; seat of government; government office 2.（府第）official residence; mansion 3.（对方住宅）your home

【府绸】 fǔchóu poplin; popeline

【府上】 fǔ·shàng 1.（指对方家庭）your home; your family 2.（指对方老家）your native place

俯（fǔ） bow (one's head)

【俯冲】 fǔchōng 〈*Aeron*.〉 dive

【俯瞰】 fǔkàn look down at; overlook：从塔上～整个公园 overlook the whole park from a pagoda

【俯身】 fǔshēn bend; bow; stoop

【俯拾即是】 fǔshí-jíshì can be found everywhere; be extremely common

【俯视】 fǔshì look down at; overlook

【俯首】 fǔshǒu bow one's head (in submission)：～听命 obey submissively

【俯卧式跳高】 fǔwòshì-tiàogāo 〈*Sports*〉 straddle jump

【俯仰】 fǔyǎng 1.（低头和抬头）a bending or lifting of the head 2.（一举一动）a simple move or action

腑（fǔ）

【腑肋】 fǔlèi （牛肉部位）sirloin and flat rib

腐（fǔ） 1.（腐败）rotten; putrid; stale; corroded 2.（豆腐）bean curd

【腐败】 fǔbài 1.（腐烂）rotten; putrid; decayed 2.（陈旧）corrupt; rotten：～透顶 rotten to the core

【腐败现象】 fǔbài xiànxiàng corruption：反对～ fight corruption

【腐化】 fǔhuà 1.（变坏）degenerate; corrupt; dissolute; depraved 2.（堕落）rot; decay

【腐烂】 fǔlàn 1.（某物败坏）decomposed; putrid 2.（腐败）corrupt; rotten

【腐乳】 fǔrǔ fermented bean curd

【腐蚀】 fǔshí 1.（消损破坏）corrode; etch 2.（堕落）corrupt; corrode

【腐蚀剂】 fǔshíjì corrosive; corrodent

【腐朽】 fǔxiǔ 1.（木料等损破）rotten; decayed 2.（陈腐；堕落；败坏）decadent; degenerate

【腐朽没落】 fǔxiǔ mòluò decadent and declining; rotten to the core and declining

父（fù） father

【父老】 fùlǎo elders (of a country or district)

【父母】 fùmǔ father and mother; parents

【父亲】 fù·qīn father

【父兄】 fùxiōng 1.（父亲和哥哥）father and elder brothers 2.（泛指家长）head of a family

【父子关系】 fùzǐ guānxì set membership

讣（fù） obituary

【讣告】 fùgào 1.（报丧）announce sb's death 2.（报丧文告）obituary (notice)

赴（fù） go to; attend：～英留学 go to study in England

【赴任】 fùrèn go to one's post; be on the way to one's post

【赴汤蹈火】 fùtāng-dǎohuǒ go through fire and water

【赴宴】 fùyàn attend a banquet

【赴约】 fùyuē go to fulfill an appointment

付（fù） 1.（交给）hand over to; turn over to; commit to 2.（支付）pay：～房租 pay rent / 逾期未～ fail to pay on time

【付出】 fùchū pay; expend

【付方】 fùfāng credit side; credit

【付款】 fùkuǎn pay a sum of money：分期～ pay by instalments

【付讫】 fùqì (of a bill) paid

【付清】 fùqīng pay in full; pay off; clear (a bill)：一次～ pay off in one lump sum

【付税】 fùsuì pay taxes

【付现】 fùxiàn pay in cash; cash

【付印】 fùyìn 1.（准备出版）send to the press 2.（交付印刷）put into print; turn over to the printing shop (after proofreading)

【付邮】 fùyóu take to the post; post

【付账】 fùzhàng pay a bill

【付之一炬】 fùzhī-yījù commit to the flames

【付之一笑】 fùzhī-yīxiào laugh away; dismiss with a laugh

【付诸东流】 fùzhū-dōngliú thrown into the eastward flowing stream; all one's efforts wasted; irrevocably lost

【付诸实施】 fùzhū shíshī put into effect

【付诸行动】 fùzhū xíngdòng put into practice
【付梓】 fùzǐ put into print
附［坿］(fù) 1.（附带）add; attach; enclose 2.（靠近）get close to; be near 3.（依从）agree to
【附笔】 fùbǐ postscript; additional note
【附表】 fùbiǎo attached list; attached chart
【附带】 fùdài 1.（顺便）in passing: ～说一下 by the way 2.（附加）attach: 不～任何条件 never to attach any conditions 3.（非主要的）subsidiary; supplementary
【附带条件】 fùdài tiáojiàn with conditions attached
【附和】 fùhè echo; chime in with: 随声～ echo what others say
【附会】 fùhuì draw wrong conclusions by false analogy; strain one's interpretation: 牵强～ give a strained interpretation
【附加】 fùjiā 1.（额外加上）add; attach 2.（附带的）additional; attached; appended
【附加费】 fùjiāfèi extra charges; surcharge
【附加工资】 fùjiā gōngzī extra wage
【附加税】 fùjiāshuì surtax; additional tax
【附加条款】 fùjiā tiáokuǎn additional article; memorandum clause
【附件】 fùjiàn 1.（文件的）appendix; annex 2.（书信中的）enclosure 3.〈*Mech*.〉accessory; attachment
【附近】 fùjìn 1.（靠近）nearby; neighboring 2.（附近的地方）close to; in the vicinity of: 住在公园～ live close to the park
【附录】 fùlù appendix
【附设】 fùshè have as an attached institution
【附属】 fùshǔ subsidiary; auxiliary; attached; affiliated: 医科大学～医院 a hospital attached to a medical college
【附属中学】 fùshǔ zhōngxué affiliated middle school
【附图】 fùtú attached map or drawing; figure
【附言】 fùyán postscript (P.S.)
【附议】 fùyì second a motion; support a proposal
【附庸风雅】 fùyōng-fēngyǎ (of landlords, merchants, etc.) mingle with men of letters and pose as a lover of culture
【附庸国】 fùyōngguó dependency
【附中】 fùzhōng affiliated middle school: 北大～ Middle School Affiliated to Peking University
【附注】 fùzhù notes appended to a book, etc.; annotations
【附着】 fùzhuó adhere to; cling to
驸(fù)
【驸马】 fùmǎ emperor's son-in-low
负(fù) 1.（担负）carry on the back; shoulder; bear: ～经济责任 be held economically responsible 2.（遭受）suffer 3.（享有）enjoy 4.（亏欠）owe 5.（背弃）fail in one's duty, obligation, etc.; betray 6.（失败）lose (a battle, game, etc.); be defeated 7.（小于零的）minus; negative 8.〈*Electr*.〉negative
【负担】 fùdān 1.（承当）bear (a burden); shoulder 2.（指责任）burden; load; encumbrance: 精神～ mental burden; load on one's mind / 减轻…的精神～ take a load off sb's mind
【负电】 fùdiàn negative electric charge
【负号】 fùhào minus (符号为 －)
【负荷】 fùhè 〈*Electr*.〉load: 安全～ safe load
【负极】 fùjí negative pole
【负荆请罪】 fùjīng-qǐngzuì proffer a birch and ask for a flogging; offer a humble apology
【负离子】 fùlízǐ 〈*Physics*〉anion
【负面】 fùmiàn negative
【负面效应】 fùmiàn xiàoyìng negative effect
【负气】 fùqì do sth. in a fit of pique
【负伤】 fùshāng be wounded; be injured
【负数】 fùshù 〈*Math*.〉negative number
【负隅顽抗】 fùyú-wánkàng (of an enemy or a robber) fight stubbornly with one's back to the wall; put up a desperate struggle
【负责】 fùzé 1.（担负责任）be responsible for; be in charge of 2.（认真踏实）conscientious: 对工作很～ be very conscientious in one's work
【负责干部】 fùzé gànbù cadre in charge
【负责人】 fùzérén responsible; a person in charge
【负债】 fùzhài 1.（欠人钱财）be in debt; incur debts: ～累累 be heavily in debt; be up to one's eyes in debt / ～容易还债难。It's a

lot easier to get in the hole than to get out again. 2.(资产负债表的一方) liabilities

【负债额】 fùzhàié amount of obligation; liabilities

【负重】 fùzhòng bear a heavy burden

妇[婦](fù) 1.(妇女) woman 2.(已婚女子) married woman 3.(妻) wife

【妇产科】 fùchǎnkē (department of) gynecology and obstetrics

【妇产医院】 fùchǎn yīyuàn a hospital for gynecology and obstetrics

【妇科】 fùkē 〈*Med.*〉(department of) gynecology; gynaecology; gynecological (adj.)

【妇科医生】 fùkē yīshēng gynecologist; gynaecologist

【妇联】 fùlián the Women's Federation

【妇女】 fùnǚ woman

【妇女病】 fùnǚbìng gynecological disease

【妇女节】 fùnǚjié Women's Day

【妇女用品商店】 fùnǚ yòngpǐn shāngdiàn ladies' goods store

【妇幼】 fùyòu women and children

【妇幼保健】 fùyòu bǎojiàn maternity and child care

【妇幼保健站】 fùyòu bǎojiànzhàn health center for women and children; maternity and child care center

【妇幼卫生】 fùyòu wèishēng maternity and child hygiene

服(fù) (用于中药) dose: 一~中药 a dose of medicine
(另见"服"fú)

复[複[1]、復[2-6]](fù) 1.(重复) compound; complex 2.(转过来;转过去) turn round; turn over 3.(回答) answer; reply 4.(恢复) recover; resume 5.(报复) revenge 6.(再;又) again: 日~一日 day after day

【复本】 fùběn duplicate: 留~ keep a duplicate

【复辟】 fùbì 1.(失位君主复位) restoration of a dethroned monarch: 阴谋~ plot to stage a comeback 2.(恢复旧制度) restoration of the old order

【复查】 fùchá check; reexamine

【复仇】 fùchóu revenge; avenge; take revenge

【复电】 fùdiàn telegram in reply (to one received)

【复发】 fùfā have a relapse; recur

【复返】 fùfǎn return: 一去不~ gone never to return

【复方】 fùfāng 〈*Pharm.*〉 complex prescription; compound

【复方阿司匹林】 fùfāng āsīpǐlín 〈*Pharm.*〉 compound aspirin

【复方甘草合剂】 fùfāng gāncǎo héjì 〈*Pharm.*〉 brown mixture

【复工】 fùgōng return to work (after a strike)

【复古】 fùgǔ back to the ancients

【复果】 fùguǒ multiple fruit

【复合】 fùhé compound; complex; composite

【复合肥料】 fùhé féiliào compound fertilizer

【复合维生素B】 fùhé wéishēngsù B vitamin B compound

【复合型人才】 fùhéxíng réncái compound talent

【复核】 fùhé 1.(核对) check: 把报表~一下 check the report forms 2.〈*Law*〉 review a case in which a death sentence has been passed by a lower court

【复婚】 fùhūn restoration of a marriage; resume matrimonial relation

【复活】 fùhuó 1.(死而复活) bring back to life; revive 2.(耶稣复活日) Resurrection

【复活节】 fùhuójié Easter

【复活节彩蛋】 fùhuójié cǎidàn Easter egg

【复交】 fùjiāo reestablish diplomatic relations

【复刊】 fùkān resume publication

【复利】 fùlì 〈*Econ.*〉 compound interest

【复赛】 fùsài 〈*Sports*〉 intermediary heat

【复审】 fùshěn 1.(再一次审查) reexamine 2.〈*Law*〉(再一次审理) review a case

【复视】 fùshì 〈*Med.*〉 diplopia; double vision

【复述】 fùshù 1.(重说一遍) repeat 2.(语言教学用语) retell

【复数】 fùshù 1.(多数) plural 2.(复合数) complex number

【复苏】 fùsū 1.(苏醒) come back to life or consciousness; resuscitate 2.(经济恢复) recovery

【复位】 fùwèi 1.(回到原位) restore; re-

storation (n.) 2.〈*Computer*〉reset
【复息】 fùxī compound interest
【复习】 fùxí review; revise: ～功课 review lessons
【复线】 fùxiàn 〈*Transport*〉multiple track
【复线铁路】 fùxiàn tiělù double-tracking railways
【复写】 fùxiě make carbon copies; duplicate
【复写纸】 fùxiězhǐ carbon paper
【复信】 fùxìn 1.(答复来信) write a letter in reply 2.(回信) letter in reply; reply
【复兴】 fùxīng revive; resurge; rejuvenate
【复姓】 fùxìng compound surname; two-character surname
【复学】 fùxué go back to school
【复业】 fùyè 1.(恢复旧业) resume one's occupation; reestablish one's business 2.(恢复营业) reopen
【复议】 fùyì reconsider (a decision)
【复印】 fùyìn 〈*Printing*〉duplicate; xerox
【复印机】 fùyìnjī duplicator; duplicating machine; photocopier; xerox machine
【复印纸】 fùyìnzhǐ duplicating paper
【复员】 fùyuán demobilize; demobilization (n.)
【复员军人】 fùyuán jūnrén ex-serviceman; demobilized soldier
【复原】 fùyuán 1.(病后恢复健康) recover from an illness; be restored to health 2.(恢复原状) restore; rehabilitate
【复杂】 fùzá complicated; complex: ～多变的国际形势 complex and volatile world situation / ～的局面 complicated situation / ～的心情 mixed feelings
【复杂化】 fùzáhuà make sth. more difficult; complicate; complication (n.): 使国际形势～ complicate the international situation
【复照】 fùzhào sent a note in reply
【复诊】 fùzhěn further consultation (with a doctor); subsequent visit
【复职】 fùzhí resume one's post; be reinstated
【复制】 fùzhì duplicate; reproduce; make a copy of
【复制品】 fùzhìpǐn replica; reproduction
【复种】 fùzhòng 〈*Agric.*〉multiple cropping
【复种面积】 fùzhòng miànjī multiple cropping area

腹 (fù) belly; abdomen; stomach
【腹部】 fùbù abdomen
【腹带】 fùdài binder: 乳罩和～ bra and binder
【腹地】 fùdì hinterland; interior
【腹稿】 fùgǎo mental notes; mental draft: 打～ make mental draft
【腹股沟】 fùgǔgōu 〈*Anat.*〉groin
【腹肌】 fùjī 〈*Anat.*〉abdominal muscle
【腹膜】 fùmó 〈*Anat.*〉peritoneum
【腹膜炎】 fùmóyán 〈*Med.*〉peritonitis
【腹鳍】 fùqí 〈*Zool.*〉pelvic fin
【腹水】 fùshuǐ 〈*Med.*〉ascites
【腹痛】 fùtòng abdominal pain
【腹泻】 fùxiè diarrhea
【腹主动脉】 fù zhǔdòngmài 〈*Anat.*〉abdominal aorta

蝮 (fù)
【蝮蛇】 fùshé viper; Pallas pit viper

覆 (fù) 1.(遮盖) cover 2.(翻过来;歪倒) overturn; upset
【覆盖】 fùgài 1.(遮盖) cover 2.(植被的保护作用) plant cover; vegetation
【覆灭】 fùmiè destruction; complete collapse
【覆没】 fùmò 1.(翻沉) capsize and sink 2.(被消灭) be overwhelmed; be annihilated
【覆亡】 fùwáng fall (of an empire, nation, etc.)
【覆辙】 fùzhé the track of an overturned cart: 重蹈～ take the same disastrous road

馥 (fù) fragrance; fragrant (adj.)
【馥郁】 fùyù fragrance; sweet and pleasant smell

副 (fù) 1.(居第二位的) deputy; assistant; vice: ～部长 vice-minister / ～经理 assistant manager / ～主席 vice-chairman / ～总理 vice-premier 2.(辅助的) auxiliary; subsidiary; secondary 3.(符合) correspond to; fit
【副本】 fùběn duplicate; transcript; copy
【副标题】 fùbiāotí subheading; subtitle
【副博士】 fùbóshì candidate doctor
【副裁判】 fùcáipàn 〈*Volleyball*〉umpire

【副产品】 fùchǎnpǐn by-product
【副词】 fùcí 〈*Gram.*〉 adverb; adverbial (adj.)
【副官】 fùguān aide; adjutant; aide-de-camp (ADC)
【副虹】 fùhóng 〈*Meteorol.*〉 secondary bow
【副教授】 fùjiàoshòu associate professor
【副刊】 fùkān supplement: 文学～ literary supplement
【副品】 fùpǐn substandard goods
【副热带】 fùrèdài 〈*Meteorol.*〉 subtropical belt
【副热带高压】 fùrèdài gāoyā 〈*Meteorol.*〉 subtropical high; horse latitude high
【副伤寒】 fùshānghán 〈*Med.*〉 paratyphoid
【副食】 fùshí non-staple food; non-staple foodstuffs
【副食商店】 fùshí shāngdiàn grocery; grocer's
【副手】 fùshǒu assistant
【副研】 fùyán associate research fellow
【副业】 fùyè sideline; sideline production; side occupation
【副油箱】 fùyóuxiāng 〈*Aeron.*〉 auxiliary fuel tank
【副作用】 fùzuòyòng 1.(附带发生的坏作用) side effect; by-effect: 没有～ be free from side effects 2.〈*Mech.*〉 secondary action

富 (fù) rich; wealthy; abundant: 脱贫致～ shake off poverty and set out on the road to prosperity / 先～起来 grow rich first
【富贵】 fùguì riches and honor; wealth and rank
【富贵荣华】 fùguì-rónghuá riches; honor and splendor
【富国】 fùguó rich country
【富豪】 fùháo rich and powerful people
【富矿】 fùkuàng rich ore; high-grade ore
【富丽】 fùlì gorgeous; magnificent
【富丽堂皇】 fùlì-tánghuáng sumptuous; gorgeous; splendid
【富农】 fùnóng rich peasant; rich farmer
【富强】 fùqiáng prosperous and strong: ～民主文明的社会主义现代化国家 a prosperous, strong, democratic, culturally advanced and modern socialist country
【富饶】 fùráo richly endowed; fertile; abundant: 美丽～的国家 a beautiful and richly endowed country
【富翁】 fùwēng man of wealth; man of fortune
【富有】 fùyǒu 1.(有大量财产) rich; wealthy 2.(大量具有) rich in; full of: ～朝气 full of vigor
【富裕】 fùyù prosperous: 共同～ common prosperity / 同步～ become prosperous simultaneously
【富余】 fù·yu have enough and to spare; have more than needed
【富足】 fùzú plentiful; abundant; rich

赋 (fù) 1.(给予) bestow on; endow with; vest with: ～予新的意义 give a new meaning 2.(税) tax: 田～ land tax
【赋税】 fùshuì taxes
【赋闲】 fùxián (of an official, etc.) be unemployed
【赋有】 fùyǒu possess (naturally); be gifted (with): ～才能 possess talents; be gifted with talents

缚 (fù) tie up; bind fast
【缚鸡之力】 fùjī-zhīlì strength for binding a chicken

G

ga

夹[夾](gā)

【夹肢窝】 gā·zhiwō armpit

(另见"夹"jiā, jiá)

胳(gā)

【胳肢窝】 gā·zhiwō armpit

(另见"胳"gē, gé)

旮(gā)

【旮旯儿】 gālár **1.**(角落) nook; corner **2.**(狭窄偏僻处) out-of-the-way place

咖(gā)

【咖喱】 gālí curry: ～牛肉 beef curry

【咖喱粉】 gālífěng curry powder

(另见"咖"kā)

嘎(gā)

【嘎巴】 gābā **1.**〈*onomat.*〉 crack **2.**(粘, 糊) crust

【嘎巴儿】 gābar crust: 饭～ rice crust

【嘎嘣脆】 gā·bēngcuì crisp

【嘎嘎】 gāgā 〈*onomat.*〉 quack: 鸭子开始～叫。The duck started quacking.

【嘎渣儿】 gā·zhar **1.**(痂) scab; crust: 结～ form a scab **2.**(锅巴) rice crust

【嘎吱】 gāzhī 〈*onomat.*〉 creak

钆(gá) 〈*Chem.*〉 gadolinium (元素符号 Gd)

尜(gá)

【尜尜儿】 gá·gar top: 抽～ whip a top

gai

该(gāi) **1.**(应该) ought to; should; probably: 如果他在 9 点钟出发, 现在～到那里了。If he started at nine, he ought to be there by now. **2.**(轮到) be sb's turn to do sth.: 现在～你了。It's your turn. **3.**(理该如此) deserve: ～挨罚 deserve punishment **4.**(该欠) owe: 我～他 100 元钱。I owe a hundred yuan to him. **5.**(此) this; that; the said; the above-mentioned: ～医院 that hospital

【该当】 gāidāng **1.**(应受) deserve **2.**(应当) should: 这是大家的, 我们～尽力。It's for everybody and we should do our best.

【该死】 gāisǐ Go to hell!: 这雨天真～! Blame this rainy weather!

【该账】 gāizhàng be in debt

改(gǎi) **1.**(改变) change; transform **2.**(修改) alter; revise **3.**(改正) correct; rectify; put right: ～作文 correct students' compositions

【改编】 gǎibiān **1.**(指作品) adapt; rearrange; revise **2.**(指编制) reorganize; redesignate

【改变】 gǎibiàn **1.**(发生变化) change; transform **2.**(改换) alter; change; convert: ～航线 alter the course / ～经济体制 change the economic structure / ～主意 change one's mind

【改道】 gǎidào **1.**(指路线) change one's route **2.**(指河流) change its course

【改掉】 gǎidiào give up; drop: ～坏习惯 give up bad habits

【改订】 gǎidìng reformulate; rewrite: ～税则 revise the tariff

【改动】 gǎidòng change; alter; modify

【改革】 gǎigé reform: 价格～ the pricing reform / 政治体制～ reform of political structure / 锐意～ work hard to carry out reform / 深化～ deepen the reform

【改革开放】 gǎigé kāifàng reform and the opening to the outside world

【改观】 gǎiguān change the appearance; get

a new look; take on a new look

【改过】 gǎiguò mend one's ways; correct one's mistakes: ～自新 correct one's errors and make a fresh start; mend one's ways; turn over a new leaf

【改行】 gǎiháng change one's profession; change to new occupation

【改换】 gǎihuàn change over to; change: ～会议日期 change the date of meeting

【改悔】 gǎihuǐ regret; repent and reform; 死不～ absolutely unrepentant; be a real diehard

【改嫁】 gǎijià (of a woman) remarry

【改建工程】 gǎijiàn gōngchéng reconstruction project

【改进】 gǎijìn improve; make better: ～方法 improve one's methods / ～工作作风 improve one's work style

【改口】 gǎikǒu correct oneself; change one's tone

【改良】 gǎiliáng 1.(使更适合要求) improve; ameliorate: ～品种 improve the breed 2.(改善) reform

【改良主义】 gǎiliáng zhǔyì reformism; reformist (adj.)

【改期】 gǎiqī change the date: 会议～了。The date for the meeting has been changed.

【改日】 gǎirì another day; some other day: 咱们～再去吧! Let's go another day.

【改善】 gǎishàn improve; ameliorate: ～工作条件 improve working conditions

【改天】 gǎitiān some other day; another day: ～见。See you some other day.

【改天换地】 gǎitiān-huàndì transform heaven and earth; change the world; remake nature

【改弦更张】 gǎixián-gēngzhāng change over to new ways; make a fresh start

【改邪归正】 gǎixié-guīzhèng give up evil and return to good; turn over a new leaf

【改写】 gǎixiě rewrite; adapt

【改选】 gǎixuǎn reelect: 每四年～一次 hold elections one every four years

【改造】 gǎizào transform; reform; remold; remake: ～老企业 transforming outmoded enterprises

【改正】 gǎizhèng correct; amend; put right: ～拼写错误 correct one's wrong spellings

【改装】 gǎizhuāng 1.(指服装) change one's costume or dress 2.(指包装) repackage; repack 3.(指装置) reequip; refit: ～一辆卡车 refit a truck

【改锥】 gǎizhuī screwdriver

【改组】 gǎizǔ reorganize; reshuffle: ～政府部门 reshuffle the government departments

钙 (gài) 〈*Chem*.〉 calcium (元素符号 Ca)

【钙片】 gàipiàn calcium tablet

芥 (gài)
(另见"芥"jiè)

【芥菜】 gàicài 〈*Bot*.〉 leaf mustard

【芥蓝】 gàilán 〈*Bot*.〉 cabbage mustard

盖[葢] (gài) 1.(盖子) lid; cover: 箱子～the lid of a box 2.(甲壳) shell (of a tortoise, crab, etc.) 3.(伞状盖) canopy 4.(覆盖) cover 5.(盖印) affix (a seal) 6.(超过;压倒) surpass; top 7.(建筑) build

【盖房】 gàifáng build a house

【盖浇饭】 gàijiāofàn rice served with meat and vegetables on top

【盖世】 gàishì unparalleled; matchless; peerless: ～无双 without equal in the world

【盖世太保】 Gàishìtàibǎo Gestapo (Geheime Staatspolizei)

【盖章】 gàizhāng affix one's seal; seal; stamp: 由收件人～ to be sealed by the recipient

【盖子】 gài·zi 1.(指器物的) lid; cover; cap; top 2.(甲壳) shell (of a tortoise, etc.)

概[槩[1,2]] (gài) 1.(大略) general; approximate 2.(无例外) without exception; categorically 3.(气概) spirit; deportment

【概不赊欠】 gàibù-shēqiàn no credit allowed to anybody

【概不追究】 gàibù-zhuījiū no action will be taken (against sb. for his past offenses)

【概况】 gàikuàng general situation; survey

【概括】 gèikuò 1.(总括) summarize; generalize; epitomize: ～起来说 to sum up 2.(扼要) briefly; in broad outline: ～地说 to put it briefly

【概括性】 gàikuòxìng generality: 这篇文章的～很强。This article is a succinct summary.

【概率】 gàilǜ probability
【概率分析】 gàilǜ fēngxī probability analysis
【概率误差】 gàilǜ wùchā probable error
【概略】 gàilüè 1.(大概情况) outline; summary 2.(大致) generally
【概论】 gàilùn (多用于书名) outline; introduction
【概莫能外】 gàimò-néngwài admit of no exception whatever
【概念】 gàiniàn concept; conception; notion; idea: 形成一个～ form a concept
【概念化】 gàiniànhuà deal in generalities; write or speak in abstract terms
【概述】 gàishù general introduction
【概要】 gàiyào (多用于书名) essentials; outline

gan

干[乾1-4](gān) 1.(干燥) dry: 水塘快～了。The pound is running dry./衣服在外面～得快。The clothes dried quickly outside. 2.(干食品) dried food: 水果～ dried fruit 3.(空虚) empty; hollow; dry 4.(徒然)(do sth.) for nothing; futilely 5.(相干) have to do with; be concerned with; be implicated in: 这个问题与你无～。This problem has nothing to do with you.
(另见"干"gàn)
【干巴】 gān·ba 1.(无水分) dry 2.(枯燥) uninteresting
【干巴巴】 gānbābā 1.(无水分) dry 2.(不生动) dull and dry; insipid; dull as dishwater
【干白葡萄酒】 gānbái pú·táojiǔ dry white wine
【干杯】 gānbēi drink a toast; toast to a person's health: 提议～ propose a toast to / 为公司的成功～ toast the success of a company
【干贝】 gāibèi scallop; dried scallop
【干瘪】 gāibiě 1.(指物) shrivelled; wizened 2.(指内容) empty and dull
【干冰】 gānbīng dry ice
【干菜】 gāncài dried vegetable
【干草】 gāncǎo hay
【干船坞】 gānchuánwū dry dock
【干脆】 gāncuì 1.(直截了当) clear-cut; straightforward; not mince one's words 2.(爽快) simply; just; altogether
【干电池】 gāndiànchí dry cell; dry battery
【干戈】 gāngē weapons of war; arms; war: 动～ take up arms; go to war
【干戈四起】 gāngē-sìqǐ civil war breaks out in the country; fighting broke out all over the country
【干果】 gānguǒ 1.(硬壳果) dry fruit (e.g. nuts) 2.(晒干的果子) dried fruit
【干旱】 gānhàn arid; dry: 战胜～ conquer drought
【干旱地区】 gānhàn dìqū arid area
【干涸】 gānhé dry up; run dry: 湖泊～。The lake dried up.
【干红葡萄酒】 gānhóng pú·táojiǔ dry red wine
【干净】 gānjìng 1.(清洁) clean; neat and tidy: 把房间打扫～ sweep the room clean 2.(完全) completely; totally
【干净利落】 gānjìng-lì·luo neat and tidy; neat; efficient: 她办事～。She's very efficient.
【干酒】 gānjiǔ dry wine
【干枯】 gānkū dried-up; withered; shrivelled; wizened
【干酪】 gānlào cheese
【干垒】 gānlěi 〈*Archit.*〉 drystone
【干垒墙】 gānlěiqiáng dry wall; drystone wall
【干冷】 gānlěng dry and cold: 天气～。The weather is dry and cold.
【干粮】 gān·liáng solid food (prepared for a journey); rations for a journey
【干裂】 gāliè be dry and cracked
【干啤酒】 gānpíjiǔ dry beer
【干扰】 gānrǎo 1.(扰乱) disturb; interfere; obstruct: ～某人的工作 interfere with sb's work / 排除～ remove interference 2.(无线电干扰) jam; interference (n.): 外国广播的～ interference from foreign broadcasting station / 广播经常受到～。The radio broadcasts were regularly jammed.
【干扰素】 gānrǎosù interferon
【干热风】 gānrèfēng 〈*Meteorol.*〉 hot dry wind
【干涉】 gānshè 1.(插手) interfere; inter-

vene; meddle: 外来～ external interference from outside / 武装～ armed intervention / 互不～内政 nonintervention in each other's internal affairs 2.〈*Physics*〉 interference

【干尸】 gānshī mummy: 吐鲁番～ mummies of Turpan

【干瘦】 gānshòu skinny; bony

【干洗】 gānxǐ dry-clean; dry cleaning

【干洗店】 gānxǐdiàn dry cleaner's

【干笑】 gānxiào hollow laugh

【干薪】 gānxīn 1.(挂名而领的) salary drawn for a sinecure 2.(纯工资) net salary

【干蓄电池】 gān xùdiànchí dry battery

【干与】 gānyù 同"干预"

【干预】 gānyù intervene; interpose; meddle

【干燥】 gānzào 1.(无水分或少水分) dry; arid: ～的气候 arid climate 2.(无趣味) dull; uninteresting

【干燥剂】 gānzàojì drier; drying agent; desiccating agent

【干着急】 gānzháojí be anxious but unable to do anything

杆 (gān) pole; staff: 电话线～ a telephone pole / 旗子挂在～上。The flag hangs on a staff.
(另见"杆"gǎn)

【杆子】 gān·zi pole: 电线～ electricity pole

肝 (gān) liver; hepatic (adj.)

【肝癌】 gān'ái 〈*Med.*〉 cancer of the liver

【肝胆】 gāndǎn 1.(肝与胆) liver and gall 2.(勇气) heroic spirit; courage: ～过人 unsurpassed in valor 3.(真心相见) openheartedness; sincerity

【肝胆相照,荣辱与共】 gāndǎn-xiāngzhào, róngrǔ-yǔgòng treat each other with all sincerity and share weal or woe

【肝功能】 gāngōngnéng liver function

【肝火】 gānhuǒ irascibility: 动～ get worked up; fly into a rage

【肝炎】 gānyán 〈*Med.*〉 hepatitis: 甲型～ hepatitis A / 乙型～ hepatitis B / 病毒性～ virus hepatitis / 传染性～ epidemic hepatitis; infectious hepatitis

【肝硬变】 gānyìngbiàn 〈*Med.*〉 cirrhosis (of the liver)

【肝脏】 gānzàng liver

矸 (gān)

【矸石】 gānshí waste rock

竿 (gān) pole; rod: 渔～ fishing rod / 竹～ bamboo pole

甘 (gān) 1.(甜) sweet; pleasant 2.(乐于) willingly; of one's own accord: 不～落后 unwilling to lag behind / ～当小学生 make oneself a willing pupil

【甘草】 gāncǎo 1.〈*Bot.*〉 licorice 2.〈*Chin. Pharm.*〉 licorice root

【甘苦】 gānkǔ 1.(指处境) sweetness and bitterness; weal and woe: 同～ share the joys and sorrows 2.(指体验) hardships and difficulties experienced in work: 深知其中～ know well the taste of it; know well what it is like

【甘霖普降】 gānlín-pǔjiàng seasonable rain has fallen everywhere

【甘泉】 gānquán sweet spring water

【甘薯】 gānshǔ sweet potato

【甘心】 gānxīn 1.(愿意) willingly; readily 2.(称心满意) be reconciled to; resign oneself to; be content with

【甘心情愿】 gānxīn-qíngyuàn willing-hearted; willing and pleased

【甘休】 gānxiū be willing to give up; be content with the present situation

【甘油】 gānyóu 〈*Chem.*〉 glycerine

【甘于】 gānyú be willing to; be ready to; be happy to

【甘愿】 gānyuàn willingly; readily: ～冒风险 be willing to take the risk / ～效劳 be glad to offer one's services; be glad to do sth. for sb.

【甘蔗】 gān·zhe sugarcane

【甘孜】 gānzī 〈plane〉 Garze

坩 (gān)

【坩埚】 gānguō 〈*Chem.*〉 crucible: 石墨～ graphite crucible

泔 (gān)

【泔水】 gānshuǐ swill; slops; hogwash; pigwash; wash

柑 (gān) mandarin orange

【柑橘】 gānjú 1.（橙；红橘）oranges and tangerines 2.（柑橘）citrus

疳(gān) 〈*Med*.〉infantile malnutrition

尴[尷、尲](gān)

【尴尬】 gāngà awkward; embarrassed: 感到～ feel awkward; feel embarrassed

杆[桿](gǎn) the shaft or arm of sth.（另见“杆”gān）

【杆菌】 gǎnjūn 〈*Microbiol*.〉bacillus: 结核～ tubercle bacillus

秆[稈](gǎn) stalk: 高粱～ sorghum stalk

【秆子】 gǎn·zi stalk

赶[趕](gǎn) 1.（追赶）catch up with; overtake 2.（紧追）try to catch; make a dash for; rush for: ～头班车 catch the first bus 3.（加快）hurry through: ～任务 rush through one's job 4.（驾御）drive: ～车 drive a cart 5.（驱逐）drive away: ～下台 drive (sb.) off the stage; oust (sb.) from office 6.（碰巧）happen to; find oneself in; avail oneself of

【赶超】 gǎnchāo catch up with and surpass: ～世界先进水平 catch up with and surpass the world's advanced levels

【赶集】 gǎnjí go to market; go to a fair

【赶紧】 gǎnjǐn lose no time; hasten

【赶快】 gǎnkuài 1.（催促）hurry up; be quick 2.（急忙）at once; quickly: ～回家 go home at once

【赶路】 gǎnlù hurry on with one's journey

【赶忙】 gǎnmáng hurry; hasten; make haste

【赶巧】 gǎnqiǎo happen to; it so happened that

【赶上】 gǎnshàng 1.（追上）overtake; catch up with; keep pace with: ～末班车 catch the last bus 2.（碰上）run into: 没～公共汽车 miss the bus 3.（及时）be in time for: ～午饭 be in time for lunch 4.（差不多一样）about as ... as

【赶时髦】 gǎnshímáo follow the fashion; try to be in the swim

【赶走】 gǎnzǒu drive away

擀[扞](gǎn) roll

【擀面】 gǎnmiàn make dough

【擀面条】 gǎnmiàntiáo make noodles

敢(gǎn) 1.（有勇气，有胆量）bold; courageous; daring: 果～ courageous and resolute; daring 2.（有胆量做）dare: ～想～干 dare to think and dare to act 3.（有把握）have the confidence to; be certain 4.（请求）make bold; venture

【敢死队】 gǎnsǐduì dare-to-die corps

【敢于】 gǎnyú dare to; be bold in; have the courage to: ～面对现实 have the courage to face reality / ～实践 dare to experiment

【敢作敢为】 gǎnzuò-gǎnwéi dare to do everything; be afraid of no difficulties

橄(gǎn)

【橄榄】 gǎnlǎn 1.（青果）Chinese olive; the fruit of the canary tree 2.（油橄榄）olive

【橄榄绿】 gǎnlǎnlǜ olive green

【橄榄球】 gǎnlǎnqiú rugby; rugby football: 美式～ American Football

【橄榄油】 gǎnlǎnyóu olive oil

【橄榄枝】 gǎnlǎnzhī olive branch

感(gǎn) 1.（感觉到）feel; sense: 略～不适 not feel very well; feel a bit unwell; be under the weather; be out of sorts 2.（感动）move; touch; affect 3.（感谢）be grateful; be obliged 4.〈*Chin*. *Med*.〉be affected: 外～风寒 be affected by the cold; have a cold 5.（感觉）sense; feeling: 安全～ feeling of security / 荣誉～ sense of honor / 责任～ sense of responsibility

【感触】 gǎnchù thoughts and feelings; feeling

【感到】 gǎndào feel; sense: ～高兴 feel happy / ～委曲 feel oneself wronged

【感动】 gǎndòng 1.（受影响而激动）move; touch; affect: 听众深为～。The audience was deeply affected. 2.（给深刻印象）impress

【感恩】 gǎn'ēn feel grateful; be thankful: ～不尽 be everlastingly grateful

【感官】 gǎnguān sense organ; sensory organ

【感光】 gǎnguāng 〈*Photog*.〉sensitize; sensitization (n.)

【感光材料】 gǎnguāng cáiliào 〈*Photog*.〉sensitive material

【感光片】 gǎnguángpiàn 〈*Photog*.〉 sensitive film

【感光纸】 gǎnguángzhǐ 〈*Photog*.〉 sensitive paper

【感激】 gǎn·jī feel grateful; be thankful; feel indebted: ～不尽 be indebted forever; be very grateful

【感觉】 gǎnjué 1.（感觉）sense perception; sensation; feeling 2.（觉得）feel; perceive; become aware of: 你～怎么样? How do you feel now?

【感觉器官】 gǎnjué qìguān sense organ; sensory organ

【感慨】 gǎnkǎi sigh with emotion

【感慨系之】 gǎnkǎi-xìzhī sigh with deep feeling

【感冒】 gǎnmào 1.（伤风）common cold: 患～ catch cold; have a cold / 流行性～ influenza; the flu 2.（患感冒）catch cold; contract a cold

【感情】 gǎnqíng 1.（心理反应）emotion; feeling; sentiment 2.（关切、喜爱之情）affection; attachment; love

【感情不合】 gǎnqíng bùhé incompatibility

【感情冲动】 gǎnqíng chōngdòng act on a momentary impulse; emotional impulse

【感情破裂】 gǎnqíng pòliè 1.（朋友间的）rupture a friendship 2.（夫妻间的）rupture a marriage

【感情投资】 gǎnqíng tóuzī emotional investment

【感情用事】 gǎnqíng yòngshì act impetuously; give away to one's feeling; be swayed by one's emotions

【感染】 gǎnrǎn 1.（受到传染）infect 2.（引起同感）influence; infect; affect

【感染力】 gǎnrǎnlì appeal; fascination; magnetism

【感人肺腑】 gǎnrén-fèifǔ touch one deeply in the heart; touch the chords of one's heart

【感受】 gǎnshòu 1.（受到）be affected by: ～风寒 catch cold 2.（体会）experience; feel: 使…～很深 be deeply impressed by

【感叹】 gǎntàn sigh with feeling

【感叹词】 gǎntàncí interjection; exclamation

【感叹号】 gǎntànhào exclamation point; exclamation mark（符号为：!）

【感叹句】 gǎntànjù exclamatory sentence

【感想】 gǎnxiǎng impressions; reflections; thoughts: 你对此事有什么～? What are your feelings about this matter?

【感谢】 gǎnxiè thank; be grateful: 表示衷心的～ express heartfelt thanks

【感谢信】 gǎnxièxìn thank-you note

【感性】 gǎnxìng perceptual

【感性认识】 gǎnxìng rèn·shi perceptual knowledge

【感应】 gǎnyìng 1.（引起相应感情或动作）response; reaction; interaction 2.〈*Biol*.〉 irritability 3.（电磁感应）induction: 电磁～ electromagnetic induction

【感召】 gǎnzhào move and inspire; impel

干［幹、榦[1,2]］（gàn） 1.（主体）trunk; main part: 树～ tree-trunk; trunk 2.（干部）cadre; leading cadre 3.（做）do; work: 实～ do solid work / 有好多事情要～。There's a lot to do. 4.（斗争）fight; strike 5.（能干的）capable; able

（另见"干"gān）

【干部】 gànbù 1.（机关人员）public official; government functionary 2.（领导干部）cadre; leading cadre: 基层～ leading personnel at the basic level / 高级～ high level cadre

【干部学校】 gànbù xuéxiào cadre school

【干才】 gàncái 1.（办事才能）ability; qualification; competence 2.（有办事才能的人）a capable person; a competent person

【干道】 gàndào main road

【干掉】 gàndiào kill; get rid of; put sb. out of the way

【干活】 gànhuó work; work on a job

【干架】 gànjià 1.（吵架）quarrel 2.（动手打架）come to blows

【干将】 gànjiàng capable person; go-getter

【干劲】 gànjìn drive; vigor; enthusiasm: ～十足 be full of enthusiasm

【干尽坏事】 gànjìn huàishì do every evil; do all manner of evil; stop at no evil

【干警】 gànjǐng officers and policemen of public security

【干练】 gànliàn capable and experienced

【干流】 gànliú main stream; master stream

【干吗】 gànmá 1.（为什么）why on earth; whatever for 2.（干什么）what to do
【干群】 gànqún leading cadres and masses
【干事】 gànshi a secretary in charge of sth.: 文娱～ person in charge of recreational activities
【干线】 gànxiàn main line; trunk line; artery: 公路～ arterial or main highway
【干校】 gànxiào cadres' school; schools for training cadres
【干休所】 gànxiúsuǒ rest house for veteran cadres
【干员】 gànyuán a capable official
绀（gàn） dark purple
【绀青】 gànqīng dark purple; prune purple

gang

冈［岡］（gāng） ridge (of a hill): 山～ low hill; hillock
【冈底斯山】 gāngdǐsīshān 〈plane〉 Gangdise
刚［剛］（gāng） 1.（刚强） firm; strong; indomitable 2.（刚好） just; exactly: ～合适 just fit 3.（仅仅） barely; only just 4.（刚刚） only a short while ago; just: 他～回来。He's just come back.
【刚才】 gāngcái just now; a moment ago: 他比～好一点了。He is a little better than he was a short while ago.
【刚刚】 gāng·gāng 1.（正好） just; only; exactly 2.（刚才） a moment ago; just now
【刚好】 gānghǎo 1.（正合适） just; exactly 2.（正巧） happen to; it so happened that
【刚劲有力】 gāngjìn-yǒulì (the calligraphy) is powerful and vigorous; vigorous and forcible
【刚强】 gāngqiáng firm; staunch; unyielding
【刚毅】 gāngyì resolute and steadfast
【刚正】 gāngzhèng upright; honorable; principled
【刚正不阿】 gāngzhèng-bù'ē upright and never stooping to flattery
纲［綱］（gāng） 1.（网绳） the headrope of a fishing net 2.（总纲） key link; guiding principle 3.（大纲） outline; program 4.（动植物分类） class: 哺乳动物～ the class of mammals
【纲领】 gānglǐng program; guiding principle
【纲领性文件】 gānglǐngxìng wénjiàn programmatic document
【纲目】 gāngmù （多用于书名） detailed outline; outline
【纲要】 gāngyào 1.（提纲） outline; sketch 2.（书名、文件名） essentials; compendium
钢［鋼］（gāng） steel: 不锈～ stainless steel / 合金～ alloy steel / 锰～ manganese steel / 弹簧～ spring steel （另见"钢"gàng）
【钢板】 gāngbǎn 1.（板状钢材） steel plate; plate: 薄～ steel sheet; sheet steel 2.（汽车片状弹簧） spring
【钢镚儿】 gāngbèngr coin
【钢笔】 gāngbǐ pen; fountain pen
【钢材】 gāngcái steel products; steels; rolled steel
【钢尺】 gāngchǐ steel rule
【钢带】 gāngdài steel band; steel belt; steel strip
【钢锭】 gāngdìng steel ingot
【钢管】 gāngguǎn steel tube: 无缝～ seamless steel tube
【钢管椅】 gāngguǎnyǐ tubular steel chair
【钢轨】 gāngguǐ rail; track
【钢化玻璃】 gānghuà bōlí toughened glass
【钢结构】 gāngjiégòu 〈*Archit.*〉 steel structure; steel construction
【钢筋】 gāngjīn reinforcing bar
【钢筋混凝土】 gāngjīn hùnníngtǔ reinforced concrete
【钢筋铁骨】 gāngjīn-tiěgǔ body strong as iron; muscles of steel
【钢锯】 gāngjù hacksaw
【钢卷尺】 gāngjuǎnchǐ tape; steel tape; steel measuring tape
【钢盔】 gāngkuī (steel) helmet
【钢坯】 gāngpī billet; bloom
【钢瓶】 gāngpíng steel cylinder
【钢钎】 gāngqiān drill rod; drill steel
【钢琴】 gāngqín piano: 弹～ play the piano
【钢琴伴奏】 gāngqín bànzòu piano accompaniment
【钢琴凳】 gāngqíndèng piano stool
【钢琴独奏】 gāngqín dúzòu piano recital
【钢琴家】 gāngqínjiā pianist

【钢琴调音师】 gāngqín tiáoyīnshī piano tuner
【钢水】 gāngshuǐ molten steel
【钢丝】 gāngsī (steel) wire：走～ walk the wire；walk the tightrope；high-wire walking
【钢丝床】 gāngsīchuáng spring bed
【钢丝钳】 gāngsīqián pliers
【钢丝绳】 gāngsīshéng steel cable；wire rope
【钢铁】 gāngtiě **1.**(钢和铁) iron and steel；steel **2.**(比喻坚强) firm；resolute
【钢铁厂】 gāngtiěchǎng steelworks
【钢铁工业】 gāngtiě gōngyè iron and steel industry
【钢铁公司】 gāngtiě gōngsī iron and steel company
【钢铁联合企业】 gāngtiě liánhé qǐyè integrated iron and steel works；iron and steel complex
【钢印】 gāngyìn **1.**(硬印) steel seal；embossing seal **2.**(印痕) embossed stamp
【钢渣】 gāngzhā slag
【钢珠】 gāngzhū steel ball；ball bearing；ball

缸[甌] (gāng) **1.**(器皿) vat；jar；crock **2.**(汽缸) cylinder：六～发动机 a six-cylinder engine
【缸管】 gāngguǎn earthen pipe
【缸瓦】 gāngwǎ material for making earthware
【缸砖】 gāngzhuān clinker (tile)；quarry tile
【缸子】 gāng·zi mug；bowl

肛 (gāng) anus；anal (adj.)
【肛道】 gāngdào anal passage
【肛瘘】 gānglòu anal fistula
【肛门】 gāngmén anus；anal (adj.)
【肛门括约肌】 gāngmén kuòyuējī anal sphincter

岗[崗] (gǎng) **1.**(山岗) hillock；mound **2.**(岗位；岗哨) sentry；guard **3.**(长的隆起物) ridge
【岗警】 gǎngjǐng policeman on point duty
【岗楼】 gǎnglóu watchtower
【岗哨】 gǎngshào **1.**(岗位) lookout post **2.**(放哨人) sentry；sentinel：设置～ post sentries
【岗亭】 gǎngtíng sentry box；police box
【岗位】 gǎngwèi one's post；one's position：坚守～ stand fast at one's post；stick to one's position / 走上新的～ take up a new post；take on a new job
【岗位津贴】 gǎngwèi jīntiē job subsidy；duty allowance
【岗位责任制】 gǎngwèi zérènzhì system of post responsibility
【岗子】 gǎng·zi **1.**(小山) mound；hillock **2.**(长的隆起物) ridge；wale；welt

港 (gǎng) **1.**(港口) port；harbor：不冻～ ice-free port / 天然～ natural harbor/ 自由～ free port **2.**(香港) Hong Kong
【港澳同胞】 Gǎng-Ào tóngbāo compatriots in Hong Kong and Macao
【港币】 gǎngbì Hong Kong dollar；H. K. dollar
【港府】 gǎngfǔ the Hong Kong government
【港化】 gǎnghuà Hong Kongnization
【港口】 gǎngkǒu port；harbor：沿海～ coastal port
【港口吞吐量】 gǎngkǒu tūntǔliàng port capacity
【港区】 gǎngqū port area；port district
【港人】 gǎngrén Hong Kong people
【港人治港】 gǎngrén zhìgǎng administration of Hong Kong by Hong Kong people
【港商】 gǎngshāng merchant from Hong Kong；Hong Kong merchant
【港台歌星】 Gǎng-Tái gēxīng famous singer from Hong Kong and Taiwan
【港湾】 gǎngwān harbor
【港湾式停车站】 gǎngwānshì tíngchēzhàn rest stop (AmE.)；lay-by (BrE.)
【港务监督】 gǎngwù jiāndū harbor superintendency administration
【港务局】 gǎngwùjú port office；harbor bureau
【港纸】 gǎngzhǐ 〈*dial.*〉 H.K. dollar

杠[槓] (gàng) **1.**(粗棍子) thick stick；stout carrying pole **2.**(体育器械) bar：单～ horizontal bar / 双～ parallel bars **3.**(标记线) thick line **4.**(把错字勾出) cross out；delete：把错字～掉 cross out the wrong word
【杠杆】 gànggǎn **1.**〈*Mech.*〉 lever；pry bar **2.**(比喻起平衡作用) lever：经济～ economic levers
【杠杠】 gàng·gang limit；regulations：按照

年龄～ in accordance with age limits
【杠铃】 gànglíng 〈*Sports*〉 barbell
【杠子】 gàng·zi 1.（粗棍子）thick stick; stout carrying pole 2.（体育用品）bar
钢［鋼］（gàng） sharpen; whet; strop: ～一下剃刀 sharpen a razor（另见"钢"gāng）
【钢刀布】 gàngdāobù strop; razor strop

gao

高（gāo） 1.（与"低"相反）tall; high: ～矮不一 some tall and some short 2.（指等级）of a high level; of a high degree; above the average: ～年级 higher grades / ～质量 high quality 3.（大声）loud: ～喊 shout loudly 4.（价高）high-priced; dear; expensive
【高矮】 gāo'ǎi height: 她们俩～差不多。They two are about the same height.
【高昂】 gāo'áng 1.（高高扬起）hold high (one's head, etc.) 2.（向上高起）high; elated; exalted: ～的情绪 high spirits 3.（昂贵）dear; expensive; exorbitant
【高傲】 gāo'ào supercilious; arrogant; haughty
【高保真】 gāobǎozhén high fidelity; hi-fi
【高堡状积云】 gāobǎozhuàng jíyún 〈*Meteorol.*〉 altocumulus castellanus
【高层云】 gāocéngyún 〈*Meteorol.*〉 altostratus
【高产】 gāochǎn high yield; high production: ～稳产 high and stable yield; stable high yield
【高产田】 gāochǎntián high yield field; high yield plot
【高唱】 gāochàng 1.（高声唱）sing loudly; sing with spirit 2.（大声叫喊）talk glibly about; call out loudly for
【高超】 gāochāo superb; excellent: 技艺～ superb skill
【高潮】 gāocháo 1.（最高潮位）high tide; high water 2.（发展顶点）upsurge; climax; high tide: 全剧的～ the climax of the play
【高大】 gāodà 1.（又高又大）tall and big; tall: 身材～ be of great stature 2.（崇高的）lofty
【高蛋白】 gāodànbái high protein
【高档】 gāodàng top grade; high grade; superior quality
【高档商品】 gāndàng shāngpǐn high-grade goods; expensive goods of high quality
【高等】 gāoděng higher
【高等教育】 gāoděng jiàoyù higher education
【高等数学】 gāoděng shùxué higher mathematics; advanced mathematics
【高等院校】 gāotěng yuànxiào institutions of higher learning; colleges and universities
【高低】 gāodī 1.（高低程度）height 2.（高下）relative superiority or inferiority 3.（深浅轻重）sense of propriety; discretion
【高低杠】 gāodīgàng 〈*Sports*〉 uneven bars
【高地】 gāodì 1.（高处之地）highland; upland; elevation 2.〈*Mil.*〉 height
【高调】 gāodiào lofty tone; high-sounding words: 唱～ say fine-sounding things
【高度】 gāodù 1.（高低程度）altitude; height: 飞行～ flying altitude / 山的～ the height of a mountain 2.（程度高）high; high degree; highly: ～评价 attach immense significance to / ～赞扬 speak highly of; praise highly / ～重视 put great effort into
【高度表】 gāodùbiǎo altimeter; altitude meter
【高度计】 gāodùjì altimeter
【高尔夫俱乐部】 gāo'érfū jùlèbù golf club
【高尔夫球】 gāo'ěrfūqiú 1.（指项目）golf 2.（指球）golf ball
【高尔夫球场】 gāo'ěrfū qiúchǎng golf course
【高尔夫球球杆车】 gāo'ěrfūqiú qiúgānchē golf trolley
【高尔夫球球员】 gāo'érfūqiú qiúyuán golfer
【高法】 gāofǎ the Supreme People's Court
【高分辨率】 gāofēnbiànlǜ high-resolution
【高分低能】 gāofēn dīnéng having high scores in study but poor ability to do things
【高分子】 gāofēnzǐ 〈*Chem.*〉 high polymer; macromolecule
【高分子化学】 gāofēnzǐ huàxué (high) polymer chemistry
【高分子聚合物】 gāofēnzǐ jùhéwù high polymer
【高风亮节】 gāofēng-liàngjié exemplary con-

duct and nobility of character; have a sharp sense of integrity
【高峰】 gāofēng 1.(指山峰) peak; summit 2.(比喻最高点) height; top: 攀登科学～ scale the heights of science
【高峰时间】 gāofēng shíjiān peak hours: 在～行人车辆很多。There's a lot traffic at peak hours
【高浮雕】 gāofúdiāo high relief
【高干】 gāogàn leading cadre of high rank; high level cadre
【高个子】 gāogè·zi a tall person
【高跟鞋】 gāogēnxié high-heeled shoes
【高工】 gāogōng senior engineer
【高贵】 gāoguì 1.(指道德水平) noble; high: ～品质 noble quality 2.(贵重) precious; valuable 3.(指地位) highly privileged; elitist
【高积云】 gāojīyún 〈*Meteorol.*〉 altocumulus
【高级】 gāojí 1.(级别高) senior; high-ranking; high-level; high: ～干部 leading cadre of high rank / ～将领 high-ranking general officer 2.(质量、水平高) high-grade; high-quality; advanced: ～墨水 high-quality ink
【高级人民法院】 gāojí rénmín fǎyuàn higher people's court
【高级职称】 gāojí zhíchēng title of a senior professional post
【高级中学】 gāojí zhōngxué senior middle school
【高技术】 gāojìshù high technology
【高价】 gāojià high price: ～出让 go off at high price / ～收买 buy over at a high price / 索要～ demand extortionate prices
【高架公路】 gāojià gōnglù flyover; skyway
【高架桥】 gāojiàqiáo viaduct
【高架铁路】 gāojià tiělù overhead railway; elevated railway
【高检】 gāojiǎn the Supreme People's Procuratorate
【高见】 gāojiàn your opinion: 有何～? What do you think of it?
【高脚杯】 gāojiǎobēi goblet; cocktail glass
【高教】 gāojiào higher education
【高精尖】 gāojīngjiān high-grade, precision and advanced: ～设备 advanced equipment of high grade and precision
【高举】 gāojǔ hold high; hold aloft: ～红旗 hold high the red banner
【高峻】 gāojùn high and steep
【高亢】 gāokàng loud and sonorous; resounding
【高考】 gāokǎo the university entrance examination
【高科技产品】 gāokējì chǎnpǐn Hi-tech product
【高科技产业】 gāokējì chǎnyè Hi-tech industry
【高科技开发区】 gāokējì kāifāqū Hi-tech development zone
【高空】 gāokōng high altitude; upper air
【高空作业】 gāokōng zuòyè work high above the ground
【高栏】 gāolán 〈*Sports*〉 high hurdles
【高利】 gāolì high interest
【高利贷】 gāolìdài usury; usurious loan: 放～ practice usury
【高利贷者】 gāolìdàizhě usurer
【高粱】 gāo·liang Chinese sorghum
【高粱酒】 gāo·liangjiǔ sorghum liquor
【高龄】 gāolíng advanced age; venerable age: 80～ the advanced age of 80
【高楼大厦】 gāolóu-dàshà high buildings and large mansions
【高炉】 gāolú 〈*Metall.*〉 blast furnace
【高帽子】 gāomào·zi 1.(纸帽) tall paper hat (worn as a sign of humiliation) 2.(恭维话) flattery
【高锰酸钾】 gāoměngsuānjiǎ 〈*Chem.*〉 potassium permanganate
【高明】 gāomíng 1.(高超) brilliant; wise; intelligent 2.(高明的人) wise person; skillful person: 另请～。Find someone better qualified (than myself).
【高难】 gāonán high-leveled and difficult
【高攀】 gāopān make friends or claim ties of kinship with someone of a higher social position
【高频】 gāopín high frequency: 超～ ultrahigh frequency (UHF) / 甚～ very high frequency (VHF)
【高气压】 gāoqìyā high atmospheric pressure
【高强】 gāoqiáng excel in; be master of
【高强度】 gāoqiángdù high strength

【高跷】 gāoqiāo stilts：踩～ walk on stilts

【高清晰度电视】 gāoqīngxīdù diànshì high definition television（HDTV）

【高人一等】 gāorén-yīděng a cut above other people

【高山病】 gāoshānbìng mountain sickness

【高山族】 Gāoshānzú Gaoshan（中国少数民族，主要分布在台湾及福建）

【高尚】 gāoshàng noble；lofty：～的品质 noble character

【高烧】 gāoshāo high fever：发～ have a high fever

【高射机关枪】 gāoshè jīguānqiāng antiaircraft automatic

【高射炮】 gāoshèpào antiaircraft gun

【高深】 gāoshēn advanced；profound；recondite：～的造诣 high attainment

【高深莫测】 gāoshēn-mòcè too profound to be understood

【高手】 gāoshǒu past master；master-hand；ace

【高寿】 gāoshòu 1.（长寿）longevity；long life 2.〈*politeness*〉your venerable age：您今年～？May I ask how old you are?

【高耸】 gāosǒng stand tall and erect；tower：～入云 reach to the sky

【高速】 gāosù high speed：～发展 develop at top speed / ～行驶 go at high speed

【高速公路】 gāosù gōnglù highway（AmE.）；motorway（BrE.）；autoroute（Fr.）；autorostrada（Ital.）

【高谈阔论】 gāotán-kuòlùn indulge in loud and empty talk；talk volubly or bombastically；harangue

【高温】 gāowēn high temperature

【高温气候】 gāowēn qìhòu megathermal climate

【高温作业】 gāowēn zuòyè high-temperature operation

【高下】 gāoxià relative superiority；better：不分～ come out even；neck and neck

【高消费】 gāoxiāofèi high consumption

【高小】 gāoxiǎo higher primary school

【高校】 gāoxiào colleges and universities of higher learning

【高效】 gāoxiào high efficiency

【高效农业】 gāoxiào nóngyè highly efficient agriculture

【高新技术开发区】 gāoxīn jìshù kāifāqū new and high-tech development zone

【高薪】 gāoxīn high salary

【高薪阶层】 gāoxīn jiēcéng high-salary stratum

【高兴】 gāoxìng 1.（愉快）glad；happy；cheerful 2.（喜欢做）be willing to；be happy to

【高血压】 gāoxuèyā 〈*Med*.〉hypertension

【高压】 gāoyā 1.（高气压）high pressure 2.（高电压）high tension；high voltage 3.（残酷迫害）high-handed：～手段 high handed measure 4.（高血压）maximum pressure

【高压电】 gāoyādiàn high-tension electric current；high-voltage electric current

【高压锅】 gāoyāguō pressure cooker

【高压线】 gāoyāxiàn high-tension line；high-tension wire

【高雅】 gāoyǎ noble；elegant；exquisite

【高雅艺术】 gāoyǎ yìshù noble arts

【高音】 gāoyīn 1.〈*Music*〉high pitch；high-pitched voice 2.（演唱者）男～ tenor / 女～ soprano

【高音喇叭】 gāoyīn lǎ·ba tweeter；loudspeaker

【高音拾音器】 gāoyīn shíyīnqì 〈*Music*〉trebel pick-up；lead pick-up

【高原】 gāoyuán plateau；highland；tableland

【高瞻远瞩】 gāozhān-yuǎnzhǔ stand high and see far；take a broad and long-term view；show great foresight

【高涨】 gāozhǎng rise；upsurge；run high：情绪～ be in high spirits

【高招】 gāozhāo brilliant idea；clever suggest

【高着】 gāozhāo brilliant idea

【高枕无忧】 gāozhěn-wúyōu shake up the pillow and have a good sleep；sit back and relax

【高知】 gāozhī the intellectuals with senior professional titles

【高中】 gāozhōng senior middle school

【高姿态】 gāozītài high attitude

膏（gāo） 1.（脂肪；油）fat；grease；oil 2.（糊状物）paste；cream；ointment（另见“膏”gào）

【膏药】 gào·yao plaster：贴～ apply a plaster to

篙(gāo) punt-pole; barge-pole

羔(gāo) lamb; kid; fawn

【羔皮】 gāopí lambskin; kidskin; kid

【羔羊】 gāoyáng lamb; kid

糕[餻](gāo) cake; pudding

【糕饼】 gāobǐng 〈*dial.*〉cake

【糕点】 gāodiǎn cake; pastry

睾(gāo)

【睾丸】 gāowán testis; testicle

搞(gǎo) 1.(做;干) do; carry on; be engaged in: 他是～法律的。He is in the law. 2.(弄) cause; make; produce; work out: ～一个计划 draw up a plan 3.(搞出) set up; start; organize 4.(取得) get; get hold of; secure: ～到一批原材料 get a batch of raw materials

【搞臭】 gǎochòu discredit; put to shame

【搞出】 gǎochū work out; achieve; produce: 把方案～来 work out a plan

【搞错】 gǎocuò mistake: 我把他们两人～了。I mistook the one for the other.

【搞掉】 gǎodiào get rid of; do away with

【搞鬼】 gǎoguǐ play tricks; be up to some mischief

【搞好】 gǎohǎo make a good job of; do well: ～关系 build good relations (with sb.)

【搞坏】 gǎohuài damage; impair; spoil: 把身体～ impair one's health

【搞活】 gǎohuó invigorate; enliven: ～经济 invigorate the economy

【搞活市场】 gǎohuó shìchǎng enliven the market

【搞垮】 gǎokuǎ disrupt; undermine

【搞乱】 gáoluàn confuse; muddle; mess up: 把秩序～了 get the order confused

【搞上去】 gǎoshàngqù work together for still greater successes in

【搞卫生】 gǎowèishēng do cleaning

【搞糟】 gǎozāo mess up; make a mess (of)

镐(gǎo) pick; pickaxe

稿[稾](gǎo) 1.(谷物的茎) stalk of grain; straw 2.(草稿) rough copy; draft; sketch 3.(稿子) manuscript; original text

【稿费】 gǎofèi author's remuneration; contribution fee; payment for an article or book written

【稿件】 gǎojiàn manuscript; contribution

【稿纸】 gǎozhǐ paper for copying manuscripts

【稿子】 gǎo·zi 1.(草稿) draft; sketch 2.(稿件) manuscript; contribution 3.(腹稿) idea; plan

告(gào) 1.(陈述、解说) tell; inform; notify 2.(控告) accuse; go to law against; bring an action against 3.(为某事而请求) ask for; request; solicit 4.(表明) declare; announce

【告别】 gàobié 1.(离别) leave; part from 2.(向死者诀别) bid farewell to; say good-bye to: 向遗体～ pay one's last respects to the deceased

【告别仪式】 gàobié yíshì farewell ceremony

【告成】 gàochéng accomplish; complete: 大功～ the important task is accomplished

【告吹】 gàochuī fizzle out; fail: 野餐的计划～了。The plans for the picnic fizzled out.

【告辞】 gàocí take leave of; say good-bye

【告发】 gàofā report (an offender); inform against; lodge an accusation against; delate

【告急】 gàojí 1.(情况紧急) be in an emergency 2.(请求援救) report an emergency; ask for emergency help

【告假】 gàojià ask for leave

【告捷】 gàojié 1.(取得胜利) win victory 2.(报告得胜消息) report a victory

【告诫】【告戒】 gàojiè warn; admonish; exhort: ～某人要… exhort sb. to ...

【告竣】 gàojùn accomplish; finish; complete

【告老还乡】 gàolǎo-huánxiāng retire on account of old age and return to one's native place

【告密】 gàomì inform against sb.

【告示】 gào·shi official notice; bulletin; placard: 安民～ notice to reassure the people

【告诉】 gàosù tell; let know: ～某人某事 tell sb. (about) sth.; inform sb. of sth.

【告台湾同胞书】 Gào Táiwān Tóngbāoshū A Message to the Compatriots in Taiwan

(1979)
【告知】 gàozhī inform; notify
【告终】 gàozhōng come to an end; end up: 以失败～ end in failure
【告状】 gàozhuàng **1.**(到法院) go to law against sb.; bring a lawsuit against sb. **2.**(向上级或长辈诉说) lodge a complaint against sb. with his superior

诰 (gào) imperial mandate
【诰命】 gàomìng imperial mandate

锆 (gào) 〈*Chem.*〉 zirconium (元素符号 Zr)

膏 (gào) lubricate; oil (另见"膏"gāo)
【膏油】 gàoyóu lubricate; oil: 给轮子～ oil the axle of wheels /铰链得～了。The hinges need lubricating.

ge

戈 (gē)
【戈比】 gēbǐ copeck (俄罗斯辅币)
【戈壁】 gēbì Gobi

仡 (gē)
【仡佬族】 Gēlǎozú Gelao (中国少数民族, 主要分布在贵州)

疙 (gē)
【疙疸】 gē·da 同"疙瘩"
【疙瘩】 gē·da **1.**(疣或树瘤) a swelling on the skin; pimple; lump **2.**(团块状物) lump; knot **3.**(难解决的事) a knot in one's heart; hang-up

咯 (gē) (另见"咯"kǎ)
【咯噔】 gēdēng 〈*onomat.*〉 click: 听到～一声 hear a click
【咯咯】 gēgē **1.**(指母鸡叫声) cluck; chuckle; cackle: 母鸡一边～叫, 一边四处刨着。The hens were clucking and scratching around. **2.**(指笑声) chuckle; titter
【咯吱】 gēzhī 〈*onomat.*〉 creak; groan: 门～一声开了。The door creaked open.

胳[肐] (gē) (另见"胳"gā, gé)
【胳臂】 gē·bei arm
【胳膊】 gē·bo arm
【胳膊肘儿】 gē·bo zhǒur elbow

搁 (gē) **1.**(放) put: 他把杯子～在桌子上了。He put the cups on the table. **2.**(搁置) put aside; leave over; shelve
【搁浅】 gēqiǎn **1.**(指船) run aground; be stranded **2.**(遇阻停顿) be held up; be at a deadlock; reach a deadlock: 会谈～了。The negotiations have come to a deadlock.
【搁置】 gēzhì shelve; lay aside; pigeonhole

哥 (gē) (elder) brother
【哥哥】 gē·ge (elder) brother
【哥们儿】 gē·menr **1.**(弟兄们) brothers **2.**(用于朋友间) buddies; pals

歌 (gē) **1.**(歌曲) song: 民～ folk song **2.**(唱) sing
【歌唱】 gēchàng sing
【歌唱家】 gēchàngjiā singer; vocalist
【歌词】 gēcí words of a song
【歌功颂德】 gēgōng-sòngdé sing the praises of sb.; eulogize sb's virtues and achievements
【歌剧】 gējù opera
【歌谱】 gēpǔ music of a song
【歌曲】 gēqǔ song
【歌声】 gēshēng singing; song of singing
【歌手】 gēshǒu singer; vocalist
【歌颂】 gēsòng sing the praises of; extol; eulogize
【歌坛】 gētán circles of vocal music
【歌舞】 gēwǔ song and dance
【歌星】 gēxīng famous singer
【歌谣】 gēyáo ballad; folk song; nursery rhyme
【歌咏】 gēyǒng singing: ～比赛 singing contest

鸽 (gē) pigeon; dove: 信～ carrier pigeon; homing pigeon
【鸽子】 gē·zi pigeon; dove

割 (gē) cut: ～草 cut the grass / 他～破了手指。He cut his finger.
【割爱】 gē'ài give away one's beloved thing
【割除】 gēchú cut off; cut out; excise
【割断】 gēduàn sever; cut off: ～联系 sever relations; cut off connections (with)

【割胶】 gējiāo tap rubber; rubber tapping (n.)

【割据】 gējù set up a separatist regime by force of arms: 军阀～ separatist warlord regimes

【割礼】 gēlǐ 〈*Islam*〉 circumcision

【割裂】 gēliè cut apart; separate; isolate: 把问题～开来看 look at the problem in isolation

【割让】 gēràng cede: ～领土 cede territory

【割绒】 gēróng 〈*Textiles*〉 cut velvet

【割舍】 gēshě give up; part with

革 (gé) 1.(皮革) leather; hide: ～制品 leather goods / 人造～ imitation leather 2.(改变) change; transform 3.(开除) remove from office; expel

【革除】 géchú 1.(去掉) abolish; get rid of 2.(开除) expel; dismiss; remove from office

【革命】 gémìng 1.(社会变革) revolution; revolutionary (adj.) 2.(根本改革) revolution; reform: 工业～ industrial revolution

【革命导师】 gémìng dǎoshī a teacher of the revolution

【革命公墓】 gémìng gōngmù cemetery for revolutionaries

【革命化】 gémìnghuà revolutionize; revolutionization (n.)

【革命烈士】 gémìng lièshì revolutionary martyr

【革命英雄主义】 gémìng yīngxióng zhǔyì revolutionary heroism

【革新】 géxīn innovation: 技术～ technological innovation

【革新派】 géxīnpài reform party; reformers

【革职】 gézhí remove from office; cashier

蛤 (gé) clam
(另见"蛤"há)

【蛤蚧】 géjiè red-spotted lizard

【蛤蜊】 gé·lí clam

胳 (gé)
(另见"胳"gā, gē)

【胳肢】 gé·zhi tickle sb.; give sb. a tickle

阁 (gé) 1.(亭) pavilion 2.(内阁) cabinet: 组～ form a cabinet

【阁楼】 gélóu attic; penthouse; garret

【阁下】 géxià 1.(直接称呼) Your Excellency 2.(间接称呼) His or Her Excellency

格 (gé) 1.(方格) squares formed by crossed lines; check 2.(格子) division (horizontal or otherwise) 3.(格式) standard; pattern; style: 别具一～ have a style of its own

【格调】 gédiào 1.(指作品的) style: 文学～ literary style / 艺术～ artistic style 2.(指人的) one's style of work as well as one's moral quality

【格斗】 gédòu wrestling; fistfight

【格尔木】 Gé'ěrmù 〈place〉 Golmud

【格格不入】 gégé-bùrù incompatible with; out of tune with; out of one's element; like a square peg in a round hole

【格局】 géjú pattern; setup; structure: 经济循环新～ a new pattern of circulation / 两极～ bipolar structure

【格林尼治时间】 Gélínnízhì shíjiān Greenwich mean time

【格式】 gé·shi form; pattern: 文件～ the form of an document

【格式化】 géshìhuà 〈*Computer*〉 format

【格外】 géwài 1.〈*adv.*〉 especially; all the more 2.(额外) extra; additional

【格言】 géyán maxim; motto; aphorism

【格纸】 gézhǐ ruled paper

【格子】 gé·zi check; chequer: 打～ draw chequers

【格子布】 gé·zibù checked fabric

【格子花呢】 gé·zi huāní tartan

隔[隔] (gé) 1.(隔开) separate; partition; stand or lie between 2.(间隔) at a distance from; after or at an interval of: 相～甚远 at a great distance from each other

【隔壁】 gébì next door: ～邻居 next-door neighbor

【隔断】 géduàn cut off; separate; obstruct

【隔断】 gé·duan 〈*Archit.*〉 partition (wall, board, etc.)

【隔行】 géháng different in profession

【隔行如隔山】 géháng rú géshān difference in profession makes one feel worlds apart

【隔阂】 géhé 1.(指思想上的) estrangement; misunderstanding: 消除～ remove the misunderstanding 2.(指语言上的) barrier: 语

言的～ language barrier
【隔绝】 géjué completely cut off; isolated: 音信～ (with) all news cut off
【隔离】 gélí keep apart; isolate; segregate
【隔离舱】 gélícāng 〈*Naut*.〉 cofferdam
【隔膜】 gémó **1.** (情意不相通) lack of mutual understanding **2.** (外行) unfamiliar with
【隔墙有耳】 géqiáng-yǒuěr walls have ears; beware of eaves-droppers
【隔音】 géyīn sound insulation
【隔音材料】 géyīn cáiliào acoustic material; soundproof material
【隔音室】 géyīnshì soundproof room

嗝 (gé) **1.** (饱嗝) belch **2.** (呃逆) hiccup: 打～ have the hiccups

膈 (gé) 〈*Anat*.〉 diaphragm

【膈膜】 gémó 〈*Anat*.〉 diaphragm

镉 (gé) 〈*Chem*.〉 cadmium (元素符号 Cd)

【镉电池】 gédiànchí cadmium cell

个 [個、箇] (gè) **1.** 〈*classifier*〉 10～苹果 ten apples / 一～玩具汽车 a toy car **2.** (单独的) individual

【个别】 gèbié **1.** (单个) individual; specific: ～辅导 individual coaching **2.** (极少数) very few; one or two; exceptional: ～现象 exceptional phenomenon
【个别项目】 gèbié xiàngmù end item
【个儿】 gèr **1.** (大小) size; height; stature **2.** (一个个的人、物) persons or things taken singly
【个人】 gèrén **1.** (一个人) individual (person): 以她～的名义 in her own name **2.** (自称) I
【个人财产】 gèrén cháichǎn personal property
【个人崇拜】 gèrén chóngbài cult of the individual; personality cult
【个人得失】 gèrén déshī personal gains or losses
【个人负责】 gèrén fùzé individual responsibility
【个人迷信】 gèrén míxìn cult of the individual; personality cult
【个人名誉】 gèrén míngyù personal reputation
【个人收入】 gèrén shōurù personal income
【个人所得税】 gèrén suǒdéshuì individual income tax; personal income tax
【个人卫生】 gèrén wèishéng personal hygiene
【个人野心】 gèrén yěxīn personal ambition
【个人责任】 gèrén zérèn personal liability
【个人主义】 gèrén zhǔyì individualism
【个体】 gètǐ individual
【个体户】 gètǐhù self-employed individual or household; private businessman
【个体经济】 gètǐ jīngjì individual economy
【个体劳动者】 gètǐ láodòngzhě self-employed laborer
【个体所有制】 gètǐ shuǒyǒuzhì individual ownership
【个性】 gèxìng individual character; individuality; personality
【个展】 gèzhǎn individual exhibition; individual exposition
【个子】 gè·zi height; stature; build: ～高 tall of stature

各 (gè) each; every; various; different

【各半】 gèbàn half and half; fifty-fifty
【各别】 gèbié **1.** (区别) distinct; different: ～对待 treat differently; treat each on its (his, etc.) own merits **2.** (特殊) peculiar; out of the ordinary
【各不相同】 gèbù-xiāngtóng have nothing in common with each other
【各持己见】 gèchí-jǐjiàn each sticks to his own view
【各得其所】 gèdé-qísuǒ each is in his proper place; each is properly provided for
【各个】 gègè **1.** (每个) each; every; various **2.** (分别) one by one; separately: ～解决 piecemeal solution
【各行各业】 gèháng-gèyè all trades and professions; the various walks of life
【各级】 gèjí all or different levels
【各界】 gèjiè all walks of life; all circles: ～朋友 friends of various circles
【各尽其责】 gèjìn-qízé each one does his duty
【各就各位】 gèjiù-gèwèi on your marks
【各拉丹东峰】 Gèlādān dōngfēng 〈plane〉 Geladaindong
【各人】 gèrén each one; everyone

【各色】 gèsè of all kinds; of every description: ～货物 goods of all kinds

【各抒己见】 gèshū-jǐjiàn each airs his own views

【各位】 gèwèi **1.**（大家）everybody **2.**（每个）every

【各行其是】 gèxíng-qíshì each does what he thinks is right; each goes his own way

【各有所长】 gèyǒu-suǒcháng each has his own strong points

【各执一词】 gèzhí-yìcí each sticks to his own version or argument

【各自】 gèzì each; respective

【各自为政】 gèzì-wéizhèng each does things in his own way

硌（gè） hurt; rub against: 砂子～我脚。The grit hurts my foot.

【硌窝儿鸡蛋】 gèwōr jīdàn cracked egg

铬（gè） 〈*Chem.*〉chromium（元素符号 Cr）

【铬钢】 gègāng 〈*Metall.*〉chromium steel; chrome steel

gei

给（gěi） **1.**（送给）give; grant: ～某人某物 give sb. sth. **2.**（交给）书已经交～她了。I' ve handed the book to her. **3.**（为）for; for the benefit of **4.**（让）let; allow: ～我看看。Let me have a look.

（另见"给"jǐ）

【给以】 gěiyǐ give; grant: ～帮助 give help / ～好评 give good opinions; accord commendation

gen

根（gēn） **1.**〈*Bot.*〉root: 树～ root of a tree / 连～拔 pull up by the root **2.**〈*Math.*〉root: 立方～ cube root / 平方～ square root **3.**〈*Chem.*〉radical **4.**（下部；基部）root; foot; base: 墙～ the foot of a wall **5.**（本原）cause; origin; source; root: 祸～ the root of trouble **6.**（彻底）thoroughly; completely

【根本】 gēnběn **1.**（最重要的）basic; fundamental; essential; cardinal: 维护…～利益 defend the fundamental interests **2.**（从来）at all: 这～行不通。This is utterly impracticable. **3.**（彻底）radically; thoroughly: ～否定 condemn fundamentally

【根本法】 gēnběnfǎ fundamental law

【根除】 gēnchú thoroughly do away with; eradicate; root out; eliminate

【根底】 gēndǐ **1.**（基础）foundation: 汉语～好 have a solid foundation in Chinese **2.**（底细）cause; root

【根基】 gēnjī foundation; basis: 打好～ lay a solid foundation

【根据】 gēnjù **1.**（依据）on the basis of; according to; in the light of; in line with: ～初步测算 according to an initial estimate / ～天气预报 according to the weather forecast **2.**（作为根据的事）basis; grounds; foundation: 说话要有～。One should avoid making assertions without good grounds.

【根据地】 gēnjùdì base area; base

【根绝】 gēnjué stamp out; eradicate; exterminate

【根深蒂固】 gēnshēn-dìgù have deep roots in ...

【根由】 gēnyóu cause; origin

【根源】 gēnyuán source; origin; root: 社会～ social cause

【根治】 gēnzhì effect a radical cure; cure once and for all; bring under permanent control

【根子】 gēn·zi root; source; origin

跟（gēn） **1.**（脚跟）heel: 左脚～ heel of the left foot **2.**（跟随）follow **3.**〈*conj.*〉and

【跟班】 gēnbān （work）on shifts with workers

【跟风】 gēnfēng follow the trend

【跟骨】 gēngǔ 〈*Anat.*〉calcaneum; heelbone

【跟脚】 gēnjiǎo **1.**（鞋穿着合适）fit well **2.**（随即）close upon sb's heels

【跟前】 gēnqián **1.**（附近）in front of; close to; near: 在窗户～ in front of the window **2.**（身边）living with one: 他～只有一女。He has only a daughter living with him.

【跟上】 gēn·shang keep pace with; catch up with; keep abreast of: ～形势 keep abreast of the current situation

【跟随】 gēnsuí 1.(在后面跟着行动) follow; go after: ～左右 follow one wherever one goes 2.(随从人员) retinue

【跟头】 gēn·tou 1.(摔倒) fall: 摔～ have a fall 2.(指体操动作) somersault: 翻个～ turn somersault

【跟踪】 gēnzōng follow the tracks of

【跟踪调查】 gēnzōng diàochá follow-up survey

【跟踪站】 gēnzōngzhàn tracking station

亘[亙](gèn) extend; stretch

【亘古及今】 gèngǔ-jíjīn from time immemorial down to the present day

【亘古未有】 gèngǔ-wèiyǒu There was none ever since the beginning of the age.

geng

更(gēng) 1.(更换) change; replace 2.(经历) experience

(另见"更"gèng)

【更迭】 gēngdié alternate; change

【更动】 gēngdòng change; alter

【更改】 gēnggǎi change; alter

【更换】 gēnghuàn change; replace; substitute

【更年期】 gēngniánqī climacteric; menopause

【更深】 gēngshēn in the dead of night

【更生】 gēngshēng 1.(重新得到生命) regenerate; revive 2.(再生) renew

【更替】 gēngtì replace

【更新】 gēngxīn renew; replace: ～观念 renew one's concept / ～设备 replace the equipment

【更新改造】 gēngxīn gǎizhào make replacements and technical innovations

【更新换代】 gēngxīn-huàndài replace sth. old with sth. new; replace a product with one of new generation: 产品～ production renewal and change

【更衣】 gēngyī change one's clothes

【更衣室】 gēngyīshì change-room; changing room; locker room

【更正】 gēngzhèng make corrections: 作必要的～ make necessary corrections

耕(gēng) plough; till

【耕畜】 gēngchù farm animal

【耕地】 gēngdì 1.(翻松土地) plough; till 2.(农田) cultivated land: 休～ fallow land / ～面积 area under cultivation; cultivated area

【耕具】 gēngjù tillage implements

【耕牛】 gēngniú farm cattle

【耕耘】 gēngyún ploughing and weeding; cultivation

【耕者有其田】 gēngzhě yǒu qí tián land to the tiller

【耕种】 gēngzhòng till; cultivate

【耕作】 gēngzuò tillage; cultivation; farming

羹(gēng) thick soup: 鸡蛋～ egg custard / 水果～ thick fruit soup

【羹匙】 gēngchí spoon; soupspoon

埂(gěng) 1.(田埂) a low bank of earth between fields 2.(泥筑的堤防) an earth dike 3.(小山丘) a long, narrow mound

哽(gěng) choke (with emotion); feel a lump in one's throat

【哽咽】 gěngyè choke with sobs

梗(gěng) 1.(植物枝茎) stalk; stem: 茶叶～ tea stalks 2.(挺直) straighten 3.(阻碍) obstruct; block: 从中作～ place obstacles in the way

【梗概】 gěnggài broad outline; main idea; gist: 影片的故事～ the gist of a film

【梗塞】 gěngsè 1.(阻塞) block; obstruct; clog: 道路～ with the road blocked up / 交通～ traffic jam 2.(动脉堵塞) infarction: 心肌～ myocardial infarction

【梗咽】 gěngyè choke with sobs

【梗直】 gěngzhí honest and frank; upright

【梗阻】 gěngzǔ 1.(拦挡) block; obstruct; hamper 2.〈*Med.*〉 obstruction: 肠～ intestinal obstruction / 幽门～ pyloric obstruction

耿(gěng) 1.(光明) bright 2.(耿耿) dedicated 3.(耿直) honest and just; upright

【耿耿】 gěnggěng 1.(忠诚) devoted; dedicated: 忠心～ loyal and faithful 2.(有心事) have sth. on one's mind; be troubled

【耿耿于怀】 gěnggěng-yúhuái brood on; take sth. to heart

【耿直】 gěngzhí honest and frank; upright: 秉性～ be upright by nature

更(gèng) 1.(更加) more; still more; even more: 这样～好。It's better this

way 2.(再；又) further; furthermore; what is more：～进一步地调查此事 inquire further into the matter
(另见"更"gēng)

【更加】 gèngjiā more; still more; even more：情况～复杂了。The situation became even more complicated.

【更上一层楼】 gèngshàng yīcénglóu achieve an even higher goal; score even greater achievements

【更有甚者】 gèngyǒushènzhě What is more

gong

工 (gōng) 1.(工人) worker; workman 2.(工人阶级) the working class 3.(工作) work; labor 4.(工程) (construction) project 5.(工业) industry 6.(一个劳动日的工作) man-day 7.(技术和技术修养) skill; craftsmanship 8.(善于) be versed in; be good at 9.(工程师) engineer：张～ engineer Zhang

【工本】 gōngběn cost (of production)：不惜～ spare no expense

【工本费】 gōngběnfèi cost of production

【工兵】 gōngbīng engineer

【工厂】 gōngchǎng factory; mill; plant; works

【工场】 gōngchǎng workshop

【工潮】 gōngcháo worker's demonstration; strike movement

【工程】 gōngchéng engineering; project：电机～ electrical engineering / "骨干"～ 'backbone' projects / 社会系统～ social systems engineering / 水利～ water conservancy project / 土木～ civil engineering

【工程兵】 gōngchéngbīng 1.(工兵) engineer 2.(工程兵部队) engineer troops; engineer units

【工程承包】 gōngchéng chéngbāo contract engineering; project contract

【工程技术人员】 gōngchéng jìshù rényuán engineers and technicians

【工程师】 gōngchéngshī engineer：总～ chief engineer

【工地】 gōngdì building site; construction site

【工读】 gōngdú 1.(半工半读) part work and part study 2.(工读教育) reformatory

【工读生】 gōngdúshēng 1.(半工半读的学生) part-time student 2.(工读学校学生) student of a reformatory school

【工读学校】 gōngdú xuéxiào reformatory school; approved school

【工段】 gōngduàn 1.(施工单位) a section of a construction project 2.(车间下的单位) workshop section

【工段长】 gōngduànzhǎng section chief

【工蜂】 gōngfēng worker bee

【工夫】 gōng·fu 1.(时间) time：需要一个月的～ will take a month's time 2.(本领) workmanship; skill; art 3.(化学费) work; labor; effort 4.(指武术) kung fu

【工会】 gōnghuì trade union; labor union

【工会会员】 gōnghuì huìyuán member of a trade union

【工价】 gōngjià labor cost

【工间操】 gōngjiāncāo work-break exercises

【工件】 gōngjiàn workpiece; work

【工匠】 gōngjiàng craftsman; artisan

【工交战线】 gōngjiāo zhànxiàn the industry and transportation and communications front; industry and communications

【工具】 gōngjù tool; means; instrument; implement

【工具包】 gōngjùbāo saddlebag

【工具书】 gōngjùshū reference book

【工具箱】 gōngjùxiāng toolbox; tool kit; workbox

【工科】 gōngkē engineering course

【工科大学】 gōngkē dàxué college of engineering

【工矿企业】 gōngkuàng qǐyè industrial and mining enterprises

【工龄】 gōnglíng length of service; standing; seniority：一个有 20 年～ 的工人 a worker of twenty years' standing

【工农】 gōngnóng workers and peasants

【工农业】 gōngnóngyè industry and agriculture

【工农业总产值】 gōngnóngyè zǒngchǎnzhí gross output value of industry and agriculture

【工期】 gōngqī time limit for a project

【工钱】 gōng·qian 1.(作零活的报酬) money paid for odd jobs; charge for a service 2.(工

资）wages; pay

【工人】 gōng·rén worker; workman: 产业～ industrial worker / 农业～ farm worker

【工人阶级】 gōngrén jiējí the working class

【工人俱乐部】 gōngrén jùlèbù worker's club

【工人运动】 gōngrén yùndòng labor movement

【工伤】 gōngshāng injury suffered on the job; industrial injury

【工伤事故】 gōngshāng shìgù industrial accident

【工商行】 gōngshāngháng the Bank of Industry and Commerce of China

【工商界】 gōngshāngjiè industrial and commercial circles; business circles

【工商界人士】 gōngshāngjiè rénshì industrialists and businessmen

【工商联】 gōngshānglián association of industry and commerce

【工商业】 gōngshāngyè industry and commerce: 私营～ privately owned industrial and commercial enterprises

【工商业者】 gōngshāngyèzhě industrialists and businessmen

【工时】 gōngshí man-hour

【工事】 gōngshì fortifications; defense works: 防御～ defense works

【工头】 gōngtóu overseer; foreman

【工效】 gōngxiào work efficiency

【工序】 gōngxù working procedure; process

【工学院】 gōngxuéyuàn engineering college

【工业】 gōngyè industry; industrial (adj.): 基础～ basic industry / 加工～ processing industry / 汽车～ automobile industry

【工业国】 gōngyèguó industrialized country

【工业化】 gōngyèhuà industrialization; industrialize (v.); industrialized (adj.): ～国家 industrialized countries

【工业品】 gōngyèpǐng industrial products; manufactured goods

【工业企业】 gōngyè qǐyè industrial enterprise

【工业园区】 gōngyè yuánqū industrial park

【工业总产值】 gōngyè zǒngchǎnzhí gross value of industrial output

【工艺】 gōngyì **1.**（加工的工艺）technology; technological (adj.) **2.**（手工艺）handicraft

【工艺流程】 gōngyì liúchéng technological process

【工艺品】 gōngyìpǐng handicraft article; handiwork; handicraft

【工贼】 gōngzéi scab

【工长】 gōngzhǎng foreman; section chief

【工整】 gōngzhěng carefully and neatly done: 字迹～ neatly lettered

【工种】 gōngzhǒng type of work in production

【工资】 gōngzī wages; pay: 浮动～ floating wages / 基本～ basic wages / 计件～ piece rate wage / 计时～ payment by the hour; time wage / 发～ pay sb. the wages; give sb. the pay / 补发～ give the back pay due to . . .

【工资表】 gōngzībiǎo payroll; pay sheet

【工资袋】 gōngzīdài pay envelope (AmE.); pay packet (BrE.)

【工资级别】 gōngzī jíbié wage scale

【工资增长机制】 gōngzī zēngzhǎng jīzhì mechanism for normal increase of wages

【工字钢】 gōngzìgāng I-steel

【工作】 gōngzuò **1.**（人劳动；机器运行）work **2.**（职业）job: 分配～ assign jobs **3.**（任务）task

【工作餐】 gōngzuòcān working lunch; working dinner

【工作访问】 gōngzuò fǎngwèn working visit

【工作服】 gōngzuòfú work clothes; boiler suit

【工作狂】 gōngzuòkuáng workaholic

【工作经验】 gōngzuò jīngyàn work experience

【工作量】 gōngzuòliàng amount of work; work load

【工作人员】 gōngzuò rényuán working personnel; staff member; functionary

【工作日】 gōngzuòrì **1.**（一天中工作的时间）man-day **2.**（非休息日）workday; working day

【工作台】 gōngzuòtái working table

【工作午餐】 gōngzuò wǔcān working lunch

【工作语言】 gōngzuò yǔyán working language

【工作早餐】 gōngzuò zǎocān working breakfast

【工作站】 gōngzuòzhàn workstation

【工作者】 gōngzuòzhě worker: 教育～ educational worker / 文艺～ literary and art workers; writers and artists

【工作证】 gōngzuòzhèng employee's card; I. D. card

功 (gōng) 1.(功劳) meritorious service; merit; exploit 2.(功效) achievement; result: 事半～倍 half the amount of work brings double the results 3.(技术修养) skill 4.〈*Physics*〉 work

【功败垂成】 gōngbài-chuíchéng suffer defeat on the verge of success; fall in the last hurdle; fail before a success

【功臣】 gōngchén a person who has rendered outstanding service

【功成身退】 gōngchéng-shēntuì retire from political life after winning tremendous successes, retire from public life after a great work is done

【功大于过】 gōngdàyúguò one's achievements outweigh one's errors

【功到自然成】 gōngdào zìránchéng constant effort yields sure success

【功夫】 gōng·fu 1.(时间) time: 需要一个月的～ will take a month's time 2.(本领) workmanship; skill; art 3.(花费力气) work; labor; effort 4.(指武术) kung fu

【功夫茶】 gōng·fuchá kung fu tea

【功夫片】 gōng·fupiàn kung fu movie; kung fu film

【功过不分】 gōngguò-bùfēn no distinction is made between merits and demerits

【功过相抵】 gōngguò xiāngdǐ merits offset faults; deserts equal faults

【功绩】 gōngjì merits and achievements; contribution

【功课】 gōngkè schoolwork; homework: 做～ do one's homework

【功劳】 gōng·láo contribution; meritorious service; credit: 立下了～ have great achievements to one's credit

【功利】 gōnglì 1.(功效和利益) utility; material gain 2.(功名利禄) position and wealth

【功率】 gōnglǜ 〈*Physics*〉 power: 这台发动机的～有多大? What is the power of this engine?

【功名】 gōngmíng scholarly honor or official rank (in feudal times)

【功能】 gōngnéng function; functional (adj.)

【功效】 gōngxiào efficacy; effect

【功勋】 gōngxūn exploit; meritorious service: 立下了不朽的～ have performed immortal feats

【功业】 gōngyè exploits; achievements

【功用】 gōngyòng function; use

攻 (gōng) 1.(攻打) attack; take the offensive: ～城 attack a city 2.(指责) accuse; charge 3.(致力研究) study; specialize in

【攻打】 gōngdǎ attack; assault; assail

【攻读】 gōngdú 1.(勤奋学习) assiduously study; diligently study 2.(钻研) specialize in

【攻关】 gōngguān 1.(攻打要隘) storm a strategic pass 2.(解决关键性问题) tackle key problems; solve a key problem: 技术～ surmount a technical difficulty

【攻击】 gōngjī 1.(进攻) attack; assault; launch an offensive: 发起～ launch a offensive 2.(恶意指摘) accuse; charge; vilify: 人身～ personal attack

【攻击区】 gōngjīqū 〈*Volleyball*〉 attack area

【攻击手】 gōngjìshǒu 〈*Hondball*〉 attacker

【攻击线】 gōngjìxiàn 〈*Volleyball*〉 attack line

【攻坚】 gōngjiān 1.(攻打敌人坚固工事) storm fortifications; assault fortified positions 2.(比喻解决难题) tackle key problem

【攻克】 gōngkè capture; take: ～城池 capture a city / ～技术难关 solve a difficult technical problem

【攻破】 gōngpò break through

【攻其不备】 gōngqí-búbèi strike where or when the enemy is unprepared; take sb. by surprise; catch sb. unawares

【攻其一点,不及其余】 gōng qí yī diǎn, bù jí qí yǔ attack sb. for a single fault without considering his other aspects; seize upon one point and ignore the overall picture

【攻势】 gōngshì offensive: 采取～ take the offensive / 冬季～ winter offensive

【攻守同盟】 gōng shǒu tóngméng an agreement made to conceal each other's crime

【攻陷】 gōngxiàn capture; storm

【攻占】 gōngzhàn attack and occupy; storm and capture

弓（gōng） 1.（箭弓）bow：拉～ pull the bow 2.（使弯曲）bend; arch; bow：～着背走路 **walk with one's back bent forward** 3.（弓子）anything bow-shaped：小提琴的～ bow of a violin

【弓背】 gōngbèi 1.（弓的背儿）back of a bow 2.（曲背）hunchbacked; stooping

【弓箭】 gōngjiàn bow and arrow

【弓锯】 gōngjù bow saw

【弓弦】 gōngxián bowstring

【弓弦乐器】 gōngxián yuèqì bowed stringed instrument; bowed string instrument

【弓形】 gōngxíng 1.〈*Math*.〉segment of a circle 2.（像弓的形状）bow-shaped; arched; curved

【弓子】 gōng·zi 1.（箭弓）bow 2.（弓形物）anything bow-shaped

躬［躳］（gōng） 1.（亲自）personally 2.（弯下）bend forward; bow

【躬亲】 gōngqīn attend to personally：事必～ attend to everything personally

【躬行实践】 gōngxíng shíjiàn practice what one preaches

公（gōng） 1.（国家或集体的）public; state-owned; collective：交～ turn over to the authorities 2.（共同的）common; general 3.（公制的）metric 4.（使公开）make public 5.（公平；公正）equitable; impartial; fair; just：秉～办理 handle affairs equitably 6.（公事）public affairs; official business：因～外出 be away on official business 7.（雄性的）male（animal）

【公安部】 gōng'ānbù the Ministry of Public Security

【公安机关】 gōng'ān jīguān public security organs

【公安局】 gōng'ānjú public security bureau

【公安人员】 gōng'ān rényuán public security officer

【公办】 gōngbàn state-run; state owned

【公报】 gōngbào communiqué; bulletin：新闻～ press communiqué

【公布】 gōngbù announce; publish; make public：～开会日期 announce the date of the meeting / ～名单 publish a name list

【公厕】 gōngcè public lavatory; latrine

【公差】 gōngchā 1.〈*Math*.〉common difference 2.〈*Mech*.〉tolerance

【公差】 gōngchāi 1.（临时公务）public errand; noncombatant duty：出～ go on a public errand; go on official business; perform noncombatant duty 2.（差役）a person on a public errand

【公尺】 gōngchǐ meter; metre（m.）

【公出】 gōngchū be away on official business

【公畜】 gōngchù male animal; stud

【公道】 gōngdào 1.（正义）justice：主持～ uphold justice 2.（公平）fair; just; reasonable; impartial：办事～ be evenhanded; be impartial / 价钱～。The price is reasonable.

【公房商品化】 gōngfáng shāngpǐnhuà commercializing public housing

【公费】 gōngfèi government-funded; at public expense

【公费留学生】 gōngfèi liúxuéshēng state-funded student

【公费医疗】 gōngfèi yīliáo free medical service; public health services

【公愤】 gōngfèn public indignation; popular anger：引起～ arouse public indignation

【公干】 gōnggàn important business

【公告】 gōnggào announcement; proclamation

【公格尔九别峰】 Gōnggé'ěrjiǔbiéfēng〈place〉Kongur Tobe Feng

【公格尔山】 Gōnggé'ěrshān〈place〉Kongur Shan

【公公】 gōng·gong 1.（丈夫之父）husband's father; father-in-law 2.（祖父）grandfather 3.（尊称年老男子）grandpa; grandad

【公共】 gōnggòng public; common; communal

【公共财产】 gōnggòng cáichǎn public property

【公共福利】 gōnggòng fúlì public welfare

【公共关系】 gōnggòng guān·xì public relations

【公共交通】 gōnggòng jiāotōng mass transit; public transit

【公共汽车】 gōnggòng qìchē bus

【公共汽车站】 gōnggòng qìchēzhàn bus stop

【公共汽车站牌】 gōnggòng qìchēzhànpái bus stop sign

【公共汽车专用车道】 gōnggòng qìchē

zhuānyòng chēdào bus lane
【公共卫生】 gōnggòng wèishēng public health
【公共秩序】 gōnggòng zhìxù public order
【公关】 gōngguān public relations
【公关小姐】 gōngguān xiǎojiě public relations miss; public relations officer
【公馆】 gōngguǎn residence; mansion
【公海】 gōnghǎi high seas
【公害】 gōnghài **1.**（环境污染）environmental pollution **2.**（对公众有害）social effects of pollution：消除～ eliminate the public hazard
【公函】 gōnghán official letter
【公积金】 gōngjījīn accumulation fund
【公家】 gōng·jia the state; the public; the organization
【公检法】 gōngjiǎnfǎ public security organs, procuratorial organs and people's courts
【公交】 gōngjiāo public transit
【公教人员】 gōngjiào rényuán government employees and teachers
【公斤】 gōngjīn kilogram (kg.); kilo
【公爵】 gōngjué **1.**（指人）duke; duchess (f.); ducal (adj.) **2.**（指爵位）dukedom
【公开】 gōngkāi **1.**（不加隐蔽）open; overt; public：～的秘密 an open secret **2.**（使秘密公开）make public; make known to the public
【公开化】 gōngkāihuà be brought into the open; come out into the open
【公开信】 gōngkāixìn open letter
【公开招标】 gōngkāi zhāobiāo competitive bidding; open tender
【公筷】 gōngkuài serving chopsticks
【公款】 gōngkuǎn public money; public funds：挥霍～ squander public funds / 挪用～ misappropriate public funds
【公款旅游】 gōngkuǎn lǚyóu travel at public expense
【公款请客】 gōngkuǎn qǐngkè squander public money on feasting
【公里】 gōnglǐ kilometer (km.)
【公理】 gōnglǐ **1.**（公认的道理）generally acknowledged truth; self-evident truth **2.** 〈*Math.*〉 axiom
【公历】 gōnglì the Gregorian calendar
【公立】 gōnglì public; established and maintained by the government：～学校 public school
【公粮】 gōngliáng agricultural tax paid in grain：缴～ pay agricultural tax in grain
【公路】 gōnglù highway; road：高速～ highway; motorway
【公路桥】 gōnglùqiáo highway bridge
【公路运输】 gōnglù yùnshū highway transportation
【公论】 gōnglùn public opinion; verdict of the masses
【公民】 gōngmín citizen
【公民权】 gōngmínquán civil rights; citizenship; citizen's rights
【公民投票】 gōngmín tóupiào plebiscite
【公亩】 gōngmǔ are (a.)
【公墓】 gōngmù cemetery
【公派】 gōngpài sent by the state; sent by a unit
【公判】 gōngpàn public trial; open trial
【公平】 gōng·píng fair; just; impartial; equitable：～待人 deal fairly with someone / ～合理 fair and reasonable / ～交易 fair deal / 买卖～ be fair in buying and selling; buy and sell at reasonable prices
【公婆】 gōngpó parents-in-law; husband's father and mother
【公仆】 gōngpú public servant
【公勤人员】 gōngqín rényuán service personnel in an office; office attendants
【公顷】 gōngqǐng hectare (ha.)
【公然】 gōngrán 〈*derog.*〉 openly; undisguisedly; brazenly：～反对 openly oppose
【公认】 gōngrèn established; universally accepted; generally acknowledged：～的国际法准则 established principles of international law / ～的国际关系原则 generally-accepted principles of international relations
【公社】 gōngshè **1.**（原始公社）primitive commune **2.**（政权形式）commune：人民～ people's commune
【公审】 gōngshěn 〈*Law*〉 public trial
【公使】 gōngshǐ envoy; minister
【公使馆】 gōngshǐguǎn legation
【公使衔参赞】 gōngshǐxián cānzàn counsellor with the rank of minister; minister-counsel-

lor

【公式】 gōngshì 1.〈*Math.*〉formula：一个数学～ a mathematical formula 2.（泛指固定的方式方法）formulistic method

【公事】 gōngshì 1.（公家的事）public affairs; official business 2.（公文）official document

【公事包】 gōngshìbāo briefcase; portfolio

【公事公办】 gōngshì gōngbàn do official business according to official principles; not let personal considerations interfere with one's execution of public duty

【公式化】 gōngshìhuà 1.（文艺创作中的一种倾向）formulism 2.（用固定方式处理问题）formulistic; stereotyped

【公署】 gōngshǔ government office：（地区）专员～ prefectural commissioner's office

【公司】 gōngsī company; corporation：保险～ insurance company / 进出口～ import and export corporation

【公私分明】 gōng-sī fēnmíng be scrupulous in separating public from private interests

【公私合营】 gōng-sī héyíng joint state-private ownership

【公私兼顾】 gōng-sī jiāngù give consideration to both public and private interests

【公诉】 gōngsù 〈*Law*〉public prosecution：提起～ institute prosecution; prefer a public charge

【公诉人】 gōngsùrén 〈*Law*〉public prosecutor; the prosecution

【公文】 gōngwén official document

【公文箱】 gōngwénxiāng briefcase

【公务】 gōngwù public affairs; official business

【公务护照】 gōngwù hùzhào service passport

【公务人员】 gōngwù rényuán government functionary

【公务员】 gōngwùyuán 1.（政府机关工作人员）public servant 2.（勤杂人员）orderly

【公物】 gōngwù public property

【公休】 gōngxiū general holiday; official holiday

【公演】 gōngyǎn perform in public; give a performance

【公益】 gōngyì public good; public welfare

【公益劳动】 gōngyì láodòng labor for public good

【公用】 gōngyòng for public use; public; communal

【公用电话】 gōngyòng diànhuà public telephone

【公用电话亭】 gōngyòng diànhuàtíng telephone kiosk; telephone box

【公用事业】 gōngyòng shìyè public utilities

【公有】 gōngyǒu publicly-owned; public：～财产 public property

【公有化】 gōngyǒuhuà socialize; transfer to public ownership; socialization (n.)

【公有制】 gōngyǒuzhì public ownership (of means of production)

【公寓】 gōngyù 1.（公寓住宅楼）flats; apartment house 2.（公寓旅馆）lodging house

【公元】 gōngyuán the Christian era：～前 28 年 28 B.C. / ～1997 年 A.D. 1997

【公园】 gōngyuán park：逛～ walk and play in the park / 中山～ Zhongshan Park; Dr. Sun Yat-sen Park / 北海～ Beihai Park; the Winter Palace

【公约】 gōngyuē 1.（条约名称）convention; pact：日内瓦～ the Geneva Convention 2.（共同遵守的章程）joint pledge：服务～ service pledge

【公允】 gōngyǔn just and sound; fair and equitable; evenhanded

【公债】 gōngzhài (government) bonds; public debt：经济建设～ economic construction bonds / 发行～ issue bonds

【公债券】 gōngzhàiquàn bonds

【公章】 gōngzhāng official seal

【公正】 gōngzhèng just; fair; impartial; fair-minded：～的裁决 true verdict

【公证】 gōngzhèng notary; notarization; notarize (v.); notarial (adj.)：经～的合同 notarized contract

【公证处】 gōngzhèngchù notary office; notary public office

【公证人】 gōngzhèngrén notary public; notary

【公证书】 gōngzhèngshū authentic act; notarial deed

【公证证书】 gōngzhèng zhèngshū notarial certificate

【公职】 gōngzhí public office; public employment：开除～ discharge from public employment

【公制】 gōngzhì the metric system：折成～ convert into the metric system

【公众】 gōngzhòng the public

【公众形象】 gōngzhòng xíngxiàng public image

【公众舆论】 gōngzhòng yúlùn public opinion

【公诸于众】 gōngzhū yúzhòng make public

【公主】 gōngzhǔ princess

【公转】 gōngzhuàn 〈*Aeron*.〉 revolution

【公子】 gōngzǐ son of a feudal prince or high official

【公子哥儿】 gōngzǐgēr a pampered son of a wealthy or influential family

供(gōng) 1.(供应；供给) supply; feed 2.(供…之用) for：仅～参考 for your reference only

(另见"供"gòng)

【供不应求】 gōngbùyìngqiú supply falls short of demand; demand exceeds supply

【供电】 gōngdiàn power supply

【供电局】 gōngdiànjú power supply bureau

【供电系统】 gōngdiàn xìtǒng system of power supply

【供给】 gōngjǐ supply; provide; furnish

【供过于求】 gōngguòyúqiú drug on the market; supply exceeds demand

【供暖】 gōngnuǎn 〈*Archit*.〉 heating; supply of heat：热水～ hot water heating

【供暖系统】 gōngnuǎn xìtǒng heating system

【供求】 gōngqiú supply and demand：～关系 the relation between supply and demand; relationships between supply and demand

【供求平衡】 gōngqiú pínghéng equilibrium of supply and demand

【供水】 gōngshuǐ water supply

【供销】 gōngxiāo supply and marketing

【供销社】 gōngxiāoshè supply and marketing cooperative

【供需】 gōngxū supply and demanding

【供需见面】 gōngxū jiànmiàn direct contact between the supplying and demanding

【供养】 gōngyǎng provide for (one's parents or elders); support

【供应】 gōngyìng supply：～充足 be in liberal supply / 敞开～ can be bought without any restriction / 计划～ planned supply

肱(gōng) the upper arm

【肱二头肌】 gōng'èrtóujī 〈*Anat*.〉 musclus biceps feroris

【肱骨】 gōnggǔ 〈*Anat*.〉 humerus

宫(gōng) 1.(宫殿) palace 2.(庙宇名称) temple 3.(文化娱乐场所) a place for cultural activities and recreation：少年～ Children's Palace 4.(子宫) womb; uterus

【宫灯】 gōngdēng palace lantern

【宫殿】 gōngdiàn palace

【宫颈】 gōngjǐng 〈*Anat*.〉 cervix; cervical (adj.)

【宫颈糜烂】 gōngjǐng mílàn 〈*Med*.〉 cervical erosion

【宫内节育器】 gōngnèi jiéyùqì intrauterine device (IUD)

【宫廷】 gōngtíng 1.(帝王住所) palace 2.(封建统治集团) royal court; imperial court; court

【宫廷政变】 gōngtíng zhèngbiàn palace coup

恭(gōng) respectful; reverent：洗耳～听 listen respectfully with attentive ears

【恭贺】 gōnghè congratulate

【恭贺新禧】 gōnghè xīnxǐ Happy New Year; with best wishes for a happy New Year

【恭候】 gōnghòu 〈*politensee*〉 await respectfully

【恭敬】 gōngjìng respectful; with great respect

【恭桶】 gōngtǒng toilet; lavatory

【恭桶盖】 gōngtǒnggài toilet cover

【恭桶座圈】 gōngtǒng zuòquān toilet seat

【恭维】 gōng·wei flatter; compliment

【恭喜】 gōngxǐ congratulations

巩[鞏](gǒng) consolidate; consolidation (n.)

【巩固】 gǒnggù 1.(使坚固) consolidate; strengthen; solidify; consolidation (n.)：～国防 consolidate the national defense 2.(坚固；不易动摇) steadily consolidated; strong; solid; stable

【巩膜】 gǒngmó 〈*Anat*.〉 sclera; sclerotica

【巩乃斯】 Gǒngnǎisī 〈place〉 Kunes

汞(gǒng) 〈*Chem*.〉 mercury (元素符号 Hg)

【汞灯】 gǒngdēng mercury lamp

拱(gǒng) 1.(拱手) cup one hand in the other before the chest 2.(环绕) surround 3.(弯成弧形) hump up; arch 4.〈*Archit.*〉 arch 5.(推撞) push without using one's hands 6.(植物出土) sprout up through the earth

【拱地】 gǒngdì 1.(指猪) dig earth with the snout 2.(指蚯蚓等) wriggle through the earth

【拱梁】 gǒngliáng arched girder

【拱门】 gǒngmén arched door

【拱桥】 gǒngqiáo 〈*Archit.*〉 arch bridge

【拱手称谢】 gǒngshǒu-chēngxiè join one's hands together in salute and thank

【拱手相让】 gǒngshǒu-xiāngràng surrender sth. submissively

共(gòng) 1.(相同) common; general 2.(共同) share: ～患难 share hardship 3.(一起;一齐) doing the same thing; together 4.(共计) altogether; in all; all told: ～8万字 a total of eighty thousand words; eighty thousand words altogether 5.(共产党) the Communist Party: 中～ the CPC (the Communist Party of China)

【共产党】 gòngchǎndǎng the Communist Party: 中国～ The Communist Party of China

【共产党员】 gòngchǎndǎngyuán member of the Communist Party

【共产主义】 gòngchǎn zhǔyì communism; communist (adj.): ～战士 fighter for communism

【共产主义风格】 gòngchǎn zhǔyì fēnggé communist style

【共产主义建设】 gòngchǎn zhǔyì jiànshè communist construction

【共产主义觉悟】 gòngchǎn zhǔyì juéwù communist consciousness

【共处】 gòngchǔ coexist; coexistence (n.): 和平～五项原则 the five principles of peaceful coexistence

【共存】 gòngcún coexist; survive together; coexistence (n.): 多种经济成分～ coexistence of the diversified economic sectors

【共和】 gònghé republicanism; republic

【共和国】 gònghéguó republic

【共计】 gòngjì amount to; add up to; total

【共建】 gòngjiàn establish with joint efforts; build jointly: 军民～文明单位 model communities and units established jointly by the army and the people

【共勉】 gòngmiǎn mutual encouragement

【共鸣】 gòngmíng 1.(引起相同情绪) sympathetic response: 引起～ arouse sympathy; strike a sympathetic chord 2.〈*Physics*〉 resonance

【共谋】 gòngmóu 〈*Law*〉 collusion; conspire

【共青团】 gòngqīngtuán the Communist Youth League

【共青团员】 gòngqīngtuányuán member of the Communist Youth League

【共生】 gòngshēng 〈*Biol.*〉 intergrowth

【共识】 gòngshí common understanding: 增进～ improve common understanding

【共事】 gòngshì work together (at the same organization); be fellow workers: ～多年 have been colleagues for many years

【共同】 gòngtóng 1.(属于大家的) common: ～关心的问题 matters of common concern; issues of common interest 2.(大家一起) together; jointly: ～对敌 fight the enemy jointly

【共同富裕】 gòngtóng fùyù common prosperity: 逐步实现～ gradually bring about common prosperity

【共同市场】 gòngtóng shìchǎng the Common Market

【共同体】 gòngtóngtǐ community: 欧洲经济～ the European Economic Community

【共同行动】 gòngtóng xíngdòng joint action

【共同语言】 gòngtóng yǔyán common language

【共享】 gòngxiǎng enjoy together; share: ～甘苦 share the sweet and the bitter together

【共性】 gòngxìng general character

【共叙友情】 gòngxù yǒuqíng exchange sentiments of friendship with sb.

【共振】 gòngzhèn 〈*Physics*〉 resonance

供(gòng) 1.(供奉) lay (offerings) 2.(供品) offerings: 上～ offer sacrifices in worship 3.(供认) confess; own up 4.(供词) confession; deposition: 串～ act in collusion with others to make confessions tally

(另见"供"gōng)

【供词】 gòngcí confession; a statement made under examination

【供奉】 gòngfèng enshrine and worship; consecrate

【供认】 gòngrèn confess: ～不讳 confess everything

【供职】 gòngzhí hold office

贡 (gòng) tribute: 进～ pay tribute

【贡嘎】 Gònggǎ 〈place〉 Gonggar

【贡品】 gòngpǐn articles of tribute

【贡献】 gòngxiàn 1.（指行为）contribute; dedicate; devote: ～自己的一份力量 contribute one's share; do one's bit (for) / 对某事有所～ contribute to sth. 2.（指所做的事）contribution: 作出～ make contributions

gou

勾[句] (gōu) 1.（勾除）cancel; cross out; strike out; tick off 2.（勾画）delineate; draw 3.（勾抹）fill up the joints of brickwork with mortar or cement; point 4.（勾兑）thicken 5.（勾起）induce; evoke; call to mind: 这件事～起了他的回忆。This incident called forth his reminiscences. 6.（勾结）collude with; gang up with

（另见"勾"gòu）

【勾搭】 gōu·da 1.（串通）gang up with 2.（勾引）seduce

【勾兑】 gōuduì thicken

【勾画】 gōuhuà draw the outline of; delineate; sketch

【勾结】 gōujié collude with; collaborate with; gang up with

【勾勒】 gōulè 1.（画出轮廓）draw the outline of; sketch the contours of 2.（写出大致情况）give a brief account of; outline

【勾描】 gōumiáo delineate; draw

【勾芡】 gōuqiàn thicken soup

【勾销】 gōuxiāo liquidate; write off; strike out: ～一笔债务 liquidate a debt

【勾心斗角】 gōuxīn dòujiǎo intrigue against each other; jockey for position

【勾引】 gōuyǐn tempt; entice; seduce: ～女青年 seduce a young woman

沟[溝] (gōu) 1.（沟渠）ditch; channel; trench: 阴～ sewerage 2.（沟槽）groove; rut; furrow 3.（沟壑）冲～ gully / 河～ ravine

【沟壑】 gōuhè gully; ravine

【沟渠】 gōuqú irrigation canals and ditches

【沟通】 gōutōng link up: ～两国文化 link the cultures of the two countries

钩[鉤] (gōu) 1.（钩子）hook: 窗～ window catch / 挂衣～ clothes-hook 2.（钩形符号）check mark; tick 3.（钩住）secure with a hook; hook: 围巾给树枝～住了。The scarf was caught by the branches. 4.（用针粗缝）sew with large stitches 5.（用钩针编织）crochet

【钩虫病】 gōuchóngbìng hookworm disease

【钩心斗角】 gōuxīn dòujiǎo intrigue against each other; jockey for position

【钩形扳手】 gōuxíng bān·shou claw wrench; hook key; hook spanner

【钩针】 gōuzhēn crochet hook

【钩子】 gōu·zi hook

佝 (gōu)

【佝偻】 gōu·lóu hunch-back

【佝偻病】 gōu·lóubìng rickets

篝 (gōu)

【篝火】 gōuhuǒ bonfire; campfire: 燃起～ make a campfire

鞲 (gōu)

【鞲鞴】 gōubèi 〈*Mech*.〉 piston

苟 (gǒu) careless; negligent; indifferent (to right or wrong): 不～言笑 be not indiscreet in speech and manner; be solemn and dignified / 一丝不～ be not the least bit negligent; be scrupulous about every detail

【苟安一时】 gǒu'ān-yīshí seek security for a time; gain some respite for oneself; seek

【苟合】 gǒuhé illicit sexual relations

【苟且】 gǒuqiě 1.（得过且过）drift along; be resigned to circumstances 2.（敷衍了事）perfunctorily; carelessly 3.（不正当的）illicit (sexual relations); improper

【苟且偷生】 gǒuqiě-tōushēng drag out an ignoble existence; keep alive without serious

ambition
【苟全】 gǒuquán preserve (one's own life) at all costs
【苟同】 gǒutóng agree without giving serious thought; readily subscribe to (sb's view): 不敢～ can hardly agree; cannot agree
【苟延残喘】 gǒuyán-cánchuǎn be on one's last legs; linger on in a steadily worsening condition

狗 (gǒu) 1.(犬) dog: 猎～ hunting dog / 母～ bitch / 野～ wild dog 2.(骂人话) damned; cursed
【狗胆包天】 gǒudǎn-bāotiān monstrous audacity
【狗急跳墙】 gǒují-tiàoqiáng a cornered beast will do something desperate
【狗娘养的】 gǒuniáng yǎng·de (骂人话) sun of a bitch
【狗皮膏药】 gǒupí gāo·yao 1.(涂在狗皮上的膏药) dogskin plaster 2.(骗人货色) quack medicine
【狗屁】 gǒupì horseshit; rubbish; nonsense: ～不通 unreadable rubbish; mere trash
【狗食】 gǒushí dog food
【狗头军师】 gǒutóu jūnshī 1.(出坏主意的人) a person who offers bad advice; inept adviser 2.(极坏的顾问) villainous adviser
【狗腿子】 gǒutuǐ·zi 〈*colloq*.〉 hired thug; lackey; henchman
【狗熊】 gǒuxióng 1.(黑熊) black bear 2.(懦夫) coward
【狗咬狗】 gǒuyǎogǒu dog-eat-dog; dogfight
【狗仗人势】 gǒuzhàng-rénshì like a dog threatening people on the strength of its master's power; be a bully under the protection of a powerful person

枸 (gǒu)
【枸杞】 gǒuqǐ 〈*Bot*.〉 Chinese wolfberry
【枸杞子】 gǒuqǐzǐ 〈*Chin. Pharm*.〉 fruit of Chinese wolfberry

勾[句] (gòu) (另见"勾"gōu)
【勾当】 gòu·dàng business; deal: 肮脏～ a dirty deal / 罪恶～ criminal activities / 不可告人的～ a sinister trick

构[構] (gòu) 1.(构成) construct; form; compose 2.(结成) fabricate; make up
【构成】 gòuchéng constitute; form; compose; make up: ～威胁 constitute a threat
【构成部分】 gòuchéng bùfèn component part
【构件】 gòujiàn 1.〈*Archit*.〉 (structural) member; component 2.〈*Mech*.〉 component (part)
【构思】 gòusī 1.(设计作品) work out the plot of a literary work or the composition of a painting 2.(想像) conception: 大胆的～ boldness of conception / ～新颖 original in conception
【构图】 gòutú 〈*Arts*〉 composition (of a picture)
【构想】 gòuxiǎng tentative idea; conception
【构造】 gòuzào 1.(结构) structure; construction 2.〈*Geog*.〉 tectonic; structural
【构筑】 gòuzhù construct (military works); build

购[購] (gòu) purchase; buy: 订～ place an order / 赊～ buy on credit; sales on credit
【购货单】 gòuhuòdān order form; order
【购买】 gòumǎi purchase; buy
【购买力】 gòumǎilì 1.(支付能力) purchasing power 2.(单位货币的购买能力) buying power of money
【购买欲】 gòumǎiyù desire to buy; desire to purchase
【购物袋】 gòuwùdài shopping bag
【购物中心】 gòuwù zhōngxīn shopping center
【购销】 gòuxiāo purchase and sale; buying and selling: ～两旺 brisk buying and selling
【购置】 gòuzhì purchase (durables)

诟 (gòu) shame; humiliation
【诟骂】 gòumà abuse; vilify

垢 (gòu) 1.(污秽) dirty; filthy 2.(脏东西) dirt; filth 3.(耻辱) disgrace; humiliation; insults

够[夠] (gòu) 1.(足够) enough; sufficient; adequate: ～两天的粮食 provisions enough for two days 2.(达到) reach; be up to (a certain standard, etc.): ～得着吗? Can you reach it? 3.(确实的;真的) quite; rather; really: 这场足球赛可真～意思。That football match was really something.

【够本】 gòuběn make enough money to cover the cost; break even

【够格】 gòugé be qualified; be up to standard: 她当教师很～。She is highly qualified to be a teacher.

【够朋友】 gòu péng·you deserve to be called a true friend; be a friend indeed

【够呛】 gòuqiàng unbearable; terrible

【够戗】 gòuqiàng unbearable; terrible

【够受的】 gòushòu·de quite an ordeal; hard to bear

【够数】 gòushù sufficient in quantity; enough

【够条件】 gòu tiáojiàn reach the standard; be qualified

【够意思】 gòu yì·si 1.(好极了) really something; terrific 2.(大方) generous; really kind

媾 (gòu) 1.(结为婚姻) wed 2.(友好) reach agreement 3.(交配) copulate

【媾和】 gòuhé make peace; negotiate for peace: 单独～ make a separate peace

gu

估 (gū) estimate; appraise: ～一～损失多少 assess the damages

【估计】 gūjì estimate; appraise; reckon: 约略的～ a rough estimate

【估价】 gūjià 1.(评价) appraise; evaluate 2.(估计价格) appraised price

【估量】 gū·liáng appraise; estimate; assess: 不可～的损失 an immeasurable loss

【估算】 gūsuàn estimate; appraise

咕 (gū)

【咕咚】 gūdōng 〈*onomat.*〉 thud; splash; plump

【咕嘟】 gū·du 1.〈*onomat.*〉 bubble; gurgle 2.(长时间煮) boil for a long time

【咕噜】 gūlū 1.〈*onomat.*〉 rumble; roll 2.(小声说话) murmur; whisper

【咕哝】 gū·nong murmur; mutter; grumble

沽 (gū) 1.(买) buy 2.(卖) sell: 待价而～ wait to sell at a good price; wait for the highest bid

【沽名钓誉】 gūmíng-diàoyù fish for fame and compliments

姑 (gū) 1.(姑母) father's sister; aunt 2.(丈夫的姐妹) husband's sister; sister-in-law 3.(出家的妇女) nun: 尼～ Buddhist nun 4.(姑且) tentatively; for the time being

【姑表】 gūbiǎo cousinship

【姑父】 gū·fu the husband of one's father's sister; uncle

【姑母】 gūmǔ father's sister (married); aunt

【姑娘】 gū·niang 1.(未婚女子) girl 2.(女儿) daughter

【姑且】 gūqiě tentatively; for the moment: ～不谈 leave sth. aside for the moment

【姑且不论】 gūqiě-bùlùn let us not go into the question now; let's not discuss it for the present

【姑息】 gūxī appease; indulge; tolerate

【姑爷】 gū·ye son-in-law

轱 (gū) wheel

【轱辘】 gū·lu 1.(轮子) wheel 2.(滚动) roll

菇 (gū) mushroom

辜 (gū) guilt; crime: 无～ guiltless; innocent

【辜负】 gūfù be unworthy of; disappoint; let down; fail to live up to: 我们决不要～老师的谆谆教导。We must never be unworthy of our teachers' untiring and sincere teachings

孤 (gū) 1.(孤儿)(of a child) fatherless; orphaned 2.(孤单) solitary; isolated; alone

【孤本】 gūběn the only existing copy

【孤单】 gūdān 1.(单身无靠) alone 2.(孤寂) lonely; friendless

【孤岛】 gūdǎo an isolated island

【孤独】 gūdú lonely; solitary

【孤儿】 gū'ér orphan: ～寡母 orphan and widow

【孤儿院】 gū'éryuàn orphanage

【孤寡】 gūguǎ orphans and widows

【孤家寡人】 gūjiā-guǎrén a person in solitary splendor; a person who has no mass support; a loner

【孤军】 gūjūn an isolated force: ～作战 fight in isolation

【孤苦】 gūkǔ orphaned and miserable
【孤苦伶仃】 gūkǔ-língdīng orphaned and helpless; friendless and wretched
【孤立】 gūlì 1.(与其他事物无联系) isolated: ～无援 isolated and cut off from help 2.(使得不到同情、支援) isolate
【孤零零】 gūlínglíng solitary; lone; all alone
【孤僻】 gūpì unsociable and eccentric
【孤身一人】 gūshēn-yìrén be all on one's own
【孤注一掷】 gūzhù-yīzhì stake everything on a single throw; risk everything on a single venture; put all one's eggs in one basket

骨 (gū)
(另见"骨"gǔ)
【骨朵儿】 gū·duor flower bud
【骨碌】 gū·lu roll: 从床上一～爬起来 roll out of bed

箍 (gū) 1.(圈儿) hoop; band: 铁～ hoop iron 2.(圈住) bind round; hoop: 用铁丝把桶～上 band a bucket with wire

古 (gǔ) ancient; age-old; paleo-
【古板】 gǔbǎn old-fashioned and inflexible
【古代】 gǔdài ancient times; antiquity: ～文化 ancient civilization
【古代史】 gǔdàishǐ ancient history
【古典】 gǔdiǎn 1.(典故) classical allusion 2.(经典的) classical
【古典式摔跤】 gǔdiǎnshì shuāijiāo Greed-Roman wrestling
【古典文学】 gǔdiǎn wénxué classical literature
【古典艺术】 gǔdiǎn yìshù classical art
【古典音乐】 gǔdiǎn yīnyuè classical music
【古董】 gǔdǒng 1.(指器物) antique; curio 2.(守旧的人) old fogey
【古都】 gǔdū ancient capital
【古尔邦节】 Gǔ'ěrbāngjié 〈*Islam*〉 Corban
【古怪】 gǔguài eccentric; odd; strange: 举止～ eccentric behaviors
【古国】 gǔguó ancient country
【古籍】 gǔjí ancient books
【古迹】 gǔjì historic site; place of historic interest
【古今中外】 gǔjīn zhōngwài ancient and modern, Chinese and foreign; at all times and in all countries
【古兰经】 Gǔlánjīng 〈*Islam*〉 the Koran
【古老】 gǔlǎo ancient; age-old: ～的传说 legend
【古朴】 gǔpǔ simple and unsophisticated; of primitive simplicity
【古琴】 gǔqín *guqin*; 7-stringed Chinese zither
【古人】 gǔrén the ancients; our forefathers
【古色古香】 gǔsè-gǔxiāng antique; quaint
【古生物学】 gǔshēngwùxué paleontology; paleontological (adj.)
【古生物学家】 gǔshēngwù xuéjiā paleontologist
【古时候】 gǔshíhòu in ancient times; in olden days
【古书】 gǔshū ancient books
【古铜色】 gǔtóngsè bronze-colored
【古玩】 gǔwán antique; curio
【古往今来】 gǔwǎng-jīnlái through the ages; of all ages; since time immemorial
【古为今用】 gǔwéi-jīnyòng make the past serve the present
【古文】 gǔwén ancient style prose; ancient Chinese prose
【古稀】 gǔxī seventy years of age: 年近～ getting on for seventy
【古雅】 gǔyǎ of classic elegance
【古已有之】 gǔyǐyǒuzhī have existed since ancient times
【古筝】 gǔzhēng *guzheng*; 25-stringed Chinese zither
【古装】 gǔzhuāng in ancient costume
【古装戏】 gǔzhuāngxì play in ancient costume

钴 (gǔ) 〈*Chem.*〉 cobalt (元素符号 Co)
【钴 60 疗法】 gǔliùshí liáofǎ cobalt 60 therapy
【钴铁】 gǔtiě ferro-cobalt

谷[**穀**[2,3]] (gǔ) 1.(山谷) valley; gorge 2.(谷類) cereal; grain 3.(粟) millet
【谷氨酸鈉】 gǔānsuānnà sodium glutamate
【谷倉】 gǔcáng granary; barn
【谷草】 gǔcǎo 1.(谷秆) millet straw 2.(稻草) rice straw
【谷殼】 gǔké husk (of rice)
【谷類】 gǔlèi cereal; grain
【谷類作物】 gǔlèi zuòwù cereal crops

【谷物】 gǔwù cereal; grain
【谷雨】 gǔyǔ the Grain Rain (4 月 19-21 日交節)
【谷子】 gǔ·zi 1.(粟) millet 2.(稻子) unhusked rice

股 (gǔ) 1.(大腿) thigh 2.(绳线的股) strand; ply: 三～的绳子 a rope of three strands 3.(股份) share: 法人～ corporate share / 内部～ internal share / 普通～ common stock / 优先～ preference shares; preferred stock / 赠送～ donated stock

【股本】 gǔběn capital stock: ～折价 discount on capital stock
【股东】 gǔdōng shareholder; stockholder
【股东产权】 gǔdōng chǎnquán stockholder's equity
【股动脉】 gǔdòngmài 〈*Anat*.〉 femoral artery
【股分】 gǔfèn share; stock
【股份】 gǔfèn share; stock: 投资公司将认购40% 的～。The investment company will subscribe to 40% of the shares.
【股份公司】 gǔfèn gōngsī joint-stock company; stock company
【股份认购】 gǔfèn rèngòu stock subscription
【股份有限公司】 gǔfèn yǒuxiàn gōngsī limited-liability company; limited company (Ltd.)
【股份责任制】 gǔfèn zérènzhì system of share-holding responsibility
【股份制】 gǔfènzhì share-holding system
【股份转让】 gǔfèn zhuǎnràng share transfer; stock transfer
【股骨】 gǔgǔ 〈*Anat*.〉 thighbone; femur
【股价回升】 gǔjià huíshēng recovery of stock
【股价上涨】 gǔjià shàngzhǎng rise stock in stock
【股价下落】 gǔjià xiàluò reduction in stock
【股金】 gǔjīn money paid for shares
【股民】 gǔmín stockholder; shareholder
【股票】 gǔpiào share certificate; share; stock: 不上市～ unlisted stock / 发行～ issue share; issue stock / 热门～ blue chip
【股票交易所】 gǔpiào jiāoyìsuǒ stock exchange
【股票经纪人】 gǔpiào jīngjìrén stockbroker; stockjobber
【股票热】 gǔpiàorè stock crazy
【股票认购证】 gǔpiào rèngòuzhèng stock warrant
【股票市场】 gǔpiào shìchǎog stock market
【股权】 gǔquán equity share; stock right
【股市】 gǔshì the stock market
【股市牌价】 gǔshì páijià stock quotations
【股市指数】 gǔshì zhǐshù stock index; stock exchange index
【股息】 gǔxī dividend

骨 (gǔ) 1.(骨头) bone 2.(架子) skeleton; framework 3.(品质;气概) character; spirit
(另见"骨"gū)

【骨癌】 gǔ'ái osteocarcinoma; cancer in the bones
【骨刺】 gǔcì 〈*Med*.〉 spur
【骨粉】 gǔfěn bone meal; bone dust
【骨干】 gǔgàn 1.(长骨的主要部分) diaphysis 2.(主要作用) backbone; mainstay: 起～作用 be a mainstay
【骨干企业】 gǔgàn qǐyè key enterprises
【骨骼】 gǔgé skeleton
【骨鲠在喉】 gǔgěng zàihóu have a lump in the throat
【骨灰】 gǔhuī 1.(骨头烧成的灰) bone ash 2.(火葬的骨灰) ashes of the dead
【骨灰安放仪式】 gǔhuī ānfàng yíshì ceremony of laying ashes to rest
【骨灰盒】 gǔhuīhé cinerary casket
【骨架】 gǔjià skeleton; framework: 房屋的～ the framework of a house
【骨科】 gǔkē orthopedics
【骨科医生】 gǔkē yīshēng orthopedist
【骨盆】 gǔpén pelvis
【骨气】 gǔqì strength of character; back bone; moral integrity
【骨肉】 gǔròu flesh and blood; kindred: 亲生～ one's own flesh and blood / ～团聚 a family reunion / ～兄弟 blood brothers; one's own brothers
【骨髓】 gǔsuǐ marrow
【骨头】 gǔ·tou 1.(骨骼) bone 2.(喻人的品质) character; a person of a certain character: 懒～ lazybones / 软～ a spineless creature
【骨头架子】 gǔ·tou jià·zi 1.(骨架) skeleton 2.(极瘦的人) a bag of bones; skin and

bones：瘦得成了一副～ be all skin and bone

【骨折】 gǔzhé 〈*Med*.〉 fracture：粉碎性～ comminuted fracture

【骨子】 gǔ·zi frame；ribs：伞～ umbrella frame；the ribs of an umbrella

【骨子里】 gǔ·zilǐ in one's heart of hearts

蛊［蠱］(gǔ) a legendary venomous insect

【蛊惑】 gǔhuò poison and bewitch

【蛊惑人心】 gǔhuò-rénxīn resort to demagoguery；confuse and poison people's minds：～的作品 demagogic writings

鼓 (gǔ) **1**.〈*Music*〉drum：定音～ kettle drum **2**.(使发声) beat；strike；sound **3**.(煽) blow with bellows，etc. **4**.(发动；振奋) rouse；agitate；pluck up：～起勇气 pluck up one's courage **5**.(隆起) bulge；swell

【鼓吹】 gǔchuī **1**.(宣传提倡) advocate **2**.(吹嘘) preach；advertise；play up

【鼓槌】 gǔchuí stick；drumstick

【鼓动】 gǔdòng **1**.(激发情绪) agitate；arouse：～群众 arouse the masses **2**.(唆使) incite；instigate

【鼓风机】 gǔfēngjī air-blower

【鼓励】 gǔlì encourage；urge：～先进 encourage the advanced

【鼓铃】 gǔlíng jingles

【鼓楼】 gǔlóu drum-tower

【鼓膜】 gǔmó 〈*Anat*.〉 tympanic membrane；eardrum

【鼓起】 gǔqǐ call up；muster up；pluck up：～精神 stir up one's spirit / ～勇气 pluck up one's courage；muster up one's courage

【鼓式制动器】 gǔshì zhìdòngqì drum brake

【鼓舞】 gǔwǔ **1**.(使振作) inspire；hearten：～斗志 inspire the fighting spirit / ～士气 enhance troop morale **2**.(振作) feel excited：受到…的极大～ have been a great encouragement to

【鼓噪】 gǔzào make an uproar；raise a hubbub；clamor

【鼓掌】 gǔzhǎng clap one's hands；applaud：热烈～ warmly applaud / ～通过 approve by acclamation

【鼓足勇气】 gǔzú yǒngqì call up all one's courage；muster (up) one's courage

故 (gù) **1**.(事故) incident；happening **2**.(缘故) reason；cause：无～缺勤 be absent without reason **3**.(故意) on purpose；intentionally：明知～犯 willfully violate (a law or rule) / ～作镇静 pretend to be calm **4**.(所以) hence；therefore；consequently；for this reason **5**.(从前的；旧的) former；old **6**.(朋友) friend；acquaintance：非亲非～ neither relative nor friend；a perfect stranger **7**.(亡故) die：病～ die of illness

【故步自封】 gùbù zìfēng stand still and refuse to make progress；be complacent and conservative

【故地】 gùdì old haunt

【故都】 gùdū onetime capital

【故宫】 Gùgōng the Imperial Palace

【故宫博物院】 Gùgōng Bówùyuàn the Palace Museum

【故伎】 gùjì stock trick；old tactics：重演～ play the same old trick

【故居】 gùjū former residence；former dwelling place

【故人】 gùrén **1**.(老朋友；旧友) old friend **2**.(死去的人) the died

【故事】 gù·shi **1**.(例行的事) old practice；routine：奉行～ follow established practice mechanically **2**.(gù·shi)(一种文学形式) story；tale：民间～ folktale；folk story **3**.(故事性) plot

【故事片】 gù·shipiàn feature film

【故事影片】 gù·shi yǐngpiàn 见“故事片”

【故土】 gùtǔ native land

【故乡】 gùxiāng native place；hometown；birthplace

【故意】 gùyì intentionally；willfully；deliberately；on purpose：～刁难 place obstacles in sb's way

【故障】 gùzhàng trouble；breakdown；stoppage；hitch：排除～ clear away a trouble

【故作姿态】 gùzuò-zītài make a deliberate gesture；strike an attitude on purpose

固 (gù) **1**.(牢固) solid；firm：加～ make sth. more solid **2**.(坚决地) firmly；resolutely **3**.(使坚固) solidity；consolidate；strengthen **4**.(原本) originally；in the first place；as a matter of course **5**.(固然) admittedly；no doubt

【固氮】 gùdàn 〈*Bot*.〉 nitrogen fixation

【固定】 gùdìng 1.（不变动）fixed; regular: 电视台的～节目 a regular TV program 2.（使固定）fix; regularize

【固定工】 gùdìnggōng regular worker; permanent worker

【固定工资】 gùdìng gōngzī regular pay; fixed wage

【固定价格】 gùdìng jiàgé regular price; fixed price

【固定资产】 gùdìng zīchǎn fixed assets

【固件】 gùjiàn 〈*Computer*〉 firmware

【固然】 gùrán no doubt; it is true; true; of course; admittedly

【固守】 gùshǒu 1.（坚守）defend tenaciously 2.（固执地遵循）adhere to; stick to: ～成法 stick to the regulations

【固体】 gùtǐ solid body; solid

【固体电路】 gùtǐ diànlù solid-state circuit

【固有】 gùyǒu intrinsic; inherent; innate: ～矛盾 intrinsic contradictions

【固执】 gù·zhí 1.（不肯改变）obstinate; stubborn 2.（坚持己见）persist in; cling to

【固执己见】 gù·zhí jǐjiàn stubbornly adhere to one's opinions

痼（gù） chronic

【痼疾】 gùjí chronic illness

【痼习】 gùxí deeply-rooted habits

顾［顧］（gù） 1.（转过头看）turn round and look at; look at: 环～ look around / 回～ look back; retrospect / 左～右盼 look to the left and to the right 2.（照顾）attend to; take into consideration: 兼～ give consideration to both 3.（拜访）visit; call on

【顾此失彼】 gùcǐ-shībǐ be unable to attend to everything at once

【顾及】 gùjí take into account; attend to; give consideration to: 无暇～ have no time to attend to the matter

【顾忌】 gùjì scruple; misgiving: 不能不有所～ have to think twice (before doing sth.); be unable to overcome certain misgivings / 毫无～ without scruple; have no scruples

【顾客】 gùkè customer; shopper; client

【顾虑】 gùlǜ misgiving; apprehension; worry: 打消～ dispel one's misgivings

【顾虑重重】 gùlǜ-chóngchóng be full of worries; have no end of misgivings; have scruples

【顾面子】 gùmiàn·zi care for sb's reputation

【顾名思义】 gùmíng-sīyì seeing the name of a thing one thinks of its function; just as its name implies; as the term suggests

【顾盼自如】 gùpàn-zìrú gaze round as one wishes; free and easy

【顾全】 gùquán show consideration for and take care to preserve: ～大局 take the interests of the whole into account / ～名誉 take into consideration one's reputation

【顾问】 gùwèn adviser; advisor; consultant: 法律～ legal adviser / 经济～ economic adviser / 军事～ military adviser

【顾惜】 gùxī 1.（顾全爱惜）take good care of: 要～你的身体 take good care of your health 2.（照顾怜惜）sympathize with

【顾主】 gùzhǔ customer; client; patron

雇［僱］（gù） hire; employ: ～车 hire a car

【雇工】 gùgōng 1.（雇用工人）hire labor; hire hands 2.（受雇工人）hired laborer

【雇农】 gùnóng farmhand; farm laborer

【雇佣】 gùyōng employ; hire

【雇佣军】 gùyōngjūn mercenary army

【雇用】 gùyòng employ

【雇员】 gùyuán employee

【雇主】 gùzhǔ employer

gua

瓜（guā） melon; watermelon; gourd

【瓜分】 guāfēn carve up; divide up; partition

【瓜葛】 guāgé connection; implication; association: 不难看出他们之间是有～的。It was not hard to see that they got entangled with each other.

【瓜果】 guāguǒ melon and fruit

【瓜熟蒂落】 guāshú-dìluò when a melon is ripe it falls off its stem; things will be easily settled when conditions are ripe

【瓜子儿】 guāzǐr melon seeds

【瓜子儿脸】 guāzǐrliǎn oval face

呱(guā)

【呱呱】 guāguā quack; croak; caw

【呱呱叫】 guāguājiào tiptop; top-notch

刮[颳[4]](guā) 1.(用刀刮掉)scrape: 把锈都～掉 scrape all the rust off 2.(涂)smear with (paste, etc.) 3.(搜刮)plunder; fleece; extort 4.(刮风)blow

【刮风】 guāfēng blow

【刮胡刀】 guāhúdāo razor

【刮胡子】 guāhú·zi shave the face

【刮脸】 guāliǎn shave the face

【刮脸刀】 guāliǎndāo razor

【刮目相看】 guāmù-xiāngkàn look at sb. with new eyes; treat sb. with increased respect

栝(guā)

【栝楼】 guālóu 〈*Bot.*〉snakegourd; Mongolian snakegourd

剐[剮](guǎ) 1.(凌迟)cut to pieces (a form of capital punishment in a ancient times); dismember: 千刀万～ be cut to pieces 2.(刺破)cut; slit: 手上～了个口子 cut one's hand

寡(guǎ) 1.(少)few; scant 2.(淡而无味)tasteless 3.(寡妇)widowed: 守～ live in widowhood

【寡不敌众】 guǎbùdízhòng be hopelessly outnumbered

【寡妇】 guǎ·fu widow

【寡廉鲜耻】 guǎlián-xiǎnchǐ lost to shame; shameless

【寡头】 guǎtóu oligarch: 金融～ financial oligarchy; financial magnates

【寡言】 guǎyán of few words; taciturn; sparing of words

挂[掛](guà) 1.(悬挂)hang; put up 2.(钩)hitch; get caught 3.(挂上电话)ring off 4.(打电话)call up; put sb. through to 5.(牵挂)be concerned about: 我会把这事～在心上。I shall keep the matter in mind. 6.(糊)be covered with; be coated with 7.(登记)register (at a hospital, etc.): ～外科 register for surgery

【挂彩】 guàcǎi 1.(结彩)decorate with colored silk festoons; decorate for festive occasions 2.(负伤)be wounded in action

【挂车】 guàchē trailer

【挂齿】 guàchǐ mention: 此事不足～。This matter is not worth mentioning.

【挂挡】 guàdǎng put into gear

【挂钩】 guàgōu 1.(连接车辆)couple (two railway coaches); articulate 2.(联系)link up with; establish contact with; get in touch with

【挂号】 guàhào 1.(在医院登记)register (at a hospital, etc.) 2.(寄挂号信)send by registered mail

【挂号处】 guàhàochù registration office

【挂号费】 guàhàofèi registration fee

【挂号信】 giàhàoxìn registered letter

【挂花】 guàhuā be wounded in action

【挂记】 guà·ji worry about; miss

【挂靠】 guàkào link themselves up with

【挂历】 guàlì wall calendar; hanging calendar

【挂零】 guàlíng odd: 50～ fifty odd

【挂面】 guàmiàn fine dried noodles; vermicelli

【挂名】 guàmíng titular; nominal; only in name

【挂念】 guàniàn worry about sb. who is absent; miss: 非常～ miss sb. very much

【挂牌开业】 guàpái kāiyè put one's plate in (a certain street)

【挂失】 guàshī report the loss of (identity papers, checks, etc.)

【挂帅】 guàshuài be in command; assume command; assume leadership: 亲自～ take command in person

【挂锁】 guàsuǒ padlock

【挂毯】 guàtǎn tapestry

【挂图】 guàtú 1.(指地图)wall map 2.(指图表)hanging chart

【挂心】 guàxīn keep in mind; be concerned about

【挂衣钩】 guàyīgōu clothes-hook

【挂职】 guàzhí 1.(保留职务)reserved post; retained post 2.(临时担任)entrusted with responsibility and authority

【挂钟】 guàzhōng wall clock

褂(guà)

【褂子】 guà·zi coat; short gown

guai

乖 (guāi) 1.（听话）well-behaved (child); good; dear 2.（伶俐）clever; shrewd; alert

【乖戾】 guāilì perverse

【乖僻】 guāipì queer; eccentric

【乖巧】 guāiqiǎo 1.（机灵）clever 2.（讨人喜欢）cute; lovely

拐[枴[3]] (guǎi) 1.（轉彎）turn: ～過街角 turn the corner / 向右～ turn to the right 汽車一～就不見了。The car turned the corner and disappeared from sight. 2.（瘸）limp: 一～一～地走 walk with a limp 3.（拐杖）crutch 4.（綁架）abduct; kidnap 5.（拐騙）swindle; make off with

【拐帶兒童】 guǎidài értóng child-stealing

【拐棍】 guǎigùn walking stick

【拐角】 guǎijiǎo corner; turning: 在大街的～ at the corner of the street

【拐款潛逃】 guǎikuǎn qiántáo abscond with funds

【拐賣人口】 guǎimài rénkǒu kidnap and sell people

【拐騙】 guǎipiàn 1.（用于財物）swindle: ～錢財 swindle money (out of sb.) 2.（用于人）abduct: ～婦女 abduct women

【拐彎】 guǎiwān 1.（指行路）turn a corner; turn 2.（指思路、語言等）turn round; pursue a new course 3.（拐角）corner

【拐彎抹角】 guǎiwān mòjiǎo talk in a roundabout way; beat about the bush

【拐杖】 guǎizhàng walking stick

怪[恠] (guài) 1.（奇怪）strange; odd; queer; bewildering: 一点儿也不～ not at all strange 2.（觉得奇怪）find sth. strange; wonder at 3.（很;非常）quite; rather 4.（妖怪）monster; demon; evil being 5.（责怪）blame

【怪不得】 guài·bu·de 1.（难怪）no wonder; so that's why; that explains why: 她管那么多事，～老是很忙。No wonder she's always busy, she has so many things to attend to. 2.（不能责备）not to blame

【怪话】 guàihuà cynical remark; grumble; complaint

【怪模怪样】 guàimú-guàiyàng queer-looking; grotesque

【怪僻】 guàipì eccentric behavior

【怪声怪气】 guàishēng guàiqì (speak in a) strange voice or affected manner

【怪物】 guài·wu 1.（妖怪）monster; monstrosity; freak 2.（古怪的人）an eccentric person

guan

关[關、関] (guān) 1.（关闭）shut; close: 随手～门 please shut the door after you 2.（禁闭）lock up; shut in: 老虎～在笼子里。The tiger is shut in the cage. 3.（切断）turn off: ～灯 switch off the light / ～电视机 turn off the TV set 4.（关张）close down 5.（关隘）pass 6.（海关）customhouse 7.（关键之处）barrier; critical juncture 8.（关系）concern; involve

【关闭】 guānbì 1.（合拢）close; shut 2.（歇业）close down; shut down: 工厂～ the closing down of factories

【关怀】 guānhuái show loving care for; show solicitude for

【关键】 guānjiàn hinge; key; crux: 问题的～ the key to the question / ～时刻 the crucial moment

【关节】 guānjié 1.〈*Anat.*〉joint 2.（关键环节）key links; links

【关节炎】 guānjiéyán 〈*Med.*〉arthritis: 风湿性～ rheumatic arthritis

【关口】 guānkǒu 1.（要冲）pass: 把守～ guard the pass 2.（关头）moment

【关联】 guānlián be related; be connected: 互相～ be interrelated

【关门】 guānmén 1.（停业）close 2.（没有商量余地）slam the door on sth.; refuse discussion or consideration 3.（不愿容纳）behind closed doors

【关切】 guānqiè be deeply concerned; show one's concern over

【关税】 guānshuì customs duty; tariff: 保护～ protective tariff

【关税壁垒】 guānshuì bìlěi tariff barrier

【关税配额】 guānshuì pèi'é customs quota system

【关税同盟】 guānshuì tóngméng customs union

【关停并转】 guāntíng bìngzhuǎn shut down and suspend production, merge with other business and shift to other products

【关头】 guāntóu juncture; moment: 紧要～ a critical moment

【关系】 guān·xi 1.(相互关系) relation; relationship: 外交～ diplomatic relations / 理顺…～ straighten out the relation; smooth the relations of ... / 发展和平友好、平等互利、长期稳定的～ develop relations of peace and friendship, equality and mutual benefit, and prolonged stability 2.(有影响) bearing; impact; significance 3.(关联;牵涉) concern; affect; have a bearing on; have to do with 4.(组织关系) credentials showing membership in an organization

【关系户】 guān·xihù connections; individuals or units connected with and improperly benefited from each other

【关系网】 guān·xìwǎng network of social connections; system of interconnected and cooperating individuals or units

【关系正常化】 guān·xi zhèngchánghuà normalization of relations

【关心】 guānxīn be concerned with; show solicitude for; be interested in; care for: 双方共同～的问题 matters of interest to both sides / 共同～的问题 questions of common interest

【关押】 guānyā put in prison; be kept in jail

【关于】 guānyú 〈*prep.*〉 about; on; with regard to; concerning

【关照】 guānzhào 1.(关心照顾) look after; keep an eye on 2.(口头通知) notify by word of mouth

【关注】 guānzhù attention; concern

观[觀] (guān) 1.(观看) look at; watch; observe: 以～后效 see how the offender behaves in future 2.(景象) sight; view: 奇～ wonderful sight / 壮～ impressive sight 3.(看法) outlook; view; concept: 正确的人生～ a correct outlook on life

【观测】 guāncè 1.(观察测量) observe: ～气象 make weather observations 2.(观察测度) survey: ～敌情 keep watch over the enemy's movement

【观察】 guānchá observe; watch; survey: ～动静 watch what is going on / ～形势 observe the situation; examine the situation

【观察员】 guāncháyuán observer; inspector

【观点】 guāndiǎn view; point of view; viewpoint; standpoint: ～一致 identity of views / 阐明～ explain one's position

【观感】 guāngǎn impressions

【观光】 guānguāng go sightseeing; visit; tour

【观光团】 guānguāngtuán visiting group; sight-seeing party

【观看】 guānkàn watch; view: ～足球比赛 watch a football match

【观礼】 guānlǐ attend a celebration or ceremony

【观礼台】 guānlǐtái reviewing stand; visitors' stand

【观摩】 guānmó inspect and learn from each other's work; view and emulate

【观摩教学】 guānmó jiàoxué demonstration lecture

【观摩演出】 guānmó yǎnchū performance staged purposely to invite comments from fellow artists

【观念】 guānniàn sense; idea; concept: 更新～ renew one's concept / 传统～ traditional concept / 道德～ moral concept

【观赏】 guānshǎng view and admire; enjoy the sight of

【观赏植物】 guānshǎng zhíwù ornamental plant

【观望】 guānwàng 1.(犹豫) wait and see; look on (from the sidelines): ～不前 hesitating and stalling 2.(张望) look around: 四下～ look around in all directions

【观望态度】 guānwàng tàidù wait-and-see attitude

【观瞻】 guānzhān 1.(给人的印象) the appearance of a place and the impressions it leaves: 有碍～ be repugnant to the eye; offend the eye 2.(瞻望;观赏) sight; view

【观众】 guānzhòng spectator; viewer; audience

官 (guān) 1.(公职人员) government official; officer; officeholder: 外交～ diplomat; diplomatic officer 2.（政府的或公家的）government-owned; government-sponsored; official; public 3.（器官）organ：感～ sense organ

【官办】 guānbàn run by the government; operated by official bodies

【官兵】 guānbīng officers and soldiers; officers and men

【官场】 guānchǎng officialdom; official circles

【官倒】 guāndǎo 1.（指行为）bureaucrat profiteering 2.（指人）profiteering official; bureaucratic profiteer

【官邸】 guāndǐ official residence; official mansion：大使～ ambassador's residence

【官方】 guānfāng of or by the government; official：～人士 official quarters / ～消息 news from government sources; official sources

【官复原职】 guānfù-yuánzhí restore an official to his original post; be reinstated

【官价】 guānjià official price

【官价汇率】 guānjià huìlǜ official rate of exchange

【官架子】 guānjià·zi the airs of an official; bureaucratic airs

【官僚】 guānliáo bureaucrat

【官僚主义】 guānliáo zhǔyì bureaucracy ‖ 官僚主义者 bureaucrat

【官僚主义作风】 guānliáo zhǔyì zuòfēng bureaucratic style of work; bureaucratic way of doing things

【官僚资本】 guānliáo zīběn bureaucrat capital

【官僚资本主义】 guānliáo zīběn zhǔyì bureaucrat capitalism

【官腔】 guānqiāng bureaucratic tone; official jargon：打～ speak in a bureaucratic tone; stall with official jargon

【官商】 guānshāng bureaucratic merchant

【官司】 guān·si lawsuit：和人打～ go to law against sb.

【官衔】 guānxián official title

【官员】 guānyuán official：外交～ diplomatic official

【官职】 guānzhí government post; official position

棺（guān） coffin

【棺材】 guān·cai coffin

冠（guān） 1.（帽子）hat 2.（冠状物）corona; crown：花～ corolla / 王～ crown 3.（鸟冠）crest; comb
（另见"冠"guàn）

【冠冕堂皇】 guānmiǎn-tánghuáng highfalutin; high-sounding

【冠心病】 guānxīnbìng 〈*Med*.〉 coronary heart disease

【冠状动脉】 guānzhuàng dòngmài 〈*Anat*.〉 coronary artery

【冠状动脉硬化】 guānzhuàng dòngmài yìnghuà 〈*Med*.〉 coronary arteriosclerosis

鳏（guān） wifeless

【鳏夫】 guānfū widower; bachelor

【鳏寡孤独】 guānguǎ gūdú widowers, widows, orphans and the childless

馆［館］（guǎn） 1.（招待宾客的处所）accommodation for guests：宾～ guest house / 旅～ hotel 2.（大使馆）embassy 3.（商店名称）shop：茶～ teahouse / 饭～ restaurant / 酒～ wineshop / 咖啡～ coffee house; cafe / 理发～ barbershop / 照相～ photo studio 4.（公共场所）a place for cultural activities：博物～ museum / 美术～ art gallery / 体育～ gymnasium / 图书～ library / 文化～ cultural center / 展览～ exhibition hall

【馆子】 guǎn·zi restaurant; eating house：下～ eat at a restaurant

管（guǎn） 1.（管子）tube; pipe：试～ test tube / 水～ water pipe 2.（管乐器）wind instrument 3.（管状电子器件）valve; tube：电子～ electron tube 4.（管理）manage; run; be in charge of：这事我～不了。I'm not in a position to take care of this business. 5.（管教）subject sb. to discipline 6.（过问）bother about; mind 7.（负责供给）provide; guarantee：～饭 provide meals

【管保】 guǎnbǎo 1.（保证）guarantee; assure 2.（肯定）certainly; surely

【管材】 guǎncái tubes; pipes

【管道】 guǎndào 1.（管子）pipeline; piping; conduit; tubing：煤气～ gas piping 2.（渠道，途径）channel

【管风琴】 guǎnfēngqín 〈*Music*〉 organ

【管家】 guǎn·jiā 1.（仆人）steward; butler 2.（管财物的人）manager; housekeeper
【管教】 guǎnjiào 1.（管保）certainly; surely 2.（约束教育）subject sb. to discipline
【管界】 guǎnjiè extent of jurisdiction
【管窥】 guǎnkuī look at sth. through a bamboo tube; have a restricted view
【管理】 guǎnlǐ 1.（从事管理）manage; run; administer; supervise: ～生产 manage production 2.（照管约束）take care of; keep control of
【管理方法】 guǎnlǐ fāngfǎ management techniques
【管理水平】 guǎnlǐ shuǐpíng managerial skills
【管片】 guǎnpiàn section of jurisdiction
【管区】 guǎnqū area of jurisdiction
【管事】 guǎnshì 1.（负责）run affairs; be in charge 2.（管用）efficacious; effective; of use 3.（管总务的人）manager; steward
【管辖】 guǎnxiá have jurisdiction over; administer
【管辖范围】 guǎnxiá fànwéi compass of competency; extent of jurisdiction; sphere of jurisdiction
【管弦乐】 guǎnxiányuè orchestral music
【管弦乐队】 guǎnxián yuèduì orchestra
【管用】 guǎnyòng efficacious; effective; in good repair
【管乐队】 guǎnyuèduì wind band; band
【管乐器】 guǎnyuèqì wind instrument
【管制】 guǎnzhì 1.（强制管理）control: 外汇～ foreign exchange control / 交通～ traffic control / 军事～ military control 2.（对罪犯强制管束）put under surveillance
【管制劳动】 guǎnzhì láodòng labor under surveillance
【管中窥豹】 guǎnzhōng-kuībào look at a leopard through a bamboo tube; have limited view of sth.
【管子】 guǎn·zi tube; pipe
【管子工】 guǎn·zigōng plumber; pipe fitter

贯（guàn） 1.（贯通）pass through; pierce 2.（连贯）be linked together; follow in a continuous line 3.（籍贯）birthplace; native place
【贯彻】 guànchè carry out; implement; put into effect: 全面～ carry out . . . in all respects / ～始终 prosecute to the end
【贯穿】 guànchuān run through; penetrate: 这条公路～十几个城镇。This highway runs through a dozen towns.
【贯通】 guàntōng 1.（透彻了解）have a thorough knowledge of; be well versed in 2.（接通）link up; thread together: 这条铁路已全线～。The whole railway line has been joined up.
【贯注】 guànzhù 1.（集中）concentrate on; be absorbed in: 全神～ be wholly absorbed; be rapt 2.（连贯；贯穿）be connected in meaning or feeling

惯（guàn） 1.（习惯）be used to; be in the habit of 2.（纵容）indulge; spoil: 孩子要管不要～。Children should be disciplined and not indulged.
【惯盗】 guàndào common thief; habitual robber; incorrigible thief
【惯犯】 guànfàn habitual offender; hardened criminal; recidivist; repeater
【惯匪】 guànfěi hardened bandit; professional brigand
【惯技】 guànjì old trick
【惯例】 guànlì 1.（常规）usual practice: 国际～ international practice / 外交～ diplomatic practice / 按照～ according to the practice 2.〈*Law*〉convention; conventional (adj.)
【惯偷】 guàntōu confirmed thief; habitual thief
【惯性】 guànxìng 〈*Physics*〉inertia
【惯性销售】 guànxìng xiāoshòu 〈*Trade*〉negative marketing; inertia selling
【惯用】 guànyòng 1.（惯于使用）habitually practice; consistently use 2.（惯用的）habitual; customary: ～伎俩 customary tactics / ～手法 habitual practice
【惯用法】 guànyòngfǎ usage

冠（guàn） 1.（把帽子戴在头上）put on a hat 2.（加名号或文字）precede; crown with 3.（居第一位）first place; the best （另见“冠”guān）
【冠军】 guànjūn champion; gold medalist
【冠军赛】 guànjūnsài championships; tournament

盥（guàn）

【盥洗】 guànxǐ wash one's hands and face
【盥洗室】 guànxǐshì washroom
【盥洗用具】 guànxǐ yòngjù toilet articles

灌 (guàn) 1.(浇) irrigate 2.(倒进;装进) fill; pour: 往游泳池里～水 fill the swimming pool with water
【灌肠】 guàncháng 〈*Med*.〉 enema
【灌肠】 guàn·chang sausage
【灌唱片】 guànchàngpiān make a gramophone record; cut a disc
【灌溉】 guàngài irrigate; irrigation (n.)
【灌溉面积】 guàngài miànjí irrigated area
【灌溉系统】 guàngài xìtǒng irrigation system
【灌录】 guànlù record; make a record
【灌木】 guànmù bush; shrub
【灌渠】 guànqú feed ditch
【灌输】 guànshū instill into; inculcate; imbue with
【灌醉】 guànzuì get sb. drunk
【灌制】 guànzhì cut (a disc)
【灌注】 guànzhù pour into

鹳 (guàn) 〈*Zool*.〉 stork

罐[鑵] (guàn) jar; pot; tin
【罐车】 guànchē tank car; tank truck; tanker
【罐头】 guàn·tou tin; can: 肉类～ canned meat / 水果～ canned fruit / 蔬菜～ canned vegetables / 鱼类～ canned fish
【罐头牛肉】 guàn·tou niúròu tinned beef
【罐头食品】 guàn·tou shípǐn tinned food
【罐子】 guàn·zi pot; jar; pitcher; jug: 玻璃～ glass pot; glass jar

guang

光 (guāng) 1.(光线) light; ray 2.(光亮) brightness; luster 3.(光荣) honor; glory 4.(景物) scenery 5.(光滑) smooth; glossy; polished 6.(一点不剩) used up; nothing left 7.(光着) bare; naked 8.(只;单) solely; only; merely; alone
【光膀子】 guāngbǎng·zi stripped to the waist
【光笔】 guāngbǐ light gun; light pen
【光标】 guāngbiāo 〈*Computer*〉 cursor
【光波】 guāngbō light wave
【光彩】 guāngcǎi 1.(颜色和光泽) luster; splendor; radiance 2.(光荣) honorable; glorious
【光彩夺目】 guāngcǎi duómù bright and glittering
【光导纤维】 guāngdǎo xiānwéi optical fiber; light-transmitting fiber
【光电】 guāngdiàn 〈*Physics*〉 photoelectricity
【光电管】 guāngdiànguǎn photocell; phototube
【光度】 guāngdù luminosity
【光度计】 guāngdùjì photometer
【光辐射】 guāngfúshè ray radiation
【光复】 guāngfù recover; recovery
【光复失地】 guāngfù shīdì recover lost territory; regain possession of lost territory
【光杆儿】 guānggǎnr 1.(花叶尽落) a bare trunk or stalk 2.(失去家属的人) a man who has lost his family 3.(失去群众的领导) a person without a following: ～司令 a general without an army; a leader without a following
【光棍儿】 guānggùnr unmarried man; bachelor
【光合作用】 guānghé zuòyòng 〈*Biol*.〉 photosynthesis
【光滑】 guāng·huá smooth; glossy; sleek
【光辉】 guānghuī 1.(耀眼的光) radiance; brilliance; glory 2.(光明;灿烂) brilliant; magnificent; glorious: ～的一生 a glorious life / ～形象 magnificent images
【光辉灿烂】 guānghuī cànlàn shine with great splendor; shine with increasing splendor
【光洁】 guāngjié bring and clean
【光洁度】 guāngjiédù 〈*Mech*.〉 smooth finish; fineness: ～高 highly polished
【光解作用】 guāngjiě zuòyòng 〈*Physics*〉 photolysis
【光景】 guāngjǐng 1.(情景) scene 2.(景况) circumstances; conditions: ～越来越好 the life is becoming better and better 3.(大约) about; around
【光缆】 guānglǎn optical cable
【光亮】 guāngliàng 1.(明亮) bright; luminous; shiny 2.(亮光) light
【光临】 guānglín 〈*politeness*〉 presence (of a guest, etc.): 敬请～。Your presence is cor-

dially requested.

【光溜溜】 guāngliūliū 1.(光滑) smooth; slippery 2.(无遮盖) bare; naked

【光芒】 guāngmáng rays of light; brilliant rays; radiance

【光明】 guāngmíng 1.(亮光) light: 重见～ see the light again 2.(明亮) bright; promising: ～前途 bright prospects; brilliant future 3.(没有私心) openhearted; guileless

【光明磊落】 guāngmíng-lěiluò open and aboveboard; frank and openhearted

【光明正大】 guāngmíng-zhèngdà open and aboveboard; just and honorable

【光年】 guāngnián 〈*Astron*.〉 light-year (1光年＝94,605亿公里)

【光谱】 guāngpǔ 〈*Physics*〉 spectrum; spectral (adj.)

【光圈】 guāngquān 〈*Photog*.〉 aperture; diaphragm

【光圈环】 guāngquānhuán 〈*Photog*.〉 aperture ring

【光荣】 guāngróng honor; glory; credit: ～称号 a title of honor / ～人家 honorable family

【光荣榜】 guāngróngbǎng honor roll

【光速】 guāngsù light speed

【光天化日】 guāngtiān huàrì broad daylight; the light of day

【光头】 guāngtóu 1.(不戴帽子) bareheaded 2.(秃头) shaven head; shaven-headed

【光秃秃】 guāngtūtū bare; bald: ～的山 a bald hill / 这山～的没有树。The hill is bare of trees.

【光鲜】 guāngxiān 1.(明亮鲜艳) bright 2. honorable; glorious

【光纤】 guāngxiān optical fiber; light-transmitting fiber

【光纤通信】 guāngxiān tōngxìn optical fiber communication; optical fiber telecommunication

【光线】 guāngxiàn light; ray

【光学】 guāngxué optics; optical (adj.)

【光学玻璃】 guāngxué bō·li optical glass

【光学工程】 guāngxué gōngchéng optical engineering

【光学仪器】 guāngxué yíqì optical instrument

【光阴】 guāngyīn time: ～虚度 lose one's time by trifling / ～似箭。Time flies like an arrow.

【光源】 guāngyuán light source; illuminant

【光泽】 guāngzé luster; gloss; sheen

【光照】 guāngzhào 〈*Bot*.〉 illumination

【光照度】 guāngzhàodù illuminance

【光针】 guāngzhēn 〈*Med*.〉 laser acupuncture

【光柱】 guāngzhù light beam

【光子】 guāngzǐ 〈*Physics*〉 photon

【光子火箭】 guāngzǐ huǒjiàn photon rocket

【光宗耀祖】 guāngzōng yàozǔ bring honor to one's ancestors

咣 (guāng) 〈*onomat*.〉 bang

【咣当】 guāngdāng bang: 窗户～一声关上了。The window closed with a bang.

桄 (guāng)

【桄榔】 guāngláng 1.〈*Bot*.〉 gomuti palm 2.(果实) seeds of gomuti palm

胱 (guāng)

【胱氨酸】 guāng'ānsuān 〈*Med*.〉 cystine

广[廣] (guǎng) 1.(宽阔) wide; vast; extensive: 地～人稀 a vast and densely populated country 2.(多) numerous: 她在大庭～众之下出了丑。She made a fool of herself in public. 3.(扩大) expand; spread: ～为流传的民间故事 a widely spread folk-tale

【广板】 guǎngbǎn 〈*Music*〉 largo

【广播】 guǎngbō broadcast; be on the air: 开始～ go on the air / 实况～ live broadcast; live transmissions over the radio or television / 足球赛的～ the broadcast of a football match / ～新闻 broadcast the news

【广播波段】 guǎngbō bōduàn broadcast band

【广播电台】 guǎngbō diàntái broadcasting station

【广播发射机】 guǎngbō fāshèjī broadcast transmitter

【广播发射台】 guǎngbō fāshètái broadcast transmitting station

【广播稿】 guǎngbōgǎo broadcast message

【广播讲话】 guǎngbō jiǎnghuà broadcast speech; radio talk

【广播教学】 guǎngbō jiàoxué distance teaching

【广播节目】 guǎngbō jiémù broadcast program

【广播剧】 guǎngbōjù radio play

【广播喇叭】 guǎngbō lǎbā loudspeaker

【广播频率】 guǎngbō pīnlǜ broadcasting frequency

【广播时间】 guǎngbō shíjiān airtime

【广播室】 guǎngbōshì studio

【广播体操】 guǎngbō tǐcāo setting-up exercises to radio music

【广播网】 guǎngbōwǎng diffusion network

【广播信道】 guǎngbō xìndào broadcast channel

【广播员】 guǎngbōyuán (radio) announcer; broadcaster

【广播站】 guǎngbōzhàn broadcasting station; rediffusion station

【广播装置】 guǎngbō zhuāngzhì broadcaster; loudspeaker system

【广博】 guǎngbó extensive; wide: 学识～ have extensive knowledge / 她在这一学科上知识～。Her knowledge of the subject is extensive.

【广场】 guǎngchǎng 1.(城市中宽广的场地) square; public square: 天安门～ Tian An Men Square / 在～上听乐队的演奏 listen to the band playing in the square 2.(源于西班牙语,转义指商业建筑群) plaza

【广场音乐会】 guǎngchǎng yīnyuèhuì promenade; promenade concert ‖ 广场音乐会听众 promenader

【广大】 guǎngdà 1.(宽阔) vast; wide; extensive: 幅员～ vast in territory 2.(巨大) large-scale; wide spread 3.(众多) numerous: ～读者 the reading public

【广度】 guǎngdù scope; range: 社会变革的～和深度 deep and widespread social changes

【广而言之】 guǎng'éryánzhī speaking generally; in a general sense

【广泛】 guǎngfàn extensive; wide-ranging; widespread: ～的影响 widespread influence / ～的贸易关系 far-flung trade connections / 这则报导引起了～的兴趣。This news aroused wide interest.

【广泛抽样】 guǎngfàn chōuyàng extensive sampling

【广柑】 guǎnggān a kind of orange

【广告】 guǎnggào advertisement; advertise (v.); ad.: 车身～ transportation advertising / 灯光～ illuminated signs; electric sign advertising / 分类～ classified advertisements / 在报纸上做～ put an advertisement in the newspaper / 我们公司耗巨资为产品做～。Our company spends a large amount of money advertising our products. / 公司登～招聘一名新秘书。The company advertised for a new secretary.

【广告布局】 guǎnggào bùjú layout: ～设计 layout design

【广告部】 guǎnggàobù advertising department

【广告插页】 guǎnggào chāyè insert

【广告大战】 guǎnggào dàzhàn advertising campaign

【广告代理人】 guǎnggào dàilǐrén advertising agent

【广告费】 guǎnggàofèi advertising fee

【广告经纪人】 guǎnggào jīnjìrén advertising broker; advertising agent

【广告栏】 guǎnggàolán advertisement column

【广告妙语】 guǎnggào miàoyǔ attention-getter

【广告牌】 guǎnggàopái billboard; show-card sign

【广告片】 guǎnggàopiān advertising film

【广告人】 guǎnggàorén advertiser; adman

【广告色】 guǎnggàosè poster color; poster paint

【广告社】 guǎnggàoshè advertising agency

【广告设计】 guǎnggào shèjì advertising design

【广告识别标记】 guǎnggào shíbié biāojì logotype

【广告时间】 guǎnggào shíjiān time spot

【广告效果】 guǎnggào xiàoguǒ effectiveness of advertising; demonstration effect

【广告效果检验法】 guǎnggào xiàoguǒ jiǎnyànfǎ aided recall

【广告效果研究】 guǎnggào xiàoguǒ yánjiū analysis of advertising results

【广告心理学】 guǎnggào xīnlǐxué advertising

psychology
【广告宣传】 guǎnggào xuānchuán advertising
【广告研究】 guǎnggào yánjiū advertising research
【广告艺术家】 guǎnggào yìshùjiā commercial artist
【广告邮件】 guǎnggào yóujiàn junk mail; advertisement matter
【广告预算】 guǎnggào yùsuàn advertising budget
【广告正文】 guǎnggào zhèngwén body text
【广告撰稿人】 guǎnggào zhuàngǎorén copywriter
【广告咨询费】 guǎnggào zīxúnfèi cost of inquiry
【广寒宫】 guǎnghángōng the Moon Palace (the mythical palace in the moon)
【广藿香】 guǎnghuòxiāng 〈*Bot*.〉 patchouli
【广见博识】 guǎnjiàn-bóshí have a rich experience and extensive knowledge
【广交四海】 guǎngjiāo-sìhǎi make-friends extensively
【广角镜头】 guǎngjiǎo jìngtóu wide angle lens
【广开才路】 guǎngkāi-cáilù open all avenues for people of talent
【广开眼界】 guǎngkāi-yǎnjiè one's field of vision is vastly enlarged; widen one's horizon
【广口瓶】 guǎngkǒupíng wide-necked bottle
【广阔】 guǎngkuò vast; wide; broad: ～的前景 broad prospects / ～天地 a wide world; a vast new world
【广绫】 guǎnglíng Canton satin
【广漠】 guǎngmò vast and bare: 在～的沙滩上 on the bare expanse of the beach
【广纳贤士】 guǎngnà-xiánshì send far and wide to invite men of ability
【广食性】 guǎngshíxìng euryphagy; euryphagous (adj.)
【广温性】 guǎngwēnxìng eurytherm
【广盐性】 guǎngyánxìng eurysalinity; eurysaline (adj.)
【广盐性鱼类】 guǎngyánxìng yúlèi eurysaline fishes
【广延】 guǎngyán 〈*Physics*〉 extension; extensive (adj.)
【广延宾客】 guǎngyán-bīnkè keep open house
【广延参量】 guǎngyán cānliàng extensive parameter
【广延量】 guǎngyánliàng extensive quantity
【广义】 guǎngyì 1.(范围较宽的定义) broad sense: 从～上说 in a broad sense; broadly speaking 2.〈*Physics*〉 generalized
【广义函数】 guǎngyì hánshù distribution
【广义积分】 guǎngyì jífēn improper integral
【广义空间】 guǎngyì kōngjiān generalized space
【广义理论】 guǎngyì lǐlùn generalized theory
【广义速度】 guǎngyì sùdù generalized velocity
【广义相对论】 guǎngyì xiāngduìlùn general theory of relativity
【广义坐标】 guǎngyì zuòbiāo generalized coordinates
【广征博引】 guǎngzhēn-bóyǐn quote and prove fully
【广种薄收】 guǎngzhòng-bóshōu extensive cultivation

犷[獷] (guǎng) rustic; rude; unmannerly
【犷悍】 guǎnghàn tough and valiant

逛 (guàng) stroll; saunter; ramble; roam: ～大街 stroll around the streets; saunter in the street / ～公园 stroll in the park; walk and play in the park

gui

归[歸] (guī) 1.(返回) go back to; return: 胜利～来 return victoriously 2.(归还) give back to; return sth. to: 物～原主 return a thing to its rightful owner 3.(趋向于;集中于) converge; come together 4.(由谁负责) turn over to; put in sb's charge: 这件事～我。Leave this to me.
【归案】 guīàn bring to justice
【归并】 guībìng 1.(合并到) incorporate into; merge into: 把一家公司～到另一家公司 merge one company into another 2.(合并在一起;归拢) lump together; add up
【归程】 guīchéng return journey
【归档】 guīdàng place on file; file
【归队】 guīduì 1.(回原部队) rejoin one's unit; return to the ranks 2.(重干本行) return

to the profession one was trained for
【归根结底】 guīgēn-jiédǐ in the final analysis; come down to bedrock
【归公】 guīgōng be made a public possession; go to the public
【归功于】 guīgōngyú attribute the success to; give the credit to
【归国】 guīguó return to one's country: ～观光 return to one's homeland on a sightseeing tour
【归还】 guīhuán return; revert; send back; give back
【归结】 guījié 1.(总括) sum up; put in a nutshell 2.(结局) end (of a story, etc.): 故事的～ the end of the story
【归咎】 guījiù impute to; attribute a fault to; put the blame on: ～于你 the blame falls entirely on you
【归口】 guīkǒu belong under
【归口单位】 guīkǒu dānwèi specified administrative department
【归来】 guīlái go back; return
【归拢】 guīlǒng put together
【归纳】 guīnà 1.(归并) sum up; conclude; induce: ～报告的要点 sum up the main points of the report 2.(一种推理方法) inductive method; induction
【归期】 guīqī date of return
【归侨】 guīqiáo returned overseas national; returned overseas Chinese
【归入】 guīrù classify; include
【归属】 guīshǔ belong to; come under the jurisdiction of
【归顺】 guīshùn submit to; yield to; pledge allegiance
【归宿】 guīsù a home to return to: 人生～ destination of one's life voyage / 找到人生～ find the place where one belongs
【归途】 guītú homeward journey; one's way home
【归心似箭】 guīxīn sìjiàn be anxious to return home
【归于】 guīyú 1.(属于) belong to; be attributed to 2.(趋向于) tend to; result in; end in: 我们的看法～一致。Our views tend to be the same.
【归总】 guīzǒng put (items, etc.) together; sum up: ～一句话 to put it in a nutshell
【归罪】 guīzuì put the blame on; impute to
【归罪于】 guīzuìyú impute; incriminate; inculpate

圭 (guī)

【圭表】 guībiǎo ancient Chinese sundial

闺 (guī)

【闺房】 guīfáng boudoir
【闺女】 guī·nü 1.(未婚女子) girl; maiden 2.(女儿) daughter

硅 (guī) 〈*Chem.*〉 silicon (元素符号 Si)

【硅二极管】 guī'èrjíguǎn silicon detector; silicon diode
【硅肺】 guīfèi 〈*Med.*〉 silicosis
【硅钢】 guīgāng silicon steel
【硅化】 guīhuà silification
【硅化物】 guīhuàwù silicide
【硅可控整流器】 guīkěkòng zhěngliúqì 〈*Electr.*〉 silicon controlled rectifier
【硅酸盐】 guīsuānyán 〈*Chem.*〉 silicate
【硅酸盐工业】 guīsuānyán gōngyè silicate industry
【硅酸盐水泥】 guīsuānyán shuǐní portland cement

鲑 (guī) salmon

【鲑鱼】 guīyú salmon

龟[**龜**] (guī) tortoise; turtle (另见"龟"jūn)

【龟板】 guībǎn 〈*Chin. Pharm.*〉 tortoise-shell
【龟甲】 guījiǎ tortoise-shell
【龟缩】 guīsuō huddle up like a turtle drawing in its head and legs
【龟头】 guītóu 〈*Anat.*〉 glans penis

规[**槼**] (guī) 1.(圆规) compasses; dividers 2.(规则; 成例) regulation; rule 3.(劝告) admonish; advise 4.(谋划) plan; map out 5.〈*Mech.*〉 gauge

【规避】 guībì evade; dodge; avoid: ～义务 evade obligations
【规程】 guīchéng rules; regulations: 操作～ rules of operation
【规定】 guīdìng 1.(所做的决定) stipulate;

provide 2.（所规定的内容）fix；set；formulate：在～的时间内 within the fixed time

【规范】 guīfàn 1.（标准）standard；norm：用法不～ not conform with regular usage 2.（合乎规范）standard；normal 3.（使合乎规范）standardize：～市场行为 standardize market activities

【规范化】 guīfànhuà standardize；standardization

【规格】 guīgé specifications；standards；norms

【规划】 guīhuà 1.（计划）program；plan：城市～ a city plan / 市政～ a plan of the municipal administration 2.（做规划）make a plan；make a program：做出全面～ make a comprehensive program

【规矩】 guī·ju 1.（法则）rule；established practice；custom：守～ follow the custom 2.（端正老实）well-behaved；well-disciplined

【规律】 guīlǜ law；regular pattern：客观～ objective law / 历史发展的～ law of the development of history / 自然～ law of nature / 生活有～ live a regular life

【规模】 guīmó scale；scope；dimensions：大～的调查 investigation of wide scope

【规劝】 guīquàn admonish；advise

【规约】 guīyuē 1.（条款）stipulations of an agreement 2.（限制，约束）restrain；restrict

【规则】 guīzé 1.（章则）rule；regulation：交通～ traffic regulations 2.（规律；法则）law 3.（整齐）regular：～四边形 regular quadrangle

【规章】 guīzhāng rules；regulations：～制度 rules and regulations

皈 (guī)

【皈依】 guīyī be converted to (a religion)

瑰 (guī)

【瑰宝】 guībǎo rarity；treasure；gem：艺术～ artistic treasure

【瑰丽】 guīlì surpassingly beautiful；magnificent：天山山脉的～景色 the scenic splendor of the Tianshan Mountains

【瑰丽多彩】 guīlì-duōcǎi extraordinarily beautiful and magnificent

轨 (guǐ) 1.（路轨）rail；track：出～ be derailed 2.（规矩、秩序等）course；path：纳入正～ put on the right track / 越～ violate the rule

【轨道】 guǐdào 1.（路轨）track：地铁～ underground railway track 2.（运行路线）orbit；trajectory 3.（规则；范围）course；path

【轨道地球物理观测卫星】 guǐdào dìqiú wùlǐ guāncè wèixīng O. G. O.；Orbiting Geophysical Observatory

【轨道站】 guǐdàozhàn 〈*Astron.*〉 orbit station

【轨迹】 guǐjì 1.（移动路线）locus 2.（天体轨道）orbit 3.（发展道路）course；path

【轨距】 guǐjù 〈*Railroad*〉 gauge：标准～ standard gauge

【轨枕】 guǐzhěn 〈*Railroad*〉 sleeper；tie；crosstie

诡 (guǐ) 1.（奸诈）deceitful；tricky；cunning：～称 say deceitfully；falsely allege；pretend 2.（奇异）weird；eerie

【诡辩】 guǐbiàn sophistry；sophism；quibbling

【诡计】 guǐjì crafty plot；cunning scheme；trick；ruse：～多端 have a whole bag of tricks；be very crafty

【诡谲多诈】 guǐjué-duōzhà be sly and shrewd

【诡秘】 guǐmì surreptitious；secretive

【诡诈】 guǐzhà crafty；cunning；treacherous

鬼 (guǐ) 1.（迷信的人认为人死后的灵魂）ghost；spirit；apparition：～故事 ghost stories 2.（不光明）stealthy；surreptitious 3.（不可告人的勾当）sinister plot；dirty trick：心里有～ have a guilty conscience 4.（恶劣）terrible；damnable 5.（机灵）clever；smart；quick

【鬼点子】 guǐdiǎn·zi wicked idea；trick

【鬼怪】 guǐguài ghosts and monsters；monsters of all kinds；forces of evil

【鬼鬼祟祟】 guǐguǐ-suìsuì sneaking；furtive；stealthy

【鬼话】 guǐhuà lies；empty words：这份报告通篇是～。The report is a peak of lies.

【鬼魂】 guǐhún ghost；spirit；apparition

【鬼混】 guǐhùn 1.（糊里糊涂地过活）lead an aimless existence 2.（与他人过不正当的生活）hang around with sb.

【鬼脸】 guǐliǎn 1.（脸部表情滑稽）funny face；wry face；grimace 2.（假面具）mask

used as a toy
【鬼迷心窍】 guǐmí-xīnqiào be possessed; be obsessed
【鬼胎】 guǐtāi sinister design; ulterior motive: 心怀～ harbor sinister designs
【鬼蜮】 guǐyù evil spirit; demon; treacherous person: ～伎俩 devilish stratagem; evil tactics
【鬼主意】 guǐzhǔ·yi evil plan; wicked idea
【鬼子】 guǐ·zi devil: 洋～ foreign devil; foreign invaders

柜[櫃](guì) cupboard; cabinet
【柜台】 guìtái counter; bar: 玻璃～ show case / 站～ serve behind the counter
【柜子】 guì·zi cupboard; cabinet; chest

刽[劊](guì) cut off; chop off
【刽子手】 guì·zishǒu **1.**(执行死刑的人) executioner; headsman **2.**(屠杀人民的人) slaughterer; butcher

贵(guì) **1.**(价格高) expensive; costly; dear: 价钱很～ very expensive **2.**(值得重视) highly valued; valuable; precious: ～在坚持。The important thing is perseverance. / 人～有自知之明。It is a good thing for one to be able to have a proper appraisal of oneself. **3.**(地位优越) of high rank; noble **4.**〈*politeness*〉 your: ～国 your country / ～国人民 your people
【贵宾】 guìbīn honored guest; distinguished guest
【贵宾席】 guìbīnxí seats for distinguished guests
【贵客】 guìkè distinguished guest
【贵客盈门】 guìkè yíngmén The house was full of distinguished guests
【贵姓】 guìxìng your name: 您～? What's your name, please?
【贵重】 guìzhòng valuable; precious: ～珠宝 valuables jewels
【贵族】 guìzú noble; aristocrat

桂(guì) **1.**(肉桂) cassia bark tree **2.**(月桂) laurel; bay tree
【桂冠】 guìguān laurel
【桂花】 guìhuā sweet-scented osmanthus
【桂皮】 guìpí cassia bark
【桂圆】 guìyuán longan

跪(guì) kneel; go down on one's knees
【跪拜】 guìbài kowtow; bow and kneel to
【跪撑摔】 guìchēngshuāi 〈*Wrestle*〉 on-the-ground wrestling
【跪倒】 guìdǎo throw oneself on one's knees; prostrate oneself; grovel: ～在地 go down on one's knee / ～在…的脚下 throw oneself at sb's feet
【跪射】 guìshè 〈*Mil.*〉 kneeling fire
【跪姿】 guìzī kneeling position

gun

滚[滾](gǔn) **1.**(滚动) roll; trundle: ～下山去 roll down the hill **2.**(走开) get away; beat it: 你给我～! Get away with you! **3.**(沸腾) boil: 用～水泡茶 make tea with boiling water **4.**(缝纫方法) bind; trim: 袖口上～一道花边 make an embroidered hem on the cuff
【滚齿机】 gǔnchǐjī hob; gear-hobbing machine
【滚蛋】 gǔndàn 〈*offens.*〉 scram; get away
【滚动】 gúndòng roll; trundle
【滚瓜烂熟】 gǔnguā lànshú (recite, etc.) fluently; (know sth.) pat
【滚滚】 gǔngǔn **1.**(急速滚动或翻腾) billow; roll: ～的浓烟 billowing smoke **2.**(连续不断) roll; surge: ～而来 roll in; come in torrents
【滚雷】 gǔnléi 〈*Mil.*〉 rolling mine
【滚式跳高】 gǔnshì tiàogāo Western layout
【滚烫】 gǔntàng boiling hot; burning hot
【滚筒】 gǔntǒng cylinder; roll
【滚雪球】 gǔnxuěqiú snowball
【滚圆】 gǔnyuán round as a ball; ball-shaped
【滚轴滑冰】 gǔnzhóu huábīng roller skate; roller skating (n.)
【滚轴滑冰场】 gǔnzhóu huábīngchǎng roller skating rink
【滚轴滑冰鞋】 gǔnzhóu huábīngxié roller skate
【滚珠】 gǔnzhū 〈*Mech.*〉 ball
【滚珠轴承】 gǔnzhū zhóuchéng ball bearing
【滚柱轴承】 gǔnzhù zhóuchéng roller bearing

【滚装船】 gǔnzhuāngchuán roll-on-roll-off ship

磙［磙］(gǔn) 1.（磙子）roller; stone roller 2.（用磙子轧）level with a roller

【磙子】 gǔn·zi roller; stone roller

辊(gǔn) 〈*Mech.*〉 roller

【辊子】 gǔn·zi roller

棍(gùn) 1.（棍子）rod; stick 2.（无赖）scoundrel; rascal: 恶～ ruffian; rascal

【棍棒】 gùnbàng 1.（武术器械）club; cudgel 2.（体操器械）a stick or staff used in gymnastics

【棍子】 gǔn·zi rod; stick: 打～ criticize arbitrarily and unfoundedly

guo

锅［鍋］(guō) 1.（炊事用具）pot; pan; boiler; caldron; etc.: 大～ caldron / 煎～ frying-pan / 压力～ pressure cooker / 煮～ saucepan; stewpan 2.（器物上像锅的部分）bowl (of a pipe, etc.)

【锅巴】 guōbā crust of cooked rice; rice crust

【锅把】 guōbǎ handle

【锅耳】 guō'ěr handle

【锅盖】 guōgài cover; lid

【锅炉】 guōlú boiler

【锅炉房】 guōlúfáng boiler room

【锅炉给水】 guōlú jǐshuǐ boiler feedwater

【锅炉效率】 guōlú xiàolǜ boiler efficiency

【锅台】 guōtái the top of a kitchen range

【锅贴儿】 guōtiēr lightly fried dumpling

【锅子】 guō·zi 1.（锅）pot; caldron 2.（器物上像锅的部分）bowl (of a pipe, etc.) 3.（火锅）chafing dish

蝈［蟈］(guō)

【蝈蝈儿】 guō·guor katydid; long-horned grasshopper

聒(guō) noise

【聒耳】 guō'ěr a piercing noise

【聒噪】 guōzào noisy; clamorous

国［國、囯］(guó) 1.（国家）country; state; nation 2.（代表国家的）of the state; national 3.（指我国的）of our country; Chinese

【国宝】 guóbǎo national treasure

【国宾】 guóbīn state guest

【国宾馆】 guóbīnguǎn state guest house

【国策】 guócè the basic policy of a state; national policy

【国产】 guóchǎn made in our country; made in China

【国产货】 guóchǎnhuò domestic products; domestic goods

【国产品】 guóchǎnpǐn national products; domestic products

【国耻】 guóchǐ national humiliation

【国粹】 guócuì the quintessence of Chinese culture

【国道】 guódào state road

【国都】 guódū national capital; capital

【国度】 guódù country; state; nation

【国法】 guófǎ national law

【国法无情】 guófǎ-wúqíng the law is no respecter of persons

【国防】 guófáng national defense

【国防部】 guófángbù the Ministry of National Defense

【国防工业】 guófáng gōngyè national defense industry

【国歌】 guógē national anthem

【国格】 guógé dignity of the nation; national dignity

【国画】 guóhuà traditional Chinese painting

【国徽】 guóhuī national emblem

【国会】 guóhuì 1.（议会）parliament 2.（美国议会）Congress 3.（日本议会）the Diet

【国货】 guóhuò national products; domestic products

【国籍】 guójí 1.（个人的）nationality: 双重～ dual nationality / 无～ statelessness; stateless / 申请加入～ apply for naturalization 2.（船舶、飞机等的）registration in a certain country: 不明～的飞机 unidentified aircraft

【国计民生】 guójì-mínshēng the national economy and the people's livelihood

【国际】 guójì international: ～地位 international status / ～关系 international relations / ～事务 international affairs / ～形势 the international situation

【国际奥委会】 Guójì Àowěihuì the International Olympic Committee (IOC)

【国际标准】 guójì biāozhǔn international standard

【国际标准期刊编号】 guójì biāozhǔn qīkān biānhào International Standard Serial Number; ISSN

【国际标准书号】 guójì biāozhǔn shūhào International Standard Book Number; ISBN

【国际博览会】 guójì bólǎnhuì international fair

【国际单位制】 guójì dānwèizhì International Unit System

【国际地球物理年】 guójì dìqiú wùlǐnián International Geophysical Year (IGY)

【国际儿童节】 Guójì Értóngjié International Children's Day

【国际法】 guójìfǎ international law; the law of nations

【国际法准则】 guójìfǎ zhǔnzé norms of international law; an established principle of international law

【国际歌】 Guójìgē The Internationale

【国际公法】 guójì gōngfǎ international public law

【国际公约】 guójì gōngyuē international convention

【国际共运】 guójì gōngyùn international communist movement

【国际惯例】 guójì guànlì international practice; international usage

【国际环境】 guójì huánjìng international environment: 和平的～ peaceful international environment

【国际货币基金组织】 Guójì Huòbì Jījīn Zǔzhī International Monetary Fund (IMF)

【国际监督】 guójì jiāndū international control

【国际经济新秩序】 guójì jīngjì xīnzhìxù a new international economic order

【国际警察组织】 Guójì Jǐngchá Zǔzhī Interpol

【国际劳动妇女节】 Guójì Láodòng Fùnǚjié International Working Women's Day

【国际劳动节】 Guójì Láodòngjié International Labor Day; May Day

【国际列车】 guójì lièchē international train

【国际日期变更线】 guójì rìqī biàngēngxiàn international date line; date-line

【国际收支】 guójì shōuzhī balance of (international) payments: ～不平衡 disequilibrium of balance of payments

【国际书籍标准编号】 guójì shūjí biāozhǔn biānhào International Standard Book Number; ISBN

【国际水域】 guójì shuǐyù international waters

【国际私法】 guójì sīfǎ international private law

【国际象棋】 guójì xiàngqí chess

【国际新秩序】 guójì xīnzhìxù new international order

【国际形势】 guójì xíngshì international situation

【国际音标】 guójì yīnbiāo the International Phonetic Alphabet

【国际直拨】 guójì zhíbō international direct dial (IDD)

【国际制】 guójìzhì International Unit System

【国际主义】 guójì zhǔyì internationalism ‖ 国际主义者 internationalist

【国际主义义务】 guójì zhǔyì yìwù internationalist duty

【国际组织】 guójì zǔzhī international organization

【国家】 guójiā country; state; nation: 第三世界～ Third World countries / 发达～ advanced country / 发展中～ developing countries / 友好～ friendly country / 中等发达～ moderately developed country / 周边～ surrounding countries / ～不分大小, 应该一律平等。All countries, big or small, should be equal.

【国家大事】 guójiā dàshì national affairs

【国家队】 guójiāduì national team

【国家二级企业】 guójiā èrjí qǐyè second-class state enterprise

【国家关系】 guójiā guānxì state relations: 建立正常的～ establish normal state relations

【国家合并】 guójiā hébìng merger of states

【国家机关】 guójiā jīguān state organs; government offices

【国家机关工作人员】 guójiā jīguān gōngzuò rényuán personnel of organs of state; state personnel

【国家机密】 guójiā jīmì state secrets

【国家机器】 guójiā jīqì state apparatus

【国家奖】 guójiājiǎng state award of honor; state prize

【国家统配】 guójiā tǒngbèi direct state distribution

【国家兴亡,匹夫有责】 guójiā-xīngwáng, pǐfū-yǒuzé The rise and fall of the nation is the concern of every citizen. (或: All men share a common responsibility for the fate of their country.)

【国家元首】 guójiā yuānshǒu head of state

【国家重点工程】 guójiā zhòngdiǎn gōngchéng key state project

【国家主权】 guójiā zhǔquán national sovereignty: 保卫～和民族资源 safeguard national sovereignty and national resources

【国家资本主义】 guójiā zīběn zhǔyì state capitalism

【国脚】 guójiǎo football star; national champion in football

【国界】 guójiè national boundaries

【国境】 guójìng border

【国境线】 guójìngxiàn boundary line

【国库】 guókù national treasury

【国库券】 guókùquàn state treasury bonds; treasury bill (T. B.): 发行～ issue treasury bills / 两年期～ two-year state treasure bonds

【国立】 guólì state-maintained; state-run

【国立大学】 guólì dàxué national university

【国民】 guómín national: ～经济 national economy / ～收入 national income

【国民党】 guómíndǎng the Kuomintang (KMT); nationalist party

【国民党革命委员会】 guómíndǎng gémìng wěiyuánhuì Revolutionary Committee of Kuomintang

【国民生产总值】 guómín shēngchǎn zǒngzhí gross national product (GNP)

【国内】 guónèi internal; domestic; home

【国内贸易】 guónèi màoyì domestic trade

【国内生产总值】 guónèi shēngchǎn zǒngzhí gross domestic product (GDP)

【国内市场】 guónèi shìchǎng domestic market

【国内新闻】 guónèi xīnwén home news

【国内战争】 guónèi zhànzhēng civil war: 第一次国内革命战争 the First Revolutionary Civil War

【国内直拨】 guónèi zhíbō domestic direct dial (DDD)

【国旗】 guóqí national flag: 升～ raise the national flag / 各成员国的～在总部外迎风飘扬。Flags of all the member countries are flying outside the headquarters.

【国情】 guóqíng the condition of a country; national conditions: 不合～ out of keeping with country's conditions

【国庆节】 guóqìngjié National Day

【国事】 guóshì national affairs

【国事访问】 guóshì fǎngwèn state visit

【国是】 guóshì affairs of state; matters of national importance: 共商～ hold discussions on affairs of state

【国书】 guóshū letter of credence; credentials: 递交～ present one's credentials

【国泰民安】 guótài-mín'ān the country is prosperous and the people live in peace

【国土】 guótǔ territory; land

【国外】 guówài external; overseas; abroad

【国外代理行】 guówài dàilǐháng foreign agency

【国外市场】 guówài shìchǎng overseas market

【国外投资】 guówài tóuzī external assets

【国王】 guówáng king

【国威】 guówēi national strength; power of a nation

【国务会议】 guówù huìyì state conference: 最高～ the Supreme State Conference

【国务卿】 guówùqīng (美国外交部长) Secretary of State

【国务委员】 guówù wěiyuán State councillor

【国务院】 guówùyuàn 1. (国家最高行政机关) the State Council 2. (美国外交部) the State Department

【国务院副总理】 guówùyuàn fùzǒnglǐ vice-premier

【国务院总理】 guówùyuàn zǒnglǐ premier; prime minister

【国宴】 guóyàn state banquet: 设～招待 hold the state banquet in honor of sb.

【国营】 guóyíng state-operated; state-run

【国营经济】 guóyíng jīngjì state sector of the

economy; state-owned economy

【国营农场】 guóyíng nóngchǎng state farm

【国营企业】 guóyíng qǐyè state enterprise

【国优产品】 guóyōu chǎnpǐn products of the best quality in a country; the nation's best product

【国有化】 guóyǒuhuà nationalize; nationalise; nationalization (n.)：将煤炭工业、钢铁工业和铁路实行～ nationalize the coal and steel industries and the railways

【国有经济】 guǒyǒu jīngjì state-owned economy：非～ non-state-owned economy

【国有企业】 guóyǒu qǐyè state-owned enterprises：大中型～ large and medium-sized state-owned enterprises

【国资】 guózī state funds; state capital

果 (guǒ) 1.(果实) fruit：干～ dry fruit / 鲜～ fresh fruit / 开花后,不久就结～。After blossoming, it will soon bear fruit. 2.(结果,后果) result; consequence：恶～ a disastrous result 3.(果断) resolute; determined：言必信,行必～ true to one's word and resolute in action 4.(果然) really; as expected; sure enough：～不出所料 just as one expected 5.(果真) if indeed; if really：～有所见,不妨实说。If you should have any opinion, you might as well tell us frankly.

【果不其然】 guǒ·buqírán as expected; not unexpectedly; indeed：～,下了雨。As expected, it rained.

【果冻儿】 guǒdòngr jelly

【果断】 guǒduàn resolute; decisive：办事～ handle affairs in a decisive manner

【果脯】 guǒfǔ preserved fruit; candied fruit

【果敢】 guǒgǎn courageous and resolute

【果酱】 guǒjiàng jam

【果酒】 guǒjiǔ fruit wine

【果洛】 guǒluò 〈place〉 Golog

【果木】 guǒmù fruit tree

【果农】 guǒnóng orchard worker; orchardman

【果皮】 guǒpí rind

【果品】 guǒpǐn fruit：干鲜～ fresh and dried fruit

【果然】 guǒrǎn really; as expected; sure enough

【果仁儿】 guǒ·rénr kernel

【果实】 guǒshí 1.(果子) fruit 2.(收获) gains; fruits：劳动～ fruits of labor

【果实累累】 guǒshí lěilěi fruit growing in close clusters; fruit hanging heavy on the trees

【果树】 guǒshù fruit tree

【果树栽培】 guǒshù zāipéi cultivation of fruit tree

【果园】 guǒyuán orchard

【果真】 guǒzhēn if indeed; if really：～如此 if this is really true

【果汁】 guǒzhī fruit juice

【果汁机】 guǒzhījī fruit and vegetable juice extractor

【果子】 guǒ·zi fruit

裹 (guǒ) 1.(包扎) bind; wrap：用绷带把伤口～好 bind up the wound with a bandage 2.(卷入带走) carry off

【裹腿】 guǒ·tui puttee：打～ fix the puttee

【裹胁】 guǒxié force to take part; coerce

【裹挟】 guǒxié 1.(卷入带走) carry off 2.(把人卷进去) sweep sb. along 3.(裹胁) force to take part; coerce

【裹足不前】 guǒzú bùqián hesitate to move forward

过[過] (guò) 1.(通过) cross; pass：他们二人刚刚～去。They two have just passed by. 2.(穿过) across; past; through; over：～马路 cross the street / ～桥 go over a bridge 3.(度过) spend (time); pass (time)：～冬 pass the winter / 假期～得怎样? How did you spend your holiday? 4.(过去) after; past 5.(使经过) undergo a process; go through; go over 6.(超过) exceed; go beyond 7.(过于;过分;太) excessively; unduly：雨水～多 excessive rainfall 8.〈*Chem.*〉〈*Physics*〉 per-; super-; over- 9.(过失) fault; mistake 10.〈*classifier*〉 time：被单漂了三～儿了。The sheet have been rinsed three times.

【过磅】 guòbàng weigh (on the scales)

【过不去】 guò·buqù 1.(不能通过) cannot get through; be unable to get by; be impassable 2.(为难) be hard on; make it difficult for; embarrass：他有意跟我～。He deliberately made things difficult for me. 3.(过意不去) feel sorry

【过场】 guòchǎng 1.(贯场的表演) interlude 2.(从舞台上穿过) cross the stage 3.(做样子,敷衍) 走～ do sth. as a mere formality; go through the motions

【过程】 guòchéng course; process: 在发展～中 in the process of development / 在制作～中 in the process of manufacture

【过秤】 guòchèng weigh (on the steelyard)

【过从】 guòcóng have friendly intercourse; associate: ～甚密 be in close association with sb.

【过错】 guòcuò fault; mistake

【过道】 guòdào passageway; corridor

【过得去】 guò·deqù 1.(可通过) be able to pass; can get through 2.(不坏) passable; tolerable; so-so; not too bad 3.(多用于反问) feel at ease

【过冬】 guòdōng pass the winter; winter

【过度】 guòdù excessive; undue; over-: 饮酒～ drink to excess / ～疲劳 be exhausted; be overtired

【过渡】 guòdù transition; interim: ～时期 a period of transition; a transitional period

【过分】 guòfèn excessive; undue; over-: 做得太～ go too far; overdo sth. / 无论怎么强调…也不～。It cannot be emphasized enough that ...

【过分自信】 guòfèn zìxìn overconfidence in oneself

【过关】 guòguān 1.(通过关口) pass a barrier; go through an ordeal 2.(指通过检验) pass a test; reach a standard

【过后】 guòhòu afterwards; later: 这事我们～再谈。Let's talk about it later.

【过活】 guòhuó make a living; live: 勉强～ make a bare living; live from hand to mouth

【过火】 guòhuǒ go too far; go to extremes; overdo

【过激】 guòjī too drastic; extremist: ～的言论 extremist opinions

【过继】 guòjì 1.(把亲属的孩子过继来) adopt a young relative 2.(把自己的孩子过继给亲属) have one's child adopted by a relative

【过奖】 guòjiǎng overpraise

【过街天桥】 guòjiē tiānqiáo pedestrian overpass; pedestrian bridge

【过节】 guòjié celebrate a festival

【过境】 guòjìng pass through the territory of a country; be in transit

【过境货物】 guòjìng huòwù transit goods

【过境旅客】 guòjìng lǚkè transit passenger

【过境贸易】 guòjìng màoyì transit trade

【过境签证】 guòjìng qiānzhèng transit visa

【过来】 guò·lái 1.(向着自己方向) come over; come up 2.(回到正常状态) round: 他醒～了。He woke up; He came round. 3.(有充分时间、能力) can manage

【过来人】 guò·láirén a person who has had the experience

【过量】 guòliàng excessive; over-dose; surfeit

【过磷酸钙】 guòlínsuāngài 〈*Chem.*〉 lime superphosphate; calicium superphosphate

【过路】 guòlù pass by on one's way

【过路人】 guòlùrén passerby

【过虑】 guòlǜ be over-anxious; worry overmuch; worry unnecessarily

【过滤】 guòlǜ filter; filtrate

【过滤器】 guòlǜqì filter

【过滤嘴】 guòlǜzuǐ filter tip

【过滤嘴香烟】 guòlǜzuǐ xiāngyān cigarettes with filters

【过敏】 guòmǐn 1.〈*Med.*〉 irritability; allergy 2.(过于敏感) hypersensitivity; hypersensitive

【过目】 guòmù look over (papers, lists, etc.) so as to check or approve

【过目不忘】 guòmù-búwàng be able to remember what one has read; have a camera eye

【过年】 guònián 1.(过新年) celebrate the New Year; spend the New Year: ～好! Happy New Year! 2.(明年) next year

【过期】 guòqī exceed the time limit; be overdue: ～作废 in valid after the specified date

【过期胶卷】 guòqī jiāojuǎn expired film

【过期票据】 guòqī piàojù pass due note; overdue bill

【过去】 guò·qù 1.(以前) in or of the past; formerly; previously: 现在和～不同了。Now it is different from the past. / ～的事就让它过去吧。Let bygones be bygones. 2.(趋向) go over; pass by 3.(去世) pass away

【过热】 guòrè over heated：～经济增长 excessive economic growth

【过人】 guòrén surpass; excel：精力～ surpass many others in energy

【过日子】 guòrì·zi live; get along：会～ can manage to get along quite well

【过筛子】 guòshāi·zi sift out

【过山车】 guòshānchē roller coaster

【过剩】 guòshèng excess; surplus

【过失】 guòshī **1.**（错误）fault; slip; error **2.**〈*Law*〉unpremeditated crime; offense：疏忽大意的～ careless and inadvertent negligence

【过失犯罪】 guòshī fànzuì 〈*Law*〉 criminal negligence; involuntary crime

【过时】 guòshí **1.**（陈旧）out-of-date; outmoded; obsolete; antiquated; out of fashion：～的观念 antiquated ideas **2.**（错过规定时间）past the appointed time

【过时不候】 guòshí-bùhòu no waiting after the set time

【过世】 guòshì pass away

【过堂风】 guòtángfēng draught：门一开就有～。There's a draught every time that door is opened.

【过头】 guòtóu go beyond the limit; overdo

【过往】 guòwǎng **1.**（来去）come and go **2.**（交往；来往）have friendly intercourse with; associate with

【过问】 guòwèn concern oneself with; take an interest in; bother about：亲自～ take up matter personally; take a personal interest in a matter / 无人～ not be attended to by anybody; be nobody's business

【过细】 guòxì meticulous; careful; with meticulous care

【过夜】 guòyè pass the night; put up for the night; stay overnight

【过意不去】 guòyì bùqù feel apologetic; feel sorry

【过瘾】 guòyǐn satisfy a craving; enjoy oneself to the full; do sth. to one's heart's content

【过硬】 guòyìng have a perfect mastery of sth.; be really up to the mark：技术上～ have a thorough mastery of the operational technique / 军事上～ be competent militarily

【过犹不及】 guòyóubùjí going too far is as bad as not going far enough too much for granted

【过于】 guòyú too; excessively：～自信 take sth. too much for granted

【过载】 guòzài **1.**（换船、换车转装）transship **2.**（超载）overload

【过账】 guòzhàng transfer items

H

ha

哈 (hā) （哈气）blow one's breath; breathe out (with the mouth open): ～了一口气 breathe out a breath 2.（表示笑声）ha; ha-ha

（另见"哈"hǎ, hà）

【哈尔滨】 Hā'ěrbīn 〈place〉 Harbin

【哈哈镜】 hāhājìng mirror of distortion

【哈拉苏】 Hālāsū 〈place〉 Har Us

【哈喇】 hā·la rancid: 黄油～了。The butter is rancid.

【哈尼族】 Hānízú Hani（中国少数民族，主要分布在云南）

【哈气】 hāqì breathe out

【哈欠】 hā·qian yawn: 打～ give a yawn

【哈萨克斯坦】 Hāsàkèsītǎn Kazakhstan ‖ 哈萨克人 kazakh ‖ 哈萨克语 kazakh (language)

【哈萨克族】 Hāsàkèzú Kazak（中国少数民族，主要分布在新疆）‖ 哈萨克人 kazak ‖ 哈萨克语 kazak (language)

【哈腰】 hāyāo 1.（弯腰）bend one's back; stoop 2.（鞠躬）bow: 点头～ bow unctuously; bow and scrape

铪 (hā) 〈*Chem.*〉 hafnium（元素符号 Hf）

蛤 (há)

（另见"蛤"gé）

【蛤蟆】 há·má 1.（青蛙）frog 2.（蟾蜍）toad

哈 (hǎ)

（另见"哈"hā, hà）

【哈巴狗】 hǎ·bagǒu 1.（狮子狗）peke 2.（奴才）toady; sycophant

【哈达】 hǎdá hada

哈 (hà)

（另见"哈"hā, hǎ）

【哈什蚂】 hà·shimǎ 〈*Zool.*〉 Chinese forest frog

hai

嗨 (hāi)

【嗨哟】 hāiyō 〈*int.*〉 heave ho; yo-heave-ho; yo-ho

还[還] (hái) 1.（仍旧）still; yet: ～早 still early / 他～没有来。He has not come yet. 2.（更加）even more; still more: 今天比昨天～冷。Today is even colder than yesterday. / 这个问题～要困难。This problem is still more difficult. 3.（另外）also; too; as well; in addition: 我们看了一个故事片，～看了一个动画片。We saw a cartoon in addition to a feature film. 4.（勉强过得去）passably; fairly 5.（尚且）even

（另见"还"huán）

【还好】 háihǎo 1.（不坏）not bad; passable 2.（幸运）fortunately

【还是】 hái·shi 1.（仍旧）still; nevertheless; all the same: 尽管如此，～要谢谢你。Thank you all the same. 2.（表示希望）had better: 要下雨了，你～带把伞吧。It looks like rain, you'd better take an umbrella with you. 3.（表示选择）or: 你早上去，～下午去? Are you going in the morning or in the afternoon?

孩 (hái) child: 小女～儿 a little girl / 她生了一个男～。She gave birth to a boy.

【孩提】 háití early childhood

【孩子】 hái·zi 1.（儿童）child: 男～ boy / 女～ girl 2.（子女）children; son or daughter

【孩子气】 hái·ziqì childishness: 别再～啦。Don't be childish any more.

海 (hǎi) 1.（海洋）sea: 渤～ Bohai Sea / 黄～ Yellow Sea / 东～ East China Sea / 南～ South China Sea / 地中～ the Mediterranean Sea / 出～ put out to sea / 趁大潮出～ put out to sea on high tide / 长江在上海附近入～。Yangtze River flows into the sea near Shanghai. / 我们在～里游泳。We were swimming in the sea. **2.**（大湖）big lake：草～ Cao Hai / 黄旗～ Huangqi Hai **3.**（多）a great number of people or things coming together：人～ a sea of people; crowds of people **4.**（大）extra large; of great capacity

【海岸】 hǎi'àn seacoast; coast; seashore; coastal (adj.)：沿～航行 sail along the coast

【海岸线】 hǎi'ànxiàn coastline

【海拔】 hǎibá height above sea level; elevation：珠穆朗玛峰顶～高度为 8848 米。The top of Qomolangma is 8848 meters above sea level.

【海报】 hǎibào playbill：张贴～ put up a playbill

【海豹】 hǎibào seal

【海豹皮】 hǎibàopí sealskin

【海滨】 hǎibīn seashore; seaside：去～度假 go to the seaside for one's holidays

【海滨浴场】 hǎibīn yùchǎng seaside resort

【海冰】 hǎibīng sea ice

【海菜】 hǎicài edible seaweed

【海草】 hǎicǎo seaweed

【海产】 hǎichǎn marine products

【海产品】 hǎichǎnpǐn 〈*Food*〉 seafood

【海程】 hǎichéng voyage; distance travelled by sea

【海带】 hǎidài kelp

【海胆】 hǎidǎn 〈*Zool.*〉 sea urchin

【海岛】 hǎidǎo island (in the sea)

【海岛居民】 hǎidǎo jūmín islander

【海盗】 hǎidào pirate; sea rover; corsair; piratical (adj.)

【海盗船】 hǎidàochuán pirate (ship); sea rover

【海盗行为】 hǎidào xíngwéi piracy

【海堤】 hǎidī sea wall

【海底】 hǎidǐ seabed; sea floor; the bottom of the sea

【海防】 hǎifáng coast defense

【海防前线】 hǎifáng qiánxiàn coastal front

【海匪】 hǎifěi pirate

【海风】 hǎifēng sea breeze; sea wind

【海港】 hǎigǎng seaport; harbor

【海沟】 hǎigōu 〈*Geog.*〉 oceanic trench

【海狗】 hǎigǒu 〈*Zool.*〉 fur seal; ursine seal

【海关】 hǎiguān customhouse; customs

【海关检查】 hǎiguān jiǎnchá customs inspection：通过～ go through customs

【海关检查站】 hǎiguān jiǎncházhàn customs inspection post

【海关检疫】 hǎiguān jiǎnyì customs quarantine control

【海关人员】 hǎiguān rényuán customs officer

【海关申报单】 hǎiguān shēnbàodān customs declaration

【海关税则】 hǎiguān shuìzé customs tariff

【海龟】 hǎiguī green turtle; sea turtle

【海魂衫】 hǎihúnshān sailor's striped unit

【海货】 hǎihuò marine products

【海疆】 hǎijiāng coastal areas and territorial seas

【海角天涯】 hǎijiǎo tiānyá (go to) the ends of the earth; the corner of the world; far-off regions

【海进】 hǎijìn 〈*Geog.*〉 transgression

【海景画】 hǎijǐnghuà 〈*Arts*〉 seascape：特纳画了许多～。Turner painted many seascapes.

【海军】 hǎijūn navy; naval (adj.)：我兄弟在～服役。My brother is in the Navy.

【海军航空兵】 hǎijūn hángkōngbīng naval air force

【海军基地】 hǎijūn jīdì naval base

【海军陆战队】 hǎijūn lùzhànduì marine corps; marines

【海军呢】 hǎijūnní navy cloth

【海口】 hǎikǒu 1.（河流入海口）river mouth **2.**（港口）seaport **3.**（说大话）boast about what one can do; talk big

【海况】 hǎikuàng state of sea

【海葵】 hǎikuí 〈*Zool.*〉 sea anemone

【海阔天空】 hǎikuò-tiānkōng **1.**（大自然的广阔）as boundless as the sea and sky; unrestrained and far-ranging **2.**（说话无拘束、无边际）discursive; rambling

【海拉尔】 Hǎilā'ěr 〈place〉 Hailar

【海蓝】 hǎilán sea blue

【海里】 hǎilǐ nautical mile; sea mile (= 1.852 km)

【海路】 hǎilù 1.（海上路线）sea lane; seaway **2.**（走海路）by sea：走～ travel by sea

【海轮】 hǎilún seagoing vessel; oceangoing vessel
【海螺】 hǎiluó conch
【海洛因】 hǎiluòyīn heroin
【海马】 hǎimǎ 〈*Zool.*〉 seahorse
【海米】 hǎimǐ dried shrimps
【海绵】 hǎimián **1.**(低等多细胞动物) sponge **2.**(橡塑制品) foam rubber or plastic; sponge
【海绵池】 hǎimiánchí moistener
【海绵底球鞋】 hǎimiándǐ qiúxié sponge-insoled shoes
【海绵垫】 hǎimiándiàn **1.**(床上用的) foam-rubber cushion **2.**〈*Sports*〉 foam rubber mat
【海面】 hǎimiàn sea surface
【海难】 hǎinàn perils of the sea
【海内】 hǎinèi within the four seas; throughout the country
【海鸟】 hǎiniǎo seabird
【海鸟粪】 hǎiniǎofèn guano
【海鸥】 hǎiōu seagull; gull
【海平面】 hǎipíngmiàn sea level: 平或低于～ lay at or below sea level
【海平面气压】 hǎipíngmiàn qìyā sea-level pressure
【海侵】 hǎiqīn 〈*Geog.*〉 transgression
【海区】 hǎiqū sea area
【海上】 hǎishàng at sea; on the sea: ～风暴 a storm at sea
【海上霸权】 hǎishàng bàquán maritime hegemony
【海上封锁】 hǎishàng fēngsuǒ naval blockade
【海上劫持】 hǎishàng jiéchí seajack
【海上救助】 hǎishàng jiùzhù salvage
【海上油田】 hǎishàng yóutián offshore oil field
【海上遇险信号】 hǎishàng yùxiǎn xìnhào signal of distress; SOS
【海上钻井平台】 hǎishàng zuànjǐn píngtái offshore drilling platform
【海上钻探】 hǎishàng zuàntàn offshore drilling
【海参】 hǎishēn sea cucumber; sea slug; trepang
【海狮】 hǎishī 〈*Zool.*〉 sea lion
【海市蜃楼】 hǎishì-shènlóu mirage
【海事】 hǎishì marine affairs
【海事仲裁】 hǎishì zhòngcái maritime arbitration
【海誓山盟】 hǎishì-shānméng (make) a solemn pledge of love
【海水】 hǎishuǐ seawater; brine; the sea
【海水淡化】 hǎishuǐ dànhuà desalination of sea water; desalinate (v.)
【海水养殖】 hǎishuǐ yǎngzhí sea-water aquiculture
【海水浴】 hǎishuǐyù sea-water bath; sea bathing
【海损】 hǎisǔn **1.**(指货物) average **2.**(指船舶) sea damage
【海獭】 hǎitǎ 〈*Zool.*〉 sea otter
【海滩】 hǎitān seabeach; beach; perils of the sea
【海棠】 hǎitáng **1.**〈*Bot.*〉 crabapple tree **2.**(果实) crabapple
【海棠花】 hǎitánghuā 〈*Bot.*〉 Chinese flowering crabapple
【海兔】 hǎitù 〈*Zool.*〉 sea hare
【海退】 hǎituì 〈*Geog.*〉 regression
【海豚】 hǎitún 〈*Zool.*〉 dolphin
【海豚式蝶泳】 hǎitúnshì diéyǒng dolphin butterfly stroke
【海外】 hǎiwài overseas; abroad: ～华侨 overseas Chinese / ～同胞 countryman residing abroad / ～侨胞 Chinese nationals residing in foreign countries
【海外版】 hǎiwàibǎn overseas edition
【海外关系】 hǎiwài guān·xì **1.**(指关系) relation with relatives or friends abroad **2.**(指人) relatives or friends living abroad
【海外倾销】 hǎiwài qīngxiāo dumping abroad
【海湾】 hǎiwān bay; gulf
【海湾地区】 hǎiwān dìqū gulf areas
【海湾国家】 hǎiwān guójiā gulf states
【海王星】 hǎiwángxīng 〈*Astron.*〉 Neptune
【海味】 hǎiwèi choice seafood
【海雾】 hǎiwù sea fog
【海峡】 hǎixiá **1.**(泛指) strait; channel **2.**(特指台湾海峡) the Taiwan Strait: ～两岸 both sides of the Strait
【海鲜】 hǎixiān seafood
【海相】 hǎixiàng 〈*Geog.*〉 sea facies; marine facies
【海相沉积】 hǎixiàng chénjī 〈*Geog.*〉 marine deposit

【海象】 hǎixiàng 〈*Zool.*〉 walrus; sea elephant
【海啸】 hǎixiào tsunami
【海蟹】 hǎixiè sea crab
【海寻】 hǎixún nautical fathom (= 1.852 meter)
【海盐】 hǎiyán sea salt
【海洋】 hǎiyáng seas and oceans; ocean; oceanic (adj.)
【海洋工程】 hǎiyáng gōngchéng oceanographic engineering
【海洋性气候】 hǎiyángxìng qìhòu marine climate
【海洋学】 hǎiyángxué oceanography
【海洋资源】 hǎiyáng zīyuán marine resources; maritime resources
【海鱼】 hǎiyú sea fish
【海域】 hǎiyù sea area; maritime space
【海员】 hǎiyuán seaman; sailor; mariner
【海员俱乐部】 hǎiyuán jùlèbù seamen's club
【海运】 hǎiyùn sea transportation; ocean shipping; ocean carriage; seaborne (adj.)
【海藻】 hǎizǎo marine alga; seaweed; kelp
【海战】 hǎizhàn sea warfare; naval battle
【海蜇】 hǎizhé 〈*Zool.*〉 jellyfish
【海蜇皮】 hǎizhépí umbrella of jellyfish
【海蜇头】 hǎizhétóu oral arms of jellyfish

骇 (hài) be astonished; be shocked
【骇怕】 hàipà be afraid; be scared
【骇然】 hàirán be overwhelmed with amazement
【骇人听闻】 hàirén tīngwén shocking; appalling; fabulous: ～的事件 astounding event / ～的消息 shocking news
【骇异】 hàiyì be shocked; be astonished: 不胜～ be greatly shocked; be greatly surprised

氦 (hài) 〈*Chem.*〉 helium (元素符号 He)
【氦灯】 hàidēng helium lamp

害 (hài) **1.** (祸害; 害处) evil; harm; calamity: 为～不浅 do great harm; cause much damage **2.** (有害的) harmful; destructive; injurious: ～鸟 harmful bird / ～兽 harmful animal **3.** (使受害) do harm to; impair; cause trouble to **4.** (杀害) kill; murder: 他遇～身亡了。He was murdered. **5.** (生病) contract (an illness); suffer from: ～眼 suffer from eye disease **6.** (发生不安的情绪) feel (ashamed, afraid, etc.)
【害病】 hàibìng suffer from an illness
【害虫】 hàichóng injurious insect: 除～ get rid of insects
【害处】 hài·chu harm: 饮酒过多对健康有～。Excessive drinking is harmful to one's health.
【害怕】 hàipà fear; be afraid; be scared; be frightened: 突然感到～ felt suddenly afraid / 我～这只大狗。I was scared of the big dog. / 他～得直发抖。He was shaking with fear.
【害群之马】 hàiqúnzhīmǎ black sheep; one who bring disgrace on his group
【害人非浅】 hàirén-fēiqiǎn cause deep injury to someone; do people great harm; cause infinite harm to people
【害人害己】 hàirén-hàijǐ bite off one's own head; curses come home to roost
【害臊】 hàisào feel ashamed; be bashful; be ashamed of
【害羞】 hàixiū be bashful; be shy: 在生人面前显得～ be shy in presence of strangers

han

鼾 (hān) snore: 打～ snore
【鼾声】 hānshēng sound of snoring
【鼾睡】 hānshuì sound, snoring sleep

蚶 (hān) blood clam
【蚶子】 hān·zi blood clam

酣 (hān) **1.** (饮酒尽兴) (drink, etc.) to one's heart's content; to the full **2.** (泛指尽量、痛快等) fully; heartily; profound; soundly
【酣畅】 hānchàng **1.** (指饮酒) merry and lively **2.** (指睡眠) sound **3.** (指文艺作品) with ease and verve; fully
【酣眠】 hānmián sleep soundly; be fast asleep; sopor
【酣然入睡】 hānrán-rùshuì fall into a profound sleep
【酣睡】 hānshuì sleep soundly; be fast

asleep; sopor

【酣饮】 hānyǐn drink to intoxication

【酣战】 hānzhàn hard-fought battle; bloody battle

【酣醉】 hānzuì be dead drunk

憨(hān) 1.(傻) foolish; silly 2.(朴实;天真) straightforward; naive; ingenuous

【憨厚】 hān·hòu simple and honest; straightforward and good-natured

【憨笑】 hānxiào smile fatuously; simper

含(hán) 1.(衔在口中) keep in the mouth: ～着润喉片 have a throat tablet in the mouth 2.(藏在里面;包含) contain 3.(不露出来) nurse; cherish; harbor

【含胡】 hán·hu 同"含糊"

【含糊】 hán·hu 1.(不清晰;不明确) ambiguous; vague 2.(马虎) careless; perfunctory: ～了事 finish a job carelessly

【含糊其辞】 hán·hu-qící talk evasively

【含混】 hánhùn indistinct; ambiguous

【含量】 hánliàng content

【含片】 hánpiàn lozenge: 止咳～ cough lozenge

【含情脉脉】 hánqíng-mòmò (soft eyes) exuding tenderness and love

【含沙射影】 hánshā-shèyǐng attack by innuendo; make insinuations

【含笑】 hánxiào have a smile on one's face

【含羞】 hánxiū with a shy look; bashfully

【含蓄】 hánxù 1.(包含) contain; embody 2.(不直接说出) implicit; veiled: ～的批评 implicit criticism 3.(不外露) reserved

【含义】 hányì meaning; implication

【含有】 hányǒu contain; have: ～盐分 contain salt

【含冤】 hányuān suffer a wrong

焓(hán) 〈*Physics*〉 heat content; total heat

【焓熵图】 hánshāngtú enthalpy-entropy diagram

函[圅](hán) 1.(匣;封套) case; envelope 2.(信件) letter: 复～ reply by letter; write a letter in reply

【函大】 hándà correspondence university

【函电】 hándiàn letters and telegrams

【函告】 hángào inform by letter

【函购】 hángòu purchase by mail; mail order

【函件】 hánjiàn letters; correspondence

【函授】 hánshòu teach by correspondence; give a correspondence course

【函授部】 hánshòubù correspondence department (of a school)

【函授教育】 hánshòu jiàoyù correspondence education

【函授生】 hánshòushēng correspondence student

【函授学校】 hánshòu xuéxiào correspondence school

【函数】 hánshù 〈*Math.*〉 function

【函数表】 hánshùbiǎo 〈*Math.*〉 function table

【函索】 hánsuǒ request by letter: 备有书目,～即寄。A catalogue is available on request.

涵(hán) 1.(包容) contain 2.(涵洞) culvert

【涵洞】 hándòng culvert

【涵养】 hányǎng 1.(修养) ability to control oneself; self restraint 2.(蓄积) conserve: ～水源 conserve water through afforestation

寒(hán) 1.(冷) cold: 受～ catch a cold 2.(害怕;畏惧) tremble (with fear) 3.(穷困) poor; needy

【寒潮】 háncháo 〈*Meteorol.*〉 cold wave; cold-air outbreak

【寒伧】 hán·chen 同"寒碜"

【寒碜】 hán·chen 1.(难看) ugly; unsightly: 长得不～ not bad-looking 2.(丢脸;不体面) shabby; disgraceful: 这有什么～。There's nothing to be ashamed of. 3.(讥笑) ridicule; put to shame: 叫人～了一顿 be ridiculed by sb.

【寒带】 hándài 〈*Geog.*〉 frigid zone

【寒冬】 hándōng severe winter

【寒冬腊月】 hándōng-làyuè severe winter; dead of winter

【寒风】 hánfēng cold wind

【寒假】 hánjià winter vacation; winter vac: 放～ have winter vacation; be in winter vacation / 你们什么时候放～? When is your winter vacation?

【寒噤】 hánjìn shiver (with cold or fear): 打～ send cold shivers down one's back

【寒苦】 hánkǔ poverty-stricken

【寒冷】 hánlěng cold; frigid: ～的气候 a

cold climate

【寒流】 hánliú 1.〈*Geog*.〉 cold current (of water) 2.〈*Meteorol*.〉 cold wave; cold current (or air)

【寒露】 hánlù the Cold Dew (10月8-9日交节)

【寒毛】 hán·máo fine hair (on the human body)

【寒气】 hánqì cold air; cold draught; cold

【寒热】 hánrè chills and fever: 发～ have a fever

【寒暑表】 hánshǔbiǎo thermometer

【寒酸】 hánsuān miserable and shabby; humble and ragged: 一副～相 a looking miserable and shabby

【寒心】 hánxīn 1.(痛心) be bitterly disappointed 2.(害怕) be frightened

【寒暄】 hánxuān exchange of conventional greetings; exchange of amenities; exchange a few words of greeting with

【寒战】 hánzhàn shiver; tremble (with cold or fear)

【寒颤】 hánzhàn 同"寒战"

罕 (hǎn) rarely; seldom

【罕见】 hǎnjiàn seldom seen; rare: 一场～的大旱 an exceptionally serious drought

【罕有】 hǎnyǒu rare; unusual; exceptional: ～的机会 a rare opportunity / ～的现象 an exceptional phenomenon

喊 (hǎn) 1.(大声叫) shout; cry out; yell 2.(叫) call (a person)

【喊话】 hǎnhuà shout propaganda at enemy soldiers

【喊叫】 hǎnjiào shout; cry out: 大声～ shout at the top of one's voice

【喊冤叫屈】 hǎnyuān-jiàoqū cry out about one's grievances; complain loudly about an alleged injustice

汉[漢] (hàn) 1.(汉语) Chinese (language) 2.(男子) man: 老～ an old man

【汉白玉】 hànbáiyù white marble

【汉堡包】 hànbǎobāo hamburger; burger; beefburger

【汉奸】 hànjiān traitor (to China)

【汉显】 hànxiǎn 〈*Computer*〉 Chinese display

【汉学】 hànxué sinology; sinological (adj.)

【汉学家】 hànxuéjiā sinologue; sinologist

【汉语】 hànyǔ Chinese (language)

【汉语拼音】 Hànyǔ pīnyīn the Chinese Phonetic Alphabet

【汉子】 hàn·zi 1.(男子) man; fellow 2.(丈夫) husband

【汉字】 hànzì Chinese character: 简化～ simplify (simplified) Chinese characters

【汉字显示装置】 hànzì xiǎnshì zhuāngzhì Chinese display

【汉族】 Hànzú Han (中国民族,分布在全国各地)

汗 (hàn) sweat; perspiration: 出～ sweat; perspire / 发～ induce perspiration

【汗背心】 hànbèixīn sleeveless undershirt; vest; singlet

【汗脚】 hànjiǎo feet that sweat easily; sweaty feet

【汗流浃背】 hànliú-jiābèi streaming with sweat (from fear or physical exertion)

【汗马功劳】 hànmǎ-gōngláo 1.(战功) distinctions won in battle; war exploits 2.(工作中的贡献) one's contributions in work

【汗毛】 hànmáo fine hair (on the human body)

【汗如雨下】 hànrú-yǔxià sweat profusely; the sweat runs down like raindrops

【汗衫】 hànshān undershirt; T-shirt

【汗腾格里峰】 Hànténggélǐfēng 〈place〉 Hantengri Feng

【汗腺】 hànxiàn 〈*Anat*.〉 sweat gland

【汗珠子】 hànzhū·zi beads of sweat

【汗渍】 hànzì sweat stain

旱 (hàn) 1.(降水少;无降水) dry spell; drought: 抗～ combat drought 2.(非水田的) dryland 3.(陆地交通) on land

【旱冰鞋】 hànbīngxié 1.(四轮旱冰鞋) roller skates 2.(单排四轮旱冰鞋) rollerblade

【旱稻】 hàndào upland rice; dry rice

【旱地】 hàndì nonirrigated farmland; dry land

【旱季】 hànjì dry season

【旱涝保收】 hànlào-bǎoshōu ensure stable yields despite drought or excessive rain

【旱路】 hànlù overland route: 走～ travel by land

【旱桥】 hànqiáo overpass; flyover

【旱情】 hànqíng damage to crops by drought：～已趋缓和。The drought has eased up.
【旱生植物】 hànshēng zhíwù xerophilous plant；xerophite
【旱獭】 hàntǎ 〈*Zool.*〉 marmot
【旱田】 hàntián dry farmland；dry land
【旱灾】 hànzāi drought

捍(hàn) defend；guard
【捍卫】 hànwèi defend；guard；protect：～国家主权 uphold state sovereignty / ～胜利成果 safeguard the fruits of triumph

悍(hàn) **1.**(勇猛) brave；bold **2.**(凶狠；蛮横) fierce；ferocious：凶～ fierce and tough；ferocious
【悍然】 hànrán outrageously；brazenly；flagrantly：～宣布 brazenly declare

焊[銲、釬](hàn) weld；solder：电～ electric welding / 电弧～ arc welding / 气～ gas welding / 锡～ solder
【焊缝】 hànfèng welding seam；weld line
【焊工】 hàngōng **1.**(焊接工作) welding；soldering **2.**(焊接工人) welder；solderer
【焊机】 hànjī welder；welding machine
【焊接】 hànjiē welding；soldering：许多公司在制造汽车时现已采用机器人进行～。Many companies now use robots for welding involved in car manufacture.
【焊料】 hànliào solder
【焊枪】 hànqiāng welding torch；(welding) blowpipe
【焊条】 hàntiáo welding rod
【焊锡】 hànxī soldering tin；tin solder
【焊油】 hànyóu soldering paste

撼(hàn) shake
【撼动】 hàndòng shake；vibrate
【撼天动地】 hàntiān-dòngdì cause a great sensation

憾(hàn) regret：引以为～ deem it regrettable
【憾事】 hànshì a matter for regret；regretful matter

hang

夯[硶](hāng) **1.**(砸地基的工具) rammer；tamper：木～ wooden ram / 打～ pound the ground with a rammer **2.**(用夯砸) ram；tamp；pound：把土～实 ram the earth
【夯土机】 hāngtǔjī rammer；tamper

行(háng) **1.**(行列) line；row：排成三～ be arranged in three rows **2.**(行业) trade；profession；line of business：改～ change one's profession **3.**(营业机构) business firm：分～ branch **4.**(排行) seniority among brothers and sisters
(另见"行"xíng)
【行行出状元】 hángháng chūzhuàngyuán one may distinguish himself in any trade
【行话】 hánghuà jargon；cant
【行会】 hánghuì guild：服装设计师～ the fashion designer's guild
【行家】 háng·jia expert；connoisseur：～里手 experts and master hands
【行列】 hángliè ranks：参加研究与设计的～ join the ranks for research and design
【行情】 hángqíng quotations；prices：市场～ quotations on the market
【行市】 háng·shi prices
【行业】 hángyè trade；profession；industry：服务～ service trades
【行业暗语】 hángyè ànyǔ lingo
【行业不正之风】 hángyè bùzhèng zhīfēng unhealthy tendencies in some trades
【行长】 hángzhǎng president (of a bank)

绗(háng) sew with long stitches：～被子 sew the cover onto the quilt with long stitches

杭(háng)
【杭锦】 hángjǐn 〈place〉 Hanggin
【杭育】 hángyō 〈*onomat.*〉 heave ho；yo-ho

航(háng) **1.**(船) boat；ship **2.**(航海，航空) navigate；navigation (n.)
【航班】 hángbān flight；scheduled flight；flight number：变更～ change the flight / 我们将乘CA1302～于星期一返回。We'll be arriving back on Monday on flight number CA1302.
【航标】 hángbiāo 〈*Naut.*〉 beacon；buoy

【航测】 hángcè aerial survey
【航程】 hángchéng voyage；passage；range
【航船】 hángchuán boat that plies regularly between inland towns
【航次】 hángcì 1.（船舶出航次第）the sequence of voyages；voyage number 2.（船舶出航次数）the number of voyages made 3.（飞机出航次第）the sequence of flights；flight number 4.（飞机出航次数）the number of flights made
【航道】 hángdào channel；lane；course：主～ the main channel
【航海】 hánghǎi navigation
【航海家】 hánghǎijiā navigator；voyager
【航海日志】 hánghǎi rìzhì logbook；log
【航海学】 hánghǎixué navigation
【航空】 hángkōng aviation：民用～ civil aviation
【航空兵】 hángkōngbīng 1.（指兵种）air arm 2.（指飞行员）airman
【航空港】 hángkōnggǎng airport
【航空工业】 hángkōng gōngyè aviation industry
【航空公司】 hángkōng gōngsī airlines；airways
【航空煤油】 hángkōng méiyóu aviation kerosene
【航空模型】 hángkōng móxíng model airplane
【航空母舰】 hángkōng mǔjiàn aircraft carrier：直升机～ helicopter carrier
【航空汽油】 hángkōng qìyóu aviation gas；aviation petrol
【航空器】 hángkōngqì aircraft
【航空燃料】 hángkōng ránliào aviation fuel；aircraft fuel
【航空线】 hángkōngxiàn airline；airway
【航空信】 hángkōngxìn airmail letter；air letter；airmail
【航空邮简】 hángkōng yōujiǎn aerogramme；aerogram
【航空邮件】 hángkōng yōujiàn airmail
【航速】 hángsù speed of a ship or plane：（船的）～为 16 节 sail at a speed of 16 knots
【航天】 hángtiān spaceflight；aerospace
【航天飞机】 hángtiān fēijī space shuttle
【航天服】 hángtiānfú space suit
【航天器】 hángtiānqì spacecraft
【航天员】 hángtiānyuán astronaut
【航线】 hángxiàn 1.（航空线）airline；airway：你飞哪条～？What airline did you fly？2.（航海线）shipping line；route
【航向】 hángxiàng course（of a ship or plane）：改变～ change course
【航行】 hángxíng 1.（空中行驶）navigate by air；fly 2.（水中行驶）navigate by water；sail：逆风～ sail to windward / 顺风～ sail before the wind；sail downwind
【航运】 hángyùn shipping
【航运公司】 hángyùn gōngsī shipping company

沆（hàng）

【沆瀣一气】 hàngxiè-yīqì act in collusion with；wallow in the mire with；like attracts like

巷（hàng）
（另见“巷”xiàng）

【巷道】 hàngdào 〈*Mineral*.〉 tunnel

hao

蒿（hāo）

【蒿子】 hāo·zi 〈*Bot*.〉 wormwood；artemisia
【蒿子杆】 hāo·zigǎn 〈*Bot*.〉 annual chrysanthemum

薅（hāo） pull up

【薅草】 hāocǎo weed：在菜园～ weed the vegetable garden

号［**號**］（háo） 1.（号叫）howl；yell：北风怒～。A north wind is howling. 2.（大声哭）wail
（另见“号”hào）

【号叫】 háojiào howl；yell
【号哭】 háokū wail
【号啕】 háotáo cry loudly；wail：～大哭 cry one's eyes out

嗥［**嘷**］（háo） howl：狼～ the howl of a wolf

【嗥叫】 háojiào howl

蚝［**蠔**］（háo） 〈*Zool*.〉 oyster

【蚝油】 háoyóu oyster oil

毫（háo） 1.（毛）fine long hair：狼～ wolf's hair 2.（毛笔）writing brush 3.（一

点儿）in the least; at all 4.（千分之一）milli- 5.（辅币）10 cents

【毫不动摇】 háobù-dòngyáo firmly; not waver in the least: ～地坚持 firmly adhere to

【毫不含糊】 háobù-hánhū make a clear and definite commitment

【毫不犹豫】 háobù-yóuyù without the least hesitation

【毫克】 háokè milligram（mg.）

【毫厘】 háolí the least bit; an iota: ～不差 without the slightest error; just right

【毫毛】 háomáo soft hair on the body: 不准你动他一根～。Don't you dare do him the slightest harm.

【毫米】 háomǐ millimeter; millimetre（mm.）

【毫升】 háoshēng milliliter; millilitre（ml.）

【毫无道理】 háowú-dàolǐ utterly unjustifiable; for no reason whatsoever

【毫无二致】 háowú-èrzhì without the slightest difference; just the same; identical

【毫无顾虑】 háowú-gùlǜ free from all inhibitions

【毫无例外】 háowú-lìwài admit of no exception

【毫无用处】 háowú-yòngchù good for nothing

貉（háo） raccoon dog; racoon dog
（另见“貉”hé）

【貉子】 háo·zi raccoon dog; racoon dog

豪（háo） 1.（豪杰）a person of extraordinary powers or endowments 2.（气魄大；爽快）bold and unconstrained; unrestrained; forth-right 3.（强横）despotic; bullying

【豪放】 háofàng bold and unconstrained

【豪华】 háohuá luxurious; sumptuous; de luxe

【豪华本】 háohuáběn de luxe

【豪华车】 háohuáchē luxurious car

【豪华轿车】 háohuá jiàochē limousine

【豪华型】 háohuáxíng de luxe

【豪杰】 háojié person with unusual courage and ability

【豪迈】 háomài bold and generous; heroic

【豪门】 háomén rich and powerful family

【豪气】 háoqì heroism; heroic spirit

【豪强】 háoqiáng 1.（强横）despotic; tyrannical 2.（强横的人）despot; bully

【豪情】 háoqíng lofty sentiments: ～满怀 full of lofty aspiration

【豪爽】 háoshuǎng frank and straightforward

【豪言壮语】 háoyán-zhuàngyǔ brave words

【豪饮】 háoyǐn drink a lot

【豪雨】 háoyǔ torrential rain

【豪猪】 háozhū 〈*Zool.*〉porcupine

壕（háo） 1.（护城河）moat 2.（壕沟）trench: 防空～ air-raid shelter

【壕沟】 háogōu 1.〈*Mil.*〉trench 2.（沟）ditch

嚎（háo） howl; wail

【嚎啕】 háotáo cry loudly; wail: ～大哭 cry bitter tears; cry loudly with abandon

好（hǎo） 1.（优良的）good; fine; nice: ～主意 good idea 2.（友好）friendly; kind 他们俩很要～。They are on friendly terms. 3.（健康；痊愈）be in good health; get well 4.（表示赞许等）ok; well 5.（容易）be easy（to do）; be convenient 6.（便于）so as to; so that 7.（用在形容词前，表示程度深、数量多、时间长等）what; how
（另见“好”hào）

【好办】 hǎobàn be easy to handle; be easily arranged

【好比】 hǎobǐ can be compared to; may be likened to; be just like

【好不容易】 hǎobù róngyì with great difficulty; have a hard time（doing sth.）

【好吃】 hǎochī good to eat; tasty; delicious

【好处】 hǎochù be easy to get along with

【好处】 hǎo·chu 1.（益处）good; benefit; advantage 2.（利益）gain; profit

【好处费】 hǎochùfèi reward; middleman's fee

【好歹】 hǎodǎi 1.（好和坏）good and bad; what's good and what's bad 2.（危险）mishap; disaster 3.（无论如何）in any case; at any rate; anyhow 4.（将就）no matter in what way; anyhow

【好多】 hǎoduō a good many; a good deal; a lot of: 有～事要做 have a good many things to do

【好感】 hǎogǎn（have）good opinion; favorable impression: 博得～ leave good impression on

【好过】 hǎoguò 1.（日子容易过）have an easy time; be in easy circumstances: 日子很不～ have a very hard time 2.（好受）fell well; fell better

【好汉】 hǎohàn brave man; true man; hero: ～不吃眼前亏。A wise man does not right when the odds are against him.

【好好】 hǎohǎo well; all out; to one's heart's content: ～想一想 think it over carefully / ～休息一下 have a good rest

【好话】 hǎohuà 1.（有益的话；赞扬的话）a good word; word of praise 2.（漂亮话）fine words

【好家伙】 hǎojiā·huo （表示惊讶或赞叹）good god; good heavens; good gracious

【好久】 hǎojiǔ for a long time

【好看】 hǎokàn 1.（美观）good-looking; nice 2.（使人感兴趣）interesting 3.（脸上有光彩）honored 4.（难堪）be in a fix; in an embarrassing situation; on the spot

【好评】 hǎopíng favorable comment; high opinion: 博得～ be well received by

【好人】 hǎorén 1.（品质好的人）good person 2.（健康的人）a healthy person 3.（老好人）a person who tries to get along with everyone

【好日子】 hǎorì·zi 1.（结婚的日子）wedding day 2.（美好的生活）good days; happy life

【好容易】 hǎoróngyì with great difficulty; have a hard time (doing sth.)

【好生】 hǎoshēng 1.（多么；很）quite; exceedingly 2.（好好儿地）carefully; properly

【好使】 hǎoshǐ be convenient to use; work well: 这台录像机很～。This video tape recorder is very reliable.

【好事】 hǎoshì 1.（好事情）good deed; good turn 2.〈*Religion*〉an act of charity 3.（喜庆事）anything that deserves celebration

【好事多磨】 hǎoshì-duōmó 1.（指常遇波折）the road to happiness is strewn with setbacks 2.（指常经历曲折）the course of true love never did run smooth

【好手】 hǎoshǒu good hand; past master

【好受】 hǎoshòu feel better; feel more comfortable: 我有些不～。I'm not feeling quite well.

【好似】 hǎosì seem; be like

【好天儿】 hǎotiānr fine day; lovely weather

【好听】 hǎotīng 1.（指声音）pleasant to her 2.（指言语）pleasing; satisfying

【好玩儿】 hǎowánr amusing; interesting

【好戏】 hǎoxì 1.（好的戏剧）good play 2.〈*iron.*〉great fun

【好下场】 hǎoxiàchǎng good end

【好像】 hǎoxiàng seem; be like: 我看～要下雨。It seems to me that it will rain.

【好笑】 hǎoxiào laughable; funny; ridiculous

【好些】 hǎoxiē quite a lot; a good deal of

【好心】 hǎoxīn good intention

【好样儿的】 hǎoyàngr·de example; great fellow

【好意】 hǎoyì good intention; kindness: 出于～ with good intention / 不怀～ harbor malicious intentions

【好意思】 hǎoyì·si （多用在反问句中）have the nerve to do sth.

【好在】 hǎozài fortunately; luckily

【好转】 hǎozhuǎn take a turn for the better; take a favorable turn; improve: 经济形势正在～。The economic situation is taking a turn for the better.

号[號] (hào) 1.（名称）name 2.（别号；字）assumed name; alternative name 3.（商店）business house 4.（信号）mark; sign; signal 5.（次第）number（符号为 ＃）6.（服装号码）size 7.（日期）date 8.（号令）order 9.（号角）horn 10.（号声）bugle call; any call made on a bugle: 吹冲锋～ sound the call to charge

（另见"号"háo）

【号兵】 hàobīng 〈*Mil.*〉trumpeter

【号称】 hàochēng 1.（以…著称）be known as 2.（名义上是）claim to be

【号角】 hàojiǎo 1.（喇叭等）bugle; horn 2.（号角声）bugle call

【号令】 hàolìng verbal command; order

【号码】 hàomǎ number: 电话～ telephone number

【号码机】 hàomǎjī numbering machine

【号脉】 hàomài 〈*Chin. Med.*〉feel the pulse

【号手】 hàoshǒu trumpeter; bugler

【号外】 hàowài extra; extra issue (of a newspaper)

【号召】 hàozhào call; appeal: 发出～ issue a call / 响应…的～ respond to the call of

好 (hào) 1.（喜爱）like; love; be fond of: ～学 be eager to learn 2.（易于）be liable

to：～晕车 be liable to carsickness
（另见"好"hǎo）

【好出风头】 hàochū-fēngtóu like to get into the limelight；be fond of the limelight

【好大喜功】 hàodà-xǐgōng crave for greatness and success；have a fondness for the grandiose

【好高骛远】 hàogāo-wùyuǎn reach for what is beyond one's grasp；aim too high；bite off more than one can chew

【好客】 hàokè be hospitable；keep open house

【好奇】 hàoqí be curious；be full of curiosity

【好奇心】 hàoqíxīn curiosity

【好强】 hàoqiáng eager to do well in everything

【好色】 hàosè letch；lech；lechery（n.）；lecherous（adj.）

【好胜】 hàoshèng seek to do others down

【好事】 hàoshì meddlesome；officious

【好事之徒】 hàoshìzhītú busybody

【好为人师】 hàowéirénshī be fond of teaching others；like to be a master to others

【好恶】 hàowù likes and dislikes；taste

【好学】 hàoxué be studious；be eager to learn

【好逸恶劳】 hàoyì-wùláo love ease and hate work

【好战】 hàozhàn bellicose；warlike

【好战分子】 hàozhàn fènzǐ warlike elements；warmongers

耗（hào） 1.（消耗）consume；cost 2.（拖延）waste time；dawdle 3.（坏消息）bad news

【耗电量】 hàodiànliàng power consumption

【耗费】 hàofèi consume；expend：～人力物力 consume manpower and material resources

【耗尽】 hàojìn exhaust；use up：～体力 use up all one's strength

【耗能】 hàonéng power consumption

【耗能大户】 hàonéng dàhù a big power consumer

【耗损】 hàosǔn consume；waste；lose：机器～ wear and tear of machinery

【耗资】 hàozī money spent；money cost：～近亿元 spend nearly 100 million dollars

【耗子】 hào·zi mouse；rat

【耗子药】 hào·ziyào ratsbane；rat poison

浩（hào） great；vast；grand

【浩大】 hàodà very great；huge；vast：工程～ an extremely big project

【浩荡】 hàodàng 1.（水势大）vast and mighty：～的长江 the mighty Yangtze River 2.（广阔或壮大）vast and numerous：～的游行队伍 an enormous parading procession

【浩瀚】 hàohàn 1.（水势盛大）vast 2.（广大；繁多）vast；numerous

【浩浩荡荡】 hàohào-dàngdàng go forward with great strength and vigor

【浩劫】 hàojié great calamity；catastrophe；havoc

【浩淼】 hàomiǎo vast；extending into the distance

【浩渺】 hàomiǎo 同"浩淼"

【浩气】 hàoqì noble spirit：～长存 imperishable noble spirit

【浩气凛然】 hàoqì-lǐnrán full of noble spirit and dignity

【浩然正气】 hàorán-zhèngqì awe-inspiring righteousness

【浩如烟海】 hàorú-yānhǎi vast as the open sea；tremendous amount of

【浩特】 hàotè hot；city

皓［皜］（hào） 1.（白）white 2.（明亮）bright

【皓齿】 hàochǐ white teeth

【皓月】 hàoyuè bright moon

he

呵［訶[2]］（hē） 1.（呼氣）breathe out（with the mouth open）2.（呵斥）scold

【呵斥】 hēchì berate；excoriate：～孩子 scold a child in a loud voice

【呵護】 hēhù bless

【呵欠】 hē·qiàn yawn：我不停地打～，一定是太困了。I can't stop yawning — I must be tired.

【呵責】 hēzé scold sb. severely；give sb. a dressing down

嗬（hē） 〈*int.*〉 ah；oh：～，真是奇迹！Oh，what a wonder!

喝［欲］（hē） 1.（饮）drink：～茶 drink tea 2.（饮酒）drink alcoholic liquor

（另见"喝"hè）

【喝水不忘掘井人】 hēshuǐ bú wàng juéjǐngrén When you drink the water, think of those who dug the well.

【喝汤】 hētāng eat soup

【喝西北风】 hē xīběifēng drink the northwest wind; have nothing to eat

【喝醉】 hēzuì get drunk：他～了。He is drunk.

禾（hé） standing grain (esp. rice)

【禾本科】 héběnkē 〈*Bot.*〉 the grass family

【禾苗】 hémiáo seedlings of cereal crops

和［龢1－4］（hé） 1.（平和）gentle; mild; kind 2.（和睦）harmonious; on good terms 3.（和平）peace：讲～ make peace 4.（比赛和局）draw; tie 5.（连带）together with 6.（表示相关、比较等）with 7.〈*conj.*〉 and：你～我 you and I 8.〈*Math.*〉 sum 9.（和，及）ampersand = and（符号为 & ）

（另见"和"hè, hú, huó, huò）

【和蔼】 hé'ǎi kindly; affable; amiable：～的教师 a kindly teacher

【和风】 héfēng 1.（温和的风）soft breeze 2.〈*Meteorol.*〉 moderate breeze

【和风细雨】 héfēng-xìyǔ like a gentle breeze and a mild rain; in a gentle and mild way

【和好】 héhǎo 1.（和睦）harmony; concord; amity 2.（恢复感情）become reconciled; restore good relations

【和缓】 héhuǎn 1.（平和）gentle; mild：态度～ a mild attitude; a gentle manner 2.（使缓和）ease up; relax

【和解】 héjiě become reconciled

【和局】 héjú drawn game; draw; tie

【和睦】 hémù harmony; concord; amity：～相处 live in harmony

【和暖】 hénuǎn pleasantly warm; genial：～的阳光 warm sunshine / ～宜人 pleasantly warm

【和盘托出】 hépán-tuōchū tell the whole truth; reveal everything

【和平】 hépíng 1.（无战争状态）peace 2.（温和）mild：药性～。The medicine is mild. 3.（平静；宁静）calm; tranquil; serene

【和平队】 Hépíngduì the Peace Corps (of U.S)

【和平鸽】 hépínggē dove of peace

【和平攻势】 hépíng gōngshì peace offensive

【和平共处】 hépíng gòngchǔ peaceful coexistence

【和平共处五项原则】 hépíng gòngchǔ wǔxiàng yuánzé the Five Principles of Peaceful Coexistence ‖ 互相尊重主权和领土完整 mutual respect for sovereignty and territorial integrity; 互不侵犯 mutual non-aggression; 互不干涉内政 non-interference in each other's internal affairs; 平等互利 equality and mutual benefit; 和平共处 peaceful coexistence

【和平时期】 hépíng shíqī peacetime

【和平谈判】 hépíng tánpàn peace negotiations

【和平统一】 hépíng tǒngyī reunify peacefully：争取～祖国的方针 policy of striving to reunify the motherland peacefully

【和平演变】 hépíng yǎnbiàn peaceful evolution

【和平中立政策】 hépíng zhōnglì zhèngcè policy of peace and neutrality

【和棋】 héqí a draw in chess or other board games

【和气】 hé·qi 1.（指态度）gentle; polite; amiable; kind 2.（指气氛）harmony; friendship; friendly feelings：有伤～。That might hurt sb's feelings.

【和气生财】 héqì-shēngcái Friendliness is conducive to business success.

【和善】 héshàn kind and gentle; genial：～的面容 benign faces / ～的笑容 genial smiles

【和尚】 hé·shang Buddhist monk

【和声】 héshēng 〈*Music*〉 harmony

【和事佬】 héshìlǎo peacemaker

【和谈】 hétán peace talks

【和田】 Hétián 〈place〉 Hotan

【和谐】 héxié harmonious：～的气氛 a harmonious atmosphere / ～一致 in perfect harmony

【和煦】 héxù pleasantly warm; genial：～的阳光 genial sunshine / 春风～。The spring breeze is pleasantly warm.

【和颜悦色】 héyán-yuèsè with kind and

pleasant countenance

【和叶尔阿木德】 Héyèěrāmùdé 〈place〉 Hoyor Amt

【和约】 héyuē peace treaty

合 (hé) 1.(合拢) close; shut: 请把书～上。Close your book, please. 2.(结合) join; combine 3.(全) whole 4.(符合) suit; agree 5.(折合) be equal to; add up to 6.(应当;应该) proper

【合办】 hébàn jointly run

【合抱】 hébào measuring sth. by putting one's arms around it: 五人～的大树 a huge tree that needs five people to put their arms around it to encircle it

【合并】 hébìng 1.(合到一起) merge; amalgamate 2.(同时发生) concurrently suffering from two of more illnesses: 麻疹～肺炎 concurrently suffering from measles and pneumonia

【合并处罚】 hébìng chǔfá mixed punishments

【合唱】 héchàng chorus: 大～ cantata / 童声～ children's chorus

【合唱队】 héchàngduì chorus

【合唱团】 héchàngtuán chorus

【合成】 héchéng 1.(由部分组成) compose; compound 2.〈*Chem.*〉 synthesize; synthetize; synthesization (n.)

【合成氨】 héchéngān synthetic ammonia

【合成洗涤剂】 héchéng xǐdíjì synthetic detergent

【合成洗衣粉】 héchéng xǐyīfěn synthetic detergent powder

【合成纤维】 héchéng xiānwéi synthetic fiber

【合成橡胶】 héchéng xiàngjiāo synthetic rubber; synthal

【合订本】 hédìngběn one-volume edition; bound volume

【合法】 héfǎ legal; lawful; legitimate; rightful: ～政府 the legal government

【合法地位】 héfǎ dìwèi legal status

【合法斗争】 héfǎ dòuzhēng legal struggle

【合法化】 héfǎhuà legalize; legitimize; legalization (n.)

【合法继承人】 héfǎ jìchéngrén rightful heir

【合法权利】 héfǎ quánlì legitimate right; lawful right

【合法权益】 héfǎ quányì legitimate rights and interests

【合法收入】 héfǎ shōurù lawful earned income

【合法途径】 héfǎ tújìng legal means

【合格】 hégé qualified; up to standard: 政治上～ be qualified politically

【合格产品】 hégé chǎnpǐn qualified products

【合股】 hégǔ 1.(合资经营) pool capital; form a partnership 2.〈*Textiles*〉 plying

【合股公司】 hégǔ gōngsī joint-stock company

【合乎】 héhū conform with; correspond to; accord with; tally with: ～规格 up to the specifications / ～事实 tally with the facts / ～自然规律 in conformity with the laws of nature

【合伙】 héhuǒ form a partnership: ～经营 run a business in partnership

【合集】 héjí intersection of (符号为 ∪)

【合计】 hé·jì (总共) amount to; add up to; total

【合计】 hé·ji 1.(盘算) consider; deliberate 2.(商量) consult; discuss

【合剂】 héjì 〈*Pharm.*〉 mixture: 复方甘草～ brown mixture / 咳嗽～ cough mixture

【合金】 héjīn alloy: 黄铜是铜和锡的～。Brass is an alloy of copper and zinc.

【合金钢】 héjīngāng alloy steel

【合刊】 hékān combined issue (of a periodical)

【合口】 hékǒu 1.(指伤口) heal up 2.(指口味) be to one's taste

【合理】 hélǐ rational; reasonable; equitable: ～的价格 a reasonable price / ～拉开收入差距 widen differences in personal income to a reasonable degree / ～利用资源 make rational use of resources

【合理分工】 héhǐ fēngōng rational division of labor

【合理负担】 hélǐ fùdān equitable distribution of burden

【合理化】 hélǐhuà rationalize; rationalization (n.)

【合理化建议】 hélǐhuà jiànyì rationalization proposal

【合龙】 hélóng 1.(指堤坝等) closure 2.(指桥梁等) join the two sections of a bridge, etc.

【合谋】 hémóu 1.（共同策划）conspire; plot together 2.〈*Law*〉conspiracy

【合拍】 hépāi 1.（协调一致）in time; in step; in harmony 2.（合作拍摄）co-produce; co-production (n.) 3.（在一起拍照）take a group photo

【合拍片】 hépāipiān 〈*Cinematog.*〉co-production：电影《末代皇帝》是一部～。The film *Last Emperor* is a co-production.

【合情合理】 héqíng-hélǐ fair and reasonable; fair and sensible

【合群】 héqún get along well with others; be in good terms with others

【合身】 héshēn fit; be the right size：这件体恤衫很～。This T-shirt fits well.

【合适】 héshì 1.（符合要求）suitable; appropriate; becoming; right 2.（合身）fit：这大衣我穿着正～。The coat fits me perfectly.

【合算】 hésuàn 1.（划得来）paying; worthwhile 2.（算计）reckon up

【合体】 hétǐ fit; be the right size

【合同】 hé·tong contract：签订～ sign a contract / 撕毁～ tear up a contract

【合同法】 hé·tongfǎ contract law

【合同工】 hé·tonggōng contract worker

【合同期限】 hé·tong qīxiàn contract period

【合同条款】 hé·tong tiáokuǎn contract terms

【合同制工人】 hé·tongzhì gōngrén contract system worker

【合意】 héyì suit; be to one's liking; be acceptable

【合议庭】 héyìtíng 〈*Law*〉collegiate bench

【合营】 héyíng jointly owned; jointly operated

【合营企业】 héyíng qǐyè joint venture

【合影】 héyǐng 1.（照合影）take a group photo：～留念 have a group photo taken to mark the occasion 2.（合影照片）group photo

【合照】 hézhào group photo

【合著】 hézhù 1.（合作著书）write in collaboration with 2.（合著者）coauthor

【合资】 hézī joint venture

【合资经营】 hézī jīngyíng joint venture

【合资企业】 hézī qǐyè joint venture

【合奏】 hézòu instrumental ensemble

【合作】 hézuò cooperate; collaborate; work together：技术～ technological cooperation / 多党～ multiparty cooperation / 实行新老干部的～和交替 encourage cooperation between young and old cadres and gradually replace the old with the young

【合作经济】 hézuò jīngjì cooperative economy

【合作拍片】 hézuò pāipiān 〈*Cinematog.*〉co-pruduce; co-production (n.)

【合作企业】 hézuò qǐyè co-operative enterprise

【合作社】 hézuòshè cooperative; co-op

【合作医疗】 hézuò yīliáo cooperative medical service

盒 (hé) box; case

【盒带】 hédài cassette tape; cassette

【盒带录音机】 hédài lùyīnjī cassette tape recorder

【盒饭】 héfàn packed lunch; box lunch

【盒子】 hé·zi box; case; casket

颌 (hé) 〈*Anat.*〉jaw：上～ upper jaw / 下～ lower jaw

【颌骨】 hégǔ jawbone

何 (hé) ～时 what time; when

【何必】 hébì why; there is no need：～多此一举。Why do you carry water to the river?

【何等】 héděng 1.（什么样的）what kind：～人物 what kind of person 2.（多么）how; what

【何妨】 héfáng why not; might as well：试试又～? Why not have a try?（或：You might as well have a try.）

【何故】 hégù why; for what reason：不知～ not know why

【何苦】 hékǔ why bother; is it worth the trouble：～自寻烦恼? Why worry yourself sick?

【何况】 hékuàng 〈*conj.*〉much less; let alone

【何去何从】 héqù-hécóng what course to follow

【何以】 héyǐ how; why

【何在】 hézài where：用心～? What's the motive?

【何止】 hézhǐ far more than：石油的用途～这些。The uses of oil are by no means limited to those.

【何足轻重】 hézú-qīngzhòng Of what consequence is it?

河 (hé) river

【河岸】 hé'àn river bank

【河叉】 héchà fork：北～ north fork / 南～ south fork

【河床】 héchuáng river bed

【河道】 hédào river course; river channel

【河堤】 hédī dike; river wall

【河沟】 hégōu brook; stream

【河谷】 hégǔ valley

【河口】 hékǒu river mouth

【河狸】 hélí 〈*Zool*.〉 beaver

【河狸鼠】 hélíshǔ 〈*Zool*.〉 nutria

【河流】 héliú river：通航～ navigable river

【河流断面】 héliú duànmiàn cross section of river

【河马】 hémǎ 〈*Zool*.〉 hippopotamus; hippo

【河泥】 héní river silt

【河螃蟹】 hépángxiè river crab; fresh-water crab

【河曲】 héqū bend (of a river)

【河渠】 héqú rivers and canals; waterways

【河山】 héshān rivers and mountains; territory; land：祖国～美丽如画。Our native land is as pretty as a picture.

【河滩地】 hétāndì flood land

【河套】 hétào the bend of a river

【河豚】 hétún 〈*Zool*.〉 estuarine puffer; globefish

【河外星系】 héwài xīngxì 〈*Astron*.〉 extragalactic system

【河外星云】 héwài xīngyún 〈*Astron*.〉 extragalactic nebula

【河网】 héwǎng a network of waterways

【河系】 héxì river system

【河蟹】 héxiè river crab; fresh-water crab

【河鱼】 héyú river fish

【河源】 héyuán river head; river source

【河源湖】 héyuánhú source lake

【河运】 héyùn river transport

荷 (hé) lotus (另见“荷”hè)

【荷包蛋】 hé·bāodàn fried eggs; poached eggs

【荷花】 héhuā lotus

【荷兰豆】 hélándòu 〈*Vagetables*〉 garden pea

【荷叶】 héyè lotus leaf

核［覈[3]］(hé) **1**.（果核；果仁）pit; stone **2**.（核状物）nucleus **3**.（查对）examine; check **4**.（核动力的）nuclear-powered

【核爆炸】 hébàozhà nuclear explosion

【核查】 héchá check; examine and verify

【核磁共振】 hécí gòngzhèn nuclear magnetic resonance (NMR)

【核大国】 hédàguó nuclear power

【核弹】 hédàn nuclear bomb

【核弹头】 hédàntóu nuclear warhead

【核电站】 hédiànzhàn nuclear power station

【核定】 hédìng check and ratify; appraise and decide

【核动力】 hédònglì nuclear power

【核对】 héduì check; check up：～事实 check the facts / ～账目 check the accounts

【核讹诈】 hé'ézhà nuclear blackmail

【核发】 héfā approve and issue

【核反应】 héfǎnyìng nuclear reaction

【核反应堆】 héfǎnyìngduī nuclear reactor

【核辐射】 héfúshè nuclear radiation

【核果】 héguǒ 〈*Bot*.〉 stone fruit; drupe

【核计】 héjì calculate

【核扩散】 hékuòsàn nuclear proliferation

【核力】 hélì nuclear force

【核垄断】 hélǒngduàn nuclear monopoly

【核能】 hénéng nuclear energy

【核能源】 hénéngyuán nuclear power source

【核潜艇】 héqiántǐng nuclear-powered submarine

【核仁】 hérén **1**.〈*Biol*.〉 nucleolus **2**.（果仁）kernel (of a fruit-stone)

【核实】 héshí verify; check

【核试验】 héshìyàn nuclear test：地下～ underground nuclear test

【核算】 hésuàn business accounting：成本～ cost accounting / 独立～ keep separate accounts

【核算单位】 hésuàn dānwèi accounting unit：独立～ independent accounting unit

【核桃】 hé·tao **1**.（核果）walnut **2**.（树）walnut tree

【核威慑力量】 héwēishè lìliàng nuclear deterrent (power)

【核威胁】 héwēixié nuclear threat

【核武库】 héwǔkù nuclear arsenal

【核武器】 héwǔqì nuclear weapon：战略～ strategic nuclear weapon / 全面禁止和彻底销毁～ complete prohibition and thorough destruction of nuclear weapons
【核物理】 héwùlǐ nuclear physics
【核泄露】 héxièlòu nuclear leakage
【核心】 héxīn nucleus；core；kernel：领导～ the core of leadership / 以…为～ with ... at the core
【核心家庭】 héxīn jiātíng nuclear family
【核心力量】 héxīn lìliàng force at the core
【核心人物】 héxīn rénwù key figure
【核心问题】 héxīn wèntí key problem
【核原料】 héyuánliào nuclear fuel material
【核战争】 hézhànzhēng nuclear war
【核准】 hézhǔn examine and approve；check and approve
【核子】 hézǐ 〈*Physics*〉 nucleon

貉 (hé) 〈*Zool.*〉 raccoon dog；racoon dog (另见"貉"háo)

和 (hè) 1.(跟着唱) join in the singing 2.(和诗) compose a poem in reply (另见"和"hé, hú, huó, huò)

贺 (hè) congratulate

【贺词】 hècí speech of congratulation；message of congratulation；congratulations；greetings：新年～ New Year message
【贺电】 hèdiàn message of congratulation
【贺卡】 hèkǎ card
【贺礼】 hèlǐ gift (as a token of congratulation)：生日～ birthday present
【贺年】 hènián extend New Year greetings；pay a New Year call
【贺年卡】 hèniánkǎ New Year card
【贺喜】 hèxǐ congratulate sb. on a happy occasion
【贺信】 hèxìn congratulatory letter；letter of congratulation

荷 (hè) carry on one's shoulder (另见"荷"hé)

【荷枪】 hèqiāng carry a rifle
【荷载】 hèzài load

喝 (hè) shout loudly (另见"喝"hē)

【喝彩】 hècǎi acclaim；cheer：～叫好 a shout of applause
【喝倒彩】 hèdàocǎi make catcalls；hoot；boo

褐 (hè) brown

【褐煤】 hèméi brown coal；lignite

赫 (hè) 1.(显著) conspicuous；grand 2.(赫兹) hertz (hz)

【赫赫】 hèhè illustrious；very impressive：～战功 illustrious military exploits；brilliant military success
【赫然】 hèrán 1.(突然呈现) impressively；awesomely 2.(大怒) terribly (angry)
【赫哲族】 Hèzhézú Hezhen (中国少数民族，主要分布在黑龙江)
【赫兹】 hèzī 〈*Electr.*〉 hertz

鹤 (hè) 〈*Zool.*〉 crane

【鹤立鸡群】 hèlì-jīqún stand head and shoulders above others；be preeminent

壑 (hè) valley；gully；ravine

hei

黑 (hēi) 1.(黑色) black：她穿了一身～。She is dressed in black. 2.(黑暗) dark 3.(秘密) secret；shady 4.(坏) wicked；sinister

【黑暗】 hēi'àn dark：～的房间 a dark room
【黑暗面】 hēi'ànmiàn the seamy side；a dark aspect：生活的～ the seamy side of life
【黑白】 hēibái 1.(黑和白) black and white：～分明 in sharp contrast between black and white 2.(正与错) right and wrong：～鲜明 right and wrong is clearly obvious
【黑白电视】 hēibái diànshì black-and-white television
【黑白电视机】 hēibái diànshìjī black-and-white television receiver；monochrome TV receiver
【黑板】 hēibǎn blackboard
【黑板报】 hēibǎnbào blackboard newspaper
【黑板擦】 hēibǎncā eraser
【黑帮】 hēibāng reactionary gang；sinister gang
【黑豹】 hēibào black panther
【黑冰】 hēibīng 〈*Transport*〉 black ice
【黑洞】 hēidòng 〈*Astron.*〉 black hole

【黑洞洞】 hēidòngdòng pitch-dark
【黑格】 hēigé 〈*Chess*〉 black square
【黑管】 hēiguǎn 〈*Music*〉 clarinet
【黑糊糊】 hēihūhū 1.（颜色发黑）black blackened 2.（光线昏暗）rather dark；dusky 3.（模糊不清）indistinctly observable in the distance
【黑话】 hēihuà 1.（强盗的）argot 2.（盗贼的）cant 3.（隐晦的话）double talk；malicious words
【黑货】 hēihuò 1.（走私货）smuggled goods；contraband 2.（违禁物）sinister stuff；trash
【黑客】 hēikè 〈*Computer*〉 hacker
【黑马】 hēimǎ dark horse
【黑名单】 hēimíngdān blacklist
【黑幕】 hēimù inside story of a plot：揭穿～ expose a sinister project
【黑钱】 hēiqián black money
【黑人】 Hēirén Black people；Black；Negro：美国～ Black American；Afro-American
【黑色】 hēisè black
【黑色火药】 hēisè huǒyào black powder
【黑色金属】 hēisè jīnshǔ ferrous metal
【黑色经济】 hēisè jīngjì black economy
【黑色幽默】 hēisè yōumò black humor
【黑纱】 hēishā black armband：佩戴～ wear black armband
【黑社会】 hēishèhuì underworld；criminal world；criminal society
【黑市】 hēishì black market
【黑市汇率】 hēishì huìlǜ black market rate
【黑市价格】 hēishì jiàgé black rate
【黑市交易】 hēishì jiāoyì off-the-books deal
【黑势力】 hēishìlì forces of evil
【黑手】 hēishǒu evil backstage manipulator
【黑死病】 hēisǐbìng 〈*Med.*〉 black death；bubonic plague
【黑穗病】 hēisuìbìng 〈*Agric.*〉 smut
【黑桃】 hēitáo 〈*Cards*〉 spade
【黑土】 hēitǔ black earth
【黑匣子】 hēixiázi 〈*Aeron.*〉 black box：～揭示了飞机坠毁的原因。The black box showed why the plane had crashed.
【黑心】 hēixīn 1.（狠毒心肠）blackheartedness；evil-mindedness；viciousness 2.（阴险狠毒）blackhearted；evil-minded；vicious
【黑猩猩】 hēixīng·xing 〈*Zool.*〉 chimpanzee
【黑熊】 hēixióng black bear
【黑压压】 hēiyāyā a dense mass of；a dark mass of
【黑腰带】 hēiyāodài 〈*Judo*〉 black belt
【黑夜】 hēiyè night
【黑油油】 hēiyōuyōu jet-black；shiny black
【黑黝黝】 hēiyōuyōu 1.（黑得发亮）shiny black：～的脸 swarthy face 2.（光线昏暗）dim；dark
【黑鱼】 hēiyú 〈*Zool.*〉 snakeheaded fish；snakeheaded
【黑枣】 hēizǎo dateplum persimmon
【黑种】 Hēizhǒng the black race
【黑子】 hēizǐ 1.〈*Chess*〉 black pieces 2.〈*Astron.*〉 sunspot

hen

痕（hén） mark；trace
【痕迹】 hénjì mark；trace；vestige；imprint；print：不露～ make no sign / 留下～ leave a trace
【痕量】 hénliàng 〈*Chem.*〉 trace
【痕量元素】 hénliàng yuánsù 〈*Chem.*〉 trace element
很（hěn） 〈*adv.*〉 very；quite；awfully：～久以前 long ago / ～可能 very likely / ～有意义 highly significant
狠（hěn） 1.（凶狠）ruthless；relentless 2.（坚决）firm；resolute
【狠毒】 hěndú vicious；venomous：用心～ with vicious intent
【狠心】 hěnxīn 1.（狠着心）suppress one's feelings；harden the heart 2.（残忍）cruel-hearted；heartless
恨（hèn） 1.（仇视）hate：～得要命 hate intensely；bitterly hate / ～之入骨 hate sb. to the very marrow of one's bones 2.（悔恨；不称心）regret
【恨入骨髓】 hènrùgǔsuǐ hate bitterly；hate to the very marrow of one's bones

heng

亨（hēng） 1.（亨通）go smoothly 2.〈*Physics*〉 henry（符号为：H）

【亨利】 hēnglì 〈*Physics*〉 henry（符号为：H）
【亨通】 hēngtōng go smoothly; to sb's satisfaction：万事～。Everything is going smoothly.（或：Everything is running satisfactorily.）

哼（hēng） 1.（鼻子发出的声音）snort 2.（低声吟唱）hum; croon 3.（发出呻吟声）groan
（另见"哼"hng）
【哼哧】 hēngchī 〈*onomat.*〉 puff hard：～～地直喘 be puffing and blowing
【哼哼哈哈】 hēnghēng-hāhā hem and ham

恒［恆］（héng） 1.（永恒）permanent; lasting 2.（恒心）perseverance：持之以～ persevere in（doing sth.）3.（平常;经常）usual; common
【恒等式】 héngděngshì 〈*Math.*〉 identical equation; identity
【恒久】 héngjiǔ permanent; eternal; everlasting
【恒生指数】 Héngshēng zhǐshù Hang Seng index
【恒温】 héngwēn constant temperature
【恒温车间】 héngwēn chējiān constant temperature workshop
【恒温器】 héngwēnqì calorstat; thermostat
【恒温设备】 héngwēn shèbèi thermostatic equipment
【恒心】 héngxīn perseverance; constancy of purpose
【恒星】 héngxīng 〈*Astron.*〉（fixed）star
【恒星年】 héngxīngnián 〈*Astron.*〉 sidereal year
【恒星系】 héngxīngxì 〈*Astron.*〉 stellar system
【恒牙】 héngyá 〈*Anat.*〉 permanent teeth

桁（héng） purlin; purline
【桁架】 héngjià truss

衡（héng） 1.（秤杆）the graduated arm of a steelyard 2.（称重量）weighing apparatus 3.（衡量）weigh; measure; judge
【衡量】 héng·liáng weight; measure; judge
【衡器】 héngqì weighing apparatus
【衡情度理】 héng qíng dù lǐ take everything into consideration; judge the situation carefully

横（héng） 1.（与地面平行的）horizontal; transverse 2.（从左到右或从右到左）across; sideways：～过街道 across the street / ～写 write words sideways 3.（把东西横过来）move crosswise; traverse 4.（纵横杂乱）unrestrainedly; turbulently 5.（蛮横）violently; fiercely; flagrantly
（另见"横"hèng）
【横冲直撞】 héngchōng-zhízhuàng push one's way by shoving or humping; jostle and elbow one's way
【横道线】 héngdàoxiàn zebra crossing; pedestrian crossing; crosswalk
【横笛】 héngdí 〈*Music*〉 flute
【横渡】 héngdù traverse; sail across
【横断面】 héngduànmiàn cross section
【横队】 héngduì rank; row
【横幅】 héngfú banner; streamer
【横杆】 hénggān 〈*Sports*〉 bar
【横格纸】 hénggézhǐ lined paper
【横膈膜】 hénggémó 〈*Anat.*〉 diaphragm
【横加干涉】 héngjiā·gānshè flagrantly interfere; deliberately intrude
【横加指责】 héngjiā-zhǐzé blame unscrupulously
【横结肠】 héngjiécháng 〈*Anat.*〉 transverse colon
【横截面】 héngjiémiàn cross section
【横跨】 héngkuà stretch over; stretch across
【横梁】 héngliáng 1.〈*Archit.*〉 crossbeam 2.〈*Auto*〉 cross member
【横七竖八】 héngqī-shùbā in disorder; at sixes and sevens：过道里～地放着各种东西。The passage was cluttered up with all sorts of things.
【横肉】 héngròu 一脸～ look ugly and ferocious
【横扫】 héngsǎo 1.（扫除）sweep away; make a clean sweep of 2.（扫荡）wipe out：～千军 wipe out the enemy forces
【横生】 héngshēng 1.（杂乱生）grow wild 2.（层出不穷）be overflowing with; be full of 3.（意外发生）happen unexpectedly
【横生枝节】 héngshēng-zhījié 1.（意外插进来的问题）side issues of new problems unexpectedly crop up 2.（提出难题）raise obstacles; deliberately complicate an issue
【横向】 héngxiàng lateral; extend sideways

【横向经济联系】 héngxiàng jīngjì liánxì horizontal economic ties; lateral economic ties

【横向联系】 héngxiàng liánxì horizontal ties; lateral ties

【横心】 héngxīn steel one's heart; become desperate

【横行】 héngxíng run wild; run amuck; be on a rampage: ～一时 run wild for a time

【横行霸道】 héngxíng-bàdào ride roughshod; play the tyrant; tyrannize; domineer

横 (hèng) 1.(粗暴无理的) harsh and unreasonable; perverse: 发～ act in an unreasonable way 2.(意外的) unexpected

(另见"横"héng)

【横暴】 hèngbào perverse and violent; brutal; barbarous

【横财】 hèngcái ill-gotten wealth: 发～ get rich by foul means

【横祸】 hènghuò unexpected calamity; sudden misfortune: 飞来～ an unforeseen disaster

hng

哼 (hng) humph: ～,我才不请他呢! Humph, I won't invite him.

(另见"哼"hēng)

hong

轰[轟、揈] (hōng) 1.〈*onomat.*〉 bang; boom: 炮～声 boom of guns 2.(击;鸣) rumble; bombard; explode 3.(赶) shoo away; drive off

【轰动】 hōngdòng cause a sensation; make a stir; make a sensation: ～一时 cause a sensation

【轰动效应】 hōngdòng xiàoyìng sensational effect

【轰轰烈烈】 hōnghōng-lièliè on a grand and spectacular scale; vigorous; dynamic: ～的场面 vigorous situation

【轰击】 hōngjī 1.(用炮打) shell; bombard; bombardment (n.): ～城市造成几百人的死伤 bombard the city killing and injuring hundreds 2.〈*Physics*〉 bombard: ～原子核 bombard the atomic nucleus

【轰隆】 hōnglóng 〈*onomat.*〉 rumble; roll

【轰鸣】 hōngmíng thunder; roar

【轰下台】 hōngxiàtái 1.(轰下讲台) hoot sb. off the platform 2.(使失去职务或权力) oust sb. from office or power

【轰炸】 hōngzhà bomb: ～一目标 bomb a target

【轰炸机】 hōngzhàjī bomber: 地面进攻得到了～的空中支援。The offensive on land was supported by bombers in the air.

哄 (hōng) 1.(大笑声) roars of laughter 2.(嘈杂) hubbub

(另见"哄"hǒng, hòng)

【哄传】 hōngchuán (of rumors) circulate widely

【哄动】 hōngdòng cause a sensation; make a stir

【哄然】 hōngrán boisterous; uproarious: ～而散 disperse with great noise and hubbub

【哄抬】 hōngtái drive up (prices): ～物价 inflate prices; jack up prices

【哄堂大笑】 hōngtáng-dàxiào the whole room rocking with laughter: 引起～ set the room in a roar

烘 (hōng) 1.(烤热;烤干) warm by the fire; dry by the fire 2.(衬托) set off

【烘干】 hōnggān dry: 在滚桶中～ tumble dry

【烘干机】 hōnggānjī dryer; drier: 滚桶式～ tumble dryer; tumble drier

【烘托】 hōngtuō 1.(画法) add shading around an object to make it stand out 2.(使明显突出) set off by contrast; throw into sharp relief

【烘箱】 hōngxiāng oven: 普通～ a conventional oven

弘 (hóng) 1.(大) great; grand; grandiose 2.(使光大) enlarge; expand

【弘大】 hóngdà great; grand; magnificent

【弘图】 hóngtú great plan; grandiose plan; grand prospect

【弘扬】 hóngyáng carry forward; develop

【弘愿】 hóngyuàn great aspiration; noble ambition

红 (hóng) 1.(红色) red: 穿着～衣服 dressed in red 2.(革命) revolutionary; red 3.(顺利;成功) symbol of success: 他唱戏唱～了。He has won success as an actor. 4.(红利) bonus; dividend: 分～ distribute or draw dividends

【红白喜事】 hóng-bái xǐshì weddings and funerals
【红榜】 hóngbǎng honor roll
【红宝石】 hóngbǎoshí ruby
【红茶】 hóngchá black tea
【红尘】 hóngchén human world
【红带】 hóngdài red tape
【红灯】 hóngdēng 〈*Transport*〉 red light; traffic light
【红灯区】 hóngdēngqū red-light district
【红地毯】 hóngdìtǎn red carpet：铺～ roll out the red carpet / 他受到了铺～的礼遇。He was given the red carpet treatment.
【红方】 hóngfāng red side
【红汞】 hónggǒng 〈*Pharm.*〉 mercurochrome
【红巨星】 hóngjùxīng 〈*Astron.*〉 red giant
【红军】 Hóngjūn 1.（中国工农红军）the Chinese Workers' and Peasants' Red Army (1928-1937); the Red Army 2.（红军战士）Red Army man
【红利】 hónglì bonus; extra dividend
【红脸】 hóngliǎn 1.（害羞）blush 2.（发怒）flush with anger; get angry
【红领巾】 hónglǐngjīn 1.（红色领巾）red scarf 2.（少先队员）Young Pioneer
【红绿灯】 hónglǜdēng traffic light; traffic signal
【红帽子】 hóngmào·zi red cap
【红霉素】 hóngméisù 〈*Pharm.*〉 erythromycin
【红木】 hóngmù 〈*Bot.*〉 mahogany
【红牌】 hóngpái 〈*Sports*〉 red card：出示～ show the red card / 被出示～（即被罚出场）be sent off
【红其拉甫】 Hóngqílāfǔ 〈place〉 Kunjirap
【红其拉甫达坂】 Hóngqílāfǔdábǎn 〈place〉 Kunjirap Daban
【红旗】 hóngqí red flag; red banner：～招展。Red flags are fluttering gaily in the wind.
【红旗单位】 hóngqí dānwèi red-banner unit; advanced unit
【红热】 hóngrè red hot; red-hot (adj.)
【红人】 hóngrén a favorite with sb. in power
【红日子】 hóngrì·zi red-letter day
【红润】 hóngrùn ruddy; rosy：脸色～ ruddy complexion
【红色】 hóngsè 1.（红颜色）red 2.（象征革命）red; revolutionary
【红色肉类】 hóngsè ròulèi red meat（指牛羊猪等的肉）
【红杉】 hóngshān 〈*Bot.*〉 redwood
【红烧】 hóngshāo braise in soy sauce
【红十字会】 Hóngshízìhuì the Red Cross：中国～ the Red Cross Society of China
【红薯】 hóngshǔ sweet potato
【红糖】 hóngtáng brown sugar
【红桃】 hóngtáo 〈*Cards*〉 heart
【红通通】 hóngtōngtōng bright red; glowing：～的晚霞 evening glow
【红铜】 hóngtóng red bronze
【红外线】 hóngwàixiàn 〈*Physics*〉 infrared ray
【红外线报警装置】 hóngwàixiàn bàojǐng zhuāngzhì infrared warning device
【红外线遥控器】 hóngwàixiàn yáokòngqì infrared remote controller
【红细胞】 hóngxìbāo red blood cell; red corpuscle
【红新月会】 Hóngxīnyuèhuì Red Crescent
【红星】 hóngxīng 1.（红五角星）red star 2.（走红的明星）very popular star
【红血球】 hóngxuèqiú red blood cell; erythrocyte
【红眼】 hóngyǎn 1.（眼疾）blood-shot eye 2.（发怒）see red; become infuriated 3.（眼红）be jealous of sb.
【红眼病】 hóngyǎnbìng 1.（眼疾）conjunctivitis 2.（眼红）be jealous of others' talent or becoming wealthy
【红药水】 hóngyàoshuǐ 〈*Med.*〉 mercurochrome
【红移】 hóngyí 〈*Sports*〉 redshift
【红运】 hóngyùn good luck; good fortune：走～ have good luck
【红晕】 hóngyùn blush; flush
【红妆】 hóngzhuāng 同"红装"
【红装】 hóngzhuāng 1.（女装）gay feminine attire 2.（青年妇女）young woman
【红子】 hóngzǐ 〈*Chess*〉 red pieces

虹 (hóng) 〈*Meteorol.*〉 rainbow

【虹膜】 hóngmó 〈*Anat.*〉 iris
【虹吸管】 hóngxīguǎn siphon

鸿 (hóng) 1.（鸿雁）swan goose 2.（书信）letter 3.（大）great; grand

【鸿沟】 hónggōu wide gap; chasm
【鸿毛】 hóngmáo a goose feather; sth. very light or insignificant：轻如～ as light as a

feather
【鸿图】 hóngtú great plans; grand prospects
【鸿雁】 hóngyàn swan goose; wild goose

宏(hóng) great; grand; magnificent

【宏病毒】 hóngbìngdú 〈*Computer*〉 macro virus
【宏程序设计】 hóngchéngxù shèjì 〈*Computer*〉 macroprogramming
【宏大】 hóngdà grand; great: 规模～ on a grand scale
【宏定义】 hóngdìngyì 〈*Computer*〉 macro definition
【宏观】 hóngguān macroscopic; macro-
【宏观经济学】 hóngguān jīngjìxué macroeconomics
【宏观调控】 hóngguān tiáokòng macro-control: 对经济的～ macroeconomic control; macro-control of the economy
【宏观指导】 hóngguān zhǐdǎo centralize guidance
【宏汇编程序】 hónghuì biān chéngxù 〈*Computer*〉 macro assembler
【宏汇编语言】 hónghuì biān yǔyán 〈*Computer*〉 macro assembly language
【宏论】 hónglùn intelligent view; brilliant idea
【宏命令】 hóngmìnglìng 〈*Computer*〉 macro command
【宏图】 hóngtú great plan; grandiose plan; great goal; grand prospect: 大展～ realize one's aspiration / 实现振兴中华的～ accomplish the great goal of making China prosperous and strong
【宏伟】 hóngwěi magnificent; grand: ～的计划 magnificent plan / ～前景 grand prospects
【宏扬】 hóngyáng carry forward; develop
【宏旨】 hóngzhǐ main theme; leading idea of an article
【宏指令】 hóngzhǐlìng 〈*Computer*〉 macro order

洪(hóng) 1.(大) big; vast 2.(洪水) flood: 防～ control or prevent flood / 分～ flood diversion; reduce flood; mitigate flood / 山～ mountain torrents; freshet

【洪峰】 hóngfēng flood peak
【洪亮】 hóngliàng loud and clear; sonorous
【洪流】 hóngliú mighty torrent; powerful current: 不可抗拒的革命～ irresistible current of revolution
【洪水】 hóngshuǐ flood; floodwater

哄(hǒng) 1.(哄骗) fool; cheat 2.(哄逗) coax; soothe; humor
(另见"哄"hōng, hòng)

【哄逗】 hǒngdòu coax; soothe; humor
【哄骗】 hǒngpiàn fool; cheat

哄[閧](hòng) uproar; clamor; hubbub: 一～而散 break up in an uproar
(另见"哄"hōng, hǒng)

hou

侯(hóu) marquis

【侯爵】 hóujué marquis; marquess (f.)

喉(hóu) larynx; throat

【喉结】 hóujié Adam's apple
【喉咙】 hóu·lóng throat: ～痛 have a sore throat
【喉舌】 hóushé 1.(发声器官) speech organs 2.(指宣传工具) mouthpiece
【喉头】 hóutóu larynx; throat

猴(hóu) 1.(猴子) monkey 2.(机灵) clever boy; smart chap

【猴皮筋】 hóupíjīn rubber band: 跳～ skip rubber band
【猴戏】 hóuxì monkey show
【猴子】 hóu·zi monkey

吼(hǒu) roar; howl

【吼声】 hǒushēng roar; howl: 大炮的～ the roar of the cannon

后[後1-3](hòu) 1.(后面的) behind; back; rear: 请往～站! Stand back, please! 2.(未来的;较晚的) after; afterwards; later 3.(后代的人) offspring 4.(君主的妻子) empress; queen

【后半】 hòubàn later half; second half
【后半生】 hòubànshēng the later half of one's life
【后半天】 hòubàntiān afternoon

【后半夜】 hòubànyè after midnight
【后保险杠】 hòu bǎoxiǎngàng 〈*Auto*〉 rear bumper
【后备】 hòubèi reserve: ～力量 reserve forces / 留有～ keep sth. in reserve
【后备基金】 hòubèi jījīn reserve fund
【后备军】 hòubèijūn 1.(预备役军人) reserves 2.(补充力量) reserve force
【后辈】 hòubèi 1.(年轻的或资历浅的人) juniors 2.(后代) younger generation 3.(子孙) posterity
【后场】 hòuchǎng 〈*Tennis & Basketball*〉 back court
【后尘】 hòuchén 步某人～ follow in sb.'s footsteps; follow an example set by sb.
【后窗】 hòuchuāng 〈*Auto*〉 rear window
【后代】 hòudài 1.(以后的时代) later periods (in history); later ages 2.(后代的人) later generations; descendants; posterity
【后盾】 hòudùn backing; backup force
【后方】 hòufāng rear; rear area
【后方留守处】 hòufāng liúshǒuchù rear headquarters
【后方医院】 hòufāng yīyuàn base hospital; rear hospital
【后父】 hòufù stepfather
【后跟】 hòugēn heel: 鞋～ heel / 袜子～ heel of a sock
【后顾】 hòugù 1.(回头照看) turn back (to take care of sth.) 2.(回忆) look back (on the past)
【后顾之忧】 hòugùzhīyōu fear of disturbance in the rear; trouble back at home
【后滚翻】 hòugǔnfān 〈*Sports*〉 backward roll
【后果】 hòuguǒ consequence; aftermath: 前因～ cause and effect / 严重～ serious consequence
【后患】 hòuhuàn future trouble
【后患无穷】 hòuhuàn-wúqióng no end of trouble for the future
【后悔】 hòuhuǐ regret; repent: 一点不～ have no regrets at all
【后会有期】 hòuhuì-yǒuqī we'll meet again some day
【后记】 hòujì postscript; afterword
【后继】 hòujì succeed; carry on: ～乏人 lack worthy successors / ～有人 have qualified successors; successors will come
【后腱子】 hòujiàn·zi 1.(羊肉部位) hind leg 2.(牛肉部位) hind shank
【后脚爪】 hòujiǎozhuǎ hind foot
【后襟】 hòujīn the back of a Chinese gown
【后进】 hòujìn 1.(学习差) not learned; less educated 2.(落后) legging behind; less advanced
【后劲】 hòujìn 1.(指作用) delayed effect; aftereffect 2.(指力量) reserve strength; stamina; staying power: ～不足 lack of staying power
【后来】 hòulái 1.(然后) afterwards; later 2.(后来的人) latecomer
【后来居上】 hòulái-jūshàng the latecomers surpass the old-timers; the new generation will surpass the old
【后路】 hòulù 1.(退路) communication lines to the rear; route of retreat 2.(回旋余地) room for maneuver; a way of escape
【后轮】 hòulún rear wheel; back wheel
【后门】 hòumén 1.(后面的门) back door; back gate 2.〈*Auto*〉 rear door 3.(舞弊途径) back door influence: 走～ by the back door
【后门工程】 hòumén gōngchéng back door project
【后面】 hòu·mian 1.(指位置) at the back; in the rear; behind 2.(指次序) later
【后母】 hòumǔ stepmother
【后脑勺】 hòunǎosháo the back of the head
【后年】 hòunián the year after next
【后怕】 hòupà fear after the event
【后排】 hòupái back row: ～座位 back row seats
【后期】 hòuqī later stage; later period: 抗日战争～ the later part of the Anti-Japanese War
【后起之秀】 hòuqǐzhīxiù an up-and-coming youngster; a promising young person
【后桥】 hòuqiáo 〈*Auto*〉 rear axle; back axle
【后勤】 hòuqín rear service; logistics
【后勤部】 hòuqínbù logistics department
【后勤部队】 hòuqín bùduì rear-service units; rear services
【后勤机关】 hòuqín jīguān logistics department; rear-service department
【后区】 hòuqū 〈*Volleyball*〉 back zone

【后人】 hòurén 1.（后代之人）later generations 2.（子孙）posterity；descendants
【后任】 hòurèn successor
【后事】 hòushì 1.（以后的事情）what happened afterwards 2.（丧事）funeral affairs：料理～ make arrangements for a funeral
【后视镜】 hòushìjìng 〈*Auto*〉wing mirror
【后视图】 hòushìtú back view；rearview
【后手】 hòushǒu 1.（被动的形势）defensive position（in chess）2.（后路）room for maneuver；a way of escape
【后嗣】 hòusì offspring；descendant
【后台】 hòutái 1.（舞台后部）backstage 2.（背后操纵和支持的人）backstage supporter
【后台老板】 hòutái lǎobǎn backstage boss
【后蹄膀】 hòutíbǎng trotter
【后天】 hòutiān 1.（明天的明天）the day after tomorrow：大～ three days from today 2.（与先天相对）postnatal；acquired：～失调 lack of proper care after one's birth
【后腿】 hòutuǐ 〈*Zool.*〉leg
【后退】 hòutuì draw back；fall back；retreat
【后卫】 hòuwèi 1.〈*Mil.*〉rear guard 2.〈*Football*〉back；full back 3.〈*Basketball*〉guard
【后遗症】 hòuyízhèng sequelae；after-effect：小儿麻痹～ sequelae of infantile paralysis / 病愈没有～ recover without any after-effect
【后裔】 hòuyì descendant；offspring
【后影】 hòuyǐng the outline of sb's back
【后院】 hòuyuàn backyard
【后闸】 hòuzhá back brake
【后者】 hòuzhě the latter
【后坐力】 hòuzuòlì 〈*Mil.*〉recoil
【后座】 hòuzuò 〈*Auto*〉back seat；rear seat

厚（hòu） 1.（与薄相对）thick：～纸 thick paper 2.（深）deep；profound 3.（厚道）kind；magnanimous 4.（大）large；generous：～薪 high pay 5.（浓）rich or strong in flavor 6.（优待；推崇）favor；stress
【厚爱】 hòu'ài your kindness
【厚薄】 hòubó thickness
【厚此薄彼】 hòucǐ-bóbǐ favor one more than another；treat with partiality
【厚道】 hòu·dao honest and kind
【厚度】 hòudù thickness
【厚古薄今】 hòugǔ-bójīn stress the past，not the present
【厚今薄古】 hòujīn-bógǔ stress the present，not the past
【厚礼】 hòulǐ generous gift：收到一份～ be given a generous gift
【厚利】 hòulì a large profit
【厚脸皮】 hòuliǎnpí thick-skinned；brazen；cheeky
【厚实】 hòu·shi thick and solid
【厚望】 hòuwàng great expectations
【厚颜无耻】 hòuyán-wúchǐ impudent；brazen；shameless
【厚意】 hòuyì kindness；benefaction；generosity：承蒙～ thank you for your kindness
【厚着脸皮】 hòu·zhe liǎnpí have the nerve to
【厚重】 hòuzhòng heavily：～织物 heavily fabric

候（hòu） 1.（等候）wait；await 2.（问候）inquire after 3.（时节）time；season 4.（情况）condition；state
【候补】 hòubǔ be a candidate（for a vacancy）；be an alternate
【候补委员】 hòubǔ wěiyuán alternate member
【候车室】 hòuchēshì waiting room（in a railway or bus station）
【候机室】 hòujīshì airport lounge；waiting room
【候鸟】 hòuniǎo migratory bird；migrant
【候选人】 hòuxuǎnrén candidate：提出～ nominate candidates
【候选人名单】 hòuxuǎnrén míngdān list of candidates
【候选人资格】 hòuxuǎnrén zīgé qualifications for nomination
【候诊】 hòuzhěn wait to see the doctor
【候诊室】 hòuzhěnshì waiting room（in a hospital）

hu

呼（hū） 1.（吐气）breathe out；exhale 2.（大声喊）shout；cry out 3.（叫）call
【呼哧】 hūchī puff；gasp；pant：我跑了这么远之后直～。I was puffing after running so far.
【呼风唤雨】 hūfēng-huànyǔ 1.（使刮风下雨）summon wind and rain；control the forces of

nature 2.（煽动）stir up trouble

【呼喊】 hūhǎn call out; shout: 大声～ raise a cry / 高兴得～起来 exclaim with delight

【呼号】 hūháo （哭叫）wail; cry out in distress

【呼号】 hūhào 1.〈*Telecom.*〉call sign; call letters 2.（专用的口号）catchword (of an organization)

【呼和浩特】 Hūhéhàotè 〈place〉Hohhot

【呼唤】 hūhuàn 1.（召唤）call; shout to 2.（呼喊）call out; shout

【呼叫】 hūjiào 1.（呼喊）call out; shout 2.〈*Telecom.*〉call

【呼救】 hūjiù call for help

【呼啦】 hūlā 〈*onomat.*〉旗子在风中～～地飘。The flag flapped in the wind.

【呼喇】 hūlā 同"呼啦"

【呼拉圈】 hūlāquān hula hoop; hula

【呼噜】 hū·lu 1.（呼噜声）gurgle; wheeze 2.（打鼾）snore: 打～ snore / 他是个特能打～的人。He is a terrible snorer.

【呼伦贝尔】 Hūlúnbèiěr 〈place〉Hulun Buir

【呼伦湖】 Hūlúnhú 〈place〉Hulun Nur

【呼声】 hūshēng 1.（呼喊的声音）cry; voice 2.（民众要求）voice: 发出正义的～ give the cry of justice

【呼吸】 hūxī breathe; respire; respiration (n.): ～急促 be short of breath 人工～ artificial respiration

【呼吸器官】 hūxī qìguān respiratory organs

【呼吸系统】 hūxī xìtǒng respiratory system

【呼啸】 hūxiào whistle; scream; whizz: 寒风～。A cold wind is whistling.

【呼应】 hūyìng echo; work in concert with: 遥相～ echo each other over a distance

【呼吁】 hūyù appeal; call on: 发出紧急～ make an urgent appeal

【呼吁书】 hūyùshū letter of appeal; appeal

忽 (hū) 1.（不注意）neglect; overlook; ignore 2.（忽然）suddenly

【忽而】 hū'ér now ..., now ...: 天气～冷～热。The weather is now hot, now cold.

【忽忽】 hūhū before we notice it

【忽略】 hūlüè ignore; neglect; overlook; lose sight of: 不要～枝节问题。Don't neglect minor issues

【忽然】 hūrán 〈*adv.*〉suddenly; all of a sudden

【忽闪】 hūshǎn 1.（闪光）flash: 远处有灯光～一亮。A light flashed in the distance. 2.（闪动）blink; wink: 小姑娘～着眼睛看着妈妈。The girl winked at her mother.

【忽视】 hūshì ignore; overlook; neglect: ～经济效益 neglect economic results / 不可～的力量 a force not to be ignored; a force to be reckoned with

糊 (hū) plaster; spread; paper
（另见"糊"hú, hù）

囫 (hú)

【囫囵觉】 hú·lunjiào 1.（整夜的好觉）a good night's sleep 2.（完整的好觉）uninterrupted sleep

【囫囵吞枣】 húlún-tūnzǎo swallow dates whole; lap up information without digesting it; read without understanding

和 (hú) complete a set (in mah-jong); win at cards
（另见"和"hē, hè, huó, huò）

狐 (hú) fox

【狐步舞】 húbùwǔ foxtrot

【狐臭】 húchòu body odor; bromhidrosis; hircus

【狐狸】 hú·li fox

【狐狸精】 hú·lijīng alluring woman; seductive woman

【狐狸尾巴】 hú·li wěi·ba fox's tail; cloven hoof

【狐朋狗友】 húpéng-gǒuyǒu evil associates

【狐疑不决】 húyí-bùjué be wavering and unable to decide; indecisive in one's mind; suspicious and undecided

弧 (hú) 〈*Math.*〉arc

【弧度】 húdù 〈*Math.*〉radian; radian measure

【弧光】 húguāng arc light; arc

【弧光灯】 húguāngdēng arc lamp; arc light

【弧形】 húxíng arc; curve

胡[鬍²] (hú) 1.（胡乱）recklessly; wantonly; outrageously 2.（胡子）moustache, beard or whiskers

【胡扯】 húchě 1.（胡说）talk nonsense; drivel 2.（闲谈）chat; small talk

【胡蜂】 húfēng wasp; hornet

【胡搞】 húgǎo 1.（胡来）mess things up; meddle with sth. 2.（乱搞男女关系）carry on an affair with sb.; be promiscuous

【胡瓜】 húguā zucchini; courgette

【胡椒】 hújiāo 1.〈Bot.〉pepper; peppery (adj.) 2.（果实）peppercorn

【胡椒粉】 hújiāofěn ground pepper：黑～ black ground pepper

【胡搅蛮缠】 hújiǎo-mánchán harass sb. with unreasonable demands; pester sb. endlessly

【胡来】 húlái 1.（任意乱做）mess things up; fool with sth. 2.（胡闹）run wild; make trouble

【胡里胡涂】 hú·li-hútú confused in one's thinking; with one's mind in a haze

【胡乱】 húluàn carelessly; casually; at random：～猜测 make wild guesses

【胡萝卜】 húluó·bo carrot

【胡萝卜素】 húluó·bosù carrotene

【胡闹】 húnào run wild; be mischievous

【胡琴】 hú·qin 〈*Music*〉 *huqin*; 2-stringed Chinese violin

【胡说】 húshuō 1.（瞎说）talk nonsense; drivel：别～！Don't talk rot! / 他～些什么？What's he drivelling about? 2.（无道理的话）nonsense

【胡说八道】 húshuō-bādào 1.（胡说）talk nonsense：他的发言全是～。His speech was all rot. 2.（无价值的话）sheer nonsense; rubbish

【胡思乱想】 húsī-luànxiǎng imagine things; go off into wild flights of fancy; let one's imagination run away with one

【胡桃】 hútáo 1.〈Bot.〉walnut tree 2.（核果）walnut

【胡同儿】 hú·tòngr lane; alley

【胡须】 húxū beard, moustache or whiskers

【胡言乱语】 húyán-luànyǔ talk nonsense; rave

【胡诌】 húzhōu fabricate wild tales; cook up

【胡子】 hú·zi beard; moustache; whiskers

【胡子工程】 hú·zi gōngchéng bearded project; a project delayed long before completed

【胡作非为】 húzuò-fēiwéi act wildly in defiance of the law or public opinion; commit all kinds of outrages

葫（hú）

【葫芦】 hú·lu 1.〈Bot.〉calabash 2.（容器）bottle gourd; calabash

猢（hú）

【猢狲】 húsūn 1.（一种猕猴）macaque; rhesus monkey 2.（猴）monkey

湖（hú） lake

【湖滨】 húbīn lakeside; the shore of a lake

【湖光山色】 húguāng-shānsè a landscape of lakes and mountains

【湖泊】 húpō lakes

【湖色】 húsè light green

煳（hú） (of food) burnt：饭烧～了。The rice is burnt.

蝴（hú）

【蝴蝶】 húdié butterfly

【蝴蝶花】 hǔdiéhuā fringed iris

糊（hú） 1.（浆糊）paste 2.（粘住）stick with paste; paste up：～窗户 paste up a window 3.（焦）(of food) burnt：饭～了。The rice is burnt.

（另见"糊"hū, hù）

【糊口】 húkǒu keep body and soul together; eke out one's livelihood

【糊墙纸】 húqiángzhǐ wall paper

【糊涂】 hú·tu muddled; confused; bewildered

【糊涂观念】 hú·tu guānniàn muddled idea

壶［壺］（hú） 1.（容器）kettle; pot：茶～ teakettle; teapot 2.（瓶）bottle; flask：暖～ thermos bottle

槲（hú） 〈Bot.〉Mongolian oak

【槲寄生】 hújìshēng 〈Bot.〉mistletoe

【槲栎】 húlì 〈Bot.〉oriental white oak

虎（hǔ） 1.（老虎）tiger; tigress (f.); tigerish (adj.) 2.（威武；勇猛）brave; vigorous

【虎骨酒】 hǔgǔjiǔ tiger-bone liquor

【虎口】 hǔkǒu 1.（危险地方）tiger's mouth; jaws of death 2.（拇指与食指之间）part of the hand between the thumb and the index

finger
【虎口余生】 hǔkǒu-yúshēng have a narrow escape; survive a disaster
【虎钳】 hǔqián vice：万能～ universal vice
【虎鲨】 hǔshā bullhead shark
【虎视眈眈】 hǔshì-dāndān glare like a tiger eyeing its prey; eye covetously
【虎牙】 hǔyá protruding canine tooth

琥（hǔ）
【琥珀】 hǔpò amber
【琥珀酸】 hǔpòsuān butanedioic acid

户（hù） 1.（门户）door 2.（人家；住户）household; family 3.（户头）（bank）account 4.（门第）family status：门当～对 matched in family status
【户口】 hùkǒu 1.（住户和人口）number of households and total population 2.（户籍）registered permanent residence：临时～ temporary resident / 报～ register one's residence; apply for residence / 迁～ re-register for change of residence
【户口簿】 hùkǒubù （permanent）residence booklet
【户头】 hùtóu （bank）account：开～ open an account
【户主】 hùzhǔ head of a household

护［護］（hù） 1.（保护）protect; guard; shield 2.（袒护）be partial to; shield from censure：～孩子 be partial to one's child
【护壁板】 hùbìbǎn 〈*Archit.*〉skirting board; baseboard
【护城河】 hùchénghé city moat
【护创胶布】 hù chuàng jiāobù 〈*Med.*〉sticking plaster
【护裆】 hùdāng 〈*Baseball*〉supporter
【护堤】 hùdī protect a dike
【护短】 hùduǎn shield a shortcoming or fault
【护法】 hùfǎ protect the constitution
【护发素】 hùfǎsù hair conditioner
【护封】 hùfēng book jacket; jacket
【护航】 hùháng escort; convoy
【护航舰】 hùhángjiàn convoy ship
【护肩球衫】 hùjiān qiúshān 〈*Rugby Football*〉padded jersey
【护理】 hùlǐ nurse; tend and protect：～受伤的人 nurse the wounded
【护理人员】 hùlǐ rényuán nursing staff
【护林】 hùlín protect a forest
【护林员】 hùlínyuán forest ranger
【护路】 hùlù 1.（指铁路）patrol and guard a railway 2.（指公路）patrol and guard a road 3.（维护公路）road maintenance
【护帽】 hùmào 〈*Baseball*〉helmet
【护面】 hùmiàn 1.〈*Rugby Football*〉face guard 2.〈*Baseball*〉mask
【护目镜】 hùmùjìng goggles
【护身符】 hùshēnfú 1.（护符）amulet; protective talisman 2.（保护自己的人和物）a person or thing that protects on from punishment or censure; shield
【护士】 hù·shi （hospital）nurse
【护士学校】 hù·shi xuéxiào nurses' school
【护士长】 hù·shizhǎng head nurse
【护送】 hùsòng escort; convoy
【护田林】 hùtiánlín windbreak forest; windbreak belt
【护腿】 hùtuǐ 1.〈*Baseball*〉leg protector 2.〈*Field Hockey*〉pad 3.〈*Ice Hockey*〉shin pad; shin guard
【护卫】 hùwèi 1.（保护）protect; guard 2.（保护者）guard; bodyguard
【护卫舰】 hùwèijiàn escort vessel
【护膝】 hùxī 〈*Field Hockey*〉knee-pad
【护胸】 hùxiōng 〈*Baseball*〉chest protector
【护音板】 hùyīnbǎn 〈*Music*〉pick guard
【护照】 hùzhào passport：外交～ diplomatic passport / 公务～ service passport / 持中国～ on a Chinese passport / 查验～ examine one's passport / 出示～ show one's passport / 取得～签证 get one's passport visaed

戽（hù） bail：～出船里的水 bail water out of a boat
【戽斗】 hùdǒu bailing bucket

扈（hù） retinue; retainer
【扈从】 hùcóng retinue; retainer

互（hù） mutual; each other：～教～学 teach and learn from each other
【互不干涉内政】 hùbùgānshè nèizhèng non-interference in each other's internal affairs
【互不侵犯】 hùbùqīnfàn mutual non-aggression
【互补】 hùbǔ complementary

【互补色】 hùbǔsè complementary color
【互导】 hùdǎo 〈*Electr.*〉 mutual conductance
【互访】 hùfǎng exchange visits
【互感】 hùgǎn 〈*Electr.*〉 mutual inductance
【互换】 hùhuàn exchange：～大使 exchange ambassadors / ～记者 exchange correspondents / ～批准书 exchange instruments of ratification
【互惠】 hùhuì mutually beneficial; reciprocal：～待遇 reciprocal treatment / ～关税 mutually preferential tariff
【互见】 hùjiàn **1.**（互相参见）cross-reference **2.**（两者都有）exist side by side
【互利】 hùlì mutually beneficial; of mutual benefit：在平等～的基础上 on the basis of equality and mutual benefit
【互谅互让】 hùliàng-hùràng mutually understanding and mutual accommodation
【互通有无】 hùtōng-yǒuwú exchange of needed goods; each supplies what the other needs; help supply each other's needs
【互相】 hùxiāng 〈*adv.*〉 mutual; each other：～帮助 help each other / ～勾结 work in collusion / ～利用 each using the other for his own ends / ～配合 work in coordination
【互相承认】 hùxiāng chéngrèn mutual recognition
【互相渗透】 hùxiāng shèntòu interpenetrate
【互相制约】 hùxiāng zhìyuē mutually condition
【互相转化】 hùxiāng zhuǎnghuà mutual transformation
【互相尊重主权和领土完整】 hùxiāng zūnzhòng zhǔquán hé lǐngtǔ wánzhěng mutual respect for sovereignty and territorial integrity
【互助】 hùzhù help each other：～合作 mutual aid and cooperation

怙（hù） rely on; depend on
【怙恶不悛】 hùè-bùquān incorrigible; irredeemable; hopeless

糊（hù） paste：面～ flour paste
（另见"糊"hū, hú）
【糊弄】 hù·nong **1.**（欺骗）fool; deceive; palm sth. off on **2.**（将就）go through the motions; be slipshod in work

瓠（hù） 〈*Bot.*〉 hispid bottle gourd
【瓠瓜】 hùguā 〈*Bot.*〉 majubi bottle gourd
【瓠子】 hù·zi 〈*Bot.*〉 hispid bottle gourd

hua

哗［嘩］（huā） 〈*onomat.*〉大雨～～地下。The rain came down in torrents
（另见"哗"huá）
【哗啦】 huālā 〈*onomat.*〉风吹得树叶～～地响。The leaves rustled in the wind. / 雨～～地下个不停。The rain kept pouring down.

花（huā） **1.**（花朵）flower; blossom; bloom：摘一朵～ pluck a flower / 种～ cultivate flowers **2.**（烟花）fireworks **3.**（花纹）pattern; design **4.**（有花纹的）multicolored; colored; variegated **5.**（模糊迷乱）blurred; dim **6.**（棉花）cotton **7.**（精华）flower：文艺之～ flower of literature and art **8.**（花费）spend; expend：～很大精力 expend great energies / 他赚多少就～多少。He spends all he earns.
【花把势】 huābǎ·shi gardener
【花白】 huābái grey; grizzled：头发～ with grey hair; grey-haired
【花瓣】 huābàn petal
【花边】 huābiān **1.**（带花纹的边）decorative border **2.**（编织物）lace **3.**（印刷用语）fancy borders in printing
【花边新闻】 huābiān xīnwén box news
【花布】 huābù cotton print; print
【花草】 huācǎo flowers and plants
【花茶】 huāchá scented tea：茉莉～ jasmine tea
【花池子】 huāchí·zi flower bed
【花丛】 huācóng flowering shrubs; flowers in clusters
【花灯】 huādēng festive lantern (as displayed on the Lantern Festival)
【花店】 huādiàn florist shop
【花雕】 huādiāo yellow rice wine; millet wine
【花朵】 huāduǒ flower
【花萼】 huā'è 〈*Bot.*〉 calyx
【花房】 huāfáng greenhouse; glasshouse
【花费】 huāfèi **1.**（用法）spend; expend; cost **2.**（费用）money spent; expenditure; expenses

【花粉】 huāfěn 〈*Bot*.〉 pollen
【花岗岩】 huāgāngyán granite
【花岗岩头脑】 huāgāngyán tóunǎo ossified thinking
【花骨朵】 huāgū·duo (flower) bud
【花冠】 huāguān 〈*Bot*.〉 corolla
【花好月圆】 huāhǎo-yuèyuán perfect conjugal bliss
【花红】 huāhóng 1.〈*Bot*.〉 Chinese pearleaf crabapple 2.(喜庆礼物) gift for a happy occasion 3.(红利) bonus; dividend 4.(赏钱) money reward
【花花公子】 huāhuā-gōngzǐ play boy
【花花绿绿】 huāhuā-lǜlǜ brightly colored; colorful
【花环】 huāhuán garland; floral hoop
【花卉】 huāhuì 1.(花草) flowers and plants 2.〈*Arts*〉 painting of flowers and plants in traditional Chinese style
【花甲】 huājiǎ sixty years ago: 年过～ be over sixty
【花架子】 huājià·zi pose; affectation; mannerism
【花匠】 huājiàng gardener
【花轿】 huājiào bridal sedan chair
【花街柳巷】 huājiē-liǔxiàng red-light district
【花镜】 huājìng presbyopic glasses
【花卷】 huājuǎn steamed twisted roll
【花篮】 huālán 1.(献花用的) a basket of flowers 2.(装饰美丽的篮子) gaily decorated basket
【花里胡哨】 huā·lihúshào 1.(过于鲜艳) gaudy; garish 2.(华而不实) showy; without solid worth
【花柳病】 huāliǔbìng venereal disease (V.D.)
【花露水】 huālùshuǐ toilet water
【花蜜】 huāmì nectar
【花名册】 huāmíngcè personnel roster; membership roster; muster roll: 造～ make a personnel roster
【花木】 huāmù flowers and trees (in parks or gardens)
【花呢】 huāní fancy suiting; fancy woolen cloth
【花鸟】 huāniǎo 〈*Arts*〉 painting of flowers and birds in traditional Chinese style
【花农】 huānóng flower grower
【花盘】 huāpán 1.(花托部分) flower disc 2.〈*Mech*.〉 disc chuck
【花炮】 huāpào fireworks and firecrackers
【花盆】 huāpéng flowerpot ‖ 把…栽到花盆里 pot (v.) ‖ 给花换花盆 repot (v.)
【花瓶】 huāpíng flower vase; vase
【花圃】 huāpǔ flower nursery; greenhouse
【花圈】 huāquān (floral) wreath: 向…墓献～ place a wreath at the tomb of
【花蕊】 huāruǐ 〈*Bot*.〉 pistil; stamen
【花色】 huāsè 1.(花纹色彩) design and color: ～好看 be beautiful in design and color 2.(品种) (of merchandise) variety of designs, sizes, colors, etc.: ～齐备 have a rich assortment of goods 3.(纸牌花色) suit
【花色品种】 huāsè pǐnzhǒng colors and patterns; range of goods
【花哨】 huā·shao 1.(颜色鲜艳) garish; gaudy; showy: ～的衣服 showy dress 2.(花样多) full of flourishes; flowery
【花生】 huāshēng peanut; groundnut
【花生酱】 huāshēngjiàng peanut butter
【花生米】 huāshēngmǐ shelled peanut; peanut kernel
【花生油】 huāshēngyóu peanut oil
【花饰】 huāshì ornamental design
【花束】 huāshù a bunch of flowers; bouquet
【花坛】 huātán (raised) flower bed; flower terrace
【花托】 huātuō 〈*Bot*.〉 receptacle
【花纹】 huāwén decorative pattern; figure
【花线】 huāxiàn 1.〈*Electr*.〉 flexible cord; flex 2.(绣花的彩线) colored thread
【花消】 huā·xiao expense; cost
【花序】 huāxù 〈*Bot*.〉 florescence
【花絮】 huāxù titbits (of news); interesting sidelights
【花芽】 huāyá 〈*Bot*.〉 flower bud
【花言巧语】 huāyán-qiǎoyǔ sweet words; blandishments
【花眼】 huāyǎn presbyopia
【花样】 huāyàng 1.(花纹) pattern; variety: ～翻新 the same old thing in a new guise 2.(花招) trick: 玩～ play tricks
【花样冰鞋】 huāyàng bīngxié figure skate
【花样刀】 huāyàngdāo figure skate
【花样滑冰】 huāyàng huábīng figure skating

【花药】 huāyào 〈*Bot*.〉 anther
【花椰菜】 huāyēcài cauliflower
【花园】 huāyuán flower garden; garden: 屋顶～ roof garden
【花招】 huāzhāo 1.(武术动作) showy movement in *wushu*; flourish 2.(骗人的手段等) trick; game: 玩弄政治～ resort to political maneuver
【花着】 huāzhāo 同"花招"
【花烛】 huāzhú candles lit at a bridal chamber
【花柱】 huāzhù 〈*Bot*.〉 style
【花砖】 huāzhuān tile
【花子】 huā·zi beggar

划[劃[2]] (huá) 1.(拨水前进) paddle; row 2.(擦;割) scratch; cut the surface of 3.(合算) be to one's profit; pay (另见"划"huà)
【划不来】 huá·bulái It is not worthwhile. (或: It won't pays.)
【划得来】 huá·delái It is worthwhile. (或: It pays.)
【划算】 huásuàn 1.(盘算) calculate; weigh 2.(合算) be to one's profit; pay: 做某事～。It is worthwhile doing sth.
【划艇】 huátǐng 〈*Sports*〉 canoe; Canadian canoe
【划艇运动】 huátǐng yùndòng 〈*Sports*〉 canoeing; rowing ‖ 划艇运动员 canoeist
【划子】 huá·zi small rowboat

华[華] (huá) 1.(光辉灿烂) magnificent; splendid 2.(繁盛) prosperous; flourishing 3.(精华) best part; cream 4.(奢华) flashy; extravagant 5.(花白) grizzled; grey 6.(中国) China: 驻～大使 ambassador to China 7.(中文) Chinese
【华表】 huábiǎo Cloud Pillar; Marble Pillar
【华达呢】 huádání gabardine
【华而不实】 huá'érbùshí flashy and without substance; superficially clever
【华尔兹】 huá·ěrzī waltz ‖ 跳华尔兹 waltz (v.)
【华贵】 huáguì 1.(豪华) luxurious; sumptuous 2.(珍贵) costly
【华丽】 huálì magnificent; resplendent; gorgeous
【华侨】 huáqiáo overseas Chinese: 归国～ returned overseas Chinese
【华人】 huárén Chinese: 外籍～ Chinese of foreign nationality / 美籍～ an American Chinese
【华氏温标】 Huáshì wēnbiāo Fahrenheit thermometric scale
【华氏温度】 Huáshì wēndù degree Fahrenheit; Fahrenheit
【华文】 Huáwén Chinese; Chinese language
【华裔】 huáyì foreign citizen of Chinese origin
【华语】 huáyǔ Chinese; Chinese language

哗[嘩、譁] (huá) noise; clamor (另见"哗"huā)
【哗变】 huábiàn mutiny; mutinous (adj.) ‖ 哗变者 mutineer
【哗然】 huárán in an uproar; in commotion: ～起哄 rising up in an uproar (of protest)
【哗众取宠】 huázhòng-qǔchǒng try to please the public with claptrap

滑 (huá) 1.(光滑) slippery; smooth 2.(滑动) slip; slide: 在冰上～着走 slide on the ice 3.(奸滑) cunning; crafty; slippery
【滑板】 huábǎn 1.(指项目) skateboarding 2.(指器材) skateboard
【滑板运动】 huábǎn yùndòng skateboarding
【滑冰】 huábīng ice-skating; skating; skate (v.): 花样～ figure skating / 滚轴～ roller skating
【滑冰场】 huábīngchǎng skating rink
【滑冰鞋】 huábīngxié skate: 花样～ figure skate / 滚轴～ roller skate
【滑旱冰】 huáhànbīng roller skate; roller skating (n.)
【滑稽】 huá·jī 1.(引人发笑) funny; amusing; comical 2.〈*Quyi*〉 farce; comic talk
【滑稽演员】 huá·jī yǎnyuán farce actor; comic talk performer
【滑轮】 huálún pulley; block
【滑轮组】 huálúnzǔ set of pulleys
【滑坡】 huápō 1.(山体下滑) landslide; landslip 2.(指生产下降) descending; dropping; declining (of the industrial production)
【滑水】 huáshuǐ water skiing
【滑水橇】 huáshuǐqiāo water ski
【滑水运动员】 huáshuǐ yùndòngyuán water skier

【滑梯】 huátī (children's) slide
【滑头】 huátóu 1.(不老实的人) slippery fellow; sly customer 2.(油滑) slippery; shifty; slick 3.(不老实) foxy; cunning
【滑腿】 huátuǐ 〈*Skating*〉 tracing leg
【滑翔】 huáxiáng glide: 悬挂式～ hang gliding
【滑翔机】 huáxiángjī glider; sailplane
【滑行】 huáxíng 1.(滑动前进) slide 2.(飞机在地面前进) taxi 3.(向下滑动) coast
【滑行道】 huáxíngdào 〈*Aeron.*〉 taxiway
【滑雪】 huáxuě skiing; ski (v.): 高山～ alpine skiing / 跳台～ ski jump / ～下山 ski down the hill / ～穿过森林 ski past the forest
【滑雪板】 huáxuěbǎn ski: 一副新的～ a new pair of skis
【滑雪场】 huáxuěchǎng skifield
【滑雪车】 huáxuěchē skibob
【滑雪衫】 huáxuěshān ski suit; skiwear
【滑雪跳台】 huáxuě tiàotái ski jump
【滑雪靴】 huáxuěxuē ski boots
【滑雪运动员】 huáxuě yùndòngyuán skier
【滑雪杖】 huáxuězhàng ski pole; ski stick
【滑音】 huáyīn 1.〈*Music*〉 portamento 2.〈*Gram.*〉 glide

化 (huà) 1.(变化) change; turn; transform: ～悲痛为力量 transform grief into strength 2.(教化) convert; influence 3.(融化) melt; dissolve: 冰～了。The ice has melted. 4.(消化) digest 5.(火化) burn up 6.(化学) chemistry; chemical (adj.) 7.(词尾) -ize; -ify: 电气～ electrify / 现代～ modernize
【化冻】 huàdòng thaw; melt
【化肥】 huàféi chemical fertilizer; artificial fertilizer
【化工】 huàgōng chemical industry
【化工产品】 huàgōng chǎnpǐn chemical products
【化工厂】 huàgōngchǎng chemical plant
【化工原料】 huàgōng yuánliào industrial chemicals
【化合】 huàhé 〈*Chem.*〉 chemical combination
【化合物】 huàhéwù chemical compound: 高分子～ high polymer; highly polymerized compound
【化疗】 huàliáo 〈*Med.*〉 chemotherapy
【化名】 huàmíng 1.(使用假名) use an assumed name; use an alias 2.(假名) assumed name; alias
【化脓】 huànóng fester; suppurate
【化身】 huàshēn 1.(个人化身) incarnation; personification 2.(比喻的形象) embodiment; manifestation: 正义的～ the embodiment of justice
【化石】 huàshí fossil: 变成～ become fossilized
【化为灰烬】 huàwéi-huījìn turn to dust and ashes; reduced to ashes
【化为泡影】 huàwéi-pàoyǐng vanish like soap bubbles; melt into thin air
【化纤】 huàxiān chemical fiber; synthetic fiber
【化险为夷】 huàxiǎn-wéiyí turn danger into safety; head off a disaster
【化学】 huàxué chemistry; chemical (adj.): 生物～ biochemistry / 无机～ inorganic chemistry / 有机～ organic chemistry / 应用～ applied chemistry
【化学反应】 huàxué fǎnyìng chemical reaction
【化学方程式】 huàxué fāngchéngshì chemical equation
【化学分析】 huàxué fēnxì chemical analysis
【化学键】 huàxuéjiàn chemical bond
【化学武器】 huàxué wǔqì chemical weapon
【化学药品】 huàxué yàopǐn chemicals
【化学元素】 huàxué yuánsù chemical element
【化验】 huàyàn chemical examination; laboratory test
【化油器】 huàyóuqì carburetor
【化缘】 huàyuán 〈*Religion*〉 beg alms
【化整为零】 huàzhěngwéilíng break up the whole into parts
【化装】 huàzhuāng 1.(装扮角色) (of actors) make up 2.(假扮) disguise oneself
【化妆】 huàzhuāng put on makeup; make up
【化妆品】 huàzhuāngpǐn cosmetics: ～工业 cosmetics industry

桦[樺] (huà) 〈*Bot.*〉 birch
【桦树】 huàshù birch

划［劃］(huà) 1.(划分) delimit; differentiate 2.(划拨) transfer; assign 3.(计划) plan: 筹～ plan and prepare 4.(划线作标记) draw; mark; delineate: ～出书中要点 mark the main points in the book

(另见"划"huá)

【划拨】 huàbō 1.(转入另一户头) appropriate; transfer: ～一笔款子 appropriate a sum 2.(分出来拨给) assign; allot

【划定】 huàdìng delimit; designate: ～边界 delimit a boundary line

【划分】 huàfēn 1.(分成部分) divide: ～行政区域 divide a country into administrative areas 2.(区别) differentiate

【划归】 huàguī put under (sb's administration, etc.); incorporate into

【划款】 huàkuǎn transfer money

【划清】 huàqīng draw a clear line of demarcation; make a clear distinction: ～界限 draw a demarcation line with sb.; draw clear distinction

【划时代】 huàshídài epoch-making: ～的大事 an epoch-making event

【划一】 huàyī 1.(一致) uniform; standardized 2.(使一致) standardize

画［畫］(huà) 1.(绘画) draw; paint: ～油画 paint in oil 2.(成品画) drawing; painting; picture: 壁～ mural painting / 风景～ landscape painting/ 年～ New Year picture 3.(用画装饰的) be decorated with paintings or pictures

【画板】 huàbǎn drawing board

【画报】 huàbào illustrated magazine or newspaper; pictorial

【画笔】 huàbǐ painting brush; brush

【画布】 huàbù canvas (for painting)

【画册】 huàcè an album of paintings; picture album

【画幅】 huàfú 1.(图画总称) picture; painting 2.(画的尺寸) size of a picture

【画工】 huàgōng painter

【画家】 huàjiā painter; artist

【画具】 huàjù painter's paraphernalia

【画刊】 huàkān 1.(报刊上的画报栏) pictorial section of a newspaper 2.(画报) pictorial

【画廊】 huàláng 1.(有图画的走廊) painted corridor 2.(画展走廊) (picture) gallery; art-gallery

【画龙点睛】 huàlóng-diǎnjīng 1.(使画更生动) bring the painted dragon to life by putting in the pupils of its eyes; add the touch that brings a work of art to life; add the finishing touch 2.(在文章关键处加重要的话) add a word or two to clinch the point

【画眉】 huàméi 〈*Zool.*〉 thrush

【画面】 huàmiàn 1.(画上的形象) general appearance of a picture; tableau 2.〈*Cinematog.*〉 frame

【画皮】 huàpí disguise or mask of an evildoer

【画片】 huàpiàn picture; a miniature reproduction of a painting

【画圈】 huàquān draw a circle; draw a circle round one's name to show having read it or one's approval

【画蛇添足】 huàshé-tiānzú draw a snake and add feet to it; ruin the effect by adding sth. superfluous

【画十字】 huà shízì 1.(在签名处) make one's cross in place of a signature 2.(在胸前) cross; make the sign of the cross: 在胸口～ cross oneself

【画室】 huàshì studio

【画坛】 huàtán painting circle

【画图】 huàtú 1.(画各种图形) draw designs, maps, etc. 2.(图画) picture

【画外音】 huàwàiyīn 〈*Cinematog.*〉 offscreen voice

【画像】 huàxiàng 1.(画人像) draw a portrait; portray 2.(画成的人像) portrait; portrayal

【画展】 huàzhǎn art exhibition; exhibition of paintings

话 (huà) 1.(说或写的话) word; talk 2.(说;谈) talk about; speak about

【话别】 huàbié say a few parting words; say good-bye

【话柄】 huàbǐng subject for ridicule; handle: 成为～ become the joke of the town / 抓住～ make sth. serve as a handle

【话锋】 huàfēng thread of discourse; topic of conversation: 避开～ change the subject

【话剧】 huàjù modern drama; stage play: 演出～ put on a play; perform a play

【话剧演员】 huàjù yǎnyuán actor；actress (f.)

【话里有话】 huà·li-yǒuhuà the words mean more than they say

【话题】 huàtí subject of a talk；topic of conversation

【话筒】 huàtǒng 1.（麦克风）microphone 2.（电话发话器）telephone transmitter 3.（传声筒）megaphone

【话务员】 huàwùyuán 〈*Telecom.*〉operator

【话音】 huàyīn 1.（说话声音）one's voice in speech 2.（言外之意）tone；implication：听他的～，他准是反对的。Judging from his tone，there's no doubt he is against it.

【话语】 huàyǔ words；talk；speech

huai

怀［懷］(huái) 1.（胸部或胸前）bosom：～里的孩子 baby in one's arms 2.（胸怀）mind 3.（心里存有）keep in mind；cherish：～有恶意 harbor malice / ～有希望 cherish hopes 4.（怀念）think of；yearn for 5.（怀孕）conceive (a child)

【怀抱】 huáibào 1.（抱在怀里）bosom 2.（心里存有）cherish

【怀表】 huáibiǎo pocket watch

【怀才不遇】 huáicái-bùyù have unrecognized talents；have talent but no opportunity to use it

【怀恨】 huáihèn have a hatred of；harbor resentment

【怀恨在心】 huáihènzàixīn harbor resentment in one's bosom；have resentment rankling in one's mind

【怀旧】 huáijiù remember past times

【怀旧感】 huáijiùgǎn sense of nostalgia

【怀念】 huáiniàn cherish the memory of；think of：～故乡 yearn for one's native land

【怀胎】 huáitāi be pregnant

【怀疑】 huáiyí 1.（疑惑）distrust；doubt；suspect：引起～ raise doubts；arouse suspicion 2.（猜测）guess；suppose：我～今天她不来了。I suppose she won't come today.（或：I don't suppose she'll come today.）

【怀孕】 huáiyùn conception；in the family way；be pregnant

槐 (huái) 〈*Bot.*〉pagoda tree；sophora

【槐树】 huáishù 〈*Bot.*〉pagoda tree；sophora

踝 (huái) ankle

【踝关节】 huáiguānjié 〈*Anat.*〉ankle joint

【踝子骨】 huái·zigǔ 〈*Anat.*〉ankle bone

坏［壞］(huài) 1.（不好）bad：～天气 a bad weather / ～透了 downright bad 2.（变坏；有害）go bad；spoil；ruin：机器～了。The machinery broke down. 3.（程度深）badly；awfully；very：吓～了 be badly scared 4.（坏主意）evil idea；dirty trick：使～ play a dirty trick

【坏处】 huài·chu harm；disadvantage：这对你没～。It will do you no harm.

【坏蛋】 huàidàn bad egg；scoundrel；bastard

【坏话】 huàihuà 1.（恶意的）malicious remarks；vicious talk 2.（不好听的）unpleasant words

【坏人】 huàirén 1.（品质不好的人）dishonest person；cheater 2.（坏分子）bad person；evildoer；scoundrel

【坏事】 huàishì 1.（不好的事）bad thing；evil deed 2.（把事搞坏）ruin sth.；make things worse

【坏死】 huàisǐ 〈*Med.*〉necrosis；gangrene

【坏心眼】 huàixīnyǎn evil intention；evil will

【坏血病】 huàixuèbìng 〈*Med.*〉scurvy；scorbutus

【坏账】 huàizhàng a bad debt

huan

欢［歡、懽］(huān) 1.（快乐）joyous；merry；jubilant 2.（起劲；活跃）vigorously；with great drive；in full swing

【欢畅】 huānchàng jubilant；overjoyed；elated

【欢度】 huāndù spend (an occasion) joyfully；celebrate with jubilation

【欢呼】 huānhū hail；cheer；acclaim：～伟大的胜利 hail the great victory

【欢呼声】 huānhūshēng shouts of joy；cheer

【欢聚】 huānjù happily gather together；have a happy get-together：～一堂 have a happy

get-together; have a happy reunion
【欢快】 huānkuài cheerful and light-hearted; lively: ～的音乐 merry music
【欢乐】 huānlè happy; joyous; gay: ～的歌声 merry songs / ～的景象 a scene of great joy
【欢庆】 huānqìng celebrate joyously
【欢送】 huānsòng see off; send off: ～客人 see the guests off cordially
【欢送会】 huānsònghuì farewell meeting; send-off meeting
【欢腾】 huānténg great rejoicing; jubilation
【欢喜】 huānxǐ **1.**(快乐) joyful; happy; delighted: 满心～ be filled with joy **2.**(喜欢) like; fond of; delight in
【欢笑】 huānxiào laugh heartily
【欢心】 huānxīn favor; liking; love
【欢欣鼓舞】 huānxīn-gǔwǔ be filled with exultation; be elated: 为我们的成就而～ rejoice over our achievements
【欢宴】 huānyàn give banquet in honor of sb.
【欢迎】 huānyíng **1.**(高兴地迎接) welcome; greet **2.**(乐意接受) welcome; favorably receive: 受到观众～ be warmly received by the audience
【欢迎词】 huānyíngcí welcoming speech; address of welcome
【欢迎会】 huānyínghuì a party to welcome sb.

獾[貛](huān) 〈*Zool.*〉 badger
【獾油】 huānyóu 〈*Pharm.*〉 badger fat

还[還](huán) **1.**(回) go back; come back **2.**(归还) give back; return; repay **3.**(回报别人对自己的行动) give or do sth. in return
(另见"还"hái)
【还本付息】 huánběn fùxī repay capital with interest: 延期～ delayed repayment of capital and interest
【还击】 huánjī fight back; return fire: 进行自卫～ fight in self-defense
【还价】 huánjià counter-offer; counter-bid; abate a price
【还礼】 huánlǐ **1.**(回答敬礼) return a salute **2.**(回赠礼物) present a gift in return
【还清】 huánqīng pay off: ～债务 pay off one's debts
【还手】 huánshǒu strike back; return a blow
【还乡】 huánxiāng return to one's native place
【还原】 huányuán **1.**(恢复原状) return to the original condition or shape; restore **2.**〈*Chem.*〉 reduction
【还愿】 huányuàn **1.**(酬神) redeem a vow to a god **2.**(实践诺言) fulfill one's promise
【还债】 huánzhài pay one's debt; repay a debt
【还账】 huánzhàng pay bills (on credit sales); settle account on credit sales

环[環](huán) **1.**(环子) ring; hoop **2.**(环节) link **3.**(围绕) surround; encircle; hem in: ～渤海地区 around the perimeter of Bohai Bay / 四面～山 be surrounded by mountains **4.**〈*Sports*〉 ring
【环保】 huánbǎo environmental protection
【环抱】 huánbào surround; encircle; hem in: 群山～的湖泊 a lake nestling among the hills
【环城】 huánchéng around the city
【环顾】 huángù look about: ～四周 look all round
【环礁】 huánjiāo atoll
【环节】 huánjié link: 主要～ a key link / 中心～ central link
【环节动物】 huánjié dòngwù annelid
【环境】 huánjìng **1.**(指地方) environment; environmental (adj.) 保护～免遭污染 protect environment from pollution **2.**(指情况和条件) environment; surroundings; circumstances: 自然～ natural environment / 完善投资～ improve the investment environment / 争取有利的国际～ create a favorable international environment
【环境保护】 huánjìng bǎohù environmental protection
【环境保护主义】 huánjìng bǎohù zhǔyì environmentalism ‖ 环境保护主义者 environmentalist
【环境监测】 huánjìng jiāncè environmental monitoring
【环境卫生】 huánjìng wèishēng environmental sanitation; general sanitation
【环境污染】 huánjìng wūrǎn pollution of the environment; environmental pollution
【环流】 huánliú 〈*Meteorol.*〉 circulation; ring

current

【环球】 huánqiú 1.(围绕地球) round the world: ～旅行 travel round the world 2.(整个地球) the earth; the whole world

【环绕】 huánrào surround; encircle; revolve around: 地球～太阳运行。The earth revolves round the sun.

【环食】 huánshí 〈*Astron.*〉 annular eclipse

【环视】 huánshì look around

【环卫】 huánwèi environmental sanitation; general sanitation

【环线】 huánxiàn 〈*Transport*〉 a circular route

【环行】 huánxíng going in a ring

【环行铁路】 huánxíng tiělù circuit railway; belt line

【环形】 huánxíng annular; ringlike; ring form

【环形交叉】 huánxíng jiāochā 〈*Transport*〉 traffic circle (AmE.); roundabout (BrE.)

【环形山】 huánxíngshān 〈*Astron.*〉 crater

【环氧树脂】 huányǎng shùzhǐ 〈*Chem.*〉 epoxy resin

【环宇】 huányǔ the earth; the whole world

【环状软骨】 huánzhuàng ruǎngǔ 〈*Anat.*〉 annular cartilage

【环子】 huán·zi ring; link

寰 (huán) extensive region

【寰球】 huánqiú the earth; the whole world

【寰宇】 huányǔ the earth; the whole world

缓 (huǎn) 1.(缓慢) slow; unhurried 2.(延缓) delay; postpone; put off 3.(缓和) not tense; relaxed 4.(恢复) recuperate; revive; come to

【缓兵之计】 huǎnbīngzhījì stratagem to gain a respite; stalling tactics

【缓冲】 huǎnchōng buffer; cushion

【缓冲地带】 huǎnchōng dìdài buffer zone

【缓冲区】 huǎnchōngqū 〈*Computer*〉 buffers

【缓冲作用】 huǎnchōng zuòyòng cushioning effect

【缓和】 huǎnhé 1.(变和缓) relax; ease up; mitigate; alleviate: ～紧张局势 relax the tension 2.(使和缓) détente

【缓急】 huǎnjí 1.(和缓与急迫) pressing or otherwise; of greater or lesser urgency 2.(急迫的事) emergency

【缓建】 huǎnjiàn have been postponed

【缓解】 huǎnjiě 1.(缓和,减轻) ease; alleviate; make sth. less difficult: 该地区的紧张局势开始～。The tension in the area began to ease. / 那些药丝毫也没有～她的病痛。The drugs did nothing to alleviate her suffering. 2.(使缓解) alleviate: ～交通紧张 alleviate traffic congestion / 这笔钱可以～我们的财政问题。This money should alleviate our financial problems.

【缓慢】 huǎnmàn slow: 进展～ make slow progress / 行动～ slow in action; slow moving

【缓坡】 huǎnpō gentle slope: 这儿有很好的～,我们可以滑雪下去。There are some nice gentle slopes that we can ski down.

【缓期】 huǎnqī postpone a deadline; suspend: 判处死刑,～二年执行 condemned to death with the sentence suspended for two years

【缓气】 huǎnqì win a bit of breathing time; get a breather

【缓刑】 huǎnxíng probation: ～二年 two years of probation

【缓征】 huǎnzhēng postpone the imposition of a tax

幻 (huàn) 1.(不真实) unreal; imaginary; illusory 2.(奇异地变化) magical; changeable

【幻灯】 huàndēng 1.(幻灯节目) slide show: 放～ show slides 2.(幻灯机) slide projector

【幻灯机】 huàndēngjī slide projector; epidiascope

【幻灯片】 huàndēngpiān (lantern) slide

【幻景】 huànjǐng illusion; mirage

【幻境】 huànjìng dreamland; fairyland

【幻觉】 huànjué hallucination; illusion: 产生～ hallucinate; undergo hallucination

【幻灭】 huànmiè vanish into thin air: 希望～ one's hope is dashed

【幻想】 huànxiǎng illusion; fancy; fantasy: 存有～ cherish illusions

【幻影】 huànyǐng mirage; hallucinatory vision

换 (huàn) 1.(交换) exchange; barter; trade: 用一匹马～一头牛 barter a horse (with sb.) for a cow 2.(变换) change: 把

10美元～成人民币 change a ten US dollar into RMB yuan / 她把衣服拿回商店又～了一件。She took the dress back to the shop and changed it for another. 3.（球赛时换人）substitute：下半场比赛时，他被王勇～了下来。He was substituted for Wang Yong in the second half of the match.

【换班】 huànbān 1.（替换）change shifts 2.（交接班）relieve a person on duty

【换车】 huànchē change trains or buses

【换代】 huàndài 1.（改换朝代）change of regime or dynasty 2.（工业产品更新换代）change of generation; replacement; innovation

【换挡】 huàndǎng 〈*Auto*〉 shift gears

【换发球】 huànfāqiú 〈*Sports*〉 change of service

【换防】 huànfáng 〈*Mil.*〉 relieve a garrison

【换岗】 huàngǎng relieve a sentry; relieve a guard

【换汇】 huànhuì exchange for foreign currency; gain foreign exchange

【换货】 huànhuò exchange goods; barter

【换季】 huànjì change garments according to the season; wear different clothes for a new season

【换气】 huànqì take a breath (in swimming)

【换钱】 huànqián 1.（兑换钱）change money 2.（卖）sell

【换取】 huànqǔ exchange sth. for; get in return：～外汇 gain foreign exchange

【换人】 huànrén 〈*Sports*〉 substitute; make a substitution：看来好像教练要～。It looks as though the coach is going to make a substitution.

【换算】 huànsuàn conversion

【换算表】 huànsuànbiǎo conversion chart; conversion table

【换文】 huànwén exchange notes; change of notes：就发展贸易关系～ exchange notes on the development of trade

【换型】 huànxíng change of model; replacement of a product

【换休】 huànxiū change the day off

【换牙】 huànyá (of a child) grow permanent teeth

唤 (huàn) call out

【唤起】 huànqǐ 1.（号召）arouse 2.（引起）call; recall：～对往事的回忆 evoke past memories

【唤醒】 huànxǐng 1.（叫醒）wake up; awaken 2.（使醒悟）rouse; arouse

涣 (huàn) melt; vanish

【涣散】 huànsàn 1.（散漫）lax; low; slack off：士气～。Their morale is low. 2.（使涣散）～士气 breaking up of morale; lose morale

焕 (huàn) shining; glowing

【焕发】 huànfā shine; glow; irradiate：～青春 fresh with vigor

【焕然一新】 huànrán-yīxīn take on an entirely new look; look brand-new

宦 (huàn) 1.（官员）official 2.（宦官）eunuch

【宦官】 huànguān eunuch

【宦海】 huànhǎi officialdom; official circles

浣[澣] (huàn) wash

【浣熊】 huànxióng raccoon; racoon

患 (huàn) 1.（祸患）trouble; peril; disaster：有备无～ be prepared; is to keep out of trouble 2.（忧虑）anxiety; worry 3.（害病）contract; suffer from：～头痛 suffer from headaches

【患病】 huànbìng suffer from an illness; fall ill; be ill

【患病率】 huànbìnglǜ disease rate

【患得患失】 huàndé-huànshī worry about personal gains and losses; be swayed by considerations of gain and loss

【患难】 huànnàn trials and tribulations; adversity; trouble：～之交 friend in adversity; tested friend

【患难与共】 huànnàn-yǔgòng go through thick and thin together

【患者】 huànzhě sufferer; patient：结核病～ a TB patient

豢 (huàn)

【豢养】 huànyǎng 1.（喂养牲畜）feed; raise 2.（收买利用）keep

huang

荒（huāng） 1.（荒芜）waste 2.（荒地）wasteland; uncultivated land：开～ open up wasteland 3.（荒凉）desolate; barren 4.（荒歉）famine; crop failure 5.（荒疏）neglect; be out of practice 6.（缺乏）shortage; scarcity：水～ water shortage

【荒诞】 huāngdàn fantastic; absurd; incredible：～的故事 an incredible story

【荒地】 huāngdì wasteland; uncultivated land：开垦大批～ reclamate a lot of wasteland

【荒废】 huāngfèi 1.（不耕种）leave uncultivated; lie waste 2.（没利用）fall into disuse 3.（荒疏）neglect; be out of practice

【荒废学业】 huāngfèi xuéyè neglect one's studies

【荒郊】 huāngjiāo desolate place outside a town; wilderness

【荒凉】 huāngliáng bleak and desolate; wild：～的景象 a scene of desolation

【荒乱】 huāngluàn in great disorder; in turmoil

【荒谬】 huāngmiù absurd; preposterous

【荒谬绝伦】 huāngmiù-juélún utterly absurd; absolutely preposterous

【荒年】 huāngnián famine year

【荒僻】 huāngpì desolate; deserted; abandoned

【荒山】 huāngshān barren mountain：～秃岭 bare hills and mountains / 绿化～ clothe barren mountains with greenery

【荒疏】 huāngshū out of practice; unpracticed; rusty

【荒唐】 huāng·táng 1.（荒谬）absurd; fantastic; preposterous 2.（放荡）dissipated; loose; intemperate：～的生活 a dissipated life

【荒无人烟】 huāngwúrényān desolate and uninhabited

【荒野】 huāngyě wilderness; wildland; the wilds

【荒淫】 huāngyín dissolute; licentious; debauched：～无耻 dissipated and unashamed / ～无度 be vicious beyond measure

【荒原】 huāngyuán wasteland; wilderness

慌（huāng） 1.（慌张）flurried; flustered; confused 2.（表示难以忍受）awfully; unbearably：饿得～ be awfully hungry

【慌里慌张】 huāng·lihuāngzhāng in a hurried and confused manner; all in a fluster; lose one's head

【慌乱】 huāngluàn flurried; alarmed and bewildered

【慌忙】 huāngmáng in a great rush; in a flurry; hurriedly：～赶到现场 rush to the spot / ～离去 leave hurriedly

【慌张】 huāng·zhāng flurried; flustered; confused

皇（huáng） emperor; sovereign; empress (f.)

【皇帝】 huángdì emperor

【皇宫】 huánggōng palace; imperial palace

【皇冠】 huángguān imperial crown

【皇后】 huánghòu empress

【皇历】 huáng·li almanac

【皇企鹅】 huángqǐ'é 〈*Zool.*〉 emperor penguin

【皇权】 huángquán imperial power; imperial authority

【皇上】 huáng·shang the emperor; the throne; the reigning sovereign

【皇室】 huángshì imperial family

【皇太后】 huángtàihòu empress dowager

【皇太子】 huángtàizǐ crown prince

【皇天】 huángtiān heaven

【皇天后土】 huángtiān-hòutǔ Heaven and Earth

【皇族】 huángzú imperial kinsman

惶（huáng） fear; anxiety; trepidation

【惶惶】 huánghuáng in a state of anxiety; on tenterhooks; alarmed：人心～～。People are disquieted (on tenterhooks).

【惶惶不安】 huánghuáng-bùān be on tenterhooks; be greatly upset; live in terror and uncertainty

【惶惶不可终日】 huánghuáng bùkě zhōngrì be on tenterhooks; be in a constant state of anxiety

【惶惑】 huánghuò perplexed and alarmed; apprehensive

【惶恐】 huángkǒng terrified

蝗 (huáng) locust

【蝗虫】 huángchóng locust：一群～ a swarm of locusts

【蝗灾】 huángzāi plague of locusts

鳇 (huáng) 〈*Zool.*〉 huso strugeon

【鳇鱼】 huángyú huso strugeon

黄 (huáng) 1.（颜色）yellow; sallow：一条～裙子 a yellow skirt / 过了好多年，报纸发～了。The newspaper had become yellow over the years. 2.（中断，失败）fizzle out; fall through 3.（色情）porn; porno; pornographic; pornography (n.)：扫～ anti-porn campaign; a campaign against pornography

【黄柏】 huángbò 〈*Bot.*〉 corktree

【黄疸】 huángdǎn 〈*Med.*〉 jaundice

【黄道】 huángdào 〈*Astron.*〉 ecliptic

【黄道十二宫】 huángdào shí'èrgōng 〈*Astron.*〉 signs of the Zodiac ‖ 白羊宫 Aries / 金牛宫 Taurus / 双子宫 Gemeni / 巨蟹宫 Cancer / 狮子宫 Leo / 室女宫 Virgo / 天秤宫 Libra / 天蝎宫 Scorpio / 人马宫 Sagittarius / 摩羯宫 Capricorn / 宝瓶宫 Aquarius / 双鱼宫 Pisces

【黄澄澄】 huángdēngdēng glistening yellow; golden

【黄豆】 huángdòu soya bean; soybean

【黄豆芽】 huángdòuyá soybean sprouts

【黄蜂】 huángfēng wasp

【黄瓜】 huáng·gua cucumber：酸～ pickled cucumber

【黄褐色】 huánghèsè yellowish-brown; tawny

【黄花】 huánghuā 1.（菊花）chrysanthemum 2.（黄花菜）day lily

【黄花鱼】 huánghuāyú yellow croaker

【黄昏】 huánghūn dusk; sunset; nightfall

【黄金】 huángjīn 1.（金）gold 2.（喻宝贵）golden

【黄金储备】 huángjīn chǔbèi gold reserve

【黄金分割】 huángjīn fēngē golden section

【黄金时代】 huángjīn shídài 1.（指社会时期）the most prosperous period; the golden age 2.（指人生）the primer of life; the best years of one's life

【黄金时间】 huángjīn shíjiān prime time; golden hour

【黄金水道】 huángjīn shuǐdào golden waterway

【黄酒】 huángjiǔ yellow rice wine; millet wine

【黄鹂】 huánglí 〈*Zool.*〉 oriole; forest oriole

【黄连】 huánglián 〈*Chin. Pharm.*〉 Chinese goldthread

【黄连木】 huángliánmù 〈*Bot.*〉 Chinese pistachio; Chinese pistache

【黄粱美梦】 huángliáng-měimèng Golden Millet Dream; fond dream; pipe dream

【黄栌】 huánglú smoke tree

【黄麻】 huángmá jute

【黄鸟】 huángniǎo oriole

【黄牛】 huángniú 1.（牛）ox; cattle 2.（靠倒卖取利的人）profiteer

【黄牌】 huángpái 〈*Sports*〉 yellow card：出示～ show the yellow card / 被～警告 be booked

【黄热病】 huángrèbìng 〈*Med.*〉 yellow fever

【黄色】 huángsè 1.（颜色）yellow 2.（色情的）porn; porno; decadent; obscene; pornographic：～电影 porn movies / ～杂志 porn magazines

【黄色人种】 huángsè rénzhǒng the yellow race

【黄色炸药】 huángsè zhàyào trinitrotoluene (TNT); trinol

【黄鳝】 huángshàn ricefield eel; finless eel

【黄鼠狼】 huángshǔláng Siberian weasel; yellow weasel

【黄铜】 huángtóng brass

【黄土】 huángtǔ 〈*Geog.*〉 loess

【黄土高原】 huángtǔ gāoyuán loess plateau

【黄线】 huángxiàn 〈*Transport*〉 yellow line

【黄羊】 huángyáng Mongolian gazelle

【黄页】 huángyè 〈*Telecom.*〉 yellow pages（电话号簿的工商户部分）

【黄莺】 huángyīng 同"黄鹂"

【黄油】 huángyóu 1.（奶油）butter 2.〈*Chem.*〉 grease

【黄鼬】 huángyòu 〈*Zool.*〉 Siberian weasel; yellow weasel

【黄鱼】 huángyú yellow croaker; croaker

【黄种】 huángzhǒng the yellow race

磺(huáng) sulphur

【磺胺】 huáng'àn sulphanilamide (SN); sulfanilamite: 长效～ sulfamethoxypyridazine (SMP)

簧(huáng) 1.〈*Music*〉 reed 2.〈*Mech*.〉 spring

恍(huǎng) 1.(恍然) all of a sudden; suddenly 2.(与“如”、“若”等字连用) seem; as if

【恍忽】 huǎng·hū 同“恍惚”

【恍惚】 huǎng·hū 1.(精神不集中) in a trance; absentminded: 精神～ be in a trance 2.(不真切;不清楚) dimly; faintly; seemingly: ～记得 faintly remember

【恍然大悟】 huǎngrán-dàwù suddenly see the light; suddenly realize what has happened: 一经指点,～。At the hint, he suddenly saw the light.

晃(huǎng) 1.(闪耀) dazzle: 汽车灯亮得～我眼。The bright light of the car dazzled me. 2.(很快闪过) flash past; pass in a flash

(另见“晃”huàng)

【晃眼】 huǎngyǎn dazzle

幌(huǎng)

【幌子】 huǎng·zi 1.(招牌) shop sign; signboard 2.(假借的名义) pretense; cover; front: 在…的～下 under the cover of

谎(huǎng) lie; falsehood

【谎报】 huǎngbào lie about sth.; give false information; make a false report of

【谎话】 huǎnghuà lie; falsehood: ～连篇 tell a pack of lie / 说～ tell a lie; lie

【谎言】 huǎngyán lie; falsehood: ～总是站不住脚的。Lies have short legs.

晃[搃](huàng) shake; sway: 像钟摆似地～着 swing like a pendulum

(另见“晃”huǎng)

【晃荡】 huàng·dang rock; shake; sway: 来回～ swing to and fro

【晃动】 huàngdòng shake; rock; sway: 不要～桌子。Don't wobble the table.

【晃悠】 huàng·you shake from side to side; wobble stagger

hui

灰(huī) 1.(灰烬) ash 2.(灰尘) dust 3.(石灰) lime; (lime) mortar 4.(颜色) grey 5.(消沉) disheartened; discouraged

【灰暗】 huī'àn murky grey; gloomy: ～的天空 a gloomy sky

【灰白】 huībái greyish white; ashen; pale: 脸色～ look pale

【灰尘】 huīchén dust; dirt: 掸掉桌上的～ dust the table

【灰度】 huīdù 〈*Computer*〉 grey level; grey scale

【灰分】 huīfèn ash content

【灰姑娘】 Huīgū·niang Cinderella

【灰黄霉素】 huīhuángméisù 〈*Pharm*.〉 griseofulvin

【灰浆】 huījiāng 〈*Archit*.〉 mortar

【灰烬】 huījìn ashes: 化为～ be reduced to ashes

【灰领】 huīlǐng grey collar (指服务行业职工)

【灰溜溜】 huīliūliū gloomy; dejected; crestfallen: 他总是～的。He always looked dejected.

【灰蒙蒙】 huīmēngmēng dusky; overcast: ～的天空 a dusky sky

【灰锰氧】 huīměngyǎng potassium permanganate

【灰泥】 huīní 〈*Archit*.〉 plaster

【灰色】 huīsè 1.(颜色) grey; ashy 2.(颓废) pessimistic; gloomy 3.(暧昧) obscure; ambiguous

【灰市】 huīshì grey market

【灰鼠】 huīshǔ squirrel

【灰土】 huītǔ dust

【灰心】 huīxīn lose heart; be discouraged: 不要～! Don't be discouraged!

【灰心丧气】 huīxīn-sàngqì daunted; discouraged; disheartened

【灰质】 huīzhì 〈*Anat*.〉 grey matter

诙(huī)

【诙谐】 huīxié humorous; jocular: 言语～ sb's remarks are full of humor

恢(huī) extensive; vast

【恢复】 huīfù 1.(恢复原样) resume; renew:

～邦交 resume diplomatic relations / ～青春 renew one's youth **2**.(使恢复原样) recover; regain: ～健康 recover one's health / ～知觉 regain consciousness; come to **3**.(使失去的复得) restore; reinstate; rehabilitate: ～一个文件 restore a file / ～原职务 reinstate sb. in his post

【恢恢】 huīhuī 〈*written*〉 extensive; vast: 天网～,疏而不漏。The net of Heaven has large meshes, but it lets nothing through.

挥(huī) **1**.(挥舞) wave; wield **2**.(抹掉) wipe off **3**.(指挥) command (an army) **4**.(散出) scatter; disperse

【挥笔】 huībǐ wield the brush; put pen to paper

【挥动】 huīdòng brandish; wave

【挥发】 huīfā volatilize; volatilization (n.)

【挥发油】 huīfāyóu volatile oil

【挥汗如雨】 huīhàn-rúyǔ drip with sweat; perspiration came down like raindrops; sweat like a trooper

【挥霍】 huīhuò spend freely; squander: ～浪费 spend extravagantly / ～无度 spend without restraint

【挥泪】 huīlèi wipe away tears; wipe one's eyes: ～而别 part in tears

【挥手】 huīshǒu wave one's hand; wave: ～告别 wave good bye to sb.

【挥舞】 huīwǔ wave; wield; brandish: ～大棒 wave the big stick at ... / ～拳头 brandish one's fist

辉[煇](huī) **1**.(光彩) brightness; splendor **2**.(照耀) shine

【辉煌】 huīhuáng brilliant; splendid; glorious: ～的成就 brilliant achievements / ～的文化 splendid civilization

徽(huī) emblem; badge; insignia

【徽章】 huīzhāng badge; insignia

回[囘、囬、迴[1]、廻[1]](huí) **1**.(曲折环绕) circle; wind **2**.(还;返回) return; go back: ～国 return to one's native country **3**.(回转) turn round **4**.(回答) answer; reply **5**.(次) time **6**.(小说的章回) chapter

【回报】 huíbào **1**.(报告) report on what has been done **2**.(报答) repay; reciprocate; requite **3**.(报复) retaliate; revenge oneself

【回避】 huíbì **1**.(躲开) evade; dodge; avoid (meeting sb.): ～问题 evade the question **2**.〈*Law*〉 withdraw

【回肠】 huícháng 〈*Anat*.〉 ilenum

【回潮】 huícháo resurgence; renaissance; revival

【回程】 huíchéng **1**.(返回的路程) return trip **2**.〈*Mech*.〉 return stroke

【回春】 huíchūn **1**.(冬尽春来) return of spring **2**.(起死回生) bring back to life

【回答】 huídá answer; reply; response: ～问题 answer a question

【回电】 huídiàn wire back

【回访】 huífǎng pay a return visit

【回复】 huífù reply (to a letter)

【回顾】 huígù look back; review: ～过去,展望未来 review the past and look forward to the future

【回顾展】 huígùzhǎn retrospective exhibition; retrospective show

【回归】 huíguī return; regression: 台湾～祖国实现祖国统一 return of Taiwan to the motherland for the realization of China's unification

【回归线】 huíguīxiàn 〈*Geog*.〉 tropic: 北～ the Tropic of Cancer / 南～ the Tropic of Capricorn

【回合】 huíhé round; bout

【回话】 huíhuà **1**.(回答) reply; answer **2**.(回音) message: 请你给他带个～。Please take a message to him by way of reply

【回环】 huíhuán winding encirclement

【回击】 huíjī fight back; return fire

【回家】 huíjiā return home

【回见】 huíjiàn see you later; see you

【回教】 Huíjiào Islam; Islamic (adj.)

【回敬】 huíjìng return a compliment; do or give sth. in return: ～一杯 drink a toast in return / ～一拳 return a blow

【回绝】 huíjué decline; refuse

【回扣】 huíkòu rebate; sales commission

【回来】 huí·lái (返回) return; come back; be back

【回来】 ·huí·lái (用在动词后表示回到原地) back; backward: 跑～ run back / 把箱子拿～ carry the box back; get the box back

【回廊】 huíláng winding corridor

【回老家】 huílǎojiā die

【回礼】 huílǐ 1.(回答敬礼) return a salute 2.(回赠礼物) give a gift in return; present a gift in return

【回流】 huíliú backward flow

【回笼】 huílóng 1.(再蒸) steam again 2.(货币回笼) withdrawal (of currency) from circulation

【回暖】 huínuǎn get warm again after a cold spell

【回请】 huíqǐng return hospitality; give a return banquet

【回去】 huí·qù (用作动词) return; go back; be back

【回去】 ·huí·qù (用在动词后) back: 带～ take back

【回升】 huíshēng rise again (after a fall); pick up: 汇率～。The exchange rate has gone up again.

【回生】 huíshēng 1.(死后复生) bring back to life; restore to life 2.(感到生疏) get rusty; forget through lack of practice

【回声】 huíshēng echo

【回收】 huíshōu retrieve; recover; reclaim: ～废品 recover waste / ～人造卫星 retrieve the man-made satellite

【回手】 huíshǒu 1.(转身顺手) turn round and stretch out one's hand: ～把门关上 turn round and close the door 2.(还击) hit back; return a blow

【回首】 huíshǒu 1.(回头) turn one's head; turn round 2.(回忆) look back; call to mind: 不堪～ can't bear to think of the past

【回天乏术】 huítiān-fáshù unable to save the situation

【回条】 huítiáo receipt

【回头】 huítóu 1.(掉转头) turn one's head; turn round 2.(悔悟) repent 3.(等一会) later: ～见! See you later!

【回头路】 huítóulù the road back to one's former position; the road of retrogression

【回味】 huíwèi 1.(食后余味) aftertaste 2.(回想中体会) call sth. to mind and ponder over it

【回乡】 huíxiāng return to one's home village

【回响】 huíxiǎng 1.(回声) echo 2.(响应) resound; reverberate

【回想】 huíxiǎng think back; recollect; recall

【回心转意】 huíxīn-zhuǎnyì change one's views; come around

【回信】 huíxìn 1.(写复信) write in reply; write back 2.(复信) a letter in reply 3.(答复的话) a verbal message in reply; reply

【回形针】 huíxíngzhēn paper clip

【回旋】 huíxuán 1.(盘旋) circle round; circling overhead 2.(进退) (room for) maneuver: 没有～的余地。There are no room for maneuver.

【回忆】 huíyì call to mind; recollect; recall: 往事的～ recollections of the past

【回忆录】 huíyìlù reminiscences; memoirs; recollections

【回音】 huíyīn 1.(回声) echo 2.(回信) reply

【回执】 huízhí receipt

【回转】 huízhuǎn turn round

【回转椭圆体】 huízhuǎn tuǒyuántǐ ellipsoid of revolution

【回族】 Huízú Hui (中国少数民族, 主要分布在宁夏、甘肃、河南、青海、云南、河北、山东、安徽、辽宁、北京、内蒙古、天津、黑龙江、陕西、吉林、江苏、贵州等地)

【回嘴】 huízuǐ answer back; talk back; retort

茴 (huí)

【茴香】 huíxiāng 〈*Bot.*〉 fennel; aniseed

洄 (huí) whirl

【洄游】 huíyóu migrate; migration (n.): 幼年的大麻哈鱼长距离～还是要回到乌苏里江。Young salmon migrate long distances but return to Wusuli River.

蛔[蚘、蛕] (huí)

【蛔虫】 huíchóng roundworm; ascarid

悔 (huǐ) regret; repent

【悔不当初】 huǐbùdāngchū regret having done sth.

【悔改】 huǐgǎi repent and mend one's ways: 决心～ be determined to mend one's ways

【悔过】 huǐguò repent one's error; be repentant; penitence

【悔过书】 huǐguòshū statement of repentance

【悔过自新】 huǐguò-zìxīn repent and start anew; repent and turn over a new leaf; repent and make a fresh start
【悔恨】 huǐhèn regret deeply; be bitterly remorseful: ～交加 mixed feeling of remorse and shame
【悔悟】 huǐwù realize one's error and show repentance: 毫无～之意 show no sign of repentance

毁[燬[2]、譭[3]] (huǐ) 1.(破坏掉) destroy; ruin; damage 2.(焚烧掉) burn up 3.(诽谤) defame; slander
【毁谤】 huǐbàng slander; malign; calumniate
【毁坏】 huǐhuài destroy; damage; break; deface
【毁灭】 huǐmiè destroy; exterminate
【毁誉参半】 huǐyù-cānbàn 1.(对人) get both praise and censure 2.(对书等文艺作品) have a mixed reception
【毁约】 huǐyuē 1.(食言) break one's promise 2.(撕毁合约、契约) scrap a contract; scrap a treaty

汇[滙、匯、彙[2,3]] (huì) 1.(汇合) converge 2.(聚集) gather together 3.(聚集而成的东西) things collected; assemblage; collection 4.(寄) remit: ～钱 remit money to 5.(指外汇) foreign exchange
【汇报】 huìbào 1.(向上级汇报) report; give an account of 2.(汇报材料) report; summary: 写～ write a report
【汇编】 huìbiān compilation; collection; corpus: 法规～ the corpus of laws and regulations
【汇兑】 huìduì remittance; exchange
【汇费】 huìfèi remittance fee
【汇合】 huìhé converge; join
【汇合点】 huìhédiǎn point; point of convergence
【汇集】 huìjí 1.(聚集) collect; compile: ～材料 collect all relevant data 2.(集合) come together; converge; assemble
【汇价】 huìjià exchange rate
【汇款】 huìkuǎn 1.(寄出款) remit money; make a remittance 2.(汇寄的款项) remittance: 收到～ receive a remittance
【汇款单】 huìkuǎndān money order
【汇款人】 huìkuǎnrén remitter
【汇率】 huìlǜ exchange rate; the rate of exchange
【汇票】 huìpiào draft; bill of exchange; money order
【汇演】 huìyǎn joint performance
【汇总】 huìzǒng gather; collect; pool
【汇总表】 huìzǒngbiǎo statement

会[會] (huì) 1.(会聚) get together; assemble 2.(会见) meet; see 3.(会议) meeting; gathering; party; conference 4.(团体) association; society; union 5.(庙会) a temple fair 6.(都会) chief city; capital 7.(时机) opportunity; occasion 8.(通晓;熟习) can; be able to 9.(会做) be good at; be skillful in; be likely to; be sure to 10.(可能实现) be likely to; be sure to: 假使你早一些来,就～看到他了。If you had come earlier, you would have seen him.
(另见"会"kuài)
【会标】 huìbiāo conference emblem
【会餐】 huìcān dine together; have a dinner party
【会场】 huìchǎng meeting-place; conference hall
【会费】 huìfèi membership dues: 工会～ membership dues of a trade union
【会风】 huìfēng current tendency at meetings; tendencies appearing at meetings
【会馆】 huìguǎn guild hall
【会海】 huìhǎi sea of meetings; innumerable meetings
【会合】 huìhé join; meet; converge; assemble
【会话】 huìhuà conversation
【会话手册】 huìhuà shǒucè a handbook of conversation
【会徽】 huìhuī emblem
【会籍】 huìjí membership (of an association)
【会见】 huìjiàn meet with: ～外宾 meet with a foreign visitor
【会聚】 huìjù assemble; flock together
【会考】 huìkǎo nation-wide or city-wide examination for graduation qualification
【会客】 huìkè receive a visitor
【会客室】 huìkèshì reception room
【会面】 huìmiàn meet: 近来,我同他不常～。

I have not seen much of him lately.

【会期】 huìqī 1.（开会日期）the time fixed for a conference; the date of a meeting：确定～ fix a date for the meeting 2.（会议天数）the duration of a meeting

【会签】 huìqiān countersign：把文件送三个部门～ send a document to three departments to countersign

【会商】 huìshāng hold a conference or consultation

【会审】 huìshěn 1.（共同审理）joint hearing; joint trial 2.（公同审查）do a joint checkup; give a joint checkup

【会师】 huìshī join forces; effect a junction：胜利～ join forces triumphantly

【会谈】 huìtán talks：双边～ bilateral talks / 非正式～ unofficial talks

【会谈纪要】 huìtán jìyào minutes of talks; notes on talks; summary of a conversation

【会堂】 huìtáng assembly hall; hall

【会晤】 huìwù meet

【会心】 huìxīn understanding; knowing：～的微笑 an knowing smile

【会演】 huìyǎn joint performance：文艺～ theatrical festival

【会厌】 huìyàn 〈*Anat.*〉 epiglottis

【会议】 huìyì 1.（会）meeting; conference：筹备～ preparatory meeting / 全体～ plenary session / 小组～ group meeting / 圆桌～ round-table conference / 正式～ official meeting / 最高级～ summit conference 2.（机构）council：部长～ Council of Ministers / 中国人民政治协商～ the Chinese People's Political Consultative Conference

【会议室】 huìyìshì meeting room; council chamber

【会意】 huìyì understanding; knowing

【会员】 huìyuán member：正式～ full member

【会员国】 huìyuánguó member state

【会员证】 huìyuánzhèng membership card

【会战】 huìzhàn 1.（主力决战）meet for a decisive battle 2.（集中力量突击）join in a battle; launch a mass campaign

【会长】 huìzhǎng the president of an association or society

【会账】 huìzhàng pay a bill

【会诊】 huìzhěn 〈*Med.*〉 consultation of doctors;（group）consultation：中西医～ hold group consultations of doctors practicing Chinese and Western medicine

【会址】 huìzhǐ 1.（协会地址）the site of an association or society 2.（开会的地方）the site of a conference or meeting

荟［薈］（huì） 〈*written*〉 luxuriant growth（of plants）

【荟萃】 huìcuì gather together; assemble

绘［繪］（huì） paint; draw

【绘画】 huìhuà drawing; painting

【绘画室】 huìhuàshì studio

【绘声绘色】 huìshēng-huìsè vivid; lively

【绘图】 huìtú mapping

【绘图板】 huìtúbǎn drawing board

【绘图笔】 huìtúbǐ border pen

【绘图室】 huìtúshì drawing room

【绘图纸】 huìtúzhǐ drawing paper

【绘图员】 huìtúyuán draftsman; draftswoman（f.）

【绘制】 huìzhì draw：～图表 draw a diagram

烩［燴］（huì） braise：～菠菜 braised spinach

讳［諱］（huì） 1.（忌讳）avoid as taboo 2.（忌讳的事情） forbidden word; taboo

【讳莫如深】 huìmòrúshēn closely guard a secret; not breathe a word to a soul; not utter a single word about sth.

【讳言】 huìyán dare not or would not speak up

诲（huì） teach; instruct

【诲人不倦】 huìrén-bùjuàn be tireless in teaching; teach with tireless zeal

【诲淫诲盗】 huìyín-huìdào propagate sex and violence; stir up the base passions

晦（huì） 1.（昏暗）dark; obscure; gloomy 2.（夜晚）night

【晦暗】 huì'àn dark; gloomy; obscure

【晦气】 huì·qì unlucky; unfortunate

【晦涩】 huìsè hard to understand; obscure：语言～ with obscure language

贿（huì） bribe：受～ accept bribes / 行～ practice bribery; bribe

【贿赂】 huìlù 1.(行贿) bribe; buy off 2.(行贿物) bribery
【贿买】 huìmǎi buy over; suborn

彗[篲](huì)

【彗星】 huìxīng 〈*Astron*.〉 comet

慧(huì) intelligent; bright

【慧眼独具】 huìyǎn-dújù can see what others cannot
【慧眼识英雄】 huìyǎn shí yīngxióng discerning eyes can tell greatness from mediocrity

秽[穢](huì) 1.(肮脏) dirty; filthy 2.(丑恶) ugly; abominable; immoral

【秽行】 huìxíng scandalous behavior; immoral conduct

惠(huì) 1.(恩惠) favor; kindness 2.(给人好处) benefit 3.〈*politeness*〉 your

【惠存】 huìcún 〈*politeness*〉 please keep (sth. as a souvenir)
【惠顾】 huìgù 〈*politeness*〉 your patronage
【惠临】 huìlín 〈*politeness*〉 your presence

喙(huì) 1.(鸟嘴) beak 2.(动物嘴) snout 3.(人嘴) mouth: 不容置～ no refuse letting others talk

hun

昏(hūn) 1.(黄昏) dusk 2.(昏暗) dark; dim 3.(头脑迷糊) confused; muddled 4.(失去知觉) lose consciousness; faint

【昏暗】 hūn'àn dim; dusky: ～的天色 gloomy skies
【昏沉】 hūnchén 1.(昏暗) murky: 暮色～ murky twilight 2.(昏乱) dazed; befuddled: 睡得昏昏沉沉 be stupid with sleep
【昏倒】 hūndǎo fall into a swoon; go off into a faint; fall unconscious
【昏黑】 hūnhēi dusky; dark
【昏花】 hūnhuā dim-sighted: 老眼～。The old man's eyesight is failing.
【昏黄】 hūnhuáng pale yellow; faint; dim: ～的灯光 a dim light
【昏昏欲睡】 hūnhūn-yùshuì drowsy; sleepy
【昏厥】 hūnjué faint; swoon; faint away
【昏聩】 hūnkuì decrepit and muddle-headed; senile and stupefied
【昏迷】 hūnmí stupor; coma: ～不醒 remain unconscious
【昏迷状态】 hūnmí zhuàngtài comatose state
【昏睡】 hūnshuì lethargic sleep; lethargy
【昏天黑地】 hūntiān-hēidì 1.(指天色) pitch-dark; in pitch darkness 2.(指神志) dizzy 3.(指生活) loose; perverted; decadent 4.(指社会) dark rule and social disorder
【昏头昏脑】 hūntóu-hūnnǎo 1.(头脑糊涂) addlebrained; addleheaded; muddleheaded 2.(好忘事) absentminded; forgetful
【昏庸】 hūnyōng fatuous; muddleheaded; stupid

婚(hūn) 1.(结婚) wed; marry: 晚～ marry at a mature age / 未～ unmarried / 已～ married 2.(婚姻) marriage; wedding: 晚～ late marriage; deferred marriage / 早～ early marriage

【婚检】 hūnjiǎn pre-martial check-ups
【婚礼】 hūnlǐ wedding ceremony; wedding: 参加～ attend the wedding of A and B
【婚恋】 hūnliàn marriage and love affair
【婚龄】 hūnlíng 1.(结婚年数) years of marriage 2.(法定结婚年龄) legally marriageable age: 她还没到～。She is not of marriageable age.
【婚前检查】 hūnqián jiǎnchá pre-martial check-ups
【婚事】 hūnshì marriage; wedding
【婚外恋】 hūnwàiliàn love affair outside marriage; extramarital relation
【婚姻】 hūnyīn marriage; matrimony
【婚姻登记】 hūnyīn dēngjì marriage registration
【婚姻法】 hūnyīnfǎ law of marriage; marriage law
【婚姻介绍所】 hūnyīn jièshàosuǒ matchmaking service
【婚姻状况】 hūnyīn zhuàngkuàng marital status
【婚约】 hūnyuē marriage contract; engagement: 解除～ break off one's engagement

荤(hūn) meat or fish

【荤菜】 hūncài meat dishes
【荤腥】 hūnxīng meat or fish
【荤油】 hūnyóu lard

浑 (hún) 1.(浑浊) muddy; turbid: 把水搅～ muddle the water 2.(不明事理) foolish; stupid 3.(天然的) simple and natural; unsophisticated 4.(全;满) whole; all over

【浑蛋】 húndàn 〈*derog.*〉 blackguard; bastard; wretch

【浑厚】 húnhòu 1.(指人) simple and honest 2.(指艺术风格) simple and vigorous

【浑话】 húnhuà a foolish talk

【浑球儿】 húnqiúr 〈*derog.*〉 blackguard; bastard; wretch

【浑然】 húnrán integrated; whole; complete: ～一体 an integral whole

【浑身】 húnshēn from head to foot; all over: ～发痒 itch all over / 使出～解数 use all one's skill to do sth.

【浑水摸鱼】 húnshuǐ-mōyú fish in troubled waters

【浑天仪】 húntiānyí 〈*Astron.*〉 1.(浑仪) armillary sphere 2.(浑象) celestial glove

【浑象】 húnxiàng 〈*Astron.*〉 celestial glove

【浑仪】 húnyí 〈*Astron.*〉 armillary sphere

【浑浊】 húnzhuó muddy; turbid

馄 (hún)

【馄饨】 hún·tún dumpling soup

混 (hún) 1.(浑浊) muddy; turbid: 把水搅～ muddle the water 2.(不明事理) foolish; stupid

(另见"混"hùn)

【混蛋】 húndàn 〈*derog.*〉 blackguard; bastard; wretch

【混球儿】 húnqiúr 〈*derog.*〉 blackguard; bastard; wretch

【混水摸鱼】 húnshuǐ-mōyú fish in troubled waters

魂 (hún) 1.(灵魂) soul 2.(精神) mood; spirit 3.(国家、民族崇高精神) the lofty spirit of a nation

【魂不附体】 húnbùfùtǐ as if the soul had left the body; as if one's mind was unhinged

【魂不守舍】 húnbùshǒushè one's mind is somewhat unhinged

【魂飞魄散】 húnfēi-pòsàn be frightened out of one's wits; almost swooning with fright

诨 (hùn) joke; jest; gag

【诨名】 hùnmíng nickname

混 (hùn) 1.(搀杂) mix; confuse 2.(蒙混) pass for; pass off as 3.(苟且) muddle along; drift along: ～日子 drift along aimlessly 4.(相处) get along with sb.

(另见"混"hún)

【混充】 hùnchōng pass off as; palm off as: ～内行 pass oneself off as an expert

【混沌】 hùndùn 1.(指宇宙形成前) chaos 2.(无知) innocent; ignorant

【混纺】 hùnfǎng 〈*Textiles*〉 blending: 棉毛～ fabric of wool and cotton

【混合】 hùnhé mix; blend; mingle: 把水和酒精～起来 mingle water and alcohol

【混合双打】 hùnhé shuāngdǎ 〈*Sports*〉 mixed double

【混合饲料】 hùnhé sìliào mixed fodder

【混交林】 hùnjiāolín mixed forest

【混进】 hùnjìng infiltrate; sneak into; worm one's way into

【混乱】 hùnluàn confusion; chaos: ～不堪 in utter disorder

【混凝土】 hùnníngtǔ concrete

【混凝土搅拌机】 hùnníngtǔ jiǎobànjī concrete mixer

【混凝土结构】 hùnníngtǔ jiégòu concrete structure

【混同】 hùntóng confuse; mix up: 把"价值"和"价格"～了 confuse value with price

【混为一谈】 hùnwéiyītán lump together; confuse sth. with sth. else

【混淆】 hùnxiáo obscure; blur; confuse; mix up: ～是非 confuse right and wrong / ～视听 mislead the public; confuse public opinion

【混血儿】 hùnxuè'ér a person of mixed blood; human hybrid

【混杂】 hùnzá mix; mingle; intermix

【混战】 hùnzhàn tangled warfare; tangled fight

【混浊】 hùnzhuó muddy; turbid: ～的空气 foul air / ～的水 turbid water

huo

豁 (huō) 1.(裂开) slit; break; crack 2.(狠心付出代价) give up; sacrifice

(另见"豁"huò)

【豁出去】 huō·chu·qu go ahead regardless;

be ready to risk everything

【豁口】 huōkǒu opening; break; breach: 城墙～ an opening in the city wall

【豁子】 huō·zi 1.（豁口）opening; break; breach 2.（豁嘴的人）a harelipped person

和（huó） mix（powder）with water, etc.（另见"和"hē, hè, hú, huò）

【和面】 huómiàn knead dough; mix flour

活（huó） 1.（生存）live: 他～到90岁。He lived to be ninety. 2.（活着的）alive; living: ～鱼 live fish 3.（救活）save 4.（灵活）vivid; lively: 描写得很～ be depicted quite vividly 5.（活动的）movable; moving: ～水 flowing water 6.（真正）exactly; simply 7.（工作）work: 苦～ sweated labor / 零～ odd jobs 8.（产品）product

【活扳子】 huóbān·zi adjustable wrench; adjustable spanner

【活版】 huóbǎn 〈*Printing*〉 typography; letterpress

【活到老,学到老】 huódàolǎo, xuédàolǎo It is never too old to learn.（或: Live and learn.）

【活动】 huódòng 1.（运动）move about; exercise: 站起来～～ stand up and move about 2.（动摇）shaky; unsteady: 这颗牙～了。This tooth's loose. 3.（不固定）movable; mobile; flexible 4.（行动）activity; maneuver: 户外～ outdoor activities 5.（说情）use personal influence or irregular means

【活动车顶轿车】 huódòng chēdǐng jiàochē sliding roof limousine

【活动车篷汽车】 huódòng chēpéng qìchē convertible

【活动范围】 huódòng fànwéi sphere of activities; scope of operation

【活动房】 huódòngfáng mobile house

【活动房屋】 huódòng fángwū prefabricated house

【活动家】 huódòngjiā activist; public figure

【活法儿】 huófǎr way of life

【活该】 huógāi 〈*collog.*〉 serve sb. right: ～倒楣 be destined to come to grief

【活工资】 huógōngzī fluctuating wage; conditional wage

【活活】 huóhuó 1.（活着）while still alive: ～烧死 be burnt alive 2.（简直）absolutely

【活火山】 huóhuǒshān active volcano

【活计】 huó·ji 1.（指手工艺、体力劳动）handicraft work; manual labor 2.（手工制品）work; handiwork

【活检】 huójiǎn 〈*Med.*〉 biopsy

【活见鬼】 huójiànguǐ it's sheer fantasy; you're imagining thing

【活结】 huójié slipknot: 打个～ tie a slipknot

【活局子】 huójú·zi trap

【活力】 huólì vigor; vitality; energy

【活灵活现】 huólíng-huóxiàn vivid; lifelike; lively

【活路】 huólù 1.（维生办法）means of subsistence; way out: 找个～ look for a means of subsistence 2.（行得通的办法）workable method

【活络】 huóluò 1.（活动）loose 2.（话不肯定）noncommittal; indefinite

【活络扳手】 huóluò bān·shou adjustable wrench; adjustable spanner

【活埋】 huómái bury alive

【活门】 huómén valve; piston

【活命】 huómìng 1.（维持生命）earn a bare living; scrape along; eke out an existence 2.（救活性命）save sb's life 3.（性命）life

【活泼】 huó·po lively; vivacious; vivid: 生动～的政治局面 vigorous and lively political situation

【活期】 huóqī current

【活期储蓄】 huóqī chǔxù current deposit

【活塞】 huósāi 〈*Mech.*〉 piston

【活塞环】 huósāihuán packing ring; piston ring

【活生生】 huóshēngshēng 1.（实际生活中的）in real life; actual; real; living 2.（活活）while still alive

【活受罪】 huóshòuzuì 〈*collog.*〉 have a hell of a life

【活水】 huóshuǐ flowing water; running water

【活体检查】 huótǐ jiǎnchá 〈*Med.*〉 biopsy

【活体解剖】 huótǐ jiěpōu vivisection

【活像】 huóxiàng look exactly like; be the spit and image of; be an exact replica of: 那女孩～她的妈妈。The girl looks exactly like her mother.

【活性】 huóxìng 〈*Chem.*〉 active; activated

【活性炭】 huóxìngtàn active carbon
【活血】 huóxuè 〈*Chin. Med.*〉 invigorate the circulation of blood
【活页】 huóyè loose-leaf
【活页文选】 huóyè wénxuǎn loose-leaf selections
【活页纸】 huóyèzhǐ paper for a loose-leaf notebook
【活跃】 huóyuè **1.**（活泼；热烈）brisk; active; dynamic：讨论会开得很～。The discussion was very lively. **2.**（使活跃）enliven; animate; invigorate：～农村经济 activate rural economy / ～市场 enliven the market
【活捉】 huózhuō catch alive
【活字】 huózì 〈*Printing*〉type; letter
【活字版】 huózìbǎn 〈*Printing*〉original form
【活字印刷】 huózì yìnshuā 〈*Printing*〉movable-type printing

火（huǒ） **1.**（光焰）fire：着～ be on fire **2.**（炮火）firearms; ammunition **3.**〈*Chin. Med.*〉internal heat **4.**（红色）fiery; flaming **5.**（紧急）urgent; pressing **6.**（发怒）anger; temper：把人惹～了 make sb. angry
【火把】 huǒbǎ torch
【火棒儿】 huǒbàngr 〈*Sports*〉lighted torch
【火并】 huǒbìng open fight between factions
【火柴】 huǒchái match; matchstick：划～ strike a match
【火柴棍】 huǒcháigùn matchstick
【火柴盒】 huǒcháihé matchbox
【火场】 huǒchǎng the scene of a fire
【火车】 huǒchē train：乘～ go by train
【火车渡轮】 huǒchē dùlún train ferry
【火车票】 huǒchēpiào railway ticket
【火车时刻表】 huǒchē shíkèbiǎo railway timetable; train schedule
【火车头】 huǒchētóu locomotive; engine
【火车站】 huǒchēzhàn railway station
【火炽】 huǒchì heated; vigorous; exciting
【火电站】 huǒdiànzhàn thermal power station
【火罐儿】 huǒguànr 〈*Chin. Med.*〉cupping jar：拔～ cupping
【火光】 huǒguāng flame; blaze
【火锅】 huǒguō chafing dish
【火海】 huǒhǎi a sea of fire：一片～ a sea of fire
【火红】 huǒhóng **1.**（火一样红）red as fire **2.**（旺盛或热烈）fiery; flaming; glowing
【火候】 huǒ·hou **1.**（火力大小、时间长短）duration and degree of heating, cooking, smelting, etc. **2.**（功夫深浅）level of attainment **3.**（紧急时刻）a crucial moment
【火花】 huǒhuā spark
【火化】 huǒhuà cremation
【火鸡】 huǒjī turkey ‖ 雄火鸡 tom / 幼火鸡 poult
【火急】 huǒjí urgent; pressing：十万～ most urgent
【火箭】 huǒjiàn rocket：发射～ fire a rocket
【火箭部队】 huǒjiàn bùduì rocket troops
【火箭弹】 huǒjiàndàn rocket projectile
【火箭发射场】 huǒjiàn fāshèchǎng rocket launching site
【火箭炮】 huǒjiànpào rocket gun
【火警】 huǒjǐng fire alarm
【火炬】 huǒjù torch
【火炬点燃仪式】 huǒjù diǎnrán yíshì flame-lighting ceremony
【火炬计划】 huǒjù jìhuà torch program
【火炕】 huǒkàng heatable brick bed
【火坑】 huǒkēng fiery pit; pit of hell; abyss of suffering
【火辣辣】 huǒlālā burning
【火力】 huǒlì **1.**（指煤、石油等作燃料的动力）thermal power **2.**〈*Mil.*〉firepower; fire：发扬～ make full use of firepower / ～封锁 interdiction barrage / ～掩护 fire cover / ～支援 fire support
【火力发电厂】 huǒlì fādiànchǎng thermal power plant
【火炉】 huǒlú (heating) stove
【火冒三丈】 huǒmào-sānzhàng fly into a rage; fly into a towering passion：使人～ make sb's blood boil
【火苗】 huǒmiáo a tongue of flame; flame
【火棉】 huǒmián celloidin; pyroxyin
【火炮】 huǒpào cannon; gun
【火盆】 huǒpén fire pan; brazier
【火拼】 huǒpīn open fight between factions
【火漆】 huǒqī sealing wax
【火气】 huǒqì **1.**〈*Chin. Med.*〉internal heat **2.**（脾气）anger; temper
【火器】 huǒqì 〈*Mil.*〉firearm
【火热】 huǒrè **1.**（非常热）burning hot; fervent; fiery **2.**（十分亲近的）intimate：打得

～ carry on intimately with; be as thick as thieves

【火山】 huǒshān volcano; volcanic：活～ active volcano / 死～ extinct volcano / 休眠～ dormant volcano/ 正在喷发的～ volcano in eruption

【火山灰】 huǒshānhuī volcanic ash

【火山口】 huǒshānkǒu crater

【火伤】 huǒshāng burn

【火上加油】 huǒshàng-jiāyóu pour oil on the fire; add fuel to the flames

【火烧】 huǒ·shao 〈*Food*〉 baked wheaten cake

【火烧火燎】 huǒshāo-huǒliǎo **1.**（热得难受）feeling terribly hot **2.**（焦急）restless with anxiety

【火烧眉毛】 huǒshāo-méi·mao the fire is singeing the eyebrows; a desperate situation; a matter of the utmost urgency

【火舌】 huǒshé tongues of flame

【火石】 huǒshí flint

【火势】 huǒshì power of fire：～很猛。The fire is blazing.

【火速】 huǒsù at top speed; posthaste

【火烫】 huǒtàng **1.**（非常热）very hot; scalding hot **2.**（用火烫发）curl sb's hair with curling irons

【火头】 huǒtóu **1.**（火焰）flame **2.**（火候）duration and degree of heating, cooking, smelting, etc. **3.**（怒气）fit of anger; blaze of temper

【火腿】 huǒtuǐ ham

【火险】 huǒxiǎn 〈*Insurance*〉 fire insurance

【火线】 huǒxiàn **1.**（战场前沿）battle line **2.** 〈*Electr.*〉 live wire

【火星】 huǒxīng **1.**〈*Astron.*〉 Mars **2.**（小的火）spark

【火眼】 huǒyǎn 〈*Med.*〉 pinkeye

【火焰】 huǒyàn flame

【火焰喷射器】 huǒyàn pēnshèqì flamethrower

【火药】 huǒyào gunpowder; powder

【火药库】 huǒyàokù powder magazine

【火药桶】 huǒyàotǒng powder keg

【火药味】 huǒyàowèi the smell of gunpowder

【火印】 huǒyìn burned mark; brand

【火油】 huǒyóu kerosene; kerosine

【火灾】 huǒzāi fire (as a disaster); conflagration：发生了～。A fire breaks out.

【火葬】 huǒzàng cremation

【火葬场】 huǒzàngchǎng crematory; crematorium

【火中取栗】 huǒzhōng-qǔlì pull sb's chestnuts out of the fire; be a cat's-paw

【火种】 huǒzhǒng kindling material; kindling; tinder; live cinders kept for starting a new fire

【火烛】 huǒzhú things that are likely to start a fire：小心～！Beware of fires.

伙 (huǒ) **1.**（伙食）mess; board; meals **2.**（同伴）partner; mate **3.**（集体）partnership; company **4.**〈*classifier*〉 group; crowd; band **5.**（共同；联合）combine; join

【伙伴】 huǒbàn partner; companion

【伙伴关系】 huǒbàn guānxì partnership; companionship

【伙房】 huǒfáng kitchen (in a school, factory, etc.)

【伙计】 huǒ·ji **1.**（合伙人）partner **2.**（同伴）fellow; mate **3.**（店员）salesman; salesclerk; shop assistant

【伙食】 huǒ·shí mess; food; meals

【伙食费】 huǒ·shífèi money spent on meals; board expenses

【伙同】 huǒtóng in league with; gang up with sb.

钬 (huǒ) 〈*Chem.*〉 holmium（元素符号 Ho）

夥 (huǒ) **1.**（多）much; a great deal; many; numerous **2.**（同伴）partner; mate **3.**（集体）partnership; company **4.**〈*classifier*〉 group; crowd; band **5.**（共同；联合）combine; join

【夥伴】 huǒbàn partner; companion

【夥伴关系】 huǒbàn guānxì partnership; companionship

【夥计】 huǒ·ji **1.**（合伙人）partner **2.**（同伴）fellow; mate **3.**（店员）salesman; salesclerk; shop assistant

【夥同】 huǒtóng in league with; gang up with sb.

或 (huò) **1.**（也许；或许）perhaps; maybe; probably **2.**（或者）or; either . . . or . . .

【或大或小】 huòdà-huòxiǎo either large or small

【或去或留】 huòqù-huòliú go or stay
【或然率】 huòránlǜ 〈*Math.*〉 probability
【或许】 huòxǔ 〈*adv.*〉 perhaps; maybe
【或者】 huòzhě 1.〈*adv.*〉 perhaps; maybe 2.〈*conj.*〉 or; either ... or ...

惑 (huò) 1.(迷惑) be puzzled; be bewildered 2.(使迷惑) delude; mislead: 造谣～众 fabricate rumors to mislead people

和 (huò) mix; blend: 把水泥、沙和石子～在一起 mix cement, sand and pebbles (另见"和"hē, hè, hú, huó)

【和稀泥】 huòxīní try to mediate differences at the sacrifice of principle; try to smooth things over

货 (huò) 1.(货物) goods; commodity: 定～ order goods; place and order for goods / 发～ deliver goods / 交～ deliver goods / 接～ receive goods / 理～ tally goods / 盘～ take stock / 卸～ discharge (cargo) 2.(钱) money

【货币】 huòbì money; currency
【货币贬值】 huòbì biǎnzhí (currency) devaluation; (currency) depreciation
【货币回笼】 huòbì huílóng withdrawal of currency from circulation
【货舱】 huòcāng (cargo) hold; cargo bay (of a plane)
【货场】 huòchǎng goods yard
【货车】 huòchē 1.(货运列车) goods train; freight train 2.(敞车) stockcar; open goods wagon 3.(闷罐车) boxcar; covered goods van 4.(运货卡车) truck; lorry
【货船】 huòchuán freighter; cargo ship; cargo vessel
【货柜】 huòguì container
【货柜车】 huòguìchē container car
【货柜船】 huòguìchuán container ship
【货机】 huòjī 〈*Aeron.*〉 cargo aircraft; cargo plane; air truck
【货价】 huòjià price of goods; commodity price
【货架】 huòjià goods shelves
【货款】 huòkuǎn money for buying; money for selling goods; payment for goods
【货轮】 huòlún cargo ship; freighter
【货色】 huòsè 1.(货物) goods: 上等～ quality goods 2.(贬义指人、言论等) stuff; trash; rubbish: 你知道他是什么～吗? Don't you know what stuff he is made of?
【货摊】 huòtān stall; stand
【货物】 huòwù goods; commodity; merchandise
【货箱】 huòxiāng packing box
【货源】 huòyuán source of goods; supply of goods
【货运】 huòyùn freight transport
【货运量】 huòyùnliàng volume of goods transported: 铁路～ volume of rail freight
【货栈】 huòzhàn warehouse
【货真价实】 huòzhēn-jiàshí 1.(货非冒牌,价钱实在) genuine goods at a fair price 2.(贬义,指一点不假的) out-and-out; through and through: ～的骗子 an out-and-out swindler
【货主】 huòzhǔ owner of cargo

获[獲[1,2]、穫[3]] (huò) 1.(抓获) capture; catch 2.(获得) obtain; win; reap 3.(收获) reap; harvest

【获得】 huòdé gain; obtain; acquire; win; achieve: ～独立 gain independence / ～信任 gain sb's confidence
【获得性免疫缺损综合征】 huòdéxìng miǎnyì quēsǔn zōnghézhēng 〈*Med.*〉 Acquired Immune Deficiency Syndrome (AIDS) (艾滋病)
【获奖】 huòjiǎng win a prize; be given a prize: ～小说 prize-winning novel / ～作家 prize-winning writer
【获奖人】 huòjiǎngrén prize winner
【获救】 huòjiù be rescued
【获胜】 huòshèng win victory; be victorious; triumph: 甲队以四比一～。Team A won the match four to one.
【获释】 huòshì be released; be set free; get off
【获悉】 huòxī learn (of an event); be aware of
【获准】 huòzhǔn have permission; be permitted; be given permission

祸[禍] (huò) 1.(祸事) misfortune; disaster; calamity: 惹～ cause trouble 2.(损害) bring disaster upon; ruin

【祸不单行】 huòbùdānxíng misfortunes never come singly

【祸从口出】 huòcóngkǒuchū out of the mouth comes evil

【祸从天降】 huòcóngtiānjiàng disaster comes from sky

【祸根】 huògēn the root of the trouble; the cause of ruin; bane: 铲除～ uproot the evil / 种下～ sow the seeds of misfortune

【祸国殃民】 huòguó-yāngmín bring calamity to the country and the people

【祸害】 huòhài 1.(祸事) disaster; curse; scourge 2.(引起灾难的人或事) scourge; curse; bone 3.(损害) bring disaster to; wreck; ruin

【祸首】 huòshǒu chief culprit

【祸水】 huòshuǐ scourge; culprit; curse

【祸心】 huòxīn evil intent; malicious intentions: 怀有～ with malicious intentions

【祸殃】 huòyāng disaster; misfortune

霍 (huò) suddenly; quickly

【霍城】 Huòchéng 〈place〉 Korgas

【霍地】 huòdì 〈*adv.*〉 suddenly

【霍乱】 huòluàn 1.〈*Med.*〉 cholera 2.〈*Chin. Med.*〉 acute gastroenteritis

【霍然】 huòrán 1.〈*adv.*〉 suddenly; all of a sudden; quickly 2.(疾病很快消除) be cured quickly; suddenly recover from an illness

藿 (huò)

【藿香】 huòxiāng 〈*Bot.*〉 gianthyssop; agastache

豁 (huò) 1.(通达) clear; open; open-minded; generous 2.(免除) exempt; remit

(另见"豁"huō)

【豁达】 huòdá open-minded

【豁达大度】 huòdá-dàdù be generous and open-minded

【豁亮】 huò·liàng 1.(宽敞明亮) roomy and bright: 这屋子又干净,又～。The room is clean, bright and spacious. 2.(响亮) sonorous; resonant: 嗓音～ have a sonorous voice

【豁免】 huòmiǎn exempt; remit

【豁然】 huòrán broad; through

【豁然开朗】 huòrán-kāilǎng suddenly see the light; be suddenly enlightened

J

ji

几[幾²](jī) 1.(小矮桌) a small table 2.(几乎,差不多) nearly; almost; practically

(另见 "几"jǐ)

【几不欲生】 jībùyùshēng almost did not desire to live

【几乎】 jīhū 1.(将近) about; around; close to 2.(差点儿) nearly; almost; practically

【几率】 jīlǜ 〈*Math.*〉 probability

【几于完备】 jīyú wánbèi approximate perfection

讥[譏](jī) ridicule; mock; satirize

【讥讽】 jīfěng ridicule; satirize; throw out innuendoes against

【讥笑】 jīxiào ridicule; laugh at; sneer at; deride: ～的口吻 in a scornful sneer

叽[嘰](jī)

【叽咕】 jī·gu talk in a low voice; whisper; mutter

【叽叽喳喳】 jī·ji-zhāzhā 〈*onomat.*〉 chirp; twitter

【叽里咕噜】 jī·ligūlū 1.(说话不清楚) gabble; jabber; talk in an indistinct manner 2.(滚动的声音) rumble

饥[饑²](jī) 1.(饥饿) be hungry; starve; famish 2.(饥荒) famine; crop failure

【饥不择食】 jībùzéshí a hungry person is not choosy about his food; all food is delicious to the starving

【饥饿】 jī'è hunger; starvation; be hungry; starve

【饥寒交迫】 jīhán-jiāopò suffer hunger and cold; live in hunger and cold; suffer from cold and hunger

【饥荒】 jī·huang 1.(指收成) famine; crop failure 2.(指经济困难) be hard up; be hard pressed for money; be short of money 3.(债) debt

【饥馑】 jījǐn famine; crop failure

【饥民】 jīmín famine victim; famine refugee

机[機](jī) 1.(机器) machine; engine: 缝纫～ sewing machine 2.(飞机) aircraft; airplane; aeroplane; plane 3.(重要环节) crucial point; pivot; key link 4.(机会) chance; occasion; opportunity: 良～ good chance; good opportunity 5.(生活机能) organic 6.(灵活) flexible; quick-witted

【机播】 jībō machine sowing

【机不可失】 jībùkěshī can't afford to lose the opportunity; not let the opportunity slip through one's fingers

【机舱】 jīcāng 1.(船舶的机器房) engine room: ～上层建筑 engine room superstructure 2.(飞机客舱) passenger compartment; cabin

【机场】 jīchǎng airport; airfield; aerodrome: 国际～ international airport

【机场费】 jīchǎngfèi airport fee: 交纳～ pay an airport fee / 免收～ be exempt from the airport fee

【机场候机楼】 jīchǎng hòujīlóu departure hall

【机场酒店】 jīchǎng jiǔdiàn airtel

【机场税】 jīchǎngshuì airport tax

【机场主楼】 jīchǎng zhǔlóu terminal building

【机车】 jīchē 〈*Railroad*〉 locomotive; engine: 电力～ electric locomotive

【机床】 jīchuáng machine tool

【机电产品】 jīdiàn chǎnpǐn mechanical and electrical products

【机动】 jīdòng 1.(机器开动的) motor-driven; motorized 2.(灵活) flexible; expedient; mobile 3.(随时可调用的) keep in reserve; for emergency use

【机动车】 jīdòngchē motor vehicle
【机断】 jīduàn act on one's own judgment in an emergency
【机帆船】 jīfānchuán motor sailboat; motorized junk
【机房】 jīfáng 1.(安有动力设备的房间) generator room; motor room 2.(船舶机舱) engine room 3.(计算机机房) computer room
【机耕】 jīgēng 〈*Agric*.〉 tractor-ploughing
【机工】 jīgōng mechanic; machinist
【机构】 jīgòu 1.〈*Mech*.〉 mechanism 2.(机关团体) organ; organization; institution; setup 3.(机关团体内部组织) the internal structure of an organization: ～臃肿 inflated departments; overexpansion of organizations
【机关】 jīguān 1.〈*Mech*.〉 mechanism; gear 2.(机械控制的) machine-operated 3.(办事部门) office; organ; body 4.(指计谋) stratagem; scheme; intrigue: 识破～ see through a trick
【机关枪】 jīguānqiāng machine gun
【机会】 jī·huì chance; opportunity: 好～ good opportunity / 错过～ let a chance slip by; lose an opportunity
【机会均等】 jīhuì jūnděng principle of equal opportunity for all; equal opportunity
【机会主义】 jīhuì zhǔyì opportunism; opportunist (adj.) ‖ 机会主义者 opportunist
【机件】 jījiàn 〈*Mech*.〉 parts; works
【机井】 jījǐng motor-pumped well
【机警】 jījǐng alert; sharp-witted; vigilant
【机具】 jījù machines and tools
【机理】 jīlǐ mechanism
【机灵】 jī·ling clever; smart; sharp; intelligent
【机密】 jīmì 1.(秘密) secret; classified; confidential: ～文件 classified papers; confidential documents 2.(机密的事) secret: 国家～ state secrets
【机敏】 jīmǐn alert and resourceful
【机能】 jīnéng 〈*Biol*.〉 function: 生理～ physiological function
【机票】 jīpiào 〈*Aeron*.〉 passenger ticket
【机器】 jī·qì 1.(指设备) machine; machinery; apparatus 2.(比喻) apparatus: 表决～ voting apparatus
【机器翻译】 jī·qì fānyì machine translation
【机器人】 jī·qìrén robot
【机枪】 jīqiāng machine gun
【机枪手】 jīqiāngshǒu machine gunner
【机巧】 jīqiǎo adroit; ingenious; dexterous
【机群】 jīqún a group of planes; a fleet of planes
【机上服务】 jīshàng fúwù in-flight service
【机身】 jīshēn 〈*Aeron*.〉 fuselage
【机体】 jītǐ 1.〈*Biol*.〉 organism 2.〈*Aeron*.〉 airframe
【机头】 jītóu 〈*Aeron*.〉 nose
【机尾】 jīwěi 〈*Aeron*.〉 tail
【机务人员】 jīwù rényuán 1.(维修人员) maintenance personnel 2.(航空地勤人员) ground crew
【机械】 jīxiè 1.(装置) machinery; mechanism; machine 2.(死板;刻板) mechanical; inflexible; rigid
【机械厂】 jīxièchǎng machinery plant
【机械化】 jīxièhuà mechanize; mechanization (n.)
【机械手】 jīxièshǒu 〈*Mech*.〉 manipulator
【机械运动】 jīxiè yùndòng 〈*Physics*〉 mechanical movement
【机心】 jīxīn 〈*Clock*〉 movement
【机型】 jīxíng 1.(飞机型号) type 2.(机器型号) model
【机要】 jīyào confidential: ～秘书 confidential secretary
【机宜】 jīyí principles of action
【机翼】 jīyì 〈*Aeron*.〉 wing; aircraft wing
【机油】 jīyóu engine oil; machine oil
【机遇】 jīyù favorable circumstances; opportunity
【机缘】 jīyuán good luck; lucky chance
【机载导弹】 jīzǎi dǎodàn air-launched missile
【机长】 jīzhǎng pilot; aircraft commander; captain of an airplane
【机制】 jīzhì 1.(机器制造或加工的) machine-made; machine-processed 2.(机理) mechanism 3.(过程和方式) mechanism: 竞争～ competition / 运行～ operating mechanism
【机智】 jīzhì quick-witted; resourceful
【机组】 jīzǔ 1.〈*Mech*.〉 unit; set 2.(飞机乘务员) aircrew; flight crew; aircraft crew

肌 (jī) muscle; flesh; muscular (adj.): 腹～ abdominal muscle / 胸～ pectoral muscle

【肌肤】 jīfū 〈*written*〉(human) skin

【肌腱】 jījiàn 〈*Anat.*〉 tendon

【肌痉挛】 jījìngluán 〈*Med.*〉 muscle spasmus

【肌理】 jīlǐ 〈*written*〉 skin texture

【肌肉】 jīròu muscle; muscular (adj.): 面部～ facial muscles / ～发达的身材 a muscular body

【肌肉萎缩症】 jīròu wěisuōzhèng 〈*Med.*〉 muscular dystrophy

【肌体】 jītǐ human body; organism

【肌炎】 jīyán 〈*Med.*〉 myositis; myonitis

击[擊] (jī) **1.**(击打) beat; hit; strike **2.**(攻打) attack; assault **3.**(碰击) come in contact with; bump into

【击败】 jībài defeat; beat; vanquish

【击毙】 jībì shoot dead; strike dead

【击沉】 jīchén bombard and sink; send (a ship) to the bottom

【击穿】 jīchuān 〈*Electr.*〉 puncture; breakdown

【击发】 jīfā 〈*Mil.*〉 percussion

【击毁】 jīhuǐ smash; wreck; shatter; destroy

【击剑】 jījiàn 〈*Sports*〉 fencing; fence (v.): ～比赛 a fencing tournament / ～时要戴防护面具。You wear a protective mask when you fence. ‖ 击剑运动员 fencer

【击溃】 jīkuì rout; put to flight; defeat utterly; smash

【击落】 jīluò shoot down; bring down; down

【击跑员】 jīpǎoyuán 〈*Baseball*〉 batter-runner

【击破】 jīpò break up; destroy; rout

【击球棒】 jīqiúbàng 〈*Baseball*〉 bat

【击球员】 jīqiúyuán 〈*Baseball*〉 batter; hitter

【击球员区】 jīqiúyuánqū 〈*Baseball*〉 batter's position

【击伤】 jīshāng wound; injure (a person); damage (a plane, etc.)

【击退】 jītuì beat back; repel; repulse

【击一猛掌】 jīyīměngzhǎng give sb. a shove; give a sharp warning

【击中】 jīzhòng hit: ～要害 hit sb's vital point

鸡[鷄、雞] (jī) **1.**(家禽) chicken ‖ 公鸡 cock, rooster / 母鸡 hen / 小鸡 chick / 统称 brood **2.**(指街头妓女) streetwalker

【鸡雏】 jīchú chick

【鸡蛋】 jīdàn (hen's) egg

【鸡蛋里挑骨头】 jīdàn·li tiāo gǔ·tou look for a bone in an egg; look for a flaw where there is none; find fault; nitpick

【鸡飞蛋打】 jīfēi-dàndǎ the hen has flown away and the eggs in the coop are broken; all is lost

【鸡冠】 jīguān cockscomb; pea comb

【鸡冠花】 jīguānhuā 〈*Bot.*〉 cockscomb

【鸡奸】 jījiān sodomy; buggery; sodomize (v.)

【鸡毛】 jīmáo chicken feather

【鸡毛掸子】 jīmáo dǎn·zi feather duster

【鸡毛蒜皮】 jīmáo-suànpí chicken feathers and garlic skins; trifles; trivialities

【鸡皮疙瘩】 jīpí gē·da gooseflesh; goose skin

【鸡犬不宁】 jīquǎn-bùníng even fowls and dogs are not left in peace; general turmoil

【鸡肉】 jīròu chicken (as food)

【鸡舍】 jīshè chicken coop

【鸡食】 jīshí chicken feed

【鸡汤】 jītāng chicken broth

【鸡腿】 jītuǐ drumstick

【鸡尾酒】 jīwěijiǔ cocktail

【鸡尾酒会】 jīwěi jiǔhuì cocktail party

【鸡瘟】 jīwēn chicken pest; fowl plague; fowl pest

【鸡窝】 jīwō chicken coop; henhouse; roost

【鸡心】 jīxīn **1.**(指形状) heart-shaped **2.**(首饰) a heart-shaped pendant

【鸡心领】 jīxīnlǐng V-neck

【鸡胸】 jīxiōng 〈*Med.*〉 pigeon breast; chicken breast

【鸡眼】 jīyǎn 〈*Med.*〉 corn; clavus

【鸡爪】 jīzhuǎ shank

奇 (jī) odd (number)
(另见"奇"qí)

【奇数】 jīshù odd number; uneven number

犄 (jī)

【犄角】 jījiǎo (角;角落) corner: 桌子～ the corner of a table

【犄角】 jī·jiao (动物的角) horn: 牛～ ox horn

畸 (jī) **1.**(偏) lopsided; unbalanced **2.**(不正常;不规则) irregular; abnormal

【畸变】 jībiàn 1.（不正常）aberration 2.（失真）distortion
【畸胎】 jītāi monster; teratism
【畸形】 jīxíng 1.〈*Med.*〉deformity; malformation 2.（不正常）lopsided; unbalanced; abnormal

唧（jī） spurt; squirt

【唧唧】 jījī （形容虫叫声）chirp
【唧哝】 jī·nong talk in a low voice; whisper
【唧筒】 jītǒng pump

积［積］（jī） 1.（积累）amass; store up; accumulate 2.（积累下来的）age-old; long-standing; long-pending 3.〈*Chin. Med.*〉indigestion 4.〈*Math.*〉product

【积案】 jī'àn a long-pending case
【积弊】 jībì long-standing abuse; age-old malpractice
【积储】 jīchǔ store up
【积存】 jīcún store up; lay up; stockpile
【积德】 jīdé accumulate virtue
【积淀】 jīdiàn accumulation and waiting
【积肥】 jīféi collect manure; farmyard manure; store compost
【积分】 jīfēn 〈*Math.*〉integral（符号为 ∫ ）
【积分学】 jīfēnxué 〈*Math.*〉integral calculus
【积极】 jījí 1.（正面的）positive: 调动～因素 mobilize positive factors 2.（热心的）active; energetic; vigorous: ～参加企业管理 take an active part in the management of one's own enterprises
【积极分子】 jījí fènzǐ activist; enthusiast
【积久】 jījiǔ accumulate in the course of time
【积聚】 jījù gather; accumulate; build up: ～力量 build up strength
【积劳成疾】 jīláo-chéngjí break down from constant overwork; fall sick from overwork
【积累】 jīlěi accumulate: ～资金 accumulate funds / 妥善处理～与消费的关系 determine the correct ratio of consumption to accumulation
【积木】 jīmù building blocks; toy bricks
【积年】 jīnián 〈*written*〉for many years
【积欠】 jīqiàn 1.（历次欠下）have one's debts piling up 2.（所积下的亏欠）outstanding debts; arrears: ～股利 dividends in arrear
【积少成多】 jīshǎo-chéngduō many a little makes a mickle; a penny saved is a penny earned
【积习】 jīxí old habit; long-standing practice: ～难改。A settled practice is hard to reform.
【积蓄】 jīxù 1.（储蓄）put aside; save; accumulate 2.（存款）savings: 辛苦得来的～ hard-earned savings / ～一笔钱 save a sum of money
【积雪】 jīxuě accumulated snow; accumulation of snow; snows
【积压】 jīyā keep long in stock; overstock
【积压商品】 jīyā shāngpǐn goods kept too long in stock; overstocked merchandise
【积雨云】 jīyǔyún 〈*Meteorol.*〉cumulonimbus
【积怨】 jīyuàn accumulated rancor
【积云】 jīyún 〈*Meteorol.*〉cumulus
【积重难返】 jīzhòng-nánfǎn bad old practices die hard; old habits are difficult to get rid of

基（jī） 1.（基础）base; foundation 2.（基本的）basic; key; primary; cardinal 3.〈*Chem.*〉radical; base; group: 烃～ hydroxyl group

【基本】 jīběn 1.（根本的）basic; fundamental: ～国策 the country's basic policies / ～规律 basic law 2.（主要的）main; essential: ～国情 fundamental reality / ～色调 key color / ～特征 essential features 3.（基础的）elementary; rudimentary: ～知识 elementary knowledge 4.（大体上）basically; in the main; on the whole; by and large
【基本单位】 jīběn dānwèi fundamental unit
【基本法】 jīběnfǎ basic law
【基本工资】 jīběn gōngzī basic wage; basic salary
【基本功】 jīběngōng basic training; basic skill; essential technique: 苦练～ practice hard in basic skill
【基本国策】 jīběn guócè basic state policy
【基本建设】 jīběn jiànshè capital construction
【基本建设投资】 jīběn jiànshè tóuzī investment in capital construction
【基本权利】 jīběn quánlì fundamental rights
【基本上】 jīběn·shang 1.（主要）mainly 2.（大体上）on the whole; in the main
【基层】 jīcéng 1.（各种组织的最底一层）ba-

sic level; primary level 2.（最低层组织）grass-roots unit：深入～ go down to the grass-roots unit

【基层单位】 jīcéng dānwèi basic unit

【基层干部】 jīcéng gànbù cadre at the basic level

【基层领导】 jīcéng lǐngdǎo basic-level leadership

【基层组织】 jīcéng zhǔzhī primary organization

【基础】 jīchǔ 1.（根本，起点）foundation; base; basis：互利～ mutually beneficial basis / 经济～ economic base; economic basis / 契约～ contract basis / 物质～ material base 2.（基本的）fundamental; primary; basic：～工业 basic industry

【基础产业】 jīchǔ chǎnyè basic industry

【基础代谢】 jīchǔ dàixiè 〈*Biol.*〉 basal metabolism

【基础科学】 jīchǔ kēxué basic science

【基础课】 jīchǔkè basic courses

【基础设施】 jīchǔ shèshī infrastructural facilities; basic infrastructure; infrastructure

【基地】 jīdì base：海军～ naval base / 空军～ air base / 导弹～ missile base

【基点】 jīdiǎn 1.（基础）basic point; starting point; center 2.〈*Surveying*〉 base point (BP)

【基调】 jīdiào 1.〈*Music*〉 fundamental key; main key 2.（主要精神）keynote

【基督】 jīdū 〈*Relig.*〉 Christ

【基督教】 jīdūjiào Christianity; the Christian religion

【基督徒】 jīdútú Christian

【基干】 jīgàn backbone; hard core

【基价】 jījià base price

【基建】 jījiàn capital construction

【基建项目】 jījiàn xiàngmù capital project

【基金】 jījīn fund; foundation; pool：教育～ education fund / 建立～ establish a pool

【基金会】 jījīnhuì foundation

【基诺族】 Jīnuòzú Jino（中国少数民族，主要分布在云南）

【基期】 jīqī 〈*Statistics*〉 base period

【基石】 jīshí foundation stone; cornerstone

【基数】 jīshù 1.〈*Math.*〉 cardinal number 2.〈*Statistics*〉 base

【基数词】 jīshùcí 〈*Math.*〉 cardinal number

【基态】 jītài 〈*Physics*〉 ground state

【基体】 jītǐ matrix

【基线】 jīxiàn 〈*Surveying*〉 datum line; base line

【基因】 jīyīn 〈*Biol.*〉 gene

【基因工程】 jīyīn gōngchéng genetic engineering

【基于】 jīyú because of; in view of; on account of

【基质】 jīzhì matrix; substrate

【基准】 jīzhǔn 1.〈*Surveying*〉 datum 2.（标准）standard; criterion

箕（jī） 1.（撮垃圾的簸箕）dustpan 2.（簸粮食的簸箕）winnowing basket 3.（一种指纹）loop

【箕斗】 jīdǒu 1.〈*Mineral.*〉 skip 2.（指纹）fingerprint; loops and whorls

稽（jī）1.（考核）check; examine; investigate 2.（停留）delay; procrastinate

【稽查】 jīchá 1.（检查）check; inspect 2.（检查人员）inspector; customs officer

【稽核】 jīhé check; examine; audit

【稽考】 jīkǎo 〈*written*〉 ascertain; verify

【稽留】 jīliú 〈*written*〉 delay; detain

缉（jī） seize; arrest

【缉捕】 jībǔ seize; arrest

【缉捕人员】 jībǔ rényuán hounds of law

【缉拿】 jīná seize; arrest; apprehend：～归案 bring (a criminal) to justice

【缉私】 jīsī seize smugglers; smuggled goods; suppress smuggling; search for smuggler

【缉私船】 jīsīchuán anti-smuggling patrol boat

【缉私人员】 jīsī rényuán anti-contraband personnel

跻［**躋**］（jī） ascend; mount

【跻身】 jīshēn ascend; mount

激（jī） 1.（水向上涌）wash; surge; dash 2.（冷水刺激得病）fall ill from getting wet：他被雨～着了。He caught a chill from getting in the rain. 3.（使激动）arouse; stimulate; excite：～起生产热潮 arouse a great upsurge in production 4.（急剧）sharp; fierce; violent

【激昂】 jī'áng roused; aroused; excited and

indignant; be emotionally wrought up: 情绪～ sb's feeling is aroused
【激变】 jībiàn violent change; cataclysm
【激荡】 jīdàng agitate; surge; rage
【激动】 jīdòng 1.(使冲动) excite; stir; agitate 2.(令人激动的) exciting; stirring; inspiring
【激发】 jīfā 1.(使奋发) arouse; stimulate; set off; stir up: ～学生的学习积极性 encourage students to display more initiative in study 2.〈*Physics*〉 excitation
【激奋】 jīfèn be roused to action; be stirred into activity
【激愤】 jīfèn wrathful; indignant; enraged
【激光】 jīguāng 〈*Physics*〉 laser
【激光报警器】 jīguāng bàojǐngqì laser avoidance device
【激光唱机】 jīguāng chàngjī compact disc player
【激光唱片】 jīguāng chàngpiān compact disc; CD
【激光视盘】 jīguāng shìpán laser disc; LD
【激光印字机】 jīguāng yìnzìjī laser printer; laser-jet printer
【激化】 jīhuà intensify; sharpen; become acute; intensification (n.): 矛盾的～ intensification of contradictions
【激活】 jīhuó activate; activation (n.)
【激将】 jījiàng prod sb. into action; goad sb. into action
【激将法】 jījiàngfǎ prodding sb. into action; goading sb. into action
【激进】 jījìn radical
【激进分子】 jījìn fènzǐ radicals
【激进派】 jījìnpài radicals
【激剧】 jījù 1.(激烈) intense; sharp; fierce; violent; acute 2.(急剧) rapid; sharp; sudden
【激励】 jīlì 1.(鼓励) encourage; impel; urge; inspire: ～士气 give a boost to the morale of the army 2.〈*Electr.*〉 excitation; drive
【激烈】 jīliè 1.(剧烈) intense; sharp; fierce; violent; acute: ～的竞争 keen competition 2.(激奋) be roused to action; be stirred into activity
【激流】 jīliú torrent; rapids; turbulent current: 闯过～ shoot the rapids
【激怒】 jīnù enrage; infuriate; exasperate: ～某人 provoke sb. to anger
【激起】 jīqǐ arouse; evoke; stir up
【激切】 jīqiè 〈*written*〉 impassioned; vehement
【激情】 jīqíng intense emotion; fervor; passion; enthusiasm: 满怀～ be filled with enthusiasm
【激素】 jīsù hormone; hormonal (adj.): 性～ sex hormone
【激素取代疗法】 jīsù qǔdài liáofǎ 〈*Med.*〉 HRT, hormone replacement therapy
【激于义愤】 jīyúyìfèn be stirred by righteous indignation
【激越】 jīyuè intense; vehement; loud and strong
【激增】 jīzēng increase sharply; soar; shoot up; rapid growth
【激战】 jīzhàn fierce fighting; fierce battle; pitched battle: ～竟日 a bitter battle was fought the whole of the day

羁［覊］(jī) 1.(马笼头) bridle; headstall 2.(拘束) control; restrain 3.(停留) stay; delay; detain
【羁绊】 jībàn 〈*written*〉 trammels; fetters; yoke: 摆脱…的～ shake off the yoke of
【羁留】 jīliú 1.(在外地停留) stay; stop over: 短期～哈尔滨 short sojourn at Harbin 2.(拘留) keep in custody; detain
【羁押】 jīyā 〈*written*〉 detain; take into custody

及 (jí) 1.(达到) reach; come up to: 力所能～ within one's ability 2.(赶上) in time for 3.〈*conj.*〉 and
【及格】 jígé pass: 考试～ pass an examination / 考核～ pass a test
【及格赛】 jígésài qualifying event; qualifying trials
【及龄】 jílíng reach the required age: ～儿童 children reaching the required age
【及时】 jíshí 1.(正赶上) timely; in time; seasonable: ～的举措 timely measures 2.(立即) promptly; without delay: 要～治疗 need prompt medical treatment
【及时雨】 jíshíyǔ a timely rain
【及早】 jízǎo at an early date; as soon as possible; before it is too late: ～做好准备 be

prepared as soon as possible

【及至】 jízhì 〈*conj.*〉 up to; until

岌 (jí)

【岌岌可危】 jíjí-kěwēi in imminent danger; in precarious situation

汲 (jí) draw (water)

【汲取】 jíqǔ draw; derive

级 (jí) 1.(等级) level; rank; grade: 高～干部 cadres of higher rank 2.(年级) course; grade; class; form: 留～ repeat the year's work; stay down / 升～ promoted to a higher grade 3.(台阶) step: 拾～而上 climb the steps 4.〈*classifier*〉 step; stage 5.〈*Gram.*〉 degree

【级别】 jíbié rank; level; grade; scale

【级差】 jíchā differential; graded

【级间】 jíjiān interstage

【级数】 jíshù 〈*Math.*〉 progression; series

极[極] (jí) 1.(顶点) the utmost point; extreme; pole: 两～分化 polarize; polarization (n.) 2.(地极) pole; polar (adj.): 北～ the North Pole / 南～ the South Pole 3.(电极, 磁极) pole; polar (adj.): 正～ positive pole / 负～ negative pole 4.(最) extremely; exceedingly; utmost

【极大】 jídà maximum

【极地】 jídì polar region

【极地航空】 jídì hángkōng polar aviation

【极点】 jídiǎn the limit; the extreme; the utmost: 混乱到了～ in a state of utmost confusion

【极度】 jídù extreme; exceeding; to the utmost: ～疲劳 be extremely tired

【极端】 jíduān 1.(顶点) extreme: 走～ go to extremes 2.(达到极点的) extreme; exceeding: ～愚蠢 be exceedingly foolish

【极而言之】 jí'éryánzhī talk in extreme terms

【极光】 jíguāng 〈*Astron.*〉 aurora; polar lights

【极乐鸟】 jílèniǎo bird of paradise

【极乐世界】 jílè shìjiè 〈*Buddhism*〉 Sukhavati; Pure Land

【极力】 jílì do one's utmost; spare no effort

【极目】 jímù look as far as the eye can see

【极品】 jípǐn highest grade; best quality

【极其】 jíqí 〈*adv.*〉 most; extremely; exceedingly

【极圈】 jíquān 〈*Geog.*〉 polar circle: 北～ the Arctic Circle

【极权】 jíquán be totalitarian

【极权主义】 jíquán zhǔyì totalitarianism; totalitarian (adj.) ‖ 极权主义者 totalitarian

【极盛】 jíshèng heyday; zenith; acme: ～时期 golden age; prime

【极限】 jíxiàn 1.(最高限) the limit; the maximum; the ultimate 2.〈*Math.*〉 limit

【极限值】 jíxiànzhí limit value

【极小】 jíxiǎo minimum

【极刑】 jíxíng capital punishment; the death penalty; extreme penalty: 处以～ sentence to capital punishment

【极右】 jíyòu ultra-Right

【极左】 jízuǒ ultra-Left

吉 (jí) lucky; auspicious; propitious

【吉卜赛人】 Jíbǔsàirén Gypsy

【吉兰泰】 Jílántài 〈place〉 Jartai

【吉利】 jílì lucky; auspicious; propitious

【吉普车】 jípǔchē jeep: 北京～ Beijing Jeep

【吉期】 jíqī wedding day; lucky day

【吉庆】 jíqìng auspicious; propitious; happy

【吉人天相】 jírén-tiānxiàng heaven helps a good man

【吉日】 jírì lucky date

【吉他】【吉它】 jítā 〈*Music*〉 guitar: 声学～ acoustic guitar / 电～ electric guitar / 弹～ play the guitar / 信手拨弄～ strum the guitar

【吉他手】 jítāshǒu 〈*Music*〉 guitarist: 古典～ a classical guitarist / 民谣～ a folk guitarist / 摇滚～ a rock guitarist

【吉他音箱】 jítā yīnxiāng amp; amplifier

【吉屋招租】 jíwū zhāozū house for rent; house to let

【吉祥】 jíxiáng lucky; auspicious; propitious

【吉祥如意】 jíxiáng-rúyì good fortune as one wishes

【吉祥物】 jíxiángwù mascot: 把一个玩具熊作为他的～ adopt a teddy bear as his mascot

【吉星】 jíxīng the lucky star

【吉星高照】 jíxīng-gāozhào the lucky star shines bright

【吉凶】 jíxiōng good or ill luck

【吉凶未卜】 jíxiōng-wèibǔ cannot predict the outcome, good or bad; no one knows how it will turn out

【吉兆】 jízhào good omen; propitious sign

佶 (jí)

【佶屈聱牙】 jíqū-áoyá in a lumpish style; difficult to read or comprehend

诘 (jí)
(另见"诘"jié)

【诘屈聱牙】 jíqū áoyá in a lumpish style; difficult to read or comprehend

即 (jí) 1.(靠近) approach; reach; be near 2.(当时) at present; in immediate future 3.(对此) prompted by the occasion 4.(就是) be; mean; namely 5.(就便) promptly; at once; immediately; in no time 6.(即使) even; even if

【即便】 jíbiàn even; even if; even though

【即插即用】 jíchā-jíyòng 〈*Computer*〉 plug and play; PNP

【即或】 jíhuò 见"即便"

【即将】 jíjiāng be about to; be on the point of; soon

【即景生情】 jíjǐng-shēngqíng the scene brings back memories; the scene touches a chord in one's heart

【即刻】 jíkè at once; immediately; instantly; right away

【即令】 jílìng even; even if; even though

【即期】 jíqī 〈*Econ.*〉 immediate; spot: ～交货 deliver goods on spot

【即期付现】 jíqī fùxiàn 〈*Econ.*〉 immediate cash payment

【即期汇票】 jíqī huìpiào 〈*Econ.*〉 demand bill; demand draft

【即期交货】 jíqī jiāohuò 〈*Econ.*〉 delivery on spot

【即期票据】 jíqī piàojù 〈*Econ.*〉 demand note; not at sight

【即日】 jírì 1.(当天) this or that very day 2.(近日) within the next few days

【即时】 jíshí immediately; forthwith

【即时反馈】 jíshí fǎnkuì immediate feedback

【即时付款】 jíshí fùkuǎn immediate payment

【即时记忆】 jíshí jìyì immediate memory

【即时交货】 jíshí jiāohuò prompt delivery

【即食】 jíshí instant

【即使】 jíshǐ even; even if; even though: ～乘出租车，你也得误机。Even if you take a taxi, you'll still miss your flight.

【即位】 jíwèi ascend the throne

【即席】 jíxí 1.(未准备的) impromptu; offhand; extemporaneous: ～发言 give an offhand talk; give a talk offhand; make an extemporaneous speech 2.(入席) take one's seat

【即兴】 jíxìng impromptu; extemporaneous

【即兴表演】 jíxìng biǎoyǎn improvisation

【即兴购物】 jíxìng gòuwù impulse buying

亟 (jí) 〈*written*〉 urgently; anxiously; earnestly: ～待解决 have to be settled urgently; need prompt solution

急 (jí) 1.(着急) impatient; anxious: ～着要答复 be impatient for a reply 2.(使着急) worry: 什么事使你着～? What's worrying you? 3.(急躁) irritated; annoyed; nettled 4.(急促) fast; rapid; violent 5.(急迫；紧急) urgent; pressing 6.(急事) urgency; emergency: 当务之～ the urgent task at present; the urgent matter confronting us / 告～ appeal for emergency help 7.(赶快帮助) be eager to help

【急病】 jíbìng acute disease

【急不可待】 jíbùkědài too impatient to wait; extremely anxious

【急驰而过】 jíchí'érguò whirl away

【急促】 jícù 1.(快而短促) hurried; rapid: 呼吸～ be short of breath 2.(时间短促) short; pressing

【急电】 jídiàn urgent telegram; urgent cable

【急风暴雨】 jífēng-bàoyǔ violent storm; hurricane

【急功近利】 jígōng-jìnlì too eager to be successful that one sees only the immediate advantages

【急件】 jíjiàn urgent document; urgent dispatch

【急进】 jíjìn radical

【急救】 jíjiù first aid; emergency treatment: 你在学校学过～吗? Did you learn any first aid at school?

【急救车】 jíjiùchē emergency ambulance; breakdown van

【急救人员】 jíjiù rényuán first-aider
【急救医学】 jíjiù yīxué emergency medicine
【急救站】 jíjiùzhàn first-aid station
【急剧】 jíjù rapid; sharp; sudden: ～上涨 steep rise; sharp rise / ～增加 rapid increase
【急遽】 jíjù rapid; sharp; sudden
【急流】 jíliú 1.(指水流) torrent; rapid stream; rapids 2.〈*Meteorol.*〉 jet stream; jet flow
【急流勇进】 jíliú-yǒngjìn forge ahead against a swift current; press on in the teeth of difficulties
【急流勇退】 jíliú-yǒngtuì resolutely retire at the height of one's official career
【急忙】 jímáng in a hurry; in haste; hurriedly; hastily
【急迫】 jípò urgent; pressing; imperative
【急起直追】 jíqǐ-zhízhuī rouse oneself to catch up; make amends while there is yet time
【急切】 jíqiè 1.(迫切) eager; impatient; urgent; imperative 2.(仓猝) in a hurry; in haste
【急如星火】 jírúxīnghuǒ extremely pressing; posthaste; most urgent; most hurriedly
【急刹车】 jíshāchē 1.(紧急制动) slam the brakes on 2.(突然中止) bring to a halt
【急速】 jísù very fast; at high speed; rapidly
【急弯】 jíwān 1.(陡弯) sharp turn 2.(急转弯) turn suddenly: 汽车拐了个～。The car turned abruptly. 3.〈*Geog.*〉 elbow
【急务】 jíwù urgent task
【急行军】 jíxíngjūn rapid march
【急性】 jíxìng 〈*Med.*〉 acute: ～阑尾炎 acute appendicitis
【急性病】 jíxìngbìng 1.〈*Med.*〉 acute disease 2.(急于求成) impetuosity: 犯～ become impetuous
【急性通货膨胀】 jíxìng tōnghuò péngzhàng galloping inflation
【急性子】 jíxìng·zi 1.(指性情) of impatient disposition; impetuous 2.(指人) an impetuous person
【急需】 jíxū 1.(迫切需要) be badly in need of 2.(紧急需要) urgent need: 提供～的资金 provide much-needed funds
【急用】 jíyòng urgent need
【急于】 jíyú eager; anxious; impatient: ～求成 be impatient for success
【急躁】 jízào 1.(好激动烦躁) irritable; irascible 2.(性急) impetuous; rash; impatient
【急诊】 jízhěn emergency call; emergency treatment: 挂～ register for emergency treatment
【急诊室】 jízhěnshì emergency ward
【急中生智】 jízhōng-shēngzhì suddenly hit upon a way out of a predicament; show resourcefulness in an emergency
【急转弯】 jízhǎnwān 1.(急剧转弯) take a sudden turn 2.(大转变) make a radical change
【急转直下】 jízhuǎn-zhíxià take a sudden turn and then develop rapidly

疾 (jí) 1.(疾病) disease; sickness; illness 2.(疾苦) suffering; pain; difficulty 3.(疾恨) hate; abhor 4.(疾速) fast; quick: ～驶 whirl away / ～走 walk fast
【疾病】 jíbìng disease; illness
【疾驰】 jíchí run quickly; run fast
【疾恶如仇】 jí'è-rúchóu hate evil as much as one hates an enemy; hate evil like an enemy
【疾风】 jífēng 1.(强劲的风) strong wind; gale 2.〈*Meteorol.*〉(指7级风) moderate gale
【疾风知劲草】 jífēng zhī jìngcǎo the force of the wind tests the strength of the grass; strength of character is tested in a crisis
【疾苦】 jíkǔ sufferings; hardships; difficulties: 关心人民的～ be concerned about the sufferings of the people
【疾驶】 jíshǐ speed: ～而过 speed past / 巡逻艇破浪～。The patrol boat sped across the waves.
【疾言厉色】 jíyán-lìsè harsh words and stern looks; sudden outpourings and fierce looks

蒺 (jí)
【蒺藜】 jí·lí 〈*Bot.*〉 puncture vine

嫉 (jí) 1.(妒忌) be jealous; be envious 2.(憎恨) hate
【嫉妒】 jídù be jealous of; be envious of; envy (n.)
【嫉恨】 jíhèn envy and hate; hate out of jealousy

嵴 (jí) ridge (of a mountain or hill)

瘠(jí) 1.(瘦弱) lean; thin and weak 2.(瘠薄) barren; poor; lean

【瘠薄】 jíbó barren; unproductive

【瘠田】 jítián barren land

棘(jí) 1.(酸枣) sour jujube 2.(荆棘) thorn bushes; brambles 3.(刺) spine; spina

【棘刺】 jící quill

【棘轮】 jílún 〈*Mech*.〉 ratchet

【棘手】 jíshǒu thorny; troublesome; knotty

【棘爪】 jízhuǎ 〈*Mech*.〉 pawl; detent; pallet

集(jí) 1.(聚集) gather; collect; assemble 2.(集市) country fair; market 3.(集子) collection; anthology: 地图~ atlas / 歌曲~ song book / 选~ selected works 4.(书、影片的部分) volume; part: 上~ first part; part one / 下~ second part; part two 5.〈*Math*.〉 set

【集成电路】 jíchéng diànlù 〈*Electr*.〉 integrated circuit

【集大成】 jídàchéng be a comprehensive expression of; be an agglomeration of; epitomize

【集电杆】 jídiàngān current collector

【集合】 jíhé 1.(聚集) gather; assemble; muster; call together 2.(口令) Fall in!

【集会】 jíhuì assembly; rally; gathering; meeting

【集结】 jíjié mass; concentrate; build up: ~兵力 concentrate armed forces

【集锦】 jíjǐn a collection of choice specimens: 图片~ collection of choice pictures

【集聚】 jíjù gather; collect; assemble

【集控】 jíkòng centralized control

【集贸市场】 jímào shìchǎng fair trade market

【集权】 jíquán centralization of state power: 中央~ centralized / 个人过分~ over-concentration of power in the hands of individuals

【集日】 jírì market day

【集散地】 jísàndì collecting and distributing center; distributing center

【集少成多】 jíshǎo-chéngduō many a little makes a mickle

【集市】 jíshì country fair; market

【集市贸易】 jíshì màoyì country fair trade; village fair trade

【集市贸易价】 jíshì màoyìjià rural fair price

【集思广益】 jísī-guǎngyì draw on collective wisdom and absorb all useful ideas; pool the wisdom of the masses

【集体】 jítǐ collective: 有偿转让给~或个人 be sold to collectives or individuals

【集体工作】 jítǐ gōngzuò group work

【集体观念】 jítǐ guānniàn collective spirit

【集体化】 jítǐhuà collectivize; collectivization (n.)

【集体婚礼】 jítǐ hūnlǐ collective wedding ceremony

【集体经济】 jítǐ jīngjì collective economy

【集体领导】 jítǐ lǐngdǎo collective leadership: 实行~ exercise collective leadership

【集体粘合性】 jítǐ niánhéxìng group cohesive

【集体农场】 jítǐ nóngchǎng collective farm

【集体企业】 jítǐ qǐyè collective enterprise

【集体所有制】 jítǐ suǒyǒuzhì collective ownership

【集体舞】 jítǐwǔ group dancing

【集体照】 jítǐzhào group picture

【集体主义】 jítǐ zhǔyì collectivism

【集团】 jítuán group; consortium; circle; bloc: 军事~ a military group / ~成员间的分歧 dispute among consortium members

【集团犯罪】 jítuán fànzuì organized crime

【集团军】 jítuánjūn group army

【集训】 jíxùn assemble for training

【集训队】 jíxùnduì 〈*Sports*〉 team of athletes in training

【集邮】 jíyóu 1.(指此项活动) stamp collecting; philately 2.(指行为) collect stamps

【集邮爱好者】 jíyóu àihàozhě stamp collector; philatelist

【集邮册】 jíyóucè stamp-album

【集约经营】 jíyuē jīngyíng intensive farming

【集约农业】 jíyuē nóngyè intensive agriculture

【集镇】 jízhèn town; market town

【集中】 jízhōng concentrate; centralize; focus; amass; put together: ~精力 concentrate one's energy / ~注意力 focus one's attention on

【集中营】 jízhōngyíng concentration camp

【集注】 jízhù 1.(集中) focus 2.(集释) variorum

【集注本】 jízhùběn variorum edition

【集装箱】 jízhuāngxiāng 〈*Transport*〉 container：往～里装货 load a container

【集装箱车】 jízhuāngxiāng chē container car; container truck

【集装箱堆放场】 jízhuāngxiāng duīfàngchǎng container pool; container yard

【集装箱化】 jízhuāngxiānghuà containerize; containerization (n.)

【集装箱货轮】 jízhuāngxiāng huòlún container ship

【集装箱列车】 jízhuāngxiāng lièchē container train

【集装箱码头】 jízhuāngxiāng mǎtóu container terminal

【集装箱运输】 jízhuāngxiāng yùnshū containerized traffic

【集资】 jízī raise funds; collect money; pool resources; fund raising

【集子】 jí·zi collection; collected works; anthology

辑 (jí) **1.**(编辑) collect; compile; edit **2.**(丛书的部分) part; volume; division

【辑录】 jílù compile

【辑要】 jíyào summary; abstract

蕺 (jí)

【蕺菜】 jícài heartleaf houttuynia

籍 (jí) **1.**(书籍) book; record **2.**(籍贯) native place; home town; birthplace **3.**(国籍) nationality; citizenship：美～华人 American Chinese **4.**(组织关系) membership

【籍贯】 jíguàn the place of one's birth or origin native place：她的～是陕西。Her native place is Shaanxi.

几［幾］(jǐ) **1.**(多少) how many：今天～号？What's the date today? **2.**(几个) a few; several; some：～天 several days

(另见"几"jī)

【几番风雨】 jǐfān-fēngyǔ the devastation of a few storms and gusts

【几分】 jǐfēn a bit; somewhat; rather

【几何】 jǐhé **1.**(多少) how much; how many **2.**(几何学) geometry

【几何级数】 jǐhé jíshù geometric progression

【几何学】 jǐhéxué geometry; geometric; geometrical (adj.)

【几历沧桑】 jǐlì cāngsāng marked by vicissitudes

【几时】 jǐshí what time; when

虮［蟣］(jǐ)

【虮子】 jǐ·zi nit; the egg of a louse

麂 (jǐ) 〈*Zool.*〉 muntjac; muntjak

【麂皮】 jǐpí chamois (leather); chammy

【麂子】 jǐzi muntjac; barking deer

己 (jǐ) (自己) oneself：舍～为人 sacrifice oneself for others **2.**(自己的) one's own; personal

【己方】 jǐfāng one's own side

【己见】 jǐjiàn one's own opinion; one's own view：固执～ stick to one's own opinion; adhere to one's own view

【己所不欲，勿施于人】 jǐ suǒ bù yù, wù shī yú rén Do not do to others what you would not have them do to you. (或：Do as you would be done by.)

挤［擠］(jǐ) **1.**(拥挤) crowd; pack; cram; throng **2.**(挤开) jostle; push against **3.**(挤压) squeeze; press

【挤兑】 jǐduì a run on a bank

【挤对】 jǐ·dui force into submission

【挤眉弄眼】 jǐméi-nòngyǎn make eyes; wink

【挤奶】 jǐnǎi milk (a cow, etc.)

【挤时间】 jǐshíjiān find time; try to find time to do sth.

【挤压】 jǐyā 〈*Metall.*〉 extruding; extrusion

济［濟］(jǐ)

(另见"济"jì)

【济济】 jǐjǐ (of people) many; numerous：人才～ an abundance of capable people

【济济一堂】 jǐjǐ-yītáng gather together under the same roof

给 (jǐ) **1.**(供给) supply; provide **2.**(富裕) ample; well provided for

(另见"给"gěi)

【给排水设备】 jǐpáishuǐ shèbèi plumbing equipment

【给水】 jǐshuǐ **1.**〈*Archit.*〉 water supply **2.**〈*Mech.*〉 feed water

【给水站】 jǐshuǐzhàn water supply station

【给养】 jǐyǎng provisions; victuals; rations

【给予】 jǐyǔ 〈*written*〉 give; render; offer: ～补助 give subsidies to / ～折扣 discount granted

脊 (jǐ) 1.(脊骨) spine; backbone; vertebra 2.(脊状物) ridge: 屋～ the ridge of a roof

【脊背】 jǐbèi 1.(背) back 2.(猪肉部位) fat back 3.(牛肉部位) loin

【脊梁】 jǐ·liang back (of the human body)

【脊梁骨】 jǐ·lianggǔ backbone; spine

【脊神经】 jǐshénjīng spinal nerve

【脊髓】 jǐshuí spinal cord

【脊髓灰质炎】 jǐshuí huīzhìyán 〈*Med.*〉 polio; poliomyelitis

【脊柱】 jǐzhù spinal column; vertebral column; backbone; spine

【脊椎】 jǐzhuī vertebra

计 (jì) 1.(计算) count; compute; calculate; number 2.(仪器) meter; gauge: 体温～ clinical thermometer 3.(计策) idea; ruse; stratagem; plan: 缓兵之～ stalling tactics; stratagem to gain a respite

【计策】 jìcè stratagem; plan: 对付某人的～ stratagem for dealing with sb.

【计程表】 jìchéngbiǎo (出租汽车) taximeter

【计程仪】 jìchéngyí 〈*Naut.*〉 log

【计出万全】 jìchū-wànquán a foolproof plan or scheme

【计费单位】 jìfèi dānwèi charge unit

【计划】 jìhuà 1.(拟定的计划) plan; project; program: 五年～ five-year plan / 制定～ make a plan; draw up a plan; work out a plan 2.(做计划) map out; plan

【计划单列】 jìhuà dānliè specifically designated in the state plan

【计划单列市】 jìhuà dānlièshì city listed independently in the state plan

【计划经济】 jìhuà jīngjì planned economy

【计划生育】 jìhuà shēngyù family planning; birth control

【计划体制】 jìhuà tǐzhì planning system

【计划外怀孕】 jìhuàwài huáiyùn unplanned pregnancy

【计划外指标】 jìhuàwài zhǐbiāo plan targets

【计价】 jìjià valuation

【计价器】 jìjiàqì (出租汽车) taximeter

【计件】 jìjiàn reckon by the piece

【计件工资】 jìjiàn gōngzī piece rate wage

【计件工资制】 jìjiàn gōngzīzhì piecework system

【计较】 jìjiào 1.(在乎) bother about; haggle over; fuss about: 不～个人得失 not to care personal loss 2.(争论) argue; dispute: 我现在不同你～。I won't dispute with you now. 3.(打算) think over; plan: 日后再作～。Let's think it over later.

【计量】 jìliàng measure; calculate; estimate

【计谋】 jìmóu scheme; stratagem; plot

【计日工资】 jìrì gōngzī daily wage

【计时】 jìshí reckon by time

【计时工资】 jìshí gōngzī payment by the hour; time wage

【计时工资制】 jìshí gōngzīzhì time-rate wage system

【计时器】 jìshíqì timer; hour-counter; chronometer

【计时赛】 jìshísài (自行车项目) time trial

【计时学】 jìshíxué chronometry

【计时员】 jìshíyuán 〈*Sports*〉 timekeeper

【计数】 jìshù count

【计数器】 jìshùqì counter

【计算】 jìsuàn 1.(求未知数) count; compute; calculate; reckon: ～生产成本 calculate the cost of production 2.(考虑;筹划) consideration; planning

【计算尺】 jìsuànchǐ slide rule

【计算机】 jìsuànjī computer: 电子～ electronic computer / 个人～ personal computer (PC)

【计算机病毒】 jìsuànjī bìngdú virus; computer virus

【计算机程序】 jìsuànjī chéngxù computer program

【计算机辅助教学】 jìsuànjī fǔzhù jiàoxué 〈*Computer*〉 CAI, computer-aided instruction

【计算机辅助设计】 jìsuànjī fǔzhù shèjì 〈*Computer*〉 CAD, computer-aided design

【计算机软件】 jìsuànjī ruǎnjiàn computer software

【计算机网络】 jìsuànjī wǎngluò computer network

【计算机硬件】 jìsuànjī yìngjiàn computer

hardware

【计算机桌】 jìsuànjīzhuō typing desk

【计算器】 jìsuànqì calculator

【计算中心】 jìsuàn zhōngxīn computation center; calculating center

【计议】 jìyì deliberate; talk over; consult: 从长～ give the matter further consideration and discuss it later

记 (jì) 1. (记得) remember; bear in mind; commit to memory: 如果我没～错的话 if I remember right; if my memory serves me 2. (记下来) write down; record; jot down; take down: ～笔记 take notes / ～电话号码 jot down the telephone number 3. (记录) notes; record 4. (标记) mark; sign 5. (胎记) birthmark 6. 〈*classifier*〉 一～耳光 a slap in the face

【记仇】 jìchóu bear grudges; harbor bitter resentment

【记得】 jì·de remember; recall; call back to mind; keep in memory

【记分】 jìfēn 1. (比赛时) keep the score; record the points (in a game) 2. (在学校) register a student's marks

【记分牌】 jìfēnpái scoreboard; score indicator: 电动～ electric scoreboard

【记分员】 jìfēnyuán 〈*Sports*〉 scorer

【记功】 jìgōng cite sb. for meritorious service; record a merit

【记挂】 jìguà be concerned about; keep thinking about; miss

【记过】 jìguò record a demerit

【记号】 jì·hao mark; sign: 打～ make a mark

【记恨】 jì·hèn bear grudges

【记录】 jìlù 1. (写下来) take notes; keep the minutes; record 2. (所记录下来的材料) minutes; notes; record: 会谈～ a transcript of talks 3. (记录者) notetaker; recorder 4. (最高成绩) record: 国家～ national record / 世界～ world record / 创～ set a record; chalk up a record / 打破～ break a record / 平～ equal a record; match a record / 刷新～ improve a record

【记录片】 jìlùpiàn documentary film: 大型～ full length documentary film

【记录速度】 jìlù sùdù recording speed; writing speed

【记名】 jìmíng put down one's name; sign

【记名债券】 jìmíng zhàiquàn registered bounds

【记起】 jìqǐ recall; recollect

【记取】 jìqǔ remember; bear in mind: ～这个教训 bear firmly in mind this lesson

【记入】 jìrù post

【记时器】 jìshíqì chronoscope; timer; calculagraph

【记事】 jìshì 1. (记录事情) keep a record of events; make a memorandum 2. (记述的历史) account; record of events; chronicles

【记事本】 jìshìběn notepad

【记事儿】 jìshìr begin to remember things

【记述】 jìshù record and narrate; give an account of

【记诵】 jìsòng commit to memory and be able to recite; learn by heart

【记性】 jì·xing memory: ～好 have a good memory / ～不好 have a bad memory

【记叙】 jìxù narrate

【记叙文】 jìxùwén narration

【记忆】 jìyì 1. (想起) remember; recall 2. (记住的印象) memory: ～犹新 remain fresh in one's memory; the memory is still fresh

【记忆力】 jìyìlì the faculty of memory; memory

【记载】 jìzǎi 1. (写下来) put down in writing; record 2. (记事文章) record; account

【记账】 jìzhàng keep accounts; keep books; charge to an account

【记者】 jìzhě reporter; correspondent; newsman; journalist

【记住】 jìzhù remember; learn by heart; bear in mind; commit to memory

纪 (jì) 1. (纪律) discipline 2. (记录下来) put down in writing; record 3. (世纪) age; epoch; century

【纪检】 jìjiǎn discipline inspection

【纪录】 jìlù 同"记录"

【纪录片】 jìlùpiàn 同"记录片"

【纪律】 jìlǜ discipline: ～松弛 discipline is lax / 遵守～ keep discipline / 接受～约束 subject oneself to discipline

【纪律处分】 jìlǜ chǔfèn disciplinary award; disciplinary treatment

【纪律检查委员会】 jìlǜ jiǎnchá wěiyuánhuì commission for discipline inspection：中央～ Central Commission for Discipline Inspection

【纪年】 jìnián 1.(记年代) a way of numbering the years 2.(史书) chronological record of events; annals

【纪念】 jìniàn 1.(表示怀念) commemorate; mark 2.(纪念物) souvenir; keepsake; memento 3.(周年；纪念日) commemoration day; anniversary：10 周年～ the tenth anniversary 4.(作为纪念) commemorative

【纪念碑】 jìniànbēi monument; memorial

【纪念币】 jìniànbì commemorative coin

【纪念册】 jìniàncè autograph book; autograph album; commemorative album

【纪念馆】 jìniànguǎn memorial hall; museum in memory of：鲁迅～ the Lu Xun Museum

【纪念品】 jìniànpǐn souvenir; keepsake; memento

【纪念日】 jìniànrì commemoration day; red-letter day

【纪念塔】 jìniàntǎ memorial tower; monument

【纪念堂】 jìniàntáng memorial hall; commemoration hall; mausoleum：毛主席～ Chairman Mao's Mausoleum / 中山～ Sun Yat-sen's Memorial Hall

【纪念邮票】 jìniàn yóupiào commemorative stamp

【纪念章】 jìniànzhāng souvenir badge

【纪实】 jìshí record of actual events; on-the-spot report

【纪委】 jìwěi commission for discipline inspection

【纪行】 jìxíng travel notes; notes on a trip

【纪要】 jìyào summary of minutes; summary

【纪元】 jìyuán 1.(纪年开始) the beginning of an era 2.(时代) epoch; era

【纪传体】 jìzhuàntǐ history presented in a series of biographies

忌 (jì) 1.(忌妒) be jealous of; envy 2.(顾忌) fear; dread; scruple 3.(禁忌) avoid; shun; abstain from：婴儿～服 not to be taken by babies / ～油腻 avoid having greasy food

【忌辰】 jìchén the anniversary of the death of one's parent ...

【忌妒】 jì·du be jealous of; envy：出于～ out of jealousy

【忌讳】 jì·huì 1.(禁忌) taboo：犯～ violate a taboo; break a taboo 2.(避免) avoid as harmful; abstain from

【忌口】 jìkǒu avoid certain food; be on a diet

【忌嘴】 jìzuǐ avoid certain food; be on a diet

伎 (jì) skill; ability; trick

【伎俩】 jìliǎng trick; intrigue; maneuver; foul means：惯用的～ one's favorite trick

技 (jì) skill; ability; trick; technique

【技改资金】 jìgǎizījīn funds for technical reform

【技工】 jìgōng skilled worker; mechanic; technician

【技工学校】 jìgōng xuéxiào skilled workers' school

【技能】 jìnéng technical ability; mastery of a skill or technique：同类专业～ similar qualification

【技巧】 jìqiǎo skill; technique; craftsmanship：掌握～ master the technique of

【技巧运动】 jìqiǎo yùndòng acrobatic gymnastics; sports acrobatics; tumbling

【技师】 jìshī technician

【技术】 jìshù technology; skill; technique：科学～ science and technology / 高新～产业开发区 the development zones for industries using high and new technology

【技术操作规程】 jìshù cāozuò guīchéng technical operations

【技术成果有偿转让】 jìshù chéngguǒ yǒucháng zhuǎnràng transfer of technological achievements with compensation

【技术改造】 jìshù gǎizhào technical innovation; technical transformation; technological innovation

【技术更新】 jìshù gēngxīn technological renovation

【技术合作】 jìshù hézuò technological cooperation

【技术交流】 jìshù jiāoliú exchange of technical know-how; technical exchange

【技术经济论据】 jìshù jīngjì lùnjù feasibility report; feasibility study

【技术决策】 jìshù juécè technical solution
【技术科学】 jìshù kēxué engineering science
【技术力量】 jìshù lìliàng technical force; technical personnel
【技术密集型企业】 jìshù mìjíxíng qǐyè technology-intensive enterprise
【技术市场】 jìshù shìchǎng technological market; technical market
【技术维修站】 jìshù wéixiūzhàn maintenance depot
【技术性】 jìshùxìng technical; of a technical nature
【技术学校】 jìshù xuéxiào technical school
【技术员】 jìshùyuán technician
【技术战术讲解】 jìshù zhànshù jiǎngjiě chalk talk
【技术职称】 jìshù zhíchēng title for technical personnel
【技术指导】 jìshù zhǐdǎo 1.(技术上的指导) technological guidance; technical guidance 2.(担任指导的人) technical adviser
【技术转让】 jìshù zhuǎnràng technical transfer; transfer of technology
【技校】 jìxiào technical school
【技艺】 jìyì skill; artistry: ～超群 one's skill in mechanical arts is above the average

妓

(jì) prostitute

【妓女】 jìnǚ prostitute; harlot; whore
【妓院】 jìyuàn brothel; whorehouse

系[繫]

(jì) tie; fasten; do up; button up: ～鞋带 tie one's shoe laces
(另见"系"xì)

【系泊】 jìbó moor (a boat)
【系泊浮筒】 jìbó fútǒng mooring buoy
【系留】 jìliú moor (a balloon or airship)

际[際]

(jì) 1.(边缘或分界处) border; boundary; edge 2.(彼此之间) between; among; inter-: 夏秋之～ between summer and autumn/ 洲～导弹 intercontinental missile 3.(时候) occasion; time: 危急之～ at a critical moment 4.(正当) on the occasion of

【际遇】 jìyù 〈*written*〉 favorable or unfavorable turns in life; spells of good or bad fortune

季

(jì) 1.(季节) season: 淡～ an off season / 旺～ a busy season / 雨～ rainy season 2.(种植次数) crop: 种两～ reap two crops a year 3.(第三) third; last

【季报】 jìbào quarterly reports
【季春】 jìchūn the last month of spring; the third month of lunar calendar
【季冬】 jìdōng the last month of winter; the last month of lunar calendar
【季度】 jìdù quarter (of a year): ～预算 quarterly budget
【季风】 jìfēng 〈*Meteorol.*〉 monsoon
【季节】 jìjié season
【季节工】 jìjiégōng seasonal worker
【季节性】 jìjiéxìng seasonal
【季节性差价】 jìjiéxìng chājià seasonal variations in price
【季节性折扣】 jìjiéxìng zhékòu seasonal discount
【季军】 jìjūn 〈*Sports*〉 bronze medalist; bronze medalist
【季刊】 jìkān quarterly publication; quarterly
【季秋】 jìqiū the last month of fall; the ninth month of lunar calendar
【季夏】 jìxià the last month of summer; the sixth month of lunar calendar

剂[劑]

(jì) 1.(药剂, 制剂) preparation: 滴鼻～ nasal drops / 化学制～ a chemical preparation / 药～ a pharmaceutical preparation 2.〈*Chem.*〉 agent: 催化～ catalyst; catalytic agent 3.〈*classifier*〉(用于中药) dose

【剂量】 jìliàng 〈*Pharm.*〉 dosage; dose: 有效～ effective dose
【剂量学】 jìliàngxué dosimetry
【剂型】 jìxíng 〈*Pharm.*〉 the form of a drug

荠[薺]

(jì)

【荠菜】 jìcài 〈*Bot.*〉 shepherd's purse

济[濟]

(jì) 1.(帮助) help; aid: 扶贫～困 help those who are in difficulty 2.(渡河) cross the river 3.(有益) be of help; benefit
(另见"济"jǐ)

【济贫】 jìpín relieve the poor; help the poor

霁[霽]

(jì) 1.(放晴) clear up: 雪后初～。It is clearing up after the snow. 2.(怒气消除) calm down

鲚[鱭]

(jì) 〈*Zool.*〉 tapertail anchovy

【鲚鱼】 jìyú （凤尾鱼） tapertail anchovy

迹［跡、蹟］(jì) 1.（痕迹） mark; trace 2.（遗迹） remains; ruins; vestige 3.（形迹） an outward sign; indication

【迹象】 jìxiàng sign; indication

既(jì) 1.（已经） already 2.（既然） since; as; now that 3.（与"且""又""也"等副词连用） both ... and; as well as: ～好又便宜 both good and cheap

【既不…，又不…】 jìbù…，yòubù… neither... nor

【既成事实】 jìchéng-shìshí accomplished fact; fait accompli

【既得利益】 jìdé lìyì vested interest

【既定】 jìdìng set; fixed; established: ～目标 set objective; fixed goal

【既而】 jì'ér soon afterwards; later; subsequently

【既然】 jìrán 〈*conj.*〉 since; as; now that: ～如此 since it is so; under these circumstances

【既是】 jìshì 〈*conj.*〉 since; as; now that

【既往不咎】 jìwǎng-bùjiù forgive sb's past misdeeds; let bygones be bygones

暨(jì) 1.（和，及） and 2.（到，至） up to; till

【暨今】 jìjīn up till now

鲫(jì) crucian carp

【鲫鱼】 jìyú crucian carp

觊［覬］(jì)

【觊觎】 jìyú 〈*written*〉 covet; cast greedy eyes on; cast one's covetous eyes on

继［繼］(jì) 1.（接续） continue; succeed; follow: 日以～夜 day and night 2.（继而） then; afterwards

【继承】 jìchéng 1.〈*Law*〉 inherit: ～财产 inherit property 2.（继续前人的事业等） succeed; carry on

【继承法】 jìchéngfǎ inheritance act; law of succession

【继承权】 jìchéngquán right of succession; right of inheritance

【继承人】 jìchéngrén inheritor; heir; successor

【继电器】 jìdiànqì 〈*Electr.*〉 relay

【继而】 jì'ér 〈*adv.*〉 then; afterwards

【继父】 jìfù stepfather

【继父母】 jìfùmǔ stepparent

【继母】 jìmǔ stepmother

【继女】 jìnǚ stepdaughter

【继任】 jìrèn succeed sb. in a post

【继嗣】 jìsì 1.（过继） be adopted 2.（嗣子） adopted son

【继往开来】 jìwǎng-kāilái carry forward the cause and forge ahead into the future; carry on the past and open a way for future

【继位】 jìwèi succeed to the throne

【继续】 jìxù 1.（延续） continue; go on (with); keep on; proceed: ～有效 remain valid; remain in force 2.（某事的继续） continuation

【继续教育】 jìxù jiàoyù continuing education

【继子】 jìzǐ stepson; stepchild

【继子女】 jìzǐnǚ stepchildren

寄(jì) 1.（邮寄） send; post; mail: ～信 post a letter; mail a letter 2.（寄托） entrust; deposit; place; park 3.（依附） depend on; attach oneself to

【寄存】 jìcún deposit; leave with; check: ～行李 deposit one's luggage; check one's luggage

【寄放】 jìfàng leave with; leave in the care of

【寄费】 jìfèi postage

【寄件人】 jìjiànrén sender

【寄居】 jìjū live away from home

【寄卖】 jìmài consign for sale on commission; put up for sale in a secondhand shop

【寄卖商店】 jìmài shāngdiàn commission store; secondhand shop

【寄卖商品】 jìmài shāngpǐn consignment goods

【寄人篱下】 jìrén-líxià depend on another person for support

【寄生】 jìshēng 1.〈*Biol.*〉 parasitism 2.（靠别人生活） parasitic: ～生活 parasitic life

【寄生虫】 jìshēngchóng 1.〈*Biol.*〉 parasite 2.（过寄生生活者） anyone who lives a parasitic life

【寄售】 jìshòu consign for sale; put up for sale in a secondhand shop

【寄售人】 jìshòurén consignor

【寄售商店】 jìshòu shāngdàn commission

store; secondhand shop
【寄售商品】 jìshòu shāngpǐn consignment stock
【寄宿】 jìsù 1.(借宿) lodge; put up 2.(住校) board
【寄宿生】 jìsùshēng resident student; boarder
【寄宿学校】 jìsù xuéxiào boarding school
【寄托】 jìtuō 1.(托付) entrust to the care of sb.; leave with sb. 2.(寄予) place (hope, etc.) on; repose
【寄信】 jìxìn post a letter
【寄信人】 jìxìnrén sender
【寄养】 jìyǎng entrust one's child to the care of sb.; ask sb. to bring up one's child
【寄予】 jìyǔ 1.(寄托) place (hope, etc.) on: ～希望 place hopes on; put one's hopes on 2.(给予) show; give; express: ～关怀 show; concern for sb.
【寄语】 jìyǔ 〈*written*〉 send word: ～同窗 send verbal message to a fellow-student

祭 (jì) 1.(祭奠) hold a memorial ceremony for 2.(祭祀) offer a sacrifice to: ～祖 offer a sacrifices to an ancestor
【祭奠】 jìdiàn hold a memorial ceremony for
【祭礼】 jìlǐ 1.(祭祀仪式) sacrificial rites 2.(祭奠仪式) memorial ceremony 3.(祭品) sacrificial offerings
【祭品】 jìpǐn sacrificial offerings; oblation
【祭器】 jìqì sacrificial utensil
【祭祀】 jì·sì offer sacrifices to gods or ancestors
【祭坛】 jìtán altar; sacrificial altar
【祭文】 jìwén funeral oration; elegiac address
【祭献】 jìxiàn sacrifice

寂 (jì) 1.(寂静) quiet; still; silent 2.(寂寞) lonely; lonesome; solitary: 枯～ bored and lonely
【寂静】 jìjìng quiet; still; silent: ～无声。It is deadly still.
【寂寞】 jìmò 1.(孤单冷清) lonely; lonesome 2.(寂静) quiet; still; silent
【寂时损失】 jìshí sǔnshī dead-time loss

绩 (jì) 1.(用麻搓成线) twist hempen thread 2.(业绩,功绩;成绩) merit; accomplishment; achievement: 功～ merits and achievements; contributions

蓟 (jì) 〈*Bot.*〉 thistle

髻 (jì) hair done in a bun or coil: 挽～ wear one's hair in a bun or coil

冀 (jì) hope

jia

加 (jiā) 1.(加在一起) add; plus: 二～七等于九。Two plus seven makes nine.(或: Two and seven is nine.) 2.(增加) increase; augment 3.(添加) put in; add; append: ～点热水 add some hot water to / ～注解 add some notes
【加班】 jiābān work overtime; work an extra shift: ～工作 work overtime
【加班费】 jiābānfèi overtime pay
【加倍】 jiābèi 1.(增加一倍) double; be twice as much 2.(程度深) double; redouble: ～努力 redouble one's efforts
【加车】 jiāchē 1.(增加车辆) put on extra buses or trains 2.(增加的车辆) extra bus; extra train
【加法】 jiāfǎ 〈*Math.*〉 addition
【加格达奇】 Jiāgēdáqí 〈place〉 Jagdaqi
【加工】 jiāgōng 1.(加工过程) process: 来料～ processing of investor's raw materials; processing raw materials on client's demands / 来样～ processing according to investor's samples 2.〈*Mech.*〉 machining; working
【加工渔船】 jiāgōng yúchuán factory trawler
【加固】 jiāgù reinforce; consolidate
【加害】 jiāhài injure; do harm to
【加号】 jiāhào 〈*Math.*〉 plus sign (符号为 +)
【加护病房】 jiāhù bìngfáng intensive care unit (ICU)
【加价】 jiājià increase of price
【加紧】 jiājǐn step up; speed up; intensify
【加劲】 jiājìn put more energy into; make a greater effort
【加剧】 jiājù aggravate; intensify; exacerbate: ～紧张局势 aggravate tension
【加快】 jiākuài quicken; speed up; accelerate; pick up speed: ～国产化进程 increase

the proportion of domestic goods more quickly / ～和深化改革 accelerate and deepen the reform / ～经济体制改革 speed up the restructuring of economic systems / 使用特殊的化学物质～作物生长 use special chemical substances to accelerate the growth of crops

【加宽】 jiākuān broaden; widen

【加料】 jiāliào 1.(进料) feed in raw material 2.(用优质原料或多用原料制成的) reinforced

【加仑】 jiālún gallon (美制 = 3.785 升,英制 = 4.546 升)

【加码】 jiāmǎ 1.(指价格) raise the price of commodities; overcharge 2.(指赌注) raise the stakes in gambling 3.(指指标) raise the quota

【加盟】 jiāméng become a member of an union

【加冕】 jiāmiǎn coronation; crowning

【加冕礼】 jiāmiǎnlǐ coronation

【加农榴弹炮】 jiānóng liúdànpào gunhowitzer

【加农炮】 jiānóngpào gun; canon

【加气混凝土】 jiāqì hùnníngtǔ aerocrete

【加强】 jiāqiáng strengthen; enhance; augment; reinforce: ～企业的专业化 increase the degree of specialization of enterprises / ～社会主义法制 strengthen socialist legal system

【加热】 jiārè heat; heating (n.)

【加入】 jiārù 1.(加上) add; mix; put in 2.(参加) join; accede to: ～条约 accede to a treaty

【加塞儿】 jiāsāir 〈*collog.*〉 push into a queue out of turn; jump a queue; queue-jump

【加深】 jiāshēn deepen: ～了解 promote mutual understanding

【加湿】 jiāshī humidify; humidification: 如果房间里的空气太干燥,你可以在暖气旁放一碗水～。If the air in the room is too dry, you can put a bowl of water near the radiator to humidify it.

【加湿器】 jiāshīqì humidifier: ～使房间里的干燥空气变潮湿。The humidifier makes dry air in a room wetter.

【加数】 jiāshù 〈*Math.*〉 addend

【加速】 jiāsù quicken; speed up; accelerate; expedite: 小轿车～超过了公共汽车。The car accelerated to overtake the bus.

【加速度】 jiāsùdù 〈*Physics*〉 acceleration

【加速器】 jiāsùqì 〈*Physics*〉 accelerator

【加速踏板】 jiāsù tàbǎn 〈*Auto*〉 accelerator pedal

【加糖】 jiātáng sugaring

【加刑】 jiāxíng 〈*Law*〉 increase of penalty; infliction

【加压】 jiāyā pressurization

【加以】 jiāyǐ 1.(表示对待、处理或进行) should be; must be 2.(加上) in addition; moreover

【加意】 jiāyì with special care; with close attention: ～防范 guard with watchful care

【加油】 jiāyóu 1.(加润滑油) oil; lubricate 2.(加燃料油) refuel; oil 3.(加劲) make a greater effort; make an extra effort

【加油泵】 jiāyóubèng gasoline pump; petrol pump

【加油量】 jiāyóuliàng volume read-out

【加油枪】 jiāyóuqiāng nozzle

【加油添醋】 jiāyóu-tiāncù exaggerate embellishment to a story

【加油站】 jiāyóuzhàn service station; petrol station; gas station (AmE.); filling station (BrE.)

【加重】 jiāzhòng 1.(增加重量) make or become heavier; increase the weight of 2.(增加程度) make or become more serious; aggravate: ～负担 increase one's load

枷 (jiā) cangue

【枷锁】 jiāsuǒ yoke; chains; shackles; fetters: 摆脱…～ shake off the yoke of

痂 (jiā) scab; crust: 结～ form a scab; crust

袈 (jiā)

【袈裟】 jiāshā 〈*Buddhism*〉 kasaya

嘉 (jiā) 1.(美好) good; fine 2.(夸奖) praise; commend: 精神可～ a praiseworthy spirit

【嘉宾】 jiābīn honored guest; welcome guest

【嘉奖】 jiājiǎng 1.(奖励) commend; commendation (n.); cite; citation (n.): 传令～ cite sb. for meritorious service / 呈请～ request for commendation / 因…得到司令员～

be to receive citations from commander for sth. 2.（称赞的话，奖品）awards; praises
【嘉奖令】 jiājiǎnglìng citation
【嘉勉】 jiāmiǎn 〈*written*〉 praise and encourage

夹[夾]（jiā） 1.（夹住）press from both sides; place in between; clip; clamp; pinch：把文件～在一起 clip papers together 2.（夹杂）mix; mingle; intersperse 3.（夹子）clip; clamp; folder
（另见"夹"gā, jiá）
【夹板】 jiābǎn 1.（夹东西的木板）boards for pressing sth. or holding things together 2.〈*Med.*〉 splint
【夹背锯】 jiābèijù back saw; tenon saw
【夹层】 jiācéng mezzanine
【夹层玻璃】 jiācéng bō·li sandwich glass; double-glazed window
【夹带】 jiādài 1.（走私）carry secretly; smuggle 2.（考试作弊的材料）notes smuggled into an examination hall
【夹道】 jiādào 1.（狭窄通道）a narrow lane; passageway 2.（排在道路两旁）line both sides of the street：～欢迎 line the street to welcome; welcoming crowds lining the streets
【夹缝】 jiāfèng a narrow space between two adjacent things; crack; crevice
【夹攻】 jiāgōng attack from both sides; converging attack; pincer attack：内外～ attack from within and outside
【夹击】 jiājī converging attack; pincer attack
【夹金山】 Jiājīnshān 〈place〉 Kya'gyu Shan
【夹克】 jiākè jacket
【夹七夹八】 jiāqī-jiābā incoherent; confused; cluttered (with irrelevant remarks)
【夹钳】 jiāqián clamp
【夹生】 jiāshēng half-cooked; half-baked
【夹生饭】 jiāshēngfàn half-cooked rice
【夹馅】 jiāxiàn stuffed (pastry, etc.)
【夹心】 jiāxīn with filling
【夹心饼干】 jiāxīn bǐnggān sandwich biscuits
【夹心肉】 jiāxīnròu （猪肉部位）picnic shoulder
【夹杂】 jiāzá be mixed up with; be mingled with
【夹竹桃】 jiāzhútáo 〈*Bot.*〉 oleander
【夹注】 jiāzhù interlinear notes
【夹子】 jiā·zi 1.（夹东西的）clip; tongs; bulldog clip：头发～ hair clips 2.（夹文件、钱等的）folder; wallet

佳（jiā） good; fine; beautiful：风景绝～ beautiful scenery
【佳宾】 jiābīn distinguished guest
【佳话】 jiāhuà a deed praised far and wide; a story on everybody's lips; a much-told tale
【佳节】 jiājié happy festival time; festival
【佳期】 jiāqī wedding day; nuptial day
【佳肴】 jiāyáo delicacies
【佳音】 jiāyīn welcome news; favorable reply; good news
【佳作】 jiāzuò a fine piece of writing; an excellent work

家（jiā） 1.（家庭）family; household：养～ support one's family 2.（住所）home：回～ go home / 他的～很远。His home is far away. 3.（行家）expert; a specialist in a certain field 4.（流派）a school of thought; school：儒～ the Confucian School 5.（饲养的）domestic; tame 6.〈*politeness*〉 my：～父 my father ⑦〈*classifier*〉 三～饭馆 three restaurants
【家财】 jiācái family property
【家产】 jiāchǎn family property
【家常】 jiācháng the daily life of a family; domestic trivia
【家常便饭】 jiācháng biànfàn 1.（普通饭菜）homely food; simple meal 2.（常事）common occurrence; routine; all in the day's work; usual practice
【家常菜】 jiāchángcài home cooking
【家丑】 jiāchǒu family scandal; the skeleton in the cupboard closet
【家丑不可外扬】 jiāchǒu bùkě wàiyáng Don't wash your dirty linen in public.
【家畜】 jiāchù domestic animal; livestock
【家传】 jiāchuán handed down from the older generations of the family
【家道】 jiādào family financial situation：～小康 be comfortably off
【家底】 jiādǐ family property accumulated over a long time; resources：～厚 with substantial resources; financially solid
【家电】 jiādiàn household appliances
【家访】 jiāfǎng a visit to the parents of

school-children or young workers
【家父】 jiāfù my father
【家鸽】 jiāgē pigeon
【家和万事兴】 jiāhé wànshìxīng If the family lives in harmony, all affairs will prosper.
【家伙】 jiā·huo 1.（指工具、武器等）tool; utensil; weapon 2.（指人）fellow; guy
【家计】 jiājì 〈*written*〉family livelihood
【家家户户】 jiājiā-hùhù each and every family; every household; all households without exception
【家教】 jiājiào 1.（家庭教育）family education; upbringing 2.（家庭教师）coach; tutor; private teacher 3.（进行家庭辅导）coach：她常给一些学生～英语，好让他们应付考试。She coaches students in English, usually for exam.
【家景】 jiājǐng family financial situation; family circumstances
【家境】 jiājìng family financial situation; family circumstances：～清寒 with one's family in straitened circumstances
【家具】 jiājù furniture：组合～ unit furniture
【家眷】 jiājuàn 1.（家属）wife and children; one's family 2.（妻子）wife
【家口】 jiākǒu members of a family; the number of people in a family
【家累】 jiālěi family burden; family cares：～重 be encumbered with a large family
【家母】 jiāmǔ my mother
【家贫如洗】 jiāpín-rúxǐ utterly destitute; penniless
【家破人亡】 jiāpò-rénwáng family ruined; with one's family broken up, some gone away, some dead
【家谱】 jiāpǔ family tree; genealogical tree; genealogy
【家禽】 jiāqín domestic fowl; poultry
【家人】 jiārén one's family
【家什】 jiā·shi utensils, furniture, etc.
【家史】 jiāshǐ family history
【家室】 jiāshì 1.（家庭）wife and children; one's family 2.（妻子）wife
【家书】 jiāshū 1.（写给家里的信）a letter home 2.（家里来的信）a letter from home
【家属】 jiāshǔ family members; (family) dependents
【家私】 jiāsī family property
【家庭】 jiātíng family; household
【家庭病床】 jiātíng bìngchuáng hospital bed set up in the patient's house
【家庭出身】 jiātíng chūshēn family origin
【家庭妇女】 jiātíng fùnǚ housewife
【家庭计划】 jiātíng jìhuà （计划生育）family planning
【家庭教师】 jiātíng jiàoshī coach; tutor; private teacher
【家庭联产承包责任制】 jiātíng liánchǎn chéngbāo zérènzhì household-based system of contracted responsibility with remuneration linked to output
【家庭农场】 jiātíng nóngchǎng home farm
【家庭医生】 jiātíng yīshēng family doctor
【家庭用户】 jiātíng yònghù domestic consumer
【家庭用品】 jiātíng yòngpǐn household effects
【家徒四壁】 jiātú-sìbì have nothing but the bare walls in one's house; be utterly destitute
【家务】 jiāwù housework; household duties：料理～ do housework; do household chores
【家务女工】 jiāwù nǚgōng home help
【家乡】 jiāxiāng hometown; native place
【家小】 jiāxiǎo wife and children
【家信】 jiāxìn 1.（写给家里的信）a letter home 2.（家里来的信）a letter from home
【家兄】 jiāxiōng my brother
【家养】 jiāyǎng domestic
【家业】 jiāyè family property; property
【家蝇】 jiāyíng 〈*Zool.*〉housefly
【家用】 jiāyòng family expenses; housekeeping money
【家用电脑】 jiāyòng diànnǎo home computer
【家用电器】 jiāyòng diànqì household appliances：大件～ white goods
【家喻户晓】 jiāyù-hùxiǎo widely known; known to all; known to every family：做到～ make known to every family
【家园】 jiāyuán home; homeland：重建～ rebuild one's homeland
【家宅】 jiāzhái homestead
【家长】 jiāzhǎng 1.（一家之长）the head of a family; patriarch 2.（父母或监护人）the parent or guardian of a child
【家长会】 jiāzhǎnghuì a parents' meeting

【家长作风】 jiāzhǎng zuòfēng patriarchal behavior
【家政学】 jiāzhèngxué home economics
【家资】 jiāzī family property
【家子】 jiā·zi home
【家族】 jiāzú clan; family
镓 (jiā) 〈*Chem.*〉 gallium (元素符号 Ga)
夹[夹、袷、袷] (jiá) double-layered; lined
(另见"夹"gā, jiā)
【夹袄】 jiá'ǎo lined jacket
荚[荚] (jiá) pod: 豌豆～ pea pods / 结～ bear pods
【荚果】 jiáguǒ 〈*Bot.*〉 pod; legume
颊[頰] (jiá) cheek: 两～红润 with rosy cheeks
蛱[蛺] (jiá)
【蛱蝶】 jiádié 〈*Zool.*〉 brush-footed butterfly
戛[戞] (jiá)
【戛然而止】 jiárán ér zhǐ (of a sound) stop abruptly
甲 (jiǎ) 1.(第一) first 2.(甲壳) shell; carapace: 龟～ tortoise shell 3.(指甲) nail 4.(装甲;盔甲等) armor
【甲板】 jiǎbǎn deck
【甲虫】 jiǎchóng beetle
【甲等】 jiǎděng first-class; first-rate
【甲骨文】 jiǎgǔwén inscriptions on bones or tortoise shells
【甲基】 jiǎjī 〈*Chem.*〉 methyl
【甲基溴】 jiǎjīxiù 〈*Chem.*〉 methyl bromide
【甲级】 jiǎjí first division; first class
【甲壳】 jiǎqiào crust
【甲壳动物】 jiǎqiào dòngwù crustacean
【甲醛】 jiǎquán 〈*Chem.*〉 formaldehyde
【甲型肝炎】 jiǎxíng gānyán 〈*Med.*〉 hepatitis A
【甲鱼】 jiǎyú soft-shelled turtle
【甲状腺】 jiǎzhuàngxiàn 〈*Anat.*〉 thyroid gland
【甲子】 jiǎzǐ a cycle of sixty years
岬 (jiǎ) 1.(岬角) cape; promontory 2.(两山之间) a narrow passage between mountains
【岬角】 jiǎjiǎo cape; promontory
钾 (jiǎ) 〈*Chem.*〉 potassium (元素符号 K)
【钾肥】 jiǎféi potash fertilizer
【钾碱】 jiǎjiǎn potash
【钾缺乏】 jiǎquēfá potassium deficiency
假 (jiǎ) 1.(跟"真"相对) false; fake; sham; phoney; artificial 2.(假借) borrow; avail oneself of; make use of 3.(假如) if; suppose
(另见"假"jià)
【假案】 jiǎ'àn feigned case
【假扮】 jiǎbàn disguise oneself as; dress up as
【假充】 jiǎchōng pretend to be; pose as
【假大空】 jiǎdàkōng lying, boasting and emptiness
【假道】 jiǎdào via; by way of: ～阿布扎比去法兰克福 go to Frankfurt via Abu Dhabi
【假定】 jiǎdìng 1.(假设) suppose; assume; grant; presume 2.(科学假说) hypothesis
【假定成本】 jiǎdìng chéngběn assumed cost; hypothetical cost
【假动作】 jiǎdòngzuò fake; feint deception
【假发票】 jiǎfāpiào false invoice: 提供～ provide false invoices
【假发】 jiǎfà wig: 戴黑色～ wear a black wig
【假分数】 jiǎfēnshù 〈*Math.*〉 improper fraction
【假公济私】 jiǎgōng-jìsī use public office for private gain; practice jobbery; work for one's own ends in public affairs
【假供词】 jiǎgòngcí false statement
【假花】 jiǎhuā artificial flower
【假话】 jiǎhuà lie; falsehood: 说～ tell lies
【假借】 jiǎjiè make use of: ～…的名义 in the name of; under false pretenses
【假冒】 jiǎmào pass oneself off as; palm off: 谨防～。Beware of imitations.
【假冒签名】 jiǎmào qiānmíng forged signature
【假冒商标】 jiǎmào shāngbiāo counterfeit trademark
【假面具】 jiǎmiànjù 1.(化装面具) mask 2.(虚伪的外表) mask; false front; hypocrisy: 揭穿其～ expose sb.'s hypocrisy; tear off sb.'s mask
【假面舞会】 jiǎmiàn wǔhuì masquerade
【假名】 jiǎmíng 1.(非真名;笔名) pseudonym

2.（日语字母）kana：平～ hiragana / 片～ katakana

【假仁假义】 jiǎrén jiǎyì pretended benevolence and righteousness; hypocrisy; be a wolf in sheep's skin

【假如】 jiǎrú if; supposing; in case

【假若】 jiǎruò if; supposing; in case

【假嗓子】 jiǎsǎng·zi falsetto

【假山】 jiǎshān rockery; rockwork

【假设】 jiǎshè 1.（假定）suppose; assume; grant; presume 2.（科学假说）hypothesis 3.（虚构）invent; invention

【假使】 jiǎshǐ if; in case; in the event that

【假释】 jiǎshì 〈*Law*〉 release on parole; conditional release; free a prisoner on probation; parole provisional release

【假释犯】 jiǎshìfàn 〈*Law*〉 parolee

【假手】 jiǎshǒu do sth. through sb. else; make a cat's-paw of sb.

【假说】 jiǎshuō hypothesis

【假死】 jiǎsǐ 1.〈*Med.*〉 suspended animation 2.（装死）play dead; feign death

【假腿】 jiǎtuǐ artificial leg; leg prosthesis

【假托】 jiǎtuō 1.（推托）on the pretext of 2.（假借别人名义）under sb. else's name 3.（凭借）by means of; through the medium of

【假想】 jiǎxiǎng 1.（想像；假设）imagination; hypothesis; supposition 2.（想像的；假定的）imaginary; hypothetical; fictitious

【假想敌】 jiǎxiǎngdí imaginary enemy

【假相】 jiǎxiàng 同"假象"

【假象】 jiǎxiàng 1.（与事实不符的表面现象）false appearance：识破～ see through a false appearance 2.〈*Geog.*〉 pseudomorph

【假惺惺】 jiǎxīng·xīng hypocritically; unctuously

【假牙】 jiǎyá dental prosthesis; false tooth

【假眼】 jiǎyǎn ocular prosthesis; artificial eye

【假意】 jiǎyì 1.（指心意）unction; insincerity; hypocrisy 2.（故意装作）pretend; put on：～奉承 cheap flattery

【假造】 jiǎzào 1.（伪造）forge; counterfeit 2.（捏造）invent; fabricate

【假肢】 jiǎzhī artificial limb

【假装】 jiǎzhuāng pretend; simulate; make believe：～糊涂 pretend to be confused

价［價］（jià） 1.（价格）price：成本～ cost price / 出厂～ producer's price / 批发～ wholesale price / 市～ market price / 议～ negotiated price / 变相涨～ price to be raised in a disguised form / 擅自提～ price to be raised without permission / 削～ reduced price / 要～ ask a price 2.（价值）value：等～交换 exchange of equal values / 估～ estimate the value of 3.〈*Chem.*〉 valence

【价格】 jiàgé price：商品～ prices of commodities / 浮动～ sliding price / 零售～ retail price / 放开～ relax the control over the prices / 哄抬～ inflated prices / 批发～ wholesale price

【价格表】 jiàgébiǎo price current

【价格折扣】 jiàgé zhékòu price rebate; discount from price

【价款】 jiàkuǎn cost; money paid for sth. purchased or received for sth. sold

【价目】 jiàmù marked price; price

【价目表】 jiàmùbiǎo price list

【价签】 jiàqiān price tag

【价钱】 jià·qian price：～公道 a fair price; a decent price; a reasonable price / 讲～ bargain

【价值】 jiàzhí 1.〈*Econ.*〉 value：剩余～ surplus value 2.（值多少钱）cost; be worth：毫无～ be completely worthless 3.（重要作用）worth; value：有～的著作 valuable works / 有实用～ with practical value

【价值观念】 jiàzhí guānniàn values; concepts of value; moral standards of behavior

【价值规律】 jiàzhí guīlǜ law of value

【价值连城】 jiàzhí liánchéng worth several cities; invaluable; priceless

【价值量】 jiàzhíliàng measure of value

【价值取向】 jiàzhí qǔxiàng value orientation

【价值形态】 jiàzhí xíngtài form of value

驾（jià） 1.（套牲口）harness; draw; yoke 2.（驾驶）drive; pilot; sail：～车 drive a car / ～船 sail a boat / ～机 pilot a plane 3.〈*politeness*〉 大～ your good self

【驾临】 jiàlín 〈*politeness*〉 your arrival; your esteemed presence

【驾驶】 jiàshǐ drive; pilot; driving (n.)：I learnt to drive when I was forty. 我 40 岁时

学习驾驶(汽车)。

【驾驶舱】 jiàshǐcāng control cabin; cockpit; pilot's cockpit; pilot's compartment

【驾驶桥楼】 jiàshǐ qiáolóu 〈*Naut*.〉 navigating bridge

【驾驶学校】 jiàshǐ xuéxiào driving school

【驾驶员】 jiàshǐyuán 1.〈*Auto*〉 driver: 公共汽车～ a bus driver 2.〈*Aeron*.〉 pilot: 班机～ an airline pilot / 直升机～ a helicopter pilot

【驾驶执照】 jiàshǐ zhízhào driver's license (AmE.); driving licence (BrE.); driver's licence (AuE.)

【驾校】 jiàxiào driving school

【驾驭】 jiàyù 1.(赶车,使马) drive 2.(控制) control; master; dominate

【驾辕】 jiàyuán pull a cart or carriage from between the shafts; be hitched up

架 (jià) 1.(架子) frame; rack; shelf; stand 2.(支承) put up; erect 3.(招架) fend off; ward off; withstand 4.(支持) support; prop; help 5.(绑架) kidnap; take sb. away forcibly 6.(殴打;争吵) fight; quarrel

【架次】 jiàcì sortie: 飞行 20 个～ fly twenty sorties

【架构】 jiàgòu 1.(构筑) build; construct 2.(框架) framework 3.(结构) structure; construction

【架空】 jiàkōng 1.(离地) built on stilts; overhead; aerial 2.(没有基础) impracticable; unpractical 3.(使徒具虚名) make sb. a mere figurehead; render unfeasible

【架空索道】 jiàkōng suǒdào 〈*Transport*〉 cableway

【架空线】 jiàkōngxiàn 〈*Transport*〉 overhead wires

【架桥】 jiàqiáo bridge; build a bridge; bridging (n.): 一千四百年前,在河上用石块架起了桥。The river had been bridged with slabs of rock 1,400 years ago.

【架设】 jiàshè set up; erect: ～电话线 put up telephone lines

【架势】 jià·shi 1.(姿势;姿态) posture; stance; manner 2.(势头) circumstances

【架线工】 jiàxiàngōng lineman

【架子】 jià·zi 1.(放置物品的架子) frame; stand; rack; shelf 2.(框架,结构) framework; skeleton; outline 3.(指作风) airs; haughty manner: 官僚～ bureaucratic airs 4.(架式) posture; stance

【架子工】 jià·zigōng 〈*Archit*.〉 scaffolder

假 (jià) 1.(假期) holiday; vacation 2.(休假) leave of absence; furlough: 请～ ask for leave / 休～ be on leave; be on furlough (另见"假"jiǎ)

【假期】 jiàqī 1.(放假期间) vacation 2.(休假期间) period of leave

【假日】 jiàrì holiday; day off

【假条】 jiàtiáo 1.(请假条) application for leave 2.(准假条) leave permit: 病～ doctor's certificate

嫁 (jià) 1.(出嫁) marry 2.(转嫁) shift; transfer

【嫁祸于人】 jiàhuò-yúrén shift the misfortune onto sb. else; put the blame on sb. else; shift the blame to sb. else

【嫁接】 jiàjiē 〈*Bot*.〉 graft: 这些植物是～的,还是用种子栽培的? Are these plants grafted or grown from seed?

【嫁娶】 jiàqǔ marriage

【嫁妆】 jià·zhuang dowry; trousseau

jian

笺[箋、牋[1,2]] (jiān) 1.(书写纸) writing paper; note paper 2.(信函) letter 3.(注解) annotation

尖 (jiān) 1.(末端) point; tip; top 2.(尖削的) pointed; tapering 3.(刺耳) shrill; piercing 4.(敏锐) sharp; acute 5.(出类拔萃) the best of its kind; the pick of the bunch

【尖兵】 jiānbīng 1.〈*Mil*.〉 point 2.(开创者) trailblazer; pathbreaker; pioneer; vanguard

【尖刀】 jiāndāo sharp knife; dagger

【尖顶式】 jiāndǐngshì ogival

【尖端】 jiānduān 1.(顶端) pointed end; acme; peak 2.(发展最高的) most advanced; sophisticated

【尖端产品】 jiānduān chǎnpǐn highly sophisticated products

【尖端科学】 jiānduān kēxué most advanced branches of science

【尖刻】 jiānkè acrimonious; caustic; biting:

～的讽刺 poignant satire

【尖利】 jiānlì 1.（锋利）sharp; keen; cutting 2.（刺耳）shrill; piercing

【尖锐】 jiānruì 1.（锋利）sharp-pointed 2.（敏锐）penetrating; incisive; sharp; keen 3.（刺耳）shrill; piercing 4.（激烈）intense; acute; sharp: ～的批评 acute criticism

【尖酸】 jiānsuān acrid; acrimonious; tart

【尖牙】 jiānyá 〈*Anat.*〉 canine tooth

【尖子】 jiān·zi the best part; the finest

【尖子生】 jiān·zishēng top student

奸[姦[4]]（jiān） 1.（奸诈）wicked; evil; treacherous: ～计 an evil plot 2.（背叛国家或民族的人）traitor: 汉～ traitor to the Chinese nation 3.（自私;取巧）self-seeking and wily: 那个人才～哪。That chap is just a self-seeker. 4.（非法性关系）liaison; illicit sexual relations

【奸臣】 jiānchén treacherous court official

【奸夫】 jiānfū intrigant; paramour

【奸妇】 jiānfù paramour

【奸猾】 jiānhuá treacherous; crafty; deceitful

【奸佞】 jiānnìng 1.（奸邪）crafty and fawning 2.（奸佞的人）crafty sycophant

【奸商】 jiānshāng unscrupulous merchant; profiteer; dishonest trader

【奸污】 jiānwū 1.（强奸）rape: ～妇女 rape a woman 2.（诱奸）seduce

【奸细】 jiān·xi spy; enemy agent

【奸险】 jiānxiǎn wicked and crafty; treacherous; malicious

【奸笑】 jiānxiào sinister smile; villainous smile

【奸邪】 jiānxié 1.（奸诈、邪恶）crafty and evil; treacherous 2.（奸诈邪恶的人）a crafty and evil person

【奸雄】 jiānxióng a person who achieves high position by unscrupulous scheming; arch-careerist

【奸淫】 jiānyín 1.（非法性行为）illicit sexual relations; adultery 2.（奸污）rape; seduce

【奸诈】 jiānzhà fraudulent; crafty; treacherous

歼[殲]（jiān） annihilate; wipe out; destroy

【歼击机】 jiānjījī fighter plane; fighter

【歼灭】 jiānmiè annihilate; wipe out; destroy

【歼灭战】 jiānmièzhàn battle of annihilation

坚[堅]（jiān） 1.（坚固）hard; solid; firm; strong 2.（阵地）a heavily fortified point; fortification; strong-hold 3.（坚定;坚决）firmly; steadfastly; resolutely

【坚壁】 jiānbì hide supplies to prevent the enemy from seizing them; place in a cache

【坚不可摧】 jiānbùkěcuī indestructible; impregnable

【坚持】 jiānchí persist in; persevere in; uphold; insist on; stick to; adhere to: ～错误 persist in one's errors / ～原则 adhere to principle / ～真理 uphold the truth

【坚持不懈】 jiānchí-bùxiè unremitting

【坚定】 jiāndìng 1.（坚强）firm; staunch; steadfast 2.（使坚定）strengthen: ～信念 strengthen one's conviction

【坚定不移】 jiāndìng-bùyí resolute and firm

【坚固】 jiāngù firm; solid; sturdy; strong: ～耐用 sturdy and durable

【坚果】 jiānguǒ 〈*Bot.*〉 nuts

【坚决】 jiānjué firm; resolute; determined; resolved: 采取～措施 take resolute measures / ～要求 request sth. resolutely / ～支持 support firmly

【坚苦卓绝】 jiānkǔ-zhuōjué showing the utmost fortitude; endure hardship being prominent above all

【坚强】 jiānqiáng 1.（强固有力）strong; firm; staunch: ～的意志 strong will 2.（加强）strengthen

【坚忍】 jiānrěn steadfast and persevering (in face of difficulties)

【坚忍不拔】 jiānrěn-bùbá firm and indomitable; stubborn and unyielding

【坚韧】 jiānrèn tough and tensile; firm and tenacious

【坚韧不拔】 jiānrèn-bùbá firm and indomitable; persistent and dauntless

【坚如磐石】 jiānrúpánshí solid as a rock; rock-firm

【坚实】 jiānshí solid; substantial: 打下～的基础 lay a solid foundation

【坚守】 jiānshǒu stick to; hold fast to; stand fast

【坚挺】 jiāntǐng 〈*Econ.*〉 strong

【坚信】 jiānxìn firmly believe; be firmly convinced; be fully confident of
【坚毅】 jiānyì firm and persistent; with unswerving determination; with inflexible will
【坚硬】 jiānyìng hard; solid
【坚贞】 jiānzhēn faithful; constant
【坚贞不屈】 jiānzhēn-bùqū remain faithful and unyielding; stand firm and unbending

间[閒] (jiān) 1.(中间) between; among 2.(在…期间) within a definite time or space; in; during: 假期～ during the vacation 3.(房间) room
(另见“间”jiàn)
【间不容发】 jiānbùróngfà not a hair's breadth in between; the situation is extremely critical
【间距】 jiānjù span
【间量】 jiān·liang the area of a room; floor space
【间奏曲】 jiānzòuqǔ intermezzo

肩 (jiān) 1.(肩膀) shoulder 2.(担负) take on; undertake; shoulder; bear
【肩膀】 jiānbǎng shoulder
【肩负】 jiānfù take on; undertake; shoulder; bear: ～重任 undertake a important task
【肩胛】 jiānjiǎ 1.(肩膀) shoulder 2.〈*Med*.〉 scapula
【肩胛骨】 jiānjiǎgǔ scapula; shoulder blade
【肩挑背负】 jiāntiāo-bèifù carry on the shoulder and back
【肩章】 jiānzhāng epaulet; epaulette; shoulder loop

艰[艱] (jiān) difficult; hard
【艰巨】 jiānjù arduous; formidable; onerous
【艰苦】 jiānkǔ arduous; difficult; hard; tough
【艰苦奋斗】 jiānkǔ fèndòu struggle arduously
【艰难】 jiānnán difficult; hard; arduous
【艰涩】 jiānsè involved and abstruse; intricate and obscure
【艰深】 jiānshēn difficult to understand; abstruse
【艰危】 jiānwēi difficulties and dangers (confronting a nation)
【艰险】 jiānxiǎn hardships and dangers; perilous: 不畏～ defy difficulties and dangers / 历尽～ experience all kinds of hardships and dangers
【艰辛】 jiānxīn hardships

监[監] (jiān) 1.(监视) supervise; inspect; watch 2.(牢狱) prison; jail: 女～ women's prison
【监测】 jiāncè monitor; monitoring (n.): 环境～ environmental monitoring
【监测器】 jiāncèqì monitor
【监察】 jiānchá supervise; control
【监察委员会】 jiānchá wěiyuánhuì control commission
【监察制度】 jiānchá zhìdù supervisory system
【监督】 jiāndū 1.(察看、督促) supervise; superintend; control: 国际～ international control / 法律～机关 legal supervisory organ / 群众～制度 system of supervision by the masses / 行使～职能 exercise supervision 2.(监督人) supervisor
【监督权】 jiāndūquán authority to supervise
【监犯】 jiānfàn prisoner; convict
【监工】 jiāngōng 1.(监督工作) supervise work; oversee 2.(监工者) overseer; supervisor
【监管】 jiānguǎn supervise; keep watch on; supervision (n.): 由海关～ be under the supervision of the customs
【监护】 jiānhù 1.〈*Law*〉 guardianship; tutelage 2.〈*Med*.〉 intensive care
【监护权】 jiānhùquán guardianship
【监护人】 jiānhùrén guardian; guarder
【监禁】 jiānjìn take into custody; imprison; put in jail; put in prison; imprisonment
【监考】 jiānkǎo proctor (AmE.); invigilate (BrE.): 王先生将～我们的历史考试。Mister Wang will be proctoring (或 invigilating) our history exam.
【监考人】 jiānkǎorén proctor (AmE.); invigilator (BrE.)
【监控】 jiānkòng monitor; monitoring (n.)
【监控方式】 jiānkòng fāngshì monitor mode
【监牢】 jiānláo prison; jail
【监票】 jiānpiào scrutinize balloting
【监票人】 jiānpiàorén scrutineer
【监视】 jiānshì keep watch on; keep a lookout over; guard: ～某人 place sb. under surveillance

【监视雷达】 jiānshì léidá surveillance radar equipment
【监视器】 jiānshìqì monitor：单色～ monochromatic monitor / 彩色～ color monitor
【监守】 jiānshǒu have custody of；guard；take care of
【监守自盗】 jiānshǒu-zìdào steal what is entrusted to one's care；custodian turned thief
【监听】 jiāntīng monitor；monitoring (n.)
【监外执行】 jiānwài zhíxíng 〈*Law*〉 execute outside prison
【监狱】 jiānyù prison；jail
【监狱长】 jiānyùzhǎng warden
【监制】 jiānzhì supervise the manufacture of

兼 (jiān) 1.（两倍的）double；twice 2.（同时具有）simultaneously；concurrently：身～数职 hold several positions simultaneously
【兼备】 jiānbèi have both ... and：德才～ be both virtuous and talented
【兼并】 jiānbìng annex；merger；annexation (n.)
【兼程】 jiānchéng travel at double speed：～而往 travel by long stages
【兼而有之】 jiān'éryǒuzhī have both at the same time
【兼顾】 jiāngù give consideration to (take account of) two or more things：公私～ give consideration to both public and private interests / ～双方的利益 take the interests of both sides into consideration
【兼管】 jiānguǎn be concurrently in charge of；also look after
【兼课】 jiānkè 1.（指在本职以外）do some teaching in addition to one's main occupation 2.（指两种或两种以上）hold two or more teaching jobs concurrently
【兼课教师】 jiānkè jiàoshī part-time teacher
【兼任】 jiānrèn 1.（同时担任）hold a concurrent post 2.（非专职）part-time
【兼容】 jiānróng 〈*TV*〉 compatible
【兼容性】 jiānróngxìng compatibility
【兼收并蓄】 jiānshōu-bìngxù incorporate things of diverse nature；take in everything
【兼职】 jiānzhí 1.（指同时担任）hold two on more posts concurrently 2.（指在本职外）concurrent post；part-time job：减少～ reduce concurrent posts / 辞去～ resign one's part-time job

煎 (jiān) 1.（油煎）fry：～鸡蛋 fry the eggs 2.（用文火煮）simmer in water；decoct
【煎熬】 jiān'áo suffering；torture；torment
【煎饼】 jiān·bing thin pancake made of millet flour
【煎锅】 jiānguō frying pan

缄 (jiān) seal；close
【缄默】 jiānmò keep silent；be reticent

拣［揀］(jiǎn) 1.（挑拣）choose；select；pick out 2.（拣拾）pick up；collect；gather
【拣拾】 jiǎnshí pick up；collect；gather
【拣选】 jiǎnxuǎn select；choose

茧［繭］(jiǎn) 1.（蚕茧）cocoon；silkworm cocoon 2.（老趼）callus；thick callus
【茧绸】 jiǎnchóu pongee；tussah silk

柬 (jiǎn) card；note；letter：请～ invitation card；invitation
【柬帖】 jiǎntiě note；short letter

俭［儉］(jiǎn) thrifty；frugal
【俭朴】 jiǎnpǔ thrifty and simple；economical
【俭省】 jiǎnshěng economical；thrifty；frugal；sparing

捡［撿］(jiǎn) pick up；collect；gather
【捡破烂儿】 jiǎn pòlànr pick odds and ends from refuse heaps
【捡拾】 jiǎnshí pick up；collect；gather

检［檢］(jiǎn) 1.（检查）check up；inspect；examine 2.（检点）restrain oneself；be careful in one's conduct：行为不～ depart from correct conduct
【检波】 jiǎnbō 〈*Electr.*〉 detection
【检波器】 jiǎnbōqì detector
【检测】 jiǎncè detection
【检测极限】 jiǎncè jíxiàn limit of detection
【检测能力】 jiǎncè nénglì detectability
【检查】 jiǎnchá 1.（查看）check up；inspect；examine：定期～ periodical examination / ～身体 have a health check；have a medical

check-up / ～行李 examine sb's luggage / ～账目 audit the account; check the account / ～质量 check on the quality of sth. / 拒绝进行～ waive the inspection 2.(检讨) self-criticism

【检查井】 jiǎnchájǐng 〈*Urban Construction*〉 manhole

【检查框】 jiǎnchákuāng 〈*Computer*〉 check boxes

【检查团】 jiǎnchátuán inspection party

【检查站】 jiǎncházhàn checkpoint; checkpost; inspection station

【检察】 jiǎnchá procuratorial work

【检察院】 jiǎncháyuàn procuratorate

【检察长】 jiǎncházhǎng chief procurator

【检点】 jiǎndiǎn 1.(查看) examine; check 2.(注意约束) be cautious (about what one says or does): 有失～ be indiscreet in one's speech and conduct

【检举】 jiǎnjǔ report (an offense) to the authorities; inform against (an offender); accuse

【检举信】 jiǎnjǔxìn letter of accusation; written accusation

【检录员】 jiǎnlùyuán clerk of the course

【检索】 jiǎnsuǒ retrieve; search

【检讨】 jiǎntǎo self-criticism: 做～ make a self-criticism

【检修】 jiǎnxiū examine and repair; overhaul: 他们出售的旧汽车，全部要先彻底～过。All the used cars they sell are completely overhauled first.

【检验】 jiǎnyàn test; examine; inspect; verify: 商品～ commodity inspection / ～产品质量 examine the quality of the production

【检疫】 jiǎnyì quarantine: 必须通过～以防传染 have to be quarantined to prevent the infection

【检阅】 jiǎnyuè review (troops, etc.); inspect: ～仪仗队 review the guard of honor

【检阅台】 jiǎnyuètái reviewing stand

【检字表】 jiǎnzìbiǎo index of Chinese characters

睑[瞼](jiǎn) eyelid

【睑炎】 jiǎnyán blepharitis

减[減](jiǎn) 1.(减掉) subtract: 七～三得四。Seven minus three is four.(或: Three from seven is four.) 2.(降低) reduce; decrease; cut

【减半】 jiǎnbàn reduce by half

【减产】 jiǎnchǎn reduction of output; drop in production

【减低】 jiǎndī reduce; lower; bring down; cut: ～10% be lowered by ten per cent

【减法】 jiǎnfǎ subtraction

【减肥】 jiǎnféi slim; slimming (n.): 在最近几个月，她的确减了肥。She's really slimmed down over the last few months.

【减肥体操】 jiǎnféi tǐcāo slimnastics

【减肥丸】 jiǎnféiwán diet pill

【减肥者】 jiǎnféizhě slimmer: 节食～ dieter

【减幅】 jiǎnfú decrease; range of decrease

【减股盈余】 jiǎngǔ yíngyú surplus from cancellation of stock

【减号】 jiǎnhào 〈*Math.*〉 minus sign (符号为 −)

【减缓】 jiǎnhuǎn retard; slow down

【减价】 jiǎnjià reduce the price; mark down: ～30 元 reduce 30 yuan form the price; be marked down by 30 yuan

【减免】 jiǎnmiǎn 1.(指刑罚) mitigate a punishment; annul a punishment 2.(指捐税、债务等) reduce; remit (taxation, etc.): ～学费 reduce or remit one's tuition

【减免税】 jiǎnmiǎnshuì tax cuts and exemptions; tax break

【减轻】 jiǎnqīng lighten; ease; alleviate; mitigate

【减轻农民负担】 jiǎnqīng nóngmín fùdān reduce farmer's burdens

【减轻债务负担】 jiǎnqīng zhàiwù fùdān reduction or cancellation of debts

【减弱】 jiǎnruò weaken; abate: 风势～了。The wind has abated.

【减色】 jiǎnsè 1.(退色) fade 2.(精彩成分降低) lose luster; impair the excellence of; detract from the merit of

【减少】 jiǎnshǎo reduce; decrease; lessen; cut down: ～层次 eliminate duplication / ～到最低限度 be reduced to a minimum / ～非生产性开支 reduce nonproductive expenditure / ～疾病 reduce the incidence of disease / ～损失 reduce the loss / 犯罪行为大大～。The crime rate have declined significantly.

【减数】 jiǎnshù 〈*Math.*〉 subtrahend
【减税】 jiǎnshuì abatement of tax; tax abatement; tax reduction
【减速】 jiǎnsù slow down; decelerate; retard
【减缩】 jiǎnsuō reduce; cut down; retrench
【减退】 jiǎntuì drop; go down; abate; subside; decrease: 热度～ one's fever has abated; one's fever be come down
【减刑】 jiǎnxíng 〈*Law*〉 reduce a penalty; commute a sentence; mitigate a sentence
【减刑特赦】 jiǎnxíng tèshè 〈*Law*〉 commutation pardon
【减压】 jiǎnyā reduce pressure; decompress
【减压舱】 jiǎnyācāng decompression chamber
【减音器】 jiǎnyīnqì muffler; baffler; deafener
【减员】 jiǎnyuán depletion of numbers (in the armed forces): 非战斗～ non-battle casualties
【减震】 jiǎnzhèn shock absorption; damping
【减震式前叉】 jiǎnzhènshì qiánchā 〈*Motorcycle*〉 front hydraulic fork
【减阻】 jiǎnzǔ anti-drag
【减罪】 jiǎnzuì palliate a crime

碱[鹼、堿] (jiǎn) **1.**〈*Chem.*〉 alkali **2.** (碳酸钠) soda **3.** (盐基) base
【碱处理】 jiǎnchǔlǐ alkali treatment
【碱地】 jiǎndì alkaline land
【碱化】 jiǎnhuà alkalize; basilify; alkalization (n.)
【碱水洗涤】 jiǎnshuǐ xǐdí soda lye wash
【碱土】 jiǎntǔ alkaline earth
【碱土金属】 jiǎntǔ jīnshǔ alkaline-earth metal
【碱性】 jiǎnxìng basicity; alkalinity
【碱液】 jiǎnyè lye

剪 (jiǎn) **1.** (剪刀) scissors; shears; clippers **2.** (剪断) cut (with scissors); clip; trim: ～发 have one's hair cut / 她给他～头发。She trimmed his hair. **3.** (除去) wipe out; exterminate; annihilate
【剪报】 jiǎnbào newspaper cutting; newspaper clipping
【剪裁】 jiǎncái **1.** (指衣料) cut out (a garment); tailor **2.** (指文字材料) cut out unwanted material (from a piece of writing); prune
【剪彩】 jiǎncǎi cut the ribbon (at an opening ceremony): 为展览会～ cut the ribbon at the opening of an exhibition
【剪除】 jiǎnchú wipe out; annihilate; exterminate
【剪刀】 jiǎndāo scissors; shears
【剪刀差】 jiǎndāochā scissors differential; disparity; scissors movement of prices; scissors difference: 价格上的～ price scissors
【剪掉】 jiǎndiào cut off; scissor off
【剪断】 jiǎnduàn cut off; nip; snip
【剪辑】 jiǎnjí **1.**〈*Cinematog.*〉 montage; film editing **2.** (剪裁重编) editing and rearrangement: 电影录音～ highlights of a live recording of a film
【剪接】 jiǎnjiē 〈*Cinematog.*〉 montage; film editing
【剪开】 jiǎnkāi cut open
【剪毛】 jiǎnmáo 〈*Herd*〉 shearing; clipping
【剪票】 jiǎnpiào punch a ticket
【剪票员】 jiǎnpiàoyuán puncher
【剪式跳高】 jiǎnshì tiàogāo 〈*Sports*〉 Eastern layout
【剪贴】 jiǎntiē **1.** (剪贴资料) clip and paste (sth. out of a newspaper, etc.) in a scrapbook or on cards **2.** (儿童手工) cutting out
【剪贴簿】 jiǎntiēbù scrapbook
【剪影】 jiǎnyǐng **1.** (剪纸像) paper-cut silhouette **2.** (轮廓) outline; sketch
【剪纸】 jiǎnzhǐ paper-cut; scissor-cut
【剪子】 jiǎn·zi scissors; shears; clippers

简 (jiǎn) **1.** (简单) simple; simplified; brief: 从～ conform to the principle of simplicity **2.** (竹片) bamboo slips **3.** (信件) letter
【简报】 jiǎnbào bulletin; brief report
【简本】 jiǎnběn abridged edition
【简编】 jiǎnbiān (多用于书名) short course; concise edition; abridged edition
【简便】 jiǎnbiàn simple and convenient; handy
【简称】 jiǎnchēng **1.** (名称的简化) the abbreviated form of a name; abbreviation; shorter form **2.** (使名称简化) be called sth. for short
【简单】 jiǎndān **1.** (不复杂) simple; uncom-

plicated 2.（平凡，多用否定式）commonplace; ordinary：不～ not simple; fairly complicated; remarkable 3.（不细致）casual; oversimplified：～从事 do things in a casual way

【简单化】 jiǎndānhuà oversimplify; oversimplification (n.)

【简单劳动】 jiǎndān láodòng simple work

【简单商品生产】 jiǎndān shāngpǐn shēngchǎn simple production

【简单再生产】 jiǎndān zàishēngchǎn simple reproduction

【简短】 jiǎnduǎn brief; short

【简化】 jiǎnhuà simplify; simplification (n.)：～手续 simplify the procedures / 你能把你刚才说的～一下吗？Could you simplify what you've just said?

【简化字】 jiǎnhuàzì simplified Chinese characters

【简洁】 jiǎnjié succinct; terse; pithy; concise

【简捷】 jiǎnjié simple and direct; forthright

【简介】 jiǎnjiè brief introduction; synopsis; summarized account

【简括】 jiǎnkuò brief but comprehensive; compendious; briefly; compendiously

【简历】 jiǎnlì biographical notes; curriculum vitae; resume

【简练】 jiǎnliàn terse; succinct; pithy

【简陋】 jiǎnlòu simple and crude：～的设备 simple and crude equipment

【简略】 jiǎnlüè simple (in content); brief; sketchy

【简码】 jiǎnmǎ brevity code

【简慢】 jiǎnmàn negligent

【简明】 jiǎnmíng simple and clear; concise：～词典 a concise dictionary / ～新闻 news in brief

【简朴】 jiǎnpǔ simple and unadorned; plain

【简谱】 jiǎnpǔ 〈*Music*〉 numbered musical notation

【简体字】 jiǎntǐzì simplified Chinese character

【简图】 jiǎntú sketch; diagram; abbreviated drawing; simplified schematic

【简写】 jiǎnxiě 1.（简写字）write a Chinese character in simplified form 2.（文字浅显）simplify a book for beginners

【简写本】 jiǎnxiěběn simplified edition

【简讯】 jiǎnxùn news in brief

【简要】 jiǎnyào concise and to the point; brief

【简易】 jiǎnyì 1.（简单容易）simple and easy 2.（设备不完备）simply constructed; simply equipped; unsophisticated

【简易病房】 jiǎnyì bìngfáng simply equipped ward

【简易公路】 jiǎnyì gōnglù simply road; rough road; simply-built highway

【简约】 jiǎnyuē 1.（简略）brief; concise; sketchy 2.（节俭）economy

【简章】 jiǎnzhāng general regulations：招生～ general enrollment regulations

【简直】 jiǎnzhí 〈*adv.*〉 simply; at all; virtually：～不堪想像 virtually unimaginable

【简装本】 jiǎnzhuāngběn brochure

见［見］(jiàn) 1.（看见）see; catch sight of：亲眼所～ see with one's own eyes; see for oneself 2.（遇到）meet with; be exposed to：一～如故 become fast friends at the first meeting 3.（看得出）show evidence of; appear to be 4.（参见；参看）refer to; see; vide：～第224页 see page 224 5.（会见）meet; call on; see：明天～。See you tomorrow! 6.（见解）view; opinion：依我之～ in my opinion

【见报】 jiànbào appear in the newspapers; be carried in the newspapers

【见不得】 jiàn·bu·dé 1.（不能遇见）not to be exposed to; unable to stand 2.（见不得人的）not fit to be seen or revealed

【见长】 jiàncháng be good at; be expert in：以音乐～ be good at music

【见地】 jiàndì insight; judgment

【见多识广】 jiànduō shíguǎng experienced and knowledgeable; with rich experience and extensive knowledge

【见风使舵】 jiànfēng shǐduò trim one's sails; swap horses when crossing a stream

【见怪】 jiànguài mind; take offense

【见鬼】 jiànguǐ 1.（离奇古怪）fantastic; preposterous; absurd 2.（灭亡；毁灭）go to hell

【见好】 jiànhǎo get better; mend：病情～。The patient's condition is turning for the better.

【见机】 jiànjī as the opportunity; as befits the occasion; according to circumstances
【见机行事】 jiànjī-xíngshì act according to circumstances; do as one sees fit
【见教】 jiànjiào 〈*politeness*〉 favor me with your advice; instruct me: 有何～? Is there sth. you want to see me about?
【见解】 jiànjiě view; opinion; understanding; idea: 这是我的个人～。This is my own opinion.
【见景生情】 jiànjǐng-shēngqíng Memories revive at the sight of familiar places.
【见利忘义】 jiànlì-wàngyì forget honor at sight of money; forget all moral principles at the sight of profits
【见谅】 jiànliàng 〈*written*〉 excuse me; forgive me: 务希～。I hope you would excuse me.
【见面】 jiànmiàn **1.** (相见) meet; see **2.** (接触) contact; link leading cadres to keep frequent contacts with the masses
【见面礼】 jiànmiànlǐ a present given to sb. on first meeting him
【见仁见智】 jiànrén-jiànzhì different people, different views; opinions differ
【见识】 jiàn·shi **1.** (扩大见闻) widen one's knowledge; enrich one's experience **2.** (见闻知识) experience; knowledge; sensibleness: 长～ widen one's knowledge
【见世面】 jiàn shìmiàn see the world; enrich one's experience; face the world
【见死不救】 jiànsǐ-bújiù see someone in mortal danger without lifting a finger to save him
【见外】 jiànwài regard sb. as an outsider
【见闻】 jiànwén what one sees and hears; knowledge; information: ～广 be knowledgeable
【见习】 jiànxí learn on the job; be on probation
【见习驾驶员】 jiànxí jiàshǐyuán learner driver; learner
【见习生】 jiànxíshēng probationer
【见习医生】 jiànxí yīshēng intern
【见效】 jiànxiào become effective; produce the desired result
【见笑】 jiànxiào **1.** 〈*politeness*〉 laugh at me; laugh at us **2.** (被人笑话) be laughed at
【见义勇为】 jiànyì-yǒngwéi ready to take up the cudgels for a just cause; never hesitate to do what is righteous; gallantry rise to the occasion
【见异思迁】 jiànyì-sīqiān change one's mind the moment one sees something new; be inconstant; be irresolute; be like a rolling stone
【见长】 jiànzhǎng grow perceptibly
【见证】 jiànzhèng witness; testimony
【见证人】 jiànzhèngrén eyewitness; witness

舰[艦] (jiàn) warship; man-of-war; naval vessel
【舰队】 jiànduì fleet; naval force
【舰队司令】 jiànduì sīlìng admiral
【舰首】 jiànshǒu bow
【舰首炮】 jiànshǒupào bow chaser
【舰艇】 jiàntǐng naval ships and boats; naval vessels
【舰尾】 jiànwěi stern
【舰尾炮】 jiànwěipào stern chaser
【舰位】 jiànwèi berth
【舰载导弹】 jiànzǎi dǎodàn ship-based missile
【舰载飞机】 jiànzǎi fēijī carrier-based aircraft
【舰载直升机】 jiànzǎi zhíshēngjī carrier-based helicopter
【舰长】 jiànzhǎng captain (of a warship)
【舰只】 jiànzhī warships; naval vessels

件 (jiàn) **1.** 〈*classifier*〉 piece **2.** (零件) piece **3.** (文书) letter; correspondence; paper; document: 来～ a letter received; a document received

间[閒] (jiàn) **1.** (空隙) space in between; opening **2.** (相隔) separate **3.** (离间) sow discord; drive a wedge between
(另见"间"jiān)
【间谍】 jiàndié spy: 捕获一名外国～ arrest a foreign spy / 她在德国情报部门工作时给华盛顿当～。She spied for Washington while serving in German intelligence.
【间谍活动】 jiàndié huódòng espionage: 进行～ be engaged in espionage
【间谍网】 jiàndiéwǎng espionage network
【间谍卫星】 jiàndié wèixīng spy satellite
【间断】 jiànduàn be disconnected; be interrupted
【间隔】 jiàngé interval; intermission; gap;

spacing
【间或】 jiànhuò occasionally; now and then; sometimes; once in a while
【间接】 jiànjiē indirect; secondhand
【间接成本】 jiànjiē chéngběn indirect cost; overhead
【间接选举】 jiànjiē xuǎnjǔ indirect election
【间苗】 jiànmiáo thin out seedlings
【间色】 jiànsè secondary color
【间隙】 jiànxì 1.（空隙）interval; gap; space 2.〈*Mech*.〉clearance
【间歇】 jiànxiē intermittence; intermission
【间歇河】 jiànxiēhé 〈*Geog*.〉intermittent river
【间歇泉】 jiànxiēquán 〈*Geog*.〉intermittent spring
【间歇热】 jiànxiērè 〈*Med*.〉intermittent fever
【间植】 jiànzhí inter-planting
【间作】 jiànzuò 〈*Agric*.〉intercropping; interplant

饯［餞］(jiàn) 1.（饯行）give a farewell dinner 2.（蜜饯）candied fruit; preserved fruit
【饯行】 jiànxíng give a farewell dinner

贱［賤］(jiàn) 1.（价格低）low-priced; inexpensive; cheap 2.（地位低）lowly; humble 3.（下贱）low-down; base; despicable; mean 4.〈*politeness*〉my：～躯尚健 my mean body is still strong
【贱骨头】 jiàngǔ·tou miserable wretch
【贱买贵卖】 jiànmǎi guìmài buy low and sell high
【贱买贱卖】 jiànmǎi jiànmài buy and sell at low price

践［踐］(jiàn) 1.（踩）trample; tread 2.（履行）act on; carry out
【践踏】 jiàntà 1.（踩）tread on; trample underfoot：请勿～草坪。Keep off the grass. 2.（违反）violate：～国际法准则 violate the international law
【践约】 jiànyuē keep a promise; keep an appointment

溅［濺］(jiàn) splash; spatter; sputter：把凉水～到他脸上 splash his face with cold water / ～了一身泥 be spattered with mud / 咖啡～到计算机上了。A stream of coffee splashed (over) the computer. / 火花飞～。Sparks flew about.
【溅落】 jiànluò splash down：航天器～了。The spacecraft splashed down.
【溅落点】 jiànluòdiǎn splash point
【溅射】 jiànshè sputtering

建(jiàn) 1.（建设）build; construct; erect 2.（建立）establish; set up; found
【建材】 jiàncái building materials
【建党】 jiàndǎng 1.（指成立）found a party 2.（指建设）Party building
【建房互助会】 jiànfáng hùzhùhuì building society
【建国】 jiànguó 1.（建立国家）found a state; establish a state 2.（建设国家）build up a country
【建交】 jiànjiāo establish diplomatic relations
【建军】 jiànjūn 1.（建立军队）found an army 2.（建设军队）army building
【建立】 jiànlì 1.（成立）build; set up：～新的工业基地 set up a new industrial base 2.（产生,形成）form; establish：～正常的国家关系 establish normal state relations
【建设】 jiànshè build; construct; construction (n.)：社会主义～ socialist construction / ～有中国特色的社会主义 build socialism with Chinese characteristics
【建设性】 jiànshèxìng constructive：～意见 constructive suggestions
【建设周期】 jiànshè zhōuqī construction period
【建树】 jiànshù 〈*written*〉make a contribution; contribute; score an achievement
【建议】 jiànyì 1.（提建议）propose; suggest; recommend 2.（所提建议）proposal; suggestion; recommendation：合理化～ rationalization proposal / 我想提个～。I'd like to make a suggestion.
【建造】 jiànzào build; construct; make
【建制】 jiànzhì organizational system
【建筑】 jiànzhù 1.（建造）build; construct; erect 2.（建筑物）building; structure; edifice：新医院是一座很大的～。The new hospital is a big building. 3.（建筑学）architecture
【建筑工地】 jiànzhù gōngdì construction site
【建筑工人】 jiànzhù gōngrén builder

【建筑面积】 jiànzhù miànjī floorage
【建筑师】 jiànzhùshī architect
【建筑业】 jiànzhùyè construction industry

健(jiàn) 1.(强健) healthy; strong 2.(使强健) strengthen; toughen; invigorate 3.(善于) be strong in; be good at
【健步】 jiànbù walk with vigorous strides
【健儿】 jiàn'ér 1.(健儿) valiant fighter 2.(运动员) good athlete; skilled athlete
【健将】 jiànjiàng master sportsman; master sportswoman; top-notch player
【健康】 jiànkāng 1.(指身体) in good health; sound; fit: 身体～ be in good health 2.(情况正常) healthy; wholesome; sound
【健康证明书】 jiànkāng zhèngmíngshū health certificate
【健美】 jiànměi strong and handsome; vigorous and graceful
【健美表演】 jiànměi biǎoyǎn a vigorous and graceful performance
【健美操】 jiànměicāo aerobics exercises; slimming exercise
【健美裤】 jiànměikù body stocking; leotard
【健美运动】 jiànměi yùndòng body building
【健全】 jiànquán 1.(强健无缺陷) sound; perfect 2.(完善) regular; perfect 3.(使完善) perfect; improve; strengthen: ～规章制度 improve rules and regulations / ～社会主义法制 perfect the socialist legal system
【健身】 jiànshēn be healthy
【健身操】 jiànshēncāo body-building exercise
【健身房】 jiànshēnfáng gymnasium; gym
【健身球】 jiànshēnqiú ball for health
【健身运动】 jiànshēn yùndòng body-building
【健谈】 jiàntán be a good talker; be talkative
【健忘】 jiànwàng be forgetful; have a poor memory
【健忘症】 jiànwàngzhèng 〈*Med*.〉 amnesia
【健旺】 jiànwàng healthy and vigorous
【健在】 jiànzài be still living and in good health
【健壮】 jiànzhuàng healthy and strong; robust

毽(jiàn) shuttlecock
【毽子】 jiàn·zi shuttlecock: 踢～ kick the shuttlecock

腱(jiàn) 〈*Anat*.〉 tendon
【腱鞘】 jiànqiào 〈*Anat*.〉 tendon sheath
【腱鞘炎】 jiànqiàoyán 〈*Med*.〉 tenosynovitis; tendovaginitis

键(jiàn) 1.〈*Mech*.〉 key 2.(按键) key: 钢琴～ the keys of a piano 3.〈*Chem*.〉 bond
【键盘】 jiànpán keyboard; fingerboard: 标准～ QWERTY keyboard / 计算机～ the keyboard of a computer / 用～输入 key in; keyboard (v.)
【键盘乐器】 jiànpán yuèqì keyboard instrument

荐[薦](jiàn) recommend
【荐举】 jiànjǔ propose sb. for an office; recommend

剑[劍、劒](jiàn) sword
【剑拔弩张】 jiànbá-nǔzhāng with swords drawn and bows bent; at daggers drawn
【剑道】 jiàndào kendo (Jap.)
【剑客】 jiànkè swordsman
【剑麻】 jiànmá 〈*Bot*.〉 sisal hemp
【剑眉】 jiànméi straight eyebrows slanting upwards and outwards; dashing eyebrows
【剑术】 jiànshù art of fencing; swordplay
【剑舞】 jiànwǔ sword dance

鉴[鑒、鑑](jiàn) 1.(照) reflect; mirror: 光可～人 so shining and bright that it can serve as a looking glass 2.(教训) warning; object lesson 3.(仔细看;审察) inspect; scrutinize; examine
【鉴别】 jiànbié distinguish; differentiate; discriminate; discern; identify: ～真伪 discern the false from the genuine
【鉴定】 jiàndìng 1.(评语) appraisal: 书面～ written appraisal 2.(评定) appraise; identify; authenticate; determine: ～产品质量 appraise the quality of a product / 科研成果的～ evaluation of research results
【鉴定人】 jiàndìngrén expert; identifier; surveyor
【鉴定委员会】 jiàndìng wěiyuánhuì appraisal committee

【鉴戒】 jiànjiè warning; object lesson
【鉴赏】 jiànshǎng appreciate; appreciation
【鉴赏家】 jiànshǎngjiā connoisseur：艺术～ an art connoisseur
【鉴赏力】 jiànshǎnglì ability to appreciate
【鉴于】 jiànyú in view of; seeing that; in consideration of

渐 (jiàn) gradually; by degrees：天气～暖。The weather is getting warmer.
【渐变】 jiànbiàn 1.(逐渐变化) gradual change 2.〈*Evolution*〉 anamorphism; anamorphosis
【渐次】 jiàncì 〈*written*〉 gradually; one after another
【渐渐】 jiànjiàn gradually; by degrees; little by little：那船～远去。The ship gradually vanishes in the distance.
【渐进】 jiànjìn advance gradually; progress step by step：循序～ advance gradually in due order

箭 (jiàn) arrow：射～ shoot an arrow
【箭靶子】 jiànbǎzi target for archery
【箭步】 jiànbù quick jump：一个～ a quick jump forward
【箭杆】 jiàngān arrow shaft
【箭号】 jiànhào arrow (符号为 →)
【箭模】 jiànmó model rocket
【箭头】 jiàntóu 1.(箭的头) arrowhead; arrow tip; arrow point; head of arrow 2.(箭头形符号) arrow
【箭在弦上】 jiànzàixiánshàng like an arrow on the bowstring; there can be no turning back
【箭镞】 jiànzú metal arrowhead

jiang

江 (jiāng) 1.(河流) river 2.(长江) the Changjiang River; the Yangtze River
【江岸】 jiāng'àn river bank
【江防】 jiāngfáng defense works along the Yangtze River
【江河日下】 jiānghé-rìxià go from bad to worse; be on the decline; decline steadily
【江湖】 jiānghú 1.(河流;湖泊) rivers and lakes 2.(四方各地) all corners of the country：走～ tramp from place to place to make a living
【江湖骗子】 jiānghú piàn·zi swindler; charlatan
【江湖医生】 jiānghú yīshēng quack
【江湖艺人】 jiānghú yìrén itinerant entertainer
【江湖义气】 jiānghú yìqì brotherhood：讲～ be loyal to brotherhood
【江口】 jiāngkǒu estuary
【江轮】 jiānglún river steamer
【江米】 jiāngmǐ polished glutinous rice
【江米酒】 jiāngmǐjiǔ fermented glutinous rice
【江畔】 jiāngpàn river bank; beside the river
【江山】 jiāngshān 1.(江河山川) rivers and mountains; land; landscape 2.(国家;国家政权) country; state power：打～ fight to win state power
【江心岛】 jiāngxīndǎo ait

豇 (jiāng)
【豇豆】 jiāngdòu cowpea; blackeye bean

将[將] (jiāng) 1.(将要) be going to; be about to; will; shall 2.〈*Chess*〉 check 3.(用言语相激) incite sb. to action; challenge; prod 4.(拿;用) with; by means of; by：～功补过 make amends for one's faults by good service 5.(把)～某人捉拿归案 bring sb. to justice
(另见"将"jiàng)
【将错就错】 jiāngcuò-jiùcuò make the best of a mistake without correcting it
【将功补过】 jiānggōng-bǔguò make amends for one's faults by good deeds
【将功赎罪】 jiānggōng-shúzuì atone for a crime by good deeds; redeem sins by good deeds
【将计就计】 jiāngjì-jiùjì turn sb's trick against him; beat sb. at his own game
【将近】 jiāngjìn close to; nearly; almost：～中午 towards noon
【将就】 jiāng·jiu make do with; make the best of; put up with
【将军】 jiāngjūn 1.〈*Mil.*〉 general 2.〈*Chess*〉 check：你的王被我的马～了。Your king is in check from my knight. 3.(使人为难) put sb. on the spot; embarrass; challenge

【将来】 jiānglái future：美好的～ happy future

【将死】 jiāngsǐ 〈*Chess*〉 checkmate；mate：他常常能在 20 步之内～我。He can always checkmate me within twenty moves.

【将心比心】 jiāngxīn-bǐxīn feel for others；judge other people's feelings by one's own；compare one's feeling with other's

【将信将疑】 jiāngxìn-jiāngyí half believing，half doubting；take with a grain of salt；half believe and half doubt

【将养】 jiāngyǎng rest；recuperate

【将要】 jiāngyào be going to；will；shall；be about to

浆［漿］(jiāng) 1.（浆水）thick liquid 2.（上浆）starch：～衣服 starch clothes

【浆果】 jiāngguǒ 〈*Bot.*〉 berry

【浆洗】 jiāngxǐ wash and starch：～衣服 wash and starch clothes

姜［薑］(jiāng) 〈*Bot.*〉 ginger

【姜黄】 jiānghuáng 〈*Bot.*〉 turmeric

【姜汤】 jiāngtāng ginger soup

【姜汁啤酒】 jiāngzhī píjiǔ ginger beer

僵［殭[1]］(jiāng) 1.（僵硬）stiff；numb 2.（僵局）deadlocked：把事情搞～ lead the things to a deadlock

【僵持】 jiāngchí （of both parties）refuse to budge；be stalemated；refuse to give in

【僵化】 jiānghuà become rigid；ossify：思想～ a rigid way of thinking；an ossified way of thinking

【僵局】 jiāngjú deadlock；impasse；stalemate：陷入～ have reached an impasse / 打破～ break a deadlock

【僵尸】 jiāngshī corpse：政治～ a political mummy

【僵死】 jiāngsǐ dead；ossified

【僵硬】 jiāngyìng 1.（不能活动）stiff 2.（呆板）rigid；inflexible

【僵直】 jiāngzhí stiff and rigid

疆(jiāng) boundary；border：边～ frontier；borderland

【疆场】 jiāngchǎng battlefield

【疆界】 jiāngjiè boundary；border；frontier

【疆土】 jiāngtǔ territory

【疆域】 jiāngyù territory；domain

缰［繮］(jiāng) reins；halter

【缰绳】 jiāng·shéng reins；halter

讲［講］(jiǎng) 1.（说）speak；say；tell；talk about：～西班牙语 speak Spanish 2.（讲解）explain；make clear；interpret 3.（商量）discuss；negotiate：～条件 negotiate the terms；insist on the fulfillment of certain conditions 4.（讲求）stress；lay emphasis on；pay special attention to；be particular about：～团结 pay a attention to unity 5.（就某方面说）as far as sth. is concerned；when it comes to；as to；with regard to；as regards：从效果来～ with regard to effects

【讲稿】 jiǎnggǎo 1.（讲话稿）the draft or text of a speech 2.（讲课稿）lecture notes

【讲和】 jiǎnghé make peace；settle a dispute；become reconciled

【讲话】 jiǎnghuà 1.（说话）speak；talk；address 2.（讲演）speech；talk：广播～ broadcast speech；radio talk 3.（用作书名）guide；introduction：《语法～》*An Introduction to Grammar*

【讲价】 jiǎngjià bargain；haggle over the price

【讲价钱】 jiǎngjiàqián 1.（讨价）bargain；haggle over the price 2.（讲条件）negotiate the terms

【讲解】 jiǎngjiě explain；interpret；expound

【讲解员】 jiǎngjiěyuán 1.（展览会等的）guide；interpreter；stand-attendant 2.（体育比赛的）announcer

【讲究】 jiǎng·jiu 1.（讲求）be particular about；pay attention to；stress；strive for：～经济效益 take into consideration the economic effect 2.（精美）exquisite；tasteful；elegant 3.（推敲）careful study：有～ be worthy of careful study

【讲课】 jiǎngkè teach；lecture：今天我准备给学生～。I am going to lecture to my students today.

【讲理】 jiǎnglǐ 1.（评是非）reason with sb.；argue 2.（服从道理）listen to reason；be amenable to reason；be reasonable；be sensible：不～ be unreasonable

【讲明】 jiǎngmíng explain; make clear; state explicitly

【讲排场】 jiǎng pái·chǎng go in for pomp; hanker after vainglory

【讲评】 jiǎngpíng comment on and appraise

【讲情】 jiǎngqíng intercede; plead for sb.

【讲求】 jiǎngqiú be particular about; pay attention to; stress; strive for

【讲师】 jiǎngshī lecturer

【讲师团】 jiǎngshītuán teaching corps

【讲授】 jiǎngshòu lecture; instruct; teach; give a lecture

【讲述】 jiǎngshù tell about; give an account of; narrate; relate

【讲台】 jiǎngtái platform; dais; rostrum

【讲坛】 jiǎngtán 1.(讲台) platform; rostrum 2.(讨论场所) forum

【讲堂】 jiǎngtáng lecture room; classroom

【讲题】 jiǎngtí subject of a lecture; topic of a speech

【讲习】 jiǎngxí 1.(讲授和学习) lecture and study 2.(研习) research and study

【讲学】 jiǎngxué give lectures; discourse on an academic subject

【讲演】 jiǎngyǎn lecture; speech

【讲义】 jiǎngyì teaching materials: 油印～ mimeographed teaching materials

【讲座】 jiǎngzuò a course of lectures: 电视～ lectures by television

奖［奬］(jiǎng) 1.(奖赏) encourage; praise; reward; award 2.(奖品; 奖状; 奖金) award; prize; reward: 一等～ first prize

【奖杯】 jiǎngbēi cup (as a prize)

【奖惩】 jiǎngchéng rewards and punishments; bonus-penalty

【奖惩条例】 jiǎngchéng tiáolì regulations concerning rewards and disciplinary sanctions

【奖金】 jiǎngjīn money award; bonus; premium: 发～ issue bonuses

【奖励】 jiǎnglì encourage and reward; award; reward: ～有成就的教师 reward school teachers who have distinguished themselves

【奖牌】 jiǎngpái medal

【奖品】 jiǎngpǐn prize; award; trophy

【奖勤罚懒】 jiǎngqín fálǎn award the diligent and punish the lazy

【奖券】 jiǎngquàn lottery ticket

【奖赏】 jiǎngshǎng award; reward

【奖售】 jiǎngshòu 1.(用奖鼓励出售) encourage sales 2.(作为奖励售给) prize sale; reward for selling award; reward

【奖学金】 jiǎngxuéjīn scholarship; fellowship; stipend: 有权获得～ be eligible for a stipend

【奖掖】 jiǎngyè 〈written〉 reward and promote; encourage by promoting and rewarding

【奖章】 jiǎngzhāng medal; decoration: 金质～ gold medal / 铜质～ bronze medal / 银质～ silver medal

【奖状】 jiǎngzhuàng certificate of merit; certificate of award; honorary credential; diploma

桨［槳］(jiǎng) oar; scull; paddle

【桨手】 jiǎngshǒu rower

匠(jiàng) craftsman; artisan

【匠人】 jiàngrén artisan; craftsman

【匠心】 jiàngxīn 〈written〉 ingenuity; craftsmanship

降(jiàng) fall; drop; lower: 温度～到零下。The temperature fell below zero degrees Centigrade

(另见"降"xiáng)

【降班】 jiàngbān send to a lower grade

【降半旗】 jiàngbànqí fly a flag at half-mast; lower the flag to half-mast

【降半音】 jiàngbànyīn 〈Music〉 flat

【降低】 jiàngdī reduce; cut down; drop; lower: ～生产成本 reduce production costs / ～消耗 cut down the consumption

【降调】 jiàngdiào 〈Music〉 falling intonation; falling tone

【降幅】 jiàngfú range of decrease

【降格】 jiànggé 〈written〉 lower one's standard or status: ～以求 accept a second best

【降号】 jiànghào 〈Music〉 flat

【降级】 jiàngjí 1.(降低级别) reduce to a lower rank; demote 2.(留级) send to a lower grade

【降价】 jiàngjià lower prices

【降结肠】 jiàngjiécháng 〈Anat.〉 descending colon

【降解】 jiàngjiě 1.〈*Biol*.〉 catabolism 2.〈*Chem*.〉 degradation

【降临】 jiànglín 〈*written*〉 befall; arrive; come

【降落】 jiàngluò descend; land; landing (n.); touch down; touchdown (n.): 飞机将在5分钟后～。The plan will land in five minutes. / 飞机的一个轮胎在～时爆了。One of the plane's tires burst on touchdown. / 他能在紧急时候把飞机～在水面上。He can land a plane on water in an emergency.

【降落伞】 jiàngluòsǎn parachute

【降旗】 jiàngqí lower a flag: 傍晚～ lower a flag at nightfall

【降生】 jiàngshēng be born

【降升】 jiàngshēng falling-rising

【降水】 jiàngshuǐ 〈*Meteorol*.〉 precipitation: 人工～ artificial precipitation

【降水量】 jiàngshuǐliàng 〈*Meteorol*.〉 precipitation

【降水区】 jiàngshuǐqū 〈*Meteorol*.〉 precipitation area

【降温】 jiàngwēn 1.(降低温度) lower the temperature 2.〈*Meteorol*.〉 drop in temperature; cool down

【降压】 jiàngyā 1.〈*Electr*.〉 step-down 2.〈*Med*.〉 bring high blood pressure down

【降压片】 jiàngyāpiàn 〈*Pharm*.〉 hypertension pill

【降雨量】 jiàngyǔliàng rainfall: 年～ annual rainfall

【降雨期】 jiàngyǔqī flush period

绛 (jiàng) deep red; crimson

【绛紫】 jiàngzǐ dark reddish purple

将［將］(jiàng) 1.(将军) general (请参见"一级上将、上将、中将、少将"各条) 2.(统兵者) commander in chief 3.(带兵) lead; command

(另见"将"jiāng)

【将官】 jiàngguān high-ranking army officer

【将领】 jiànglǐng generals: 高级～ high-ranking military officer

【将士】 jiàngshì 〈*written*〉 officers and men: 全体～ all the officers and soldiers

【将帅】 jiàngshuài high-ranking military officer

【将相】 jiàngxiàng generals and ministers of state

【将遇良才】 jiàngyùliángcái a Roland for an Oliver

酱［醬］(jiàng) 1.(豆酱;面酱) a thick sauce made from soya beans, flour, etc. 2.(用酱或酱油腌、煮) cooked or pickled in soy sauce 3.(像酱的食品) paste; jam; jelly; butter: 番茄～ tomato paste / 鱼～ fish paste / 草莓～ strawberry jam / 苹果～ apple jelly / 花生～ peanut butter

【酱菜】 jiàngcài vegetables pickled in soy sauce; pickles

【酱豆腐】 jiàngdòu·fu fermented bean curd

【酱色】 jiàngsè dark reddish brown

【酱油】 jiàngyóu soy sauce; soy: 辣～ pungent sauce

【酱园】 jiàngyuán a shop making and selling sauce, pickles, etc.

【酱紫】 jiàngzǐ dark reddish purple

强［強、彊］(jiàng) stubborn; unyielding

(另见"强"qiáng, qiǎng)

【强嘴】 jiàngzuǐ reply defiantly; answer back; talk back

犟［勥］(jiàng) obstinate; stubborn; self-willed; bullheaded

【犟脾气】 jiàngpí·qi be obstinate in disposition

糨［浆、糡］(jiàng) thick

【糨糊】 jiàng·hu paste: 打～ make paste

jiao

交 (jiāo) 1.(交出;交付;交纳) hand in; hand over; give up; deliver 2.(相交) meet; join: 夏秋之～ when summer is changing into autumn 3.(交叉) cross; intersect: AB和CD两线相～于E点。Line AB intersects line CD at E. 4.(交往;交谊) friend; acquaintance; friendship; relationship; relation: 患难之～ tested friend / 建～ establish diplomatic relations 5.(性交) have sexual intercourse 6.(交配) mate; breed 7.(互相) mutual; reciprocal; each other 8.(一齐;同

进）together; simultaneous **9**.（交易）deal; bargain; business transaction **10**.（同“跤”）fall

【交白卷】 jiāo báijuàn **1**.（没回答试题）hand in a blank examination paper; hand in an unanswered examination paper **2**.（没完成任务）fail to carry out an assignment; completely fail to accomplish a task

【交班】 jiāobān hand over to the next shift; turn over one's duty

【交兵】 jiāobīng 〈*written*〉 be at war; wage war

【交叉】 jiāochā **1**.（互相穿过）intersect; cross; crisscross **2**.（相重）overlapping：两个方案中～的部分 the overlapping parts of the two plans **3**.（间隔穿插）alternate; stagger

【交叉学科】 jiāochā xuékē interdiscipline

【交差】 jiāochāi report on one's mission; report on the fulfillment of one's duty

【交出】 jiāochū surrender; hand over

【交存】 jiāocún deposit; hand in for safekeeping

【交错】 jiāocuò **1**.（交叉）interlock; crisscross; interlace：管道纵横～ ducts and pipes crisscross **2**.〈*Mech*.〉staggered

【交代】 jiāodài **1**.（移交）turn over; hand over; transfer：～任务 assign and explain a task **2**.（嘱咐）tell; leave words; order：已～得清清楚楚 have given clear-cut orders **3**.（说明）explain; make clear; brief **4**.（说清楚）account for; justify oneself **5**.（坦白）confess：彻底～ make a clean breast of

【交待】 jiāodài **1**.（说明）explain; make clear; brief **2**.（完结）be finished

【交底】 jiāodǐ tell sb. what one's real intentions are; put all one's cards on the table

【交点】 jiāodiǎn **1**.〈*Math*.〉point of intersection **2**.〈*Astron*.〉node

【交电】 jiāodiàn transport vehicles and electrical household appliances

【交叠】 jiāodié overlap

【交锋】 jiāofēng cross swords; engage in a battle or contest; fight with; struggle with

【交付】 jiāofù **1**.（付钱）pay：～定金 down payment **2**.（交给）turn over; hand over; deliver; consign：～使用 has been made available to the users

【交割】 jiāogē **1**.（结清手续）complete a business transaction **2**.（移交）turn over; hand over; transfer

【交工】 jiāogōng hand over a completed project

【交公】 jiāogōng hand over to the collective or the state

【交媾】 jiāogòu sexual intercourse; copulation; coitus

【交好】 jiāohǎo （of people or states）be on friendly terms; be friendly with

【交合】 jiāohé **1**.（连在一起）join; link up **2**.（性交）have sexual intercourse

【交互】 jiāohù **1**.（互相）each other; mutual **2**.（替换着）alternately; in turn **3**.〈*Computer*〉interactive

【交互电视】 jiāohù diànshì interactive television

【交换】 jiāohuàn **1**.（互换）exchange; swap; interchange：～场地 change of courts / 与…～礼物 exchange gifts with sb. / ～名片 exchange visiting cards / ～意见 exchange views / 以…作为～ in exchange for sth. / 当你看完你的画报，我也看完我的时，咱们能～一下吗？When you've finished reading your pictorial, and I've finished mine, shall we swap? **2**.（商品交换）exchange：等价～ exchange of equal value / 商品～ exchange of commodities

【交换台】 jiāohuàntái 〈*Telecoms*.〉exchange

【交汇】 jiāohuì join; converge：汉水在武汉与长江～在一起。The Hanshui River joins the Yangtze River at Wuhan.

【交会】 jiāohuì join; converge

【交火】 jiāohuǒ fight

【交货】 jiāohuò delivery：～及时 timely delivery guaranteed / ～迅速 prompt delivery

【交集】 jiāojí （of different feelings）be mixed; occur simultaneously

【交际】 jiāojì social intercourse; communication：～很广 have a large circle of acquaintances / 忙于～ be busy with social activities

【交加】 jiāojiā 〈*written*〉（of two things）accompany each other; occur simultaneously

【交接】 jiāojiē **1**.（连接）join; connect **2**.（移交）hand over and take over **3**.（结交）associate with; make friends with

【交界】 jiāojiè have a common border; border on: 法国和西班牙～。France borders Spain.

【交卷】 jiāojuàn 1.(交考卷) hand in an examination paper 2.(完成任务) complete one's task; carry out an assignment; finish up one's job

【交口称誉】 jiāokǒu-chēngyù praise sb. or sth. unanimously

【交流】 jiāoliú 1.(沟通) exchange; interflow; interchange; bilateral exchange: 文化～ cultural exchange / ～经验 exchange experiences 2.〈*Electr*.〉 alternating

【交流道】 jiāoliúdào 〈*Transport*〉 ramp (AmE.); slip road (BrE.)

【交流电】 jiāoliúdiàn alternating current; A. C.

【交流发电机】 jiāoliú fādiànjī alternating current generator; alternator

【交流声】 jiāoliúshēng 〈*Electr*.〉 backdrop; hum noise

【交纳】 jiāonà pay (to the state or an organization); hand in: ～会费 pay membership dues / ～所得税 pay income tax

【交配】 jiāopèi mate; mating (n.); copulation:

【交情】 jiāo·qing friendship; friendly relation

【交融】 jiāoróng blend; mingle: 水乳～ be in perfect harmony

【交涉】 jiāoshè negotiate; make representations; take up with: 与某人～ negotiate with sb. on sth.

【交手】 jiāoshǒu fight hand to hand; be engaged in a hand-to-hand fight; come to grips

【交售】 jiāoshòu sell (to the state)

【交谈】 jiāotán talk with each other; converse; chat; have a conversation: 亲切～ have a heart-to-heart talk

【交替】 jiāotì 1.(接替) supersede; replace: 新老～ the new replace the old; the old gives place to the new 2.(替换着) alternately; take place by turn; in turn: 昼夜～ day alternates with night

【交通】 jiāotōng traffic; communications: ～便利 have transport facilities

【交通安全】 jiāotōng ānquán traffic safety

【交通标志】 jiāotōng biāozhì road sign

【交通规则】 jiāotōng guīzé traffic regulations

【交通警】 jiāotōngjǐng traffic police

【交通事故】 jiāotōng shìgù traffic accident

【交通事故多发地段】 jiāotōng shìgù duōfā dìduàn black spot

【交通信号灯】 jiāotōng xìnhàodēng traffic lights

【交通信号灯柱】 jiāotōng xìnhào dēngzhù traffic light post

【交通信号牌】 jiāotōng xìnhàopái traffic sign

【交通要道】 jiāotōng yàodào vital communication line

【交头接耳】 jiāotóu-jiēěr speak in each other's ears; to bill and coo

【交往】 jiāowǎng association; contact; associate with; be in contact with: 加强国际～ increase international contacts

【交往自由】 jiāowǎng zhìyóu freedom of communication

【交尾】 jiāowěi mate; mating; pairing; coupling

【交恶】 jiāowù fall foul of each other; become enemies

【交响诗】 jiāoxiǎngshī symphonic poem; tone poem

【交响乐】 jiāoxiǎngyuè symphony; symphonic music

【交响乐队】 jiāoxiǎng yuèduì philharmonic orchestra; symphony orchestra

【交心】 jiāoxīn lay one's heart bare; open one's heart to

【交学费】 jiāoxuéfèi 1.(指交上学的费用) pay the tuition fee 2.(把浪费国家资财比喻为"交学费") pay one's dues

【交易】 jiāoyì business; deal; trade; transaction: 黑市～ black market bargain / 现金～ cash transaction / 有利可图的～ profitable business / 政治～ a political deal

【交易额】 jiāoyì'é volume of trade

【交易会】 jiāoyìhuì trade fair

【交易所】 jiāoyìsuǒ exchange: 证券～ stock exchange

【交谊】 jiāoyì friendship; friendly relations

【交游】 jiāoyóu make friends

【交战】 jiāozhàn be at war; fight; wage war

【交战国】 jiāozhànguó belligerent countries

【交战状态】 jiāozhàn zhuàngtài state of war; belligerency
【交账】 jiāozhàng 1.(移交账目)hand over the accounts 2.(说明原因)account for
【交织】 jiāozhī interweave; intertwine; mingle

郊(jiāo) suburbs; outskirts: 市～ outskirts of a city / 西～ the western suburbs
【郊区】 jiāoqū suburban district; suburbs; outskirts
【郊外】 jiāowài the countryside around a city; outskirts
【郊游】 jiāoyóu outing; excursion

胶[膠](jiāo) 1.(黏性物)glue; gum: 树～ gum / 鱼～ fish glue 2.(用胶粘)stick with glue; glue 3.(黏的)gluey; sticky; gummy 4.(橡胶)rubber
【胶版】 jiāobǎn offset plate
【胶版纸】 jiāobǎnzhǐ offset paper
【胶布】 jiāobù 1.(涂有胶的布)rubberized fabric 2.(指橡皮膏)adhesive plaster
【胶带】 jiāodài adhesive tape; gummed tape
【胶带架】 jiāodàijià tape holder
【胶合】 jiāohé glue together; veneer
【胶合板】 jiāohébǎn plywood; veneer board
【胶结】 jiāojié glued; cemented
【胶卷】 jiāojuǎn film; film roll: 彩色～ color film / 全色～ panchromatic film
【胶粒】 jiāolì micelle; colloidal particle
【胶轮】 jiāolún rubber tire
【胶轮车】 jiāolúnchē rubber-tired cart
【胶木】 jiāomù bakelite
【胶囊】 jiāonáng capsule
【胶泥】 jiāoní clay
【胶片】 jiāopiàn film: 彩色～ color film / 电影～ cinefilm / 全色～ panchromatic film
【胶乳】 jiāorǔ 〈*Chem.*〉 latex
【胶水】 jiāoshuǐ mucilage; glue
【胶鞋】 jiāoxié rubber overshoes; galoshes; rubbers; rubber-soled shoes; tennis shoes
【胶靴】 jiāoxuē high rubber overshoes; galoshes
【胶印】 jiāoyìn offset printing; offset lithography; offset
【胶印机】 jiāoyìnjī offset press; offset (printing) machine
【胶质】 jiāozhì colloid
【胶着】 jiāozhuó deadlocked; stalemated: ～状态 deadlock; stalemate; impasse

跤(jiāo) 1.(跌跤)fall: 跌～ trip and fall; stumble an fall / 我在木头上绊了一下跌了～。I stumbled on a log and fell. 2.〈*Sports*〉 wrestle

浇[澆](jiāo) 1.(洒)pour liquid on; sprinkle: ～水 sprinkle water on 2.(浇灌)irrigate; water: ～花 water flowers 3.(浇铸)cast
【浇灌】 jiāoguàn 1.(灌溉)water; irrigate 2.(灌进模子内)pour: ～混凝土 pour concrete
【浇冷水】 jiāolěngshuǐ throw cold water on
【浇注】 jiāozhù pour: ～混凝土 pour concrete
【浇铸】 jiāozhù 〈*Metall.*〉 casting; pouring

娇[嬌](jiāo) 1.(柔嫩)tender; lovely; charming 2.(虚弱)fragile; frail; delicate 3.(娇气)squeamish 4.(娇惯)pamper; spoil
【娇滴滴】 jiāodīdī delicately pretty; affectedly sweet
【娇惯】 jiāoguàn pamper; coddle; spoil
【娇贵】 jiāo·gui enervated; pampered
【娇憨】 jiāohān young and ignorant
【娇媚】 jiāomèi 1.(撒娇献媚)coquettish 2.(妩媚)sweet and charming
【娇嫩】 jiāo·nen 1.(柔嫩)tender and lovely 2.(柔弱)fragile; delicate
【娇气】 jiāo·qì squeamish; finicky
【娇娆】 jiāoráo enchantingly beautiful
【娇生惯养】 jiāoshēng-guànyǎng pampered by doting parents; brought up in clover
【娇声娇气】 jiāoshēng-jiāoqì speak in a seductive tone
【娇艳】 jiāoyàn delicate and charming; tender and beautiful
【娇纵】 jiāozòng indulge (a child); pamper; spoil

骄[驕](jiāo) proud; arrogant; conceited
【骄傲】 jiāo'ào 1.(自大)arrogant; conceited: ～自满 conceited and self-satisfied; arrogant and complacent 2.(自豪)be proud; take pride in: 值得～ worth feeling proud of 3.(值得自豪的人或物)pride: 儿子是她的～和快乐。Her son is her pride and joy.

【骄兵必败】 jiāobīng-bìbài An army puffed up with pride is bound to lose.
【骄横】 jiāohèng arrogant and imperious; overbearing
【骄矜】 jiāojīn 〈written〉 self-important; proud; haughty
【骄气】 jiāoqì overbearing airs; arrogance
【骄奢淫逸】 jiāoshē-yínyì wallowing in luxury and pleasure; extravagant and dissipated
【骄阳】 jiāoyáng 〈written〉 blazing sun; scorching sun
【骄纵】 jiāozòng arrogant and willful

教 (jiāo) teach; instruct: ～英语 teach English / ～某人游泳 teach sb. to swim / 谁～你开车的? Who taught you to drive?
(另见"教"jiào)
【教书】 jiāoshū teach school; teach
【教书匠】 jiāoshūjiàng teacher
【教书育人】 jiāoshū-yùrén impart knowledge and educate people
【教学】 jiāoxué teach school; teach

椒 (jiāo) hot spice plants; pepper; chili; red pepper
【椒盐】 jiāoyán spiced salt

焦 (jiāo) 1.(烧焦) burnt; scorched; charred: ～味 smell of burning 2.(焦炭) coke 3.(心焦) worried; anxious
【焦斑】 jiāobān focal spat
【焦点】 jiāodiǎn 1.〈Physics〉 focal point; focus: ～对准 in focus / ～没对准 out of focus 2.(注意点) central issue; point at issue: 矛盾的～ focal points of contradictions / 成为关注的～ be the focus of attention
【焦点平面快门】 jiāodiǎn píngmiàn kuàimén 〈Photog.〉 focal plane shutter
【焦点问题】 jiāodiǎn wèntí focal issue
【焦耳】 jiāoěr 〈Physics〉 joule
【焦耳定律】 jiāoěr dìnglǜ 〈Physics〉 Joule's law
【焦化】 jiāohuà 〈Chem.〉 coking
【焦黄】 jiāohuáng sallow; brown
【焦急】 jiāojí anxious; worried
【焦距】 jiāojù 〈Physics〉 focal distance; focal length: 调节～ focus (v.)
【焦渴】 jiāokě terribly thirsty; parched; dying of thirst
【焦枯】 jiāokū shrivelled; dried up; withered
【焦虑】 jiāolǜ feel anxious; have worries and misgivings
【焦虑反应】 jiāolǜ fǎnyìng anxiety reaction
【焦煤】 jiāoméi coking coal
【焦炭】 jiāotàn coke: 沥青～ pitch coke
【焦头烂额】 jiāotóu-lànè in a terrible fix; be bruised and battered
【焦土】 jiāotǔ scorched earth; ravages of war
【焦土政策】 jiāotǔ zhèngcè scorched earth policy
【焦油】 jiāoyóu 〈Chem.〉 tar: 煤～ coal tar
【焦躁】 jiāozào restless with anxiety; impatient

蕉 (jiāo) banana; plantain

礁 (jiāo) reef: 珊瑚～ coral reefs / 触～ strike a reef
【礁石】 jiāoshí reef; rock: 油轮驶上水下～, 900万加仑的原油泄漏出来。Nine million gallons of oil were dumped when the tanker ran into an underwater reef.

嚼 (jiáo) masticate; chew; munch
【嚼舌】 jiáoshé 1.(搬弄是非) wag one's tongue; chatter away; gossip 2.(无谓争论) argue senselessly; squabble
【嚼烟】 jiáoyān chewing tobacco
【嚼子】 jiáo·zi bit (of a bridle)

角 (jiǎo) 1.(动物的角) horn 2.(号角) bugle; horn 3.(岬角) cape; promontory; headland: 好望～ Cape of Good Hope / 合恩～ Cape de Hornas 4.(角落) corner 5.〈Math.〉 angle; angular (adj.): 直～ right angle / 锐～ acute angle / 钝～ obtuse angle / 补～ complementary angle / 90度～ angle of 90 degrees / 成30度～ at 30 degree angle (符号为 ∠) 6.(人民币辅币) jiao (1 yuan = 10 jiao = 100 fen): 5角的邮票 a stamp of 5 jiao
(另见"角"jué)
【角度】 jiǎodù 1.〈Math.〉 angle: 给照相机换个～ angle a camera 2.(看问题的出发点) point of view; angle: 从各个～考虑这个问题 consider all angles of the question / 从另一个～看问题 regard the issue from another point of view / 为了取悦领导, 他改变了报告的～。He angled his reports to please his di-

rector.
【角度计】 jiǎodùjì goniometer; angle gauge
【角钢】 jiǎogāng 〈*Metall.*〉 angle steel; angle bar; angle iron
【角力桥】 jiǎolìqiáo 〈*Wrestle*〉 bridge
【角楼】 jiǎolóu watchtower
【角落】 jiǎoluò corner; nook: 在房间～ in the corner of the room
【角门】 jiǎomén small side door
【角膜】 jiǎomó 〈*Anat.*〉 cornea
【角膜接触镜】 jiǎomó jiēchùjìng contact lens
【角膜炎】 jiǎomóyán 〈*Med.*〉 keratitis; ceratitis
【角膜移植】 jiǎomó yízhí 〈*Med.*〉 corneal transplantation
【角球】 jiǎoqiú 〈*Football*〉 corner (kick); corner ball
【角铁】 jiǎotiě angle iron
【角质】 jiǎozhì 〈*Biol.*〉 cutin; keratin

侥[僥] (jiǎo)

【侥幸】 jiǎoxìng lucky; by luck; by a fluke: ～得免 escape by good fortune

佼 (jiǎo) 〈*written*〉 handsome; beautiful

【佼佼】 jiǎojiǎo 〈*written*〉 above average; outstanding

狡 (jiǎo) crafty; foxy; cunning

【狡辩】 jiǎobiàn quibble; indulge in sophistry
【狡猾】 jiǎohuá sly; crafty; cunning; tricky
【狡计】 jiǎojì crafty trick; ruse
【狡赖】 jiǎolài deny (by resorting to sophistry)
【狡黠】 jiǎoxiá 〈*written*〉 sly; crafty; cunning
【狡诈】 jiǎozhà deceitful; crafty; cunning

饺 (jiǎo) dumpling

【饺子】 jiǎo·zi dumpling
【饺子粉】 jiǎo·zifěn dumpling flour
【饺子皮】 jiǎo·zipí dumpling wrapper
【饺子馅】 jiǎo·zixiàn filling for dumplings; stuffing

绞 (jiǎo) 1.(绞扭在一起) twist; wring; entangle: 心如刀～ feel as if a knife were being twisted in one's heart 2.(转动轮轴) wind 3.(绞刑) hang by the neck 4.〈*Mech.*〉 reaming 5.〈*classifier*〉 skein; hank

【绞车】 jiǎochē winch; windlass
【绞架】 jiǎojià gallows
【绞尽脑汁】 jiǎojìn-nǎozhī rack one's brains; beat one's brains
【绞盘】 jiǎopán capstan
【绞肉机】 jiǎoròujī meat mincer; mincing machine
【绞杀】 jiǎoshā 1.(勒死) strangle; hang; garrotte 2.(压制、摧残) strangle; throttle
【绞死】 jiǎosǐ gibbet
【绞索】 jiǎosuǒ (the hangman's) noose
【绞痛】 jiǎotòng 〈*Med.*〉 angina: 心～ angina pectoris
【绞刑】 jiǎoxíng hanging; sentence to be hung; sentence to the gallows
【绞刑架】 jiǎoxíngjià gallows

铰 (jiǎo) 1.(剪) cut with scissors 2.(用铰刀切削) bore with a reamer; ream

【铰刀】 jiǎodāo reamer
【铰接】 jiǎojiē 〈*Mech.*〉 join with a hinge; articulate
【铰接式公共汽车】 jiǎojiēshì gōnggòng qìchē articulated bus
【铰链】 jiǎoliàn hinge: 我们得把门从～上拆下来，才能让这写字台进房间。We had to take the door off its hinges to get this desk into the room.

皎 (jiǎo) clear and bright

【皎皎】 jiǎojiǎo very clear and bright; glistening white
【皎皎者易污】 jiǎojiǎozhě yìwū the immaculate stains easily
【皎洁】 jiǎojié (of moonlight) bright and clear

矫[矯] (jiǎo) 1.(矫正) rectify; straighten out; correct 2.(强壮；勇武) strong; brave

【矫健】 jiǎojiàn strong and vigorous
【矫捷】 jiǎojié vigorous and nimble; brisk
【矫揉造作】 jiǎoróu-zàozuò affected; artificial
【矫饰】 jiǎoshì feign in order to conceal sth.; dissemble
【矫枉过正】 jiǎowǎng-guòzhèng exceed the

proper limits in righting a wrong; overcorrect; overdo in righting a wrong
【矫形】 jiǎoxíng 〈*Med.*〉 orthopedic
【矫形术】 jiǎoxíngshù orthopedics
【矫形外科】 jiǎoxíng wàikē orthopedic surgery
【矫形外科医生】 jiǎoxíng wàikē yīshēng orthopedic surgeon
【矫正】 jiǎozhèng correct; put right; rectify
【矫正视力】 jiǎozhèng shìlì **1.**(指行为) correct defects of vision; rectify one's eyesight **2.**(指视力) corrected eyesight; rectified vision

脚[腳](jiǎo) **1.**(足) foot **2.**(东西的最下部) foot; base
【脚背】 jiǎobèi instep
【脚本】 jiǎoběn script; scenario: 电影～ film script
【脚脖子】 jiǎobó·zi ankle
【脚步】 jiǎobù step; pace: 加快～ hasten one's steps
【脚步声】 jiǎobùshēng footstep: 听到～ hear sb's steps
【脚灯】 jiǎodēng footlight
【脚蹬子】 jiǎodēng·zi pedal; treadle
【脚底】 jiǎodǐ sole
【脚夫】 jiǎofū porter
【脚根】 jiǎogēn heel
【脚跟】 jiǎogēn heel: 站稳～ stand firm
【脚尖】 jiǎojiān the tip of a toe; tiptoe: 踮着～走 walk on tiptoe
【脚扣】 jiǎokòu foot clasp
【脚镣】 jiǎoliào fetters; shackles
【脚面】 jiǎomiàn instep
【脚蹼】 jiǎopǔ 〈*Swimming*〉 flipper; fin
【脚气】 jiǎoqì **1.**〈*Med.*〉 beriberi **2.**(脚癣) athlete's foot
【脚钱】 jiǎo·qian payment to a porter
【脚刹车】 jiǎoshāchē foot brake
【脚手架】 jiǎoshǒujià 〈*Archit.*〉 scaffold; falsework
【脚踏板】 jiǎotàbǎn 〈*Auto*〉 running board
【脚踏开关】 jiǎotà kāiguān floor push
【脚踏开关插口】 jiǎotà kāiguān chākǒu 〈*Guitar*〉 foot-switch input
【脚踏实地】 jiǎotà-shídì have one's feet planted on solid ground; stand on solid ground
【脚踏式变速杆】 jiǎotàshì biànsùgǎn 〈*Motorcycle*〉 foot gear-change control
【脚踏制动器】 jiǎotà zhìdòngqì foot brake
【脚腕子】 jiǎowàn·zi ankle
【脚误裁判员】 jiǎowù cáipànyuán 〈*Tennis*〉 foot-fault judge
【脚心】 jiǎoxīn arch (of the foot)
【脚癣】 jiǎoxuǎn 〈*Med.*〉 tinea pedis; athlete's foot
【脚印】 jiǎoyìn footprint; footmark; track
【脚掌】 jiǎozhǎng sole (of the foot)
【脚指】 jiǎozhǐ toe
【脚指甲】 jiǎozhǐjiǎ toenail
【脚趾】 jiǎozhǐ toe
【脚注】 jiǎozhù footnote: 加一个～ make a footnote

搅[攪](jiǎo) **1.**(搅拌) stir; mix **2.**(搅扰) disturb; annoy
【搅拌】 jiǎobàn stir; agitate; mix
【搅拌车】 jiǎobànchē truck mixer: 混凝土～ truck mixer
【搅拌机】 jiǎobànjī mixer; blender
【搅拌器】 jiǎobànqì stirrer; agitator
【搅打机】 jiǎodǎjī beetle
【搅动】 jiǎodòng mix; stir
【搅和】 jiǎo·huo **1.**(混合) mix; blend; mingle: 把水泥和沙石～在一起 mix cement, sand and pebbles **2.**(扰乱) mess up; spoil
【搅乱】 jiǎoluàn confuse; throw into disorder; mess up: ～了计划 mess up the plan / 把人心～ disturb people's feeling
【搅扰】 jiǎorǎo disturb; annoy; cause trouble

缴(jiǎo) **1.**(交出) pay; hand over; hand in: 上～ turn over to the higher authorities **2.**(迫使交出) capture
【缴获】 jiǎohuò capture; seize
【缴纳】 jiǎonà pay: ～会费 pay membership dues / ～所得税 pay income tax
【缴税】 jiǎoshuì pay taxes
【缴销】 jiǎoxiāo hand in for cancellation
【缴械】 jiǎoxiè **1.**(解除武装) disarm **2.**(被迫交出武器) surrender one's weapons; lay down one's arms

剿[勦](jiǎo) put down; send armed forces to suppress
【剿匪】 jiǎofěi suppress bandits; put down

bandits

【剿灭】 jiǎomiè exterminate; wipe out

叫[吅](jiào) 1.(发出声音) cry; shout 2.(招唤) call; greet 3.(雇车;点菜;买煤) hire; order: ～出租汽车 hire a taxi; call a taxi 4.(称为) name; call: 他～什么? What's his name? 5.(吩咐) ask; order; make: 医生～我好好休息。The doctor ordered me to have a good rest. 6.(被)书～谁拿走了? Who took the book?

【叫喊】 jiàohǎn shout; yell; howl

【叫好】 jiàohǎo applaud; shout 'Bravo!'; shout 'Well done!'

【叫号电话】 jiàohào diànhuà station to station call

【叫化子】 jiàohuā·zi beggar

【叫花子】 jiàohuā·zi beggar

【叫唤】 jiào·huan 1.(大声叫) cry out; call out 2.(啼叫) cry; shout; sound

【叫苦】 jiàokǔ complain of hardship or suffering; moan and groan: ～连天 one's cry for bitterness is heavenly high; ventilate one's endless grievances

【叫骂】 jiàomà shout curses

【叫卖】 jiàomài cry one's wares; peddle; hawk

【叫门】 jiàomén call at the door to be let in

【叫屈】 jiàoqū complain of being wronged; protest against an injustice

【叫嚷】 jiàorǎng shout; howl; clamor; raise a hue and cry

【叫人电话】 jiàorén diànhuà person to person call

【叫嚣】 jiàoxiāo clamor; raise a hue and cry

【叫醒】 jiàoxǐng wake up; awake: 他7点钟～了我。He awoke me at seven.

【叫座】 jiàozuò draw a large audience; draw well; appeal to the audience: 这部电影很～。The film draws well.

【叫做】 jiàozuò be called; be known as

轿[轎](jiào) sedan (chair)

【轿车】 jiàochē 1.(马拉轿车) (horse-drawn) carriage 2.(汽车) bus; car; sedan; saloon: 小～ car; sedan; saloon / 大～ bus / 高级～ limousine

【轿子】 jiào·zi sedan (chair)

觉[覺](jiào) sleep: 睡一～ have a sleep / 一～醒来 wake up after a sound sleep

(另见"觉"jué)

校(jiào) check; proofread; collate: 二～ the second proof

(另见"校"xiào)

【校订】 jiàodìng check against the authoritative text

【校对】 jiàoduì 1.(核对) proofread; proof; proofreading (n.): 许多错误是在～阶段改正的。Most of the errors were corrected at the proofreading stage. 2.(校对人) proofreader 3.(核准) check against a standard; calibrate

【校改】 jiàogǎi read and correct proofs

【校勘】 jiàokān collate

【校勘学】 jiàokānxué textual criticism

【校样】 jiàoyàng 〈*Printing*〉 proof sheet; proof

【校阅】 jiàoyuè 1.(审阅校订) read and revise 2.(检阅) review

【校正】 jiàozhèng proofread and correct; rectify

【校正器】 jiàozhèngqì corrector; adjuster

【校正液】 jiàozhèngyè correcting fluid

【校准】 jiàozhǔn 〈*Mech.*〉 calibration

【校准器】 jiàozhǔnqì calibrator

较(jiào) 1.(比较) compare; as compare with; in comparison with 2.(一定程度的) comparatively; relatively; fairly; quite; rather: 取得～大进步 make considerable progress 3.(明显) clear; obvious; marked

【较比】 jiàobǐ comparatively; relatively; fairly; quite

【较差】 jiàochà relatively poor

【较好】 jiàohǎo fairly good; quite good

【较量】 jiàoliàng 1.(比高低) measure one's strength with; have a contest; have a trial of strength 2.(计较) haggle; argue; dispute

教(jiào) 1.(教导) teach; instruct 2.(宗教) religion: 信～ believe in a religion; be religious

(另见"教"jiāo)

【教案】 jiào'àn teaching plan; lesson plan

【教鞭】 jiàobiān (teacher's) pointer

【教材】 jiàocái teaching material; textbook

【教程】 jiàochéng course (of study)：简明～ a concise course

【教导】 jiàodǎo 1.(教育指导) instruct; teach; give guidance 2.(学说，指引) teaching; guidance

【教导员】 jiàodǎoyuán political instructor

【教父】 jiàofù god-father

【教改】 jiàogǎi educational reform; reform in education

【教工】 jiàogōng teaching and administrative staff (of a school)

【教官】 jiàoguān drillmaster; instructor

【教规】 jiàoguī 〈*Relig.*〉 canon

【教皇】 jiàohuáng 〈*Relig.*〉 pope; pontiff; pontifical (adj.)：～信谕 a pontifical letter

【教会】 jiàohuì 〈*Relig.*〉 church

【教会学校】 jiàohuì xuéxiào missionary school

【教诲】 jiàohuì teaching; instruction

【教具】 jiàojù teaching aid：直观～ audio-visual aids; aids to object teaching

【教科书】 jiàokēshū textbook

【教练】 jiàoliàn 1.(训练) train; drill; coach 2.(教练员) coach; instructor：足球～ football coach

【教练机】 jiàoliànjī trainer plane

【教龄】 jiàolíng length of teaching

【教母】 jiàomǔ god-mother

【教女】 jiàonǚ god-daughter

【教派】 jiàopài 〈*Relig.*〉 religious sect; denomination

【教区】 jiàoqū parish

【教师】 jiàoshī teacher; school teacher：特级～ special-class teacher

【教师节】 jiàoshījié Teachers' Day

【教士】 jiàoshì 〈*Relig.*〉 priest; clergyman (m.); clergy-woman (f.)

【教室】 jiàoshì classroom; schoolroom：阶梯～ lecture theater

【教授】 jiàoshòu 1.(指职称) professor：客座～ visiting professor; guest professor / 副～ associate professor 2.(讲授) instruct; teach：～得法 have tact in teaching

【教授职称】 jiàoshòu zhíchēng title of professor (of the first, second or third grade)

【教唆】 jiàosuō instigate; abet; put sb. up to sth.

【教唆犯】 jiàosuōfàn instigator; abetter

【教唆犯罪】 jiàosuō fànzuì 1.(教唆他人犯罪) instigate to crime 2.(被人教唆犯罪) subornation

【教坛】 jiàotán educational circle; educational world

【教堂】 jiàotáng church; cathedral

【教条】 jiàotiáo dogma; doctrine; creed; tenet

【教条主义】 jiàotiáo zhǔyì dogmatism; doctrinairism

【教廷】 jiàotíng the Vatican; the Holy See

【教廷大使】 jiàotíng dàshǐ nuncio

【教廷公使】 jiàotíng gōngshǐ internuncio

【教徒】 jiàotú believer (follower) of a religion

【教务】 jiàowù educational administration

【教务处】 jiàowùchù Dean's Office

【教务长】 jiàowùzhǎng Dean of Studies

【教学】 jiàoxué teaching; education

【教学大纲】 jiàoxué dàgāng teaching program; academic program

【教学法】 jiàoxuéfǎ teaching methodology; pedagogy

【教学方针】 jiàoxué fāngzhēn principles of teaching

【教学工作量】 jiàoxué gōngzuòliàng faculty load

【教学机】 jiàoxuéjī teaching machine

【教学玩具】 jiàoxué wánjù didactical doll

【教学相长】 jiàoxué xiāngzhǎng teaching benefits teacher and student alike; teaching benefits teachers as well as students; teaching and learning promote and enhance each other

【教学中心】 jiàoxué zhōngxīn training center

【教学资料】 jiàoxué zīliào resources material

【教训】 jiào·xun 1.(鉴戒) lesson; moral：血的～ a lesson paid for with blood 2.(教育训诫) teach sb. a lesson; give sb. a talking-to; chide

【教研室】 jiàoyánshì teaching and research section

【教养】 jiàoyǎng 1.(教育和培养) bring up; train; educate 2.(文化品德修养) upbringing; education; culture; breeding 3.〈*Law*〉 correction

【教养员】 jiàoyǎngyuán teacher

【教义】 jiàoyì 〈*Religion*〉 religious doctrine; creed

【教益】　jiàoyì　〈*written*〉 benefit gained from sb's wisdom; enlightenment

【教育】　jiàoyù　1.(指各种教育) education: 高等～ higher education / 职业～ vocational education 2.(教导) teach; educate; inculcate

【教育程度】　jiàoyù chéngdù　level of education

【教育方针】　jiàoyù fāngzhēn　policy for education; educational policy

【教育费附加】　jiàoyùfèi fùjiā　additional education funds

【教育家】　jiàoyùjiā　educationist; educator

【教育界】　jiàoyùjiè　educational circles; educational world

【教员】　jiàoyuán　teacher; instructor

【教员任期】　jiàoyuán rènqī　academic tenure

【教员休息室】　jiàoyuán xiūxīshì　staff room; common room

【教长】　jiàozhǎng　〈*Relig.*〉 dean

【教职员】　jiàozhíyuán　teaching and administrative staff

【教主】　jiàozhǔ　the founder of a religion

【教子】　jiàozǐ　god-son

酵 (jiào)　ferment; leaven

【酵母】　jiàomǔ　yeast: 鲜～ yeast cake

【酵母菌】　jiàomǔjūn　yeast; saccharomycete

窖 (jiào)　1.(地窖) cellar or pit for storing things: 菜～ vegetable cellar 2.(收藏在窖里) store sth. in a cellar or pit

【窖藏】　jiàocáng　store sth. in a cellar

jie

节[節] (jiē)
(另见"节"jié)

【节骨眼】　jiē·guyǎn　1.(关键时刻) critical juncture; at the critical moment; in the nick of time 2.(紧要环节) vital link

疖[癤] (jiē)

【疖子】　jiē·zi　1.〈*Med.*〉 furuncle; boil 2.〈*Bot.*〉 knot (in wood)

阶[階、堦] (jiē)　1.(台阶) steps; stairs 2.(等级) rank

【阶层】　jiēcéng　(social) stratum: 特权～ the privileged stratum

【阶段】　jiēduàn　stage; phase; period: 历史～ historical period

【阶级】　jiējí　1.(台阶) step 2.(社会阶级) class; social class: 工人～ the working class / 有产～ propertied class / 无产～ proletariat / 剥削～ exploiting class / 被剥削～ exploited class / 中产～ middle class; middle bourgeoisie / 资产～ bourgeoisie; capitalist class

【阶级成分】　jiējí chéngfèn　class status

【阶级冲突】　jiējí chōngtū　class conflict

【阶级斗争】　jiējí dòuzhēng　class struggle

【阶级对抗】　jiējí duìkàng　class antagonism

【阶级感情】　jiējí gǎnqíng　class feeling

【阶级觉悟】　jiējí juéwù　class consciousness

【阶级立场】　jiējí lìchǎng　class stand

【阶级矛盾】　jiējí máodùn　class contradictions

【阶级性】　jiējíxìng　class character; class nature

【阶级意识】　jiējí yìshí　class consciousness

【阶梯】　jiētī　a flight of stairs; ladder

【阶梯教室】　jiētī jiàoshì　lecture theater

【阶下囚】　jiēxiàqiú　prisoner; captive

皆 (jiē)　all; each and every

【皆大欢喜】　jiēdà-huānxǐ　everybody is happy; to the satisfaction of all; everybody is satisfied

结 (jiē)　bear; form; produce: ～果 bear fruit / ～籽 form seeds
(另见"结"jié)

【结巴】　jiē·ba　1.(口吃) stammer; stutter 2.(口吃的人) stammerer; stutterer

【结果】　jiēguǒ　bear fruit: 开花～ be in blossom and then bear fruit

【结果树】　jiēguǒshù　bearing-age tree

【结实】　jiēshí　(结出果实) bear fruit; fructify; fruit

【结实】　jiē·shi　1.(坚固耐用) solid; sturdy; durable 2.(健壮) strong; sturdy; tough; robust

【结籽】　jiēzǐ　set seeds; seed-setting

秸[稭] (jiē)　stalks; straw: 豆～ bean stalks / 麦～ wheat straw / 秫～ sorghum stalks

【秸秆】　jiēgǎn　straw

【秸秆肥】　jiēgǎnféi　compost made of stalks

接 (jiē)　1.(接近) come into contact with; come close to 2.(继续) continue: ～下页

be continued on next page 3.(连接;使连接) connect; join; put together: ~管子 join two pipes together 4.(托住;承受) catch; take hold of: ~球 catch the ball 5.(接受;接到) receive; take: 他~到一封信。He received a letter. 6.(迎接) meet; welcome: 到机场~人 go to the airport to meet sb. 7.(接替) take over

【接班】 jiēbān 1.(接上一班) take one's turn on duty 2.(接替) take over from; succeed to; carry on: 他接父亲的班,当了推销员。He succeeded his father as traveling salesman.

【接班人】 jiēbānrén successor: 谁将被指定为经理的~? Who will be appointed as the manager's successor?

【接触】 jiēchù 1.(交往) come into contact with; get in touch with 2.(冲突) engage 3.(挨上;碰着) contact: ~不良 loose contact

【接触眼镜】 jiēchù yǎnjìng contact lens

【接待】 jiēdài receive; admit: 镇上的人非常高兴地~了归来的战士。The townspeople received the returning soldiers with great cheers. / 这旅馆大约能~三百人。The hotel admits about 300 people.

【接待人员】 jiēdài rényuán reception personnel

【接待室】 jiēdàishì reception room

【接待站】 jiēdàizhàn reception center

【接地】 jiēdì 1.〈*Electr.*〉 ground connection; grounding; earthing 2.〈*Aeron.*〉 touchdown; ground contact

【接二连三】 jiēèr-liánsān one after another; in quick succession; repeatedly; continuously

【接防】 jiēfáng relieve a garrison; relieve; take over the defense

【接风】 jiēfēng give a dinner for a visitor from afar; give a reception in honor of a guest from afar: ~洗尘 give a dinner of welcome

【接骨】 jiēgǔ set a fracture

【接管】 jiēguǎn take over

【接合】 jiēhé joint; join; link

【接济】 jiējì give material assistance to; give financial help to; offer pecuniary aid to

【接见】 jiējiàn receive sb.; grant an interview to

【接近】 jiējìn be close to; near; approach: ~最高水平 approach the topmost level

【接客】 jiēkè 1.(接待客人) receive guests 2.(妓女接客) have sex with; prostitute

【接口】 jiēkǒu 〈*Computer*〉 interface

【接口盖】 jiēkǒugài 〈*Astron.*〉 access flap

【接力】 jiēlì relay; relay race

【接力棒】 jiēlìbàng relay baton

【接力区】 jiēlìqū take-over zone

【接力赛跑】 jiēlì sàipǎo relay race; relay: 我们队赢得400米~的金牌。Our team won the gold for the 400 meters relay.

【接连】 jiēlián on end; in a row; in succession; running: ~好几天 for days on end / ~提出许多问题 raise one question after another

【接纳】 jiēnà 1.(接受) admit (into); take in: 他被~为学会会员。He was admitted as a member of the society. 2.(采纳) adopt; accept

【接洽】 jiēqià take up a matter with; arrange with; consult with: 来~工作 be here to talk business

【接球】 jiēqiú 1.(接到传来的球) catch a ball 2.〈*Football*〉 take a pass

【接球员】 jiēqiúyuán 〈*Table Tennis & Tennis*〉 receiver

【接壤】 jiērǎng border on; be contiguous to; be bounded by: 加拿大和美国~。Canada borders the United States.

【接壤地区】 jiērǎng dìqū contiguous areas

【接任】 jiērèn take over a job; replace; succeed

【接入】 jiērù cut-in

【接生】 jiēshēng deliver a child; practice midwifery

【接生员】 jiēshēngyuán midwife

【接收】 jiēshōu 1.(收受) receive: ~订货 receive orders for 2.(接管) take over; expropriate 3.(接纳) admit

【接收合同】 jiēshōu hé·tong receipt of contract

【接收机】 jiēshōujī receiver: 电视~ TV receiver / 无线电~ wireless receiver

【接收器】 jiēshōuqì receiver

【接手】 jiēshǒu 1.(接管) take over (duties, etc.); take up matters 2.〈*Baseball*〉 catcher

【接手手套】 jiēshǒu shǒutào 〈*Baseball*〉

catcher's glove

【接受】 jiēshòu accept; take; embrace: ～定货 execute an order / ～客户定货 accept orders according to customers' requirements / ～…的邀请 accept the invitation of sb. / ～教训 learn a lesson / ～考验 face up to a test; be ready for a test / ～意见 take sb's advice / ～任务 accept an assignment; accept a task / ～批评 accept criticism / ～群众监督 subject oneself to supervision by the masses / ～贿赂 accept bribes; take bribes; on the take

【接替】 jiētì take over; replace; succeed; take the place of: 他去年退休了,我～了他的工作。He retired last year and I took over from him.

【接通】 jiētōng put through: 电话～了吗? Have you got through?

【接头】 jiētóu 1.(连接起来) connect; join; joint 2.(找人联系) contact; get in touch with 3.(了解情况) know about; have knowledge of: 这事她不～。She doesn't know anything about it. 4.〈*Mech.*〉 connection; joint; junction: 万向～ universal joint

【接吻】 jiēwěn kiss

【接线】 jiēxiàn 1.〈*Electr.*〉 wiring 2.(接通线路) work a telephone switchboard

【接线插口】 jiēxiàn chākǒu 〈*Guitar*〉 jack-plug socket

【接线员】 jiēxiànyuán telephone operator

【接续】 jiēxù continue; follow

【接应】 jiēyìng 1.(配合) coordinate with; come to sb's aid 2.(供应) supply

【接站】 jiēzhàn go to the railway station to meet sb.

【接着】 jiē·zhe 1.(用手接) catch: 给你一个苹果,～! Here's an apple for you. Catch! 2.(连着;紧跟着) follow; carry on; go on (with); proceed

【接踵】 jiēzhǒng 〈*written*〉 following on sb's heels: ～而至 come one after another; follow hard at heel

【接种】 jiēzhòng 〈*Med.*〉 have an inoculation; inoculate: ～牛痘疫苗 be vaccinated

揭 (jiē) 1.(揭下来) tear off; take off 2.(揭开) uncover; lift (the lid, etc.) 3.(揭露) expose; show up; bring to light

【揭不开锅】 jiē·bukāiguō have nothing in the pot; go hungry

【揭穿】 jiēchuān expose; lay bare; show up: ～…的阴谋 expose sb's scheme / ～谎言 expose a lie

【揭短】 jiēduǎn rake up sb's faults; disclose sb's shortcomings

【揭发】 jiēfā expose; unmask; bring to light; lay open: ～罪行 expose a crime

【揭盖子】 jiēgài·zi take the lid off

【揭开】 jiēkāi uncover; reveal; open; disclose: ～内幕 reveal the inside story of; get to the bottom of / ～序幕 raise the curtain on sth.

【揭老底】 jiēlǎodǐ make known sb. s old secret

【揭露】 jiēlù expose; ferret out; uncover; disclose; show up; bring to light: ～矛盾 expose contradictions / ～问题 reveal the problem

【揭幕】 jiēmù unveil (a monument, etc.); inaugurate

【揭示】 jiēshì 1.(公布) announce; promulgate; proclaim 2.(使人看到) reveal; bring to light

【揭晓】 jiēxiǎo announce; make known; publish: 足球赛的结果已～。The result of the football match has been announced.

嗟 (jiē) 〈*written*〉 sigh; lament

【嗟来之食】 jiēláizhīshí food handed out in contempt; a handout

街 (jiē) street: 他住在宽～。He lives in Wide Street. / 我在～上遇见了她。I met her in the street.

【街道】 jiēdào 1.(路) street 2.(街道地区) residential district; neighborhood

【街道办事处】 jiēdào bànshìchù subdistrict office; subdistrict government

【街道居民委员会】 jiēdào jūmín wěiyuánhuì neighborhood committee

【街灯】 jiēdēng street lamp; road lamp

【街坊】 jiē·fang neighbor

【街垒】 jiēlěi street barricade

【街市】 jiēshì downtown streets

【街谈巷议】 jiētán-xiàngyì street gossip; rumors; common talk

【街头】 jiētóu street corner; street: 涌上～ pour into the streets

【街头巷尾】 jiētóu-xiàngwěi streets and lanes; street corners and alleys

【街头信誉】 jiētóu xìnyù street credit; street credibility

【街巷手册】 jiēxiàng shǒucè street dictionary

【街心花园】 jiēxīn huāyuán garden at the intersection

孑 (jié) 〈*written*〉 lonely; all alone

【孑孓】 jiéjué wiggler; wriggler

【孑然】 jiérán 〈*written*〉 solitary; lonely; alone: ～一身 all alone in the world

节［節］(jié) **1**.（各段的相连处）joint; node; knot: 脱～ out of joint **2**.（段落）division; part **3**.〈*classifier*〉 section; length: 第三章第二～ Chapter Three, Section Two **4**.（节日）festival; red-letter day; holiday **5**.（删节）abridge **6**.（节约;节制）economize; save **7**.（节操）moral integrity; chastity: 晚～ integrity in one's later year **8**.（船速单位）knot（1 节 ＝ 每小时 1 海里）

（另见"节"jiē）

【节哀】 jié'āi restrain one's grief

【节本】 jiéběn abridged edition; abbreviated version

【节操】 jiécāo high moral principle; moral integrity

【节点】 jiédiǎn node; nodal point

【节假日】 jiéjiàrì festivals and holidays

【节俭】 jiéjiǎn thrifty; frugal

【节节】 jiéjié successively; steadily: ～胜利 win one victory after another; win many victories in succession / ～败退 retreat in defeat again and again; keep on retreating

【节流】 jiéliú **1**.（节约开支）reduce expenditure **2**.〈*Mech*.〉 throttle

【节录】 jiélù extract; excerpt

【节略】 jiélüè **1**.（摘要）summary; abstract **2**.（省略）omission **3**.〈*Foreign Affairs*〉 diplomatic note

【节目】 jiémù program; item; number

【节目单】 jiémùdān program; playbill

【节目预告】 jiémù yùgào program parade

【节目主持人】 jiémù zhǔchírén host; presenter; master of ceremonies

【节能】 jiénéng energy saving

【节拍】 jiépāi 〈*Music*〉 meter

【节拍器】 jiépāiqì 〈*Music*〉 metronome

【节气】 jié·qi solar terms

【节日】 jiérì festival; red-letter day; holiday: ～送礼的佳品 ideal gift for occasions

【节省】 jiéshěng economize; save; use sparingly; cut down on: ～时间 save time / ～人力 use manpower sparingly / ～篇幅 save space

【节食】 jiéshí eat and drink moderately

【节选】 jiéxuǎn select; selection (n.)

【节衣缩食】 jiéyī-suōshí economize on clothing and food; live frugally

【节余】 jiéyú surplus: 略有～ with a slight surplus

【节育】 jiéyù birth control: ～措施 birth-control method

【节育环】 jiéyùhuán intrauterine device (IUD); the loop

【节约】 jiéyuē practice thrift; economize; save: ～用水 economize on water / ～用电 economize on electricity / ～开支 cut down expenses

【节支】 jiézhī cut down expenses; retrench

【节制】 jiézhì **1**.（限制；控制）control; check; be moderate in **2**.（克制）temperance; abstinence

【节制闸】 jiézhìzhá check gate

【节奏】 jiézòu rhythm: ～明快 lively rhythm

劫［刦[1]、刧[1]、刼[1]］(jié) **1**.（抢劫）rob; plunder; raid **2**.（灾难）calamity; disaster; misfortune: 遭～ meet a disaster; suffer a disaster **3**.〈*Buddhism*〉 kalpa

【劫持】 jiéchí kidnap; hold under duress; hijack; abduction: ～飞机 hijack an airplane

【劫夺】 jiéduó seize by force

【劫机者】 jiéjīzhě air pirate; skyjacker; hijacker

【劫掠】 jiélüè plunder; loot

【劫数】 jiéshù 〈*Buddhism*〉 inexorable doom; predestined fate

【劫数难逃】 jiéshù-nántáo a fatal lot is unavoidable

【劫狱】 jiéyù break into a jail and rescue a prisoner; jail delivery

杰［傑］(jié) 1.（杰出）outstanding; prominent; distinguished 2.（杰出的人）outstanding person; hero

【杰出】 jiéchū outstanding; remarkable; prominent; brilliant: ～人物 a prominent person; a brilliant person

【杰作】 jiézuò masterpiece

桀(jié)

【桀骜不驯】 jiéào-būxùn 〈*written*〉 stubborn and intractable; obstinate and unruly

诘(jié) 〈*written*〉 closely question; interrogate; interrogation (n.)
(另见"诘"jí)

【诘问】 jiéwèn closely question; interrogate; cross-examine

拮(jié)

【拮据】 jiéjū short of money; hard up; in straitened circumstances: 手头～ be short of money

洁［潔］(jié) clean

【洁白】 jiébái spotlessly white; pure white

【洁净】 jiéjìng clean; spotless

【洁身自好】 jiéshēn-zìhào 1.（独善其身）refuse to be contaminated by evil influence; preserve one's purity; exercise self-control so as to protect oneself from immorality 2.（不招惹是非）keep to one's own business; mind one's own business in order to keep out of trouble

结(jié) 1.（编织）tie; knit; knot; weave 2.（结子）knot 3.（结合）tie; form: ～为夫妇 be tied in wedlock 4.（凝结）congeal; form 5.（结束；了结）settle; conclude 6.（保证负责的字据）written guarantee; affidavit 7.〈*Electr.*〉junction 8.〈*Biol.*〉node
(另见"结"jiē)

【结案】 jié'àn wind up a case; close a case; settle a lawsuit

【结疤】 jiébā 1.〈*Metall.*〉scab 2.〈*Med.*〉become scarred

【结拜】 jiébài become sworn brothers or sisters: ～为兄弟 become sworn brothers

【结伴】 jiébàn go with; go in a group

【结冰】 jiébīng freeze; ice up; ice over

【结彩】 jiécǎi be decorated with festoons; be festooned with decorations

【结肠】 jiécháng 〈*Anat.*〉 colon: 升～ ascending colon / 横～ transverse colon / 降～ descending colon / 乙状～ sigmoid colon

【结肠癌】 jiécháng'ái 〈*Med.*〉 carcinoma of colon

【结成】 jiéchéng form: ～深厚的友谊 form a profound friendship

【结仇】 jiéchóu start a feud; become enemies; breed enmity with; incur hatred of

【结存】 jiécún 1.（指款项）cash on hand; balance 2.（指货物）goods on hand; inventory

【结党营私】 jiédǎng-yíngsī form a clique to pursue selfish interests; gang together for clandestine and illegal activities

【结缔组织】 jiédì zǔzhī 〈*Anat.*〉 connective tissue

【结发夫妻】 jiéfà fūqī husband and wife by the first marriage

【结构】 jiégòu 1.（组织）structure; composition; construction: 经济～ economic structure / 产业～ structure of production / 消费～ structure of consumption / ～严谨 be compact and well organized 2.〈*Archit.*〉structure; construction: 钢筋混凝土～ reinforced concrete structure 3.〈*Geog.*〉texture

【结构式】 jiégòushì 〈*Chem.*〉 structural formula

【结关】 jiéguān customs clearance: 采取～措施 take measures on customs clearance

【结果】 jiéguǒ 1.（结局）result; outcome; ending 2.（最终）finally; at last: ～，他们打赢了。Finally, they won the game. 3.（杀死）kill; finish of

【结合】 jiéhé 1.（相互密切联系）combine; unite; integrate; link: 产销～ integrate production and sale / 劳逸～ arrange work and rest properly; alternate work with recreation 2.（结为夫妻）marry; be united in wedlock; be tied in wedlock

【结核】 jiéhé 1.〈*Med.*〉tuberculosis: 肺～ pulmonary tuberculosis 2.〈*Mineral.*〉nodule

【结核病院】 jiéhé bìngyuàn tuberculosis sanatorium

【结汇】 jiéhuì settlement of exchange

【结婚】 jiéhūn marry; get married

【结婚登记】 jiéhūn dēngjì marriage registration

【结婚证书】 jiéhūn zhèngshū marriage certificate

【结伙】 jiéhuǒ gang: ~抢劫 gang robbery

【结交】 jiéjiāo make friends with; associate with

【结晶】 jiéjīng 1.（析出晶体）crystallize 2.（晶体）crystal 3.（成果）crystallization; fruit; product; quintessence: 智慧的~ a crystallization of wisdom

【结局】 jiéjú final result; outcome; ending

【结论】 jiélùn 1.〈*Logic*〉conclusion (of a syllogism) 2.（最后论断）conclusion; verdict: 匆忙下~ jump to a conclusion

【结盟】 jiéméng form an alliance; ally; align: 不~国家 nonaligned countries

【结膜】 jiémó 〈*Anat.*〉conjunctiva

【结膜炎】 jiémóyán 〈*Med.*〉conjunctivitis

【结亲】 jiéqīn 1.（结婚）marry; get married 2.（结成姻亲）become related by marriage

【结清】 jiéqīng settle; square up: ~债务 settle a debt

【结社】 jiéshè form an association; establish a society

【结石】 jiéshí 〈*Med.*〉stone; calculus: 胆~ gall stone / 肾~ kidney stone

【结识】 jiéshí get acquainted with sb.; get to know sb.

【结束】 jiéshù end; finish; conclude; wind up; close

【结束位】 jiéshùwèi 〈*Computer*〉stop bits

【结束语】 jiéshùyǔ concluding remarks

【结算】 jiésuàn settle accounts; close an account; wind up an account: 用人民币~ use RMB for settling accounts

【结算日】 jiésuànrì account day

【结网】 jiéwǎng 1.（编网）weave a net; 2.（蜘蛛结网）weave a web

【结尾】 jiéwěi 1.（结束）winding-up stage; ending 2.〈*Music*〉coda

【结业】 jiéyè complete a course; wind up one's studies

【结余】 jiéyú 1.（结算后余下）balance 2.（结算后余下的钱）surplus; cash surplus; balance

【结缘】 jiéyuán form ties (of affection, friendship, etc.); become attached to; take a fancy to

【结怨】 jiéyuàn contract enmity; incur hatred

【结扎】 jiézā 〈*Med.*〉ligation; ligature: 输精管~术 vasoligation / 输卵管~术 ligation of oviduct

【结账】 jiézhàng settle accounts; square accounts; balance the books; closing accounts

捷[**捷**] (jié) 1.（敏捷）prompt; nimble; quick; agile 2.（胜利）victory; triumph

【捷报】 jiébào news of victory; report of a success: ~频传。Good news reached us one after another.

【捷径】 jiéjìng shortcut: 走~ take a shortcut

【捷足先登】 jiézú-xiāndēng the swift-footed arrive first; the race is to the swiftest; the early bird catches the worms

睫 (jié) eyelash; lash

【睫毛】 jiémáo eyelash; lash

竭 (jié) exhaust; use up

【竭诚】 jiéchéng wholeheartedly; with all one's heart

【竭尽】 jiéjìn use up; exhaust: ~造谣诬蔑之能事 exhaust every means to spread lies and slanders

【竭力】 jiélì do one's utmost; spare no efforts: ~反对 oppose strongly; actively oppose

【竭泽而渔】 jiézé-éryú drain the pond to get all the fish; kill the goose that lays the golden eggs

截 (jié) 1.（截断）cut; sever 2.〈*classifier*〉section; chunk; length 3.（阻拦）stop; check; stem; intercept 4.（截止）by; up to

【截断】 jiéduàn 1.（切断）cut off; block 2.（打断；拦住）cut short; interrupt

【截稿线】 jiégǎoxiàn deadline

【截获】 jiéhuò intercept and capture: ~情报 intercept (enemy) information

【截击】 jiéjī intercept: ~敌轰炸机 intercept enemy bombers

【截击导弹】 jiéjī dǎodàn interceptor missile; interception missile
【截击机】 jiéjījī interceptor
【截击球】 jiéjīqiú 〈*Tennis*〉 volley
【截流】 jiéliú stop; obstruct (running water in the water course)
【截留】 jiéliú hold back: ～国家财政收入 hold back state revenue
【截取】 jiéqǔ cut out
【截然】 jiérán sharply; completely; entirely: ～相反 completely contradict / ～不同 differ radically; be different entirely
【截瘫】 jiétān 〈*Med.*〉 paraplegia
【截肢】 jiézhī 〈*Med.*〉 amputation
【截止】 jiézhǐ **1.** (停止) end; close **2.** 〈*Electr.*〉 cut-off
【截止期】 jiézhǐqī closing date; dead line
【截至】 jiézhì by (a specified time); up to: ～目前为止 up to now / ～本月底 by the end of this month

姐 (jiě) elder sister; sister

【姐夫】 jiě·fu brother-in-law; elder sister's husband
【姐姐】 jiě·jie elder sister; sister
【姐妹】 jiěmèi sisters

解[鮮] (jiě) **1.** (分开) separate; divide **2.** (打开，松开) untie; undo **3.** (解除) allay; alleviate; dispel; dismiss: ～热 allay a fever / ～痛 alleviate pain **4.** (解释) explain; interpret; solve problem **5.** (了解；明白) understand; comprehend: 费～ hard to understand; obscure **6.** (解手) relieve oneself **7.** 〈*Math.*〉 solution: 求～ find the solution
(另见"解"jiè, xiè)

【解馋】 jiěchán satisfy a craving for good food; satisfy an appetite for good food
【解嘲】 jiěcháo try to explain things away when ridiculed; try to get out of a scrape when ridiculed
【解除】 jiěchú remove; relieve; get rid of: ～合同 terminate a contract; dissolution of contract / ～警报 sound the all clear / ～职务 remove sb. from his position
【解答】 jiědá answer; explain: ～问题 answer a question
【解冻】 jiědòng **1.** (融化) thaw; unfreeze **2.** (解除冻结) unfreeze (funds, assets, etc.): 在烹调之前给鸡完全～ defrost the chicken thoroughly before cooking **3.** (关系缓和) thaw: 两国关系的～ a thawing of the relations between the two countries
【解毒】 jiědú **1.** 〈*Med.*〉 detoxify; detoxicate **2.** 〈*Chin. Med.*〉 relieve internal heat or fever
【解毒药】 jiědúyào antidote
【解乏】 jiěfá recover from fatigue; refresh oneself
【解放】 jiěfàng **1.** (解除束缚) liberate; liberation (n.); emancipate; emancipation (n.): ～生产力 liberate the production forces / ～思想 emancipate the mind **2.** (推翻反动统治) liberate; liberation (n.): ～前 before liberation / ～后 after liberation
【解放军】 jiěfàngjūn **1.** (泛指) liberation army **2.** (中国人民解放军) the Chinese People's Liberation Army; the PLA **3.** (解放军战士) PLA man
【解放区】 jiěfàngqū liberated area
【解放战争】 jiěfàng zhànzhēng war of liberation
【解雇】 jiěgù discharge; dismiss; fire; give the sack
【解雇书】 jiěgùshū termination slip
【解恨】 jiěhèn vent one's hatred; have one's hatred slaked
【解教】 jiějiào release of reeducation through labor
【解禁】 jiějìn lift a ban; cancel an existing prohibition
【解救】 jiějiù save; rescue; deliver
【解决】 jiějué **1.** (处理) solve; resolve; settle: ～困难 overcome a difficulty / ～矛盾 resolve a contradiction / 和平～争端 settle a dispute by peaceful means / ～吃饭问题 solve the problem of feeding / ～就业问题 solve the problem of employing the population / ～温饱问题 solve the problem of food and clothing **2.** (消灭) finish off; dispose of: ～了敌人一个连 have finished off a company of enemy troops
【解开】 jiěkāi untie; undo; unfasten: ～上衣 unbutton one's jacket

【解渴】 jiěkě quench one's thirst
【解困】 jiěkùn overcome difficulties
【解闷】 jiěmèn divert oneself (from boredom)
【解囊】 jiěnáng 〈*written*〉 open one's purse
【解聘】 jiěpìn dismiss an employee
【解剖】 jiěpōu 1.〈*Med.*〉 dissect; dissection (n.): 人体～ human dissection / 在生物课上我们常～老鼠。In biology classes we used to dissect rats. 2.(分析;剖析) analyse; anatomise; dissect
【解剖刀】 jiěpōudāo 〈*Med.*〉 scalpel
【解剖学】 jiěpōuxué 〈*Med.*〉 anatomy
【解气】 jiěqì vent one's spleen; work off one's anger; vent one's spite upon sb.
【解劝】 jiěquàn soothe; mollify; comfort
【解散】 jiěsàn 1.(集合的人分散开) dismiss 2.(口令) Dismiss! 3.(取消) dissolve; disband: ～国会 dissolve a parliament
【解释】 jiěshì explain; expound; interpret: ～合同 interpretation of contract
【解释性报导】 jiěshìxìng bàodǎo interpretative reporting
【解手】 jiěshǒu relieve oneself; go to the toilet
【解说】 jiěshuō explain orally; comment
【解说词】 jiěshuōcí 1.(口头的) commentary 2.(书面的) caption
【解说员】 jiěshuōyuán commentator; announcer
【解体】 jiětǐ 1.(分解) disintegrate; break up: 油轮～ breakup of an oil tanker / 奥斯曼帝国～成一批小国家。The Ottoman Empire disintegrated into lots of small states. 2.(崩溃) collapse
【解脱】 jiětuō 1.(摆脱) free oneself from; get rid of; extricate oneself 2.(开脱) exonerate; absolve 3.〈*Buddhism*〉 mukti; vimukta
【解围】 jiěwéi 1.(解除包围) force an enemy to raise a siege; rescue sb. from a siege; come to the rescue of the besieged 2.(摆脱窘境) help sb. out of a predicament; save sb. from embarrassment; get sb. out of a fix
【解析几何】 jiěxī jǐhé analytic geometry
【解疑】 jiěyí 1.(消除疑虑) clear one's mind of doubt; clear up one's suspicion 2.(解释疑难) explain the meaning (of a word, etc.)
【解职】 jiězhí dismiss from office; discharge; relieve sb. of his post

介 (jiè) 1.(在两者中间) be situated between; interpose 2.(介意) take seriously; take to heart; mind
【介词】 jiècí 〈*Gram.*〉 preposition
【介入】 jièrù intervene; interpose; get involved
【介绍】 jièshào 1.(使相识) introduce; present: 自我～ introduce oneself 2.(推荐) recommend; suggest: 为某人～工作 recommend sb. for a position 3.(使了解) let know; brief; give information; provide information: ～经验 pass on experience
【介绍人】 jièshàorén 1.(组织介绍者) introducer; sponsor 2.(婚姻介绍人) matchmaker
【介绍信】 jièshàoxìn 1.(介绍认识的书信) letter of introduction 2.(推荐信) letter of recommendation
【介意】 jièyì (多用于否定词后) take offense; mind; get annoyed; care about: 区区小事,何必～。Never mind such trifles.
【介质】 jièzhì medium
【介子】 jièzǐ 〈*Physics*〉 meson; mesotron

芥 (jiè) mustard (另见"芥"gài)
【芥菜】 jiècài leaf mustard
【芥菜疙瘩】 jiècài gēdā rutabaga
【芥蒂】 jièdì 〈*written*〉 ill feeling; unpleasantness; grudge: 不存～ bear no grudge / 心存～ bear a grudge
【芥末】 jiè·mo mustard
【芥子气】 jièzǐqì 〈*Chem.*〉 mustard gas
【芥子气中毒】 jièzǐqì zhòngdú mustard gas poisoning

界 (jiè) 1.(界线) boundary; border: 国～ the boundary of the country 2.(范围) bounds; scope; extend 3.(社会各界) circles; world: 各～人士 people of all walks of life; all sections of the people 4.(自然界类别) primary division; kingdom: 植物～ the plant kingdom / 动物～ the animal kingdom / 矿物～ the mineral kingdom
【界碑】 jièbēi boundary tablet; boundary marker
【界标】 jièbiāo post; boundary monument
【界尺】 jièchǐ ungraduated ruler

【界河】 jièhé boundary river
【界湖】 jièhú boundary lake
【界面】 jièmiàn interface
【界内地区】 jiènèi dìqū 〈*Baseball*〉 fair territory
【界内球】 jiènèiqiú 〈*Sports*〉 in bounds; in
【界山】 jièshān boundary mountain
【界石】 jièshí boundary stone; boundary tablet
【界外地区】 jièwài dìqū 〈*Baseball*〉 foul territory
【界外球】 jièwàiqiú out-of-bounds
【界限】 jièxiàn **1.**（分界）demarcation line; dividing line; limits; bounds：打破行业～ break the bounds of different trades **2.**（限度）limit; end
【界线】 jièxiàn **1.**（分界线）boundary line **2.**（界限）demarcation line; dividing line; limits
【界桩】 jièzhuāng boundary stone; boundary marker; boundary post

疥（jiè） scabies
【疥疮】 jièchuāng 〈*Med.*〉 scabies; psora

戒（jiè） **1.**（戒备）guard against; avoid **2.**（警告）exhort; admonish; warn **3.**（戒除）give up; drop; stop：～酒 give up drinking **4.**（佛教戒律）Buddhist monastic discipline **5.**（戒指）ring：钻～ diamond ring
【戒备】 jièbèi **1.**（警戒防备）guard; be on the alert; keep a sharp lookout **2.**（对人有戒心）take precautions
【戒除】 jièchú give up; drop; leave off; stop：～恶习 abandon a bad habit
【戒骄戒躁】 jièjiāo-jièzào guard against arrogance and rashness; be on guard against conceit and impetuosity; guard against pride and haste
【戒心】 jièxīn vigilance; wariness; alertness
【戒严】 jièyán enforce martial law; cordon off an area; impose a curfew：宣布～ proclaim martial law
【戒严令】 jièyánlìng order of martial law
【戒指】 jiè·zhi (finger) ring：订婚～ engagement ring / 结婚～ wedding ring / 她的手指戴了只金～。She wore a gold ring on her finger.

届（jiè） **1.**（到）fall due **2.**〈*classifier*〉session：第八～全国人大 the Eighth National People's Congress
【届满】 jièmǎn expiration; at the expiration of one's term of office
【届时】 jièshí when the time comes; at the appointed time; on the occasion

借［藉[3,4]］（jiè） **1.**（借进）borrow：～钱 borrow money from sb. **2.**（借出）lend **3.**（凭借）make use of; take advantage of：～此机会 take this opportunity to **4.**（假托）use as a pretext **5.**（借阅图书）～出 in circulation; out / 不外～ not for circulation / 续～ renewal
【借贷】 jièdài **1.**（借钱）borrow or lend money **2.**（借方和贷方）debit and credit sides
【借调】 jièdiào temporarily transfer; be on loan
【借读】 jièdú study at a school on a temporary basis
【借端】 jièduān use as a pretext; find a pretext; invent an excuse：～寻衅 make use of anything as a pretext for seeking a quarrel
【借方】 jièfāng 〈*Econ.*〉 debit; debit side
【借故】 jiègù find an excuse：～不去开会 absent oneself from a meeting on some pretext
【借光】 jièguāng 〈*politeness*〉 excuse me
【借火】 jièhuǒ ask for a light
【借鉴】 jièjiàn use for reference; draw lessons from; draw on the experience of; have successful experiences of others to go by：学习和～外国经验 learn from foreign countries and draw on their experience
【借据】 jièjù receipt for a loan (IOU); certificate of indebtedness; debt on bond; evidence of debt
【借口】 jièkǒu **1.**（以某事为理由）use as an excuse; on the pretext of; on the excuse of **2.**（假托的理由）excuse; pretext：制造～ cook up a pretext / 寻找～ find an excuse
【借款】 jièkuǎn **1.**（借入）borrow money; ask for a loan **2.**（贷出）lend money; offer a loan **3.**（借用的钱）loan：偿还～ pay off a loan; repay a loan
【借书处】 jièshūchù loan desk (of a library)
【借书证】 jièshūzhèng library card; reader's card; admission card

【借宿】 jièsù stay overnight at sb. else's place; put up for the night

【借题发挥】 jiètí-fāhuī make use of a subject as a pretext for one's flown talk; seize on an incident to exaggerate matters

【借条】 jiètiáo receipt for a loan (IOU)

【借问】 jièwèn 〈*politeness*〉 may I ask

【借以】 jièyǐ so as to; for the purpose of; by way of

【借用】 jièyòng **1.**（借来使用）borrow; have the loan of **2.**（用于别种用途）use sth. for another purpose

【借债】 jièzhài borrow money; raise (contract) a loan

【借支】 jièzhī obtain an advance on one's salary; ask for an advance on one's pay

【借重】 jièzhòng rely on for support; enlist sb.'s help; count on for support

【借助】 jièzhù have the aid of; draw support from; with the help of

解［觧］(jiè) send under guard (另见"解"jiě, xiè)

【解送】 jièsòng send under guard: ～犯人 send criminals under guard

jin

巾 (jīn) towel; scarf; kerchief: 毛～ towel / 餐～ napkin / 湿纸～ towelette / 围～ scarf / 纸～ paper towel

【巾帼】 jīnguó woman

【巾帼英雄】 jīnguó yīngxióng heroine

斤［觔］(jīn) **1.**（市斤）jin (= 0.5 kilogram) **2.**（公斤）kilo; kilogram

【斤斤】 jīnjīn fuss about; haggle over

【斤斤计较】 jīnjīn-jìjiào haggle over every ounce; be calculating

【斤两】 jīnliǎng weight

今 (jīn) **1.**（现今）present-day; modern; now; nowadays **2.**（今天）today: ～晨 this morning / ～晚 tonight; this evening **3.**（当前）this (year); of this year

【今非昔比】 jīnfēixībǐ The present cannot compare with the past.

【今后】 jīnhòu from now on; in the days to come; henceforth; hereafter; in future

【今年】 jīnnián this year

【今日】 jīnrì **1.**（今天）today **2.**（当前）present; now

【今生】 jīnshēng this life

【今世】 jīnshì **1.**（今生）this life **2.**（当代）this age; the contemporary age

【今天】 jīntiān **1.**（今日）today **2.**（目前）today; present; now

【今昔】 jīnxī the present and the past; today and yesterday

【今译】 jīnyì modern-language version; modern translation

矜 (jīn) **1.**（怜悯）pity; sympathize with **2.**（自尊自大）self-important; conceited **3.**（矜持）restrained; reserved

【矜持】 jīnchí restrained; reserved

【矜夸】 jīnkuā conceited and boastful

【矜重】 jīnzhòng reserved and dignified

金 (jīn) **1.**（金属）metals **2.**（钱）money: 现～ cash; ready money **3.**（黄金）gold（元素符号 Au）**4.**（金色的）golden: ～发 golden hair

【金杯】 jīnbēi golden cup

【金本位】 jīnběnwèi gold standard

【金笔】 jīnbǐ fountain pen; fountain pen with a gold nib

【金笔厂】 jīnbǐchǎng pen factory

【金币】 jīnbì gold coin

【金碧辉煌】 jīnbì-huīhuáng looking splendid in green and gold; magnificent and splendid

【金边债券】 jīnbiān zhàiquàn gilt-edged shares; gilt-edged stock; gilt-edged securities

【金箔】 jīnbó goldleaf; gold foil

【金蝉脱壳】 jīnchán-tuōqiào escape by cunning maneuvering; a disappearance act from an entangled situation

【金雕】 jīndiāo 〈*Zool.*〉 golden eagle

【金额】 jīn'é amount of money

【金刚砂】 jīngāngshā emery; diamond grit

【金刚石】 jīngāngshí diamond

【金刚石钻头】 jīngāngshí zuàntóu diamond bit

【金工】 jīngōng metalworking; metal processing

【金光】 jīnguāng golden light: ～闪闪 glittering, glistening

【金龟】 jīnguī tortoise

【金龟子】 jīnguīzǐ 〈*Insect*〉 beetle
【金衡】 jīnhéng troy (weight)
【金衡制】 jīnhéngzhì troy weight; troy
【金黄】 jīnhuáng golden yellow; golden: ~的天空 a golden sky
【金婚】 jīnhūn golden wedding
【金鸡】 jīnjī golden pheasant
【金鸡纳霜】 jīnjīnàshuāng 〈*Pharm.*〉 quinine
【金奖】 jīnjiǎng gold medal
【金匠】 jīnjiàng goldsmith
【金戒指】 jīnjiè·zi gold ring: 在手指上戴着个~ wear a gold ring on one's finger
【金橘】 jīnjú 〈*Bot.*〉 kumquat
【金库】 jīnkù national (state) treasury; exchequer
【金块】 jīnkuài gold bullion
【金矿】 jīnkuàng gold mine
【金矿区】 jīnkuàngqū goldfield
【金銮殿】 jīnluándiàn emperor's audience hall; throne room
【金霉素】 jīnméisù 〈*Pharm.*〉 aureomycin
【金牛宫】 Jīnniúgōng 〈*Astron.*〉 Taurus (4 月 21 日至 5 月 22 日): 生于~ be born under Taurus
【金牛座】 Jīnniúzuò 〈*Astron.*〉 Taurus
【金牌】 jīnpái 〈*Sports*〉 gold medal
【金牌得主】 jīnpái dézhǔ 〈*Sports*〉 gold medalist
【金器】 jīnqì gold vessel
【金钱】 jīnqián money
【金枪鱼】 jīnqiāngyú 〈*Zool.*〉 tuna
【金融】 jīnróng finance; banking; financial (adj.)
【金融机构】 jīnróng jīgòu financial institution; banking institution
【金融界】 jīnróngjiè financial circles
【金融紧缩】 jīnróng jǐnsuō tight money policy; deflationary policy
【金融市场】 jīnróng shìchǎng financial market; money market
【金融体制】 jīnróng tǐzhì monetary system
【金融投机】 jīnróng tóujī monetary speculation
【金融衍生物】 jīnróng yǎnshēngwù financial derivatives
【金融中心】 jīnróng zhōngxīn financial center; banking center
【金融资本】 jīnróng zīběn financial capital
【金色】 jīnsè golden
【金石】 jīnshí **1.** (坚硬的东西) metal and stone; a symbol of hardness and strength **2.** (铜器、石碑上的铭刻) inscriptions on ancient bronzes and stone tablets
【金属】 jīnshǔ metal: 有色~ nonferrous metals / 黑色~ ferrous metal
【金属板】 jīnshǔbǎn 〈*Music*〉 metal bar
【金属分币】 jīnshǔ fēnbì coin; small denomination coin
【金属管】 jīnshǔguǎn 〈*Music*〉 tubular metal resonator
【金属加工】 jīnshǔ jiāgōng metal processing
【金属陶瓷】 jīnshǔ táocí cermet; ceramic metal
【金属整流罩】 jīnshǔ zhěngliúzhào metal fairings
【金丝猴】 jīnsīhóu golden monkey; snub-nosed monkey
【金丝雀】 jīnsīquè canary
【金条】 jīntiáo gold bar
【金星】 jīnxīng **1.** 〈*Astron.*〉 Venus **2.** (金黄色五角星) golden star **3.** (星状小点) spark; star: 两眼冒~ see stars
【金银财宝】 jīnyín-cáibǎo treasures
【金鱼】 jīnyú goldfish
【金玉】 jīnyù 〈*written*〉 gold and jade; precious stone and metals; treasures: ~其外, 败絮其中 fair without, foul within; a rotten interior beneath a fine exterior
【金元】 jīnyuán gold dollar
【金针】 jīnzhēn **1.** (针) needle **2.** 〈*Chin. Med.*〉 acupuncture needle **3.** (金针菜) day lily
【金针菜】 jīnzhēncài day lily
【金子】 jīn·zi gold
【金字塔】 jīnzìtǎ pyramid
【金字招牌】 jīnzì zhāopái **1.** (商店招牌) gold-lettered signboard **2.** (炫耀的称号) vainglorious title

津 (jīn) **1.** (唾液) saliva **2.** (汗) sweat **3.** (渡口) ferry crossing; ford: 要~ important position
【津津乐道】 jīnjīn-lèdào take delight in talking about; dwell upon with great relish; talk with great relish

【津津有味】 jīnjīn-yǒuwèi with relish; with gusto; with keen pleasure

【津贴】 jīntiē subsidy; allowance

【津要】 jīnyào 1.（指地点）important position; important place 2.（指职位）important post

【津液】 jīnyè 1.〈*Chin. Med.*〉body fluid 2.（唾液）saliva

筋［觔］（jīn） 1.（韧带）tendon; sinew 2.（可看见的皮下静脉）vein：青～ blue veins 3.（像筋的东西）anything resembling a tendon or vein：钢～ reinforcing steel; steel reinforcement

【筋斗】 jīndǒu 1.（跟斗）somersault 2.（跌跤）fall; tumble (over)

【筋骨】 jīngǔ muscles and bones; physique

【筋疲力竭】 jīnpí-lìjié be completely exhausted; have used up all energy

【筋疲力尽】 jīnpí-lìjìn utterly exhausted; played out; worn out; tired out; dead tired

【筋肉】 jīnròu muscles

禁（jīn） 1.（禁受）bear; stand; endure：涤纶～洗。Polyester bears lot of washing. 2.（忍住）restrain oneself; contain oneself：不～失笑 cannot help giggling
（另见"禁"jìn）

【禁不起】 jīn·buqǐ be unable to stand (tests, trials, etc.); cannot withstand; cannot bear：～考验 fail to stand tests; cannot pass tests

【禁不住】 jīn·buzhù 1.（承受不住）be unable to bear or endure：～折磨 can't endure torture 2.（抑制不住）can't help (doing sth.); can't refrain from

【禁得起】 jīn·deqǐ be able to stand (tests, trials, etc.)：～各种考验 be able to stand all tests

【禁得住】 jīn·dezhù be able to bear or endure

【禁受】 jīnshòu bear; stand; endure

襟（jīn） front of a garment

【襟怀】 jīnhuái 〈*written*〉 bosom; (breadth of) mind：～坦白 openhearted and aboveboard; have an open heart

【襟门】 jīnmén shield：装有拉锁的～ zipper shield

【襟兄】 jīnxiōng husband of one's wife's elder sister

【襟翼】 jīnyì 〈*Aeron.*〉 flap

仅［僅］（jǐn） 〈*adv.*〉 only; merely; barely; simply; solely

【仅次于】 jǐncìyú second only to; next to

【仅供参考】 jǐn gōng cānkǎo This is for your reference only.

【仅仅】 jǐnjǐn 〈*adv.*〉 only; merely; barely; simply; just; alone：这～是时间问题。It is merely a matter of time.

尽［儘］（jǐn） 1.（尽量）to the greatest extent 2.（不超过）within the limits of; no more than：～着150元花。Don't spend more than one hundred and fifty yuan. 3.（尽先）give priority to; first：～着女士们先坐。Let ladies sit down first. 4.（最）at the furthest end of; most：～底下 at the very bottom

【尽管】 jǐnguǎn 1.〈*adv.*〉（不必考虑别的）feel free to; not hesitate to：你～直说。Just speak out. 2.〈*conj.*〉（虽然）though; even though; in spite of; despite; notwithstanding：～如此 in spite of that

【尽可能】 jǐnkěnéng as far as possible; to the best of one's ability

【尽快】 jǐnkuài as early as possible

【尽量】 jǐnliàng to the best of one's ability; as far as possible：～利用时间 make the best of one's time

【尽先】 jǐnxiān give first priority to; in the first instance

【尽早】 jǐnzǎo as early as possible; at your earliest convenience

紧［緊］（jǐn） 1.（不松）tight; taut; close 2.（牢固）fast; firm 3.（贴近）close：～靠墙 close against the wall 4.（厉害）hard; heavily; violently：风刮得很～。The wind blow hard. 5.（紧急）urgent; pressing; tense：时间很～。Time is pressing. 6.（拮据）short of money; hard up：银根～ money is tight

【紧逼】 jǐnbī press hard; close in on

【紧凑】 jǐncòu compact; terse; well-knit; tight：情节～ have a well-knit plot

【紧跟】 jǐngēn keep up with; tread on the heels of; follow closely; keep in step with：～时代步伐 keep in step with the times

【紧急】 jǐnjí urgent; pressing; critical; emergent: ～措施 emergency measures / ～会议 emergency meeting / ～任务 urgent task / 情况～。The situation is critical.

【紧紧】 jǐnjǐn closely; firmly; tightly: ～盯着 watch closely; stare fixedly; gaze steadfastly

【紧密】 jǐnmì 1.(密切) inseparable; close together: ～联系 be closely connected 2.(密集) thick and fast; rapid and intense

【紧迫】 jǐnpò pressing; urgent; imminent: 时间～。The time presses.

【紧迫感】 jǐnpògǎn sense of urgency: 有～ have a sense of urgency

【紧俏】 jǐnqiào well sold and in short supply

【紧俏商品】 jǐnqiào shāngpǐn commodities in short supply

【紧缺】 jǐnquē in short supply; tight short of (sth.)

【紧身】 jǐnshēn close-fitting vest; undershirt; close-fitting undergarment

【紧身健美服】 jǐnshēn jiànměifú corset

【紧身女内衣】 jǐnshēn nǚnèiyī body stocking

【紧缩】 jǐnsuō reduce; retrench; tighten; cut down: ～开支 reduce expenses; cut down expenses

【紧要】 jǐnyào critical; crucial; vital: ～关头 critical moment / 无关～ of no consequence

【紧张】 jǐnzhāng 1.(指精神) nervous; keyed up: 神情～ look nervous 2.(紧迫) tense; intense; strained: ～局势 a tense situation 3.(供应不足) in short supply; tight: 供应～ be in short supply

谨 (jǐn) 1.(谨慎) careful; cautious; circumspect: ～守诺言 carefully keep one's promise 2.(郑重) solemnly; sincerely: ～启 yours respectfully

【谨防】 jǐnfáng guard against; beware of; be alert to; be cautious of: ～假冒。Beware of imitations.

【谨上】 jǐnshàng (用于书信具名后) sincerely yours

【谨慎】 jǐnshèn prudent; careful; cautious; circumspect: 言行～ be prudent in one's words and deeds / ～从事 act with caution

【谨小慎微】 jǐnxiǎo-shènwēi overcautious; timorous and punctilious; cautious and meticulous

【谨严】 jǐnyán careful and precise

锦 (jǐn) 1.(丝织品) brocade 2.(鲜明华丽) bright and beautiful

【锦标赛】 jǐnbiāosài championship contest; championships

【锦缎】 jǐnduàn brocade

【锦纶】 jǐnlún 〈*Textiles*〉 polyamide fiber; jinlun

【锦旗】 jǐnqí silk banner (as an award or a gift)

【锦上添花】 jǐnshàng-tiānhuā make perfection still more perfect; gild refined gold

【锦绣】 jǐnxiù as beautiful as brocade; beautiful; splendid: ～山河 a beautiful land; a beautiful landscape

尽［盡］ (jìn) 1.(完) exhausted; finished: 取之不～ inexhaustible 2.(到头) to the utmost; to the limit; to the full 3.(用完) use up; exhaust: 一言难～ it can't be expressed in a few words 4.(全部使出) try one's best; put to the best use; exert oneself; do one's best: ～全力 do one's best; exert one's utmost; do all in one's power / 人～其才 make the best possible use of men 5.(全;所有的) all; completely; exhaustive

【尽欢而散】 jìnhuānérsàn leave only after each has enjoyed himself to the utmost

【尽力】 jìnlì do all one can; try one's best; do sth. to the best of one's ability: ～而为 do one's best; do everything in one's power

【尽量】 jìnliàng (drink or eat) to the full

【尽其所长】 jìnqísuǒcháng work or endeavor to the best of one's ability

【尽情】 jìnqíng to one's heart's content; as much as one likes: ～款待 treat with the utmost kindness

【尽人皆知】 jìnrén-jiēzhī be common knowledge; be known to all

【尽善尽美】 jìnshàn-jìnměi the acme of perfection; perfect; perfectly satisfactory

【尽是】 jìnshì full of; all; without exception

【尽头】 jìntuó end

【尽心】 jìnxīn with all one's heart; put one's heart and soul into: ～竭力 (do sth.) with all one's heart and all one's might

【尽兴】 jìnxìng to one's heart's content; enjoy oneself to the full

【尽义务】 jìnyìwù 1.(尽责任) do one's duty; fulfill one's obligation 2.(无报酬) be a volunteer; work for no reward; work without reward

【尽早】 jìnzǎo with the least delay; at one's earliest convenience; as soon as possible

【尽责】 jìnzé do one's duty

【尽职】 jìnzhí fulfill one's duty; discharge one's duty

进[進](jìn) 1.(前进) advance; move forward; move ahead 2.(进入) enter; come into; go into; get into: ～房间 enter a room 3.(收入) receive: ～货 lay in a new stock of goods / ～款 income 4.(进食) eat; drink; take 5.(呈上) submit; present 6.(进到里面) into; in: 走～客厅 walk into the hall 7.(进球) score a goal

【进逼】 jìnbī close in on; advance on; press on towards

【进步】 jìnbù 1.(向前发展) advance; progress; improve: ～取决于个人是否努力 progress depends on individual effort 2.(先进的)(politically) progressive: 思想～ have progressive ideas

【进步人士】 jìnbù rénshì progressive personages

【进餐】 jìncān have a meal; have a dinner

【进场】 jìnchǎng 1.(进入场地) march into the arena 2.(飞机进入机场) approach

【进城】 jìnchéng 1.(到城里去) go into town; go to town 2.(到城市生活和工作) enter the big cities

【进程】 jìnchéng course; process; progress

【进出】 jìnchū 1.(进来和出去) pass in and out; get in and out 2.(收入和支出) receipts and payments; turnover

【进出口】 jìnchūkǒu 1.(商品进出口) imports and exports 2.(出入的门口) exits and entrances; exit

【进出口公司】 jìnchūkǒu gōngsī import and export corporation

【进出口贸易】 jìnchūkǒu màoyì import and export trade; foreign trade

【进度】 jìndù 1.(工作进行的速度) rate of progress; rate of advance 2.(工作进行的计划) planned speed; schedule

【进度表】 jìndùbiǎo progress chart

【进发】 jìnfā set out; start

【进犯】 jìnfàn intrude into; invade

【进攻】 jìngōng attack; assault; offensive

【进化】 jìnhuà evolution

【进化论】 jìnhuàlùn the theory of evolution

【进货】 jìnhuò stock (a shop) with goods; lay in a stock of merchandise

【进军】 jìnjūn march; advance; move: 向现代化～ march towards the modernization

【进口】 jìnkǒu 1.(船只进港) enter port; sail into a port 2.(外贸进口) import: 从澳大利亚～羊毛 import wool from Australia 3.(入口) entrance

【进口货】 jìnkǒuhuò import; importation; imported goods

【进口配额】 jìnkǒu pèi'é import quota

【进口商】 jìnkǒushāng importer

【进口税】 jìnkǒushuì import duty

【进口许可证】 jìnkǒu xǔkězhèng import license

【进款】 jìnkuǎn 1.(收进款项) earn; receive 2.(指款项) income; receipts

【进来】 jìn·lái 1.(到里面来) come in; get in; enter 2.(到里面) in: 走～ walk in

【进料加工】 jìnliào jiāgōng processing imported materials

【进门】 jìnmén enter; come in

【进取】 jìnqǔ be eager to make progress; keep forging ahead; be enterprising

【进取心】 jìnqǔxīn enterprising spirit; initiative; gumption; push

【进去】 jìn·qù 1.(进入) go in; get in; enter 2.(到里面去) in: 闯～ break in / 鞋太小,他穿不～。The shoes are too small for him.

【进入】 jìnrù get into; enter

【进食】 jìnshí take food; have one's meal

【进水管】 jìnshuǐguǎn inlet tube

【进退】 jìntuì 1.(进和退) advance and retreat: ～维谷 to be in a cleft stick; between the devil and the deep blue sea 2.(分寸) sense of propriety

【进退两难】 jìntuì-liǎngnán in a dilemma

【进项】 jìn·xiang income; receipts

【进行】 jìnxíng 1.(开展) be in progress; go on; be underway: 会谈正在顺利～中。The talks are in good progress. 2.(从事) carry on; carry out; conduct; make: 经济上～改

革 carry out economic reform / ～处分 take disciplinary action 3.（前进）be on the march; march; advance

【进行曲】 jìnxíngqǔ march: 义勇军～ March of the Volunteers

【进修】 jìnxiū engage in advanced studies; take a refresher course: 在职～ in-service training

【进修生】 jìnxiūshēng trainee

【进一步】 jìnyībù go a step further; further: ～深化改革 take further steps to deepen the reform / 提出～要求 make a further demand

【进展】 jìnzhǎn make progress; make headway: 事情～得怎么样? How are things going? / 会谈～顺利。Good progress has been made in the talks.

【进占】 jìnzhàn attack and occupy; attack and capture; capture

【进站】 jìnzhàn get in; pull in; draw up at a station

【进账】 jìnzhàng income; receipts

【进驻】 jìnzhù enter and be stationed in; enter and garrison; march into (a place) and station there

近 (jìn) 1.（指距离或时间）near; close; immediate: ～距离 short distance 2.（接近）approaching; approximately; come near to; close to: 年～八十 approaching eighty; getting on for eighty 3.（亲密）intimate; closely related 4.（浅显）easy to understand

【近便】 jìn·bian close and convenient; close at hand

【近代】 jìndài modern times

【近代史】 jìndàishǐ modern history

【近道】 jìndào shortcut: 抄～ take a shortcut

【近地点】 jìndìdiǎn 〈*Astron*.〉 perigee

【近东】 Jìndōng the Near East

【近海】 jìnhǎi coastal waters; inshore; offshore

【近海油田】 jìnhǎi yóutián offshore oilfield

【近乎】 jìn·hu 1.（接近于）close to; little short of; near; almost; approximately: ～不可能 almost impossible 2.（指关系）intimate; friendly: 套～ try to be friendly with; try to chum up with

【近郊】 jìnjiāo outskirts of a city; suburbs; environs

【近景】 jìnjǐng 〈*Photog*.〉 close shot

【近距离】 jìnjùlí close quarter; at short range

【近况】 jìnkuàng recent developments; how things stand: 她的～怎么样? How are things with her?

【近来】 jìnlái recently; of late; lately

【近邻】 jìnlín near neighbor

【近路】 jìnlù shortcut

【近旁】 jìnpáng nearby; near

【近期】 jìnqī in the near future; short term

【近亲】 jìnqīn close relative; near relation

【近亲繁殖】 jìnqīn fánzhí inbreeding

【近亲结婚】 jìnqīn jiéhūn consanguineous marriage

【近日】 jìnrì 1.（指过去）recently; in the past few days 2.（指将来）within the next few days

【近日点】 jìnrìdiǎn 〈*Astron*.〉 perihelion

【近视】 jìnshì 1.（指视力）myopia; myopic (adj.); near-sightedness; short-sightedness 2.（指人眼睛近视）be myopic; be near-sightedned; be short-sighted 3.（喻目光短浅）without foresight; be near-sighted; be short-sighted

【近视眼】 jìnshìyǎn 1.（指患有近视症）be myopic; be near-sightedness; be short-sighted 2.（形容目光短浅）without foresight; be near-sighted; be short-sighted

【近似】 jìnsì approximate; similar

【近似值】 jìnsìzhí approximate value

【近因】 jìnyīn immediate cause

【近于】 jìnyú bordering on; little short of: ～荒唐 little short of preposterous

【近月点】 jìnyuèdiǎn 〈*Astron*.〉 perilune

【近战】 jìnzhàn 1.（近距离战斗）fighting at close quarters; close combat 2.〈*Boxing*〉 in-fighting

【近作】 jìnzuò a new work; a recent work

劲［勁、劤］(jìn) 1.（strength; energy: 没～ feel weak 2.（情绪）vigor; spirit; drive; zeal 3.（神情）air; manner; expression 4.（趣味）interest; relish; gusto; mood: 打麻将没～。Playing mah-jong is no fun.
（另见"劲"jìng）

【劲头】 jìntóu 1.（strength; energy 2.（情绪）vigor; spirit; drive; zeal: ～十足 full of enthusiasm

晋［晉］(jìn) 1.(进) enter; advance 2.(提高) promote

【晋级】 jìnjí rise in rank; be promoted

【晋见】 jìnjiàn call on (sb. holding high office); have an audience with

【晋升】 jìnshēng promote to a higher office; promotion (n.)

【晋谒】 jìnyè 〈*Written*〉 call on (sb. holding high office); have an audience with

浸(jìn) soak; steep; immerse; immersion (n.): 把头～入水中 immerse one's head in the water

【浸膏】 jìngāo 〈*Pharm.*〉 extract

【浸剂】 jìnjì 〈*Pharm.*〉 infusion

【浸礼】 jìnlǐ 〈*Christ*〉 baptism; immersion

【浸没】 jìnmò 1.(淹没) flood; inundate 2.(沉浸) immerse

【浸泡】 jìnpào soak; immerse: 把脏衣服～在水里 soak the dirty clothes in water

【浸染】 jìnrǎn 1.(染色) dip-dye 2.(逐渐沾染) be gradually tainted with; be contaminated; be gradually influenced

【浸入】 jìnrù immerse; immersion (n.)

【浸入式热水器】 jìnrùshì rèshuǐqì (热得快) immersion heater

【浸软】 jìnruǎn macerate

【浸润】 jìnrùn 1.(渐渐渗入) soak; infiltrate 2.〈*Med.*〉 infiltration

【浸湿】 jìnshī soak

【浸蚀】 jìnshí erosion: 雨水～土壤 soil erosion by rain

【浸透】 jìntòu soak; saturate; steep; infuse

【浸种】 jìnzhǒng 〈*Agric.*〉 seed soaking (in water); water treatment

【浸渍】 jìnzì soak; ret; macerate

禁(jìn) 1.(禁止) prohibit; forbid; ban 2.(监禁) imprison; detain 3.(禁止的事项) what is forbidden by law or custom; a taboo (另见"禁"jīn)

【禁闭】 jìnbì confinement (as a punishment)

【禁赌】 jìndǔ prohibit gambling; suppress gambling; prohibition of gambling

【禁火期】 jìnhuǒqī closed fire-season

【禁锢】 jìngù 1.(禁止异己做官) debar from holding office 2.(监禁) keep in custody; imprison; put in jail 3.(强制束缚) confine; shackle

【禁忌】 jìnjì 1.(忌讳) taboo 2.〈*Med.*〉 contraindication 3.(戒) avoid; abstain from

【禁酒】 jìnjiǔ prohibition against alcoholic drinks

【禁令】 jìnlìng prohibition; ban

【禁区】 jìnqū 1.(禁止进入的地区) forbidden zone; restricted zone; out-of-bounds area 2.(自然保护区) preserve; reserve; natural park 3.〈*Football*〉 penalty area 4.〈*Basketball*〉 restricted area

【禁书】 jìnshū official banned book; banned book

【禁运】 jìnyùn embargo: 取消～ lift embargo / 实行～ impose embargo

【禁止】 jìnzhǐ prohibit; ban; forbid

【禁止标志】 jìnzhǐ biāozhì prohibitory sign ‖ 禁止超车 no overtaking; no passing / 禁止大型货车通行 no trucks / 禁止调头 no U turn / 禁止垂钓 no fishing / 禁止非机动车通行 no bicycles / 禁止倾倒垃圾 no garbage here / 禁止入内 no admittance / 禁止驶入 one-way traffic; do not enter / 禁止停车 no parking / 禁止通行 no thoroughfare; closed to traffic / 禁止吸烟 no smoking / 禁止行人通行 no entry / 禁止游泳 no swimming / 禁止右转弯 no right turn / 禁止招贴 post no bills / 禁止左转弯 no left turn

【禁止性关税】 jìnzhǐxìng guānshuì prohibitive duty

噤(jìn) 1.(不做声) keep silent 2.(冷得哆嗦) shiver: 寒～ shiver with cold

【噤若寒蝉】 jìnruò-hánchán as silent as a cicada in cold weather; keep quiet out of fear

觐(jìn) 1.(朝见) present oneself before 2.(朝拜) go on a pilgrimage

【觐见】 jìnjiàn present oneself before (a monarch); go to court; have an audience with

jing

茎［莖］(jīng) stem (of a plant); stalk

【茎稿】 jīnggǎo straw

泾［涇］(jīng)

【泾渭分明】 Jīng Wèi fēnmíng be quite distinct from each other; make a clear distinction between purity and impurity; entirely different

经[經](jīng) 1.〈*Textiles*〉warp 2.〈*Chin. Med.*〉channels 3.〈*Geog.*〉longitude; longitudinal (adj.): 东～ east longitude / 西～ west longitude 4.(经营) manage; deal in; engage in 5.(经久不变) constant; regular 6.(经典) scripture; canon; classics: 佛～ Buddhist sutra; Buddhist scripture / 圣～ the Bible 7.(月经) menses; menstruation 8.(途经) pass through; via; by way of; undergo: ～新加坡回国 return home via Singapore 9.(经过) as a result of; after; through: ～法律许可 authorized by law / ～双方同意 by mutual consent / ～水陆联运 through transport by land and water / ～第三者调解 through the mediation of a third party 10.(经受) stand; bear; endure

【经常】 jīngcháng 1.(平常) day-to-day; everyday; daily 2.(常常) often; frequently; constantly; regularly: ～保持联系 often keep in contact with sb.

【经典】 jīngdiǎn 1.(权威著作) classics: ～作家 author of classics 2.(宗教教义著作) scriptures 3.(具有权威性的) classical: ～著作 classical works

【经度】 jīngdù longitude

【经费】 jīngfèi funds; outlay: 教育～ funds for education

【经费包干】 jīngfèi bāogān take responsibility for one's surplus or deficits

【经管】 jīngguǎn be in charge of: ～出口业务 be in charge of imports and exports

【经过】 jīngguò 1.(途经) pass; go through; go by 2.(通过) as a result of; after; through 3.(过程;经历) process; course

【经纪】 jīngjì 1.(经营) manage (a business) 2.(经纪人) manager; broker

【经纪人】 jīngjìrén broker; middleman; agent

【经济】 jīngjì 1.〈*Econ.*〉economy: 国民～ national economy / 国营～ the state sector of the economy / 民族～ national economy / 易货～ barter economy / 规模～ economy of scale / 泡沫～ bubble economy 2.(对国民经济有利的) economic; of industrial value; of economic value 3.(个人生活费用) financial condition; income: ～宽裕 be well-off 4.(节省的) economical; thrifty; economically (adv.): 乘公共汽车比乘出租汽车～。Going by bus is more economical than going by taxi.

【经济包装】 jīngjì bāozhuāng economy-size

【经济崩溃】 jīngjì bēngkuì economic collapse

【经济舱】 jīngjìcāng economy class

【经济发展】 jīngjì fāzhǎn economic development

【经济封锁】 jīngjì fēngsuǒ economic blockade

【经济改革】 jīngjì gǎigé economic reform

【经济杠杆】 jīngjì gànggǎn economic levers

【经济过热】 jīngjì guòrè overheated economy; over-stimulated economy

【经济核算】 jīngjì hésuàn economic accounting

【经济滑坡】 jīngjì huápō economic slump

【经济环境】 jīngjì huánjìng economic environment: 改善～ improve the economic environment

【经济基础】 jīngjì jīchǔ economic base; economic basis

【经济技术开发区】 jīngjì jìshù kāifāqū the economic and technological development zones

【经济开放区】 jīngjì kāifàngqū economic area

【经济昆虫】 jīngjì kūnchóng economic insects

【经济林】 jīngjìlín economic forest

【经济贸易区】 jīngjì màoyìqū financial and trade zone

【经济模式】 jīngjì móshì economic model

【经济赔偿】 jīngjì péicháng economic compensation; financial reimbursement

【经济平衡】 jīngjì pínghéng economic equilibrium

【经济起飞】 jīngjì qǐfēi economic 'take-off'

【经济实惠】 jīngjì shíhuì economy; economical and practical: 买成品鞋～,因为它们更经穿。It is good economy to buy well-made shoes, as they will last longer.

【经济实体】 jīngjì shítǐ economic entity

【经济手段】 jīngjì shǒuduàn means of controlling economic activity

【经济特区】 jīngjì tèqū special economic zone

【经济体系】 jīngjì tǐxì economic system

【经济体制】 jīngjì tǐzhì economic structure：加快～改革 speed up the restructuring of economic systems
【经济危机】 jīngjì wēijī economic crisis
【经济效果】 jīngjì xiàoguǒ economic effect：讲究～ take into consideration the economic effect / 以最少的消耗取得最大的～ obtain the maximum economic results at minimum costs
【经济效益】 jīngjì xiàoyì economic efficiency；economic benefits；economic results：讲究～ take into consideration the economic efficiency
【经济协作区】 jīngjì xiézuòqū economic coordination region
【经济学】 jīngjìxué economics：政治～ political economy ‖ 经济学家 economist
【经济一体化】 jīngjì yītǐhuà economic integration
【经济援助】 jīngjì yuánzhù economic aid
【经济运行机制】 jīngjì yùnxíng jīzhì economic operational mechanism；economic operation mechanism
【经济运营】 jīngjì yùnyíng economic operation
【经济责任制】 jīngjì zérènzhì system of economic responsibility
【经济指标】 jīngjì zhǐbiāo economic norms
【经济秩序】 jīngjì zhìxù economic order：整顿～ rectify the economic order
【经济制裁】 jīngjì zhìcái economic sanctions
【经济制度】 jīngjì zhìdù economic system
【经济状况】 jīngjì zhuàngkuàng economic state：～很好 be in a good economic state / ～不佳 be in a bad economic state
【经济作物】 jīngjì zuòwù industrial crops
【经久】 jīngjiǔ 1.（经过长时间）prolonged 2.（耐久）durable
【经久耐用】 jīngjiǔ nàiyòng durable；able to last for a long time
【经理】 jīnglǐ 1.（经营管理）handle；manage 2.（负责人）manager；director：总～ general manager / 副总～ deputy general manager 3.（项目、部门负责人或工作人员）manager：销售～ marketing manager；marketing and sales manager / 地区～ regional manager
【经历】 jīnglì 1.（亲身体验）go through；undergo；experience 2.（经历之事）experience：共同的～ a common experience
【经络】 jīngluò 〈*Chin. Med.*〉 channels and subsidiary channels
【经贸】 jīngmào economy and trade
【经期】 jīngqī 〈*Physiol.*〉 period；menstrual period
【经纱】 jīngshā 〈*Textiles*〉 warp
【经商】 jīngshāng engage in trade；be in business；go into business
【经手】 jīngshǒu handle；deal with
【经手人】 jīngshǒurén a person who handles the job in question
【经受】 jīngshòu undergo；experience；stand；weather；withstand：～锻炼 be tempered / ～考验 stand severe tests
【经售】 jīngshòu sell on commission；deal in；distribute；sell
【经纬度】 jīngwěidù longitude and latitude
【经纬仪】 jīngwěiyí theodolite；transit
【经线】 jīngxiàn 1.〈*Textiles*〉 warp 2.〈*Geog.*〉 meridian (line)
【经销】 jīngxiāo sell on commission；deal in；distribute；sell
【经销处】 jīngxiāochù agency；sales agency；distributor
【经销店】 jīngxiāodiàn sales agency；distributor
【经销商】 jīngxiāoshāng sales agent；distributor
【经心】 jīngxīn careful；mindful；conscientious
【经验】 jīngyàn 1.（指知识或技能）experience：～丰富 have much experience；be experienced 2.（经历）go through；experience
【经验主义】 jīngyàn zhǔyì empiricism；empiricist (adj.) ‖ 经验主义者 empiricist
【经营】 jīngyíng manage；run；engage in：承包～责任制 contract system of managerial responsibility / 集约～ intensive management / 合资～ joint venture
【经营方式】 jīngyíng fāngshì methods of operating
【经营机制】 jīngyíng jīzhì operating mechanism
【经营决策】 jīngyíng juécè management decisions

【经营战略】 jīngyíng zhànlüè business strategy
【经营职能】 jīngyíng zhínéng function of management
【经营自主权】 jīngyíng zhìzhǔquán make their own decisions about production
【经由】 jīngyóu via; by way of: 由北京～天津去上海 travel from Beijing to Shanghai via Tianjin
【经援】 jīngyuán economic aid

京（jīng） 1.（首都）the capital (of a country) 2.（北京）Beijing: 进～ go to Beijing
【京白梨】 jīngbáilí Beijing pear
【京城】 jīngchéng the capital of a country
【京都】 jīngdū the capital of a country
【京胡】 jīnghú *jinghu*; 2-stringed Chinese violin for Beijing Opera
【京郊】 jīngjiāo the suburbs of Beijing; the outskirt of Beijing
【京剧】 jīngjù Beijing opera; Peking opera
【京剧团】 jīngjùtuán Beijing opera troupe
【京族】 Jīngzú Gin（中国少数民族，主要分布在广西）

惊［**驚**］（jīng） 1.（惊恐）start; be frightened: ～叫 give a cry of alarm 2.（惊动）surprise; shock; alarm 3.（动物受惊）shy; stampede
【惊动】 jīngdòng 1.（使吃惊）startle; alarm; shock 2.（使警惕）alert 3.（惊扰）disturb; bother: 不要～病人 don't disturb the patient
【惊弓之鸟】 jīnggōngzhīniǎo a panic-stricken person
【惊骇】 jīnghài 〈*written*〉 frightened; panic-stricken
【惊呼】 jīnghū cry out in alarm
【惊慌】 jīnghuāng alarmed; scared; panic-stricken: ～失措 be frightened out of one's wits
【惊悸】 jīngjì palpitate with terror; have the heart in the mouth
【惊厥】 jīngjué 1.（因害怕而晕过去）faint from fear 2.〈*Med.*〉convulsions
【惊恐】 jīngkǒng alarmed and panicky; seized with terror; terrified: ～失色 be so terrified that one turns pale
【惊雷】 jīngléi a sudden clap of thunder
【惊奇】 jīngqí wonder; be surprised; be amazed
【惊扰】 jīngrǎo alarm; agitate: 自相～ raise a false alarm
【惊人】 jīngrén astonishing; amazing; alarming: ～的成就 astonishing achievements
【惊叹】 jīngtàn wonder at; marvel at; exclaim (with admiration)
【惊叹号】 jīngtànhào exclamation; exclamation mark（符号为！）
【惊涛骇浪】 jīngtāo-hàilàng 1.（大风浪）terrifying waves; stormy sea; fearful storm 2.（险恶环境或遭遇）a situation or life full of perils; perilous situation
【惊天动地】 jīngtiān-dòngdì sky-rocking and earth shaking; shaking heaven and earth
【惊悉】 jīngxī be shocked to learn of
【惊喜】 jīngxǐ pleasantly surprised
【惊吓】 jīngxià frighten; scare; shock
【惊险】 jīngxiǎn breathtaking; thrilling; alarmingly dangerous
【惊险片】 jīngxiǎnpiān 〈*Cinematog.*〉 thriller
【惊险小说】 jīngxiǎn xiǎoshuō thriller
【惊心动魄】 jīngxīn-dòngpò soul-stirring; profoundly affecting; struck with fright or horror
【惊醒】 jīngxǐng 1.（受惊醒来）wake up with a start 2.（使醒来）cause to wake up; rouse suddenly from sleep; awaken 3.（容易醒来）sleep lightly; easily roused from sleep
【惊讶】 jīngyà surprised; amazed; astonished
【惊异】 jīngyì surprised; amazed; astonished; astounded
【惊蛰】 Jīngzhé the Waking of Insects (3月5-7日交节)

鲸（jīng） whale: 抹香～ sperm whale ‖ 雄鲸 bull whale / 雌鲸 cow whale / 幼鲸 whale calf ‖ 捕鲸船 whaler
【鲸蜡】 jīnglà spermaceti
【鲸肉】 jīngròu whalemeat
【鲸鲨】 jīngshā whale shark
【鲸吞】 jīngtūn swallow like a whale; annex (territory): ～蚕食 take by force and encroach upon land or territory
【鲸须】 jīngxū baleen; whalebone
【鲸油】 jīngyóu whale oil; blubber
【鲸鱼】 jīngyú whale
【鲸脂】 jīngzhī blubber

荆(jīng) chaste tree; vitex

【荆棘】 jīngjí thistles and thorns; brambles; thorny under-growth

精(jīng) 1.(精选) refined; picked; choice 2.(精华) essence; extract 3.(完美;最好) perfect; excellent 4.(精细) meticulous; fine; precise 5.(机灵心细) smart; sharp; clever; shrewd 6.(精通) skilled; conversant; proficient: ～于武术 be proficient at *kung fu* 7.(精神;精力) energy; spirit 8.(精液;精子) sperm; semen; seed; seminal (adj.): 遗～ seminal emission 9.(非常;十分) extremely; very 10.(妖精) goblin; spirit; demon

【精兵】 jīngbīng picked troops; crack troops

【精兵简政】 jīngbīng-jiǎnzhèng better troops and simpler administration; streamlined administration

【精彩】 jīngcǎi brilliant; splendid; wonderful; marvellous

【精巢】 jīngcháo 〈*Anat*.〉 spermary; testis

【精粹】 jīngcuì succinct; pithy; terse

【精打细算】 jīngdǎ-xìsuàn careful calculation and strict budgeting; to use one's calculating funds with meticulous care

【精度】 jīngdù precision: 高～ high precision

【精纺】 jīngfǎng 〈*Textiles*〉 fine spinning

【精干】 jīnggàn 1.(指人少而精) small in number but highly trained; crack 2.(精明强干) keen-witted and capable

【精光】 jīngguāng 1.(一无所有) with nothing left 2.(光洁) shiny; bright

【精悍】 jīnghàn 1.(精明能干) capable and vigorous 2.(精练犀利) pithy and poignant

【精华】 jīnghuá cream; essence; quintessence

【精简】 jīngjiǎn retrench; simplify; reduce: ～编制 reduce the staff / ～非生产人员 reduce nonproductive personnel / ～机构 streamlining the government and squeeze out inefficiency

【精力】 jīnglì energy; vigor; vim: ～充沛 be energetic; full of vitality

【精练】 jīngliàn concise; succinct; terse

【精炼】 jīngliàn 1.〈*Metall*.〉 refine; purify 2.(精练) concise; succinct; terse

【精良】 jīngliáng excellent; superior; of the best quality

【精灵】 jīng·ling 1.(鬼怪) spirit; demon 2.(机灵) clever; smart; intelligent

【精美】 jīngměi exquisite; elegant: ～的装潢 excellent finish

【精密】 jīngmì precise; accurate

【精密度】 jīngmìdù precision

【精密仪器】 jīngmì yíqì precision instrument

【精明】 jīngmíng astute; shrewd; sagacious

【精囊】 jīngnáng 〈*Anat*.〉 seminal vesicle

【精疲力竭】 jīngpí-lìjié exhausted; worn out; tired out; spent

【精疲力尽】 jīngpí-lìjìn spirit and strength totally used up; extremely fatigued

【精辟】 jīngpì penetrating; incisive

【精品】 jīngpǐn 1.(指艺术作品) fine works 2.(指商品) quality goods

【精巧】 jīngqiǎo exquisite; ingenious

【精确】 jīngquè accurate; exact; precise: ～的定义 a precise definition

【精肉】 jīngròu lean meat

【精锐】 jīngruì crack; picked: ～部队 crack troops

【精深】 jīngshēn profound: 博大～ have both extensive knowledge and profound scholarship

【精神】 jīngshén 1.(心理状态) spirit; mind 2.(宗旨) essence; gist; spirit; substance

【精神】 jīng·shen 1.(活力) vigor; vitality; drive: 振作～ bestir oneself; summon up one's energy; get up steam 2.(有生气) lively; spirited; vigorous: 那孩子怪～的。The child is full of life.

【精神病】 jīngshénbìng mental disease; mental disorder; psychosis

【精神分裂症】 jīngshén fēnlièzhèng 〈*Med*.〉 schizophrenia

【精神分析】 jīngshén fēnxī psychoanalysis

【精神衰弱】 jīngshén shuāiruò athopia; psychasthenia

【精神文明】 jīngshén wénmíng spiritual civilization; cultural and ideological progress; culture and ideology

【精神文明建设】 jīngshén wénmíng jiànshè cultural and ideological progress

【精神污染】 jīngshén wūrǎn spiritual contamination; spiritual pollution

【精饲料】 jīngsìliào concentrated feed; concentrate
【精髓】 jīngsuǐ marrow; pith; quintessence
【精邃】 jīngsuì profound
【精通】 jīngtōng be proficient in; have a good command of; master: ～业务 be proficient in professional work
【精细】 jīngxì 1.(细致) meticulous; fine: 做工～ of exquisite workmanship 2.(精心) careful
【精细化工】 jīngxì huàgōng fine chemical industry
【精心】 jīngxīn meticulously; painstakingly: ～培育 take pains to foster
【精选】 jīngxuǎn 1.〈*Mineral*.〉 concentration 2.(精心挑选) carefully chosen; choice
【精选品】 jīngxuǎnpǐn select items
【精盐】 jīngyán refined salt
【精研】 jīngyán careful study or consideration
【精液】 jīngyè 〈*Physiol*.〉 seminal fluid; semen
【精益求精】 jīngyìqiújīng constantly improve sth.; keep improving; always endeavor to do still better; strive for perfection
【精英】 jīngyīng 1.(精华) essence; flower 2.(出类拔萃的人) elite
【精英政治】 jīngyīng zhèngzhì elitism
【精湛】 jīngzhàn consummate; exquisite
【精制】 jīngzhì make with extra care; refine
【精制品】 jīngzhìpǐn refined product
【精致】 jīngzhì fine; exquisite; delicate
【精装】 jīngzhuāng (of books) clothbound; hardback; hardcover
【精装本】 jīngzhuāngběn de luxe edition
【精壮】 jīngzhuàng able-bodied; strong
【精子】 jīngzǐ 〈*Physiol*.〉 sperm; spermatozoon
【精子库】 jīngzǐkù 〈*Med*.〉 sperm bank
【精子数】 jīngzǐshù 〈*Med*.〉 sperm count

旌(jīng) an ancient type of banner

【旌旗】 jīngqí banners and flags

晶(jīng) 1.(光亮) brilliant; glittering 2.(水晶) quartz; (rock) crystal 3.(晶体) any crystalline substance

【晶体】 jīngtǐ crystal
【晶体管】 jīngtǐguǎn transistor
【晶体管收音机】 jīngtǐguǎn shōuyīnjī transistor radio
【晶莹】 jīngyíng sparkling; clear and transparent

兢(jīng)

【兢兢业业】 jīngjīng-yèyè cautious and conscientious; highly responsible

腈(jīng) 〈*Chem*.〉 nitrile

【腈纶】 jīnglún acrylic fibers

井(jǐng) 1.(水井) well: 打～ sink a well; drill a well 2.(形状像井的) well; sth. in the shape of a well: 矿～ pit; mine / 油～ oil well 3.(整齐) neat; orderly

【井场】 jǐngchǎng 〈*Petroleum*〉 well site
【井架】 jǐngjià 1.〈*Petroleum*〉 derrick 2.〈*Mineral*.〉 headframe; headgear; pitheadframe 3.(水井架) well head
【井井有条】 jǐngjǐng-yǒutiáo in perfect order; shipshape; methodical; well-arranged
【井口】 jǐngkǒu 1.(水井口) the mouth of a well 2.〈*Mineral*.〉 pithead 3.〈*Petroleum*〉 wellhead
【井喷】 jǐngpēn 〈*Petroleum*〉 blowout
【井然】 jǐngrán 〈*written*〉 orderly; neat and tidy; well-organized
【井下】 jǐngxià in the pit; under the shaft
【井涌量】 jǐngyǒngliàng well yield

肼(jǐng) 〈*Chem*.〉 hydrazine

颈[頸](jǐng) neck: 瓶～ bottle-neck

【颈动脉】 jǐngdòngmài 〈*Anat*.〉 carotid artery
【颈内静脉】 jǐngnèi jìngmài 〈*Anat*.〉 jugular vein
【颈浅淋巴结】 jǐngqiǎn línbājié 〈*Med*.〉 superficial cervial lymph node
【颈肉】 jǐngròu 1.(羊肉、猪肉部位) neck 2.(牛肉部位) chuck
【颈项】 jǐngxiàng neck
【颈椎】 jǐngzhuī 〈*Anat*.〉 cervical vertebra
【颈总动脉】 jǐng zǒngdòngmài 〈*Anat*.〉 common carotid artery

景(jǐng) 1.(风景) view; scenery; scene: 夜～ night view 2.(景况) situation; con-

dition 3.〈*Theatre*〉scenery; scene: 第一幕第二～ Act I, scene 2 4.(景仰) admire; revere; respect
【景点】 jǐngdiǎn scenic spots
【景观】 jǐngguān 〈*Geog.*〉landscape; scenery
【景况】 jǐngkuàng situation; circumstances; condition
【景慕】 jǐngmù esteem; revere
【景旁】 jǐngpáng 〈*Theatre*〉a piece of scenery
【景颇族】 Jǐngpōzú Jingpo (中国少数民族，主要分布在云南)
【景气】 jǐngqì prosperity; boom: 不～ depression; slump
【景区】 jǐngqū scenic spot
【景色】 jǐngsè scenery; view; scene; landscape: ～宜人 attractive scenery / 山里的～非常美。The scenery in the mountains is very beautiful.
【景深】 jǐngshēn 〈*Photog.*〉depth of field
【景泰蓝】 jǐngtàilán cloisonne enamel; cloisonne
【景物】 jǐngwù scenery: ～宜人 delightful scenery
【景象】 jǐngxiàng scene; sight; picture
【景仰】 jǐngyǎng respect and admire; hold in deep respect: ～大名 look up to your great name
【景遇】 jǐngyù 〈*written*〉circumstances; one's lot
【景致】 jǐngzhì view; scenery; scene

儆 (jǐng) warn; admonish: 以～效尤 so as to deter anyone from committing the same mistake

警 (jǐng) 1.(警戒) alert; vigilant 2.(使人警惕) warn; alarm 3.(危险紧急的情况) alarm: 火～ fire alarm 4.(警察) police: 去报～! Call the police! 5.(警察人员) policeman (m.); police-woman (f.): 巡～ patrolman; cop on the beat
【警报】 jǐngbào alarm; warning; alert
【警备】 jǐngbèi guard; garrison
【警备区】 jǐngbèiqū garrison command
【警备司令】 jǐngbèi sīlìng garrison commander
【警察】 jǐngchá 1.(总称) police; police force: 人民～ the people's police 2.(警察人员) policeman (m.); policewoman (f.); cop: 便衣～ policeman in plain clothes
【警察分局】 jǐngchá fēnjú police station
【警察国家】 jǐngchá guójiā police state
【警察局】 jǐngchájú police office
【警车】 jǐngchē patrol wagon
【警笛】 jǐngdí 1.(警哨) police whistle 2.(警报汽笛) siren
【警告】 jǐnggào 1.(告诫) warn; caution; admonish 2.(处分) warning: ～处分 punishment of warning
【警官】 jǐngguān police officer
【警棍】 jǐnggùn baton; truncheon
【警徽】 jǐnghuī police emblem
【警戒】 jǐngjiè 1.(告诫) warn; admonish 2.〈*Mil.*〉be on the alert against; guard against; keep a close watch on: ～森严 the caution is stern
【警戒部队】 jǐngjiè bùduì outpost troops; security force; security detachment
【警戒色】 jǐngjièsè 〈*Zool.*〉warning color
【警戒水位】 jǐngjiè shuǐwèi warning line; warning water level; warning stage
【警戒线】 jǐngjièxiàn cordon; security line
【警句】 jǐngjù aphorism; epigram
【警觉】 jǐngjué vigilance; alertness
【警铃】 jǐnglíng alarm bell
【警犬】 jǐngquǎn police dog; patrol dog
【警探】 jǐngtàn police-spy
【警惕】 jǐngtì be on guard against; watch out for; be vigilant; be on the alert: 提高～ heighten one's vigilance / 时刻保持～ be alert at all times
【警亭】 jǐngtíng police kiosk
【警卫】 jǐngwèi 1.(警戒保卫) security guard; safeguards 2.(警卫员) guardsman
【警卫团】 jǐngwèituán guards regiment
【警卫员】 jǐngwèiyuán guardsman; bodyguard
【警衔】 jǐngxián police rank
【警醒】 jǐngxǐng be a light sleeper
【警钟】 jǐngzhōng alarm bell; tocsin

劲[勁] (jìng) strong; powerful; sturdy
(另见"劲"jìn)
【劲敌】 jìngdí 1.(指敌人) powerful enemy 2.(指对手) formidable rival; strong opponent

【劲旅】 jìnglǚ strong contingent; crack force: 棒球～ strong baseball team

径[徑、逕 1-3](jìng) 1.(小路) footpath; path; track: 山～ mountain path 2.(途径) way; means: 捷～ an easy way 3.(径直) directly; straightaway: ～回西安 go straight back to Xi'an 4.(直径) diameter

【径赛】 jìngsài 〈*Sports*〉 track

【径赛项目】 jìngsài xiàngmù track events

【径庭】 jìngtíng 〈*written*〉 very unlike: 大相～ entirely different; poles apart

【径行办理】 jìngxíng bànlǐ handle sth. straight; deal with the matter straight

【径直】 jìngzhí 〈*adv.*〉 straight; directly; straightaway

【径自】 jìngzì 〈*adv.*〉 without leave; without consulting anyone

胫[脛](jìng) 〈*Anat.*〉 shin

【胫骨】 jìnggǔ 〈*Anat.*〉 shin bone; tibia

痉[痙](jìng)

【痉挛】 jìngluán convulsion; spasm; cramp

净[淨](jìng) 1.(洁净) clean: ～水 clean water 2.(一点没有) completely; up: 吃～ eat up / 用～ use up 3.(纯净) net: ～出口 net export / ～进口 net import / ～收入 net income / ～收益 net earnings 4.(没有别的) only; merely; nothing but

【净产值】 jìngchǎnzhí net output value

【净高】 jìnggāo 〈*Archit.*〉 clear height

【净化】 jìnghuà purify; purification (n.): 水的～ purification of water / ～污水 purify waste water

【净化器】 jìnghuàqì purifier: 空气～ air purifier / 水～ water purifier

【净化塔】 jìnghuàtǎ purifying column

【净尽】 jìngjìn completely; utterly

【净空】 jìngkōng 〈*Archit.*〉 clearance; headroom

【净跨】 jìngkuà 〈*Archit.*〉 clear span

【净宽】 jìngkuān 〈*Archit.*〉 clear width

【净亏】 jìngkuī net loss; net deficiency

【净利】 jìnglì net profit

【净投资】 jìngtóuzī net investment

【净效益】 jìngxiàoyì net efficiency

【净余】 jìngyú remainder; surplus

【净值】 jìngzhí net worth; net value: 出口～ net export value / 进口～ net import value

【净重】 jìngzhòng net weight

【净赚】 jìngzhuàn net earnings

竞[競](jìng) compete; contest; vie

【竞渡】 jìngdù 1.(划船比赛) boat race 2.(游泳比赛) swimming race

【竞技】 jìngjì sports; athletics

【竞技场】 jìngjìchǎng arena

【竞技状态】 jìngjì zhuàngtài form (of an athlete)

【竞赛】 jìngsài contest; competition; emulation; race

【竞选】 jìngxuǎn enter into an election contest; campaign for (office); stand for; run for

【竞争】 jìngzhēng compete; vie; contend: 自由～ free competition / 不正当～ illegitimate competition; unfair competition

【竞争对手】 jìngzhēng duìshǒu competitor

【竞争机制】 jìngzhēng jīzhì competitive mechanism; competition: 把～引进科技领域 introduce competition into science and technology

【竞争价格】 jìngzhēng jiàgé competitive price

【竞争能力】 jìngzhēng nénglì capacity of competition: 在国际市场上有～ become competitive internationally; be competitive on the world market

【竞争性】 jìngzhēngxìng competitiveness

【竞走】 jìngzǒu 〈*Sports*〉 walking; walking race; heel-and-toe walking

竟(jìng) 1.(完毕) finish; complete 2.(从头到尾) throughout; whole: ～日 throughout the day; all day long 3.(终于) in the end; eventually 4.(竟然;出于意料之外) go so far as to; unexpectedly; actually

【竟然】 jìngrán 〈*adv.*〉 1.(表示有点出乎意外) to one's surprise; unexpectedly; actually 2.(居然) go so far as to; go to the length of; have the impudence to

境(jìng) 1.(边境) border; boundary: 国～ national boundary / 迁移出～ emigrate; emigration / 驱逐出～ deport sb. 2.(地方) place; area; territory; land 3.(境况)

condition; situation; circumstances: 在逆～中 in adverse circumstances

【境地】 jìngdì condition; circumstances

【境界】 jìngjiè 1.(地界) boundary 2.(情况; 程度) extent reached; plane attained; state; realm

【境况】 jìngkuàng condition; circumstances: 家庭～ family circumstances

【境域】 jìngyù 1.(境地) condition; circumstances 2.(境界) area; realm

【境遇】 jìngyù circumstances; one's lot

镜 (jìng) 1.(镜子) looking glass; mirror 2.(视镜) lens; glass

【镜架】 jìngjià spectacles frame

【镜框】 jìngkuāng 1.(相片框) picture frame 2.(眼镜架) spectacles frame

【镜片】 jìngpiàn lens: 隐形～ contact lens

【镜台】 jìngtái dressing table

【镜头】 jìngtóu 1.(光学透镜) lens; camera lens: 可变焦距～ zoom lens 2.(画面) shot; scene: 特技～ special effect shot; trick shot / 抢～ steal the scene / 外景～是在内蒙古拍摄的。The exterior shots were taken in Inner Mongolia.

【镜子】 jìng·zi 1.(各种面镜) mirror; looking glass: 照～ look at oneself in the glass 2.(眼镜) glasses; spectacles

静 (jìng) 1.(不动) still; calm; motionless: ～立 stand still / ～卧 lie motionless 2.(没有声响) silent; quiet: 请～一～。Please be quiet.

【静电】 jìngdiàn 〈*Physics*〉 static electricity

【静化器】 jìnghuàqì staticizer

【静力学】 jìnglìxué statics

【静脉】 jìngmài 〈*Anat.*〉 vein: 肺～ pulmonary vein / 颈～ jugular vein / 有些药品要直接注射到患者的～里。Some drugs have to be injected directly into patients' veins.

【静脉注射】 jìngmài zhùshè 〈*Med.*〉 intraveous injection

【静谧】 jìngmì 〈*written*〉 quiet; still; tranquil

【静默】 jìngmò 1.(不出声) become silent: ～无声 absolute quietness 2.(肃立悼念) mourn in silence; observe silence: 为…～致哀 mourn in silence for

【静穆】 jìngmù solemn and quiet

【静悄悄】 jìngqiāoqiāo very quiet

【静水】 jìngshuǐ dead water

【静态】 jìngtài 〈*Physics*〉 static state

【静听】 jìngtīng listen quietly

【静物】 jìngwù still life

【静物画】 jìngwùhuà still life

【静养】 jìngyǎng rest quietly to recuperate; have a good rest to recuperate

【静止】 jìngzhǐ static; motionless; at a standstill: 不要～地孤立地看待事物。Don't view things as static and isolated.

【静坐】 jìngzuò 1.(疗养办法) sit quietly 2.(示威) sit still as a form of therapy

【静坐示威】 jìngzuò shìwēi 1.(示威) sit-in 2.(抗议) sit-down

敬 (jìng) 1.(尊敬) respect; honor 2.(恭敬) respectfully: ～请光临 May I have the honor of your presence at ... 3.(有礼貌地送上) serve; offer politely

【敬爱】 jìng'ài respect and love; esteemed and beloved

【敬辞】 jìngcí term of respect; polite expression

【敬贺】 jìnghè congratulate sb. on sth.; offer congratulations

【敬酒】 jìngjiǔ propose a toast; toast

【敬老院】 jìnglǎoyuàn home for the aged; nursing home for the aged

【敬老尊贤】 jìnglǎo-zūnxián respect the aged and the virtuous

【敬礼】 jìnglǐ 1.(行礼) salute; give a salute 2.(致敬意) extend one's greetings 3.(用于书信结尾)此致～ with high respect; with best wishes

【敬佩】 jìngpèi esteem; admire; express admiration for; have a great esteem for

【敬上】 jìngshàng (用于书信结尾) truly yours; yours truly

【敬挽】 jìngwǎn (用于挽联、花圈等的落款) with deep condolences from sb.

【敬畏】 jìngwèi hold in awe and veneration; revere

【敬仰】 jìngyǎng revere; venerate; admire; look up to

【敬意】 jìngyì respect; tribute; regards: 顺致崇高的～ pay high tribute to

【敬赠】 jìngzhèng respectfully presented by

【敬重】 jìngzhòng highly esteem; look up to

with great respect; have great respect for

jiong

迥 (jiǒng) 〈*written*〉 widely different

【迥然】 jiǒngrán far apart; widely different: ～不同 not in the least alike; diametrically different

炯 (jiǒng) bright; shining

【炯炯】 jiǒngjiǒng 〈*written*〉(of eyes) bright; shining: 目光～ sparkling eyes; piercing eyes

窘 (jiǒng) 1.(穷困) in straitened circumstances; hard up; poorly off; in financial straits 2.(为难) awkward; embarrassed; ill at ease 3.(使为难) embarrass; disconcert

【窘境】 jiǒngjìng awkward situation; plight; predicament

【窘困潦倒】 jiǒngkùn-liáodǎo be miserably poor and greatly disappointed

【窘迫】 jiǒngpò 1.(非常困难) poverty-stricken; very poor; in poverty 2.(十分为难) hard pressed; embarrassed; in a predicament

【窘态】 jiǒngtài embarrassed look

jiu

纠 (jiū) 1.(纠缠) entangle 2.(纠集) gather together 3.(纠正) correct; rectify; put right

【纠察】 jiūchá 1.(维持秩序) maintain order at a public gathering 2.(维持秩序者) picket

【纠察队】 jiūcháduì pickets

【纠察线】 jiūcháxiàn picket line

【纠缠】 jiūchán 1.(绕在一起) get entangled; be in a tangle: ～不清 too tangled up to unravel 2.(捣麻烦) nag; worry; pester

【纠纷】 jiūfēn dispute; issue: 挑起～ stir up trouble / 调解～ mediate an issue

【纠葛】 jiūgé entanglement; dispute; complication

【纠合】 jiūhé get together; gather; muster

【纠集】 jiūjí 〈*derog.*〉 get together; muster; draw together: ～一伙流氓 get together a bunch of hoodlums

【纠结】 jiūjié be entangled with; be intertwined with

【纠偏】 jiūpiān rectify a deviation; correct an error

【纠正】 jiūzhèng correct; put right; redress; rectify; set right: ～错误 correct a mistake / ～不正之风 check unhealthy tendencies; amend unwholesome ways

赳 (jiū)

【赳赳】 jiūjiū valiant; gallant: ～武夫 a soldier of dauntless courage

究 (jiū) 1.(追究) study careful; go into; investigate 2.(用在问句中,究竟) actually; really; after all

【究办】 jiūbàn investigate and deal with

【究竟】 jiūjìng 1.(原委) outcome; what actually happened: 每个人都想知道个～。Everybody wants to know what actually happened. 2.(用于问句,表示追究) actually; exactly: 你～要干什么? What exactly do you want to do? 3.(毕竟) after all; in the end: 他～是生手。He is new to the job after all.

阄[鬮] (jiū) lot: 抓～ draw lots

揪 (jiū) 1.(紧紧地抓) hold tight; seize: ～头发 tear sb.'s hair / ～住不放 hold in a tight grip 2.(拽) pull; tug; drag; give a hard tug

【揪辫子】 jiūbiàn·zi seize upon sb.'s weak points

【揪出】 jiūchū uncover; ferret out

【揪心】 jiūxīn 1.(放不下心) anxious; worried 2.(疼痛难忍) heartrending; agonizing; gnawing

九 (jiǔ) 1.(数目) nine; ninth 2.(从冬至起每九天为一个九) each of the nine-day periods after the Winter Solstice: 三～ the third nine-day period after the Winter Solstice; the coldest days of winter 3.(多次;多数) many; numerous

【九百】 jiǔbǎi nine hundred; nine-hundredth

【九边形】 jiǔbiānxíng nonagon; nonagonal (adj.)

【九分之一】 jiǔfēnzhīyī a ninth; one ninth

【九牛二虎之力】 jiǔ niú èr hǔ zhī lì the

strength of nine bulls and two tigers; tremendous effort

【九牛一毛】 jiǔniú-yīmáo a single hair out of nine ox hides; a drop in the ocean

【九千】 jiǔqiān nine thousand; nine thousandth

【九曲桥】 jiǔqǔqiáo a zigzag bridge

【九泉】 jiǔquán 〈*written*〉 grave; the nether world: ～之下 in the nether regions; after death

【九十】 jiǔshí ninety; ninetieth

【九死一生】 jiǔsǐ-yīshēng a narrow escape from death; survival after many hazards

【九万】 jiǔwàn ninety thousand; ninety thousandth

【"九五"计划】 "jiǔwǔ" jìhuà the ninth five-year plan

【"九五"期间】 "jiǔwǔ" qījiān the enforcement period of the ninth five-year plan

【九霄云外】 jiǔxiāoyúnwài beyond the highest heavens; beyond the nine clouds; far, far away

【九月】 jiǔyuè September; Sept

【九折】 jiǔzhé ten per cent discount

久 (jiǔ) **1.**(时间长) for a long time; long: 很～以前 long ago **2.**(时间的长短) of a specified duration: 三周之～ for as long as three weeks

【久别重逢】 jiǔbié-chóngféng meet again after a long separation

【久而久之】 jiǔérjiǔzhī in the course of time; as time passes; in the long run

【久经风霜】 jiǔjīng-fēngshuāng have experienced all sorts of hardships

【久经考验】 jiǔjīng-kǎoyàn a long-tested; seasoned

【久久】 jiǔjiǔ for a long, long time

【久违】 jiǔwéi 〈*politeness*〉 how long it is since we last met; I haven't seen you for ages

【久闻大名】 jiǔwén-dàmíng I've long heard of your great name.

【久享盛名】 jiǔxiǎng-shèngmíng with a long standing reputation

【久仰】 jiǔyǎng 〈*politeness*〉 I'm very pleased to meet you; I have long desired to know you

【久远】 jiǔyuǎn far back; ages ago; remote: 年代～ of the remote past

玖 (jiǔ) nine; ninth

灸 (jiǔ) 〈*Chin. Med.*〉 moxa treatment; moxibustion

韭［**韮**］(jiǔ) tuber onion: 青～ young tuber onion; tuber onion seedlings

【韭菜】 jiǔcài tuber onion

【韭黄】 jiǔhuáng hotbed tuber onion

酒 (jiǔ) alcoholic drink; wine; liquor; spirits

【酒吧】 jiǔbā bar: 旅馆～ hotel bar

【酒吧凳】 jiǔbādèng barstool

【酒吧老板】 jiǔbā lǎobǎn barkeeper; barkeep

【酒吧女郎】 jiǔbā nǚláng bar girl

【酒吧招待】 jiǔbā zhāodài bartender; barman (m.); barmaid (f.)

【酒杯】 jiǔbēi wineglass; wine bowl

【酒菜】 jiǔcài **1.**(酒和菜) food and drink **2.**(下酒的菜) food to go with liquor

【酒厂】 jiǔchǎng brewery; winery; distillery

【酒店】 jiǔdiàn **1.**(酒类商店) wineshop; public house **2.**(大旅馆;饭店) hotel: 花园～ The Garden Hotel

【酒逢知己千杯少】 jiǔ féng zhījǐ qiān bēi shǎo When drinking with a bosom friend, a thousand cups will still be too little.

【酒馆】 jiǔguǎn public house; tavern; pub

【酒鬼】 jiǔguǐ drunkard; alkie

【酒后驾驶】 jiǔhòu jiàshǐ drinking and driving: ～是极危险的。Drinking and driving is dangerous.

【酒壶】 jiǔhú wine pot; flagon

【酒会】 jiǔhuì cocktail party

【酒家】 jiǔjiā restaurant

【酒窖】 jiǔjiào wine cellar

【酒精】 jiǔjīng alcohol; ethyl alcohol; alcoholic (adj.): 含～的饮料 an alcoholic drink

【酒精灯】 jiǔjīngdēng spirit lamp; alcohol lamp

【酒精炉】 jiǔjīnglú alcohol stove

【酒精中毒】 jiǔjīng zhòngdú 〈*Med.*〉 alcoholism; alcoholic (adj.)

【酒具】 jiǔjù flagon and wine cups; drinking vessels

【酒量】 jiǔliàng capacity for liquor; one's drinking capacity

【酒囊】 jiǔnáng wineskin
【酒囊饭袋】 jiǔnáng-fàndài wine skin and rice bag; useless person good only for feasting and drinking
【酒酿】 jiǔniàng fermented glutinous rice
【酒肉朋友】 jiǔròu-péngyǒu fair-weather friends
【酒色】 jiǔsè wine and women
【酒色财气】 jiǔsè-cáiqì wine, women, avarice and pride; the four cardinal vices
【酒水】 jiǔshuǐ drinks
【酒肆】 jiǔsì tavern
【酒提】 jiǔtí wine dipper
【酒涡】 jiǔwō dimple
【酒窝】 jiǔwō dimple
【酒席】 jiǔxí feast; banquet
【酒意】 jiǔyì a tipsy feeling
【酒糟鼻】 jiǔzāobí acne rosacea; brandy nose
【酒盅】 jiǔzhōng a small handleless wine cup
【酒醉】 jiǔzuì drunkenness

旧[舊] (jiù) 1.(过去的) past; bygone; old: ～风俗 old customs 2.(用过的) used; worn; old; secondhand: ～家具 timeworn furniture / ～鞋子 old shoes 3.(以前的) former; onetime 4.(老朋友) old friendship; old friend: 故～ old acquaintances
【旧病复发】 jiùbìng-fùfā have a recurrence of an old illness; have a relapse
【旧大陆】 jiùdàlù Old World
【旧恶】 jiùwù old grievance; old wrong
【旧货】 jiùhuò secondhand goods; junk
【旧货店】 jiùhuòdiàn secondhand shop; junk shop
【旧货市场】 jiùhuò shìchǎng flea market
【旧交】 jiùjiāo old acquaintance
【旧居】 jiùjū former residence; old home
【旧框框】 jiùkuāngkuāng convention
【旧历】 jiùlì the lunar calendar
【旧日】 jiùrì former days; old days
【旧社会】 jiùshèhuì old society
【旧诗】 jiùshī old-style poetry; classical poetry
【旧时】 jiùshí old times; old days
【旧式】 jiùshì old-type; conventional; old-fashion: ～服装 old-fashioned dresses
【旧事重提】 jiùshì chóngtí repetition of the old tale; bring up a matter of the past
【旧书】 jiùshū 1.(破旧的书籍) secondhand book; used book; old book 2.(古书) books by ancient writers
【旧书店】 jiùshūdiàn secondhand bookstore
【旧俗】 jiùsú old customs
【旧习】 jiùxí old habits and customs
【旧友】 jiùyǒu old friend; old acquaintance
【旧约】 jiùyuē 〈*Christ*〉 the Old Testament
【旧址】 jiùzhǐ former site

臼 (jiù) 1.(石臼) mortar: 石～ stone mortar 2.(形状像臼的) any mortar-shaped thing 3.(关节) joint (of bones): 脱～ dislocation (of joints)
【臼齿】 jiùchǐ molar; molar tooth

舅 (jiù) 1.(舅父) mother's brother; uncle 2.(妻子的弟兄) wife's brother; brother-in-law
【舅父】 jiùfù mother's brother; uncle
【舅母】 jiù·mu wife of mother's brother; aunt

咎 (jiù) 1.(过失) fault; blame: 引～辞职 take the blame and resign 2.(责备) censure; punish; blame: 既往不～ forgive sb's past misdeeds; let bygones be bygones
【咎由自取】 jiùyóuzìqǔ have only oneself to blame; that serves him right; he asked for it; deserving reproof

疚 (jiù) 〈*written*〉 remorse: 感到内～ have a guilty conscience

救[捄] (jiù) 1.(使摆脱危险或灾难) rescue; save; salvage; help: 呼～ call out for help; send out SOS signals 2.(援助) help; relieve; succor
【救兵】 jiùbīng relief troops; reinforcements
【救国】 jiùguó save the nation; save the country
【救护】 jiùhù give first aid; rescue: ～伤员 give first aid to the wounded
【救护车】 jiùhùchē ambulance
【救活】 jiùhuó bring sb. back to life
【救火】 jiùhuǒ fire fighting; firefight
【救急】 jiùjí help sb. to cope with an emergency; help meet an urgent need
【救济】 jiùjì relieve; succor: ～灾区人民 provide relief to the people in a disaster area
【救济金】 jiùjìjīn relief payment; relief fund; raise

【救济粮】 jiùjìliáng relief grain; relief food
【救济物资】 jiùjì wùzī relief: 给水灾灾民运去～ send relief to flood victims
【救命】 jiùmìng 1.(救人) save sb's life 2.(呼救声) Help!
【救生】 jiùshēng lifesaving
【救生圈】 jiùshēngquān lifebelt; life buoy
【救生索】 jiùshēngsuǒ lifeline
【救生艇】 jiùshēngtǐng lifeboat
【救生衣】 jiùshēngyī life jacket
【救生员】 jiùshēngyuán lifeguard; lifesaver
【救世主】 Jiùshìzhǔ 〈*Christ*〉 the Savior; the Redeemer
【救死扶伤】 jiùsǐ-fúshāng heal the wounded and rescue the dying
【救亡】 jiùwáng save the nation from extinction
【救星】 jiùxīng liberator; emancipator; savior; deliverer
【救援】 jiùyuán rescue; come to sb's help
【救灾】 jiùzāi provide disaster relief; help the people tide over a natural disaster; relieve the victims of a disaster
【救治】 jiùzhì bring a patient out of danger; treat and cure
【救助】 jiùzhù help sb. in danger or difficulty; succor

厩[庣、廄](jiù) stable; cattleshed; pen
【厩肥】 jiùféi 〈*Agric.*〉 barnyard manure
【厩蝇】 jiùyíng stable fly

就(jiù) 1.(靠近) come near; move towards 2.(开始从事) go to; take up; undertake; engage in; enter upon 3.(造就) accomplish; make 4.(就着吃喝) go with: 花生仁～酒 have peanuts to go with liquor 5.(按照) with regard to; concerning; on; in the light of; as far as: ～共同关心的问题进行会谈 hold talks on questions of common interest 6.(立刻) at once; right away; in a moment: 我这～来。I'm coming right away. 7.(已经) as early as; already: 大风早晨～停了。The wind has already subsided in the morning. 8.(表示数量大、能力强等) as much as; as many as: 一个月～节约了20吨煤 save as much as 20 tons of coal in one month 9.(表示在时间上紧接着) as soon as; no sooner ... than; right after: 说干～干 act without delay 10.(仅仅) only; merely; just: ～等你一个了。You're the only one we're waiting for.
【就便】 jiùbiàn at sb's convenience; while you're at it
【就餐】 jiùcān have a meal; go to the dining room
【就地】 jiùdì on the spot: ～正法 carry out the execution on the spot / ～取材 gather materials on the spot
【就范】 jiùfàn submit; give in: 不肯～ refuse to give in
【就近】 jiùjìn nearby; within reach; at close quarters
【就寝】 jiùqǐn 〈*written*〉 retire for the night; go to bed
【就任】 jiùrèn to assume one's post
【就事论事】 jiùshì-lùnshì take the matter as it stands; confine oneself merely to facts as they are
【就是】 jiùshì 1.(即使) even if; even: 你～送来,我也不要。Even if you bring it to me, I won't take it. 2.(表示强调) exactly; precisely: 我要的～这一个。What I want is exactly this one. 3.(表示同意) right; yes: ～, ～,你说的对。All right, all right, you're right.
【就手】 jiùshǒu while you're at it: 请～把门关上。Close the door behind you, please.
【就位】 jiùwèi take one's place
【就绪】 jiùxù be in order; be ready
【就学】 jiùxué go to school
【就学人数】 jiùxuě rénshù school enrollment
【就要】 jiùyào be about to; be going to; be on the point of
【就业】 jiùyè obtain employment; take up an occupation; get a job: 广开～门路 open new avenues of employment; provide job opportunities through various channels
【就业前职业培训】 jiùyèqián zhíyè péixùn pre-employment training
【就业人口】 jiùyè rénkǒu population of employment
【就业指导】 jiùyè zhǐdǎo vocational counsel
【就医】 jiùyī seek medical advice; go to a doctor
【就义】 jiùyì be executed for championing a

just cause; die a martyr
【就职】 jiùzhí assume office: 宣誓～ take the oath of office; be sworn in
【就职典礼】 jiùzhí diǎnlǐ inaugural ceremony; inauguration
【就职演说】 jiùzhí yǎnshuō inaugural speech
【就座】 jiùzuò take one's seat; be seated: 请大家～! Please take your seat!
鹫 (jiù) 〈*Zool.*〉 vulture

ju

车[車] (jū) 1.(中国象棋的) chariot 2.(国际象棋的) rook; castle
狙 (jū)
【狙击】 jūjī snipe
【狙击手】 jūjīshǒu sniper
【狙击战】 jūjīzhàn sniping action
拘 (jū) 1.(拘捕) arrest; detain 2.(限制) restrain; restrict; limit; constrain: 大小不～ regardless of size 3.(不变通) inflexible
【拘捕】 jūbǔ arrest; capture
【拘捕权】 jūbǔquán power of arrest
【拘谨】 jūjǐn overcautious; reserved
【拘禁】 jūjìn take into custody; put under arrest
【拘礼】 jūlǐ be punctilious; stand on ceremony
【拘留】 jūliú detain; hold in custody; intern; detention; provisional apprehension
【拘留所】 jūliúsuǒ bridewell; house of detention
【拘泥】 jū·nì be a stickler for; rigidly adhere to: ～于形式 rigidly adhere to form; be formalistic
【拘票】 jūpiào warrant; arrest warrant
【拘束】 jūshù 1.(限制) restrain; restrict 2.(不自然) constrained; awkward; ill at ease: 显得～ look ill at ease / 不要～ make yourself at home
【拘押】 jūyā take into custody
驹 (jū) 1.(少壮的马) colt 2.(小马) foal: 怀～ be in foal; be with foal
居 (jū) 1.(居住) reside; dwell; live 2.(居所) residence; house: 故～ former residence 3.(处于;在) be in; occupy: ～同类产品之魁首 rank first among similar products / 身～要职 hold an important post 4.(当;任) claim; assert: 以专家自～ be a self-styled expert 5.(积蓄) store up; lay by 6.(停留;固定) stay put; be at a standstill
【居安思危】 jū'ān-sīwēi be prepared for danger in times of peace; be vigilant in peace time; provide against danger while living in peace
【居功】 jūgōng claim credit for oneself
【居积】 jūjī store up; lay by
【居间】 jūjiān (mediate) between two parties
【居间贸易】 jū jiān màoyì intermediary trade
【居留】 jūliú reside; residence (n.)
【居留权】 jūliúquán right of residence
【居留证】 jūliúzhèng residence permit
【居民】 jūmín resident; inhabitant
【居民点】 jūmíndiǎn residential area
【居然】 jūrán 1.(竟然) unexpectedly; to one's surprise: 他～会相信这件事! Fancy his believing it! 2.(甚至于) go so far as to; have the impudence to; have the effrontery to: 敌人～使用了毒气。The enemy went so far as to use poison gas.
【居室】 jūshì room
【居所】 jūsuǒ residence; house
【居委会】 jūwěihuì the neighborhood committee
【居心】 jūxīn intentions; intents: ～不良 harbor evil intentions
【居心叵测】 jūxīn-pǒcè with hidden intent; with ulterior motives
【居中】 jūzhōng 1.(在当中) between two parties: ～调解 mediate between two parties 2.(当中) in the middle 3.〈*Printing*〉 be placed in the middle
【居住】 jūzhù live; reside; dwell: 在城里～ take up residence in a town
【居住国】 jūzhùguó country of residence
【居住环境】 jūzhù huánjìng residential environment
【居住面积】 jūzhù miànjī living space; floor space
【居住期限】 jūzhù qīxiàn length of residence
【居住条件】 jūzhù tiáojiàn housing conditions
鞠 (jū) rear; bring up

【鞠躬】 jūgōng bow; make a bow
【鞠躬尽瘁】 jūgōng-jìncuì bend oneself to a task and exert oneself to the utmost; fag oneself to death
【鞠养】 jūyǎng bring up

锔［鋸］(jū) mend with cramps (另见"锔"jú)

【锔子】 jū·zi cramps

局(jú) 1.（机关）office; bureau：邮～ post office / 政治～ Political Bureau 2.〈*Table Tennis*〉game; set：第一～ the first game; the first set 3.〈*Baseball*〉innings：第一～ the first innings 4.（局势）situation; state of affairs 5.（聚会）gathering：饭～ a dinner party; a banquet 6.（圈套）ruse; trap：骗～ fraud; trap; swindle 7.（局部）part; portion

【局部】 júbù part; partial
【局部地区】 júbù dìqū 1.（一些地区）some areas 2.（某地区的一些部分）parts of an area
【局部利益】 júbù lìyì partial and local interests
【局部麻醉】 júbù mázuì local anesthesia
【局部战争】 júbù zhànzhēng local war; partial war
【局促】 júcù 1.（狭小）narrow; cramped 2.（短促）short 3.（拘谨）feel or show constraint：～不安 ill at ease
【局面】 júmiàn aspect; phase; situation; prospects
【局势】 júshì situation：国际～ the international situation
【局外人】 júwàirén outsider; looker-on
【局限】 júxiàn limit; confine
【局限性】 júxiànxìng limitations

锔(jú) 〈*Chem.*〉curium（人造元素，符号Cm）(另见"锔"jū)

菊(jú) chrysanthemum

【菊花】 júhuā chrysanthemum; florists chrysanthemum
【菊苣】 jújù chicory
【菊展】 júzhǎng chrysanthemum show

橘(jú) tangerine

【橘红】 júhóng 1.（颜色）tangerine (color); reddish orange 2.〈*Chin. Med.*〉dried tangerine peel
【橘皮】 júpí orange peel; tangerine peel
【橘汁】 júzhī orange juice
【橘子】 jú·zi tangerine

矩［榘］(jǔ) 1.（曲尺）carpenter's square; square 2.（规矩）rules; regulations 3.〈*Physics*〉moment

【矩尺】 jǔchǐ carpenter's square
【矩形】 jǔxíng rectangle; rectangular (adj.)
【矩阵】 jǔzhèn matrix

咀(jǔ) chew

【咀嚼】 jǔjué 1.（嚼食物）masticate; chew 2.（反复体会）mull over; ruminate; chew the cud

沮(jǔ)

【沮丧】 jǔsàng dejected; depressed; dispirited; disheartened

龃(jǔ)

【龃龉】 jǔyǔ the upper and lower teeth not meeting properly; disagreement; discord

举［舉、擧］(jǔ) 1.（举起）lift; raise; hold up：～杯 raise one's glass (to propose a toast) 2.（举动）act; deed; move：善～ good deed 3.（兴起；起）start 4.（推举）elect; choose：我们公～他作代表。We chose him for our representative. 5.（列举）cite; enumerate; take; give 6.（全）whole; entire：～座 all those present

【举办】 jǔbàn conduct; hold; run：～音乐会 give a concert / ～展览会 hold an exhibition
【举报】 jǔbào report to; inform against; accuse; accusation (n.)
【举报电话】 jǔbào diànhuà telephone of accusation
【举报信】 jǔbàoxìn letter of accusation
【举报中心】 jǔbào zhōngxīn reporting center
【举杯】 jǔbēi raise one's glass：～祝贺 drink a toast
【举措】 jǔcuò behave; move; act
【举动】 jǔdòng movement; move; act; activity
【举国】 jǔguó whole nation; entire nation：～欢腾。The whole nation is jubilant.

【举荐】 jǔjiàn recommend (a person); recommendation: 经他～我去了这家公司。I went to the firm on his recommendation.

【举例】 jǔlì give an example; cite an instance: ～说明 cite example to show; illustrate with examples

【举目】 jǔmù raise the eyes; look: ～无亲 have no one to turn to (for help); find oneself in a forlorn position

【举棋不定】 jǔqí-bùdìng be unable to make up one's mind

【举世】 jǔshì all over the world; the world over; throughout the world; universally: ～瞩目 become the focus of world attention

【举手】 jǔshǒu raise one's hand; put up one's hands: ～表决 vote by a show of hands / ～通过 vote by a show of hands to pass the verdict

【举手礼】 jǔshǒulǐ hand salute

【举手之劳】 jǔshǒuzhīláo lift a finger

【举行】 jǔxíng hold; stage: ～会谈 hold talks / ～婚礼 have a wedding / ～宴会 give a banquet; host a banquet

【举一反三】 jǔyī-fǎnsān learn by analogy; make an inferential judgement

【举证】 jǔzhèng put to the proof

【举止】 jǔzhǐ bearing manner; mien: ～大方 have poise; have an easy manner; be gentle of mien; have a dignified air / ～轻浮 behave frivolously

【举重】 jǔzhòng weight lifting ‖ 举重运动员 weight lifter

【举足轻重】 jǔzú-qīngzhòng hold the balance; play a decisive role

踽 (jǔ)

【踽踽】 jǔjǔ alone; by oneself: ～独行 walk alone; walk by oneself

巨[钜] (jù) huge; tremendous; gigantic

【巨变】 jùbiàn great change; radical change

【巨擘】 jùbò authority; expert: 文坛～ authority of writers

【巨大】 jùdà huge; tremendous; enormous; gigantic; immense

【巨额】 jù'é a huge sum; a big amount: ～财富 immense amount of treasure / ～利润 enormous profits / ～资金 a huge sum of money; an enormous fund

【巨匠】 jùjiàng 〈*written*〉 great master; consummate craftsman

【巨款】 jùkuǎn a huge sum of money

【巨浪】 jùlàng billow; surge; mountainous waves

【巨流】 jùliú a mighty current

【巨轮】 jùlún **1.** (大轮船) a large ship **2.** (比喻大轮子) a large wheel: 历史～ the wheel of history

【巨人】 jùrén giant; colossus

【巨头】 jùtóu magnate; tycoon: 金融～ financial magnate

【巨细】 jùxì big and small: 事无～ all matters, big and small

【巨蟹宫】 Jùxiègōng 〈*Astron.*〉 Cancer (6月22日至7月22日): 生于～ be born under Cancer

【巨蟹座】 Jùxièzuò 〈*Astron.*〉 Cancer

【巨型】 jùxíng giant; heavy; mammoth; colossal: ～客机 a giant liner

【巨制】 jùzhì monumental work; great work

【巨著】 jùzhù monumental work; great work: 历史～ a magnum opus of historic significance

【巨子】 jùzǐ giant

拒 (jù) **1.** (抵抗) resist; repel **2.** (拒绝) refuse; reject: ～不收礼 refuse a gift / ～不执行 refuse to implement

【拒捕】 jùbǔ resist arrest

【拒敌】 jùdí resist the enemy; fight back the enemy

【拒腐蚀】 jù fǔshí repel the corrupting influence; ward off the corrosive influence

【拒付】 jùfù refuse payment; dishonor (a check)

【拒绝】 jùjué refuse; reject; turn down; decline: ～批评 reject other people's criticism

【拒收】 jùshōu dishonor

炬 (jù) **1.** (火炬) torch **2.** (烧掉) fire: 付之一～ be burnt down; be committed to the flames

距 (jù) **1.** (距离) distance: 行～ the distance between rows of plants **2.** (相距) be apart from; away from; be at a distance from: 相～不远 not far from each other/ ～

机场40公里 40 kilometers from the airport **3.**（鸡距）spur

【距离】 jùlí **1.**（相距）be apart from; away from; be at a distance from: ～约三百公里 be about 300 kilometers apart from each other **2.**（相隔）distance; range; gap: 保持～ keep at a distance; keep one's distance / 从学校到火车站的距离是 20 公里。The distance from the school to the railways station is 20 kilometers. / 你我的看法有～。Your view is different from mines.

句（jù） sentence

【句点】 jùdiǎn period

【句法】 jùfǎ **1.**（句子结构）sentence structure **2.**〈*Gram.*〉syntax

【句号】 jùhào full stop; full point; period（符号为 . 或。）

【句型】 jùxíng sentence pattern

【句型练习】 jùxíng liànxí pattern drills

【句子】 jù·zi sentence

具（jù） **1.**（用具）utensil; tool: 文～ writing materials; stationery / 渔～ fishing tackle **2.**（具有）possess; have

【具备】 jùbèi possess; have; be provided with: ～申请资格 have qualifications for application / ～必要的条件 be endowed with all the necessary qualifications

【具结】 jùjié sign an undertaking; binding over; enter into recognizances: 责令～悔过 instructed to write a statement of repentance

【具名】 jùmíng put one's name to a document, etc.; affix one's signature

【具体】 jùtǐ **1.**（非抽象的）concrete: 采取～措施 take the concrete measures **2.**（特定的）specific; particular: 他有他的～工作。He has his own specific duty.

【具文】 jùwén only a formality; a mere formality

【具有】 jùyǒu possess; have; be provided with: ～传统风味特色 distinctive for its traditional properties / ～深远的历史意义 have profound historical significance

俱（jù） all; complete; entirely: 面面～到 pay attention to all sides of a matter

【俱乐部】 jùlèbù club: 足球～ football club

【俱全】 jùquán complete in all varieties: 一应～ be available in all varieties

惧［**懼**］（jù） fear; dread

【惧怕】 jùpà fear; dread

【惧色】 jùsè a look of fear: 面有～ look scared

飓（jù）

【飓风】 jùfēng hurricane

剧［**劇**］（jù） **1.**（戏剧）theatrical work; drama; play; opera: 悲～ tragedy / 独幕～ one-act play / 歌～ opera / 广播～ radio play / 话～ play; stage play / 京～ Beijing opera / 舞～ dance drama **2.**（剧烈）acute; severe; intense

【剧本】 jùběn play; drama: 电影～ scenario

【剧变】 jùbiàn a violent change

【剧场】 jùchǎng theater; theatre

【剧烈】 jùliè violent; acute; severe; fierce: ～的社会变动 radical social changes

【剧目】 jùmù a list of plays or operas

【剧评】 jùpíng dramatic criticism

【剧情】 jùqíng the plot of a play or opera: ～复杂 intricate plot

【剧情简介】 jùqíng jiǎnjiè synopsis

【剧坛】 jùtán theatrical circles

【剧痛】 jùtòng a severe pain

【剧团】 jùtuán theatrical company; opera troupe

【剧务】 jùwù **1.**（排演、演出等事务）stage management **2.**（负责剧务的人）stage manager

【剧院】 jùyuàn **1.**（剧场）theater; theatre **2.**（剧团）theatrical company; opera troupe

【剧照】 jùzhào stage photo; still: 电影～ still

【剧中人】 jùzhōngrén characters in a play or opera

【剧终】 jùzhōng the end; curtain

【剧种】 jùzhǒng type of drama; genre of drama

【剧组】 jùzǔ a play staff

【剧作】 jùzuò theatrical work; drama; play

【剧作家】 jùzuòjiā playwright; dramatist

倨（jù）

【倨傲】 jù'ào arrogant; conceited; haughty

据［**據**］（jù） **1.**（占据）occupy; seize; take possession of; lay hold of:

～为已有 take forcible possession of 2.（凭借）rely on; depend on 3.（依据）according to; on the grounds of: ～实相告 tell according to facts 4.（证据;凭据）evidence; proof; grounds: 言之有～ have good grounds in what one says

【据传】 jùzhuàn a story is going around that; rumor has it that

【据此】 jùcǐ on these grounds; in view of the above; accordingly

【据点】 jùdiǎn strongpoint; fortified point; stronghold

【据守】 jùshǒu guard; be entrenched in

【据说】 jùshuō it is said; they say; allegedly: ～情况如此。This is allegedly the case.

【据闻】 jùwén it is said; they say

【据悉】 jùxī it is reported

锯（jù） 1.（工具）saw: 钢～ hacksaw / 夹背～ back saw; tenon saw / 链～ chain saw / 手～ handsaw / 圆～ circular saw 2.（用锯锯开）saw; cut with a saw: 他把木头～成四块。He sawed the wood into four pieces.

【锯齿】 jùchǐ teeth; sawteeth

【锯末】 jùmò sawdust

【锯条】 jùtiáo saw blade

【锯子】 jùzi saw

聚（jù） assemble; gather; get together

【聚变】 jùbiàn 〈*Physics*〉 fusion: 核～ nuclear fusion

【聚变反应堆】 jùbiàn fǎnyìngduī fusion reactor

【聚丙烯】 jùbǐngxī 〈*Chem.*〉 polypropyrene

【聚丙烯腈】 jùbǐngxījīng 〈*Chem.*〉 polyacrylonitrile

【聚餐】 jùcān dine together; have a dinner party

【聚赌】 jùdǔ gambling in group; group gambling

【聚光灯】 jùguāngdēng spotlight

【聚光灯天桥】 jùguāngdēng tiānqiáo 〈*Cinematog.*〉 spotlight catwalk

【聚光镜】 jùguāngjìng condensing lens; condenser

【聚合】 jùhé 1.（聚集到一起）get together 2. 〈*Chem.*〉 polymerization

【聚合果】 jùhéguǒ 〈*Bot.*〉 aggregate fruits; compound fruit

【聚合物】 jùhéwù 〈*Chem.*〉 polymer

【聚花果】 jùhuāguǒ 〈*Bot.*〉 collective fruits

【聚会】 jùhuì 1.（聚集）get together; meet 2.（聚会的事）party; meeting

【聚积】 jùjī accumulate; collect; build up

【聚集】 jùjí gather; assemble; collect: ～和融通资金 collect and circulate funds

【聚歼】 jùjiān round up and annihilate; annihilate en masse

【聚焦】 jùjiāo 〈*Physics*〉 focus; focusing (n.)

【聚焦圈】 jùjiāoquān 〈*Physics*〉 focusing circle; focusing ring

【聚精会神】 jùjīng-huìshén concentrate one's attention; be all attention

【聚居】 jùjū inhabit a region; live in a compact community: 少数民族～的地方 areas where people of the minority nationalities live in compact communities

【聚敛】 jùliǎn amass wealth by heavy taxation; levy heavy taxes

【聚拢】 jùlǒng gather together

【聚氯乙烯】 jùlǜyǐxī 〈*Chem.*〉 polyvinyl chloride (PVC)

【聚乙烯】 jùyǐxī 〈*Chem.*〉 polyethylene; polythene

【聚酯】 jùzhǐ 〈*Chem.*〉 polyester

【聚众】 jùzhòng gather a crowd: ～斗殴 gather a crowd to engage in an affray

遽（jù） 1.（匆忙;急）hurriedly; hastily 2.（惊慌）frightened; alarmed

【遽然】 jùrán 〈*written*〉 suddenly; abruptly: ～变色 suddenly change countenance

juan

捐（juān） 1.（舍弃）relinquish; abandon 2.（捐助）contribute; donate; subscribe: ～钱 contribute money / ～资办学 donate money for school 3.（税收）tax: 房～ housing tax / 上～ pay a tax

【捐办】 juānbàn contribute money to initiate sth.

【捐款】 juānkuǎn 1.（捐助款项）contribute money 2.（所捐款项）contribution; donation; subscription: 给医院的～ a donation of

money to the hospital
【捐弃】 juānqì 〈*written*〉 relinquish; abandon
【捐弃前嫌】 juānqì-qiánxián forget previous ill will; throw away the past resentment
【捐躯】 juānqū sacrifice one's life: 为国～ lay down one's life for one's country
【捐税】 juānshuì taxes and levies
【捐献】 juānxiàn contribute; donate; present
【捐援国】 juānyuánguó donor country
【捐赠】 juānzèng contribute (as a gift); donate; present: 公司向学校～了30台计算机。The company donated 30 computers to the school.
【捐助】 juānzhù offer; contribute; donate: ～食品和衣物救济水灾灾民 contribute food and clothing for the relief of the victims of a flood
【捐资】 juānzī contribute money: ～助学 contribute money for school

涓 (juān) 〈*written*〉 a tiny stream
【涓滴】 juāndī 〈*written*〉 a tiny drop; dribble; driblet: ～归公 turn in every cent of public money
【涓涓】 juānjuān 〈*written*〉 trickling sluggishly

娟 (juān) 〈*written*〉 beautiful; graceful
【娟秀】 juānxiù 〈*written*〉 beautiful; graceful

圈 (juān) **1.** (围起来) shut in a pen; pen in: 把鸡～起来 pen the chickens / The sheep were penned behind the barn. 羊～在谷仓后面。**2.** (监禁) jail; put in jail: 他被～了两年。He was jailed for two years.
(另见"圈"juàn, quān)

镌[鐫] (juān) 〈*written*〉 engrave
【镌刻】 juānkè 〈*written*〉 engrave

卷[捲] (juǎn) **1.** (裹成圆筒形) roll up; coil; curl; furl: ～地图 roll up a map **2.** (裹走) sweep off; carry along; swirl **3.** (裹成圆筒的东西) cylindrical mass of sth.; roll **4.** 〈*classifier*〉 roll; spool; reel: 一～胶卷 a roll of film
(另见"卷"juàn)
【卷笔刀】 juǎnbǐdāo pencil sharpener
【卷层云】 juǎncéngyún 〈*Meteorol.*〉 cirrostratus
【卷尺】 juǎnchǐ tape measure; band tape
【卷积云】 juǎnjīyún 〈*Meteorol.*〉 cirrocumulus
【卷片手柄】 juǎnpiàn shǒubǐng 〈*Photog.*〉 film advance lever
【卷片旋钮】 juǎnpiàn xuánniǔ 〈*Photog.*〉 film winder
【卷刃】 juǎnrèn (of a knife blade) be turned
【卷入】 juǎnrù be drawn into; be involved in: ～纠纷 be involved in a dispute
【卷逃】 juǎntáo abscond with valuables: 携款～ abscond with funds
【卷土重来】 juǎntǔ-chónglái stage a comeback; bounce back; bob up
【卷心菜】 juǎnxīncài cabbage
【卷烟】 juǎnyān cigarette
【卷扬机】 juǎnyángjī hoist; hoister
【卷云】 juǎnyún 〈*Meteorol.*〉 cirrus
【卷轴】 juǎnzhóu reel: 天线～ aerial reel
【卷子】 juǎn·zi steamed roll

卷 (juàn) **1.** (书本) book: 画～ scroll of painting / 手不释～ always have a book in one's hand; be a diligent reader **2.** (书籍册数) volume: 第一～ Volume One **3.** (考卷) examination paper **4.** (案卷) file; dossier
(另见"卷"juǎn)
【卷次】 juàncì volume
【卷子】 juàn·zi examination paper
【卷宗】 juànzōng **1.** (纸夹子) folder **2.** (文件) file; dossier

倦 (juàn) weary; tired
【倦容】 juànróng look tired; a look of tiredness
【倦色】 juànsè look tired; a look of tiredness
【倦意】 juànyì tiredness; weariness; sleepiness

圈 (juàn) pen; fold; sty: 猪～ a pig pen / 羊～ a sheep pen
(另见"圈"juān, quān)
【圈肥】 juànféi 〈*Agric.*〉 barnyard manure
【圈养】 juànyǎng rear livestock in pens

隽[雋] (juàn) pen; fold; sty
【隽永】 juànyǒng meaningful; interesting

绢(juàn) thin, tough silk

【绢纺】 juànfǎng silk spinning

【绢花】 juànhuā 〈*Arts*〉 silk flower

【绢画】 juànhuà classical Chinese painting on silk

【绢丝】 juànsī spun silk (yarn)

眷［睠²］(juàn) **1.**（眷属）family dependant：女～ female members of a family **2.**（关心；怀念）have tender feeling for

【眷恋】 juànliàn 〈*written*〉 be sentimentally attached to

【眷念】 juànniàn think fondly of; feel nostalgic about

【眷属】 juànshǔ **1.**（家眷；亲属）family dependants; family members **2.**（夫妻）husband and wife

jue

撅［撧²］(juē) **1.**（翘起）stick up **2.**（折断）break (sth. long and narrow); snap：把铅笔～成两段 break the pencil in two

【撅嘴】 juēzuǐ pout

决［決］(jué) **1.**（决定）decide; determine：悬而未～ be undecided; be awaiting decision / 犹豫不～ be in a state of indecision **2.**（一定，用在否定词前面）definitely; certainly; under any circumstances：～无此事 no such things ever happened **3.**（执行死刑）execute a person by shooting **4.**（决口）be breached; burst：全堤溃～。The bank burst and totally collapsed.

【决策】 juécè **1.**（决定策略或办法）make policy; make a strategic decision; decide a policy **2.**（决定的策略或办法）policy decision; decision of strategic importance：战略～ strategic decision / 重大～ very important decision

【决策风险】 juécè fēngxiǎn the risk of decision-making

【决策机构】 juécè jīgòu policy-making body

【决策人】 juécèrén policymaker

【决定】 juédìng **1.**（做出主张）decide; resolve; make up one's mind：我们～不去。We conclude not to go. **2.**（决定的事项）decision; resolution：这项～行得通。The decision will be carried out effectively. **3.**（起决定作用）determine; decide：内容～形式。Content determines form. **4.**（起决定作用的）determinant; decisive：～因素 decisive factor

【决定权】 juédìngquán power to make decisions

【决定性】 juédìngxìng determinant; decisive：～胜利 a decisive victory

【决斗】 juédòu **1.**（格斗）duel **2.**（斗争）decisive struggle

【决断】 juéduàn **1.**（做决定）make a decision **2.**（有魄力）resolution; resolve; decisiveness

【决非偶然】 jué fēi ǒurán by no means accidental

【决计】 juéjì **1.**（主意已定）have decided; have made up one's mind：我～明天就走。I've decided to go tomorrow. **2.**（一定）definitely; certainly：～不会错 definitely can't go wrong

【决口】 juékǒu **1.**（出现裂口）burst; be breached **2.**（裂口）breach; break：堵住～ close up a breach

【决裂】 juéliè break with; rupture

【决然】 juérán **1.**（坚决）resolutely; determinedly; decidedly; firmly：毅然～地 determinedly; decidedly **2.**（必然）definitely

【决赛】 juésài 〈*Sports*〉 finals：进入～ enter the finals

【决胜】 juéshèng decide the issue of the battle; determine the victory

【决胜局】 juéshèngjú 〈*Sports*〉 deciding game; deciding set

【决死】 juésǐ life-and-death

【决算】 juésuàn final accounts; final accounting of revenue and expenditure

【决心】 juéxīn **1.**（坚定的意志）determination; resolution **2.**（一心一意）be determined; be resolute

【决心书】 juéxīnshū written pledge; statement of one's determination

【决一雌雄】 juéyīcíxióng fight to see who is the stronger; fight it out

【决一胜负】 juéyīshèngfù fight it out

【决一死战】 juéyīsǐzhàn wage a life-and-death battle

【决议】 juéyì resolution：通过一项～ pass a resolution

【决议草案】 juéyì cǎoàn draft resolution

【决意】 juéyì have one's mind made up; be determined

【决战】 juézhàn decisive battle; decisive engagement

诀 (jué) 1.（口诀）rhymed formula 2.（诀窍）knack; tricks of the trade 3.（诀别）bid farewell; part

【诀别】 juébié bid farewell; part

【诀窍】 juéqiào secret of success; tricks of the trade; knack; know-how：工艺的～ technological know-how / 生意的～ the tricks of the trade

抉 (jué) 〈*written*〉 pick out; single out

【抉择】 juézé choose：作出～ make one's choice / 面临严重的～ have a very difficult choice to make

角 (jué) 1.（角色）role; part; character：主～ leading role; principal role; main character 2.（演员）actor; actress：名～ a famous actor; a famous actress 3.（竞赛；斗争）contend; wrestle：口～ quarrel; bicker（另见"角"jiǎo）

【角斗】 juédòu wrestle

【角斗场】 juédòuchǎng wrestling ring

【角力】 juélì have a trial of strength; wrestle

【角色】 juésè 1.（扮演的人物）role; part 2.（生活中的某类人）role

【角逐】 juézhú 1.（武力竞争）tussle 2.（竞争或竞赛）contend; enter into rivalry：进行～ enter into rivalry

觉［覺］(jué) 1.（感觉）sense; feel：触～ touch; sense of touch; tactile sensation / 错～ illusion 2.（睡醒）wake (up); awake：大梦初～ awake from a dream 3.（觉悟）become aware; become awakened（另见"觉"jiào）

【觉察】 juéchá detect; become aware of; perceive：～到有危险 become aware of the danger

【觉得】 jué·de 1.（感觉）feel：一点不～累 not feel tired at all 2.（认为）think; feel; find：你～这部电影怎样？How do you think of the film?（或：How do you like the film?）

【觉悟】 juéwù 1.（认识程度）consciousness; awareness：政治～ political consciousness 2.（醒悟）come to understand; become aware of; become politically awakened

【觉醒】 juéxǐng awaken; awake

绝 (jué) 1.（断绝）cut off; sever 2.（穷尽）exhausted; used up; finished 3.（走不通的）desperate; hopeless 4.（独一无二）unique; superb; matchless：她的书画可称双～。Her calligraphy as well as her painting can be rated as superb works of art. 5.（极；最）extremely; most 6.（绝对，用在否定词前）absolutely; in the least; by any means; on any account：～不可能 absolutely impossible 7.（穷尽）leaving no leeway; making no allowance; uncompromising; definitive：不要把话说～ don't be too definitive in what you say

【绝笔】 juébǐ 1.（遗书）last words written before one's death 2.（最后作品）the last work of an author or painter

【绝壁】 juébì precipice

【绝唱】 juéchàng 1.（诗文创作的顶峰）the peak of poetic perfection 2.（生前最后的歌唱）last song

【绝处逢生】 juéchù-féngshēng be unexpectedly rescued from a desperate situation; find one's way out from an impasse

【绝代】 juédài 〈*written*〉 unique among one's contemporaries; peerless

【绝代佳人】 juédài-jiārén beauty of beauties

【绝顶】 juédǐng 1.（极端）extremely; utterly：～荒谬 utterly ridiculous / ～聪明 extremely clever 2.（最高峰）peak; summit; zenith

【绝对】 juéduì 1.（没有任何条件；不受任何限制）absolute：～优势 absolute predominance 2.（完全）absolutely; perfectly; definitely

【绝对多数】 juéduì duōshù absolute majority

【绝对零度】 juéduì língdù absolute zero (273.15 ℃)

【绝对湿度】 juéduì shīdù absolute humidity

【绝对温度】 juéduì wēndù absolute temperature

【绝对真理】 juéduì zhēnlǐ absolute truth

【绝对值】 juéduìzhí absolute value

【绝后】 juéhuò 1.(没有后代) without offspring; without issue 2.(今后不会再有) never to be seen again

【绝户】 jué·hu 1.(没有后代) without offspring; without issue 2.(没有后代的人) a childless person

【绝活】 juéhuó unique skill; consummate skill

【绝迹】 juéjì disappear; vanish; be stamped out

【绝技】 juéjì unique skill; consummate skill

【绝交】 juéjiāo 1.(朋友间) cut off friendship 2.(国家间) sever diplomatic relations

【绝经】 juéjīng 〈*Physiol.*〉 menopause; climacteric

【绝境】 juéjìng 1.(与外界隔绝) be isolated 2.(无出路) hopeless situation; impasse; blind alley; cul-de-sac: 濒于～ face an impasse

【绝口】 juékǒu 1.(住口,只用在"不"字后) stop talking: 赞不～ be profuse in praise; praise profusely 2.(因回避而不开口) keep one's mouth shut: ～不提 never say a single word about; avoid all mention of

【绝路】 juélù 1.(走不通的路) road to ruin; blind alley; impasse; disaster: ～逢生 be alive in desperation 2.(断绝出路) no way out

【绝伦】 juélún unsurpassed; unequalled; peerless: 荒谬～ utterly absurd; utterly preposterous

【绝密】 juémì top-secret; most confidential

【绝妙】 juémiào extremely clever; excellent; perfect

【绝命】 juémìng commit suicide

【绝命书】 juémìngshū 1.(自杀前的) suicide note 2.(死刑前的) note written on the eve of one's execution

【绝食】 juéshí go on a hunger strike; fast: 宣布～ declare a hunger strike

【绝望】 juéwàng give up all hope; despair; lose all hope of

【绝无仅有】 juéwú-jǐnyǒu the only one of its kind; unique; singular of its kind

【绝育】 juéyù 〈*Med.*〉 sterilization

【绝育手术】 juéyù shǒushù sterilization operation

【绝缘】 juéyuán 1.〈*Electr.*〉 insulation 2.(与外界不接触) be cut off from; be isolated from

【绝招】 juézhāo 1.(绝技) unique skill 2.(最后一招) unexpected tricky move (as a last resort)

【绝着】 juézhāo 同"绝招"

【绝症】 juézhèng incurable disease; fatal illness

【绝种】 juézhǒng become extinct; die out: ～的动物 extinct animal

倔 (jué)
(另见"倔"juè)

【倔强】 juéjiàng stubborn; unbending; unyielding

掘 (jué) dig: ～井 dig a well / 自～坟墓 dig one's own grave

【掘进】 juéjìn 〈*Mineral.*〉 driving; tunnelling

【掘墓人】 juémùrén gravedigger

【掘土机】 juétǔjī excavator; power shovel

崛 (jué) rise abruptly

【崛起】 juéqǐ 1.(突起) rise abruptly; rise sharply; suddenly appear on the horizon: 群山～。Mountains rise abruptly (over the plain). 2.(兴起) rise; spring up

谲 (jué) 〈*written*〉 cheat; swindle

【谲诈】 juézhà cunning; crafty

爵 (jué) the rank of nobility; peerage

【爵士】 juéshì 1.(封号) knight 2.(称呼) Sir

【爵士摇滚乐】 juéshì yáogǔnyuè jazz-rock

【爵士乐】 juéshìyuè jazz: 你喜欢～吗? Do you like listening to jazz?

【爵士乐队】 juéshì yuèduì jazz band ‖ 爵士乐手 jazzman

【爵士乐小号】 juéshìyuè xiǎohào jazz trumpet

【爵位】 juéwèi the rank of nobility; title of nobility

矍 (jué)

【矍铄】 juéshuò 〈*written*〉 hale and hearty

攫 (jué) seize; grab

【攫取】 juéqǔ seize; grab

【攫为己有】 juéwéijǐyǒu seize possession of; appropriate

蹶[蹷](juě)

【蹶子】 juě·zi kick：尥～ kick

倔(juè) gruff；surly；blunt：说话～ be blunt of speech / 他脾气够～的。He's surly enough.

(另见“倔”jué)

jun

军(jūn) 1.(军队) armed forces；army；troops：参～ join the army / 陆海空三～ army, navy and airforce 2.〈*Mil.*〉 corps 3.(军人的；军队的) military 4.(队伍) army；contingent：劳动大～ labor army；contingent of labor forces

【军备】 jūnbèi armament；arms：常规～ conventional armament / ～竞赛 armament race / ～控制 arms control

【军部】 jūnbù corps headquarters

【军操】 jūncāo military drill

【军车】 jūnchē military vehicle

【军刀】 jūndāo soldier's sword；saber；sabre

【军地两用人才】 jūndì liǎngyòng réncái personnel trained for both military and civilian services

【军队】 jūnduì armed forces；army；troops

【军阀】 jūnfá warlord

【军法】 jūnfǎ military criminal code；military law

【军法审判】 jūnfǎ shěnpàn court-martial

【军费】 jūnfèi military expenditure：消减～ reduce military expenditure / 增加～ increase military expenditure

【军分区】 jūnfēnqū military sub-command；military subarea

【军风纪】 jūnfēngjì soldier's bearing and discipline

【军服】 jūnfú military uniform；uniform

【军港】 jūngǎng naval port；navy yard

【军工】 jūngōng 1.(军事工业) war industry 2.(军事工程) military project

【军工生产】 jūngōng shēngchǎn war production

【军功】 jūngōng military exploit

【军官】 jūnguān officer

【军管】 jūnguǎn military control：实行～ exercise military control

【军管会】 jūnguǎnhuì military control commission

【军国主义】 jūnguó zhǔyì militarism；militarist (adj.) ‖ 军国主义者 militarist

【军号】 jūnhào bugle

【军徽】 jūnhuī army emblem

【军火】 jūnhuǒ munitions；arms and ammunition：贩卖～ peddle munitions

【军火工业】 jūnhuǒ gōngyè munitions industry；armament industry

【军火库】 jūnhuǒkù arsenal

【军火贸易】 jūnhuǒ màoyì arms trade

【军火商】 jūnhuǒshāng arms dealer；merchant of death；munitions merchant

【军火走私】 jūnhuǒ zǒusī gunrunning

【军机】 jūnjī 1.(军事机宜) military plan：贻误～ delay the fulfillment of a military plan 2.(军事秘密) military secret：泄漏～ leak a military secret

【军籍】 jūnjí military status；one's name on the army roll：开除～ strike sb's name off the army roll；discharge sb. from the army

【军纪】 jūnjì military discipline

【军舰】 jūnjiàn warship；naval vessel

【军阶】 jūnjiē (military) rank；grade

【军界】 jūnjiè military circles；the military

【军垦】 jūnkěn reclamation of wasteland by an army unit

【军垦农场】 jūnkěn nóngchǎng army farm

【军礼】 jūnlǐ military salute：行～ give a salute；make a salute

【军粮】 jūnliáng army provisions；grain for the army

【军列】 jūnliè military train

【军龄】 jūnlíng length of military service

【军令】 jūnlìng military orders：～如山 military orders cannot be disobeyed or revoked

【军令状】 jūnlìngzhuàng a pledge of carrying out a military order

【军帽】 jūnmào army cap；service cap

【军民共建】 jūnmín gòngjiàn joint efforts of the army and the people

【军品】 jūnpǐn products for military use；military products

【军旗】 jūnqí army flag；colors；ensign

【军情】 jūnqíng military situation; war situation

【军区】 jūnqū military region; (military) area command

【军人】 jūnrén soldier; serviceman; armyman: 转业～ demobilized soldier

【军容】 jūnróng soldier's discipline, appearance and bearing

【军师】 jūn·shī military counsellor; army adviser

【军士】 jūnshì 见"专业军士"

【军士长】 jūnshìzhǎng **1.**(陆军) Master Sergeant **2.**(空军) Air Master Sergeant **3.**(海军) Chief Petty Officer

【军事】 jūnshì military affairs

【军事化】 jūnshìhuà militarize; place on a war footing: 过～的生活 follow a military routine

【军事基地】 jūnshì jīdì military base

【军属】 jūnshǔ soldier's dependants; armyman's family

【军体】 jūntǐ 〈*Sports*〉 military sports

【军团】 jūntuán army group

【军威】 jūnwēi might of an army

【军委】 jūnwěi **1.**(中央军委) the Central Military Commission **2.**(中共中央军事委员会) the Military Commission of the Central Committee of the Communist Party of China

【军务】 jūnwù military affairs; military task

【军衔】 jūnxián military rank

【军衔制度】 jūnxián zhìdù system of military ranks

【军饷】 jūnxiǎng soldier's pay and provisions

【军校】 jūnxiào military school; military academy

【军械】 jūnxiè ordnance; armament

【军心】 jūnxīn morale of the troops; soldiers' morale: 振奋～ heighten the morale of the troops

【军需】 jūnxū **1.**(军用物资) military supplies; arms supplies **2.**(军需官) quartermaster

【军需官】 jūnxūguān quartermaster

【军需品】 jūnxūpǐn military supplies; arms supplies

【军训】 jūnxùn military training

【军医】 jūnyī medical officer; military surgeon

【军医大学】 jūnyī dàxué army medical college

【军营】 jūnyíng military camp; barracks

【军用】 jūnyòng for military use; military

【军用地图】 jūnyòng dìtú military map

【军用飞机】 jūnyòng fēijī warplane; military aircraft

【军用列车】 jūnyòng lièchē military train

【军用物资】 jūnyòng wùzī military supplies

【军援】 jūnyuán military aid

【军乐】 jūnyuè martial music; military music

【军乐队】 jūnyuèduì military band

【军长】 jūnzhǎng army commander

【军政】 jūnzhèng **1.**(军事和政治) military-political: ～大学 military and political college **2.**(军队和政府) army and government: ～当局 civil and military authorities

【军政府】 jūnzhèngfǔ military government

【军职】 jūnzhí official post in the army; military appointment

【军种】 jūnzhǒng (armed) services: 各～兵种 all services and arms

【军转民】 jūnzhuǎnmín switched from manufacturing military products to goods for civilian use

【军装】 jūnzhuāng military uniform; army uniform

均 (jūn) **1.**(均匀) equal; even: 分得不～ not evenly divided **2.**(全部) without exception; all: 诸事～已办妥。All things have been properly arranged.

【均等】 jūnděng equal; impartial; fair: 机会～ equal opportunity / 势力～ balance of power

【均分】 jūnfēn divide equally; share out equally

【均衡】 jūnhéng balanced; proportionate; harmonious; even: ～速度 balancing speed

【均势】 jūnshì balance of power; equilibrium of forces; parity

【均摊】 jūntān share equally; share alike

【均匀】 jūnyún even; well-distributed; uniform; regular: ～的呼吸 even breathing

龟[龜] (jūn) (另见"龟"guī)

【龟裂】 jūnliè **1.**(田地干裂) be full of cracks

2.（皲裂）chap

君（jūn） 1.（君主）monarch；sovereign；supreme ruler 2.（尊称）gentleman；Mr.

【君权】 jūnquán monarchical power

【君权神授】 jūnquán shénshòu divine right of kings

【君王】 jūnwáng king；lord

【君主】 jūnzhǔ monarch；sovereign

【君主国】 jūnzhǔguó monarchical state；monarchy

【君主立宪】 jūnzhǔ lìxiàn constitutional monarchy

【君主制】 jūnzhǔzhì monarchy

【君子】 jūnzǐ gentleman；a man of noble character

【君子兰】 jūnzǐlán scarlet kafirlily

【君子协定】 jūnzǐ xiédìng gentlemen's agreement

菌（jūn） 1.（细菌）bacterium 2.（真菌）fungus：食用～ mushroom

（另见"菌"jùn）

【菌肥】 jūnféi bacterial manure

【菌落】 jūnluò colony

俊［隽²、儁］（jùn） 1.（指相貌）handsome；pretty 2.（才智出众的人）a person of outstanding talent

【俊杰】 jùnjié a person of outstanding talent；hero

【俊美】 jùnměi pretty；handsome

【俊俏】 jùnqiào pretty and charming

【俊秀】 jùnxiù pretty；of delicate beauty

峻（jùn） 1.（高大）high：高山～岭 high mountains / 险～ precipitous 2.（严厉）harsh；severe；stern

【峻峭】 jùnqiào high and steep

骏（jùn） fine horse；steed

【骏马】 jùnmǎ fine horse；steed；gallant horse

竣（jùn） complete；finish

【竣工】 jùngōng be completed；come to a successful end

菌（jùn） mushroom

（另见"菌"jūn）

【菌子】 jùn·zi mushroom

K

ka

咖 (kā) (见“咖”gā)

【咖啡】 kāfēi coffee：速溶～ instant coffee / 煮～ make coffee / 请来两杯～！Two coffee, please!

【咖啡馆】 kāfēiguǎn cafe；coffee bar

【咖啡壶】 kāfēihú coffee pot

【咖啡色】 kāfēisè coffee (color)

【咖啡因】 kāfēiyīn 〈*Pharm*.〉 caffeine；caffeinum

【咖啡桌】 kāfēizhuō coffee table

喀 (kā) noise made in coughing or vomiting

【喀嚓】 kāchā 〈*onomat*.〉 crack；snap：竹竿～一声断了。The bamboo broke with a crack.

【喀拉昆仑】 Kālākūnlún 〈place〉 Karakorum

【喀喇沁】 Kālāqìn 〈place〉 Harqin

【喀什】 Kāshí 〈place〉 Kaxgar；Kashi

卡 (kǎ) 1.（扣住；阻挡）block；check：～住所有的出口 block all the exits 2.（卡路里）calorie 3.（卡片）card：分类～ classified card
（另见“卡”qiǎ）

【卡车】 kǎchē truck (AmE.)；lorry (BrE.)：40吨～ 40-ton lorry / 重型～ heavy lorries

【卡车司机】 kǎchē sījī trucker；truck driver；lorry driver；turckie (AuE.)：长途～ long-distance lorry driver

【卡尺】 kǎchǐ callipers；sliding callipers

【卡带】 kǎdài cassette

【卡介苗】 kǎjièmiáo Bacille Calmette-Guerin；BCG vaccine

【卡拉 OK】 kǎlā ōukèi Karaoke

【卡路里】 kǎlùlǐ 〈*Physics*〉 calorie

【卡片】 kǎpiàn card

【卡片柜】 kǎpiànguì card cabinet

【卡片教学法】 kǎpiàn jiàoxuéfǎ card system

【卡片目录】 kǎpiàn mùlù card catalogue

【卡片索引】 kǎpiàn suǒyǐn card index

【卡通】 kǎtōng 1.（动画）cartoon；animated cartoon 2.（漫画）caricature；cartoon

【卡纸】 kǎzhǐ card paper

咔 (kā)

【咔叽布】 kǎjībù 〈*Textiles*〉 khaki

胩 (kǎ) 〈*Chem*.〉 carbyl amine

咯 (kǎ) cough up
（另见“咯”gē）

【咯痰】 kǎtán cough up phlegm

【咯血】 kǎxiě spit blood；hemoptysis

开[開] (kāi) 1.（打开）open；turn on；be on：～灯 turn on the light / ～窗 open the window / ～门 open the door / ～锁 open a lock；unlock 2.（开通；开辟）make an opening；open up；reclaim 3.（张开）open out；come loose：花～了 the flowers are out 4.（开冻）thaw；become navigable：河～了 the river is navigable now 5.（开动；操纵）start；operate；drive；pilot；run；work：～机器 operate a machine / ～汽车 drive a car 6.（军队开拔）set out；move 7.（开办）set up；run 8.（开始）begin；start 9.（召开）hold；run：～运动会 hold an athletic meet；hold a sports-meet 10.（写出）write out；make out；draw：～药方 write out a prescription / ～发票 make out a receipt / ～支票 make out a check 11.（沸腾）boil：水～时，就变成了蒸汽。When the water boils, it changes into steam. 12.（十分之几的比例）percentage；proportion：三七～ in the proportion of three to seven 13.（开本）format；book size 14.（黄金纯度）carat；karat：24～金 24-carat gold

【开拔】 kāibá move；set out

【开办】 kāibàn open；set up；start；found；

establish：～工厂 start a factory
【开办费】 kāibànfèi initial cost; start-up cost; moving cost
【开本】 kāiběn 〈*Printing*〉 format; book size：新～ a new format
【开标】 kāibiāo open sealed tenders
【开采】 kāicǎi mine; extract; exploit：～海底石油 exploit the oil under the sea / 他们～锡矿。They were mining for tin.
【开场】 kāichǎng begin; opening of a show; open; start
【开场白】 kāichǎngbái **1**.〈*Theatre*〉prologue **2**.（文章等的开始）opening speech; introductory remarks
【开车】 kāichē **1**.（开动车辆）drive; start：～进城 drive to town / 她～送我去机场。She drove me to the airport. / 你会～吗？Can you drive? **2**.（发动机器）set a machine going
【开诚布公】 kāichéng-bùgōng frankly and sincerely
【开除】 kāichú expel; discharge; dismiss; fire; sack：～公职 expel sb. from public employment / ～党籍 expel sb. from the Party
【开船】 kāichuán sail; set sail
【开创】 kāichuàng start; initiate; found; set up; pioneer; open
【开春】 kāichūn beginning of spring
【开刀】 kāidāo **1**.（医生动手术）perform an operation; operate on：给病人～ operate on a patient **2**.（让医生给动手术）have an operation; be operated on **3**.（先从某方面下手）make sb. the first target of attack
【开导】 kāidǎo help sb. to see what is right or sensible; help sb. to straighten out his wrong or muddled thinking; give guidance to
【开道】 kāidào clear the away
【开倒车】 kāidàochē turn the clock back; turn back the wheel of history; return to the past
【开动】 kāidòng **1**.（开行运转）start; set in motion：～机器 start a machine / 汽车～时，千万不能下车。You must not get out of the car when it is in motion. **2**.（开拔前进）move; march; be on the move
【开动脑筋】 kāidòng nǎojīn use one's brains
【开冻】 kāidòng thaw：湖泊很快就～了。The lake is thawing fast.
【开端】 kāiduān beginning; start
【开恩】 kāi'ēn show mercy; bestow favors
【开尔文】 kāiěrwén 〈*Physics*〉kelvin
【开发】 kāifā **1**.（开拓）develop; exploit; open up：～山区 develop mountain areas / ～实业 open up industries **2**.（发现并利用）develop
【开发公司】 kāifā gōngsī development company
【开发区】 kāifāqū new area; developing zone：经济～ economic development zone
【开饭】 kāifàn **1**.（准备吃饭）lay the table for a meal **2**.（开始供应饭菜）begin to serve a meal
【开方】 kāifāng extraction of a root; evolution
【开放】 kāifàng **1**.（开花）come into bloom **2**.（解除封锁、限制等）lift a ban; lift a restriction：**3**.（对外开放）open; opening to the outside world：沿海～城市 open coastal cities / 实行～政策 adopt an open policy **4**.（允许通行）open to traffic; open to public use **5**.（接待游人、参观者等）be open to the public：展览会将 于4月24日起～。The exhibition is going to open to the public on April 24.
【开放城市】 kāifàng chéngshì the open cities
【开放地带】 kāifàng dìdài the open regions
【开放港】 kāifànggǎng open port
【开放经济】 kāifàng jīngjì open economy
【开放政策】 kāifàng zhèngcè the policy of opening to the world
【开赴】 kāifù march to; be bound for
【开工】 kāigōng **1**.（开始生产）go into operation; start operation; come on stream; be put into operation：～不足 be operating under capacity **2**.（开始修建）start; begin construction; begin building
【开工率】 kāigōnglǜ utilization of capacity
【开关】 kāiguān switch; button：墙上有一个电灯～。There is a switch on the wall for turning on the lights.
【开关键】 kāiguānjiàn 〈*Guitar*〉 on & off switch
【开罐器】 kāiguànqì can opener
【开国】 kāiguó found a state
【开国大典】 kāiguó dàdiǎn founding ceremony（of a state）
【开国元勋】 kāiguó yuánxūn a founding fa-

ther of a country

【开航】 kāiháng 1.(开始通航) become open for navigation; be open to navigation 2.(船只启程) sail; set sail: 他们的船今天～。Their ship sails today.

【开河】 kāihé 1.(河流开冻) thaw; defreeze 2.(挖运河) construct a canal; open up a waterway

【开后门】 kāihòumén open the back door

【开户】 kāihù open an account; establish an account

【开户行】 kāihùháng bank of deposit

【开花】 kāihuā 1.(花朵开放) flower; bloom; blossom; be in flower; come into flower: 玫瑰要～了。The roses are blooming. 2.(传播开来) be shared by many others: 他的经验已经遍地～。People all over the country have benefited from his advanced experience. 3.(裂开;炸开) explode

【开花结果】 kāihuā jiēguǒ blossom and bear fruit; yield positive results

【开化】 kāihuà become civilized

【开怀】 kāihuái to one's heart's content: ～畅饮 drink to one's heart's content

【开荒】 kāihuāng open up wasteland; reclaim wasteland

【开会】 kāihuì hold a meeting; have a meeting; go to a meeting: 去～ go to a meeting / 现在我们～。Let's start the meeting.

【开荤】 kāihūn end a meatless diet

【开火】 kāihuǒ 1.(放枪发炮) fire; shoot; open fire 2.(喻抨击) attack; criticize

【开机】 kāijī 1.(开动机器) start a machine 2.〈*Cinematog*.〉 start filming; start shooting 3.(电影导演术语) camera

【开价】 kāijià 1.(要价) state a price; make a quotation 2.(开出的价格) opening price; initial price

【开架】 kāijià open shelves: ～借阅 open book shelves to borrowers

【开架阅览室】 kāijià yuèlǎnshì open-shelf reading room

【开胶】 kāijiāo come unglued; come unstuck

【开襟汗衫】 kāijīn hànshān cardigan sweater

【开禁】 kāijìn lift a ban; cancel an exiting prohibition

【开卷】 kāijuàn open a book; read: ～有益 Reading is always profitable.

【开卷考试】 kāijuàn kǎoshì open-book examination

【开掘】 kāijué dig: ～运河 dig a canal

【开课】 kāikè 1.(开始上课) school begins 2.(教授某一课程) give a course; teach a subject

【开垦】 kāikěn open up wasteland; reclaim wasteland; bring under cultivation: ～荒地 reclaim wasteland; bring wasteland under cultivation

【开口】 kāikǒu 1.(开口说话) open one's mouth; start to talk; begin to speak: 难～ find it difficult to bring the matter up 2.(开刃) put the first edge on a knife

【开口销】 kāikǒuxiāo split pin

【开口信件】 kāikǒu xìnjiàn unsealed letter

【开口子】 kāikǒu · zi 1.(堤岸决口) break; burst 2.(皮肤裂口) chap 3.(打开缺口) break an opening in; burst; give free rein to

【开快车】 kāikuàichē 1.(快速开车) speed 2.(加快机器速度) speed up a machine 3.(加快工作学习速度) make short work of a job

【开矿】 kāikuàng open up a mine; exploit a mine

【开阔】 kāikuò 1.(宽广) open; wide 2.(乐观、畅快) tolerant 3.(使开阔) widen: ～眼界 broaden one's outlook

【开阔地】 kāikuòdì open terrain

【开朗】 kāilǎng 1.(指地方) open and clear 2.(指人) sanguine; optimistic: 性情～ always cheerful

【开列】 kāiliè draw up (a list); list: ～清单 draw up a list; make out a list

【开路】 kāilù 1.(开辟道路) open a way; blaze a trail; open a new road; break a fresh path 2.〈*Electr*.〉 open circuit

【开路先锋】 kāilù xiānfēng pioneer

【开绿灯】 kāilǜdēng give the green light to; give free rein to

【开门】 kāimén 1.(打开门) open the door 2.(开始营业) open a store to begin business 3.(公开地) open-door

【开门见山】 kāimén-jiànshān come straight to the point; declare one's intention right at the outset

【开明】 kāimíng enlightened; liberal: ～人士 enlightened persons

【开幕】 kāimù 1.(演出开始) the curtain rises; begin the performance 2.(会议、展览等开始) open; inaugurate
【开幕词】 kāimùcí opening speech; inaugural address: 致～ deliver an opening speech; give an inaugural address
【开幕式】 kāimùshì opening ceremony; inaugural ceremony; inauguration
【开拍】 kāipāi 〈*Cinematog.*〉 start filming; start shooting
【开盘】 kāipán 〈*Econ.*〉 opening quotation
【开盘汇率】 kāipán huìlǜ opening rate
【开盘价格】 kāipán jiàgé opening price
【开炮】 kāipào 1.(发射炮弹) open fire with artillery; fire; bombard 2.(严厉批评) fire criticism at sb.; severely criticize
【开辟】 kāipì 1.(打开道路) open up; hew out; break: ～新航线 open a new air route 2.(创立;建设) open up; set up; establish: ～历史发展的新阶段 open up a new period of development in the history 3.(开发) open up; develop: ～财源 tap new financial resources / ～贸易途径 explore trade channels
【开票】 kāipiào 1.(指选举时) open the ballot box and count the ballots 2.(开发票) make out an invoice
【开启】 kāiqǐ open
【开瓶费】 kāipíngfèi corkage
【开枪】 kāiqiāng open fire; shoot; fire with a rifle, pistol, etc.: ～还击 return fire
【开窍】 kāiqiào have one's ideas straightened out; enlighten
【开球】 kāiqiú 〈*Football*〉 kick off; kick-off (n.)
【开球区】 kāiqiúqū 〈*Golf*〉 teeing ground
【开塞钻】 kāisàizuàn corkscrew
【开赛】 kāisài begin a match
【开设】 kāishè 1.(设立) open; set up; found 2.(设置) offer: ～一门新课 offer a new course
【开审】 kāishěn sit at session
【开审日期】 kāishěn rìqī hearing time
【开始】 kāishǐ 1.(从头起) begin; start; commence: 从头～ start from the very beginning / 从每页的第二行～写 start each page on the second line / 电影7点钟～。The film begins at seven o'clock. 跑了500米之后,我～感到累了。After running half a kilometer, I began to feel tired. 2.(开始阶段) initial stage; beginning; outset: 一～ at the initial stage; at the beginning
【开氏温标】 kāishì wēngbiāo Kelvin's thermodynamic scale
【开市】 kāishì 1.(开始营业) reopen after a cessation of business 2.(每天第一次成交) the first transaction of a day's business
【开市行情】 kāishì hángqíng opening quotation
【开释】 kāishì 〈*Law*〉 set free; release
【开涮】 kāishuàn crack a joke; make fun of; at sb's expense: 他想卖弄小聪明拿我～。He tried to be clever at my expense.
【开水】 kāishuǐ 1.(正开着的水) boiling water 2.(已烧开的水) boiled water
【开司米】 kāisīmǐ cashmere
【开膛】 kāitáng draw: 给鸡～ draw a chicken
【开天辟地】 kāitiān-pìdì 1.(开辟天地) the creation of the world; genesis 2.(有史以来) since the dawn of history; since the beginning of history
【开庭】 kāitíng open a court session; call the court to order; hold a court
【开通】 kāitōng 1.(打开通路) remove obstacles from; dredge clear 2.(使不闭塞) enlighten 3.(不守旧) open-minded; liberal; enlightened; broad-minded
【开头】 kāitóu 1.(开始) start; begin: 你先开个头。Would you make a start. 2.(开始阶段) initial stage; beginning; outset: 一～ at the initial stage; at the beginning
【开脱】 kāituō absolve sb. from; exculpate: 给某人～罪名 absolve sb. from guilt
【开拓】 kāituò 1.(开辟) open up; reclaim: ～荒地 reclaim wasteland 2.〈*Mineral.*〉 developing; opening
【开拓精神】 kāituò jīngshén pioneering spirit
【开外】 kāiwài over; above; more than: 他已五十～了。He is already over fifty.
【开玩笑】 kāiwánxiào crack a joke; joke; make fun of
【开往】 kāiwǎng leave for; be bound for
【开胃】 kāiwèi whet the appetite; stimulate one's appetite
【开胃酒】 kāiwèijiǔ aperitif

【开销】 kāi·xiāo 1.（支付）pay expenses 2.（费用）expense：你搬家的～有多少？What are your expenses of moving house?

【开小差】 kāixiǎochāi 1.（当逃兵）desert 2.（思想不集中）be absentminded

【开小灶】 kāixiǎozào open a small canteen

【开心】 kāixīn 1.（快乐）feel happy; rejoice; joyful; be delighted 2.（戏弄别人）amuse oneself at sb's expense; make fun of sb.

【开心果】 kāixīnguǒ pistachio (nut)

【开学】 kāixué school opens; term begins

【开学典礼】 kāixué diǎnlǐ school commencement ceremony

【开眼】 kāiyǎn open one's eyes; widen one's view; widen one's horizons; broaden one's mind

【开演】 kāiyǎn begin; start：戏今晚7点～。The play begins at 7 p.m. this evening.

【开业】 kāiyè 1.（指商店）start business; open for business 2.（指律师、医生等）open a private practice：～行医 practice medicine

【开夜车】 kāiyèchē work late into the night

【开源节流】 kāiyuán-jiéliú increase income and decrease expenditure; tap new resources and economize on expense

【开凿】 kāizáo dig; cut：～运河 dig a canal

【开斋】 kāizhāi 1.（恢复吃荤）resume a meat diet 2.〈*Islam*〉come to the end of Ramadan

【开斋节】 Kāizhāijié Lasser Bairam

【开展】 kāizhǎn 1.（使展开）develop; launch; unfold; carry out：～贸易 develop trade /～批评与自我批评 carry out criticism and self-criticism 2.（开朗）open-minded; politically progressive 3.（开始展出）be open to the public

【开战】 kāizhàn 1.（打仗）make war; open hostilities 2.（与…斗争）battle：向顽固势力～ battle against conservative forces

【开绽】 kāizhàn come unsewn

【开张】 kāizhāng 1.（开始营业）open a business; begin doing business 2.（做第一笔交易）the first transaction of a day's business

【开张大吉】 kāizhāng-dàjí auspicious beginning of a new enterprise

【开仗】 kāizhàng 1.（开战）make war 2.（打架）fight

【开账】 kāizhàng 1.（开列账单）make out a bill 2.（付款）pay the bill

【开支】 kāizhī 1.（支付）pay (expenses); spend 2.（费用）expenses; expenditure; spending：军费～ military spending / 意外～ incidental expenses / 节省～ reduce expenses / 缩减～ cut down expenses 3.（发工资）pay wages; pay salaries; get the pay

【开足马力】 kāizú mǎlì put into high gear; go full steam ahead; open the throttle; switch to top gear

锎 (kāi) 〈*Chem.*〉californium（人造元素，符号Cf）

揩 (kāi) wipe：～汗 wipe sweat / ～眼泪 wipe out one's tears

【揩拭】 kāishì clean; wipe：～桌面 wipe the table

【揩油】 kāiyóu get petty advantages at the expense of other people or the state; scrounge

凯［凱］(kǎi) 1.（胜利的乐曲）triumphant strains 2.（胜利的）triumphal; triumphant; victorious

【凯歌】 kǎigē a song of triumph; paean

【凯旋】 kǎixuán to return in triumph; triumphal return (n.)

【凯旋门】 kǎixuánmén triumphal arch

楷 (kǎi) 1.（楷模）model; pattern 2.（楷书）regular script：小～ regular script in small characters

【楷模】 kǎimó model; pattern; good example

【楷书】 kǎishū regular script

【楷体】 kǎitǐ 1.（楷书）regular script 2.（印刷体字母）block letter

慨［嘅²］(kǎi) 1.（愤激）indignant：对某事感到愤～ be indignant at sth. 2.（感慨）deeply; touched 3.（慷慨）generous

【慨然】 kǎirán 1.（感慨地）with emotion; with deep feeling 2.（慷慨地）generously; without stint：～相助 help without stint / ～相赠 generously give sth. to sb.

【慨叹】 kǎitàn sigh with regret

kan

刊［栞］(kān) 1.（排印出版）print; publish 2.（期刊）periodical; publication：期～ journal; periodical / 双月

～ bimonthly / 双周～ fortnightly; biweekly / 特～ special issue / 月～ monthly / 周～ weekly / 增～ supplement 3.（削除；修改）delete; correct

【刊大】 kāndà periodical university

【刊登】 kāndēng publish in; carry

【刊授】 kānshòu give courses through periodical

【刊物】 kāiwù publication：定期～ periodical

【刊物出版日期】 kāiwù chūbǎn rìqī cover date

【刊载】 kāizǎi publish; carry

看（kān） 1.（照看）look after; take care of; tend：～孩子 look after children 2.（守护）guard; keep watch on：～仓库 guard the warehouse 3.（监视；看押）keep under surveillance

（另见"看"kàn）

【看场】 kānchǎng guard the threshing floor (during the harvest season)

【看管】 kānguǎn 1.（照管）look after; attend to：～行李 take care of the luggage 2.（看守）guard; watch

【看护】 kānhù nurse; look after; take care of; tend; attend on

【看家】 kānjiā look after the house

【看家狗】 kānjiāgǒu watchdog

【看门】 kānmén 1.（看管大门）guard the entrance; act as doorkeeper 2.（看家）look after the house

【看守】 kānshǒu 1.（守卫；照料）watch; guard 2.（监视管理犯人）guard：～犯人 guard prisoners 3.（监狱看守人员）jailor; gaoler (BrE.); warder (m.); wardress (f.)：～用一把大钥匙打开了牢房门。The jailor opened the cell door with a large key.

【看守内阁】 kānshǒu nèigé caretaker cabinet

【看守所】 kānshǒusuǒ detention house

【看押】 kānyā take into custody; detain

勘（kān） 1.（校勘）read and correct the text of; collate 2.（勘测）investigate; survey

【勘测】 kāncè survey：在新的铁路建成之前，线路经过了认真的～。Before the new railway was built, its route was carefully surveyed.

【勘察】 kānchá 1.（实地调查）reconnaissance 2.〈*Geog*.〉prospecting

【勘探】 kāntàn explore; prospect; exploration (n.)：地震～ seismic prospecting / 煤田地质和～ coal geology and exploration

【勘探队】 kāntànduì exploration team

【勘误】 kānwù correct errors in printing

【勘误表】 kánwùbiǎo errata; corrigenda

堪（kān） 1.（可以）may; can; be capable of 2.（能忍受）bear; endure：不～回首 cannot bear to look back

坎［埳[2]］（kǎn） 1.（台阶状的东西）bank; ridge 2.〈*written*〉（坑）pit; hole

【坎德拉】 kǎndélā 〈*Physics*〉candela

【坎肩】 kǎnjiān sleeveless jacket

【坎坷】 kǎnkě 1.（坑坑洼洼）bumpy; rough 2.（不得志）full of frustrations

砍（kǎn） 1.（用刀斧砍）cut; chop; hack; hew：～倒 cut down; chop down 2.（去掉）cut (down)：把这篇文章～去一半。Cut the article down to half its length.

【砍大山】 kǎndàshān 同"侃大山"

【砍伐】 kǎnfá fell：～树木 fell trees

【砍头】 kǎntóu chop off the head; behead

莰（kǎn） 〈*Chem*.〉camphane

侃（kǎn）

【侃大山】 kǎndàshān discursive chat; rambling talk

【侃侃而谈】 kǎnkǎn'értán speak with fervor and assurance; talk with ease and fluency

看（kàn） 1.（观看）see; look at; watch：～电视 watch TV / ～电影 see a film; go to the movies / ～球赛 watch a ball game / ～戏 go to the theater; see a play, an opera, etc. / 老师叫我们～黑板。The teacher told us to look at the blackboard. 2.（阅读）read：～报 read a newspaper / ～书 read (a book) 3.（观察并加以判断）think; consider; view; observe; judge 4.（访问）call on; visit; go to see：～朋友 visit a friend; call on a friend 5.（诊治）treat：她正在～病。She is under medical treatment. 6.（照料）look after：～孩子 look after children 7.（取决于）depend on 8.（表示试一试）等等～ wait and see

（另见"看"kān）

【看病】 kànbìng 1.(医生治病) see a patient; treat; attend; give medical advice 2.(病人就医) see a doctor; consult a doctor; go to a doctor; receive medical; advice: 请医生来～ send for a doctor / 去医院～ go to a hospital to see a doctor

【看不惯】 kàn·buguàn cannot bear the sight of; frown upon

【看不起】 kàn·buqǐ look down upon; scorn; despise; disdain; hold in contempt

【看成】 kànchéng look upon as; regard as; treat as; consider as: 不要把幻想～事实。Don't regard fantasies as truth.

【看出】 kànchū make out; see; perceive; find out; be aware of

【看穿】 kànchuān 1.(透彻地了解) understand thoroughly; gain an insight into 2.(透彻地认识) see through; penetrate 3.(喻失望)我什么都～了。I feel disillusioned at everything.

【看待】 kàndài look upon; regard; treat: 一律～ treat alike

【看到】 kàndào 1.(看见) see; catch sight of: 看不到 fail to see; lose sight of / 我可以～港口有两艘油轮。I can see two tankers in the harbor. 2.(注意到) notice; note; be aware of

【看得起】 kàn·deqǐ think highly of

【看法】 kàn·fǎ a way of looking at a thing; view: 这种～是很有道理的。There is much to be said for this view.

【看风使舵】 kànfēng-shǐduò trim one's sails; adapt oneself to circumstances

【看顾】 kàngù look after; take care of: ～孩子 look after the children

【看见】 kànjiàn catch sight of; see: 我注意了,但什么也没～。I looked but saw nothing.

【看开】 kànkāi see through

【看看】 kànkān see; look: ～谁在门口哪。Please see who is at the door. / ～这本书。Have a look at this book.

【看来】 kànlái it seems; it appears; it looks as if: ～那是部有意思的电影。That looks like an interesting film.

【看破】 kànpò see through

【看齐】 kànqí 1.(口令) dress: 向右～! Dress right, dress! 2.(作为榜样) keep abreast with; keep up with; emulate

【看轻】 kànqīng underestimate; look down upon

【看清】 kànqīng 1.(看清楚) see clearly 2.(认识清楚) realize

【看上】 kàn·shàng like; take a fancy to; settle on

【看台】 kàntái 1.(泛指看台) bleachers; stand 2.(指正面看台) grandstand

【看透】 kàntòu 1.(透彻了解) understand thoroughly; gain an insight into 2.(透彻认识) see through; penetrate 3.(喻失望)我是什么都～了。I feel disillusioned at everything.

【看图识字】 kàntú shízì learn to read with the aid of pictures

【看望】 kàn·wàng call on; visit; see

【看样定货】 kànyàng dìnghuò sample order

【看涨】 kànzhǎng be expected to rise

【看中】 kànzhòng take a fancy to; take to; settle on

【看重】 kànzhòng 1.(重视) regard as important; set store by 2.(估计过高) overestimate

【看准】 kànzhǔn be certain (about sth.)

【看做】 kànzuò look upon as; regard as

kang

康(kāng) well-being; health

【康拜因】 kāngbàiyīn combine; combine harvester

【康采恩】 kāngcǎi'ēn 〈*Econ*.〉 concern

【康复】 kāngfù 1.(恢复健康) recuperate one's health; be restored to health; recover; recovery (n.): 术后～ recover from the operation / 卧床一个月后,他完全～了。After a month in bed, he was fully restored to health. / 我们祝您早日～。We wish you a speedy recovery from your illness. 2.(恢复身体机能) rehabilitate; rehabilitation (n.): 我们要给事故的伤者进行～治疗。We want to rehabilitate the victims of the accident.

【康复器械】 kāngfù qìxiè rehabilitation apparatus and instruments

【康复中心】 kāngfù zhōngxīn rehabilitation center

【康健】 kāngjiàn healthy; in good health
【康乐】 kānglè peace and happiness
【康乐球】 kānglèqiú caroms
【康乐室】 kānglèshì recreation room
【康乃馨】 kāngnǎixīng （麝香石竹）carnation
【康平纳】 kāngpíngnà 〈*Econ.*〉 combinatus
【康庄大道】 kāngzhuāng dàdào broad road; main road; wide free road

慷［忼］（kāng）
【慷慨】 kāngkǎi **1.**（激昂）vehement; fervent **2.**（不吝惜）generous; liberal: ～解囊 help sb. generously with money
【慷慨悲歌】 kāngkǎi-bēigē chant in a heroic but mournful tone
【慷慨激昂】 kāngkǎi-jī'áng impassioned; vehement: ～的演说 vehement speech
【慷慨就义】 kāngkǎi-jiùyì go to one's death like a hero; die a martyr's death; die a hero
【慷他人之慨】 kāng tārén zhī kǎi be generous at other people's expense

糠［穅］（kāng） **1.**（麦、谷的皮壳）chaff; bran; husk **2.**（萝卜变空）spongy: 萝卜～了。The radish has gone spongy.

扛（káng） carry on the shoulder
【扛枪】 kángqiāng shoulder a gun; bear arms

亢（kàng） **1.**（高）high; haughty **2.**（过度；极；很）excessive; extreme
【亢奋】 kàngfèn stimulated; excited
【亢进】 kàngjìn 〈*Med.*〉 hyperfunction

伉（kàng）
【伉俪】 kànglì married couple; husband and wife

抗（kàng） **1.**（抵抗；抵挡）resist; combat; fight: ～敌 fight the enemy **2.**（拒绝；抗拒）refuse; defy **3.**（对等）contend with; be a match for
【抗暴】 kàngbào combat violence
【抗爆】 kàngbào anti-knock
【抗辩】 kàngbiàn **1.**（进行辩护）contradict **2.**〈*Law*〉 counterplea; demurrer ‖ 抗辩者 opposing counsel
【抗辩者】 kàngbiànzhě 〈*Law*〉 opposing counsel
【抗病】 kàngbìng 〈*Agric.*〉 disease-resistant
【抗毒素】 kàngdúsù antitoxin
【抗干扰】 kànggānrǎo anti-interference
【抗干扰素】 kànggānrǎosù anti-interferon
【抗旱】 kànghàn fight a drought
【抗旱作物】 kànghàn zuòwù drought-resistant crops
【抗衡】 kànghéng contend with; match; rival be evenly matched with
【抗洪】 kànghóng fight a flood; combat a flood: ～抢险 combat a flood and go to the rescue hurriedly
【抗击】 kàngjī resist; beat back; fight: ～侵略者 resist the aggressors
【抗拒】 kàngjù resist; defy
【抗菌素】 kàngjūnsù antibiotic
【抗涝】 kànglào fight a waterlogging; combat a waterlogging
【抗疲劳剂】 kàngpíláojì antifatigue
【抗日战争】 Kàng-Rì Zhànzhēng the War of Resistance Against Japan (1937-1945)
【抗诉】 kàngsù counterappeal; lodge a protest against court judgments; oppose an action
【抗台】 kàngtái 见"抗台风"
【抗台风】 kàngtáifēng combat typhoon
【抗体】 kàngtǐ 〈*Biol.*〉 antibody
【抗压】 kàngyā resistance to compression
【抗议】 kàngyì **1.**（强烈反对）protest; remonstrate: 向…提出～ lodge a protest with sb. / ～集会 protest rally / ～照会 note of protest **2.**〈*Law*〉 object; objection (n.)
【抗原】 kàngyuán 〈*Med.*〉 antigen
【抗噪声】 kàngzàoshēng antinoise
【抗战】 kàngzhàn **1.**（抵抗外国侵略）war of resistance against aggression **2.**（抗日战争）Anti-Japanese War (1937-1945): ～时期 period of the War of Resistance Against Japan
【抗震】 kàngzhèn anti-seismic: ～救灾 earthquake relief work

炕（kàng） kang; a heatable brick bed
【炕席】 kàngxí mat

钪（kàng） 〈*Chem.*〉 scandium（元素符号 Sc）

kao

尻(kāo) buttocks; bottom

【尻子】 kāo·zi buttocks; bottom

考[攷](kǎo) 1.(考试) examine; give an examination; take an examination; test; examination (n.): 统～ the unified state examination 2.(检查) check; inspect 3.(研究) study; investigate; verify

【考查】 kǎochá examine; test; check

【考察】 kǎochá 1.(实地调查) inspect; investigate: 出国～ go abroad on a tour of investigation 2.(细致深刻观察) observe and study

【考察报告】 kǎochá bàogào report on an investigation

【考察团】 kǎochátuán investigation group

【考察组】 kǎocházǔ study group

【考场】 kǎochǎng examination hall; examination room

【考古】 kǎogǔ 1.(研究古代历史) engage in archaeological studies 2.(考古学) archeology: 在大学教授～ teach archeology at the university

【考古学】 kǎogǔxué archaeology; archeological (adj.) ‖ 考古学者 archeologist

【考核】 kǎohé examine; check; assess (sb's proficiency): 技术～ assess technical proficiency / 对专业人员业务水平的～ the assessment of the competence of professional personnel / ～干部 assess cadre's achievements

【考绩制度】 kǎojì zhìdù merit system

【考究】 kǎo·jiu 1.(查考) observe and study; investigate; examine closely 2.(讲究) care about; fastidious; particular: 穿衣服过于～ be too particular about dress 3.(精美) exquisite; fine

【考卷】 kǎojuàn examination paper

【考虑】 kǎolǜ think over; take into account; consider: ～问题 think about an issue / 不～个人得失 disregard personal gains and losses / 反复～过后, 他决定不买汽车了。After much thought he decided not to buy the car.

【考评】 kǎopíng assessment; evaluation; examination

【考勤】 kǎoqín check on work attendance

【考勤簿】 kǎoqínbù attendance record

【考勤卡】 kǎoqínkǎ check card

【考勤钟】 kǎoqínzhōng time clock

【考取】 kǎoqǔ pass (an entrance) examination; be admitted to school or college: ～清华大学 be admitted to Tsinghua University

【考生】 kǎoshēng candidate for an entrance examination; examinee

【考试】 kǎoshì examination; test; exam: 大学入学～ college entrance examination / 期末～ end-of-term examination / 毕业～ graduation examination / ～不及格 fail an examination / 我今天通过了驾驶～。I passed my driving test today. / 上个月的～你通过了吗? Have you passed the examination you took last month?

【考题】 kǎotí examination questions; examination paper: 出～ set an examination paper

【考问】 kǎowèn examine orally; question

【考验】 kǎoyàn test; trial; ordeal: 经受～ go through a test; experience a trial

【考证】 kǎozhèng textual criticism; textual research

拷(kǎo) flog; beat; torture

【拷贝】 kǎobèi 〈*Cinematog.*〉 copy

【拷打】 kǎodǎ flog; beat; torture: 严刑～ severely torture sb.

【拷花】 kǎohuā 〈*Textiles*〉 embossing

【拷问】 kǎowèn torture sb. during interrogation; interrogate with torture

烤(kǎo) 1.(烤熟, 烤干) bake; roast; toast: ～蛋糕 bake a cake / ～鸡 roast a chicken / ～面包 toast bread / ～羊肉串 roast mutton cubes on a skewer 2.(太热) scorching: 这个炉子太～人。This stove is really scorching

【烤电】 kǎodiàn 〈*Med.*〉 diathermy

【烤火】 kǎohuǒ warm oneself by a fire

【烤炉】 kǎolú oven

【烤面包】 kǎomiànbāo toast: 一片～ a slice of toast

【烤肉】 kǎoròu roast meat; roast

【烤肉叉】 kǎoròuchā spit; skewer

【烤箱】 kǎoxiāng toaster

【烤鸭】 kǎoyā roast duck

【烤鱼】 kǎoyú roast fish; grill

铐 (kào) 1.(手铐) handcuffs 2.(戴手铐) put handcuffs on; handcuff (v.): 他被～着带到公安局。He was taken to the police station in handcuffs.

【铐子】 kào·zi handcuffs: 戴着～ in handcuffs

犒 (kào) reward with food and drink

【犒劳】 kào·láo reward with food and drink; give food and drink for meritorious service

【犒赏】 kàoshǎng reward with money or gifts

靠 (kào) 1.(依着) lean against; lean on; rest against: 把它～在墙上 lean it against a wall / 她～在他的肩上。She leaned against his shoulder. 2.(沿着) keep to; get near; come up to: 火车都～左走。All trains should keep to the left. 3.(挨近) near; by: 书店～大学。The bookstore stands by a university. 4.(依靠) depend on; rely on: 农业发展一～政策,二～科学。Agricultural growth hinges first on policy and second on science. 5.(信赖) trust: 可～ reliable; trustworthy

【靠背】 kàobèi back (of a chair)

【靠边】 kàobiān keep to the side

【靠不住】 kào·buzhù unreliable; untrust-worthy

【靠窗座位】 kàochuāng zuòwèi window seat

【靠得住】 kào·dezhù reliable; trust-worthy; dependable: 这消息～。The information is reliable.

【靠垫】 kàodiàn (backrest) cushion

【靠近】 kàojìn 1.(挨近) near; close to; by 2.(靠拢) draw near; approach

【靠拢】 kàolǒng draw close; close up

【靠山】 kàoshān backer; patron; backing

【靠椅】 kàoyǐ arm-chair

【靠走廊座位】 kàozǒuláng zuòwèi aisle seat

ke

坷 (kē) a clod of earth

【坷垃】 kē·lā a clod of earth

苛 (kē) severe; exacting

【苛待】 kēdài treat harshly; be hard upon

【苛捐杂税】 kējuān-záshuì multifarious taxes and levies

【苛刻】 kēkè harsh: 待人～ treat others harshly; treat others unfeelingly

【苛求】 kēqiú make excessive demands; be over-critical

【苛责】 lēzé criticize severely; excoriate

珂 (kē)

【珂罗版】 kēluóbǎn 〈*Printing*〉 collotype

柯 (kē)

【柯尔克孜族】 Kē'érkèzīzú Kirgiz (中国少数民族,主要分布在新疆)

科 (kē) 1.(学科) branch of (academic) study: 理～ the sciences / 文～ the humanities 2.(机关单位) department; section: 销售～ sales section / 总务～ general affairs section 3.〈*Biol*.〉 family: 豆～植物 bean family; legume / 猫～ the cat family / 犬～动物 animals of the dog family 4.(判定) pass a sentence

【科班】 kēbān regular professional training

【科班出身】 kēbān chūshēng a man with professional training

【科尔沁】 Kērqìn 〈place〉 Horqin

【科工贸一体化】 kēgōngmào yìtǐhuà integration of trade and industry and technology

【科幻】 kēhuàn scientific fiction

【科幻小说】 kēhuàn xiǎoshuō sci-fi; science fiction

【科技】 kējì science and technology: ～攻关 tackle key problems in science and technology

【科技成果转化】 kējì chéngguǒ zhuǎnhuà commercialize research results

【科技大学】 kējì dàxué university of science and technology

【科技工作者】 kējì gōngzuòzhě scientific and technical worker

【科技馆】 kējìguǎn science and technological museum

【科技规划】 kējì guīhuà program for the development of science and technology

【科技户】 kējìhù household using new technique

【科技界】 kējìjiè scientific and technological circles

【科技情报】 kējì qíngbào scientific and technical information

【科技人才】 kējì réncái skilled personnel

【科技人员】 kējì rényuán scientists and technicians：合理使用～ make proper use of the talents of scientists and technicians

【科技术语】 kējì shùyǔ scientific and technical terminology

【科教片】 kējiàopiān popular science film; science and educational film

【科盲】 kēmáng illiteracy of science

【科目】 kēmù 1.（学科）subject（in a curriculum）; course：必修～ compulsory courses 2.（会计账目）headings（in an account book）：会计～ headings in an account book

【科普】 kēpǔ popular science; popularization of science：～读物 popular science readings / ～工作 job of popularizing scientific knowledge

【科室】 kēshì administrative or technical offices

【科室人员】 kēshì rényuán office staff; office personnel

【科学】 kēxué science; scientific knowledge; scientific（adj.）：自然～ natural science / 社会～ social science / 纯～ pure science / 应用～ applied science / 现代～ modern science

【科学城】 kēxuéchéng scientific town

【科学工作者】 kēxué gōngzuòzě scientific worker; scientist

【科学公园】 kēxué gōngyuán science park

【科学管理】 kēxué guǎnlǐ scientific management

【科学技术】 kēxué jìshù science and technology：～是生产力。Science and technology are part of the productive forces.

【科学家】 kēxuéjiā scientist：核～ nuclear scientist

【科学理论】 kēxué lǐlùn scientific theory

【科学社会主义】 kēxué shèhuì zhǔyì scientific socialism

【科学实验】 kēxué shíyàn scientific experiment

【科学文献】 kēxué wénxiàn scientific literature

【科学研究】 kēxué yānjiū scientific research; scientific studies

【科学仪器】 kēxué yíqì scientific instruments; scientific apparatus

【科学院】 kēxuéyuàn academy of sciences

【科研】 kēyán scientific research：～要走在前面。Scientific research should be given priority.

【科研单位】 kēyán dānwèi scientific research institutions

【科研机制】 kēyán jīzhì scientific research mechanism

【科研计划】 kēyán jìhuà plans for scientific research

【科研经费】 kēyán jīngfèi research fund

【科研人员】 kēyán rényuán scientific research personnel：～的职称 professional titles of scientific research personnel

【科研项目】 kēyán xiàngmù scientific research item

【科研中心】 kēyán zhōngxīn scientific research center

【科长】 kēzhǎng section chief; section manager

蝌（kē）

【蝌蚪】 kēdǒu tadpole; polliwog

窠（kē） nest; burrow

【窠穴】 kēxuè pattern：不落～ show originality; be unconventional

颗（kē）

【颗粒】 kēlì 1.（小圆粒）pellet; anything small and roundish 2.（粮食）grain

【颗粒肥料】 kēlì féiliào granulated fertilizer

【颗粒饲料】 kēlì sìliào pellet

磕［搕］（kē） 1.（磕碰）knock 2.（磕打）rap

【磕巴】 kē·ba 1.（口吃）stammer; stutter 2.（口吃的人）stammerer; stutterer

【磕打】 kē·da knock sth. out of a vessel, container, etc.; knock out

【磕碰】 kēpèng knock against; collide with; bump against

【磕头】 kētóu kowtow; make a kowtou to sb.

瞌（kē）

【瞌睡】 kēshuì sleepy; drowsy：打～ doze off; nod; fall into a doze

壳［殼］（ké） shell：鸡蛋～ egg shell（另见“壳”qiào）

咳（ké） cough：干～ dry cough / ～得利害 have a bad cough

【咳嗽】 ké·sou cough

【咳嗽糖浆】 ké·sou tāngjiāng cough syrup

【咳痰】 kétán expectoration

可（kě） 1.（同意）approve 2.（许可；可能）can；may：～供效法 it may serve as a model 3.（值得）need（doing）；be worth（doing）4.（适合）fit；suit：这帽子你～心吗？Does the hat suit you? 5.（可是）but；yet

【可爱】 kě'ài lovable；likable；lovely

【可悲】 kěbēi sad；lamentable

【可比价格】 kěbǐ jiàgé 〈*Econ*.〉 fixed price；constant price

【可比较】 kěbǐjiào comparable

【可鄙】 kěbǐ contemptible；despicable；mean

【可变】 kěbiàn variable

【可变成本】 kěbiàn chéngběn variable cost

【可变电容】 kěbiàn diànróng variable capacitance

【可变电容器】 kěbiàn diànróngqì variable capacitor

【可变翼】 kěbiànyì 〈*Aeron*.〉 adjustable wing

【可采储量】 kěcǎi chǔliàng recoverable reserves

【可操纵】 kěcāozòng controllable

【可拆除】 kěchāichú dismountable

【可拆开】 kěchāikāi removable；detachable

【可乘之机】 kěchéngzhījī an opportunity that can be exploited to sb's advantage

【可持续发展】 kěchíxù fāzhǎn sustainable development

【可耻】 kěchǐ shameful；disgraceful；ignominious

【可充电】 kěchōngdiàn chargeable

【可待因】 kědàiyīn 〈*Pharm*.〉 codeine

【可的松】 kědìsōng 〈*Pharm*.〉 cortisone

【可读性】 kědúxìng worth reading；readability

【可兑换】 kěduìhuàn convertible；exchangeable

【可兑换债券】 kěduìhuàn zhàiquàn convertible debenture

【可兑换证券】 kěduìhuàn zhèngquàn convertible bond

【可伐林】 kěfálín open wood

【可分辨】 kěfēnbiàn distinguishable

【可分离】 kěfēnlí separable

【可歌可泣】 kěgē-kěqì move one to song and tears

【可耕地】 kěgēngdì arable land；cultivable land

【可观】 kěguān considerable；impressive；sizable：成绩很～ considerable achievements

【可贵】 kěguì valuable；praiseworthy；commendable

【可恨】 kěhèn hateful；detestable；abominable

【可换股份】 kěhuàn gǔfèn convertible stock

【可见】 kějiàn 1.（可看见）visible：隐约～ barely visible 2.（可以想见）it is thus clear that；it is thus evident that：由此～，… It is thus clear that . . .

【可见度】 kějiàndù degree of visibility

【可惊】 kějīng surprising；startling

【可敬】 kějìng worthy of respect；respected

【可卡因】 kěkǎyīn 〈*Pharm*.〉 cocaine

【可靠】 kěkào reliable；dependable；trustworthy：～消息 reliable news / 为人～ be reliable

【可靠性】 kěkàoxìng reliability

【可靠账户】 kěkào zhànghù reliable account

【可可】 kěkě cocoa

【可可粉】 kěkěfěn cocoa powder

【可可奶】 kěkěnǎi milky cocoa

【可可西里】 Kěkěxīlǐ 〈place〉 Hoh Xil

【可控制】 kěkòngzhì controllable

【可口】 kěkǒu good to eat；nice；tasty；palatable

【可口可乐】 kěkǒu kělè Coca Cola

【可兰经】 Kělánjīng 〈*Islam*〉 the Koran

【可乐】 kělè Coke；Coca Cola：百事～ Pepsi Cola

【可怜】 kělián 1.（值得怜悯）pitiful；pitiable；poor；pathetic 2.（怜悯）pity；have pity on；take compassion on 3.（不值一提）meager；wretched；miserable；pitiful：少得～ pathetically meager

【可能】 kěnéng 1.（可以实现）possible；probable；can；may：～达到的国民生产总值 potential gross national product / 团结一切～团结的力量 unite all the forces that can be united 2.（或许）probably；maybe：她～在教室里。Maybe she is in the classroom. 3.

（可能性）possibility：甲队没有获胜的～。Team A has no chance of winning.

【可能性】 kěnéngxìng possibility

【可逆性】 kěnìxìng invertibility；reversibility

【可怕】 kěpà fearful；frightful；terrible；terrifying

【可气】 kěqì annoying；exasperating

【可巧】 kěqiǎo as luck would have it；by a happy coincidence；it happened that

【可取】 kěqǔ desirable；advisable；commendable：她的建议有～之处。Her proposal has something to recommend it.

【可燃】 kěrán combustibility；combustible (adj.)

【可是】 kěshì 〈*conj.*〉 but；yet；however

【可视电话】 kěshì diànhuà visual telephone

【可塑】 kěsù plasticity；compliance

【可谓】 kěwèi one may well say；it may be said；it may be called

【可恶】 kěwù hateful；abominable；detestable：～之极 utterly detestable

【可惜】 kěxī it's a pity；unfortunately；it is to be regretted

【可喜】 kěxǐ gratifying；heartening：～可贺 you are to be congratulated

【可想而知】 kěxiǎng'érzhī you can imagine

【可笑】 kěxiào 1.（滑稽）laughable；ridiculous；funny；ludicrous 2.（荒唐）absurd

【可卸侧面板】 kěxiè cèmiànbǎn 〈*Motorcycle*〉 removable side panel

【可心】 kěxīn satisfying；to the satisfaction of；to the liking of

【可信】 kěxìn credible；dependable

【可信性】 kěxìnxìng credibility

【可行】 kěxíng feasible；practicable；workable

【可行性】 kěxíngxìng feasibility

【可行性研究】 kěxíngxìng yánjiū feasibility study

【可疑】 kěyí suspicious；dubious；questionable

【可疑分子】 kěyí fènzǐ a suspect；a suspicious character

【可以】 kěyǐ 1.（能够）can；may：我～在这里吸烟吗？May I smoke here? 2.（好；不坏）passable；pretty good；not bad：她的俄语还～。Her Russian is pretty good. 3.（利害）awful：她那张嘴真～。What a sharp tongue she has got!

【可以预订】 kěyǐ yùdìng bookable

【可有可无】 kěyǒu-kěwú not essential；not indispensable；may or may not be needed

【可知性】 kězhīxìng 〈*Philos.*〉 knowability

【可转让证券】 kězhuǎnràng zhèngquàn negotiable instruments

渴（kě） 1.（口渴）thirsty：解～ quench one's thirst 2.（迫切地）yearningly；thirstily；eagerly

【渴念】 kěniàn yearn for；long for

【渴求】 kěqiú eager to get；long for

【渴望】 kěwàng thirst for；long for；yearn for：～求知 be thirsty for knowledge

可（kè）

【可汗】 kèhàn 〈*Hist.*〉 khan

克［尅[3-5]、剋[3-5]］（kè） 1.（能）can；be able to 2.（克服；克制）restrain 3.（攻下；战胜）overcome；subdue；capture：攻无不～ be invincible 4.（消化）digest 5.（严格限定期限）set a time limit：～期完工 set a date for completing the work 6.〈*classifier*〉 gram (g.)

【克当量】 kèdāngliàng 〈*Chem.*〉 gram equivalent

【克敌制胜】 kèdí-zhìshèng vanquish the enemy；conquer the enemy

【克分子】 kèfēnzǐ 〈*Chem.*〉 gram molecule

【克分子体积】 kèfēnzǐ tǐjī 〈*Chem.*〉 gram-molecular volume

【克服】 kèfú 1.（战胜）surmount；overcome；conquer：～教育脱离实际的倾向 overcome the tendency to divorce education from reality / ～软弱涣散的状态 overcome weakness and laxity 2.（克制；忍受困难）put up with

【克复】 kèfù retake；recapture；recover

【克格勃】 Kègébó KGB (Komitet gosudarstvennoy bezopasnosti)

【克己奉公】 kèjǐ-fènggōng wholehearted devotion to public duty；work selflessly for the public interest

【克扣】 kèkòu embezzle part of what should be issued

【克拉】 kèlā carat：一～的钻石 a one-carat diamond

【克拉玛依】 Kèlāmǎyí 〈place〉 Karamay

【克里姆林宫】 Kèlǐmǔlíngōng the Kremlin

【克隆】 kèlóng 〈*Genetics*〉 clone

【克期】 kèqī set a time limit

【克勤克俭】 kèqín-kèjiǎn be industrious and frugal; be able to practice diligence and frugality

【克制】 kèzhì restrain; exercise restraint: 自我～ restrain oneself

氪 (kè) 〈*Chem.*〉 krypton (元素符号 Kr)

刻 (kè) 1.(雕刻) carve; engrave; cut 2.(15 分钟) quarter: 7 点一～ a quarter past seven; seven fifteen 3.(时间) moment: 稍等片～。Wait a moment. 4.(程度深) in the highest degree; profound 5.(刻薄) cutting; penetrating

【刻板】 kèbǎn 1.(刻底版) cut blocks for printing 2.(呆板) mechanical; stiff; inflexible

【刻薄】 kèbó unkind; harsh; mean

【刻不容缓】 kèbùrónghuǎn brook no delay; demand immediate attention; be of great urgency

【刻度】 kèdù graduation

【刻度盘】 kèdùpán graduation disc

【刻骨】 kègǔ deeply ingrained; deep-rooted

【刻画】 kèhuà 1.(刻和画) engrave and paint 2.(描绘,表现) depict; portray; describe

【刻苦】 kèkǔ 1.(很能吃苦) assiduous; hardworking; painstaking 2.(俭朴) simple and frugal

【刻期】 kèqī set a time limit

【刻意】 kèyì painstakingly; sedulously: ～求精 perfect one's skill assiduously; do one's every best to achieve perfection

【刻字】 kèzì carve characters on a seal

恪 (kè) scrupulously and respectfully

【恪守】 kèshǒu scrupulously abide by; maintain: ～一个中国的立场 maintain one-China position

客 (kè) 1.(客人) visitor; guest; caller: 常～ a frequenter; a frequent visitor / 贵～ a distinguished guest / 稀～ a rare visitor / 远～ a visitor from afar / 会～ receive a visitor / 送～ see a visitor off 2.(旅客) traveller; passenger 3.(寄居或迁居外地) settle or live a strange place; be a stranger 4.(客商) travelling merchant 5.(顾客) customer: 房～ boarder; lodger 6.(客观) objective

【客舱】 kècāng passenger cabin

【客车】 kèchē 1.(指铁路列车) coach; passenger train 2.(指列车车厢) passenger car; passenger coach 3.(大轿车) bus; coach

【客船】 kèchuán passenger ship; passenger boat

【客串】 kèchuàn play a part in a professional performance; be a guest performer

【客店】 kèdiàn inn; tavern

【客队】 kèduì 〈*Sports*〉 visiting team

【客饭】 kèfàn 1.(供客人的饭) a meal specially prepared for visitors at a canteen 2.(份儿饭) set meal

【客房】 kèfáng guest room

【客房服务员】 kèfáng fúwùyuán room-service waiter (m.); chambermaid (f.)

【客房经理】 kèfáng jīnglǐ resident manager

【客观】 kèguān objective: ～规律 objective law / ～世界 objective world

【客户】 kèhù client; customer

【客机】 kèjī passenger plane; airliner

【客籍】 kèjí 1.(寄居本地的外地人) a settler from another province 2.(寄居的籍贯) the province into which settlers move

【客轮】 kèlún passenger liner

【客满】 kèmǎn sold out; full house

【客票】 kèpiào passenger ticket

【客气】 kè·qi 1.(说客气话;做出客气的动作) polite; courteous: 请不要～。(对客人说时用) Please don't stand on ceremony. (或: Make yourself at home.); (对主人说时用) Please don't bother. 2.(对人谦让) modest: 您太～了。You are being too modest.

【客人】 kè·rén 1.(宾客) visitor; guest: 招待～ receive the guests; entertain the guests / 我们有两位～来吃饭。We have two guests to dinner. 2.(车船乘客) passenger 3.(旅馆宾客) guest

【客商】 kèshāng travelling trader; travelling merchant

【客套】 kètào 1.(客套话) polite formula; ceremonial 2.(说客气话) use polite formula in conversation: 互相～了几句。They exchanged some polite greetings. polite formu-

la；civilities
【客套话】 kètàohuà polite greetings
【客厅】 kètīng drawing room；parlor
【客运】 kèyùn passenger transport；passenger traffic
【客运列车】 kèyùn lièchē passenger train
【客栈】 kèzhàn inn
【客座】 kèzuò 1.（客人座位）seats for guests 2.（不在编的应邀者）guest：～演员 guest actor；guest actress
【客座教授】 kèzuò jiàoshòu guest professor；visiting professor

课（kè） 1.（教学科目）subject；course：基础～ basic course / 选修～ option courses / 专业～ specialized courses 2.（教学时间）class：讲～ give a lecture / 上～ go to class / 听～ visit a class；sit in on a class 3.〈*classifier*〉lesson：这本教科书共有16～。This textbook contain 16 lessons. 4.（征收）levy
【课本】 kèběn textbook：自学～ textbook for self-study
【课表】 kèbiǎo school timetable
【课程】 kèchéng course；curriculum：学完大学～ complete all the courses set in the curriculum
【课程表】 kèchéngbiǎo school timetable
【课程设置】 kèchéng shèzhì course offered
【课间操】 kèjiāncāo exercises during the break
【课时】 kèshí class hour；period
【课税】 kèshuì levy duty；charge duty
【课堂】 kètáng classroom；schoolroom
【课题】 kètí 1.（研究或讨论的问题）a question for study or discussion 2.（急待解决的问题）problem；task
【课题计划】 kètí jìhuà project planning
【课外】 kèwài extracurricular；outside class；after school
【课外活动】 kèwài huódòng extracurricular activities
【课外阅读】 kèwài yuèdú outside reading
【课外作业】 kèwài zuòyè homework：做～ do homework
【课文】 kèwén text
【课业】 kèyè lessons；schoolwork
【课椅】 kèyǐ tablet chair
【课余】 kèyú after school；after class
【课桌】 kèzhuō （school）desk

溘（kè） suddenly
【溘然】 kèrán suddenly：～长逝 pass away suddenly；die suddenly

ken

肯（kěn） 1.（同意）agree；consent 2.（乐意；愿意）be willing to；be ready to
【肯定】 kěndìng 1.（承认）affirm；confirm；approve；regard as positive 2.（正面的）positive；affirmative：她的回答是～的。Her answer is in the affirmative. 3.（明确的）definite；sure：～的答复 a definite answer 4.（一定；无疑问）certainly；undoubtedly；definitely：我们～能按时完成任务。We can certainly have the job finished on time.

啃［龈］（kěn） gnaw；nibble；bite：～骨头 gnaw a bone
【啃书本】 kěnshūběn delve into books

垦［墾］（kěn） cultivate；reclaim
【垦荒】 kěnhuāng reclaim wasteland；bring wasteland under cultivation；open up virgin soil
【垦区】 kěnqū reclamation area
【垦殖】 kěnzhí reclaim and cultivate wasteland

恳［懇］（kěn） 1.（诚恳）earnestly；sincerely 2.（请求）request；beseech；entreat
【恳切】 kěnqiè earnest；sincere：～陈词 make a statement earnestly
【恳请】 kěnqǐng earnestly request；cordially invite
【恳求】 kěnqiú implore；entreat；beseech：～再三 repeatedly beg for
【恳谈会】 kěntánhuì earnest talks
【恳挚】 kěnzhì 〈*written*〉earnest；sincere

keng

坑（kēng） 1.（洼下去的地方）hole；pit；hollow：沙～ jumping pit / 土～（sunken）pit / 挖～种树 dig a hole to plant the tree 2.（地洞；地道）tunnel；pit 3.（坑害）trap；cheat：～人 trap sb.；set a trap for sb.

【坑道】 kēngdào 1.〈*Mineral*.〉 gallery 2.〈*Mil*.〉 tunnel
【坑害】 kēnghài lead into a trap; entrap; scheme to do harm; make false accusation against sb.
【坑坑洼洼】 kēng · kēng-wāwā bumps and hollows: 路上～。The road is full of bumps and hollows.
【坑蒙拐骗】 kēngmēng-guǎipiàn swindle
【坑骗】 kēngpiàn cheat

吭 (kēng) utter a sound or a word: 一声不～ without saying a word
【吭哧】 kēng · chi 1.(因用力而发出声音) puff and blow 2.(吞吞吐吐) hum and haw 3.(费力) work hard; toil
【吭气】 kēngqì utter a sound or a word
【吭声】 kēngshēng utter a sound or a word

铿[**鏗**] (kēng) 〈*onomat*.〉 clang; clatter
【铿锵】 kēngqiāng ring; clang; jingle: ～有力 be sonorous and forceful

kong

空 (kōng) 1.(里面没东西) empty; hollow; void; vacant: ～屋 an empty room / 这楼是～的,没有人住。The building is empty, no one is living there. 2.(天空) sky; air: 领～ territorial sky; territorial air / 晴～ a clear sky; blue sky 3.(白白地;没有结果的) for nothing; in vain
(另见"空"kòng)
【空肠】 kōngcháng 〈*Anat*.〉 jejunum
【空挡】 kōngdǎng 〈*Auto*〉 neutral: 踩下离合器踏板,从～换到一挡。Press the clutch pedal down and change from neutral into first gear.
【空荡荡】 kōngdàngdàng empty; deserted
【空洞】 kōngdòng 1.(物体内的窟窿) cavity 2.(无内容) empty; hollow; devoid of content; vague and general: ～的议论 vague and general proposal
【空泛】 kōngfàn vague and general; not specific
【空房】 kōngfáng empty room
【空防】 kōngfáng air defense
【空腹】 kōngfù on an empty stomach
【空话】 kōnghuà empty talk; empty words; empty promises: 讲～ give an empty talk / 不能只讲～ can't afford to be satisfied with empty promises
【空集】 kōngjí 〈*Math*.〉 empty set
【空间】 kōngjiān space: 外层～ outer space
【空间站】 kōngjiānzhàn space station
【空降】 kōngjiàng airborne
【空降兵】 kōngjiàngbīng airborne force; parachute landing force
【空降部队】 kōngjiàng bùduì air-borne troop
【空姐】 kōngjiě stewardess; airline hostess; air hostess
【空军】 kōngjūn air force
【空军部队】 kōngjūn bùduì air (force) unit
【空军基地】 kōngjūn jīdì air base
【空军司令】 kōngjūn sīlìng commander of the air force
【空军司令部】 kōngjūn sīlìngbù general headquarters of the air force; air command
【空空如也】 kōngkōngrúyě absolutely empty; all empty; having nothing in it
【空口无凭】 kōngkǒu-wúpíng A mere verbal statement is no guarantee.(或: Oral expressions cannot be taken as proof.): ～,立字为证。Words of mouth being no guarantee, a written statement is hereby given.
【空旷】 kōngkuàng open; spacious
【空论】 kōnglùn empty talk
【空难】 gōngnàn aviation accident; airplane crash
【空飘】 kōngpiāo drifted by wind
【空气】 kōngqì 1.(大气) air; atmosphere: 新鲜的～ fresh air 2.(气氛) atmosphere: 政治～ political atmosphere / ～紧张 a tense atmosphere
【空气滤清器】 kōngqì lǜqīngqì 〈*Auto*〉 air cleaner
【空气污染】 kōngqì wūrǎn air pollution
【空前】 kōngqián unprecedented; unparalleled: ～的孤立 be more isolated than ever before / ～的规模和速度 on an unprecedented scale and with unprecedented speed
【空前绝后】 kōngqián-juéhòu without both precedent and following up; unique
【空勤】 kōngqín air duty
【空勤人员】 kōngqín rényuán aircrew; flight

crew
【空手】 kōngshǒu empty-handed：～而归 return empty
【空手道】 kōngshǒudào 〈*Sports*〉 karate ‖ 空手道运动员 karateka
【空谈】 kōngtán 1.（只说不做）indulge in empty talk 2.（不切实际的言论）empty talk; idle talk; prattle
【空调】 kōngtiáo air-condition：带～的卧室 an air-conditioned bedroom
【空调车】 kōngtiáochē air-conditioned coach
【空调机】 kōngtiáojī air conditioner
【空头】 kōngtóu 1.〈*Econ*.〉 bear; short-seller：～市场 bear market 2.（有名无实）nominal; phony：～政治家 armchair politician
【空头支票】 kōngtóu zhīpiào 1.（不兑现的支票）dud check; rubber check; 2.（不实践的诺言）empty promise; lip service
【空投】 kōngtóu airdrop; paradrop：向灾区～大量救灾物资 airdrop great numbers of relief supplies to the stricken areas
【空文】 kōngwén ineffective law, rule, etc.：一纸～ a mere scrap of paper
【空袭】 kōngxí air raid; air attack
【空袭警报】 kōngxí jǐngbào air raid alarm
【空袭警报器】 kōngxí jǐngbàoqì air raid siren
【空想】 kōngxiǎng idle dream; fantasy
【空想家】 kōngxiǎngjiā dreamer; visionary
【空想社会主义】 kōngxiǎng shèhuì zhǔyì utopian socialism ‖ 空想社会主义者 utopian socialist
【空心】 kōngxīn hollow
【空心菜】 kōngxīncài water spinach; swamp cabbage
【空心砖】 kōngxīnzhuān airbrick; hollow brick
【空虚】 kōngxū hollow; void：思想～ be impractical in one's thinking / 感到～ suffer from spiritual emptiness
【空邮】 kōngyóu air mail
【空邮签条】 kōngyóu qiāntiáo air mail sticker
【空运】 kōngyùn air transport; air freight; airlift
【空运保险】 kōngyùn bǎoxiǎn air transportation insurance
【空运单】 kōngyùndān airway bill (of lading)
【空运货物】 kōngyùn huòwù airfreight; air cargo
【空载】 kōngzǎi weight empty：～运费 dead freight
【空战】 kōngzhàn air battle; air action; aerial combat
【空中】 kōngzhōng in the sky; in the air; aerial; overhead：鸟儿在～飞翔。Birds fly in the air.
【空中补给线】 kōngzhōng bǔjǐxiàn airlift
【空中乘务员】 kōngzhōng chèngwùyuán flight attendant; steward; stewardess (f.)
【空中打击】 kōngzhōng dǎjī air strike
【空中飞人演员】 kōngzhōng fēirén yǎnyuán aerialists; flyers
【空中广告】 kōngzhōng guǎnggào sky writing
【空中加油】 kōngzhōng jiāyóu air refueling; inflight refueling
【空中交通管制员】 kōngzhōng jiāotōng guǎnzhìyuán air traffic controller
【空中劫持】 kōngzhōng jiéchí aerial hijacking; air piracy
【空中禁区】 kōngzhōng jìnqū restricted airspace; airspace reservation
【空中客车】 kōngzhōng kèchē airbus
【空中力量】 kōngzhōng lìliàng air power
【空中楼阁】 kōngzhōng lóugé castles in the air
【空中桥梁】 kōngzhōng qiáoliáng air bridge
【空中小姐】 kōngzhōng xiǎojiě stewardess; airline hostess; air hostess
【空中优势】 kōngzhōng yōushì air superiority
【空中侦察】 kōngzhōng zhēnchá aerial reconnaissance
【空中支援】 kōngzhōng zhīyuán air support
【空中走廊】 kōngzhōng zǒuláng air corridor; air lane
【空竹】 kōngzhú diabolo：抖～ juggle with a diabolo
【空转】 kōngzhuàn 1.（机器无负荷运转）race; idle 2.（轮子打滑）spin; turn without moving forward

孔 (kǒng) hole; opening; aperture：穿个～ perforate a hole
【孔道】 kǒngdào duct; drill way; passage; pass
【孔洞】 kǒngdòng opening or hole in a uten-

sil, etc.

【孔方兄】 kǒngfāngxiōng money

【孔孟之道】 Kǒng-Mèng zhī dào the doctrine of Confucius and Mencius

【孔庙】 Kǒngmiào Confucian temple

【孔雀】 kǒng·què peacock; peafowl; peahen (f.)

【孔雀河】 Kǒng·quèhé 〈place〉 Konqi He

【孔雀石】 kǒng·quèshí malachite

【孔隙】 kǒngxì small opening; hole

【孔穴】 kǒngxuè hole; cavity

【孔眼】 kǒngyǎn hole

恐 (kǒng) 1.(害怕) fear; dread 2.(使害怕) terrify; intimidate 3.(恐怕) I'm afraid: ～非原意。I'm afraid it was not the original intent.

【恐怖】 kǒngbù terror; terroristic

【恐怖分子】 kǒngbù fènzǐ terrorist

【恐怖片】 kǒngbùpiān horror film

【恐怖主义】 kǒngbù zhǔyì terrorism; terrorist: 反对国际～ fight international terrorism ‖ 恐怖主义者 terrorist

【恐怖组织】 kǒngbù zǔzhī terroristic organization

【恐吓】 kǒnghè threaten; intimidate; cow; menace; frighten

【恐吓信】 kǒnghèxìn letter of intimidation

【恐慌】 kǒnghuāng panic; scare; fright: 引起～ cause panic

【恐惧】 kǒngjù fear; dread; be afraid of: 无所～ fear nothing; feel no fear

【恐龙】 kǒnglóng 〈*Palaeont.*〉 dinosaur

【恐怕】 kǒngpà 〈*adv.*〉 1.(表示估计、担心) I'm afraid; fear: ～不成。I'm afraid it won't do. 2.(表示估计) perhaps; I think; probably: ～要下雪。It looks like snow.

倥 (kǒng)

【倥偬】 kǒngzǒng 1.(急迫匆忙) pressing; urgent: 戎马～ burdened with pressing military duties 2.(穷困) poverty-stricken; destitute

空 (kòng) 1.(腾出来;使空) leave empty; leave blank; vacate: ～出一个抽屉 empty a drawer / ～出一个座位 vacate a seat 2.(没被利用的) unoccupied; vacant; blank: ～行 blank line / ～座位 unoccupied seat 3.(尚未占用的地点) empty space; room 4.(尚未占用的时间) free time; spare time; leisure; free hours: 你有～吗? Are you free? (另见"空"kōng)

【空白】 kòngbái blank space; gap; margin

【空白点】 kòngbáidiǎn blank spot; gap; blank

【空白票据】 kòngbái piàojù blank bill

【空白支票】 kòngbái zhīpiào blank check

【空当】 kòngdāng space; interval

【空地】 kòngdì vacant lot; open ground; open space

【空额】 kòng'é vacancy: 补三个～ fill three vacancies

【空房】 kòngfáng vacant room; vacancy: 这家旅馆有～吗? Are there any rooms vacant in this hotel? 对不起,没～了。Sorry, no vacancies.

【空格】 kònggé blank space (on a form)

【空格键】 kònggéjiàn space (key)

【空缺】 kòngquē vacant position; vacancy: 我们有一个打字员的～。We have vacancy for a typist.

【空隙】 kòngxì 1.(时间上的) interval 2.(空间上的) gap; space: 填补～ fill up a gap / 留出～ leave some space

【空暇】 kòngxiá free time; spare time; leisure

【空闲】 kòngxián 1.(无事) idle; free 2.(空着的时间) free time; spare time; leisure 3.(空着不用) vacancy; vacant (adj.)

【空闲号码】 kòngxián hàomǎ 〈*Telecom.*〉 vacant number

【空线】 kòngxiàn disengaged line

【空子】 kòng·zi 1.(空隙) gap; opening 2.(可乘之机) chance; opportunity; loophole: 钻法律的～ find a loophole in the law

控 (kòng) 1.(控告) accuse; charge 2.(控制) control; dominate 3.(控水) turn (a container) upside down to let the liquid trickle out: 把瓶子～一～。Turn the bottle upside down to empty it.

【控告】 kònggào charge; accuse; complain

【控购】 kònggòu control purchase; purchase certain goods in a controlled way

【控股公司】 kònggǔ gōngsī holding company

【控诉】 kòngsù accuse; denounce; make a

complaint against：提出～ bring an accusation against

【控诉方】 kòngsùfāng accusing party；complainant

【控诉人】 kòngsùrén accuser

【控诉要点】 kòngsù yàodiǎn gravamen；heads of a charge

【控诉状】 kòngsùzhuàng bill of complaint

【控制】 kòngzhì control；dominate；command：对固定资产进行严格～ exercise tight control over the fixed assets / ～基本建设规模 control capital construction scale / ～人口增长 control population growth / ～需求 control demand / ～局势 have the situation under control

【控制论】 kòngzhìlùn cybernetics；kybernetics

【控制面板】 kòngzhì miànbǎn control panel

【控制权】 kòngzhìquán control power；mastery

【控制室】 kòngzhìshì control cubicle；control room

【控制数字】 kòngzhì shùzì control figure

【控制塔】 kòngzhìtǎ control tower（of an airport）

【控制台】 kòngzhìtái control power；mastery

【控制系统】 kòngzhì xìtǒng control system

【控制中心】 kòngzhì zhōngxīn control center

kou

抠［摳］（kōu） 1.（挖）dig or dig out with a finger or sth. pointed；scratch；pick；scrape 2.（雕刻）carve；cut 3.（不必要的深究）delve into；study meticulously 4.（吝啬）stingy；miserly

口（kǒu） 1.（嘴）mouth 2.（容器口）mouth；rim：信箱～ the slit of a letter box 3.（出入口）opening；entrance；inlet；outlet；exit：出～ entrance；outlet；exit / 洞～ the mouth of a cave / 入～ entrance；inlet 4.（口子）cut；hole；opening 5.（刀口）edge；blade 6.（驴、马等的年龄）the age of a draft animal：这匹马～还轻。This horse is still young.

【口岸】 kǒu'àn port；seaport；river port：通商～ commercial port / ～检查机关 inspection office at the port

【口杯】 kǒubēi cup；glass

【口才】 kǒucái eloquence：有～ be eloquent

【口吃】 kǒuchī stutter；stammer

【口齿】 kǒuchǐ 1.（发音）enunciation：～清楚 have clear enunciation 2.（说话本领）ability to speak：～伶俐 be clever and fluent

【口臭】 kǒuchòu halitosis；bad breath；ozostomia

【口袋】 kǒu·dai 1.（衣兜）pocket 2.（用具）bag；sack：纸～ paper bag

【口对口】 kǒuduìkǒu mouth to mouth

【口服】 kǒufú 1.（口头信服）profess to be convinced：～心不服 pretend to be convinced 2.（内服）oral；take orally

【口福】 kǒufú gourmet's luck；the luck to get sth. very nice to eat

【口供】 kǒugòng a statement made by the accused under examination；oral confession：问～ question for oral confession

【口号】 kǒuhào slogan；watchword：呼～ shout slogans

【口红】 kǒuhóng lipstick：涂～ wear lipstick；lipstick

【口技】 kǒujì vocal mimicry；vocal imitation ‖ 口技演员 vocal mimicry performer

【口讲指画】 kǒujiǎng-zhǐhuà gesticulate

【口角】 kǒujiǎo corner of the mouth

【口紧】 kǒujǐn tight-lipped

【口径】 kǒujìng 1.（直径）bore；caliber：～105毫米的炮 105 mm. gun 2.（说法）statement：统一～ unify statement；unify each other's statement

【口诀】 kǒujué a pithy formula

【口角】 kǒujué quarrel；bicker；wrangle；spat：因某事与某人～ quarrel with sb. about sth.；have a quarrel with sb. over sth.

【口渴】 kǒukě thirsty

【口口声声】 kǒu·kou-shēngshēng say again and again；keep on saying；repeatedly declare：她～说不知道。She kept on pleading ignorance.

【口粮】 kǒuliáng grain ration

【口令】 kǒulìng 1.（口头命令）word of command；word；command 2.（口头暗号）password；watch-word；countersign：～问答 challenge and reply

【口气】 kǒu·qì 1.（感情色彩）tone；note：埋怨的～ a tone of complaint 2.（言外之意）what is actually meant；implication：听他的～ judging by the way he spoke；from the implication of his statement 3.（说话的气势）manner or speaking：好大的～！ What high-sounding sentiments!

【口腔】 kǒuqiāng 〈*Anat.*〉oral cavity

【口腔科】 kǒuqiāngkē department of stomatology

【口腔卫生】 kǒuqiāng wèishēng oral hygiene

【口腔医院】 kǒuqiāng yīyuàn stomatological hospital

【口琴】 kǒuqín harmonica；mouth organ

【口轻】 kǒuqīng 1.（味道不咸）not salty 2.（爱吃淡的）be fond of food that is not salty 3.（驴、马等年龄小）young

【口若悬河】 kǒuruò-xuánhé with an easy flow of language

【口哨儿】 kǒushàor a whistle：吹～ whistle

【口舌】 kǒushé 1.（争吵）quarrel；dispute；exchange of words 2.（言语）talking round；words；talking：白费～ waste one's talking

【口实】 kǒushí a cause for gossip；handle

【口试】 kǒushì oral examination；oral test；oral quiz：参加～ take oral examination

【口是心非】 kǒushì-xīnfēi say yes and mean no；say one thing and mean another；affirm with one's lips but deny in one's heart

【口授】 kǒushòu 1.（口头传授）oral instruction；pass on (sth.) through oral instruction 2.（口说由别人代写）dictate：向秘书～信稿 dictate a letter to a secretary

【口授遗嘱】 kǒushòu yízhǔ oral testament

【口述】 kǒushù oral account

【口水】 kǒushuǐ saliva：流～ slobber

【口蹄疫】 kǒutíyì 〈*Veterinary*〉foot-and-mouth disease

【口头】 kǒutóu 1.（用说话方式）oral；verbal 2.（口头上）in words；in speech；on one's lips；verbal：～上赞成 agree in words

【口头汇报】 kǒutóu huìbào oral report

【口头声明】 kǒutóu shēngmíng oral statement

【口头协议】 kǒutóu xiéyì oral contract

【口味】 kǒuwèi 1.（对味道的偏好）a person's taste：合～ suit one's taste / 不合～ not be to one's taste 2.（食品味道）flavor；taste of food：～鲜美 delicious in taste

【口吻】 kǒuwěn 1.〈*Zool.*〉muzzle；snout 2.（口气）tone；note

【口香糖】 kǒuxiāngtáng chewing gum

【口信】 kǒuxìn oral message；message；word

【口译】 kǒuyì 1.（口头翻译）oral interpretation；interpret 2.（口译译员）interpreter

【口音】 kǒuyīn 1.（声调）voice 2.（方音）accent：她讲英语带法国～。She speaks English with an French accent.

【口语】 kǒuyǔ 1.（口头语言）colloquial language；colloquialism 2.（与“书面语言”相对）spoken language

【口语体】 kǒuyǔtǐ colloquial style

【口罩】 kǒuzhào gauze mask；mouth-muffle

【口重】 kǒuzhòng 1.（味道咸）salty 2.（爱吃咸的）be fond of salty food

【口诛笔伐】 kǒuzhū-bǐfá condemn both in speech and in writing；denounce by tongue and pen

【口子】 kǒu·zi opening；hole；cut；tear

叩 (kòu) 1.（敲；打）knock：～门 knock at a door 2.（磕头）kowtow

【叩头】 kòutóu kowtow

【叩问】 kòuwèn 〈*written*〉make inquiries

【叩诊】 kòuzhěn 〈*Med.*〉percussion

扣［釦[5]］(kòu) 1.（套住；搭住）button up；buckle；fasten 2.（器物口朝下）place a cup，bowl，etc. upside down；cover with an inverted cup，bowl，etc.：把碗～在盘子上 turn the bowl bottom upward on the plate 3.（扣留；扣押）detain；take into custody；arrest 4.（扣减）deduct；discount；take off 5.（纽扣）knot；button；buckle 6.（扣动）press；pull：～动扳机 press the trigger 7.（用力猛击）smash (the ball)：猛～一球 smash the ball forcefully

【扣除】 kòuchú deduct；take off：～费用的 20% deduct 20% from the expenses

【扣缴】 kòujiǎo withhold

【扣款】 kòukuǎn deduct a part of the money

【扣留】 kòuliú detain arrest；hold in custody

【扣帽子】 kòu mào·zi put a label on sb.；label sb. as

【扣球】 kòuqiú smash；spike

【扣人心弦】 kòurénxīnxián exciting；thrilling；soul-stirring；very touching：～的

歌 a soul-stirring song

【扣式瓶盖】 kòushì pínggài squeeze cap

【扣压】 kòuyā withhold; pigeonhole: ～信件 withhold letters

【扣押】 kòuyā 1.(扣留) detain; hold in custody 2.〈*Law*〉 distrain; detention; levy on

【扣眼】 kòuyǎn buttonhole

【扣子】 kòu·zi 1.(纽扣) button: 扣～ do up the buttons; fasten the buttons / 解开～ undo the buttons; unfasten the buttons 2.(皮带扣) buckle 3.(结) knot

寇 (kòu) 1.(强盗) bandit; robber 2.(侵略者) invader; enemy: 敌～ the invading enemy 3.(侵犯) invade

ku

枯 (kū) 1.(枯萎) withered: ～树 a withered tree / ～枝 a dead branch 2.(没有水) dried up 3.(枯燥) dull; uninteresting

【枯槁】 kūgǎo 1.(枯萎) withered 2.(憔悴) haggard; wizened: 面容～ look haggard

【枯竭】 kūjié 1.(干涸) dried up; drain 2.(体力、资财等用尽) exhausted: 财源～ financial resources were exhausted

【枯木逢春】 kūmù féngchūn spring comes to the withered tree; good fortune that comes after a long spell of bad luck; get a new lease of lift

【枯水】 kūshuǐ low water

【枯水期】 kūshuǐqī dry season

【枯萎】 lūwěi be withered: 干热风使植物～了。The hot dry wind withered the plants.

【枯燥】 kūzào dull and dry; uninteresting; insipid

骷 (kū)

【骷髅】 kūlóu 1.(人的尸骨) human skeleton 2.(死人头骨) human skull; death's-head

哭 (kū) cry; weep; sob; blubber; wail

【哭哭啼啼】 kū · ku-títí endlessly weep and wail; weep and sniffle; blubber

【哭泣】 kūqì cry; weep; sob

【哭丧着脸】 kū·sang·zhe liǎn look down-in-the-mouth; pull a long face

【哭诉】 kūsù complain with tears

【哭笑不得】 kūxiào-bùdé not know whether to laugh or to cry; find sth. both funny and annoying

窟 (kū) 1.(洞穴) hole; cave: 石～ cave; grotto 2.(坏人聚集场所) den: 赌～ a gambling-den / 匪～ robbers' den; bandit's den

【窟窿】 kū·long 1.(洞) hole; cavity 2.(亏空) deficit; debt: 填～ make up a deficit

苦 (kǔ) 1.(味苦) bitter: 这药～得很。This medicine tastes very bitter. 2.(难受;痛苦) hardship; suffering; pain; bitterness 3.(使痛苦;使难受) cause sb. suffering; give sb. a hard time 4.(苦于) suffer from; be troubled by 5.(苦苦地) painstakingly; doing one's utmost: ～留 try hard to ask sb. to stay

【苦楚】 kǔchǔ suffering; misery; distress

【苦处】 kǔ·chu 1.(苦难) suffering; hardship 2.(困难) difficulty

【苦干】 kǔgàn work hard

【苦工】 kǔgōng hard work; hard labor

【苦功】 kǔgōng hard work; painstaking effort: 下～ take pains; hard work; make painstaking efforts

【苦瓜】 kǔguā 〈*Bot.*〉 balsam pear

【苦果】 kǔguǒ 1.(坏的结果) bitter fruit: 尝到…的～ taste the bitter fruits of sth. 2.(必须接受的坏结果) bitter pill; bitter swallow; bitter medicine: 吞下…的～ swallow the bitter pill of sth.

【苦海】 kǔhǎi sea of bitterness; abyss of misery

【苦海无边】 kǔhǎi wú biān boundless sea of hardship

【苦尽甘来】 kǔjìn-gānlái sweet are the fruits of labor, luck turns after hardship

【苦口】 kǔkǒu 1.(反复恳切地说) (admonish) in earnest 2.(引起苦的味觉) bitter to the taste

【苦口婆心】 kǔkǒu-póxīn urge sb. time and again with good intentions; advice in earnest words and with good intention

【苦练】 kǔliàn practice hard; drill diligently

【苦闷】 kǔmèn depressed; dejected; feeling low

【苦命】 kǔmìng hard lot

【苦命人】 kǔmìngrén a luckless person
【苦难】 kǔnàn suffering; misery; distress: 受尽～ suffer all kinds of hardships
【苦恼】 kǔnǎo worried; distressed; tormented; troubled
【苦日子】 kǔrì·zi days of hardship
【苦涩】 kǔsè 1.(又苦又涩) bitter and astringent 2.(内心痛苦) pained; agonized; anguished
【苦水】 kǔshuǐ 1.(味道苦的水) bitter water 2.(吐出的苦水) gastric secretion, etc. rising to the mouth 3.(内心痛苦) suffering
【苦思冥想】 kǔsī-míngxiǎng cudgel one's brains (to evolve an idea)
【苦头】 kǔtóu (指味道) bitter taste
【苦头】 kǔ·tóu (苦痛) suffering; hardship: 吃～ suffer hardships
【苦笑】 kǔxiào forced smile; wry smile
【苦心】 kǔxīn 1.(心思或精力) trouble taken; pains 2.(费尽心思) do sth. with great effort: ～经营 carry an enterprise painstaking efforts
【苦心孤诣】 kǔxīn-gūyì do sth. with painstaking efforts
【苦役】 kǔyì hard labor; penal servitude
【苦于】 kǔyú suffer from: ～时间紧迫 hard pressed for time
【苦战】 kǔzhàn wage an arduous struggle; struggle hard
【苦衷】 kǔzhōng difficulties: 她也许有她的～。She might have her own difficulties.
【苦中作乐】 kǔzhōng-zuòlè find joy amid hardship; enjoy in adversity
【苦主】 kǔzhǔ the family of the victim in a murder case

库(kù) 1.(仓库,库房;车库) warehouse; storehouse; depository; depot: 国～ state treasury / 家具～ a warehouse for furniture / 车～ garage 2.〈*Computer*〉 library
【库藏】 kùcáng have in storage
【库存】 kùcún stock; reserve: 有大量～ have a large stock
【库存量】 kùcúnliàng storage
【库尔勒】 Kùěrlè 〈place〉 Korla
【库房】 kùfáng storehouse; storeroom
【库容】 kùróng 〈*Water Conservancy*〉 storage capacity
【库文件】 kùwénjiàn 〈*Computer*〉 library file

裤(kù) trousers; pants: 牛仔～ jeans / 长～ trousers
【裤衩】 kùchǎ underpants; undershorts: 比基尼三角～ bikini briefs / 三角～ briefs
【裤长】 kùcháng outside length of trousers
【裤带】 kùdài waist-belt
【裤裆】 kùdāng crotch (of trousers)
【裤兜】 kùdōu trouser pocket
【裤缝】 kùfèng seam; seams of a trouser leg
【裤管】 kùguǎn trouser legs
【裤脚】 kùjiǎo bottom of a trouser leg
【裤口】 kùkǒu cuff
【裤料】 kùliào trousering
【裤腿】 kùtuǐ trouser legs
【裤线】 kùxiàn creases (of trousers)
【裤腰】 kùyāo waistband; waist of trousers
【裤子】 kù·zi trousers; pants

酷(kù) 1.(残酷) cruel; brutal; oppressive 2.(程度深) very; extremely
【酷爱】 kùài ardently love; be very fond of
【酷热】 kùrè extremely hot (weather)
【酷暑】 kùshǔ the intense heat of summer
【酷似】 kùsì be the very image of; be exactly like; bear a strong resemblance to
【酷刑】 kùxíng cruel torture; savage torture; brutal corporal punishment; excruciation

kua

夸[誇](kuā) 1.(夸大) exaggerate; overstate; boast 2.(夸奖) praise: 自～ sing one's own praises
【夸大】 kuādà exaggerate; exaggeration (n.); overstate; overstatement (n.); aggrandize: ～病情 exaggerate an illness / ～成绩 exaggerate one's achievements / ～的重要性 overstate the importance of sth.
【夸大其词】 kuādà-qící make an overstatement; exaggerate: ～的报告 an exaggerated report
【夸奖】 kuājiǎng praise; commend; compliment; extol; speak well of: 值得～ be worth praising
【夸克】 kuākè 〈*Physics*〉 quark
【夸口】 kuākǒu boast; brag; talk big
【夸夸其谈】 kuākuā-qítán indulge in exagger-

ations; talk big; a big screed full of bombast

【夸耀】 kuāyào brag about; show off; flaunt; boast of: ～自己的学识 boast of one's learning

【夸赞】 kuāzàn speak highly of; commend; praise

【夸张】 kuāzhāng exaggerate; overstate

垮 (kuǎ) collapse; fall; break down; crack up: 她身体～了。Her health has broken down.

【垮台】 kuǎtái collapse; fall from power

挎 (kuà) 1.(挂在胳膊上) carry on the arm; sling; hang 2.(挂在肩头、脖颈或腰里) carry sth. over one's shoulder or at one's side: ～着照相机 have a camera slung over one's shoulder

【挎包】 kuàbāo satchel

【挎斗】 kuàdǒu 〈*Motorcycle*〉 sidecar

【挎斗摩托车】 kuàdǒu mótuōchē sidecar machine

胯 (kuà) hip

【胯骨】 kuàgǔ hipbone; innominate bone

跨 (kuà) 1.(迈步) step; stride: ～进学校大门 step into the college gate 2.(跨骑) bestride; straddle; ride astride: ～上马 mount a horse; bestride a horse 3.(跨越) cut across; go beyond

【跨部门】 kuàbùmén trans-department

【跨地区】 kuàdìqū transregional: ～交流 transregional exchange

【跨度】 kuàdù 〈*Archit.*〉 span; fly-past; stretch

【跨国】 kuàguó transnational

【跨国公司】 kuàguó gōngsī transnational corporation; TNC

【跨行业公司】 kuàhángyè gōngsī conglomerate

【跨栏赛跑】 kuàlán sàipǎo hurdles; hurdle race

【跨栏运动员】 kuàlán yùndòngyuán hurdler; hurdle runner

【跨年度】 kuà niándù go beyond the year: ～预算 a budget that covers the next year's needs

【跨世纪工程】 kuàshìjì gōngchéng century-crossing project; turn-of-the-century project

【跨文化研究】 kuàwénhuà yānjiū cross-culture study

【跨线桥】 kuàxiànqiáo 1.〈*Transport*〉 overpass (AmE.); flyover (BrE.) 2.〈*Electr.*〉 overline bridge

【跨学科】 kuàxuékē interdiscipline; interdisciplinary (adj.): ～领域 interdisciplinary field

【跨洋】 kuàyáng transoceanic

【跨音速】 kuàyīnsù transonic speed; transonic (adj.): ～飞行 transonic flight

【跨越】 kuàyuè stride across; leap over; cut across: ～时空 leap over space-time

kuai

会[會] (kuài) (另见"会"huì)

【会计】 kuài·jì 1.(会计工作) accounting; accountancy: 财务～ financial accounting / 成本～ cost accounting / 工业～ industrial accounting / 税务～ tax accounting 2.(会计人员) accountant; bookkeeper

【会计报表】 kuàijì bàobiǎo accounting statement

【会计核算】 kuàijì hésuàn book records

【会计师】 kuàijìshī accountant: 总～ chief accountant

【会计学】 kuàijìxué accounting

脍[膾] (kuài)

【脍炙人口】 kuàizhì-rénkǒu win universal praise; enjoy great popularity; be on everybody's lips

块[塊] (kuài) 1.(成块的东西) piece; lump; chunk; block: 木～ wood block / 糖～ lumps of sugar 2.〈*classifier*〉一～肥皂 a cake of soap

【块茎】 kuàijīng 〈*Bot.*〉 stem tuber; root tuber

【块煤】 kuàiméi lump coal; torbanite; bitumenite

【块状构造】 kuàizhuàng gòuzào massive structure; block structure

快 (kuài) 1.(速度快) fast; quick; rapid; swift; speedy: 动作～ be quick in action / 这表～了一分钟。The watch is a minute fast. **2.**（速度）speed：这公共汽车能跑多～？How fast can this bus go? **3.**（赶快）hurry up；make haste：～，开开门！Quickly, open the door! **4.**（快要）soon；before long；be about to：春天～来了。Spring is coming. **5.**（灵敏）quick-witted；ingenious：她脑子～。She understands things quickly. **6.**（锋利）sharp；keen **7.**（爽快；痛快）straightforward；forthright；plainspoken **8.**（愉快）pleased；happy；gratified

【快班】 kuàibān advanced class

【快板歌】 kuàibǎngē rap song；rap music

【快报】 kuàibào bulletin；stop-press news；newsflash

【快步】 kuàibù quick step：～穿过大街 walk quickly across the street

【快步舞】 kuàibùwǔ quickstep

【快餐】 kuàicān fast food；quick meal

【快餐店】 kuàicāndiàn fast food restaurant

【快餐馆】 kuàicānguǎn fast food restaurant

【快车】 kuàichē express train；express bus；fast train：直达～ through express / 特别～ special express

【快车道】 kuàichēdào fast traffic lane；fast lane

【快递】 kuàidì express delivery；special delivery

【快递费】 kuàidìfèi express fee

【快递邮件】 kuàidì yóujiàn express mail

【快干】 kuàigàn quick-drying

【快感】 kuàigǎn pleasant sensation；delight

【快活】 kuài·huo happy；cheerful；joyful；joyous

【快件】 kuàijiàn express mail

【快乐】 kuàilè happy；joyful；cheerful；gay

【快慢】 kuàimàn speed

【快慢针】 kuàimànzhēn index lever；regulator pin

【快门】 kuàimén 〈*Photog.*〉 shutter

【快门按钮】 kuàimén ànniǔ 〈*Photog.*〉 shutter release

【快门速度】 kuàimén sùdù 〈*Photog.*〉 shutter speed

【快门速度调节钮】 kuàimén sùdù tiáojiéniǔ 〈*Photog.*〉 shutter-speed selector

【快门线】 kuàiménxiàn 〈*Photog.*〉 cable release

【快事】 kuàishì pleasure；delightful event；delight

【快速】 kuàisù fast；quick；high-speed；speedy

【快速部队】 kuàisù bùduì mobile force；mobile troops；mobile units

【快速格式化】 kuàisù géshìhuà 〈*Computer*〉 quick formatting

【快速烹调】 kuàisù pēngtiáo flash-cook

【快速眼动】 kuàisù yǎndòng 〈*Psycho.*〉 rapid eye movement；REM

【快艇】 kuàitǐng speedboat；motor boat：鱼雷～ torpedo boat

【快慰】 kuàiwèi feel much delighted；feel pleased

【快信】 kuàixìn express letter

【快要】 kuàiyào be about to；be going to；be on the verge of：他们～出发了。They are about to start.

【快意】 kuàiyì pleased；satisfied；comfortable

【快照】 kuàizhào snap；snapshot

筷（kuài） chopsticks

【筷子】 kuài·zi chopsticks

kuan

宽［寬］（kuān） **1.**（跟"窄"相对）wide；broad：～脸 a broad face **2.**（宽度）width；breadth：4 米～ four meters in breadth **3.**（放宽）relax；relieve：心里～多了 be greatly relieved **4.**（放宽限期）extend：期限放～两天。The deadline will be extended two days. **5.**（宽大）generous；lenient **6.**（宽裕；宽绰）comfortably off；well-off：手头～多了 have more money than before；be better off than before

【宽敞】 kuān·chang spacious；roomy；commodious

【宽畅】 kuānchàng free from worry；happy；cheerful；carefree：胸怀～ be cheerful in one's mind

【宽绰】 kuān·chuo **1.**（宽阔）spacious；commodious **2.**（松缓）relax；relieve：心里～多了 feel greatly relieved **3.**（富余）comfortably off；well-off

【宽大】 kuāndà 1.（面积或容积大）roomy; spacious; wide：一间～的客厅 a spacious sitting room 2.（从宽处理）lenient; magnanimous

【宽大政策】 kuāndà zhèngcè lenient policy

【宽待】 kuāndài treat with leniency; treat liberally; accord lenient treatment：～战俘 treat the POWs liberally; give lenient treatment to prisoners of war

【宽贷】 kuāndài pardon; forgive

【宽度】 kuāndù width; breadth

【宽广】 kuānguǎng broad; extensive; vast

【宽宏大量】 kuānhóng dàliàng large-minded; magnanimous; generous

【宽厚】 kuānhòu 1.（宽而厚）wide and tick 2.（宽容厚道）generous; lenient; kind

【宽旷】 kuānkuàng extensive; vast

【宽阔】 kuānkuò broad; wide

【宽容】 kuānróng tolerant; lenient; bear with

【宽恕】 kuānshù forgive; pardon; excuse：得到～ obtain clemency from

【宽松】 kuānsōng 1.（宽绰；不拥挤）no crowded 2.（宽畅）spacious; roomy; commodious 3.（放松）feel relieved; be free from worry 4.（宽舒；松快）relaxed：～的社会环境 relaxed social environment 5.（宽裕）well-to-do; well-off; ample：手头～ be in easy circumstances 6.（肥大）loose and comfortable

【宽松的】 kuānsōng·de relaxed：～的社会环境 relaxed social environment

【宽慰】 kuānwèi comfort; console

【宽限】 kuānxiàn extend a time limit; grace

【宽限期】 kuānxiànqī grace period; period of grace

【宽限日期】 kuānxiàn rìqī days of grace

【宽心】 kuānxīn feel relieved; find relief; be relaxed; be at ease

【宽心丸儿】 kuānxīnwánr story told to make people relax

【宽以待人】 kuānyǐdàirén be lenient with others

【宽银幕电影】 kuānyīnmù diànyǐng wide-screen film

【宽裕】 kuānyù well-to-do; well-off; ample：经济～ in easy circumstances

【宽纵】 kuānzòng indulge

髋［髖］（kuān） hip

【髋骨】 kuāngǔ hipbone; innominate bone

款［欵］（kuǎn） 1.（诚恳）sincere 2.（招待；款待）receive with hospitality; entertain 3.（条款）section; paragraph; item：第十条第二～ Article 10, Section 2 4.（款项）a sum of money; fund; money：拨～ set aside a sum / 捐～ contribute money 5.（书画的上下款）上～ the name of recipient / 下～ the signature 6.（缓；慢）leisurely; slow

【款待】 kuǎndài treat cordially; receive cordially：～客人 entertain guests; receive guests cordially

【款留】 kuǎnliú offer to put up a visitor; kindly urge a friend to stay

【款式】 kuǎnshì pattern; style; design; form：～新颖 be of a new design

【款项】 kuǎnxiàng 1.（一笔钱）a sum of money; fund 2.（指支出）item of expenditure 3.（条款）item

【款子】 kuǎn·zi a sum of money：大笔～ a big sum of money

kuang

匡（kuāng） 1.（纠正）rectify; correct 2.（救；帮助）assist; save：～我不逮 help me to overcome my shortcomings

【匡谬】 kuāngmiù correct mistakes

【匡正】 kuāngzhèng rectify; correct

诓（kuāng） deceive; hoax

【诓骗】 kuāngpiàn deceive; hoax; dupe; cheat; swindle

哐（kuāng） 〈*onomat.*〉 crash; bang：～的一声掉在地上 fall with a crash

【哐啷】 kuānglāng 〈*onomat.*〉 crash：～一声关上门 bang the door shut

筐（kuāng） 1.（竹筐，柳条筐）basket; crate 2.〈*classifier*〉 basketful

【筐子】 kuāng·zi small basket; crate

狂（kuáng） 1.（疯狂）mad; crazy; mania; insanity：发～ go mad; become mad; run mad 2.（猛烈；声势大）violent; wild：～饮

drink heavily 3.（纵情、无拘束地）wild; delirious; raving; unrestrained: ～怒 raving with fury / ～喜 be wild with joy; be delirious with delight 4.（狂妄）arrogant; overbearing

【狂暴】 kuángbào violent; wild; frantic; rabid

【狂放】 kuángfàng live wildly and freely

【狂风】 kuángfēng 1.〈*Meteorol.*〉 whole gale 2.（猛烈的风）fierce wind; wild wind: ～巨浪 wild winds and huge waves

【狂轰滥炸】 kuánghōng lànzhà bomb indiscriminately and wantonly

【狂欢】 kuánghuān revelry; carnival

【狂欢节】 kuánghuānjié carnival

【狂澜】 kuánglán raging waves; roaring waves: 力挽～ do one's utmost to save a desperate situation

【狂犬病】 kuángquǎnbìng hydrophobia; rabies

【狂热】 kuángrè fanaticism; fanatical; feverish; rabid

【狂人】 kuángrén madman; maniac

【狂妄】 kuángwàng wildly arrogant; unbridled; wanton: ～无知 conceited and ignorant / ～自大 arrogant and conceited

【狂喜】 kuángxǐ wild with joy

【狂想曲】 kuángxiǎngqǔ 〈*Music*〉 rhapsody

【狂笑】 kuángxiào laugh wildly; wild laugh; roars of laughter

【狂言】 kuángyán wild language; crazy talk; crazy remarks; extravagant language

旷［曠］(kuàng) 1.（空旷）vast; spacious 2.（心境开阔）free from worries and petty ideas 3.（荒废）neglect; waste 4.（过于肥大;间隙过大）loose-fitting

【旷达】 kuàngdá broad-minded; open-minded

【旷废】 kuàngfèi neglect

【旷工】 kuànggōng stay away from work without leave or good reason

【旷古】 kuànggǔ 1.（自古以来）from time immemorial 2.（远古）history: ～未闻 never heard of in history; unprecedented in history

【旷课】 kuàngkè cut school; cut classes

【旷日持久】 kuàngrì-chíjiǔ long-drawn-out; protracted; prolonged: ～的谈判 long-drawn-out negotiations

【旷世】 kuàngshì outstanding; without peer in one's generation: ～奇才 a remarkable talent of many ages; a genius without peer in one's generation

【旷野】 kuàngyě wilderness; open field; open country

矿［礦、鑛］(kuàng) 1.（矿床）ore deposit; mineral deposit 2.（开采场所）mine: 露天～ an open pit / 铁～ iron mine 3.（矿石）ore: 选～ ore dressing / 他们开采银～。They were mining for silver.

【矿藏】 kuàngcáng mineral resources; mineral reserves; ore deposits

【矿藏量】 kuàngcángliàng ore reserves

【矿产】 kuàngchǎn mineral products; minerals: ～资源的合理开发 rational exploitation of mineral resources

【矿场】 kuàngchǎng mine

【矿床】 kuàngchuáng mineral deposit; ore deposit; deposit

【矿灯】 kuàngdēng miner's lamp; cap-lamp

【矿工】 kuànggōng miner

【矿化】 kuànghuà mineralize; mineralization (n.)

【矿井】 kuàngjǐng shaft; mine; pit

【矿坑】 kuàngkēng pit

【矿口发电厂】 kuàngkǒu fādiànchǎng mine mouth power plant

【矿脉】 kuàngmài mineral ore; mineral vein; lode

【矿泥】 kuàngní sludge; slime; slurry

【矿区】 kuàngqū mining area; minefield

【矿区铁路】 kuàngqū tiělù mine railway

【矿泉】 kuàngquán mineral spring

【矿泉水】 kuàngquánshuǐ mineral water; bottled water: 喝～ drink mineral water

【矿山】 kuàngshān mine; mining area

【矿山机械】 kuàngshān jīxiè mining machinery

【矿石】 kuàngshí ore; mineral: 铁～ iron ore / 高品位～ high grade ore / 低品位～ low grade ore

【矿物】 kuàngwù mineral

【矿物界】 kuàngwùjiè mineral kingdom

【矿物学】 kuàngwùxué mineralogy

【矿物油】 kuàngwùyóu mineral oil
【矿业】 kuàngyè mining industry
【矿业学院】 kuàngyè xuéyuàn mining institute
【矿渣】 kuàngzhā slag
【矿长】 kuàngzhǎng barmaster

况［況］（kuàng） 1.（情况）condition; situation: 近～ recent condition / 窘～ predicament; difficult situation 2.（比较）compare: 每～愈下 from bad to worse
【况且】 kuàngqiě moreover; besides; in addition; furthermore

框（kuàng） 1.（框子）frame; circle; case: 窗～ window frame; window case / 镜～儿 picture frame 2.（加框）circumscribe; draw a frame round 3.（约束;限制）put in a strait-jacket
【框架】 kuàngjià frame
【框架建筑】 kuàngjià jiànzhù framed building
【框框】 kuàngkuàng 1.（周围的圈）frame; circle 2.（固有格式;传统做法）convention; restriction; set pattern: 打破旧～ break through the conventions; throw convention to the winds

眶（kuàng） orbit; socket (of the eye); eye socket: 热泪盈～ one's eyes filling with tears / 夺～而出 burst into tears

kui

亏［虧］（kuī） 1.（受损失;亏折）lose (money, etc.); have a deficit: 吃大～ suffer heavy losses / 转～为盈 show a turn from loss to profit 2.（欠缺;短少）short of; deficient 3.（亏负）treat unfairly 4.（多亏;幸亏）fortunately; luckily; thanks to: ～得是你。Luckily it is you.
【亏本】 kuīběn lose money in business; lose one's capital: ～生意 a losing proposition
【亏待】 kuīdài 1.（不公平）treat unfairly; treat shabbily 2.（不尽心）treat unobligingly
【亏负】 kuīfù let sb. suffer; let sb. down
【亏空】 kuīkōng 1.（欠人财物）be in debt; be in the red; can't make both ends meet 2.（所欠财物）debt; deficit: 巨额～ a great deficit
【亏空公款】 kuīkōng gōngkuǎn embezzle
【亏欠】 kuīqiàn have a deficit; be in arrears
【亏蚀】 kuīshí 1.（日蚀;月蚀）eclipse of the sun; eclipse of the moon 2.（亏本）lose money in business
【亏损】 kuīsǔn 1.（支出超过收入）loss; deficit: 净～ dead loss / 年度～ losses in a (tax) year / 严重～的企业 enterprises which run at a heavy loss 2.（身体虚弱）general debility
【亏损企业】 kuīsǔn qǐyè enterprise in the red; deficit-ridden enterprise
【亏损总额】 kuīsǔn zǒngé total loss
【亏心】 kuīxīn have a bad conscience
【亏心事】 kuīxīnshì sth. with a bad conscience

岿［巋］（kuī）
【岿然】 kuīrán towering; lofty: ～不动 remain firm; remain unmoved / ～屹立 tower; stand towering

盔（kuī） helmet; headpiece: 钢～ steel helmet
【盔甲】 kuījiǎ a suit of armor; helmet and armor

窥［窺］（kuī） peep; spy
【窥豹一斑】 kuībào-yībān see segment of a whole
【窥测】 kuīcè spy out: ～时机 bide one's time
【窥见】 kuījiàn get a glimpse of; catch a glimpse of; detect: ～一斑 see segment of a whole
【窥视】 kuīshì peep at; spy on; watch stealthily; take a furtive glance
【窥视镜】 kuīshìjìng peephole; eyehole; spyhole: 门上有个～。There's a peephole in the door.
【窥伺】 kuīsì lie in wait for; be on watch for
【窥探】 kuītàn spy upon; pry about; pry into; poke one's nose into: ～秘密 pry into sb.'s secret

奎（kuí）
【奎宁】 kuíníng 〈*Pharm.*〉 quinine

魁（kuí） 1.（为首的）chief; head: 罪～ chief criminal; arch-criminal 2.（匪首）chieftain 3.（身体高大）of stalwart build

【魁首】 kuíshǒu the brightest and best：文章～ outstanding writer of the day
【魁伟】 kuíwěi big and tall
【魁梧】 kuí·wú tall and strong；big and tall

葵（kuí）

【葵花】 kuíhuā sunflower
【葵花油】 kuíhuāyóu sunflower oil
【葵花籽】 kuíhuāzhǐ sunflower seeds
【葵花鹦鹉】 kuíhuā yīngwǔ cockatoo
【葵扇】 kuíshàn palm-leaf fan

睽（kuí）

【睽睽】 kuíkuí stare；gaze：众目～之下 in the public eye

傀（kuǐ）

【傀儡】 kuǐlěi puppet
【傀儡政府】 kuǐlěi zhèngfǔ puppet government
【傀儡政权】 kuǐlěi zhèngquán puppet regime

匮（kuì） deficient

【匮乏】 kuìfá short (of supplies)；deficient：劳动力～ a scarcity of labor / 资源～ want of natural resources

馈［餽］（kuì） make a present of

【馈电】 kuìdiàn feed；infeed
【馈电盘】 kuìdiànpán feeder panel
【馈入】 kuìrù 〈*Electr.*〉 feed-in
【馈送】 kuìsòng present：～礼品 make a present
【馈线】 kuìxiàn feeder
【馈赠】 kuìzèng present (a gift)；make a present of sth.

溃（kuì） **1.**（河水冲破堤坝）burst **2.**（突破包围）break through：～围西奔 break through the encirclement and head west **3.**（溃败）be defeated；be routed **4.**（肌肉组织腐烂）fester；ulcerate

【溃败】 kuìbài be defeated；be routed
【溃决】 kuìjué burst；break
【溃烂】 kuìlàn fester；ulcerate；ulceration (n.)
【溃灭】 kuìmiè crumble and fall；collapse and perish
【溃散】 kuìsàn be defeated and dispersed；collapse in disorder；scatter
【溃逃】 kuìtáo escape in disorder；fly pell-mell；flee helter-skelter；break and flee
【溃退】 kuìtuì beat a precipitate retreat；retreat in disorder
【溃疡】 kuìyáng 〈*Med.*〉 ulcer：胃～ gastric ulcer

愧［媿］（kuì） **1.**（惭愧）ashamed **2.**（不安）embarrassed；uneasy：～不敢当 embarrassed by undeserved praise

【愧恨】 kuìhèn ashamed and remorseful
【愧色】 kuìsè ashamed look；sign of shame：面有～ look ashamed

kun

坤（kūn） female；feminine

【坤包】 kūnbāo woman's bag
【坤表】 kūnbiǎo woman's watch

昆（kūn）

【昆布】 kūnbù **1.**〈*Chin. Pharm.*〉 kelp **2.**〈*Bot.*〉 laminaria
【昆虫】 kūnchóng insect
【昆虫防治】 kūnchóng fángzhì insect control
【昆虫学】 kūnchóngxué entomology；insectology ‖ 昆虫学家 entomologist

醌（kūn） 〈*Chem.*〉 quinone

捆［綑］（kǔn） **1.**（捆扎）tie；bind；bundle up；truss：～干草 truss hay **2.**〈*classifier*〉 bundle；sheaf；truss：两～柴 two bundles of firewood

【捆绑】 kǔnbǎng truss up；bind；tie up
【捆扎】 kǔnzā tie up；bundle up

困［睏⁴］（kùn） **1.**（困扰）be stranded；be hard pressed；be distressed；be beset：内外交～ be beset with troubles both at home and abroad **2.**（围困）surround；pin down；besiege；hem in；encircle **3.**（疲乏）tired；weary；fatigued **4.**（疲乏想睡）sleepy：她～了。She felt sleepy.

【困顿】 kùndùn **1.**（劳累）tired out；exhausted；fatigued；weary；worn-out **2.**（生活艰难）in financial straits；hard up；in straitened circumstances

【困乏】 kùnfá feel tired; feel fatigued

【困惑】 kùnhuò perplexed; puzzled; bewildered; at a loss

【困境】 kùnjìng difficult position; straits; dilemma; predicament; plight: 陷于～ land oneself in a fix / 摆脱～ free oneself from a difficult position

【困窘】 kùnjiǒng in straitened circumstances; in a difficult position; embarrassed

【困倦】 kùnjuàn sleepy; drowsy

【困苦】 kùnkǔ hardship; privation; deep poverty: 生活～ live in poverty; live a miserable life

【困难】 kùn·nan 1.(有阻碍) difficulty: 克服～ overcome difficulties 2.(生活穷困) financial difficulties; straitened circumstances

【困难补助】 kùn·nan bǔzhù financial subsidies for the poor

【困扰】 kùnrǎo perplex; puzzle: 为…所～ be puzzled by

【困守】 kùnshǒu defend against a siege; stand a siege: ～一隅 be hemmed in a corner

kuo

扩[擴](kuò) expand; enlarge; extend

【扩充】 kuòchōng expand; strengthen; augment; enlarge; extend: ～设备 augment the equipment

【扩充接口】 kuòchōng jiēkǒu extended interface

【扩大】 kuòdà enlarge; expand; extend; broaden; widen: ～企业自主权 enhance the power of decision of enterprises / ～营业 extend one's business / ～再生产 expanded reproduction

【扩大化】 kuòdàhuà broaden the scope; magnify; magnification (n.)

【扩建】 kuòjiàn extend; expand; build on: 医院的这部分是后来～的。This part of the hospital was built on later.

【扩军】 kuòjūn arms expansion; armaments expansion

【扩权】 kuòquán extend power

【扩散】 kuòsàn spread; diffuse; proliferate: 核～ nuclear proliferation

【扩音机】 kuòyīnjī amplifier

【扩音器】 kuòyīnqì 1.(扬声器) loud-speaker 2.(话筒) microphone; megaphone

【扩印】 kuòyìn 〈*Photog.*〉 enlarge; enlargement (n.): ～照片 enlarge a photograph

【扩展】 kuòzhǎn expand; spread; extend; develop: 那座城市将～到河那里。That city will extend as far as to the river.

【扩张】 kuòzhāng 1.(扩大) expand; enlarge; extend; spread; aggrandize: 领土～ territorial expansion; territorial aggrandizement 2.〈*Med.*〉 dilate

括(kuò) 1.(扎;束) draw together; contract 2.(包括) include

【括号】 kuòhào brackets: 大～ braces / 方～ brackets / 圆～ parentheses

【括弧】 kuòhú parentheses

【括约肌】 kuòyuējī 〈*Anat.*〉 sphincter

蛞(kuò)

【蛞蝓】 kuòyú 〈*Zool.*〉 slug

阔[闊](kuò) 1.(宽广) wide; broad; vast 2.(有钱) rich; wealthy

【阔别】 kuòbié have not seen each other for a long time

【阔步】 kuòbù take big strides; make great strides: ～前进 advance in giant strides; stride forward

【阔绰】 kuòchuò ostentatious; liberal with money

【阔老】 kuòlǎo rich man

【阔气】 kuò·qi luxurious; extravagant; lavish; showily rich: 摆～ display one's wealth

【阔人】 kuòrén rich man

L

la

垃(lā)

【垃圾】 lājī garbage; trash; rubbish; refuse (matter): 倒～ put the rubbish out

【垃圾车】 lājīchē garbage truck; dust-cart; dustbin lorry

【垃圾处理】 lājī chǔlǐ garbage disposal

【垃圾袋】 lājīdài garbage bag; dustbin bag; litter bag; rubbish bag

【垃圾堆】 lājīduī garbage heap; rubbish heap; refuse dump

【垃圾焚化炉】 lājī fénhuàlú destructor; incinerator

【垃圾箱】 lājīxiāng garbage can; dustbin; ash can

拉(lā) 1.(牵引,拽) pull; draw; tug; drag: ～车 pull a cart 2.(用车运输) transport by vehicle; haul: 去～肥料 haul back the fertilizer 3.(带领军队转移) move troops to a place 4.(牵累) drag in; implicate: 这事与他无关,不要～上他。He has nothing to do with it, don't drag him into trouble. 5.(拉拢;联络) draw in; win over; canvass 6.(演奏) play: ～小提琴 play the violin 7.(拖长) drag out; draw out; space out: ～长声音说话 drawl 8.(帮助) give a helping hand; help: 我们应当～他一把。We should help him out. 9.(排泄) empty the bowels 10. 〈*dial*.〉(闲谈) chat: ～家常 have a chat (另见"拉"lá)

【拉扯】 lā·che 1.(拉) drag; pull 2.(抚养) take great pains to bring up 3.(牵涉;牵扯) implicate; drag in 4.(闲谈) chat

【拉出去】 lāchūqù pull out; drag out

【拉倒】 lādǎo drop it; forget about it: 她不来就～。Since she won't come let's forget about it.

【拉丁字母】 lādīng zìmǔ the Latin alphabet

【拉肚子】 lā dù·zi suffer from diarrhea; have loose bowels

【拉关系】 lā guān·xi try to establish a relationship with sb.; cotton up to

【拉后腿】 lā hòutuǐ hold sb. back; be a drag on sb.

【拉祜族】 Lāhùzú Lahu (中国少数民族,主要分布在云南)

【拉交情】 lā jiāo·qing try to form ties with; cotton up to

【拉锯】 lājù 1.(拉大锯) work a two-handed saw 2.(来回往复的) be locked in a seesaw struggle

【拉锯战】 lājùzhàn seesaw match; seesaw battle

【拉开】 lākāi 1.(打开) pull open; draw back 2.(增加间隔距离) increase the distance between; space out: 合理～收入差距 widen differences personal income to a reasonable degree

【拉客】 lākè 1.(旅馆、餐馆招揽顾客) solicit guests; solicit diners 2.(出租汽车载运乘客) take on passengers 3.(妓女拉客) solicit

【拉拉扯扯】 lālā-chěchě 1.(动手动脚) pull sb. about; drag sb. about: 别～的! Take your hands off me! 2.(拉拢吹拍) exchange flattery and favors

【拉拉队】 lālāduì cheering squad; rooters

【拉链】 lāliàn zipper; zip-fastener: 拉上衣服的～ zip up one's dress

【拉拢】 lā·lǒng draw sb. over to one's side; rope in

【拉买卖】 lā mǎi·mai act as a broker; solicit business

【拉美】 Lāměi Latin America; Latin American (adj.)

【拉皮条】 lāpítiáo act as a procurer; act as a pimp

【拉平】 lāpíng bring to the same level; even

up：把比分～ even the score up

【拉纤】 lāqiàn 1.（用纤绳拉船）tow a boat 2.（充当中间人）act as go-between

【拉萨】 Lāsà 〈place〉 Lhasa

【拉生意】 lā shēngyì 1.（促成交易）solicit trade; canvass trade 2.（为…招徕顾客）tout for：为旅馆～ tout for hotels

【拉屎】 lāshǐ empty the bowels; shit

【拉手】 lāshǒu （握手）shake hands

【拉手】 lā·shou （把手）handle：门～ door-knob

【拉锁儿】 lāsuǒr zipper; zip-fastener

【拉稀】 lāxī have loose bowels; have diarrhea

【拉下脸】 lāxià liǎn 1.（不高兴）pull a long face; look displeased; put on a stern expression 2.（打破情面）not spare sb's sensibilities

【拉下水】 lāxià shuǐ drag sb. into the mire; make an accomplice of sb.; corrupt sb.

【拉线】 lāxiàn bracing wire; span wire

【拉选票】 lā xuǎnpiào canvass votes for sb.

【拉主顾】 lā zhǔgù attract customers; solicit customers

邋 (lā)

【邋遢】 lā·tā 〈*colloq.*〉 slovenly; sloppy

拉[剌] (lá)

（割）slash; slit; cut; make a gash in：～成小块 cut it into pieces

（另见“拉”lā）

喇 (lǎ)

【喇叭】 lǎ·ba 1.（唢呐）*suona*, a woodwind instrument 2.（管乐器）brass-wind instruments in general：吹～ blow a trumpet 3.（扬声器）speaker; loudspeaker 4.〈*Auto*〉 horn

【喇叭花】 lǎ·bahuā （牵牛）morning glory

【喇叭口】 lǎ·bakǒu bell (of a wind instrument)

【喇叭裤】 lǎ·bakù flared trousers; bell-bottoms

【喇叭筒】 lǎ·batǒng megaphone

【喇嘛】 lǎ·ma 〈*Relig.*〉 lama

【喇嘛教】 Lǎ·majiào Lamaism

【喇嘛教徒】 lǎ·ma jiàotú lamaist; lamaite

【喇嘛庙】 lǎ·mamiào lamasery

辣 (là)

1.（辣味）hot; peppery; pungent：闻到一股～味 notice a pungent smell 2.（狠毒）vicious; ruthless

【辣根】 làgēn 〈*Bot.*〉 horse-radish

【辣酱】 làjiàng thick chili sauce

【辣酱油】 làjiàngyóu pungent sauce

【辣椒】 làjiāo red pepper; chili hot pepper

【辣椒粉】 làjiāofěn chili powder

【辣椒油】 làjiāoyóu chili oil

【辣手】 làshǒu 1.（毒辣的手段）ruthless method; vicious device 2.（手段毒辣）vicious; ruthless 3.（棘手；难办）troublesome; thorny; knotty

【辣子】 là·zi red pepper; cayenne pepper; chili

落 (là)

1.（遗漏）leave out; be missing：～了几个字。A few words are left out. 2.（遗忘）leave behind; forget to bring：把书～在家里 leave one's book at home 3.（跟不上）lag behind; fall behind; drop behind：～了一周的课 miss a week's lessons

（另见“落”lào, luò）

腊[臘、臈] (là)

【腊肠】 làcháng sausage

【腊梅】 làméi 〈*Bot.*〉 wintersweet

【腊肉】 làròu cured meat; bacon

蜡[蠟] (là)

1.（石蜡等）wax：给地板打～ wax the floor 2.（蜡烛）candle：点～ light a candle

【蜡黄】 làhuáng wax yellow; waxen; sallow：面色～ a waxen complexion

【蜡染】 làrǎn 〈*Textiles*〉 wax printing

【蜡染壁画】 làrǎn bìhuà wax printing hanger

【蜡染服饰】 làrǎn fúshì wax-printing costumes and ornaments

【蜡人】 làrén waxwork

【蜡人馆】 làrénguǎn waxworks

【蜡丸】 làwán wax-wrapped pill

【蜡像】 làxiàng waxen image; waxen statue

【蜡像馆】 làxiàngguǎn waxworks

【蜡纸】 làzhǐ 1.（包装用）wax paper 2.（油印用）stencil paper; stencil

【蜡烛】 làzhú candle

lai

来[來] (lái)

1.（来到）come; arrive：她～了吗？Has she come yet? /

邮件每天什么时候～? What time does the mail usually arrive? **2**.(发生) crop up; take place **3**.(代替意义更具体的动词) 我自己～吧。Let me do it myself. (指做事) Let me do it myself. / (指吃东西) I'll help myself. **4**.(跟"得"或"不"连用) 他答不上～。He couldn't come up with an answer. / 车进得～么? Can the car get in? **5**.(表示要做某事) 大家～想个办法。Let's pool out ideas and see what to do. **6**.(表示来做某事)他回学校看望大家～了。He's come back to the college to see us folks. **7**.(表示目的)怎么～帮助他呢? How are you going to help him? **8**.(未来的) future; coming; next: ～年 the coming year; next year **9**.(以来) ever since: 十几年～ for the last ten years and more **10**.(表示概数) about; around: 三十～岁 about thirty (years old)

【来宾】 láibīn guest; visitor

【来宾席】 láibīnxí seats for guests

【来不及】 lái·bu jí there's not enough time (to do sth.); it's too late

【来到】 láidào arrive; come

【来得及】 lái·de jí there's still time; be able to do sth. in time; be able to make it: 你赶末班车还～。You'll be in time for the last bus.

【来电】 láidiàn **1**.(发来的电报) incoming telegram; your telegram; your message: ～收到。Your telegram received. **2**.(发电报来) send a telegram here

【来犯】 láifàn come to attack us; invade our territory

【来访】 láifǎng come to visit; come to call

【来复枪】 láifùqiāng rifle

【来复线】 láifùxiàn rifling

【来稿】 láigǎo incoming manuscripts; a contribution received by an editor

【来鸿】 láihóng incoming letter

【来回】 láihuí **1**.(往复一次) make a round trip; make a return journey; go to a place and come back: 打～儿 make a round trip **2**.(往复多次) back and forth; to and fro: ～摇摆 oscillate; vacillate

【来回票】 láihuípiào a return ticket

【来件】 láijiàn letter received; parcel received

【来件装配】 láijiàn zhuāngpèi assemble with parts supplied by foreign firms

【来劲】 láijìn **1**.(有劲头) full of enthusiasm; in high spirits: 她越干越～。The longer she worked at it, the more enthusiastic she became. **2**.(使烦恼) jest with; annoy; offend **3**.(有意思) exciting; thrilling: 这么大的宴会! 可真～! What a grand party! How thrilling!

【来客】 láikè guest; visitor

【来来往往】 láilái-wǎngwǎng coming and going in great number

【来历】 láilì origin; source; antecedents; background; past history: ～不明 of unknown origin (指事物); of dubious background (指人)

【来料加工】 láiliào jiāgōng process raw materials supplied by foreign firms; processing on order; processing raw materials on client's demands

【来临】 láilín arrive; come; approach

【来龙去脉】 láilóng-qùmài origin and development; cause and effect

【来路】 láilù (向这里来的路) incoming road; approach

【来路】 láilu (来历) origin; antecedents: (某人)～不正 of dubious background / (某物)～不正 of questionable origin

【来年】 láinián the coming year; next year

【来去】 láiqù come and go back

【…来…去】 …lái…qù (表示动作的不断反复) back and forth; over and over again: 考虑～考虑～ turn sth. over and over again in one's mind / 挑～挑～ pick and choose

【来去自由】 láiqù zìyóu come and go freely

【来人】 láirén bearer; messenger: 请将回执交～带回。Please give your receipt to the messenger to take back.

【来日方长】 láirì-fāngcháng there will be ample time; there is a long time ahead

【来生】 láishēng next life

【来势】 láishì the force with which sth. breaks out; oncoming force

【来头】 lái·tou **1**.(背景) connections; background; backing **2**.(来由) the motive behind cause: 他说这些话是有～的。He didn't say these words without a motive.

【来往】 lái·wang **1.**（来和去）come and go **2.**（交际往来）dealings; contact; intercourse: 促进商业～ promote commercial intercourse

【来文】 láiwén document received

【来信】 láixìn **1.**（寄信来）send a letter here **2.**（寄来的信）incoming letter

【来意】 láiyì one's purpose in coming

【来由】 láiyóu reason; cause

【来源】 láiyuán **1.**（所出自的地方）source; origin: 经济～ source of income **2.**（起源）originate; stem from

【来者不拒】 láizhě-bùjù refuse nobody; refuse nobody's request or offer

【来之不易】 láizhī-bùyì it has not come easily; hard-earned

莱［萊］(lái)

【莱菔】 láifú （萝卜）radish

【莱塞】 láisè **1.**（激光）laser **2.**（激光器）laser

铼［錸］(lái) 〈*Chem.*〉rhenium（元素符号 Re）

赖(lài) **1.**（依靠）rely; depend **2.**（赖着不走）hang on in a place; drag out one's stay in a place; hold on to a place **3.**（抵赖）deny one's error or responsibility; go back on one's word **4.**（诬赖）blame sb. wrongly; put the blame on sb. else **5.**（责怪）blame **6.**（不好）not good, poor

【赖氨酸】 làiānsuān 〈*Biochem.*〉lysine

【赖皮】 làipí rascally; shameless; unreasonable

【赖账】 làizhàng **1.**（赖债）repudiate a debt **2.**（食言）go back on one's word

【赖子】 lài·zi rascal; scoundrel; villain

癞(lài) **1.**（麻风）leprosy **2.**（黄癣）favus of the scalp

【癞蛤蟆】 làihá·ma toad

【癞皮狗】 làipígǒu **1.**（患疥癣的狗）mangy dog **2.**（讨厌的人）loathsome creature

lan

兰［蘭］(lán) **1.**（兰）cymbidium **2.**（红门兰）orchid

【兰草】 láncǎo fragrant thoroughwort

【兰花】 lánhuā **1.**（春兰）cymbidium; goering cymbidium **2.**（建兰）swordleaf cymbidium

拦［攔］(lán) bar; block; hold back: ～住去路 bar the way / ～一辆车 stop a car

【拦挡】 lándǎng block; obstruct

【拦河坝】 lánhébà a dam across a river; dam

【拦洪坝】 lánhóngbà regulating dam; flood-control dam

【拦击】 lánjī intercept and attack

【拦劫】 lánjié intercept and rob

【拦截】 lánjié intercept: ～敌机 intercept an enemy plane

【拦路】 lánlù block the way: ～抢劫 waylay; hold up

【拦路虎】 lánlùhǔ obstacle; stumbling block

【拦网】 lánwǎng 〈*Volleyball*〉block

【拦腰】 lányāo by the waist; round the middle

【拦住】 lánzhù hold up; keep away

【拦阻】 lánzǔ block; hold back; obstruct

栏［欄］(lán) **1.**（栏杆）fence; railing; balustrade; hurdle **2.**（畜圈）pen; shed: 羊～ sheep pen; sheepfold **3.**〈*Printing*〉column

【栏杆】 lán'gān railing; banisters; balustrade

【栏目】 lánmù column

阑(lán) **1.**（将尽）late **2.**（栏杆）railing; balustrade

【阑珊】 lánshān 〈*written*〉coming to an end; waning

【阑尾】 lánwěi 〈*Anat.*〉appendix: 他的～已切除了。He had his appendix out.

【阑尾穿孔】 lánwěi chuānkǒng 〈*Med.*〉appendicular perforation

【阑尾切除术】 lánwěi jiēchúshù 〈*Med.*〉appendectomy

【阑尾炎】 lánwěiyán 〈*Med.*〉appendicitis

谰(lán) calumniate; slander

【谰言】 lányán calumny; slander: 无耻～ a shameless slander

镧(lán) 〈*Chem.*〉lanthanum（元素符号 La）

蓝［藍］(lán) **1.**（蓝色）blue: 穿一身～ be dressed in blue **2.**（蓼蓝）indigo plant

【蓝宝石】 lánbǎoshí sapphire

【蓝本】 lánběn 1.（主要原始资料）writing upon which later work is based; chief source 2.（指底本）original version（of a literary work）

【蓝布】 lánbù blue cloth

【蓝黑】 lánhēi blue-black

【蓝鲸】 lánjīng 〈*Zool.*〉blue whale

【蓝盔部队】 lánkuī bùduì blue helmet

【蓝领】 lánlǐng blue-collar worker

【蓝领工人】 lánlǐng gōngrén blue-collar worker

【蓝皮书】 lánpíshū blue book

【蓝铅笔】 lánqiānbǐ blue-pencil

【蓝色】 lánsè blue

【蓝图】 lántú blueprint

褴［襤］（lán）

【褴褛】 lánlǚ ragged; shabby: 衣衫～ be dressed in rags; shabbily dressed; out at elbows

篮［籃］（lán） 1.（篮子）basket: 提～ hand basket; hamper / 网～ net-covered basket 2.（篮球球篮）goal; basket: 补～ tap in; rebound shot; tip-in; follow-up shot / 扣～ dunk shot / 上～ lay up / 投～ shoot a basket; shoot; shooting

【篮板】 lánbǎn 〈*Basketball*〉backboard; bank

【篮板球】 lánbǎnqiú 〈*Basketball*〉rebound: 抢～ back-board recovery

【篮架】 lánjià 〈*Basketball*〉basket support

【篮筐】 lánkuāng 〈*Basketball*〉basket

【篮球】 lánqiú 1.〈*Sports*〉basketball: 打～ play basketball 2.（指球）basketball

【篮球场】 lánqiúchǎng basketball court

【篮球队】 lánqiúduì basketball team; quintet

【篮球队员】 lánqiú duìyuán basketball player; basketballer

【篮球赛】 lánqiúsài basketball match

【篮圈】 lánquān 〈*Basketball*〉ring

【篮坛】 lántán the basketball circles

【篮子】 lán·zi basket

览［覽］（lǎn） 1.（看）look at; see; view 2.（阅读）read

揽［攬］（lǎn） 1.（用胳膊围住）pull sb. into one's arms; take into one's arms: 把孩子～在怀里 clasp the child to one's bosom 2.（拢住）fasten with a rope 3.（拉到自己方面）take on; take upon oneself; canvass: ～买卖 canvass business orders 4.（把持）grasp; monopolize

缆［纜］（lǎn） 1.（缆绳）hawser; mooring rope; cable 2.（钢缆等）thick rope; cable: 钢～ steel cable

【缆车】 lǎnchē cable car

【缆道】 lǎndào cableway

【缆绳】 lǎnshéng hawser

【缆索】 lǎnsuǒ thick rope; cable

【缆索铁道】 lǎnsuǒ tiědào funicular（railway）

懒［嬾］（lǎn） 1.（懒惰）lazy; indolent; slothful 2.（没力气 sluggish; languid

【懒惰】 lǎnduò lazy; have laziness

【懒汉】 lǎnhàn sluggard; idler; lazybones

【懒汉鞋】 lǎnhànxié loafer

【懒散】 lǎnsǎn sluggish; negligent; indolent

【懒洋洋】 lǎnyāngyāng languid; listless

【懒于】 lǎnyú too lazy to do sth.; not enthusiastic about sth.

烂［爛］（làn） 1.（松软）sodden; mashed; pappy: 雨后地上都是～泥。The ground was sodden after the rain. 2.（腐烂）rot; spoil; fester; decay; putrefy 3.（破烂）worn-out 4.（头绪乱）messy

【烂漫】 lànmàn 1.（鲜明美丽）bright-colored; brilliant 2.（坦率自然）unaffected

【烂泥】 lànní mud; slush

【烂泥塘】 lànnítáng a muddy pond

【烂熟】 lànshú 1.（肉菜十分熟）thoroughly cooked 2.（十分熟悉）know sth. thoroughly: 课文背得～ learn one's text thoroughly

【烂摊子】 làntān·zi a shambles; an awful mess

【烂醉】 lànzuì be dead drunk

滥［濫］（làn） 1.（泛滥）overflow; flood 2.（过度）excessive; indiscriminate: ～收费 charge excessively

【滥调】 làndiào hackneyed tune; worn-out theme

【滥发钞票】 lànfā chāopiào issue banknotes excessively

【滥发奖金】 lànfā jiǎngjīn distribute bonuses

indiscriminately

【滥伐】 lànfá 〈*Forestry*〉 denudation; deforestation

【滥用】 lànyòng abuse; misuse; use indiscriminately: ～公款 irregularities in use of public funds / ～职权 abuse one's power; misuse one's authority

【滥竽充数】 lànyú-chōngshù pass oneself off as one of the players in an ensemble; be there just to make up the number

lang

廊 (láng) porch; corridor; veranda: 长～ the Long Corridor (in the Summer Palace, Beijing) / 画～ picture gallery

【廊子】 láng·zi veranda; corridor

狼 (láng) 1.〈*Zool.*〉 wolf: 幼～ wolfkin / 喊"～来了" cry wolf 2.(指某种人)色～ wolf / 披着羊皮的～ a wolf in sheep's clothing

【狼狈】 lángbèi in a tight corner; in a difficult position

【狼狈为奸】 lángbèi-wéijiān act in collusion with each other

【狼疮】 lángchuāng 〈*Med.*〉 lupus

【狼狗】 lánggǒu wolf dog

【狼孩】 lánghái wolf child

【狼藉】 lángjí in disorder; scattered about in a mess: 声名～ be notorious; be discredited

【狼群】 lángqún wolf pack

【狼吞虎咽】 lángtūn-hǔyàn wolf down; gobble up; devour ravenously

【狼心狗肺】 lángxīn-gǒufèi 1.(心肠狠毒) rapacious as a wolf and savage as a cur; cruel and unscrupulous; brutal and cold-blooded 2.(忘恩负义) ungrateful

【狼子野心】 lángzǐ-yěxīn wolfish ambition; wicked intention

锒 (láng)

【锒铛】 lángdāng 1.(铁锁链) iron chains: ～入狱 be chained and thrown into prison 2.(金属撞击声) chank; clang

朗 (lǎng) 1.(明亮) light; bright 2.(响亮) loud and clear

【朗读】 lǎngdú read aloud; read loudly and clearly

【朗朗】 lǎnglǎng 1.(读书声) the sound of reading aloud 2.(明亮) bright; light

【朗诵】 lǎngsòng recite; deliver a recitation

浪 (làng) 1.(波浪) wave; breaker; ripple: 大～ rough sea / 巨～ very rough sea 2.(放纵) unrestrained; dissolute

【浪潮】 làngcháo tide; wave: 抗议～ a wave of protest

【浪荡】 làngdàng 1.(游荡) loiter about; loaf about 2.(不检点) dissolute; dissipated

【浪费】 làngfèi waste; squander; be extravagant: ～时间 waste one's time / 有些企业～惊人。The waste in some enterprises is appalling.

【浪花】 lànghuā spray; spindrift

【浪迹天涯】 làngjì-tiānyá roam freely all over the world

【浪漫】 làngmàn romantic

【浪漫主义】 làngmàn zhǔyì romanticism

【浪头】 làng·tou 1.(波浪) wave 2.(潮流) trend

【浪子】 làngzǐ prodigal; loafer; wastrel: ～回头 return of the prodigal son

【浪子回头金不换】 làngzǐ huítóu jīn·bùhuàn A prodigal who returns is more precious than gold.

lao

捞[撈] (lāo) 1.(打捞) drag for; dredge up; fish for; scoop up from the water 2.(攫取) get by improper means; gain 3.(得到机会) get the opportunity

【捞稻草】 lāo dàocǎo 1.(捞好处) take advantage of sth. 2.(做无益的挣扎) clutch at a straw

【捞面】 lāomiàn drain the pasta

【捞取】 lāoqǔ fish for; gain: ～资本 make capital out of / ～政治资本 fish for political advantage

【捞网】 lāowǎng scoop net

【捞一把】 lāo yībǎ reap some profit; profiteer

劳[勞] (láo) 1.(劳动) work; labor 2.(烦劳) put sb. to the trouble of

3.(劳苦) fatigue; toil: 积～成疾 break down from constant overwork 4.(功劳) meritorious deed; distinction; service 5.(慰劳) express one's appreciation reward

【劳保】 láobǎo 1.(劳动保险) labor insurance 2.(劳动保护) labor protection

【劳保条例】 láobǎo tiáolì labor insurance regulations

【劳保用品】 láobǎo yòngpǐn appliances for labor protection

【劳动】 láodòng 1.(指人类的活动) work; labor: ～创造世界。Labor creates the world. 2.(体力劳动) physical labor; manual labor: 参加体力～ take part in manual labor

【劳动保护】 láodòng bǎohù labor protection

【劳动保险】 láodòng bǎoxiǎn labor insurance

【劳动报酬】 láodòng bàochóu payment for labor

【劳动服务公司】 láodòng fúwù gōngsī labor service company; company providing labor services

【劳动改造】 láodòng gǎizào reform through labor

【劳动观点】 láodòng guāndiǎn attitude to labor

【劳动合同制】 láodòng hétong·zhì labor contract system

【劳动纪律】 láodòng jìlǜ labor discipline

【劳动节】 Láodòngjié International Labor Day

【劳动力】 láodònglì 1.(人力) labor force; labor 2.(劳动能力) capacity for physical labor: 丧失～ lose one's ability to labor 3.(有劳动力的人) able-bodied person; manpower: 缺乏～ lack of manpower

【劳动密集】 láodòng mìjí labor intensive

【劳动密集型产业】 láodòng mìjíxíng chǎnyè labor-intensive production

【劳动强度】 láodòng qiángdù labor intensity

【劳动群众】 láodòng qúnzhòng working people; laboring masses

【劳动人民】 láodòng rénmín laboring people; working people

【劳动日】 láodòngrì workday; working day

【劳动生产率】 láodòng shēngchǎnlǜ labor productivity

【劳动收入】 láodòng shōurù income from work

【劳动态度】 láodòng tàidù attitude towards labor

【劳动效率】 láodòng xiàolǜ labor efficiency

【劳动用工制度】 láodòng yònggōng zhìdù the employment

【劳动者】 láodòngzhě laborer; worker

【劳方】 láofāng labor: ～与资方 labor and capital

【劳改】 láogǎi reform through labor

【劳改产品】 láogǎi chǎnpǐn products made by prison labor

【劳改队】 láogǎiduì group sentenced to reform through labor

【劳改犯】 láogǎifàn prisoner sentenced to reform through labor

【劳改农场】 láogǎi nóngchǎng reform through labor farm

【劳工】 láogōng laborer; worker

【劳驾】 láojià 1.(请求让路) Excuse me. 2.(请求别人做事) May I trouble you?

【劳教】 láojiào reeducation through labor

【劳教所】 láojiàosuǒ house of reeducation through labor

【劳苦】 láokǔ toil; hard work

【劳苦大众】 láokǔ dàzhòng toiling masses; working people

【劳苦功高】 láokǔ gōnggāo have worked hard and achieved great things

【劳累】 láolèi tired; run-down; overworked: ～过度 be overworked

【劳力】 láolì 1.(人力) labor force; labor 2.(有劳动力的人) able-bodied person; manpower: 缺乏～ lack of manpower 3.(从事体力劳动) labor or work with one's strength

【劳碌】 láolù work hard; toil

【劳民伤财】 láomín-shāngcái tire the people and drain the treasury; waste money and manpower

【劳模】 láomó model worker

【劳神】 láoshén be a tax on (one's mind); bother; trouble

【劳损】 láosǔn 〈*Med.*〉 strain

【劳务】 láowù services; labor services

【劳务出口】 láowù chūkǒu export of labor services

【劳务范围】 láowù fànwéi range of service

【劳务费】 láowùfèi cost of service

【劳务合同】 láowù hé·tong contract of service
【劳务市场】 láowù shìchǎng service market
【劳务输出】 láowù shūchū export of labor services
【劳心】 láoxīn work with one's mind or brains
【劳逸】 láoyì labor and rest
【劳逸结合】 láoyì jiéhé alternate work with rest and recreation
【劳资】 láozī labor and capital：～两利 benefit both labor and capital
【劳资关系】 láozī guānxì relations between labor and capital
【劳资纠纷】 láozī jiūfēng trouble between labor and management
【劳资协议】 láozī xiéyì labor agreement
【劳资争议】 láozī zhēngyì labor dispute

铹［鐒］（láo）〈*Chem.*〉lawrencium（人造元素，符号 Lr）

痨［癆］（láo）〈*Med.*〉tuberculosis：肺～ pulmonary tuberculosis
【痨病】 láobìng tuberculosis；consumptive disease

牢（láo） **1.**（监牢）jail；prison：坐～ be in prison **2.**（牢固）firm：～～记住 firmly bear in mind
【牢不可破】 láobùkěpò unbreakable；indestructible
【牢房】 láofáng cell；ward：单人～ single cell
【牢固】 láogù firm；secure：～的基础 solid foundation
【牢记】 láojì keep firmly in mind；remember well：～在心 keep sth. in one's mind
【牢靠】 láo·kao **1.**（牢固；稳固）firm；strong；sturdy **2.**（稳妥可靠）dependable；reliable
【牢笼】 láolóng **1.**（鸟兽笼）cage **2.**（束缚）bonds **3.**（圈套）trap；snare
【牢骚】 láo·sāo **1.**（牢骚话）discontent；grumbles；complaint：听到关于饭食的～ hear grumbles about food **2.**（发牢骚）grumble；complaint
【牢狱】 láoyù prison；jail

唠［嘮］（láo）
【唠叨】 lǎo·dao chatter；be garrulous

老（lǎo） **1.**（年岁大）old；aged **2.**（老年人）old people：扶～携幼 bring along the old and the young **3.**（历史久）of long standing；old：～朋友 an old friend **4.**（陈旧）outdated：～机器 outmoded machine / ～习惯 outdated customs **5.**（火候大）overdone；tough **6.**（蔬菜长过了时）overgrown **7.**（颜色深）dark **8.**（经常）always；constantly：她～是在家里。She always stays at home. **9.**（很）very **10.**（排行最末的）the youngest：～姑娘 the youngest daughter
【老百姓】 lǎobǎixìng common people；ordinary people；civilians
【老板】 lǎobǎn boss；proprietor；shopkeeper
【老板娘】 lǎobǎnniáng shopkeeper's wife；proprietress
【老伴儿】 lǎobànr husband；wife
【老本】 lǎoběn principal；capital
【老兵】 lǎobīng old soldier；veteran
【老伯】 lǎobó uncle
【老成】 lǎochéng experienced；steady：少年～ be young but mature
【老处女】 lǎochùnǚ old maid
【老粗】 lǎocū uneducated person；rough and ready chap
【老大】 lǎodà **1.**（排行第一）eldest child **2.**（木船上的船夫）master of a sailing vessel **3.**（很）greatly；very
【老大娘】 lǎodà·niáng〈*respects*〉aunty；granny
【老大爷】 lǎodà·yé〈*respects*〉uncle；grandpa
【老当益壮】 lǎodāngyìzhuàng old but vigorous
【老弟】 lǎodì young man；young fellow；my boy
【老掉牙】 lǎodiàoyá old：～的故事 the same old story
【老调】 lǎodiào hackneyed theme；platitude
【老夫老妻】 lǎofū-lǎoqī an old couple
【老干部】 lǎogànbù veteran cadre
【老革命】 lǎogémìng veteran revolutionary
【老古董】 lǎogǔdǒng **1.**（指物）antique；old-fashioned article **2.**（指人）old fogey
【老汉】 lǎohàn **1.**（老年男人）old man **2.**（自称）an old fellow like me
【老好人】 lǎohǎorén a benign and uncontentious person who is indifferent to matters

of principle; one who tries never to offend anybody

【老狐狸】 lǎohú·li 1.(老的狐狸) old fox 2.(非常狡猾的人) crafty scoundrel

【老虎】 lǎohǔ 1.(虎) tiger; tigress (f.) 2.(能源或材料消耗大户) a big consumer: 电～ electric tiger; a big power-consumer 3.(喻凶恶的人) tiger; tigress (f.): 她简直是个母～。She is a real tigress.

【老花镜】 lǎohuājìng presbyopic glasses

【老化】 lǎohuà 1.〈*Chem*.〉 aging; ageing 2.(老年人的比重增大) aging; ageing; become old: 人口～ aging of population 3.(知识等陈旧) become outdated: 产品～ products old-fashioned

【老话】 lǎohuà 1.(流传已久的话) old saying 2.(过去的事) remarks about past events: ～重提 mention again the remarks about a past event

【老家】 lǎojiā 1.(故乡) native place; old home; hometown: 回～ go back to one's hometown 2.(原籍) birthplace

【老奸巨猾】 lǎojiān-jùhuá a past master of machination and maneuver; a wily old fox

【老茧】 lǎojiǎn callosity; callus

【老将】 lǎojiàng veteran; old-timer

【老交情】 lǎojiāo·qing long-standing friendship; an old friend

【老老实实】 lǎolǎo-shíshí honestly; conscientiously; in earnest

【老练】 lǎoliàn seasoned; experienced

【老龄】 lǎolíng the aged; people of old age

【老路】 lǎolù old road; beaten track

【老迈】 lǎomài aged; senile

【老年】 lǎonián old age

【老年斑】 lǎoniánbān senile plaque

【老年人】 lǎoniánrén old people; the aged

【老年性痴呆】 lǎoniánxìng chīdāi senile dementia

【老年医学】 lǎonián yīxué gerontology

【老农】 lǎonóng 1.(泛指农民) farmer; peasant 2.(年老有经验的农民) old farmer; experienced peasant

【老牌】 lǎopái old brand

【老朋友】 lǎopéngyǒu old friend

【老气横秋】 lǎoqì-héngqiū 1.(摆老资格) arrogant on account of one's seniority 2.(没有朝气) lacking in youthful vigor

【老前辈】 lǎoqiánbèi one's senior; one's elder

【老区】 lǎoqū old liberated area

【老人】 lǎo·rén 1.(老年人) old man or woman; the aged; the old 2.(上了年纪的父母) one's aged parents 2.(上了年纪的祖父母) one's aged grandparents

【老人家】 lǎo·ren·jia grand old man

【老人星】 Lǎorénxīng 〈*Astron*.〉 Canopus (船底座 α)

【老弱】 lǎoruò the old and weak

【老弱病残】 lǎoruò-bìngcán the old, weak, sick and disabled

【老生常谈】 lǎoshēng-chángtán commonplace; platitude

【老师】 lǎoshī teacher

【老师傅】 lǎoshī·fu 〈*respects*〉 master craftsman; experienced worker

【老实】 lǎo·shi 1.(诚实) honest; frank 2.(规矩) well-behaved; good: 你～点! Behave yourself! 3.(不聪明) simpleminded; naive; easily taken in

【老式】 lǎoshì old-fashioned; outmoded: ～服装 outmoded clothes

【老手】 lǎoshǒu old hand; old stager; veteran

【老鼠】 lǎoshǔ mouse; rat

【老帅】 lǎoshuài old marshal; veteran marshal

【老太婆】 lǎotàipó old lady; old woman

【老太太】 lǎotài·tai 1.(年老的妇女) old lady 2.(对人称自己的母亲) my mother 3.(尊称对方的母亲) your mother

【老太爷】 lǎotàiyé 1.(年老的男子) elderly gentleman 2.(对人称自己的父亲) my father 3.(尊称对方的父亲) your father

【老天爷】 lǎotiānyé God; Heavens

【老头子】 lǎotóu·zi old man

【老外】 lǎowài 1.(外行) layman; non-professional 2.(外国人) foreigner; nonlocal

【老乡】 lǎoxiāng fellow-townsman; fellow-villager

【老小】 lǎoxiǎo grown-ups and children; one's family

【老兄】 lǎoxiōng brother; man; old chap

【老羞成怒】 lǎoxiū-chéngnù fly into a rage

out of shame; be shamed into anger
【老朽】 lǎoxiǔ decrepit and behind the times; old and useless: ～昏庸 old, worthless, dull and mean
【老眼光】 lǎoyǎnguāng old ways of looking at things; old views
【老眼昏花】 lǎoyǎn-hūnhuā can't see clearly; dim-sighted from old age
【老爷】 lǎo·ye 1.(官僚) master; bureaucrat; lord: 做官当～ act as lords and masters 2.(外祖父) grandfather; grandpa
【老爷兵】 lǎoyébīng pampered soldier
【老爷们】 lǎoyémen man
【老爷爷】 lǎoyé·ye 1.(曾祖父) great grandfather 2.(小孩尊称年老的男子) grandpa
【老爷子】 lǎoyé·zi 1.(年老的男子) elderly gentleman 2.(对人称自己的父亲) my father 3.(尊称对方的父亲) your father
【老一辈】 lǎoyībèi older generation: ～无产阶级革命家 proletarian revolutionaries of the older generation; veteran proletarian revolutionaries
【老一套】 lǎoyītào the same old stuff; the same old story
【老鹰】 lǎoyīng black-eared kite; hawk; eagle
【老玉米】 lǎoyù·mi corn
【老丈人】 lǎozhàngrén a man's father-in-law
【老账】 lǎozhàng 1.(旧账) old debts; long-standing debts 2.(喻很久的事) a past event
【老主顾】 lǎozhǔgù regular customer
【老资格】 lǎozīgé old-timer; veteran
【老子】 lǎo·zi 1.(父亲) father 2.(自称) I; myself
【老祖宗】 lǎozǔzōng ancestor; forefather

佬 (lǎo) 〈*derog.*〉 man; guy; fellow: 阔～ a rich guy / 美国～ Yankee

姥 (lǎo)

【姥姥】 lǎo·lao grandmother; grandma
【姥爷】 lǎo·ye grandfather; grandpa

铑 (lǎo) 〈*Chem.*〉 rhodium (元素符号 Rh)

烙 (lào) 1.(烫;熨) brand; iron 2.(烤熟) bake in a pan: ～两张饼 bake a couple of cakes

【烙饼】 làobǐng a kind of pancake
【烙铁】 lào·tie 1.(烫衣服的) flatiron; iron 2.(焊接的) soldering iron
【烙印】 làoyìn 1.(不易磨灭的痕迹) brand 2.(烫成痕迹) make brands (on animals with a hot iron)

落 (lào) (另见"落"là, luò)

【落价】 làojià a fall in price: 电视～了。The price of TV has gone down.
【落色】 làoshǎi discolor; fade
【落枕】 làozhěn have a stiff neck

酪 (lào) 1.(奶酪) junket 2.(果酱) fruit jelly 3.(干酪) cheese 4.(干果酪) sweet paste made from crushed nuts; sweet nut paste

涝[澇] (lào) waterlogging: 防～ prevent waterlogging / 排～ drain waterlogged areas

【涝灾】 làozāi damage or crop failure caused by waterlogging

le

勒 (lè) 1.(勒住缰绳) rein in: ～马 rein in a horse 2.(强制;逼迫) force; coerce (另见"勒"lēi)

【勒逼】 lèbī force; coerce
【勒克斯】 lèkèsī 〈*Physics*〉 lux
【勒令】 lèlìng compel (by legal authority); order: ～停业 be closed down by order
【勒索】 lèsuǒ extort; blackmail: 向老妇人～钱财 extort money from the old lady
【勒诈】 lèzhà extort; blackmail: 他们企图向我～钱财。They tried to blackmail me into giving them the money.

乐[樂] (lè) 1.(快乐) happy; cheerful; joyful: ～得跳起来 jump with delight 2.(乐于) be glad to; find pleasure in; enjoy 3.(笑) laugh; be amused (另见"乐"yuè)

【乐不可支】 lèbùkězhī overwhelmed with joy; be beside oneself with happiness
【乐此不疲】 lècǐbùpí always enjoy it; never be bored with it
【乐而忘返】 lè'ěrwàngfǎn be a slave of pleasure
【乐观】 lèguān optimistic; hopeful; sanguine

【乐观主义】 lèguān zhǔyì optimism ‖ 乐观主义者 **optimist**

【乐极生悲】 lèjí-shēngbēi extreme joy begets sorrow

【乐趣】 lèqù delight; pleasure; joy: 生活～ joys of life

【乐事】 lèshì pleasure; delight: 以助人为～ find pleasure in helping others

【乐天】 lètiān carefree; happy-go-luck

【乐天派】 lètiānpài an easy going person

【乐土】 lètǔ land of happiness; paradise

【乐意】 lèyì 1.(甘心愿意) be willing to; be ready to 2.(满意;高兴) pleased; happy: 心里～ feel happy / 心里不～ feel unhappy

【乐于】 lèyú be happy to; take delight in: ～助人 be happy to render helps to other

【乐园】 lèyuán paradise; Eden: 冒险家的～ paradise of the adventures

lei

勒 (lēi) tie or strap sth. tight: ～紧裤腰带 tighten one's belt
(另见"勒"lè)

【勒死】 lēisǐ strangle sb. to death

累［纍］(léi)
(另见"累"lěi, lèi)

【累累】 léiléi 1.(连成串) clusters of; heaps of: 果实～ fruit hanging in clusters; fruit hanging heavy 2.(憔悴颓丧) haggard; gaunt: ～若丧家之犬 wretched as a stray cur

【累赘】 léi·zhui 1.(多余;麻烦) burdensome; cumbersome 2.(不简洁) wordy; verbose 3.(使人感到多余、麻烦的事物) encumbrance; burden; nuisance

雷 (léi) 1.(打雷) thunder 2.(爆炸武器) mine: 地～ mine; land mine / 水～ mine / 鱼～ torpedo / 布～ lay mines / 扫～ sweep mines / 探～ detect mines

【雷暴】 léibào 〈*Meteorol.*〉 thunderstorm

【雷场】 léichǎng 〈*Mil.*〉 mine field

【雷达】 léidá radar

【雷达兵】 léidábīng radar operator; radarman

【雷达测速器】 léidá cèsùqì 〈*Transport*〉 radar trap

【雷达抛物面天线】 léidá pāowùmiàn tiānxiàn radar dish

【雷达网】 léidáwǎng radar fence

【雷达系统】 léidá xìtǒng radar system

【雷达预警机】 léidá yùjǐngjī radar picket

【雷达站】 léidázhàn radar station

【雷电】 léidiàn thunder and lightning: ～交加 lightning accompanied by rolls of thunders

【雷动】 léidòng thunderous: 欢声～ thunderous cheers

【雷管】 léiguǎn detonator; detonating cap; blasting cap; primer

【雷击】 léijī be struck by lightning

【雷厉风行】 léilì-fēngxíng with the power of a thunderbolt and the speed of lightning; vigorously and speedily

【雷鸣】 léimíng thunderous; thundery: ～般的掌声 thunderous applause

【雷区】 léiqū 〈*Mil.*〉 mine field

【雷声】 léishēng thunderclap; thunder

【雷司令】 Léisīlìng (干白葡萄酒) Riesling

【雷霆】 léitíng 1.(霹雳) thunderclap; thunderbolt 2.(威力或怒气) thunder-like power or rage; wrath: 大发～ fly into a rage

【雷同】 léitóng 1.(附和) echoing what others have said 2.(相同) duplicate; identical: 内容～ with identical contents

【雷雨交加】 léiyǔ-jiāojiā storm accompanied by peals of thunder

【雷阵雨】 léizhènyǔ thunder shower

镭 (léi) 〈*Chem.*〉 radium (元素符号 Ra)

【镭射气】 léishèqì 〈*Chem.*〉 radium emanation

垒［壘］(lěi) 1.(砌;筑) build by piling up bricks, stones, earth, etc.: ～墙 build a wall 2.(壁垒) rampart 3.〈*Baseball & Softball*〉 base: 安全上～ safe / 本～ home base / 滑～ sliding / 跑～ base running / 偷～ stealing

【垒垫】 lěidiàn 〈*Baseball & Softball*〉 bag

【垒球】 lěiqiú softball: 打～ play softball

【垒球棒】 lěiqiúbàng softball bat

【垒球场】 lěiqiúchǎng softball field

累［纍1,2］(lěi) 1.(积累) pile up; accumulate 2.(屡次;连续) continuous; repeated; running 3.(牵扯) involve; get sb. into

（另见“累”léi, lèi）
【累次】 lěicì repeatedly; several times
【累犯】 lěifàn 1.（指行为）recidivism 2.（指人）recidivist
【累积】 lěijī accumulate
【累及】 lěijí implicate; involve; drag in：～无辜 involve the innocents
【累计】 lěijì 1.（加算）add up 2.（合计）grand total; accumulative total
【累进】 lěijìn progression; progressive (adj.)
【累进税】 lěijìnshuì progressive tax; progressive taxation
【累累】 lěilěi 1.（屡屡）again and again; many times 2.（累积得多）innumerable; countless：～罪行 countless crimes

磊（lěi）
【磊落】 lěiluò open and upright：光明～ open and aboveboard

蕾（lěi） flower bud; bud：花～ flower bud
【蕾铃】 lěilíng 〈*Bot.*〉cotton buds and bolls

肋（lèi） 1.（肋条）rib 2.（胸部的侧面）costal region
【肋骨】 lèigǔ rib
【肋膜】 lèimó 〈*Anat.*〉pleura
【肋膜炎】 lèimóyán 〈*Med.*〉pleurisy
【肋条】 lèi·tiáo 1.（肋骨）rib 2.（排骨）pork ribs

泪［淚］（lèi） tear; teardrop：流～ shed tear
【泪痕】 lèihén tear stains
【泪花】 lèihuā tears in one's eye
【泪流满面】 lèiliú-mǎnmiàn tears cover one's face
【泪如泉涌】 lèirúquányǒng tears welling up like a fountain
【泪水】 lèishuǐ tear; teardrop
【泪汪汪】 lèiwāngwāng with watery eyes; brimming with tears
【泪眼】 lèiyǎn tearful eyes
【泪珠】 lèizhū teardrop

类［類］（lèi） 1.（种类）kind; type; class; category：各～ all sorts of 2.（类似）resemble; be similar to 3.（构词成分）quasi-
【类别】 lèibié classification; category
【类地行星】 lèidì xíngxīng 〈*Astron.*〉terrestrial planet
【类固醇】 lèigùchún 〈*Biol.*〉steroids
【类固醇激素】 lèigùchún jīsù steroid hormone
【类木行星】 lèimù xíngxīng 〈*Astron.*〉govian planet
【类人猿】 lèirényuán anthropoid
【类似】 lèisì similar; analogous
【类推】 lèituī analogize; reason by analogy：依此～ on the analogy of this
【类星体】 lèixīngtǐ 〈*Astron.*〉quasi-stellar object
【类型】 lèixíng type; pattern

累（lèi） 1.（疲劳）tired; fatigued; weary 2.（使疲劳）tire; strain; wear out 3.（操劳）work hard; toil：从早到晚～了一天 have been working hard all day
（另见“累”léi, lěi）

擂（lèi） beat
【擂台】 lèitái ring; arena：摆～ give an open challenge / 打～ take up the challenge

leng

棱［稜］（léng） 1.（两平面的连接部分）arris; edge 2.（条状凸起）corrugation; ridge
【棱角】 léngjiǎo 1.（棱和角）edges and corners 2.（锋芒）edge; pointedness
【棱镜】 léngjìng 〈*Physics*〉prism：三～ triangular prism
【棱柱】 léngzhù prism
【棱锥】 léngzhuī pyramid

冷（lěng） 1.（温度低）cold：～得发抖 shiver with cold 2.（不热情）cold in manner; frosty：～若冰霜 frosty in manner 3.（寂静）unfrequented; deserted：屋里～清清的。The house looked deserted. 4.（乘人不备）shot from hiding
【冷冰冰】 lěngbīngbīng ice cold; icy; frosty：～的态度 icy manners
【冷不防】 lěng·bufáng all of a sudden; by surprise
【冷不防电话】 lěng·bufáng diànhuà cold call
【冷餐】 lěngcān buffet
【冷餐招待会】 lěngcān zhāodàihuì buffet re-

ception

【冷藏】 lěngcáng refrigeration; cold storage

【冷藏车】 lěngcángchē refrigerator car; refrigerator van

【冷藏库】 lěngcángkù cold storage; freezer

【冷藏汽车】 lěngcáng qìchē cold storage truck

【冷藏设备】 lěngcáng shèbèi refrigerating equipment

【冷藏箱】 lěngcángxiāng refrigerator; freezer

【冷场】 lěngchǎng 1.（演员失误）awkward silence on the stage when an actor enters late or forgets his lines 2.（开会没人发言）awkward silence at a meeting

【冷嘲热讽】 lěngcháo-rèfěng freezing irony and burning satire

【冷处理】 lěngchǔlǐ cold treatment

【冷淡】 lěngdàn 1.（不热闹）cheerless; desolate 2.（不热情）cold; indifferent：表示～ show indifference towards sth. 3.（招待不热情）treat coldly; cold-shoulder; slight：～的接待（give sb.）a cool reception

【冷冻】 lěngdòng freeze; freezing (n.)

【冷冻厂】 lěngdòngchǎng cold storage plant

【冷冻剂】 lěngdòngjì refrigerant

【冷冻食物】 lěngdòng shíwù frozen food

【冷冻手术】 lěngdòng shǒushù 〈*Med.*〉 cryosurgery

【冷风机】 lěngfēngjī air-cooler

【冷锋】 lěngfēng 〈*Meteorol.*〉 cold front

【冷敷】 lěngfū 〈*Med.*〉 cold compress

【冷宫】 lěnggōng cold palace：被打入～ be consigned to limbo

【冷柜】 lěngguì refrigerator; freezer

【冷汗】 lěnghàn cold sweat：出～ break out in a cold sweat

【冷荤】 lěnghūn cold meat; cold buffet

【冷加工】 lěngjiāgōng cold working

【冷箭】 lěngjiàn an arrow shot from hiding; sniper's shot：～伤人 injure a person by hidden arrows

【冷静】 lěngjìng sober; calm; in cold blood：保持～ remain calm / ～下来 cool it

【冷聚变】 lěngjùbiàn 〈*Physics*〉 cold fusion

【冷空气】 lěngkōngqì cold air

【冷酷】 lěngkù unfeeling; callous; grim：～的现实 grim reality / ～无情 be cold-blooded; be cold-hearted

【冷冷清清】 lěnglěng-qīngqīng cold and cheerless; desolate

【冷落】 lěngluò 1.（不热闹）unfrequented; desolate 2.（使受冷淡待遇）treat coldly; cold-shoulder：遭到～ leave out in the cold

【冷门】 lěngmén 1.（不时兴）a profession, trade or branch of learning that receives little attention 2.（意想不到的）an unexpected winner; dark horse

【冷漠】 lěngmò cold and detached; unconcerned; indifferent：～无情 sternly cool and unmoved

【冷凝】 lěngníng 〈*Meteorol.*〉 solidification

【冷暖】 lěngnuǎn changes in temperature

【冷盘】 lěngpán cold dish; hors d'oeuvre

【冷僻】 lěngpì 1.（冷落偏僻）out-of-the-way; deserted 2.（不常见的）unfamiliar; rare：～的字眼 rarely used words

【冷气】 lěngqì air conditioning

【冷气机】 lěngqìjī air conditioner

【冷气设备】 lěngqì shèbèi air-cooling system

【冷枪】 lěngqiāng sniper's shot：打～ shoot at sb. from a hiding place; injure sb. by underhand means

【冷清】 lěngqīng cold and cheerless; desolate; lonely; deserted

【冷却】 lěngquè cool; cooling (n.)

【冷却剂】 lěngquèjì coolant; cooler

【冷却器】 lěngquèqì cooler

【冷却塔】 lěngquètǎ cooling tower

【冷却装置】 lěngquè zhuāngzhì cooling installation; cooling equipment

【冷若冰霜】 lěngruòbīngshuāng as cold as ice in manner; frosty in manner

【冷色】 lěngsè 〈*Arts*〉 cool color

【冷杉】 lěngshān 〈*Bot.*〉 fir

【冷食】 lěngshí cold drinks and snacks

【冷水】 lěngshuǐ 1.（凉水）cold water：～浇头 throw cold water on / 泼～ dampen sb's enthusiasm 2.（生水）unboiled water

【冷水浴】 lěngshuǐyù cold bath

【冷烫】 lěngtàng have one's hair done by chemicals

【冷笑】 lěngxiào sneer; laugh grimly

【冷血动物】 lěngxuě dòngwù 1.〈*Zool.*〉

cold-blooded animal 2.（冷酷的人）cold-blooded person; cold-hearted person

【冷言冷语】 lěngyán-lěngyǔ sarcastic comments; ironical remarks

【冷眼】 lěngyǎn 1.（冷静客观）coldly 2.（冷淡的待遇）cold-shoulder

【冷眼旁观】 lěngyǎn-pángguān 1.（冷静观察）look on coldly; stay aloof 2.（挑剔）look on with a critical eye

【冷饮】 lěngyǐn cold drink

【冷遇】 lěngyù cold reception; cold shoulder: 遭到～ be given the cold shoulder; be left out in the cold

【冷凿】 lěngzáo cold chisel

【冷轧】 lěngzhá 〈*Metall.*〉 cold rolling

【冷战】 lěngzhàn cold war

【冷战】 lěng·zhan shiver: 打～ shiver with cold

愣（lèng） 1.（失神）distracted; stupefied; blank 2.（鲁莽）rash; reckless; foolhardy

【愣神儿】 lèngshénr stare blankly; be in a daze

【愣头愣脑】 lèngtóu-lèngnǎo rash; impetuous; reckless

【愣小子】 lèngxiǎo·zi rash young fellow; young hothead

li

厘［釐］（lí） 1.（利率）a unit of monthly interest rate（＝0.1%；1‰）：月利 6～ a monthly interest of 6‰ 2.（一点儿）a fraction; the least: 分～不差 without the slightest error; just right

【厘米】 límǐ centimeter

离［離］（lí） 1.（分离）leave; part from; be away from: 火车 6 点～站。The train leaves the station at six. 2.（相距）off; away; from: 机场～我们学校有 25 公里路。The airport is twenty-five kilometers from our university. 3.（缺少）without; independent of: 植物生长～不了阳光。Plants generally can't grow without sunlight. 4.（离婚）divorce: 他们结婚才六个月就～了。They got divorced after only six months of marriage.

【离岸价格】 lí'àn-jiàgé free on board（FOB）

【离别】 líbié part（for a longish period）; leave; bid farewell: ～故园 part from home district

【离不开】 lí·bukāi 1.（不可缺）can't do without 2.（太忙走不开）too busy to get away

【离港楼】 lígǎnglóu 〈*Aeron.*〉 departure building

【离馆规定时间】 líguǎn guīdìng shíjiān check-out time

【离馆手续】 líguǎn shǒuxù check-out procedure

【离合器】 líhéqì 〈*Mech.*〉 clutch

【离合器踏板】 líhéqì tàbǎn 〈*Auto*〉 clutch pedal: 踩下～ press the clutch pedal down

【离合器握把】 líhéqì wòbǎ 〈*Motorcycle*〉 clutch lever

【离婚】 líhūn divorce; break a marriage: 他们上个月～了。They got divorced last month. / 去年他和她离了婚。He got a divorce from her last year. / 是李先生要和他妻子～，还是他妻子要和他～？Did Mr Lee divorce his wife or did she divorce him?

【离婚判决】 líhūn pànjué divorce decree

【离婚申请书】 líhūn shēnqǐngshū divorce petition

【离婚诉讼】 líhūn sùsòng divorce proceedings; matrimonial action: 提出～ take divorce proceedings

【离婚调解】 líhūn tiáojiě divorce conciliation; divorce mediation

【离婚者】 líhūnzhě 1.（男方）divorcee; divorcé 2.（女方）divorcée

【离婚证书】 líhūn zhèngshū bill of divorcement

【离婚自由】 líhūn zìyóu freedom to divorce

【离间】 líjiàn sow discord; drive a wedge between; set one party against another

【离间计】 líjiànjì the scheme of sowing dissension

【离境】 líjìng leave a country or place

【离境签证】 líjìng qiānzhèng exit visa

【离境许可证】 líjìng xǔkězhèng exit permit

【离开】 líkāi leave; depart from; deviate from: 我们今晚～。We leave tonight.

【离谱】 lípǔ far away from what is normal; far off the beam

【离奇】 líqí odd; fantastic; bizarre: ～的传闻 strange rumor

【离弃】 líqì abandon; desert
【离群索居】 líqún-suǒjū live in solitude
【离任】 lírèn leave one's post: ～回国 leave one's post for home
【离散】 lísàn dispersed; scattered about; separated from one another
【离题】 lítí digress from the subject; stray from the point
【离土不离乡】 lítǔ bùlíxiāng leave the field but not the village
【离乡背井】 líxiāng-bèijǐng tear oneself away from one's native place
【离心】 líxīn 1.(不是一条心) be at odds with the community or the leadership 2.(离开中心) centrifugal
【离心泵】 líxīnbèng centrifugal pump
【离心离德】 líxīn-lídé dissension and discord; disunity
【离心力】 líxīnlì centrifugal force
【离心作用】 líxīn zuòyòng centrifugation
【离休】 líxiū leave office for rest
【离休干部】 líxiū gànbù prerogative retired officials
【离异】 líyì separate; divorce: ～,无子女 divorced, without child
【离职】 lízhí 1.(暂时离职) leave one's job temporarily 2.(离开工作岗位) leave office
【离子】 lízǐ 〈*Physics*〉 ion
【离子键】 lízǐjiàn 〈*Chem.*〉 ionic bond
【离子交换树脂】 lízǐ jiāohuàn shùzhǐ ion exchange resin

篱[籬] (lí) hedge; fence

【篱笆】 lí·ba bamboo fence; twig fence: 给一块地围上～ fence in a field / 扎一圈～把邻居家的狗挡在花园外头 build a fence to keep the neighbor's dog out of the garden
【篱笆墙】 lí·baqiáng wattled wall

梨[棃] (lí) pear

【梨膏】 lígāo 〈*Chin. Pharm.*〉 pear syrup
【梨花】 líhuā pear flower
【梨树】 líshù pear tree
【梨园】 líyuán the operatic circle
【梨园子弟】 líyuán zǐdì operatic players

犁[犂] (lí) 1.(农具) plow; plough 2.(用犁耕地) plow; work with a plough: ～地 plow the field / 把庄稼茬儿～进地里增加土壤肥力 plow in (或 back) the remains of a crop to help fertilize the earth
【犁沟】 lígōu ditch dug with a plow
【犁铧】 líhuá plowshare; ploughshare; share

黎 (lí)

【黎民】 límín the common people; the multitude
【黎明】 límíng dawn; daybreak: 我们～时出发了。We left at dawn.
【黎族】 Lízú Li (中国少数民族,主要分布在海南)

罹 (lí)

【罹难】 línàn 1.(遇灾) die in a disaster 2.(遇险) die in an accident 3.(被害) be murdered

礼[禮] (lǐ) 1.(仪式) ceremony; rite: 婚～ wedding; marriage ceremony / 丧～ funeral ceremony; funeral 2.(敬礼) courtesy; etiquette; manners: 行～ (give a) salute 3.(礼物) gift; present: 送～ give a present; send a gift

【礼拜】 lǐnbài 1.(向神行礼) religious service: 做～ go to church; be at church 2.(星期) week: 下～ next week 3.(星期天) Sunday
【礼拜二】 lǐbàièr Tuesday
【礼拜六】 lǐbàiliù Saturday
【礼拜日】 lǐbàirì Sunday
【礼拜三】 lǐbàisān Wednesday
【礼拜四】 lǐbàisì Thursday
【礼拜寺】 lǐbàisì 〈*Islam*〉 mosque
【礼拜堂】 lǐbàitáng 〈*Christianity*〉 church
【礼拜天】 lǐbàitiān Sunday
【礼拜五】 lǐbàiwǔ Friday
【礼拜一】 lǐbàiyī Monday
【礼宾司】 lǐbīnsī the Department of Protocol; the Protocol Department
【礼单】 lǐdān list of presents
【礼多人不怪】 lǐ duō rén bù guài civility costs nothing
【礼服】 lǐfú ceremonial dress; full dress; formal attire
【礼花】 lǐhuā fireworks display
【礼教】 lǐjiào feudal ethics; old moral code
【礼节】 lǐjié courtesy; etiquette; protocol;

ceremony：社交～ social etiquette / 外交～ diplomatic protocol
【礼金】 lǐjīn cash gift
【礼帽】 lǐmào ceremonial hat; formal hat
【礼貌】 lǐmào courtesy; politeness; manners：讲～ observe good manners
【礼炮】 lǐpào salvo; (gun) salute：21 响～ 21 gun salute; a salvo of 21 guns
【礼品】 lǐpǐn gift; present
【礼聘】 lǐpìn cordially invite the service of
【礼券】 lǐquàn gift taken; gift voucher
【礼让】 lǐràng give precedence to sb. out of courtesy or thoughtfulness; comity：安全～ yield right of way for safety's sake
【礼尚往来】 lǐshàng-wǎnglái 1.（礼节往来） courtesy demands reciprocity 2.（以其人之道还治其人之身） deal with a man as he deals with you; pay a man back in his own coin
【礼所当然】 lǐ suǒ dāngrán etiquette requires it
【礼堂】 lǐtáng assembly hall; auditorium
【礼物】 lǐwù gift; present：他给了她一个～。He gave her a present.
【礼仪】 lǐyí etiquette; rite; protocol
【礼仪电报】 lǐyí diànbào greeting telegram
【礼仪之邦】 lǐyí zhī bāng a state of ceremonies
【礼遇】 lǐyù courteous reception; cordial reception

李（lǐ） plum
【李代桃僵】 lǐdàitáojiāng 1.（用一种事物取代另一种） substitute one thing for another; substitute this for that 2.（代替别人受过） sacrifice oneself for another person
【李子】 lǐ·zi plum

里［裏[1,2,3,6]、裡[1,2,3,6]］（lǐ） 1.（衣服里子） lining; inside：衣服～儿 the lining of a garment 2.（里边） in; inside; within：在房间～ in the room / 在学校～ in school / 手～ in one's hands / 在城～ within the city / 把钱放到包～ put the money inside one's bag 3.（里边的） inner：～屋 inner room 4.（街坊） neighborhood：邻～ people of the neighborhood 5.（家乡） hometown; native place：故～ native place 6.（里面） in; inside：手～ in one's hands 7.（长度单位） li, 0.5 kilometer
【里边】 lǐ·bian in; inside; within：房间～ the inside of the room / 她正好站在大门～。She was standing just inside the gate. / 盒子～有一本词典。There is a dictionary in the box. / 在这些古城墙～曾经有过一座城市。Within these ancient walls there was once a town.
【里程】 lǐchéng 1.（路程） mileage 2.（发展过程） course of development; course：生命的～ one's lifetime
【里程碑】 lǐchéngbēi milestone：历史的～ a milestone in history
【里程表】 lǐchéngbiǎo odometer
【里脊】 lǐ·ji tenderloin
【里脊肉】 lǐ·jiròu 见"里脊"
【里里外外】 lǐlǐ-wàiwài inside and outside
【里面】 lǐmiàn inside; interior
【里弄】 lǐlòng lanes and alleys; neighborhood
【里圈】 lǐquān 〈*Sports*〉 inside lane; inner lane
【里手】 lǐshǒu 1.（左边） the left-hand side 2.（内行） expert; old hand
【里通外国】 lǐtōng-wàiguó have illicit relations with a foreign country
【里屋】 lǐwū inner room
【里应外合】 lǐyìng-wàihé act from inside in coordination with forces attacking from outside; collaborate from within with forces from without
【里子】 lǐ·zi lining：活～ detachable lining
【里仔盖】 lǐzǐgài （牛肉部位） round

俚（lǐ） vulgar
【俚俗】 lǐsú vulgar; unrefined; uncultured
【俚语】 lǐyǔ slang

理（lǐ） 1.（纹理） texture; grain 2.（道理） reason; logic; truth 3.（自然科学） natural science 4.（物理学） physics：数～化 mathematics, physics and chemistry 5.（管理；治理） manage; run 6.（整理） put in order; tidy up：～东西 put things in order 7.（理睬） pay attention to; acknowledge
【理财】 lǐcái manage money matters; conduct financial transactions：～之道 the way of managing financial affair
【理睬】 lǐcǎi pay attention to; show interest

in：不予～ take no notice of
【理发】 lǐfà haircut；hairdressing
【理发馆】 lǐfàguǎn barbershop；barber's；hairdresser's
【理发师】 lǐfàshī barber；hairdresser；woman barber
【理工科】 lǐgōngkē science and engineering
【理工科大学】 lǐgōngkē dàxué college of science and engineering；university of science and engineering
【理会】 lǐhuì 1.（理解）understand；comprehend 2.（理睬）take notice of；pay attention to：不予～ take no notice of 3.（理论）argue；debate 4.（照料；处理）take care of；deal with
【理解】 lǐjiě understand；comprehend
【理解力】 lǐjiělì faculty of understanding；understanding；comprehension
【理解性记忆】 lǐjiěxìng jìyì intelligent memory
【理科】 lǐkē 1.（指学科）science department in a college 2.（自然科学）science；natural science
【理科博士】 lǐkē bóshì Doctor of Science（D. Sc）
【理科硕士】 lǐkē shuòshì Master of Science（M. Sc）
【理科学士】 lǐkē xuéshì Bachelor of Science（B. Sc）
【理亏】 lǐkuī be in the wrong
【理疗】 lǐliáo 〈*Med*.〉physiotherapy
【理论】 lǐlùn 1.（认识）theory：马克思列宁主义～ Marxist-Leninist theory / ～联系实际 unite theory with practice / 建设有中国特色社会主义的～ the theory of building socialism with Chinese characteristics / 关于月球的一种～ one theory about the moon 2.（理会）argue；debate
【理论家】 lǐlùnjiā theoretician；theorist
【理论水平】 lǐlùn shuǐpíng theoretical level
【理屈词穷】 lǐqū-cíqióng fall silent on finding oneself bested in argument；be unable to advance any further arguments to justify oneself
【理事】 lǐ·shì member of a council；director：常务～ permanent member of a council
【理事会】 lǐshìhuì council；board of directors
【理事长】 lǐshìzhǎng chairman of the board of directors
【理顺】 lǐshùn rationalize；straighten out：～关系 rationalize relations between ...；straighten out relationships / ～价格关系 rationalize prices
【理所当然】 lǐsuǒdāngrán of course；naturally
【理想】 lǐxiǎng ideal
【理想化】 lǐxiǎnghuà idealize；idealization（n.）
【理想家】 lǐxiǎngjiā idealists；dreamers
【理想主义】 lǐxiǎng zhǔyì idealism ‖ 理想主义者 idealist
【理性】 lǐxìng 1.（与"感性"相对）rational 2.（控制行为能力）reason：恢复～ come to one's senses
【理性认识】 lǐxìng rèn·shi rational knowledge
【理应】 lǐyīng ought to；should
【理由】 lǐyóu reason；ground；argument：有充足的～ have every reason；there are sufficient reasons
【理直气壮】 lǐzhí-qìzhuàng with justice；justly and forcefully
【理智】 lǐzhì reason；intellect：丧失～ lose one's reason；lose one's senses

锂（lǐ） 〈*Med*.〉lithium（元素符号 Li）

【锂电池】 lǐdiànchí lithium cell

鲤（lǐ） carp

【鲤鱼】 lǐyú carp
【鲤鱼钳】 lǐyúqián slip-joint pliers；combination pliers

力（lì） 1.（力量）power；strength；ability：创造～ creative power / 兵～ military strength；military capabilities / 电～ electric power / 记忆～ strength of memory / 能～ ability；capability / 魄～ drive and decisiveness；boldness / 人～ manpower / 视～ power of vision / 物～ material resources 2.（物理作用）force：磁～ magnetic force / 分～ component force / 浮～ buoyancy force / 合～ composite force / 拉～ tractive force / 离心～ centrifugal force / 弹～ elastic force / 向心～ centripetal force / 引～ attraction force / 张～ tension force / 阻～ resisting force 3.（体力）physical strength 4.（努力；尽

力）do all one can；make every effort
【力不从心】 lìbùcóngxīn ability not equal to one's ambition；ability falling short of one's wishes
【力场】 lìchǎng 〈*Physics*〉 field of force
【力挫】 lìcuō try hard to defeat
【力度】 lìdù 1.（力量大小）force；strength：加大～ strengthen；give force to；increase the strength of 2.〈*Music*〉 dynamics
【力竭声嘶】 lìjié-shēngsī exhausted from effort
【力戒】 lìjiè strictly avoid；do everything possible to avoid；guard against：～骄傲 guard against arrogance
【力量】 lì·liang 1.（力气）physical strength 2.（能力）power；force；strength：国防～ defense capability / ～悬殊 disparity in strength 3.（效力）effect；efficacy
【力气】 lì·qi physical strength；effort：用尽～ bring all one's strength into play
【力求】 lìqiú make every effort to；do one's best to；strive to
【力所不及】 lìsuǒbùjí beyond one's power；out of one's ability
【力所能及】 lìsuǒnéngjí in one's power
【力图】 lìtú try hard to；strive to
【力挽狂澜】 lìwǎn-kuánglán make vigorous efforts to turn the tide
【力学】 lìxué mechanics；mechanic (adj.)：材料～ mechanics of materials
【力争】 lìzhēng 1.（争取）work hard for；do all one can to 2.（争辩）contend vigorously；argue strongly：据理～ argue strongly on just grounds
【力争上游】 lìzhēng-shàngyóu strive for the best
【力作】 lìzuò a major piece of writing

荔 (lì)

【荔枝】 lìzhī litchi；lychee

历［歷、曆[4]、厤[4]］ (lì)

1.（经历）undergo；go through；experience 2.（过去的各个或各次）all previous 3.（遍）covering all；one by one 4.（历法）calendar：阴～ lunar calendar
【历程】 lìchéng course；experience：人生的～ life's journey
【历次】 lìcì all previous
【历代】 lìdài 1.（过去的各个朝代）successive dynasties；past dynasties：～名画 famous paintings through the ages 2.（过去的许多世代）past generations 3.（经历各个时期）through the periods
【历法】 lìfǎ 〈*Astron.*〉 calendar
【历届】 lìjiè all previous：～内阁 successive cabinets / ～政府 successive governments / ～人民代表 all the previous members of the People's Congress
【历尽艰辛】 lìjìn-jiānxīn have gone through all kinds of hardships and difficulties
【历来】 lìlái always；constantly；all long：～如此。It has always been so.
【历历】 lìlì distinctly；clearly：～在目 come clearly into view
【历年】 lìnián 1.（过去多少年）over the years：～积蓄 savings over the years 2.（历法年）calendar year
【历任】 lìrèn 1.（相继担任）have successively held the posts of；have served successively as 2.（过去各任）successive：这所大学的～校长 all the successive presidents of this university
【历时】 lìshí last；take
【历史】 lìshǐ 1.（发展史）history；historical (adj.)：中国～ history of China / 两位领导人具有～意义的会见 a historical meeting between the two leaders 2.（过去的记载）past records：～最高水平 highest standard on records / ～清白 have a good record 3.（过去的经历）past experience：这早已成为～了。This event is history now. 4.（历史学）history；historical (adj.)：学校的～课 a history lesson at school
【历史博物馆】 lìshǐ bówùguǎn history museum；historical museum
【历史潮流】 lìshǐ cháoliú the tide of history；historical trend
【历史地图】 lìshǐ dìtú historical atlas
【历史记载】 lìshǐ jìzǎi historical records
【历史阶段】 lìshǐ jiēduàn historical stage
【历史剧】 lìshǐjù historical play
【历史人物】 lìshǐ rénwù historical personage；historical figure
【历史唯物主义】 lìshǐ wéiwù zhǔyì historical

materialism

【历史唯心主义】 lìshǐ wéixīn zhǔyì historical idealism

【历史文献】 lìshǐ wénxiàn historical documents

【历史问题】 lìshǐ wèntí question of a political nature in sb's history

【历史性】 lìshǐxìng historic; of historic significance

【历史遗产】 lìshǐ yíchǎn legacy of history; historical heritage

【历史遗留问题】 lìshǐ yíliú wèntí question left over by history; problem left over by history

【历书】 lìshū almanac

【历数】 lìshǔ count one by one; enumerate

沥[瀝](lì) 1.(滴落) drip; trickle 2.(液体的滴) drop

【沥青】 lìqīng pitch; asphalt; bitumen

【沥水板】 lìshuǐbǎn drainboard (AmE.); draining board (BrE.)

厉[厲](lì) 1.(严格) strict; rigorous 2.(严肃) stern; severe

【厉兵秣马】 lìbīng-mòmǎ sharpen the weapons and feed the horses; get ready for battle

【厉害】 lì·hai 1.(严厉的) severe; sharp; fierce 2.(极度的) terrible: 病得～ be seriously ill

【厉色正言】 lìsè-zhèngyán speak with stern countenance

【厉声】 lìshēng in a stern voice; talk harshly; shout angrily

【厉行】 lìxíng strictly enforce; rigorously enforce; make great efforts to carry out: ～节约 practice strict economy

励[勵](lì) encourage

【励精图治】 lìjīng-túzhì rouse oneself for vigorous efforts to make the country prosperous

立(lì) 1.(站立) stand 2.(竖立) erect; set up: ～纪念碑 erect a monument 3.(直立的) upright; erect; vertical 4.(建立;制定) found; establish; set up 5.(自立) exist; live 6.(立刻) immediate; instantaneous

【立案】 lì'àn 1.(备案) register; put on record 2.(设立专案) place a case on file for investigation and prosecution

【立案注册】 lì'àn zhùcè register and make a record of

【立叉】 lìchā 〈*Bicycle*〉 seat stays

【立场】 lìchǎng 1.(态度) position; stand; standpoint: 坚持～ stick to one's position 2.(阶级立场) class stand

【立春】 lìchūn the Beginning of Spring (3 月 3-5 日交节)

【立定】 lìdìng 1.(停下立正) halt 2.(站稳) stand firm 3.(牢固地确定) establish

【立冬】 lìdōng the Beginning of Winter (11 月 7-8 日交节)

【立法】 lìfǎ legislation: 经济～ economic legislation / 加强～工作 improve legislation

【立法机关】 lìfǎ jīguān legislative body; legislature

【立法权】 lìfǎquán legislative power

【立法委员会】 lìfǎ wěiyuánhuì legislation committee; legislative council

【立方】 lìfāng 1.〈*Math.*〉四的立方: cube of 4; 4^3 2.(立方体) cube 3.(量词, 立方米) cubic meter

【立方米】 lìfāngmǐ cubic meter: 一～写作 m^3。A cubic meter is written m^3.

【立竿见影】 lìgān-jiànyǐng set up a pole and see its shadow; get instant results

【立功】 lìgōng render meritorious service; do a deed of merit; make contributions

【立管】 lìguǎn 〈*Bicycle*〉 seat tube

【立柜】 lìguì clothes closet; wardrobe; hanging cupboard

【立国】 lìguó 1.(建国) establish a state 2.(建设国家) build a country

【立国之本】 lìguó zhī běn fundamental to the building of the country

【立合同】 lìhé·tong sign a contract; conclude a contract

【立户】 lìhù 1.(立户口) register for a household residence card; register for permanent residence 2.(建立银行户头) open an account with the bank

【立即】 lìjí immediately; at once; promptly

【立交】 lìjiāo grade separation

【立交桥】 lìjiāoqiáo overpass; gallop bridge: 人行～ pedestrian overpass / 下行式铁路～ railway underpass project

【立脚点】 lìjiǎodiǎn 1.(观察、判断的角度)

standpoint; position; point of view 2.（生存的地方）foot-hold; footing; position
【立井】 lìjǐng 〈*Mineral*.〉vertical shaft
【立据】 lìjù deed
【立克次氏体】 lìkècìshìtǐ 〈*Med*.〉rickettsia
【立刻】 lìkè immediately; at once; right away
【立领】 lìlǐng stand-up collar
【立论】 lìlùn 1.（提出看法）set forth one's views; present one's argument 2.（表示意见）argument; position; line of reasoning
【立马】 lìmǎ immediately; at once; right away
【立米】 lìmǐ cubic meter
【立秋】 lìqiū the Beginning of Autumn（8月7-9日交节）
【立誓】 lìshì take an oath; vow
【立体】 lìtǐ 1.（三维的）three-dimensional 2.（几何体）solid 3.（上下多层次）cubic 4.（有立体感的）stereo; stereoscopic
【立体电视】 lìtǐ diànshì stereoscopic television; three dimensional television
【立体电影】 lìtǐ diànyǐng stereoscopic film
【立体感】 lìtǐgǎn three-dimensional effect
【立体几何学】 lìtǐ jǐhéxué solid geometry
【立体交叉】 lìtǐ jiāochā grade separation
【立体声】 lìtǐshēng stereo; stereophony: 环绕～ surround-sound
【立体声磁带录音机】 lìtǐshēng cídài lùyīnjī stereo tape recorder
【立体声收音机】 lìtǐshēng shōuyīnjī stereo receiver
【立体声系统】 lìtǐshēng xìtǒng stereophonic sound system
【立体战争】 lìtǐ zhànzhēng triphibious warfare
【立夏】 lìxià the Beginning of Summer（5月5-7日交节）
【立宪】 lìxiàn constitutionalism: 君主～ constitutional monarchy
【立言】 lìyán expound one's ideas in writing; achieve glory by writing
【立业】 lìyè embark on a career
【立遗嘱】 lì yízhǔ make a will
【立意】 lìyì 1.（打定主意）be determined; make up one's mind 2.（命意）conception; approach
【立于不败之地】 lìyú bù bài zhī dì remain invincible; be in an impregnable position
【立约】 lìyuē make a contract
【立约当事人】 lìyuē dāngshìrén contracting party
【立账】 lìzhàng open an account with sth.
【立正】 lìzhèng stand at attention
【立志】 lìzhì resolve; be determined: ～改革 be determined to carry out reforms
【立柱】 lìzhù column
【立足】 lìzú 1.（站住脚）have a foothold; keep a foothold: ～中国实际 base ourselves on China's realities 2.（处于某种立场）base oneself upon

莅［蒞、涖］(lì) 〈*written*〉arrive; be present
【莅场】 lìchǎng be present on the occasion
【莅会】 lìhuì be present at a meeting
【莅临】 lìlín arrive; be present: 敬请～指导。Your presence and guidance are requested.

粒 (lì) 1.（颗粒）grain; granule; pellet: 米～儿 grains of rice 2.〈*classifier*〉dosage: 每服3～ 3 pills each time
【粒状】 lìzhuàng granular
【粒子】 lìzǐ 〈*Physics*〉particle: 高能～ energetic particle
【粒子加速器】 lìzǐ jiāsùqì 〈*Physics*〉particle accelerator

丽［麗］(lì) beautiful
【丽人】 lìrén a beauty: ～如云 beauties are numerous like clouds
【丽日和风】 lìrì-héfēng bright sun and pleasant breezes

俪［儷］(lì) 1.（成双的）pair; couple 2.（指夫妻）husband and wife; married couple
【俪影】 lìyǐng heart-warming sight of a couple in love

利 (lì) 1.（锋利）sharp 2.（顺利）favorable: 不顺～ be unfavorable 3.（利益）advantage; benefit: 这对双方都不～。Neither side would benefit from that. 4.（利润或利息）profit; interest 5.（使有利）do good to; benefit
【利弊】 lìbì advantages and disadvantages; pros and cons: 这样做利多弊少。That would

produce far more gains than losses.

【利钝】 lìdùn 1.(锋利或不锋利) sharp or blunt 2.(成或败) advantages or disadvantages; successes or failures: 成败～ advantages or disadvantages; successes or failures

【利改税】 lìgǎishuì switch from profit delivery to tax

【利滚利】 lìgǔnlì at compound interest

【利国利民】 lìguó-lìmín benefit the nation and the people

【利害】 lìhài advantages and disadvantages; gains and losses: 对他们讲清～ explain clearly to them what is beneficial and what is harmful

【利害】 lì·hai terrible; formidable

【利害冲突】 lìhài chōngtū conflict of interest

【利己主义】 lìjǐ zhǔyì egoism: 民族～ national egoism ‖ 利己主义者 egoist

【利令智昏】 lìlìng-zhìhūn be blinded by lust for gain

【利禄】 lìlù wealth and position

【利率】 lìlǜ 〈*Econ*.〉 rate of interest; interest rate: 高～ high interest / 过高的～ excessive interest / 优惠～ concessionary interest rate

【利落】 lì·luo 1.(敏捷) agile; nimble; dexterous 2.(整齐) neat; orderly: 房间干净～。 The room is neat and tidy. 3.(完毕) settled; finished: 事情总算办～了。 The matter has been all settled.

【利尿】 lìniào 〈*Med*.〉 diuresis

【利尿剂】 lìniàojì 〈*Pharm*.〉 diuretic; emictoria

【利器】 lìqì 1.(锐利武器) sharp weapon 2.(有效的工具) good tool; efficient instrument

【利钱】 lì·qian interest

【利权】 lìquán 1.(经济权力) economic rights 2.(财政权利) financial power: ～外溢 vested rights overflow outwardly

【利刃】 lìrèn sharp weapon

【利润】 lìrùn profit; interest: 超额～ superprofit / 企业～留成收入 portion of the profits kept by the enterprises for their own use / 上交～ profit turned into the state; that part of the profit turned over to the state / 税后～ after-tax profit / 投资～ return on capital

【利润法则】 lìrùn fǎzé capitalist principle of profit-seeking

【利润分成】 lìrùn fēnchéng proportional profit retention

【利润率】 lìrùnlǜ profit margin; profit rate

【利税】 lìshuì profit and tax

【利税分流】 lìshuì fēnliú a system whereby enterprises pay tax plus a percentage of profits

【利他主义】 lìtā zhǔyì altruism

【利息】 lìxī interest: 不包括～ excluding interest / 取得～ receive interest

【利益】 lìyì interest; benefit; profit: 根本～ fundamental interest / 切身～ vital interest / 触及许多人的～ affect the interests of countless individuals

【利用】 lìyòng 1.(使发挥效用) use; utilize; make use of: ～国外资金 utilize foreign capital 2.(利用手段) take advantage of; exploit: ～地位，追求特权 use one's position to seek personal privileges

【利用率】 lìyònglǜ utilization ratio

【利诱】 lìyòu lure by promise of gain

【利欲熏心】 lìyù-xūnxīn be blinded by greed; be overcome by covetousness; be obsessed with the desire for gain

痢 (lì) dysentery

【痢疾】 lì·ji dysentery: 恶性～ malignant dysentery / 细菌性～ bacillary dysentery

【痢特灵】 lìtèlíng 〈*Pharm*.〉 furazolidone

例 (lì) 1.(例子) example; instance: 举～ give an example; cite an instance 2.(先例) precedent: 破～ break all precedents; make an exception 3.(事例) case; instance 4.(规则) rule; regulation: 旧～ an old rule 5.(照成规办的) regular; routine

【例会】 lìhuì regular meeting

【例假】 lìjià 1.(规定假日) official holiday; legal holiday 2.(指月经) menstruation: 来～ menstruate 3.(指月经期) menstrual period; period

【例句】 lìjù example sentence

【例如】 lìrú for instance; for example (e.g.); such as

【例题】 lìtí example

【例外】 lìwài exception: 毫无～ without exception

【例行公事】 lìxíng gōngshì 1.(常规公事)

routine; routine business 2.(形式主义的工作) mere formality

【例行检查】 lìxíng jiǎnchá routine inspection

【例证】 lìzhèng illustration; example; case in point

【例子】 lì·zi example; case; instance: 举一个～ cite an instance; give an example / 这～很说明问题。This example pinpoints the problem.

隶［隸、隷］(lì) 1.(附属) be subordinate to; be under 2.(被奴役的) a person in servitude: 奴～ slave

【隶属】 lìshǔ be subordinate to; be under the jurisdiction or command of

砾［礫］(lì) gravel; shingle

【砾石】 lìshí gravel

【砾石路】 lìshílù gravel road

【砾岩】 lìyán 〈*Geol*.〉 conglomerate

栗(lì) 1.(栗子树) chestnut 2.(发抖) tremble; shudder

【栗色】 lìsè chestnut color; maroon

【栗子】 lì·zi chestnut

傈(lì)

【傈僳族】 Lìsùzú Lisu (中国少数民族，主要分布在云南)

lia

俩［倆］(liǎ) 1.(两个) two: 咱～ we two; both of us; the two of us / 哥儿～ both brothers 2.(不多;几个) some; several: 接济他～钱儿。Help him with some money.

lian

连(lián) 1.(连接) link; join; connect: 这两句～不上。The two sentences are disconnected. 2.(连续) in succession; one after another; repeatedly: ～发两封信 send two letters in succession 3.(包括) include: ～你20人 twenty people including you / ～皮10公斤。It weighs 10 kilos, including packing. 4.(连队) company 5.(甚至) even: 这个我～想都没想过。I haven't even thought of it.

【连本带利】 liánběn-dàilì both the principal and the interest

【连鬓胡子】 liánbìn hú·zi whiskers

【连串】 liánchuàn consecutive

【连词】 liáncí 〈*Gram*.〉 conjunction

【连带】 liándài 1.(互相关联) related; joint; contributory 2.(牵连) involve in 3.(附带) by the way

【连…带…】 lián…dài… 1.(表示包括前后两项) and; as well as: ～工～料，一共多少钱? How much is it, with material and labor all together? 2.(表示同时发生) and while

【连带关系】 liándài guānxì relationship; connection; link

【连带责任】 liándài zérèn joint liability: ～的债务 obligation establishing joint and several

【连带债务人】 liándài zhàiwùrén joint and several debtor

【连队】 liánduì 〈*Mil*.〉 company

【连根拔】 liángēnbá tear up by the roots; uproot

【连贯】 liánguàn 1.(连接贯通) link up; piece together; hang together 2.(首尾一致) coherent; consistent

【连贯性】 liánguànxìng coherence; continuity

【连环】 liánhuán 1.(一环套一环) chain of rings 2.(系列) a series of; a set of

【连环画】 liánhuánhuà picture-story book

【连击】 liánjī 〈*Sports*〉 double hit

【连接】 liánjiē 1.(相接) joined; linked; connected 2.(使相接) join; link up; connect

【连接号】 liánjiēhào hyphen; dash (符号为：-)

【连接项目】 liánjiē xiàngmù interlocking item

【连结】 liánjié 同"联结"

【连累】 liánlèi implicate; involve; get sb. into trouble

【连连】 liánlián 〈*colloq*.〉 repeatedly; again and again

【连忙】 liánmáng promptly; at once

【连袂】 liánmèi 同"联袂"

【连绵】 liánmián continuous; unbroken; uninterrupted

【连年】 liánnián in successive years; in consecutive years; for years running; for years on end

【连篇】 liánpiān 1.(充满篇幅) throughout a piece of writing; page after page: 废话～

pages and pages of nonsense 2.(一篇接一篇) one article after another; a multitude of articles
【连篇累牍】 liángpiān-lěidú lengthy and tedious; at great length
【连任】 liánrèn be reappointed or reelected consecutively; renew one's term of office: ～总统 be reelected president
【连日】 liánrì for days on end; day after day
【连衫裤】 liánshānkù combinations
【连署】 liánshǔ be a witness
【连署人】 liánshǔrén witness
【连锁店】 liánsuǒdiàn chain store
【连锁反应】 liánsuǒ fǎnyìng 1.〈*Physics*〉 chain reaction 2.(形容像连锁反应一样的效果) ripple effect
【连锁学习】 liánsuǒ xuéxí chain learning
【连天】 liántiān 1.(形容与天空相接) reaching the sky 2.(连续几天) incessantly
【连同】 liántóng together with; along with
【连袜裤】 liánwàkù tights; panty hose
【连写】 liánxiě write a disyllabic or polysyllabic word as one word
【连续】 liánxù continuous; successive; in a row; running: ～三个夜晚 for three nights running
【连续剧】 liánxùjù serial
【连续弯路】 liánxù wānlù 〈*Transport*〉 winding road
【连续性】 liánxùxìng continuity; continuance: 现行政策的～ the continuity of the current policy
【连续纸】 liánxùzhǐ continuous paper
【连夜】 liányè 1.(整夜) all through the night 2.(连续几个夜晚) for nights running
【连衣裙】 liányīqún a woman's dress
【连载】 liánzǎi publish in instalments; serialize
【连载小说】 liánzǎi xiǎoshuō serial story; continued story
【连长】 liánchǎng 〈*Mil.*〉 company commander
【连指手套】 liánzhǐ shǒutào mitten
【连珠炮】 liánzhūpào continuous firing; drumfire
【连属】 liánzhǔ joined; linked; connected
【连柱廊】 liánzhùláng arcade
【连缀】 liánzhuì 1.(联结) join together; put together 2.(辅音或元音群) cluster
【连字符】 liánzìfú 同"连字号"
【连字号】 liánzìhào hyphen; dash (符号为-)

莲 (lián) 〈*Bot.*〉 lotus
【莲花】 liánhuā lotus flower; lotus
【莲蓬】 lián·peng seedpod of the lotus
【莲蓬头】 lián·pengtóu shower nozzle; shower head injector
【莲子】 liánzǐ lotus seed

涟 (lián)
【涟漪】 liányī 〈*written*〉 ripples

鲢 (lián) silver carp
【鲢鱼】 liányú silver carp

怜[憐] (lián) sympathize with; pity
【怜爱】 lián'ài love tenderly; have tender affection for
【怜才】 liáncái have sympathy for talented persons
【怜悯】 liánmǐn pity; take pity on; have compassion for
【怜贫】 liánpín pity or commiserate the poor
【怜惜】 liánxī take pity on; have pity for

帘[簾²] (lián) 1.(布望子) flag as shop sign: 酒～ wineshop sign 2.(帘子) curtain: 窗～ window curtain
【帘布】 liánbù cord fabric
【帘子】 lián·zi (hanging) screen; curtain

联[聯] (lián) 1.(联合) ally oneself with; unite; join 2.(对联) antithetical couplet: 春～ Spring Festival couplets
【联办】 liánbàn establish, run or hold sth. with joint efforts
【联邦】 liánbāng federation; union; commonwealth
【联邦共和国】 liánbāng gònghéguó federal republic; federated republic
【联邦议会】 liánbāng yìhuì federal parliament
【联邦制】 liánbāngzhì federal system; federalism
【联播】 liánbō simulcast; radio hookup; broadcast over a radio network
【联播节目】 liánbō jiémù simulcast; network

program

【联播节目时间】 liánbō jiémù shíjiān network time

【联产承包责任制】 liánchǎn chéngbāo zérènzhì the contracted responsibility system with remuneration linked to output

【联产计酬】 liánchǎn jìchóu method of paying remuneration according to output

【联大】 liándà the United Nations General Assembly

【联队】 liánduì 〈*Mil.*〉 wing (of an air force)

【联防】 liánfáng joint defense; joint command of defense forces

【联号商店】 liánhào shāngdiàn chain store

【联合】 liánhé **1.** (结合) unite; ally **2.** (结合在一起) alliance; union; coalition **3.** (共同) joint; combined **4.** 〈*Anat.*〉 symphysis

【联合公报】 liánhé gōngbào joint communiqué

【联合公司】 liánhé gōngsī allied company

【联合国】 Liánhéguó the United Nations (U. N.)

【联合国安理会】 Liánhéguó Ānlǐhuì the U. N. Security Council

【联合国大会】 Liánhéguó Dàhuì the United Nations General Assembly

【联合国军事观察组】 Liánhéguó Jūnshì Guāncházǔ a U. N. arm inspection team

【联合国秘书处】 Liánhéguó Mìshūchù the United Nations Secretariat

【联合国宪章】 Liánhéguó Xiànzhāng the Charter of the United Nations

【联合会】 liánhéhuì federation; union: 妇女～ women's federation

【联合经营】 liánhé jīngyíng coordinated management

【联合联络小组】 liánhé liánluò xiǎozǔ joint liaison group

【联合企业】 liánhé qǐyè integrated complex; joint venture

【联合声明】 liánhé shēngmíng joint statement

【联合收割机】 liánhé shōugējī combine harvester; combine

【联合投资】 liánhé tóuzī joint investment

【联合王国】 Liánhé wángguó the United Kingdom

【联合政府】 liánhé zhèngfǔ coalition government

【联欢】 liánhuān have a get-together; have a party

【联欢会】 liánhuānhuì get-together; party

【联欢节】 liánhuānjié festival

【联接】 liánjiē 〈*Aeron.*〉 mate

【联结】 liánjié bind; tie; join

【联军】 liánjūn allied forces; united army

【联络】 liánluò **1.** (联系) get in touch with; come into contact with: ～感情 make friendly contacts / 失去～ lose contact with **2.** (接上关系) contact; liaison

【联络部】 liánluòbù liaison department

【联络处】 liánluòchù liaison office

【联络点】 liánluòdiǎn contact point

【联络员】 liánluòyuán liaison man

【联盟】 liánméng alliance; coalition; league; union

【联袂】 liánmèi hand in hand; together

【联名】 liánmíng jointly signed; jointly: ～发起 initiate jointly; sponsor jointly

【联翩】 liánpiān successively; continued: 浮想～。Many thoughts cross one's mind.

【联赛】 liánsài 〈*Sports*〉 league matches: 足球～ league football matches

【联手】 liánshǒu joint; combined

【联席会议】 liánxí huìyì joint conference; joint meeting

【联系】 liánxì **1.** (接上关系) contact; touch; connection; relation: 对外经济～ foreign economic relation / 科技～ scientific and technical links / 商业～ trade contacts / 取得～ get in touch with; establish contact with **2.** (使结合) integrate; relate; link; get in touch with: 与物质利益～起来 be linked to increases or reductions in material benefits / ～群众 make friends with the people

【联想】 liánxiǎng associate; connect in the mind

【联谊】 liányí promote friendship through contacts

【联谊会】 liányíhuì friendship society

【联姻】 liányīn joint people in marriage; unite by marriage: 与有钱人家～ ally oneself with a rich family

【联营】 liányíng joint operation

【联营企业】 liányíng qǐyè company of joint operation

【联运】 liányùn 〈*Transport*〉 through transport; through traffic：水陆～ through transport by land and water
【联展】 liánzhǎn joint exhibition
【联属】 liánzhǔ 同“连属”
【联缀】 liánzhuì 同“连缀”

廉［**亷**］(lián) 1.（廉洁）honest and clean 2.（便宜）low-priced; inexpensive; cheap
【廉耻】 liánchǐ sense of honor; sense of shame
【廉价】 liánjià low price; cheap; low-priced (adj.)：～出售 sell at a low price; sell cheap
【廉价出售】 liánjià chūshòu sell at a low price; sell cheap
【廉价劳动力】 liánjià láodònglì cheap labor
【廉价书】 liánjiàshū cheap book
【廉洁】 liánjié honest：～奉公 be honest in performing one's official duties; honestly perform one's duties
【廉洁政治】 liánjié zhèngzhì clean government
【廉明】 liánmíng incorruptible and intelligent; cleanhanded and clearheaded
【廉政】 liánzhèng clean and honest government
【廉政建设】 liánzhèng jiànshè construction of a clean and honest government; construction of a clean and trustworthy government

镰［**鎌**］(lián) sickle
【镰刀】 liándāo sickle

臁(lián) shank
【臁疮】 liánchuāng ulcer on the shank

敛［**斂**］(liǎn) 1.（收起）hold back; restrain 2.（收集）collect：横征暴～ extort heavy taxes and levies
【敛财】 liǎncái accumulate wealth by unfair means
【敛迹】 liǎnjì lie low; hide so as to avoid being discovered
【敛容】 liǎnróng 〈*written*〉 assume a serious expression
【敛足】 liǎnzú withdraw one's footsteps

脸［**臉**］(liǎn) 1.（面部）face; countenance 2.（物体的前部）front：(商店)门～儿 the front of a shop
【脸蛋儿】 liǎndànr cheeks; face
【脸红】 liǎnhóng 1.（由于害羞等）blush with shame; blush 2.（由于愤怒等）flush with anger; get excited; get worked up
【脸面】 liǎnmiàn face; self-respect; sb.'s feelings
【脸盆】 liǎnpén washbasin; washbowl
【脸皮】 liǎnpí 1.（脸上的皮肤）face; cheek 2.（情面）sense of shame：～厚 shameless; thick-skinned/ ～薄 sensitive; thin-skinned
【脸谱】 liǎnpǔ types of facial makeup in operas
【脸色】 liǎnsè 1.（气色）complexion; look 2.（表情）facial expression

练［**練**］(liàn) 1.（白绢）white silk 2.（把生丝煮熟）boil and scour raw silk 3.（练习）practice; train; drill 4.（经验多）experienced; skilled; seasoned
【练兵】 liànbīng 1.（训练军队）troop training 2.（训练各种人员）training
【练操】 liàncāo drill
【练队】 liànduì drill in formation
【练功】 liàngōng practice one's skill
【练功房】 liàngōngfáng gymnasium; exercise room
【练气功】 liànqìgōng do breathing exercises
【练球】 liànqiú practice a ball game
【练武】 liànwǔ do weapon practice; practice martial arts
【练习】 liànxí 1.（反复学习）practice：～讲英语 practice spoken English 2.（习题、作业）exercise
【练习本】 liànxíběn exercise-book

炼［**煉、鍊**］(liàn) 1.（熔炼；精炼）smelt; refine 2.（锤炼）temper with fire 3.（琢磨）polish
【炼钢】 liàngāng steelmaking; steel-smelting
【炼钢炉】 liàngānglú steelmaking furnace; steel-smelting furnace
【炼焦】 liànjiāo coking
【炼乳】 liànrǔ condensed milk
【炼糖厂】 liàntángchǎng sugar refinery
【炼铁】 liàntiě iron-smelting
【炼铁炉】 liàntiělú iron-smelting furnace
【炼油】 liànyóu 1.（分馏石油）oil refining 2.（提炼动、植物油）extract oil by heat 3.（加热食用油）heat edible oil

【炼油厂】 liànyóuchǎng (oil) refinery
【炼制】 liànzhì refine：石油～ petroleum refining

恋[戀] (liàn) 1.(恋爱) love：初～ be in love for the first time；first love / 热～ be passionately in love 2.(想念；不忍分离) long for；feel attached to
【恋爱】 liàn'ài love：谈～ be in love；fall in love / 甲与乙～。A and B are in love with each other.
【恋歌】 liàngē a love song
【恋旧】 liànjiù 1.(留恋过去) yearn for the past；to long for the good old days 2.(怀念老朋友) yearn for old friends
【恋恋不舍】 liànliàn-bùshě be reluctant to part with；hate to see sb. go
【恋情】 liànqíng love affair
【恋人】 liànrén a sweetheart；a lover

殓[殮] (liàn) encoffin：给某人入～ put sb's corpse in a coffin

链[鏈] (liàn) 1.(链子) chain 2.(海程单位) cable's length (＝185.2 m.)
【链锯】 liànjū chain saw
【链轮】 liànlún 〈*Bicycle*〉 chain wheel
【链霉素】 liànméisù 〈*Pharm.*〉 streptomycin
【链球】 liànqiú 1.〈*Sports*〉 hammer-throwing 2.(指器械) hammer：掷～ hammer throw
【链球菌】 liànqiújūn 〈*Biol.*〉 streptococcus
【链套】 liàntào 〈*Bicycle*〉 chain case
【链条】 liàntiáo chain；roller chain
【链罩】 liànzhào 〈*Bicycle*〉 chain guard；chain cover
【链子】 liàn·zi chain

liang

良 (liáng) 1.(好) good；fin 2.(善良的人) good people
【良材】 liángcái 1.(好木料) good timber 2.(有能力的人) able person
【良策】 liángcè good plan；sound strategy
【良方】 liángfāng 1.(好药方) effective prescription；good recipe 2.(好计划) good plan；sound strategy
【良港】 liánggǎng good harbor
【良好】 liánghǎo good；well：树立～的作风 foster a good style of work
【良机】 liángjī 〈*written*〉 good opportunity：坐失～ let a good chance slip by
【良久】 liángjiǔ 〈*written*〉 a good while；a long time
【良师益友】 liángshī-yìyǒu good teacher and helpful friend
【良田】 liángtián good field；fertile farmland
【良心】 liángxīn conscience：凭～ be fair
【良性】 liángxìng benign
【良性循环】 liángxìng xúnhuán a healthy cycle
【良性肿瘤】 liángxìng zhǒngliú a benign tumor
【良药苦口】 liángyào-kǔkǒu good medicine tastes bitter
【良医】 liángyī good doctor
【良友】 liángyǒu beneficial friend
【良莠不齐】 liángyǒu-bùqí some good and some bad；with the good and the bad mixed up
【良缘】 liángyuán happy match；harmonious union
【良种】 liángzhǒng 1.(指作物品种) improved variety：玉米～ improved varieties of corn 2.(指牲畜品种) fine breed：～马 a horse of fine breed
【良种场】 liángzhǒngchǎng seed multiplication farm

粮[糧] (liáng) 1.(粮食) grain；food；provisions：粗～ coarse grain / 商品～ marketable grain / 细～ refined grain 2.(农业税) grain tax paid in kind
【粮仓】 liángcāng granary；barn
【粮草】 liángcǎo army provisions；rations and forage
【粮店】 liángdiàn grain shop
【粮囤】 liángtún bulk grain tank
【粮库】 liángkù grain depot
【粮秣】 liángmò army provisions；rations and forage；grain and fodder：～被服 grain, fodder, bedding and clothing
【粮秣库】 liángmòkù ration depot
【粮票】 liángpiào grain coupon
【粮食】 liáng·shi grain；cereals；food：～问题还没有真正解决。The problem of grain has not really been solved yet.
【粮食作物】 liáng·shi zuòwù cereal crops；grain crops

【粮站】 liángzhàn grain supply center

【粮栈】 liángzhàn grain depot; wholesale grain store

凉［涼］(liáng) 1.（冷）cool; cold 2.（灰心）discouraged; disappointed
（另见"凉"liàng）

【凉白开】 liángbáikāi cold boiled water

【凉拌】 liángbàn cold and dressed with sauce

【凉拌面】 liángbànmiàn cold noodles in sauce

【凉菜】 liángcài cold dish

【凉快】 liángkuài 1.（指天气）nice and cool; pleasantly cool 2.（纳凉）cool oneself; cool off

【凉帽】 liángmào summer hat

【凉棚】 liángpéng mat-awning; mat shed

【凉伞】 liángsǎn parasol; sunshade

【凉爽】 liángshuǎng nice and cool; pleasantly cool

【凉水】 liángshuǐ 1.（冷水）cold water 2.（生水）unboiled water

【凉飕飕】 liángsōusōu chilly; chill

【凉台】 liángtái balcony; veranda

【凉亭】 liángtíng wayside pavilion; summer house; kiosk

【凉席】 liángxí bed-mat for summer; summer sleeping mat

【凉鞋】 liángxié sandals

梁［樑］(liáng) 1.（房梁）roof beam 2.（桥）bridge 3.（中间隆起的长条部分）ridge

【梁桥】 liángqiáo beam bridge

【梁上君子】 liángshàng-jūnzǐ gentleman on the beam; thief; burglar

【梁状结构】 liángzhuàng jiégòu beam texture

量(liáng) measure: ～尺寸 take sb.'s measurements / ～体温 take sb.'s temperature / ～体重 weigh oneself
（另见"量"liàng）

【量杯】 liángbēi measuring glass; graduate

【量度】 liángdù measurement

【量角器】 liángjiǎoqì protractor

【量具】 liángjù measuring tool

【量块】 liángkuài gauge block; block gauge

【量瓶】 liángpíng measuring flask; graduated flask

【量筒】【量桶】 liángtǒng graduated cylinder; graduate

【量雪尺】 liángxuěchǐ 〈*Meteorol.*〉 snow scale

【量雨筒】 liángyǔtǒng 〈*Meteorol.*〉 precipitation gauge

两［兩］(liǎng) 1.（二）two: ～本书 two books / ～层楼房 a two-story house 2.（双方）both (sides); either (side): ～者缺一不可 neither is dispensable 3.（不定数目）a few; some: 我过～天再来。I'll come again in a few days.

【两岸】 liǎngàn 1.（泛指）right bank and left bank; right shore and left shore 2.（特指台湾海峡两岸）on both sides of Taiwan Strait

【两败俱伤】 liǎngbài-jùshāng both sides suffer neither side gains

【两倍】 liǎngbèi twofold; double; twice as much

【两边】 liǎngbiān 1.（两个边）both sides 2.（两处）both places 3.（两个方向）both direction 4.（双方）both parties; both sides

【两侧】 liǎngcè bilateral

【两重】 liǎngchóng double; dual; twofold

【两重性】 liǎngchóngxìng dual nature; duality

【两弹】 liǎngdàn two types of bombs; atomic bomb and hydrogen bomb

【两弹一星】 liǎngdàn yīxīng two types of bomb and a satellite; atomic bomb, hydrogen bomb and man-made satellite

【两党】 liǎngdǎng bipartisan: ～会谈 bipartisan talks

【两党制】 liǎngdǎngzhì two-party system; bipartisan system

【两点论】 liǎngdiǎnlùn 〈*Philos.*〉 the doctrine that everything has two aspects

【两分法】 liǎngfēnfǎ law of one dividing into two

【两个基本点】 liǎnggè jīběndiǎn two focal points

【两个文明】 liǎnggè wénmíng material civilization and cultural and ideological progress

【两极】 liǎngjí 1.（地球的两极）the two poles of the earth: ～地区 polar regions 2.（阴、阳两极）the two poles

【两极分化】 liǎngjí fēnhuà 1.（两个极端；两个对立面）polarization; division into two opposing extremes; polarize (v.): 社会的贫富

～能在纽约、伦敦、东京…看得一清二楚。The polarization of society into rich and poor can clearly be seen in New York, London, Tokyo, etc. **2.**(分成两极) polarize; produce a polarization of

【两件套】 liǎngjiàntào two-piece

【两可】 liǎngkě both will do; either will do: ～之间 not knowing which to choose

【两口儿】 liǎngkǒur husband and wife; the couple

【两利】 liǎnglì be good for both sides; benefit both

【两码事】 liǎngmǎshì two different matters; entirely different

【两面】 liǎngmiàn **1.**(正反面) two sides; both sides; two aspects; both **2.**(具有两面性) having a dual character; dual; double

【两面派】 liǎngmiànpài **1.**(要两面手法的人) double- dealer **2.**(两面手法) double-dealing

【两面三刀】 liǎngmiàn-sāndāo double-dealing; play a double game

【两面性】 liǎngmiànxìng dual character

【两幕喜剧】 liǎngmù xǐjù double act

【两难】 liǎngnán face a difficult choice: 进退～ be in a dilemma

【两旁】 liǎngpáng both sides; either side

【两栖】 liǎngqī amphibious

【两栖部队】 liǎngqī bùduì amphibious forces; amphibious units

【两栖动物】 liǎngqī dòngwù amphibious animal; amphibian

【两栖植物】 liǎngqī zhíwù amphibious plants

【两栖作战】 liǎngqī zuòzhàn amphibious warfare; amphibious operations

【两讫】 liǎngqì 〈*Trade*〉 the goods are delivered and the bill is paid

【两全】 liǎngquán be satisfactory to both parties; have regard for both sides

【两全其美】 liǎngquánqíměi satisfy both sides; satisfy rival claims

【两权分离】 liǎngquán fēnlí separation of the two powers; two separate powers: 实行企业所有权、经营权～的原则 the principle of the separation of enterprise ownership from managerial power

【两手】 liǎngshǒu dual tactics: 作～准备 prepare oneself for both eventualities

【两手抓】 liǎngshǒuzhuā paired tactics

【两头】 liǎngtóu **1.**(两端) both ends; either end **2.**(双方) both parties; both sides **3.**(两个地方) both

【两位数】 liǎngwèishù double figures

【两厢】 liǎngxiāng **1.**(两面的厢房) wing-rooms on either side of a one-story house **2.**(两旁) both sides

【两相】 liǎngxiāng 〈*Electr.*〉 two-phase

【两相情愿】 liǎngxiāng-qíngyuàn both parties are willing

【两性】 liǎngxìng **1.**(两种性别) both sexes; bisexual (adj.) **2.**(两种性质) amphiprotic; amphoteric

【两性关系】 liǎngxìng guānxì sexual relations

【两袖清风】 liǎngxiù-qīngfēng remain uncorrupted; have clean hands

【两样】 liǎngyàng not the same; different: 没什么～ make no different

【两翼】 liǎngyì 〈*Mil.*〉 both wings; both flanks

【两用】 liǎngyòng dual purpose: 培养军地～人才 train people for both military and civilian jobs

【两用炉】 liǎngyònglú dual-purpose stove

【两用衫】 liǎngyòngshān reversible jacket

【两院制】 liǎngyuànzhì two-chamber system; bicameral system; bicameralism

【两种文字对照】 liǎngzhǒng wénzhì duìzhào bilingual

【两足动物】 liǎngzú dòngwù biped

亮 (liàng) **1.**(明亮) bright; light: 天开始～了。It's beginning to get light. **2.**(使响亮) loud and clear **3.**(开朗) enlightened: 心里～了 be enlightened **4.**(发光) shine **5.**(显示) show: ～出入证 show one's pass

【亮丑】 liàngchǒu make one's errors public

【亮度】 liàngdù brightness; brilliance

【亮光】 liàngguāng light

【亮节】 liàngjié integrity; uprightness

【亮晶晶】 liàngjīngjīng glittering; sparkling; glistening: ～的眼睛 sparkling eyes

【亮堂】 liàng·tang **1.**(敞亮) light; bright: 这房间很～。The room is well lighted. **2.**(清楚) clear; enlightened: 她一讲,大家心里都～了。What she said enlightened all of us. **3.**(响亮) resounding; loud and distinct

【亮相】 liàngxiàng 1.（指舞台表演方式）strike a pose on the stage 2.（表明态度、观点）declare one's position; state one's views 3.（出现）appear in public：一种新型洗衣机在市场上～了。A new model of washing machine has appeared on the market.

凉[涼]（liàng） make cool; become cool
（另见“凉”liáng）

谅（liàng） 1.（原谅）forgive; understand：尚希见～。I hope you will excuse me. 2.（料想）I think; I suppose; I expect

【谅必】 liàngbì most likely; probably

【谅解】 liàngjiě understand; make allowance for：达成～ come to an understanding

【谅解备忘录】 liàngjiě bèiwànglù memorandum of understanding

晾（liàng） 1.（晾干）dry in the air; air：～床单 air the sheets 2.（晒）dry in the sun; sun

【晾干】 liànggān dry by airing; dry in the air

【晾晒】 liàngshài sun; dry in the sun

靓（liàng） beautiful; pretty

【靓女】 liàngnǚ a pretty girl

【靓仔】 liàngzǎi a handsome young man

量（liàng） 1.（容纳限度）capacity：载重～ loading capacity 2.（数量）quantity; amount; volume：保质保～ guarantee both quantity and quality 3.（估量）estimate; measure
（另见“量”liáng）

【量变】 liàngbiàn 〈*Philos.*〉 quantitative change

【量才录用】 liàngcái-lùyòng assign jobs to people according to their abilities

【量词】 liàngcí 〈*Gram.*〉 classifier measure word

【量化】 liànghuà quantification

【量力】 liànglì estimate one's own strength or ability (and act accordingly)

【量力而为】 liànglì'érwéi estimate one's strength before acting

【量入为出】 liàngrù-wéichū plan expenditures in the light of one's income

【量体裁衣】 liàngtǐ-cáiyī act according to actual circumstances

【量刑】 liàngxíng 〈*Law*〉 measurement of penalty

【量子】 liàngzǐ 〈*Physics*〉 quantum

【量子力学】 liàngzǐ lìxué 〈*Physics*〉 quantum mechanics

踉（liàng）

【踉跄】 liàngqiàng stagger; limp：～而行 walk unsteadily

liao

撩（liāo） 1.（掀）hold up：～起裙子 hold up the skirt 2.（用手洒）sprinkle：～水 sprinkle water
（另见“撩”liáo）

辽[遼]（liáo） distant; faraway

【辽阔】 liáokuò vast; extensive

【辽远】 liáoyuǎn distant; faraway

疗[療]（liáo） treat; cure; treatment (n.)：电～ electrotherapy; electrical treatment / 泥～ mud-bath treatment / 水～ hydrotherapy; hydropathic treatment / 诊～ make a diagnosis and give treatment / 治～ treat (a patient); give medical care to

【疗程】 liáochéng period of treatment

【疗法】 liáofǎ therapy; treatment：保守～ conservative treatment / 放射～ radiotherapy / 封闭～ block therapy / 化学～ chemotherapy / 药物～ medicinal treatment / 放射～ radiotherapy / 物理～ physiotherapy; physical therapy / 饮食～ dietotherapy / 针刺～ acupuncture treatment / 综合～ composite treatment

【疗效】 liáoxiào curative effect：具有良好的～ produce a good curative effect

【疗养】 liáoyǎng recuperate; convalesce

【疗养地】 liáoyǎngdì health resort

【疗养院】 liáoyǎngyuàn sanatorium; convalescent hospital

聊（liáo） 1.（姑且）merely; just 2.（略微）a little; slightly 3.（闲谈）chat：～一～ have a chat

【聊赖】 liáolài something to live for; something to rely upon

【聊胜于无】 liáoshèngyúwú Half a loaf is

better than no bread.

【聊天儿】 liáotiānr chat

【聊以塞责】 liáoyǐsèzé merely to avoid the charge of dereliction of duty

【聊以自慰】 liáoyǐzìwèi just to console oneself

【聊以卒岁】 liáoyǐzúsuì just to tide over the year

僚 (liáo) 1.（官吏）official 2.（同一官署的官吏）an associate in office; colleague

【僚机】 liáojī 1.（跟随长机的飞机）wing plane; wingman 2.（僚机飞行员）wingman

【僚舰】 liáojiàn 〈*Mil.*〉 consort

【僚属】 liáoshǔ subordinate; aide; assistant

撩 (liáo) 1.（逗引）tease; tantalize 2.（拨动）provoke; stir up

（另见"撩"liāo

【撩拨】 liáobō 1.（挑逗）tease; banter 2.（招惹）incite; provoke

【撩逗】 liáodòu provoke; entice

嘹 (liáo)

【嘹亮】 liáoliàng resonant; loud and clear: 歌声～ sonorous sound of songs

獠 (liáo)

【獠牙】 liáoyá long, sharp, protruding teeth

潦 (liáo)

【潦草】 liáocǎo 1.（不工整）hasty and careless; illegible: 字迹～ careless handwriting 2.（不仔细）sloppy; slovenly

【潦倒】 liáodǎo be frustrated

缭 (liáo) 1.（缠绕）entangled 2.（缝纫方法）sew with slanting stitches

【缭乱】 liáoluàn confused; in a turmoil; in a confused state of

【缭绕】 liáorào curl up; wind around

燎 (liáo) burn

（另见"燎"liǎo）

【燎泡】 liáopào blister raised by a burn or scald

【燎原】 liáoyuán set the prairie ablaze: 星星之火，可以～。A single spark can start a prairie fire.

【燎原计划】 liáoyuán jìhuà prairie fire program

寥 (liáo) 1.（稀少）few; scanty: ～～几行 just a few lines 2.（静寂）silent; deserted

【寥廓】 liáokuò boundless; vast

【寥寥无几】 liáoliáo-wújǐ very few

【寥落】 liáoluò very few; sparse; scanty

【寥若晨星】 liáoruòchénxīng as sparse as the morning stars; few and far between

了［**瞭**[1]］ (liǎo) 1.（明白）know clearly; understand 2.（完了）end; finish; settle; dispose of 3.（在动词之后，表示可能）can: 来不～ could not come

【了不得】 liǎo·bu·dé 1.（非常）terrific; extraordinary: 多得～ in terrific number 2.（情况严重）terrible; awful: 真是～的大祸啊! What a terrible disaster!

【了不起】 liǎo·buqǐ amazing; terrific; extraordinary: 没什么～ nothing extraordinary

【了此一生】 liǎocǐyīshēng to end this life

【了断】 liǎoduàn finish; bring to an end

【了结】 liǎojié finish; settle; wind up; bring to an end: ～一场官司 settle a lawsuit; end a lawsuit

【了解】 liǎojiě 1.（知道得清楚）understand; comprehend: 增进～ increase mutual understanding 2.（打听；调查）find out; acquaint oneself with: ～情况 go and find out what's going on

【了局】 liǎojú 1.（结局）end 2.（解决办法）solution; settlement

【了却】 liǎoquè settle; solve: ～一桩心事 take a load off one's mind

【了然】 liǎorán understand; be clear: 一目～ learn at a glance; see at a glance

【了如指掌】 liǎorúzhǐzhǎng know sth. like the palm of one's hand; have sth. at one's fingertips

【了事】 liǎoshì get sth. over; get through sth.: 草草～ complete sth. in great haste

钌 (liǎo) 〈*Chem.*〉 ruthenium（元素符号 Ru）

（另见"钌"liào）

燎 (liǎo) singe; burn lightly

（另见"燎"liáo）

瞭 (liào) watch from a height or a distance

【瞭望】 liàowàng watch from a height or a distance; keep a lookout

【瞭望哨】 liàowàngshào stand sentry; stand

sentinel
【瞭望台】 liàowàngtái observation tower; lookout tower

钌(liào) hasp and staple
(另见"钌"liǎo)

【钌铞】 liàodiào hasp and staple

尥(liào)

【尥蹶子】 liào juě·zi kick

料(liào) 1.(预料) expect; anticipate 2.(原料) material; stuff 3.(精饲料) grain meal 4.(适合做某事的人) makings; stuff: 他不是跳舞的～。He hasn't got the makings of a dancer.

【料仓】 liàocāng feed bin
【料酒】 liàojiǔ cooking wine
【料理】 liàolǐ 1.(办理) arrange; manage; attend to; take care of: ～家务 manage household affairs 2.(日本餐) Japanese dish; Japanese cooking
【料器】 liàoqì glassware
【料峭】 liàoqiào 〈*written*〉 chilly: 春寒～。There is a chill in the air in early spring.
【料事如神】 liàoshì-rúshén predict like a prophet; foretell with miraculous accuracy
【料想】 liàoxiǎng expect; think; presume
【料子】 liào·zi 1.(指布料) material for making clothes 2.(指毛料) woolen fabric: ～裤 trousers made of woolen fabric

撂[撩](liào) 1.(放;搁) put down; leave behind: ～下饭碗 put down one's rice bowl 2.(弄倒) throw down; knock down; shoot down

【撂荒地】 liàohuāngdì black fallow
【撂挑子】 liàotiāo·zi throw up one's job

镣(liào) fetters

【镣铐】 liàokào fetters and handcuffs; irons; chains; shackles

lie

咧(liē)
(另见"咧"liě)

【咧咧】 liēliē 1.(乱说) babble 2.(小儿哭) baby's crying sound

咧(liě)
(另见"咧"liē)

【咧嘴】 liězuǐ grin: 疼得直～ grin with pain

列(liè) 1.(排列) arrange; line up 2.(列入) list; enter in a list 3.(行列) row; file; rank 4.(类) kind; sort 5.(各) various; each and every

【列兵】 lièbīng 1.(陆军) recruit 2.(空军) airman recruit 3.(海军) seaman recruit
【列车】 lièchē train: 国际～ international train / 旅客～ passenger train
【列车时刻表】 lièchē shíkèbiǎo train schedule; timetable
【列岛】 lièdǎo a chain of islands; archipelago
【列队】 lièduì line up; form into a row: ～欢迎 line up to welcome sb.
【列国】 lièguó the various states or nations
【列举】 lièjǔ enumerate; list
【列宁主义】 Lièníng zhǔyì Leninism; Leninist (adj.) ‖ 列宁主义者 Leninist
【列强】 lièqiáng various powers
【列位】 lièwèi all the ladies and gentlemen present
【列席】 lièxí attend as a nonvoting delegate: ～旁听 attend the meeting as an observer
【列席代表】 lièxí dàibiǎo nonvoting delegate; observer
【列支】 lièzhī be itemized as expenditure
【列传】 lièzhuàn collected biographies

烈(liè) 1.(强烈) strong; violent; intense: ～酒 strong drink 2.(暴烈) fiery: ～马 fiery steed 3.(为正义而死的) sacrificing oneself for a just cause

【烈度】 lièdù intensity: 地震～ earthquake intensity
【烈火】 lièhuǒ raging fire; raging flames
【烈日】 lièrì burning sun; scorching sun
【烈士】 lièshì martyr: 革命～ revolutionary martyr
【烈士纪念碑】 lièshì jìniànbēi a monument to revolutionary martyrs
【烈士陵园】 lièshì língyuán cemetery of revolutionary martyrs
【烈士墓】 lièshìmù the grave of a revolutionary martyr
【烈属】 lièshǔ members of a revolutionary martyr's family
【烈性】 lièxìng 1.(指性情) spirited: ～女子 a woman of character 2.(指性质) strong; vi-

olent：～炸药 high explosives

裂 (liè) split；crack；rend：～成两半 be rent in two / 分～ split；break up / 冻～ be frozen open

【裂变】 lièbiàn 〈*Physics*〉fission：核～ nuclear fission

【裂缝】 lièfèng rift；crevice；crack；fissure

【裂果】 lièguǒ 〈*Bot*.〉dehiscent fruit

【裂痕】 lièhén rift；crack；fissure

【裂化】 lièhuà 〈*Petroleum*〉cracking

【裂解】 lièjiě 〈*Chem*.〉splitting decomposition

【裂开】 lièkāi split open；rend

【裂口】 lièkǒu 1.（裂开的口）breach；gap；split 2.（火山口）vent

【裂纹】 lièwén crackle

【裂隙】 lièxì crack；crevice；fracture

趔 (liè)

【趔趄】 liè·qie stagger；reel

劣 (liè) bad；inferior；of low quality

【劣等】 lièděng of inferior quality；low-grade；poor

【劣等货】 lièděnghuò goods of inferior quality

【劣根性】 liègēnxìng deep-rooted bad habits

【劣迹】 lièjì misdeed；evil doing

【劣迹昭著】 lièjì-zhāozhù be notorious

【劣绅】 lièshēn evil gentry：土豪～ local tyrants and evil gentry

【劣势】 lièshì inferior strength；inferior position；disadvantageous position：处于～ be in a disadvantageous position

【劣质】 lièzhì of poor quality；of low quality；inferior

【劣种】 lièzhǒng inferior strain

猎[獵] (liè) hunt：～狐 fox hunting / 去打～ go hunting

【猎场】 lièchǎng hunting ground；hunting field

【猎刀】 lièdāo hunting knife

【猎狗】 liègǒu hunting dog；hound

【猎户】 lièhù hunter；huntsman

【猎获】 lièhuò capture or kill in hunting；bag

【猎奇】 lièqí hunt for novelty；seek novelty

【猎潜舰】 lièqiánjiàn submarine chaser

【猎枪】 lièqiāng shotgun；hunting rifle

【猎取】 lièqǔ 1.（打猎获得）hunt 2.（夺取）pursue；seek；hunt for

【猎犬】 lièquǎn hunting dog

【猎人】 lièrén hunter；huntsman

【猎手】 lièshǒu hunter

【猎物】 lièwù prey；quarry；game

【猎鹰】 lièyīng falcon

【猎装】 lièzhuāng a hunting dress

鬣 (liè) mane

【鬣狗】 liègǒu 〈*Zool*.〉hyena；striped hyena

lin

拎 (līn) carry；lift：她～着一个篮子。She was carrying a basket.

邻[鄰、隣] (lín) 1.（邻居）neighbor：睦～政策 good-neighbor policy 2.（邻近的）neighboring；near；adjacent：～村 neighboring village / ～国 neighboring country / ～县 neighboring county / ～座 an adjacent seat

【邻邦】 línbāng neighboring country

【邻接】 línjiē border on；be next to；be contiguous to；adjoin

【邻近】 línjìn 1.（紧挨着）near；close to；adjacent to 2.（附件）nearby；at close quarters

【邻居】 línjū neighbor

【邻里】 línlǐ 1.（乡里）neighborhood 2.（同一乡里的人）people of the neighborhood；neighbors

林 (lín) 1.（树林或竹林）forest；woods：防风～ windbreaks；windbreak forest / 防沙～ sand-breaks / 风景～ ornamental plantation / 松～ pine forest / 天然～ natural forest / 用材～ timber forest；timberland / 竹～ bamboo groves / 伐～ cut down a forest / 护～ protect forests；protect a forest / 造～ afforestation 2.（界，圈）circles：艺～ art circles / 自立于世界民族之～ stand independently among the peoples of the world 3.（林业）forestry

【林产品】 línchǎnpǐn forest products

【林场】 línchǎng 1.（指单位）forest farm 2.（指地方）forestry center

【林丛】 líncóng grove

【林带】 líndài forest belt：防沙～ sandbreaks

【林副产品】 línfùchǎnpǐn minor forest produce

【林冠】 línguān 〈*Forestry*〉 crown canopy; crown cover

【林海】 línhǎi immense forest

【林卡】 Línkǎ 〈place〉 Lingka

【林立】 línlì stand in great numbers：烟囱～ a forest of chimneys

【林木】 línmù **1**.（树林）forest; woods：经济～ trees of economic value / 油料～ oil-yielding shrubs **2**.（森林中的树木）forest tree

【林木线】 línmùxiàn timberline

【林区】 línqū forest zone; forest region; forest：营造～ afforested area

【林学】 línxué forestry

【林业】 línyè forestry

【林业工人】 línyè gōngrén forest worker; forester

【林业学院】 línyè xuéyuàn forestry institute

【林阴路】 línyīnlù boulevard; avenue

【林园】 línyuán wooden land; a park of trees and vegetation

【林芝】 Línzhī 〈place〉 Nyingchi

【林中空地】 lín zhōng kòngdì clearance

【林周】 Línzhōu 〈place〉 Lhunzhub

【林子】 lín·zi 〈*colloq*.〉 woods; grove; forest

淋（lín） pour; drench（另见"淋"lìn）

【淋巴】 línbā 〈*Anat*.〉 lymph

【淋巴管】 línbāguǎn 〈*Anat*.〉 lymphatic vessel

【淋巴结】 línbājié 〈*Anat*.〉 lymph node

【淋巴结结核】 línbājié jiéhé 〈*Med*.〉 scrofula; tuberculous lymphadenitis

【淋巴结肿大】 línbājié zhǒngdà 〈*Med*.〉 lymph node enlargement

【淋巴细胞】 línbā xìbāo lymphocyte

【淋巴腺】 línbāxiàn 〈*Anat*.〉 lymphatic gland

【淋漓】 línlí **1**.（往下滴）dripping wet：大汗～ sweat all over; drip with sweat **2**.（形容畅快）free from inhibition

【淋漓尽致】 línlí-jìnzhì incisively and vividly; thoroughly

【淋漓柯】 línlíkē 〈*Bot*.〉 urai tanoak

【淋淋】 línlín dripping：湿～的衣服 dripping clothes

【淋湿】 línshī be soaked; splashed wet

【淋洗】 línxǐ 〈*Chem*. *Fibre*〉 drip washing

【淋雨】 línyǔ get wet in the rain; be exposed to the rain

【淋浴】 línyù shower bath; shower：洗个～ take a shower bath

【淋浴莲蓬头】 línyù lián·pengtóu shower bath head

【淋浴喷头】 línyù pēntóu shower

【淋浴室】 línyùshì shower bathroom; shower room

琳（lín） 〈*written*〉 beautiful jade

【琳琅满目】 línláng-mǎnmù a superb collection of beautiful things; a feast for the eyes

霖（lín） continuous heavy rain

【霖雨】 línyǔ continuous heavy rain

临［臨］（lín） **1**.（临近）face; overlook：南～大海 border on the sea in the south **2**.（来到）arrive; be present：亲～ come personally **3**.（将要）on the point of; just before; be about to **4**.（摹仿）copy

【临本】 línběn copy（of a painting）

【临别】 línbié at parting; just before parting

【临别赠言】 línbié zèngyán parting advice; parting words

【临产】 línchǎn about to give birth; parturient

【临场教练员】 línchǎng jiàoliànyuán bench coach

【临床】 línchuáng 〈*Med*.〉 clinical

【临床观察】 línchuáng guānchá clinical observation

【临床检查】 línchuáng jiǎnchá clinical examination

【临床心理学】 línchuáng xīnlǐxué clinical psychology

【临床学】 línchuángxué clinical medicine

【临床医生】 línchuáng yīshēng clinician

【临床应用】 línchuáng yīngyòng clinical practice

【临床诊断】 línchuáng zhěnduàn clinical diagnosis

【临到】 líndào **1**.（接近）be about to; just before; on the point of 2.(落到) befall; happen to: 万一这种不幸～他头上 in case such misfortune should happen to him

【临界】 línjiè 〈*Physics*〉 critical

【临界点】 línjièdiǎn critical point

【临界角】 línjièjiǎo critical angle

【临界速度】 línjiè sùdù critical speed

【临界温度】 línjiè wēndù critical temperature

【临近】 línjìn close to; close on

【临摹】 línmó copy; imitate

【临时】 línshí 1.(事到临头) at the time when sth. happens 2.(暂时的) temporary; provisional; for a short time

【临时抱佛脚】 línshí bào fójiǎo 1.(指考试前仓促复习) cramming 2.(指事到临头仓促准备) make a frantic last-minute effort

【临时代办】 línshí dàibàn chargé d'affaires ad interim

【临时代理人】 línshí dàilǐrén acting agent

【临时工】 línshígōng casual laborer; temporary worker

【临时户口】 línshí hùkǒu temporary residence permit

【临时拘留】 línshí jūliú temporary detention

【临时扣押】 línshí kòuyā interim attachment

【临时停火】 línshí tínghuǒ suspension of arms

【临时舞台】 línshí wǔtái makeshift stage

【临时协议】 línshí xiéyì interim agreement; provisional agreement

【临时演员】 línshí yǎnyuán atmosphere person

【临时议程】 línshí yìchéng provisional agenda

【临时用户】 línshí yònghù casual user

【临时证书】 línshí zhèngshū temporary credentials; temporary papers

【临时政府】 línshí zhèngfǔ provisional government; interim government

【临时执照】 línshí zhízhào provisional certificate; temporary licence

【临死】 línsǐ on one's deathbed

【临头】 líntóu befall; happen: 大难～ be faced with imminent disaster

【临危】 línwēi 1.(病重将死) be dying 2.(面临危险) facing death or deadly peril; in the hour of danger: ～不惧 be undaunted in face of periles; be composed in times of emergency

【临危授命】 línwēi-shòumìng give a very important assignment in time of a national emergency

【临刑】 línxíng just before execution

【临阵】 línzhèn on the eve of a battle

【临阵脱逃】 línzhèn-tuōtáo desert on the eve of a battle; sneak away at a critical juncture

【临终】 línzhōng approaching one's end; immediately before one's death; on one's deathbed: ～遗言 deathbed will; deathbed words

【临终关怀医院】 línzhōng guānhuái yīyuàn hospice

粼 (lín)

【粼粼】 línlín clear and bright: 碧波～ dazzling green ripples

嶙 (lín)

【嶙峋】 línxún 1.(指山石) jagged; rugged; craggy 2.(指人) bony; thin: 瘦骨～ be emaciated

遴 (lín)

【遴选】 línxuǎn 1.(选拔) select sb. for a post 2.(挑选) select; choose

辚 (lín)

【辚辚】 línlín rattle; clank: 车～。The cart rattled along.

磷[**燐**] (lín) 〈*Chem.*〉 phosphorus (元素符号 P)

【磷肥】 línféi phosphate fertilizer

【磷火】 línhuǒ will-o'-the wisp; phosphorescent light

【磷酸】 línsuān 〈*Chem.*〉 phosphoric acid

【磷酸铵】 línsuān'ān 〈*Chem.*〉 ammonium phosphate

【磷虾】 línxiā krill

【磷中毒】 lín zhòngdú phosphorism

鳞 (lín) 1.(鱼鳞) scale: 刮鱼～ scrape the scale off the fish; scale the fish 2.(像鱼鳞的) like the scales of a fish

【鳞次栉比】 líncì-zhìbǐ row upon row of (buildings)

【鳞茎】 línjīng 〈*Bot.*〉 bulb

【鳞片】 línpiàn 1.(鱼鳞) scale 2.(植物芽上的鳞片) bud scale

【鳞伤】 línshāng a mass of bruises：遍体～ be covered with bruises

凛[凜](lǐn) 1.（冷）cold 2.（严肃）strict; stern; severe 3.（畏惧）afraid; apprehensive

【凛冽】 lǐnliè piercingly cold; biting cold

【凛凛】 lǐnlǐn 1.（寒冷）cold 2.（严肃）stern; awe-inspiring：威风～ majestic-looking; with an awe-inspiring

【凛然】 lǐnrán stern; awe-inspiring：正气～ awe-inspiring righteousness

【凛若冰霜】 lǐnruò-bīngshuāng cold as ice and dew

檩[檁](lǐn) 〈*Archit.*〉 purlin

【檩条】 lǐntiáo 〈*Archit.*〉 purlin

吝(lìn) stingy; mean; closefisted

【吝啬】 lìnsè stingy; niggardly; miserly; mean

【吝啬鬼】 lìnsèguǐ miser; niggard; skinflint

【吝惜】 lìnxī grudge; stint：～财物 be sparing with money and goods, not willing to spend

赁(lìn) rent; hire：～借 hire; borrow / ～书 borrow books for reading / ～屋 rent a house / ～租 rent / 房屋出～ house to let

【赁费】 lìnfèi rent; rental

淋(lìn) strain; filter：～一下药 strain the herbal medicine
（另见"淋"lín）

【淋病】 lìnbìng 〈*Med.*〉 clap; gonorrhea

膦(lìn) 〈*Chem.*〉 phosphine

ling

〇(líng) zero：一九九～年 1990; nineteen ninety / 二～～～年 2000; two thousand

伶(líng)

【伶仃】 língdīng 1.（孤独）left alone without help; lonely：孤苦～ alone and uncared for 2.（瘦弱）skinny; frail

【伶俐】 línglì clever; bright; quick-witted：～乖巧 clever and tricky / 口齿～ have a glib tongue

【伶牙俐齿】 língyá-lìchǐ have the gift of the gab; have a glib tongue

囹(líng)

【囹圄】 língyǔ prison; jail; gaol：身陷～ be sent to prison; be imprisoned

玲(líng)

【玲琅】 língláng tinkling of jades

【玲珑】 línglóng 1.（精巧细致）ingeniously and delicately wrought; exquisite 2.（灵活敏捷）clever and nimble

【玲珑剔透】 línglóng-tītòu 1.（指器物）exquisitely carved; beautifully wrought 2.（指人）clever and tricky

铃(líng) 1.（响器）bell：摇～ ring the bell 2.（铃状物）anything in the shape of a bell 3.（蕾铃）boll; bud：棉～ cotton boll

【铃铛】 líng·dang small bell

【铃鼓】 línggǔ 〈*Music*〉 tambourine

【铃兰】 línglán 〈*Bot.*〉 lily of the valley

【铃声】 língshēng the tinkle of bells

聆(líng) 〈*written*〉 listen; hear

【聆听】 língtīng listen

【聆悉】 língxī learn; hear

羚(líng) antelope; gazelle ‖ 大羚羊 oryx / 小羚羊 duiker; forest duiker / 小岩羚 steenbok / 岩羚羊 chamois / 印度羚 blackbuck

【羚牛】 língniú takin

【羚羊】 língyáng gazelle

【羚羊角】 línyángjiǎo antelope's horn

零(líng) 1.（数字）zero sign (0); nought：二～四二号 No. 2042 / ～点～四五 0.045 2.（放在两数之间）两年～十天 two years and ten days / 七十二元～七分 seventy dollars and seven cents 3.（零头）odd; with a little extra：年纪八十有～ a little more than eighty years old / 四千挂～ four thousand odd 4.（没有数量）nought; zero; nil：他们的努力结果等于～。Their effort came to nought. 5.（零度）zero：～下二十摄氏度 20 degrees below zero centigrade; minus twenty degrees centigrade 6.（零碎）fractional; part 7.（枯萎而落下）wither and fall 8.（体育零分）nil; love：～比～ no score; love all

【零部件】 língbùjiàn spare part

【零存整取】 língcún zhěngqǔ deposit small sums of money every month and draw out both the principal and interest in a lump sum when the specified time comes up
【零蛋】 língdàn zero; love
【零点】 língdiǎn 1.(零度) zero point 2.(零时) zero hour; 0:00 a.m.
【零度】 língdù zero
【零儿】 língr small change; coins: 找～ give change; make change
【零分】 língfēn zero; no marks; scoreless
【零工】 línggōng 1.(指短工) odd job; short-term hired labor: 打～ do odd jobs 2.(做零工的人) odd-job man; casual laborer
【零花】 línghuā 1.(零碎地花钱) incidental expenses 2.(零用钱) pocket money
【零活】 línghuó odd jobs; temporary work
【零件】 língjiàn spare parts; spares
【零落】 língluò 1.(脱落) withered and fallen 2.(衰败) decayed; desolate 3.(稀疏) scattered; sporadic: ～的来访者 a scattering of visitors
【零卖】 língmài 1.(不成批地卖) retail; sell retail 2.(零散地卖) sell by the piece or in small quantities
【零七八碎】 língqī-bāsuì 1.(零碎而纷乱) scattered and disorderly 2.(杂事,杂物) miscellaneous and trifling things; odds and ends
【零钱】 língqián 1.(面值小的钱) small change; coins 2.(零用钱) pocket money 3.(小费收入) tip; gratuity
【零敲碎打】 língqiāo-suìdǎ do sth. bit by bit, off and on; adopt a piecemeal approach
【零散】 líng·sǎn dispersed; scattered
【零时】 língshí zero hour; 0:00 a.m.
【零食】 língshí between-meal nibbles; snacks
【零售】 língshòu retail; sell retail
【零售店】 língshòudiàn retail shop; retail store
【零售额】 língshòu'é turnover
【零售价格】 língshòu jiàgé retail price
【零售商】 língshòushāng retail dealer; retail trader; retailer
【零售市场】 língshòu shìchǎng retail market
【零售总额】 língshòu zǒng'é total volume of retail sales
【零数】 língshù odd amount in addition to the round number
【零碎】 língsuì 1.(琐碎) scrappy; piecemeal; fragmentary 2.(零碎的事物) odds and ends; oddments; bits and pieces
【零头】 língtóu 1.(零碎数量) odd: 3 米～ the odd three meters 2.(剩余的部分) remnant
【零星】 língxīng 1.(零碎的) fragmentary; odd: ～材料 fragmentary material 2.(零散) sporadic
【零星小雨】 língxīng xiǎoyǔ occasional drizzles
【零用】 língyòng 1.(小额费用) small incidental expenses 2.(零用钱) pocket money
【零用钱】 língyòngqián pocket money
【零值经济增长】 língzhí jīngjì zēngzhǎng zero economic growth
【零值人口增长】 língzhí rénkǒu zēngzhǎng zero population growth

龄 (líng) 1.(岁数) age; years 2.(年限) length of time; duration: 工～ length of service; number of years worked; years of service

灵[靈、霛] (líng) 1.(灵活) quick; clever; sharp: 耳朵很～ have sharp ears / 脑筋不～ one's brain doesn't seem to be working well 2.(灵验) efficacious; effective 3.(精神;灵魂) spirit; intelligence: 英～ the spirit of the brave departed 4.(关于神仙的) fairy; sprite; elf 5.(关于死人的) of the deceased; bier: 守～ stand as guards at the bier
【灵便】 líng·bian 1.(灵活) nimble; agile: ～的手指 agile fingers 2.(工具轻巧) easy to handle; handy: 这辆车开起来很～。The car handles well.
【灵车】 língchē hearse
【灵床】 língchuáng bier
【灵丹妙药】 língdān-miàoyào miraculous cure; panacea
【灵感】 línggǎn inspiration
【灵魂】 línghún 1.(迷信说法) soul; spirit 2.(心灵) inmost thoughts: ～深处 inmost; innermost 3.(良心) soul; principle; conscience: 出卖～ sell one's soul 4.(决定性因素) deciding factor; determining factor
【灵活】 línghuó 1.(敏捷) nimble; agile;

quick：他的脑筋比较～。His minds are more flexible 2.（善于随机应变）flexible；elastic：～措施 flexible measures / ～运用 apply in a flexible way

【灵活关税】 línghuó guānshuì flexible tariff

【灵活性】 línghuóxìng flexibility；adaptability；mobility

【灵机】 língjī sudden inspiration；brain wave：～一动 have a brain wave；a sudden inspiration

【灵柩】 língjiù a coffin containing a corpse；bier

【灵敏】 língmǐn sensitive；keen；agile；acute

【灵敏度】 língmǐndù sensitivity

【灵气】 língqì anima

【灵巧】 língqiǎo dexterous；skillful；ingenious

【灵堂】 língtáng mourning hall

【灵通】 língtōng well-informed；having quick access to information：消息～人士 well-informed sources

【灵位】 língwèi memorial tablet

【灵性】 língxìng intelligence

【灵验】 língyàn 1.（有奇效）efficacious；effective 2.（应验）accurate；right：她说的话果然～。What she said is proved to be correct.

棂［欞、櫺］（líng） lattice；latticework：窗～ window lattice

凌［淩$^{1-3}$］（líng） 1.（欺侮）insult 2.（逼近）approach 3.（升高）rise high；tower aloft 4.（冰凌）icicle

【凌波】 língbō ride the waves

【凌晨】 língchén in the small hours；before dawn

【凌驾】 língjià place oneself above；override：～他人 oppress another in order to advance oneself

【凌空】 língkōng be high up in the air；soar or tower aloft：～高飞的鸟 bird soaring to the skies

【凌厉】 línglì swift and fierce：～的攻势 a swift and fierce attack

【凌乱】 língluàn in disorder；in a mess；in a state of confusion

【凌辱】 língrǔ insult；humiliate

【凌侮】 língwǔ insult；humiliate

【凌汛】 língxùn ice run

【凌云】 língyún reach the clouds；soar to the skies：～壮志 lofty aspiration

陵（líng） 1.（丘陵）hill；mound 2.（陵墓）imperial tomb；mausoleum：中山～ the Sun Yat-sen Mausoleum

【陵居】 língjū live on the highland

【陵墓】 língmù mausoleum；tomb

【陵寝】 língqǐn emperor's mausoleum

【陵园】 língyuán tombs surrounded by a park；cemetery：烈士～ cemetery of revolutionary martyrs

菱（líng） 〈*Bot*.〉 water chestnut；water caltrop

【菱角】 líng·jiao water chestnut；water caltrop

【菱形】 língxíng rhomboid；rhombus；lozenge

绫（líng） a very fine silk fabric；damask silk：～罗绸缎 silks and satins

【绫子】 líng·zi thin satin；damask silk

令（lǐng） 〈*classifier*〉 ream（of paper）：一～纸 a ream of paper
（另见"令"lìng）

岭［嶺］（lǐng） 1.（山）mountain；ridge：崇山峻～ high mountain ridges / 翻山越～ cross over mountain after mountain 2.（山脉）mountains；mountain range：大兴安～ Da Xingganling Mountains / 小兴安～ Xiao Xingganling Mountains 3.（专指南岭）Nan Ling Mountains：～南 south of Nan Ling Mountains

领（lǐng） 1.（颈）neck 2.（衣领）collar；neck；neckband：翻～ reverse collar / 高～ cowl collar / 鸡心～ V-neck / 立～ stand-up collar / 松紧～ neck of a jumper / 圆高～ turtleneck；polo neck；roll neck / 折～ turn-down collar / 舟型～ boat neck 3.（要领）outline；main point 4.〈*classifier*〉一～席 a mat 5.（带；引）lead；usher：把客人～到会客室去 usher the guests into the reception room 6.（领有）have jurisdiction over；be in possession of 7.（领取）receive；draw；get：～工资 take one's wages 8.（领会）understand；comprehend；grasp

【领班】 lǐngbān foreman；head waiter

【领兵】 lǐngbīng lead troops；a military offi-

cer
【领唱】 lǐngchàng 1.〈*Music*〉lead a chorus 2.(领唱者) leading singer
【领带】 lǐngdài tie; necktie
【领带夹】 lǐngdàijiā a tie clip
【领带扣针】 lǐngdài kòuzhēn tiepin
【领导】 lǐngdǎo 1.(率领前进) lead; exercise leadership: 集体～ collective leadership 2.(领导者) leader; head; chief
【领导班子】 lǐngdǎo bān·zi leading group
【领导方法】 lǐngdǎo fāngfǎ method of leadership
【领导干部】 lǐngdǎo gànbù leading cadre
【领导核心】 lǐngdǎo héxīn leading nucleus
【领导机关】 lǐngdǎo jīguān leading body
【领导集团】 lǐngdǎo jítuán leading group
【领导权】 lǐngdǎoquán leadership; authority; overall control
【领导人】 lǐngdǎorén leader
【领导艺术】 lǐngdǎo yìshù the art of leadership
【领导职务】 lǐngdǎo zhíwù leading post: 担任～ take up a post of leadership
【领导职务终身制】 lǐngdǎo zhíwù zhōngshēnzhì life tenure of leading posts
【领导作风】 lǐngdǎo zuòfēng work style of the leadership
【领地】 lǐngdì 1.(封建主的领地) manor 2.(领土) territory
【领队】 lǐngduì 1.(率领队伍) lead a group 2.(领队的人) the leader of a group, sports team, etc.
【领港】 lǐnggǎng 1.(引导船舶进出港) pilot a ship into or out of a harbor 2.(领港员) pilot
【领港费】 lǐnggǎngfèi pilotage
【领钩】 lǐnggōu hook
【领钩环】 lǐnggōuhuán eye
【领海】 lǐnghǎi territorial waters; territorial sea
【领海范围】 lǐnghǎi fànwéi extent of territorial waters; limits of territorial sea
【领海管辖权】 lǐnghǎi guǎnxiáquán jurisdiction within territorial water
【领海宽度】 lǐnghǎi kuāndù breadth of the territorial sea
【领海权】 lǐnghǎiquán maritime domain
【领海线】 lǐnghǎixiàn boundary line of territorial waters
【领航】 lǐngháng 1.(引导船舶或飞机航行) navigate; pilot 2.(领航员) navigator; pilot
【领航飞机】 lǐngháng fēijī pathfinder aircraft
【领航权】 lǐnghángquán pilotage
【领航设备】 lǐngháng shèbèi navigation equipment
【领航图】 lǐnghángtú pilotage chart
【领航员】 lǐnghángyuán navigator
【领会】 lǐnghuì understand; comprehend; grasp: ～文件精神 grasp the essence of the document
【领奖】 lǐngjiǎng receive a prize
【领教】 lǐngjiào 1.(客气话) thanks; much obliged 2.(请教) ask advice 3.(经历过) experience; encounter
【领结】 lǐngjié bow tie
【领巾】 lǐngjīn scarf; neckerchief: 红～ red scarf
【领进】 lǐngjìn usher into; lead to; introduce into
【领空】 lǐngkōng territorial sky; territorial air space; territorial air
【领空权】 lǐngkōngquán jurisdiction within space
【领口】 lǐngkǒu 1.(衣服领口) collarband; neckband: 敞着～ with the collar unbottoned / ～太小了。The neckband is too small. 2.(领子两头相合处) the place where the two ends of a collar meet
【领扣】 lǐngkòu collar button; collar stud
【领款】 lǐngkuǎn draw money
【领款人】 lǐngkuǎnrén payee
【领陆】 lǐnglù territory
【领路】 lǐnglù lead the way
【领略】 lǐnglüè have a taste of; realize; appreciate: ～粤菜风味 taste Guangdong dishes
【领情】 lǐngqíng feel grateful to sb.; appreciate the kindness
【领取】 lǐngqǔ draw; receive
【领事】 lǐngshì 〈*Foreign Affairs*〉consul: 建立～关系 establish consular relations
【领事处】 lǐngshìchù consular section
【领事馆】 lǐngshìguǎn consulate
【领事豁免权】 lǐngshì huòmiǎnquán consular immunity
【领事签证】 lǐngshì qiānzhèng consular in-

voice
【领事特权】 lǐngshì tèquán consular privileges
【领事条例】 lǐngshì tiáolì consular act
【领受】 lǐngshòu accept (kindness, etc.); receive
【领水】 lǐngshuǐ territorial waters
【领头】 lǐngtóu take the lead; be the first to do sth.
【领土】 lǐngtǔ territory：钓鱼岛是中国～。Diaoyu Islands is Chinese territory.
【领土管辖权】 lǐngtǔ guǎnxiáquán territorial jurisdiction; jurisdiction within territory
【领土扩张】 lǐngtǔ kuòzhāng territorial expansion; territorial aggrandizement
【领土毗连】 lǐngtǔ pílián territorial contiguity
【领土完整】 lǐngtǔ wánzhěng territorial integrity：捍卫我国～ defend our territorial integrity
【领土要求】 lǐngtǔ yāoqiú territorial claim：向…提出～ make territorial claims to . . .
【领悟】 lǐngwù comprehend; grasp
【领先】 lǐngxiān 1.(走在最前面) be in the lead; lead 2.(处于最前列) leading
【领衔】 lǐngxián be the first on a name list; head the list of signers
【领衔主演】 lǐngxián zhǔyǎn star in
【领袖】 lǐngxiù leader
【领养】 lǐngyǎng adopt; adoption (n.)：～的子女 adopted children / 她～了一个孩子。She had the child adopted. / 这对夫妇～了两个孤儿。They couple adopted two orphans.
【领养人】 lǐngyǎngrén adopter
【领域】 lǐngyù 1.(指国家领土) territory; domain; realm：～广大 the domain is vast 2.(范围) field; sphere; domain; realm：科学～ the field of science / 意识形态～ the ideological sphere
【领章】 lǐngzhāng collar badge; collar insignia
【领子】 lǐng·zi collar

另 (lìng) other; another; separate：付款条例～议。The terms of payment are to be arranged.
【另案】 lìng'àn the other case
【另册】 lìngcè the other register
【另搞一套】 lìnggǎo yītào do what suits oneself; go one's own way
【另函】 lìnghán a separate letter; write another letter
【另寄】 lìngjì post separately; post under separate cover
【另立户头】 lìnglì hùtóu open another bank account
【另谋生路】 lìngmóu shēnglù find another way of living
【另起炉灶】 lìngqǐ lúzào set up a separate kitchen; make a fresh start; start all over again
【另请高明】 lìngqǐng gāomíng find someone better qualified
【另外】 lìngwài in addition; moreover; besides：～你还要些什么? Would you like anything else?
【另行】 lìngxíng separately：～通知 be notified later; till further notice
【另眼相看】 lìngyǎn xiāngkàn 1.(指不同于一般) regard sb. with special respect 2.(指不同于过去) view sb. in a new, more favorable light; see sb. in a new light
【另议】 lìngyì be discussed separately

令 (lìng) 1.(命令) command; order; decree：下～ issue an order 2.(使) make; cause 3.(时节) season：夏～时间 summer time 4.〈*respects*〉 your：～亲 your parents 5.(酒令) drinking game 6.(美好) good：～德 good character; high virtue / ～誉 good reputation
【令爱】 lìng'ài your daughter
【令嫒】 lìng'ài 同"令爱"
【令郎】 lìngláng your son
【令人】 lìng rén make one：～发指 make one's hair stand on end / ～费解 elude the understanding / ～鼓舞 inspiring / ～怀疑 open to suspicion / ～泪下 bring the tears to one's eyes / ～满意 satisfactory; satisfying / ～捧腹 make one burst out laughing / ～钦佩 admirable / ～神往 fire one's imagination / ～深省 make one deep in thought / ～痛心 cut one to the heart / ～厌烦 bore one to tears / ～作呕 make one sick
【令堂】 lìngtáng your mother
【令行禁止】 lìngxíng-jìnzhǐ strict execution of orders and prohibitions

【令尊】 lìngzūn your father

liu

溜(liū) 1.(往下滑) slide; glide: 从滑梯上～下来 slide down a children's slide 2.(滑溜) smooth 3.(溜走) sneak off; slip away; glide
(另见"溜"liù)

【溜冰】 liūbīng 1.(滑冰) slide on the ice; skating 2.(溜旱冰) roller-skating

【溜冰场】 liūbīngchǎng skating rink

【溜冰鞋】 liūbīngxié 1.(冰刀鞋) skating shoes 2.(四轮旱冰鞋) roller skates 3.(单排四轮旱冰鞋) rollerblade

【溜达】 liū·da stroll; saunter; go for a walk

【溜须拍马】 liūxū-pāimǎ fawn on; toady to; shamelessly flatter

【溜之大吉】 liūzhīdàjí sneak away; slink off

【溜走】 liūzǒu leave stealthily; slip away

熘[溜](liū) sauté; quick-fry: ～肝尖 liver sauté / ～鱼片 fish slices sauté

刘[劉](liú)

【刘海儿】 liúhǎir bang; fringe

浏[瀏](liú)

【浏览】 liúlǎn glance over; skim through; browse: ～报纸上的大标题 take a glance at the newspaper headlines

留[畱](liú) 1.(不离去) stay; remain: ～在亲戚家里 stay with a relative 2.(留下) ask sb. to stay; keep sb. where he is: ～朋友吃饭 ask one's friend to stay for dinner 3.(保留) reserve; keep; save: ～座位 reserve a seat for sb. 4.(留着继续长) let grow; grow; wear: ～胡子 grow a beard 5.(收下) accept; take 6.(遗留) leave

【留步】 liúbù 〈*politeness*〉 don't bother to see me out; don't bother to come any further

【留成】 liúchéng portion (of the profits); kept (by the enterprise)

【留成外汇】 liúchéng wàihuì retain a portion of one's foreign exchange

【留存】 liúcún 1.(保存) preserve; keep 2.(存在) remain; be extant

【留待】 liúdài wait until

【留党察看】 liúdǎng chákàn be placed on probation within the Party

【留芳百世】 liúfāng-bǎishì have a niche in the temple of fame

【留级】 liújí fail to go up to the next grade; repeat the year's work

【留级生】 liújíshēng repeater

【留空】 liúkòng leave a blank; leave a space in writing

【留兰香】 liúlánxiāng 〈*Bot.*〉 spearmint

【留连忘返】 liúlián-wàngfǎn so enchanted as to forget about home

【留恋】 liúliàn 1.(不忍离开) be reluctant to leave (a place); can't bear to part: ～家乡 be unwilling to leave one's hometown 2.(缅怀过去) recall with nostalgia

【留名】 liúmíng leave behind a good reputation

【留难】 liúnàn make things difficult for sb.: 百般～ pose all kinds of obstacles; create obstructions of every description

【留念】 liúniàn accept or keep as a souvenir; accept as a memento

【留情】 liúqíng show mercy or forgiveness: 手下～ show mercy / 毫不～ show no mercy

【留任】 liúrèn retain a post; remain in office

【留神】 liúshén be careful; take care

【留声电话机】 liúshēng diànhuàjī telegraphone

【留声机】 liúshēngjī phonograph

【留守】 liúshǒu stay behind to take care of things; stay behind for garrison or liaison duty

【留守处】 liúshǒuchù rear office

【留守人员】 liúshǒu rényuán rear personnel

【留宿】 liúsù 1.(留客人住宿) put up a guest for the night 2.(留下来住宿) stay over night; put up for the night

【留校察看】 liúxiào chákàn be kept in school but placed under surveillance

【留心】 liúxīn be careful; take care

【留学】 liúxué study abroad

【留学生】 liúxuéshēng 1.(指仍在外者) student studying abroad: 公费～ state-funded student 2.(指归来者) returned student 3.(指外国的) foreign student

【留言】 liúyán leave one's comments; leave a

message

【留言簿】 liúyánbù visitors' book

【留意】 liúyì be careful; look out; keep one's eyes open

【留影】 liúyǐng take a photo as a memento; have a picture taken as a souvenir

【留用】 liúyòng continue to employ; keep on

【留余地】 liúyúdì allow for unforeseen circumstances; leave some leeway

【留职】 liúzhí retain office

【留职停薪】 liúzhí tíngxīn stop payment of salary but retain office

【留种】 liúzhǒng 〈*Agric.*〉 reserve seed for planting; have seed stock

【留种地】 liúzhǒngdì 〈*Agric.*〉 seed-plot; seedbed

馏 (liú) (另见"馏"liù)

【馏出油】 liúchūyóu 〈*Petroleum*〉 distillate oil

【馏份】 liúfèn 〈*Petroleum*〉 fraction; cut: 轻～ light fraction / 重～ heavy fraction

榴 (liú)

【榴弹】 liúdàn high explosive shell

【榴弹炮】 liúdànpào howitzer

【榴莲】 liúlián durian; civet durian

【榴霰弹】 liúsǎndàn shrapnel; canister

镏 (liú)

【镏金】 liújīn gold-plating: ～银器 gilded silverware

瘤 (liú) tumor: 恶性～ malignant tumor / 良性～ benign tumor / 肉～ sarcoma / 纤维～ fibroma / 腺～ adenoma

【瘤胃】 liúwèi rumen

【瘤子】 liú·zi tumor

流 (liú) 1.(流动) flow; run 2.(移动不定) moving from place to place; drifting; wandering 3.(流传) spread; circulate 4.(向坏的方向转变) change for the worse; degenerate 5.(流放) banish; send into exile 6.(水流) stream of water: 顺～ with the current 7.(似水流的) sth. resembling a stream of water; current: 电～ electric current / 气～ air current 8.(品类; 等级) class; rate; grade: 第一～的旅馆 first-class hotel / 第一～的作家 a first-rate writer / 二～演员 second-rate actor

【流弊】 liúbì corrupt practices; abuses

【流产】 liúchǎn 1.(指胎儿不足月产出) abortion; miscarriage: 人工～ induced abortion; artificial abortion 2.(指计划落空) miscarry; fall through; frustrate

【流畅】 liúchàng easy and smooth

【流程】 liúchéng 1.(工艺程序) technological process 2.〈*Mineral.*〉 circuit

【流程图】 liúchéngtú flow chart; flow diagram

【流传】 liúchuán spread; circulate; hand down

【流窜】 liúcuàn flee hither and thither: ～作案 flee hither and thither to commit offenses

【流窜犯】 liúcuànfàn migratory criminal

【流弹】 liúdàn stray bullet

【流动】 liúdòng 1.(移动) flow: 人才合理～ rational flow of trained personnel 2.(经常变换位置) going from place to place; on the move; mobile

【流动汇率】 liúdòng huìlǜ floating rate of exchange

【流动基金】 liúdòng jījīn circulating fund

【流动人口】 liúdòng rénkǒu floating population

【流动售货车】 liúdòng shòuhuòchē shop-on-wheels

【流动性】 liúdòngxìng mobility; fluidity

【流动资本】 liúdòng zīběn circulating capital; floating capital; circulation funds

【流动资产】 liúdòng zīchǎn floating assets; current assets

【流毒】 liúdú 1.(毒害的流传) exert a pernicious influence 2.(流传的毒害) pernicious influence; baneful influence

【流芳百世】 liúfāng bǎishì leave a good name for a hundred generations; leave a reputation which will go down to posterity

【流放】 liúfàng 1.(流放犯人) banish; send into exile 2.(把原木放在河里运输) float (logs) downstream: ～木材 float logs

【流放地】 liúfàngdì penal colony

【流感】 liúgǎn flu; influenza

【流寇】 liúkòu roving bandits; roving rebel bands

【流浪】 liúlàng roam about; lead a vagrant life

【流浪儿】 liúlàngr waif; street urchin; homeless child

【流浪汉】 liúlànghàn tramp; vagrant

【流浪者】 liúlàngzhě vagabond; vagrant

【流离失所】 liúlí-shīsuǒ become destitute and homeless; be forced to leave home and wander about

【流里流气】 liúlǐliúqì rascally

【流利】 liúlì 1.（指说话）fluent; smooth：讲一口～的英语 speak fluent English 2.（指书写）flowing; graceful：书写～ write in flowing handwriting

【流连忘返】 liúlián-wàngfǎn enjoy oneself so much as to forget to go home; linger on, forgetting to return

【流量】 liúliàng rate of flow; flow; discharge

【流露】 liúlù reveal; betray; show unintentionally：真情的～ a revelation of one's true feelings

【流落】 liúluò wander about destitute

【流氓】 liúmáng 1.（指人）rogue; hoodlum; hooligan; gangster 2.（指手段）immoral behavior; indecency：耍～ behave like a hoodlum; take liberties with women; act indecently

【流氓团伙】 liúmáng tuánhuǒ hoodlum gangs; gangs of hooligans

【流明】 liúmíng 〈*Physics*〉lumen

【流脑】 liúnǎo 〈*Med.*〉meningitis

【流年】 liúnián 1.（光阴）fleeting time 2.（运道）prediction of a person's luck in a given year

【流派】 liúpài school; sect

【流沙】 liúshā drift sand; quicksand; shifting sand

【流失】 liúshī 1.（流掉）run off; be washed away：水土～ loss of water and erosion of soil; soil erosion 2.（流散失去）loss 3.（喻人员离失）drain：人才～ brain drain 4.（喻中途退学）drop out

【流失率】 liúshīlǜ dropout rate

【流失生】 liúshīshēng school dropout

【流逝】 liúshì pass; elapse：光阴～ time flows away

【流水】 liúshuǐ 1.（流动的水）running water 2.（商店销售额）turnover

【流水线】 liúshuǐxiàn assembly line

【流水账】 liúshuǐzhàng 1.（每天的账目）day-to-day account; current account 2.（喻叙述或记载）

【流水作业】 liúshuǐ zuòyè flow process; assembly line method; conveyer system

【流速】 liúsù 1.〈*Mech.*〉velocity of flow 2.〈*Water Conservancy*〉current velocity

【流速计】 liúsùjì current meter

【流体】 liútǐ 〈*Physics*〉fluid

【流体力学】 liútǐ lìxué hydromechanics; fluid mechanics

【流体压力计】 liútǐ yālìjì manometer

【流通】 liútōng 1.（泛指）flow; circulation：空气～ circulation of air 2.（指商品、货币）circulate：搞活物资～ enliven the circulation of commodities

【流通费用】 liútōng fèiyòng circulation costs

【流通货币】 liútōng huòbì currency

【流通领域】 liútōng lǐngyù the field of circulation

【流通手段】 liútōng shǒuduàn medium of circulation

【流通证券】 liútōng zhèngquàn negotiable instrument

【流亡】 liúwáng be forced to leave one's native land; go into exile

【流亡政府】 liúwáng zhèngfǔ government-in-exile

【流线型】 liúxiànxíng streamline：～汽车 streamlined car

【流向】 liúxiàng current direction

【流星】 liúxīng meteor; shooting star

【流行】 liúxíng prevalent; fashionable; in vogue

【流行病】 liúxíngbìng epidemic disease

【流行服装】 liúxíng fúzhuāng stylish garment

【流行歌曲】 liúxíng gēqǔ popular song

【流行色】 liúxíngsè color in fashion; fashionable color

【流行性】 liúxíngxìng 〈*Med.*〉epidemic

【流行性感冒】 liúxíngxìng gǎnmào influenza; flu

【流行性乙型脑炎】 liúxíngxìng yǐxíng nǎoyán epidemic encephalitis B

【流血】 liúxuè bleed; shed blood：尽量避免～ do one's best to avoid shedding blood / 企图制造～事件 attempt to provoke bloodshed

【流言】 liúyán rumor; gossip: ～飞语 rumors and slanders / 散布～ spread a rumor
【流于形式】 liúyú xíngshì become a mere formality
【流域】 liúyù valley; river basin; drainage area
【流转】 liúzhuǎn 1.(流动转移) wander about; roam; be on the move 2.(周转) circulation (of goods or capital)

琉[瑠](liú)
【琉璃】 liú·lí colored glaze
【琉璃塔】 liú·litǎ glazed pagoda
【琉璃瓦】 liú·liwǎ glazed tile
【琉璃瓦屋顶】 liú·liwǎ wūdǐng glazed roof

硫(liú)〈*Chem*.〉sulphur (元素符号 S)
【硫化】 liúhuà 〈*Chem*.〉vulcanizate; vulcanization
【硫磺】 liúhuáng 〈*Chem*.〉sulphur
【硫磺泉】 liúhuángquán sulphur spring
【硫酸】 liúsuān 〈*Chem*.〉sulphuric acid
【硫酸钙】 liúsuāngài calcium sulfate

柳(liǔ) willow: 垂～ weeping willow
【柳暗花明】 liǔàn-huāmíng dense willow trees and bright flowers; enchanting sight in spring time
【柳眉】 liǔméi the eyebrows of a beautiful woman
【柳丝】 liǔsī fine willow branches
【柳条】 liǔtiáo willow twig; osier; wicker
【柳条筐】 liǔtiáokuāng wicker basket
【柳条制品】 liǔtiáo zhìpǐn wicker; wickerwork
【柳絮】 liǔxù (willow) catkin
【柳阴】 liǔyīng shade of willow trees
【柳枝】 liǔzhī withy; willow branch

绺(liǔ) 〈*classifier*〉tuft; lock; skein: 一～丝线 a skein of silk thread / 一～头发 a lock of hair

六(liù) six; sixth: ～年 six years / 排成～个一组 arranged by sixes / 她穿～号衣服。She wears a six. / 找到了～个。Six were found. / 这里有～个。Six are there.
【六百】 liùbǎi six hundred; six-hundredth
【六边形】 liùbiānxíng hexagon; hexagonal (adj.)
【六畜兴旺】 liùchù xīngwàng the domestic animals are all thriving
【六分之一】 liùfēnzhīyī a sixth; one sixth
【六角螺母】 liùjiǎo luómǔ hex nut; full nut
【六面体】 liùmiàntǐ hexahedron
【六亲】 liùqīn the six relations; one's kin: ～无靠 nobody to turn to
【六神无主】 liùshén-wúzhǔ all six vital organs failing to function; in a state of utter stupefaction
【六十】 liùshí sixty; sixtieth: ～倍的增长 a sixtyfold increase
【六弦琴】 liùxiánqín guitar
【六一国际儿童节】 Liù-Yī Guójì Értóngjié International Children's Day (June 1)
【六月】 liùyuè June
【六折】 liùzhé forty percent discount

陆[陸](liù) six; sixth (另见"陆"lù)

碌(liù) (另见"碌"lù)
【碌碡】 liù·zhóu stone roller

馏(liù) heat up in a steamer: 把馒头～一～ heat up the cold steamed bread

溜[霤[2,3]](liù) 1.(湍流) swift current; turbulent flow 2.(房顶流下来的水) rainwater from the roof 3.(檐沟) roof gutter 4.(排) row: 一～房屋 a row of houses 5.(附近) surroundings neighborhood: 这一～有许多工厂。There are many factories in the neighborhood. 6.(填塞) fill (另见"溜"liū)
【溜子】 liù·zi 〈*Mineral*.〉scraper-trough conveyer

遛(liù) 1.(散步) saunter; stroll: 出去～～。Let's go for a stroll. 2.(遛牲口) walk (a horse, etc.)
【遛遛】 liù·liu take a walk
【遛马】 liùmǎ walk a horse
【遛鸟】 liùniǎo walk with caged birds
【遛弯儿】 liùwānr take a walk; go for a stroll

long

龙[龍](lóng) 1.(传说中的动物) dragon 2.(帝王的) imperial

【龙船】 lóngchuán dragon boat：赛～ a dragon-boat race
【龙胆】 lóngdǎn 〈*Bot*.〉 gentian
【龙灯】 lóngdēng dragon lantern
【龙飞凤舞】 lóngfēi-fèngwǔ like dragons flying and phoenixes dancing; lively and vigorous flourishes in calligraphy
【龙凤呈祥】 lóngfèng-chéngxiáng prosperity brought by the dragon and the phoenix; in extremely good fortune
【龙宫】 lónggōng the palace of the Dragon King
【龙井】 lónglǐng longjing tea; Dragon Well tea
【龙卷】 lóngjuǎn 〈*Meteorol*.〉 spout：水～ spout of water; waterspout
【龙卷风】 lóngjuǎnfēng tornado; whirlwind; twister
【龙门刨床】 lóngmén bàochuáng 〈*Mech*.〉 double hosing planer
【龙门铣床】 lóngmén xǐchuáng 〈*Mech*.〉 planer-type miller
【龙门钻床】 lóngmén zuànchuáng 〈*Mech*.〉 planer drilling machine
【龙盘虎踞】 lóngpán-hǔjù like a coiling dragon and crouching tiger; a forbidding strategic point
【龙舌兰】 lóngshélán 〈*Bot*.〉 agave
【龙腾虎跃】 lóngténg-hǔyuè dragons rising and tigers leaping; a scene of bustling activity
【龙头】 lóngtóu **1**.（旋塞）faucet; tap; cock：打开～ turn on the tap / 关上～ turn off the tap **2**.（自行车把）handlebar
【龙王】 lóngwáng the Dragon King
【龙舞】 lóngwǔ dragon dance
【龙虾】 lóngxiā lobster
【龙眼】 lóngyǎn 〈*Bot*.〉 longan
【龙争虎斗】 lóngzhēng-hǔdòu a fierce struggle between two evenly-matched opponents
【龙钟】 lóngzhōng decrepit; senile：老态～ doddering; senile
【龙舟】 lóngzhōu dragon boat

茏［蘢］(lóng)
【茏葱】 lóngcōng verdant; luxuriantly green

聋［聾］(lóng) deaf; hard of hearing
【聋哑】 lóngyǎ deaf and dumb; deaf-mute
【聋哑人】 lóngyǎrén deaf-mute
【聋哑学校】 lóngyǎ xuéxiào school for deaf-mutes
【聋子】 lóng·zi a deaf person

笼［籠］(lóng) **1**.（笼子）cage; coop **2**.（笼屉）steamer; steambox（另见"笼"lǒng）
【笼屉】 lóngtì food steamer
【笼养】 lóngyǎng cage culture
【笼养法】 lóngyǎngfǎ cage system
【笼子】 lóng·zi **1**.（鸡笼，鸟笼）cage; coop **2**.（篮子）basket; container

隆(lóng) **1**.（盛大）grand **2**.（兴盛）prosperous; thriving **3**.（深厚）intense; deep **4**.（凸出）swell; bulge
【隆冬】 lóngdōng midwinter; the depth of winter
【隆隆】 lónglóng 〈*onomat*.〉 rumble：雷声～～ the rumble of thunder
【隆起】 lóngqǐ rise; swell; bulge
【隆重】 lóngzhòng grand; solemn; ceremonious：～的接待 a grand reception / ～开幕 open ceremoniously

垄［壟、壠］(lǒng) **1**.（地垄）ridge：打～ make into ridges **2**.（田地的分界）raised path between fields
【垄断】 lǒngduàn monopolize; monopolization (n.)：～市场 monopolize the market
【垄断集团】 lǒngduàn jítuán monopoly group
【垄断价格】 lǒngduàn jiàgé monopoly price
【垄断利润】 lǒngduàn lìrùn monopolist profits
【垄断资本】 lǒngduàn zīběn monopoly capital
【垄断资本主义】 lǒngduàn zīběn zhǔyì monopoly capitalism
【垄断资产阶级】 lǒngduàn zīchǎn jiējí monopoly capitalist class
【垄沟】 lǒnggōu field ditch; furrow

拢［攏］(lǒng) **1**.（靠近）approach; reach **2**.（总共）add up; sum up：～一～账 sum up the accounts **3**.（合上）hold together：用绳子把竹竿～住 tie bamboo poles in a bundle **4**.（梳）comb：～头发 comb hair
【拢共】 lǒnggòng altogether; all told; in all
【拢头】 lǒngtóu comb hair
【拢子】 lǒng·zi a fine-toothed comb

【拢总】 lǒngzǒng amount to; add up to; total

笼[籠](lǒng) 1.(笼罩) envelop; cover 2.(笼子) a large box or chest; trunk
(另见"笼"lóng)

【笼括】 lǒngkuò encompass; seize all

【笼络】 lǒngluò win sb. over by any means; draw over; rope in

【笼统】 lǒngtǒng general; sweeping: 说得很～ speak in very general terms

【笼罩】 lǒngzhào envelop; shroud: ～着阴影 over-shadowed

【笼子】 lǒng·zi a large box or chest; trunk

弄(lòng)
(另见"弄"nòng)

【弄堂】 lòngtáng lane; alley; alley-way

lou

搂[摟](lōu) 1.(聚拢过来) gather up; rake together: ～草 rake up hay / ～到一块儿 gather in a heap; heap up 2.(用手拢着提起) hold up; tuck up: ～袖子 tuck up one's sleeves 3.(搜刮) squeeze; extort; tort: ～钱 extort money 4.(向自己方向拨) pull
(另见"搂"lǒu)

娄[婁](lóu)

【娄子】 lóu·zi trouble; blunder: 捅～ make a blunder; get into trouble

楼[樓](lóu) 1.(楼房) a storied building 2.(楼房的每层) floor; story (AmE.); storey (BrE.): 一～ first floor (AmE.); ground floor (BrE.) / 二～ second floor (AmE.); first floor (BrE.) / 三～ third floor (AmE.); second floor (BrE.) 3.(塔楼) tower: 鼓～ drum-tower

【楼板】 lóubǎn floor; floorslab

【楼层】 lóucéng floor; story; storey

【楼道】 lóudào corridor; passageway

【楼房】 lóufáng a building of two or more stories

【楼面】 lóumiàn 〈*Archit.*〉 floor

【楼面面积】 lóumiàn miànjī floor area

【楼上】 lóushàng upstairs: 睡在～ sleep upstairs

【楼梯】 lóutī stairs; staircase; stairway: 太平～ fire-escape / 上～ go up the stairs; climb the stairs / 下～ go down the stairs

【楼梯灯】 lóutīdēng stair light

【楼梯间】 lóutījiān stairway; stairwell

【楼梯井】 lóutījǐng stairwell

【楼下】 lóuxià downstairs

喽[嘍](lóu)

【喽罗】 lóu·luó 1.(强盗的部下) the rank and file of a band of outlaws 2.(仆从) underling; lackey

蝼[螻](lóu)

【蝼蛄】 lóugū mole cricket

【蝼蚁】 lóuyǐ mole crickets and ants; nobodies

搂[摟](lǒu) hold in one's arms; hug; embrace: 小女孩紧～着妈妈。The little girl gave her mother a big hug.
(另见"搂"lōu)

【搂抱】 lǒubào hug; embrace; cuddle

篓[簍](lǒu) basket: 竹～ bamboo basket

【篓子】 lǒu·zi basket

陋(lòu) 1.(不好看) plain; ugly 2.(狭小) humble; mean 3.(不文明) vulgar; corrupt; undesirable 4.(见闻少) scanty; limited; shallow; superficial

【陋规】 lòuguī objectionable practices; corrupt practices

【陋室】 lòushì a humble room; a room totally without decoration

【陋俗】 lòusú undesirable customs

【陋习】 lòuxí corrupt customs; bad habits

瘘[瘻、瘺](lòu) fistula: 肛～ anal fistula

镂[鏤](lòu) engrave; carve

【镂花】 lòuhuā 〈*Arts and Crafts*〉 ornamental engraving

【镂刻】 lòukè engrave; carve

【镂空】 lòukōng 〈*Arts and Crafts*〉 hollow out: ～的象牙球 hollowed-out ivory ball

漏(lòu) 1.(渗漏) leak: 管子～气。The pipe leaks gas. 2.(泄露) divulge; leak; leak information 3.(遗漏) missing; leave

out：～了一页。A page is missing.
【漏报】 lòubào fail to report sth.; fail to declare
【漏电】 lòudiàn leakage of electricity
【漏洞】 lòudòng **1.**（小孔）leak **2.**（破绽）flaw; hole; loophole：～百出 full of loopholes / 寻找法律的～ find a loophole in the law
【漏斗】 lòudǒu funnel
【漏斗车】 lòudǒuchē 〈*Railway*〉 hopper car
【漏光】 lòuguāng **1.**（封闭不严而走光）light leak **2.**（漏完）水～了。All the water has leaked out.
【漏花织物】 lòuhuā zhīwù off-patterned cloth
【漏检错误率】 lòujiǎn cuòwùlǜ residual error rate; undetected error rate
【漏孔】 lòukǒng a small hole through which air or water leaks out
【漏勺】 lòusháo strainer; colander
【漏税】 lòushuì evade payment of a tax; evade taxation
【漏网】 lòuwǎng escape unpunished; slip through the net：～之鱼 fish that has escape the net
【漏泄】 lòuxiè leak
【漏子】 lòu·zi **1.**（漏斗）funnel **2.**（漏洞）flaw; hole; loophole

露（lòu）〈*colloq.*〉 reveal; show（另见"露"lù）
【露丑】 lòuchǒu be disgraced
【露出】 lòuchū show; reveal
【露出破绽】 lòuchū-pòzhàn show one's slip
【露底】 lòudǐ betray a confidence; let out the whole story
【露脸】 lòuliǎn look good as a result of receiving honor or praise
【露马脚】 lòumǎjiǎo give oneself away; let the cat out of the bag
【露面】 lòumiàn show one's face; appear on public occasions
【露头】 lòutóu **1.**（露出头部）show one's head **2.**（刚出现）appear; emerge
【露馅儿】 lòuxiànr let the cat out of the bag; give the game away; spill the beans
【露一手】 lòuyīshǒu make an exhibition of one's abilities or skills; show off

lu

卢［盧］（lú）
【卢比】 lúbǐ rupee
【卢布】 lúbù rouble

鸬［鸕］（lú）
【鸬鹚】 lúcí 〈*Zool.*〉 great cormorant

颅［顱］（lú） cranium; skull
【颅骨】 lúgǔ 〈*Anat.*〉 skull
【颅腔】 lúqiāng 〈*Anat.*〉 cranial cavity

鲈［鱸］（lú） 〈*Zool.*〉 perch
【鲈鱼】 lúyú freshwater perch

芦［蘆］（lú） 〈*Bot.*〉 reed
【芦荡】 lúdàng reed marshes
【芦根】 lúgēn 〈*Chin. Pharm.*〉 reed rhizome
【芦花】 lúhuā reed catkins
【芦荟】 lúhuì 〈*Bot.*〉 aloe; Chinese aloe
【芦笙】 lúshēng a reed-pipe wind instrument
【芦笋】 lúsǔn 〈*Bot.*〉 asparagus
【芦苇】 lúwěi reed
【芦苇荡】 lúwěidàng reed marshes
【芦席】 lúxí reed mat
【芦竹】 lúzhú 〈*Bot.*〉 giantreed

炉［爐、鑪］（lú） **1.**（炉子）stove; furnace：壁～ wall oven / 柴～ wood stove / 电～ electric stove / 火～ household stove / 鼓风～ blast furnace / 炼焦～ coke oven / 煤～ coal stove / 煤气～ gas heater; gas stove / 煤油～ kerosene stove **2.**（炼钢炉次）heat：一～钢 a heat of steel
【炉灰】 lúhuī ashes of a stove
【炉火纯青】 lúhuǒ-chúnqīng pure blue flame; high degree of technical or professional proficiency
【炉龄】 lúlíng 〈*Metall.*〉 furnace life
【炉身】 lúshēn 〈*Metall.*〉 shaft; furnace stack
【炉膛】 lútáng the chamber of a stove or furnace
【炉条】 lútiáo fire bars; grate
【炉温】 lúwēn 〈*Metall.*〉 furnace tempera-

ture
【炉灶】 lúzào kitchen range; cooking range: 另起～ make a fresh start
【炉渣】 lúzhā slag; cinder
【炉子】 lú·zi stove; furnace: 生～ light a stove / 围着～烤火 sit round a fire to get warm

卤［鹵、滷］(lǔ) 1.(盐卤) bittern 2.(卤素) halogen: ～族 halogen family 3.(卤制) stew in soy sauce: ～蛋 spiced corned eggs / ～鸡 spiced corned chicken / ～牛肉 spiced corned beef 4.(卤汁) thick gravy used as a sauce for noodles: ～面 noodles served with thick gravy
【卤化】 lǔhuà 〈*Chem*.〉 halogenate; halogenation (n.)
【卤水】 lǔshuǐ 1.(卤) bittern 2.(盐水) brine
【卤味】 lǔwèi pot-stewed fowl, meat, etc.
【卤制】 lǔzhì stew in soy sauce
【卤族】 lǔzú 〈*Chem*.〉 halogen family

虏［虜］(lǔ) 1.(俘获) take prisoner 2.(战俘) captive; prisoner of war; POW
【虏获】 lǔhuò 1.(俘虏敌人) capture 2.(俘获的敌人和武器) men and arms captured

掳［擄］(lǔ) carry off; capture
【掳掠】 lǔlüè pillage; loot

鲁(lǔ) 1.(迟钝) stupid; dull 2.(莽撞) rash; rough; rude
【鲁钝】 lǔdùn dull-witted; obtuse; stupid
【鲁莽】 lǔmǎng crude and rash; rash

橹［櫓、艪、艣］(lǔ) scull; sweep

镥(lǔ) 〈*Chem*.〉 lutetium (元素符号 Lu)

陆［陸］(lù) land: 水～交通 land and water communications
(另见"陆"liù)
【陆地】 lùdì dry land; land
【陆风】 lùfēng land breeze
【陆海空三军】 lù-hǎi-kōng sānjūn the army, navy and air force
【陆军】 lùjūn ground force; land force; army
【陆军医院】 lùjūn yīyuàn army hospital
【陆路】 lùlù land route: ～交通 land communication / 走～ travel by land
【陆桥】 lùqiáo land bridge
【陆上练习】 lùshàng liànxí 〈*Swimming*〉 land drill
【陆线】 lùxiàn 〈*Telecom*.〉 land line
【陆相】 lùxiàng 〈*Geol*.〉 land facies
【陆相沉积】 lùxiàng chénjī 〈*Geol*.〉 continental deposit
【陆续】 lùxù one after another; in succession
【陆运】 lùyùn land transportation
【陆战队】 lùzhànduì 〈*Mil*.〉 marine corps; marines: 海军～ marine corps

录［錄］(lù) 1.(记录) record; write down; copy: 抄～ copy down 2.(采取;任用) employ; hire: 收～ take sb. on the staff 3.(录音) tape-record: 把演讲～下来 record a speech 4.(文章或书的名称) record; register; collection: 回忆～ memoirs
【录放】 lùfàng record and play
【录供】 lùgòng 〈*Law*〉 take down a confession or testimony during an interrogation
【录取】 lùqǔ enroll; recruit; admit: ～新生 enroll students / 择优～ admit only those who are best qualified
【录取名单】 lùqǔ míngdān list of enrollees
【录取名额】 lùqǔ míng'é number of enrollees
【录取通知书】 lùqǔ tōngzhīshū admission notice
【录像】 lùxiàng 1.(录制图像) video recording 2.(录像带) video tape
【录像带】 lùxiàngdài video cassette; video tape
【录像机】 lùxiàngjī video recorder; video tape recorder
【录像片】 lùxiàngpiàn film or telefilm recorded on the videotape
【录像视盘】 lùxiàng shìpán video disk
【录音】 lùyīn recording: 放～ play back the recording
【录音报告】 lùyīn bàogào tape-recorded speech
【录音车】 lùyīnchē recording van
【录音带】 lùyīndài tape; magnetic tape
【录音电话】 lùyīn diànhuà dictaphone; telegraphone
【录音机】 lùyīnjī recorder: 双声道～ double-track recorder
【录音师】 lùyīnshī 〈*Cinematog*.〉 recording

engineer

【录音室】 lùyīnshì recording room

【录影】 lùyǐng 1.(录制图像) video recording 2.(录像带) video tape

【录用】 lùyòng employ; take sb. on the staff

【录制】 lùzhì record and duplicate; make recording and reproduction

绿(lù)

【绿林】 lùlín 1.(绿林英雄) heroes of the greenwood; forest outlaws 2.(强盗集团) a band of bandits entrenched in a mountain stronghold; brigands

(另见"绿"lǜ)

禄(lù) official's salary in feudal China; emolument: 高官厚～ high position and handsome salary

碌(lù) 1.(平凡) commonplace; mediocre 2.(事务繁杂) busy

(另见"碌"liù)

【碌碌】 lùlù 1.(平庸) mediocre; commonplace; incompetent: ～无能 incompetent; incapable / ～庸才 very mediocre person / ～庸人 a rough and commonplace person 2.(辛苦) busy with miscellaneous work: ～半生 toil half a lifetime / ～无奇 rough and not wonderful

鹿(lù) deer: 梅花～ sika deer / 麋～ milu; David's deer / 马～ red deer; wapiti / 驯～ rein deer; caribou

【鹿角】 lùjiǎo 1.(鹿的角) deerhorn antler 2.(鹿砦) abatis

【鹿角胶】 lùjiǎojiāo 〈*Chin. Pharm.*〉 deerhorn glue

【鹿圈】 lùjuàn deer enclosure; deer pen

【鹿皮】 lùpí deerskin

【鹿茸】 lùróng 〈*Chin. Pharm.*〉 pilose antler

【鹿肉】 lùròu venison

【鹿死谁手】 lùsǐshuíshǒu at whose hand will the deer die; who will win the prize; who will gain supremacy: ～,尚难逆料 it's still hard to tell who will emerge victorious

【鹿跳】 lùtiào 〈*Skating*〉 stag jump

【鹿砦】 lùzhài 〈*Mil.*〉 abatis

辘(lù)

【辘轳】 lù·lú windlass; winch

【辘辘】 lù·lù 〈*onomat.*〉 rumble: 饥肠～ so hungry that one's stomach rumbles

麓(lù) 〈*written*〉 the foot of a hill or mountain: 天山～ the foot of the Tianshan mountains

路(lù) 1.(道路) road; path; way: 公～ highway / 混凝土～ concrete road / 沥青～ asphalt road / 汽车～ motor road / 碎石～ macadam road / 土～ dirt road / 迷～ lose one's way / 引～ lead the way 2.(路程) journey; distance: 走很远的～ walk a long distance; make a long journey 3.(途径) way; means: 走邪～ go the wrong way / 走正～ go the right way 4.(条理) sequence; line; logic 5.(路线) route: 332～公共汽车 No. 332 bus 6.(种类) sort; grade; class: 二三～角色 second-rate role 7.(指铁路) railroad; railway

【路霸】 lùbà overlord of road

【路标】 lùbiāo 1.(交通标志) road sign 2.(联络标志) route marking; route sign

【路不拾遗】 lùbùshíyí no one picks up and pockets anything lost on the road; descriptive of a high moral standard in society

【路程】 lùchéng distance travelled; journey: 两天的～ a two-day journey

【路灯】 lùdēng street lamp; road lamp

【路灯灯柱】 lùdēng dēngzhù lamp post

【路堤】 lùdī embankment

【路段】 lùduàn a section of a highway or railway

【路费】 lùfèi travelling expenses

【路轨】 lùguǐ 1.(钢轨) rail 2.(轨道) track; railroad track; railway track

【路过】 lùguò pass by or through

【路基】 lùjī roadbed; bed: 铁路～ the bed of a railway

【路劫】 lùjié highway robbery; holdup; mugging

【路警】 lùjǐng railway police

【路径】 lùjìng 1.(道路) route; way 2.(门路) method; ways and means

【路考】 lùkǎo driving test

【路口】 lùkǒu crossing; intersection

【路面】 lùmiàn road surface; pavement: 柏油～ asphalt road surface

【路牌】 lùpái street nameplate

【路堑】 lùqiàn 〈*Transport*〉cutting

【路人】 lùrén passerby; stranger：视若～ treat sb. like a passerby

【路上】 lù·shang **1.**（道路上面）on the road **2.**（在途中）on the way：在我回家的～ on my way home

【路数】 lùshù **1.**（途径）way; approach **2.**（着数）a movement in martial arts **3.**（底细）exact details; inside story

【路透社】 Lùtòushè Reuters; Reuter's News Agency

【路途】 lùtú **1.**（路）road; path **2.**（路程）way; journey; distance：～遥远。It's a long distance.

【路线】 lùxiàn **1.**（所经道路）route; itinerary：旅行的～ the route of a journey **2.**（所遵循的途径）line：基本～ basic line / 群众～ the mass line

【路砟】 lùzhǎ 〈*Railway*〉road-metal

【路障】 lùzhàng roadblock：设～ put up roadblock / 警察在所有出城的道路设置～。Police set up roadblocks on all roads out of the town.

【路子】 lù·zi way; approach

鹭（lù）〈*Zool.*〉egret; heron：白～ little egret / 苍～ gray heron / 池～ Chinese pond-heron / 大白～ great egret / 黑～ black egret / 雪～ snowy egret / 岩～ Eastern reef heron

【鹭鸶】 lùsī 〈*Zool.*〉little egret

露（lù） **1.**（露水）dew：～珠 dew drop **2.**（饮料）syrup **3.**（显露）show; reveal betray

（另见"露"lòu）

【露骨】 lùgǔ thinly veiled; undisguised; barefaced; flagrant：～的干涉 flagrant interference

【露酒】 lùjiǔ alcoholic drink mixed with fruit juice

【露水】 lù·shui dew

【露宿】 lùsù sleep in the open

【露天】 lùtiān in the open; outdoors

【露天采矿】 lùtiān cǎikuàng opencast mining

【露天电影院】 lùtiān diànyǐngyuàn open-air cinema

【露天开采】 lùtiān kāicǎi surface mining

【露天看台】 lùtiān kàntái bleachers

【露天矿】 lùtiānkuàng opencut; opencast; open-pit; strip mine

【露天煤矿】 lùtiān méikuàng opencut coal mine

【露天舞会】 lùtiān wǔhuì open-air dance

【露营】 lùyíng camp; encamp; bivouac

【露珠】 lùzhū dewdrop

戮［**剹**²］（lù） **1.**（杀）kill; slay：杀～ slaughter **2.**（并；合）unite; join

【戮力同心】 lùlì-tóngxīn 〈*written*〉join hands; unite in a concerted effort; make concerted efforts

lü

驴［**驢**］（lǘ） donkey; ass：野～ wild ass / 公～ donkey / 母～ jenny ass

【驴唇不对马嘴】 lǘchún bù duì mǎzuǐ donkeys' lips don't match horses' jaws; incongruous; irrelevant：这个例子有点～。The example is rather farfetched.

【驴骡】 lǘluó hinny

【驴年马月】 lǘnián-mǎyuè a time that will never come

【驴皮胶】 lǘpíjiāo donkey-hide gelatin

【驴子】 lǘ·zi donkey; ass

铝（lǚ）〈*Chem.*〉aluminum; aluminium（元素符号 Al）

【铝箔】 lǚbó aluminum foil

【铝锅】 lǚguō aluminum pot

【铝热法】 lǚrèfǎ aluminothermic process

【铝热剂】 lǚrèjì 〈*Chem.*〉thermite

【铝土矿】 lǚtǔkuàng bauxite

【铝线】 lǚxiàn aluminum steel; aluminum wire

【铝制品】 lǚzhìpǐn aluminum products

捋（lǚ） stroke; smooth out：～胡子 stroke one's beard

（另见"捋"luō）

旅（lǚ） **1.**（旅行）travel; stay away from home **2.**〈*Mil.*〉brigade **3.**（泛指军队）troops; force

【旅伴】 lǚbàn traveling companion; fellow traveller

【旅程】 lǚchéng route; itinerary

【旅店】 lǚdiàn inn; hotel

【旅费】 lǚfèi traveling expenses

【旅馆】 lǚguǎn hotel
【旅馆业】 lǚguǎnyè hotel business; the accommodations industry
【旅居】 lǚjū reside abroad; sojourn: ～海外的侨胞 Chinese nationals residing abroad
【旅客】 lǚkè hotel guest; traveller; passenger
【旅客登机桥】 lǚkè dēngjīqiáo 〈*Aeron.*〉 passenger loading bridge
【旅客登记簿】 lǚkè dēngjìbù hotel register
【旅社】 lǚshè hotel
【旅途】 lǚtú journey; trip
【旅行】 lǚxíng travel; journey; tour: ～经验丰富的人 a traveled man; a travelled man
【旅行包】 lǚxíngbāo traveling bag
【旅行车】 lǚxíngchē station wagon; estate car
【旅行袋】 lǚxíngdài valise
【旅行轿车】 lǚxíng jiàochē station wagon; estate car
【旅行平安险】 lǚxíng píngānxiǎn travel accident insurance
【旅行社】 lǚxíngshè travel service; travel agency
【旅行团】 lǚxíngtuán touring party
【旅行推销员】 lǚxíng tuīxiāoyuán traveler; traveling salesman
【旅行信用证】 lǚxíng xìnyòngzhèng travellers letter of credit
【旅行者】 lǚxíngzhě tourist; traveler (AmE.); traveller (BrE.)
【旅行证】 lǚxíngzhèng travel certificate
【旅行支票】 lǚxíng zhīpiào traveler's check (AmE.); traveller's cheque (BrE.)
【旅行指南】 lǚxíng zhǐnán guidebook
【旅游】 lǚyóu tour; tourism: 他们去～了。They have gone on a tour.
【旅游车】 lǚyóuchē coach; motor coach
【旅游热线】 lǚyóu rèxiàn tourist hotline
【旅游旺季】 lǚyóu wàngjì tourist rush season; peak tourist season
【旅游鞋】 lǚyóuxié trainers; running shoes
【旅游意外保险】 lǚyóu yìwài bǎoxiǎn travel-accident insurance
【旅游者】 lǚyóuzhě tourist; traveler (AmE.); traveller (BrE.)
【旅长】 lǚzhǎng brigadier; brigade commander

膂 (lǚ)
【膂力】 lǚlì muscular strength; physical strength; brawn

屡[屢] (lǚ) repeatedly; time and again: ～建奇功 make unusual contributions repeatedly
【屡次】 lǚcì time and again; repeatedly: ～破世界纪录 repeatedly break the world record
【屡次三番】 lǚcì-sānfān again and again; over and over again; many times
【屡见不鲜】 lǚjiàn-bùxiān common occurrence; nothing new
【屡教不改】 lǚjiào-bùgǎi refuse to mend one's ways despite repeated admonition

缕[縷] (lǚ) 1.(线) thread: 金～ gold thread 2. 〈*classifier*〉 wisp; strand; lock 3.(详详细细) detailed; in detail
【缕解】 lǚjiě explain in detail; go into particulars
【缕缕】 lǚlǚ continuously

履 (lǚ) 1.(鞋) shoe 2.(踩;踏) tread on; walk on 3.(脚步) footstep 4.(履行) carry out; honor; fulfill
【履带】 lǚdài 〈*Mech.*〉 caterpillar tread; track
【履带式牵引车】 lǚdàishì qiānyǐnchē truck tractor
【履历】 lǚlì personal details; antecedents
【履历表】 lǚlìbiǎo résumé; CV; curriculum vitae: 请按上述地址寄函和～。Send a letter and CV to the above address. / 她给 20 家外国公司寄了～,但没一家要她面试。She sent her résumé to twenty foreign companies, but didn't even get an interview.
【履行】 lǚxíng perform; fulfill; carry out: ～合同 carry a contract; discharge a contract / ～合约 meet one's engagements / ～诺言 keep one's word; fulfill one's promise / ～契约 execute one's promises / ～期限 deadline for performance / ～条约 execution of treaty / ～义务 duty of performance / ～债务 fulfill obligation / ～职责 do one's duty
【履约】 lǚyuē execute a treaty; discharge a contract

律 (lǜ) 1.(法律) law: 按～处治 punish according to law 2.(规律) law: 因果～ law of causation 3.（约束）discipline; restrain; keep under control

【律己】 lǜjǐ discipline oneself; self-restraint: 严于～ be strict with oneself

【律例】 lǜlì laws, statutes and precedents

【律师】 lǜshī lawyer; attorney (AmE.); solicitor (BrE.): 出庭～ barrister; barrister-in-law / 请～ employ a lawyer

【律师费】 lǜshīfèi counsel fee

【律师留置权】 lǜshī liúzhìquán lawyer's lien

【律师事务所】 lǜshī shìwùsuǒ law office

【律师协会】 lǜshī xiéhuì bar association

虑［慮］(lǜ) 1.（思考）consider; ponder; think over 2.（担忧；发愁）concern; anxiety; worry: 不必过～ need not worry overmuch; need not be over-anxious

滤［濾］(lǜ) strain; filter

【滤波电容】 lǜbō diànróng 〈*Electr.*〉 filter capacitor

【滤波器】 lǜbōqì 〈*Electr.*〉 wave filter

【滤光镜】 lǜguāngjìng 〈*Photog.*〉 filter

【滤过】 lǜguò filter; filtration (n.)

【滤过性病毒】 lǜguòxìng bìngdú filterable virus

【滤器】 lǜqì filter: 粗～ strainer

【滤色镜】 lǜsèjìng 〈*Photog.*〉 (color) filter

【滤液】 lǜyè 〈*Chem.*〉 filtrate

【滤油器】 lǜyóuqì 〈*Auto*〉 oil filter

【滤纸】 lǜzhǐ 〈*Chem.*〉 filter paper; filter

【滤嘴】 lǜzuǐ filter tip: 香烟～ cigarette filter

率 (lǜ) rate; proportion; ratio: 出勤～ rate of attendance / (外汇)兑换～ rate of exchange / 利～ rate of interest; interest rate / 利用～ utilization ratio / 人口增长～ the rate of population increase / 贴现～ discount rate / 银行贴现～ bank rate / 圆周～ ratio of circumference

(另见"率"shuài)

绿 (lǜ) green: 碧～ bright green / 嫩～ vivid green

(另见"绿"lù)

【绿宝石】 lǜbǎoshí emerald

【绿茶】 lǜchá green tea

【绿灯】 lǜdēng 1.〈*Transport*〉 green light 2.（准许前进）permission to go ahead with some project; green light: 开～ give the green light to

【绿地】 lǜdì green land; green field

【绿豆】 lǜdòu mung bean; green gram

【绿肥】 lǜféi green manure

【绿肥作物】 lǜféi zuòwù green manure crop

【绿化】 lǜhuà make green by planting trees, flowers, etc.; afforest

【绿卡】 lǜkǎ green card

【绿卡持有者】 lǜkǎ chíyǒuzhě green-carder

【绿篱】 lǜlí hedge; hedgerow

【绿色长城】 lǜsè chángchéng green Great Wall; forest belt

【绿色革命】 lǜsè gémìng green revolution

【绿色企业】 lǜsè qǐyè green enterprises

【绿色食品】 lǜsè shípǐn green food

【绿色植物】 lǜsè zhíwù evergreen plant

【绿松石】 lǜsōngshí 〈*Mineral.*〉 turquoise

【绿野】 lǜyě the green field

【绿阴】 lǜyīn shade of a tree

【绿茵场】 lǜyīnchǎng green field; green pitch

【绿油油】 lǜyōuyōu glossy and green; shiny green

【绿洲】 lǜzhōu oasis

氯 (lǜ)〈*Chem.*〉 chlorine (元素符号 Cl)

【氯丙嗪】 lǜbǐngqín 〈*Pharm.*〉 chlorpromazine; wintermine

【氯仿】 lǜfǎng 〈*Chem.*〉 chloroform

【氯化钠】 lǜhuànà common salt; sodium chloride

【氯化物】 lǜhuàwù 〈*Chem.*〉 chloride

【氯化银】 lǜhuàyín 〈*Chem.*〉 silver chlorate

【氯纶】 lǜlún 〈*Textiles*〉 polyvinyl chloride fiber

【氯霉素】 lǜméisù 〈*Pharm.*〉 chloromycetin

【氯气】 lǜqì 〈*Chem.*〉 chlorine

luan

峦［巒］(luán) mountains; mountain range: 重～叠嶂 range upon range of mountains

孪［孿］(luán) twin

【孪生】 luánshēng twin: ～姐妹 twin sisters / ～兄弟 twin brothers

挛[攣](luán) contract; contracture

【挛缩】 luánsuō contract; contracture

卵(luǎn) ovum; egg; spawn

【卵巢】 luǎncháo 〈*Anat*.〉 ovary

【卵泡】 luǎnpāo 〈*Biol*.〉 follicle; follicular (adj.)

【卵生】 luǎnshēng 〈*Zool*.〉 oviparity

【卵生动物】 luǎnshēng dòngwù oviparous animal; ovipara

【卵石】 luǎnshí cobble; pebble; shingle

【卵形】 luǎnxíng egg-shape

【卵翼】 luǎnyì cover with wings as in brooding; shield: ～之下 under the wings of; under the shield of

【卵子】 luǎnzǐ **1**.〈*Biol*.〉 ovum; egg **2**.〈*dial*.〉 testis

乱[亂](luàn) **1**.(无秩序) in disorder; in a mess; in confusion: ～跑 run about / 屋子里～作一团。There was great confusion in the house. **2**.(心绪不宁) be confused; be upset; be disturbed: 心烦意～ be confused in mind **3**.(使混乱) confuse; upset; throw sb. into chaos: ～了手脚 be thrown into chaos **4**.(任意;随便) indiscriminate; random; arbitrary: ～花钱 spend money extravagantly **5**.(不正当男女关系) promiscuous sexual behavior; promiscuity **6**.(战乱) disorder; upheaval; chaos; riot; unrest; turmoil: 内～ internal unrest / 叛～ armed rebellion; mutiny

【乱成一团】 luànchéngyītuán in great confusion

【乱罚款】 luànfákuǎn mete out unjustified punishment

【乱纷纷】 luànfēnfēn disorderly; confused; chaotic

【乱哄哄】 luànhōnghōng in noisy disorder; in a hubbub; tumultuous; in an uproar: 街上～的 the street being in a hubbub

【乱伦】 luànlún commit incest

【乱蓬蓬】 luànpēngpēng dishevelled; tangled; jumbled: ～的胡子 unkempt beard

【乱七八糟】 luànqībāzāo at sixes and sevens; in a mess; in a muddle

【乱世】 luànshì troubled times; turbulent days

【乱收费】 luànshōufèi collect illegally extra charge or fares

【乱说】 luànshuō speak carelessly; make irresponsible remarks; gossip

【乱弹琴】 luàntánqín talk nonsense

【乱糟糟】 luànzāozāo **1**.(事物杂乱) hubbub; cluttered: 桌上～地堆满了书报。The desk is cluttered with books and papers. **2**.(心里烦乱) confused; troubled; perturbed: 心里～的 feel very perturbed

【乱真】 luànzhēn **1**.(模仿得很像) look genuine: 以假～ pass off a fake as genuine **2**.〈*Physics*〉 spurious

【乱子】 luàn·zi disturbance; trouble; disorder

lue

掠(lüè) **1**.(掠夺) plunder; pillage; sack **2**.(掠过) sweep past; brush past; graze; skim over

【掠夺】 lüèduó plunder; rob; pillage

【掠夺性战争】 lüèduóxìng zhànzhēng predatory warfare

【掠夺者】 lüèduózhě plunderer; looter

【掠过】 lüèguò sideswipe; fly past

【掠取】 lüèqǔ seize; grab; plunder

略[畧](lüè) **1**.(简略) brief; sketchy: 简～ sketchy; simple **2**.(略微) slightly; a little; somewhat: ～知一二 know sth. about; have only a smattering of **3**.(简叙) summary; brief account; outline **4**.(略去) omit; delete; leave out: 从～ be omitted **5**.(谋略) strategy; plan; scheme: 雄才大～ great talent and bold vision; rare gifts and bold strategy **6**.(夺取) capture; seize

【略表寸心】 lüèbiǎo-cùnxīn just to show my gratitude

【略见一斑】 lüèjiàn-yībān catch a glimpse of; get a rough idea of

【略去】 lüèqù omit; leave out

【略胜一筹】 lüèshèng-yīchóu a notch above; slightly better

【略图】 lüètú sketch map; sketch

【略微】 lüèwēi slightly; a little; somewhat: ～懂一点意大利语 know a little Italian

【略有节余】 lüèyǒu-jiéyú with a slight surplus

【略语】 lüèyǔ 〈*Gram*.〉abbreviation; shortening

lun

抡[掄](lūn) brandish; swing: 拔出刀向敌人～去 draw one's sword and brandish it at his enemy

伦[倫](lún) 1.(人伦) human relations 2.(条理) logic; order 3.(同类;同等) peer; match

【伦巴舞】 lúnbāwǔ rumba

【伦比】 lúnbǐ 〈*written*〉 rival; equal: 无与～ unrivaled; unequalled; peerless

【伦次】 lúncì coherence; logical sequence: 语无～ speak incoherently; babble like an idiot

【伦理】 lúnlǐ ethics; moral principles

【伦理学】 lúnlǐxué ethics

【伦琴】 lúnqín 〈*Physics*〉 roentgen: ～射线 roentgen rays

沦[淪](lún) 1.(沉没) sink 2.(陷入) fall; be reduced to: ～为乞丐 be reduced to begging

【沦落】 lúnluò 1.(流落) fall low; come down in the world; be reduced to poverty: ～异乡 sinking in a strange district 2.(没落;衰落) decline; wane 3.(沉沦) sink into degradation

【沦入风尘】 lúnrùfēngchén fall into professions not socially respectable

【沦丧】 lúnsàng be lost or ruined

【沦亡】 lúnwáng 1.(失陷) be annexed; be occupied; be subjugated 2.(沦落) decline; wane

【沦陷】 lúnxiàn be occupied by the enemy; fall into enemy hands

【沦陷区】 lúnxiànqū enemy-occupied area

纶[綸](lún) 1.(青丝带子) black silk ribbon 2.(钓丝) fishing line 3.(合成纤维) synthetic fiber: 涤～ polyester fiber / 锦～ polyamide fiber / 腈～ acrylic fiber / 氯～ polyvinyl chloride fiber

轮[輪](lún) 1.(轮子) wheel 2.(像轮子的东西) sth. resembling a wheel; disc; ring: (树的)年～ annual ring 3.(轮船) steamboat; steamer 4.(轮流) take turns; in turn: ～着看护病人 take turns to watch the sick 5.(次,圈等) round: 举行新的一～会谈 hold a new round of talks

【轮班】 lúnbān in shifts; in relays; in rotation: ～工作 work in shifts

【轮班制】 lúnbānzhì rotation system; relay system

【轮船】 lúnchuán steamer; steamship; steamboat

【轮渡】 lúndù ferry: 火车～ train ferry

【轮番】 lúnfān take turns: ～轰炸 bomb in waves

【轮毂罩】 lúngǔzhào 〈*Auto*〉 hubcap

【轮换】 lúnhuàn rotate; take turns

【轮机】 lúnjī 1.(涡轮机) turbine 2.(轮船发动机) motorship engine; engine

【轮机室】 lúnjīshì engine room

【轮机员】 lúnjīyuán engineer

【轮机长】 lúnjīzhǎng chief engineer

【轮奸】 lúnjiān violation of a woman by several men in turn

【轮空】 lúnkōng 〈*Sports*〉 bye: 在第一轮比赛中～ be a bye in the first round of the tournament

【轮廓】 lúnkuò 1.(外形) outline; contour; rough sketch: ～分明 sharp outline 2.(概况) general situation

【轮流】 lúnliú take turns; do sth. in turn: ～执政 ruling the country in turn

【轮圈】 lúnquān 〈*Auto*〉 wheel rim

【轮式旱冰鞋】 lúnshì hànbīngxié 1.(双排四轮的) roller skate 2.(单排) rollerblade

【轮胎】 lúntāi tire; tyre

【轮辋】 lúnwǎng rim; felloe

【轮休】 lúnxiū have holidays by turns; rotate days off; stagger holidays

【轮训】 lúnxùn train in rotation; training in rotation

【轮椅】 lúnyǐ wheelchair

【轮轴】 lúnzhóu 1.(差动滑轮) wheel and axle 2.(轮子的轴) wheel axle; wheel spindle

【轮子】 lún·zi wheel

【轮作】 lúnzuò 〈*Agric*.〉 crop rotation

论[論](lùn) 1.(论理) discuss; talk about; discourse: 就事～事 talk about a matter in isolation 2.(话或文章) view; opinion; statement 3.(文章题目) dissertation; essay: 《矛盾～》 *On Contradiction*

4.(学说) theory: 相对～ the theory of relativity 5.(说;看待) mention; regard; consider: 相提并～ mention in the same breath 6.(衡量) decide on; determine: 按质～价 determine the price according to the quality 7.(按照) by; in terms of: ～件 by piece / ～天 by day / ～月发工资 pay wages by the month

【论处】 lùnchǔ decide on sb's punishment; punish: 以…～ be punished for ...

【论点】 lùndiǎn argument; thesis: 基本～ the main argument / 提出～ put forward an argument

【论调】 lùndiào view; argument

【论断】 lùnduàn inference; judgment; thesis

【论功行赏】 lùngōng-xíngshǎng grant awards according to merit

【论件计酬】 lùnjiàn-jìchóu payment by the piece

【论据】 lùnjù grounds of argument; argument: ～不足 insufficient grounds

【论理】 lùnlǐ 1.(按理说) normally; as things should be 2.(逻辑) logic; be logical

【论述】 lùnshù discuss; expound

【论说】 lùnshuō 1.(议论) exposition and argumentation 2.(按理说) normally

【论坛】 lùntán forum; tribune: 文学～ forum on literature

【论题】 lùntí 〈*Logic*〉 proposition

【论文】 lùnwén thesis; dissertation: 学术～ academic thesis / 博士～ thesis for the Doctorate; doctoral dissertation

【论文答辩】 lùnwén dábiàn thesis defense

【论文集】 lùnwénjí symposium

【论战】 lùnzhàn polemic; debate

【论证】 lùnzhèng 1.(论述过程) demonstration; proof 2.(论述证明) expound and prove: 经济～ technical and economic assessments 3.(论据) grounds of argument; argument

【论著】 lùnzhù treatise; work; book

【论资排辈】 lùnzī-páibèi (the idea of) giving priority only to seniority

【论罪】 lùnzuì be considered as an offense

luo

捋 (luō) rub one's palm along (sth. long): ～起袖子 push up one's sleeve (另见"捋"lǚ)

【捋虎须】 luō hǔxū stroke a tiger's whiskers; do sth. very daring; run great risks

啰[囉] (luō)

【啰嗦】 luōsuō 1.(繁复) long-winded; wordy 2.(琐碎;麻烦) overelaborate; troublesome: 这件事真～。The matter is really troublesome.

罗[羅] (luó) 1.(捕鸟的网) a net for catching birds 2.(张网捕鸟) catch birds with a net 3.(搜集) collect; gather together 4.(陈列) display; spread out 5.(细筛) sieve; sift 6.(丝织品) a kind of silk gauze 7.(量词, 12打) twelve dozen; a gross

【罗布泊】 Luóbùpō 〈place〉 Lop Nur

【罗布麻】 luóbùmá 〈*Bot.*〉 dogbane

【罗锅】 luóguō 1.(驼背) hunchback; humpback 2.(驮背者) hunchbacked; humpbacked

【罗汉】 luóhàn 〈*Buddhism*〉 arhat; disciple of Buddha

【罗汉松】 luóhànsōng 〈*Bot.*〉 podocarpus; yellow wood

【罗经】 luójīng 〈*Naut.*〉 compass

【罗口灯泡】 luókǒu dēngpào screw socket bulb

【罗口灯头】 luókǒu dēngtóu screw socket

【罗列】 luóliè 1.(分布) spread out; set out: ～珍品 set out precious things in order 2.(列举) enumerate: ～事实 enumerate the facts

【罗马教皇】 Luómǎ Jiàohuáng the Pope

【罗马数字】 Luómǎ shùzì Roman numerals

【罗盘】 luópán compass

【罗圈腿】 luóquāntuǐ bowlegs; bandy legs

【罗网】 luówǎng net; trap: 布下～ spread a net / 自投～ fall into a trap; walk right into the trap

【罗帷】 luówéi a gauze curtain

【罗音】 luóyīn 〈*Med.*〉 rale

【罗帐】 luózhàng curtain of thin silk

【罗织】 luózhī frame up: ～成狱 frame up a crime / ～罪名 cook up charges

【罗致】 luózhì enlist the services of; collect; gather together: ～人才 enlist the services of talents

萝[蘿] (luó) trailing plants: 藤～ Chinese wistaria

【萝卜】 luó·bo radish
【萝卜干】 luó·bogān dried radish

逻［邏］(luó) patrol

【逻辑】 luójí logic; logical (adj.): 形式～ formal logic
【逻辑思维】 luójí sīwéi logical thinking
【逻辑推理】 luójí tuīlǐ logical deduction
【逻辑学】 luójíxué logic; logical (adj.) ‖ 逻辑学家 logician

箩［籮］(luó) a square-bottomed bamboo basket

【箩筐】 luókuāng a large bamboo basket; a large wicker basket

锣［鑼］(luó) gong: 敲～ beat a gong

【锣鼓】 luógǔ 1.(锣和鼓) gong and drum 2.(泛指传统打击乐器) traditional percussion instruments

骡［贏］(luó) mule; hinny: 驴～ hinny / 马～ mule

【骡子】 luó·zi mule; hinny

螺(luó) 1.(软体动物) spiral shell; snail: 田～ field snail 2.(螺旋形指纹) whorl

【螺钉】 luódīng screw: 木～ wood screw; screwnail / 把～拧松 loosen a screw
【螺杆】 luógǎn shank
【螺号】 luóhào conch; shell trumpet
【螺帽】 luómào head
【螺母】 luómǔ 〈Mech.〉 nut: 蝶形～ wing nut
【螺母垫圈】 luómǔ diànquān nut collar
【螺栓】 luóshuān 〈*Mech*.〉 bolt
【螺丝】 luósī screw: 上～ tighten up a screw
【螺丝刀】 luósīdāo screwdriver: 用～把螺丝上紧 tighten a screw with a screwdriver
【螺丝钉】 luósīdīng screw
【螺丝扣】 luósīkòu thread
【螺丝母】 luósīmǔ nut
【螺纹】 luówén 1.(指纹) whorl; spiral 2.〈*Mech*.〉 thread; screw thread: 公制～ metric thread
【螺旋】 luóxuán 1.(像螺壳纹理的曲线形) spiral; helix 2.〈*Physics*〉 screw
【螺旋桨】 luóxuánjiǎng 〈*Mech*.〉 propeller; screw: 涡轮～ turbo-propeller
【螺旋桨式飞机】 luóxuánjiǎngshì fēijī propeller-driven aircraft

裸［躶、羸］(luǒ) bare; naked; exposed: 赤～～ stark-naked; undisguised / 正面全～ full frontal nudity

【裸导线】 luǒdǎoxiàn bare conductor
【裸机】 luǒjī bare bones; bare machine
【裸露】 luǒlù uncovered; exposed: ～在阳光下 exposed to the sun
【裸体】 luǒtǐ naked; nude; in the nude; nudity (n.)
【裸体画】 luǒtǐhuà nude; nudity
【裸体模特】 luǒtǐ mótè nude model
【裸线】 luǒxiàn 〈*Electr*.〉 bare wire

瘰(luǒ)

【瘰疬】 luǒlì scrofula; struma

荦［犖］(luò)

【荦荦】 luòluò 〈*written*〉 conspicuous; apparent; obvious: ～大者 the most essential points

骆(luò)

【骆驼】 luò·tuo camel: 双峰～ Bactrian camel / 单峰～ dromedary camel
【骆驼绒】 luò·tuoróng camel hair cloth

络(luò) 1.(网状物) sth. resembling a net: 丝瓜～ loofah 2.(用网状物兜住) hold sth. in place with a net 3.(缠绕) twine; wind

【络腮胡子】 luòsāi-hú·zi whiskers; full beard
【络纱】 luòshā winding yarn; spooling
【络绎不绝】 luòyì-bùjué in an endless stream

珞(luò)

【珞巴族】 Luòbāzú Lhoba (中国少数民族,主要分布在西藏)

落(luò) 1.(掉下) fall; drop: 西红柿价格～了。The price of tomatoes has dropped. 2.(下降) go down; set: 洪水～了。The flood is low. 3.(使下降) lower: ～帆 lower a sail 4.(衰败) decline; come down; sink: 衰～ decline; go downhill 5.(遗留在后边) lag behind; fall behind 6.(留下) leave behind; stay behind: ～一个好名声 leave a good name 7.(下落) whereabouts 8.(聚居

地) settlement 9.(归属) fall onto; rest with: 这个任务就 ～在我们肩上了。The task rested squarely on our shoulders. 10.(得到) get; have; receive
(另见"落"là, lào)
【落榜】 luòbǎng flunk a competitive examination for a job or school admission
【落笔】 luòbǐ put pen to paper; start to write
【落泊】 luòbó 1.(潦倒) be in dire straits; be down and out 2.(豪迈) unconventional; unusual
【落魄】 luòbó 同"落泊"
【落差】 luòchā 1.(水位的差数) drop 2.(蓄水高度) head
【落潮】 luòcháo ebb tide
【落成】 luòchéng complete; completion (n.)
【落成典礼】 luòchéng diǎnlǐ inauguration ceremony
【落得】 luò·de get; end in
【落地】 luòdì 1.(落在地上) fall to the ground 2.(婴儿出生) be born
【落地窗】 luòdìchuāng French window
【落地灯】 luòdìdēng floor lamp; standard lamp
【落地电扇】 luòdì diànshàn electric fan with adjustable stand
【落地式收音机】 luòdìshì shōuyīnjī console (radio) set
【落点】 luòdiǎn 1.〈*Sports*〉 placement (of a ball): ～准 accuracy in placement 2.(火炮的落点) point of fall
【落后】 luòhòu 1.(落在后面) fall behind; lag behind: 认识到～,才能改变～。Backwardness must be recognized before it can be changed. 2.(比原计划慢) develop more slowly than scheduled: 比原计划～了五个月 five months behind the plan 3.(不先进) backward: 技术～ backward in technique / 经济～ backward in economy
【落后地区】 luòhòu dìqū backward areas; underdeveloped areas
【落后分子】 luòhòu fēnzǐ backward element
【落户】 luòhù 1.(在他乡定居) settle; make one's home: 安家～ make a place one's home and settle down there / 她已在南京～。She has settled in Nanjing. 2.(登记户籍) register one's residence
【落花流水】 luòhuā-liúshuǐ like fallen flowers carried away by the flowing water; utterly routed: 把…打得～ put sb. to rout
【落花生】 luò·huashēng 1.〈*Bot.*〉 peanut; groundnut 2.(花生果) peanut
【落价】 luòjià fall in price; drop in price
【落脚】 luòjiǎo stay; stop over; put up
【落脚处】 luòjiǎochù temporary lodging
【落井下石】 luòjǐng-xiàshí drop stones on someone who has fallen into a well; hit a person when he's down
【落空】 luòkōng come to nothing; fail; fall through: 这事有～的危险。There is a danger that nothing will come of it.
【落款】 luòkuǎn write the names of the sender and the recipient on a letter, etc.; inscribe
【落泪】 luòlèi shed tears; weep
【落落大方】 luòluò-dàfāng natural and graceful
【落难】 luònàn meet with misfortune; be in distress
【落聘】 luòpìn fail to be engaged
【落魄】 luòpò 1.(潦倒) be in dire straits; be down and out 2.(豪迈) unconventional; unusual
【落日】 luòrì setting sun
【落石】 luòshí 〈*Transport*〉 falling rocks
【落实】 luòshí 1.(切合实际) practicable; workable: 采取～的措施 adopt workable measures 2.(确定) fix in advance; ascertain; make sure 3.(实现) carry out; fulfill; implement; put into effect: ～政策 implement the policies
【落水】 luòshuǐ 1.(掉在水里) fall into water 2.(堕落) go astray; degenerate: 拖人～ lead sb. astray
【落水管】 luòshuǐguǎn sink drain
【落汤鸡】 luòtāngjī like a drowned rat; wet through: 淋得像～ be wet through in the rain; through in the rain
【落体】 luòtǐ 〈*Physics*〉 falling body: 自由～ freely falling body
【落网】 luòwǎng fall into the net; be caught; be captured
【落伍】 luòwǔ 1.(掉队) fall behind the ranks; straggle; drop behind; drop out 2.(落后) backward: 产品设计上～ backward in product design
【落选】 luòxuǎn fail to be chosen; lose an election
【落叶】 luòyè 1.(落下的树叶) fallen leaves

2.(每年落叶的) deciduous leaf

【落叶林】 luòyèlín deciduous forest

【落叶树】 luòyèshù deciduous tree

【落叶松】 luòyèsōng 〈*Bot.*〉 larch

摞(luò) **1.**(堆积) pile up; stack up: 把书~起来 stack up the books **2.**〈*classifier*〉 pile; stack: 一~杂志 a stack of magazines

M

ma

妈(mā) **1**.(母亲) ma; mum; mummy; mother **2**.(大妈) aunt; auntie

【妈妈】 mā·ma ma; mummy; mother

抹[擵[2]](mā) **1**.(擦) wipe: 把泥～去 wipe the mud off / ～去眼泪 wipe one's tears away **2**.(抹下来) rub sth. down; slip sth. off
(另见"抹"mǒ, mò)

【抹布】 mābù rag

【抹脸】 māliǎn straighten one's face; put on a stern expression: 抹下脸来 show anger or displeasure suddenly

麻[蔴[1,2]](má) **1**.(麻类植物) fiber crops ‖ 大麻 hemp / 黄麻 jute / 剑麻 sisal-hemp / 罗布麻 dogbane / 亚麻 flax / 苎麻 ramie; ramee **2**.(芝麻) sesame **3**.(不光滑) rough; coarse **4**.(麻子) pocked; pockmarked; pitted; spotty **5**.(麻木) have pins and needles; tingle **6**.(麻醉) anesthesia: 局～ local anesthesia / 全～ general anesthesia

【麻包】 mábāo gunny bag; gunny sack

【麻痹】 mábì **1**.〈*Med*.〉 paralysis: 全身～ general paralysis **2**.(使丧失警惕) benumb; lull; blunt: ～大意 be off one's guard **3**.(疏忽) lower one's guard; be off one's guard

【麻布】 mábù **1**.(粗麻布) gunny (cloth) **2**.(夏布) linen

【麻袋】 mádài gunny bag; gunny sack; sack

【麻烦】 má·fan **1**.(费事) troublesome: 带来～ make troubles / 自找～ look for trouble **2**.(使费事) put sb. to trouble; trouble sb.; bother sb.

【麻纺厂】 máfǎngchǎng flax mill

【麻风病】 máfēngbìng 〈*Med*.〉 lepra; leprosy

【麻风病患者】 máfēngbìng huànzhě leper

【麻花】 máhuā fried dough twist

【麻将】 májiàng mah-jong: 打～ play mah-jong

【麻酱】 májiàng sesame paste

【麻利】 má·li quick and neat; dexterous; deft: 干事～的人 quick and neat worker

【麻木】 mámù **1**.(失去知觉) numb: 两腿～得一时站不起身来 one's legs are too numb to get up at once **2**.(麻木的感觉) apathetic; insensitive **3**.(思想迟钝) slow (in thought)

【麻木不仁】 mámù-bùrén apathetic; insensitive; unfeeling

【麻雀】 máquè sparrow

【麻纱】 máshā **1**.(麻纤维) yarn of linen; flax **2**.(棉麻织品) cambric; hair cords

【麻绳】 máshéng rope made of gunny

【麻线】 máxiàn linen thread

【麻药】 máyào anesthetic

【麻油】 máyóu sesame oil

【麻疹】 mázhěn 〈*Med*.〉 measles

【麻织品】 mázhīpǐn linen fabrics

【麻子】 má·zi **1**.(天花疤痕) pockmarks **2**.(指有麻子的人) a person with a pockmarked face

【麻醉】 mázuì **1**.〈*Med*.〉 anesthesia; narcosis: 低温～ hypothermic anesthesia / 脊髓～ spinal anesthesia / 药物～ drug anesthesia / 针刺～ acupuncture anesthesia **2**.(使人认识模糊) anesthetize; poison: ～自己 hypnotize oneself; give oneself over to

【麻醉剂】 mázuìjì anesthetic; narcotic

【麻醉品】 mázuìpǐng narcotic; drug

【麻醉品管制】 mázuìpǐng guǎnzhì narcotic control

【麻醉师】 mázuìshī anesthetist

【麻醉药】 mázuìyào narcotic; anesthetics

【麻醉针】 mázuìzhēng anesthetic needle

马[馬](mǎ) **1**.(家畜) horse: 骑～ ride a horse / 有三个士兵骑着～。There are three soldiers on horseback. ‖

公马 stallion / 母马 mare / 幼马 foal / 阉马 gelding 2.〈*Chess*〉knight
【马鞍】 mǎ'ān saddle
【马鞍形】 mǎ'ānxíng the shape of a saddle
【马背】 mǎbèi horseback
【马鞭】 mǎbiān horsewhip
【马不停蹄】 mǎbùtíngtí without a stop; non-stop
【马槽】 mǎcháo manger
【马车】 mǎchē 1.（载人的）carriage 2.（拉货的）cart
【马刺】 mǎcì spur
【马达】 mǎdá motor
【马大哈】 mǎdàhā 1.（粗心大意）careless; forgetful 2.（粗心大意的人）a careless person; scatterbrain
【马刀】 mǎdāo saber
【马到成功】 mǎdào-chénggōng be accomplished quickly and easily; gain an immediate victory
【马灯】 mǎdēng barn lantern; lantern
【马镫】 mǎdèng stirrup
【马丁炉】 mǎdīnglú 〈*Metall.*〉Martin furnace; open-hearth furnace
【马队】 mǎduì 1.（运货的马队）caravan; a train of horses carrying goods 2.（骑兵部队）mounted troops; cavalry
【马尔萨斯主义】 Mǎ'ěrsàsī zhǔyì Malthusianism; Malthusianist (adj.)
【马粪纸】 mǎfènzhǐ strawboard
【马蜂】 mǎfēng hornet; wasp
【马蜂窝】 mǎfēngwō hornet's nest: 捅～ stir up a hornet's nest
【马倌】 mǎguān groom
【马海毛】 mǎhǎimáo 〈*Textiles*〉mohair
【马赫数】 mǎhèshù 〈*Physics*〉Mach number
【马后炮】 mǎhòupào belated action or advice; belated effort: ～式的声明 a belated statement
【马虎】 mǎ·hu careless; casual: 工作～ be careless in one's work
【马糊】 mǎ·hu 同"马虎"
【马甲】 mǎjiǎ waists-coat
【马脚】 mǎjiǎo one's concealed true character: 露了～ give oneself away
【马厩】 mǎjiù stable
【马克思列宁主义】 Mǎkèsī-Lièníng zhǔyì Marxism-Leninism; Marxist-Leninist (adj.) ‖ 马克思列宁主义者 Marxist-Leninist
【马克思主义】 Mǎkèsī zhǔyì Marxism; Marxist (adj.): ～哲学 Marxist philosophy / ～政治经济学 Marxist political economy ‖ 马克思主义者 Marxist
【马口铁】 mǎkǒutiě tinplate; galvanized iron
【马裤】 mǎkù riding breeches
【马裤呢】 mǎkùní 〈*Textiles*〉whipcord; cavalry twill
【马拉松】 mǎlāsōng 1.〈*Sports*〉marathon: ～运动员 a marathon runner 2.（时间冗长的）marathon: ～会议 a marathon session
【马拉松赛跑】 mǎlāsōng sàipǎo marathon race (42.195 km.)
【马兰】 mǎlán 〈*Bot.*〉kalimeris
【马蓝】 mǎlán 〈*Bot.*〉conehead
【马力】 mǎlì 〈*Physics*〉horsepower (HP; hp): 1～=0.735 千瓦 1 horsepower = 0.735 kW / 240～的柴油发动机 a 240-horsepower diesel engine
【马力小时】 mǎlì xiǎoshí horsepower-hour
【马蔺】 mǎlìn 〈*Bot.*〉Chinese iris
【马铃薯】 mǎlíngshǔ potato: 煮～ boiled potatoes / 烤～ roasted potatoes / 煎～ fried potatoes / ～泥 mashed potato / 炸～片 potato chip; potato crisp / 削～ peel the potato
【马路】 mǎlù road; street; avenue: 柏油～ an asphalt road / 过～时先向两边看一下 look both ways before crossing the road
【马路画家】 mǎlù huàjiā pavement artist
【马鹿】 mǎlù 〈*Zool.*〉red deer
【马骡】 mǎluó 〈*Zool.*〉mule
【马马虎虎】 mǎmǎ-hūhū 1.（不仔细）careless; casual 2.（勉强可以）not so bad; just passable; so-so
【马奶】 mǎnǎi mare's milk
【马棚】 mǎpéng stable
【马匹】 mǎpǐ horses
【马前卒】 mǎqiánzú pawn; cat's-paw
【马枪】 mǎqiāng carbine
【马球】 mǎqiú 1.〈*Sports*〉polo 2.（球）polo ‖ 马球运动员 polo player
【马赛克】 mǎsàikè 〈*Archit.*〉mosaic

【马赛克贴面】 mǎsàikè tiēmiàn mosaic pavement

【马上】 mǎshàng immediately; straight away; at once; right away：她让他～离开办公室。She told him to leave the office at once.

【马术】 mǎshù horsemanship

【马术师】 mǎshùshī horseman (m.); horsewoman (f.)

【马蹄】 mǎtí horse's hoof

【马蹄表】 mǎtíbiǎo alarm clock

【马蹄铁】 mǎtítiě 1.(铁掌) horseshoe 2.(马蹄形的磁铁) U-shaped magnet; horseshoe magnet

【马蹄形】 mǎtíxíng the shape of a hoof; U-shaped

【马铁】 mǎtiě 〈*Metall.*〉 malleable iron

【马桶】 mǎtǒng nightstool; closestool; commode

【马尾巴】 mǎwěi·ba horsetail

【马尾松】 mǎwěishōng 〈*Bot.*〉 masson pine

【马戏】 mǎxì circus

【马戏棚】 mǎxìpéng circus tent

【马戏团】 mǎxìtuán circus; circus troupe

【马靴】 mǎxuē riding boots

【马蝇】 mǎyíng 〈*Zool.*〉 horsefly

【马掌】 mǎzhǎng 1.(马蹄下部的角质物) horse's hoof 2.(马蹄铁) horseshoe：钉～ put a horseshoe on; horseshoe

【马鬃】 mǎzōng horse's mane; horsehair

【马醉木】 mǎzuìmù 〈*Bot.*〉 pieris

吗 (mǎ)

【吗啡】 mǎfēi 〈*Pharm.*〉 morphine

玛 (mǎ)

【玛钢】 mǎgāng 〈*Metall.*〉 malleable iron

【玛纳斯】 Mǎ'nàsī 〈place〉 Manas

【玛瑙】 mǎ'nǎo agate：～念珠 agate beads

码 (mǎ) 1.(数目符号) a sign or thing indicating number：尺～ size / 页～ page number 2.(堆叠) pile up; stack 3.(英美制长度单位) yard (yd.) 4.(代码) code

【码放】 mǎfàng pile up; stack

【码头】 mǎ·tou wharf; dock; quay; pier：安全～ safe berth / 储油～ oil wharf; petrol wharf / 浮～ pontoon / 货运～ cargo berth / 客运～ passenger wharf

【码头工人】 mǎ·tou gōngrén docker; stevedore; longshoreman

【码头交货价格】 mǎ·tou jiāohuò jiàgé ex dock

【码头税】 mǎ·toushuì pierage

【码头停泊时间】 mǎ·tou tíngbō shíjiān lay days

蚂 (mǎ)

【蚂蟥】 mǎhuáng 〈*Zool.*〉 leech

【蚂蚁】 mǎyǐ ant

骂［**罵**］(mà) 1.(咒骂) abuse; curse; swear; call names：不～人 never swear at people 2.(斥责) condemn; rebuke; reprove; scold：小～大帮忙 scold a little but help a great deal

【骂街】 màjiē shout abuses in the street; call people names in public

【骂骂咧咧】 mà·ma-liēliē intersperse one's talk with curses; be foul-mouthed

【骂名】 màmíng bad name; infamy：留下～ earn oneself infamy

【骂人话】 màrénhuà abusive language; swearword

mai

埋 (mái) cover up; bury：把树根用土～起来 cover up the roots of the tree with earth
(另见"埋"mán)

【埋藏】 máicáng 1.(藏在地里) lie hidden in the earth; bury：～着丰富的矿藏。Rich mineral resources lie hidden in the earth. 2.(隐藏) hide; conceal：把秘密～在心底 hide the secret deep in one's heart 3.(在皮下埋入制剂) plant some medicine under one's skin

【埋藏物】 máicángwù treasure trove

【埋单】 máidān pay bill

【埋伏】 mái·fú 1.(秘密布置兵力) ambush; lie in ambush：设～ lay an ambush / 中～ fall into an ambush 2.(潜伏) hide; lie low：～着失败的因素 bear the seed of defeat

【埋伏圈】 mái·fúquān ambuscade

【埋名】 máimíng conceal one's name; live incognito

【埋没】 máimò 1.(埋起来) bury; cover up

2.(使显不出来) neglect; stifle: ～人才 stifle real talents

【埋汰】 mái·tai dirty

【埋头】 máitóu immerse oneself in; be engrossed in

【埋葬】 máizàng 1.(掩埋尸体) bury: 他昨天被～。He was buried yesterday. 2.(喻使完结) eliminate; finish

买[買] (mǎi) buy; purchase: ～票 buy a ticket; purchase a ticket / ～书 buy books / ～一幅凡高的画儿 purchase a painting by Van Gogh / 给女友～花 buy some flowers for his girlfriend

【买办】 mǎibàn comprador

【买办资产阶级】 mǎibàn zīchǎn jiējí comprador bourgeoisie

【买不起】 mǎibùqǐ cannot afford it

【买断】 mǎiduàn buy a thing outright

【买方】 mǎifāng buyer; the buying party: ～负担风险 let the buyer beware

【买方市场】 mǎifāng shìchǎng buyer's market

【买方样品】 mǎifāng yàngpǐn buyer's sample

【买好】 mǎihǎo ingratiate oneself with; play up to

【买价】 mǎijià buying price

【买进】 mǎijìng buy in

【买空卖空】 mǎikōng-màikōng buy long and sell short; speculate

【买路钱】 mǎilùqián money paid to bandits for passage

【买卖】 mǎimài buying and selling; buy and sell: ～公平 buying and selling at reasonable prices

【买卖合同】 mǎi·mai hé·tong contract note

【买卖黄金者】 mǎi · mai huángjīnzhě gold trafficker

【买卖婚姻】 mǎi·mai hūnyīn mercenary marriage

【买卖】 mǎi·mai 1.(做生意) business; deal: ～清淡。Business is dull. 2.(商店) shop; business: 他在南京有一家～。He has a business in Nanjing.

【买卖人】 mǎi · mairén businessman; trader; merchant

【买入汇率】 mǎirù huìlǜ buying rate

【买通】 mǎitōng bribe; buy over; buy off

【买下来】 mǎixiàlái settle a purchase; contract a purchase

【买一送一】 mǎiyī-sòngyī buy one get one free

【买账】 mǎizhàng (多用于否定) respect for; show respect for

【买主】 mǎizhǔ buyer; customer

【买主垄断市场】 mǎizhǔ lǒngduàn shìchǎng monopsony

【买主自己动手工具】 mǎizhǔ zìjǐ dòngshǒu gōngjù do-it-yourself kit

迈[邁] (mài) 1.(跨过) step; stride: ～过钢轨 step over the rail 2.(老迈) advanced in years; old: 在他老～之年 in his old age 3.(英里的音译) mile

【迈步】 màibù take a step; make a step; step forward: ～走向讲台 step up to the platform

【迈进】 màijìn stride forward; forge ahead; advance with big strides: 向着四个现代化的宏伟目标～ forge ahead toward the great goal of the four modernization

麦[麥] (mài) 1.(麦类统称) wheat; barley; etc.: 春小～ spring wheat / 大～ barley / 黑～ rye / 荞～ buckwheat / 小～ wheat / 燕～ oats / 莜～ naked oats / 割～ reap wheat / 种～ raise wheat 2.(专指小麦) wheat

【麦草】 màicǎo wheat grass

【麦粉】 màifěn flour

【麦麸】 màifū wheat bran

【麦秸】 màijiē wheat straw

【麦秸工艺】 màijiē gōngyì wheat straw handicrafts

【麦秸画】 màijiēhuà straw patchwork

【麦酒】 màijiǔ beer

【麦克风】 màikèfēng microphone; mike

【麦浪】 màilàng rippling wheat; billowing wheat fields

【麦粒肿】 màilìzhǒng 〈*Med*.〉 sty

【麦芒】 màimáng awn of wheat

【麦苗】 màimiáo wheat seedling

【麦片】 màipiàn wheat flakes; oatmeal

【麦片粥】 màipiànzhōu oatmeal porridge; oatmeal

【麦乳精】 màirǔjīng malted milk; extract of malt and milk

【麦收】 màishōu wheat harvest

【麦穗】 màishuì ear of wheat; wheat head

【麦芽】 màiyá malt
【麦芽糖】 màiyátáng malt sugar; maltose
【麦子】 mài·zi wheat

卖[賣](mài) 1.(出售) sell: 票全～完了。All tickets were sold out. / 我的书～了3元。I sold my book for 3 dollars. 2.(出卖) betray: ～友求荣 betray one's friend to obtain promotion 3.(卖劲儿) exert to the utmost; not spare 4.(卖弄) show off
【卖唱】 màichàng sing for a living: ～过活 maintain life by singing
【卖大号】 màidàhào sell retail goods as wholesale; sell retail goods in large quantity
【卖方】 màifāng the selling party; seller: ～负担风险 let the seller beware
【卖方市场】 màifāng shìchǎng seller's market
【卖方样品】 màifāng yàngpǐn seller's sample
【卖关子】 màiguān·zi keep people guessing
【卖国】 màiguó betray one's country: ～通敌 sell the country and communicate with the enemy
【卖国集团】 màiguó jítuán traitorous clique
【卖国条约】 màiguó tiáoyuē traitorous treaty
【卖国行为】 màiguó xíngwéi treasonable act
【卖国贼】 màiguózéi traitor (to one's country)
【卖国主义】 màiguó zhǔyì national betrayal
【卖价】 màijià selling price
【卖劲】 màijìn exert all one's strength; spare no effort
【卖绝】 màijué sell a thing outright
【卖空】 màikōng short sales
【卖力】 màilì exert all one's strength; spare no effort; do all one can
【卖力气】 mài lì·qi 1.(尽量出力) exert all one's strength; exert oneself to the utmost 2.(出卖劳动力) make a living by manual labor
【卖命】 màimìng 1.(拼命干活) work oneself to the bone for sb. 2.(送死) die unworthy for
【卖弄】 mài·nong show off; parade: ～小聪明 show off one's smartness
【卖弄风情】 mài·nong-fēngqíng flirt and coquet
【卖俏】 màiqiào play the coquette; coquette
【卖身】 màishēn 1.(卖自己或家人) sell oneself or a member of one's family 2.(出卖灵魂或肉体) sell one's body; sell one's soul
【卖身契】 màishēnqì an indenture by which one sells oneself or a member of one's family
【卖身投靠】 màishēn-tóukào sell out oneself to the enemy; joint the enemy camp for sheer profit
【卖艺】 màiyì make a living as a performer
【卖淫】 màiyín prostitute; prostitution (n.)
【卖淫女】 màiyínnǚ prostitute
【卖主】 màizhǔ bargainer; seller
【卖座】 màizuò draw large audiences; attract large numbers of customers: 这部影片很～。The film draws well.

脉[脈、衇](mài) 1.(动脉和静脉) arteries and veins 2.(脉搏) pulse: 号～ feel sb's pulse 3.(矿脉, 叶脉) vein: 金矿～ vein of gold / 矿～ ore vein; mineral vein / 叶～ veins in a leaf (另见"脉"mò)
【脉搏】 màibó pulse: 时代的～ the pulse of present era / ～微弱 have a weak pulse
【脉冲】 màichōng 〈*Physics*〉 pulse
【脉冲发生器】 màichōng fāshēngqì pulser
【脉冲计数器】 màichōng jìshùqì pulse counter
【脉冲雷达】 màichōng léidá pulse radar
【脉冲信号】 màichōng xìnhào pulse signal
【脉冲星】 màichōngxīng 〈*Astron.*〉 pulsar
【脉络】 màiluò 1.(对静脉和动脉的统称) arteries and veins 2.(条理) thread of thought; sequence of ideas: ～分明 clear line of thought
【脉弱】 màiruò 〈*Med.*〉 weak pulse
【脉息】 màixī pulse: ～微弱 have a weak pulse

唛(mài) mark
【唛头】 màitóu mark

man

颟[顢](mān)
【颟顸】 mān·hān muddleheaded and careless

埋(mán) (另见"埋"mái)
【埋怨】 mányuàn complain of; murmur at;

blame：过多的～ a surfeit of complaints / ～他人 blame others

蛮［蠻］(mán) 1.（野蛮）rough; fierce; reckless; unreasoning：野～ savage 2.（很；挺）quite; pretty：～好 pretty good

【蛮不讲理】 mánbùjiǎnglǐ be impervious to reason; persist in being unreasonable

【蛮干】 mángàn act rashly; act recklessly; be foolhardy

【蛮横】 mánhèng rude and unreasonable; arbitrary：～无理 be impervious to reason

蔓(mán)（另见"蔓"màn, wàn）

【蔓菁】 mán·jing 〈*Bot*.〉 turnip

馒(mán)

【馒头】 mán · tou steamed bun; steamed bread

鳗(mán) eel

【鳗鲡】 mánlí 同"鳗鱼"

【鳗鱼】 mányū eel

瞒［瞞］(mán) hide the truth from：～不了人 can't deceive others / 别～我 don't hide it from me

【瞒报】 mánbào give a false report

【瞒哄】 mánhǒng deceive; pull the wool over sb's eyes

【瞒上欺下】 mánshàng-qīxià deceive those above and bully those below

【瞒天过海】 mántiān-guòhǎi cross the sea by a trick; practice deception

【瞒心昧己】 mánxīn-mèijǐ blot out one's conscience; deceive oneself

满［滿］(mǎn) 1.（充满）full; filled; packed：～～一箱书 a full case of book / 她的眼里噙～泪水。Her eyes were full of tears. / 公共汽车上挤～了人。The bus was packed with people. / 杯子～了，盛～了牛奶。The glass is full — it is full of milk. 2.（使满）fill：把杯子斟～啤酒 fill a glass with beer / 给水桶装～水 fill (up) the bucket with water 3.（达到一定期限）expire; reach the limit：不～两年 in less than two years / 年～35 岁的公民 citizen who have reached the age of 35 4.（全）completely; entirely; perfectly 5.（满足）satisfied：不～ not satisfied

【满不在乎】 mǎnbùzài·hu not worry at all; not care in the least; give no heed; take no heed

【满城风雨】 mǎnchéng-fēngyǔ the talk of the town

【满点】 mǎndiǎn get to enough working hours

【满额】 mǎn'é fulfill the quota

【满而不溢】 mǎn'érbùyì full without flowing over

【满分】 mǎnfēn full marks

【满腹】 mǎnfù be full of; have one's mind filled with

【满腹经纶】 mǎnfù-jīnglún an encyclopedic mind

【满怀】 mǎnhuái 1.（心中充满） have one's heart filled with; be imbued with：～深情 be imbued with deep love / ～信心 with full confidence 2.（整个前胸）bosom：撞了个～ bump into sb. 3.（母畜全部怀孕）all with young

【满口】 mǎnkǒu speak profusely：～胡说 talk nonsense

【满脸】 mǎnliǎn all over the face：～风尘 a faceful of traveling dust / ～晦气 look very depressed / ～雀斑 freckled face / ～俗气 look very vulgar / ～通红 face reddens all over / ～笑容 be all smiles / ～皱纹 full of wrinkles

【满门】 mǎnmén the whole family

【满面】 mǎnmiàn have one's face covered with：～怒容 red with anger

【满目】 mǎnmù meet the eye on every side：～疮痍 misery and suffering greets the eyes everywhere

【满拧】 mǎnnǐng completely contrary; totally different

【满期】 mǎnqī expire; come to deadline

【满期通知书】 mǎnqī tōngzhīshū expiration notice

【满腔】 mǎnqiāng have one's bosom filled with：～热忱 filled with ardor and sincerity

【满勤】 mǎnqín full attendance

【满身】 mǎnshēng have one's body covered with; be covered all over with

【满师】 mǎnshī finish serving one's time;

serve out one's apprenticeship：他尚未～。He is not yet out of his apprenticeship.

【满世界】 mǎnshì·jie everywhere

【满堂灌】 mǎntángguàn full-class instillation; full-class feeding

【满堂喝彩】 mǎntáng-hècǎi universal applause

【满堂红】 mǎntánghóng 1.（全面胜利）success in every field 2.〈*Cards*〉full house

【满天】 mǎntiān all over the sky

【满头大汗】 mǎntóu-dàhàn head covered with big drops of perspiration

【满心】 mǎnxīn have one's heart filled with sth.：～欢喜 filled with joy

【满眼】 mǎnyǎn 1.（充满眼睛）have one's eyes filled with 2.（充满视野）meet the eyes on every side

【满意】 mǎnyì satisfied; pleased：～之至 satisfied to the utmost degree / 她的答复令人十分～。Her answer is most satisfactory.

【满园春色】 mǎnyuán-chūnsè the garden is filled with the brightness of spring

【满员】 mǎnyuán 1.（军队达到规定人数）at full strength 2.（乘客满了）all seats taken

【满月】 mǎnyuè 1.（望月）full moon 2.（小孩满月）a baby's completion of its first month of life

【满载】 mǎnzài 1.（装满）loaded to capacity; fully loaded; laden with：～的火车 a full train / 一辆～煤炭的卡车 a truck fully loaded with coal 2.（满负荷）full load

【满载而归】 mǎnzàiérguī come back with fruitful results; return from a rewarding journey

【满招损，谦受益】 mǎn zhāo sǔn, qiān shòu yì one loses by pride and gains by modesty

【满足】 mǎnzú 1.（觉得足够）satisfied; content; contented：切不可～于这些数目字。Never be satisfied with such figures. 2.（使满足）satisfy; meet：～读者的需要 meet the reader's demands

【满族】 Mǎnzú Man（中国少数民族，主要分布在辽宁及黑龙江、吉林、河北、内蒙古、北京等地）

【满座】 mǎnzuò capacity audience; capacity house; full house：场场～ have a capacity audience for every show

螨［蟎］（mǎn）〈*Zool.*〉acarid; mite

曼（màn） 1.（柔和）graceful：～舞 graceful dances 2.（长）prolonged; long-drawn-out

【曼陀林】 màntuólín 〈*Music*〉mandolin

【曼陀罗】 màntuóluó 〈*Bot.*〉datura

【曼延】 mànyán draw out (in length); stretch：小路～好几公里。The footpath stretches for kilometers.

谩（màn） disrespectful; rude

【谩骂】 mànmà hurl invectives; fling abuses; rail

墁（màn） pave with stone or brick-paved：小路用砖～成了图案。The path is paved with bricks set in patterns.

蔓（màn）
（另见"蔓"mán, wàn）

【蔓草】 màncǎo creeping weed

【蔓延】 mànyán creep; spread：大火从工厂～到附近的住宅。The fire spread from the factory to the houses near by.

幔（màn） curtain; screen：布～ cotton curtain

【幔帐】 mànzhàng curtain; screen; canopy

慢（màn） 1.（速度慢）slow：把汽车开～ slow down a car / 对…反应～ be slow to react to sth. / 表～了两分钟。The watch is two minutes slow. / 这里的服务太～了，一杯咖啡我等了15分钟。The service in here is so slow — I've been waiting for a coffee for fifteen minutes! / 他的影片情节发展太～。His films are slow. 2.（从缓）postpone; defer 3.（态度冷淡）supercilious; rude

【慢班】 mànbān adjustment class

【慢车】 mànchē slow train; local train：乘～ take the slow train

【慢车道】 mànchēdào slow-traffic lanes

【慢待】 màndài treat rudely or discourteously

【慢动作】 màndòngzuò 〈*Cinematog.*〉slow motion; slow-mo; slo-mo

【慢镜头】 mànjìngtóu 〈*Cinematog. & TV*〉slow motion; slow-mo; slo-mo：放射门的～ show the goal in slow motion

【慢镜头重放】 mànjìngtóu chóngfàng 〈*TV*〉instant replay

【慢慢】 mànmàn 1.(速度慢) slowly; leisurely: ～讲 speak slowly 2.(逐渐地) gradually: ～积累 accumulate gradually
【慢跑】 mànpǎo jog: 我每天清早在饭前～20分钟。I jog for twenty minutes every morning before breakfast.
【慢坡】 mànpō gentle slope
【慢手慢脚】 mànshǒu-mànjiǎo slow in doing things; slow moving
【慢腾腾】 màntēngtēng at a leisurely pace; unhurriedly; sluggishly: ～地念 read unhurriedly
【慢条斯理】 màntiáo-sīlǐ leisurely; unhurriedly; very slow
【慢吞吞】 màntūntūn irritatingly slow; exasperatingly slow
【慢行线】 mànxíngxiàn 〈*Transport*〉 slow lane (of the motorway)
【慢性】 mànxìng 1.(发作得慢) slow in taking effect 2.(拖得长久) chronic: ～病 chronic disease / ～阑尾炎 chronic appendicitis
【慢性子】 mànxìng·zi 1.(性情迟缓) phlegmatic temperament 2.(性情迟缓的人) slow poke; slow coach
【慢悠悠】 mànyōuyōu unhurriedly; without haste
【慢中子】 mànzhōngzǐ 〈*Physics*〉 slow neutron; low-speed neutron
【慢走】 mànzǒu 1.(不要着急走) don't go yet; stay; wait a minute 2.(用于送别时) good-bye; take care

漫 (màn) 1.(溢出) overflow; brim over; flood; inundate: 由于大雨，河水有～过堤岸的危险。Because a heavy rain, there is a danger that the river will overflow its banks. / 啤酒～出了杯子。Beer overflows the glass. 2.(到处都是) all over the place; everywhere 3.(自由;随便) free; casual; unrestrained
【漫笔】 mànbǐ informal essay; literary notes
【漫不经心】 mànbùjīngxīn careless; casual; negligent
【漫步】 mànbù stroll; ramble; roam
【漫长】 màncháng very long; endless
【漫画】 mànhuà caricature; cartoon
【漫画家】 mànhuàjiā cartoonist; caricaturist
【漫骂】 mànmà abuse wildly; slander with
【漫漫】 mànmàn very long; boundless
【漫山遍野】 mànshān-biànyě all over the mountains and plains; over hill and dale
【漫射柔光屏】 mànshè róuguāngpíng 〈*Cinematog.*〉 diffusing screen
【漫谈】 màntán random talk; informal discussion: ～中国文学 random talk on Chinese literature
【漫天】 màntiān 1.(布满天空) filling the whole sky; all over the sky 2.(无限度的) boundless; limitless
【漫无边际】 mànwúbiānjì 1.(无边际的) boundless; limitless 2.(离题甚远) straying far from the subject; rambling; discursive
【漫延】 mànyán stretch; draw out (in length)
【漫游】 mànyóu go on a pleasure trip; roam; wander: ～世界 roam about the world

镘[**槾**] (màn) trowel

mang

芒 (máng) awn; beard; arista
【芒果】 mángguǒ 〈*Bot.*〉 mango
【芒种】 mángzhòng the Grain in Ear (6月5-7日交节)

忙 (máng) 1.(事情多) busy; fully occupied: 尽管～但很快活 be busy but happy / ～得不可开交 be swamped with work / ～于工作 be busy with one's work / ～于准备考试 be busy preparing for the examination / 他现在很～。He is busy now. 2.(匆忙) hurry; hasten; make haste: 你～什么? What's the hurry?
【忙蜂音】 mángfēngyīn busy-buzz
【忙里偷闲】 mánglǐ-tōuxián snatch a little leisure from a busy life
【忙碌】 mánglù be busy; bustle about: ～的一天 a busy day / 一天到晚忙忙碌碌 be busy all day long
【忙乱】 mángluàn be in a rush and a muddle; tackle a job in a hasty and disorderly manner
【忙人】 mángrén busy person
【忙音】 mángyīn busy back tone; busy tone
【忙音信号】 mángyīn xìnhào busy-back signal

【忙中有错】 mángzhōng-yǒucuò haste makes waste

盲(máng) blind：偏～ hemianopsia / 色～ color-blindness / 夜～ night blindness

【盲肠】 mángcháng 〈*Anat.*〉 cecum；caecum

【盲肠炎】 mángchángyán 〈*Med.*〉 appendicitis；cecitis

【盲从】 mángcóng follow blindly

【盲点】 mángdiǎn 〈*Med.*〉 blind spot

【盲动】 mángdòng act blindly；act rashly

【盲动主义】 mángdòng zhǔyì putschism

【盲降】 mángjiàng 〈*Aeron.*〉 blind landing

【盲流】 mángliú blind inflow into；blind influx

【盲目】 mángmù blind：～抄袭 blind imitation / ～追随(某人) follow sb. blindly

【盲目飞行】 mángmù fēixíng blind flight；instrument flying

【盲目轰炸】 mángmù hōngzhà blind bombing

【盲目性】 mángmùxìng blindness：克服～ curb blindness in action；refrain from blindfold action

【盲目着陆】 mángmù zháolù 〈*Aeron.*〉 blind landing

【盲区】 mángqū blind area

【盲人】 mángrén blind person

【盲文】 mángwén braille：～书籍 books printed in braille

【盲校】 mángxiào schools for the blind

茫(máng) 1.(没有边际) boundless and indistinct 2.(无所知) ignorant；in the dark

【茫茫】 mángmáng boundless and indistinct；vast：～大海 a vast sea

【茫然】 mángrán ignorant；in the dark；at a loss：感到～ be at a loss what to do

【茫无头绪】 mángwútóuxù be confused like a tangle of flax；not know where to begin

硭(máng)

【硭硝】 mángxiāo mirabilite；Glauber's salt

莽(mǎng) 1.(密生的草) rank grass 2.(鲁莽) rash

【莽苍】 mǎngcāng 1.(原野) open country 2.(景色迷茫) misty；hazy

【莽汉】 mǎnghàn a boorish fellow；a boor

【莽莽】 mǎngmǎng 1.(草木茂盛) luxuriant；rank 2.(无边无际) vast；boundless：～草原 boundless grasslands / ～原野 vast fields

【莽原】 mǎngyuán wilderness overgrown with grass

【莽撞】 mǎngzhuàng crude and impetuous；rash

蟒(mǎng) boa；python

【蟒蛇】 mǎngshé boa；python

mao

猫［**貓**］(māo) cat：波斯～ Persian cat / 虎斑～ tabby cat ‖ 公猫 tomcat / 母猫 catta / 小猫 kitten (另见"猫"máo)

【猫洞】 māodòng cat flap；cat door

【猫耳洞】 māo'ěrdòng cat's-ear-shaped cave

【猫叫】 māojiào mew；miaow：猫在门外喵喵叫。A cat was miaowing outside the door.

【猫科动物】 māokē dòngwù cats

【猫哭老鼠】 māokūlǎoshǔ shed crocodile tears

【猫头鹰】 māotóuyīng owl

【猫眼】 māoyǎn 〈*Electr.*〉 cat eye

【猫眼道钉】 māoyǎn dàodīng 〈*Transport*〉 reflector；cat's eye

毛(máo) 1.(毛发) hair；feather；down 2.(羊毛) wool；woolen 3.(霉) mildew：长～ be covered with mildew 4.(粗糙的；未加工的) semifinished 5.(不纯净的) gross 6.(小) little；small 7.(粗心) careless；crude；rash 8.(惊慌) panicky；scared；flurried：心里发～ feel frightened 8.(货币贬值) depreciate；devaluate

【毛笔】 máobǐ writing brush

【毛笔画】 máobǐhuà brush drawing

【毛病】 máobìng 1.(疾病) illness；disease：老～ inveterate disease 2.(故障) trouble：这台机器有点～。The machine does not work properly. 3.(缺点) shortcoming；defect：思想上的～ ideological malady / 作文中的～ faults in a composition 4.(坏习惯) bad habit

【毛玻璃】 máobō·li frosted glass

【毛糙】 máo·cao crude；coarse；careless

【毛虫】 máochóng 〈*Insect*〉 caterpillar

【毛豆】 máodòu young soya bean

【毛发】 máofà hair
【毛发鉴定】 máofà jiàndìng identification by hair
【毛纺】 máofǎng wool spinning：～工业 woolen industry
【毛估】 máo·gu rough estimation
【毛骨悚然】 máogǔ-sǒngrán with one's hair standing on end; absolutely terrified
【毛孩子】 máohái·zi a little boy
【毛校样】 máojiàoyàng roughs
【毛巾】 máojīn towel：洗脸～ hand towel / 洗澡～ bath towel / 用～擦干头发 towel one's hair dry
【毛巾被】 máoyīnbèi toweling coverlet
【毛巾布】 máoyīnbù toweling
【毛巾架】 máoyīnjià towel rack (AmE.); towel rail (BrE.)
【毛巾浴衣】 máojīn yùyī toweling bath robe
【毛孔】 máokǒng 〈*Anat.*〉 pore
【毛裤】 máokù long woolen underwear
【毛利】 máolì gross profit
【毛利率】 máolìlǜ rate of margin; rate of gross profit
【毛料】 máoliào woolen cloth; woolens：～裤子 woolen trousers
【毛驴】 máolǘ donkey
【毛毛雨】 máo·maoyǔ **1.**(很小的雨) drizzle：下了一整天～。It's been drizzling all day **2.**(放出风声) spread news; leak certain information
【毛南族】 Máonánzú Maonan (中国少数民族,主要分布在广西)
【毛坯】 máopī **1.**(砖瓦等的坯) semifinished product **2.**(坯料) blank
【毛皮】 máopí fur; pelt：～大衣 a fur coat
【毛皮兽】 máopíshòu fur-bearing animal
【毛片】 máopiān **1.**〈*Cinematog.*〉 workprint **2.**(指色情片) blue film; skin film; pornographic film
【毛茸茸】 máorōngrōng hairy; downy
【毛纱】 máoshā 〈*Textiles*〉 wool yarn
【毛收入】 máoshōurù gross income
【毛手毛脚】 máoshǒu-máojiǎo careless
【毛遂自荐】 Máo Suì zìjiàn recommend oneself to a post
【毛笋】 máosǔn (edible) bamboo shoots
【毛损】 máosǔn gross loss
【毛毯】 máotǎn woolen blanket
【毛细管】 máoxìguǎn **1.**(非常细的管子) capillary **2.**〈*Anat.*〉 blood capillary
【毛细管水】 máoxìguǎn shuǐ 〈*Agric.*〉 capillary water
【毛细现象】 máoxì xiànxiàng 〈*Physics*〉 capillarity
【毛细血管】 màoxì xuěguǎn 〈*Anat.*〉 blood capillary
【毛虾】 máoxiā shrimp
【毛线】 máoxiàn wool; knitting wool：用～织手套 knit some gloves / 她爱打～。She enjoys knitting.
【毛线手套】 máoxiàn shǒutào hand-knitted gloves
【毛线套头衫】 máoxiàn tàotóushān knitted jumper
【毛线针】 máoxiànzhēng knitting needle：织羊毛衫需要 8 号～ need size eight knitting needles to make the cardigan
【毛丫头】 máoyā·tou a little girl
【毛衣】 máoyī woolen sweater; sweater; woolly
【毛躁】 máo·zao **1.**(急躁) short-tempered; irritable **2.**(不细心) rush and careless
【毛泽东思想】 Máo Zédōng sīxiǎng Mao Zedong Thought
【毛毡】 máozhān felt
【毛织品】 máozhīpǐn **1.**(毛料) wool fabric; woolens **2.**(编织物) woolen knitwear
【毛重】 máozhòng gross weight
【毛竹】 máozhú mao bamboo; moso bamboo
【毛主席纪念堂】 Máozhǔxí Jìniàntáng Chairman Mao's Mausoleum

牦[犛] (máo)

【牦牛】 máoniú yak

矛 (máo) lance; pike; spear

【矛盾】 máodùn **1.**(自相抵触) contradictory：相互～的因素 contradictory elements / 自相～的推论 inconsequent reasoning **2.**〈*Philos. & Logic*〉 contradiction
【矛盾人格】 máodùnréngé conflicting personality
【矛头】 máotóu spearhead：～针对 be spearheaded at / 把～指向某人 direct the spear-

head at sb.

茅(máo) 〈*Bot*.〉 cogongrass

【茅草】 máocǎo 〈*Bot*.〉 cogongrass

【茅草棚】 máocǎopéng thatched shed; thatched shack

【茅坑】 máokēng **1**.(厕所的便坑) latrine pit **2**.(厕所) latrine

【茅棚】 máopéng thatched shed; thatched shack

【茅塞顿开】 máosè-dùnkāi be suddenly enlightened; become suddenly aware of the real state of affairs

【茅舍】 máoshè 〈*written*〉 thatched cottage

【茅屋】 máowū thatched cottage

蟊(máo) harmful insect

【蟊贼】 máozéi vermin; a person who harms the country and people

猫[貓](máo) (另见"猫"māo)

【猫腰】 máoyāo arch one's back; bend down

锚(máo) anchor: ～链 anchor chain / 抛～ drop anchor; cast anchor / 起～ weigh anchor

【锚泊】 máobó anchor; come to an anchor

【锚地】 máodì anchorage: 这个海湾是公认的安全～。The bay is well-known as a safety anchorage.

【锚链】 máoliàn anchor chain; anchor cable

【锚链孔】 máoliànkǒng hawsehole

【锚位】 máowèi anchorage point

【锚爪】 máozhuǎ fluke

卯(mǎo)

【卯劲儿】 mǎojìnr make a sudden all-out effort

【卯榫】 mǎosǔn mortise and tenon

【卯眼】 mǎoyǎn mortise

铆(mǎo) 〈*Mech*.〉 rivet: 飞机的许多部位都是～上的。Many parts of an aircraft are riveted together.

【铆钉】 mǎodīng rivet

【铆钉枪】 mǎodīngqiāng riveting gun

【铆工】 mǎogōng **1**.(铆接) riveting **2**.(指操作的人) riveter

【铆接】 mǎojiē riveting; rivet joint; rivet (v.)

茂(mào) **1**.(茂盛) luxuriant; exuberant; profuse **2**.(丰富精美) rich and splendid

【茂密】 màomì dense; thick: 叶子～的树 trees thick with leaves

【茂盛】 màoshèng luxuriant; exuberant; flourishing: 草木～ luxuriant vegetation

冒(mào) **1**.(向外冒;往上升) emit; send out; give off: ～出水来 emit water / ～臭味 give off an unpleasant smell / 眼前～金星 see stars / 伤口还在～血。Blood was still oozing from the wound. **2**.(不顾) risk; brave: ～着风雨 brave the storm / ～着生命危险救人 risk one's life to save another **3**.(冒失;冒昧) boldly; rashly **4**.(冒充) falsely; fraudulently: ～领 falsely claim sth. as one's own

【冒充】 màochōng pretend to be; pass sb. or sth. off as

【冒充者】 màochōngzhě jactitator; fraud

【冒顶】 màodǐng 〈*Mineral*.〉 roof fall

【冒犯】 màofàn offend; affront: ～尊严 violate the sanctity

【冒风险】 màofēngxiǎn run risks

【冒富】 màofù become better off

【冒号】 màohào colon (符号为 :)

【冒火】 màohuǒ burn with anger; get angry; flare up: 他心里直～。He was burning with anger in his heart.

【冒尖儿】 màojiānr **1**.(装得溢出) piled high above the brim **2**.(超过一点) a little over; a little more than: 10 公斤刚～ a little over ten kilos **3**.(突出) stand out; be conspicuous **4**.(露出苗头) begin to crop up

【冒尖户】 màojiānhù conspicuous household; conspicuous person

【冒进】 màojìn premature advance; rash advance

【冒领】 màolǐng falsely claim as one's own

【冒昧】 màomèi 〈*politeness*〉 make bold; venture; take the liberty: ～陈辞 make bold to express my views; venture an opinion

【冒名】 màomíng go under sb. else's name; assume another's name

【冒名顶替】 màomíng-dǐngtì substitute for another by assuming latter name; take falsely the place of another

【冒名顶替者】 màomíng dǐngtìzhě imposter; impostor

【冒牌】 màopái fake; imitation; infringe a well-known trade mark

【冒牌货】 màopáihuò imitation; fake: 这画看上去年代久远，实际上是最近的～。The painting looked old but was a recent fake.

【冒牌医生】 màopái yīshēng fake doctor

【冒然闯入】 màorán chuǎngrù butt in

【冒失】 mào·shi rash; abrupt: ～的行为 rash action / ～从事 act abruptly

【冒失鬼】 mào·shiguǐ harumscarum; cool hand

【冒天下之大不韪】 mào tiānxià zhī dà bùwěi defy world opinion; risk universal condemnation

【冒险】 màoxiǎn take a risk; run a risk

【冒险家】 màoxiǎnjiā adventurer

【冒险政策】 màoxiǎn zhèngcè adventurist policy

【冒险主义】 màoxiǎn zhǔyì adventurism; adventurist (adj.)

【冒烟】 màoyān smoke; smoky (adj.): 这火～太大。The fire's very smoky. / 这烟筒怎么冒这么多烟? Why is the chimney smoking so much?

【冒用商标】 màoyòng shāngbiāo infringement

帽 (mào) 1. (帽子) headgear; hat; cap: 安全～ safety helmet / 贝蕾～ beret / 便～ cap; sports cap / 草～ straw hat / 大檐～ peaked cap / 貂皮～ mink hat / 宽檐～ wide-brimmed hat / 礼～ hat; trilby hat / 呢～ woolen cap / 女～ bonnet / 皮～ fur cap / 绒线～ woolen hat / 游泳～ swimming cap / 毡～ felt hat 2. (帽状物) cap-like cover for sth.: 钢笔～儿 the cap of a fountain pen

【帽翅】 màochì brim

【帽带】 màodài hatband; chinstrap

【帽徽】 màohuī insignia (on a cap)

【帽架】 màojià hat rack

【帽舌】 màoshé peak (of a cap); visor

【帽檐】 màoyán 1. (帽子前面的檐) peak 2. (帽子四周的边) brim (of a hat)

【帽子】 mào·zi 1. (帽子) headgear; hat; cap: 戴着～ wear a hat / 戴上～ put on a hat / 摘下～ take off a hat 2. (罪名或名义) label; tag; brand: 扣～ put a label on sb.; hurl an epithet at sb. / 摘～ rid of the label; remove the label

贸 (mào) trade: 外～ foreign trade / 内～ internal trade

【贸然】 màorán rashly; hastily; without careful consideration: ～说出 speak out precipitately

【贸易】 màoyì trade: 补偿～ compensation trade / 对外～ foreign trade / 国际～ international trade / 国内～ domestic trade / 集市～ village fair / 特惠～ preferential trade / 沿海～ cabotage; coasting trade / 易货～ barter trade / 直接～ direct trade / 工业品～ trade in manufactured goods / 石油～ trade in oil / 开展～ develop trade / 建立经常～关系 establish regular trade relations / 与其他国家进行～ trade with others countries

【贸易保护主义】 màoyì bǎohù zhǔyì trade protectionism

【贸易壁垒】 màoyì bìlěi trade barriers: 把～作为控制进口的手段 introduce trade barriers as a way of controlling imports

【贸易差额】 màoyì chā'é trade balance; balance of trade

【贸易额】 màoyì'é volume of trade; turnover

【贸易法】 màoyìfǎ law of trade

【贸易港】 màoyìgǎng a trading port; a commercial port

【贸易公司】 màoyì gōngsī a trading company; a trading firm

【贸易伙伴】 màoyì huǒbàn trade partner; trading partner

【贸易货栈】 màoyì huòzhàn trade warehouse

【贸易积极性】 màoyì jījíxìng trade activity

【贸易禁运】 màoyì jìnyùn commercial embargo

【贸易逆差】 màoyì nìchā trade deficit; unfavorable balance of trade: 上个月～有所减少。The trade deficit narrowed last month.

【贸易区】 màoyìqū trade area

【贸易顺差】 màoyì shùnchā trade surplus; favorable balance of trade

【贸易条件】 màoyì tiáojiàn term of trade

【贸易条约】 màoyì tiáoyuē commercial treaty

【贸易往来】 màoyì wǎnglái trade contacts

【贸易限制】 màoyì xiànzhì restriction of trade

【贸易协定】 màoyì xiédìng trade agreement：两国签订了一个为期 5 年的～。The two countries have signed a trade agreement for five years.
【贸易议定书】 màoyì yìdìngshū trade protocol
【贸易中心】 màoyì zhōngxīn trade center
【贸易自由】 màoyì zìyóu freedom of trade
【贸易总额】 màoyì zhǒng'é total volume of trade

貌 (mào) looks; appearance：古城新～ the new look of an old city
【貌不惊人】 màobùjīngrén look mediocre
【貌合神离】 màohé-shénlí seemingly in harmony but actually at variance; be friendly in name only
【貌似】 màosì seemingly; in appearance

mei

没 (méi)
(另见"没"mò)
【没出息】 méichūxī not promising; good for nothing
【没词儿】 méicír 1.（没有说的）can find nothing to say 2.（不知说什么合适）be at a loss for words; be stuck for an answer
【没错儿】 méicuòr 1.（我确信）I'm quite sure; you can rest assured 2.（不会错）can't go wrong
【没大没小】 méidà-méixiǎo ill-mannered or rude to one's elders
【没道理】 méi dàolǐ unreasonable; not justified
【没地儿】 méidìr no seat for; no place for
【没多少】 méiduōshǎo not much; not many
【没关系】 méiguān·xi it doesn't matter; that's all right; never mind
【没见过世面】 méijiànguò shìmiàn green and inexperienced
【没见识】 méijiànshí inexperienced and ignorant
【没劲儿】 méijìnr have no interest in anything; listless
【没精打采】 méijīng-dǎcǎi listless; in low spirits; out of sorts; lackadaisical
【没开过眼】 méikāiguòyǎn rustic; unsophisticated; have seen little of the world
【没脸】 méiliǎn too shame to; lose face
【没良心】 méiliángxīn without conscience; unconscionable; ungrateful
【没…没…】 méi…méi… 1.（用在两个同义词前面，强调没有）～皮～脸 shamelessly / ～亲～故 without any relatives or friends / ～完～了 endless; without end / ～心～肺 inattentive 2.（用在两个反义词前面，表示应区别而未区别）～日～夜 day and night / ～早～晚 without regard to time of day
【没门儿】 méiménr 1.（没有门路）have no access to sth.; have no means of doing sth. 2.（表示不可能）impossible 3.（表示不同意）no go; nothing doing
【没命】 méimìng 1.（死亡）lose one's life; die 2.（拼命地）recklessly; desperately; like mad; for all one's worth
【没皮没脸】 méipí-méiliǎn shameless; shamelessly
【没谱儿】 méipǔr without any standard or criterion
【没趣】 méiqù feel put out; feel snubbed：自讨～ ask for a snub
【没什么】 méi shén·me it doesn't matter; it's nothing; that's all right; never mind
【没事】 méishì 1.（在闲着）have nothing to do; be free; be at leisure 2.（没关系）it doesn't matter; it's nothing; that's all right; never mind
【没事找事】 méishì-zhǎoshì 1.（自找麻烦）ask for trouble 2.（找碴）find fault with
【没王法】 méi wángfǎ lawless; without justice; act lawless
【没心没肺】 méixīn-méifèi careless; inattentive
【没羞】 méixiū unabashed; unblushing
【没有】 méiyǒu 1.（无）not have; there is not：～办法 it can't be helped / ～别的选择 there is no alternative 2.（不及；不如）not so ... as：你～他高。You are not as tall as he. 3.（不到）less than 4.（未）not：我今早～见到他。I didn't see him this morning.
【没有出路】 méiyǒu cūlù find oneself in a blind alley; without a way out
【没有说的】 méiyǒushuō·de 1.（没有缺点）really good; excellent 2.（不成问题）without

question; needless to say; it goes without saying

【没辙】 méizhé can find no way out; be at the end of one's rope

【没指望】 méizhǐwàng hopeless

【没志气】 méizhìqì without ambition; defeatist

【没主意】 méizhǔ·yi lose one's head; cannot make up one's mind

玫 (méi)

【玫瑰】 méi·gui 〈*Bot.*〉 rose; rugosa rose

枚 (méi) 〈*classifier*〉 20～古币 twenty ancient coin / 两～纪念章 two badges / 不胜～举 too numerous to enumerate

眉 (méi) 1.（眉毛）eyebrow; brow: 浓～ bushy eyebrows 2.（书眉）the top margin of a page

【眉笔】 méibǐ eyebrow pencil

【眉飞色舞】 méifēi-sèwǔ with dancing eyebrows and radiant face; enraptured

【眉睫】 méijié 1.（眉毛和睫毛）the eyebrows and eyelashes 2.（近在眼前）urgent; imminent

【眉开眼笑】 méikāi-yǎnxiào be all smiles; beam with joy

【眉来眼去】 méilái-yǎnqù make eyes at each other; flirt with each other

【眉毛】 méi·mao eyebrow; brow: 拔～ pluck one's eyebrow

【眉毛胡子一把抓】 méi·mao hú·zi yībǎzhuā try to attend to big and small matters all at once

【眉目】 méimù 1.（面貌）features; looks 2.（条理）logic; sequence of ideas: ～不清 not well organized 3.（纲要）essential

【眉目】 méi·mu （头绪）sign of a positive outcome; prospect of a solution: 那件事渐渐有了～。That matter is settling into shape.

【眉目传情】 méimù-chuánqíng flash amorous glances; make eyes at sb.

【眉头】 méitóu brows: ～不展 with knitted brows

楣 (méi) 〈*Archit.*〉 lintel

镅 (méi) 〈*Chem.*〉 americium（人造元素，符号 Am）

梅［楳、槑］(méi) plum

【梅毒】 méidú 〈*Med.*〉 syphilis

【梅花】 méihuā 1.（梅树的花）plum blossom 2.（腊梅）wintersweet 3.〈*Cards*〉 club

【梅花扳手】 méihuā bān·shou box wrench; ring spanner

【梅花鹿】 méihuālù sika; sika deer

【梅里雪山】 Méilǐxuěshān 〈place〉 Moirigkawagarbo

【梅雨】 méiyū 〈*Meteorol.*〉 plum rains

【梅子】 méi·zi plum

酶 (méi) 〈*Biol.*〉 enzyme; ferment

霉［黴］(méi) mold; mildew: 发～ go moldy; mildew

【霉病】 méibìng 〈*Agric.*〉 mildew

【霉菌】 méijūn mold; mildew

【霉烂】 méilàn mildew and rot

【霉天】 méitiān hot and humid weather

媒 (méi) 1.（媒人）go-between; matchmaker: 做～ act as a matchmaker 2.（媒介）intermediary: 虫～ insect-pollination / 风～ wind-pollination

【媒介】 méijiè intermediary; medium; vehicle: 授粉～ pollination medium

【媒婆】 méipó woman match-maker

【媒人】 méi·ren match-maker; go-between

【媒妁婚姻】 méishuò hūnyīn arranged marriage

【媒妁之言】 méishuòzhīyán the words of a match-maker

【媒体】 méitǐ medium; media (pl.): 新闻～ the medium of the press

煤 (méi) coal: 褐～ lignite / 焦～ coking coal / 泥～ peat / 无烟～ anthracite / 烟～ bituminous coal

【煤仓】 méicāng coal bunker

【煤藏】 méicáng coal deposits; coal reserves

【煤层】 méicéng coal seam; coal bed

【煤场】 méichǎng coal yard

【煤尘】 méichén coal dust

【煤尘爆炸】 méichén bàozhà coal-dust explosion

【煤斗】 méidǒu coal scuttle; scuttle

【煤斗车】 méidǒuchē hopper car

【煤矸石】 méigānshí gangue; coal gangue

【煤耗】 méihào coal consumption
【煤灰】 méihūi coal ash
【煤焦油】 méijiāoyóu coal tar
【煤精】 méijīng jet; black amber
【煤矿】 méikuàng coal mine; colliery: 露天～ open coal mine
【煤矿工人】 méikuàng gōngrén coal miner
【煤矿企业管理】 méikuàng qǐyè guǎnlǐ coal enterprise management
【煤气】 méiqì gas; coal gas
【煤气厂】 méiqìchǎng gasworks; gashouse
【煤气灯】 méiqìdēng gas lamp; gas light
【煤气公司查表员】 méiqì gōngsī chábiǎoyuán gasman
【煤气管】 méiqìguǎn gas pipe
【煤气管线】 méiqì guǎnxiàn gas-pipe line
【煤气罐】 méiqìguàn gas tank; gas container
【煤气净化系统】 méiqì jìnghuà xìtǒng gas cleaning system
【煤气热水器】 méiqì rèshuǐqì gas water heater; gasboiler
【煤气灶】 méiqìzào gas range; gas cooker
【煤气中毒】 méiqì zhòngdú carbon monoxide poisoning; gas poisoning
【煤气总管】 méiqì zhǒngguǎn gas main
【煤球】 méiqiú briquet
【煤炭】 méitàn coal
【煤炭工业】 méitàn gōngyè coal industry
【煤田】 méitián coal field
【煤田地质学】 méitián dìzhìxué coal geology
【煤屑】 méixiè nickings; coal dust
【煤烟】 méiyān 1.（烧煤产生的烟）smoke from burning coal 2.（烟灰）soot
【煤烟污染】 méiyān wūrǎn smoke pollution
【煤窑】 méiyáo coal pit
【煤油】 méiyóu kerosene; paraffin
【煤油灯】 méiyóudēng kerosene lamp
【煤油炉】 méiyóulú kerosene stove
【煤渣】 méizhā coal cinder
【煤渣路】 méizhālù cinder road
【煤渣跑道】 méizhā pǎodào cinder track

糜［穈、穈］(méi) broom corn millet
（另见“糜”mí）
【糜子】 méi·zi broom corn millet

每(měi) 1.（各个）every; each; per: ～个人 every one; each one / ～隔一段时间 at set intervals / ～人一架录音机 a recorder for each person / ～周两次 twice a week 以～小时 120 公里的速度行驶 drive at 120 kilometers an hour 2.（反复）every; often: ～逢星期天 on Sundays / ～会必到 be present at every meeting
【每笔交易总价】 měibǐ jiāoyì zǒngjià cost per sale
【每次】 měicì at every turn
【每单位】 měidānwèi per unit
【每当】 měidāng whenever; every time
【每逢佳节倍思亲】 měiféng jiājié bèi sīqīn on festive occasions more than ever we think of our dear ones far away
【每个角落】 měi gè jiǎoluò every nook and cranny
【每况愈下】 měikuàngyùxià go downhill; go from bad to worse; out of the flying-pan into the fire
【每每】 měiměi often: ～推故 often make some excuse / ～如此。It is often like this.
【每日天气图】 měirì tiānqìtú daily weather chart
【每日允许摄入量】 měirì yǔnxǔ shèrùliàng acceptable daily intake
【每时每刻】 měishí-měikè all the time; at all times

美(měi) 1.（美丽）beautiful; pretty: 大自然的～ beauty of nature 2.（好）very satisfactory; good: 味道～ good taste 3.（得意）be pleased with oneself 4.（美洲）America; American (adj.) 5.（美国）the United States of America; American (adj.)
【美不胜收】 měibùshèngshōu The fine things are too many to see.
【美差】 měichāi cushy job
【美称】 měichēng laudatory title; good name
【美德】 měidé virtue; moral excellence: ～无价 virtue is beyond price
【美发】 měifà hairdressing
【美发师】 měifàshī hairdresser
【美发厅】 měifàtīng hair salon; hairdresser's; hairdresser's salon
【美感】 měigǎn aesthetic feeling; sense of beauty
【美工】 měigōng 1.（指工作）art designing 2.（指人）art designer

【美观】 měiguān pleasing to the eye; beautiful to look at: ～大方 beautiful and dignified; elegant and in good taste / ～实用 both artistic and practical

【美国】 Měiguó the United States of America (U.S.A.; U.S.); American (adj.) ‖ 美国人 American

【美国梦】 Měiguómèng American dream

【美国生活方式】 Měiguó shēnghuó fāngshì American way of life

【美国之音】 Měiguózhīyīn Voice of America (VOA)

【美好】 měihǎo fine; happy; glorious: ～的景色 fine view / ～的理想 glorious ideals

【美化】 měihuà beautify; prettify; embellish: ～校园 beautify the campus

【美籍华人】 měijí huárén Chinese-American

【美金】 měijīn U.S. dollar

【美景】 měijǐng beautiful scenery: ～良辰 beautiful scenery and pleasant morning; an enjoyable situation

【美丽】 měilì beautiful: ～的花朵 beautiful flowers

【美满】 měimǎn happy; perfectly satisfactory: ～的家庭 a good and perfect family

【美貌】 měimào 1.(指容貌) beautiful look; good-looking features 2.(指人) beautiful; pretty

【美梦】 měimèng fond dream

【美妙】 měimiào beautiful; splendid; wonderful: ～的歌喉 sweet voice

【美名】 měimíng good name; good reputation: ～胜于财富 a good name is better than riches

【美男子】 měinánzǐ handsome man; very good-looking man

【美女】 měinǚ beauty; beautiful woman; pretty girl

【美其名曰】 měiqímíngyuē call it by the fine-sounding name of

【美人】 měirén beauty; beautiful woman

【美人计】 měirénjì sex-trap; use of a woman to ensnare a man

【美人蕉】 měirénjiāo 〈*Bot.*〉 India canna

【美容】 měiróng 1.(使容貌美丽) improve one's looks 2.(整容) cosmetology

【美容师】 měiróngshī beautician

【美容术】 měiróngshù cosmetology

【美容院】 měiróngyuàn beauty parlor; beauty shop

【美容专家】 měiróng zhuānjiā cosmetologist

【美声】 měishēng 〈*Music*〉 Western style of singing

【美食家】 měishíjiā epicure; gourmet; gourmand

【美食节】 měishíjié food festival

【美式橄榄球】 měishì gǎnlǎnqiú American football

【美式英语】 měishì yīngyǔ American English

【美术】 měishù 1.(造型艺术) the fine arts; art: 舞台～ stage design 2.(绘画) painting

【美术工作者】 měishù gōngzuòzhě art worker; artist

【美术馆】 měishùguǎn art gallery

【美术家】 měishùjiā artist

【美术明信片】 měishù míngxìnpiàn picture postcard

【美术片】 měishùpiàn 〈*Cinematog.*〉 cartoons; puppet films

【美术品】 měishùpǐn artistic products

【美术设计】 měishù shèjì artistic designing

【美术学校】 měishù xuéxiào art school

【美术学院】 měishù xuéyuàn academy of fine arts

【美术展览会】 měishù zhǎnlǎnhuì art exhibition

【美术字】 měishùzì artistic calligraphy; art lettering

【美谈】 měitán a story passed on with approval

【美味】 měiwèi 1.(佳肴) delicious food; delicacy: 品尝应时～ enjoy the delicacies of the season 2.(味美) delicious dainty: ～清香 delicious and fragrant

【美学】 měixué esthetics (AmE.); aesthetics (BrE.); esthetic (adj.)

【美学原理】 měixué yuánlǐ elements of esthetics

【美言】 měiyán put in a good word for sb.

【美意】 měiyì kindness

【美育】 měiyù aesthetic education; art education

【美元】 měiyuán American dollar; U.S. dollar

【美元短缺】 měiyuán duǎnquē dollar gap
【美元区】 měiyuánqū dollar area
【美展】 měizhǎn art exhibition
【美制】 měizhì 1.（美国单位制）American system 2.（美国制造）made in U.S.
【美中不足】 měizhōng-bùzú a fly in the ointment
【美洲】 Měizhōu America; American (adj.): 北～ North American / 南～ South American ‖ 美洲人 American
【美洲豹】 měizhōubào jaguar
【美洲虎】 měizhōuhǔ 即“美洲豹”
【美洲狮】 měizhōushī puma; cougar
【美洲鸵】 měizhōutuó rhea; greater rhea
【美洲野牛】 měizhōu yěniú American bison
【美滋滋】 měizīzī self-satisfied; complacent

镁 (měi)〈*Chem.*〉magnesium（元素符号 Mg）
【镁光】 měiguāng magnesium light
【镁光灯】 měiguāngdēng flash lamp magnesium lamp
【镁合金】 měihéjīn magnesium alloy; Dow metal

妹 (mèi) younger sister; sister
【妹夫】 mèi·fu brother-in-law; younger sister's husband
【妹妹】 mèi·mei sister; younger sister

昧 (mèi) 1.（糊涂）have hazy notions about; be ignorant of 2.（隐藏）hide; conceal: ～着良心 do nothing against one's conscience
【昧心】 mèixīn against one's conscience: 不说～话 never say anything against one's conscience

寐 (mèi) sleep: 夜不能～ unable to fall asleep at night

魅 (mèi) evil spirit; demon
【魅惑】 mèihuò cast a glamor over
【魅力】 mèilì glamor; charm; enchantment; fascination: 领袖人物的超凡～ charisma

媚 (mèi) 1.（取悦于人）fawn on; curry favor with; flatter; toady to: ～上 fawn on superiors 2.（美好）charming; fascinating; enchanting
【媚骨】 mèigǔ obsequiousness
【媚态】 mèitài coquetry; subservience: ～娇容 a seductive appearance and attractive manner
【媚外】 mèiwài fawn on foreign powers: 崇洋～ worship foreign things and fawn on foreign powers

men

闷 (mēn) 1.（气闷）stuffy; stifling; close: 房间里很～。It is stifling in the room. 2.（使不透气）cover closely; cover tightly 3.（不响亮）muffled 4.（呆在家）shut oneself or sb. indoors: ～在家里 confine oneself indoors
（另见“闷”mèn）
【闷气】 mēnqì stuffy; close
【闷热】 mēnrè hot and suffocating; sultry; muggy: ～的天气 sultry weather
【闷声不响】 mēnshēng bùxiǎng remain silent; be dumb

门［門］(mén) 1.（出入口）entrance; door; gate: 单扇～ univalve door / 后～ back door / 拉～ sliding door / 炉～ stove door / 双扇～ bivalve door / 校～ school gate / 旋转～ revolving doors / 正～ front entrance / 关～ close/shut the door / 叫～ call at the door / 进～ get in through the door / 开～ open the door / 敲～ knock at the door; knock on the door / 应～ answer the door 2.（开关）valve; switch: 电～ switch / 气～ air valve / 水～ water valve 3.（门径）way to do sth.; knack 4.（家族）family 5.（派别）sect; school: 佛～子弟 Buddhist follower / 会道～ superstitious sects 6.（类别）field; sphere; branch: ～～精通 be proficient in all subjects / 分～别类 classify according to categories / 一～知识 a field of knowledge / 一～技术 a special kind of skill 7.〈*Biol.*〉phylum
【门巴族】 Ménbāzú Monba（中国少数民族，主要分布在西藏）
【门把手】 ménbǎ·shou 1.（长形的）door handle 2.（球形的）doorknob
【门板】 ménbǎn 1.（木板门）door plank 2.（店门板）shutter
【门掣】 ménchè doorstop; doorstopper

【门齿】 ménchǐ front tooth; incisor

【门当户对】 méndāng hùduì a marriage between the families that are of equal socioeconomic status

【门道】 méndào doorway：我看到他站在～里。I looked up and saw him standing in the doorway.

【门到门】 méndàomén door-to-door

【门第】 méndì family status：书香～ intellectual family / ～相称 families related by marriage equal in social status

【门洞】 méndòng 〈*Archit.*〉 archway

【门房】 ménfáng 1.(看门人的房子) gate house; janitor's room; porter's lodge 2.(看门人) gatekeeper; doorman; janitor; porter

【门缝】 ménfèng a crack between a door and its frame

【门岗】 méngǎng gate sentry

【门钩】 méngōu gate stop

【门户】 ménhù 1.(门) door 2.(必经地) gateway; important passageway 3.(派别) faction; sect：～之见 parochial prejudice; sectarian bias 4.(门第) family status：～相当 be well-matched in family status

【门户开放】 ménhù kāifàng 'Open Door'：～政策 'Open Door' policy

【门环】 ménhuán doorknocker

【门将】 ménjiàng goalkeeper in ballgames

【门警】 ménjǐng police guard at an entrance

【门静脉】 ménjìngmài 〈*Anat.*〉 portal vein

【门径】 ménjìng access; key; way

【门镜】 ménjìng peephole; eyehole; spyhole

【门槛】 ménkǎn threshold

【门可罗雀】 ménkěluóquè where visitors are few and far between

【门口】 ménkǒu entrance; doorway：送到～ show sb. to the door / 不要站在～。Don't stand in the doorway. / 你在～等我好吗? Will you wait at the door?

【门框】 ménkuàng doorframe

【门廊】 ménláng porch; portico

【门类】 ménlèi class; kind; category

【门帘】 ménlián door curtain; portiére

【门脸】 ménliǎn 1.(城门附近的地方) the vicinity of a city gate 2.(商店门面) the facade of a shop; shop front：三间～ a three-bay shop front

【门铃】 ménlíng 1.(铃铛) the doorbell 2.(电铃) buzzer

【门路】 mén·lu 1.(途径) pull; social connections：找～ solicit help from potential backers 2.(诀窍) knack; way; know-how：学到做生意的～ acquire the knack for business; learn the tricks of the trade

【门面】 mén·mian 1.(店面) shop front 2.(外表) appearance; facade：为了装～ for appearance's sake

【门牌】 ménpái house number：她家～是几号? What's the number of her house?

【门票】 ménpiào entrance ticket; admission ticket：不收～ free admission

【门前三包】 ménqián shānbāo system of three responsibilities in front of gate

【门扇】 ménshàn door leaf

【门式起重机】 ménshì qǐzhòngjī portal crane

【门市】 ménshì retail sales

【门市部】 ménshìbù retail department; sales department

【门闩】 ménshuān bolt; bar

【门栓】 ménshuān 同"门闩"

【门锁】 ménsuǒ door lock

【门厅】 méntīng 〈*Archit.*〉 entrance hall; vestibule

【门厅镜】 méntīngjìng hall mirror

【门庭若市】 méntíng-ruòshì a much visited place

【门徒】 méntú disciple; follower; devotee

【门外汉】 ménwàihàn layman; laic

【门卫】 ménwèi guard; entrance guard

【门牙】 ményá front tooth; incisor

【门诊】 ménzhěn outpatient service

【门诊病人】 ménzhěn bìngrén outpatient; clinic patient

【门诊部】 ménzhěnbù clinic; outpatient department

【门诊时间】 ménzhěn shíjiān consulting hours

【门诊所】 ménzhěnsuǒ clinic; ambulatorium

扪 (mén) 〈*written*〉 touch; stroke

【扪心自问】 ménxīn-zìwèn examine one's conscience

钔 (mén) 〈*Chem.*〉 mendelevium (人造元素,符号 Md)

闷 (mèn) 1.(心情不舒畅) bored; depressed; in low spirits 2.(密闭) tightly

closed; sealed
(另见"闷"mēn)

【闷罐车】 mènguànchē 〈*Railway*〉 boxcar; covered goods van

【闷棍】 mèngùn staggering blow

【闷葫芦】 mènhú·lu mystery; puzzle; riddle: 打开～ solve the puzzle

【闷雷】 mènléi **1.**(低沉的雷) dull thunder **2.**(精神打击) unpleasant surprise; shock

【闷闷不乐】 mènmèn-bùlè out of humor; be very much bored; feel depressed

【闷气】 mènqì the sulks: 生～ be in the sulks

【闷子车】 mèn·zichē 〈*Railway*〉 boxcar; covered goods van

焖 (mèn) braise; boil in a covered pot over a slow fire: ～饭 cook rice over a slow fire

【焖牛肉】 mènniúròu braised beef

【焖羊肉】 mènyángròu braised mutton

meng

蒙[**矇**[1,2]] (mēng) **1.**(欺骗) cheat; deceive; hoodwink; swindle: 你～人。You are cheating. **2.**(瞎猜) make a wild guess **3.**(昏迷) unconscious; senseless
(另见"蒙"méng, měng)

【蒙蒙亮】 mēngmēngliàng first glimmer of dawn; daybreak: 天～就出发 leave up at daybreak

【蒙骗】 mēngpiàn deceive; cheat; hoodwink; delude

【蒙头转向】 mēngtóu-zhuànxiàng lose one's bearings; be utterly confused: 使某人～ make sb. utterly confused

虻[**蝱**] (méng) horsefly; gadfly

萌 (méng) **1.**(芽) sprout; shoot forth; bud **2.**(生芽) sprout; germinate; shoot; bud

【萌动】 méngdòng begin or start an action; bud: ～待时 waiting for the budding

【萌发】 méngfā **1.**(发芽) sprout; germinate; shoot; bud: 玫瑰～新枝。The rose sprouted new buds. **2.**(喻事物发生) spring up; come forth

【萌生】 méngshēng produce; conceive

【萌芽】 méngyá **1.**(植物生芽) sprout; germinate; shoot; bud **2.**(新生事物) spring up; rudiment; shoot; germ: ～时期 in embryo; in the rudimentary stage

盟 (méng) **1.**(同盟) alliance: 与…结～ enter into alliance with **2.**(内蒙古自治区的行政区域) meng; league: 呼伦贝尔～ Hunlun Buir Meng **3.**(结拜兄弟) sworn brothers

【盟邦】 méngbāng allied country; ally

【盟国】 méngguó allied country; ally

【盟军】 méngjūn allied forces; allies

【盟誓】 méngshì **1.**(盟约) oath of alliance **2.**(发誓) take an oath; make a pledge

【盟友】 méngyǒu ally

【盟员】 méngyuán a member of an alliance

【盟约】 méngyuē oath of alliance; treaty of alliance

【盟主】 méngzhǔ the leader of an alliance

蒙 (méng) **1.**(遮盖) cover **2.**(受) receive; meet with: ～不白之冤 suffer underdressed injustice **3.**(蒙昧) ignorant; illiterate
(另见"蒙"mēng, měng)

【蒙蔽】 méngbì hoodwink; deceive; hide the truth from; pull the wool over sb's eyes: ～某人 pull wool over sb's eye

【蒙哄】 ménghǒng deceive; hoodwink; swindle; cheat

【蒙混】 ménghùn deceive or mislead people: ～过关 bluff it out

【蒙胧】 ménglóng drowsy; sleepy; half asleep; somnolent: ～睡去 doze off

【蒙昧】 méngmèi **1.**(未开化的) barbaric; uncivilized; uncultured **2.**(无知) ignorant; benighted; unenlightened

【蒙昧时代】 méngmèi shídài age of barbarism

【蒙昧主义】 méngmèi zhǔyì obscurantism

【蒙蒙】 méngméng **1.**(雨点很细小) drizzly; misty: ～小雨 a fine drizzle **2.**(模糊不清) indistinct; no clear

【蒙面盗】 méngmiàndào a masked bandit; a masked burglar

【蒙难】 méngnàn be confronted by danger

【蒙受】 méngshòu suffer; sustain: ～巨大损失 sustain a great loss

【蒙太奇】 méngtàiqí 〈*Cinematog.*〉 montage

【蒙在鼓里】 méngzàigǔlǐ be in the dark

朦(méng)

【朦胧】 ménglóng 1.(月光不明) dim moonlight; hazy moonlight 2.(不清楚) obscure; dim; hazy: ～不清 not bright and not clear

猛(měng) 1.(猛烈) fierce; violent; energetic; vigorous: ～狮 a fierce lion / 价格～跌 a sharp drop in the price / 越干越～ work with ever growing energy 2.(猛然) suddenly; abruptly: ～一拐弯 turn a corner suddenly / ～一刹车 apply the brake suddenly

【猛冲】 měngchōng onrush: 猛打～ go full blast ahead

【猛攻】 měnggōng onslaught; fierce attack

【猛进】 měngjìn advance forward vigorously: 突飞～ advance swiftly and vigorously; make rapid progress

【猛力】 měnglì vigorously; with sudden force: ～冲刺 make a dash with all one's strength

【猛力侧踢】 měnglì cètī 〈*Karate*〉 side thrust kick

【猛烈】 měngliè 1.(力量大) fierce; vigorous; violent: ～的风暴 a violent storm / ～轰炸 heavy bombing 2.(急剧) rapid; sudden; abrupt

【猛犸】 měngmǎ 〈*Palaeont.*〉 mammoth

【猛禽】 měngqín bird of prey

【猛犬】 měngquǎn fierce dogs; vicious dogs

【猛然】 měngrán suddenly; abruptly: ～想起 recall sth. suddenly

【猛士】 měngshì brave warrior

【猛兽】 měngshòu beast of prey

【猛省】 měngxǐng 同"猛醒"

【猛醒】 měngxǐng suddenly wake up

【猛增】 měngzēng increase vigorously

【猛追】 měngzhuī give a hot pursuit

锰(měng) 〈*Chem.*〉 manganese (元素符号 Mn)

【锰钢】 měnggāng manganese steel

【锰结核】 měngjiéhé manganese nodule

【锰矿】 měngkuàng manganese mine

【锰铁】 měngtiě ferromanganese

蒙(měng) Mongolia; Mongolian (另见"蒙"mēng, méng)

【蒙古】 Měnggǔ Mongolia; Mongolian

【蒙古包】 měnggǔbāo yurt; ger

【蒙古高原】 Měnggǔ Gāoyuán Mongolian Plateau

【蒙古人】 Měnggǔrén Mongolian

【蒙古人种】 Měnggǔ rénzhǒng the Mongolian stock

【蒙古语】 Měnggǔyǔ Mongol

【蒙古族】 Měnggǔzú Mongol (中国少数民族,主要分布在内蒙古、辽宁、新疆、黑龙江、吉林、青海、河北、河南等地)

蠓(měng) 〈*Zool.*〉 midge

懵[懞](měng) muddled; ignorant

【懵懂】 měngdǒng muddled; ignorant; muddleheaded: ～无知 ignorant and dull

孟(mèng) 1.(农历每个季的第一月) the first month of a season 2.(兄弟中排行第一者) eldest brother

【孟春】 mèngchūn the first month of spring; the first month of lunar calendar

【孟冬】 mèngdōng the first month of winter; the tenth month of lunar calendar

【孟浪】 mènglàng rash; impetuous; impulsive: ～之谈 a rough and wasteful talk

【孟秋】 mèngqiū the first month of fall; the seventh month of lunar calendar

【孟什维克】 Mèngshíwéikè Menshevik

【孟夏】 mèngxià the first month of summer; the fourth month of lunar calendar

【孟子】 Mèngzǐ Mencius

梦[夢](mèng) dream: 从～中醒来 awake from a dream / 做了一个～ had a dream

【梦话】 mènghuà 1.(睡梦中说的话) words uttered in one's sleep; somniloquy 2.(胡言乱语) daydream; nonsense

【梦幻】 mènghuàn illusion; dream; reverie

【梦见】 mèngjiàn see in a dream; dream about

【梦境】 mèngjìng dreamland; dreamworld; dream

【梦寐】 mèngmèi dream; sleep: ～以求 crave for; try to find even in sleep

【梦乡】 mèngxiāng dreamland

【梦想】 mèngxiǎng 1.(妄想) dream of; vainly hope 2.(渴望) fond dream; earnest wish: 他的～实现了。His dream has come true.

【梦遗】 mèngyí 〈*Med.*〉 nocturnal emission; wet dream

【梦呓】 mèngyì 1.(梦话) somniloquy 2.(胡言乱语) rigmarole

【梦中愿望满足】 mèng zhōng yuànwàng mǎnzú dream wish-fulfillment

mi

咪(mī)

【咪咪】 mīmī 1.(猫叫声) mew; miaow 2.(笑貌) smilingly: 笑～ be all smiles

眯[瞇](mī) 1.(眯着眼) narrow one's eyes 2.(小睡) nap; take a nap: ～一会儿 take a short nap; have forty winks

【眯缝】 mī·feng narrow: ～着眼看 squint at; look with narrowed eyes

弥[彌](mí) 1.(遍; 满) full; overflowing 2.(填满) cover; fill 3.(更加) more

【弥补】 míbǔ make up; remedy; make good: ～差额 make up the difference / ～赤字 make up a deficit / ～过失 smooth over a fault / ～损失 make up for the loss; compensate for the loss

【弥缝】 míféng fill cracks; cover up mistakes: ～差错 patch up mistakes

【弥合】 míhé close; bridge

【弥留】 míliú 〈*written*〉 be dying: ～遗言 words uttered when there is no hope of recovery / ～之际 on one's deathbed

【弥漫】 mímàn fill the air; spread all over the place: ～浊气 a boundless and foul air

【弥撒】 mí·sa 〈*RC Ch.*〉 Mass: 去望～ go to Mass / 为…做～ say Mass for sb.

【弥散】 mísàn scatter

【弥天大谎】 mítiān-dàhuǎng monstrous lie

【弥天大罪】 mítiān-dàzhuì monstrous crime; heinous crime

猕[獼](mí)

【猕猴】 míhóu macaque; rhesus monkey

【猕猴桃】 míhóutáo 〈*Bot.*〉 yangtao; yangtao actinidia; kiwi fruit

迷(mí) 1.(迷失) be confused; be lost: ～了路 lose one's way 2.(入迷) be fascinated by; be crazy about: 看电影入了～ be crazy about movies 3.(爱好者) fan; enthusiast; fiend: 电影～ film fan 4.(使看不清) confuse; perplex; fascinate; enchant: 被音乐～住 be bewitched by music

【迷彩】 mícǎi camouflage; camouflage pattern

【迷彩服】 mícǎifú camouflage suit; camouflage uniform

【迷宫】 mígōng labyrinth; maze

【迷航】 míháng drift off course; lose one's course; get lost

【迷糊】 mí·hu 1.(看不清) misted; blurred; dimmed 2.(神志不清) dazed; confused; muddled

【迷惑】 míhuò puzzle; confuse; perplex; baffle: ～舆论 throw dust in the eyes of the public

【迷离】 mílí blurred; misted: ～恍惚 be in a stupor

【迷恋】 míliàn be infatuated with; madly cling to

【迷路】 mílù 1.(迷失道路) lose one's way; get lost 2.(迷失方向) go astray 3.(内耳) inner ear; labyrinth

【迷漫】 mímàn vague; hazy; indistinct

【迷茫】 mímáng 1.(广阔而看不清) vast and hazy: 远处一片～。It's vast and hazy in the distance. 2.(迷离恍惚) confused; perplexed; dazed: ～的神情 a confused look

【迷梦】 mímèng pipe dream; fond illusion

【迷迷糊糊】 mí·mi-hūhū in a daze, difficult to make out

【迷你】 mínǐ mini

【迷你裙】 mínǐqún miniskirt

【迷人】 mírén charming; fascinating; enchanting; bewitching

【迷失】 míshī lose: ～方向 lose one's bearings

【迷途】 mítú 1.(迷失道路) lose one's way 2.(错误的道路) wrong path: 引入～ lead sb. astray

【迷途羔羊】 mítú gāoyáng astray lamb

【迷途知返】 mítú zhīfǎn recover one's bearings and return to the fold; realize one's errors and mend one's ways

【迷惘】 míwǎng be perplexed; be at a loss

【迷惘的一代】 míwǎng de yīdài lost generation

【迷雾】 míwù 1.(浓厚的雾) dense fog 2.(使人迷失方向的事物) anything that misleads people

【迷信】 míxìn 1.(迷信鬼神) superstition; superstitious belief; blind faith; blind worship: 搞～职业活动 make a living by playing on people's superstitions 2.(盲目崇拜) have blind faith in; make a fetish of: 个人～ cult of the individual; personality cult

谜(mí) 1.(谜语) riddle; conundrum: 猜～ guess a riddle 2.(没弄清的事物) enigma; mystery; puzzle: 不解之～ insoluble mystery; unfathomable enigma / 世界之～ mysteries of the world / 警察发现手枪后，这个～终于解开了。The mystery was solved when the police discovered the pistol.

【谜底】 mídǐ 1.(谜语答案) answer to a riddle 2.(真相) truth

【谜语】 míyǔ riddle; conundrum: 出～ ask a riddle / 猜释～ guess and explain riddles

醚(mí) 〈*Chem*.〉 ether; aether

【醚醇】 míchún 〈*Chem*.〉 ether alcohol

【醚化】 míhuà 〈*Chem*.〉 etherificate; etherification

【醚酯】 mízhǐ 〈*Chem*.〉 ether-ether

糜(mí) 1.(粥) gruel 2.(烂) rotten 3.(浪费) wasteful; extravagant
(另见"糜"méi)

【糜费】 mífèi waste; dissipation: ～精力 dissipate energy

【糜烂】 mílàn 1.(腐化堕落) rotten to the corn; corrupted; profligate; debauched: 生活～ lead a fast life 2.〈*Med*.〉 maceration; erosion

靡(mí) waste: 奢～ wasteful; extravagant
(另见"靡"mǐ)

【靡费】 mífèi waste; spend extravagantly

麋(mí) elk

【麋鹿】 mílù mi-lu; David's deer

米(mǐ) 1.(稻米) rice: ～粒 grain of rice / 精白～ polished rice 2.(去壳的种子) shelled seed; husked seed: 花生～ peanut seed; peanut kernel 3.(长度单位) meter (AmE.); metre (BrE.)

【米饭】 mǐfàn rice

【米粉】 mǐfěn 1.(大米粉) ground rice; rice flour 2.(米粉条) rice-flour noodles

【米价】 mǐjià the price of rice

【米酒】 mǐjiǔ rice wine

【米糠】 mǐkāng rice bran

【米糠油】 mǐkāngyóu rice bran oil

【米色】 mǐsè cream-colored

【米汤】 mǐtāng 1.(煮饭时的汤) water in which rice has been cooked 2.(薄稀饭) thin rice or millet gruel; rice water 3.(甜言蜜语) flattering words

【米制】 mǐzhì the metric system

【米粥】 mǐzhōu congee; rice gruel

脒(mǐ) 〈*Chem*.〉 amidine

靡(mǐ) 1.(顺风倒下) blown away by the wind: 所向披～ sweep all before one; carry all before one 2.(无) no; not
(另见"靡"mí)

【靡丽】 mǐlì extravagant

【靡靡之音】 mǐmǐzhīyīn soft and decadent music

觅[覔](mì) look for; hunt for; seek: ～食 look for food

【觅致人才】 mìzhìréncái on the lookout for proper personnel

泌(mì) secrete

【泌尿科】 mìniàokē 〈*Med*.〉 urological department

【泌尿器官】 mìniào qìguān 〈*Anat*.〉 urinary organs

【泌尿系统】 mìniào xìtǒng 〈*Anat*.〉 urinary system

秘[祕](mì) 1.(秘密的) secret; confidential 2.(保守秘密) keep sth. secret; hold sth. back

【秘方】 mìfāng secret recipe

【秘诀】 mìjué secret (of success): 他成功的～是什么? What is the secret of his success?

【秘密】 mìmì secret; clandestine; confidential: ～结社 form a secret society / 揭开宇宙的～ unravel the secrets of the universe

【秘密警察】 mìmì jǐngchá secret police
【秘密入境】 mìmì rùjìng clandestine immigration
【秘密条约】 mìmì tiáoyuē secret treaty
【秘密投票】 mìmì tóupiào secret ballot; Australian ballot
【秘密外交】 mìmì wàijiāo secret diplomacy
【秘密文件】 mìmì wénjiàn secret papers; confidential document
【秘密消息】 mìmì xiāoxi classified information
【秘史】 mìshǐ secret history; inside story
【秘书】 mìshū secretary; secretarial (adj.): 国务～ secretary of state
【秘书处】 mìshūchù secretariat
【秘书长】 mìshūzhǎng secretary general

密 (mì) 1.(稠密) close; dense; thick: 人口很～ densely populated / 头发很～ thick hair 2.(亲密) intimate; close: 与某人来往很～ be on intimate terms with sb. 3.(精致;细致) fine; meticulous 4.(秘密) secret: ～件 confidential document; classified material / 保～ keep sth. secret
【密闭】 mìbì airtight; hermetic
【密播】 mìbō heavy seeding; dense sowing
【密布】 mìbù densely covered: 战云～ gathering war clouds
【密电】 mìdiàn 1.(密码电报) cipher telegram 2.(秘密电告) secretly telegraph sb.
【密电码】 mìdiànmǎ cipher code
【密度】 mìdù 1.(密的程度) density; thickness: 人口～ population density 2.(物质密度) density: 大气～ atmospheric density / 电流～ current density
【密度计】 mìdùjì densimeter
【密访】 mìfǎng pay a secret visit; make investigation by traveling incognito
【密封】 mìfēng seal up; seal airtight; seal hermetically: ～的罐头 sealed tin
【密封舱】 mìfēngcāng sealed cabin; airtight cabin
【密封垫圈】 mìfēng diànquān sealing washer
【密集】 mìjí concentrated; crowded together
【密集队形】 mìjí duìxíng close formation; tight formation
【密集轰炸】 mìjí hōngzhà mass bombing
【密件】 mìjiàn confidential paper; confidential letter: 亲启～ private and confidential
【密林】 mìlín dense forest
【密令】 mìlìng a secret order
【密码】 mìmǎ cipher; cipher code; secret code
【密码本】 mìmǎběn code book
【密码电报】 mìmǎ diànbào cipher telegram
【密码机】 mìmǎjī cipher machine; cryptograph
【密码锁】 mìmǎsuǒ trick lock
【密码通讯】 mìmǎ tōngxùn communicate with code telegram
【密码箱】 mìmǎxiāng cipher box
【密码信】 mìmǎxìng message in cipher
【密码信息】 mìmǎ xìngxī encrypted message
【密码员】 mìmǎyuán cryptographer
【密密麻麻】 mì·mi-mámá close and numerous; thickly dotted
【密谋】 mìmóu conspire; plot; scheme: ～策划 conspire
【密切】 mìqiè 1.(关系近) close; intimate: ～合作 be hand in glove with / ～相关 go hand in hand with 2.(仔细) carefully; intently; closely: ～注视 pay close attention to
【密如蛛网】 mìrúzhūwǎng as fine as a spider's web
【密使】 mìshǐ secret emissary; secret envoy
【密室】 mìshì a room used for secret purposes
【密谈】 mìtán secret talk; talk behind closed doors
【密探】 mìtàn secret agent; spy
【密纹唱片】 mìwéng chàngpiàn micro-groove record
【密友】 mìyǒu friend; bosom friend
【密约】 mìyuē secret agreement; secret treaty
【密植】 mìzhí 〈*Agric*.〉 close planting: 合理～ rational close planting
【密装】 mìzhuāng closely packed

嘧 (mì)
【嘧啶】 mìdìng 〈*Chem*.〉 pyrimidine

蜜 (mì) 1.(蜂蜜) honey 2.(甜美) honeyed; sweet: 甜如～ honey-sweet; as sweet as honey
【蜜蜂】 mìfēng bee; honeybee
【蜜柑】 mìgān mandarin orange; tangerine

orange
【蜜饯】 mìjiàn 1.（指制作）make candied fruit 2.（指果品）candied fruit; preserved fruit
【蜜橘】 mìjú tangerine
【蜜月】 mìyuè honeymoon: ～旅行 honeymoon trip / 他们在度～。They are on their honeymoon.
【蜜枣】 mìzǎo candied date; jujube
幂［冪］(mì) 1.〈*Math*〉power: 五次～ the fifth power 2.（盖东西的布）cloth cover

mian

眠(mián) 1.（睡眠）sleep 2.（冬眠）dormancy
【眠尔通】 mián'ěrtōng 〈*Pharm.*〉miltown
【眠目静思】 miánmù-jìngsī closing the eyes and meditating
绵［緜］(mián) 1.（丝棉）silk floss 2.（绵延）continuous: ～长 long; lengthy 3.（柔软）soft
【绵薄】 miánbó 〈*politeness*〉window's mite; humble effort: 愿尽～。I'll do what little I can.
【绵绸】 miánchóu fabric made from waste silk
【绵亘】 miángèn stretch in an unbroken chain: ～数千里 stretching for thousands of miles
【绵力】 miánlì 〈*written*〉humble effort: 略尽～。I'll do what little I can.
【绵绵】 miánmián continuous; unbroken: ～不绝 continuing forever
【绵软】 miánruǎn 1.（柔软）soft 2.（身体无力）weak
【绵延】 miányán be continuous; stretch long and unbroken: ～几百公里的林带 forest belt extending a thousand kilometers
【绵羊】 miányáng sheep: 一群～ a flock of sheep ‖ 雄～ ram; 雌～ ewe; 幼～ lamb; ～群 flock; 肉用～ mutton
【绵纸】 miánzhǐ tissue paper
棉(mián) 1.（棉类统称）cotton 长绒～ long staple cotton / 海岛～ sea island cotton / 陆地～ upland cotton / 木～ bombax; common bombax / 爪哇木～ kapok; silk cotton 2.（棉花）cotton: 皮～ ginned cotton / 脱脂～ absorbent cotton / 原～ raw cotton / 籽～ unginned cotton / 纯～衬衣 a shirt made of pure cotton 3.（衬有棉花的）cotton-padded; quilted: ～大衣 cotton-padded overcoat
【棉袄】 mián'ǎo cotton-padded jacket
【棉被】 miánbèi a quilt with cotton wadding
【棉饼】 miánbǐng cottonseed cake
【棉布】 miánbù cotton cloth; cotton: ～衣服 cotton dress
【棉纺】 miánfǎng cotton spinning
【棉纺厂】 miánfǎngchǎng cotton mill
【棉纺织品】 miánfǎngzhīpǐn cotton textiles
【棉花】 mián·hua cotton
【棉花签】 mián·huaqiān (cotton) swab; cotton bud; Q-tip
【棉花胎】 mián·huatāi cotton batting
【棉裤】 miánkù cotton-padded trousers
【棉铃】 miánlíng cotton boil
【棉毛】 miánmáo interlock
【棉毛交织物】 miánmáo jiāozhīwù half-wool
【棉毛裤】 miánmáokù cotton (interlock) trousers
【棉毛衫】 miánmáoshān cotton (interlock) jersey
【棉帽】 miánmào cotton-padded cap
【棉农】 miánnóng cotton grower
【棉签】 miánqiān cotton swab; cotton bud; Q-tip
【棉球】 miánqiū cotton balls; cotton wool
【棉绒】 miánróng cotton velvet
【棉绒布】 miánróngbù 〈*Textiles*〉winsey
【棉纱】 miánshā cotton yarn
【棉纱头】 miánshātóu (cotton) waste
【棉毯】 miántǎn cotton blanket
【棉桃】 miántáo cotton boll
【棉套】 miántào cotton batting
【棉田】 miántián cotton field
【棉线】 miánxiàn cotton thread; cotton
【棉鞋】 miánxié cotton-padded shoes
【棉絮】 miánxù 1.（棉花纤维）cotton fiber 2.（棉胎）cotton batting
【棉衣】 miányī cotton-padded clothes
【棉织厂】 miánzhīchǎng cotton textile mill
【棉织品】 miánzhīpǐn cotton goods; cotton

textiles; cotton fabrics
【棉籽】 miánzǐ cottonseed
【棉籽饼】 miánzǐbǐng cottonseed cake
【棉籽油】 miánzǐyǒu cottonseed oil

免 (miǎn) 1.(去掉) excuse sb. from sth.; exempt; dispense with: ～受攻击 immune against attacks / 互相～办签证 mutual exemption of visas 2.(避免) avoid; avert; escape: ～了一场灾祸 avert an accident / 以～误会 avoid misunderstanding 3.(不可) not allowed; forbidden: 闲人～进。No admittance except on business.

【免不了】 miǎn·buliǎo unavoidable; inevitable
【免除】 miǎnchú 1.(免去) prevent; avoid: ～某人职务 remove sb. from office 2.(免掉) remit; excuse; exempt; relieve: ～罚金 relief against forfeiture / ～劳役 dispensing with service / ～债务 remit a debt
【免得】 miǎn·de so as not to; avoid: ～引起误会 avoid misunderstanding
【免费】 miǎnfèi free of charge; free; gratis
【免费参观】 miǎnfèi cānguān admission free
【免耕农业】 miǎngēng nóngyè till-less agriculture
【免冠】 miǎnguān 1.(脱帽) take one's hat off 2.(不戴帽子) without a hat on; bareheaded
【免检】 miǎnjiǎn exempt from customs examination
【免开尊口】 miǎnkāi-zūnkǒu you had better shut up
【免票】 miǎnpiào 1.(免费的票) free ticket 2.(免费) free of charge
【免试】 miǎnshì be excused from an examination
【免税】 miǎnshuì exempt from taxation; tax-free; duty free
【免税单】 miǎnshuìdān duty free slips
【免税进口】 miǎnshuì jìnkǒu duty free importation
【免税进口货物】 miǎnshuì jìnkǒu huòwù free goods
【免税贸易区】 miǎnshuì màoyìqū tax-free trade zone
【免税入境许可证】 miǎnshuì rùjìng xǔkězhèng permission for duty
【免税商店】 miǎnshuì shāngdiàn duty free shop
【免税商品】 miǎnshuì shāngpǐn free commodities; free goods
【免税执照】 miǎnshuì zhízhào duty free certificate
【免烫】 miǎntàng non-ironing: 快干～ wash and wear
【免刑】 miǎnxíng 〈*Law*〉 exempt from punishment
【免验】 miǎnyàn pass without examination (P.W.E.)
【免验证】 miǎnyànzhèng laissez-passer
【免疫】 miǎnyì 〈*Med.*〉 immunity: 先天～ congenital immunity
【免疫力】 miǎnyìlì 〈*Med.*〉 natural immunity; inquired immunity
【免予处罚】 miǎnyú chǔfá remit; be exempt from punishment
【免予公诉】 miǎnyú gōngsù immunity from prosecution
【免予起诉】 miǎnyú qǐsù exemption from prosecution; immunity from suit
【免职】 miǎnzhí remove sb. from office; relieve sb. of his post
【免罪】 miǎnzuì exempt from punishment

勉 (miǎn) 1.(努力) exert oneself; strive 2.(勉励) encourage; urge; exhort 3.(尽力做) strive to do what is beyond one's power

【勉尽力量】 miǎnjìn lìliàng do one's best
【勉励】 miǎnlì encourage; urge: ～上进 incite one to make progress / ～学生努力学习 encourage the students to study with still greater efforts
【勉强】 miǎnqiǎng 1.(尽力) manage with an effort; do with difficulty 2.(不心甘情愿) with bad grace; reluctantly; grudgingly: 毫不～地同意 agree without reluctance 3.(强迫) force sb. to do sth.: 要是她不答应,不要～她。In case she doesn't agree, don't try to force her to. 4.(牵强) inadequate; unconvincing; farfetched; strained 5.(刚刚够) barely enough: ～糊口 eke out a living / 他～赶上火车。He barely caught the train.
【勉为其难】 miǎnwéiqínán try to do a difficult job as best one can

娩[挽](miǎn) delivery; childbirth

【娩出】 miǎnchū deliver a baby

冕(miǎn) 1.(冠冕) crown 2.〈*Astron.*〉 corona; coronal (adj.)

【冕珥】 miǎn'ěr 〈*Astron.*〉 coronal prominence

湎(miǎn)

【湎于酒色】 miǎnyú jiǔsè indulging in wine and lewdness

缅(miǎn) remote; far back

【缅怀】 miǎnhuái cherish the memory of; recall: ～往事 recall past events

【缅想】 miǎnxiǎng think of (past events); recall: ～前尘 think of the past affairs

腼(miǎn)

【腼腆】 niǎn·tiǎn shy; bashful

面[靣、麪[9,10]、麵[9,10]](miàn) 1.(脸) face: ～有难色 wear an embarrassed look 2.(向着) face 3.(表面) surface; top; face: 地～ the surface of the earth 4.(当面) personally; directly; face to face: ～谈 speak to sb. face to face / ～谢 thank sb. in person 5.(皮; 面) the right side; cover; outside 6.〈*Math.*〉 surface: 球～ curved surface 7.(方面) side; aspect: 右～ right side / 左～ left side 8.(范围) extend; range; scale; scope 9.(面粉) wheat flour; flour 10.(面条) noodles: 一碗～ a bowl of noodles / 中午吃～ have noodles for lunch

【面案】 miàn'àn breadboard

【面板】 miànbǎn 〈*Guitar*〉 sounding board

【面包】 miànbāo bread: 切片～ sliced bread / 法式～(棍子～) French bread / 全麦～ wholewheat bread / 一个～ a loaf of bread / 烤一个～ bake a loaf of bread

【面包车】 miànbāochē minibus; wagon

【面包房】 miànbāofáng bakery

【面包干】 miànbāogān rusk

【面包圈】 miànbāoquān bagel

【面不改色】 miànbùgǎishè not change countenance; remain calm; without turning a hair

【面部】 miànbù the face; facial

【面部表情】 miànbù biǎoqíng facial expression

【面陈】 miànchén report in person; deliver sth. to a superior in person

【面辞】 miàncí go to say good-bye to sb.; take leave of sb.

【面带病容】 miàndài bìngróng one's face shows sickly countenance

【面带愁容】 miàndài chóuróng with a sad air

【面的】 miàndí 〈*Transport*〉 miandi; minicab; minibus taxi

【面对】 miànduì face; confront: ～现实 face the reality / 我们～困难不退缩。We will never flinch from difficulties.

【面对面】 miànduìmiàn facing each other; face to face: ～地坐着 sit face to face; sit vis-a-vis

【面额】 miàn'é 〈*Econ.*〉 denomination: ～为 100 元的人民币 Renminbi in 100-yuan notes

【面访】 miànfǎng interview; a face to face talk

【面粉】 miànfěn flour; wheat flour: 全麦～ wholewheat flour

【面粉厂】 miànfěnchǎng flour mill

【面告】 miàngào tell in person

【面红耳赤】 miànhóng-ěrchì be red in the face; be flushed

【面黄肌瘦】 miànhuáng jīshòu pale and emaciated; lean and haggard

【面积】 miànjī area: 建筑～ built-up area / 居住～ dwelling area; floor space / 大～丰收 bumper harvest over an extensive area

【面颊】 miànjiá cheek

【面交】 miànjiāo hand over in person

【面巾】 miànjīn towel

【面巾纸】 miànjīnzhǐ face tissues

【面筋】 miàn·jin gluten

【面具】 miànjù mask: 戴～ wear a mask

【面孔】 miànkǒng face: 和蔼的～ amiable countenance

【面料】 miànliào surface fabric

【面临】 miànlín be faced with; be confronted with; be up against: ～重重困难 be confronted with numerous difficulties / ～严峻的挑战 be faced with formidable challenges

【面貌】 miànmào 1.(相貌) face; features;

looks：～清秀 have delicate looks 2.（面目）appearance；look；aspect：城市～ the appearance of a city

【面面俱到】 miànmiàn-jùdào attend to each and every aspect of a matter

【面面相觑】 miànmiàn-xiāngqù look at each other in blank dismay；gaze at each other in speechless despair

【面膜】 miànmó face film；facial film

【面目】 miànmù 1.（相貌）face；features；visage：～清秀 have delicate looks / ～狰狞 sinister in appearance 2.（面貌）appearance；look；aspect：显出庐山真～ show one's true colors 3.（面子）self-respect；honor；sense of shame；face

【面目一新】 miànmù-yīxīn take on an entirely new look；present a completely new appearance；assume a new aspect

【面庞】 miànpáng face；contours of the face

【面盆】 miànpén wash basin；hand basin

【面洽】 miànqià face to face talk；consult personally

【面前】 miànqián face of；in front of；before

【面请】 miànqǐng request in person

【面容】 miànròng facial features；face

【面如土色】 miànrútǔsè look ashen；look pale：吓得～ turn pale with fright

【面色】 miànsè 1.（气色）complexion：～黝黑 have a dark complexion 2.（神色）facial expression：～骤变 one's countenance suddenly changed

【面纱】 miànshā 1.（纱巾）veil；a face-veil 2.（掩盖）veil；mask

【面商】 miànshāng discuss with sb. face to face；consult personally

【面生】 miànshēng look unfamiliar；look a stranger

【面食】 miànshí cooked wheaten food

【面世】 miànshì come into being；come out；be published

【面试】 miànshì an oral quiz；an audition

【面授】 miànshòu 1.（当面传授）instruct sb. in person 2.（在课堂讲授）classroom teaching

【面授机宜】 miànshòu jīyí give confidential briefing

【面熟】 miànshú look familiar

【面霜】 miànshuāng face cream

【面谈】 miàntán speak to sb. face to face

【面条】 miàntiáo noodles

【面团】 miàntuán dough

【面向】 miànxiàng 1.（朝着）turn one's face to；turn in the direction of；face：～国旗庄严敬礼 stand facing the national flag and salute solemnly 2.（使适合）be geared to the needs of；cater to：～广大读者 be geared to the needs of reading public

【面谢】 miànxiè thank sb. in person

【面议】 miànyì discuss with sb. face to face

【面有难色】 miànyǒu-nánsè appear to be reluctant；wear an embarrassed look

【面罩】 miànzhào face guard

【面值】 miànzhí 1.（票面价值）par value；face value；nominal value 2.（纸币单位）denomination

【面砖】 miànzhuān 〈*Archit.*〉 face brick

【面子】 miàn·zi 1.（物体表面）outer part；outside；face 2.（体面）reputation；prestige；face：～问题 questions of one's reputation / 不讲～ have no consideration for sb's sensibilities

【面子工程】 miàn·zi gōngchéng face-saving project

miao

喵（miāo） mew；miaow

【喵喵叫】 miāomiāojiào mew；miaow：猫～，要吃饭。The cat was mewing for its supper.

苗（miáo） 1.（幼苗）young plant；seedling：禾～ rice shoots / 间～保～ thin out and protect young plants 2.（初生的动物）the young of some animals：鱼～ fry 3.（疫苗）vaccine：牛痘～（bovine）vaccine 4.（形状像苗的）sth. resembling a young plant：火～儿 flame

【苗床】 miáochuáng seedbed

【苗木】 miáomù 〈*Forestry*〉 nursery stock

【苗圃】 miáopǔ nursery（of young plants）

【苗期】 miáoqī 〈*Agric.*〉 seedling stage

【苗条】 miáo·tiao slender；slim：～身材 slender and graceful in stature

【苗头】 miáo·tou symptom of a trend；suggestion of a new development：露出～ show indications of a new development

【苗子】 miáo·zi 1.（苗）young plant; seedling 2.（指事业继承人）young successor

【苗族】 Miáozú Miao（中国少数民族，主要分布在贵州、云南、湖南、四川、广西、湖北等地）

描（miáo） 1.（照底样画）trace; copy：这画是你自己画的，还是你～的？Did you draw this picture yourself, or did you trace? 2.（重复涂抹）touch up; retouch

【描红】 miáohóng trace out the letters

【描画】 miáohuà draw; paint; depict; describe：～出幸福的未来 picture a happy future

【描绘】 miáohuì depict; describe; portray

【描金】 miáojīn trace a design in gold

【描摹】 miáomó depict; portray; delineate

【描述】 miáoshù describe：文章生动地～了该地区的山色。The article vividly describes the area's mountain scenery.

【描图】 miáotú trace; make a tracing of sth.; tracing (n.)

【描图员】 miáotúyuán tracer

【描图纸】 miáotúzhǐ tracing paper：用～复制一张地图 copy a map using tracing paper

【描写】 miáoxiě describe; depict; portray

瞄（miáo） concentrate one's gaze on; take aim：～得准 take good aim

【瞄准】 miáozhǔn aim; take aim; train on：～黄环 aim at the yellow circle / 他举枪，～，开火，整个是一连贯动作。He raised his gun, took aim and fired, all in one smooth movement.

秒（miǎo） second：他用 4 分 12～跑完全程。He completed the race in 4 minutes 12 seconds.（符号为″）

【秒摆】 miǎobǎi second pendulum

【秒表】 miǎobiǎo stopwatch; chronograph

【秒针】 miǎozhēn second hand (of a clock or watch)

渺（miǎo） 1.（渺茫）vast; distant and indistinct; vague：～无希望 have slim hopes 2.（渺小）tiny; insignificant

【渺茫】 miǎománg 1.（模糊不清）distant and indistinct; vague 2.（难以预期）uncertain：～得很 completely at sea; uncertain

【渺小】 miǎoxiǎo tiny; negligible; insignificant

淼（miǎo） vast

【淼茫】 miǎománg stretch as far as the eye can see

藐（miǎo） 1.（小）small; petty 2.（轻视）slight; despise

【藐视】 miǎoshì despise; look down upon：～法律 defiance of law / ～法庭 contempt of court

【藐小】 miǎoxiǎo tiny; negligible; insignificant; paltry

妙（miào） 1.（美妙）wonderful; excellent; fine：～极了！It is simply wonderful! 2.（巧妙）ingenious; clever; subtle：～语 clever remarks

【妙不可言】 miàobùkěyán too wonderful for words; most intriguing

【妙计】 miàojì excellent plan; brilliant scheme

【妙句】 miàojù a quotable quote

【妙龄】 miàolíng young; youthful

【妙论】 miàolùn extraordinary argument; convincing discourse; sparkling discourse

【妙品】 miàopǐn 1.（高质商品）fine quality goods 2.（精致工艺品）fine work of art

【妙趣横生】 miàoqù-héngshēng full of wit and humor; very witty

【妙手回春】 miàoshǒu-huíchūn effect a miraculous cure and bring the dying back to life

【妙用】 miàoyòng magical effect

【妙语】 miàoyǔ witty remark; witticism：～双关 a clever double-extender

庙［廟］（miào） 1.（庙宇）temple; shrine：龙王～ Temple of the Dragon King / 昭～ the Bright Temple 2.（庙会）temple fair

【庙会】 miàohuì temple fair：赶～ go to the temple fair

【庙宇】 miàoyǔ temple

mie

乜（miē）

【乜斜】 miē·xie 1.（眯着眼斜看）squint 2.（眼睛眯成缝）half-closed：～着的眼睛 half-closed eyes

灭［滅］(miè) 1.（熄灭）go out：灯～了。The light goes out. 2.（使熄灭）extinguish；put out；turn off：～灯 turn off the light 3.（淹没）submerge；drown 4.（消灭）destroy；exterminate；wipe out：～蚊 kill mosquito

【灭草剂】 miècǎojì herbicide

【灭顶之灾】 mièdǐngzhīzāi the woe of falling into river；disaster of being drowned

【灭火】 mièhuǒ 1.（把火弄灭）put out a fire；extinguish a fire 2.（使发动机熄火）cut out an engine

【灭火剂】 mièhuǒjì fire-extinguishing chemical

【灭火器】 mièhuǒqì fire extinguisher

【灭火沙】 mièhuǒshā sand for extinguishing fire

【灭迹】 mièjì destroy the evidence

【灭绝】 mièjué become extinct：～净尽 totally exterminated

【灭绝人性】 mièjué rénxìng inhuman；savage；cannibalistic

【灭绝种族】 mièjué zhǒngzú genocide；genocidal（adj.）：～的杀戮 a genocidal killing

【灭菌】 mièjūn sterilization；disinfection

【灭口】 mièkǒu do away with a witness or accomplice

【灭门之祸】 mièménzhīhuò the calamity of exterminating a family

【灭鼠】 mièshǔ deratization

【灭亡】 mièwáng be destroyed；become extinct；die out：注定要～ be doomed to perish

【灭蚤】 mièzǎo depulization

【灭族】 mièzú extermination of an entire family

蔑［衊³］(miè) 1.（轻视）slight；disdain 2.（无）nothing；none 3.（诽谤）smear

【蔑弃】 mièqì despise and cast away

【蔑视】 mièshì despise；show contempt for；scorn：～世俗 have a contempt for custom

篾(miè) 1.（薄竹片）thin bamboo strip 2.（苇子、高粱的篾）the rind of reed or sorghum

【篾匠】 mièjiàng a craftsman who makes articles from bamboo strips

【篾片】 mièpiàn thin bamboo strip

【篾席】 mièxí a mat made of thin bamboo strips

min

民(mín) 1.（人民）the people：为国为～ for the country and the people 2.（民间的）of the people；folk 3.（非军用的）civilian

【民安国泰】 mín'ān guótài the masses are in peace and the country is prosperous

【民办】 mínbàn run by the local people；collectively owned

【民办教师】 mínbàn jiàoshī teachers of school run by local people

【民办小学】 mínbàn xiǎoxué a primary school run by the local people

【民兵】 mínbīng 1.（指组织）militia；people's militia 2.（指个人）militiaman（m.）；militiawoman（f.）

【民不聊生】 mínbùliáoshēng the people have no way of making a living

【民代国储】 míndàiguóchǔ people store grain instead of the state

【民法】 mínfǎ civil law

【民法通则】 mínfǎ tōngzé general rule of the civil law

【民法学】 mínfǎxué science of civil law ‖ 民法学家 civil jurist；civilian

【民房】 mínfáng a house owned by a citizen

【民愤】 mínfèn the people's wrath；popular indignation

【民风】 mínfēng folkway；folk custom

【民风淳朴】 mínfēng chúnpǔ the people are simple, honest and unspoiled

【民歌】 míngē folk song：唱～ sing a folk song

【民歌手】 míngēshǒu folk-singer

【民工】 míngōng 1.（公益劳动的）a laborer working on a public project 2.（进城打工农民）peasant worker

【民航】 mínháng civil aviation

【民航飞机】 mínháng fēijī civil aircraft；civil airplane

【民间】 mínjiān 1.（人民之间的）among the people；popular；folk 2.（非官方的）non-

governmental; people-to-people
【民间传说】 mínjiān chuánshuō popular legend; folk legend; folklore
【民间故事】 mínjiān gùshì folktale; folk story
【民间纠纷】 mínjiān jiūfēn dispute among the people
【民间文学】 mínjiān wénxué folk literature
【民间舞】 mínjiānwǔ folk dance
【民间协定】 mínjiān xiédìng nongovernmental agreement
【民间艺术】 mínjiān yìshù folk art
【民间音乐】 mínjiān yīnyuè folk music
【民警】 mínjǐng people's police; people's policeman
【民居】 mínjū a house owned by a citizen
【民力】 mínlì financial resources of the people
【民品】 mínpǐn products for civilian use
【民气】 mínqì the people's morale; popular morale
【民情】 mínqíng 1.(指情况) condition of the people 2.(指心情、愿望) feeling of the people; public feeling
【民穷财尽】 mínqióng-cáijìn the means of the people have been used up
【民权】 mínquán civil rights; civil liberties; democratic rights
【民生】 mínshēng the people's livelihood
【民事】 mínshì 〈*Law*〉 relating to civil law; civil
【民事案件】 mínshì ànjiàn civil case
【民事法庭】 mínshì fǎtíng civil court
【民事纠纷】 mínshì jiūfēn civil dispute
【民事立法】 mínshì lìfǎ civil legislation
【民事赔偿】 mínshì péicháng civil compensation
【民事审判庭】 mínshì shěnpàntíng the civil division of a people's court; civil court
【民事诉讼】 mínshì sùsòng civil action
【民事诉讼法】 mínshì sùsòngfǎ civil procedure act
【民事调解】 mínshì tiáojiě civil mediation
【民事责任】 mínshì zérèn civil liability
【民俗】 mínsú folk custom; folkways
【民俗文化村】 mínsú wénhuàcūn local culture village
【民俗学】 mínsúxué folklore
【民心】 mínxīn popular feelings; popular sentiments: 深得～ enjoy popular supports
【民谣】 mínyáo folk rhyme
【民以食为天】 mín yǐ shí wéi tiān hunger breeds discontentment
【民意】 mínyì popular opinion
【民意测验】 mínyì cèyàn public opinion poll; public poll; poll
【民营】 mínyíng privately managed
【民用】 mínyòng for civil use; civil
【民用航空】 mínyòng hángkōng civil aviation
【民用机场】 mínyòng jīchǎng civil airport
【民用建筑】 mínyòng jiànzhù civil architecture
【民乐】 mínyuè (instrumental) folk music
【民宅】 mínzhái private residence
【民政】 mínzhèng civil administration
【民政部】 mínzhèngbù ministry of civil affairs
【民政机关】 mínzhèng jīguān civil administration organ
【民政事务】 mínzhèng shìwù civil affairs
【民脂民膏】 mínzhī-míngāo flesh and blood of the people
【民众】 mínzhòng the masses of the people; the common people
【民主】 mínzhǔ 1.(民主权利) democracy; democratic rights: 社会主义～ socialist democracy 2.(用于民主原则) democratic
【民主党派】 mínzhǔ dǎngpài democratic party
【民主改革】 mínzhǔ gǎigé democratic reform
【民主革命】 mínzhǔ gémìng democratic revolution
【民主共和国】 mínzhǔ gònghéguó democratic republic
【民主管理】 mínzhǔ guǎnlǐ democratic management
【民主国家】 mínzhǔ guójiā democratic state
【民主集中制】 mínzhǔ-jízhōngzhì democratic centralism: ～的原则 principles of democratic centralism
【民主权利】 mínzhǔ quánlì democratic rights
【民主人士】 mínzhǔ rénshì democratic personages
【民主生活】 mínzhǔ shēnghuó democratic life
【民主协商】 mínzhǔ xiéshāng democratic consultation

【民主制度】 mínzhǔ zhìdù democratic system
【民族】 mínzú nation; nationality; national (adj.): 少数～ minority nationality; national minority / 中华～ the Chinese nation
【民族大家庭】 mínzú dàjiātíng the great family of nationalities
【民族独立】 mínzú dúlì national independence
【民族对立】 mínzú duìlì national antagonism
【民族复兴】 mínzú fùxīng revival of nationhood; national rejuvenation
【民族感情】 mínzú gǎnqíng national sentiments
【民族隔阂】 mínzú géhé national estrangement
【民族共同语】 mínzú gòngtóngyǔ common national language
【民族解放运动】 mínzú jiěfàng yùndòng national liberation movement
【民族经济】 mínzú jīngjì the national economy: 发展～ develop the national economy
【民族民主革命】 mínzú mínzhǔ gémìng national-democratic revolution
【民族区域自治】 mínzú qūyù zìzhì regional autonomy of minority nationalities; regional national autonomy
【民族同化】 mínzú tónghuà national assimilation
【民族统一战线】 mínzú tǒngyī zhànxiàn national united front
【民族团结】 mínzú tuánjié national unity
【民族心理学】 mínzú xīnlǐxué folk psychology
【民族虚无主义】 mínzú xūwú zhǔyì national nihilism
【民族学】 mínzúxué ethnology
【民族压迫】 mínzú yāpò national oppression
【民族遗产】 mínzú yíchǎn national heritage
【民族意识】 mínzú yì·shí national consciousness
【民族英雄】 mínzú yīngxióng national hero
【民族运动】 mínzú yùndòng national movement
【民族政策】 mínzú zhèngcè policy towards nationalities
【民族主义】 mínzú zhǔyì nationalism; nationalist (adj.) ‖ 民族主义者 nationalist
【民族资本】 mínzú zīběn national capital
【民族资产阶级】 mínzú zīchǎn jiējí national bourgeoisie
【民族自决】 mínzú zìjué national self-determination
【民族自信心】 mínzú zìxìnxīn national confidence
【民族自尊心】 mínzú zìzhūnxīn national pride; national self-respect

悯 (mǐn) commiserate; pity

【悯恻于怀】 mǐncèyúhuái pity in the heart

抿 (mǐn) 1.(用小刷子抹头) smooth with a wet brush 2.(稍稍合拢) close lightly; furl; tuck: ～翅 furl the wings 3.(稍沾) sip: ～一口威士忌 take a sip of the whisky

【抿子】 mǐn·zi small hairbrush

泯 (mǐn) vanish; die out

【泯灭】 mǐnmiè die out; disappear; vanish
【泯没】 mǐnmò vanish; sink into oblivion; become lost: ～无闻 dead and forgotten

敏 (mǐn) quick; nimble; agile

【敏感】 mǐngǎn sensitive; susceptible: 人们对此很～。People are very sensitive to it.
【敏感地区】 mǐngǎn dìqū sensitive area
【敏感区】 mǐngǎnqū 〈*Physiol*.〉 sensitizing range
【敏感性】 mǐngǎnxìng sensitiveness
【敏感元件】 mǐngǎn yuánjiàn sensor; sensitive unit
【敏感中心】 mǐngǎn zhōngxīn sensitivity center
【敏慧】 mǐnhuì clever; sharp-witted; keen
【敏捷】 mǐnjié quick; nimble; agile: 才思～ quick in thought
【敏锐】 mǐnruì sharp; acute; keen: ～的见解 a sagacious perception

ming

名 (míng) 1.(名字;名称) name; title: 人～ name of a person / 书～ title of a book / 您尊姓大～? May I ask your name? 2.(不带姓的名字) given name 3.(名声) fame; reputation; renown 4.(有名声的) famous; well-known; noted: ～城 well-known city /

～画家 celebrated painter; noted painter / ～医 famous physician

【名不副实】 míngbùfùshí of a short; of shorts; the name falls short of the reality; be sth. more in name than in reality

【名不虚传】 míngbùxūchuán have a well-deserved reputation; true to one's name

【名册】 míngcè register; roll

【名产】 míngchǎn famous product; specialty goods

【名场失意】 míngchǎng-shīyì be disappointed in examination for degrees

【名称】 míngchēng name: 发明～ denomination of invention / 你能叫出花园里所有花草树木的～吗? Can you name all the plants and trees in the garden?

【名垂青史】 míngchuí-qīngshǐ go down in history; be crowned with eternal glory

【名词】 míngcí 1.〈*Gram.*〉 noun; substantive 2.(术语) term; phrase: 科学～ scientific terms

【名次】 míngcì position in a name list; place in a competition

【名存实亡】 míngcún-shíwáng cease to exist except in name; exist in name only

【名单】 míngdān name list: 候选人～ the name list of the candidates

【名额】 míng'é the number of people assigned or allowed; quota of people

【名副其实】 míngfùqíshí the name matches the reality; be sth. in reality as well as in name; be worthy of the name: ～的专家 be an expert worthy of the name

【名贵】 míngguì famous and precious; rare: ～的古玩 rare curious

【名家】 míngjiā 1.(思想流派) the School of Logicians 2.(著名专家) a person of academic or artistic distinction; famous expert; master: ～手笔 the handwritings of celebrities

【名将】 míngjiàng famous general; great soldier

【名利】 mínglì fame and gain; fame and wealth: 不计个人～ not care for personal fame and gain

【名利双收】 mínglì shuāngshōu gain both honor and money; gain both fame and wealth

【名列前茅】 mínglìè-qiánmáo come out in front; be among the best of the successful candidates

【名流】 míngliú distinguished personages; celebrities

【名录】 mínglù name list

【名目】 míngmù names of things; items

【名牌】 míngpái 1.(著名商标) famous brand; top brand: ～进口服装 top brand imported garment 2.(写有人名、厂名的牌子) nameplate; name tag: 你可以根据门上的～找到我的办公室。You will know my office by the nameplate on the door.

【名牌产品】 míngpái chǎnpǐn famous brand product

【名片】 míngpiàn visiting card; business card; calling card: 请,这是我的～。Here, let me give you my business card.

【名气】 míng·qi reputation; fame; name: ～大的人 man of great reputation

【名曲】 míngqǔ a masterpiece in music

【名人】 míngrén famous person; eminent person; celebrity; notable: 历史～ great names in history

【名人访谈】 míngrén fǎngtán talk show

【名人效应】 míngrén xiàoyìng celebrity effect

【名山大川】 míngshān dàchuān famous mountains and great rivers

【名声】 míngshēng reputation; repute; fame; name: ～好 have a good reputation / ～不好 have a bad reputation / 他有诚实的～。He has a name of honesty.

【名胜】 míngshèng famous sites

【名胜古迹】 míngshèng gǔjì places of historic interest and scenic beauty

【名手】 míngshǒu a famous artist, player, etc.: 象棋～ famous chess player

【名数】 míngshù 〈*Math.*〉 concrete number

【名堂】 míng·tang 1.(成就;成果) result; achievement: 他们会搞出～来的。They'll certainly accomplish something. 2.(道理;内容) reason 3.(花样) item; variety: 搞不出～来 accomplish nothing remarkable

【名望】 míngwàng fame and prestige; good reputation; renown: ～颇高 one's reputation is fairly high

【名位】 míngwèi fame and position

【名闻中外】 míngwén zhōngwài well-known both at home and abroad

【名下】 míngxià under sb's name; belonging or related to sb.

【名衔】 míngxián title

【名言】 míngyán well-known saying; celebrated dictum; famous remark

【名扬四海】 míngyángshìhǎi well-known in the world; become famous all over the world; world-renowned

【名义】 míngyì 1.(名称或称号) name: 盗用…的～ usurp the name of ... / 他以他父亲的～赴会。He came to the meeting in the name of his father. 2.(表面上) nominal; titular; in name

【名优】 míngyōu famous-brand and high-quality: ～产品 famous-brand and high-quality goods

【名誉】 míngyù 1.(名声) fame; reputation: ～扫地 be discredited / 破坏某人～ damage sb's reputation 2.(名义上的) honorary: ～顾问 honorary advisor / ～主席 honorary chairman; honorary president

【名誉损害赔偿】 míngyù sǔnhài péicháng indemnity for defamation

【名噪一时】 míngzào-yìshí gain considerable fame among one's contemporaries

【名正言顺】 míngzhèng-yánshùn come within one's jurisdiction; be perfectly justifiable

【名著】 míngzhù famous book; famous work: 英国文学～ masterpieces in English literature

【名字】 míng·zi 1.(人名) name: 那人的～叫什么? What is the name of that man? 2.(事物名称) name; title: 影片的～ title of a film

铭 (míng) 1.(器物上刻的文字) inscription 2.(铭记) engrave

【铭记】 míngjì engrave on one's mind; always remember: ～心头 be engraved on one's mind

【铭刻】 míngkè 1.(刻在器物上的文字) inscription 2.(铭记) engrave on one's mind

【铭牌】 míngpái data plate; nameplate

【铭文】 míngwén inscription; epigraph

【铭谢】 míngxiè show gratefulness

【铭心】 míngxīn imprint on one's mind

明 (míng) 1.(明亮) bright; brilliant; light 2.(明白;清楚) clear; distinct: 说～自己的意思 make one's meaning clear 3.(公开的) open; overt; explicit: ～里暗里支持 give both overt and covert support 4.(眼力好) sharp-eyed; clear-sighted: 眼～心亮 be sharp-eyed and clear-headed 5.(心地光明) aboveboard; honest 6.(视觉) sight 7.(懂得) understand; know: 深～大义 understand perfectly where righteousness lies 8.(次于今年或今天的) immediately following in time: ～晨 tomorrow morning / ～年 next year

【明白】 míng·bai 1.(清楚;明确) clear; obvious; plain 2.(懂得) know; understand: 把真相讲～ explain the actual situation in explicit terms 3.(公开的;不含糊的) frank; unequivocal; explicit 4.(懂道理) sensible; reasonable: 他是一个～人。He is a sensible person.

【明摆着】 míngbǎi·zhe obvious; clear; plain

【明辨是非】 míngbiàn-shìfēi make a clear distinction between right and wrong

【明补】 míngbǔ visible subsidy

【明察秋毫】 míngchá-qiūháo be perceptive of the minutest detail

【明澈】 míngchè bright and limpid; transparent

【明处】 míngchù 1.(明亮的地方) where there is light 2.(公开场合) in the open; in public

【明灯】 míngdēng bright lamp; beacon

【明断】 míngduàn clear and fair judgement

【明矾】 míngfán alum

【明沟】 mínggōu open drain

【明晃晃】 mínghuānghuāng gleaming; shining

【明火执仗】 mínghuǒ-zhízhàng conduct evil activities openly

【明胶】 míngjiāo gelatin

【明净】 míngjìng bright and clean; clear and tranquil

【明镜】 míngjìng bright mirror

【明快】 míngkuài 1.(明白通畅) lucid and lively; sprightly 2.(性格爽朗) straightforward; forthright

【明朗】 mínglǎng 1.(光亮) bright and clear: ～的早晨 a bright morning 2.(明显) clear; obvious: 形势逐渐～了。The situation was becoming clear. 3.(开朗爽快) forthright;

bright and cheerful：色彩～ in bright and gay colors

【明亮】 míngliàng 1.（光线足）light；well-lit；bright：在～的灯光下 under a bright lamp 2.（发亮的）bright；shining 3.（明白）become clear

【明了】 míngliǎo 1.（清楚地懂得）clearly understand；be clear about：～党的政策 understand clearly the Party's policies 2.（清晰）clear；plain：简单～ simple and clear

【明令】 mínglìng explicit order；formal decree：～禁止 prohibited by official order

【明码】 míngmǎ 1.（通用电码）plain code：～电报 plain code telegram 2.（标明售价）with prices marked；with prices indicated

【明媚】 míngmèi bright and beautiful；radiant and enchanting

【明明】 míngmíng 〈*adv*.〉obviously；plainly

【明目张胆】 míngmù-zhāngdǎn brazenly；flagrantly

【明渠】 míngqú open canal；open trench

【明确】 míngquè 1.（明白确定）clear and definite；explicit；clear-cut；unequivocal：～的承诺 definite undertaking / ～的分工 clear division of work / 有～的目的 with a definite purpose 2.（使明白确定）make clear and definite：～讨论的目的 make clear the purpose of the discussion

【明日】 míngrì 1.（明天）tomorrow 2.（不久的将来）the near future

【明三联式浴缸水嘴】 míngsānliánshì yùgāng shuǐzuǐ faucet；mixer tap

【明十三陵】 Míng Shísānlíng Ming Tombs

【明示】 míngshì express：～保释 express bailment / ～承认 express recognition / ～担保 express guaranteeship / ～放弃 express waiver / ～和解 express arrangement / ～合同 express contract / ～交付 express delivery / ～拒绝履行 express renunciation / ～诺言 express promise / ～条件 express condition / ～条款 express terms / ～同意 express consent / ～信托 express trust / ～引渡 express extradition

【明天】 míngtiān 1.（明日）tomorrow 2.（不久将来）the near future

【明铁盖】 Míngtiěgài 〈place〉Mingteke

【明铁盖达坂】 Míngtiěgài Dábǎn 〈plane〉Mingteke Daban

【明文】 míngwén proclaimed in writing

【明晰】 míngxī distinct；clear

【明细】 míngxì clear and detailed

【明细表】 míngxìbiǎo bill；list；schedule：货物受损～ inspection record

【明显】 míngxiǎn clear；obvious；evident；distinct：～的成效 tangible result

【明线】 míngxiàn 〈*Electr*.〉open-wire line；open wire

【明信片】 míngxìnpiàn postcard：他从巴黎给我寄了张～。He sent me a postcard from Paris.

【明星】 míngxīng star：电影～ film star；movie star / 足球～球员 football star；star players of a soccer team

【明星制】 míngxīngzhì star system

【明哲保身】 míngzhé-bǎoshēn be worldly wise and play safe

【明争暗斗】 míngzhēng-àndòu both open strife and veiled struggle

【明证】 míngzhèng clear proof

【明知】 míngzhī know perfectly well；be fully aware

【明知故犯】 míngzhī-gùfàn break knowingly；violate deliberately

【明知故问】 míngzhī-gùwèn ask while knowing the answer

【明智】 míngzhì sensible；sagacious；wise

【明珠】 míngzhū bright pearl；jewel

鸣（míng） 1.（鸣叫）the cry of birds，animals or insects：鸟～ chirping of birds / 蛙～ croaking of a frog 2.（发声）ring；sound：雷～ pealing of the thunder 3.（表达）express；voice；air

【鸣笛】 míngdí whistle：旧式蒸汽火车～。The old-fashioned steam train whistled.

【鸣笛水壶】 míngdí shuǐhú whistling kettle

【鸣礼炮】 mínglǐpào fire a salute：～21响 fire a salute of 21 guns

【鸣枪】 míngqiāng fire rifles into the air；fire a shot：～示警 fire a warning shot

【鸣禽】 míngqín singing bird；songbird

【鸣谢】 míngxiè express one's thanks formally；express gratitude

【鸣冤叫屈】 míngyuān-jiàoqū complain and call for redress

冥 (míng) 1.(昏暗) dark; obscure 2.(深沉) deep; profound: ～想 be deep in thought 3.(阴间) underworld; the nether world 4.(糊涂) dull; stupid

【冥府】 míngfǔ Hades; the nether world; underworld

【冥思苦想】 míngsī-kǔxiǎng think long and hard; cudgel one's brains

【冥顽】 míngwán 〈*written*〉 thickheaded; stupid

【冥王星】 Míngwángxīng 〈*Astron.*〉 Pluto

【冥想】 míngxiǎng deep meditation: 苦思～ think long and hard; cudgel one's brains

瞑 (míng)

【瞑目】 míngmù close one's eyes in death; die content: 死不～ die with one's wishes not fulfilled

螟 (míng) snout moth's larva

【螟虫】 míngchóng snout moth's larva

【螟蛾】 míng'é snout moth

【螟蛉】 mínglíng 1.(小虫) corn earworm 2.(比喻义子) adopted son

酩 (mǐng)

【酩酊】 mǐngdǐng get drunk

【酩酊大醉】 mǐngdǐng dàzuì be dead drunk

命 (mìng) 1.(生命) life: 救～ save sb's life / 丧～ lose one's life 2.(命运) lot; fate; destiny: 苦～ hard lot / 听天由～ resign to fate; submit oneself to fate 3.(命令) order; command: 不肯听～于人 refuse to take orders from anybody 4.(给与) assign

【命案】 mìng'àn homicide case

【命根子】 mìnggēn·zi one's very life; lifeblood: 这女孩子是她母亲的～。The girl is the lifeblood of her mother.

【命令】 mìnglìng 1.(下命令) order; command; give an order: 上尉～他的人开火。The captain commanded his men to shoot. / 他～他们停下。He ordered them to stop. 2.(下的命令) order; command: 服从～ obey command / 下～ give a command; issue an order

【命脉】 mìngmài lifeblood; lifeline: 经济～ economic lifelines

【命名】 mìngmíng name: 这个海峡是以它的发现者～的。The strait was named after its discoverer.

【命题】 mìngtí 1.(提出题目) assign a topic; set a question 2.〈*Logic & Math.*〉 proposition

【命运】 mìngyùn 1.(指生死、贫富等) destiny; fate; lot: 受～的摆布 be controlled by one's fate 2.(指前途) future; destiny; fate: 关心公司的～ be concerned about the future of the company / 决定自己的～ determine one's own destiny; decide one's own fate

【命在旦夕】 mìngzàidànxī death may come any minute; be dying

【命中】 mìngzhòng hit the target; score a hit: ～目标 hit the mark

【命中率】 mìngzhònglǜ percentage of hits

miu

谬 (miù) wrong; false; erroneous; mistaken

【谬传】 miùchuán a false report

【谬错】 miùcuò error; mistake

【谬论】 miùlùn fallacy; false theory; falsehood

【谬说】 miùshuō false theory; falsehood

【谬误】 miùwù falsehood; error; mistake

【谬种】 miùzhǒng error; fallacy: ～流传 the dissemination of error

mo

摸 (mō) 1.(触摩) touch; feel; stroke: ～起来很平滑 smooth to the touch 2.(摸索) feel for; grope for; fumble: 在口袋里～钥匙 fumble in one's pocket for the key 3.(试着了解) get to know; find out; sound out: ～一下他对这个问题的意见 sound her out about this matter

【摸不透】 mō·butòu wonder; be puzzled

【摸彩】 mōcǎi draw lot; cast lot

【摸底】 mōdǐ 1.(了解底细) know the real situation 2.(打听底细) try to find out the real intention or situation; sound sb. out

【摸底测验】 mōdǐ cèyàn assessment test

【摸高】 mōgāo 〈*Sports*〉 sargent jump

【摸黑儿】 mōhēir in the dark: ～走路 grope

one's way in the dark

【摸清底细】 mōqīng-dǐxì get to the bottom of the story; ascertain the actual situation

【摸索】 mōsuǒ 1.(试探着) grope; feel about; fumble: ～而行 feel one's way; grope one's way 2.(寻找) try to find out: 不断～,掌握技能 learn technical skills through trial and error

模(mó) 1.(规范) pattern; standard 2.(仿效) imitate 3.(模范) model: 劳～ model worker 4.(模特儿) model: 超级名～ supermodel

(另见"模"mú)

【模范】 mófàn exemplary; model; fine example: 劳动～ model worker

【模仿】 mófǎng imitate; copy; model oneself on

【模糊】 mó·hu 1.(不清楚) dim; vague; indistinct; obscure: ～的景象 obscure view 2.(混淆) blur; obscure; confuse; mix up: ～二者的界限 confuse the distinction between the two 3.〈*Computer*〉 fuzzy

【模糊逻辑控制】 mó·hu luójì kòngzhì fuzzy logic control

【模糊数学】 mó·hu shùxué fuzzy mathematics

【模糊信息】 mó·hu xìnxī fuzzy message

【模糊语言】 mó·hu yǔyán fuzzy language

【模棱两可】 móléng-liǎngkě equivocal; ambiguous: ～的话 equivocality; hedge

【模模糊糊】 mómó-hūhū unintelligible

【模拟】 mónǐ imitate; simulate

【模拟飞行】 mónǐ fēixíng simulated flight

【模拟计算机】 mónǐ jìsuànjī analogue computer

【模拟考试】 mónǐ kǎoshì practice test

【模拟器】 mónǐqì emulator; imitator; simulator

【模拟设计】 mónǐ shèjì board design

【模拟试验】 mónǐ shìyàn simulated test

【模拟战】 mónǐzhàn mock battle; mimic warfare

【模式】 móshì model; pattern; type; schema: 工作～ working model

【模式化】 móshìhuà standardize; standardization (n.)

【模式学派】 móshì xuépài model school

【模式语法】 móshì yǔfǎ pattern grammar

【模特儿】 mótèr model: 裸体～ nude model / 时装～ fashion model / 男～ male model / 为画家当～ model for an artist / 她在一家商厦当时装～。She models dresses for a plaza.

【模特衣架】 mótè yījià dummy

【模效】 móxiào imitate; copy; model oneself on

【模型】 móxíng 1.(仿制实物) model; pattern: 飞机～ a model aircraft 2.(制砂型的工具) mold; pattern

摹(mó) copy; trace

【摹本】 móběn facsimile; copy

【摹拟】 mónǐ mimic; imitate: ～某人声音、姿势和举止 imitate sb's voice, gestures and manners

【摹效】 móxiào imitate; copy; model oneself on

【摹写】 móxiě 1.(照样子写) copy; imitate the calligraphy of 2.(描写) describe; depict

膜(mó) 1.(皮组织) membrane: 粘～ mucous membrane 2.(薄皮儿) film: 塑料薄～ plastic film / 水面上的一层油～ a film of oil on water

【膜拜】 móbài prostrate oneself worship: 顶礼～ prostrate oneself in worship

【膜片】 mópiàn diaphragm

摩(mó) 1.(摩擦) rub; scrape; touch 2.(研究,切磋) mull over; study

【摩擦】 mócā 1.(摩动) rub; scrape 2.〈*Physics*〉 friction; frictional (adj.) 3.(冲突) friction; conflict; clash: 内部～ internal friction

【摩擦力】 mócālì frictional force; friction

【摩登】 módēng modern; fashionable: ～式样 modern fashion

【摩肩接踵】 mójiān-jiēzhǒng jostle each other in a crowd

【摩羯宫】 Mójiégōng 〈*Astron.*〉 Capricorn (12月23日至1月20日): 生于～ be born under Capricorn

【摩羯座】 Mójiézuò 〈*Astron.*〉 Capricorn

【摩氏硬度表】 Móshì yìngdùbiǎo 〈*Mineral.*〉 Mohs scale; Mohs' scale ‖ 1.滑石 talk; 2.石膏 gypsum; 3.方解石 calcite; 4.莹石 fluorite; 5. 磷灰石 apatite; 6.长石 orthoclase;

7.石英 quartz; 8.黄玉 topaz; 8.刚石 corundum; 10.金刚石 diamond

【摩丝】 mósī mousse: 定型～ styling mousse

【摩天】 mótiān skyscraping

【摩天楼】 mótiānlóu skyscraper

【摩托】 mótuō **1.**(发动机) motor **2.**(摩托车) motor cycle

【摩托车】 mótuōchē motorcycle; motor bicycle; motor-bike: 单人～ solo; solomachine / 低座～ scooter; motor scooter / 三轮～ motor tricycle; motor tri-wheeler

【摩托化】 mótuōhuà motorized; motorised: ～步兵 motorized infantry / ～部队 motorized troops / ～团 a motorized regiment

【摩托艇】 mótuōtǐng motorboat; motor launch: ～运动 motorboating; powerboating

【摩托巡逻队】 mótuō xúnluóduì motor patrol

【摩托越野赛】 mótuō yuèyěsài motocross

【摩托运动】 mótuō yùndòng motorcycling

【摩托运动员】 mótuō yùndòngyuán motorcyclist

磨(mó) **1.**(摩擦) rub; wear: 裤子上～出一个洞 wear a hole in one's trousers **2.**(磨东西) grind; polish sharpen: ～刀 whet a knife / ～墨 rub an ink stick **3.**(折磨) wear down; wear out: 她给病～垮了。She was totally worn down by the disease. **4.**(纠缠) trouble; pester; worry: ～着某人要某物 worry sb. for sth. **5.**(拖延;耗时间) dawdle; waste time: ～时间 dawdle away one's time **6.**(消灭;磨灭) obliterate; die out (另见"磨"mò)

【磨蹭】 mó·ceng **1.**(轻微摩擦) lightly rub **2.**(行动缓慢) dawdle; move slowly

【磨床】 móchuáng 〈*Mech.*〉 grinding machine; grinder

【磨刀石】 módāoshí whetstone; grindstone

【磨光】 móguāng polish

【磨耗】 móhào wear and tear

【磨合】 móhé break in; run in: 我还在～这车,所以不能开快。I'm still breaking the car in, so I won't drive fast.

【磨练】 móliàn put oneself through the mill; temper oneself; steel oneself: 在实际工作中～自己 steel oneself in practical work

【磨轮】 mólún emery wheel; grinding wheel; abrasive wheel

【磨面革】 mómiàngé buff; buff leather

【磨灭】 mómiè wear away; efface; obliterate: 留下不可～的印象 leave an indelible impression

【磨难】 mónàn tribulation; hardship; suffering

【磨漆画】 móqīhuà polish lacquer paintings

【磨拳擦掌】 móquán-cāzhǎng ready for fight

【磨砂玻璃】 móshā bō·li frosted glass

【磨砂灯泡】 móshā dēngpào frosted bulb

【磨石】 móshí burr; burrstone; rub stone

【磨蚀】 móshí abrasion

【磨碎】 mósuì ground

【磨碎机】 mósuìjī grinding drum

【磨损】 mósǔn wear and tear

【磨牙】 móyá **1.**(睡觉时咬牙) grind one's teeth in sleep **2.**(多费口舌) indulge in idle talk; argue pointlessly **3.** 〈*Anat.*〉 molar (teeth)

【磨洋工】 móyánggōng loaf on the job; dawdle along

蘑(mó) mushroom: 干～ dried mushroom

【蘑菇】 mó·gu **1.**(食用蕈类) mushroom: 野生～ wild mushroom / 种植～ cultivated mushroom / 食用～ edible mushroom / 有毒～ poisonous mushroom / 采～ go to gather mushrooms; go to mushroom **2.**(故意纠缠) worry; pester; keep on at **3.**(拖延时间) dawdle; dillydally

【蘑菇云】 mó·guyún mushroom cloud

魔(mó) **1.**(魔鬼) devil; demon; evil spirit **2.**(神奇) magic; mystic

【魔法】 mófǎ magic; wizardry; witchcraft

【魔法师】 mófǎshī magician; conjurer; conjuror

【魔方】 mófāng Rubik's cube

【魔鬼】 móguǐ devil; demon; monster

【魔力】 mólì magic power; magic; charm

【魔术】 móshù magic; conjuring; sleight of hand

【魔术师】 móshùshī magician; conjurer

【魔术演员】 móshù yǎnyuán magician; conjurer

【魔王】 mówáng **1.**(恶鬼) Prince of the Devils **2.**(凶暴的人) tyrant; despot; fiend

【魔掌】 mózhǎng devil's clutches; evil

hands：落入～ fall into the devil's clutches

【魔爪】 mózhǎo devil's talons；claws；tentacles

抹（mǒ） 1.（涂抹）put on；apply；smear；plaster：～粉 put on powder 2.（擦去）wipe off：～去额头的汗水 wipe the sweat off one's forehead 3.（去掉）erase；strike out；delete；blot out；cross out：～掉磁盘上的文件 erase the file from a disc

（另见"抹"mā，mò）

【抹掉】 mǒdiào erase；wipe away：～一行 erase a line

【抹黑】 mǒhēi blacken sb's name；bring shame on

【抹杀】 mǒshā blot out；obliterate；write off：～是非界线 blur out distinctions between right and wrong

【抹煞】 mǒshā 同"抹杀"

【抹稀泥】 mǒxīní mediate between two parties to smooth things over

末（mò） 1.（东西的梢）tip；end 2.（不是根本的）nonessentials；minor details 3.（最后）end；last stage：月～ at the end of the month 4.（粉末）powder；dust：研成～ grind to powder；pulverize

【末班车】 mòbānchē 1.（最后一班车）last bus 2.（最后机会）last time；last chance

【末代】 mòdài the last reign of a dynasty：～皇帝 the last emperor of a dynasty

【末读数】 mòdúshù final reading

【末端】 mòduān end；terminal

【末节】 mòjié minor details；nonessentials

【末了】 mòliǎo finally；at last；in the end

【末路】 mòlù dead end；impasse

【末期】 mòqī last phase；final phase；last stage：60 年代～ in the last sixties / 20 世纪～ towards the end of the twentieth century

【末日】 mòrì 1.（基督教指世界末日）Day of Judgment；Judgment Day；doomsday：～审判 Last Judgment 2.（死亡或灭亡的日子）end；doom：～可数 one's days are numbered

【末梢】 mòshāo tip；end：神经～ nerve endings

【末梢神经】 mòshāo shénjīng nerve endings

【末世】 mòshì last phase (of an age)

【末尾】 mòwěi 1.（最后部分）end：在信的～ at the end of the letter / 站在～ stand at the end of a line 2.〈*Music*〉fine；end

【末叶】 mòyè last years：20 世纪～ the end of the 20th century

【末子】 mò·zi powder；dust：煤～ coal powder

茉（mò）

【茉莉】 mò·lì 〈*Bot.*〉jasmine

【茉莉花茶】 mò·lì huāchá jasmine tea

抹（mò） 1.（涂上灰泥再抹平）daub；plaster：～墙 plaster a wall 2.（紧挨着绕过）skirt；bypass

（另见"抹"mā，mǒ）

【抹不开】 mò·bu kāi 1.（脸上下不来）feel embarrassed 2.（不好意思）for fear of hurting sb's feelings

【抹灰】 bòhuī 〈Archit.〉plaster；plastering (n.)

【抹灰工】 mòhuīgōng plasterer

沫（mò） foam；froth：啤酒～ beer froths

【沫子】 mò·zi foam；froth

秣（mò） 1.（牲口的饲料）fodder 2.（喂牲口）feed animals

【秣马厉兵】 mòmǎ-lìbīng feed the horses and drill the soldiers

没（mò） 1.（沉下，沉没）sink；submerge：船沉～了。The ship sank. 2.（漫过，高过）overflow；rise beyond：水深～膝。The water is knee-deep. 3.（隐没）disappear；hide 4.（没收）confiscate；take possession of 5.（尽；终）till the end

（另见"没"méi）

【没顶】 mòdǐng be drowned：水深～。The water goes above a man's head.

【没落】 mòluò decline；wane：～贵族 declining aristocrat

【没奈何】 mònàihé be utterly helpless；have no way out

【没世】 mòshì through one's life-time；till the end of one's life：～不忘 I shall not forget it in my life

【没收】 mòshōu confiscate；expropriate

陌（mò） 1.（田间小路）a path between fields 2.（泛指道路）road

【陌路】 mòlù stranger：视同～ regard as a stranger

【陌生】 mòshēng strange; unfamiliar

【陌生人】 mòshēngrén stranger

脉[脈] (mò) (另见"脉"mài)

【脉脉】 mòmò affectionately; lovingly; amorously: ～含情 quietly sending the message of love

莫 (mò) **1.**(不) no; not **2.**(不要) don't: ～管闲事。Don't poke your nose into other's business.

【莫不】 mòbù there's no one who doesn't or isn't: ～发指。There were none who were not angry with him.

【莫测高深】 mòcè-gāoshēn unfathomable; enigmatic

【莫大】 mòdà greatest; utmost

【莫尔斯电码】 Mò'ěrsī diànmǎ Morse code: 用～发出电报 tap out a message in Morse code

【莫非】 mòfēi 〈*adv*.〉 can it be that; is it possible that: ～写错了? Could it be that it was written wrongly?

【莫怪】 mòguài no wonder that ...

【莫过于】 mòguòyú nothing is more ... than; nothing is better than

【莫名其妙】 mòmíng-qímiào **1.**(没人能说明其奥妙) be unable to make head or tail of sth.; be baffled **2.**(奇怪的事) without rhyme or reason; inexplicable; odd: 她～地生起气来。She got angry without rhyme or reason.

【莫逆】 mònì very friendly; intimate

【莫逆之交】 mònìzhījiāo intimate friends

【莫惹是非】 mò rě shìfēi Let sleeping dogs lie.

【莫须有】 mòxūyǒu unwarranted; groundless; fabricated: ～的罪名 an unwarranted charge

【莫衷一是】 mòzhōngyīshì unable to agree or decide which is right

漠 (mò) **1.**(沙漠) desert **2.**(冷淡地) indifferent; unconcerned

【漠不关心】 mòbùguānxīn indifferent; unconcerned

【漠然】 mòrán indifferently; apathetically; with unconcern: ～不动 completely indifferent

【漠然处之】 mòránchùzhī adopt an indifferent attitude towards

【漠视】 mòshì ignore; overlook; treat with indifference; pay no attention to

蓦 (mò) suddenly

【蓦地】 mòdì suddenly; unexpectedly; all of a sudden: ～惊叫 give a sudden scream

【蓦然】 mòrán suddenly

貘[貊] (mò) 〈*Zool*.〉 tapir

墨 (mò) **1.**(写字、绘画用的墨) China ink; ink stick: 一块～ an ink stick **2.**(字画) handwriting or painting **3.**(学识) learning **4.**(黑) black; dark

【墨宝】 mòbǎo **1.**(贵重字画) treasured scrolls of calligraphy or painting; valued pieces of calligraphy or painting **2.**(尊称) your beautiful handwriting or painting

【墨斗鱼】 mòdǒuyú (乌贼) cuttlefish

【墨黑】 mòhēi pitch-dark

【墨迹】 mòjì **1.**(墨的痕迹) ink mark: ～犹新 the trace of ink is still fresh **2.**(亲笔字画) sb's writing or painting

【墨镜】 mòjìng sunglasses

【墨绿】 mòlǜ blackish green

【墨守成规】 mòshǒu-chéngguī stick to established practice; get into a rut

【墨水】 mòshuǐ **1.**(墨汁) prepared Chinese ink **2.**(钢笔用的水) ink: 红～ red ink / 蓝～ blue ink **3.**(学问) book learning

【墨水瓶】 mòshuǐpíng ink bottle

【墨汁】 mòzhī prepared Chinese ink

默 (mò) **1.**(不说话) silent; tacit: ～坐 sit in silence **2.**(默写) write from memory: ～英语单词 write the English words from memory

【默哀】 mò'āi stand in silent tribute

【默读】 mòdú read silently

【默剧】 mòjù pantomime

【默默】 mòmò quietly; silently: ～无言 without saying a word

【默默无闻】 mòmò-wúwén unknown to the public; without attracting public attention

【默念】 mòniàn read silently

【默片】 mòpiàn 〈*Cinematog*.〉 silent film

【默契】 mòqì **1.**(心照不宣) tacit agreement;

tacit understanding：配合～ good team work 2.（秘密协定）secret agreement：双方早有～。The two parties reached a secret agreement long ago.
【默然】 mòrán silent；speechless
【默认】 mòrèn give tacit consent to；tacitly approve；acquiesce in：～既成事实 acquiesce in the fait accompli
【默示】 mòshì imply
【默诵】 mòsòng read silently
【默算】 mòsuàn 1.（心中盘算）calculate；figure 2.（心算）calculate mentally
【默写】 mòxiě write from memory
【默许】 mòxǔ tacitly consent to；acquiesce in：～所求 tacit permission of a request

磨（mò） 1.（磨子）mill；millstones：咖啡～ coffee mill / 胡椒～ pepper mill / 推～ turn a millstone 2.（磨碎）mill；grind 3.（磨成小块）grate：～干酪 grate the cheese 4.（掉转）turn about：把汽车～过来 turn about the car
（另见"磨"mó）
【磨不开】 mò·bu kāi 1.（脸上下不来）feel embarrassed 2.（不好意思）for fear of hurting sb's feelings
【磨坊】 mòfáng mill：风～ windmill / 水～ watermill
【磨面机】 mòmiànjī flour-milling machine
【磨盘】 mòpán 1.（底盘）nether millstone 2.（磨）mill；millstone
【磨扇】 mòshàn millstone
【磨碎】 mòsuì grate

mou

哞（móu） moo：牛～～叫。The cow mooed.

牟（móu） try to gain；seek；obtain
【牟利】 mōulì seek profit
【牟取】 mōuqǔ try to gain；seek；obtain：～暴利 seek exorbitant profits

眸（móu） pupil；eye：回～ glance back
【眸子】 móuzǐ pupil；eye

谋（móu） 1.（主意）stratagem；plan；scheme 2.（谋求）work for；seek；plot：～私利 pursue private ends 3.（商议）consult
【谋财害命】 móucái-hàimìng murder sb. for his money
【谋刺】 móucì plot to assassinate；make an attempt on sb's life
【谋反】 móufǎn conspire against the state；plot a rebellion：～叛逆 plot and rebel
【谋害】 móuhài 1.（阴谋杀害）plot to murder 2.（阴谋陷害）plot a frame-up against
【谋划】 móuhuà plan；scheme；try to find a solution
【谋利】 móulì profit；turn something to profit
【谋略】 móulüè astuteness and resourcefulness；strategy
【谋求】 móuqiú seek；strive for；be in quest-tion of：～霸权 seek hegemony
【谋取】 móuqǔ try to gain；seek；obtain：～私利 play one's own game；trying to abstain profit for oneself
【谋杀】 móushā murder
【谋杀案】 móushā'àn case of murder
【谋杀罪】 móushāzuì offense of murder
【谋生】 móushēng seek a livelihood；make a living：～乏术 having no means of getting a livelihood
【谋事】 móushì 1.（计划事情）plan matters 2.（找职业）look for a job
【谋私】 móusī pursue private ends
【谋职】 móuzhí look for a job

某（mǒu） 1.（指一定的人或事）certain：～些产品 certain products 2.（指不定的人或事）some：～地 some place / ～人 somebody
【某部】 mǒubù a certain unit：解放军～ a certain unit of the P.L.A.
【某某】 mǒumǒu so-and-so：～先生 Mr. so-and-so
【某些】 mǒuxiē certain；a few

mu

模（mú） mold（AmE.）；mould（BrE.）；pattern；matrix
（另见"模"mó）
【模板】 múbǎn 〈*Archit.*〉 formwork；shuttering

【模具】 mújù mold (AmE.); mould (BrE.); matrix; pattern
【模块】 múkuài mold block; module
【模样】 múyàng 1.(长相) appearance; look: 这女孩子的～很讨人喜欢。The girl has a pleasing appearance. 2.(约略) approximately; about; around: 这女孩有十岁～。The girl is around ten.
【模子】 mú · zi mold (AmE.); mould (BrE.); matrix; pattern

母 (mǔ) 1.(母亲) mother: ～女俩 the mother and the daughter 2.(长辈女性) one's female elders: 姨～ aunt / 祖～ grandmother 3.(雌性的) female 4.(指能产生其他事物者) origin; parent
【母爱】 mǔ'ài mother love; maternal love
【母板】 mǔbǎn 〈*Computer*〉 motherboard
【母本】 mǔběn 〈*Bot.*〉 female parent
【母畜】 mǔchù dam
【母带】 mǔdài original tape
【母公司】 mǔgōngsī parent company
【母机】 mǔjī 1.(工作母机) machine tool 2.〈*Aeron.*〉 mother aircraft; launching aircraft
【母鸡】 mǔjī hen
【母舰】 mǔjiàn depot ship
【母金】 mǔjīn capital; capital fund
【母老虎】 mǔlǎohǔ 1.(雌老虎) tigress 2.(泼妇) vixen; shrew; termagant
【母亲】 mǔqīn mother
【母亲节】 Mǔqīnjié Mother's Day
【母权制】 mǔquánzhì matriarchy
【母乳】 mǔrǔ breast milk; mother's milk
【母乳喂养】 mǔrǔ wèiyǎng breast-feeding
【母树】 mǔshù 〈*Forestry*〉 elite stand; seed stand
【母系】 mǔxì 1.(属于母亲血统的) maternal side 2.(母女相承的) matriarchal
【母系亲属】 mǔxì qīnshǔ maternal relatives
【母系社会】 mǔxì shèhuì matriarchal society
【母线】 mǔxiàn 1.〈*Electr.*〉 bus; bus bar 2.〈*Math.*〉 generatrix; generator
【母校】 mǔxiào one's old school; Alma Mater
【母性】 mǔxìng maternal instinct
【母液】 mǔyè 〈*Chem.*〉 mother liquid; mother solution
【母语】 mǔyǔ 1.(本族语) mother tongue 2.(某些语言的共同来源) parent language; linguistic parent
【母株】 mǔzhū 〈*Bot.*〉 maternal plant
【母子】 mǔzǐ mother and baby

拇 (mǔ)
【拇指】 mǔzhǐ 1.(手的) thumb 2.(脚的) big toe
【拇指索引】 mǔzhǐ suǒyǐn thumb index
【拇指印】 mǔzhǐyìn thumbprint
【拇指指甲】 mǔzhǐ zhǐjiā thumbnail
【拇趾】 mǔzhǐ big toe

牡 (mǔ) male
【牡丹】 mǔ·dan peony; tree peony
【牡蛎】 mǔlì 〈*Zool.*〉 oyster

亩[畝] (mǔ) *mu*: 1 公顷 = 15 ～ 1 hectare = 15 *mu*
【亩产】 mǔchǎn per *mu* yield

木 (mù) 1.(树木) tree: 花～ flowers and trees 2.(木头) timber; wood; log 3.(木制的) made of wood; wooden: ～梳 wooden comb 4.(麻木) numb; wooden
【木板】 mùbǎn plank; board
【木板床】 mùbǎnchuáng plank bed
【木本植物】 mùběn zhíwù 〈*Bot.*〉 xylophyta; woody plant
【木材】 mùcái wood; timber; lumber
【木材厂】 mùcáichǎng timber mill
【木材工业】 mùcái gōngyè timber industry
【木柴】 mùchái firewood: 劈～ chop wood
【木船】 mùchuán wooden boat
【木槌】 mùchuí mallet
【木雕】 mùdiāo wood statue; idol carved in wood
【木耳】 mù'ěr an edible fungus
【木筏】 mùfá raft
【木工】 mùgōng 1.(木工工作) woodwork; carpentry 2.(做木工活的人) woodworker; carpenter
【木匠】 mù·jiang carpenter
【木结构】 mùjiégòu 〈*Archit.*〉 timber structure; wood construction
【木刻】 mùkè woodcut; wood engraving
【木兰花】 mùlánhuā 〈*Bot.*〉 mangnolia
【木料】 mùliào timber; lumber
【木螺丝】 mùluósī wood screw

【木马】 mùmǎ 1.〈*Sports*〉vaulting horse; pommelled horse 2.(像马的儿童玩具) hobbyhorse; rocking horse

【木棉】 mùmián 〈*Bot.*〉bombax; common bombax: 爪哇～(美洲～) kapok; silk cotton

【木乃伊】 mùnǎiyī mummy

【木讷】 mùnè simple-minded; plain: ～寡言 plain and quiet

【木偶】 mùǒu 1.(木头偶像) wooden image; carved figure 2.(做戏的木人) puppet; marionette

【木偶剧】 mùǒujù puppet show; puppet play

【木偶片】 mù'ǒupiàn 〈*Cinematog.*〉puppet film

【木排】 mùpái raft: 扎～ make a raft / 放～ raft; raft-towing

【木盆】 mùpén tub

【木器】 mùqì wooden furniture; wooden articles

【木琴】 mùqín 〈*Music*〉xylophone

【木然】 mùrán stupefied; stunned

【木炭】 mùtàn charcoal

【木头】 mù·tou wood; log; timber

【木屋】 mùwū log cabin

【木屋区】 mùwūqū shanty town

【木犀】 mù·xi 1.(桂花) sweet-scented osmanthus 2.(指鸡蛋) egg beaten and then cooked

【木犀肉】 mù·xiròu pork fried with scrambled eggs

【木犀汤】 mù·xitāng eggdrop soup

【木屑】 mùxiè saw dust

【木星】 Mùxīng 〈*Astron.*〉Jupiter

【木已成舟】 mùyǐchéngzhōu What is done is done.

【木鱼】 mùyú wooden clapper

【木枕】 mùzhěn 〈*Railway*〉sleeper; wood sleeper

【木蛀虫】 mùzhùchóng wood borer

沐 (mù) wash one's hair

【沐浴】 mùyù 1.(洗澡) have a bath 2.(沉浸) bathe; immerse: ～在阳光中 be bathed in the sunshine

目 (mù) 1.(眼睛) eye: ～语 communicate with the eyes 2.(看) look; regard: ～为奇事 regard as something strange 3.(项目) item 4.〈*Biol.*〉order 5.(目录) list; catalogue

【目标】 mùbiāo 1.(对象) target; objective: 打不中～ miss one's aim 2.(目的) goal; aim; objective: 怀着崇高的～ with a lofty end in mind

【目不识丁】 mùbùshídīng not know one's ABC; be totally illiterate

【目不斜视】 mùbùxiéshì look steadily forward

【目不转睛】 mùbùzhuǎnjīng look with fixed eyes; watch with the utmost concentration

【目测】 mùcè range estimation

【目次】 mùcì contents; table of contents

【目瞪口呆】 mùdèng-kǒudāi gaping; stupefied; dumbstruck

【目的】 mùdì purpose; aim; goal; objective; end

【目的地】 mùdìdì destination

【目的站】 mùdìzhàn point of destination

【目睹】 mùdǔ see with one's eyes; witness

【目光】 mùguāng 1.(眼光) sight; vision; view 2.(神采) gaze; look: ～呆滞 one's eye-sight is restrained

【目光短浅】 mùguāng-duǎnqiǎn be short-sighted

【目光如豆】 mùguāngrúdòu of narrow vision; shortsighted

【目击】 mùjī see with one's own eyes; witness

【目击者】 mùjīzhě eyewitness; witness

【目镜】 mùjìng 〈*Physics*〉eyepiece; ocular

【目空一切】 mùkōngyīqiè consider everybody and everything beneath one's notice; be supercilious

【目力】 mùlì eyesight; vision

【目录】 mùlù 1.(事物名录) catalogue; list: 分类～ classified catalogue 2.(篇章目录) table of contents; contents

【目录室】 mùlùshì catalogue room

【目前】 mùqián present; at the moment: 就～情况看 as matters stand; as things are at the moment

【目送】 mùsòng follow sb. with one's eyes; watch sb. go

【目无法纪】 mùwúfǎjì disregard law and discipline

【目无组织】 mùwú-zhǔzhī disregard organizational discipline
【目眩】 mùxuàn dizzy; dazzled
【目中无人】 mùzhōng-wúrén consider everyone beneath one's notice; be supercilious

苜 (mù)

【苜蓿】 mù·xu 〈*Bot.*〉 lucerne; alfalfa

睦 (mù) peaceful; harmonious

【睦邻】 mùlín good-neighborliness
【睦邻政策】 mùlín zhèngcè good-neighbor policy

钼 (mù) 〈*Chem.*〉 molybdenum (元素符号 Mo)

仫 (mù)

【仫佬族】 Mùlǎozú Mulam (中国少数民族，主要分布在广西)

牧 (mù) herd; tend

【牧草】 mùcǎo herbage; forage grass
【牧场】 mùchǎng grazing land; pastureland; pasture; livestock farm
【牧笛】 mùdí reed pipe
【牧放】 mùfàng herd; tend; put out to pasture
【牧歌】 mùgē 1.(乡村题材诗歌、乐曲) pastoral song; pastoral 2.〈*Music*〉 madrigal
【牧工】 mùgōng hired herdsman
【牧民】 mùmín herdsman (m.); herdswoman (f.)
【牧区】 mùqū pastoral area
【牧犬】 mùquǎn shepherd dog; collie
【牧师】 mù·shi 〈*Christianity*〉 pastor; minister; clergyman
【牧童】 mùtóng shepherd boy; buffalo boy
【牧畜】 mùxù livestock breeding; animal husbandry
【牧羊犬】 mùyángquǎn shepherd dog; sheep dog; collie
【牧羊人】 mùyángrén shepherd (m.); shepherdess (f.)
【牧业】 mùyè animal husbandry; stock raising
【牧主】 mùzhǔ herd owner

募 (mù) raise; collect; enlist; recruit: ～款 raise money

【募兵制】 mùbīngzhì mercenary system
【募捐】 mùjuān solicit contributions; collect donations

墓 (mù) grave; tomb; mausoleum: 烈士～ tombs of revolutionary martyrs

【墓碑】 mùbēi tombstone; gravestone
【墓地】 mùdì graveyard; burial ground; cemetery
【墓祭】 mùjì pay respect to a dead person at his tomb
【墓穴】 mùxué coffin pit; open grave
【墓茔】 mùyíng grave; tomb
【墓葬】 mùzàng 〈*Archaeol.*〉 grave
【墓葬群】 mùzàngqún graves
【墓志】 mùzhì inscription on the memorial tablet within a tomb
【墓志铭】 mùzhìmíng inscription on the memorial tablet within a tomb; epitaph

幕 (mù) 1.(幕布) curtain; screen: 在夜～的掩护下 under screen of night 2.〈*Theatre*〉 act: 五～悲剧 a tragedy in five acts

【幕布】 mùbù curtain; screen
【幕后】 mùhòu behind the scenes; backstage: ～新闻 behind-the-scenes news / 退居～ retire back-stage
【幕间休息】 mùjiān xiū·xi interval; intermission
【幕僚】 mùliáo aides and staff

暮 (mù) 1.(傍晚) dusk; evening; sunset 2.(时间将尽) towards the end; late: ～春 late spring

【暮霭】 mù'ǎi evening mist
【暮春】 mùchūn the late spring; the third month of lunar calendar
【暮年】 mùnián declining years
【暮气沉沉】 mùqì-chénchén lethargic; apathetic
【暮秋】 mùqiū the late fall; the ninth month of lunar calendar
【暮色】 mùsè dusk; twilight; gloaming: ～朦胧 glimmering twilight
【暮岁】 mùsuì 1.(年终) towards the end of the year 2.(老年) old age

慕 (mù) admire; look for; yearn for

【慕名】 mùmíng out of admiration for a famous person ～而来 be attracted to a place by its reputation as a scenic spot

【慕尼黑阴谋】 Mùníhēi yīnmóu the Munich conspiracy

【慕士塔格山】 Mùshìtǎgéshān 〈place〉 Muztagata

穆（mù） solemn；reverent：肃～ solemn

【穆斯林】 mùsīlín Moslem；Muslim

N

na

南 (nā)
(另见“南”nán)

【南无】 nāmó 〈*Buddhism*〉 Namas：～阿弥陀佛 Namas Amithabha

拿［拏］(ná) 1.(用手拿) hold; take; bring; fetch; get：～起武器 take up arms / 把箱子～上楼 take the box upstairs 2.(强力夺取) seize; capture：～下敌人要塞 capture an enemy fort 3.(掌握;把握) be sure of; have a firm grasp of; be able to do：～不准 feel uncertain 4.(用) with：～铅笔写字 write with a pencil 5.(把)～朋友当敌人 take a friend for foe

【拿不出手】 nábùchūshǒu not be presentable

【拿获】 náhuò apprehend; catch：～凶手 catch the murder

【拿架子】 ná jià·zi put on airs

【拿摩温】 námówēn number one

【拿开】 nákāi take away

【拿权】 náquán control power

【拿人】 nárén 1.(刁难) make things difficult for others; put sb. in difficult position 2.(捉人) catch sb.; capture sb. 3.(吸引人) attract; attractive (adj.)

【拿手】 náshǒu adept; expert; good at

【拿手好戏】 náshǒuhǎoxì one's specialty

【拿稳】 náwěn hold steadily; predict with confidence

【拿主意】 ná zhǔ·yi make a decision; make up one's mind

【拿住】 názhù hold firmly; put under arrest

镎 (ná) 〈*Chem.*〉 neptunium (元素符号 Np)

哪［那］(nǎ) 1.(表示疑问) which; what：你们中间～一位是赵先生? Which one of you is Mr. Zhao? / 你最喜欢～种音乐? What is your favorite kind of music? 2.(泛指) any：今年的收成比以往～一年都好。This year's crop is better than any other year's. 3.(表示反问)～会有这种事? How can there be things as such?

【哪个】 nǎ·ge 1.(哪一个) which：你要～? Which do you want? / 然后我按～按钮? Which bottom do I press next? 2.(谁) who：这话你是听～讲的? Who told you so? 3.(泛指) whichever：你们之中随便～要,我都给。I'll give it to whichever of you wants it.

【哪会儿】 nǎhuìr 1.(问时间) when：你～能来? When can you come? 2.(泛指时间) whenever; any time：你～方便就～来吧。Come at any time that is convenient to you.

【哪里】 nǎlǐ 1.(问处所) where：你到～去? Where are you going? 你从～来? Where are you from? 2.(泛指任何处所) wherever; where：无论你去～,我都去。Wherever you go, I go too. 3.(表示否定)～,～,你过奖了。Oh, it's nothing! You are flattering me.

【哪能】 nǎnéng how can：她～说谎? How can she tell lies?

【哪怕】 nǎpà 〈*conj*〉 even; even if; even though; no matter how：～失败,我也要试一下。I will have a try even though I should fail.

【哪儿】 nǎr 1.(哪里) where：你从～来? Where are you from? 2.(泛指任何地方) wherever; anywhere：在家,在学校,随便在～ at home, at school, or wherever

【哪些】 nǎxiē which; who; what：～人是你的亲戚? Who are your relatives?

【哪样】 nǎyàng 1.(用于问话) what kind of; which 2.(泛指) any kind of：你挑选～颜色都行。You can choose any color you like.

那 (nà) 1.(那个) that 2.(那么) then; in that case

【那边】 nàbiān there; over there

【那儿】 nàr 1.(那里) that place; there：他

将在～呆到3月份。He will stay there till March. 2.(那时候) that time; then: 打～起… since then ...

【那个】 nà·ge that: 你认识～女孩吗? Do you know that girl?

【那会儿】 nàhuìr 〈*collog.*〉 at that time; then: 我们～住在乡下。We lived in country then.

【那里】 nà·li that place; there

【那么】 nà·me 1.(如此) like that; in that way 2.(表示估计) about; or so: 再有～五六十元钱就够了。Another fifty or sixty yuan will probably be enough. 3.(这样) then; in that case; such being the case

【那么着】 nà·me·zhe do that; do so: ～也许会好一些。Perhaps it'll be better that way.

【那曲】 Nàqǔ 〈地名〉 Nag Qu

【那时】 nàshí at that time; then; in those days

【那些】 nàxiē those: 你把～照片带来了吗? Did you bring those photos?

【那样】 nàyàng of that kind; like that; such; so: 像雪～白 as white as snow

【那阵儿】 nàzhènr at that time; then

呐 (nà)

【呐喊】 nàhǎn shout loudly; cry out

纳 (nà) 1.(收进来) receive; admit 2.(接受) accept; take in: 不～忠言 not accept any advice; refuse to take in admonishment 3.(享受) enjoy; take delight or pleasure in life 4.(交付) pay; offer

【纳粹】 Nàcuì Nazi ‖ 纳粹分子 Nazi

【纳贿】 nàhuì 1.(受贿) take bribes 2.(行贿) offer bribes

【纳凉】 nàliáng enjoy the cool

【纳闷儿】 nàmènr feel puzzled; be perplexed; wonder

【纳木错】 Nàmùcuò 〈place〉 Nam Co

【纳米技术】 nàmǐ jìshù nano-technology

【纳入】 nàrù bring into; fit into: ～正轨 bring sth. onto the right track

【纳税】 nàshuì pay taxes: 应～的所得额 taxable income / 每月从工资中～ pay tax out of one's salary every month

【纳税年度】 nàshuì niándù tax year

【纳税凭证】 nàshuì píngzhèng tax payment receipt

【纳税人】 nàshuìrén taxpayer

【纳税申报单】 nàshuì shēnbàodān tax return

【纳税收据】 nàshuì shōujù duty receipt

【纳税义务】 nàshuì yìwù duty to pay taxes; obligation to pay tax

【纳西族】 Nàxīzú Naxi (中国少数民族, 主要分布在云南)

【纳降】 nàxiáng accept the enemy's surrender

钠 (nà) 〈*Chem.*〉 sodium (元素符号 Na): 氯化～ sodium chloride

【钠玻璃】 nàbō·li soda-lime glass

【钠灯】 nàdēng sodium lamp

【钠钙玻璃】 nàgài bō·li soda-lime glass

【钠钾玻璃】 nàjiǎ bō·li soda potash glass

【钠缺乏】 nà quēfá sodium deficiency

nai

乃[迺、廼] (nǎi) 1.(是) be 2.(于是) then; hence; therefore: ～有此名 hence comes the name 3.(才) only then 4.(你的) your: ～父 your father / ～兄 your brother

【乃至】 nǎizhì and even

奶[嬭] (nǎi) 1.(乳房) breasts 2.(乳汁) milk: 全脂～ whole milk / 脱脂～ skimmed milk 3.(哺乳) suckle; breast-feed: 给婴儿喂～ feed the baby at the breast

【奶茶】 nǎichá tea with milk

【奶粉】 nǎifěn milk powder; powdered milk; dried milk: 全脂～ whole milk powder / 脱脂～ skimmed milk powder

【奶酪】 nǎilào cheese

【奶奶】 nǎi·nai 1.(祖母) grandmother; grandma 2.(称老年妇女) grandma; granny

【奶牛】 nǎiniú milch cow; milk cow; cow

【奶品】 nǎipǐn milk products; dairy products

【奶瓶】 nǎipíng 1.(喂婴儿用) feeding bottle; nursing bottle; baby's bottle 2.(盛奶用) milk bottle

【奶脯】 nǎipū flank (猪肉部位) flank

【奶水】 nǎishuǐ milk

【奶糖】 nǎitáng toffee; toffy

【奶头】 nǎitóu 1.(乳头) nipple; teat 2.(奶嘴) teat (of a feeding bottle)

【奶羊】 nǎiyáng milch goat
【奶油】 nǎiyóu cream：～蛋糕 cream cake
【奶油分离器】 nǎiyóu fēnlíqì cream separator
【奶油色】 nǎiyóusè cream-colored
【奶罩】 nǎizhào brassiere；bra
【奶嘴】 nǎizuǐ nipple (of a feeding bottle)

氖 (nǎi) 〈*Chem.*〉 neon (元素符号 Ne)

【氖灯】 nǎidēng neon lamp；neon light；neon
【氖气】 nǎiqì neon

奈 (nài)

【奈何】 nàihé 1.(反问) how；to no avail 2.(拿某人怎么办) do sth. to a person：你～不了他。You can do nothing to him.

萘 (nài) 〈*Chem.*〉 naphthalene

耐 (nài) be able to bear or endure：～用 be endurable

【耐不住】 nàibùzhù unable to bear；unable to stand
【耐烦】 nàifán patient
【耐风雨】 nàifēngyǔ weather proof
【耐寒】 nàihán cold-resistant
【耐寒作物】 nàihán zuòwù cold-resistant crop
【耐火】 nàihuǒ fire-resistant；refractory
【耐火材料】 nàihuǒ cáiliào refractory, fireproof material
【耐火砖】 nàihuǒzhuān refractory brick；firebrick
【耐久】 nàijiǔ lasting long；durable
【耐久力】 nàijiǔlì durability；endurance
【耐久试验】 nàijiǔ shìyàn durability test；endurance test
【耐劳】 nàiláo able to endure hard work
【耐力】 nàilì endurance；staying power；stamina
【耐磨】 nàimó wear-resisting；wearproof
【耐磨性】 nàimóxìng wearability；wear resistance
【耐热】 nàirè heat-resisting；heatproof
【耐热性】 nàirèxìng heat resistance
【耐人寻味】 nàirénxúnwèi afford food for thought
【耐酸】 nàisuān acidproof；acid-resisting
【耐缩】 nàisuō anti-shrink
【耐心】 nàixīn patience；patient (adj.)：有～ have patience；be patient / 没～ be impatient / ～等待 be patient and wait for sth. / ～点，公共汽车快来了。Have patience, the bus will come soon.
【耐性】 nàixìng patience；endurance
【耐用】 nàiyòng durable：～消费品 durable consumer goods / 非～品 nondurable products

nan

男 (nán) 1.(男性) man；male：～扮女装 a man disguised as a woman；crossdress / ～服 men's clothing 2.(儿子) son；boy：没～没女 has neither sons nor daughters

【男厕所】 náncèsuǒ men's lavatory；Gentlemen；Men；Gents
【男盗女娼】 nándào-nǚchāng behave like thieves and whores
【男低音】 nándīyīn 〈*Music*〉 bass
【男儿】 nán'ér man：～本色 the manliness of a man
【男方】 nánfāng the bridegroom's or husband's side
【男服务员】 nán fúwùyuán 〈*Aeron.*〉 steward
【男高音】 nángāoyīn 〈*Music*〉 tenor
【男孩】 nánhái boy
【男婚女嫁】 nánhūn-nǚjià a man should take a wife and a woman should take a husband
【男女】 nánnǚ men and women：～青年 young men and women / 不分～ irrespective of sex
【男女混合双打】 nánnǚ hǔnhé shuāngdǎ mixed double
【男女老少】 nánnǚ-lǎoshào men and women, old and young：～皆宜 suitable for men, women and children
【男女平等】 nánnǚ-píngděng equality of men and women；equality of the sexes
【男女平等权】 nánnǚ píngděngquán equal rights for both sexes
【男女有别】 nánnǚ-yǒubié Males and females should be treated differently.
【男人】 nánrén 1.(男子) man 2.(丈夫) husband
【男生】 nánshēng man student；boy student；

schoolboy
【男声】 nánshēng 〈*Music*〉 male voice
【男声合唱】 nánshēng héchàng men's chorus; male chorus
【男士】 nánshì man; gentleman
【男士用品商店】 nánshì yòngpǐn shāngdiàn menswear shop; men's wear
【男睡衣】 nánshuìyī pajamas; pyjamas
【男性】 nánxìng 1.(性别) the male sex 2.(男人) man
【男性不育症】 nánxìng bùyùzhèng male sterility
【男性同性恋】 nánxìng tóngxìngliàn men homosexuality
【男友】 nányǒu boyfriend; boy friend
【男中音】 nánzhōngyīn 〈*Music*〉 baritone
【男主角】 nánzhǔjué leading man; chief actor; hero
【男装】 nánzhuāng men's clothing
【男子】 nánzǐ man; male
【男子单打】 nánzǐ dāndǎ men's singles
【男子更年期】 nánzǐ gēngniánqī male menopause
【男子汉】 nánzǐhàn man: 我们怎么才能使他成为～? How can we make a man of him?
【男子双打】 nánzǐ shuāngdǎ men's doubles

南 (nán) south; southern: ～岸 south coast / ～屋 a room with a northern exposure / 正～偏东 south by east
(另见"南"nā)
【南半球】 nánbànqiú the Southern Hemisphere
【南北】 nánběi 1.(南和北) north and south 2.(从南到北) from north to south: 大江～ on both sides of the Changjiang River
【南北对话】 Nán-Běi duìhuà North-South dialog; dialog between developing and developed countries
【南部】 nánbù southern part; south
【南方】 nánfāng 1.(南) south; southern 2.(南部地区) the southern part of the country
【南方话】 nánfānghuà southern dialect
【南方人】 nánfāngrén Southerner
【南风】 nánfēng south wind
【南风窗】 nánfēngchuāng the south wind window
【南瓜】 nánguā pumpkin; cushaw
【南瓜子】 nánguāzǐ pumpkin seeds
【南海】 Nánhǎi the South China Sea
【南海诸岛】 Nánhǎi zhūdǎo South China Sea Islands
【南回归线】 Nánhuíguīxiàn 〈*Geog.*〉 Tropic of Capricorn
【南极】 nánjí 1.(南极地区) the South Pole; the Antarctic Pole 2.(南磁极) the south magnetic pole
【南极光】 nánjíguāng southern lights; aurora australis
【南极海】 Nánjíhǎi Antarctic Ocean
【南极圈】 Nánjíquān Antarctic Circle
【南极洲】 Nánjízhōu Antarctic Continent; Antarctica
【南美洲】 Nánměizhōu South America; South American (adj.) ‖ 南美洲人 South American
【南南合作】 Nán-Nán hézuò South-South Cooperation
【南腔北调】 nánqiāng-běidiào a mixed accent
【南太平洋】 Nántàipíngyáng southern Pacific Ocean; South Sea; South Seas
【南纬】 nánwěi south latitude
【南亚】 Nányà South Asia; South Asian (adj.)
【南亚次大陆】 Nányà cìdàlù the South Asian Subcontinent
【南征北战】 nánzhēng-běizhàn fight north and south on many fronts

喃 (nán)
【喃喃】 nánnán 〈*onomat.*〉 mutter; murmur

楠[枏] (nán)
【楠木】 nánmù 1.〈*Bot.*〉 phoebe 2.(指其木材) phoebe wood; nanmu wood

难[難] (nán) 1.(不易) difficult; hard; troublesome: 这山很～爬。This hill is hard to climb. 2.(使感到困难) put sb. into a difficult position 3.(不大可能) hardly possible 4.(不好) bad; unpleasant: ～闻 smell bad
(另见"难"nàn)
【难保】 nánbǎo cannot say for sure: 明天～不下雪。You can't say for sure that it won't snow tomorrow.
【难产】 nánchǎn 1.〈*Med.*〉 difficult labor; dystocia 2.(不易完成) be difficult of fulfill-

ment

【难处】 nánchǔ hard to get along with sb.

【难处】 nán·chu difficulty; trouble：各家有各家的～。Each family has its own difficulties.

【难倒】 nándǎo daunt; baffle; beat

【难道】 nándào surely it doesn't mean that ...; could it be said that ...：～这是办不到的吗? Could it be said that it is impossible of attainment?

【难得】 nándé 1.（不易得到）hard to come by; rare：～的机会 a rare chance 2.（不常发生）seldom; rarely：她～到这里来。She seldom comes here.

【难点】 nándiǎn difficult point; difficulty

【难懂】 nándǒng difficult to comprehend; hard to understand

【难度】 nándù degree of difficulty; difficulty

【难度系数】 nándù xìshù degree-of-difficulty factor

【难怪】 nánguài 1.（怪不得）no wonder 2.（不应当责备）understandable; pardonable

【难关】 nánguān difficulty; crisis：渡过～ tide over a difficulty

【难管】 nánguǎn difficult to govern; hard to rule

【难过】 nánguò 1.（不易过活）have a hard time 2.（难受）feel sorry; feel bad; be grieved

【难解难分】 nánjiě-nánfēn 1.（相持不下）neither would give in; neither can get the upper hand 2.（关系密切）be sentimentally attached to each other

【难堪】 nánkān 1.（难以忍受）intolerable; unbearable：～之事 a bitter pill to swallow 2.（窘）embarrassed

【难看】 nánkàn 1.（不好看）ugly; unsightly：～的帽子 an ugly hat 2.（不体面）shameful; embarrassing; disgraceful

【难免】 nánmiǎn hard to avoid：～有照顾不周的地方 be bound to overlook sth.

【难能可贵】 nánnéng-kěguì praiseworthy for one's excellent conduct; estimable; rare and commendable

【难人】 nánrén 1.（使人为难）difficulty; delicate; ticklish：～的问题 ticklish problem 2.（担当为难事情的人）a person handling a delicate matter

【难色】 nánsè appear to be embarrassed

【难上加难】 nánshàngjiānán extremely difficult

【难舍难分】 nánshě-nánfēn loath to part from each other

【难受】 nánshòu 1.（不舒服）feel unwell; feel ill; suffer pain 2.（不痛快）feel unhappy; feel bad

【难说】 nánshuō it's hard to say; you never can tell

【难逃法网】 nántáo-fǎwǎng be unable to escape the net of justice

【难题】 nántí difficult problem; a hard nut to crack; poser

【难听】 nántīng 1.（不悦耳）unpleasant to hear：～的声音 unpleasant sound 2.（粗俗刺耳）offensive; coarse：～的话 offensive language; profane language 3.（不体面）scandalous

【难忘】 nánwàng unforgettable; memorable：～的印象 indelible impression; memorable impression

【难为】 nánwéi 1.（使人为难）embarrass; press 2.（多亏）be a tough job to

【难为情】 nánwéiqíng 1.（害羞）ashamed; embarrassed; shy 2.（为难）find it difficult; disconcerting

【难闻】 nánwén smell unpleasant; smell bad

【难兄难弟】 nánxiōng-nándì 〈*iron.*〉 two of a kind

【难言之隐】 nányánzhīyǐn sth. one doesn't want to reveal; sth. embarrassing to mention

【难以】 nányǐ difficult to：～比拟 hardly match; hardly equal / ～否认 undeniable; irrefutable

【难于启齿】 nányúqǐchǐ have a bone in the throat; difficult to speak out one's mind

赧［赧］(nǎn) blushing

【赧然】 nǎnrán 〈*written*〉 blushing

【赧颜】 nǎnyán 〈*written*〉 blush; be shamefaced

难［難］(nàn) 1.（灾难）catastrophe; disaster; calamity：大～临头 be faced with imminent disaster 2.（质问）blame; reproach：非～ blame

（另见“难”nán）
【难民】 nànmín refugee
【难民营】 nànmínyíng refugee camp
【难兄难弟】 nànxiōng-nàndì fellow sufferers
【难友】 nànyǒu fellow sufferer

nang

囔（nāng）
【囔囔】 nāng·nang murmur; whisper
囊（náng） 1.（口袋）bag; pocket 2.（袋装物）anything shaped like a bag
【囊空如洗】 nángkōng-rúxǐ with empty pocket; penniless; broke
【囊括】 nángkuò include; embrace：～一切 sweep up everything
【囊肿】 nángzhǒng cyst
【囊肿病】 nángzhǒngbìng 〈*Med.*〉 cystic disease
攮（nǎng） stab; thrust; pierce：他用匕首把这妇女～死了。He stabbed the woman with a dagger and she died.
【攮子】 nǎng·zi dagger

nao

孬（nāo） 1.（坏）bad 2.（怯懦）cowardly
【孬种】 nāozhǒng coward
挠［撓］（náo） 1.（轻轻地抓）scratch：～痒 scratch an itch 2.（阻止）hinder 3.（屈服）yield; flinch
【挠钩】 náogōu long-handled hook
【挠头】 náotóu 1.（用手抓头）scratch one's head 2.（事情麻烦）difficult to tackle：令人～的事 a knotty problem
蛲［蟯］（náo）
【蛲虫】 náochóng pinworm
【蛲虫病】 náochóngbìng enterobiasis
硇［磠、硵］（náo）
【硇砂】 náoshā 〈*Mineral.*〉 sal ammoniac
恼［惱］（nǎo） 1.（生气）angry; irritated; annoyed 2.（烦闷）unhappy; worried
【恼恨】 nǎohèn resent; hate
【恼火】 nǎohuǒ annoyed; irritated; vexed：别～。Don't lose your temper.
【恼怒】 nǎonù angry; indignant; furious：因某人做某事而～ be angry at what sb. has done
【恼人】 nǎorén irritating; annoying
【恼羞成怒】 nǎoxiū-chéngnù fly into a rage from shame; be shamed into anger
脑［腦］（nǎo） brain：大～ cerebrum / 后～ hindbrain / 小～ cerebellum / 用～过度 overtax one's brain
【脑充血】 nǎochōngxuè 〈*Med.*〉 encephalemia
【脑袋】 nǎo·dai 1.〈*colloq.*〉 head 2.（脑筋）mind; thinking
【脑袋瓜】 nǎo·daiguā 〈*colloq.*〉 head
【脑电图】 nǎodiàntú 〈*Med.*〉 electroencephalogram (EEG)
【脑瓜儿】 nǎoguār 〈*colloq.*〉 head
【脑海】 nǎohǎi brain; mind：往事又浮上～。Past events flashed across my mind again.
【脑浆】 nǎojiāng brains
【脑筋】 nǎojīn 1.（指思考、记忆等能力）brains; mind; head：～灵敏 keen and sharp in thinking / 动～ use one's brains 2.（指意识）ideas：老～ outdated conventional ideas; an old fogey
【脑壳】 nǎoké 1.（头颅）skull 2.（头）head
【脑力劳动】 nǎolì láodòng mental work
【脑力劳动者】 nǎolì láodòngzhě mental worker; brain worker
【脑瘤】 nǎoliú brain tumor
【脑满肠肥】 nǎomǎn-chángféi heavy-jowled and potbellied
【脑门儿】 nǎoménr front
【脑膜】 nǎomó 〈*Anat.*〉 meninx
【脑膜炎】 nǎomóyán 〈*Med.*〉 meningitis
【脑桥】 nǎoqiáo 〈*Anat.*〉 pons
【脑死亡】 nǎosǐwáng 〈*Med.*〉 brain death
【脑髓】 nǎosuǐ 〈*Anat.*〉 brains
【脑体倒挂】 nǎotǐ-dàoguà the reversal of the relation between mental labor and physical labor
【脑炎】 nǎoyán 〈*Med.*〉 encephalitis; cerebritis：流行性乙型～ epidemic encephalitis B
【脑溢血】 nǎoyìxuè 〈*Med.*〉 cerebral hemor-

rhage

【脑震荡】 nǎozhèndàng 〈*Med*.〉 cerebral concussion; concussion of the brain

【脑汁】 nǎozhī brains: 绞尽～ rack one's brains

【脑子】 nǎo·zi 1.(脑) brain 2.(脑筋) brains; mind; head

闹[鬧] (nào) 1.(喧哗) noisy: ～中取静 a quite spot in a noisy neighborhood 2.(吵) make a noise; stir up trouble: ～翻了天 make a hell of a fuss / ～名利 be out for fame and gain 3.(发泄) give vent 4.(害;发生) suffer from; be troubled by: ～事 make trouble / ～水灾 suffer from flood 5.(干;搞) go in for; do; make: ～技术革新 make a technical innovation

【闹别扭】 nào biè·niu be difficult with sb.; be at odds with sb.

【闹病】 nàobìng fall ill; be ill

【闹翻】 nàofān fall out with sb.

【闹革命】 nào gémìng carry out revolution; make revolution; rise in revolution

【闹鬼】 nàoguǐ 1.(鬼怪作祟) be haunted 2.(在背后做坏事) play tricks behind sb's back; use underhand means

【闹哄哄】 nàohōnghōng clamorous; noisy

【闹饥荒】 nào jī·huang 1.(遇荒年) suffer from famine 2.(指经济困难) be hard up

【闹剧】 nàojù farce

【闹情绪】 nào qíngxù be disgruntled; be in low spirits

【闹市】 nàoshì busy shopping center; busy streets

【闹笑话】 nào xiào·hua make a fool of oneself; make a stupid mistake

【闹意见】 nào yìjiàn be on bad terms because of a difference of opinion

【闹意气】 nào yìqì feel resentful because sth. is not to one's liking; sulk

【闹钟】 nàozhōng alarm clock

淖 (nào) mire

【淖尔】 nāo'ěr nur; lake: 罗布～ Lop Nur

ne

讷 (nè) slow of speech

【讷讷】 nènè slow of speech: ～不出于口 slow of speech

nei

馁 (něi) 1.(饥饿) hungry; famished 2.(失掉勇气) discourage: 气～ be discouraged

内 (nèi) 1.(里头) inner; inside; within: ～附详细说明 full directions inside 2.(指妻或妻的亲属) one's wife or her relatives

【内宾】 nèibīn guests from native country; domestic gusts

【内部】 nèibù inside; internal; interior

【内部比率】 nèibù bǐlǜ internal ratio

【内部电话】 nèibù diànhuà interphone; house telephone

【内部规律】 nèibù guīlǜ inherent laws

【内部结构】 nèibù jiégòu internal structure

【内部刊物】 nèibù kānwù restricted publication

【内部审计】 nèibù shěnjì internal audit

【内参】 nèicān inside reference news

【内场】 nèichǎng 〈*Baseball*〉 infield

【内场手】 nèichǎngshǒu 〈*Baseball*〉 infielder

【内出血】 nèichūxuè 〈*Med*.〉 internal hemorrage

【内存】 nèicún 〈*Computer*〉 memory: 扩充～ expanded memory (XMS) / 扩展～ extented memory (EMS) / 装入上端～ load into upper memory

【内存条】 nèicúntiáo 〈*Computer*〉 DRAM; dynamic random access memory

【内地】 nèidì inland; interior; hinterland: ～城市 inland city / 发展～工业 promote the inland industry

【内定】 nèidìng decided at the higher level but not officially announced

【内耳】 nèi'ěr 〈*Anat*.〉 internal ear; inner ear

【内耳眩晕症】 nèi'ěr xuànyūnzhèng 〈*Med*.〉 Meniere's syndrome

【内分泌】 nèifēnmì 〈*Physiol*.〉 endocrine; internal secretion; incretion

【内封】 nèifēng title page

【内服】 nèifú be taken orally

【内港】 nèigǎng inner harbor
【内阁】 nèigé cabinet：影子～ shadow cabinet / ～改组 cabinet reshuffle / ～会议 cabinet council
【内果皮】 nèiguǒpí 〈*Bot*.〉 endocarp
【内海】 nèihǎi **1**.（内陆海） continental sea **2**.（属于一国的海） inland sea
【内涵】 nèihán **1**.〈*Logic*〉 intension；connotation **2**.（内在的涵养） virtue of patience：～很高的人 a very self-restraint person
【内行】 nèiháng **1**.（在行，精通） be expert at；be adept in：对计算机很～ be expert at computers **2**.（内行的人） expert；master：向～人学习 learn from the one who knows how
【内耗】 nèihào inside consumption
【内河】 nèihé inland river
【内河运输】 nèihé yùnshū inland water transport
【内讧】 nèihòng internal conflict；internal strife；internal dissension
【内画】 nèihuà inside-paint
【内画壶】 nèihuàhú inside-painted bottle
【内婚制】 nèihūnzhì endogamy
【内寄生】 nèijìshēng endoparasitism
【内奸】 nèijiān a secret enemy agent within one's ranks；hidden traitor
【内角】 nèijiǎo 〈*Math*.〉 interior angle
【内景】 nèijǐng 〈*Cinematog*.〉 indoor setting；interior
【内疚】 nèijiū compunction；guilty conscience
【内眷】 nèijuàn female members of a family
【内科】 nèikē 〈*Med*.〉 internal medicine
【内科病房】 nèikē bìngfáng medical ward
【内科医生】 nèikē yīshēng physician
【内控】 nèikòng the inside control
【内裤】 nèikù briefs；knickers：男～ briefs / 女～ knickers
【内窥镜】 nèikuìjìng 〈*Med*.〉 endoscope
【内联】 nèilián internal combination；be combined with other domestic enterprises
【内联外引】 nèilián wàiyǐn introduce investment from abroad and establish lateral ties at home
【内流河】 nèiliúhé inland river
【内流湖】 nèiliúhú inland lake
【内六角扳手】 nèiliùjiǎo bān·shou Allen wrench；hex wrench
【内陆】 nèilù inland；interior；landlocked
【内陆国】 nèilùguó landlocked country
【内陆河】 nèilùhé continental river；inland river
【内乱】 nèiluàn civil strife；internal disorder
【内蒙古】 Nèiměnggǔ Nei Mongol；Inner Mongolia
【内蒙古自治区】 Nèiměnggǔ zìzhìqū Nei Mongol Zizhiqu；Inner Mongolia Autonomous Region
【内幕】 nèimù what goes on behind the scenes；inside story
【内幕新闻】 nèimù xīnwén inside story；news behind the news
【内能】 nèinéng internal energy；inner energy
【内勤】 nèiqín **1**.（内部工作） office work **2**.（内勤人员） office staff
【内情】 nèiqíng inside information
【内燃机】 nèiránjī internal-combustion engine：柴油～ diesel engine
【内燃机车】 nèirán jīchē diesel locomotive
【内燃机货轮】 nèiránjī huòlún motor cargo ship
【内热】 nèirè 〈*Med*.〉 interior-heat
【内容】 nèiróng content；substance：～丰富 rich in content
【内容提要】 nèiróng tíyào synopsis；résumé
【内伤】 nèishāng 〈*Med*.〉 internal injury
【内水】 nèishuǐ internal territorial waters
【内胎】 nèitāi inner tube（of a tire）
【内外】 nèiwài **1**.（内部和外部） inside and outside；domestic and foreign：国～市场 domestic and foreign market **2**.（表示概数） around；about：二十年～ in about twenty years
【内务】 nèiwù **1**.（国内事务） internal affairs **2**.（日常事务） daily routine of sanitation tasks
【内务部】 nèiwùbù Ministry of Internal Affairs
【内线】 nèixiàn **1**.（在对方内部活动的人） planted agent **2**.〈*Mil*.〉 interior lines **3**.（电话内线） inside telephone connections
【内线自动电话机】 nèixiàn zìdòng diànhuàjī interphone
【内详】 nèixiáng name and address of sender enclosed

【内向】 nèixiàng introversion; introvert (adj.)

【内向型经济】 nèixiàngxíng jīngjì domestically oriented economy

【内销】 nèixiāo sold inside the country; for the domestic market; home trade: ～商品 commodities for the home market

【内斜视】 nèixiéshì 〈*Med.*〉 esotropia; cross-eye

【内心】 nèixīn heart; innermost being: 在～深处 in one's heart of hearts

【内省】 nèixǐng 〈*Psycho.*〉 introspection; self-examination: ～不疚 find no fault in examining one's heart

【内衣】 nèiyī underwear; underclothes

【内因】 nèiyīn 〈*Philos.*〉 internal cause

【内应】 nèiyìng a planted agent; a person operating from within in coordination with outside forces

【内忧】 nèiyōu domestic trouble

【内忧外患】 nèiyōu-wàihuàn domestic trouble and foreign invasion

【内在】 nèizài inherent; intrinsic

【内在联系】 nèizài liánxì inner link; internal relations

【内在矛盾】 nèizài máodùn inner contradictions

【内在美】 nèizàiměi inner beauty

【内在因素】 nèizài yīnsù internal factor

【内脏】 nèizàng internal organs; viscera

【内宅】 nèizhái inner chambers

【内债】 nèizhài internal debt

【内战】 nèizhàn civil war

【内招】 nèizhāo 1.(指招生) internal enrollment of students 2.(指招工) internal employment of workers

【内政】 nèizhèng internal affairs; domestic affairs

【内中】 nèizhōng inside; inner; within

【内助】 nèizhù 〈*written*〉 wife

【内装式闪光灯】 nèizhuāngshì shǎnguāngdēng 〈*Photog.*〉 built-in flash

【内传】 nèizhuàn anecdotes

【内资】 nèizī domestic capital

nen

嫩 (nèn) 1.(娇嫩) tender; delicate: ～黄瓜 young cucumber / ～芽 tender shoots 2.(烹调时间短) underdone; tender: 这些鸡蛋煮得太～了。These eggs boiled too tender. 3.(色浅) light; delicate: ～色 light color 4.(阅历浅;经验少) inexperienced; immature; green: 他做这件工作还太～。He is still green at this job.

【嫩红】 nènhóng light red

【嫩绿】 nènlǜ light green

neng

能 (néng) 1.(能力) ability; capability; skill: 无～的人 a man of small caliber 2.(能量) energy: 动～ kinetic energy / 位～ potential energy 3.(有能力的) able; capable 4.(能够;会) can; be able to; be capable of: ～吃苦耐劳 able to bear hardship

【能动】 néngdòng active; dynamic; vigorous

【能动性】 néngdòngxìng dynamic role; activity; initiative: 主观～ subjective activity

【能干】 nénggàn able; capable; competent

【能歌善舞】 nénggē-shànwǔ good at both singing and dancing

【能工巧匠】 nénggōng-qiǎojiàng skillful craftsman; dab hand

【能够】 nénggòu can; be able to; be capable of: ～独立操作 be able to operate on one's own

【能回收月球火箭】 néng huíshōu yuèqiú huǒjiàn recoverable lunar rocket

【能级】 néngjí 〈*Physics*〉 energy level

【能见度】 néngjiàndù visibility

【能力】 nénglì ability; capacity; capability: 出口创汇～ capacity to earn foreign exchange

【能量】 néngliàng 1.〈*Physics*〉 energy 2.(能力) capabilities

【能量交换】 néngliàng jiāohuàn energy exchange

【能量守恒】 néngliàng shǒuhéng conservation of energy

【能量转化】 néngliàng zhuǎnhuà energy conversion

【能耐】 néng·nai 〈*colloq.*〉 ability; capability; skill

【能…能…】 néng…néng… cannot only ... but also: ～攻～守 be good at offense and defense; be able to take the offensive or hold one's ground / ～屈～伸 be able to stoop or to stand; can take temporary setbacks

【能人】 néngrén man of large caliber; able person

【能手】 néngshǒu dab; expert; crackajack

【能说会道】 néngshuō-huìdào very eloquent; good at speaking

【能言善辩】 néngyán-shànbiàn eloquent, glib and quick-tongued in argument

【能源】 néngyuán energy resources; energy: ～危机 energy crisis

【能者多劳】 néngzhě-duōláo able people should do more work

【能者为师】 néngzhě-wéishī let those who know teach

ni

妮 (nī) girl

【妮子】 nī·zi girl

尼 (ní) Buddhist nun

【尼庵】 ní'ān Buddhist nunnery

【尼姑】 nígū Buddhist nun

【尼古丁】 nígǔdīng nicotine

【尼龙】 nílóng 〈*Textiles*〉 nylon

【尼龙搭扣】 nílóng dākòu velcro

【尼龙丝】 nílóngsī nylon yarn

【尼龙袜】 nílóngwà nylon socks

呢 (ní) wool; woolen cloth; heavy woolen cloth: 大衣～ heavy woolen cloth for overcoat / 海军～ navy cloth

【呢料】 níliào woolen material

【呢喃】 nínán 〈*onomat.*〉 twitter

【呢绒】 níróng woolen goods; wool fabric

【呢子】 ní·zi woolen cloth; heavy woolen cloth

泥 (ní) **1.** (泥巴) mud; mire: ～墙 mud wall **2.** (泥状物) mash: 蒜～ mashed garlic / 土豆～ mashed potato
(另见"泥"nì)

【泥刀】 nídāo trowel

【泥点儿】 nídiǎnr droplets of mud

【泥饭碗】 nífànwǎn clay bowl

【泥肥】 níféi mud fertilizer; sludge

【泥垢】 nígòu dirt; smut; grime

【泥浆】 níjiāng slurry; mud

【泥坑】 níkēng **1.** (烂泥坑) mud pit; mire; morass: 卡车陷在了～里。The truck got stuck in the mud. **2.** (比喻) difficult situation

【泥疗】 níliáo 〈*Med.*〉 mud therapy

【泥泞】 nínìng **1.** (有烂泥的) muddy; miry; sloppy: ～的路 a muddy road **2.** (烂泥) mud; slurry; mire

【泥鳅】 ní·qiū loach; mud fish

【泥沙】 níshā 〈*Geol.*〉 silt

【泥沙俱下】 níshā-jùxià mud and sand are carried along; there is a mingling of good and bad

【泥石流】 níshíliú 〈*Geol.*〉 mud-rock flow; debris flow

【泥水匠】 níshuǐjiàng bricklayer; tiler; plasterer

【泥塑】 nísù clay sculpture

【泥胎】 nítāi **1.** (泥像的坯) unpainted clay idol **2.** (陶坯) unfired pottery

【泥潭】 nítán mire; morass; quagmire

【泥炭】 nítàn peat

【泥土】 nítǔ **1.** (土壤) earth; soil **2.** (黏土) clay

【泥瓦匠】 níwǎjiàng bricklayer; tiler; plasterer

【泥岩】 níyán mudstone

【泥沼】 nízhǎo mire; swamp; morass; slough

铌 (ní) 〈*Chem.*〉 niobium (元素符号 Nb)

霓[蜺] (ní) 〈*Meteorol.*〉 secondary rainbow

【霓虹灯】 níhóngdēng neon lamp; neon light; neon sign; neon

鲵 (ní) 〈*Zool.*〉 salamander: 大～ Chinese giant salamander; man fish / 小～ Chinese salamander

拟[擬] (nǐ) **1.** (拟定) draw up; draft: ～电稿 draft a telegram / ～一个计划 draw up a plan **2.** (打算) intend; plan **3.** (仿效) imitate

【拟订】 nǐdìng draw up; draft; work out: ～一份决议草案 work out a draft resolution / ～一份提纲 draw up an outline

【拟稿】 nǐgǎo make a draft

【拟人】 nǐrén 〈*Gram*.〉 personification
【拟声词】 nǐshēngcí onomatopoetic word
【拟声法】 nǐshēngfǎ onomatopoeia
【拟议】 nǐyì 1.（事先的考虑）proposal; recommendation 2.（草拟）draw up; draft
【拟作】 nǐzuò 1.（模仿他人风格的作品）work done in the manner of a certain author 2.（打算）intend; plan

你（nǐ） 1.（指对方）you; your (adj.)：～和～的家人 you and yours / 这是～的词典吗？Is this your own dictionary? 2.（泛指任何人）you; one：～走～的阳关道，我走我的独木桥 you look after your own concern and leave me to my own affairs 3.（你们）you; your：～方 your side / ～厂 your factory
【你好】 nǐhǎo how do you do; how are you; hello
【你们】 nǐmén you; your：～学校 your school / ～俩准备好了吗？Are you two ready? / 把～的书放在课桌上。Put your books on your desks.
【你们自己】 nǐmén zìjǐ yourselves
【你死我活】 nǐsǐ-wǒhuó life-and-death; mortal
【你追我赶】 nǐzhuī-wǒgǎn try to overtake each other in friendly emulation
【你自己】 nǐzìjǐ yourself：会伤着～的。You will hurt yourself.

泥（nì） 1.（用土、灰等涂抹）cover with plaster; daub; plaster：～墙 plaster a wall 2.（固执）stubborn; obstinate
（另见"泥"ní）
【泥子】 nì·zi 〈*Archit*.〉 putty

昵［暱］（nì） intimate; close：亲～ very intimate; affectionate

逆（nì） 1.（方向相反）contrary; counter 2.（抵触）go against; disobey; defy 3.（叛逆）traitor
【逆差】 nìchā 〈*Trade*〉 adverse balance of trade; trade deficit：国际收支～ an adverse balance of international payments
【逆产】 nìchǎn traitor's property
【逆潮】 nìcháo head tide; countertide
【逆耳】 nì'ěr grate on the ear; be unpleasant to the ear：～的话 words unpleasant to hear
【逆反心理】 nìfǎn xīnlǐ the adverse psychology; the rebellious psychology
【逆反应】 nìfǎnyìng 〈*Chem*.〉 reverse reaction
【逆风】 nìfēng 1.（迎对风）against the wind; in the teeth of the wind 2.（跟行进方向相反的风）contrary wind; head wind; adverse wind
【逆光】 nìguāng against the light
【逆境】 nìjìng adverse circumstances; adversity
【逆来顺受】 nìlái-shùnshòu be resigned to one's fate; resign oneself to adversity
【逆料】 nìliào anticipate; foresee
【逆流】 nìliú 1.（逆水）against the current：～游泳而上 swim upstream 2.（逆潮流）adverse current; countercurrent
【逆时针方向】 nìshízhēn fāngxiàng counter-clockwise direction; anti-clockwise direction
【逆水】 nìshuǐ against the current：～而上 go up stream / ～而行 sail against the stream
【逆向】 nìxiàng inverse; adverse; contrary
【逆行】 nìxíng go in the wrong direction; go in a direction not allowed by traffic regulations
【逆转】 nìzhuǎn take a turn for the worse; reverse; become worse; deteriorate
【逆转过敏反应】 nìzhuǎn guòmǐn fǎnyìng reversed anaphylaxis
【逆子】 nìzǐ unfilial son

匿（nì） hide; conceal：逃～ escape and hide
【匿藏】 nìcáng hide; conceal
【匿伏】 nìfú be in hiding; lurk
【匿迹】 nìjì go into hiding; stay in concealment：销声～ keep silent and lie low
【匿名】 nìmíng anonymous
【匿名信】 nìmíngxìn poison-pen letter

腻（nì） 1.（食物中油脂过多）greasy; oily 2.（厌烦）be bored with; be tired of：他实在叫人～。He is so tiresome. 3.（细致）meticulous
【腻烦】 nì·fan 1.（厌烦）be bored; be fed up 2.（厌恶）loathe; hate：～油味 loathe the smell of grease
【腻歪】 nì·wai 〈*dial*.〉 get fed up
【腻味】 nì·wei 〈*dial*.〉 get fed up
【腻友】 nìyǒu 〈*written*〉 intimate friends
【腻子】 nì·zi 〈*Archit*.〉 putty

溺 (nì) 1.(淹没在水里) drown：他在翻船事故中～水。He drowned in a boating accident. 2.(沉迷不悟) be addicted to：～于利欲 indulge in profits and lust

【溺爱】 nì'ài spoil; dote on：～子女 dote on children

【溺婴】 nìyīng infanticide by drowning; drowning of infants

【溺于酒色】 nìyújiǔsè given over to wine and women

nian

拈 (niān) take; pick up

【拈花惹草】 niānhuā-rěcǎo have many affairs

【拈阄儿】 niānjiūr draw lots

【拈轻怕重】 niānqīng-pàzhòng prefer the light to the heavy; pick easy jobs and shirk hard ones

蔫 (niān) 1.(萎缩) shrivel up; wither; wilt; fade 2.(精神不振) droopy; listless; spiritless; run-down：这女孩看上去有点～。The girl seems droopy.

年[秊] (nián) 1.(时间单位) year：今～ this year / 明～ next year / 前～ year before last/ 去～ last year / 日历～ calendar year / 学～ school year; academic year 2.(每年的) annual; yearly：逐～ annually 3.(岁数) age; year：～高德昭 advanced in years and highly esteemed 4.(时期) a period of time：童～ childhood 5.(年成) harvest 6.(新年) New Year：拜～ pay a New Year visit

【年报】 niánbào annual report; annual; annals

【年变化率】 nián biànhuàlǜ annual gradient

【年表】 niánbiǎo chronological table

【年产量】 niánchǎnliàng annual production; annual out-put; annual yield

【年成】 niánchéng the year's harvest：好～ a good harvest; a rich harvest

【年初】 niánchū at the beginning of the year

【年代】 niándài 1.(时代) age; years; time 2.(10 年的时期) a decade of a century：20 世纪 90～ 1990s

【年底】 niándǐ the end of the year; year-end

【年度】 niándù year：财政～ financial year

【年度报告】 niándù bàogào annual report

【年度计划】 niándù jìhuà annual plan

【年度结算】 niándù jiésuàn annual account

【年度决算表】 niándù juésuànbiǎo annual statement

【年度收入】 niándù shōurù annual revenue

【年度统计表】 niándù tǒngjìbiǎo annual returns

【年份】 niánfèn 1.(指某一年) a particular year 2.(所经历的年代) age; time

【年富力强】 niánfù-lìqiáng in the prime of life; in one's prime

【年糕】 niángāo New Year cake

【年关】 niánguān the end of the year

【年光】 niánguāng 1.(年华) time; years 2.(收成) the year's harvest：好～ a good harvest

【年号】 niánhào reign title

【年华】 niánhuá time; years：虚度～ waste the best years of one's life

【年画】 niánhuà New Year pictures

【年会】 niánhuì annual meeting

【年货】 niánhuò special purchases for the New Year or Spring Festival

【年级】 niánjí grade; year：3～ third grade

【年纪】 niánjì age：～轻 young / 上～ aged / 上～的人 aged person

【年假】 niánjià 1.(指寒假) winter vacation 2.(新年的假期) New Year holiday 3.(春节假期) Spring Festival holiday 4.(每年的假期) annual holidays

【年鉴】 niánjiàn yearbook; almanac

【年金】 niánjīn annuity

【年景】 niánjǐng the year's harvest：好～ a good harvest

【年净利】 niánjìnglì annual net profit

【年久失修】 niánjiǔ-shīxiū worn down by the years without repair

【年均】 niánjūn the yearly average; per-year average

【年历】 niánlì a calendar with the whole year printed on one sheet; single-page calendar

【年利】 niánlì annual interest

【年利率】 niánlìlǜ annual interest rate

【年龄】 niánlíng age：～相仿 be of the similar age

【年龄段】 niánlíngduàn age bracket
【年龄结构】 niánlíng jiégòu age structure
【年龄群】 niánlíngqún age set
【年龄组】 niánlíngzǔ age group
【年率】 niánlǜ annual rate; rate per annum
【年轮】 niánlún 〈*Bot*.〉 annual ring; growth ring
【年迈】 niánmài old; aged
【年年】 niánnián every year; year after year; year by year: ～如意 New Year greetings
【年谱】 niánpǔ a chronicle of sb.'s life
【年轻】 niánqīng young: ～化、知识化和专业化 be younger on the average, better educated and better qualified professionally
【年少】 niánshào young
【年少气盛】 niánshào-qìshèng young and impetuous
【年深日久】 niánshēn-rìjiǔ with the passage of time; as the years go by
【年事】 niánshì age: ～已高 advanced in age
【年收入】 niánshōurù annual yield
【年岁】 niánsuì **1**.(年纪) age **2**.(年代) years **3**.(年成) the year's harvest
【年头】 niántóu **1**.(年代) days; times: 那～ in those days **2**.(指年份) year: 10个～ ten years **3**.(多年的时间) long time; years: 他教书有～了。He has been teaching for years. **4**.(收成) the year's harvest: 好～ a good harvest
【年尾】 niánwěi the end of the year; year-end
【年息】 niánxī annual interest
【年限】 niánxiàn fixed number of years; period
【年薪】 niánxīn annual salary
【年夜】 niányè the eve of the lunar New Year
【年幼无知】 niányòu-wúzhī young and ignorant; ignorance for being young of age
【年雨量】 niányǔliàng annual rainfall
【年月】 niányuè days; years
【年终】 niánzhōng the end of the year; year-end: ～加薪 year-end bonus / ～结算 annual closing
【年资】 niánzī seniority; age and years of service
【年资制度】 niánzī zhìdù seniority system

粘 (nián) 同"黏"
(另见"粘"zhān)

黏 (nián) sticky; glutinous
【黏不住】 nián·buzhù fail to stick; fail to adhere
【黏稠】 niánchóu stringy; viscid; thick
【黏度】 niándù 〈*Chem*.〉 viscosity
【黏附】 niánfù adhere
【黏合】 niánhé 〈*Chem*.〉 bind; bond; adhere
【黏合剂】 niánhéjì binder; adhesive; bonding agent
【黏糊】 nián·hu **1**.(黏) sticky; glutinous **2**.(缓慢) dull; languid; slow-moving: 这人真～。He is very dull.
【黏胶】 niánjiāo 〈*Chem*.〉 viscose
【黏胶纤维】 niánjiāo xiānwéi viscose fiber
【黏结】 niánjié cohere; cohesion (n.); cohesive (adj.)
【黏结力】 niánjiélì cohesive force
【黏米】 niánmǐ glutinous rice
【黏膜】 niánmó 〈*Anat*.〉 mucous membrane; mucosa
【黏膜炎】 niánmóyán 〈*Med*.〉 mucositis
【黏土】 niántǔ clay
【黏性】 niánxìng stickiness; viscidity; viscosity
【黏液】 niányè **1**.〈*Physiol*.〉 mucus **2**.〈*Bot*.〉 mucilage
【黏住】 niánzhù stick; adhere
【黏着】 niánzhuó stick together; adhere

鲇[鯰] (nián) 〈*Zool*.〉 sheatfish; catfish
【鲇鱼】 niányú sheatfish; catfish

捻[撚] (niǎn) **1**.(用手指搓) twist with the finger: ～胡子 finger the beard / ～线 twist thread **2**.(捻子) spill; wick
【捻子】 niǎn·zi **1**.(纸捻儿) spill **2**.(灯芯) wick; lampwick

撵 (niǎn) **1**.(驱逐) drive out; oust: ～走某人 drive sb. away **2**.(追赶) catch up: 我会～上你的。I'll catch up with you.

碾 (niǎn) **1**.(碾子) roller **2**.(去掉谷壳) grind or husk with a roller: ～米 husk rice **3**.(压碎) crush; pulverize; grind: 把玉米～成粉 grind corn into flour **4**.(碾平) flatten
【碾坊】 niǎnfáng mill
【碾房】 niǎnfáng mill

【碾磙子】 niǎngǔn·zi roller
【碾米机】 niǎnmǐjī rice mill
【碾盘】 niǎnpán millstone
【碾碎】 niǎnsuì pulverize
【碾子】 niǎn·zi roller：石～ stone roller

念［唸[3, 4]］(niàn) 1.（想念）think of; miss 2.（念头）thought; idea：心无杂～ have only one thing in mind 3.（读）read：请～给我听。Read to me, please. 4.（求学）study; attend school：～书 read; study
【念叨】 niàn·dao 1.（不停地说）talk about again and again in recollection or anticipation; be always talking about 2.（谈论）talk over; discuss
【念佛】 niànfó pray to Buddha; say "Amitabha"; say "Namas Amithabha"
【念经】 niànjīng recite or chant scriptures
【念旧】 niànjiù 1.（不忘旧日友谊）keep old friendships in mind 2.（怀念旧时光）for old time's sake
【念念不忘】 niànniàn-bùwàng bear in mind constantly
【念念有词】 niànniàn-yǒucí 1.（念咒）mutter incantations 2.（咕哝）mumble
【念青唐古拉山】 Niànqīngtánggǔlāshān 〈place〉 Nyainqentanglha Shan
【念书】 niànshū 1.（看着书读）read a book 2.（上学）study (in school); go to school
【念诵】 niànsòng recite; read aloud
【念头】 niàn·tou thought; idea; intention：忽然想到一个～ hit upon an idea
【念物】 niànwù souvenir
【念珠】 niànzhū beads; rosary

niang

娘［孃］(niáng) 1.（母亲）ma; mum; mother 2.（大娘）aunt 3.（年轻妇女）a young woman
【娘家】 niáng·jia the wife's family; the wife's parents' home
【娘娘】 niáng·niang 1.（皇后）empress 2.（妃子）imperial concubine 3.（女神）goddess
【娘子军】 niáng·zǐjūn detachment of women

酿［釀］(niàng) 1.（酿造）make wine; brew beer 2.（蜜蜂做蜜）make honey：～蜜 make honey 3.（逐渐形成）lead to; result in 4.（酒）wine
【酿成】 niàngchéng lead to; bring on; breed：～巨祸 bring about a great calamity / ～争端 breed strife
【酿祸】 niànghuò create trouble; ferment disturbances
【酿酒】 niàngjiǔ make wine; brew beer
【酿酒厂】 niàngjiǔchǎng winery; brewery
【酿酒业】 niàngjiǔyè wine-making industry
【酿酶】 niàngméi zymase
【酿造】 niàngzào make; brew：这种啤酒是用传统的方法～的。This beer has been brewed using traditional methods.
【酿造厂】 niàngzàochǎng winery; brewery

niao

鸟［鳥］(niǎo) bird：候～ migratory birds; birds of passage / 留～ resident birds / 雏～ young bird; birdie; nestling
【鸟粪】 niǎofèn 1.（鸟的粪）birds' droppings 2.（海鸟粪）guano
【鸟尽弓藏】 niǎojìn-gōngcáng cast sb. aside when he has served his purpose
【鸟瞰】 niáokàn 1.（从高处往下看）get a bird's eye view 2.（概括描写）general survey of a subject
【鸟类】 niǎolèi birds
【鸟笼】 niǎolóng birdcage
【鸟枪】 niǎoqiāng 1.（火枪）fowling piece 2.（气枪）airgun; shotgun
【鸟食】 niǎoshí birdseed
【鸟兽】 niǎoshòu birds and beasts; fur and feather
【鸟兽散】 niǎoshòusàn scatter like birds and beasts
【鸟葬】 niǎozàng celestial burial
【鸟嘴】 niǎozuǐ beak; bill

袅［嫋、嬝］(niǎo) slender and delicate
【袅袅】 niǎoniǎo 1.（缭绕上升）curl upwards 2.（随风摆动）wave in the wind：晨风中垂柳～。The drooping willows are waving gently in the morning breeze. 3.（延长不绝）linger
【袅袅婷婷】 niǎoniǎo-tíngtíng curvaceous and soft; lissome and graceful

【袅娜】 niǎonuó slender and graceful; willowy

尿(niào) 1.(人或动物尿) urine; uric (adj.) 2.(撒尿) urinate; make water; pass water; piss
(另见"尿"suī)

【尿布】 niàobù diaper; napkin
【尿床】 niàochuáng wet the bed; bed-wetting
【尿道】 niàodào 〈*Anat.*〉 urethra
【尿道炎】 niàodàoyán 〈*Med.*〉 urethritis
【尿毒症】 niàodúzhèng 〈*Med.*〉 uremia
【尿肥】 niàoféi 〈*Agric.*〉 urine
【尿路感染】 niàolù gǎnrǎn 〈*Med.*〉 urinary tract infections
【尿尿】 niàoniào piss
【尿盆】 niàopén chamber pot; urinal
【尿频】 niàopín 〈*Med.*〉 frequent micturition
【尿失禁】 niàoshījìn 〈*Med.*〉 urinary incontinence
【尿素】 niàosù 〈*Chem.*〉 urea; carbamide
【尿酸】 niàosuān 〈*Chem.*〉 uric acid; uric (adj.)
【尿尿】 niàosuī piss
【尿桶】 niàotǒng wooden pail for urine
【尿血】 niàoxiě 〈*Med.*〉 hematuria
【尿样】 niàoyàng 〈*Med.*〉 urine sample: 给出～ give a urine sample

脲(niào) 〈*Chem.*〉 urea; carbamide

nie

捏[揑](niē) 1.(握;捏) hold between the fingers; pinch: ～住一枚别针 hold a pin with one's fingers 2.(揉捏) mold; knead 3.(捏造) fabricate; make up

【捏估】 niē·gu 1.(私下商量) discuss in private 2.(使合到一起) mediate; act as a go-between
【捏合】 niēhé mediate; act as go-between
【捏弄】 niēnòng 1.(揉捏) play with; fiddle with 2.(摆布) manipulate 3.(私下商量) discuss in private 4.(捏造) fabricate; concoct
【捏一把汗】 niē yībǎhàn catch one's breath; hold one's breath
【捏造】 niēzào fabricate; concoct; fake; trump up: ～案情陷害某人 frame a case against sb.

涅(niè)

【涅白】 nièbái opaque white
【涅磐】 nièpán 〈*Buddhism*〉 nirvana

嗫[囁](niè)

【嗫嚅】 nièrú speak hesitatively

镊[鑷](niè)

【镊子】 niè·zi tweezers

颞[顳](niè)

【颞骨】 niègǔ 〈*Anat.*〉 temporal bone
【颞颥】 nièrú 〈*Anat.*〉 temple

蹑[躡](niè) 1.(放轻脚步) lighten one's step; walk on tiptoe 2.(追随) tread; step on; walk with

【蹑手蹑脚】 nièshǒu-nièjiǎo walk gingerly; walk on tiptoe
【蹑踪】 nièzōng follow along behind sb.; track
【蹑足】 nièzú 1.(放轻脚步走) walk on tiptoe 2.(插足) join; associate with
【蹑足其间】 nièzúqíjiān join a trade; associate with

镍(niè)〈*Chem.*〉 nickel (元素符号 Ni) ～钢 nickel steel

【镍币】 nièbì nickel coin; nickel

啮[齧、囓](niè) 〈*written*〉 gnaw

【啮齿动物】 nièchǐ dòngwù rodent
【啮合】 nièhé 1.(上下牙咬紧) clench the teeth 2.(像牙齿那样咬合) mesh; engage: 两个齿轮～。The two cogwheels engage.
【啮合齿轮】 nièhé chǐlún meshing gear

孽[孼](niè) evil; sin: 造(作)～ do evil; commit a sin

【孽根】 niègēn sinful cause; original sin
【孽海】 nièhǎi the sea of degradation
【孽障】 nièzhàng evil creature; vile spawn
【孽种】 nièzhǒng 1.(祸根) sinful cause 2.(孽障) evil creature; vile spawn

蘖(niè) tiller

【蘖枝】 nièzhī 〈*Bot.*〉 tiller; shoot of plant

nin

您(nín) 〈*politeness*〉 you; your

ning

宁[寧、甯](níng) peaceful; tranquil
(另见"宁"nìng)
【宁静】 níngjìng peaceful; tranquil; quiet: ～的小镇 a quiet little town / 拂晓前的～ the still hours before dawn
【宁人息事】 níngrén-xīshì pacify people and settle matters
【宁日】 níngrì peaceful day

拧[擰](níng) 1.(扭绞) twist; wring: ～毛巾 twist a towel 2.(捏) pinch; tweak: ～了她一下 give her a pinch
(另见"拧"nǐng, nìng)
【拧眉瞪眼】 níngméi-dèngyǎn raise one's eyebrows and stare in anger

狞[獰](níng) ferocious; hideous
【狞笑】 níngxiào grin hideously

柠[檸](níng)
【柠檬】 níngméng lemon
【柠檬茶】 níngméngchá lemon tea
【柠檬色】 níngméngsè lemon yellow
【柠檬水】 níngméngshuǐ lemonade; lemon squash
【柠檬酸】 níngméngsuān 〈*Chem*.〉 citric acid
【柠檬糖】 níngméngtáng lemon drops
【柠檬汁】 níngméngzhī lemon juice

凝(níng) 1.(凝结) congeal; curdle; coagulate 2.(注意力集中) with fixed attention
【凝冻】 níngdòng freeze: 湖水～得很结实，我们能到上面滑冰了。The lake had frozen hard, we can go skating on it.
【凝固】 nínggù 1.(由液体变成固体) solidify 2.(喻固定不变) standstill
【凝固点】 nínggùdiǎn solidifying point; freezing point
【凝固剂】 nínggùjì coagulant; coagulating agent
【凝固汽油】 nínggù qìyóu gelatinized gasoline
【凝固汽油弹】 nínggù qìyóudàn napalm bomb
【凝固热】 nínggùrè heat of solidification
【凝结】 níngjié 1.(气体变为液体) condense 2.(液体变为固体) coagulate; congeal 3.(结合) cement: ～成深厚的友谊 cement a profound friendship
【凝结剂】 níngjiéjì 〈*Chem*.〉 coagulant
【凝结力】 níngjiélì coagulability
【凝结器】 níngjiéqì condenser
【凝结物】 níngjiéwù coagulum
【凝聚】 níngjù 1.(凝结) condense; condensation (n.) 2.〈*Chem*.〉 coacerve; coacervation (n.) 3.(聚集) cohere; cohesion (n.)
【凝聚力】 níngjùlì 1.(内聚力) cohesion; cohesive force 2.(聚集到一起的力量) cohesion
【凝练】 níngliàn concise; condensed; compact
【凝眸而视】 níngmóuěrshì behold with fixed gazing; gaze fixedly at
【凝目】 níngmù gaze fixedly at
【凝神】 níngshén with fixed attention: ～思索 gaze fixedly and ponder
【凝视】 níngshì gaze fixedly; stare
【凝思】 níngsī be buried in thought; be deep in contemplation: ～默想 profounding and meditating
【凝想】 níngxiǎng be buried in thought; be deep in contemplation
【凝血药】 níngxuèyào 〈*Med*.〉 coagulant
【凝脂】 níngzhī congealed fat
【凝滞】 níngzhì stragnate; move stuggishly
【凝重】 níngzhòng 1.(庄重) dignified 2.(浑厚) deep and forceful 3.(浓重) deep; dense: ～的乌云 heavy black clouds

拧[擰](nǐng) 1.(旋转) twist; screw; wrench: ～断铁丝 twist off a piece of wire 2.(颠倒) wrong; mistaken: 全给弄～了。All is wrong. 3.(别扭) differ; disagree; be at cross-purposes
(另见"拧"níng, nìng)
【拧紧】 nǐngjǐn screw up; tighten
【拧松】 nǐngsōng screw off; unscrew

宁[寧、甯](nìng) rather; would rather; better: ～折不弯。It may break, but it will not bend.

(另见"宁"níng)

【宁可】 nìngkě would rather; better

【宁肯】 nìngkěn would rather

【宁缺毋滥】 nìngquē-wùlàn put quality before quantity; put quality first; fewer and better

【宁死不屈】 nìngsǐ-bùqū rather die than submit

【宁愿】 nìngyuàn would rather; better：我～待在家里。I would rather stay at home.

拧[擰] (nìng) obstinate; headstrong (另见"拧"níng, nǐng)

佞 (nìng)

【佞人】 nìngrén toady; sycophant; flatterer

【佞笑】 nìngxiào sinister smile

niu

妞 (niū) girl：小～ a girl; a young girl

【妞儿】 niūr girl：泡～ court girls

【妞子】 niū·zi girl; lass

牛 (niú) cattle：菜～ beef cattle / 纯种公～ pedigree bull / 公～ bull; ox / 母～ cow / 奶～ milk cow; dairy cattle / 水～ water buffalo / 小～ calf

【牛鼻子】 niúbí·zi 1.(牛的鼻子) the nose of an ox 2.(关键) key link：抓住提高企业素质的～ grasp the key link of raising the enterprise's quality

【牛车】 niúchē ox cart; bullock cart

【牛痘】 niúdòu 1.〈*Epizootio.*〉 cowpox; vaccinia 2.(豆状疱疹) smallpox pustule; vaccine pustule：种～ give or get smallpox vaccination

【牛痘苗】 niúdòumiáo bovine vaccine

【牛犊】 niúdú calf

【牛顿】 niúdùn 〈*Physics*〉 newton

【牛轭湖】 niú'èhú oxbow lake

【牛粪】 niúfèn cow excrement; shard

【牛鬼蛇神】 niúguǐ-shéshén evildoers of all description

【牛黄】 niúhuáng 〈*Chin. Pharm.*〉 bezoar

【牛角】 niújiǎo ox horn

【牛角尖】 niújiǎojiān the tip of a horn; an insoluble problem：钻～ split hairs

【牛角制品】 niújiǎo zhìpǐn horn-ware

【牛劲】 niújìn 1.(大力气) great strength; tremendous effort 2.(牛脾气) stubbornness; obstinacy; tenacity

【牛圈】 niújuàn cowshed

【牛郎星】 Niúlángxīng 〈*Astron.*〉 Altair (河鼓二,天鹰座 α)

【牛马】 niúmǎ oxen and horses; beasts of burden：当～ be a slave

【牛毛】 niúmáo ox hair：多如～ innumerable

【牛毛细雨】 niúmáo-xìyǔ drizzle; fine drizzling rain

【牛虻】 niúméng gadfly

【牛奶】 niúnǎi milk：鲜～ fresh milk

【牛奶场】 niúnǎichǎng dairy; dairy farm

【牛奶咖啡】 niúnǎi kāfēi white coffee

【牛排】 niúpái beefsteak

【牛棚】 niúpéng cowshed; ox fence

【牛皮】 niúpí 1.(牛的皮) cowhide; cattlehide; oxhide 2.(说大话) brag：吹～ talk big

【牛皮大王】 niúpí dàwáng braggart

【牛皮癣】 niúpíxuǎn 〈*Med.*〉 psoriasis

【牛皮纸】 niúpízhǐ kraft paper

【牛脾气】 niúpí·qi stubbornness; obstinacy

【牛气】 niú·qi self-conceit; pride; haughtiness

【牛肉】 niúròu beef：小～ veal

【牛市】 niúshì bullish market

【牛头不对马嘴】 niútóu bù duì mǎzuǐ incongruous; irrelevant

【牛蛙】 niúwā 〈*Zool.*〉 bullfrog

【牛瘟】 niúwēn rinderpest; cattle plague

【牛眼窗】 niúyǎnchuāng oeil-de-boeuf window

【牛饮】 niúyǐn drink heavily

【牛油】 niúyóu butter

【牛仔】 niúzǎi cowboy

【牛仔裤】 niúzǎikù jeans; blue jeans

扭 (niǔ) 1.(扭转) turn round：～过头去 turn about; turn round 2.(拧) twist; wrench：～开门 wrench the door open 3.(拧伤) sprain; wrench：～伤了手腕 sprain one's wrist 4.(走路时扭摆) roll; swing 5.(揪住) grapple with; grab; seize：两个摔跤的～在一起。The two wrestlers grappled together.

【扭摆】 niǔbǎi swing：一个酒鬼～着沿街走来。A drinker came swinging down the street.

【扭摆舞】 niǔbǎiwǔ twist：跳～ dance the twist
【扭打】 niǔdǎ wrestle；grapple
【扭干】 niǔgān wring dry
【扭结】 niǔjié twist together；tangle up
【扭亏为盈】 niǔkuī-wéiyíng turn loss into gain；turn form deficits to profits
【扭捏】 niǔ·nie unnatural；affected；pretentious
【扭扭捏捏】 niǔniǔ-niēniē unmanly in handling business
【扭曲】 niǔqū twisted；distorted
【扭伤】 niǔshāng sprain；wrench：～了腰 sprain one's back
【扭送】 niǔsòng seize and turn over；drag sb. off to：小偷被～到派出所了。The thief was seized and turned over to a police station.
【扭头】 niǔtóu turn about
【扭歪】 niǔwāi distort
【扭转】 niǔzhuǎn 1.（掉转）turn round；turn about 2.（纠正）turn back；reverse： ～社会风气 bring about a complete change in the general atmosphere in society as a whole

忸（niǔ）
【忸怩】 niǔní blushing；bashful

狃（niǔ） be bound by；be restricted by：～于成见 be blinded by prejudice／～于习俗 be bound by old customs

纽（niǔ） 1.（器物的把儿）handle；knob：门～ doorknob 2.（纽扣）button 3.（枢纽）bond；tie
【纽带】 niǔdài link；tie；bond：友谊的～ ties of friendship
【纽扣】 niǔkòu button
【纽襻】 niǔpàn button loop

钮（niǔ） 同"纽"

拗［抝］（niù） stubborn；obstinate；difficult：～不过某人 unable to dissuade sb.；unable to turn sb. away／脾气～ be of a stubborn temper
（另见"拗"ǎo，ào）

nong

农［農、辳］（nóng） 1.（农业）agriculture；farming 2.（农民）peasant；farmer：～户 peasant household
【农产品】 nóngchǎnpǐn agricultural products；farm produce
【农场】 nóngchǎng farm：国营～ state farm
【农村】 nóngcūn rural area；countryside；village
【农村城市化】 nóngcūn chéngshìhuà urbanization of villages
【农村电气化】 nóngcūn diànqìhuà electrification of the countryside
【农村集市】 nóngcūn jíshì village fair；rural market
【农村生活】 nóngcūn shēnghuó rural life
【农副产品】 nóngfù chǎnpǐn farm and sideline products
【农工】 nónggōng agricultural workers；farm workers
【农工联合企业】 nónggōng liánhé qǐyè agro-industrial complex
【农工商联合企业】 nónggōngshāng liánhé qǐyè integrated farm-industry-commerce enterprise
【农户】 nónghù peasant family；peasant household
【农活】 nónghuó farm work
【农机】 nóngjī agricultural machinery；farm machinery
【农机户】 nóngjīhù individual dealers of agricultural machines
【农家】 nóngjiā peasant family
【农家肥】 nóngjiāféi farm manure；farmyard manure
【农具】 nóngjù farm implements；farm tools
【农垦】 nóngkěn reclaim（wasteland）and cultivate（it）
【农历】 nónglì the lunar calendar
【农林牧副渔】 nóng-lín-mù-fù-yú farming, forestry, animal husbandry, side-line production and fishery
【农忙】 nóngmáng busy season；busy farming season
【农贸】 nóngmào county fair trade in farm and sideline products；farm and sideline product trade
【农贸公司】 nóngmào gōngsī rural firm
【农贸市场】 nóngmào shìchǎng rural trade market

【农民】 nóngmín peasant; peasantry
【农民起义】 nóngmín qǐyì peasant uprising
【农奴】 nóngnú serf
【农奴制度】 nóngnú zhìdù serfdom; serf system
【农奴主】 nóngnúzhǔ serf owner
【农人】 nóngrén farmer; peasant
【农舍】 nóngshè farmhouse
【农时】 nóngshí farming season
【农事】 nóngshì farm work; farming
【农田】 nóngtián farmland; cropland; cultivated land
【农田基本建设】 nóngtián jīběn jiànshè capital construction on farm-land; farmland capital construction
【农田水利建设】 nóngtián shuǐlì jiànshè construction of water conservancy works
【农闲】 nóngxián slack season
【农学】 nóngxué agronomy; agriculture
【农学家】 nóngxuéjiā agronomist
【农谚】 nóngyàn farmer's proverb; farmer's saying
【农药】 nóngyào agricultural chemical; farm chemical; pesticide
【农业】 nóngyè agriculture; farming; agricultural (adj.)
【农业保险】 nóngyè bǎoxiǎn agricultural insurance
【农业车间】 nóngyè chējiān agricultural workshop; base of production and supply of agricultural and sideline products
【农业贷款】 nóngyè dàikuǎn agricultural credit
【农业工人】 nóngyè gōngrén agricultural laborer; farm laborer; farm worker
【农业国】 nóngyèguó an agricultural country
【农业机械】 nóngyè jīxiè farm machinery; agricultural machinery
【农业机械化】 nóngyè jīxièhuà agricultural mechanization
【农业技术】 nóngyè jìshù agricultural technology
【农业经济】 nóngyè jīngjì agricultural economy
【农业科学】 nóngyè kéxué agricultural sciences
【农业气象学】 nóngyè qìxiàngxué agricultural meteorology
【农业人口】 nóngyè rénkǒu agricultural population
【农业税】 nóngyèshuì agricultural tax
【农业生态学】 nóngyè shēngtàixué agroecology
【农业现代化】 nóngyè xiàndàihuà modernization of agriculture; agricultural modernization
【农业信贷】 nóngyè xìndài agricultural credit
【农业一体化】 nóngyè yītǐhuà agricultural integration
【农业中学】 nóngyè zhōngxué agricultural school
【农业综合企业】 nóngyè zónghé qǐyè agribusiness
【农艺师】 nóngyìshī agronomist
【农艺学】 nóngyìxué agronomy
【农用】 nóngyòng agricultural
【农运会】 nóngyùnhuì the peasants' game
【农转非】 nóngzhuǎnfēi change one's rural residence to urban residence
【农庄】 nóngzhuāng farmstead
【农资】 nóngzī means of agricultural production
【农作物】 nóngzuòwù crops

哝［噥］(nóng)
【哝哝】 nóng·nong talk in a quiet voice; murmur

浓［濃］(nóng) 1.（稠密）dense; thick; concentrated: ～雾 dense fog / ～烟 dense smoke; thick smoke 2.（味道厚）strong; rich 3.（程度深）great; keen: 对此兴趣不～ take not much interest in it
【浓度】 nóngdù consistency; concentration; density
【浓厚】 nónghòu 1.（很浓）dense; thick 2.（浓重）deep; strong; pronounced: ～的民族色彩 strong national color 3.（程度深）strong: 兴趣～ with keen interest
【浓积云】 nóngjíyún 〈*Meteorol*.〉 cumular congestus
【浓烈】 nóngliè strong; heavy
【浓眉】 nóngméi heavy eyebrows; thick eyebrows
【浓密】 nóngmì dense; thick: ～相宜 proper distribution (of trees in painting)
【浓缩】 nóngsuō concentrate; enrich

【浓缩果汁】 nóngsuō guǒzhī inspissated juice
【浓缩剂】 nóngsuōjì concentrating agents
【浓缩物】 nóngsuōwù concentrate
【浓缩铀】 nóngsuōyóu enriched uranium
【浓汤】 nóngtāng thick soup
【浓雾】 nóngwù thick fog
【浓艳】 nóngyàn rich and gaudy
【浓郁】 nóngyù rich; strong: ～的香味 rich fragrance
【浓云】 nóngyún heavy clouds
【浓妆艳抹】 nóngzhuāng-yànmǒ wear heavy make up

脓［膿］(nóng) pus: 化～ suppurate; suppuration / 流～ run with pus
【脓包】 nóngbāo 1.〈*Med*.〉pustule 2.(无用的人) worthless fellow; good-for-nothing
【脓疮】 nóngchuāng running sore
【脓肿】 nóngzhǒng 〈*Med*.〉abscess

弄(nòng) 1.(戏耍) play with; fool with; trifle with: 小孩爱～水。Children like to play with water. 2.(做;干) do; make; handle: 我替你～吧。Let me do it for you. 3.(设法取得) get; fetch: 去～点酒来。Go and get some drink. 4.(玩弄) play
(另见"弄"lòng)
【弄潮儿】 nòngcháor a seaman; a beach swimmer
【弄错】 nòngcuò make a mistake; misunderstand
【弄饭】 nòngfàn prepare a meal
【弄鬼】 nòngguǐ hatch plots; play tricks behind the scene
【弄好】 nònghǎo get sth. done: 你能把我的自行车～吗? Can you get my bicycle fixed?
【弄坏】 nònghuài ruin; put out of order; make a mess of: 把事情～ make a mess of things
【弄假成真】 nòngjiǎ-chéngzhēn pretense may become reality
【弄僵】 nòngjiāng bring to a deadlock; deadlock
【弄巧成拙】 nòngqiǎo-chéngzhuō suffer from being too smart; outsmart oneself
【弄清】 nòngqīng make clear; clarify; gain a clear idea of; understand fully: ～事实真相 clarify the facts
【弄权】 nòngquán manipulate power for personal ends
【弄死】 nòngsǐ put to death; kill
【弄通】 nòngtōng get a good grasp of
【弄虚作假】 nòngxū-zuòjiǎ practice fraud; employ trickery; resort to deception
【弄脏】 nòngzāng stain; soil; pollute; smudge; smear
【弄糟】 nòngzāo make a mess of; mess up; bungle; spoil: 你把事情～了。You have spoiled the whole thing.

nu

奴(nú) 1.(受奴役的人) slave; bondservant 2.(奴役) enslave
【奴才】 nú·cai flunkey; lackey
【奴化】 núhuà enslave: ～教育 enslaving education
【奴隶】 núlì slave
【奴隶起义】 núlì qǐyì slave uprising
【奴隶社会】 núlì shèhuì slave society
【奴隶主】 núlìzhǔ slave owner; slaveholder
【奴隶主义】 núlì zhǔyì slavishness; slavish mentality
【奴仆】 núpú servant; lackey
【奴性】 núxìng servility; slavishness
【奴颜婢膝】 núyán-bìxī subservient; servile
【奴役】 núyì enslave; keep in bondage

努［抝²、呶、噜］(nǔ) 1.(使出) put forth; exert 2.(凸出) protrude; bulge: ～着嘴 protrude one's lips 3.(用力太过而使身体受伤) injure oneself through overexertion
【努力】 nǔlì make great efforts; try hard; exert oneself: ～不懈 strive without cease
【努嘴】 nǔzuǐ pout one's lips as a signal

弩(nǔ) crossbow
【弩弓】 nǔgōng crossbow
【弩箭】 nǔjiàn arrow

怒(nù) 1.(愤怒) anger; rage; fury: 大～ in great anger 2.(形容 气势很盛) in profusion; burst: 心花～放 be beside oneself with joy; be highly delighted; be exceedingly happy
【怒不可遏】 nùbùkě'è be beside oneself with anger; boil with rage

【怒潮】 nùcháo 1.(汹涌的浪潮) angry tide; raging tide 2.〈*Geog*.〉 bore
【怒叱】 nùchì angrily rebuke
【怒斥】 nùchì indignantly denounce; angrily rebuke
【怒冲冲】 nùchōngchōng in a rage; furiously
【怒发冲冠】 nùfà-chōngguān bristle with anger; be in a towering rage
【怒放】 nùfàng in full bloom: 百花～。Hundreds of flowers are blooming in profusion.
【怒号】 nùháo roar; howl
【怒吼】 nùhǒu roar; howl; bellow
【怒火】 nùhuǒ flames of fury; fury
【怒骂】 nùmà curse in rage
【怒目】 nùmù glaring eyes; fierce stare
【怒气】 nùqì anger; rage; fury: ～冲冲 boil with indignation
【怒容】 nùróng an angry look
【怒视】 nùshì glare at; glower at; scowl at
【怒涛】 nùtāo furious billows; mountainous sea
【怒族】 Nùzú Nu (中国少数民族,主要分布在云南)

nu

女 (nǚ) 1.(女子) woman; female: ～歌手 songstress / ～医生 woman doctor 2.(女儿) daughter; girl: 独生～ one's only daughter
【女扮男装】 nǚbàn-nánzhuāng a woman disguised as a man
【女厕所】 nǚcèsuǒ Ladies; Women; women's lavatory; ladies room
【女场记员】 nǚ chǎngjìyuán 〈*Cinematog*.〉 script girl
【女超人】 nǚcháorén superwoman
【女车】 nǚchē lady's bike; woman's bike; lady's bicycle
【女衬衫】 nǚchènshān blouse
【女儿】 nǚ'ér daughter; girl
【女方】 nǚfāng the bride's side; the wife's side
【女飞行员】 nǚfēixíngyuán female pilot; aviatrix
【女服务员】 nǚfúwùyuán 1.(飞机上的) air hostess; stewardess 2.(餐馆的) waitress
【女高音】 nǚgāoyīn 〈*Music*〉 soprano
【女工】 nǚgōng woman worker
【女孩】 nǚhái girl
【女皇】 nǚhuáng empress
【女将】 nǚjiàng able woman; strong woman
【女眷】 nǚjuàn the womenfolk of a family
【女郎】 nǚláng young woman; maiden; girl: 封面～ cover girl
【女帽】 nǚmào bonnet
【女秘书】 nǚmìshū female secretary
【女强人】 nǚqiángrén powerful woman
【女权】 nǚquán women's rights
【女权主义】 nǚquán zhǔyì feminism; feminist (adj.)
【女人】 nǚrén 1.(女性) woman 2.(妻子) wife
【女色】 nǚsè woman's charms: 好～ be fond of women
【女神】 nǚshén goddess
【女生】 nǚshēng woman student; schoolgirl; girl student
【女声】 nǚshēng 〈*Music*〉 female voice
【女声合唱】 nǚshēng héchàng women's chorus; female chorus
【女士】 nǚshì lady
【女售货员】 nǚshòuhuòyuán saleswoman; shopgirl
【女睡衣】 nǚshuìyī nightdress
【女王】 nǚwáng queen
【女校友】 nǚxiàoyǒu alumna
【女性】 nǚxìng 1.(性别) the female sex 2.(妇女) woman
【女性同性恋】 nǚxìng tóngxìngliàn lesbianism; sapphism
【女修道院】 nǚxiūdàoyuàn convent
【女婿】 nǚ·xu son-in-law
【女演员】 nǚyǎnyuán actress
【女英雄】 nǚyīngxióng heroine
【女友】 nǚyǒu girl friend
【女招待】 nǚzhāodài waitress; girl
【女中音】 nǚzhōngyīn 〈*Music*〉 mezzo-soprano
【女主角】 nǚzhǔjué feminine lead; leading lady; 〈*Cinematog*.〉 actress
【女主人】 nǚzhǔ·ren hostess; woman of the house
【女主人公】 nǚzhǔréngōng heroine
【女装】 nǚzhuāng women's costume
【女装店】 nǚzhuāngdiàn dress shop

【女子】 nǚzǐ woman; female
【女子单打】 nǚzǐ dāndǎ women's singles
【女子双打】 nǚzǐ shuāngdǎ women's doubles
【女子团体赛】 nǚzǐ tuántǐsài women's team event
【女子学校】 nǚzǐ xuéxiào girl's school
【女子足球】 nǚzǐ zúqiú women's football game

钕 (nǚ) 〈*Chem*.〉 neodymium (元素符号 Nd)

nuan

暖[煖、焕、暝] (nuǎn) 1.(暖和) warm; genial 2.(使温暖) warm up: 烤火取～ warm oneself at fire / 烤火～～手 warm one's hands by the fire
【暖房】 nuǎnfáng greenhouse; hothouse
【暖风机】 nuǎnfēngjī electric fan heater
【暖锋】 nuǎnfēng 〈*Meteorol*.〉 warm front
【暖烘烘】 nuǎnhōnghōng nice and warm
【暖壶】 nuǎnhú 1.(热水瓶) thermos flask; thermos bottle 2.(汤壶) hotwater bottle
【暖和】 nuǎn·huo 1.(气候不冷) warm; nice and warm: 天气～了。It's getting warm. 2.(使暖和) warm up: 进屋来,到火旁边～～吧。Come in and warm yourself up near the fire.
【暖流】 nuǎnliú 〈*Geol*. & *Meteorol*.〉 warm current
【暖气】 nuǎnqì central heating
【暖气片】 nuǎnqìpiàn (heating) radiator
【暖气装置】 nuǎnqì zhuāngzhì heating installation
【暖融融】 nuǎnróngróng nice and warm
【暖色】 nuǎnsè warm color
【暖水瓶】 nuǎnshuǐpíng thermos flask; thermos bottle
【暖洋洋】 nuǎnyángyáng warm; warmful

nue

疟[瘧] (nüè) malaria
【疟疾】 nüè·ji malaria; ague
【疟蚊】 nüèwén malarial mosquito
【疟原虫】 nüèyuánchóng malarial parasite

虐 (nüè) cruel; tyrannical
【虐待】 nüèdài maltreat; ill-treat
【虐杀】 nüèshā kill sb. with maltreatment

nuo

挪 (nuó) move; shift
【挪动】 nuó·dong move; shift
【挪借】 nuójiè borrow money for a short time; get a short-term loan
【挪开】 nuókāi move away
【挪移】 nuóyí 1.(挪借) borrow money for a short time 2.(挪动) move
【挪用】 nuóyòng 1.(把钱移作别用) divert 2.(私自动用) misappropriate; embezzle: ～公款 misappropriate public funds

诺 (nuò) 1.(许诺) promise; assent; nod 2.(答应的声音) yes; yep
【诺贝尔奖金】 Nuòbèiěr jiǎngjīn Nobel Prize
【诺贝尔奖金获得者】 Nuòbèiěr jiǎngjīn huòdézhě Nobelist
【诺亚方舟】 Nuòyà fángzhóu Noah's ark
【诺言】 nuòyán promise: 守～ keep promises / 违背～ break promises

锘 (nuò) 〈*Chem*.〉 nobelium (人造元素,符号 No)

懦 (nuò) cowardly; weak
【懦夫】 nuòfū coward; craven; weakling
【懦怯】 nuòquè cowardly
【懦弱】 nuòruò cowardly; weak: 性格～ be weak in character

糯[稬、稬] (nuò) glutinous
【糯米】 nuòmǐ polished glutinous rice

O

ou

讴[謳]（ōu） 1.（歌唱）sing 2.（民歌）folk songs; ballads

【讴歌】 ōugē sing the praises of; celebrate in song; eulogize

欧[歐]（ōu） Europe; European

【欧安会】 Ōu'ānhuì the Security and Cooperation Conference of Europe

【欧化】 ōuhuà Europeanize; westernize

【欧几里得几何】 Ōujǐlǐdé jǐhé 〈*Math*.〉 Euclidean geometry

【欧美】 Ōu-Měi Europe and America; Western; the West

【欧姆】 ōumǔ 〈*Electr*.〉 ohm

【欧姆表】 ōumǔbiǎo 〈*Electr*.〉 ohmmeter

【欧佩克】 Ōupèikè Organization of Petroleum Exporting Countries; OPEC（石油输出国组织）

【欧氏管】 ōushìguǎn 〈*Anat*.〉（咽鼓管）eustachian tube

【欧亚大陆】 Ōu-Yà dàlù Eurasia; Euroasian (adj.)

【欧元】 Ōuyuán Euro

【欧洲】 Ōuzhōu Europe; European (adj.)

【欧洲共同市场】 Ōuzhōu Gòngtóng Shìchǎng Euromarket; European Common Market

【欧洲货币】 Ōuzhōu huòbì Euro-currency

【欧洲货币联盟】 Ōuzhōu huòbì liánméng the European Monetary System

【欧洲经济共同体】 Ōuzhōu jīngjì gòngtóngtǐ the European Economic Community (E. E. C.)

【欧洲经济共同体官员】 Ōuzhōu jīngjì gòngtóngtǐ guānyuán Eurocrat

【欧洲美元】 Ōuzhōu měiyuán Eurodollar

【欧洲议会】 Ōuzhōu yìhuì European Parliament

【欧洲议会议员】 Ōuzhōu yìhuì yìyuán Euro-MP; Member of the European Parliament

【欧洲自由贸易联盟】 Ōuzhōu zìyóu màoyì liánméng European Free Trade Association (EFTA)

殴[毆]（ōu） beat up; hit：～伤 beat and injure

【殴打】 ōudǎ beat up; hit

鸥[鷗]（ōu） gull：海～ sea gull

呕[嘔]（ǒu） vomit; throw up

【呕吐】 ǒutù vomit; throw up; be sick

【呕心沥血】 ǒuxīn-lìxuè shed one's heart's blood; take infinite pains; work one's heart out

【呕血】 ǒuxuè 1.〈*Med*.〉 hematemesis 2.（吐血）spill blood; spit up blood

偶（ǒu） 1.（木雕或泥塑人像）image; idol：木～ puppet 2.（双数）even; in pairs 3.（配偶）mate; spouse 4.（偶然）by chance; by accident; once in a while; occasionally：～遇 meet by chance

【偶氮染料】 ǒudàn-rǎnliào 〈*Chem*.〉 azo dye

【偶尔】 ǒu'ěr once in a while; occasionally

【偶发】 ǒufā accidental; chance; fortuitous：～事件 a chance occurrence

【偶合】 ǒuhé coincidence

【偶或】 ǒuhuò occasionally

【偶然】 ǒurán accidental; fortuitous; chance：～误差 accidental error

【偶然性】 ǒuránxìng contingency; fortuity; chance

【偶生成本】 ǒushēng chéngběn non-recurring cost

【偶生收益】 ǒushēng shōuyì non-recurring income

【偶数】 ǒushù 〈*Math*.〉 even number

【偶数页】 ǒushùyè even page

【偶蹄动物】 ǒutí dòngwù artiodactyl

【偶像】 ǒuxiàng idol; image

【偶像崇拜】 ǒuxiàng chóngbài idolatry ‖ 偶像崇拜者 idolater

【偶像化】 ǒuxiànghuà idolize

耦（ǒu）

【耦合】 ǒuhé 〈*Physics*〉 coupling

藕[蕅]（ǒu） lotus root

【藕断丝连】 ǒuduàn-sīlián the lotus root snaps but its fibers stay joined; apparently severed, actually still connected

【藕粉】 ǒufěn lotus root starch

【藕荷】 ǒuhé pale pinkish purple

【藕灰】 ǒuhuī pale pinkish grey

【藕色】 ǒusè pale pinkish grey

怄［慪］（òu） 1.（使怄气）irritate; annoy 2.（怄气）be irritated

【怄气】 òuqì be difficult and sulky

沤［漚］（òu） soak; steep; macerate: ～麻 ret hemp

【沤肥】 òuféi 1.（沤成肥料）make compost 2.（沤成的肥料）wet compost; waterlogged compost

P

pa

趴(pā) 1.(脸朝下卧倒) lie on one's stomach; lie prone; lie prostrate: ～下 lie down / ～在地上 lie on the ground 2.(身体向前靠) bend over; lean over; lean on: ～在桌上 lean over a desk

派(pā)
(另见"派"pài)

【派司】 pā·si 1.(通行证) pass 2.(准予通过) pass; allow sb. to pass

啪(pā) 〈*onomat.*〉 bang

【啪嚓】 pāchā 〈*onomat.*〉 crash

葩(pā) flower: 奇～ exotic flower

扒(pá) 1.(用手或耙子搂) gather up; rake up; rake together: 把干草～在一起 rake together the hay 2.(煨烂) stew; braise: ～鸡 stewed chicken
(另见"扒"bā)

【扒灰】 páhuī 同"爬灰"

【扒窃】 páqiè pick sb's pocket; steal things out of pockets

【扒手】 páshǒu pickpocket; shoplifter: 留神～! Beware pickpockets!

爬(pá) 1.(爬行) crawl; creep: 婴儿向他母亲～去。The baby crawled towards his mother. / 树上～了虫子。The tree is crawling with worms. 2.(攀登) climb; clamber; scramble: ～山 climb a mountain / ～绳 climb a rope / ～树 climb a tree

【爬竿】 págān 1.〈*Sports*〉 pole-climbing 2.(所爬的竿) climbing pole

【爬高】 págāo climb; ascent

【爬格子】 págé·zi working on squared papers

【爬灰】 páhuī commit incest with one's daughter-in-law

【爬犁】 pá·li sledge; sleigh

【爬坡】 pápō climb a mountain slope: 朝着建立外向型经济奋力～ be doing their best in establishing their export-oriented economy

【爬墙虎】 páqiánghǔ 〈*Bot.*〉 同"爬藤榕"

【爬山虎】 páshānhǔ 〈*Bot.*〉 creeper; Boston ivy

【爬上】 páshàng climb up: ～山 climb up the hill / ～树 climb up the tree / ～河堤 climb up to the top of the dike

【爬升】 páshēng climb

【爬绳】 páshéng 1.〈*Sports*〉 rope climbing 2.(所爬的绳) climbing rope

【爬藤榕】 páténgróng 〈*Bot.*〉 Martin fig

【爬梯】 pátī rope ladder

【爬行】 páxíng crawl; creep

【爬行动物】 páxíng dòngwù reptile; creeper

【爬泳】 páyǒng 〈*Sports*〉 the crawl; crawl stroke

耙[钯](pá) 1.(耙子) rake: 钉～ an iron rake 2.(耙平;耙拢) rake; make smooth with a rake
(另见"耙"bà)

【耙网】 páwǎng scraper

【耙子】 pá·zi rake

帕(pà) 1.(手帕) handkerchief: 手～ handkerchief 2.〈*Physics*〉 Pascal (符号为: P; Pa)

【帕金森氏病】 Pàjīnsēnshìbìng 〈*Med.*〉 Parkinson's disease

【帕米尔】 Pàmǐ'ěr 〈place〉 Pamir

【帕斯卡】 pàsīkǎ 〈*Physics*〉 Pascal (符号为: P, Pa)

怕(pà) 1.(害怕) fear; dread; be afraid of: ～负责任 be afraid of shouldering responsibility / ～伤了和气 be afraid of hurting people's feelings 2.(估计) I'm afraid; I suppose; perhaps: 会议～要延期了。I'm afraid the meeting will be postponed. 3.（担心）be afraid of; for fear; fear lest: 她～把孩子吵醒。She was afraid of waking the child.

【怕前怕后】 pàqián-pàhòu timid and apprehensive of everything

【怕人】 pàrén 1.（见人害怕）shy; timid 2.（可怕）terrible; terrific; awful

【怕生】 pàshēng （of a child）be shy with strangers

【怕事】 pàshì be afraid of getting into trouble; be afraid of being involved

【怕死】 pàsǐ fear death; be afraid of death

【怕羞】 pàxiū coy; shy; bashful: 这女孩～。The girl is shy.

pai

拍（pāi） 1.（拍打）clap; pat; beat; slap: ～手 clap one's hands / ～掉衣服上的灰尘 beat the dust off one's clothes 2.（球拍）bat; racket: 网球～ tennis racket 3.〈*Music*〉beat; time: 一小节四～ four beats in a bar 4.（拍摄）take（a picture）; shoot: ～电影 make a film 5.（拍发）send: ～电报 send a telegram 6.（拍马屁）flatter; fawn on: 能吹会～ be good at boasting and toadying

【拍案】 pāi'àn strike the table: ～叫绝 express admiration by thumping the table

【拍板】 pāibǎn 1.〈*Music*〉clappers 2.（打拍板）beat time with clappers 3.〈*Trade*〉rap the gavel deal 4.（做出决定）have the final say; give the final verdict 5.〈*Cinematog.*〉clapper

【拍打】 pāi·da 1.（轻轻地打）pat; beat; slap 2.（扇动翅膀）flap: ～翅膀 flap the wings

【拍档】 pāidàng partner

【拍发】 pāifā send: ～电报 send a telegram

【拍花】 pāihuā kidnap children by narcotics

【拍马】 pāimǎ flatter; fawn on

【拍马屁】 pāimǎpì lick sb's boots; flatter; fawn on

【拍卖】 pāimài 1.（拍卖）auction; sell sth. at auction: 他把他的邮票～了。He auctioned off his stamps. 2.（甩卖）sale; selling off goods at reduced prices

【拍卖锤】 pāimàichuí gavel

【拍卖行】 pāimàiháng auctioneer's

【拍卖价格】 pāimài jiàgé auction price

【拍卖人】 pāimàirén auctioneer

【拍卖商】 pāimàishāng auctioneer

【拍摄】 pāishè take（a picture）; shoot: ～照片 take photo

【拍手】 pāishǒu clap one's hands; applaud: ～称快 express one's joy by clapping hands

【拍胸脯】 pāi xiōngpú pat one's chest to show confidence（of a challenge or responsibility）

【拍照】 pāizhào take a picture; photograph: 为别人～ take a picture of sb. / 请别人为自己～ get one's photo taken

【拍纸簿】 pāizhǐbù pad; notepad

【拍子】 pāi·zi 1.（球拍）bat; racket 2.〈*Music*〉beat; time: 打～ beat time

俳（pái） farce; comic performance

【俳句】 páijù haiku（Jap.）

排（pái） 1.（排列）arrange; put in order: ～节目单 arrange the program 2.（排成的行列）row; line; rank: 坐在后～ sit in the back row 3.〈*Mil.*〉platoon 4.（排演）rehearse 5.（竹排；木排）raft 6.（排除）exclude; eject; discharge 7.（馅饼）pie: 苹果～ apple pie 8.（西餐）chop; rib: 牛～ beef chop / 羊～ lamb chop / 猪～ pork chop

【排版】 páibǎn composing; typesetting

【排比】 páibǐ parallelism

【排笔】 páibǐ broad brush comprising a row of penshaped brushes

【排场】 páichǎng ostentation and extravagance: 讲～ go in favor for ostentation and extravagance

【排斥】 páichì repel; exclude; reject: ～异己 exclude outsiders; discriminate against those who hold different views

【排出】 páichū discharge; exhaust; transpiration

【排除】 páichú get rid of; remove; eliminate: ～万难 surmount all difficulties

【排除法】 páichúfǎ exclusive method

【排挡】 páidǎng gear: 这部车有5个～。This is a car with five gears.

【排档】 páidàng 〈*dial.*〉stand; booth

【排队】 páiduì form a line; line up; queue

up：～等公共汽车 queue for the bus

【排放】 páifàng emit; emission (n.)

【排放管】 páifàngguǎn delivery pipe

【排风扇】 páifēngshàn extractor fan

【排骨】 páigǔ spareribs; ribs

【排灌】 páiguàn irrigation and drainage

【排灌站】 páiguànzhàn irrigation and drainage pumping station

【排行】 páiháng seniority among brothers and sisters：她～第二。She is the second child.

【排行榜】 páihángbǎng the charts：在～上名列前茅的唱片 the records high up in the charts / 那张唱片在～上是第几名？What number did that record get to in the charts?

【排挤】 páijǐ push aside; push out; squeeze out; elbow out：～某人 push sb. aside

【排检】 páijiǎn list and index

【排解】 páijiě 1.（调解）mediate; reconcile; intervene 2.（排遣）divert oneself from; dispel

【排涝】 páilào drain flooded fields; drain waterlogged land

【排雷】 páiléi 〈*Mil.*〉removal of mines

【排练】 páiliàn rehearse：～节目 have a rehearsal

【排列】 páiliè 1.（按顺序放）arrange; range; put in order：按字母顺序～ arrange in alphabetical order / 把商品整齐地～在商店橱窗里 range the goods neatly on the shop window 2.〈*Math.*〉permutation：～和组合 permutations and combinations

【排卵】 páiluǎn ovulate; ovulation (n.)

【排卵期】 páiluǎnqī period of ovulation

【排名】 páimíng list names; number：他～第一。He's been number one.

【排难解纷】 páinàn-jiěfēn mediate a dispute; pour oil on troubled waters

【排尿】 páiniào urinate; urination (n.); micturate; micturition (n.)

【排尿困难】 páiniào kùn·nan 〈*Med.*〉dysuria; difficulty in urination

【排气】 páiqì 〈*Mech.*〉exhaust

【排气阀】 páiqìfá exhaust valve

【排气管】 páiqìguǎn 〈*Auto*〉tailpipe; exhaust (pipe)

【排气装置】 páiqì zhuāngzhì air exhausting device

【排遣】 páiqiǎn divert oneself from; distract one's mind from

【排球】 páiqiú 〈*Sports*〉volleyball：打～ play volleyball

【排球场】 páiqiúchǎng volleyball court

【排球赛】 páiqiúsài volleyball match

【排球网】 páiqiúwǎng volleyball net

【排球主攻手】 páiqiú zhǔgōngshǒu ace spiker

【排山倒海】 páishān-dǎohǎi topple the mountains and over-turn the seas; overwhelming or sweeping：以～之势 with the momentum of an avalanche

【排水】 páishuǐ drain off water; drain away water; dewater：开沟～ dig trenches to drain water off

【排水工程】 páishuǐ gōngchéng drainage works

【排水管】 páishuǐguǎn drain pipe

【排水量】 páishuǐliàng 1.（船舶的）displacement; delivery：～20万吨的油轮 a tanker of 200,000 tons displacement 2.（河流的）discharge capacity

【排闼】 páità push：～直入 push the door open and go straight in; break into room unceremoniously

【排坛】 páitán volleyball circle

【排外】 páiwài exclusive; antiforeign

【排泄】 páixiè 1.（排水）drain：～不畅 drainage difficulty 2.〈*Physiol.*〉excrete; excretion (n.)

【排泄器官】 páixiè qìguān excretory organ

【排泄物】 páixièwù excreta; excrement

【排泄系统】 páixiè xìtǒng excretory system

【排烟】 páiyān discharge fume

【排烟设备】 páiyān shèbèi fume extractor

【排演】 páiyǎn rehearse：～一出戏 rehearse a play

【排印】 páiyìn type and print; typesetting and printing

【排忧解难】 páiyōu-jiěnàn remove difficulties and danger and alleviate sufferings

【排长】 páizhǎng 〈*Mil.*〉platoon leader

【排字】 páizì compose; typeset; composing (n.)

【排字车间】 páizì chējiān composing room

【排字工人】 páizì gōngrén compositor; typesetter

徘 (pái)

【徘徊】 páihuái 1.(来回走) pace up and down; walk back and forth 2.(犹豫不决) hesitate; waver; hover 3.〈*Econ.*〉 fluctuate

【徘徊不前】 páihuáibùqián hesitate to press forward

牌 (pái) 1.(标志牌) plate; tablet; board; placard: 布告～ notice board / 车～ number plate on a vehicle 2.(商标) brand 3.(娱乐用品) cards; dominoes: 一副～ a deck of cards; a pack of cards / 打～ play cards; have a game of cards / 发～ deal the cards; deal the cards out / 洗～ shuffle the cards / 摊～ lay/put one's cards on the table

【牌匾】 páibiǎn board; tablet

【牌坊】 páifāng memorial archway; memorial gateway; honorific arch

【牌号】 páihào 1.(商店字号) the name of a shop; shop sign 2.(商标) trademark

【牌价】 páijià 1.(标出价格) list price 2.(市价) market quotation; prevailing price: 有利～ favorable rate

【牌九】 páijiǔ Chinese domino

【牌楼】 pái·lou 1.〈*Archit.*〉 pailou; decorative gateway; decorated archway 2.(临时搭的) temporary ceremonial gateway

【牌位】 páiwèi memorial tablet

【牌照】 páizhào license plate (AmE.); number plate (BrE.): 自行车～ bicycle number plate

【牌照灯】 páizhàodēng 〈*Auto*〉 license plate light; number plate light

【牌照税】 páizhàoshuì licence tax

【牌子】 pái·zi 1.(标志板) plate; sign 2.(商标) brand; trademark: 我们有各种最好～的酒。We have the best brands of wines.

迫[**廹**] (pǎi) (另见"迫"pò)

【迫击炮】 pǎijīpào mortar

派 (pài) 1.(派别) group; school; faction; clique 2.(作风;风度) style; manner and air 3.(派遣;委派) send; dispatch; assign; appoint: ～人出国留学 send people abroad for advanced study
(另见"派"pā)

【派别】 pàibié group; school; faction; factional (adj.): 进行～活动 engage in factional activity

【派出机构】 pàichū jīgòu agency

【派出所】 pàichūsuǒ police substation; local police station

【派饭】 pàifàn assigned meal

【派购】 pàigòu assigned purchase

【派力司】 pàilìsī 〈*Textiles*〉 palace

【派遣】 pàiqiǎn send; dispatch: ～代表团参加会议 send a delegation to the conference

【派遣期限】 pàiqiǎn qīxiàn term of service abroad

【派生】 pàishēng derive; derivation (n.); derivative (adj.)

【派生词】 pàishēngcí derivative

【派头】 pàitóu style; manner

【派系】 pàixì factions; clique; factional (adj.): ～斗争 factional dispute; factional struggle

【派驻】 pàizhù accredit: 大使是本国～外国的代表。An ambassador is accredited as the representative of his own country in a foreign land.

哌 (pài) 〈*Chem.*〉 piperazine

【哌嗪】 pàiqín 〈*Chem.*〉 piperazine

蒎 (pài) 〈*Chem.*〉 pinane

pan

攀 (pān) 1.(攀登) climb; clamber: ～着铁索往上爬 climb up a cable hand over hand 2.(高攀) seek connections in high places 3.(牵扯) involve; implicate

【攀比】 pānbǐ vying; compete in climbing to see who is superior: 避免相互～,竞相涨价 avoid wide-spread competition in price raising

【攀比风】 pānbǐfēng craze to vie with each other; craze to follow suit

【攀扯】 pānchě implicate (sb. in a crime)

【攀登】 pāndēng climb; clamber; scale: ～高峰 scale the heights

【攀附】 pānfù 1.(往上爬) climb; creep 2.(投靠有权势者) seek connections with influential officials

【攀高枝儿】 pān gāozhīr 1.（攀交）make friends with sb. of a higher social position 2.（与地位高者攀亲）claim kinship with sb. of a higher social position

【攀供】 pāngòng offer a false testimony to implicate sb.

【攀交】 pānjiāo make friends with sb. of a higher social position

【攀亲】 pānqīn 1.（拉亲戚关系）claim kinship 2.（议婚）arrange a match; seek a match; ask for a match

【攀禽】 pānqín scansorial birds

【攀谈】 pāntán engage in small talk; chitchat：跟朋友～ have a chat with a friend

【攀诬】 pānwū implicate and frame sb.

【攀援】 pānyuán 同"攀缘"

【攀缘】 pānyuán 1.（抓着东西往上爬）climb; clamber：由树上～而下 climb down a tree 2.（攀附投靠）climb the social ladder through pull

【攀折】 pānzhé pull down and break off：请勿～花木！Please don't pluck the flowers!

【攀枝花】 pānzhīhuā 〈*Bot.*〉 bombax; common bombax

盘［盤］（pán） 1.（盘子）dish; plate; tray：古瓷～ old china plate / 茶～ tea plate 2.（磁盘，激光盘）disk：软～ floppy disk / 光～ compact disk 3.（商品行情）market quotation 4.（回旋地绕）coil; wind; twist 5.（盘问）check; examine; interrogate 6.（转让）transfer 7.（垒、砌、搭灶或炕）build 8.〈*Sports*〉 game; set：下一～棋 play a game of chess

【盘剥】 pánbō practice usury; exploit：～取利 be a Shylock

【盘查】 pánchá interrogate and examine; question; examine thoroughly：～行人 question the passers-by

【盘缠】 pán·chan travelling expenses; passage money

【盘秤】 pánchèng a steelyard with a pan

【盘存】 páncún take inventory

【盘点】 pándiǎn check; make an inventory of：今日～，明日照常营业。Stock-taking today. Business as usual tomorrow.

【盘费】 pán·fei travelling expenses; passage money

【盘根错节】 pángēn-cuòjié with twisted roots and gnarled branches; complicated and difficult to deal with; deep-rooted

【盘桓】 pánhuán stay; linger

【盘货】 pánhuò make an inventory of stock on hand; take stock

【盘诘】 pánjié cross-examine; question

【盘究】 pánjiū interrogate; question; examine narrowly

【盘踞】 pánjù illegally or forcibly occupy; be entrenched; settle in：～要津 hold a place of importance

【盘库】 pánkù make an inventory of goods in a warehouse

【盘片】 pánpiàn 〈*Computer*〉 disk; disc

【盘曲】 pánqū entwine

【盘绕】 pánrǎo twine; coil; wreathe

【盘山】 pánshān wind through the mountain

【盘山公路】 pánshān gōnglù winding mountain road

【盘式制动器】 pánshì zhìdòngqì 〈*Motorcycle*〉 disk brake

【盘算】 pánsuàn calculate; figure; plan

【盘梯】 pántī winding staircase; spiral staircase

【盘腿】 pántuǐ cross one's legs

【盘问】 pánwèn cross-examine; interrogate：～可疑的人 interrogate a suspicious person

【盘香】 pánxiāng incense coil

【盘旋】 pánxuán 1.（环绕着飞或走）spiral; circle; wheel; hover：飞机降落前在机场上空～。The plane spiraled the airport before. 2.（徘徊；逗留）linger; stay

【盘羊】 pányáng 〈*Zool.*〉 argali

【盘运】 pányùn transport; move; carry

【盘账】 pánzhàng check accounts; audit accounts; examine accounts

【盘子】 pán·zi 1.（器皿）dish; plate：纸～ paper plate / 塑料～ plastic plate / 把豆儿放到～里 put the beans in/on a dish 2.（一盘子的量）plateful：他吃了一整～的马铃薯。He ate the whole plateful of potatoes. 3.（行情）quotations on the market

磐（pán）

【磐石】 pánshí huge rock; bedrock：安如～ as stable as bedrock

蟠 (pán)

【蟠曲】 pánqū entwine

【蟠桃】 pántáo 1.〈*Bot*.〉flat peach 2.(果实) flat peach 3.〈神话〉peach of immortality

蹒[蹣] (pán)

【蹒跚】 pánshān walk haltingly; stagger; dodder:～着向门口走去 limp to the door

判 (pàn) 1.(判别) distinguish; discriminate 2.(明显) obviously (different) 3.(评定) appraise; give a mark 4.(判决) judge; decide 5.(判处) sentence; condemn:～死刑 sentence sb. to death

【判别】 pànbié differentiate; distinguish:～是非 distinguish right from wrong

【判处】 pànchǔ sentence; condemn:～三年徒刑 sentence sb. to three years' imprisonment

【判定】 pàndìng judge; decide; determine

【判断】 pànduàn 1.(断定) judge; decide; determine:逻辑的～ logical judgment / 科学的～ scientific judgment 2.〈*Logic*〉judgment

【判断力】 pànduànlì judgment

【判分】 pànfēn appraise; give a mark

【判决】 pànjué 1.〈*Law*〉court decision; judgment:～无罪 pronounce sb. not guilty / 仲裁～ arbitration award 2.(判断) judge; decide; determine

【判决书】 pànjuéshū court verdict; written judgment

【判例】 pànlì 〈*Law*〉legal precedent; judicial precedent; case law

【判明】 pànmíng distinguish; ascertain; draw a clear distinction

【判刑】 pànxíng sentence sb. to

【判罪】 pànzuì declare guilty; convict

叛 (pàn) betray; rebel against

【叛变】 pànbiàn betray one's country; turn traitor; turn renegade; defect

【叛党】 pàndǎng betray one's political party

【叛匪】 pànfěi rebel bandit; bandit rebels

【叛国】 pànguó betray one's country; commit treason

【叛国分子】 pànguó fènzǐ traitor to one's country

【叛军】 pànjūn rebel army; rebel forces; insurgent troops

【叛乱】 pànluàn armed rebellion; insurrection; revolt; mutiny:镇压～ suppress a rebellion; put down a rebellion

【叛卖】 pànmài betray; sell

【叛卖活动】 pànmài huódòng traitorous activity; acts of treason

【叛逆】 pànnì 1.(指行为) rebel against; revolt against 2.(指人) rebel

【叛逃】 pàntáo betray and flee

【叛徒】 pàntú traitor; renegade; turncoat; rebel

畔 (pàn) 1.(旁,边) side; bank 2.(田地边界) boundary; border:田～ the border of a field

盼 (pàn) 1.(盼望) hope for; long for; expect; yearn for; look forward to:～家信 look forward to hearing from one's family 2.(看) look

【盼头】 pàn·tou sth. hoped for and likely to happen; good prospects:这下子可有～了。There is hope then.

【盼望】 pànwàng hope for; long for; look forward to:～佳音 long for your good voice

袢 (pàn) 同"襻"

襻 (pàn) 1.(纽襻) a loop for fastening a button 2.(像纽襻的东西) sth. shaped like a button loop or used for a similar purpose 3.(绕上) tie; fasten:～上几针 put a few stitches in

pang

乓 (pāng) 〈*onomat*.〉bang:他～的一声关上了门。He closed the door with a bang.

滂 (pāng)

【滂湃】 pāngpài (of water) roaring and rushing:～的急流 rushing torrent

【滂沱】 pāngtuó torrential; pouring:大雨～。It's raining in torrents.

膀[髈] (pāng) swell (另见"膀"bǎng, páng)

【膀肿】 pāngzhǒng swollen; bloated

彷[徬](páng)

【彷徨】 pánghuáng walk back and forth, not knowing which way to go; hesitate about which way to go; hesitate

庞[龐、厖[1,2]](páng) 1.(庞大) huge; tremendous; immense 2.(庞杂) innumerable and disordered 3.(脸庞) face

【庞大】 pángdà huge; enormous; colossal; gigantic; big; immense: ～的代表团 a large delegation / ～的预算 huge budget

【庞然大物】 pángrán dà wù huge monster; colossus; formidable giant; monstrous creature

【庞杂】 pángzá numerous and jumbled; multi-farious and disorderly; in a cumbersome jumble: 内容～ the contents are multifarious and disorderly

旁(páng) 1.(旁边) side 2.(其他;另外) other; else: ～的事 other thing

【旁白】 pángbái aside (in a play)

【旁边】 pángbiān side

【旁顾】 pánggù attend to other things

【旁观】 pángguān look on; be an onlooker

【旁观者】 pángguānzhě bystander; onlooker; spectator

【旁观者清】 pángguānzhěqīng the spectator sees most clearly; the onlooker sees the game best; the onlooker is clear-headed

【旁落】 pángluò pass into others' hands

【旁敲侧击】 pángqiāo-cèjī attack by innuendo; make oblique thrusts

【旁人】 pángrén other people; others

【旁若无人】 pángruòwúrén act as if there was no one else present; self-assured; supercilious; act as if there was no one else present

【旁听】 pángtīng be a visitor at a meeting, in a school class, etc.; audit

【旁听生】 pángtīngshēng auditor

【旁听席】 pángtīngxí visitors' seats; public gallery

【旁系】 pángxì collateral line

【旁系继承人】 pángxì jìchéngrén collateral heir

【旁系亲属】 pángxì qīnshǔ collateral; collateral consanguinity; collateral relative

【旁系血亲】 pángxì xuèqīn collateral relatives by blood

【旁征博引】 pángzhēng-bóyǐn quote copiously from many sources

【旁证】 pángzhèng circumstantial evidence; extraneous evidence; side witness

膀(páng)
(另见"膀"bǎng, pāng)

【膀胱】 pángguāng 〈*Anat.*〉 urinary bladder

【膀胱结石】 pángguāng jiéshí 〈*Med.*〉 urinary calculus; cystolith; vesical calculus

【膀胱炎】 pángguāngyán 〈*Med.*〉 cystitis; urocystitis

磅(páng)
(另见"磅"bàng)

【磅礴】 pángbó 1.(广大) boundless; majestic; vast; widespread; tremendous: 气势～ of tremendous momentum 2.(充满) fill; permeate

螃(páng)

【螃蟹】 pángxiè crab

耪(pǎng) loosen soil with a hoe: ～地 loosen soil with a hoe

胖[肨](pàng) fat; stout; plump: 矮～的人 a man of stout build / 长～ get fat; put on weight

【胖乎乎】 pànghūhū plump; chubby; pudgy: ～的脸蛋 plump cheeks; chubby cheeks

【胖头鱼】 pàngtóuyú bighead; variegated carp

【胖子】 pàng·zi fat person; fatty

pao

抛[拋](pāo) 1.(扔) throw; toss; fling: ～救生圈 throw a life buoy 2.(丢下) leave behind; cast aside: 被时代～在后面 be tossed to the rear by the times

【抛光】 pāoguāng 〈*Mech.*〉 polish; buff: ～零件 polish parts

【抛锚】 pāomáo 1.(下锚) drop anchor; cast anchor: 这船在岸边抛下了锚。The ship anchored along the shore. 2.(发生故障) break down; be out of order: 汽车在路上～了。

The car broke down on the way.

【抛弃】 pāoqì abandon; forsake; cast away; cast aside; discard: ～坏习惯 forsake bad habits; give up bad habits / ～官僚主义作风 get rid of bureaucratic ways of doing things

【抛却】 pāoquè abandon; forsake

【抛射】 pāoshè project; projection (n.)

【抛售】 pāoshòu undersell; dump; sell sth. in big quantities

【抛售价】 pāoshòujià closeout rate

【抛物面】 pāowùmiàn 〈*Physics*〉 paraboloid; paraboloidal (adj.)

【抛物面镜】 pāowù miànjìng paraboloidal mirror

【抛物面天线】 pāowùmiàn tiānxiàn paraboloid antenna; dish antenna

【抛物线】 pāowùxiàn 〈*Physics*〉 paracurve; parabola; parabolic (adj.)

【抛掷】 pāozhì throw; cast; toss

泡 (pāo) 1.(大而松软) sth. puffy and soft 2.(虚而松软) spongy
(另见"泡"pào)

【泡货】 pāohuò bulky cargo

【泡桐】 pāotóng 〈*Bot*.〉 paulownia: 兰考～ elongate paulownia

刨 (páo) 1.(挖掘) dig; excavate 2.(减去) excluding; not counting; minus
(另见"刨"bào)

【刨除】 páochú exclude; not count

【刨根问底】 páogēn-wèndǐ get to the root of the matter; get to the bottom of things

咆 (páo)

【咆哮】 páoxiào roar; thunder

狍[麅] (páo)

【狍子】 páo·zi 〈*Zool*.〉 roe deer

炮 (páo)
(另见"炮"pào)

【炮制】 páozhì 1.〈*Chin. Med*.〉 prepare (Chinese medicine) 2.(捣出) concoct; cook up

袍 (páo) robe; gown: 棉～ cotton-padded robe

【袍子】 páo·zi robe; gown

匏 (páo)

【匏瓜】 páoguā 〈*Bot*.〉 bottle gourd

跑 (páo) paw: ～地 paw the ground; paw at the ground
(另见"跑"pǎo)

跑 (pǎo) 1.(迅速前进) run: 火车通常1小时～120公里。The train usually goes 120 kilometers in one hour. 2.(逃走) run away; escape; flee: 别让坏蛋～了。Don't let the rascal escape. 3.(奔走) run about doing sth.; run errands traveller 4.(挥发) evaporate: 瓶里的汽油～了。The gasoline in the bottle has evaporated. 5.(接在动词后面,表示离开原有位置) away; off
(另见"跑"páo)

【跑遍】 pǎobiàn go around; travel all over

【跑表】 pǎobiǎo stopwatch

【跑步】 pǎobù run; march at the double

【跑车】 pǎochē 1.(汽车) sports car 2.(自行车) racing bike

【跑刀】 pǎodāo 〈*Skating*〉 speed skate

【跑道】 pǎodào 1.〈*Aeron*.〉 runway 2.〈*Sports*〉 track; athletic track 3.(赛马场的) raceway; racetrack

【跑电】 pǎodiàn leakage of electricity; electric leakage

【跑狗】 pǎogǒu a dog race

【跑来跑去】 pǎolái-pǎoqù run back and forth

【跑垒员】 pǎolěiyuán 〈*Baseball*〉 runner; base-runner

【跑龙套】 pǎolóngtào 1.(扮演群众角色) play a bit role 2.(从事无关紧要的工作) be a utility man

【跑马】 pǎomǎ 1.(骑着马跑) run a horse; have a ride on a horse 2.(赛马) horse race 3.(遗精) emission

【跑马场】 pǎomǎchǎng racecourse; the turf

【跑买卖】 pǎomǎi·mai be a commercial traveler

【跑冒滴漏】 pǎo-mào-dī-lòu evaporate, emit, drip, leak: 严肃财政纪律,堵塞～ strictly keep financial discipline, and stop up draining on funds

【跑跑颠颠】 pǎopǎo-diāndiān bustle about; be on the go

【跑墒】 pǎoshāng 〈*Agric*.〉 evaporation of water in soil

【跑生意】 pǎoshēng·yi be a commercial traveler

【跑题】 pǎotí digress from the subject

【跑腿儿】 pǎotuǐr do legwork：他有一个助手给他～。He has an assistant who does the legwork.

【跑外】 pǎowài act as a traveling salesman

【跑鞋】 pǎoxié track shoes

泡 (pào) 1.（气泡）bubble 2.（泡状物）sth. shaped like a bubble：脚上起了～ get blisters on one's feet 3.（浸泡）steep；soak 4.（故意耗时间）dawdle；dillydally
（另见"泡"pāo）

【泡菜】 pàocài pickles；sauerkraut：朝鲜～ kimchi

【泡茶】 pàochá make tea

【泡沫】 pàomò foam；froth

【泡沫经济】 pàomò jīngjì bubble economy

【泡沫灭火器】 pàomò mièhuǒqì foam extinguisher

【泡泡纱】 pàopàoshā seersucker：格子～ seersucker gingham

【泡泡糖】 pàopàotáng bubble gum；chewing gum

【泡影】 pàoyǐng visionary hope, plan, scheme, etc.；bubble：化为～ go up in smoke；come to nothing；end up in smoke

【泡状卵泡】 pàozhuàng luǎnpào 〈*Anat*.〉 follicle with ovum

炮［砲、礮］(pào) 1.（火炮）big gun；cannon；artillery piece：火～ artillery / 火箭～ rocket artillery / 多管火箭～ multibarrel rocket launcher / 加农～ cannon / 无后坐力～ recoilless rifle / 迫击～ mortar / 高射～ antiaircraft gun / 反坦克～ antitank artillery；AT gun；tank destroyer / 自行火～ self-propelled gun / 听到远处打～的声音 hear the noise of the big guns firing in the distance 2.〈*Chess*〉 cannon
（另见"炮"páo）

【炮兵】 pàobīng artillery；artillerymen

【炮兵部队】 pàobīng bùduì artillery (troops)

【炮兵阵地】 pàobīng zhèndì artillery position

【炮弹】 pàodàn (artillery) shell：毒气～ gas shell / 迫击～ mortar shell

【炮管】 pàoguǎn tube；gun tube

【炮轰】 pàohōng bombard；shell

【炮灰】 pàohuī cannon fodder：充当～ be used as cannon fodder

【炮火】 pàohuǒ artillery fire；gunfire

【炮击】 pàojī bombard；shell

【炮舰】 pàojiàn gunboat

【炮舰外交】 pàojiàn wàijiāo gunboat diplomacy

【炮舰政策】 pàojiàn zhèngcè gunboat policy

【炮口】 pàokǒu gun muzzle

【炮楼】 pàolóu blockhouse：炸毁敌人～ blow up the enemy blockhouse

【炮声】 pàoshēng thunder of guns；report of artillery；roar of guns

【炮手】 pàoshǒu gunner；artilleryman

【炮艇】 pàotǐng gunboat

【炮筒子】 pàotǒng·zi 1.（炮管）tube；gun tube 2.（急躁口快的人）person who shoots off his mouth

【炮眼】 pàoyǎn 1.〈*Mil*.〉 porthole；embrasure 2.〈*Mineral*.〉 blasthole；dynamite hole；borehole

【炮战】 pàozhàn artillery action；artillery engagement

疱［皰］(pào) blister；bleb

【疱疹】 pàozhěn 1.（天花、水痘等的症状）bleb 2.（皮肤病）herpes

pei

呸 (pēi) pah；bah；pooh

胚［肧］(pēi) 〈*Biol*.〉 embryo

【胚层】 pēicéng 〈*Biol*.〉 germ-layer；germinal layer

【胚根】 pēigēn 〈*Bot*.〉 radicle

【胚胎】 pēitāi 〈*Biol*.〉 embryo；embryon

【胚芽】 pēiyá 〈*Bot*.〉 germ；plumule

【胚珠】 pēizhū 〈*Bot*.〉 ovule

陪 (péi) accompany；keep sb. company：请～我散散步。Please accompany me on my walk. / 我～你回家。I'll accompany you home.

【陪伴】 péibàn for company；keep sb. company

【陪衬】 péichèn 1.（衬托）serve as a contrast

or foil; set off **2.**（陪衬物）foil; setoff

【陪吃】 péichī accompany a guest at a dinner party

【陪床】 péichuáng stay at the bed-side of a patient

【陪读】 péidú accompany and look after a person while he is studying at school

【陪护】 péihù keep sb. company and nurse him

【陪客】 péikè **1.**（主人请来陪客人的人）a guest invited to help entertain the guest of honor at a dinner party **2.**（陪伴客人）accompany a guest; with a guest for company

【陪审】 péishěn act as an assessor; serve as an assessor; serve on a jury

【陪审团】 péishěntuán jury

【陪审席】 péishěnxí box

【陪审员】 péishěnyuán juror; juryman

【陪审制】 péishěnzhì jury system

【陪同】 péitóng accompany; be in the company of: 在…～下 in the company of ...; accompanied by ...

【陪夜】 péiyè stay at the bed-side of a patient at night

【陪葬】 péizàng be buried with the dead

【陪葬物】 péizàngwù objects buried together with the dead

培（péi） **1.**（在根部培土）bank up with earth; earth up **2.**（培养）cultivate; foster; train

【培土】 péitǔ hill up; earth up; bank up with earth; ridge: 给植物或它的根～ earth up a plant or its root

【培训】 péixùn cultivate; train

【培训班】 péixùnbān training class

【培养】 péiyǎng **1.**（教育和训练）foster; train; develop; educate; cultivate: ～人才 train men for profession **2.**〈*Biol.*〉culture; cultivate

【培养出】 péiyǎngchū turn sb. out

【培育】 péiyù cultivate; foster; breed; nurture; rear: 意志的～ cultivation of one's will power

【培植】 péizhí **1.**（栽种）cultivate; foster **2.**（培养）foster; train; educate: ～亲信 foster faithful followers

赔（péi） **1.**（赔偿）compensate; pay for: 损坏东西要～。Pay for anything you damage. **2.**（亏本）stand a loss

【赔本】 péiběn sustain losses in business; lose one's outlay; lose one's capital: ～的买卖 losing business

【赔不是】 péi bù·shi apologize

【赔偿】 péicháng **1.**（赔偿损失）compensate; pay for **2.**（赔偿费）damages

【赔偿范围】 péicháng fànwéi extent of compensation

【赔偿合同】 péicháng hétóng indemnity contract

【赔偿名誉】 péicháng míngyù indemnity for defamation

【赔偿条款】 péicháng tiáokuǎn indemnity clause

【赔偿协定】 péicháng xiédìng reparations agreement

【赔偿责任】 péicháng zérèn liability to pay compensation

【赔款】 péikuǎn **1.**（赔偿损失）pay an indemnity; pay reparations **2.**（赔偿费）indemnity; amends; reparations

【赔款额】 péikuǎn'é amount of damages

【赔礼】 péilǐ offer an apology; apologize: ～道歉 offer an apology

【赔钱】 péiqián money-losing

【赔情】 péiqíng apologize

【赔笑】 péixiào smile obsequiously or apologetically

【赔账】 péizhàng pay for the loss of cash or goods entrusted to one

【赔罪】 péizuì apologize

锫（péi） 〈*Chem.*〉berkelium（人造元素，符号 Bk）

沛（pèi） copious; plentiful; abundant

【沛然】 pèirán abundant; plentiful

佩（pèi） **1.**（佩带）wear (at the waist): ～着剑 wear a sword at the waist **2.**（佩服）admire: 他的精神可～。His spirit is admirable.

【佩带】 pèidài wear; bear; carry: ～纪念章 wear a souvenir badge

【佩戴】 pèidài 同"佩带"

【佩服】 pèifú admire; have admiration for:

～他的工作能力 admire his capacity for work

【佩剑】 pèijiàn saber; sabre ‖ 佩剑运动员 saber fencer

配(pèi) 1.(两性结合) match sb. with sb.; join in marriage; pair off with sb.: 婚～ marry 2.(使动物交配) mate: ～猪 mate pigs 3.(按比例合在一起) blend; compound; mix 4.(按计划地分派) distribute according to plan; apportion 5.(补足;配齐) fit; complete: ～成一套 complete the set 6.(相配) match: 这顶帽子与外衣很相～。The hat is a match for the coat. 7.(够得上) deserve; be worthy of; be qualified: 他不～做一名教师。He is not qualified to be a teacher.

【配备】 pèibèi 1.(根据需要提供) allocate; provide; fit out: ～干部 provide cadres 2.(布置) dispose (troops, etc.); deploy 3.(成套器物等) outfit; equipment

【配餐】 pèicān mixed food: 大力发展～、快餐 make big efforts to develop mixed food and quick meal

【配电】 pèidiàn (power) distribution

【配电盘】 pèidiànpán distributor

【配电站】 pèidiànzhàn power distribution station

【配殿】 pèidiàn side hall in a palace or temple

【配对】 pèiduì 1.(配成双) pair; make a pair 2.(动物交配) mate

【配对题】 pèiduìtí matching

【配额】 pèi'é quota: ～限制 quota restrictions

【配额制】 pèi'ézhì quota system

【配发】 pèifā publish a concerted article: ～的评论 the concerted commentator's article

【配方】 pèifāng 1.(配药) make up a prescription; fill a prescription 2.(配制方法) formula: 止咳合剂的～ a formula for cough mixture 3.〈*Math.*〉 compete square

【配合】 pèihé coordinate; cooperate; concert: ～得宜 be in harmony with one another

【配货提单】 pèihuò tídān order blank

【配给】 pèijǐ ration; allotment; allocate

【配给品】 pèijǐpǐn rationed goods

【配给制】 pèijǐzhì ration system; allotment system

【配件】 pèijiàn 1.(零件;部件) fittings; parts: 汽车～ spare parts of a car 2.(新换上的零件) a replacement

【配角】 pèijué 1.(共同主演) appear with another leading player; costar 2.(次要角色) supporting role; minor role: 男～ a supporting actor / 女～ a supporting actress

【配料】 pèiliào 〈*Metall.*〉 burden

【配偶】 pèiǒu spouse; consort

【配器】 pèiqì 〈*Music*〉 orchestrate; orchestration (n.): 这个曲子已经配了器。The piece of music is orchestrated.

【配色】 pèisè match colors; harmonize colors

【配套】 pèitào form a complete set

【配套措施】 pèitào cuòshī supplementary measure; supporting measure

【配套单位】 pèitào dānwèi complete unit

【配套工程】 pèitào gōngchéng conveyance system

【配套器材】 pèitào qìcái necessary accessories

【配套饰物】 pèitào shìwù parure

【配戏】 pèixì support a leading actor; play a supporting role

【配药】 pèiyào make up a prescription

【配音】 pèiyīn dub: 给一部外国电影～ dub a foreign films

【配音演员】 pèiyīn yǎnyuán dubber

【配乐】 pèiyuè dub in background music

【配制】 pèizhì compound; make up

【配置】 pèizhì dispose; deploy: ～兵力 dispose forces

【配种】 pèizhǒng breed; mate

【配种期】 pèizhǒngqī breeding season

【配种站】 pèizhǒngzhàng breeding station; breeding ground

【配子】 pèizǐ 〈*Biol.*〉 gamete

【配子体】 pèizǐtǐ 〈*Biol.*〉 gametophyte

辔(pèi)

【辔头】 pèitóu bridle

pen

喷(pēn) 1.(喷射) spurt; spout; gush; jet: 消防队员把水～进着火的房子。The

fireman sent jets of water into the burning house. / 伤口～血。Blood spouts from wound. **2.**（喷洒）spray; sprinkle：给玫瑰花～点水 sprinkle some water on the roses
（另见"喷"pèn）

【喷播】 pēnbō sow grass seeds by duster

【喷薄】 pēnbó gush; spurt：一轮～欲出的红日 the emerging sun with all its shimmering rays

【喷发胶】 pēnfàjiāo hair spray

【喷灌】 pēnguàn sprinkling irrigation; spray irrigation：机械化～ mechanized spray irrigation

【喷壶】 pēnhú watering can; sprinkling can

【喷火器】 pēnhuǒqì flamethrower; flame projector

【喷浆】 pēnjiāng 〈*Archit.*〉 **1.**（粉刷）whitewashing **2.**（灌混凝土）guniting

【喷墨式印字机】 pēnmòshì yìnzìjī ink-jet printer

【喷漆】 pēnqī spray paint; spray lacquer

【喷气发动机】 pēnqì fādòngjī jet engine

【喷气燃料】 pēnqì ránliào jet fuel

【喷气式】 pēnqìshì jet-propelled

【喷气式轰炸机】 pēnqìshì hōngzhàjī jet bomber

【喷气式客机】 pēnqìshì kèjī jet airliner; jetliner

【喷气推进】 pēnqì tuī jìn jet propulsion; jet-propelled (*adj.*)

【喷枪】 pēnqiāng spray gun

【喷泉】 pēnquán fountain

【喷泉式饮水器】 pēnquánshì yǐnshuǐqì fountain

【喷洒】 pēnsǎ spray; sprinkle：～农药 spray insecticide

【喷射】 pēnshè spray; spurt; jet

【喷射剂】 pēnshèjì propellant

【喷水池】 pēnshuǐchí fountain

【喷水口】 pēnshuǐkǒu water jet

【喷嚏】 pēntì sneeze：打～ sneeze

【喷头】 pēntóu **1.**（淋浴喷头）shower nozzle **2.**（洒水车喷头）sprinkler head

【喷涂】 pēntú spray

【喷雾】 pēnwù spray

【喷雾器】 pēnwùqì sprayer; atomizer

【喷雾作用】 pēnwù zuòyòng nebulization

【喷涌】 pēyǒng jet：水～而出。The water jetted out.

【喷嘴】 pēnzuǐ spray nozzle; spray head

盆（pén） basin; tub; pot：花～ flowerpot / 洗～里的衣服 wash the clothes in a tub / 把（花等）栽到～里 pot a plant / 给（花等）换～ repot a plant

【盆地】 péndì basin

【盆花】 pénhuā potted flower

【盆景】 pénjǐng potted landscape; miniature trees and rockery

【盆腔】 pénqiāng 〈*Anat.*〉 pelvic cavity

【盆腔炎】 pénqiāngyán 〈*Med.*〉 pelvic infection

【盆浴】 pényù bath in a tub; tub

【盆栽】 pénzāi pot culture

【盆栽植物】 pénzāi zhíwù potted plant; pot culture

喷（pèn）
（另见"喷"pēn）

【喷香】 pènxiāng **1.**（香气浓）fragrant **2.**（味美）delicious; appetizing

peng

抨（pēng）

【抨击】 pēngjī attack (in speech or writing); assail; lash out at; flay：～某人 assail sb.

【抨弹】 pēngtán **1.**（抨击）assail **2.**（弹劾）impeach

怦（pēng） thump; pit-a-pit：～然心动 sb's heart be palpitating with (excitement, joy, etc.); palpitation of the heart

烹（pēng） **1.**（用水煮）boil; cook **2.**（用油烹）fry quickly in hot oil and stir in sauce

【烹饪】 pēngrèn cooking; culinary art

【烹饪比赛】 pēngrèn bǐsài cook-off

【烹饪法】 pēngrènfǎ cookery; culinary arts; cuisine

【烹饪讲座】 pēngrèn jiǎngzuò cook-in

【烹饪学】 pēngrènxué gastronomy; gastronomic (adj.)

【烹调】 pēngtiáo cook (dishes)：他的妻子精于～。His wife is a good cook.

【烹调法】 pēngtiáofǎ cookery; culinary arts; cuisine

朋(péng) friend

【朋友】 péng·you 1.(朋友) friend：与…交～ make friends with sb. 2.(恋爱对方) friend：男～ boy friend / 女～ girl friend

棚(péng) 1.(竹棚，木棚) booth; awning; canopy：茶～ tea booth 2.(棚屋) shed; shack：草～ straw mat shed

【棚车】 péngchē 1.〈*Railway*〉 box wagon; boxcar 2.(带篷卡车) covered truck

【棚户】 pénghù slum-dwellers; shack-dwellers

【棚户区】 pénghùqū shanty town

【棚饲】 péngsì shelf rearing

【棚子】 péng·zi shed; shack

硼(péng) 〈*Chem*.〉 boron (元素符号 B)

【硼钢】 pénggāng boron steel

【硼砂】 péngshā borax; sodium borate

【硼砂玻璃】 péngshā bō·lí borax glass

【硼酸】 péngsuān boric acid

【硼酸盐】 péngsuānyán borate

【硼铁】 péngtiě ferro-boron

鹏(péng) roc

【鹏程万里】 péngchéng-wànlǐ (make) a roc's flight of 10,000 li; have a bright future

澎(péng) splash; spatter

【澎湃】 péngpài 1.(指波涛) surge; be in an upsurge：波涛～ wages surge high 2.(指声势) powerful; great in strength

膨(péng)

【膨大】 péngdà expand; inflate

【膨化】 pénghuà pop; popped (adj.)

【膨松剂】 péngsōngjì leavening agent

【膨体纱】 péngtǐshā 〈*Textiles*〉 bulk yarn

【膨胀】 péngzhàng 1.(指物体) expand; expansion (n.); dilate; dilatation (n.)：金属受热则～。Metals expand when they are heated. 2.(比喻) inflate; inflation (n.)：通货～ inflation

【膨胀率】 péngzhànglǜ 〈*Physics*〉 expansion rate

蓬(péng) 1.〈*Bot*.〉 bitter fleabane 2.(蓬乱) fluffy; dishevelled：～着头 with dishevelled hair

【蓬勃】 péngbó vigorous; flourishing; full of vitality：技术市场～兴起 technology markets spring up / 经济获得了空前的～发展。The economy has grown more vigorously than ever before.

【蓬莱】 pénglái a fabled abode of immortals

【蓬乱】 péngluàn fluffy; dishevelled：～的头发 dishevelled hair

【蓬松】 péngsōng fluffy; puffy：把枕头弄～ fluffy the pillows up/out

【蓬头垢面】 péngtóu-gòumiàn with dishevelled hair and a dirty face; unkempt

篷(péng) 1.(篷子) covering; awning：车～ awning on a car 2.(船帆) sail：落～ drop sails

【篷布】 péngbù tarpaulin

【篷帐】 péngzhàng tent：搭～ erect a tent

【篷子】 péng·zi covering

捧(pěng) 1.(用双手托) hold or carry in both hands：～着一个大碗 hold a big bowl in both hands 2.(奉承；吹捧) boost; exalt; extol; flatter

【捧场】 pěngchǎng 1.(在剧场喝彩) be a member of a claque 2.(吹嘘) boost; sing the praises of; flatter

【捧腹】 pěngfù split one's sides with laughter

【捧杀】 pěngshā terminate sb. by exalting

碰[掽、踫](pèng) 1.(碰击) touch; bump：～得头破血流 knock one's head against a brick wall 2.(碰见) meet; run into 3.(试探) take one's chance

【碰杯】 pèngbēi clink glasses

【碰壁】 pèngbì run up against a stone wall; meet a rebuff; be rebuffed; have one's nose put out of joint

【碰钉子】 pèng dīng·zi meet with a rebuff; run into snags

【碰痕】 pènghén bruise mark

【碰见】 pèngjiàn meet unexpectedly; encounter; run into; come across：在街上～一个熟人 run into an acquaintance in the street

【碰面】 pèngmiàn meet：我们商定星期五～。We agreed to meet on Friday.

【碰碰车】 pèngpèngchē bumper car; dodgem; dodgem car：去玩～ go on the dodgems

【碰碰船】 pèngpèngchuán bumper boat; dodgem boat

【碰巧】 pèngqiǎo by chance; by coincidence; happen to

【碰软】 pèngruǎn deal with soft tactics

【碰锁】 pèngsuǒ 1.（碰簧锁）spring lock 2.（没遇到要找的人）have not meet sb.

【碰头】 pèngtóu 1.（开短会）meet and discuss; put (our, your, their) heads together 2.（见面）see each other

【碰头会】 pèngtóuhuì brief meeting (mainly to exchange information)

【碰硬】 pèngyìng face up to the tough

【碰撞】 pèngzhuàng 1.（猛然碰上）collide; knock against; run foul of; crash: 互相～ran foul of each other 2.〈*Physics*〉collision; impact

pi

坯[坏] (pī) 1.（坯件）base; semifinished product; blank: 铜～ cooper base; cooper blank 2.（砖坯;土坯）unburned brick; earthen brick; adobe

【坯布】 pībù grey cloth; grey

【坯件】 pījiàn blank

【坯料】 pīliào blank

【坯模】 pīmó mold

【坯胎】 pītāi mold

【坯子】 pī·zi semifinished product; base; blank

批 (pī) 1.（用手掌打）slap 2.（批判）criticize; refute 3.（批示）write instructions or comments on (a report from a subordinate, etc.) 4.（大量买卖）wholesale 5.〈*classifier*〉batch; lot; group: 一～货物 a batch of goods 6.（线批;麻批）fibers of cotton, flax, etc. ready to be drawn and twisted

【批驳】 pībó 1.（否决）veto an opinion or a request from a subordinate body 2.（批评）refute; criticize; rebut

【批处理文件】 pīchǔlǐ wénjiàn 〈*Computer*〉 autoexec. bat file

【批发】 pīfā 1.（成批销售）wholesale 2.（批准发布）be authorized for dispatch

【批发部】 pīfābù wholesale department

【批发价格】 pīfā jiàgé wholesale price

【批发商】 pīfāshāng wholesaler

【批发市场】 pīfā shìchǎng terminal market

【批复】 pīfù give an official, written reply to a subordinate body

【批改】 pīgǎi correct; mark: ～作业 correct students' papers

【批件】 pījiàn an official, written reply to a subordinate body

【批量】 pīliàng batch; lot: ～生产 batch process

【批零】 pīlíng wholesale and retail

【批判】 pīpàn criticize; repudiate: ～地继承 inherit in a critical way

【批判现实主义】 pīpàn xiànshí zhǔyì critical realism

【批评】 pīpíng criticize: 他的论调受到了严厉的～。His argument were severely criticized.

【批示】 pīshì 1.（批语）written instructions; written comments 2.（发表书面意见和指示）make comments and instructions

【批售】 pīshòu whole sale

【批条】 pītiáo written instruction or comments on a slip of paper

【批条子】 pītiáo·zi write a slip of paper; make instructions on a scrap of paper

【批文】 pīwén 1.（指文件）an official, written reply to a subordinate body 2.（指文字）written instructions or comments

【批语】 pīyǔ 1.（批示）comments and instructions 2.（对文章的评语）remarks

【批阅】 pīyuè read over; read and amend or comment on; read over and give remarks: ～文件 read and comment on documents

【批注】 pīzhù 1.（加批语和注释）annotate and comment on 2.（批语和注释）annotations and commentaries; marginalia; headnote

【批准】 pīzhǔn ratify; approve; sanction; authorize: 计划需经～ the plan is subject to approval

【批准书】 pīzhǔnshū instrument of ratification: 交存～ deposit the instruments of ratification

纰 (pī) (of cloth, thread, etc.) become unwoven or untwisted; be spoilt

【纰漏】 pīlòu careless mistake; small accident; slip: 出了～ make a small error; make a slip

【纰缪】 pīmiù error; mistake

砒(pī) arsenic

【砒霜】 pīshuāng (white) arsenic

披(pī) 1.(搭在肩、背上) drape over; wrap around; throw on; spread: ～着大衣 have an overcoat draped over one's shoulders / ～着…的外衣 under the cloak of; be clothed in; disguised as 2.(打开) open; unroll; spread out: ～卷 open a book 3.(裂开) split open; crack; break

【披风】 pīfēng cloak; mantle: 穿一件红～ wear a red cloak

【披红】 pīhóng drape a band of red silk over sb's shoulders

【披肩】 pījiān 1.(无袖短外衣) cape 2.(女用披巾) shawl

【披巾】 pījīn shawl

【披荆斩棘】 pījīng-zhǎnjí clear away obstacles in one's way; hack one's way through difficulties

【披露】 pīlù 1.(发表;公布) publish; announce; make public 2.(表露) reveal; show; disclose

【披靡】 pīmǐ 1.(随风倒下) be swept by the wind; be blown about by the wind 2.(溃散) be routed; flee; put to rout: 望风～ flee pell-mell at the sight of the opponent army

【披散】 pī·san hang down loosely: ～着头发 hang one's hair down loosely

【披头散发】 pītóu-sànfà with hair dishevelled; with hair in disarray; wear hair dishevelled

【披屋】 pīwū penthouse

【披星戴月】 pīxīng-dàiyuè under the canopy of the moon and the stars; work or travel night and day

【披阅】 pīyuè open and read (a book); peruse

劈(pī) 1.(用刀斧破开) split; chop; cleave: 把木头～成两块 cleave/split a block of wood in two pieces 2.(正对着;冲着) right against 3.(雷击) strike: 被雷电～了 have been struck by lightning 4.〈*Physics*〉(尖劈) wedge
(另见"劈"pǐ)

【劈波斩浪】 pībō-zhǎnlàng cleave through the waves

【劈刺】 pīcì 〈*Mil*.〉 saber or bayonet fighting

【劈刀】 pīdāo 1.(刀背厚的刀) chopper 2.〈*Mil*.〉 saber fighting

【劈脸】 pīliǎn right in the face: 一个球～向她打来。A ball came hurtling towards her face.

【劈山】 pīshān level off hilltops; blast cliffs: ～筑路 blast cliffs to build highways

【劈手】 pīshǒu make a sudden snatch: ～抢来 grab sth. in a flash

【劈头】 pītóu 1.(迎头) straight on the head; right in the face 2.(开头) at the very start; right at the beginning

【劈头盖脸】 pītóu-gàiliǎn right in the face; direct to one's head and face: ～地提了许多问题 shower a lot of questions upon sb.; fire a volley of questions at sb.

【劈胸】 pīxiōng right against the chest; straight on the breast

霹(pī)

【霹雷】 pīléi thunderbolt; thunderclap

【霹雳舞】 pīlìwǔ break dance

皮(pí) 1.(外皮) skin 2.(皮革) leather; hide 3.(毛皮) fur: 上等的狐～ a fine fox fur 4.(书皮) cover; wrapper 5.(表面) surface 6.(薄片状物) a broad, flat piece (of some thin material); sheet 7.(发皮) become soft and soggy 8.(顽皮;调皮) naughty 8.(无所谓) indifferent: 他老挨罚,都～了。He gets punished so often that he no longer cares.

【皮袄】 pí'ǎo fur-lined jacket

【皮包】 píbāo leather handbag; briefcase; purse; portfolio

【皮包公司】 píbāo gōngsī dummy corporation; paper company

【皮包骨头】 píbāogǔtóu skinny: 瘦得～ be only skin and bone

【皮便鞋】 píbiànxié loafers

【皮尺】 píchǐ tape measure; tape

【皮带】 pídài 1.(腰带) belt; leather belt 2.(传动带) belt

【皮带环】 pídàihuán keeper
【皮带孔】 pídàikǒng punch holes
【皮带扣】 pídàikòu belt fastener; belt buckle
【皮带襻】 pídàipàn belt loop
【皮蛋】 pídàn preserved egg
【皮筏】 pífá skin raft
【皮肤】 pífū skin
【皮肤病】 pífūbìng skin disease; dermatosis
【皮肤科】 pífūkē dermatological department; dermatology; dermatological (adj.) ‖ 皮肤科医生 dermatologist
【皮革】 pígé leather; hide: 黑色～ black leather coat
【皮货】 píhuò fur; pelt
【皮货店】 píhuòdiàn fur shop
【皮货商】 píhuòshāng furrier; fur trader
【皮夹子】 píjiā·zi wallet; pock etbook
【皮匠】 píjiàng 1.(制鞋的) cobbler; shoemaker 2.(制革或鞣皮的) tanner
【皮胶】 píjiāo hide glue
【皮筋儿】 píjīnr rubber band; elastic band
【皮开肉绽】 píkāi-ròuzhàn the skin is torn and the flesh gapes open; badly bruised from flogging
【皮毛】 pímáo 1.(带毛兽皮) fur 2.(表面的知识) smattering; superficial knowledge: 略知～ have only a superficial knowledge
【皮棉】 pímián ginned cotton; lint (cotton)
【皮腔】 píqiāng 〈*Photog.*〉 bellows
【皮球】 píqiú rubber ball; ball
【皮肉】 píròu human body
【皮肉生涯】 píròu shēngyá prostitution: 从事～ prostitute herself
【皮艇】 pítǐng kayak: 单人～ single kayak; kayak single / 双人～ double kayak; kayak pair / 四人～ kayak four
【皮艇运动】 pítǐng yùndòng kayaking
【皮艇运动员】 pítǐng yùndòngyuán kayaker
【皮箱】 píxiāng leather suitcase; leather trunk
【皮鞋】 píxié leather shoes
【皮鞋油】 píxiéyóu shoe polish
【皮炎】 píyán dermatitis; cutitis; dermitis
【皮衣】 píyī 1.(毛皮的) fur clothing 2.(皮革的) leather clothing: 毛皮领子的棕色～ a brown leather coat with a fur collar
【皮影戏】 píyǐngxì leather-silhouette show; shadow play
【皮疹】 pízhěn 〈*Med.*〉 rash
【皮脂腺】 pízhīxiàn 〈*Anat.*〉 sebaceous glands
【皮质】 pízhì 〈*Anat.*〉 cortical substance
【皮重】 pízhòng tare
【皮子】 pí·zi 1.(皮革) leather; hide 2.(毛皮) fur

铍 (pí) 〈*Chem.*〉 beryllium (元素符号 Be)

疲 (pí) tired; weary; exhausted: 精～力尽 be tired out

【疲惫】 píbèi tired out; exhausted
【疲乏】 pífá weary; tired
【疲倦】 píjuàn tired; weary; fatigued
【疲劳】 píláo 1.(指人) tired; fatigued; weary: ～过度 excessive fatigue 2.(指机体等) fatigue; strain: 肌肉～ muscular fatigue / 听觉～ auditory fatigue 3.〈*Physics*〉 fatigue: 金属～ metal fatigue
【疲劳试验】 píláo shìyàn fatigue test
【疲软】 píruǎn 1.(疲乏无力) fatigued and weak 2.〈*Econ.*〉 weaken; slump: 市场～ bearish market
【疲塌】 pítā slack; negligent: 工作～ be slack at one's work
【疲于奔命】 píyú-bēnmìng be kept constantly on the run; be tired from running around; be weighed down with work

枇 (pí)

【枇杷】 pí·pá 〈*Bot.*〉 loquat

毗 [毘] (pí) adjoin; be adjacent to

【毗连】 pílián adjoin; border on; be adjacent to: 墨西哥与美国～。Mexico adjoins United States.
【毗邻】 pílín 同"毗连"
【毗邻水域】 pílín shuǐyù adjacent waters

蚍 (pí)

【蚍蜉】 pífú ant: ～撼大树 an ant trying to shake a big tree; ridiculously overrating one's own strength

琵 (pí)

【琵琶】 pí·pá *pipa*; 4-stringed Chinese lute

【琵琶桶】 pí·pátǒng barrel

啤 (pí)

【啤酒】 píjiǔ beer; beery (adj.): 黑～ porter; brown ale; dark beer / 生～ draught beer / 桶装～ keg beer / 一听(罐)～ a can of beer; a tin of beer / 喝～ beer

【啤酒厂】 píjiǔchǎng brewery

【啤酒馆】 píjiǔguǎn 1.(室内的) beer bar 2.(露天的) beer garden

【啤酒花】 píjiǔhuā 〈*Bot.*〉 hops

【啤酒桶】 píjiǔtǒng barrel of beer

脾 (pí) spleen

【脾气】 pí·qi 1.(性情) temperament; disposition: ～急躁 have a hot temper 2.(易怒) bad temper: 发～ lose one's temper; flare up 3.(特性) behavior; characteristic

【脾胃】 píwèi taste: ～相投 have similar likes and dislikes

【脾性】 píxìng nature

【脾脏】 pízàng 〈*Anat.*〉 spleen

【脾脏切除】 pízàng qiēchú 〈*Med.*〉 splenectomy

匹[疋²] (pǐ)

1.(匹敌) be equal to; be a match for 2.〈*classifier*〉 bolt: 两～布 two bolts of cloth 3.〈*classifier*〉两～马 two horses

【匹敌】 pǐdí be equal to; be well matched: 无可～ be without a rival

【匹夫】 pǐfū 1.(平常人) ordinary man 2.(无学识、智谋者) an ignorant person

【匹配】 pǐpèi 1.〈*written*〉 mate; marry 2.〈*Electr.*〉 matching

痞 (pǐ)

1.(痞块) a lump in the abdomen 2.(流氓) ruffian; riffraff: 地～ local ruffian

【痞子】 pǐ·zi ruffian; riffraff

劈 (pǐ)

1.(分开) divide; split 2.(剥;分裂) break off; strip off: ～莴苣叶 strip the outer leaves off lettuces

(另见"劈"pī)

【劈叉】 pǐchà do the splits

【劈柴】 pǐchái kindling; firewood

癖 (pǐ)

addiction; weakness for: 成～ be addicted to sth.

【癖好】 pǐhào favorite hobby; fondness for; weakness for; partiality for: 种玫瑰花是她的～。Growing roses is her hobby.

【癖习】 pǐxí natural inclination

【癖性】 pǐxìng natural inclination; proclivity; propensity

屁 (pì)

wind (from bowels); fart: 放～ break wind; fart

【屁股】 pì·gu 1.(人的) buttocks; bottom; behind; backside: 在右～上打一针 have an injection in the right buttock 2.(动物的) rump; haunch; hindquarters 3.(物体的尾部) end; butt: 香烟～ cigarette butt

【屁股蛋儿】 pì·gudànr buttocks; bottom; behind; backside

【屁话】 pìhuà shit; nonsense; rubbish

辟[闢] (pì)

1.(开辟) open up; break; lay out 2.(精辟) penetrating; incisive 3.(驳斥) refute; repudiate

【辟谣】 pìyáo refute a rumor

僻 (pì)

1.(偏僻) out-of-the-way; secluded 2.(怪僻) eccentric 3.(不常见的) rare

【僻静】 pìjìng secluded; lonely

【僻壤】 pìrǎng an out-of-the-way place; little known region: 穷乡～ remote and undeveloped place

譬 (pì) example; analogy

【譬方】 pìfāng for example; for instance; such as

【譬如】 pìrú for example; for instance; such as

【譬喻】 pìyù metaphor; simile; figure of speech

媲 (pì)

【媲美】 pìměi compare favorably with; rival

pian

片 (piān)

(另见"片"piàn)

【片儿】 piānr (构成词的组成部分,用于以下各例)唱～ record; disc; phonograph record / 电影～ film; movie / 故事～ feature film / 画～ picture / 相～ photo; photograph

【片子】 piān·zi 1.(电影胶片) a roll of film 2.(影片) film; movie: 电视台正在我们镇

上拍～。The television station is filming in our town. **3.**（唱片）gramophone record; disc **4.**（爱克斯光片）X-ray; radiograph:（给病人）拍～ take an X-ray /（自己接受）拍～ have an X-ray taken

偏 (piān) **1.**（倾斜）inclined to one side; slanting; leaning: 方向略～ in a slight slanting direction **2.**（偏向）partial; prejudiced

【偏爱】 piān'ài have a preference for; love one more than another

【偏安】 piān'ān be content to retain sovereignty over a part of the country

【偏差】 piānchā **1.**（偏离方向）deviation; declination **2.**（工作差错）deviation; error: 防止～ guard against deviations

【偏方】 piānfāng folk prescription

【偏废】 piānfèi do one thing and neglect another; emphasize one thing at the expense of another

【偏航】 piānháng going off course; off-course; yaw

【偏护】 piānhù show partiality for; take sides with

【偏激】 piānjī extreme: 她这个人比较～。She tends to go to extremes.

【偏见】 piānjiàn prejudice; bias; preconception; partial opinion: 对某人有～ have a prejudice against sb.; be biased against sb.

【偏离】 piānlí deviate; diverge: ～航线 drift off the course

【偏盲】 piānmáng 〈*Med.*〉 hemianopia; hemianopsia

【偏僻】 piānpì remote; out-of-the-way; far-off: 这是个～的地方。It is an out-of-the-way place.

【偏偏】 piānpiān **1.**（故意）just opposite; deliberately; but **2.**（正相反）happen to; it so happened that **3.**（单单）alone

【偏巧】 piānqiǎo it so happened that; as luck would have it; by chance; fortunately

【偏食】 piānshí **1.**〈*Astron.*〉 partial eclipse: 月～ partial lunar eclipse **2.**〈*Med.*〉 partiality for a particular kind of food

【偏瘫】 piāntān 〈*Med.*〉 hemiplegia; hemiparalysis

【偏袒】 piāntǎn be partial to and side with; show partiality for; take sides with: ～某人 bias for sb.

【偏听偏信】 piāntīng-piānxìn heed and trust only one side; listen only to one side; believe in one-side story

【偏头痛】 piāntóutòng 〈*Med.*〉 migraine; hemicrania

【偏析】 piānxī 〈*Physics*〉 segregation

【偏向】 piānxiàng **1.**（错误倾向）erroneous tendency; deviation **2.**（袒护）be partial to: ～某人 be partial to sb. **3.**（偏于赞成）be inclined to; prefer; side with

【偏心】 piānxīn **1.**（不公正）partiality; bias **2.**〈*Mech.*〉 eccentric

【偏心眼儿】 piānxīnyǎnr partiality

【偏移】 piānyí deviate; deviation (n.)

【偏远】 piānyuǎn remote; faraway: ～的山村 a remote village

【偏振】 piānzhèn 〈*Physics*〉 polarize; polarization (n.)

【偏振光】 piānzhènguāng 〈*Physics*〉 polarized light

【偏振片】 piānzhènpiān 〈*Physics*〉 polarized filter

【偏执】 piānzhí extreme and obstinate

【偏重】 piānzhòng lay particular stress on; one-sidedly emphasize

篇 (piān) **1.**（篇章）a piece of writing **2.**（单张纸）sheet (of paper) **3.**〈*classifier*〉 piece; sheet

【篇幅】 piānfú **1.**（文章长短）length (of a piece of writing) **2.**（指书刊篇幅）space: 限于～ due to limited space

【篇目】 piānmù **1.**（标题）list of articles; chapter heading **2.**（目录）table of contents; contents

【篇章】 piānzhāng sections and chapters; writings: 人类历史的新～ a new chapter of human history

翩 (piān)

【翩翩】 piānpiān **1.**（轻快飞舞）dance lightly: ～起舞 dance trippingly **2.**（风流洒脱）elegant; smart

【翩跹】 piānxiān lightly; trippingly

便 (pián)（另见"便"biàn）

【便宜】 pián·yi 1.（价格低）cheap; inexpensive: 东西买得～ buy a thing cheap 2.（好处）small advantages; petty gain: 贪小～ out for small advantages; on the fiddle 3.（使得到好处）let sb. off lightly

【便宜货】 pián·yihuò goods sold at bargain prices

胼 (pián)

【胼胝】 piánzhī callosity; callus

片 (piàn) 1.（薄片）a flat, thin piece; slice; flake: 面包～ slices of bread; sliced break 2.（较小的地区）part of a place 3.（切成薄片）cut into slices 4.（零星的）incomplete; fragmentary; partial; brief 5.〈*classifier*〉两～药 two tablets of medicine / 一～草地 a tract of meadow

（另见"片"piān）

【片酬】 piànchóu 〈*Cinematog.*〉 remuneration for movie actors

【片段】 piànduàn part; passage; extract; fragment

【片儿警】 piànrjǐng section police

【片剂】 piànjì tablet

【片假名】 piànjiǎmíng katakana (Jap.)

【片甲不存】 piànjiǎ-bùcún the army is completely wiped out; have not even a fragment of armor remaining

【片刻】 piànkè a short while; an instant; a moment; a little while; a minute

【片面】 piànmiàn 1.（单方面）unilateral; one-sided 2.（不全面）one-sided; lopsided: ～的观点 lopsided view / ～夸大 one-sided exaggeration; exaggerate certain aspects of

【片面性】 piànmiànxìng one-sidedness

【片头】 piàntóu 〈*Cinematog.*〉 titles

【片言】 piànyán a few words; a phrase or two

【片言只字】 piànyán-zhīzì a few words and phrases

【片纸只字】 piànzhǐ-zhīzì fragments of writing; a brief note or letter

【片状】 piànzhuàng lamellar; lamellate; flaky

【片子】 piàn·zi 1.（薄片）flat, thin piece; slice; flake; scrap 2.（名片）visiting card

骗 (piàn) 1.（欺骗）deceive; fool; hoodwink: ～某人去做某事 deceive sb. into doing sth. / 他～她,使她相信他会开车。He deceiver her into thinking he could drive a car. 2.（骗取）cheat; swindle: ～钱 cheat sb. out of his money; swindle money out of sb.

【骗局】 piànjú fraud; hoax; swindle: 和谈～ a peace talk swindle

【骗取】 piànqǔ gain sth. by cheating; cheat sb. out of sth.; swindle; defraud: ～信任 gain sb's confidence by cheating

【骗人】 piànrén deceive people

【骗术】 piànshù deceitful trick; ruse; hoax

【骗子】 piàn·zi swindler; cheat; trickster; fraudulent person: 政治～ political swindler

piao

剽 (piāo) 1.（抢劫）rob 2.（动作敏捷）nimble; swift

【剽悍】 piāohàn agile and brave; quick and fierce

【剽窃】 piāoqiè plagiarize; lift; plagiarism (n.): ～别人的著作 plagiarize the work of others

漂 (piāo) float; drift: 船～到海里去了。The boat drifted out to sea. / 木头～在水上。Wood floats on water.

（另见"漂"piǎo, piào）

【漂泊】 piāobó 1.（指船等）drift; be driven by the current 2.（生活无定）lead a wandering life; rove; wander: ～江湖 lead a wandering life all over the country

【漂浮】 piāofú 1.（在水上漂）float: 树叶～在水上。Leaves were floating on the water. 2.（工作不踏实）showy; superficial

【漂流】 piāoliú 1.（在水面上漂）be driven by the current; drift about: 随波～ drift with the tide / 随风～ drift with the wind 2.（漂泊）lead a wandering life; rove; drift 3.〈*Oceanog.*〉drift current; wind-driven current

【漂网】 piāowǎng drift-net

【漂游】 piāoyóu drift; wander: 一块木头在顺水～。A piece of wood was drifting down the river.

缥 (piāo)

【缥缈】 piāomiǎo dimly discernible; misty:

虚无～ visionary; illusory

飘[飄] (piāo) wave to and fro; float (in the air); flutter: 灰尘～在空中。Dust floats in the air. / 从厨房～出阵阵香味。Delicious smells were emanating from the kitchen.

【飘尘】 piāochēng floating dust

【飘带】 piāodài streamer; ribbon

【飘荡】 piāodàng 1.(在风中飘动) float in the air 2.(在水中漂动) drift; wave: 几只小船随波～。A few boats were drifting with the tide. 3.(漂泊) lead a wandering life; rove; wander

【飘动】 piāodòng float (in the air); fly; flutter: 迎风～ fly in the wind

【飘浮】 piāofú 同"漂浮"

【飘忽】 piāohū 1.(轻轻移动) move swiftly; fleet 2.(摇摆) mobile; uncertain

【飘零】 piāolíng 1.(凋谢) faded and fallen 2.(失去依靠) wandering; adrift; homeless

【飘流】 piāoliú 同"漂流"

【飘落】 piāoluò drift and fall slowly

【飘缈】 piāomiǎo 同"缥缈"

【飘飘然】 piāopiāorán 1.(轻飘飘地) lightly: 脚下有些～ like tread on air 2.(很得意) smug; self-satisfied; complacent: 心中～ feel quite self-satisfied

【飘然】 piāorán 1.(飘摇) floating in the air 2.(轻快) lightly 3.(轻松愉快) happy and relaxed

【飘洒】 piāosǎ 1.(飘扬) float; drift 2.(指姿态) suave 3.(指书法) facile and graceful

【飘散】 piāosàn drift away: 浓雾～了。The heavy fog drifted away.

【飘舞】 piāowǔ wave in the wind

【飘扬】 piāoyáng wave; flutter; fly: 红旗迎风～。The red flag fluttered in the wind.

【飘摇】 piāoyáo sway; shake; totter

【飘移】 piāoyí draft: 大陆～ continental draft

【飘逸】 piāoyì 1.〈*written*〉 possessing natural grace; elegant 2.(飘散) drift away

【飘溢】 piāoyì drift about

【飘悠】 piāo·you drift slowly and leisurely

嫖[闞] (piáo) visit prostitutes; go whoring

【嫖娼】 piáochāng go whoring; visit a prostitute

【嫖客】 piáokè brothel visitor; whorehouse visitor

瓢 (piáo) gourd ladle; wooden dipper

【瓢虫】 piáochóng ladybird

【瓢泼大雨】 piáopō-dàyǔ heavy rain; torrential rain; torrential downpour

【瓢子】 piáo·zi gourd ladle; wooden dipper

漂 (piǎo) 1.(漂白) bleach 2.(用水冲净) rinse

(另见"漂"piāo, piào)

【漂白】 piǎobái bleach: 这块桌布你～了吗? Did you bleach this tablecloth?

【漂白粉】 piǎobáifěn bleaching powder

【漂洗】 piǎoxǐ rinse: 我把洗过的衣服～干净。I rinsed the clothes I had washed.

瞟 (piǎo) look sidelong at; glance sideways at; look askance at

票 (piào) 1.(车票、戏票等) ticket: 来回～ return ticket; round trip ticket / 买～ get a ticket; buy a ticket 2.(选票) ballot: 反对～ negative vote / 废～ spoilt vote 3.(钞票) bill; bank note 4.(票友) amateur performer 5.(绑票) sb. kidnaped: 绑～ kidnap sb.

【票霸】 piàobà ticket monopolize

【票额】 piào'é the sum stated on a check or bill; denomination; face value

【票贩子】 piàofàn·zi ticket-speculator

【票房】 piàofáng 1.(车站等的) booking office 2.(戏院等的) box office

【票房价值】 piàofáng jiàzhí box-office value

【票根】 piàogēn counterfoil; stub

【票价】 piàojià the price of a ticket; admission fee; entrance fee

【票据】 piàojù 1.(支付凭证) bill; note: ～托收 collection on bill 2.(出纳或货运凭证) voucher; receipt

【票据交换】 piàojù jiāohuàn bank clearing

【票据交换所】 piàojù jiāohuànsuǒ clearing house

【票据贴现】 piàojù tiēxiàn bill discounted

【票面】 piàomiàn face value; par value; nominal value: ～价值 face value; par (value)

【票期】 piàoqī usance

【票箱】 piàoxiāng ballot box
【票友】 piàoyǒu amateur performer
【票证】 piàozhèng coupons and booklets
【票子】 piào·zi bank note; paper money; bill

漂 (piào)
(另见"漂"piāo, piǎo)

【漂亮】 piào·liang 1.(好看) handsome; beautiful; pretty; good-looking: 把自己打扮得漂漂亮亮 trim oneself up 2.(出色) smart; remarkable; brilliant; splendid; beautiful: 法语讲得很～ speak French beautifully

pie

氕 (piē) 〈*Chem*.〉 protium (符号为: H^1)

撇 (piē) 1.(丢弃,抛弃) cast aside; throw overboard; neglect: 我们不能～下他不管。We should not ignore him. 2.(在液面上舀取) skim off
(另见"撇"piě)

【撇开】 piēkāi leave aside; bypass: ～次要问题 bypass questions of minor importance
【撇弃】 piēqì cast away; abandon; desert

瞥 (piē) shoot a glance at; dart a look at

【瞥见】 piējiàn get a glimpse of; catch sight of
【瞥视】 piēshì shoot a glance at

苤 (piě)

【苤蓝】 piě·lan 〈*Bot*.〉 kohlrabi

撇 (piě) throw; fling; cast
(另见"撇"piē)

【撇嘴】 piězuǐ curl one's lip; twitch one's mouth

pin

拼[拚] (pīn) 1.(合在一起) put together; piece together: 把两件～成一件 put the two together to form one piece 2.(不顾一切) be ready to risk one's life (in fighting, work, etc.); go all out in work

【拼版】 pīnbǎn 〈*Printing*〉 makeup
【拼搏】 pīnbó fight with all one's might for the victory in a battle or competition
【拼刺】 pīncì 1.(军事训练) bayonet drill; bayonet practice 2.(枪刺格斗) bayonet charge
【拼凑】 pīncòu piece together; knock together; rig up: ～小集团 knock together a clique
【拼接】 pīnjiē joggle joint
【拼命】 pīnmìng 1.(冒生命危险) risk one's life; defy death; go all out regardless of danger to one's life: ～抵抗 risk the life in resistance 2.(尽最大力量) exerting the utmost strength; for all one is worth; with all one's might; desperately
【拼盘】 pīnpán assorted cold dishes; hors d'oeuvres
【拼死】 pīnsǐ risk one's life; defy death; fight desperately
【拼图测验】 pīntú cèyàn picture arrangement test
【拼写】 pīnxiě spell; transliterate: 你的名字怎样～? How do you spell your name?
【拼写法】 pīnxiěfǎ spelling; orthography
【拼音】 pīnyīn combine sounds into syllables
【拼音文字】 pīnyīn wénzì alphabetic (system of) writing
【拼音字母】 pīnyīn zìmǔ phonetic alphabet; phonetic letters

姘 (pīn) have illicit relations with

【姘夫】 pīnfū live-in lover; cohabitant; cohabitee
【姘妇】 pīnfù mistress; paramour
【姘居】 pīnjū cohabit; live illicitly as husband and wife
【姘头】 pīn·tou mistress; paramour

贫 (pín) 1.(贫穷) poor; impoverished: 脱～致富 cast off poverty and become prosperous 2.(缺少) be deficient in; be poor in; be scanty of 3.(絮烦讨厌) garrulous; loquacious

【贫病交集】 pínbìng-jiāojí sick and in straits
【贫病交迫】 pínbìng-jiāopò sick as well as poor; be beset by poverty and illness
【贫病相连】 pínbìng-xiānglián poverty and sickness are closely connected with

【贫乏】 pínfá poor; short; lacking: 内容～ devoid of matter

【贫富不均】 pínfù-bùjūn too much difference between the rich and the poor; gap between the rich and the poor

【贫富两极分化】 pínfù liǎngjí fēnhuà polarization between the rich and the poor

【贫富悬殊】 pínfù-xuánshū extreme disparity between the rich and the poor; wide gap between the rich and the poor

【贫寒】 pínhán poor; poverty-stricken: 出身～ be born poor; came from a poor family

【贫瘠】 pínjí barren; infertile; poor: ～的土壤 poor soil

【贫贱】 pínjiàn poor and lowly; in straitened and humble circumstances: ～不能移 not to be shaken or modified by one's poverty or destitution

【贫苦】 pínkǔ poor; poverty-stricken; badly off

【贫矿】 pínkuàng lean ore; low grade ore

【贫困】 pínkùn poor; impoverished; in straitened circumstances: 摆脱～ lift oneself out of poverty; cast off poverty

【贫困地区】 pínkùn dìqū poverty-stricken area

【贫困线】 pínkùnxiàn subsistence level; poverty level; poverty line

【贫民】 pínmín poor people; pauper

【贫民窟】 pínmínkū slum

【贫民区】 pínmínqū slum area; slum district

【贫农】 pínnóng poor peasant

【贫气】 pín·qi 1.（小气）stingy; miserly; mean 2.（絮烦讨厌）garrulous; loquacious

【贫穷】 pínqióng poor; needy; impoverished

【贫弱】 pínruò poor and weak

【贫血】 pínxuè anemia: 再生障碍性～ aplastic anemia

【贫铀弹】 pínyóudàn depleted uranium projectile

【贫嘴】 pínzuǐ garrulous; loquacious: 耍～ be talkative; be a loquacious

频（pín） 1.（屡次）frequently; repeatedly 2.〈*Physics*〉frequency

【频传】 pínchuán keep pouring in: 捷报～ reports of new victories keep pouring in

【频带】 píndài frequency band

【频道】 píndào frequency channel: 35～ channel 35; channel thirty five

【频段】 pínduàn frequency range

【频段分配】 pínduàn fēnpèi frequency allocation

【频繁】 pínfán frequently; often: ～交往 frequent contacts

【频率】 pínlǜ frequency: 低～ low frequency / 高～ high frequency

【频频】 pínpín again and again; repeatedly

【频谱】 pínpǔ frequency spectrum

品（pǐn） 1.（物品）article; product: 生活必需～ daily necessities 2.（品位；品级）grade; class; rank: 上～ top grade 3.（品质）character; quality: 人～ moral quality 4.（品评）taste sth. with discrimination; sample; savor: ～茶 sample tea

【品标】 pǐnbiāo 〈*Guitar*〉 position marks

【品尝】 pǐncháng taste; sample; savor

【品德】 pǐndé moral character; morality: ～教育 character education

【品格】 pǐngé 1.（品性；品行）one's character and morals: ～高雅 high character 2.（作品质量和风格）quality and style

【品红】 pǐnhóng 1.（颜色）pinkish red 2.（染料）magenta; fuchsine

【品级】 pǐnjí grade; class

【品类】 pǐnlèi category; class; variety: ～繁多 a great variety

【品貌】 pǐnmào 1.（相貌）looks; appearance: ～端正 well-shaped figure and decorous appearance 2.（人品和相貌）character and looks; conduct and appearance: ～端庄 one's bearing is respectable

【品名】 pǐnmíng the name of an article; the name or description of a commodity

【品目】 pǐnmù names of things; items: ～繁多 numerous names; names and descriptions of articles are numerous

【品评】 pǐnpíng judge; comment on

【品头论足】 pǐntóu-lùnzú 1.（评人外表）make frivolous remarks about a woman's appearance 2.（挑剔）find fault with; be overcritical

【品脱】 pǐntuō pint: 1 pint = 0.4732 liter 或 0.5683 litre

【品位】 pǐnwèi 1.〈*Mineral.*〉 grade 2.（品质）

quality

【品味】 pǐnwèi 1.(品尝) taste; savor 2.(玩味) savor; ponder; chew 3.(品质) quality

【品系】 pǐnxì 〈*Biol*.〉 strain

【品行】 pǐnxíng conduct; behavior: ～不良 having bad conduct; ill-behaved

【品性】 pǐnxìng moral character

【品议】 pǐnyì judge; comment on

【品质】 pǐnzhì 1.(人品) character; quality: 道德～ moral character 2.(质量) quality: ～高 of the best quality

【品质管制】 pǐnzhì guǎnzhì quality control

【品质检验】 pǐnzhì jiǎnyàn quality restriction

【品质证明书】 pǐnzhì zhèngmíngshū certificate of quality

【品种】 pǐnzhǒng 1.〈*Biol*.〉 breed; strain; variety: 优良～ improved breeds 2.(产品种类) variety; assortment

聘 (pìn) 1.(聘请) engage: ～某人为教授 engage sb. as a professor 2.(定亲) betroth

【聘金】 pìnjīn betrothal money (for the bride's family)

【聘礼】 pìnlǐ betrothal presents; bride-price

【聘期】 pìnqī allotted time of employment

【聘请】 pìnqǐng engage; invite; employ: ～律师 brief a barrister / ～一个新秘书 engage a new secretary

【聘任】 pìnrèn engage; appoint to a position: ～她为经理 appoint her to be manager

【聘任制】 pìnrènzhì appointive employment

【聘书】 pìnshū letter of appointment; contract

【聘用】 pìnyòng engage; appoint to a position; assign sb. to a post

【聘用条件】 pìnyòng tiáojiàn conditions for employment

【聘约】 pìnyuē contract of employment

ping

乒 (pīng) table tennis; ping-pong

【乒联】 pīnglián table tennis federation

【乒乓球】 pīngpāngqiú 1.〈*Sports*〉 table tennis; ping-pong: 打～ play ping-pong 2.(指球) table tennis ball; ping-pong ball

【乒乓球拍】 pīngpāngqiúpāi table tennis bat

【乒乓球台】 pīngpāngqiútái table tennis table

【乒乓球网】 pīngpāngqiúwǎng table tennis net

【乒乓球运动】 pīngpāngqiú yùndòng table tennis; ping-pong

【乒坛】 pīngtán table tennis circles

【乒协】 pīngxié table tennis association

平 (píng) 1.(不斜,无凹凸) flat; level; even; smooth: 把衣服弄～ smooth one's dress / 躺～ lie stretched out; lie flat / 这块地相当～。This piece of ground is flat enough. 2.(使平) level; even: ～一～地面 level the ground; even the land 3.(高度相同) be on the same level; be on a par; equal: ～全国纪录 equal a national record 4.(平局) make the same score; tie; draw: 双方踢成二～。The two teams tied at 2-2. 5.(平均;公平) equal; fair; impartial 6.(平静) calm; peaceful; quiet: 风～浪静 the sea was calm 7.(平定) put down; suppress: ～乱 suppress a riot 8.(平常的) average; common

【平安】 píng'ān safe and sound; without mishap; well: ～康泰 peaceful and well-being

【平安险】 píng'ānxiǎn free of particular average (F.P.A.)

【平白】 píngbái 1.(无缘无故) for no reason; gratuitously 2.(浅显) plain; obvious; easy to understand

【平板】 píngbǎn dull and stereotyped; flat; monotonous: 写得～ written in a dull style

【平板玻璃】 píngbǎn bō·li plate glass

【平板车】 píngbǎnchē 1.(人力货运三轮车) flatbed tricycle 2.(货运汽车) platform trailer; flatbed; flatbed truck

【平辈】 píngbèi of the same generation

【平布】 píngbù plain cloth

【平步青云】 píngbù-qīngyún rapidly go up in the world; have a meteoric rise

【平产】 píngchǎn be equal in output; have the same output

【平常】 píngcháng 1.(普通) ordinary; common: 她穿着～的衣服。She is in ordinary dress. 2.(平时) generally; usually; ordinarily; as a rule: 到得比～晚 arrive later than

usual 3.（不出色）average; mediocre: 他的才能很～。He is a man of average ability.
【平车】 píngchē 〈*Railway*〉 flatcar; flat wagon
【平川】 píngchuān level land; flat, open country; plain: 一马～ a vast stretch of flat land
【平淡】 píngdàn flat; insipid; prosaic; pedestrian; dull: ～无奇 prosaic; pedestrian; nothing exciting
【平等】 píngděng equality; equal (adj.): 在～的基础上 on an equal footing
【平等待遇】 píngděng dàiyù equal treatment
【平等关系】 píngděng guānxì relations on an equal basis
【平等互惠】 píngděng hùhuì reciprocal favored treatment
【平等互利】 píngděng hùlì equality and mutual benefit
【平等权利】 píngděng quánlì equal rights
【平等协商】 píngděng xiéshāng consultation on the basis of equality
【平地】 píngdì 1.（平整土地）level the land; level the ground; rake the soil smooth 2.（平坦的土地）level ground; flat ground
【平地风波】 píngdì fēngbō a sudden storm on a calm sea; a sudden, unexpected turn of events; unforeseen trouble
【平定】 píngdìng 1.（平稳安定）calm down 2.（平息）suppress; put down: ～叛乱 put down a rebellion
【平凡】 píngfán ordinary; common; commonplace: ～的工作 ordinary work
【平反】 píngfǎn redress (a mishandled case); rehabilitate: ～错案 redress a mishandled case / ～冤案 redress of a grievance
【平方】 píngfāng 1.〈*Math.*〉 square; X squared (符号为 X^2): 九是三的～。Nine is the square of three. 2.（平方米）square meter: 15～米的房间 a room of fifteen square meters
【平方根】 píngfānggēn root; square root
【平房】 píngfáng single-story house; one-story house
【平分】 píngfēn divide equally; share and share alike; go halves; go fifty-fifty
【平分秋色】 píngfēn qiūsè have equal shares; share on a fifty-fifty basis; divide the cheerful countenance equally
【平复】 píng·fu 1.（恢复平静）calm down; subside; be pacified 2.（痊愈）be cured; be healed
【平光】 píngguāng zero diopter; plain glass
【平光眼镜】 píngguāng yǎnjìng plain glass spectacles
【平和】 pínghé 1.（温和）gentle; mild; moderate; placid 2.（药性温和）mild 3.（平静）calm; quiet; tranquil
【平衡】 pínghéng balance; equilibrium: 综合～ overall balance / 收支～ balance between income and expenditure
【平衡表演】 pínghéng biǎoyǎn balancing act
【平衡杆】 pínghénggān balancing pole
【平衡轮】 pínghénglún 〈*Bicycle*〉 stabilizer
【平衡木】 pínghéngmù 1.〈*Sports*〉 balance beam exercise 2.（指器械）balance beam
【平滑】 pínghuá level and smooth; smooth
【平滑肌】 pínghuájī 〈*Anat.*〉 smooth muscle
【平缓】 pínghuǎn 1.（平坦）gently 2.（平稳）mild; placid; gentle 3.（平和）calm; quiet; tranquil
【平假名】 píngjiǎmíng hiragana (Jap.)
【平价】 píngjià 1.（利润低的价格）fair price 2.〈*Econ.*〉 par; parity: 固定～ fixed parity / 汇兑～ par of exchange / 官方～ official parity
【平价商店】 píngjià shāngdiàn fair-price shop
【平静】 píngjìng calm; quiet; tranquil: ～的生活 a quiet life
【平局】 píngjú draw; tie: 以～结束 end in a draw
【平均】 píngjūn 1.（按份均算）average; mean 2.（没有轻重区别）equally; share and share alike
【平均分摊】 píngjūn fēntān share out equally
【平均高度】 píngjūn gāodù average height
【平均价格】 píngjūn jiàgé average price
【平均利润】 píngjūn lìrùn average profit
【平均年龄】 píngjūn niánlíng composite life; average age
【平均收入】 píngjūn shōurù average income
【平均寿命】 píngjūn shòumìng average life span; life expectancy
【平均数】 píngjūnshù average; mean: 取其～

take the mean

【平均速度】 píngjūn sùdù average speed; mean velocity

【平均无故障时间】 píngjūn wúgùzhàng shíjiān mean time between failure

【平均支付额】 píngjūn zhīfù'é average payoff

【平均值】 píngjūnzhí average value; mean: 取其～ take the mean

【平均主义】 píngjūn zhǔyì equalitarianism; egalitarianism

【平列】 píngliè place side by side; place on a par with each other; put on a par with

【平流】 píngliú 〈*Meteorol.*〉 advection

【平流层】 píngliúcéng 〈*Meteorol.*〉 stratosphere

【平米】 píngmǐ square meter: 12～米的房间 a room of twelve square meters

【平面】 píngmiàn plane; plane surface; level surface

【平面几何】 píngmiàn jǐhé plane geometry

【平面交叉】 píngmiàn jiāochā 〈*Transport*〉 level crossing

【平面图】 píngmiàntú 1.(平面图形) plane 2.(垂直投影图形) plane figure

【平民】 píngmín common people; common man; the populace

【平年】 píngnián 1.〈*Astron.*〉 non-leap year; common year 2.(平常年景) average year

【平平】 píngpíng average; mediocre; indifferent: ～无奇 be average and not clever

【平铺直叙】 píngpū-zhíxù 1.(简单直接叙述) tell in a simple, straightforward way; narrate in a simple direct way 2.(不讲求修辞) speak or write in a dull, flat style

【平起平坐】 píngqǐ-píngzuò sit as equals at the same table; be on an equal footing

【平权】 píngquán (enjoy) equal rights

【平绒】 píngróng 〈*Textiles*〉 velveteen

【平生】 píngshēng all one's life; one's whole life: ～大事 the biggest events in all one's life

【平时】 píngshí 1.(日常) at ordinary times; in normal times; usually 2.(非战时) in peacetime

【平顺】 píngshùn smooth-going; plain sailing

【平素】 píngsù usually; customarily

【平台】 píngtái terrace; platform

【平坦】 píngtǎn level; even; smooth

【平头】 píngtóu 1.(男子发式) closely cropped hair; crop; crew cut 2.(普通的) common; ordinary

【平头百姓】 píngtóu bǎixìng common people

【平头螺帽】 píngtóu luómào flat head

【平纹】 píngwén plain weave

【平纹织物】 píngwén zhīwù plain cloth

【平稳】 píngwěn 1.(没波动) smooth: ～过渡 smooth transition 2.(不摇晃) smooth and steady; smooth; stable: 飞行～ have a smooth flight

【平息】 píngxī 1.(平静) calm down; quiet down; subside 2.(平定) put down; suppress; quell: ～暴乱 suppress a riot

【平心而论】 píngxīn'érlùn in all fairness; to give sb. his due; objectively speaking

【平心静气】 píngxīn-jìngqì calmly; dispassionately; cool-headed

【平信】 píngxìn 1.(非挂号信) ordinary mail 2.(非航空信) surface mail

【平行】 píngxíng 1.(等级相同) of equal rank; on an equal footing; parallel; of the same level 2.(同时进行的) simultaneous; parallel 3.〈*Math.*〉 parallel: 相互～ be parallel to each other

【平行四边形】 píngxíng sìbiānxíng parallelogram

【平胸球】 píngxiōngqiú 〈*Football*〉 chest-high ball

【平移】 píngyí 〈*Physics*〉 translation; translational (adj.)

【平抑】 píngyì stabilize through checking measures

【平易】 píngyì 1.(谦逊和蔼) unassuming; amiable: ～近人 amiable and easy of approach; easy to approach; unassuming and approachable 2.(浅近易懂) easy; plain

【平庸】 píngyōng mediocre; indifferent; commonplace

【平邮】 píngyōu 1.(不挂号的) ordinary mail 2.(非航空的) surface mail: 这个包裹你是想空邮还是～? Would you like this parcel sent by air or surface mail?

【平原】 píngyuán plain: 冲积～ alluvial plain

【平展】 píngzhǎn 1.(平坦、宽敞) open and flat 2.(平而舒展) unruffled

【平展展】 píngzhǎnzhǎn unruffled
【平整】 píngzhěng 1.（整地）level：～土地 level the land 2.（平而整齐）neat；smooth
【平正】 píngzhèng straight and even
【平装】 píngzhuāng paperback；paper-cover
【平装本】 píngzhuāngběn paperback；paperback edition
【平足】 píngzú flatfoot

评（píng） 1.（评论；批评）comment；criticize；review 2.（评判）judge；appraise
【评比】 píngbǐ appraise through comparison；compare and assess
【评定】 píngdìng pass judgment on；evaluate；assess；rate
【评分】 píngfēn give a mark；mark（students' papers，etc.）；grade；score
【评分标准】 píngfēn biāozhǔn standards of grading
【评功】 pínggōng evaluate achievements；appraise sb's merits：～授奖 announce commendations and issue awards
【评估】 pínggū evaluate and appraise
【评级】 píngjí grade；rate
【评价】 píngjià 1.（进行评价）appraise；evaluate；assess：～过低 rate sth. unreasonably low / 高度～ highly appraise 2.（所给的评价）appraisal；evaluation；assessment：给予很高的～ give a highly appraisal
【评奖】 píngjiǎng decide on awards through discussion
【评介】 píngjiè review：～一本新书 review a new book
【评卷】 píngjuàn read and appraise examination papers
【评理】 pínglǐ judge between right and wrong；decide which side is right
【评论】 pínglùn 1.（批评或议论）comment on；discuss：～是非 discuss right and wrong / 大家都在～她的皮大衣。Everyone commented on her fur coat. 2.（批评文章，议论文章）comment；commentary；review：时事～ comments on current events / 无关紧要的～ insignificant remarks / 对…发表～ make a comment about sth.
【评论员】 pínglùnyuán commentator：电视～ television commentator
【评判】 píngpàn pass judgment on；judge
【评判员】 píngpànyuán 1.（体育、演讲等的）judge 2.（音乐等的）adjudicator
【评聘】 píngpìn evaluate and appointed to a position
【评审】 píngshěn evaluate and pass judgment；judge and determine
【评书】 píngshū story telling
【评述】 píngshù comment on
【评头论足】 píngtóu-lùnzú find fault with；criticize from head to feet；comment from head to feet
【评析】 píngxī make commentary analyze
【评选】 píngxuǎn choose through public appraisal；discuss and elect
【评议】 píngyì appraise sth. through discussion；deliberate：～确定 be discussed and determined by the masses
【评议会】 píngyìhuì appraisal meeting
【评语】 píngyǔ comment；remark
【评阅】 píngyuè read and appraise
【评职称】 píngzhíchēng evaluate the title of a technical or professional post
【评注】 píngzhù 1.（评论并注释）make commentary and annotation 2.（作出的评论和注释）notes and commentary
【评传】 píngzhuàn critical biography

坪（píng） level ground：草～ lawn / 停机～ aircraft park；apron

苹［蘋］（píng）
【苹果】 píngguǒ 1.〈*Bot.*〉apple；apple tree 2.（果实）apple
【苹果脯】 píngguǒfǔ preserved apple
【苹果干】 píngguǒgān dried apple slices
【苹果花】 píngguǒhuā apple flower
【苹果酱】 píngguǒjiàng apple jam
【苹果酒】 píngguǒjiǔ cider；applejack
【苹果绿】 píngguǒlǜ apple green
【苹果树】 píngguǒshù apple tree
【苹果园】 píngguǒyuán apple orchard
【苹果汁】 píngguǒzhī cider
【苹果种籽】 píngguǒ zhǒng·zǐ apple kernel

萍［蓱］（píng） duckweed
【萍水相逢】 píngshuǐ-xiāngféng meet by chance like patches of drifting duckweed

鲆（píng） flounder：斑～ flounder / 大菱～ turbot / 菱～ brill / 牙～ bastard halibut

【鲆鱼】 píngyú flounder

凭[凴、凴] (píng) 1.(靠着) lean on; lean against 2.(依靠) rely on; depend on 3.(证据) certification; evidence; proof: 以此为～。This will serve as certification. 4.(根据) go by; base on; take as the basis: ～表面现象判断 on the face of it 5.(任凭) no matter: ～你是谁 no matter who you may be

【凭单】 píngdān voucher; indenture; a certificate for drawing money, goods, etc.

【凭单索引】 píngdān suǒyǐn vouchers index

【凭单制度】 píngdān zhìdù voucher system

【凭吊】 píngdiào visit (a historical site) and ponder on the past

【凭借】 píngjiè rely on; depend on: ～经验 by virtue of experience

【凭据】 píngjù evidence; proof

【凭空】 píngkōng out of the void; without foundation; out of thin air: ～杜撰 create groundless rumors / ～捏造 a mere lie

【凭眺】 píngtiào enjoy a distant view from a height; gaze from a high place into the distance

【凭信】 píngxìn trust; believe: 他的话不足～。His words are not to be trusted.

【凭依】 píngyī base oneself on; rely on; have sth. to go by

【凭仗】 píngzhàng rely on; depend on

【凭证】 píngzhèng proof; evidence; certificate; voucher: 付款～ paying voucher / 收款～ receiving voucher

屏 (píng) 1.(屏风) screen 2.(遮挡) shield; screen

(另见"屏"bǐng)

【屏蔽】 píngbì shield; screen

【屏风】 píngfēng screen

【屏幕】 píngmù screen: 电视～ telescreen; screen

【屏条】 píngtiáo a set of hanging scrolls

【屏障】 píngzhàng protective screen; shelter; barrier: 天然～ natural barrier; natural defense

瓶[缾] (píng) bottle; vase; jar; flask: 醋～ vinegar cruet / 胡椒～ pepper-box; pepper pot / 酒～ wine bottle / 花～ flower vase / 酱油～ sauce cruet / 芥末～ mustard pot / 奶～ milk bottle / 热水～ thermos; vacuum flask / 塑料～ plastic bottle / 盐～ saltcellar; saltshaker / 一～啤酒 a bottle of beer

【瓶胆】 píngdǎn glass liner

【瓶盖】 pínggài cap

【瓶盖起子】 pínggài qǐ·zi bottle cap opener

【瓶颈】 píngjǐng bottleneck

【瓶塞】 píngsāi bottle stopper: 软木～ cork

【瓶装】 píngzhuāng bottled; in bottles: ～啤酒 beer in bottle / ～液化气 bottled gas; bugas

【瓶子】 píng·zi bottle: 给～装满水,然后盖紧瓶盖儿。Fill the bottle with water and put the cap on firmly.

po

钋 (pō) 〈*Chem.*〉 polonium (元素符号 Po)

坡 (pō) 1.(斜坡) slope: 山～ a mountain slope; hillside / 上～ uphill / 下～ downhill 2.(倾斜) sloping; slanting: 把梯子放～一点。Slope the ladder a bit.

【坡地】 pōdì hillside fields; sloping fields; land on the slopes

【坡度】 pōdù slope; gradient: 30 度的～ a slope of 30 degrees

颇 (pō) 1.(偏颇;不正) inclined to one side; oblique 2.(很;相当地) quite; rather; considerably: ～感兴趣 have considerable interest

泼[潑] (pō) 1.(泼水) sprinkle; splash; spill: 用水～地 splash the floor with water 2.(撒泼) rude and unreasonable; shrewish

【泼妇】 pōfù shrew; vixen

【泼辣】 pō·la 1.(凶悍不讲理) rude and unreasonable; shrewish; vixenish; fierce and unreasonable 2.(文章有力) pungent; forceful 3.(有魄力) bold and vigorous: 工作～ be bold and vigorous in one's work

【泼冷水】 pō lěngshuǐ pour cold water on; dampen the enthusiasm of; put a dumper on; discourage

【泼墨】 pōmò splash-ink

【泼洒】 pōsǎ sprinkle; splash; spill

【泼水节】 Pōshuǐjié the Water-Sprinkling Festival

婆 (pó) 1.(老年妇女) old woman 2.(丈夫的母亲) mother-in-law; husband's mother

【婆家】 pó·jia husband's family

【婆母】 pómǔ mother-in-law

【婆婆】 pó·po 1.(丈夫的母亲) husband's mother; mother-in-law 2.(祖母或外祖母) grandmother 3.(比喻上级机关或领导) higher authority; chief

【婆娑】 pósuō whirling; dancing

叵 (pǒ) impossible

【叵测】 pǒcè unfathomable; unpredictable: 居心～ with hidden intent / 心怀～ harbor dark designs; nurse evil intentions

钷 (pǒ) 〈*Chem.*〉 promethium (元素符号 Pm)

笸 (pǒ)

【笸箩】 pǒ·luo shallow basket

迫［廹］(pò) 1.(逼迫;强迫) compel; force; press: 被～撤退 be forced to retreat 2.(急迫) urgent; pressing: 从容不～ calm and unhurried 3.(迫近) approach; go towards; go near

(另见"迫"pǎi)

【迫不得已】 pòbùdéyǐ have no alternative (but to); be forced to; be compelled compelled by circumstances

【迫不及待】 pòbùjídài unable to hold oneself back; too impatient to wait; brook no delay

【迫害】 pòhài persecute: 政治～ political persecution

【迫降】 pòjiàng forced landing; distress landing

【迫近】 pòjìn approach; draw near; be imminent: 死亡～ be faced with imminent death

【迫切】 pòqiè urgent; pressing; imperative: ～要求 urgent request

【迫切陈词】 pòqiè chéncí urge to give a statement

【迫使】 pòshǐ force; compel; coerce: ～某人做某事 force sb. to do sth.; force sb. into doing sth. / 大雨～我们待在家里。The rain compelled us to stay indoors.

【迫降】 pòjiàng force the enemy to surrender; for the enemy into surrender

【迫在眉睫】 pòzàiméijié 1.(临近眼前) imminent; stare sb. in the face 2.(紧迫) extremely urgent; extremely urgent and near

魄 (pò) 1.(魂魄) soul: 魂飞～散 (be frightened) out of one's wits 2.(魄力) vigor; spirit

【魄力】 pò·lì daring and resolution; boldness: 很有～的人 man with plenty of guts

破 (pò) 1.(破旧) broken; damaged; torn; worn-out 2.(破开) break; split; cleave; cut: 把百元的票子～开 break a hundred yuan note 3.(使破损) break; break down; damage: 小心别打～杯子。Be careful not to break the cup. 4.(突破) break; break through: ～世界纪录 break the world record 5.(破除) get rid of; destroy; break with: ～旧立新 destroy the old and establish the new 6.(打败;攻克) defeat; capture 7.(揭穿) expose the truth of; lay bare; see through 8.(讥讽质量不好) poor; paltry; lousy; shabby: 谁看那个～电影! Who wants to see that poor film!

【破案】 pò'àn solve a case; clear up a case; unravel a case

【破案率】 pò'ànlǜ detection rate; clear-up rate

【破败】 pòbài 1.(残破) ruined; dilapidated; tumble-down 2.(衰败) declined; be at a low ebb

【破冰船】 pòbīngchuán icebreaker

【破财】 pòcái suffer unexpected personal financial losses

【破产】 pòchǎn 1.〈*Law*〉 go bankrupt; become insolvent; bankruptcy (n.): 银行～ bank failure / 濒于～ on the verge of bankruptcy / 宣告～ declare bankruptcy / 公司已经～。The company is bankrupt. 2.(丧失全部财产) become impoverished 3.(失败) go bankruptcy; fall through; come to naught: 阴谋～了。The plot has fallen through.

【破产法】 pòchǎnfǎ insolvent law; law of bankruptcy

【破除】 pòchú do away with; get rid of;

eradicate; break with：～恶习 break with foul habits / ～迷信 do away with superstitions

【破费】 pòfèi spend money; go to some expense

【破釜沉舟】 pòfǔ-chénzhōu break the caldrons and sink the boats (after crossing); cut off all means of retreat; burn one's boats

【破格】 pògé break a rule; make an exception：～使用优秀人才 employ excellent, qualified person by bypassing the conventional rules

【破格录用】 pògé lùyòng break a rule to engage sb.

【破格提升】 pògé tíshēng make an exceptional promotion

【破坏】 pòhuài **1**.（损毁）destroy; wreck：～铁路 wreck railways **2**.（使受损）do great damage to; damage; disrupt：～社会秩序 disrupt public order **3**.（变革）destroy; demolish; change completely：～旧秩序 demolish the old order **4**.（违反）violate; break; breach：～合同 breach of contract **5**.（物体的组织损坏）decompose; destroy：～维生素 C destroy vitamin C

【破坏分子】 pòhuài fènzǐ saboteur

【破坏活动】 pòhuài huódòng sabotage

【破坏力】 pòhuàilì destructive power

【破坏性】 pòhuàixìng destructiveness; destructive (adj.)

【破坏性试验】 pòhuàixìng shìyàn destructive test

【破获】 pòhuò unearth; uncover; ferret out：～一个间谍组织 unearth a spy ring

【破旧】 pòjiù old and shabby; worn-out; dilapidated

【破口大骂】 pòkǒu-dàmà shout abuse; let loose a torrent of abuse; hurl all kinds of abuse

【破烂】 pòlàn **1**.（残破的）tattered; worn-out; ragged：～东西 worm-out stuff **2**.（废品）junk; scrap

【破烂货】 pòlànhuò worthless stuff; rubbish; trash

【破例】 pòlì break a rule; make an exception

【破裂】 pòliè **1**.（出现裂缝）crack; split **2**.（指感情、关系等）break down; break up; rupture; fall through：谈判～了。The negotiations broke down. / 他们的婚姻～了。Their marriage has broken up.

【破落】 pòluò **1**.（由盛而衰）decline (in wealth and position); fall into reduced circumstances; be reduced to poverty **2**.（破败）ruined; dilapidated; tumble-down

【破落户】 pòluòhù a family that has gone down in the world; impoverished family

【破门】 pòmén **1**.（砸开门）force open the door; break into **2**.〈*Football*〉kick a goal; make a goal; score a goal

【破灭】 pòmiè be shattered; be disillusioned; fall through; evaporate：幻想～ ruin of an illusion

【破伤风】 pòshāngfēng 〈*Med*.〉tetanus

【破碎】 pòsuì **1**.（破成碎块的）tattered; broken：～的纸 paper in tatters **2**.（使破成碎块）smash sth. to pieces; break into pieces; crush

【破碎机】 pòsuìjī crusher; breaker

【破损】 pòsǔn damage; breakage：避免～ avoid breakage

【破损险】 pòsǔnxiǎn risk of breakage

【破天荒】 pòtiānhuāng occur for the first time; be unprecedented; without precedent：～的大事 the biggest event without any precedent

【破土】 pòtǔ **1**.（挖地动工）break ground：～建新的图书馆。The ground was broken for a new library. **2**.（开始耕种）start spring ploughing **3**.（种子发芽出土）break through the soil

【破晓】 pòxiǎo dawn; daybreak：～时分 at dawn; at the peep of day

【破鞋】 pòxié loose woman

【破译】 pòyì recognize and interpret

【破绽】 pò·zhàn **1**.（衣服开线）a burst seam **2**.（漏洞）flaw; weak point：～百出 be full of flaws

【破折号】 pòzhéhào dash (符号为 —)

pou

剖 (pōu) **1**.（破开）cut open; rip open：把鸡肚子～开 cut open the belly of a chicken 2.(剖析) analyse; examine; dissect

【剖白】 pōubái explain oneself; vindicate oneself: ～心迹 explain what one thinks

【剖腹】 pōufù 1.(剖腹自杀) harakiri 2.〈*Med*.〉 cut open the abdomen

【剖宫产】 pōugōngchǎn 1.(指分娩) Caesarean birth 2.(指手术) Caesarean operation

【剖解】 pōujiě analyse; dissect

【剖面】 pōumiàn section; sectional (adj.)

【剖面图】 pōumiàntú sectional drawing; section

【剖明事理】 pōumíng-shìlǐ analyse the whys and wherefores

【剖视图】 pōushìtú cut-away view; cut-open view

【剖析】 pōuxī analyse; dissect: ～失败的原因 analyse the cause of failure

pu

仆 (pū) fall forward; fall prostrate: 前～后继 one stepping into the breach as another falls

(另见"仆"pú)

扑[撲] (pū) 1.(冲向) throw oneself on; pounce on: 警察突然向罪犯～过去。Policeman pounced on the criminal. 2.(全力以赴) devote: 一心～在癌症的研究上 devote oneself heart and soul to the research on cancer 3.(攻打) rush at; attack: 直～匪巢 swoop down on the bandits' lair 4.(拍打) flap; flutter

【扑鼻】 pūbí assail the nostrils

【扑打】 pūdǎ swat: ～苍蝇 swat a fly

【扑打】 pū·da beat; pat

【扑粉】 pūfěng 1.(化妆用香粉) face powder 2.(爽身粉) talcum powder 3.(搽粉) apply powder; put on powder

【扑救】 pūjiù put out a fire to save life and property

【扑克】 pūkè playing cards; poker: 打～ play cards

【扑空】 pūkōng come away empty-handed; fail to get or achieve what one wants

【扑面】 pūmiàn blow on one's face; against one's face

【扑灭】 pūmiè 1.(扑打消灭) stamp out; put out; extinguish 2.(消灭;灭亡) exterminate; wipe out: ～虫害 exterminate insect pests

【扑簌】 pūsù (of tears) trickling down: 眼泪～地往下掉 tears trickled down one's cheeks

【扑腾】 pūtēng 〈*onomat*.〉 thump; thud

【扑腾】 pū·teng move up and down; throb; palpitate

【扑通】 pūtōng 〈*onomat*.〉 flop; thump; splash; pit-a-pat

【扑翼】 pūyì flapping wing

铺 (pū) 1.(展开;摊平) spread; extend; unfold 2.(铺设) pave; lay: ～地板 lay down a floor

(另见"铺"pù)

【铺陈】 pūchén narrate in detail; elaborate

【铺衬】 pū·chen small pieces of cloth used for patches

【铺床】 pūchuáng make the bed

【铺地砖】 pūdìzhuān floor tile; paving tile

【铺盖】 pū·gai bedding; bedclothes

【铺轨】 pūguǐ lay a railway track

【铺轨机】 pūguǐjī track-laying machine; tracklayer

【铺路】 pūlù 1.(铺设道路) pave a road; pave the way; surface a road 2.(预作安排;排除障碍) pave the way for: 那个条约是为进一步的合作～。The treaty paved the way to still closer forms of joint action.

【铺路机】 pūlùjī paver

【铺平】 pūpíng pave nicely; smooth out: ～道路 pave the way for

【铺砌】 pūqì pave: 用卵石～的小路 a path paved with pebbles

【铺设】 pūshè 1.(铺铁轨、管线) lay; build: ～铁轨 lay a railway track 2.(布置;安排) arrange; decorate

【铺天盖地】 pūtiān-gàidì blot out the sky and cover up the earth; in an overwhelming manner

【铺叙】 pūxù narrate in detail; elaborate

【铺展】 pūzhǎn spread out; sprawl

【铺张】 pūzhāng extravagant; wasteful

【铺张浪费】 pūzhāng làngfèi extravagance and waste: 反对～ oppose extravagance and waste

噗 (pū) 〈*onomat*.〉 puff

【噗通】 pūtōng 同“扑通”

蒲(pú) 〈*Bot.*〉 cattail

【蒲包】 púbāo cattail bag; rush bag

【蒲草】 púcǎo the stem or leaf of cattail

【蒲福风级】 Púfú fēngjí 〈*Meteorol.*〉 Beaufort scale ‖ 参见“风级”

【蒲公英】 púgōngyīng dandelion

【蒲绒】 púróng cattail wool

【蒲扇】 púshàn cattail leaf fan

【蒲式耳】 púshìěr bushel (1 bushel ＝ 35.2 liters in the US or 36.4 liters in Britain)

【蒲团】 pútuán cattail hassock; rush cushion

【蒲席】 púxí cattail mat; rush mat

仆[僕](pú) servant：公～ public servant

(另见“仆”pū)

【仆从】 púcóng footman; retainer; henchman

【仆从国】 púcóngguó vassal country

【仆人】 púrén (domestic) servant

匍(pú)

【匍匐】 púfú 1.(爬行) crawl; creep：～前进 crawl forward 2.(趴) lie prostrate

【匍匐植物】 púfú zhíwù creeper

葡(pú)

【葡萄】 pú·táo grape

【葡萄干】 pú·táogān raisin

【葡萄架】 pú·táojià grape trellis

【葡萄酒】 pú·táojiǔ (grape) wine：白～ white wine / 红～ red wine / 干白～ dry white wine / 干红～ dry red wine

【葡萄酒杯】 pú·táojiǔ bēi wineglass

【葡萄胎】 pú·táotāi 〈*Med.*〉 vesicular mole; hudatidiform mole

【葡萄藤】 pú·táoténg grapevine

【葡萄园】 pú·táoyuán vineyard; grapery

【葡萄糖】 pú·táotáng glucose; grape sugar; dextrose

【葡萄柚】 pú·táoyòu 〈*Bot.*〉 grapefruit

【葡萄汁】 pú·táozhī grape juice

菩(pú)

【菩萨】 púsà 1.〈*Religion*〉 Bodhisattva 2.(佛；神) Buddha; Buddhist idol 3.(心肠慈善的人) a kindhearted person

【菩提】 pútí 〈*Buddhism*〉 bodhi; supreme

【菩提树】 pútíshù pipal; bo-tree; bodhi tree

镤(pú) 〈*Chem.*〉 protactinium (元素符号 Pa)

朴[樸](pǔ) simple; plain

【朴实】 pǔshí 1.(朴素) simple; plain 2.(踏实) down-to-earth; sincere and honest; guileless

【朴素】 pǔsù 1.(不华丽) plain; simple; unadorned 2.(不奢侈) frugal; economical; thrifty 3.(朴实) down-to-earth; sincere and honest：～的语言 unaffected language

【朴素唯物主义】 pǔsù wéiwù zhǔyì naive materialism

【朴直】 pǔzhí honest and straightforward

【朴质】 pǔzhì simple and unadorned; natural

圃(pǔ) garden：花～ flower nursery

浦(pǔ) water side; shore

【浦东开发区】 Pǔdōng kāifāqū Pudong New Area

【浦东开发规划】 Pǔdōng kāifā guīhuà Pudong development project

普(pǔ) general; universal

【普遍】 pǔbiàn universal; common; general; widespread：～的要求 universal demand

【普遍裁军】 pǔbiàn cáijūn universal disarmament

【普遍规律】 pǔbiàn guīlǜ universal law

【普遍性】 pǔbiànxìng universality

【普遍真理】 pǔbiàn zhēnlǐ universal truth

【普查】 pǔchá general investigation; general survey：地质～ reconnaissance survey

【普法】 pǔfǎ popularize law

【普及】 pǔjí 1.(推广) popularize; disseminate; spread 2.(普遍传到) universal; popular

【普及本】 pǔjíběn popular edition

【普及教育】 pǔjí jiàoyù universal education

【普教】 pǔjiào general education

【普兰】 Pǔlán 〈place〉 Purang

【普米族】 Pǔmǐzú Primi (中国少数民族，主要分布在云南)

【普天同庆】 pǔtiān-tóngqìng the whole world or nation joins in the jubilation; universal or national celebration
【普天下】 pǔtiānxià everywhere in the world; in all the world; all over the world
【普通】 pǔtōng ordinary; common; average: 劳动人民的～一员 an ordinary member of the working people
【普通法】 pǔtōngfǎ common law
【普通股】 pǔtōnggǔ common stock; ordinary share
【普通话】 pǔtōnghuà common spoken Chinese
【普通会计学】 pǔtōng kuàijìxué general accounting
【普通基金】 pǔtōng jījīn general fund
【普通教育】 pǔtōng jiàoyù elementary education
【普通劳动者】 pǔtōng láodòngzhě ordinary laborer
【普通礼服】 pǔtōng lǐfú morning dress
【普通税则】 pǔtōng shuìzé general tariff
【普通条款】 pǔtōng tiáokuǎn general clause
【普通心理学】 pǔtōng xīnlǐxué general psychology
【普通照会】 pǔtōng zhàohuì verbal note
【普选】 pǔxuǎn general election
【普选权】 pǔxuǎnquán universal suffrage
【普照】 pǔzhào illuminate all things

谱(pǔ) 1.(参考书) book; register: 菜～ cookery book 2.(练习用书) manual; guide: 棋～ chess manual 3.(乐谱;曲谱) music score; music 4.(谱曲) set to music; compose: 把一首诗～成歌曲 set a poem to music 5.(把握) sth. to count on; a fair amount of confidence
【谱表】 pǔbiǎo 〈*Music*〉 stave; staff
【谱号】 pǔhào 〈*Music*〉 clef: 低音～ bass clef / 高音～ treble clef / 中音～ alto clef
【谱系】 pǔxì 〈*Biol.*〉 pedigree; lineage
【谱写】 pǔxiě compose (music)
【谱子】 pǔ·zi music score; music

镨(pǔ) 〈*Chem.*〉 praseodymium (元素符号 Pr)

蹼(pǔ) web
【蹼趾】 pǔzhǐ webbed toe
【蹼足】 pǔzú webfoot; palmate foot

铺[舖](pù) 1.(店铺) shop; store 2.(床铺) plank bed
(另见"铺"pū)
【铺板】 pùbǎn bed board; bed plank
【铺面】 pùmiàn shop front
【铺面房】 pùmiànfáng shop building
【铺位】 pùwèi bunk; berth
【铺子】 pù·zi shop; store

瀑(pù) waterfall
【瀑布】 pùbù waterfall; falls; cataract

曝[暴](pù)
(另见"曝"bào)
【曝晒】 pùshài solarize; solarization (n.)

Q

qi

七(qī) seven; seventh: 十～ seventeen; seventeenth / 乱～八糟 at sixes and sevens

(在本词典中"七"统注 qī)

【七百】 qībǎi seven hundred; seven-hundredth

【七边形】 qībiānxíng heptagon; septlateral

【七重唱】 qīchóngchàng septet

【七分之一】 qīfēnzīyī a seventh; one seventh

【七绝】 qījué a four-line verse with seven characters to a line

【七律】 qīlǜ an eight-line verse with seven characters to a line

【七扭八歪】 qīniǔ-bāwāi crooked; uneven; irregular; in a state of great disorder

【七拼八凑】 qīpīn-bācòu piece together; knock together; rig up; scrape together

【七平八稳】 qīpíng-bāwěn balanced; stable

【七千】 qīqiān seven thousand; seven thousandth

【七巧板】 qīqiǎobǎn seven-piece puzzle; tangram

【七窍】 qīqiào the seven apertures in the human head

【七情】 qīqíng the seven human emotions

【七情六欲】 qīqíng-liùyù the seven emotions and the six sensory pleasures

【七上八下】 qīshàng-bāxià an unsettled state of mind; be agitated; be perturbed

【七十】 qīshí seventy; seventieth

【七十二行】 qīshí'èrháng all the professions and avocations

【七手八脚】 qīshǒu-bājiǎo with everybody lending a hand; in a bustle

【七大洋】 qīdàyáng the seven seas

【七国集团】 qīguó jítuán G7; Group of Seven (包括美德日英法意加)

【七十七国集团】 qīshíqī guó jítuán Group of 77

【七一】 Qīyī July 1 (anniversary of the founding of the Communist Party of China)

【七月】 qīyuè July

【七嘴八舌】 qīzuǐ-bāshé all talking at once; lively discussion with everybody trying to get a word in

柒(qī) seven; seventh

沏(qī) infuse: ～茶 infuse tea; make tea

漆(qī) 1.(涂料) lacquer; paint 2.(涂漆) paint; lacquer; varnish; coat with paint: 把门～成红色 paint the door red

【漆包线】 qībāoxiàn enamel-insulated wire; enameled wire

【漆布】 qībù varnished cloth

【漆革】 qīgé patent leather

【漆工】 qīgōng 1.(指工作) lacquering; painting 2.(指人) lacquerer; lacquer man; painter

【漆黑】 qīhēi 1.(光线很暗) pitch-dark: ～的夜 pitch-dark night 2.(非常黑) pitch-black; jet-black

【漆黑一团】 qīhēi-yītuán 1.(非常黑暗) pitch-dark; complete darkness: 把…说得～ paint a dark picture of 2.(一无所知) be entirely ignorant of; be in the dark

【漆画】 qīhuà lacquer painting

【漆匠】 qījiàng lacquerer; painter

【漆皮】 qīpí 1.(一层漆) coat of paint 2.(虫胶清漆) shellac

【漆片】 qīpiàn color chips

【漆器】 qīqì lacquerware; lacquerwork

【漆树】 qīshù lacquer tree; varnish tree

妻(qī) wife: 夫～ husband and wife / 娶某人为～ take sb. to wife

【妻管严】 qīguǎnyán wife keeps husband under strict control; husband is in dread of wife

at home
【妻舅】 qījiù brother-in-law
【妻离子散】 qīlí-zǐsàn be separated from one's wife and children; breaking up or scattering of one's family; family broken up
【妻子】 qī·zi **1**.(男子的配偶) wife **2**. qīzǐ (妻子和儿女) wife and children

凄[淒[1,2]、悽[3]](qī) **1**.(寒冷) chilly; cold **2**.(冷落寂静) bleak and desolate: ～清 lonely and sad **3**.(悲伤难过) sad; wretched; miserable: ～楚 miserable
【凄惨】 qīcǎn wretched; miserable; tragic
【凄风苦雨】 qīfēng-kǔyǔ miserable conditions; wailing wind and weeping rain; wretched circumstances
【凄厉】 qīlì sad and shrill
【凄凉】 qīliáng dreary; desolate; miserable: ～的地方 desolate place
【凄切】 qīqiè plaintive; mournful
【凄然】 qīrán sad; mournful; in sadness

萋(qī)
【萋萋】 qīqī luxuriant; verdant: 芳草～ a luxuriant growth of grass

栖[棲](qī) **1**.(停在树上) perch **2**.(居住,停留) dwell; stay
【栖身】 qīshēn stay; sojourn: 暂作～之计 plan to make a stay for a time
【栖息】 qīxī perch; rest

戚[慼[2]](qī) **1**.(亲戚) relative **2**.(悲哀) sorrow; woe: 休～相关 share joys and sorrows; share weal and woe

期(qī) **1**.(一段时间) a period of time; phase; stage: 服役～ term of military service / 危险～ critical phase / 学～ school term **2**.(预定时日) designated time; scheduled time: 到～ fall date / 过～ be overdue; become overdue **3**.〈*classifier*〉 issue; number; term: 最近一～《大学英语》the current issue of *College English* **4**.(约定时日) make an appointment: 约～会晤 appoint a date for interview **5**.(期盼) expect
【期待】 qīdài anticipate; await; expect; look forward to: 我们殷切地～你早日光临。We eagerly await your early arrival.
【期货】 qīhuò 〈*Econ*.〉 futures: 小麦～以最高价出售。Wheat futures are selling at high prices.
【期货合同】 qīhuò hé·tong forward contract; futures contract
【期货汇率】 qīhuò huìlǜ forward exchange rate
【期货价格】 qīhuò jiàgé forward price
【期货交易】 qīhuò jiāoyì forward business
【期货交易所】 qīhuò jiāoyìsuǒ forward exchange
【期货市场】 qīhuò shìchǎng forward market; futures market
【期间】 qījiān time; period; course; duration: 在讨论～ in the course of discussion
【期刊】 qīkān periodical
【期考】 qīkǎo end-of-term examination; terminal examination
【期满】 qīmǎn expire; run out; come to an end: 合同～ when the contract expires
【期票】 qīpiào promissory note; term bill: 黄金～ gold note / 商业～ commercial bill
【期权】 qīquán options
【期望】 qīwàng hope; expectation: ～成功 hope to succeed / 对某人寄予很大的～ place high hopes on sb.
【期限】 qīxiàn allotted time; time limit; deadline: 一个星期的～ a time limit of one week / ～一星期 set a deadline of one week
【期中决算表】 qīzhōng juésuànbiǎo interim statements
【期中考试】 qīzhōng kǎoshì midterm examination
【期终考试】 qīzōng kǎoshì term examination; end-of-term examination; final examination

欺(qī) **1**.(欺骗) deceit; deceive **2**.(欺负) bully; take advantage of: 可～ can be taken advantage of
【欺负】 qī·fu bully; browbeat; treat sb. rough: 他总是～比他小的男孩儿。He's always bullying smaller boys.
【欺行霸市】 qīháng-bàshì dominate the market
【欺凌】 qīlíng bully and humiliate: 任人～ allow oneself to be trodden upon; allow others to tread on one's neck
【欺瞒】 qīmán hoodwink; dupe; pull the

wool over sb's eyes; cover up the truth to deceive

【欺蒙】 qīméng hoodwink; dupe; pull wool over sb's eyes; befool

【欺骗】 qīpiàn deceive; cheat; dupe; swindle; defraud; take in: ～无知的人 dupe the ignorant people

【欺骗案】 qīpiàn'àn case of victimization

【欺骗行为】 qīpiàn xíngwéi act of swindling; fraudulent act

【欺人之谈】 qīrénzhītán a lie

【欺辱】 qīrǔ insult; humiliate; disgrace

【欺软怕硬】 qīruǎn-pàyìng bully the weak and fear the strong; meek towards the brutal and brutal towards the meek

【欺上瞒下】 qīshàng-mánxià deceive one's superiors and delude one's subordinates

【欺生】 qīshēng **1.**（指人）bully or cheat strangers **2.**（指马、驴等）be ungovernable by strangers

【欺世盗名】 qīshì-dàomíng gain fame by deceiving the public; angle for undeserved fame

【欺侮】 qīwǔ bully; treat sb. high-handedly

【欺压】 qīyā bully and oppress; ride roughshod over

【欺诈】 qīzhà fraud; cheat; swindle

【欺诈行为】 qīzhà xíngwéi fraudulent conduct

【欺诈意图】 qīzhà yìtú fraudulent intention

【欺诈罪】 qīzhàzuì crime of false pretenses

蹊（qī）

【蹊跷】 qīqiāo odd; queer; fishy

七（qí） seven; seventh:（请见"七"qī）

齐［齊］（qí） **1.**（整齐）neat; even; uniform; well arranged; in good order: 把椅子摆～ arrange the chairs in an orderly way **2.**（达到）on a level with; be flush with; on the same plane with: 河水～岸。The river is flush with its banks. **3.**（同样，一致）alike; similar: 心～ think alike; think in similar way **4.**（一块儿，同时）together; simultaneously: 师生～动手。Teachers and students all pitched in. **5.**（完备，全）all ready; all present: 人都～了。All are present. **6.**（取齐）along: ～根切 cut to the roots

【齐备】 qíbèi all ready; complete: 商店里货色～。The store carries a complete stock.

【齐步走】 qíbùzǒu （口令）Quick time, march!

【齐唱】 qíchàng singing in unison; unison

【齐集】 qíjí assemble; gather; collect

【齐家治国】 qíjiā-zhìguó regulate the family and rule the state

【齐名】 qímíng enjoy equal popularity; be equally famous

【齐齐哈尔】 qíqíhāěr 〈place〉 Qiqihar

【齐全】 qíquán complete; all in readiness: 货物～ have a satisfactory variety of goods / 设施～的办公室 office with all appliances

【齐射】 qíshè 〈*Mil.*〉 salvo; volley

【齐声】 qíshēng in chorus; in unison: ～附和 second with one voice

【齐头并进】 qítóu-bìngjìn advance side by side; do two or more things at once; go forward together

【齐心】 qíxīn be of one mind: ～协力 work as one; pull together

【齐整】 qízhěng neat; uniform

【齐奏】 qízòu 〈*Music*〉 playing (instruments) in unison; unison

脐［臍］（qí） **1.**〈*Anat.*〉 navel; umbilicus **2.**（蟹脐）the abdomen of a crab

【脐橙】 qíchéng navel orange

【脐带】 qídài 〈*Anat.*〉 umbilical cord

祈（qí） **1.**（祈祷）pray: ～年 pray for a good harvest **2.**（祈求）entreat

【祈祷】 qídǎo pray; say one's prayers

【祈求】 qíqiú earnestly hope; pray for

【祈使句】 qíshǐjù 〈*Gram.*〉 imperative sentence

【祈望】 qíwàng hope; wish

颀（qí）

【颀长】 qícháng tall; of imposing stature

岐（qí） **1.**（岔道）fork; branch **2.**（不相同，不一致）divergent; different

【岐点】 qídiǎn bifurcation point

【岐化】 qíhuà 〈*Chem.*〉 disproportionate

【岐路】 qílù branch road; forked road

【岐视】 qíshì discriminate against; discrimination (n.)：～妇女 discriminate against women / ～妇女是不能允许的。Discrimination against women is not allowed.

【歧途】 qítú wrong road：被引入～ be led astray

【歧义】 qíyì different meanings; various interpretations

【歧异】 qíyì divergence; divergent (adj.)

其 (qí) 1.(他的;她的;它的;他们的;她们的;它们的) his; her; its; their：～母 his mother 2.(他;她;它;他们;她们;它们) he; she; it; they：听～自然 let it alone 3.(那个;那样) that; such：查无～事。It is found that there was no such thing. 4.(与"大"连用,虚指)大请～客 feast many guests; entertain lavishly; invite many guests to dinner

【其次】 qícì 1.(指次第) next; secondly; then：他首先发言,～轮到我。He will speak first, and I next. 2.(指地位) secondary：主要是内容,～才是形式。Content comes first, form second.

【其间】 qíjiān between them; between which; among them; among which

【其人其事】 qírénqíshì the man and his deeds; a biographic sketch

【其实】 qíshí 〈*adv.*〉 actually; in fact; as a matter of fact; really; in reality：～他是个很聪明的人。He's really a very clever man.

【其他】 qítā other; else

【其余】 qíyú the others; the rest; the remainder：～的不用说了。The rest needs no telling.

【其中】 qízhōng among which; among them; in which; in it：他爸爸给他六个苹果,～有一个是坏的。His father gave him six apples. There was a bad one among them.

棋[棊、碁] (qí) chess or any board game：国际象～ chess / 跳～ Chinese checkers / 围～ go / 象～ Chinese chess / 一副～ a chess set / 下～ play chess / 走～ move

【棋逢对手】 jíféng-duìshǒu meet one's match in a chess tournament; diamond cut diamond

【棋迷】 qímí chess fan; chess enthusiast

【棋盘】 qípán chessboard; checkerboard

【棋谱】 qípǔ chess manual; chess book

【棋赛钟】 qísàizhōng chess clock

【棋手】 qíshǒu chess player

【棋子】 qízǐ piece (in a board game); chessman

綦 (qí) very

【綦切】 qíqiè ardent; eager; earnest

麒 (qí)

【麒麟】 qílín 〈*Mythol.*〉 Chinese unicorn

奇 (qí) 1.(奇特的) strange; queer; rare; uncommon; unusual：～事 peculiar things; strange things 2.(出人意料) unexpected; unpredictable：出～制胜 win victory through unexpected moves 3.(惊奇) surprise; wonder; astonish：不足为～ be nothing surprising; nothing to be surprised at 4.(非常) extremely; exceeding：～冷 extremely cold; exceedingly cold / ～痛 unbearably painful
(另见"奇"jí)

【奇兵】 qíbīng an army suddenly appearing from nowhere; an ingenious military move

【奇才】 qícái unusual talent; remarkable talent

【奇耻大辱】 qíchǐ-dàrǔ galling shame and humiliation; deep disgrace; burning shame

【奇功】 qígōng outstanding service

【奇怪】 qíguài 1.(奇特) odd; queer; strange; surprising：～的风俗 odd customs 2.(出人意料) surprising：这没有什么可～的。There's nothing to be surprised at.

【奇观】 qíguān marvellous spectacle; wonder; wonderful sight

【奇花异草】 qíhuā-yìcǎo exotic flowers and rare herbs

【奇货可居】 qíhuò-kějū 1.(囤积) hoard as a rare commodity 2.(囤积的货) a rare commodity worth boarding

【奇迹】 qíjī miracle; wonder; marvel：科学上的～ a marvel of science / 创造～ create miracles

【奇景】 qíjǐng wonderful view; extraordinary sight

【奇妙】 qímiào marvellous; wonderful; intriguing

【奇谋】 qímóu a very clever strategy

【奇女子】 qínǚzǐ a remarkable woman

【奇葩】 qípā exotic flowers
【奇人】 qírén 1.（奇怪的人）a queer person; a strange person 2.（有非凡才能的人）a person of unusual ability
【奇谈】 qítán strange tale; absurd argument: ～怪论 strange tales and absurd arguments
【奇特】 qítè peculiar; queer; singular: ～的服装 peculiar dress / ～的习惯 queer habits
【奇文】 qíwén 1.（精美的文章）a remarkable piece of writing 2.（荒谬文章）preposterous piece of writing; queer writing
【奇闻】 qíwén sth. unheard-of; a thrilling, fantastic story: ～逸事 a strange news and an extraordinary affair
【奇袭】 qíxī surprise attack; raid
【奇效】 qíxiào special effect
【奇形怪状】 qíxīng-guàizhuàng grotesque or fantastic in shape or appearance; of strange or grotesque shapes and sizes
【奇异】 qíyì 1.（奇怪）queer; strange; bizarre; odd 2.（惊异）surprising; curious: 用～的眼光看人 look at sb. in surprise; look at sb. with curious eyes
【奇遇】 qíyù 1.（指相逢）happy encounter; fortuitous meeting 2.（指遭遇）adventure
【奇装异服】 qízhuāng-yìfú exotic costume; bizarre dress; outlandish clothes

崎（qí）

【崎岖】 qíqū rugged; rough: ～的山路 a rugged mountain path
【崎岖不平】 qíqū-bùpíng rugged and rough

骑（qí） 1.（跨坐）ride; sit on the back of: ～马 ride a horse; be on horseback / ～自行车 ride a bicycle 2.（骑兵）cavalryman; cavalry: 铁～ cavalry
【骑兵】 qíbīng cavalryman; cavalry
【骑虎难下】 qíhǔ-nánxià ride a tiger and find it hard to get off; have no way to back down; irrevocably committed
【骑墙】 qíqiáng sit on the fence; straddle: 在争论中采取～态度 sit on the fence in the argument
【骑墙派】 qíqiángpài fence-sitter
【骑士】 qíshì knight; cavalier
【骑手】 qíshǒu rider: 有一个～从马上摔了下来。One of the riders was thrown off his horse.
【骑术】 qíshù horsemanship; equestrian skill

耆（qí） over sixty years of age

【耆老】 qílǎo very old people; seniors

鳍（qí） 〈*Zool*.〉 fin: 背～ dorsal fin / 胸～ pectoral fin / 腹～ pelvic fin / 臀～ anal fin / 尾～ caudal fin
【鳍足】 qízú 〈*Zool*.〉 clasper

旗［斿[1]］（qí） 1.（旗子）flag; banner; standard: 国～ the national flag / 白～ white flag / 红～ red flag / 升～ raise a flag / 摇～（助威）wave the flag; show the flag; fly the flag / 下半～致哀 hoist a flag half-mast high 2.（内蒙古自治区的县级行政单位）qi; banner: 太仆寺～ Taibus Qi
【旗杆】 qígān 1.（泛指）flagpole; flag post 2.〈*Golf*〉 flagstick
【旗鼓相当】 qígǔ-xiāngdāng be well-matched; be equal in match or contest strength
【旗号】 qíhào 〈*derog*.〉 banner; flag: 打着…的～ flaunt the banner of; under the signboard of
【旗舰】 qíjiàn flagship
【旗舰舰长】 qíjiàn jiànzhǎng flag captain
【旗开得胜】 qíkāi-déshèng win victory in the first battle
【旗袍】 qípáo *chi-pao*; cheongsam
【旗手】 qíshǒu standard-bearer
【旗语】 qíyǔ semaphore; flag signal: 用～通信 flag a message / 打～ to flag
【旗帜】 qízhì 1.（旗子）flag; banner; standard 2.（象征）stand; colors
【旗帜鲜明】 qízhì xiānmíng have a clear-cut stand
【旗子】 qí·zi flag; banner; pennant; standard: ～迎风招展。Flags were flapping.

畦（qí） plot of land: 菜～ a vegetable bed

【畦灌】 qíguàn border method of irrigation
【畦田】 qítián ridge-bordered plots

乞（qǐ） beg (for alms, etc.); supplicate: ～食 beg for food / 行～ go begging
【乞丐】 qǐgài beggar
【乞和】 qǐhé sue for pity

【乞怜】 qǐlián beg for pity; beg for mercy
【乞灵】 qǐlíng resort to; seek help from
【乞求】 qǐqiú beg for; supplicate; implore: ～宽恕 beg for pardon
【乞讨】 qǐtǎo beg; go begging
【乞降】 qǐxiáng beg to surrender
【乞援】 qǐyuán ask for assistance; beg for aid

岂[豈](qǐ)

【岂不】 qǐbù (表示反问)Isn't that; Doesn't that; Hasn't that; Won't that: 这样～更好些? Wouldn't that be better?
【岂但】 qǐdàn not only
【岂敢】 qǐgǎn you flatter me; I don't deserve such praise or honor
【岂能】 qǐnéng how could; how is it possible
【岂有此理】 qǐyǒucǐlǐ preposterous; outrageous

杞(qǐ)

【杞人忧天】 Qǐrén-yōutiān entertain imaginary or groundless fears; with unwarranted anxiety

企(qǐ) 1.(踮着脚) stand on tiptoe 2.(企盼) anxiously expect sth.; look forward to
【企鹅】 qǐ'é penguin
【企盼】 qǐpàn anxiously expect sth.; look forward to
【企求】 qǐqiú desire to gain; seek for; hanker after
【企图】 qǐtú attempt; seek; try
【企望】 qǐwàng hope for; look forward to
【企业】 qǐyè enterprise; business: 村办～ village-run enterprise / 改造老～ transform outmoded enterprises
【企业承包经营责任制】 qǐyè chéngbāo jīngyíng zérènzhì enterprise-related system of contracted managerial responsibilities
【企业倒闭】 qǐyè dǎobì business failure
【企业发展基金】 qǐyè fázhǎn jījīn venture expansion fund
【企业法】 qǐyèfǎ law of enterprises; enterprise law
【企业集团】 qǐyè jítuán enterprise group: 联合兼并成～ join or amalgamate into an enterprise group
【企业家】 qǐyèjiā entrepreneur; enterpriser
【企业经营机制】 qǐyè jīngyíng jīzhì managerial mechanisms of enterprises
【企业自主权】 qǐyè zìzhǔquán decision-making power of enterprises; right of autonomy for enterprises

启[啟、啓](qǐ) 1.(开) open: ～门 open the door / ～幕 raise the curtain 2.(开始) start; initiate 3.(开导) enlighten; awaken 4.(陈述) state; inform
【启程】 qǐchéng set out; start on a journey
【启齿】 qǐchǐ open one's mouth; start to talk about sth.
【启迪】 qǐdí open and enlighten
【启动】 qǐdòng start (a machine, etc.); switch on
【启动成本】 qǐdòng chéngběn start-up cost; moving cost
【启动机】 qǐdòngjī 〈*Auto*〉 starter motor
【启发】 qǐfā arouse; inspire; enlighten: 从…中得到～ draw inspiration from
【启发式】 qǐfāshì elicitation method (of teaching); heuristic method
【启发式教学】 qǐfāshì jiàoxué heuristic mode of teaching
【启封】 qǐfēng 1.(除去封印、封条) unseal; break the seal; remove the seal 2.(拆信;拆包) open an envelop or wrapper
【启航】 qǐháng set sail; weigh anchor
【启蒙】 qǐméng 1.(使学到入门知识) impart rudimentary knowledge to beginners; initiate 2.(使摆脱愚昧、迷信) enlighten; free sb. from prejudice or superstition
【启蒙运动】 qǐméng yùndòng the Enlightenment; enlightenment campaign
【启明星】 Qǐmíngxīng 〈*Astron.*〉 Venus
【启示】 qǐshì enlightenment; inspiration
【启事】 qǐshì notice; announcement: 他们的结婚～已见报了。The announcement of their marriage appeared in the newspaper.
【启用】 qǐyòng start using
【启用前检查】 qǐyòngqián jiǎnchá 〈*Computec*〉 readiness review
【启运】 qǐyùn start shipment

起(qǐ) 1.(站起;坐起) rise; get up; stand up: 早睡早～ early to bed early to rise 2.

(起出，拔出，挖出) draw out; remove; extract; pull: ～地雷 clear mines **3**. (长出) appear; raise: 背上～痱子 heat rash rises on one's back **4**. (发生) rise; grow: ～风。The wind rose. **5**. (拟定) draft; work out: ～草 draft **6**. (建立) build; set up: ～伙 set up a mess **7**. (开始) start; begin: 从今天～ starting from today **8**. 〈*classifier*〉(件；次) case; instance; batch; group; lot: 两～火警 two cases of fire alarm

【起岸】 qǐ'àn bring (cargo from ship) to land; unship a cargo; unload a ship

【起爆】 qǐbào detonate

【起爆剂】 qǐbàojì detonating agent; primer

【起爆帽】 qǐbàomào detonating cap

【起笔】 qǐbǐ **1**. (第一笔) the first stroke of a Chinese character **2**. (每笔的开始) the start of each stroke in writing a Chinese character

【起搏器】 qǐbóqì pacemaker; artificial pacemaker

【起步】 qǐbù **1**. (开始走) start to walk **2**. (开始进行) start: ～较晚 started late

【起草】 qǐcǎo draft; draw up: ～一个文件 do a draft of the document / ～了一个计划 draw up a plan in draft / 你～一个提案，然后我们可以在会上进行讨论。Draft a proposal and we can discuss it at the meeting.

【起草人】 qǐcǎorén draftsman (m.); draftwoman (f.)

【起草委员会】 qǐcǎo wěiyuǎnhuì drafting committee

【起程】 qǐchéng leave; set out; start on a journey

【起初】 qǐchū originally; at first; at the outset; in the beginning

【起床】 qǐchuáng get up; get out of bed; rise

【起点】 qǐdiǎn starting point: 赛跑的～ the starting mark of a race

【起点运费】 qǐdiǎn yùnfèi minimum freight

【起电】 qǐdiàn electrification; charge

【起飞】 qǐfēi **1**. (飞机升空) take off; takeoff (n.): 飞机～5分钟后坠毁了。The plane crashed five minutes after takeoff. **2**. (从落后状态迅猛发展) develop very rapidly: 经济～ economic takeoff / 电视广播事业～很快。The television broadcasting business has been developing very rapidly.

【起伏】 qǐfú rise and fall; undulate: 波涛～ waves rise and fall

【起稿】 qǐgǎo make a draft; draft

【起航】 qǐháng set sail

【起哄】 qǐhòng **1**. (胡闹) gather together to create a disturbance; gather together to stir up trouble **2**. (开玩笑) jeer; boo and hoot

【起火】 qǐhuǒ **1**. (失火) fire breaking out; outbreak of a fire **2**. (做饭) cook meals; prepare meals; do cooking

【起货】 qǐhuò unload; landing

【起家】 qǐjiā build up; grow and thrive: 白手～ start from nothing

【起价】 qǐjià price starts at: 从10元～。Prices start at 10 yuan.

【起见】 qǐjiàn for the purpose of; in order to: 为醒目～ in order to make it stand out clearly

【起劲】 qǐjìn vigorously; energetically; enthusiastically

【起居】 qǐjū daily life

【起居室】 qǐjūshì living room

【起来】 qǐ·lái **1**. (站起；坐起) stand up; sit up; rise to one's feet **2**. (起床) get up; get out of bed **3**. (奋起) rise; arise; revolt: ～反抗 rise in revolt **4**. (表示动作向上) 把孩子抱～ take a child up in one's arms **5**. (表示动作开始并继续) 唱～ start to sing **6**. (表示印象或看法) 听～没什么问题。It sounds quite all right.

【起立】 qǐlì stand up; rise to one's feet: 全体～! Stand up!

【起落】 qǐluò rise and fall; up and down

【起落滑橇】 qǐluò huáqiāo 〈*Aeron*.〉 landing skids

【起落架】 qǐluòjià 〈*Aeron*.〉 landing gear; alighting gear; undercarriage

【起落架轮】 qǐluòjiàlún 〈*Aeron*.〉 undercarriage wheel

【起码】 qǐmǎ **1**. (最低的；初步的) minimum; rudimentary; elementary: ～资格 minimum qualification **2**. (最低限度) at least: 最～的酬劳 the least reward

【起锚】 qǐmáo weigh anchor; set sail

【起名】 qǐmíng name; give a name: 他们给孩子～建国。They named the child Jianguo.

【起跑】 qǐpǎo 〈*Sports*〉 start of a race

【起跑线】 qǐpǎoxiàn 〈*Sports*〉 starting line; starting mark

【起泡】 qǐpào 1.(起水泡) blister; bubble 2.(起泡沫) foam; bead

【起泡剂】 qǐpàojì blowing agent; foaming agent

【起讫】 qǐqì the beginning and the end

【起色】 qǐsè improvement; pickup: 工作有～ there's some improvement in the work

【起身】 qǐshēn 1.(起床) get up; get out of bed 2.(动身) leave; set out; get off

【起事】 qǐshì start armed struggle; rise in rebellion

【起誓】 qǐshì take an oath; swear

【起死回生】 qǐsǐ-huíshēng (of a doctor's skill) bring the dying back to life; snatch a patient from the jaws of death; restore the dying to life

【起诉】 qǐsù bring a suit against sb.; bring an action against sb.; sue; prosecute

【起诉人】 qǐsùrén suitor; prosecutor

【起诉书】 qǐsùshū indictment; bill of complaint; statement of charges

【起诉资格】 qǐsù zīgé standing to sue

【起跳】 qǐtiào 〈*Sports*〉 take off

【起跳板】 qǐtiàobǎn take-off board

【起跳线】 qǐtiàoxiàn take-off line; take-off mark

【起头】 qǐtóu 1.(开始;发起) start; originate; initiate: 这件事都是他～的。It was he who started all this. 2.(开始的时候) at first; in the beginning; originally 3.(开始;开端) beginning: 万事～难。Everything is hard in the beginning.

【起先】 qǐxiān at first; in the beginning

【起义】 qǐyì uprising; insurrection; revolt: 农民～ peasant uprising / 武装～ armed uprising / 举行～ rise in revolt; start a uprising 镇压～ crush the insurrection; put down the revolt

【起意】 qǐyì 〈*derog.*〉 conceive a design

【起因】 qǐyīn cause; origin

【起用】 qǐyòng 1.(重新任用) reinstate a retired official; reinstate a dismissed official 2.(提拔使用) promote; promotion (n.): ～三名自学成才的技师 promoted three technicians who had become professionals through independent study

【起源】 qǐyuán 1.(根源) origin: 文明的～ the origin of civilization 2.(开始发生) originate from; stem from; come from: 舞蹈～于劳动。Dancing originates from labor.

【起运】 qǐyùn start shipment

【起运地点】 qǐyùn dìdiǎn starting place for shipping; place of dispatch

【起赃】 qǐzāng track down and recover stolen goods

【起早贪黑】 qǐzǎo-tānhēi start work early and knock off late; work from down to dusk

【起止】 qǐzhǐ the beginning and the end

【起重机】 qǐzhòngjī hoist; crane; derrick

【起绉】 qǐzhòu wrinkle; crumple

【起绉工艺】 qǐzhòu gōngyì 〈*Textiles*〉 creping

【起子】 qǐ·zi 1.(开瓶盖的) bottle opener 2.(螺丝刀) screwdriver 3.(发酵粉) baking powder

【起坐间】 qǐzuòjiān living room

【起作用】 qǐzuòyòng 1.(有影响) play a part (in) 2.(产生效果) take effect

绮 (qǐ) 1.(丝织品) figured woven silk material; damask 2.(美丽) beautiful; gorgeous

【绮丽】 qǐlì beautiful; gorgeous: 风景～ beautiful scenery

气[氣] (qì) 1.(气体) gas: 废～ waste gas / 尾～ tail gas 2.(空气) air: 到室外透透～ go out and take some fresh air 3.(气息) breath: 喘不过～来 lose one's breath; gasp for breath 4.(天气) weather 5.(味儿) smell; odor: 臭～ bad odor; foul smell / 香～ sweet smell 6.(精神状态) spirit; morale: 垂头丧～ in low spirits 7.(作风;习气) airs; manner; style: 孩子～ childish / 书生～ bookish; pedantic 8.(使人生气) make angry; enrage 9.(生气;发怒) get angry; be enraged: ～得发抖 tremble with anger 10.(欺压) bully; insult

【气冲冲】 qìchōngchōng furious; beside oneself with rage

【气喘】 qìchuǎn asthma: 阵发性～ spasmodic asthma

【气喘吁吁】 qìchuǎn-xūxū puff; gasp; pant: 到达山顶时,她～。She was panting when she reached the top of the hill.

【气窗】 qìchuāng transom (window); fanlight

【气垫】 qìdiàn air cushion

【气垫车】 qìdiànchē air cushion car; hovercraft

【气垫船】 qìdiànchuán hovercraft

【气垫运载器】 qìdiàn yùnzǎiqì air cushion machine

【气度】 qìdù tolerance; bearing: ～不凡 in a laudable tolerant spirit

【气短】 qìduǎn **1.** (呼吸短促) breathe hard; be short of breath; pant **2.** (泄气) lose heart; be discouraged

【气氛】 qìfēn atmosphere; air: 节日～ festive air / 诚挚友好的～ an atmosphere of cordiality and friendship / 亲切友好的～ cordial and friendly atmosphere

【气愤】 qìfèn indignant; furious

【气概】 qìgài lofty quality; mettle; spirit: 革命～ revolutionary spirit / 英雄～ heroic spirit

【气干法】 qìgānfǎ air drying

【气缸】 qìgāng 〈*Mech.*〉 air cylinder; cylinder

【气功】 qìgōng *qigong*; breathing exercises: ～疗法 traditional Chinese breathing exercise

【气管】 qìguǎn 〈*Anat.*〉 windpipe; trachea

【气管炎】 qìguǎnyán **1.** 〈*Med.*〉 tracheitis **2.** (喻'妻管严') wife keeps husband under strict control

【气贯长虹】 qìguàn-chánghóng imbued-with a spirit as lofty as the rainbow spanning the sky; full of noble aspiration and daring

【气候】 qìhòu **1.** 〈*Geol.*〉 climate: 赤道～ equatorial climate / 大陆性～ continental climate / 高原～ plateau climate / 海岸～ coastal climate / 海洋性～ oceanic climate / 改良～条件 improve weather conditions / 调节～ regulate the climate **2.** (局势) climate; situation: 政治～ political climate **3.** (结果; 成就) successful development: 成不了～ will not amount to anything

【气呼呼】 qìhūhū in a huff; panting with rage

【气化】 qìhuà gasify; gasification (n.)

【气急败坏】 qìjí-bàihuài flustered and exasperated; utterly discomfited; be in exasperation

【气节】 qìjié integrity; moral courage: 民族～ national integrity

【气井】 qìjǐng 〈*Petroleum*〉 gas well

【气可鼓而不可泄】 qì kě gǔ ér bùkě xiè morale should be boosted, not dampened

【气孔】 qìkǒng **1.** 〈*Bot.*〉 stoma **2.** 〈*Zool.*〉 spiracle **3.** 〈*Metall.*〉 gas hole **4.** 〈*Archit.*〉 air hole

【气浪】 qìlàng blast (of an explosion)

【气力】 qìlì effort; energy; strength: 费很大～ exert great efforts

【气流】 qìliú **1.** 〈*Meteorol.*〉 air current; airflow; airstream **2.** 〈*Gram.*〉 breath

【气轮机】 qìlúnjī gas turbine

【气煤】 qìméi gas-coal; bottle coal

【气门】 qìmén **1.** (轮胎气门) (air) valve of a tire **2.** 〈*Zool.*〉 spiracle; stigma

【气门盖】 qìméngài valve cap

【气门心】 qìménxīn **1.** (气门) valve inside **2.** (气门的橡胶管) valve rubber tube

【气恼】 qìnǎo get angry; take offense; be ruffled; be peeved: 因某事～ be peeved over sth.

【气馁】 qìněi become dejected; be discouraged; lose heart

【气派】 qìpài **1.** (气势) manner; style; air: 学者～ scholarly manner **2.** (神气) arrogant; cocky

【气泡】 qìpào bubble; air bubble

【气瓶】 qìpíng gas cylinder

【气魄】 qìpò boldness of vision; breadth of spirit; daring: 有扭转乾坤的～ have the daring to reverse the course of events

【气枪】 qìqiāng air gun; pneumatic gun

【气球】 qìqiú balloon: 彩色～ colored balloon / 测风～ pilot balloon

【气球飞翔运动】 qìqiú fēixiáng yùndòng ballooning

【气球飞翔运动员】 qìqiú fēixiáng yùndòngyuán balloonist

【气色】 qìsè complexion; color: ～好 have a good complexion; be in good looks / ～不好 look pale; be off color

【气势】 qìshì momentum; imposing manner: ～雄伟的建筑 imposing building

【气势汹汹】 qìshì xiōngxiōng fierce; truculent; overbearing; in a threatening manner
【气数已尽】 qì·shu-yǐjìn spell of good fortune has run out; His days are numbered.
【气态】 qìtài gaseous state
【气体】 qìtǐ gas
【气体舱】 qìtǐcáng gas tank
【气体动力学】 qìtǐ dònglìxué aerodynamics; aerodynamic (adj.)
【气体发生器】 qìtǐ fāshēngqì gas generator
【气体分离器】 qìtǐ fēnlíqì gas separator
【气体力学】 qìtǐ lìxué pneumatics; pneumatic (adj.)
【气体燃料】 qìtǐ ránliào gaseous fuel
【气体燃烧器】 qìtǐ ránshāoqì gas burner
【气田】 qìtián 〈*Petroleum*〉 gas field
【气筒】 qìtǒng inflator; bicycle pump; air pump
【气团】 qìtuán 〈*Meteorol.*〉 air mass: 冷～ cold air mass
【气团变性】 qìtuán biànxìng air-mass modification
【气吞山河】 qìtūn-shānhé imbued with a spirit that can conquer mountains and rivers; full of daring
【气味】 qìwèi **1.** (味儿) smell; odor; flavor **2.** (性格;志趣) smack; taste: ～相投 congenial to each other; have the same tastes and temperament; be two of a kind
【气温】 qìwēn air temperature; atmospheric temperature
【气雾剂】 qìwùjì aerosol
【气息】 qìxī **1.** (呼吸) breath: ～奄奄 at one's last gasp; at the point of death; like a person who is sinking fast **2.** (色彩) flavor; smell: 具有强烈的生活～ have the rich flavor of life / 时代～ the spirit of the times
【气象】 qìxiàng **1.** (大气现象) meteorological phenomena **2.** (气象学) meteorology; meteorological (adj.) **3.** (情景) atmosphere; scene **4.** (气势) manner; style; air
【气象部门】 qìxiàng bùmén meteorological department
【气象工作者】 qìxiàng gōngzuòzhě a worker in meteorology
【气象观测】 qìxiàng guāncè meteorological observation
【气象火箭】 qìxiàng huǒjiàn meteorological rocket
【气象哨】 qìxiàngshào weather post
【气象台】 qìxiàngtái meteorological observatory
【气象图】 qìxiàngtú meteorological map
【气象万千】 qìxiàng-wànqiān majestic in all its variety; things change in countless ways; spectacular
【气象卫星】 qìxiàng wèixīng meteorological satellite; weather satellite
【气象学】 qìxiàngxué meteorology; meteorological ‖ 气象学家 meteorologist
【气象预报】 qìxiàng yùbào weather forecast
【气象员】 qìxiàngyuán weatherman (m.); weatherwoman (f.)
【气象站】 qìxiàngzhàn weather station; climatological station
【气吁吁】 qìxūxū panting; gasping for breath
【气虚】 qìxū deficiency of vital energy
【气压】 qìyā atmospheric pressure; barometric pressure: 高～ high pressure
【气压表】 qìyābiǎo barometer
【气焰】 qìyàn arrogance; bluster: ～嚣张 be swollen with arrogance
【气宇轩昂】 qìyǔ-xuān'áng dignified; exalted; manly
【气质】 qìzhì **1.** (个性特点) temperament; disposition **2.** (风格) qualities; makings: 革命英雄的～ qualities of a revolutionary hero
【气壮山河】 qìzhuàng-shānhé full of power and grandeur; magnificent: 一篇～的宣言 a magnificent manifesto

汽 (qì) vapor; steam

【汽车】 qìchē car; automobile; motor car: 公共～ bus; autobus / 微型～ baby car; mini car / 小～ car; sedan / 小型公共～ minibus / 越野～ cross-country car / 载重～ truck; heavy-duty truck / 自卸～ dump truck / 开～ drive a car
【汽车保险】 qìchē bǎoxiǎn automobile insurance
【汽车队】 qìchēduì motor transport corps; fleet of cars; fleet of trucks
【汽车渡轮】 qìchē dùlún car ferry

【汽车工业】 qìchē gōngyè auto industry; automobile industry; automotive industry
【汽车混凝土搅拌机】 qìchē hùnníngtǔ jiǎobànjī motor-truck concrete mixer
【汽车驾驶执照】 qìchē jiàshǐ zhízhào driver's licence
【汽车库】 qìchēkù garage
【汽车拉力赛】 qìchē lālìsài rally
【汽车旅馆】 qìchē lǚguǎn motel
【汽车赛】 qìchēsài automobile racing
【汽车速度测速站】 qìchē sùdù cèsùzhàn speed trap
【汽车越野赛】 qìchē yuèyěsài autocross
【汽车制造厂】 qìchē zhìzàochǎng automobile factory; motor works
【汽船】 qìchuán steamship; steamer
【汽锤】 qìchuí steam hammer
【汽灯】 qìdēng gas lamp
【汽笛】 qìdí steam whistle; siren; hooter
【汽缸】 qìgāng cylinder: 八个～的发动机 a eight-cylinder engine
【汽缸盖】 qìgānggài cylinder head; cylinder cap
【汽缸体】 qìgāngtǐ cylinder body
【汽化】 qìhuà 〈*Physics*〉 vaporize; vaporization (n.)
【汽化器】 qìhuàqì 1.〈*Mech.*〉 carburetor 2.〈*Chem.*〉 vaporizer
【汽酒】 qìjiǔ light sparkling wine
【汽轮发电机】 qìlún fádiànjī (steam) turbogenerator
【汽轮机】 qìlúnjī steam turbine
【汽水】 qìshuǐ aerated water; soft drink; soda water
【汽艇】 qìtǐng motorboat
【汽油】 qìyóu petrol; gasoline; gas: 航空～ aviation gasoline / 加氧～ oxygenated gasoline / 抗爆～ anti-knock gasoline / 凝固～ napalm / 人造～ synthetic petroleum

讫 (qì) 1.(完结) settled; completed: 银货两～ delivered and paid 2.(截止) end: 起～ the beginning and the end

迄 (qì) 1.(直到) up to; till 2.(用于"未"或"无"前) so far; all along: ～未见效。So far there hasn't been any result.
【迄今】 qìjīn up to now; to this day; to date; so far

弃[棄] (qì) throw away; discard; abandon; give up: ～城而逃 abandon the city and flee
【弃暗投明】 qì'àn-tóumíng forsake darkness for light; leave the reactionary side and cross over to the side of progress; give oneself up to the government
【弃短取长】 qìduǎn-qǔcháng forget someone's shortcomings and make use of his strong points
【弃旧图新】 qìjiù-túxīn turn over a new leaf; change new for the old
【弃权】 qìquán 1.(放弃权利) abstain from voting; abstention (n.): 四票～ four abstentions 2.〈*Sports*〉 waive the right (to play); forfeit
【弃世】 qìshì pass away; die
【弃置】 qìzhì discard; throw aside

泣 (qì) 1.(哭) weep; whimper; sob 2.(眼泪) tears
【泣不成声】 qìbùchéngshēng choke with sobs

契[栔] (qì) 1.(文书;凭证) contract; deed: 房地～ title deed for real property 2.(投合) agree; get along well: 默～ tacit agreement; tacit understanding
【契合】 qìhé 1.(符合) agree with; tally with; correspond to 2.(合得来) be in good terms
【契机】 qìjī 1.〈*Physics*〉 moment 2.(转化关键) turning point; juncture
【契据】 qìjù deed; contract; receipt
【契友】 qìyǒu close friend; bosom friend
【契约】 qìyuē contract; deed; charter: 以～形式 in the form of contracts
【契约当事人】 qìyuē dāngshìrén contracting parties
【契约法】 qìyuēfǎ contract law
【契约生效】 qìyuē shēngxiào validity of contract; execution of contract
【契约条款】 qìyuē tiáokuǎn contract terms

砌 (qì) build by laying bricks or stones: ～墙 build a wall (with bricks, stones, etc.) / ～烟囱 build a chimney / ～砖 lay bricks

器[噐] (qì) 1.(器具) implement; utensil; ware: 瓷～ chinaware; china; porcelain / 玉～ jade article / 乐～

musical instrument 2.(器官) organ：生殖～ reproductive organs; generative organs; genitals 3.(才能) capacity; talent

【器材】 qìcái equipment; material：体育～ sports equipment

【器度不凡】 qìdù-bùfán uncommon personality

【器官】 qìguān organ; apparatus：呼吸～ breathing apparatus / 眼睛是视觉～。The eyes are the organs of sight.

【器件】 qìjiàn parts of an apparatus or appliance

【器具】 qìjù utensil; implement; appliance

【器量】 qìliàng tolerance：～大 broad-minded

【器皿】 qìmǐn household utensils; containers esp. for use in the house

【器物】 qìwù implements; utensils

【器械】 qìxiè 1.(器具) apparatus; appliance; instrument：医疗～ medical appliances 2.(武器) weapon; weaponry

【器械体操】 qìxiè tǐcāo gymnastics on apparatus

【器宇】 qìyǔ bearing; deportment：～不凡 with unusual deportment

【器乐】 qìyuè instrumental music

【器乐曲】 qìyuèqǔ composition for an instrument

【器质性精神病】 qìzhìxìng jīngshénbìng organic psychosis

【器重】 qìzhòng think highly of; regard highly; have a high opinion of

qia

掐 (qiā) 1.(用手指捏或截断) pinch; nip：～花 nip off the flowers 2.(用手紧卡住) clutch：～死 choke to death; throttle

【掐断】 qiāduàn nip off; cut off

【掐算】 qiāsuàn count sth. on one's fingers

【掐头去尾】 qiātóu-qùwěi break off both ends; leave out the beginning and the end; remove the superfluous part

卡 (qiǎ) 1.(夹在中间) wedge; get stuck; be jammed; become tightly wedged：～在冰中间的船 a ship jammed in the ice 2.(卡子) clip; fastener：发～ hairpin 3.(关卡) checkpost：关～ checkpost

【卡壳】 qiǎké 1.〈*Mil.*〉 jamming of cartridge or shell case 2.(遇到障碍) get stuck; be held up; have a temporary stoppage

【卡口灯泡】 qiǎkǒu dēngpào bayonet-socket bulb

【卡口灯头】 qiǎkǒu dēngtóu bayonet socket

【卡子】 qiǎ·zi 1.(器具) clip; fastener 2.(关卡) checkpost

恰 (qià) 1.(恰当) appropriate; proper 2.(恰恰) just; exactly

【恰当】 qiàdàng proper; suitable; appropriate; fitting：找～的人担任这项工作 try to get a suitable man for the job

【恰好】 qiàhǎo just right; as luck would have it：这里的气候～宜于种植水稻。The climate here is just right for planting rice.

【恰恰】 qiàqià just; exactly; precisely

【恰恰舞】 qiàqiàwǔ cha-cha; cha-cha-cha

【恰巧】 qiàqiǎo by chance; fortunately; as chance would have it; happen to：我～在路上遇见了她。I met her by chance on the way.

【恰如其分】 qiàrú-qífèn apt; appropriate; just right

【恰似】 qiàsì exactly like

洽 (qià) 1.(融洽) be in harmony; agree：融～ be in harmony 2.(接洽) consult; arrange with

【洽谈】 qiàtán make arrangements with; talk over with：与某人～某事 talk sth. over with sb.

髂 (qià)

【髂骨】 qiàgǔ 〈*Anat.*〉 ilium

qian

千 (qiān) 1.(数目) thousand; thousandth 2.(很多) a great amount of; a great number of; a thousand

【千变万化】 qiānbiàn-wànhuà ever changing; change in thousands of ways; volatile

【千差万别】 qiānchā-wànbié differ in thousands of ways; be in endless variety

【千锤百炼】 qiānchuí-bǎiliàn 1.(经过多次斗争和考验) thoroughly tempered; well-seasoned; much-steeled **2**.(经过多次精细修改) be polished again and again; be revised and rewritten many times; be highly finished

【千方百计】 qiānfáng-bǎijì in a thousand and one ways; by every possible means; by hook or by crook; use every conceivable stratagem

【千分之…】 qiānfēnzhī… per milli (符号为 ‰)

【千分之一】 qiānfēnzhīyī one thousandth

【千夫】 qiānfū numerous people: ～所指 be universally condemned

【千伏】 qiānfú kilovolt (Kv.)

【千伏安】 qiānfú'ān kilovolt-ampere (KVA)

【千古】 qiāngǔ **1**.(很长的时间) through the ages; eternal; for all time: ～奇冤 the most appalling injustice through the ages **2**.(用于挽联、花圈上款) 王先生～! Eternal repose to Mr. Wang!

【千赫】 qiānhè kilohertz (KHz): 1040～ 1040 kilohertz

【千回百转】 qiānhuí-bǎizhuǎn a thousand twists and a hundred turns

【千娇百媚】 qiānjiāo-bǎimèi beauty of beauties; the pinnacle of beauty and charms

【千斤】 qiānjīn **1**.(千斤顶) hoisting jack; jack **2**.〈*Mech.*〉 pawl **3**.(责任重) very heavy; weighty: ～重担 an exceptionally heavy load or responsibility

【千金】 qiānjīn **1**.(很多钱) a thousand pieces of gold; a lot of money **2**.(指女儿) daughter

【千斤顶】 qiānjīndǐng **1**.〈*Mech.*〉 jack; hoisting jack **2**.〈*Auto*〉 jack; screw jack

【千军万马】 qiānjūn-wànmǎ like the charge of a powerful army which no force can stop; a large number of mounted and foot soldiers

【千钧一发】 qiānjūn-yīfà a hundredweight hanging by a hair; be in an extremely critical situation

【千克】 qiānkè kilogram (kg.)

【千里】 qiānlǐ a thousand li; a long distance: ～迢迢 a far distance; from afar

【千里之行,始于足下】 qiānlǐ zhī xíng, shǐ yú zú xià a thousand-li journey is started by taking the first step

【千米】 qiānmǐ kilometer (km.)

【千难万险】 qiānnán-wànxiǎn innumerable hazards and hardships

【千篇一律】 qiānpiān-yīlǜ stereotyped; following the same pattern; thousand pieces of the same tune

【千奇百怪】 qiānqí-bǎiguài all kinds of strange things; an infinite variety of fantastic phenomena; a great variety of fantasies

【千秋】 qiānqiū a thousand years; centuries: ～万代 for all generations to come

【千山万水】 qiānshān-wànshuǐ numerous mountains and rivers; a long and arduous journey

【千丝万缕】 qiānsī wànlǚ countless ties; a thousand and one links; interrelated in innumerable ways

【千头万绪】 qiāntóu-wànxù thousands of strands and loose ends; a multitude of things; a thousand and one things to attend to

【千瓦】 qiānwǎ kilowatt (KW)

【千瓦小时】 qiānwǎ xiǎoshí kilowatt-hour (KWh)

【千万】 qiānwàn **1**.(数目) ten million; millions upon millions **2**.(务必) be sure so; do: 这事你～记着。Be sure to bear this in mind.

【千辛万苦】 qiānxīn-wànkǔ innumerable trials and tribulations; untold hardships

【千言万语】 qiānyán-wànyǔ thousands and thousands of words; innumerable words

【千载难逢】 qiānzǎi-nánféng occurring only once in a thousand years; very rare; once in a blue moon: ～的机会 a golden opportunity

【千真万确】 qiānzhēn-wànquè absolutely true; very real

仟 (qiān) thousand; thousandth

阡 (qiān) a footpath between fields, running north and south

【阡陌】 qiānmò crisscross footpaths between fields: ～纵横。The crisscross paths on a farmland.

扦 (qiān) a short slender pointed piece of metal, bamboo, etc.: 竹～ bamboo spike

【扦子】 qiān·zi **1**.(竹扦) bamboo spike **2**.(取样器) a sharp-pointed metal tube used to extract samples of grains, etc. from sacks

迁[遷] (qiān) **1**.(迁移) move: ～出 move out / ～入 move in **2**.(转变) change

【迁建】 qiānjiàn move out from the old and have new buildings constructed

【迁就】 qiānjiù accommodate oneself to; yield to: 过于～ excessively accommodating

【迁居】 qiānjū move (house); change residence

【迁怒】 qiānnù vent one's anger on sb. who's not to blame; take it out on sb.: ～他人 transfer one's anger to others

【迁徙】 qiānxǐ move; migrate; change one's residence

【迁延】 qiānyán delay; defer; procrastinate

【迁移】 qiānyí move; remove; migrate

钎 (qiān) drill rod; drill steel; borer

【钎子】 qiān·zi hammer drill; rock drill

签[簽、籤 3-6] (qiān) 1.(签名) sign; autograph: ～合同 sign a contract / ～支票 sign a check/ 他在信的末尾～上了他的名字。He signed his name at the end of the letter. 2.(签署意见) make brief comments on a document 3.(竹签) bamboo slips used for divination or drawing lots: 抽～ draw lots 4.(书签) label; sticker 5.(竹木制小细棍) a slender pointed piece of bamboo or wood: 取食～ cocktail stick / 牙～ tooth pick 6.(粗粗地缝) tack

【签到】 qiāndào sign in; register one's attendance at a meeting or at an office

【签到簿】 qiāndàobù attendance book

【签到处】 qiāndàochù sign-in desk

【签订】 qiāndìng conclude and sign: ～租约 sign a lease / 为某事与某人～合同 sign a contract with sb. for sth.

【签发】 qiānfā sign and issue (a document)

【签合同】 qiānhé·tong sign a contract

【签名】 qiānmíng sign one's name; autograph

【签名运动】 qiānmíng yùndòng signature drive

【签收】 qiānshōu sign after receiving sth.; sign to acknowledge the receipt of sth.; sign for

【签署】 qiānshǔ sign; affix; subscribe: ～联合公报 sign a joint communiqué / ～协议 sign an agreement

【签署人】 qiānshǔrén under-signed

【签约】 qiānyuē sign on; sign a contract; signing (n.)

【签约方】 qiānyuēfāng contract party

【签约人】 qiānyuērén parties to a contract

【签约日期】 qiānyuē rìqī date of contract

【签证】 qiānzhèng 1.〈*Diplomacy*〉 visa: 出境～ exit visa / 过境～ transit visa / 入境～ entry visa 2.(给予签证) give the visa; grant the visa: 拒绝～ refuse to give the visa; refuse to grant the visa

【签证机关】 qiānzhèng jīguān visa-granting office

【签证费】 qiānzhèngfèi certificate fee

【签注】 qiānzhù attach a slip of paper to a document with comments on it; write comments on a document

【签字】 qiānzì 1.(签上名字) sign; affix one's signature: 请在这里～。Sign here, please. 2.(所签的名字) signature (n.): 有某人的～ bear a signature

【签字国】 qiānzìguó signatory state; signatory

【签字权】 qiānzìquán signing authority

【签字认证】 qiānzì rènzhèng authentication

【签字仪式】 qiānzì yíshì signing ceremony

牵[牽] (qiān) 1.(拉) lead along; pull: ～着狗散步 take one's dog for a walk 2.(牵连) involve

【牵肠挂肚】 qiāncháng-guàdù feel deep anxiety about; be very worried about; be deeply concerned

【牵扯】 qiānchě involve; implicate; drag in: 他不愿意～在里头。He didn't want to get involved in it.

【牵掣】 qiānchè 1.(阻碍) hold up; impede 2.(牵制) pin down; check; contain

【牵动】 qiāndòng affect; influence

【牵挂】 qiānguà worry; care: 没有～ free from care

【牵累】 qiānlěi 1.(因牵制受累) tie down: 受家务～ be tied down by household chores 2.(连累) implicate; involve (in trouble)

【牵连】 qiānlián involve (in trouble); implicate; tie up with

【牵连犯】 qiānliánfàn implicated offender; act related to a crime

【牵牛】 qiānniú （喇叭花）morning glory
【牵强】 qiānqiǎng forced；farfetched：～附会 give a strained interpretation；stretch of language
【牵涉】 qiānshè concern；drag in；involve：营业上的这些变动～到所有股东的利益。These changes in the business involve the interests of all owners.
【牵头】 qiāntóu initiate；take the lead；be the first to do and take the responsibility of sth.
【牵线】 qiānxiàn 1.（幕后操纵）pull strings；pull wires；control from behind the scenes 2.（充当介绍人）act as go-between
【牵线搭桥】 qiānxiàn-dāqiáo act as go-between
【牵线人】 qiānxiànrén wirepuller；go-between
【牵引】 qiānyǐn tow；draw；haul
【牵引车】 qiānyǐnchē tractor；tractor truck
【牵引犁】 qiānyǐnlí trailed plough
【牵引力】 qiānyǐnlì traction force；traction；pulling force
【牵引炮】 qiānyǐnpào towed artillery
【牵引器】 qiānyǐnqì tractor
【牵引式滑翔机】 qiānyǐnshì huáxiángjī towed glider
【牵制】 qiānzhì pin down；tie up；check；contain
【牵制行动】 qiānzhì xíngdòng containing action
【牵制性攻击】 qiānzhìxìng gōngjī diversionary attack

铅（qiān） 1.〈*Chem.*〉 lead；leaden（adj.）（元素符号 Pb） 2.（铅笔心） lead；black lead
【铅版】 qiānbǎn 〈*Printing*〉 stereotype
【铅笔】 qiānbǐ pencil
【铅笔刀】 qiānbǐdāo small knife for sharpening pencils；pen-knife
【铅笔盒】 qiānbǐhé pencil-case
【铅笔画】 qiānbǐhuà pencil drawing
【铅笔心】 qiānbǐxīn lead（in a pencil）；black lead
【铅玻璃】 qiānbō·li lead glass
【铅灰色】 qiānhuīsè leaden（color）：～的天空 leaden sky / ～的云 leaden clouds
【铅球】 qiānqiú 1.〈*Sports*〉 shot：推～ shot put；putting the shot 2.（指器械） shot
【铅球运动员】 qiānqiú yùndòngyuán shot-putter
【铅丝】 qiānsī 1.（镀锌铁丝） galvanized wire 2.〈*Electr.*〉 lead wire
【铅印】 qiānyìn letterpress printing；typographic printing
【铅印本】 qiānyìnběn typographic copy
【铅中毒】 qiānzhòngdú lead-poisoning
【铅字】 qiānzì type；letter

悭［慳］（qiān）
【悭吝】 qiānlìn stingy；miserly
【悭吝人】 qiānlìnrén miser

谦（qiān） modest
【谦卑】 qiānbēi humble；modest
【谦辞】 qiāncí 1.（谦虚的言辞） self-depreciatory expression 2.（谦让推辞） modestly decline
【谦恭】 qiāngōng modest and courteous；modest and polite：～有礼 respectful and polite
【谦谦君子】 qiānqiān jūnzǐ 1.（谦虚的人） a modest，self-disciplined gentleman 2.（故作谦虚的人） a hypocritically modest person
【谦让】 qiānràng modestly decline
【谦受益，满招损】 qiān shòu yì，mǎn zhāo sǔn the modest receive benefit，while the conceited reap failure
【谦虚】 qiānxū 1.（虚心） modest；self-effacing：～谨慎 modest and prudent 2.（说话谦虚） make modest remarks
【谦逊】 qiānxùn modest；unassuming

愆（qiān） crime；fault：前～ past crimes

荨［蕁、薟］（qián）（另见"荨"xún）
【荨麻】 qiánmá nettle

钤（qián） 1.（印章） seal 2.（盖印章） affix a seal to
【钤印】 qiányìng affix a seal to；put a seal to

黔（qián）
【黔驴技穷】 Qiánlǘ-jìqióng the proverbial donkey in ancient Guizhou has exhausted its

tricks; at one's wit's end

【黔驴之技】 Qiánlǘzhījì tricks not to be feared; cheap tricks; one's low skill is disclosed

前(qián) 1.(正面的) front; frontal (adj.):～部 front part / ～门 front door / ～院 front courtyard 2.(向前) forward; ahead: 向～看 look forward / 一直朝～走到河边。Walk straight ahead until you reach the river. 3.(以前) ago; before; preceding: ～一阶段 the preceding stage / 30 年～ thirty years ago / 春节的～一天 a day previous to Spring Festival 4.(从前的) former; formerly: ～市长 former mayor; ex-mayor 5.(次序在先的) first: ～三名 the first three places

【前半夜】 qiánbànyè the first half of the night

【前保险杠】 qián bǎoxiǎngāng 〈*Auto*〉 front bumper

【前辈】 qiánbèi senior (person); elder; the older generation

【前臂】 qiánbì forearm

【前边】 qián·bian 1.(在前面) in front; ahead: 他走在我们的～。He walk ahead of us. 2.(从前) above; preceding

【前舱】 qiáncāng forecabin; forehold

【前叉】 qiánchā 〈*Bicycle*〉 front forks

【前场】 qiánchǎng 〈*Sports*〉 fore court

【前车之鉴】 qiánchēzhījiàn warning taken from the overturned cart ahead; lessons drawn from other's mistakes; a lesson from the failure of one's predecessor

【前程】 qiánchéng future; prospect: ～远大 have brilliant prospects

【前导】 qiándǎo 1.(引路) march in front; lead the way; precede 2.(引路的人) a person who leads the way; guide

【前灯】 qiándēng headlight

【前敌】 qiándí front line

【前敌委员会】 qiándí wěiyuánhuì front committee

【前额】 qián'é forehead

【前方】 qiánfāng 1.(前面) ahead 2.(前线) the front: 支援～ support the front

【前锋】 qiánfēng 1.(先头部队) vanguard 2.〈*Sports*〉 forward

【前夫】 qiánfū 1.(离了婚的) former husband; ex-husband 2.(死去的) late husband

【前赴后继】 qiánfù-hòujì advance wave upon wave

【前功尽弃】 qiángōng-jìnqì all that has been achieved is spoiled; all one's previous efforts are wasted; all the former tasks have been thrown away

【前管】 qiánguǎn 〈*Bicycle*〉 head tube

【前后】 qiánhòu 1.(时间接近) around; about: 十点～ around 10 o'clock 2.(自始至终) from start to finish; from beginning to end; altogether 3.(前面和后面) in front and behind

【前呼后拥】 qiánhū-hòuyōng with many attendants crowding round; with a large retinue

【前腱子】 qiánjiàn·zi 1.(羊肉部位) shank; foreshank 2.(牛肉部位) shin

【前脚】 qiánjiǎo 1.(先迈的脚) the forward foot in a step 2.(与"后脚"连用,表示时间靠近) no sooner ... than; the moment (when); hardly ... when: 你～走,她后脚就来了。She arrived the moment you had left.(或: No sooner had you left than she arrived.)

【前脚爪】 qiánjiǎozhuǎ (猪肉部位) forefoot

【前襟】 qiánjīn the front part of a Chinese robe or jacket

【前进】 qiánjìn advance; go forward; forge ahead; make progress: 他～速度很慢。His advance was slow.

【前景】 qiánqǐng 1.〈*Photog.*〉 foreground 2.(未来的景象) prospect; vista; perspective

【前科】 qiánkē criminal record; pedigree: ～的证据 evidence of previous convictions

【前科犯】 qiánkēfàn ex-convict; ex-prisoner; criminal with previous conviction; pedigreeman

【前科记录】 qiánkē jìlù record of previous crime

【前科罪】 qiánkēzuì previous crime

【前例】 qiánlì precedent: 有～可援 have precedents to go by

【前列】 qiánliè front row; front rank; forefront; van

【前列腺】 qiánlièxiàn 〈*Anat.*〉 prostate

(gland)

【前轮】 qiánlún front wheel

【前轮驱动】 qiánlún qūdòng 〈*Auto*〉 front wheel driving

【前门】 qiánmén front door

【前面】 qiánmiàn **1.** (指位置) front; in front; at the head; ahead: 在商店～ in front of the shop / 老师把那男孩叫到～。The teacher called the boy to the front. / 在一列小汽车的～是辆公共汽车。At the head of the line of cars was a bus. **2.** (指次序) above; preceding: ～提到的事 the facts mentioned above

【前磨牙】 qiánmóyá 〈*Anat.*〉 premolar

【前年】 qiánnián the year before last

【前怕狼,后怕虎】 qián pà láng, hòu pà hǔ fear wolves ahead and tigers behind; be full of fears

【前排】 qiánpái front row: 在主席台～就座 be seated in the front row on the rostrum

【前仆后继】 qiánpū-hòujì no sooner has one fallen than another steps into the breach

【前妻】 qiánqī **1.** (离了婚的) former wife; ex-wife **2.** (死去的) late wife

【前期】 qiánqī earlier stage; early days

【前期损益】 qiánqī sǔnyì profit and loss for the previous period

【前起落架】 qián qǐluòjià 〈*Aeron.*〉 nose landing gear unit

【前前后后】 qiánqián-hòuhòu the whole story; the ins and outs; from front to rear

【前桥】 qiánqiáo 〈*Auto*〉 front axle

【前驱】 qiánqū forerunner; vanguard; precursor

【前驱动】 qiánqūdòng 〈*Auto*〉 front wheel driving

【前人】 qiánrén forefathers; predecessors: ～开路后人行。One generation opens the road upon which another generation travels.

【前任】 qiánrèn predecessor: ～总统 ex-president

【前日】 qiánrì the day before yesterday

【前哨】 qiánshào outpost; advance guard

【前哨阵地】 qiánshào zhèndì outpost position

【前身】 qiánshēn **1.** (原来的) predecessor **2.** (衣服的) front part

【前世】 qiánshì previous existence; previous life

【前事不忘,后事之师】 qiánshì bù wàng, hòushì zhī shī past experience, if not forgotten, is a guide for the future; the past is the prologue

【前思后想】 qiánsī-hòuxiǎng think over again and again; turn over in one's mind

【前松后紧】 qiánsōng-hòujǐn be slack at the beginning and have to speed up towards the end

【前所未闻】 qiánsuǒwèiwén never heard before

【前所未有】 qiánsuǒwèiyǒu hitherto unknown; unprecedented: 取得～的成果 have received unprecedented results / 遇到～的困难 encounter greater difficulties than ever

【前台】 qiántái **1.** (舞台) proscenium **2.** (公开) (on) the stage

【前提】 qiántí **1.** 〈*Logic*〉 premise **2.** (必要条件) prerequisite; presupposition: 以安定团结为～ on the basis of stability and unity

【前蹄髈】 qiántípǎng (猪肉部位) trotter

【前天】 qiántiān the day before yesterday: ～早晨 the morning before last

【前厅】 qiántīng antechamber; vestibule

【前途】 qiántú future; prospect: 国家的～和命运 the future and destiny of our nation / 他们的～似难预测。Their future seems very uncertain.

【前腿】 qiántuǐ **1.** (先迈的腿) foreleg **2.** (牛肉部位) leg **3.** (羊肉部位) shoulder

【前往】 qiánwǎng go to; leave for; proceed to: 经上海～东京 go to Tokyo via Shanghai

【前卫】 qiánwèi **1.** 〈*Mil.*〉 advance guard; vanguard **2.** 〈*Sports*〉 halfback: 左～ left halfback; left half

【前无古人】 qiánwúgǔrén without parallel in history; unprecedented; have no predecessors

【前夕】 qiánxī eve: 节日～ holiday eve; on the eve of a festival

【前嫌】 qiánxián past grudge

【前线】 qiánxiàn front; frontline: 上～ go to the front

【前项】 qiánxiàng preceding paragraph; former term

【前言】 qiányán preface; foreword; introduction

【前沿】 qiányán forward position：～阵地 forward position / ～指挥所 forward command post

【前言不搭后语】 qiányán bù dā hòuyǔ utter words that do not hang together; talk incoherently; self-contradictory

【前沿科学】 qiányán kēxué front-line science

【前仰后合】 qiányǎng-hòuhé rock (with laughter)：笑得～ shake with laughter

【前夜】 qiányè eve：第二次世界大战～ on the eve of the Second World War

【前因后果】 qiányīn-hòuguǒ cause and effect; the entire process; the ways and wherefores

【前闸】 qiánzhā front brake

【前兆】 qiánzhào omen; forewarning; premonition：地震的～ warning signs of an earthquake

【前者】 qiánzhě the former

【前肢】 qiánzhī forelimb

【前置词】 qiánzhìcí 〈*Gram.*〉 preposition

【前置词宾语】 qiánzhìcí bīnyǔ prepositional object

【前置词短语】 qiánzhìcí duǎnyǔ prepositional phrase

【前轴】 qiánzhóu front axle

【前缀】 qiánzhuì prefix

【前奏】 qiánzòu 1.（前奏曲）prelude 2.（事情的先声）prelude; vestibule

【前奏曲】 qiánzòuqǔ 〈*Music*〉 prelude

【前座】 qiánzuò 〈*Auto*〉 front seat

虔 (qián) pious; sincere

【虔诚】 qiánchéng pious; devout：～的基督徒 a devout Christian

【虔敬】 qiánjìng reverent

钱［錢］(qián) 1.（硬币）coin; cash：古～ ancient coins 2.（钱财）money; wealth; riches：有～人家 wealthy family / 有～有势 both rich and influential / 挣～ make money / 有～能使鬼推磨。Money can move the gods. 3.（款项）fund; sum

【钱包】 qiánbāo wallet; purse; moneybag

【钱币】 qiánbì coin

【钱财】 qiáncái wealth; money：～身外物。Money is not an inherent part of the human being.

【钱柜】 qiánguì money-box; money locker

【钱庄】 qiánzhuāng private bank

钳［箝、拑[2]］(qián) 1.（钳子）pincers; pliers; tongs 2.（用钳子夹）grip; clamp

【钳工】 qiángōng 1.（工种）benchwork 2.（工人）fitter

【钳制】 qiánzhì clamp down on; suppress：～舆论 muzzle public opinion

【钳子】 qián·zi pliers; pincers; forceps

乾 (qián)

【乾坤】 qiánkūn heaven and earth; the universe

掮 (qián)

【掮客】 qiánkè broker：房地产～ real estate broker / 政治～ political broker

潜［潛］(qián) 1.（隐藏的）latent; hidden：～能 latent energy 2.（秘密的）secretly; stealthily; on the sly

【潜藏】 qiáncáng hide; go into hiding

【潜伏】 qiánfú hide; conceal; lie low

【潜伏期】 qiánfúqī 〈*Med.*〉 incubation period

【潜伏性病毒感染】 qiánfúxìng bìngdú gǎnrǎn latent-virus infection

【潜航】 qiánháng submerge

【潜科学】 qiánkēxué embryonic science

【潜力】 qiánlì latent capacity; potential：挖掘～ exploit potentialities; tap potentials

【潜流】 qiánliú 〈*Geol.*〉 undercurrent; underflow

【潜热】 qiánrè 〈*Physics*〉 latent heat

【潜入】 qiánrù 1.（偷偷进入）slip into; steal in; sneak into 2.（钻进水中）dive into; go under (water); submerge：他～水中，救出溺水的小孩。He dived into the water and rescued the drowning boy.

【潜水】 qiánshuǐ go under water; dive

【潜水艇】 qiánshuǐtǐng submarine; U-boat

【潜水员】 qiánshuǐyuán diver; frogman

【潜台词】 qiántáicí 〈*Theatre*〉 unspoken words in a play left to the understanding of the audience or reader

【潜逃】 qiántáo abscond; go away secretly：携款～ abscond with an amount of money

【潜听装置】 qiántīng zhuāngzhì listening-in

device

【潜艇】 qiántǐng submarine：核～ nuclear-powered submarine

【潜望镜】 qiánwàngjìng periscope

【潜心】 qiánxīn with great concentration; devote oneself to sth.：～研究 concentrate on studies

【潜行】 qiánxíng 1.（在水下行动）move under water 2.（秘密行走）move stealthily; slink

【潜移默化】 qiányí-mòhuà exert a subtle influence on sb's character, thinking, etc.; imperceptibly influence; a silent transforming influence

【潜意识】 qiányìshí the subconscious; subconsciousness

【潜影】 qiányǐng 〈*Photog.*〉 latent image

【潜泳】 qiányǒng underwater swimming; skin-diving

【潜在】 qiánzài latent; potential：～的力量 potential force / ～的社会不稳定因素 potential social instability / ～的危险 potential danger

【潜在竞争】 qiánzài jìngzhēng potential competition

【潜在市场】 qiánzài shìchǎng potential market

【潜在效用】 qiánzài xiàoyòng potential utility

【潜在需要】 qiánzài xūyào potential demand

【潜在资本】 qiánzài zīběn latent capital

浅［淺］（qiǎn） 1.（跟"深"相对）shallow：～盘 shallow dish / ～水 shallow water / 这里的海水很～。The sea is shallow here. 2.（浅显）simple; easy：这课书很～。This text is very easy. 3.（浅薄）superficial：～薄的知识 superficial knowledge 4.（感情不深）not intimate; not close 5.（颜色淡）light：～红 pale red / ～黄 pale yellow / ～绿 light green 6.（时间短）not long in time

【浅薄】 qiǎnbó 1.（缺乏学识或修养）shallow; superficial; meager; limited：～的议论 shallow argument 2.（感情不深）not intimate; not close 3.（轻浮）frivolous

【浅尝辄止】 qiǎncháng-zhézhǐ stop after getting a little knowledge of a subject or about sth.; be satisfied with a smattering of a subject; do not study further or deeper

【浅耕】 qiǎngēng 〈*Agric.*〉 shallow plowing

【浅海】 qiǎnhǎi 〈*Geol.*〉 shallow sea; epeiric sea

【浅见】 qiǎnjiàn superficial view; humble opinion

【浅近】 qiǎnjìn simple; plain; easy to understand

【浅陋】 qiǎnlòu shallow; meager; mean：～不堪 very shallow and detestable

【浅明】 qiǎnmíng easy and clean

【浅色】 qiǎnsè light color

【浅水池】 qiǎnshuǐcí 〈*Swimming*〉 non-swimmer's pool

【浅说】 qiǎnshuō elementary introduction

【浅滩】 qiǎntān shoal; shallows

【浅显】 qiǎnxiǎn plain; easy to read and understand：～的科普读物 simple popular scientific literature

【浅易】 qiǎnyì simple and easy

遣（qiǎn） 1.（派遣）send; dispatch; designate 2.（排遣）dispel; expel：无以自～ have no diversion

【遣愁】 qiǎnchóu drove away melancholy

【遣词造句】 qiǎncí-zàojù choice of words and building of sentences; wording and phrasing

【遣返】 qiǎnfǎn repatriate：～战俘 repatriate prisoners of war

【遣散】 qiǎnsàn disband; dismiss; send away

【遣散费】 qiǎnsànfèi termination pay; release pay

【遣送】 qiǎnsòng send back; repatriate

【遣送出境】 qiǎnsòng chūjìng deport; deportation：一名非法移民被～。An illegal immigrant was deported.

谴（qiǎn）

【谴责】 qiǎnzé condemn; denounce; censure; reprimand; condemnation：～恐怖行动 condemn the terrorist action / 受到广泛的～ receive universal condemnation

欠（qiàn） 1.（未还）owe; be behind with：～租 be behind with the rent / 食品要 30 元,我只付了 25 元,所以我还～5 元。The food cost 30 yuan, but I only paid 25 yuan so I still owe 5 yuan. 2.（不够;缺少）insufficient; not enough; lacking; wanting：～慎重

lack of prudence **3.**（欠身）raise slightly **4.**（呵欠）yawn

【欠安】 qiàn'ān fell unwell; indisposed

【欠产】 qiànchǎn shortfall in output; a bad crop

【欠发达】 qiànfādá less-developed：～的内陆地区 less-developed inland province

【欠款】 qiànkuǎn money that is owing; arrears; balance due; debt

【欠情】 qiànqíng owe sb. a debt of gratitude; be indebted to sb.

【欠缺】 qiànquē **1.**（不够）be deficient in; be short of **2.**（不够的地方）shortcoming; deficiency

【欠身】 qiànshēn raise oneself slightly; half rise from one's seat：～倾听 bend one's body slightly forward to listen

【欠条】 qiàntiáo IOU; a bill signed in acknowledgement of debt

【欠妥】 qiàntuǒ not proper; inadequate; improper

【欠债】 qiànzhài **1.**（欠别人的钱）be in debt; run into debt **2.**（所欠的债）debt due; outstanding accounts：还清～ clear off all one's debt

【欠账】 qiànzhàng bills due; outstanding accounts

【欠资】 qiànzī 〈*Post*〉postage due

【欠资通知单】 qiànzī tóngzhīdān notice for postage due

【欠资信】 qiànzīxìn postage-due letter

芡（qiàn） 〈*Bot.*〉Gorgon euryale

【芡粉】 qiànfěn **1.**（芡实的粉）the seed powder of Gorgon euryale **2.**（勾芡用的淀粉）any starch used in cooking

【芡实】 qiànshí Gorgon fruit

嵌（qiàn） inlay; embed; set：～有宝石的王冠 a crown embedded with jewels

【嵌板】 qiànbǎn panel; fielded panel

【嵌花地面】 qiànhuā dìmiàn a mosaic pavement

【嵌甲】 qiànjiǎ ingrowing nail

纤［縴］（qiàn） a rope for towing a boat; tow line：拉～ track（a boat）
（另见"纤"xiān）

【纤夫】 qiànfū boat tracker

【纤路】 qiànlù towpath; towing path; track road

【纤绳】 qiànshéng towline; towrope

【纤手】 qiànshǒu go-between; middleman

茜［蒨］（qiàn） **1.**（茜草）madder **2.**（红色）red

【茜草】 qiàncǎo 〈*Bot.*〉madder

【茜素】 qiànsù 〈*Chem.*〉alizarin

倩（qiàn） pretty; beautiful

【倩影】 qiànyǐng pretty silhouette; beautiful silhouette

堑（qiàn） moat; chasm：天～ natural chasm

【堑壕】 qiànháo trench; entrenchment：～工事 entrenchment works

歉（qiàn） **1.**（歉收）poor harvest **2.**（抱歉）apology; sorry; ill at ease：迟复为～。I feel sorry for not giving you a quick reply.

【歉年】 qiànnián lean year

【歉收】 qiànshōu crop failure; poor harvest：因遭旱灾而～ have a bad harvest due to natural drought

【歉意】 qiànyì apology; regret：表示～ express one's regret; offer an apology

qiang

羌（qiāng）

【羌笛】 qiāngdí Qiang flute

【羌族】 Qiāngzú Qiang（中国少数民族，主要分布在四川）

蜣（qiāng）

【蜣螂】 qiāngláng dung beetle

呛［嗆］（qiāng） choke
（另见"呛"qiàng）

【呛着】 qiāng·zhe choke; be choked; get choked by water：这水～着我了。The water choked me.

枪［槍、鎗］（qiāng） **1.**（兵器）rifle; gun; firearm：步～ rifle / 冲锋～ sub-machine gun / 机～ machine gun / 卡宾～ carbine; machine carbine / 手～ pistol / 信号～ flare pistol; ground signal projector / 左轮手～ revolver / 开～ open fire; fire with rifle 2.(工具) gun: 润滑～ a grease gun 3.(旧式兵器) spear

【枪靶】 qiāngbǎ target; mark

【枪把】 qiāngbà the small of the stock; pistol grip

【枪毙】 qiāngbì execute by shooting: ～一杀人犯 execute a murderer

【枪刺】 qiāngcì bayonet

【枪弹】 qiāngdàn cartridge; bullet

【枪法】 qiāngfǎ marksmanship

【枪管】 qiāngguǎn barrel (of a gun)

【枪机】 qiāngjī rifle bolt

【枪击】 qiāngjī shoot

【枪决】 qiāngjué execute by shooting

【枪口】 qiāngkǒu 1.(枪管口) muzzle 2.(比喻) gunpoint: 在～之下 at gunpoint

【枪林弹雨】 qiānglín-dànyǔ a hail of bullets; storm of shots and shells

【枪榴弹】 qiāngliúdàn rifle grenade

【枪炮】 qiāngpào firearms; arms; guns

【枪杀】 qiāngshā shoot dead; gun killing

【枪伤】 qiāngshāng bullet wound

【枪声】 qiāngshēng report of a gun; shot; crack

【枪手】 qiāngshǒu marksman; gunner: 神～ an expert marksman; a crack shot

【枪栓】 qiāngshuān rifle bolt

【枪膛】 qiāngtáng bore (of a gun)

【枪托】 qiāngtuō (rifle) butt; buttstock; gunstock

【枪乌贼】 qiāngwūzéi (鱿鱼) squid

【枪械】 qiāngxiè firearms

【枪眼】 qiāngyǎn 1.(射击孔) embrasure; loophole 2.(枪弹打的洞) bullet hole

【枪战】 qiāngzhàn gunfight; gunplay: 在逃犯和警察之间展开了一场～。A gunfight broke out between the escaped convicts and police officers.

【枪支】 qiāngzhī firearms

【枪支弹药】 qiāngzhī dànyào firearms and ammunition

戗[戧] (qiāng) 1.(方向相对) in an opposite direction 2.(言语冲突) clash; be at loggerheads with

【戗风】 qiāngfēng against the wind

戕 (qiāng) kill; murder: 自～ commit suicide

【戕害】 qiānghài kill; murder

腔 (qiāng) 1.(体腔) cavity 2.(话) speech 3.(乐曲调子) tune; pitch: 高～ high pitched tune / 花～ coloratura 4.(说话腔调) accent: 说话南～北调 speak with a mixture of accents

【腔调】 qiāngdiào 1.(曲调) tune 2.(口音、语调) accent; intonation

锖 (qiāng)

【锖色】 qiāngsè tarnish

镪 (qiāng)

【镪水】 qiāngshuǐ strong acid: 硝～ nitric acid

强[強、彊] (qiáng) 1.(力量大;健壮) strong; powerful: ～有力的人物 a powerful man 2.(强迫) by force 3.(优越;好) better than; surpass; excel: 一代更比一代～。Each generation surpasses the preceding one. 4.(程度高) slightly more than; plus: 四分之一～ slightly more than one fourth 5.(大国) power: 世界列～ the great world powers

(另见"强"jiàng, qiǎng)

【强暴】 qiángbào 1.(强横凶暴) violent; brutal 2.(强暴势力) ferocious adversary 3.(强奸) indecent assault: ～妇女 indecent assault on women

【强大】 qiángdà big and powerful; powerful; formidable

【强盗】 qiángdào robber; bandit; pirate; highwayman

【强盗逻辑】 qiángdào luójí gangster logic

【强盗头子】 qiángdào tóu·zi gang boss; bandit chieftain

【强盗遇着贼打劫】 qiángdào yù·zhe zéi dǎjié robbers are plundered by thieves

【强电流】 qiángdiànliú heavy current

【强调】 qiángdiào stress; emphasize; underline: ～指出 point out emphatically

【强调成分】 qiángdiào chéngfèn intensifier

【强度】 qiángdù 1.(指作用力) intensity 2.(指能力) strength: 抗震～ shock strength

【强渡】 qiángdù fight one's way across a river; force a river

【强夺】 qiángduó grab

【强风】 qiángfēng strong breeze
【强攻】 qiánggōng take by storm; storm: ～该城 storm the city
【强固】 qiánggù strong; solid
【强国】 qiángguó powerful nation; power: 现代化～ modern, powerful country
【强悍】 qiánghàn intrepid; doughty; valiant
【强横】 qiánghèng tyrannical; insolent; brutal and unreasonable; overbearing
【强化】 qiánghuà strengthen; intensify; consolidate: ～企业自我约束机制 strengthen the self-discipline of enterprises
【强击机】 qiángjījī attack plane
【强加】 qiángjiā impose; force: ～于人 force one's views on others
【强奸】 qiángjiān rape; violate: 女孩被从车里拖出来～了。The girl was dragged from the car and raped.
【强奸犯】 qiángjiānfàn rapist; raper: 警察抓到了～。The police have caught the rapist.
【强奸民意】 qiángjiān mínyì defile public opinion
【强奸罪】 qiángjiānzuì forcible rape; offense of rape; rape
【强健】 qiángjiàn strong and healthy: ～的游泳运动员 a strong swimmer
【强劲】 qiángjìng powerful; forceful: 功率～的发动机 a powerful engine
【强力】 qiánglì 1.(力量强大) powerful 2.(强度) strength
【强力霉素】 qiánglìméisù 〈*Pharm.*〉 doxycycline
【强烈】 qiángliè 1.(很强) strong; intense; powerful: ～的反应 strong reaction / ～的光线 forceful rays / ～的愿望 a strong desire / 洋葱有～的味道。Onions have a powerful smell. 2.(鲜明) striking; clear; clear-cut: ～的对比 striking contrast 3.(强硬) vigorously; vehemently: ～谴责 vehemently condemn; vigorously denounce
【强买强卖】 qiángmǎi-qiángmài buy or sell under coercion
【强弩之末】 qiángnǔzhīmò an arrow at the end of its fight; a spent force
【强取豪夺】 qiángqǔ-háoduó rapacity; rapacious (adj.)
【强权】 qiángquán power; might
【强权政治】 qiángquán zhèngzhì power politics
【强人】 qiángrén strongman (m.); strongwoman (f.)
【强盛】 qiángshèng powerful and prosperous: ～时期 the powerful and prosperous period
【强手】 qiángshǒu strong opponent; high-level and capable man
【强似】 qiángsì be better than; be superior to
【强项】 qiángxiàng 〈*Sports*〉 strong sports
【强心剂】 qiángxīnjì cardiac stimulant; cardiotonic
【强行】 qiángxíng force: ～进入… make a forcible entry into
【强行军】 qiángxíngjūn forced march
【强行摊派】 qiángxíng tānpài arbitrary levies
【强行推销】 qiángxíng tuīxiāo hard sell
【强硬】 qiángyìng strong; tough; unyielding: 用～的手段 with a high hand
【强硬路线】 qiángyìng lùxiàn tough line; hard line
【强硬派】 qiángyìngpài hardliner
【强有力】 qiángyǒulì strong; vigorous; forceful
【强占】 qiángzhàn forcibly occupy; seize
【强震】 qiángzhèn strong shock
【强震区】 qiángzhènqū meizoseismal area
【强直】 qiángzhí 〈*Med.*〉 tetanic
【强制】 qiángzhì force; compel; compulsory (adj.); coerce; coercive (adj.): ～保险 compulsory insurance / ～措施 coercive measures / ～机关 institutions of coercion / ～劳动 forced labor / ～手段 compulsory means; coercive measure
【强制性】 qiángzhìxìng mandatory: ～命令 mandatory order / ～法规 mandatory rules of law / ～规定 mandatory provision / ～条款 mandatory term / ～制裁 mandatory sanction
【强制执行】 qiángzhì zhíxíng enforce
【强壮】 qiángzhuàng strong; sturdy; robust: 身体～的人 a strong man
【强壮剂】 qiángzhuàngjì roborant; tonic

墙[墻、牆] (qiáng) wall: 围～ surrounding wall / 砖～ brick wall / 挡水～ a wall of waterproof /

把画挂在～上 hang the picture on the wall / 隔～有耳。Walls have ear.

【墙板】 qiángbǎn wallboard

【墙报】 qiángbào wall newspaper

【墙壁】 qiángbì wall：我们把所有的～都涂成了白色。We have painted all the walls white.

【墙倒众人推】 qiáng dǎo zhòngrén tuī when a wall is about to collapse, everybody gives it a push; everybody hits a man who is down

【墙根】 qiánggēn the foot of a wall

【墙角】 qiángjiǎo a corner formed by two walls

【墙角家具】 qiángjiǎo jiājù corner furniture

【墙脚】 qiángjiǎo 1.(墙根) the foot of a wall 2.(基础) foundation：挖～ cut the ground (from under sb's feet); undermine the foundation of

【墙面涂料】 qiángmiàn túliào wall covering

【墙内灯】 qiángnèidēng build-in lamp

【墙裙】 qiángqún 〈*Archit*.〉 dado; wainscot

【墙上插头】 qiángshàng chātóu wall outlet

【墙头】 qiángtóu the top of a wall

【墙纸】 qiángzhǐ 〈*Archit*.〉 wallpaper ‖ 贴墙纸 wallpaper (v.)

蔷[薔](qiáng)

【蔷薇】 qiángwēi rose

樯[檣、艢](qiáng) 〈*Naut*.〉 mast：前～ foremast

抢[搶](qiǎng) 1.(抢劫) rob; loot：～了某人的钱 rob a man of his money 2.(抢夺) snatch; grab：从某人手中把信～了过去 snatch away the letter from a person's hand 3.(抢先；争先) vie for; scramble for 4.(赶紧；突击) rush in：～运 rush-transport sth. 5.(刮掉) scrape; scratch

【抢白】 qiǎngbái reprove or satirize sb. to his face

【抢渡】 qiǎngdù speedily cross (a river)

【抢夺】 qiǎngduó snatch; wrest; seize：～战略基地 grab strategic places

【抢购】 qiǎnggòu rush to purchase

【抢购风】 qiǎnggòufēng purchasing spree; panic-buying

【抢劫】 qiǎngjié rob; loot; plunder：～银行 rob the bank / ～一空 loot to the last pin

【抢劫犯】 qiǎngjiéfàn robber; looter; plunderer

【抢劫罪】 qiǎngjiézuì crime of pillage; offense of robbery

【抢救】 qiǎngjiù rescue; save; salvage：～遇险矿工 rescue trapped miners / ～无效。All rescue measures proved ineffectual.

【抢跑】 qiǎngpǎo 〈*Sports*〉 jump the gun

【抢时间】 qiǎngshíjiān race against time

【抢收】 qiǎngshōu rush in the harvest; get the harvest in quickly

【抢手货】 qiǎngshǒuhuò commodities that are popular and customers rush to buy

【抢先】 qiǎngxiān try to be the first to do sth.; anticipate; forestall; do sth. before others have a chance to

【抢险】 qiǎngxiǎn rush to deal with an emergency

【抢险队】 qiǎngxiǎnduì emergency squad

【抢修】 qiǎngxiū rush to repair; do rush repairs; make urgent repair on：～公路和桥梁 make urgent repair on highway and bridges

【抢运】 qiǎngyùn rush transport

【抢占】 qiǎngzhàn race to control; seize; grab

【抢种】 qiǎngzhòng rush-planting

羟[羥](qiǎng)

【羟基】 qiǎngjī 〈*Chem*.〉 hydroxyl; hydroxyl group

强[強、彊](qiǎng) make an effort; strive

(另见"强"jiàng, qiáng)

【强逼】 qiǎngbī compel; force

【强辩】 qiǎngbiàn defend oneself by sophistry

【强词夺理】 qiǎngcí-duólǐ use lame arguments; resort to sophistry; reason fallaciously; argue irrationally

【强记】 qiǎngjì strain to memorize sth.; cram sth. into one's memory

【强迫】 qiǎngpò force; compel; coerce：～包办婚姻 compulsory marriage on account of an arrangement / ～卖淫 force harlotry / ～命令 resort to coercion and command

【强迫劳动】 qiǎngpò láodòng forced labor

【强求】 qiǎngqiú insist on; impose

【强人所难】 qiǎngrénsuǒnán try to make sb. do sth. which he won't or can't
【强使】 qiǎngshǐ force; compel
【强笑】 qiǎngxiào forced smile
【强颜欢笑】 qiǎngyán-huānxiào put on an air of cheerfulness; try to look happy when one is sad; a forced countenance with a smile

襁［繈］(qiǎng)
【襁褓】 qiǎngbǎo swaddling clothes
【襁褓中】 qiǎngbǎo zhōng be in one's infancy

呛［嗆］(qiàng) irritate (respiratory organs): 辣椒味～鼻子 the smell of red pepper irritates the nose
(另见"呛"qiāng)

跄［蹌］(qiàng)
【跄踉】 qiàngliàng stagger; totter; stumble

qiao

悄 (qiāo)
(另见"悄"qiǎo)
【悄悄】 qiāoqiāo 1.(低声或几乎无声) quietly; on the quiet; with as little noise as possible: ～地告诉 tell sb. quietly 2.(不让人知道) without being noticed: ～地拿走 take away sth. without being noticed

跷［蹺］(qiāo) 1.(抬起) lift up; hold up: ～起腿 lift up a leg / ～起大拇指 hold up one's thumb 2.(踮起) on tiptoe 3.(高跷) stilts
【跷蹊】 qiāo·qi fishy; dubious
【跷跷板】 qiāoqiāobǎn seesaw: 玩～ play on a seesaw

锹［鍫］(qiāo) spade

劁 (qiāo) geld; castrate
【劁猪】 qiāozhū castrate a pig

敲 (qiāo) knock; beat; strike: 谁～门? Who is knocking?
【敲打】 qiāodǎ 1.(击打) beat; rap; tap 2.(用言语刺激) say sth. to irritate sb.
【敲定】 qiāodìng determine: 方案～了。The plan was determined.
【敲骨吸髓】 qiāogǔ-xīsuǐ break the bones and suck the marrow; cruel, bloodsucking exploitation; suck the lifeblood
【敲锣打鼓】 qiāoluó-dǎgǔ beat drums and strike gongs
【敲门砖】 qiāoménzhuān a stepping-stone to success
【敲诈】 qiāozhà extort; blackmail; racketeer: ～勒索 blackmail and impose exactions on; extort and racketeer
【敲竹杠】 qiāozhúgàng take advantage of sb's being in a weak position to overcharge him; fleece
【敲竹杠的场所】 qiāozhúgàng de chǎngsuǒ gyp joint

橇 (qiāo) sledge; sled; sleigh

乔［喬］(qiáo) 1.(高大) tall 2.(假扮) disguise
【乔戈里峰】 Qiáogēlǐfēng 〈place〉 Mount Qogir
【乔木】 qiáomù arbor; tree
【乔其纱】 qiáoqíshā 〈*Textiles*〉 georgette; crepe georgette
【乔迁】 qiáoqiān 1.(指搬家) move to a better place: ～之喜。Best wishes for your new home. 2.(指升官) have a promotion
【乔装】 qiáozhuāng disguise; dress up: ～男人 disguise oneself as a man

侨［僑］(qiáo) 1.(侨居) live abroad 2.(侨民) a person living abroad: 华～ overseas Chinese / 外～ foreign residents
【侨胞】 qiáobāo countrymen residing abroad: 海外～ Chinese nationals residing in foreign countries
【侨汇】 qiáohuì overseas remittance
【侨居】 qiáojū live abroad; emigration
【侨居国】 qiáojūguó country of one's residence
【侨眷】 qiáojuàn relatives of nationals living abroad
【侨民】 qiáomín a national of a particular country residing abroad
【侨务】 qiáowù affairs concerning nationals living abroad
【侨乡】 qiáoxiāng hometown of overseas

Chinese

荞[蕎](qiáo)

【荞麦】 qiáomài buckwheat

【荞麦面】 qiáomàimiàn buckwheat flour

桥[橋](qiáo) bridge：高架～ viaduct / 公路～ highway bridge / 弓弦式桁架～ bow-string girder bridge / 拱～ arch bridge / 桁架～ truss bridge / 跨线～ overline bridge / 立交～ grade separation / 平～ level bridge; flat bridge / 人行～ foot bridge; pedestrian bridge / 双层～ double-deck bridge / 铁路～ railway bridge / 铁路公路两用～ combined bridge; rail and highway bridge / 悬索～ suspension bridge / 引～ approach / 预应力混凝土～ pre-stressed concrete bridge / 在河上架～ bridge the river; put up a bridge across the river / 开车过～ drive across the bridge; drive over the bridge / 武汉长江大～从汉阳到武昌横跨长江。The Wuhan Changjiang River Bridge spans the Changjiang River from Hanyang to Wuchang.

【桥洞】 qiáodòng bridge opening

【桥墩】 qiáodūn (bridge) pier：水下～ underwater foundation

【桥墩破冰构造】 qiáodūn bò bīng gòuzào ice guard

【桥拱】 qiáogǒng bridge arch

【桥孔】 qiáokǒng bridge opening

【桥栏杆】 qiáolángān bridge railings

【桥梁】 qiáoliáng 1.(桥) bridge：～工程 bridge work 2.(比喻) bridge; connection：起～作用 serve as a connection

【桥门】 qiáomén portal

【桥面】 qiáomiàn road of bridge; bridge floor

【桥牌】 qiáopái bridge：打～ play bridge

【桥塔】 qiáotǎ bridge tower

【桥台】 qiáotái abutment

【桥头】 qiáotóu either end of a bridge

【桥头堡】 qiáotóubǎo 1.〈*Mil.*〉 bridgehead 2.〈*Archit.*〉 bridge tower

翘[翹](qiáo) 1.(抬起) raise (one's head) 2.(翘棱) become warped (另见"翘"qiào)

【翘棱】 qiáo·leng become warped：板子～了。The board become warped.

【翘首】 qiáoshǒu raise one's head and look：～以待 raise one's head and look forward to

【翘望】 qiáowàng 1.(抬头看) raise one's head and look 2.(盼望) look forward to

憔(qiáo)

【憔悴】 qiáocuì 1.(指人) wan and sallow; thin and pallid：面容～ haggard face 2.(指花木) withered：花已显得～。The flowers are withering away.

瞧(qiáo) look; see; glance at：～报 read a newspaper / ～一～ take a look at; have a look at / 东～西～ look about

【瞧病】 qiáobìng 1.(就医) see a doctor; consult a doctor 2.(诊病) see a patient; examine a patient

【瞧不起】 qiáo·buqǐ look down upon; hold in contempt; look down one's nose at

【瞧不上眼】 qiáo·bushàngyǎn consider beneath one's notice; turn one's nose up at; not worth so much a look at; not at all appealing to the eye; beneath notice

【瞧得起】 qiáo·deqǐ think much of; look up to; see much in

【瞧见】 qiáojiàn see; catch sight of

巧(qiǎo) 1.(灵巧) skillful; ingenious; clever：手～(指手) a dab hand; a clever hand; (指人) clever with one's hands; dexterous / 嘴～ silver-tongued; have a nimble tongue 2.(虚浮不实) cunning; deceitful; artful 3.(恰巧) opportunely; coincidentally; as it happens; as luck would have it：来得真～ have come at a most opportune moment

【巧辩】 qiǎobiàn plausible argument; ingenious argument

【巧夺天工】 qiǎoduó-tiāngōng wonderful workmanship excelling nature; superb craftsmanship excelling nature

【巧干】 qiǎogàn work ingeniously; do sth. in a clever way

【巧合】 qiǎohé coincidence：真是～! What a happy coincidence!

【巧计】 qiǎojì clever device; artful scheme

【巧匠】 qiǎojiàng clever artisan; skilled workman

【巧克力】 qiǎokèlì chocolate：牛奶～ milk

chocolate / 纯～ plain chocolate; white chocolate

【巧立名目】 qiǎolì-míngmù concoct various pretexts; invent all sorts of names

【巧妙】 qiǎomiào ingenious; clever

【巧取豪夺】 qiǎoqǔ-háoduó extort by trick or by force; grab through deceit or by force; take by art and plunder by force

【巧事】 qiǎoshì coincidence

【巧言令色】 qiǎoyán-lìngsè clever talk and an ingratiating manner

【巧遇】 qiǎoyù chance encounter

悄 (qiǎo) quiet; silent; low-voiced (另见"悄"qiāo)

【悄寂】 qiǎojì quiet; silent

【悄然】 qiǎorán **1.**(忧愁) sorrowfully; sadly **2.**(无声) quietly; softly

【悄声】 qiǎoshēng quietly; in a low voice

壳[殼] (qiào) shell; hard surface (另见"壳"ké)

俏 (qiào) **1.**(俊俏) pretty; smart; good-looking; handsome **2.**(走俏) sell well; be in great demand: 这些商品很走～。These goods are selling well.

【俏货】 qiàohuò goods in high demand; fast-selling goods

【俏皮】 qiào·pi **1.**(俊俏) good-looking; smart **2.**(活泼风趣) lively and delightful; witty

【俏皮话】 qiào·pihuà **1.**(歇后语) witty remark; witticism; wisecrack **2.**(讽刺) sarcastic remark

峭[陗] (qiào) **1.**(山势高陡) high and steep; precipitous **2.**(严厉) severe; stern

【峭拔】 qiàobá **1.**(指山) high and steep **2.**(指文笔) vigorous

【峭壁】 qiàobì cliff; precipice; steep

【峭立】 qiàolì rise steeply

鞘 (qiào) sheath; scabbard: 刀～ the sheath of a sword

窍[竅] (qiào) **1.**(孔洞) aperture **2.**(窍门) a key to sth.

【窍门】 qiàomén key (to a problem); knack: 找～ try to find the key to a problem

翘[翹、翹] (qiào) stick up; hold up; bend upwards; turn upwards (另见"翘"qiáo)

【翘辫子】 qiào biàn·zi turn up one's toes; kick up one's heels

【翘尾巴】 qiào wěi·ba be cocky; get stuck-up

撬 (qiào) prize; pry: ～锁 pick a lock / ～开箱子 prize open a box / ～起一块地板 pry up a floorboard

【撬杆】 qiàogǎn pinch bar

【撬杠】 qiàogàng crowbar

【撬棍】 qiàogùn crowbar

qie

切 (qiē) **1.**(用刀分开) cut; slice: ～成两半 cut into halves; cut in two / ～蛋糕 cut a cake / 把黄瓜～成片 slice the cucumber / 把圆白菜～成丝 shred the cabbage / 把洋葱～碎 chop the onion **2.**〈*Math.*〉 tangency (另见"切"qiè)

【切除】 qiēchú 〈*Med.*〉 excision; resection: ～扁桃腺 removal of tonsils

【切磋】 qiēcuō learn from each other by exchanging views; compare notes

【切丁】 qiēdīng dice: 把胡萝卜切成丁 dice the carrot

【切断】 qiēduàn cut off: ～水源 cut off the water supply

【切风窗】 qiēfēngchuāng 〈*Auto*〉 windbreaker

【切割】 qiēgē cut: ～金属 cut through metal

【切割机】 qiēgējī cutting machine; cutter

【切割线】 qiēgēxiàn line of cut

【切汇】 qiēhuì intercept foreign exchange

【切开】 qiēkāi **1.**(用刀子) cut open; cut apart: ～西瓜 cut open a water melon **2.**〈*Med.*〉 incision: ～引流 incision and drainage

【切口】 qiēkǒu incision

【切块】 qiēkuài 〈*Food*〉 stripping and slicing

【切面】 qiēmiàn **1.**〈*Math.*〉 tangent plane **2.**(剖面) section **3.**(面条) cut noodles; machine-made noodles

【切片】 qiēpiàn **1.**(切成片) slice; cut into slices: 把面包切成片 slice the bread **2.**

〈*Med*.〉section：～检查 cut sections for microscopic examination

【切丝】 qiēsī shred

【切碎】 qiēsuì cut up；chop

【切削】 qiēxiāo 〈*Mech*.〉cut；cutting：高速～ high-speed cutting

【切牙】 qiēyā 〈*Anat*.〉incisors

【切纸机】 qiēzhǐjī slitter；paper cutting machine；paper cutter

茄(qié) eggplant；aubergine

【茄汁】 qiézhī tomato juice：～牛肉 tomato sauce fried beef

【茄子】 qié·zi eggplant；aubergine

且(qiě) **1**.(暂且) just；for the time being：～等一会儿 just wait a while **2**.(经久) for a long time：这种鞋～穿呢。These shoes will last long. **3**.(尚且) even **4**.(并且) both . . . and . . . ；as well (as)：既智～勇 be both brave and clever

【且慢】 qiěmàn wait a moment；not go or do so soon

【且…且…】 qiě…qiě… while；as：～战～退 carry on the fight while beating a retreat

切(qiè) **1**.(切合；符合) correspond to；be close to：不～实际 not correspond to reality **2**.(迫切；急切) eager；anxious：回家心～ be anxious to return home **3**.(切实；千万要) be sure to：～勿悲观 hope for the best / ～勿迟延 be sure not to delay

(另见"切"qiē)

【切齿】 qièchǐ gnash one's teeth：～之仇 bitter hatred that gnashes the teeth

【切肤之痛】 qièfūzhītòng pain of cutting one's body；keenly-felt pain

【切合】 qièhé suit；fit in with；correspond with：～实际 be geared to actual circumstances

【切记】 qièjì be sure to keep in mind；must always remember

【切忌】 qièjì must guard against；avoid by all means：～饮酒过度 by all means avoid excessive drinking

【切脉】 qièmài 〈*Chin*. *Med*.〉feel the pulse

【切切】 qièqiè **1**.(务必) be absolutely sure to：～不可过份 be absolutely sure not go too far **2**.(用于布告)～此令。This order is to be observed. **3**.(声音细小，同"窃窃") in small voice：～私语 a private talk in small voice

【切身】 qièshēn **1**.(跟自己关系密切) of immediate concern to oneself：～利益 one's immediate interests **2**.(亲身) personal：～体验 one's own experience

【切实】 qièshí **1**.(切合实际) feasible；practical；realistic：～可行的办法 practical ways **2**.(实实在在) conscientiously；earnestly；in real earnest

【切题】 qiètí keep to the point；be relevant to the subject；be pertinent to the subject

【切勿】 qièwù be sure not to：～倒置 do not turn over；keep upright

【切诊】 qièzhěn 〈*Chin*. *Med*.〉pulse-feeling and palpation

【切中要害】 qièzhòng yàohài hit the mark；strike home

窃[竊](qiè) **1**.(偷窃) steal；pilfer：失～ be stolen / 行～ steal；practice theft **2**.(偷偷地) secretly；surreptitiously；furtively：～笑 laugh secretly；laugh up one's sleeve

【窃案】 qiè'àn larceny；burglary

【窃盗险】 qièdàoxiǎn burglary insurance

【窃国】 qièguó usurp state power

【窃据】 qièjù usurp；unjustly occupy：～要位 usurp a high post

【窃窃】 qièqiè **1**.(声音小) in small voice：～私语 a private talk in small voice **2**.(暗地里) in secret

【窃取】 qièqǔ usurp；steal；grab：～胜利果实 steal the fruits of victory

【窃听】 qiètīng eavesdrop；wiretap；bug

【窃听电话】 qiètīng diànhuà tap phone

【窃听器】 qiètīngqì bug；tapping device；listening-in device

【窃贼】 qièzéi thief；burglar；pilferer

妾(qiè) concubine

怯(qiè) timid；cowardly；nervous

【怯场】 qièchǎng have stage fright

【怯懦】 qiènuò timid and overcautious

【怯弱】 qièruò timid and weak-willed

【怯生】 qièshēng shy with strangers

【怯阵】 qièzhèn **1**.(临阵胆怯) feel nervous

when going into battle; be battle-shy **2**.(怯场) have stage fright

挈 (qiè) **1**.(带领) take along **2**.(举;提) lift; raise; take up: 提纲～领 concentrate on the main points

【挈带】 qièdài take along; bring along with sb.

锲 (qiè) carve; engrave

【锲而不舍】 qiè'érbùshě keep on carving unflaggingly; work with perseverance

惬[愜、㥦] (qiè) be satisfied

【惬意】 qièyì be pleased; be satisfied

qin

钦 (qīn) **1**.(敬重) admire; respect **2**.(皇帝亲自) by the emperor himself: ～赐 granted by an emperor

【钦差】 qīnchāi imperial envoy; imperial commissioner

【钦定】 qīndìng made by imperial order

【钦敬】 qīnjìng admire and respect

【钦佩】 qīnpèi admire; esteem: 使我们十分～ command our great admiration

侵 (qīn) **1**.(侵入) invade; intrude into; infringe upon: 入～之敌 invading enemy; invaders **2**.(接近) approaching

【侵犯】 qīnfàn **1**.(侵入) invade; intrude into: ～领空 intrude into a country's air space **2**.(非法损害) encroach on; infringe upon; violate: ～版权 infringe a copyright / ～主权 violate a country's sovereignty

【侵害】 qīnhài **1**.(造成损害) encroach on; make inroads on **2**.(非法损害) infringe; invade; infringement (n.): ～他人的权益 invade another person's rights / ～公民权利的行为 infringement of the rights of citizens

【侵略】 qīnlüè aggression; aggressive (adj.); invasion; invade (v.): 帝国主义～ imperialist aggression

【侵略军】 qīnlüèjūn aggressor troops; invading army

【侵略行为】 qīnlüè xíngwéi act of aggression

【侵略战争】 qīnlüè zhànzhēng war of aggression

【侵略者】 qīnlüèzhě aggressor; invader

【侵权】 qīnquán tort; infringe

【侵权人】 qīnquánrén infringer

【侵权行为】 qīnquán xíngwéi act of tort; infringement act

【侵权责任】 qīnquán zérèn liability for tort

【侵扰】 qīnrǎo invade and harass

【侵入】 qīnrù **1**.(侵犯) invade; intrude into; made incursions into: 敌军～了这个城市。The enemy army invaded the city. **2**.(比喻) invade: 病菌～人体。Germs have invaded the human body.

【侵蚀】 qīnshí corrode; erode: 土壤～ soil erosion

【侵吞】 qīntūn **1**.(非法占有) embezzle; peculate: ～税款 embezzle tax funds **2**.(武力吞并) swallow up; annex: ～别国领土 annex another country's territory

【侵袭】 qīnxí make inroads on; invade and attack; hit

【侵占】 qīnzhàn invade and occupy; seize: ～一边境城镇 seize a border town

亲[親] (qīn) **1**.(父母) parent **2**.(血亲) blood relation; next of kin **3**.(亲属) relative; kinsfolk **4**.(婚姻) marriage; match: 成～ be married / 定～ be engaged; be betrothed to **5**.(新娘) bride **6**.(亲密) close; intimate; dear: ～如手足 as dear to each other as brothers **7**.(亲自) in person; oneself ～临出事现场 visit the scene of the accident in person **8**.(吻) kiss **9**.(接近,倾向) pro-: ～华 pro-Chinese / ～美 pro-American / ～日 pro-Japanese

(另见"亲"qìng)

【亲爱】 qīn'ài dear; beloved

【亲本】 qīnběng 〈*Bot*.〉 parent; parent plant

【亲笔】 qīnbǐ **1**.(亲笔写) in one's own handwriting; in one's own hand **2**.(亲笔写的字) one's own handwriting

【亲笔签名】 qīnbǐ qiānmíng one's own signature; autograph

【亲笔签名簿】 qīnbǐ qiānmíngbù autograph album

【亲笔信】 qīnbǐxìn an autograph letter

【亲笔遗嘱】 qīnbǐ yízhǔ holographic will

【亲近】 qīnjìn be close to; be on intimate terms with: 我们之间很～。We are on intimate terms.

【亲眷】 qīnjuàn one's relatives
【亲口】 qīnkǒu (say sth.) personally: ～答应 make a promise personally
【亲临】 qīnlín in person
【亲密】 qīnmì close; intimate: ～的朋友 a close friend; a intimate friend / ～无间 be very close to; be close-knit
【亲昵】 qīnnì very intimate
【亲朋】 qīnpéng relatives and friends
【亲戚】 qīn·qi relative; kinsman (m.); kinswoman (f.)
【亲戚关系】 qīn·qi guānxì relationship: 你知道他和那女孩有～吗? Do you know his relationship to that girl?
【亲启】 qīnqǐ be opened personally; confidential
【亲切】 qīnqiè cordial; kind
【亲热】 qīnrè 1. (亲密) affectionate; intimate; warmhearted 2. 〈*euphem.*〉 intimacy
【亲人】 qīnrén 1. (亲属) one's parents, spouse, children, etc.; one's family members 2. (关系密切的人) dear ones; those dear to one
【亲如手足】 qīnrúshǒuzú as close as brothers
【亲善】 qīnshàn goodwill (between countries)
【亲上加亲】 qīnshàngjiāqīn cement old ties by marriage as marriage between cousins, etc.
【亲身】 qīnshēn personal; firsthand: ～感受 personal experiences
【亲生】 qīnshēng one's own: ～儿女 one's own children / ～父母 one's own parents
【亲事】 qīn·shi marriage
【亲手】 qīnshǒu with one's own hands; personally; one-self: ～交付 deliver sth. personally
【亲属】 qīnshǔ kinsfolk; relatives; kinsman (m.); kinswoman (f.): 直系～ blood relations; directly-related relatives
【亲属关系】 qīnshǔ guānxì kinship
【亲痛仇快】 qīntòng-chóukuài sadden one's own people and gladden the enemy; grieve one's friends and gladden one's enemies
【亲王】 qīnwáng prince
【亲信】 qīnxìn trusted follower
【亲眼】 qīnyǎn with one's own eyes; personally: ～目睹 see with one's own eyes
【亲友】 qīnyǒu relatives and friends; kith and kin
【亲鱼】 qīnyú 〈*Fishery*〉 parent fish
【亲自】 qīnzì personally; in person; oneself: ～参加 take part in person
【亲嘴】 qīnzuǐ kiss

芹 (qín)

【芹菜】 qíncài celery

琴 (qín) musical instrument: 钢～ piano / 提～ violin / 口～ harmonica / 弹钢～ play the piano / 拉小提～ play the violin / 拉手风～ play the accordion / 吹口～ play the harmonica
【琴凳】 qíndèng music stool
【琴弓】 qíngōng 〈*Music*〉 violin bow
【琴肩】 qínjiān 〈*Music*〉 shoe brace; heel
【琴键】 qínjiàn 〈*Music*〉 piano key
【琴键开关】 qínjiàn kāiguān key switch
【琴颈】 qínjǐng 〈*Music*〉 neck
【琴楼】 qínlóu 〈*Music*〉 pedal tower
【琴马】 qínmǎ 1. 〈*Music*〉 bridge 2. (吉他的) bridge base
【琴鸟】 qínniǎo 〈*Zool.*〉 lyrebird
【琴身】 qínshēng 〈*Music*〉 body
【琴师】 qínshī music master; accompanist
【琴头】 qíntóu 1. 〈*Music*〉 scroll 2. (吉他的) head
【琴弦】 qínxuán 1. 〈*Music*〉 strings 2. (钢琴的) piano strings
【琴弦板】 qínxuánbǎn 〈*Music*〉 tail piece
【琴枕】 qínzhěn 〈*Music*〉 nut
【琴槌】 qínchuí 〈*Music*〉 hammer

秦 (qín)

【秦艽】 qínjiāo 〈*Bot.*〉 largeleaf gentian
【秦始皇兵马俑】 Qínshǐhuáng bīngmǎyǒng Qin Shi Huang's Buried Sculpture Legion
【秦俑馆】 Qínyǒngguǎn Museum of Qin Shi Huang's Buried Sculpture Legion

禽 (qín) birds: 家～ (domestic) fowls; poultry / 猛～ birds of prey / 鸣～ song birds / 涉～ wading birds
【禽兽】 qínshòu 1. (鸟兽) birds and beasts 2. (指人) beasts; brutes: 衣冠～ a beast in human clothing

擒 (qín) capture; catch; seize: 生～ capture alive

【擒获】 qínhuò capture; catch; seize
【擒拿】 qínná arrest; catch
【擒纵自如】 qínzòng-zìrú arrest and release at will; in perfect control of situation
【擒纵机】 qínzòngjī 〈*Mech.*〉 escapement
【擒纵轮】 qínzònglún 〈*Mech.*〉 escape wheel

噙 (qín) hold in the mouth or the eyes: ～着眼泪 with tears in one's eyes

勤 (qín) **1.** (勤劳) diligent; industrious; hardworking **2.** (经常) often; frequently; regularly: 她来得最～。She comes here more often than any other. **3.** (勤务) duty; attendance: 内～ office work / 外～ field work / 值～ be on duty
【勤奋】 qínfèn diligent; assiduous; industrious
【勤工俭学】 qíngōng-jiǎnxué part-work and part-study system; work-study program
【勤工助学】 qíngōng-zhùxué part-time work in order to pay one's school expenses
【勤俭】 qínjiǎn hardworking and thrifty: ～持家 be industrious and thrifty in managing one's household / 办任何事情都要～。Be thrifty and hardworking in whatever undertaking you are to start on.
【勤恳】 qínkěn diligent and conscientious; earnestly and assiduously: 乐于为教学～地服务 be ready to work diligently in the service of teaching
【勤快】 qínkuài diligent; hardworking
【勤劳】 qínláo diligent; hardworking; industrious and courageous: ～致富是正当的。It is only fair that people should become prosperous through their own hard work
【勤勉】 qínmiǎn diligent; assiduous
【勤务】 qínwù duty; service
【勤务兵】 qínwùbīng orderly
【勤务员】 qínwùyuán odd-jobman; servant
【勤学苦练】 qínxué-kǔliàn diligent study and hard training

寝［寑］ (qǐn) **1.** (睡) sleep: 入～ fall asleep **2.** (卧室) bedroom: 就～ go to bed; turn in; retire to bed **3.** (寝宫) coffin chamber
【寝具】 qǐnjù bedding
【寝食】 qǐnshí sleeping and eating: ～不安 be worried waking or sleeping
【寝室】 qǐnshì bedroom; dormitory

沁 (qìn) ooze; seep; exude: 汗珠～了出来。Beads of perspiration oozed out.
【沁人心脾】 qìnrén-xīnpí gladdening the heart and refreshing the mind; mentally refreshing; refreshing

qing

青 (qīng) **1.** (青色) blue; green **2.** (黑色) black **3.** (青草) green grass **4.** (未熟的庄稼) young crops **5.** (年轻) young (people)
【青菜】 qīngcài **1.** (蔬菜) green vegetables; greens: 新鲜～ fresh vegetable; young vegetable **2.** (小白菜) pakchoi; Chinese cabbage
【青草】 qīngcǎo green grass
【青出于蓝而胜于蓝】 qīngchūyúlán ér shèngyúlán indigo blue is extracted from the indigo plant but is bluer than the plant it comes from; the pupil surpasses the master; the pupil excels the teacher
【青春】 qīngchūn youth; youthful; youthfulness: ～的活力 youthful vigor; youthful energy
【青春期】 qīngchūnqī puberty
【青葱】 qīngcōng verdant; fresh green
【青翠】 qīngcuì verdant; fresh and green
【青豆】 qīngdòu green soya bean
【青工】 qīnggōng young worker
【青黄不接】 qīnghuáng-bùjiē when the new crop is still in the blade and the old one is all consumed; temporary shortage
【青椒】 qīngjiāo green pepper
【青筋】 qīngjīn blue veins
【青稞】 qīngkē highland barley
【青睐】 qīnglài favor; good graces: 获得某人的～ find favor in sb's eyes
【青绿】 qīnglǜ dark green
【青梅】 qīngméi green plum
【青梅竹马】 qīngméi-zhúmǎ the games of childhood; the period when a boy and a girl grew up together
【青霉素】 qīngméisù penicillin
【青苗】 qīngmiáo young crops; green shoots of (food) grains
【青年】 qīngnián **1.** (指年龄) youth; young (adj.): ～教师 young teacher / 他～时当过

兵。In his youth he was a soldier. **2.**(指人) young; youth; young people

【青年宫】 qīngniángōng young palace

【青年节】 qīngniánjié Youth Day

【青山】 qīngshān green hill

【青少年】 qīngshàonián young boys and girls; teen-agers; youngsters

【青少年犯】 qīng-shàoniánfàn young-offender

【青史】 qīngshǐ annals of history: 永垂～ go down in the annals of history

【青饲料】 qīngsìliào green fodder; greenfeed

【青松】 qīngsōng pine

【青蒜】 qīngsuàn garlic sprouts

【青苔】 qīngtái moss

【青天】 qīngtiān **1.**(蓝天) blue sky **2.**(指清官) a just judge; an upright magistrate

【青天霹雳】 qīngtiān-pīlì a bolt from the blue

【青铜】 qīngtóng bronze

【青铜器】 qīngtóngqì bronze ware

【青铜时代】 qīngtóng shídài the Bronze Age

【青蛙】 qīngwā frog

【青鱼】 qīngyú black carp

【青玉】 qīngyù gray jade

【青云】 qīngyún high official position

【青贮】 qīngzhù 〈*Agric.*〉 ensile; ensiling (n.)

【青贮窖】 qīngzhùjiào silo

【青贮饲料】 qīngzhù sìliào ensilage; silage

【青贮作物】 qīngzhù zuòwù silo crop; silage crop

【青砖】 qīngzhuān blue brick

清(qīng) **1.**(纯净) unmixed; clear **2.**(清静) quiet **3.**(清楚) distinct; clarified: 查～事实 check up on the facts **4.**(一点不留) completely; thoroughly: 扫～障碍 sweep away the obstacles completely **5.**(使组织纯洁) clean up **6.**(还清;结清) settle; clear up: ～账 clear up an account **7.**(清点) count

【清白】 qīngbái pure; clean; stainless

【清白历史】 qīngbái lìshǐ clean sheet; clean slate

【清白人家】 qīngbái rénjiā a decent family

【清仓】 qīngcāng make an inventory of the stock in the storehouse

【清仓查库】 qīngcāng chákù make an inventory of warehouses

【清册】 qīngcè inventory; detailed list: 材料～ detailed list of materials / 编制～ work out a detailed list of sth.

【清茶】 qīngchá **1.**(绿茶) green tea **2.**(只有茶水,没有点心) tea served without refreshments

【清查】 qīngchá **1.**(查对) check: ～账目 check the accounts **2.**(查出) ferret out; uncover; comb out

【清产核资】 qīngchǎn-hézī checkup on enterprise assets

【清偿】 qīngcháng pay off; clear off: ～损失额 liquidated damages

【清唱】 qīngchàng sing opera arias (without makeup and acting)

【清彻】 qīngchè 同"清澈"

【清澈】 qīngchè limpid; clear: ～的眼睛 clear eyes / ～透明 as clear as crystal

【清晨】 qīngchén early morning

【清除】 qīngchú clear away; eliminate; get rid of; sweep away: ～不良工作作风 get rid of the bad working style

【清楚】 qīng·chu **1.**(容易了解、辨认) clear; distinct: 一清二楚 (as) clear as daylight **2.**(不糊涂) clear; lucid: 头脑～的思想家 a clear thinker **3.**(了解) be clear about; understand

【清脆】 qīngcuì **1.**(指声音) clear and melodious **2.**(指食物) crisp and refresh

【清单】 qīngdān detailed list; detailed account

【清淡】 qīngdàn **1.**(不浓烈) light; weak; delicate: 一杯～的茶 a cup of weak tea **2.**(不油腻) not greasy or strongly flavored; light **3.**(清新淡雅) refresh and elegant **4.**(萧条) dull; slack: ～季节 slack season

【清点】 qīngdiǎn check; make an inventory; sort and count: ～人数 check the number of people

【清炖】 qīngdùn boiled in clear soup

【清风】 qīngfēng cool breeze; refreshing breeze

【清福】 qīngfú an easy and carefree life

【清高】 qīnggāo aloof from politics and material pursuits; above politics and worldly interests

【清官】 qīngguān honest and upright official

【清规】 qīngguī 〈*Buddhism*〉 monastic rules

for Buddhists
【清规戒律】 qīngguī-jièlǜ 1.〈*Relig.*〉 regulations, taboos and commandments 2.(规章制度) restrictions and fetters
【清寒】 qīnghán 1.(清贫) poor; in straitened circumstances 2.(明亮、有寒意) cold and clear
【清户】 qīnghù close an account
【清剿】 qīngjiǎo clean up; suppress; eliminate
【清洁】 qīngjié clean: 保持～。Keep it clean and tidy.
【清洁队】 qīngjiéduì cleaning squad
【清洁工】 qīngjiégōng cleaner: 街道～ street cleaner
【清洁剂】 qīngjiéjì cleanser; cleaner
【清劲风】 qīngjìngfēng 〈*Meteorol.*〉 fresh breeze
【清净】 qīngjìng 1.(无打扰) peace and quiet 2.(清澈) limpid; clear
【清静】 qīngjìng quiet; secluded: ～的地方 a quiet spot
【清酒】 qīngjiǔ sake (Jap.)
【清朗】 qīnglǎng 1.(清澈晴朗) clear and bright 2.(清楚响亮) clear; ringing; clear and resounding: ～的声音 clear voice 3.(清净明亮) limpid; clear and bright 4.(清新明快) refresh
【清冷】 qīnglěng 1.(微寒) chilly 2.(冷清) deserted; desolate
【清理】 qīnglǐ put in order; check up; clear; sort out: ～仓库 take store
【清丽】 qīnglì a clear and attractive style
【清廉】 qīnglián honest and upright; free from corruption
【清凉】 qīngliáng cool and refreshing: ～饮料 cold and refreshing drinks
【清凉油】 qīngliángyóu cooling ointment; essential balm
【清亮】 qīng·liang clear and bright
【清明】 qīngmíng 1.(清澈明朗) clear and bright 2.(心里明白、镇静) sober and calm 3.(节气) the Pure Brightness (4 月 4-6 日交节)
【清贫】 qīngpín be poor
【清平世界】 qīngpíng shìjiè a peaceful and orderly world
【清漆】 qīngqī varnish
【清热】 qīngrè 〈*Chin. Med.*〉 antipyretic
【清瘦】 qīngshòu thin; lean; spare: 面容～ meager face
【清爽】 qīngshuǎng 1.(清洁凉爽) fresh and cool; brisk; refreshing: 空气～ fresh air 2.(轻松爽快) easy; light; relieved; relaxed: 心里～了一些 feel relaxed; be in an easier state of mind 3.(清淡爽口) not greasy; refresh
【清算】 qīngsuàn 1.〈*Econ.*〉 clear (accounts); square: 国际～ international payment / 划拨～ clearing payment / 现金～ cash clearance 2.(清算罪恶) settle accounts; expose and criticize: ～罪行 expose and criticize the crimes
【清算协定】 qīngsuàn xiédìng clearing agreement
【清算银行】 qīngsuàn yínháng clearing bank
【清算债务】 qīngsuàn zhàiwù settle a claim
【清算账户】 qīngsuàn zhànghù clearing account
【清谈】 qīngtán idle talk; empty talk: ～误国 pure theories and talks without action will get the nation into trouble
【清汤】 qīngtāng clear soup; light soup
【清晰】 qīngxī distinct; clear: 发音～ pronounce distinctly / ～的照片 a clear photograph
【清晰度】 qīngxīdù 1.(电视的) clarity: 彩色～ acuteness of color 2.(传声的) articulation
【清洗】 qīngxǐ 1.(洗净) rinse; wash; clean: ～口腔 rinse the mouth 2.(清除) purge; comb out: ～坏分子 comb out the bad elements
【清闲】 qīngxián at leisure; idle
【清香】 qīngxiāng delicate fragrance; faint scent; refreshing fragrance: ～扑鼻 a sweet scent assails the nostrils / ～爽口 pleasant to the palate
【清新】 qīngxīn 1.(清爽而新鲜) pure and fresh; fresh: 空气～ pure and fresh air; crisp air 2.(新颖雅致) new and elegant
【清心】 qīngxīn 〈*Chin. Med.*〉 clear away heart-fire
【清心寡欲】 qīngxīn-guǎyù purge one's mind of desires and ambitions

【清醒】 qīngxǐng 1.（清楚）clear-headed; sober：～的估计 clear-headed appraisal 2.（神志恢复正常）come to; come round; regain consciousness

【清秀】 qīngxiù delicate and pretty：山清水秀 beautiful landscape

【清雅】 qīngyǎ 1.（清新高雅）elegant; refined 2.（清秀文雅）delicate and pretty

【清一色】 qīngyīsè 1.（同一颜色）all of the same color; uniform; homogeneous：穿着～的白衣服 all dressed alike in white 2.（完全一致）uniform; identical：～的看法 identical views 3.（牌同一花色）all of the same suit

【清音】 qīngyīn 〈*Phonet*.〉voiceless sound

【清幽】 qīngyōu （of a landscape）quiet and beautiful

【清早】 qīngzǎo early in the morning; early morning

【清账】 qīngzhàng square an account; clear an account

【清障】 qīngzhàng clear away obstacles

【清障车】 qīngzhàngchē tow truck; breakdown truck

【清真】 qīngzhēn Islamic; Muslim

【清真食堂】 qīngzhēn shítáng Muslims' canteen

【清真寺】 qīngzhēnsì mosque

【清蒸】 qīngzhēng steamed in clear soup

蜻 (qīng)

【蜻蜓】 qīngtíng dragonfly

【蜻蜓点水】 qīngtíng-diǎnshuǐ like a dragonfly skimming the surface of the water; touch on sth. without going into it deeply

鲭 (qīng) 〈*Zool*.〉mackerel

【鲭鱼】 qīngyú Atlantic mackerel

轻[輕] (qīng)

1.（重量小）light：～如鸿毛 as light as a feather / 这箱子很～，我可以很容易地拿起来。The suitcase is very light; I can easily pick it up. 2.（数量少；程度浅）small in number, degree, etc., slight; not serious：某人的病很～ one's illness is not at all serious 3.（不重要）not important 4.（轻松）light; relaxed：～音乐 light music 5.（用力不猛）gently; softly; lightly 6.（轻率）rashly 7.（轻视）belittle; make light of：文人相～。Men of letters tend to despise one another.

【轻便】 qīngbiàn 1.（轻型的，便携的）light; portable：一双～鞋 a pair of light shoes / ～黑板 light blackboard 2.（容易）light; easy：干～活儿 do light work

【轻薄】 qīngbó given to philandering; frivolous：举止～ frivolous behavior; philandering act

【轻车简从】 qīngchē-jiǎncóng travel with light luggage and few attendants for quick movements

【轻敌】 qīngdí take the enemy lightly

【轻而易举】 qīng'éryìjǔ easy to do; easy to accomplish

【轻放】 qīngfàng put down gently

【轻风】 qīngfēng light wind：～徐徐。A light wind was blowing.

【轻浮】 qīngfú frivolous; flighty; light：～的女人 a light woman

【轻歌剧】 qīnggējù light opera

【轻歌曼舞】 qīnggē-mànwǔ sing merrily and dance gracefully; soft music and graceful dances

【轻工业】 qīnggōngyè light industry

【轻轨铁路】 qīngguǐ tiělù light railway

【轻忽】 qīnghū neglect; overlook

【轻活】 qīnghuó light work; soft job：干～ do light work

【轻机枪】 qīngjīqiáng light machine gun

【轻健】 qīngjiàn spry and light

【轻捷】 qīngjié spry and light; nimble; brisk

【轻举妄动】 qīngjǔ-wàngdòng act rashly; take reckless action

【轻快】 qīngkuài 1.（不费力）brisk; spry 2.（轻松愉快）relaxed; lively

【轻狂】 qīngkuáng extremely frivolous

【轻慢】 qīngmàn treat sb. without proper respect

【轻描淡写】 qīngmiáo-dànxiě touch on lightly; mention casually; describe with a delicate touch

【轻蔑】 qīngmiè scornful; disdainful; contemptuous

【轻泡货】 qīngpāohuò light cargo

【轻飘】 qīngpiāo 1.（轻飘飘）light buoyant

2.(不踏实) unsteady; undependable; of two minds

【轻飘飘】 qīngpiāopiāo 1.(轻快) light; buoyant 2.(如同驾云) as if treading on air

【轻骑】 qīngqí 1.(指骑兵) light cavalryman 2.(轻便摩托车) light motorcycle

【轻巧】 qīngqiǎo 1.(轻便) light and handy 2.(轻松灵巧) deft; dexterous: ～的双手 dexterous hands 3.(简单容易) easy; simple: 说起来～,做起来难。Easier said than done.

【轻轻】 qīngqīng lightly; gently; softly: ～地走 walk with light steps

【轻取】 qīngqǔ beat easily; win an easy victory; win hands down: ～三局 win three sets easily

【轻柔】 qīngróu soft; gentle

【轻伤】 qīngshāng slight wound; minor wound

【轻伤员】 qīngshāngyuán walking wounded; ambulant patient

【轻生】 qīngshēng make light of one's life; commit suicide

【轻声】 qīngshēng in a soft voice; softly

【轻视】 qīngshì despise; look down on; make light of; take things lightly: ～困难 make light of difficulties

【轻手轻脚】 qīngshǒu-qīngjiǎo gently; softly

【轻率】 qīngshuài rash; hasty; indiscreet: ～的决定 a rash decision / ～的行动 indiscreet act

【轻水】 qīngshuǐ light water

【轻松】 qīngsōng light; relaxed; light-hearted: ～愉快 happy and relaxed

【轻佻】 qīngtiāo frivolous; skittish; giddy: ～的女子 coquettish woman

【轻微】 qīngwēi light; slight; trifling; to a small extent

【轻武器】 qīngwǔqì light weapons

【轻信】 qīngxìn be credulous; readily place trust in; readily believe

【轻型】 qīngxíng light-duty; light: ～飞机 light aircraft

【轻熏】 qīngxūn mild smoke

【轻扬】 qīngyáng lightly float; lightly drift

【轻易】 qīngyì 1.(简单;容易) easily; readily 2.(随随便便地) lightly; rashly: ～下结论 draw hasty conclusions

【轻音乐】 qīngyīnyuè light music

【轻盈】 qīngyíng slim and graceful: 体态～ with a slim and graceful figure

【轻油】 qīngyóu light oil

【轻于鸿毛】 qīngyúhóngmáo lighter than a goose feather

【轻重】 qīngzhòng 1.(重量大小) weight: ～相等 equal in weight 2.(指程度) degree of seriousness; relative importance: 无足～ a matter of no consequence 3.(限度) propriety: 做事不知～ not know the proper way to act

【轻舟】 qīngzhōu a small light boat

【轻装】 qīngzhuāng 1.(指行装) with light packs 2.(指武装) light weapons

【轻装上阵】 qīngzhuāng-shàngzhèn go into battle with a light pack; take part in a political movement with nothing on one's conscience

【轻罪】 qīngzuì 〈*Law*〉 misdemeanor; minor offense; minor crime

氢[氫] (qīng) 〈*Chem.*〉 hydrogen (元素符号 H)

【氢弹】 qīngdàn hydrogen bomb

【氢离子浓度指数】 qīnglízǐ nóngdù zhǐshù 〈*Chem.*〉 hydrogen ionexponent

【氢气】 qīngqì hydrogen

【氢气球】 qīngqìqiú hydrogen balloon

【氢氧根】 qīngyǎnggēn 〈*Chem.*〉 hydroxyl

【氢氧化物】 qīngyǎnghuàwù 〈*Chem.*〉 hydroxide

倾 (qīng) 1.(歪斜) incline; lean; bend 2.(倾向) deviation; tendency 3.(倒塌) collapse 4.(尽数倒出) overturn and pour out; empty 5.(用尽力量) do all one can; use up all one's resources: ～全力 exert oneself to the utmost to do sth.

【倾巢】 qīngcháo (of the enemy or bandits) turn out in full force: ～出动 turn out in full strength

【倾城倾国】 qīngchéng-qīngguó so beautiful as to overrun cities and ruin states; exceedingly beautiful

【倾倒】 qīngdǎo 1.(歪斜倒下) topple and fall; topple over; topple down 2.(十分佩服) greatly admire; be overwhelmed with admiration for sb.

【倾倒】 qīngdào tip; dump; empty; pour out: ～垃圾 dump rubbish
【倾覆】 qīngfù overturn; topple; capsize
【倾家荡产】 qīngjiā-dàngchǎn lose a family fortune; be reduced to poverty and ruin; be brought to total ruin
【倾慕】 qīngmù have a strong admiration for; adore
【倾囊相助】 qīngnáng-xiāngzhù empty one's purse to help; give generous financial support; give one's all to help
【倾盆大雨】 qīngpén-dàyǔ heavy downpour; torrential rain: 下起了～。It was pouring.
【倾诉】 qīngsù pour out; pour forth
【倾塌】 qīngtā topple over; topple down
【倾听】 qīngtīng listen attentively to; lend an attentive ear to
【倾吐】 qīngtǔ say what is on one's mind without reservation
【倾向】 qīngxiàng 1.(趋势) tendency; trend; inclination; deviation: 有害～ harmful tendency 2.(偏于赞成) incline to; prefer: 我～另一观点。I incline to another point of view. / 我们～于她的方案。I prefer her plan.
【倾向性】 qīngxiàngxìng tendentiousness; tendencies
【倾销】 qīngxiāo dump: ～货物 dump goods
【倾销价格】 qīngxiāo-jiàgé dumping price
【倾斜】 qīngxié 1.(歪斜) tilt; incline; slope; slant: 地势向海面～。The ground slopes down to the sea. 2.(偏向) incline to: 向基础科学～ incline to basic sciences
【倾泻】 qīngxiè come down in torrents
【倾卸车】 qīngxièchē dump truck; dumper truck
【倾心】 qīngxīn 1.(爱慕) admire; fall in love with; lose one's heart to 2.(真诚) cordial; heart-to-heart: ～交谈 have a heart-to-heart talk
【倾轧】 qīngyà engage in internal strife: 互相～ jostle against one another
【倾注】 qīngzhù 1.(注入) pour into; stream down into 2.(集中于) devote to; direct to; throw into: 把精力～在工作上 devote all one's energies to work; throw all one's energy into one's work

情 (qíng) 1.(感情) feeling; affection; sentiment 2.(情面) favor; kindness; sensibilities; feelings: 求～ ask for a favor; beg for leniency 3.(爱情) love; passion: 谈～说爱 be courting; talk love 4.(情形;情况) situation; circumstances; condition: 实～ actual state of affairs
【情爱】 qíng'ài 1.(爱情) love; passion 2.(感情) feeling; affection; sentiment
【情报】 qíngbào intelligence; information: 互通～ exchange information
【情报处】 qíngbàochù intelligence department
【情报处理】 qíngbào chùlǐ information processing
【情报机关】 qíngbào jīguān intelligence agency
【情报局】 qíngbàojú intelligence bureau
【情报人员】 qíngbào rényuán intelligence personnel; intelligence agent
【情报系统】 qíngbào xìtǒng intelligence channel
【情报资料】 qíngbào zīliào intelligence data
【情不自禁】 qíngbùzìjìn cannot refrain from; be seized with a sudden impulse to
【情操】 qíngcāo sentiment: 高尚的～ elevated sentiments
【情场失意】 qíngchǎng-shīyì frustrated in love; unlucky in love
【情敌】 qíngdí rival in love
【情调】 qíngdiào sentiment; flavor; emotional appeal: 异国～ exotic flavor
【情窦初开】 qíngdòu-chūkāi (of a young girl) first awakening of love; reach puberty
【情分】 qíng·fèn mutual affection: 夫妻～ marital affection; marital relationship
【情夫】 qíngfū lover
【情妇】 qíngfù mistress
【情感】 qínggǎn 1.(心理反应) feeling; affection; affective (adj.) 2.(感情) emotion; emotional (adj.); sentiment; sentimental (adj.): 易动～ emotional; sentimental
【情感曲线】 qínggǎn qǔxiàn feeling curve
【情感投资】 qínggǎn tóuzī emotional investment
【情歌】 qínggē love song
【情话】 qínghuà 1.(表示爱情的) lovers' prattle; lover's honeyed words 2.(知心话) heart-to-heart talk

【情怀】 qínghuái feelings

【情节】 qíngjié 1.(内容) plot; story: 动人的～ fascinating story 2.(事实经过) circumstances: ～相同 with similar details

【情结】 qíngjié 〈*Psycho.*〉 complex: 恋父～ Electra complex / 恋母～ Oedipus complex

【情景】 qíngjǐng scene; sight; circumstances

【情景交融】 qíngjǐng-jiāoróng feeling and setting happily blended

【情景喜剧】 qíngjǐng xǐjù sitcom; situation comedy

【情况】 qíngkuàng 1.(情形) circumstances; situation; condition; state of affairs: 健康～ health condition / 全部～ the whole circumstances / 这辆车～良好。This car is in very good condition. 2.(变化) military situation

【情理】 qínglǐ reason; sense: ～难容 contrary to reason or common sense

【情侣】 qínglǚ sweethearts; lovers

【情面】 qíngmiàn feelings; sensibilities: 不讲～ not spare sb's feelings; not give any respect

【情趣】 qíngqù 1.(性情志趣) temperament and interest: 我们～相投。We are temperamentally compatible. 2.(情调趣味) interest; appeal; delight: 生活～ delight of life

【情人】 qíngrén lover; sweetheart

【情杀】 qíngshā crime passionnel

【情深似海】 qíngshēnsìhǎi love is as deep as the sea

【情诗】 qíngshí love poetry

【情势】 qíshì situation; trend of events; circumstances: ～不妙 the trend of events being unfavorable

【情书】 qíngshū love letter

【情思】 qíngsī 1.(情感) affection; feelings 2.(情绪) morale; sentiment

【情愫】 qíngsù 1.(感情) feelings; sentiment 2.(真实感情) real sentiment

【情态】 qíngtài spirit; mood

【情态动词】 qíngtài dòngcí modal verb

【情同手足】 qíngtóng-shǒuzú like brothers; with brotherly love for each other; be attached to each other like brothers

【情投意合】 qíngtóu-yìhé find each other congenial; hit it off perfectly; be congenial

【情网】 qíngwǎng snares of love: 堕入～ be caught in the snares of love

【情形】 qíng·xing circumstances; situation; condition; state of affairs

【情绪】 qíngxù 1.(心理状态) morale; sentiments; feeling; mood: 对立～ antagonistic sentiments 2.(不愉快) depression; moodiness; the sulks: 有～ be in a bad mood

【情义】 qíngyì feelings; ties of friendship; tie of comradeship: 夫妻～ true feelings between husband and wife

【情谊】 qíngyì friendly sentiments; friendly feelings: 深厚的～ deep friendly feelings

【情意】 qíngyì tender regards; affection; goodwill: ～绵绵 lingering sentiments; everlasting love

【情由】 qíngyóu the hows and whys

【情欲】 qíngyù sexual passion; lust; erotic feeling

【情愿】 qíngyuàn 1.(愿意) be willing to; be consent to 2.(宁愿) prefer; would rather; had rather

晴 (qíng) fine; clear: ～天 fine day / ～转多云 change from fine to cloudy

【晴好】 qínghǎo fine; sunny

【晴和】 qínghé warm and fine

【晴空】 qíngkōng clear sky; cloudless sky: ～万里 a cloudless sky

【晴朗】 qínglǎng fine; sunny: ～的天 bright day

【晴天】 qíngtiān fine day; sunny day

【晴天霹雳】 qíngtiān-pīlì a bolt from the blue

【晴雨表】 qíngyǔbiǎo barometer; weather-glass

氰 (qíng) 〈*Chem.*〉 cyanogen; dicyanogen (分子式为 $(CN)_2$)

【氰化钾】 qínghuàjiǎ potassium cyanide

【氰化物】 qínghuàwù cyanide

擎 (qíng) prop up; hold up; lift up: 高～火炬 hold aloft the torch/ 高～红旗 hold aloft the red flag

苘[**檾、蘔**] (qǐng)

【苘麻】 qǐngmá 1.〈*Bot.*〉 abutilon; piemarker 2.(麻) abutilon hemp; piemarker hemp

顷 (qǐng) 1.(公顷) hectare 2.(顷刻) moment; instant; a little while; in a momen 3.(不久前) just; just now: ～接大札。I have just received your letter.

【顷刻】 qǐngkè in a moment; in an instant; instantly: ～消失 vanish in an instant

请(qǐng) 1.(请求) request; ask: ～勿动手。Keep your hands off. 2.(邀请) invite; engage: ～外国学者来华讲学 invite foreign scholars to lecture in China 3.〈*respects*〉 please: ～坐。Sit down, please.（或：Please be seated.）

【请便】 qǐngbiàn do as you wish; please yourself

【请调】 qǐngdiào ask for a transfer to some other post

【请功】 qǐnggōng ask the higher level to record sb's meritorious deeds

【请假】 qǐngjià ask for leave: 请病假 ask for a sick leave

【请假条】 qǐngjiàtiáo written request for leave (of absence)

【请柬】 qǐngjiǎn invitation card: 一张参加聚会的～ an invitation card to the party

【请教】 qǐngjiào ask for advice; consult: 向某人～ ask for sb's advice; ask advice of sb.

【请客】 qǐngkè stand treat; invite sb. to dinner: 这回我～。This is to be my treat.

【请命】 qǐngmìng plead on sb's behalf: 为民～ plead on behalf of the people

【请求】 qǐngqiú ask; request: ～某人帮忙 ask a favor of sb. / ～一项贷款 request a loan

【请示】 qǐngshì ask for instructions

【请帖】 qǐngtiě invitation card; invitation

【请问】 qǐngwèn 1.〈*respects*〉(用于请对方回答问题) excuse me; please: ～,到机场怎么走? Excuse me, but could you tell me how to get to the airport? 2.(用于向对方提出问题) we should like to ask; it may be asked; one may ask

【请勿】 qǐngwù please don't: ～迟到。You are requested to come on time.

【请降】 qǐngxiáng beg to surrender

【请愿】 qǐngyuàn present a petition; petition: 为某事向某人～ petition sb. for sth.

【请愿书】 qǐngyuànshū petition

【请战】 qǐngzhàn ask for a battle assignment

【请罪】 qǐngzuì 1.(请求处分) admit one's error and ask for punishment 2.(道歉) apologize; humbly apologize

庆[慶](qìng) 1.(庆祝;庆贺) celebrate; congratulate 2.(庆祝日) occasion for celebration: 国～ National Day / 校～ anniversary of the founding of a school

【庆大霉素】 qìngdàméisù 〈*Pharm.*〉 gentamycin

【庆典】 qìngdiǎn celebration; a ceremony to celebrate

【庆功会】 qìnggōnghuì victory meeting

【庆功论赏】 qìnggōng-lùnshǎng confer honors according to merits in service while celebrating a success or victory

【庆贺】 qìnghè congratulate; celebrate: 向朋友～生日 congratulate my friend on his birthday

【庆幸】 qìngxìng rejoice; congratulate oneself: 你真该为自己的外表而～。You really should congratulate yourself on your appearance. / 可～的是,大家都平安地回到家里。Happily, all have returned safe and sound.

【庆祝】 qìngzhù celebrate: ～生日 celebrate one's birthday / 这个计划一运行,咱们得特别地～一下。If this plan works, we'll celebrate in style.

亲[親](qìng)(另见"亲"qīn)

【亲家】 qìng·jia 1.(儿子的岳父母或女儿的公婆) parents of one's daughter-in-law or son-in-law 2.(儿女婚配而形成的亲戚关系) relatives by marriage

罄(qìng) use up; exhaust; empty: 告～ be all used up; be exhausted; run out

【罄尽】 qìngjìn with nothing left; all used up

【罄其所有】 qìngqísuǒyǒu use up all that is available; offer all one has

【罄竹难书】 qìngzhú-nánshū too numerous to record

qiong

穷[窮](qióng) 1.(贫穷) poor; poverty-stricken; badly off: 人～志不～。One may be poor but never ceases to be ambitious. 2.(穷尽) limit; end: 智～ at one's wit's end 3.(彻底) thoroughly 4.

（极端）extremely

【穷光蛋】 qióngguāngdàn pauper; poor wretch; a penniless vagrant

【穷极思变】 qióngjí-sībiàn one will start thinking about changes when he is in extreme poverty

【穷极无聊】 qióngjí-wúliáo 1.（感到厌烦）be utterly bored 2.（令人讨厌）absolutely senseless; disgusting

【穷尽】 qióngjìn limit; end：知识是无～的。Knowledge knows no bounds.

【穷寇】 qióngkòu hard-pressed enemy; tottering foe：～勿追。The stag at bay is a dangerous foe.

【穷苦】 qióngkǔ poverty-stricken; impoverished

【穷困】 qióngkùn poverty-stricken; destitute; in straitened circumstances

【穷期】 qióngqī termination; end

【穷人】 qióngrén poor people; the poor

【穷日子】 qióngrì·zi straitened circumstances; days of poverty

【穷奢极欲】 qióngshē-jíyù extremely extravagant and luxurious; go to the extremes of extravagance：过着～的生活 wallow in luxury

【穷酸】 qióngsuān poor and pedantic

【穷途末路】 qióngtú-mòlù have come to a dead end; be driven into an impasse

【穷乡僻壤】 qióng-xiāng-pìrǎng a remote, backward place; obscure village

【穷凶极恶】 qióngxiōng-jí'è extremely violent and wicked; extremely vicious; utterly evil; atrocious; diabolical

【穷于应付】 qióngyú-yìng·fu be hard put to cope with

【穷则思变】 qióngzésībiàn poverty gives rise to a desire for change

【穷追】 qióngzhuī go in hot pursuit：～不舍 run down a convict

茕［煢、惸］(qióng) 1.（孤单）solitary; alone 2.（忧愁）dejected

【茕茕】 qióngqióng all alone; lonely：～孑立，形影相吊 standing all alone, body and shadow comforting each other

穹 (qióng) 1.（穹隆）vault; dome 2.（天空）the sky

【穹苍】 qióngcāng the vault of heaven; the firmament; the sky; the heavens

【穹顶】 qióngdǐng 〈*Archit*.〉dome

【穹隆】 qiónglóng vault; arched roof

【穹形】 qióngxíng vaulted; arched

琼［瓊］(qióng) fine jade

【琼浆玉液】 qióngjiāng-yùyè nectar

【琼楼玉宇】 qiónglóu-yùyǔ a richly decorated jade palace; a magnificent building; a splendid building

【琼筵】 qióngyàn luxurious dinner; sumptuous banquet

【琼脂】 qióngzhī agar-agar; agar

qiu

丘 (qiū) 1.（小土山）mound; hillock：沙～ a sand dune 2.（坟）grave

【丘陵】 qiūlíng hills：～地带 hilly country; hilly land

【丘疹】 qiūzhěn 〈*Med*.〉papule

蚯 (qiū)

【蚯蚓】 qiūyǐn earthworm

秋［秌］(qiū) 1.（秋季）autumn; fall (AmE.); autumnal (adj.) 2.（庄稼成熟季节）harvest time 3.（年）year 4.（时期）time; period; a period of time：危急存亡之～ at a critical time of survival or extinction

【秋波】 qiūbō bright eyes of a beautiful woman：送～ make eyes; cast amorous glances

【秋播】 qiūbō autumn sowing

【秋分】 qiūfēn 1.〈*Astron*.〉autumn equinox; autumnal equinox 2.（节气）the Autumnal Equinox（9月22-24日交节）

【秋分点】 qiūfēndiǎn 〈*Astron*.〉autumnal equinoctial point

【秋耕】 qiūgēng autumn ploughing

【秋海棠】 qiūhǎitáng begonia

【秋毫无犯】 qiūháo-wúfàn not commit the slightest offense against the civilians; not encroach on the interests of the people to the slightest degree

【秋季】 qiūjì autumn; fall (AmE.)

【秋季作物】 qiūjì zuòwù autumn crops
【秋景】 qiūjǐng 1.（景色）autumnal scenery; autumnal landscape 2.（收成）prospects for the autumn harvest
【秋凉】 qiūliáng cool autumn days
【秋令】 qiūlìng 1.（秋季）autumn 2.（秋季气候）autumn weather
【秋千】 qiūqiān 1.（玩具）swing：打～ have a swing 2.〈*Circus*〉trapeze：一男一女在～上表演高空节目。A man and woman performed on the flying trapeze.
【秋千台板】 qiūqiān táibǎn trapeze platform
【秋色】 qiūsè autumn scenery; autumnal landscape
【秋收】 qiūshōu autumn harvest
【秋水】 qiūshuǐ limpid eyes (of a woman)：～伊人 thinking of an old acquaintance on seeing a familiar scene
【秋天】 qiūtiān autumn; fall (AmE.)
【秋游】 qiūyóu travel in the autumn
【秋雨】 qiūyǔ autumn rains; autumnal rain
【秋种】 qiūzhòng autumn planting
【秋庄稼】 qiūzuāng·jia autumn crops
【秋子梨】 qiūzǐlí Ussurian pear

楸 (qiū) 〈*Bot.*〉catalpa; Chinese catalpa

犰 (qiú)

【犰狳】 qiúyú 〈*Zool.*〉armadillo

囚 (qiú) 1.（囚禁）imprison 2.（囚犯）prisoner; convict

【囚车】 qiúchē prison van; black maria; prisoners' van
【囚犯】 qiúfàn prisoner; convict
【囚禁】 qiújìn imprison; put in jail; keep in captivity
【囚牢】 qiúláo prison; jail
【囚室】 qiúshì prison cell
【囚徒】 qiútú convict; prisoner

泅 (qiú) swim

【泅渡】 qiúdù swim across
【泅水】 qiúshuǐ swim

求 (qiú) 1.（请求）ask; beg; request; entreat; beseech：我～你一件事。I must ask you a favor. 2.（追求；探求；寻求）strive for; seek; try：～得公平合理的解决 seek a fair and reasonable solution 3.（需求）demand：供不应～。Supply falls short of demand.

【求爱】 qiú'ài pay court to; woo; court
【求成】 qiúchéng hope for success：急于～ be impatient for success
【求大同,存小异】 qiú dàtóng, cún xiǎoyì seek common ground on major issues while reserving differences on minor ones
【求告】 qiúgào 1.（求得帮助、支持）solicit; petition 2.（求情、求恕）implore; entreat; supplicate
【求和】 qiúhé 1.（请求停战）sue for peace 2.（设法作成平局）try to draw a match
【求婚】 qiúhūn make an offer of marriage; propose
【求见】 qiújiàn ask to see; request an interview; beg for an audience
【求教】 qiújiào ask for advice
【求救】 qiújiù ask sb. to come to the rescue; cry for help
【求救呼号】 qiújiù hūhào distress call; SOS
【求偶】 qiú'ǒu courtship
【求乞】 qiúqǐ beg
【求亲】 qiúqīn seek a marriage alliance
【求亲靠友】 qiúqīn-kàoyǒu ask favors of relatives and friends
【求情】 qiúqíng plead; intercede; ask for a favor; beg for leniency：向某人～ plead with sb.
【求全】 qiúquán 1.（要求完美无缺）demand perfection 2.（希望事情成全）try to round sth. off; try to bring sth. to a satisfactory conclusion：委曲～ make concessions to achieve one's purpose
【求饶】 qiúráo beg for mercy; ask for pardon
【求人】 qiúrén ask for help
【求生】 qiúshēng seek to live on
【求胜】 qiúshèng strive for victory
【求实】 qiúshí be realistic; be practical-minded
【求实精神】 qiúshí jīngshén matter-of-fact attitude; realistic approach; down-to-earth approach
【求同存异】 qiútóng-cúnyì put aside minor differences so as to seek common ground; seek common ground while reserving differ-

ences
【求降】 qiúxiáng beg to surrender; hang out the white flag
【求学】 qiúxué **1.**(在学校学习) go to school; attend school **2.**(探求学问) pursue one's studies; seek knowledge
【求医】 qiúyī seek medical advice; go to a doctor
【求援】 qiúyuán ask for help; request reinforcements
【求之不得】 qiúzhībùdé all that one could wish for; most welcome
【求知】 qiúzhī seek knowledge
【求知欲】 qiúzhīyù thirst for knowledge
【求职】 qiúzhí job wanted
【求治】 qiúzhì seek medical advice; go to a doctor
【求助】 qiúzhù turn to sb. for help; seek help
【求助程序】 qiúzhù chéngxù 〈*Computer*〉 help program

球[毬²](qiú) **1.**〈*Math.*〉 sphere **2.**〈*Sports*〉 ball: 高尔夫～ golf / 篮～ basketball / 排～ volleyball / 网～ tennis / 足～ football **3.**(球形物) ball; anything shaped like a ball: 一～毛线 a ball of wool / 拇趾～ the ball of the foot / 线已经绕成～了。The threads are wound into a ball. **4.**(地球) the globe; the earth
【球场】 qiúchǎng **1.**(排、篮、网、羽毛球场) court: 室内～ in-door court **2.**(足、棒、垒球场) field
【球蛋白】 qiúdànbái 〈*Biol.*〉 globulin
【球队】 qiúduì (ball game) team
【球杆】 qiúgān 〈*Golf*〉 club
【球罐】 qiúguàn sphere
【球果】 qiúguǒ 〈*Bot.*〉 cone
【球籍】 qiújí one's or a country's identity of living on the earth
【球技】 qiújì ball game skills
【球菌】 qiújūn 〈*Biol.*〉 coccus
【球类运动】 qiúlèi yùndòng ball games
【球门】 qiúmén 〈*Sports*〉 goal; goalmouth: 守～ keep the goal
【球门球】 qiúménqiú 〈*Sports*〉 goal kick
【球门区】 qiúménqū 〈*Sports*〉 goal area
【球门网】 qiúménwǎng 〈*Sports*〉 goal net
【球门线】 qiúménxiàn 〈*Sports*〉 goal line
【球门员】 qiúményuán 〈*Sports*〉 goalkeeper; goalie
【球门柱】 qiúménzhù 〈*Sports*〉 goalpost
【球迷】 qiúmí (ball game) fan: 足～ football fan
【球面】 qiúmiàn spherical surface; sphere; spherical (adj.)
【球面度】 qiúmiàndù 〈*Math.*〉 steradian; spherical degree
【球面角】 qiúmiànjiǎo 〈*Math.*〉 spherical angle
【球面镜】 qiúmiànjìn 〈*Physics*〉 spherical mirror
【球磨机】 qiúmójī ball crusher; ball mill
【球墨铸铁】 qiúmò zhùtiě 〈*Metall.*〉 nodular cast iron; spherical graphite cast iron
【球幕电影】 qiúmù diànyǐng spherical screen stereoscopic film
【球拍】 qiúpāi **1.**(网球、羽毛球拍) racket **2.**(乒乓球拍) bat
【球拍夹】 qiúpáijiā 〈*Tennis*〉 racket press
【球赛】 qiúsài ball game; match
【球台】 qiútái table
【球坛】 qiútán the ball-playing world; ball-playing circles; ball-players
【球体】 qiútǐ **1.**(圆球) sphere; spherical (adj.) **2.**(球形体) spheroid: 地球是个～。The Earth is a spheroid.
【球网】 qiúwǎng net (for ball games)
【球鞋】 qiúxié gym shoes; tennis shoes; sneakers
【球星】 qiúxīng ball game star
【球形】 qiúxíng spherical; globular; round
【球艺】 qiúyì skills in playing a ball game; ball game skills
【球座】 qiúzuò 〈*Golf*〉 tee

裘(qiú) fur coat
【裘皮】 qiúpí fur: ～大衣 fur coat

酋(qiú) **1.**(酋长) chief of a tribe **2.**(首领) chieftain
【酋长】 qiúzhǎng **1.**(部落首领) chief of a tribe **2.**(酋长国首领) emir
【酋长国】 qiúzhǎngguó emirate

巯[巰](qiú) 〈*Chem.*〉 mercapto

【巯基】 qiújī 〈*Chem.*〉 sulfydryl; hydrosulphonyl; mercaptol group

qu

区［區］（qū） 1.（地区；区域）area; district; region; zone：禁止吸烟～ smokeless zone / 经济开发～ open economic areas / 邮～ a postal district / 战～ a war zone 2.（行政区划）district; region; division：郊～ suburban district / 市～ urban district / 行政～ administrative division / 她不住在这个～。She doesn't live in this district. 3.（区别；划分）distinguish; classify; subdivide 4.（球场的特定区域）area; zone：端～ end zone / 攻～ attacking zone / 球门～ goal area; goal crease / 守～ defending zone

【区别】 qūbié 1.（区分）distinguish; differentiate; make a distinction between：～不同情况 distinguish among differing cases 2.（差别）difference：主要～ the main distinction

【区分】 qūfēn differentiate; distinguish：你能～出正在演奏的各种乐器吗？Can you distinguish the different musical instruments playing now?

【区划】 qūhuà division into districts：行政～ administrative divisions

【区间】 qūjiān interval

【区间车】 qūjiānchē a bus travelling only part of its normal route

【区间贸易】 qūjiān màoyì inter-regional trade

【区区】 qūqū trivial; trifling：～之数 this is a petty amount

【区时】 qūshí zone time

【区域】 qūyù region; area; district; regional (adj.)：我们准备在这个～建一所医院。We are going to build a hospital in this area.

【区域会议】 qūyù huìyì regional conference; local conference

【区域性】 qūyùxìng regional：～公约 regional convention / ～同盟 regional alliance / ～问题 a matter of regional significance / ～战争 regional war

【区域自治】 qūyù zìzhì regional autonomy

驱［驅、敺］（qū） 1.（赶牲口；驾车）drive：～马前进 urge a horse on 2.（驱除；驱散）expel; disperse 3.（快跑）run quickly：长～直入 drive deep into; drive straight in

【驱策】 qūcè 1.（用鞭子赶）drive; whip on 2.（驱使）order about

【驱车】 qūchē drive：～进城 drive to town / 他～送我去机场。He drove me to the airport.

【驱除】 qūchú drive out; get rid of

【驱动】 qūdòng 〈*Mech.*〉 drive：前轮～ front-wheel drive / 四轮～ four-wheel drive

【驱动器】 qūdòngqì 〈*Computer*〉 drive

【驱赶】 qūgǎn 1.（赶车）drive 2.（赶走）drive away

【驱散】 qūsàn disperse; dispel; break up：风不久就把雾～了。The wind soon dispelled the fog.

【驱使】 qūshǐ 1.（迫使；使唤）order about 2.（推动）urge; spur on; be prompted by：是什么～你做出这种事来的？What prompted you to do such a thing?

【驱逐】 qūzhú drive out; expel; banish：～出境 deport; expel

【驱逐机】 qūzhújī pursuit plane

【驱逐舰】 qūzhújiàn destroyer：导弹～ guided missile destroyer / 护航～ escort destroyer

躯［軀］（qū） the human body

【躯干】 qūgàn trunk; torso

【躯壳】 qūqiào the body; outer form

【躯体】 qūtǐ body

曲［麯⁴、粬⁴］（qū） 1.（弯曲）bent; crooked 2.（弯曲处）bend：河～ bend of a river 3.（理亏）wrong; unjustifiable 4.（发酵剂）leaven; yeast

（另见“曲”qǔ）

【曲别针】 qūbiézhēn paper clip

【曲柄】 qūbǐng 〈*Mech.*〉 crank

【曲柄钻】 qūbǐngzuàn brace; hand brace

【曲尺】 qūchǐ carpenter's square

【曲棍球】 qūgùnqiú 1.〈*Sports*〉 field hockey 2.（曲棍球用球）hockey ball

【曲棍球棒】 qūgùnqiúbàng hockey stick

【曲棍球场】 qūgùnqiúchǎng field hockey field

【曲棍球运动员】 qūgùnqiú yùndòngyuán hockey player
【曲解】 qūjiě misinterpret; twist: 他～了我的话。He twisted what I said.
【曲颈甑】 qūjǐngzèng 〈*Chem*.〉 retort
【曲面】 qūmiàn curved surface
【曲曲弯弯】 qūqū-wānwān full of twists and turns: ～的小路 winding path
【曲线】 qūxiàn curve; curvilinear (adj.)
【曲线板】 qūxiànbǎn 〈*Math*.〉 French curve; curve board
【曲线图】 qūxiàntú diagram (of curves)
【曲线运动】 qūxiàn yùndòng curvilinear motion
【曲折】 qūzhé 1.(弯曲) tortuous; winding: 长期～的斗争 protracted tortuous struggle 2.(复杂、不顺当的情节) complications; complicated (adj.): 故事的情节是～的。The story has a complicated plot.
【曲直】 qūzhí right and wrong: ～不分 not distinguish between right and wrong
【曲轴】 qūzhóu 〈*Mech*.〉 bent axle
【曲轴箱】 qūzhóuxiāng 〈*Mech*.〉 crankcase

蛐 (qū)

【蛐蛐】 qūqu 〈*Zool*.〉 cricket

屈 (qū) 1.(弯曲) bend; bow; crook: ～伸自如 bend and stretch the limbs freely 2.(屈服) subdue; submit 3.(委曲) wrong; injustice 4.(理亏) in the wrong
【屈才】 qūcái do work unworthy of one's talents; put sb. on a job unworthy of his talents
【屈从】 qūcóng submit to; yield to; knuckle under to
【屈打成招】 qūdǎ-chéngzhāo confess to false charges under torture; beat a man in order to extort a confession
【屈服】 qūfú surrender; yield; knuckle under: 迫使敌人～ force the enemy to give in
【屈就】 qūjiù condescend to take a post offered
【屈居】 qūjū reluctant to accept a place
【屈辱】 qūrǔ humiliation; mortification: 感到～ feel mortified at
【屈死】 qūsǐ be wronged and driven to death; be persecuted to death
【屈体】 qūtǐ 〈*Sports*〉 picked
【屈膝】 qūxī go down on one's knees; bend one's knees: ～求和 bow the knees and sue for peace
【屈膝礼】 qūxīlǐ leg: 行～ made a leg
【屈折】 qūzhé flexion
【屈折变化】 qūzhé biànhuà inflection
【屈折语言】 qūzhé yǔyán inflected language
【屈指】 qūzhǐ count on one's fingers: ～一算 count on one's fingers
【屈指可数】 qūzhǐ-kěshǔ can be counted on one's fingers; very few: 他的日子～了。His days are numbered.
【屈尊】 qūzūn condescend

祛 (qū) dispel; remove; drive away

【祛除】 qūchú dispel; get rid of; drive out
【祛风】 qūfēng 〈*Chin. Med*.〉 dispel the wind; relieve rheumatic pains, colds, etc.
【祛痰】 qūtán make expectoration easy
【祛痰剂】 qūtánjì expectorant
【祛疑】 qūyí remove suspicion or doubts
【祛淤】 qūyū 〈*Chin. Med*.〉 remove blood stasis

蛆 (qū) maggot

黢 (qū) black; dark

【黢黑】 qūhēi pitch-black; pitch-dark

趋[**趨**] (qū) 1.(快走) hasten; hurry along 2.(趋向) tend towards; tend to become: 日～繁荣 be getting prosperous with every passing day
【趋奉】 qūfèng toady to; fawn on: ～权贵 dance attendance on a nobleman
【趋附】 qūfù ingratiate oneself with; curry favor with: ～权贵 be a hanger-on of high officials
【趋势】 qūshì trend; tendency: 营业有改善的～。Business is showing a tendency to improve.
【趋向】 qūxiàng 1.(向…发展) tend to; incline to: ～完善 tend to reach perfection 2.(趋势) trend; direction: 物价的～是仍在上涨。The trend of prices is still upwards.
【趋炎附势】 qūyán-fùshì curry favor with the powerful; play up to those in power; be fol-

lower of the rich and powerful

渠 (qú) canal; ditch; channel：干～ main canal / 沟～ ditches / 排水～ drainage ditch / 引水 ～ inlet channel

【渠道】 qúdào 1.（灌渠）irrigation ditch; canal; channel 2.（途径）medium; channel：通过各种～ through various channels

【渠灌】 qúguàn canal irrigation

蠼 (qú)

【蠼螋】 qúsōu 〈*Zool*.〉 earwig

衢 (qú) boulevard：通～大道 thoroughfare

曲 (qǔ) 1.（歌曲）song; tune; melody 2.（歌谱；乐谱）music

（另见"曲"qū）

【曲调】 qǔdiào tune (of a song); melody：古老～ old melody / 流行～ popular tune

【曲高和寡】 qǔgāo-hèguǎ caviar to the general; melodies of superior taste find few to join in chorus

【曲艺】 qǔyì *quyi*; Chinese folk art forms

【曲子】 qǔ·zi song; tune; melody

苣 (qǔ)

【苣荬菜】 qǔ·mǎicài 〈*Bot*.〉 sowthistle

取 (qǔ) 1.（拿来）take; get; fetch：～款 draw on an account; draw money 2.（得到；招致）aim at; seek 3.（采取；选取）adopt; assume; choose：～中立态度 adopt a neutral attitude

【取保】 qǔbǎo get sb. to go bail for one

【取材】 qǔcái draw materials：～于 have drawn sth. from / 就地～ draw on local materials

【取长补短】 qǔcháng-bǔduǎn learn from other's strong points to offset one's weaknesses; overcome one's weaknesses by acquiring other's strong points

【取代】 qǔdài replace; substitute for; supersede; supplant：公共汽车已经～了电车。Buses have replaced trams.

【取代反应】 qǔdài fǎnyìn substitution reaction

【取道】 qǔdào by way of; via

【取得】 qǔdé gain; acquire; obtain：～成绩 achieve a feat / ～律师资格 call to the bar

【取缔】 qǔdì outlaw; ban; suppress：～非法组织 ban illegal organization

【取而代之】 qǔ'érdàizhī replace sb.; supersede sb.; take it over

【取法】 qǔfǎ take as one's model; follow the example of

【取经】 qǔjīng 1.（求佛取经）go on a pilgrimage for Buddhist scriptures 2.（吸取经验）learn from sb. else's experience

【取景】 qǔjǐng find a view

【取景器】 qǔjǐngqì view-finder

【取决】 qǔjué be decided by; depend on; hinge on：这完全～于你如何应付这个问题。It all depends on how you tackle the problem.

【取乐】 qǔlè seek pleasure; find amusement; amuse oneself; make merry

【取名】 qǔmíng name; give name; entitle：他们给孩子～小雪。They named the baby Xiaoxue.

【取暖】 qǔnuǎn warm oneself (by a fire, etc.)

【取暖装置】 qǔnuǎn zhuāngzhì heating installation

【取齐】 qǔqí 1.（使相等）make even; even up：我来付车钱，这样花费就～了。I'll pay for the taxi, to even expenses up. 2.（聚齐；集合）assemble; meet each other

【取巧】 qǔqiǎo resort to trickery to serve oneself：投机～ be opportunistic

【取人之长】 qǔrénzhīcháng suck a person's brains

【取舍】 qǔshě accept or reject; make one's choice

【取舍权】 qǔshěquán option

【取胜】 qǔshèng win victory; score a success

【取食签】 qǔshíqiān cocktail stick

【取向】 qǔxiàng orientation

【取消】 qǔxiāo cancel; call off; abolish：～定货 cancel an order / ～比赛资格 debar sb. from

【取销】 qǔxiāo 同"取消"

【取笑】 qǔxiào ridicule; make fun of; poke fun at

【取信于民】 qǔxìnyúmín win the people's confidence

【取样】 qǔyàng sample; sampling (n.)：～

办法 sampling method

【取悦】 qǔyuè try to please; ingratiate oneself with sb.

【取证】 qǔzhèng obtain evidence

娶(qǔ) marry (a woman); take a wife

【娶妻】 qǔqī take a wife

【娶亲】 qǔqīn get married

龋(qǔ)

【龋齿】 qǔchǐ 1.〈*Med*.〉dental caries 2.(蛀齿) decayed tooth

去(qù) 1.(离开某地到某地) go; leave: ～游泳 go swimming / ～广州 go to Guangzhou / 从北京～上海 leave Beijing for Shanghai / 到泰国～旅游 go out to Thailand / 我要到呼和浩特去。I'm going to Huhhot. 2.(除去) remove; get rid of: ～掉几个字 take off some words 3.(距离) be apart from: ～今三十多年 more than thirty years ago 4.(去年的) of last year: ～秋 last autumn

【去臭】 qùchòu deodorize

【去处】 qùchù 1.(去的地方) place to go; whereabouts: 他的～不明。His present whereabouts is unknown. 2.(场所; 地方) place; site: 这是一个极好的避暑～。This is a very nice place for summer.

【去粗取精】 qùcū-qǔjīng discard the dross and select the essential

【去恶务尽】 qù'èwùjìn do away with evil and must do it wholly

【去骨】 qùgǔ debone; deboned (adj.)

【去火】 qùhuǒ reduce internal heat

【去壳】 qùké shell; de-carapace

【去路】 qùlù the way along which one is going; outlet: 挡住某人的～ block one's way

【去沫】 qùmò skimming; defoaming

【去年】 qùnián last year

【去皮】 qùpí 1.(去掉皮) remove the peel 2.(净重) net weight

【去任】 qùrèn no longer hold the post

【去日】 qùrì last day

【去世】 qùshì die; pass away

【去势】 qùshì 〈*Veterinary*〉castrate; castration (n.)

【去伪存真】 qùwěi-cúnzhēn eliminate the false and retain the true

【去污】 qùwū decontamination

【去污粉】 qùwūfěn household cleanser; cleanser

【去污剂】 qùwújì detergent; stain remover

【去向】 qùxiàng the direction in which sb. or sth. has gone: ～不明 whereabouts unknown

【去雄】 qùxióng 〈*Bot*.〉emasculate; emasculation (n.)

【去职】 qùzhí no longer hold the post

阒(qù) quiet; silent; still

【阒无一人】 qùwúyīrén profoundly quiet

趣(qù) 1.(趣味) interest; delight 2.(有趣味的) interesting

【趣事】 qùshì interesting stores; an interesting episode

【趣味】 qùwèi 1.(有趣的) interest; delight 2.(爱好) taste; liking; preference: 迎合低级～ cater to vulgar tastes

【趣闻】 qùwén interesting news

觑[覰、覻](qù) look; gaze: 面面相～ gaze at each other in speechless despair

quan

悛(quān) repent; make amends: 怙恶不～ be steeped in evil and refuse to repent

圈(quān) 1.(环形) circle; ring: 钥匙～儿 key ring / 北极～ the Arctic Circle / 围成一～ form a ring / 他们围着火,坐成一～儿。They sat in a circle round the fire. 2.(范围) circle; group: 文化～ cultural circle / 影视～ movie and TV circles 3.(围) enclose; encircle: 足球场被墙～起来了。The football field is enclosed by a wall. 4.(画圈儿) mark with a circle 5.(跑道的一圈) lap: 五～赛跑 a five lap race / 领先一～ lap (v.) 6.(打牌的一轮儿) trick: 打一～ take a trick / 赢一～ win a trick / 输一～ lose a trick (另见"圈"juān, juàn)

【圈点】 quāndiǎn 1.(加标点) punctuate 2.(标出应注意的语句) mark words and phrases for special attention

【圈定】 quāndìng circle the name of a candidate

【圈套】 quāntào snare; trap: 设～ lay a snare; set a trap / 落入～ be caught in a trap / 他设～骗走了我的钱。He got the money from me by a trick.

【圈椅】 quānyǐ round-backed armchair

【圈阅】 quānyuè make a circle round one's name listed on a document after reading it

【圈子】 quān·zi 1.(环形) circle; ring: 兜～ go all around the circle / 说话绕～ speak in a roundabout way 2.(范围) circle; group: 她的活动～很小。She moves in a very small circle.

权[權] (quán) 1.(权利) right: 选举～ the right to vote / 特～ special right and privilege 2.(权力) power; authority: 3.(有利形势) advantageous position 4.(权衡) weigh up 5.(权且) tentatively; for the time being; temporarily 6.(权变;权宜) expediency

【权变】 quánbiàn adaptability in tactics; tact; adaptation to circumstances

【权柄】 quánbǐng power; authority

【权倒】 quándǎo power profiteering

【权贵】 quánguì influential officials; bigwigs

【权衡】 quánhéng weigh; balance: ～得失 weigh gains and losses

【权力】 quánlì power; authority: ～过于集中 power is overconcentrated

【权力分享】 quánlì fēnxiǎng power-sharing

【权力机构】 quánlì jīgòu organ of power

【权利】 quánlì right: 公民的～和义务 rights and duties of citizens / 依照自己的～ in one's own right

【权利能力】 quánlì nénglì legal capacity

【权利人】 quánlìrén obligee

【权利证书】 quánlì zhèngshū document of title; letter of authorization

【权谋】 quánmóu (political) tactics; trickery

【权能】 quánnéng powers and functions

【权且】 quánqiě for the time being; as a temporary measure

【权势】 quánshì power and influence: 依仗～ use one's influence

【权术】 quánshù political trickery; shifts in politics: 玩弄～ play politics; resort to political trickery

【权威】 quánwēi 1.(指人) authority; a person of authority 学术～ an academic authority 2.(权威性的) authoritative: ～意见 authoritative opinion

【权限】 quánxiàn limits of authority; extent of authority; extent of power: ～范围 extent of competence / 超越～ exceed one's powers

【权宜】 quányí expedient: ～之计 an expedient measure; makeshift (device)

【权益】 quányì rights and interests: 合法～ lawful rights and interests

【权诈】 quánzhà trickery; craftiness

全 (quán) 1.(完备;齐全) complete: 获得～胜 win complete victory 2.(保全;使完整不缺) make perfect or complete; keep intact 3.(整个) all; whole; entire; full; total: ～人类 all mankind / ～班人都在那儿。The entire class will be there. / 道路～被大雪覆盖了。The road is all covered with snow. 4.(完全;都) entirely; completely

【全包】 quánbāo all-in: ～价格 an all-in price / ～10日游 an all-in 10-day tour

【全本】 quánběn full-length

【全部】 quánbù whole; complete; total; all: ～保险 full insurance / ～付讫 payment in full / ～真相 the whole truth; the full truth

【全才】 quáncái a versatile person; all-rounder

【全场】 quánchǎng 1.(全部在场者) the whole audience; all those present: 博得～喝彩 bring down the house 2.〈*Sports*〉 full-court; all-court: ～紧逼 all-court press; full-court press

【全称】 quánchēng full name

【全程】 quánchéng whole journey; whole course

【全等】 quánděng 〈*Math.*〉 congruent

【全等于号】 quánděngyúhào is equivalent to (符号为 ≡)

【全都】 quándōu all; without exception

【全方位】 quánfāngwèi omnibearing; all-inclusive; in all domains; comprehensive: 实行～开放 lift all restrictions

【全副】 quánfù complete: ～武装 fully armed

【全国】 quánguó 1.(整个国家) the whole nation; the whole country 2.(全国各地) throughout the country 3.(全国性的) national; nationwide

【全国冠军】 quánguó guànjūn national champion

【全国记录】 quánguó jìlù national record

【全国人大】 quánguó réndà the National People's Congress (NPC)

【全国人大常委会】 quánguó réndà chángwěihuì the Standing Committee of the National People's Congress

【全国人口普查】 quánguó rénkǒu pǔchá nationwide census

【全国人民代表大会】 quánguó rénmín dàibiǎo dàhuì the National People's Congress

【全国性】 quánguóxìng national; nationwide: ～报纸 a national newspaper; a newspaper with a nationwide circulation

【全会】 quánhuì plenary meeting; plenary session: 十一届三中～ the Third Plenary Session of the Eleventh Central Committee

【全集】 quánjí complete works; collected works:《列宁～》The Collected Works of Lenin / 莎士比亚戏剧～ an entire set of Shakespeare's plays

【全家福】 quánjiāfú 1.（全家人的合影）a photograph of the whole family 2.（一种菜肴）hotch-potch

【全景】 quánjǐng panorama; full view; whole scene

【全景电影】 quánjǐng diànyǐng cinerama

【全景画】 quánjǐnghuà panorama

【全景摄影机】 quánjǐng shèyǐngjī panoramic camera

【全局】 quánjú situation as a whole; overall situation: ～利益 interests of the whole; general interests

【全军】 quánjūn the whole army; the entire army

【全军覆没】 quánjūn fùmò completely annihilated; total destruction of an army; the whole army was annihilated

【全力】 quánlì with all one's strength; all-out; sparing no effort: ～攻打 a full-scale attack / ～以赴 go all out; spare no effort / ～支持 give all-out support

【全粒】 quánlì wholegrain

【全麦】 quánmài wholewheat

【全毛】 quánmáo 〈*Textiles*〉 all woolen

【全貌】 quánmào complete picture; full view

【全棉】 quánmián 〈*Textiles*〉 all cotton

【全面】 quánmiàn overall; comprehensive; all-round: ～发展 all-round development / ～规划 overall planning / ～强制性制裁 comprehensive mandatory sanctions

【全面战争】 quánmiàn zhànzhēng a full-scale war

【全面质量管理】 quánmiàn zhìliàng guǎnlǐ Total Quality Control (TQC)

【全民】 quánmín the whole people; the entire people; all the people

【全民公决】 quánmín gōngjué national referendum

【全民所有制】 quánmín suǒyǒuzhì ownership by the whole people

【全名】 quánmíng full name

【全明星】 quánmíngxīng all-star

【全明星队】 quánmíngxīngduì 〈*Sports*〉 all-star

【全能】 quánnéng 〈*Sports*〉 all-round: ～冠军 all-round champion / 五项～ pentathlon / 十项～ decathlon

【全能运动员】 quánnéng yùndòngyuán all-round athlete; all-round sportsman (m.); all-round sportswoman (f.)

【全年】 quánnián annual; yearly

【全盘】 quánpán overall; comprehensive; wholesale: ～接受 swallow sth. whole / ～考虑 give overall consideration

【全盘西化】 quánpán xīhuà wholesale Westernization

【全频道】 quánpíndào multichannel: ～电视机 a multi-channel television set

【全勤】 quánqín full attendance

【全球】 quánqiú the whole world; global (adj.): ～战略 global strategy

【全权】 quánquán 1.（完全的权力）full powers; plenipotence 2.（有全权的）plenipotentiary

【全权代表】 quánquán dàibiǎo plenipotentiary

【全然】 quánrán completely; entirely: ～不顾个人安危 give no thought to one's own safety

【全日制】 quánrìzhì full-time: ～教育 full-time schooling / ～学校 full-time school

【全色】 quánsè 〈*Photog.*〉 panchromatic：～胶片 panchromatic film

【全身】 quánshēn the whole body; all over (the body)

【全神贯注】 quánshén-guànzhù be absorbed in; be engrossed in; be preoccupied with：～地听着 be all ears

【全盛】 quánshèng flourishing; in full bloom：～时期 period of full bloom; prime; heyday

【全食】 quánshí 〈*Aeron.*〉 total eclipse

【全食带】 quánshídài path of total eclipse; belt of totality; zone of totality

【全数】 quánshù total number; whole amount：～付讫 have paid the whole amount; paid in full

【全速】 quánsù full speed; maximum speed; top speed

【全损】 quánsǔn 〈*Insurance*〉 total loss

【全损险】 quánsǔnxiǎn total loss only (T. L. O.)

【全套】 quántào complete set：～设备 a complete set of equipment

【全体】 quántǐ all; entire; whole：～出席 full attendance / ～同意。All are agreed.

【全天】 quántiān all-day

【全天候】 quántiānhòu all-weather：～飞机 all-weather aircraft / ～公路 all-weather road

【全托】 quántuō put one's child in a boarding nursery

【全托托儿所】 quántuō tuō'érsuǒ boarding nursery

【全文】 quánwén full text：～发表 publish in full / ～如下。Following is the full text.

【全无头绪】 quánwútóuxù make neither head nor tail of it

【全无章法】 quánwúzhāngfǎ utterly without a literary style

【全息】 quánxī holographic

【全息电影】 quánxī diànyǐng holographic movie

【全息摄影】 quánxī shèyǐng holography

【全息照相】 quánxī zhàoxiàng hologram：激光～ laser hologram

【全息照相存储器】 quánxī zhàoxiàng cúnchǔqì holographic memory

【全息照相术】 quánxī zhàoxiàngshù holography

【全线】 quánxiàn all fronts; the whole line; the entire length：～出击 launch attacks on all fronts / ～通车 whole line opened to traffic

【全向导航】 quánxiàng dǎoháng omnirange; omnidirectional range

【全向天线】 quánxiàng tiānxiàn omnidirectional antenna

【全心全意】 quánxīn-quányì wholeheartedly; heart and soul; full-hearted：～为人民服务。Serve the people wholeheartedly.

【全休】 quánxiū complete rest

【全休止符】 quánxiūzhǐfú 〈*Music*〉 semibreve rest

【全音】 quányīn 〈*Music*〉 whole tone

【全优】 quányōu all-round excellent

【全员抵押承包】 quányuán dǐyā chéngbāo all-member mortgage contract

【全员劳动生产率】 quányuán láodòng shēngchǎnlǜ overall labor productivity

【全运会】 quányùnhuì the national games

【全正面】 quánzhèngmiàn full-frontal

【全脂奶粉】 quánzhī nǎifěn whole milk powder

【全植物式营养】 quán zhíwùshì yīngyǎng holophytic nutrition

【全自动高质量翻译】 quánzìdòng gāozhìliàng fānyì Full Automatic High-Quality Translation

【全座席】 quánzuòxí all-seater：～体育场 all-seater stadium

诠 (quán)

【诠释】 quánshì annotation; explanatory notes

【诠注】 quánzhù notes and commentary

痊 (quán) recover from an illness

【痊愈】 quányù fully recover from an illness; be fully recovered：祝你早日～。I wish you a speedy recovery.

醛 (quán) 〈*Chem.*〉 aldehyde：乙～ acetaldehyde; ethanal

【醛醇】 quánchún 〈*Chem.*〉 aldehyde alcohol

【醛酸】 quánsuān 〈*Chem.*〉 aldehydic acid

【醛糖】 quántáng 〈*Chem.*〉 aldose

【醛酯】 quánzhǐ 〈*Chem.*〉 aldehydo-ester

泉 (quán) spring：矿～ mineral spring / 喷～ fountain / 温～ hot spring

【泉华】 quánhuá 〈*Geol.*〉 sinter

【泉水】 quánshuǐ spring water; spring

【泉眼】 quányǎn the mouth of a spring; spring

【泉源】 quányuán 1.（水源）fountainhead; springhead; wellspring 2.（来源）source：知识的～ source of knowledge

拳 (quán) 1.（拳头）fist：握～ clench one's fist; close a fist 2.（拳术）boxing; pugilism：打～ do Chinese boxing

【拳打脚踢】 quándǎ-jiǎotī cuff and kick; beat up; strike and kick

【拳击】 quánjī boxing; pugilism

【拳击比赛】 quánjī bǐsài boxing match

【拳击手套】 quánjī shǒutào boxing glove

【拳击台】 quánjītái boxing ring

【拳击运动员】 quánjī yùndòngyuán boxer

【拳曲】 quánqū curl; twist; bend：～着身子 curl oneself up

【拳师】 quánshī boxing coach; pugilist

【拳术】 quánshù Chinese boxing

【拳头】 quán·tou fist

【拳头产品】 quán·tou chǎnpǐn hit product; key product：发展～ develop hit products

蜷［踡］(quán) curl up; huddle up

【蜷伏】 quánfú curl up; huddle up; lie with the knees drawn up

【蜷曲】 quánqū curl; coil; twist：一条蛇～在树枝上。A snake coiled round the branch.

【蜷缩】 quánsuō roll up; huddle up; curl up：把身体～成一团 huddle oneself up

鬈 (quán) curly; wavy：～发 curly hair

【鬈曲】 quánqū 〈*Textiles*〉 crimp; crinkle; curl

颧 (quán) cheekbone

【颧骨】 quán·gǔ cheekbone; zygomatic bone

犬 (quǎn) dog：猎～ hunting dog; hound / 警～ police dog

【犬齿】 quǎnchǐ 〈*Anat.*〉 canine tooth

【犬马之劳】 quǎnmǎzhīláo serve like a dog or a horse：效～ serve one's master faithfully; be at sb's beck and call

【犬牙】 quǎnyá 1.（犬齿）canine tooth 2.（狗牙）fang

【犬牙交错】 quǎnyá-jiāocuò jigsaw-like; interlocking：～的战争 jigsaw pattern warfare

【犬子】 quǎnzǐ my son

劝［勸］(quàn) 1.（说服）advise; urge; try to persuade：～某人做某事 try to persuade sb. to do sth. / 她～我穿上最好的衣服。She advised me to wear my best clothes. 2.（勉励）encourage

【劝导】 quàndǎo try to persuade; advise; induce

【劝告】 quàngào advise; urge; exhort：～他不要多喝酒 advise him not to drink excessively / 听他的～，我卧床休息。On his advice I am staying in bed.

【劝架】 quànjià try to reconcile parties to a quarrel; try to stop people from fighting each other; mediate between two quarrelling parties; mediate

【劝解】 quànjiě 1.（劝导宽解）help sb. to get over his worries, etc. 2.（劝架）mediate; make peace between; bring people together

【劝戒】 quànjiè admonish; expostulate

【劝酒】 quànjiǔ urge sb. to drink (at a banquet)

【劝勉】 quànmiǎn advise and encourage

【劝说】 quànshuō persuade; advise; talk (sb.) into; persuasion (n.)：经过一再～，她同意去了。After a lot of persuasion, she agreed to go.

【劝退】 quàntuì persuade sb. to retire

【劝慰】 quànwèi console; soothe

【劝降】 quànxiáng induce to capitulate

【劝诱】 quànyòu induce; prevail upon

【劝阻】 quànzǔ dissuade sb. from; advise sb. not to; warn sb. against; talk sb. out of：你最好～她别这样早结婚。You'd better dissuade her from marrying so early.

券 (quàn) certificate; ticket：国库～ treasure bill / 奖～ lottery ticket / 外汇兑换～ foreign exchange certificate / 入场～ admission ticket / 赠～ free ticket

que

炔 (quē) 〈*Chem.*〉 alkyne：乙～ acetylene

缺（quē） 1.（缺乏；缺少）be short of；lack；shortage：～水 a shortage of water / 你～钱用吗？Are you short of money？2.（残缺）incomplete；imperfect 3.（该到而未到）be absent 4.（空额）vacancy：补～ supply a vacancy；fill a vacancy

【缺德】 quēdé mean；wicked；villainous

【缺点】 quēdiǎn shortcoming；defect；weakness

【缺额】 quē'é vacancy

【缺乏】 quēfá be short of；lack；be wanting in；be deficient in：他～勇气。He lacks courage.

【缺货】 quēhuò be in short supply；be out of stock

【缺课】 quēkè be absent from school；miss a class：～两天 be absent from school for two days

【缺口】 quēkǒu 1.（裂口）breach；gap：打开～ make a breach；open a breach 2.（不足；缺额）insufficiency 3.〈*Mech*.〉notch

【缺门】 quēmén gap（in a branch of learning，etc.）

【缺勤】 quēqín absence from work

【缺勤率】 quēqínlǜ absence rate

【缺少】 quēshǎo lack；be short of：～人手 be short of hands；be shorthanded

【缺损】 quēsǔn defect

【缺席】 quēxí absent（from a meeting，etc）：无故～ be absent without excuse / 他因事～。He is absent on business.

【缺席判决】 quēxí pànjué judgment by default

【缺席审判】 quēxí shěnpàn trial by default

【缺席投票人】 quēxí tóupiàorén absentee voter

【缺陷】 quēxiàn defect；drawback；flaw；blemish：他在性格上有～。There is something lacking in his character.

【缺医少药】 quēyī shǎoyào be short of medical services and supplies

【缺雨区】 quēyǔqū anhyetism

阙（quē） fault；error

【阙如】 quērú be wanting

【阙疑】 quēyí leave the question open

瘸（qué） be lame；limp：右腿～了 be lame in the right leg

【瘸腿】 quétuǐ lame

【瘸子】 qué·zi a lame person；cripple

却［卻］（què） 1.（退却）step back；fall back 2.（使退却）drive back；repulse 3.（推却）decline；refuse；reject；turn down

【却病】 quèbìng prevent or cure a disease：～延年 prevent disease and prolong life；banish illness and increase long life

【却步】 quèbù step back（from）；hang back（from）：～而行 walk stepping backwards

【却而不受】 què'érbùshòu refuse to accept

【却之不恭】 quèzhībùgōng it would be impolite to decline

确［確、塙、碻］（què） 1.（确实）true；reliable；authentic 2.（坚固；坚定）firmly

【确保】 quèbǎo ensure；guarantee

【确定】 quèdìng 1.（使确定）define；fix；determine；ascertain：各单位要～编制。Each unit should determine its appropriate size and structure. 2.（明确而肯定）definite；certain；for sure

【确乎】 quèhū really；indeed：～有效 really effective

【确立】 quèlì establish：～他的领导地位 establish his leadership

【确切】 quèqiè definite；exact；precise：～的答复 a definite reply / 我们把下次开会的～日期定下来吧。Let's fix a definite date for the next meeting.

【确认】 quèrèn affirm；confirm；acknowledge：～所陈属实 confirm the statement

【确实】 quèshí 1.（真实可靠）true；reliable：～的消息 reliable information 2.（的确）really；indeed：～太晚了。Indeed，it's too late.

【确信】 quèxìn firmly believe；be convinced；be sure：～无疑 firmly believe sth. to be true / 我～她看到我了。I'm certain she saw me.

【确凿】 quèzáo conclusive；authentic；irrefutable：证据～ irrefutable evidence；verified evidence；valid evidence

【确诊】 quèzhěn make a definite diagnosis；diagnose

【确证】 quèzhèng ironclad proof；conclusive evidence

雀 (què) sparrow

【雀斑】 quèbān freckle

【雀儿山】 Què'érshān 〈place〉 Chola Shan

【雀跃】 quèyuè jump for joy

鹊 (què) magpie

榷[搉] (què) discuss：商～ discuss；deliberate over

qun

裙[帬] (qún) skirt：百褶～ pleated skirt / 超短～ miniskirt / 衬～ slip；petticoat

【裙带】 qúndài nepotism；connected through one's female relatives：通过～关系 with the help of one's female relatives

【裙裤】 qúnkù divided skirt

【裙子】 qún·zi skirt

群[羣] (qún) 1.（聚在一起）crowd；group：人们三五成～地散立着。People were standing about in small groups. 2.〈*classifier*〉group；herd；flock：一～孩子 a group of children / 一～狼 a pack of wolves / 一～马 a drove of horses

【群策群力】 qúncè-qúnlì pool the wisdom and efforts of everyone；work with collective wisdom and concerted efforts

【群岛】 qúndǎo archipelago；islands

【群而不党】 qún'érbùdǎng be social, but not clannish

【群芳】 qúnfāng beautiful and fragrant flowers；all kinds of flowers

【群婚】 qúnhūn group marriage；communal marriage

【群集】 qúnjí aggregation

【群居】 qúnjū living in groups；gregarious；social

【群聚】 qúnjù bunching

【群控制】 qúnkòngzhì group control

【群龙无首】 qúnlóng-wúshǒu a host of dragons without a head；a group without a leader

【群论】 qúnlùn 〈*Math*.〉 theory of groups

【群落】 qúnluò 〈*Bot*.〉 community

【群魔乱舞】 qúnmóluànwǔ a host of demons dancing in riotous revelry；rogues of all kinds running wild

【群起而攻之】 qúnqǐ ér gōng zhī all rise against sb.；rally together to attack sb.

【群青】 qúnqīng 〈*Chem*.〉 ultramarine

【群情】 qúnqíng public sentiment；feelings of the masses：～激昂。Popular feeling ran high.

【群体】 qúntǐ 1.〈*Biol*.〉 colony 2.〈*Sociology*〉 group：次属～ secondary group / 首属～ primary group / 小～ small group / 指涉～ reference group

【群众】 qúnzhòng 1.（人民大众）the masses 2.（非党内的）non-Party member 3.（老百姓）populace

【群众路线】 qúnzhòng lùxiàn the mass line：走～ follow the mass line

【群众性】 qúnzhòngxìng of a mass character：～体育活动 mass sports activities

麇[麕] (qún) flock together

【麇集】 qúnjí swarm；flock together

R

ran

然(rán) 1.(对) right; correct 2.(如此；这样) so; like that 3.〈*written*〉〈*conj*.〉 but; nevertheless; however

【然而】 rán'ér 〈*conj*.〉 yet; but; however: 他已年老，～记忆力还好。He is aged, but his memory is still good.

【然后】 ránhòu 〈*adv*.〉 then; after that; afterwards: 学～知不足。One discovers his ignorance only through learning.

燃(rán) burn; ignite; light

【燃点】 rándiǎn 1.(使燃烧) ignite; kindle; set fire to 2.(燃烧的最低温度) ignition point

【燃放】 ránfàng set off: ～烟花 set off fireworks

【燃料】 ránliào fuel

【燃料库】 ránliàokù fuel depot; fuel reservoir

【燃料油】 ránliàoyóu fuel oil

【燃眉之急】 ránméizhījí a matter of extreme urgency; a pressing need

【燃气】 ránqì fuel gas

【燃气轮机】 ránqìlúnjī gas turbine

【燃气热水器】 ránqì rèshuǐqì gas water heater

【燃烧】 ránshāo 1.(烧) burn; kindle 2.〈*Chem*.〉 combustion; inflammation

【燃烧弹】 ránshāodàn incendiary bomb

【燃烧剂】 ránshāojì incendiary agent

【燃烧瓶】 ránshāopíng Molotov cocktail

【燃烧室】 ránshāoshì combustion chamber; blast chamber; combustor

【燃烧性能】 ránshāo xìngnéng combustibility

【燃烧值】 ránshāozhí fuel value

【燃烧终止】 ránshāo zhōngzhǐ fire end

【燃油舱】 rányóucāng oil fuel tank

【燃油炉】 rányóulú oil burner

冉[**冄**](rǎn) 〈*written*〉 slowly

【冉冉】 rǎnrǎn slowly; gradually: ～而上 go up slowly / ～上升 rise slowly

染(rǎn) 1.(着色) dye: 把白衣服～成蓝色 dye a white dress blue / 她把头发～黑了。She dyed her hair black. 2.(感染) catch (a disease): ～上了流感 have caught flu; become infected with influenza 3.(沾染) acquire (a bad habit, etc.); soil; contaminate: ～上恶习 acquire a bad habit

【染病】 rǎnbìng catch an illness; be infected with a disease

【染布】 rǎnbù dye cloth

【染厂】 rǎnchǎng dye-work

【染发】 rǎnfà dye hair

【染缸】 rǎngāng dye vat; dye jigger

【染料】 rǎnliào dyestuff; dye

【染色】 rǎnsè dyeing; coloring

【染色法】 rǎnsèfǎ decoration method; staining

【染色剂】 rǎnsèjì coloring agent

【染色体】 rǎnsètǐ 〈*Biol*.〉 chromosome; chromosomal (adj): 性～ sex chromosome

【染色性】 rǎnsèxìng dyeability

【染印法】 rǎnyìnfǎ 〈*Cinematog*.〉 dye transfer process

【染印法彩色电影】 rǎnyìnfǎ cǎisè diànyǐng color film made by the dye transfer process; technicolor

【染指】 rǎnzhǐ take a share of sth. one is not entitled to; encroach on

【染指甲】 rǎnzhǐ·jia paint fingernails

【染指择肥】 rǎnzhǐ-zéféi dip one's finger in the pie and claim the lion's share

rang

嚷(rāng)
(另见"嚷"rǎng)

【嚷嚷】 rāngrāng 1.（喧哗）shout; yell; make an uproar：外面人们在～。People are shouting outside. 2.（声张）make widely known：这事暂时不要～出去。Don't breathe a word about this for the time being.

禳（ráng） avert a misfortune by praying

【禳灾】 rángzāi pray in order to avert a disaster

瓤（ráng） 1.（瓤子）pulp; flesh; pith：南瓜～ the pulp of a pumpkin 2.（泛指里面的东西）the interior part of certain things：光剩了个空信封，里头没有信～儿。There's only an empty envelope with nothing in it.

【瓤子】 ráng·zi pulp; flesh; pith

壤（rǎng） 1.（土壤）soil 2.（地）earth 3.（地区）area：接～ have a common border

【壤土】 rǎngtǔ 〈*Agric*.〉 loam

攘［纕[3]］（rǎng） 1.（排斥）reject; resist 2.（抢）seize; grab 3.（捋起）push up one's sleeves

【攘臂】 rǎngbì 〈*written*〉 push up one's sleeves and bare one's arms (in excitement or agitation)

【攘除】 rǎngchú 〈*written*〉 get rid of; weed out; reject

【攘夺】 rǎngduó 〈*written*〉 seize; grab

【攘外】 rǎngwài resist foreign invasion

嚷（rǎng） shout; yell; make an uproar：她在～什么？What's she shouting about?（另见"嚷"rāng）

让［讓］（ràng） 1.（不争，给别人）give way; give ground; yield; give up 2.（请，招待）invite; offer 3.（叫，允许）let; allow; make：～我试一试。Let me have a try. 4.（出让；转让）let sb. have sth. at a fair price：我可以按半价把这本词典～给你。I can let you have this dictionary at half its price. 5.〈*prep*.〉我～雨淋着了。I was caught in the rain.

【让步】 ràngbù make a concession; give in; give way; yield：在原则问题上不～ make no concession in matters of principle

【让车道】 ràngchēdào passing bay

【让车线】 ràngchēxiàn passing track

【让干路车先行】 ràng gànlùchē xiānxíng 〈*Transport*〉 yield

【让价】 ràngjià price concession：给予～ grant price concession

【让开】 ràngkāi get out of the way; step aside; make way

【让利】 rànglì reduce own interest

【让路】 rànglù make way for sb. or sth.; give way; give sb. the right of way

【让球】 ràngqiú concede points：他～她五个球。He conceded her five points.

【让位】 ràngwèi 1.（指王位、职位）resign sovereign authority; abdicate 2.（指座位）offer one's seat to sb.

【让贤】 ràngxián yield one's position to amore talented person

【让贤与能】 ràngxiányǔnéng retire and give room to better men

【让座】 ràngzuò 1.（让座位）offer one's seat to sb.; give up one's seat to another 2.（请客人入座）invite guests to be seated

rao

饶［饒］（ráo） 1.（富饶）rich; plentiful 2.（饶恕）have mercy on; let sb. off; forgive：～他这回吧。Let him off this time. 3.（另外添）give sth. extra; let sb. have sth. into the bargain 4.〈*colloq*.〉〈*conj*.〉although; in spite of the fact that：～这么细心核对，还是有遗漏。In spite of careful checking there are still omission.

【饶命】 ráomìng spare sb's life

【饶舌】 ráoshé 1.（唠叨）too talkative; garrulous 2.（多嘴）say more than is proper; shoot off one's mouth

【饶恕】 ráoshù forgive; pardon

桡［橈］（ráo） oar

【桡动脉】 ráodòngmài 〈*Anat*.〉 radial artery

【桡骨】 ráogǔ 〈*Anat*.〉 radius

【桡神经】 ráoshéngjīng 〈*Anat*.〉 nervus radialis

扰［擾］（rǎo） 1.（扰乱）harass; trouble：～人清梦 disturb one's sweet dream 2.（客套话）trespass on sb's hospitality

【扰动】 rǎodòng 1.（动荡）perturbation motion; disturb 2.（干扰）interfere; disturb

【扰动气流】 rǎodòng qìliú rough air
【扰动速度】 rǎodòng sùdù disturbance velocity
【扰动中心】 rǎodòng zhōngxīn center of disturbance
【扰流板】 rǎoliúbǎn 〈*Motorcycle*〉 spoiler
【扰乱】 rǎoluàn harass; disturb; create confusion: ～边境 harass the border of a country / ～社会治安 disturb public order
【扰攘】 rǎorǎng hustle and bustle; noisy confusion; tumult

绕［繞、遶[2,3]］(rào) **1.**（缠绕）wind; coil **2.**（围着转）move round; circle; revolve: 月球～地球运行。The moon revolves round the earth. **3.**（迂回）make a detour; bypass; go round **4.**（纠缠）confuse; baffle; befuddle
【绕场一周】 ràochǎng yīzhōu **1.**（指动作）go round the stadium **2.**（指荣誉）lap of honor
【绕道】 ràodào make a detour; go by a roundabout route: ～而行 take a devious route; go in a roundabout way
【绕接】 ràojiē solderless wrapped connection; wire-wrap connection
【绕口令】 ràokǒulìng tongue twister
【绕圈子】 rào quān·zi **1.**（走迂回路）circle; go round and round **2.**（不直说）take a circuitous route; make a detour
【绕弯儿】 rào wānr **1.**（散步）go for a stroll **2.**（不照直说）talk in a roundabout way; beat about the bush: 你直说吧，别～了。You might come straight to the point. Don't beat about the bush.
【绕远儿】 rào yuǎnr go the long way round
【绕月火箭】 ràoyuè huǒjiàn circumlunar rocket
【绕嘴】 ràozuǐ not be smooth; be difficult to articulate

re

惹 (rě) **1.**（引起）cause; invite; ask for: ～人注意 attract attention / 别～我发火。Don't make me lose my temper. **2.**（招惹）offend; provoke; tease: 别～他。Don't offend him. **3.**（引逗）attract; cause
【惹草拈花】 rěcǎo-niānhuā stir bushes and pick flowers; have a fancy for prostitutes
【惹火烧身】 rěhuǒ-shāoshēn stir a fire only to burn oneself; court disaster; ask for trouble
【惹祸】 rěhuò court disaster; stir up trouble
【惹乱子】 rě luàn·zi cause trouble
【惹麻烦】 rě máfán cause trouble; make trouble; look trouble
【惹气】 rěqì get angry
【惹事】 rěshì stir up trouble
【惹是生非】 rěshì-shēngfēi provoke a dispute; stir up trouble

热［熱］(rè) **1.**〈*Physics*〉heat: 导～性 heat conductivity **2.**（温度高）hot: ～水 hot water / ～天 hot weather / 请喝点～茶。Here is some hot tea for you. **3.**（加热）heat up; warm up; warm: 把汤～一下 heat up the soup **4.**（体温高）fever; temperature: 发～ have a fever **5.**（情意深）ardent; warmhearted **6.**（受欢迎）in great demand; popular **7.**（热潮）craze; fad: 汉语～ crazy for Chinese (language) **8.**（羡慕）envious; eager: 眼～ feel envious at the sight of sth. **9.**（放射性强）thermal; thermo-
【热爱】 rè'ài ardently love; have deep love for: ～科学 take a keen interest in science
【热病】 rèbìng pyreticosis; fever
【热波】 rèbō thermal wave
【热补】 rèbǔ vulcanize (tire, etc.)
【热层】 rècéng 〈*Meteorol.*〉thermosphere
【热潮】 rècháo great mass fervor; upsurge
【热忱】 rèchén zeal; warmheartedness; enthusiasm and devotion
【热诚】 rèchéng warm and sincere; cordial: ～欢迎 cordially welcome
【热成形】 rèchéngxíng thermosetting
【热处理】 rèchǔlǐ 〈*Mech.*〉 heat treatment; thermal treatment
【热传导】 rèchuándǎo heat conduction; egress
【热带】 rèdài the torrid zone; the tropics
【热带草原】 rèdài cǎoyuán savanna
【热带雨林】 rèdài yǔlín selva; tropical rainforest
【热带植物】 rèdài zhíwù tropical plants
【热带作物】 rèdài zuòwù tropical crops
【热当量】 rèdāngliàng heat equivalent
【热导体】 rèdǎotǐ 〈*Physics*〉heat conductor

【热得快】 rè·dekuài immersion heater
【热点】 rèdiǎn hot point; hot spot: 读者最关心的～ the reader's most concerned hot point
【热点问题】 rèdiǎn wèntí hot issue
【热电】 rèdiàn 〈*Physics*〉 pyroelectricity; thermoelectricity; thermoelectric (adj.)
【热电厂】 rèdiànchǎng heat and power plant
【热电偶】 rèdiànǒu thermocouple
【热度】 rèdù **1.**(冷热程度) degree of heat; heat **2.**(高于正常体温) fever; temperature: 他的～退了吗? Has his temperature come down? **3.**(热情) enthusiasm
【热风】 rèfēng 〈*Meteorol.*〉 hot wind; hot-blas-air
【热风炉】 rèfēnglú 〈*Metall.*〉 hot-blast stove
【热敷】 rèfū 〈*Med.*〉 hot compress
【热辐射】 rèfúshè 〈*Med.*〉 heat radiation; thermal radiation
【热狗】 règǒu hot dog
【热管】 règuǎn heat pipe
【热耗】 rèhào heat rate
【热核】 rèhé thermonuclear
【热核爆炸】 rèhé bàozhà thermonuclear explosion
【热核弹头】 rèhé dàntóu thermonuclear warhead
【热核反应】 rèhé fǎnyìng 〈*Physics*〉 thermonuclear reaction: 受控～ controlled thermonuclear reaction
【热核反应堆】 rèhé fǎnyìngduī thermonuclear reactor
【热核武器】 rèhé wǔqì thermonuclear weapon
【热烘烘】 rèhōnghōng very warm
【热乎】 rè·hu **1.**(热) warm; nice and warm **2.**(亲热) warm and friendly; chummy; thick
【热乎乎】 rèhūhū warm: 她的话使我心里感到～的。Her words warmed my heart.
【热呼呼】 rèhūhū 同"热乎乎"
【热火朝天】 rèhuǒ-cháotiān in full swing; buzzing with activity
【热货】 rèhuò goods in great demand
【热机】 rèjī 〈*Mech.*〉 heat engine
【热加工】 rèjiāgōng 〈*Mech.*〉 hot-work; hot-working
【热空气气球】 rèkōngqì qìqiú montgolfier
【热扩散】 rèkuòsàn 〈*Physics*〉 thermal diffusion
【热辣辣】 rèlālā burning hot; scorching: 觉得脸上～的 feel one's cheeks burning
【热浪】 rèlàng **1.**〈*Meteorol.*〉 heat wave; hot wave **2.**(指热烈场面等) warm wave
【热老化】 rèlǎohuà heat ageing; heat aging
【热泪盈眶】 rèlèi yíngkuàng one's eyes brimming with tears
【热离子管】 rèlízǐguǎn thermionic valve
【热利用】 rèlìyòng heat utilization
【热力】 rèlì 〈*Mech.*〉 heating power
【热力学】 rèlìxué thermodynamics
【热恋】 rèliàn be passionately in love; be head over heels in love
【热量】 rèliàng 〈*Physics*〉 quantity of heat
【热量单位】 rèliàng dānwèi thermal unit
【热量计】 rèliàngjì calorimeter
【热烈】 rèliè warm; enthusiastic; ardent: ～的欢迎 warm welcome
【热流】 rèliú **1.**〈*Meteorol.*〉 thermal current **2.**(指感受) warm current **3.**(热潮) great mass fervor; upsurge
【热门】 rèmén in great demand; popular
【热门货】 rèménhuò goods in great demand; goods which sell well; hot item
【热门音乐】 rèmén yīnyuè hot music
【热闹】 rènào **1.**(繁盛活跃) lively; bustling with noise and excitement: ～的市场 a busy market **2.**(使欢跃愉快) liven up; have a jolly time: 晚会开始～起来了。The evening party is beginning to liven up. **3.**(热闹景象) a scene of bustle and excitement
【热能】 rènéng 〈*Physics*〉 heat energy
【热膨胀】 rèpéngzhàng thermal energy
【热平衡】 rèpínghéng thermal equilibrium; heat balance
【热气】 rèqì steam; heat
【热气球】 rèqìqiú hot air balloon: 乘坐～ fly a hot air balloon
【热切】 rèqiè fervent; earnest: ～地希望 earnestly hope
【热情】 rèqíng **1.**(热烈的感情) enthusiasm; zeal; warmth **2.**(有热情) warm; fervent; enthusiastic; warmhearted: ～欢迎 a warm welcome / ～接待 give sb. a warm reception
【热情奔放】 rèqíng-bēnfàng an outburst of

enthusiasm; bubbling with enthusiasm
【热情洋溢】 rèqíng-yángyì glowing with enthusiasm; brimming over with enthusiasm: ～的讲话 a speech brimming with warm feeling
【热容量】 rèróngliàng 〈*Physics*〉 heat capacity; thermal capacity
【热身】 rèshēn warm-up
【热身赛】 rèshēnsài warm-up competition: 参加一场～ participate in a warm-up competition
【热身运动】 rèshēn yùndòng warm-up; warm-up exercise: 比赛开始前先做～ warm up before entering a game
【热水袋】 rèshuǐdài hot-water bottle
【热水瓶】 rèshuǐpíng 〈*colloq.*〉 thermos bottle; thermos; vacuum bottle
【热水器】 rèshuǐqì water heater: 电～ electric water heater / 燃气～ gas water heater
【热腾腾】 rètēngtēng steaming hot
【热天】 rètiān hot weather; hot season; hot days
【热调节器】 rètiáojiéqì heat regulator
【热望】 rèwàng 1.(热烈盼望) fervently hope; ardently wish 2.(热切的希望) fervent hope; ardent wish
【热污染】 rèwūrǎn thermal pollution
【热线】 rèxiàn 1.〈*Physics*〉 heat ray 2.(直通电话线路) hotline 3.(旅游线路) hot route
【热线电话】 rèxiàn diànhuà telephone hotline
【热销】 rèxiāo be in great demand; commodities that are popular and sell well
【热销货】 rèxiāohuò fast-selling commodities
【热效率】 rèxiàolǜ thermal efficiency; heat efficiency
【热效应】 rèxiàoyìng fuel factor; heat effect; thermal results
【热心】 rèxīn warm-hearted; enthusiastic; ardent; earnest: ～科学 eager to promote science
【热心肠】 rèxīncháng 〈*collog.*〉 warmheartedness; warm heart
【热心人】 rèxīnrén enthusiast; zealot
【热学】 rèxué 〈*Physics*〉 heat (a branch of physics)
【热血】 rèxuè 1.(指血液) warm blood 2.(指热情) righteous ardor
【热血动物】 rèxuè dòngwù warm-blooded animal; warm blood
【热血沸腾】 rèxuè fèiténg hot-blooded
【热压】 rèyā 〈*Chem.*〉 hot pressing
【热饮】 rèyǐn hot drinks
【热源】 rèyuán 〈*Physics*〉 heat source
【热轧】 rèzhá 〈*Metall.*〉 hot-rolling
【热轧机】 rèzhájī hot-rolling mill
【热战】 rèzhàn hot war; shooting war
【热胀冷缩】 rèzhàng-lěngsuō expand with heat and contract with cold; expansion caused by heat and contraction caused by cold; heat makes something expand and cold makes it contract
【热中】 rèzhōng 1.(急切想望) hanker after; crave 2.(十分爱好) be fond of; be keen on: ～于游泳 be very fond of swimming
【热衷】 rèzhōng 同"热中"

ren

人 (rén) 1.(泛指) man; person; people; human being: 城里～ townman / 好～ good person / 普通～ man in the street / 不受欢迎的～ persona non grata / 我们需要有个～帮忙。We need a person to help us. 2.(成年人) adult; grown-up 3.(别人) people; other people 4.(人品;性格) personality; character: 为～谦恭 modest in character 5.(人的身体或意识) state of one's health; how one feels: 送到医院时,～已经死了。When the patient was taken to hospital, he had already died. 6.(每人) everybody; each; all 7.(人手;人才) manpower; hand: 我们这里还缺～。We are still short of hands.
【人不可貌相】 rén bù kě mào xiàng Men cannot be judged by their looks.
【人不为己,天诛地灭】 rén bù wèi jǐ, tiān zhū dì miè unless a man looks out for himself, Heaven and Earth will destroy him; everyone for himself and the devil take the hindmost
【人不知,鬼不觉】 rén bù zhī, guǐ bù jué without a soul knowing anything about it
【人才】 réncái 1.(指人) a person of ability; a talented person; talent; qualified personnel: 科技～ qualified scientists and techni-

cians 2.(指相貌) handsome appearance

【人才辈出】 réncái-bèichū people of talent coming forth in large numbers

【人才出众】 réncái-chūzhòng a person of exceptional ability or striking appearance

【人才济济】 réncái-jǐjǐ a galaxy of talent

【人才交流】 réncái jiāoliú the interchange of talents

【人才交流服务中心】 réncái jiāoliú fúwù zhōngxīn talent exchange service center; personnel exchange center

【人才库】 réncáikù reserve of talented people

【人才流动】 réncái liúdòng mobility of the talents; flow of the talents

【人才培养】 réncái péiyǎng personnel training

【人才外流】 réncái wàiliú brain drain

【人才造就】 réncái zàojiù talent accomplishment

【人财两旺】 rén-cái liǎngwàng prosperous both in family and purse

【人称】 rénchēng 〈*Gram.*〉 person: 第一~ the first person

【人称代词】 rénchēng dàicí personal pronoun

【人次】 réncì person-time; man-time

【人大】 réndà the National People's Congress (NPC)

【人大常委会】 réndà chángwěihuì the Standing Committee of the NPC

【人大代表】 réndà dàibiǎo deputy to the NPC

【人道】 réndào 1.(指道德) humanity; human sympathy 2.(仁慈的) human; humane: ~的待遇 humane treatment

【人道主义】 réndào zhǔyì humanitarianism; humanitarian (adj.)

【人地比率】 rén-dì bǐlǜ man-land ratio

【人地生疏】 rén-dì shēngshū be unfamiliar with the place and the people; be a complete stranger

【人丁】 réndīng population; family number

【人定胜天】 réndìngshèngtiān man can conquer nature; man will triumph over nature

【人盾】 réndùn human shield

【人多势众】 rénduō-shìzhòng overwhelm with numerical strength; many hands provide great strength

【人多智广】 rénduō-zhìguǎng More people means more ideas.

【人多嘴杂】 rénduō-zuǐzá Agreement is difficult if there are too many people.

【人贩子】 rénfàn·zi trader in human beings

【人防】 rénfáng people's air defense; civil air defense

【人防工程】 rénfáng gōngchéng civil air defense constructions and installations

【人浮于事】 rénfúyúshì have more hands than needed; be overstaffed

【人格】 réngé 1.(人品) personality; character; moral quality: ~高尚 have a noble character 2.(尊严) human dignity 3.(资格) human rights

【人格化】 réngéhuà personification

【人格教育】 réngé jiàoyù personal education

【人格类型学】 réngé lèixíngxué personality typology

【人格权】 réngéquán human rights

【人格学】 réngéxué personology

【人工】 réngōng 1.(人为的) man-made; artificial 2.(人力) manual work; work done by hand: 用机器代替~ install machines to replace manual labor 3.(指工作量) manpower; man-day: 修这座桥要多少~? How many man-days will be needed to construct this bridge?

【人工草场】 réngōng cǎochǎng artificially sown pastures

【人工繁殖】 réngōng fánzhí artificial propagation

【人工孵化】 réngōng fūhuà artificial incubation

【人工海浪】 réngōng hǎilàng artificial waves

【人工海浪泳池】 réngōng hǎilàng yǒngchí swimming pool with artificial waves

【人工合成蛋白质】 réngōng héchéng dànbáizhì synthetic protein

【人工呼吸】 réngōng hūxī artificial respiration

【人工湖】 réngōnghú man-made lake

【人工降水】 réngōng jiàngshuǐ artificial rainmaking; artificial precipitation

【人工降雨】 réngōng jiàngyǔ artificial rainfall

【人工降雨装置】 réngōng jiàngyǔ zhuāngzhì artificial rain device; sprinkler

【人工流产】 réngōng liúchǎn induced abortion

【人工器官】 réngōng qìguān artificial organs

【人工肾】 réngōngshèn artificial kidney

【人工授粉】 réngōng shòufěn artificial pollination

【人工授精】 réngōng shòujīng artificial insemination

【人工心肺机】 réngōng xīnfèijī heart-lung machine; extra-corporeal circulation apparatus

【人工智能】 réngōng zhìnéng artificial intelligence

【人公里】 réngōnglǐ 〈*Transport*〉 passenger-kilometer

【人海】 rénhǎi a sea of faces; a huge crowd (of people)

【人和】 rénhé unity and coordination within one's own ranks; support of the people

【人欢马叫】 rénhuān-mǎjiào people bustling and horses neighing; a busy, prosperous country scene

【人寰】 rénhuán 〈*written*〉 man's world; the world

【人机对话】 rén-jī duìhuà man-machine interaction

【人机联系】 rén-jī liánxì man-machine interface

【人机模拟】 rén-jī mónǐ man-machine simulation

【人迹】 rénjì human footmarks; traces of human presence

【人际】 rénjì between people; among people: 幽默经常被用作～交往的润滑剂。Humor is often used to play the role of lubricating.

【人家】 rénjiā 1.（住户）household: 10 户～ ten households 2.（家庭）family

【人家】 rén·jia 1.（别人）other; another: ～都这么说。That's the common opinion of others. 2.（指某个人或某些人）he; she; they: 把书给～送去。Take the book to him. 3.（指说话者本人）I: ～这会儿忙着呢! I am busy just now!

【人间】 rénjiān man's world; the world: ～乐园 earthly paradise

【人杰】 rénjié an outstanding personality: ～地灵 a place propitious for giving birth to great men; the greatness of a man lends glory to a place

【人尽其才】 rénjìnqícái make the best possible use of men

【人均】 rénjūn per capita; average per capita

【人口】 rénkǒu 1.（居民总数）population: 常住～ resident population; permanent population / 城市～ urban population / 控制～数量 control the population quantitatively / 提高～质量 improve the quality of the population / 这个城市的～有多少? What is the population of this city? 2.（家庭人数）number of people in a family 3.（泛指人）person; people; human being

【人口爆炸】 rénkǒu bàozhà population explosion

【人口稠密】 rénkǒu chóumì populous; thickly populated: ～的城市 a thickly populated city

【人口出生率】 rénkǒu chūshēnglǜ human fertility

【人口断层】 rénkǒu duàncéng population gap

【人口分布】 rénkǒu fēnbù population distribution

【人口负增长】 rénkǒu fùzēngzhǎng NPG; negative population growth

【人口更替】 rénkǒu gēngtì population replacement

【人口过剩】 rénkǒu guòshèng overpopulation

【人口基数】 rénkǒu jīshù population base

【人口激增】 rénkǒu jīzēng explosive population growth

【人口减少】 rénkǒu jiǎnshǎo population decline; population decrease

【人口结构】 rénkǒu jiégòu population structure

【人口老化】 rénkǒu lǎohuà aging of population

【人口理论】 rénkǒu lǐlùn population theory

【人口零点增长】 rénkǒu língdiǎn zēngzhǎng ZPG; zero population growth

【人口密度】 rénkǒu mìdù density of population; population density

【人口普查】 rénkǒu pǔchá census; population census

【人口生育力】 rénkǒu shēngyùlì human fecundity

【人口死亡率】 rénkǒu sǐwánglǜ human mortality

【人口统计】 rénkǒu tǒngjì vital statistics; population statistics

【人口学】 rénkǒuxué demography ‖ 人口学家 demographer

【人口预测】 rénkǒu yùcè population projection

【人口增长】 rénkǒu zēngzhǎng population growth

【人口自然增长】 rénkǒu zìrán zēngzhǎng natural growth of the population

【人困马乏】 rénkùn-mǎfá the men weary, their steeds spent; the entire force was exhausted

【人老识广】 rénlǎo-shíguǎng The devil knows many things because he is old.

【人老心不老】 rénlǎo-xīnbùlǎo be old in age, but young in mind; though old, still young in heart

【人老珠黄】 rénlǎo-zhūhuáng one getting old like the pearl becoming yellow; lose one's looks; no longer held in esteem

【人类】 rénlèi mankind; humanity

【人力】 rénlì manpower; labor power: 爱惜～物力 treasure manpower and material resources

【人力车】 rénlìchē 1.(人力拉或推的车) two-wheeled vehicle drawn by man 2.(人拉的载客的车) rickshaw

【人力开发】 rénlì kāifā development of manpower

【人力投资】 rénlì tóuzī human capital investment

【人力资本】 rénlì zīběn human capital

【人链】 rénliàn human chain

【人流】 rénliú 1.(指人) stream of people 2.(人工流产) artificial abortion

【人伦】 rénlún human relations

【人马】 rénmǎ 1.(军队) forces; troops: 大队～ a large group of people 2.(人员) personnel; staff: 原班～ the former staff

【人马宫】 Rénmǎgōng 〈*Astron*.〉 Sagittarius (11月22日至12月22日): 生于～ be born under Sagittarius

【人马座】 Rénmǎzuò 〈*Astron*.〉 Sagittarius

【人满为患】 rénmǎnwéihuàn The house is crowded in every part. (或: The place is packed.)

【人们】 rén·men people; men; the public

【人面兽心】 rénmiàn-shòuxīn have the face of a man but the heart of a beast; a beast in human shape

【人民】 rénmín the people; popular (adj.): 世界各国～ peoples of the world / ～之间的联系和交流 people-to-people contacts and exchanges

【人民币】 rénmínbì Renminbi (RMB)

【人民大会堂】 Rénmín Dàhuìtáng Great Hall of the People

【人民代表大会】 rénmín dàibiǎo dàhuì people's congress

【人民法院】 rénmín fǎyuàn people's court

【人民法院院长】 rénmín fǎyuàn yuànzhǎng president of the people's court

【人民检察院】 rénmín jiǎncháyuàn people's procuratorate

【人民检察院检察长】 rénmín jiǎncháyuàn jiǎncházhǎng chief procurator of the people's procuratorate

【人民警察】 rénmín jǐngchá the people's police

【人民来信】 rénmín láixìn letters from the masses

【人民民主专政】 rénmín mínzhǔ zhuānzhèng people's democratic dictatorship

【人民陪审员】 rénmín péishěnyuán people's assessor

【人民群众】 rénmín qúnzhòng the masses

【人民团体】 rénmín tuántǐ mass organization; people's organization

【人民武装部】 rénmín wǔzhuāngbù people's armed forces department

【人民性】 rénmínxìng affinity to the people

【人民英雄纪念碑】 Rénmín Yīngxióng Jìniànbēi Monument to the People's Heroes

【人民战争】 rénmín zhànzhēng people's war

【人民政府】 rénmín zhèngfǔ the People's Government

【人民资本主义】 rénmín zīběn zhǔyì people's capitalism

【人命】 rénmìng life; human life

【人命案子】 rénmìng àn·zi a case of homicide; a case of murder

【人品】 rénpǐn 1.(人的品质) moral standing; moral quality; character 2.(仪表) looks; bearing: ～端庄 have good looks

【人情】 rénqíng 1.(人之常情) human feelings; human sympathy; sensibilities 2.（情面）human relationship 3.（恩惠）favor：空头～ lip service / 做～ do sb. a favor 4.（礼物）gift; present：送～ send gifts; make a gift of sth.

【人情礼】 rénqínglǐ human relationship gift

【人情世故】 rénqíng-shìgù worldly wisdom

【人情味】 rénqíngwèi human touch; human interest

【人穷志不穷】 rén qióng zhì bù qióng though one is poor, he has lofty aspirations; poor but with lofty ideas

【人穷志短】 rénqióng-zhìduǎn poverty chills ambition

【人权】 rénquán human rights; rights of man

【人权法】 rénquánfǎ Human Right Act

【人权宣言】 rénquán xuānyán 1.（法国的）Declaration of the Rights of Man and of the Citizen（1789）2.（联合国的）Declaration of Human Rights

【人群】 rénqún crowd; throng; multitude

【人人】 rénrén everybody; everyone：～平等。Everyone is equal.（或：All men are equal.）

【人人为我,我为人人】 rénrén-wèiwǒ, wǒwèi-rénrén All for one and one for all.

【人山人海】 rénshān-rénhǎi huge crowds of people; a sea of people：观众～ a bumper audience

【人身】 rénshēn living body of a human being; person

【人身安全】 rénshēn ānquán personal safety

【人身保护】 rénshēn bǎohù physical protection

【人身保险】 rénshēn bǎoxiǎn personal insurance

【人身不可侵犯】 rénshēn bùkě qīnfàn inviolability of the person; personal abuse

【人身攻击】 rénshēn gōngjī personal attack; personal abuse

【人身事故】 rénshēn shìgù personal injury caused by an accident

【人身侮辱】 rénshēn wǔrǔ personal insult

【人身虐待】 rénshēn nüèdài body persecution

【人身自由】 rénshēn zìyóu freedom of person; personal freedom

【人参】 rénshēn ginseng：～酒 ginseng liquor

【人生】 rénshēng life; existence

【人声】 rénshēng voice：～鼎沸 a hubbub of voices

【人生观】 rénshēngguān outlook on life

【人士】 rénshì personage; public figure：党外～ people outside the Party / 官方～ official quarters / 民主～ democratic personage

【人世】 rénshì this world; the world：～沧桑 tremendous changes in the world

【人事】 rénshì 1.（人的处境）human affairs; occurrences in human life 2.（人员调动、安排等）personnel matters：～调动 transfer of personnel 3.（事理人情）ways of the world 4.（人的意识）consciousness of the outside world：不省～ lose consciousness 5.（人力能做到的事）what is humanly possible

【人事变动】 rénshì biàndòng personnel change

【人事部门】 rénshì bùmén personnel department

【人事档案】 rénshì dàng'àn personal file

【人事更迭】 rénshì gēngdié change of staff

【人事关系】 rénshì guānxì organizational affiliation

【人事管理】 rénshì guǎnlǐ personal administration

【人事制度】 rénshì zhìdù personnel system; personnel scheme

【人手】 rénshǒu manpower; hand

【人手一册】 rénshǒu yīcè every one has a copy

【人寿保险】 rénshòu bǎoxiǎn life insurance

【人梯】 réntī human ladder：甘当～ offered to do whatever one can

【人体】 réntǐ human body

【人体残骸】 réntǐ cánhái human remains

【人体骨骼】 réntǐ gǔgé skeleton

【人体模型】 réntǐ móxíng manikin; mannequin

【人体生物钟】 réntǐ shēngwùzhōng biological clock

【人体消化系统】 réntǐ xiāohuà xìtǒng 〈*Physiol.*〉 digestion; digestive system

【人同此心,心同此理】 rén tóng cǐ xīn, xīn tóng cǐ lǐ everybody feels the same about this

【人头】 réntóu 1.（人数）the number of people：按～分 distribute according to the number of people **2.**（和人的关系）relations with people：～熟 know a lot of people **3.**（品质）moral quality；character：～儿次 be not much of a person **4.**（人的头）head

【人微言轻】 rénwēi-yánqīng the words of the lowly carry little weight

【人为】 rénwéi artificial；man-made：～的污染 artificial pollution

【人为财死，鸟为食亡】 rén wèi cái sǐ, niǎo wèi shí wáng Human beings die in pursuit of wealth, and birds die in pursuit of food.（或：The wages of avarice is death.）

【人为刀俎，我为鱼肉】 rén wéi dāozǔ, wǒ wéi yúròu be meat on sb's chopping block；be at sb's mercy

【人文科学】 rénwén kēxué the humanities；humane studies

【人文主义】 rénwén zhǔyì humanism；humanist（adj.）‖人文主义者 humanist

【人物】 rénwù **1.**（指有代表性的人）figure；personage：历史～ a historical figure / 大～ VIP；very important person **2.**（指文艺作品中的人）person（in literature）；character：反面～ negative character / 正面～ positive character **3.**〈*Arts*〉figure painting

【人像】 rénxiàng portrait；image；figure

【人心】 rénxīn **1.**（指感情等）popular feeling；public feeling；the will of the people **2.**（指心地）human feelings；human reason：不得～ unpopular；unreasonable

【人心不古】 rénxīn-bùgū Human heart are not what they were in the old days.

【人心各异，犹如其面】 rénxīn gè yì, yóurú qí miàn Several men, several minds.

【人心叵测】 rénxīn-pǒcè One's heart is past finding out.

【人心所向】 rénxīn-suǒxiàng the popular sentiment；the feelings of the people

【人心向背】 rénxīn-xiàngbèi the feelings of the people

【人行便道】 rénxíng biàndào sidewalk（AmE.）；pavement（BrE.）

【人行道】 rénxíngdào 同"人行便道"

【人行过街地道】 rénxíng guòjiē dìdào pedestrian underpass

【人行横道】 rénxíng héngdào crosswalk（AmE.）；zebra crossing（BrE.）

【人行桥】 rénxíngqiáo footbridge；pedestrian bridge

【人行天桥】 rénxíng tiānqiáo pedestrian overpass；footbridge；pedestrian bridge

【人性】 rénxìng **1.**（人的本性）human nature；humanity **2.**（正常感情和理性）normal human feelings；reason；human（adj.）：毫无～ unfeeling；inhumane / 他的残忍表明他没有～。His cruelty suggests that he is less than human.

【人性论】 rénxìnglùn the theory of human nature

【人选】 rénxuǎn person selected；choice of persons

【人烟】 rényān signs of human habitation：～稀少 with a sparse population / ～稠密 be densely populated

【人言可畏】 rényán-kěwèi gossip is a fearful thing

【人仰马翻】 rényǎng-mǎfān men and horses thrown off their feet；utterly routed

【人样】 rényàng **1.**（人形）human appearance **2.**（有作为的人）a successful person

【人影儿】 rényǐngr **1.**（人的影子）the shadow of a human figure **2.**（人的踪影）the trace of a person's presence；figure：大街上看不到一个～。Not a soul was seen in the street.

【人员】 rényuán personnel；staff：教学～ the teaching staff；the faculty / 专业技能～ efficient staff

【人缘儿】 rényuánr relations with people；popularity

【人云亦云】 rényún-yìyún echo the views of others；parrot

【人造】 rénzào artificial；man-made；imitation

【人造宝石】 rénzào bǎoshí imitation jewel

【人造冰】 rénzàobīng artificial ice

【人造材料】 rénzào cáiliào man-made material

【人造革】 rénzàogé imitation leather；leatherette

【人造黄油】 rénzào huángyóu margarine

【人造棉】 rénzàomián staple rayon

【人造石油】 rénzào shíyóu artificial petroleum

【人造丝】 rénzàosī artificial silk；rayon

【人造卫星】 rénzào wèixīng artificial satellite
【人造纤维】 rénzào xiānwéi artificial fiber
【人造橡胶】 rénzào xiàngjiāo artificial rubber; synthetic rubber
【人造羊毛】 rénzào yángmáo artificial wool
【人造障碍】 rénzào zhàng'ài 〈*Golf*〉 bunker
【人证】 rénzhèng 〈*Law*〉 testimony of a witness：～物证 human testimony and material evidence
【人之常情】 rénzhīchángqíng the way of the world; what is natural and normal (in human relationships)
【人治】 rénzhì rule by man; rule of man：解决法治和～的问题 solve the problem of the rule of law as opposed to the rule of man
【人质】 rénzhì hostage：被扣作～ be held as a hostage
【人中】 rénzhōng 〈*Anat.*〉 philtrum
【人种】 rénzhǒng ethnic group; race; ethnic (adj.)：蒙古～ the Mongolian race
【人种史】 rénzhǒngshǐ ethnography; ethnographical (adj.)
【人种史学者】 rénzhǒngshǐ xuézhě ethnographer
【人种学】 rénzhǒngxué ethnology; ethnics; ethnologic (adj.); ethnological (adj.)
【人种学者】 rénzhǒng xuézhě ethnologist
【人字呢】 rénzìní 〈*Textiles*〉 herringbone

仁 (rén) 1.（仁爱）benevolence; kindheartedness; humanity 2.（敏感）sensitive 3.（果仁）kernel
【仁爱】 rén'ài kindheartedness
【仁慈】 réncí benevolent; merciful; kind
【仁人君子】 rénrén jūnzǐ public-spirited people; benevolent gentlemen
【仁人志士】 rénrén zhìshì people with lofty ideals
【仁兄】 rénxiōng my dear friend
【仁义道德】 rényì dàodé humanity, justice and virtue; virtue and morality
【仁者见仁，智者见智】 rénzhě jiàn rén, zhìzhě jiàn zhì the benevolent see benevolence and the wise see wisdom; different people look at a thing in different way
【仁政】 rénzhèng policy of benevolence; benevolent government
【仁至义尽】 rénzhì-yìjìn do everything called for by humanity and duty; do what is humanly possible to help; show extreme forbearance

忍 (rěn) 1.（忍耐；忍受）bear; endure; tolerate; put up with 2.（忍心）be hard-hearted enough to; have the heart to
【忍不住】 rěn·buzhù unable to bear; cannot help (doing sth.)：～笑 cannot refrain from laughing
【忍饥挨饿】 rěnjī-ái'è stay one's stomach; endure the torments of hunger
【忍俊不禁】 rěnjùn-bùjīn cannot help laughing
【忍耐】 rěnnài exercise patience; exercise restraint; restrain oneself：～不住 cannot restrain oneself from
【忍气吞声】 rěnqì-tūnshēng swallow an insult; submit to humiliation
【忍让】 rěnràng exercise forbearance; be forbearing and conciliatory
【忍辱负重】 rěnrǔ-fùzhòng endure humiliation in order to carry out an important mission
【忍辱偷生】 rěnrǔ-tōushēng live on, bearing one's shame
【忍受】 rěnshòu bear; endure; stand：～侮辱 pocket an insult
【忍痛】 rěntòng very reluctantly：～削价出售 reluctantly sell sth. at a discount
【忍无可忍】 rěnwúkěrěn be driven beyond (the limits of) forbearance; come to the end of one's patience
【忍心】 rěnxīn have the heart to; be hard-hearted enough to：不～ cannot bear to; cannot stand the sight of

荏 (rěn) 1.（软弱）weak; weak-kneed：色厉内～ threatening in manner but cowardly at heart 2.〈*Bot.*〉 common perilla
【荏苒】 rěnrǎn 〈*written*〉 elapse quickly; slip by; pass imperceptibly

稔 (rěn) 1.（庄稼成熟）harvest 2.（熟悉）be familiar with sb.
【稔知】 rěnzhī know well; be quite familiar with

刃［刄］(rèn) 1.（刀刃）the edge of a knife; blade：刀～ knife-edge 2.（刀）sword; knife 3.（用刀杀）kill with a sword or knife
【刃具】 rènjù 〈*Mech.*〉 cutting tool

纫 (rèn) 1.（缝）sew; stitch 2.（纫针）thread (a needle)

【纫针】 rènzhēn thread a needle

韧［靭、靱］(rèn) pliable but strong; tenacious; tough

【韧带】 rèndài 〈*Anat*.〉 ligament

【韧劲】 rènjìn tenacity

【韧性】 rènxìng toughness; tenacity

认［認］(rèn) 1.（认识）recognize; know; make out; identify: 他变化太大，几乎让人～不出了。He had changed so much that one could hardly recognize him. 2.（建立关系）enter into a certain relationship with; adopt 3.（承认）admit; recognize; own 4.（应承）undertake to do sth. ～捐一笔款项 undertake to contribute a sum 5.（认吃亏）accept as unavoidable; resign oneself to: 这房子一定要建，多花钱我也～了。I simply must have the house built, even if I have to spend a lot of money.

【认错】 rèncuò acknowledge a mistake; make an apology; admit a fault

【认得】 rèn·de know; recognize: 我～她。I know her.

【认敌为友】 rèndí-wéiyǒu regard enemies as friends; take the enemy for one's own people; take a foe for a friend

【认定】 rèndìng firmly believe; maintain; hold: 我～这是错的。I maintained that it was wrong.

【认罚】 rènfá admit that one deserve punishment

【认购】 rèngòu offer to buy; subscribe: ～股票 subscribe for shares

【认股特权】 rèngǔ tèquán subscription right

【认股证书】 rèngǔ zhèngshū warrant; stock warrants

【认可】 rènkě approve; accept; confirm

【认了】 rèn·le 1.（接受）accept; tolerate; resign oneself to what is inevitable 2.（承认）admit; acknowledge

【认领】 rènlǐng 1.（辨认并领取）claim: ～失物 claim a lost article 2.（领来抚养）adopt: ～两个孤儿 adopt two orphans

【认明】 rènmíng see clearly; recognize

【认命】 rènmìng accept fate; resign oneself to destiny

【认赔】 rènpéi admit an obligation to pay

【认清】 rènqīng see clearly; recognize; get a clear understanding of: ～形势 get a clear understanding of the situation

【认生】 rènshēng (of a child) be shy with strangers

【认识】 rèn·shi 1.（认得，熟悉）know; understand; recognize: ～某人 know somebody 2.〈*Philos*.〉 understanding; knowledge; cognition: 理性～ rational knowledge / ～来源于实践。Knowledge originates in practice.

【认识功能】 rèn·shi gōngnéng recognizing ability

【认识过程】 rèn·shi guòchéng process of cognition

【认识论】 rèn·shilùn epistemology; theory of knowledge

【认识能力】 rèn·shi nénglì cognitive ability

【认识水平】 rèn·shi shuǐpíng level of understanding

【认识系统】 rèn·shi xìtǒng recognition system

【认输】 rènshū admit defeat; throw in the sponge; give up

【认同】 rèntóng identity: 社会～ social identity

【认为】 rènwéi think; consider; hold; deem: 我不～这是真的。I don't believe it to be true. / 他～美与善是一致的。He identifies beauty with goodness.

【认贼作父】 rènzéizuòfù take the foe for one's father; regard the enemy as kith and kin

【认账】 rènzhàng acknowledge a debt; admit what one has said or done

【认真】 rènzhēn 1.（不马虎）conscientious; earnest; serious: ～执行政策 carry out the policy conscientiously 2.（当真）take seriously; take to heart: 我是说着玩儿的，他就～了。I was only joking, but he took it to heart.

【认证】 rènzhèng 〈*Law*〉 attestation; authentication

【认知】 rènzhī 〈*Physiol*.〉 cognition

【认知测验】 rènzhī cèyàn apperception test

【认知学习】 rènzhī xuéxí cognitive learning

【认字】 rènzì know or learn how to read

【认罪】 rènzuì admit one's guilt; plead guilty

【认罪书】 rènzuìshū statement of confession

【认罪态度】 rènzuì tàidù attitude toward admission of guilt

任 (rèn) 1.(任用) appoint: 新～的市长 the newly appointed mayor of the city 2.(担任) assume a post; take up a job: ～教 take up teaching; work as a teacher 3.(职务) official post; office: 返～ resume charge of the office; return to one's post / 赴～ proceed to take up one's post 4.〈*classifier*〉做过两～大使 have twice been ambassador 5.(听凭) let; allow; give free rein to 6.(无论) no matter (how, what, etc.): ～他怎么说,也别信他。Don't trust him, no matter what he says.

【任便】 rènbiàn as you like; as you see fit: 你去不去～。You may go or not as you see fit.

【任何】 rènhé any; whichever; whatever: 你可以从两个中间挑～一个。You may take either of the two.

【任教】 rènjiào take up teaching or training; work as a teacher

【任劳任怨】 rènláo-rènyuàn work hard and not be upset by criticism; bear responsibility without grudge

【任免】 rènmiǎn appoint and remove

【任免事项】 rènmiǎn shìxiàng appointments and removals

【任命】 rènmìng appoint; commission; designate: ～大使 appoint an ambassador / ～一个委员会 appoint a committee

【任凭】 rènpíng 1.(听凭) at one's convenience; at one's discretion 2.(不管) no matter (how, what, etc.)

【任期】 rènqī term of office; tenure of office

【任情】 rènqíng to one's heart's content

【任人摆布】 rènrén-bǎibù allow oneself to be ordered about

【任人唯亲】 rènrén-wéiqīn appoint people by favoritism

【任人唯贤】 rènrén-wéixián appoint people on their merits; appoint people according to their political integrity and ability

【任人宰割】 rènrén-zǎigē allow oneself to be trampled upon; be partitioned by others at will

【任务】 rènwù task; job; assignment; mission: 光荣而艰巨的～ a glorious but arduous task

【任性】 rènxìng capricious; self-willed; wayward; headstrong: ～恣意 indulge in emotions

【任意】 rènyì 1.(无拘束) wantonly; arbitrarily; willfully 2.(无条件) arbitrary

【任意球】 rènyìqiú 1.〈*Football*〉 free kick 2.〈*Handball*〉 free throw

【任用】 rènyòng appoint; assign sb. to a post

【任择条款】 rènzé tiáokuǎn 〈*Econ.*〉 optional clause

【任职】 rènzhí hold a post; be in office: ～期满 expiration of one's term of office

【任重道远】 rènzhòng-dàoyuǎn the burden is heavy and the road is long; shoulder heavy responsibilities

妊[姙] (rèn) be pregnant

【妊妇】 rènfù pregnant woman

【妊娠】 rènshēn gestation; pregnancy

【妊娠反应】 rènshēn fǎnyìng pregnancy reaction

【妊娠期】 rènshēnqī gestational period; gestation period

【妊娠试验】 rènshēn shìyàn pregnancy tests

【妊娠中毒症】 rènshēn zhòngdúzhèng toxemias of pregnancy

reng

扔 (rēng) 1.(抛) throw; toss; cast: 把球～给某人 toss a ball to sb. 2.(抛弃) throw away; cast aside: 把旧杂志～掉 throw away old magazines

【扔下】 rēngxià abandon; put aside; leave behind: 那个男人～了老婆和孩子。The man abandoned his wife and child.

仍 (réng) 1.(仍旧) remain: 他们～是朋友。They remain friends. / 我进了城,但我兄弟～留在家。I went to the city, but my brother remained at home. 2.(仍然) still; yet: 那事～未解决。The matter is still unsettled.

【仍旧】 réngjiù 1.(照旧) remain the same 2.(仍然) still; yet: ～乐观 be still optimistic

【仍然】 réngrán 〈*adv.*〉 still; yet：他～很忙。He is still busy. / 我父亲～记得他上学的那一天。My father still remembers his first day at school.

ri

日 (rì) **1.**（太阳）sun **2.**（白天）daytime; day：夜以继～ day and night **3.**（天）day：今～ today **4.**（每天）daily; every day; with each passing day：～渐好转 get better every day **5.**（泛指一段时间）time：往～ former days / 工作～ working day / 通知之～ reporting day

【日班】 rìbān day shift：上～ be on the day shift

【日报】 rìbào daily paper; daily：中国～ *China Daily*

【日本】 rìběn Japan; Japanese ‖ 日本人 Japanese

【日本海】 rìběnhǎi Sea of Japan

【日产量】 rìchǎnliàng daily output

【日常】 rìcháng everyday; daily：～开支 daily expenditure / ～食品 daily bread / ～用品 articles for daily use

【日场】 rìchǎng day show; daytime performance

【日程】 rìchéng program; schedule：访问～ itinerary of a visit

【日程表】 rìchéngbiǎo schedule

【日出】 rìchū sunrise; sun-up

【日戳】 rìchuō **1.**（戳子）date stamp; dater **2.**（印记）datemark

【日耳曼人】 Rì'ěrmànrén German; Germanic people

【日工】 rìgōng **1.**（白天的活儿）daywork **2.**（临时工作）day labor **3.**（临时工）day laborer

【日光】 rìguāng **1.**（太阳光）sunlight; sunbeam; daylight **2.**（时光）time

【日光灯】 rìguāngdēng fluorescent lamp; daylight lamp

【日光疗法】 rìguāng liáofǎ heliotherapy

【日光温室】 rìguāng wēnshì heliogreenhouse

【日光浴】 rìguāngyù sunbathe：我喜欢在上午～。I like to sunbathe in the morning.

【日光浴室】 rìguāng yùshì solarium

【日规】 rìguī 同"日晷"

【日晷】 rìguǐ sundial

【日后】 rìhòu in the future; in days to come

【日积月累】 rìjī-yuèlěi accumulate over a long period

【日记】 rìjì diary

【日记本】 rìjìběn diary

【日记账】 rìjìzhàng journal; day book

【日间】 rìjiān in the daytime; during the day

【日间休息】 rìjiān xiūxī day off

【日见】 rìjiàn with each passing day; day by day：～好转 get better every day

【日渐】 rìjiàn with each passing day; day by day：～壮大 be growing steadily

【日界线】 rìjièxiàn International Date Line

【日久】 rìjiǔ with the passing of time; in (the) course of time：～天长 in (the) course of time

【日久见人心】 rìjiǔ jiàn rénxīn time reveals a person's heart; it takes time to know a person

【日喀则】 Rìkāzé 〈place〉 Xigaze

【日刊】 rìkān a daily publication; daily newspaper

【日理万机】 rìlǐ-wànjī attend to numerous affairs of state every day; be occupied with a myriad of state affairs

【日历】 rìlì calendar

【日历表】 rìlìbiǎo 同"日历手表"

【日历年度】 rìlì niándù calendar year

【日历日】 rìlìrì calendar day

【日历手表】 rìlì shǒubiǎo calendar watch

【日落】 rìluò sunset; sundown

【日冕】 rìmiǎn 〈*Astron.*〉 (solar) corona

【日暮途穷】 rìmù-túqióng the day is waning and the road is ending

【日内】 rìnèi in a few days; in a day or two; in a couple of days

【日期】 rìqī date：出生～ date of birth / 发函的～ date of letter / 生效～ effective date / 邮戳～ date of postmark

【日前】 rìqián a few days ago; the other day

【日趋】 rìqū with each passing day; gradually; day by day：～衰落 decline day by day

【日上三竿】 rìshàng-sāngān the sun is three poles high; it's late in the morning

【日射病】 rìshèbìng sunstroke

【日食】 rìshí 〈*Astron*.〉 solar eclipse：日环食 annular eclipse / 日偏食 partial solar eclipse / 日全食 total solar eclipse

【日头】 rì·tou sun

【日托】 rìtuō day care

【日托托儿所】 rìtuō tuō'érsuǒ day nursery

【日心轨道】 rìxīn guǐdào 〈*Astron*.〉 heliocentric orbit

【日心视差】 rìxīn shìchā 〈*Astron*.〉 heliocentric parallax

【日心说】 rìxīnshuō 〈*Astron*.〉 heliocentric theory

【日新月异】 rìxīn-yuèyì change with each passing day：祖国面貌～。The face of our motherland has been changing with each passing day.

【日夜】 rìyè day and night；night and day；round the clock：我们～兼程。We travelled day and night without stopping.

【日夜不宁】 rìyè-bùníng be restless by day and sleepless by night

【日夜操劳】 rìyè-cāoláo work indefatigably day and night

【日夜商店】 rìyè shāngdiàn a shop open night and day；a 24-hour-service shop

【日以继夜】 rìyǐ-jìyè night and day；round the clock

【日益】 rìyì increasingly；day by day：～壮大 getting stronger day by day

【日用】 rìyòng **1**.（生活费用）daily expenses **2**.（日常应用的）of everyday use

【日用必需品】 rìyòng bìxūpǐn daily necessities；household necessities

【日语】 rìyǔ Japanese（language）

【日元】 rìyuán 同“日圆”

【日圆】 rìyuán Yen

【日月】 rìyuè **1**.（日子）life；livelihood **2**.（时间）time

【日月合璧】 rìyuè-hébì High in the sky hang sun and moon.

【日月经天】 rìyuè-jīng tiān be as everlasting as the sun and the moon

【日月如梭】 rìyuè-rúsuō the sun and the moon move back and forth like a shuttle；time flies

【日月同辉】 rìyuè-tónghuī shine forever like the sun and the moon

【日月星辰】 rìyuè-xīngchén the sun, the moon and the stars；the heavenly bodies

【日晕】 rìyùn 〈*Meteorol*.〉 solar halo：～主雨。A solar halo means rain.

【日照】 rìzhào sunshine

【日照计】 rìzhàojì sunshine recorder

【日照时间】 rìzhào shíjiān sunshine time

【日臻】 rìzhēn day by day

【日臻完善】 rìzhēn wánshàn becoming better and approaching perfection day by day

【日志】 rìzhì daily record；journal

【日中】 rìzhōng 〈*written*〉 noon；midday

【日子】 rì·zi **1**.（日期）day；date **2**.（天数）days；time **3**.（生活）life；livelihood：～好过 enjoy a happy life

【日坐愁城】 rìzuò-chóuchéng in deep worry every day

rong

戎（róng） 〈*written*〉 army；military affairs：投笔从～ cast aside the pen to join the army

【戎马】 róngmǎ army horse

【戎马倥偬】 róngmǎ-kǒngzǒng soldier and horses are in great haste；busily engaged in warfare

【戎马生涯】 róngmǎ-shēngyá army life

【戎装】 róngzhuāng martialattire

绒［羢、毧］（róng） **1**.（绒毛）fine hair；down：羽～ eiderdown **2**.（绒布）cloth with pile：长毛～ plush **3**.（刺绣用丝）fine floss for embroidery

【绒布】 róngbù flannelette；cotton flannel

【绒布寺】 Róngbùsì 〈place〉 Rongpu Si

【绒裤】 róngkù sweat pants

【绒毛】 róngmáo **1**.（软毛）fine hair；down **2**.〈*Textiles*〉 nap；pile

【绒线】 róngxiàn **1**.（粗丝线）floss for embroidery **2**.（纯毛线）knitting wool

【绒线刺绣】 róngxiàn cìxiù crewelwork

【绒线衫】 róngxiànshāng woolen sweater

【绒绣】 róngxiù 〈*Arts & Crafts*〉 woolen needlepoint tapestry；woolen embroidery

【绒绣地毯】 róngxiù dìtǎn finished needlepoint carpet

【绒衣】 róngyī sweat shirt

茸（róng） 1.（茸茸）fine and soft; downy 2.（鹿茸）young pilose antler

【茸茸】 róngróng fine, soft and thick; downy：绿茵～ a carpet of green grass

荣[榮]（róng） 1.（茂盛）grow luxuriantly; flourish 2.（光荣）honor; glory：他的父母以他为～。He's an honor to his parents.

【荣归】 rónguī return in glory：～故里 return to one's native place with honor

【荣华富贵】 rónghuá-fùguì glory, splendor, wealth and rank; high position and great wealth

【荣获】 rónghuò have the honor to get or win：～金质奖章 be awarded a gold medal

【荣任】 róngrèn be honored with a post

【荣辱】 róngrǔ honor or disgrace; weal or woe

【荣辱与共】 róngrǔ-yǔgòng share weal or woe：肝胆相照，～ treat each other with all sincerity and share weal or woe

【荣升】 róngshēng be honored by promotion to a higher post

【荣幸】 róngxìng be honored：我～地通知你… I have the honor to inform you that ...

【荣耀】 róngyào honor; glory

【荣誉】 róngyù honor; credit; glory; honorary (adj.)：为祖国争得～ win honor for one's motherland / 你是贵队的～。You're credit to your team.

【荣誉称号】 róngyù chēnghào honorary title：获得～ win the honorary title

【荣誉感】 róngyùgǎn sense of honor

【荣誉奖】 róngyùjiǎng prize of honor; honorable mention

【荣誉军人】 róngyù jūnrén disabled soldier (wounded in revolutionary war)

【荣誉学位】 róngyù xuéwèi honorary degrees

蝾[蠑]（róng）

【蝾螈】 róngyuán 〈*Zool.*〉 newt; fire-bellied newt

容（róng） 1.（容纳）hold; contain：这个阅览室能～100 人。The reading room can hold a hundred people. 2.（宽容）tolerate 3.（容许）permit; allow：不～耽搁 allow of no delay 4.（容貌）facial expression 5.（景象，状态）appearance; looks

【容差】 róngchā allowance; tolerance

【容光焕发】 róngguāng-huànfā one's face glowing with health

【容华绝代】 rónghuá-juédài be endowed with a rare and radiant beauty

【容积】 róngjī volume：这个罐的～是 5 立方米。The volume of this tank is 5 cubic meters.

【容量】 róngliàng capacity：那个容器的～是 30 升。That container has a capacity of 30 liters.

【容貌】 róngmào appearance; looks

【容貌流盼】 róngmào-liúpàn have alluring eyes and exquisite features

【容貌秀丽】 róngmào-xiùlì be of charming appearance; pretty

【容纳】 róngnà hold; have a capacity of; accommodate：一套住房可～一个四口之家。One flat can accommodate a family of four.

【容器】 róngqì container; vessel

【容情】 róngqíng show mercy：我们对坏人是决不～的。We never show mercy to bad people.

【容人】 róngrén tolerant towards others; magnanimous; broad-minded：～之过 be tolerant of other's faults

【容忍】 róngrěn tolerate; put up with; condone

【容身】 róngshēn shelter oneself：～之地 a place to stay

【容许】 róngxǔ 1.（许可）tolerate; permit; allow：如条件～ if conditions permit / 如果我的健康情况～的话 if my health permits 2.（或许）possibly; perhaps

【容颜】 róngyán appearance; looks

【容易】 róngyì 1.（不难）easy; ease (n.)：～处理的局面 a situation easy to handle / ～做的活儿 easy job / 很～跳过去 jump over with ease 2.（可能性大）easily; likely; liable; apt：～发生事故 be prone to accidents

【容重】 róngzhòng unit weight

溶（róng） dissolve：盐～于水。Salt dissolves in water.

【溶出】 róngchū 〈*Cinematog.*〉 dissolve out

【溶化】 rónghuà 1.（溶解）dissolve 2.（融化）melt; thaw; thawing (n.)

【溶剂】 róngjì 〈*Chem.*〉 solvent; dissolvent; menstruum

【溶解】 róngjiě dissolve：水～盐。Water dissolve salt.

【溶解度】 róngjiědù solubility：～曲线 solubility curve

【溶解热】 róngjiěrè heat of solution

【溶菌酶】 róngjūnméi 〈*Biol.*〉 lysozyme; muramidase

【溶菌素】 róngjūnsù 〈*Biol.*〉 bacteriolysin

【溶媒】 róngméi menstruum; resolver

【溶入】 róngrù 〈*Cinematog.*〉 dissolve in

【溶蚀】 róngshí denude; corrosion (n.)

【溶血】 róngxuè 〈*Med.*〉 hemolysis

【溶血现象】 róngxuè xiànxiàng hemolysis

【溶液】 róngyè 〈*Chem.*〉 solution

【溶质】 róngzhì 〈*Chem.*〉 solute

榕 (róng) 〈*Bot.*〉 fig; fig tree

【榕树】 róngshù small fruit fig：孟加拉～ banyan; Indian wild fig

熔 (róng) melt; fuse; smelt

【熔点】 róngdiǎn 〈*Physics*〉 melting point

【熔度】 róngdù meltability

【熔断】 róngduàn 〈*Electr.*〉 fusing

【熔断器】 róngduànqì fuse (box)

【熔化】 rónghuà melt：热使铁～。Heat will melt iron. / 铁烧得很热时，它就～了。Iron will melt when it is made very hot.

【熔剂】 róngjì 〈*Metall.*〉 flux

【熔解】 róngjiě 〈*Physics*〉 fuse; fusion

【熔解热】 róngjiěrè heat of fusion

【熔炼】 róngliàn **1.**（熔化炼制）smelt **2.**（喻锻炼）temper

【熔炉】 rónglú **1.**（熔炼金属的）smelting furnace **2.**（比喻）crucible; furnace：在革命的～中经受锻炼 be tempered in the furnace of revolution

【熔融】 róngróng 〈*Chem.*〉 melt

【熔性】 róngxìng fusibility

【熔岩】 róngyán 〈*Geol.*〉 lava

【熔渣】 róngzhā 〈*Metall.*〉 molten slag

【熔铸】 róngzhù founding; casting

【熔铸工】 róngzhùgōng smelter

融 (róng) **1.**（融化）melt; thaw：阳光使冰消雪～。The sun thawed the ice and melted the snow. **2.**（融合）blend; fuse; be in harmony：水乳交～ be in perfect harmony

【融合】 rónghé mix together; fuse; merge

【融和】 rónghé **1.**（暖和）warm **2.**（融洽）harmonious; on friendly terms **3.** 同"融合"

【融化】 rónghuà melt; thaw; thawing (n.)：有太阳照射时，冰就～。The ice will melt when the sun shines on it.

【融会贯通】 rónghuì-guàntōng achieve mastery through a comprehensive study of the subject

【融解】 róngjiě melt; thaw

【融洽】 róngqià harmonious; on friendly terms：～感情 blend with mutual feeling(s) and understanding

【融融】 róngróng **1.**（和睦快乐）happy and harmonious **2.**（暖和）warm

【融通】 róngtōng **1.**（使流通）circulate **2.**（融会贯通）achieve mastery through a comprehensive study of the subject **3.**（沟通）link up

【融通资金】 róngtōng zījīn circulate necessary funds

【融资】 róngzī **1.**（融通资金）finance; circulate necessary funds; financing (n.) **2.**（指资金）fund

【融资公司】 róngzī gōngsī finance company; finance house

冗［宂］(rǒng) **1.**（多余的）superfluous; redundant：～词 superfluous words **2.**（烦琐）full of trivial details **3.**（繁忙的事）busyness：拨～ find time in the midst of one's work

【冗长】 rǒngcháng tediously long; lengthy; long-winded; prolix

【冗词赘句】 rǒngcí-zhuìjù superfluous words and redundant sentences; verbose

【冗余】 rǒngyú redundancy

【冗员】 rǒngyuán redundant personnel

【冗杂】 rǒngzá many and diverse; miscellaneous

【冗赘】 rǒngzhuì verbose; diffuse：～的句子 a redundant sentence

rou

柔 (róu) **1.**（柔软）soft; supple; flexible **2.**（使变软）soften **3.**（柔和）gentle; yielding; mild

【柔肠寸断】 róucháng-cùnduàn the heart breaks thinking of one's love; brokenhearted

【柔道】 róudào 〈*Sports*〉 judo：他是～六段。(他在～中束黑色横带。) He's a black belt in/at judo.

【柔道运动员】 róudào yùndòngyuán judoka

【柔道摔】 róudàoshuāi 〈*Judo*〉 judo throw

【柔和】 róuhé **1.**(不强烈) soft; gentle; mild：～的灯光 soft light **2.**(柔软) soft

【柔毛】 róumáo pubescence

【柔媚】 róuméi gentle and lovely

【柔嫩】 róunèn tender; delicate：～的皮肤 delicate skin; soft skin

【柔能克刚】 róunéngkègāng softness can overcome the hardest; the soft can conquer the hard

【柔情】 róuqíng tender feelings; tenderness：～似水 tender and soft as water

【柔韧】 róurèn pliable and tough

【柔软】 róuruǎn soft; lithe

【柔弱】 róuruò weak; delicate

【柔术】 róushù 〈*Sports*〉 jujitsu; jiujitsu

【柔顺】 róushùn gentle and agreeable; meek

揉 (róu) **1.**(揉搓) rub：～眼睛 rub one's eyes **2.**(揉成团) knead：～面 knead the dough

【揉此万邦】 róucǐwànbāng subdue all other states; gain domination by war or force

【揉搓】 róucuō rub; knead

糅 (róu) mix; mingle

【糅合】 róuhé mix; form a mixture

蹂 (róu)

【蹂躏】 róulìn trample on; ravage; make havoc of; devastate

鞣 (róu) tan：～皮子 tan hides

【鞣革】 róugé tan; tanning (n.)

【鞣革工人】 róugé gōngrén tanner

【鞣革作坊】 róugé zuō·fang tannery

【鞣料】 róuliào tanning material

【鞣料浸膏】 róuliào jìngāo tanning extract

【鞣酸】 róusuān 〈*Chem.*〉 tannic acid

【鞣制】 róuzhì tan：～皮革 tan leather

肉 (ròu) **1.**(人、动物的肉) meat：肥～ fat meat; fat / 净～ dressed carcass; dressed meat / 生～ raw meat / 瘦～ lean meat / 鲜～ fresh meat / 鸡～ chicken / 牛～ beef / 羊～ mutton / 猪～ pork / 熏～ smoked meat / 吃～ eat meat ‖ 注意：meat 不包括鱼和禽鸟的肉 **2.**(果肉) pulp; flesh (of fruit)

【肉案子】 ròu'àn·zi **1.**(卖肉的) meat counter **2.**(厨房的) meat table

【肉饼】 ròubǐng meat pie

【肉搏】 ròubó fight hand-to-hand

【肉搏战】 ròubózhàn hand-to-hand fight

【肉店】 ròudiàn butcher's (shop)

【肉丁】 ròudīng diced meat

【肉冻】 ròudòng meat jelly; aspic

【肉感】 ròugǎn sexy

【肉桂】 ròuguì 〈*Bot.*〉 Chinese cassia tree; cinnamon

【肉鸡】 ròujī fryer

【肉类加工厂】 ròulèi jiāgōngchǎng meat-packing plant

【肉林酒池】 ròulín-jiǔchí live in the world of wine and women; steeped in wine and surrounded by women

【肉瘤】 ròuliú 〈*Med.*〉 sarcoma

【肉麻】 ròumá nauseating; sickening; disgusting

【肉末】 ròumò minced meat; ground meat

【肉牛】 ròuniú beef cattle

【肉排】 ròupái steak

【肉皮】 ròupí pork skin

【肉片】 ròupiàn sliced meat

【肉禽】 ròuqín butcher's beast; table poultry

【肉色】 ròusè yellowish pink

【肉食】 ròushí **1.**(肉类食物) meat **2.**(以肉类为食物) carnivorous：～动物 carnivorous animal; carnivore

【肉丝】 ròusī shredded meat

【肉丝炒面】 ròusī chǎomiàn julienne pork fried noodles

【肉丝面】 ròusīmiàn noodles with shredded meat

【肉松】 ròusōng dried meat floss

【肉汤】 ròutāng broth

【肉体】 ròutǐ the human body; flesh

【肉丸子】 ròuwán·zi meatball

【肉馅】 ròuxiàn meat stuffing; chopped meat

【肉刑】 ròuxíng corporal punishment

【肉芽】 ròuyá 〈*Med.*〉granulation
【肉眼】 ròuyǎn naked eye：～看不到 be invisible to the naked eye
【肉眼检查】 ròuyǎn jiǎnchá macrography
【肉用鸡】 ròuyòngjī fryer
【肉用家禽】 ròuyòng jiāqín butcher's beast; table poultry
【肉用牛】 ròuyòngniú beef cattle
【肉用羊】 ròuyòngyáng mutton sheep
【肉用仔鸡】 ròuyòng zǐjī broiler
【肉欲】 ròuyù carnal desire
【肉汁】 ròuzhī gravy; (meat) juice
【肉质果】 ròuzhìguǒ 〈*Bot.*〉fleshy fruit
【肉质水果】 ròuzhì shuǐguǒ pulpy fruit
【肉中刺】 ròuzhōngcì a thorn in one's flesh
【肉猪】 ròuzhū pork
【肉赘】 ròuzhuì wart

ru

如(rú) **1.**(依照) in compliance with; according to：～数付清 pay in full **2.**(如同) like; as; as if **3.**(比得上) can compare with; be as good as：我不～她。I'm no match for her. **4.**(比如) for instance; such as; as **5.** 〈*conj.*〉if：～遇火警,即按警铃。In case of fire, ring the alarm bell.
【如常】 rúcháng as usual
【如出一辙】 rúchūyīzhé be exactly the same as; be no different from; be cut from the same cloth
【如此】 rúcǐ so; such; in this way; like that：～等等 and so on and so forth
【如此而已】 rúcǐ éryǐ that's what it all adds up to; that's all there is to it
【如次】 rúcì as follows：原文～。The text is as follows.
【如堕烟海】 rúduòyānhǎi as if lost on a misty sea; all at sea; completely at a loss
【如法炮制】 rúfǎ-páozhì prepare herbal medicine by the prescribed method; follow a set pattern; follow suit
【如飞】 rúfēi like flying; quickly; swiftly
【如风过耳】 rúfēng-guò'ěr turn a deaf ear to
【如夫人】 rúfūrén a concubine
【如鲠在喉】 rúgěng-zàihóu like a fish bone getting stuck in the throat; necessary to give vent to one's pent-up feelings
【如故】 rúgù **1.**(和原来一样) as before **2.**(就像老朋友一样) like old friends：一见～ feel like old friends at the first meeting
【如果】 rúguǒ 〈*conj.*〉if; in case; in the event of：～她来的话,告诉我一声。In case she comes, let me know.
【如何】 rúhé how; what：你近来情况～? How are things with you?
【如虎添翼】 rúhǔtiānyì like a tiger that has grown wings; with might redoubled
【如花似玉】 rúhuā-sìyù as pretty as a flower; as pretty as flower and jade
【如火如荼】 rúhuǒ-rútú like a raging fire
【如获至宝】 rúhuòzhìbǎo as if one had found a treasure
【如饥似渴】 rújī-sìkě as if thirsting or hungering for sth.; eagerly：～地学习 study with great eagerness
【如胶似漆】 rújiāo-sìqī stick to each other like glue or lacquer; remain glued to each other; be deeply attached to each other
【如今】 rújīn nowadays; now：～人们乘飞机旅行。Nowadays people travel by plane. / 他原来是教师,但～搞出版。He used to be a teacher, but now he works in publishing.
【如旧】 rújiù as usual
【如来】 Rúlái 〈*Buddhism*〉Tathagata; Buddha
【如临大敌】 rúlíndàdí as if faced with a formidable enemy
【如履薄冰】 rú lǚ bóbīng as though treading on thin ice; be very careful; acting with extreme caution
【如梦初醒】 rúmèngchūxǐng as if awakening from a dream; beginning to see the light
【如鸟兽散】 rúniǎoshòusàn flee helter-skelter; be utterly routed
【如牛负重】 rúniúfùzhòng like an ox carrying a heavy load
【如期】 rúqī as scheduled; by the scheduled time; on schedule：～完成 finish on schedule
【如其】 rúqí 〈*conj.*〉if
【如切如磋】 rúqiē-rúcuō like 'cutting and grinding' stones; to learn from each other
【如日中天】 rúrìzhōngtiān like the sun at high noon; at the zenith of one's power, career,

etc.

【如入无人之境】 rú rù wú rén zhī jìng like entering an unpeopled land; breaking all resistance

【如若】 rúruò 〈*conj.*〉 if: ～不然 if not; otherwise

【如丧家之犬】 rú sàng jiā zhī quǎn like a dog with the tail between the legs; like a dog without its master

【如丧考妣】 rúsàngkǎobǐ look as if one had lost one's parents; look utterly wretched

【如上】 rúshàng as above

【如实】 rúshí strictly according to the facts; as things really are

【如释重负】 rúshìzhòngfù as if relieved of a heavy load

【如数家珍】 rúshǔjiāzhēn as if enumerating one's family valuables; very familiar with one's subject

【如数】 rúshù exactly the number or amount; in full: ～偿还 recompense in full

【如同】 rútóng like; as: ～草芥 be no more than the weeds by the roadside

【如下】 rúxià as follows: 发表～声明 make the following statement

【如新】 rúxīn brand as if it were new

【如一】 rúyī without change; consistent

【如意】 rúyì as one wishes: 称心～ after one's own heart

【如意算盘】 rúyì-suàn·pan wishful thinking: 打～ indulge in wishful thinking

【如蝇逐臭】 rúyíngzhúchòu run after filth, as flies swarm around garbage; like flies taking to rottenness; like flies swarming about a bit of filth

【如影随形】 rúyǐngsuíxíng like the shadow following the person; very closely associated with each other

【如鱼得水】 rúyúdéshuǐ feel just like fish in water; be in one's element

【如愿】 rúyuàn as one wishes; as one expected

【如愿以偿】 rúyuàn-yǐcháng have one's wish fulfilled; achieve what one wishes

【如约】 rúyuē as agreed upon

【如之奈何】 rúzhīnàihé What can be done about it?

【如坐针毡】 rúzuòzhēnzhān be on pins and needles; be on tenterhooks

茹 (rú) 〈*written*〉 eat

【茹毛饮血】 rúmáo-yǐnxuè eat birds and animals raw

铷 (rú) 〈*Chem.*〉 rubidium (元素符号 Rb)

儒 (rú) **1.** (儒家) Confucianism; Confucianist; Confucian (adj.) **2.** (旧指读书人) scholar; learned man: 腐～ pedantic scholar

【儒艮】 rúgèn 〈*Zool.*〉 dugong; sea cow

【儒家】 rújiā the Confucian school; the Confucianists; Confucian (adj.)

【儒教】 Rújiào Confucianism

【儒略历】 Rúlüèlì Julian calendar

【儒学】 rúxué the Confucian school

濡 (rú) **1.** (沾湿) immerse; moisten **2.** (迟滞) linger

【濡染】 rúrǎn immerse; imbue

【濡湿】 rúshī soak; make wet

孺 (rú) child: 妇～ women and children

【孺子】 rúzǐ 〈*written*〉 child

【孺子可教】 rúzǐ-kějiào The young man is worthy to be taught.

蠕 [蝡] (rú) wriggle; squirm

【蠕变】 rúbiàn creep; creep deformation

【蠕虫】 rúchóng worm; helminth

【蠕动】 rúdòng **1.** (爬动) wriggle; squirm **2.** 〈*Physiol.*〉 peristalsis; peristaltic (adj.) **3.** 〈*Geol.*〉 creep

【蠕动波】 rúdòngbō 〈*Geol.*〉 peristaltic wave

【蠕动消失】 rúdòng xiāoshī 〈*Physiol.*〉 loss of peristalsis

【蠕动音】 rúdòngyīn 〈*Physiol.*〉 peristaltic sound

【蠕蠕】 rúrú wriggling; squirming: ～而动 crawl out

汝 (rǔ) you; your

【汝等】 rǔděng you; yours

乳 (rǔ) **1.** (乳房) breast **2.** (奶汁) milk: 炼～ condensed milk **3.** (像奶汁的东西) any milk-like liquid: 豆～ bean milk / 发～

hair cream / 洗面～ face-washing milk **4.** (初生的) newborn (animal); sucking: ～猪 sucking pig; suckling pig
【乳白】 rǔbái milky white; cream color
【乳齿】 rǔchǐ milk tooth; deciduous tooth
【乳儿】 rǔ'ér nursing infant; suckling
【乳房】 rǔfáng **1.** (指人的) breast; mamma **2.** (指动物的) udder
【乳房切除】 rǔfáng qiēchú 〈*Med.*〉 mastectomy
【乳剂】 rǔjì 〈*Chem.*〉 emulsion
【乳胶】 rǔjiāo 〈*Chem.*〉 emulsion
【乳胶漆】 rǔjiāoqī emulsion paint; latex paint
【乳酪】 rǔlào cheese
【乳名】 rǔmíng infant name; child's pet name
【乳母】 rǔmǔ wet nurse
【乳牛】 rǔniú dairy cattle; milch cow
【乳牛场】 rǔniúchǎng dairy farm
【乳品】 rǔpǐn milkings
【乳品业】 rǔpǐnyè dairy
【乳酸】 rǔsuān lactic acid
【乳酸钙】 rǔsuāngài calcium lactate
【乳糖】 rǔtáng milk sugar; lactose
【乳糖酶】 rǔtángméi lactase
【乳头】 rǔtóu **1.** (奶头) nipple; teat; mammilla **2.** (奶头状物) papilla: 视神经～ optic papilla
【乳头轮】 rǔtóulún 〈*Anat.*〉 areola
【乳头状瘤】 rǔtóuzhuàngliú papilloma
【乳腺】 rǔxiàn 〈*Anat.*〉 mammary gland
【乳腺癌】 rǔxiàn'ái 〈*Med.*〉 breast cancer
【乳腺瘤】 rǔxiànliú 〈*Med.*〉 mastadenoma
【乳腺炎】 rǔxiànyán 〈*Med.*〉 mastitis
【乳香】 rǔxiāng frankincense
【乳臭未干】 rǔxiù-wèigān still smell of one's mother's milk; be young and inexperienced; be wet behind the ears
【乳牙】 rǔyá milk tooth; deciduous tooth
【乳罩】 rǔzhào brassiere; bra
【乳汁】 rǔzhī milk
【乳脂】 rǔzhī butterfat
【乳脂糖】 rǔzhītáng toffee; taffy
【乳制品】 rǔzhìpǐn dairy products

辱 (rǔ) **1.** (耻辱) disgrace; dishonor **2.** (使受辱) bring disgrace to; insult
【辱骂】 rǔmà abuse; call sb. names; hurl insults
【辱命】 rǔmìng fail to accomplish a mission
【辱没】 rǔmò bring disgrace to; be unworthy of

入 (rù) **1.** (进入) enter: ～冬以来 since winter has set in / ～夜 at nightfall **2.** (加入) join; be admitted into; become a member of: ～党 be admitted into Chinese Communist Party; join the Party **3.** (收入) income; means **4.** (合乎) conform to; agree with
【入不敷出】 rùbùfūchū run behind one's expenses; income falling short of expenditure; one's income is not adequate to one's needs
【入仓】 rùcāng be stored in a barn; be put in storage
【入场】 rùchǎng enter; entrance (n.); admit; admission (v.)
【入场费】 rùchǎngfèi entrance fee; price of admission
【入场券】 rùchǎngquàn (admission) ticket
【入超】 rùchāo unfavorable balance of trade; import surplus
【入定】 rùdìng 〈*Buddhism*〉 sit quietly and meditate
【入肚】 rùdù eat; enter the stomach
【入耳】 rù'ěr pleasant to the ear: 不堪～ offensive to the ear
【入伏】 rùfú beginning of the hottest part of the summer: ～以来 since the dog days began
【入港】 rùgǎng **1.** (进港) enter a port **2.** (谈得投机) in full agreement; in perfect harmony
【入彀】 rùgòu in full agreement; in perfect harmony
【入股】 rùgǔ buy a share; become a shareholder
【入骨】 rùgǔ to the marrow: 恨之～ bear a bitter hatred for sb. or sth.
【入国问禁】 rùguó-wènjìn ask about taboos and bans upon arrival in a foreign country
【入国问禁,入乡随俗】 rùguó-wènjìn, rùxiāng-suísú When in Rome do as the Romans do.
【入画】 rùhuà suitable for a painting; picturesque: 黄山山景,处处可以～。Every bit of Huangshan Mountain scenery is worth painting.

【入伙】 rùhuǒ **1.**（加入某集团）join a gang; join in partnership **2.**（入集体伙食）join a mess

【入籍】 rùjí naturalize; naturalization (n.)

【入籍者】 rùjízhě naturalized person

【入寂】 rùjì 〈*Buddhism*〉 dead

【入境】 rùjìng enter a country

【入境登记】 rùjìng dēngjì entrance registration

【入境护照】 rùjìng hùzhào entry passport

【入境口岸】 rùjìng kǒu'àn port of entry

【入境签证】 rùjìng qiānzhèng entry visa

【入境申报单】 rùjìng shēnbàodān customs declaration made at the time of entry

【入境手续】 rùjìng shǒuxù entry formalities; entry procedures

【入境问俗】 rùjìng-wènsú on entering a country, inquire about its customs

【入境许可证】 rùjìng xǔkězhèng entry permit

【入境证书】 rùjìng zhèngshū entry certificate

【入口】 rùkǒu **1.**（入嘴）enter the mouth **2.**（进入的门）entrance：车站～ entrance to the station **3.**（进口）import; importation (n.)

【入口处通道】 rùkǒuchù tōngdào access road

【入寇】 rùkòu invade

【入库】 rùkù be put in storage; be laid up：正常～ normal storage

【入款】 rùkuǎn income; receipts

【入殓】 rùliàn put a corpse in a coffin; encoffin

【入列】 rùliè 〈*Mil.*〉 take one's place in the ranks; fall in

【入寐】 rùmèi fall asleep

【入门】 rùmén **1.**（初步学会）cross the threshold; learn the rudiments of a subject **2.**（指初级读物）elementary course; ABC：《摄影～》*The ABC of Photography*

【入梦】 rùmèng **1.**（入睡）fall asleep **2.**（出现在梦中）appear in one's dream

【入迷】 rùmí be fascinated; be enchanted

【入眠】 rùmián fall asleep

【入魔】 rùmó be infatuated; be spellbound

【入木三分】 rùmù-sānfēn **1.**（书法有力）written in a forceful hand. **2.**（议论深刻）penetrating; profound; keen

【入脑】 rùnǎo be accepted willingly by and left a deep impression on the people

【入侵】 rùqīn invade; intrude; make an incursion

【入情入理】 rùqíng-rùlǐ be fair and reasonable; perfectly logical and reasonable

【入射口】 rùshèkǒu entrance port

【入神】 rùshén **1.**（兴趣浓厚）be entranced; be enthralled：那紧张的故事使他看得～了。He was enthralled by the exciting story. **2.**（精妙）superb; marvellous

【入时】 rùshí fashionable; becoming

【入手】 rùshǒu start with; begin with; proceed from; take as the point of departure：从基本训练～ start with the basic training

【入睡】 rùshuì go to sleep; fall asleep

【入土】 rùtǔ be buried; be interred

【入土为安】 rùtǔwéi'ān be laid to rest; have one's bones buried; burial brings peace to the deceased

【入托】 rùtuō start going to a nursery

【入微】 rùwēi in every possible way; in a subtle way：体贴～ show every possible consideration

【入围】 rùwéi enter the final contest; be selected or elected as one of the few

【入味】 rùwèi **1.**（有滋味）tasty **2.**（有趣味）interesting

【入伍】 rùwǔ enlist in the armed forces; join up

【入席】 rùxí take one's seat at a banquet, ceremony, etc.

【入乡随俗】 rùxiāng-suísú While in Rome, do as the Romans do.

【入选】 rùxuǎn be selected; be chosen

【入学】 rùxué **1.**（开始上小学）start school **2.**（开始进学校）enter a school

【入学考试】 rùxué kǎoshì entrance exam; entrance examination

【入学年龄】 rùxué niánlíng school age

【入眼】 rùyǎn pleasing to the eye

【入药】 rùyào 〈*Chin. Pharm.*〉 be used as medicine

【入夜】 rùyè at nightfall

【入狱】 rùyù be put in prison; be sent to jail

【入院】 rùyuàn be admitted to hospital; be hospitalized

【入账】 rùzhàng enter an item in an account;

enter into the account book
【入赘】 rùzhuì marry into and live with one's bride's family
【入坐】 rùzuò set down
【入座】 rùzuò 同"入坐"
溽(rù) 〈*written*〉 humid; damp
【溽暑】 rùshǔ sweltering summer weather
缛(rù) elaborate; cumbersome: 繁文～节 unnecessary and overelaborate formalities; red tape
褥(rù) cotton-padded mattress
【褥疮】 rùchuāng 〈*Med.*〉 bedsore; decubitus ulcer; pressure sore
【褥单】 rùdān bed sheet
【褥套】 rùtào **1.**(布套) bedding sack **2.**(褥子的棉花胎) cotton padding for a bedtick **3.**(褥子的布罩) mattress cover
【褥子】 rù·zi cotton-padded mattress

ruan

阮(ruǎn) 〈*Music*〉 *ruan*; a plucked stringed instrument
【阮囊羞涩】 ruǎnnáng-xiūsè embarrassingly short of money; lacking sufficient funds to meet necessary expenses
软[輭](ruǎn) **1.**(与"硬"相反) soft; flexible; supple; pliable: ～床 soft bed / ～椅 soft chair **2.**(柔和) soft; mild; gentle **3.**(软弱) weak; feeble: 她两腿发～。Her legs felt weak. **4.**(差) poor: 货色～ poor in quality / 能力～ poor in ability **5.**(容易动摇) easily moved or influenced: 耳朵～ credulous and pliable
【软百叶窗】 ruǎnbǎiyèchuāng 〈*Archit.*〉 venetian blind
【软包装】 ruǎnbāozhuāng soft packing
【软磁盘】 ruǎncípán disk; floppy disk: 双面高密～ double sided, high density disk
【软磁盘系统】 ruǎncípán xìtǒng floppy disk system
【软贷款】 ruǎndàikuǎn soft loan
【软刀子】 ruǎndāo·zi soft knife; a way of harming people imperceptibly
【软底鞋】 ruǎndǐxié soft sole
【软电线】 ruǎndiànxiàn cord
【软缎】 ruǎnduàn soft silk fabric in satin weave
【软腭】 ruǎn'è 〈*Anat.*〉 soft palate
【软耳朵】 ruǎn'ěr·duo easy of belief
【软风】 ruǎnfēng **1.**(和风) gentle breeze **2.**〈*Meteorol.*〉 light air
【软膏】 ruǎngāo ointment; paste
【软骨】 ruǎngǔ 〈*Anat.*〉 cartilage
【软骨瘤】 ruǎngǔliú 〈*Med.*〉 chondroma
【软骨头】 ruǎngǔ·tou a weak-kneed person; a spineless person; a coward
【软管】 ruǎnguǎn flexible pipe; flexible tube; hose: 铠装～ armored hose
【软化】 ruǎnhuà **1.**(变软) soften **2.**(变为动摇) win over by soft tactics **3.**〈*Tan*〉 bating
【软化栽培】 ruǎnhuà zāipéi 〈*Agric.*〉 blanching culture
【软话】 ruǎnhuà gentle words
【软环境】 ruǎnhuánjìng soft environment: 开发区的～日臻完善。In developing region the soft environment is being perfected.
【软和】 ruǎn·huo **1.**(柔软) soft **2.**(柔和) gentle; kind; soft: 说几句～话 say some kind words
【软货物】 ruǎnhuòwù soft goods
【软件】 ruǎnjiàn 〈*Computer*〉 software
【软件包】 ruǎnjiànbāo 〈*Computer*〉 software package
【软件跟踪方式】 ruǎnjiàn gēnzōng fāngshì software trace mode
【软件工程师】 ruǎnjiàn gōngchéngshī software engineer
【软件公司】 ruǎnjiàn gōngsī software house
【软件开发】 ruǎnjiàn kāifā software development
【软件库】 ruǎnjiànkù software library
【软件模型化】 ruǎnjiàn móxínghuà software modularity
【软禁】 ruǎnjìn put sb. under house arrest; house arrest; house confinement
【软科学】 ruǎnkēxué soft science
【软肋骨】 ruǎnlèigǔ 〈*Anat.*〉 costal cartilage
【软绵绵】 ruǎnmiánmián **1.**(柔软) soft **2.**(软弱无力) weak
【软磨】 ruǎnmó use soft tactics
【软木】 ruǎnmù cork

【软木画】 ruǎnmùhuà cork patchwork
【软木塞】 ruǎnmùsāi cork (as a stopper)
【软盘】 ruǎnpán 〈*Computer*〉 disk; floppy disk
【软皮本】 ruǎnpíběn 〈*Printing*〉 softback
【软皮鞋】 ruǎnpíxié loafer shoes
【软片】 ruǎnpiàn (a roll of) film
【软铅笔】 ruǎnqiānbǐ soft pencil
【软任务】 ruǎnrènwù soft task
【软弱】 ruǎnruò **1.**(无力) weak; feeble: 我生病时很～。I felt feeble when I was ill. **2.**(不坚强) weak; flabby: ～可欺 be weak and easy to bully
【软商品】 ruǎnshāngpǐn soft merchandise: 技术成果和信息被称为～ technical achievements and information are called the soft merchandise
【软食】 ruǎnshí soft diet; soft food; pap
【软式推销法】 ruǎnshì tuīxiāofǎ soft sell
【软水】 ruǎnshuǐ soft water
【软糖】 ruǎntáng soft sweets; jelly drops
【软梯】 ruǎntī 〈*colloq.*〉 rope ladder
【软体动物】 ruǎntǐ dòngwù mollusk; mollusc
【软通货】 ruǎntōnghuò soft currency
【软卧】 ruǎnwò soft sleeper
【软武器】 ruǎnwǔqì soft weapons
【软席】 ruǎnxí 〈*Transport*〉 soft seat or berth; cushioned seat or berth
【软席车厢】 ruǎnsí chēxiāng railway carriage with soft seats or berths
【软性肥皂】 ruǎnxìng féizào soft soap
【软饮料】 ruǎnyǐnliào soft drink; non-alcoholic beverage
【软硬兼施】 ruǎnyìng jiānshī use both hard and soft tactics; couple threats with promises
【软语温存】 ruǎnyǔ-wēncún have many caressing and affectionate words to say to one another
【软脂】 ruǎnzhī palmitin
【软脂酸】 ruǎnzhīsuān palmitic acid; palmic acid
【软指标】 ruǎnzhǐbiāo soft target; soft index
【软着陆】 ruǎnzhuólù soft landing
【软组织】 ruǎnzǔzhī 〈*Anat.*〉 soft tissue

rui

蕊[蕋、橤] (ruǐ) 〈*Bot.*〉 stamen; pistil: 雌～ pistil / 雄～ stamen

锐 (ruì) **1.**(锐利) sharp; keen; acute **2.**(急剧) radical; sharp **3.**(锐气) vigor; fighting spirit
【锐不可当】 ruìbùkědāng can't be held back; be irresistible
【锐减】 ruìjiǎn sharp decline; rapid decrease
【锐角三角形】 ruìjiǎo sānjiǎoxíng acute-angled triangle
【锐利】 ruìlì sharp; keen: ～的眼光 sharp-eyed; sharp-sighted
【锐敏】 ruìmǐn sensitive; keen
【锐器伤】 ruìqìshāng 〈*Law*〉 injury from sharp utensil; sharp instrument injury
【锐气】 ruìqì dash; drive: 青年人的～ dashing spirit of young people
【锐意改革】 ruìyì gǎigé have been working hard to carry out reform; reform with keen determination

瑞 (ruì) auspicious; lucky
【瑞雪】 ruìxuě timely snow; auspicious snow
【瑞雪纷飞】 ruìxuě-fēnfēi Snow falls thick and fast.
【瑞雪兆丰年】 ruìxuě zhào fēngnián A fall of seasonable snow gives promise of a fruitful year.

run

闰 (rùn) 〈*Astron.*〉 intercalary
【闰年】 rùnnián leap year; intercalary year
【闰月】 rùnyuè intercalary month; leap month

润 (rùn) **1.**(细腻光滑) moist; smooth; sleek **2.**(加油或水) moisten; lubricate **3.**(使有光彩) embellish; touch up **4.**(好处) profit; benefit
【润笔】 rùnbǐ remuneration for a writer, painter or calligrapher
【润肤洗液】 rùnfū xǐyè skin toning lotion
【润滑】 rùnhuá lubricate: 汽车发动机需要用油很好地～。A car engine needs to be well lubricated with oil.
【润滑系统】 rùnhuá xìtǒng lubricating system; lubrication system

【润滑油】 rùnhuáyóu lubricating oil; lubrication oil

【润滑脂】 rùnhuázhī (lubricating) grease

【润色】 rùnsè polish; touch up: 我想这篇文章得～～。I thought the article had been touched up.

【润泽】 rùnzé 1.(滋润) moist; smooth; sleek: 2.(使滋润) moisten; lubricate: 用油～轮轴 oil the axle

ruo

若 (ruò) 1.(好像) like; seem; as if 2.(如果) if

【若不然】 ruòbùrán if not; otherwise

【若非】 ruòfēi if not; were it not for: ～我那时亲眼看到, 我是不会相信的。Were it not for the fact that I saw it with my own eyes, I wouldn't believe it.

【若干】 ruògān 1.(一些) several; a number of; certain 2.(多少) how many; how much

【若即若离】 ruòjí-ruòlí be neither friendly nor aloof; maintain a lukewarm relationship; keep sb. at arm's length

【若明若暗】 ruòmíng-ruò'àn have an indistinct picture of; have a hazy notion about

【若是】 ruòshì 〈*conj.*〉 if: 我～你, 我就去。If I were you, I would go.

【若无其事】 ruòwúqíshì as if nothing had happened; calmly; casually

【若要人不知, 除非己莫为】 ruò yào rén bù zhī, chúfēi jǐ mò wéi if you don't want others to know about it, don't do it

【若隐若现】 ruòyǐn-ruòxiàn partly hidden and partly visible; appear indistinctly

【若有所失】 ruòyǒusuǒshī feel as if sth. were missing; look distracted

【若有所思】 ruòyǒusuǒsī as if thinking of something; as if deep in thought; seem lost in thought

偌 (ruò) such; so

【偌大】 ruòdà 1 of such a size; so big

箬[篛] (ruò)

【箬竹】 ruòzhú 〈*Bot.*〉 indocalamus

弱 (ruò) 1.(软弱) weak; feeble: ～国 a weak nation 2.(年幼) young 3.(差) inferior 4.(略少) a little less than: 五分之一～ a little less than one-fifth

【弱不禁风】 ruòbùjīnfēng too weak to stand a gust of wind; extremely delicate; fragile

【弱不胜衣】 ruòbùshèngyī too frail to bear the weight of one's clothes

【弱点】 ruòdiǎn weakness; weak point; failing: 人类的～ human weakness / 她的主要～是花钱太多。Spending too much money is her main weakness.

【弱读式】 ruòdúshì weak form

【弱化】 ruòhuà be weakening and disappearing: 农民式的乡土观念日益～。Peasant provincialism is weakening and disappearing.

【弱肉强食】 ruòròu-qiángshí the weak are the prey of the strong; the law of the jungle

【弱视】 ruòshì amblyopia; weak sight

【弱项】 ruòxiàng 〈*Sports*〉 weak sports

【弱小】 ruòxiǎo small and weak: ～国家 a small and weak country

【弱音器】 ruòyīnqì 〈*Music*〉 mute

【弱智】 ruòzhì mental retardation

【弱智儿童】 ruòzhì értóng mentally retarded children; mentally impaired children

S

sa

撒(sā) 1.(放开) cast; let go; let out: ～腿就跑 make off at once; take off at once / 往水里～网 cast a net into the water 2.(尽量施展) throw off all restraint; let oneself go: ～泼 be shrewish and make a scene
(另见“撒”sǎ)

【撒谎】 sāhuǎng 〈*colloq.*〉 tell a lie; lie: 你在～。You are telling lies.

【撒娇】 sājiāo act like a spoiled child

【撒娇装嗔】 sājiāo-zhuānchēn act as a spoiled child; act in a pettishly charming manner

【撒拉族】 Sālāzú Salar (中国少数民族,主要分布在青海、甘肃等地)

【撒赖】 sālài make a scene; act shamelessly; raise hell

【撒尿】 sāniào 〈*colloq.*〉 piss; pee

【撒气】 sāqì 1.(轮胎等漏气) leak; go soft; get a flat: 前带～了。The front tire has got a puncture. 2.(拿他人发泄怒气) vent one's anger or ill temper: 你别拿他～。Don't take it out on him.

【撒手】 sāshǒu let go one's hold; let go: 抓住绳子,别～。Hold the rope tight. Don't let it go.

【撒手归西】 sāshǒu-guīxī go to the Western Heaven; to die; pass away; pay the debt of nature

【撒野】 sāyě act wildly; behave atrociously: 对人～ be rude to sb.

洒[灑](sǎ) sprinkle; spray; spill; shed: 墨水～在书桌上了。The ink has spilt on the desk.
(另见“撒”sā)

【洒粉】 sǎfěn powder; powdering (n.)

【洒泪】 sǎlèi shed tears

【洒扫】 sǎsǎo sprinkle water and sweep the floor; sweep: ～庭院 sweep the courtyard

【洒水】 sǎshuǐ sprinkle water: ～扫地 sprinkle water and sweep the floor

【洒水车】 sǎshuǐchē watering car; sprinklers; spraying car; water-barrow

【洒水机】 sǎshuǐjī water sprayer

【洒脱】 sǎ·tuo free and easy: 举止～ have an easy and unaffected manner

撒(sǎ) 1.(散布) scatter; sprinkle; spread: ～化肥 spread chemical fertilizer / 往食物上～盐 sprinkle food with salt / 把糖～在蛋糕上 sprinkle sugar on the cake 2.(洒落) spill; drop: 别把咖啡～了。Don't spill the coffee.

【撒播】 sǎbō broadcast sowing

【撒播机】 sǎbōjī broadcast seeder; broadcaster

【撒胡椒面】 sǎ hújiāomiàn sprinkle pepper: 用～的办法不能取得好的经济效益 good economic results cannot be achieved by ‘sprinkling pepper’

【撒施】 sǎshī 〈*Agric.*〉 spread fertilizer over the fields; broadcast (fertilizer)

【撒种】 sǎzhǒng scatter seeds; spread seeds

卅(sà) thirty; thirtieth

飒(sà)

【飒然】 sàrán 〈*written*〉 soughing

【飒飒】 sàsà 〈*onomat*〉 sough; rustle

【飒爽】 sàshuǎng 〈*written*〉 of martial bearing; valiant: ～英姿 bright and brave

脎(sà) 〈*Chem.*〉 osazone

萨[薩](sà)

【萨克管】 sàkèguǎn 〈*Music*〉 saxophone

【萨克号】 sàkèhào 〈*Music*〉 saxhorn

【萨克斯】 sàkèsī 同“萨克管”

sai

腮[顋](sāi) cheek

【腮帮子】 sāibāng·zi 〈*colloq*.〉 cheek

【腮托】 sāituō 〈*Music*〉 chin rest

【腮腺】 sāixiàn 〈*Anat*.〉 parotid gland

【腮腺炎】 sāixiànyán parotitis：流行性～ mumps

鳃(sāi) gills

【鳃盖】 sāigài gill cover

塞(sāi) 1.(堵住;填入) fill in; squeeze in; stuff：把东西～进箱子 stuff things into a trunk / 管子被脏东西～住了。The pipe was clogged with dirt. 2.(塞子) stopper
(另见"塞"sài, sè)

【塞车】 sāichē traffic jam; jam (v.)：我们因～给堵了两个小时。We were stuck in a traffic jam for two hour. / 路上～有好几公里。The traffic was jammed up for kilometers.

【塞环】 sāihuán ring of plug

【塞套】 sāitào plug sleeve

【塞条】 sāitiáo 〈*Med*.〉 tent

【塞子】 sāi·zi stopper; cork; plug; spigot

噻(sāi)

【噻吩】 sāifēn 〈*Chem*.〉 thiophene

【噻唑】 sāizuò 〈*Chem*.〉 thiazole

塞(sài) a place of strategic importance; fortress
(另见"塞"sāi, sè)

【塞北】 sàiběi beyond the Great Wall

【塞外】 sàiwài beyond the Great Wall：～风光 a northern-frontier scene

【塞翁失马,安知非福】 sàiwēng shī mǎ, ān zhī fēi fú a loss may turn out to be a gain; a blessing in disguise

赛(sài) 1.(比赛) match; game; competition; contest：安慰～ consolation event / 半决～ semi-finals / 表演～ exhibition match / 对抗～ dual meet / 锦标～ championship contest / 决～ finals / 淘汰～ elimination / 田径～ field events / 团体～ team competition / 循环～ round match / 邀请～ invitation tournament / 友谊～ friendly competition / 预～ preliminary trials / 足球～ football match; football game 2.(胜过) be comparable to; surpass

【赛场】 sàichǎng competition ground

【赛车】 sàichē 1.(自行车比赛) cycle racing 2.(比赛用自行车) racing bike; racing cycle 3.(汽车比赛) motorcycle race; automobile race 4.(比赛用汽车) racing car

【赛车场】 sàichēchǎng racetrack; racecourse

【赛车手】 sàichēshǒu racing driver

【赛程】 sàichéng 1.(比赛距离) competition distance 2.(比赛日程) competition schedule

【赛风】 sàifēn competition style

【赛狗】 sàigǒu dog race

【赛过】 sàiguò overtake; be better than; surpass; exceed：上次比赛他～我了。He was better than me in the last contest.

【赛会】 sàihuì a grand sports meet

【赛季】 sàijì sports competition season

【赛马】 sàimǎ 1.(指活动) horse race; horse racing; the races：平道～ flat racing / 我星期六参加～。I'm racing my horse on Saturday. 2.(指马) racehorse

【赛马场】 sàimǎchǎng racecourse; race ground

【赛马跑道】 sàimǎ pǎodào race track

【赛跑】 sàipǎo race; running：百米～ 100-meter dash / 长距离～ long-distance race; distance race / 短距离～ sprint; dash / 接力～ relay race; relay / 跨栏～ hurdles; hurdle race / 马拉松～ Marathon (race) / 越野～ cross-country race / 障碍～ steeplechase / 与时间～ run a race against time

【赛跑运动员】 sàipǎo yùndòngyuán runner

【赛区】 sàiqū competition area

【赛事】 sàishì competition

【赛艇】 sàitǐng 1.〈*Sports*〉 rowing 2.(比赛用艇) racing boat; shell

san

三(sān) 1.(数目) three; third：～倍 three times; threefold; triple / ～幕喜剧 comedy in three acts / ～岁小孩 a child of three 2.(多数;多次) more than two; several; many

【三八妇女节】 Sān-bā Fùnǚjié International Working Women's Day (March 8)
【三八红旗手】 sān-bā hóngqíshǒu 'March 8th' Red Banner Winners
【三百】 sānbǎi three hundred; three-hundredth
【三班制】 sānbānzhì three-shift system
【三包】 sānbāo (包修包换包退) three guarantees; guarantees for repair, replacement or compensation of fault products
【三胞胎】 sānbāotāi triples
【三保三压】 sānbǎo sānyā three guarantees and three cut-down
【三保一挂】 sānbǎo yīguà three guarantees and one link-up: 实行～综合承包 implement the 'three guarantees and one link-up' multiple contract system
【三北】 Sānběi three Norths; North-East, North-West and North of China
【三部曲】 sānbùqǔ trilogy
【三不政策】 sānbùzhèngcè the three nots
【三彩】 sāncǎi 〈*Archaeol.*〉 three-color glazed pottery: 唐～ three-color glazed pottery of the Tang Dynasty
【三叉戟】 sānchājǐ trident
【三叉神经】 sānchā shénjīng 〈*Anat.*〉 trigeminal nerve
【三叉神经痛】 sānchā shénjīngtòng 〈*Med.*〉 trigeminal neuralgia
【三岔路口】 sānchà lùkǒu a fork in the road; a junction of three roads
【三春】 sānchūn the three months in spring
【三次方程】 sāncì fāngchéng 〈*Math.*〉 cubic equation
【三从四德】 sāncóng-sìdé the three obediences and the four virtues
【三寸不烂之舌】 sāncùn bù làn zhī shé have a silver tongue
【三等秘书】 sānděng mìshū 〈*Foreign Affairs*〉 third secretary
【三点式】 sāndiǎnshì 见"三点式游泳衣"
【三点式游泳衣】 sāndiǎnshì yóuyǒngyī bikini (suit)
【三发中程客机】 sānfā zhōngchéng kèjī tri-jet medium haul airliner
【三番五次】 sānfān-wǔcì over and over again; repeatedly; again and again; time and again
【三方】 sānfāng three parts; tripartite (adj.)
【三废】 sānfèi the three wastes; waste gas, waste water, and industrial residue
【三分之一】 sānfēnzhīyī a third; one third
【三伏】 sānfú **1.** (初、中、末伏总称) the three ten-day periods of the hot season: ～天 dog days **2.** (末伏) the last of the three periods of the hot season
【三纲五常】 sāngāng-wǔcháng the three cardinal guides and the five constant virtues as specified in the feudal ethical code
【三好】 sānhǎo triple-A
【三好学生】 sānhǎo xuéshēng triple-A pupil
【三合板】 sānhébǎn three-ply board; plywood
【三合一】 sānhéyī three-in-one
【三级跳远】 sānjí tiàoyuǎn 〈*Sports*〉 hop, step and jump; triple jump
【三级跳远运动员】 sānjí tiàoyuǎn yùndòngyuán triple jumper
【三极管】 sānjíguǎn 〈*Electr.*〉 triode
【三尖瓣】 sānjiānbàn 〈*Anat.*〉 tricuspid valve
【三件套】 sānjiàntào three-pieces; three-piece suit
【三角】 sānjiǎo **1.** (三角形东西) triangle **2.** (三角学) trigonometry
【三角板】 sānjiǎobǎn set square
【三角带】 sānjiǎodài V belt; triangle belt
【三角钢琴】 sānjiǎo gāngqín grand piano
【三角函数】 sānjiǎo hánshù trigonometric function
【三角恋爱】 sānjiǎo liàn'ài love triangle
【三角贸易】 sānjiǎo màoyì triangular trade
【三角铁】 sānjiǎotiě **1.** (角钢) L-iron **2.** (打击乐器) triangle
【三角形】 sānjiǎoxíng 〈*Math.*〉 triangle (符号为 △): 不等边～ scalene triangle / 等边～ equilateral triangle / 等腰～ isosceles triangle / 直角～ right-angled triangle
【三角学】 sānjiǎoxué 〈*Math.*〉 trigonometry; trigonometric (adj.)
【三角债】 sānjiǎozhài triangle debt chain; debt chain
【三角洲】 sānjiǎozhōu 〈*Geog.*〉 delta: 珠江～ delta of Zhujiang River

【三脚架】 sānjiǎojià tripod; tripod mounting; trivet

【三教九流】 sānjiào-jiǔliú 1.(指儒、佛、道三教及其它各家) the three religions and the nine schools of thought 2.(指各宗教、学术流派) various religious sects and academic schools 3.(泛指江湖各种人) people in various trades; people of all sorts

【三九】 sānjiǔ the third nine-day period after the winter solstice; coldest days of winter

【三九天】 sānjiǔtiān 同"三九"

【三局二胜制】 sān jú liǎng shèng zhì best of three games; two out of three sets

【三卷本】 sānjuànběn three-decker

【三军】 sānjūn 1.(指军队) the army 2.(陆、海、空三军) the three armed services

【三来一补】 sānláiyībǔ the three processing industries and one compensation; processing raw materials on client's demands, assembling parts for the client, processing according to the client's samples and compensation trade in foreign trade business

【三垒】 sānlěi 〈*Baseball*〉 third base

【三垒手】 sānlěishǒu 〈*Baseball*〉 third baseman

【三连冠】 sānliánguàn be the champion for three times in succession; triple crown; three successive championship

【三联单】 sānliándān triplicate form

【三棱尺】 sānléngchǐ three-square rule; triangular scale

【三棱镜】 sānléngjìng 〈*Physics*〉(triangular) prism

【三棱柱】 sānléngzhù triangular prism

【三令五申】 sānlìng-wǔshēn repeated injunctions

【三乱】 sānluàn indiscriminate apportionment, charge and fine

【三轮车】 sānlúnchē tricycle; pedicab

【三轮摩托车】 sānlún mótuōchē motor tricycle; 挎斗～ sidecar machine

【三轮汽车】 sānlún qìchē three-wheeled automobile

【三昧】 sānmèi 1.〈*Buddhism*〉 samadhi 2.(诀要) secret; knack

【三门干部】 sānmén gànbù the three-door cadre

【三民主义】 sānmín zhǔyì the Three People's Principles; nationalism, democracy and people's livelihood

【三明治】 sānmíngzhì sandwich: 火腿～ ham sandwich / 鸡肉～ chicken sandwich

【三拍子】 sānpāi·zi 〈*Music*〉 triple time

【三千】 sānqiān three thousand; three thousandth

【三秋】 sānqiū 〈*Agric.*〉 the three autumn jobs

【三人行,必有我师】 sān rén xíng, bì yǒu wǒ shī If three of us are walking together, at least one of the other two is good enough to be my teacher.

【三三两两】 sānsān-liǎngliǎng in twos and threes; by twos and threes

【三色堇】 sānsèjǐn 〈*Bot.*〉 pansy

【三十】 sānshí thirty; thirtieth

【三思而行】 sānsī'érxíng think thrice before you act; look before you leap; Think before you act.

【三天打鱼,两天晒网】 sān diān dǎ yú, liǎng tiān shài wǎng go fishing for three days and dry the nets for two; work by fits and starts; lack perseverance

【三天两头】 sāntiān-liǎngtóu every other day; almost every day

【三通】 sāntōng 1.〈*Mech.*〉 tee; tee joint 2.(指通邮、通商、通航) exchanges of mails, trade, air and shipping services

【三头六臂】 sāntóu-liùbì (with) three heads and six arms; superhuman powers

【三万】 sānwàn thirty thousand; thirty thousandth

【三围】 sānwéi vital statistics: 女子的～是胸围、腰围和臀围。A woman's vital statistics are the measurements of her breasts, waist and hips.

【三维】 sānwéi three-dimensional

【三维动画】 sānwéi dònghuà three-dimensional animation

【三维空间】 sānwéi kōngjiān three-dimensional space

【三位一体】 sānwèi-yītǐ 1.〈*Christianity*〉 the Trinity 2.(三者联为一体) trinity; three forming an organic whole; three in one

【三五成群】 sānwǔ-chéngqún in threes and

fours; in knots
【三夏】 sānxià 〈*Agric.*〉 the three summer jobs
【三弦】 sānxián 〈*Music*〉 *sanxian*; 3-stringed Chinese guitar
【三线】 sānxiàn the third front
【三相】 sānxiàng 〈*Electr.*〉 three-phase
【三相变压器】 sānxiàng biànyāqì three-phase transformer
【三相插座】 sānxiàng chāzuò three-phase socket
【三心二意】 sānxīn-èryì **1.**(犹豫不决) be of two minds; shilly-shally **2.**(非全心全意) half-hearted
【三星】 sānxīng three stars
【三言两语】 sānyán-liǎngyǔ in a few words; in one or two words
【三月】 sānyuè March
【三战两胜】 sānzhàn-liǎngshèng 〈*Sports*〉 the best of three games
【三资企业】 sānzī qǐyè the three kinds of ventures (Chinese-foreign joint ventures, co-operative enterprises and exclusively foreign-owned enterprises)

叁 (sān) three; third

伞[傘、繖[1]] (sǎn) **1.**(雨伞;旱伞) umbrella: 缩折～ extension umbrella / 阳～ parasol / 打开～ put the umbrella up / 收～ put down the umbrella **2.**(伞状物) sth. shaped like an umbrella: 降落～ parachute
【伞兵】 sǎnbīng paratrooper; parachuter
【伞兵部队】 sǎnbīng bùduì parachute troops; paratroops
【伞架】 sǎnjià umbrella stand
【伞投】 sǎntóu drop by parachute; parachute
【伞投救济品】 sǎntóu jiùjìpǐn parachute relief
【伞形天线】 sǎnxíng tiānxiàn umbrella antennas
【伞衣】 sǎnyī canopy

散 (sǎn) **1.**(松开) come loose; fall apart; not hold together: 行李～了。The luggage has got loosened. **2.**(分散) scattered: ～～落落 scattered about **3.**〈*Chin. Pharm.*〉 medicine in powder form; medicinal powder: 健胃～ digestive powder
(另见"散"sàn)
【散兵】 sǎnbīng 〈*Mil.*〉 skirmisher
【散兵游勇】 sǎnbīng-yóuyǒng stragglers and disbanded soldiers
【散淡】 sǎndàn lead an idle life
【散光】 sǎnguāng astigmatism; astigmatic (adj.)
【散光眼镜】 sǎnguāng yǎnjìng astigmatic glasses
【散货】 sǎnhuò bulk cargo
【散货集装箱】 sǎnhuò jízhuāngxiāng solid bulk container
【散记】 sǎnjì random notes; sidelights
【散剂】 sǎnjì 〈*Pharm.*〉 powder; pulvis
【散架】 sǎnjià **1.**(散开) fall apart; fall to pieces **2.**(累极) (feel as if) all one's limbs are out of joint
【散居】 sǎnjū live scattered; live separately
【散漫】 sǎnmàn **1.**(随便) undisciplined; careless and sloppy **2.**(分散) unorganized; scattered
【散射】 sǎnshè 〈*Physics*〉 scatter
【散射波】 sǎnshèbō scattered wave
【散射层】 sǎnshècéng scattering layer
【散射光】 sǎnshèguāng scattered light
【散射粒子】 sǎnshè lìzǐ scattering particles
【散射通信】 sǎnshè tōngxìn scatter communication
【散射线】 sǎnshèxiàn scattered rays
【散文】 sǎnwén prose
【散文诗】 sǎnwénshī prose poem
【散运】 sǎnyùn loan in bulk
【散装】 sǎnzhuāng bulk; in bulk

馓 (sǎn)
【馓子】 sǎn·zi *sanzi*; deep-fried dough net

散 (sàn) **1.**(由聚集而分离) break up; disperse: ～会。A meeting breaks up. / 会后,人们三三两两地～了。After the meeting, people drifted away in twos and threes. **2.**(散布) distribute; tribute; give out **3.**(排除) dispel; let out
(另见"散"sǎn)
【散播】 sànbō disseminate; spread: ～谣言 spread rumors
【散布】 sànbù spread; disseminate; scatter; diffuse: ～流言蜚语 spread slanderous ru-

mors

【散步】 sànbù take a walk; go for walk; go for a stroll

【散布存储】 sànbù cúnchǔ scatter storage

【散布误差】 sànbù wùchā dispersion error

【散场】 sànchǎng empty after the show

【散发】 sànfā 1.（发出）send out; send forth; diffuse; emit 2.（分发）distribute; issue; give out

【散会】 sànhuì (of a meeting) be over; break up

【散伙】 sànhuǒ (of a group, body or organization) dissolve; disband

【散开】 sànkāi spread out or apart; disperse; scatter

【散裂】 sànliè 〈*Physics*〉 spallation

【散热】 sànrè heat loss; rejection of heat：～系统 cooling system / ～装置 heat abstractor

【散热器】 sànrèqì radiator：管式～ tubular radiator

【散热器护栅】 sànrèqì hùshān 〈*Auto*〉 radiator grille

【散失】 sànshī 1.（分散遗失）scatter and disappear; be lost; be missing 2.（消散失去）be lost; vaporize; dissipate; evaporate：田里的水分～了。The soil moisture in the fields was evaporated.

【散摊子】 sàntān·zi (of a group, body or organization) dissolve; disband; break up

【散心】 sànxīn drive away one's cares; relieve boredom

【散逸】 sànyì 〈*Physics*〉 dissipation：热～ heat dissipation

sang

丧[喪、丧] (sāng) funeral; mourning

(另见"丧"sàng)

【丧服】 sāngfú mourning apparel

【丧礼】 sānglǐ obsequies; funeral：参加～ attend a funeral

【丧事】 sāngshì funeral arrangements

【丧葬】 sāngzàng burial; funeral

【丧葬承办人】 sāngzàng chéngbànrén funeral director

【丧葬费】 sāngzàngfèi funeral expenses

【丧钟】 sāngzhōng funeral bell; death knell; knell：敲响～ sound the death knell

桑 (sāng) white mulberry; mulberry

【桑蚕】 sāngcán silkworm

【桑蚕丝】 sāngcánsī mulberry silk

【桑木】 sāngmù mulberry

【桑拿浴】 sāngnáyù sauna; sauna bath

【桑树】 sāngshù white mulberry; mulberry

【桑园】 sāngyuán mulberry field

【桑梓】 sāngzǐ 〈*written*〉 one's native place：～故里 one's native village

嗓 (sǎng) 1.（嗓子）throat; larynx 2.（嗓音）voice

【嗓门儿】 sǎngménr voice：提高～ raise one's voice

【嗓音】 sǎngyīn voice

【嗓子】 sǎng·zi 1.（喉咙）throat; larynx 2.（嗓音）voice：一副好～ a good voice / 清一清～ clear one's throat / 我～哑了。I've lost my voice.

丧[喪、丧] (sàng) lose

(另见"丧"sāng)

【丧胆】 sàngdǎn be terror-stricken; be smitten with fear：闻风～ be panic-stricken at the news (of)

【丧魂落魄】 sànghún-luòpò be driven to distraction

【丧家之犬】 sàngjiāzhīquǎn stray dog; homeless dog

【丧尽天良】 sàngjìn-tiānliáng utterly devoid of conscience; conscienceless; heartless

【丧命】 sàngmìng meet one's death; get killed

【丧偶】 sàng'ǒu be bereft of one's spouse

【丧气】 sàngqì 1.（情绪低落）feel disheartened; lose heart; become crest fallen 2.（倒霉；不吉利）be unlucky; be out of luck; have bad luck

【丧气话】 sàngqìhuà demoralizing words

【丧权辱国】 sàngquán-rǔguó humiliate the country and forfeit its sovereignty; surrender a country's sovereign rights under humiliating terms

【丧生】 sàngshēng meet one's death; get killed

【丧失】 sàngshī lose; forfeit：～国格 forfeit

national dignify; at the expense of the dignity of one's state / ～人格 forfeit personal dignity; at the expense of one's own moral integrity

【丧心病狂】 sàngxīn-bìngkuáng frenzied; perverse; lose one's senses

sao

搔 (sāo) scratch: ～痒 scratch where it itches

【搔到痒处】 sāodàoyǎngchù scratch where it itches; to hit the nail on the head; scratch at the place that itches

【搔首】 sāoshǒu scratch one's head

【搔头弄姿】 sāotóu-nòngzī 〈*written*〉 be coquettish; stroke one's hair in coquetry

【搔痒】 sāoyǎng **1.** (挠痒痒) scratch where it itches **2.** 〈*Med.*〉 pruritus

骚 (sāo) **1.** (扰乱) disturb; upset **2.** (诗文) literary writings: ～人 poet **3.** (举止轻佻) coquettish

【骚动】 sāodòng **1.** (扰乱) disturbance; commotion; ferment **2.** (动乱) be in a tumult; become restless: 全城～。The whole city was in a tumult.

【骚客】 sāokè 〈*written*〉 poet

【骚乱】 sāoluàn disturbance; riot; chaos: 街上发生～,有人被打伤了。There has been a disturbance in the street; somebody has been hurt.

【骚扰】 sāorǎo harass; molest; harassment (n.): 性～ sexual harassment / ～侵略军 harass the occupying army / 那女孩常遭到继父的～。The girl had been molested frequently by her stepfather.

【骚人墨客】 sāorén-mòkè 〈*written*〉 men of letters; a poet; literati

缫［缲］ (sāo) reel silk from cocoons; reel

【缫丝】 sāosī silk reeling; filature

臊 (sāo) the smell of urine; foul smell (另见"臊"sào)

【臊气】 sāoqì foul smell; the smell of urine

扫［掃］ (sǎo) **1.** (打扫) sweep: ～雪 sweep away the snow **2.** (很快地移动) pass quickly along or over; sweep: 眼光～过人群 sweep one's eyes over the crowd **3.** (归拢在一起) put all together (另见"扫"sào)

【扫除】 sǎochú **1.** (清除) cleaning; cleanup **2.** (消除) clear away; remove; wipe out: ～障碍 remove the obstacles

【扫荡】 sǎodàng **1.** (用武力) mop up **2.** (扫荡行动) mopping-up operation: 粉碎日寇的～ smash the Japanese aggressors' mopping-up operations **3.** (清除) eliminate; finish off: ～海盗 sweep the seas of pirates

【扫地】 sǎodì **1.** (打扫) sweep the floor **2.** (丧失名誉等) reach rock bottom; be dragged in the dust

【扫地出门】 sǎodì-chūmén drive sb. out of his house and deprive him of everything; drive out sb. in dire poverty

【扫黄】 sǎohuáng anti-porn campaign; anti-porno campaign

【扫黄运动】 sǎohuáng yùndòng campaign against the spread of pornography

【扫雷】 sǎoléi mine sweeping

【扫雷机】 sǎoléijī mine-dredger

【扫雷舰】 sǎoléijiàn minesweeper

【扫雷器】 sǎoléiqì mine-sweeping apparatus; minesweeper

【扫盲】 sǎománg eliminate illiteracy; wipe out illiteracy

【扫描】 sǎomiáo 〈*Electr.*〉 scan; scanning (n.)

【扫描器】 sǎomiáoqì scanner

【扫墓】 sǎomù sweep a grave; pay respects to a dead person at his tomb

【扫平】 sǎopíng put down; crush; suppress

【扫清】 sǎoqīng clear away: ～道路 clear the path / ～障碍 clear away the obstacles; remove the obstacles

【扫射】 sǎoshè **1.** (用枪) strafe; rake **2.** (用目光、灯光等) sweep

【扫视】 sǎoshì sweep one's eyes over

【扫尾】 sǎowěi wind up; round off

【扫尾工作】 sǎowěi gōngzuò rounding-off work

【扫兴】 sǎoxìng have one's spirits dampened; feel disappointed

【扫雪车】 sǎoxuěchē snow removal truck

嫂 (sǎo) **1.** (哥哥的妻子) elder brother's wife; sister-in-law **2.** (大嫂) sister

【嫂嫂】 sǎo·sao 见“嫂子”
【嫂子】 sǎo·zi sister-in-law; elder brother's wife

扫[掃](sào)(另见“扫”sǎo)
【扫帚】 sào·zhou broom
【扫帚星】 sào·zhouxīng comet

臊(sào) shy; bashful: 害～ be bashful (另见“臊”sāo)

se

色(sè) 1.(颜色) color (AmE.); colour (BrE.); colored (adj.): 白～ white / 黑～ black / 红～ red / 黄～ yellow / 蓝～ blue / 绿～ green / 彩～ color / 全～ panchromatic / 无～ colorless / 原～ primary color ‖ …～的 -colored: 一件乳白～的衣服 a cream-colored dress 2.(神色) look; countenance; expression: 面无惧～ not look at all afraid / 面有难～ show reluctance 3.(种类) kind; description 4.(景色) scene; scenery 5.(质量) quality (of precious metals, goods, etc.) 6.(妇女美貌) woman's looks 7.(色欲) carnal pleasure: 好～ lech; lechery (n.); lecherous (adj.) 8.〈*Buddhism*〉 material appearance of things (另见“色”shǎi)
【色饱和度】 sè bǎohédù color saturation
【色标】 sèbiāo color code
【色彩】 sècǎi 1.(颜色) color; hue; tint; shade: ～奇异大方 in plain, fancy color / ～鲜明 in bright gay color / ～协调 matching in color 2.(倾向) color; flavor: 时代～ the flavor of the day
【色带】 sèdài ribbon
【色带盒】 sèdàihé ribbon cartridge
【色调】 sèdiào tone; hue; shade: 暖～ warm tones
【色度】 sèdù chromaticity; chrominance; colority
【色度计】 sèdùjì 〈*Physics*〉 colorimeter: 光电～ photoelectric colorimeter
【色鬼】 sèguǐ a satyr; a lecher
【色觉测验】 sèjué cèyàn color vision test
【色拉】 sèlā salad: 火腿～ ham salad / 鸡～ chicken salad / 素～ vegetable salad
【色拉酱】 sèlājiàng mayonnaise
【色拉油】 sèlāyóu salad oil
【色狼】 sèláng wolf; sexual offender
【色厉内荏】 sèlì-nèirěn fierce of mien but faint of heart
【色盲】 sèmáng 〈*Med.*〉 achromatopsia; color blindness; color-blind (adj.)
【色品】 sèpǐn 〈*Physics*〉 chroma; chromaticity
【色谱】 sèpǔ chromatogram; color spectrum
【色情】 sèqíng pornographic; sexy
【色情电影】 sèqíng diànyǐng pornofilm; wet dream
【色情狂】 sèqíngkuáng 〈*Med.*〉 erotomania
【色情文学】 sèqíng wénxué pornography
【色情作品】 sèqíng zuòpǐn erotica
【色素】 sèsù 〈*Biol.*〉 pigment
【色素沉着】 sèsù chénzhuó 〈*Med.*〉 pigmentation
【色素细胞】 sèsù xìbāo chromatophere
【色温度】 sèwēndù color temperature
【色香味美】 sèxiāng-wèiměi good in color, smell and taste
【色相】 sèxiàng 1.(女色) look; charm: 出卖～ sell her charms 2.〈*Physics*〉 hue
【色泽】 sèzé color and luster: ～和谐 the colors match well
【色纸】 sèzhǐ colored paper
【色痣】 sèzhì mole

铯(sè)〈*Chem.*〉 caesium (元素符号 Cs)

涩[澀、澁](sè) 1.(麻木味) puckery; astringent: 这柿子太～了。The persimmon is very puckery. 2.(不滑润) unsmooth; hard-going: 轮轴发～。The axle doesn't work smoothly. 3.(难读、难懂) obscure; difficult
【涩味】 sèwèi acerbity

瑟(sè) 〈*Music*〉 *se*; 25-stringed Chinese horizontal harp
【瑟瑟】 sèsè rustle: 秋风～。The autumn wind is rustling soughing.
【瑟缩】 sèsuō curl up with cold; cower

塞(sè)(另见“塞”sāi, sài)
【塞责】 sèzé not do one's job conscientiously: 敷衍～ perform one's duty in a perfunc-

tory manner

sen

森（sēn） 1.（树多）full of trees 2.（众多）multitudinous；in multitudes 3.（阴暗）dark；gloomy

【森林】 sēnlín forest；forestal（adj.）：原始～ primeval forest；virgin forest

【森林保护区】 sēnlín bǎohùqū forestry reserve

【森林保护员】 sēnlín bǎohùyuán forest ranger

【森林采伐权】 sēnlín cǎifáquán forest concession

【森林调查】 sēnlín diàochá forest survey

【森林法】 sēnlínfǎ forestry act；law of forestry

【森林风】 sēnlínfēng forest wind

【森林抚育】 sēnlín fǔyù tending of woods

【森林覆被率】 sēnlín fùbèilǜ percentage of forest cover

【森林覆盖率】 sēnlín fùgàilǜ 同"森林覆被率"

【森林工业】 sēnlín gōngyè timber industry

【森林火灾】 sēnlín huǒzāi forest fire

【森林警察】 sēnlín jǐngchá forest ranger

【森林生态学】 sēnlín shēngtàixué forest ecology

【森林学】 sēnlínxué forestry

【森林资源】 sēnlín zīyuán forest reserves

【森然】 sēnrán 1.（繁茂直立）dense；thick 2.（森严可畏）awe-inspiring

【森森】 sēnsēn dense；thick；luxuriant

【森严】 sēnyán stern；strict；forbidding：门卫～ with the entrances closely guarded

【森严壁垒】 sēnyán-bìlěi closely guarded；strongly fortified

seng

僧（sēng） Buddhist monk；monk：托钵～ fakir／行脚～ palmer／云水～ wandering monk

【僧多粥少】 sēng duō zhōu shǎo There are too many（Buddhist）monks and too little gruel；cannot meet the needs of the people.（或：The monks are many and the supply of gruel is meager；not enough to go around.）

【僧侣】 sēnglǚ monks and priests；clergy

【僧俗】 sēngsú monks and laymen

【僧徒】 sēngtú Buddhist monks

【僧院】 sēngyuàn Buddhist temple；Buddhist monastery

sha

杀［殺］（shā） 1.（杀死）kill；slaughter：他～ homicide／误～ manslaughter／自～ suicide 2.（战斗）fight；go into battle 3.（削弱）weaken；reduce；abate：～威风 deflate the arrogance 4.（程度深）extremely；to death

【杀病毒程序】 shābìngdú chéngxù 〈*Computer*〉 killer

【杀虫粉】 shāchóngfěn insect powder

【杀虫剂】 shāchóngjì 〈*Agric.*〉 insecticide；pesticide

【杀敌】 shādí fight the enemy；engage in battle

【杀风景】 shāfēngjǐng spoil the fun；be a wet blanket

【杀害】 shāhài murder；kill

【杀回马枪】 shā huímǎqiāng give sb. a back thrust；wheel around and hit back

【杀鸡取卵】 shājī-qǔluǎn kill the hen to get the eggs；kill the goose that lays the golden eggs

【杀鸡用牛刀】 shā jī yòng niúdāo break a fly upon a wheel；use a steam-hammer to crack nuts

【杀价】 shājià offer to buy sth. cheap, knowing the seller needs cash

【杀菌】 shājūn disinfect；sterilize

【杀菌剂】 shājūnjì germicide；bactericide

【杀戮】 shālù massacre；slaughter

【杀气】 shāqì 1.（凶恶）murderous look 2.（出气）vent one's ill feeling

【杀人】 shārén kill a person；murder

【杀人案】 shārén'àn homicide case

【杀人本性】 shārén běnxìng killer instinct

【杀人不见血】 shārén bù jiàn xuě kill without spilling blood；kill by subtle means

【杀人不眨眼】 shārén bù zhǎyǎn kill without batting an eyelid；kill without blinking an eye

【杀人犯】 shārénfàn murderer; manslayer; homicide; mankiller
【杀人放火】 shārén-fànghuǒ murder and arson: ～,无恶不作 commit murder, arson and every crime imaginable
【杀人灭口】 shārén-mièkǒu do away with a witness; murder sb. to prevent divulgence of one's secrets
【杀人越货】 shārén-yuèhuò kill a person and seize his goods
【杀伤】 shāshāng kill and wound; inflict casualties on
【杀身】 shāshēn be killed; be murdered
【杀身成仁】 shāshēn-chéngrén die to achieve virtue; die for a just cause
【杀身之祸】 shāshēnzhīhuò a fatal disaster
【杀手】 shāshǒu killer
【杀手锏】 shāshǒujiǎn deadly weapon
【杀头】 shātóu behead; decapitate
【杀一儆百】 shāyī-jǐngbǎi execute one as a warning to a hundred; execute one man to warn a hundred

刹 (shā) put on the brakes; stop; check: ～住歪风 check an unhealthy tendency / 司机突然把车～住。The driver put on the brake suddenly.
(另见"刹"chà)
【刹把】 shābǎ 〈*Mech.*〉 brake clank
【刹车】 shāchē **1.** (停车) brake a car; stop a car; put on the brakes: 司机突然～。The driver suddenly applied his brakes. / 我急忙～,但是已经晚了。I slammed on the brake but it was too late. **2.** (停机) stop a machine by cutting off the power; turn off a machine **3.** (指制动机件) brake: 防抱锁～ anti-lock brakes **4.** (制止) stop; check
【刹车灯】 shāchēdēng 〈*Auto*〉 brake light
【刹车鼓】 shāchēgǔ 〈*Auto*〉 brake drum
【刹车片】 shāchēpiàn 〈*Auto*〉 brake shoe

杉 (shā) 〈*Bot.*〉 Chinese fir
(另见"杉"shān)
【杉篙】 shāgāo 〈*Archit.*〉 fir pole
【杉木】 shāmù Chinese fir

沙 (shā) **1.** (沙子) sand: 在路上铺～ sand the road **2.** (像沙子的) granulated; powdered **3.** (不清脆) hoarse; husky
【沙包】 shābāo sandbag
【沙暴】 shābào sandstorm
【沙场】 shāchǎng battlefield; battleground
【沙尘暴】 shāchénbào sand storm
【沙槌】 shāchuí 〈*Music*〉 maracas
【沙袋】 shādài **1.** (沙包) sandbag **2.** 〈*Boxing*〉 punch bag
【沙丁鱼】 shādīngyú sardine
【沙发】 shāfā sofa; settee: 长～ sofa; settee / 单人～ armchair
【沙发床】 shāfāchuáng sofa bed
【沙岗】 shāgǎng sand hill
【沙锅】 shāguō earthenware pot; casserole
【沙化】 shāhuà fertile farmland tend to become desert
【沙荒】 shāhuāng sandy wasteland; sandy waste
【沙皇】 shāhuáng tzar; tsar; czar ‖ 女沙皇 tzarina; tsarina; czarina
【沙鸡】 shājī sandgrouse
【沙棘】 shājí sea buckthorn; sallow thorn
【沙金】 shājīn alluvial gold; placer gold
【沙坑】 shākēng 〈*Sport*〉 jumping pit; sandpit
【沙拉】 shālā 同"色拉"
【沙里淘金】 shālǐ-táojīn wash grains of gold out of the sands; extract the essential from a large mass of material; get small returns for great effort
【沙粒】 shālì grains of sand; sand
【沙砾】 shālì grit
【沙龙】 shālóng salon: 文艺～ literary salon
【沙漏】 shālòu sandglass
【沙漠】 shāmò desert: 塔克拉玛干～ Taklimakan desert / 腾格里～ Tengger desert / 撒哈拉大～ the Sahara desert
【沙漠化】 shāmòhuà desertification
【沙漠绿洲】 shāmò lǜzhōu oasis
【沙漠靴】 shāmòxuē desert boot
【沙鸥】 shā'ōu gull
【沙盘】 shāpán 〈*Mil.*〉 sand table
【沙丘】 shāqiū dune; sand-dune: 流动～ moving dunes
【沙球】 shāqiú 〈*Boxing*〉 punch ball
【沙瓤】 shāráng mushy watermelon pulp
【沙壤土】 shārǎngtǔ sandy loam
【沙沙】 shāshā 〈*onomat.*〉 rustle: 树叶在风中～作响。The leaves rustled in the wind. /

风把树叶吹得～响。The wind rustled the leaves.
【沙滩】 shātān sandy beach; sand beach; sea beach
【沙土】 shātǔ sandy soil
【沙文主义】 shāwén zhǔyì chauvinism; chauvinist (adj.): 大国～ great-nation chauvinism
【沙哑】 shāyǎ hoarse; husky; raucous: 声音～ have a husky voice
【沙眼】 shāyǎn trachoma
【沙浴】 shāyù sand bath
【沙钟】 shāzhōng 见"沙漏"
【沙洲】 shāzhōu shoal; sandbar; sandbank
【沙子】 shā·zi 1.(细沙) sand; grit 2.(像沙的东西) small grains; pellets

痧 (shā) sunstroke; heatstroke: 发～ suffer sunstroke
【痧子】 shā·zi 〈*Chin. Med.*〉 measles: 出～ have measles

鲨 (shā) shark
【鲨鱼】 shāyú shark

纱 (shā) 1.(线) yarn: 粗支～ low count yarn / 细支～ fine count yarn / 中支～ medium count yarn / 棉～ cotton yarn 2.(经纬线很稀的织物) gauze; sheer: 窗～ gauze curtain
【纱包线】 shābāoxiàn cotton-covered wire
【纱布】 shābù gauze: ～绷带 gauze bandage
【纱厂】 shāchǎng cotton mill
【纱橱】 shāchú screen cupboard
【纱窗】 shāchuāng screen window
【纱灯】 shādēng gauze lantern
【纱锭】 shādìng 〈*Textiles*〉 spindle
【纱巾】 shājīn gauze kerchief
【纱笼】 shālǒng sarong
【纱罗】 shāluó 〈*Textiles*〉 gauze
【纱染】 shārǎn yarn-dyed
【纱线】 shāxiàn yarn
【纱罩】 shāzhào 1.(罩食物的) gauze; screen covering (over food) 2.(煤气灯的) mantle

砂 (shā) sand; grit: 往米里掺～ sand the rice
【砂布】 shābù emery cloth; abrasive cloth
【砂浆】 shājiāng 〈*Archit.*〉 mortar
【砂晶】 shājīng sand crystal
【砂矿】 shākuàng placer deposit; placer
【砂砾】 shālì gravel; grit
【砂轮】 shālún 〈*Mech.*〉 emery wheel; grinding wheel; abrasive wheel
【砂轮机】 shālúnjī grinder
【砂囊】 shānáng 〈*Zool.*〉 gizzard; vesica arenae
【砂皮】 shāpí sand skin
【砂糖】 shātáng granulated sugar
【砂田】 shātián sandy land
【砂土】 shātǔ sandy soil; sand
【砂岩】 shāyán 〈*Mineral.*〉 sandstone
【砂眼】 shāyǎn 〈*Metall.*〉 sand holes; blowholes; slag pin hole
【砂样】 shāyàng 〈*Petroleum*〉 drilling mud cuttings
【砂纸】 shāzhǐ abrasive paper; sand paper

煞 (shā) 1.(停;结束) stop; halt; check; bring to a close 2.(勒紧) tighten (另见"煞"shà)
【煞笔】 shābǐ 1.(停笔) concluding lines of an article; ending of a piece of writing 2.(结束语) write the final line
【煞车】 shāchē 1.同"刹车" 2.(把车上的货用绳索捆紧) firmly fasten a load; secure with rope; lash down the load
【煞风景】 shāfēngjǐng 同"杀风景"
【煞尾】 shāwěi 1.(收尾) finish off; round off; wind up 2.(最后一段) final stage; end; ending

啥 (shá) 1.(什么) what: 你找～? What are you looking for? 2.(表示不肯定的事物) anything: 她～也没说。She didn't say anything. 3.(用在"也"或"都"前面,表示没有例外) ～用处也没有 be quite worthless 4.(两个"什么"前后照应,前者决定后者) 有～说～ say what one has in mind
【啥地方】 shádì·fang where
【啥人】 shárén who
【啥时候】 sháshí·hou when: 你～见到她的? When did you see her?

傻[傻] (shǎ) 1.(糊涂) stupid; muddleheaded: 装～ pretend not to know 2.(死心眼) think or act mechanically; tactless: 他为人太～,不知怎样与人交往。He has no tact in dealing with people.
【傻瓜】 shǎguā fool; blockhead; simpleton

【傻瓜像机】 shǎguā xiàngjī automatic miniature camera; foolproof camera
【傻呵呵】 shǎhēhē simpleminded; not very clever
【傻乎乎】 shǎhūhū simpleminded; not very clever
【傻劲儿】 shǎjìnr 1.(傻气) foolishness; stupidity 2.(单凭力气干) with sheer enthusiasm; be foolhardy
【傻帽儿】 shǎmàor fool; blockhead; simpleton
【傻笑】 shǎxiào laugh foolishly; giggle; smirk
【傻眼】 shǎyǎn be dumbfounded; be stunned; get a nasty shock
【傻子】 shǎ·zi fool; blockhead; simpleton

厦[廈](shà) mansion; tall building: 商～ plaza

歃(shà) 〈*written*〉 suck
【歃血】 shàxuè smear the blood of a sacrifice on the mouth; an ancient form of swearing an oath
【歃血为盟】 shàxuèwéiméng smear the blood as a sign of the oath; smear the mouth with blood and swear fidelity

煞(shà) 1.(凶神) evil spirit; goblin 2.(很) very
(另见"煞"shā)
【煞白】 shàbái ghastly pale; deathly pale; pallid
【煞费苦心】 shàfèi-kǔxīn rack one's brains; take great pains
【煞有介事】 shàyǒujièshì make a great show of being in earnest; pretend to be serious (about doing sth.)

霎(shà) a very short time; moment; instant
【霎时】 shàshí 见"霎时间"
【霎时间】 shàshíjiān in a twinkling; in a split second; in a jiffy

shai

筛[篩](shāi) 1.(筛子) sieve; sifter; screen 2.(筛东西) sift; sieve; screen; riddle: ～糖粉 sift the icing sugar
【筛分】 shāifēn screen; sieve
【筛析】 shāixì screen analysis
【筛选】 shāixuǎn 1.(用筛子选) sieve; screen 2.(挑选) screen; chose; select: 这部电影是经过层层～评选出来的。This film has been chosen through competition and elimination at various levels.
【筛子】 shāi·zi sieve; sifter; screen: 煤～ coal screen

色(shǎi) 〈*colloq.*〉 color (AmE.); colour (BrE.): 这布掉～。This cloth fade.
(另见"色"sè)
【色酒】 shǎijiǔ color wine
【色子】 shǎi·zi dice: 掷～ play dice
【色子桶】 shǎi·zitǒng dice cup

晒[曬](shài) 1.(日照) shine upon 2.(在阳光下晒) dry in the sun; bask: 我们在阳光充足的海滩上～太阳。We basked ourselves on the sunny beach.
【晒熟】 shàishóu sunburn
【晒台】 shàitái flat roof; terrace
【晒太阳】 shài tàiyáng sunbathe; bask
【晒图】 shàitú make a blueprint; blueprint
【晒图员】 shàitúyuán blueprinter
【晒图纸】 shàitúzhǐ blueprint paper
【晒像灯】 shàixiàngdēng printing lamp
【晒烟】 shàiyān sun-cured tobacco
【晒盐】 shàiyán evaporate brine in the sun to make salt
【晒盐场】 shàiyánchǎng salt field

shan

山(shān) 1.(山脉,山峰) hill; mountain: 慕士塔格～ Mt. Muztagata / 爬上～ mount a hill 2.(像山的) anything resembling a mountain: 冰～ iceberg 3.(蚕蔟) bushes in which silkworms spin cocoons
【山坳】 shān'ào col
【山崩】 shānbēng landslide; landslip
【山茶】 shānchá 〈*Bot.*〉 camellia
【山茶花】 shānchā huā camellia
【山城】 shānchéng mountain city
【山川】 shānchuān mountains and rivers; land
【山村】 shāncūn mountain village
【山带】 shāndài mountain belts

【山道】 shāndào mountain pass
【山道年】 shāndàonián 〈Pharm.〉 santonin
【山地】 shāndì 1.(多山地带) mountainous region; hilly area; hilly country 2.(山上的农田) fields on a hill
【山地草原】 shāndì cǎoyuán upland meadow
【山地车】 shāndìchē mountain bike
【山顶】 shāndǐng mountain's summit; hill top
【山顶洞人】 Shāndǐngdòngrén Upper Cave Man
【山顶山口】 shāndǐng shānkǒu summit crater
【山洞】 shāndòng cave; cavern
【山峰】 shānfēng peak; mountain; mountain peak: 珠穆朗玛峰是世界上最高的～。Mt. Qomolangma is the highest mountain in the world.
【山冈】 shāngāng low hill; hillock
【山高水长】 shāngāo-shuǐcháng as high as the hills and as long as the rivers; of lasting influence
【山高水低】 shāngāo-shuǐdī death; unexpected misfortune; sth. unfortunate
【山歌】 shāngē folk song
【山沟】 shāngōu 1.(流水沟) gully; ravine 2.(山谷) mountain valley 3.(指山区) mountainous area: 穷～ poor mountainous area
【山谷】 shāngǔ mountain valley
【山河】 shānhé mountains and rivers; the land of a country: 锦绣～ beautiful land
【山核桃】 shānhé·tao 〈Bot.〉 cathay hickory
【山洪】 shānhóng mountain torrents
【山货】 shānhuò 1.(山区土产) mountain products 2.(用竹、木、麻、瓷等日用品) household utensils made of wood, bamboo, clay, etc.
【山脊】 shānjǐ ridge (of a mountain or hill)
【山涧】 shānjiàn mountain stream
【山脚】 shānjiǎo the foot of a hill
【山口】 shānkǒu mountain pass; pass: 乌兹别里～ Uzbel Shankou
【山梁】 shānliáng ridge (of a mountain or hill)
【山林】 shānlín mountain forest; wooded mountain
【山林所有权】 shānlín suǒyǒuquán ownership of mountains
【山岭】 shānlǐn mountain ridge
【山路】 shānlù mountain road; mountain path
【山麓】 shānlù the foot of a mountain
【山峦】 shānluán chain of mountains
【山脉】 shānmài mountain range; mountain chain: 阿尔泰～ Mts. Altay Shan / 昆仑～ Mts. Kunlun Shan / 喜马拉雅～ Himalayas
【山盟海誓】 shānméng-hǎishì (make) a solemn pledge of love
【山明水秀】 shānmíng-shuǐxiù green hills and clear waters; picturesque scenery
【山南海北】 shānnán-hǎiběi far and wide; all over the land; south of the mountains and north of the seas
【山坡】 shānpō hillside; mountain slope
【山墙】 shānqiáng 〈Archit.〉 gable
【山穷水尽】 shānqióng-shuǐjìn where the mountains and the rivers end; at the end of one's rope
【山区】 shānqū mountain area
【山泉】 shānquán mountain spring
【山雀】 shānquè 〈Zool.〉 tit
【山水】 shānshuǐ 1.(山上流下的水) water from mountain 2.(山和水) mountains and rivers; scenery with hills and waters 3.〈Arts〉 traditional Chinese painting of mountains and waters; landscape
【山水画】 shānshuǐhuà mountains-and-waters painting; landscape painting
【山田】 shāntián hillside plot
【山头】 shāntóu 1.(山的上部) hilltop; the top of a mountain 2.(宗派) faction
【山乡】 shānxiāng mountain area
【山响】 shānxiǎng deafening; thunderous
【山杏】 shānxìng 〈Bot.〉 ansu apricot
【山崖】 shānyá cliff
【山羊】 shānyáng 1.(羊的一品种) goat ‖ 公羊 billy / 母羊 nanny / 小羊 kid 2.〈Sports〉 buck
【山杨】 shānyáng 〈Bot.〉 David poplar
【山腰】 shānyāo mountainside; half way up the mountain
【山药】 shān·yao 1.〈Bot.〉 Chinese yam 2.(甘薯) sweet potato
【山药蛋】 shān·yaodàn 〈dial.〉 potato
【山雨欲来风满楼】 shānyǔ yù lái fēng mǎn lóu

the wind sweeping through the tower heralds a rising storm in the mountains; the rising wind forebodes the coming storm

【山岳】 shānyuè lofty mountains

【山楂】 shānzhā 1.〈*Bot*.〉 Chinese hawthorn 2.（山楂的果实）haw

【山楂糕】 shānzhāgāo haw jelly

【山寨】 shānzhài mountain fastness; fortified mountain village

【山珍海味】 shānzhēn-hǎiwèi delicacies from land and sea; dainties of every kind

【山中无老虎,猴子称大王】 shānzhōng wú lǎohǔ, hóu·zi chēng dàwáng The monkey reigns in the mountains when the tiger is not there.（或：Among the blind the one-eyed man is king.）

【山庄】 shānzhuāng mountain villa

舢（shān）

【舢板】 shānbǎn sampan

杉（shān） 〈*Bot*.〉 Chinese fir; China fir（另见"杉"shā）

【杉树】 shānshù Chinese fir

钐（shān）〈*Chem*.〉 samarium（元素符号Sm）

（另见"钐"shàn）

删［刪］（shān） delete; leave out：把长故事～短 cut a long story short / 有几个字被～掉了。Several words had been deleted.

【删除】 shānchú delete; strike out; cut off; cut out; leave out

【删繁就简】 shānfán-jiùjiǎn simplify sth. by cutting out the superfluous

【删改】 shāngǎi delete and change; revise; finalized

【删节】 shānjié abridge; abbreviate：这是由原本～的。It was abridged from the original work.

【删节本】 shānjiéběn abridged edition; abbreviated version

【删节号】 shānjiéhào ellipsis; suspension points; ellipsis dots（符号为：……，…或...）

姗［姍］（shān）

【姗姗来迟】 shānshān-láichí be slow in coming; be late

珊［珊］（shān）

【珊瑚】 shānhú coral：～项链 coral necklace

【珊瑚岛】 shānhúdǎo coral island

【珊瑚礁】 shānhújiāo coral reef

栅［柵］（shān） （另见"栅"zhà）

【栅级】 shānjí 〈*Electr*.〉 grid; grid electrode

扇［搧］（shān） 1.（扇风）fan：用报纸～扇子 fan oneself with the newspaper 2.（鼓动）incite; instigate; fan up; stir up

（另见"扇"shàn）

【扇动】 shāndòng 1.（摇动）fan; flap 2.（鼓动坏事）instigate; incite; stir up; whip up：～叛乱 incite a rebellion

【扇风点火】 shānfēng-diǎnhuǒ fan the flames; inflame and agitate people; stir up trouble

煽（shān） incite; instigate; fan up; stir up

【煽动】 shāndòng instigate; incite; stir up; whip up：～叛乱 incite a rebellion

潸［潸］（shān） 〈*written*〉 in tears; tearfully

【潸然泪下】 shānrán-lèixià shed silent tears; drop a few silent tears

膻（shān） the smell of mutton：这羊肉味太～。This mutton has got a strong smell.

闪（shǎn） 1.（闪避）dodge; get out of the way：～到树后 dodge behind a tree / 东躲西～ dodge about 2.（扭伤）twist; sprain 3.（闪电）lightning 4.（突然出现）flash; sparkle; shine 5.（丢下）leave behind

【闪避】 shǎnbì dodge; sidestep

【闪挫】 shǎncuō 〈*Chin*. *Med*.〉 sudden strain or contusion of a muscle; sprain

【闪电】 shǎndiàn lightning：一道～，接着就是隆隆的雷声。There was a flash of lightning and then a loud peal of thunder.

【闪电式罢工】 shǎndiànshì bàgōng lightning strike

【闪电式进攻】 shǎndiànshì jìngōng lightning attack：发动～ make a lightning attack

【闪电战】 shǎndiànzhàn lightning war; blitzkrieg; blitz

【闪光】 shǎnguāng 1.（突然一现的光亮）flash of light：流星像一道～划过夜空。Like a flash of lightning, the meteor shot across the sky. 2.（闪闪发光）gleam；glisten；glitter：星星的～ twinkling of stars

【闪光触点】 shǎnguāng chùdiǎn 〈*Photog.*〉hot-shoe flash contact

【闪光灯】 shǎnguāngdēng 〈*Photog.*〉flash lamp；photoflash；flashlight

【闪光装置】 shǎnguāng zhuāngzhì flasher

【闪击战】 shǎnjīzhàn lightning war；blitzkrieg；blitz

【闪开】 shǎnkāi get out of the way；jump aside；dodge

【闪闪】 shǎnshǎn sparkle；glisten；glitter

【闪身】 shǎnshēn 1.（闪避）dodge 2.（侧身）sideways

【闪失】 shǎnshī mishap；accident

【闪烁】 shǎnshuò 1.（光亮摇摆不定）twinkle；glimmer；glisten：湖水在月光下～。The lake glistens in the moonlight. 2.（不直说）evasive；vague；noncommittal：～其词 speak evasively；dodge about；evade issues 3.〈*Electr.*〉scintillation

【闪现】 shǎnxiàn flash before one：～在眼前 flash before one's eyes

【闪耀】 shǎnyào glitter；shine；radiate

陕［陝］（shǎn） Shaanxi

【陕甘宁边区】 Shǎn-Gān-Níng biānqū the Shaanxi-Gansu-Ningxia Border Region

【陕西】 Shǎnxī Shaanxi

讪（shàn） 1.（讥笑）mock；ridicule 2.（难为情）embarrassed；awkward；shamefaced：～～地坐下 sit down feeling abashed

【讪笑】 shànxiào ridicule；mock；deride

疝（shàn） 〈*Med.*〉hernia

【疝气】 shànqì 〈*Med.*〉hernia

【疝气带】 shànqìdài 〈*Med.*〉hernia band；truss

苫（shàn） cover (with a straw mat, tarpaulin, etc.)：把麦子～上 cover up the wheat

【苫布】 shànbù tarpaulin

钐［繕、鐥］（shàn） 〈*dial.*〉cut with a sickle

（另见"钐"shān）

【钐镰】 shànlián scythe

禅［禪］（shàn）
（另见"禅"chán）

【禅让】 shànràng abdicate and hand over the crown to another person

扇（shàn） 1.（扇子）fan：芭蕉～ palm-leaf fan / 电～ electric fan / 宫～ mandarin fan / 绢～ silk fan / 葵～ palm fan / 檀香～ sandalwood fan / 羽毛～ feather fan / 折～ folding fan / 通风～ draft fan 2.（板状物）leaf：门～ door leaf 3.〈*classifier*〉一～窗 a window

（另见"扇"shān）

【扇贝】 shànbèi 〈*Zool.*〉scallop

【扇车】 shànchē winnowing machine；winnower

【扇面儿】 shànmiànr the covering of a fan

【扇形】 shànxíng 1.（扇子的形状）fan-shaped：～窗子 fan-shaped window 2.〈*Math.*〉sector

【扇子】 shàn·zi fan

骟（shàn） 1.（割掉睾丸）castrate：～马 castrate a horse 2.（切除卵巢）spay：～母马 spay a mare

善（shàn） 1.（善良）good 2.（良好）satisfactory；good 3.（办好；弄好）make a success of；perfect 4.（友善）be friendly；be kind and helpful 5.（擅长）be good at；be expert in：～经营 be good at management 6.（好好地）properly 7.（容易；易于）be apt to

【善罢甘休】 shànbà-gānxiū （多用于否定）leave the matter at that；let it go at that；willing to let it go

【善本】 shànběn reliable text；good edition

【善策】 shàncè a wise policy；the best policy

【善处】 shànchù 〈*written*〉deal discreetly with；conduct oneself well

【善恶】 shàn'è good and evil

【善后】 shànhòu cope with the aftermath of a disaster

【善后事宜】 shànhòu-shìyí rehabilitation works；matters concerning reconstruction

【善举】 shànjǔ 〈*written*〉philanthropic act or project

【善良】 shànliáng good and honest；kindhearted：～守法 good and lawful

【善男信女】 shànnán-xìnnǚ devotees to Buddha; devout men and women

【善人】 shànrén philanthropist; charitable person

【善始善终】 shànshǐ-shànzhōng start well and end well; do well from start to finish; see sth. through

【善心】 shànxīn mercy; benevolence

【善意】 shànyì good intentions; bona fides; good faith

【善有善报，恶有恶报】 shàn yǒu shànbào, è yǒu èbào good will be rewarded with good, and evil with evil

【善于】 shànyú be good at; be adept in: ～辞令 one is skillful in making statement; eloquent in speech

【善终】 shànzhōng die a natural death; die in one's bed

【善自保重】 shànzìbǎozhòng take good care of yourself

缮 (shàn) 1.（修缮）repair; mend: 房屋修～ house repairing 2.（缮写）copy; write out: ～清 make a fair copy

【缮写】 shànxiě write out; copy

膳［饍］(shàn) meals; board

【膳费】 shànfèi board expenses

【膳食】 shànshí meals; food: 流质～ liquid diet

【膳宿】 shànsù board and lodging

【膳务长】 shànwùzhǎng chief steward

鳝［鱓］(shàn) 〈*Zool.*〉 ricefield eel; Fluta alba ‖ 注：有人译为 eel 或 finless eel。eel 是鳗鱼，鳗鱼属鳗鲡科，而鳝鱼属合鳃科。

擅 (shàn) 1.（擅自）arrogate to oneself; do sth. on one's own authority: ～作主张 make a decision without authorization 2.（善于）be good at; be expert in

【擅长】 shàncháng be good at; be expert in; be skilled in: 他～画山水。He is good at landscape painting.

【擅离职守】 shànlí-zhíshǒu be absent from one's post without leave; leave one's post without permission; unauthorized departure from official duty

【擅自】 shànzì do sth. without authorization: ～决定 make arbitrary decisions / ～行动 act arbitrarily; take an arbitrary action

嬗 (shàn) replace; change

【嬗变】 shànbiàn develop; evolve

赡 (shàn) 1.（赡养）support; provide for: ～家养口 support a family 2.（丰富；充足）sufficient; abundant

【赡养】 shànyǎng support; provide for: ～父母 support one's parents

【赡养费】 shànyǎngfèi alimony; cost of support; maintenance

【赡养义务】 shànyǎng yìwù duty of maintenance; duty to support

shang

伤［傷］(shāng) 1.（受的伤）wound; injury: 枪～ a gun wound / 致命～ mortal wound; fatal wound / 头部受～ suffer injuries to the head 2.（受伤）wound; injure: 他胳膊受～了。He was wounded in the arm. / 在车祸中有两个人受了～。There was two people injured in the car accident. 3.（伤害）injure; hurt; wound: ～了她的自尊心 injure her price; wound to her pride 4.（悲伤）be distressed 5.（厌烦）get sick of sth.; develop an aversion to sth. 6.（妨碍）be harmful to; hinder: 无～大雅 involving no major principle; not matter much

【伤疤】 shāngbā scar

【伤兵】 shāngbīng wounded soldier

【伤病员】 shāngbìngyuán noneffectives; the sick and wounded

【伤残】 shāngcán permanent disability

【伤残人】 shāngcánrén disabled man

【伤风】 shāngfēng catch cold; have a cold

【伤风败俗】 shāngfēng-bàisú offend public decency; corrupt public morals; breach of morality

【伤感】 shānggǎn sick at heart; sentimental

【伤害】 shānghài injure; harm; hurt: ～他人身体 do an injury to sb.

【伤害保险】 shānghài bǎoxiǎn injury insurance

【伤寒】 shānghán 1.〈*Med.*〉 typhoid fever; typhoid 2.〈*Chin. Med.*〉 diseases caused by

harmful cold factors; febrile diseases; fevers
【伤寒杆菌】 shānghán gǎnjūn typhoid bacillus
【伤痕】 shānghén scar; bruise; hack
【伤筋动骨】 shāngjīn-dònggǔ have a fracture; be injured in the sinews or bones
【伤科】 shāngkē 〈*Chin. Med.*〉(department of) traumatology
【伤口】 shāngkǒu wound; cut: 腿上的～ a cut on the leg
【伤脑筋】 shāngnǎojīn knotty; troublesome; bothersome: 这事真～。It's rather troublesome.
【伤神】 shāngshén overtax one's nerves; be nerve-racking
【伤势】 shāngshì the condition of an injury
【伤天害理】 shāngtiān-hàilǐ flagrantly wrongful; grossly unjust; do things offensive to God and reason
【伤亡】 shāngwáng injuries and deaths; casualties
【伤心】 shāngxīn **1.**(伤心的) sad; grieved; broken-hearted **2.**(使伤心) sadden; grieve: 儿子的忘恩负义使她很～。She was saddened by her son's ingratitude. / 她仍在为死去的丈夫而～。She is still grieving for her dead husband.
【伤员】 shāngyuán wounded personnel; the wounded: 重～ seriously wounded

商 (shāng) **1.**(商量) discuss; consult: 面～ discuss with sb. personally **2.**(商业) trade; commerce; business: 经～ be in business **3.**(商人) merchant; businessman; dealer; trader: 零售～ retailer / 批发～ wholesaler / 水果～ a fruit merchant / 奸～ profiteer **4.**〈*Math.*〉 quotient
【商标】 shāngbiāo trade mark; brand: 注册～ trade-mark registered
【商标法】 shāngbiāofǎ trademark law
【商标名称】 shāngbiāo míngchēng brand name; trade name
【商标权】 shāngbiāoquán trade mark privileges; trademark right
【商标所有权】 shāngbiāo suǒyǒuquán ownership of trademark
【商标所有者】 shāngbiāo suǒyǒuzhě grantee of trade-mark
【商标注册】 shāngbiāo zhùcè trade mark registration
【商标注册人】 shāngbiāo zhùcèrén trademark registrant
【商标专用权】 shāngbiāo zhuānyòngquán exclusive right to use trademark
【商场】 shāngchǎng **1.**(指购物中心) shopping center; plaza **2.**(指大型百货商店) department store **3.**(指商界) business circles; commercial circles: ～如战场。The business circles are like the battlefield.
【商城】 shāngchéng shopping center; plaza
【商船】 shāngchuán merchantman; merchant ship
【商船队】 shāngchuánduì merchant marine (AmE.); merchant navy (BrE.)
【商店】 shāngdiàn shop; store
【商店橱窗】 shāngdiàn chúchuāng shop window
【商店招牌】 shāngdiàn zhāopái shop sign
【商调】 shāngdiào transfer sb. to another post through discussion of the two parties concerned
【商定】 shāngdìng decide through consultation; agree: 双方～了谈判的日期。The two sides have agreed on the date of negotiations.
【商队】 shāngduì a company of travelling merchants; trade caravan
【商法】 shāngfǎ 〈*Law*〉 commercial law; commercial act
【商贩】 shāngfàn small retailer; pedlar
【商港】 shānggǎng commercial port
【商行】 shāngháng trading company; commercial firm
【商号】 shānghào shop; store; business establishment; corporate name
【商会】 shānghuì chamber of commerce
【商检】 shāngjiǎn commodity inspection
【商检证明书】 shāngjiǎn zhèngmíngshū commodity inspection certificate
【商界】 shāngjiè business circles; commercial circles
【商量】 shāng·liáng consult; discuss; talk over
【商贸】 shāngmào commerce and trade
【商品】 shāngpǐn commodity; goods; merchandise: 呆滞～ slow-selling goods / 对路

～ marketable commodities / 市场紧俏～ products that are in short supply
【商品房】 shāngpǐnfáng commodity house; commercial apartment
【商品化】 shāngpǐnhuà commercialize; commercialization
【商品价格】 shāngpǐn jiàgé commodity price
【商品检验】 shāngpǐn jiǎnyàn commodity inspection
【商品交换】 shāngpǐn jiāohuàn exchange of commodities
【商品交易所】 shāngpǐn jiāoyìsuǒ commodity exchange
【商品经济】 shāngpǐn jīngjì commodity economy
【商品库存】 shāngpǐn kùcún commodity stocks
【商品粮】 shāngpǐnliáng marketable grain
【商品粮基地】 shāngpǐnliáng jīdì commodity grain base
【商品流通】 shāngpǐn liútōng circulation of commodities; commodity circulation
【商品目录】 shāngpǐn mùlù commodity list
【商品生产】 shāngpǐn shēngchǎn commodity production
【商品生产基地】 shāngpǐn shēngchǎng jīdì bases for the production of commodities
【商品税】 shāngpǐnshuì commodity tax
【商品销售市场】 shāngpǐn xiāoshòu shìchǎng outlet for goods
【商品运输】 shāngpǐn yùnshū transportation of goods
【商品展览】 shāngpǐn zhǎnlǎn trade show
【商品住宅楼】 shāngpǐn zhùzháilóu commercial residential buildings
【商洽】 shāngqià arrange with sb.; take up (a matter) with sb.
【商情】 shāngqíng market conditions
【商榷】 shāngquè discuss; deliberate
【商人】 shāngrén business person; merchant; trader; businessman (m.); businesswoman (f.)
【商厦】 shāngshà shopping center; plaza
【商事】 shāngshì commercial affairs
【商事法庭】 shāngshì fǎtíng commercial act
【商事纠纷】 shāngshì jiūfēn commercial dispute
【商事诉讼】 shāngshì sùsòng commercial action; commercial causes
【商事行为】 shāngshì xíngwéi commercial act
【商事仲裁】 shāngshì zhòngcái commercial arbitration
【商数】 shāngshù 〈*Math*.〉 quotient
【商谈】 shāngtán exchange views; confer; discuss; negotiate
【商讨】 shāngtǎo discuss; deliberate over
【商务】 shāngwù commercial affairs; business affairs
【商务参赞】 shāngwù cānzàn commercial counsellor
【商务处】 shāngwùchù commercial counsellor's office
【商务代表】 shāngwù dàibiǎo commercial representative; trade representative
【商务代表处】 shāngwù dàibiǎochù office of a trade delegation; trade representative's office
【商务责任】 shāngwù zérèn commercial liability
【商务仲裁】 shāngwù zhòngcái commercial arbitration
【商务专员】 shāngwù zhuānyuán commercial attaché
【商学院】 shāngxuéyuàn business college
【商业】 shāngyè commerce; trade; business; commercial (adj.); mercantile (adj.)
【商业包装】 shāngyè bāozhuāng commercial packing
【商业部门】 shāngyè bùmén commercial departments
【商业贷款】 shāngyè dàikuǎn commercial loans
【商业道德】 shāngyè dàodé business ethics; commercial morality
【商业电视】 shāngyè diànshì sponsored television
【商业对策】 shāngyè duìcè business game
【商业法】 shāngyèfǎ business law; commercial law
【商业惯例】 shāngyè guànlì business practice
【商业广播】 shāngyè guǎngbō commercial broadcasting
【商业行话】 shāngyè hánghuà business jargon
【商业化】 shāngyèhuà commercialization;

commercialize：棒球在美国已经～了。Baseball has been commercialized in America.

【商业机构】 shāngyè jīgòu business organization; commercial undertaking

【商业街】 shāngyèjiē commercial area; commercial district; shopping streets：地下～ subterranean commercial area; underground commercial district

【商业秘密】 shāngyè mìmì trade secrets; business secrets

【商业票据】 shāngyè piàojù commercial bill; trade bill

【商业区】 shāngyèqū business quarter; commercial district; business district; shopping part of town

【商业事务】 shāngyè shìwù business affair

【商业网】 shāngyèwǎng commercial network; network of trading establishments

【商业往来】 shāngyè wǎnglái commercial intercourse

【商业信贷】 shāngyè xìndài mercantile credit

【商业信用卡】 shāngyè xìnyòngkǎ commercial letter of credit

【商业银行】 shāngyè yínháng commercial bank

【商业预测】 shāngyè yùcè business forecasting

【商业中心】 shāngyè zhōngxīn commercial center; trading center; shopping center

【商业注册】 shāngyè zhùcè business registration

【商业资本】 shāngyè zīběn commercial capital; merchant capital

【商议】 shāngyì confer; discuss

【商约】 shāngyuē commercial treaty

【商酌】 shāngzhuó discuss and consider; deliberate over

墒［**暘**］(shāng) 〈*Agric.*〉 moisture in the soil：保～ preserve the moisture of the soil

【墒情】 shāngqíng soil moisture content

熵 (shāng) 〈*Physics*〉 entropy; thermal charge

晌 (shǎng) 1.(一会儿) part of the day 2.(中午) noon

【晌午】 shǎng·wu midday; noon

赏 (shǎng) 1.(奖赏) grant a reward; award：有～有罚 mete out rewards or punishments as the case demands 2.(奖赏之物) reward; award：领～ receive a reward 3.(欣赏) admire; enjoy; appreciate：～花 admire the beauty of flowers

【赏赐】 shǎngcì grant a reward; award

【赏罚】 shǎngfá rewards and punishments; deserving award and punishment

【赏功罚罪】 shǎnggōng-fázuì give rewards for good service and punishments for faults

【赏光】 shǎngguāng 〈*politeness*〉务请～ request the pleasure of your company

【赏鉴】 shǎngjiàn appreciate

【赏金】 shǎngjīn money reward; pecuniary reward

【赏识】 shǎngshí recognize the worth of; appreciate：受到某人的～ be in sb's good graces

【赏玩】 shǎngwán admire the beauty of sth.; delight in; enjoy

【赏心悦目】 shǎngxīn-yuèmù find the scenery pleasing to both the eye and the mind

【赏月】 shǎngyuè enjoy the glorious full moon

上 (shàng) 1.(与"下"相对) upper; up; upward; upwards：～身 the upper part of the body / ～嘴唇 upper lip / 树向～长。The tree grows upwards. / 人们都向～看。The people were all looking upwards. 2.(次序在前的) first (part); last; previous：～半年 the first half of the year / ～星期 last week 3.(等级高的) higher; superior; better：中～水平 above the average; better than the average 4.(到高的地方) go up; mount; board; get on：～车 get on a car / ～船 go on board; go aboard a ship / ～楼 go upstairs; go up the stairs / ～山 go up a hill; go up a mountain 5.(到；去) go to; leave for：～北京 leave for Beijing / 你～哪儿去? Where are you going? 6.(向前进) forge ahead; go ahead：快～!(指打球等) Go ahead. Quick! (指上车等) Hurry up and get on! 7.(比赛时上场) enter the court or field：前半时你～。You play the first half. 8.(加添) fill; supply; serve：～货 replenish the stock of goods 9.(安上) place sth. in position; set; fix：～螺丝 drive a screw (into sth.) / 给窗子～玻璃 to glaze a window

10.(涂；搽) apply; paint; smear：他把墙漆～黄色。He painted the wall yellow. 11.(登载) be carried; appear：她的名字～了报。Her name has appeared on the newspaper. 12.(拧紧) wind; screw; tighten：表该～了。The watch needs winding. 13.(达到) up to; as many as：～百人 up to a hundred people 14.(在…之上) on; above：在地板～ on the floor / 在墙～ on the wall / 在桌子～ on the table / 你衣服～有油漆。There's paint on your clothes. / 我上星期在电视～看过这部影片。I saw this film on television last week. / 那球员踩在了边线～。That player trampled on the boundary line. / 那座山高高地耸立在平原之～。The mountain towered above the plain. 15.(在…范围、范畴) in：在世界～ in the world / 在报纸～ in the newspaper / 在历史～ in history

【上岸】 shàng'àn ashore; land; go ashore：每到一个港口他都～。He went ashore at every port.

【上岸证明书】 shàng'àn zhèngmíngshū landing certificate

【上班】 shàngbān go to work; start work; be on duty：我今天两点～。My work start at two in today's afternoon.

【上板儿】 shàngbǎnr put up the shutters

【上半场】 shàngbànchǎng 同"上半时"

【上半时】 shàngbànshí first half (of a game)

【上报】 shàngbào 1.(登载) appear in the newspapers：这篇文章～了。This article has appeared on the newspaper. 2.(向上级报告) report to a higher body; report to the leadership

【上臂】 shàngbì the upper arm

【上膘】 shàngbiāo become fat; fatten：这牛在卖之前上了膘。This cattle are being fattened up before being sold.

【上表】 shàngbiǎo wind (up) the watch; wind (up) the clock：我忘～了。I've forgotten to wind my watch (up) again.

【上宾】 shàngbīn distinguished guest; guest of honor

【上不封顶，下不保底】 shàng bù fēngdǐng, xià bù bǎodǐ no ceiling above, no protection below

【上操】 shàngcāo go out to drill; be drilling

【上策】 shàngcè the best plan; the best way out; the best thing to do

【上层】 shàngcéng 1.(指领导层) upper strata; upper levels 2.(双层汽车的上层) upper deck

【上层分子】 shàngcéng fènzǐ members of the upper strata; upper-class elements

【上层建筑】 shàngcéng jiànzù 1.(指具体的) superstructure：船舶的～ superstructure of a ship / 新医院的基础已经完工，但～还未开工。The foundations are finished and work has now begun on building the superstructure of the new hospital. 2.(指抽象的) superstructure：～与经济基础 superstructure and economic base

【上层人士】 shàngcéng rénshì upper circles

【上层社会】 shàngcéng shèhuì upper classes of society; upper-class society

【上场】 shàngchǎng 1.(演员出场) appear on the stage; enter：她在第二幕时才～。She doesn't go on until the second act. 2.(运动员出场) enter the court or field; join in a contest; take part in the competition：这后半时你～。You play this second half.

【上场门】 shàngchǎngmén 〈*Theatre*〉 entrance

【上乘】 shàngchéng a work of a high order

【上床】 shàngchuáng 1.(去睡觉) go to bed; bed down：昨晚你几点～睡觉的？What time did you go to bed last night? 2.(与…发生性行为) go to bed with sb.

【上唇】 shàngchún upper lip; labrum

【上窜下跳】 shàngcuān xiàtiào run around on sinister errands

【上达】 shàngdá reach the higher authorities：下情～ make the situation at the lower level known to the higher authorities

【上单翼单发飞机】 shàngdānyì dānfā fēijī high-wing monoplane

【上当】 shàngdàng be duped by sb.; be taken in; be fooled：～受骗 swallow a gudgeon; be tricked / 这是个阴谋，他～了。It was a put-up job and he'd been duped.

【上当的人】 shàngdàng·derén dupe

【上等】 shàngděng first-class; first-rate; superior

【上等兵】 shàngděngbīng 1.(陆军) Private 2.(空军) Airman 3.(海军) Seaman
【上等品】 shàngděngpǐn superior quality
【上帝】 shàngdì God
【上吊】 shàngdiào hang oneself
【上调】 shàngdiào 1.(指调动工作) be transferred to post at a higher-level organ 2.(上级调用物资或资金) transfer goods or funds
【上冻】 shàngdòng freeze：湖水～了，我们可以去滑冰了。The lake had frozen, we can go skating.
【上端内存】 shàngduān nèicún 〈Computer〉 upper memory
【上颚】 shàng'è the upper jaw
【上房】 shàngfáng main rooms
【上访】 shàngfǎng apply for an audience with the higher authorities to appeal for help
【上坟】 shàngfén visit the grave; visit the tomb
【上风】 shàngfēng 1.(风刮来的那一方) windward：站在～打农药 spray insecticide on-the windward side 2.(优势) advantage; superior position; upper hand：占～ get the upper hand; have the upper hand; win an advantage
【上腹部】 shàngfùbù upper abdomen
【上岗】 shànggǎng take up a post; take on a job; begin to work
【上告】 shànggào complain to the higher authorities or appeal to a higher court
【上工】 shànggōng 1.(去工作) go to work; get to work 2.(雇工开始工作) start work as an employee
【上供】 shànggòng 1.(摆祭祀物品) offer up a sacrifice 2.(喻为拉关系送钱物) give dinners; send gifts
【上钩】 shànggōu rise to the bait; swallow the bait; get hooked
【上钩拳】 shànggōuquán 〈Boxing〉 uppercut
【上古】 shànggǔ ancient times; remote ages
【上管】 shàngguǎn 〈Bicycle〉 top tube
【上光】 shàngguāng glazing; polishing
【上光机】 shàngguāngjī glazing machine; glazer
【上光蜡】 shàngguānglà wax polish
【上轨道】 shàngguǐdào get on the right track; begin to work smoothly：一切都已～了。Everything is in good order now.
【上好】 shànghǎo first-class; best-quality; tip-top
【上颌】 shànghé 〈Anat.〉 the upper jaw; maxilla
【上颌骨】 shànghégǔ 〈Anat.〉 maxilla; upper jawbone
【上呼吸道】 shànghūxīdào 〈Anat.〉 the upper respiratory tract
【上呼吸道感染】 shànghūxīdào gǎnrǎn 〈Med.〉 infection of the upper respiratory tract
【上火】 shànghuǒ 1.〈dial.〉 get angry 2.〈Chin. Med.〉 suffer from excessive internal heat
【上级】 shàngjí higher level; higher authorities
【上级法院】 shàngjí fǎyuàn court above; higher court; superior court
【上级机关】 shàngjí jīguān higher bodies; higher authorities
【上将】 shàngjiàng 1.(陆军) General 2.(空军) Air General 3.(海军) Admiral ‖ 一级上将 1.(陆军) Senior General 2.(空军，海军) General First Grade
【上交】 shàngjiāo hand in; turn over to the higher authorities
【上缴】 shàngjiǎo turn over to the higher authorities
【上缴利润】 shàngjiǎo lìrùn that part of the profits turned over to the state
【上接】 shàngjiē be continued from
【上街】 shàngjiē 1.(到街上去) go into the street：～买东西 go on to the streets and shopping 2.(购物) go shopping
【上届】 shàngjiè previous term or session; last：～毕业生 last year's graduates
【上进】 shàngjìn go forward; make progress：力求～ do one's best to advance
【上进心】 shàngjìnxīn the desire to do better; the urge for improvement
【上劲】 shàngjìn energetically; with gusto; with great vigor
【上课】 shàngkè 1.(学生听课) attend class; go to class：他昨天没来～。He didn't come to class yesterday. 2.(教师讲课) conduct a class; give a lesson
【上空】 shàngkōng in the sky; overhead

【上空装】 shàngkōngzhuāng topless dress：着～ **go topless**

【上口】 shàngkǒu fluent; smooth：他把那首诗念得琅琅～。He can recite the poem fluently.

【上款】 shàngkuǎn the name of the recipient

【上来】 shànglái 1.（表示从下到上）up, upward：跑～ come up by running / 坐电梯～ come up by elevator 2.（表示动作完成）影迷围～要他签名留念。The film fans gathered around him and asked for his autographs. 3.（表示能成功）这个问题你一定答得～。I'm sure you can answer this question.

【上联】 shànglián the first line of a couplet on a scroll

【上梁】 shàngliáng 1.（自行车的）cross bar; top tube 2.（建筑物的）upper beam

【上梁不正下梁歪】 shàngliáng bù zhèng xiàliáng wāi When those above behave unworthily, those below will do the same.

【上列】 shàngliè the above-listed; the above

【上流】 shàngliú 1.（上游）upper reaches（of a river）2.（指社会地位）belonging to the upper circles; upper-class：～社会 high society; polite society; upper crust

【上路】 shànglù 1.（开始行程）set out on a journey 2.（上轨道）start off

【上马】 shàngmǎ 1.（骑上马背）mount a horse 2.（口令）To horse! 3.（着手办事）start

【上门】 shàngmén 1.（登门）come or go to see sb.; call; drop in; visit：～服务 come knocking at sb's door to offer one's service; make house calls 2.（关门）shut the door for the night; bolt the door 3.（打烊）close for the night; put up the shutters 4.（入赘）marry into and live with one's bride's family

【上面】 shàng·mian 1.（在另一物正上方）above; over; on top of; on the surface of：河～有座桥。There is a bridge over the river. 2.（前面提到的）above-mentioned; aforesaid; foregoing 3.（上级）the higher authorities; the higher-ups：这是～的指示。These are the instructions from above. 4.（方面）aspect; respect; regard

【上脑】 shàngnǎo 1.（牛肉部位）neck 2.（猪肉部位）shoulder butt

【上皮组织】 shàngpí zǔzhī 〈*Anat.*〉epithelial tissue

【上品】 shàngpǐn highest grade; top grade

【上坡】 shàngpō 1.（爬坡）uphill 2.（上坡路标志）hill

【上坡路】 shàngpōlù 1.（通向高处的路）uphill road; ascent; upward slope 2.（向好的方向发展）upward trend; steady progress

【上铺】 shàngpù upper berth

【上气不接下气】 shàngqì bù jiē xiàqì gasp for breath; be out of breath

【上腔静脉】 shàngqiāng jìngmài 〈*Anat.*〉superior vena cava

【上情下达】 shàngqíng-xiàdá the situation at a higher level made know to a lower level

【上去】 shàngqù go up：登着梯子～ go up a ladder / 爬～ climb up

【上任】 shàngrèn 1.（赴任）take up an official post; assume office 2.（前任）predecessor

【上色】 shàngsè color（a picture, map, etc.）

【上山】 shàngshān 1.（到山上去）go up a hill; go up a mountain 2.（到山区去）go to mountainous area

【上上】 shàngshàng 1.（最好的）the very best：～策 the best plan 2.（比"上"再往前的）before last：～月 the month before last

【上身】 shàngshēn 1.（身体上半部）the upper part of the body 2.（上衣）upper outer garment; shirt; blouse; jacket 3.（初次穿）start wearing

【上升】 shàngshēng 1.（往上升起）move upward; ascend 2.（升高，增加）ascend; increase; rise：气温～。The temperature rises.

【上升段】 shàngshēngduàn 〈*Astron.*〉ascent stage

【上士】 shàngshì 1.（陆军）Sergeant First Class 2.（空军）Air Sergeant First Class 3.（海军）Petty Officer First Class

【上市】 shàngshì 1.（指蔬菜水果等）appear on the market; be on the market 2.（指证券）list; be listed 3.（去市场）go to the market

【上市公司】 shàngshì gōngsī listed company

【上市条件】 shàngshì tiáojiàn listing requirements

【上市证券】 shàngshì zhèngquàn listed securities

【上手】 shàngshǒu 1.(上首) left-hand seat; seat of honor 2.(开始) start; begin: 今天的球一～就打得很顺利。Today we were doing fine right after the game started.

【上书】 shàngshū submit a written statement to a higher authority; send in a memorial

【上述】 shàngshù above-mentioned; aforementioned; aforesaid

【上水】 shàngshuǐ 1.(向上游航行) sail upstream: ～船 upriver boat 2.(加水) feed water: 给蒸汽机车～ feed water to a steam engine

【上税】 shàngshuì pay taxes

【上司】 shàngsī superior; boss

【上诉】 shàngsù 〈*Law*〉 appeal (to a higher court): 不服判决而～ appeal to a higher court; appeal against a decision

【上诉程序】 shàngsù chéngxù procedure for appeal

【上诉法院】 shàngsù fǎyuàn appellate court

【上诉费用】 shàngsù fèiyòng costs of appeal

【上诉理由】 shàngsù lǐyóu grounds of appeal

【上诉权】 shàngsùquán right of appeal

【上诉人】 shàngsùrén petitioner; appellant

【上诉审】 shàngsùshěn trial on appeal; retrial on appeal

【上诉书】 shàngsùshū instrument of appeal

【上诉文件】 shàngsù wénjiàn instrument of appeal

【上溯】 shàngsù 1.(逆水前进) go upstream 2.(指年代) trace back: ～到 1840 年 trace back to the 1840

【上算】 shàngsuàn paying; worthwhile: 不～ be not worth-while

【上台】 shàngtái 1.(登台) go up onto the platform; appear on the stage: ～演奏 go up onto the platform and play 2.(掌权) assume power; come to power

【上膛】 shàngtáng 1.〈*Mil.*〉 load; be loaded: 上了膛的枪 a loaded gun / 给子弹～ load a gun; put bullets into a gun 2.(腭) palate

【上天】 shàngtiān 1.(上苍) Heaven; Providence; God 2.(升到天空) go up to the sky; fly sky-high: 人造卫星～。An artificial satellite has been launched.

【上天无路,入地无门】 shàngtiān wú lù, rùdì wú mén there is no road to heaven and no door into the earth; no way of escape; in desperate straits

【上调】 shàngtiáo raise: ～工资 raise wages / ～物价 raise prices / ～租金 raise the rent

【上吐下泻】 shàngtù-xiàxiè vomit and have watery stools; vomiting and being purged

【上尉】 shàngwèi 1.(陆军) Captain 2.(空军) Air Captain 3.(海军) Lieutenant

【上文】 shàngwén foregoing paragraphs or chapters; preceding part of the text: 见～ see above

【上午】 shàngwǔ forenoon; morning

【上下】 shàngxià 1.(职务、辈分上的高低) high and low; old and young: 举国～ the whole nation 2.(从上到下) from top to bottom; up and down: ～打量 look sb. up and down 3.(从高到低或从低到高) go up and down 4.(程度高低) relative superiority or inferiority: 难分～ hard to tell which is better 5.(大约) about; or so; or thereabouts: 三十岁～ about thirty years old; thirty or so 6.(上去和下来) go up and come down

【上下班时间】 shàngxiàbān shíjiān commuter time

【上下文】 shàngxiàwén context

【上弦】 shàngxián 1.〈*Astron.*〉 first quarter (of the moon) 2.(上钟表发条) wind up a clock or watch

【上弦月】 shàngxiányuè the moon at the first quarter

【上限】 shàngxiàn upper limit

【上校】 shàngxiào 1.(陆军) Colonel 2.(空军) Air Colonel 3.(海军) Captain

【上鞋】 shàngxié sole a shoe; stitch the sole (to the upper)

【上刑】 shàngxíng put sb. to torture; torture

【上行】 shàngxíng 1.〈*Railway*〉 up; upgoing: ～列车 the up train 2.(指船) upriver; upstream: ～船 upriver boat

【上行下效】 shàngxíng-xiàxiào those in subordinate positions will follow the example set by their superiors

【上学】 shàngxué 1.(去学校) go to school 2.(开始读小学) be at school

【上旬】 shàngxún the first ten-day period of a month：三月～ the first ten-day period of the March

【上演】 shàngyǎn put on the stage；perform：不日～ will be performed very soon

【上眼睑】 shàngyǎnjiǎn 〈*Anat*.〉 upper eyelid

【上衣】 shàngyī upper outer garment；jacket

【上议院】 shàngyìyuàn upper house；the House of Lords（of Britain）

【上瘾】 shàngyǐn be addicted（to sth.）；get into the habit（of doing sth.）：这东西吃多了会～吗？Is this habit-forming?

【上映】 shàngyìn show（a film）；screen；be on；run：这部影片已～5天。The film has run for five days.

【上游】 shàngyóu **1**.（指河流的前段）upper reaches **2**.（先进）advanced position：力争～ strive for the best

【上有政策，下有对策】 shàng yǒu zhèngcè, xià yǒu duìcè the higher authority has policies and the locality has his counter-measures

【上涨】 shàngzhǎng rise；go up：河水～的很快。The river rises rapidly. / 物价在～。The prices are going up. / 房价～了。House prices have risen.

【上账】 shàngzhàng make an entry in an account book；enter sth. in an account

【上阵】 shàngzhèn go into battle；pitch into the work

【上肢】 shàngzhī upper limbs

【上装】 shàngzhuāng **1**.（演员化装）make up（for a theatrical performance）**2**.（上衣）upper outer garment；jacket

【上座】 shàngzuò **1**.（指上首座位）seat of honor **2**.（吸引观众）draw an audience **3**.（指观众）audience

【上座率】 shàngzuòlǜ attendance；audience attendance：～高 a high attendance

尚（shàng） **1**.〈*adv*.〉（还）still；yet：时机～未成熟。The time is not yet ripe. **2**.（尊崇）esteem；value；set great store by

【尚付阙如】 shàng fù quērú still wanting；not yet done

【尚且】 shàngqiě 〈*conj*.〉 even：小孩～懂得。Even a child can understand it.

【尚武】 shàngwǔ set great store by military affairs or martial arts：～精神 encourage a military spirit；militarism

绱［鞝］（shàng）

【绱鞋】 shàngxié 同“上鞋”

shao

捎（shāo） take along sth. to or for sb.；bring to sb.：请把这本词典～给他。Take this dictionary to him, please.

【捎带】 shāodài incidentally；in passing：～把这点提一下 mention this point in passing

梢（shāo） tip；the thin end of a twig, etc.：树～ the top of a tree / 头发～ the end of a braid

【梢公】 shāogōng 同“艄公”

【梢头】 shāotóu **1**.（树枝顶端）the tip of a branch **2**.〈*Forestry*〉 top log

稍（shāo） 〈*abv*.〉 a little；a bit；slightly；a trifle：～待片刻 stay a minute / ～事休息 have a short interval
（另见“稍”shào）

【稍稍】 shāoshāo 〈*abv*.〉 a little；a bit

【稍微】 shāowēi 〈*abv*.〉 a little；a bit；slightly；a trifle：觉得～有点冷 feel a bit cold / 他比他妹妹～高一点。He's slightly taller than his sister.

【稍许】 shāoxǔ 〈*abv*.〉 a little；a bit

【稍纵即逝】 shāozòng-jíshì transient；fleeting：～的机会 a fleeting opportunity

艄（shāo） **1**.（船尾）stern **2**.（舵）helm：掌～ take the helm；be at the helm

【艄公】 shāogōng helmsman

烧［燒］（shāo） **1**.（燃烧）burn：～煤的船 ships that burn coal / 房子～起来了。The house is burning. **2**.（烧毁）burn：他把熨衣板～了一个洞。He burned a hole on the ironing board. **3**.（加热，使熟）cook；bake；heat；boil：～水 boil water / 在炉子上～汤 heat the soup on the cooker / 我还没～好饭呢。I haven't cooked the dinner. **4**.（烹调方法）stew after frying or fry after stewing：～羊肉 stewed mutton / 红～肉 stewed pork with brown sauce **5**.（烤）roast：～鹅 roasted goose / ～鸡 roasted chicken **6**.（发烧）run a fever；have a temperature：有点儿～ have a slight fever **7**.（身

体热度）fever：高～ a burning fever / ～退了。The fever went down.

【烧饼】 shāo·bing sesame seed cake

【烧穿】 shāochuān burn out; burn through

【烧锅】 shāoguō cooking pot

【烧化】 shāohuà 1.（烧掉尸体）cremate 2.（烧掉）burn（paper, etc. as an offering to the dead）

【烧坏】 shāohuài burn out; burn up

【烧毁】 shāohuǐ 1.（焚烧毁坏）burn down：他～了所有的文件。He burnt all his papers. 2.〈*Electr.*〉burn out; burn-through; overburning

【烧火】 shāohuǒ make a fire; light a fire; tend the kitchen fire

【烧结】 shāojié sintering; agglomeration

【烧焦】 shāojiāo singe; scorch

【烧酒】 shāojiǔ spirit; white

【烧烤】 shāokǎo barbecue; Bar-B-Q; barbie; barbecue（v.）

【烧麦】 shāomài 〈*Food*〉a steamed dumpling with the dough gathered at the top

【烧瓶】 shāopíng 〈*Chem.*〉flask

【烧伤】 shāoshāng 〈*Med.*〉burn：他手上的～ burns on his hand

【烧香】 shāoxiāng 1.（拜佛）burn joss sticks（before an idol）：～上供 burn joss sticks and offer up a sacrifice 2.（请客求关照）give dinners 3.（送礼请求关照）send gifts

【烧心】 shāoxīn 1.〈*Med.*〉heartburn 2.（菜心发黄）turn yellow at the heart

【烧砖】 shāozhuān bake bricks; fire bricks

【烧灼】 shāozhuó burn; scorch; singe

勺［杓[1]］（sháo） 1.（餐具）spoon; ladle：长柄～ ladle; dipper / 木～ wooden spoon / 汤～ soup spoon 2.（一勺的量）spoonful：一～糖 a spoonful of sugar

【勺状软骨】 sháozhuàng ruǎngǔ 〈*Anat.*〉arytenoidea cartilago

【勺子】 sháo·zi ladle; scoop

芍（sháo）

【芍药】 sháo·yao 〈*Bot.*〉Chinese herbaceous peony; common peony

韶（sháo） 〈*written*〉splendid; beautiful

【韶光】 sháoguāng 1.（指春光）beautiful springtime 2.（指青年时代）glorious youth

【韶光易逝】 sháoguāng yìshì Time passes quickly.

【韶华虚度】 sháohuá-xūdù pouring one's life in the sand; wasting one's youth; idling one's youth away

少（shǎo） 1.（数量小）few; little; less：～劳～得 the less the contribution, the lower the pay / 我的时间太～了，完成不了这项工作。I have too little time to finish this work. / 实际困难比我想像得要～。There is much less difficulty than I thought. 谁的错儿～？Who has fewest mistakes? 2.（缺少）be short; lack：人手～ be short of hands 3.（丢失）lose; be missing 4.（暂时）a little while; a moment：请～等。Wait a moment, please. 5.（不要）stop; quit：～管闲事。Mind your own business.

【少不得】 shǎo·budé cannot do without; cannot dispense with：学英语，词典是～的。Dictionaries are indispensable in English study.

【少不了】 shǎo·buliǎo cannot do without; cannot dispense with

【少而精】 shǎo'érjīng smaller quantity, better quality; fewer but better

【少见】 shǎojiàn rare; exceptional：虎在这个国家已经很～了。The tiger is very rare in this country.

【少见多怪】 shǎojiàn-duōguài comment excitedly on a commonplace thing; consider sth. remarkable simply because one has not seen it before

【少刻】 shǎokè after a little while; a moment later

【少量】 shǎoliàng a small amount; a little; a few

【少陪】 shǎopéi if you'll excuse me; I'm afraid I must be going now

【少顷】 shǎoqǐng 〈*written*〉after a short while; after a few moments; presently

【少时】 shǎoshí after a little while; a moment later

【少食多餐】 shǎoshí-duōcān have more meals a day but less food at each

【少数】 shǎoshù small number; few; minority

【少数民族】 shǎoshù mínzú minority nationality; national minority
【少数民族地区】 shǎoshù mínzú dìqū areas inhabited by the minority nationalities; minority nationality regions
【少数民族干部】 shǎoshù mínzú gànbù minority nationality cadres
【少数民族区域自治】 shǎoshù mínzú qūyù zìzhì regional autonomy of minority nationalities
【少许】 shǎoxǔ 〈*written*〉 a little; a few; a modicum
【少有】 shǎoyǒu rare; exceptional; seldom
【少云】 shǎoyún 〈*Meteorol.*〉 partly cloudy

少 (shào) 1.(年纪轻) young: 男女老～ men and women, old and young 2.(少爷) son of a rich family; young master
【少白头】 shàobáitóu 1.(指头发) be prematurely grey 2.(指人) a young person with greying hair
【少不更事】 shàobùgēngshì young and inexperienced; green
【少儿】 shào'ér baby
【少妇】 shàofù young married woman
【少将】 shàojiàng 1.(陆军) Major General 2.(空军) Air Major General 3.(海军) Rear Admiral
【少男】 shàonán young boy
【少年】 shàonián 1.(指人生阶段) early youth 2.(指人) juvenile; young person
【少年读物】 shàonián dúwù juvenile books; books for young people
【少年法庭】 shàonián fǎtíng children's court; juvenile court
【少年犯】 shàoniánfàn juvenile offender; juvenile delinquent
【少年犯管教所】 shàoniánfàn guǎnjiàosuǒ juvenile offender correctional institution
【少年犯罪】 shàonián fànzuì juvenile delinquency; juvenile crime; crime of children
【少年犯罪案件】 shàonián fànzuì ànjiàn juvenile case
【少年宫】 shàoniángōng Children's Palace
【少年老成】 shàonián-lǎochéng 1.(年轻老练) an old head on young shoulders; young but prudent and capable 2.(年轻但缺乏朝气) a young person lacking in vigor and drive
【少年业余体校】 shàonián yèyú tǐxiào children's sparetime sports school
【少年运动员】 shàonián yùndòngyuán juvenile athlete
【少年之家】 shàonián zhī jiā Children's Center; Children's Club
【少女】 shàonǚ young girl
【少尉】 shàowèi 1.(陆军) Second Lieutenant 2.(空军) Air Second Lieutenant 3.(海军) Ensign
【少先队】 shàoxiānduì 〈*brief*〉 Young Pioneers
【少先队辅导员】 shàoxiānduì fǔdǎoyuán Young Pioneer counsellor
【少先队员】 shàoxiān duìyuán Young Pioneer
【少校】 shàoxiào 1.(陆军) Major 2.(空军) Air Major 3.(海军) Lieutenant Commander
【少爷】 shào·ye 1.(主人的儿子) young master of the house 2.(尊称别人的儿子) your son
【少壮】 shàozhuàng young and vigorous: ～不努力,老大徒伤悲。If one does not exert oneself in youth, one will regret it in old age.
【少壮派】 shàozhuàngpài young guard

哨 (shào) 1.(哨所) sentry post; post: 岗～ sentry post / 放～ on sentry-go 2.(鸟叫) warble; chirp 3.(哨子) whistle: 老师吹～,开始赛跑。The teacher blew a whistle to start the race.
【哨兵】 shàobīng sentry; sentinel; guard
【哨所】 shàosuǒ post; sentry post
【哨位】 shàowèi post
【哨子】 shào·zi whistle; blew a whistle

稍 (shào) (另见"稍"shāo)
【稍息】 shàoxī 1.〈*Mil.*〉 stand at ease 2.(口令) At ease!

潲 (shào) 1.(雨斜着落下来) slant in: 西边～雨。The rain is driving in from the west. 2.(洒水) sprinkle

she

奢 (shē) 1.(奢侈) luxurious; extravagant 2.(过分的) excessive; inordinate; extravagant

【奢侈】 shēchǐ luxurious; extravagant; wasteful：～浪费 luxury and waste

【奢侈品】 shēchǐpǐn luxury goods; luxuries

【奢侈品税】 shēchǐpǐnshuì luxury tax

【奢华】 shēhuá luxurious; sumptuous; extravagant：～的旅馆 de luxe hotel

【奢靡】 shēmí extravagant; wasteful

【奢求】 shēqiú extravagant claims; excessive demands

【奢望】 shēwàng extravagant hopes

【奢想】 shēxiǎng extravagant hopes

赊(shē) buy or sell on credit

【赊供】 shēgōng deliver on credit; supply on credit

【赊购】 shēgòu buy on credit; purchase on credit

【赊欠】 shēqiàn buy or sell on credit; give or get credit

【赊售】 shēshòu credit sale

【赊销】 shēxiāo sell on credit; charge sales

【赊账】 shēzhàng on credit; on account：～交易 transaction on credit

畲(Shē) She nationality distributed Fujian, Zhejiang provinces etc., Chine

【畲族】 shēzú She (中国少数民族，主要分布在福建、浙江等地)

猞(shē) buy or sell on credit

【猞猁】 shēlì 〈*Zool*.〉 lynx

舌(shé) 1.(舌头) tongue 2.(舌形物) sth. shaped like a tongue：火～ tongues of flame / 钟～ tongue of bell

【舌癌】 shé'ái 〈*Med*.〉 tongue cancer

【舌尖】 shéjiān the tip of the tongue

【舌苔】 shétāi 〈*Chin. Med*.〉 coating on the tongue; fur

【舌头】 shé·tou 1.(舌) tongue 2.(为获情报捉来的俘虏) an enemy soldier or official captured for the purpose of extracting information

【舌战】 shézhàn argue heatedly; have a verbal battle with

【舌诊】 shézhěn 〈*Chin. Med*.〉 lingual diagnosis

折(shé) 1.(断) break; snap：腿骨～了 have broken one's leg / 小提琴的弦～了。The violin string snapped. 2.(亏损) lose money in business：把本钱都～光了 have lost the capital altogether
(另见"折"zhē, zhé)

【折本】 shéběn lose money in business：～生意 a losing business

【折耗】 shéhào damage; loss

蛇[虵](shé) snake; serpent：蝮～ viper / 蟒～ python / 响尾～ rattlesnake / 眼镜～ cobra / 眼镜王～ King cobra / 她怕被～咬。She's terrified of being bitten by a snake. / 有些～是有毒的。Some snakes are poisonous. / 有些山路上～很多。Some of the mountains roads are very snaky.

【蛇毒】 shédú snake venom; venin

【蛇皮革】 shépígé snakeskin

【蛇伤】 shéshāng snakebite

【蛇蜕】 shétuì snake slough

【蛇蝎】 shéxiē snakes and scorpions; vicious people：毒如～ as vicious as a viper

【蛇行】 shéxíng crawl; move with the body on the ground

【蛇形】 shéxíng snakelike; S-shaped; serpentine

【蛇形浮动】 shéxíng fúdòng 〈*Econ*.〉 snake; currency snake

【蛇形管】 shéxíngguǎng coiled pipe coiler

【蛇药】 shéyào antidote for snake-bites

【蛇足】 shézú feet added to a snake by an ignorant artist; sth. superfluous

舍[捨](shě) 1.(舍弃) give up; abandon：～下妻子儿女 abandon one's wife and children 2.(施舍) give alms; dispense charity
(另见"舍"shè)

【舍本逐末】 shěběn-zhúmò attend to trifles to the neglect of essentials

【舍不得】 shě·bu·de hate to part with or use; grudge：～花钱 hate to part with one's money

【舍得】 shě·de be willing to part with; not grudge：～下功夫 not grudge time spent on practice

【舍己为人】 shějǐ-wèirén sacrifice one's own interests for the sake of others

【舍近求远】 shějìn-qiúyuǎn seek far and wide for what lies close at hand

【舍命】 shěmìng risk one's life; sacrifice oneself

【舍弃】 shěqì give up; abandon: ～个人利益 give up one's own interests

【舍去】 shěqù 〈*Math.*〉 rounding; truncation

【舍入】 shěrù 〈*Math.*〉 rounding off

【舍入常数】 shěrù chángshù round-off constant

【舍入误差】 shěrù wùchā rounding error; round-off error

【舍入指令】 shěrù zhǐlìng round-off order

【舍入字符】 shěrù zìfú separating character

【舍身】 shěshēn give one's life; sacrifice oneself: ～报国 sacrifice oneself for the country

【舍生取义】 shěshēng-qǔyì lay down one's life for a just cause

【舍死忘生】 shěsǐ-wàngshēng disregard one's own safety; risk one's life

设 (shè) **1.** (设立) set up; establish; found: ～个圈套 set a trap / ～一所学校 establish a school / 总公司～在上海 set up the head office in Shanghai **2.** (筹划) work out **3.** (假设) given; suppose; if **4.** (倘若;假如) if; in case

【设备】 shèbèi equipment; installation; facilities: 现代化～ modern facilities / ～的正常运转 normal operation of equipment / 更新～ update the equipment / 拒绝接受有缺陷的～ reject defective equipment

【设备更新】 shèbèi gēngxīn updating equipment

【设备利用率】 shèbèi lìyònglǜ utilization rate of equipment and installations

【设备明细表】 shèbèi míngxìbiǎo equipment nomenclature

【设备使用和保养说明书】 shèbèi shǐyòng hé bǎoyǎng shuōmíngshū operation and maintenance instructions

【设备性能】 shèbèi xìngnéng equipment characteristic

【设法】 shèfǎ think of a way; try; do what one can

【设防】 shèfáng set up defenses; fortify; garrison

【设计】 shèjì design; plan: 服装～ dress design / 基础～ basic engineering / 结构～ structural design / 软件～ software design / 施工～ construction designing / 这一系列的服装是专门为矮个子妇女～的。This range of clothes is specially designed for shorter women. / 这机器的～很差。This machine is of bad design. / 是谁～的这座大楼? Who designed the building?

【设计方案】 shèjì fāng'àn design approach

【设计师】 shèjìshī designer

【设计图】 shèjìtú design; design drawing: 一所新房子的～ designs for a new house

【设计院】 shèjìyuàn designing institute

【设雷地带】 shèléi dìdài carpet of mines

【设立】 shèlì establish; set up; found: ～基金救助地震灾民 set up a fund for victims of the earthquake

【设身处地】 shèshēn-chǔdì put oneself in sb. else's position; be considerate

【设施】 shèshī installation; facilities: 文化教育～ cultural and educational institutions / 医疗～ medical facilities

【设想】 shèxiǎng **1.** (想像) imagine; envisage; conceive; assume; imagination (n.): 不堪～ beyond imagination **2.** (想法) tentative plan; tentative idea **3.** (着想) have consideration for

【设宴】 shèyàn give a banquet; fête: ～欢送 give sb. a send-off dinner

【设置】 shèzhì **1.** (设立) set up; establish: ～一个专门委员会 set up a special committee **2.** (安设) put up; install: ～重重障碍 place all sorts of obstacles (for sth.)

社 (shè) organized body; agency; society: 出版～ publishing house; press / 广告～ advertising agency / 旅行～ travel agency / 通讯～ news agency

【社会】 shèhuì society; social (adj.): 工业～ industrial society / 农业～ agricultural society / 社会主义～ socialist society / 资本主义～ capitalist society

【社会保险】 shèhuì bǎoxiǎn social insurance

【社会保障】 shèhuì bǎozhàng social security

【社会必要劳动】 shèhuì bìyào láodòng socially necessary labor

【社会弊病】 shèhuì bìbìng social evil

【社会财富】 shèhuì cáifù wealth of society; public wealth

【社会丑恶现象】 shèhuì chǒu'è xiànxiàng vile social practice
【社会党】 shèhuìdǎng Socialist Party
【社会地位】 shèhuì dìwèi social position; social status
【社会调查】 shèhuì diàochá social investigation; social survey
【社会发展】 shèhuì fāzhǎn social development
【社会发展史】 shèhuì fāzhǎnshǐ history of social development; history of development of society
【社会分工】 shèhuì fēngōng division of labor in society
【社会分配不公】 shèhuì fēnpèi bùgōng unfair distribution of social wealth
【社会风气】 shèhuì fēngqì the standards of social conduct; tendency in society: 良好的～ healthy tendency in society
【社会福利】 shèhuì fúlì social welfare; public welfare
【社会福利救济工作】 shèhuì fúlì jiùjì gōngzuò social work
【社会福利救济工作者】 shèhuì fúlì jiùjì gōngzuòzhě social worker
【社会福利事业】 shèhuì fúlì shìyè social and welfare services
【社会工作】 shèhuì gōngzuò work, in addition to one's regular job, done for the collective
【社会公德】 shèhuì gōngdé social morals
【社会公证】 shèhuì gōngzhèng notarization
【社会关系】 shèhuì guānxì 1.（相互的）human relations in society; social relations 2.（个人的）one's social connections
【社会化】 shèhuìhuà socialization
【社会环境】 shèhuì huánjìng social environment: 净化～ purify social environment
【社会活动】 shèhuì huódòng social activities; public activities
【社会基础】 shèhuì jīchǔ social base; social basis
【社会集团购买力】 shèhuì jítuán gòumǎilì group purchasing power
【社会集资】 shèhuì jízī social fund raising
【社会交往】 shèhuì jiāowǎng social interaction
【社会焦点】 shèhuì jiāodiǎn social focus
【社会阶级】 shèhuì jiējí social class
【社会结构】 shèhuì jiégòu social structure
【社会、经济制度】 shèhuì jīngjì zhìdù socio-economic system
【社会进化】 shèhuì jìnhuà social evolution
【社会科学】 shèhuì kēxué social sciences; social studies
【社会力量】 shèhuì lìliàng societal forces
【社会名流】 shèhuì míngliú socialite; noted public figures
【社会群体】 shèhuì qúntǐ social groups
【社会认同】 shèhuì rèntóng social identity
【社会实践】 shèhuì shíjiàn social practice
【社会体系】 shèhuì tǐxì social system
【社会问题】 shèhuì wèntí social problem
【社会贤达】 shèhuì xiándá community leaders
【社会效益】 shèhuì xiàoyì social benefit
【社会心理学】 shèhuì xīnlǐxué social psychology
【社会新闻栏】 shèhuì xīnwénlán social column
【社会行为】 shèhuì xíngwéi social action
【社会学】 shèhuìxué sociology
【社会一体化】 shèhuì yītǐhuà social integration
【社会舆论】 shèhuì yúlùn public opinion
【社会责任】 shèhuì zérèn community responsibility
【社会治安】 shèhuì zhì'ān security of society: ～综合治理 comprehensive governance of social order and security
【社会制度】 shèhuì zhìdù social system
【社会秩序】 shèhuì zhìxù social order; the public order
【社会主义】 shèhuì zhǔyì socialism; socialist (adj.): 有中国特色的～ socialism with Chinese characteristics / 发展～的商品生产和商品交换 promote commodity production and exchange on a socialist basis
【社会主义初级阶段】 shèhuì zhǔyì chūjí jiēduàn the primary stage of socialism
【社会主义道路】 shèhuì zhǔyì dàolù socialist road
【社会主义法制】 shèhuì zhǔyì fǎzhì socialist legality
【社会主义国家】 shèhuì zhǔyì guójiā socialist

state
【社会主义精神文明建设】 shèhuì zhǔyì jīngshén wénmíng jiànshè building a socialist society that is culturally and ideologically advanced
【社会主义生产关系】 shèhuì zhǔyì shēngchǎn guānxì socialist relations of production
【社会主义市场体系】 shèhuì zhǔyì shìchǎng tǐxì socialist market system; market system of socialism
【社会主义制度】 shèhuì zhǔyì zhìdù socialist system
【社会资本】 shèhuì zīběn social capital
【社会总产值】 shèhuì zǒngchǎnzhí total social output value
【社会总需求】 shèhuì zǒngxūqiú the total social demand
【社会组织】 shèhuì zǔzhī social organization
【社交】 shèjiāo social intercourse; social contact
【社交聚会】 shèjiāo jùhuì party
【社交秘书】 shèjiāo mìshū social secretary
【社交生活】 shèjiāo shēnghuó social life
【社控】 shèkòng united allocation and control by the society
【社论】 shèlùn editorial; leading article; leader
【社区】 shèqū community
【社团】 shètuán body of persons; corporation
【社团法人】 shètuán fǎrén commonalty; juridical association
【社戏】 shèxì village theatrical performance given on religious festivals in old times
【社长】 shèzhǎng chief-of-staff

舍 (shè) 1.(房舍) house; shed; hut: 校~ school buildings 2.〈*politeness*〉 my: ~弟 my younger brother
(另见"舍"shě)
【舍间】 shèjiān 〈*politeness*〉 my humble abode; my house
【舍利】 shèlì 〈*Buddhism*〉 Buddhist relics
【舍利塔】 shèlìtǎ stupa; pagoda for Buddhist relics; Buddhist shrine
【舍亲】 shèqīn 〈*politeness*〉 my relative
【舍下】 shèxià 〈*politeness*〉 my humble abode; my house

射 (shè) 1.(发射) shoot; fire: ~靶 shoot at the target 2.(喷射) discharge in a jet 3.(放出) send out (light, heat, etc.) 4.(有所指) allude to sth. or sb.; insinuate
【射程】 shèchéng range (of fire): 有效~ effective range
【射电望远镜】 shèdiàn wàngyuǎnjìng radio telescope
【射击】 shèjī 1.(开枪、开炮) shoot; fire: 她用枪向他们~。She fired her gun at them. 2.〈*Sports*〉 shooting: 飞碟~ clay-pigeon shooting / 多向飞碟~ transhooting / 双向飞碟~ skeet shooting
【射击场】 shèjīchǎng shooting range
【射击技术】 shèjī jìshù marksmanship
【射击孔】 shèjīkǒng embrasure
【射击区域】 shèjī qūyù sector of fire
【射击运动员】 shèjī yùndòngyuán shooter
【射箭】 shèjiàn 1.(用弓把箭射出) shoot an arrow 2.〈*Sports*〉 archery ‖ 射箭运动员 archer; bow-man
【射箭场】 shèjiànchǎng archery range
【射箭手】 shèjiànshǒu archer; bow-man
【射角】 shèjiǎo angle of fire; elevation
【射界】 shèjiè area of fire; firing area
【射精】 shèjīng 〈*Physiol.*〉 ejaculate; ejaculation (n.)
【射精管】 shèjīngguǎn 〈*Anat.*〉 ejaculatory ducts
【射猎】 shèliè hunting with bow and arrow or firearms
【射门】 shèmén 〈*Football*〉 shoot (at the goal); shot (n.): 反弹~ bounce shot / 跳起~ jump shot / 鱼跃~ dive shot / 转身~ turn-around shot; pivot shot
【射门得分】 shèmén défēn 〈*Football*〉 scoring; goalscoring: 失掉一次~机会 miss a goalscoring opportunity
【射频】 shèpín 〈*Electr.*〉 radio frequency
【射手】 shèshǒu 1.(射箭、放枪炮的人) shooter; marksman 2.(射门得分的人) scorer; goalscorer; goal getter: 主~ leading goalscorer
【射速】 shèsù firing rate
【射线】 shèxiàn 〈*Physics*〉 ray: 宇宙~ cosmic rays

麝 (shè) 1.〈*Zool.*〉 musk deer 2.(麝香) musk
【麝袋鼠】 shèdàishǔ 〈*Zool.*〉 musk rat-kan-

garoo

【麝馥兰香】 shèfùlánxiāng breath of musk and the scent of orchids

【麝牛】 shèniú 〈*Zool.*〉 musk ox

【麝鼠】 shèshǔ 〈*Zool.*〉 muskrat

【麝香】 shèxiāng musk

涉 (shè) **1.** (趟水走) wake; ford **2.** (经历) go through; experience **3.** (涉及) involve

【涉及】 shèjí involve; relate to; touch upon: ～重大原则性问题 involve major matters of principle

【涉猎】 shèliè do desultory reading; read cursorily

【涉世不深】 shèshìbùshēn have scanty experience of life; have seen little of the world

【涉讼】 shèsòng be involved in a lawsuit

【涉讼人】 shèsòngrén person involved in lawsuit

【涉外】 shèwài concerning foreign affairs; concerning foreign nationals: ～案件 foreign case

【涉外婚姻】 shèwài hūnyīn Chinese marriage with foreigners

【涉嫌】 shèxián be suspected of being involved; be a suspect; inviting suspicion

【涉足】 shèzú 〈*written*〉 set foot in: ～仕途 start an official career; join the civil service

赦 (shè) remit (a punishment); pardon: 大～ general pardon; amnesty / 特～ special pardon

【赦令】 shèlìng decree for pardon

【赦免】 shèmiǎn remit (a punishment); pardon; absolve; excuse

【赦免权】 shèmiǎnquán power of absolution

【赦罪】 shèzuì absolve sb. from guilt; pardon sb.

摄 [攝] (shè) **1.** (吸收) absorb; assimilate **2.** (摄影) take a photograph of; shoot **3.** (保养) conserve (one's health) **4.** (代理) act for

【摄取】 shèqǔ **1.** (吸收) absorb; assimilate; take in **2.** (拍摄) take a photograph of; shoot

【摄食】 shèshí ingest

【摄食量】 shèshíliàng food ration

【摄食习性】 shèshí xíxìng eating habit

【摄氏度】 Shèshìdù degree centigrade; Celsius: 温度是用～还是华氏度? Are the temperatures given in Celsius or Fahrenheit? (符号为 ℃)

【摄氏温标】 Shèshì wēnbiāo Celsius' thermometric scale

【摄氏温度】 Shèshì wēndù centigrade

【摄氏温度计】 Shèshì wēndùjì centigrade thermometer; Celsius thermometer

【摄像机】 shèxiàngjī video camera; pickup camera: 电视～ television camera

【摄影】 shèyǐng **1.** (照相) take a photograph: 红外～ infrared photography **2.** (拍电影) shoot a film; film **3.** (指摄影师) cameraman

【摄影场】 shèyǐngchǎng studio

【摄影机】 shèyǐngjī camera: 电影～ cinecamera

【摄影记者】 shèyǐng jìzhě cameraman; press photographer

【摄影棚】 shèyǐngpéng studio; film studio

【摄影升降机】 shèyǐng shēngjiàngjī 〈*Cinematog.*〉 camera crane

【摄影师】 shèyǐngshī **1.** 〈*Photog.*〉 photographer **2.** 〈*Cinematog.*〉 cameraman

【摄影室】 shèyǐngshì photographic studio; photo studio

【摄影术】 shèyǐngshù photography: photographic (adj.)

【摄影展览】 shèyǐng zhǎnlǎn photographic exhibition; photo exhibition

【摄政】 shèzhèng act as regent

【摄政王】 shèzhèngwáng prince regent

【摄制】 shèzhì 〈*Cinematog.*〉 produce: ～影片 produce a film

【摄制组】 shèzhìzǔ 〈*Cinematog.*〉 production unit

慑 [懾、慴] (shè) 〈*written*〉 fear; be awed: ～于淫威 be awed by authority

【慑服】 shèfú **1.** (顺从) submit because of fear; succumb **2.** (使服从) cow sb. into submission

shei

谁 (shéi) **1.** (什么人) who; whose (adj.): 她是～? Who is she? / 这是～的自行车?

Whose bike is this? **2.**（任何人）somebody; someone; anybody; anyone; whoever：你有困难时～都会帮助你。Anyone will help you when you meet with difficulties. / 不论～经营，这生意都会成功。The business would be a success, whoever owned it.
（又读"谁" shuí）

【谁边】 shéibiān where

【谁个】 shéigè who：～不知？Everybody knew.

【谁人】 shéirén who：～不晓？Everybody knew.

【谁谁】 shéishéi so-and-so：你知道吗。～要生孩子，～才买了辆汽车。You know, so-and-so is having a baby and so-and-so's just bought a car.

shen

申（shēn） state; express; explain：重～如下规定 reiterate the rules as follows

【申办】 shēnbàn bid for：～冬季奥运会 bid for the Winter Olympic Games

【申报】 shēnbào **1.**（向上级）report to a higher body **2.**（向海关）declare sth. (to the customs)：你有什么要～的吗？Have you anything to declare?

【申报出生】 shēnbào chūshēng declaration of birth

【申报单】 shēnbàodān declaration form：海关～ customs declaration form / 入境旅客物品～ baggage declaration for inward passengers

【申报价值】 shēnbào jiàzhí declared value

【申辩】 shēnbiàn defend oneself; explain oneself; argue one's case：～无罪 exculpate

【申斥】 shēnchì rebuke; reprimand

【申饬】 shēnchì **1.**（告诫）warn; admonish **2.**（申斥）rebuke; reprimand

【申敕】 shēnchì warn; admonish

【申领】 shēnlǐng apply and receive

【申明】 shēnmíng declare; state; avow：～立场 declare one's stand

【申请】 shēnqǐng apply for：～出境签证 apply for an exit visa

【申请国】 shēnqǐngguó applicant country

【申请回避】 shēnqǐng huíbì withdrawal by petition

【申请离婚】 shēnqǐng líhūn petition for a divorce

【申请人】 shēnqǐngrén applicant

【申请书】 shēngqǐngshū 〈*written*〉 application; petition

【申请作出判决】 shēnqǐng zuòchū pànjué motion for decree

【申述】 shēnshù state; explain in detail

【申诉】 shēnsù appeal：～的权利 right of petition

【申诉人】 shēnsùrén declarant

【申讨】 shēntǎo openly condemn; denounce

【申冤】 shēnyuān **1.**（洗雪冤屈）redress an injustice; right a wrong **2.**（申诉冤屈）appeal for redress of a wrong

伸（shēn） stretch; extend：～出友谊之手 stretch out a hand of friendship to sb. / 他把手～向那本书。He stretched out his hand towards the book.

【伸长】 shēncháng elongate; elongation (n.)

【伸手】 shēnshǒu **1.**（伸出手）stretch out one's hand：～拿书 reach out for the book **2.**（向别人要东西）ask for help, etc.

【伸缩】 shēnsuō **1.**（引长和缩短）stretch out and draw back; expand and contract; lengthen and shorten：～自如 be capable of expansion and contraction **2.**（规模、数量的变动）flexible; elastic; adjustable：没有～余地 leave one no latitude

【伸腿】 shēntuǐ **1.**（伸出腿）stretch one's legs **2.**（插足）step in (to gain an advantage) **3.**（死亡）kick the bucket; turn up one's toes

【伸延】 shēnyán extend; stretch

【伸腰】 shēnyāo straighten oneself up; straighten one's back

【伸展】 shēnzhǎn spread; extend; stretch

【伸张】 shēnzhāng uphold; promote：～正义 let justice prevail

呻（shēn）

【呻吟】 shēnyín groan; moan

绅（shēn） gentry

【绅士】 shēnshì gentleman

【绅士风度】 shēnshì fēngdù gentility; gentlemanly (adj.)

砷 (shēn)〈*Chem.*〉arsenic (元素符号 As)

【砷中毒】 shēnzhòngdú arseniasis; arsenic poisoning

身 (shēn) **1.**(身体) body:～高 1.85 米 1.85m. in height **2.**(生命) life:终～会员 a life member / 以～殉职 die a martyr at one's post **3.**(自己;本身) oneself; personally:以～作则 set a good example with one's own conduct **4.**(品格和修养) one's moral character and conduct:立～处世 conduct oneself in society **5.**(主体部分) the main part of a structure; body:车～ body / 机～ fuselage **6.**〈*classifier*〉suit:一～新衣服 a new suit / 一～三件套 a three-piece suit

【身败名裂】 shēnbài-mínglìe lose all standing and reputation; bring disgrace and ruin upon oneself; be utterly discredited

【身板】 shēnbǎn〈*dial.*〉body; bodily health

【身边】 shēnbiān **1.**(身旁) at one's side **2.**(随身;身上) (have sth.) on one; with one

【身不由己】 shēnbùyóujǐ involuntarily; in spite of oneself

【身材】 shēncái stature; figure:～矮小 a person of short and small stature / ～高大 a person of imposing stature

【身长】 shēncháng **1.**(人体高度) height **2.**(衣服长度) length

【身段】 shēnduàn **1.**(女子身姿) figure:～优美 have a graceful carriage **2.**〈*Theatre*〉posture

【身分】 shēn·fen 同"身份"

【身份】 shēn·fen **1.**(指社会、法律地位) status; capacity; identity **2.**(指受人尊敬) dignity:有失～ lose one's dignity

【身份证】 shēn·fenzhèng identity card; identification card; certificate of identification

【身高】 shēngāo height (of a person):～两米 two meters in height

【身后】 shēnhòu after one's death:～无出 die without issue; without progeny after one's death

【身价】 shēnjià **1.**(社会地位) social status **2.**(人身卖价) the selling price of a slave

【身教】 shēnjiào teach others by one's example

【身经百战】 shēnjīngbǎizhàn have fought a hundred battles

【身历声】 shēnlìshēng **1.**(立体声) stereo **2.**(环绕立体声) stereo surround

【身临其境】 shēnlínqíjìng be personally on the scene

【身强力壮】 shēnqiáng-lìzhuàng strong; robust; tough sturdy

【身躯】 shēnqū body; stature

【身上】 shēn·shang **1.**(身体上) on one's body:～不舒服 do not feel well **2.**(随身) (have sth.) on one; with one:我～没带名片。I haven't got calling cards with me.

【身世】 shēnshì one's life experience; one's lot

【身势语】 shēnshìyǔ body language

【身手】 shēnshǒu skill; talent:显～ display one's talents; exhibit one's skill

【身受】 shēnshòu experience (personally)

【身体】 shēntǐ **1.**(人身) body; human body:～上的伤害 infliction of body / 锻炼～ do physical exercises **2.**(健康) health:～好,学习好,工作好 keep fit, study well and work hard

【身体力行】 shēntǐ-lìxíng earnestly practice what one advocates

【身体素质】 shēntǐ sùzhì fitness; physical attribute

【身条儿】 shēntiáor figure

【身外之物】 shēnwàizhīwù external things; mere worldly possessions

【身无长物】 shēnwúchángwù have nothing

【身无寸功】 shēnwúcùngōng have no merit

【身无分文】 shēnwúfēnwén be stone-broke; without a cash in one's pocket

【身无己出】 shēnwújǐchū have no children of one's own

【身先士卒】 shēnxiānshìzú lead one's men in a charge

【身陷囹圄】 shēnxiàn-língyǔ be thrown into jail

【身心】 shēnxīn body and mind:～愉快 be in a good mood

【身心交瘁】 shēnxīn-jiāocuì be mentally and physically exhausted; in a state of complete bodily and mental prostration

【身影】 shēnyǐng a person's silhouette;

form; figure

【身孕】 shēnyùn pregnancy; pregnant：她已有六个月的～。She's six months pregnant.

【身在福中不知福】 shēn zài fú zhōng bù zhī fú not appreciate the happy life one enjoys

【身子】 shēn·zi 1.（身体）body 2.（身孕）pregnancy

参［参、蓡、葠］（shēn） ginseng：人～ ginseng; Asiatic ginseng / 西洋～ American ginseng（另见"参"cān, cēn）

【参茸】 shēnróng ginseng and young pilose antler

莘（shēn）

【莘莘】 shēnshēn 〈*written*〉 numerous：～学子 a great number of disciples; large numbers of students; numerous students

深（shēn） 1.（与"浅"相反）deep：这个池塘～约五米。The pond is about five meters deep. 2.（深奥）difficult; profound 3.（深刻；深入）thoroughgoing; penetrating; profound：印象很～ have a deep impression of 4.（深厚）close; intimate 5.（浓）dark; deep：～棕 dark brown 6.（晚）late：～秋 late autumn 7.（很；十分）very; greatly; deeply：～知 know very well

【深奥】 shēn'ào abstruse; profound; recondite：这是一本～的书。This is a deep book.

【深不可测】 shēnbùkěcè have no bottom; too deep to be fathomable

【深层】 shēncéng 1.（深层次）deep; depth（n.）2.（深入）thorough; deepgoing; profound

【深层语法】 shēncéng yǔfǎ deep grammar

【深长】 shēncháng profound：意味～ significant

【深沉】 shēnchén 1.（程度深）dark; deep：在～的暮色中 in the deepening dusk 2.（低沉）deep; heavy; dull：～的声音 dull sound 3.（思想感情不外露）concealing one's real feelings：～的人 man of great depth

【深仇大恨】 shēnchóu-dàhèn bitter and deep-seated hatred; profound hatred

【深处】 shēnchù depths; recesses：在内心～ in the depths of the heart

【深度】 shēndù 1.（深浅程度）depth; degree of depth 2.（触及事物本质的程度）profundity; depth：一篇表现出思想～的文章 an article that shows depth of thought

【深度报导】 shēndù bàodǎo in-depth reports

【深度冻结】 shēndù dòngjié deep freezing

【深更半夜】 shēngēng-bànyè at dead of night; in the depth of night; in the middle of the night

【深耕】 shēngēng 〈*Agric.*〉 deep ploughing

【深海】 shēnhǎi deep sea

【深海平原】 shēnhǎi píngyuán abyssal plain

【深海区】 shēnhǎiqū abyssal region

【深海资源】 shēnhǎi zīyuán deep-sea resources

【深厚】 shēnhòu 1.（浓厚）deep; profound：～的感情 deep feelings 2.（坚实）solid; deep seated：～的基础 a solid foundation

【深呼吸】 shēnhūxī deep breathing

【深化】 shēnhuà deepen：～改革 deepen reform

【深加工】 shēnjiāgōng deeply process; finely process

【深加工产品】 shēnjiāgōng chǎnpǐn deeply processed products

【深交】 shēnjiāo 1.（指友情）close friendship; deep friendship 2.（指交往）establish a profound friendship

【深景电影】 shēnjǐng diànyǐng Vistavision

【深究】 shēnjiū go into（a matter）seriously; get to the bottom of（a matter）：～原因何在 get to the bottom of it

【深居简出】 shēnjū-jiǎnchū live in the seclusion of one's own home; live a secluded life

【深刻】 shēnkè deep; profound; deepgoing：～的批评 incisive criticism

【深明大义】 shēnmíng-dàyì understand the important principle thoroughly; know clearly the right thing to do and the principles to follow

【深谋远虑】 shēnmóu-yuǎnlǜ think deeply and plan carefully; be circumspect and far-sighted

【深浅】 shēnqiǎn 1.（深浅程度）depth：你知道这河水的～吗？Do you know how deep the river is? 2.（分寸）proper limits（for speech or action）; sense of propriety：说话没～ speak without thought and often inappropriately 3.(颜色浓淡) shade

【深切】 shēnqiè heartfelt; deep; profound

【深情】 shēnqíng 1.(指感情) deep feeling; deep love: ～厚谊 profound sentiments of friendship 2.(指怀着深厚感情) with deep feeling

【深秋】 shēnqiū late autumn

【深入】 shēnrù 1.(达到事物内部) go deep into; penetrate into; go down to 2.(深刻) thorough; deepgoing

【深入浅出】 shēnrù-qiǎnchū explain profound theories in simple language

【深色】 shēnsè deep color

【深山】 shēnshān remote mountains

【深深】 shēnshēn profoundly; deeply; keenly

【深受欢迎】 shēnshòu huānyíng win warm praise from

【深水】 shēnshuǐ deepwater

【深水泊位】 shēnshuǐ bówèi deep-water berths

【深水池】 shēnshuǐchí 〈*Swimming*.〉 swimminer's pool

【深水港】 shēnshuǐgǎng deepwater port

【深水码头】 shēnshuǐ mǎtóu deepwater wharf

【深思】 shēnsī think deeply about; ponder deeply over: ～练达 thoughtful and clear-headed

【深思熟虑】 shēnsī-shúlǜ careful consideration

【深邃】 shēnsuì 1.(上下或里外距离大) deep 2.(深奥) profound; abstruse; recondite

【深谈】 shēntán discuss thoroughly; go deeply into

【深文周纳】 shēnwén-zhōunà use every means to have an innocent person pronounced guilty; convict sb. by deliberately misinterpreting the law; frame up and punish severely

【深恶痛绝】 shēnwù-tòngjué have a deep-seated hatred; hate bitterly; abhor; detest

【深信】 shēnxìn deeply believe; be deeply convinced

【深省】 shēnxǐng wake up to reality: 发人～ set people thinking; call for deep thought

【深醒】 shēnxǐng 同"深省"

【深夜】 shēnyè late at night; in the small hours of the morning

【深渊】 shēnyuān abyss: 无底～ bottomless abyss

【深远】 shēnyuǎn profound and lasting; far-reaching: ～的影响 far-reaching influence

【深造】 shēnzào take up advanced studies; take a more advanced course of study or training; take further education

【深湛】 shēnzhàn profound and thorough

【深重】 shēnzhòng very grave; extremely serious: 危机～ be in the grip of a crisis

什[甚] (shén) (另见"什"shí)

【什么】 shén·me 1.(问事物) what: 你找～? What are you looking for? 2.(表示不肯定的事物) any; anything: ～书都行。Any book will do. / 她～也没说。She didn't say anything. / 随便～都能把门弄开。Anything will do to keep the door open. 3.(用在"也"或"都"前面,表示没有例外) ～用处也没有 be quite worthless 4.(两个"什么"前后照应,前者决定后者)有～说～ say what one has in mind / ～人说～话。Each people speaks its own language.

【什么的】 shén·me·de and so on; and so forth; and the like; and others; and what not: 她在菜市场买了些猪肉、土豆、青菜～。She bought at the market pork, potatoes, green vegetables and the like

【什么地方】 shén·me dìfāng where: 你是～的? Where are you from? / 在家、在学校,在随便～ at home, at school, or wherever

【什么人】 shén·merén who: ～给你的那本书。Who gave you that book?

【什么时候】 shén·me shíhòu when: 你～能来? When can you come? / 星期一、星期二或随便～ on Monday, Tuesday or whenever

神 (shén)

1.(神灵) god; deity; divinity: 尼普顿是海～。Neptune was the god of the sea. 2.(特别) supernatural; magical: ～效 magical effect 3.(精神) spirit; mind: 养～ rest one's mind / 走～ be absentminded 4.(神气) expression; look 5.(机灵;聪明) smart; clever; incredible

【神不守舍】 shénbùshǒushè have ants in one's pants; out of one's mind

【神不知,鬼不觉】 shén bù zhī, guǐ bù jué unknown to god or ghost; (do sth.) without anybody knowing it; in great secrecy

【神采】 shéncǎi expression; look: ～奕奕 with a radiant look; with health and radiating vigor

【神出鬼没】 shénchū-guǐmò come and go like a ghost; appear and disappear mysteriously

【神父】 shénfù 见"神甫"

【神甫】 shén·fu Catholic father; priest

【神乎其神】 shénhūqíshén fantastic; wonderful; miraculous: 吹得～ laud sth. or sb. to the skies

【神化】 shénhuà deify

【神话】 shénhuà myth; mythology; fairy tale: 希腊罗马～ Greek and Roman myth

【神魂】 shénhún state of mind; mind: ～颠倒 be infatuated

【神机妙算】 shénjī-miàosuàn wonderful foresight (in military operations, etc.)

【神经】 shénjīng 1.〈*Anat*.〉nerve 2.(精神失常) mental disorder

【神经病】 shénjīngbìng 1.〈*Med*.〉neuropathy 2.(俗称精神病) mental disorder: 你简直是～。You are simply not in your right mind.

【神经冲动】 shénjīng chōngdòng nerve impulse

【神经官能症】 shénjīng guānnéngzhèng 〈*Med*.〉neurosis; neurotic (adj.) ‖ 神经官能症患者 neurotic

【神经过敏】 shénjīng guòmǐng 1.〈*Med*.〉neuroticism 2.(多疑) neurotic; oversensitive

【神经衰弱】 shénjīng shuāiruò 〈*Med*.〉neurasthenia; neurosism

【神经损害】 shénjīng sǔnhài nervous lesion

【神经系统】 shénjīng xìtǒng nervous system

【神经战】 shénjīngzhàn war of nerves

【神经质】 shénjīngzhì nervousness

【神经中枢】 shénjīng zhōngshū nerve center

【神龛】 shénkān a shrine for idols or ancestral tablets

【神来之笔】 shénláizhībǐ an inspired passage; a stroke of genius

【神力】 shénlì superhuman strength; extraordinary power

【神聊】 shénliáo discursive chat; rambling talk

【神灵】 shénlíng gods; deities; divinities

【神秘】 shénmì mysterious; mystical

【神秘感】 shénmìgǎn mystery: 充满～的故事 stories full of mystery

【神秘化】 shénmìhuà make a mystery of

【神秘主义】 shénmì zhǔyì mysticism

【神妙】 shénmiào wonderful; marvellous; ingenious

【神明】 shénmíng gods; deities; divinities: 奉若～ worship sb. or sth.; make a fetish of sth.

【神女】 shénnǚ 1.(女神) goddess 2.(指妓女) prostitute

【神奇】 shénqí magical; mystical; miraculous

【神气】 shénqì 1.(神情) expression; air; manner 2.(精神饱满) spirited; vigorous 3.(骄傲得意) putting on airs; cocky; overweening: ～活现 very cocky; as proud as a peacock / ～十足 very arrogant

【神枪手】 shénqiāngshǒu sharp-shooter; good shot

【神情】 shénqíng expression; look: ～自若 with an easy grace

【神权】 shénquán 1.(神灵权力) religious authority; theocracy 2.(神赋予的权力) rule by divine right

【神权统治】 shénquán tǒngzhì thearchy; thearchic (adj.)

【神权政治】 shénquán zhèngzhì theocracy; theocratic (adj.)

【神人共鉴】 shénrén gòngjiàn May it be taken as evidence both by gods and men.

【神色】 shénsè expression; look: ～自若 be calm and poised

【神神叨叨】 shénshén-dāodāo 见"神神道道"

【神神道道】 shénshén-dāodāo odd: 她妈妈是个～的人。Her mother was an odd woman.

【神圣】 shénshèng sacred; holy: ～权利 sacred right / ～义务 sacred duty

【神圣不可侵犯】 shénshèng bùkě qīnfàn sacred and inviolable; holy and inviolable

【神圣罗马帝国】 Shénshèng Luómǎ Dìguó Holy Roman Empire

【神思】 shénsī state of mind; mental state: ～恍惚 be lost in a reverie

【神似】 shénsì be alike in spirit; be an excellent likeness

【神速】 shénsù marvellously quick；with amazing speed：收效～ obtain instant results

【神态】 shéntài expression；manner；bearing；mien：～自若 look perfectly calm

【神通】 shéntōng remarkable ability；magical power：～广大 be infinitely resourceful

【神童】 shéntóng child prodigy

【神往】 shénwǎng be carried away；be rapt；be charmed：为之～ be enchanted with

【神物】 shénwù 1.（神奇的东西）wonder；prodigy；phenomenon 2.（神仙）supernatural being；deity

【神仙】 shénxiān supernatural being；celestial being；immortal：～下凡 a fairy becomes incarnate

【神像】 shénxiàng the picture or statue of a god or Buddha

【神学】 shénxué 〈*Religion*〉theology；theological（adj.）‖ 神学家 theologian

【神学院】 shénxuéyuàn theological college

【神医】 shényī highly skilled doctor；miracle-working doctor

【神异】 shényì 1.（神怪）gods and spirits 2.（神奇）magical；mystical；miraculous

【神职人员】 shénzhí rényuán clergy

【神志】 shénzì consciousness；senses；mind：～不清 obnubilation

【神州】 shénzhōu the Divine Land；Cathay

审［審］（shěn） 1.（详细；周密）careful：～察 careful observation 2.（审查）examine；go over：～稿 go over a manuscript 3.（审讯）interrogate；try：公～ put sb. on public trial / 他因谋杀而受～。He's being tried for murder.

【审察】 shěnchá （with）careful observation

【审查】 shěnchá examine；investigate：提交…～ submit to ... for examination

【审查证书】 shěnchá zhèngshū 〈*Foreign Affairs*〉examination of credentials

【审处】 shěnchù 1.（审判处理）try and punish 2.（审查处理）deliberate and decide

【审订】 shěndìng examine and revise：～教材 revise teaching materials

【审定】 shěndìng examine and approve：由委员会～ be examined and approved by the committee

【审干】 shěngàn examination of cadres

【审核】 shěnhé examine and verify

【审计】 shěnjì audit

【审计报告】 shěnjì bàogào audit report

【审计员】 shěnjìyuán auditor

【审计制度】 shěnjì zhìdù auditing system

【审结】 shěnjié completion of investigation

【审理】 shěnlǐ 〈*Law*〉try；hear：～案件 hear a case / ～诉案 hold pleas

【审美】 shěnměi appreciation of the beauty

【审美观念】 shěnměi guānniàn aesthetic standards

【审美能力】 shěnměi nénglì aesthetic judgment

【审判】 shěnpàn bring to trial；try；trial（n.）：公开～ an open trial

【审判程序】 shěnpàn chéngxù judicial procedure

【审判对象】 shěnpàn duìxiàng object of adjudication

【审判工作】 shěnpàn gōngzuò administration of justice

【审判规则】 shěnpàn guīzé adjudication rule

【审判机关】 shěnpàn jīguān judicial organ

【审判监督】 shěnpàn jiāndū adjudication supervision

【审判权】 shěnpànquán judicial authority；jurisdiction

【审判员】 shěnpànyuán judge；judicial officer

【审判长】 shěnpànzhǎng presiding judge；chief judge

【审批】 shěnpī examine and approve

【审慎】 shěnshèn cautious；careful；circumspect

【审时度势】 shěnshí-duóshì judge the hour and size up the situation

【审问】 shěnwèn interrogate；question；examine；hear；try：～被告 interrogate the accused

【审讯】 shěnxùn 〈*Law*〉interrogate；try

【审议】 shěnyì consideration；deliberation；discussion；consider：提交…～ submit to ... for consideration；submit to ... for discussion

【审阅】 shěnyuè check and approve

婶［嬸］（shěn） 1.（婶母）aunt；wife of father's younger brother 2.（大

婶）aunt；auntie

【婶母】 shěnmǔ wife of father's younger brother；aunt

肾［腎］（shèn） 1.〈*Anat*.〉kidney 2.〈*Chin*. *Med*.〉testis；testicle

【肾病】 shènbìng nephrosis

【肾功能】 shèngōngnéng 〈*Med*.〉kidney function

【肾结石】 shènjiéshí 〈*Med*.〉kidney stone；renal calculus

【肾上腺】 shènshàngxiàn 〈*Anat*.〉adrenal gland；suprarenal gland；adrenal

【肾上腺功能亢进】 shènshàngxiàn gōngnéng kàngjìn 〈*Med*.〉hyperadrenalism

【肾上腺素】 shènshàngxiànsù 〈*Biochem*.〉adrenaline；epinephrine

【肾衰竭】 shènshuāijié 〈*Anat*.〉kidney failure；renal failure

【肾下垂】 shènxiàchuí 〈*Anat*.〉nephroptosis

【肾炎】 shènyán 〈*Anat*.〉nephritis

【肾移植】 shènyízhí 〈*Anat*.〉kidney transplant

【肾盂】 shènyú 〈*Anat*.〉renal pelvis

【肾盂肾炎】 shènyú shènyán 〈*Med*.〉pyelonephritis

【肾脏】 shènzàng kidney

【肾盏】 shènzhǎn 〈*Anat*.〉renal calyx

甚（shèn） 1.（很；极）very；extremely 2.（超过；胜过）more than：日～一日 get intensified with each passing day 3. 同"什么"

【甚而】 shèn'ér 〈*conj*.〉even；(go) so far as to

【甚高频】 shèngāopín very-high-frequency (VHF)

【甚或】 shènhuò 〈*written*〉〈*conj*.〉even；(go) so far as to；so much so that

【甚嚣尘上】 shènxiāo-chénshàng cause a temporary clamor；make a great noise

【甚至】 shènzhì 〈*conj*.〉even；(go) so far as to；so much so that：她～连"再见"都没说就走了。She left without so much as saying 'good-bye'.

胂（shèn） 〈*Chem*.〉arsine

渗［滲］（shèn） ooze；seep：～水了。The water has oozed. / 雨水从屋顶往下～。Rain seeped through the roof.

【渗出】 shènchū seep；exude；ooze

【渗沟】 shèngōu sewer

【渗坑】 shènkēng seepage pit

【渗漏】 shènlòu seepage；leakage

【渗入】 shènrù 1.（慢慢流入）permeate；seep into：～地下 permeate the ground；seep into the ground 2.（侵入）(of influence, etc.) penetrate；infiltrate

【渗碳】 shèntàn 〈*Metall*.〉carburize；carburization (n.)

【渗透】 shèntòu 1.〈*Physics*〉osmosis 2.（透过）permeate；seep：鲜血～了绷带。Blood soaked through the bandage. 3.（逐渐侵入）penetrate；infiltrate：经济～ economic infiltration

【渗析】 shènxī dialysis

蜃（shèn） 〈*Zool*.〉clam

【蜃景】 shènjǐng 〈*Meteorol*.〉mirage

慎（shèn） careful；cautious

【慎重】 shènzhòng cautious；careful；prudent；discreet：～处理 be prudent in dealing with sth. / 采取～态度 adopt a prudent policy / 经过～考虑 after careful consideration / 说话～ be prudent in speech

sheng

升［昇[1,2]、陞[2]］（shēng） 1.（升起）rise；hoist；go up；ascend：～帆 hoist a sail / 太阳～起。The sun rises. 2.（提升）promote：～为教授 be promoted professor 3.（容量单位）liter (l.)

【升班】 shēngbān go up (one grade in school)

【升调】 shēngdiào 〈*Phonet*.〉rising tune or tone

【升幅】 shēngfú rate of increase

【升高】 shēnggāo 1.（向上升）go up；ascend 2.（等级提高）go up；promote；raise：温度～了。The temperature has gone up.

【升格】 shēnggé promote；upgrade：外交关系～ upgrade diplomatic relations

【升官发财】 shēngguān fācái win promotion and get rich；(be out for) power and money

【升华】 shēnghuā 1.〈*Physics*〉sublimation 2.（提高）raising of things to a higher level; distillation; sublimation

【升华热】 shēnghuārè 〈*Physics*〉heat of sublimation

【升级】 shēngjí 1.（晋升）upgrade 2.（学生升级）go up (one grade, etc.) 3.（战争规模扩大）escalate：使战争～ escalate the war

【升降机】 shēngjiàngjī elevator; lift

【升降舵】 shēngjiàngduò 〈*Aeron.*〉elevator

【升结肠】 shēngjiécháng 〈*Anat.*〉ascending colon

【升空】 shēngkōng 〈*Aeron.*〉lift-off; blast-off; blast off (v.)：太空船（发射）～了。The spaceship blasted off.

【升力】 shēnglì 〈*Physics*〉lift; ascensional force

【升幂】 shēngmì 〈*Math.*〉ascending power

【升平】 shēngpíng peace：～世界 peaceful world

【升旗】 shēngqí hoist a flag; raise a flag

【升旗典礼】 shēngqí diǎnlǐ flag-raising ceremony

【升迁机会】 shēngqiān jīhuì chance of promotion

【升水】 shēngshuǐ 〈*Econ.*〉premium

【升腾】 shēngténg leap up; rise

【升天】 shēngtiān 1.（指死）ascension 2.（升空）lift-off; blast-off

【升温】 shēngwēn raise of temperature

【升学】 shēngxué go to a school of a higher grade; enter a higher school

【升学率】 shēngxuélǜ proportion of students entering schools of a higher grade

【升压】 shēngyā 〈*Electr.*〉step up; boost

【升值】 shēngzhí 1.〈*Econ.*〉revalue 2.（提高价值）appreciate

生 (shēng) 1.（出生）be born：他～于1970年。He was born in 1970. 2.（生长）grow 3.（产生；发生）get; have 4.（生育）give birth to; bear：她～了一个女孩。She has borne a girl. 5.（生存；活）existence; life：栩栩如～ to the life / 有～之年 the remaining years of one's life 6.（活的）living 7.（生计）livelihood：以开汽车为～ make a living as a driver 8.（使燃烧）light (a fire)：～火 light a fire 9.（未成熟）unripe; green：～瓜 unripe watermelon 10.（未煮熟的）raw; uncooked：吃～虾 eat shrimps raw 11.（生疏）unfamiliar; unacquainted; strange 12.（学生）pupil; student：师～关系 teacher-student relations 13.（未炼制的）unprocessed; crude; unrefined：～石灰 quicklime 14.（生硬）stiff; mechanical 15.（很）very

【生搬硬套】 shēngbān yìngtào copy mechanically in disregard of specific conditions; apply of copy mechanically

【生病】 shēngbìng fall ill; get ill

【生不逢辰】 shēngbùféngchén it is unlucky to be born at such a time; be born under an unlucky star

【生财有道】 shēngcái-yǒudào expertly in making money

【生菜】 shēngcài （叶用莴苣）lettuce; garden lettuce

【生产】 shēngchǎn 1.（制造）produce; manufacture：～拖拉机 produce tractors 2.（生孩子）give birth to a child：他妻子快～了。His wife will be having her baby soon.

【生产厂家】 shēngchǎn chǎngjiā manufacturer

【生产成本】 shēngchǎn chéngběn cost of production

【生产单位】 shēngchǎn dānwèi production unit

【生产定额】 shēngchǎn dìng'é production quota

【生产方式】 shēngchǎn fāngshì mode of production

【生产费用】 shēngchǎn fèiyòng expense of production

【生产工具】 shēngchǎn gōngjù tool of production

【生产关系】 shēngchǎn guānxì relations of production; production relations

【生产管理】 shēngchǎn guǎnlǐ production management

【生产过程】 shēngchǎn guòchéng process of production

【生产过剩】 shēngchǎn guòshèng overproduction

【生产基地】 shēngchǎn jīdì production base

【生产教学车间】 shēngchǎn jiàoxué chējiān

vocational training workshops; industrial practice workshops

【生产力】 shēngchǎnlì productive forces

【生产领域】 shēngchǎn lǐngyù sphere of production

【生产率】 shēngchǎnlǜ 1.(劳动生产率) productivity; labor productivity 2.(机器效率) efficiency

【生产能力】 shēngchǎn nénglì production capacity

【生产潜力】 shēngchǎn qiǎnlì productive potentialities; latent productive capacity

【生产设备】 shēngchǎn shèbèi production facilities

【生产线】 shēngchǎnxiàn production line

【生产手段】 shēngchǎn shǒuduàn means of production

【生产效率】 shēngchǎn xiàolǜ production efficiency

【生产要素】 shēngchǎn yàosù factor of production

【生产责任制】 shēngchǎn zérènzhì system of production responsibility

【生产指标】 shēngchǎn zhǐbiāo production quota

【生产指数】 shēngchǎn zhǐshù index of production

【生产资料】 shēngchǎn zīliào means of production

【生产自主权】 shēngchǎn zìzhǔquán production autonomy

【生产总值】 shēngchǎn zǒngzhí total output value

【生辰】 shēngchén birthday

【生成】 shēngchéng 1.(形成) generate; produce; generative (adj.) 2.(天生的) inborn; be born with

【生成语法】 shēngchéng yǔfǎ generative grammar

【生成语义学】 shēngchéng yǔyìxué generative semantics

【生词】 shēngcí new word

【生存】 shēngcún subsist; exist; live

【生存竞争】 shēngcún jìngzhēng struggle for existence

【生存空间】 shēngcún kōngjiān vivosphere

【生存农业】 shēngcún nóngyè subsistence farming

【生地】 shēngdì 1.(生荒地) virgin soil; uncultivated land 2.〈*Chin. Med.*〉 the dried rhizome of rehmannia

【生动】 shēngdòng lively; vivid: ～的描写 lively description

【生动活泼】 shēngdòng huópō lively; vivid and vigorous: ～的语言 vivid language

【生动记忆】 shēngdòng jìyì photographic memory

【生儿育女】 shēng'ér yùnǚ bear sons and daughters; bear children

【生发油】 shēngfàyóu hair oil

【生父】 shēngfù one's own father

【生根】 shēnggēn take root; strike root

【生花妙笔】 shēnghuāmiàobǐ (straight from) a gifted pen; (written with) a graphic pen

【生荒地】 shēnghuāngdì virgin soil; uncultivated land

【生活】 shēnghuó 1.(日常生活) life; living: 高水准的～ high standards of living / 改善～待遇 improve one's living standard / 过上温饱～ have secured a life with enough food and clothing / 过上小康～ lead a fairly comfortable life 2.(生存) live: 靠工资～ live on one's wages 3.(衣、食、住) livelihood: ～俭朴 lead a thrifty and simple life

【生活必需品】 shēnghuó bìxūpǐn necessaries of life; daily necessities

【生活标准】 shēnghuó biāozhǔn standard of living

【生活方式】 shēnghuó fāngshì way of life; life style

【生活费】 shēnghuófèi 1.(生活费用) cost of living; living expenses 2.〈*Law*〉 alimony

【生活费用】 shēnghuó fèiyòng living expenses; cost of living

【生活福利】 shēnghuó fúlì welfare; welfare benefits

【生活环境】 shēnghuó huánjìng surroundings; environment

【生活津贴】 shēnghuó jīntiē living allowance

【生活经验】 shēnghuó jīngyàn experience of life

【生活来源】 shēnghuó láiyuán source of income

【生活水平】 shēnghuó shuǐpíng living standard

【生活条件】 shēnghuó tiáojiàn living conditions

【生活污水】 shēnghuó wūshuǐ domestic sewage

【生活习惯】 shēnghuó xíguàn habits and customs

【生活用品】 shēnghuó yòngpǐn articles for daily use

【生活用水】 shēnghuó yòngshuǐ domestic water

【生活指导】 shēnghuó zhǐdǎo life guidance

【生活指数】 shēnghuó zhǐshù index of living

【生活资料】 shēnghuó zīliào means of subsistence; means of livelihood

【生活作风】 shēnghuó zuòfēng behavior; conduct

【生火】 shēnghuǒ make a fire; light a fire

【生机】 shēngjī 1.(生存机会) lease of life: 一线～ last hope of recovery 2.(生命力) life; vitality; vital (adj.): 充满～ full of vigor and vitality / 使充满～ vitalize

【生计】 shēngjì means of livelihood; livelihood

【生就】 shēngjiù be born with; be gifted with

【生来】 shēnglái come with birth; be born with

【生老病死】 shēnglǎo-bìngsǐ birth, age, illness and death

【生冷】 shēnglěng raw or cold food

【生离死别】 shēnglí-sǐbié part never to meet again; part for ever

【生理】 shēnglǐ physiology; physiological (adj.) ‖ 生理学家 physiologist

【生理缺陷】 shēnglǐ quēxiàn physiological defect; physiological deficiency

【生理心理学】 shēnglǐ xīnlǐxué physiological psychology

【生理需要】 shēnglǐ xūyào physiological need

【生力军】 shēnglìjūn 1.〈*Mil.*〉 fresh troops 2.(新参加的人) fresh activists; new force

【生灵】 shēnglíng 〈*written*〉 the people: ～涂炭 the people are plunged into an abyss of misery

【生龙活虎】 shēnglóng-huóhǔ doughty as a dragon and lively as a tiger; full of vim and vigor

【生路】 shēnglù means of livelihood; way out

【生闷鸡】 shēngmènjī braised chicken

【生米煮成熟饭】 shēngmǐ zhǔchéng shúfàn the rice is cooked; what's done can't be undone

【生蜜】 shēngmì unripe honey

【生面孔】 shēngmiànkǒng strange faces

【生命】 shēngmìng life

【生命科学】 shēngmìng kēxué life sciences

【生命力】 shēngmìnglì life-force; vitality

【生命维持系统】 shēngmìng wéichí xìtǒng 〈*Aeron.*〉 life support system

【生命线】 shēngmìngxiàn lifeline; lifeblood: 贸易是大多数现代国家的～。Trade is the lifeblood of most modern states.

【生母】 shēngmǔ one's own mother

【生怕】 shēngpà for fear that; so as not to; lest

【生啤酒】 shēngpíjiǔ draft beer

【生僻】 shēngpì uncommon; rare: ～词汇 rarely used words

【生平】 shēngpíng 1.(一生整个过程) all one's life; biography 2.(有生以来) in one's whole life

【生漆】 shēngqī raw lacquer

【生气】 shēngqì 1.(不愉快) take offense; get angry 2.(生命力) life; vitality: ～勃勃 dynamic; vigorous; full of vitality

【生前】 shēngqián during one's lifetime; before one's death

【生前友好】 shēngqián yǒuhǎo friends of the deceased

【生擒】 shēngqín capture alive; arrest alive

【生趣】 shēngqù joy of life: ～盎然 overflowing with joy of life

【生人】 shēngrén stranger; strange face

【生日】 shēng · ri birthday: 过～ have a birthday celebration; give a birthday party / 祝你～快乐。Happy birthday to you.

【生日蛋糕】 shēng·ri dàngāo birthday cake

【生日礼物】 shēng·ri lǐwù birthday present

【生色】 shēngsè add color to; add luster to; give added significance to

【生涩】 shēngsè jerky; choppy; not smooth: 文字～ jerky style of writing

【生杀予夺】 shēngshā-yǔduó hold power over sb's life and property; have sb. completely

in one's power
【生身父母】 shēngshēn fùmǔ one's own parents
【生石灰】 shēngshíhuī quick lime
【生事】 shēngshì make trouble; create a disturbance: 造谣～ spread rumors and make trouble
【生手】 shēngshǒu new hand; sb. new to a job
【生疏】 shēngshú 1.(不熟悉) not familiar: 业务还～ be still not familiar with one's profession 2.(不熟练) out of practice; rusty: 他的俄语有点～了。His Russian is getting rusty. 3.(疏远) be not as close as before
【生水】 shēngshuǐ unboiled water
【生丝】 shēngsī raw silk
【生死】 shēngsǐ life and death
【生死存亡】 shēngsǐ-cúnwáng grave crisis between life and death
【生死关头】 shēng-sǐ guāntóu at the critical moment
【生态】 shēngtài organisms' habits, modes of life and relation to their environment; ecology; ecological (adj.): 加强～环境的保护 do a better job of protecting the ecological balance
【生态灭绝】 shēngtài mièjué ecocide
【生态平衡】 shēngtài pínghéng ecological balance
【生态学】 shēngtàixué ecology; ecological (adj.) ‖ 生态学家 ecologist
【生铁】 shēngtiě pig iron
【生吞活剥】 shēngtūn-huóbō swallow sth. raw and whole; accept sth. uncritically
【生物】 shēngwù living things; living beings; organisms
【生物工程】 shēngwù gōngchéng bio-engineering; genetic engineering
【生物圈】 shēngwùquān biosphere; vivosphere
【生物体】 shēngwùtǐ organism
【生物学】 shēngwùxué biology; biological (adj.) ‖ 生物学家 biologist
【生物战】 shēngwùzhàn 〈*Mil.*〉 biological warfare
【生物钟】 shēngwùzhōng biological clock; biochronometer; living clock
【生息】 shēngxī 1.(取得利息) bear interest 2.(生活;生存) live; grow; propagate: 休养～ rest and build up one's strength
【生息资本】 shēngxī zīběn interest-bearing capital
【生鲜运销】 shēngxiān yùnxiāo distributing in fresh
【生肖】 shēngxiāo animal year; animal sign
【生效】 shēngxiào go into effect; become effective: 签字后立即～ become effective immediately upon signature
【生性】 shēngxìng natural disposition: ～固执 be stubborn by nature
【生锈】 shēngxiù get rusty; rust: 汽车翼子板已经～了。The fender of the car had rusted.
【生涯】 shēngyá career; profession: 舞台～ a stage career
【生疑】 shēngyí be suspicious; begin to suspect
【生意】 shēng·yi 1.(生机) tendency to grow; life and vitality 2.(买卖) business; trade: 做～ do business
【生意经】 shēng·yijīng the knack of doing business; shrewd business sense
【生硬】 shēngyìng stiff; rigid; harsh: 态度～ be stiff in manner
【生油】 shēngyóu 1.(没熬过的油) unboiled oil 2.(花生油) peanut oil
【生于忧患,死于安乐】 shēng yú yōuhuàn, sǐ yú ānlè thrive in calamity and perish in soft living; life springs from sorrow and calamity, death comes from ease and pleasure
【生育】 shēngyù give birth to; bear: 计划～ family planning; planned parenthood
【生育高峰】 shēngyù gāofēng baby boom
【生育率】 shēngyùlǜ fertility-rate; fertility
【生源】 shēngyuán source of students
【生造】 shēngzào coin (words and expressions)
【生长】 shēngzhǎng 1.(长大) grow: 水稻～良好。The rice is growing well. 2.(出生和成长) grow up; be brought up: 她～在城市。She was born and brought up in the city.
【生殖】 shēngzhí reproduction; reproductive (adj.): 无性～ asexual reproduction

【生殖器】 shēngzhíqì reproductive organs; genitals

【生殖器崇拜】 shēngzhíqì chóngbài phallicism

【生殖系统】 shēngzhí xìtǒng reproductive system

【生猪】 shēngzhū 〈*Trade*〉 live pig; pig; hog; pork on the hoof

【生字】 shēngzì new word

【生字表】 shēngzìbiǎo (a list of) new words

牲 (shēng) 1.(家畜) domestic animal 2.(祭神用牲畜) animal sacrifice

【牲畜】 shēngchù livestock; domestic animals

【牲口】 shēng·kou draught animals; beasts of burden

笙 (shēng) 〈*Music*〉 *sheng*; Chinese wind pipe

甥 (shēng) sister's son; nephew

【甥女】 shēngnǚ sister's daughter; niece

声[聲] (shēng) 1.(声音) sound; voice: 传～ propagation of sound / 大～ in a loud voice / 发～ production of sound / 高～ in a high voice / 歌～ singing; sound of singing / 雷～ thunder / 立体～ stereo / 小～ in a low voice / 雨～ the sound of raindrops / 原～ primary sound / 异口同～ with one voice 2.(发出声音) make a sound: 不～不响 not utter a word; keep quiet; making no sound 3.(声名) reputation

【声辩】 shēngbiàn argue; justify; explain away

【声波】 shēngbō 〈*Physics*〉 sound wave; acoustic wave

【声部】 shēngbù 〈*Music*〉 part (in concerted music)

【声场】 shēngchǎng sound field

【声称】 shēngchēng profess; claim; assert: ～实有其事 assert that it is true

【声带】 shēngdài 1.〈*Anat.*〉 vocal cords 2.〈*Cinematog.*〉 sound track

【声调】 shēngdiào 1.(音调) tone; note 2.〈*Phonet.*〉 the tone of a Chinese character

【声东击西】 shēngdōng-jīxī make a feint to the east and attack in the west; make a noise in the east while attacking in the west

【声干扰】 shēnggānrǎo acoustic noise

【声光表演】 shēngguāng biǎoyǎn sound-and-light show; son et lumiere

【声画同步】 shēnghuà tóngbù sound and picture synchronization

【声价】 shēngjià reputation; prestige: ～百倍 hold a very good reputation

【声控】 shēngkòng sound control; voice control

【声控机器人】 shēngkòng jīqìrén televox

【声浪】 shēnglàng voice; clamor: 抗议的～ a wave of protest

【声泪俱下】 shēnglèi-jùxià shedding tears while speaking; in a tearful voice

【声名】 shēngmíng reputation: ～远扬 one's fame spread far and wide

【声明】 shēngmíng 1.(公开表明) state; declare; announce: 口头～ a verbal statement / ～作废 declare invalid 2.(文告) statement; declaration: 联合～ joint statement

【声名狼藉】 shēngmíng-lángjí disrepute; have a bad name; be notorious

【声明书】 shēngmíngshū declaration; statement

【声纳】 shēngnà 〈*Physics*〉 sonar; sound navigation and ranging

【声频】 shēngpín audio frequency; sonic frequency

【声气】 shēngqì 1.(消息) information: 互通～ exchange information; keep in contact with each other 2.(语气、声音) voice; tone: 小声小气地 in a low voice; in undertones

【声情】 shēngqíng voice and expression: ～并茂 be remarkable for both voice and expression

【声色】 shēngsè 1.(声音和脸色) voice and countenance: 不动～ remain composed 2.(歌舞和女色) woman and song

【声色俱厉】 shēngsè-jùlì stern in voice and countenance

【声色犬马】 shēngsè-quǎnmǎ drown oneself in sex and pleasure

【声色自娱】 shēngsè-zìyù have one's fling; indulge oneself in song and with women

【声势】 shēngshì impetus; momentum: 虚张～ make pretenses of power and influence

【声势凌人】 shēngshì-língrén overwhelm the

weaker with excessively strong language

【声势煊赫】 shēngshì-xuānhè one's influence is majestic and powerful

【声嘶力竭】 shēngsī-lìjié shout oneself hoarse; shout oneself blue in the face

【声速】 shēngsù 〈*Physics*〉 velocity of sound

【声讨】 shēngtǎo denounce; condemn; condemnation (n.)

【声望】 shēngwàng popularity; prestige: ～日盛 one's reputation becomes more and more impressive

【声威】 shēngwēi renown; prestige

【声响】 shēngxiǎng sound; noise

【声学】 shēngxué acoustics; acoustic (adj.)

【声音】 shēngyīn sound; voice

【声誉】 shēngyù reputation; fame; prestige: ～扫地 fall into discredit

【声援】 shēngyuán express support for; support

【声乐】 shēngyuè 〈*Music*〉 vocal music

【声韵学】 shēngyùnxué 〈*Gram.*〉 phonology

【声张】 shēngzhāng make public; disclose

【声障】 shēngzhàng sound barrier; sonic barrier

【声震】 shēngzhèn sonic bang; sonic boom

绳[繩] (shéng) **1**.(绳子) rope; cord; string: 粗～ thick rope / 麻～ hemp rope / 钢丝～ steel cable / 包装用的～ packing string **2**.(约束;制裁) restrict; restrain

【绳索】 shéngsuǒ rope; cord

【绳梯】 shéngtī rope ladder

【绳之以法】 shéngzhīyǐfǎ restrain by law; punish sb. according to law; bring sb. to justice

【绳子】 shéng·zi cord; rope; string: 包裹用～捆着。The parcel was tied with string.

省 (shěng) **1**.(节约) economize; save: ～力 save labor / ～钱 save money; economize money **2**.(省去) omit; leave out: 这个句子可以～去。This sentence can be omitted. **3**.(省份) province: 山西～ province of Shanxi; Shanxi Province / 台湾～ province of Taiwan; Taiwan Province / 陕西～ province of Shaanxi; Shaanxi Province (另见"省"xǐng)

【省城】 shěngchéng provincial capital

【省吃俭用】 shěngchī-jiǎnyòng skimp and save; live frugally; save money on food and expenses

【省得】 shěng·de so as to save; so as to avoid: 我再说一遍，～你忘了。Let me remind you once again so that you won't forget.

【省份】 shěngfèn province

【省工】 shěnggōng labor-saving

【省会】 shěnghuì provincial capital

【省界】 shěngjiè provincial boundaries

【省力】 shěnglì save effort; save labor; economize labor

【省略】 shěnglüè **1**.(除去) leave out; omit **2**.〈*Gram.*〉 ellipsis

【省略号】 shěnglüèhào **1**.(...或…) ellipsis; suspension points; ellipsis dots **2**.(') apostrophe

【省略值】 shěnglüèzhí default value

【省钱】 shěngqián save money; be economical

【省却】 shěngquè **1**.(节省) economize; save **2**.(除去) omit; leave out

【省事】 shěngshì **1**.(减少手续) save trouble; simplify matters **2**.(方便) it's more convenient to: 在快餐店就餐～。It's more convenient to eat in the fast food restaurant.

【省属】 shěngshǔ directly under the jurisdiction of a provincial government

【省委】 shěngwěi provincial Party committee

【省心】 shěngxīn save worry

【省优】 shěngyōu be rated as provincial-level standard products of quality

圣[聖] (shèng) **1**.(最崇高的) sage; saint **2**.(神圣的) holy; sacred: 神～领土 sacred territory **3**.(帝王) emperor: ～上 His Majesty; Her Majesty

【圣餐】 shèngcān 〈*Religion*〉 Holy Communion

【圣城】 Shèngchéng the Holy City

【圣诞】 shèngdàn the birthday of Jesus Christ

【圣诞节】 Shèngdànjié Christmas Day

【圣诞节贺片】 Shèngdànjié hèpiān Christmas card

【圣诞节礼物】 Shèngdànjié lǐwù Christmas present; Christmas box

【圣诞节前夜】 Shèngdànjié qiányè Christmas

Eve

【圣诞卡】 shèngdànkǎ Christmas card

【圣诞老人】 Shèngdàn Lǎorén Santa Claus; Santa Klaus

【圣诞树】 shèngdànshù Christmas tree

【圣地】 shèngdì 1.〈*Religion*〉the Holy Land 2.(比喻) sacred place; shrine: 革命～ a sacred place of the revolution

【圣殿】 shèngdiàn 〈*Judaism*〉Temple of God

【圣父】 Shènfù the Father

【圣洁】 shèngjié holy and pure

【圣经】 Shèngjīng the Holy Bible; the Bible; Holy Writ

【圣灵】 shènglíng the Holy Ghost; the Holy Spirit

【圣母】 Shèngmǔ 1.(女神) a female deity; goddess 2.(圣母马利亚) the (Blessed) Virgin Mary; Madonna

【圣母堂】 Shèngmǔtáng the Chapel of Our Lady

【圣人】 shèngrén sage; wise man: ～也有三分错。Sages, however wise, are human and can make mistakes.

【圣坛】 shèngtán chancel

【圣贤】 shèngxián sages and men of virtue: 人非～,孰能无过? Men are not saints, how can they by free from faults?

【圣旨】 shèngzhǐ imperial edict

【圣子】 shèngzǐ the Son of God

胜[**勝**] (shèng) 1.(胜利) victory; success: 获～ win; emerge the victor 2.(优越) surpass; be superior to; get the better of 3.(优美的) superb; wonderful; lovely 4.(能承担或承受) be equal to; can bear

【胜败】 shèngbài victory or defeat; success or failure

【胜败未卜】 shèngbài wèi bǔ It is uncertain whether (he) will succeed or fail.

【胜不骄,败不馁】 shèng bù jiāo, bài bù něi not to get conceited because of victory or disheartened in case of defeat

【胜地】 shèngdì famous scenic spot: 避暑～ summer resort / 游览～ a scenic spot for tourists

【胜负】 shèngfù victory or defeat; success or failure

【胜迹】 shèngjì famous historical site

【胜利】 shènglì 1.(获胜) victory; triumph: 外交上的～ a diplomatic triumph 2.(达到目的) successfully; triumphantly: ～完成任务 successfully carry out one's task

【胜利者】 shènglìzhě winner

【胜券】 shèngquàn confidence in victory: 操～ be sure to win

【胜任】 shèngrèn competent; qualified; equal to

【胜似】 shèngsì be better than; surpass

【胜诉】 shèngsù win a lawsuit; carry the cause; recover; win over

【胜算】 shèngsuàn 〈*written*〉a stratagem which ensures success: 操～ be sure of success

【胜友如云】 shèngyǒurúyún a cloud of good friends; a great many good friends

【胜仗】 shèngzhàng victorious battle; victory

盛 (shèng) 1.(繁盛) flourishing; prosperous: 菊花～开。The chrysanthemums bloom luxuriantly. 2.(旺盛) vigorous; energetic 3.(盛大) magnificent; grand 4.(深厚) abundant; plentiful 5.(盛行) popular; common; wide spread 6.(程度深) greatly; deeply
(另见"盛"chéng)

【盛产】 shèngchǎn abound in; teem with: 这条河～鱼虾。This river is teeming with fish and shrimps.

【盛传】 shèngchuán be widely rumored

【盛大】 shèngdà grand; magnificent: ～的场面 a spectacular scenes

【盛典】 shèngdiǎn grand ceremony

【盛会】 shènghuì distinguished gathering; grand meeting: 体育～ a magnificent sports meet

【盛极一时】 shèngjí-yīshí be in fashion for a time; be all the rage at the moment

【盛况】 shèngkuàng grand occasion; magnificent occasion; spectacular event: ～空前 unprecedentedly magnificent occasion

【盛名】 shèngmíng great reputation: 负有～的人 man of great reputation

【盛怒】 shèngnù rage; fury

【盛气凌人】 shèngqì-língrén domineering; arrogant; overbearing

【盛情】 shèngqíng great kindness; boundless hospitality
【盛世】 shèngshì flourishing age; heyday; prospering period
【盛暑】 shèngshǔ sweltering summer heat; the dog days
【盛衰】 shèngshuāi prosperity and decline; rise and fall; ups and downs
【盛衰荣辱】 shèngshuāi-róngrǔ prosperity and decline, glory and humiliation; rise and fall; ups and downs
【盛夏】 shèngxià the height of summer; midsummer
【盛行】 shèngxíng be current; be in vogue
【盛宴】 shèngyàn grand banquet; sumptuous dinner: ～难再 difficult to have such a grand feast again
【盛意】 shèngyì great kindness; generosity
【盛誉】 shèngyù great fame; high reputation
【盛赞】 shèngzàn highly praise; speak of sb. in glowing terms
【盛装】 shèngzhuāng splendid attire; rich dress

剩［賸］(shèng) surplus; remnant; leave (over): 20 减 4～16。4 from 20 leaves 16.
【剩下】 shèng·xia be left (over); remain: 桌上～的饭菜 remains of a meal on the table / 只～一个问题。There is only one problem left unsolved.
【剩余】 shèngyú surplus; remainder: ～产品 surplus products / ～劳动力 surplus labor

shi

尸［屍］(shī) corpse; dead body; remains: 死～ dead body; corpse
【尸斑】 shībān cadaveric ecchymoses
【尸骨】 shīgǔ 1.(尸体骨头) skeleton 2.(尸体) corpse; dead body
【尸骸】 shīhái skeleton
【尸横遍野】 shīhéngbiànyě a field littered with corpses
【尸检】 shījiǎn necropsy; postmortem examination
【尸僵】 shījiāng cadaveric rigidity; rigor mortis
【尸身】 shīshēn 同"尸首"
【尸首】 shī·shou corpse; dead body; remains
【尸体】 shītǐ corpse; dead body; remains
【尸体检验】 shītǐ jiǎnyàn necropsy; postmortem examination
【尸体鉴定】 shītǐ jiàndìng identification of the dead
【尸体解剖】 shītǐ jiěpōu autopsy; postmortem (examination)
【尸位素餐】 shīwèi-sùcān hold down a job without doing a stroke of work

失(shī) 1.(丢失) lose: 得～ gain and loss / 迷～方向 lose one's bearings 2.(错过) miss; let slip: 机不可～ don't let slip an opportunity 3.(没有达到目的) fail to achieve one's end 4.(过失;错误) mishap; defect; mistake 5.(改变) deviate from the normal 6.(背弃) break (a promise); go back on (one's word)
【失败】 shībài 1.(被打败) be defeated; lose: 我们队足球赛～了。Our team lost the football match. 2.(没有成功) fail; failure (n.): 计划已经～。The plan fell through. / ～是成功之母。Failure is the mother of success.
【失策】 shīcè unwise; inexpedient
【失察】 shīchá neglect one's supervisory duties
【失常】 shīcháng not normal; odd: 举动～ act oddly; behave strangely
【失宠】 shīchǒng fall into disfavor; be out of favor; be in disgrace
【失传】 shīchuán not be handed down from past generations; be lost
【失聪】 shīcōng become deaf; be deaf
【失措】 shīcuò lose one's presence of mind; lose one's head: 惊慌～ be frightened out of one's wits
【失单】 shīdān a list of lost articles
【失当】 shīdàng improper; inappropriate: 举止～ behave inappropriately
【失道寡助】 shīdào-guǎzhù an unjust cause finds scant support
【失地】 shīdì lost territory: 收复～ recover the lost territory
【失掉】 shīdiào 1.(失去) lose 2.(错过) miss: ～机会 miss a chance

【失和】 shīhé be in discord; become estranged

【失衡】 shīhéng be in a state of imbalance; lose one's balance

【失魂落魄】 shīhún-luòpò driven to distraction; lose one's mind

【失火】 shīhuǒ catch fire; be on fire: 大楼～了。The building caught fire.

【失脚】 shījiǎo lose one's footing; slip: ～跌倒 lose one's footing and fall

【失节】 shījié **1.** (指气节) forfeit one's integrity; be disloyal **2.** (指贞操) lose one's chastity

【失禁】 shījìn 〈*Med.*〉 incontinence: 大小便～ incontinence of feces and urine

【失敬】 shījìng 〈*politeness*〉 sorry; sorry I didn't recognize you

【失控】 shīkòng out of control; runaway: ～的通货膨胀 runaway inflation

【失礼】 shīlǐ breach of etiquette; impoliteness; discourtesy

【失利】 shīlì suffer a setback; suffer a loss: 进攻～ suffer setback in attack

【失恋】 shīliàn be disappointed in a love affair

【失灵】 shīlíng not work; not work properly; be out of order: 刹车～。The brake doesn't work.

【失落】 shīluò lose

【失落感】 shīluògǎn sense of alienation

【失密】 shīmì give away official secrets due to carelessness

【失眠】 shīmián (suffer from) insomnia; have a sleepless night

【失明】 shīmíng lose one's sight; go blind

【失陪】 shīpéi 〈*politeness*〉 excuse me, but I must be leaving now

【失窃】 shīqiè have things stolen; suffer loss by theft

【失去】 shīqù **1.** (失掉) lose: 对那个计划我们已经～兴趣了。We've lost interest in that project. **2.** (错过) miss: ～机会 miss a chance

【失却】 shīquè lose

【失散】 shīsàn be separated from and lose touch with each other; be scattered

【失色】 shīsè **1.** (指脸色) turn pale: 大惊～ turn pale with fright **2.** (指色彩) be eclipsed; be outshone

【失身】 shīshēn **1.** (指少女) lose one's virginity **2.** (失节) lose one's chastity

【失神】 shīshén **1.** (疏忽) inattentive; absent-minded **2.** (精神不振) out of sorts; in low spirits

【失慎】 shīshèn **1.** (疏忽) not cautious; careless **2.** (失火) cause a fire through carelessness

【失声】 shīshēng **1.** (情不自禁地出声) cry out involuntarily **2.** (哭不出声) lose one's voice: 痛哭～ be choked with tears **3.** (失音) aphonia

【失时】 shīshí miss the season; let slip the opportunity

【失实】 shīshí inconsistent with the facts: 报导～。The report gave a false picture of the situation.

【失势】 shīshì lose power and influence; fall into disgrace

【失事】 shīshì (have an) accident; wreck: 飞机～ aviation accident; airplane crash

【失收】 shīshōu have no harvest

【失手】 shīshǒu **1.** (非故意) accidentally drop **2.** (喻失利) suffer a setback; suffer a loss

【失守】 shīshǒu fall; be taken: 城市～ the fall of a city

【失算】 shīsuàn miscalculate; be injudicious

【失态】 shītài forget oneself: 酒后～ forget oneself in one's cups

【失调】 shītiáo **1.** (失去平衡) imbalance; dislocation: 经济比例～ there are disproportions in economy; economy has been plagued with disproportions / 生产与消费的～ mal-adjustment in production and consumption **2.** (失去调养) lack of proper care (after an illness, etc.): 产后～ lack of proper care after childbirth **3.** 〈*Radio*〉 mal-adjustment; detuning

【失望】 shīwàng **1.** (感到无望) lose hope **2.** (希望落空而不快) be disappointed: 对他感到～ be disappointed in him / 对某事感到～ be disappointed at sth. / 当她最需要朋友的时候,他们却令她～。Her friends failed her when she most needed them.

【失物】 shīwù lost article; lost property

【失物招领处】 shīwù zhāolǐngchù Lost and Found Office; Lost Property Office

【失误】 shīwù 1.(指打球、下棋) fault; muff: 发球～ faulty service / 接球～ muff a ball 2.(指差错) slip up: 工作中有不少～。There are not a few failings in one's work.

【失陷】 shīxiàn fall; fall into enemy hands

【失效】 shīxiào 1.(失去效力) lose efficacy; cease to be effective: 药品～。The medicine has lost its efficacy. 2.(无效) be no longer in force; become invalid: 这张证明已～。This certificate is invalid.

【失笑】 shīxiào laugh in spite of oneself; cannot help laughing

【失信】 shīxìn break one's promise; go back on one's word

【失修】 shīxiū be in bad repair; fall into disrepair: 年久～ have been neglected for years

【失学】 shīxué be deprived of education; be unable to go to school; be obliged to discontinue one's studies

【失血】 shīxuè lose blood

【失言】 shīyán make an indiscreet remark

【失业】 shīyè lose one's job; be out of work; be unemployed: ～工人 unemployed workers

【失业保险】 shīyè bǎoxiǎn unemployment insurance

【失业津贴】 shīyè jīntiē unemployment benefit

【失业救济】 shīyè jiùjì unemployment relief

【失业率】 shīyèlǜ rate of unemployment

【失宜】 shīyí 〈*written*〉 inappropriate

【失意】 shīyì be dejected; be frustrated; be disappointed

【失音】 shīyīn 〈*Med.*〉 aphonia

【失迎】 shīyíng 〈*politeness*〉 fail to meet (a guest)

【失语】 shīyǔ 〈*Med.*〉 aphasia

【失约】 shīyuē fail to keep an appointment

【失真】 shīzhēn 1.(与原来的有出入) lack fidelity; not be true to the original 2.〈*Radio*〉 distortion

【失之交臂】 shīzhī-jiāobì just miss the person or opportunity

【失职】 shīzhí neglect one's duty; dereliction of duty

【失职罪】 shīzhízuì offense of misconduct in office

【失重】 shīzhòng 〈*Physics*〉 weightlessness; zero gravity; weight loss: ～状态 the state of weightlessness

【失主】 shīzhǔ owner of lost property

【失踪】 shīzōng disappear; absence; be missing

【失足】 shīzú 1.(跌倒) lose one's footing; slip: ～落水 slip and fall into the water 2.(堕落或犯罪) take a wrong step in life

【失足青年】 shīzú qīngnián juvenile delinquent; young offender

师[師](shī) 1.(老师) teacher; master 2.(榜样) model; example 3.(某一等级的专门人才) a person skilled in a certain profession: 工程～ engineer 4.(同一师傅的) of one's master; of one's teacher 5.〈*Mil.*〉 division 6.(军队) troops; army

【师表】 shībiǎo 〈*written*〉 a person of exemplary virtue: 为人～ be a paragon of virtue and learning

【师部】 shībù 〈*Mil.*〉 division headquarters

【师出无名】 shīchū-wúmíng dispatch troops without just cause

【师弟】 shīdì 1.(指同一师傅的) junior fellow apprentice of same master 2.(指师傅的儿子) the son of one's master (younger than oneself) 3.(指父亲的徒弟) father's apprentice (younger than oneself) 4.(对上述三种人的称呼) brother

【师法】 shīfǎ 1.(效法) model oneself after (a great master); imitate 2.(指学问、技术) knowledge or technique handed down by one's master

【师范】 shīfàn 1.(培养师资的) teacher-training; pedagogical: ～大学 teachers university 2.(师范学校) normal school

【师父】 shīfù 1.(师傅) master; master worker 2.(对僧、尼等的尊称) master

【师傅】 shī·fu master worker

【师姐】 shījiě 1.(指同一师傅的) senior female fellow apprentice of same master 2.(指师傅的女儿) the daughter of one's master (older than oneself) 3.(指父亲的女弟子) father's apprentice (older than oneself) 4.

（对上述三种人的称呼）sister
【师妹】 shīmèi 1.（指同一师傅的）junior female fellow apprentice of same master 2.（指师傅的女儿）the daughter of one's master (younger than oneself) 3.（指父亲的女弟子）father's apprentice (younger than oneself) 4.（对上述三种人的称呼）sister
【师母】 shīmǔ 1.（老师或师傅之妻）the wife of one's teacher or master 2.（称呼）mother
【师娘】 shīniáng 同"师母"
【师生】 shīshēng teachers and students
【师生关系】 shīshēng guānxì teacher-student relationship
【师徒】 shītú master and apprentice
【师团】 shītuán 〈*Mil*.〉division
【师兄】 shīxiōng 1.（指同一师傅的）senior fellow apprentice of same master 2.（指师傅的儿子）the son of one's master (older than oneself) 3.（指父亲的徒弟）father's apprentice (older than oneself) 4.（对上述三种人的称呼）big brother
【师爷】 shī·ye private adviser
【师长】 shīzhǎng 1.〈*respect*〉teacher 2.〈*Mil*.〉division commander; divisional commander
【师专】 shīzhuān teachers training school; normal school
【师资】 shīzī persons qualified to teach; teachers
【师资力量】 shīzī lìliàng teacher staff：充实～ strengthen the teaching staff

狮［獅］(shī) 〈*Zool*.〉lion (m.); lioness (f.)：美洲～ puma
【狮身人面像】 shīshēn-rénmiànxiàng sphinx
【狮子】 shī·zi lion (m.); lioness (f.)
【狮子宫】 Shī·zigōng 〈*Astron*.〉Leo (7月23日至8月22日)：生于～ be born under Leo
【狮子狗】 shī·zigǒu pug-dog
【狮子舞】 shī·ziwǔ lion dance
【狮子座】 Shī·zizuò 〈*Astron*.〉Leo

诗(shī) poetry; verse; poem; poetic (adj.)：自由～ free verse / 他写了一首关于战争的～。He wrote a poem about war.
【诗风】 shīfēng style of poems
【诗歌】 shīgē poems and songs; poetry
【诗话】 shīhuà notes on poets and poetry; notes on classical poetry
【诗集】 shījí collection of poems; poetry anthology
【诗经】 Shījīng *The Book of Songs*
【诗句】 shījù verse; line
【诗剧】 shījù drama in verse; poetic drama
【诗礼传家】 shīlǐ-chuánjiā a family of scholars
【诗篇】 shīpiān 1.（总称）poem 2.（比喻）inspiring story：壮丽～ a magnificent epic (of)
【诗情画意】 shīqíng-huàyì a quality suggestive of poetry or painting
【诗人】 shīrén poet
【诗书门第】 shīshū-méndì a scholarly family
【诗坛】 shītán the circles of poets
【诗兴】 shīxìng urge for poetic creation; poetic inspiration; poetic mood
【诗意】 shīyì poetic quality or flavor
【诗韵】 shīyùn 1.（做诗的韵）rhyme 2.（韵书）rhyming dictionary
【诗作】 shīzuò poetry; poems and songs

虱［蝨］(shī) 〈*Zool*.〉louse
【虱子】 shī·zi louse

施(shī) 1.（施行）execute; carry out 2.（给予）bestow; grant; hand out 3.（施加）exert; impose 4.（施用）use; apply：～肥 apply fertilizer
【施暴】 shībào 1.（施以暴力）resort to violence 2.（强奸）rape; violate：对妇女～ rape a woman
【施放】 shīfàng discharge; fire：～烟幕 throw up a smokescreen
【施肥】 shīféi spread manure; apply fertilizer
【施工】 shīgōng construct; construction (n.); build; building (n.)：新机场仍在～中。The new airport is still under construction.
【施加】 shījiā exert; bring to bear on：～压力 exert pressure / ～影响 exercise influence
【施礼】 shīlǐ salute
【施舍】 shīshě give alms; give in charity
【施威】 shīwēi exhibit one's power; show severity
【施行】 shīxíng 1.（执行）put in force; execute; apply：自公布之日起～ come into force upon promulgation 2.（做；实行）per-

form：～手术 perform a surgical operation

【施行细则】 shīxíng xìzé rules for implementation

【施用】 shīyòng use；employ；apply：～化肥 apply fertilizer

【施展】 shīzhǎn put to good use；give free play to：～才能 display one's ability

【施政】 shīzhèng administration

【施政方针】 shīzhèng fāngzhēn administrative politics

【施政纲领】 shīzhèng gānglǐng administrative program

【施政演说】 shīzhèng yǎnshuō policy address

【施主】 shīzhǔ 1.（施舍财物的人）alms giver；benefactor 3.〈*Physics*〉donor

湿［溼、溼］（shī） wet；damp；humid：～空气 humid air；moist air / ～衣服 wet clothes / 在雨中淋～ be damped in the rain / 这里太～。There is too much damp.

【湿材】 shīcái green lumber

【湿地】 shīdì 1.〈*Geog.*〉wetland 2.（湿了的地）wet ground

【湿度】 shīdù humidity；moisture

【湿度表】 shīdùbiǎo humidometer

【湿度计】 shīdùjì hygrometer；succulometer

【湿度调节器】 shīdù tiáojiéqì humidistat

【湿季】 shījì wet season

【湿淋淋】 shīlínlín dripping wet；drenched：浑身～的 get dripping wet

【湿漉漉】 shīlūlū wet；damp

【湿气】 shīqì 1.（水蒸气）moisture；dampness 2.〈*Chin. Med.*〉eczema；fungus infection of hand or foot

【湿润】 shīrùn moist

【湿润剂】 shīrùnjì wetting agent

【湿透】 shītòu wet through；drenched：她被雨淋得浑身～。She was drenched through with rain.

【湿疹】 shīzhěn 〈*Med.*〉eczema

【湿纸巾】 shīzhǐjīn towelette：用～擦手 wipe one's hands on the towelette

蓍（shī）

【蓍草】 shīcǎo 〈*Bot.*〉yaroow；common yarrow

嘘（shī） 〈*onomat.*〉sh；hush；hiss（v.）：被～下台 be hissed off the stage / ～，别说话！Hush！Stop talking！（另见"嘘"xū）

十（shí） 1.（数目）ten；tenth 2.（达到顶点）topmost

【十八】 shíbā eighteen；eighteenth

【十边形】 shíbiānxíng decagon

【十成】 shíchéng 100 per cent

【十冬腊月】 shídōng-làyuè the cold months of the year

【十恶不赦】 shí'è-bùshè unpardonable evil；guilty beyond forgiveness

【十二】 shí'èr twelve；twelfth

【十二进制】 shí'èrjìnzhì duodecimal notation

【十二月】 shí'èryuè December

【十二指肠】 shí'èrzhǐcháng 〈*Anat.*〉duodenum

【十分】 shífēn 〈*abv.*〉very；fully；utterly；extremely：～流行的运动项目 big-time game / ～有害 extremely harmful

【十佳】 shíjiā the top-ten

【十锦】 shíjǐn 同"什锦"

【十进制】 shíjìnzhì 〈*Math.*〉the decimal system

【十九】 shíjiǔ nineteen；nineteenth

【十六】 shíliù sixteen；sixteenth

【十拿九稳】 shíná-jiǔwěn 90 per cent sure；be very sure of；practically certain；in the bag：这冠军，我们是～了。We're sure of winning the championship.

【十年寒窗】 shínián-hánchuāng persevere ten years in one's studies in spite of hardships

【十年九不遇】 shí nián jiǔ bù yù be very rare；not occur once in ten years

【十年树木，百年树人】 shí nián shù mù, bǎi nián shù rén 〈*Proverb*〉it takes ten years to grow trees, but a hundred to rear people

【十七】 shíqī seventeen；seventeenth

【十全十美】 shíquán-shíměi be perfect in every way；be the acme of perfection；leave nothing to be desired：世上没有～的东西。Nothing in the world is flawless and perfect.

【十三】 shísān thirteen；thirteenth

【十四】 shísì fourteen；fourteenth

【十万】 shíwàn one hundred thousand；one hundred thousandth

【十万八千里】 shíwàn bāqiān lǐ very far away：相差～ differ greatly

【十万火急】 shíwàn-huǒjí most urgent; extra-urgent

【十五】 shíwǔ fifteen; fifteenth

【十五个吊桶打水,七上八下】 shíwǔ gè diàotǒng dǎ shuǐ, qī shàng bā xià One's heartis like a well in which seven buckets are drawn up and eight dropped down.

【十项全能运动】 shíxiàng quánnéng yùndòng 〈*Sports*〉 decathlon

【十项全能运动员】 shíxiàng quánnéng yùndòngyuán decathlete

【十一】 shíyī **1.**(数目) eleven; eleventh **2.**(十月一日) October 1 (National Day)

【十一月】 shíyīyuè November

【十亿】 shíyì billion (AmE.); thousand million (BrE.); billionth (AmE.); thousand millionth (BrE.)

【十月】 shíyuè October

【十之八九】 shí zhī bājiǔ in eight or nine cases out of ten; most probably; very likely

【十指连心】 shízhǐ-liánxīn The nerves of the fingertips are linked with the heart. (或: What happens to children is of vital interest to parents.)

【十字】 shízì cross: 红~ Red Cross / 蓝~ Blue Cross / 划~ make the sign of the cross; cross

【十字槽螺帽】 shízìcáo luómào Phillips head

【十字镐】 shízìgǎo pick; pickax; mattock

【十字架】 shízìjià cross: 在脖子上戴了一个金的~ wear a gold cross around one's neck

【十字街头】 shízì-jiētóu crisscross streets

【十字军】 Shízìjūn **1.**〈*Hist.*〉 the Crusades **2.**(指英美某种社会改革运动) crusade **3.**(指参加者) crusader

【十字路口】 shízì lùkǒu crossroads: 到下一个~往右拐。Turn right at the next crossroads.

【十足】 shízú **1.**(纯粹的) out-and-out; sheer; 100 per cent; downright: ~的黄金 pure gold / ~的骗局 a sheer fraud **2.**(十分充足) full of: 官气~ assuming the airs of a mandarin

什 (shí) **1.**(多种的) assorted; varied; miscellaneous **2.**(用于分数或倍数) ten; tenth: ~一 one-tenth

(另见"什"shén)

【什锦】 shíjǐn 〈*Food*〉 assorted; mixed

【什锦锉】 shíjǐncuò assorted set of files

【什物】 shíwù articles for daily use; odds and ends; sundries

石 (shí) **1.**(岩石) stone; rock **2.**(石刻) stone inscription: 金~ inscriptions on ancient bronzes and stone tablets

【石斑鱼】 shíbānyú 〈*Zool.*〉 grouper

【石板】 shíbǎn **1.**(建筑用的) flagstone; slabstone **2.**(写字用的) slate; slate writing board

【石碑】 shíbēi stone tablet; stele; stela

【石笔】 shíbǐ slate pencil

【石沉大海】 shíchéndàhǎi like a stone dropped into the sea; disappear for ever

【石雕】 shídiāo **1.**(在石头上雕刻) stone carving **2.**(石雕艺术品) carved stone

【石方】 shífāng **1.**(一立方米石料) cubic meter of stone **2.**(石方工程) stonework

【石膏】 shígāo gypsum; plaster stone

【石膏像】 shígāoxiàng plaster statue

【石工】 shígōng **1.**(指活计) masonry **2.**(指人) stonemason; mason

【石拱桥】 shígǒngqiáo stone arch bridge

【石化】 shíhuà **1.**〈*Geol.*〉 petrify; petrification (n.) **2.**(石油化工) petrochemical industry; petrochemical (adj.)

【石灰】 shíhuī lime; limy (adj.): 生~ quicklime / 熟~ slaked lime

【石灰水】 shíhuīshuǐ limewash

【石灰岩】 shíhuīyán limestone

【石灰窑】 shíhuīyáo limekiln

【石级】 shíjí stone steep

【石匠】 shí·jiang stonemason; mason

【石刻】 shíkè **1.**(指石碑、石壁等) carved stone **2.**(指所刻文字、图画) stone inscription

【石窟】 shíkū rock cave; grotto

【石块】 shíkuài stone; rock

【石蜡】 shílà paraffin wax

【石林】 shílín stone forest

【石榴】 shí·liu 〈*Bot.*〉 pomegranate

【石煤】 shíméi bone coal

【石棉】 shímián asbestos

【石棉瓦】 shímiánwǎ asbestos tile

【石墨】 shímò graphite

【石磨】 shímò stone mill

【石破天惊】 shípò-tiānjīng remarkably original and forceful (music, writing, etc.); great vibration or shock

【石器】 shíqì 1.(石制工具、器具) stone implement; stone artifact 2.(石制品) stone vessel; stoneware

【石器时代】 shíqì shídài the Stone Age

【石笋】 shísǔn 〈*Geog.*〉 the stalagmite

【石头】 shí·tou stone; rock

【石头子儿】 shí·touzǐr pebble; cobblestone

【石英】 shíyīng quartz

【石英表】 shíyīngbiǎo quartz watch

【石油】 shíyóu petroleum; oil: 勘探～ prospect for oil / 开采～ exploit the oil

【石油产品】 shíyóu chǎnpǐn petroleum products

【石油工业】 shíyóu gōngyè oil industry; petroleum industry

【石油管路】 shíyóu guǎnlù petroleum pipeline

【石油化工】 shíyóu huàgōng petrochemical industry; petrochemical (adj.)

【石油化工产品】 shíyóu huàgōng chǎnpǐn petrochemical products; petrochemicals; petroleum chemicals

【石油化工厂】 shíyóu huàgōngchǎng petrochemical works

【石油化学产品】 shíyóu huàxué chǎnpǐn petroleum chemicals

【石油勘探】 shíyóu kāntàn petroleum prospecting

【石油沥青】 shíyóu lìqīng petroleum pitch

【石油美元】 shíyóu měiyuán oil dollar; petrodollars

【石油气】 shíyóuqì petroleum gas: 液化～ liquefied petroleum gas (LPG)

【石油输出国组织】 shíyóu shūchūguó zǔzhī (欧佩克) the Organization of Petroleum Exporting Countries (OPEC)

【石钟乳】 shízhōngrǔ stalactite

【石竹】 shízú 〈*Bot.*〉 pink

【石子儿】 shízǐr pebble; cobblestone

【石子儿路】 shízǐrlù pebbled path; cobbled path

时[時] (shí) 1.(一段时间) time; times; days: 古～ in ancient times 2.(规定时刻) fixed time: 火车准～到达。The train arrived on time. 3.(季节) season 4.(计时单位) hour: 从十～到十二～ from 10 to 12 / 上午九～ 9 a.m. 5.(当前) current; at present 6.(时机) opportunity; chance: 失～ lose the opportunity 7.(时常) now and then; occasionally; from time to time 8.(叠用) now... now...; sometimes... sometimes...: ～快～慢 sometimes fast, sometimes slow 9.〈*Gram.*〉 tense: 过去～ the past tense

【时不我待】 shíbùwǒdài Time will not wait for me. (或: Time waits for no man.)

【时不宜迟】 shíbùyíchí There's no time to be lost.

【时差】 shíchā 1.(两地的时间差) time difference 2.〈*Astron.*〉 equation of time

【时差反应】 shíchā fǎnyìng jet lag

【时常】 shícháng frequently; often:

【时代】 shídài 1.(时期) times; age; era; epoch: 铜器～ bronze age / 太空旅行～ the era of space travel / 划～的大事 the epoch-making event / 顺应～潮流 go with the current of the times 2.(生命中的时期) a period in one's life: 青年～ youth / 在我读书的～ in my school days

【时代感】 shídàigǎn sense of modern times

【时代精神】 shídài jīngshén spirit of the times

【时段】 shíduàn time

【时而】 shí'ér 1.(重复发生) from time to time; sometimes: 蔚蓝色的天空中,～飘过几朵白云。Sometimes several clusters of white clouds drift across the blue sky. 2.(叠用) now ... now ...; sometimes ... sometimes ...: 天气～热～冷。It is sometimes warm and sometimes cold.

【时分】 shífèn time: 黄昏～ at dusk; at twilight

【时乖运蹇】 shíguāi-yùnjiǎn be very hard up, and (in fact) be at a loose end; run into bad luck

【时光】 shíguāng 1.(光阴) time 2.(时期) times; years; days 3.(日子) day

【时过境迁】 shíguò-jìngqiān Circumstances change with the passage of time. (或: Once on shore, we pray no more.)

【时候】 shí·hou 1.(一段时间) (the duration of) time 2.(某一时间) (a point in) time; moment

【时机】 shíjī an opportune moment; opportunity：把握～ catch an opportunity / 错过～ lose an opportunity; miss an opportunity

【时价】 shíjià current price

【时间】 shíjiān time; hour：上课～ school hours / 屏幕～ screen time / 没有～ have no time / 你在家里怎么打发～? How do you spend your time at home?

【时间表】 shíjiānbiǎo timetable; schedule

【时间方位】 shíjiān fāngwèi time azimuth

【时间共享】 shíjiān gòngxiǎng 〈*Computer*〉 time-share

【时间间隔】 shíjiān jiāngé time separation

【时间效率】 shíjiān xiàolǜ time efficiency

【时间性】 shíjiānxìng timeliness

【时节】 shíjié **1**.（季节）season **2**.（时候）time：那～我们每年夏天都去游泳。At that time we used to go swimming every summer.

【时局】 shíjú the current political situation：～动荡。The current situation is turbulent.

【时刻】 shíkè **1**.（某一时间）time; hour; moment：关键～ critical moment; crucial moment / 一生中最幸福的～ the happiest hour of one's life **2**.（每时每刻）constantly; always：～保持清醒头脑 constantly keep a cool head

【时刻表】 shíkèbiǎo timetable; schedule：列车～ train schedule

【时空】 shíkōng space-time; space-time continuum

【时控】 shíkòng timed

【时控装置】 shíkòng zhuāngzhì timed unit

【时来运转】 shílái-yùnzhuǎn Fortune is smiling.

【时令】 shílìng season; seasonal (adj.)：～正当 be in season

【时令河】 shílìnghé seasonal river

【时令湖】 shílìnghú seasonal lake

【时令商品】 shílìng shāngpǐn seasonal commodities

【时髦】 shímáo fashionable; stylish; in vogue：赶～ follow the fashion

【时期】 shíqī period：和平～ peacetime / 全盛～ the most prosperous period

【时区】 shíqū time zone：从北京到罗马要跨七个～。If you go from Beijing to Rome, you cross seven time zones.

【时时】 shíshí often; constantly

【时势】 shíshì the current situation; the trend of the times; the way things are going：～造英雄。The times produce their heroes

【时事】 shíshì current events; current affairs

【时速】 shísù speed per hour：～限制：30 公里/小时 Speed Limit：30 Km/h

【时态】 shítài 〈*Gram.*〉 tense

【时务】 shíwù current affairs; the trend of the times：不识～ show no understanding of the times

【时鲜】 shíxiān in season：～果品 fruits in season

【时限】 shíxiàn time limit

【时效】 shíxiào **1**.（指作用）effectiveness for a given period of time **2**.〈*Law*〉 prescription

【时效期限】 shíxiào qīxiàn length of limitation period; limitation period

【时效性】 shíxiàoxìng timeliness

【时效中断】 shíxiào zhōngduàn interruption; interruption of prescription

【时效终止】 shíxiào zhōngzhǐ lapse of time

【时新】 shíxīn stylish; trendy

【时兴】 shíxīng fashionable; in vogue; be in fashion

【时序】 shíxù sequence in time

【时宜】 shíyí what is appropriate to the occasion：不合～ be inopportune; be inappropriate / 改革不合～的人事制度 reform outmoded personnel system

【时疫】 shíyì epidemic

【时运】 shíyùn luck; fortune：～不济 have bad luck

【时针】 shízhēn **1**.（钟表的针）hands of a clock or watch **2**.（钟、表的短针）hour hand

【时至今日】 shízhìjīnrì at this late hour

【时钟】 shízhōng clock

【时装】 shízhuāng fashionable dress; the latest fashion

【时装表演】 shízhuāng biǎoyǎn fashion show

【时装模特儿】 shízhuāng mótèr fashion model

【时装设计师】 shízhuāng shèjìshī fashion designer

【时装杂志】 shízhuāng zázhì fashion magazine

识[識] (shí) **1**.（认识）know：一字不～ not know a single character;

absolutely illiterate 2.（知识）knowledge：学～ learning; knowledge

【识别】 shíbié identify; distinguish; discern; spot: 这些标记模糊不清，难以～。The markings are so blurred that it is difficult to identify.

【识别标记】 shíbié biāojì identification marking

【识大体，顾大局】 shí dàtǐ, gù dàjú have the cardinal principles in mind and take the overall situation into account

【识货】 shíhuò know all about the goods; be able to tell good from bad; know what's what

【识家】 shíjiā who know what's what

【识破】 shípò see through; penetrate：～机关 see through a plot / ～阴谋 see through an intrigue

【识趣】 shíqù know how to behave in a delicate situation：不～ be insensible

【识时务者为俊杰】 shí shíwù zhě wéi jùnjié Those who suit their actions to the time are wise.

【识途老马】 shítú-lǎomǎ an old horse which knows the way; a person of rich experience; a wise old bird

【识文断字】 shíwén-duànzì able to read; literate

【识字】 shízì learn to read; become literate

实［實］（shí） 1.（实心）solid：铁条是～心的，管子是空心的。An iron bar is solid, a pipe is hollow. 2.（真实）true; real; honest：情况属～。It's true. 3.（实际）reality; fact：名～相副 in reality as well as in name 4.（果实）fruit; seed：结～ bear fruit

【实词】 shící 〈*Gram.*〉 notional word

【实弹】 shídàn 〈*Mil.*〉 live shell; live ammunition

【实弹射击】 shídàn shèjī firing practice; range practice

【实弹演习】 shídàn yǎnxí practice with live ammunition

【实得工资】 shídé gōngzī take-home pay

【实地】 shídì 1.（在现场）on the spot：～勘测 field exploring 2.（实实在在）sincere; honest

【实地考察】 shídì kǎochá make an on-the-spot investigation

【实干】 shígàn get right on the job; do solid work：有～精神 with a spirit of working in earnest

【实干家】 shígànjiā man of action

【实话】 shíhuà truth：说～ to tell the truth

【实惠】 shíhuì 1.（实际好处）material benefit：人民可以得到更多～ yield more substantial benefits to the people 2.（有实际好处）substantial; solid：经济～的饭菜 inexpensive but substantial meals

【实际】 shíjì 1.（客观存在）reality; practice：作出符合～的分析 make an accurate analysis 2.（实有的）practical; realistic：～经验 practical experience 3.（合乎事实的）real; actual; concrete：我不能举出～数字。I cannot give the actual figures.

【实际成本】 shíjì chéngběn actual cost; real cost

【实际工资】 shíjì gōngzī real wages

【实际汇价】 shíjì huìjià effective rate

【实际价值】 shíjì jiàzhí actual value

【实际控制线】 shíjì kòngzhìxiàn line of actual control

【实际利率】 shíjì lìlǜ actual rate of interest

【实际利润】 shíjì lìrùn real profit

【实际伤害】 shíjì shānghài actual harm; real injury

【实际收入】 shíjì shōurù real income

【实际消费】 shíjì xiāofèi actual consumption

【实际债务】 shíjì zhàiwù actual debts

【实际支付】 shíjì zhīfù actual delivery

【实际资本】 shíjì zīběn actual capital

【实绩】 shíjì real achievement; gain

【实价】 shíjià actual price

【实践】 shíjiàn 1.〈*Philos.*〉 practice：～是检验真理的唯一标准。Practice is the sole criterion for testing truth. 2.（实行）put into practice; carry out; live up to：～诺言 keep one's word; make good one's promise

【实据】 shíjù substantial evidence; substantial proof：查无～ investigations show no evidence

【实况】 shíkuàng live; what is actually happening

【实况广播】 shíkuàng guǎngbō live broadcast

【实况录音】 shíkuàng lùyīn on-the-spot recording; live recording

【实况转播】 shíkuàng zhuǎnbō live broadcast; live telecast

【实力】 shílì actual strength; strength: 扩充～ expand power

【实力地位】 shílì dìwèi position of strength

【实力政策】 shílì zhèngcè realpolitik; power policy

【实例】 shílì living example; example

【实情】 shíqíng the true state of affairs; the actual situation; truth

【实权】 shíquán real power; actual power: 掌～ have the real power

【实施】 shíshī put into effect; implement; carry out

【实施法规】 shíshī fǎguī enforcement regulations

【实施机构】 shíshī jīgòu enforcement body

【实施条例】 shíshī tiáolì enforcement regulations

【实施细则】 shíshī xìzé rules for implementation

【实事】 shíshì facts

【实事求是】 shíshì-qiúshì seek truth from facts; be practical and realistic

【实数】 shíshù 1.(实在数字) the actual amount or number 2.〈*Math*.〉real number: 整数、有理数和无理数都是～。Integers, rational numbers, and irrational numbers are all real.

【实体】 shítǐ entity: 真正独立的经济～ really independent economic entities

【实物】 shíwù 1.(具体之物) material object 2.(代款之物) in kind 3.(应用之物) the things in actual use

【实物工资】 shíwù gōngzī wages in kind

【实物化】 shíwùhuà the form of material

【实物交易】 shíwù jiāoyì barter

【实物赔偿】 shíwù péicháng reparations in kind

【实物税】 shíwùshuì tax paid in kind

【实物证据】 shíwù zhèngjù tangible evidence

【实习】 shíxí practice; fieldwork; field trip: 你们有护理病人的～吗? Have you had any practice in nursing the sick?

【实习工厂】 shíxí gōngchǎng factory attached to a school

【实习生】 shíxíshēng trainee

【实习医生】 shíxí yīshēng intern

【实线】 shíxiàn hard-wire; actual line; real line

【实现】 shíxiàn realize; achieve; bring about: ～四个现代化 accomplish the four modernizations

【实效】 shíxiào actual effect; substantial results

【实心】 shíxīn 1.(心地诚实) sincere: ～实意 honest and sincere 2.(内部是实的) solid: 垒球是～的。The softball is solid.

【实心眼儿】 shíxīnyǎnr a sincere person

【实行】 shíxíng put into practice; carry out; practice; implement: ～对外开放,搞活经济的政策 carry out the policies of opening to the out-side world and enlivening the domestic economy / ～集体领导 exercise collective leadership

【实学】 shíxué real learning; sound scholarship: 真才～ real ability and learning

【实验】 shíyàn experiment; test; experimental (adj.): 科学～ scientific experimentation / 我们可以通过～看到油与水是不相溶的。We can learn by experiment that oil and water will not mix.

【实验报告】 shíyàn bàogào laboratory report

【实验动物】 shíyàn dòngwù animal used as a subject of experiment

【实验室】 shíyànshì laboratory: 设备齐全的～ equipped laboratory

【实验员】 shíyànyuán laboratory technician

【实业】 shíyè industry and commerce; industry

【实业家】 shíyèjiā industrialist

【实音】 shíyīn flatness

【实用】 shíyòng 1.(正在使用的) be in use 2.(有实用价值的) practical; pragmatic; functional: ～、有效、廉价、方便 practical, efficient, economical and convenient for use

【实用主义】 shíyòng zhǔyì 〈*Philos*.〉pragmatism

【实在】 shízài 1.(真实的) true; real; honest; dependable: ～的本事 real ability 2.(的确) indeed; really; honestly: ～太好了 very good indeed 3.(其实) in fact; as a matter of fact：他装懂，～并没懂。He pretends to understand, but as a matter of fact he doesn't. 4.（扎实）well-done; done carefully：工作做得很～。The work is well-done.

【实则】 shízé actually; in fact; in reality

【实战】 shízhàn actual combat

【实质】 shízhì substance; essence

【实质性变更】 shízhìxìng biàngēng material alteration

【实质性陈述】 shízhìxìng chénshù material representation

【实质性条款】 shízhìxìng tiáokuǎn substantive provision

【实质性证据】 shízhìxìng zhèngjù material evidence

【实足】 shízú full; solid：～年龄 exact age

拾（shí） 1.（捡拾）pick up (from the ground); collect：～一块石头 pick up a stone 2.（十）ten; tenth

【拾波】 shíbō pick-up

【拾掇】 shí·duo 1.（整理）put in order; set in order 2.（修理）repair; fix：～收音机 repair a radio 3.（惩治）punish

【拾荒】 shíhuāng glean and collect scraps (to eke out an existence)

【拾级而上】 shíjí'érshàng ascend the stairs

【拾金不昧】 shíjīn-bùmèi not pocket the money one picks up

【拾球员】 shíqiúyuán 〈*Sports*〉 ball boy

【拾取】 shíqǔ pick up; collect

【拾人牙慧】 shírényáhuì pick up phrases from sb. and pass them off as one's own

【拾遗】 shíyí 1.（拾取失物）appropriate lost property：路不～。No one pockets anything found on the road. 2.（补充遗漏）make good omissions：～补阙 make good omissions and deficiencies

【拾音】 shíyīn pick up

【拾音器】 shíyīnqì pick-up

【拾音器选择开关】 shíyīnqì xuǎnzé kāiguān pick-up selector

【拾音头】 shíyīntóu pick-up head

食［蚀[5]］（shí） 1.（吃；吃饭）eat：废寝忘～（be so absorbed as to）forget to sleep and eat 2.（食物）meal; food：流～ liquid diet / 面～ food made of flour / 肉～ meat 3.（饲料）feed：鸡～ hen feed / 猪～ pig feed 4.（可食用的）edible 5.（日食，月食）eclipse：环～ annular eclipse / 偏～ partial eclipse / 全～ total eclipse / 日～ solar eclipse / 月～ lunar eclipse

【食不甘味】 shíbùgānwèi have no appetite for food (in deep sorrow); eat food but without knowing its taste

【食不果腹】 shíbùguǒfù have little food to eat; have not sufficient food to eat

【食不厌精】 shíbùyànjīng One does not object to the finest food.

【食道】 shídào 〈*Anat.*〉 gullet; esophagus; oesophagus

【食道癌】 shídào'ái 〈*Med.*〉 cancer of the esophagus

【食分】 shífēn 〈*Astron.*〉 degree obscuration; magnitude of eclipse

【食管】 shíguǎn 〈*Anat.*〉 gullet; esophagus; oesophagus

【食管炎】 shíguǎnyán 〈*Med.*〉 esophagitis

【食既】 shíjì 〈*Astron.*〉 second contact of an eclipse

【食具】 shíjù tableware; dinner service

【食客】 shíkè 1.（寄食者）a hanger-on of an aristocrat 2.（餐馆顾客）a customer of a restaurant

【食利者】 shílìzhě rentier

【食粮】 shíliáng grain; food：精神～ spiritual food

【食量】 shíliàng capacity for eating; appetite

【食疗】 shíliáo dietotherapy; dietetic treatment

【食品】 shípǐn foodstuff; food; provisions

【食品保鲜】 shípǐn bǎoxiān food fresh keeping

【食品部】 shípǐnbù food department

【食品厂】 shípǐnchǎng bakery and confectionery; food products factory

【食品袋】 shípǐndài plastic food bag

【食品工业】 shípǐn gōngyè food industry

【食品公司】 shípǐn gōngsī food company

【食品加工】 shípǐn jiāgōng food processing

【食品加工机】 shípǐn jiāgōngjī food processor

【食品街】 shípǐnjiē restaurant strip

【食品商店】 shípǐn shāngdiàn food store; provisions shop

【食品添加剂】 shípǐn tiānjiājì food additive

【食品营养价值】 shípǐn yíngyǎng jiàzhí food value
【食谱】 shípǔ recipes; cookbook
【食甚】 shíshèn 〈*Astron.*〉 middle of eclipse
【食宿】 shísù board and lodging
【食堂】 shítáng dining room; mess hall; canteen
【食糖】 shítáng sugar
【食物】 shíwù food; eatables; edibles
【食物链】 shíwùliàn food chain
【食物中毒】 shíwù zhòngdú food poisoning
【食言】 shíyán go back on one's word; break one's promise: ～而肥 fail to make good one's promise
【食盐】 shíyán table salt; salt
【食蚁兽】 shíyǐshòu 〈*Zool.*〉 anteater
【食用】 shíyòng edible; comestible
【食用色素】 shíyòng sèsù food coloring
【食油】 shíyóu edible oil; cooking oil
【食欲】 shíyù appetite
【食指】 shízhǐ **1.**（第二指）index finger; forefinger **2.**（家庭人口）household; family members: ～众多 large family index finger; forefinger

蚀(shí) **1.**（损失）lose: 亏～ lose (money) in business **2.**（腐蚀）erode; corrode: 风雨侵～ erosion by wind and rain **3.**（同"食 5."）eclipse
【蚀本】 shíběn lose one's capital: ～出售 sell at a loss
【蚀变】 shíbiàn alteration
【蚀刻】 shíkè etch on; etch upon; etching (n.): 把名字～在一块金属板上 etch one's name on a metal plate / The design on the glass was produced by etching. 玻璃杯上的图案是～上去的。
【蚀刻机】 shíkèjī etching machine
【蚀刻剂】 shíkèjì etchant
【蚀刻印刷】 shíkè yìnshuā etch printing

莳［蒔］(shí)
【莳萝】 shíluó 〈*Bot.*〉 dill

鲥［鰣］(shí)
【鲥鱼】 shíyú seasonal shad; Reeves' shad

史(shǐ) history; historical (adj.): 古代～ ancient history / 近代～ modern history / 现代～ contemporary history
【史册】 shǐcè history; annals: 永垂～ make history / 载入～ go down in history; be recorded in history
【史籍】 shǐjí history; historical records
【史迹】 shǐjì historical site or relics
【史剧】 shǐjù historical play
【史料】 shǐliào historical data; historical materials
【史前】 shǐqián prehistoric: ～时代 prehistoric age
【史诗】 shǐshī epic
【史实】 shǐshí historical facts
【史书】 shǐshū history; historical records
【史无前例】 shǐwúqiánlì without precedent in history; unprecedented
【史学】 shǐxué the science of history; historical science; historiography
【史学家】 shǐxuéjiā historian; historiographer

驶(shǐ) **1.**（开动）sail; drive: ～出港口 sail out the harbor / 临时停～ suspension of service **2.**（飞快地跑）speed: 疾～而过 speed by; fly past

矢(shǐ) **1.**（箭）arrow **2.**（发誓）vow; swear
【矢口否认】 shǐkǒu-fǒurèn flatly deny; deny by oath; deny stoutly
【矢如雨下】 shǐrúyǔxià The arrows come down like a shower.
【矢志不移】 shǐzhì-bùyí one's resolve is unshaken; vow to adhere to one's chosen course

使(shǐ) **1.**（派遣）send; tell sb. to do sth.: ～人去请医生 send sb. for a doctor **2.**（用）use; employ; apply: ～尽一切办法 employ all available means **3.**（致使）make; cause; enable: ～企业遭到巨大损失 cause enormous losses to the enterprise / 鸟的翅膀～鸟能飞。A bird's wings enable it to fly. / 他将～她幸福。He will make her happy. **4.**（使者，大使）envoy; messenger; ambassador: 大～ ambassador / 密～ emissary **5.**（假如）if; supposing
【使不得】 shǐbu·de **1.**（不能用）can't be use **2.**（不可以）won't do; must not
【使出】 shǐchū use; exert: ～全身本事 use

all one's skill
【使得】 shǐ·de 1.(可用) can be used; usable 2.(能行) will do; workable; feasible: 这个计划可～? Is the plan workable? 3.(致使) make; cause; render
【使乖弄巧】 shǐguāi-nòngqiǎo use strategy
【使馆】 shǐguǎn embassy; diplomatic mission: 我驻美～ our embassy in U.S.
【使唤】 shǐ·huan 1.(指使) order about: 爱～人 be in the habit of ordering people about; be bossy 2.(使用) use; handle
【使节】 shǐjié diplomatic envoy; ambassador: 各国外交～ diplomatic envoys of various countries / 驻华～ foreign ambassadors in China
【使劲】 shǐjìn exert all one's strength: 再使把劲 put in more effort
【使领馆】 shǐlǐngguǎn diplomatic and consular missions; embassies and consulates
【使命】 shǐmìng mission: 历史～ historical mission
【使命感】 shǐmìnggǎn sense of mission
【使团】 shǐtuán diplomatic corps
【使团团长】 shǐtuán tuánzhǎng dean of the diplomatic corps
【使性子】 shǐxìng·zi get angry; lose one's temper
【使眼色】 shǐyǎnsè tip sb. the wink; wink
【使用】 shǐyòng make use of; use; employ; apply; maintenance: ～贷款 utilization of credit / 学会～微机 learn to use a personal computer
【使用费】 shǐyòngfèi use fee
【使用价值】 shǐyòng jiàzhí use value
【使用率】 shǐyònglǜ rate of utilization; utilization ratio
【使用面积】 shǐyòng miànjī usable floor area
【使用年限】 shǐyòng niánxiàn tenure of use
【使用权】 shǐyòngquán right of use; right to use a thing
【使用寿命】 shǐyòng shòumìng service life (of machines)
【使用税】 shǐyòngshuì royalties
【使用说明书】 shǐyòng shuōmíngshū operation instructions
【使者】 shǐzhě emissary; envoy; messenger; ambassador: 和平的～ ambassador of peace

始 (shǐ) 1.(开始) beginning; start: 自～至终 from beginning to end; from A to Z 2.〈*written*〉〈*abv*.〉 only then; not ... until
【始发港】 shǐfāgǎng port of departure
【始发站】 shǐfāzhàn starting station
【始末】 shǐmò beginning and end; the whole story
【始业】 shǐyè the beginning of the school year
【始终】 shǐzhōng from beginning to end; from start to finish; all along; throughout: ～保持国家的活力 ensure the continuing vitality of the state
【始终不渝】 shǐzhōng-bùyú unswerving; consistently
【始终如一】 shǐzhōng-rúyī constant; consistent; persistent; (forever) true to oneself
【始祖】 shǐzǔ first ancestor; earliest ancestor

屎 (shǐ) 1.(粪) excrement; feces; dung; droppings: 拉～ empty the bowels; shit 2.(眼、耳等的分泌物) secretion: 耳～ earwax

士 (shì) 1.(士人;读书人) scholar 2.(军士) noncommissioned officer (NCO) 3.(某些初级技术人员) a person trained in a certain field: 护～ nurse 4.(美称) (commendable) person: 烈～ martyr / 勇～ brave fighter; warrior 5.(象棋子) bodyguard
【士别三日,刮目相看】 shì bié sān rì, guā mù xiāng kàn A scholar who has been away three days must be looked at with new eyes.
【士兵】 shìbīng rank-and-file soldiers; privates
【士可杀,不可辱】 shì kě shā, bùkě rǔ A scholar prefers death to humiliation.
【士女】 shìnǚ young men and women: ～如云。Men and women gathered like clouds.
【士气】 shìqì morale: ～大振。The martial spirit has been roused greatly.
【士绅】 shìshēn gentry
【士为知己者死】 shì wéi zhījǐzhě sǐ The scholar dies for his bosom friend.
【士卒】 shìzú soldiers; privates

仕 (shì) 1.(做官) be an official; fill an office: 学而优则～。A good scholar will make an official. 2.(象棋子) bodyguard

【仕女】 shìnǚ 〈*Arts*〉 traditional Chinese painting of beautiful women

【仕途】 shìtú 〈*written*〉 official career

氏（shì） 1.（姓）family name; surname: 王～兄弟 the Wang brothers 2.（旧称已婚妇女）née: 夫人李～ one's wife, née Li

【氏族】 shìzú clan

【氏族公社】 shìzú gōngshè clan commune

【氏族社会】 shìzú shèhuì clan society

【氏族制度】 shìzú zhìdù clan system

舐（shì）

【舐犊情深】 shìdú-qíngshēn very affectionate toward one's children

【舐犊之爱】 shìdú zhī'ài parental love; the love of licking shown by cow for its calf

示（shì） show; notify; express; instruct: 暗～ hint; drop a hint / 以～关怀 as an expression of solicitude

【示波器】 shìbōqì 〈*Electr.*〉 oscillograph; oscilloscope (OSC)

【示范】 shìfàn set an example; demonstrate: 进行～教学 teach by demonstration

【示范飞行】 shìfàn fēixíng demonstration flight

【示分牌】 shìfēnpái flash card

【示警】 shìjǐng give a warning; warn: 鸣枪～ fire a warning shot; give a warning by firing a shot

【示宽灯】 shìkuāndēng 〈*Auto*〉 sidemarker lamp

【示例】 shìlì give typical examples; give a demonstration

【示人】 shìrén show sth. to sb.

【示弱】 shìruò give the impression of weakness; take sth. lying down: 不甘～ not to be outdone

【示威】 shìwēi 1.（表示抗议或要求）demonstrate; hold a demonstration 2.（显示力量）put on a show of force; display one's strength

【示威游行】 shìwēi yóuxíng demonstration; parade; march

【示悉】 shìxī Your letter has been received.

【示性式】 shìxìngshì 〈*Chem.*〉 rational formula

【示意】 shìyì signal; hint; motion

【示意图】 shìyìtú diagrammatic sketch; abridged general view; sketch map; schematic diagram: 发动机～ diagram of the engine

【示众】 shìzhòng publicly expose; put before the public: 游街～ parade sb. through the streets

世［卋］（shì） 1.（人的一辈子）lifetime; life: 一生一～ one's whole life; all one's life 2.（一代又一代）generation 3.（有世交关系）～叔 younger friend of one's father / ～兄 son of one's friend 4.（时代）age; era 5.（世界）world: 举～闻名 well known all over the world; world-famous

【世仇】 shìchóu 1.（指冤仇）family feud 2.（指仇人）bitter enemy (in a family feud)

【世传】 shìchuán be handed down through generations: ～秘方 secret recipe handed down from generation to generation

【世代】 shìdài 1.（好几辈子）for generations; from generation to generation; generation after generation: ～相传 pass on from generation to generation 2.〈*Biol.*〉 generation

【世道】 shìdào the manners and morals of the time

【世风日下】 shìfēng-rìxià The moral degeneration of the world is getting worse day by day.

【世故】 shìgù the ways of the world

【世故】 shì·gu worldly-wise: 这人很～。This chap is quite a smooth character.

【世纪】 shìjì century: 21～ twenty-first century

【世家】 shìjiā 1.（官僚人家）aristocratic family 2.（有某种专长的家族）old and well-known family: 梨园～ family of Beijing opera actors

【世交】 shìjiāo 1.（指交情）friendship spanning two or more generations 2.（指人或人家）old family friends

【世界】 shìjiè world: 第三～ the Third World / ～天天发生变化。The world is changing every day.

【世界霸权】 shìjiè bàquán world domination; world supremacy

【世界版权公约】 shìjiè bǎnquán gōngyuē U-

niversal Copyright Convention
【世界杯】 shìjièbēi 〈*Football*〉 World Cup
【世界博览会】 shìjiè bólǎnhuì World's Fair
【世界大战】 shìjiè dàzhàn world war; war of global proportions: 第二次～ World War II; the Second World War
【世界格局】 shìjiè géjú world pattern: 多极化～ multipolar world pattern
【世界观】 shìjièguān world outlook
【世界冠军】 shìjiè guànjūn world champion
【世界级】 shìjièjí world-class
【世界纪录】 shìjiè jìlù world record: 保持～ hold the world record / 创造新的～ set a new world record; establish a new world record / 打破～ break the world record; smash the world record
【世界价格】 shìjiè jiàgé world-price
【世界贸易】 shìjiè màoyì world commerce
【世界奇观】 shìjiè qíguān wonders of the world
【世界市场】 shìjiè shìchǎng world market
【世界水平】 shìjiè shuǐpíng world standard; world caliber; international level
【世界银行】 Shìjiè Yínháng World Bank
【世界语】 Shìjièyǔ Esperanto
【世界舆论】 shìjiè yúlùn world opinion
【世面】 shìmiàn various aspects of society; society; world; life: 见过～ have seen the world; have experienced life
【世人】 shìrén common people
【世上】 shìshàng in the world; on earth
【世事】 shìshì affairs of human life
【世俗】 shìsú 1.(流俗) common customs 2.(非宗教的) secular; worldly
【世态】 shìtài the ways of the world
【世态炎凉】 shìtài-yánliáng inconstancy of human relationships
【世袭】 shìxí hereditary
【世袭制度】 shìxí zhìdù the hereditary system
【世系】 shìxì pedigree; genealogy

市 (shì) 1.(市场) market: 菜～ vegetable market / 上～ be on the market; be in season 2.(城市) city; municipality; municipal (adj.): ～中心 the heart of the city; city center; downtown
【市场】 shìchǎng 1.(指场所) market house; bazaar; market place: 花卉～ flower market / 跳蚤～ flea market / ～上的蔬菜和水果比超市便宜得多。Vegetables and fruits are much cheaper in/on the market than in supermarket. 2.(指领域) market: 股票～ stock market / 信用～ credit market / 证券～ stock market / 资本～ capital market / 打入～ penetrate into the market / 控制～ command the market / 多方位地开拓国际～ open up new markets in different parts of the world
【市场调查】 shìchǎng diàochá market research; market survey
【市场定价】 shìchǎng dìngjià price be fixed by the market
【市场分析】 shìchǎng fēnxī market analysis
【市场行情】 shìchǎng hángqíng market condition
【市场环境】 shìchǎng huánjìng market environment
【市场活跃】 shìchǎng huóyuè brisk market; active market
【市场机制】 shìchǎng jīzhì a market mechanism; the market force: 强化～ intensify the market force
【市场价格】 shìchǎng jiàgé market price
【市场坚挺】 shìchǎng jiāntǐng 〈*Econ.*〉 market strong
【市场经济】 shìchǎng jīngjì market economy; market-directed economy: 社会主义～ socialist market economy
【市场疲软】 shìchǎng píruǎn sluggish market
【市场潜力】 shìchǎng qiǎnlì market potential
【市场索赔】 shìchǎng suǒpéi market claim
【市场体系】 shìchǎng tǐxì the market system
【市场调节】 shìchǎng tiáojié market regulation
【市场占有率】 shìchǎng zhànyǒulǜ the market share
【市电】 shìdiàn commercial power
【市花】 shìhuā flower of a city
【市徽】 shìhuī emblem of a city
【市集】 shìjí 1.(集市) fair 2.(市镇) small town
【市际】 shìjì interurban
【市价】 shìjià market price
【市郊】 shìjiāo suburb; outskirts: 他住在北京～,在城里工作。He lives in the suburb of

Beijing and works in the city.

【市井】 shìjǐng 〈*written*〉 marketplace; town

【市侩】 shìkuài sordid merchant: ～习气 sordid merchants' ways; philistinism

【市面】 shìmiàn **1.**（街面上）in the city; in the town **2.**（指商业活动）market conditions; business: ～呆滞 sick market / ～繁荣。The business is prospering.

【市民】 shìmín residents of a city; townspeople

【市内电话网】 shìnèi diànhuàwǎng district telephone net work

【市内电话中心局】 shìnèi diànhuà zhōngxīnjú local central office

【市内呼叫】 shìnèi hūjiào exchange call

【市内交通】 shìnèi jiāotōng city traffic

【市内中继线路】 shìnèi zhōngjì xiànlù local junction circuit

【市区】 shìqū city proper; urban district

【市容】 shìróng the appearance of a city

【市树】 shìshù tree of a city

【市委】 shìwěi municipal Party committee

【市长】 shìzhǎng mayor (m.); mayoress (f.)

【市镇】 shìzhèn small towns; towns; market town

【市政】 shìzhèng municipal administration; municipal affairs; municipal (adj.)

【市政府】 shìzhèngfǔ municipal government

【市政工程】 shìzhèng gōngchéng municipal works; municipal engineering

柿［梯］(shì) persimmon

【柿饼】 shìbǐng dried persimmon

【柿子】 shì·zi persimmon

【柿子椒】 shì·zijiāo sweetbell redpepper; sweet redpepper

铈 (shì)〈*Chem.*〉cerium（元素符号 Ce）

式 (shì) **1.**（样式）type; style; model: 发～ a hair style / 欧～建筑 a building in European style / 新～汽车 a car of new model **2.**（格式）pattern; form **3.**（仪式）ceremony; ritual: 开幕～ opening ceremony / 闭幕～ closing ceremony / 结业～ graduation ceremony **4.**〈*Math. & Chem.*〉formula: 方程～ equation / 分子～ molecular formula / 公～ formula **5.**〈*Phonet.*〉mood; mode

【式样】 shìyàng style; type; model: 各种～的服装 clothes in different styles / ～美观 attractive in fashion; graceful looking / ～新颖大方 modern and elegant in fashion / 那套服装是最新～的。That dress is in the latest style.

【式子】 shì·zi **1.**（姿势）posture **2.**〈*Math.*〉〈*Chem.*〉formula

试 (shì) **1.**（试着做）try; test; attempt: 尝～ try one's hand at / 让我～一下。Let me have a try. / 她～着做饭。She made an attempt to cook the dinner. **2.**（考试，检查）examination; test: 笔～ written examination / 他在买下这辆车之前先开了一下～～。Before he bought the car, he drove it to test it.

【试办】 shìbàn run an enterprise as an experiment; run a pilot scheme

【试表】 shìbiǎo take sb's temperature

【试播】 shìbō trial broadcast

【试唱】 shìchàng audition

【试车】 shìchē 〈*Mech.*〉test run; trial run

【试点】 shìdiǎn **1.**（指试验）make experiments; conduct tests at selected points; launch a pilot project **2.**（指地点）a place where an experiment is made; experimental unit

【试电笔】 shìdiànbǐ test pencil; voltage tester

【试读】 shìdú probation study

【试读生】 shìdúshēng student on probation

【试飞】 shìfēi test flight; trial flight

【试飞员】 shìfēiyuán test pilot

【试工】 shìgōng probation

【试管】 shìguǎn 〈*Chem.*〉test tube: 把化学药品放到～里 put chemicals in test tube

【试管婴儿】 shìguǎn yīng'ér test-tube baby

【试航】 shìháng **1.**（用作名词）trial trip; trial run: 船舶～ trial voyage; shakedown cruise / 飞机～ trial flight; shakedown flight **2.**（用作动词）shake down: 船舶～ shake down a ship / 飞机～ shake down a plain

【试剂】 shìjì 〈*Chem.*〉reagent

【试金石】 shìjīnshí touchstone: 检验友谊的～ the touchstone to test friendship

【试卷】 shìjuàn test paper; examination paper

【试探】 shìtàn sound out; feel out; probe; explore

【试探性】 shìtànxìng trial; exploratory; probing

【试探性气球】 shìtànxìng qìqiú trial balloon

【试题】 shìtí examination questions; test questions

【试跳】 shìtiào **1.**（田径）trial jump **2.**（跳水）trial dive

【试听】 shìtīng audition

【试图】 shìtú attempt; try

【试问】 shìwèn we should like to ask; it may well be asked; may we ask

【试想】 shìxiǎng （用于质问）just think：～他竟然对那件事一无所知！To think of his not knowing anything about it!

【试销】 shìxiāo trial marketing; trial sale：～商品 commodities for trial marketing

【试行】 shìxíng try out：～股份制 implement a system of shares on a trial basis

【试验】 shìyàn trial; experiment; test：核～ nuclear test

【试验场】 shìyànchǎng proving ground; testing ground

【试验成本】 shìyàn chéngběn experimentation cost

【试验费用】 shìyàn fèiyòng testing expenses

【试验田】 shìyàntián experimental plot

【试验系统】 shìyàn xìtǒng pilot system

【试样】 shìyàng （test）sample

【试映】 shìyìng 〈*Cinematog.*〉 preview

【试用】 shìyòng on trial; try out; on probation：请拿去～。Please take it on trial.

【试用品】 shìyòngpǐn trial products

【试用期】 shìyòngqī probation period; trial period

【试用人员】 shìyòng rényuán person on probation

【试运行】 shìyùnxíng pilot run; test run; trial run

【试运转】 shìyùnzhuǎn 〈*Mech.*〉 test run; running-in

【试纸】 shìzhǐ 〈*Chem.*〉 test paper

【试制】 shìzhì trial-produce; trial-manufacture：加强新产品的～工作 do more trial-production of new items

【试种】 shìzhòng plant experimentally

拭（shì） wipe away; wipe：～泪 wipe away tears

【拭目以待】 shìmùyǐdài wait and see; rub one's eyes and wait

弑（shì） murder; kill

【弑父】 shìfù murder one's own father; patricide（n.）

【弑君】 shìjūn murder one's sovereign; regicide（n.）

【弑母】 shìmǔ murder one's own mother; matricide（n.）

似（shì）
（另见"似"sì）

【似的】 shì·de as if; as though：她和我说话的神情，好像早就认识我～。She spoke to me as if she knew me.

势［勢］（shì） **1.**（势力）power; force; influence：以～压人 overwhelm others with one's power **2.**（趋势）momentum; tendency：以其不可阻挡之～ with irresistible momentum **3.**（自然状况）the outward appearance of a natural object：地～ physical features of the land; terrain **4.**（形势）situation; state of affairs; circumstances **5.**（姿态）sign; gesture **6.**（雄性生殖器）male genitals：去～ castration

【势必】 shìbì certainly will; be bound to：～如此。It is bound to come like this.

【势不可挡】 shìbùkědǎng irresistible

【势不两立】 shìbùliǎnglì irreconcilable; extremely antagonistic

【势成骑虎】 shìchéngqíhǔ Circumstances make it difficult for one to back down.

【势均力敌】 shìjūn-lìdí match each other in strength

【势力】 shì·li force; power; influence; powerful（adj.）：进步～ progressive forces

【势力范围】 shì·li fànwéi sphere of influence

【势利】 shì·li snobbery; snobbish（adj.）

【势利小人】 shì·li xiǎorén snob

【势利眼】 shì·liyǎn **1.**（势利）snobbish attitude; snobbishness; snobbery **2.**（势利之人）snob

【势难从命】 shìnáncóngmìng Circumstances make it difficult for me to comply with your request.

【势如累卵】 shìrúlěiluǎn be in a very perilous position; hazardous like a pile of eggs

【势如破竹】 shìrúpòzhú like splitting a bamboo; like a hot knife cutting through butter; with irresistible force

【势态】 shìtài situation; circumstances: ～危急。The situation is critical.

【势头】 shìtóu 1.(情势) impetus; momentum: 保持良好～ maintain good momentum 2.(形势) tendency; the look of things

【势要】 shìyào powerful

【势在必行】 shìzàibìxíng be imperative (under the circumstances)

事 (shì) 1.(事情) matter; affair; thing; business: 公～ public business / 私～ private business; private affair / 一件怪～ a strange business / 我有件重要的～要和你谈谈。I have an important matter to talk to you about. 2.(事故) trouble; accident: 他出～了,被一辆小汽车撞倒了。He had an accident: he's been knocked down by a car. 3.(职业) job; work: 找～ look for a job 4.(关系或责任) responsibility; involvement 5.(侍奉) wait upon; serve 6.(从事) be engaged in: 无所～～ doing nothing; loafing

【事半功倍】 shìbàn-gōngbèi get twice the result with half the effort

【事倍功半】 shìbèi-gōngbàn get half the result with twice the effort

【事必躬亲】 shìbìgōngqīn see to everything oneself; take care of every single thing personally

【事变】 shìbiàn 1.(重大事件) incident 2.(重大变化) emergency; exigency 3.(泛指变化) the course of events; events

【事不关己,高高挂起】 shì bù guān jǐ, gāogāo guàqǐ To let things drift if they do not affect one personally.

【事不宜迟】 shìbùyíchí one must lose no time in doing it; we must attend to the matter immediately; the matter brooks no delay

【事出有因】 shìchū-yǒuyīn there is good reason for it; it is by no means accidental

【事到临头】 shìdàolíntóu when things come to a head; when the situation becomes critical; at the last moment

【事到如今】 shìdàorújīn under the circumstances

【事典】 shìdiǎn dictionary

【事端】 shìduān disturbance; incident: 昨晚有些醉汉在街上制造～。Some drunken men made a great disturbance yesterday evening.

【事非经过不知难】 shì fēi jīngguò bù zhī nán You never know how hard a task is until you have done it yourself.

【事故】 shìgù accident: 交通～ road accidents / 防止恶性～ guard against fatal accident

【事故险】 shìgùxiǎn 〈*Insurance*〉 accident insurance

【事过境迁】 shìguò-jìngqiān the affair is over and the situation has changed; the incident is over and the circumstances are different

【事后】 shìhòu after the event; afterwards

【事后承诺】 shìhòu chéngnuò after consent

【事后从犯】 shìhòu cóngfàn accessory after the fact

【事后审计】 shìhòu shěnjì past audit

【事后追认】 shìhòu zhuīrèn subsequent ratification

【事迹】 shìjì deed; achievement: 生平～ one's lifetime deeds

【事假】 shìjià leave of absence (to attend to private affairs); compassionate leave

【事件】 shìjiàn incident; event; thing: 边境～ frontier incident / 这起谋杀案是一次令人发指的～。The murder was a terrible thing.

【事理】 shìlǐ reason; logic

【事例】 shìlì example; instance

【事略】 shìlüè biographical sketch; short biographical account

【事前】 shìqián before the event; in advance; beforehand: ～准备好 be prepared beforehand

【事前从犯】 shìqián cóngfàn accessory before the fact

【事前故意】 shìqián gùyì antecedent intent; intent before the fact

【事前审计】 shìqián shěnjì pre-audit

【事情】 shì·qing 1.(泛指) affair; matter; thing; business: 重要的～ an affairs of great moment 2.(事故) trouble; accident 3.(职

业）job; word

【事实】 shìshí fact：歪曲～ distort the facts / ～胜于雄辩。Facts speak louder than words.

【事实错误】 shìshí cuòwù error of fact; mistake of fact

【事实含糊】 shìshí hánhú ambiguity upon the factum

【事实上】 shìshí·shang in fact; in reality; actually; de facto

【事实真相】 shìshí zhēnxiàng sober truth

【事实证据】 shìshí zhèngjù factual evidence

【事实证明】 shìshí zhèngmíng factual proof

【事事】 shìshì everything

【事态】 shìtài state of affairs; situation：～有所缓和。Things are smoothing down a bit.

【事无巨细】 shìwújùxì All matters, big and small, (were handled by him).

【事务】 shìwù 1.（事情）work; affairs; routine：外交～ foreign affairs 2.（总务）general affairs

【事务所】 shìwùsuǒ agency; office; business agency

【事务性工作】 shìwùxìng gōngzuò routine work; daily routine

【事务员】 shìwùyuán office clerk

【事务主义】 shìwù zhǔyì routinism

【事物】 shìwù thing; object; matter

【事先】 shìxiān in advance; beforehand; prior

【事项】 shìxiàng item; matter：章程中规定的～ items stipulated in the regulations

【事业】 shìyè 1.（指活动）cause; undertaking: 文化教育～ cultural and educational undertakings 2.（指单位）enterprise; facilities：集体福利～ collective welfare facilities or services

【事业单位】 shìyè dānwèi institution

【事业费】 shìyèfèi operating expenses

【事业心】 shìyèxīn devotion to one's work; dedication

【事宜】 shìyí matters concerned; arrangements：商谈技术合作～ discuss matters relating to technical cooperation

【事由】 shìyóu 1.（事情原委）the origin of an incident; particulars of a matter 2.（公文用语）main content 3.（理由）pretext 4.（职业）job; work

【事与愿违】 shìyǔyuànwěi things go contrary to one's wishes; thing do not always turn out the way one wishes

【事在人为】 shìzàirénwéi it all depends on human effort; it is the man who disposes

【事主】 shìzhǔ the victim of a crime

侍 (shì) wait upon; attend upon; serve：～立一旁 stand at sb's side in attendance

【侍从】 shìcóng attendant; guard

【侍奉】 shìfèng wait upon; attend upon; serve：～父母 look after one's parents

【侍候】 shìhòu wait upon; look after; attend：病人有护士～。The patient has a nurse attending (on) him.

【侍立】 shìlì stand

【侍女】 shìnǚ maidservant; maid

【侍卫】 shìwèi 1.（护卫）guard 2.（指人）imperial bodyguard

【侍者】 shìzhě attendant; servant; waiter

恃 (shì) rely on; depend on：～势 rely on one's position

【恃才傲物】 shìcái-àowù be inordinately proud of one's ability; be conceited and contemptuous

【恃德者昌】 shìdézhě chāng Those who rely on virtue will thrive.

【恃强凌弱】 shìqiáng-língruò use one's strength to bully the weak

【恃势凌人】 shìshì-língrén trust to one's power and insult people; use one's power to bully others

饰 (shì) 1.（装饰）decorations; ornaments：服～ clothes and ornaments 2.（修饰）adorn; dress up; polish; cover up 3.（扮演）play the role of; act the part of; impersonate：他～老头儿很出色。He played the part of old people very well. 4.（电影字幕用字）as：赵丹～林则徐 Zhao Dan as Lin Zexu

【饰词】 shìcí excuse; pretext

【饰品】 shìpǐn jewelry; jewels

【饰物】 shìwù 1.（首饰）jewelry; articles for personal adornment 2.（装饰品）ornaments; decorations

视［眡、眎］(shì) 1.（看）look at 2.（看待）regard; look upon：～为知己 look upon sb. as one's bosom friend 3.（考察）inspect；watch

【视差】 shìchā 〈*Physics*〉 parallax；optical parallax

【视察】 shìchá inspect；inspection（n.）

【视程】 shìchéng visual range

【视而不见】 shì'érbùjiàn look but see not；turn a blind eye to

【视角】 shìjiǎo angle of view；visual angle

【视觉】 shìjué 〈*Physiol.*〉 visual sense；vision；sense of sight

【视觉辨认】 shìjué biànrèn visuognosis

【视觉疲劳】 shìjué píláo visual fatigue

【视觉器官】 shìjué qìguān visual organs

【视觉缺陷】 shìjué quēxiàn defects of vision

【视觉污染】 shìjué wūrǎn visual pollution

【视觉误差】 shìjué wùchā collimation error

【视觉信息】 shìjué xìnxī visual information

【视觉障碍】 shìjué zhàng'ài dysopia；paropsia

【视力】 shìlì vision；sight

【视力表】 shìlìbiǎo visual chart

【视亮度】 shìliàngdù 〈*Astron.*〉 apparent brightness

【视盘】 shìpán video disc；video disk

【视盘机】 shìpánjī video disc player；video disk player

【视频】 shìpín 〈*Physics*〉 video frequency

【视频显示】 shìpín xiǎnshì video display

【视频显示终端】 shìpín xiǎnshì zhōngduān video display terminal

【视如粪土】 shìrú-fèntǔ look upon as filth and dirt；consider as beneath contempt

【视若草芥】 shìruò-cǎojiè regard as worthless

【视若无睹】 shìruòwúdǔ take no notice of what one sees；shut one's eyes to；turn a blind eye to；ignore

【视神经】 shìshénjīng 〈*Anat.*〉 optic nerve

【视事】 shìshì （of officials）attend to business after assuming office；assume office

【视死如归】 shìsǐrúguī look upon death as going home；look death calmly in the face；face death unflinchingly

【视听】 shìtīng seeing and hearing；what is seen and heard：混淆～ confuse the public

【视听广告设备】 shìtīng guǎnggào shèbèi audiovisual sales aids

【视听教材】 shìtīng jiàocái audiovisuals

【视听教具】 shìtīng jiàojù audiovisual aids

【视听教育】 shìtīng jiàoyù audiovisual education

【视听率】 shìtīnglǜ audience rating

【视同儿戏】 shìtóng-érxì treat（a serious matter）as a trifle；trifle with

【视同路人】 shìtóng-lùrén regard as a stranger

【视网膜】 shìwǎngmó 〈*Anat.*〉 retina

【视线】 shìxiàn 1.（眼睛和事物的假想连线）line of vision；line of sight 2.（喻注意力）attention

【视野】 shìyě view；field of vision：这座房子面向大海，～开阔。The house has a view over the sea.

【视域】 shìyù 见"视阈"

【视阈】 shìyù 1.〈*Physiol.*〉 visual threshold 2.（视野）field of vision

是（shì） 1.（对；正确）correct；right 2.（表示答应）yes；right：～，我就来。Yes, I'm coming right now. 3.（作同位语）be：我～一个教师。I am a teacher. 4.（表示存在）be；exist：宿舍前面～花园。There is a garden in front of the dormitory. 5.（表示适合）the right：～时侯 at just the right time / 不～地方 not in the right place 6.（表示"凡是"、"任何"）all；every；any：～人总要犯错误。Every man is liable to error. 7.（表示坚决肯定）certainly；really 8.（认为正确）praise；justify

【是的】 shì·de yes；right；that's it

【是非】 shìfēi 1.（正确与错误）right and wrong：明辨～ distinguish clearly between right and wrong 2.（口舌）quarrel；dispute：惹起～ stir up trouble；provoke a dispute

【是非颠倒】 shìfēi-diāndǎo confound right and wrong

【是非曲直】 shìfēi-qūzhí rights and wrongs；truth and falsehood：不问～ not bother to look into the rights and wrongs of a case

【是非题】 shìfēití true and false

【是非之地】 shìfēizhīdì a place where one is apt to get into trouble

【是否】 shìfǒu whether or not；whether；if

【是可忍，孰不可忍】 shì kě rěn, shú bùkě rěn If this can be tolerated, what cannot?

适［適］(shì) 1.（适合）fit; suitable; proper: ～于儿童观看的影片 a film suitable for children 2.（合适）right; opportune 3.（舒适）comfortable; well 4.（去,往）go; follow; pursue: 无所～从 be at a loss what to do

【适才】 shìcái 〈*dial.*〉 just now

【适当】 shìdāng suitable; proper; appropriate: ～的场合 suitable occasion / 采取～措施 take some appropriate measures

【适得其反】 shìdé-qífǎn run counter to one's desire; be just the opposite to what one wished

【适度】 shìdù appropriate measure; moderate degree: ～规模经营 manage on a fairly large scale; fairly large-scale management

【适逢其会】 shìféng-qíhuì happen to be present at the right moment

【适合】 shìhé suit; fit: ～做这项工作 be fit for the job

【适可而止】 shìkě'érzhǐ stop before going too far; know when or where to stop; not overdo it

【适口】 shìkǒu agreeable to the taste; palatable

【适量】 shìliàng the proper amount; the appropriate amount

【适龄】 shìlíng of the right age

【适龄儿童】 shìlíng értóng children of school age

【适时】 shìshí at the right moment; in good time; opportune; timely: ～的劝告 timely advice

【适销】 shìxiāo sell well in the market

【适销对路】 shìxiāo duìlù satisfy the customer's needs and sell well in the market: ～产品 commodities that satisfy the customer's needs and sell well in the market

【适宜】 shìyí suitable; fit; appropriate: 这水不～饮用。The water is not fit to drink.

【适意】 shìyì agreeable; enjoyable; comfortable

【适应】 shìyìng suit; adapt; fit: ～人民购买力的提高 meet the people's rising purchasing power / ～现代化大生产的需要 suit the needs of modern large-scale production

【适用】 shìyòng suit; apply to: ～范围 scope of application; sphere of application

【适者生存】 shìzhě shēngcún 〈*Biol.*〉 survival of the fittest

【适值】 shìzhí just when

【适中】 shìzhōng 1.（适度）moderate: 大小～的房间 room of moderate size 2.（指位置）well situated: 地点～ be conveniently situated; be nicely located

室(shì) room: 办公～ office / 起居～ living room / 卧～ bedroom / 浴～ bathroom

【室间隔】 shìjiāngé 〈*Anat.*〉 ventricular septum

【室内】 shìnèi indoor; interior: 进入～ go indoors

【室内空调设备】 shìnèi kōngtiáo shèbèi room conditioning

【室内溜冰场】 shìnèi liūbīngchǎng indoor skating rink

【室内网球】 shìnèi wǎngqiú real tennis

【室内游戏】 shìnèi yóuxì indoor games

【室内游泳池】 shìnèi yóuyǒngchí indoor swimming pool

【室内乐】 shìnèiyuè 〈*Music*〉 chamber music

【室内运动】 shìnèi yùndòng indoor sport

【室内照明】 shìnèi zhàomíng interior illumination

【室内植物】 shìnèi zhíwù houseplants; indoor plants

【室内装饰】 shìnèi zhuāngshì interior decoration

【室内装修】 shìnèi zhuāngxiū interior decoration

【室内装修师】 shìnèi zhuāngxiū shī interior expert

【室女宫】 Shìnǚgōng 〈*Astron.*〉 Virgo (8月23日至9月22日): 生于～ be born under Virgo

【室女座】 Shìnǚzuò 〈*Astron.*〉 Virgo

【室如悬磬】 shìrúxuánqìng One's house is like an empty jar hanging up.

【室外】 shìwài outdoor; outside

【室外天线】 shìwài tiānxiàn open aerial; open antenna

【室外停车场】 shìwài tíngchēchǎng motor pool

【室温】 shìwēn room temperature

【室友】 shìyǒu room-mate

逝(shì) 1.(过去) pass 2.(死) die; pass away: 病～ die of illness

【逝世】 shìshì pass away; die

【逝水年华】 shìshuǐ-niánhuá Time passes like flowing water.

誓(shì) 1.(决心实行) swear; vow; pledge: ～夺丰收 pledge to strive for bumper harvest 2.(决心) oath; vow: 发～ take an oath / 证人宣过了～。The witness is on oath. / 我发～不把你的秘密告诉任何人。I swear I won't tell anyone your secret.

【誓不罢休】 shìbùbàxiū swear not to stop; swear not to rest

【誓不两立】 shìbùliǎnglì swear not to coexist with one's enemy; resolve to destroy the enemy or die in the attempt; be irreconcilable

【誓词】 shìcí oath; pledge

【誓师】 shìshī 1.(指军队) a rally to pledge resolution before going to war 2.(指民众) take a mass pledge

【誓师大会】 shìshī dàhuì a meeting to pledge mass effort; an oath-taking rally

【誓死】 shìsǐ pledge one's life; dare to die

【誓言】 shìyán oath; pledge

【誓约】 shìyuē vow; pledge; solemn promise

释[釋](shì) 1.(解释) explain; elucidate 2.(消释) clear up; dispel 3.(放开) let go; be relieved of 4.(释放) release; set free

【释放】 shìfàng 1.〈*Law*〉 release; set free: 取保～ be released on bail; be bailed out / 刑满～ be released after one has served one's sentence 2.〈*Physics*〉 release

【释放裁定书】 shìfàng cáidìngshū rulings of acquittal

【释放程序】 shìfàng chéngxù release procedure

【释放出狱令】 shìfàng chūyùlìng order of release

【释放令】 shìfànglìng order for discharge; order of acquittal

【释放囚犯】 shìfàng qiúfàn discharge of prisoner; release a prisoner

【释放证书】 shìfàng zhèngshū release certificate

【释古行今】 shìgǔ-xíngjīn justify one's own wishes and desires by abandoning ancient

【释迦牟尼】 Shìjiāmóní 〈*Buddhism*〉 Sakyamuni

【释教】 Shìjiào Buddhism

【释梦】 shìmèng dream interpretation

【释然】 shìrán 〈*written*〉 feel relieved; feel at ease

【释疑】 shìyí clear up doubts

【释义】 shìyì definition

嗜(shì) have a liking for; be addicted to

【嗜好】 shìhào hobby; addiction; habit: 她的～是打网球。Her hobby is playing tennis.

【嗜酒】 shìjiǔ be addicted to drink

【嗜眠】 shìmián somnolence

【嗜血】 shìxuè bloodthirsty; bloodsucking

【嗜血成性】 shìxuè-chéngxìng kill without batting an eyelid; be fond of killing

噬(shì) bite

shou

收[収](shōu) 1.(收到;接受) receive; accept: ～到礼物 receive gifts / 我们不～小费。We don't accept gratuities. 2.(收拢) put away; take in: 把东西～起来 put the things away 3.(收取) collect: ～税 collect taxes 4.(收入) money received; receipts; income: 税～ tax revenue 5.(收获) harvest; gather in 6.(收缩) close 7.(结束) bring to an end; stop: ～操 bring drill to an end 8.(约束) restrain; control: ～心 concentrate on more serious things

【收报】 shōubào receive a telegram

【收兵】 shōubīng 1.(撤回军队) withdraw troops; call off a battle 2.(喻结束工作) finish; complete

【收藏】 shōucáng collect; store up: ～艺术珍品 collect art curiosities

【收藏家】 shōucángjiā collector (of books, antiques, etc.)

【收场】 shōuchǎng 1.(结束) wind up; end up; stop: 草草～ wind up a matter hastily 2.(结局) end; ending: 戏快～了。The play is coming to an end.

【收车】 shōuchē return to the garage

【收成】 shōu·cheng harvest; crop: 获得好～ reap a good harvest
【收储】 shōuchǔ handle savings
【收存】 shōucún receive and keep
【收到】 shōudào receive; get; achieve; obtain: ～良好效果 achieve good results / 你今天～信了吗? Did you receive any letter today? / 我～了他送的礼物,但我不准备接受。I've received a gift from him, but I'm not going to accept it.
【收发】 shōufā 1.(指工作) receive and dispatch 2.(指人) dispatcher
【收发报机】 shōufābàojī transmitter-receiver; transceiver
【收发室】 shōufāshì office for incoming and outgoing mail
【收方】 shōufāng 〈*Accounting*〉 debit; debit side
【收费】 shōufèi collect fees; charge: 不～ free of charge
【收费标准牌】 shōufèi biāozhǔnpái fee indicator
【收费厕所】 shōufèi cèsuǒ pay toilet
【收费电话】 shōufèi diànhuà charged call
【收费电视】 shōufèi diànshì pay TV
【收费生】 shōufèishēng fee-paying student
【收费亭】 shōufèitíng toll booth
【收费学校】 shōufèi xuéxiào fee-paying school
【收费站】 shōufèizhàn toll booth
【收复】 shōufù recover; recapture: ～失地 recover lost land; recover lost territory
【收割】 shōugē reap; harvest; gather in: ～小麦 reap the wheat
【收割机】 shōugējī harvester; reaper
【收工】 shōugōng stop work for the day; knock off
【收购】 shōugòu purchase; buy
【收购价格】 shōugòu jiàgé purchasing price
【收购站】 shōugòuzhàn purchasing station
【收归国有】 shōuguī guóyǒu be taken over by the state; be nationalized
【收回】 shōuhuí 1.(取回) take back; call in; regain; recall 2.(撤销) withdraw; countermand: ～成命 countermand an order; revoke a command
【收货凭单】 shōuhuò píngdān consignment sheet
【收货人】 shōuhuòrén consignee: ～的支付能力 consignee's solvency / ～过失 consignee's fault
【收获】 shōuhuò 1.(指农作物) gather in the crops; harvest 2.(成果) results; gains; fruits: 不下苦功,便无～。No pains, no gains.
【收获量】 shōuhuòliàng harvest yield
【收集】 shōují collect; gather: ～民歌 collect folk songs / ～情报 collect information / ～资料 gather data
【收监】 shōujiān take into custody; commit to prison
【收件人】 shōujiànrén addressee; consignee
【收缴】 shōujiǎo 1.(缴获) take over; capture 2.(征收) purchase
【收紧】 shōujǐn tighten up
【收据】 shōujù receipt: 保管～ trust receipt / 临时～ interim receipt
【收据簿】 shōujùbù receipt book
【收看率】 shōukànlǜ viewing rate
【收口】 shōukǒu 1.(伤口愈合) close up; heal 2.(编织物收口) binding off
【收款处】 shōukuǎnchù cashier's
【收款人】 shōukuǎnrén payee
【收敛】 shōuliǎn 1.(减弱或消失) weaken or disappear: 他～了笑容。Her smile vanished. 2.(约束言行) restrain oneself; hold back 3.〈*Math.*〉 convergence 4.〈*Med.*〉 astringent
【收敛剂】 shōuliǎnjì 〈*Med.*〉 astringent
【收殓】 shōuliàn lay a body in a coffin
【收留】 shōuliú take sb. in; have sb. in one's care
【收拢】 shōulǒng draw sth. in: 把网～ draw the net in
【收录】 shōulù 1.(吸收任用) employ; recruit; take on 2.(编入集子) include: 这本小说集～了他的作品。His works are included in this anthology of stories. 3.(录音) listen in and take down; take down; record
【收录机】 shōulùjī radio cassette player
【收录两用机】 shōulù liǎngyòngjī radio cassette player
【收罗】 shōuluó collect; gather; enlist: ～人才 recruit qualified personnel

【收买】 shōumǎi 1.（收购）purchase; buy in 2.（笼络）buy over; bribe: ～人心 buy popular support

【收盘】 shōupán 〈*Econ.*〉 closing quotation (on the exchange, etc.)

【收盘汇率】 shōupán huìlǜ closing rate

【收盘价】 shōupánjià closing price; final quotation

【收片轴】 shōupiànzhóu 〈*Photog.*〉 take-up spool

【收起】 shōuqǐ pack up; cut out; stop

【收讫】 shōuqì 1.（收清）payment received; paid 2.（如数收到）(on a bill of lading, an invoice, etc.) all the above goods received; received in full

【收清】 shōuqīng received in full

【收容】 shōuróng take in; accept; house: ～难民 house refugees

【收容所】 shōuróngsuǒ collecting post; detention center

【收入】 shōurù 1.（收进来的钱）income; revenue; receipts; earnings; proceeds: 纯～ net profit / 合理拉开～差距 widen the differences in personal income to a reasonable degree 2.（收进）take in; include

【收审】 shōushěn take in and examine; detain and investigate

【收视】 shōushì view

【收视率】 shōushìlǜ viewing rate: ～最高的节目之一 one of the most extensively viewed items

【收拾】 shōu・shi 1.（整理）put in order; tidy; clear away: ～房间 tidy up the room 2.（准备）get things ready; pack: ～行李 pack one's luggage 3.（修理）repair; mend: ～自行车 repair a bicycle 4.（整治）settle with; punish: 不出这个星期我们要～他。We'll settle with him before the week's out.

【收受】 shōushòu receive; accept; take: ～贿赂 take bribes / ～礼物 accept gifts

【收束】 shōushù 1.（约束）bring together; collect 2.（结束）bring to a close 3.（收拾）pack (for a journey)

【收缩】 shōusuō 1.（由大变小，由长变短）contract; shrink: 金属遇冷～。Metal contracts as it cools. 2.（紧缩）concentrate one's forces; draw back 3.〈*Physiol.*〉 systole

【收缩性】 shōusuōxìng contractibility

【收缩压】 shōusuōyā 〈*Physiol.*〉 systolic pressure

【收条】 shōutiáo receipt: 给某人打～ give a receipt to sb.

【收听】 shōutīng listen in: ～天气预报 listen in to the weather forecast

【收尾】 shōuwěi 1.（结束）wind up 2.（文章末尾）ending: 一篇文章的～ ending of an article

【收文】 shōuwén incoming dispatches

【收效】 shōuxiào yield results; produce effects; bear fruit: 这方法很快就～了。The method quickly took effects.

【收心】 shōuxīn 1.（把心收起来）get into the frame of mind for work; concentrate on more serious things 2.（改变坏念头）have a change of heart

【收信人】 shōuxìnrén the recipient of a letter; addressee

【收押】 shōuyā take into custody; detain

【收养】 shōuyǎng take in and bring up; adopt

【收养法与遗嘱法】 shōuyǎngfǎ yǔ yízhǔfǎ law of adoption and of wills

【收养关系】 shōuyǎng guānxì adoptive relationship

【收养继承人】 shōuyǎng jìchéngrén heir by adoption

【收养人】 shōuyǎngrén consignee

【收益】 shōuyì income; profit; avails; gains

【收益率】 shōuyìlǜ return: 这种股票的～很高。These shares return a good rate of interest.

【收益债券】 shōuyì zhàiquàn income bonds

【收益账户】 shōuyì zhànghù income account

【收音】 shōuyīn 1.（收听广播）reception 2.（拢音）have good acoustics

【收音电唱两用机】 shōuyīn diànchàng liǎngyòngjī radiogramophone

【收音机】 shōuyīnjī radio (set); wireless (set): 落地式～ console set / 便携式～ portable radio

【收支】 shōuzhī revenue and expenditure; income and expenses: 国际～逆差 unfavorable balance of international payments / 国际～

顺差 favorable balance of international payments

【收支逆差】 shōuzhī nìchā balance of payments deficit

【收支预算】 shōuzhī yùsuàn budget for revenues and expenditures

【收支账目】 shōuzhī zhàngmù income and expenditure account

【收执】 shōuzhí 1.(收下并保存)(of a certificate, etc.) be issued to the person concerned for safekeeping 2.(凭证) receipt (issued by a government agency)

【收治】 shōuzhì take in and give treatment

熟 (shóu) (见"熟"shú)

手 (shǒu) 1.(人的手) hand: ～拉～ hand in hand / 伸出友谊之～ stretch out the hand of friendship / 与某人握～ shake hands with sb. 2.(拿着) have in one's hand; hold: 人～一册。Everyone has a copy. 3.(方便的) handy; convenient 4.(亲手) personally 5.(擅长某种技能的人) a person doing or good at a certain job: 歌～ singer / 水～ seaman

【手背】 shǒubèi the back of the hand

【手笔】 shǒubǐ 1.(写的字) sb's own handwriting or painting 2.(造诣) literary skill: 大～ a well-known writer; master

【手臂】 shǒubì arm: ～挽着～ arm in arm

【手边】 shǒubiān on hand; at hand

【手表】 shǒubiǎo watch; wrist watch

【手柄】 shǒubǐng handle

【手柄钻】 shǒubǐngzuàn gimlet

【手不释卷】 shǒubùshìjuàn always have a book in one's hand; be very studious

【手册】 shǒucè handbook; manual; guide: 用户～ user's guide

【手抄本】 shǒuchāoběn hand-written copy

【手车】 shǒuchē handcart; wheelbarrow

【手大】 shǒudà handsome

【手到病除】 shǒudào-bìngchú bring back life to a patient; illness departs at a touch of the hand

【手电筒】 shǒudiàntǒng flashlight; electric torch

【手动】 shǒudòng direct manual control

【手动控制】 shǒudòng kòngzhì hand control

【手段】 shǒuduàn 1.(方法) means; medium; measure; method: 不择～ by fair means or foul; by hook or by crook; unscrupulously / 强制～ coercive method; coercion 2.(不正当的方法) trick; artifice: 耍～ play tricks

【手法】 shǒufǎ 1.(技巧) produce; technique; results: 独特的～ unique technique 2.(不正当的方法) trick; gimmick: 惯用～ habitual practice

【手风琴】 shǒufēngqín accordion: 六角～ concertina ‖ 手风琴手 accordion player

【手扶拖拉机】 shǒufú tuōlājī walking tractor

【手感】 shǒugǎn 〈*Textiles*〉 feel; handle

【手稿】 shǒugǎo original manuscript ; manuscript

【手工】 shǒugōng 1.(手做的工作) handwork 2.(用手操作) by hand; manual: 这玩具是～制做的。The toy was made by hand. 3.(手工费) charge for a piece of handwork: ～是多少? How much did you pay for this?

【手工编织】 shǒugōng biānzhī hand-knit; hand-knitted

【手工业】 shǒugōngyè handicraft industry; handicraft

【手工业工人】 shǒugōngyè gōngrén handicraftsman; handicraft worker

【手工业品】 shǒugōngyèpǐn handicrafts; handiwork

【手工艺】 shǒugōngyì handicraft art; handicraft

【手工艺品】 shǒugōngyìpǐn arts and handicrafts; handicraft products

【手机】 shǒujī 1.(电话手机) receiver; handset 2.(移动电话) mobile phone

【手疾眼快】 shǒují-yǎnkuài quick of eye and deft of hand

【手迹】 shǒujì 1.(指字) sb.'s original handwriting 2.(指画) sb.'s original painting

【手脚】 shǒujiǎo 1.(动作) movement of hands or feet; motion: ～利落 nimble; agile 2.(暗中的行动) underhand method; trick: 做了～ have juggled things

【手巾】 shǒujīn towel

【手巾架】 shǒujīnjià towel rail; towel rack

【手紧】 shǒujǐn closefisted; tightfisted

【手锯】 shǒujù handsaw

【手绢】 shǒujuàn handkerchief

【手铐】 shǒukào handcuffs; cuffs: 戴上～ be handcuffed

【手快】 shǒukuài deft of hand

【手榴弹】 shǒuliúdàn 1.〈*Mil.*〉 hand grenade; grenade 2.(军体器材) hand grenade 3.(军体项目) hand grenade throw

【手慢】 shǒumàn slow in movements

【手忙脚乱】 shǒumáng-jiǎoluàn running around in circles; in a frantic rush; in a muddle

【手民】 shǒumín 〈*written*〉 typesetter

【手帕】 shǒupà handkerchief; handkie

【手气】 shǒuqì luck at gambling, card playing, etc.

【手枪】 shǒuqiāng pistol: 左轮～ revolver

【手巧】 shǒuqiǎo skillful with one's hands; deft; dexterous: 心灵～ clever and deft

【手勤】 shǒuqín diligent; industrious; hard-working

【手轻】 shǒuqīng not use too much force; handle gently

【手球】 shǒuqiú 1.〈*Sports*〉 handball ‖ 手球运动员 handball player 2.(指球) handball 3.〈*Football*〉 handling

【手球场】 shǒuqiúchǎng handball field; rink

【手软】 shǒuruǎn be irresolute; be softhearted

【手刹车】 shǒushāchē hand brake

【手势】 shǒushì gesture; sign; signal: 打～ make gesture; gesticulate

【手书】 shǒushū 1.(亲笔写) write in one's own hand 2.(手札) personal letter

【手术】 shǒushù surgical operation; operation: (医生)动～ perform an operation / (病人)动～ have an operation

【手术室】 shǒushùshì operating room; operating theatre

【手术台】 shǒushùtái operating table

【手松】 shǒusōng freehanded; openhanded

【手套】 shǒutào gloves; mittens

【手提】 shǒutí portable: ～打字机 portable typewriter

【手提包】 shǒutíbāo handbag; bag

【手提箱】 shǒutíxiāng suitcase

【手提行李】 shǒutí xínglǐ hand luggage; carry-on luggage

【手头】 shǒutóu 1.(手够得到的地方) right beside one; on hand; at hand: ～工作很忙 have one's hands full 2.(经济状况) one's financial condition at the moment: ～紧 be short of money; be hard up

【手推车】 shǒutuīchē handcart; wheelbarrow

【手腕儿】 shǒuwànr artifice; finesse; stratagem

【手腕子】 shǒuwàn·zi wrist

【手纹】 shǒuwén lines of the hand

【手纹鉴定】 shǒuwén jiàndìng verification of hand-print

【手无寸铁】 shǒuwúcùntiě bare-handed; defenseless

【手舞足蹈】 shǒuwǔ-zúdǎo dance for joy

【手下】 shǒuxià 1.(领导之下) under the leadership of; under: 在他～当工程师 be an engineer under him 2.(手头) at hand 3.(动手时) at the hands of sb.

【手下败将】 shǒuxià-bàijiàng one's defeated opponent

【手下留情】 shǒuxià-liúqíng show mercy; be lenient

【手相学】 shǒuxiàngxué chirognomies; chirognosy

【手写体】 shǒuxiětǐ handwritten form; script

【手心】 shǒuxīn 1.(手掌心) the palm of the hand 2.(控制范围) control: 他逃不出我们的～。He cannot escape from our control.

【手续】 shǒuxù procedures; formalities: 地方～ local formalities / 海关～ customs formalities / 检疫～ quarantine formalities

【手续费】 shǒuxùfèi commission: 收取～ charge commission / 银行～ banker's commission

【手续费标准】 shǒuxùfèi biāozhǔn commission rates

【手痒】 shǒuyǎng one's fingers itch; have an itch to do sth.

【手艺】 shǒuyì 1.(指技术) craftsmanship; workmanship: ～高 be highly skilled 2.(手工艺) handicraft; trade: 学一门～ learn a trade

【手淫】 shǒuyín masturbate; masturbation (n.)

【手印】 shǒuyìn 1.(指痕迹) an impression of the hand 2.(按在契约上的) thumb print; fingerprint

【手札】 shǒuzhá 〈*written*〉 personal letter
【手闸】 shǒuzhá hand brake; brake lever
【手掌】 shǒuzhǎng palm; palm of the hand
【手杖】 shǒuzhàng stick; walking stick
【手纸】 shǒuzhǐ toilet paper
【手指】 shǒuzhǐ finger
【手指甲】 shǒuzhǐ·jia finger nail
【手重】 shǒuzhòng use too much force; heavy-handed
【手镯】 shǒuzhuó bracelet
【手足】 shǒuzú brothers: ～之情 brotherly affection
【手足无措】 shǒuzú-wúcuò all in a fluster; at a loss what to do; be bewildered
【手钻】 shǒuzuàn manual drill

守 (shǒu) **1.** (防守) guard; defend: ～土有责 be duty-bound to defend the territory of one's country **2.** (守候) keep watch: ～了一天 keep watch for the whole day **3.** (遵守) observe; serve; abide by: ～纪律 observe the rules / ～信用 keep one's promise **4.** (靠近) close to; near: ～着这样好的老师，你为什么不学英语? Why don't you learn English when you have such a good teacher at your side?

【守备】 shǒubèi perform garrison duty; be on garrison duty; garrison
【守备部队】 shǒubèi bùduì garrison force
【守财奴】 shǒucáinú miser
【守场员】 shǒuchǎngyuán 〈*Baseball*〉 fielder
【守场员手套】 shǒuchǎngyuán shǒutào 〈*Baseball*〉 fielder's glove
【守法】 shǒufǎ abide by the law; keep the law
【守寡】 shǒuguǎ remain a widow; live in widowhood
【守恒】 shǒuhéng conservation
【守恒定律】 shǒuhéng dìnglǜ conservation law
【守候】 shǒuhòu **1.** (等待) wait for; expect: ～机会 wait for one's opportunity **2.** (看护) keep watch; attend
【守护】 shǒuhù guard; defend: 狗～着房子。The dog guarded the house.
【守护神】 shǒuhùshén patron saint
【守节】 shǒujié preserve chastity after the death of her husband; not remarry
【守旧】 shǒujiù adhere to past practices; stick to old ways; be conservative
【守旧派】 shǒujiùpài old liners
【守军】 shǒujūn defending troops; defenders
【守口如瓶】 shǒukǒu-rúpíng keep one's mouth shut; breathe not a single word; be tight-mouthed
【守垒员】 shǒulěiyuán 〈*Baseball*〉 baseman
【守灵】 shǒulíng stand as guards at the bier; keep vigil beside the coffin
【守门】 shǒumén **1.** (看门) be on duty at the door or gate **2.** 〈*Sports*〉 keep goal
【守门员】 shǒuményuán goalkeeper; goaltender; goalie
【守势】 shǒushì defensive: 采取～ be on the defensive
【守岁】 shǒusuì stay up late or all night on New Year's Eve
【守土】 shǒutǔ 〈*written*〉 defend the territory of one's country
【守望】 shǒuwàng keep watch
【守望台】 shǒuwàngtái watchtower
【守望相助】 shǒuwàng-xiāngzhù (of neighboring villages) keep watch and help defend each other; give mutual help and protection
【守卫】 shǒuwèi guard; defend: ～海岛 defend the island
【守孝】 shǒuxiào observe mourning for one's parent
【守信】 shǒuxìn keep one's word; abide by one's word
【守业】 shǒuyè maintain what has been achieved by one's forefathers or predecessors; safeguard one's heritage
【守夜】 shǒuyè keep watch at night; spend the night on watch
【守则】 shǒuzé rules; regulations: 学生～ students regulations
【守株待兔】 shǒuzhū-dàitù stand by a stump waiting for more hares to come and dash themselves against it; trust to chance and windfalls

首 (shǒu) **1.** (头) head **2.** (第一) first: ～播 broadcast or show for the first time / ～批 the first batch **3.** (首领) leader; head; chief: 祸～ chief culprit **4.** (出头告发) bring charges against sb.; inform against sb.

【首倡】 shǒuchàng initiate; start
【首车】 shǒuchē first bus
【首创】 shǒuchuàng initiate; originate; pioneer: ～一种学说 initiate a doctrine
【首创精神】 shǒuchuàng jīngshén initiative
【首次】 shǒucì for the first time; first: ～上映的影片 first run film; first showing of a film
【首当其冲】 shǒudāng-qíchōng be the first to be affected (by a disaster, etc.); bear the brunt
【首都】 shǒudū capital: 北京是中国的～。Beijing is the capital of China.
【首恶】 shǒu'è chief criminal; principal culprit: ～必办，胁从不问，立功受奖。The chief criminals shall be punished without fail, those who are accomplices under duress shall go unpunished and those who perform deeds of merit shall be rewarded.
【首发式】 shǒufāshì ceremony held for the first issuing of books or magazines
【首犯】 shǒufàn chief criminal
【首府】 shǒufǔ capital
【首级】 shǒují head
【首肯】 shǒukěn nod approval; nod assent; approve; consent
【首领】 shǒulǐng chieftain; leader; head
【首脑】 shǒunǎo head: 国家～ head of state / 政府～ head of government
【首脑会议】 shǒunǎo huìyì conference of heads of state or government; summit conference
【首脑人物】 shǒunǎo rénwù leading figure
【首屈一指】 shǒuqū-yīzhǐ come first on the list; be second to none
【首任】 shǒurèn the first to be appointed to an office: ～驻华大使 the first ambassador accredited to China
【首日封】 shǒurìfēng first day cover
【首饰】 shǒu·shi ornaments; jewelry; jewels: 戴～ wear jewels
【首尾】 shǒuwěi 1.(开头和末尾) the head and the tail; the beginning and the end 2.(始终) from beginning to end
【首位】 shǒuwèi the first place
【首席】 shǒuxí 1.(最高席位) seat of honor 2.(职位最高的) chief: ～代表 chief representative / ～法官 chief judge; chief justice / ～检察官 chief inspector; chief procurator
【首先】 shǒuxiān 1.(最先) first: 兰兰是～到的。Lanlan was the first to arrive. 2.(第一) in the first place; first of all; above all: ～把你的名字告诉我。First of all tell me your name.
【首相】 shǒuxiàng prime minister
【首演场观众】 shǒuyǎnchǎng guānzhòng first-nighter
【首要】 shǒuyào 1.(最重要的) of the first importance; first: ～原因 first cause 2.(首脑) head
【首映】 shǒuyìng show for the first time
【首映式】 shǒuyìngshì premiere; ceremony held for the first show
【首战】 shǒuzhàn 1.〈*Mil.*〉 the first battle 2.〈*Sports*〉 the first game
【首战告捷】 shǒuzhàn-gàojié 1.(第一仗获胜) win the first battle 2.〈*Sports*〉 score a victory in the first game
【首长】 shǒuzhǎng leading cadre; senior officer
【首座】 shǒuzuò seat of honor

寿[壽、夀] (shòu) 1.(长命) longevity 2.(生命;年岁) life; age: 长～ long life 3.(寿辰) birthday: 祝～ congratulate sb. on his birthday
【寿比南山，福如东海】 shòu bǐ nánshān, fú rú dōnghǎi May your age be as Mountain Tai and your happiness as the Eastern Sea
【寿材】 shòucái coffin prepared before one's death
【寿辰】 shòuchén birthday (of an elderly person)
【寿礼】 shòulǐ birthday present (for an elderly person)
【寿面】 shòumiàn birthday noodles
【寿命】 shòumìng life-span; life
【寿桃】 shòutáo (peach-shaped) birthday cake
【寿星】 shòuxīng 1.(老人星) the god of longevity 2.(被祝寿的老人) an elderly person whose birthday is being celebrated
【寿衣】 shòuyī graveclothes; shroud; cerements
【寿终正寝】 shòuzhōng-zhèngqǐn die in bed of

old age; die a natural death

受 (shòu) 1.(接受) receive; accept 2.(忍受) stand; endure; bear: 你～得住这疼痛吗? Can you stand the pain? / 真够～的。It's really unbearable. 3.(遭受) suffer; be subjected to: ～损失 suffer losses 4.(适合) be pleasant: ～看 be pleasant to look at

【受病】 shòubìng catch a disease; fall ill

【受潮】 shòucháo be affected with damp; become damp

【受宠若惊】 shòuchǒng-ruòjīng feel extremely flattered; be overwhelmed by an unexpected favor

【受挫】 shòucuò be foiled; be baffled; be thwarted; suffer a setback

【受罚】 shòufá be punished

【受粉】 shòufěn 〈*Bot*.〉 be pollinated

【受害】 shòuhài suffer injury; fall victim; be affected

【受害国】 shòuhàiguó the country that's been wronged; victimized country

【受害人】 shòuhàirén aggrieved party

【受害者】 shòuhàizhě victim; suffer

【受寒】 shòuhán catch a chill; catch cold

【受话器】 shòuhuàqì (telephone) receiver

【受话人】 shòuhuàrén callee

【受欢迎】 shòuhuānyíng be well received; be well liked

【受欢迎的人】 shòuhuānyíng·de rén 〈*Foreign Affairs*〉 persona grata ‖ 不受欢迎的人 persona non grata

【受贿】 shòuhuì accept bribes; bribery (n.)

【受贿行为】 shòuhuì xíngwéi act of accepting bribe

【受贿者】 shòuhuìzhě bribee; grafter

【受贿罪】 shòuhuìzuì acceptance of bribes

【受惠国】 shòuhuìguó favored nation

【受奖】 shòujiǎng be rewarded

【受教育】 shòujiàoyù receive an education

【受戒】 shòujiè 〈*Buddhism*〉 be initiated into monkhood or nunhood

【受尽】 shòujìn suffer enough from; suffer all kinds of; have one's fill of: ～千辛万苦 undergo all kinds of hardships

【受惊】 shòujīng be frightened; be startled

【受精】 shòujīng be fertilized

【受精卵】 shòujīngluǎn 〈*Biol*.〉 zygote

【受窘】 shòujiǒng be embarrassed; be in an awkward position

【受控】 shòukòng be controlled

【受苦】 shòukǔ suffer (hardships); have a rough time

【受累】 shòulěi (受到牵累) get involved on account of sb. else

【受累】 shòulèi (受劳累) be put to much trouble; be inconvenienced

【受理】 shòulǐ 1.(接受并办理) accept and attend 2.〈*Law*〉 accept and hear a case: ～案件 accept and hear a case / ～控诉 accept a complaint / ～申诉 hear a claim / ～诉状 hear a complaint; receive a petition

【受礼】 shòulǐ accept gifts

【受凉】 shòuliáng catch cold; get a cold

【受命】 shòumìng receive instructions

【受难】 shòunàn suffer calamities or disasters; be in distress

【受骗】 shòupiàn be deceived; be taken in

【受聘】 shòupìn accept an appointment; be appointed to

【受气】 shòuqì be bullied; suffer wrong

【受权】 shòuquán be authorized: ～发表声明如下 be authorized to issue the following statement

【受热】 shòurè 1.(受高温影响) be heated 2.(受暑) be affected by the heat; have heatstroke; suffer from sunstroke

【受辱】 shòurǔ be insulted; be disgraced; be humiliated

【受伤】 shòushāng be injured; be wounded; sustain an injury

【受审】 shòushěn stand trial; be tried; be on trial

【受暑】 shòushǔ suffer from heatstroke

【受损】 shòusǔn suffer losses

【受损程度】 shòusǔn chéngdù extent of damage

【受胎】 shòutāi become pregnant; be impregnated; conceive

【受胎率】 shòutāilǜ 〈*Husbandry*〉 conception rate

【受托】 shòutuō be commissioned; be entrusted (with a task): ～办理某事 be entrusted with sth. / ～代行业务 be asked to manage sb's business

【受委屈】 shòuwěiqū be upset by some unkindness

【受洗】 shòuxǐ 〈*Christianity*〉 be baptized; receive baptism

【受降】 shòuxiáng accept a surrender

【受刑】 shòuxíng be tortured; be put to torture

【受讯问】 shòuxúnwèn subject to cross-examination

【受训】 shòuxùn receive training

【受遗赠人】 shòuyízèngrén 〈*Law*〉 devisee; legatee

【受益】 shòuyì profit by; benefit from; be benefited

【受用】 shòuyòng benefit from; profit by; enjoy: ～不尽 benefit from sth. all one's life

【受援】 shòuyuán receive aid

【受援国】 shòuyuánguó recipient country

【受阅】 shòuyuè be reviewed

【受孕】 shòuyùn become pregnant; be impregnated; conceive

【受灾】 shòuzāi be hit by a natural adversity: 严重～地区 badly stricken area

【受震强度】 shòuzhèn qiángdù seismicity

【受之无愧】 shòuzhī-wúkuì deserve it; be worthy of it

【受之有愧】 shòuzhī-yǒukuì receive it with shame; I don't deserve it.

【受罪】 shòuzuì endure hardships, tortures, rough conditions, etc.; have a hard time

授 (shòu) **1.**(交付;给予) award; vest; confer; give: ～以全权 vest sb. with full authority **2.**(传授) teach; instruct

【授粉】 shòufěn 〈*Bot.*〉 pollination

【授计】 shòujì confide a stratagem to sb.; tell sb. the plan of action

【授奖】 shòujiǎng award a prize; present awards

【授精】 shòujīng inseminate; insemination (n.): 人工～ artificial insemination

【授课】 shòukè give lessons; give instruction

【授命】 shòumìng give orders: ～组阁 authorize sb. to form a cabinet

【授旗】 shòuqí present (sb. with) a flag

【授权】 shòuquán empower; authorize; warrant: 经～的官员 authorized officer

【授权书】 shòuquánshū letter of authority

【授时】 shòushí **1.**(报告精确时间) time service **2.**(颁行历书) (in former times) issue the official calendar

【授时信号】 shòushí xìnhào time signal

【授受】 shòushòu grant and receive; give and accept: ～不亲 no physical contact between a man and a woman except between man and wife

【授勋】 shòuxūn confer orders or medals; award a decoration

【授意】 shòuyì incite sb. to do sth.; inspire; suggest: 某人～写的文章 inspired articles

【授予】 shòuyǔ confer; award; grant; endow: ～金质奖章 award a gold medal; give a gold medal

绶 (shòu)

【绶带】 shòudài ribbon (attached to an official seal or a medal)

狩 (shòu) 〈*written*〉 hunt; hunting (n.)

【狩猎】 shòuliè hunt; hunting (n.)

售 (shòu) **1.**(卖) sell: 鸡蛋每公斤～6元。Eggs sell at six yuan a kilo. / 票全部～完了。All tickets were sold out. **2.**(施展) make (one's plan, trick, etc.) work; carry out (intrigues): 以～其奸 achieve one's treacherous purpose

【售出】 shòuchū put on sale

【售后服务】 shòuhòu fúwù post sale service

【售后免费服务】 shòuhòu miǎnfèi fúwù after-sale service; after service

【售货】 shòuhuò sell goods

【售货合同】 shòuhuò hétóng sales contract

【售货机】 shòuhuòjī vending machine

【售货经理】 shòuhuò jīnglǐ sales manager

【售货亭】 shòuhuòtíng kiosk

【售货员】 shòuhuòyuán salesclerk; salesperson; shop assistant; salesman (m.); saleswoman (f.)

【售价】 shòujià selling price; price

【售票处】 shòupiàochù **1.**(火车站的) ticket office; booking office **2.**(剧院等的) box office

【售票口】 shòupiàokǒu wicket

【售票员】 shòupiàoyuán **1.**(公共汽车的) ticket seller; conductor **2.**(火车站的) booking office clerk 3.（剧院等的）box office clerk

【售完】 shòuwán be sold out

兽[獸]（shòu） 1.（哺乳动物）beast; animal: 野～ wild animal 2.（野蛮）beastly; bestial

【兽类】 shòulèi beasts; animals

【兽行】 shòuxíng 1.（野蛮行为）brutal act; brutality 2.（指泄欲）bestiality; ferocious sexual acts

【兽性】 shòuxìng brutish nature; barbarity

【兽医】 shòuyī veterinary surgeon; veterinarian; vet

【兽医学】 shòuyīxué veterinary medicine; veterinary science

【兽医站】 shòuyīzhàn veterinary station

【兽疫学】 shòuyìxué epizootiology

【兽欲】 shòuyù animal desire

瘦（shòu） 1.（肉少）thin; emaciated: ～得皮包骨头 be only skin and bones 2.（脂肪少）lean 3.（窄小）tight: 这件上衣他穿～了一点。This jacket is a little too tight for him. 4.（不肥沃）not fertile; poor

【瘦长】 shòucháng long and thin; tall and thin; lanky

【瘦骨嶙峋】 shòugǔ-línxún become as emaciated as a fowl; a bony appearance

【瘦肉】 shòuròu lean meat

【瘦弱】 shòuruò thin and weak; emaciated

【瘦小】 shòuxiǎo thin and small; slight

【瘦削】 shòuxuē very thin; gaunt

【瘦子】 shòu·zi a lean person

shu

书[書]（shū） 1.（书写）write: 大～特～ record in letters of gold 2.（字体）style of calligraphy; script: 楷～ regular script 3.（书籍）book: 写～ write a book 4.（信）letter: 家～ a letter to or from home 5.（文件）document: 证～ certificate

【书包】 shūbāo satchel; schoolbag

【书报】 shūbào books and newspapers

【书本】 shūběn book

【书本知识】 shūběn zhīshí book knowledge

【书边空白】 shūbiān kòngbái margin

【书橱】 shūchú bookcase

【书呆子】 shūdāi·zi pedant; bookworm

【书店】 shūdiàn bookshop; bookstore; bookseller's

【书法】 shūfǎ handwriting; penmanship; calligraphy

【书法家】 shūfǎjiā calligrapher

【书房】 shūfáng study

【书稿】 shūgǎo manuscript

【书柜】 shūguì bookcase

【书号】 shūhào book number: 国际标准～ ISBN; International Standard Book Number

【书后】 shūhòu postscript

【书画】 shūhuà painting and calligraphy

【书画展】 shūhuàzhǎn painting and calligraphy display

【书籍】 shūjí books; works; literature

【书脊】 shūjǐ spine (of a book)

【书记】 shū·ji 1.（党团主要负责人）secretary: 总～ general secretary 2.（文牍员）clerk

【书记处】 shū·jichù secretariat

【书记员】 shū·jiyuán clerk (of a court)

【书架】 shūjià bookshelf; book case

【书柬】 shūjiǎn 同"书简"

【书简】 shūjiǎn letters; correspondence

【书局】 shūjú publishing house; press

【书刊】 shūkān books and periodicals

【书面】 shūmiàn written; in written form; in writing: ～报告 reading report / ～裁决 written decision

【书名】 shūmíng the title of a book; title

【书名号】 shūmínghào French quotes（符号为《》）

【书目】 shūmù booklist; title catalogue: 参考～ a list of reference books; bibliography

【书皮】 shūpí book cover; book jacket; dust cover; cover: 塑料～ plastic cover

【书评】 shūpíng book review

【书签】 shūqiān 1.（夹在书中的）book-mark 2.（线装书封面上的）title label

【书商】 shūshāng bookman

【书社】 shūshè press; publishing house

【书生】 shūshēng intellectual; scholar

【书生气】 shūshēngqì bookishness: ～十足 be bookish and naive

【书市】 shūshì book-market; book fair

【书摊】 shūtān bookstall; bookstand

【书套】 shūtào slipcase
【书亭】 shūtíng book-kiosk；bookstall
【书香门第】 shūxiāng-méndì scholar-gentry families；a scholarly family；family of scholars
【书写】 shūxiě write
【书写纸】 shūxiězhǐ writing paper
【书信】 shūxìn letter；written message
【书信集】 shūxìnjí collected letters
【书信体】 shūxìntǐ epistolary style
【书信往来】 shūxìn wǎnglái correspondence
【书页】 shūyè page
【书院】 shūyuàn academy of classical learning
【书札】 shūzhá 〈*written*〉 letters；correspondence
【书斋】 shūzhāi study
【书展】 shūzhǎn exhibition of books
【书桌】 shūzhuō desk；writing desk

抒（shū） express；give expression to；convey：各～己见 each airs his own views
【抒发】 shūfā express；voice；give expression to
【抒情】 shūqíng express one's emotion
【抒情歌曲】 shūqíng gēqǔ lyric songs
【抒情散文】 shūqíng sǎnwén lyric prose
【抒情诗】 shūqíngshī lyric poetry；lyrics
【抒写】 shūxiě express；describe

舒（shū） **1.**（展开，宽解）stretch；unfold：～了一口气 heave a sigh of relief **2.**（缓慢）easy；leisurely；in no hurry
【舒畅】 shūchàng happy；entirely free from worry
【舒服】 shū·fu **1.**（轻松愉快）comfortable **2.**（无病）be well：我觉得不大～。I am not feeling very well.
【舒卷】 shūjuǎn 〈*written*〉 roll back and forth
【舒适】 shūshì comfortable；cosy；snug
【舒坦】 shū·tan comfortable；at ease
【舒展】 shūzhǎn **1.**（不卷着）unfold；extend；smooth out：～展目 lift one's eyebrows and open one's eyes **2.**（使舒适）limber up；stretch

枢［樞］（shū） pivot；hub；center
【枢杆】 shūgǎn hinged arm
【枢接】 shūjiē pin joint
【枢纽】 shūniǔ pivot；hub；axis；key position：交通～ axis of communication
【枢纽工程】 shūniǔ gōngchéng multi-purpose project；pivotal project
【枢轴】 shūzhóu pivot；king journal；weigh bar shaft

叔（shū） **1.**（叔父）uncle；father's younger brother；uncle **2.**（与父亲同辈的男人）uncle **3.**（丈夫之弟）husband's younger brother
【叔伯】 shū·bai relationship between cousins of the same grandfather or great-grandfather：～兄弟 first or second cousins on the paternal side；cousins
【叔父】 shūfù uncle；father's younger brother
【叔母】 shūmǔ aunt；wife of father's younger brother
【叔叔】 shū·shu **1.**（叔父）uncle；father's younger brother **2.**（与父亲同辈的男人）uncle

菽［尗］（shū） beans

殊（shū） **1.**（不同）different **2.**（特殊）outstanding；special；remarkable：特～ remarkable efficacy **3.**（很）very much；extremely；really
【殊不知】 shūbùzhī little imagine；hardly realize
【殊荣】 shūróng special honor
【殊深轸念】 shūshēn-zhěnniàn express deep solicitude；feel deeply concerned
【殊死】 shūsǐ desperate；life-and-death
【殊途同归】 shūtú-tóngguī reach the same goal by different routes
【殊勋】 shūxūn distinguished service；outstanding merit

倏［儵］（shū） swiftly
【倏忽】 shūhū swiftly；in the twinkling of an eye
【倏然】 shūrán swiftly

梳（shū） **1.**（梳子）comb：电热～ electric heat comb **2.**（梳理）comb：～头发 comb one's hair
【梳洗】 shūxǐ wash and dress

【梳妆】 shūzhuāng dress and make up：～打扮 get dressed and made up

【梳妆凳】 shūzhuāngdèng dressing stool

【梳妆台】 shūzhuāngtái dressing table ～用具 toilet articles; toilet set

【梳子】 shū·zi comb

疏[踈] (shū) 1.(疏浚) dredge 2.(疏落) thin; sparse; scattered 3.(关系远) distant 4.(不熟悉) not familiar with：人地生～ be unfamiliar with the place and the people; be a complete stranger 5.(疏忽) neglect 6.(空虚) scanty：才～学浅 have little talent and less learning 7.(分散) disperse; scatter

【疏不间亲】 shūbùjiànqīn A merest acquaintance should not say anything to estrange somebody from one who is dear to him.

【疏导】 shūdǎo 1.(疏浚) dredge 2.(引导) guide; direct; show the way

【疏忽】 shū·hu carelessness; negligence; oversight

【疏忽大意】 shū·hu-dàyì be neglectful and careless; inattentive and heedless

【疏浚】 shūjùn dredge：～航道 dredge a channel

【疏漏】 shūlòu careless omission; slip; oversight：笔头～ slip of the pen / 口头～ slip of the tongue

【疏落】 shūluò sparse; scattered; oversight

【疏密】 shūmì density; spacing

【疏散】 shūsàn 1.(疏落的) scattered; dispersed; sparse：～的村落 scattered villages 2.(使分散) evacuate：～人口 evacuate inhabitants

【疏松】 shūsōng 1.(松散) loose 2.(使松散) loosen：～土壤 loosen the soil

【疏通】 shūtōng 1.(疏浚) dredge：～河流 dredge a river 2.(沟通；调解) mediate between two parties

【疏远】 shūyuǎn drift apart; become estranged

蔬 (shū) vegetables

【蔬菜】 shūcài vegetables; greens; greenstuff

【蔬菜栽培】 shūcài zāipéi vegetable growing; vegetable farming

摅[攄] (shū) express; give expression to; convey：各～己见 each airs his own views

输 (shū) 1.(运输) transport; convey：把电～往山区 transmit the electricity to the mountain regions 2.(失败) lose; be beaten; be defeated：～了一局 lose one game in the set

【输不起的人】 shū·buqǐ·derén a sore loser

【输出】 shūchū 1.(指从里到外) feed out; send off; transport out 2.(指商品等) export：资本～ export of capital / ～商品 export of commodities 3.〈*Electr.*〉 output

【输出港】 shūchūgǎng delivery port; outport

【输出功率】 shūchū gōnglǜ output power

【输出口岸】 shūchū kǒu'àn loading port

【输出数据】 shūchū shùjù dataout; output date

【输出限额】 shūchū xiàn'é export quota

【输出许可证】 shūchū xǔkězhèng export licence

【输电】 shūdiàn transmit electricity

【输家】 shūjiā loser

【输金点】 shūjīndiǎn gold point

【输精管】 shūjīngguǎn 〈*Anat.*〉 spermatic duct; deferent duct

【输精管结扎】 shūjīngguǎn jiézhā 〈*Med.*〉 vasoligation

【输理】 shūlǐ be in the wrong

【输卵管】 shūluǎnguǎn 〈*Anat.*〉 oviduct; Fallopian tube

【输卵管结扎】 shūluǎnguǎn jiézhā 〈*Med.*〉 tubal ligation

【输尿管】 shūniàoguǎn 〈*Anat.*〉 ureter

【输尿管炎】 shūniàoguǎnyán 〈*Med.*〉 ureteritis

【输入】 shūrù 1.(指从外到内) feed in; transport in 2.(指商品等) import：资本～ import of capital / ～商品 import of commodities 3.〈*Electr.*〉 input：同步～ simultaneous input

【输入插孔】 shūrù chākǒng instrument input

【输入程序】 shūrù chéngxù input routine; loading routine

【输入额】 shūrù'é amount of imports

【输入功率】 shūrù gōnglǜ input power

【输入数据】 shūrù shùjù data-in

【输入数字】 shūrù shùzì input digit
【输入税】 shūrùshuì import duty
【输入文件】 shūrù wénjiàn input file
【输入限额】 shūrù xiàn'é import quota
【输入许可证】 shūrù xǔkězhèng import licence
【输入字段】 shūrù zìduàn input field
【输入字块】 shūrù zìkuài input block
【输送】 shūsòng carry; transport; convey
【输血】 shūxuè 1.〈*Med*.〉blood transfusion: 医生给他～。The doctor give him a blood transfusion. / 她输了血。She was given a blood transfusion. 2.(给以支援) give aid and support; bolster up; give sb. a shot in the arm
【输氧】 shūyǎng 〈*Med*.〉oxygen therapy
【输液】 shūyè 〈*Med*.〉infusion; transfusion: 病人需要～。The patient will need regular infusions.
【输赢】 shūyíng 1.(输或赢) lose or win 2.(指数额) losses and winnings
【输油管】 shūyóuguǎn petroleum pipeline

秫 (shú) *kaoliang*; sorghum

【秫秸】 shújiē *kaoliang* stalk

孰 (shú) 1.(谁) which; who: ～是～非? Who is right and who is wrong? 2.(什么) what: 是可忍,～不可忍? If this can be tolerated, what cannot?

塾 (shú) private school: 私～ private school

【塾师】 shúshī private tutor

熟 (shú) 1.(成熟) ripe: 这果子还没～,不能吃。This fruit isn't ripe yet — we can't eat it. 2.(煮熟的) cooked; done: ～肉 cooked meat 3.(加工过的) processed 4.(知道得清楚) familiar: 我和他不太～。I'm not on familiar terms with him. 5.(精通) skilled; experienced; practiced 6.(程度深) deeply
(也读作"熟"shóu)

【熟谙】 shú'ān be familiar with; be good at
【熟菜】 shúcài cooked food; prepared food
【熟地】 shúdì cultivated land
【熟记】 shújì learn by heart; memorize; commit to memory
【熟客】 shúkè frequent visitor
【熟练】 shúliàn skilled; practiced; proficient
【熟练程度】 shúliàn chéngdù competence: 提高～ raise the skill
【熟路】 shúlù familiar route; beaten track
【熟能生巧】 shúnéngshēngqiǎo skill comes from practice; practice makes perfect
【熟年】 shúnián a year of good harvests
【熟人】 shúrén acquaintance; friend
【熟石膏】 shúshígāo plaster of Paris
【熟食】 shúshí prepared food; cooked food
【熟食店】 shúshídiàn delicatessen
【熟识】 shú·shi be well acquainted with; know well: 彼此很～ know each other very well
【熟视无睹】 shúshì-wúdǔ pay no attention to a familiar sight; turn a blind eye to; ignore
【熟手】 shúshǒu skilled hand; experienced hand
【熟睡】 shúshuì sleep soundly; be fast asleep
【熟思】 shúsī ponder deeply; consider carefully
【熟悉】 shúxī know well; be familiar with; have an intimate knowledge of
【熟习】 shúxí be skillful at; have the knack of; be practiced in
【熟语】 shúyǔ idiom; idiomatic phrase
【熟知】 shúzhī know very well; know intimately
【熟字】 shúzì words already learned; familiar words

赎[贖] (shú) 1.(用钱物换回) redeem; ransom: ～回被绑架的人 ransom a kidnapped person 2.(抵销) atone for (a crime)

【赎当】 shúdàng redeem sth. pawned
【赎价】 shújià ransom price; ransom
【赎金】 shújīn ransom money; ransom
【赎买】 shúmǎi redeem; buy out
【赎买政策】 shúmǎi zhèngcè a policy of redemption
【赎身】 shúshēn redeem oneself; buy back one's freedom
【赎罪】 shúzuì atone for one's crime: 立功～ perform merits to atone for one's crime

暑 (shǔ) heat; hot weather: 我们在盛～之时不能工作。We can't work in the heat.

【暑假】 shǔjià summer vacation
【暑期】 shǔqī summer vacation time
【暑期学校】 shǔqī xuéxiào summer school
【暑气】 shǔqì summer heat; heat
【暑热】 shǔrè hot summer weather
【暑天】 shǔtiān hot summer days; dog days

署 (shǔ) 1.(办公处所) a government office 2.(布置) make arrangements for; arrange 3.(签署) sign; put one's signature to: 签～合同 sign a contract
【署理】 shǔlǐ handle by proxy; act as deputy: ～部务 handle the ministry's affairs during the minister's absence
【署名】 shǔmíng sign; put one's signature to: ～画押 sign one's name and affix one's seal to a document

薯［藷］(shǔ) potato: 白～ sweet potato / 马铃～ potato
【薯莨】 shǔliáng 〈*Bot*.〉 shouliang yam
【薯蓣】 shǔyù 〈*Bot*.〉 yam

曙 (shǔ) 〈*written*〉 daybreak; dawn
【曙光】 shǔguāng first light of morning; dawn
【曙色】 shǔsè light of early dawn

属［屬］(shǔ) 1.(类别) category 2. 〈*Biol*.〉 genus: 亚～ subgenus 3.(隶属) under; subordinate to and departments 4.(属于) belong to: 我们两国同～发展中国家。Both our countries belong to developing countries. 5.(亲属) family members; dependents 6.(是) be 7.(用属相记生年) be born in the year of (one of the twelve animals): 我姐姐～马。My sister was born in the year of the horse.
(另见"属"zhǔ)
【属地】 shǔdì possession; dependency; colony
【属国】 shǔguó vassal state; dependent state
【属性】 shǔxìng attribute; quality; characteristic
【属于】 shǔyú belong to; be part of

蜀 (shǔ)
【蜀葵】 shǔkuí 〈*Bot*.〉 hollyhock

鼠 (shǔ) mouse; rat
【鼠辈】 shǔbèi mean creatures; scoundrels
【鼠标器】 shǔbiāoqì 〈*Computer*〉 mouse; Genius mouse
【鼠窜】 shǔcuàn scamper off like a rat; scurry away like frightened rats: ～狼奔 run higher and thither like rats and wolves
【鼠肚鸡肠】 shǔdù-jīcháng suffer affronts without resentment; lacking courage or endurance
【鼠目寸光】 shǔmù-cùnguāng a mouse can see only an inch; see only what is under one's nose; be shortsighted
【鼠窃狗盗】 shǔqiè-gǒudào filch like rats and snatch like dogs; play petty tricks on the sly
【鼠疫】 shǔyì the plague

数［數］(shǔ) 1.(查点) count: 倒着～count down / 学～数 learn how to count 2.(突出) be reckoned as exceptionally 3.(列举) enumerate; list
(另见"数"shù, shuò)
【数不胜数】 shǔbùshèngshǔ beyond count
【数不着】 shǔ·buzháo not count as outstanding, important, etc.
【数九】 shǔjiǔ the nine periods (of nine days each) following the winter solstice
【数落】 shǔ·luo 1.(指责) scold sb. by enumerating his wrong-doings; reprove 2.(列举) enumerate; cite one example after another
【数秒】 shǔmiǎo count the seconds
【数一数二】 shǔyī-shǔ'èr be as one of the best; ranking very high

术［術］(shù) 1.(技艺) art; skill; technique 2.(方法) method; tactics
【术语】 shùyǔ technical terms; terminology

述 (shù) state; relate; narrate: 如上所～ as stated above; as mentioned above
【述而不作】 shù'érbùzuò pass on the ancient culture without adding anything new to it
【述评】 shùpíng review; commentary: 时事～ commentary on current affairs
【述说】 shùshuō state; recount; narrate
【述职】 shùzhí report on one's work; report

戍 (shù) defend; garrison
【戍边】 shùbiān garrison the frontiers

束 (shù) 1.(捆;系) bind; tie: ～紧皮带 tighten one's belt 2.〈*classifier*〉 bundle;

bunch; sheaf: 一～花 a bunch of flowers 3.（约束）control; restrain: ～手～脚 timid and hesitant

【束缚】 shùfù tie; bind up; fetter: 受传统的～ be fettered by tradition / 摆脱～ do away with the shackles

【束身藏拙】 shùshēn-cángzhuō hide one's inadequacy by keeping quiet

【束手】 shùshǒu have one's hands tied; be helpless

【束手待毙】 shùshǒu-dàibì helplessly wait for death; resign oneself to extinction

【束手就擒】 shùshǒu-jiùqín allow oneself to be seized without putting up a fight

【束手无策】 shùshǒu-wúcè be at a loss what to do; feel quite helpless; be at one's wit's end

【束之高阁】 shùzhīgāogé bundle sth. up and place it on the top shelf; lay aside and neglect; shelve; pigeonhole

树［樹］(shù) 1.（树木）tree: 爬～ climb up the tree / 植～ plant trees 2.（栽培）plant; cultivate 3.（树立）set up; establish; up-hold: ～正气 uphold healthy tendencies 4.〈*Computer*〉tree

【树碑立传】 shùbēi-lìzhuàn 〈*derog.*〉glorify sb. by erecting a monument to him and writing his biography; build up sb's public image

【树杈】 shùchà crotch (of a tree)

【树丛】 shùcóng grove; thicket

【树大招风】 shùdà-zhāofēng 〈*Proverb*〉a tall tree catches the wind; a person in a high position is liable to be attacked

【树倒猢狲散】 shù dǎo húsūn sàn When an influential person falls from power, his hangers-on disperse.

【树敌】 shùdí make an enemy of sb.; set others against oneself; antagonize

【树墩】 shùdūn stump; tree stump

【树干】 shùgàn trunk; tree trunk

【树高千丈,叶落归根】 shù gāo qiānzhàng, yè luò guī gēn a person residing away from home eventually returns to his native soil

【树根】 shùgēn root; tree root

【树冠】 shùguān crown (of a tree); treetop

【树胶】 shùjiāo gum of the tree

【树立】 shùlì set up; establish: ～一个榜样 set up a model / ～法制观念 acquire a sense of the rule of law

【树林】 shùlín woods; grove

【树苗】 shùmiáo sapling; seedling

【树木】 shùmù wood; trees: 只见～不见森林 can't see the wood for the trees

【树目录】 shùmùlù 〈*Computer*〉tree directory

【树皮】 shùpí bark: 剥～ bark (v.)

【树皮画】 shùpíhuà bark picture

【树梢】 shùshāo the tip of a tree; treetop

【树身】 shùshēn trunk; tree trunk

【树形】 shùxíng tree-form; arborescence

【树形检索】 shùxíng jiǎnshuǒ 〈*Computer*〉tree search

【树形结构】 shùxíng jiégòu 〈*Computer*〉tree structure

【树形图】 shùxíngtú arborescence

【树叶】 shùyè leaf

【树叶饲料】 shùyè sìliào leaf-feeder

【树阴】 shùyīn shade (of a tree)

【树欲静而风不止】 shù yù jìng ér fēng bù zhǐ the tree may prefer calm, but the wind will not subside

【树枝】 shùzhī branch; twig

【树脂】 shùzhī resin: 合成～ synthetic resin

【树桩】 shùzhuāng slump; tree slump

竖［豎、竪］(shù) 1.（垂直的）vertical; upright; perpendicular: ～着放 place sth. vertically 2.（竖立）set upright; erect; stand: ～电线杆 erect a wire pole / ～帐篷 erect a tent

【竖井】 shùjǐng 〈*Mineral.*〉shaft; vertical shaft

【竖立】 shùlì erect; set upright; stand

【竖起】 shùqǐ hold up; erect: ～衣领 turn up the collar

【竖琴】 shùqín 〈*Music*〉harp ‖ 竖琴手 harper; harpist

【竖子】 shùzǐ 1.（童仆）boy; lad 2.（小子）mean fellow; fellow

恕 (shù) 1.（宽恕）forgive; pardon; excuse 2.（请求原谅）excuse me; beg your pardon: ～我打扰。Excuse my troubling you.

【恕不奉陪】 shùbùfèngpéi I'm sorry but I

cannot keep you company.（或：Excuse me for not keeping you company.）

【恕不拘礼】 shùbùjūlǐ Pardon me for not standing on ceremony.

【恕难从命】 shùnáncóngmìng We regret that we cannot comply with your wishes.

【恕罪】 shùzuì pardon an offense; forgive a sin

庶（shù） 1.（多）abundant; numerous; multiple 2.（几乎）so that; in order to

【庶民】 shùmín the multitude; the public

【庶务】 shùwù 1.（杂务）business matter; general affairs 2.（指从事庶务的人）clerk

数［數］（shù） 1.（数目）number; figure: 基～ cardinal number / 序～ ordinal number / 图书馆里的书～以千计。The books in the library numbers in the thousands. 2.〈*Gram*.〉number: 单～ singular number / 复～ plural number 3.（几，几个）several; a few: ～日 a few days

（另见"数"shǔ，shuò）

【数词】 shùcí 〈*Gram*.〉numeral: 基～ cardinal numbers; cardinal numerals / 序～ ordinal numbers; ordinal numerals

【数额】 shù'é number; amount

【数据】 shùjù data: 科学～ scientific data

【数据操作语言】 shùjù cāozuò yǔyán data manipulation language

【数据处理】 shùjù chǔlǐ data processing

【数据存储系统】 shùjù cúnchǔ xìtǒng data-storage system

【数据分析】 shùjù fēnxī data analysis

【数据管理系统】 shùjù guǎnlǐ xìtǒng data management system

【数据检查】 shùjù jiǎnchá data checks

【数据库】 shùjùkù data base

【数据输入】 shùjù shūrù data entry; data input

【数据终端】 shùjù zhōngduān data terminal

【数控】 shùkòng 〈*Mech*.〉numerical control

【数量】 shùliàng quantity; amount

【数码】 shùmǎ 1.（数字）numeral 2.（数目字）number; amount

【数码相机】 shùmǎ xiàngjī digital camera

【数目】 shùmù number; amount

【数学】 shùxué mathematics; maths; mathematic (adj.): 高等～ advanced mathematics ‖ 数学家 mathematician

【数学符号】 shùxué fúhào numerical symbols

【数学图形】 shùxué túxíng shapes

【数值】 shùzhí 〈*Math*.〉numerical value

【数轴】 shùzhóu 〈*Math*.〉number axis

【数珠】 shùzhū 〈*Buddhism*〉beads

【数字】 shùzì 1.（数目字）numeral; figure; digit: 阿拉伯～ Arabic numeral / 罗马～ Roman numeral 2.（数量）quantity; amount: 控制～ controlled quantity

【数字编码】 shùzì biānmǎ digital coding; numeric coding

【数字光盘】 shùzì guāngpán CD; compact disc: 只读～ CD-ROM; compact disc read-only memory

【数字计算机】 shùzì jìsuànjī digital computer

【数字控制】 shùzì kòngzhì numerical control

【数字控制系统】 shùzì kòngzhì xìtǒng numerical control system

【数字伺服系统】 shùzì sìfú xìtǒng digital servo system

【数字显示】 shùzì xiǎnshì digital display; digital presentation

【数罪并罚】 shùzuì bìngfá concurrent punishment for several crimes; cumulative punishment

漱（shù） gargle; rinse

【漱口】 shùkǒu rinse the mouth; gargle: 牙医递给我一杯水，要我用它漱漱口。The dentist handed me a glass of water to swill my mouth out with.

shua

刷［唰[5]］（shuā） 1.（刷子）brush: 衣～ clothes brush 2.（用刷子刷）brush; scrub: ～地板 brush the floor / 把我的大衣～一～。Give my coat a brush. 3.（涂抹）daub; paste up 4.（淘汰）eliminate; remove 5.〈*onomat*.〉swish; rustle: 杨树叶子被风吹得～～响。The poplar leaves rustled in the wind.

（另见"刷"shuà）

【刷掉】 shuādiào brush off: 这个脏点儿很容易～。The dirt will brush off easily.

【刷痕】 shuāhén brush mark

【刷墙】 shuāqiáng whitewash the wall

【刷去】 shuāqù brush off：这个脏点儿很容易～。The dirt will brush off easily.

【刷洗】 shuāxǐ scrub：把平锅～干净 scrub out a pan

【刷新】 shuāxīn 1.（刷洗一新）renovate；refurbish：～一张旧桌子 refurbish an old table 2.（创出新的）break：～全国纪录 break a national record / ～世界纪录 break a world record

【刷牙】 shuāyá brush one's teeth

【刷子】 shuā·zi brush

耍（shuǎ） 1.（玩）play：小男孩在院子里～。The boy is playing in the courtyard. 2.（玩弄）play with；flourish 3.（耍花招）play（tricks）

【耍把戏】 shuǎbǎxì 1.（玩杂耍）juggle（with）2.（耍花招）play tricks；be up to one's tricks

【耍笔杆】 shuǎbǐgǎn wield a pen；be skilled in literary tricks

【耍花招】 shuǎhuāzhāo 1.（卖弄武术技巧）display showy movements in *wushu*, etc. 2.（欺诈）play tricks

【耍滑】 shuǎhuá try to shirk work or responsibility；act in a slick way

【耍赖】 shuǎlài act shamelessly；be perverse

【耍流氓】 shuǎliúmáng behave like a hoodlum；take liberties with women；act indecently

【耍弄】 shuǎnòng 1.（玩弄）play with；flourish 2.（戏弄）make fun of；make a fool of；deceive

【耍脾气】 shuǎpíqì wreak one's bad temper；show temper

【耍贫嘴】 shuǎpínzuǐ 〈*dial.*〉 be garrulous

【耍人】 shuǎrén make fun of；make a fool of；deceive

【耍手腕】 shuǎshǒuwàn play tricks；maneuver

【耍威风】 shuǎwēifēng make a show of authority

【耍无赖】 shuǎwúlài act shamelessly；be perverse

【耍笑】 shuǎxiào 1.（随意说笑）joke；have fun 2.（戏弄）make fun of；play a joke on sb.

【耍心眼儿】 shuǎxīnyǎnr exercise one's wits for personal gain；be calculating；pull a smart trick

【耍嘴皮子】 shuǎ zuǐpí·zi 1.（卖弄口才）show off one's eloquence；talk glibly；be a slick talker 2.（只说不做）merely chatter idly；mere empty talk；lip service

刷（shuà） select；pick up（另见"刷"shuā）

【刷白】 shuàbái white；pale：月亮把大地照得～。The earth turned white under the moon.

shuai

衰（shuāi） decline；wane：～运 declining fortune / 年老力～ decrepit / 兴～ rise and decline

【衰败】 shuāibài decline；wane；be at a low ebb

【衰变】 shuāibiàn 〈*Physics*〉 decay：核～ nuclear decay

【衰耗】 shuāihào pad control

【衰减】 shuāijiǎn 〈*Electr.*〉 attenuation

【衰竭】 shuāijié 〈*Med.*〉 exhaustion；prostration

【衰老】 shuāilǎo old and feeble；decrepit；senile；slow death；senescence

【衰老期】 shuāilǎoqī senescence phase

【衰落】 shuāiluò decline；be on the wane；go downhill

【衰弱】 shuāiruò 1.（指精力）weak；feeble：病人很～。The patient is very weak. 2.（指事物）slack off；weaken

【衰世之秋】 shuāishìzhīqiū in the time of the age of decadence

【衰颓】 shuāituí weak and degenerate

【衰退】 shuāituì fail；decline：记忆力～ lessen one's memory / 经济～ economic recession

【衰亡】 shuāiwáng become feeble and die；decline and fall；wither away

【衰朽】 shuāixiǔ 〈*written*〉 feeble and decaying；decrepit

摔［踤[1]］（shuāi） 1.（跌倒）fall；tumble；lose one's balance：～倒在地 fall down 2.（跌落）hurtle down；plunge 3.（打破）cause to fall and break；break：～得粉碎 break into pieces 4.（扔）cast；throw；fling

【摔打】 shuāi·da 1.（磕打）beat；knock 2.

(磨炼) rough it; temper oneself: 他经历了多年的～，如今更老练了。Tempered through years' hardships, he has grown much more experienced than ever.

【摔跟头】 shuāi gēn·tou 1.(跌倒) tumble; trip and fall 2.(犯错误) trip up; come a cropper; make a blunder.

【摔跤】 shuāijiāo 1.(跌倒) tumble; trip and fall 2.(犯错误) trip up; come a cropper; blunder 3.〈*Sports*〉 wrestling: 古典式～ Greco-Roman wrestling / 自由式～ free-style wrestling ‖ 摔跤运动员 wrestler

【摔跤台】 shuāijiāotái platform

甩 (shuǎi) 1.(挥) swing; move backward and forward: 把辫子往后一～ throw back one's plait 2.(扔) throw; fling; toss: 把某物～出窗外 throw sth. out of the window / ～手榴弹 throw a hand grenade 3.(抛开) leave sb. behind; throw off

【甩卖】 shuǎimài off a clearance sale; sale at a reduced price

【甩手】 shuǎishǒu 1.(摆动手) swing one's arms 2.(扔下不管) refuse to do; wash one's hand of: 你可不能～不管。You can't wash your hands of this.

帅[帥、率[2]] (shuài) 1.〈*Mil.*〉 commander in chief: 统～ supreme commander / 元～ marshal 2.(漂亮) beautiful; graceful; smart: 字写得～ write a beautiful hand 3.(棋子) commander in chief

率 (shuài) 1.(率领) lead; command: ～代表团前往… head a delegation to leave for ... 2.(轻易) rash; hasty 3.(爽直) frank; straightforward

(另见"率"lǜ)

【率领】 shuàilǐng lead; head; command: ～军队进攻敌人 head the troops to attack the enemy

【率土之滨】 shuàitǔzhībīn all this land; all within the boundaries; within the territory of a state

【率先】 shuàixiān take the lead in doing sth.; be the first to do sth.

【率真】 shuàizhēn forthright and sincere

【率直】 shuàizhí straightforward; unreserved; blunt

shuan

闩[櫎] (shuān) 1.(门闩) bolt; latch: 门～ door bolt 2.(用闩关好) fasten with a bolt or latch: 把门～好 bolt the door

拴 (shuān) tie; fasten: 把马～在树上 tie a horse to a tree

栓 (shuān) 1.(机件) bolt; plug: 消火～ fire hydrant; fireplug 2.(塞子) stopper; cork

【栓剂】 shuānjì 〈*Pharm.*〉 suppository

【栓皮】 shuānpí (软木) cork

【栓皮栎】 shuānpílì 〈*Bot.*〉 oriental oak

【栓塞】 shuānsè 〈*Med.*〉 embolism

涮 (shuàn) 1.(漂洗) rinse; swill: ～瓶子 rinse a bottle / ～一下衣服 rinse the clothes 2.(烫一下就吃) boil thin slices of meat instantly; instant-boil: ～羊肉 instant-boiled mutton

【涮锅子】 shuànguō·zi instant-boil slices of meat and vegetables in a chafing dish

shuang

双[雙、雙] (shuāng) 1.(两个) two; twin; both; dual 2.〈*classifier*〉 pair: 一～鞋 a pair of shoes 3.(偶数的) even: ～号座位 even-numbered seats 4.(加倍的) double; twofold

【双胞胎】 shuāngbāotāi twins

【双边】 shuāngbiān bilateral: ～贸易 bilateral trade; two-way trade / ～和多边经济合作 bilateral and multilateral economic cooperation

【双钹】 shuāngbó 〈*Music*〉 high-hat cymbals

【双层】 shuāngcéng double-deck; having two layers; of two thicknesses

【双层玻璃】 shuāngcéng bō·li double glazing

【双层床】 shuāngcéngchuáng bunk beds

【双层公共汽车】 shuāngcéng gōnggòng qìchē double-deck bus; double decker

【双层汽车运输车】 shuāngcéng qìchē yùnshūchē 〈*Railway*〉 double-deck car carrier

【双重】 shuāngchóng double; dual; twofold: ～任务 double task; twofold task / 她受着

疾病和贫穷的～困扰。She is doubly troubled, by illness and poverty.

【双重标准】 shuāngchóng biāozhǔn double standard

【双重代表权】 shuāngchóng dàibiǎoquán dual representation

【双重国籍】 shuāngchóng guójí dual nationality

【双重汇率】 shuāngchóng huìlǜ dual rate

【双重间谍】 shuāngchóng jiàndié double agent

【双重控制】 shuāngchóng kòngzhì dual control

【双重人格】 shuāngchóng réngé duality of character; dual personality

【双重征税】 shuāngchóng zhēngshuì double taxation

【双打】 shuāngdǎ 〈*Sports*〉 doubles：男子～ men's doubles / 男女混合～ mixed doubles / 女子～ women's doubles

【双打边线】 shuāngdǎ biānxiàn 〈*Tennis*〉 doubles sideline

【双点号】 shuāngdiǎnhào tandem colon（符号为¨）

【双发】 shuāngfā 〈*Aeron.*〉 twin-engined：～飞机 a twin-engined plane

【双方】 shuāngfāng both sides; the two parties：缔约国～ both signatory states; the contracting parties

【双峰驼】 shuāngfēngtuó 〈*Zool.*〉 bactrian camel

【双扶】 shuāngfú give aid to two kinds of families

【双幅】 shuāngfú double width

【双缸洗衣机】 shuānggāng xǐyījī two-tub washing machine

【双杠】 shuānggàng 〈*Sports*〉 parallel bars

【双股】 shuānggǔ two-ply; bifilar

【双关】 shuāngguān having a double meaning

【双关语】 shuāngguānyǔ pun：带有性内容的～ double entendre / 使用～ play on pun; pun (v.)

【双管齐下】 shuāngguǎn-qíxià paint a picture with two brushes at the same time; work along both lines

【双轨】 shuāngguǐ 〈*Transport*〉 double track

【双轨铁路】 shuāngguǐ tiělù double-track railway

【双轨制】 shuāngguǐzhì double-track system; dual track system：价格～ the double-track system in commodity price

【双号】 shuānghào even numbers (of tickets, seats, etc.)

【双簧管】 shuānghuángguǎn 〈*Music*〉 oboe

【双季稻】 shuāngjìdào double harvest rice

【双镜头反光照相机】 shuāngjìngtóu fǎnguāng zhàoxiàngjī twin-lens reflex camera

【双联合同】 shuānglián hé·tong indented deed; indenture

【双料】 shuāngliào of reinforced material; extra quality

【双螺旋】 shuāngluóxuán 〈*Biochem.*〉 double helix

【双门冰箱】 shuāngmén bīngxiāng two-door refrigerator

【双面】 shuāngmiàn double side

【双面绣】 shuāngmiànxiù double-faced embroidery

【双目失明】 shuāngmù shīmíng lose one's eyesight; lose the sight of both eyes

【双亲】 shuāngqīn (both) parents; father and mother

【双全】 shuāngquán complete in both respects; possessing both：智勇～ possessing both wisdom and courage

【双人床】 shuāngrénchuáng double bed

【双人房间】 shuāngrén fángjiān double room

【双人滑】 shuāngrénhuá 〈*Skating*〉 pair skaters

【双人舞】 shuāngrénwǔ dance for two people; pas de deux

【双日】 shuāngrì even-numbered days

【双生】 shuāngshēng twin

【双生子】 shuāngshēngzǐ twins

【双手】 shuāngshǒu both hands

【双数】 shuāngshù even numbers

【双双】 shuāngshuāng in pairs

【双喜】 shuāngxǐ double happiness：～临门。A double blessing has descended upon the house.

【双线号】 shuāngxiànhào parallel（符号为‖）

【双线索道】 shuāngxiàn suǒdào bicable tramway

【双向】 shuāngxiàng two-way

【双向电视】 shuāngxiàng diànshì two-way television
【双向飞碟射击】 shuāngxiàng fēidié shèjī skeet shooting
【双向开关】 shuāngxiàng kāiguān two-way switch
【双向选择】 shuāngxiàng xuǎnzé two-way choose; the two-way selection
【双薪】 shuāngxīn double pay
【双学位】 shuāngxuéwèi double degree
【双眼皮】 shuāngyǎnpí double-fold eyelid
【双翼机】 shuāngyìjī biplane
【双引号】 shuāngyǐnhào double quotation marks（符号为“”）
【双拥】 shuāngyōng the two support
【双鱼宫】 Shuāngyúgōng 〈*Astron.*〉 Pisces（2月19日至3月20日）：生于～ be born under Pisces
【双鱼座】 Shuāngyúzuò 〈*Astron.*〉 Pisces
【双语】 shuāngyǔ bilingual; two different languages：～词典 a bilingual dictionary
【双元音】 shuāngyuányīn 〈*Gram.*〉 diphthong
【双月刊】 shuāngyuèkān bimonthly
【双增双节】 shuāngzhēng-shuāngjié two increases and two reductions
【双职工】 shuāngzhígōng man and wife both at work; working couple
【双子宫】 Shuāngzǐgōng 〈*Astron.*〉 Gemini（5月23日至6月21日）：生于～ be born under Gemini
【双子座】 Shuāngzǐzuò 〈*Astron.*〉 Gemini
【双座】 shuāngzuò **1.**〈*Auto*〉 two-seater; double-seater **2.**〈*Motorcycle*〉 twin seat
【双座汽车】 shuāngzuò qìchē two-seater

霜（shuāng） **1.**〈*Meteorol.*〉 frost：地上有～。There is frost on the ground. **2.**（霜状物）frostlike powder **3.**（白色）white; hoar
【霜冻】 shuāngdòng frost
【霜害】 shuānghài frostbite; frost injury
【霜降】 shuāngjiàng the Frost's Descent（10月23－24日交节）
【霜期】 shuāngqī 〈*Meteorol.*〉 frost season
【霜叶】 shuāngyè red leaves; autumn maple leaves

孀（shuāng） widow
【孀妇】 shuāngfù widow
【孀居】 shuāngjū be a widow; live in widowhood

爽（shuǎng） **1.**（明朗）bright; clear; crisp **2.**（率直）frank; straightforward; openhearted **3.**（舒服）feel well **4.**（不合）deviate
【爽口】 shuǎngkǒu tasty and refreshing：这道菜很～。This dish tastes very refreshing.
【爽快】 shuǎng·kuai **1.**（舒服痛快）refreshed; comfortable：心里很～ be quite at ease **2.**（直爽）frank; straightforward; outright **3.**（痛快）with alacrity; readily and briskly
【爽朗】 shuǎnglǎng **1.**（指天气）bright and clear **2.**（指人等）hearty; candid; frank and open; straightforward：～的笑声 hearty laughter
【爽利】 shuǎnglì brisk and neat; efficient and able
【爽然若失】 shuǎngrán-ruòshī 〈*written*〉 not know what to do
【爽身粉】 shuǎngshēnfěn talcum powder
【爽约】 shuǎngyuē 〈*written*〉 an appointment
【爽直】 shuǎngzhí frank; straightforward; candid

shui

谁（shuí）（见“谁”shéi）

水（shuǐ） **1.**（水）water：工业用～ service water / 饮用～ drinking water / 供应～ supply water / 给街上洒～ water a street / 往牛奶里掺～ water down the milk **2.**（江、河、湖、海）water; rivers, lakes, seas, etc.：～陆运输 land and water transportation **3.**（稀的汁）a liquid
【水坝】 shuǐbà dam
【水泵】 shuǐbèng water pump
【水笔】 shuǐbǐ **1.**（小楷笔）a stiff-haired writing brush **2.**（水彩画笔）water-color paintbrush
【水表】 shuǐbiǎo water meter
【水兵】 shuǐbīng seaman; sailor; bluejacket
【水波】 shuǐbō waves
【水玻璃】 shuǐbō·li water glass
【水彩】 shuǐcǎi watercolor

【水彩画】 shuǐcǎihuà watercolor painting
【水彩颜料】 shuǐcǎi yánliào watercolors
【水草】 shuǐcǎo 1.（水源和草）water and grass 2.（水生植物）waterweeds; water plants
【水产】 shuǐchǎn aquatic product
【水产品】 shuǐchǎnpǐn aquatic product
【水产养殖】 shuǐchǎn yǎngzhí aquaculture
【水产业】 shuǐchǎnyè aquatic products industry
【水产资源】 shuǐchǎn zīyuán aquatic resources
【水车】 shuǐchē 1.（灌溉用）waterwheel 2.（运水用）watercart; water wagon
【水池】 shuǐchí pond; pool; cistern
【水处理】 shuǐchǔlǐ 〈*Chem.*〉 water treatment
【水床】 shuǐchuáng water bed
【水到渠成】 shuǐdào-qúchéng where water flows, a channel is formed; when conditions are ripe, success will come
【水道】 shuǐdào 1.（河道）water course 2.（水路）waterway; water route 3.〈*Sports*〉 lane; course: 自己的～ own water
【水道标志】 shuǐdào biāozhì 〈*Sports*〉 marking of course
【水稻】 shuǐdào paddy (rice); rice
【水滴石穿】 shuǐdī-shíchuān dripping water wears through rock; constant effort brings success
【水底电缆】 shuǐdǐ diànlǎn submarine cable; subaqueous cable
【水底生物】 shuǐdǐ shēngwù benthon; benthos
【水底植物】 shuǐdǐ zhíwù benthophytes; phytobenthos
【水电】 shuǐdiàn water and electricity
【水电费】 shuǐdiànfèi charges for water and electricity
【水电站】 shuǐdiànzhàn hydroelectric (power) station; hydropower station
【水痘】 shuǐdòu 〈*Med.*〉 varicella; chicken pox
【水费】 shuǐfèi water-rate
【水粉】 shuǐfěn soaked bean-noodles
【水粉画】 shuǐfěnhuà gouache
【水分】 shuǐfèn 1.（物体中含的水）moisture content 2.（夸大成分）exaggeration: 有～ be inflated
【水沟】 shuǐgōu ditch; drain; gutter
【水垢】 shuǐgòu scale; incrustation
【水管】 shuǐguǎn waterpipe
【水果】 shuǐguǒ fruit
【水果运输船】 shuǐguǒ yùnshūchuán fruit-carrier
【水壶】 shuǐhú 1.（烧水用的）kettle 2.（军用的）canteen 3.（浇水用的）watering can
【水葫芦】 shuǐhú·lu 〈*Bot.*〉 water hyacinth
【水花】 shuǐhuā spray
【水患】 shuǐhuàn flood; inundation
【水回收设备】 shuǐhuíshōu shèbèi water-recovery apparatus
【水火】 shuǐhuǒ 1.（水和火）fire and water: ～不相容 be incompatible as fire and water 2.（灾难）extreme misery
【水火无情】 shuǐhuǒ-wúqíng floods and fires have no mercy for anybody
【水货】 shuǐhuò commodities sold through abnormal channel
【水碱】 shuǐjiǎn scale; incrustation
【水浇地】 shuǐjiāodì 〈*Agric.*〉 irrigated land
【水饺】 shuǐjiǎo boiled dumplings
【水解】 shuǐjiě 〈*Chem.*〉 hydrolysis
【水晶】 shuǐjīng crystal; rock crystal
【水晶玻璃】 shuǐjīng bō·li crystal (glass)
【水晶宫】 shuǐjīnggōng the Crystal Palace (of the Dragon King)
【水晶棺】 shuǐjīngguān crystal sarcophagus
【水晶体】 shuǐjīngtǐ 〈*Anat.*〉 crystalline lens
【水井】 shuǐjǐng well
【水净化】 shuǐjìnghuà water purification
【水坑】 shuǐkēng puddle; pool; water hole
【水库】 shuǐkù reservoir
【水牢】 shuǐláo water dungeon
【水涝】 shuǐlào waterlogging
【水涝地】 shuǐlàodì waterlogged land
【水雷】 shuǐléi 〈*Mil.*〉 (submarine) mine
【水冷】 shuǐlěng water-cooling; water-cooled (adj.)
【水冷式发动机】 shuǐlěngshì fādòngjī water-cooled engine
【水冷式反应堆】 shuǐlěngshì fǎnyìngduī water-cooled reactor
【水力】 shuǐlì waterpower; hydraulic power

【水力发电站】 shuǐlì fādiànzhàn hydroelectric (power) station

【水力学】 shuǐlìxué hydraulics

【水力资源】 shuǐlì zīyuán hydroelectric resources; waterpower resources

【水利】 shuǐlì 1.(水力资源的利用) water conservancy 2.(水利工程) irrigation works; water conservancy project: 兴修～ build irrigation works

【水利工程】 shuǐlì gōngchéng water conservancy project; irrigation works

【水利灌溉网】 shuǐlì guàngàiwǎng irrigation network

【水利枢纽】 shuǐlì shūniǔ key water control project

【水利资源】 shuǐlì zīyuán water resources; hydro-power resources; water resources

【水疗】 shuǐliáo 〈*Med.*〉 hydrotherapy

【水灵】 shuǐ·ling 1.(指水果等) fresh and juicy 2.(指人) bright and beautiful; radiant and vivacious

【水流】 shuǐliú 1.(江河) rivers; streams; waters 2.(水的流速) current; flow

【水龙】 shuǐlóng fire hose

【水龙卷】 shuǐlóngjuǎn 〈*Meteorol.*〉 waterspout

【水龙头】 shuǐlóngtóu (water) tap; faucet; bibcock

【水陆】 shuǐlù land and water

【水陆交通线】 shuǐlù jiāotōngxiàn land and water communication lines

【水陆联运】 shuǐlù liányùn water-land transshipment

【水陆联运码头】 shuǐlù liányùn mǎtóu a dock for joint land and water transport service

【水陆两用】 shuǐlù liǎngyòng amphibious: ～车 amphibious vehicle / ～汽车 amphibian automobile; amphibious car / ～坦克 amphibious tank

【水陆运输】 shuǐlù yùshū transportation by land and water

【水路】 shuǐlù waterway; water route

【水轮机】 shuǐlúnjī hydraulic turbine

【水萝卜】 shuǐluó·bo summer radish

【水落管】 shuǐluòguǎn downpipe; downspout

【水落石出】 shuǐluò-shíchū when the water subsides the rocks emerge; the whole thing comes to light: 把事情辩个～ argue a matter out

【水门】 shuǐmén 1.(阀门) water valve 2.(水闸) water gate

【水磨石】 shuǐmóshí 〈*Archit.*〉 terrazzo: ～地面 terrazzo floor

【水磨】 shuǐmò 1.(水力磨) water mill 2.(加水细磨) grind grain, etc. fine while adding water: ～年糕 New Year cake made from finely ground rice flour

【水墨画】 shuǐmòhuà ink and wash; wash painting

【水母】 shuǐmǔ 〈*Zool.*〉 medusa

【水泥】 shuǐní cement: 高标号～ high-mark cement

【水鸟】 shuǐniǎo aquatic bird; water bird

【水牛】 shuǐniú buffalo; water buffalo; water ox

【水暖工】 shuǐnuǎngōng plumber

【水泡】 shuǐpào 1.(水泡泡) bubble 2.(水疱) blister

【水疱】 shuǐpào blister

【水培养】 shuǐpéiyǎng water culture

【水平】 shuǐpíng 1.(与水面平行) horizontal; level 2.(某一高度) standard; level: 文化～ level of culture / 相应～ appropriate level / 达到小康～ achieve a relatively comfortable standard of living

【水平测试】 shuǐpíng cèshì proficiency test

【水平飞行】 shuǐpíng fēixíng horizontal flight

【水平轰炸】 shuǐpíng hōngzhà horizontal bombing; level bombing

【水平贸易】 shuǐpíng màoyì horizontal trade

【水平面】 shuǐpíngmiàn horizontal plane; level (surface)

【水平同步】 shuǐpíng tóngbù horizontal synchronization

【水平尾翼】 shuǐpíng wěiyì 〈*Aeron.*〉 horizontal tail

【水平线】 shuǐpíngxiàn horizontal line

【水平仪】 shuǐpíngyí level

【水汽】 shuǐqì vapor; steam; moisture

【水枪】 shuǐqiāng 〈*Mineral.*〉 giant; (hydraulic) monitor

【水橇】 shuǐqiāo 〈*Sports*〉 water ski

【水禽】 shuǐqín 〈*Zool.*〉 waterfowl; water bird

【水情】 shuǐqíng 〈*Water Conservancy*〉 regimen
【水球】 shuǐqiú 1.〈*Sports*〉 water polo 2.(指球) water polo ball ‖ 水球运动员 water poloist
【水球场】 shuǐqiúchǎng 〈*Sports*〉 playing pool; bath
【水球球门】 shuǐqiú qiúmén 〈*Sports*〉 cage
【水渠】 shuǐqú ditch; canal
【水乳交融】 shuǐrǔ-jiāoróng as well blended as milk and water; in complete harmony
【水上芭蕾】 shuǐshàng bālěi water ballet; aquathenics; synchronized swimming
【水上城市】 shuǐshàng chéngshì aquapolis
【水上房屋】 shuǐshàng fángwū lake dwelling
【水上飞机】 shuǐshàng fēijī seaplane; hydroplane
【水上飞行】 shuǐshàng fēixíng overwater flight
【水上交通】 shuǐshàng jiāotōng water borne traffic
【水上警察】 shuǐshàng jǐngchá harbor police; waterside police
【水上居民】 shuǐshàng jūmín boat dwellers
【水上派出所】 shuǐshàng pàichūsuǒ water police station
【水上人家】 shuǐshàng rénjiā boat dwellers; boatnik
【水上运动】 shuǐshàng yùndòng aquatic sports; water sports
【水上运动会】 shuǐshàng yùndònghuì aquatic sports meet
【水上运输】 shuǐshàng yùnshū water transport; water-borne transport
【水上杂技】 shuǐshàng zájì water aerobatics
【水深】 shuǐshēn depth of water
【水深火热】 shuǐshēn-huǒrè deep water and scorching fire; an abyss of suffering; extreme misery
【水生动物】 shuǐshēng dòngwù aquatic animal
【水生植物】 shuǐshēng zhíwù water plant; aquatic plant; hydrophyte
【水势】 shuǐshì flow of water; rise and fall of floodwater: ～汹涌。The current is turbulent.
【水手】 shuǐshǒu seaman; sailor
【水手长】 shuǐshǒuzhǎng boatswain
【水塔】 shuǐtǎ water tower
【水獭】 shuǐtǎ 〈*Zool.*〉 otter
【水潭】 shuǐtán puddle; pool
【水塘】 shuǐtáng pool; pond
【水天一色】 shuǐtiān-yīsè The waters and skies are of one color.
【水田】 shuǐtián paddy field; irrigated field
【水桶】 shuǐtǒng pail; bucket
【水头】 shuǐtóu 1.(落差) head of water 2.(洪峰) flood peak; peak of flow
【水土】 shuǐtǔ 1.(水和土) water and soil: ～保持 water and soil conservation 2.(环境和气候) natural environment and climate: 不服～ not acclimatized
【水洼】 shuǐwā paddle; waterpocket
【水汪汪】 shuǐwāngwāng 1.(形容充满水) full of water 2.(指眼睛) bright and intelligent
【水网】 shuǐwǎng a network of rivers
【水位】 shuǐwèi 1.(水面高度) water level: 警戒～ warning line 2.(地下水位) water table
【水温表】 shuǐwēnbiǎo 1.(量水温的温度表) water-thermometer 2.〈*Auto*〉 engine temperature gauge
【水文】 shuǐwén hydrology; hydrologic (adj.)
【水文站】 shuǐwénzhàn hydrologic station; hydrometric station
【水污染】 shuǐwūrǎn water pollution; pollution of water
【水系】 shuǐxì river system; water system
【水下】 shuǐxià underwater
【水下运载工具】 shuǐxià yùnzǎi gōngjù submersible vehicle
【水仙】 shuǐxiān 〈*Bot.*〉 narcissus
【水险】 shuǐxiǎn marine insurance; marine risk
【水线】 shuǐxiàn 1.(船舶的) waterline 2.〈*Swimming*〉 rope with cork floats
【水乡】 shuǐxiāng a region of rivers and lakes
【水箱】 shuǐxiāng water tank
【水箱盖】 shuǐxiānggài tank lid
【水泻】 shuǐxiè 〈*Med.*〉 watery diarrhea
【水泄不通】 shuǐxiè-bùtōng not even a drop of water could trickle through; be watertight

【水榭】 shuǐxiè waterside pavilion; pavilion on the water

【水星】 Shuǐxīng 〈Astron.〉 Mercury

【水性】 shuǐxìng 1.（游泳、潜水技能）ability in swimming：～很好 be a good swimmer 2.（水的深浅）the depth, currents and other characteristics of a river, lake, etc.

【水性杨花】 shuǐxìng-yánghuā vamp; vampiness

【水锈】 shuǐxiù 1.（水垢）scale; incrustation 2.（水迹）watermark（in water vessels）

【水压】 shuǐyā hydraulic pressure

【水压机】 shuǐyājī hydraulic press

【水烟】 shuǐyān shredded tobacco for water pipes

【水烟袋】 shuǐyāndài water pipe

【水眼】 shuǐyǎn spring

【水翼船】 shuǐyìchuán hydrofoil; hydrofoil boat

【水银】 shuǐyín 〈Chem.〉 mercury; quicksilver

【水银灯】 shuǐyíndēng mercury-vapor lamp

【水印】 shuǐyìn 1.〈Arts〉 watercolor block printing 2.（纸内的隐影图案）watermark

【水域】 shuǐyù waters; water area; body of water：内陆～ inland waters

【水源】 shuǐyuán 1.（河流发源地）the source of a river; headwaters; water head 2.（用水来源）source of water

【水运】 shuǐyùn water transport; waterborne（adj.）

【水灾】 shuǐzāi flood; inundation

【水葬】 shuǐzàng water burial

【水藻】 shuǐzǎo 〈Bot.〉 algae

【水闸】 shuǐzhá sluice; water gate; water lock

【水涨船高】 shuǐzhǎng-chuángāo when the river rises the boat goes up

【水蒸汽】 shuǐzhēngqì steam; water vapor

【水质】 shuǐzhì water quality

【水蛭】 shuǐzhì 〈Zool.〉 leech

【水中捞月】 shuǐzhōng-lāoyuè fish for the moon in the water; make impractical or vain efforts

【水肿】 shuǐzhǒng 〈Med.〉 edema; dropsy

【水柱】 shuǐzhù water column

【水状液】 shuǐzhuàngyè 〈Anat.〉 aqueous humor

【水准】 shuǐzhǔn 1.〈Geol.〉 level 2.（水平）level; standard

【水准点】 shuǐzhǔndiǎn bench mark

【水准面】 shuǐzhǔnmiàn level surface; level plane

【水准器】 shuǐzhǔnqì spirit level

【水准仪】 shuǐzhǔnyí surveyor's level; levelling instrument

【水族】 Shuǐzú Sui（中国少数民族，主要分布在贵州）

【水族】 shuǐzú aquatic animals

【水族馆】 shuǐzúguǎn aquarium

税（shuì） tax; duty：超额累进～ progressive tax of the income from wages and salaries in excess of specific amounts / 出口～ export duty / 地方～ local tax / 房地产～ housing and land tax / 附加～ additional tax / 港口～ harbor dues / 工资所得～ wage tax / 国～ state tax / 间接～ indirect tax / 进口～ import duty / 累进～ progressive tax / 所得～ income tax / 特别～ special tax / 遗产～ estate duty / 营业～ business tax / 直接～ direct tax / 避～ tax avoidance / 减～ reduce a tax; reduction of a tax / 免～ tax-free; duty-free; free of tax; free of duty; exemption from a tax / 纳～ pay taxes / 逃～ evade tax; tax evasion / 偷～ evade taxes; tax evasion / 征～ levy a tax

【税单】 shuìdān tax receipt

【税额】 shuì'é the amount of tax to be paid

【税法】 shuìfǎ law of tax; tax law

【税后个人所得】 shuìhuò gèrén shuǒdé disposable personal income

【税后扣除】 shuìhòu kòuchú after-tax deduction

【税后利润】 shuìhòu lìrùn after-tax profit

【税后所得】 shuìhòu suǒdé income after tax

【税款】 shuìkuǎn tax payment; taxation

【税率】 shuìlǜ tax rate; rate of taxation; tariff rate

【税目】 shuìmù tax items; taxable items

【税收】 shuìshōu tax revenue

【税收政策】 shuìshōu zhèngcè tax policy

【税务】 shuìwù tax business

【税务机关】 shuìwù jīguān tax authority

【税务稽查员】 shuìwù jīcháyuán inspector of

taxes

【税务局】 shuìwùjú tax bureau

【税务员】 shuìwùyuán tax collector; taxman

【税则】 shuìzé tax regulations

【税制】 shuìzhì tax system; taxation

【税制改革】 shuìzhì gǎigé reform of tax system

【税种】 shuìzhǒng categories of taxes

睡 (shuì) sleep: ～得好 sleep well / ～得晚 stay up late / 早～早起 early to bed and early to rise / 他～了两个小时。He slept for two hours.

【睡袋】 shuìdài sleeping bag

【睡觉】 shuìjiào 1.(睡眠) sleep; have a sleep; go to bed 2.(性交) sleep with; go to bed with

【睡帽】 shuìmào nightcap

【睡梦】 shuìmèng sleep; slumber: ～状态 dream state

【睡眠】 shuìmián sleep: ～不足 not have enough sleep

【睡眠疗法】 shuìmián liáofǎ physiological sleep therapy

【睡醒】 shuìxǐng wake up

【睡衣】 shuìyī night clothes; pajamas

【睡衣裤】 shuìyīkù pajamas

【睡意】 shuìyì sleepiness; drowsiness

【睡着】 shuìzháo be sleeping; be asleep; go to sleep: 他在 10 点时～了。He went sleep at ten o'clock.

shun

吮 (shǔn) suck

【吮吸】 shǔnxī suck: 婴儿～着母亲的奶水。The baby was sucking milk from its mother.

顺 (shùn) 1.(向同一方向) in the same direction as; with 2.(沿着) along: ～着大街走 follow the main street / 我们～着河走。We walked along the river. 3.(理顺) arrange; put in order 4.(适合) suitable; agreeable 5.(趁便) take the opportunity to: ～致最崇高的敬意。I avail myself of this opportunity to renew to you the assurances of my highest consideration. 6.(依次) in sequence

【顺便】 shùnbiàn conveniently; in passing; by the way

【顺差】 shùnchā favorable balance; surplus: 贸易～ favorable balance of trade

【顺产】 shùnchǎn 〈*Med*.〉 natural labor

【顺畅】 shùnchàng smooth; unhindered

【顺次】 shùncì in order; in succession; in proper sequence

【顺从】 shùncóng obey; yield to; act in submission to: ～他的意愿 yield to his wishes

【顺当】 shùn·dang smoothly; without a hitch

【顺耳】 shùn'ěr pleasing to the ear

【顺风】 shùnfēng 1.(与风同方向) have a favorable wind; have a tail wind: 一路～ a pleasant journey; bon voyage 2.(顺利) favorable wind; tail wind

【顺风转舵】 shùnfēng-zhuǎnduò trim one's sails; take one's cue from changing conditions

【顺杆儿爬】 shùngānrpá follow sb's cue and do everything to please him; readily fall in with other people's wishes

【顺境】 shùnjìng favorable circumstances: 处于～ be in favorable circumstances

【顺口】 shùnkǒu 1.(流畅) read smoothly 2.(未经考虑) speak casually; say offhandedly: ～答应 promise thoughtlessly / ～说出 say sth. offhandedly 3.(可口) suit one's taste; like the taste

【顺口溜】 shùnkǒuliū doggerel; jingle

【顺理成章】 shùnlǐ-chéngzhāng to do some work well, you must follow a rational line

【顺利】 shùnlì smoothly; successfully; without a hitch

【顺流而下】 shùnliú'érxià downstream; downriver: 水带着她～。The current carried her downstream.

【顺路】 shùnlù 1.(顺着同一路线) on the way: ～到朋友家看看 call on one's friend on the way 2.(不绕远) direct route; regular route

【顺时针方向】 shùnshízhēn fāngxiàng clockwise; in a clockwise direction: ～旋转把手 turn the knob clockwise

【顺势】 shùnshì take advantage of an opportunity (as provided by an opponent's reckless move)

【顺手】 shùnshǒu 1.（顺利）smoothly; without difficulty; without a hitch 2.（随手）conveniently; without extra trouble 3.（顺便）do sth. as a natural sequence; do sth. simultaneously 4.（合用）handy; convenient and easy to use

【顺手牵羊】 shùnshǒu-qiānyáng lead away a goat in passing; pick up sth. on the sly; walk off with sth.

【顺水】 shùnshuǐ downstream; with the stream; downriver

【顺水人情】 shùnshuǐ-rénqíng a favor done at little cost to oneself

【顺水推舟】 shùnshuǐ-tuīzhōu push the boat along with the current; make use of an opportunity to gain one's end

【顺藤摸瓜】 shùnténg-mōguā follow the vine to get the melon; track down sb. or sth. by following clues

【顺天应人】 shùntiān-yìngrén follow the mandate of heaven and comply with the popular wishes of the people

【顺我者昌，逆我者亡】 shùnwǒzhě chāng, nìwǒzhě wáng those who submit will prosper, those who resist shall perish

【顺心】 shùnxīn satisfactory; satisfaction (n.)

【顺序】 shùnxù 1.（次序）sequence; order: 按年代～ in chronological sequence / 按字母～ in alphabetical order 2.（依次）in proper order; in turn: ～前进 advance in proper order

【顺延】 shùnyán postpone: 遇雨～ subject to postponement in case of rain

【顺眼】 shùnyǎn pleasing to the eye

【顺意】 shùnyì satisfactory; satisfaction (n.)

【顺应】 shùnyìng comply with; conform to: ～民心 comply with the aspirations of the people

瞬 (shùn) wink; twinkling: 一～间 in a twinkling

【瞬间】 shùnjiān twinkling

【瞬时】 shùnshí instantaneous

【瞬息】 shùnxī twinkling: ～万变 undergoing a myriad changes in the twinkling of an eye; fast changing

shuo

说 (shuō) 1.（说话）speak; talk; say: ～某人好话 speak well of sb. / 她～过想搬到天津去。He talked of moving to Tianjin. / 用英语再～一遍。Say it again in English. 2.（解释）explain: 怎么也～不明白。You can't make it clear, no matter how hard you try to explain. 3.（言论，主张）theory; teachings; doctrine 4.（责备）scold: 爸爸～了他几句。Daddy gave him a talking-to

【说不得】 shuō·bu·de 1.（不能说）unspeakable; unmentionable 2.（无从说起）scandalous

【说不定】 shuō·budìng perhaps; maybe: ～我们队会赢。Perhaps our team will win.

【说不过去】 shuō·buguòqù be hardly justified; cannot be explained away

【说不来】 shuō·bulái cannot get along (with sb.): 我跟他～。I don't see eye to eye with him.

【说长道短】 shuōcháng-dàoduǎn indulge in idle gossip; make captious comments

【说穿】 shuōchuān tell what sth. really is; reveal; disclose

【说大话】 shuōdàhuà brag; boast; talk big: 他只是在～罢了。He's just boasting.

【说到底】 shuōdàodǐ in the final analysis; at bottom

【说到痛处】 shuōdào tòngchù sting to the quick

【说到做到】 shuōdào-zuòdào do what one says; match one's deeds to one's words; live up to one's word

【说得过去】 shuō·deguòqù justifiable; passable

【说得来】 shuō·delái can get along; be on good terms

【说定】 shuōdìng settle; agree on: 我们已～由谁买单。We have settled who will pay for the meal.

【说东道西】 shuōdōng-dàoxī chatter away on a variety of things

【说法】 shuō·fa 1.（措词）way of saying a thing; wording: ～不妥 inappropriate wording 2.（意见）statement; version; argument:

～不一 have different versions 3.（道理）reason; argument

【说服】 shuōfú persuade; convince; prevail on; talk sb. over

【说合】 shuō·he 1.（从中介绍）bring two（or more）parties together 2.（商议）talk over; discuss

【说和】 shuō·he mediate a settlement; compose a quarrel

【说话】 shuōhuà 1.（用话表达）speak; talk; say：有～的权利 have the right to speak 2.（闲谈）chat; talk：找人～ have a chat with sb. 3.（指责）gossip; talk：你这样干，人家要～的。Considering what you've done, people will talk. 4.（很短的时间）in a minute; in no time

【说谎】 shuōhuǎng lie; tell a lie：你为什么要向我～？Why did you tell me a lie?

【说教】 shuōjiào deliver a sermon; preach

【说客】 shuōkè a person often sent to win sb. over or enlist his support through persuasion; a persuasive talker

【说来话长】 shuōlái-huàcháng it's a long story

【说理】 shuōlǐ 1.（说明）argue; reason things out 2.（讲理）be reasonable

【说漏嘴】 shuōlòuzuǐ inadvertently blurt out

【说媒】 shuōméi act as matchmaker

【说明】 shuōmíng 1.（解释明白）explain; illustrate; show 2.（说明文字）explanation; directions; caption 3.（证明）prove; verify：事实本身就是很好的～。Facts speak for themselves.

【说明书】 shuōmíngshū 1.（文字说明）（a booklet of）directions 2.（技术说明）manual; technical manual：技术～ technical specification 3.（影剧说明书）synopsis

【说亲】 shuōqīn act as matchmaker

【说情】 shuōqíng plead for mercy for sb.; intercede for sb.

【说三道四】 shuōsān-dàosì make carding comments; make irresponsible remarks

【说实在的】 shuōshízài·de to tell the truth ...

【说头儿】 shuō·tour 1.（可谈之处）sth. to talk about; things to discuss 2.（辩解的理由）excuse

【说妥】 shuōtuǒ come to an agreement

【说戏】 shuōxì explain the play

【说笑】 shuōxiào chatting and laughing

【说笑话】 shuō xiàohuà tell a joke

【说一不二】 shuōyī-bùèr mean what one says; stand by one's word

烁[爍]（shuò） bright; shining：闪～ twinkle; glimmer

【烁烁】 shuòshuò glitter; sparkle

朔（shuò） 1.（新月）new moon 2.（朔日）the first day of the lunar month 3.（北）north; northern

【朔方】 shuòfāng north

【朔风】 shuòfēng north wind

【朔日】 shuòrì the first day of the lunar month

【朔望】 shuòwàng the first and the fifteenth day of the lunar month; syzygy

【朔望月】 shuòwàngyuè lunar month; synodic month

【朔月】 shuòyuè new moon

蒴（shuò）

【蒴果】 shuòguǒ 〈*Bot.*〉capsule

硕（shuò） large

【硕大】 shuòdà large; big

【硕大无朋】 shuòdà-wúpéng of unparalleled size; gigantic; exceptionally large

【硕果】 shuòguǒ 1.（大的果实）big fruit 2.（指成果）rich fruits; great achievements：～累累 have achieved great success

【硕果仅存】 shuòguǒ-jǐncún rare survival

【硕士】 shuòshì Master：理科～ Master of Science

【硕士学位】 shuòshì xuéwèi master's degree

【硕学鸿儒】 shuòxué-hóngrú a great learned literate

数[數]（shuò） frequently; repeatedly（另见"数"shǔ, shù）

【数见不鲜】 shuòjiàn-bùxiān encountered with many times; common occurrence; nothing new

si

私（sī） 1.（个人的）personal; private：～信 personal letter; private letter 2.（私

心) selfish：不要自～自利。Don't be selfish. 3.(暗地里) secret; private 4.(非法的) illicit; illegal：～卖 illicit sale

【私奔】 sībēn elope; elopement (n.)

【私弊】 sībì corrupt practices

【私藏】 sīcáng unlawfully possess oneself of

【私藏毒品】 sīcáng dúpǐn unlawful possession of drug

【私藏武器】 sīcáng wǔqì unlawful possession of weapons

【私产】 sīchǎn private property

【私娼】 sīchāng unlicensed prostitute

【私仇】 sīchóu personal enmity; personal grudge

【私出版物】 sī chūbǎnwù self-publication

【私倒】 sīdǎo personal profiteering

【私邸】 sīdǐ private residence

【私第】 sīdì private residence

【私法】 sīfǎ 〈*Law*〉 private law

【私贩鸦片】 sīfàn yāpiàn opium trafficking

【私方】 sīfāng private side; private party

【私房】 sī·fang 1.(个人积蓄) private savings 2.(不愿让外人知道) confidential：说～话 exchange confidences

【私愤】 sīfèn personal spite：泄～ vent personal spite

【私货】 sīhuò smuggled goods; contraband goods

【私交】 sījiāo personal friendship; personal friend

【私立】 sīlì 1.(私人设立) privately run 2.(私立的) private：～学校 private school

【私利】 sīlì private interests; personal gain：谋～ seek personal gains

【私了】 sīliǎo 1.〈*Law*〉 compound; compounding (n.) 2.(私下了结) solve sth. privately; settle a case out of court

【私囊】 sīnáng private purse：中饱～ line one's pockets

【私情】 sīqíng 1.(私人之间的) personal relationships：不徇～ not swayed by personal considerations 2.(男女间的) illicit love

【私人】 sīrén 1.(个人的) private; personal：～朋友 personal friend 2.(私人之间的) personal：～感情 personal affection / ～关系 personal relation 3.(自己的人) one's own man：任用～ fill a post with one's own man; practice nepotism

【私人财产】 sīrén cáichǎn private property; private goods and chattels

【私人代表】 sīrén dàibiǎo personal representative

【私人动产】 sīrén dòngchǎn personal chattels

【私人公司】 sīrén gōngsī private company; private-owned firm

【私人股】 sīréngǔ private share

【私人借款】 sīrén jièkuǎn private loan

【私人经济】 sīrén jīngjì private sector of the economy

【私人秘书】 sīrén mìshū private secretary

【私人企业】 sīrén qǐyè private enterprise

【私人信件】 sīrén xìnjiàn personal correspondence

【私人侦探】 sīrén zhēntàn private detective

【私人资本】 sīrén zīběn private capital

【私商】 sīshāng businessman; merchant; trader

【私生活】 sīshēnghuó private life

【私生子】 sīshēngzǐ illegitimate child; natural child; bastard

【私事】 sīshì privacy; private affairs; personal affairs

【私塾】 sīshú old-style private school

【私逃】 sītáo abscond

【私通】 sītōng 1.(私下勾结) have secret communication with 2.(通奸) illicit intercourse; adultery; fornication

【私通案件】 sītōng ànjiàn case of fornication

【私下】 sīxià 1.(背地) in secret：～商议 discuss in secret 2.(自己做) in private; privately：～活动 act in private

【私下和解】 sīxià héjiě compounding

【私相授受】 sīxiāngshòushòu privately give and privately accept; make an illicit transfer

【私心】 sīxīn 1.(内心) in one's heart; in one's mind 2.(为自己打算) selfish motives; selfishness：～杂念 selfish ideas and personal considerations

【私刑】 sīxíng lynch; illegal punishment (meted out by a kangaroo court)

【私蓄】 sīxù private savings

【私营】 sīyíng privately owned; privately operated; private：～经济 private economics

【私营企业】 sīyíng qǐyè private enterprise

【私有】 sīyǒu privately owned; private: ～财富 private wealth
【私有财产】 sīyǒu cáichǎn private property
【私有观念】 sīyǒu guānniàn private ownership mentality
【私有化】 sīyǒuhuà personalize; personalization (n.)
【私有制】 sīyǒuzhì private ownership
【私语】 sīyǔ **1.**（小声说）whisper: 切切～ talk in whispers **2.**（私下说的话）confidence
【私欲】 sīyù selfish desire
【私运进口】 sīyùn jìnkǒu smuggle goods into a port
【私运军火】 sīyùn jūnhuǒ gun-running
【私运鸦片】 sīyùn yāpiàn opium smuggling
【私章】 sīzhāng personal seal; signet
【私自】 sīzì privately; secretly; without permission: ～逃跑 escape secretly

司（sī） **1.**（主管）take charge of; attend to; manage: 各～其职。Each attends to his own duties. **2.**（部下的一级部门）department: 外交部礼宾～ the Protocol Department of the Ministry of Foreign Affairs / 新闻～ Information Department
【司法】 sīfǎ administration of justice; judicature
【司法部门】 sīfǎ bùmén judicial departments; judiciary
【司法程序】 sīfǎ chéngxù judicial process; judicial procedure
【司法独立】 sīfǎ dúlì judicial independence
【司法机关】 sīfǎ jīguān judicial office
【司法鉴定】 sīfǎ jiàndìng expert testimony
【司法警察】 sīfǎ jǐngchá judicial police
【司法权】 sīfǎquán judicial powers
【司法行为】 sīfǎ xíngwéi judicial act
【司法仲裁】 sīfǎ zhòngcái judicial arbitration
【司号员】 sīhàoyuán bugler; trumpeter
【司机】 sījī driver: 公共汽车～ a bus driver / 卡车～ a truck driver / 出租汽车～ a taxi driver
【司机室】 sījīshì cab
【司空见惯】 sīkōng-jiànguàn a common sight; a common occurrence; a matter of repeated occurrence
【司库】 sīkù cashier; treasurer: 名誉～ honorary treasurer
【司垒裁判员】 sīlěi cáipànyuán 〈*Baseball*〉 base umpire
【司令】 sīlìng commander; commanding officer: 总～ commander in chief
【司令部】 sīlìngbù headquarters; command
【司令员】 sīlìngyuán commander; commanding officer
【司炉】 sīlú stoker; fireman; chief stoker
【司球裁判员】 sīqiú cáipànyuán 〈*Baseball*〉 plate umpire
【司网裁判员】 sīwǎng cáipànyuán 〈*Tennis*〉 net-cord judge
【司务长】 sīwùzhǎng company quartermaster
【司线员】 sīxiànyuán 〈*Sports*〉 linesman
【司药】 sīyào pharmacist; druggist; chemist
【司仪】 sīyí master of ceremonies
【司钻】 sīzuàn (head) driller

丝［絲］（sī） **1.**（丝绸;蚕丝）silk **2.**（丝状物）a threadlike thing: 钢～ steel wire **3.**（极少、极小的量）a tiny bit; trace: 一～不差 not a bit of difference
【丝绸】 sīchóu silk cloth; silk
【丝绸之路】 sīchóu zhī lù the Silk Road
【丝带】 sīdài silk ribbon; silk braid; silk sash
【丝糕】 sīgāo steamed corn cake
【丝瓜】 sīguā **1.**〈*Bot.*〉 towel gourd; dishcloth gourd **2.**（丝瓜筋）loofah; luffa; dishcloth gourd
【丝光】 sīguāng the silky luster of mercerized cotton fabrics
【丝毫】 sīháo the slightest amount or degree; a bit; a particle; a shred; an iota: ～不差 fit it to a hair; not err by a hair's breadth; tally in every detail; be just right
【丝路】 sīlù the silk road
【丝绵】 sīmián silk floss; silk wadding
【丝绒】 sīróng velvet; velour
【丝丝入扣】 sīsī-rùkòu all threads neatly tied up; (done) with meticulous care and flawless artistry
【丝网印刷】 sīwǎng yìnshuā silk-screen printing
【丝弦】 sīxián 〈*Music*〉 silk string
【丝线】 sīxiàn silk thread (for sewing); silk yarn
【丝织画】 sīzhīhuà stevengraph
【丝织品】 sīzhīpǐn **1.**（指布料）silk fabrics **2.**

（指衣物）silk knit goods
【丝状】 sīzhuàng filiform

思（sī） 1.（想，考虑）think; consider; deliberate 2.（思念）think of; long for 3.（思路）thought; thinking
【思潮】 sīcháo 1.（思想潮流）trend of thought; ideological trend：社会～ social trend of thought; social ideological trends / 文艺～ trend of thought in literature and art 2.（思想活动）thoughts
【思忖】 sīcǔn 〈*written*〉 ponder; consider
【思考】 sīkǎo think deeply; ponder over; reflect on：你在～什么？What are you pondering over? / 反复～后，他决定不买房子了。After much thought he decided not to buy the house.
【思量】 sīliàng consider; turn sth. over in one's mind
【思路】 sīlù train of thought; thinking：～断了 lose the train of thought / 打断～ interrupt the train of thought
【思虑】 sīlǜ consider carefully; contemplate; deliberate
【思慕】 sīmù think of sb. with respect; admire
【思念】 sīniàn think of; long for; miss
【思索】 sīsuǒ think deeply; ponder：不假～ without stopping to reflect
【思维】 sīwéi 1.〈*Philos.*〉 thought; thinking 2.（进行思维）think about; give thought to sth.
【思贤若渴】 sīxián-ruòkě desire greatly to win the support of the wise; One's love for able men is equal to one's thirst for water.
【思想】 sīxiǎng 1.〈*Philos.*〉 thought; thinking; idea; ideology; ideological（adj.） 2.（想法）plan; intention
【思想包袱】 sīxiǎng bāo·fu sth. weighing on one's mind
【思想迟钝】 sīxiǎng chídùn bradyphrenia
【思想动向】 sīxiǎng dòngxiàng ideological trend
【思想斗争】 sīxiǎng dòuzhēng ideological struggle; mental struggle
【思想方法】 sīxiǎng fāngfǎ method of thinking
【思想感情】 sīxiǎng gǎnqíng thoughts and feelings; minds and sentiments
【思想工作】 sīxiǎng gōngzuò ideological work
【思想家】 sīxiǎngjiā thinker
【思想僵化】 sīxiǎng jiānghuà mental stagnation
【思想解放】 sīxiǎng jiěfàng ideological emancipation
【思想境界】 sīxiǎng jìngjiè ideological level
【思想库】 sīxiǎngkù brain trust
【思想体系】 sīxiǎng tǐxì ideological system; ideology
【思想性】 sīxiǎngxìng ideological content
【思想意识】 sīxiǎng yìshí ideology
【思绪】 sīxù 1.（思路）train of thought; thinking 2.（情绪）feeling：～不宁 feel perturbed

锶（sī）〈*Chem.*〉 strontium（元素符号 Sr）

斯（sī） 1.（这，此）this 2.（于是，就）then; thus
【斯拉夫人】 Sīlāfūrén Slav
【斯拉夫语】 Sīlāfūyǔ Slavic; Slavic language
【斯文】 sī·wen refined; gentle：举止～ refined in manner
【斯文扫地】 sīwén-sǎodì disgrace one's scholarly dignity; a scholar's misbehavior; have the educated humbled to the dust

厮［廝］（sī） 1.（男仆）male servant 2.（蔑称）fellow; guy 3.（互相）with each other; together
【厮打】 sīdǎ come to blows; exchange blows; tussle
【厮混】 sīhùn fool around together
【厮杀】 sīshā fight at close quarters

撕（sī） tear; rip：～下布告 tear down the notice / ～下一张日历 tear off a leaf from a calendar / 大风～破了船帆。The wind ripped the sail.
【撕毁】 sīhuǐ 1.（用手撕碎）tear up and destroy 2.（单方面背弃）tear up; tear to shreds：～合同 tear up a contract / ～协定 tear up an agreement; tear an agreement to shreds
【撕裂】 sīliè lacerate; laceration（n.）; tear; tearing（n.）
【撕破脸皮】 sīpò liǎnpí no longer spare sb's

sensibilities

【撕脱】 sītuō avuse; avulsion (n.)

嘶 (sī) 1.(叫) neigh: 马～ horses neigh 2.(嘶哑) hoarse: 声～力竭 hoarse and exhausted

【嘶哑】 sīyǎ hoarse: ～的嗓音 a hoarse voice

死 (sǐ) 1.(死亡) die; pass away: 病～ die of illness 2.(坚决) to the death 3.(达到极点) extremely; to death: ～要面子 save face at all costs / 我们要笑～了。We were killing ourselves laughing. 4.(不可调和的) implacable; deadly: ～对头 deadly enemy; irreconcilable opponent 5.(死板) fixed; rigid; inflexible 6.(不能通过) impassable; closed: 堵～ plug; stop up

【死板】 sǐbǎn 1.(指人) rigid; stiff; stiff-necked 2.(指办事) rigid; inflexible; mechanical: 做事～ work in a mechanical manner

【死不】 sǐbù stubbornly refuse to; would rather die than: ～要脸 be utterly shameless

【死不瞑目】 sǐbùmíngmù not close one's eyes when one dies; die with a grievance or everlasting regret

【死产】 sǐchǎn 〈*Med.*〉 stillbirth

【死党】 sǐdǎng sworn followers; diehard followers

【死得其所】 sǐdéqísuǒ die a worthy death

【死敌】 sǐdí deadly enemy; mortal enemy; implacable foe

【死地】 sǐdì a fatal position; deathtrap: 置之～ confront a person with the danger of death

【死而后已】 sǐ'érhòuyǐ until one's dying day; to the end of one's days: 鞠躬尽瘁，～ have dedicated one's life to a cause; bend one's back to the task until one's dying day

【死光】 sǐguāng death ray

【死鬼】 sǐguǐ devil: 你这个～ You devil!

【死胡同】 sǐhútòng blind alley; dead end

【死缓】 sǐhuǎn 〈*Law*〉 stay of execution; death sentence with reprieve: 两年～ death sentence with a two-year reprieve

【死灰复燃】 sǐhuī-fùrán dying embers glowing again; resurgence; revival

【死活】 sǐhuó 1.(死或活) life or death; fate: 不知～ have no idea of death or danger 2.(无论如何) anyway; simply: 他～不承认。He simply won't admit it

【死火山】 sǐhuǒshān extinct volcano

【死记】 sǐjì memorize mechanically; learn by rote

【死记硬背】 sǐjì-yìngbèi mechanical memorizing

【死寂】 sǐjì 〈*written*〉 deathly stillness

【死角】 sǐjiǎo 1.(影响达不到的地方) a spot as yet untouched by sth. 2.〈*Mil.*〉 dead angle; blind angle; dead space

【死校】 sǐjiào 〈*Printing*〉 proofread strictly

【死结】 sǐjié fast knot

【死里逃生】 sǐlǐ-táoshēng escape from the jaws of death; have a narrow escape; barely escape with one's life

【死力】 sǐlì 1.(最大力量) all one's strength; one's utmost effort 2.(使出最大力量) with all one's strength; with might and main

【死路】 sǐlù 1.(走不通的路) blind alley 2.(喻毁灭) the road to ruin: ～一条 a way to ruin / 自寻～ court self-destruction; bring ruin upon oneself

【死面】 sǐmiàn unleavened dough

【死命】 sǐmìng 1.(指命运) doom; death: 致人于～ bring doom to sb. 2.(拼命) desperately: ～挣扎 struggle desperately

【死难】 sǐnàn die in a misfortune; die in a political incident: ～烈士 martyr / 地震～同胞 compatriots died in the earthquake

【死皮赖脸】 sǐpí-làiliǎn thick-skinned and hard to shake off; brazen-faced and unreasonable

【死棋】 sǐqí a dead piece in a game of chess; a hopeless case; a stupid move

【死气沉沉】 sǐqì-chénchén lifeless; spiritless; stagnant

【死契】 sǐqì irrevocable title deed

【死囚】 sǐqiú a convict sentenced to death; a convict awaiting execution; condemned prisoner

【死球】 sǐqiú 〈*Sports*〉 dead ball

【死去活来】 sǐqù-huólái half dead; half alive; hovering between life and death

【死人】 sǐrén a dead person; the dead; (the) defunct

【死生由命】 sǐ-shēng yǒu mìng Life and death are foreordained.

【死尸】 sǐshī corpse; dead body

【死守】 sǐshǒu 1.（拼死守住）defend to the death; defend to the last; make a last-ditch defense：～该城 defend the city to the death 2.（墨守）obstinately cling to; rigidly adhere to

【死水】 sǐshuǐ stagnant water

【死胎】 sǐtāi 〈*Med*.〉 stillborn fetus; stillbirth

【死亡】 sǐwáng death; doom

【死亡保险】 sǐwáng bǎoxiǎn insurance against death; mortality insurance

【死亡抚恤金】 sǐwáng fǔxùjīn death benefits

【死亡鉴定】 sǐwáng jiàndìng verification of death

【死亡率】 sǐwánglǜ death rate; mortality rate

【死亡诊断】 sǐwáng zhěnduàn medical diagnosis on death

【死亡证明书】 sǐwáng zhèngmíngshū death certificate; certificate of death

【死无对证】 sǐwúduìzhèng the dead cannot bear witness

【死无葬身之地】 sǐ wú zhàngshēn zhī dì die without a burial place; come to a bad end

【死心】 sǐxīn drop the idea forever; have no more illusions about the matter

【死心塌地】 sǐxīn-tādì be dead set; be hell-bent

【死心眼儿】 sǐxīnyǎnr 1.（固执）stubborn; as obstinate as a mule 2.（指人）a person with a one-track mind

【死信】 sǐxìn 1.（无法投递的信）dead letter 2.（死讯）news of sb's death

【死刑】 sǐxíng 〈*Law*〉 death penalty; death sentence; capital punishment; nameless death

【死旋】 sǐxuán 〈*Skating*〉 death spiral

【死讯】 sǐxùn news of sb's death

【死一般】 sǐyībān deathly：～苍白 deathly pale / ～的沉寂 deathly silence

【死因】 sǐyīn cause of death

【死硬】 sǐyìng 1.（呆板）stiff; inflexible 2.（顽固）very obstinate; die-hard

【死硬派】 sǐyìngpài diehards; extreme conservative

【死有余辜】 sǐyǒuyúgū even death would be too good for him; even death would not expiate all his crimes

【死于非命】 sǐyú-fēimìng die an unnatural death

【死者】 sǐzhě the dead; the deceased; the departed

【死罪】 sǐzuì capital crime; capital offense

祀 (sì) make an offering as a sacrifice to a god

【祀天】 sìtiān make a sacrifice to Heaven

四 (sì) four; forth：第～号 Number Four / 第～卷 Volume Four; the Fourth Volume

【四百】 sìbǎi four hundred; four-hundredth

【四倍】 sìbèi quadruple; quadruplicate; quadruplication (n.)

【四边】 sìbiān (on) four sides; all sides

【四边形】 sìbiānxíng quadrilateral

【四不像】 sìbùxiàng 1.（麋鹿）David's deer; *mi-lu* 2.（不伦不类的东西）nondescript; neither fish nor fowl

【四冲程】 sìchōngchéng 〈*Mech*.〉 four-stroke

【四冲程内燃机】 sìchōngchéng nèiránjī 〈*Mech*.〉 four-stroke engine

【四重唱】 sìchóngchàng 〈*Music*〉 (vocal) quartet

【四重奏】 sìchóngzòu 〈*Music*〉 (instrumental) quartet

【四处】 sìchù all around; in all directions; everywhere：～奔走 go hither and thither

【四次】 sìcì quartic

【四二一综合症】 sì-èr-yī zōnghézhèng the 'four two one' multiple symptom

【四发远程客机】 sìfā yuǎnchéng kèjī four-jet long haul airliner

【四方】 sìfāng 1.（各处）the four directions (north, south, east, west); all sides; all quarters 2.（正方形）square 3.（立方体的）cubic

【四方步】 sìfāngbù big and leisure steps

【四分五裂】 sìfēn-wǔliè fall apart; be rent by disunity; be all split up; disintegrate

【四分之一】 sìfēnzhīyī a quarter; one quarter; one-fourth

【四分之一决赛】 sìfēnzhīyī juésài quarter-final
【四个现代化】 sìgè xiàndàihuà the four modernizations: 实现～ achieve the four modernizations (of agriculture, industry, national defense, and science and technology)
【四海】 sìhǎi the four seas; the whole country; the whole world: ～之内皆兄弟。All within the Four Seas are brothers.
【四害】 sìhài the four pests
【四合院】 sìhéyuàn *siheyuan*, a compound with houses around a courtyard
【四胡】 sìhú 〈*Music*〉 *sihu* ; 4-stringed Chinese violin
【四环素】 sìhuánsù 〈*Pharm.*〉 tetracycline
【四级考试】 sìjí kǎoshì Band Four Test
【四季】 sìjì the four seasons
【四季豆】 sìjìdòu kidney bean
【四郊】 sìjiāo suburbs; outskirts
【四开】 sìkāi 〈*Printing*〉 quarto
【四棱柱】 sìléngzhù quadratic prism
【四棱锥】 sìléngzhuī quadrilateral pyramid
【四邻】 sìlín one's near neighbors
【四轮驱动】 sìlún qūdòng 〈*Auto*〉 four-wheel drive
【四面】 sìmiàn (on) four sides; (on) all sides: ～出击 hit out in all directions
【四面八方】 sìmiàn-bāfāng all directions; all quarters; all around; far and near
【四面楚歌】 sìmiàn-chǔgē be besieged on all sides; be utterly isolated; land oneself in a tight spot
【四旁】 sìpáng 1.(前后左右) back and front, left and right; all around 2.(四周) the 'four sides'
【四平八稳】 sìpíng-bāwěn 1.(稳当) very steady; well organized: 办事～ be dependable in work 2.(缺乏创新精神) lacking in initiative and overcautious
【四起】 sìqǐ rise from all directions: 音乐声～。Sounds of music were heard from all around.
【四千】 sìqiān four thousand; four thousandth
【四散】 sìsàn scatter in all directions
【四舍五入】 sìshě-wǔrù 〈*Math.*〉 rounding (off); to the nearest whole number
【四十】 sìshí forty; fortieth
【四十五转唱片】 sìshíwǔzhuàn chàngpiàn forty-five
【四时】 sìshí the four seasons
【四通八达】 sìtōng-bādá extend in all directions
【四万】 sìwàn forty thousand; forty thousandth
【四项基本原则】 sìxiàng jīběn yuánzé Four Fundamental Principles; the four cardinal principles ‖ the socialist road, the people's democratic dictatorship, Marxism-Leninism and Mao Zedong Thought, and the leadership of the Communist Party of China
【四小龙】 sìxiǎolóng the four little dragons
【四野】 sìyě the surrounding country; a vast expanse of open ground
【四月】 sìyuè April
【四则】 sìzé 〈*Math.*〉 the four fundamental operations of arithmetic: ～运算 arithmetic; four fundamental rules
【四肢】 sìzhī the four limbs; arms and legs
【四肢麻痹】 sìzhī mábì 〈*Med.*〉 quadriplegia
【四周】 sìzhōu all around

驷 (sì)

【驷马】 sìmǎ 〈*written*〉 a team of four horses: 一言既出，～难追。Even four horses cannot take back what one has said.

寺 (sì) 1.〈*Buddhism*〉 temple: 白塔～ White Pagoda Temple / 碧云～ the Temple of Azure Clouds 2.〈*Ialam*〉 mosque: 清真～ mosque
【寺观】 sìguàn temple
【寺庙】 sìmiào temple
【寺院】 sìyuàn temple; monastery

似 (sì) 1.(像) similar; like: 白～雪 as white as snow 2.(似乎) seem; appear: ～曾相识 seem to have met before 3.(超过) 生活一年胜～一年。Life has been getting better year by year.
(另见"似"shì)
【似懂非懂】 sìdǒngfēidǒng have only vague idea
【似海绵状】 sìhǎimiánzhuàng spongy
【似乎】 sìhū it seems; as if; seemingly: ～

要下雨了。It looks like rain
【似是而非】 sìshì'érfēi apparently right but actually wrong; specious
【似水流年】 sìshuǐliúnián As a fleeting wave, youth passes.
【似笑非笑】 sìxiàofēixiào a faint smile on one's face; with a spurious smile

伺(sì) watch; await
(另见“伺”cì)
【伺服】 sìfú servo
【伺服传动】 sìfú chuándòng servodrive
【伺服电动机】 sìfú diàndòngjī servomotor
【伺服机构】 sìfú jīgòu servomechanism
【伺服控制】 sìfú kòngzhì servocontrol
【伺机】 sìjī watch for one's chance; wait for a opportunity
【伺隙】 sìxì wait for a opportunity

饲(sì) raise; rear
【饲槽】 sìcáo feeding trough
【饲草】 sìcǎo forage grass
【饲料】 sìliào forage; fodder; feed: 精～(fodder) concentrates; fine fodder / 青贮～silage; ensilage / 猪～ pig feed
【饲养】 sìyǎng raise; rear: ～绵羊 rear sheep
【饲养场】 sìyǎngchǎng feed lot; dry lot; farm
【饲养员】 sìyǎngyuán 1.(饲养牲畜的) stockman; breeder 2.(饲养家禽的) poultry raiser 3.(动物园的) animal keeper (in a zoo)

嗣(sì) 1.(继承) succeed; inherit 2.(子孙) heir; descendant
【嗣后】 sìhòu hereafter; subsequently; afterwards; later on
【嗣位】 sìwèi succeed to the throne

俟[竢](sì) watch for; wait for
【俟机】 sìjī watch for one's chance; wait for a opportune

肆(sì) 1.(肆意) wanton; unbridled: 大～攻击 wantonly vilify; launch an unbridled attack against 2.(铺子) shop: 茶楼酒～ teahouses and wineshops 3.(四) four; forth
【肆口谩骂】 sìkǒu-mànmà rail and swear at wildly
【肆虐】 sìnüè indulge in wanton massacre or persecution; wreak havoc
【肆无忌惮】 sìwújìdàn unbridled; brazen; unscrupulous: ～地攻击 make unbridled attacks
【肆意】 sìyì wantonly; recklessly; willfully: ～攻击 attack wantonly / ～挥霍 freely squander

song

松[鬆 2－6](sōng) 1.(松树) pine; pinetree: 红～ Korean pine / 马尾～ masson pine / 油～ Chinese pine 2.(松散) loose; slack: 你的鞋带～了。Your shoelace has come loose. 3.(使松) loosen; relax; slacken: ～一～螺丝 loosen the screw a little 4.(经济宽裕) not hard up; be better off 5.(不坚实) light and flaky; soft: 这里的土质很～。The soil here is very loose. 6.(碎末食品) dried meat floss; dried minced meat: 猪肉～ dried minced pork
【松柏长青】 sōng-bǎi chángqīng remain evergreen as the pine and cypress; the pine and cypress stay evergreen
【松柏园】 sōngbǎiyuán pinetum
【松绑】 sōngbǎng untie a person
【松弛】 sōngchí 1.(不坚实) limp; flabby; slack: 肌肉～ flaccid muscles 2.(不紧张) lax: 纪律～ lax discipline
【松动】 sōngdòng 1.(不拥挤) become less crowded 2.(经济宽裕) not hard up 3.(有所放松) become flexible: 禁运在很大程度上有了～。The embargo was considerably relaxed. 4.(活动) shaky; unsteady; loose: 这牙有点～了。The tooth is a bit loose.
【松果】 sōngguǒ pine cone
【松果体】 sōngguǒtǐ 〈*Anat.*〉 pineal body; pineal gland; pineal (adj.)
【松果腺】 sōngguǒxiàn 〈*Anat.*〉 pineal gland; pineal (adj.)
【松花】 sōnghuā preserved egg
【松花蛋】 sōnghuādàn 同“松花”
【松节油】 sōngjiéyóu 〈*Chem.*〉 turpentine (oil)
【松紧】 sōngjǐn 1.(松紧程度) degree of tightness 2.(伸缩) elasticity

【松紧带】 sōngjǐndài elastic webbing; elastic cord; elastic

【松劲】 sōngjìn relax one's efforts; slacken (off)

【松口】 sōngkǒu 1.(张口放开) relax one's bite and release what is held 2.(不坚持) become less intransigent; soften; relent

【松快】 sōng·kuai 1.(不拥挤) less crowded 2.(轻松爽快) feel relieved 3.(宽畅) relax

【松明】 sōngmíng pine torch

【松球】 sōngqiú pine cone

【松仁】 sōngrén pine seed

【松软】 sōngruǎn 1.(指物) soft; spongy 2.(指肢体) loose

【松散】 sōngsǎn 1.(指结构) loose 2.(指精神) inattentive

【松散】 sōng·san relax; take one's ease

【松手】 sōngshǒu loosen one's grip; let go; release one's hold

【松鼠】 sōngshǔ squirrel

【松树】 sōngshù pine; pinetree

【松松垮垮】 sōng·sōng-kuǎkuǎ behave in a lax, undisciplined way; be slack and perfunctory

【松涛】 sōngtāo the soughing of the wind in the pines

【松土】 sōngtǔ 〈*Agric.*〉 loosen the soil; scarify the soil

【松土机】 sōngtǔjī loosener; scarifier

【松香】 sōngxiāng resin; colophony

【松懈】 sōngxiè relax; slacken; slack: 纪律～ loosen discipline / 学习～ slack off in one's studies

【松心】 sōngxīn feel relieved

【松针】 sōngzhēn pine needle

【松脂】 sōngzhī rosin; pine resin

【松子】 sōngzǐ 1.(松果) pine nut 2.(松仁) pine seed; pine nut kernel

【松嘴】 sōngzuǐ 见"松口"

怂［慫］(sǒng)

【怂恿】 sǒngyǒng instigate; incite; egg sb. on; abet

耸［聳］(sǒng)

1.(耸立) towering; lofty 2.(使人吃惊) alarm; shock: 危言～听 exaggerate things just to frighten people

【耸动】 sǒngdòng 1.(向上动) shrug (one's shoulders) 2.(使人震动) create a sensation

【耸肩】 sǒngjiān shrug one's shoulders

【耸立】 sǒnglì tower aloft

【耸人听闻】 sǒngréntīngwén deliberately exaggerate so as to create a sensation

【耸入云霄】 sǒngrù-yúnxiāo tower to the skies

悚(sǒng)

【悚惧】 sǒngjù fear; dread; be afraid

【悚然】 sǒngrán terrified; horrified: ～而立 stand up terrified

讼(sòng)

1.(打官司) bring a case to court 2.(争辩) dispute; argue

【讼棍】 sònggùn pettifogger; shyster; inferior lawyer

【讼事】 sòngshì lawsuit; litigation

颂(sòng)

1.(颂扬) praise; extol; eulogize; laud: 歌～ sing the praises of 2.(颂歌) song; ode; paean; eulogy: 《祖国～》 *Ode to Our Motherland*

【颂词】 sòngcí 1.(称赞) complimentary address; panegyric; eulogy: 致～ make complimentary address 2.〈*Foreign Affairs*〉 a speech delivered by an ambassador on presentation of his credentials

【颂歌】 sònggē song; ode

【颂古非今】 sònggǔ-fēijīn eulogize the past and condemn the present; extol the past to negate the present

【颂扬】 sòngyáng sing sb's praises; laud; extol; eulogize

送(sòng)

1.(运送) deliver; carry: ～报 deliver newspaper / ～信 deliver a letter / 孩子把书～回书架。The boy carried back the book to the shelf. 2.(赠送) give as a present; give: ～本书留作纪念 give sb. a book as a souvenir 3.(伴送) see sb. off or out; accompany; escort: ～孩子上托儿所 take a child to the nursery / ～朋友去机场 accompany a friend to the airport

【送别】 sòngbié see sb. off: 握手～ shake hands to say good-bye

【送殡】 sòngbìn attend a funeral; take part in a funeral procession

【送餐到房服务】 sòngcān dàofáng fúwù room

service
【送达】 sòngdá service：及时～ timely delivery / 迅速～ express delivery / 逾期～ delay in delivery
【送达传票】 sòngdá chuánpiào service of summons
【送达地址】 sòngdá dìzhǐ address for service
【送达日期】 sòngdá rìqī date of service
【送达文件】 sòngdá wénjiàn document for service
【送达证书】 sòngdá zhèngshū certificate of delivery
【送电】 sòngdiàn power transmission
【送话器】 sònghuàqì 〈*Electr.*〉 microphone
【送还】 sònghuán give back；return：把书～图书馆。Return the book to the library.
【送货】 sònghuò deliver goods
【送货回单】 sònghuò huídān delivery receipt
【送交】 sòngjiāo deliver；hand over
【送旧迎新】 sòngjiù-yíngxīn see off the old and welcome the new；ring out the Old Year and ring in the New
【送客】 sòngkè see a visitor out
【送礼】 sònglǐ give sb. a present；present a gift to sb.
【送命】 sòngmìng lose one's life；get killed；go to one's doom
【送人情】 sòngrénqíng **1.**（给人好处）do favors at no great cost to oneself **2.**（送礼）make a gift of sth.
【送丧】 sòngsāng attend a funeral；take part in a funeral procession
【送死】 sòngsǐ 〈*colloq.*〉 court death
【送往迎来】 sòngwǎng-yínglái see off those who depart and welcome those who arrive；speed the parting guests and welcome the new arrivals
【送信】 sòngxìn deliver letters：今天不～。There is no delivery of letters today.
【送信儿】 sòngxìnr 〈*colloq.*〉 send word；go and tell
【送行】 sòngxíng **1.**（送别）see sb. off；wish sb. bon voyage：到机场给人～ go to the airport to see sb. off **2.**（饯行）give a send-off party
【送葬】 sòngzàng take part in a funeral procession
【送站】 sòngzhàn go to the railway station to see sb. off
【送终】 sòngzhōng attend upon a dying parent or other senior member of one's family；bury a parent

诵（sòng） **1.**（读出声来）read aloud；chant **2.**（背诵）recite
【诵读】 sòngdú read aloud；chant

sou

搜［蒐］（sōu） search：他们～遍了林子的每个地方。They searched every part of the forest.
【搜捕】 sōubǔ track down and arrest
【搜查】 sōuchá search；ransack；rummage；seek：～赃物 search for stolen goods
【搜查证】 sōucházhèng document of search；search warrant
【搜刮】 sōuguā claw；extort；plunder；expropriate；fleece：～人民 fleece the people
【搜集】 sōují collect；gather：～情报 collect information / ～数据 gather data / ～资料 collect materials
【搜罗】 sōuluó collect；gather；recruit：～人才 recruit qualified persons；scout for talent
【搜身】 sōushēn frisk；make a body search；search the person
【搜索】 sōusuǒ hunting；search for；hunt for；scout around
【搜索枯肠】 sōusuǒ-kūcháng rack one's brains（for fresh ideas or apt expressions）
【搜寻】 sōuxún search for；look for；seek；frisk
【搜腰包】 sōuyāobāo search sb's pockets；search sb. for money and valuables
【搜章摘句】 sōuzhāng-zhāijù search for chapters and pick sentences

嗖［颼］（sōu） 〈*onomat.*〉 whiz：炮弹～的一声飞过去了。A shell whizzed past.

馊（sōu） sour；spoiled：菜～了。The dish has spoiled.
【馊主意】 sōuzhú·yi rotten idea；lousy idea

嗾（sǒu）

【嗾使】 sǒushǐ instigate; abet: ～某人犯罪 abet sb. in a crime / ～某人干坏事 instigate sb. to do evil

嗽 (sòu) cough: 干～ emit dry coughs

su

苏［蘇、甦[1]］(sū) 1.(苏醒) revive; come to; come back to life 2.(苏维埃) Soviet

【苏打】 sūdá soda

【苏打水】 sūdáshuǐ soda water

【苏区】 Sūqū Chinese Soviet area

【苏维埃】 Sūwéiāi Soviet

【苏醒】 sūxǐng revive; regain consciousness; come to; come round

【苏绣】 sūxiù Suzhou embroidery

酥 (sū) 1.(松脆) crisp; short 2.(点心) short pastry; shortbread 3.(肢体酥软) limp; weak; soft

【酥脆】 sūcuì crisp: ～的饼干 crisp biscuit

【酥麻】 sūmá limp and numb

【酥软】 sūruǎn limp; weak; soft

【酥糖】 sūtáng crunchy candy

【酥油】 sūyóu butter

【酥油茶】 sūyóuchá buttered tea

【酥油花】 sūyóuhuā buttered sculpture

俗 (sú) 1.(风俗) custom; convention 2.(普遍的) popular; common: 未能免～ have to do what others are doing 3.(庸俗) vulgar 4.(未皈依佛门的人) secular; lay: 僧～ monks and laymen; clergy and laity

【俗不可耐】 súbùkěnài unbearably vulgar

【俗称】 súchēng vulgar tongue; informal term

【俗词语】 súcíyǔ vulgarism

【俗话】 súhuà common saying; proverb

【俗名】 súmíng 1.(通俗的名称) popular name; local name 2.(未出家前的名字) original name

【俗气】 sú·qi vulgar; in poor taste

【俗曲】 súqǔ popular song

【俗人】 súrén 1.(一般人) civilian; ordinary people 2.(庸俗的人) vulgar person

【俗套】 sútào conventional pattern; convention: 不落～ conform to no conventional pattern

【俗文学】 súwénxué vulgar literature

【俗语】 súyǔ common saying; folk adage

夙 (sù) 1.(早) early in the morning 2.(素有的) old; long-standing

【夙世冤家】 sùshì-yuānjiā a bitter enemy; an enemy of former life

【夙兴夜寐】 sùxīng-yèmèi rise early and retire late; hard at work night and day

【夙夜】 sùyè morning and night

【夙怨】 sùyuàn old grudge

【夙愿】 sùyuàn long-cherished wish; constant wish: ～已偿 have one's long-cherished hope realized

【夙志】 sùzhì long-cherished ambition

诉 (sù) 1.(说给人听) tell; relate; inform: 告～ tell 2.(倾吐) complain; accuse: 控～ accuse / 倾～ pour out; unburden oneself of 3.(控告) appeal to; resort to: 上～ appeal to a higher court

【诉苦】 sùkǔ vent one's grievances; pour out one's woes

【诉述】 sùshù tell; relate; recount

【诉说】 sùshuō tell; relate; recount

【诉讼】 sùsòng lawsuit; litigation: 专利～ patent action / 损失赔偿～ action for damage

【诉讼案件】 sùsòng ànjiàn contentious case; court case

【诉讼保险】 sùsòng bǎoxiǎn insurance against litigation

【诉讼程序】 sùsòng chéngxù contentious procedure

【诉讼代理人】 sùsòng dàilǐrén law-agent; process attorney

【诉讼法】 sùsòngfǎ procedural law: 刑事～ criminal procedure law

【诉讼费】 sùsòngfèi costs; court costs

【诉讼合并】 sùsòng hébìng joinder of causes of action

【诉讼价值】 sùsòng jiàzhí amount of a claim

【诉讼权】 sùsòngquán right of action

【诉讼条例】 sùsòng tiáolì rules of procedure

【诉讼文书】 sùsòng wénshū charging document

【诉讼形式】 sùsòng xíngshì form of action

【诉讼自由】 sùsòng zìyóu freedom of action
【诉因】 sùyīn cause; cause of action
【诉冤】 sùyuān inform
【诉诸法律】 sùzhū fǎlǜ go to law; have recourse to law
【诉诸武力】 sùzhū wǔlì resort to force; appeal to arms; have recourse to force
【诉状】 sùzhuàng 〈*Law*〉 plaint; indictment

肃[肅](sù) 1.(恭敬) reverent; respectful 2.(严肃) solemn; serious; grave 3.(肃清) eliminate; mop up: ～贪 eliminate corruption
【肃反】 sùfǎn eliminate counter-revolutionaries
【肃静】 sùjìng solemn silence
【肃立】 sùlì stand as a mark of respect
【肃穆】 sùmù solemn and respectful
【肃清】 sùqīng eliminate; clean up; mop up: ～残敌 wipe out the remnants of the enemy
【肃然起敬】 sùrán-qǐjìng be filled with deep veneration
【肃然生畏】 sùrán-shēngwèi be struck with awe

素(sù) 1.(白色,本色) white: ～绢 white silk 2.(不花哨) plain; simple; quiet 3.(蔬菜瓜果等) vegetable: 吃～ be a vegetarian 4.(本来的) native 5.(基本物质) basic element 6.(向来) usually; habitually; always
【素不相识】 sùbùxiāngshí be strangers to each other; have never met before: 我与她～。I don't know her at all.
【素材】 sùcái material: 搜集～ gather material
【素菜】 sùcài vegetable dish
【素餐】 sùcān 1.(指饮食) vegetarian meal 2.(指人) be a vegetarian 3.(不干事白吃饭) not work for one's living: 尸位～ hold down a job without doing a stroke of work
【素常】 sùcháng usually; ordinarily
【素淡】 sùdàn quiet (color)
【素服】 sùfú white clothing (as a sign of mourning)
【素净】 sù·jing plain and neat; quiet (color)
【素酒】 sùjiǔ 1.(指酒) wine served at a vegetarian feast 2.(指筵席) vegetarian feast
【素来】 sùlái always; usually; all along: 他～守法。He always abides by the law.
【素昧平生】 sùmèi-píngshēng have never met before
【素描】 sùmiáo 1.〈*Arts*〉 sketch 2.〈*Literature*〉 literary sketch
【素日】 sùrì generally; usually
【素食】 sùshí 1.(指饮食、点心) vegetarian diet 2.(指人) be a vegetarian
【素食者】 sùshízhě vegetarian
【素席】 sùxí vegetarian feast
【素雅】 sùyǎ simple but elegant; unadorned and in good taste
【素养】 sùyǎng accomplishment; attainment: 文学～ literary attainments
【素油】 sùyóu vegetable oil
【素有大志】 sùyǒudàzhì have always cherished a yearning for high enterprise
【素愿】 sùyuàn long-cherished wish; constant wish
【素质】 sùzhì 1.(指事物) quality; nature 2.(素养) accomplishment; attainment; level of competence: 科学文化～ cultural and scientific levels 3.〈*Psycho.*〉 diathesis

嗉[膆](sù)
【嗉子】 sù·zi crop: 鸡～ crop of a chicken

速(sù) 1.(迅速) fast; rapid; quick; speedy: ～去～回。Go and return quickly. 2.(速度) speed; velocity: 风～ wind speed / 声～ velocity of sound / 高～ high speed / 低～ low speed 3.(邀请) invite: 不～之客 uninvited guest; gate-crasher
【速成】 sùchéng quick method; express: ～教学 quick method of teaching; speeded-up educational program
【速冻】 sùdòng quick-freeze
【速动】 sùdòng quick acting
【速度】 sùdù 1.〈*Physics*〉 speed; velocity 2.(快慢) speed; rate; pace: 加快～ build up speed 3.〈*Music*〉 tempo
【速度表】 sùdùbiǎo autometer
【速度计】 sùdùjì speed indicator; speedometer
【速度计附里程表】 sùdùjì fù lǐchéngbiǎo (汽车路码表) speedometer and trip odometer
【速滑】 sùhuá 〈*Sports*〉 speed skating

【速滑冰鞋】 sùhuá bīngxié speed skate

【速记】 sùjì 1.(用速记法记录) make notes in shorthand; make shorthand notes 2.(速记法) shorthand; stenography

【速记符号】 sùjì fúhào shorthand; stenograph

【速记员】 sùjìyuán shorthand writer; stenographer

【速决】 sùjué quick decision

【速决战】 sùjuézhàn war of quick decision

【速率】 sùlǜ speed; rate

【速遣费】 sùqiǎnfèi dispatch; despatch: 支付～ payment of dispatch

【速遣费余额】 sùqiǎnfèi yú'é dispatch sum

【速溶】 sùróng instant

【速溶咖啡】 sùróng kāfēi instant coffee

【速食面】 sùshímiàn instant noodles

【速算】 sùsuàn rapid calculation

【速效】 sùxiào quick results

【速写】 sùxiě 1.〈*Arts*〉 sketch 2.(一种文体) literary sketch

【速战速决】 sùzhàn-sùjué fight a quick battle to force a quick decision

宿 (sù) 1.(住宿) lodge for the night; stay overnight: 借～ ask for a night's lodging 2.(旧有的) long-standing; old 3.(经历多的;年老的) veteran; old: ～将 veteran general

(另见"宿"xiǔ)

【宿娼】 sùchāng sleep with a prostitute

【宿仇】 sùchóu long-standing enmity

【宿敌】 sùdí old enemy

【宿根】 sùgēn 1.(多年生植物的根) perennial root 2.(二年生植物的根) biennial root

【宿疾】 sùjí chronic complaint; old trouble

【宿命论】 sùmìnglùn 〈*Philos*.〉 fatalism ‖ 宿命论者 fatalist

【宿舍】 sùshè hostel; living quarters; dormitory

【宿营】 sùyíng take up quarters; camp

【宿营地】 sùyíngdì camping site

【宿怨】 sùyuàn old grudge; old scores

【宿愿】 sùyuàn long-cherished wish; constant wish

【宿债】 sùzhài long-standing debt

塑 (sù) model; mold (AmE.); mould (BrE.)

【塑胶】 sùjiāo plastic cement

【塑胶跑道】 sùjiāo pǎodào Rekortan track

【塑料】 sùliào plastics; plastic (adj.): 工程～ engineering plastics / 泡沫～ foam plastics

【塑料薄膜】 sùliào báomó plastic film

【塑料工业】 sùliào gōngyè plastics industry

【塑料垃圾袋】 sùliào lājīdài plastic garbage bag

【塑料凉鞋】 sùliào liángxié plastic sandals

【塑料炸弹】 sùliào zhàdàn plastic bomb

【塑像】 sùxiàng 1.(塑造人像) mold a statue 2.(塑成的人像) statue

【塑造】 sùzào 1.(造型) model; mold: ～石膏像 mold a plaster figure 2.(描写) portray: ～典型形象 create typical characters

溯[泝、遡] (sù) 1.(逆水行进) go against the stream 2.(追溯) trace back; recall: 回～往事 recall past events

【溯流而上】 sùliú'érshàng going up a river; go upstream

【溯源】 sùyuán trace to the source: 追本～ track down the origin; trace to the source

簌 (sù)

【簌簌】 sùsù 1.〈*onomat*.〉 rustle: 风吹树叶～响。The leaves are rustling in the wind. 2.(眼泪纷纷落下) (tears) streaming down

suan

酸[痠[5]] (suān) 1.〈*Chem*.〉 acid: 硫～ sulfuric acid / 硝～ nitric acid / 盐～ hydrochloric acid 2.(酸味) sour; tart 3.(悲痛;伤心) sick at heart; grieved; distressed: 令人辛～的往事 sad memories 4.(迂腐) pedantic; impractical 5.(酸痛) tingle; ache: 腰～背痛 have a pain in the back; have a backache

【酸菜】 suāncài Chinese sauerkraut; pickled Chinese cabbage

【酸楚】 suānchǔ grieved; distressed

【酸碱度】 suānjiǎndù pH value

【酸辣汤】 suānlàtāng vinegar-pepper soup

【酸溜溜】 suānliūliū 1.(酸味) tart; sour 2.(酸痛) pain; tingle; ache: 周身～ have a vague feeling of pain all over **3**.（心里难过）sad; mournful **4**.（说话尖刻）sharp-tongued; acrimonious **5**.（迂腐）pedantic

【酸梅】 suānméi smoked plum; dark plum

【酸梅汤】 suānméitāng sweet-sour plum juice

【酸牛奶】 suānniúnǎi yoghurt; sour milk

【酸软】 suānruǎn aching and limp

【酸甜苦辣】 suān-tián-kǔ-là sour, sweet, bitter, hot; joys and sorrows of life

【酸痛】 suāntòng ache：四肢～ have aches in the limbs

【酸味】 suānwèi tart flavor; acidity

【酸性】 suānxìng 〈*Chem*.〉 acidity

【酸烟】 suānyān acid fume

【酸雨】 suānyǔ acid rain

【酸枣】 suānzǎo wild jujube

【酸中毒】 suānzhòngdú acidosis

蒜（suàn） garlic：大～ garlic / 青～ garlic sprout

【蒜黄】 suānhuáng blanched garlic leaves

【蒜苗】 suānmiáo garlic bolt

【蒜泥】 suānní mashed garlic

【蒜头】 suāntóu the head of garlic

【蒜油】 suānyóu garlic oil

算［祘］（suàn） **1**.（计算）calculate; reckon; compute; figure：～一下生产成本 calculate the cost of production / 她～出了我们欠她的钱。She reckoned the money we owed her. **2**.（计算进去）include; count **3**.（谋划）plan; calculate **4**.（推测）think; suppose：我～他今天会来。I think he will come today. **5**.（当作）consider; regard as; count as **6**.（算数）carry weight; count：不应该由一两个人说了～。One or two persons should not have the final say. / 他说了不～。His words do not count. **7**.（总算）at long last; in the end; finally

【算法】 suànfǎ 〈*Math*.〉 algorithm

【算法语言】 suànfǎ yǔyán algorithmic language; ALGOL

【算计】 suàn·ji **1**.（计算）calculate; reckon **2**.（考虑）consider; plan **3**.（估计）expect; figure; guess：我～他很快回来。I figure he'll be back soon. **4**.（暗中谋划）scheme; plot：～人 scheme against others

【算了】 suàn·le let it be; let it pass：～，别说了。That's enough! Let it go at that.

【算命】 suànmìng fortune-telling

【算命先生】 suànmìng xiān·sheng fortune-teller

【算盘】 suànpán **1**.（珠算）abacus：打～ use an abacus **2**.（个人打算）selfish calculations：他老打个人小～。He is always calculating.

【算盘珠】 suànpánzhū abacus ball

【算是】 suànshì at last

【算术】 suànshù arithmetic

【算术题】 suànshùtí arithmetic exercises

【算数】 suànshù count; hold; stand：我说话是～的。I mean what I say.

【算学】 suànxué **1**.（数学）mathematics **2**.（算术）arithmetic

【算账】 suànzhàng **1**.（计算账目）do accounts; balance the books; make out bills：～算得快 be quick at accounts **2**.（清算）square accounts with sb.; get even with sb.：我回头找你～。I will get even with you.

sui

尿（suī） urine; piss：尿～（niàosuī）piss (v.)

（另见"尿"niào）

【尿脬】 suīpāo bladder; urinary bladder

虽［雖］（suī） **1**.〈*conj*.〉 though; although：他～很努力，但没成功。For all his efforts, he didn't succeed. **2**.（纵然）even if; even though

【虽然】 suīrán 〈*conj*.〉 though; although

【虽死犹荣】 suīsǐ-yóuróng honored though dead; have died a glorious death

【虽死犹生】 suīsǐ-yóushēng live on in spirit

【虽则】 suīzé 〈*conj*.〉 though; although

绥（suí） **1**.（安好）peaceful **2**.（安抚）pacify

【绥靖】 suíjìng pacify; appease

【绥靖政策】 suíjìng zhèngcè policy of appeasement

随［隨］（suí） **1**.（跟随）follow：孩子～着母亲进了房间。The child followed his mother into the room. **2**.（顺从）comply with; adapt to **3**.（任凭）let (sb. do as he likes) **4**.（顺便）along with **5**.（相像）look like; resemble：她～妈妈。She looks like her mother.

【随笔】 suíbǐ **1**.（指文体）informal essay;

jotting 2.（笔记） short notes

【随便】 suíbiàn 1.（按某人意愿）anyhow; any：请～坐。Sit anywhere. / 随你的便。Do as you like. / 你～什么时候来都行。You may come any time you like. 2.（不加限制）casual; random; informal 3.（不拘礼）do as one pleases 4.（不加考虑）careless; slipshod：说话～ not be careful about the way one talks 5.（任意）wanton; willful; arbitrary：～歪曲事实 make willful distortion of the facts

【随波逐流】 suíbō-zhúliú drift with the tide

【随常】 suícháng ordinary; common

【随处】 suíchù everywhere; anywhere：～可见 can be seen everywhere

【随从】 suícóng 1.（跟随上司）accompany; attend 2.（随员）retinue; suite; entourage

【随带】 suídài 1.（随同带去）going along with 2.（随身携带）have sth. taken along with one

【随地】 suídì anywhere; everywhere：请勿～吐痰。No spitting.

【随风转舵】 suífēng-zhuǎnduò trim one's sails; take one's cue from changing conditions

【随行就市】 suíháng-jiùshì fluctuate along with market changes

【随和】 suí·he amiable; obliging; easy to approach

【随后】 suíhòu 〈*abv.*〉 soon afterwards

【随机】 suíjī 1.〈*Computer*〉 random 2.〈*Math.*〉 stochastic

【随机存储器】 suíjī cúnchǔqì 〈*Computer*〉 random access memory (RAM)

【随机存取】 suíjī cúnqǔ 〈*Computer*〉 random access; random-access (adj.)

【随机事件】 suíjī shìjiàn random event

【随机现象】 suíjī xiànxiàng chance phenomenon

【随机应变】 suíjī yìngbiàn adapt oneself to changing conditions; act according to circumstances

【随即】 suíjí immediately; presently：她～就来了。She came immediately.

【随叫随到】 suíjiào-suídào be on call at any hour

【随军】 suíjūn with an army

【随口】 suíkǒu speak thoughtlessly; blurt out whatever comes into one's head：～答应 say 'yes' absentmindedly; agree without thinking

【随人俯仰】 suírén-fǔyǎng be at sb's beck and call; follow sb. servilely

【随身】 suíshēn (carry) on one's person; (take) with one

【随身听】 suíshēntīng walkman

【随身行李】 suíshēn xíng·li personal luggage

【随声附和】 suíshēng-fùhè echo what others say; chime in with others

【随时】 suíshí 1.（任何时候）at any time; at all times 2.（有需要时）whenever necessary; as the occasion demands：～调节温度 regulate the temperature whenever necessary

【随时随地】 suíshí-suídì at all times and places

【随手】 suíshǒu conveniently; without extra trouble：请～关门。Close the door after you. / 勿忘～关灯。Don't forget turn the light off.

【随俗】 suísú comply with convention; do as everybody else does

【随同】 suítóng be in company with

【随心所欲】 suíxīnsuǒyù follow one's inclinations; have one's own way; do as one pleases

【随行人员】 suíxíng rényuán entourtage; suite; party

【随意】 suíyì at will; as one pleases：请～! Help yourselves! Please!

【随意肌】 suíyìjī 〈*Anat.*〉 voluntary muscle

【随遇而安】 suíyù'ér'ān feel at home wherever one is; be able to adapt oneself to different circumstances

【随员】 suíyuán 1.（随行人员）suite; retinue; entourage 2.〈*Foreign Affairs*〉 attaché

【随着】 suí·zhe along with; in the wake of; in pace with：～生产的发展 with the growth of production

髓 (suí) 1.（骨髓）marrow 2.（像骨髓之物）sth. like marrow：脊～ spinal cord 3.（精髓）pith

岁［歳、嵗、歲］(suì) 1.（年）year 2.（年龄）year

(of age)：七～的女孩儿 a seven-year-old girl; a little girl seven years old / 你几～了? How old are you? 3.(年成) year (for crops)

【岁差】 suìchā 〈*Astron.*〉 precession of the equinoxes

【岁出】 suìchū annual expenditure

【岁寒三友】 suìhán-sānyǒu three durable plants of winter

【岁寒知松柏】 suìhán zhī sōngbǎi only when the year grows cold do we see the qualities of the pine and the cypress; adversity reveals virtue

【岁末】 suìmò the end of the year

【岁暮】 suìmù 1.〈*written*〉 the close of the year：～天寒 Cold weather sets in as the year draws to its close. 2.(喻年老) old age

【岁入】 suìrù revenue; annual income

【岁首】 suìshǒu the beginning of the year

【岁数】 suì·shu age; years：您多大～了? May I know your age?

【岁月】 suìyuè years：～如流。Time is fleeting.

碎 (suì) 1.(破碎) break to pieces; smash：玻璃杯打～了。The glass is smashed to pieces. 2.(不完整的) broken; fragmentary：～玻璃 bits of broken glass 3.(唠叨) garrulous; gabby

【碎步儿】 suìbùr quick short steps

【碎层云】 suìcéngyún 〈*Meteorol.*〉 fractostratus

【碎积云】 suìjīyún 〈*Meteorol.*〉 fractocumulus

【碎米】 suìmǐ broken rice

【碎片】 suìpiàn scrap; broken pieces

【碎尸万段】 suìshī-wànduàn tear sb. to shreds; cut sb. to pieces

【碎石】 suìshí 〈*Archit.*〉 crushed stones; broken stones

【碎石混凝土】 suìshí hùnníngtǔ crushed stone concrete

【碎石机】 suìshíjī stone crusher

【碎石路】 suìshílù broken stone road; macadam road

【碎石术】 suìshíshù 〈*Med.*〉 lithotrity

【碎屑】 suìxiè bits; scraps; extremely small bits

遂 (suì) 1.(顺心,如意) satisfy; fulfill 2.(成功) succeed：功成名～ have one's work done and one's name recognized 3.(于是,就) then; thereupon

【遂心】 suìxīn after one's own heart; to one's liking

【遂心所欲】 suìxīnsuǒyù one's liking; satisfy one's desire

【遂意】 suìyì to one's liking

【遂愿】 suìyuàn have one's wish fulfilled

隧 (suì)

【隧道】 suìdào tunnel：如果你驾车走山路，得穿过许多～。If you drive on the mountain road, you'll go through a lot of tunnels.

【隧洞】 suìdòng tunnel

穗 (suì) 1.(庄稼的穗) the ear of grain; spike：麦～儿 the ear of wheat 2.(装饰品) tassel; fringe

【穗子】 suì·zi tassel; fringe

邃 (suì) 〈*written*〉 remote; ancient; distant

sun

孙[孫] (sūn) 1.(孙子) grandson (m.); granddaughter (f.)：祖～ grandfather and grandson 2.(孙子以后各代) generations below that of the grandchild：玄～ great-great-grandson / 曾～ great-grandson 3.(植物再生的) second growth of plants

【孙女】 sūnnǚ granddaughter

【孙子】 sūn·zi grandson

损 (sǔn) 1.(减少) decrease; lose 2.(损害) harm; damage：有益无～ can only do good, not harm 3.(挖苦人) sarcastic; cutting; make caustic remarks 4.(恶毒;刻薄) mean; shabby

【损兵折将】 sǔnbīng-zhéjiàng suffer heavy casualties

【损公肥私】 sǔngōng-féisī injure the public interest to benefit one's private interests; seek private gain at public expense; feather one's nest at public expense

【损害】 sǔnhài harm; damage; injure; damnify：～国家利益 harm the interests of the state

【损害保险】 sǔnhài bǎoxiǎn insurance of damage

【损害程度】 sǔnhài chéngdù extent of damage
【损害赔偿】 sǔnhài péicháng compensation for damages; damages
【损害赔偿金】 sǔnhài péichángjīn damages
【损害赔偿诉讼】 sǔnhài péicháng sùsòng damage suit
【损耗】 sǔnhào 1.（损失消耗）loss; wear and tear 2.〈*Trade*〉wastage; spoilage
【损坏】 sǔnhuài breakdown; damage; injure; spoil: 发现～ detect a fault / 清理～ clear a fault
【损毁】 sǔnhuǐ damage; injure
【损人】 sǔnrén make caustic remarks
【损人利己】 sǔnrén-lìjǐ harm others to benefit oneself; benefit oneself at the expense of others
【损伤】 sǔnshāng 1.（伤害）damnify; harm; damage; injure; damnification 2.（损失）loss
【损失】 sǔnshī 1.（失去）lose: 使国家～大量外汇 cause the country heavy losses in foreign exchange 2.（失去的东西）loss: 赔偿～ compensate for a loss / 我的～很大。My losses have been very great.
【损失补偿保险】 sǔnshī bǔcháng bǎoxiǎn indemnity insurance
【损失额】 sǔnshī'é amount of loss
【损失赔偿】 sǔnshī péicháng compensation for damages
【损失赔偿金】 sǔnshī péichángjīn indemnification for loss
【损益】 sǔnyì 1.（减少和增加）increase and decrease: 斟酌～ consider making necessary adjustments 2.（赔和赚）profit and loss; gains and losses: ～相抵。The gains offset the losses.

笋［筍］(sǔn) bamboo shoot: 竹～ bamboo shoot
【笋干】 sǔngān dried bamboo shoots
【笋鸡】 sǔnjī young chicken; broiler
【笋尖】 sǔnjiān tender tips of bamboo shoots

隼 (sǔn) 〈*Zool.*〉falcon: 猎～ saker falcon

榫 (sǔn) tenon
【榫接】 sǔnjiē joggle; mortise joint
【榫头】 sǔn·tou tenon
【榫眼】 sǔnyǎn mortise

suo

莎 (suō)
【莎草】 suōcǎo 1.〈*Bot.*〉flatsedge 2.〈*Bot.*〉（香附子）nutglass flatsedge

唆 (suō) instigate; abet: 教～ instigate; abet
【唆使】 suōshǐ instigate; abet

梭 (suō) shuttle: 无～织机 shuttleless loom
【梭标】 suōbiāo spear
【梭巡】 suōxún 〈*written*〉patrol; move around to watch and guard
【梭子】 suō·zi 1.〈*Textiles*〉shuttle 2.（子弹夹）cartridge clip 3.〈*classifier*〉clip: 一～子弹 a whole clip of ammunition
【梭子蟹】 suō·zixiè swimming crab

睃 (suō) look askance at

羧 (suō) 〈*Chem.*〉carboxyl
【羧酸】 suōsuān 〈*Chem.*〉carboxylic acid; carboxylic (adj.)

蓑［簑］(suō)
【蓑衣】 suōyī straw rain cape; palm-bark rain cape

缩 (suō) 1.（收缩）contract; shrink: 热胀冷～ expand with heat and contract with cold 2.（退缩）draw back; withdraw; recoil: 把手～回 withdraw one's hand back
【缩编】 suōbiān reduce the staff
【缩尺】 suōchǐ scale
【缩短】 suōduǎn shorten; curtail; cut down: ～假期 curtail one's holidays / ～距离 diminish the distance / ～期限 shorten the duration
【缩格】 suōgé indent; leave an indentation: 每一段的开头都要～。Each new paragraph should be indented.
【缩减】 suōjiǎn reduce; cut: ～行政人员 retrench administrative staff
【缩进】 suōjìn indent; indentation (n.)
【缩膜包装】 suōmó bāozhuāng shrink-wrap:

～的词典 a shrink-wrapped dictionary
【缩手】 suōshǒu 1.（手缩回来）draw back one's hand 2.（不敢再做下去）shrink（from doing sth.）
【缩手缩脚】 suōshǒu-suōjiǎo 1.（指因冷）shrink with cold 2.（指做事）be over-cautious
【缩水】 suōshuǐ shrink：这衣服我洗后～了。The dress shrank when I washed it.
【缩水率】 suōshuǐlǜ shrinkage
【缩头缩脑】 suōtóu-suōnǎo 1.（畏缩）recoil in fear; be timid; be fainthearted 2.（不敢负责）shrink from responsibility
【缩微】 suōwēi micro; micrify
【缩微胶片】 suōwēi jiāopiàn micro-fiche
【缩小】 suōxiǎo reduce; lessen; shrink
【缩写】 suōxiě 1.〈*Gram*.〉abbreviate; abbreviation（n.）2.（缩短篇幅）abridge
【缩写本】 suōxiěběn abridged edition; abridged version
【缩印】 suōyìn reprint in a reduced format
【缩印本】 suōyìnběn reduction
【缩影】 suōyǐng epitome; miniature
【缩折式天线】 suōzhéshì tiānxiàn telescopic aerial; telescopic antenna

所［**听**］（suǒ） 1.（处所）place：住～dwelling place / 居无定～ without definite residence 2.（机构名称）研究～research institute 3.〈*classifier*〉一～大学 a college / 一～房子 a house
【所部】 suǒbù troops under one's command
【所长】 suǒzhǎng what one is good at; one's strong point; one's forte
【所得】 suǒdé income; earnings; gains
【所得税】 suǒdéshuì income tax
【所见所闻】 suǒjiàn-suǒwén what one sees and hears; all that one saw and heard
【所属】 suǒshǔ 1.（统属之下的）what is subordinate to one or under one's command：通令～一体遵照。All the units are to be informed that the instructions should be carried out. 2.（自己隶属的）affiliated with
【所谓】 suǒwèi 1.（所说的）what is called 2.（某些人所说的）so-called
【所向披靡】 suǒxiàng-pīmǐ carry all before one; sweep away all obstacles
【所向无前】 suǒxiàng-wúqián be invincible; be irresistible; break all enemy resistance
【所以】 suǒyǐ 1.（因此）so; therefore; as a result; hence 2.（指情由、举动）truth; facts：不知～ not know the truth 3.〈*Math*.〉hence（符号为 ∴）
【所以然】 suǒyǐrán the reason why：知其然而不知其～ know what is done but not why it is done
【所有】 suǒyǒu 1.（拥有）own; possess：这老人死后家产归谁～？Who did the property go to when the old man died? 2.（领有的东西）possessions：完全～ absolute property / 毗邻～ adjoining property / 尽其～ give everything one has; give one's all 3.（一切；全部）all; whole：～的学生 all the students
【所有格符号】 suǒyǒugé fúhào apostrophe（符号为 ’）
【所有权】 suǒyǒuquán proprietary rights; ownership; title
【所有制】 suǒyǒuzhì ownership; system of ownership
【所在】 suǒzài 1.（处所）place; location 2.（存在的地方）where：这就是问题的～。That is where the question arises.
【所在地】 suǒzàidì location; seat; site
【所致】 suǒzhì be caused by; be the result of

索（suǒ） 1.（大绳，大链）large rope 2.（搜寻）search 3.（要；取）demand; ask; exact 4.（孤单）all alone; all by oneself：离群～居 live all alone 5.（没有意味）dull; insipid
【索车】 suǒchē cable car
【索道】 suǒdào cableway; ropeway：高架～telpher
【索价】 suǒjià ask a price; charge
【索具】 suǒjù rigging
【索赔】 suǒpéi claim indemnity; claim damages：合法的～要求 lawful claim / 满足～的要求 meet a claim
【索赔期限】 suǒpéi qīxiàn deadline for demanding compensation
【索赔权】 suǒpéiquán right of claim
【索赔时限】 suǒpéi shíxiàn time limit for filing claims
【索赔证件】 suǒpéi zhèngjiàn claims document; document for claims
【索取】 suǒqǔ ask for; demand; exact; ex-

tort

【索然】 suǒrán dull; dry; insipid: 兴致～ have no interest at all

【索性】 suǒxìng may as well; just; simply

【索要】 suǒyào demand; ask

【索引】 suǒyǐn index: 书目～ title index

【索债】 suǒzhài demand payment of a debt

唢 (suǒ)

【唢呐】 suǒnà *suona*; Chinese cornet

琐 (suǒ) trivial; petty

【琐罗亚斯德教】 Suǒluóyàsīdéjiào 〈*Religion*〉 Zoroastrianism; Zoroastrian (adj.)

【琐事】 suǒshì trifles; trivial matters: 家庭～ household chores

【琐碎】 suǒsuì trifling; trivial

【琐闻】 suǒwén bits of news; scraps of information

【琐细】 suǒxì trifling; trivial

锁 (suǒ) **1.** (锁具) lock: 开～ open a look; unlock **2.** (上锁) lock up: ～门 lock a door / ～得好好地 under lock and key / ～在屋内 lock in / ～在屋外 lock out / 大门没～上。The gate wasn't locked. / 这门～不住。This door won't lock. **3.** (皱眉) knit **4.** (缝纫法) lockstitch: ～扣眼 do a lockstitch on a buttonhold

【锁臂缠腿】 suǒbì chántuǐ 〈*Wrestling*〉 bar arm with grapevine

【锁骨】 suǒgǔ 〈*Anat.*〉 clavicle; collarbone; clavian (adj.)

【锁骨下动脉】 suǒgǔ xià dòngmài 〈*Anat.*〉 subclavian artery

【锁骨下静脉】 suǒgǔ xià jìngmài 〈*Anat.*〉 subclavian vein

【锁簧】 suǒhuáng 〈*Mech.*〉 locking spring

【锁匠】 suǒjiàng locksmith

【锁紧】 suǒjǐn 〈*Mech.*〉 locking: 自～ self-locking

【锁紧螺母】 suǒjǐn luómǔ locknut

【锁孔】 suǒkǒng lockhole; keyhole

【锁链】 suǒliàn chain; shackles; fetters; chains

【锁眼】 suǒyǎn **1.** (锁孔) keyhole **2.** (缝扣眼) do a lockstitch on a buttonhold

【锁钥】 suǒyuè **1.** (关键) key: 解决问题的～ a key to the problem **2.** (军事要地) strategic gateway

T

ta

他(tā) 1.(男性第三人) he; his: ～在这里。He is here. / 我听见～在唱歌。I heard him sing. / 这本书是～的,不是我的。This book is his, not mine. 2.(其他的) other; another; some other: 别无～法 have no other way; there's no other way

【他方】 tāfāng 1.(另一方) the other party 2.(别的地方) other places: ～求食 seek a livelihood in another region

【他们】 tā·men they; their; theirs: ～的狗丢了。They have lost their dog. / ～我都认识。I know both of them. / 这所房子是～的。The house is theirs.

【他们自己】 tā·men zìjǐ themselves: ～并不知道发生了什么事。They themselves had no knowledge of what was happening.

【他人】 tārén another person; other: 不仅要想到你自己,也还要想到～。Think of others as well as yourself.

【他日】 tārì some other day; another day

【他杀】 tāshā homicide

【他乡】 tāxiāng a place far away from home; an alien land

【他自己】 tāzìjǐ himself: 就～住在一所大房子里。He lives by himself in a very large house.

她(tā) 1.(女性第三人) she; her; hers: ～最爱读的书 her favorite book / ～是中等个儿。She is of medium height. / ～把糖放进茶里并搅了搅。She put sugar in her tea and stirred it. / 这是他的还是～的? Is this his or hers? 2.(指国家、汽车等敬爱或珍爱之事物) she; her; hers: 这是我的新汽车,～很漂亮。This is my new car — she's beautiful.

【她或他】 tāhuòtā she/he

【她们】 tā·men they; their; theirs

【她们自己】 tā·men zìjǐ themselves

【她自己】 tāzìjǐ herself: 救孩子时～受了伤。She hurt herself while rescuing the child.

它[牠](tā) it; its: 请把～拿去试试。Please take it on trial. / 这狗～的爪子伤了。The dog hurt its paw.

【它们】 tā·men they; their

【它自己】 tāzìjǐ itself

铊(tā) 〈*Chem*.〉 thallium (元素符号 Tl)

趿(tā)

【趿拉】 tā·la wear shoes with the backs trodden down

踏(tā)
(另见"踏"tà)

【踏实】 tā·shi 1.(不浮躁) dependable; steady and sure: 工作～ be steadfast in one's work 2.(安定) free from anxiety: 睡得～ have a sound sleep

塌(tā) 1.(倒塌) collapse; fall down; cave in: 这座旧房子的屋顶～了。The roof of the old house collapsed. 2.(凹下) sink; droop 3.(安定) settle down; calm down

【塌方】 tāfāng 1.(地层结构的) landslide; landslip 2.(修筑上的) cave in; collapse

【塌棵菜】 tākēcài 〈*Bot*.〉 broadbeaked mustard

【塌实】 tā·shi 1.(切实) steady and sure; dependable 2.(安定) free from anxiety; having peace of mind

【塌陷】 tāxiàn subside; sink; cave in

溻(tā) become soaked with sweat: 太热了,我的衣服都～了。It's too hot and my clothes become soaked with sweat.

塔[墖](tǎ) 1.(佛塔) pagoda; dagoba: 白～ the White Pagoda; the White Dagoba 2.(塔形建筑;塔形物) tower: 纪念～ memorial tower / 水～ water tower / 象牙～ tower of ivory 3.〈*Chem*.〉 column;

tower
【塔吊】 tǎdiào tower crane
【塔吉克族】 Tǎjíkèzú Tajik（中国少数民族，主要分布在新疆）
【塔克拉玛干】 Tǎkèlāmǎgān 〈place〉 Taklimakan
【塔里木】 Tǎlǐmù 〈place〉 Tarim
【塔楼】 tǎlóu tower
【塔什库尔干】 Tǎshíkù'ěrgān 〈place〉 Taxkorgan
【塔塔尔族】 Tǎtǎ'ěrzú Tatar（中国少数民族，主要分布在新疆）
【塔台】 tǎtái 〈*Aeron*.〉 control tower

獭（tǎ） 〈*Zool*.〉 otter：旱～ marmot / 水～ otter; river otter

鳎（tǎ） 〈*Zool*.〉 sole

拓［搨］（tà） make rubbings（另见"拓"tuò）
【拓本】 tàběn a book of rubbings
【拓片】 tàpiàn rubbing
【拓印】 tàyìn rub; make rubbings

踏（tà） **1**.（踩）step on; tread; stamp：～上故土 set foot on one's native land **2**.（去现场）go to the spot（另见"踏"tā）
【踏板】 tàbǎn **1**.（机器等的）treadle; footboard; footrest **2**.（乐器的）pedal：钢琴～ piano pedal
【踏板挡】 tàbǎndǎng 〈*Music*〉 pedal bracket
【踏步】 tàbù mark time：～不前 make no headway
【踏勘】 tàkān make an on-the-spot; survey; investigate carefully
【踏看】 tàkàn go to the spot to make an investigation
【踏青】 tàqīng go for a walk in the country in spring

榻（tà） couch：卧～ couch

tai

苔（tāi） 〈*Physiol*.〉 coating on the tongue（另见"苔"tái）

胎（tāi） **1**.（幼体）fetus（AmE.）; foetus（BrE.）; embryo **2**.（生育次数）birth：头～ firstborn; first baby **3**.（棉胎等）padding; stuffing; wadding **4**.（坯子）roughcast：泥～ unfired pottery **5**.（轮胎）tire（AmE）.; tyre（BrE.）
【胎儿】 tāi'ér fetus（AmE.）; foetus（BrE.）; embryo
【胎记】 tāijì 〈*Med*.〉birthmark
【胎教】 tāijiào antenatal training; intelligence education of fetus
【胎盘】 tāipán 〈*Anat*.〉 placenta
【胎生】 tāishēng 〈*Zool*.〉 viviparity; viviparous（adj.）
【胎生动物】 tāishēng dòngwù viviparous animal; vivipara
【胎位】 tāiwèi 〈*Med*.〉 position of a fetus
【胎位不正】 tāiwèi bùzhèng 〈*Med*.〉 fetus in wrong position

台［臺、檯[4]、枱[4]］（tái） **1**.（平台）platform; stage; terrace **2**.（座子）stand; support **3**.（窗台等）sill; platform：窗～ windowsill; window sill **4**.（桌子）table; desk：写字～ writing desk **5**.〈*classifier*〉一～机器 a machine **6**.（台湾省）Taiwan; Taiwan province
【台胞】 táibāo compatriot of Taiwan
【台本】 táiběn a playscript with stage directions
【台布】 táibù tablecloth
【台秤】 táichèng platform scale; platform balance
【台词】 táicí actor's lines：背～ learn the lines by heart
【台灯】 táidēng desk lamp; table lamp; reading lamp
【台风】 táifēng 〈*Meteorol*.〉 typhoon
【台海两岸】 táihǎi liǎng'àn on both sides of the Taiwan Strait
【台阶】 táijiē **1**.（踏级）flight of steps **2**.（转义）step：上几个～ vault several steps **3**.（摆脱窘境的机会）chance：下～ extricate oneself from an awkward position
【台历】 táilì desk calendar; desk diary
【台钳】 táiqián vise; vice
【台球】 táiqiú **1**.（指游戏）billiards：打～ play billiards **2**.（指球）billiard ball **3**.（乒乓球）table tennis; ping-pong
【台球桌】 táiqiúzhuō billiard table

【台扇】 táishàn desk fan
【台商】 táishāng businessman from Taiwan
【台属】 táishǔ Taiwan compatriots' relatives in the mainland
【台湾海峡】 Táiwān Hǎixiá the Taiwan Strait：～两岸 on both sides of the Taiwan Strait
【台资】 táizī funds put in by Taiwan compatriots

苔（tái） 〈*Bot*.〉 liver mosses（另见"苔"tāi）
【苔藓】 táixiǎn moss；bryphyte
【苔原】 táiyuán 〈*Geol*.〉 tundra

抬［擡］（tái） **1**.（举起） lift up；raise：你能帮我把桌子～起一点儿来吗？Could you help me lift this table a bit，please？ **2**.（搬运） carry：～担架 carry sb. on a stretcher
【抬杠】 táigàng **1**.（争辩） argue for the sake of arguing；bicker；wrangle **2**.（抬运灵柩） carry a coffin on stout poles
【抬高】 táigāo raise：～价格 raise prices
【抬价】 táijià raise prices
【抬举】 táijǔ praise or promote sb. to show favor；favor sb.：不识～ not know how to appreciate favors
【抬头】 táitóu **1**.（昂起头） raise one's head：～挺胸 chin up and chest out **2**.（不受压制） rise；look up；gain ground **3**.（单据的抬头） name of the buyer or payee

跆（tái）
【跆拳道】 táiquándào 〈*Sports*〉 tae kwon do；taekwondist（adj.）
【跆拳道手】 táiquándàoshǒu taekwondist

鲐（tái） 〈*Zool*.〉 mackerel
【鲐鱼】 táiyú macherel

薹（tái） **1**.〈*Bot*.〉 sedge **2**.（菜薹） bolt：油菜～ bolt of bird rape

太（tài） **1**.〈*abv*.〉（过于） too；over：～忙 overbusy / ～晚 too late / 天～热。It's too hot. / 她～细心了。She is overcareful. / 他开车～快了。He drives too fast. **2**.（程度极高） too；extremely：～好了！It's wonderful！ **3**.（最，极） highest；greatest；remotest
【太古】 tàigǔ remote ancient times；remote antiquity
【太后】 tàihòu empress dowager；mother of an emperor
【太极】 tàijí tai ji；ta'i chi
【太极拳】 tàijíquán tai ji quan；ta'i chi chu'an；tai ji quan boxing：打～ exercise tai ji quan
【太监】 tàijiān eunuch
【太空】 tàikōng space；outer space；spatial（adj.）；spacial（adj.）
【太空船】 tàikōngchuán a space craft；space ship
【太空服】 tàikōngfú a space suit
【太空人】 tàikōngrén spaceman（m.）；spacewoman（f.）
【太空时代】 tàikōng shídài the space age
【太空舞】 tàikōngwǔ space dance
【太平】 tàipíng peace and tranquility
【太平盛世】 tàipíng shèngshì piping times of peace
【太平斧】 tàipíngfǔ ax；axe
【太平间】 tàipíngjiān mortuary；reposing room
【太平门】 tàipíngmēn exit
【太平鸟】 tàipíngniǎo 〈*Zool*.〉 waxwing
【太平洋】 Tàipíngyáng the Pacific Ocean；the Pacific；Pacific（adj.）
【太仆寺旗】 Tàipǔshìqí 〈place〉 Taibus Qi
【太上皇】 tàishànghuáng **1**.（皇帝父亲的称号） arch-emperor（emperor's father who abdicated in favor of his son） **2**.（幕后的掌实权者） overlord；supreme ruler
【太太】 tài·tai **1**.（称呼） Mrs.；madame **2**.（尊称） madame；lady **3**.（妻子） wife
【太阳】 tàiyáng **1**.〈*Astron*.〉 the sun；solar（adj.） **2**.（太阳光） sunshine；sunlight：晒～ bask in the sun；sun oneself **3**.（太阳穴） temple
【太阳灯】 tàiyángdēng sunlamp
【太阳电池】 tàiyáng diànchí 〈*Astron*.〉 solar cell
【太阳风】 tàiyángfēng 〈*Astron*.〉 solar wind
【太阳黑子】 tàiyáng hēizǐ 〈*Astron*.〉 sunspot
【太阳镜】 tàiyángjìng sunglasses
【太阳历】 tàiyánglì solar calendar
【太阳能】 tàiyángnéng solar energy
【太阳能电池板】 tàiyángnéng diànchíbǎn solar panel
【太阳能电池组】 tàiyángnéng diànchízhǔ solar

battery
【太阳能热水器】 tàiyángnéng rèshuǐqì solar water heater
【太阳年】 tàiyángnián solar year
【太阳鸟】 tàiyángniǎo sunbird
【太阳神经丛】 tàiyáng shéngjīngcóng 〈*Anat.*〉 solar plexus
【太阳窝】 tàiyángwō temple
【太阳系】 tàiyángxì 〈*Astron.*〉 solar system
【太阳穴】 tàiyángxué 〈*Anat.*〉 temple
【太医】 tàiyī royal doctor
【太阴】 tàiyīn moon
【太阴历】 tàiyīnlì lunar calendar
【太子】 tàizǐ crown prince

肽 (tài) 〈*Chem.*〉 peptide

态［態］(tài) **1.**（状态）form; appearance; condition: 形～ shape; morphology **2.**（态度）view; attitude: 表～ express one's view **3.**〈*Physics*〉 state: 固～ solid state / 气～ gaseous state / 液～ liquid state **4.**〈*Phonet.*〉 voice
【态度】 tài·du **1.**（举止）manner; bearing; how one conducts oneself: ～大方 have an easy manner **2.**（看法，立场）attitude; vies; approach: 劳动～ attitude towards labor
【态势】 dàishì state; situation; posture: 军事～ military posture

钛 (tài) 〈*Chem.*〉 titanium（元素符号 Ti）
【钛钢】 dàigāng titanic steel

酞 (tài) 〈*Chem.*〉 phthalein

泰 (tài) **1.**（平安）safe; peaceful **2.**（极；最）extreme; most
【泰斗】 tàidǒu an outstanding authority
【泰然】 tàirán calm; composed; self-possessed: ～处之 take sth. calmly; bear sth. with equanimity
【泰然自若】 dàirán-zìruò keep composure; remain perfectly calm
【泰山】 dàishān father-in-law
【泰水】 dàishuǐ mother-in-law

tan

坍［坍］(tān) collapse; fall; tumble
【坍缩】 tānsuō collapse
【坍缩星】 tānsuōxīng 〈*Astron.*〉 collapsar
【坍塌】 tāntā cave in; collapse: 那建筑～了。The building collapsed.

贪 (tān) **1.**（贪污）corrupt; venal **2.**（求多）greedy; have an insatiable desire for: ～睡 hate to get up **3.**（贪图）covet; hanker for: ～小便宜 keen on gaining petty advantages
【贪财】 tāncái be greedy for money
【贪得无厌】 tāndé-wúyàn be insatiably avaricious
【贪官】 tānguān corrupt official
【贪官污吏】 tānguān-wūlì corrupt officials
【贪婪】 tānlán 〈*written*〉 avaricious; greedy; rapacious
【贪恋】 tānliàn be reluctant to leave
【贪求】 tānqiú covet; hanker for
【贪色】 tānsè lech; lechery (n.); lecherous (adj.)
【贪生怕死】 tānshēng-pàsǐ cravenly cling to life instead of braving death
【贪图】 tāntú seek; hanker after; covet: ～安逸 seek ease and comfort / ～名利 hanker after personal fame and gain
【贪污】 tānwū embezzle; embezzlement (n.); practice graft; graft (n.): ～和受贿 graft and bribery / 她因～公司的钱而被捕。She was arrested for embezzlement of company funds.
【贪污分子】 tānwū fènzǐ a person guilty of corruption; grafter; embezzler
【贪污腐化】 tānwū-fǔhuà graft and corruption; guilt of corruption and accepting bribery
【贪小】 tānxiǎo keen on gaining petty advantages
【贪心】 tānxīn **1.**（欲望）greed; avarice; rapacity **2.**（不知足）greedy; avaricious; insatiable; voracious
【贪赃】 tānzāng take bribes; practice graft: ～枉法 take bribes and bend the law; pervert justice for a bribe
【贪嘴】 tānzuǐ greedy for food

摊［攤］(tān) **1.**（摆开，铺平）spread out; unfold **2.**（分担）take a share in **3.**（摊子）vendor's stand; booth;

stall：报～ news-stand **4.**（一种烹饪方法）fry batter in a thin layer：～鸡蛋 make an omelet

【摊点】 tāndiǎn stands and places

【摊贩】 tānfàn street pedlar

【摊开】 tānkāi spread out；unfold：～地图 unfold the map

【摊牌】 tānpái lay/put one's cards on the table；show one's hand；have a showdown

【摊派】 tānpài apportion；quotas；charges and devotions

【摊位】 tānwèi stand：在展览会设有～ have stands at the exhibition

【摊主】 tānzhǔ owner of the stand；owner of the booth

【摊子】 tān·zi **1.**（售货摊）vendor's stand；booth；stall **2.**（规模）the structure of an organization；setup

滩［灘］（tān） **1.**（沙滩）beach；sands：海～ seabeach / 沙～ sandy beach **2.**（险滩）shoal：险～ shoal

【滩头】 tāntóu beachhead

瘫［癱］（tān） paralyze；paralysis（n.）；paralytic（adj.）

【瘫痪】 tānhuàn **1.**〈*Med.*〉paralyze（AmE.）；paralyse（BrE.）；paralysis（n.）；palsy（n.）；paralytic（adj.）：下肢～ paralysis of one's legs / 他全身～。He has been totally paralyzed. **2.**（机构涣散）be paralyzed；break down；be at a standstill：机构～ the organ is paralyzed

【瘫痪病人】 tānhuàn bìngrén paralytic

坛［壇$^{1-3}$、壜^{4}、罎^{4}、墰^{4}、罈^{4}］（tán） **1.**（祭台）altar **2.**（土台）a raised plot of land：花～ flower bed **3.**（某些组织）circles；world：影～ movie circles **4.**（坛子）earthen jar；jug

【坛子】 tán·zi earthen jar

昙［曇］（tán） covered with clouds

【昙花】 tánhuā 〈*Bot.*〉broadleaved epiphyllum

【昙花一现】 tánhuā-yīxiàn flower briefly as the broadleaved epiphyllum；last briefly；be a flash in the pan

谈（tán） **1.**（说话）talk；chat；discuss：我想和你～～你的工作。I want to discuss your work with you. **2.**（说的话）what is said or talked about：无稽之～ fantastic talk

【谈锋】 tánfēng volubility；eloquence

【谈话】 tánhuà **1.**（说话）converse；talk；conversation（n.）：和某人～ converse with sb. / 和某人进行了长时间的～ have a long conversation with sb. / 两个人在～。The two men were talking. **2.**（发表意见）statement；talk：发表～ make a statement；give a talk

【谈论】 tánlùn discuss；talk about：他们一晚上都在～流行音乐。They talked about pop music all evening

【谈判】 tánpàn negotiations；talks；negotiate（v.）：和平～ negotiation for peace；peace talks / 对等～ hold talks on a reciprocal basis / 和某人进行～ carry on negotiations with sb. / 通过外交途径进行～ negotiate through diplomatic channels

【谈天】 tántiān chat；make conversation

【谈吐】 tántǔ style of conversation：～文雅 have a refined style of conversation

【谈笑风生】 tánxiào-fēngshēng talk cheerfully and humorously

【谈心】 tánxīn heart-to-heart talk

【谈资】 tánzī subject of a talk

痰（tán） phlegm；sputum：请勿随地吐～。No spitting.

【痰盂】 tányú spittoon；cuspidor

弹［彈］（tán） **1.**（弹射）shoot；send forth **2.**（使变松）fluff；tease：～棉花 fluff cotton **3.**（弹出）flick；flip：～烟灰 flick the ash off the end of one's cigarette **4.**（拨弄）play；pluck：～钢琴 play the piano **5.**（弹回）leap；spring **6.**（有弹性）elastic **7.**（抨击）accuse；impeach
（另见"弹"dàn）

【弹拨乐器】 tánbō yuèqì plucked instrument

【弹冠相庆】 tánguān-xiāngqìng congratulate each other and dust off their old official's hats；congratulate each other on the prospect of getting good appointments

【弹劾】 tánhé impeach；impeachment（n.）：总统因一件丑闻受到～。The president was impeached for a scandal.

【弹劾权】 tánhéquán power to impeach
【弹簧】 tánhuáng spring：沙发的～断了。The springs have gone in the sofa.
【弹簧秤】 tánhuángchèng spring balance；spring scale
【弹力】 tánlì elastic force；elasticity；resilience
【弹射】 tánshè 〈*Mil.*〉 launch；catapult；shoot off；eject
【弹射座舱】 tánshè zuòcāng ejection capsule
【弹跳】 tántiào bounce；spring
【弹性】 tánxìng **1.**（弹力）elasticity；resilience **2.**（事物的伸缩性）elastic；flexible
【弹性工作时间】 tánxìng gōngzuò shíjiān flextime；flexitime
【弹性外交】 tánxìng wàijiāo elastic diplomacy
【弹压】 tányā suppress；quell
【弹指】 tánzhǐ a snap of the fingers：～之间 in a flash；in an instant
【弹奏】 tánzòu play；pluck

潭（tán） **1.**（深水池）deep pool；pond **2.**（坑）pit

檀（tán） 〈*Bot.*〉 whinghackberry：青～ whinghackberry / 紫～ padauk
【檀香】 tánxiāng **1.**〈*Bot.*〉 sandalwood；sandalwood tree **2.**（檀香木）sandalwood
【檀香扇】 tánxiāngshàn sandalwood fan
【檀香皂】 tánxiāngzhào sandal soap

忐（tǎn）
【忐忑】 tǎntè perturbed；mentally disturbed：～不安 uneasy；fidgety

坦（tǎn） **1.**（平坦）level；smooth **2.**（坦白）open；candid **3.**（心里安定）calm；composed
【坦白】 tǎnbái **1.**（直率）honest；frank；candid：襟怀～ honest and aboveboard **2.**（如实说出）confess；make a confession；own up
【坦诚】 tǎnchéng frank and honest
【坦荡】 tǎndàng **1.**（指道路）broad and level **2.**（指心地）bighearted；magnanimous
【坦克】 tǎnkè tank：扫雷～ mine exploder / 重型～ heavy tank / 主战～ capital tank
【坦克兵】 tǎnkèbīng **1.**（指兵种）tank forces **2.**（指单兵）tankman
【坦然】 tǎnrán calm；unperturbed；having no misgivings：～自若 calm and confident；completely at ease
【坦率】 tǎnshuài candid；frank；straightforward；outspoken
【坦途】 tǎntú level road；highway

钽（tǎn） 〈*Chem.*〉 tantalum（元素符号 Ta）

袒（tǎn） **1.**（袒露）leave uncovered；expose；bare **2.**（袒护）give unprincipled protection to；shield；shelter：偏～ give unprincipled support to；be partial to
【袒护】 tǎnhù be partial to；shield
【袒露】 tǎnlù expose；bare
【袒胸露背】 tǎnxiōng-lùbèi expose too much cleavage

毯（tǎn） blanket；rug；carpet：地～ rug；carpet / 挂～ tapestry

叹［嘆、歎］（tàn） **1.**（叹气）sigh **2.**（赞叹）exclaim in admiration：赞～ highly praise
【叹词】 tàncí 〈*Gram.*〉 interjection；exclamation
【叹服】 tànfú gasp in admiration
【叹气】 tànqì sigh；heave a sigh
【叹赏】 tànshǎng admire；acclaim；greatly appreciate
【叹为观止】 tànwéi-guānzhǐ acclaim sth. as the acme of perfection
【叹惜】 tànxī sigh with regret；lament
【叹息】 tànxī heave a sigh；sigh

炭［炭］（tàn） charcoal：木～ charcoal
【炭画】 tànhuà 〈*Arts*〉 charcoal drawing；charcoal
【炭火】 tànhuǒ charcoal fire
【炭精】 tànjīng 〈*Electr.*〉 carbon
【炭精棒】 tànjīngbàng carbon stick；carbon
【炭精电极】 tànjīng diànjí carbon electrode
【炭盆】 tànpén charcoal brazier
【炭窑】 tànyáo charcoal kiln；charcoal burner

碳（tàn） 〈*Chem.*〉 carbon（元素符号 C）
【碳黑】 tànhēi 〈*Chem.*〉 carbon black
【碳化】 tànhuà 〈*Chem.*〉 carbonize；carbonization（n.）
【碳化钙】 tànhuàgài 〈*Chem.*〉 calcium carbide

【碳化硅】 tànhuàguī 〈*Chem.*〉carborundum; silicon carbide

【碳化物】 tànhuàwù 〈*Chem.*〉carbide

【碳氢化合物】 tànqīng huàhéwù 〈*Chem.*〉hydrocarbon

【碳水化合物】 tànshuǐ huàhéwù 〈*Chem.*〉carbohydrate

【碳素测定】 tànsù cèdìng 〈*Archaeol.*〉carbon dating

【碳酸】 tànsuān 〈*Chem.*〉carbonic acid; carbonic (adj.)

【碳酸钙】 tànsuāngài 〈*Chem.*〉calcium carbonate

【碳酸钠】 tànsuānnà 〈*Chem.*〉sodium carbonate; soda

【碳酸气】 tànsuānqì 〈*Chem.*〉carbon dioxide; carbonic gas

【碳酸盐】 tànsuānyán 〈*Chem.*〉carbonate

探 (tàn) **1.**(探索) try to find out; explore; sound: ～路 explore the way **2.**(看望) visit; pay a call on **3.**(向前伸出) stretch out; stretch forward **4.**(探员) scout; spy

【探病】 tànbìng visit the sick; visit a patient

【探测】 tàncè survey; sound; probe

【探查】 tànchá look over; examine; explore: ～伤处 explore sb's injuries

【探察】 tànchá watch; look carefully at; observe

【探访】 tànfǎng **1.**(搜寻) seek by inquiry or search **2.**(探望) call on; visit; pay a visit

【探戈舞】 tàngēwǔ tango

【探监】 tànjiān visit a prisoner

【探井】 tànjǐng **1.**〈*Mineral.*〉prospect pit; exploring shaft **2.**〈*Petroleum*〉test well; exploratory well

【探究】 tànjiū make a thorough inquiry; investigate

【探空气球】 tànkōng qìqiú sounding-balloon

【探矿】 tànkuàng go prospecting; prospect

【探亲】 tànqīn go home to visit one's family; go to visit one's relatives

【探亲假】 tànqīnjià home leave

【探求】 tànqiú seek; pursue; search after: ～真理 seek after the truth

【探伤】 tànshāng flaw detection; crack detection

【探伤器】 tànshāngqì flaw detector

【探身】 tànshēn stretch out; stretch forward

【探深竿】 tànshēngān sounding-rod

【探深绳】 tànshēnshéng sounding-line

【探视】 tànshì visit: ～病人 visit a patient

【探视时间】 tànshì shíjiān visiting hours

【探索】 tànsuǒ explore; probe: ～人性之深处 probe deeply into human nature / ～宇宙 explore the outer space

【探讨】 tàntǎo inquire into; probe into

【探听】 tàntīng try to find out; make inquiries: ～消息 make inquiries about sb. or sth.; fish for information

【探头】 tàntóu probe

【探望】 tànwàng **1.**(看望) visit; pay a visit to; call on; look in **2.**(伸出头去看) look about

【探问】 tànwèn **1.**(试探着问) make cautious inquiries about **2.**(问候) inquire after

【探险】 tànxiǎn explore; make explorations; venture into the unknown

【探险队】 tànxiǎnduì exploring party; expedition

【探险家】 tànxiǎnjiā explorer

【探友】 tànyǒu visit friends

【探照灯】 tànzhàodēng searchlight

【探子】 tàn·zi **1.**(指人) scout **2.**(指用具) a thin tube used to extract samples of food grains, etc.

tang

汤[湯] (tāng) **1.**(热水) hot water; boiling water **2.**(温泉) hot springs **3.**(食物) soup; broth: 番茄～ tomato soup / 肉～ meat broth

【汤匙】 tāngchí tablespoon; soupspoon

【汤壶】 tānghú metal or earthenware hot-water bottle

【汤面】 tāngmiàn noodles in soup

【汤勺】 tāngsháo soup ladle

【汤碗】 tāngwǎn soup bowl

【汤药】 tāngyào 〈*Chin. Med.*〉a decoction of medicinal ingredients

【汤圆】 tāngyuán stuffed dumplings made of glutinous rice flour served in soup

耥 (tāng) 〈*Agric.*〉weed or loosen the soil with a harrow

（又读"耥" tǎng）

镗（tāng） 〈*onomat.*〉 dong; clang
（另见"镗"tàng）

趟（tāng） **1.**（趟水）wade; ford: ～过河 wade across the river **2.**〈*Agric.*〉 turn the soil and dig up weeds
（另见"趟"tàng）

羰（tāng） 〈*Chem.*〉 carbonyl

【羰基】 tāngjī 〈*Chem.*〉 carbonyl; carbonyl group

唐（táng） pompous; ostentatious

【唐古拉山】 Tánggǔlāshān 〈place〉 Dangla Shan

【唐棣】 tángdì 〈*Bot.*〉 Chinese serviceberry

【唐人街】 Tángrénjiē Chinatown

【唐三彩】 tángsāncǎi 〈*Archaeol.*〉 tri-colored glazed pottery of the Tang Dynasty

【唐诗】 tángshī Tang poetry

【唐突】 tángtū brusque; rude; offensive: ～的语言 offensive language

塘（táng） **1.**（堤岸）dike; embankment **2.**（水塘）pool; pond: 鱼～ fish pond **3.**（浴池）hot-water bathing pool: 澡～ public baths; bathhouse

【塘肥】 tángféi pond sludge used as manure

【塘泥】 tánní pond sludge; pond silt

【塘堰】 tányàn small reservoir

搪（táng） **1.**（抵挡）ward off; keep out **2.**（搪塞）evade; do sth. perfunctorily **3.**（给炉灶抹膛儿）spread over; daub **4.**〈*Mech.*〉 bore; boring (n.)

【搪床】 tángchuáng 〈*Mech.*〉 boring machine; boring lathe; borer

【搪瓷】 tángcí enamel; porcelain enamelling

【搪瓷器皿】 tángcí qìmǐn enamel ware; enamelware

【搪塞】 tángsè stall sb. off; do sth. perfunctorily: ～之词 a statement of excuse

糖［醣[3]］（táng） **1.**（食糖）sugar: 白～ white sugar / 冰～ icing sugar / 红～ brown sugar / 精制～ caster sugar; castor sugar / 砂～ granulated sugar / 你的咖啡放～吗？ Do you take sugar in your coffee? **2.**（糖果）candy; sweets: 口香～ chewing-gum **3.**（碳氢化合物）carbohydrate: 麦芽～ maltose

【糖厂】 tángchǎng sugar refinery

【糖醋】 tángchù sugar and vinegar; sweet and sour: ～鱼 fish in sweet and sour sauce

【糖弹】 tángdàn sugar-coated bullet

【糖果】 tángguǒ sweets; candy; sweetmeats

【糖果店】 tánguǒdiàn sweet shop; candy store; confectionery

【糖葫芦】 tánghú·lu sugarcoated haws on a stick

【糖浆】 tángjiāng syrup: 止咳～ anti-cough syrup

【糖精】 tángjīng saccharin; gluside

【糖萝卜】 tángluó·bo **1.**（甜菜）beet **2.**（蜜饯胡萝卜）preserved carrot

【糖蜜】 tángmì molasses

【糖尿病】 tángniàobìng diabetes ‖ 糖尿病患者 diabetic

【糖食】 tángshí sweetmeats; sugar

【糖水】 tángshuǐ syrup

【糖蒜】 tángshuàn sweetened garlic; garlic in syrup

【糖业】 tángyè a sugar industry

【糖衣】 tángyī sugar-coat; sugarcoating

【糖衣炮弹】 tángyī pàodàn sugar-coated bullet

【糖汁】 tángzhī syrup

堂（táng） **1.**（大厅）hall **2.**（正房）the main room of a house **3.**（堂兄弟、姐妹）relations between cousins **4.**（公堂）court of law

【堂而皇之】 táng'érhuángzhī a dignified bearing

【堂皇】 tánghuáng **1.**（形容气势）grand; stately; magnificent **2.**（冠冕堂皇）with strict etiquette and decorum; high-sounding

【堂会】 tánghuì home party; private party: 唱～ perform at the private party

【堂姐妹】 tángjiěmèi cousins (f.)

【堂堂】 tángtáng **1.**（形容容貌）dignified; impressive: 仪表～ dignified in appearance **2.**（形容气魄）having high aspirations and boldness of vision **3.**（形容阵容）imposing; awe inspiring; formidable

【堂堂大国】 tángtáng-dàguó a great, powerful nation

【堂堂正正】 tángtáng-zhèngzhèng **1.**（指为

人）open and above-board 2.（指身材）impressive or dignified in personal appearance

【堂屋】 tángwū central room

【堂戏】 tángxì 见“堂会”

【堂兄弟】 tángxiōngdì cousins (m.)

膛（táng） 1.（胸膛）thorax; chest 2.（器物的膛儿）an enclosed space inside sth.; chamber: 炉～ the chamber of a stove

镗（táng） 〈*Mech.*〉 bore; boring (n.)（另见“镗”tāng）

【镗床】 tángchuáng 〈*Mech.*〉 boring machine; boring lathe; borer

螳（táng） mantis

【螳臂当车】 tángbì-dāngchē overrate oneself and attempt sth. impossible; a mantis trying to stop a chariot

【螳螂】 tángláng 〈*Zool.*〉 mantis

棠（táng）

【棠棣】 tángdì 〈*Bot.*〉 Chinese serviceberry

【棠梨】 tánglí birchleaf pear

倘［儻］（tǎng） 〈*coni.*〉 if; supposing; in case: ～有困难 if there should be any difficulty

【倘若】 tǎngruò if; in case; supposing: ～下雨我们就不能去了。In case of rain we can't go.

【倘使】 tǎngshǐ if; in case; supposing

淌（tǎng） drip; shed; trickle: ～血 shed blood

耥（tǎng） 见“耥”(tāng)

躺（tǎng） lie; lie down; recline: 他正～在树阴下。He was lying in the shade of the tree. / 她～到她的床上。She lay down on her bed.

【躺倒】 tǎngdǎo lie down

【躺椅】 tǎngyǐ deck chair; sling chair

烫［燙］（tàng） 1.（烫痛）scald; burn: 我把一壶开水弄洒了，～了我的腿。I dropped a kettle of boiling water and scalded my leg. 2.（加热）warm; heat: ～酒 warm the wine 3.（温度高）boiling hot: 滚～的水 boiling hot water 4.（熨）iron; press: ～裤子 iron trousers 5.（烫发）perm; have one's hair permed

【烫发】 tàngfà perm; give or have a permanent wave

【烫金】 tàngjīn 〈*Printing*〉 gilding bronzing

【烫伤】 tàngshāng 〈*Med.*〉 scald

【烫手】 tàngshǒu scald the hand

【烫头】 tàngtóu perm; give or have a permanent wave

趟（tàng） 1.（次）number of times 2.（行）line

（另见“趟”tāng）

tao

叨（tāo） be favored with; get the benefit of

【叨光】 tāoguāng 〈*politeness*〉 much obliged to you

【叨教】 tāojiào 〈*politeness*〉 many thanks for your advice

【叨扰】 tāorǎo 〈*politeness*〉 thank you for your hospitality

涛［濤］（tāo） great waves; billows: 惊～骇浪 furious waves and terrific billows

【涛声】 the howling of the surging waves

绦［縧、絛、縚］（tāo） silk ribbon; silk braid

【绦虫】 tāochóng tapeworm; cestode

【绦子】 tāo·zi silk ribbon; silk braid

掏［搯］（tāo） 1.（拿出来）draw out; pull out; fish out: ～钱 fish out some money 2.（挖）dig; scoop out; hollow out: ～一个洞 scoop out a hole 3.（扒窃）steal from sb's pocket

【掏井】 tāojǐng dredge a well

【掏腰包】 tāoyāobāo 1.（出钱）pay; pay out of one's own pocket 2.（偷窃）pick sb's pocket

滔（tāo） inundate; flood

【滔滔】 tāotāo 1.（大水滚滚）surging; torrential; billowy 2.（话多）keeping up a constant flow of words: ～雄辩 a torrent of eloquence

【滔天】 tāotiān 1.（形容波浪）dash to the skies; billowy 2.（形容罪恶、灾祸等）heinous; monstrous: ～大祸 a disaster like foaming billows dashing to the skies; a terrible disaster / ～大罪 a monstrous crime; a heinous crime

韬[韜、弢](tāo)

【韬晦】 tāohuì conceal one's true features or intentions; lie low

【韬略】 tāolüè military strategy

饕(tāo)

【饕餮】 tāotiè 1.(凶恶贪婪的人) a fierce and cruel person 2.(贪吃的人) voracious eater; glutton; gourmand

逃[迯](táo) 1.(逃跑) run away from; escape from; flee; take flight 2.(逃避) evade; dodge; shirk; escape

【逃奔】 táobèn run away to: ～他乡 run away to another place

【逃避】 táobì escape; evade; shirk: ～现实 try to escape reality / ～债务 dodge a creditor / ～责任 evade one's responsibility / ～职责 evade doing a duty

【逃兵】 táobīng 1.(军队的) army deserter; deserter 2.(逃脱者) deserter; fugitive

【逃窜】 táocuàn run away; flee in disorder: 四处～ flee in all directions

【逃遁】 táodùn flee; escape; evade: 无处～ can find no hiding-place

【逃犯】 táofàn escaped criminal; escape convict; fugitive from justice

【逃荒】 táohuāng flee from famine; get away from a famine-stricken area

【逃课】 táokè cut school; cut classes

【逃命】 táomìng run for one's life

【逃难】 táonàn flee from a calamity; be a refugee

【逃匿】 táonì escape and hide; go into hiding

【逃跑】 táopǎo run away; flee; take flight; take to one's heels: 警铃一响，窃贼们就～了。The burglars ran away when the alarm sounded.

【逃散】 táosàn become separated in flight

【逃生】 táoshēng flee for one's life; escape with one's life: 死里～ barely escape with one's life; have a narrow escape; have a close shave

【逃税】 táoshuì evade a tax; tax evasion; evasion of taxation

【逃税人】 táoshuìrén tax dodger

【逃脱】 táotuō make good one's escape; get clear of: ～责任 run away from one's responsibilities

【逃亡】 táowáng become a fugitive; flee from home: ～国外 go into exile

【逃亡者】 táowángzhě escapee; fugitive

【逃学】 táoxué play truant; cut class

【逃逸】 táoyì escape; run away; abscond

【逃逸速度】 táoyì sùdù escape velocity

【逃债】 táozhài dodge a creditor

【逃之夭夭】 táozhīyāoyāo decamp; make one's getaway; show a clean pair of heels

【逃走】 táozǒu run away; flee; take flight; take to one's heels; make one's escape

桃(táo) 1.(桃树;桃子) peach 2.(像桃的东西) a peach-shaped thing

【桃红】 táohóng pink

【桃花】 táohuā peach blossom

【桃李】 táolǐ peaches and plums; one's pupils or disciples: ～满天下 have pupils everywhere

【桃仁】 táorén 1.(桃核) stone of a peach 2.(核桃仁) walnut

【桃色新闻】 táosè xīnwén news of illicit love

【桃树】 táoshù peach (tree)

【桃子】 táo·zi peach

陶(táo) 1.(陶器) pottery; earthenware 2.(制造陶器) make pottery 3.(熏陶) cultivate; mold; educate 4.(快乐) contented; happy

【陶瓷】 táocí pottery and porcelain; ceramics

【陶瓷业】 táocíyè ceramics; ceramic industry

【陶器】 táoqì pottery; earthenware

【陶然】 táorán happy and carefree

【陶土】 táotǔ potter's clay; pottery clay; *kaolin*

【陶冶】 táoyě 1.(指器皿和金属) make pottery and smelt metal 2.(指对思想等) exert a favorable influence; mold: ～性情 mold a person's temperament

【陶醉】 táozuì be intoxicated; revel in

淘(táo) 1.(洗去) wash: ～米 wash rice 2.(舀出) clean out; dredge 3.(耗费) tax 4.(淘气) naughty

【淘金】 táojīn 〈*Mineral*.〉pan out; pan off; pan gold

【淘金热】 táojīnrè gold rush

【淘金者】 táojīnzhě gold-digger

【淘气】 táoqì naughty; mischievous: 爱～ be fond of pranks

【淘神】 táoshén 〈*colloq*.〉trying; bothersome: ～费力 worrying the mind and wasting energy

【淘汰】 táotài eliminate through selection or competition; be sifted out

【淘汰赛】 táotàisài elimination series

讨(tǎo) 1.(讨伐) send armed forces to suppress; send a punitive expedition against 2.(索取) demand; ask for 3.(娶) marry: ～老婆 take a wife 4.(招惹) incur; invite: ～人喜欢 make happy 5.(讨论) discuss; study: 研～ deliberate

【讨伐】 tǎofá send armed forces to suppress; send a punitive expedition against

【讨饭】 tǎofàn beg for food; be a beggar

【讨好】 tǎohǎo 1.(迎合) ingratiate oneself with; fawn on; curry favor with 2.(得到好效果) be rewarded with a fruitful result; get good result: 费力不～ put in a lot of work without pleasing anybody; waste energy and come to nothing

【讨还】 tǎohuán get sth. back

【讨价】 tǎojià ask a price; set a price

【讨价还价】 tǎojià-huánjià bargain; haggle: 我一向不～。I'm not used to haggling over price. / 她和卖主～,最后他把水果很便宜地卖给了她。She bargained with the trader till he sold her the fruit cheaply.

【讨教】 tǎojiào ask for advice

【讨论】 tǎolùn discuss; talk over

【讨论会】 tǎolùnhuì symposium; discussion

【讨论题】 tǎolùntí a topic for discussion

【讨便宜】 tǎo pián·yi seek undue advantage; try to gain sth. at the expense of others; look for a bargain

【讨饶】 tǎoráo beg for mercy; ask for forgiveness

【讨嫌】 tǎoxián disagreeable; annoying

【讨厌】 tǎoyàn 1.(惹人厌烦) disagreeable; disgusting; repugnant 2.(事情难办) hard to handle; troublesome; nasty 3.(厌恶) dislike; loathe; be disgusted with

【讨债】 tǎozhài demand repayment of a loan

【讨账】 tǎozhàng 1.(讨债) demand repayment of a loan 2.(索还) get sth. back

套(tào) 1.(套子) sheath; case; cover; sleeve: 椅子～ covering of a chair 2.(河套) the bend of a river 3.(罩上) cover with; slip on 4.(衔接或重叠) interlink; overlap 5.(模仿) model on; copy 6.〈*classifier*〉set; suit; suite: 一～衣服 a suit of clothes 7.(绳套) knot; loop; noose 8.(俗套子) convention; formula 9.(引出) coax a secret out of sb.; pump sb. about sth. 10.(拉拢) try to win: ～交情 try to get in good with sb.

【套餐】 tàocān set meal; table d'hote

【套车】 tàochē harness an animal to a cart; hitch up

【套房】 tàofáng 1.(套间) the inner room 2.(一套住房) flat; apartment

【套服】 tàofú a suit; a suit of clothes

【套购】 tàogòu fraudulently purchase: ～物资 illegally by up goods

【套红】 tàohóng rubric

【套话】 tàohuà polite formula; polite remarks

【套汇】 tàohuì arbitrage of exchange; illegal procurement of foreign exchange

【套汇交易】 tàohuì jiāoyì arbitrage transaction

【套间】 tàojiān inner room; a small room opening off another

【套拉拢】 tào lālǒng try to get in good with sb.

【套曲】 tàoqǔ 〈*Music*〉divertimento

【套曲形式】 tàoqǔ xíngshì cyclical form

【套裙】 tàoqún matching skirt

【套衫】 tàoshān pullover

【套数】 tàoshù 1.(指曲子) a cycle of songs in a traditional opera 2.(指技巧和手法) a series of skills and tricks

【套索】 tàosuǒ lasso; noose

【套筒扳手】 tàotǒng bānshǒu socket wrench; socket set

【套问】 tàowèn find out by asking seemingly casual questions; tactfully sound sb. out

【套用】 tàoyòng apply mechanically

【套语】 tàoyǔ polite formula; polite remarks

【套种】 tàozhòng 〈*Agric*.〉 interplant; interplanting

【套装】 tàozhuāng a suit of clothes

【套子】 tào·zi **1**.(罩子) sheath; case; cover **2**.(棉花套) cotton padding; batting **3**.(应酬时说的话) conventionality; conventional remark

te

铽 (tè) 〈*Chem*.〉 terbium (元素符号 Tb)

特 (tè) **1**.(特殊) special; particular; peculiar; exceptional **2**.(特别) special; particular; unusual; exceptional: 能力～强 unusually capable **3**.(特地) for a special purpose; specially **4**.(特务) secret agent; spy

【特别】 tèbié **1**.(与众不同) special; particular; out of the ordinary: ～的式样 peculiar style / 这封信里没有什么～重要的内容。There was nothing in the letter of particular importance. **2**.(格外) especially; particularly: 质量～好 be of extra fine quality / 他不是～聪明，而是工作很努力。He is not specially clever, but he works hard. **3**.(特地) specially; in particular **4**.(尤其) especially; particularly: 今天～热。It is particularly hot today. / 我喜欢北京，～是秋天。I love Beijing, especially in autumn.

【特别案件】 tèbié ànjiàn extraordinary case

【特别保险】 tèbié bǎoxiǎn specific insurance

【特别法】 tèbiéfǎ special law

【特别法庭】 tèbié fǎtíng special tribunal

【特别开支】 tèbié kāizhī special expenses

【特别快车】 tèbié kuàichē express train; express

【特别留置权】 tèbié liúzhìquán particular lien

【特别诉讼程序】 tèbié sùsòng chéngxù special proceedings

【特别提款权】 tèbié tíkuǎnquán special drawing rights (SDR 或 SDRs)

【特别条款】 tèbié tiáokuǎn special clause

【特别行政区】 tèbié xíngzhèngqū special administrative region

【特别许可证】 tèbié xǔkězhèng special license

【特别预算】 tèbié yùsuàn special budget

【特别账户】 tèbié zhànghù special account

【特产】 tèchǎn special local product; specialty; speciality: 木雕是该村的～。Wood carving are a speciality of this village.

【特长】 tècháng what one is skilled in; strong point; speciality

【特出】 tèchū outstanding; prominent; extraordinary

【特大】 tèdà especially big; the most: ～喜讯 excellent news / ～丰收 an exceptionally rich harvest

【特等】 tèděng special grade; top grade; de luxe

【特等舱】 tèděngcāng stateroom; de luxe cabin

【特等功臣】 tèděng gōngchén special-class hero

【特地】 tèdì 〈*adv*.〉 for a special purpose; specially: 我是～来问你一个问题的。I came here specially to ask you a question.

【特点】 tèdiǎn characteristic; peculiarity; trait; distinguishing feature

【特定】 tèdìng **1**.(特别指定的) specially appointed; specially designated **2**.(某一个) given; specified; specific

【特定管辖权】 tèdìng guǎnxiáquán limited jurisdiction; special jurisdiction

【特定继承人】 tèdìng jìchéngrén particular successor

【特定期限】 tèdìng qīxiàn definite term

【特定信用状】 tèdìng xìnyòngzhuàng special credit

【特定证据】 tèdìng zhèngjù particular evidence

【特定罪行】 tèdìng zuìxíng particular crime

【特工】 tègōng **1**.(指工作) secret service **2**.(指人员) special agent

【特护】 tèhù 〈*Med*.〉 intensive care

【特惠】 tèhuì preferential: ～关税 preferential tariff / ～条款 preferential clause / ～制度 preferential system

【特混舰队】 tèhùn jiànduì task force

【特级】 tèjí special grade; superfine

【特级教师】 tèjí jiàoshī teacher of a special classification; special-class teacher

【特急】 tèjí extra urgent

【特急电】 tèjídiàn extra urgent telegram;

flash message
【特辑】 tèjí 1.(指报刊) special number of a periodical 2.(电影专辑) a special collection of short films
【特技】 tèjì 1.(特殊技能) stunt; trick 2.〈*Cinematog*.〉 special effects
【特技飞行】 tèjì fēixíng stunt flying; aerobatics
【特技镜头】 tèjì jìngtóu 〈*Cinematog*.〉 trick shot
【特技摄影】 tèjì shèyǐng trick photography
【特技跳伞】 tèjì tiàosǎn trick parachuting
【特技效果】 tèjì xiàoguǒ 〈*Cinematog*.〉 special effects
【特价】 tèjià special offer; bargain price: ～出售 sell at a bargain price
【特刊】 tèkān special issue; special
【特克斯】 Tèkèsī 〈place〉 Tekes
【特快】 tèkuài 〈*Railway*〉 express
【特快专递】 tèkuài zhuāndì Express Mail Service (EMS)
【特命全权大使】 tèmìng quánquán dàshǐ ambassador extraordinary and plenipotentiary
【特派】 tèpài specially appointed
【特派记者】 tèpài jìzhě special correspondent; accredited journalist
【特派员】 tèpàiyuán special messenger; accredited representative
【特遣部队】 tèqiǎn bùduì task force
【特区】 tèqū special zone: 经济～ special economic zone
【特权】 tèquán privilege; prerogative: ～地位 privileged position / 外交～ diplomatic privileges
【特权阶层】 tèquán jiēcéng privileged stratum
【特权思想】 tèquán sīxiǎng the idea that prerogatives and privileges go with position; the 'special privilege' mentality
【特权专利】 tèquán zhuānlì special privilege monopoly
【特色】 tèsè characteristic; distinguishing feature: 有中国～的社会主义 socialism with Chinese characteristics
【特赦】 tèshè special pardon; special amnesty
【特赦令】 tèshèlìng decree of special pardon
【特使】 tèshǐ special envoy; accredited representative
【特殊】 tèshū special; particular; peculiar; exceptional: ～的气味儿 a peculiar smell / 这本书有～的价值。This book has a peculiar value. / 今天是我国历史上一个～的日子。This is a special day in the history of our country.
【特殊化】 tèshūhuà have privileges
【特殊性】 tèshūxìng articularity; specific characteristics
【特殊折扣】 tèshū zhékòu channel discount
【特务】 tèwù 1.(特殊任务) special task 2.(情报人员) special agent; spy
【特务活动】 tèwù huódòng espionage
【特务机关】 tèwù jīguān secret service; espionage agency
【特务连】 tèwùlián 〈*Mil*.〉 special-task company
【特务组织】 tèwù zǔzhī secret service; spy organization
【特效】 tèxiào specially good effect; special efficacy
【特效药】 tèxiàoyào specific drug; specific; effective cure
【特写】 tèxiě 1.〈*Literature*〉 feature article or story; feature 2.〈*Cinematog*.〉 close-up
【特写镜头】 tèxiě jìngtóu 〈*Cinematog*.〉 close-up shot
【特性】 tèxìng specific property; peculiarity
【特许】 tèxǔ special permission
【特许法人】 tèxǔ fǎrén chartered corporation
【特许权】 tèxǔquán chartered right
【特许权使用费】 tèxǔquán shǐyòngfèi royalty
【特许经营】 tèxǔ jīngyíng franchise
【特许证书】 tèxǔ zhèngshū special permit; letters patent
【特邀】 tèyāo specially invite
【特邀代表】 tèyāo dàibiǎo specially invited representative
【特异】 tèyì 1.(特别优异) exceptionally good; excellent; superfine 2.(特殊) peculiar; distinctive
【特异功能】 tèyì gōngnéng peculiar function; exceptional function; superfunction
【特意】 tèyì specially; for a special purpose
【特有】 tèyǒu peculiar; characteristic: ～财

产 peculiar property
【特约】 tèyuē engage by special arrangement
【特约稿】 tèyuēgǎo special contribution
【特约记者】 tèyuē jìzhě special correspondent
【特约经售处】 tèyuē jīngshòuchù special sales agency
【特约维修店】 tèyuē wéixiūdiàn special repair shop
【特约演员】 tèyuē yǎnyuán guest actor
【特征】 tèzhēng characteristic; feature; trait: 基本～ essential features
【特指】 tèzhǐ refer in particular to
【特制】 tèzhì specially made; made to order
【特种】 tèzhǒng special type; particular kind
【特种兵】 tèzhǒngbīng the special arms; the special forces
【特种技术部队】 tèzhǒng jìshù bùduì special technical units
【特种诉讼案件】 tèzhǒng sùsòng ànjiàn special conditions of an action
【特种销售税】 tèzhǒng xiāoshòushuì special sale tax
【特种战争】 tèzhǒng zhànzhēng special warfare

teng

疼 (téng) **1.**（痛）ache; pain; sore: 头～ have a headache / 牙～ have a toothache / 我背～。My back aches. / 我胃～。My stomach aches. **2.**（疼爱）love dearly; be fond of; dote on
【疼爱】 téng'ài be very fond of; love dearly
【疼痛】 téngtòng pain; ache; soreness
腾 (téng) **1.**（奔跑）gallop **2.**（跳跃）jump **3.**（腾飞）rise; soar **4.**（腾空）make room; clear out; vacate: ～地方 clear some space; make room / 把办公桌的抽屉都～出来 turn out all the drawers in one's desk **5.**（表示反复）折～ turn over and over
【腾飞】 téngfēi **1.**（飞腾）soar **2.**（迅速发展）develop rapidly: 经济～ exceptionally fast growth in economy
【腾格里沙漠】 Ténggélǐ shāmò 〈place〉Tengger Desert
【腾空】 téngkōng **1.**（把地方空出来）make room; clear out; vacate **2.**（向天上飞）ascend high into the air; rise to the sky
【腾挪】 téngnuó **1.**（指款项）transfer to other use **2.**（指地方）move sth. to make room
【腾腾】 téngténg steaming; seething: 一杯热气～的咖啡 a cup of steaming coffee
【腾跃】 téngyuè **1.**（奔腾跳跃）gallop and jump **2.**（指物价）go up; rise
【腾越】 téngyuè jump over
【腾云驾雾】 téngyún-jiàwù **1.**〈*Mythol.*〉mount the clouds and ride the mist; speed across the sky **2.**（奔驰迅速）speed on as if flying in the air **3.**（头脑发胀）feel dizzy; feel giddy
誊[謄] (téng) transcribe; copy out
【誊清】 téngqīng make a fair copy of
【誊清稿】 téngqīnggǎo fair copy
【誊写】 téngxiě transcribe; copy out
藤[籐] (téng) **1.**（藤制的）cane; rattan: ～椅 cane chair; rattan chair / ～制品 rattan work **2.**（像藤的细茎）vine
【藤本植物】 téngběn zhíwù vine
【藤编】 téngbiān rattan work
【藤篮】 ténglán rattan basket
【藤萝】 téngluó **1.**〈*Bot.*〉villous wisteria **2.**（紫藤）Chinese wisteria
【藤球】 téngqiú 〈*Sports*〉codeball
【藤条】 téngtiáo rattan

ti

体[體] (tī)（另见"体"tǐ）
【体己】 tī·ji **1.**（亲近的）intimate; confidential **2.**（私房钱）private savings
【体己话】 tī·jihuà things one says only to one's intimates
剔 (tī) **1.**（刮）pick; clean with a pointed instrument **2.**（剔除）pick out and throw away; reject
【剔除】 tīchú reject; get rid of: 选出好苹果，～坏的 choose the good apples and reject the bad ones
踢 (tī) kick: 孩子们正在～足球。The children were playing football.
【踢脚板】 tījiǎobǎn 〈*Archit.*〉skirtboard

【踢皮球】 tīpíqiú 1.(儿童游戏) play children's football 2.(推卸责任) pass the buck：互相～ pass the buck to each other

【踢踏舞】 tītàwǔ step dance; tap dance

梯 (tī) 1.(梯子) ladder：绳～ rope ladder / 竹～ bamboo ladder 2.(阶梯) steps 3.(楼梯) stairs：电～ lift; elevator / 电动扶～ escalator 4.(像楼梯的) shaped like a staircase; terraced

【梯队】 tīduì 〈*Mil.*〉 echelon formation; echelon

【梯恩梯】 tī'ēntī 〈*Chem.*〉 trinitrotoluene (TNT)

【梯恩梯当量】 tī'ēntī dāngliàng TNT equivalent

【梯级】 tījí stair; step

【梯级船闸】 tījí chuánzhá chain of locks

【梯己】 tī·ji 同"体己"

【梯田】 tītián 〈*Agric.*〉 terraced fields; terrace

【梯形】 tīxíng 1.(像梯子的) ladder-shaped 2.〈*Math.*〉 trapezoid (AmE.); trapezium (BrE.)

【梯子】 tī·zi ladder; stepladder：爬上～ climb up a ladder

锑 (tī) 〈*Chem.*〉 antimony; stibium (元素符号 Sb)

鹈 (tí)

【鹈鹕】 tíhú 〈*Zool.*〉 pelican

提 (tí) 1.(垂手拿着) carry in one's hand 2.(由下往上) lift; raise; promote 3.(提出) put forward; bring up; raise：～抗议 enter a protest / ～个问题 ask a question; bring up a question / ～意见 make a criticism; make comments or suggestions 4.(提取) draw out; extract：从账号上～款 draw money from one's account 5.(带犯人) bring a criminal to trial：～犯人 bring a criminal in custody to trial 6.(谈起) mention; refer to; bring up：重～往事 make mention of a past event 7.(提子) dipper：酒～ wine dipper / 油～ oil dipper
(另见"提"dī)

【提案】 tí'àn motion; proposal; draft resolution

【提案国】 tí'ànguó sponsor country; sponsor

【提案审查委员会】 tí'àn shěnchā wěiyuánhuì motions examination committee

【提拔】 tíbá promote; promotion (n.)：他被～了。He has got a promotion.

【提白】 tíbái 〈*Theatre*〉 prompt

【提白员】 tíbáiyuán 〈*Theatre*〉 prompter

【提包】 tíbāo handbag; shopping bag; bag; valise

【提倡】 tíchàng advocate; promote; encourage; recommend：～节约 advocate strict economy / ～晚婚 advocate late marriage / ～一对夫妇生一个孩子 advocate one child of one couple

【提成】 tíchéng 1.(按百分比提出来) deduct a percentage; draw a percentage (from a sum of money) 2.(提成数) deductions

【提成权】 tíchéngquán 〈*Econ.*〉 drawing rights

【提出】 tíchū put forward; advance; pose; raise：～报价 submit an offer / ～控告 lodge a complaint against / ～证据 adduce evidence

【提词】 tící 〈*Theatre*〉 prompt ‖ 提词人 prompter

【提单】 tídān bill of lading (B/L)：海运～ ocean bill of lading / 外运～ outward bill of lading

【提单内容】 tídān nèiróng contents of bill of lading

【提单条件】 tídān tiáojiàn terms of bill of lading

【提到】 tídào mention; refer to

【提法】 tífǎ the way sth. is put; formulation; wording

【提干】 tígàn promote; promotion (n.)

【提纲】 tígāng outline：发言～ an outline for a speech

【提纲挈领】 tígāng-qièlǐng take a net by the headrope or a coat by the collar; concentrate on the main points; bring out the essentials

【提高】 tígāo raise; heighten; enhance; increase; improve：～工资 increase sb's pay / ～积极性 lift morale / ～劳动生产率 raise labor productivity / 大幅度～ be increased by a big margin

【提供】 tígòng provide; supply; furnish; offer：～成套设备和材料 delivery of complete equipment and materials / ～开发资金 development financing / ～援助 render assistance / ～证据 give evidence / ～咨询 giving consultations

【提花】 tíhuā 〈*Textiles*〉 jacquard weave

【提花织物】 tíhuā zhīwù 〈*Textiles*〉 jacquard

【提货】 tíhuò pick up goods; take delivery of goods

【提货单】 tíhuòdān bill of lading (B/L)

【提级】 tíjí promote; promotion (n.)

【提交】 tíjiāo submit to; refer to: ～单据 surrender of documents / ～仲裁 dispute to arbitration / 把草案～大会讨论 submit the draft to the plenary session for discussion

【提款权】 tíkuǎnquán 〈*Econ.*〉 drawing rights

【提炼】 tíliàn extract and purify; abstract; refine

【提名】 tímíng nominate; designate

【提起】 tíqǐ 1.(提到) mention; speak of 2.(激起) raise; arouse; brace up

【提前】 tíqián 1.(往前移) shift to an earlier date; move up; advance 2.(事先) in advance; ahead of time; beforehand: ～出发 set off ahead of schedule / ～释放 release before the sentence expires

【提亲】 tíqīn a match-making; talk about a marriage

【提琴】 tíqín 〈*Music*〉 violin

【提请】 tíqǐng submit sth. to

【提取】 tíqǔ 1.(取出) draw; pick up; collect: ～利润 derive a profit 2.(提炼) extract; abstract; recover

【提取器】 tíqǔqì extractor

【提取塔】 tíqǔtǎ extraction column

【提神】 tíshén refresh oneself; give oneself a lift

【提审】 tíshěn 1.(提出来审讯) bring before the court; bring to trial 2.(由上一级法院审判) take over by a higher court; review

【提升】 tíshēng 1.(提高职级) promote; promotion (n.): 我们的老师已被～为校长了。Our teacher has promoted to headmaster. 2.(向高处运) hoist; elevate

【提升机】 tíshēngjī hoist; elevator

【提示】 tíshì point out; prompt

【提问】 tíwèn put questions to; quiz

【提箱】 tíxiāng suitcase

【提携】 tíxié 1.(领着走) lead by the hand 2.(扶植) guide and support; give guidance and help to

【提心吊胆】 tíxīn-diàodǎn be breathless with anxiety; have one's heart in one's mouth

【提醒】 tíxǐng remind; warn; call attention to

【提选】 tíxuǎn select; choose

【提要】 tíyào summary; abstract; epitome; synopsis

【提议】 tíyì 1.(提出主张) propose; suggest; move 2.(所提主张) proposal; motion

【提子】 tí·zi dipper: 酒～ wine dipper / 油～ oil dipper

【提足】 tízú 〈*Skating*〉 holding the foot

啼［嗁］(tí) 1.(啼哭) cry; weep aloud 2.(叫) crow; caw

【啼哭】 tíkū cry; wail

【啼笑皆非】 tíxiào-jiēfēi not know whether to laugh or cry

蹄［蹏］(tí) hoof

【蹄关节】 tíguānjié coffin joint

【蹄筋】 tíjīn 1.(牛蹄筋) tendons of beef 2.(羊蹄筋) tendons of mutton 3.(猪蹄筋) tendons of pork

【蹄铁钢】 títiěgāng 〈*Metall.*〉 horseshoe bar

【蹄子】 tí·zi hoof

题 (tí) 1.(题目) topic; subject; title; problem: 话～ subject of one's talk 2.(写上) inscribe

【题材】 tícái subject matter; theme

【题词】 tící 1.(题写) write an inscription 2.(题写的字) inscription 3.(序文) foreword

【题解】 tíjiě 1.(详细解答) key to exercises or problems 2.(解释性文字) explanatory notes on the title or background of a book

【题名】 tímíng 1.(写姓名) autograph 2.(题目) title; subject 3.(题写书名) inscribe: 一本～的书 an inscribed book

【题目】 tímù 1.(标题) title; subject; topic 2.(习题) exercise problems; examination questions

【题字】 tízì 1.(题写的字) inscription; autograph 2.(题写) inscribe

体［體、躰］(tǐ) 1.(身体) body; part of the body 2.(物

体) substance; state of a substance: 固～ solid / 流～ fluid / 气～ gas; air / 液～ liquid 3.(体裁) form; style: 文～ literary form 4.〈*Math.*〉 shape: 几何～ geometric shape 5.(亲身经验) personally do or experience sth.; put oneself in another's position 6.(系统) system: 政～ system of government
(另见"体"tī)

【体裁】 tǐcái types or forms of literature

【体操】 tǐcāo gymnastics; gymnastic (adj.)

【体操表演】 tǐcāo biǎoyǎn gymnastic exhibition

【体操服】 tǐcāofú gym outfit

【体操器械】 tǐcāo qìxiè gymnastic apparatus

【体操运动员】 tǐcāo yùndòngyuán gymnast

【体察】 tǐchá experience and observe

【体察民情】 tǐchá mínqíng be streetwise; observe the people's condition

【体罚】 tǐfá corporal punishment; physical punishment

【体格】 tǐgé physique; build; health

【体格检查】 tǐgé jiǎnchá health checkup; physical examination

【体会】 tǐhuì 1.(领会) know from experience; realize 2.(领会到的) what one has learned; experiences: 交流～ exchange views

【体积】 tǐjī volume; bulk

【体力】 tǐlì physical strength; physical power

【体力劳动】 tǐlì láodòng physical labor; manual labor

【体例】 tǐlì stylistic rules and layout; style

【体谅】 tǐliàng show understanding and sympathy for; make allowances for

【体面】 tǐmiàn 1.(体统) dignity; face: 有失～ fail to keep face 2.(光荣) honorable; creditable; respectable: 不～的行为 disgraceful conduct; indecent behavior 3.(好看) handsome; good-looking: 小姑娘长得很～。The girl is good-looking.

【体内】 tǐnèi in vivo

【体魄】 tǐpò physique; build; constitution: 锻炼～ build up one's physique

【体弱】 tǐruò weak; delicate; frail

【体式】 tǐshì 1.(文字式样) form of characters or letters 2.(体裁) style: 史诗～ the epic style

【体态】 tǐtài posture; carriage

【体态情感】 tǐtài qínggǎn 〈*Psycho.*〉 attitudinal feeling

【体贴】 tǐtiē show consideration for; give every care to: ～入微 look after with meticulous care; have the greatest concern for

【体统】 tǐtǒng decorum; propriety; decency: 一件多么有失～的事啊! What a disgraceful thing to do!

【体外受精】 tǐwài shòujīng 〈*Zool.*〉 external fertilization

【体外循环】 tǐwài xúnhuán extracorporal circulation

【体位】 tǐwèi 〈*Med.*〉 position

【体味】 tǐwèi appreciate; savor

【体温】 tǐwēn temperature: 量～ take one's temperature

【体温计】 tǐwēnjì thermometer

【体无完肤】 tǐwúwánfū 1.(浑身受伤) have cuts and bruises all over the body; be a mass of bruises 2.(被驳倒) be thoroughly refuted

【体系】 tǐxì system; setup: 经济～ economic system / 思想～ ideological system

【体现】 tǐxiàn embody; incarnate; reflect

【体校】 tǐxiào physical culture school

【体形】 tǐxíng bodily form; build: 我们俩～相同。We are of the same build.

【体型】 tǐxíng type of build or figure; bodily form

【体恤】 tǐxù understand and sympathize with; show solicitude for

【体恤衫】 tǐxùshān T-shirt

【体验】 tǐyàn learn through one's personal experience; learn through practice

【体液】 tǐyè body fluid

【体育】 tǐyù 1.(体育教育) physical culture 2.(体育运动) sports

【体育比赛】 tǐyù bǐsài sports tournament

【体育场】 tǐyùchǎng stadium

【体育道德】 tǐyù dàodé sportsmanship

【体育锻炼】 tǐyù duànliàn physical training

【体育锻炼标准】 tǐyù duànliàn biāozhǔn standards for physical training

【体育馆】 tǐyùguǎn gymnasium; gym

【体育活动】 tǐyù huódòng sports activities

【体育记者】 tǐyù jìzhě scribe

【体育节目播音员】 tǐyù jiémù bōyīnyuán sports-caster

【体育解说员】 tǐyù jiěshuōyuán sports reporter
【体育界】 tǐyùjiè the sporting world
【体育课】 tǐyùkè physical education（PE）
【体育疗法】 tǐyù liáofǎ physical exercise therapy
【体育系】 tǐyùxì department of physical education
【体育消息】 tǐyù xiāoxī sport-cast
【体育用品】 tǐyù yòngpǐn sports goods；sports requisites
【体育运动】 tǐyù yùndòng sports；physical culture；physical education
【体育中心】 tǐyù zhōngxīn sports center；indoor stadium
【体制】 tǐzhì system of organization；system；structure；structural（adj.）：～改革 structural reforms / 领导～ system of leadership / 建立新经济～ establish a new economic structure
【体质】 tǐzhì physique；constitution：增强～ build up the physique
【体重】 tǐzhòng weight；body weight

屉［**屜**］（tì） 1.（笼屉）steamer tray 2.（抽屉）drawer

剃（tì） shave
【剃刀】 tìdāo razor
【剃光头】 tìguāngtóu 1.（剃成光头）have one's head shaved 2.（一分未得）score no points
【剃头】 tìtóu 1.（剃光头）have one's head shaved 2.（理发）have one's hair cut；have a haircut
【剃须刀】 tìxūdāo shaver：电动～ electric shaver
【剃须刀插座】 tìxūdāo chāzuò shaver outlet；shaver point
【剃须膏】 tìxūgāo shaving cream

涕（tì） 1.（眼泪）tears 2.（鼻涕）mucus of the nose；snivel
【涕泣】 tìqì weep：～沾襟 wet the front part of one's garment with tears

倜（tì） cautious
【倜傥】 tìtǎng easy and unembarrassed：风流～ be talented and gallant

惕（tì） cautious
【惕厉】 tìlì watchful；on guard；vigilant
【惕励】 tìlì 见"惕厉"

替（tì） 1.（代替）take the place of；replace；substitute for：谁～张华，他病了。Who will take the place of Zhang Hua? He is ill. 2.（为）for；on behalf of：我真～她高兴。I share her joy.
【替补】 tìbǔ replace；replacement（n.）
【替补队员】 tìbǔ duìyuán 〈*Sports*〉 replacement；reserve；spare；sub；substitute
【替代】 tìdài substitute for；replace；supersede：～能源 substitute energy resources
【替代法】 tìdàifǎ method of substitution
【替代品】 tìdàipǐn substitute；succedaneum
【替工】 tìgōng 1.（替别人做工）work as a substitute 2.（替工的人）temporary substitute（worker）
【替换】 tìhuàn replace；substitute for；displace；take the place of：～测验 duplicate test
【替身】 tìshēn 1.（替身演员）substitute；stand-in；replacement 2.（替罪羊）scapegoat
【替身机器人】 tìshēn jīqìrén augmentor
【替罪羊】 tìzuìyáng scapegoat

嚏（tì）
【嚏喷】 tì·pen sneeze：打～ sneeze

tian

天（tiān） 1.（天空）sky；heaven 2.（一昼夜；白天）day：第二～ the next day；the following day / 第三～ the third day / 雨好几～都没停。It hasn't stopped raining for days 3.（在上面的）overhead 4.（时间）time；a period of time in a day 5.（季节）season：春～ spring / 夏～ summer 5.（天气）weather：～晴了。It's fine. 7.（天然的）naturarl 8.（天生的）natural；innate 9.（指大自然）nature 10.（神）God；Heaven
【天安门】 Tiān'ānmén Tian An Men；Tiananmen；Gate of Heavenly Peace
【天安门城楼】 Tiān'ānmén Chénglóu Tiananmen Gate Tower
【天安门广场】 Tiān'ānmén Guǎngchǎng

Tian'anmen Square

【天边】 tiānbiān 1.(天际) horizon 2.(很远的地方) the ends of the earth; remotest places

【天才】 tiāncái 1.(才能) genius; talent; gift: 有艺术～ have a genius for arts 2.(有天才的人) man of genius

【天长日久】 tiāncháng-rìjiǔ after a considerable period of time

【天车】 tiānchē 〈*Astron.*〉 shop traveller; crown block

【天秤宫】 Tiānchènggōng 〈*Astron.*〉 Libra (9月23日至10月22日): 生于～ be born under Libra

【天秤座】 Tiānchèngzuò 〈*Astron.*〉 Libra

【天赤道】 tiānchìdào 〈*Astron.*〉 celestial equator

【天窗】 tiānchuāng 〈*Archit.*〉 skylight

【天从人愿】 tiāncóngrényuàn Heaven grants man's wish; by the grace of God

【天敌】 tiāndí natural enemy

【天地】 tiāndì 1.(天和地) heaven and earth; universe; world 2.(活动范围) field of activity; scope of operation: ～间 in this world 3.(地步,境地) condition; circumstances

【天地良心】 tiāndì-liángxīn from the bottom of my heart

【天地万物】 tiāndì-wànwù works of God

【天电】 tiāndiàn 〈*Electr.*〉 atmospherics; static

【天电干扰】 tiāndiàn gānrǎo statics; static disturbances

【天顶】 tiāndǐng 〈*Astron.*〉 zenith

【天鹅】 tiān'é swan

【天鹅绒】 tiān'éróng 〈*Textiles*〉 velvet

【天翻地覆】 tiānfān-dìfù heaven and earth turning upside down

【天分】 tiānfèn special endowments; natural gift; talent: 绘画的～ a talent for drawing

【天府之国】 tiānfǔzhīguó the land of abundance; the land of plenty

【天赋】 tiānfù 1.(自然赋予) inborn; innate; endowed by nature 2.(天资) natural gift; talent; endowments

【天赋人权论】 tiānfù rénquánlùn the theory of natural rights

【天赋资源】 tiānfù zīyuán natural endowment

【天高地厚】 tiāngāo-dìhòu 1.(指恩情) profound; deep 2.(复杂性) immensity of the universe; complexity of things: 不知～ not understand things

【天工】 tiāngōng work of nature; formed by nature: 巧夺～ art beats nature; one's works of art may overcome nature

【天国】 tiānguó 1.〈*Christianity*〉 the Kingdom of Heaven 2.(理想世界) paradise

【天寒地冻】 tiānhán-dìdòng the weather is cold and the ground is frozen

【天河】 tiānhé 〈*Astron.*〉 the Milky Way; the Galaxy

【天候】 tiānhòu weather

【天花】 tiānhuā 〈*Med.*〉 smallpox

【天花板】 tiānhuābǎn ceiling

【天花乱坠】 tiānhuā-luànzhuì as if it were raining flowers; give an extravagantly colorful description

【天昏地暗】 tiānhūn-dì'àn 1.(指景象) a murky sky over a dark earth; dark all around: ～日月无光 a mass of murkiness which neither sunlight nor moonlight can penetrate 2.(政治腐败) in a state of chaos and darkness 3.(指程度) terribly

【天机】 tiānjī 1.(秘密) nature's mystery; something inexplicable 2.(天意) God's design; secret

【天极】 tiānjí 1.〈*Astron.*〉 celestial pole 2.(天际) horizon

【天际】 tiānjì horizon

【天经地义】 tiānjīng-dìyì unalterable principle; right and proper; perfectly justified

【天井】 tiānjǐng 1.(院中空地) small yard; courtyard 2.(天窗) skylight 3.〈*Mineral.*〉 raise

【天空】 tiānkōng the sky; the heavens: ～蔚蓝晴朗。The sky was blue and clean.

【天蓝】 tiānlán sky blue; azure

【天狼星】 Tiānlángxīng 〈*Astron.*〉 Sirius; Dog Star (大犬座 α)

【天老爷】 tiānlǎo·ye God

【天理】 tiānlǐ justice: ～良心 the course of nature and one's conscience

【天良】 tiānliáng conscience: 丧尽～ conscienceless

【天亮】 tiānliàng daybreak; dawn

【天灵盖】 tiānlínggài top of the skull; crown
【天伦】 tiānlún 〈*written*〉 the natural bonds and ethical relationships between members of a family: 享受～之乐 enjoy family happiness
【天罗地网】 tiānluó-dìwǎng an inescapable dragnet; nets above and snares below
【天马行空】 tiānmǎ-xíngkōng a heavenly steed soaring across the skies; a powerful and unconstrained style
【天明】 tiānmíng daybreak; dawn
【天命】 tiānmìng God's will; the mandate of heaven; destiny; fate
【天幕】 tiānmù **1.**(天空) the canopy of the heavens **2.**〈*Theatre*〉 backdrop
【天南地北】 tiānnán-dìběi **1.**(距离远) far apart **2.**(地区不同) from different places or areas
【天南海北】 tiānnán-hǎiběi **1.**(到处) all over the country **2.**(东拉西扯) discursive; rambling
【天年】 tiānnián natural span of life; one's allotted span
【天牛】 tiānniú 〈*Zool.*〉 longicorn; longhorned beetle
【天疱疮】 tiānpàochuāng 〈*Med.*〉 pemphigus
【天棚】 tiānpéng **1.**(房屋顶棚) ceiling **2.**(凉棚) awning or canopy; mat awning
【天棚灯】 tiānpéngdēng ceiling lamp
【天平】 tiānpíng balance; scales
【天气】 tiānqì **1.**〈*Meteorol.*〉 weather: 这个星期～干燥。The weather has been dry this week. / ～多好哇! What heavenly weather! **2.**(时间,时候) time
【天气图】 tiānqìtú synoptic chart; weather map
【天气学】 tiānqìxué synoptic meteorology
【天气预报】 tiānqì yùbào weather forecast
【天气预报员】 tiānqì yùbàoyuán weatherman; weatherwoman
【天堑】 tiānqiàn natural moat: 长江～ the natural moat of the Yangtze River
【天桥】 tiānqiáo overline bridge; platform bridge: 人行～ pedestrian bridge; overhead walkway
【天穹】 tiānqióng the vault of heaven
【天球】 tiānqiú 〈*Astron.*〉 celestial sphere
【天然】 tiānrán natural
【天然堤岸】 tiānrán-dī'àn natural levee
【天然港】 tiānrángǎng natural harbor
【天然气】 tiānránqì natural gas
【天然嗓音】 tiānrán sǎngyīn natural voice
【天然丝】 tiānránsī natural silk
【天然橡胶】 tiānrán xiàngjiāo natural rubber
【天壤之别】 tiānrǎngzhībié a world of difference; poles apart
【天日】 tiānrì the sky and the sun; light
【天色】 tiānsè color of the sky; time of the day: ～已晚 It's getting late.
【天神】 tiānshén god; deity
【天生】 tiānshēng born; inborn; inherent; innate: ～才子 born great artist; a genius
【天时】 tiānshí **1.**(气候) weather climate **2.**(时机) timeliness; opportunity
【天使】 tiānshǐ 〈*Religion*〉 angel
【天书】 tiānshū a book from heaven; abstruse writing; illegible writing
【天数】 tiānshù 〈*Superstition*〉 the will of God
【天坛】 Tiāntán Temple of Heaven
【天堂】 tiāntáng paradise; heaven
【天体】 tiāntǐ 〈*Astron.*〉 celestial body
【天体物理学】 tiāntǐ wùlǐxué 〈*Astron.*〉 astrophysics
【天天】 tiāntiān every day; daily; day in, day out
【天王星】 Tiānwángxīng 〈*Astron.*〉 Uranus
【天网恢恢】 tiānwǎng-huīhuī The net of Heaven stretches everywhere; nobody escape the judgment of Heaven
【天文】 tiānwén astronomy; astronomical (adj.)
【天文导航】 tiānwén dǎoháng astronavigation
【天文观测】 tiānwén guāncè astronomical observation
【天文馆】 tiānwénguǎn planetarium
【天文数字】 tiānwén shùzì astronomical figure; enormous figure
【天文台】 tiānwéntái (astronomical) observatory
【天文图】 tiānwéntú the star atlas
【天文望远镜】 tiānwén wàngyuǎnjìng astronomical telescope
【天文学】 tiānwénxué astronomy ‖ 天文学家 astronomer

【天文仪器】 tiānwén yíqì astronomical instruments

【天无绝人之路】 tiān wú jué rén zhī lù God will not close all doors; Heaven will always leave a door open

【天下】 tiānxià 1.（指中国）China; land under heaven: ～大治 great order across the land 2.（统治权）rule; domination: 打～ seize state power

【天仙】 tiānxiān 1.（仙女）goddess 2.（美女）a beauty

【天险】 tiānxiǎn natural barrier

【天线】 tiānxiàn aerial; antenna: 室外～ outside aerial; outside antenna

【天象】 tiānxiàng 〈*Astron*.〉 astronomical phenomena; celestial phenomena

【天象仪】 tiānxiàngyí 〈*Astron*.〉 planetarium

【天晓得】 tiānxiǎo·de God knows.

【天蝎宫】 Tiānxiēgōng 〈*Astron*.〉 Scorpio（10月23日至11月21日）: 生于～ be born under Scorpio

【天蝎座】 Tiānxiēzuò 〈*Astron*.〉 Scorpio

【天性】 tiānxìng natural instincts; nature; natural disposition; natural temperaments

【天涯】 tiānyá the end of the world; the remotest corner of the earth: ～海角 the remotest regions of the earth; faraway

【天衣无缝】 tiānyī-wúfèng a seamless heavenly robe; flawless; without a trace

【天意】 tiānyì God's will; the will of Heaven

【天有不测风云】 tiān yǒu bùcè fēngyún a storm may arise from a clear sky; sth. unexpected may happen any time: ～，人有旦夕祸福 Human fortunes are as unpredictable as the weather.

【天灾】 tiānzāi natural disaster: ～人祸 natural disaster and man-made calamity

【天真】 tiānzhēn 1.（单纯）innocent; artless; naive 2.（头脑简单）childish; inexperienced

【天知道】 tiānzhīdào God knows.

【天职】 tiānzhí bounden duty; vocation

【天轴】 tiānzhóu 1.〈*Astron*.〉 celestial axis 2.〈*Mech*.〉 line shaft

【天诛地灭】 tiānzhū-dìmiè stand condemned by God; be destroyed by heaven and earth

【天主】 Tiānzhǔ God

【天主教】 Tiānzhǔjiào Catholicism

【天主教会】 Tiānzhǔ Jiàohuì the Roman Catholic Church

【天主教徒】 tiānzhǔ jiàotú Catholic

【天资】 tiānzī natural gift; talent; natural endowments; inborn intellectual capacity

【天子】 tiānzǐ the Son of Heaven; the emperor

【天作之合】 tiānzuòzhīhé a heaven-made match; a match blessed by God

添（tiān） add; increase; have more: 为…～光彩 add luster to sth.

【添补】 tiān·bu replenish; get more

【添彩】 tiāncǎi add luster

【添丁】 tiāndīng have a baby; give birth to a baby

【添加】 tiānjiā add to; increase

【添加剂】 tiānjiājì 〈*Chem*.〉 additive

【添置】 tiānzhì add to one's possessions; acquire: ～一套家具 buy a set of furniture

田（tián） 1.（农田）field; farmland; cropland: 麦～ a field of wheat 2.（油田、煤田等）field: 煤～ coalfield / 气～ gas field / 油～ oil field

【田产】 tiánchǎn real estate

【田地】 tiándì 1.（农田）field; farmland 2.（地步）plight; wretched situation; condition

【田埂】 tiángěng a low bank of earth between fields; ridge

【田鸡】 tiánjī frog

【田间】 tiánjiān field; farm

【田间管理】 tiánjiān guǎnlǐ field management

【田径】 tiánjìng 〈*Sports*〉 track and field

【田径裁判长】 tiánjìng cáipànzhǎng chief judge at the finish

【田径场】 tiánjìngchǎng athletic field

【田径队】 tiánjìngduì track and field team

【田径服】 tiánjìngfú track suit

【田径赛】 tiánjìngsài track and field meet

【田径赛项目】 tiánjìngsài xiàngmù track and field events

【田径十项全能运动】 tiánjìng shíxiàng quánnéng yùndòng decathlon

【田径运动】 tiánjìng yùndòng track and field sports; athletics ‖ 田径运动员 athlete

【田螺】 tiánluó river snail

【田赛】 tiánsài 〈*Sports*〉 field events

【田鼠】 tiánshǔ 〈*Zool*.〉 vole

【田野】 tiányě field; open country
【田园】 tiányuán fields and gardens; countryside; rural
【田园诗】 tiányuánshī pastoral poetry; idyll ‖ 田园诗人 pastoral poet; idyllist
【田园文学】 tiányuán wénxué pastoral literature; idyllic literature
【田庄】 tiánzhuāng country estate

恬(tián)

【恬不知耻】 tiánbùzhīchǐ not feel ashamed; totally devoid of sense of shame; brazen-faced
【恬淡】 tiándàn 1.(淡泊名利) indifferent to fame or gain 2.(恬静) quiet; peaceful; tranquil
【恬静】 tiánjìng quiet; peaceful; tranquil
【恬然】 tiánrán 〈*written*〉 unperturbed; nonchalant; unhurried; calm

甜(tián) 1.(指味道) sweet; honeyed 2.(睡得塌实) sound

【甜菜】 tiáncài 1.(经济作物) beet 2.(甜菜的根) beetroot
【甜菜糖】 tiáncàitáng beet sugar
【甜橙】 tiánchéng sweet orange
【甜点】 tiándiǎn dessert
【甜点心】 tiándiǎn·xin 见“甜点”
【甜瓜】 tiánguā muskmelon; sweet melon
【甜活儿】 tiánhuór cushy job
【甜酒】 tiánjiǔ sweet wine
【甜美】 tiánměi 1.(甜) sweet; luscious 2.(愉快;舒服) pleasant; refreshing
【甜蜜】 tiánmì sweet; happy
【甜面酱】 tiánmiànjiàng sweet flour paste
【甜食】 tiánshí sweet food; sweetmeats; dessert
【甜水】 tiánshuǐ 1.(不苦的水)fresh water 2.(指幸福) happiness; comfort
【甜丝丝】 tiànsīsī 1.(有甜味) pleasant sweet 2.(感到愉快) quite pleased; gratified; happy
【甜酸】 tiánsuān sweet-and-sour
【甜酸苦辣】 tiánsuān-kǔlà all sorts of joys and sorrows
【甜头】 tián·tou 1.(指味道) sweet taste; pleasant flavor 2.(好处) good; benefit: 尝到～ get a benefit
【甜味】 tiánwèi sweet taste
【甜言蜜语】 tiányán-mìyǔ fine-sounding words; flattery; sweet words and honeyed phrases

填(tián) 1.(垫平;塞满) fill up; stuff 2.(填写) fill in; write: 请在支票上～好你的名字。Fill in your name on this check.

【填报】 tiánbào fill in a form and submit it to the leadership
【填表】 tiánbiǎo fill in a form
【填补】 tiánbǔ fill: ～空白 fill in the gaps
【填充】 tiánchōng 1.(一种测验) fill in the blanks 2.(填补) fill up; stuff
【填充材料】 tiánchōng cáiliào filled composite
【填充题】 tiánchōngtí blank-filling; completion; cloze
【填充物】 tiánchōngwù filler
【填词】 tiáncí compose a *ci* poem
【填空】 tiánkòng 1.(填补) fill a vacant position; fill a vacancy 2.(填空测验) fill in the blanks: 选择～ cloze
【填平】 tiánpíng fill and level up
【填塞】 tiánsè fill up; stuff
【填写】 tiánxiě fill in; write: ～所得税申报表 fill in one's income tax form
【填鸭】 tiányā 1.(一种养鸭法) to stuff the duck 2.(此法养的鸭子) force-fed duck
【填鸭式教学方法】 tiányāshì jiàoxuéfāngfǎ cramming method of teaching
【填字游戏】 tiánzì yóuxì cross-word puzzle

舔(tiǎn) lick; lap: ～盘子 lick the plate / 狗～水喝。The dog lapped its water up.

腆(tiǎn) 1.(丰盛) sumptuous; rich 2.(凸出) protrude; thrust out

tiao

挑(tiāo) 1.(挑选) choose; select; pick: 为什么偏偏～中我? Why pick on me? 2.(挑剔) pick; find 3.(挑担) shoulder; carry on the shoulder with a pole
(另见“挑”tiǎo)

【挑错】 tiāocuò find faults; pick flaws
【挑错测验】 tiāocuò cèyàn absurdity test
【挑担】 tiāodàn carry a load
【挑肥拣瘦】 tiāoféi-jiǎnshòu to be very par-

ticular in one's selection; choose whichever is to one's personal advantage

【挑夫】 tiāofū porter

【挑拣】 tiāojiǎn pick; pick and choose

【挑三拣四】 tiāosān-jiǎnsì pick and choose; be choosy

【挑食】 tiāoshí be choosy about food

【挑剔】 tiāo·ti nitpick; be hypercritical; be fastidious; to find fault with sb. or sth.: 无可～ invulnerable / 她对吃的很～。She's very choosy about food.

【挑选】 tiāoxuǎn choose; select; pick out: ～接班人 choose successors

【挑选试验】 tiāoxuǎn shìyàn percent test

【挑子】 tiāo·zi carrying pole with its load; load carried on a shoulder pole; load

【挑字眼儿】 tiāo zìyǎnr find fault with the choice of words

条[條] (tiáo) 1.(细长树枝) twig 2.(狭长的东西) a long narrow piece; strip; slip: 布～ a strip of cloth 3.(项目) item; article: 第 24～ article 24 4.(层次) order 5.〈*classifier*〉一～裤子 a pair of trousers / 两～鱼 two fishes

【条案】 tiáo'àn a long narrow table

【条播】 tiáobō 〈*Agric.*〉 drill; drilling (n.)

【条播机】 tiáobōjī seed drill; drill

【条幅】 tiáofú a vertically-hung scroll; scroll

【条件】 tiáojiàn 1.(客观因素) condition; factor; terms: 不对等～ non-reciprocal terms / 经济～ economical terms / 可行性～ feasibility conditions / 在对等的～下给予优厚待遇 give preferential treatment on a reciprocal basis 2.(要求) requirement; prerequisite; qualification: 提谈判～ list the prerequisites for negotiation / 先决～ precondition; requirements 3.(状况) condition; situation; state: 这个工厂设备～很好。This factory is well equipped.

【条件刺激】 tiáojiàn cìjī 〈*Physiol.*〉 conditioned stimulus

【条件反射】 tiáojiàn fǎnshè 〈*Physiol.*〉 conditioned reflex

【条款】 tiáokuǎn clause; article; provision; chapter; section: 地方立法～ domestic law conditions

【条理】 tiáolǐ orderliness; method; reasonable; proper arrangement or presentation: 没有～ be in a state of disorder

【条例】 tiáolì regulations; rules; ordinances

【条令】 tiáolìng 〈*Mil.*〉 regulations

【条目】 tiáomù 1.(词典的) entry: 6 万个～ 60,000 entries 2.(规章的) clauses and subclauses

【条绒】 tiáoróng corduroy

【条条框框】 tiáotiáo-kuàngkuàng rules and regulations; conventions

【条文】 tiáowén article; clause; regulation: 法律～ legal provisions / 政策～ the content of the policy

【条纹】 tiáowén stripe; streak

【条纹布】 tiáowénbù striped cloth; stripe

【条形码】 tiáoxíngmǎ bar code

【条约】 tiáoyuē treaty; pact: 边界～ boundary treaty / 多边～ multilateral pact / 技术合作～ technological cooperation treaty / 双边～ bilateral treaty / 通商航海～ treaty of commerce and navigation / 友好合作～ treaty of friendship and cooperation / 友好和互不侵犯～ treaty of friendship and mutual non-aggression / 订立～ conclude a treaty / 签订～ sign a treaty

【条子】 tiáo·zi 1.(长条) strip 2.(便条) a brief informal note

迢 (tiáo) far; remote

【迢迢】 tiáotiáo far away; remote: 千里～～ from afar; from a remote place

【迢远】 tiáoyuǎn distant; remote; faraway

笤 (tiáo)

【笤帚】 tiáo·zhou broom; besom

调 (tiáo) 1.(调配) suit well; fit in perfectly 2.(调合) mix; adjust: 妻子给他～了一杯热饮。His wife mixed him a hot drink. 3.(调解) mediate 4.(挑逗) tease; provoke
(另见"调"diào)

【调拨】 tiáobō 见"挑拨"

【调程序】 tiáochéngxù 〈*Computer*〉 debug; debugging

【调处】 tiáochù mediate; arbitrate

【调挡】 tiáodǎng 〈*Mech.*〉 gear shift

【调幅】 tiáofú 〈*Radio*〉 amplitude modulation

【调羹】 tiáogēng spoon
【调和】 tiáohé 1.(配合适当) be in harmonious proportion; harmonize 2.(调解) mediate; reconcile 3.(妥协) compromise; make concessions
【调和漆】 tiáohéqī ready-mixed paint
【调级】 tiáojí adjust a wage scale
【调剂】 tiáojì 1.(配制药物) make up a prescription 2.(调整) adjust; regulate: ～物资 adjust the distribution of materials
【调价】 tiáojià readjust prices
【调焦】 tiáojiāo 〈*Photog.*〉 focusing
【调焦环】 tiáojiāohuǎn 〈*Photog.*〉 focusing ring
【调焦镜头】 tiáojiāo jìngtóu 〈*Photog.*〉 focusing lens
【调节】 tiáojié regulate; adjust: 市场～ market regulation
【调节器】 tiáojiéqì regulator; conditioner
【调节税】 tiáojiéshuì regulating taxes
【调解】 tiáojiě mediate; make peace: ～纠纷 arbitrate a dispute; adjust a dispute
【调解程序】 tiáojiě chéngxù conciliation proceedings
【调解法庭】 tiáojiě fǎtíng conciliation court
【调解人】 tiáojiěrén intermediator; bridge builder
【调解协议】 tiáojiě xiéyì reconciliation agreement
【调侃】 tiáokǎn scoff; mock; jeer
【调控】 tiáokòng regulate; regulation (n.): 重视宏观的经济～ pay attention to macroeconomic regulation
【调理】 tiáolǐ 1.(调养) nurse one's health; recuperate 2.(照料) look after; take care of
【调料】 tiáoliào condiment; seasoning; flavoring
【调配】 tiáopèi mix; blend
【调皮】 tiáopí 1.(顽皮) naughty; mischievous 2.(不驯服) unruly; tricky 3.(耍小聪明) play tricks
【调频】 tiáopín 〈*Radio*〉 frequency modulation
【调频广播】 tiáopín guǎngbō frequency modulation broadcasting
【调频收音机】 tiáopín shōuyīnjī FM receiver
【调情】 tiáoqíng flirt; coquet
【调色】 tiáosè 〈*Arts*〉 mix colors
【调色板】 tiáosèbǎn 〈*Arts*〉 palette
【调色剂】 tiáosèjì toner
【调试】 tiáoshì 〈*Computer*〉 debug; debugging
【调试程序】 tiáoshì chéngxù 〈*Computer*〉 debugging routine
【调唆】 tiáosuō incite; instigate
【调停】 tiáotíng 1.(调解) mediate; intervene 2.(安排) arrange
【调味】 tiáowèi flavor; season
【调味品】 tiáowèipǐn flavoring; seasoning; condiment
【调温】 tiáowēn adjust temperature
【调戏】 tiáoxì take liberties with; assail with obscenities
【调弦器】 tiáoxiánqì 〈*Music*〉 tuning machine
【调弦器钮】 tiáoxiánqì niǔ 〈*Music*〉 tuning pegs; tuning keys
【调笑】 tiáoxiào make fun of; poke fun at; tease
【调谐】 tiáoxié 1.(和谐) harmonious 2. 〈*Electr.*〉 turning
【调谐范围】 tiáoxié fànwéi 〈*Electr.*〉 tuning range
【调谐旋钮】 tiáoxié xuánniǔ 〈*Electr.*〉 tuning knob
【调养】 tiáoyǎng take good care of oneself; build up one's health by rest and by taking nourishing food; be nursed back to health
【调音】 tiáoyīn 〈*Music*〉 tuning
【调音螺丝】 tiáoyīn luósī 〈*Music*〉 tension screws
【调音台】 tiáoyīntái 〈*Music*〉 console table
【调匀】 tiáoyún mix evenly
【调整】 tiáozhěng adjust; regulate; revise: 工资～ adjustment of wages / ～供求关系 regulate supply and demand / ～价格 readjust prices
【调制】 tiáozhì modulate; modulation (n.)
【调制解调器】 tiáozhì jiětiáoqì 〈*Computer*〉 modem; modulator demodulator
【调资】 tiáozī adjust the wage; adjustment of wages (n.)

挑 (tiǎo) 1.(支起) push sth. up with a pole or stick; raise 2.(挑开) poke; pick 3.(挑拨;挑动) stir up; instigate

(另见"挑"tiāo)

【挑拨】 tiǎobō instigate; incite; sow discord: ～离间 stir up ill-will or bad feelings

【挑动】 tiǎodòng 1.(引起) provoke; stir up; incite 2.(煽动) provoke; incite: ～战争 provoke a war

【挑逗】 tiǎodòu provoke; tease; tantalize; seduce

【挑花】 tiǎohuā cross-stitch work

【挑弄】 tiǎonòng 1.(挑拨) instigate; incite; sow discord 2.(戏弄) tease; make fun of

【挑弄是非】 tiǎonòng-shìfēi arouse ill-will between two parties; stir up one side against the other

【挑起】 tiǎoqǐ provoke; stir up; instigate: ～争端 provoke dispute

【挑唆】 tiǎosuō incite; abet; instigate

【挑衅】 tiǎoxìn provoke; provocation (n.); provocative (adj.): 武装～ armed provocation

【挑衅行为】 tiǎoxìn xíngwéi provocative act

【挑衅者】 tiǎoxìnzhě provocateur

【挑战】 tiǎozhàn 1.(挑衅) throw down the gauntlet; challenge to battle 2.(提出竞赛) challenge to a contest; challenge: 提出～ issue a challenge to sb. to do sth. / 响应～ accept a challenge

【挑战书】 tiǎozhànshū letter of challenge; challenge

【挑战者】 tiǎozhànzhě challenger

眺 (tiào) look into the distance from a high place: 远～ look far into the distance

【眺望】 tiàowàng look into the distance from a high place

跳 (tiào) 1.(跳跃) jump; leap; spring; bounce; hop: 他～上公共汽车。He jumped into the bus. / 他～过了篱笆。He made a leap over the fence. 2.(跳动) move up and down; beat: 我眼睛直～是不是有什么事? Is the twitch in my eye noticeable? 3.(跳过) skip; make omissions: ～了一行 skip over one line

【跳班】 tiàobān skip a grade

【跳板】 tiàobǎn 1.(供人走的) gangplank 2.(跳水用的) springboard; diving board 3.(跷跷板) seesaw

【跳槽】 tiàocáo abandon one occupation in favor of another; get a new employment

【跳道】 tiàodào 〈*Sports*〉 track; course

【跳动】 tiàodòng move up and down; beat; pulsate

【跳高】 tiàogāo 〈*Sports*〉 high jump: 背越式～ back style; Fosbury flop; flop / 撑竿～ pole vault; pole jump / 俯卧式～ straddle jump / 滚式～ Western layout / 剪式～ Eastern layout ‖ 跳高运动员 high jumper

【跳高架】 tiàogāojià 〈*Sports*〉 jumping standard

【跳行】 tiàoháng 1.(漏去一行) skip a line 2.(改行) change to a new occupation

【跳级】 tiàojí skip a grade

【跳级生】 tiàojíshēng accelerated student

【跳栏】 tiàolán 〈*Sports*〉 hurdle race; the hurdles

【跳梁小丑】 tiàoliáng xiǎochǒu a buffoon who performs antics; contemptible scoundrel

【跳马】 tiàomǎ 1.(指器械) vaulting horse 2.(指项目) horse-vaulting

【跳棋】 tiàoqí Chinese checkers; Chinese draughts

【跳起顶球】 tiàoqǐ dǐngqiú 〈*Football*〉 flying header

【跳起射门】 tiàoqǐ shèmén 〈*Handball*〉 jump shot

【跳球】 tiàoqiú 〈*Basketball*〉 jump ball

【跳伞】 tiàosǎn 1.(用降落伞往下跳) parachute; bale out 2.(指项目) parachute jumping: 定点～ accuracy jump; precision landing / 特技～ style jump / 造型～ relative work ‖ 跳伞运动员 parachutist; parachuter

【跳伞区】 tiàosǎnqū parachute drop zone

【跳伞塔】 tiàosǎntǎ parachute tower

【跳伞氧气调节器】 tiàosǎn yǎngqì tiáojiéqì parachute oxygen regulator

【跳绳】 tiàoshéng 〈*Sports*〉 rope skipping; rope jumping

【跳水】 tiàoshuǐ 〈*Sports*〉 dive; diving: 跳板～ springboard diving / 跳台～ platform diving ‖ 跳水运动员 diver

【跳水池】 tiàoshuǐchí diving pool

【跳台】 tiàotái diving tower; diving platform

【跳台滑雪】 tiàotái huáxuě ski jumping

【跳舞】 tiàowǔ dance: 我们随着音乐～。We

danced to the music.
【跳箱】 tiàoxiāng box horse; vaulting box
【跳远】 tiàoyuǎn 〈*Sports*〉 long jump; broad jump: 三级～ hop, step and jump ‖ 跳远运动员 broad jumper; long jumper
【跳跃】 tiàoyuè jump; leap; bound
【跳蚤】 tiào·zao flea
【跳蚤市场】 tiào·zao shìchǎng flea market
【跳闸】 tiàozhá tripping operation
粜［糶］(tiào) sell (grain): ～粮 sell grain

tie

帖［貼］(tiē) **1.** (服从) submissive; obedient **2.** (妥当) well-settled; well-placed
(另见“帖”tiě, tiè)
贴(tiē) **1.** (粘) paste; stick; glue: 在信封上～邮票 put a stamp on the envelope **2.** (紧挨) keep close to; nestle closely to: ～着墙 close to the wall **3.** (津贴) subsidies; allowance **4.** 〈*classifier*〉 一～膏药 a piece of medicated plaster
【贴边】 tiēbiān hem
【贴标签】 tiēbiāoqiān label; put label on: 给箱子贴上发往上海的标签 label the trunk for Shanghai
【贴补】 tiēbǔ **1.** (从经济上帮助) give a financial support **2.** (用积蓄补日常开支) subsidize; help out financially: ～家用 help out with domestic expenses
【贴花】 tiēhuā 〈*Textiles*〉 appliqué
【贴换】 tiēhuàn trade sth. in; trade-in
【贴己】 tiējǐ **1.** (亲近) intimate; confidential **2.** (私房钱) private savings
【贴金】 tiējīn **1.** (贴金箔) cover with gold leaf; gild **2.** (美化) touch up; prettify; put feathers in: 往自己脸上～ put a feather in one's cap
【贴近】 tiējìn press close to; nestle up against
【贴切】 tiēqiè apt; suitable; appropriate; proper
【贴身】 tiēshēn **1.** (挨着皮肤的) next to the skin **2.** (合身) fit; be the right size **3.** (跟随在身边) close companion
【贴水】 tiēshuǐ 〈*Trade*〉 agio
【贴题】 tiētí relevant; pertinent; to the point: 不～ irrelevant; beside the point
【贴息】 tiēxī **1.** 〈*Trade*〉 pay interest (in the form of a deduction when selling a bill of exchange, etc.) **2.** (付出的利息) interest so deducted; discount
【贴现】 tiēxiàn 〈*Trade*〉 discount
【贴现贷款】 tiēxiàn dàikuǎn discount loan
【贴现率】 tiēxiànlǜ discount rate
【贴现银行】 tiēxiàn yínháng discount bank
【贴现值】 tiēxiànzhí discounted value
【贴心】 tiēxīn intimate; close
【贴心话】 tiēxīnhuà confidential talk
萜(tiē) 〈*Chem.*〉 terpenes
帖(tiě) **1.** (帖子) invitation: 请～ invitation **2.** (字条) note; card: 谢～ card of thanks **3.** 〈*classifier*〉 一～药 a dose of herbal medicine
(另见“帖”tiē, tiè)
铁［鐵、銕］(tiě) **1.** 〈*Chem.*〉 iron (元素符号 Fe) **2.** (指刀枪等) arms; weapon **3.** (坚硬的) hard or strong as iron **4.** (确定不移的) firm; indisputable; irrefutable; unalterable: ～的事实 indisputable fact; irrefutable evidence **5.** (下决心) resolve; determine
【铁案如山】 tiě'ànrúshān borne out by ironclad evidence
【铁板】 tiěbǎn iron plate; sheet iron
【铁笔】 tiěbǐ **1.** (刻图章的) cutting tool **2.** (刻蜡纸用) stencil pen
【铁饼】 tiěbǐng **1.** 〈*Sports*〉 discus throw **2.** (指器械) discus ‖ 铁饼运动员 discus thrower
【铁窗】 tiěchuāng **1.** (有铁栅的窗) a window with iron grating **2.** (监狱) prison bars; prison
【铁锤】 tiěchuí hammer
【铁道】 tiědào railroad; railway
【铁道兵】 tiědàobīng railway corps
【铁道路口】 tiědào lùkǒu railroad crossing
【铁道炮兵】 tiědào pàobīng railway artillery
【铁饭碗】 tiěfànwǎn iron rice bowl; a secure job
【铁工】 tiěgōng **1.** (指工人) ironworker; blacksmith **2.** (指工作) ironwork

【铁工厂】 tiěgōngchǎng ironworks
【铁管】 tiěguǎn iron pipe; iron tube
【铁轨】 tiěguǐ rail
【铁合金】 tiěhéjīn 〈*Metall*.〉 ferroalloy; iron alloy
【铁黑】 tiěhēi 1.（氧化铁）iron oxide black 2.（一种颜色）iron black
【铁蒺藜】 tiějí·li barb; barbed wire; caltrop
【铁甲】 tiějiǎ 1.（装甲的）armored 2.（铠甲）armor; mail
【铁甲车】 tiějiǎchē armored vehicle; armored car
【铁甲船】 tiějiǎchuán an ironclad
【铁匠】 tiějiàng blacksmith; ironsmith
【铁匠铺】 tiějiàngpù smithy; blacksmith's shop
【铁矿】 tiěkuàng iron mine
【铁矿石】 tiěkuàngshí iron ore
【铁链】 tiěliàn iron chain; shackles
【铁路】 tiělù railway; railroad
【铁路电气化】 tiělù diànqìhuà railway electrification
【铁路干线】 tiělù gànxiàn trunk railway
【铁路公路两用桥】 tiělù gōnglù liǎngyòngqiáo combined bridge
【铁路路基】 tiělù lùjī railway bed
【铁路网】 tiělùwǎng railway network
【铁路线】 tiělùxiàn railway line
【铁路运费】 tiělù yùnfèi railage
【铁路职工】 tiělù zhígōng railman
【铁门】 tiěmén 1.（铁制的门）iron gate 2.（铁花格）grille
【铁面无私】 tiěmiàn-wúsī impartial and incorruptible
【铁皮】 tiěpí iron sheet
【铁器】 tiěqì ironware
【铁器时代】 tiěqì shídài the Iron Age
【铁锹】 tiěqiāo spade; shovel
【铁青】 tiěqīng ashen; livid; ghastly pale
【铁拳】 tiěquán iron fist
【铁砂】 tiěshā 1.（铁矿砂）iron sand 2.（猎枪子弹）shot; pellets
【铁石心肠】 tiěshí-xīncháng be ironhearted; have a heart of stone; be hardhearted
【铁树】 tiěshù 〈*Bot*.〉 sago cycas
【铁水】 tiěshuǐ molten iron
【铁丝】 tiěsī iron wire
【铁丝网】 tiěsīwǎng wire netting; wire fence
【铁索】 tiěsuǒ cable; iron chain
【铁索吊车】 tiěsuǒ diàochē cable car
【铁索桥】 tiěsuǒqiáo chain bridge
【铁塔】 tiětǎ 1.（钢铁造的塔）iron tower; iron pagoda 2.（高压线铁塔）pylon; transmission tower
【铁蹄】 tiětí iron heel; cruel oppression of the people
【铁桶】 tiětǒng metal pail; metal bucket; drum
【铁头球杆】 tiětóu qiúgān 〈*Golf*〉 iron
【铁腕】 tiěwàn iron hand
【铁腕人物】 tiěwàn rénwù an ironhanded person; strong man
【铁锨】 tiěxiān shovel; spade
【铁屑】 tiěxiè iron filings; iron chippings and shavings
【铁锈】 tiěxiù rust
【铁渣】 tiězhā iron slag
【铁砧】 tiězhēn anvil
【铁证】 tiězhèng ironclad proof; irrefutable evidence: ～如山 irrefutable, conclusive evidence

帖 (tiè) a book of models: 字～ a copybook of models of calligraphy
（另见"帖"tiē, tiě）

ting

厅［廳、庁］(tīng) 1.（大房间）hall 2.（政府部门）office; department: 办公～ general office / 公安～ Department of Public Security

听［聽、聴］(tīng) 1.（耳听）listen; hear: ～音乐 listen to music / 去～重金属滚石乐队 go to hear a heavy metal rock group 2.（听从）heed; obey; listen: 如果你想学的话，必须～老师的。You should listen to the teacher if you want to learn. 3.（听凭）allow; let: ～其自然 let things take their own course 4.〈*classifier*〉 tin; can: 一～啤酒 a tin of beer
【听便】 tīngbiàn as you please; as you like
【听从】 tīngcóng obey; heed; comply with; conform: ～劝告 take sb's advice; conform to sb's ideas

【听候】 tīnghòu wait for; pending
【听话】 tīnghuà heed what an elder or superior says; be obedient
【听见】 tīngjiàn hear: 听得见 can hear / 我～一声巨响。I heard a loud noise.
【听讲】 tīngjiǎng 1.(听讲课, 听讲演) listen to a talk; attend a lecture 2.(听说) be told; hear of; hear about
【听觉】 tīngjué 〈*Physiol.*〉 sense of hearing: 他的～很灵敏。His hearing is very sharp.
【听觉教具】 tīngjué jiàojù audio-visual aid
【听觉器官】 tīngjué qìguān 〈*Anat.*〉 organs of hearing
【听课】 tīngkè attend a lecture; sit in on a class
【听课证】 tīngkèzhèng class card
【听力】 tīnglì 1.(听的能力) hearing 2.(听力课) aural comprehension 3.(听力材料) comprehension
【听力测定】 tīnglì cèdìng audiometry
【听命】 tīngmìng take orders from; be at sb's command
【听凭】 tīngpíng allow; let
【听其言观其行】 tīng qí yán guān qí xíng listen to what a person says and watch what he does; judge people by their deeds, not just by their words
【听其自然】 tīngqízìrán let things take their own course; let matters slide
【听取】 tīngqǔ listen to; hear: ～工作报告 listen to a report on the work / ～证词 hear witnesses
【听任】 tīngrèn allow; let
【听说】 tīngshuō be told; hear of; hear about: 我～她病了。I heard that she was ill. / 我们从未～有人做过那种事。We've never heard of anyone doing that.
【听说法】 tīngshuōfǎ audio-visual approach
【听说技能】 tīngshuō jìnéng audio-lingual skills
【听天由命】 tīngtiān-yóumìng submit to the will of Heaven; resign oneself to one's fate; trust to luck
【听筒】 tīngtǒng 1.(电话听筒) receiver 2.(耳机) headphone; earphone 3.(听诊器) stethoscope
【听写】 tīngxiě 〈*Education*〉 dictation
【听信】 tīngxìn 1.(等候消息) wait for information 2.(听到而相信) believe; believe what one hears: ～谗言 hear and believe slanders
【听阈】 tīngyù auditory threshold
【听诊】 tīngzhěn 〈*Med.*〉 auscultation
【听诊器】 tīngzhěnqì 〈*Med.*〉 stethoscope
【听证】 tīngzhèng hear; hearing of argument (n.)
【听证会】 tīngzhènghuì hearing: 就某事举行～ hold a hearing into sth.
【听之任之】 tīngzhī-rènzhī let sth. go unchecked; take a laissez-faire attitude; let matters drift
【听众】 tīngzhòng audience; listeners
【听装】 tīngzhuāng tinned; canned: ～水果 tinned fruit

烃[烴] (tīng) 〈*Chem.*〉 hydrocarbon
【烃基】 tīngjī hydrocarbon radical

庭 (tíng) 1.(庭院) front courtyard; front yard 2.(法院) law court
【庭园】 tíngyuán flower garden; grounds
【庭院】 tíngyuàn courtyard
【庭长】 tíngzhǎng 〈*Law*〉 the president of a court

亭 (tíng) 1.(亭子) pavilion; kiosk 2.(商亭) kiosk: 电话～ telephone booth; telephone box / 书～ bookstall; bookstand
【亭亭玉立】 tíngtíng-yùlì 1.(形容妇女) slim and graceful 2.(形容花木) tall and erect
【亭子】 tíng·zi pavilion; kiosk

停 (tíng) 1.(停止) stop; cease; halt; pause: 跑上小山, 他～下来休息了一会儿。When he had run up the hill, he paused for a minute to rest. 2.(停留) stop over; stay 3.(停放) be parked 4.(停泊) lie at anchor 5.(电影导演术语) cut: "～!", 导演大声说。"Cut!" shouted the director.
【停办】 tíngbàn close down
【停播信号】 tíngbō xìnhào off-the-air signal
【停泊】 tíngbó anchor; come to an anchor; berth: 船在新加坡～, 这样我们花一天的时间游览了这个城市。The ship berthed at Singapore and so we spent a day touring the city.
【停泊处】 tíngbóchù anchorage; berth; dock

【停泊港】 tíngbógǎng port of call
【停泊时间】 tíngbó shíjiān lay-time
【停泊税】 tíngbóshuì keelage
【停产】 tíngchǎn stop production
【停产期】 tíngchǎnqī idling period
【停车】 tíngchē 1.(停驶) stop; pull up 2.(停放) park：不准～！No Parking! 3.(停止转动) stall; stop working
【停车场】 tíngchēchǎng car park; parking lot; parking area：收费～ fee park
【停车灯】 tíngchēdēng 〈*Auto*〉parkinglight
【停车灯和尾灯】 tíngchēdēng hé wěidēng 〈*Auto*〉stop and tail light
【停车线】 tíngchēxiàn stop line
【停当】 tíng·dang ready; prepared; in a go condition
【停电】 tíngdiàn power cut; power failure
【停顿】 tíngdùn 1.(停止) stop; halt; pause 2.(说话的间歇) pause：她进来时，谈话～了一下。There was a pause in the talk when she came in.
【停放】 tíngfàng park; place
【停飞】 tíngfēi 〈*Mil.*〉grounding of aircraft
【停工】 tínggōng stop work; shut down
【停航】 tíngháng suspend air or shipping service
【停火】 tínghuǒ cease fire; armistice (n.)
【停机】 tíngjī 1.〈*Cinematog.*〉stop 2.(停放飞机) park
【停机坪】 tíngjīpíng 〈*Aeron.*〉apron; aircraft parking area
【停刊】 tíngkān stop publication
【停靠】 tíngkào stop; berth
【停靠港】 tíngkàogǎng port of call
【停课】 tíngkè suspend classes
【停留】 tíngliú stay for a time; stop; remain
【停手】 tíngshǒu stop; cease
【停水】 tíngshuǐ cut off the water supply; cut off the water
【停息】 tíngxī stop; cease
【停歇】 tíngxiē 1.(歇业) close down; stop doing business 2.(停止) stop; cease 3.(停下休息) stop for a rest; rest
【停薪留职】 tíngxīn-liúzhí stop payment of salary but retain office
【停学】 tíngxué stop going to school; drop out of school; suspend sb. from school
【停业】 tíngyè 1.(暂时的) suspend; shut up 2.(永久的) stop doing business; close down
【停业甩卖】 tíngyè shuǎimài closing sales
【停战】 tíngzhàn cease-fire; armistice; truce; cessation of hostilities
【停战令】 tíngzhànlìng order to cease-fire
【停战谈判】 tíngzhàn tánpàn armistice talks
【停战协定】 tíngzhàn xiédìng truce agreement; armistice
【停职】 tíngzhí suspend sb. from his duties：～检查 be temporarily relieved of one's post for self-examination
【停止】 tíngzhǐ stop; cease; halt; suspend; call off：～呼吸 stop breathing
【停止兑现】 tíngzhǐ duìxiàn suspension of specie payment
【停止设备】 tíngzhǐ shèbèi arrestment
【停止信号】 tíngzhǐ xìnhào break alarm
【停滞】 tíngzhì stagnate; be at a standstill; bog down：～不前 be at a standstill

葶 (tíng)

【葶苈】 tínglì 〈*Bot.*〉draba; woolly draba

挺 (tǐng) 1.(硬而直) straight; erect; stiff 2.(伸直) straighten up; stick out 3.(勉强支持) endure; stand; hold out 4.(很) very; rather; quite：～好 very well

【挺拔】 tǐngbá 1.(直立而高耸) tall and straight 2.(坚强有力) forceful
【挺进】 tǐngjìn boldly drive on; press onward; push forward
【挺举】 tǐngjǔ 〈*Weight-lifting*〉clean and jerk
【挺立】 tǐnglì stand upright; stand firm
【挺身】 tǐngshēn straighten one's back
【挺秀】 tǐngxiù tall and graceful
【挺直】 tǐngzhí straight and upright

铤 (tǐng) (run) quickly

【铤而走险】 tǐng'érzǒuxiǎn risk danger in desperation

艇 (tǐng) a light boat：快～ motor boat / 潜～ submarine / 橡皮～ rubber dinghy

tong

通 (tōng) 1.(通行) open; through：这列火车直～九龙。The train goes through to

Jiulong (Kowloon). 2.(使通) open up; clean out; clear out: ～下水道 clean out a drainage 3.(有路通到) lead to; go to: 这条铁路～昆明。This railway leads to Kunming. 4.(相通) connect; communicate: 互～信息 exchange information 5.(通知) notify; tell 6.(懂得;了解) understand; know: 不～人情 not amenable to reason 7.(专家) authority; expert: 北京～ an expert of Beijing 8.(通顺) logical; coherent 9.(普通) general; common 10.(整个) all; whole

【通报】 tōngbào 1.(书面通知) circulate a notice 2.(文件) circular 3.(刊物) bulletin; journal: 化学～ journal of the Chemistry 4.(说出姓名等) notify; report

【通病】 tōngbìng common failing; common mistake

【通才】 tōngcái an all-round person; a universal genius

【通常】 tōngcháng general; usual; normal

【通畅】 tōngchàng 1.(运行无阻) unobstructed; clear: 道路～。The road is clear. 2.(流畅) easy and smooth: 他文字～。He writes easily and smoothly.

【通车】 tōngchē 1.(开始行车) be open to traffic 2.(有车来往) have transport service

【通称】 tōngchēng 1.(通常叫做) be generally called; be generally known as 2.(通常的名字) a general term; common name; popular name

【通达】 tōngdá understand: ～事理 be reasonable; be sensible

【通道】 tōngdào thoroughfare; passageway; passage: 绿色～ green passage

【通敌】 tōngdí collaborate with the enemy; act in collusion with the enemy

【通电】 tōngdiàn 1.(通电流) set up an electric circuit; electrify; energize; be charged with electricity 2.(公开发表电报) send a circular telegram: ～全国 publish an open telegram to the nation 3.(该电报) circular telegram

【通牒】 tōngdié diplomatic note: 最后～ ultimatum

【通读】 tōngdú read over

【通风】 tōngfēng 1.(使空气流通) ventilate; air 2.(透气) be well ventilated 3.(透露消息) divulge information; tip-off

【通风管道】 tōngfēng guǎndào ventilating duct

【通风机】 tōngfēngjī ventilator; fanner

【通风井】 tōngfēngjǐng ventilation shaft; air shaft

【通风孔】 tōngfēngkǒng air hole

【通风口】 tōngfēngkǒu vent

【通风设备】 tōngfēng shèbèi ventilation system

【通风系统】 tōngfēng xìtǒng system of ventilation

【通风贮藏】 tōngfēng zhùcáng air-cooler storage

【通风装置】 tōngfēng zhuāngzhì ventilation installation

【通告】 tōnggào 1.(普遍通知) give public notice; announce 2.(文告) public notice; circular; announcement

【通共】 tōnggòng in all; altogether; all told

【通过】 tōngguò 1.(穿过) pass through; get past; traverse: 船～了马六甲海峡。The ship passed the Strait of Malacca. / 街上的人很多,车辆无法～。Because of the large crowd in the street the carriage was unable to pass through. 2.(同意) adopt; pass; carry: ～一项决议 adopt a resolution / 他考试～了。He passed in examination. 3.(指方式) by means of; by way of; by; through: ～外交途径 through diplomatic channels / 小偷是～窗户进来的。The thief got in through the window. / 他～努力工作而致富。He became rich through hard work. 4.(征得同意) ask the consent or approval of

【通航】 tōngháng 1.(指海上航线) be open to navigation 2.(指空中航线) be open to air traffic

【通红】 tōnghóng very red; red through and through

【通话】 tōnghuà 1.(通电话) communicate by telephone 2.(彼此交谈) converse; talk with sb; hold conversation

【通婚】 tōnghūn be related by marriage; intermarry

【通货】 tōnghuò 〈*Econ.*〉 currency; current money

【通货回笼】 tōnghuò huílóng 〈*Econ.*〉 recall

currency
【通货膨胀】 tōnghuò péngzhàng 〈*Econ.*〉 inflation
【通货收缩】 tōnghuò shōusuō 〈*Econ.*〉 deflation
【通货稳定】 tōnghuò wěngdìng 〈*Econ.*〉 currency stabilization
【通货自由兑换】 tōnghuò zìyóu duìhuàn 〈*Econ.*〉 currency convertibility
【通缉】 tōngjī order the arrest of a criminal at large; list as wanted
【通缉犯】 tōngjīfàn a criminal wanted by the law
【通缉令】 tōngjīlìng order for arrest
【通集】 tōngjí union of (符号为 ∩)
【通奸】 tōngjiān commit adultery; fornicate; fornication (n.) ‖ 通奸者 fornicator
【通奸罪】 tōngjiānzuì crime of adultery
【通栏标题】 tōnglán biāotí banner headline; banner
【通力】 tōnglì concerted effort: ～合作 give full cooperation to; make a concerted effort
【通例】 tōnglì general rule; usual practice
【通联】 tōnglián communications and liaison
【通令】 tōnglìng 1. (发出同一命令) issue a general order: ～全国 issue a general order to the whole nation 2. (该命令) a general order
【通路】 tōnglù 1. (往来的大路) thoroughfare; highway; highroad; route 2. (途径) passage; access
【通论】 tōnglùn 1. (通达的议论) a sensible argument; a well-rounded argument 2. (全面论述) a general survey; an introduction
【通名】 tōngmíng 1. (通常的名称) a general term; common name; popular name 2. (通报姓名) notify; report
【通明】 tōngmíng well-illuminated; brightly lit
【通盘】 tōngpán overall; all-round; comprehensive: ～考虑 give an overall consideration; consider every possible angle
【通票】 tōngpiào through ticket
【通气】 tōngqì 1. (使通空气) ventilate; aerate 2. (互通声气) be in touch with each other; keep each other informed; have communication with
【通气孔】 tōngqìkǒng air vent; orifice; airflow
【通情达理】 tōngqíng-dálǐ showing good sense; reasonable
【通融】 tōngróng 1. (给人方便) make an exception in sb's favor; stretch rules, get around regulations, etc., to accommodate sb. 2. (短期借钱) accommodate sb. with a short-term loan
【通融票据】 tōngróng piàojù accommodation notes
【通商】 tōngshāng have trade relations
【通商口岸】 tōngshāng kǒu'àn trading port
【通商贸易关系】 tōngshāng màoyì guān·xì trade relations
【通商许可】 tōngshāng xǔkě licence to trade
【通史】 tōngshǐ comprehensive history; general history
【通顺】 tōngshùn clear and coherent; smooth: 文理～ in a coherent and flowing style
【通俗】 tōngsú popular; common
【通俗读物】 tōngsú dúwù books for popular consumption; popular literature
【通俗歌曲】 tōngsú gēqǔ popular song
【通俗化】 tōngsúhuà popularize; popularization (n.)
【通俗小说】 tōngsú xiǎoshuō popular fiction
【通天】 tōngtiān 1. (形容非常之高) exceedingly high; exceedingly great 2. (与上层有联系) direct access to the highest authorities
【通条】 tōngtiáo poker; clean rod
【通通】 tōngtōng all; entirely; totally
【通途】 tōngtú 〈*written*〉 thoroughfare
【通宵】 tōngxiāo all night; the whole night; throughout the night: ～达旦 all through the night
【通宵服务部】 tōngxiāo fúwùbù a shop that is open all night; an all-night shop
【通晓】 tōngxiǎo thoroughly understand; be well versed in; be proficient in: ～世故 be perfectly familiar with the ways of the world
【通心粉】 tōngxīnfěn macaroni
【通信】 tōngxìn communicate by letter; correspond
【通信保密】 tōngxìn bǎomì communication security

【通信兵】 tōngxìnbīng signal corps; signalman
【通信处】 tōngxìnchù mailing address
【通信调查】 tōngxìn diàochá questionnaire mail
【通信鸽】 tōngxìngē homing pigeon; carrier pigeon
【通信连】 tōngxìnlián signal company
【通信频带】 tōngxìn píndài communication band
【通信犬】 tōngxìnquǎn messenger dog
【通信枢纽】 tōngxìn shūniǔ signal center
【通信卫星】 tōngxìn wèixīng communication satellite; radio relay satellite; Telsatar
【通信员】 tōngxìnyuán messenger; orderly
【通行】 tōngxíng 1.（通过）pass through 2.（通用）current; general：～的办法 the current practice
【通行费】 tōngxíngfèi toll
【通行能力】 tōngxíng nénglì traffic capacity
【通行权】 tōngxíngquán right of way
【通行税】 tōngxíngshuì transit duty
【通行证】 tōngxíngzhèng pass; permit; safe-conduct：出示～ show the pass to sb.
【通讯】 tōngxùn 1.（传递消息）communication 2.（报道）news report; news dispatch; correspondence; newsletter
【通讯方法】 tōngxùn fāngfǎ means of communication
【通讯稿】 tōngxùngǎo press release
【通讯联络】 tōngxùn liánluò signal communication; communications and liaison
【通讯录】 tōngxùnlù address book
【通讯社】 tōngxùnshè news agency：新华～ Xinhua News Agency
【通讯设备】 tōngxùn shèbèi communication apparatus
【通讯网络】 tōngxùn wǎngluò communication network
【通讯线路】 tōngxùn xiànlù communication line
【通讯员】 tōngxùnyuán reporter; correspondent
【通讯自由】 tōngxùn zìyóu freedom of correspondence
【通用】 tōngyòng 1.（普遍使用）in common use; current general; general 2.（可换用）interchangeable
【通用插件】 tōngyòng chājiàn universal card
【通用车辆】 tōngyòng chēliàng general-purpose vehicle
【通用电机】 tōngyòng diànjī general-purpose machine
【通用货币】 tōngyòng huòbì current money
【通用软件】 tōngyòng ruǎnjiàn common software
【通用应用程序】 tōngyòng yīngyòng chéngxù general purpose application program
【通用语种】 tōngyòng yǔzhǒng commonly used languages
【通用月票】 tōngyòng yuèpiào a monthly ticket for all urban and suburban lines
【通邮】 tōngyóu accessible by postal communication
【通邮、通商、通航】 tōngyóu、tōngshāng、tōngháng exchanges of mails, trade, air and shipping services
【通则】 tōngzé general rule; general provisions
【通知】 tōngzhī 1.（告知）notify; inform; give notice; let know 2.（通知文件或口信）notice; circular; notification：发一个～ send a notice; send out a circular
【通知单】 tōngzhīdān advice note; letter of notice; notification
【通知人】 tōngzhīrén notifier
【通知书】 tōngzhīshū advertisement; information; advice notice：贷方～ credit advice / 当月～ at a month's notice / 短期～ at short notice / 付款～ advice of payment / 借方～ debit advice

同（tóng） 1.（相同）same; alike; similar 大～小异 alike with minor differences 2.（跟…相同）be the same as 你的钢笔～我的一样。Your pen is the same as mine. 3.（共同）together; in common 4.（同"跟"）with：我们～你一起去。We'll go with you. 5.（同"和"）and; with
【同案犯】 tóng'ànfàn a accomplice
【同案犯证言】 tóng'ànfàn zhèngyán testimony of accomplice
【同班】 tóngbān 1.（在一个班级）in the same class 2.（同班同学）classmate
【同伴】 tóngbàn companion

【同胞】 tóngbāo 1.（同一父母的）born of the same parents 2.（本国或本民族的）fellow countryman; compatriot: 台湾～ compatriots in Taiwan

【同辈】 tóngbèi of the same generation

【同病相怜】 tóngbìng-xiānglián those who have the same illness sympathize with each other; fellow sufferers commiserate with each other

【同步】 tóngbù 1.〈*Physics*〉synchronize; be in of sync; synchronous (adj.) 2.（同时，协调一致）simultaneous

【同步广播】 tóngbù guǎngbō synchronized broadcast

【同步卫星】 tóngbù wèixīng synchronous satellite

【同步信号】 tóngbù xìnhào sync; synch; sync signal

【同仇敌忾】 tóngchóu-díkài share a bitter hatred of the enemy

【同窗】 tóngchuāng 1.（在同一学校学习）study in the same school 2.（同学）schoolmate

【同床异梦】 tóngchuáng yìmèng share the same bed but dream different dreams; be strange bedfellows

【同等】 tóngděng of the same class, rank, or status; on an equal basis

【同等学力】 tóngděng xuélì of the same educational level

【同房】 tóngfáng 1.（家族中同一支的）of the same branch of a family 2.（夫妻过性生活）sleep together; have sexual intercourse

【同父异母兄弟】 tóngfù yìmǔ xiōngdì consanguineous brothers

【同甘共苦】 tónggān-gòngkǔ share weal and woe; share comforts and hardships

【同感】 tónggǎn the same feeling

【同庚】 tónggēng of the same age

【同工异曲】 tónggōng-yìqǔ different tunes rendered with equal skill; different in approach but equally satisfactory results

【同归于尽】 tóngguī-yújìn perish together; end in common ruin

【同行】 tóngháng 1.（指行业）of the same trade or occupation 2.（指人）a person of the same trade or occupation

【同行工会】 tóngháng gōnghuì craft union

【同呼吸，共命运】 tóng hūxī, gòng mìngyùn share a common fate; throw in one's lot with sb.

【同化】 tónghuà 1.（逐渐融合）assimilate; assimilation (n.) 2.〈*Gram.*〉assimilation

【同化政策】 tónghuà zhèngcè the policy of national assimilation

【同化作用】 tónghuà zuòyòng 〈*Biol.*〉assimilation

【同伙】 tónghuǒ 1.（共同参加）be in partnership; collude with 2.（伙伴）partner; associate; confederate

【同居】 tóngjū 1.（住在一起）live together 2.（未婚同居）cohabit; cohabitation (n.)

【同类】 tónglèi of the same kind; similar

【同龄】 tónglíng of the same age

【同流合污】 tóngliú-héwū wallow in the mire with sb.; associate with an evil person

【同路】 tónglù go the same way

【同路人】 tónglùrén fellow traveller

【同盟】 tóngméng 1.（结盟）ally with; unite with 2.（联合体）alliance; league; union

【同名】 tóngmíng of the same name

【同谋】 tóngmóu 1.（参与谋划）conspire; be of complicity 2.（参与谋划的人）accomplice; confederate; conspirator

【同谋犯】 tóngmóufàn accomplice

【同年】 tóngnián 1.（同一年）the same year 2.（同岁）of the same age

【同期】 tóngqī 1.（同一时期）the corresponding period 2.（同一届）of the same term

【同情】 tóngqíng sympathize with; show sympathy for

【同情心】 tóngqíngxīn sympathy; fellow feeling

【同人】 tóngrén colleague; fellow member (of an organization)

【同仁】 tóngrén 同"同人"

【同色】 tóngsè homochromy

【同上】 tóngshàng ditto; idem （符号为〃）

【同声传译】 tóngshēng chuányì simultaneous interpretation

【同生现象】 tóngshēng xiànxiàng 〈*Biol.*〉consortism

【同时】 tóngshí 1.（在同一时候）at the same time; simultaneously; meanwhile; in the meantime：大家不要～讲话。Don't all speak together. / ～发出的两声枪响听起来像是一声。The two simultaneous shots sounded like one. 2.（并且）moreover；besides：我不喜欢滑冰，～冰也太薄。I don't like skating；moreover，the ice is too thin.

【同时联播】 tóngshí liánbō simulcast

【同事】 tóngshì 1.（在同一单位）work in the same place；work together 2.（同一单位的人）colleague；fellow worker

【同岁】 tóngsuì of the same age

【同位素】 tóngwèisù 〈*Chem.*〉isotope；isotopic（adj.）：放射性～ radio-isotope

【同位素检查】 tóngwèisù jiǎnchá isotope examination

【同位素量】 tóngwèisùliàng isotopic content

【同位素扫描器】 tóngwèisù sǎomiáoqì radioisotope scanner

【同位素探伤仪】 tóngwèisù tànshāngyí isoscope

【同位语】 tóngwèiyǔ 〈*Gram.*〉appositive

【同乡】 tóngxiāng a person from the same village，town or province；a fellow villager；a townsman

【同心】 tóngxīn 1.（齐心）with one heart：～同德 with one heart and one mind；with one idea and will 2.（具同一中心的）concentric

【同心协力】 tóngxīn-xiélì work in full cooperation and with unity of purpose；work together with one heart；make concerted efforts

【同心圆】 tóngxīnyuán concentric circles

【同行】 tóngxíng travel together

【同性】 tóngxìng 1.（指性别）of the same sex 2.（指性质）of the same nature or character

【同性恋】 tóngxìngliàn homosexuality；homosexual（adj.）‖ 同性恋者 homosexual

【同姓】 tóngxìng of the same surname

【同学】 tóngxué 1.（在同校学习）be in the same school；be a schoolmate of sb. 2.（在同校学习的人）fellow student；schoolmate

【同样】 tóngyàng same；equal；similar：～大小 of the same size

【同一】 tóngyī same；identical：～竞争规则 compete under the same rules / 请明天～时间和我见面。Meet me at the same time tomorrow.

【同义词】 tóngyìcí synonym

【同意】 tóngyì agree；consent；approve：取得～ obtain sb's consent

【同意书】 tóngyìshū letter of consent

【同意照会】 tóngyì zhàohuì note of approval

【同音词】 tóngyīncí homonym；homophone

【同音异义词】 tóngyīn yìyìcí homonym

【同志】 tóngzhì comrade

【同舟共济】 tóngzhōu-gòngjì cross a river in the same boat；people in the same boat help each other

【同轴电缆】 tóngzhóu diànlǎn coax；coaxial cable

【同族语言】 tóngzú yǔyán cognate language；related language

茼（tóng）

【茼蒿】 tónghāo 〈*Bot.*〉chrysanthemum；crowndaisy chrysanthemum

桐（tóng） 1.（泡桐）paulownia 2.（油桐）tung tree；tung oil tree 3.（梧桐）phoenix tree

【桐油】 tóngyóu tung oil

铜（tóng） 〈*Chem.*〉copper（元素符号 Cu）‖ 黄铜 brass / 青铜 bronze / 紫铜 red copper

【铜版】 tóngbǎn 〈*Printing*〉copperplate

【铜版画】 tóngbǎnhuà copperplate etching；copperplate

【铜版纸】 tóngbǎnzhǐ art paper

【铜币】 tóngbì copper coin

【铜鼓】 tónggǔ bronze drum

【铜管乐队】 tóngguǎn yuèduì brass band

【铜管乐器】 tóngguǎn yuèqì brass-wind instrument；brass wind

【铜活】 tónghuó bronze；brass ware；copper ware

【铜匠】 tóngjiàng coppersmith

【铜镜】 tóngjìng 〈*Archaeol.*〉bronze mirror

【铜矿】 tóngkuàng copper mine

【铜绿】 tónglǜ 〈*Chem.*〉verdigris

【铜模】 tóngmú 〈*Printing*〉matrix；mold

【铜牌】 tóngpái bronze medal

【铜器】 tóngqì bronze；brass ware；copper ware

【铜钱】 tóngqián copper cash

【铜墙铁壁】 tóngqiáng-tiěbì bastion of iron；

impregnable fortress
【铜像】 tóngxiàng bronze statue
【铜臭】 tóngxiù the stink of money; smell like copper coin
【铜元】 tóngyuán copper coin; copper

酮(tóng) 〈*Chem*.〉 ketont

童(tóng) 1.(儿童) child 2.(未婚的) unmarried; virgin: ～男 virgin boy / ～女 maiden; virgin 3.(秃的) bare; bald; barren
【童工】 tónggōng child laborer
【童话】 tónghuà children's stories; fairy tales
【童话世界】 tónghuà shìjiè fairy-tale world
【童年】 tóngnián childhood; boyhood (m.); girlhood (f.)
【童声】 tóngshēng child's voice
【童声合唱】 tóngshēng héchàng children's chorus
【童心】 tóngxīn childlike innocence; childishness
【童谣】 tóngyáo children's rhymes
【童贞】 tóngzhēn virginity
【童真】 tóngzhēn childlike
【童装】 tóngzhuāng children's garments
【童子】 tóngzǐ boy; lad

瞳(tóng) pupil
【瞳孔】 tóngkǒng 〈*Anat*.〉 pupil
【瞳孔开大】 tóngkǒng kāidà 〈*Med*.〉 mydriasis
【瞳孔缩小】 tóngkǒng suōxiǎo 〈*Med*.〉 myosis
【瞳人】 tóngrén 〈*Anat*.〉 pupil
【瞳仁】 tóngrén 同"瞳人"

统(tǒng) 1.(关系) interconnected system: 系～ system 2.(全部) all; together 3.(总括) gather into one; unite 4.(衣物的筒) a tube-shaped part of
【统编】 tǒngbiān centralized compilation
【统舱】 tǒngcāng steerage
【统测】 tǒngcè unified test
【统称】 tǒngchēng 1.(总起来叫) be called by a joint name 2.(总的名称) a general designation
【统筹】 tǒngchóu plan as a whole
【统筹规划】 tǒngchóu guīhuà overall planning
【统筹兼顾】 tǒngchóu jiāngù take the interests of all those concerned into consideration before making an overall plan
【统分结合】 tǒngfēn jiéhé the household contract responsibility system supplemented by unified management
【统共】 tǒnggòng altogether; in all
【统购】 tǒnggòu state monopoly for purchase
【统购统销】 tǒnggòu tǒngxiāo state monopoly for purchase and marketing
【统货】 tǒnghuò gradeless and uniformly-priced goods
【统计】 tǒngjì 1.(统计学) statistics; statistical (adj.) 2.(总括地计算) add up; count: 据初步～ according to preliminary counting
【统计抽样】 tǒngjì chōuyàng statistical sampling
【统计地图】 tǒngjì dìtú statistical map
【统计经济学】 tǒngjì jīngjìxué statistical economics
【统计力学】 tǒngjì lìxué statistical mechanics
【统计数列】 tǒngjì shùliè statistical series
【统计数字】 tǒngjì shùzhì statistical figures; statistics
【统计图表】 tǒngjì túbiǎo statistical graph
【统计推断】 tǒngjì tuīduàn statistical inference
【统计误差】 tǒngjì wùchā statistical uncertainty
【统计学】 tǒngjìxué statistics; statistical (adj.) ‖ 统计学家 statistician
【统计语言学】 tǒngjì yǔyánxué statistical linguistics
【统计员】 tǒngjìyuán statistician
【统计资料】 tǒngjì zīliào statistical data
【统考】 tǒngkǎo unified examination; general examination with a common test paper
【统铺】 tǒngpù a wide bed for a number of people
【统率】 tǒngshuài command
【统帅】 tǒngshuài 1.(军队最高领导人) commander in chief; commander 2.(统辖率领) command
【统帅部】 tǒngshuàibù supreme command
【统辖】 tǒngxiá have under one's command
【统一】 tǒngyī 1.(联成整体) unify; unite; integrate: 完成祖国～大业 accomplish the

great cause of national reunification 2.(一致的;整体的) unified; unitary; centralized

【统一币制】 tǒngyī bìzhì unification of the currency

【统一战线】 tǒngyī zhànxiàn united front

【统战】 tǒngzhàn united front

【统战部】 tǒngzhànbù the united front work department

【统治】 tǒngzhì rule; dominate; domination (n.)

【统治阶级】 tǒngzhì jiējí ruling class

【统治权】 tǒngzhìquán dominion; sovereignty

【统治者】 tǒngzhìzhě ruler

【统制】 tǒngzhì control: 经济～ economic control / 军事～ military control

捅[㨔] (tǒng) 1.(戳;扎) poke; stab: 他用刀子把这妇女～死了。He stabbed the women with a knife and she died. 2.(碰;触动) poke; stir up: 他用一根棍子～火。He poked the fire with a stick. 3.(揭露) disclose; give away; let out: 把真相～了出去 disclose the truth

【捅娄子】 tǒng lóu·zi make a mess of sth.; get into trouble

【捅马蜂窝】 tǒng mǎfēngwō stir up a hornets' nests

桶 (tǒng) 1.(容器) tub; pail; bucket; keg; barrel: 啤酒～ barrel of beer / 汽油～ drum of oil 2.(量词,用于石油) barrel

筒[筩] (tǒng) 1.(粗竹管) a section of thick bamboo 2.(器物) a thick tube-shaped: 烟～ chimney / 邮～ pillar box 3.(衣服等的管状部分) the tube-shaped part of an article of clothing 4.〈*classifier*〉 tin; can: 一～可乐 a can of coke

【筒裙】 tǒngqún tight skirt

【筒子】 tǒng·zi tube; tube-shaped object

【筒子楼】 tǒng·zilóu tube-shaped department

痛 (tòng) 1.(疼痛) ache; pain 2.(悲伤) sorrow; sadness: 悲～ deep sorrow 3.(尽情地) extremely; deeply; bitterly: ～饮 drink one's fill

【痛不欲生】 tòngbùyùshēng grieve to the extent of wishing to die; be overwhelmed with sorrow

【痛斥】 tòngchì bitterly attack; scathingly denounce

【痛楚】 tòngchǔ pain; anguish; suffering

【痛处】 tòngchù sore spot; tender spot

【痛打】 tòngdǎ beat soundly; belabor

【痛点】 tòngdiǎn pain spot

【痛改前非】 tònggǎi-qiánfēi sincerely mend one's ways; thoroughly rectify one's errors

【痛感】 tònggǎn keenly feel

【痛恨】 tònghèn hate bitterly; utterly detest

【痛击】 tòngjī strike a severe blow: 迎头～ give sb. a bad knock on the head; repulse a frontal attack

【痛经】 tòngjīng 〈*Med*.〉 dysmenorrhea

【痛哭】 tòngkū cry bitterly; wail

【痛哭流涕】 tòngkū-liútì cry and shed bitter tears; set one's eyes at flow

【痛苦】 tòngkǔ pain; suffering; agony

【痛快】 tòngkuài 1.(高兴) very happy; delighted; joyful: 感到～ be filled with joy 2.(尽兴) to one's heart's content; to one's great satisfaction 3.(爽快) simple and direct; forthright; straightforward

【痛骂】 tòngmà scold severely; curse roundly; give a good scolding

【痛惜】 tòngxī deeply regret; deplore

【痛心】 tòngxīn pained; distressed; grieved

【痛心疾首】 tòngxīn jíshǒu with bitter hatred

【痛痒】 tòngyǎng 1.(疾苦) sufferings; difficulties 2.(紧要的事) importance; consequence: 无关～ a matter of no consequence

tou

偷 (tōu) 1.(偷窃) steal; pilfer; thieve; make off with: 谁～了我的钱包? Who stole my wallet? 2.(偷偷) stealthily; secretly; on the sly 3.(抽时间) find (time): ～空 take time off

【偷安】 tōu'ān seek temporary ease

【偷盗】 tōudào steal; pilfer

【偷渡】 tōudù cross the border illegally

【偷看】 tōukàn peek; peep: 从窗户～ peep out of a window / 在镜子里～某人 steal a glance at sb. in the mirror

【偷懒】 tōulǎn loaf on the job; be lazy: 干活～ be lazy in one's work

【偷猎】 tōuliè poach

【偷窃】 tōuqiè steal; pilfer; thieve

【偷情】 tōuqíng carry on a clandestine love affair

【偷生】 tōushēng drag out an ignoble existence

【偷税】 tōushuì evade taxes

【偷听】 tōutīng eavesdrop; bug; tap: 他们～了使馆里的全部谈话。They've been eavesdropping on all conversations in the Embassy. / 他在～电话的丑闻之后辞去了部长职务。He resigned as minister after phone-tapping scandal.

【偷偷】 tōutōu stealthily; secretly; covertly; on the sly: 她～溜出了房间。She stole out of the room.

【偷偷摸摸】 tōutōu-mōmō furtively; surreptitiously; covertly

【偷袭】 tōuxī sneak attack; sneak raid; surprise attack

【偷闲】 tōuxián 1.(挤出空闲) snatch a moment of leisure: 忙里～ allow oneself a bit of time 2.(偷懒) loaf on the job; be idle

【偷越国境】 tōuyuè guójìng illegally cross the national border

头[頭] (tóu) 1.(脑袋,头部) head 2.(发式) hair; hair style: 梳～ comb the hair / 分～ parted hair / 光～ skinhead 3.(顶端或末梢) head; top; end: 锤子～ the head of a hammer / 床～ headboard 4.(起点或终点) beginning or end 5.(残留部分) stub; remnant; stump; end 6.(头目) head; chief; boss 7.(方面) side; aspect 8.(第一;前面的) first: ～胎 firstborn / ～一遍 the first time 9.(领头的) leading 10.〈*classifier*〉 head: 三～牛 three head of cattle

【头版】 tóubǎn front page

【头部】 tóubù head

【头彩】 tóucǎi the first prize

【头寸】 tóucùn 1.(银行款项) cash 2.(银根) money market; money supply: 缺～ be in want of money supply

【头戴耳机】 tóudài ěrjī headphone; can

【头灯】 tóudēng 〈*Mineral*.〉 head lamp

【头等】 tóuděng 1.(一等) first-class; first-rate 2.(重要) prime importance; primary importance: ～大事 things of primary importance

【头等舱】 tóuděngcāng first-class cabin

【头等品】 tóuděngpǐn first-rate goods

【头顶】 tóudǐng the top of the head; the crown of the head

【头发】 tóu·fa hair

【头号】 tóuhào 1.(第一号) number one; size one 2.(最好的) first-rate; top quality: ～面粉 the best flour

【头号新闻】 tóuhào xīnwén headline news; lead story in a paper

【头昏】 tóuhūn dizzy; giddy

【头角】 tóujiǎo brilliance; talent: 初露～ begin to show one's talent

【头巾】 tóujīn scarf; kerchief; turban

【头靠】 tóukào 〈*Auto*〉 head rest

【头盔】 tóukuī helmet: 骑摩托车的人戴了一顶～。The man on the motorcycle wore a helmet.

【头里】 tóu·li 1.(前面) in front: ahead 2.(事先) in advance; beforehand

【头颅】 tóulú 1.(颅骨) skull 2.(头) head: 抛～ lay down one's life

【头面人物】 tóumiàn rénwù bigwig; big shot; prominent figure: 我们被邀与当地的～共进午餐。We were invited to a lunch with local bigwigs.

【头目】 tóumù head of a gang; ringleader; chieftain

【头脑】 tóunǎo 1.(脑筋) head; brains; mind: ～清醒 have a clear mind / 没有数学～ a poor head for mathematics 2.(头绪) main threads; clue

【头年】 tóunián 1.(第一年) the first year 2.(去年) last year

【头皮】 tóupí 1.(头上的皮肤) scalp 2.(头皮屑) dandruff; scurf

【头皮屑】 tóupíxiè dandruff; scurf

【头皮癣】 tóupíxuǎn ringworm of scalp

【头破血流】 tóupò-xuèliú head broken and bleeding; hurt one's head badly

【头前】 tóuqián 1.(前面) in front: ahead 2.(以前) before; previously

【头球】 tóuqiú 〈*Football*〉 header

【头生】 tóushēng 1.(第一次生育) the first birth 2.(第一胎) the first-born

【头饰】 tóushì headdress

【头胎】 tóutāi the first-born

【头套】 tóutào actor's headgear

【头疼】 tóuténg headache; have a headache: 她～。Her head aches. (或: She has a headache.)

【头条新闻】 tóutiáo xīnwén top news; top-line news

【头痛】 tóutòng headache: 他～。He has a headache.

【头衔】 tóuxián title

【头像】 tóuxiàng 1.(塑像) head sculpture 2.(画像) head portrait

【头绪】 tóuxù main threads: 理出～ arrange things in order

【头油】 tóuyóu hair oil; pomade

【头晕】 tóuyūn dizzy; giddy

【头重脚轻】 tóuzhòng-jiǎoqīng top-heavy

【头子】 tóu·zi chieftain; chief; boss

投 (tóu) 1.(投掷) throw; fling; hurl: 他把球～给我,我接住了。He threw the ball to me, and I caught it. / 他用力把砖头从窗户～了进去。He hurled the brick through the window. 2.(投入) put in; drop 3.(跳进去) throw oneself into: ～河自尽 drown oneself in a river; commit suicide by throwing oneself into the river 4.(投射) project; cast 5.(投寄) send; deliver: ～书 deliver a letter / ～信 send a letter 6.(迎合) fit in with; agree with; cater to: 意气相～ find each other congenial

【投案】 tóu'àn give oneself up to the police: ～自首 voluntary surrender to court

【投保】 tóubǎo insure: 给房屋～火险 insure one's house against fire

【投保单】 tóubǎodān insurance application; insurance cover note

【投保价值】 tóubǎo jiàzhí insured value

【投保人】 tóubǎorén insurant; the insured: ～的责任 liability of the insurant / ～的权利 right of the insured

【投奔】 tóubèn go to for shelter

【投笔从戎】 tóubǐ-cóngróng throw aside the writing brush and join the army; renounce the pen for the sword

【投币式公用电话机】 tóubìshí gōngyòng diànhuàjī prepay-set

【投币式自动售货机】 tóubìshí zìdòng shòuhuòjī slot machine

【投标】 tóubiāo tender; submit a tender; enter a bid: 在～阶段 at the tender stage

【投标递价】 tóubiāo dìjià bid; tender

【投标人】 tóubiāorén bidder; tenderer

【投标委员会】 tóubiāo wěiyuánhuì tender committee

【投产】 tóuchǎn go into operation; put into production; commissioning; bring into service

【投诚】 tóuchéng surrender; cross over

【投弹】 tóudàn 1.(空投炸弹) drop a bomb 2.(投掷手榴弹) throw a hand grenades

【投弹高度】 tóudàn gāodù release altitude

【投弹角】 tóudànjiǎo dropping angle

【投弹器】 tóudànqì bomb rack control; bomb release mechanism

【投弹手】 tóudànshǒu bombardier; grenadier

【投敌】 tóudí go over to the enemy; defect to the enemy

【投递】 tóudì deliver: ～信件 deliver letters

【投递员】 tóudìyuán postman; letter carrier; mail carrier; mailman

【投放】 tóufàng 1.(放进) throw in; put in 2.(提供资金) put (money) into circulation 3.(供应商品) put (goods) on the market

【投稿】 tóugǎo contribute; submit a piece of writing for publication

【投稿人】 tóugǎorén contributor

【投合】 tóuhé 1.(合得来) agree; get along 2.(迎合) cater to

【投机】 tóujī 1.(见解相同) congenial; agreeable 2.(谋取私利) speculate

【投机倒把】 tóujī-dǎobǎ speculate; engage in speculation

【投机分子】 tóujī fènzǐ opportunist; political speculator

【投机贸易】 tóujī màoyì speculative trade

【投机取巧】 tóujī qǔqiǎo do things by irregular ways

【投机商】 tóujīshāng speculator; profiteer

【投机事业】 tóujī shìyè speculative enterprise

【投考】 tóukǎo sign up for an examination

【投靠】 tóukào go and seek refuge with sb.; go to live under the roof of sb.

【投篮】 tóulán 〈*Sports*〉 shoot; shoot at the basket; shot: ～不中 miss a shot; miss the basket / ～得分 shoot a basket / 近距离～ close-in shot / 远距离～ long shot

【投料试生产】 tóuliào shìshēngchǎn commission test run

【投票】 tóupiào vote; cast a vote: 无记名～ secret ballot / ～表决 decide by ballot / ～反对 vote against / ～赞成 vote for; vote in favor of

【投票日】 tóupiàorì polling day

【投票箱】 tóupiàoxiāng ballot box

【投票站】 tóupiàozhàn polling booth; the polls

【投亲】 tóuqīn go and live with relatives; seek refuge with relatives

【投入】 tóurù 1.(进入) put in; throw in: ～生产 bring into production / ～战斗 engage oneself in the battle 2.(聚精会神) with rapt attention; attentive 3.(指资金) input: 教育～ educational input / ～和产出 input and output

【投入资本】 tóurù zīběng invested capital; vested capital

【投射】 tóushè 1.(扔;掷) throw; cast 2.(指光线等) project; cast

【投射点】 tóushèdiǎn incident point

【投射角】 tóushèjiǎo angle of incidence

【投射器】 tóushèqì projector

【投射物】 tóushèwù projectile

【投身】 tóushēn throw oneself into

【投师】 tóushī seek instruction from a master: ～访友 learn from a master and call on friends to exchange knowledge or skills

【投石问路】 tóushí-wènlù throw a stone to clear the road

【投手】 tóushǒu 〈*Baseball & Softball*〉 pitcher

【投手板】 tóushǒubǎn 〈*Baseball*〉 pitcher's plate

【投手犯规】 tóushǒu fànguī 〈*Baseball & Softball*〉 balk

【投手坡】 tóushǒupō 〈*Baseball*〉 pitcher's mound

【投手圈】 tóushǒuquān 〈*Softball*〉 pitcher's circle

【投鼠忌器】 tóushǔ-jìqì hesitate to pelt a rat for fear of smashing the dishes beside it; spare the rat to save the dishes; Burn not your horse to rid it of the mouse.

【投诉】 tóusù complaint; make a complaint

【投诉信】 tóusùxìn letter of complaint

【投宿】 tóusù seek temporary lodging; put up for the night

【投胎】 tóutāi reincarnate; reincarnation (n.)

【投降】 tóuxiáng surrender; capitulate; capitulation (n.): 无条件～ unconditional surrender / 有条件～ capitulation / 他们宁死也不～。They would rather die than surrender. / 体育部长在要求他辞职的呼声中今天宣布～。The sports minister today capitulated to calls for his resignation.

【投降派】 tóuxiángpài 1.(指派别) capitulationist clique 2.(指个人) capitulator

【投降主义】 tóuxiáng zhǔyì capitulationism; capitulationist (adj.)

【投医】 tóuyī go to a doctor

【投影】 tóuyǐng project; projection (n.)

【投影图】 tóuyǐngtú projection drawing

【投影仪】 tóuyǐngyí projecting apparatus

【投掷】 tóuzhì throw; hurl: ～70米远 a throw of 70 meters

【投掷区】 tóuzhìqū 〈*Sports*〉 throwing sector

【投掷圈】 tóuzhìquān 〈*Sports*〉 throwing circle

【投掷项目】 tóuzhì xiàngmù 〈*Sports*〉 distance throw

【投资】 tóuzī 1.(投入资金) invest; put money into 2.(指资金) investment; money invested: 外商～ investment by foreign businessman

【投资保障协议】 tóuzī bǎozhàng xiéyì an investment protection agreement

【投资场所】 tóuzī chǎngsuǒ outlet for investment

【投资方向】 tóuzī fāngxiàng investment orientation

【投资公司】 tóuzī gōngsī investment company

【投资环境】 tóuzī huánjìng investment environment; investment climate: 改善～ improve the investment climate

【投资回收率】 tóuzī huíshōulǜ return on investment

【投资基金】 tóuzī jījīn investment funds

【投资热点】 tóuzī rèdiǎn hot spot for foreign investment

【投资少,收效快】 tóuzī shǎo, shōuxiào kuài

require less investment while yielding quicker results

【投资市场】 tóuzī shìchǎng investment market

【投资收益】 tóuzī shōuyì income from investment; income on investment

【投资效益】 tóuzī xiàoyì deficiency of investment

【投资信用】 tóuzī xìnyòng investment credit

【投资银行】 tóuzī yínháng investment bank

【投资总量】 tóuzī zǒngliàng aggregate investment

骰（tóu）

【骰子】 tóu·zi dice：掷～ throw; throw dice; roll dice

透（tòu） 1.（透过）penetrate; pass through; seep through 2.（透露）tell secretly 3.（透彻）fully; thoroughly; in a penetrating way 4.（显露）appear; show

【透彻】 tòuchè penetrating; thorough; incisive

【透顶】 tòudǐng extremely; downright; out and out

【透风】 tòufēng 1.（让风通过）let in air; ventilate 2.（透露风声）divulge a secret; leak

【透光】 tòuguāng pervious to light

【透光度】 tòuguāngdù transmittance; transmittancy

【透镜】 tòujìng 〈*Physics*〉 lens：凹～ concave lens / 凹凸～ convex-concave lens / 分光～ beam-splitting lens / 复合～ compound lens / 凸～ convex lens

【透亮】 tòuliàng 1.（明亮）bright; transparent 2.（明白）perfectly clear

【透漏】 tòulòu divulge; leak; reveal

【透露】 tòulù divulge; leak; disclose; reveal：～机密 reveal the secret

【透明】 tòumíng transparency; transparent (adj.)

【透明度】 tòumíngdù 1.〈*Physics*〉 transparency; diaphaneity 2.（公开程度）openness：政治～ open politics; openness of the politics

【透明胶带】 tòumíng jiāodài scotch tape; Sellotape

【透明漆】 tòumíngqī celluloid paint; clear lacquer

【透明体】 tòumíngtǐ transparent body

【透气】 tòuqì 1.（空气通过）ventilate 2.（呼吸空气）breathe freely

【透气性】 tòuqìxìng gas permeability

【透视】 tòushì 1.〈*Arts*〉 perspective 2.〈*Med.*〉 fluoroscopy; roentgenoscopy 3.（看穿）see through; see the inside of; penetrate

【透水】 tòushuǐ 1.（让水透过来）let in water 2.（水透过来）seep in; permeate

【透析】 tòuxī 〈*Med.*〉 dialysis; dialysis therapy

【透析机】 tòuxījī 〈*Med.*〉 dialyser

【透信】 tòuxìn divulge; disclose; reveal

【透支】 tòuzhī 1.〈*Econ.*〉 overdraw; make an overdraft：这个信用卡允许～。This credit card offers overdrafts. / 该账户已经～。The account was overdrawn. 2.（预支工资）draw one's salary in advance：～薪金 anticipate one's pay

【透支户】 tòuzhīhù overdrawn account

tu

凸（tū） protruding; raised

【凸凹不平】 tū'āo bùpíng rough and uneven in surface

【凸版纸】 tūbǎnzhǐ printing paper

【凸出】 tūchū bulge; protrude; project

【凸镜】 tūjìng convex mirror; convex lens

【凸面镜】 tūmiànjìng 〈*Physics*〉 convex mirror

【凸透镜】 tūtòujìng 〈*Physics*〉 convex lens

秃（tū） 1.（无毛发）bald; bare 2.（无树木;无枝叶）bare 3.（失去尖端的）blunt; without a point 4.（结构不完整）incomplete; unsatisfactory

【秃笔】 tūbǐ 1.（指笔）worn-out writing brush; bald writing brush 2.（指写作能力）poor writing ability

【秃顶】 tūdǐng 1.（指人）bald; baldheaded：～的老人 a bald old man 2.（指头）bald head

【秃鹫】 tūjiù 〈*Zool.*〉 condor

【秃瓢】 tūpiáo shaken head

【秃头】 tūtóu 1.（秃顶）bald head 2.（光头）shaven head 3.（秃顶的人）bald; baldheaded

4.（没戴帽子的）bareheaded; hatless

【秃子】 tū·zi bald; baldheaded

突（tū） 1.（猛冲）dash forward; charge 2.（突然）sudden; abrupt 3.（突起；突出）projecting; sticking out

【突变】 tūbiàn 1.（突然变化）sudden change; unexpected change 2.〈*Biol*.〉mutation

【突出】 tūchū 1.（冲出）break out: ～重围 break out through the siege 2.（鼓出来）protrude; project; stick out: 他的牙太～了。His teeth protrude too far. 3.（明显；出众）outstanding; prominent: ～的表现 outstanding performance / 一个很～的学生 an outstanding pupil 4.（强调）stress; highlight; give prominence to: ～个人 push oneself forward / ～重点 lay stress on the key points

【突飞猛进】 tūfēi-měngjìn develop rapidly; advance at top speed

【突击】 tūjī 1.（急速攻击）make a sudden and violent attack; assault 2.（加快完成）make a concentrated effort to finish a job quickly: ～任务 do a crash job

【突击点】 tūjīdiǎn point of assault

【突击队】 tūjīduì shock brigade

【突击任务】 tūjī rènwù rush job; shock work

【突击手】 tūjīshǒu shock worker

【突击战术】 tūjī zhànshù shock tactics

【突破】 tūpò 1.（打开缺口）break through; make a breakthrough: ～封锁 break through the blockade 2.（打破）surmount; break; top: ～定额 overfulfil a quota 3.〈*Football*〉break through a defense

【突破口】 tūpòkǒu breakthrough point

【突起】 tūqǐ 1.（突然发生）break out; suddenly appear 2.（高耸）rise high; tower

【突然】 tūrán sudden; abrupt; unexpected: 她的病很～，昨天就好了。Her illness was very sudden — she was well yesterday. / 由于价格走向的～变化，买主已退出市场。Buyers have withdrawn from the market in view of the abrupt turn of the trend of prices.

【突如其来】 tūrúqílái arise suddenly; come all of a sudden

【突围】 tūwéi break out of an encirclement

【突兀】 tūwù 1.（高耸）rise high; tower 2.（突然发生）break out; suddenly appear

【突袭】 tūxí surprise attack; sudden assault

图［圖］（tú） 1.（图画）picture; drawing; chart; map: 地～ map / 示意～ sketch; sketch map 2.（谋划）scheme; plan; attempt 3.（贪图）pursue; seek 4.（意图）intention; intent

【图案】 tú'àn pattern; design

【图饱私囊】 túbǎo-sīnáng planning to fill one's own pocket

【图表】 túbiǎo chart; diagram; graph: 统计～ statistical chart

【图财害命】 túcái-hàimìng murder for money

【图钉】 túdīng drawing pin; thumbtack

【图画】 túhuà drawing; picture; painting

【图解】 tújiě 1.（用图形分析、演算）figure; diagram; graph 2.〈*Math*.〉graphic solution 3.（有图、表的）pictorial; illustrated: ～词典 pictorial dictionary

【图景】 tújǐng view; prospect

【图利】 túlì desire to make money or profit; plan to make money

【图例】 túlì legend; key; brief description

【图名】 túmíng seek fame; for the sake of prestige

【图谋】 túmóu 1.（谋划）plot; scheme; conspire: ～私利 plot for personal gain 2.（计谋）plot; scheme; conspiracy

【图片】 túpiàn picture; photograph

【图片社】 túpiànshè photo house

【图片新闻】 túpiàn xīnwén art photo journalism

【图穷匕首见】 tú qióng bǐshǒu xiàn when the map was unrolled, the dagger was revealed; the real intention is revealed in the end

【图示】 túshì graphic representation

【图示法】 túshìfǎ graphic method

【图示仪】 túshìyí graphic instrument

【图书】 túshū book

【图书馆】 túshūguǎn library: 大学～ university library / 公共～ public library ‖ 图书馆馆员 librarian

【图书馆学】 túshūguǎnxué library science

【图书目录】 túshū mùlù catalogue of books; library catalogue

【图书室】 túshūshì a reading room

【图腾】 túténg totem

【图腾崇拜】 túténg chóngbài totemism

【图像】 túxiàng picture; image

【图像显示】 túxiàng xiǎnshì pictorial display
【图形】 túxíng 1.（画的形状）graph；figure 2.（几何图形）geometric figure
【图形字符】 túxíng zìfú graphic character
【图样】 túyàng pattern；design；draft；drawing
【图章】 túzhāng 1.（章）seal；stamp：盖～ affix a seal；put one's seal 2.（印记）seal；stamp；chop
【图纸】 túzhǐ blueprint；drawing：建筑施工～ construction blueprint

荼（tú）

【荼毒】 túdú 〈*written*〉afflict with great suffering；torment：～生灵 plunge the people into the depths of suffering

涂［塗］（tú） 1.（涂抹）spread on；apply；smear 2.（抹去）blot out；cross out 3.（乱写）scribble；scrawl
【涂布】 túbù coat
【涂层】 túcéng paint-coat；coat
【涂改】 túgǎi alter；make over
【涂改液】 túgǎiyè correction pen
【涂料】 túliào coating；paint
【涂抹】 túmǒ 1.（涂在东西上）daub；smear；paint 2.（乱写；乱画）scribble；scrawl
【涂炭】 tútàn 〈*written*〉utter misery；misery and suffering：生灵～ the people are plunged into an abyss of misery
【涂写】 túxiě scribble；scrawl
【涂鸦】 túyā poor handwriting；scrawl
【涂脂抹粉】 túzhī-mǒfěn prettify；apply powder and paint

途（tú） way；road；route

【途经】 tújīng by way of；via：～西安 by way of Xi'an / 从北京～天津去上海 travel from Beijing to Shanghai via Tianjin
【途径】 tújìng way；channel：通过外交～进行谈判 negotiate through diplomatic channels

酴（tú） leaven；yeast

徒（tú） 1.（步行）on foot 2.（空的）empty；bare 3.（仅仅）merely；only 4.（徒然）in vain；to no avail 5.（徒弟）apprentice；pupil
【徒步】 túbù on foot：～旅行 travel on foot
【徒弟】 túdì apprentice；disciple
【徒工】 túgōng apprentice；apprentice worker
【徒劳】 túláo futile effort；fruitless labor：～往返 make a futile trip；hurry back and forth for nothing
【徒劳无益】 túláo-wúyì flog a dead horse
【徒然】 túrán 1.（白白）in vain；to no avail 2.（仅仅）merely；only
【徒手】 túshǒu bare-handed；unarmed
【徒刑】 túxíng 〈*Law*〉imprisonment；sentence：无期～ life sentence / 判5年有期～ sentence sb. to five years' imprisonment
【徒有其名】 túyǒu-qímíng nominal；in name only
【徒有虚名】 túyǒu-xūmíng nominal；in name only
【徒子徒孙】 túzǐ-túsūn 〈*derog.*〉disciples and followers

屠（tú） 1.（宰杀）slaughter 2.（屠杀）massacre；slaughter

【屠城】 túchéng massacre the inhabitants of a captured city
【屠刀】 túdāo 1.（屠户的）butcher's knife 2.（泛指杀人武器）massacre weapon
【屠夫】 túfū 1.（屠户）butcher 2.（屠杀人民的人）a ruthless ruler
【屠户】 túhù butcher
【屠戮】 túlù 〈*written*〉slaughter；massacre
【屠杀】 túshā massacre；slaughter：大～ massacre；mass slaughter
【屠宰】 túzǎi butcher；slaughter
【屠宰场】 túzǎichǎng butcher house；slaughter house

土（tǔ） 1.（土壤）soil；earth 2.（土地）land；ground 3.（地方性的）local；native 4.（民间的）homemade；indigenous 5.（不合潮流的）unrefined；unenlightened

【土包子】 tǔbāo·zi clodhopper；bumpkin
【土崩瓦解】 tǔbēng-wǎjiě disintegrate；crumble；fall apart；collapse like a house of cards
【土布】 tǔbù handwoven cloth；homespun cloth
【土产】 tǔchǎn 1.（地方生产的）produced locally 2.（地 方产品）local product
【土地】 tǔdì 1.（田地）land；soil；ground：～

的征用 expropriation of land / ～很旱,好久没下雨了。The land is very dry; there has been no rain. 2.(疆域) territory
【土地法】 tǔdìfǎ land law; agrarian law
【土地分红】 tǔdì fēnhóng dividend on land shares
【土地改革】 tǔdì gǎigé land reform; agrarian reform
【土地集中】 tǔdì jízhōng concentration of landholdings
【土地纠纷】 tǔdì jiūfēn land disputes
【土地税】 tǔdìshuì land tax
【土地所有人】 tǔdì shuǒyǒurén landholder; landowner
【土地制度】 tǔdì zhìdù land system
【土地转让】 tǔdì zhuǎnràng land transfer
【土豆】 tǔdòu potato
【土豆片】 tǔdòupiàn potato chips
【土方】 tǔfāng 1.(民间药方) traditional cure; folk recipe 2.(土方工程) earthwork 3.(计量单位) cubic meter of earth
【土匪】 tǔfěi bandit; brigand
【土贵乌拉】 Tǔguìwūlā 〈place〉 Togrog Ul
【土豪】 tǔháo local lord: ～劣绅 local lords and evil gentry
【土话】 tǔhuà local dialect; localism; colloquial expressions
【土家族】 Tǔjiāzú Tujia (中国少数民族,主要分布在湖北、湖南、四川等地)
【土霉素】 tǔméisù 〈*Pharm.*〉 terramycin; oxytetracycline
【土木】 tǔmù building; construction: 大兴～ go into great scale of construction
【土木工程】 tǔmù gōngchéng civil engineering
【土木工程师】 tǔmù gōngchéngshī civil engineer
【土坯】 tǔpī adobe
【土气】 tǔqì rustic; uncouth; countrified
【土壤】 tǔrǎng soil: 白垩质～ chalky soil / 沙质～ sandy soil / 肥沃的～ fertile soil
【土壤保持】 tǔrǎng bǎochí soil conservation
【土壤肥力】 tǔrǎng féilì soil fertility
【土壤改良】 tǔrǎng gǎiliáng soil improvement; soil amelioration
【土壤结构】 tǔrǎng jiégòu soil structure
【土壤普查】 tǔrǎng pǔchá general survey of soil
【土壤湿度】 tǔrǎng shīdù soil moisture
【土壤温度】 tǔrǎng wēndù soil temperature
【土壤学】 tǔrǎngxué soil science; pedology ‖ 土壤学家 pedologist
【土色】 tǔsè ashen; pale
【土生土长】 tǔshēng-tǔzhǎng locally born and bred; born and brought up on one's native soil
【土特产】 tǔtèchǎn local specialty; local speciality
【土星】 Tǔxīng 〈*Astron.*〉 Saturn
【土音】 tǔyīn local accent
【土语】 tǔyǔ local, colloquial expressions; local dialect
【土葬】 tǔzàng burial in the ground
【土政策】 tǔzhèncè local policy
【土质】 tǔzhì soil property
【土著】 tǔzhù aboriginals; natives
【土著人】 tǔzhùrén original inhabitants; natives; aborigines
【土族】 Tǔzú Tu (中国少数民族,主要分布在青海)

吐 (tǔ) 1.(吐出来) spit: ～痰 spit; expectorate 2.(长出来,露出来) put: ～穗 sprout ears; be earing 3.(说出) say; tell; pour out
(另见"吐"tù)
【吐故纳新】 tǔgù-nàxīn get rid of the stale and take in the fresh
【吐鲁番】 Tǔlǔfān 〈place〉 Turpan
【吐露】 tǔlù reveal; tell: ～真情 reveal the truth
【吐气】 tǔqì 1.(松口气) feel elated after unburdening oneself of resentment; feel elated and exultant: 扬眉～ feel elated and exalted; hold one's head high 2.〈*Phonet.*〉 aspirated
【吐穗】 tǔsuì 〈*Agric.*〉 ear; sprout ears
【吐字】 tǔzì articulate: ～清楚 articulate clearly

钍 (tǔ) 〈*Chem.*〉 thorium (元素符号 Th)

吐 (tù) 1.(呕吐) vomit; throw up; spit: 他吃了变质的肉后～了。He vomited after eating the bad meat. / 孩子把吃的东西都～出来了。The child spat out its food. 2.(被迫退还) give up unwillingly; disgorge: ～出

赃款 disgorge ill-gotten gains
（另见“吐”tǔ）

【吐沫】 tù·mo saliva; spittle; spit

【吐血】 tùxiě 1.（呕出血）spit out blood; hematemesis（n.）2.（强迫退出）be forced to return; be forced to give back

【吐泻】 tù-xiè vomiting and diarrhea

兔［兎］（tù） hare; rabbit：家～ rabbit / 野～ hare; wild rabbit / 雄～ buck

【兔唇】 tùchún 〈*Med*.〉 harelip

【兔毛衫】 tùmáoshān angora sweater

【兔子】 tù·zi hare; rabbit

菟（tù）

【菟丝子】 tùsīzǐ 〈*Bot*.〉 dodder; Chinese dodder

tuan

湍（tuān）

【湍急】 tuānjí rapid; torrential

【湍流】 tuānliú 1.（急流）swift current; rushing waters; torrent; rapids：～滚下 torrents of water rolling down 2.（汹涌）turbulent flow; turbulence

团［團、糰[2]］（tuán） 1.（圆形的）round; circular; roundish 2.（团子）sth. shaped like a ball 3.（揉成球形）roll sth. into a ball; roll 4.（团体）group; society; organization 5.（团结）unite; conglomerate 6.〈*Mil*.〉 regiment

【团拜】 tuánbài mass greetings; mass congratulations

【团队】 tuánduì corps

【团伙】 tuánhuǒ gang; band

【团籍】 tuánjí the League membership

【团结】 tuánjié 1.（联合）unite; rally; unity（n.）：加强～ consolidate unity 2.（和睦）accordant; harmonious; friendly

【团聚】 tuánjù reunite; reunion：亲人～ reunite with one's family and relatives

【团脐】 tuánqí female crab

【团体】 tuántǐ organization; group; team：社会～ social organization

【团体保险】 tuántǐ bǎoxiǎn group insurance

【团体操】 tuántǐcāo group calisthenics

【团体冠军】 tuántǐ guànjūn team title

【团体票】 tuántǐpiào group ticket

【团体赛】 tuántǐsài team competition

【团团】 tuántuán round and round; all round：～围住 encircle; surround completely

【团团转】 tuántuánzhuàn round and round

【团鱼】 tuányú soft-shelled turtle

【团员】 tuányuán 1.（共青团员）League member 2.（代表团成员）member of a delegation

【团圆】 tuányuán 1.（团聚）reunion 2.（圆形的）round

【团长】 tuánzhǎng 1.〈*Mil*.〉 regimental commander 2.（代表团的）head：代表团～ head of a delegation

【团子】 tuán·zi dumpling

tui

忒（tuī） very; too

推（tuī） 1.（向前推）push; shove：～车 push a cart / 把船～到水里 shove a boat into the water / 他们把大门～开了。They pushed the gate open. / 她使劲一～，门开了。She gave a hard push, and the door opened. 2.（磨、碾粮食）turn a mill; turn a grindstone; grind millstone 3.（剪；削）cut; pare：～头 have a haircut; cut sb's hair 4.（推动）push forward; promote; advance 5.（推断）infer; deduce 6.（推卸）push away; shirk; shift 7.（推迟）put off; postpone 8.（推选）elect; choose 9.（推崇）hold in esteem; praise highly

【推波助澜】 tuībō-zhùlán fan the fire; aggravate a complicate situation

【推测】 tuīcè infer; conjecture; guess

【推陈出新】 tuīchén-chūxīn weed through the old to bring forth the new

【推迟】 tuīchí put off; postpone; defer：我们把比赛从9月5日～到9月15日。We postponed the match from September 5th to September 15th.

【推崇】 tuīchóng hold in esteem; praise highly：～备至 have the greatest esteem for

【推出】 tuīchū 1.（推）push to 2.（介绍给公

众) present sth. 3.(投放市场) put out：～新产品 launch the new product

【推辞】 tuīcí decline

【推倒】 tuīdǎo 1.(使倒下) push over; overturn 2.(推翻) repudiate; cancel; reverse

【推动】 tuīdòng push forward; promote; give impetus to：～工作 push the work forward

【推动力】 tuīdònglì motive force; driving force

【推断】 tuīduàn 1.(推测断定) deduce; infer：从已知的事实～出未知的事实 infer an unknown fact from a known fact 2.(所作的结论) deduction; inference

【推翻】 tuīfān 1.(打垮) overthrow; overturn; topple 2.(根本否定) repudiate; cancel; reverse：～原计划 reverse the original plan

【推广】 tuīguǎng popularize; spread; extend

【推广品种】 tuīguǎng pǐnzhǒng commercial variety

【推击球杆】 tuījī qiúgān 〈*Golf*〉 putter

【推击区草坪】 tuījīqū cǎopíng 〈*Golf*〉 green

【推荐】 tuījiàn recommend; propose; recommendation (n.)：你能～一本好词典吗? Can you recommend a good dictionary?

【推进】 tuījìn 1.(推动前进) push on; carry forward; advance; give impetus to 2.〈*Mil.*〉 move forward; push; drive

【推进力】 tuījìnlì propulsive force; driving power

【推进器】 tuījìnqì propeller

【推究】 tuījiū examine; study

【推举】 tuījǔ 1.(推选) elect; choose 2.〈*Weight-lifting*〉 clean and press; press

【推理】 tuīlǐ 〈*Logic*〉 inference; reasoning

【推理小说】 tuīlǐ xiǎoshuō inference novel

【推力】 tuīlì thrust

【推论】 tuīlùn inference; deduction; corollary

【推拿】 tuīná 〈*Med.*〉 massage

【推铅球】 tuīqiānqiú 〈*Sports*〉 shot put

【推敲】 tuīqiāo weigh; deliberate

【推求】 tuīqiú inquire into; ascertain

【推却】 tuīquè refuse; decline

【推让】 tuīràng decline

【推算】 tuīsuàn calculate; reckon

【推算价】 tuīsuànjià computed price

【推土机】 tuītǔjī bulldozer

【推托】 tuītuō offer as an excuse; plead：～之词 words that make excuses

【推脱】 tuītuō evade; shirk：～责任 shirk responsibility / ～职责 evade doing a duty

【推委】 tuīwěi shift responsibility onto others：～责任 shift responsibility onto others

【推想】 tuīxiǎng imagine; guess; reckon

【推销】 tuīxiāo promote sales; market; peddle：提供～后的服务 give after-sale service

【推销员】 tuīxiāoyuán salesperson; salesman (m.); saleswoman (f.)

【推销政策】 tuīxiāo zhèngcè promotion policy

【推卸】 tuīxiè shirk：～责任 shirk responsibility

【推心置腹】 tuīxīn-zhìfù repose full confidence in sb.; confide in sb.

【推行】 tuīxíng carry out; pursue; practice

【推选】 tuīxuǎn elect; choose

【推移】 tuīyí 1.(时间发展) elapse; pass 2.(形势变化) develop; evolve

【推重】 tuīzhòng have a high regard for; hold in respect

【推子】 tuī·zi clippers; hair-clippers：电～ electric clippers

颓 (tuí) 1.(坍塌) ruined; dilapidated 2.(衰败) declining; decadent 3.(委靡) dejected; dispirited

【颓败】 tuíbài degenerating; declining; decadent

【颓废】 tuífèi dispirited; decadent

【颓废派】 tuífèipài the decadent school; the decadents

【颓然】 tuírán 〈*written*〉 dejected; disappointed

【颓丧】 tuísàng dejected; dispirited; listless

【颓势】 tuíshì declining tendency

【颓唐】 tuítáng dejected; dispirited：～失意 failing and disappointing

腿 (tuǐ) 1.(下肢) leg: 2.(似腿的东西) leg; a leglike support：桌子～ legs of a table 3.(火腿) ham

【腿肚子】 tuǐdù·zi calf

【腿脚】 tuǐjiǎo legs and feet; ability to walk

【腿肉】 tuǐròu thigh

【腿腕子】 tuǐwàn·zi ankle

退 (tuì) 1.(后退) move back; retreat: 在战斗受挫时，士兵们不得不向后撤～。They had to retreat when they were beaten in battle. 2.(使向后退) cause to move back; withdraw; remove: ～兵 withdraw the troops 3.(退出) withdraw from; quit 4.(减退) decline; recede; ebb: 烧已～了。The fever has come down. 5.(退还) return; give back; refund: ～稿 return the manuscript / ～货 return merchandise 6.(撤消) cancel; break off

【退避】 tuìbì withdraw and keep off; keep out of the way

【退避三舍】 tuìbì-sānshè keep sb. at arm's length

【退兵】 tuìbīng 1.(撤退) retreat; withdrawal 2.(使敌军撤退) force the enemy to retreat: ～之计 a plan for repulsing the enemy

【退步】 tuìbù 1.(落后) lag behind; retrogress 2.(后路) room for maneuver; leeway: 留个～ leave some leeway

【退潮】 tuìcháo ebb tide; ebb

【退出】 tuìchū withdraw from; secede; quit: ～会场 leave the meeting

【退后】 tuìhòu move back; retreat

【退化】 tuìhuà 1.〈*Biol*.〉degeneration 2.(由好变坏) degenerate; deteriorate; retrograde

【退还】 tuìhuán return; give back

【退换】 tuìhuàn exchange a purchase

【退回】 tuìhuí 1.(退还) return; send back 2.(返回原地) go back

【退婚】 tuìhūn break off an engagement

【退货】 tuìhuò return of goods; returned purchase

【退货报告】 tuìhuò bàogào return sales report

【退货单据】 tuìhuò dānjù returned purchase invoice

【退居二线】 tuìjū èrxiàn leave the leading position

【退款】 tuìkuǎn reimburse

【退路】 tuìlù 1.(退回去的道路) route of retreat 2.(回旋余地) room for maneuver; leeway

【退赔】 tuìpéi return what one has unlawfully taken or pay compensation for it

【退票】 tuìpiào 1.(退掉已购的票) refund a ticket; get a refund for a ticket 2.(别人多余的票) spare ticket: 等～ wait for spare ticket

【退却】 tuìquè 1.〈*Mil*.〉retreat; withdraw 2.(畏难后退) hang back; shrink back; flinch

【退让】 tuìràng 1.(向后退) retreat 2.(让步) make a concession; give in; yield

【退色】 tuìsè fade

【退烧】 tuìshāo bring down a fever

【退烧药】 tuìshāoyào antipyretic

【退税】 tuìshuì drawback

【退缩】 tuìsuō shrink back; flinch; cower

【退位】 tuìwèi give up the throne; abdicate

【退伍】 tuìwǔ retire or be discharged from active military service; be demobilized; leave the army

【退伍军人】 tuìwǔ jūnrén ex-serviceman; demobilized soldier; veteran

【退席】 tuìxí 1.(退出宴席) leave a banquet 2.(退出会场) walk out

【退休】 tuìxiū retire: 提前～ early retirement

【退休金】 tuìxiūjīn retirement pay; pension

【退休年龄】 tuìxiū niánlíng retirement age

【退休制度】 tuìxiū zhìdù retirement system

【退学】 tuìxué leave school; discontinue one's schooling

【退役】 tuìyì retire from military service; be released from military service

【退役军官】 tuìyì jūnguān retired officer

【退役军人】 tuìyì jūnrén ex-serviceman

【退赃】 tuìzāng give up ill-gotten gains

【退职】 tuìzhí resign from office; be discharged from office; quit working

煺［燵、㷟］(tuì) scald

【煺毛】 tuìmáo remove the hairs of feathers: 给鸡～ remove the feathers of a chicken

褪 (tuì) 1.(脱衣服) take off 2.(脱色) fade 3.(脱毛) shed (feathers)
(另见"褪"tùn)

【褪毛】 tuìmáo shed feathers

【褪色】 tuìsè color fading

蜕 (tuì) 1.(脱皮) slough off; exuviate; molt 2.(脱下的皮) exuviae

【蜕变】 tuìbiàn change qualitatively; transform; transmute

【蜕化】 tuìhuà 1.(脱皮) slough off; exuviate

2.(腐化堕落) degenerate
【蜕化变质分子】 tuìhuà biànzhì fènzǐ degenerate element; degenerate
【蜕皮】 tuìpí 〈*Zool*.〉 cast off a skin; exuviate

tun

吞 (tūn) 1.(整个咽下) swallow; gulp down: 一口～下一杯酒 gulp down a cup of wine / 她～下了几口牛奶。She swallowed some milk. 2.(并吞) take possession of; annex
【吞并】 tūnbìng annex; gobble up; swallow up
【吞没】 tūnmò 1.(据为已有) take possession; embezzle; misappropriate 2.(淹没) swallow up; engulf
【吞食】 tūnshí swallow; devour
【吞噬】 tūnshì swallow; gobble up; engulf
【吞吐】 tūntǔ 1.(大量进出) swallow and spit; take in and send out in large quantities 2.(含混不清) hem and haw; mince one's words: ～其辞 hum and haw one's words
【吞吐量】 tūntǔliàng handling capacity; the volume of freight handled
【吞吞吐吐】 tūntūn-tǔtǔ hesitate in speech; hem and haw
【吞咽】 tūnyàn 〈*Med*.〉 ingurgitation
【吞云吐雾】 tūnyún-tǔwù blow a cloud

屯 (tún) 1.(储存) collect; store up 2.(驻扎) station; quarter 3.(村庄) village
【屯兵】 túnbīng station troops
【屯垦】 túnkěn station troops to open up wasteland
【屯粮】 túnliáng hoard up grains; store up grain

囤 (tún) store up; hoard: ～货 store goods
【囤积】 túnjī hoard for speculation; corner: ～居奇 hoarding and cornering; hoarding and speculation

臀 (tún) buttocks
【臀部】 túnbù buttocks
【臀尖】 túnjiān (猪肉部位) fat end
【臀鳍】 túnqí 〈*Zool*.〉 anal fin

褪 (tùn) slip out of sth.
(另见"褪"tuì)

tuo

托[託[4－7]] (tuō) 1.(托着) hold in the palm; support with the hand or palm 2.(托子) sth. serving as a support 3.(衬托) serve as a foil; set off 4.(委托) ask; entrust 5.(推托) plead; give as a pretext 6.(依托) rely upon; owe to 7.(托儿所) nursery
【托病】 tuōbìng on pretext of illness; plead illness
【托词】 tuōcí 1.(找借口) find a pretext; make an excuse 2.(借口) pretext; excuse; subterfuge
【托辞】 tuōcí 同"托词"
【托儿所】 tuō'érsuǒ nursery; child-care center
【托福】 tuōfú 1.(客套话) thanks to you 2.(指 TOEFL) Test of English as a Foreign Language
【托付】 tuōfù entrust; commit sth. to sb's care
【托付单】 tuōfùdān payment order
【托故】 tuōgù give a pretext; make an excuse
【托管】 tuōguǎn trust; trusteeship: 被～ be in trust
【托管地】 tuōguǎndì trust territory; trusteeship zone
【托管国】 tuōguǎnguó trustee
【托管理事会】 tuōguǎn lǐshìhuì Trusteeship Council
【托管领土】 tuōguǎn lǐngtǔ trust territory
【托管制度】 tuōguǎn zhìdù trusteeship
【托克托】 Tuōkètuō 〈place〉 Togtoh
【托克逊】 Tuōkèxùn 〈place〉 Toksun
【托拉斯】 tuōlāsī 〈*Econ*.〉 trust
【托盘】 tuōpán tray; service tray
【托收】 tuōshōu collection; collection of payments: 寄送～单据 forward documents for collection / 收到～单据 undertake the collection of documents
【托收单】 tuōshōudān collection order; order for collection
【托收人】 tuōshōurén drawer
【托收条件】 tuōshōu tiáojiàn term of collection
【托运】 tuōyùn consign for shipment; check

【托运单】 tuōyùndān booking note
【托运人】 tuōyùnrén consignor
【托子】 tuō·zi base; support: 花瓶～ vase support

拖 (tuō) 1.(牵引) pull; drag; haul: 马～着重载。The horse was dragging a heavy load. / 他们用力把船～上了岸。They hauled the boat up onto the shore. 2.(拖延) delay; drag on; procrastinate

【拖把】 tuōbǎ mop
【拖布】 tuōbù mop
【拖长】 tuōcháng 1.(拉长) lengthen 2.(拖延) drag on
【拖车】 tuōchē trailer
【拖船】 tuōchuán tugboat; tug; towboat
【拖斗】 tuōdǒu trailer
【拖后腿】 tuōhòutuǐ hinder sb.; hold sb. back
【拖拉】 tuōlā dilatory; slow; sluggish
【拖拉机】 tuōlājī tractor ‖ 拖拉机手 tractor driver
【拖累】 tuōlěi 1.(成为负担) encumber; be a burden on 2.(牵连) implicate; involve
【拖欠】 tuōqiàn be behind in payment; be in arrears
【拖欠工资】 tuōqiàn gōngzī be in arrears with salary; be behind in one's salary
【拖沓】 tuōtà dilatory; sluggish; laggard
【拖网】 tuōwǎng trawlnet; trawl; dragnet
【拖网渔船】 tuōwǎng yúchuán trawler
【拖鞋】 tuōxié slippers
【拖延】 tuōyán delay; put off; procrastinate: ～时间 gain time; play for time
【拖曳】 tuōyè drag; pull; tow
【拖纸架】 tuōzhǐjià 〈*Computer*〉 tractor

脱 (tuō) 1.(脱落) shed; come off; peel 2.(脱去) take off; cast off: ～鞋 take off one's shoes / ～衣 take off one's clothes 3.(脱离) escape from; get out of: ～榫 be out of joint 4.(脱漏) miss out: ～误 omissions and errors

【脱班】 tuōbān 1.(上班迟到) be late for work 2.(车、船、飞机误点) be behind schedule
【脱产】 tuōchǎn be released from production or one's regular work to take on other duties
【脱发】 tuōfà 〈*Med.*〉 trichomadesis
【脱肛】 tuōgāng 〈*Med.*〉 prolapse of the anus
【脱稿】 tuōgǎo be completed
【脱轨】 tuōguǐ derail
【脱节】 tuōjié come apart; be disjointed; be out of line with
【脱臼】 tuōjiù 〈*Med.*〉 dislocation
【脱口而出】 tuōkǒu'érchū say sth. unwittingly; blurt out; let slip
【脱口秀】 tuōkǒuxiù (电视访谈节目) talk show
【脱离】 tuōlí separate oneself from; break away from; be divorced from
【脱粒】 tuōlì 〈*Agric.*〉 thresh; shell
【脱粒机】 tuōlìjī 〈*Agric.*〉 thresher; sheller
【脱漏】 tuōlòu be left out; be omitted; be missing
【脱落】 tuōluò drop; fall off; come off: 油漆～。The paint is coming off.
【脱毛】 tuōmáo lose hair; lose feathers; shed
【脱帽】 tuōmào take off one's hat: ～致敬 take off one's hat in salutation
【脱敏】 tuōmǐn desensitization; hyposensitization
【脱皮】 tuōpí decortication
【脱贫】 tuōpín be lifted out of poverty and backwardness
【脱贫致富】 tuōpín zhìfù shake off poverty and set out on the road to prosperity; shake off poverty and become prosperous; get rid of poverty and become better off
【脱色】 tuōsè 1.(去色) decolor; decolorize 2.(退色) fade
【脱色剂】 tuōsèjì decolorant; decolorizer
【脱身】 tuōshēn get away; get free; extricate oneself: ～之计 a plan that helps one to slip away
【脱手】 tuōshǒu 1.(脱开手) slip out of the hand 2.(卖出) get off one's hands
【脱水】 tuōshuǐ 1.〈*Med.*〉 deprivation of body fluids; dehydration; dehydrate (v.) 2.〈*Chem.*〉 dehydration; dewatering; dehydrate (v.)
【脱水机】 tuōshuǐjī whizzer; hydroextractor
【脱水剂】 tuōshuǐjì dehydrating agent
【脱水蔬菜】 tuōshuǐ shūcài dehydrated vegetables
【脱俗】 tuōsú free from vulgarity; refined
【脱胎】 tuōtāi emerge from the womb of; be born out off
【脱胎换骨】 tuōtāi-huàngǔ be reborn; cast off one's old self; thoroughly remold oneself
【脱逃】 tuōtáo run away; escape; flee: 临阵

～ flee from battle; turn back at the critical moment
【脱位】 tuōwèi 〈*Med.*〉 dislocation
【脱险】 tuōxiǎn be out of danger; escape danger: 他现在已～了。He is now out of danger.
【脱销】 tuōxiāo out of stock; sold out: 新产品～了。The new products were sold out.
【脱盐】 tuōyán desalinize; desalinate
【脱氧】 tuōyǎng 〈*Chem.*〉 deoxidation; deoxidization
【脱氧剂】 tuōyǎngjì deoxidizer; deoxidant
【脱衣舞】 tuōyīwǔ striptease: 跳～ do a striptease; striptease
【脱颖而出】 tuōyǐng'érchū An able man cannot be kept down as an awl.
【脱羽】 tuōyǔ lose feathers; shed
【脱脂】 tuōzhī de-fat; degrease
【脱脂棉】 tuōzhīmián absorbent cotton
【脱脂奶粉】 tuōzhī nǎifěn de-fatted milk powder; nonfat dried milk
【脱脂器】 tuōzhīqì separator

驮 (tuó) carry on the back (另见"驮"duò)
【驮畜】 tuóchù pack animal
【驮马】 tuómǎ pack horse

陀 (tuó)
【陀螺】 tuóluó top

驼 (tuó) 1.（骆驼）camel: 单峰～ dromedary; Arabian camel / 双峰～ camel; Bactrian camel 2.（后背弯曲）hunchback; humpback
【驼背】 tuóbèi 1.（背弯）hunchback; humpback 2.（驼背的人）hunchbacked; humpbacked
【驼峰】 tuófēng 1.（骆驼背）hump 2. 〈*Railway*〉 hump: ～调车 hump switching
【驼鹿】 tuólù 〈*Zool.*〉 elk; moose
【驼绒】 tuóróng 1.（骆驼绒毛）camel's hair 2.（骆驼绒布）camel hair cloth
【驼色】 tuósè the color of camel's hair; light tan

柁 (tuó) 〈*Archit.*〉 girder

砣[鉈] (tuó) weight; the sliding weight of a steelyard

鸵 (tuó) ostrich
【鸵鸟】 tuóniǎo ostrich
【鸵鸟政策】 tuóniǎo zhèngcè ostrichism; ostrich policy

橐[槖] (tuó) 1.（口袋）bag 2. 〈*onomat*〉 tread
【橐驼】 tuótuó amel

鼍[鼉] (tuó) （扬子鳄）Chinese alligator

妥 (tuǒ) 1.（妥当）appropriate; proper 2.（齐备;停当）ready; settled; finished
【妥当】 tuǒ·dang appropriate; proper
【妥善】 tuǒshàn appropriate; proper; well arranged: ～处理 handle properly
【妥帖】 tuǒtiē appropriate; fitting; proper
【妥协】 tuǒxié come to terms; compromise
【妥协分子】 tuǒxié fènzǐ an appeaser
【妥协性】 tuǒxiéxìng a tendency towards compromise

椭[橢] (tuǒ)
【椭圆】 tuǒyuán 〈*Math.*〉 ellipse
【椭圆规】 tuǒyuánguī ellipsograph; elliptic trammel
【椭圆截面】 tuǒyuán jiémiàn oval cross section
【椭圆星云】 tuǒyuán xīngyún elliptical nebula
【椭圆柱面】 tuǒyuán zhùmiàn elliptic cylinder
【椭圆锥面】 tuǒyuán zhuīmiàn elliptic cone

拓 (tuò) open up; develop (另见"拓"tà)
【拓荒】 tuòhuāng reclaim wasteland; open up virgin soil
【拓荒者】 tuòhuāngzhě pioneer; pathbreaker; trailblazer
【拓扑学】 tuòpūxué 〈*Math.*〉 topology
【拓展】 tuòzhǎn expand; extend; develop

唾 (tuò) 1.（唾液）saliva; spittle 2.（用力吐唾沫）spit
【唾骂】 tuòmà spit on and curse; revile
【唾沫】 tuò·mo saliva; spittle
【唾弃】 tuòqì cast aside; spurn
【唾手可得】 tuòshǒu-kědé be extremely easy to obtain
【唾液】 tuòyè saliva
【唾液腺】 tuòyèxiàn 〈*Anat.*〉 salivary gland

W

wa

挖(wā) dig; excavate; scoop (out): ～洞 make a hole; make a cave; scoop out a hole / 隧道是用重型机械～的。The tunnel was dug with the aid of heavy machinery.

【挖掉】 wādiào dig up

【挖耳朵】 wā'ěr·duo pick ears

【挖掘】 wājué excavate; unearth; excavation (n.): 参加了兵马俑的～工作 take part in excavations of clay figures of warriors and horses

【挖掘机】 wājuéjī excavator; steam shovel

【挖掘潜力】 wājué qiǎnlì exploit potentialities; tap potentials

【挖空心思】 wākōng-xīnsī rack one's brains; cudgel one's brains

【挖苦】 wā·ku speak sarcastically; speak ironically

【挖苦话】 wā·kuhuà ironical remarks; verbal thrusts

【挖泥船】 wāníchuán dredger

【挖潜】 wāqiǎn work out the potentialities

【挖墙脚】 wāqiángjiǎo undermine the foundation of (sb. or sth.)

【挖土机】 wātǔjī excavator; steam shovel

哇(wā)

【哇啦】 wālā yelling; uproar; hullabaloo: ～～乱叫 raise a hullabaloo

【哇喇】 wālā 同"哇啦"

洼[窪](wā) 1.(凹陷) hollow; low-lying 2.(凹陷的地方) low-lying area; depression

【洼地】 wādì depression; low-lying land

【洼陷】 wāxiàn (of ground) be sunken; be low-lying

蛙[鼃](wā) frog: 牛～ bull frog / 青～ green frog / 雨～ green tree-frog

【蛙人】 wārén frogman

【蛙泳】 wāyǒng breaststroke

娃(wá) 1.(小孩) baby; child 2.(小动物) newborn animal: 猪～ piglet

【娃娃】 wá·wa baby; child

瓦(wǎ) 1.(屋瓦) tile 2.(陶土烧成的) made of baked clay: ～罐 earthen jar; pottery container / ～盆 earthen basin / ～器 earthenware 3.〈*Electr*.〉 watt (另见"瓦"wà)

【瓦房】 wǎfáng tile-roofed house

【瓦工】 wǎgōng 1.(砌砖、盖瓦) bricklaying, tiling or plastering 2.(建筑工人) bricklayer; tiler; plasterer

【瓦匠】 wǎjiàng bricklayer; tiler; plasterer

【瓦解】 wǎjiě 1.(崩溃) disintegrate; collapse; crumble: 土崩～ collapse; crumble down 2.(使崩溃) disintegrate; break up: ～敌人 disintegrate the enemy

【瓦块】 wǎkuài fragment of a tile

【瓦楞纸】 wǎléngzhǐ corrugated paper

【瓦砾】 wǎlì rubble; debris

【瓦砾堆】 wǎlìduī rubble pile

【瓦时】 wǎshí watt-hour

【瓦数】 wǎshù 〈*Electr*.〉 wattage

【瓦斯】 wǎsī gas: 催泪～ tear-gas bomb

【瓦斯爆炸】 wǎsī bàozhà gas explosion

【瓦斯煤层】 wǎsī méicéng gassy seam

【瓦斯筒】 wǎsītǒng gas cylinder

【瓦特】 wǎtè 〈*Electr*.〉 watt

【瓦特计】 wǎtèjì wattmeter

佤(wǎ)

【佤族】 Wǎzú Va (我国少数民族，主要分布在云南)

瓦(wà) cover (a roof) with tiles; tile: ～瓦 (wà wǎ): cover with tiles

（另见“瓦”wǎ）
【瓦刀】 wàdāo （bricklayer's）cleaver
袜［襪、韈］（wà） socks；stockings；hose：长～ long socks / 短～ socks / 连裤～ pantyhose；pantihose / 毛～ woolen socks / 男～ men's socks / 尼龙～ nylon socks / 女～ ladies' stockings / 丝～ silk stockings / 线～ cotton socks / 她穿了一双尼龙长～。She wore nylon stockings.
【袜带】 wàdài suspenders；garters
【袜底】 wàdǐ sole of a stocking
【袜套】 wàtào socks；ankle socks
【袜筒】 wàtǒng the leg of a stocking
【袜子】 wà·zi socks；stockings；hose：一双～ a pair of socks；a pair of stockings
腽（wà）
【腽肭】 wànà obese
【腽肭脐】 wànàqí 〈*Chin. Pharm.*〉 the penis and testicles of an ursine seal
【腽肭兽】 wànàshòu 〈*Zool.*〉 fur seal；ursine seal

wai

歪（wāi） 1.（不正；斜）askew；inclined；slanting 2.（不正当的）devious；underhand；crooked
【歪风】 wāifēng evil wind；unhealthy trend：～邪气 evil winds and noxious influences；unhealthy trends and evil practices
【歪理】 wāilǐ erroneous reasoning
【歪门邪道】 wāimén-xiédào crooked ways；crooked means；dishonest practices
【歪曲】 wāiqū distort；misrepresent；twist；mutilate
【歪诗】 wāishī inelegant verses；doggerel
【歪斜】 wāixié crooked；askew；aslant
外（wài） 1.（外边；外边的）outer；outward；outside 2.（此地以外的）other：～省 other provinces 3.（外国）foreign；external：～商 foreign merchants 4.（外戚）（relatives）of one's mother，sisters or daughters 5.（关系疏远的）not of the same organization，class，etc.；not closely related 6.（另外）besides；in addition；beyond 7.（非正式的）unofficial
【外币】 wàibì foreign currency
【外币存款】 wàibì cúnkuǎn deposit in foreign currency；foreign currency deposit
【外币兑换】 wàibì duìhuàn foreign currency exchange
【外币汇票】 wàibì huìpiào foreign currency bill
【外边】 wài·bian 1.（与“里边”相对）outside；out；exterior：门～ outside the door / 房子～ the exterior of the house 2.（外地）another place；a place other than where one lives or works 3.（表面）exterior；outside
【外表】 wàibiǎo outward appearance；exterior；surface
【外宾】 wàibīn foreign guest；foreign visitor
【外埠】 wàibù nonlocal；other ports；towns or cities other than where one is
【外部】 wàibù 1.（范围以外）outside；external 2.（表面）exterior；outside；surface：～特征 surface features
【外部设备】 wàibù shèbèi external device
【外部条件】 wàibù tiáojiàn external condition
【外层空间】 wàicéng kōngjiān outer space
【外场】 wàichǎng 〈*Baseball & Softball*〉 outfield ‖ 外场手 outfielder
【外出】 wàichū go out；get out：～5个月之后 after an absence of five months
【外出血】 wàichūxuè 〈*Med.*〉 external hemorrhage
【外带】 wàidài 1.（外胎）tire（cover）2.（又加上）as well；besides；into the bargain
【外裆】 wàidāng （猪肉部位）leg
【外敌】 wàidí foreign enemy；enemy from outside
【外地】 wàidì other places；nonlocal；parts of the country other than where one is
【外地学生】 wàidì xué·sheng extra district student
【外电】 wàidiàn dispatches from foreign news agencies
【外调】 wàidiào 1.（把…调出）transfer（materials or personnel）to other localities 2.（外出调查）investigation mission outside the city or town
【外耳】 wài'ěr 〈*Anat.*〉 external ear
【外耳炎】 wài'ěryán 〈*Med.*〉 otitis external

【外分泌】 wàifēnmì 〈*Med*.〉 exocrine
【外敷】 wàifū 〈*Med*.〉 apply (ointment, etc.)
【外敷药】 wàifūyào medicine for external application
【外副翼】 wàifùyì 〈*Aeron*.〉 outer aileron
【外感】 wàigǎn 〈*Chin*. *Pharm*.〉 diseases caused by external factors
【外港】 wàigǎng outport
【外公】 wàigōng maternal grandfather
【外观】 wàiguān outward appearance; exterior
【外观检查】 wàiguān jiǎnchá outer inspection
【外国】 wàiguó foreign country
【外国法人】 wàiguó fǎrén foreign juristical person; foreign juridic person
【外国公司】 wàiguó gōngsī foreign company; foreign corporation; alien corporation
【外国汇票】 wàiguó huìpiào foreign bill of exchange
【外国货】 wàiguóhuò foreign goods; foreign product
【外国留学生】 wàiguó liúxuéshēng international students
【外国侨民】 wàiguó qiáomín foreign immigrant
【外国人】 wàiguórén foreigner: 他不是这个国家的人,他是～。He is not from this country, he is foreigner.
【外国人居留证】 wàiguórén jūliúzhèng residence permit for foreigners
【外国人入境许可】 wàiguórén rùjìng xǔkě admission of alien
【外国投资】 wàiguó tóuzī foreign investment
【外国投资者】 wàiguó tóuzīzhě foreign investor
【外国语】 wàiguóyǔ foreign language
【外国语学院】 wàiguóyǔ xuéyuàn foreign language institute
【外国支票】 wàiguó zhīpiào foreign check
【外国驻华机构】 wàiguó zhùhuá jīgòu foreign institutions in China
【外国专家】 wàiguó zhuānjiā foreign specialist
【外国资本】 wàiguó zīběn foreign capital
【外果皮】 wàiguǒpí 〈*Bot*.〉 exocarp
【外海】 wàihǎi open waters; open sea
【外行】 wàiháng 1.(不懂) lay; nonprofessional 2.(外行的人) layman; nonprofessional
【外行话】 wàihánghuà lay language; a mere dabbler's opinion
【外号】 wàihào nickname
【外患】 wàihuàn foreign aggression
【外汇】 wàihuì 1.〈*Econ*.〉 foreign exchange 2.(外币) foreign currency
【外汇波动】 wàihuì bōdòng foreign exchange fluctuation
【外汇偿付能力】 wàihuì chángfù nénglì ability to repay in foreign exchange
【外汇储备】 wàihuì chǔbèi foreign exchange reserve
【外汇钉住】 wàihuì dīngzhù peg; pegging (n.)
【外汇兑换率】 wàihuì duìhuànlǜ rate of exchange
【外汇兑换券】 wàihuì duìhuànquàn foreign exchange certificate (FEC)
【外汇官价】 wàihuì guānjià official exchange rate
【外汇管制】 wàihuì guǎnzhì (foreign) exchange control
【外汇行情】 wàihuì hángqíng exchange quotations
【外汇黑市】 wàihuì hēishì dark exchange
【外汇交易】 wàihuì jiāoyì foreign exchange transaction
【外汇结存】 wàihuì jiécún foreign balance
【外汇结算】 wàihuì jiésuàn exchange payment
【外汇牌价】 wàihuì páijià foreign exchange rate: 操纵～ manipulate the rates of exchange between the currencies
【外汇牌价表】 wàihuì páijiàbiǎo list of exchange rate quotations
【外汇配给】 wàihuì pèijǐ rationing of exchange
【外汇平价】 wàihuì píngjià par of exchange; exchange parity
【外汇期货交易】 wàihuì qīhuò jiāoyì forward exchange transaction
【外汇市场】 wàihuì shìchǎng foreign exchange market
【外汇收入】 wàihuì shōurù foreign exchange

earnings; foreign exchange income
【外汇损失】 wàihuì sǔnshī exchange losses
【外汇调剂】 wàihuì tiáojì foreign currency swap
【外汇限制】 wàihuì xiànzhì exchange restriction
【外汇业务】 wàihuì yèwù exchange business
【外汇资金】 wàihuì zījīn foreign exchange
【外婚】 wàihūn exogamy
【外货】 wàihuò foreign goods; imported goods
【外货进口报单】 wàihuò jìnkǒu bàodān application for import of foreign goods
【外籍】 wàijí foreign nationality
【外籍华人】 wàijí huárén Chinese of foreign nationality
【外籍职工】 wàijí zhígōng foreign staff and workers
【外加】 wàijiā more; additional; extra
【外交】 wàijiāo diplomacy; foreign affairs: 穿梭～ shuttle diplomacy
【外交庇护】 wàijiāo bìhù diplomatic asylum
【外交部】 wàijiāobù the Ministry of Foreign Affairs; the Foreign Ministry
【外交部长】 wàijiāo bùzhǎng Minister of Foreign Affairs; Foreign Minister
【外交辞令】 wàijiāo cílìng diplomatic language; diplomatic parlance
【外交代表】 wàijiāo dàibiǎo diplomatic representative
【外交代表机构】 wàijiāo dàibiǎo jīgòu diplomatic mission
【外交关系】 wàijiāo guānxì diplomatic relations: 建立～ establishment of diplomatic relations / 建立大使级的～关系 establish diplomatic relations at ambassadorial level / ～升格 upgrade diplomatic relations / 断绝～ sever diplomatic relations / 中断～ suspend diplomatic relations / 恢复～ resume diplomatic relations
【外交官】 wàijiāoguān diplomat; diplomatist
【外交官衔】 wàijiāo guānxián diplomatic rank
【外交惯例】 wàijiāo guànlì diplomatic practice; diplomatic usage
【外交护照】 wàijiāo hùzhào diplomatic passport
【外交豁免】 wàijiāo huòmiǎn diplomatic immunities
【外交豁免权】 wàijiāo huòmiǎnquán diplomatic immunities
【外交家】 wàijiāojiā diplomat
【外交礼节】 wàijiāo lǐjié diplomatic protocol
【外交签证】 wàijiāo qiānzhèng diplomatic visa
【外交人员】 wàijiāo rényuán diplomatic personnel
【外交使节】 wàijiāo shǐjié diplomatic envoy
【外交使团】 wàijiāo shǐtuán diplomatic corps
【外交使团团长】 wàijiāo shǐtuán tuánzhǎng doyen of the diplomatic corps; dean of the diplomatic corps
【外交事务】 wàijiāo shìwù foreign affairs
【外交特权】 wàijiāo tèquán diplomatic privileges; diplomatic prerogatives
【外交途径】 wàijiāo tújìng diplomatic channels: 通过～进行谈判 negotiate through diplomatic channels
【外交信使】 wàijiāo xìnshǐ diplomatic courier
【外交邮袋】 wàijiāo yōudài diplomatic bag; diplomatic pouch
【外角】 wàijiǎo 〈*Math.*〉 exterior angle
【外界】 wàijiè 1.(指社会) the external world; the outside world 2.(指空间) outside
【外景】 wàijǐng 〈*Cinematog.*〉 exterior; outdoor scene: 拍～ be on location
【外景地】 wàijǐngdì 〈*Cinematog.*〉 location: 找～ hunt the location; location hunting
【外径】 wàijìng outer diameter; o.d.
【外科】 wàikē surgical department
【外科病房】 wàikē bìngfáng surgical ward
【外科手术】 wàikē shǒushù surgical operation; surgery
【外科学】 wàikēxué surgery; surgical (adj.)
【外科医生】 wàikē yīshēng surgeon
【外壳】 wàiké outer covering; outer casing; shell; case
【外快】 wàikuài extra income: 捞～ go after extra income
【外来】 wàilái outside; external; foreign
【外来语】 wàiláiyǔ word of foreign origin; foreign word
【外来种】 wàiláizhǒng exotic species; adventitious species

【外廊式】 wàilángshì 〈*Archit*.〉 gallery type; balcony access type
【外力】 wàilì 1.(外部力量) outside force 2.〈*Physics*〉 external force
【外流】 wàiliú outflow; drain: 人才～ brain drain
【外轮】 wàilún foreign ship
【外卖】 wàimài take-away
【外卖餐馆】 wàimài cānguǎn take-away
【外貌】 wàimào appearance; exterior; looks
【外贸】 wàimào foreign trade; external trade
【外贸经营权】 wàimào jīngyíngquán the power to engage in foreign trade
【外贸仲裁】 wàimào zhòngcái foreign trade arbitration
【外贸自主权】 wàimào zìzhǔquán autonomy in foreign trade
【外面】 wàimiàn outward appearance; exterior; surface
【外面】 wài·mian outside; out: 这盒子的～是红的,里面是白的。The box was red outside and white inside.
【外婆】 wàipó maternal grandmother
【外墙】 wàiqiáng outer wall; external wall: 这所房子的～是砖的。The outer wall of the house were made of brick.
【外强中干】 wàiqiáng-zhōnggān strong in appearance but weak in reality; a colossus with feet of clay
【外侨】 wàiqiáo foreign national; alien
【外侨身份】 wàiqiáo shēnfèn alienism
【外勤】 wàiqín 1.(室外工作) outwork 2.(野外工作) field-work 3.(外勤人员) field personnel; field-worker
【外勤人员】 wàiqín rényuán out worker; field personnel; field-worker
【外圈】 wàiquān 〈*Sports*〉 outside lane; outer lane
【外人】 wàirén 1.(局外人) stranger; outsider 2.(外地人) non-native; outlander 3.(外国人) foreigner; alien
【外柔内刚】 wàiróu-nèigāng velvet glove
【外商】 wàishāng foreign tradesman
【外伤】 wàishāng an injury or wound; trauma
【外伤学】 wàishāngxué traumatology
【外甥】 wài·sheng sister's son; nephew
【外甥女】 wài·shengnǚ sister's daughter; niece
【外事】 wàishì foreign affairs; external affairs
【外事部门】 wàishì bùmén foreign affairs section
【外孙】 wàisūn grandson; daughter's son
【外孙女】 wàisūnnǚ granddaughter; daughter's daughter
【外胎】 wàitāi tire (cover)
【外逃】 wàitáo 1.(潜逃别处) flee to some other place 2.(逃到国外) flee the country
【外套】 wàitào 1.(大衣) overcoat 2.(外衣) loose coat; outer garment
【外围】 wàiwéi 1.(周围) periphery; outerring 2.(外围的) peripheral; outlying; subordinate
【外围设备】 wàiwéi shèbèi peripheral equipment
【外文】 wàiwén foreign language
【外侮】 wàiwǔ foreign aggression; external aggression
【外务】 wàiwù 1.(职务外的事) matters outside one's job 2.(外交) foreign affairs; external affairs
【外线】 wàixiàn 1.〈*Mil*.〉 exterior lines 2.(指电话) outside (telephone) connections
【外乡】 wàixiāng other parts of the country
【外乡人】 wàixiāngrén non-native; people from other parts of the country
【外向】 wàixiàng 1.(供出口的) export-oriented 2.(指性格) extrovert
【外向型经济】 wàixiàngxíng jīngjì export-oriented economy
【外向型企业】 wàixiàngxíng qǐyè export-oriented enterprise
【外销】 wàixiāo for sale abroad or in another part of the country
【外销部】 wàixiāobù export department
【外销产品】 wàixiāo chǎnpǐn export goods; products for export; articles for sale in other areas
【外心】 wàixīn 1.(不忠于配偶) unfaithful intentions 2.〈*Math*.〉 circumcenter
【外星人】 wàixīngrén extraterrestrial; saucerman
【外形】 wàixíng appearance; external form;

contour

【外形尺寸】 wàixíng chǐcùn outline dimension; overall dimension

【外姓】 wàixìng （people） not of the same surname

【外衣】 wàiyī **1.**（外套）coat; jacket; outer clothing; outer garment **2.**（遮盖物）semblance; appearance; garb: 披着…的～ in the grab of sth.; under the cloak of sth.

【外溢】 wàiyì spillover

【外阴】 wàiyīn 〈*Anat.*〉 vulva

【外阴部】 wàiyīnbù 〈*Anat.*〉 genitalia

【外因】 wàiyīn external cause

【外引内联】 wàiyǐn-nèilián introduce investment from abroad and establish lateral ties at home; import from abroad and linkage at home

【外用】 wàiyòng 〈*Pharm.*〉 external use; external application

【外语】 wàiyǔ foreign language

【外语教学】 wàiyǔ jiàoxué foreign language teaching

【外语学院】 wàiyǔ xuéyuàn foreign languages institute

【外语专业】 wàiyǔ zhuānyè faculty of foreign languages

【外遇】 wàiyù affair; extramartial relations: 她发现丈夫有～。She discovered that her husband was having an affair.

【外援】 wàiyuán foreign aid; outside help; external assistance

【外在】 wàizài external; extrinsic: ～因素 external factor

【外债】 wàizhài external debt; foreign debt

【外长】 wàizhǎng Foreign Minister; Minister of Foreign affairs

【外罩】 wàizhào **1.**（衣服）outer garment; dustcoat; overall **2.**（罩子）cover; shade

【外痔】 wàizhì 〈*Med.*〉 external hemorrhoids; external piles

【外传】 wàizhuàn unofficial biography

【外资】 wàizī foreign capital: 利用～ introduce foreign investment

【外资企业】 wàizī qǐyè foreign-owned enterprise

【外祖父】 wàizǔfù （maternal） grandfather; grandpa

【外祖母】 wàizǔmǔ （maternal） grandmother; grandma

wan

弯［彎］（wān） **1.**（弯曲）curved; tortuous; crooked; bent **2.**（使弯曲）bend; flex **3.**（弯子）turn; curve; bend: 急～ blind bend / 险～ dangerous bend; hairpin bend / 转～ turn

【弯道】 wāndào 〈*Sports*〉 curve; bend; turn

【弯路】 wānlù **1.**（不直的道路）winding course; crooked road; tortuous path: 连续～ consecutive curves **2.**（冤枉功夫）round-about way; detour: 走～ take a round-about way; make a detour

【弯曲】 wānqū winding; meandering; zigzag; crooked; curved

【弯弯曲曲】 wānwān-qūqū having many bends or curves

【弯子】 wān·zi turn; twist; curve

湾［灣］（wān） **1.**（河流的）a bend in a stream **2.**（海湾）gulf; bay; bight: 北部～ Beibu Gulf / 墨西哥～ Gulf of Mexico / 孟加拉～ Bay of Bengal / 贝宁～ Bight of Benin **3.**（使船停住）cast anchor; moor

【湾泊】 wānbó cast anchor; moor

【湾流】 wānliú Gulf Stream

剜（wān） cut out; gouge out; scoop out

【剜肉补疮】 wānròu-bǔchuāng resort to a stopgap measure detrimental to a long-term interests

蜿（wān）

【蜿蜒】 wānyán **1.**（蛇爬）wriggle **2.**（弯弯曲曲）wind; zigzag; meander: 一条～的道路 a zigzag road

豌（wān）

【豌豆】 wāndòu pea

丸（wán） **1.**（小球）ball; pellet **2.**（丸药）pill; bolus

【丸剂】 wánjì pill

【丸药】 wányào pill of Chinese medicine; bolus of Chinese medicine

【丸子】 wán·zi ball; a round mass of food: 肉～ meatball

芄(wán)

【芄兰】 wánlán 〈*Bot.*〉 schoenorchis

纨(wán) fine silk fabrics

【纨绔子弟】 wánkù zǐdì profligate son of the rich; fop; dandy; playboy

完(wán) 1.(全;完整) intact; whole; unharmed 2.(用完) exhaust; finish; use up; run out: The coffee is low. 咖啡快～了。3.(完结) finish; complete; be over; be through: 这项工作还没～。The work is not completed yet. 4.(交纳) pay: ～税 pay taxes

【完备】 wánbèi complete; perfect: 品种～ have every variety of sth.

【完毕】 wánbì finish; complete; end; be done

【完成】 wánchéng accomplish; complete; fulfill; bring to success: ～任务 accomplish one's task; complete one's task

【完蛋】 wándàn be finished; go to smash: 彻底～ be completely finished

【完稿】 wángǎo finish a piece of writing; complete the manuscript

【完工】 wángōng complete a project, etc.; finish doing sth.; get through

【完好】 wánhǎo intact; whole; in good condition: ～无损 excellent without damage

【完婚】 wánhūn (of a man) get married; marry; conclusion of marriage

【完结】 wánjié end; be over; finish

【完满】 wánmǎn satisfactory; successful

【完美】 wánměi perfect: ～无缺 perfect; flawless / 他们努力使舞蹈更加～。They worked hard to perfect their dance.

【完全】 wánquán 1.(不缺;齐全) complete; whole 2.(全部) completely fully; wholly; entirely; absolutely: 我～同意。I totally agree.

【完全市场】 wánquán shìchǎng perfect market

【完善】 wánshàn perfect; consummate

【完事】 wánshì finish; wind up

【完事大吉】 wánshì-dàjí finish everything successfully

【完税】 wánshuì pay tax; pay duty

【完税凭证】 wánshuì píngzhèng duty-paid proof

【完形说】 wánxíngshuō 〈*Education*〉 configuration theory

【完整】 wánzhěng complete; integrated; intact: 领土～ territorial integrity

玩[顽[1,2]、翫[3,4]](wán) 1.(玩耍) play; have fun; amuse oneself: 孩子们在～球。The children were playing with a ball. 2.(玩弄) employ; resort to 3.(玩忽) trifle with; treat lightly; toy with 4.(玩赏) enjoy; find pleasure in; appreciate

【玩忽】 wánhū neglect; trifle with; ignore: ～职守 neglect of duty; ignore one's duty

【玩火自焚】 wánhuǒ-zìfén He who plays with fire will get burnt.(或: Sow the wind and reap the whirlwind.)

【玩具】 wánjù toy; plaything

【玩具店】 wánjùdiàn toy shop

【玩具熊】 wánjùxióng teddy; teddy bear

【玩弄】 wánnòng 1.(调戏) dally with; flirt with 2.(搬弄) play with; juggle with: ～词藻 play with words 3.(施展) resort to; employ: ～两面手法 employ the two-faced tactics

【玩偶】 wán'ǒu doll; toy figurine

【玩赏】 wánshǎng enjoy; take pleasure in

【玩世不恭】 wánshì-bùgōng be cynical; disdain worldly affairs

【玩耍】 wánshuǎ play; have fun; amuse oneself: 孩子们在院子里～。The children were at play in the yard.

【玩味】 wánwèi ponder; ruminate; contemplate

【玩物】 wánwù plaything; toy

【玩物丧志】 wánwù-sàngzhì riding a hobby saps one's will to make progress; excessive attention to trivia saps the will; be a playboy without ambitions

【玩笑】 wánxiào joke; jest: 开～ play a joke; make a joke; in jest / 请不要和我开～。Please don't jest with me.

【玩意儿】 wányìr 1.(玩具) toy; plaything 2.(指东西) thing

顽(wán) 1.(迟钝;愚笨) stupid; dense; insensate 2.(顽固) stubborn; obstinate 3.(顽皮) naughty; mischievous
【顽固】 wángù 1.(思想保守) obstinate; stubborn; headstrong 2.(立场反动) bitterly opposed to change; die-hard
【顽固分子】 wángù fènzǐ diehard
【顽疾】 wánjí obstinate disease; pertinacious illness
【顽抗】 wánkàng resist stubbornly; oppose obstinately
【顽皮】 wánpí naughty; mischievous: 班上最～的孩子 the naughtiest boy in the class
【顽强】 wánqiáng indomitable; staunch; tenacious: 学习～ study tenaciously
【顽石】 wánshí hard rock; insensate stone
【顽童】 wántóng naughty child; urchin
【顽症】 wánzhèng chronic and stubborn disease; persistent ailment

烷(wán) 〈*Chem*.〉 alkane
【烷基】 wánjī 〈*Chem*.〉 alkyl
【烷烃】 wántīng 〈*Chem*.〉 alkane; paraffin

宛(wǎn) 1.(曲折) winding; tortuous 2.(仿佛) as if
【宛然】 wǎnrán as if
【宛如】 wǎnrú just like; as if
【宛若】 wǎnruò just like; as if
【宛似】 wǎnsì just like; as if
【宛转】 wǎnzhuǎn 1.见"辗转" 2.同"婉转"

惋(wǎn) sigh
【惋惜】 wǎnxī feel sorry for sb. or about sth.; sympathize with; regret

婉(wǎn) 1.(婉转) gentle; gracious; tactful 2.(美好) beautiful; graceful; elegant
【婉辞】 wǎncí 1.(婉言) gentle words; euphemism 2.(婉言谢绝) graciously decline; politely refuse
【婉言】 wǎnyán gentle words; tactful expressions: ～谢绝 graciously decline; politely refuse
【婉约】 wǎnyuē graceful and restrained
【婉转】 wǎnzhuǎn 1.(曲折) mild and indirect; tactful; euphemistic: ～的说法 euphemistic way of speaking 2.(抑扬动听) sweet and agreeable

碗[椀、盌](wǎn) bowl: 一～水 a bowl of water
【碗橱】 wǎncú cupboard

莞(wǎn)
【莞尔】 wǎněr smile: ～而笑 give a soft smile

挽[輓[3]](wǎn) 1.(拉) draw; pull 2.(向上卷) roll up: ～袖子 roll up one's sleeves 3.(哀悼) lament sb.'s death 4.(盘绕) coil up
【挽畜】 wǎnchù draft animal
【挽歌】 wǎngē dirge; elegy
【挽回】 wǎnhuí retrieve; redeem
【挽救】 wǎnjiù save; remedy; rescue: ～某人的生命 save sb's life
【挽联】 wǎnlián elegiac couplet
【挽留】 wǎnliú urge sb. to stay; persuade sb. to stay
【挽马】 wǎnmǎ draft horse
【挽诗】 wǎnshī elegy

晚(wǎn) 1.(晚上) evening; night 2.(时间靠后) late; far on in time: 她来～了。She arrived late. / 天很～了，我得上床了。It is very late — I should be in bed. 3.(后来的) younger; junior
【晚安】 wǎn'ān good night
【晚班】 wǎnbān night shift: 上～ be on the night shift
【晚报】 wǎnbào evening news; evening paper
【晚辈】 wǎnbèi the younger generation; one's juniors
【晚餐】 wǎncān supper; dinner
【晚场】 wǎnchǎng evening show; evening performance
【晚潮】 wǎncháo evening tide
【晚车】 wǎnchē night train
【晚春】 wǎnchūn late spring; late in the spring
【晚稻】 wǎndào late rice
【晚点】 wǎndiǎn late; behind schedule: ～10分钟 10 minutes behind schedule
【晚饭】 wǎnfàn supper; dinner: 吃～ have supper
【晚会】 wǎnhuì an evening of entertainment; social evening; evening party: 音乐～ a mu-

sic evening
【晚婚】 wǎnhūn marry at a mature age; late marriage
【晚间】 wǎnjiān (in the) evening; (at) night
【晚节】 wǎnjié integrity in one's later years: 保持～ keep one's integrity in one's later years
【晚年】 wǎnnián old age; one's remaining years; one's latter years
【晚期】 wǎnqī later period; terminal (adj.)
【晚期癌】 wǎnqī'ái terminal cancer
【晚秋】 wǎnqiū late autumn; late in the autumn
【晚秋作物】 wǎnqiū zuòwù late-autumn crops
【晚上】 wǎn·shang (in the) evening; (at) night: 我们每星期六～都去看电影。Saturday is our cinema night.
【晚熟】 wǎnshú late-maturing
【晚熟品种】 wǎnshú pǐnzhǒng late variety
【晚霜】 wǎnshuāng late frost
【晚、稀、少】 wǎn-xī-shǎo late, spaced and few; deferred marriage, spaced and fewer number of births
【晚霞】 wǎnxiá sunset glow; sunset clouds
【晚育】 wǎnyù late childbirth
【晚造】 wǎnzào late harvest

万[萬] (wàn) 1.(数目) ten thousand; ten thousandth 2.(很多) a very great number; myriad 3.(很;极;绝对) absolutely; by all means
【万般】 wànbān 1.(各种各样) all the different kinds 2.(非常) utterly; extremely: ～无奈 have no alternative (but to); absolutely bored
【万次闪光灯】 wàncì shǎnguāngdēng 〈*Photog.*〉 electronic flash
【万吨轮】 wàndūnlún 10,000 tonner
【万恶】 wàn'è extremely evil; absolutely vicious: ～之源 the source of all evil
【万方】 wànfāng 1.(各地) all places 2.(多种多样) extremely; incomparably
【万分】 wànfēn very much; extremely; enormously: 我～感谢你的帮助。I'm enormously grateful for your help.
【万分之一】 wànfēnzhīyī one ten-thousandth
【万福】 wànfú boundless blessings
【万古】 wàngǔ through the ages; eternally; forever: ～流芳 will be remembered throughout the ages; leave a good name that will live forever
【万古长青】 wàngǔ-chángqīng remain fresh forever; be everlasting
【万贯家私】 wànguàn-jiāsī very wealthy; very rich
【万国】 wànguó all countries; the world; international (adj.)
【万花筒】 wànhuātǒng kaleidoscope
【万金油】 wànjīnyóu 1.(一种药) a balm for treating headaches, scalds and other minor ailments 2.(什么都会,但都不擅长) Jack of all trades; Jack of all trades and master of none
【万籁俱寂】 wànlài-jùjì All is quiet.(或:Silence reigns everywhere.)
【万里长城】 wànlǐ chángchéng the Great Wall
【万里长征】 wànlǐ chángzhēng a long march of ten thousand *li*
【万里无云】 wànlǐ wúyún cloudless
【万马奔腾】 wànmǎ-bēnténg ten thousand horses galloping ahead; going full steam ahead
【万马齐喑】 wànmǎ-qíyīn ten thousand horses stand mute
【万民】 wànmín millions of people; the multitude
【万难】 wànnán 1.(非常难于) extremely difficult; utterly impossible: ～照办 impossible to do as requested 2.(各种困难) all difficulties: 排除～ surmount all difficulties
【万能】 wànnéng 1.(无所不能的) omnipotent; all-powerful 2.(多用途的) universal; all-purpose
【万能胶】 wànnéngjiāo all-purpose adhesive
【万能钥匙】 wànnéng yào·shi master-key; skeleton key
【万年】 wànnián ten thousand years; all ages; eternity: 遗臭～ leave a bad name for generations to come
【万年历】 wànniánlì perpetual calendar
【万千】 wànqiān multifarious; myriad
【万全】 wànquán perfectly sound; surefire
【万全之策】 wànquánzhīcè prudential policy
【万人空巷】 wànrén-kōngxiàng the whole

town turns out

【万世】 wànshì all ages; generation after generation: ～师表 an exemplary teacher for all ages

【万事】 wànshì all things; everything: ～大吉。Everything is just fine. (或: All's well with the world.) / ～休矣。All is lost.

【万事通】 wànshìtōng know-all; know-it-all

【万寿无疆】 wànshòu-wújiāng (wish sb.) a long life; many happy returns of the day to eternity

【万死】 wànsǐ die ten thousand deaths

【万死不辞】 wànsǐ-bùcí willing to risk any danger to do one's duty

【万岁】 wànsuì 1.(祝愿) long live 2.(指皇帝) the emperor 3.(对皇帝的直接称呼) Your Majesty 4.(对皇帝的间接称呼) His Majesty

【万万】 wànwàn 1.(绝对,用于否定) absolutely; wholly 2.(数字;亿) hundred million

【万无一失】 wànwúyīshī no danger of anything going wrong; no risk at all; perfectly safe; surefire

【万物】 wànwù all things on earth

【万向】 wànxiàng 〈*Mech.*〉 universal

【万向接头】 wànxiàng jiētóu joint coupling

【万向节】 wànxiàngjié universal joint; cardan joint

【万象】 wànxiàng every phenomenon on earth; all manifestations of nature: ～更新 everything takes on a completely new look; all things appear fresh and gay

【万幸】 wànxìng very lucky; very fortunate; by sheer luck

【万一】 wànyī 1.(可能性极小的假设) just in case; if by any chance: ～有什么事 just in case sth. should happen 2.(可能性很小的意外) contingency; eventuality: 以防～ ready for any contingency 3.(极小的一部分) one ten-thousandth; a very small percentage

【万有引力】 wànyǒu yǐnlì 〈*Physics*〉(universal) gravitation

【万有引力定律】 wànyǒu yǐnlì dìnglǜ the law of universal gravitation

【万丈】 wànzhàng lofty or bottomless: ～光芒 shine with boundless radiance; shine in all its splendor

【万众】 wànzhòng millions of people; the multitude: ～一心 millions of people all of one mind

【万状】 wànzhuàng in the extreme; extremely: 惊恐～ be frightened out of one's senses

【万紫千红】 wànzǐ-qiānhóng a riot of color; a blaze of color; innumerable flowers of purple and red

腕 (wàn) wrist

【腕骨】 wàngǔ 〈*Anat.*〉 carpus

【腕力】 wànlì wrist strength

【腕子】 wàn·zi wrist: 手～ wrist / 掰～ hand wrestling

蔓 (wàn) vine; tendriled vine

(另见"蔓"mán, màn)

wang

汪 (wāng) 1.(液体聚集) collect; accumulate 2.〈*classifier*〉 puddle; pool: 一～水 a puddle of water

【汪汪】 wāngwāng 1.(充满眼泪) tears welling up; tearful: 泪～的 with tearful eyes 2.〈*onomat.*〉 bark; yap; bowwow

【汪洋】 wāngyáng vast; boundless: ～大海 vast ocean

亡[亾] (wáng) 1.(逃亡) flee; run away 2.(丢失;失去) lose; be gone 3.(死亡) die; perish 4.(死去的) deceased: ～夫 deceased husband 5.(灭亡) conquer; subjugate

【亡故】 wánggù die; pass away; decease

【亡国】 wángguó 1.(灭亡一国家) subjugate a nation; let a state perish 2.(灭亡了的国家) a conquered nation

【亡国奴】 wángguónú a slave of a foreign power; a slave without a country; a conquered people

【亡灵】 wánglíng the soul of a deceased person; ghost; specter

【亡命】 wángmìng 1.(逃亡) flee; seek refuge; go into exile 2.(不顾性命) desperate: ～之徒 desperado

王 (wáng) king; monarch

【王八】 wáng·ba 1.（鳖）soft-shelled turtle 2.〈*coarse*〉cuckold

【王八蛋】 wángbādàn 〈*coarse*〉bastard; son of bitch

【王朝】 wángcháo 1.（朝廷）imperial court; royal court 2.（朝代）dynasty

【王储】 wángchǔ crown prince

【王道】 wángdào kingly way; benevolent government

【王法】 wángfǎ the law of the land; the law: 目无～ be defiant of laws

【王妃】 wángfēi queen consort

【王公】 wánggōng princes and dukes; the nobility

【王公贵族】 wánggōng guìzú the nobility

【王宫】 wánggōng (imperial) palace

【王冠】 wángguān imperial crown; royal crown

【王国】 wángguó 1.（国家）kingdom 2.（领域）realm; domain: 自由～ realm of freedom

【王侯】 wánghóu princes and marquises; the nobility

【王后】 wánghòu 1.（国王之妻）queen consort; queen 2.〈*Chess & Cards*〉Queen

【王浆】 wángjiāng royal jelly

【王牌】 wángpái trump card; the elite

【王牌军】 wángpáijūn elite troops; crack units

【王室】 wángshì 1.（王族）royal family: ～成员 members of the royal family 2.（朝廷）imperial court; royal court

【王水】 wángshuǐ aqua regia

【王位】 wángwèi throne

【王子】 wángzǐ 1.（国王之子）king's son; prince 2.〈*Cards*〉Jack

【王族】 wángzú persons of royal lineage

网［網］(wǎng) 1.（网子）net 2.（系统）network: 广播～ a network of broadcasting stations / 输电～ power network 3.（用网捕捉）net; catch with a net: 用～捕鸟 net birds 4.（笼罩）cover or enclose as with a net

【网点】 wǎngdiǎn 1.（系统）network and points: 零售～ retail network and shops 2.〈*Printing*〉dot; microdot

【网兜】 wǎngdōu string bag

【网罗】 wǎngluó 1.（网）a net for catching fish or birds; trap 2.（搜寻招致）enlist

【网络】 wǎngluò 〈*Electr.*〉network; electric network

【网络分析】 wǎngluò fēnxī network analysis

【网球】 wǎngqiú 1.（指项目）tennis 2.（指用的球）tennis ball

【网球场】 wǎngqiúchǎng tennis court

【网球拍】 wǎngqiúpāi tennis racket

【网球球网】 wǎngqiú qiúwǎng tennis net

【网眼】 wǎngyǎn mesh

【网眼织物】 wǎngyǎn zhīwù open-meshed fabric

【网柱】 wǎngzhù 〈*Volleyball*〉net post

【网状】 wǎngzhuàng reticular; retiform; netlike

【网子】 wǎng·zi 1.（网）net 2.（发网）hairnet

枉(wǎng) 1.（不合正道）crooked; wrong: 矫～ straighten sth. crooked; right a wrong 2.（歪曲）twist; pervert 3.（冤屈）treat unjustly; wrong 4.（枉然）in vain; to no avail; vainly

【枉法】 wǎngfǎ pervert the law: 贪赃～ take bribes and break the law

【枉费】 wǎngfèi waste; try in vain; be of no avail: ～心机 rack one's brains in vain; scheme without avail

【枉然】 wǎngrán in vain; to no avail; to no purpose

罔(wǎng) 1.（蒙蔽）deceive; cheat 2.（没有）no; not: 置若～闻 take no heed of; turn a deaf ear to

惘(wǎng) frustrated

【惘然】 wǎngrán frustrated; disappointed

辋(wǎng) rim: 轮～ rim of a wheel

魍(wǎng)

【魍魉】 wǎngliǎng demons and monsters

往(wǎng) 1.（到；去）go 2.（向）in the direction of; toward; to: ～右拐 turn to the right / 到交叉路口，你走～北的那条路。At the junction, take the road that tends north. 3.（过去的）former; past; previous: ～事 the past

【往常】 wǎngcháng habitually in the past; as one used to do formerly

【往返】 wǎngfǎn 1.（来回）go there and back：我能一天～吗？Can I go there and back in one day? 2.（反复）journey to and fro

【往返票】 wǎngfǎnpiào 〈*Railway*〉 return ticket; roundtrip ticket

【往返运费】 wǎngfǎn yùnfèi freight out and home

【往后】 wǎnghòu from now on; in the future; later on

【往还】 wǎnghuán contact; dealings; intercourse

【往来】 wǎnglái 1.（去和来）come and go 2.（互访）contact; dealings; intercourse：贸易～ trade contacts; commercial intercourse

【往来账户】 wǎnglái zhànghù current account; running account; open account

【往来资产】 wǎnglái zīchǎn quick assets

【往年】 wǎngnián （in）former years

【往日】 wǎngrì （in）former days;（in）bygone days

【往时】 wǎngshí in the past

【往事】 wǎngshì past events; the past：～不要再提了。Let bygones be bygones.

【往往】 wǎngwǎng often; frequently; more often than not

【往昔】 wǎngxī in the past; in ancient times; in olden times

旺（wàng） prosperous; flourishing; vigorous

【旺季】 wàngjì peak period; busy season

【旺盛】 wàngshèng vigorous; exuberant：士气～ have a high morale

【旺月】 wàngyuè busy month（in business）

望（wàng） 1.（向远处看）gaze into the distance; look over; look far ahead 2.（探望）call on; visit 3.（盼望；希望）hope; expect; look forward to; anticipate 4.（名望）reputation; prestige 5.（月相）full moon

【望尘莫及】 wàngchén-mòjí so far behind that one can only see the dust of the rider ahead; too far behind to catch up; too inferior to bear comparison

【望而生畏】 wàng'érshēngwèi be terrified by the sight of sb. or sth.; inspire awe even from distance

【望风】 wàngfēng keep watch; be on watch

【望风披靡】 wàngfēng-pīmǐ flee pell-mell at the mere sight of the oncoming force; flee at sight

【望见】 wàngjiàn see

【望楼】 wànglóu watchtower; lookout tower

【望梅止渴】 wàngméi-zhǐkě quench one's thirst by thinking of plums; console oneself with false hopes; feed on fancies

【望日】 wàngrì 〈*Astron.*〉 the 15th day of the lunar month

【望文生义】 wàngwén-shēngyì take the words too literally; interpret without real understanding

【望洋兴叹】 wàngyáng-xīngtàn lament one's littleness before the vast ocean; bemoan one's inadequacy in the face of a great task; feel powerless and frustrated

【望远镜】 wàngyuǎnjìng telescope：观剧～ opera-glasses / 野外双筒～ field-glasses

【望远镜头】 wàngyuǎnjìngtóu 〈*Photog.*〉 telephoto lens

【望月】 wàngyuè 〈*Astron.*〉 full moon

【望子成龙】 wàngzǐ-chénglóng hope one's children will have a bright future

【望子】 wàng·zi signboard; trade marker：酒～ signboard of a tavern

【望族】 wàngzú distinguished family; prominent family

妄（wàng） 1.（荒谬）absurd; preposterous 2.（胡乱）presumptuous; rash：～加评论 make improper comments

【妄动】 wàngdòng rash action; reckless action：轻举～ take rash action; take reckless action

【妄念】 wàngniàn wild fancy; improper thought

【妄求】 wàngqiú inappropriate request; presumptuous demand

【妄图】 wàngtú try in vain; vainly attempt

【妄想】 wàngxiǎng 1.（妄图）try in vain; vainly hope 2.（指想法）vain hope; wishful thinking：痴心～ be obsessed with fantastic ideas

【妄想狂】 wàngxiǎngkuáng nympholepsy;

paranoia

【妄语】 wàngyǔ 1.(胡说) tell lies; talk nonsense 2.(虚妄的话) wild talk; rant

【妄自菲薄】 wàngzì-fěibó improperly belittle oneself; unduly humble oneself; underestimate one's own capabilities

【妄自尊大】 wàngzì-zūndà have too high an opinion of oneself; be overweening; be self-important

忘 (wàng) 1.(忘记) forget; escape one's memory: ～不了 will not forget / 别～了带箱子。Don't forget the cases. 2.(忽略) overlook; neglect

【忘本】 wàngběn forget one's class origin; forget one's past suffering

【忘掉】 wàngdiào forget; let slip from one's mind

【忘恩负义】 wàng'ēn-fùyì devoid of gratitude; ungrateful; be ungrateful and act contrary to justice

【忘乎所以】 wànghū-suǒyǐ forget oneself

【忘怀】 wànghuái forget; dismiss from one's mind

【忘记】 wàngjì 1.(不记得) forget; slip from one's memory 2.(忽略) forget; overlook; neglect; dismiss from one's mind: 她～寄这封信了。She forgot to post the letter.

【忘了】 wàng·le have forgotten

【忘年交】 wàngniánjiāo 1.(指友情) friendship between generations 2.(指人) good friends despite great difference in age

【忘情】 wàngqíng 1.(无动于衷) be unruffled by emotion; be unmoved; be indifferent 2.(情不自禁) let oneself go

【忘却】 wàngquè forget

【忘我】 wàngwǒ oblivious of oneself; selfless

【忘形】 wàngxíng have one's head turned; forget oneself: 得意～ lose all bearings in moment of pride and satisfaction

【忘性】 wàngxìng forgetfulness; absent-mindedness

【忘忧】 wàngyōu forget cares and worries

【忘忧草】 wàngyōucǎo day-lily

wei

危 (wēi) 1.(危险) danger; peril 2.(危及) endanger; imperil: ～及生命 endanger one's life 3.(病危) dying: 病～ be critically ill; be dying 4.(高) high; precipitous: ～楼 a high tower 5.(端正) properly

【危害】 wēihài harm; endanger; jeopardize: ～公共秩序 jeopardize public order

【危害程度】 wēihài chéngdù extent of injury

【危害公共安全罪】 wēihài gōnggòng ānquánzuì offense against public security

【危害社会秩序罪】 wēihài shèhuì zhìxùzuì offense against social order

【危害性】 wēihàixìng harmfulness; perniciousness

【危机】 wēijī crisis: 财政～ financial crisis / 货币～ exchange crisis / 金融～ monetary crisis / 经济～ economic crisis / 能源～ energy crisis / 信贷～ credit crisis / 周期性～ cyclic crisis 转嫁～ shift a crisis onto others

【危急】 wēijí critical; in imminent danger; in a desperate situation

【危局】 wēijú a dangerous situation; a critical situation; a desperate situation

【危惧】 wēijù worry and fear; be apprehensive

【危楼】 wēilóu a high building

【危难】 wēinàn danger and disaster; calamity

【危亡】 wēiwáng in peril; at stake

【危险】 wēixiǎn 1.(险) danger: 充满了～ be full of danger / 脱离～ be out of danger / 临头的～ sword of Damocles 2.(危险的) dangerous; perilous: 在这个湖里游泳～。This lake is dangerous for swimmers.

【危险地带】 wēixiǎn dìdài danger zone

【危险职业】 wēixiǎn zhíyè dangerous occupation

【危言耸听】 wēiyán-sǒngtīng say frightening things just to raise an alarm; exaggerate things just to scare people; use lofty words to excite one to listen

【危在旦夕】 wēizàidànxī on the verge of death or destruction; in imminent danger

【危坐】 wēizuò sit properly

逶 (wēi)

【逶迤】 wēiyí winding; meandering

巍 (wēi) towering; lofty

【巍峨】 wēi'é towering; lofty: ～的群山

lofty mountains

【巍然】 wēirán towering; lofty; majestic; imposing: ～屹立 stand lofty and firm

【巍巍】 wēiwēi towering; lofty

威 (wēi) impressive strength; might; power

【威逼】 wēibī threaten by force; coerce; intimidate: ～利诱 combine threats with inducements

【威风】 wēifēng 1.(气派) power and prestige; high prestige backed up with power 2.(有威风) imposing; impressive; awe-inspiring; majestic looking

【威风凛凛】 wēifēng-lǐnlǐn majestic looking; awe-inspiring

【威风扫地】 wēifēng-sǎodì with every shred of one's prestige swept away

【威吓】 wēihè intimidate; threaten; bully

【威赫】 wēihè majestic looking; awe-inspiring

【威力】 wēilì power; formidable force; might: 军事～ military power

【威名】 wēimíng prestige; renown; fame based on great strength or military exploits

【威慑】 wēishè terrorize with military force; deter

【威慑力量】 wēishè lìliàng deterrent force; deterrent

【威慑政策】 wēishè zhèngcè deterrence policy

【威士忌】 wēishìjì whisky: 苏格兰～ Scottish whisky

【威望】 wēiwàng prestige; renown: 崇高的～ high prestige

【威武】 wēiwǔ 1.(权势;武力) might; force; power: ～不能屈 not to be subdued by force 2.(力量强大) powerful; mighty

【威胁】 wēixié threaten; menace; imperil

【威胁利诱】 wēixié lìyòu intimidation and bribery; coercion and bribery

【威信】 wēixìn prestige; popular trust; prestigious: ～扫地 cause a loss of prestige; completely discredited / 丧失～ lose one's prestige

【威严】 wēiyán 1.(指样子) dignified; stately; majestic; awe-inspiring 2.(威风) awe; prestige; dignity

【威仪】 wēiyí impressive and dignified manner

偎 (wēi) snuggle up to; lean close to

【偎抱】 wēibào hug; cuddle

【偎依】 wēiyī snuggle up to; lean close to

煨 (wēi) 1.(慢火煮) stew; cook over a small fire 2.(用炭灰烤) roast in fresh cinders

微 (wēi) 1.(细微) minute; tiny 2.(精深) profound; abstruse: 精～ subtle 3.(衰落) decline 4.(百万分之一) one millionth part of; micro-: ～米 micron (μ)

【微波】 wēibō 〈*Electr.*〉 microwave

【微波炉】 wēibōlú microwave oven

【微波通信】 wēibō tōngxìn microwave communication

【微薄】 wēibó meager; scanty

【微不足道】 wēibùzúdào insignificant; inconsiderable; not worth mentioning; negligible

【微处理机】 wēichǔlǐjī 〈*Computer*〉 microprocessing unit; microprocessor

【微电脑】 wēidiànnǎo microcomputer

【微电子】 wēidiànzǐ microelectronics; microelectronic (adj.): ～技术 microelectronic technology

【微雕】 wēidiāo microscopic carving

【微分】 wēifēng 〈*Math.*〉 differential

【微分学】 wēifēnxué differential calculus

【微风】 wēifēng 〈*Meteorol.*〉 gentle breeze

【微观】 wēiguān microcosmic

【微观搞活】 wēiguān gǎohuó micro-flexibility

【微观经济学】 wēiguān jīngjìxué microeconomics

【微观世界】 wēiguān shìjiè microcosmos

【微乎其微】 wēihūqíwēi very little; next to nothing; as trifling as it is

【微机】 wēijī 〈*Computer*〉 microcomputer; personal computer

【微粒】 wēilì 1.(微小的颗粒) particle 2.〈*Physics*〉 corpuscle

【微量】 wēiliàng trace; micro-

【微量元素】 wēiliàng yuánsù trace element

【微米】 wēimǐ micron (μ)

【微秒】 wēimiǎo microsecond

【微妙】 wēimiào delicate; subtle: 关系～

subtle relations
【微末】 wēimò trifling; insignificant
【微热】 wēirè 〈*Med*.〉 low-grade fever
【微弱】 wēiruò 1.(小而弱) slender; small: ～多数 slender majority 2.(衰弱) faint; feeble; weak
【微生物】 wēishēngwù microorganism; microbe
【微生物学】 wēishēngwùxué microbiology
【微缩胶片】 wēisuō jiāopiàn microfiche
【微缩照片】 wēisuō zhàopiān microphotograph
【微调】 wēitiáo 〈*Electr*.〉 fine-tune; fine tuning (n.)
【微微】 wēiwēi slightly; faintly: ～一笑 smile slightly
【微细】 wēixì very small; tiny
【微小】 wēixiǎo small; little
【微笑】 wēixiào smile: 她看见我时露出～。She smiled when she saw me.
【微笑服务】 wēixiào fúwù service-with-a-smile
【微型】 wēixíng miniature; mini-
【微型出租汽车】 wēixíng chūzū qìchē minicab
【微型公共汽车】 wēixíng gōnggòng qìchē minibus
【微型汽车】 wēixíng qìchē baby car; midget car; mini
【微型照相机】 wēixíng zhàoxiàngjī miniature camera; minicam
【微血管】 wēixuèguǎn 〈*Anat*.〉 (blood) capillary
【微循环】 wēixúnhuán 〈*Biol*.〉 microcirculation
【微恙】 wēiyàng slight illness; indisposition
【微震】 wēizhèn 1.(微小震动) slight shock 2.〈*Geog. & Physics*〉 microseism

围[圍](wéi) 1.(环绕) enclose; surround: 团团～住 besiege tightly / 她在脖子上～了条围巾。She put a scarf around her neck. 2.(四周) all round; around
【围脖儿】 wéibór scarf; muffler
【围捕】 wéibǔ surround and catch; fish in a circle
【围攻】 wéigōng 1.(攻击) besiege; lay siege to 2.(用言语攻击) jointly speak or write against sb.; jointly attack sb.: 遭到～ come under attacked from all sides
【围观】 wéiguān rubberneck
【围观者】 wéiguānzhě rubberneck
【围歼】 wéijiān surround and annihilate
【围剿】 wéijiǎo encircle and suppress
【围巾】 wéijīn muffler; scarf: 围上～ put a scarf round the neck
【围垦】 wéikěn build dikes to reclaim land from marshes; enclose tideland for cultivation
【围困】 wéikùn besiege; hem in; pin down
【围拢】 wéilǒng crowd around; come closer
【围棋】 wéiqí go; *wei qi*: 下～ play *wei qi*
【围墙】 wéiqiáng enclosure; enclosing wall
【围裙】 wéiqún apron
【围绕】 wéirào 1.(围着转) round; around 2.(以…为中心) center on; revolve round
【围绳】 wéishéng 〈*Boxing*〉 rope
【围网】 wéiwǎng purse seine; purse net
【围堰】 wéiyàn coffer-dam
【围子】 wéi·zi 1.(村庄周围的墙) defensive wall; stockade surrounding a village 2.(帷子) curtain
【围嘴儿】 wéizuǐr bib

帏[幃](wéi) curtain

违[違](wéi) 1.(违背,违反) disobey; violate: ～约 break a contract 2.(离别) be separated; part with: 久～了。I haven't seen you for ages.
【违碍】 wéi'ài taboo; prohibition
【违拗】 wéi'ào disobey; defy
【违背】 wéibèi violate; go against; run counter to: ～诺言 violate one's promise
【违法】 wéifǎ break the law; be illegal; against the law: ～乱纪 malfeasance; violate the law and discipline
【违反】 wéifǎn violate; run counter to; transgress; infringe: ～法律 breach of law; contrary to law; disregard of law / ～合同 breach of contract; infringement of contract / ～合同所规定的义务 break one's obligations under the contract / ～交通规则 infringe traffic regulations; contravene the traffic regulations
【违犯】 wéifàn violate; infringe; act con-

trary to：～宪法 violation of the constitution
【违禁】 wéijìn violate a ban
【违禁品】 wéijìnpǐn contraband；contraband goods；prohibited products
【违抗】 wéikàng disobey；defy：～法律 defy law
【违例】 wéilì 1.〈*Sports*〉breach of rules 2.〈*Basketball*〉violation
【违误】 wéiwù （公文用语）disobey orders and cause delay
【违宪行为】 wéixiàn xíngwéi unconstitutional act
【违心】 wéixīn against one's will；contrary to one's convictions
【违约】 wéiyuē 1.（违反条约、契约等）break a contract；violate a treaty 2.（失约）break one's promise；break off an engagement
【违章】 wéizhāng break rules and regulations
【违章建筑】 wéizhāng jiànzhù illegal construction
【违章停车罚款通知单】 wéizhāng tíngchē fákuǎn tōngzhīdān parking-ticket
【违章肇事者】 wéizhāng zhàoshìzhě delinquent
为［爲］（wéi） 1.（做）do；act：事在人～。It all depends on human effort. 2.（充当）act as；serve as 3.（成为）become 4.（是；合）be；mean；make
（另见"为"wèi）
【为非作歹】 wéifēi-zuòdǎi do evil；commit crimes；perpetrate outrages
【为富不仁】 wéifù-bùrén be rich and cruel；be one of the heartless rich
【为害】 wéihài do harms；imperil
【为难】 wéinán 1.（难以对付）feel embarrassed；feel awkward：左右～ be in an embarrassed situation 2.（刁难）make things difficult for：故意～某人 deliberately make things difficult for sb.
【为期】 wéiqī （to be completed）by a definite date
【为人】 wéirén behave；conduct oneself：～正直 be honest
【为生】 wéishēng make a living：无以～ have nothing to live on
【为首】 wéishǒu with sb. as the leader；headed by；led by：以某人～的代表团 delegation headed by sb.
【为数】 wéishù amount to；number：～不多 have only a small number
【为所欲为】 wéisuǒyùwéi do as one pleases；do whatever one likes；have one's own way
【为伍】 wéiwǔ associate with
【为限】 wéixiàn be within the limit of；not exceed；be good for . . . only
【为止】 wéizhǐ up to；till：到今天～ till today；up to now
【为重】 wéizhòng attach most importance to：以友谊～ value the friendship highly
【为主】 wéizhǔ give first place to；give priority to；take sth. as the principal thing
圩（wéi） 1.（堤岸）dike；bank 2.（围子）defensive wall；stockade surrounding a village
（另见"圩"xū）
【圩田】 wéitián embanked paddy field
桅（wéi） mast
【桅灯】 wéidēng 1.（船用的）mast head light；range light 2.（马灯）barn lantern
【桅杆】 wéigān mast
【桅杆式天线】 wéigānshì tiānxiàn flagpole antennas
【桅樯】 wéiqiáng mast
唯（wéi） 1.（单单，同"惟"）only；alone 2.（答应的声音）yea；yes
【唯独】 wéidú 见"惟独"
【唯恐】 wéikǒng 见"惟恐"
【唯利是图】 wéilì-shìtú 见"惟利是图"
【唯命是从】 wéimìng-shìcóng 见"惟命是从"
【唯唯诺诺】 wéiwéi-nuònuò be a yes-man；be obsequious
【唯我独尊】 wéiwǒ-dúzūn 见"惟我独尊"
【唯我主义】 wéiwǒ zhǔyì 〈*Philos.*〉solipsism；egotism
【唯武器论】 wéiwǔqìlùn the theory that weapons alone decide the outcome of war
【唯物辩证法】 wéiwù biànzhèngfǎ 〈*Philos.*〉materialist dialectics
【唯物论】 wéiwùlùn 〈*Philos.*〉materialism
【唯物主义】 wéiwù zhǔyì 〈*Philos.*〉materialism；materialist（adj.）：辩证～ dialectical materialism / 机械～ mechanical materialism / 历史～ historical materialism ‖ 唯物

主义者 materialist
【唯心论】 wéixīnlùn 〈*Philos.*〉 idealism
【唯心主义】 wéixīn zhǔyì 〈*Philos.*〉 idealism
【唯一】 wéiyī 见"惟一"
【唯意志论】 wéiyìzhìlùn 〈*Philos.*〉 panthelism; voluntarism

帷 (wéi) curtain
【帷幕】 wéimù heavy curtain
【帷幄】 wéiwò army tent：运筹～ devise strategies within a command tent
【帷子】 wéi·zi curtain

惟 (wéi) **1.**（单单）only; alone **2.**（只是）but; only that **3.**（思惟）thinking; thought
【惟独】 wéidú only; alone
【惟恐】 wéikǒng for fear that; lest
【惟利是图】 wéilì-shìtú be bent solely on profit; put profit-making first; interested only in material gain
【惟妙惟肖】 wéimiào-wéixiào absolutely lifelike; remarkably true to life
【惟命是从】 wéimìng-shìcóng always do as one is told; be absolutely obedient; receive absolutely one's instruction
【惟我独尊】 wéiwǒ-dúzūn overweening; extremely conceited; no one is noble but me
【惟一】 wéiyī only; sole; unique：～合法政府 sole legal government / 你是～能了解我的人。You're the only person that can know me.
【惟有】 wéiyǒu only; alone

维 (wéi) **1.**（维系）tie up; hold together：～系 hold together; maintain **2.**（维持）maintain; safeguard; preserve **3.**（思维）thinking; thought **4.**〈*Math.*〉dimension：三～空间 three-dimensional space
【维持】 wéichí keep; maintain; preserve：～边界现状 maintain the status quo of the border / ～秩序 keep order / 这些给养还够～一个月。These supplies should last for a month.
【维持和平部队】 wéichí hépíng bùduì peacekeeping force
【维护】 wéihù safeguard; defend; uphold：～某人的权益 assert one's rights / ～国家独立和主权完整 safeguard national independence and the integrity of sovereignty / ～社会治安 maintain public security / ～世界和平 safeguard world peace
【维纶】 wéilún 〈*Textiles*〉 polyvinyl alcohol fiber
【维棉】 wéimián 〈*Textiles*〉 vinylon and cotton blend
【维尼纶】 wéinílún 〈*Textiles*〉 vinylon
【维生素】 wéishēngsù vitamin
【维生素 B_1】 wéishēngsùB_1 〈*Biochem.*〉 thiamine; thiamian
【维生素 B_2】 wéishēngsùB_2 （核黄素）riboflavin
【维吾尔族】 Wéiwú'ěrzú Uygur（中国少数民族，主要分布在新疆）
【维系】 wéixì hold together; maintain
【维新】 wéixīn reform; modernization
【维修】 wéixiū keep in (good) repair; service; maintain：日常～ routine maintenance

伟［偉］(wěi) big; great：～力 mighty force
【伟大】 wěidà great; big; mighty
【伟绩】 wěijì great feats; great exploits; brilliant achievements：丰功～ great achievements and abundant merits
【伟人】 wěirén a great man; a great personage
【伟业】 wěiyè great cause; exploit

苇［葦］(wěi) reed：芦～ reed
【苇荡】 wěidàng reed pond; reed marshes
【苇塘】 wěitáng reed pond
【苇席】 wěixí reed mat
【苇子】 wěi·zi reed

纬［緯］(wěi) **1.**〈*Textiles*〉 weft; woof **2.**〈*Geol.*〉 latitude
【纬度】 wěidù 〈*Geol.*〉 latitude：低～ low latitudes / 高～ high latitudes / 北京在什么纬度上？北纬 40 度。What latitude is Beijing on? — 40°N.（40°N 读作 forty degrees north 或 north latitude forty degrees）
【纬纱】 wěishā 〈*Textiles*〉 woof
【纬线】 wěixiàn **1.**〈*Geol.*〉 parallel **2.**〈*Textiles*〉 weft
【纬向】 wěixiàng broadwise

伪［僞、偽］(wěi) **1.**（虚假的）false; fake; bogus：～钞

counterfeit bank note; forged bank note 2.(不合法的) puppet; collaborationist: ～政府 illegitimate government

【伪币】 wěibì 1.(伪造的) counterfeit money; counterfeit bank note; forged bank note; spurious coin 2.(伪政府发行的) money issued by a puppet government

【伪钞】 wěichāo 见"伪币"

【伪军】 wěijūn 1.(指军队) puppet army; puppet troops 2.(指士兵) puppet soldier

【伪君子】 wěijūnzǐ hypocrite

【伪科学】 wěikēxué pseudoscience

【伪劣】 wěiliè counterfeit and inferior

【伪劣假冒产品】 wěiliè jiǎmào chǎnpǐn inferior and counterfeit products

【伪劣商品】 wěiliè shāngpǐn counterfeit and defective goods

【伪善】 wěishàn hypocritical

【伪善者】 wěishànzhě goody-goody

【伪造】 wěizào forge; falsify; fabricate; counterfeit: ～公章 forge official seals / ～文件 falsify documents

【伪造钞票罪】 wěizào chāopiào zuì offense of counterfeiting bank notes

【伪造品】 wěizàopǐn counterfeit; forgery

【伪造罪】 wěizàozuì forgery

【伪证】 wěizhèng 〈*Law*〉 perjury; false witness: 作～ bear false witness

【伪证人】 wěizhèngrén perjured witness

【伪证罪】 wěizhèngzuì offense of false evidence

【伪装】 wěizhuāng 1.(假装) pretend; feign 2.(假的装扮) disguise; guise; mask: 剥去～ strip off the disguise; remove one's musk 3.〈*Mil.*〉 camouflage: 军车被～起来了。The military vehicles were camouflaged.

【伪装网】 wěizhuāngwǎng camouflage net; garnished net

尾 (wěi) 1.(尾巴) tail 2.(末端) end 3.(未完之事) remaining part; remnant 4.(羊肉部位) dock
(另见"尾"yǐ)

【尾巴】 wěi·ba 1.(尾) tail: 狗高兴时摇～。Dog wag their tails when they are pleased. 2.(尾部) tail-like part: 风筝～ the tail of a kite 3.(随声附和的人) servile adherent; appendage 4.(尾随者) a person shadowing sb. 5.(未完之事) remaining part; remnant

【尾部】 wěibù 〈*Mech.*〉 afterbody; tail assembly: 飞机～ the tail of a plane

【尾灯】 wěidēng 〈*Auto*〉 tail light; tail lamp; rear light

【尾骨】 wěigǔ 〈*Anat.*〉 coccyx; tail bone

【尾鳍】 wěiqí 〈*Zool.*〉 tail fin; caudal fin

【尾气】 wěiqì 〈*Chem.*〉 tail gas

【尾声】 wěishēng 1.〈*Music*〉 coda 2.(与序幕相对) epilogue: 序幕和～ prologue and epilogue 3.(临近结尾) end

【尾数】 wěishù mantissa; odd amount in addition to the round number

【尾随】 wěisuí 1.(跟在后面) tail behind; tag along after; follow at sb's heels; at the tail of 2.(跟踪监视) tail; shadow: 警察一直在～着他。The police have been tailing him.

【尾旋翼】 wěixuányì 〈*Aeron.*〉 tail rotor

【尾翼】 wěiyì 〈*Aeron.*〉 tail surface; empennage

【尾翼垂直安定面】 wěiyì chuízhí āndìngmiàn 〈*Aeron.*〉 fin

【尾羽】 wěiyǔ 〈*Zool.*〉 tail feather

【尾椎】 wěizhuī 〈*Anat.*〉 caudal vertebrae

【尾追】 wěizhuī in hot pursuit; hot on the trail of

【尾座】 wěizuò 〈*Mech.*〉 tailstock

娓 (wěi)

【娓娓】 wěiwěi (talk) tirelessly: ～动听 speak with absorbing interest; sound pleasing and attractive

委 (wěi) 1.(委托) entrust; appoint: ～以重任 entrust sb. with an important task; give one the bag to hold 2.(抛弃) throw away; cast aside: ～弃 discard 3.(推委) shift: ～罪于人 shift the blame on others 4.(曲折) indirect; roundabout 5.(末尾) end: 原～ the beginning and the end 6.(不振作; 无精打采) listless; dejected: ～靡 listless; dispirited 7.(的确; 确实) actually; certainly: ～系实情。This is really the case. 8.(委员) committee member: 常～ member of a standing committee 9.(委员会) committee; commission; council: 党～ Party committee

【委顿】 wěidùn tired; weary; fagged out

【委靡】 wěimǐ listless; dispirited; dejected
【委靡不振】 wěimǐ-bùzhèn look blue; be in low spirits
【委派】 wěipài appoint; delegate; designate: ～某人代表 appoint sb. as delegate
【委屈】 wěiqū 1.(受冤屈) feel wronged; nurse a grievance 2.(冤屈人) put sb. to great inconvenience
【委曲】 wěiqū 1.(弯曲) winding; tortuous 2.(原委) truth; facts; the pros and cons
【委曲求全】 wěiqū-qiúquán compromise out of consideration for the general interest; stoop to compromise
【委曲之词】 wěiqūzhīcí an indirect statement
【委任】 wěirèn appoint; nominate
【委任状】 wěirènzhuàng certificate of appointment
【委身】 wěishēn become the wife of
【委实】 wěishí really; indeed
【委托】 wěituō entrust; trust; deliver to sb's care: ～某人为独家代理 entrust sb. with sale agency / 他～副手照管商店。He left his assistant in charge of the store.
【委托保险】 wěituō bǎoxiǎn trust insurance
【委托代理】 wěituō dàilǐ agency by agreement
【委托加工】 wěituō jiāgōng manufacturing consignment
【委托人】 wěituōrén trustee; principal: ～的利益 interest of the principal / ～的职责 obligation of the principal
【委托商店】 wěituō shāngdiàn commission house; commission shop
【委托书】 wěituōshū certificate of entrustment; letter of attorney; commission
【委婉】 wěiwǎn mild and roundabout; tactful
【委员】 wěiyuán committee member; member of a committee: 常务～ standing member of a committee / 中央～ member of the Central Committee
【委员会】 wěiyuánhuì committee; commission; council: 中央～ central committee / 仲裁～ arbitration commission
【委员长】 wěiyuánzhǎng chairman of a committee
【委罪】 wěizuì put the blame on sb. else

诿 (wěi)

【诿罪】 wěizuì put the blame on sb. else

萎 (wěi) wither; wilt; fade

【萎靡不振】 wěimǐ-bùzhèn in low spirits; dejected and apathetic
【萎缩】 wěisuō 1.(干枯) wither; shrivel; shrink 2.(经济衰退) shrink; sag; contraction 3.〈*Med*.〉 atrophy
【萎谢】 wěixiè wither; fade

痿 (wěi) flaccid paralysis: 阳～ impotence; impotent (adj.)

【痿症】 wěizhèng 〈*Chin. Med*.〉 flaccid paralysis

猥 (wěi) 1.(下流) base; obscene; salacious; indecent 2.(多; 杂) numerous; multifarious: ～杂 miscellaneous

【猥词】 wěicí obscene language; salacious words
【猥辞】 wěicí 同"猥词"
【猥琐】 wěisuǒ of wretched appearance; of dreadful appearance
【猥亵】 wěixiè 1.(下流言行) obscene; salacious 2.(做下流动作) act indecently towards (a woman)
【猥亵刊物】 wěixiè kānwù obscene publication
【猥亵行为】 wěixiè xíngwéi act of indecency; indecent conduct
【猥亵罪】 wěixièzuì crime of indecent act; indecent assault

卫[衛、衞] (wèi) defend; guard; protect

【卫兵】 wèibīng guard; bodyguard
【卫道】 wèidào defend traditional moral principles
【卫道士】 wèidàoshì apologist
【卫队】 wèiduì squad of bodyguards; armed escort
【卫护】 wèihù protect; guard
【卫矛】 wèimáo 〈*Bot*.〉 winged euonymus
【卫生】 wèishēng 1.(卫生) hygiene; sanitation; health: 讲～ pay attention to hygiene / 改善环境～ improve environmental sanitation 2.(符合卫生的) hygienic; healthy; sanitary: ～习惯 hygienic habit
【卫生部门】 wèishēng bùmén sanitary authorities

【卫生措施】 wèishēng cuòshī sanitary measures

【卫生带】 wèishēngdài sanitary towel; sanitary napkin

【卫生队】 wèishēngduì medical unit; medical team

【卫生防疫站】 wèishēng fángyìzhàn sanitation and antiepidemic station

【卫生规定】 wèishēng guīdìng sanitary rules

【卫生环境】 wèishēng huánjìng hygienic conditions

【卫生间】 wèishēngjiān toilet; bathroom

【卫生间镜箱】 wèishēngjiān jìngxiāng bathroom cabinet

【卫生检查】 wèishēng jiǎnchá sanitary inspection

【卫生教育】 wèishēng jiàoyù hygiene education

【卫生巾】 wèishēngjīn sanitary napkin; sanitary towel

【卫生局】 wèishēngjú public health bureau

【卫生科】 wèishēngkē health section

【卫生球】 wèishēngqiú camphor ball; mothball

【卫生设备】 wèishēng shèbèi sanitary equipment

【卫生室】 wèishēngshì clinic

【卫生学】 wèishēngxué hygiene; hygienics

【卫生预防措施】 wèishēng yùfáng cuòshī sanitary arrangements

【卫生员】 wèishēngyuán health worker; medical orderly; medic

【卫生院】 wèishēngyuàn local hospital

【卫生皂】 wèishēngzào toilet soap

【卫生知识】 wèishēng zhī·shi hygienic knowledge: 普及～ popularize knowledge of hygiene; popularize halth know-how

【卫生纸】 wèishēngzhǐ toilet paper; toilet roll

【卫生纸架】 wèishēngzhǐ jià toilet paper holder

【卫士】 wèishì bodyguard

【卫戍】 wèishù garrison

【卫戍部队】 wèishù bùduì garrison force

【卫戍区】 wèishùqū garrison command

【卫星】 wèixīng 1.（天体）satellite; moon 2.（人造卫星）artificial satellite; man-made satellite; sputnik (Rus.): 电视转播～ television transmission satellite / 气象～ meteorological satellite / 同步通信～ syncom; synchronous communication satellite

【卫星城】 wèixīngchéng satellite town; satellite city

【卫星地面站】 wèixīng dìmiànzhàn ground satellite station

【卫星跟踪】 wèixīng gēnzōng moontrack

【卫星国】 wèixīngguó satellite state; satellite country

【卫星通信】 wèixīng tōngxìn satellite communication

【卫星云图】 wèixīng yúntú satellite cloud picture

【卫星云图接收系统】 wèixīng yúntú jiēshōu xìtǒng satellite cloud picture receiving system

【卫星直播】 wèixīng zhíbō DBS; direct broadcasting by satellite

为[為、爲] (wèi) 1.（给；替）for; for the benefit of; in the interests of 2.（为了）for; for the sake of: ～国增光 bring credit to one's country 3.（因为）because; for; on account of
（另见“为”wéi）

【为此】 wèicǐ to this end; for this reason; for this purpose; in this connection

【为公】 wèigōng for public good

【为国捐躯】 wèiguó-juānqū lay down one's life for one's country

【为何】 wèihé why; for what reason

【为虎作伥】 wèihǔ-zuòchāng play the jackal to the tiger; help a villain do evil

【为了】 wèi·le for; for the sake of; in order to: ～生存 for existence / ～赶火车,她匆忙地做完了她的工作。In order to catch the train, she hurried through her work. / ～夜间长途行车,他喝了清咖啡。He armed himself for the long night's drive by drinking black coffee.

【为民除害】 wèimín-chúhài rid the people of an evil

【为民请命】 wèimín-qǐngmìng plead in the name of the people; plead for the people

【为名为利】 wèimíng-wèilì for fame and for wealth

【为人作嫁】 wèirén-zuòjià sew sb. else's trousseau; doing work for others with no benefit to oneself; toil just for the benefit of others

【为什么】 wèishén·me why; why is it that; how is it that

【为私】 wèisī for one's personal interest

未 (wèi) 1.(不曾) have not; did not; not yet: ～达标的工程部分 fault in workmanship 2.(不) not; no: ～见好转。It isn't any better.

【未必】 wèibì may not; not necessarily; not sure

【未必尽然】 wèibìjìnrán not always so; not necessarily so

【未便】 wèibiàn not be in a position to; find it hard to

【未卜先知】 wèibǔ-xiānzhī foresee; have foresight; be able to foresee the future

【未曾】 wèicéng have not; did not: ～有 have not happened before

【未尝】 wèicháng 1.(未曾) have not; did not 2.〈*euphem.*〉那也～不可。That should be all right.

【未尝债务】 wèicháng zhàiwù outstanding debt

【未成年】 wèichéngnián not yet of age; under age; immaturity

【未成年子女】 wèichéngnián zǐnǚ minor children

【未成年罪犯】 wèichéngnián zuìfàn minor offender

【未成熟】 wèichéngshú unripe; immature

【未点燃】 wèidiǎnrán unignited

【未定】 wèidìng uncertain; undecided; undefined

【未定稿】 wèidìnggǎo draft

【未定界】 wèidìngjiè undefined boundary

【未分配利润】 wèifēnpèi lìrùn 〈*Econ.*〉 undistributed profits

【未付】 wèifù outstanding; unpaid: ～款项 unpaid item

【未敢苟同】 wèigǎn-gǒutóng beg to differ; cannot agree

【未婚】 wèihūn unmarried; not married

【未婚夫】 wèihūnfū fiancé

【未婚妻】 wèihūnqī fiancée

【未几】 wèijǐ 1.(不久) in the near future 2.(不多) few; little

【未加工】 wèijiāgōng crude

【未竟】 wèijìng unfinished; outstanding

【未决】 wèijué unsettled; outstanding

【未决犯】 wèijuéfàn prisoner awaiting trial; culprit; unconvicted prisoner

【未可】 wèikě cannot: ～乐观 give no cause for optimism; nothing to be optimistic about

【未来】 wèilái 1.(将到来的) coming; next; future; approaching 2.(将来) future; tomorrow: 美好的～ bright future

【未来学】 wèiláixué futurology

【未老先衰】 wèilǎo-xiānshuāi prematurely senile; old before one's time

【未了】 wèiliǎo unfinished; outstanding

【未免】 wèimiǎn rather; a bit too; truly

【未能】 wèinéng fail to; cannot; haven't been able to

【未遂】 wèisuì not accomplished; abortive: ～政变 a aborted coup d'état / 谋杀～ an attempt at murder

【未遂罪】 wèisuìzuì attempted crime; attempt

【未完】 wèiwán unfinished: ～待续 to be continued

【未完成时】 wèiwánchéngshí 〈*Gram.*〉 imperfect tense

【未雨绸缪】 wèiyǔ-chóumóu repair the house before it rains; provide for a rainy day; take precautions

【未知数】 wèizhīshù 1.〈*Math.*〉 unknown number 2.(未知事物) unknown; uncertain

味 (wèi) 1.(滋味) taste; flavor: 糖有甜～。Sugar has a sweet taste. 2.(气味) smell; odor 3.(趣味) interest 4.(辨别味道) distinguish the flavor of

【味道】 wèi·dao 1.(味) taste; flavor: ～不好 not have a good taste / ～好 have a good taste / 这汤有鸡的～。This soup tastes of chicken. / 这茶的～很香。This tea tastes sweet. 2.(兴趣) interest 3.(气味) smell

【味精】 wèijīng monosodium glutamate (M.S.G.); gourmet powder

【味觉】 wèijué sense of taste

【味蕾】 wèilěi 〈*Anat.*〉 taste bud

【味素】 wèisù monosodium glutamate;

gourmet powder

【味同嚼蜡】 wèitóngjiáolà it is like chewing wax; insipid

【味鲜适口】 wèixiān-shìkǒu agreeable to taste

位 (wèi) **1.**(地点) place; location; site **2.**(地位;职位) position **3.**(王位) throne: 即～ come to the throne **4.**〈*Math.*〉 place; figure; digit: 个～ unit's place **5.**〈*classifier*〉 几～朋友 some friends

【位次】 wèicì precedence; seating arrangement

【位次卡】 wèicìkǎ place card

【位能】 wèinéng place value

【位于】 wèiyú be located; be situated; lie

【位置】 wèi·zhi **1.**(所在地方) seat; place; site; location: 地理～ geographic location / 这个街角是设加油站的好～。This corner would make a good location for a gas station. **2.**(地位) place; position: 占据重要～ occupy an important place **3.**(职位) post; position; office

【位置灯】 wèi·zhidēng 〈*Auto*〉 sidelights; parking lights

【位子】 wèi·zi seat; place

畏 (wèi) **1.**(畏惧) fear **2.**(佩服) respect

【畏避】 wèibì avoid sth. out of fear; recoil from; flinch from

【畏惧】 wèijù fear; dread: 无所～ have nothing to fear; be intrepid

【畏难】 wèinán be afraid of difficulty

【畏难情绪】 wèinán qíngxù fear of difficulty

【畏怯】 wèiqiè cowardly; timid; chicken-hearted

【畏首畏尾】 wèishǒu-wèiwěi be full of misgivings; be over-cautious

【畏缩】 wèisuō recoil; shrink; flinch: ～不前 shrink with fear; hesitate to press forward; hang back

【畏途】 wèitú a dangerous road; a perilous undertaking: 视为～ regard it as a dangerous road to take; be afraid to undertake it

【畏罪】 wèizuì dread punishment for one's crime: ～潜逃 abscond to avoid punishment / 他～自杀了。He committed suicide to avoid punishment.

喂[餵、餧] (wèi) **1.**(招呼) hello; hey: ～,是你吗?(打电话用语) Are you there? **2.**(给东西吃) feed

【喂肥】 wèiféi engross

【喂奶】 wèinǎi breast-feed; suckle; nurse

【喂饲槽】 wèisìcáo feeding rack

【喂养】 wèiyǎng feed; raise; keep: ～小鸡 keep chickens

胃 (wèi) 〈*Anat.*〉 stomach

【胃癌】 wèi'ái 〈*Med.*〉 cancer of the stomach; gastric carcinoma

【胃病】 wèibìng stomach trouble; gastric disease

【胃肠性感冒】 wèichángxìng gǎnmào gastric flu

【胃出血】 wèichūxuè 〈*Med.*〉 gastrorrhagia; gastric hemorrhage

【胃穿孔】 wèichuānkǒng 〈*Med.*〉 gastric perforation

【胃大弯】 wèidàwān 〈*Anat.*〉 greater curvature

【胃蛋白酶】 wèidànbáiméi 〈*Biochem.*〉 pepsin

【胃镜】 wèijìng 〈*Med.*〉 gastroscope

【胃镜检查】 wèijìng jiǎnchá 〈*Med.*〉 gastrocopy

【胃口】 wèikǒu **1.**(食欲) appetite: ～好 have a good appetite / ～不佳 off one's oats **2.**(兴趣) liking; preference: 对某人的～ to one's liking

【胃溃疡】 wèikuìyáng 〈*Med.*〉 gastric ulcer

【胃切除术】 wèiqiēchúshù 〈*Med.*〉 gastrectomy

【胃酸】 wèisuān 〈*Physiol.*〉 hydrochloric acid in gastric juice

【胃痛】 wèitòng 〈*Med.*〉 stomachache; gastralgia

【胃下垂】 wèixiàchuí 〈*Med.*〉 ptosis of the stomach; gastroptosis

【胃腺】 wèixiàn 〈*Anat.*〉 gastric gland

【胃小弯】 wèixiǎowān 〈*Anat.*〉 lesser curvature

【胃炎】 wèiyán 〈*Med.*〉 gastritis

【胃液】 wèiyè 〈*Physiol.*〉 gastric juice

谓 (wèi) **1.**(说) say **2.**(称) call; name **3.**(意思;意义) meaning; sense

【谓语】 wèiyǔ predicate

尉 (wèi) junior officer(请参见"上尉、中尉、少尉"各条)

【尉官】 wèiguān junior officer

蔚（wèi） 1.（茂盛；盛大）luxuriant；grand 2.（有文采）colorful

【蔚蓝】 wèilán azure；sky blue

【蔚然成风】 wèirán-chéngfēng become common practice；become the order of the day

【蔚为大观】 wèiwéi-dàguān present a splendid sight；afford a magnificent view

慰（wèi） 1.（安慰）console；comfort：～勉 comfort and encourage 2.（宽慰）be relieved；feel

【慰安】 wèi'ān soothe；comfort

【慰安妇】 wèi'ānfù comfort woman（military prostitute of Japanese army）

【慰问】 wèiwèn express sympathy and solicitude for：表示～ convey one's sympathy

【慰问团】 wèiwèntuán a group sent to convey greetings and appreciation

【慰问信】 wèiwènxìn a letter expressing one's appreciation or sympathy

【慰问演出】 wèiwèn yǎnchū a special performance as an expression of gratitude or appreciation

【慰唁】 wèiyàn condole with sb.

遗（wèi） （赠与）offer as a gift；make a gift of sth.

（另见"遗"yí）

wen

温（wēn） 1.（不冷不热）warm；lukewarm；tepid：～水 lukewarm water 2.（温度）temperature：水～ water temperature 3.（加温）warm up；heat up：～水 warm up the water 4.（温习）review；revise one's lessons

【温饱】 wēnbǎo dress warmly and eat one's fill；the basic need：基本解决～问题 assure the basic need

【温饱型】 wēnbǎoxíng simply having adequate food and clothing

【温差】 wēnchā difference in temperature；range of temperature

【温彻斯特硬盘】 Wēnchèsītè yìngpán〈*Computer*〉Winchester disk；hard disk

【温床】 wēnchuáng 1.〈*Agric.*〉hotbed；seed-bed 2.（坏事发生、发展的环境）breeding ground；hotbed

【温存】 wēncún 1.（抚慰）be attentive to；give tender attentions to 2.（体贴）affectionate；kind；gentle；tender：～体贴 tender and considerate

【温带】 wēndài temperate zone：～气候 temperate climate / ～植物 flora of the temperate zone

【温度】 wēndù temperature：最低～ minimum temperature/ 最高～ maximum temperature

【温度表】 wēndùbiǎo thermometer：华氏～ Fahrenheit thermometer / 摄氏～ centigrade thermometer；Celsius thermometer

【温度计】 wēndùjì 〈*Meteorol.*〉thermometer；thermograph

【温度调节】 wēndù tiáojié attemperation

【温度调节器】 wēndù tiáojiéqì thermoregulator；attemperator

【温故知新】 wēngù-zhīxīn gain new insights through restudying old material；reviewing the past helps one to understand the present；learn new things by reviewing old things

【温和】 wēnhé 1.（不冷不热）temperate；moderate；mild：气候～ be of mild climate 2.（平和）gentle；mild：态度～ be of gentle manner

【温和派】 wēnhépài moderates

【温厚】 wēnhòu gentle and kind；good-natured

【温乎】 wēn·hu 见"温和"（wēn·huo）

【温和】 wēn·huo lukewarm；warm：菜还～。The dish is still lukewarm.

【温暖】 wēnnuǎn 1.（暖和）warm 2.（使感到温暖）warmth；kindness

【温情】 wēnqíng 1.（指感情）tender feeling：～脉脉 full of tender feeling 2.（指态度）too softhearted

【温情主义】 wēnqíng zhǔyì excessive tenderheartedness；undue leniency

【温泉】 wēnquán hot spring

【温泉城】 wēnquánchéng spring town

【温泉浴】 wēnquányù a hot-spring bath

【温柔】 wēnróu gentle and soft

【温湿计】 wēnshījì hygrothermograph

【温室】 wēnshì hothouse；greenhouse；glasshouse；conservatory

【温室效应】 wēnshì xiàoyìng greenhouse effect

【温室植物】 wēnshì zhíwù warmhouse plant

【温水游泳池】 wēnshuǐ yóuyǒngchí heated swimming pool

【温顺】 wēnshùn docile; meek

【温文尔雅】 wēnwén-ěryǎ gentle and cultivated; refined and cultivated

【温习】 wēnxí review; revise

【温馨】 wēnxīn warm and fragrant; sweet

【温驯】 wēnxùn (of animals) docile; meek; tame

瘟 (wēn) acute communicable diseases

【瘟病】 wēnbìng seasonal febrile diseases; epidemic

【瘟神】 wēnshén god of plague

【瘟疫】 wēnyì pestilence; plague; pestilent (adj.)

文 (wén) **1.**（字）character; script; writing **2.**（文字）language：中～ Chinese language / 英～ English language **3.**（文章）literary composition; writing **4.**（文言）literary language：半～半白 half literary and half vernacular **5.**（非军事的）civilian; civil **6.**（自然界某些现象）certain natural phenomena：天～ astronomy **7.**（掩饰）cover up; paint over：～过饰非 conceal faults and gloss over wrongs **8.**〈*classifier*〉一～不名 penniless

【文本】 wénběn text; version

【文本文件】 wénběn wénjiàn 〈*Computer*〉 document file：打开～ open a document file

【文笔】 wénbǐ style of writing：～优美 write in a excellent style

【文不对题】 wénbùduìtí irrelevant to the subject; beside the point; wide of the mark

【文才】 wéncái literary talent; aptitude for writing

【文采】 wéncǎi **1.**（指色彩）rich and bright colors **2.**（指才华）literary grace; literary talent

【文词】 wéncí 同"文辞"

【文辞】 wéncí diction; language

【文牍】 wéndú official documents and correspondence

【文牍主义】 wéndú zhǔyì red tape; bureaucracy

【文法】 wénfǎ grammar; grammatical (adj.)：His grammar is bad. 他的～不通。

【文房四宝】 wénfáng sìbǎo （笔墨纸砚）the four treasures of the study (writing brush, ink stick, paper and ink slab)

【文风】 wénfēng style of writing

【文稿】 wéngǎo manuscript; draft

【文告】 wéngào proclamation; statement; message

【文工团】 wéngōngtuán song and dance ensemble; art troupe; cultural troupe

【文官】 wénguān **1.**（文职官员）civil official **2.**（总称）civil service

【文过饰非】 wénguò-shìfēi conceal faults and gloss over wrongs; gloss over one's faults; cover up one's errors; cover up and whitewash mistakes

【文豪】 wénháo literary giant; great writer; eminent writer

【文化】 wénhuà **1.**（精神财富）civilization; culture; cultural (adj.)：两国有着不同的～。These two countries have different cultures. **2.**（知识）education; educational (adj.); culture; cultural (adj.); schooling; literacy：学～ acquire an elementary education; acquire literacy; learn to read and write

【文化参赞】 wénhuà cānzàn cultural counsellor; cultural attaché

【文化程度】 wénhuà chéngdù educational level; cultural level

【文化冲击】 wénhuà chōngjī cultural shock

【文化宫】 wénhuàgōng palace of culture; cultural palace

【文化馆】 wénhuàguǎn cultural center

【文化机关】 wénhuà jīguān cultural institution

【文化交流】 wénhuà jiāoliú cultural exchange

【文化教育事业】 wénhuà jiàoyù shìyè cultural and educational work

【文化界】 wénhuàjiè cultural circles; cultured people

【文化课】 wénhuàkè literacy class; general knowledge course

【文化落后】 wénhuà luòhòu cultural lag

【文化名流】 wénhuà míngliú cultural figures

【文化侵略】 wénhuà qīnlüè cultural aggression; cultural penetration
【文化区】 wénhuàqū culture area
【文化趋同】 wénhuà qūtóng cultural convergence
【文化人】 wénhuàrén cultural worker; intellectual
【文化渗透】 wénhuà shèntòu cultural infiltration
【文化事业】 wénhuà shìyè cultural undertakings; cultural establishments
【文化水平】 wénhuà shuǐpíng cultural level; educational level
【文化素养】 wénhuà sùyǎng artistic appreciation
【文化污染】 wénhuà wūrǎn cultural pollution
【文化遗产】 wénhuà yíchǎn cultural heritage; cultural legacy
【文化用品】 wénhuà yòngpǐn stationery
【文化站】 wénhuàzhàn cultural center
【文化滞差】 wénhuà zhìchā cultural lag
【文化中心】 wénhuà zhōngxīn cultural center; culture center
【文火】 wénhuǒ slow fire; gentle heat
【文集】 wénjí collected works
【文件】 wénjiàn 1.(公文、信件) documents; papers: 机密～ classified documents / 获得～ obtain a document 2.(学术文章) professional article; academic article 3.〈*Computer*〉 file; document file
【文件备份】 wénjiàn bèifèn file backup
【文件编号】 wénjiàn biānhào the reference or serial number of a document
【文件编辑】 wénjiàn biānjí file edit
【文件查阅】 wénjiàn cháyuè file reference
【文件处理】 wénjiàn chùlǐ file processing
【文件处理机】 wénjiàn chùlǐjī file processor
【文件存储】 wénjiàn cúnchǔ filestore
【文件袋】 wénjiàndài documents pouch; dispatch case
【文件段】 wénjiànduàn file section
【文件格式】 wénjiàn géshì file layout
【文件柜】 wénjiànguì filing cabinet
【文件夹】 wénjiànjiā file
【文件名称】 wénjiàn míngchēng file name
【文件清单】 wénjiàn qīngdān list of documents
【文件识别】 wénjiàn shíbié file identification
【文件转换】 wénjiàn zhuǎnhuàn file conversion
【文教】 wénjiào culture and education
【文教界】 wénjiàojiè cultural and educational circles
【文教事业】 wénjiào shìyè cultural and educational work; culture and education
【文静】 wénjìng gentle and quiet
【文具】 wénjù writing materials; stationery
【文具店】 wénjùdiàn stationery's; stationery shop
【文科】 wénkē liberal arts
【文科学校】 wénkē xuéxiào liberal arts school
【文科院校】 wénkē yuànxiào colleges of arts
【文库】 wénkù library; a series of books (issued in a single format by a publisher)
【文理】 wénlǐ unity and coherence in writing: ～不通 be illogical and ungrammatical
【文盲】 wénmáng 1.(不识字) illiteracy: 扫除～ wipe out illiteracy 2.(不识字的人) an illiterate person
【文明】 wénmíng 1.(文化) civilization; culture: ～古国 a country with an ancient civilization / 精神～ spiritual civilization / 物质～ material civilization 2.(有较高文化的) civilized: ～社会 civilized society
【文墨】 wénmò writing: 粗通～ barely know the rudiments of writing
【文凭】 wénpíng diploma; certificate
【文人】 wénrén man of letters; scholar; literati: ～相轻。Scholars tend to scorn each other.
【文如其人】 wénrúqírén the writing mirrors the writer
【文史】 wénshǐ literature and history
【文史馆】 wénshǐguǎn Research Institute of Culture and History
【文史资料】 wénshǐ zīliào historical accounts of past events
【文书】 wénshū 1.(公文) document; official dispatch 2.(文牍人员) copy clerk; clerical staff
【文思】 wénsī the thread of ideas in writing: ～敏捷 have a ready pen; ability to think and write fast

【文坛】 wéntán the literary world; the literary arena; the literary circles; the world of letters

【文体】 wéntǐ 1.（文章体裁）type of writing; literary form; style 2.（文娱和体育）recreation and sports

【文体活动】 wéntǐ huódòng recreational and sports activities

【文武】 wénwǔ civil and military: ～双全 be well versed in both polite letters and martial arts

【文物】 wénwù cultural relic; historical relic

【文献】 wénxiàn document; literature

【文献记录片】 wénxiàn jìlùpiān documentary; documentary film

【文献检索】 wénxiàn jiǎnsuǒ literature search

【文选】 wénxuǎn selected works; literary selections; anthology

【文学】 wénxué literature; literary (adj.)

【文学家】 wénxuéjiā writer; man of letters; literati

【文学流派】 wénxué liúpài schools of literature

【文学评论】 wénxué pínglùn literary criticism

【文学语言】 wénxué yǔyán 1.〈*Linguis*.〉 standard speech 2.（文艺语言）literary language

【文雅】 wényǎ elegant; refined; cultured; polished

【文言】 wényán classical Chinese

【文言文】 wényánwén writings in classical Chinese; classical style of writing

【文艺】 wényì literature and art

【文艺创作】 wényì chuàngzuò literary and artistic creation

【文艺队伍】 wényì duìwǔ ranks of writers and artists

【文艺复兴】 wényì fùxīng the Renaissance

【文艺工作】 wényì gōngzuò work in the literary and artistic fields

【文艺工作者】 wényì gōngzuòzhě literary and art workers; writers and artists

【文艺会演】 wényì huìyǎn theatrical festival

【文艺节目】 wényì jiémù program of entertainment; theatrical items; theatrical performance

【文艺界】 wényìjiè literary and art circles; the world of literature and art

【文艺理论】 wényì lǐlùn theory of literature and art

【文艺批评】 wényì pīpíng literary or art criticism

【文艺批评家】 wényì pīpíngjiā literary or art critic

【文艺团体】 wényì tuántǐ literature and art organization; theatre company; theatre troupe

【文艺作品】 wényì zuòpǐn literary and artistic works

【文娱】 wényú cultural recreation; entertainment

【文娱活动】 wényú huódòng recreational activities

【文责】 wénzé the responsibility an author should assume for his own writings; author's responsibility: ～自负。The author takes sole responsibility for his views.

【文摘】 wénzhāi abstract; digest

【文章】 wénzhāng 1.（短篇论著）article; essay: 一篇关于船舶的～ an article about ships 2.（著作）literary works; writings 3.（暗含的意思）hidden meaning; implied meaning: 这里头大有～。There is some hidden meaning in it.

【文职】 wénzhí civilian post; civil service

【文职人员】 wénzhí rényuán nonmilitary personnel

【文质彬彬】 wénzhì-bīnbīn gentle; be cultured and gentle

【文竹】 wénzhú 〈*Bot*.〉 setose asparagus

【文字】 wénzì 1.（书写符号）characters; script; writing 2.（书面语）written language: 游戏～ play with words; juggle with terms 3.（文章形式）writing (as regards form or style): ～清通 lucid writing

【文字方程】 wénzì fāngchéng literal equation

【文字改革】 wénzì gǎigé reform of a writing system

【文字库】 wénzìkù literal pool

【文字说明】 wénzì shuōmíng caption

【文字学】 wénzìxué philology

【文字游戏】 wénzì yóuxì charade

纹 (wén) lines; veins; grain

【纹理】 wénlǐ veins; grain
【纹路】 wén·lu lines; grain; wrinkle
【纹缕】 wén·lǚ 同"纹路"
【纹丝不动】 wénsī-búdòng absolutely still; not a wrinkle was touched
【纹玉】 wényù veined jade
【纹纸】 wénzhǐ laid paper

蚊 (wén) mosquito: 按～(疟～) malaria mosquito / 库～ culex mosquito
【蚊虫】 wénchóng mosquito
【蚊香】 wénxiāng mosquito-repellent incense
【蚊帐】 wénzhàng mosquito net
【蚊帐布】 wénzhàngbù mosquito netting
【蚊子】 wén·zi mosquito

闻 (wén) 1.(听见) hear: ～讯 hear the news / 所见所～ what one sees and hears 2.(消息) news; story: 要～ important news 3.(名声) repute; reputation: 秽～ ill repute 4.(嗅) smell
【闻风而动】 wénfēng'érdòng immediately respond to a call; go into action without delay
【闻风丧胆】 wénfēng-sàngdǎn become terror-stricken at the news
【闻过则喜】 wénguò-zéxǐ feel happy when told of one's errors; be glad to have one's errors pointed out; thankful for being told of one's errors
【闻名】 wénmíng 1.(有名) well-known; famous; renowned: 以质优～ well-known for its fine quality 2.(听到名声) be familiar with sb's name; know sb. by repute: 久闻大名。I'm familiar with your name.
【闻所未闻】 wénsuǒwèiwén unheard-of; never heard of

刎 (wěn) cut one's throat

吻［脗］(wěn) 1.(嘴唇) lips 2.(接吻) kiss: 她～了女儿一下。She gave her daughter a kiss. 3.(动物的嘴) an animal's mouth
【吻合】 wěnhé be identical; coincide; tally
【吻合项目】 wěnhé xiàngmù 〈*Education*〉 dovetailing item

紊 (wěn) disorderly; confused
【紊乱】 wěnluàn disorder; chaos; confusion: 秩序～ in a state of disorder

稳［穩］(wěn) 1.(稳当;稳定) steady; firm 2.(稳妥) sure; certain: ～赢 sure to win
【稳步】 wěnbù with steady steps; steadily
【稳操胜券】 wěncāo-shèngquàn have full assurance of success; be certain to win
【稳产】 wěnchǎn stable yields
【稳当】 wěn·dang 1.(稳重妥当) reliable; secure; safe 2.(稳固牢靠) firm; stable
【稳定】 wěndìng 1.(稳固,没有变动) steady; stable: 破坏…的～ destabilize; destabilise / 物价～。Prices remain stable. / 政治形势～。The political situation is stable. 2.(使稳定) stabilize; steady: ～物价 stabilize the price
【稳定性】 wěndìngxìng stability
【稳定性选择】 wěndìngxìng xuǎnzé stabilizing process
【稳定装置】 wěndìng zhuāngzhì catcher
【稳固】 wěngù 1.(安稳) firm; stable: 政权～。The government is firm. 2.(使稳固) make firm; stabilize: ～其地位 stabilize his position
【稳健】 wěnjiàn 1.(稳而有力) firm; steady: ～的步子 firm steps 2.(稳重) steady; staid
【稳健派】 wěnjiànpài moderates
【稳妥】 wěntuǒ safe; reliable
【稳重】 wěnzhòng steady; staid; sedate

问 (wèn) 1.(询问) ask; enquire; inquire: ～路 ask the way / 向他～个问题 ask him question / 2.(问到;问候) ask after; enquire after: 询～ make enquiries about 3.(审问) interrogate; examine: 审～ interrogate 4.(追究) hold responsible 5.(感兴趣,干预) be interested in; interfere: 不～政治 be uninterested in politics 6.(向) from: 我～他借了本小说。I borrowed a novel from him.
【问安】 wèn'ān pay one's respects; wish sb. good health
【问案】 wèn'àn try a case; hear a case
【问答】 wèndá questions and answers
【问答练习】 wèndá liànxí question-and-answer drills
【问答式讲述】 wèndáshì jiǎngshù dialectical statement
【问答题】 wèndátí question-and-answer exercise

【问好】 wènhǎo send one's regards to; say hello to; extend greetings to

【问号】 wènhào 1.(标点) question mark; interrogation mark (符号为 ?) 2.(疑问) question mark; unknown factor; unsolved problem: 她是否适应这个工作还是个～。There's a question mark about her suitability for the job.

【问候】 wènhòu send one's respects to; extend greetings to

【问津】 wènjīn make inquiries (as about prices): 无人～ nobody cares to ask about sth.

【问卷】 wènjuàn condensed questionnaire

【问卷调查表】 wènjuàn diàochábiǎo questionnaire

【问世】 wènshì 1.(出版) be published; come out 2.(面市) be presented to the public

【问题】 wèntí 1.(需解答的题目) question; problem: 有争议的～ the question at issue / 提～ raise questions 2.(需解决的问题) problem; matter; question: 正在审理的～ case in point / 解决～ solve a problem / 共同关心的～ questions of common interest; question of common concern / ～是… The thing is, ... 3.(事故或意外) trouble; mishap; something wrong: 出～了。There occurred a trouble. 4.(重要之点) the point; the thing

【问题难度】 wèntí nándù problem-dimension

【问心无愧】 wènxīn-wúkuì have a clear conscience; feel no qualms upon self-examination

【问心有愧】 wènxīn-yǒukuì feel a twinge of conscience; have a guilty conscience

【问讯】 wènxùn enquire; ask

【问讯处】 wènxùnchù enquiry office; information desk

【问诊】 wènzhěn interrogation; enquiry

【问罪】 wènzuì denounce; condemn: 兴师～ send a punitive force against; denounce sb. publicly for his crimes or serious errors

weng

翁 (wēng) 1.(老头儿) old man 2.(父亲) father 3.(丈夫或妻子的父亲) father-in-law

【翁姑】 wēnggū a woman's parents-in-law

【翁牛特旗】 Wēngniútèqí 〈place〉 Ongniud Qi

【翁婿】 wēng-xù father-in-law and son-in-law

嗡 (wēng) 〈*onomat.*〉 drone; buzz; hum: 蚊子～～叫。Mosquitoes buzz.

瓮[甕、罋] (wèng) urn; earthen jar

【瓮声瓮气】 wèngshēng-wèngqì in a low, muffled voice

【瓮中之鳖】 wèngzhōngzhībiē a turtle in a jar; trapped; bottled up

【瓮中捉鳖】 wèngzhōng-zhuōbiē catch a turtle in a jar; go after an easy prey

蕹 (wèng)

【蕹菜】 wèngcài 〈*Bot.*〉 swamp morning glory

WO

莴[萵] (wō)

【莴苣】 wōjù 〈*Bot.*〉 lettuce

【莴笋】 wōsǔn asparagus lettuce

涡[渦] (wō) whirlpool; eddy

【涡动】 wōdòng eddy turbulence

【涡流】 wōliú 1.(旋涡) whirlpool; whirling fluid; eddy 2.〈*Physics*〉 eddy current; vortex flow

【涡轮】 wōlún turbine

【涡轮风扇发动机】 wōlún fēngshàn fādòngjī turbofan engine

【涡轮螺桨客机】 wōlún luójiǎng kèjī turboprop plane

窝[窩] (wō) 1.(鸟兽昆虫的窝) nest: 鸟～ bird's nest 2.(坏人聚居地) lair; den: 贼～ thieves' den 3.(人体的窝儿) a hollow part of the human body; pit: 心～ the pit of the stomach / 眼～ eye-socket 4.(窝藏) harbor; shelter: ～赃 harbor stolen goods 5.(郁积) hold in; check: ～着火儿 be simmering with anger 6.(使弯或曲折) bend 7.(量词,用于动物、家禽) litter; brood: 一～小鸡 a brood of chicken

【窝藏】 wōcáng harbor; shelter: ～罪犯 give

shelter to a criminal; harbor a criminal

【窝工】 wōgōng enforced idleness due to poor organization of work; holdup in the work through poor organization

【窝囊】 wō·nang 1.(因委屈而烦闷) feel vexed; be annoyed 2.(怯懦;无能) stupid, cowardly and timid; good-for-nothing; hopelessly stupid

【窝囊废】 wō·nangfèi good-for-nothing; worthless wretch

【窝棚】 wō·peng shed; shack; hut

【窝赃】 wōzāng house the spoils; harbor the stolen goods

【窝主】 wōzhǔ a person who harbors criminals, loot or contraband goods

蜗[蝸] (wō) snail

【蜗杆】 wōgǎn 〈*Mech.*〉 worm

【蜗居】 wōjū humble abode

【蜗轮】 wōlún 〈*Mech.*〉 worm wheel

【蜗牛】 wōniú 〈*Zool.*〉 snail

我 (wǒ) 1.(称自己) I; my: ～家 my family / 请告诉～。Tell me, please. 2.(我们) we; our: ～方 our side; we / ～国 our country 3.(自己) self: 自～牺牲 self sacrifice

【我们】 wǒ·men we; our: 今天下午～能去游泳吗? Can we go to swim this afternoon? / 他对～大家都很友好。He is friendly to us all. / ～的书在桌子上。Our books are on the table.

【我们自己】 wǒ·men zìjǐ ourselves: ～会做。We will do it ourselves.

【我向思维】 wǒxiàng sīwéi 〈*Psycho.*〉 autistic thinking

【我行我素】 wǒxíng-wǒsù persist in one's old ways; stick to one's old way of doing things

【我自己】 wǒzìjǐ myself

肟 (wò) 〈*Chem.*〉 oxime

沃 (wò) 1.(肥) fertile; rich: ～土 fertile soil; rich soil 2.(灌溉) irrigate

【沃野】 wòyě fertile land

【沃野千里】 wòyě-qiānlǐ a vast expanse of fertile land

卧[臥] (wò) 1.(躺) lie: 侧～ lie on one's side 2.(动物趴) crouch; sit 3.(睡觉用的) for sleeping in

【卧病】 wòbìng be confined to bed; be laid up

【卧车】 wòchē 1.(卧铺车厢) sleeping car; sleeping carriage; sleeper 2.(小轿车) automobile; car; limousine; sedan

【卧床】 wòchuáng lie in bed; be laid up: 绝对～ strict bed rest / 她因腿部骨折～休养。She's laid up with a broken leg.

【卧倒】 wòdǎo 1.(趴下) drop to the ground; take a prone position 2.(口令) Lie down!

【卧佛】 wòfó a statue of Buddha in lying position

【卧具】 wòjù 〈*Transport*〉 bedding

【卧铺】 wòpù sleeping berth; sleeper

【卧铺票】 wòpùpiào berth: 订～ book a berth

【卧室】 wòshì bedroom

【卧室灯】 wòshìdēng bedroom lamp

【卧榻】 wòtà bed

【卧姿】 wòzī 〈*Sports*〉 prone position

握 (wò) hold; grasp

【握别】 wòbié shake hands at parting; part

【握力】 wòlì the power of gripping; grip

【握力器】 wòlìqì spring-grip; dumb-bell

【握拍法】 wòpāifǎ 〈*Badminton*〉 grip: 反手～ backhand grip / 正手～ forehand grip

【握拳】 wòquán make a fist; clench one's fist

【握手】 wòshǒu shake hands; clasp hands: ～言欢 hold hands and chat cheerfully

龌 (wò)

【龌龊】 wòchuò dirty; filthy: 卑鄙～ sordid; foul

斡 (wò)

【斡旋】 wòxuán 1.(调解) mediate 2.〈*Foreign Affairs*〉 good offices

wu

乌[烏] (wū) 1.(乌鸦) crow 2.(黑色) black; dark

【乌骨鸡】 wūgǔjī black-bone silky fowl

【乌龟】 wūguī 1.〈*Zool.*〉 tortoise 2.(妻子

有外遇的人）cuckold
【乌合之众】 wūhézhīzhòng a disorderly band; a motley crowd; rabble; mob
【乌黑】 wūhēi pitch-black; jet-black
【乌金】 wūjīn 1.（煤）coal 2.〈*Chin. Med.*〉ink
【乌拉特】 Wūlātè 〈place〉 Urad
【乌兰布和沙漠】 Wūlánbùhé shāmò 〈place〉 Ulan Buh Shamo
【乌兰察布盟】 Wūlánchábùméng 〈place〉 Ulanqab Meng
【乌兰浩特】 Wūlánhàotè 〈place〉 Ulanhot
【乌鳢】 wūlǐ 〈*Zool.*〉 northern snakehead
【乌亮】 wūliàng glossy black; jet-black: ～的头发 dark, glossy hair; raven locks
【乌龙茶】 wūlóngchá oolong (tea)
【乌鲁木齐】 Wūlǔmùqí 〈place〉 Urumqi
【乌七八糟】 wūqī-bāzāo 1.（十分杂乱）in a horrible mess; in great disorder 2.（淫秽）obscene; dirty; filthy
【乌青眼】 wūqīngyǎn black eye
【乌纱帽】 wūshāmào 1.（比喻官位）official post: 丢～ be dismissed from office 2.（古代官帽）black gauze cap
【乌审召】 Wūshěnzhāo 〈place〉 Uxin Ju
【乌托邦】 wūtuōbāng Utopia
【乌鸦】 wūyā 〈*Zool.*〉 crow
【乌烟瘴气】 wūyān-zhàngqì foul atmosphere; pestilential atmosphere: 搞得～ foul up
【乌有】 wūyǒu nothing; naught: 化为～ come to nothing
【乌云】 wūyún black clouds; dark clouds
【乌枣】 wūzǎo smoked jujube; black jujube
【乌贼】 wūzéi 〈*Zool.*〉 cuttlefish; inkfish
【乌孜别克族】 Wūzībiékèzú Uzbek（中国少数民族，主要分布在新疆）
【乌孜别里山口】 Wūzībiélǐ shānkǒu 〈place〉 Uzbel Shankou

呜［嗚］（wū） 〈*onomat.*〉 toot; hoot; zoom
【呜呼】 wūhū 1.（表示叹息）alas; alack 2.（死亡）die: 一命～ give up the ghost
【呜呼哀哉】 wūhū-āizāi 1.（表示叹息）alas 2.（死了）dead and gone 3.（完蛋）all is lost
【呜咽】 wūyè sob; whimper

钨［鎢］（wū） 〈*Chem.*〉 wolfram; tungsten（元素符号 W）
【钨钢】 wūgāng wolfram steel; tungsten steel
【钨砂】 wūshā tungsten ore
【钨丝】 wūsī tungsten filament
【钨丝灯】 wūsīdēng tungsten lamp
【钨铁】 wūtiě ferrotungsten
【钨铁矿】 wūtiěkuàng ferberite

污［汙、汚］（wū） 1.（污垢）dirt; filth 2.（脏）dirty; filthy; foul: ～泥 mud; mire 3.（不廉洁）corrupt 4.（弄脏）defile; smear
【污点】 wūdiǎn 1.（污垢）stain; spot; blemish 2.（不光彩之处）stain; blemish; stigma: 历史～ a stigma in one's past
【污垢】 wūgòu dirt; filth
【污秽】 wūhuì filthy; foul: ～的语言 filthy language
【污迹】 wūjì stain; smear; smudge
【污蔑】 wūmiè 1.（诬蔑）slander; calumniate 2.（玷污）defile; sully; tarnish
【污泥】 wūní mud; mire; sludge
【污染】 wūrǎn pollute; pollution (n.); contaminate; contamination (n.): 空气～ air pollution / 防止～ prevent pollution / 人类应该停止对地球大气的～。Man must stop polluting the earth's atmosphere.
【污染等级】 wūrǎn děngjí class of pollution
【污染物质】 wūrǎn wùzhì pollutant
【污辱】 wūrǔ 1.（侮辱）humiliate; insult 2.（玷污）defile; sully; tarnish
【污水】 wūshuǐ sewage; foul water; polluted water; waste water; slops
【污水处理】 wūshuǐ chǔlǐ sewage disposal; sewage treatment
【污水处理厂】 wūshuǐ chǔlǐchǎng sewage treatment plant
【污水管】 wūshuǐguǎn sewage pipe; sewer (pipe); waste pipe
【污水管道】 wūshuǐ guǎndào sewage conduit; sewer line
【污水灌溉】 wūshuǐ guàngài sewage irrigation
【污水净化】 wūshuǐ jìnghuà sewage purification
【污浊】 wūzhuó dirty; muddy; foul; filthy

巫（wū） shaman; witch; wizard
【巫婆】 wūpó witch; sorceress

【巫师】 wūshī wizard; sorcerer
【巫术】 wūshù witchcraft; sorcery
【巫医】 wūyī witch doctor

诬(wū) accuse falsely

【诬告】 wūgào lodge a false accusation against; bring a false charge against
【诬告案件】 wūgào ànjiàn frame-up; trumped-up case
【诬告人】 wūgàorén maliciously false accuser
【诬告陷害罪】 wūgào xiànhàizuì crime of false charge
【诬告行为】 wūgào xíngwéi action of malicious prosecution
【诬告者】 wūgàozhě calumniator
【诬害】 wūhài injure by spreading false reports about; calumniate; malign
【诬赖】 wūlài falsely incriminate
【诬蔑】 wūmiè slander; vilify; calumniate; smear: ～不实之词 slander and libel
【诬陷】 wūxiàn frame a case against; frame sb.

屋(wū) 1.(房子) house 2.(屋子) room

【屋顶】 wūdǐng roof; housetop
【屋顶花园】 wūdǐng huāyuán roof garden
【屋顶平台】 wūdǐng píngtái terrace: 晚上我们坐在～上。We sat on the terrace in the evening.
【屋顶天线】 wūdǐng tiānxiàn roof antennas
【屋脊】 wūjǐ ridge (of a roof)
【屋子】 wū·zi room: 三间～ three rooms

无[無](wú) 1.(没有) nothing; nil; not have; without 2.(不) not: ～碍大局 not affect the situation as a whole 3.(不论) regardless of; no matter whether, what, etc.

【无暗影】 wú'ànyǐng unshadowed
【无伴奏】 wúbànzòu unaccompanied; a cappella
【无包装商品】 wúbāozhuāng shāngpǐn unpacked goods
【无孢子生殖】 wúbāozǐ shēngzhí 〈*Biol.*〉 apospory
【无比】 wúbǐ incomparable; unparalleled; matchless: ～愤怒 furiously indignant / ～高超的技能 incomparable skills
【无边无际】 wúbiān-wújì boundless; limitless; vast
【无病呻吟】 wúbìng-shēnyín moan and groan without being ill; make a fuss about an imaginary illness
【无补】 wúbǔ of no help; of no avail: 于事～ be of no help with the matter
【无补偿】 wúbǔcháng uncompensated
【无不】 wúbù all without exception; invariably: ～为之感动。None were unmoved.
【无产阶级】 wúchǎn jiējí the proletariat; proletarian (adj.)
【无产阶级专政】 wúchǎn jiējí zhuānzhèng proletarian dictatorship
【无产者】 wúchǎnzhě proletarian
【无常】 wúcháng 1.(变化无常) variable; changeable: 反复～ capricious; uncertain 2. 〈*Buddhism*〉 impermanence
【无偿】 wúcháng free; gratis; gratuitous: ～使用 use without compensation; uncompensated use / ～援助 aid given gratis; aid given gratuitously
【无偿契约】 wúcháng qìyuē naked contract
【无偿取得】 wúcháng qǔdé acquisition without consideration
【无偿让与】 wúcháng ràngyǔ voluntary conveyance
【无尘】 wúchén dust free
【无耻】 wúchǐ shameless; brazen; impudent: ～谰言 shameless slander / ～之徒 a person who has lost all sense of shame; a shameless person / ～之尤 brazen in the extreme; the height of shamelessness
【无触点】 wúchùdiǎn contactless
【无醇饮料】 wúchún yǐnliào unfermented beverage
【无从】 wúcóng have no way (of doing sth.); not be in a position (to do sth.): ～下手 have no way of doing it; not know how to start
【无党派爱国人士】 wúdǎngpài àiguó rénshì patriots without party affiliation
【无党派人士】 wúdǎngpài rénshì nonparty personage; a public figure without party affiliation
【无敌】 wúdí unmatched; invincible
【无地自容】 wúdì-zìróng can find no place to

hide oneself for shame; feel too ashamed to show one's face; look for a hole to crawl into

【无的放矢】 wúdì-fàngshǐ shoot an arrow without a target; shoot at random

【无电】 wúdiàn electroless

【无动于衷】 wúdòngyúzhōng unmoved; unconcerned; aloof and indifferent

【无独有偶】 wúdú-yǒu'ǒu it is not unique, but has its counterpart; not come singly but in pairs

【无毒】 wúdú nonpoisonous; non-toxic

【无毒蛇】 wúdúshé nonpoisonous snake

【无毒性】 wúdúxìng 〈*Bot.*〉 avirulence

【无度】 wúdù immoderate; excessive: 挥霍～ squander wantonly

【无端】 wúduān for no reason: ～侮辱 a gratuitous insult / ～争吵 quarrelled for no reason

【无恶不作】 wú'è-bùzuò stop at nothing in doing evil; stop at no evil; commit all manner of crimes

【无法】 wúfǎ unable; incapable: ～理解 unable to understand / ～想像 unable to imagine

【无法履行】 wúfǎ-lǚxíng impossibility of performance

【无法无天】 wúfǎ-wútiān defy laws human and divine; become absolutely lawless; run wild

【无方】 wúfāng not in the proper way; in the wrong way; not knowing how: 经营～ mismanagement

【无妨】 wúfáng there's no harm; may as well; might as well: 这样做并～。There is no harm in doing that.

【无非】 wúfēi nothing but; no more than; simply; only

【无风】 wúfēng 〈*Meteorol.*〉 calm

【无风带】 wúfēngdài calm belt; calm zone

【无缝钢管】 wúfèng gāngguǎn seamless steel tube

【无干扰】 wúgānrǎo jam-free

【无辜】 wúgū **1.** (没有罪) innocent **2.** (没有罪的人) an innocent person

【无故】 wúgù without cause or reason: ～迟到 be late without reason / ～旷工 absent from work without reason

【无故障】 wúgùzhàng fault-free; trouble-free: ～运行 fault-free operation

【无故障时间】 wúgùzhàng shíjiān time without failure

【无关】 wúguān be unconcerned; have nothing to do with: ～大局 not affecting the general situation; insignificant / ～紧要 of no importance

【无光】 wúguāng **1.** (暗的) dark **2.** (没有上釉的) unglazed

【无光泽】 wúguāngzé reluster

【无轨道路】 wúguǐ dàolù railless; trackless

【无轨电车】 wúguǐ diànchē trolley bus

【无国籍】 wúguójí 〈*Foreign Affairs*〉 stateless

【无国籍者】 wúguójízhě a stateless person

【无海岸国家】 wúhǎi'àn guójiā non-coastal state

【无害】 wúhài harmless; do no harm to

【无害处理】 wúhài chùlǐ sanitize; sanitization (n.)

【无害通过】 wúhài tōngguò innocent passage

【无核国】 wúhéguó non-nuclear state; nuclear-free state

【无核区】 wúhéqū nuclear-free zone: 对～承担义务 undertake obligations in respect of the nuclear-free zone

【无花果】 wúhuāguǒ fig

【无灰】 wúhuī ashless; ash-free

【无火玩具】 wúhuǒ wánjù fireless cooker

【无疾而终】 wújí-érzhōng die without known cause

【无机】 wújī 〈*Chem.*〉 inorganic

【无机肥料】 wújī féiliào inorganic fertilizer; mineral fertilizer

【无机化合物】 wújī huàhéwù inorganic compound

【无机化学】 wújī huàxué inorganic chemistry

【无机物】 wújīwù inorganic substance; inorganic matter

【无机盐】 wújīyán inorganic salts

【无稽】 wújī unfounded; fantastic; absurd: ～之谈 fantastic talk; sheer nonsense

【无级变速】 wújí biànsù stepless speed change

【无几】 wújǐ very few; very little; hardly any: 相差～ very little difference; almost the same

【无脊椎】 wújǐzhuī invertebrate：～动物 invertebrate animal

【无计可施】 wújì-kěshī at one's wits' end; at the end of one's tether

【无记名股票】 wújìmíng gǔpiào bearer stock certificate

【无记名投票】 wújìmíng tóupiào secret ballot

【无记名债券】 wújìmíng zhàiquàn bearer bonds

【无记名支票】 wújìmíng zhīpiào check to bearer; bearer check

【无济于事】 wújìyúshì of no avail; to no effect

【无家可归】 wújiā-kěguī wander about without a home to go to; be homeless

【无价之宝】 wújiàzhībǎo priceless treasure; invaluable asset

【无坚不摧】 wújiān-bùcuī overrun all fortifications; carry all before one; be all-conquering

【无间】 wújiān 1.（没有间隙）not keeping anything from each other; very close to each other：亲密～的朋友 close friends; bosom friends 2.（不间断）continuously; without interruption

【无节制】 wújiézhì intemperance

【无界线】 wújièxiàn boundless

【无尽小数】 wújìn xiǎoshù infinite decimal

【无精打采】 wújīng-dǎcǎi listless; lackadaisical; in low spirits; out of sorts

【无拘无束】 wújū-wúshù unrestrained; unconstrained; free and easy

【无菌】 wújūn asepsis; aceptic; germfree

【无可比拟】 wúkě-bǐnǐ incomparable; unparalleled

【无可辩驳】 wúkě-biànbó irrefutable：～的事实 an irrefutable fact

【无可非议】 wúkě-fēiyì beyond reproach; above criticism; blameless

【无可奉告】 wúkě-fènggào no comment

【无可厚非】 wúkě-hòufēi give no cause for much criticism

【无可讳言】 wúkě-huìyán there is no hiding the fact

【无可救药】 wúkě-jiùyào incorrigible; incurable

【无可奈何】 wúkě-nàihé have no way out; have no alternative

【无可挽回】 wúkě-wǎnhuí irretrievable; irredeemable

【无可争议】 wúkě-zhēngyì beyond controversy

【无可置疑】 wúkě-zhìyí indubitable; unquestionable

【无孔不入】 wúkǒng-bùrù get in by every opening; be all-pervasive; seize every opportunity (to do evil)

【无愧】 wúkuì feel no qualms; have a clear conscience：当之～ be worthy of the name

【无赖】 wúlài 1.（不讲道理）rascally; scoundrelly; blackguardly：耍～ act shamelessly 2.（品行不端的人）rascal

【无礼】 wúlǐ rudeness; uncivil (adj.)

【无理】 wúlǐ unreasonable; unjustifiable：～取闹 willfully make trouble; be deliberately provocative

【无理数】 wúlǐshù 〈*Math.*〉 irrational number

【无力】 wúlì 1.（指气力）lack strength; feel weak：四肢～ feel weak in one's limbs 2.（指力量）unable; incapable; powerless：～应付 unable to deal with

【无力偿付】 wúlì chángfù insolvency

【无力支付】 wúlì zhīfù financial insolvency

【无利可图】 wúlì-kětú unprofitable; unremunerative; profitless (n.)

【无量】 wúliàng measureless; immeasurable; boundless：前途～ a boundless future

【无聊】 wúliáo 1.（闲得烦闷）bored 2.（没有意义）senseless; silly; stupid

【无论】 wúlùn no matter what, how, etc.; regardless of：～什么 no matter what

【无论如何】 wúlùnrúhé at any rate; in any case：天可能要下雨，但～我得出门。It may rain, but anyhow I shall go out. / ～我要去看他。I shall go and see him anyway. / ～已经太迟了。It's too late now, in any case.

【无名】 wúmíng 1.（没有名称的）nameless 2.（不为人知的）unknown 3.（说不出原因的）indefinable; indescribable

【无名氏】 wúmíngshì an anonymous person

【无名小卒】 wúmíng xiǎozú a nobody

【无名英雄】 wúmíng yīngxióng an unknown

hero
【无名指】 wúmíngzhǐ the third finger; ring finger
【无奈】 wúnài 1.(无可奈何) cannot help but; have no alternative; have no choice: 出于～她才去。She couldn't help but go. 2.(可惜) but; however
【无能】 wúnéng incompetent; incapable: 软弱～ weak and incompetent
【无能为力】 wúnéngwéilì powerless; helpless; incapable of action
【无票面值股票】 wúpiàomiànzhí gǔpiào no par share
【无期徒刑】 wúqī túxíng life imprisonment
【无铅】 wúqiān unleaded; lead-free
【无铅汽油】 wúqiān qìyóu unleaded gas; unleaded petrol
【无情】 wúqíng 1.(指没有感情) without passions; emotionless 2.(情面) merciless; ruthless; heartless
【无穷】 wúqióng infinite; endless; boundless: ～的烦恼 endless troubles
【无穷大】 wúqióngdà infinitely great; infinity
【无穷小】 wúqióngxiǎo infinitely small; infinitesimal
【无权】 wúquán have no right
【无人】 wúrén 1.(无人驾驶的) unmanned: ～驾驶飞机 unmanned plane; pilotless plane; robot plane 2.(无人居住的) depopulated 3.(自动售货的) self-service: ～售书处 self-service bookstall
【无人驾驶】 wúrén jiàshǐ unmanned; pilotless
【无人区】 wúrénqū a depopulated zone; no man's land
【无人问津】 wúrén-wènjīn no one shows any interest in
【无色】 wúsè colorless; tintless; uncolored
【无商业价值】 wúshāngyè jiàzhí n. c. v., no commercial value
【无伤大雅】 wúshāng-dàyǎ not affect the whole; not matter much
【无上】 wúshàng supreme; paramount; highest: ～光荣 the highest honor
【无神论】 wúshénlùn atheism ‖ 无神论者 atheist
【无声】 wúshēng noiseless; silent
【无声片】 wúshēngpiàn silent film
【无声手枪】 wúshēng shǒuqiāng pistol with a silencer
【无绳电话】 wúshéng diànhuà cordless telephone (CT)
【无师自通】 wúshī-zìtōng learned without teacher
【无时无刻】 wúshí-wúkè all the time; incessantly
【无事生非】 wúshì-shēngfēi make trouble out of nothing; be deliberately provocative; make the fur fly
【无视】 wúshì ignore; disregard; defy: ～别国主权 disregard the sovereignty of other countries
【无数】 wúshù 1.(难以计算) innumerable; countless 2.(不知道底细) not know for certain; be uncertain: 心中～ be uncertain about sth.
【无双】 wúshuāng unparalleled; unrivaled; matchless: 举世～ absolutely unrivaled
【无霜期】 wúshuāngqī frost-free period
【无水】 wúshuǐ 〈*Chem*.〉 anhydrous
【无私】 wúsī selfless; disinterested; unselfish: ～才能无畏。Only the selfless can be fearless.
【无所不能】 wúsuǒbùnéng omnipotent
【无所不为】 wúsuǒbùwéi stop at nothing; do all manner of evil
【无所不在】 wúsuǒbùzài omnipresent; ubiquitous
【无所不知】 wúsuǒbùzhī omniscient
【无所不至】 wúsuǒbùzhì 1.(指地方) penetrate everywhere 2.(指坏事) spare no pains (to do evil); be capable of anything; stop at nothing
【无所事事】 wúsuǒshìshì be occupied with nothing; have nothing to do; idle away one's time; do nothing all day
【无所适从】 wúsuǒshìcóng not know what course to take; be at a loss as to what to do; don't know whose suggestion to follow
【无所畏惧】 wúsuǒwèijù fearless; dauntless; undaunted
【无所谓】 wúsuǒwèi 1.(说不上) cannot be designated as; not deserve the name of 2.(不在乎) be indifferent; not matter: 你是

去是留，我都～。It's all the same to me whether you go or stay.

【无所用心】 wúsuǒyòngxīn not give serious thought to anything

【无所作为】 wúsuǒzuòwéi attempt nothing and accomplish nothing; be in a state of inertia

【无弹性供给】 wútánxìng gōngjǐ inelastic supply

【无弹性需求】 wútánxìng xūqiú inelastic demand

【无题】 wútí no title

【无题诗】 wútíshī titleless poem

【无条件】 wútiáojiàn unconditional; absolute; without preconditions

【无条件承兑】 wútiáojiàn chéngduì absolute acceptance

【无条件担保】 wútiáojiàn dānbǎo absolute guaranty

【无条件反射】 wútiáojiàn fǎnshè unconditioned reflex

【无条件接受】 wútiáojiàn jiēshòu absolute acceptance

【无条件投降】 wútiáojiàn tóuxiáng unconditional surrender

【无条件转让】 wútiáojiàn zhuǎnràng absolute conveyance; absolute assignment

【无土农业】 wútǔ nóngyè soilless agriculture

【无往不胜】 wúwǎng-bùshèng ever-victorious; invincible

【无望】 wúwàng hopeless; without any hope

【无微不至】 wúwēi-bùzhì meticulously; in every possible way

【无味】 wúwèi 1.（没有滋味）tasteless; unpalatable 2.（没有趣味）dull; insipid; uninteresting：枯燥～ dry as dust

【无畏】 wúwèi fearless; dauntless

【无谓】 wúwèi meaningless; pointless; senseless

【无…无…】 wú… wú… ～牵～挂 have no cares / ～穷～尽 inexhaustible; endless / ～依～靠 have no one to depend on; helpless / ～影～踪 disappear completely; vanish without a trace / ～忧～虑 free from care; carefree

【无息贷款】 wúxī dàikuǎn interest-free loan

【无隙可乘】 wúxì-kěchéng no crack to get in by; no loophole to exploit; no weakness to take advantage of; no chink in sb's armor

【无暇】 wúxiá have no time; be too busy：～考虑 have no time to think it over

【无先例可循】 wúxiānlì kěxún have no precedent to go by

【无限】 wúxiàn infinite; limitless; boundless; immeasurable：～热爱 have boundless love for

【无限大】 wúxiàndà infinity（符号为 ∞ ）

【无限公司】 wúxiàn gōngsī unlimited company

【无限期】 wúxiànqī indefinite duration：～罢工 a strike of indefinite duration

【无线】 wúxiàn wireless：～电报 wireless telegram; radiotelegram

【无线电】 wúxiàndiàn 1.（指媒介）radio; wireless transmission 2.（收音机）radio

【无线电波】 wúxiàn diànbō radio wave

【无线电传真】 wúxiàndiàn chuánzhēn radiofacsimile

【无线电干扰】 wúxiàndiàn gānrǎo radio jamming

【无线电跟踪】 wúxiàndiàn gēnzōng radio tracking

【无线电广播节目】 wúxiàndiàn guǎngbō jiémù radio program

【无线电话】 wúxiàn diànhuà radiotelephone; radiophone

【无线电话机】 wúxiàn diànhuàjī bellboy

【无线电控制】 wúxiàndiàn kòngzhì radiocontrol

【无线电收发两用机】 wúxiàndiàn shōufā liǎngyòngjī transceiver

【无线电收音机】 wúxiàndiàn shōuyīnjī radio receiver

【无线电通信】 wúxiàndiàn tōngxìn radio communication

【无线电中继台】 wúxiàndiàn zhōngjìtái radio relay station

【无线寻呼机】 wúxiàn xúnhūjī pager; beeper

【无效】 wúxiào of no avail; to no avail; invalid; null and void：宣布合同～ declare a contract invalid; declare a contract null and void; invalidate a contract; nullify a contract

【无效法律行为】 wúxiào fǎlǜ xíngwéi nullity

of juristic act

【无效诉讼】 wúxiào sùsòng annulment suit

【无效条款】 wúxiào tiáokuǎn irritancy

【无懈可击】 wúxiè-kějī with no chink in one's armor; unassailable; invulnerable

【无心】 wúxīn 1.(没有心思) not be in the mood for 2.(不是故意的) not intentionally; unwittingly; inadvertently

【无形】 wúxíng 1.(无形的) invisible; intangible; incorporeal 2.(无形中的) imperceivable; unperceptible

【无形财产】 wúxíng cáichǎn incorporeal property; non-visible property

【无形出口】 wúxíng chūkǒu invisible export

【无形价值】 wúxíng jiàzhí intangible value

【无形进口】 wúxíng jìnkǒu invisible import

【无形利益】 wúxíng lìyì invisible gain

【无形贸易】 wúxíng màoyì invisible trade

【无形权利】 wúxíng quánlì intangible right

【无形商品】 wúxíng shāngpǐn intangible goods

【无形损耗】 wúxíng sǔnhào invisible waste

【无形损失】 wúxíng sǔnshī invisible loss; non-physical loss

【无形效益】 wúxíng xiàoyì intangible benefits

【无形遗产】 wúxíng yíchǎn incorporeal hereditaments

【无形中】 wúxíngzhōng imperceivably; unperceptibly

【无形资本】 wúxíng zīběn incorporeal capital

【无形资产】 wúxíng zīchǎn incorporeal asset

【无形资源】 wúxíng zīyuán intangible resources

【无性】 wúxìng 〈*Biol.*〉 asexual

【无性繁殖】 wúxìng fánzhí vegetative propagation

【无性生殖】 wúxìng shēngzhí asexual reproduction

【无性种】 wúxìngzhǒng asexual species

【无须】 wúxū need not; not have to: ～顾虑 need not worry / ～过目 not have to read it

【无需】 wúxū 同"无须"

【无烟煤】 wúyānméi anthracite

【无烟区】 wúyānqū 1.(禁止吸烟的地方) no smoking area 2.(只准许使用无烟燃料的地区) smokeless zone

【无恙】 wúyàng 〈*written*〉 in good health; well; safe

【无疑】 wúyí no doubt; beyond doubt; undoubtedly: ～他只是想帮忙,但却把我们的工作给弄糟了。No doubt he was just trying to help, but he's spoiled our work.

【无依无靠】 wúyī-wúkào have no one to depend on; be helpless

【无异】 wúyì not different from; the same as; as good as

【无益】 wúyì unprofitable; useless; no good

【无意】 wúyì 1.(无意愿) have no intention (of doing sth.); not be inclined to 2.(不是故意的) inadvertently; unwittingly; accidentally

【无意识】 wúyì·shi unconscious

【无意遗漏】 wúyì yílòu innocent omission

【无垠】 wúyín boundless; vast

【无影灯】 wúyǐngdēng 〈*Med.*〉 shadowless lamp

【无影无踪】 wúyǐng-wúzōng without a trace; no footprints left behind

【无庸讳言】 wúyōng-huìyán not need for reticence

【无用】 wúyòng useless; of no use

【无用附件】 wúyòng fùjiàn falderal; falderol

【无用输出】 wúyòng shūchū garbage-out

【无用输入】 wúyòng shūrù garbage-in

【无用数据】 wúyòng shùjù hash

【无用信息】 wúyòng xìnxī garbage; gibberish

【无忧无虑】 wúyōu-wúlǜ free from care; free from all anxieties

【无由】 wúyóu not be in a position (to do sth.); have no way (of doing sth.)

【无与伦比】 wúyǔlúnbǐ unique; without equal; incomparable; unparalleled

【无原则】 wúyuánzé unprincipled

【无缘无故】 wúyuán-wúgù without cause or reason; for no reason at all: ～地发脾气 get into a temper for no reason at all

【无源之水】 wú yuán zhī shuǐ water without a source

【无政府主义】 wúzhèngfǔ zhǔyì anarchism; anarchist (adj.) ‖ 无政府主义者 anarchist

【无知】 wúzhī ignorant: 由于～ out of ignorance

【无支付能力】 wúzhīfù nénglì insolvency

【无执照营业】 wúzhízhào yíngyè interlope ‖

无执照营业者 interloper
【无止境】 wúzhǐjìng have no limits; know no end
【无中生有】 wúzhōng-shēngyǒu purely fictitious; fabricated
【无周期性】 wúzhōuqīxìng aperiodicity
【无籽】 wúzǐ seedless
【无籽西瓜】 wúzǐ xīguā seedless watermelon
【无足轻重】 wúzúqīngzhòng of little importance; of little consequence; insignificant
【无罪】 wúzuì innocent; not guilty: ～释放 set a person free with a verdict of "not guilty"; acquitted of a charge

芜［蕪］(wú) 1.（草多而乱）overgrown with weeds: 荒～ lie waste 2.（乱草丛生）grassland: 平～ open grassland 3.（杂乱）mixed and disorderly; miscellaneous: ～词 superfluous words
【芜菁】 wújīng 〈*Bot*.〉 turnip
【芜杂】 wúzá mixed and disorderly; miscellaneous

毋(wú) （表示禁止或劝阻）no; not: ～令逃逸。You must not let him escape.
【毋宁】 wúnìng rather ... (than); (not so much ...) as
【毋庸】 wúyōng need not: ～讳言 no need for reticence / ～赘言 need not go into the details

梧(wú)
【梧桐】 wútóng 〈*Bot*.〉 phoenix tree; Chinese parasol (tree)

鼯(wú)
【鼯鼠】 wúshǔ 〈*Zool*.〉 squirrel; giant flying squirrel

蜈(wú)
【蜈蚣】 wúgōng 〈*Zool*.〉 centipede

五(wǔ) five; fifth
【五百】 wǔbǎi five hundred; five-hundredth
【五倍子】 wǔbèizǐ Chinese gall
【五边形】 wǔbiānxíng pentagon; pentagonal (adj.)
【五彩】 wǔcǎi 1.（五色）the five colors 2.（颜色多）multicolored: ～缤纷 colorful; blazing with color
【五斗橱】 wǔdǒuchú chest of drawers
【五毒】 wǔdú the five poisonous creatures
【五分之一】 wǔfēnzhīyī a fifth; one fifth
【五谷】 wǔgǔ 1.（指五种粮食）the five cereals: ～不分 cannot tell one cereal from the other 2.（粮食作物）food crops: ～丰登 an abundant harvest of all food crops
【五官】 wǔguān 1.〈*Chin. Med*.〉 the five sense organs 2.（脸上的器官）facial features
【五湖四海】 wǔhú-sìhǎi all corners of the land
【五花八门】 wǔhuā-bāmén multifarious; of a wide variety
【五花肋条】 wǔhuā lèitiáo （猪肉部位）loin
【五讲四美】 wǔjiǎng sìměi Five Stresses and Four Points of Beauty ‖ 讲文明 stress on decorum / 讲礼貌 stress on manners / 讲卫生 stress on hygiene / 讲纪律 stress on discipline / 讲道德 stress on moral / 心灵美 beautification of the mind / 语言美 beautification of language / 行为美 beautification of behaviour / 环境美 beautification of the environment
【五角大楼】 Wǔjiǎo Dàlóu （美国国防部）Pentagon
【五角星】 wǔjiǎoxīng five-pointed star
【五金】 wǔjīn 1.（五种金属）the five metals 2.（金属）metals; hardware
【五金厂】 wǔjīnchǎng hardware factory
【五金店】 wǔjīndiàn hardware store
【五金商】 wǔjīnshāng dealer in hardware; ironmonger
【五年计划】 wǔnián jìhuà Five-Year Plan
【五千】 wǔqiān five thousand; five thousandth
【五色】 wǔsè 1.（五彩）the five colors 2.（颜色多）multicolored
【五十】 wǔshí fifty; fiftieth
【五四青年节】 Wǔ-sì Qīngniánjié Youth Day (May 4)
【五四运动】 Wǔ-sì Yùndòng the May 4th Movement (1919)
【五体投地】 wǔtǐ-tóudì prostrate oneself before sb. in admiration
【五味】 wǔwèi 1.（五种味道）the five flavors 2.（各种味道）all sorts of flavors

【五线谱】 wǔxiànpǔ 〈*Music*〉 staff; stave
【五项全能运动】 wǔxiàng quánnéng yùndòng 〈*Sports*〉 pentathlon
【五项全能运动员】 wǔxiàng quánnéng yùndòngyuán pentathlete
【五星红旗】 Wǔxīng Hóngqí the Five-Starred Red Flag
【五星级饭店】 wǔxīngjí fàndiàn five stars; de luxe; luxury hotel; hotels of highest quality
【五颜六色】 wǔyán-liùsè of various colors; multicolored; colorful
【五一国际劳动节】 Wǔyī Guójì Láodòngjié May 1, International Labor Day; May Day
【五月】 wǔyuè May
【五月节】 Wǔyuèjié the Dragon Boat Festival
【五脏】 wǔzàng 〈*Chin. Med.*〉 the five internal organs
【五指】 wǔzhǐ the five fingers
【五子棋】 wǔzǐqí gobang

伍 (wǔ) 1.(五) five 2.(队伍;军队) army 3.(伙伴) company: 与…为～ associate with sb.

午 (wǔ) noon; midday; meridiam

【午餐】 wǔcān lunch
【午餐肉】 wǔcānròu pork luncheon meat: 火腿～ ham luncheon meat
【午饭】 wǔfàn midday meal; lunch: 吃～ have a lunch
【午觉】 wǔjiào afternoon nap; noontime snooze: 睡～ have a nap
【午睡】 wǔshuì 1.(午觉) afternoon nap; noontime snooze 2.(睡午觉) have a nap
【午休】 wǔxiū noon break; midday rest; noontime rest; lunch hour
【午夜】 wǔyè midnight

忤[牾] (wǔ) 1.(不顺从) disobedient: ～逆 disobedient (to parents) 2.(不和睦) uncongenial; inharmonious

妩[嫵、娬] (wǔ)

【妩媚】 wǔmèi lovely; charming

武 (wǔ) 1.(军事的) military: ～官 military officer 2.(关于技击的) connected with boxing skill, swordplay, etc. 3.(猛烈;勇猛) valiant; fierce 4.(武力) force; fight

【武昌鱼】 wǔchāngyú blunt-snout bream
【武断】 wǔduàn arbitrary decision; subjective assertion: ～的解释 an arbitrary interpretation / ～行事 execute business dogmatically
【武官】 wǔguān 1.(军官) military officer 2.〈*Foreign Affairs*〉 military attaché: 海军～ naval attaché / 空军～ air attaché
【武官处】 wǔguānchù military attaché's office
【武警】 wǔjǐng armed police
【武库】 wǔkù armory; arsenal
【武力】 wǔlì 1.(强暴的力量) force: 使用～ resort to force 2.(军事力量) military force; armed might; armed strength; force of arms: 以～相威胁 threaten with military force
【武器】 wǔqì 1.(军械) weapon; arms: 常规～ conventional weapons / 核～ nuclear weapons 2.(泛指工具) instrument; weapon: 思想～ ideological weapon
【武器输出国】 wǔqì shūchūguó arms exporter; arms exporting country
【武器输入国】 wǔqì shūrùguó arms importer; arms importing country
【武器装备】 wǔqì zhuāngbèi weaponry
【武士】 wǔshì 1.(宫廷卫士) palace guards in ancient times 2.(有勇力的人) man of prowess; warrior; knight 3.(日本武士) samurai
【武士道】 wǔshìdào bushido (Jap.)
【武士俑】 wǔshìyǒng warrior figure
【武术】 wǔshù *wushu*; martial arts
【武侠】 wǔxiá swordsman
【武侠片】 wǔxiápiàn swordsman film
【武侠小说】 wǔxiá xiǎoshuō swordsman novel
【武装】 wǔzhuāng 1.(军事装备) arms; military equipment; battle outfit: 士兵们已经全副～。The soldiers had plenty of arms and ammunition. 2.(武装力量) armed forces 3.(用武器装备) equip with arms; supply with arms
【武装部队】 wǔzhuāng bùduì armed forces
【武装冲突】 wǔzhuāng chōngtū armed conflict; armed clash
【武装带】 wǔzhuāngdài Sam Browne belt
【武装斗争】 wǔzhuāng dòuzhēng armed struggle
【武装干涉】 wǔzhuāng gānshè armed inter-

vention
【武装警察】 wǔzhuāng jǐngchá Armed Police
【武装力量】 wǔzhuāng lìliàng armed power; armed forces
【武装起义】 wǔzhuāng qǐyì armed uprising; armed insurrection

侮（wǔ） insult; bully
【侮慢】 wǔmàn slight; treat disrespectfully
【侮辱】 wǔrǔ insult; humiliate; subject sb. to indignities

捂［搗］（wǔ） seal; cover; muffle

舞（wǔ） 1.（舞蹈）dance 2.（做出舞蹈动作）move about as in a dance：雪花飞～ snowflakes dancing in the air 3.（舞动）dance with sth. in one's hands：～剑 perform a sword-dance 4.（挥舞）flourish; wield; brandish：挥～大棒 brandish the big stick
【舞伴】 wǔbàn dancing partner
【舞弊】 wǔbì malpractices; irregularities; fraudulent practices; embezzlement
【舞步】 wǔbù dance; dance pas
【舞步路线图】 wǔbù lùxiàntú floor pattern
【舞场】 wǔchǎng dance hall; ballroom
【舞池】 wǔchí dancing pit
【舞蹈】 wǔdǎo dance
【舞蹈动作】 wǔdǎo dòngzuò dance movement
【舞蹈家】 wǔdǎojiā dancer
【舞蹈设计】 wǔdǎo shèjì choreography
【舞蹈演员】 wǔdǎo yǎnyuán dancer
【舞动】 wǔdòng wave; brandish
【舞会】 wǔhuì dance; ball; dance party
【舞剧】 wǔjù dance drama; ballet
【舞弄】 wǔnòng wave; wield; brandish
【舞女】 wǔnǚ taxi dancer; dancing girl; dance-hostess
【舞曲】 wǔqǔ dance music; dance
【舞台】 wǔtái 1.（剧场的）stage; arena：搬上～ present on the stage 2.（活动场所）stage; area：历史～ historical stage / 政治～ political arena / 进入国际贸易～ enter the arena of international trade
【舞台布景】 wǔtái bùjǐng （stage）scenery; décor
【舞台工作人员】 wǔtái gōngzuò rényuán stagehand
【舞台记录片】 wǔtái jìlùpiàn stage documentary
【舞台监督】 wǔtái jiāndū 1.（指工作）stage-manage 2.（指人）stage-manager
【舞台设计】 wǔtái shèjì stage design
【舞台效果】 wǔtái xiàoguǒ stage effect
【舞台艺术】 wǔtái yìshù stagecraft
【舞台语言】 wǔtái yǔyán stage language; theatrical speech
【舞台照明】 wǔtái zhàomíng stage illumination; lighting
【舞台指导】 wǔtái zhǐdǎo stage direction
【舞厅】 wǔtīng ballroom; dance hall
【舞文弄墨】 wǔwén-nòngmò 1.（歪曲法律条文作弊）pervert the law by playing with legal phraseology 2.（玩弄文字技巧）engage in phrase-mongering

兀（wù） 1.（高高地突起）rising to a height; towering 2.（秃）bald
【兀鹫】 wùjiù 〈*Zool.*〉 vulture
【兀立】 wùlì stand upright
【兀自】 wùzì still

勿（wù） no; not：请～吸烟！ No smoking, please.

芴（wù） 〈*Chem.*〉 fluorene

物（wù） 1.（东西）thing; matter 2.（内容；实质）content; substance：言之无～ talk or writing devoid of substance
【物产】 wùchǎn products; produce
【物归原主】 wùguīyuánzhǔ return sth. to its rightful owner; things return to their proper owners
【物候】 wùhòu phenological phenomenon
【物候学】 wùhòuxué phenology; phenological (adj.)
【物极必反】 wùjí-bìfǎn things will develop in the opposite direction when they become extreme
【物价】 wùjià （commodity）prices：抬高～ boost the price
【物价波动】 wùjià bōdòng price fluctuation
【物价大检查】 wùjià dàjiǎnchá massive price inspection
【物价改革】 wùjià gǎigé price reform

【物价管制】 wùjià guǎnzhì price control
【物价政策】 wùjià zhèngcè pricing policy
【物价指数】 wùjià zhǐshù price index; index of price: 零售～ index of retail prices
【物价总水平】 wùjià zǒngshuǐpíng purchasing power unit; PuPU
【物件】 wùjiàn thing; article
【物尽其用】 wùjìnqíyòng make the best use of everything; let all things serve their proper purpose
【物理】 wùlǐ 1.(事物内在规律) innate laws of things 2.(物理学) physics; physical (adj.)
【物理变化】 wùlǐ biànhuà physical change
【物理故障】 wùlǐ gùzhàng physical fault
【物理化学】 wùlǐ huàxué physical chemistry
【物理疗法】 wùlǐ liáofǎ physiotherapy; physical therapy
【物理学】 wùlǐxué physics; physical (adj.): 核～ nuclear physics ‖ 物理学家 physicist
【物力】 wùlì material resources
【物美价廉】 wùměi-jiàlián cheap and fine; excellent quality and reasonable price; good quality and fair price
【物品】 wùpǐn article; goods: 贵重～ valuables / 有考古价值的～ things of archaeological interest
【物色】 wùsè look for; seek out; choose: ～人才 look for talented persons
【物体】 wùtǐ body; substance; object
【物物交换】 wùwù jiāohuàn barter one thing for another
【物以类聚】 wùyǐlèijù things of one kind come together; like attracts like; birds of a feather flock together
【物以稀为贵】 wù yǐ xī wéi guì When a thing is scarce, it is precious. (或: A thing is valued if it is rare.)
【物议】 wùyì criticism from the people
【物证】 wùzhèng material evidence
【物质】 wùzhì 1.(客观存在) matter; substance; material 2.(指金钱) money
【物质不灭定律】 wùzhì bùmiè dìnglǜ the law of conservation of matter
【物质财富】 wùzhì cáifù material wealth
【物质产品】 wùzhì chǎnpǐn physical product
【物质储备】 wùzhì chǔbèi reserve supply; stockpile
【物质刺激】 wùzhì cìjī material incentive
【物质鼓励】 wùzhì gǔlì material reward
【物质基础】 wùzhì jīchǔ material base
【物质奖励】 wùzhì jiǎnglì material award
【物质力量】 wùzhì lìliàng material strength; material force
【物质利益】 wùzhì lìyì material benefits; material gains
【物质生活】 wùzhì shēnghuó material life
【物质世界】 wùzhì shìjiè the material world; the physical world
【物质条件】 wùzhì tiáojiàn material conditions or prerequisites
【物质文化】 wùzhì wénhuà material culture
【物质文明】 wùzhì wénmíng material civilization
【物质享受】 wùzhì xiǎngshòu creature comforts
【物种】 wùzhǒng 〈*Biol.*〉 species
【物种起源】 wùzhǒng qǐyuán 〈*Biol.*〉 genesis; the origin of species
【物资】 wùzī goods and materials
【物资调度】 wùzī diàodù distribution of materials
【物资管理】 wùzī guǎnlǐ handling of goods and materials
【物资交流】 wùzī jiāoliú interflow of commodities
【物资消耗】 wùzī xiāohào consumption of materials

务[務](wù) 1.(事务) affair; business 2.(从事) be engaged in; devote one's efforts to: ～农 be engaged in agriculture; be a farmer 3.(务必) must; be sure to: ～请来电。Please do not fail to cable us.
【务必】 wùbì must; be sure to
【务工】 wùgōng be a worker
【务实】 wùshí deal with concrete matters relating to work
【务使】 wùshǐ make sure; ensure
【务虚】 wùxū discuss principles; discuss ideological guidelines

雾[霧](wù) 1.〈*Meteorol.*〉 fog 2.(雾状水点) fine spray
【雾灯】 wùdēng foglamp

【雾号】 wùhào foghorn
【雾化】 wùhuà atomize; atomization (n.)
【雾化器】 wùhuàqì atomizer
【雾气】 wùqì fog; mist; vapor
【雾凇】 wùsōng 〈*Meteorol.*〉 rime; soft rime

坞[塢、隖] (wù) 1.(山中凹地) a basin-like place 2.(船坞) dock: 船～ dock / 花～ sunken flower-bed

误[悮] (wù) 1.(错) mistake; error: 笔～ slip of the pen / 口～ slip of the tongue 2.(耽误) miss; fail to seize the right moment: ～车 miss the train / ～船 miss the ship / ～机 miss the airliner 3.(使受害) harm 4.(不是故意) by mistake; by accident: ～伤 accidentally injure
【误差】 wùchā error
【误传】 wùchuán misrepresent (v.); misinformation (n.)
【误导】 wùdǎo misguide
【误点】 wùdiǎn late; overdue; behind schedule
【误工】 wùgōng 1.(耽误工作) delay one's work 2.(耽误时间) loss of working time
【误会】 wùhuì 1.(误解人) misunderstand; mistake; misconstrue 2.(对人的误解) misunderstanding: 消除～ clear away misunderstanding
【误击】 wùjī mishit
【误解】 wùjiě 1.(理解错) misread; misunderstand 2.(错的理解) misunderstanding
【误入歧途】 wùrù-qítú go astray; be misled: 把～的女儿带回 bring back the errant daughter
【误伤】 wùshāng 1.(无意中伤人) accidentally injure 2.(无意中受的伤) accidental injury
【误事】 wùshì 1.(耽误事情) cause delay in work or business; hold things up 2.(把事情搞糟了) bungle matters
【误诊】 wùzhěn make a wrong diagnosis
【误中本队球门】 wùzhòng běnduì qiúmén 〈*Football*〉 own goal

恶[惡] (wù) loathe; dislike; hate: 一个人的好～ one's likes and dislikes / 可～ loathsome; hateful
(另见"恶"ě, è)

悟 (wù) realize; awaken
【悟性】 wùxìng power of understanding; comprehension

晤 (wù) meet; interview; see
【晤面】 wùmiàn meet; see
【晤谈】 wùtán meet and talk; have a talk; interview

焐 (wù) warm up

痦[瘑] (wù)
【痦子】 wù·zi mole

X

xi

夕 (xī) 1.(傍晚) sunset 2.(晚上) evening; night

【夕烟】 xīyān evening mist

【夕阳】 xīyáng the setting sun: ～如血 a lurid sunset / ～西下。The sun is setting. / ～映红了天空。The sky was aglow with setting sun.

【夕照】 xīzhào the glow of the setting sun; evening glow

矽 (xī) 〈*Chem*.〉 silicon (元素符号 Si)

【矽尘】 xīchén silicious dust

【矽肺】 xīfèi 〈*Med*.〉 silicosis; pneumosilicosis

【矽钢】 xīgāng 〈*Metall*.〉 silicon steel

西 (xī) 1.(方向) west; western 2.(西洋; 西方) Occidental; Western: ～乐 Western music

【西班牙】 Xībānyā Spain; Spanish (adj.)

【西班牙人】 Xībānyārén Spanish

【西班牙语】 xībānyāyǔ Spanish; Spanish language

【西半球】 xībànqiú the Western Hemisphere

【西北】 xīběi 1.(指方向) northwest 2.(中国西北地区) northwest China; the Northwest

【西部】 xībù West (of the United States)

【西部片】 xībùpiàn 〈*Cinematog*.〉 the Western

【西餐】 xīcān Western-style food

【西餐餐馆】 xīcān cānguǎn restaurant serving Western-style food

【西点】 xīdiǎn Western-style pastry

【西方】 xīfāng 1.(方向) the west; westward 2.(指欧美发达国家) the West; the Occident; occidental (adj.)

【西风】 xīfēng west wind; westerly wind

【西风带】 xīfēngdài 〈*Geog*.〉 westerlies

【西服】 xīfú Western-style clothes

【西服料】 xīfúliào suiting

【西瓜】 xīguā watermelon

【西瓜子】 xīguāzhǐ watermelon seed

【西红柿】 xīhóngshì tomato

【西葫芦】 xīhú·lu pumpkin

【西化】 xīhuà Occidentalize; Westernize; Westernization (n.)

【西经】 xījīng 〈*Geog*.〉 west longitude

【西拉木伦河】 Xīlāmùlúnhé 〈place〉 Xar Moron He

【西门子】 xīménzǐ 〈*Electr*.〉 siemens

【西南】 xīnán 1.(指方向) southwest 2.(中国西南地区) southwest China; the Southwest

【西南风】 xīnánfēng southwest wind; southwesterly wind

【西欧】 Xī Ōu Western Europe

【西欧共同市场】 Xī Ōu gòngtóng shìchǎng European Common Market

【西式】 xīshì Western style

【西天】 xītiān 〈*Buddhism*〉 Western Paradise

【西洋】 xīyáng the West; the Western world ‖ 西洋人 Westerner

【西洋景】 xīyángjǐng 1.(拉洋片) peep show 2.(骗人的东西) trickery; fraud: 拆穿～ expose sb's fraud

【西洋参】 xīyángshēn American ginseng

【西洋文学】 xīyáng wénxué Western literature

【西药】 xīyào Western medicine

【西医】 xīyī 1.(指医学) Western medicine 2.(指医生) a doctor trained in Western medicine

【西装】 xīzhuāng Western-style clothes

牺[犧] (xī)

【牺牲】 xīshēng 1.(祭祀用牲畜) a beast slaughtered for sacrifice; sacrifice 2.(舍弃生命) sacrifice oneself; die a martyr's death; lay down one's life 3.(放弃或损害利益) sacrifice; give up; do sth. at the expense of

【牺牲品】 xīshēngpǐn victim; prey

硒 (xī) 〈*Chem.*〉 selenium (元素符号 Se)

舾 (xī)

【舾装】 xīxuāng 〈*Naut.*〉 fitting-out

吸 (xī) 1.(引入体内) inhale; breathe in; draw 2.(吸收) absorb; suck up: 海绵～水。The sponge absorbed water. 3.(吸引) attract; draw

【吸潮器】 xīcháoqì air-breather

【吸尘器】 xīchénqì vacuum cleaner; dust catcher; dust collector: 真空～ vacuum cleaner

【吸虫】 xīchóng fluke

【吸顶灯】 xīdǐngdéng ceiling light

【吸毒】 xīdú 1.(吸食毒品) take drug; use drug 2.(通过注射静脉) mainline

【吸毒者】 xīdúzhě drug addict; drug-dependent

【吸力】 xīlì suction; attraction: 磁铁对钢有～。A magnet attracts steel.

【吸力计】 xīlìjì suction gauge

【吸滤器】 xīlǜqì suction filter

【吸墨纸】 xīmòzhǐ blotting paper

【吸气】 xīqì gas absorption; gas pick-up

【吸取】 xīqǔ absorb; draw; assimilate: ～教训 learn a lesson / ～精华 absorb the quintessence

【吸热】 xīrè absorption of heat

【吸热反应】 xīrè fǎnyìng endothermic reaction

【吸入】 xīrù soak; suck in

【吸湿剂】 xīshījì hygroscopic agent

【吸食】 xīshí suck; take in

【吸收】 xīshōu 1.(吸到内部) absorb; suck up; assimilate; imbibe; draw: ～外资 absorb foreign capital / 好学生～知识快。A good student assimilate knowledge quickly. 2.(接受) recruit; enroll; admit: ～入协会 be admitted into the association

【吸吮】 xīshǔn suck; absorb

【吸铁石】 xītiěshí magnet; lodestone

【吸血鬼】 xīxuèguǐ bloodsucker; vampire

【吸烟】 xīyān smoke: 禁止～。No smoking.

【吸烟室】 xīyānshì smoking room

【吸音板】 xīyīnbǎn sound-absorbing wall panels

【吸音材料】 xīyīn cáiliào draping

【吸引】 xīyǐn attract; draw; fascinate: ～更多的外来投资 attract more foreign investment/ 展览会～了很多参观者。The exhibition attracted many visitors.

【吸引力】 xīyǐnlì attraction; appeal: 悬念小说对我特别有～。Suspense novels hold a special attraction for me.

希 (xī) 1.(希望) hope 2.(稀少) rare; scarce; uncommon

【希罕】 xī·han 1.(希奇) rare; scarce; uncommon 2.(认为希奇) value as a rarity; cherish 3.(希罕的事物) rare thing; rarity

【希冀】 xījì hope for; wish for; aspire after

【希腊】 Xīlà Greece; Greek (*adj.*) ‖ 希腊人 Greek

【希腊罗马神话】 Xīlà Luómǎ shénhuà Greek and Roman mythology

【希腊神话】 Xīlà shénhuà Greek mythology

【希腊语】 Xīlàyǔ Greek (language)

【希腊字母】 Xīlà zìmǔ the Greek alphabet

【希奇】 xīqí rare; strange; curious

【希奇古怪】 xīqí-gǔguài rare and peculiar

【希少】 xīshǎo few; rare; sparse

【希世】 xīshì rare

【希世之珍】 xīshìzhīzhēn a rare treasure

【希图】 xītú harbor the intention of; try to; attempt to

【希望】 xīwàng hope; wish; expect: 渺茫的～ forlorn hope / 最～和平 desire peace more than anything else / 他要当演员已无～。He's finished as an actor.

【希望工程】 xīwàng gōngchéng the Hope Project

【希夏邦马峰】 Xīxiàbāngmǎfēng 〈place〉 Mount Xixabangma

烯 (xī) 〈*Chem.*〉 alkene

【烯烃】 xītīng alkene; olefin

稀 (xī) 1.(稀少) rare; scarce; uncommon: 她的头发愈来愈～了。Her hair is getting thin. 2.(稀疏) sparse; scattered: 地广人～。It is a vast area but sparsely populated. 3.(稀薄; 含水多) watery; thin: 这汤太～。This soup's too thin.

【稀薄】 xībó thin; rare: ～的雾 a thin mist

【稀饭】 xīfàn rice or millet gruel; porridge

【稀客】 xīkè rare visitor; infrequent visitor

【稀烂】 xīlàn 1.(极烂) completely mashed; pulpy 2.(极破碎) smashed to pieces; broken to bits
【稀里糊涂】 xī·lihútú not knowing what one is about; muddleheaded
【稀少】 xīshǎo few; rare; sparse: 人烟～ be sparsely populated
【稀释】 xīshì dilute; dilution (n.)
【稀疏】 xīshū few and scattered; few and far between; thin; sparse
【稀树草原】 xīshù cǎoyuán 〈*Geog.*〉 savanna
【稀土】 xītǔ 〈*Med.*〉 rare earth
【稀土元素】 xītǔ yuánsù rare-earth element
【稀有】 xīyǒu rare; unusual
【稀有金属】 xīyǒu jīnshǔ rare metal
【稀有气体】 xīyǒu qìtǐ rare gas

昔 (xī) former times; the past
【昔日】 xīrì in former days; in the past; in the old days

惜 (xī) 1.(爱惜) cherish; value highly; care for tenderly 2.(吝惜) spare; grudge; stint: 不～工本 spare no expense 3.(惋惜) have pity on sb.; feel sorry for sb.
【惜别】 xībié be reluctant to part; hate to see sb. go
【惜力】 xīlì be sparing of one's energy; not do one's best

析 (xī) 1.(分开) divide; separate 2.(分析) analyse; dissect; resolve
【析取】 xīqǔ disjunction
【析疑】 xīyí resolve a doubt; clarify a doubt; clear up a doubtful point
【析义】 xīyì analyse the meaning (of a word, etc.)

淅 (xī)
【淅沥】 xīlì 〈*onomat.*〉 the gentle sound of rain, snow, etc.
【淅淅】 xīxī 〈*onomat.*〉 the low sound of wind, rain, snow, etc.

蜥 (xī)
【蜥蜴】 xīyì 〈*Zool.*〉 lizard

膝 (xī) knee: 大雪没～。The snow was knee-deep. / 水深及～。The water was knee-deep.
【膝盖】 xīgài knee
【膝盖骨】 xīgàigǔ kneecap; patella
【膝盖囊肿】 xīgài nángzhǒng 〈*Med.*〉 housemaid's knee
【膝关节】 xīguānjié knee joint
【膝关节炎】 xīguānjiéyán gonitis; gonarthritis

息 (xī) 1.(气息) breath: 屏～ hold one's breath 2.(消息) news: 信～ news; message 3.(停止) cease; stop 4.(休息) rest 5.(滋生;繁殖) grow; multiply 6.(利息) interest: 生～ earn interest; bear interest
【息怒】 xīnù cease to be angry; calm one's anger
【息票】 xīpiào interest coupon
【息肉】 xīròu 〈*Med.*〉 polyp; polypus
【息事宁人】 xīshì-níngrén 1.(调解) patch up a quarrel and reconcile the parties concerned 2.(让步) make concessions to avoid trouble; gloss things over to stay on good terms
【息息相关】 xīxī-xiāngguān be closely linked; be closely bound up; related as closely as each breath is to the next

熄 (xī) extinguish; put out
【熄灯】 xīdēng put out the light
【熄火】 xīhuǒ 1.(熄灭) extinction 2.〈*Auto*〉 switch off the motor
【熄灭】 xīmiè go out; die out

奚 (xī)
【奚落】 xīluò scoff at; taunt; gibe

溪 (xī) small stream; brook; rivulet
【溪涧】 xījiàn mountain stream
【溪流】 xīliú brook; rivulet

蹊 (xī) footpath
(另见“蹊”qī)
【蹊径】 xījìng path; way: 另辟～ find one's own way

鼷 (xī)
【鼷鼠】 xīshǔ 〈*Zool.*〉 rat

悉 (xī) 1.(知道) know; learn; be informed of: 惊～ be shocked to learn 2.(全;尽) all; entirely: ～力 go all out; spare no effort
【悉数】 xīshù 1.(数清;列举) enumerate in full detail: 不可～ too many to enumerate 2.

(全部) all; every single one: ～奉还 return all that has been borrowed or taken away
【悉听尊便】 xītīngzūnbiàn You are free to try anything you like.
【悉心】 xīxīn devote all one's attention; take the utmost care

蟋 (xī)
【蟋蟀】 xīshuài cricket: 斗～ cricketfight

翕 (xī) smooth and peaceful
【翕动】 xīdòng open and close: 口唇～ open and close one's lips

犀 (xī) 〈*Zool*.〉 rhinoceros
【犀角】 xījiǎo rhinoceros horn
【犀利】 xīlì sharp; incisive; trenchant: 目光～ with penetrating eyesight
【犀鸟】 xīniǎo 〈*Zool*.〉 hornbill; toucan
【犀牛】 xīniú 〈*Zool*.〉 rhino; rhinoceros

锡 (xī) 〈*Chem*.〉 tin (元素符号 Sn)
【锡棒】 xībàng tin bar
【锡保鲜纸】 xībǎoxiānzhǐ tin foil
【锡伯族】 Xībózú Xibe (中国少数民族, 主要分布在辽宁、新疆、黑龙江等地)
【锡箔】 xībó tinfoil paper
【锡焊】 xīhàn solder
【锡匠】 xījiàng tinsmith
【锡矿】 xīkuàng tin ore
【锡林郭勒盟】 Xīlínguōlèméng 〈place〉 Xilin Gol Meng
【锡林浩特】 Xīlín Hàotè 〈place〉 Xilinhot
【锡器】 xīqì tinware
【锡纸】 xīzhǐ silver paper; tinfoil

熙 (xī)
【熙熙攘攘】 xīxī-rǎngrǎng bustling with activity; with people bustling about

嘻 (xī)
【嘻嘻哈哈】 xīxī-hāhā laughing and joking; laughing merrily; mirthful

嬉 (xī) play; sport
【嬉皮士】 xīpíshì hippy; hippie
【嬉皮笑脸】 xīpí-xiàoliǎn grinning cheekily; smiling and grimacing
【嬉戏】 xīxì play; sport
【嬉笑】 xīxiào be laughing and playing

习 [習] (xí) 1. (温习; 练习) practice; exercise; review 2. (熟习) get accustomed to; be used to; become familiar with 3. (习惯) habit; custom; usual practice: 陋～ bad custom
【习得特性】 xídé tèxìng acquired characteristic
【习得行为】 xídé xíngwéi acquired behavior
【习惯】 xíguàn 1. (适应) be accustomed to; be used to; be inured to 阿拉斯加人～寒冷的天气。 Alaskans are accustomed to cold weather. 2. (养成的习惯) habit; custom; usual practice: ～成自然。 Habit becomes second nature.
【习惯法】 xíguànfǎ common law; customary law
【习惯势力】 xíguàn shìlì force of habit
【习见】 xíjiàn (of things) commonly seen
【习气】 xíqì bad habit; bad practice: 官僚～ habitual practice of bureaucracy
【习俗】 xísú custom; convention: 民间～ folk custom
【习题】 xítí exercises (in school work): 做～ do exercises
【习习】 xíxí blow gently
【习性】 xíxìng habits and characteristics
【习以为常】 xíyǐwéicháng be used to sth.; be accustomed to sth.
【习用】 xíyòng habitually use
【习语】 xíyǔ idiom
【习字】 xízì practice penmanship; do exercises in calligraphy
【习字帖】 xízìtiě copybook; calligraphy model
【习作】 xízuò 1. (练习写作) do exercises in composition 2. (作业) an exercise in composition, drawing, etc.

席 [蓆][1] (xí) 1. (席子) mat: 草～ straw mat / 竹～ bamboo mat 2. (席位) seat; place: 记者～ seats for the press / 贵宾～ guest seats 3. (酒席) feast; banquet; dinner
【席次】 xícì the order of seats; seating arrangement
【席地】 xídì on the ground

【席卷】 xíjuǎn 1.（卷走）roll up like a mat; carry everything with one; take away everything: ～而去 roll the mat with everything and run away / ～一空 take away everything 2.（横扫）sweep across; engulf

【席棚】 xípēng mat shed

【席位】 xíwèi seat

袭［**襲**］（xí）1.（袭击）raid; attack: 偷～ make a surprise attack on 2.（照样做）follow the pattern of; carry on as before: 抄～ plagiarize

【袭击】 xíjī 1.〈*Mil.*〉raid; attack: 突然～ make a surprise attack on 2.（意外打击）unexpected strike: 遭到台风～ be hit by a typhoon

【袭取】 xíqǔ 1.（夺取）take by surprise 2.（袭用）take over

【袭扰】 xírǎo 〈*Mil.*〉harassing attack

【袭用】 xíyòng take over; follow

媳（xí）daughter-in-law

【媳妇】 xífù 1.（儿媳）daughter-in-law; son's wife 2.（晚辈之妻）the wife of a relative of the younger generation

檄（xí）

【檄文】 xíwén 1.（征召文书）an official call to arms 2.（声讨文书）an official denunciation of the enemy

洗（xǐ）1.（洗涤）wash; bathe: ～衣服 wash clothes / 你的衬衫～了吗？ Have you washed your shirt? / 我的衬衫正在～。My shirt is in wash. 2.〈*Religion*〉baptize: 受～ receive baptism; be baptized 3.（除去）redress; right 4.（洗劫）kill and loot; sack city 5.〈*Photog.*〉develop: ～胶卷 develop a film 6.（洗牌）shuffle: ～骨牌 shuffle the dominoes

【洗不清】 xǐbùqīng unable to vindicate oneself

【洗肠】 xǐcháng intestinal lavage

【洗尘】 xǐchén give a dinner of welcome (to a visitor from afar)

【洗涤】 xǐdí wash; cleanse

【洗涤剂】 xǐdíjì detergent

【洗耳恭听】 xǐ'ěr-gōngtīng listen with great respect and attention; be all ears

【洗发剂】 xǐfàjì shampoo: 药物～ medicated shampoo

【洗发水】 xǐfàshuǐ shampoo

【洗劫】 xǐjié loot; sack: ～一空 loot everything

【洗礼】 xǐlǐ 1.〈*Religion*〉baptism 2.（锻练和考验）severe test: 经受战斗～ go through the test of a battle

【洗脸盆】 xǐliǎnpén washbasin; washbowl

【洗煤】 xǐméi coal washing

【洗煤厂】 xǐméichǎng coal washery; coal cleaning plant

【洗煤机】 xǐméijī coal washer

【洗牌】 xǐpái shuffle playing cards

【洗盘子】 xǐpán·zi wash up dishes

【洗片】 xǐpiàn 〈*Photog.*〉develop (a film)

【洗片机】 xǐpiànjī developing machine

【洗片夹】 xǐpiànjiā film clip

【洗片架】 xǐpiànjià film hanger

【洗染店】 xǐrǎndiàn cleaners and dyers; laundering and dyeing shop

【洗手】 xǐshǒu 1.（改邪归正）stop doing evil and reform oneself 2.（不再干）wash one's hands of sth.

【洗手间】 xǐshǒujiān toilet

【洗刷】 xǐshuā 1.（用水）wash and brush; scrub 2.（除去耻辱、污点等）wash off; clear oneself of

【洗烫】 xǐtàng launder: 我得把这些脏工作服去～好。I'll have to launder these dirty work clothes.

【洗头】 xǐtóu wash one's hair; shampoo

【洗碗碟机】 xǐwǎndiéjī washed-up; washing-up machine

【洗碗机】 xǐwǎnjī dishwasher

【洗胃】 xǐwèi gastric lavage

【洗心革面】 xǐxīn-gémiàn turn over a new leaf; thoroughly reform oneself

【洗雪】 xǐxuě wipe out: ～耻辱 wipe out a disgrace

【洗衣】 xǐyī wash clothes; do one's washing

【洗衣板】 xǐyībǎn washboard

【洗衣店】 xǐyīdiàn laundry

【洗衣粉】 xǐyīfěn washing powder

【洗衣机】 xǐyījī washing machine; washer

【洗衣刷】 xǐyīshuā wash brush

【洗印】 xǐyìn 〈*Photog.*〉developing and

printing

【洗印机】 xǐyìnjī （film）processor

【洗澡】 xǐzǎo have a bath；have a wash；take a bath；bathe：洗凉水澡 take a cold bath / 你洗过澡了吗？Have you had a wash?

【洗澡间】 xǐzǎojiān bathroom

【洗澡盆】 xǐzǎopén bathtub

【洗澡塘】 xǐzǎotáng bath pool

铣（xǐ）〈*Mech.*〉mill（另见“铣”xiǎn）

【铣床】 xǐchuáng 〈*Mech.*〉miller；milling machine

【铣刀】 xǐdāo 〈*Mech.*〉milling cutter

【铣工】 xǐgōng 1.〈*Mech.*〉milling work 2.（指工人）milling machine operator

【铣削】 xǐxiāo 〈*Mech.*〉mill

徙（xǐ）move（from one place to another）

【徙居】 xǐjū move house：～内地 move up-country

喜（xǐ） 1.（高兴，快乐）happy；delighted；pleased：她又惊又～。She was agreeably surprised. 2.（喜事）happy event（esp. wedding）；occasion for celebration 3.（怀孕）pregnancy：有～ be expecting；be in the family way 4.（喜好）be fond of；like；have an inclination for：～交游 like to make friends

【喜爱】 xǐ'ài like；love；be fond of；be keen on：惹人～ lovely and cute / 他非常～古典音乐。He has an enormous appetite for classical music.

【喜报】 xǐbào a bulletin of glad tidings

【喜不自胜】 xǐbùzìshèng be in heaven；be delighted beyond measure

【喜冲冲】 xǐchōngchōng be in high spirits；be in a happy mood

【喜出望外】 xǐchūwàngwài be overjoyed；be pleasantly surprised；be extraordinary happy

【喜从天降】 xǐcóngtiānjiàng an unexpected piece of good fortune；heaven-sent fortune

【喜好】 xǐhào like；love；be fond of；be keen on

【喜欢】 xǐ·huan 1.（喜爱）like；love；be fond of；be keen on：我很～她。I like her very much. / 她非常～猫。She adores cats. 2.（高兴）happy；elated；filled with joy

【喜酒】 xǐjiǔ 1.（指酒）wine drunk at a wedding feast 2.（指酒席）wedding feast

【喜剧】 xǐjù comedy

【喜剧演员】 xǐjù yǎnyuán comedian（m.）；comedienne（f.）

【喜马拉雅山】 Xǐmǎlāyǎshān 〈place〉 Himalaya

【喜怒无常】 xǐnù-wúcháng subject to changing moods

【喜气洋洋】 xǐqì-yángyáng full of joy；jubilant

【喜庆】 xǐqìng 1.（值得庆贺）joyous；jubilant：～的日子 festival days 2.（值得庆贺的事）happy event 3.（庆贺）celebrate

【喜鹊】 xǐ·que 〈*Zool.*〉magpie

【喜人】 xǐrén gratifying；satisfactory

【喜色】 xǐsè happy expression；joyful look

【喜事】 xǐshì 1.（高兴的事）happy event；joyous occasion 2.（结婚）wedding

【喜闻乐见】 xǐwén-lèjiàn love to see and hear；love

【喜笑颜开】 xǐxiào-yánkāi be wreathed in smiles；light up with pleasure

【喜新厌旧】 xǐxīn-yànjiù love the new and loathe the old；be fickle in affection

【喜形于色】 xǐxíngyúsè be visibly pleased；light up with pleasure

【喜讯】 xǐxùn happy news；good news；glad tidings

【喜洋洋】 xǐyángyáng beaming with joy；radiant

【喜雨】 xǐyǔ seasonable rain；a welcome fall of rain

【喜雨植物】 xǐyǔ zhíwù ombrophilous plant

【喜悦】 xǐyuè happy；joyous

戏［戲、戯］（xì） 1.（游戏）play；sport：嬉～ sport；have fun 2.（戏弄）make fun of；joke：～言 say something for fun；joke 3.（戏曲，戏剧）drama；play；show：京～ Beijing opera；Peking opera

【戏词】 xìcí actor's part；actor's lines

【戏单】 xìdān theatrical bill

【戏法】 xìfǎ conjuring；juggling；tricks；magic：变～ perform tricks

【戏剧】 xìjù drama；play；theater：希腊～ the Greek theater

【戏剧编剧】 xìjù biānjù dramaturge; dramaturg
【戏剧工作者】 xìjù gōngzuòzhě people working in the theatrical circles
【戏剧化】 xìjùhuà dramatize; dramatization (n.)
【戏剧家】 xìjùjiā dramatist
【戏剧节】 xìjùjié Drama Day
【戏剧界】 xìjùjiè theatrical circles
【戏剧评论】 xìjù pínglùn dramatic criticism
【戏剧性】 xìjùxìng dramatic: ～场面 a dramatic scene / 一连串～的国际政治事件 the drama of international politics
【戏迷】 xìmí playgoer; theater fan; theatre fan
【戏目】 xìmù theatrical program
【戏弄】 xìnòng make fun of; play tricks on; tease; kid
【戏票】 xìpiào admission ticket for a play
【戏曲】 xìqǔ traditional opera: 地方～ local operas
【戏曲学校】 xìqǔ xuéxiào school of traditional opera
【戏水】 xìshuǐ play with water
【戏台】 xìtái stage
【戏谑】 xìxuè banter; crack jokes
【戏言】 xìyán joke; witticism
【戏院】 xìyuàn theater; theatre
【戏照】 xìzhào a photo of a person in stage costume
【戏装】 xìzhuāng theatrical costume; stage costume

系[係^4,6^、繫^3-5^] (xì) 1.(系统) system; series: 派～ faction 2.(高校院系) department (in a college); faculty: 外语～ foreign language department 3.(关联) relate to; bear on; have a direct bearing on 4.(牵挂) feel anxious; be concerned 5.(栓;绑) tie; fasten: ～马 tether a horse 6.(是) be: 纯～ be purely (另见"系"jì)
【系泊操纵桥楼】 xìbó cāozòng qiáolóu 〈*Naut*.〉 maneuvering bridge
【系词】 xìcí 1.〈*Logic*〉 copula 2.〈*Gram*.〉 copulative verb; linking verb
【系列】 xìliè series; set
【系列化】 xìlièhuà serialize; serialization (n.): ～产品 serialization of products
【系列片】 xìlièpiàn serialized movie; film series: 电视～片 TV series
【系念】 xìniàn be anxious about; worry about; feel concerned about
【系谱】 xìpǔ pedigree
【系谱学】 xìpǔxué genealogy
【系数】 xìshù 〈*Math*.〉 coefficient
【系统】 xìtǒng system; systematic (adj.): ～的选择方案 system alternative
【系统分析】 xìtǒng fēnxī 〈*Computing*〉 systems analysis
【系统工程】 xìtǒng gōngchéng systems engineering
【系统管理】 xìtǒng guǎnlǐ systematic management
【系统化】 xìtǒnghuà systematize; systematization (n.)
【系统性】 xìtǒngxìng systematicness
【系主任】 xìzhǔrèn dean

细 (xì) 1.(跟"粗"相对) thin; slender: ～线 fine thread / 一根～绳子 a thin piece of string 2.(颗粒小) in small particles; fine: ～沙 fine sand 3.(音量小) thin and soft 4.(精细) fine; exquisite; delicate: ～瓷 fine porcelain 5.(仔细;详细) careful; meticulous; detailed: ～看 examine carefully / ～问 ask about details 6.(细微;细小) minute; trifling: 事无巨～ a matters, big and small
【细胞】 xìbāo 〈*Biol*.〉 cell
【细胞壁】 xìbāobì 〈*Biol*.〉 cell wall
【细胞分裂】 xìbāo fēnliè 〈*Biol*.〉 cell division
【细胞构造】 xìbāo gòuzào 〈*Biol*.〉 cell structure
【细胞核】 xìbāohé 〈*Biol*.〉 cell nucleus
【细胞呼吸】 xìbāo hūxī 〈*Biol*.〉 cellular respiration
【细胞免疫】 xìbāo miǎnyì 〈*Biol*.〉 cell-mediated immunity
【细胞膜】 xìbāomó 〈*Biol*.〉 cell membrane
【细胞学】 xìbāoxué cytology
【细胞质】 xìbāozhì 〈*Biol*.〉 cytoplasm
【细长】 xìcháng long and thin; tall and slender
【细纺】 xìfǎng 〈*Textiles*〉 finespun
【细活】 xìhuó a job requiring fine workmanship or meticulous care; skilled work
【细货】 xìhuò small wares
【细嚼慢咽】 xìjiáo-mànyàn take one's time in

eating
【细节】 xìjié details; particulars: 更多～ further details (particulars) / ～上已作必要改动mutatis mutandis (Lat.)
【细菌】 xìjūn germ; bacterium
【细菌肥料】 xìjūn féiliào bacterial fertilizer
【细菌农药】 xìjūn nóngyào bacterial pesticide
【细菌武器】 xìjūn wǔqì bacteriological weapon; germ weapon
【细菌性食物中毒】 xìjūnxìng shíwù zhòngdú bacterial food poisoning
【细菌学】 xìjūnxué bacteriology; bacteriological ‖ 细菌学家 bacteriologist
【细菌战】 xìjūnzhàn bacteriological warfare; germ warfare
【细毛羊】 xìmáoyáng fine-wool sheep
【细密】 xìmì 1.(仔密) fine and closely woven; close 2.(仔细) meticulous; detailed
【细目】 xìmù detailed catalogue; detail; specific item
【细嫩】 xìnèn delicate; tender: ～的皮肤 delicate skin
【细腻】 xìnì 1.(精细光滑) fine and smooth 2.(细致入微) exquisite; minute: ～的描写 a minute description
【细巧】 xìqiǎo fine and delicate; exquisite
【细软】 xìruǎn jewelry, expensive clothing and other valuables
【细弱】 xìruò thin and delicate; slim and fragile
【细纱】 xìshā 〈*Textiles*〉 fine yarn
【细声细气】 xìshēng-xìqì in a soft voice; soft-spoken
【细绳】 xìshéng cord: 包装用～ packing cord
【细水长流】 xìshuǐ-chángliú 1.(使经常不缺) economize to avoid running short 2.(不间断地) go about sth. little by little without a let-up
【细碎】 xìsuì in small, broken bits: ～的脚步 light and hurried steps
【细微】 xìwēi slight; fine; subtle: ～差别 a fine distinction; a subtle difference
【细纹】 xìwén microgroove
【细小】 xìxiǎo very small; tiny; fine; trivial
【细心】 xìxīn careful; attentive
【细则】 xìzé detailed rules and regulations
【细账】 xìzhàng itemized account
【细枝末节】 xìzhī-mòjié minor details; nonessentials
【细致】 xìzhì careful; meticulous; painstaking

隙[隟] (xì) 1.(缝隙) crack; chink; crevice 2.(空闲) gap; interval: 农～ interval between busy seasons in farming 3.(机会) loophole; opportunity: 无～可乘 no loophole to take advantage of 4.(感情裂痕) discord; rift
【隙地】 xìdì unoccupied place; open space
【隙缝】 xìfèn crack; chink; crevice

xia

虾[蝦] (xiā) shrimp; prawn; lobster: 对～ prawn / 磷～ krill / 龙～ lobster
【虾干】 xiāgān dried shrimps
【虾钩】 xiāgóu crawfish hook
【虾酱】 xiājiàng shrimp paste
【虾米】 xiā·mi 1.(干虾仁) dried, shelled shrimps 2.(小虾) small shrimps
【虾皮】 xiāpí dried small shrimps
【虾仁】 xiārén shelled fresh shrimps; shrimp meat
【虾油】 xiāyóu shrimp sauce
【虾子】 xiāzǐ shrimp roe; shrimp eggs

瞎 (xiā) 1.(失明) blind 2.(胡乱) aimlessly; groundlessly; foolishly; to no purpose: ～猜 make a wild guess / ～干 go it blind / ～忙 bustle aimlessly / ～说 speak groundlessly
【瞎扯】 xiāchě 1.(无根据乱说) talk irresponsibly; talk rubbish 2.(无中心乱说) talk at random about anything under the sun; waffle; natter
【瞎胡弄】 xiāhúnòng fuck about; fuck around
【瞎话】 xiāhuà untruth; lie: 说～ lie; talk lies
【瞎闹】 xiānào 1.(胡闹) act senselessly; mess about 2.(无效地做) fool around; be mischievous
【瞎说】 xiāshuō talk irresponsibly; talk rubbish
【瞎子】 xiā·zi a blind person

匣 (xiá) a small box; a small case; casket

【匣子】 xiá·zi a small box; a small case; casket

狎 (xiá) be intimate with but not respectful to sb.

【狎昵】 xiánì be on intimate terms with but not respectful to sb.

侠[俠] (xiá) 1.(侠客) chivalrous person 2.(侠义) chivarlous

【侠客】 xiákè chivalrous expert swordsman

【侠义】 xiáyì chivalry; chivalrous (adj.): ～传奇文学 cloak and sword romance

峡[峽] (xiá) gorge

【峡谷】 xiágǔ gorge; canyon

狭[狹] (xiá) narrow

【狭隘】 xiá'ài 1.(窄) narrow 2.(不宽广;不宏大) narrow and limited; parochial

【狭长】 xiácháng long and narrow

【狭小】 xiáxiǎo narrow and small; narrow

【狭义】 xiáyì narrow sense

【狭窄】 xiázhǎi 1.(宽度小) narrow; cramped 2.(不宏大宽广) narrow and limited; narrow: 心地～ be narrow-minded 3. 〈*Med*.〉 stricture

遐 (xiá) 1.(远) far; distant 2.(长久) lasting; long

【遐迩】 xiá'ěr far and near: 闻名～ be well-known far and near; enjoy widespread renown

【遐龄】 xiálíng advanced age

【遐思】 xiásī reverie; daydream

【遐想】 xiáxiǎng reverie; daydream

瑕 (xiá) 1.(玉石上的斑点) flaw in a piece of jade 2.(缺点) flaw; defect; shortcoming

【瑕不掩瑜】 xiábùyǎnyú one flaw cannot obscure the splendor of the jade; the defects cannot obscure the virtues

【瑕疵】 xiácī flaw; blemish

暇 (xiá) free time; leisure

【暇日】 xiárì days of leisure

【暇时】 xiáshí in one's leisure time

霞 (xiá) rosy clouds; morning or evening glow: 彩～ (the many hues of) rosy clouds

【霞光】 xiáguāng rays of morning or evening sunlight

辖[鎋²、舝] (xiá) 1.(管辖) have jurisdiction over; administer; govern 2.(车辖) linchpin

【辖区】 xiáqū area under one's jurisdiction

黠 (xiá) crafty; sly; cunning

【黠慧】 xiáhuì crafty; sly; cunning

下 (xià) 1.(跟"上"相对) below; down; under; underneath: 树～ under the tree 2.(在后的) next; latter; second: ～册 the last of two or three volumes 3.(等级低的) lower; inferior 4.(向下面) downward; down 5.(由高处到低处) descend; alight; get off: ～床 get out of bed / ～楼 descend the stairs; go or come downstairs / ～山 descend the mountain / 她从公共汽车上～来时,没有任何人在等她。No one was waiting for her when she alighted from the bus. 6.(下达) issue; deliver; send: ～命令 issue orders; give orders 7.(去;到) go to: ～馆子 go and eat in a restaurant; eat out 8.(下场) exit; leave 9.(放入) put in; cast: ～作料 put in the condiments 10.(卸除;取下) take away; take off; dismantle; unload 11.(做出言论、判断等) form (an opinion, idea, etc.): ～定义 give a definition; define / ～决心 grit one's teeth 12.(使用) use; apply: ～力气 put forth strength; make an effort; exert oneself 13.(进行) play: ～棋 play chess 14.(动物生产) give birth to; lay: ～蛋 lay eggs / 龟一次～许多蛋。The turtle lays many eggs at one time. 15.(攻陷) capture; take: 连～数城 have captured several cities in succession 16.(退让) give in; yield: 相持不～ neither side was ready to give in 17.(结束) finish; leave off: ～课 finish class 18.(少于) be less than: 不～3000人 no less than three thousand people

【下巴】 xià·ba 1.(下颌) the lower jaw: 突出的～ lantern jaws 2.(颏) chin

【下摆】 xiàbǎi the lower hem of a dress

【下班】 xiàbān come or go off work; knock off: ～回家 return home after work

【下半场】 xiàbànchǎng 〈*Sports*〉 second half

【下半旗】 xiàbànqí fly a flag at half-mast

【下半时】 xiàbànshí 〈*Sports*〉 second half
【下半天】 xiàbàntiān afternoon
【下半夜】 xiàbànyè after midnight
【下笔】 xiàbǐ put pen to paper; begin to write or paint
【下不来】 xià·bulái **1.**（降不下来）refuse to come down **2.**（不够）cannot be accomplished **3.**（受窘）feel embarrassed
【下不为例】 xiàbùwéilì not to be taken as a precedent; not to be repeated
【下操】 xiàcāo **1.**（出操）have drills **2.**（收操）finish drilling
【下策】 xiàcè a bad plan; an unwise decision; the worst thing to do; a stupid move
【下层】 xiàcéng **1.**（指机构、组织）lower levels **2.**（指阶层）lower strata **3.**（双层公共汽车的）lower deck
【下场】 xiàchǎng **1.**〈*Theatre*〉 go off stage; exit **2.**〈*Sports*〉 leave the playing field **3.**（结局）end; fate: 不会有好～ will certainly come to no good end
【下车】 xiàchē get off a bus
【下沉】 xiàchén **1.**（沉没）sink; submerge **2.**（陷下去）subside; sink; cave in
【下厨】 xiàchú prepare food
【下垂】 xiàchuí **1.**（向下垂）hang down; droop **2.**〈*Med.*〉 prolapse: 胃～ gastroptosis
【下唇】 xiàchún lower lib; inferior labium
【下次】 xiàcì next time; next
【下达】 xiàdá make known to lower levels; transmit to lower levels: ～命令 issue an order
【下单翼单发飞机】 xiàdānyì dānfā fēijī low-wing monoplane
【下蛋】 xiàdàn lay eggs
【下等】 xiàděng low-grade; inferior
【下地】 xiàdì **1.**（到田里去）go to the fields: ～劳动 go to work in the fields **2.**（病人下床）leave a sickbed
【下定义】 xiàdìngyì define; give a definition
【下毒手】 xiàdúshǒu strike a vicious blow; lay murderous hands on sb.
【下颚】 xià'è the lower jaw; mandible
【下饭】 xiàfàn **1.**（就着菜吃）go with rice: 没有菜～。There is no dish to go with rice. **2.**（适宜就饭吃）go well with rice
【下放】 xiàfàng transfer (power) to a lower level: 权力～ transfer power to a lower level / 企业～ put an enterprise under a lower administrative level
【下放干部】 xiàfàng gànbù cadre that has been sent to work in a subordinate unit
【下飞机】 xiàfēijī deplane; get off an aircraft: 请所有旅客从后门～。Would all passengers please deplane by the rear doors.
【下风】 xiàfēng **1.**（风向下方）leeward: 在～的方向 on the leeward **2.**（不利地位）disadvantageous position: 处在～ be in an unfavorable situation
【下腹部】 xiàfùbù lower abdomen
【下岗】 xiàgǎng **1.**（指值勤岗位）come or go off sentry duty **2.**（指工作）be unemployed; be laid off
【下岗工人】 xiàgǎng gōngrén laid-off worker
【下工夫】 xiàgōng·fu put in time and energy; concentrate one's efforts
【下管】 xiàguǎn 〈*Bicycle*〉 down tube
【下跪】 xiàguì kneel down; go down on one's knees
【下海】 xiàhǎi **1.**（出海捕鱼）go to sea; put out to sea **2.**（从商）engage in trade; go to the "business sea" **3.**（票友改当专业演员）turn professional
【下颌】 xiàhé 〈*Anat.*〉 the lower jaw; mandible
【下颌骨】 xiàhégǔ 〈*Anat.*〉 lower jawbone; mandible
【下滑】 xiàhuá gliding; letting down
【下滑道】 xiàhuádào 〈*Naut.*〉 glide path
【下怀】 xiàhuái one's heart's desire: 正中～ be exactly what one wants
【下货】 xiàhuò unload goods; ship goods
【下货费】 xiàhuòfèi unloading hire
【下货港】 xiàhuògǎng unloading port
【下级】 xiàjí **1.**（指组织）lower level **2.**（指人员）subordinate
【下级法院】 xiàjí fǎyuàn court below
【下级干部】 xiàjí gànbù junior cadre
【下级机关】 xiàjí jīguān government office at a lower level
【下级军官】 xiàjí jūnguān low-ranking officer; junior officer
【下级组织】 xiàjí zǔzhī subordinate organiza-

tion

【下加线】 xiàjiāxiàn 〈*Music*〉 leger line

【下贱】 xiàjiàn low; mean; degrading

【下降】 xiàjiàng 1.(降落) descend; go down; come down 2.(降低) go down; come down; drop; fall; decline: 出生率～ a decline in the birth rate

【下脚】 xiàjiǎo 1.(插脚) get a foothold; plant one's foot 2.(下脚料) leftover bits and pieces

【下脚货】 xiàjiǎohuò inferior goods

【下脚料】 xiàjiǎoliào leftover bits and pieces (of industrial material, etc.)

【下脚棉】 xiàjiǎomián cotton waste

【下酒】 xiàjiǔ 1.(就菜喝酒) go with wine 2.(适宜就酒) go well with wine

【下酒菜】 xiàjiǔcài a dish that goes with wine

【下课】 xiàkè get out of class; finish class

【下款】 xiàkuǎn 1.(书画的) name of the donor 2.(信件的) signature at the end of a letter

【下来】 xià·lai 1.(由高到低) come down; light: 旅客们从火车上～。The passengers alighted from the train. 2.(用在动词后) down; off 3.(用在形容词后) get; grow; become

【下联】 xiàlián the second line of a couplet

【下列】 xiàliè listed below; following

【下令】 xiàlìng give orders; order

【下流】 xiàliú 1.(下游) lower reaches (of a river) 2.(卑鄙龌龊) low-down; mean; obscene; dirty: ～话 obscene language; dirty language; obscenities / ～玩笑 dirty jests; obscene jests; coarse jokes

【下落】 xiàluò 1.(人或物的所在) whereabouts: ～不明 not knowing one's whereabouts 2.(下降) drop; fall

【下马】 xiàmǎ 1.(从马上下来) get down from a horse; dismount from a horse 2.(工程停止) discontinue; abandon

【下马威】 xiàmǎwēi severity shown by an official on assuming office

【下面】 xià·mian 1.(位置低的) below; under; underneath 2.(后面的) next; following 3.(下级) lower level; subordinate

【下品】 xiàpǐn low-grade; inferior

【下坡】 xiàpó downhill

【下坡路】 xiàpólù 1.(指道路) downhill road 2.(比喻) decline: 走～ be on the decline

【下铺】 xiàpù lower berth

【下棋】 xiàqí play chess; have a game of chess

【下欠】 xiàqiàn 1.(尚欠) still owing 2.(欠的款项) a sum still owing

【下腔静脉】 xiàqiāng jìngmài 〈*Anat.*〉 inferior vena cava

【下情】 xiàqíng conditions at the lower levels; feelings or wishes of the masses: ～上达 make the situation at the lower levels known to the higher levels

【下去】 xià·qù 1.(由高往低) go down; descend 2.(用在动词后,表示由高到低) down: 太阳落～了。The sun went down. 3.(用在动词后,表示继续) on 4.(用在形容词后,表示程度继续增加) get; grow; become

【下身】 xiàshēng 1.(身体下部) the lower part of the body 2.(阴部) private parts 3.(裤子) trousers

【下士】 xiàshì 1.(陆军) Corporal 2.(空军) Air Corporal 3.(海军) Petty Officer Third Class

【下手】 xiàshǒu 1.(动手;着手) put one's hand to; start; set about; set to: 不知如何～ no know what to start 2.(下首座位) right-hand seat 3.(助手) assistant; helper

【下首】 xiàshǒu right-hand seat

【下属】 xiàshǔ subordinate

【下水】 xiàshuǐ 1.(进入水中) be launched; enter the water: (使)船～ launch a ship 2.(做坏事) take to evildoing; fall into evil ways: 拖人～ involve sb. in evildoing; entice sb. into evildoing 3.(向下游航行) down-river; downstream: ～船 downriver boat

【下水】 xià·shui offal: 猪～ pig's offal

【下水道】 xiàshuǐdào sewer; drainage

【下水道总管】 xiàshuǐdào zǒngguǎn combined sewer

【下榻】 xiàtà stay at (a place during a trip)

【下台】 xiàtái 1.(下舞台或讲台) step down from the stage or platform 2.(卸去公职) fall out of power; leave office: 被赶～ be driven out of office; be thrown out 3.(多用否定式,比喻摆脱窘境) get out of a predicament or an embarrassing situation

【下体】 xiàtǐ **1.**（身体下部）the lower part of the body **2.**（阴部）private parts
【下同】 xiàtóng （多用于附注）similarly hereinafter; the same below
【下文】 xiàwén **1.**（文章的）what follows in the passage, paragraph, article, etc. **2.**（事情的）what follows; outcome; sequel; later development：不见～ sequel unknown
【下午】 xiàwǔ afternoon：在～ in the afternoon; during the afternoon / 今天～ this afternoon / 星期一～ on Monday afternoon
【下弦】 xiàxián 〈*Astron*.〉 last quarter; third quarter
【下弦月】 xiàxiányuè the moon at the third quarter
【下限】 xiàxiàn lower limit; prescribed minimum; floor level; floor
【下乡】 xiàxiāng go to the countryside
【下行】 xiàxíng **1.**〈*Railway*〉 down：～列车 down train **2.**（指航运）downriver; downstream **3.**（指公文）to be issued to the lower levels
【下旬】 xiàxún the last ten-day period of a month
【下眼睑】 xiàyǎnjiǎn 〈*Anat*.〉 lower eyelid
【下药】 xiàyào **1.**（医生用药）prescribe medicine **2.**（下毒药）put in poison
【下野】 xiàyě retire from the political arena; be forced to relinquish power
【下义词】 xiàyìcí hyponym
【下议院】 xiàyìyuàn **1.**（众议院）lower house **2.**（英国下院）the House of Commons
【下意识】 xiàyìshí subconsciousness
【下游】 xiàyóu **1.**（河流下游）lower reaches **2.**（落后的地位）backward position
【下狱】 xiàyù throw into prison; imprison
【下月】 xiàyuè prox., proximo
【下葬】 xiàzàng bury; inter
【下肢】 xiàzhī lower limbs; legs
【下种】 xiàzhǒng sow (seeds)
【下装】 xiàzhuāng remove theatrical makeup and costume

吓［嚇］(xià) frightened; scare; intimidate：～得发抖 be trembling with fright / 一看到这恐怖场面，我们完全～呆了。We were completely aghast at the terrible sight.
【吓唬】 xià·hu frighten; scare; intimidate
【吓坏】 xiàhuài terrify：雷声把孩子～了。The thunder terrified the child.
【吓人】 xiàrén terrible

夏 (xià) summer
【夏季】 xiàjì summer; summertime
【夏历】 xiàlì the traditional Chinese calendar; the lunar calendar
【夏粮】 xiàliáng summer grain crops
【夏令】 xiàlìng **1.**（夏季）summer; summertime **2.**（夏季气候）summer weather
【夏令商品】 xiàlìng shāngpǐn commodities for summer use
【夏令时】 xiàlìngshí daylight saving time; summer time
【夏令营】 xiàlìngyíng summer camp
【夏收】 xiàshōu **1.**（指收获）summer harvest **2.**（指收成）crops harvested in summer
【夏天】 xiàtiān summer
【夏衣】 xiàyī summer clothing; summer wear
【夏至】 Xiàzhì the Summer Solstice
【夏至点】 xiàzhìdiǎn 〈*Astron*.〉 summer solstice
【夏装】 xiàzhuāng summer clothes

xian

仙［僊］(xiān) celestial being; immortal
【仙丹】 xiāndān elixir of life; cure-all
【仙姑】 xiāngū **1.**（仙女）female immortal; female celestial **2.**（女巫）sorceress
【仙鹤】 xiānhè red-crowned crane
【仙境】 xiānjìng fairyland; wonderland; paradise
【仙女】 xiānnǚ female celestial; fairy maiden
【仙人】 xiānrén celestial being; immortal
【仙人掌】 xiānrénzhǎng 〈*Bot*.〉 cactus
【仙逝】 xiānshì pass away

氙 (xiān)〈*Chem*.〉 xenon（元素符号 Xe）
【氙灯】 xiāndēng xenon lamp

籼［秈］(xiān)
【籼稻】 xiāndào long-grained nonglutinous rice; indica rice

【籼米】 xiānmǐ polished long-grained non-glutinous rice

先 (xiān) **1**. (在前的) earlier; before; first; in advance: ～富起来 become prosperous first **2**. (祖先) elder generation; ancestor: 祖～ ancestor; forefather **3**. (尊称死者) deceased; late: ～父 my late father **4**. (先前) earlier on; before

【先辈】 xiānbèi elder generation; ancestors: ～遗训 teachings of our ancestors

【先导】 xiāndǎo guide; forerunner; precursor

【先睹为快】 xiāndǔ-wéikuài consider it a pleasure to be among the first to read or see sth.

【先发制人】 xiānfā-zhìrén gain the initiative by striking first; forestall the enemy

【先锋】 xiānfēng vanguard; van

【先锋队】 xiānfēngduì vanguard

【先后】 xiānhòu **1**. (先和后) early or late; priority; order **2**. (前后相继) successively; one after another

【先见之明】 xiānjiàn-zhīmíng prophetic vision; foresight; ability to discern what is coming

【先进】 xiānjìn advanced: ～思想 advanced ideas / 吸取～技术 utilize the advanced technology

【先进工作者】 xiānjìn gōngzuòzhě advanced worker

【先进先出】 xiānjìn-xiānchū 〈*Econ.*〉 first-in first-out

【先决】 xiānjué prerequisite: ～条件 prerequisite; precondition

【先礼后兵】 xiānlǐ-hòubīng take strong measures only after courteous ones fail; try peaceful means before resorting to force

【先例】 xiānlì precedent: 开～ create a precedent; set a precedent / 无～可循 have no precedent to go by

【先烈】 xiānliè martyr

【先期】 xiānqī earlier on; in advance: ～到达 have arrived at an earlier date

【先期录制】 xiānqī lùzhì pre-record

【先前】 xiānqián before; previously

【先遣】 xiānqiǎn sent in advance

【先遣部队】 xiānqiǎn bùduì advance force; advance army unit

【先驱】 xiānqū pioneer; forerunner; harbinger

【先人】 xiānrén **1**. (祖先) ancestor; forefather **2**. (已故父亲) my late father

【先人后己】 xiānrén-hòujǐ put others before oneself; put other people's interest ahead of one's own

【先入为主】 xiānrù-wéizhǔ first impressions are strongest; preconceived ideas keep a strong hold; be prejudiced

【先声夺人】 xiānshēng-duórén forestall one's opponent by a show of strength; overawe others by displaying one's strength

【先生】 xiān·sheng **1**. (老师) teacher **2**. (称呼) mister (Mr.); gentleman; sir: 有位～要见您。A gentleman has called to see you. / ～们, 请肃静! Gentlemen, be quiet please! **3**. (医生) doctor

【先天】 xiāntiān **1**. (生来就有的) congenital; inborn: ～不足 be congenitally deficient; suffer from an inherent shortage **2**. 〈*Philos.*〉 a priori; innate

【先天性心脏病】 xiāntiānxìng xīnzhàngbìng congenital heart disease

【先头】 xiāntóu **1**. (位置在前) ahead; in advance; in front: ～部队 an advance army unit **2**. (以前) before; formerly; in the past

【先下手为强】 xiān xiàshǒu wéi qiáng he who strikes first gains the advantage; take the initiative is to gain the upper hand

【先行】 xiānxíng **1**. (走在其他人的前面) go ahead of the rest; start off before the others **2**. (预先准备) before-hand; in advance: ～通知 notify in advance

【先行者】 xiānxíngzhě forerunner

【先验】 xiānyàn 〈*Philos.*〉 a priori

【先验论】 xiānyànlùn apriorism

【先兆】 xiānzhào omen; portent; sign; indication

【先哲】 xiānzhé a great thinker of the past; sage

【先知】 xiānzhī **1**. (先知先觉的人) a person of foresight **2**. 〈*Religion*〉 prophet

【先知先觉】 xiānzhī-xiānjué **1**. (先知) a person of foresight **2**. (有预见) having foresight

酰 (xiān) acyl

【酰基】 xiānjí acyl group

纤［纖］(xiān) fine; minute (另见“纤”qiàn)

【纤尘】 xiānchén fine dust

【纤巧】 xiānqiǎo dainty; delicate

【纤柔】 xiānróu fine and soft

【纤弱】 xiānruò slim and fragile; delicate

【纤维】 xiānwéi fiber; staple: 合成～ synthetic fiber / 人造～ man-made fiber; artificial fiber / 天然～ natural fiber

【纤维板】 xiānwéibǎn fiberboard

【纤维长度】 xiānwéi chángdù fiber length; staple

【纤维蛋白】 xiānwéi dànbái fibrin

【纤维镜】 xiānwéijìng fiberscope

【纤维瘤】 xiānwéiliú 〈*Med.*〉 fibroma

【纤维植物】 xiānwéi zhíwù fiber plant

【纤细】 xiānxì very thin; slender; fine; tenuous

【纤小】 xiānxiǎo fine; tenuous

掀 (xiān) lift: ～帘子 lift the curtain

【掀动】 xiāndòng lift; start; set in motion

【掀起】 xiānqǐ **1.**(揭起) lift; raise **2.**(翻腾) surge; cause to surge **3.**(大规模兴起) set off; start

锨［杴、鍁］(xiān) shovel

祆 (xiān)

【祆教】 Xiānjiào 〈*Religion*〉 Zoroastrianism; Zoroastrian (*adj.*) ‖ 祆教教徒 Zoroastrian

鲜 (xiān) **1.**(新鲜) fresh: ～蛋 fresh eggs / ～蘑 fresh mushrooms / ～奶 fresh milk / ～肉 fresh meat **2.**(鲜明) bright-colored; bright: ～红色 bright red; scarlet **3.**(鲜美) delicious; tasty: ～汤 delicious soup / ～味 delicate flavor **4.**(鲜美的食物) delicacy: 时～ delicacies of the season **5.**(鱼虾等水产) aquatic foods: 海～ seafood
(另见“鲜”xiǎn)

【鲜果】 xiānguǒ fresh fruit

【鲜红】 xiānhóng bright red

【鲜花】 xiānhuā fresh flowers; flowers: 一束～ a bundle of fresh flowers

【鲜活货物】 xiānhuó huòwù live cargo

【鲜货】 xiānhuò **1.**(新鲜蔬菜水果) fresh fruit or vegetables **2.**(新鲜鱼虾) fresh aquatic foods

【鲜橘水】 xiānjúshuǐ orange squash

【鲜美】 xiānměi delicious; tasty

【鲜明】 xiānmíng **1.**(颜色明亮) bright: 色彩～ in bright colors; bright-colored **2.**(显著) clear-cut; distinct; distinctive: ～的对照 a striking contrast; a sharp contrast

【鲜嫩】 xiānnèn fresh and tender

【鲜血】 xiānxuè blood

【鲜艳】 xiānyàn bright-colored; gaily-colored: ～夺目 dazzlingly beautiful; resplendent

闲［閒］(xián) **1.**(没闲暇) not busy; idle; unoccupied **2.**(未使用) not in use; unoccupied; lying idle: ～房 unoccupied room; vacant room; unoccupied house; vacant house **3.**(闲空儿) spare time; free time; leisure

【闲扯】 xiánchě chat; engage in chitchat

【闲工夫】 xiángōng·fu spare time; free time; leisure

【闲逛】 xiánguàng saunter; stroll; loiter: 回家时在路上～ loiter on one's way home

【闲话】 xiánhuà **1.**(无用的话) digression **2.**(不满意的话) complaint **3.**(搬弄是非的话) gossip

【闲空】 xiánkòng free time; spare time; leisure

【闲聊】 xiánliáo chat; gossip: 他们整晚上坐着～。They sat and gossiped all evening.

【闲气】 xiánqì anger about trifles

【闲情逸致】 xiánqíng-yìzhì leisurely and carefree mood; leisure and mood for enjoyments

【闲人】 xiánrén **1.**(无工作的) an unoccupied person; idler **2.**(无关的) persons not concerned: ～免进。No admittance except on business.

【闲散】 xiánsǎn **1.**(无事可做的) free and at leisure; at a loose end **2.**(闲着不用的) unused; idle: ～劳力 idle labor / ～土地 scattered plots of unutilized land

【闲散资金】 xiánsǎn zījīn idle capital; idle funds; scattered funds

【闲事】 xiánshì **1.**(与己无关的) a matter that does not concern one; other people's business: 管～ mind other people's business;

poke one's nose into other's business 2.(无关紧要的) unimportant matter

【闲书】 xiánshū light reading

【闲谈】 xiántán chat; engage in chitchat

【闲暇】 xiánxiá leisure

【闲心】 xiánxīn leisurely mood

【闲杂】 xiázá without fixed duties

【闲杂人员】 xiánzá rényuán people without fixed duties; miscellaneous and idle personnel

【闲置】 xiánzhì leave unused; let sth. lie idle; set aside

【闲置人员】 xiánzhì rényuán laid-off workers; unemployed

【闲置设备】 xiánzhì shèbèi idle equipment; idle facilities

【闲置资金】 xiánzhì zījīng idle funds

娴[嫻](xián) 1.(文雅) refined 2.(熟练) adept; skilled

【娴静】 xiánjìng gentle and refined

【娴熟】 xiánshú adept; skilled: 技术~ adept in skills

【娴雅】 xiányǎ (of a woman) refined; elegant

贤[賢](xián) 1.(贤德) virtuous; worthy; able: 任人唯~ appoint people on their merits 2.(贤能) a worthy person; an able and virtuous person: 让~ relinquish one's post in favor of sb. better qualified

【贤达】 xiándá prominent personage; worthy: 社会~ social alite

【贤惠】 xiánhuì virtuous

【贤良】 xiánliáng 1.(有贤德) able and virtuous 2.(贤能) a worthy person; an able and virtuous person

【贤明】 xiánmíng wise and able; sagacious

【贤能】 xiánnéng a worthy person; an able and virtuous person

【贤妻良母】 xiánqī liángmǔ a good wife and loving mother

【贤人】 xiánrén a person of virtue; worthy

【贤士】 xiánshì a person of virtue; worthy

弦[絃[2]](xián) 1.(弓弦) bowstring; string 2.(乐弦) the string of a musical instrument 3.(钟表发条) spring 4.(圆周上的连线) chord 5.(直角三角形斜边) hypotenuse

【弦外之音】 xiánwàizhīyīn implied meaning; implications

【弦乐队】 xiányuèduì string orchestra; string band

【弦乐器】 xiányuèqì stringed instrument: 弓~ bowed stringed instruments/ 拨~ plucked instruments/ 击~ hammered string instruments

【弦桥】 xiánqiáo 〈*Music*〉 bridge; bridge bone; saddle

【弦枕】 xiánzhěn 〈*Music*〉 capo

【弦轴】 xiánzhōu 〈*Music*〉 peg; screw

【弦轴箱】 xiánzhōuxiáng 〈*Music*〉 pegbox

舷(xián) the side of a ship; board: 右~ starboard / 左~ port

【舷边】 xiánbiān gunwale; gunnel

【舷窗】 xiánchuāng 1.(船舶的) porthole; hole 2.(飞机的) side window

【舷梯】 xiántī 1.(船舶的) gangway ladder; accommodation ladder 2.(飞机的) ramp

【舷外发动机】 xiánwài fādòngjī outboard motor

【舷外浮木】 xiánwài fúmù outrigger

咸[鹹[1]](xián) 1.(咸味) salted; salty: ~蛋 salted egg / ~鱼 salt fish 2.(全;都) all: 老少~宜。Good for the old and the young.

【咸菜】 xiáncài salted vegetables; pickles

【咸肉】 xiánròu salt meat; bacon

【咸受其益】 xiánshòuqīyì All benefited from it.

【咸水】 xiánshuǐ salt water: salt-water (adj.)

【咸水湖】 xiánshuǐhú saltwater lake

【咸味】 xiánwèi saline taste

【咸盐】 xiányán salt

涎(xián) saliva

【涎水】 xiánshuǐ saliva

衔[啣[1,2]](xián) 1.(用嘴含) hold in the mouth 2.(存在心里) harbor; bear a grudge 3.(级别) rank; title: 公使~参赞 counsellor with rank of minister

【衔接】 xiánjiē link up; join; connect

【衔冤】 xiányuān nurse a bitter sense of wrong; have a simmering sense of injustice

嫌(xián) 1.(嫌疑) suspicion: 避~ avoid suspicion / 涉~ on sus 2.(嫌怨) enmity;

ill will; resentment; grudge: 尽释前～ remove all previous ill 3.(厌恶) dislike; mind; complain of: ～麻烦 not want to take the trouble; think it troublesome

【嫌弃】 xiánqì dislike and avoid; cold-shoulder

【嫌恶】 xiánwù detest; loathe; disgust

【嫌隙】 xiánxì feeling of animosity; enmity; ill will; grudge

【嫌疑】 xiányí suspicion: 有～ on sus

【嫌疑犯】 xiányífàn suspect

【嫌疑分子】 xiányí fènzǐ suspected person; marked man

【嫌怨】 xiányuàn grudge; resentment; enmity

铣 (xiǎn)
(另见"铣"xǐ)

【铣铁】 xiǎntiě cast iron

显［顯］(xiǎn) 1.(明显) apparent; obvious; noticeable 她的黑头发更～出她皮肤白皙。Her black hair accentuated the whiteness of her skin. 2.(表现) show; display; manifest: ～身扬名 show one's mettle and make a name 3.(显赫的) illustrious and influential

【显得】 xiǎn·de look; seem; appear: 她～很疲劳。She appears very tired.

【显而易见】 xiǎn'éryìjiàn obviously; evidently; clearly: 答案是～的。The correct answer is apparent.

【显贵】 xiǎnguì high official in ancient times

【显赫】 xiǎnhè illustrious; celebrated; powerful: ～一时 celebrated for a while / ～的战功 illustrious war exploits

【显见】 xiǎnjiàn obvious; self-evident; apparent

【显露】 xiǎnlù become visible; appear; manifest itself: ～头角 show one's promises

【显明】 xiǎnmíng obvious; manifest; distinct; marked

【显然】 xiǎnrán obvious; evident; clear; patent: 他～是在说谎。He was patently lying.

【显色】 xiǎnsè coloration

【显色管】 xiǎnsèguǎn chromoscope

【显示】 xiǎnshì 1.(明显表示) show; display; demonstrate; manifest: 温度计～26 摄氏度。The thermometer gives 26℃. 2.〈*Petroleum*〉 show; indication

【显示器】 xiǎnshìqì display: 彩色～ color display

【显微镜】 xiǎnwēijìng microscope

【显微外科】 xiǎnwēi wàikē 〈*Med.*〉 microsurgery

【显现】 xiǎnxiàn manifest oneself; reveal oneself; appear; show

【显像管】 xiǎnxiàngguǎn 〈*Electr.*〉 kinescope; picture tube: 彩色～ tricolor tube

【显形】 xiǎnxíng show one's (true) colors; betray oneself

【显性】 xiǎnxìng 〈*Biol.*〉 dominance; dominant (adj.): ～基因 dominant gene / ～性状 dominant character

【显眼】 xiǎnyǎn conspicuous; perceptible; showy

【显要】 xiǎnyào 1.(官职高、权力大) powerful and influential: ～人物 an influential figure 2.(官职高、权力大的人) influential figure; important personage; VIP

【显影】 xiǎnyǐng 〈*Photog.*〉 develop

【显影过度】 xiǎnyǐng guòdù 〈*Photog.*〉 overdevelop

【显影机】 xiǎnyǐngjī 〈*Photog.*〉 developing machine

【显著】 xiǎnzhù notable; marked; striking; remarkable; outstanding

险［險］(xiǎn) 1.(危险) danger; peril; risk; dangerous (adj.): 冒～ run a risk 2.(险要) a place difficult of access; narrow pass; defile: 天～ natural barrier 3.(阴险) sinister; vicious; venomous 4.(险些) by a hair's breadth; by inches; nearly: ～遭毒手 was nearly killed

【险隘】 xiǎn'ài strategic pass; defile

【险地】 xiǎndì 1.(险要所在) narrow pass; strategically located and difficult of access 2.(危险处境) risky situation: 处于～ be in risky situation

【险恶】 xiǎn'è 1.(凶险可怕) dangerous; perilous; ominous 2.(邪恶的;恶毒的) sinister; vicious; malicious; treacherous

【险峰】 xiǎnfēng perilous peak

【险关】 xiǎnguān narrow pass

【险境】 xiǎnjìng dangerous situation

【险峻】 xiǎnjùn 1.(山势高险) dangerously steep; precipitous 2.(危险严峻) seriously dangerous

【险区】 xiǎnqū danger zone

【险胜】 xiǎnshèng win by a narrow margin

【险滩】 xiǎntān dangerous shoal; rapids

【险象环生】 xiǎnxiàng-huánshēng signs of danger appearing everywhere

【险些】 xiǎnxiē narrowly; nearly

【险要】 xiǎnyào strategically located and difficult of access

【险阻】 xiǎnzǔ (of roads) dangerous and difficult

蚬 (xiǎn) 〈*Zool.*〉 Corbicula leana

鲜[尟、尠] (xiǎn) little; rare: ～见 rarely seen; seldom met with
(另见"鲜"xiān)

藓 (xiǎn) 〈*Bot.*〉 moss

苋 (xiàn) 〈*Bot.*〉 amaranth

【苋菜】 xiàncài three-colored amaranth; flower gentle

现[见[5]] (xiàn) 1.(现在) present; current; existing: ～况 the existing situation; the present situation / ～政府 present government 2.(临时) (do sth.) in time of need; extempore 3.(手头上有的) on hand: ～金 ready money; cash 4.(现款) cash; ready money: 付～ pay cash 5.(露出) show; appear: ～形 reveal one's true colors

【现场】 xiànchǎng 1.(出事地点) scene: 作案～ the scene of a crime 2.(工作地点) site; spot: 工作～ worksite / 试验～ testing ground

【现场表演】 xiànchǎng biǎoyǎn on-the-spot demonstration

【现场采访】 xiànchǎng cǎifǎng spot coverage

【现场查验】 xiànchǎng cháyàn view of the scene

【现场会议】 xiànchǎng huìyì on-the-spot meeting; on-sit meeting

【现场试验】 xiànchǎng shìyàn field-test

【现场消息】 xiànchǎng xiāoxī spot news

【现场演示】 xiànchǎng yǎnshì on-the-spot demonstration

【现场指导】 xiànchǎng zhǐdǎo on-the-spot guidance

【现成】 xiànchéng ready-made

【现成饭】 xiànchéngfàn cooked meal; gains without pains

【现出】 xiànchū reveal; display

【现存】 xiàncún extant; in stock

【现代】 xiàndài 1.(指现在所处时代) modern times; the contemporary age 2.(现代的) modern; contemporary: ～交通工具 modern means of communication / ～科学成就 modern scientific achievements

【现代化】 xiàndàihuà modernize; bring up to date; modernization (n.): 实现四个～ achieve the four modernizations (of agriculture, industry, national defense, and science and technology)

【现代化大都会】 xiàndàihuà dàdūhuì metropolis

【现代化设备】 xiàndàihuà shèbèi sophisticated equipment

【现代派】 xiàndàipài modernist school

【现代史】 xiàndàishǐ contemporary history

【现付】 xiànfù ready-money

【现货】 xiànhuò 〈*Trade*〉 merchandise on hand; spots

【现货供应】 xiànhuò gōngyìng off the shelf

【现货价格】 xiànhuò jiàgé spot price

【现货交易】 xiànhuò jiāoyì over-the-counter trading; spot transaction

【现货市场】 xiànhuò shìchǎng spot market

【现价】 xiànjià present price

【现今】 xiànjīn nowadays; these days

【现金】 xiànjīn 1.(现款) ready money; cash: 出售时收～ sell for cash; cash sale 2.(银行库存) cash reserve in a bank

【现金出纳机】 xiànjīn chūnàjī cash register

【现金付款】 xiànjīn fùkuǎn cash payment; payment in cash

【现金交易】 xiànjīn jiāoyì cash transaction

【现金收入】 xiànjīn shōurù cash receipts

【现金余额】 xiànjīn yú'é cash balance

【现金预算】 xiànjīn yùsuàn cash budget

【现金账】 xiànjīnzhàng cash account; cash book

【现金折扣】 xiànjīn zhékòu cash discount

【现金支出】 xiànjīn zhīchū out-of-pocket expenses

【现金支付】 xiànjīn zhīfù pay in cash
【现款】 xiànkuǎn ready money; cash
【现款交易】 xiànkuǎn jiāoyì bargain on spot; ready money business
【现买现卖】 xiànmǎi-xiànmài hand-to-mouth buying
【现钱】 xiànqián ready money; cash
【现任】 xiànrèn 1.(现在担任) at present hold the office of: 她～公司经理。At present she holds the position of company manager. 2.(现在任职的) currently in office; incumbent: ～校长是吴教授。The present president is Professor Wu.
【现时】 xiànshí now; at present
【现时购买力】 xiànshí gòumǎilì current purchasing power (CPP)
【现实】 xiànshí 1.(客观存在) reality; actuality 2.(合乎情况的) real; actual
【现实主义】 xiànshí zhǔyì realism; realistic (adj.) ‖ 现实主义者 realist
【现实主义文学】 xiànshí zhǔyì wénxué realistic literature
【现世】 xiànshì 1.(今生) this life 2.(出丑) lose face; be disgraced; bring shame on oneself
【现象】 xiànxiàng appearance; phenomenon: 社会～ social phenomenon
【现行】 xiànxíng 1.(现正有效的) currently in effect; in force; in operation: ～政策 present policies 2.(正在进行的) active
【现行法】 xiànxíngfǎ laws in effect
【现行犯】 xiànxíngfàn criminal caught in the act
【现行利率】 xiànxíng lìlǜ prevailing rate of interest
【现行罪】 xiànxíngzuì flagrant crime
【现形】 xiànxíng reveal one's true features; betray oneself
【现眼】 xiànyǎn make a spectacle of oneself; lose face
【现役】 xiànyì 1.(所服兵役) active service; active duty: 服～ be on active service 2.(正在服役的) on active service; on active duty; active: ～兵员 personnel on active service / ～军队 active military unit
【现役军官】 xiànyì jūnguān officer on the active list
【现役军人】 xiànyì jūnrén serviceman
【现有】 xiànyǒu now available; existing
【现在】 xiànzài now; at present; today
【现职】 xiànzhí present job; current post; present employment
【现值】 xiànzhí present value
【现住人口】 xiànzhù rénkǒu de facto population
【现状】 xiànzhuàng present situation; current situation; status quo; existing state of affairs: 改变～ change the status quo 维持～ maintain the status quo

县[縣] (xiàn) county
【县城】 xiànchéng county seat; county town
【县委】 xiànwěi county Party committee
【县长】 xiànzhǎng the head of a county; county magistrate
【县志】 xiànzhì general records of a county; county annals

限 (xiàn) 1.(范围;限度) limit; bounds 2.(指定范围) set a limit; limit; restrict
【限定】 xiàndìng prescribe a limit to; set a limit to; limit; restrict: ～价格 limit price
【限度】 xiàndù limit; limitation: 最大～ maximum; extreme limit / 我将有～地帮助你。I'm willing to help you, within limits.
【限额】 xiàn'é norm; limit; quota: 最大～ utmost limit / 最高～ maximum limit; top limit / 规定～ fix up quota
【限额抵押】 xiàn'é dǐyā closed mortgage
【限额交易】 xiàn'é jiāoyì rationed exchange
【限额输出】 xiàn'é shūchū ration export
【限价】 xiànjià 1.(现定价格) set a limit to the prices 2.(该价格) the fixed price
【限量】 xiànliàng 1.(限定数量) limit the quantity of; set bounds to 2.(限度) limit; limitation
【限令】 xiànlìng order sb. to do sth. within a certain time
【限期】 xiànqī 1.(限定日期) within a definite time; set a time limit 2.(限定的日期) time limit; deadline
【限速】 xiànsù speed limit: 这里～是多少? What is the speed limit?
【限于】 xiànyú be confined to; be limited to: ～水平 owing to one's limitation

【限制】 xiànzhì place restrictions on; impose restrictions on; restrict; limit; confine: ～数量 limit to a number or amount / 任何人都不能～你的合法权利。No one can abridge your legal rights. / 国家应～土地开发。The nation must limit land development.

【限制分配】 xiànzhì fēnpèi restricted distribution

【限制认付】 xiànzhì rènfù qualified acceptance

【限制物品】 xiànzhì wùpǐn restricted item

【限制性】 xiànzhìxìng restricted; restrictive: ～定语 restrictive attribute

【限制性条款】 xiànzhìxìng tiáokuǎn proviso

【限制战略武器谈判】 xiànzhì zhànlüè wǔqì tánpàn Strategic Arms Limitation Talks (SALT)

线[綫、線] (xiàn) 1.(各种线) thread; string; wire: ～团 a ball of string; a reel of thread/ 电话～ telephone lines / 钓鱼～ fishing lines 2.〈*Math.*〉 line: 平行～ parallel lines / 直～ straight line / 虚～ a dotted line / 从 A 到 B 画一条～。Draw a line from A to B. / 在拼写错了的词下面画一条～。Draw a line under the misspelled words. 3.(用棉线做的) made of cotton thread: ～毯 cotton blanket 4.(交通路线) route; line: 干～ the main line / 支～ a branch line / 铁路～ railway line 5.(边界线) demarcation line; boundary: 边界～ boundary line 6.(某种边际) brink; verge: 死亡～ the verge of death

【线材】 xiàncái wire rod

【线段】 xiànduàn 〈*Math.*〉 line segment

【线路】 xiànlù 1.〈*Electr.*〉 circuit; line 2.〈*Transport*〉 line; route: 航空～ airline

【线路图】 xiànlùtú 〈*Electr.*〉 circuit diagram

【线圈】 xiànquān 〈*Electr.*〉 coil

【线绳】 xiànshéng cotton rope

【线人】 xiànrén reporter

【线索】 xiànsuǒ clue; lead; thread: 提供～ give a clue / 警方没有一点～。The police haven't a single lead.

【线毯】 xiàntǎn cotton blanket

【线条】 xiàntiáo 1.〈*Arts*〉 line 2.(人体等的) lines: ～优美 of fine lines

【线条画】 xiàntiáohuà line drawing

【线头】 xiàntóu 1.(线的一端) the end of a thread 2.(短线) an odd piece of thread

【线团】 xiàntuán a reel of thread

【线务员】 xiànwùyuán lineman

【线闸】 xiànzhā 〈*Bicycle*〉 cable brake

【线装本】 xiànzhuāngběn 〈*Printing*〉 thread-bound edition

【线装书】 xiànzhuāngshū thread-bound Chinese book

宪[憲] (xiàn) 1.(法令) statute 2.(宪法) constitution: 制～ draw up a constitution

【宪兵】 xiànbīng military police; military policeman; gendarme

【宪兵队】 xiànbīngduì military police corps; gendarmerie

【宪法】 xiànfǎ constitution; charter

【宪章】 xiànzhāng charter: 联合国～ the United States Charter

【宪政】 xiànzhèng constitutional government; constitutionalism

陷 (xiàn) 1.(陷阱) pitfall; trap 2.(掉进;陷入) get stuck; get bogged down 3.(凹进) sink; cave in 4.(陷害) frame sb. up; incriminate sb. 5.(被攻占;被占领) be captured; fall 6.(缺点) defect; deficiency: 缺～ defect; flaw

【陷害】 xiànhài frame up; make a false charge against: ～好人 frame up an innocent person

【陷阱】 xiànjǐng 1.(捕猎用的) pitfall; pit; trap 2.(阴谋) frame-up

【陷坑】 xiànkēng pitfall; pit

【陷落】 xiànluò 1.(下陷) subside; sink in; cave in: 地壳的～ subsidence of the earth's crust 2.(沦陷) fall into enemy's hands

【陷入】 xiànrù 1.(落到不利境地) sink into; fall into; land oneself in; be caught in; get bogged down in: ～僵局 come to a deadlock; reach an impasse / ～绝境 sink into a deadlock / ～麻烦 get into: get into trouble / ～债务中 get into debt 2.(深深进入) be lost in; be immersed in; be deep in: ～沉思 be lost in thought; be deep in meditation

【陷于】 xiànyú fall into; sink into: ～孤立 be isolated / ～困境 be on a sticky wicket

馅 (xiàn) filling; stuffing

【馅儿饼】 xiànrbǐng meat pie

羡［羨］(xiàn) admire; envy

【羡慕】 xiànmù admire; be envious of：我非常～你的新车。I'm very envious of your new car.

腺 (xiàn) gland：乳～ mammary gland

【腺切除术】 xiànqiēchúshù 〈*Med.*〉 adenectomy; adenotomy

献［獻］(xiàn) 1.（奉献）offer; present; dedicate; donate：～花圈 lay a wreath 2.（表现）show; put on; display

【献宝】 xiànbǎo 1.（献宝物）present a treasure 2.（提出好建议等）offer a valuable piece of advice or one's valuable experience 3.（拿出给人看）show off what one treasures

【献策】 xiàncè offer advice; make suggestions

【献词】 xiàncí congratulatory message

【献花】 xiànhuā present a bouquet to ...

【献计】 xiànjì offer advice; make suggestions

【献技】 xiànjì show one's skill

【献礼】 xiànlǐ present a gift

【献媚】 xiànmèi try to ingratiate oneself with; make up to

【献身】 xiànshēn devote oneself to; dedicate oneself to; give one's life for：～于四个现代化 devote oneself to the four modernizations

【献血】 xiànxuè donate blood; blood donation (n.)：无偿～ blood donated gratis; blood donated gratuitously

【献血者】 xiànxuèzhě blood donor

【献殷勤】 xiàn yīnqín show sb. excessive attentions; pay one's addresses：他在舞会上对女人大～。He was very gallant at the ball.

霰 (xiàn)〈*Meteorol.*〉 graupel

【霰弹】 xiàndàn shrapnel; canister

xiang

乡［鄉］(xiāng) 1.（乡下）country; countryside; village; rural area 2.（家乡）native place; home village; home town 3.（行政单位）township

【乡巴佬】 xiāng·balǎo bumpkin; rustic

【乡村】 xiāngcūn village; countryside; rural area

【乡村音乐】 xiāngcūn yīnyuè country music; country-and-western

【乡间】 xiāngjiān village; country：～别墅 country villa

【乡里】 xiānglǐ 1.（家乡）home village; home town 2.（乡亲）fellow villager or townsman

【乡亲】 xiāngqīn 1.（同乡）a person from the same village or town; fellow villager or townsman 2.（当地群众）local people; villagers; folks

【乡土】 xiāngtǔ native soil; home village; of one's native land; local

【乡土观念】 xiāngtǔ guānniàn provincialism

【乡土音乐】 xiāngtǔ yīnyuè country music

【乡土作品】 xiāngtǔ zuòpǐn local color writing

【乡下】 xiāng·xia village; country; countryside

【乡下人】 xiāng·xiarén country folk; country cousin

【乡音】 xiāngyīn accent of one's native place; local accent

【乡邮】 xiāngyóu rural postal service

【乡邮员】 xiāngyóuyuán rural postman

【乡镇】 xiāngzhèn 1.（乡和镇）villages and towns 2.（小市镇）small towns

【乡镇企业】 xiāngzhèn qǐyè town and township enterprises

相 (xiāng) 1.（互相）each other; one another; mutually：～距不远 be not far from / 不～往来 never communicate with each other 2.（表示对另一方的动作）好言～劝 advise sb. with kind words 3.（相看）see for oneself：～女婿 take a look at one's prospective son-in-law

（另见"相"xiàng）

【相爱】 xiāng'ài love each other

【相伴】 xiāngbàn concomitant

【相比】 xiāngbǐ compare with

【相差】 xiāngchà differ; difference between：7点钟时她会在这儿的，前后～不了几分钟。She'll be here at 7 o'clock, give or take a few minutes.

【相称】 xiāngchèn match; suit; be commensurate to; be worthy of

【相持】 xiāngchí be locked in a stalemate
【相处】 xiāngchǔ get along with; live together: 和睦～ get along amiably and peacefully with sb.
【相传】 xiāngchuán 1.(传说) tradition has it that ...; according to legend 2.(传授) hand down; pass on: 世代～ pass on from generation to generation
【相当】 xiāngdāng 1.(差不多) match; balance; correspond to; be equivalent to; be equal to; be commensurate with: 得失～。The gains balance the losses. 2.(适宜;合适) suitable; fit; appropriate 3.(程度高) quite; fairly; considerably: ～困难 fairly difficult / 我上星期～忙。I was quite busy last week.
【相等】 xiāngděng be equal: 条件～ with equal terms
【相对】 xiāngduì 1.(面对面) opposite; face 2.(非绝对的) relative: ～高度 relative high / ～真理 relative truth 3.(比较的) relatively; comparatively: ～稳定 relatively stable
【相对论】 xiāngduìlùn 〈*Physics*〉 the theory of relativity; relativity
【相对性】 xiāngduìxìng relativity
【相对值】 xiāngduìzhí relative value
【相对主义】 xiāngduì zhǔyì relativism
【相反】 xiāngfǎn 1.(截然不同的) opposite; contrary; adverse; reverse: ～的决定 an adverse decision 2.(反而) on the contrary: 恰恰～ just on the contrary
【相反相成】 xiāngfǎn-xiāngchéng (of two things) be both opposite and complementary to each other; oppose each other and yet also complement each other
【相仿】 xiāngfǎng similar; much alike; more or less the same
【相逢】 xiāngféng meet (by chance); come across
【相符】 xiāngfú conform to; tally with; agree with; correspond to: 这份账单与你原来的估算不～。This bill does not agree with your original estimate. / 名实～。One's reputation corresponds to the reality.
【相辅相成】 xiāngfǔ-xiāngchéng supplement each other; complement each other
【相干】 xiānggān 1.(有关) have to do with; be concerned with 2.〈*Physics*〉 coherent
【相隔】 xiānggé be separated by; be apart; be at a distance of
【相关】 xiāngguān be interrelated; be bound up with; be related to
【相好】 xiānghǎo 1.(关系密切) be on familiar terms; be on intimate terms 2.(亲密的朋友) intimate friend 3.(不正当恋爱) have an affair with 4.(不正当恋爱的一方) lover (m.); mistress (*f*.)
【相互】 xiānghù mutual; reciprocal; each other: ～谅解 forgive each other / 该词典中～参照条目用＝或→表示。In this dictionary crossreferences are shown with ＝ or →.
【相继】 xiāngjì in succession; one after another
【相间】 xiāngjiān alternate with
【相煎太急】 xiāngjiān-tàijí torment a person too hard
【相见恨晚】 xiāngjiàn-hènwǎn regret we didn't meet sooner
【相交】 xiāngjiāo 1.(相交叉) intersect 2.(做朋友) be friends; make friends with
【相近】 xiāngjìn 1.(距离接近) close; near; in the neighborhood of 2.(相似) be similar to
【相距】 xiāngjù apart; at a distance of; away from: ～太远 too far apart / 两家旅馆～400米。The two hotels are 400 meters apart.
【相看】 xiāngkàn 1.(看) look 2.(对待) treat 3.(相亲) see for oneself
【相连】 xiānglián be linked together; be joined
【相邻】 xiānglín adjacent; adjacency (n.): 我们学校与你们学校～。Our school is adjacent to yours.
【相配】 xiāngpèi match each other: 这颜色和那裙子～。This color goes with the skirt.
【相扑】 xiāngpū sumo (Jap.) ‖ 相扑手 sumoist
【相亲】 xiāngqīn meet one's prospective son-in-law or daughter-in-law
【相亲相爱】 xiāngqīn-xiāng'ài be deeply attached to each other; love each other devotedly
【相劝】 xiāngquàn persuade; offer advice
【相容】 xiāngróng tolerate each other; endure each other

【相商】 xiāngshāng consult with；talk over with

【相识】 xiāngshí 1.(彼此认识) be acquainted with each other：我们互不～。We are not acquainted (with each other). 2.(相识的人) acquaintance

【相思】 xiāngsī yearning between lovers：单～ one-sided love

【相思病】 xiāngsībìng lovesickness

【相思鸟】 xiāngsīniǎo leiothrix

【相似】 xiāngsì resemble；be similar；be alike：这三个孩子有～之处。There is a likeness between the three boys.

【相似形】 xiāngsìxíng similar figures

【相提并论】 xiāngtí-bìnglùn mention in the same breath；place on a par

【相通】 xiāngtōng communicate with each other；be interlinked

【相同】 xiāngtóng identical；the same；alike：两个过程各不～。The two processes are not analogous (with each other).

【相同点】 xiāngtóngdiǎn similarities；features in common

【相投】 xiāngtóu be congenial；agree with each other：臭味～ be birds of a feather

【相像】 xiāngxiàng resemble；be similar；be alike：两兄弟非常～。The two brothers are very alike.

【相信】 xiāngxìn believe in；be convinced of；have faith in

【相形见绌】 xiāngxíng-jiànchū prove definitely inferior；pale by comparison；be outshone

【相依】 xiāngyī depend on each other：～为命 depend on each other for survival

【相宜】 xiāngyí suitable；fitting；appropriate：这气候对我不～。The climate doesn't agree with me.

【相应】 xiāngyìng corresponding；appropriate；relevant：采取～措施 adopt appropriate measures

【相与】 xiāngyǔ 1.(相处) get along with sb.；deal with sb. 2.(相互) with each other；together

【相约】 xiāngyuē agree (on meeting place, date, etc.)；reach agreement；make an appointment

厢[庿] (xiāng) 1.(厢房) wing；wingroom 2.(像房间的) railway carriage or compartment；(theatre) box：包～ theatre box / 车～ carriage 3.(城厢) the vicinity outside of a city gate：城～ the city proper and areas just outside its gates

【厢房】 xiāngfáng wing；wing-room

箱 (xiāng) chest；box；case；trunk

【箱子】 xiāng·zi chest；box；case；trunk

香 (xiāng) 1.(味香) fragrant；sweet-smelling；aromatic；scented：～花 fragrant flowers / 他吸一种很～的烟斗烟叶。He smokes an aromatic pipe tobacco. 2.(味道香) savory；appetizing；delicious 3.(胃口好) with relish；with good appetite 4.(睡得塌实) soundly：她睡得正～。She is sleeping soundly. 5.(受欢迎) popular；welcome 6.(香料) perfume；spice：麝～ musk 7.(烧的香) incense；joss stick：蚊～ mosquito-repellent incense

【香槟酒】 xiāngbīnjiǔ champagne

【香波】 xiāngbō shampoo

【香菜】 xiāngcài (芫荽) coriander

【香肠】 xiāngcháng sausage

【香椿】 xiāngchūn 1.〈*Bot*.〉Chinese toon 2.(香椿芽) young leaves of Chinese toon

【香榧】 xiāngfěi 1.〈*Bot*.〉Chinese torreya 2.(香榧子) Chinese torreya nut

【香粉】 xiāngfěn face powder

【香港特别行政区】 Xiānggǎng Tèbié Xíngzhèngqū Hong Kong Special Administrative Region

【香港特别行政区基本法】 Xiānggǎng Tèbié Xíngzhèngqū Jīběnfǎ the Basic Law of Hong Kong Special Administrative Region

【香菇】 xiānggū mushroom

【香菰】 xiānggū 同"香菇"

【香瓜】 xiāngguā muskmelon

【香蕉】 xiāngjiāo banana

【香精】 xiāngjīng essence

【香客】 xiāngkè pilgrim

【香料】 xiāngliào perfume；spice；condiment

【香料厂】 xiāngliàochǎng perfumery

【香炉】 xiānglú incense burner

【香喷喷】 xiāngpēnpēn 1.(好闻) sweet-smelling 2.(好吃) savory；appetizing

【香气】 xiāngqì sweet smell；fragrance；aroma

【香水】 xiāngshuǐ perfume；scent

【香甜】 xiāngtián 1.（又香又甜）fragrant and sweet 2.（睡得塌实）soundly

【香味】 xiāngwèi sweet smell; fragrance; perfume: 厨房出来的诱人～ an appetizing smell from the kitchen

【香烟】 xiāngyān 1.（卷烟）cigarette 2.（烧香的烟）incense smoke: ～缭绕 coiling incense smoke

【香烟盒】 xiāngyānhé cigarette case

【香油】 xiāngyóu sesame oil

【香皂】 xiāngzào perfumed soap; scented soap; toilet soap

【香脂】 xiāngzhī 1.（冷霜）face cream 2.（止痛用）balm; balsam

【香烛】 xiāngzhú incense and candies

襄（xiāng）assist; help

【襄理】 xiānglǐ assistant manager

【襄助】 xiāngzhù assist; help

镶（xiāng）1.（嵌入）inlay; set; mount: ～有钻石的金冠 a gold crown encrusted with diamonds 2.（围在边缘）rim; edge; border

【镶边】 xiāngbiān edge with lace

【镶木地板】 xiāngmù dìbǎn parquetry

【镶嵌】 xiāngqiàn inlay; set; mount

【镶牙】 xiāngyá 1.（指医生）put in a false tooth; insert an artificial tooth 2.（指患者）have a denture made

详（xiáng）1.（详细）detailed; minute 2.（详情）details; particulars: ～见附录。For details, see the appendix. 3.（清楚）know clearly: 其生卒年月不～ sb's dates are unknown

【详尽】 xiángjìn detailed; exhaustive; thorough

【详密】 xiángmì elaborate; meticulous

【详明】 xiángmíng full and clear; complete and explicit

【详情】 xiángqíng detailed information; details; particulars

【详实】 xiángshí full and accurate

【详谈】 xiángtán speak in detail; go into details; have a detailed discussion

【详图】 xiángtú detail (drawing)

【详细】 xiángxì detailed; minute: ～说明 detailed description / ～账目 itemized account

【详详细细】 xiángxiáng-xìxì with all the details and particulars

祥（xiáng）1.（吉祥）fortunate; lucky: 吉～ fortunate; luck 2.（吉兆）lucky omen; good omen

降（xiáng）1.（投降）surrender; capitulate; capitulation (n.) 2.（降伏）subdue; vanquish; tame
（另见"降"jiàng）

【降伏】 xiángfú subdue; vanquish; tame

【降服】 xiángfú yield; surrender

翔（xiáng）fly; circle in the air

【翔实】 xiángshí full and accurate; detailed and accurate

享（xiǎng）enjoy

【享福】 xiǎngfú enjoy a happy life; live in ease and comfort

【享乐】 xiǎnglè lead a life of pleasure; indulge in creature comforts

【享乐思想】 xiǎnglè sīxiǎng preoccupation with pleasure-seeking

【享乐主义】 xiǎnglè zhǔyì hedonism; pleasure-seeking

【享年】 xiǎngnián die at the age of

【享清福】 xiǎngqīngfú enjoy the happiness of leisure

【享受】 xiǎngshòu treat; enjoy; enjoyment (n.): 她～惯了。She had luxurious habits.

【享用】 xiǎngyòng enjoy the use of; enjoy

【享有】 xiǎngyǒu enjoy (rights, prestige, etc.): ～崇高的威信 enjoy a high prestige / ～民主和自由 enjoy democracy and freedom / ～盛名 enjoy high reputation / ～外交豁免权 enjoy diplomatic immunities

响［響］（xiǎng）1.（响声）sound; noise 2.（回声）echo: ～应 respond; answer 3.（发出声音）make a sound; sound; ring 4.（响亮）loud; noisy

【响板】 xiǎngbǎn 〈*Music*〉 castanets

【响彻】 xiǎngchè resound through

【响动】 xiǎngdòng sound of sth. astir

【响亮】 xiǎngliàng sonorous; resonant; loud and clear

【响声】 xiǎng·sheng sound; noise

【响尾蛇】 xiǎngwěishé 〈*Zool.*〉 rattlesnake

【响应】 xiǎngyìng respond; answer: ～号召 respond to the call of sb.

饷 (xiǎng) 1.（薪水）pay: 关～ get one's pay 2.（款待）treat sb. with wine and food

【饷银】 xiǎngyín pay

飨［饗］(xiǎng) treat sb. with wine and food: ～客 entertain one's guest / 以～读者 offer to the readers

想 (xiǎng) 1.（思考）think: 先～后做。Think before you act. 2.（认为）suppose; reckon; think; consider 3.（打算）want to; would like to; feel like (doing sth.): 我～见到你。I'd like to see you. / 我～今年我们到北戴河去度假。I guess we'll go to Bei Dai He on our vacation this year. 4.（想念）miss; remember with longing: ～家 have a longing to be home

【想必】 xiǎngbì presumably; most probably

【想不到】 xiǎng·budào unexpected; unexpectedly (*adv*.)

【想不开】 xiǎng·bukāi take things too hard; take a matter to heart

【想当然】 xiǎngdāngrán assume sth. as a matter of course; take for granted

【想到】 xiǎngdào think of; call to mind; have at heart: 我们没有～会这样晚。We didn't think we'd be this late.

【想得到】 xiǎng·dedào（多用于反问）think; imagine; expect

【想得开】 xiǎng·dekāi try to look on the bright side of things; not take to heart; take philosophically

【想法】 xiǎngfǎ 1.（想办法）think of a way; do what one can; try: 我从不敢有和像你这样的姑娘结婚的～。I could never think of marrying a girl like you! 2.（意见）idea; opinion; what one has in mind

【想方设法】 xiǎngfāng-shèfǎ do everything possible; try every means; try by hook or by crook

【想来】 xiǎnglái it may be assumed that; presumably

【想念】 xiǎngniàn long to see again; miss; remember with longing

【想起】 xiǎngqǐ remember; recall; think of; call to mind: 我一时想不起他的名字。I can't think of his name at the moment.

【想入非非】 xiǎngrùfēifēi indulge in fantasy; allow one's fancy to run wild

【想通】 xiǎngtōng straighten out one's thinking; become convinced; come round

【想头】 xiǎngtóu 1.（想法）idea; what one has in mind 2.（希望）hope

【想望】 xiǎngwàng 1.（希望）desire; long for; hope to be 2.（仰慕）admire

【想象】 xiǎngxiàng 同"想像"

【想像】 xiǎngxiàng 1.〈*Psycho*.〉imagination 2.（设想）imagine; fancy; visualize

【想像力】 xiǎngxiànglì imaginative power; imaginative faculty; imagination

向［嚮[1,2]］(xiàng) 1.（方向）direction: 风～ wind direction 2.（对着）face; turn towards 3.（偏袒）favor; side with; take the part of; be partial to 4.（动作方向）to; towards: ～北走 walk to the north / 从胜利走～胜利 march from victory to victory 5.（向来）always; all along: ～无此例。There's no precedent for this.

【向背】 xiàngbèi support or oppose

【向导】 xiàngdǎo 1.（带路）guide the way; show the way 2.（带路人）guide

【向后】 xiànghòu towards the back; backward

【向后转】 xiànghòuzhuǎn（口令）About face

【向来】 xiànglái always; all along

【向前】 xiàngqián forward; onward; ahead

【向前看】 xiàngqiánkàn 1.（向前方看）look ahead 2.（口令）Eyes front!

【向日葵】 xiàngrìkuí〈*Bot*.〉sunflower

【向上】 xiàngshàng upward; up

【向外】 xiàngwài outward

【向往】 xiàngwǎng yearn for; look forward to; be attracted toward: ～未来 look forward to the future

【向下】 xiàngxià downward; down

【向阳】 xiàngyáng 1.（对着太阳）exposed to the sun; sunny 2.（朝南）with a sunny exposure; with a southern exposure

【向右】 xiàngyòu 1.（向右拐）towards the right 2.（交通标志）right branch

【向右转】 xiàngyòuzhuǎn（口令）Right face!

【向隅】 xiàngyú be left alone: ～而泣 weep by himself in a corner

【向着】 xiàng·zhe 1.(朝着;对着) turn towards; face 2.(偏袒) take the part of; side with; be partial to

【向左】 xiàngzuǒ 1.(向左拐) towards the left 2.(交通标志) left branch

【向左转】 xiàngzuǒzhuǎn (口令) Left face!

项 (xiàng) 1.(后颈) nape (of the neck) 2. 〈*classifier*〉 item: 四~基本原则 four basic principles; four fundamentals 3.(款项) sum: 进~ income / 欠~ liabilities 4. 〈*Math*.〉 term: $x^2+2xy+y^2$ 有三项。The $x^2+2xy+y^2$ has three terms.

【项背】 xiàngbèi a person's back: ~相望 (walk) one after another in close succession

【项链】 xiàngliàn necklace

【项目】 xiàngmù 1.(门类) item; project: 重复~ duplicated project / 出口~ goods for export; export items / 基本建设~ capital construction project / 经营~ lines of business; lines of goods / 支出~ item of expense / 盲目上~ rashly launching new project 2. 〈*Sports*〉 event: 男子~ men's event / 女子~ women's event / 正式~ title event

【项目工程】 xiàngmù gōngchéng the construction of a project: ~的可行性 economic feasibility of the construction of a project

【项目债务】 xiàngmù zhàiwù project debt

【项圈】 xiàngquān necklace; necklet

【项值】 xiàngzhí 〈*Math*.〉 term value

巷 (xiàng) lane; alley (另见"巷"hàng)

【巷战】 xiàngzhàn street fighting

【巷子】 xiàng·zi lane; alley

相 (xiàng) 1.(相貌) looks; appearance: 可怜~ pitiful appearance; sorry figure 2.(坐立姿态) bearing; posture 3.(观察) look at and appraise 4. 〈*Electr*.〉 phase: ~位 phase position 5(照片) photograph: 照个~ take a photo; have a photo taken 6.(日本等国的部长) minister 7. 〈*Chess*〉 bishop (另见"相"xiāng)

【相册】 xiàngcè photo album

【相机】 xiàngjī 1.(察看机会) watch for an opportunity: ~行事 act as the occasion demands; do as one sees fit 2.(照相机) camera

【相机后盖】 xiàngjī hòugài 〈*Photog*.〉 camera back

【相貌】 xiàngmào facial features; looks; appearance

【相面】 xiàngmiàn practice physiognomy; tell sb's fortune by reading his face

【相面先生】 xiàngmiàn xiān·sheng physiognomist

【相片】 xiàngpiān photograph; photo

【相声】 xiàng·sheng 〈*Quyi*〉 comic dialogue; cross talk

【相纸】 xiàngzhǐ 〈*Photog*.〉 printing paper; photographic paper

象 (xiàng) 1. 〈*Zool*.〉 elephant: 非洲~ African elephant / 亚洲~ Asian elephant; Indian elephant 2.(形状;样子) appearance; shape; image 3.(仿效;摹拟) imitate: ~声 onomatopoeia 4. 〈*Chess*〉 bishop

【象鼻】 xiàngbí trunk; proboscis

【象棋】 xiàngqí (Chinese) chess: 国际~ chess

【象声】 xiàngshēng onomatopoeia

【象声词】 xiàngshēngcí onomatope

【象形文字】 xiàngxíng wénzì pictograph; hieroglyph

【象牙】 xiàngyá elephant's tusk; ivory

【象征】 xiàngzhēng 1.(意味) symbolize; signify; stand for 2.(象征物) symbol; emblem; token; symbolic (adj.): ~意义 symbolic meaning

【象征主义】 xiàngzhēng zhǔyì symbolism

像 (xiàng) 1.(图像;人像) likeness (of sb.); portrait; picture: 佛~ image of Buddha / 画~ portrait / 铜~ bronze statue 2. 〈*Physics*〉 image: 实~ real image / 虚~ virtual image 3.(相同,相似) be like; resemble; take after: 这幅画像很~你。The painting is a good likeness of you. 4.(好像) seem; look as if; appear 5.(如同) as; such as; like: 她~你一样高。She's as tall as you. / 它并不~我们想像的那么困难。It's not so/as difficult as we expected. / 这就~ABC 一样容易。It's as easy as ABC.

【像差】 xiàngchā aberration: 球面~ spherical aberration

【像框】 xiàngkuàng frame

【像素】 xiàngshù 〈*TV*〉 pixel; picture element

【像样】 xiàngyàng up to the mark; presentable; decent; sound

【像章】 xiàngzhāng badge with sb's likeness on it

橡(xiàng) 1.(橡树) oak 2.(橡胶树) rubber tree

【橡胶】 xiàngjiāo rubber：泡沫～ foam rubber

【橡胶厂】 xiàngjiāochǎng rubber plant

【橡胶海绵】 xiàngjiāo hǎimián sponge rubber

【橡胶轮胎】 xiàngjiāo lúntāi rubber tire

【橡胶树】 xiàngjiāoshù rubber tree

【橡胶制品】 xiàngjiāo zhìpǐn rubber goods

【橡胶种植园】 xiàngjiāo zhòngzhíyuán rubber plantation

【橡皮】 xiàngpí 1.(硫化橡胶) rubber 2.(文具) eraser; rubber

【橡皮搋子】 xiàngpí chuāi·zi plunger

【橡皮船】 xiàngpíchuān rubber boat

【橡皮膏】 xiàngpígāo adhesive plaster; sticking-plaster

【橡皮筋】 xiàngpíjīn rubber band; elastic band

【橡皮泥】 xiàngpíní plasticine

【橡皮圈】 xiàngpíquān 1.(游泳圈) lifebelt; lifebuoy 2.(橡皮筋) rubber band; elastic band

【橡皮手套】 xiàngpí shǒutào rubber (operating) gloves

【橡皮艇】 xiàngpítǐng pneumatic boat; rubber dinghy

【橡皮图章】 xiàngpí túzhāng rubber stamp：盖～ rubber-stamp

【橡皮制品】 xiàngpí zhìpǐn rubber goods

【橡实】 xiàngshí 〈*Bot.*〉 acorn

xiao

削(xiāo) pare with a knife; peel with a knife：～马铃薯皮 peel the potato (另见"削"xuē)

【削皮】 xiāopí peel

【削铅笔】 xiāoqiānbǐ sharpen a pencil

【削球】 xiāoqiú 〈*Table Tennis*〉 cut; chop

消(xiāo) 1.(消失) disappear; vanish 2.(消除) eliminate; remove; dispel：～愁解闷 divert oneself from boredom; dispel depression or melancholy 3.(消遣) pass the time in a leisurely way; while away (the time)：～夏 pass the summer in a leisurely way 4.(需要) need; take

【消沉】 xiāochén low-spirited; dejected; depressed; downhearted：意志～ demoralized; despondent

【消除】 xiāochú eliminate; dispel; remove; clear up：～分歧 eliminate differences / ～故障 debug / ～大城市中的煤烟 abate the smoke nuisance in big cities

【消磁】 xiāocí degauss; field discharge

【消磁器】 xiāocíqì magnetic eraser

【消毒】 xiāodú 1.(杀死病菌) disinfect; sterilize 2.(清除流毒) eliminate the pernicious influence

【消毒剂】 xiāodújì disinfectant

【消毒牛奶】 xiāodú niúnǎi sterilized milk

【消防】 xiāofáng fire control; fire fighting; fire protection

【消防车】 xiāofángchē fire engine; fire truck

【消防队】 xiāofángduì fire brigade

【消防技术】 xiāofáng jìshù fire prevention

【消防人员】 xiāofáng rényuán fire fighter

【消防设备】 xiāofáng shèbèi fire-fighting equipment

【消防水龙】 xiāofáng shuǐlóng fire hose; fire hydrant

【消防艇】 xiāofángtǐng fireboat

【消防演习】 xiāofáng yǎnxí fire-practice; fire drill

【消防业】 xiāofángyè fire service

【消防站】 xiāofángzhàn fire station

【消费】 xiāofèi consume; consumption (n.)：超前～ excessive consumption / 提前～ anticipate one's wage

【消费城市】 xiāofèi chéngshì consumer-city

【消费价格指数】 xiāofèi jiàgé zhǐshù consumer price index

【消费决策】 xiāofèi juécè consumer decision

【消费品】 xiāofèipǐn consumer goods; articles of consumption

【消费市场】 xiāofèi shìchǎng consumer market

【消费水平】 xiāofèi shuǐpíng consumption level

【消费税】 xiāofèishuì consumption tax

【消费者】 xiāofèizhě consumer; user：最终～ ultimate consumer

【消费者权益保护法】 Xiāofèizhě Quányì

Bǎohùfǎ Law on Protection of the Rights and Interests of Consumers

【消费者协会】 xiāofèizhě xiéhuì consumer's association

【消费主义】 xiāofèi zhǔyì consumerism

【消费资料】 xiāofèi zīliào means of subsistence

【消耗】 xiāohào 1.（逐渐减少）consume; use up; deplete; expend 2.（使消耗）reduce; lessen：～敌人的有生力量 reduce the enemy's active force

【消化】 xiāohuà 1.（指食物）digest; digestion (n.); digestive (adj.) 2.（指知识等）digest; absorb ‖ 难消化的 indigestible

【消化不良】 xiāohuà bùliáng 〈*Med*.〉indigestion; dyspepsia

【消化力】 xiāohuàlì digestion：～差 have a poor digestion / ～强 have a good digestion

【消化系统】 xiāohuà xìtǒng 〈*Anat*.〉digestive system

【消火栓】 xiāohuǒshuān fire hydrant; fire cock

【消极】 xiāojí 1.（负面的）negative：～影响 negative influence 2.（不求进取的）passive; inactive：～怠工 be slack in work / ～情绪 a passive attitude / ～抵抗 passive resistance

【消解】 xiāojiě clear up; dispel

【消灭】 xiāomiè 1.（消失;灭亡）perish; die out; pass away 2.（使消灭;除掉）annihilate; eliminate; abolish; exterminate; wipe out

【消磨】 xiāomó 1.（逐渐消耗）wear down; fritter away：～志气 sap one's will 2.（度过）while away; idle away：～岁月 while away the time

【消气】 xiāoqì cool down; be mollified

【消遣】 xiāoqiǎn divert oneself; while away the time; pastime; diversion：她看侦探小说～。She amused herself by reading detective stories.

【消遣性】 xiāoqiǎnxìng light：～的电影 a light movie

【消融】 xiāoróng melt

【消散】 xiāosàn scatter and disappear; dissipate：由于下了雨，城里的雾～了。With the rain, the smog lifted from the city.

【消色】 xiāosè 〈*Physics*〉achromatic

【消声】 xiāoshēng 〈*Archit*.〉noise elimination

【消声器】 xiāoshēngqì silencer; muffler; acoustical damper

【消失】 xiāoshī disappear; vanish; dissolve; fade away; die away

【消逝】 xiāoshì die away; fade away; vanish; elapse

【消释】 xiāoshì clear up; dispel：～前嫌 remove a grudge; bury the hatchet

【消受】 xiāoshòu 1.（多用于否定，享受）enjoy：无福～ not have the luck to enjoy; be unable to enjoy 2.（忍受）endure; bear

【消瘦】 xiāoshòu become thin; become emaciated

【消暑】 xiāoshǔ spend the summer in a leisurely way

【消损】 xiāosǔn 1.（消磨而损耗）wear and tear 2.（逐渐减少）wear down

【消亡】 xiāowáng wither away; die out

【消息】 xiāo·xi 1.（情况报道）news; information：非官方～ non-official information / 最新～ hot news; latest news 2.（音信）tidings; news

【消息灵通人士】 xiāo·xi língtōng rénshì a well-informed source

【消闲】 xiāoxián idle away one's free time

【消协】 xiāoxiè consumer's association

【消炎】 xiāoyán 〈*Med*.〉diminish inflammation; reduce inflammation; allay inflammation

【消炎药】 xiāoyányào antiphlogistic

【消音】 xiāoyīn amortization; erasure

【消音磁头】 xiāoyīn cítóu erase head

【消音器】 xiāoyīnqì muffler; silencer

【消长】 xiāozhǎng growth and decline

【消账】 xiāozhàng cross off account; balance account

【消肿】 xiāozhǒng 〈*Med*.〉detumescence; subsidence of a swelling

宵 (xiāo) night：良～ festival night

【宵禁】 xiāojìn curfew：实行～ impose a curfew

逍 (xiāo)

【逍遥】 xiāoyáo free and unfettered

【逍遥法外】 xiāoyáo-fǎwài go scot-free; be

(still) at large; outlawry

硝 (xiāo) 1.〈*Chem*.〉niter; saltpetre; nitric (adj.) 2.〈*Leather-Making*〉taw: ～皮 taw leathers

【硝化】 xiāohuà 〈*Chem*.〉nitrify; nitrification (n.)

【硝化甘油】 xiāohuà gānyóu nitroglycerin; nitroglycerine

【硝石】 xiāoshí 〈*Chem*.〉niter; saltpetre

【硝酸】 xiāosuān 〈*Chem*.〉nitric acid; nitric (adj.)

【硝烟】 xiāoyān smoke of gunpowder

销 (xiāo) 1.(熔化) melt 2.(除去;解除) cancel; annul: 注～ write off; cancel 3.(销售) sell; market: 畅～ sell well / 滞～ sell poorly / 自～ sales through one's own channel 4.(消费) expend; spend: 开～ expenditure 5.(销子) pin

【销毁】 xiāohuǐ destroy by melting or burning: ～核武器 the destruction of nuclear weapons

【销魂】 xiāohún be overwhelmed with sorrow or joy; feel transported

【销货】 xiāohuò sales; merchandise sales

【销货单】 xiāohuòdān sales slip

【销货定单】 xiāohuò dìngdān sales order

【销货发票】 xiāohuò fāpiào invoice for sale

【销货记录】 xiāohuò jìlù record of goods sold

【销货利润】 xiāohuò lìrùn selling profits

【销货凭证】 xiāohuò píngzhèng sales voucher

【销货收益】 xiāohuò shōuyì sales income

【销货限额】 xiāohuò xiàn'é sales quotas

【销假】 xiāojià report back after leave of absence

【销路】 xiāolù sale; market: ～很广 have a big market / ～很好 have a good sale

【销声匿迹】 xiāoshēng-nìjì keep silent and lie low; disappear from the scene

【销售】 xiāoshòu sell; market

【销售点】 xiāoshòudiǎn point of purchase

【销售额】 xiāoshòu'é sales volume

【销售费用】 xiāoshòu fèiyòng marketing expenses

【销售计划】 xiāoshòu jìhuà marketing plan

【销售价格】 xiāoshòu jiàgé selling price

【销售经理】 xiāoshòu jīnglǐ sales manager

【销售量】 xiāoshòuliàng sales volume

【销售渠道】 xiāoshòu qúdào trade channels; channels of distribution

【销售税】 xiāoshòushuì sales tax

【销售网点】 xiāoshòu wǎngdiǎn commercial networks

【销售研究】 xiāoshòu yánjiū marketing research

【销售原则】 xiāoshòu yuánzé marketing policy

【销售战略】 xiāoshòu zhànlüè marketing strategy

【销售折扣】 xiāoshòu zhékòu discount on sales

【销售总额】 xiāoshòu zǒng'é total sales; aggregate sales

【销行】 xiāoxíng sell; be on sale

【销赃】 xiāozāng disposal of stolen goods

【销账】 xiāozhàng write off; cancel or remove from an account

霄 (xiāo) 1.(云) clouds: 高入云～ towering into the clouds 2.(天空) sky; heaven

【霄汉】 xiāohàn 〈*written*〉the sky; the firmament; heavens

枭[梟] (xiāo) 1.〈*Zool*.〉owl 2.(勇猛) valiant; brave 3.(走私首领) smuggler: 毒～ smuggler of narcotics

【枭将】 xiāojiàng brave officer; courageous general

【枭雄】 xiāoxióng powerful and ambitious person

骁[驍] (xiāo) valiant; brave

【骁将】 xiāojiàng brave officer; courageous general

【骁勇】 xiāoyǒng brave; valiant

嚣[囂] (xiāo) clamor; hubbub; din: 叫～ clamor

【嚣张】 xiāozhāng rampant; arrogant; aggressive

萧[蕭] (xiāo)

【萧瑟】 xiāosè 1.(指声音) rustle in the air: 秋风～。The autumn wind is soughing. 2.(指景色) bleak; desolate

【萧索】 xiāosuǒ bleak and chilly; desolate

【萧条】 xiāotiáo 1.(毫无生气) desolate; bleak 2.〈*Econ*.〉depression: 经济～ economic depression; slump

【萧萧】 xiāoxiāo **1.**（马嘶声）neigh；whinny **2.**（风声）whistle；sough

潇［瀟］（xiāo）deep and clear

【潇洒】 xiāosǎ natural and unrestrained

【潇潇】 xiāoxiāo **1.**（刮风下雨）whistling and pattering **2.**（小雨）drizzly

箫［簫］（xiāo）〈*Music*〉*xiao*；Chinese vertical bamboo flute

淆（xiáo）confuse；mix：混～是非 confuse right and wrong

【淆惑】 xiáohuò bewilder；puzzle；baffle：～视听 bewilder the minds of the public

【淆乱】 xiáoluàn confuse；bewilder

小（xiǎo）**1.**（跟"大"相对）small；little；petty；minor：雨开始～了。The rain began to let up. **2.**（短时间）for a while；for a short time：～住 stay for a few days **3.**（年纪小）young

【小巴】 xiǎobā mini bus

【小白脸】 xiǎobáiliǎn toy boy

【小百货】 xiǎobǎihuò small articles of daily use

【小百科全书】 xiǎobǎikē quánshū micropedia；micropaedia

【小报】 xiǎobào small-sized newspaper；tabloid

【小辈】 xiǎobèi younger members of the family

【小本经营】 xiǎoběn jīngyíng business with a small capital；do business in a small way

【小便】 xiǎobiàn **1.**（排尿）urinate；pass water；make water **2.**（尿）urine：验～ urine test；have one's urine tested **3.**（男性生殖器）penis

【小便池】 xiǎobiànchí urinal

【小辫儿】 xiǎobiànr short braid

【小辫子】 xiǎobiàn·zi **1.**（小辫儿）short braid **2.**（把柄）mistake or misconduct that can be exploited by others：抓～ use sb's misconduct to discredit him

【小才大用】 xiǎocái-dàyòng a man of little ability in high capacity

【小菜】 xiǎocài **1.**（咸菜）pickled vegetables；pickles **2.**（小事情）petty thing；minor matter

【小册子】 xiǎocè·zi booklet；pamphlet；brochure

【小产】 xiǎochǎn 〈*Med.*〉miscarriage；abortion

【小长筒鼓】 xiǎochángtǒnggǔ small tom-tom

【小肠】 xiǎocháng 〈*Anat.*〉small intestine

【小车】 xiǎochē **1.**（手车）handcart；pushcart **2.**（小轿车）sedan；sedan car

【小吃】 xiǎochī **1.**（餐馆里价廉的菜）cheap dishes **2.**（非正餐）snack；refreshments **3.**（西餐冷盘）cold dish；made dish

【小吃部】 xiǎochībù snack counter；refreshment room

【小吃店】 xiǎochīdiàn snack bar；lunchroom

【小丑】 xiǎochǒu **1.**（滑稽角色）clown；buffoon **2.**（小人）a base person

【小聪明】 xiǎocōng·ming good at playing petty tricks：耍～ play petty tricks

【小刀】 xiǎo·dāo pocket knife

【小道】 xiǎodào **1.**（小路）path；trail **2.**（非官方）non-official：～消息 hearsay；gossip

【小道消息】 xiǎodào xiāo·xi grapevine；hearsay；gossip：我听～说小赵要升官了。I heard the grapevine that Xiao Zhao is to be promoted.

【小调】 xiǎodiào **1.**（民间小曲）popular tune；ditty **2.**〈*Music*〉minor

【小动作】 xiǎodòngzuò little tricks：搞～ play little tricks

【小洞不补大洞吃苦】 xiǎodòng bù bǔ dàdòng chīkǔ A stitch in time saves nine.

【小队】 xiǎoduì team；squad

【小额】 xiǎo'é petty；small：～钞票 small note / ～贷款 petty loan / ～硬币 small change / ～债券 baby bond

【小恩小惠】 xiǎoēn-xiǎohuì petty favors；small favors；economic sops；paltry charity

【小儿】 xiǎo'ér **1.**（儿童）children **2.**〈*politeness*〉my son

【小儿科】 xiǎo'érkē 〈*Med.*〉（department of）pediatrics；pediatric（adj.）‖ 小儿科医生 pediatrician

【小儿麻痹症】 xiǎo'ér mábìzhèng infantile paralysis；polio；poliomyelitis

【小贩】 xiǎofàn pedlar；vendor；hawker

【小费】 xiǎofèi tip；gratuity；pourboire：给～ tip sb.；give sb. a tip

【小分队】 xiǎofēnduì detachment；small-scale troupe

【小腹】 xiǎofù underbelly; lower abdomen
【小歌剧】 xiǎogējù operetta
【小工】 xiǎogōng unskilled laborer; helping hand
【小公共汽车】 xiǎogōnggòng qìchē mini bus
【小姑】 xiǎogū sister-in-law; husband's younger sister
【小鼓】 xiǎogǔ 〈*Music*〉 side drum; snare drum
【小规模】 xiǎoguīmó small-scale
【小孩】 xiǎohái child
【小孩床】 xiǎoháichuáng cod
【小寒】 Xiǎohán the Slight Cold (1月5-7日交节)
【小号】 xiǎohào 〈*Music*〉 trumpet
【小河】 xiǎohé creek; brook
【小户】 xiǎohù 1.(人少的家庭) small family 2.(无钱无势的家庭) family of limited means and without powerful connections
【小火车】 xiǎohuǒchē ghost train
【小伙子】 xiǎohuǒ·zi youngster; lad; young fellow
【小集团】 xiǎojítuán clique; faction
【小家鼠】 xiǎojiāshǔ rat
【小轿车】 xiǎojiàochē sedan (car): 豪华～ limousine
【小节】 xiǎojié 1.(琐碎事情) small matter; trifle: 不拘～ not bother about small matters; not be punctilious 2.〈*Music*〉 bar; measure
【小结】 xiǎojié 1.(一段时间的总结) brief summary; preliminary summary; brief sum-up; interim summary 2.(做小结) summarize briefly
【小姐】 xiǎo·jiě 1.(尊称) Miss 2.(少女) young lady
【小径】 xiǎojìng path; trail
【小舅子】 xiǎojiù·zi brother-in-law; wife's younger brother
【小剧场】 xiǎojùchǎng 〈*Theatre*〉 little theatre
【小看】 xiǎokàn underestimate; look down upon: ～人 underestimate a person
【小康】 xiǎokāng well-to-do; comfortably off; a relatively comfortable standard of living: 正在向～迈进 moving towards a relatively comfortable standard of living
【小康型】 xiǎokāngxíng being fairly well-off
【小口径】 xiǎokǒujìng small-bore
【小口径步枪】 xiǎokǒujìng bùqiāng small-bore rifle
【小两口】 xiǎoliǎngkǒu a young couple
【小龙虾】 xiǎolóngxiā 〈*Zool.*〉 crayfish
【小路】 xiǎolù by-road; by-path
【小旅行车】 xiǎolǚxíngchē minibus; wagon
【小轮摩托车】 xiǎolún mótuōchē scooter
【小麦】 xiǎomài wheat: 冬～ winter wheat
【小卖部】 xiǎomàibù 1.(小店) canteen; small shop 2.(食品小卖部) buffet; snack counter
【小满】 Xiǎomǎn the Grain Full (5月20-22日交节)
【小猫熊】 xiǎomáoxióng 〈*Zool.*〉 lesser panda; red panda
【小米】 xiǎomǐ millet
【小拇指】 xiǎomǔzhǐ little finger
【小脑】 xiǎonǎo 〈*Anat.*〉 cerebellum; little brain
【小牛肉】 xiǎoniúròu veal
【小农】 xiǎonóng small farmer
【小农经济】 xiǎonóng jīngjì small-scale peasant economy
【小女】 xiǎonǚ my daughter
【小朋友】 xiǎopéngyǒu 1.(孩子们) children 2.(小孩) little boy or girl; child
【小批生产】 xiǎopī shēngchǎn small serial production
【小便宜】 xiǎopiányì small gain; petty advantage
【小品】 xiǎopǐn a short, simple literary or artistic creation; essay; sketch
【小品文】 xiǎopǐnwén familiar essay; essay
【小气】 xiǎoqì stingy; niggardly; mean
【小气候】 xiǎoqìhòu microclimate
【小巧】 xiǎoqiǎo small and pretty; pretty and cleverly made
【小巧玲珑】 xiǎoqiǎo-línglóng small and exquisite
【小曲】 xiǎoqǔ ditty; popular tune
【小圈子】 xiǎoquān·zi 1.(生活圈子) limited social contact 2.(小集团) small circle; gang: 搞～ form a small circle; form a gang
【小人】 xiǎorén a base person; villain; vile character

【小人得志】 xiǎorén-dézhì villains holding sway
【小人物】 xiǎorénwù an unimportant person; a nobody; cipher; nonentity
【小日子】 xiǎorì·zi easy life of a small family
【小山】 xiǎoshān hill
【小商品】 xiǎoshāngpǐn small commodities
【小商品经济】 xiǎoshāngpǐn jīngjì small commodity economy
【小商品生产者】 xiǎoshāngpǐn shēngchǎnzhě small commodity producer
【小生产】 xiǎoshēngchǎn small production; small-scale production
【小生产者】 xiǎoshēngchǎnzhě small producer
【小诗】 xiǎoshī verselet
【小时】 xiǎoshí hour: 半～ half an hour
【小石子】 xiǎoshí·zi pebble
【小事】 xiǎoshì trifle; petty thing; minor matter: 为～争吵 have a quarrel over trifles
【小市民】 xiǎoshìmín urban petty bourgeois
【小饰物】 xiǎoshìwù charm; trinket
【小手工业者】 xiǎoshǒugōngyèzhě small handicraftsman
【小叔子】 xiǎoshū·zi brother-in-law; husband's younger brother
【小暑】 Xiǎoshǔ the Slight Heat (7月6-8日交节)
【小数】 xiǎoshù 〈*Math.*〉 decimal: 循环～ recurring decimal; repeating decimal
【小数点】 xiǎoshùdiǎn decimal point
【小睡】 xiǎoshuì catnap
【小说】 xiǎoshuō novel; fiction: 长篇～ novel / 短篇～ short story / 中篇～ medium-length novel; novelette
【小说家】 xiǎoshuōjiā 1.(写长篇的) novelist 2.(写中、短篇的) novella
【小苏打】 xiǎosūdá sodium bicarbonate
【小提琴】 xiǎotíqín 〈*Music*〉 violin
【小提琴手】 xiǎotíqínshǒu violinist: 第一～ first violinist
【小题大作】 xiǎotí-dàzuò make a fuss over a trifling matter; make a mountain out of a molehill
【小艇】 xiǎotǐng small boat; skiff
【小桶】 xiǎotǒng keg
【小偷】 xiǎotōu petty thief; sneak thief; pilferer
【小腿】 xiǎotuǐ shank
【小五金】 xiǎowǔjīn hardware
【小溪】 xiǎoxī rivulet
【小写】 xiǎoxiě small letter
【小写体】 xiǎoxiětǐ lower case
【小心】 xiǎoxīn take care; be careful; be cautious: ～搬运 care handle / ～玻璃 glass / ～轻放 handle with care / ～,危险! DANGER!
【小心眼】 xiǎoxīnyǎn be narrow-minded
【小心翼翼】 xiǎoxīn-yìyì with great care; cautiously: 我们～地走在新打蜡的地板上。We walked gingerly over the newly waxed floor.
【小兴安岭】 Xiǎoxīng'ānlǐng 〈place〉 Xiao Hinggan Ling
【小行星】 xiǎoxíngxīng 〈*Astron.*〉 asteroids
【小型】 xiǎoxíng small-sized; small-scale; miniature
【小型机】 xiǎoxíngjī 〈*Computer*〉 minicomputer
【小型张】 xiǎoxíngzhāng souvenir card
【小熊猫】 xiǎoxióngmáo 见"小猫熊"
【小熊座】 Xiǎoxióngzuò 〈*Astron.*〉 Little Bear
【小学】 xiǎoxué primary school; elementary school
【小学生】 xiǎoxuéshēng pupil; schoolchild; schoolboy (m.); schoolgirl (f.)
【小雪】 Xiǎoxuě the Slight Snow (11月22-23日交节)
【小业主】 xiǎoyèzhǔ small proprietor; petty proprietor
【小夜曲】 xiǎoyèqǔ 〈*Music*〉 serenade
【小姨子】 xiǎoyí·zi sister-in-law; wife's younger sister
【小于】 xiǎoyú is less than (符号为 $<$)
【小于或等于】 xiǎoyú huò děngyú is less than or equal to (符号为 $\leqslant$)
【小雨】 xiǎoyǔ 1.〈*Meteorol.*〉 light rain 2.(不大的雨) drizzle
【小灶】 xiǎozào 1.(伙食) special mess 2.(喻特殊对待) special care
【小照】 xiǎozhào small-sized photograph
【小指】 xiǎozhǐ little finger or toe
【小传】 xiǎozhuàn brief biography; bio-

graphical sketch; profile
【小转盘】 xiǎozhuànpán 〈*Transport*〉 mini-roundabout
【小资产阶级】 xiǎozīchǎ jiējí petty bourgeoisie
【小字】 xiǎozì small character
【小子】 xiǎo·zi 1.(儿子) boy 2.(用于男性,含轻蔑意) fellow; chap; bloke
【小奏鸣曲】 xiǎozhòumíngqǔ 〈*Music*〉 sonatina
【小组】 xiǎozǔ group
【小组会议】 xiǎozǔ huìyì group meeting
【小组委员会】 xiǎozǔ wěiyuánhuì subcommittee
【小组长】 xiǎozǔzhǎng group leader

晓[曉](xiǎo) 1.(天刚亮时) dawn; daybreak: 拂～ foredawn 2.(知道) know: 家喻户～ known to all 3.(使人知道) tell; let sb. know: ～以利害 warn sb. of the consequences
【晓得】 xiǎo·de know
【晓示】 xiǎoshì tell explicitly; notify

孝(xiào) 1.(孝顺) filial piety 2.(孝服) mourning: 带～ in mourning
【孝服】 xiàofú mourning (dress)
【孝敬】 xiàojìng give presents (to one's elders or superiors)
【孝顺】 xiàoshùn show filial obedience
【孝衣】 xiàoyī mourning dress
【孝子】 xiàozǐ 1.(孝顺的人) worthy progeny 2.(居丧者) son showing filial obedience
【孝子贤孙】 xiàozǐ-xiánsūn worthy progeny; true son

哮(xiào) 1.(急促喘气) heavy breathing; wheeze 2.(吼叫) roar; howl: 咆～ roar; thunder
【哮喘】 xiàochuǎn asthma
【哮喘气管炎】 xiàochuǎn qìguǎnyán asthmatic bronchitis

肖(xiào) resemble; be like: 惟妙惟～ absolutely lifelike
【肖像】 xiàoxiàng portrait; portraiture
【肖像画】 xiàoxiànghuà portrait painting

笑(xiào) 1.(欢笑) smile; laugh: 大～ burst into laughter / 冷～ smile coldly / 谁～到最后,谁～得最好。He who laughs last laughs longest. 2.(讥笑) ridicule; laugh at
【笑柄】 xiàobǐng laughing stock; butt; joke
【笑哈哈】 xiàohāhā laughingly; with a laugh
【笑话】 xiào·hua 1.(引人笑的故事) joke; jest: 说～ crack a joke 2.(讥笑) laugh at; ridicule
【笑剧】 xiàojù farce
【笑口常开】 xiàokǒu-chángkāi grinning all the time
【笑里藏刀】 xiàolǐ-cángdāo hide a dagger in a smile; with murderous intent behind one's smiles
【笑脸】 xiàoliǎn smiling face: ～相迎 greet sb. with a smile; salute one with a smile
【笑料】 xiàoliào laughing stock; joke
【笑骂】 xiàomà deride and taunt
【笑眯眯】 xiàomīmī smilingly; with a smile on one's face
【笑纳】 xiàonà kindly accept (this small gift of mine)
【笑气】 xiàoqì 〈*Chem.*〉 laughing gas; nitrous oxide
【笑容】 xiàoróng smiling expression; smile
【笑声】 xiàoshēng laugh; laughter: 响亮的～ loud laughter
【笑死】 xiàosǐ kill laughing: 我们要～了。We were killing ourselves laughing. / 那个小丑～我了。That clown kills me.
【笑谈】 xiàotán laughing stock; object of ridicule
【笑嘻嘻】 xiàoxīxī grinning; smiling broadly
【笑逐颜开】 xiàozhú-yánkāi beam with smiles; be wreathed in smiles

效[傚[2]、効[3]](xiào) 1.(效果) effect; avail: 无～ without avail 2.(仿效) imitate; follow the example of 3.(献出) devote to; render a service to
【效法】 xiàofǎ follow the example of; model oneself on; learn from
【效果】 xiàoguǒ 1.(产生的结果) effect; result: 产生～ produce some effect 2.〈*Theatre*〉 sound effects: 音响～ sound effects
【效劳】 xiàoláo work in the service of; work for
【效力】 xiàolì 1.(效劳) render a service to; serve 2.(效果) effect 3.(约束力) force; effect; avail: 具有同等～ be equally authentic
【效率】 xiàolǜ efficiency: ～低 inefficient / ～高 efficient / 工作～ work efficiency / 提高～ promote efficiency

【效命】 xiàomìng go all out to serve sb. regardless of the consequences
【效能】 xiàonéng efficacy; usefulness
【效验】 xiàoyàn intended effect; desired result
【效益】 xiàoyì beneficial result; benefit: 经济～ economic benefit
【效益工资】 xiàoyì gōngzī wages based on benefit
【效应】 xiàoyìng 1.〈*Physics*〉effect: 光电～ the effect of light and electricity 2.(泛指反应和效果) effect
【效用】 xiàoyòng effectiveness; usefulness
【效尤】 xiàoyóu knowingly follow the example of a wrongdoer: 以儆～ warn others against following a bad example
【效忠】 xiàozhōng pledge loyalty to; devote oneself heart and soul to

校 (xiào) 1.(学校) school; college; university 2.(校级军官) field officer (请参见"大校、上校、中校、少校"各条)
(另见"校"jiào)
【校办工厂】 xiàobàn gōngchǎng school-run workshop; campus workshop
【校车】 xiàochē school bus
【校风】 xiàofēng school spirit
【校官】 xiàoguān field officer; field grade officer
【校规】 xiàoguī school regulations
【校徽】 xiàohuī school badge
【校际】 xiàojì intercollegiate: ～运动赛 intercollegiate games
【校刊】 xiàokān school magazine; college journal
【校历】 xiàolì school calendar
【校庆】 xiàoqìng anniversary of the founding of a school or college
【校舍】 xiàoshè schoolhouse; school building
【校外】 xiàowài outside school; after school
【校外部】 xiàowàibù extramurl department
【校外辅导员】 xiàowài fǔdǎoyuán after-school activities counsellor
【校外活动站】 xiàowài huódòngzhàn after-school activities club
【校务】 xiàowù administrative affairs of a school or college
【校训】 xiàoxùn school motto
【校医】 xiàoyī school doctor
【校友】 xiàoyǒu alumnus (m.); alumna (f.)
【校园】 xiàoyuán campus; school yard
【校长】 xiàozhǎng 1.(大专院校的) president; chancellor 2.(中小学的) headmaster; principal; schoolmaster (m.); schoolmistress (f.)
【校址】 xiàozhǐ the location of a school or college

啸[嘯、歗] (xiào) 1.(呼啸) whistle 2.(野兽叫声) howl; roar: 虎～ the roar of a tiger
【啸聚】 xiàojù band together; gang up

xie

些 (xiē) 1.〈*classifier*〉some: 前～日子 some days ago 2.(些微) slightly; a little; a bit
【些微】 xiēwēi slightly; a little; a bit
【些许】 xiēxǔ a few; a little

楔 (xiē)
【楔子】 xiē·zi 1.(榫头) wedge 2.(木钉;竹钉) peg; wooden peg; bamboo peg 3.(戏曲、小说的引子) prologue in some modern novels

歇 (xiē) 1.(休息) have a rest 2.(停止) stop; knock off
【歇班】 xiēbān be off duty; have time off
【歇顶】 xiēdǐng get a bit thin on top; be balding
【歇工】 xiēgōng stop work; off shift; call it a day
【歇后语】 xiēhòuyǔ a two-part structured saying, consisting of a descriptive statement and its explanation
【歇脚】 xiējiǎo stop on the way for a rest
【歇晌】 xiēshǎng take a midday nap or rest
【歇斯底里】 xiēsīdǐlǐ 1.〈*Med.*〉hysteria ‖ 歇斯底里患者 hysteric 2.(举动失常) hysteria: ～大发作 go into hysterics; become hysterical
【歇息】 xiēxī 1.(休息) have a rest 2.(睡觉) go to bed; put up for the night
【歇业】 xiēyè close a business; go out of business

蝎[蠍] (xiē)〈*Zool.*〉scorpion
【蝎子】 xiē·zi scorpion

协[協](xié) 1.(共同) joint; common 2.(协助) assist

【协办】 xiébàn do sth. jointly

【协定】 xiédìng 1.(协商订立的条款) agreement; accord: 避免双重征税~ agreement on cancellation of double taxation / 冲账~ agreement to offset payments / 贷款~ loan agreement / 多边~ multilateral agreement / 国际~ international agreement / 货币~ monetary agreement / 军事停战~ armistice agreement / 君子~ gentlemen's agreement / 科学技术合作~ agreement on scientific and technical cooperation / 临时~ provisional agreement / 贸易~ trade agreement/ 停火~ cease-fire agreement / 停战~ cease-fire agreement/ 文化合作~ agreement on cultural cooperation / 一般~ general agreement / 支付~ payment agreement / 仲裁~ arbitration agreement / ~的执行 realization of an agreement / ~签字日期 the date of signing an agreement / ~条款 article of an agreement / ~有效日期 term of an agreement; validity of an agreement / ~正文 text of an agreement 2.(协商订立) reach an agreement on sth.

【协会】 xiéhuì association; society: 作家~ writer's association

【协理】 xiélǐ 1.(协助办理) assist in the management (of an enterprise, etc.) 2.(协助经理主持业务的人) assistant manager

【协力】 xiélì unite efforts; join in a common effort

【协商】 xiéshāng consult; talk things over: ~会议 consultative conference / ~一致的原则 the principle of reaching unanimity through consultation / 民主~ democratic consultation

【协调】 xiétiáo coordinate; concert; harmonize; bring into line: 共同~ overall coordination / ~发展 coordinated growth / ~技术问题 technical coordination / 采取~行动 take concerted steps / 这些窗帘和地毯不~。These curtains and rugs don't go together.

【协同】 xiétóng cooperate with; work in coordination with

【协同作战】 xiétóng zuòzhàn fight in coordination

【协议】 xiéyì 1.(协商) agree on 2.(协商一致的意见) agreement: 达成~ come to an agreement; reach an agreement / 撕毁~ tear up an agreement; violate an agreement 签署~ sign an agreement

【协议离婚】 xiéyì líhūn divorce by agreement

【协助】 xiézhù assist; help; give assistance; provide help

【协奏曲】 xiézòuqǔ 〈*Music*〉 concerto: 钢琴~ piano concerto

【协作】 xiézuò cooperate; cooperation (n.); coordinate; coordination (n.); ~的效益 efficiency of assistance / 参加~的各方 cooperating parties / 参加~的各方的责任分工 division of obligations of the cooperating parties; responsibility shares / 经济~区 economically coordinated region / 经济技术~ economic and technical assistance / 给予经济技术~ render economic and technical assistance

【协作范围】 xiézuò fànwéi sphere of assistance

【协作金额】 xiézuò jīn'é amount of assistance

【协作贸易】 xiézuò màoyì cooperating trade

【协作目的】 xiézuò mùdì purpose of assistance

胁[脅、脇](xié) 1.(上身两侧) the upper part of the side of the human body 2.(胁迫) coerce; force

【胁持】 xiéchí abduct; hold under duress

【胁从】 xiécóng 1.(被迫跟着干) be an accomplice under duress 2.(胁从分子) unwilling accomplice; reluctant follower

【胁迫】 xiépò coerce; force

邪(xié) evil; heretical; irregular: 改~归正 give up one's evil ways and return to the right path; turn over a new leaf

【邪道】 xiédào evil ways; depraved life; vice: 走~ lead a depraved life; abandon oneself to evil ways

【邪恶】 xié'è evil; wicked; vicious

【邪路】 xiélù evil way; vice

【邪门歪道】 xiémén-wāidào crooked ways; crooked means; dishonest practices; dishonest methods

【邪念】 xiéniàn evil thought; wicked idea; evil intention

【邪气】 xiéqì perverse trend; evil influence
【邪说】 xiéshuō heresy; heretical ideas; fallacy

挟［挾］(xié) 1.(用胳膊夹住) hold sth. under the arm 2.(挟制) coerce; force sb. to submit to one's will: 要～ coerce 3.(心里怀着) harbor
【挟持】 xiéchí 1.(从两旁抓住) seize sb. on both sides by the arms 2.(强迫对方服从) hold sb. under duress; coerce sb. into submission
【挟嫌】 xiéxián harbor resentment; bear a grudge: ～报复 bear resentment against sb. and retaliate
【挟制】 xiézhì take advantage of sb's weakness to enforce obedience; force sb. to do one's bidding

携［攜、擕］(xié) 1.(携带) carry; take along: ～款潜逃 abscond with funds 2.(拉着手) take sb. by the hand; hold sb. by the hand
【携带】 xiédài 1.(随身带着) carry; take along 2.(提携) support; give guidance to
【携带式电话机】 xiédàishì diànhuàjī portable telephone
【携手】 xiéshǒu 1.(手拉着手) hand in hand 2.(共同) together; jointly

斜 (xié) oblique; slanting; inclined; tilted
【斜井】 xiéjǐng 1.〈*Mineral*.〉inclined shaft; slope 2.〈*Petroleum*〉inclined well; slant hole
【斜路】 xiélù wrong path
【斜坡】 xiépō slope
【斜视】 xiéshì 1.〈*Med*.〉strabismus 2.(斜着眼看) look sideways; cast a sidelong glance: 目不～ not look sideways; refuse to be distracted
【斜纹】 xiéwén 〈*Textiles*〉twill (weave)
【斜纹布】 xiéwénbù twill; drill
【斜线】 xiéxiàn oblique line
【斜线号】 xiéxiànhào slant (符号为 /)
【斜眼】 xiéyǎn 1.〈*Med*.〉strabismus 2.(指眼睛) wall-eye or cross-eye 3.(指人) a wall-eyed or cross-eyed person
【斜阳】 xiéyáng setting sun

偕 (xié) together with; in the company of
【偕老】 xiélǎo husband and wife grow old together
【偕同】 xiétóng in the company of; accompanied by; along with

谐 (xié) 1.(和谐) in harmony; in accord; in tune: 和～ harmonious 2.(办好;商量好) settle; come to an agreement 3.(诙谐) humorous
【谐和】 xiéhé harmonious; concordant
【谐谑】 xiéxuè banter
【谐音】 xiéyīn 1.〈*Phonet*.〉homophonic 2.〈*Music*〉partials
【谐振】 xiézhèn 〈*Physics*〉resonance
【谐振器】 xiézhènqì 〈*Physics*〉resonator

鞋 (xié) shoes: 芭蕾舞舞～ ballet shoes / 半高跟～ pump (AmE.); court shoes (BrE.) / 布～ cloth shoes / 高跟～ high-heeled shoes / 胶～ sneaker (AmE.); plimsoll (BrE.) / 凉～ sandal / 旅游～ hiking boot (AmE.); walking boot (BrE.) / 皮～ leather shoes / 拖～ thong (AmE.); flip-flop (BrE.) / 相巾～ slipper / 运动～ trainer (AmE.); running shoe (BrE.) / 足球～ cleats (AmE.); football boot (BrE.)
【鞋拔子】 xiébá·zi shoehorn; shoe lifter
【鞋帮】 xiébāng upper (of a shoe)
【鞋带】 xiédài shoelace; shoestring
【鞋底】 xiédǐ sole (of a shoe)
【鞋垫】 xiédiàn shoe-pad; insole; inner sole
【鞋跟】 xiégēn heel (of a shoe)
【鞋柜】 xiéguì chest of drawers for shoes
【鞋匠】 xiéjiàng shoe maker; cobbler
【鞋扣】 xiékòu shoe buckle
【鞋面】 xiémiàn instep; vamp
【鞋刷】 xiéshuā shoe brush
【鞋楦】 xiéxuàn shoe-tree
【鞋样】 xiéyàng shoe pattern; outline of sole
【鞋油】 xiéyóu shoe polish; shoe cream

写［寫］(xiě) 1.(书写) write 2.(写作) compose; write: ～论文 write a thesis / ～日记 make an entry in one's diary; keep a diary / ～诗 compose a poem / ～信 write a letter 3.(描写) describe; depict: ～景 describe the scenery 4.(画) paint; draw: ～生 paint from life
【写稿】 xiěgǎo write for a magazine; contribute to a magazine

【写景】 xiějǐng describe a view
【写入】 xiěrù 〈*Computer*〉 read-in; write-in
【写实】 xiěshí write or paint realistically
【写实派】 xiěshípài realism: realistic (adj.)
【写信】 xiěxìn write
【写意】 xiěyì 〈*Arts*〉 freehand brushwork in traditional Chinese painting
【写照】 xiězhào portrayal; portraiture: 生活的真实～ be a true portrayal of the life
【写真】 xiězhēn 1.(画人像) portray a person; draw a portrait 2.(人像画) portraits painted 3.(如实描绘) true description of sth. 4.(裸体像) nude; nude figure
【写真集】 xiězhēnjí collection of nude figures
【写字间】 xiězìjiān office room
【写字楼】 xiězìlóu office building
【写字台】 xiězìtái writing desk; desk
【写作】 xiězuò write; compose; writing (n.)
【写作技巧】 xiězuò jìqiǎo writing technique

血 (xiě) blood
(另见"血"xuè)
【血淋淋】 xiělīnlīn dripping with blood; bloody
【血晕】 xiěyùn bruise

泄［洩］(xiè) 1.(排出；排泄) let out; discharge; release: 像个～了气的皮球 like a deflated rubber ball; dejected 2.(泄漏) let out; leak 3.(发泄) give vent to; vent
【泄底】 xièdǐ reveal the inside story; expose what is behind the screen
【泄愤】 xièfèn give vent to one's anger; vent one's resentment
【泄恨】 xièhèn give vent to one's hatred
【泄洪】 xièhóng 〈*Water Conservancy*〉 flood discharge
【泄洪道】 xièhóngdào flood-relief channel; floodway
【泄劲】 xièjìn 1.(失去信心) lose heart; feel discouraged; be disheartened 2.(失去干劲) slacken one's efforts; slack off
【泄漏】 xièlòu 1.(漏出) leak; let out; divulge; give away: 煤气～得很慢,我们勉强发现。The gas leak was so slow we barely noticed. 2.同"泄露"
【泄露】 xièlòu let out; reveal; betray; disclose: ～国家机密 betray state secrets / ～军事秘密 disclose military secrets
【泄密】 xièmì divulge a secret; betray confidential matters: ～事件 case of leakage of a secret
【泄气】 xièqì 1.(泄劲儿) lose heart; feel discouraged; be disheartened 2.(低劣或无本领) disappointing; frustrating; pathetic
【泄水】 xièshuǐ 〈*Water Conservancy*〉 sluicing
【泄水道】 xièshuǐdào sluiceway
【泄水工程】 xièshuǐ gōngchéng outlet work
【泄水孔】 xièshuǐkǒng outlet
【泄水闸】 xièshuǐzhā sluice gate; sluice

泻［瀉］(xiè) 1.(很快地流) flow swiftly; rush down; pour out 2.(腹泻) have loose bowels; have diarrhea
【泻肚】 xièdù have loose bowels; have diarrhea
【泻药】 xièyào laxative; cathartic; purgative

卸 (xiè) 1.(卸货) unload; discharge; lay down 2.(拆卸) remove; strip: ～零件 remove parts from a machine; strip a machine 3.(推卸) get rid of; shirk
【卸车】 xièchē unload (goods, etc.) from a vehicle; unload a vehicle
【卸货】 xièhuò unload cargo; discharge cargo: 平均～定额 average rate of unloading
【卸货单】 xièhuòdān landing order
【卸货等级】 xièhuò děngjí unloading scale
【卸货费】 xièhuòfèi discharging expenses; landing charges
【卸货港】 xièhuògǎng port of delivery; port of discharge
【卸货码头】 xièhuò mǎtóu landing stage
【卸料装置】 xièliào zhuāngzhì tripper
【卸任】 xièrèn be relieved of one's office
【卸责】 xièzé shirk one's duty; deny one's responsibility
【卸装】 xièzhuāng remove stage makeup and costume

屑 (xiè) 1.(碎末) bits; scraps; crumbs: 煤～ (coal) slack 2.(琐碎) trifling 3.(认为值得) 不～ disdain to do sth.

械 (xiè) 1.(器械) tool; instrument: 机～ machine; mechanism 2.(武器) weapon: 军～ weapons; arms; ordnance
【械斗】 xièdòu fight with weapons between

groups of people

亵［褻］(xiè) **1.** (轻慢) treat with irreverence; be disrespectful **2.** (淫秽) obscene; indecent

【亵渎】 xièdú blaspheme; profane; pollute: ～神明 blaspheme the gods; insult the gods

谢 (xiè) **1.** (感谢) thank **2.** (道歉,认错) apologize; make an apology **3.** (谢绝) decline **4.** (花、叶脱落) wither

【谢忱】 xièchén gratitude; thankfulness

【谢词】 xiècí thank-you speech

【谢绝】 xièjué refuse; decline: ～参观。Not open to visitors.

【谢幕】 xièmù answer a curtain call; respond to a curtain call

【谢世】 xièshì pass away; die

【谢天谢地】 xiètiān-xièdì thank goodness; thank heaven

【谢谢】 xièxie thanks; thank you: 不,～你。No, thanks. / "再来点茶吧。""不,～,我不要茶了。" Have some more tea. No, thank you, I don't want any more tea.

【谢意】 xièyì gratitude; thankfulness

【谢罪】 xièzuì apologize for an offense; offer an apology

榭 (xiè) a pavilion or house on a terrace: 歌台舞～ halls for the performance of songs and dances / 水～ waterside pavilion

解 (xiè) understand
(另见"解"jiě, jiè)

懈 (xiè) slack; lax

【懈怠】 xièdài slack; sluggish

邂 (xiè)

【邂逅】 xièhòu meet unexpectedly; run into sb.; meet by chance

蟹［蠏］(xiè) 〈*Zool.*〉 crab

【蟹粉】 xièfěn crab meat

【蟹黄】 xièhuáng the ovary and digestive glands of a crab

【蟹青】 xièqīng greenish-grey

【蟹爪】 xièzhǎo crab claw

【蟹爪兰】 xièzhǎolán 〈*Bot.*〉 schlumbergera

xin

心 (xīn) **1.** (心脏) the heart **2.** (思想、感情) heart; mind; feeling; intention: 爱国～ patriotic feeling; patriotism **3.** (中心) center; core: 核～ core; nucleus

【心爱】 xīn'ài love; treasure

【心安理得】 xīn'ān-lǐdé feel at ease and justified; have an easy conscience; heart at rest and virtue in completion

【心包】 xīnbāo 〈*Anat.*〉 pericardium

【心病】 xīnbìng **1.** (指心情) worry; anxiety **2.** (隐情或隐痛) sore point; secret trouble

【心搏】 xīnbó 〈*Physiol.*〉 heartbeat

【心搏过速】 xīnbó guòsù 〈*Med.*〉 tachycardia

【心不在焉】 xīnbùzàiyān absent-minded; inattentive; preoccupied (with sth. else)

【心肠】 xīncháng **1.** (存心) heart; intention: ～好 be kind-hearted **2.** (感情) feeling: ～软 have a soft heart **3.** (兴致) state of mind; interest; mood: 没～ be not interested in doing sth.

【心潮】 xīncháo a tidal surge of emotion; surging thoughts and emotions

【心慈手软】 xīncí-shǒuruǎn softhearted

【心胆俱裂】 xīndǎn-jùliè be frightened out of one's wits; be terror-stricken

【心得】 xīndé what one has learned from work, study, etc.

【心地】 xīndì a person's mind, character, moral nature, etc.: ～纯洁 pure in mind

【心电图】 xīndiàntú 〈*Med.*〉 electrocardiogram; ECG: 做～ have an electrocardiogram

【心电图机】 xīndiàntújī 〈*Med.*〉 electrocardiograph; ECG machine

【心动过速】 xīndòng guòsù 〈*Med.*〉 tachycardia

【心毒手辣】 xīndú-shǒulà callous and cruel

【心烦】 xīnfán be vexed; be perturbed

【心房】 xīnfáng **1.** 〈*Anat.*〉 atrium (of the heart) **2.** (内心) heart; inmost; innermost

【心浮】 xīnfú flighty and impatient; unstable

【心服】 xīnfú be genuinely convinced; acknowledge sincerely

【心腹】 xīnfù **1.** (亲信的) trusted; reliable **2.** (亲信) trusted subordinate; reliable agent **3.** (不轻易说的) confidential: ～事 a secret in the depth of one's heart

【心腹之患】 xīnfùzhīhuàn disease in one's vital organs; serious hidden trouble or danger

【心甘】 xīngān willing; ready; perfectly

【心甘情愿】 xīngān-qíngyuàn be most willing to; be perfectly happy to

【心肝】 xīngān **1.**（良心）conscience：没～ heartless **2.**（最心爱的人）darling; deary

【心黑】 xīnhēi **1.**（心狠）cruel; merciless **2.**（贪心）greedy; insatiable

【心狠】 xīnhěn cruel; merciless

【心花怒放】 xīnhuā-nùfàng burst with joy; be wild with joy; be elated

【心怀】 xīnhuái **1.**（心中存有）harbor; entertain; cherish ～鬼胎 entertain dark schemes; have ulterior motives **2.**（心意）intention; purpose **3.**（心情）state of mind; mood

【心怀叵测】 xīnhuáipǒcè entertain dark schemes; have ulterior motives

【心慌】 xīnhuāng be flustered; be nervous：～意乱 be alarmed and nervous

【心灰意懒】 xīnhuī-yìlǎn the heart dispirited and the mind indolent; be disheartened; be downhearted

【心肌】 xīnjī 〈*Anat*.〉 cardiac muscle; myocardium

【心肌梗塞】 xīnjī gěngsè 〈*Med*.〉 myocardial infarction

【心肌炎】 xīnjīyán 〈*Med*.〉 myocarditis

【心机】 xīnjī thinking; scheming

【心急】 xīnjí impatient; short-tempered

【心计】 xīnjì calculation; scheming; planning：很有～ adept at scheming

【心迹】 xīnjì the true state of one's mind; true motives or feelings：表明～ lay bare one's innermost thought

【心悸】 xīnjì **1.**〈*Med*.〉 palpitation **2.**（害怕）fright; fear：令人～ make sb. feel frightened

【心尖】 xīnjiān 〈*Anat*.〉 apex of the heart

【心焦】 xīnjiāo anxious; worried

【心绞痛】 xīnjiǎotòng 〈*Med*.〉 angina pectoris

【心惊胆战】 xīnjīng-dǎnzhàn tremble with fear; shake with fright

【心惊肉跳】 xīnjīng-ròutiào palpitate with anxiety and fear; be filled with apprehension

【心境】 xīnjìng state of mind; frame of mind; mental state; mood：～不好 be in a bad mood; be in low spirits / ～好 be in a good mood

【心静】 xīnjìng calm

【心坎】 xīnkǎn **1.**（心口）stomach; the pit of the stomach **2.**（内心）the bottom of one's heart：她的话说到了我的～上。Her words have sunken deep into my heart.

【心口】 xīnkǒu the pit of the stomach

【心口如一】 xīnkǒu-rúyī say what one thinks; be frank and unreserved

【心旷神怡】 xīnkuàng-shényí relaxed and happy; carefree and joyous

【心理】 xīnlǐ psychology; mentality

【心理发育】 xīnlǐ fāyù psychological development

【心理分析】 xīnlǐ fēnxì psychoanalysis

【心理健康】 xīnlǐ jiànkāng mental health

【心理社会危机】 xīnlǐ shèhuì wēijī psychosocial crisis

【心理卫生】 xīnlǐ wèishēng mental hygiene

【心理学】 xīnlǐxué psychology; psychological (adj.) ‖ 心理学家 psychologist

【心理因素】 xīnlǐ yīnsù psychological factor

【心理战】 xīnlǐzhàn psychological warfare

【心理障碍】 xīnlǐ zhàng'ài psychological barrier

【心理治疗】 xīnlǐ zhìliáo psychotherapy

【心里】 xīn·li **1.**（胸内）in the heart; at heart **2.**（思想里）in (the) mind：记在～ keep in mind

【心里话】 xīn·lihuà one's innermost thoughts and feelings

【心里美萝卜】 xīn·liměi luó·bo radish; sweet radish

【心力】 xīnlì mental and physical efforts：～交瘁 be mentally and physically exhausted

【心力衰竭】 xīnlì shuāijié 〈*Med*.〉 cardiac failure; heart failure; go into heart failure

【心灵】 xīnlíng **1.**（心思灵敏）clever; intelligent; quick-witted：～手巧 clever and deft **2.**（内心）heart; soul; spirit：～深处 deep in one's heart

【心领】 xīnlǐng understand tacitly

【心领神会】 xīnlǐng-shénhuì the heart receives and spirit knows it; understand tacitly; readily take a hint

【心率】 xīnlǜ 〈*Med*.〉 heart rate

【心律】 xīnlǜ 〈*Med*.〉 rhythm of the heart

【心律不齐】 xīnlǜ bùqí 〈*Med*.〉 arrhythmia
【心律失常】 xīnlǜ shīcháng 〈*Med*.〉 arrhythmia cordis
【心乱如麻】 xīnluàn-rúmá have one's mind as confused as a tangled skein; be utterly confused and disconcerted; be terribly upset
【心满意足】 xīnmǎn-yìzú be perfectly content; be fully satisfied; to one's heart's content
【心明眼亮】 xīnmíng-yǎnliàng be sharpeyed and clearheaded; see and think clearly
【心目】 xīnmù 1.(感受) mind; mental view; mind's eye 2.(看法,想法) mind; thought
【心内直视手术】 xīnnèi zhíshì shǒushù 〈*Med*.〉 open-heart surgery
【心平气和】 xīnpíng-qìhé even-tempered and good-humored; quiet in mind and peace in disposition
【心情】 xīnqíng frame of mind; state of mind; mood: ～沉重 feel sad and depressed / ～舒畅 feel happy and relaxed
【心如刀割】 xīnrúdāogē feel as if a knife were piercing one's heart
【心软】 xīnruǎn be softhearted; be tenderhearted
【心上人】 xīnshàngrén darling; deary
【心神】 xīnshén 1.(心思) mind; thought 2.(精神) state of mind: ～不定 feel uneasy
【心声】 xīnshēng heartfelt wishes; aspirations; thinking
【心室】 xīnshì 〈*Anat*.〉 ventricle
【心事】 xīnshì sth. weighing on one's mind; a load on one's mind
【心术】 xīnshù intention; design: ～不正 harbor evil intentions; harbor evil designs
【心思】 xīn·si 1.(念头) thought; idea 2.(脑筋) thinking; thoughts: 用～ do a lot of thinking; think hard 3.(心情) state of mind; mood
【心酸】 xīnsuān be grieved; feel sad
【心算】 xīnsuàn mental arithmetic; doing sums in one's head
【心疼】 xīnténg 1.(疼爱) love dearly 2.(舍不得) feel sorry; make one's heart ache
【心田】 xīntián 1.(内心) heart 2.(用心) intention
【心跳】 xīntiào palpitation; the beating of the heart
【心痛】 xīntòng 〈*Med*.〉 cardiac pain
【心头】 xīntóu mind; heart: ～恨 rankling hatred
【心细】 xīnxì careful; scrupulous
【心弦】 xīnxián heartstrings: 动人～ touch sb. to the heart
【心向往之】 xīnxiàngwǎngzhī yearning for sb. or sth.
【心心相印】 xīnxīn-xiāngyìn hearts and feelings find a perfect response; have mutual affinity; be kindred spirits
【心胸】 xīnxiōng 1.(内心深处) breadth of mind 2.(胸怀,气量) mind; heart: ～开阔 broadminded; unprejudiced / ～狭窄 narrow-minded 3.(抱负) ambition; aspiration
【心虚】 xīnxū 1.(怕人知道) afraid of being found out; with a guilty conscience: 做贼～ have a guilty conscience 2.(缺乏自信心) lacking in self-confidence; diffident
【心绪】 xīnxù state of mind: ～不宁 in a disturbed state of mind; in a flutter
【心血】 xīnxuè painstaking care; painstaking effort
【心血来潮】 xīnxuè-láicháo be prompted by a sudden impulse; be seized by a whim
【心眼儿】 xīnyǎnr 1.(内心) heart; mind 2.(心地) intention: ～好 good-natured; kindhearted 3.(聪明) intelligence; cleverness: 缺～ lack of intelligence / 我竟问出这么个问题,实在是少了个～。I was rather tactless me to ask such a question. 4.(顾虑) unfounded doubts; unnecessary misgivings: ～多 full of unnecessary misgivings; oversensitive 5.(气量) breadth of mind: ～小 oversensitive; narrow-minded
【心意】 xīnyì 1.(情意) regard; kindly feelings 2.(愿望) intention; purpose
【心硬】 xīnyìng hardhearted; stonyhearted; callous; unfeeling
【心有灵犀一点通】 xīn yǒu língxī yì diǎn tōng heart which beat in unison are linked
【心有余而力不足】 xīn yǒuyú ér lì bùzú the spirit is willing, but the flesh is weak; unable to do what one wants very much to do
【心有余悸】 xīnyǒuyújì one's heart still fluttering with fear; have a lingering fear

【心猿意马】 xīnyuán-yìmǎ restless and whimsical; fanciful and fickle; capricious; when one meant gibbon, he thinks of a horse

【心愿】 xīnyuàn cherished desire; aspiration; wish

【心悦诚服】 xīnyuè-chéngfú feel a heartfelt admiration; be completely convinced

【心脏】 xīnzàng heart

【心脏病】 xīnzàngbìng 〈*Med.*〉 heart disease; cardiopathy: 风湿性～ rheumatic heart disease / 先天性～ congenital heart disease / ～发作 heart attack

【心照】 xīnzhào understand without being told; have an understanding: ～不宣 have a tacit understanding; understood but not expressed

【心直口快】 xīnzhí-kǒukuài frank and outspoken; saying what one thinks without much deliberation

【心智缺陷者】 xīnzhì quēxiànzhě 〈*Education*〉 mental defective

【心中】 xīnzhōng in one's heart; in one's mind

【心中无数】 xīnzhōng-wúshù not know for certain; feel uncertain about sth.

【心中有数】 xīnzhōng-yǒushù have a pretty good idea of; know fairly well; know what's what

【心醉】 xīnzuì be charmed; be enchanted; be fascinated

芯 (xīn) core
(另见"芯"xìn)

【芯片】 xīnpiàn 〈*Computer*〉 chip

辛 (xīn) 1.(辣) hot (in taste, flavor, etc.); pungent 2.(辛苦) hard; laborious: 艰～ hardships 3.(痛苦) suffering

【辛迪加】 xīndíjiā 〈*Econ.*〉 syndicate

【辛苦】 xīnkǔ 1.(劳苦) hard; toilsome; laborious 2.(套语) work hard; go to great trouble; go through hardships

【辛苦费】 xīnkǔfèi "thank you" reward

【辛辣】 xīnlà pungent; hot; bitter: ～的讽刺 bitter irony; biting sarcasm

【辛劳】 xīnláo pains; toil

【辛勤】 xīnqín industrious; hardworking

【辛酸】 xīnsuān sad; bitter; miserable

【辛酸泪】 xīnsuānlèi hot and bitter tears

【辛烷】 xīnwán 〈*Chem.*〉 octane

【辛辛苦苦】 xīnxīn-kǔkǔ take a lot of trouble; take great pains; work laboriously

锌 (xīn) 〈*Chem.*〉 zinc (元素符号 Zn)

【锌版】 xīnbǎn 〈*Printing*〉 zinc plate; zincograph

【锌版印刷术】 xīnbǎn yìnshuāshù zincography

欣[訢] (xīn) glad; happy; joyful

【欣逢】 xīnféng on the happy occasion of

【欣然】 xīnrán joyfully; with pleasure

【欣赏】 xīnshǎng 1.(享受) appreciate; enjoy 2.(喜欢) admire; like

【欣慰】 xīnwèi be gratified

【欣喜】 xīnxǐ glad; joyful; happy

【欣悉】 xīnxī be glad to learn; be happy to learn; on learning with great joy

【欣欣】 xīnxīn 1.(高兴) happy; delighted 2.(茂盛) prosperous; fluorising

【欣欣向荣】 xīnxīn-xiàngróng prosperous; flourishing; thriving

新 (xīn) 1.(跟"老"或"旧"相对) new; fresh; up-to-date: ～发明 a new invention / ～技术 new technique; up-to-date technique / 最～消息 the latest news 2.(新近) newly; freshly; recently 3.(新近结婚的) recently married: ～人 newlywed

【新版】 xīnbǎn new edition

【新兵】 xīnbīng new recruit; recruit

【新陈代谢】 xīnchén-dàixiè 1.〈*Biol.*〉 metabolism; metabolize (v.) 2.(新代替旧) the new superseding the old

【新词】 xīncí new words; neologism

【新大陆】 xīndàlù the New World; the Americas

【新房】 xīnfáng bridal chamber

【新风】 xīnfēng new style

【新妇】 xīnfù bride

【新华社】 Xīnhuáshè the Xinhua News Agency

【新婚】 xīnhūn newly-married: ～燕尔 happy wedding couple; newlyweds

【新纪元】 xīnjìyuán new era; new epoch: 开创～ usher in a new epoch; open a new era

【新交】 xīnjiāo 1.(认识不久) new acquaintance 2.(新朋友) new friend

【新教】 xīnjiào 〈*Religion*〉 Protestantism ‖ 新教徒 Protestant
【新近】 xīnjìn recently; lately; in recent times: ～流行的东西 in-thing
【新旧交替】 xīnjiù-jiāotì the transition from the old to the new
【新居】 xīnjū new home; new residence
【新开发实用品】 xīnkāifā shíyòngpǐn notions
【新开户头】 xīnkāi hùtóu new account
【新来乍到】 xīnlái-zhàdào newly arrived; have just arrived
【新郎】 xīnláng bridegroom
【新浪潮派影片】 xīnlàngcháopài yǐngpiàn nouvelle vague
【新老殖民主义】 xīnlǎo zhímín zhǔyì colonialism and neo-colonialism
【新名词】 xīnmíngcí new term; new expression; vogue word; newfangled phrase
【新民主主义】 xīnmíngzhǔ zhǔyì new democracy; new-democratic (adj.)
【新民主主义革命】 xīnmíngzhǔ zhǔyì gémìng new-democratic revolution
【新年】 xīnnián New Year
【新娘】 xīnniáng bride
【新篇章】 xīnpiānzhāng new page; new chapter
【新品迭出】 xīnpǐn-diéchū new varieties are introduced one after another
【新奇】 xīnqí strange; novel; new
【新区】 xīnqū newly developed area; newly added district
【新人】 xīnrén 1.(有新品质的) people of a new type: ～新事 new people and new things 2.(新出现的) new personality; new talent 3.(新娘) bride 4.(新郎新娘) newlywed
【新生】 xīnshēng 1.(刚产生的) newborn; newly born: ～事物 newly emerging things; new things 2.(新生命) new life; rebirth; regeneration: 获得～ gain a new life 3.(新入学的学生) new student
【新生儿】 xīnshēng'ér newly-born baby; new arrival
【新式】 xīnshì new type; latest type; new-style
【新手】 xīnshǒu new hand; raw recruit
【新书】 xīnshū 1.(新的) new book 2.(刚出版的) books that are just off the press
【新四军】 Xīnsìjūn the New Fourth Army
【新投资】 xīntóuzī equity capital
【新闻】 xīnwén 1.(媒体发布的) news: 电视～ television news 2.(新发生的事) recent social events
【新闻报导】 xīnwén bàodǎo news report; news story; news coverage
【新闻编辑室】 xīnwén biānjíshì newsroom
【新闻播音员】 xīnwén bōyīnyuán newsreader; newscaster
【新闻处】 xīnwénchù press section; information service; office of information
【新闻电讯电头】 xīnwén diànxùn diàntóu dateline
【新闻发布会】 xīnwén fābùhuì news brief; briefing
【新闻法】 xīnwénfǎ press law
【新闻封锁】 xīnwén fēngsuǒ news blockout
【新闻稿】 xīnwéngǎo press release; news release
【新闻公报】 xīnwén gōngbào press communique
【新闻工作】 xīnwén gōngzuò newspapering
【新闻工作者】 xīnwén gōngzuòzhě journalist
【新闻广播】 xīnwén guǎngbō newscast
【新闻记者】 xīnwén jìzhě newsman; newspaperman; reporter; journalist
【新闻价值】 xīnwén jiàzhí news value
【新闻简报】 xīnwén jiǎnbào news summary
【新闻检查】 xīnwén jiǎnchá censorship of press
【新闻检查官】 xīnwén jiǎncháguān press censor
【新闻界】 xīnwénjiè press circles; newspaperdom; the press
【新闻片】 xīnwénpiàn newsreel; news film
【新闻评论员】 xīnwén pínglùnyuán news analyst
【新闻人物】 xīnwén rénwù news maker
【新闻司】 xīnwénsī department of information
【新禧】 xīnxǐ happy new year: 恭贺～! Happy New Year!
【新鲜】 xīn·xiān 1.(指瓜果蔬菜肉类等) fresh: ～肉 fresh meat / ～蔬菜 fresh vegetables 2.(指空气) fresh; clean: ～空气 fresh air 3.(新发生的) new; novel; strange:

～事儿 new things
【新鲜性】 xīn·xiānxìng novelty
【新兴】 xīnxīng new and developing; burgeoning: ～工业 the new and expanding industry
【新星】 xīnxīng 1.〈*Astron*.〉nova: 超～ supernova 2.(指演员或运动员) new star
【新型】 xīnxíng new type; new pattern
【新秀】 xīnxiù new star; rising star
【新摇滚乐】 xīn yáogǔnyuè new rock
【新义】 xīnyì new definition
【新意】 xīnyì new signification; new conception
【新印象派】 xīnyìnxiàngpài neo-impressionism
【新颖】 xīnyǐng new and original; novel
【新语言学】 xīnyǔyánxué neolinguistics
【新约】 Xīnyuē 〈*Christianity*〉 the New Testament
【新月】 xīnyuè 1.(农历月初的月亮) crescent 2.〈*Astron*.〉 new moon
【新针疗法】 xīnzhēnliáofǎ 〈*Chin*. *Med*.〉 new acupuncture treatment
【新枝】 xīnzhī 〈*Bot*.〉 shoot
【新殖民主义】 xīnzhímín zhǔyì neocolonialism; new colonialism; neocolonist (adj.)
【新址】 xīnzhǐ new address
【新装】 xīnzhuāng new clothes

薪 (xīn) 1.(柴火) firewood; faggot; fuel 2.(薪水) salary: 全～ full pay / 发～ pay out the salary
【薪金】 xīnjīn salary; pay
【薪水】 xīn·shui salary; pay; wages

馨 (xīn) 〈*written*〉 strong and pervasive fragrance
【馨香】 xīnxiāng 1.(芳香) fragrance 2.(烧香的香味) smell of burning incense

囟[顖] (xìn) 〈*Anat*.〉 the parietal foramen
【囟脑门】 xìnnǎomén the parietal foramen

芯[信] (xìn) core
(另见"芯"xīn)
【芯子】 xìn·zi 1.(芯儿) fuse; wick: 蜡烛～ candle wick 2.(蛇的舌头) the forked tongue of a snake

信 (xìn) 1.(确实) true 2.(信用) confidence; trust; faith: 失～ break faith; break one's promise 3.(相信) believe: ～以为真 accept sth. as true; take sth. at face value 4.(信奉) profess faith in; believe in: ～佛 profess Buddhism 5.(听凭) at will; at random; without plan 6.(凭据) sign; evidence 7.(书信) letter; mail: 送～ deliver a letter / 写～ write a letter / 寄～ post a letter; send a letter / 收到一封～ get a letter 8.(信息) message; word; information: 口～ an oral message 9.(引信) fuse
【信步】 xìnbù take a leisurely walk; walk aimlessly; stroll
【信贷】 xìndài credit: 备用～ standby credit / 偿付～ reimbursement credit / 低利～ low-interest credit / 国家～ public credit; state credit / 票据～ paper credit / 商业～ commercial credit / 提供银行～ grant bank credit
【信贷额度】 xìndài édù line of credit
【信贷风险】 xìndài fēngxiǎn credit risk
【信贷公司】 xìndài gōngsī finance company; finance house
【信贷监督】 xìndài jiāndū credit control
【信贷来源】 xìndài láiyuán credit facilities
【信贷市场】 xìndài shìchǎng credit market
【信贷收支】 xìndài shōuzhī credit receipts and payments
【信贷业务】 xìndài yèwù credit operation
【信贷资金】 xìndài zījīn credit funds; funds for extending credit: 增拨银行～ additional allocations of credit funds to the banks
【信风】 xìnfēng 〈*Geog*.〉 trade wind
【信封】 xìnfēng envelope: 防水～ waterproof envelope / 开窗～ window envelope / 开口～ open envelope
【信奉】 xìnfèng 1.(信仰) believe in: ～上帝 believe in God 2.(相信并奉行) believe in and act accordingly
【信服】 xìngfú completely accept; be convinced
【信鸽】 xìngē carrier pigeon; homing pigeon; homer
【信管】 xìnguǎn fuse
【信函】 xìnhán letters; mail
【信号】 xìnhào signal
【信号兵】 xìnhàobīng signalman
【信号刺激】 xìnhào cìjī signal stimulus
【信号弹】 xìnhàodàn signal flare

【信号灯】 xìnhàodēng signal lamp
【信号发生器】 xìnhào fāshēngqì signal generator
【信号机】 xìnhàojī semaphore; teleseme
【信号枪】 xìnhàoqiāng flare pistol; signal pistol; pyrotechnic pistol
【信号曲】 xìnhàoqǔ 〈*Broadcast*〉 theme song; theme tone
【信号装置】 xìnhào zhuāngzhì advertiser; signaller
【信汇】 xìnhuì mail-transfer (M/T)
【信笺】 xìnjiān letter paper; writing paper
【信件】 xìnjiàn letters; mail
【信教】 xìnjiào profess a religion; be religious
【信口雌黄】 xìnkǒu-cíhuáng make irresponsible remarks; wag one's tongue too freely
【信口开河】 xìnkǒu-kāihé wag one's tongue too freely; talk nonsense; talk irresponsibly; shoot one's mouth off
【信赖】 xìnlài trust; count on; have faith in
【信念】 xìnniàn faith; belief; conviction: 坚守～ strengthen one's conviction
【信任】 xìnrèn trust; have confidence in
【信任票】 xìnrènpiào vote of confidence
【信石】 xìnshí arsenic; white arsenic
【信使】 xìnshǐ courier; messenger: 外交～ diplomatic messenger
【信使证明书】 xìnshǐ zhèngmíngshū courier's credentials
【信誓旦旦】 xìnshì-dàndàn pledge in all sincerity and seriousness; vow solemnly
【信守】 xìnshǒu abide by; stand by: ～协议 abide by an agreement; stand by an agreement
【信天翁】 xìntiānwēng 〈*Zool*.〉 albatross
【信条】 xìntiáo article of creed; article of faith
【信筒】 xìntǒng pillar-box; mailbox
【信徒】 xìntú believer; disciple; follower; adherent; devotee: 佛教～ Buddhist
【信托】 xìntuō trust; entrust
【信托存款】 xìntuō cúnkuǎn trust deposits
【信托公司】 xìntuō gōngsī trust company
【信托货币】 xìntuō huòbì fiduciary money
【信托基金】 xìntuō jījīn trust fund
【信托契约】 xìntuō qìyuē deed of trust
【信托商店】 xìntuō shāngdiàn commission house; commission shop; commission agent
【信托证书】 xìntuō zhèngshū trust certification
【信物】 xìnwù authenticating object; token; keepsake
【信息】 xìnxī 1.(消息) information; news; message: 内部～ confidential information / 专利～ patent information 供求～ information on supply and demand 2.(数据) information
【信息爆炸】 xìnxī bàozhà information explosion
【信息编码】 xìnxī biānmǎ information encoding
【信息处理】 xìnxī chǔlǐ information processing
【信息传递】 xìnxī chuándì information delivery; message delivery
【信息存储器】 xìnxī cúnchǔqì information-storing device
【信息单位】 xìnxī dānwèi logan
【信息反馈】 xìnxī fǎnkuì information feedback
【信息高速公路】 xìnxī gāosù gōnglù information superhighway
【信息管理系统】 xìnxī guǎnlǐ xìtǒng information management system
【信息技术】 xìnxī jìshù information technology
【信息检索】 xìnxī jiǎnsuǒ information retrieval
【信息库】 xìnxīkù information bank
【信息论】 xìnxīlùn information theory
【信息容量】 xìnxī róngliàng information capacity
【信息社会】 xìnxī shèhuì information society
【信息市场】 xìnxī shìchǎng information market
【信息网】 xìnxīwǎng information network
【信息系统】 xìnxī xìtǒng information system
【信息中心】 xìnxī zhōngxīn information center
【信息转储】 xìnxī zhuǎnchǔ memory dump
【信箱】 xìnxiāng 1.(信筒) letter box; mailbox 2.(可租用的) post-office box (P.O.B.)
【信箱号码】 xìnxiāng hàomǎ box number
【信心】 xìnxīn confidence; faith: 满怀～ with full confidence
【信仰】 xìnyǎng faith; belief; conviction: 政治～ political belief / 宗教～ religious belief

【信仰自由】 xìnyǎng zìyóu freedom of worship; religious freedom

【信义】 xìnyì good faith; faith

【信用】 xìnyòng 1.（信任）trustworthiness; credit; reputation：讲～ keep one's promise / 无～ not trustworthy; discredited 2.〈*Econ*.〉credit

【信用额度】 xìnyòng édù line of credit

【信用放款】 xìnyòng fàngkuǎn unsecured loan; loan on credit

【信用风险】 xìnyòng fēngxiǎn credit risks

【信用汇票】 xìnyòng huìpiào credit bill

【信用卡】 xìnyòngkǎ credit card

【信用投资】 xìnyòng tóuzī fiduciary contribution

【信用债券】 xìnyòng zhàiquàn debenture bonds

【信用证】 xìnyòngzhèng letter of credit（L/C）：可转让的～ transferable letter of credit / 商业～ commercial letter of credit

【信誉】 xìnyù prestige; credit; reputation：～高 enjoy high prestige / 商业～乃经营之必须。The goodwill is to be sold with the business.

【信誉等级】 xìnyù děngjí degrees of comparison

【信纸】 xìnzhǐ letter paper; writing paper

衅［釁］（xìn）quarrel; dispute：挑～ provoke / 寻～ seek a quarrel with sb.

xing

兴［興］（xīng）1.（兴盛；流行）prosper; rise; prevail; become popular 2.（使盛行）encourage; promote 3.（开始；发动）start; begin
（另见"兴"xìng）

【兴办】 xīngbàn initiate; set up; construct：～各种经济事业 engage in various economic undertakings

【兴奋】 xīngfèn 1.（激动）be excited 2.〈*Physiol*.〉excitation

【兴奋剂】 xīngfènjì excitant; stimulant

【兴奋药丸】 xīngfèn yàowán pep pill

【兴风作浪】 xīngfēng-zuòlàng stir up trouble; make trouble; fan the flames of disorder

【兴建】 xīngjiàn build; construct

【兴利除弊】 xīnglì-chúbì promote what is beneficial and abolish what is harmful

【兴隆】 xīnglóng prosperous; thriving; flourishing; brisk

【兴起】 xīngqǐ 1.（开始）rise; spring up 2.（奋起）be on the upgrade

【兴盛】 xīngshèng prosperous; flourishing; thriving; in the ascendant

【兴师动众】 xīngshī-dòngzhòng move troops about and stir up the people; drag in many people（to do sth.）

【兴师问罪】 xīngshī-wènzuì send a punitive expedition against

【兴衰】 xīngshuāi rise and decline; ups and downs

【兴亡】 xīng-wáng rise and fall（of a nation）

【兴旺】 xīngwàng prosperous; flourishing; thriving

【兴修】 xīngxiū start construction; build：～水利 build water conservation projects

【兴许】 xīngxǔ perhaps; maybe

星（xīng）1.〈*Astron*.〉star：恒～ star; fixed star / 行～ planet 2.（细碎东西）bit; particle：火～儿 spark 3.（明星）star：球～ a star player / 影～ a movie star

【星辰】 xīngchén stars

【星斗】 xīngdǒu stars

【星光】 xīngguāng starlight

【星光灿烂】 xīngguāng cànlàn star-studded; starry

【星号】 xīnghào asterisk（*）

【星火】 xīnghuǒ 1.（微小的火）spark 2.（流星的光）shooting star; meteor：急如～ extremely urgent

【星火工程】 xīnghuǒ gōngchéng torch project

【星火计划】 Xīnghuǒ Jìhuà Spark Plan

【星火燎原】 xīnghuǒ-liáoyuán 见"星星之火，可以燎原"

【星际】 xīngjì interplanetary; interstellar：～飞行 interplanetary flight; space flight / ～空间 interstellar space

【星空】 xīngkōng starlit sky; starry sky

【星罗棋布】 xīngluó-qíbù scattered all over like stars in the sky or men on a chessboard; spread all over the place

【星期】 xīngqī 1.（一周）week：上～ last

week / 下～ next week 2.（星期日）Sunday
【星期二】 xīngqī'èr Tuesday; Tue.
【星期六】 xīngqīliù Saturday; Sat.
【星期日】 xīngqīrì Sunday; Sun.
【星期三】 xīngqīsān Wednesday; Wed.
【星期四】 xīngqīsì Thursday; Thur.
【星期五】 xīngqīwǔ Friday; Fri.
【星期一】 xīngqīyī Monday; Mon.
【星球】 xīngqiú celestial body; heavenly body
【星球大战】 xīngqiú dàzhàn strategic defense initiative（SDI）
【星探】 xīngtàn talent-scout; talent-spotter
【星图】 xīngtú 〈*Astron.*〉star map; star atlas
【星团】 xīngtuán 〈*Astron.*〉star cluster
【星系】 xīngxì 〈*Astron.*〉galaxy
【星星】 xīngxīng tiny spot
【星星】 xīng·xing star
【星星点点】 xīngxīng-diǎndiǎn tiny spots; bits and pieces
【星星之火，可以燎原】 xīngxīng zhī huǒ, kěyǐ liáoyuán A single spark can start a prairie fire.
【星夜】 xīngyè on a starlit night; on a starry night; by night
【星云】 xīngyún 〈*Astron.*〉nebula; nebulous (adj.)：蟹状～ Crab nebula
【星座】 xīngzuò 〈*Astron.*〉constellation

猩（xīng）〈*Zool.*〉orangutan
【猩红】 xīnghóng scarlet; bloodred
【猩红热】 xīnghóngrè 〈*Med.*〉scarlet fever
【猩猩】 xīng·xing 〈*Zool.*〉orangutan

惺（xīng）
【惺松】 xīngsōng (of eyes) not yet fully open on waking up：睡眼～ eyes still heavy with sleep; sleepy eyes
【惺惺】 xīngxīng 1.（清醒）clearheaded; awake 2.（聪明）wise; intelligent

腥（xīng）1.（生肉、鱼）raw meat or fish：荤～ dishes of meat or fish 2.（有腥气）having the smell of fish, seafood, etc.
【腥臭】 xīngchòu stinking smell as of rotten fish; stench
【腥风血雨】 xīngfēng-xuèyǔ sanguinary slaughter; great bloodshed
【腥气】 xīngqì 1.（腥味）the smell of fish, seafood, etc. 2.（有腥味的）stinking; fishy; stenchy
【腥臊】 xīngsāo smelling of urine; the offensive smell of a fox
【腥膻】 xīngshān smelling of fish or mutton
【腥味儿】 xīngwèir smelling of fish; fishy

刑（xíng）1.（刑罚）punishment：服～ serve one's term in prison / 缓～ on probation / 减～ commute a sentence; reduce punishment; reduction of penalty / 量～ penal discretion / 免～ exempt from punishment / 判～ sentence; pass sentence / 死～ death penalty; death sentence; capital punishment / 死～缓期执行 stay of execution; short for death penalty with a two-year reprieve and forced labor / 徒～ imprisonment; prison sentence / 已被判处死～ be under sentence of death 2.（对犯人的体罚）torture; corporal punishment：受～ suffer corporal punishment / 用～ put sb. to torture; torture
【刑场】 xíngchǎng execution ground
【刑罚】 xíngfá 〈*Law*〉penalty; punishment; criminal penalty
【刑法】 xíngfǎ 1.〈*Law*〉penal code; criminal law 2.（对犯人的体罚）corporal punishment; torture
【刑警】 xíngjǐng criminal police
【刑具】 xíngjù instruments of torture; implements of punishment
【刑律】 xínglǜ 〈*Law*〉criminal law
【刑满】 xíngmǎn expiration of the imprisonment
【刑满释放】 xíngmǎn shìfàng be released after serving the full term of a sentence; be released after serving a sentence
【刑期】 xíngqī 〈*Law*〉term of imprisonment; prison term; term of penalty
【刑期届满】 xíngqī jièmǎn expiration of the term sentence
【刑事】 xíngshì 〈*Law*〉criminal; penal：～案件 criminal case
【刑事处分】 xíngshì chǔfèn criminal sanction
【刑事法庭】 xíngshì fǎtíng criminal court
【刑事犯】 xíngshìfàn criminal offender; criminal
【刑事犯罪】 xíngshì fànzuì criminal offense; crime

【刑事管辖权】 xíngshì guǎnxiáquán criminal jurisdiction
【刑事拘留】 xíngshì jūliú criminal attachment
【刑事审判庭】 xíngshì shěnpàntíng criminal adjudication tribunal
【刑事诉讼】 xíngshì sùsòng criminal suit
【刑事诉讼法】 xíngshì sùsòngfǎ code of criminal procedure
【刑事责任】 xíngshì zérèn responsibility for a crime; criminal responsibility
【刑事侦察】 xíngshì zhēnchá criminal investigation
【刑事罪】 xíngshìzuì criminal charge; penal offense
【刑事罪犯】 xíngshì zuìfàn prisoner at the bar
【刑庭】 xíngtíng criminal court
【刑讯】 xíngxùn 〈*Law*〉 inquisition by torture
【刑侦】 xíngzhēn criminal investigation

形 (xíng) 1.(形状) form; shape 2.(形体) body; entity 3.(表现) appear; look: 喜~于色 look very pleased 4.(对照) compare; contrast: 相~见绌 prove inferior by comparison
【形成】 xíngchéng take shape; form; take form: ~风气 become a common practice
【形而上学】 xíng'érshàngxué 〈*Philos.*〉 metaphysics
【形骸】 xínghái the human skeleton; the human body
【形迹】 xíngjì 1.(举动、神色等) a person's movements and expression: ~可疑 of suspicious appearance; suspicious-looking 2.(礼貌) formality: 不拘~ without formality
【形容】 xíngróng 1.(形体和容貌) appearance; countenance 2.(描述) describe
【形容词】 xíngróngcí adjective
【形势】 xíngshì 1.(地势) terrain; topographical features: ~险要 strategically important terrain 2.(发展状况) situation; circumstances: 国际~ the international situation / 国内~ the domestic situation
【形式】 xíngshì form; shape: ~多样、讲求实效 adopt various forms so as to achieve better economic results
【形式逻辑】 xíngshì luó·ji formal logic
【形式语法】 xíngshì yǔfǎ formal grammar
【形式语言】 xíngshì yǔyán formal language
【形式主义】 xíngshì zhǔyì formalism
【形似】 xíngsì be similar in form or appearance
【形态】 xíngtài 1.(形状或表现) form; shape; pattern: 社会经济~ social-economic formation; economic formation of society 2.〈*Gram.*〉 morphology; morphological (adj.)
【形态学】 xíngtàixué morphology; morphological (*adj.*)
【形体】 xíngtǐ 1.(身体) shape (of a person's body); physique; body 2.(形状和结构) form and structure
【形同虚设】 xíngtóngxūshè exist in name only
【形象】 xíngxiàng image; form; figure: 塑造英雄~ create the image of a hero
【形象化】 xíngxiànghuà in images; figuratively
【形象思维】 xíngxiàng sīwéi thinking in (terms of) images
【形形色色】 xíngxíng-sèsè of every hue; of all shades; of all forms; of every description
【形影不离】 xíngyǐng-bùlí inseparable as body and shadow; always together
【形影相吊】 xíngyǐng-xiāngdiào body and shadow comforting each other; extremely lonely; sad and solitary
【形影相随】 xíngyǐng-xiāngsuí follow someone like his shadow
【形于辞色】 xíngyúcísè show in one's words and expression
【形状】 xíngzhuàng form; appearance; shape

型 (xíng) 1.(模子) mold 2.(样式) model; type; pattern: 流线~的 streamlined
【型钢】 xínggāng 〈*Metall.*〉 section (steel); shape
【型钢轧机】 xínggāng zhájī shape (rolling) mill
【型号】 xínghào model; type: 产品~ type of products

行 (xíng) 1.(走) go: 寸步难~ unable to move an inch; cannot go forward at all 2.(旅行) travel: 不虚此~ do not make this trip in vain 3.(临时性的) temporary; makeshift: ~灶 makeshift cooking stove 4.(流行) be current; prevail; circulate: 流~ be in fashion 5.(做;办) do; perform; carry out; engage in: 可~ can be done; be practicable; can be carried out 6.(进行)另～安排 make other arrangements 7.(行为) behavior; conduct: 言～ words and deeds 8.(可以) all right; O.K. 9.(能干) capable; competent

(另见"行"háng)

【行不通】 xíng·butōng won't do; won't work; get nowhere: 这事永远～。This will never do.

【行车】 xíngchē drive a vehicle

【行车里程】 xíngchē lǐchéng distance travelled by a vehicle; mileage

【行车速率】 xíngchē sùlǜ driving speed

【行车执照】 xíngchē zhízhào driver's license; driving license

【行程】 xíngchéng 1.(路程) route or distance of travel 2.〈*Mech*.〉 stroke; throw; travel

【行船】 xíngchuán sail (a boat); navigate

【行刺】 xíngcì assassinate ‖ 行刺者 assassin

【行道树】 xíngdàoshù shade tree (of the roadside)

【行得通】 xíng·detōng will do; workable; practicable

【行动】 xíngdòng 1.(行走;走动) move about; get about 2.(活动) act; take action: 采取～ take action / 付诸～ put into action / ～的时间到了。The time has come for action. 3.(行为;动作) action; operation: 军事～ military operations

【行动纲领】 xíngdòng gānglǐng program of action; guideline

【行动准则】 xíngdòng zhǔnzé operative norm

【行好】 xínghǎo act charitably; be merciful; be charitable

【行贿】 xínghuì bribe; offer a bribe; resort to bribery: ～受贿 offer or accept bribes

【行贿受贿罪】 xínghuì-shòuhuìzuì offense of bribery

【行将】 xíngjiāng about to; on the verge of

【行将就木】 xíngjiāng-jiùmù be getting nearer and nearer the coffin; be fast approaching death; have one foot in the grave

【行劫】 xíngjié commit robbery; rob

【行进】 xíngjìn march forward; advance

【行进路线】 xíngjìn lùxiàn route of march

【行经】 xíngjīng 1.(经过) go by; pass by 2.〈*Physiol*.〉 menstruate

【行径】 xíngjìng act; action; move: 野蛮～ barbarous act / 罪恶～ criminal act

【行军】 xíngjūn march

【行军床】 xíngjūnchuáng cot; camp bed

【行乐】 xínglè indulge in pleasures; make merry

【行礼】 xínglǐ salute

【行李】 xíng·li baggage (AmE.); luggage (BrE.): 超重～ excess baggage / 手提～ hand-baggage / 随身～ personal baggage / 托运的～ registered baggage / 五件～ five pieces of baggage / 先送交～ send the baggage in advance 免费携带～的限量 free baggage allowance

【行李标签】 xíng·li biāoqián baggage tag; luggage label

【行李舱】 xíngl·licāng 1.(轮船的) baggage cabin; baggage compartment 2.〈*Auto*〉 trunk; boot

【行李车】 xíng·lichē 1.〈*Railway*〉 baggage car; luggage van 2.(手推行李小车) baggage cart

【行李袋】 xíng·lidài duffel bag; duffle bag

【行李过磅处】 xíng·li guòbàngchù baggage check-in counter

【行李寄存处】 xíng·li jìcúnchù check-room

【行李架】 xíng·lijià 1.(放行李的架子) baggage rack; luggage rack 2.〈*Auto*〉 roof rack 3.〈*Bicycle*〉 carrier

【行李牌】 xíng·lipái baggage claim tag

【行李票】 xíng·lipiào baggage check; luggage check

【行骗】 xíngpiàn practice fraud; swindle; cheat; practice deception

【行期】 xíngqī date of departure

【行乞】 xíngqǐ beg one's bread; beg alms; beg

【行窃】 xíngqiè steal; commit theft

【行人】 xíngrén pedestrian

【行人横道】 xíngrén héngdào street crossing

【行色】 xíngsè circumstances or style of departure

【行善】 xíngshàn do good works

【行商】 xíngshāng itinerant trader; pedlar

【行尸走肉】 xíngshī-zǒuròu a walking corpse; one who vegetates; an utterly worthless person; dead-alive person

【行时】 xíngshí 1.(流行) be in vogue; be all the rage 2.(得势) be in the ascendent
【行使】 xíngshǐ exercise; perform: ～权利 exercise of rights
【行驶】 xíngshǐ go; travel
【行事】 xíngshì 1.(办事;做事) act; handle matters: 见机～ act according to circumstances 2.(行为) behavior; conduct
【行署】 xíngshǔ (行政公署) administrative office (within a province)
【行头】 xíng·tou 1.(戏装) actor's costumes and paraphernalia 2.(泛指衣服) a person's wardrobe
【行为】 xíngwéi action; behavior; conduct: 可争论的～ voidable act / 勇敢的～ a brave act / 我们将根据你的～对你作出判断,而不是根据你的许诺。We shall judge you by your actions, not by your promises.
【行为规范】 xíngwéi guīfàn code of conduct
【行为科学】 xíngwéi kēxué behavior science; behavioral science
【行为模式】 xíngwéi móshì behavior pattern
【行为能力】 xíngwéi nénglì capacity
【行为心理学】 xíngwéi xīnlǐxué behavior psychology
【行为准则】 xíngwéi zhǔnzé code of conduct; standard of conduct; norm of behavior
【行文】 xíngwén 1.(组织文字) style of writing 2.(发公文) send an official communication to other organizations
【行销】 xíngxiāo be on sale; sell: ～全国 on sale throughout the country / ～全世界 be on sale throughout the world
【行星】 xíngxīng 〈*Astron.*〉 planet
【行星齿轮】 xíngxīng chǐlún 〈*Auto*〉 synchromesh
【行刑】 xíngxíng carry out a death sentence; execute
【行刑队】 xíngxíngduì firing squad
【行凶】 xíngxiōng commit physical assault or murder; do violence: ～杀人 commit murder
【行医】 xíngyī practice medicine
【行政】 xíngzhèng administration; administrative (adj.)
【行政部门】 xíngzhèng bùmén administrative department; administrative unit; executive branch; administration
【行政处分】 xíngzhèng chǔfèn disciplinary sanction
【行政单位】 xíngzhèng dānwèi administrative unite
【行政当局】 xíngzhèng dāngjú executive authorities
【行政法】 xíngzhèngfǎ administrative law
【行政干预】 xíngzhèng gānyù administrative interference; administrative intervention
【行政管理】 xíngzhèng guǎnlǐ administration
【行政管理费】 xíngzhèng guǎnlǐfèi expenditure on administration
【行政规章】 xíngzhèng guīzhāng administrative rule
【行政机关】 xíngzhèng jīguān administrative organ
【行政监督】 xíngzhèng jiāndū administrative supervision
【行政拘留】 xíngzhèng jūliú administrative attachment
【行政命令】 xíngzhèng mìnglìng administrative decree; administrative order
【行政区】 xíngzhèngqū administrative area
【行政区域】 xíngzhèng qūyù administrative division
【行政人员】 xíngzhèng rényuán administrative personnel; administrative staff
【行政上级】 xíngzhèng shàngjí administration body
【行政摊派】 xíngzhèng tānpài administrative allocation
【行政性定价】 xíngzhèngxìng dìngjià price be fixed by the administrative organ
【行政预算】 xíngzhèng yùsuàn administrative budget
【行政责任】 xíngzhèng zérèn administrative responsibilities
【行政职务】 xíngzhèng zhíwù administrative post
【行政长官】 xíngzhèng zhǎngguān chief executive
【行之有效】 xíngzhī-yǒuxiào effective (in practice); effectual: ～的办法 effective measures / ～的疗法 effectual remedy
【行止】 xíngzhǐ 1.(行为) behavior; conduct 2.(行踪) whereabouts
【行装】 xíngzhuāng outfit for a journey; lug-

gage：整理～ prepare for a journey

【行踪】 xíngzōng whereabouts；track：～诡秘 mysterious movements / ～不定 travel around without fixed destination

【行走】 xíngzǒu walk；go on foot

省 (xǐng) 1.(自省) examine oneself critically 2.(探望；问候) visit 3.(醒悟；明白) become conscious；be aware：不～人事 lose consciousness
(另见"省"shěng)

【省察】 xǐngchá examine oneself critically；examine one's thoughts and conduct

【省亲】 xǐngqīn pay a visit to one's parents or elders (living at another place)

【省视】 xǐngshì 1.(探望) call upon；pay a visit to 2.(察看) examine carefully；inspect

醒 (xǐng) 1.(神志恢复) regain consciousness；sober up；come to 2.(睡醒) wake up；be awake：婴儿～着。The baby is awake. 3.(清醒) be clear in mind

【醒酒】 xǐngjiǔ dispel the effects of alcohol；sober up

【醒酒液】 xǐngjiǔyè hair of the dog

【醒目】 xǐngmù catch the eye；eye-catching (adj.)；attract attention；attractive (adj.)

【醒悟】 xǐngwù come to realize sth. (eg. truth, one's error, etc.)；wake up to reality

【醒眼】 xǐngyǎn 1.(醒目) eye-catching；attractive 2.(醒悟) come to realize sth.

擤[㨘] (xǐng) blow (one's nose)：～鼻涕 blow one's nose

兴[興] (xìng) mood or desire to do sth.；interest；excitement：游～很浓 be in a good mood for sight-seeing
(另见"兴"xīng)

【兴冲冲】 xìngchōngchōng (do sth.) with joy and expedition；excitedly

【兴高采烈】 xìnggāo-cǎiliè in high spirits；in great delight；jubilant

【兴趣】 xìngqù interest；taste：不感～ have no interest；be not interested in / 感～ have interest；be interested in / 对…失去～ lose interest in sb./sth.

【兴头】 xìng·tou enthusiasm；keen interest

【兴味】 xìngwèi interest：～索然 uninterested；bored stiff

【兴致】 xìngzhì interest；mood to enjoy

杏 (xìng) apricot：巴旦～ almond

【杏脯】 xìngfǔ preserved apricot

【杏红】 xìnghóng apricot pink

【杏黄】 xìnghuáng apricot yellow；apricot (color)

【杏仁】 xìngrén 1.(一般杏的) apricot kernel 2.(巴旦杏的) almond

【杏树】 xìngshù apricot (tree)

幸[倖]5 (xìng) 1.(运气好) good fortune；good luck 2.(高兴) rejoice：庆～ congratulate oneself；rejoice 3.(侥幸) fortunately；luckily 4.(希望) pray；I hope；I trust：～勿推却 please be kind enough not to decline 5.(宠幸) favor；honor：得～ gain favor

【幸存】 xìngcún survive

【幸而】 xìng'ér luckily；fortunately

【幸福】 xìngfú happiness；well-being；happy (adj.)：～生活 a happy life

【幸好】 xìnghǎo fortunately；luckily

【幸亏】 xìngkuī fortunately；luckily

【幸免】 xìngmiǎn escape by sheer luck；have a narrow escape：～于难 escape death by sheer luck；escape death by a hair's breadth

【幸事】 xìngshì good fortune；blessing

【幸运】 xìngyùn 1.(好运气) good fortune；good luck：有他在那里，真是～。It was a godsend that he was there. 2.(称心如意) fortunate；lucky

【幸运儿】 xìngyùnr fortune's favorite；lucky fellow；lucky dog

【幸灾乐祸】 xìngzāi-lèhuò take pleasure in other's misfortune；gloat over other's misfortune

悻 (xìng)

【悻悻】 xìngxìng angry；resentful

性 (xìng) 1.(性格) nature；character；disposition 2.(性能) property；quality：药～ medicinal properties 3.(性别) sex；sexual (adj.)：女～ female sex 4.(后缀，表示性质、状态、范围、方式等)可能～ possibility / 社会～ social nature / 正确～ correctness 5.(词性) gender：阳～ the masculine gender / 阴～ the feminine gender / 中～ the neuter gender

【性爱】 xìng'ài love；sexual love
【性本能】 xìngběnnéng sex instinct
【性比率】 xìngbǐlǜ sex ratio
【性变态者】 xìngbiàntàizhě pervert
【性别】 xìngbié sexual distinction；sex
【性别歧视】 xìngbié qíshì sexism
【性病】 xìngbìng venereal disease（V. D.）；sexually transmitted disease
【性病学】 xìngbìngxué venereology
【性犯罪者】 xìngfànzuìzhě sex offender
【性感】 xìnggǎn sexy；sex appeal
【性高潮】 xìnggāocháo orgasm；climax
【性格】 xìnggé nature；disposition；temperament
【性功能障碍】 xìnggōngnéng zhàng'ài sexual dysfunction
【性关系】 xìngguān · xì sexual intercourse；carnal knowledge
【性伙伴】 xìnghuǒbàn sexual partner
【性急】 xìngjí impatient；short-tempered
【性交】 xìngjiāo sexual intercourse
【性命】 xìngmìng life
【性能】 xìngnéng function；performance；property
【性器官】 xìngqìguān sexual organs；genitals
【性情】 xìngqíng disposition；temperament；temper：～暴躁 have an irascible temperament / ～平和 have a calm temper
【性染色体】 xìngrǎnsètǐ sex chromosome
【性骚扰】 xìngsāorǎo sexual harassment
【性生活】 xìngshēnghuó sexual life
【性腺】 xìngxiàn 〈*Anat.*〉 sexual gland；sex gland
【性行为】 xìngxíngwéi sex instinct act；sexual behavior
【性欲】 xìngyù sexual desire；sexual urge；sexuality：～强烈 be highly sexed
【性早熟】 xìngzǎoshú sexual precocity
【性征】 xìngzhēng sex character
【性知识】 xìngzhī·shi the facts of life
【性质】 xìngzhì quality；nature；character
【性周期】 xìngzhōuqī sexual cycle
【性状】 xìngzhuàng shape and properties；properties；character
【性子】 xìng·zi **1.**（性情）temper **2.**（酒、药等的刺激性）strength；potency
【性自由】 xìngzìyóu free love

姓（xìng） surname；family name；clan name：请问您贵～？What is your surname？我～赵。My surname is Zhao.
【姓名】 xìngmíng surname and personal name；full name
【姓氏】 xìngshì surname

xiong

凶［兇$^{3-5}$］（xiōng）**1.**（不幸的）inauspicious；ominous **2.**（年成很坏）crop failure **3.**（凶恶）fierce；ferocious **4.**（厉害）terrible；fearful **5.**（行凶）act of violence；murder：行～ commit a violent crime
【凶暴】 xiōngbào fierce and brutal
【凶残】 xiōngcán fierce and cruel；savage and cruel
【凶多吉少】 xiōngduō-jíshǎo be fraught with grim possibilities；bode ill rather than well
【凶恶】 xiōng'è fierce；ferocious；fiendish
【凶犯】 xiōngfàn one who has committed homicide or mayhem；murderer
【凶狠】 xiōnghěn **1.**（凶恶）fierce and malicious；malevolent **2.**（猛烈）violent；forceful
【凶猛】 xiōngměng violent；ferocious；terrible
【凶年】 xiōngnián a bad year
【凶器】 xiōngqì tool or weapon for criminal purposes；lethal weapon
【凶杀】 xiōngshā homicide；murder
【凶杀案】 xiōngshā'àn a case of murder；murder case
【凶神恶煞】 xiōngshén-èshà devils；fiends
【凶手】 xiōngshǒu murderer；assassin；assailant
【凶险】 xiōngxiǎn in a very dangerous state；critical
【凶相】 xiōngxiàng ferocious features；fierce look
【凶焰】 xiōngyàn ferocity；aggressive arrogance
【凶兆】 xiōngzhào ill omen；boding of evil

汹［洶］（xiōng）
【汹汹】 xiōngxiōng **1.**（波涛声）the sound of roaring waves **2.**（声势大）violent；truculent：

气势～ blustering and truculent 3.（争论的样子）tumultuous; agitated: 议论～ tumultuous debate; heated discussion

【汹涌】 xiōngyǒng tempestuous; turbulent

胸［匈］（xiōng）1.（胸部）chest; bosom; thorax; pectoral（adj.）2.（心胸）mind; heart

【胸部】 xiōngbù chest; thorax; thoracic

【胸部手术】 xiōngbù shǒushù thoracic operation

【胸骨】 xiōnggǔ 〈*Anat.*〉 sternum; breastbone

【胸怀】 xiōnghuái 1.（怀有）have at heart; keep in mind: ～全局 have the general interest at heart 2.（胸襟）mind; heart: ～宽广 be broad-minded 3.（胸部）chest; thorax

【胸肌】 xiōngjī pectoral; pectoral muscles

【胸襟】 xiōngjīn 1.（抱负）ambition 2.（心胸）mind; breadth of mind: ～开阔 be broad-minded

【胸口】 xiōngkǒu the pit of the stomach

【胸口疼】 xiōngkǒuténg pain in the chest

【胸脯】 xiōngpú 1.（胸部）chest 2.（羊肉部位）breast 3.（牛肉部位）brisket, plate, and flank

【胸鳍】 xiōngqí 〈*Zool.*〉 pectoral fin

【胸腔】 xiōngqiāng 〈*Anat.*〉 thoracic cavity

【胸腔外科】 xiōngqiāng wàikē thoracic surgery

【胸饰】 xiōngshì breast-pin; breast ornament

【胸膛】 xiōngtáng chest

【胸围】 xiōngwéi chest measurement; bust; chest circumference

【胸无大志】 xiōngwúdàzhì with no ambition at all; want of lofty aspirations

【胸无点墨】 xiōngwúdiǎnmò unlearned; unlettered

【胸像】 xiōngxiàng （sculptured）bust

【胸有成竹】 xiōngyǒuchéngzhú have a well-thought-out plan, stratagem, etc.

【胸罩】 xiōngzhào bra; brassiere

【胸针】 xiōngzhēn brooch

【胸椎】 xiōngzhuī 〈*Anat.*〉 dorsal vertebra

兄（xiōng）1.（哥哥）elder brother 2.（尊称）a courteous form of address between men

【兄弟】 xiōng·dì 1.（哥和弟）brothers 2.（兄弟般的）fraternal; brotherly: ～般的友谊 fraternal friendship

【兄弟】 xiōng·di 1.（弟）younger brother 2.（谦称）your humble servant; I

雄（xióng）1.（公的）male: ～鸡 cock 2.（有气魄）grand; imposing 3.（强有力的）powerful; mighty 4.（指人或国家）powerful person or state: 英～ hero / 称～ become a powerful country

【雄辩】 xióngbiàn 1.（辩论）convincing argument; eloquence 2.（有说服力）convincing

【雄兵】 xióngbīng a powerful army

【雄才大略】 xióngcái-dàlüè 1.（指一般人）great talent and bold vision 2.（指大人物）rare gifts and bold strategy

【雄蜂】 xióngfēng 〈*Zool.*〉 drone; drone bee

【雄厚】 xiónghòu rich; solid; abundant

【雄浑】 xiónghún vigorous and firm; forceful

【雄鸡】 xióngjī cock; rooster

【雄健】 xióngjiàn robust; vigorous; powerful

【雄赳赳】 xióngjiūjiū valiantly; gallantly

【雄鹿】 xiónglù stag; buck

【雄蕊】 xióngruǐ 〈*Bot.*〉 stamen

【雄师】 xióngshī powerful army

【雄图】 xióngtú great ambition; grandiose plan: ～大略 a great design and a big plan

【雄伟】 xióngwěi 1.（雄壮而伟大）grand; imposing; magnificent; majestic 2.（魁伟）tall and strong

【雄文】 xióngwén great works

【雄心】 xióngxīn great ambition; lofty aspiration: ～勃勃的计划 an ambitious plan / ～壮志 high hopes and great ambition; lofty aspirations and great ideals

【雄壮】 xióngzhuàng 1.（指气势）full of power and grandeur; magnificent; majestic 2.（指身体）tall and strong

【雄姿】 xióngzī majestic appearance; heroic posture

熊（xióng）1.〈*Zool.*〉 bear: 北极～ Polar bear / 黑～ Asiatic black bear / 棕～ brown bear 2.（斥责）rebuke; upbraid; scold

【熊蜂】 xióngfēng 〈*Zool.*〉 bumblebee

【熊猫】 xióngmāo panda

【熊市】 xióngshì 〈*Econ.*〉 bear market

【熊瞎子】 xióngxiā·zi bear

【熊熊】 xióngxióng flaming; ablaze; raging: ～的烈火 flaming fire

【熊掌】 xióngzhǎng bear's paw

xiu

休 (xiū) 1.(停止) stop; cease; end 2.(休息) rest 3.(不得) don't

【休耕】 xiūgēng fallow; lie fallow

【休会】 xiūhuì adjourn: ~三天 adjourn for three days / 他宣布~到明天上午10点。He adjourned the meeting until tomorrow at 10 a.m.

【休假】 xiūjià 1.(用于工人学生) have a holiday; take a vacation; go on a vacation 2.(用于士兵、在国外工作的人) be on leave; be on furlough: 他~两星期。He goes on leave for two weeks.

【休克】 xiūkè 1.〈*Med*.〉 shock 2.(发生休克) suffer a shock

【休克疗法】 xiūkè liáofǎ 〈*Med*.〉 shock therapy; shock treatment

【休眠】 xiūmián 〈*Biol*.〉 dormancy

【休眠火山】 xiūmián huǒshān dormant volcano

【休戚】 xiūqī weal and woe; joys and sorrows: 他们是~相关的。Their fortunes were interlinked.

【休戚与共】 xiūqī-yǔgòng share weal and woe; stand together through thick and thin

【休憩】 xiūqì have a rest; take a rest; rest; repose

【休息】 xiū·xi have a rest; take a rest; rest

【休息室】 xiū·xishì lounge; lobby

【休闲】 xiūxián 1.(休息) leisure 2.〈*Agric*.〉 lie fallow

【休闲地】 xiūxiándì fallow (land)

【休闲服】 xiūxiánfú leisurewear; leisure suit

【休闲中心】 xiūxián zhōngxīn leisure center

【休想】 xiūxiǎng don't imagine that it's possible

【休学】 xiūxué suspend one's schooling without losing one's status as a student

【休养】 xiūyǎng 1.(指人) recuperate; recover; convalesce 2.(指经济) recover

【休养生息】 xiūyǎng-shēngxī recuperate and multiply; rest and build up strength; rehabilitate; bring recovery

【休养所】 xiūyǎngsuǒ sanatorium; rest home

【休业】 xiūyè 1.(停止营业) suspend business; be closed down 2.(学习暂告结束) come to an end of a short-term course

【休战】 xiūzhàn truce; cease-fire; armistice

【休整】 xiūzhěng rest and reorganize; rest and reorganization (n.)

【休止】 xiūzhǐ stop; cease

【休止符】 xiūzhǐfú 〈*Music*〉 rest

修 (xiū) 1.(修饰) embellish; decorate 2.(修理;整治) repair; mend; overhaul: 大~ overhaul / 小~ minor repair / 中~ medium repair 3.(编写) write; compile 4.(学习和锻炼) study; cultivate: 进~ pursue one's studies 5.(兴建) build; construct: ~铁路 build a railway 6.(剪;削) trim; prune: ~指甲 trim one's fingernails 7.(修长) long; tall and slender

【修补】 xiūbǔ mend; patch up; repair; revamp

【修长】 xiūcháng tall and thin; slender

【修辞】 xiūcí rhetoric: ~手段 rhetoric device

【修辞学】 xiūcíxué 〈*Gram*.〉 rhetoric ‖ 修辞学家 rhetorican

【修道院】 xiūdàoyuàn 1.(男修道院) monastery 2.(女修道院) convent

【修道院院长】 xiūdàoyuàn yuànzhǎng abbot (m.); abbess (f.); the Father superior (m.); the Mother superior (f.)

【修订】 xiūdìng revise: ~条约 revise a treaty

【修订本】 xiūdìngběn revised edition

【修订者】 xiūdìngzhě reviser

【修复】 xiūfù 1.(使恢复完整) repair; restore; renovate 2.〈*Med*.〉 repair

【修改】 xiūgǎi revise; modify; amend; alter: ~一个文件 amend a document / 这个计划需要作一些~。The plan needs some amendment.

【修好】 xiūhǎo 1.(指国家之间) foster cordial relations between states 2.(行好;行善) do good works

【修剪】 xiūjiǎn prune; trim; clip: ~头发 trim one's hair

【修建】 xiūjiàn build; construct; erect: ~电气化铁路 build electric railroads / 新机场仍在~中。The new airport is still under construction.

【修脚】 xiūjiǎo pedicure
【修脚师】 xiūjiǎoshī pedicurist
【修旧利废】 xiūjiù-lìfèi repair and utilize old or discarded things
【修浚】 xiūjùn dredge
【修理】 xiūlǐ repair; mend; overhaul; fix: 紧急～ emergency repair/ 日常～ routine repair
【修理厂】 xiūlǐchǎng repair shop
【修理店】 xiūlǐdiàn fix-it shop; repair shop
【修理费】 xiūlǐfèi charge for repairs; repair cost
【修理工具包】 xiūlǐ gōngjùbāo repair kit
【修理行业】 xiūlǐ hángyè repairing trades
【修面】 xiūmiàn shave; have a shave
【修女】 xiūnǚ 〈*Religion*〉 nun; sister
【修配】 xiūpèi repair and restore to good order; make repairs and supply replacements
【修配厂】 xiūpèichǎng maintenance center
【修葺】 xiūqì repair; renovate: ～一新 take on a new look after renovation; be completely renovated
【修缮】 xiūshàn repair; renovate
【修缮工程】 xiūshàn gōngchéng repairing project
【修身】 xiūshēn cultivate one's moral character
【修士】 xiūshì 〈*Religion*〉 brother; friar
【修饰】 xiūshì 1.(装饰) decorate; adorn; embellish 2.(梳装) make up and dress up: ～边幅 beautify one's outward appearance 3.(修润文章) polish (a piece of writing) 4.〈*Gram.*〉 qualify; modify
【修心养性】 xiūxīn-yǎngxìng cultivate the heart and nature culture
【修行】 xiūxíng practice Buddhism or Taoism
【修养】 xiūyǎng 1.(知识等的水平) accomplishment; training; mastery 2.(养成) self-cultivation
【修业】 xiūyè study at school
【修业证书】 xiūyè zhèngshū certificate showing courses attended
【修造】 xiūzào 1.(修理并制造) build as well as repair 2.(建造) build
【修整】 xiūzhěng 1.(修理) repair and maintain 2.(修剪) prune; trim
【修正】 xiūzhèng 1.(改正) revise; amend; correct 2.(篡改) alter purposely
【修正案】 xiūzhèng'àn amendment
【修正主义】 xiūzhèng zhǔyì revisionism
【修枝】 xiūzhī 〈*Agric.*〉 pruning
【修筑】 xiūzhù build; construct; put up: ～飞机场 construct an airport

羞 (xiū) 1.(难为情) shy; bashful 2.(羞耻) shame; disgrace 3.(感到耻辱) feel ashamed
【羞惭】 xiūcán be ashamed
【羞耻】 xiūchǐ sense of shame; shame: ～之心 sense of shame / 不知～ be shameless; be unblushing
【羞答答】 xiūdādā coy; shy; bashful
【羞愤】 xiūfèn ashamed and resentful
【羞愧】 xiūkuì ashamed; abashed
【羞怯】 xiūqiè shy; timid; sheepish
【羞辱】 xiūrǔ 1.(耻辱) shame; dishonor; humiliation 2.(使受耻辱) humiliate; put sb. to shame
【羞臊】 xiūsào shy; bashful
【羞涩】 xiūsè shy; bashful; embarrassed

朽 (xiǔ) 1.(腐烂) rotten; decayed 2.(衰老) aged; senile
【朽木】 xiǔmù 1.(烂木头) rotten wood or tree 2.(不可造就的人) a hopeless case; a good-for-nothing

宿 (xiǔ) 〈*classifier*〉 per night: 住一～ stay for one night
(另见"宿"sù)

秀 (xiù) 1.(抽穗开花) put forth flowers or ears 2.(清秀) elegant; beautiful: 山清水～ beautiful hills and waters; lovely scenery 3.(特别优异) excellent: 优～ excellent; first-rate 4.(表演, show 的音译) show: 做～ show / 脱口～ talk show (指电视访谈节目)
【秀才】 xiù·cai scholar; skillful writer
【秀丽】 xiùlì beautiful; handsome; pretty
【秀美】 xiùměi graceful; elegant
【秀气】 xiù·qi 1.(清秀) delicate; elegant; fine 2.(文雅) refined; urbane 3.(小巧灵便) delicate and well-made
【秀色】 xiùsè beauty
【秀穗】 xiùsuì put forth ears

绣[繡] (xiù) 1.(刺绣) embroider 2.(绣品) embroidery: 机～ machine embroidery / 平～ plain embroidery / 绒线～

woolen needlepoint embroidery / 双面～ double-sided (reversible) embroidery / 丝～ silk embroidery

【绣花】 xiùhuā embroider; do embroidery

【绣花绷子】 xiùhuā bēng·zi tambor

【绣花枕头】 xiùhuā zhěn·tou 1.(刺绣枕头) a pillow with an embroidered case 2.(徒有外表的人) an outwardly attractive but worthless person

【绣球】 xiùqiú 1.(绸子结成的球) a ball made of strips of silk 2.〈*Bot*.〉 bigleaf hydrangea

【绣像】 xiùxiàng tapestry portrait; embroidered portrait

锈[鏽] (xiù) 1.(铜锈、铁锈等) rust 2.(生锈) become rusty

【锈斑】 xiùbān rusty spot

【锈病】 xiùbìng 〈*Agric*.〉 rust

【锈蚀】 xiùshí rust-eaten

袖 (xiù) 1.(衣袖) sleeve 2.(藏在袖中) tuck inside the sleeve: ～着手 with hands in sleeves

【袖标】 xiùbiāo armband

【袖长】 xiùcháng outside sleeve

【袖口】 xiùkǒu cuff (of a sleeve)

【袖扣】 xiùkòu cuff-link; sleeve buttons

【袖手旁观】 xiùshǒu-pángguān look on with folder arms; stand by with folder arms; not to stir a finger; look on unconcerned

【袖套】 xiùtào sleeve; sleeve cover

【袖章】 xiùzhāng armband

【袖珍】 xiùzhēn pocket-size; pocket: ～词典 pocket dictionary / ～计算器 pocket calculator/ ～录音机 pocket tape recorder

【袖子】 xiù·zi sleeve; arm: 这件大衣的～太长。The arms of this coat are too long.

臭 (xiù) odor; smell (另见"臭"chòu)

【臭味相投】 xiùwèi-xiāngtóu share the same rotten tastes, habits, etc.; be two of a kind

嗅 (xiù) smell; scent; sniff

【嗅觉】 xiùjué 1.〈*Physiol*.〉 (sense of) smell; scent 2.(感知力) sensitivity: 政治～ have a political sensitivity

溴 (xiù) 〈*Chem*.〉 bromine (元素符号 Br)

【溴化银】 xiùhuàyín 〈*Chem*.〉 silver bromide

xu

圩[墟] (xū) fair: 赶～ go to the fair (另见"圩"wéi)

吁 (xū) 1.(叹气) sigh 2.(表示惊异) why; oh

(另见"吁"yù)

【吁吁】 xūxū 〈*onomat*.〉 气喘～～ pant; puff hard

须[鬚 2－4] (xū) 1.(须要) must; have to 2.(胡须) beard; mustache 3.(动物的须子) palpus; feeler 4.(植物的须子) tassel

【须发】 xūfá beard and hair

【须要】 xūyào must; have to

【须臾】 xūyú moment; instant

【须臾之间】 xūyúzhījiān in a second; in an instant

【须知】 xūzhī 1.(一定要知道) one should know that; it must be understood that 2.(必须知道的事项) points for attention; notice: 客户～ notice to tenants/ 游览～ tourist guide; information for tourists

【须子】 xū·zi 1.(动物的) palpus; feeler 2.(植物的) tassel

虚 (xū) 1.(空虚) void; emptiness 2.(空着) empty; void; unoccupied: 座无～席。All seats were occupied. 3.(心虚) diffident; timid: 心～ have a guilty conscience 4.(徒然) in vain 5.(虚假) false; nominal: ～名 false reputation 6.(虚心) humble; modest: ～心 modest 7.(虚弱) weak; in poor health: 体～ be very weak physically 8.(原则、道理等) guiding principles; theory: 务～ discuss principles or ideological guidelines 9.〈*Physics*〉 virtual: ～阴极 virtual cathode

【虚报】 xūbào make a false report

【虚报税额】 xūbào shuì'é false declaration

【虚词】 xūcí 〈*Gram*.〉 function word; form word

【虚度】 xūdù spend time in vain; waste: ～年华 pass the years in vain

【虚浮】 xūfú impractical; superficial

【虚构】 xūgòu fabricate; make up: 凭空～ a sheer fabrication

【虚汗】 xūhàn abnormal sweating due to general debility：出～ be sweating abnormally due

【虚怀若谷】 xūhuái-ruògǔ have a mind as open as a valley；be very modest；be extremely open-minded

【虚幻】 xūhuàn unreal；illusory；delusive

【虚假】 xūjiǎn false；sham；unreal

【虚假繁荣】 xūjiǎ fánróng borrowed boom；borrowed prosperity

【虚假广告】 xūjiǎ guǎnggào false and misleading advertisement

【虚价】 xūjià 〈*Econ*.〉 nominal price

【虚惊】 xūjīng false alarm

【虚夸】 xūkuā exaggerative；bombastic；boastful

【虚名】 xūmíng undeserved reputation

【虚拟】 xūnǐ 1.（虚构的）invented；fictitious 2.（假设的）suppositional 3.〈*Computer*〉 virtual

【虚拟电路】 xūnǐ diànlù 〈*Computer*〉 virtual circuit

【虚拟盘】 xūnǐpán 〈*Computer*〉 virtual disk

【虚拟驱动器】 xūnǐ qūdòngqì 〈*Computer*〉 virtual drive

【虚拟市场】 xūnǐ shìchǎng dummy market

【虚胖】 xūpàng puffiness；puffy（adj.）

【虚情假意】 xūqíng-jiǎyì false display of affection；hypocritical show of friendship

【虚荣】 xūróng vanity

【虚荣心】 xūróngxīn vanity

【虚弱】 xūruò 1.（不结实）in poor health；weak；debilitated：他身体～。He is in poor health. 2.（软弱；薄弱）weak；feeble：兵力～ weak in military strength

【虚设】 xūshè nominal；existing in name only：形同～ with a nominal function

【虚实】 xūshí false or true；the actual situation（as of the opposing side）

【虚数】 xūshù 1.〈*Math*.〉 square root of any minus figures 2.（虚假的数）unreal figures；unreliable figures

【虚脱】 xūtuō 〈*Med*.〉 collapse；prostration

【虚伪】 xūwěi sham；false；hypocritical

【虚伪资本】 xūwěi zīběn fictitious capital

【虚伪资产】 xūwěi zīchǎn fictitious assets

【虚位以待】 xūwèi yǐdài leave a seat vacant for sb.；save a seat for sb.；reserve a seat for sb.

【虚文】 xūwén 1.（具文）dead letter 2.（无意义的礼节）mere formalities；empty forms：～浮礼 mere formalities；conventionalities

【虚无】 xūwú nihility；nothingness

【虚无缥缈】 xūwú-piāomiǎo purely imaginary；entirely unreal；visionary；illusory

【虚无主义】 xūwú zhǔyì nihilism；nihilist（adj.）‖虚无主义者 nihilist

【虚线】 xūxiàn 1.（非实线）dotted line；line of dashes 2.〈*Math*.〉 imaginary line

【虚心】 xūxīn with open-minded；modest

【虚虚实实】 xūxū-shíshí sometimes false, sometimes true；seemingly false and real at the same time

【虚有其表】 xūyǒuqíbiǎo look impressive but lack real worth；appear better than it is

【虚张声势】 xūzhāng-shēngshì make an empty show of strength；bluff and bluster；make a deceptive show of power

墟（xū）1.（废墟）ruins：废～ ruins 2.（集市）fair：赶～ go to the fair

嘘（xū）1.（嘘气）breathe out slowly 2.（叹气）utter a sigh 3.（被火或蒸气烫着）come into contact with sth.；scald；burn 4.〈*onomat*.〉 sh；hush
（另见“嘘”shī）

【嘘寒问暖】 xūhán-wènnuǎn inquire after sb's well-being；be solicitous about sb's health

【嘘气】 xūqì breathe out slowly

【嘘音】 xūyīn hush

需（xū）1.（需要）need；want；require 2.（需用物品）necessaries；needs

【需求】 xūqiú requirement；demand：刺激～ stimulate the demand / 有～ be in demand

【需要】 xūyào 1.（应该有）need；want；require；demand：他们什么也不～。They lacked for nothing. 2.（欲望或要求）needs：满足市场～ meet the needs of the market

徐（xú）slowly；gently

【徐步】 xúbù walk slowly；walk leisurely；stroll

【徐缓】 xúhuǎn slowly

【徐徐】 xúxú slowly；gently

许 (xǔ) 1.(称赞) praise 2.(答应) promise: ～下诺言 have made a promise 3.(允许) allow; permit 4.(也许) maybe; perhaps; possibly

【许多】 xǔduō many; much; a great deal of; a lot of: 这条街上有～书店。There are a lot bookstores on this street.

【许久】 xǔjiǔ for a long time; for ages; for long

【许可】 xǔkě permit; allow; permission (n.): 得到～ obtain permission

【许可证】 xǔkězhèng licence; permit: 出口～ an export licence / 出入境～ entry permit / 工作～ permission to work / 进口～ import licence / 临时居住～ sojourn permit / 特别～ a special permit / 一般～ bloc licence / 正式～ official permission

【许可证证书】 xǔkězhèng zhèngshū licence passport

【许诺】 xǔnuò make a promise; promise

【许配】 xǔpèi betroth one's daughter to; be betrothed to

【许愿】 xǔyuàn 1.(对神佛) make a vow (to a god) 2.(对人) promise sb. a reward

诩 (xǔ) brag; boast: 自～为… style oneself ...; boast that one is ...

栩 (xǔ)

【栩栩】 xǔxǔ vivid; lively: ～如生 lifelike; to the life

醑 (xǔ)

【醑剂】 xǔjì 〈*Chem.*〉 spirit; essence

旭 (xù) brilliance of the rising sun

【旭日】 xùrì the rising sun

序 (xù) 1.(次序) order; sequence: 按姓氏笔画为～ in the order of the number of strokes in the surnames 2.(排次序) arrange in order 3.(开头的;在正式内容之前的) introductory; initial 4.(序文) preface

【序跋】 xùbá preface and postscript

【序号】 xùhào serial number

【序列】 xùliè 1.(排好的行列) alignment; array 2.〈*Math.*〉 sequence

【序幕】 xùmù 1.〈*Theatre*〉 prologue; prelude 2.(开端) start of an important event

【序曲】 xùqǔ 1.〈*Music*〉 overture 2.(开端) beginning of an event

【序数】 xùshù ordinal number; ordinal

【序文】 xùwén preface; foreword

【序言】 xùyán preface; foreword; prefatory (adj.)

叙[敍、敘] (xù) 1.(说;谈) talk; chat: ～家常 chitchat 2.(记叙) narrate; recount; relate 3.(评议等级) assess; appraise

【叙旧】 xùjiù talk about the old days

【叙事】 xùshì narrate; recount

【叙事诗】 xùshìshī narrative poem

【叙述】 xùshù narrate; recount; relate

【叙说】 xùshuō tell; narrate

【叙谈】 xùtán chat; chitchat; talk together

恤[卹、賉] (xù) 1.(怜悯) pity; sympathize: 体～ understand and sympathize with 2.(救济) give relief; compensate: 抚～ comfort and compensate a disabled person or a bereaved family

【恤金】 xùjīn pension for a disabled person or the family of the deceased

【恤衫】 xùshān shirt: 体～ T-shirt

畜 (xù) raise (domestic animals) (另见"畜"chù)

【畜产品】 xùchǎnpǐn livestock products; animal products

【畜产业】 xùchǎnyè animal industry

【畜牧】 xùmù raise livestock; rear livestock; rear poultry

【畜牧场】 xùmùchǎng animal farm; livestock farm; stock farm

【畜牧业】 xùmùyè animal husbandry; livestock husbandry; livestock farming

【畜养】 xùyǎng raise; rear; keep

蓄 (xù) 1.(积蓄) store up; save up 2.(留着不剃) grow: ～发 wear one's hair long / ～须 grow a beard 3.(心里藏着) entertain (ideas); harbor

【蓄电池】 xùdiànchí battery; storage battery; accumulator: 备用～ spare battery

【蓄洪】 xùhóng store floodwater

【蓄洪坝】 xùhóngbà flood dam

【蓄洪工程】 xùhóng gōngchéng flood storage project

【蓄洪量】 xùhóngliàng storage capacity

【蓄积】　xùjí　store up; save up
【蓄谋】　xùmóu　premeditate：～已久 a premeditated design of
【蓄能电站】　xùnéng diànzhàn　storage plant
【蓄能器】　xùnéngqì　accumulator
【蓄热】　xùrè　accumulation of heat
【蓄水】　xùshuǐ　〈*Water Conservancy*〉retain water; store water
【蓄水池】　xùshuǐchí　cistern; reservoir
【蓄水工程】　xùshuǐ gōngchéng　(water) storage project
【蓄养池】　xùyǎngchí　stock pond
【蓄意】　xùyì　premeditated; deliberate：～犯罪 a designing criminal / ～挑衅 premeditated provocation

酗 (xù)

【酗酒】　xùjiǔ　excessive drinking：～滋事 get drunk and create a disturbance

绪 (xù) 1.（丝的头）thread 2.（开端）order in sequence or arrangement：头～ main threads (of a complicated affair); main lines 3.（心绪）mental or emotional state：心～不宁 be in a state of agitation 4.（事业）task; cause; undertaking
【绪论】　xùlùn　introduction
【绪言】　xùyán　introduction

续［續］(xù) 1.（连续）continuous; successive 2.（接续）continue; extend; join：～会 extended session; follow-up meeting 3.（添；加）add; supply more
【续编】　xùbiān　continuation (of a book); sequel
【续订】　xùdìng　renew one's subscription
【续集】　xùjí　continuation (of a book); sequel
【续假】　xùjià　extend one's leave of absence; extend leave
【续借】　xùjiè　renew
【续篇】　xùpiān　continuation
【续聘】　xùpìn　re-sign
【续弦】　xùxián　get remarried (after the death of his wife)
【续租】　xùzū　re-let

絮 (xù) 1.（棉絮）(cotton) wadding 2.（像棉絮的）sth. resembling cotton：柳～ (willow) catkin 3.（絮进棉花等）wad with cotton：～被子 wad a quilt with cotton 4.（絮叨）long-winded; garrulous
【絮叨】　xù·dao　long-winded; garrulous; wordy
【絮棉】　xùmián　cotton for wadding
【絮片】　xùpiàn　flocculus
【絮状物】　xùzhuàngwù　floccule; flocculus

婿［壻］(xù) 1.（女婿）son-in-law 2.（丈夫）husband

煦 (xù) warm; balmy：春风和～ a balmy spring breeze

xuan

轩 (xuān)

【轩昂】　xuān'áng　1.（精神饱满）dignified; imposing：气宇～ with a dignified manner 2.（高大）big and tall
【轩然大波】　xuānrán-dàbō　a great disturbance; a mighty uproar

宣 (xuān) 1.（宣布，宣告）declare; proclaim; announce 2.（疏导）lead off (liquids); drain
【宣布】　xuānbù　declare; proclaim; announce：～独立 declare independence; proclaim independence / ～无效 declare sth. invalid / ～赦免 announce amnesty / 机长～飞机就要着陆了。The captain announced that the plane was going to land.
【宣称】　xuānchēng　assert; declare; profess
【宣传】　xuānchuán　conduct propaganda; give publicity to; propagate
【宣传部】　xuānchuánbù　propaganda department
【宣传品】　xuānchánpǐn　publicity materials
【宣读】　xuāndú　read out (in public)
【宣告】　xuāngào　declare; proclaim：～破产 declare bankruptcy; go bankrupt / ～失踪 declaration of disappearance / ～无效 declare null and void
【宣礼塔】　xuānlǐtǎ　〈*Islam*〉minaret
【宣判】　xuānpàn　〈*Law*〉pronounce judgment：～无罪 pronounce sb. not guilty / ～有罪 pronounce sb. guilty / 法庭在～这个案子前查阅了判例。The justices sought precedents before adjudging the case.
【宣示】　xuānshì　declare; make known pub-

licly

【宣誓】 xuānshì take an oath; swear an oath; make a vow; make a pledge: ～就职 take an oath of office; be sworn in

【宣泄】 xuānxiè 1.(使积水流走) lead off (liquids); drain: ～洪水 drain off floodwater 2.(舒散) get sth. off one's chest; unbosom oneself

【宣言】 xuānyán declaration; manifesto: 人权～ Declaration of the Rights of Man

【宣扬】 xuānyáng publicize; propagate; advocate; advertise: ～某人的观点 air one's views

【宣战】 xuānzhàn declare war; proclaim war; levy war against: 公元前 200 年叙利亚向埃及～。In 200 BC the Syrians levied war against Egypt.

萱[蘐] (xuān)

【萱草】 xuāncǎo 〈*Bot*.〉 orange daylily

揎 (xuān) roll up

【揎拳捋袖】 xuānquán-lǚxiù roll up one's sleeve and clench one's fist

喧[諠] (xuān) noisy

【喧宾夺主】 xuānbīn-duózhǔ a presumptuous guest usurps the host's role; the secondary supersedes the primary; minor taking precedence over a major issue

【喧哗】 xuānhuá confused noise; hubbub; uproar: 请勿～! Quiet, please!

【喧闹】 xuānnào noise and excitement; bustle; racket

【喧嚷】 xuānrǎng clamor; hubbub; din; racket: 人声～ a hubbub of voices; loud confused voices

【喧扰】 xuānrǎo noise and disturbance; tumult

【喧腾】 xuānténg noise and excitement; hubbub; uproar

【喧嚣】 xuānxiāo 1.(声音杂乱) noisy: ～的车马声 the noise of dense traffic 2.(叫嚣) clamor; hullabaloo; din

暄 (xuān) 1.(温暖) warm and sunny 2.(松软) soft; fluffy

【暄和】 xuān·he soft; fluffy

【暄腾】 xuān·teng soft and springy; spongy

玄 (xuán) 1.(黑色) black; dark 2.(深奥) profound; abstruse 3.(靠不住) unreliable; incredible

【玄妙】 xuánmiào mysterious; abstruse

【玄孙】 xuánsūn great-great-grandson

【玄孙女】 xuánsūnnǚ great-great-granddaughter

【玄虚】 xuánxū deceitful trick; mystery: 故弄～ play dishonest juggling tricks

【玄学】 xuánxué 1.〈*Philos*.〉 metaphysics 2.(魏晋哲学) a philosophical sect in the Wei and Jin dynasties

悬[懸] (xuán) 1.(悬挂) hang; suspend 2.(无结果) outstanding; unresolved 3.(挂念) feel anxious; be solicitous: ～念 be anxious about (sb. who is elsewhere) 4.(凭空设想) imagine: ～拟 imagine; conjecture 5.(差距大) far apart: ～隔 be separated by a great distance 6.(危险) dangerous

【悬案】 xuán'àn 1.(指案件) unsettled law case 2.(指问题) outstanding issue; unsettled question

【悬臂桥】 xuánbìqiáo cantilever bridge

【悬灯结彩】 xuándēng-jiécǎi adorn with lanterns and festoons; hang up lanterns and festoons

【悬而未决】 xuán'érwèijué remain in suspense; unresolved

【悬浮】 xuánfú suspend; suspension (n.)

【悬浮体】 xuánfútǐ suspended substance

【悬隔】 xuángé far apart; be separated by a great distance

【悬挂】 xuánguà hang; fly: ～国旗 hang the national flag; fly the national flag

【悬挂式滑翔】 xuánguàshì huáxiáng hang gliding

【悬挂式滑翔机】 xuánguàshì huáxiángjī hang-glider

【悬空】 xuánkōng 1.(悬在空中) hang in the air; suspend in midair 2.(脱离实际) be divorced from reality

【悬空索道】 xuánkōng suǒdào aerial conveyer

【悬梁】 xuánliáng hang oneself from a beam: ～自尽 hang oneself

【悬铃木】 xuánlíngmù 〈*Bot*.〉 plane tree

【悬念】 xuánniàn 1.(挂念) be concerned

about 2.（电影、戏剧的）audience involvement 3.（文学作品的）reader involvement

【悬赏】 xuánshǎng offer a reward; post a reward: ～缉拿 reward offered for the capture of sb.

【悬殊】 xuánshū great disparity; wide gap: 贫富～ wide gap between the rich and the poor

【悬索斜拉桥】 xuánsuǒ xiélāqiáo cable suspension bridge

【悬梯】 xuántī hanging ladder

【悬想】 xuánxiǎng imagine; fancy; imagination (n.)

【悬崖】 xuányá overhanging cliff; steep cliff; precipice

【悬崖勒马】 xuányá-lèmǎ rein in at the brink of the precipice; wake up to and escape disaster at the last moment; pull back before it is too late

【悬衣架】 xuányījià clothes suspender

【悬雍垂】 xuányōngchuí 〈*Anat.*〉 uvula

旋 (xuán) 1.（旋转）revolve; circle; spin 2.（返回；归来）return; come back 3.（不久）soon

（另见"旋"xuàn）

【旋耕机】 xuángēngjī 〈*Agric.*〉 Rotavator; Rotovator

【旋即】 xuánjí very soon

【旋律】 xuánlǜ melody; melodic (adj.)

【旋钮】 xuánniǔ knob

【旋绕】 xuánrào curl up; wind around

【旋塞】 xuánsāi cock

【旋梯】 xuántī winding stair

【旋涡】 xuánwō 1.（流体的）whirlpool; vortex; eddy 2.（生活中的）matters that often get people into trouble: 生活中的～ the whirlpool of life

【旋翼】 xuányì rotary wing: 直升机～ rotary wing of helicopter

【旋翼机】 xuányìjī autogiro; autogyro; rotary wing aircraft

【旋转】 xuánzhuǎn revolve; gyrate; rotate; spin

【旋转门】 xuánzhuǎnmén revolving door

【旋转木马】 xuánzhuǎn mùmǎ merry-go-round

【旋转桥】 xuánzhuǎnqiáo swing-bridge

【旋转装置】 xuánzhuǎn zhuāngzhì swiveling mechanism

漩 (xuán) whirlpool; vortex; eddy

【漩涡】 xuánwō whirlpool; vortex; eddy

选［選］(xuǎn) 1.（挑选）select; choose; pick: 入～ be chosen; be selected; be elected 2.（选举）elect: 当～ be elected 3.（作品集）selections; anthology: 诗～ selected poems / 文～ an anthology of prose

【选拔】 xuǎnbá select; choose

【选拔赛】 xuǎnbásài (selective) trials

【选本】 xuǎnběn anthology; selected works

【选编】 xuǎnbiān select

【选材】 xuǎncái select (suitable) material

【选答题】 xuǎndátí multiple choice

【选读】 xuǎndú selected readings

【选购】 xuǎngòu pick out and buy; choose

【选集】 xuǎnjí selected works; selected writings; selections; anthology

【选举】 xuǎnjǔ elect; election (n.); electoral (adj.): 差额～ competitive election / 等额～ single-candidate election / 直接～ direct election

【选举程序】 xuǎnjǔ chéngxù electoral procedure; electoral proceedings

【选举单位】 xuǎnjǔ dānwèi electoral unit

【选举法】 xuǎnjǔfǎ electoral law

【选举结果】 xuǎnjǔ jiéguǒ election results; election returns

【选举权】 xuǎnjǔquán the right to vote; franchise ‖ 被选举权 the right to stand for election

【选举人】 xuǎnjǔrén voter; elector

【选课】 xuǎnkè curricula-variable

【选矿】 xuǎnkuàng 〈*Mineral.*〉 ore dressing; mineral separation; beneficiation

【选料讲究】 xuǎnliào jiǎngjiū high quality materials

【选美比赛】 xuǎnměi bǐsài beauty contest

【选民】 xuǎnmín 1.（指个人）voter; elector 2.（指全体）constituency; electorate

【选民证】 xuǎnmínzhèng elector's certificate; voter's card

【选派】 xuǎnpài select; detail: ～留学生 select students to be sent to study abroad

【选票】 xuǎnpiào vote; ballot; ballot ticket

【选区】 xuǎnqū electoral district; election district

【选曲】 xuǎnqǔ selected songs; selected tunes

【选取】 xuǎnqǔ select; choose

【选手】 xuǎnshǒu player; an athlete selected for a sports meet; (selected) contestant: 种子～ seeded player / 世界名～ world-famous athlete / 优秀～ ace athlete; top-ranking athlete

【选题】 xuǎntí selection of subject

【选修】 xuǎnxiū take as an elective course

【选修课】 xuǎnxiūkè elective course; selective course

【选育】 xuǎnyù 〈*Agric.*〉 seed selection; breeding

【选择】 xuǎnzé select; choose; opt: ～职业 choose one's occupation / 由我方～ at our option / 如果他想去旧金山，只能～乘飞机。If he wants to get to San Francisco, he has no alternative but to go by plane.

【选址】 xuǎnzhǐ 〈*Computer*〉 location

【选种】 zuǎnzhǒng 〈*Agric.*〉 seed selection

癣 (xuǎn) tinea; ringworm

泫 (xuàn) water drop

【泫然】 xuànrán falling water drop: ～泪下 tears falling down; tears trickling down

炫［衒²］(xuàn) 1.(晃眼) dazzle 2.(夸耀) show off; display

【炫示】 xuànshì how off; display

【炫耀】 xuànyào make a display of; show off; flaunt: ～才能 show off one's talent

眩 (xuàn) 1.(眼花) dizzy; giddy 2.(执迷) dazzled; bewildered

【眩晕】 xuànyùn dizziness

绚 (xuàn) gorgeous

【绚烂】 xuànlàn gorgeous; brilliant; radiant

【绚丽】 xuànlì gorgeous; magnificent: ～多彩 bright and colorful; gorgeous

旋［鏇²］(xuàn) 1.(旋转的) whirl 2.(转圈切削) turn sth. on a lathe; lathe; pare 3.(临时做) at the time; at the last moment
(另见"旋"xuán)

【旋风】 xuànfēng whirlwind

【旋工】 xuàngōng lathe turner

渲 (xuàn)

【渲染】 xuànrǎn play up; exaggerate; pile it on

楦［楥］(xuàn) 1.(鞋楦) shoe last 2.(楦鞋) last a shoe

【楦子】 xuàn·zi shoe last

xue

削 (xuē)(专用于合成词) pare; whittle; cut (另见"削"xiāo)

【削壁】 xuēbì cliff; precipice

【削价】 xuējià cut prices; lower the price: ～出售 sell at a reduced price

【削减】 xuējiǎn cut; cut down; reduce; slash; whittle down: ～成本 cut the cost / ～非生产性开支 cut down nonproductive expenditures; cut back on nonproductive spending / ～军费 cut down military expenditures / ～预算 slash the budget

【削减战略武器条约】 xuējiǎn zhànlüè wǔqì tiáoyuē START; Strategic Arms Reduction Treaty

【削弱】 xuēruò weaken; cripple

【削足适履】 xuēzú-shìlǚ cut the feet to fit the shoes; act in a Procrustean manner

靴［鞾］(xuē) boots

【靴子】 xuē·zi boots

穴 (xué) 1.(洞穴) cave; den; hole 2.(墓穴) grave 3.(穴位) acupuncture point; acupoint

【穴居】 xuéjū live in caves

【穴位】 xuéwèi 〈*Chin. Med.*〉 acupuncture point; acupoint

学［學、斈］(xué) 1.(学习) study; learn: ～游泳 learn to swim / 我正在～英语。I'm learning English. / 她正在～古典文学。She's studying the classical literature. 2.(模仿) imitate; mimic 3.(学问) learning; knowledge: 才疏～浅 have little talent and less learning 4.(学科) subject of study; branch of learning 5.(学校) school; college

【学报】 xuébào learned journal; journal

【学潮】 xuécháo student strike; campus upheaval
【学而不厌】 xué'érbùyàn have an insatiable desire to learn
【学阀】 xuéfá scholar-tyrant
【学非所用】 xuéfēisuǒyòng one does not do that which one has learned
【学费】 xuéfèi tuition fee; tuition
【学分】 xuéfēn credit; academic credit
【学分制】 xuéfēnzhì the credit system
【学风】 xuéfēng style of study
【学府】 xuéfǔ seat of learning; institution of higher learning: 最高～ institution of higher learning
【学好】 xuéhǎo learn from good examples; emulate good
【学会】 xuéhuì 1.(掌握) learn; master: ～滑冰 have learned to skate 2.(学术团体) society; association; learned society; institute
【学籍】 xuéjí one's status as a student; one's name on the school roll
【学究】 xuéjiū pedant
【学究气】 xuéjiūqì pedantry
【学科】 xuékē 1.(指门类) subject; course; discipline 2.(指课目) branch of learning 3.(军事科目) courses of learning in military training
【学力】 xuélì knowledge; educational level; academic attainments: 具有同等～ have the same educational level
【学历】 xuélì record of formal schooling; educational background
【学龄】 xuélíng school age
【学龄儿童】 xuélíng értóng children of school age
【学名】 xuémíng 1.(科学专名) scientific name 2.(入学时的正式名字) formal name used at school
【学年】 xuénián school year; academic year
【学派】 xuépài school of thought; school
【学期】 xuéqī school term; term; semester
【学前班】 xuéqiānbān preschool course
【学前教育】 xuéqián jiàoyù preschool education; infant school education
【学前学习】 xuéqián xuéxí preschool learning
【学前阅读技能】 xuéqián yuèdú jìnéng prereading skill
【学舌】 xuéshé 1.(模仿别人说话) mechanically repeat other people's words; parrot: 鹦鹉～ imitate mechanically; parrot 2.(嘴不严) gossipy; loosetongued
【学生】 xué·sheng 1.(在校生) student; pupil: 一个学历史的～ a student of history 2.(向人学习者) disciple; follower
【学生会】 xuéshēnghuì student union; student association
【学生俚语】 xué·sheng lǐyǔ schoolboy slang
【学生证】 xuéshēngzhèng student's identity card
【学时】 xuéshí class hour; period
【学识】 xuéshí learning; knowledge; scholarly attainments: 一个～渊博的教授 a learned professor
【学士】 xuéshì 1.(文人) scholar 2.(学位) bachelor
【学术】 xuéshù learning; science; academic (adj.): 一个优秀的历史学家应具有～头脑。A good historian must have an academic mind.
【学术带头人】 xuéshù dàitóurén leader in scientific research; pioneer in scientific research
【学术界】 xuéshùjiè academic circles
【学术刊物】 xuéshù kānwù academic publications
【学术论文】 xuéshù lùnwén thesis; scientific paper
【学术著作】 xuéshù zhùzuò academic work; academic book
【学说】 xuéshuō theory; doctrine
【学徒】 xuétú 1.(学徒工) apprentice; trainee 2.(当学徒) apprentice; work as an apprentice: 他给一位裁缝做～。He was apprenticed to a tailor.
【学位】 xuéwèi degree; academic degree: 博士～ doctor's degree; doctorate / 硕士～ Master's degree / 名誉～ honorary degree / 我获得了文学士～。I received my bachelor of arts degree.
【学问】 xué·wen learning; knowledge; scholarship
【学习】 xuéxí 1.(获得知识) study; learn 2.(效法) emulate
【学衔】 xuéxián academic rank; academic ti-

tle
【学校】 xuéxiào school; educational institution
【学业】 xuéyè one's studies; school work
【学以致用】 xuéyǐzhìyòng study for the purpose of application; study sth. in order to apply it
【学有专长】 xuéyǒuzhuānchāng have acquired a specialty from study
【学员】 xuéyuán student; trainee
【学院】 xuéyuàn college; academy; institute: 音乐～ an academy of music / 海军～ a naval academy
【学者】 xuézhě scholar; learned man; man of learning
【学制】 xuézhì 1.（教育制度）educational system; school system 2.（学习年限）length of schooling

噱 (xué)

【噱头】 xuétóu words to amuse; act meant to excite laughter

雪 (xuě) 1.〈*Meteorol*.〉snow: 降～ snow; snowfall 2.（洗掉耻辱等）wipe out; avenge

【雪白】 xuěbái snow-white; snowy white
【雪板】 xuěbǎn 〈*Sports*〉ski
【雪暴】 xuěbào snowstorm; blizzard
【雪崩】 xuěbēng snowslide; avalanche: ～把登山者给阻住了。The avalanche trapped the climbers.
【雪崩效应】 xuěbēng xiàoyìng avalanche effect
【雪耻】 xuěchǐ avenge an insult; wipe out a humiliation
【雪道】 xuědào 〈*Sports*〉trail
【雪地靴】 xuědìxuē snow boots
【雪堆】 xuěduī snow drift
【雪糕】 xuěgāo ice cream
【雪恨】 xuěhèn wreak vengeance; avenge
【雪花】 xuěhuā snowflake
【雪花膏】 xuěhuāgāo vanishing cream
【雪茄】 xuěqié cigar
【雪犁】 xuělí snowplow; snowplough
【雪里红】 xuělǐhóng potherb mustard
【雪里蕻】 xuělǐhóng 同"雪里红"
【雪莲】 xuělián snow lotus
【雪亮】 xuěliàng shiny; bright as snow
【雪盲】 xuěmáng snow blindness; snow-blind (adj.)
【雪片】 xuěpiàn snowflake
【雪橇】 xuěqiāo sled; sledge; sleigh: 机动～ snowmobile
【雪青】 xuěqīng lilac (color)
【雪球】 xuěqiú snowball: 掷～ throw snowball
【雪人】 xuěrén 1.（用雪堆成的）snowman 2.（尚不能确知的动物）yeti; Abominable Snowman
【雪山】 xuěshān snow capped mountain
【雪上汽车】 xuěshàng qìchē snowmobile
【雪松】 xuěsōng 〈*Bot*.〉cedar
【雪屋】 xuěwū igloo; iglu
【雪线】 xuěxiàn 〈*Geog*.〉snow line
【雪野】 xuěyě snowfield
【雪冤】 xuěyuān clear sb. of a false charge; redress a wrong
【雪原】 xuěyuán snowfield
【雪杖】 xuězhàng 〈*Sports*〉(ski) pole; (ski) stick
【雪中送炭】 xuězhōng-sòngtàn send charcoal in snowy weather; provide timely help

鳕 (xuě)〈*Zool*.〉cod: 大西洋～ Atlantic cod

【鳕鱼】 xuěyú cod; Pacific cod

血 (xuè) 1.（血液）blood 2.（同血统的）related by blood: ～亲 blood relation（另见"血"xiě）

【血案】 xuè'àn murder case
【血本】 xuèběn principal; original capital
【血沉】 xuèchén 〈*Med*.〉erythrocytic sedimentation rate
【血仇】 xuèchóu blood feud
【血管】 xuèguǎn 〈*Anat*.〉blood vessel
【血管瘤】 xuèguǎnliú 〈*Med*.〉hemangioma; angioma
【血管造影】 xuèguǎn zàoyǐng 〈*Med*.〉angiography
【血汗】 xuèhàn blood and sweat; sweat and toil
【血红】 xuèhóng blood red
【血红蛋白】 xuèhóng dànbái 〈*Physiol*.〉hemoglobin
【血迹】 xuèjì bloodstain: ～斑斑 blood-

stained

【血浆】 xuèjiāng 〈*Physiol*.〉(blood) plasma

【血口喷人】 xuèkǒu-pēnrén make unfounded and malicious attacks upon sb.; venomously slander

【血库】 xuèkù 〈*Med*.〉 blood bank

【血淋淋】 xuèlínlín bloody; dripping with blood

【血流成河】 xuèliú-chénghé blood flowed and has become a river

【血流如注】 xuèliú-rúzhù blood cascading down without stop; blood streaming down

【血尿】 xuèniào 〈*Med*.〉 blood in the urine; hematuria

【血泡】 xuèpào bloodstained blister: 磨出了~ there have appeared some bloodstained blisters

【血泊】 xuèpō pool of blood: 倒在~中 fall down in a pool of blood

【血气】 xuèqì **1**.(精力) animal spirits; sap; vigor: ~方刚 full of sap; full of vigor and vitality **2**.(血性) courage and uprightness

【血亲】 xuèqīn consanguinity

【血亲关系】 xuèqīn guān·xi blood ties; relationship by consanguinity

【血清】 xuèqīng 〈*Physiol*.〉(blood) serum

【血球】 xuèqiú 〈*Physiol*.〉 blood cell; blood corpuscle

【血球计数】 xuèqiú jìshù 〈*Med*.〉 blood count

【血肉】 xuèròu **1**.(肉和血) flesh and blood **2**.(密切的关系) close relationship

【血肉横飞】 xuèròu-héngfēi flesh and blood flying in all directions

【血肉模糊】 xuèròu-mó·hu badly mutilated

【血肉相连】 xuèròu-xiānglián be inseparably linked to each other

【血色】 xuèsè redness of the skin; color

【血色素】 xuèsèsù 〈*Med*.〉 hemochrome

【血书】 xuèshū a not or a letter written in one's own blood

【血栓】 xuèshuān 〈*Med*.〉 thrombus

【血栓形成】 xuèshuān xíngchéng 〈*Med*.〉 thrombosis

【血水】 xuèshuǐ blood

【血糖】 xuètáng 〈*Med*.〉 blood sugar

【血糖过高】 xuètáng guògāo 〈*Med*.〉 hyperglycemia

【血统】 xuètǒng **1**.(血亲关系) blood relationship; blood lineage **2**.(出身) family background

【血统联系】 xuètǒng liánxì blood bond

【血吸虫】 xuèxīchóng 〈*Bot*.〉 blood fluke

【血吸虫病】 xuèxīchóngbìng 〈*Med*.〉 schistosomiasis; snail fever

【血细胞】 xuèxìbāo 〈*Physiol*.〉 blood cell; corpuscle

【血小板】 xuèxiǎobǎn 〈*Physiol*.〉(blood) platelet

【血腥】 xuèxīng reeking of blood; bloody; sanguinary

【血腥味】 xuèxīngwèi smell of blood

【血型】 xuèxíng 〈*Physiol*.〉 blood group; blood type

【血性】 xuèxìng fearless and upright: 有~的人 an honest and dauntless man

【血压】 xuèyā 〈*Physiol*.〉 blood pressure: 低~ low blood pressure; hypotension / 高~ high blood pressure; hypertension / 量~ take one's blood pressure

【血压计】 xuèyājì sphygmomanometer

【血样】 xuèyàng blood sample

【血液】 xuèyè **1**.〈*Physiol*.〉 blood **2**.(主要成分或力量) key component

【血液透析】 xuèyè tòuxī dialysis

【血液循环】 xuèyè xúnhuān blood circulation

【血衣】 xuèyī bloodstained garment; clothes covered with gore

【血印】 xuèyìn bloodstain

【血雨腥风】 xuèyǔ-xīngfēng a foul wind and a rain of blood; reactionary reign of terror

【血缘】 xuèyuán ties of blood; consanguinity; blood relationship

【血晕】 xuèyùn bruise

【血债】 xuèzhài a debt of blood: 偿还~ pay debts of blood

【血战】 xuèzhàn bloody battle; sanguinary battle

【血中毒】 xuèzhòngdú blood poisoning

【血肿】 xuèzhǒng 〈*Med*.〉 hematoma

谑 (xuè) crack a joke; banter; tease: 戏~ banter; tease

【谑而不虐】 xuè'érbùnüè tease without embarrassing

xun

勋［勳］（xūn） merit; meritorious service; achievement：功～ meritorious service; contribution
【勋表】 xūnbiǎo ribbon
【勋绩】 xūnjī meritorious service; outstanding contribution
【勋爵】 xūnjué 1.（爵位）feudal title of nobility 2.（英国的）Lord
【勋章】 xūnzhāng medal; decoration：荣获一枚～ be awarded a medal

熏［燻］（xūn） 1.（用烟、气熏）smoke; fumigate 2.（熏制）treat with smoke; smoke：～肉 treat meat with smoke
【熏房】 xūnfáng chimney kiln; smoke kiln
【熏染】 xūnrǎn exert a gradual, corrupting influence on
【熏烧】 xūnshāo smolder
【熏陶】 xūntáo exert a gradual, uplifting influence on; nurture; edify
【熏鱼】 xūnyú smoked fish
【熏蒸】 xūnzhēng stifling; suffocating
【熏制】 xūnzhì smoke; fumigate sth. with jasmine; cure by smoke

旬（xún） 1.（10 日）a period of ten days 2.（10 岁）a period of ten years in a person's age

询（xún） ask; enquire; inquire
【询问】 xúnwèn 1.（征求意见）ask about; enquire 2.〈*Law*〉examination

寻［尋］（xún） look of; search; seek
【寻常】 xúncháng ordinary; usual; common：异乎～ extraordinary; unusual
【寻短见】 xúnduǎnjiàn commit suicide; take one's own life
【寻访】 xúnfǎng look for; try to locate; make inquiries about
【寻根究底】 xúngēn-jiūdǐ get to the bottom of things; inquire deeply into
【寻呼】 xúnhū page; bleep
【寻呼机】 xúnhūjī pager; beeper
【寻机】 xúnjī look for an opportunity
【寻开心】 xúnkāixīn make fun for; joke
【寻觅】 xúnmì seek; look for
【寻求】 xúnqiú seek; explore; go in quest of：我们在～解决问题的正确答案。We are groping for the right answer to the problem.
【寻思】 xún·si think sth. over; consider
【寻死】 xúnsǐ 1.（企图自杀）try to commit suicide; attempt suicide 2.（自杀）commit suicide
【寻味】 xúnwèi chew sth. over; ruminate; think over
【寻衅】 xúnxìn pick a quarrel; provoke
【寻找】 xúnzhǎo seek; look for：～机会 look for an opportunity

荨（xún）
（另见"荨"qián）
【荨麻疹】 xúnmázhěn nettle rash; urticaria

鲟［鱘、鱏］（xún）〈*Zool.*〉sturgeon：中华～ Chinese sturgeon
【鲟鱼】 xúnyú sturgeon

巡［廵］（xún） 1.（巡查；巡视）patrol; make one's rounds：～夜 go on night patrol 2.（遍数）round of drink：酒过三～。The wine has gone round three time.
【巡边员】 xúnbiānyuán 〈*Football*〉linesman
【巡查】 xúnchá go on a tour of inspection; make one's rounds
【巡航】 xúnháng cruise
【巡航导弹】 xúnháng dǎodàn cruise missile
【巡回】 xúnhuí go the rounds; tour; make a circuit of
【巡回演出】 xúnhuí yǎnchū tour; make an performance tour
【巡回展览】 xúnhuí zhǎnlǎn make an exhibition tour
【巡警】 xúnjǐng 1.（总称）patrol police 2.（人员）patrolman; cop on the beat
【巡礼】 xúnlǐ 1.（朝拜圣地）visit a sacred land; go on a pilgrimage; make a pilgrimage to a holy place 2.（观光；游览）tour; sightseeing
【巡逻】 xúnluó go on patrol; patrol
【巡逻车】 xúnluóchē patrol car; panda car
【巡逻队】 xúnluóduì patrol team; patrol group
【巡视】 xúnshì make an inspection tour; tour
【巡洋舰】 xúnyángjiàn cruiser
【巡弋】 xúnyì (of warships) cruise

循(xún) follow; abide by: ～例 follow the usual practice; follow a precedent

【循规蹈矩】 xúnguī-dǎojù follow rules docilely; conform to convention; toe the line

【循环】 xúnhuán circulate; cycle: 恶性～ vicious circle / 良性～ virtuous circle; benign cycle

【循环赛】 xúnhuánsài 〈*Sports*〉 round robin

【循环往复】 xúnhuán-wǎngfù move in circles

【循环小数】 xúnhuán xiǎoshù 〈*Math.*〉 recurring decimal

【循序】 xúnxù in proper order or sequence

【循序渐进】 xúnxù-jiànjìn progress step by step in an orderly way

【循循善诱】 xúnxún-shànyòu be good at giving systematic guidance; teach with skill and patience

训(xùn) 1.(教导;训诫) lecture; teach; train 2.(准则) standard; model; example

【训斥】 xùnchì reprimand; rebuke; dress down

【训词】 xùncí admonition; instructions

【训诫】 xùnjiè 1.(教导和告诫) admonish; advise 2.〈*Law*〉 rebuke; reprimand; be reprimanded

【训练】 xùnliàn train; drill

【训练班】 xùnliànbān training class; training course

【训练有素】 xùnliàn-yǒusù fully-fledged: ～的护士 fully-fledged nurse

【训令】 xùnlìng written instruction

驯(xùn) 1.(顺服的) tame and docile: ～象 a tame elephant 2.(使顺服) tame; domesticate: ～马 break in a horse

【驯服】 1.(顺从的) docile; tame; tractable: ～的马 a docile horse 2.(使顺从) tame; break; domesticate: ～老虎 tame a tiger 3.(控制住) control: ～洪水 bring a flood under control

【驯虎师】 xùnhǔshī a tiger tamer

【驯化】 xùnhuà domesticate; tame

【驯良】 xùnliáng tractable; docile; tame and gentle

【驯鹿】 xùnlù 〈*Zool.*〉 reindeer

【驯兽师】 xùnshòushī tamer; animal trainer

【驯顺】 xùnshùn tame and docile

【驯养】 xùnyǎng raise and train (animals); domesticate

讯(xùn) 1.(讯问) interrogate; question 2.(信息) message; dispatch

【讯问】 xùnwèn 1.(审问) interrogate; question 2.(问) ask about; enquire

【讯息】 xùnxī message

汛(xùn) flood; high water

【汛期】 xùnqī flood season; high-water season

迅(xùn) fast; swift

【迅即】 xùnjí immediately; at once

【迅疾】 xùnjí swift; rapid

【迅捷】 xùnjié fast; agile; quick

【迅猛】 xùnměng swift and violent

【迅速】 xùnsù rapid; swift; speedy; prompt

徇[狥](xùn)

【徇情】 xùnqíng act wrongly out of personal considerations; practice favoritism: ～枉法 bend the law for the benefit of relatives or friends

殉[徇²](xùn) 1.(殉葬) be buried alive with the dead 2.(牺牲) sacrifice one's life for

【殉国】 xùnguó die for one's motherland; give one's life for one's country

【殉教】 xùnjiào die for one's religious belief

【殉节】 xùnjié 1.(指战时) kill oneself because of the defeat in war 2.(指旧时妇女) kill herself

【殉难】 xùnnàn die for (a just cause); die a martyr

【殉葬】 xùnzàng be buried alive with the dead

【殉葬品】 xùnzàngpǐn funerary object; sacrificial object

【殉职】 xùnzhí die at one's post; die in the course of performing one's duty; die in line of duty

逊[遜](xùn) 1.(让位) abdicate 2.(谦虚;谦恭) modest: 出言不～ speak insolently 3.(比不上) inferior: 稍～一筹 be slightly inferior

【逊色】 xùnsè be inferior: 毫无～ be by no means inferior

【逊位】 xùnwèi abdicate; abdication (n.)

蕈(xùn) fungus; gill fungus

Y

ya

丫（yā） bifurcation；fork

【丫杈】 yāchà **1.**（树枝分开的地方）fork；crotch **2.**（形容树枝歧出）ramified；crotched；forked

【丫头】 yā·tou **1.**（女孩）girl **2.**（丫鬟）slave girl

【丫头养的】 yā·touyǎng·de （骂人话）son of a bitch

【丫丫】 yāyā （儿童用语）tootsy

压［壓］（yā） **1.**（施压力）press；push down；hold down；weigh down **2.**（使稳定）keep under control；control；keep under；quell **3.**（压制）bring pressure to bear on；suppress；daunt；intimidate **4.**（逼近）approach；be getting near **5.**（积压）pigeonhole；shelve；put aside：把问题～下来 have the problem shelved **6.**（压注）risk on sth.；stake

（另见"压"yà）

【压扁】 yābiǎn press flat；flatten

【压秤】 yāchèng be relatively heavy per unit volume

【压倒】 yādǎo overwhelm；overpower；prevail over：～多数 an overwhelming majority

【压低】 yādī bring down；lower；reduce；abate：～价格 bring down the price

【压电】 yādiàn piezoelectric：～现象 piezoelectric effect

【压服】 yāfú force sb. to submit；bring sb. to his knees

【压花】 yāhuā coining

【压坏】 yāhuài crush；squash

【压挤】 yājǐ 〈*Mech.*〉 extrude；extrusion (n.)

【压价】 yājià force prices down；demand a lower price

【压紧】 yājǐn compress tightly

【压惊】 yājīng help sb. get over a shock

【压境】 yājìng press on to the border

【压垮】 yākuǎ collapse under pressure

【压力】 yālì **1.**〈*Physics*〉 pressure **2.**（负担）overwhelming force；pressure：在舆论的～下 under the pressure of public opinion

【压力阀】 yālìfá pressure valve

【压力锅】 yālìguō pressure cooker

【压力集团】 yālì jítuán pressure group

【压路机】 yālùjī road roller；roller

【压平】 yāpíng flatten；even

【压迫】 yāpò **1.**（强制）oppress；repress **2.**（对机体施压）constrict

【压强】 yāqiáng 〈*Physics*〉 intensity of pressure；pressure

【压水反应堆】 yāshuǐ fǎnyìngduí pressurized-water reactor；PWR

【压缩】 yāsuō **1.**（使缩小）compress；condense **2.**（削减）cut down；reduce：～非生产性开支 cut down nonproductive expenses

【压缩机】 yāsuōjī compressor

【压条】 yātiáo 〈*Agric.*〉 layer

【压痛】 yātòng 〈*Med.*〉 tenderness

【压弯】 yāwān bend：树枝被雪的重量～了。The branch gave under the weight of the heavy snow.

【压蔓】 yāwàn 〈*Agric.*〉 layer

【压延】 yāyán roll

【压抑】 yāyì **1.**（指情绪、感情等）constrain；inhibit；depress；hold back：精神～ feel much depressed **2.**（憋闷）oppressive；stifling

【压榨】 yāzhà **1.**（榨汁）press；squeeze **2.**（剥削或搜刮）oppress and exploit；squeeze；bleed

【压制】 yāzhì **1.**（限制）suppress；stifle；inhibit **2.**（冲压制造）pressing

呀（yā） 1.〈*interj*.〉（表示惊异）oh；ah 2.〈*onomat*.〉creak：门～的一声开了。The door creaked open.

鸦［鴉］（yā） 〈*Zool*.〉crow

【鸦片】 yāpiàn opium：戒～ give up opium-smoking

【鸦雀无声】 yāquè-wúshēng not even a crow or sparrow can be heard；silence reigns

押（yā） 1.（抵押）give as security；mortgage；pawn；pledge 2.（扣留）detain；take into custody 3.（跟随看管）escort 4.（签字）signature：画～ mark in lieu of signature

【押车】 yāchē escort sth. in transportation

【押解】 yājiè 1.（押送）send away under escort：～俘虏 send prisoners under escort 2.（押运）escort sth. in transportation

【押金】 yājīn cash pledge；deposit；security

【押款】 yākuǎn 1.（抵押借款）borrow money on security 2.（指款项）a loan on security

【押送】 yāsòng 1.（押解）send away under escort：～犯人 send criminals under escort 2.（押运）escort sth. in transportation

【押运】 yāyùn escort sth. in transportation

【押韵】 yāyùn rhyme

【押账】 yāzhàng offer sth. as security for a loan

【押租】 yāzū rent deposit

桠［椏、枒］（yā）

【桠杈】 yāchà 1.（树杈）fork；crotch 2.（分杈）forked；crotched

【桠枝】 yāzhī branch；twig

鸭（yā） 〈*Zool*.〉duck：北京～ Beijing duck / 烤～ roast duck / 填～ force-fed duck ‖ 公鸭 drake / 母鸭 duke / 小鸭 duckling

【鸭蛋】 yādàn duck's egg

【鸭叫声】 yājiàoshēng quack

【鸭梨】 yālí pear；Hebei pear

【鸭绒】 yāróng duck's down；eider down：～被 eider down quilt；duck's down quilt

【鸭舌帽】 yāshémào peaked cap

【鸭子】 yā·zi duck

【鸭嘴笔】 yāzuǐbǐ drawing pen

【鸭嘴兽】 yāzuǐshòu 〈*Zool*.〉platypus；duck-billed platypus

牙（yá） 1.（牙齿）tooth（pl. teeth）：一副假～ a false teeth / 拔了一颗～ have a tooth taken out 2.（象牙）ivory 3.（像牙齿的东西）tooth-like thing

【牙齿】 yáchǐ tooth（pl. teeth）

【牙床】 yáchuáng 1.（齿龈）gum 2.（有牙雕的床）ivory-inlaid bed

【牙雕】 yádiāo ivory carving

【牙粉】 yáfěn tooth powder

【牙缝】 yáfèng slit between the teeth；crevice between teeth

【牙膏】 yágāo toothpaste

【牙垢】 yágòu tartar；dental calculus

【牙关】 yáguān mandibular joint：咬紧～ clench one's teeth

【牙科】 yákē 〈*Med*.〉dentistry

【牙科医生】 yákē yīshēng dentist；dental surgeon

【牙科诊疗所】 yákē zhěnliáoshuǒ dental clinic

【牙口】 yákǒu 1.（牲畜年龄）the age of a draught animal 2.（老人的咀嚼能力）the condition of an old person's teeth

【牙签】 yáqiān toothpick

【牙石】 yáshí tartar；dental calculus

【牙刷】 yáshuā toothbrush

【牙痛】 yátòng toothache

【牙线】 yáxiàn dental floss

【牙牙学语】 yáyá-xuéyǔ learn to speak；babble out one's first speech sounds

【牙医】 yáyī dentist

【牙龈】 yáyín 〈*Anat*.〉gum

【牙龈炎】 yáyínyán 〈*Med*.〉gingivitis

【牙周病学】 yázhóubìngxué 〈*Med*.〉periodontics；periodontic（adj.）

【牙周炎】 yázhóuyán 〈*Med*.〉periodontitis

芽（yá） bud；sprout；shoot：发～ sprout

【芽接】 yájiē 〈*Bot*.〉bud grafting；budding：把蔷薇～在荆棘上 bud a rose on a brier

蚜（yá）

【蚜虫】 yáchóng aphid；aphis

崖［厓、崕］（yá） precipice；cliff

【崖壁】 yábì precipice

涯（yá） margin；limit：天～海角 the remotest corners of the earth

哑［啞］（yǎ） 1.（不能说话）mute; dumb 2.（嘶哑）hoarse; husky 3.（未打响）misfire: ～炮 misfired shell

【哑巴】 yǎ·ba a dumb person; mute

【哑剧】 yǎjù dumb show; pantomime

【哑口无言】 yǎkǒu-wúyán be left without an argument; be rendered speechless; be dumb as a fish

【哑铃】 yǎlíng 〈*Sports*〉 dumbbell

【哑谜】 yǎmí puzzling remark; enigma; riddle: 打～ make a puzzling remark

【哑然失笑】 yǎrán-shīxiào unable to stifle a laugh; can't help laughing

雅（yǎ） 1.（高雅）refined; elegant; graceful 2.〈*respectness*〉～教 your esteemed opinion / ～意 your esteemed favor; your kindness 3.（合规范）standard; correct; proper

【雅观】 yǎguān refined; in good taste

【雅号】 yǎhào your name

【雅量】 yǎliàng 1.（指气度）magnanimity; generosity 2.（指酒量）great capacity for liquor

【雅鲁藏布江】 Yǎlǔzàngbùjiāng 〈place〉 Yarlung Zangbo Jiang

【雅皮士】 yǎpíshì yuppie; yuppy; young urban professional

【雅趣】 yǎqù refined tastes

【雅士】 yǎshì a refined scholar; a person of refined tastes

【雅俗共赏】 yǎsú-gòngshǎng appeal to both the more and the less cultured; suit both refined and popular tastes

【雅兴】 yǎxìng aesthetic mood

【雅致】 yǎzhì refined; tasteful

【雅座】 yǎzuò a cosy private room

轧（yà） 1.（滚压）roll; run over: ～路 roll a road surface / ～碎 roll asunder; crush to pieces 2.（机器声）铰链～～作响。The hinges squeaked.
（另见“轧”zhá）

【轧道车】 yàdàochē 〈*Railway*〉 truck inspection railcar

【轧花】 yàhuā 〈*Textiles*〉 cotton ginning

【轧花厂】 yàhuāchǎng cotton ginning mill

【轧花机】 yàhuājī cotton gin

【轧伤】 yàshāng run over and injure

【轧死】 yàsǐ run over and kill

亚［亞］（yà） 1.（差）inferior; second 2.（次于）sub-: ～科 subfamily / ～目 suborder / ～属 subgenus 3.（亚洲）Asia; Asiatic (adj.)

【亚当】 Yàdāng Adam

【亚东】 Yàdōng 〈place〉 Yadong; Chomo

【亚军】 yàjūn second place; runner-up

【亚硫酸】 yàliúsuān sulfurous acid; sulphurous acid

【亚麻】 yàmá 〈*Bot.*〉 flax

【亚麻布】 yàmábù line cloth

【亚欧大陆】 Yà-Ōu dàlù Euroasia; Euroasiatic (adj.)

【亚热带】 yàrèdài subtropical zone; subtropics; subtropical (adj.): ～园艺 subtropical gardening

【亚硝酸】 yàxiāosuān 〈*Chem.*〉 nitrous acid; nitrous (adj.)

【亚音速】 yàyīnsù 〈*Physics*〉 subsonic speed; subsonic (adj.): ～飞机 subsonic aircraft

【亚运会】 Yàyùnhuì Asian Games

【亚洲】 Yàzhōu Asia; Asian (adj.) ‖ 亚洲人 Asian

【亚洲发展银行】 Yàzhōu Fāzhǎn Yínháng Asian Development Bank (ADB)

【亚洲四小龙】 Yàzhāu sìxiǎolóng the four little dragons in Asia

【亚洲象】 yàzhōuxiàng Indian elephant

氩［氬］（yà） 〈*Chem.*〉 argon (元素符号 Ar)

压［壓］（yà）
（另见“压”yā）

【压板】 yàbǎn seesaw

【压根儿】 yàgēnr （多用否定）altogether: 他～不知道该怎么做。He's not altogether sure what to do.

揠（yà） pull up

【揠苗助长】 yàmiáo-zhùzhǎng pull up seedlings in a vain hope of helping them grow; spoil things by excessive enthusiasm

yan

咽（yān） 〈*Anat.*〉 pharynx
（另见“咽”yàn）

【咽喉】 yānhóu 1.〈*Anat.*〉pharynx and larynx; throat: ～痛 have a sore throat 2.(交通要道) key point; strategic passage
【咽镜】 yānjìng 〈*Med.*〉pharyngoscope
【咽头】 yāntóu 〈*Anat.*〉pharynx
【咽峡炎】 yānxiáyán 〈*Med.*〉angina
【咽炎】 yānyán 〈*Med.*〉pharyngitis

胭[戯](yān)

【胭红】 yānhóng carmine
【胭脂】 yān·zhi 1.(化妆品) rouge: 在脸上擦～ rouge one's cheeks 2.〈*Zool.*〉kermes
【胭脂红】 yān·zhihóng carmine
【胭脂鱼】 yān·zhiyú sucker; Chinese sucker

烟[煙、菸[4]](yān) 1.(燃烧时冒的烟) smoke 2.(像烟的东西) mist; vapor: ～霞 mist and clouds in the twilight 3.(烟刺激) be irritated by smoke 4.(烟草; 烟卷) tobacco; cigarette: 雪茄～ cigar / 戒～ give up smoking; swear off tobacco / 吸～ smoke 5.(鸦片) opium: ～枪 opium pipe
【烟波】 yānbō mist-covered waters
【烟草】 yāncǎo 1.〈*Bot.*〉tobacco 2.(烟叶) tobacco leaf
【烟尘】 yānchén fly ash
【烟囱】 yāncōng chimney; funnel
【烟囱管】 yāncōngguǎn stovepipe
【烟袋】 yāndài long pipe
【烟袋锅】 yāndàiguō the bowl of long pipe
【烟道】 yāndào 〈*Archit.*〉flue
【烟蒂】 yāndì cigarette butt
【烟斗】 yāndǒu pipe
【烟鬼】 yānguǐ 1.(烟瘾大的人) heavy smoker 2.(有鸦片烟瘾的人) opium addict
【烟海】 yānghǎi a vast sea of fog; huge and voluminous: 浩如～ a tremendous amount; voluminous
【烟盒】 yānhé cigarette case
【烟花】 yānhuā fireworks; Catherine wheel
【烟花柳巷】 yānhuā-liǔxiàng brothels
【烟灰】 yānhuī tobacco ash; cigarette ash
【烟灰缸】 yānhuīgāng ashtray
【烟火】 yānhuǒ 1.(烟和火) smoke and fire: 严禁～! No smoking and lighting fires. 2.(熟食) cooked food 3.(焰火) fireworks: 放～ set off fireworks
【烟酒专卖】 yānjiǔ zhuānmài state monopoly of sales of tobacco and alcoholic drinks
【烟具】 yānjù smoking paraphernalia; smoking set
【烟卷儿】 yānjuǎnr cigarette
【烟煤】 yānméi bituminous coal; soft coal
【烟民】 yānmín smoker
【烟幕】 yānmù smoke screen: 施放～ let go a smoke shell
【烟幕弹】 yānmùdàn 1.〈*Mil.*〉smoke shell; smoke bomb 2.(掩盖真相) smoke screen
【烟农】 yānnóng tobacco grower
【烟气】 yānqì flue gas
【烟丝】 yānsī cut tobacco; pipe tobacco
【烟筒】 yān·tong chimney; funnel; stovepipe
【烟头】 yāntóu cigarette end
【烟土】 yāntǔ crude opium
【烟雾】 yānwù smoke; mist; vapor; smog
【烟消云散】 yānxiāo-yúnsàn vanish like mist and smoke; completely vanish
【烟熏】 yānxūn smoke
【烟叶】 yānyè tobacco leaf; leaf tobacco
【烟瘾】 yānyǐn a craving for tobacco
【烟油】 yānyóu tobacco tar
【烟柱】 yānzhù column of smoke
【烟子】 yān·zi soot

恹[懨、懕](yān)

【恹恹】 yānyān languishing: 病病～ look sick and languishing

殷(yān) blackish (另见"殷"yīn)

【殷红】 yānhóng blackish red; dark red

嫣(yān)

【嫣红】 yānhóng bright red: 姹紫～ beautiful and luxuriant
【嫣然】 yānrán beautiful; sweet

阉(yān) castrate or spay

【阉割】 yāngē 1.(去势) castrate; spay 2.(抽去主要内容) emasculate; deprive a theory
【阉牛】 yānniú bullock; castrated bull; steer
【阉羊】 yānyáng wether
【阉猪】 yānzhū hog

淹[淊[1]](yān) 1.(淹没) flood; submerge; inundate 2.(被汗浸) be tingling from sweat

【淹没】 yānmò submerge; flood; inundate; drown

【淹死】 yānsǐ be drowned

腌［醃］(yān) preserve in salt; salt; pickle; cure: ～菜 pickled vegetables; pickles / ～肉 salted meat; bacon / ～鱼 salted fish

【腌熏】 yānxūn bloat

湮(yān) 1.(埋没) fall into oblivion; be forgotten 2.(淤塞) clog up

【湮灭】 yānmiè bury in oblivion; annihilate

【湮没】 yānmò 1.(埋没) fall into oblivion; be neglected; be forgotten: ～无闻 sink into oblivion; drift into obscurity 2.〈*Physics*〉 annihilation

延(yán) 1.(延长) prolong; extend; protract 2.(向后推迟) postpone; delay 3.(聘请) engage; send for: ～师 engage a teacher

【延长】 yáncháng lengthen; prolong; extend: ～期限 extend a time limit / ～索赔期 extend the time for filing claims

【延迟】 yánchí postpone; delay; put off

【延搁】 yángē procrastinate; delay

【延会】 yánhuì postpone the meeting

【延缓】 yánhuǎn delay; postpone; put off: ～执行 postpone putting sth. into execution

【延年益寿】 yánnián-yìshòu prolong life; promise longevity

【延聘】 yánpìn engage; invite; employ; invite

【延期】 yánqī postpone; defer; put off: ～付款 defer payment

【延期偿付】 yánqī chángfù moratorium

【延期交货】 yánqī jiāohuò back order

【延烧】 yánshāo begin to burn the nearby things; begin to spread

【延伸】 yánshēn extend; stretch; elongate

【延时赛】 yánshísài 〈*Sports*〉 play-off

【延髓】 yánsuí 〈*Anat.*〉 medulla oblongata

【延误】 yánwù incur loss through delay: 时间上的～ time delay / 因…过失而～ delay through sb's fault / ～班机 miss the airliner

【延续】 yánxù continue; go on; last

筵(yán) feast; banquet: 喜～ a wedding feast

【筵席】 yánxí 1.(酒宴座位) seats arranged at a banquet 2.(酒席) feast; banquet

芫(yán)
(另见“芫”yuán)

【芫荽】 yánsuī 〈*Bot.*〉 coriander

严［嚴］(yán) 1.(紧密) tight; close 2.(严格) strict; severe; stern; rigorous 3.(指父亲) father: 家～ my father

【严办】 yánbàn deal with severely; punish with severity

【严惩】 yánchěng punish severely

【严词】 yáncí in strong terms; in stern words: ～拒绝 give a stern rebuff; sternly refuse

【严打】 yándǎ take severe measures against grave illegal and criminal activities

【严冬】 yándōng severe winter

【严防】 yánfáng be strictly on guard against; take strict precautions against

【严格】 yángé strict; rigorous; rigid; stringent: ～规章制度 rigorously enforce rules and regulations / ～要求自己 set strict demands on oneself

【严寒】 yánhán severe cold; bitter cold

【严紧】 yánjǐn tight; close: 防守～ guard carefully

【严谨】 yánjǐn 1.(严密谨慎) strict; rigorous 2.(紧密) compact; well-knit

【严禁】 yánjìn strictly forbid

【严峻】 yánjùn 1.(严厉;严肃) stern; severe; rigorous; grim 2.(严重) serious; grave; critical ～的考验 acid test / ～的事实 harsh facts

【严酷】 yánkù 1.(严厉) harsh; bitter; grim 2.(冷酷) cruel; ruthless

【严控】 yánkòng strict control

【严厉】 yánlì stern; severe: ～的措施 draconian measures / 他将受到～惩罚。He's for the high jump.

【严密】 yánmì 1.(周到) careful; thorough: ～的计划 careful plan 2.(很紧) close; tight

【严明】 yánmíng strict and impartial: 纪律～ with strict discipline

【严实】 yán·shi 1.(紧密) tight; close 2.(藏得好) hide safely

【严守】 yánshǒu strictly observe; maintain strictly: ～中立 strictly observe neutrality

【严霜】 yánshuāng heavy frost

【严肃】 yánsù 1.（令人敬畏）serious; solemn; earnest: ～的声调 severe tone of voice 2.（认真）serious; earnest; grave 3.（使严肃）make more severe or strict: ～纪律 enforce the discipline

【严刑】 yánxíng cruel torture

【严刑逼供】 yánxíng-bīgòng third degree; third-degree（adj.）

【严阵以待】 yánzhènyǐdài be ready in full battle array; stand in combat readiness

【严正】 yánzhèng solemn and just; serious and principled; stern: ～警告 serious warning / ～声明 solemn statement

【严重】 yánzhòng serious; grave; critical: 这个工厂～缺乏设备。The factory has an acute shortage of equipment. / 国际形势到了～关头。The international situation has reached a point of extreme gravity.

言（yán） 1.（话）speech; word 2.（说）say; talk; speak 3.（字）character; word

【言不由衷】 yánbùyóuzhōng speak insincerely; speak with one's tongue in one's cheek

【言传】 yánchuán explain in words

【言传身教】 yánchuán-shēnjiào teach by personal example as well as verbal instruction

【言词】 yáncí 同"言辞"

【言辞】 yáncí one's words; what one says: ～恳切 speak in a sincere and earnest way

【言而无信】 yán'érwúxìn fail to keep faith; go back on one's word

【言归于好】 yánguīyúhǎo make it up with sb.; become reconciled

【言过其实】 yánguòqíshí exaggerate; overstate

【言和】 yánhé make peace; become reconciled: 握手～ shake hands and make it up

【言简意赅】 yánjiǎn-yìgāi concise and comprehensive; compendious

【言教】 yánjiào teach by word of mouth; give verbal directions: 身教胜于～。Example is better than precept.

【言路】 yánlù channels through which criticisms and suggestions may be communicated to the leadership: 广开～ provide wide opportunities for airing views

【言论】 yánlùn opinion on public affairs; expression of one's political views; speech

【言论自由】 yánlùn zìyóu freedom of speech

【言情】 yánqíng discussion of sentiments

【言情小说】 yánqíng xiǎoshuō sentimental novel

【言谈】 yántán the way one speaks or what he says: ～举止 speech and deportment

【言听计从】 yántīng-jìcóng always follow sb's advice; act upon whatever sb. says; have implicit faith in sb.

【言外之意】 yánwàizhīyì implication; what is actually meant

【言行】 yánxíng words and deeds; statements and actions

【言行一致】 yánxíng-yīzhì One's deeds match well with one's words.

【言犹在耳】 yányóuzài'ěr the words are still ringing in one's ears

【言语】 yányǔ 1.（说的话）spoken language; speech 2.（开口）speak; talk; answer: 他这个人不爱～。He is a man of few words.

【言语学】 yányǔxué glossology; glottology

妍[妍]（yán）〈*written*〉beautiful

研[研]（yán） 1.（细磨）grind; pestle 2.（研究）study

【研读】 yándú study; research

【研究】 yánjiū 1.（探讨）study; research: ～与开发 research and development 2.（商讨）consider; discuss; deliberate

【研究生】 yánjiūshēng postgraduate（student）; graduate student

【研究生院】 yánjiūshēngyuàn graduate school

【研究所】 yánjiūsuǒ research institute

【研究员】 yánjiūyuán research fellow; professor

【研磨】 yánmó 1.（研成粉末）grind; pestle 2.（磨光）abrade; polish

【研磨料】 yánmóliào abrasive: 使用砂纸或其他～ use sandpaper or some other abrasive

【研拟】 yánnǐ discuss and work out

【研评】 yánpíng research and appraise

【研讨】 yántǎo deliberate; discuss

【研讨会】 yántǎohuì symposium; seminar

【研习】 yánxí research and study

【研修】 yánxiū engage in research and advanced studies

【研制】 yánzhì prepare; manufacture; develop: ～新产品 research and produce new varieties of products

岩[巖、嵒](yán) 1.(岩石) rock 2.(岩峰) cliff; crag

【岩岸】 yán'àn rocky coast
【岩板】 yánbǎn rock beam
【岩层】 yáncéng rock stratum; rock formation
【岩洞】 yándòng grotto
【岩浆】 yánjiāng 〈*Geol*.〉 magma
【岩类学】 yánlèixué petrography
【岩羚羊】 yánlíngyáng 〈*Geol*.〉 chamois
【岩溶】 yánróng 〈*Geol*.〉 karst
【岩石】 yánshí rock
【岩心】 yánxīn core; drill core
【岩穴】 yánxué cave; cavern
【岩盐】 yányán rock salt; halite
【岩羊】 yányáng 〈*Zool*.〉 blue sheep; bharal
【岩样】 yányàng 1.(岩石标本) rock specimen 2.(矿石样品) core sample

炎(yán) 1.(极热) scorching; burning hot; blazing 2.(炎症) inflammation

【炎黄子孙】 Yán-Huáng zǐsūn the Chinese descendants; all the children of the Yellow Emperor; the Chinese people
【炎凉】 yánliáng 1.(热和冷) hot and cold 2.(势利) snobbishness: ～世态 the aspect of worldly affairs; now hot and now cold
【炎热】 yánrè scorching; blazing; burning hot: ～的天气 tropical weather
【炎暑】 yánshǔ 1.(夏天最热的日子) hot summer; sweltering summer days; dog days 2.(暑气) summer heat
【炎夏】 yánxià hot summer
【炎症】 yánzhèng 〈*Med*.〉 inflammation

沿[㳂](yán) 1.(顺着) along: ～着一条危险的小路走 tread a dangerous path / 我们～着河走。We walked along the river. 2.(依照) follow: 世代相～ be handed down from generation to generation 3.(镶边) trim 4.(物件的边) edge; border: 床～ the edge of a bed

【沿岸】 yán'àn along the bank or coast; littoral; riparian
【沿边儿】 yánbiānr trim; braid
【沿革】 yángé evolution; the process of change and development: 历史的～ the course of historical change and development
【沿海】 yánhǎi along the coast; coastal; littoral
【沿海地区】 yánhǎi dìqū coastal areas; coastland
【沿海国家】 yánhǎi guójiā coastal state; littoral state
【沿海经济开发区】 yánhǎi jīngjì kāifāqū coastal open economic zone; coastal open economic development areas
【沿海开放城市】 yánhǎi kāifàng chéngshì coastal open city
【沿海开放口岸】 yánhǎi kāifàng kǒu'àn coastal open port
【沿海贸易】 yánhǎi màoyì coasting trade; cabotage
【沿街叫卖】 yánjīe jiàomài peddle something in the streets
【沿路】 yánlù 1.(顺着路边) along the road; on the roadside 2.(一路上) on the way
【沿途】 yántú on the way; throughout a journey
【沿袭】 yánxí carry on as before; follow
【沿线】 yánxiàn along the line
【沿用】 yányòng continue to use

盐[鹽](yán) salt

【盐巴】 yánbā cake of salt
【盐层】 yáncéng salt deposit; salt bed
【盐场】 yánchǎng saltern; saltworks
【盐池】 yánchí salt pond
【盐罐】 yánguàn saltcellar
【盐湖】 yánhú salt lake
【盐碱化】 yánjiǎnhuà salinization
【盐碱土】 yànjiǎntǔ saline-alkali soil
【盐井】 yánjǐng salt well; brine pit
【盐矿】 yánkuàng salt mine
【盐卤】 yánlǔ bittern
【盐汽水】 yánqìshuǐ salt soda water
【盐泉】 yánquán brine spring; salt spring
【盐水】 yánshuǐ salt solution; brine
【盐酸】 yánsuān 〈*Chem*.〉 hydrochloric acid
【盐田】 yántián salt pan; salina
【盐渍】 yánzì salt marsh

阎(yán) gate of an inner lane

【阎罗】 Yánluó 〈*Religion*〉 Yama

【阎王】 Yán·wang 1.（阎罗）Yama；king of Hell：见～ die 2.（极凶恶的人）an extremely cruel and violent person

【阎王殿】 Yán·wangdiàn the Palace of Hell

颜（yán） 1.（脸）face；countenance 2.（体面）face；prestige 3.（颜色）color（AmE.）；colour（BrE.）

【颜料】 yánliào pigment；color；dyestuff

【颜面】 yánmiàn 1.（脸部）face 2.（体面）prestige；dignity；face：顾全～ save one's reputation

【颜色】 yánsè 1.（色彩）color 2.（脸色）countenance；facial expression 3.（颜料或染料）pigment；dyestuff

檐［簷］（yán） 1.（屋檐）eaves：廊～ the eaves of a corridor 2.（像屋檐的）ledge；brim：帽～儿 the visor of a cap；the brim of a hat

奄（yǎn）

【奄忽】 yǎnhū all of a sudden

【奄然】 yǎnrán all of a sudden

【奄奄】 yǎnyǎn feeble breathing：气息～ breathe feebly；be sinking fast

【奄奄一息】 yǎnyǎn-yīxī at one's last gasp；breathe one's last

掩［揜］（yǎn） 1.（遮盖）cover；hide 2.（关；合）shut；close：～门 shut the door 3.（被卡住）get squeezed while shutting a door, lid, etc. 4.（乘人不备进行袭击）launch a surprise attack

【掩蔽】 yǎnbì 1.（遮盖）shelter；hide；cover 2.（指地方）screen；masking

【掩蔽部】 yǎnbìbù shelter

【掩藏】 yǎncáng hide；conceal

【掩耳盗铃】 yǎn'ěr-dàolíng plug one's ears while stealing a bell；deceive oneself；bury one's head in the sand

【掩盖】 yǎngài 1.（遮盖）cover；cover up：～矛盾 cover up the contradiction 2.（隐瞒）hide；conceal

【掩护】 yǎnhù 1.〈*Mil.*〉 cover；screen；shield 2.（暗中保护）protect sb. secretly 3.（遮蔽物）shelter

【掩埋】 yǎnmái bury

【掩旗息鼓】 yǎnqí-xīgǔ stop clamoring

【掩人耳目】 yǎnrén'ěrmù deceive the public；hoodwink people

【掩饰】 yǎnshì cover up；gloss over；conceal：～缺点 cover up one's mistakes /～他的错误 gloss over his faults

【掩体】 yǎntǐ 〈*Mil.*〉 blindage；bunker

【掩映】 yǎnyìng set off：相互～ set each other off

俨［儼］（yǎn）

【俨然】 yǎnrán 1.（整齐）neatly arranged 2.（很像）just like

【俨如】 yǎnrú just like：～白昼 as bright as day

衍（yǎn） 1.（展开）develop；elaborate 2.（多余）redundant；superfluous

【衍变】 yǎnbiàn develop；evolve；evolution（n.）

【衍化】 yǎnhuà derive；derivation（n.）

【衍射】 yǎnshè diffract；diffraction（n.）

【衍生】 yǎnshēng derivate；derivation（n.）

【衍文】 yǎnwén redundancy due to misprinting or miscopying

眼（yǎn） 1.（眼睛）eye：optical（adj.）2.（小洞）small hole；aperture 3.（关键）key point：节骨～儿 critical juncture 4.〈*Weiqi*〉 trap 5.（戏曲中的拍子）an unaccented beat 6.（中心）eye：台风～ typhoon eye 7.〈*classifier*〉一～井 a well

【眼巴巴】 yǎnbābā 1.（急切盼望）eagerly；anxiously：～地等着回信 anxiously expecting a reply 2.（无可奈何地）helplessly

【眼白】 yǎnbái 〈*dial.*〉 the white of the eye

【眼波】 yǎnbō lovely look；sentimental glance（of a female）

【眼不见为净】 yǎn bù jiàn wéi jìng out of sight；out of mind

【眼馋】 yǎnchán 〈*dial.*〉 covet；be envious

【眼眵】 yǎnchī gum

【眼底镜】 yǎndǐjìng 〈*Med.*〉 ophtalmoscope

【眼底下】 yǎndǐ·xia 1.（眼前）right before one's eyes 2.（目前）at the moment

【眼福】 yǎnfú the good fortune of seeing sth. rare or beautiful

【眼高手低】 yǎngāo-shǒudī have grandiose aims but puny abilities；be fastidious but incompetent

【眼光】 yǎnguāng 1.（视线）eye; look 2.（观察力）sight; foresight; insight; vision 3.（观点）view; way of looking at things

【眼红】 yǎnhóng 1.（羡慕；嫉妒）covet; be envious; be jealous 2.（激怒的样子）furious

【眼花】 yǎnhuā have dim eyesight; have blurred vision: ～缭乱 be dazzled; dazzle the eyes

【眼尖】 yǎnjiān be sharp-eyed; have sharp eyes

【眼睑】 yǎnliǎn 〈*Anat*.〉 eyelid

【眼角】 yǎnjiǎo the corner of the eye; canthus

【眼角皱纹】 yǎnjiǎo zhòuwén crow's foot

【眼结膜】 yǎnjiémó 〈*Anat*.〉 conjunctiva

【眼结膜炎】 yǎnjiémóyán 〈*Med*.〉 conjunctivitis

【眼睫毛】 yǎnjiémáo eyelash

【眼界】 yǎnjiè field of vision; outlook: ～宽广 have a broad view

【眼睛】 yǎn·jing eye: 他～就没离开过她。He never took his eyes off her.

【眼镜】 yǎnjìng glasses; spectacles: 戴～ wear glasses; wear spectacles

【眼镜蛇】 yǎnjìngshé 〈*Zool*.〉 cobra

【眼镜蛇毒】 yǎnjìngshédú cobra venom

【眼镜王蛇】 yǎnjìng·wángshé 〈*Zool*.〉 King cobra

【眼看】 yǎnkàn 1.（马上）soon; in a moment: ～春天就要到了。Spring will come soon. 2.（听凭）watch helplessly; look on passively

【眼科】 yǎnkē 〈*Med*.〉 ophthalmology

【眼科医生】 yǎnkē yīshēng ophthalmologist; oculist; eye doctor

【眼库】 yǎnkù eye bank

【眼眶】 yǎnkuàng eye socket; orbit

【眼泪】 yǎnlèi tears; eyedrop

【眼力】 yǎnlì 1.（视力）eyesight; vision: ～好 have a good eyesight 2.（辨别力）judgment; discrimination

【眼里】 yǎn·li within one's vision; in one's eyes

【眼帘】 yǎnlián eye

【眼泡】 yǎnpāo upper eyelid

【眼皮】 yǎnpí eyelid

【眼皮底下】 yǎnpí dǐ·xia before one's eyes

【眼皮子】 yǎnpí·zi eyelid

【眼前】 yǎnqián 1.（跟前）before one's eyes 2.（目前）at the moment; at present; now

【眼前利益】 yǎnqián lìyì immediate interest

【眼球】 yǎnqiú eyeball; bulbus oculi

【眼圈】 yǎnquān eye socket

【眼圈墨】 yǎnquānmò kohl

【眼热】 yǎnrè covet; be envious

【眼色】 yǎnsè hint given with the eyes; meaningful glance; wink: 使～ tip sb. the wink; wink at sb.

【眼神】 yǎnshén 1.（神态）expression in one's eyes 2.（眼力）eyesight

【眼生】 yǎnshēng look unfamiliar

【眼熟】 yǎnshú look familiar

【眼跳】 yǎntiào twitching of the eyelid

【眼窝】 yǎnwō eye socket; eyehole

【眼下】 yǎnxià at the moment; at present; now

【眼线】 yǎnxiàn 1.（描的眼线）eye-liner 2.（线人）stool-pigeon; an informer

【眼药】 yǎnyào eye ointment; eyedrops

【眼药水】 yǎnyàoshuǐ eyedrops: 滴～ put eyedrops in one's eyes

【眼影】 yǎnyǐng eye-shadow

【眼晕】 yǎnyùn feel dizzy

【眼罩】 yǎnzhào 1.（人用的）eyeshade 2.（给牲畜用的）blinkers

【眼中钉】 yǎnzhōngdīng thorn in one's flesh: 把…看作～ regard sb. as the thorn in one's flesh

偃 (yǎn)

【偃旗息鼓】 yǎnqí xīgǔ lower the banners and muffle the drums; cease all activities

演 (yǎn) 1.（演化）develop; evolve 2.（发挥）deduce; elaborate 3.（依照程式练习或计算）drill; practice 4.（表演；上演）perform; play; act

【演变】 yǎnbiàn develop; evolve; evolution: 和平～ peaceful evolution

【演播】 yǎnbō put on a show and have it broadcasted through radio or television

【演播室】 yǎnbōshì studio

【演唱】 yǎnchàng sing (in a performance)

【演出】 yǎnchū perform; show; put on a show: 告别～ farewell performance / 登台

～ perform on the stage
【演出单位】 yǎnchū dānwèi producer
【演出队】 yǎnchūduì troupe
【演出海报】 yǎnchū hǎibào playbill
【演出节目】 yǎnchū jiémù items on the program; program
【演化】 yǎnhuà develop; evolve; evolution (n.)
【演技】 yǎnjì acting
【演讲】 yǎnjiǎng give a lecture; make a speech; lecture
【演练】 yǎnliàn drill
【演示】 yǎnshì demonstrate
【演说】 yǎnshuō 1.（发表演说）deliver a speech; make an address 2.（演说词）speech
【演说词】 yǎnshuōcí speech
【演说家】 yǎnshuōjiā speaker
【演算】 yǎnsuàn perform mathematical calculations
【演武】 yǎnwǔ practice marshal art
【演习】 yǎnxí maneuver; exercise; drill; practice
【演戏】 yǎnxì 1.（演出戏剧）put on a play; act in a play 2.（装假）playact; pretend; act
【演义】 yǎnyì historical novel; historical romance
【演艺界】 yǎnyìjiè show business; show biz
【演绎】 yǎnyì 〈*Logic*〉 deduct; deduction (n.)
【演绎法】 yǎnyìfǎ the deductive method
【演员】 yǎnyuán actor (m.); actress (f.); performer: 替身～ stunt man
【演员表】 yǎnyuánbiǎo cast
【演奏】 yǎnzòu give an instrumental performance; play a musical instrument ‖ 演奏者 executant

鼹［鼴］(yǎn) 〈*Zool.*〉 mole
【鼹鼠】 yǎnshǔ 1.〈*Zool.*〉 mole 2.（指间谍）secret agent

厌［厭］(yàn) 1.（憎恶）be disgusted with; detest 2.（厌烦）be fed up with; be bored with; be tired of 3.（满足）be satisfied
【厌烦】 yànfán be sick of; be fed up with: 令人～ make one feel sick
【厌倦】 yànjuàn be weary of; be tired of
【厌弃】 yànqì detest and reject
【厌世】 yànshì be world-weary; be pessimistic
【厌恶】 yànwù detest; abhor; abominate; be disgusted with
【厌战】 yànzhàn be weary of war; be war-weary
【厌战情绪】 yànzhàn qíngxù war-weariness

砚 (yàn) inkstone; inkslab
【砚池】 yànchí inkstone; inkslab
【砚台】 yàn·tai inkstone; inkslab

咽［嚥］(yàn) swallow（另见“咽”yān）
【咽气】 yànqì breathe one's last; die

唁 (yàn) extend condolences
【唁电】 yàndiàn telegram of condolence; message of condolence
【唁函】 yànhán letter of condolence

谚 (yàn) proverb; saying; adage; saw
【谚语】 yànyǔ proverb; saying; adage; saw

艳［艷、豔］(yàn) 1.（指色彩）gorgeous; colorful; gaudy 2.（有关爱情的）amorous: ～史 love story
【艳丽】 yànlì bright-colored and beautiful; gorgeous: ～夺目 of dazzling beauty
【艳情】 yànqíng romantic; of man and woman's love
【艳诗】 yànshī love poem in a flowery style
【艳羡】 yànxiàn extremely admire
【艳阳】 yànyáng 1.（指太阳）bright sun 2.（指天气）bright sunny weather in spring
【艳阳天】 yànyángtiān bright sunny day

宴 (yàn) 1.（请人吃饭）entertain at a banquet: ～客 entertain guests at a banquet 2.（酒席）feast; banquet: 赴～ attend a banquet
【宴会】 yànhuì banquet; feast; dinner party: 答谢～ reciprocal banquet / 欢迎～ welcoming banquet
【宴会厅】 yànhuìtīng banquet hall
【宴请】 yànqǐng entertain to a banquet; give a banquet in honor of sb.: ～贵宾 entertain the distinguished guests
【宴席】 yànxí banquet; feast

验[驗、騐]（yàn） 1.（察看）examine; check; test 2.（应验）prove effective; produce the expected result

【验电器】 yàndiànqì electroscope

【验方】 yànfāng 〈*Chin. Med.*〉 proved recipe：收集民间～ collect folk prescriptions

【验关】 yànguān customs examination

【验光】 yànguāng optometry

【验货】 yànhuò examine goods

【验货单】 yànhuòdān particular paper

【验货收款处】 yànhuò shōukuǎnchù checkstand

【验看】 yànkàn examine; check; inspect

【验明正身】 yànmíng-zhèngshēn make a positive identification of a criminal before execution; identify

【验尸】 yànshī 〈*Law*〉 postmortem; autopsy

【验尸所】 yànshīsuǒ mortuary

【验收】 yànshōu check and accept; check before acceptance; check upon delivery

【验算】 yànsuàn 〈*Med.*〉 checking computations：～公式 check formula

【验血】 yànxiě blood test：去～ have one's blood tested

【验孕】 yànyùn pregnancy test

【验证】 yànzhèng test and verify

雁[鴈]（yàn） wild goose (pl. wild geese)

【雁行】 yànháng 1.（雁的行列）formation of flying wild geese 2.（指兄弟）brothers; brotherhood

【雁阵】 yànzhèn formation of flying wild geese

赝[贋]（yàn） counterfeit; fake; sham

【赝本】 yànběn spurious edition or copy

【赝币】 yànbì counterfeit coin

【赝品】 yànpǐn counterfeit; fake; sham

焰[燄]（yàn） flame; blaze：烈～ blazing flames

【焰火】 yànhuǒ fireworks：燃放～ set off fireworks

燕[鷰]（yàn） 〈*Zool.*〉 swallow：家～ house swallow

【燕麦】 yànmài 〈*Bot.*〉 oats

【燕麦片】 yànmàipiàn oat meal

【燕雀】 yànquè brambling; bramble finch

【燕尾服】 yànwěifú swallowtail; swallow-tailed coat; tailcoat

【燕窝】 yànwō edible bird's nest

【燕子】 yàn·zi swallow

yang

央（yāng） 1.（中央）center; central (adj.) 2.（央求）entreat

【央告】 yāng·gao beg; ask earnestly

【央求】 yāngqiú beg; plead; implore

泱（yāng）

【泱泱】 yāngyāng 1.（水面广阔）vast 2.（气魄弘大）magnificent：～大国 a big country

殃（yāng） 1.（祸害）calamity; disaster; misfortune：遭～ suffer disaster 2.（使受祸害）bring disaster to：～及无辜 trouble involves the innocent people

秧（yāng） 1.（幼苗）seedling; sprout 2.（稻秧）rice seedling 3.（茎）vine; stem 4.（小动物）young; fry

【秧歌】 yāng·ge yangko, a popular rural folk dance

【秧鸡】 yāngjī 〈*Zool.*〉 water rail

【秧苗】 yāngmiáo rice shoot; rice seedling

【秧田】 yāngtián rice seedling bed

扬[揚、敭]（yáng） 1.（高举）raise：～鞭 flip the whip 2.（往上撒）throw up and scatter; winnow 3.（传播）spread; make known

【扬波】 yángbō the swelling of waves

【扬长避短】 yángcháng-bìduǎn make best use of the advantages and bypass the disadvantages; develop the strong points and avoid the weak points; foster strengths and circumvent weaknesses

【扬长而去】 yángcháng'érqù stalk off; swagger off

【扬场】 yángcháng 〈*Agric.*〉 winnow

【扬程】 yángchéng 〈*Water Conservancy*〉 lift

【扬帆】 yángfān hoist the sails; set sail

【扬花】 yánghuā 〈*Agric.*〉 flower

【扬眉吐气】 yángméi-tǔqì feel proud and elated

【扬名】 yángmíng make a name for oneself;

become famous

【扬旗】 yángqí 〈*Railway*〉 semaphore

【扬弃】 yángqì 1.〈*Physics*〉 sublate 2.(取其精华，去其糟粕) develop what is useful or healthy and discard what is not

【扬琴】 yángqín *yangqin*; Chinese dulcimer

【扬声器】 yángshēngqì loudspeaker

【扬水】 yángshuǐ pump up water

【扬汤止沸】 yángtāng-zhǐfèi try to stop water from boiling by scooping it up and pouring it back; an ineffectual remedy

【扬言】 yángyán threaten

【扬扬】 yángyáng triumphantly; complacently: ～自得 be very pleased with oneself; be complacent / 喜气～ look happy and triumphant

【扬子鳄】 yángzǐ'è 〈*Zool.*〉 Chinese alligator

杨[楊] (yáng) 〈*Bot.*〉 poplar; aspen: 大叶～ Chinese poplar / 黑～ black poplar / 毛白～ Chinese white poplar / 响叶～ Chinese aspen / 银白～ white aspen / 钻天～ Lombardy poplar

【杨柳】 yángliǔ 1.(杨树和柳树) poplar and willow 2.(柳树) willow

【杨梅】 yángméi bayberry; Chinese bayberry

【杨树】 yángshù poplar

羊 (yáng) 〈*Zool.*〉 sheep: 绵～ sheep / 山～ goat ‖ 绵羊: 公羊 ram / 母羊 ewe / 小羊 lamb / 统称 flock ‖ 山羊: 公羊 billy (goat) / 母羊 nanny (goat) / 小羊 kid / 统称 flock; herd

【羊八井】 Yángbājǐng 〈place〉 Yangbajain

【羊肠小道】 yángcháng-xiǎodào narrow winding trail; meandering footpath

【羊羔】 yánggāo 1.(绵羊) lamb 2.(山羊) kid

【羊倌】 yángguān shepherd

【羊毫】 yángháo writing brush made of goat's hair

【羊角锤】 yángjiǎochuí claw-hammer

【羊圈】 yángjuàn sheepfold; sheep pen

【羊栏】 yánglán sheepcote

【羊毛】 yángmáo sheep's wool; fleece

【羊毛衫】 yángmáoshān woolen sweater; cardigan

【羊膜】 yángmó 〈*Anat.*〉 amnion

【羊排】 yángpái mutton chop; lamb chop

【羊皮】 yángpí sheepskin

【羊皮袄】 yángpí'ǎo sheepskin jacket

【羊绒】 yángróng cashmere

【羊绒衫】 yángróngshān cashmere sweater

【羊肉】 yángròu mutton

【羊肉串】 yángròuchuàn shish kebab

【羊驼】 yángtuó 〈*Zool.*〉 *alpaca*

【羊鱼】 yángyú 〈*Zool.*〉 *surmullet*

【羊脂】 yángzhī suet

佯 (yáng) pretend; feign; sham: ～死 feign death; play dead

【佯攻】 yánggōng 〈*Mil.*〉 feign attack; make a feint

【佯言】 yángyán tell a lie

【佯装】 yángzhuāng pretend; feign

洋 (yáng) 1.(盛大) vast; multitudinous 2.(海洋) ocean; oceanic (adj.) 3.(外国的) foreign: ～房 Western-style house / ～货 imported goods 4.(现代化的) modern

【洋白菜】 yángbáicài cabbage

【洋插队】 yángchāduì stay in a foreign country for a long time

【洋厂长】 yángchǎngzhǎng foreign manager of a factory

【洋葱】 yángcōng 〈*Bot.*〉 onion

【洋葱头】 yángcōngtóu onion bulbs

【洋房】 yángfáng Western-style house

【洋服】 yángfú Western clothes; Occidental dress

【洋鬼子】 yángguǐ·zi foreign devil; foreign invader

【洋行】 yángháng foreign firm

【洋红】 yánghóng pink

【洋槐】 yánghuái 〈*Bot.*〉 black locust

【洋货】 yánghuò imported goods; foreign goods

【洋泾浜】 yángjīngbāng pidgin: ～英语 pidgin English

【洋奴】 yángnú slave of a foreign master; worshiper of everything foreign

【洋奴思想】 yángnú sīxiǎng slavish mentality towards all things foreign

【洋奴哲学】 yángnú zhéxué slavish comprador philosophy; blind worship of everything foreign

【洋气】 yángqì 1.(西洋样式) foreign flavor; Western style 2.(洋里洋气) outlandish ways

【洋钱】 yángqián silver dollar
【洋琴】 yángqín dulcimer
【洋人】 yángrén foreigner
【洋嗓子】 yángsǎng·zi a voice trained in Western style of singing
【洋娃娃】 yángwá·wa doll
【洋为中用】 yángwéi zhōngyòng make foreign things serve China
【洋文】 yángwén foreign language
【洋相】 yángxiàng silly sight; awkward behavior
【洋洋】 yángyáng 1.(多) numerous; enormous 2.(同"扬扬") triumphantly
【洋洋大观】 yángyáng-dàguān spectacular; grandiose; imposing
【洋洋得意】 yángyáng-déyì proud and happy
【洋洋万言】 yángyáng-wànyán run to ten thousand words; be very lengthy
【洋溢】 yángyì be permeated with; brim with：热情～ be saturated with warm feelings

阳[陽](yáng) 1.(太阳) the sun 2.(山的南面) south of a hill 3.(水的北面) north of a river 4.(凸出的) in relief：～文 characters cut in relief 5.(外露的) open; overt 6.〈*Physics*〉 positive 7.(与"阴"相对) masculine; positive
【阳春】 yángchūn spring
【阳春白雪】 yángchūn-báixuě 1.(古曲名) the Spring Snow 2.(高雅文艺) highbrow art and literature
【阳电】 yángdiàn positive electricity
【阳奉阴违】 yángfèng-yīnwéi overtly agree but covertly oppose; comply in public but oppose in private; feign compliance
【阳刚】 yánggāng man's qualities and character traits of firmness and persistence
【阳沟】 yánggōu open drain; ditch
【阳关道】 yángguāndào broad road; thoroughfare
【阳光】 yángguāng sunlight; sunshine
【阳光计划】 yángguāng jìhuà sunlight program
【阳光掠夺】 yángguāng lüèduó daylight robbery
【阳极】 yángjí 〈*Physics*〉 positive pole; positive electrode; anode
【阳间】 yángjiān this world
【阳历】 yánglì 1.〈*Astron.*〉 solar calendar 2.(公历) the Gregorian calendar
【阳伞】 yángsǎn parasol; sunshade
【阳台】 yángtái balcony
【阳桃】 yángtáo 〈*Bot.*〉 averrhoa; carambola
【阳痿】 yángwěi 〈*Med.*〉 impotence; impotent (adj.)
【阳性】 yángxìng 1.〈*Med.*〉 positive：～反应 positive reaction 2.〈*Phonet.*〉 masculine gender

仰(yǎng) 1.(脸向上) face upward 2.(敬慕) admire; respect; look up to：瞻～ look at with reverence; pay one's respects to 3.(依靠) rely on; depend on
【仰俯之间】 yǎngfǔzhījiān between looking up and stooping down
【仰角】 yǎngjiǎo angle of elevation
【仰面】 yǎngmiàn face upward
【仰面朝天】 yǎngmiàn-cháotiān fall flat on one's back
【仰慕】 yǎngmù admire; look up to
【仰人鼻息】 yǎngrénbíxī be dependent on the pleasure of others; be slavishly dependent
【仰视】 yǎngshì look up at; look upward
【仰天长叹】 yǎngtiān-chángtàn sign deeply; look up at heaven and lament
【仰望】 yǎngwàng 1.(抬头看) look up at 2.(敬仰) respectfully seek guidance or help from; look up to
【仰卧】 yǎngwò lie on one's back; lie supine
【仰卧起坐】 yǎngwò qǐzuò sit-up
【仰泳】 yǎngyǒng 〈*Sports*〉 backstroke：你能～吗? Can you do the backstroke?
【仰仗】 yǎngzhàng rely on; look to sb. for backing

养[養](yǎng) 1.(供养) support; provide for：～家 support a family; keep a family 2.(饲养或培植) raise; keep; grow; rear：～蜂 keep bees 3.(生育) give birth to 4.(领养的) foster; adoptive：～女 adopted daughter / ～子 adopted son 5.(培养) form; acquire; cultivate 6.(调养) rest; convalesce; recuperate one's health; heal 7.(养护) maintain; keep in good repair
【养病】 yǎngbìng take rest and nourishment

to regain one's health; recuperate
【养蚕】 yǎngcán sericulture; silkworm breeding; breed silkworms
【养成】 yǎngchéng form; grow on: ～习惯 form a habit / 我逐渐～了这个习惯。The habit grew on me.
【养分】 yǎngfèn nutrient: goodness: 牛奶里有许多～。There is a lot of goodness in milk.
【养蜂】 yǎngfēng bee-keeping; apiculture
【养父】 yǎngfù foster father
【养蛤场】 yǎnggéchǎng clam bed
【养菇原木】 yǎnggū yuánmù bed log
【养虎遗患】 yǎnghǔ-yíhuàn to rear a tiger is to court calamity; appeasement brings disaster
【养护】 yǎnghù 1.（保养维护）maintain; conserve 2.（调养护理）nurse; tend and protect
【养活】 yǎng·huo 1.（供养）support; feed 2.（饲养）raise 3.（生育）give birth to
【养鸡场】 yǎngjīchǎng chicken run; chicken farm
【养鸡业】 yǎngjīyè poultry husbandary; poultry industry
【养家】 yǎngjiā support a family; keep a family
【养家的人】 yǎngjiā·derén family man
【养家糊口】 yǎngjiā-húkǒu eke out
【养精蓄锐】 yǎngjīng-xùruì conserve strength and store up energy
【养老】 yǎnglǎo 1.（奉养老人）provide for the aged 2.（年老休养）live out one's life in retirement
【养老保险】 yǎnglǎo bǎoxiǎn endowment insurance
【养老金】 yǎnglǎojīn old-age pension
【养老院】 yǎnglǎoyuàn a home for destitute old people
【养料】 yǎngliào nutriment; nourishment
【养路】 yǎnglù maintain a road
【养路费】 yǎnglùfèi road toll
【养路工】 yǎnglùgōng 1.（公路的）roadman; road mender 2.（铁路的）platelayer
【养鹿场】 yǎnglùchǎng stag breeding
【养母】 yǎngmǔ foster mother
【养女】 yǎngnǚ adopted daughter
【养伤】 yǎngshāng recuperate from an injury
【养神】 yǎngshén rest to attain mental tranquility; repose
【养生】 yǎngshēng preserve one's health; keep in good health: ～之道 the way to keep in good health
【养兔场】 yǎngtùchǎng rabbit farm
【养鱼】 yǎngyú fish culture
【养育】 yǎngyù bring up; rear
【养殖】 yǎngzhí breed
【养殖场】 yǎngzhíchǎng farm
【养猪场】 yǎngzhūchǎng pig farm; piggery
【养子】 yǎngzǐ adopted son
【养尊处优】 yǎngzūn-chǔyōu enjoy high position and live in ease and comfort; live in clover

氧（yǎng）〈*Chem.*〉oxygen（元素符号 O）
【氧化】 yǎnghuà 〈*Chem.*〉oxidize; oxidate; oxidation（n.）
【氧化铝】 yǎnghuàlǚ alumina
【氧化镁】 yǎnghuàměi magnesia
【氧化物】 yǎnghuàwù oxide
【氧幕】 yǎngmù oxygen tent
【氧气】 yǎngqì oxygen
【氧气面罩】 yǎngqì miànzhào oxygen mask
【氧气帐篷】 yǎngqì zhàngpéng oxygen tent

痒［癢］（yǎng） itch; tickle
【痒痒】 yǎng·yang 〈*colloq.*〉itch; tickle
【痒痒挠】 yǎngyǎngnáo back-scratcher

怏（yàng）
【怏怏】 yàngyàng disgruntled; sullen

样［樣］（yàng） 1.（形状）shape; form 2.（样品）sample; model; pattern 3.〈*classifier*〉kind; type
【样板】 yàngbǎn 1.（样品）sample plate 2.（工具）templet 3.（榜样）model; example
【样本】 yàngběn 1.（商品样本）sample book 2.（样书）sample; specimen
【样机】 yàngjī sample machine
【样片】 yàngpiàn sample movie; sample telefilm
【样品】 yàngpǐn sample; specimen; design; pattern: 工业～ industrial design / 赠送的～ free sample 寄～ send a sample
【样品房】 yàngpǐnfáng show flat; show house

【样品卡片】 yàngpǐn kǎpiàn sample card
【样品室】 yàngpǐnshì sample room
【样式】 yàngshì pattern; type; style; form
【样书】 yàngshū sample book
【样图】 yàngtú master drawing
【样样】 yàngyàng every kind; each and every; all
【样子】 yàng·zi **1.**(形状) appearance; shape **2.**(神情) manner; air **3.**(模仿的标准) sample; model; pattern **4.**(趋势) tendency; likelihood
恙(yàng) ailment; illness: 安然无～ safe and sound; unscathed
漾(yàng) **1.**(水面微动) ripple **2.**(溢出) brim over

yao

幺[么](yāo) one; first
【幺蛾子】 yāo'é·zi 〈*dial.*〉 tricky idea
吆[吆](yāo)
【吆喝】 yāo·he **1.**(呼唤) cry out; call **2.**(叫卖) cry one's wares **3.**(赶牲畜) loudly urge on an animal
夭[殀](yāo) die young
【夭亡】 yāowáng die young
【夭折】 yāozhé **1.**(未成年而死) die young **2.**(中途失败) come to a premature end
妖(yāo) **1.**(妖怪) goblin; demon; evil spirit **2.**(惑人的) evil and fraudulent **3.**(指装束) bewitching; coquettish
【妖风】 yāofēng evil wind; noxious trend
【妖怪】 yāoguài monster; bogy; goblin; demon
【妖精】 yāo·jing **1.**(妖怪) evil spirit **2.**(指女人) alluring woman; seductive woman
【妖里妖气】 yāo·liyāoqì seductive and bewitching
【妖媚】 yāomèi seductively charming; bewitching
【妖魔】 yāomó evil spirit; demon
【妖魔鬼怪】 yāomó-guǐguài demons and ghosts; monsters of every description
【妖娆】 yāoráo charming and attractive
【妖术】 yāoshù black art; witchcraft; sorcery
【妖言】 yāoyán heresy; fallacy: ～惑众 spread wild rumors to mislead the public
【妖艳】 yāoyàn pretty and coquettish
【妖冶】 yāoyě pretty and coquettish
约(yāo) weigh: 给我～两公斤苹果。Please get me two kilos of apple.
(另见"约"yuē)
要(yāo) **1.**(求) demand; ask **2.**(强迫) force; coerce
(另见"要"yào)
【要求】 yāoqiú **1.**(提出要求) ask; demand; require; claim: 她母亲坚持～她11点前回家。Her mother is adamant in demanding she be home by eleven. **2.**(所提要求) requirements; needs; conditions: 满足～ satisfy sb's demand
【要挟】 yāoxié coerce; put pressure on; threaten
腰(yāo) **1.**(腰部) waist; small of the back: 齐～深 waist-deep; waist-high **2.**(裤腰) waist **3.**(指腰包) pocket **4.**(动物的腰儿) middle
【腰板儿】 yāobǎnr **1.**(人的腰和背) waist and back **2.**(体格) body
【腰包】 yāobāo purse; pocket; wallet: 掏～ take out of one's own wallet
【腰部】 yāobù waist; small of the back
【腰缠万贯】 yāochán-wànguàn very rich
【腰带】 yāodài waistband; belt; girdle: 系～ tighten one's belt
【腰杆子】 yāogǎn·zi **1.**(腰部) back **2.**(靠山) backing; support: ～硬 have strong support
【腰鼓】 yāogǔ waist drum
【腰果】 yāoguǒ **1.**〈*Bot.*〉 cashew **2.**(果实) cashew nut
【腰花】 yāohuā scalloped pork or lamb kidneys
【腰身】 yāoshēn waistline; waist; waist measurement; girth
【腰痛】 yāotòng lumbago; backache
【腰围】 yāowéi waistline
【腰窝】 yāowō flank
【腰椎】 yāozhuī 〈*Anat.*〉 lumbar vertebra
【腰子】 yāo·zi 〈*colloq.*〉 kidney

邀 (yāo) 1.（邀请）invite; request: ～客 invite guests / ～游 invite to an excursion 2.（求得）solicit; seek

【邀功】 yāogōng take credit for sb. else's achievements

【邀功请赏】 yāogōng-qǐngshǎng seek rewards by reporting other's achievement as one's own

【邀集】 yāojí invite to meet together; call together

【邀请】 yāoqǐng invite; invitation (n.): 应…～ at the invitation of ...

【邀请赛】 yāoqǐngsài invitational tournament; invitation tournament

肴［餚］(yáo) meat and fish dishes

【肴馔】 yáozhuàn sumptuous courses at a meal

窑［窰、窯］(yáo) 1.（砖瓦窑）kiln: 砖～ brickkiln 2.（煤矿）pit 3.（窑洞）cave dwelling

【窑洞】 yáodòng cave dwelling; cave-house

【窑子】 yáo·zi 〈*dial.*〉 brothel

谣 (yáo) 1.（歌谣）ballad; rhyme 2.（谣言）rumor

【谣传】 yáochuán 1.（指谣言）rumor; hearsay 2.（指传播）it is rumored

【谣言】 yáoyán rumor; groundless allegation

摇 (yáo) shake; wave; rock; turn: ～铃 ring a bell / ～旗 wave a flag / 把车窗～下/上 wind the window down/up

【摇把】 yáobà 1.〈*Mech.*〉 cranking bar; crank handle 2.〈*Guitar*〉 tremolo arm

【摇摆】 yáobǎi sway; swing; rock; vacillate

【摇摆舞】 yáobǎiwǔ rock and roll

【摇唇鼓舌】 yáochún-gǔshé flap one's lips and beat one's tongue; wag one's tongue; engage in loose talk

【摇荡】 yáodàng rock; sway

【摇动】 yáodòng 1.（摆动）wave; shake 2.（摇）sway; rock 3.（动摇）unsteady

【摇滚乐】 yáogǔnyuè big beat; rock'n'roll; rock and roll

【摇撼】 yáohàn give a violent shake to; shake to the root or foundation

【摇晃】 yáohuàng rock; sway; shake

【摇篮】 yáolán cradle

【摇篮曲】 yáolánqǔ 〈*Music*〉 lullaby; cradlesong

【摇旗呐喊】 yáoqí-nàhǎn wave flags and shout battle cries; bang the drum for sb.

【摇钱树】 yáoqiánshù a legendary tree that sheds coins when shaken; a ready source of money

【摇身一变】 yáoshēn-yībiàn give oneself a shake and change into another form; suddenly change one's identity

【摇手】 yáoshǒu 1.〈*Mech.*〉 handle 2.（摆手）wave one's hand

【摇头】 yáotóu shake one's head

【摇头摆尾】 yáotóu-bǎiwěi shake the head and wag the tail; assume an air of complacency or levity

【摇头晃脑】 yáotóu-huàngnǎo wag one's head; look pleased with oneself; assume an air of self-approbation or self-conceit

【摇头丸】 yáotóuwán ecstasy（毒品）

【摇尾乞怜】 yáowěi-qǐlián wag the tail ingratiatingly; fawn

【摇摇摆摆】 yáoyáo-bǎibǎi swagger along

【摇摇晃晃】 yáoyáo-huànghuàng vacillating and staggering

【摇摇欲坠】 yáoyáo-yùzhuì tottering; crumbling; on the verge of collapse

【摇曳】 yáoyè flicker; sway

【摇椅】 yáoyǐ rocking chair

徭［傜］(yáo) hard labor

【徭役】 yáoyì corvée

遥 (yáo)

【遥测】 yáocè telemetering

【遥感】 yáogǎn 〈*Electronics*〉 remote sensing

【遥感技术】 yáogǎn jìshù remote sensing technique

【遥感仪器】 yáogǎn yíqì remote sensing instrument

【遥见】 yáojiàn see at a distance

【遥控】 yáokòng remote control; telecontrol

【遥控器】 yáokòngqì remote controller

【遥望】 yáowàng look into the distance

【遥相呼应】 yáoxiāng-hūyìng echo each other at a distance; coordinate with each other from afar

【遥遥】 yáoyáo 1.（指距离）far away; a long way off：～领先 be far ahead; get a good lead 2.（指时间）remote：～无期 in the unforeseeable future

【遥远】 yáoyuǎn distant; remote; faraway

瑶 (yáo)

【瑶族】 Yáozú Yao（中国少数民族，主要分布在广西、湖南、云南、广东、贵州等地）

杳 (yǎo) distant and out of sight

【杳无音信】 yáowúyīnxìn have never been heard of since; there has been no news whatsoever about sb.

咬［齩、䶧］(yǎo) 1.（用牙咬）bite; snap at 2.（狗叫）bark 3.（牵扯他人）incriminate another person when blamed or interrogated; make accusation 4.（读字发音）pronounce; articulate 5.（计较字句）be nitpicking 6.（互相卡住）grip; bite

【咬定】 yǎodìng insist

【咬耳朵】 yǎo ěr·duo whisper

【咬钩】 yǎogōu bite

【咬紧牙关】 yǎojǐn yáguān grit one's teeth

【咬伤】 yǎoshāng bite

【咬文嚼字】 yǎowén-jiáozì pay excessive attention to wording

【咬牙】 yǎoyá 1.（咬紧牙关）grit one's teeth：恨得直～ gnash one's teeth in hatred 2.（熟睡时磨牙）grind one's teeth

【咬牙切齿】 yǎoyá-qièchǐ gnash one's teeth：～地咒骂 curse between one's teeth

舀 (yǎo) ladle out; spoon up; scoop up：～水 ladle out some water

【舀子】 yǎo·zi dipper; ladle; scoop

窈 (yǎo)

【窈窕】 yǎotiǎo gentle and graceful

药［藥］(yào) 1.（药物）medicine; drug; remedy：换～ change dressings / 开～ prescribe for an illness; prescribe a medicine / 给病人服～ administer the medicine to a patient / 抓～ have a prescription made up (filled) / 把～服下。Take your medicine. 2.（某些化学物质）certain chemicals 3.（用药毒死）kill with poison

【药材】 yàocái medicinal materials; crude drugs

【药草】 yàocǎo medicinal herbs

【药厂】 yàochǎng pharmaceutical factory

【药典】 yàodiǎn pharmacopeia; formulary

【药店】 yàodiàn drugstore; chemist's shop; pharmacy

【药方】 yàofāng prescription：开～ write out a prescription

【药房】 yàofáng 1.（药店）drugstore; chemist's shop; pharmacy 2.（指医院或诊所的）hospital pharmacy; dispensary

【药费】 yàofèi expenses for medicine; charges for medicine

【药粉】 yàofěn (medicinal) powder

【药膏】 yàogāo ointment; salve：上～ apply a plaster

【药剂】 yàojì medicament; drug

【药剂师】 yàojìshī pharmacist; druggist

【药剂士】 yàojìshì assistant pharmacy

【药检】 yàojiǎn drug test

【药酒】 yàojiǔ medicinal liquor

【药力】 yàolì efficacy of a drug

【药棉】 yàomián absorbent cotton

【药捻儿】 yàoniǎnr swab

【药片】 yàopiàn tablet

【药品】 yàopǐn medicines and chemical reagents

【药瓶】 yàopíng medicine bottle

【药铺】 yàopù herbal medicine shop

【药签】 yàoqiān swab

【药水】 yàoshuǐ 1.（内服的）liquid medicine; medicinal liquid 2.（外用的）lotion

【药丸】 yàowán pill

【药味】 yàowèi 1.〈*Chin. Med.*〉herbal medicines in a prescription 2.（药的味道或气味）flavor of a drug

【药物】 yàowù medicines; pharmaceuticals; medicaments

【药箱】 yàoxiāng medical kit; medicine chest

【药性】 yàoxìng property of a medicine

【药皂】 yàozào medicated soap

要 (yào) 1.（重要）important; essential：～事 an important matter 2.（希望得到）want; ask for; wish; desire：这房子你们～多少钱？What are they asking for the house?

3.(请求;要求) ask sb. to do sth. 4.(想做) want to; wish to 5.(需要) must; should; it is necessary 6.(将要) shall; will; be going to: 你看那些黑云,~来暴风雨了。Look at those black clouds — there's going to be a storm. / 她~生小孩了。She is going to have a baby. 7.(需要) need; take 8.(表示估计) might; must 9.(要是) if; suppose; in case

(另见"要"yāo)

【要隘】 yào'ài strategic pass

【要案】 yào'àn major case

【要不】 yàobù 〈*conj.*〉 otherwise; or else; or

【要不得】 yào·bu·de no good; intolerable

【要不是】 yào·bushì if it were not for; but for

【要冲】 yàochōng major juncture; transportation link

【要道】 yàodào thoroughfare: 交通~ important line of communications

【要地】 yàodì important place; strategic point: 战略~ strategic point

【要点】 yàodiǎn 1.(主要内容) main points; essentials: 他的长篇讲话的~就是他反对这一提案。The gist of his long speech was that he is against the proposal. 2.(重要据点) key strongpoint

【要犯】 yàofàn important criminal

【要饭】 yàofàn beg; go begging

【要害】 yàohài 1.(致命处) vital part; crucial point: 正中~ hit right at the vital part 2.(重要地点或部门) strategic point

【要好】 yàohǎo 1.(感情好) be on good terms; be close friends 2.(要求上进) eager to improve oneself; try hard to make progress

【要价】 yàojià ask a price; charge: ~过高 demand an exorbitant price; ask too much / 漫天~ set an unreasonable high price

【要件】 yàojiàn 1.(指文件) important document 2.(指条件) important condition

【要津】 yàojīn key post: 位居~ hold a key post

【要紧】 yàojǐn 1.(重要) important; essential 2.(严重) be critical; be serious; matter

【要领】 yàolǐng 1.(要点) main points; essentials; gist 2.(基本要求) essentials; fundamental requirements: 掌握~ acquire the basic skills

【要略】 yàolüè outline; summary

【要么】 yào·me either ... or

【要命】 yàomìng 1.(使丧生) drive sb. to his death; kill 2.(非常) extremely; awfully; terribly: 困得~ be sleepy tired 3.(令人讨厌) a nuisance

【要强】 yàoqiáng be eager to excel; be anxious to outdo others

【要人】 yàorén very important person (V.I.P.); important personage

【要塞】 yàosài fort; fortress; fortification

【要是】 yào·shi if; suppose; in case

【要死】 yàosǐ extremely; awfully; terribly: 累得~ be extremely tired

【要素】 yàosù essential factor; key element

【要闻】 yàowén important news; front-page story

【要务】 yàowù important or urgent business

【要言不烦】 yàoyán-bùfán terse; succinct

【要员】 yàoyuán top brass

【要账】 yàozhàng demand payment of a debt; press for repayment of a loan

【要知道】 yàozhīdào after all: 我知道他没有做完,不过~,他太忙了。I know he hasn't finished, but, after all, he is very busy.

【要职】 yàozhí important post

【要旨】 yàozhǐ main idea; gist

钥[鑰] (yào)

【钥匙】 yào·shi key

【钥匙包】 yào·shibāo key case

鹞 (yào) sparrow hawk

【鹞鹰】 yàoyīng sparrow hawk

【鹞子】 yào·zi 1.(雀鹰) sparrow hawk 2.(风筝) kite

耀 (yào) 1.(照耀) shine; illuminate; dazzle 2.(夸耀) boast of; laud 3.(荣耀) honor; credit

【耀武扬威】 yàowǔ-yángwēi make a show of one's strength; swagger around

【耀眼】 yàoyǎn dazzling bright; glaring: ~的汽车大灯几乎照花了我们的眼睛。The glaring headlights almost blinded us.

ye

耶(yē)

【耶和华】 Yēhéhuá 〈*Religion*〉 Yehowah

【耶稣】 Yēsū 〈*Religion*〉 Jesus

【耶稣教】 Yēsūjiào Protestantism

椰(yē) 〈*Bot.*〉 coconut palm; coconut tree; coco

【椰油】 yēyóu coconut oil; coconut butter

【椰枣】 yēzǎo 1.(椰枣树) date palm 2.(椰枣果实) date

【椰子】 yē·zi 1.(椰子树) coconut palm; coconut tree; coco 2.(椰子果实) coconut

掖(yē) tuck in; tuck up: 把你的衬衫～到裤子里。Tuck your shirt into your trousers. / 给我把被子～好。Came to tuck up in/up.
(另见"掖"yè)

噎(yē) 1.(指吃东西时) choke: ～住 choke up 2.(用话噎人) render sb. speechless; choke off

爷[爺](yé) 1.(祖父) grandfather 2.(尊称) uncle: 大～ uncle 3.(称尊者) 老～ sir; master; lord / 少～ young master 4.(称神) god: 老天～ God; Heaven

【爷们】 yé·men 1.(男人) man; menfolk: 老～ man 2.(丈夫) husband

【爷爷】 yéyé 1.(祖父) grandfather 2.(与祖父同辈的人) grandpa

揶(yé)

【揶揄】 yéyú mock at; laugh at

也(yě) 1.(同样) also; too; as well; either: 他去了澳大利亚,她～去了澳大利亚。He has been to Australia. She has also been to Australia. / 我没读过这本书,我兄弟～没读过。I haven't read this book and my brother hasn't either. 2.(叠用,表示并列或对等) as well as 3.(表示转折或让步) even if: 即使失败 10 次,我～不灰心。I'll never lose heart even if I should fail ten times. 4.(表示委婉) not but: 我～只好如此。I could not but do so. 5.(表示强调) even

【也罢】 yěbà 1.(只得如此) all right 2.(叠用,表示都可以) whether ... or ...

【也好】 yěhǎo 1.(表示容忍) it may not be a bad idea; may as well: 把情况简单说一下～。Better give a brief account of it. 2.(叠用,表示都可以) whether ... or ...; no matter whether: 你去～,不去～,情况不会改变。Whether you go or not, the situation will remain unchanged.

【也许】 yěxǔ 〈*adv.*〉 perhaps; probably; maybe

冶(yě) smelt (metal)

【冶金】 yějīn metallurgy

【冶炼】 yěliàn smelt

野[埜](yě) 1.(野外) open country; the open: 旷～ wilderness 2.(界限) limit; boundary 3.(不当政) not in power; out of office: 下～ be forced to relinquish power 4.(野生的;非驯养的) wild; uncultivated; undomesticated; untamed: ～花 wild flower 5.(蛮横;粗鲁) savage; rough; rude: 说话太～ speak rudely 6.(不受约束) unrestrained; abandoned; unruly

【野菜】 yěcài edible wild herbs

【野餐】 yěcān 1.(去野餐) picnic 2.(野餐食品) food prepared for a picnic

【野草】 yěcǎo weeds

【野地】 yědì wild country; wilderness

【野果】 yěguǒ wild fruit

【野火】 yěhuǒ prairie fire; bush fire

【野鸡】 yějī 1.〈*Zool.*〉 *pheasant* 2.(妓女) *street walker*: 当～ *walk the streets*

【野驴】 yělǘ Asiatic wild ass; kiang

【野马】 yěmǎ wild horse; mustang

【野蛮】 yěmán 1.(不文明) uncivilized; savage 2.(蛮横残暴) barbarous; cruel; brutal: ～的行为 barbarous behavior

【野炮】 yěpào field gun; field artillery

【野禽】 yěqín wild birds

【野生】 yěshēng wild; uncultivated; feral

【野生动物园】 yěshēng dòngwùyuán safari park

【野生植物】 yěshēng zhíwù wild plant

【野史】 yěshǐ unofficial history

【野兽】 yěshòu wild beast; wild animal

【野兔】 yětù hare

【野外】 yěwài open country; field

【野外作业】 yěwài zuòyè fieldwork; field operation

【野味】 yěwèi game (as food)

【野心】 yěxīn ambition; careerism: 个人～ personal ambition / ～勃勃 be overweeningly ambitious; be obsessed with ambition

【野心家】 yěxīnjiā careerist

【野心狼】 yěxīnláng a vicious wolf; a person of wicked ambition

【野性】 yěxìng wild nature; unruliness

【野鸭】 yěyā wild duck; mallard

【野营】 yěyíng camp; bivouac

【野营训练】 yěyíng xùnliàn camp and field training

【野战】 yězhàn 〈*Mil.*〉 field operations

【野战军】 yězhànjūn field army

【野猪】 yězhū wild boar

业[業] (yè) **1.** (行业) line of business; trade; industry **2.** (职业) occupation; profession; employment; job: 失～ be out of a job; be unemployed **3.** (学业) course of study: 结～ complete a course of study **4.** (事业) cause; enterprise: 创～ start an enterprise **5.** (产业) estate; property: 家～ private property **6.** (从事) engage in **7.** (已经) already: ～已核实 have already been verified **8.** 〈*Buddhism*〉 karma; deed; action

【业大】 yèdà sparetime university

【业海】 yèhǎi 〈*Buddhism*〉 sea of retribution

【业绩】 yèjì outstanding achievement; meritorious deeds

【业界】 yèjiè trade; industry

【业经】 yèjīng already

【业务】 yèwù vocational work; professional work; business: 扩大～ enlarge business; extend business / 推动～ push the business

【业务经理】 yèwù jīnglǐ office manager

【业务往来】 yèwù wǎnglái business relations: 恢复～ renew business relations

【业余】 yèyú **1.** (工作以外的) sparetime: ～时间 spare time / ～活动 sparetime recreation activities **2.** (非专业的) amateur: ～剧团 amateur troupe / ～足球赛 amateur football

【业余爱好】 yèyú àihào hobby; outside interest

【业余体育】 yèyú tǐyù amateur sports

【业主】 yèzhǔ owner; proprietor

叶[葉] (yè) **1.** (叶子) leaf; foliage **2.** (像叶子的) leaf-like thing: 百～窗 shutter; blind **3.** (世纪等的分段) part of a historical period

【叶柄】 yèbǐng 〈*Bot.*〉 petiole; leaf stalk

【叶公好龙】 Yègōng-hàolóng Lord Ye's love of dragons; professed love of what one really fears

【叶猴】 yèhóu 〈*Zool.*〉 *langur*

【叶绿素】 yèlǜsù 〈*Biochem.*〉 chlorophyll

【叶绿体】 yèlǜtǐ 〈*Biochem.*〉 chloroplast

【叶轮】 yèlún 〈*Mech.*〉 impeller; vane wheel

【叶轮泵】 yèlúnbèng vane pump

【叶落归根】 yèluò-guīgēn falling leaves settle on their roots; a person residing elsewhere finally returns to his ancestral home

【叶落植物】 yèluò zhíwù defoliate plant

【叶片】 yèpiàn **1.** 〈*Bot.*〉 blade **2.** 〈*Mech.*〉 vane

【叶肉】 yèròu 〈*Bot.*〉 mesophyll

【叶子】 yè·zi leaf

页[頁、葉、箕] (yè) **1.** (张) leaf; sheet **2.** (面) page

【页边】 yèbiān margin

【页码】 yèmǎ page number

曳[拽、抴] (yè) drag; haul; tug; tow

【曳光弹】 yèguāngdàn 〈*Mil.*〉 tracer bullet; tracer shell; tracer

夜[亱] (yè) night; evening

【夜班】 yèbān night shift: 值～ be on a night shift

【夜不安枕】 yèbù'ānzhěn toss about in bed

【夜餐】 yècān night snack

【夜长梦多】 yècháng-mèngduō a long night is fraught with dreams; a long delay means many hitches

【夜场】 yèchǎng evening show

【夜车】 yèchē **1.** (夜间开行的火车) night train **2.** (夜间工作或学习) 开～ work or study deep into the night

【夜大学】 yèdàxué evening university

【夜盗】 yèdào burglar

【夜蛾】 yè'é 〈*Zool*.〉 *noctuid*
【夜工】 yègōng night work：做～ work at night
【夜光杯】 yèguāngbēi luminous wine glass
【夜光表】 yèguāngbiǎo luminous watch
【夜航】 yèháng 1.(指飞机) night flight 2.(指船舶) night navigation
【夜壶】 yèhú po；jerry
【夜间】 yèjiān at night
【夜景】 yèjǐng night scene
【夜空】 yèkōng night sky：繁星闪烁的～ the night sky gemmed with stars
【夜郎自大】 yèláng-zìdà ludicrous conceit of the king of Yelang；parochial arrogance
【夜礼服】 yèlǐfú evening dress
【夜里】 yè·li at night
【夜盲】 yèmáng 〈*Med*.〉 nyctalopia；night blindness
【夜盲症】 yèmángzhèng 〈*Med*.〉 moon blindness；nyctalopia
【夜猫子】 yèmāo·zi 1.(猫头鹰) owl 2.(喜晚睡的人) nighthawk；nightbird
【夜幕】 yèmù curtain of night；gathering darkness
【夜尿症】 yèniàozhèng enuresis；bed-wetting
【夜曲】 yèqǔ 〈*Music*〉 nocturne：萧邦的～ Chopin's nocturnes
【夜色】 yèsè the dim light of night
【夜深】 yèshēn in the dead of night；late at night：～人静 in the dead of night
【夜生活】 yèshēnghuó night life
【夜市】 yèshì night fair；night market
【夜晚】 yèwǎn night
【夜袭】 yèxí night attack；night raid
【夜消】 yèxiāo 同"夜宵"
【夜宵】 yèxiāo food (eaten at night)：吃～ have some good late at night
【夜校】 yèxiào night school；evening school
【夜校生】 yèxiàoshēng student of an evening school
【夜行军】 yèxíngjūn night march
【夜以继日】 yèyǐjìrì day and night；round the clock
【夜莺】 yèyīng 〈*Zool*.〉 *nightingale*
【夜鹰】 yèyīng 〈*Zool*.〉 *goatsucker*；*nightjar*
【夜战】 yèzhàn 1.(夜间作战) night fighting 2.(夜间工作) work at night
【夜总会】 yèzǒnghuì nightclub；night club

掖 (yè) 1.(用手搀扶) support sb. by the arm 2.(扶助；提拔) help；assist；promote：扶～ support；help
(另见"掖"yē)

液 (yè) liquid；fluid；juice

【液化】 yèhuà 〈*Chem*.〉 liquefaction
【液化气】 yèhuàqì 〈*Physics*〉 liquid gas
【液化器】 yèhuàqì liquefier
【液化气运输船】 yèhuàqì yùnshūchuán liquid-gas tanker
【液化石油气】 yèhuà shíyóuqì liquefied petroleum gas (LPG)
【液化天然气】 yèhuà tiánránqì liquified natural gas
【液晶】 yèjīng 〈*Physics*〉 liquid crystal
【液晶显示】 yèjīng xiǎnshì LCD；liquid crystal display
【液力】 yèlì 〈*Mech*.〉 hydraulic
【液态】 yètài 〈*Physics*〉 liquid state
【液体】 yètǐ liquid
【液压】 yèyā hydraulic pressure

腋 (yè) 1.(夹肢窝) axilla；armpit：～下夹着把伞 hold an umbrella in one's armpit 2.〈*Bot*.〉 axil

【腋臭】 yèchòu underarm odor
【腋毛】 yèmáo armpit hair
【腋窝】 yèwō armpit

谒 (yè) pay a formal visit to；call on

【谒见】 yèjiàn pay a visit to sb.；call on sb.
【谒陵】 yèlíng pay homage at sb's mausoleum

yi

一 (yī) 1.(数目) one；first 2.(同一) same；one：咱们是～家人。We are of the same family. 3.(另一) also；otherwise 4.(全；满) whole；all；throughout：～年到头 all the year round 5.(专一) concentrated；whole-hearted：～心～意 heart and soul 6.(一次或短暂的动作)笑～笑 give a smile 7.(每一) every；each；per：～日三餐 three meals a day 8.(与"就""即"等字连用) once；as soon as

(在本词典中"一"统注 yī)

【一巴掌】 yībā·zhang a slap

【一把】 yībǎ a handful; a bundle; a bunch

【一把手】 yībǎshǒu 1.(一员) partner; participant; a member; a hand 2.(能干的人) a good hand; able man 3.(主要负责人) head; chief: 她曾是我们厂的～。She has been the head of our factory.

【一把抓】 yībǎzhuā 1.(什么都自己管) keep everything under one's own control 2.(不分轻重缓急) deal with all problems at the same time

【一百】 yībǎi one hundred; (one) hundredth

【一百万】 yībǎiwàn one million; one millionth

【一败涂地】 yībài-túdì suffer a crushing defeat

【一般】 yībān 1.(一样) same as; just like 2.(一种) sort; kind 3.(普通;通常) general; ordinary; common: ～常识 general knowledge / 晚餐～在 7 点用。Dinner is generally served at 7 p.m.

【一般代理人】 yībān dàilǐrén general attorney

【一般规律】 yībān guīlǜ universal law; general rule

【一般化】 yībānhuà vague generalization

【一般说来】 yībānshuōlái generally speaking: ～,女的比男的寿命长。Women, generally speaking, live longer than men.

【一般性】 yībānxìng generality; general (adj.): ～辩论 general debate

【一斑】 yībān a spot; a speck

【一板一眼】 yībǎn-yīyǎn 1.(唱得好) (sing) in an expert manner 2.(有条理性) method

【一半】 yībàn one half; half; in part

【一帮】 yībāng a gang; a band

【一包】 yībāo a parcel; a package; a pack

【一饱眼福】 yībǎoyǎnfú get an eyeful of

【一抱】 yībào an armful

【一本万利】 yīběn-wànlì a small investment brings a ten thousand-fold profit; make big profits with a small capital

【一本正经】 yīběn-zhèngjīng in all seriousness; in dead earnest

【一笔带过】 yībǐ-dàiguò underplay

【一笔勾销】 yībǐ-gōuxiāo write off at one stroke; cancel once for all: 前账～ cancel all debts

【一笔总付】 yībǐ-zǒngfù lump sum

【一臂之力】 yībìzhīlì a helping hand: 助我～ lend me a hand

【一边】 yībiān 1.(一面;一方) one side 2.(旁边) by the side; beside; aside 3.(同时发生) while; as; at the same time; simultaneously: ～走,～唱 walk while singing

【一边倒】 yībiāndǎo 1.(倾向一方) lean to one side; side with sb. without reservation 2.(一方占绝对优势) predominate; enjoy overwhelming superiority

【一表人才】 yībiǎo-réncái with the appearance of a talent; a man of striking appearance

【一并】 yībìng 〈*adv.*〉 along with all the others; in the lump: ～处理 be handled together

【一病不起】 yībìng-bùqǐ take to one's bed and never leave it again; fall ill and die

【一波三折】 yībō-sānzhé with turns and twists; with unexpected changes

【一不做,二不休】 yī bù zuò, èr bù xiū carry the thing through, whatever the consequences; in for a penny, in for a pound; stick it out

【一步不让】 yībù-bùràng not yield an inch

【一步登天】 yībù-dēngtiān reach the sky in a single bound; attain the highest level in one step; have a meteoric rise

【一步一个脚印】 yī bù yī·ge jiǎoyìn every step leaves its print; work steadily and make solid progress

【一草一木】 yīcǎo-yīmù every tree and bush

【一刹那】 yīchànà in a moment; in a split second

【一场空】 yīchángkōng come to naught; all in vain; futile: 落得～ end in futility

【一场虚惊】 yīcháng xūjīng false alarm

【一唱一和】 yīchàng-yīhè sing a duet with sb.; sing the same tune; echo each other

【一尘不染】 yīchén-bùrǎn not soiled by a speck of dust; spotless; remain uncontaminated

【一成不变】 yīchéng-bùbiàn immutable and frozen; invariable; unalterable

【一筹莫展】 yīchóu-mòzhǎn can find no way

out; be at one's wits' end; be at the end of one's tether

【一酬多挂】 yīchóu-duōguà link up payment with other factors

【一触即发】 yīchù-jífā be on the verge of breaking out; may be triggered at any moment; touch-and-go (adj.)

【一触即溃】 yīchù-jíkuì collapse at the first encounter

【一锤定音】 yīchuí-dìngyīn give the final word

【一锤子买卖】 yīchuí·zi mǎi·mai once-for-all deal

【一次】 yīcì once

【一次性】 yīcìxìng disposable; one-off: ～尿布 disposable diaper / ～毛巾和刮胡刀 disposable towels and razors

【一次性付款】 yīcìxìng fùkuǎn lump-sum payment

【一蹴而就】 yīcù'érjiù accomplish in one move

【一寸光阴一寸金】 yī cùn guāngyīn yī cùn jīn time is gold; time is precious

【一打】 yīdá a dozen: ～铅笔 a dozen of pencils

【一旦】 yīdàn 1.(很短时间) in a single day; in a very short time: 毁于～ be destroyed in one day 2.(如果某个时间) once; in case; now that: ～时机成熟 once the time is ripe

【一刀两断】 yīdāo-liǎngduàn sever at one blow; make a clean break

【一刀切】 yīdāoqiē cut everything with one knife

【一道】 yīdào together; side by side; alongside

【一得之功】 yīdé-zhīgōng just an occasional, minor success

【一等】 yīděng first-class; first-rate; top-grade

【一等功】 yīděnggōng Merit Citation, First Class

【一等秘书】 yīděng mìshū First Secretary

【一等品】 yīděngpǐn first-rate product

【一点儿】 yīdiǎnr 1.(很少的量) a bit; a little 2.(很少) little; few 3.(一点也不) not at all: 我来了～也不遗憾,我很高兴。I'm not at all sorry I came; I'm glad!

【一点一滴】 yīdiǎn-yīdī bit by bit; little by little

【一定】 yīdìng 1.(规定的) fixed; established; regular 2.(固定不变的) definite; constant 3.(必定) surely; certainly; be bound to 4.(特定的) certain; specific; given

【一度】 yīdù 1.(一次) once; at one time; for a time: 一年～ once a year; yearly; annually 2.(有过一次) on one occasion: ～失业 be out of job on one occasion

【一端】 yīduān 1.(一头) one end 2.(一个方面) one respect

【一段】 yīduàn a section; a paragraph

【一堆】 yīduī a pile; a heap

【一对】 yīduì a pair; a couple

【一对一】 yīduìyī one-to-one: ～的打斗 single combat

【一而再,再而三】 yī ér zài, zài ér sān over and over again; time and again

【一二】 yī'èr one or two; just a few: 我略知～。I know only a little about.

【一帆风顺】 yīfān-fēngshùn plain sailing

【一反常态】 yīfǎn-chángtài depart from one's normal behavior; act out of character

【一方】 yīfāng 1.(一方面) one side; a party 2.(一个地区) an area or region

【一方当事人】 yīfāng dāngshìrén one party

【一分为二】 yīfēnwéi'èr 〈*Philos.*〉 one divides into two

【一分钟小说】 yīfēnzhōng xiǎoshuō little fiction

【一夫多妻制】 yīfū-duōqīzhì polygamy; polygyny

【一夫一妻制】 yīfū-yīqīzhì monogamy; monogyny

【一副】 yīfù a pair; a set

【一概】 yīgài 〈*adv.*〉 one and all; without exception; totally; categorically: ～排斥 totally exclude

【一概而论】 yīgài'érlùn lump together all and sundry; lump under one head

【一干二净】 yīgān-èrjìng thoroughly; completely

【一竿子到底】 yī gān·zi dào dǐ carry sth. down to the grassroots level

【一个巴掌拍不响】 yī·ge bā·zhang pāi·buxiǎng

It takes two to make a quarrel.

【一个萝卜一个坑儿】 yī·ge luó·bo yī·ge kēngr each one has his own task

【一个心眼儿】 yī·ge xīnyǎnr 1.(专心一意) have one's heart set on sth.; devotedly: ～建设社会主义 devote oneself in socialist construction 2.(固执) stubbornly; inflexibly

【一个中心,两个基本点】 yī·ge zhōngxīn, liǎng·ge jīběndiǎn one central task and two main points

【一共】 yīgòng altogether; in all; all told: 在公共汽车上～有 18 个人。Altogether there were 18 people in the bus.

【一鼓作气】 yīgǔ-zuòqì press on to finish without letup; get sth. done in one vigorous effort

【一贯】 yīguàn consistent; persistent; all along: ～政策 consistent policy

【一国两制】 yīguó liǎngzhì one nation, two systems

【一晃】 yīhuǎng 1.(一闪) flash 2.(快) pass in a flash

【一会儿】 yīhuìr 1.(很短时间) a little while; mo: 请等～。Wait mo.(或 Please wait for a little while.) 2.(在很短时间内) in a while; in an instant; presently; soon 3.(叠用) now ... now ...; sometimes ... sometimes ...: 天气～热～冷。It is sometimes warm and sometimes cold.

【一伙】 yīhuǒ a gang of; a band of

【一级上将】 yījí shàngjiàng 1.(陆军) Senior General 2.(空军、海军) General First Grade

【一技之长】 yījìzhīcháng proficiency in a particular line; professional skill; speciality

【一家之言】 yījiāzhīyán statement of a school

【一价】 yījià 1.〈*Chem*. & *Biol*.〉 monovalent 2.〈*Chem*.〉 univalent

【一见如故】 yījiàn-rúgù feel like old friends at the first meeting; become intimate at the first meeting

【一箭双雕】 yījiàn-shuāngdiāo shoot two hawks with one arrow; kill two birds with one stone

【一见钟情】 yījiàn-zhōngqíng fall in love at first sight

【一经】 yījīng as soon as; once; immediately after

【一举】 yījǔ with one action; at one stroke; at one fell swoop: ～成名天下知 gain worldwide fame and success overnight

【一举两得】 yījǔ-liǎngdé kill two birds with one stone

【一举一动】 yījǔ-yīdòng any move; any action

【一绝】 yījué a special skill; a unique talent

【一蹶不振】 yījué-bùzhèn collapse after one setback; never be able to recover after a setback

【一决雌雄】 yījué-cíxióng compete for championship

【一刻】 yīkè quarter-hour; quarter: 9 点～ a quarter past nine

【一刻千金】 yīkè-qiānjīn every minute is precious

【一孔之见】 yīkǒngzhījiàn a peephole view; a narrow view; a limited view

【一口】 yīkǒu 1.(口气坚决) with certainty; readily; flatly: ～回绝 flatly refuse 2.(纯正) pure: 讲～地道的英语 speak idiomatic English 3.〈*classifier*〉 a mouthful; a bite: ～蛋糕 a bite of cake

【一口气】 yīkǒuqì 1.(一口气息) one breath: 深吸～ draw a deep breath 2.(不间断地) in one breath; without a break; at one go; at a stretch

【一块】 yīkuài a piece; a block: ～面包 a piece of bread

【一块儿】 yīkuàir 1.(同一处所) at the same place 2.(一同) together

【一览】 yīlǎn general survey; bird's-eye view

【一览表】 yīlǎnbiǎo table; schedule

【一揽子】 yīlǎn·zi wholesale; package

【一揽子计划】 yīlǎn·zi jìhuà package plan

【一揽子交易】 yīlǎn·zi jiāoyì package deal

【一劳永逸】 yīláo-yǒngyì get sth. done once and for all

【一垒】 yīlěi 〈*Baseball*〉 first base

【一垒手】 yīlěishǒu 〈*Baseball*〉 first baseman

【一连】 yīlián 〈*adv*.〉 in a row; in succession; running: ～几个月 for months in succession

【一连串】 yīliánchuàn a succession of; a series of; a chain of; a string of: ～的灾祸 a succession of disasters

【一了百了】 yīliǎo-bǎiliǎo 1.(指问题的解决) all troubles end when the main trouble ends 2.(指死结束一切) death ends all one's troubles

【一流】 yīliú first-class; first-rate; top-grade

【一溜】 yīliù a row

【一溜风】 yīliùfēng swiftly

【一楼】 yīlóu first floor (AmE.); ground floor (BrE.)

【一路】 yīlù 1.(在整个行程) all the way; throughout the journey: ～领先 lead all the way / ～多保重。Take care of yourself on the journey. 2.(同一类) of the same kind: ～货色 goods of a kind; be of the same stock 3.(一起) go the same way; take the same route

【一路平安】 yīlù píng'ān Have a pleasant journey. (或: Have a good trip.)

【一路上】 yīlù·shang all along: ～都种有树木。There are trees all along the road.

【一路纵队】 yīlù zòngduì single file; Indian file

【一律】 yīlǜ 1.(同样) same; alike; uniform: ～对待 treat in the same way 2.(无例外) all; without exception

【一卵双生】 yīluǎn shuāngshēng one-egg twin; uniovular twin

【一落千丈】 yīluò-qiānzhàng suffer a disastrous decline

【一马当先】 yīmǎ-dāngxiān take the lead; be in the forefront

【一脉相承】 yīmài-xiāngchéng come down in one continuous line; can be traced to the same origin

【一慢、二看、三通过】 yī màn、èr kàn、sān tōngguò slow down, look around, and cross

【一毛不拔】 yīmáo-bùbá unwilling to give up even a hair; very stingy

【一门心思】 yīmén-xīn·si with one's whole heart and soul

【一面】 yīmiàn 1.(物体的面) one side 2.(方面) one section; one aspect 3.(叠用) at the same time; simultaneously: ～教,～学 learn while teaching 4.〈*classifier*〉 ～鼓 a drum / ～旗 a flag

【一面之词】 yīmiànzhīcí the statement of only one of the parties

【一面之交】 yīmiànzhījiāo have met only once; be casually acquainted

【一鸣惊人】 yīmíng-jīngrén amaze the world with a single brilliant feat; set the world on fire

【一命呜呼】 yīmìng-wūhū die; kick the bucket

【一模一样】 yīmú-yīyàng exactly alike; as like as two peas

【一目了然】 yīmù-liǎorán be clear at a glance

【一年之计在于春】 yī nián zhī jì zàiyú chūn the whole year's work depends on a good start in spring

【一念之差】 yīniànzhīchā a wrong decision made in a moment of weakness; momentary slip

【一拍即合】 yīpāi-jíhé fit in readily; chime in easily

【一派胡言】 yīpài-húyán complete nonsense

【一盘棋】 yīpánqí overall point of view; overall planning

【一旁】 yīpáng by the side; beside; aside

【一批】 yīpī a batch; a shipment

【一片丹心】 yīpiàn-dānxīn a leaf of red heart

【一瞥】 yīpiē 1.(用眼一看) a quick glance: 仇恨的～ shoot a look of hatred 2.(一眼所见) a glimpse; a brief survey

【一贫如洗】 yīpín-rúxǐ penniless; in utter destitution: 老夫妇生活～。The old couple lived in abject poverty.

【一齐】 yīqí 〈*adv.*〉 simultaneously; at the same time; in unison

【一起】 yīqǐ 1.(同一处所) in the same place 2.(一同) altogether; jointly; in all: ～行动 take action jointly

【一气】 yīqì 1.(不间断的) at one go; without a break; at a stretch 2.(声气相通) of the same gang; hand in glove 3.(一阵) a spell; a fit

【一千】 yīqiān one thousand; one thousandth

【一前一后】 yīqián-yīhòu tandem; in tandem: ～地驾车 drive tandem

【一钱不值】 yīqián-bùzhí not worth a penny; mere trash; utterly worthless

【一窍不通】 yīqiào-bùtōng know nothing about; lack the slightest knowledge of; be utterly ignorant of

【一切】 yīqiè 1.(全部的) all; every 2.(全部) everything: 不惜～ at any cost

【一切向钱看】 yīqiè xiàng qián kàn put money above everything

【一清二楚】 yīqīng-èrchǔ perfectly clear; as clear as daylight

【一清早】 yīqīngzǎo early in the morning

【一丘之貉】 yīqiūzhīhé jackals from the same lair; birds of a feather

【一群】 yīqún a group; a crowd; a herd; a pack; a flock

【一人得道,鸡犬升天】 yī rén dédào, jī-quǎn shēngtiān When a man becomes powerful, all his followers are in favor.

【一日千里】 yīrì qiānlǐ a thousand *li* a day; at a tremendous pace; with giant strides

【一如既往】 yīrú-jìwǎng just as in the past; as before; as always

【一色】 yīsè 1.(一样颜色) of the same color: 水天～。The water and the sky are of one hue. 2.(全部一样) of the same type; uniform

【一霎】 yīshà in the twinkling of an eye

【一身】 yīshēn 1.(全身) the whole body; all over the body: ～冷汗 break out in cold sweat 2.(一套) a suit 3.(一个人) all alone

【一审】 yīshěn 〈*Law*〉 first instance

【一生】 yīshēng all one's life; throughout one's life

【一失足成千古恨】 yī shīzú chéng qiāngǔ hèn A single slip brings eternal regret.

【一时】 yīshí 1.(短时间) for a short while; temporary; momentary 2.(一个时期) a period of time: 此～,彼～。Times have changed. 3.(时而) now ... now ...: 天气～冷,～热。The weather is now cold, now hot.

【一时半会儿】 yīshí-bànhuìr a little while; a short time; temporarily

【一时一刻】 yīshí-yīkè for a single second; for a single moment

【一世】 yīshì 1.(一生) life; lifetime 2.(一个时代) an era

【一式三份】 yīshì sānfèn in triplicate; in three copies

【一式四份】 yīshì sìfèn in quadruplicate; in four copies: 请把这个表格填成～。Please fill out this form in quadruplicate.

【一式五份】 yīshì wǔfèn in quintuplicate; in five copies

【一视同仁】 yīshì-tóngrén treat all men alike; treat equally without discrimination

【一事无成】 yīshì-wúchéng accomplish nothing; get nowhere: 他将～。He will never achieve anything.

【一是一,二是二】 yī shì yī, èr shì èr carefully

【一手】 yīshǒu 1.(技能或本领) proficiency; skill: 露～ show off one's skill 2.(指耍手段) trick; move: 他这～真毒辣! What a vicious trick he played! 3.(一个人) single-handed; all by oneself; all alone

【一手交钱,一手交货】 yī shǒu jiāo qián, yī shǒu jiāo huò cash on delivery; transaction in cash

【一瞬】 yīshùn an instant; a flash; the twinkling of an eye: ～即逝 vanish in a flash

【一丝不苟】 yīsī-bùgǒu be rigorous; be scrupulous about every detail; be conscientious and meticulous

【一丝不挂】 yīsī-bùguà be in the nude; in a state of nature

【一胎率】 yītāilǜ the rate of the first birth

【一潭死水】 yītán-sǐshuǐ very dull and inactive

【一套】 yītào 1.(固定方式) one's set way 2.(固定内容) convention; the same stuff: 老～ old convention; the same old stuff 3.〈*classifier*〉 a set; a flat; a suite; a suit: ～房间 a suite of rooms

【一体】 yītǐ 1.(关系密切) an organic whole: 融成～ merge into an organic whole 2.(全体) all people concerned; to a man

【一体化】 yītǐhuà integration; integrated (adj.): ～的对象 object of integration / ～的效益 effect of integration / ～区域合作 integrated regional co-operation

【一天】 yītiān 1.(一昼夜) a day 2.(一个白天) one day 3.(一天到晚) the whole day; all day long; from morning till night

【一条龙】 yītiáolóng 1.(一个行列) one continuous line 2.(指过程) a connected sequence; a coordinated process

【一条心】 yītiáoxīn be of one mind; be at one: 军民～。Our fighters and people are of one mind.

【一同】 yītóng 〈*adv.*〉 together; at the same time and place

【一统】 yītǒng unify：～天下 unify the whole country

【一头】 yītóu 1.（一面…一面）at the same time; simultaneously 2.（径直）directly; headlong：～钻进公共汽车 get directly on the bus 3.（一端）end 4.（一伙）side; gang：我们是～的。We are of same side. 5.（一头的高度）a head：高～ be taller by a head

【一团和气】 yītuán-héqì keep on good terms with everyone at the expense of principle; keep on the right side of everyone

【一团漆黑】 yītuán-qīhēi pitch-dark; utterly hopeless

【一团糟】 yītuánzāo a complete mess; a chaotic state

【一万】 yīwàn ten thousand; ten thousandth

【一网打尽】 yīwǎng-dǎjìn catch the whole lot in a dragnet; round up the whole gang at one fell swoop

【一往情深】 yīwǎng-qíngshēn be passionately devoted; be head over heels in love

【一往无前】 yīwǎng-wúqián press forward with indomitable will：～的精神 indomitable spirit

【一望无际】 yīwǎng-wújì stretch as far as the eye can see; stretch to the horizon

【一味】 yīwèi 〈*adv.*〉 blindly：～蛮干 persist in acting blindly

【一味迁就】 yīwèi qiānjiù concede to sb. on endless occasions

【一文不名】 yīwén-bùmíng be penniless; be cleaned out

【一文不值】 yīwén-bùzhí not worth a cent; of no use whatsoever

【一无是处】 yīwú-shìchù without a single redeeming feature; devoid of any merit

【一无所长】 yīwú-suǒcháng have no special skill; be Jack of all trades

【一无所获】 yīwú-suǒhuò have gained nothing

【一无所有】 yīwú-suǒyǒu not own a thing in the world; not have a thing to one's name

【一无所知】 yīwú-suǒzhī know nothing about; not have the least inkling of; be absolutely ignorant of

【一五一十】 yīwǔ-yīshí systematically and in full detail

【一误再误】 yīwù-zàiwù make things worse by repeated delays

【一席之地】 yīxízhīdì a space for sb.

【一系列】 yīxìliè a series of：～措施 a series of measures

【一下】 yīxià 1.（一次）one time; once：看～ have a look 2.（短时间）in a short while; all at once; all of a sudden：需要睡～ need a little sleep

【一下子】 yīxià · zi at one go; in a short while：～就把所有的蜡烛吹灭了 blow out all the candles at one go / 问题～就解决了。The problem was solved immediately.

【一线】 yīxiàn 1.（极其细微）a ray of; a gleam of：～希望 a gleam of hope 2.（最前线）the first front

【一向】 yīxiàng 1.（某一段时间）earlier on; lately 2.（一直）consistently; all along

【一笑置之】 yīxiào-zhìzhī laugh out of court; laugh off

【一些】 yīxiē 1.〈*classifier*〉 a number of; certain 2.（数量少）some; a few; a little：有～国家 some countries

【一心】 yīxīn 1.（专心）wholeheartedly; heart and soul：～为人民谋福利 work for the people's interests heart and soul 2.（齐心）of one mind; at one：万众～。Millions of people are all of one mind.

【一新】 yīxīn a new appearance

【一星半点儿】 yīxīng-bàndiǎnr a bit of; a few; a little

【一星级旅馆】 yīxīngjí lǚguǎn one-star hotel

【一行】 yīxíng a group travelling together; party

【一言难尽】 yīyán-nánjìn it is hard to explain in a few words; it's a long story

【一眼】 yīyǎn a glance; a glimpse：看某人～ get a glimpse of sb. / ～就看出 see sth. at a glance

【一氧化碳】 yīyǎnghuàtàn 〈*Chem.*〉 carbon monoxide; white damp

【一氧化碳中毒】 yīyǎnghuàtàn zhòngdú carbon monoxide poisoning

【一样】 yīyàng the same; equally; alike; as

... as

【一一】 yīyī one by one; one after another: ～就座 seat themselves one after another

【一衣带水】 yīyīdàishuǐ a narrow strip of water: ～的邻邦 close neighbors separated only by a strip of water

【一意孤行】 yīyì-gūxíng persist in willfully and arbitrarily

【一应俱全】 yīyīng-jùquán complete in every line; everything needed is there

【一拥而上】 yīyōng'érshàng rush up in a crowd

【一隅】 yīyú a corner: ～之见 a glance from a corner

【一语双关】 yīyǔ-shuāngguān pun on a word

【一元方程】 yīyuán fāngchéng 〈*Math.*〉 equation with one unknown quantity

【一元化】 yīyuánhuà centralized; unified: ～的领导 centralized leadership

【一元论】 yīyuánlùn 1.〈*Immunity*〉 monophyletic theory 2.〈*Philos.*〉 monism

【一月】 yīyuè January

【一再】 yīzài time and again; again and again; repeatedly: ～宣称 declare time and again

【一早】 yīzhǎo early in the morning

【一张一弛】 yīzhāng-yīchí stretched and relaxed; alternate tension with relaxation

【一长制】 yīzhǎngzhì system of one-man leadership

【一朝一夕】 yīzhāo-yīxī in one day; in one morning or evening; overnight

【一针见血】 yīzhēn-jiànxiě pierce to the truth with a single pertinent remark; hit the nail on the head

【一阵】 yīzhèn in burst; a fit; a peal: ～掌声 a peal of applause

【一知半解】 yīzhī-bànjiě have scanty knowledge; have a smattering of knowledge

【一直】 yīzhí 1.(不拐弯) straight: ～走 go straight ahead; keep straight on 2.(始终) continuously; always; all along; all the way: 她打算对我～瞒到底。She intended to deceive me all along.

【一纸空文】 yīzhǐ-kōngwén a mere scrap of paper

【一致】 yīzhì showing no difference; identical; unanimous; consistent: ～决定 decide unanimously / 采取～行动 take concerted action / 与某人意见～ in accord with sb. / 与某人意见不～ out of accord with sb.

【一掷千金】 yīzhì-qiānjīn spend money extravagantly

【一专多能】 yīzhuān-duōnéng expert in one thing and good at many

【一准】 yīzhǔn 〈*adv.*〉 sure; surely; certainly

【一字槽螺帽】 yīzìcáo luómào slotted head

【一字领】 yīzìlǐng boat neck

【一字千金】 yīzì-qiānjīn Learning is more precious than gold.

【一字儿】 yīzìr in a line; in a row

【一总】 yīzǒng 1.(合并) altogether; all told; in all 2.(全部) all

伊 (yī) 1.(她) she; her 2.(他) he; his

【伊甸园】 Yīdiànyuán 〈*Christianity*〉 the Garden of Eden; paradise

【伊金霍洛旗】 Yījīnhuòluòqí 〈place〉 Ejin Horo Qi

【伊克昭盟】 Yīkèzhāoméng 〈place〉 Ih Ju Meng

【伊犁】 Yīlí 〈place〉 Ili

【伊始】 yīshǐ beginning

【伊斯兰教】 Yīsīlánjiào Islam; Islamism

【伊蚊】 yīwéng 〈*Zool.*〉 *aedes*

衣 (yī) 1.(衣服) clothing; clothes; garment 2.(包在物体外的) coating; covering

【衣钵】 yībō a Buddhist monk's mantle and alms bowl; legacy: 继承～ inherit sb's mantle

【衣不遮体】 yībùzhētǐ wear rags; wear shabby clothes

【衣橱】 yīchú wardrobe

【衣袋】 yīdài pocket

【衣兜】 yīdōu pocket

【衣服】 yī·fu clothing; clothes

【衣冠禽兽】 yīguān-qínshòu a beast in human clothing

【衣冠冢】 yīguānzhǒng a tomb containing personal effects of the deceased

【衣柜】 yīguì wardrobe; clothes closet

【衣夹】 yījiā clothes-peg; clothespin

【衣架】 yījià 1.(衣帽架) clothes stand;

clothes tree 2.（挂衣架）hanger；clothes-rack

【衣锦还乡】 yījǐn-huánxiāng return to one's hometown in silken robes；return home after making good

【衣料】 yīliào material for clothing；dress material

【衣领】 yīlǐng collar

【衣帽钩】 yīmàogōu coat hook

【衣帽间】 yīmàojiān cloakroom；checkroom

【衣衫】 yīshān clothing；clothes

【衣衫褴褛】 yīshān lánlǚ be dressed in rags

【衣裳】 yī·shang clothing；clothes

【衣身】 yīshēng body

【衣食住行】 yī-shí-zhù-xíng food, clothing, shelter and transportation；basic necessities of life

【衣刷】 yīshuā clothes brush

【衣物】 yīwù clothing and other articles of daily use

【衣箱】 yīxiāng suitcase；trunk

【衣着】 yīzhuó clothing, headgear and footwear：～整洁 be neatly dresse

依 (yī) 1.（依靠）depend on；rely on 2.（依从）comply with；listen to；yield to 3.（按照）according to；in the light of；judging by

【依傍】 yībàng 1.（依靠）rely on；depend on 2.（模仿）imitate；emulate

【依此类推】 yīcǐ-lèituī the rest may be deduced by analogy；and so on and so forth

【依次】 yīcì in proper order；successively：～进来 come in one by one

【依从】 yīcóng comply with；yield to

【依存】 yīcún depend on sb. or sth. of existence

【依法】 yīfǎ according to law；by operation of law

【依法惩处】 yīfǎ-chéngchǔ be punished according to law

【依附】 yīfù depend on；attach oneself to；become an appendage to：～权贵 attach oneself to bigwigs

【依合同】 yīhé·tong by contract

【依旧】 yījiù as before；still

【依据】 yījù 1.（根据）according to；in the light of；on the basis of；judging by 2.（基础）basis；foundation

【依靠】 yīkào 1.（凭借）rely on；depend on：～工资生活 live on one's wages / ～群众 rely on the masses 2.（可依靠人或物）sth. to fall back on；support；backing

【依赖】 yīlài 1.（依靠）rely on 2.（互不可分）be dependent on：互相～ be dependent on each other

【依赖思想】 yīlài sīxiǎng the dependent mentality

【依赖性】 yīlàixìng dependence

【依恋】 yīliàn be reluctant to leave；feel regret at parting from

【依凭】 yīpíng rely on；depend on

【依然】 yīrán still；as before：～有效 still hold good；remain valid

【依然故我】 yīrán-gùwǒ 1.（情况没变）one's circumstances haven't changed much 2.（仍和从前一样）one is still one's same old self

【依顺】 yīshùn be obedient：百依百顺 be all obedience

【依托】 yītuō 1.（依靠）rely on；depend on 2.（假借名义）support；prop；backing

【依稀】 yīxī vaguely；dimly：～记得 remember vaguely / ～可见 faintly visible / ～如旧 similarly as old

【依依】 yīyī reluctant to part：～不舍 be reluctant to part；cannot bear to part

【依仗】 yīzhàng count on；rely on：～权势 rely on one's power and position；count on one's powerful connections

【依照】 yīzhào according to；in the light of：～法律 according to the law

铱 (yī) 〈*Chem.*〉iridium（元素符号 Ir）

【铱金笔】 yījīnbǐ iridium-point pen

医［醫、毉］(yī) 1.（医生）doctor；physician 2.（医学）medical science；medical service；medicine：3.（医治）cure；treat：头痛～头，脚痛～脚 take stopgap measures

【医道】 yīdào skill of a doctor；medical skill

【医德】 yīdé medical ethics

【医护】 yīhù medical treatment and nursing

【医护人员】 yīhù rényuán doctors and nurses

【医科】 yīkē medical courses in general；medicine

【医科大学】 yīkē dàxué medical university
【医理】 yīlǐ principles of medical science; medical knowledge
【医疗】 yīliáo medical treatment：公费～ public health services
【医疗队】 yīliáoduì medical team
【医疗服务】 yīliáo fúwù medical aid
【医疗机构】 yīliáo jīgòu medical establishment
【医疗器械】 yīliáo qìxiè medical apparatus and instruments
【医疗事故】 yīliáo shìgù unskillful and faulty medical or surgical treatment; malpractice
【医疗事故保险】 yīliáo shìgù bǎoxiǎn malpractice insurance
【医疗站】 yīliáozhàn medical station; health center
【医龄】 yīlíng length of service as a medical worker
【医生】 yīshēng doctor; medical man：全科～ general practitioner / 外科～ surgeon / 请～ send for a doctor
【医师】 yīshī doctor：公共卫生～ public health doctor
【医士】 yīshì practitioner (with secondary medical school education)
【医书】 yīshū medical book
【医术】 yīshù medical skill; art of healing
【医务】 yīwù medical matters
【医务人员】 yīwù rényuán medical personnel; public health worker
【医务室】 yīwùshì clinic
【医务所】 yīwùsuǒ clinic
【医学】 yīxué medical science; medicine
【医学博士】 yīxué bóshì Doctor of Medicine
【医学科学院】 yīxué kēxuéyuàn academy of medical sciences
【医学文献】 yīxué wénxiàn medical literature
【医学学士】 yīxué xuéshì Bachelor of Medicine
【医学遗产】 yīxué yíchǎn medical heritage
【医学院】 yīxuéyuàn college of medicine
【医药】 yīyào medicine
【医药常识】 yīyào chángshí general medical knowledge
【医药费】 yīyàofèi medical expenses
【医院】 yīyuàn hospital：送～ send to hospital
【医治】 yīzhì cure; treat; heal：～无效 fail to respond to any medical treatment
【医嘱】 yīzhǔ doctor's advice; doctor's orders

壹［弌］(yī) one; first

揖(yī) salute by bowing with clasped hands

【揖让】 yīràng pay respect to others by bowing with clasped hands

一(yí) one; first
(请见"一"yī)

仪［儀］(yí) 1.(人的外表) appearance; bearing 2.(礼节;仪式) ceremony; rite：司～ master of ceremonies 3.(礼物) present; gift：贺～ present for birthday, wedding, etc 4.(仪器) apparatus; instrument

【仪表】 yíbiǎo 1.(人的外表) appearance; bearing：～堂堂 noble and dignified 2.(各种测定仪) meter; instrument
【仪表盘】 yíbiǎopán 〈*Auto*〉 dashboard
【仪器】 yíqì instrument; apparatus
【仪容】 yíróng looks; appearance
【仪式】 yíshì ceremony; rite; function：协定签字～ a ceremony for signing an agreement
【仪态】 yítài 〈*written*〉 bearing; deportment：～万方 appear in all her glory
【仪仗队】 yízhàngduì guard of honor; honor guard：陆海空三军～ a guard of honor of the three services / 检阅～ review the guard of honor

夷(yí) 1.(平安) smooth; safe：化险为～ turn danger into safety 2.(摧毁建筑) raze：～为平地 level to the ground; raze 3.(夷灭) exterminate 4.(旧指外国人或外国) foreigner; foreign country

姨(yí) 1.(姨母) aunt; one's mother's sister 2.(妻子的姐妹) sister-in-law; one's wife's sister

【姨表】 yíbiǎo maternal cousin：～姐妹 female maternal cousins / ～兄弟 male maternal cousins
【姨表亲】 yíbiǎoqīn family members of maternal cousins
【姨父】 yí·fu uncle; the husband of one's maternal aunt

【姨母】 yímǔ aunt; maternal aunt
【姨太太】 yítài·tai 〈colloq.〉 concubine
胰 (yí) 1.〈Anat.〉 pancreas 2.(肥皂) soap
【胰岛素】 yídǎosù 〈Pharm.〉 insulin
【胰脏】 yízàng 〈Anat.〉 pancreas
【胰子】 yí·zi soap
饴 (yí) maltose
【饴糖】 yítáng maltose; malt sugar
怡 (yí) happy; cheerful; joyful
【怡然】 yírán happy; contented: ～自得 happy and pleased with oneself
【怡神醒脑】 yíshén-xǐngnǎo production of an effect against refreshment
贻 (yí) 1.(赠送) make a gift to sth.; present 2.(遗留) leave behind: ～患 sow seeds of disaster
【贻害】 yíhài leave a legacy of trouble: ～无穷 entail untold troubles
【贻误】 yíwù affect adversely; bungle
【贻笑大方】 yíxiào-dàfāng make a laughing-stock of oneself before experts; incur the ridicule of experts
【贻赠】 yízèng present; leave something to posterity
宜 (yí) 1.(合适) suitable; appropriate; fitting: 适～ fitting and proper 2.(应当) should; ought to: 不～强加于人。You should not force your view on others.
【宜人】 yírén pleasant; delightful: 气候～ pleasant weather
移 (yí) 1.(移动) move; remove; shift 2.(改变) change; alter
【移动】 yídòng move; shift
【移动电话】 yídòng diànhuà mobile telephone
【移风易俗】 yífēng-yìsú change prevailing habits and customs; transform social traditions
【移行】 yíháng division into syllable
【移花接木】 yíhuā-jiēmù 1.(嫁接) graft one twig on another; graft 2.(暗中更换) stealthily substitute one thing for another
【移交】 yíjiāo 1.(转移) turn over; transfer 2.(转给他人) deliver into sb's custody; hand over one's job to a successor
【移解】 yíjiè transfer (a criminal)
【移居】 yíjū move one's residence; migrate
【移居入境】 yíjū rùjìng immigration
【移民】 yímín 1.(迁移至外地或外国) migrate; emigrate 2.(从外地或外国移入) immigrate 3.(迁入的人) migrant; immigrant 4.(迁出的人) emigrant
【移民点】 yímíndiǎn settlement
【移民法】 yímínfǎ immigration laws
【移民局】 yímínjú immigration office
【移民签证】 yímín qiānzhèng immigrant visa
【移民政策】 yímín zhèngcè immigration policy
【移植】 yízhí 1.〈Agric.〉 transplant; transplantation (n.) 2.〈Med.〉 transplant; graft; transplantation (n.): 角膜～ corneal transplantation / 外科医生从患者的背上取皮～到他烧伤的臂上。The surgeon grafted skin from the patient's back onto his burned arm.
颐 (yí) 1.(保养) keep fit 2.(腮; 颊) cheek: 支～ cheek in palm
【颐和园】 Yíhéyuán the Summer Palace
【颐养】 yíyǎng take care of oneself
遗 (yí) 1.(遗失) lose; miss 2.(遗失的东西) sth. lost: 路不拾～。No one pockets anything found on the road. 3.(遗漏) omit; slip over: 巨细无～ slip over nothing whether big or small 4.(留下) leave behind; keep back; not give: 不～余力 spare no efforts 5.(死者留下的) leave behind at one's death; bequeath; hand down: ～骨 remains / ～作 posthumous work 6.(遗精) emission: 梦～ nocturnal emission
(另见"遗"wèi)
【遗产】 yíchǎn legacy; inheritance; heritage: 继承～ inherit a legacy
【遗产承受人】 yíchǎn chéngshòurén legatee
【遗臭万年】 yíchòu-wànnián leave a stink for ten thousand years; go down in history as a byword of infamy
【遗传】 yíchuán 〈Biol.〉 heredity; inheritance
【遗传工程】 yíchuán gōngchéng genetic engineering
【遗传密码】 yíchuán mìmǎ 〈Biol.〉 genetic code

【遗传学】 yíchuánxué genetics; genetic (adj.)
【遗风】 yífēng a custom left by a preceding generation
【遗骸】 yíhái remains
【遗憾】 yíhàn 1.(遗恨) eternal regret 2.(惋惜) regret; pity: 对此表示～ express regret over the matter
【遗恨】 yíhèn eternal regret: 死无～ die without any regret
【遗迹】 yíjì historical remains; vestige; traces: 历史～ historical remains
【遗教】 yíjiào instructions left by the dead
【遗精】 yíjīng 〈*Med.*〉 emission
【遗老】 yílǎo old fogy; old diehard; old adherent of the past dynasty
【遗留】 yíliú leave over; hand down: 历史上～下来的边界问题 boundary questions left over by history
【遗留问题】 yíliú wèntí remaining problem
【遗漏】 yílòu omit; leave out
【遗墨】 yímò letters; manuscripts, scrolls of painting or calligraphy, etc. left behind by the deceased
【遗尿】 yíniào 〈*Med.*〉 enuresis; bed-wetting
【遗弃】 yíqì abandon; forsake; cast off
【遗容】 yíróng 1.(指容貌) remains: 瞻仰～ pay one's respect to the remains of sb. 2.(遗像) a portrait of the deceased
【遗少】 yíshào young man with the mentality of an old fogy; young diehard
【遗失】 yíshī lose
【遗事】 yíshì 1.(前代的事迹) incidents of the past ages 2.(前人的事迹) deeds of those now dead
【遗书】 yíshū 1.(指著作) posthumous papers; writings of an author now dead 2.(指遗嘱等) a letter or note left by one immediately before death
【遗孀】 yíshuāng widow; relict
【遗体】 yítǐ 1.(人的) remains; corpse: 向～告别 pay one's last respect to sb's remains 2.(动植物的) remains
【遗忘】 yíwàng forget
【遗忘症】 yíwàngzhèng amnesia
【遗物】 yíwù things left behind by the deceased
【遗像】 yíxiàng a portrait of a dead person
【遗训】 yíxùn teachings of the deceased
【遗言】 yíyán words of the deceased; last words
【遗业】 yíyè business or career left behind by one's ancestors
【遗愿】 yíyuàn unfulfilled wish of the deceased; last wish; behest
【遗赠】 yízèng bequeath
【遗址】 yízhǐ ruins; relics
【遗志】 yízhì unfulfilled wish; behest; work bequeathed by the deceased
【遗嘱】 yízhǔ testament; will; dying words: 立～ make a will
【遗著】 yízhù posthumous work

疑 (yí) 1.(怀疑) doubt; disbelieve; suspect: 无可置～ beyond doubt; undoubtedly 2.(未能确定的) doubtful; uncertain: 存～ leave the question open
【疑案】 yí'àn 1.(指案件) disputed case 2.(指事件) mystery
【疑点】 yídiǎn doubtful point
【疑惑】 yíhuò feel uncertain; not be convinced
【疑惧】 yíjù apprehensions; misgivings
【疑虑】 yílǜ misgivings; doubt: 消除心中的～ clear one's mind of doubt; free sb. from doubts and misgivings
【疑难】 yínán difficult; knotty: ～问题 a knotty problem
【疑似】 yísì could be; suspected to be
【疑团】 yítuán doubts and suspicions: 解除～ clear up one's doubts and suspicions
【疑问】 yíwèn query; question; doubt: 毫无～ without any doubt; without any question
【疑心】 yíxīn 1.(有怀疑) suspicious: 起～ become suspicious 2.(怀疑) suspect; doubt
【疑心病】 yíxīnbìng with a suspicious mind
【疑义】 yíyì doubt; doubtful point
【疑云】 yíyún misgivings or suspicion clouding one's mind

彝[彛] (yí)
【彝族】 Yízú Yi(中国少数民族,主要分布在云南、四川、贵州等地)

乙 (yǐ) second

【乙醇】 yǐchún 〈*Chem.*〉 ethanol; alcohol
【乙等】 yǐděng the second grade; Grade B
【乙醚】 yǐmí 〈*Chem.*〉 ether
【乙醛】 yǐquán 〈*Chem.*〉 acetaldehyde; aldehyde
【乙炔】 yǐquē 〈*Chem.*〉 acetylene; ethyne
【乙烯】 yǐxī 〈*Chem.*〉 ethylene: 聚～ polyethylene; polythene
【乙型肝炎】 yǐxíng gānyán 〈*Med.*〉 hepatitis B
【乙型脑炎】 yǐxíng nǎoyán 〈*Med.*〉 encephalitis B; Japanese encephalitis
【乙状结肠】 yǐzhuàng jiécháng 〈*Anat.*〉 sigmoid colon

钇 (yǐ) 〈*Chem.*〉 yttrium (元素符号 Y)

已 (yǐ) **1.** (停止) stop; cease; end **2.** (已经) already
【已付】 yǐfù paid; pd
【已故】 yǐgù deceased; late
【已婚】 yǐhūn be married: ～有偶 currently married
【已缴资本】 yǐjiǎo zīběn paid-in capital
【已经】 yǐ·jing already: 那部电影他～看过两次了。He has seen that film twice already.
【已然】 yǐrán already
【已往】 yǐwǎng before; previously; in the past
【已知数】 yǐzhīshù 〈*Math.*〉 known number

以 (yǐ) **1.** (用;拿) use; take: ～全速 at full speed / ～理服人 convince people by reasoning / ～10 美元购进商品再～12 美元售出 buy articles at 10 dollars and sell them at 12 dollars **2.** (依) according to **3.** (因) because of **4.** (表示目的) in order to; so as to: ～应急需 in order to answer an urgent need **5.** (表示界限) 50～内 less than fifty
【以饱私囊】 yǐ bǎo sīnáng fill one's pocket
【以便】 yǐbiàn so that; in order to; so as to; with the aim of; for the purpose of
【以此】 yǐcǐ for this reason; on this account: ～为戒 take this as a lesson
【以德报怨】 yǐdé-bàoyuàn return good for evil; requite ingratitude with kindness
【以点带面】 yǐdiǎn-dàimiàn fan out from point to area; use the experience of selected units to promote work in the entire area
【以毒攻毒】 yǐdú-gōngdú combat poison with poison; use poison as an antidote for poison
【以杜后患】 yǐdù-hòuhuàn forestall future trouble
【以讹传讹】 yǐ'é-chuán'é incorrectly relay an erroneous message
【以罚代刑】 yǐfá-dàixíng replacing imprisonment for criminal offense with lighter punishment
【以法律为准绳】 yǐ fǎlǜ wéi zhǔnshéng take law as the criterion
【以防万一】 yǐfáng wànyī be ready for any eventuality; be prepared for all contingencies
【以丰补歉】 yǐfēng-bǔqiàn store up in fat years to make up for lean ones
【以攻为守】 yǐgōng-wéishǒu attack in order to defend; use attack as a means of defense
【以古非今】 yǐgǔ-fēijīn disparage the present by extolling the past
【以观后效】 yǐguān hòuxiào see how the offender behaves
【以后】 yǐhòu after; afterwards; later; hereafter: 三天～ three days later / 他星期四生病,两天～就死了。He fell ill on Thursday and died two days later. / 我到学校～就给他打电话。I'll call him after I get to the school.
【以及】 yǐjí as well as; along with; and
【以及其他人】 yǐjí qítārén et al: 音乐会上演出了柴可夫斯基～的作品。The concert included works by Tchaikovsky et al.
【以己度人】 yǐjǐ-duórén judge others by oneself; measure other's corn by one's own bushel
【以…计算】 yǐ … jìsuàn in ... terms; in terms of: 以货币计算 in terms of money / 以数量计算 in terms of volume
【以假乱真】 yǐjiǎ-luànzhēn mix the spurious with the genuine
【以儆效尤】 yǐjǐng-xiàoyóu to warn others against following a bad example; as a warning to others
【以旧换新】 yǐjiù-huànxīn trade-in; trade in: 把旧车折价～买新车 trade an old car in for a new one

【以来】 yǐlái since：自古～ since the ancient times

【以礼相待】 yǐlǐ-xiāngdài treat sb. with due respect

【以理服人】 yǐlǐ-fúrén convince people by reasoning

【以邻为壑】 yǐlín-wéihè use one's neighbor's field as a drain; shift one's troubles onto others

【以貌取人】 yǐmào-qǔrén judge people solely by their appearance

【以免】 yǐmiǎn in order to avoid; so as not to; lest

【以内】 yǐnèi within; less than; inside of：两星期～ within two weeks

【以前】 yǐqián before; formerly; previously：很早～ a long time ago / 三年～ three years ago

【以勤补拙】 yǐqín-bǔzhuō amend stupidity by diligence

【以求】 yǐqiú in order to; in an attempt to：梦寐～ crave for; long-dreamed of

【以权谋私】 yǐquán-móusī abusing power for personal gains

【以上】 yǐshàng 1.（某点以上）more than; over; above：十吨～ over ten tons / 五年～ over five years 2.（前面的）the above; the foregoing; the above-mentioned：～各章 the above chapters

【以身试法】 yǐshēn-shìfǎ defy the law; challenge the law personally

【以身殉职】 yǐshēn-xùnzhí die at one's post

【以身作则】 yǐshēn-zuòzé set an example

【以事实为根据】 yǐshìshí wéi gēnjù base on fact

【以外】 yǐwài beyond; outside; other than; except：除此～ except this; beside this

【以往】 yǐwǎng before; formerly; in the past

【以为】 yǐwéi think; believe; consider

【以下】 yǐxià 1.（某点之下）below; under：零度～ below zero; sub-zero 2.（指下面的）the following：～各章 the following chapters

【以销定产】 yǐxiāo-dìngchǎn base production on sales prospects; produce according to sales

【以逸待劳】 yǐyì-dàiláo wait at one's ease for an exhausted enemy or opponent

【以言代法】 yǐyán-dàifǎ arbitrary intervention by persons in authority

【以怨报德】 yǐyuàn-bàodé return evil for good; requite kindness with ingratitude

【以正视听】 yǐzhèng-shìtīng in order to ensure a correct understanding of the facts

【以至】 yǐzhì 1.（表示延伸）down to; up to 2.（表示结果）to such an extent as to . . . ; so . . . that . . .

【以致】 yǐzhì so that; as a result; with the result that; consequently

【以资】 yǐzī as a means of：～鼓励 as an encouragement

苡 (yǐ) 〈*Bot.*〉 Job's tears

【苡米】 yǐmǐ 见"薏米"

【苡仁】 yǐrén 见"薏米"

尾 (yǐ) 1.（马尾上的毛）hairs on a horse's tail 2.（蟋蟀的尾）spikelets on a cricket's tail

（另见"尾"wěi）

迤［迆］(yǐ) extend towards

【迤逦】 yǐlǐ winding; coiling; twisting

蚁［蟻、螘］(yǐ) 〈*Zool.*〉 ant：兵～ soldier ant / 工～ worker ant / 雌～ gyne / 雄～ aner

【蚁巢】 yǐcháo ant nest

【蚁丘】 yǐqiū anthill

【蚁酸】 yǐsuān 〈*Chem.*〉 formic acid; formic (adj.)

倚 (yǐ) 1.（靠）lean on or against; rest on or against：～墙 lean against the wall 2.（仗恃）rely on; count on：～势欺人 take advantage of one's position to bully people 3.（歪；偏）biased; partial：不偏不～ unbiased; impartial

【倚靠】 yǐkào lean on or against; rest on or against

【倚老卖老】 yǐlǎo-màilǎo take advantage of one's seniority

【倚仗】 yǐzhàng rely on; count on：～权势 rely on one's power and position; count on one's powerful connections

椅 (yǐ) chair

【椅子】 yǐ·zi chair：给～换新套子 re-cover a chair

【椅子扶手】 yǐ·zi fúshǒu armrest；the arms of a chair

【椅子套】 yǐ·zitào loose cover

旖 (yǐ)

【旖旎】 yǐnǐ gentle and lovely：～的风光 a gentle and lovely scene

酏 (yǐ)

【酏剂】 yǐjì 〈*Chem*.〉 elixir

一 (yì) one；first
(请见"一"yī)

义［義］ (yì) 1.（正义）justice；righteousness：仁～ benevolence and righteousness **2**.（正义的）righteous；equitable；just：～战 just war **3**.（情谊）human ties；relationship **4**.（抚养或拜认的）adopted；adoptive：～父 adoptive father **5**.（意义）meaning；significance：词～ the meaning of a word **6**.（人工制造的）artificial；false：～齿 false tooth

【义不容辞】 yìbùróngcí have an unshirkable duty；be duty- bound

【义愤】 yìfèn righteous indignation；moral indignation：～填膺 be filled with righteous indignation

【义举】 yìjǔ a magnanimous act undertaken for the public good

【义卖】 yìmài a sale of goods for charity or other worthy causes；charity bazaar

【义母】 yìmǔ adoptive mother

【义女】 yìnǚ adopted daughter；foster daughter

【义旗】 yìqí the banner of an army fighting a just war；banner of righteousness

【义气】 yì·qi code of brotherhood；personal loyalty；be loyal to one's friends

【义无反顾】 yìwúfǎngù honor permits no turning back；be duty-bound not to turn back

【义务】 yìwù 1.（责任）duty；obligation；liability：保险～ insurance liability / 契约～ contractual obligation 不承担～ make no commitment to sth. / 承担～ incur a liability / 尽～ do one's duty / 履行～ meet liability **2**.（不要报酬的）volunteer；voluntary：～劳动 voluntary labor

【义务兵】 yìwùbīng compulsory serviceman

【义务兵役制】 yìwù bīngyìzhì compulsory military service；conscription

【义形于色】 yìxíngyúsè with indignation written on one's face

【义演】 yìyǎn benefit performance

【义勇军】 yìyǒngjūn army of volunteers；volunteers

【义勇军进行曲】 Yìyǒngjūn Jìnxíngqǔ March of the Volunteers

【义正词严】 yìzhèng-cíyán speak sternly out of a sense of justice；speak with the force of justice

【义肢】 yìzhī artificial lamb

【义子】 yìzǐ foster son；adopted child

议［議］ (yì) 1.（意见）opinion；view **2**.（商议）discuss；exchange views on；talk over：～而不决 discuss sth. without reaching a decision

【议案】 yì'àn proposal；motion：提出～ make a proposal

【议程】 yìchéng agenda：列入～ place on the agenda / 你今天的～是什么？What's on your agenda today?

【议订】 yìdìng negotiate：～和约 negotiate a peace treaty

【议定】 yìdìng agree

【议定书】 yìdìngshū protocol：附加～ additional protocol / 贸易～ trade protocol

【议和】 yìhé negotiate peace

【议会】 yìhuì parliament；legislative assembly

【议价】 yìjià 1.（议定价格）negotiate a price **2**.（议定的价格）negotiated price

【议决】 yìjué resolve after deliberation；pass a resolution

【议论】 yìlùn 1.（发表意见）comment；talk；discuss：～纷纷 make all sorts of comments **2**.（所发表的意见）comments；opinions：发表～ make comments；give one's opinions

【议论文】 yìlùnwén argumentation；argumentative writing

【议事】 yìshì discuss official business

【议事日程】 yìshì rìchéng agenda：提到～ place on the agenda

【议题】 yìtí subject under discussion；topic

for discussion

【议席】 yìxí seat in legislative assembly

【议员】 yìyuán 1.(泛指) member of a legislative assembly 2.(美国的) Congressman (m.); Congresswoman (f.) 3.(英国的) Member of Parliament

【议院】 yìyuàn legislative assembly; parliament; congress

【议长】 yìzhǎng speaker; president

【议政】 yìzhèng discuss political affairs and other major and important matters

亿[億] (yì) a hundred million

【亿万】 yìwàn hundreds of millions; millions upon millions

【亿万富翁】 yìwàn fùwēng billionaire; zillionaire

艺[藝] (yì) 1.(技能) skill 2.(艺术) art

【艺妓】 yìjì geisha; geisha girl (Jap.)

【艺龄】 yìlíng length of sb's artistic career

【艺名】 yìmíng stage name

【艺人】 yìrén 1.(演员) actor or artist 2.(手工艺工人) artisan; handicraftsman

【艺术】 yìshù 1.(文艺) art 2.(方法) skill; art; craft: 领导～ art of leadership 3.(指形状) conforming to good taste

【艺术水准】 yìshù shuǐzhǔn artistic standard: 这座博物馆有很高的～。The museum has high artistic standards.

【艺术体操】 yìshù tǐcāo rhythmic gymnastics

【艺术型】 yìshùxíng artistic type

【艺术性】 yìshùxìng artistic quality; artistry: 鲜花的布置很有～。The flower arrangement is very artistic.

【艺术造诣】 yìshù zàoyì artistic attainment

【艺苑】 yìyuàn the realm of art and literature; art and literary circles

忆[憶] (yì) recall; recollect

【忆及】 yìjí call to mind; remember

【忆旧】 yìjiù recollect the past; recall the bygone days with nostalgia

【忆起】 yìqǐ call to mind; remember; recall

呓[囈、嚚] (yì)

【呓语】 yìyǔ 1.(梦话) talk in one's sleep 2.(胡言乱语) crazy talk; ravings

屹 (yì)

【屹立】 yìlì stand towering like a giant; stand erect

亦 (yì) also; too

【亦步亦趋】 yìbù-yìqū ape sb. at every step; imitate sb's every move; blindly follow suit

【亦即】 yìjí that is; i.e.; namely; viz.

奕 (yì)

【奕奕】 yìyì radiating power and vitality: 神采～ glowing with health and radiating vitality

异[異] (yì) 1.(不同) different: 求同存～ seek common ground while reserving differences 2.(奇异) strange; unusual; extraordinary: ～事 strange happening 3.(惊异) surprise 4.(另外的) other; another: ～地 a strange land 5.(分离) separate: 离～ divorce

【异邦】 yìbāng a foreign country

【异彩】 yìcǎi 1.(指光彩) extraordinary splendor 2.(指成就) extraordinary achievement: 大放～ a display of a variety of remarkable achievements

【异常】 yìcháng 1.(不寻常) unusual; abnormal: ～现象 abnormal phenomena 2.(非常) extremely; exceedingly; particularly: ～困难 extremely difficult

【异地】 yìdì strange land; strange place

【异端】 yìduān heterodoxy; heresy

【异端邪说】 yìduān-xiéshuō unorthodox preaching

【异父兄弟】 yìfù xiōngdì half brothers

【异国】 yìguó foreign country; exotic (adj.): ～情调 an exotic atmosphere

【异乎寻常】 yìhū-xúncháng unusual; extraordinary; off-the-wall: 10月份下了一场～的大雪。An abnormal amount of snow fell in October.

【异化】 yìhuà 1.〈*Philos.*〉 alienation 2.〈*Phonet.*〉 dissimilation

【异己】 yìjǐ dissident; alien

【异教】 yìjiào paganism; heathenism

【异教徒】 yìjiàotú pagan; heathen

【异军突起】 yìjūn-tūqǐ a new force suddenly coming to the fore
【异口同声】 yìkǒu-tóngshēng with one voice; in unison
【异曲同工】 yìqǔ-tónggōng different tunes rendered with equal skill; different in approach but equally satisfactory in result
【异同】 yìtóng similarities and differences
【异味】 yìwèi 1.(指美味) rare delicacy 2.(指气味) peculiar smell
【异物】 yìwù 1.〈*Med.*〉 foreign matter; foreign body 2.(指物品) rarity
【异乡】 yìxiāng foreign land; strange land
【异想天开】 yìxiǎng-tiānkāi indulge in the wildest fantasy; have a very fantastic idea
【异型】 yìxíng allotype
【异姓】 yìxìng different in surname
【异性】 yìxìng 1.(指性别) the opposite sex 2.(指性质) different in nature
【异性按摩】 yìxìng ànmó massage by opposite sex
【异言】 yìyán 〈*written*〉 dissenting words
【异样】 yìyàng 1.(不同) difference 2.(不寻常) unusual; peculiar
【异议】 yìyì objection; dissent: 持～ have different views / 提出～ raise an objection to
【异族】 yìzú different race or nation
【异族人】 yìzúrén people from different race or nation

抑 (yì) 1.(压制) restrain; repress; curb 2.(可是) but 3.(或是) or
【抑扬】 yìyáng rise and fall; modulate: ～顿挫 cadence; modulation in tone
【抑郁】 yìyù depressed; despondent; gloomy
【抑郁不欢】 yìyù-bùhuān depressed and unhappy
【抑止】 yìzhǐ restrain; check
【抑制】 yìzhì 1.(控制) restrain; control; check: ～价格 check price / ～通货膨胀 control the inflation / ～需求 restrain demand 2.〈*Physiol.*〉 inhibition: 中枢～ central inhibition

轶 (yì)
【轶事】 yìshì anecdote
【轶闻】 yìwén officially unrecorded events

役 (yì) 1.(出劳力的事) labor; service: 劳～ forced labor 2.(兵役) military service: 现～军人 soldiers on service 3.(役使) use as a servant 4.(战役) battle
【役畜】 yìchù draught animal; beast of burden
【役龄】 yìlíng 1.(指年龄) enlistment age 2.(指年数) years on service
【役使】 yìshǐ work (an animal); enslave

疫 (yì) epidemic disease; pestilence
【疫病】 yìbìng epidemic disease
【疫苗】 yìmiáo 〈*Med.*〉 vaccine
【疫情】 yìqíng information about and appraisal of an epidemic; epidemic situation
【疫水】 yìshuǐ infected water

毅 (yì) firm; resolute: 刚～ fortitude
【毅力】 yìlì willpower; will; stamina
【毅然】 yìrán resolutely; firmly; determinedly

译[譯] (yì) translate; interpret
【译本】 yìběn translation
【译电】 yìdiàn 1.(把文字译成电码) encipher; encode 2.(把电码译成文字) decipher; decode
【译电员】 yìdiànyuán decoder; code clerk; cryptographer
【译码】 yìmǎ decode; decipher
【译名】 yìmíng translated term or name
【译述】 yìshù translate freely
【译文】 yìwén translated text; translation
【译意风】 yìyìfēng simultaneous interpretation equipment
【译音】 yìyīn transliteration
【译员】 yìyuán 1.(口译的) interpreter 2.(笔译的) translator
【译者】 yìzhě translator
【译制】 yìzhì dub
【译制片】 yìzhìpiàn dubbed film
【译注】 yìzhù translate and annotate
【译作】 yìzuò translations

驿[驛] (yì)
【驿道】 yìdào post road
【驿站】 yìzhàn post

易 (yì) 1.(容易) easy: ～学 easy to learn 2.(平易) amiable: 平～近人 amiable and easy of access 3.(改变) change: 移风～俗

change customs and habits; transform social traditions 4.（交换）exchange：以货～货 barter

【易腐商品】 yìfǔ shāngpǐn perishable commodity

【易货】 yìhuò barter

【易货方式】 yìhuò fāngshì barter system

【易货贸易】 yìhuò màoyì barter; barter trade

【易货协定】 yìhuò xiédìng barter arrangement

【易拉罐】 yìlāguàn pop-top can; ring-pull tin

【易拉罐式的】 yìlāguànshì·de pop-top; ring-pull

【易磨损部件】 yìmósǔn bùjiàn quick wearing parts

【易燃】 yìrán inflammable; combustible：～货物 inflammable cargo / 我们切不可带～物品上车。We must not take combustible goods aboard.

【易如反掌】 yìrúfǎnzhǎng as easy as turning one's hand over; as easy as falling off a log

【易手】 yìshǒu change hands

【易碎】 yìsuì breakable

【易损】 yìsǔn fragile

【易销货物】 yìxiāo huòwù marketable goods

【易帜】 yìzhì change the flag

诣（yì） 1.（看望）call on（sb. one respects）; visit 2.（造诣）（academic or technical）attainments

翌（yì） next：～晨 next morning / ～年 next year / ～日 next day

翼（yì） 1.（翅膀）wing 2.（机翼）wing：副～ aileron / 襟～ wing flap / 三角形～ delta wing / 水平尾～ tail plane / 右～ starboard wing / 左～ port wing 3.（侧）flank

【翼侧】 yìcè 〈*Mil.*〉 flank

【翼轨】 yìguǐ 〈*Railway*〉 wing rail

【翼形螺母】 yìxíng luómǔ wing nut; butterfly nut

【翼翼】 yìyì cautiously：小心～ with exceptional caution; very carefully

【翼展】 yìzhǎn 〈*Aeron.*〉 wingspread; wingspan

【翼子板】 yìzǐbǎn 〈*Auto*〉 fender（AmE.）; wing（BrE.）

益（yì） 1.（好处）benefit; profit; advantage：受～良多 derive much benefit 2.（增加）increase：延年～寿 prolong life 3.（更加）all the more; increasingly：多多～善 the more the better 4.（有益的）beneficial

【益虫】 yìchóng beneficial insect

【益处】 yì·chu benefit; profit; good

【益发】 yìfā increasingly; all the more

【益加】 yìjiā increasingly

【益母草】 yìmǔcǎo 〈*Bot.*〉 motherwort

【益鸟】 yìniǎo beneficial bird

【益寿】 yìshòu lengthen one's life

【益友】 yìyǒu friend and mentor：良师～ good teacher and helpful friend

溢（yì） 1.（溢出）overflow; spill over 2.（过分）excessive

【溢出】 yìchū overflow; spill over

【溢价】 yìjià at a premium; premium price

【溢美】 yìměi undeserved praise; compliment

【溢美之言】 yìměizhīyán words of fulsome praise

【溢于言表】 yìyú-yánbiǎo shows between the lines; in overtones

逸（yì） 1.（安逸）ease; leisure：劳～结合 strike a proper balance between work and leisure; alternate work with relaxation 2.（逃跑）escape; flee 3.（散失）be lost 4.（超过一般）excel all others：～群 excel all others

【逸乐】 yìlè comfort and pleasure

【逸失良机】 yìshī liángjī let slip an opportunity

【逸事】 yìshì anecdote

【逸文】 yìwén ancient writings no longer extant

【逸闻】 yìwén officially unrecorded events

意（yì） 1.（意思）meaning; idea 2.（心愿）wish; desire; intention：好～ good will 3.（料想）expect; anticipate：出其不～ catch sb. unawares 4.（暗示）suggestion; hint; trace：颇有秋～ make one feel that autumn has set in

【意大利】 Yìdàlì Italy; Italian（adj.）‖ 意大利人 Italian

【意大利面条】 Yìdàlì miàntiáo spaghetti

【意大利馅饼】 Yìdàlì xiànbǐng pizza

【意大利语】 Yìdàlìyǔ Italian（language）

【意会】 yìhuì sense：只可～ can be sensed

【意简言赅】 yìjiǎn-yángāi a few simple ideas

succinctly expressed

【意见】 yì·jian 1.(看法或想法)idea；view；opinion；suggestion：一点～ some advice / 一条～ a piece of advice / 发表～ express one's opinion / 交换～ exchange views / 征求～ collect others' opinions 2.(反对或不满意)objection；differing opinion；complaint：我对她很有～。I have a lot of complaints about her.

【意见簿】 yì·jianbù visitor's book；customers' book

【意见箱】 yì·jianxiāng suggestion box

【意境】 yìjìng artistic conception

【意料】 yìliào anticipate；expect：～之外 unexpected happening

【意念】 yìniàn idea；thought

【意气】 yìqì 1.(意志和气概)will and spirit：～昂扬 in high spirits 2.(志趣和性格)disposition；temperament：～相投 be congenial with each other 3.(不正常情绪)personal feelings：～之争 a dispute caused by personal feelings / 闹～ give vent to one's emotional feelings

【意气风发】 yìqì-fēngfā high-spirited and vigorous；daring and energetic

【意趣】 yìqù interest and charm

【意识】 yì·shí 1.〈*Philos.*〉consciousness；sense：当代～ modern sense 2.(觉察)be conscious of；awake to；realize：我没有～到这个问题的严重性。I was not aware of the seriousness of this matter. / 他～到机会来了。He awoke to his opportunities.

【意识流】 yì·shíliú stream of consciousness

【意识流小说】 yì·shíliú xiǎoshuō the stream of consciousness

【意识形态】 yì·shí xíngtài 〈*Philos.*〉ideology；ideologic (adj.)

【意思】 yì·si 1.(语义)meaning；idea 2.(意见,愿望)opinion；wish；desire 3.(心意)a token of affection, appreciation, gratitude, etc. 4.(趋势)look like；seem：天有点要下雨的～。It looks like rain. 5.(情趣)interest；fun：游泳很有～。Swimming is a lot of fun.

【意图】 yìtú intention；intent

【意外】 yìwài 1.(意料之外)unexpected；unforeseen：～的消息 unexpected news；be taken by surprise 2.(不幸事件)accident；mishap：～事件 an accident

【意外保险】 yìwài bǎoxiǎn accident insurance；casualty insurance

【意味】 yìwèi 1.(内含)meaning；significance；implication：～深长 be of great significance 2.(情趣)interest；overtone；flavor

【意味着】 yìwèi·zhe mean；show；indicate；signify

【意想】 yìxiǎng imagine；expect

【意向】 yìxiàng intention；purpose

【意向书】 yìxiàngshū letter of intention；letter of intent

【意义】 yìyì 1.(意思)meaning；sense：在某种～上 in a sense 2.(价值；作用)significance；importance：现实～ realistic significance

【意译】 yìyì free translation

【意愿】 yìyuàn wish；desire；aspiration

【意旨】 yìzhǐ intention；wish；will：违背某人的～ do against the instruction of sb.

【意志】 yìzhì will；willpower：～坚强 with a strong and firm will

【意中人】 yìzhōngrén the person one is in love with；person of one's heart

薏 (yì)

【薏米】 yìmǐ the seed of Job's tears

【薏仁米】 yìrénmǐ 同"薏米"

【薏苡】 yìyǐ 〈*Bot.*〉Job's tears

臆[肊] (yì) 1.(胸)chest 2.(主观的)subjectively

【臆测】 yìcè conjecture；surmise；guess

【臆断】 yìduàn assume；suppose

【臆说】 yìshuō assumption；supposition

【臆想】 yìxiǎng imagine subjectively

【臆造】 yìzào fabricate

镱 (yì) 〈*Chem.*〉ytterbium (元素符号 Yb)

癔 (yì)

【癔病】 yìbìng 〈*Med.*〉hysteria

肄 (yì) study

【肄业】 yìyè study in school；study at college

熠 (yì) bright；brilliant

【熠熠】 yìyì glistening; dazzling: ～生辉 shine dazzlingly

懿（yì） virtuous; exemplary

【懿德】 yìdé admirable virtue

【懿旨】 yìzhǐ the empress's decree

yin

因（yīn） 1.（原因）cause; reason: 内～ internal cause / 外～ external cause 2.（因为）because of; as a result of; for

【因病】 yīnbìng due to illness; because of illness: ～请假 ask for leave due to illness

【因材施教】 yīncái-shījiào teach students in accordance with their aptitude

【因此】 yīncǐ therefore; for this reason: 他摔坏了腿，～没能来。He has broken his leg and therefore he could not come.

【因地制宜】 yīndì-zhìyí suit measures to local conditions: ～地积极发展农业机械工业 energetically develop farm machinery industry in the light of local conditions

【因而】 yīn'ér thus; as a result; with the result that

【因公】 yīngōng on duty; on business: ～殉职 death in line of duty

【因果】 yīnguǒ 1.（原因和结果）cause and effect 2.〈*Religion*〉karma; preordained fate

【因果报应】 yīnguǒ-bào·ying 〈*Buddhism*〉 karma; retribution for sin; punitive justice

【因祸得福】 yīnhuò-défú profit from a misfortune

【因陋就简】 yīnlòu-jiùjiǎn make do with whatever is available; do things simply and thriftily

【因纽特人】 Yīnniǔtèrén Inuit; N. American Eskimo

【因式】 yīnshì 〈*Math.*〉 factor

【因势利导】 yīnshì-lìdǎo adroitly guide action according to circumstances

【因数】 yīnshù 〈*Math.*〉 factor

【因素】 yīnsù 1.（指成分）element 2.（指条件）element: 不安定～ unstable factors; destabilizing factors / 不利～ unfavorable factors / 决定性～ decisive factor / 调动一切积极～ bring every positive factors into play

【因为】 yīn·wèi 1.〈*conj.*〉because; for; on account of 2.〈*Math.*〉since; because（符号为∵）

【因袭】 yīnxí follow; copy

【因小失大】 yīnxiǎo-shīdà try to save a little only to lose a lot

【因循】 yīnxún 1.（沿袭）follow; continue in the same old rut 2.（迟延拖拉）procrastinate

【因循守旧】 yīnxún-shǒujiù stick to old ways; follow the beaten path

【因噎废食】 yīnyē-fèishí give up eating for fear of choking; refrain from doing sth. necessary for fear of a slight risk

【因缘】 yīnyuán 1.〈*Buddhism*〉cause; principal and subsidiary causes 2.（缘分）predestined relationship

【因子】 yīnzǐ 1.（因数）factor 2.（因式）factor

茵［裀］（yīn） mattress: 绿草如～ a carpet of green glass

洇［湮］（yīn） absorb and spread

姻［婣］（yīn） 1.（婚姻）marriage: 联～ connect by marriage 2.（姻亲关系）relation by marriage: ～兄弟 brother-in-law

【姻亲】 yīnqīn relation by marriage: ～关系 relationship by marriage; affinity

【姻缘】 yīnyuán the happy fate which brings lovers together

氤（yīn）

【氤氲】 yīnyūn dense; thick: 烟云～ a thick layer of smoke

铟（yīn） 〈*Chem.*〉indium（元素符号 In）

阴［陰、隂］（yīn） 1.（指天气）overcast; cloudy 2.（无阳光处）shade: 在树～下 under the shade of trees 3.（隐藏不露）hidden; secret; sinister 4.（带负电的）negative: ～离子 negative ion; anion 5.（山之北）north of a hill 6.（水之南）south of a river 7.（指月亮）the moon; lunar 8.（凹的）intaglio: ～文 characters cut in intaglio 9.（阴部）private parts; pudenda 10.（阴阳之一）*yin*

【阴暗】 yīn'àn dark; gloomy: ～的角落 dark corners

【阴暗面】 yīn'ànmiàn the dark side of things

【阴部】 yīnbù 〈*Anat.*〉 private parts; pudenda

【阴沉】 yīnchén cloudy; overcast; gloomy; somber

【阴沉沉】 yīnchénchén cloudy; overcast; gloomy; somber: 天色～的。It looks gloomy.

【阴唇】 yīnchún 〈*Anat.*〉 labium; lip of the pudendum

【阴错阳差】 yīncuò-yángchā a strange combination of circumstances

【阴道】 yīndào 〈*Anat.*〉 vagina

【阴道隔膜】 yīndào gémó （女用避孕用品） Dutch cap

【阴蒂】 yīndì 〈*Anat.*〉 clitoris

【阴电】 yīndiàn 〈*Physics*〉 negative electricity

【阴风】 yīnfēng **1.**（寒风）chilly wind **2.**（阴暗处来的风）sinister wind

【阴干】 yīngān be placed in the shade to dry; dry in the shade

【阴沟】 yīngōu sewer; drain

【阴晦】 yīnhuì shady; dark; dismal

【阴魂】 yīnhún soul; spirit

【阴极】 yīnjí negative pole; negative electrode; cathode

【阴间】 yīnjiān the nether world

【阴茎】 yīnjīng 〈*Anat.*〉 penis; penes

【阴茎包皮】 yīnjīng bāopí 〈*Anat.*〉 prepuce

【阴茎头】 yīnjīngtóu 〈*Anat.*〉 glans penis

【阴茎头冠】 yīnjīngtóuguān 〈*Anat.*〉 corona

【阴冷】 yīnlěng **1.**（阴沉寒冷）gloomy and cold; raw **2.**（阴沉冷酷）somber; glum

【阴离子】 yīnlízǐ negative ion

【阴历】 yīnlì lunar calendar

【阴凉】 yīnliáng **1.**（凉爽）shady and cool **2.**（阴凉的地方）cool place; shade

【阴霾】 yīnmái haze

【阴谋】 yīnmóu **1.**（指策划）plot secretly; conspire: ～推翻政府 conspire to overthrow the government **2.**（指计谋）plot; scheme; conspiracy: ～诡计 schemes and intrigues

【阴谋集团】 yīnmóu jítuán conspiratorial clique

【阴谋家】 yīnmóujiā schemer; intriguer; conspirator

【阴谋推翻政府罪】 yīnmóu tuīfān zhèngfǔzuì offense of conspiring to overthrow the government

【阴谋武装叛乱罪】 yīnmóu wǔzhuāng pànluànzuì offense of plotting an armed rebellion

【阴囊】 yīnnáng 〈*Anat.*〉 scrotum

【阴囊炎】 yīnnángyán 〈*Med.*〉 scrotitis

【阴平】 yīnpíng high and level tone

【阴森】 yīnsēn gloomy; gruesome; ghastly

【阴私】 yīnsī shameful secret

【阴天】 yīntiān overcast sky; cloudy day

【阴文】 yīnwén characters cut in intaglio

【阴险】 yīnxiǎn sinister; insidious; treacherous

【阴性】 yīnxìng **1.**〈*Med.*〉 negative: ～反应 negative reaction **2.**〈*Phonet.*〉 feminine gender

【阴阳】 yīnyáng *yin* and *yang*; the two opposing principles in nature

【阴阳怪气】 yīnyáng-guàiqì **1.**（指说话方式）mystifying; enigmatic; deliberately ambiguous **2.**（指人）eccentric; queer; cynical

【阴阳先生】 yīnyáng xiānshēng geomancer

【阴影】 yīnyǐng **1.**（影子）shadow **2.**〈*Med.*〉 spot; shadow

【阴雨】 yīnyǔ overcast and rainy; cloudy and rainy

【阴雨天】 yīnyǔtiān cloudy and rainy day

【阴郁】 yīnyù gloomy; dismal; depressed

【阴云】 yīnyún dark clouds: ～密布。The sky is covered with dark clouds.

音（yīn） **1.**（声音）sound: 隔～ soundproof / 调～ tune up **2.**（消息）news; tidings **3.**（音质）tone: 纯～ pure tone; simple tone / 复～ complex tone

【音标】 yīnbiāo phonetic alphabet; phonetic symbol: 国际～ the International Phonetic Alphabet

【音波】 yīnpō sound wave

【音叉】 yīnchā 〈*Music*〉 diapason; tuning fork

【音带】 yīndài **1.**（录音带）tape; magnetic tape; cassette **2.**〈*Anat.*〉 the vocal cords

【音调】 yīndiào **1.**〈*Music*〉 tone; tonal (adj.) **2.**〈*Physics*〉 pitch

【音读】 yīndú pronunciation

【音符】 yīnfú 〈*Music*〉 note：二全～ breve / 全～ semi-breve / 二分～ half note；minim / 四分～ quarter note；crotchet / 八分～ eighth note；quaver 十六分～ sixteenth note；semi-quaver / 三十二分～ thirty-second note；demisemi-quaver
【音管】 yīnguǎn 〈*Music*〉 pipes
【音阶】 yīnjiē 〈*Music*〉 scale
【音节】 yīnjié 〈*Phonet.*〉 syllable；syllabic (adj.)
【音节文字】 yīnjié wénzì syllabic language
【音孔】 yīnkǒng 〈*Music*〉 sound hole
【音孔花圈】 yīnkǒng huāquān 〈*Music*〉 rosette
【音量】 yīnliàng volume
【音量控制】 yīnliàng kòngzhì volume control
【音频】 yīnpín 〈*Physics*〉 audio frequency
【音品】 yīnpǐn 〈*Music*〉 frets
【音强】 yīnqiáng the loudness of a sound
【音儿】 yīnr 1.(声音) voice 2.(话里的含意) implication：听话听～ listen for the meaning behind sb's words
【音容】 yīnróng 〈*written*〉 the likeness of the deceased：～笑貌 one's lovely voice and happy countenance
【音色】 yīnsè tone color；timbre
【音色键】 yīnsèjiàn 〈*Music*〉 stop lever
【音色旋钮】 yīnsè xuánniǔ 〈*Music*〉 tone control
【音素】 yīnsù 〈*Phonet.*〉 phoneme
【音速】 yīnsù 〈*Physics*〉 velocity of sound；sonic (adj.)：超～ supersonic / 高超～ hypersonic / 跨～ transonic / 亚～ subsonic
【音位】 yīnwèi 〈*Phonet.*〉 phoneme
【音位学】 yīnwèixué 〈*Phonet.*〉 phonology
【音箱】 yīnxiāng speaker；loudspeaker box
【音箱护栅】 yīnxiāng hùshān grille
【音箱箱体】 yīnxiāng xiāngtǐ cabinet
【音响】 yīnxiǎng 1.(声音) sound；acoustics 2.(音响设备) stereo；hi-fi；music center
【音响系统】 yīnxiǎng xìtǒng sound system
【音响效果】 yīnxiǎng xiàoguǒ sound effects；acoustics：这座新音乐厅的～非常好。The acoustics of the new concert hall are excellent.
【音像】 yīnxiàng audio and video；sound and video recording
【音像商店】 yīnxiàng shāngdiàn video shop
【音像市场】 yīnxiàng shìchǎng tape market
【音信】 yīnxìn mail；message；news：互通～ communicate with each other；be in correspondence with each other
【音译】 yīnyì transliterate；transliteration (n.)
【音域】 yīnyù 〈*Music*〉 diapason；range
【音乐】 yīnyuè music
【音乐茶座】 yīnyuè cházuò music tea-cafe
【音乐电视】 yīnyuè diànshì Music TV (MTV)
【音乐会】 yīnyuèhuì concert
【音乐家】 yīnyuèjiā musician
【音乐厅】 yīnyuètíng concert hall；music hall
【音乐小丑】 yīnyuè xiǎochǒu musical clown
【音韵学】 yīnyùnxué phonology
【音障】 yīnzhàng 〈*Aeron.*〉 sound barrier；sonic barrier
【音质】 yīnzhì 1.(指属性) tone quality 2.(指逼真程度) acoustic fidelity

喑[瘖] (yīn)

【喑哑】 yīnyǎ lose one's voice

殷 (yīn) 1.(丰富) abundant；rich 2.(殷切) eager；deep；ardent 3.(殷勤) eagerly；keenly；enthusiastically
(另见"殷"yān)
【殷富】 yīnfù well-off；rich
【殷富人家】 yīnfù rénjiā well-off family
【殷富之人】 yīnfùzhīrén a man of ample means
【殷切】 yīnqiè ardent；eager
【殷勤】 yīnqín eagerly；keenly；with hospitality
【殷实】 yīnshí well-off；substantial

吟[唫] (yín) 1.(吟咏) chant；recite 2.(古诗) song, a type of classical poetry 3.(动物叫声) the cry of certain animals
【吟诗】 yínshī recite poems；hum verse
【吟诵】 yínsòng chant；recite
【吟味】 yínwèi recite with relish；recite with appreciation
【吟咏】 yínyǒng recite with a cadence；chant

银 (yín) 1.〈*Chem.*〉 silver：纯～ sterling silver (元素符号 Ag) 2.(跟货币有关的) currency；money 3.(银色的) silver-colored

【银白】 yínbái silvery white
【银币】 yínbì silver coin
【银箔】 yínbó silver paper
【银耳】 yín'ěr tremella
【银发】 yínfà silver hair
【银根】 yíngēn 〈*Econ.*〉 money market; money：～紧 tight / ～松 easy
【银行】 yínháng bank：中国～ China Bank / 中国工商～ Industrial and Commercial Bank of China / 中国建设～ China Construction Bank / 中国人民～ People's Bank of China / 中国农业～ Agricultural Bank of China
【银行家】 yínhángjiā banker
【银行信用卡】 yínháng xìnyòngkǎ bank card; banker's card; bank credit card
【银行账户】 yínháng zhànghù bank account
【银河】 Yínhé 〈*Astron.*〉 Galaxy; the Milky Way
【银河系】 Yínhéxì 〈*Astron.*〉 galaxy; galactic (adj.)
【银狐】 yínhú silver fox
【银灰】 yínhuī silver grey
【银婚】 yínhūn silver wedding
【银匠】 yínjiàng silversmith
【银矿】 yínkuàng silver mine
【银两】 yínliǎng tael
【银楼】 yínlóu silverware shop
【银幕】 yínmù screen; projection screen：宽～ wide screen
【银牌】 yínpái silver medal
【银屏】 yínpíng 1.（电视屏幕）television screen 2.（电视）television
【银器】 yínqì silverware
【银钱】 yínqián money：～交易 deal in cash
【银色】 yínsè silvery
【银鼠】 yínshǔ 〈*Zool.*〉 *weasel*; *least weasel*
【银条】 yíntiáo silver bar; silver bullion
【银团】 yíntuán finance group formed by bank
【银锌电池】 yínxīn diànchí smee cell
【银杏】 yínxìng 〈*Bot.*〉 ginkgo
【银鱼】 yínyú 〈*Zool.*〉 *icefish*; *Cuvier's icefish*
【银元】 yínyuán 同"银圆"
【银圆】 yínyuán silver dollar
【银质奖章】 yínzhì jiǎngzhāng silver medal
【银朱】 yínzhū 〈*Chem.*〉 vermilion
【银子】 yín·zi silver

淫[婬[3,4]] (yín) 1.（过多）excessive：～雨 excessive rains 2.（放纵）loose; wanton：骄奢～逸 lordly, luxurious, loose and idle; wallowing in luxury and pleasure 3.（色情的）obscene; pornographic：～画 obscene picture / ～书 pornographic book 4.（淫荡）licentious; lewd; lascivious：～心 sexual lust
【淫荡】 yíndàng licentious; lewd; lascivious
【淫妇】 yínfù licentious woman
【淫棍】 yíngùn lewd man
【淫秽】 yínhuì 1.（淫乱）promiscuous; licentious; salacious 2.（色情）pornographic; obscene
【淫乱】 yínluàn promiscuous; licentious; salacious
【淫威】 yínwēi abuse of power; despotic power

霪 (yín) excessive
【霪雨】 yínyǔ excessive rains

引 (yǐn) 1.（牵引）draw; stretch 2.（引导）lead; guide：～路 lead the way 3.（离开）leave：～避 make way for; keep clear of 4.（伸着）stretch：～项 crane one's neck 5.（引起）cause; make 6.（用来作证）quote; cite：～某人的话 quote sb. 7.（勾引）lure; attract：～入圈套 lure into a trap; ensnare
【引爆】 yǐnbào ignite; detonate
【引柴】 yǐnchái kindling
【引产】 yǐnchǎn induced labor
【引出】 yǐnchū draw forth; lead to：～结论 draw a conclusion
【引导】 yǐndǎo 1.（指引）guide; lead 2.〈*Computer*〉boot：重新～ reboot
【引导扇区】 yǐndǎo shànqū 〈*Computer*〉 boot section
【引逗】 yǐndòu 1.（挑逗）tantalize; tease 2.（引诱）lure; entice
【引渡】 yǐndù 〈*Law*〉 extradite; extradition (n.)
【引渡方式】 yǐndù fāngshì form of extradition
【引渡请求书】 yǐndù qǐngqiúshū demandant of extradition
【引渡人】 yǐndùrén deliverer

【引渡逃犯】 yǐndù táofàn surrender of fugitive
【引渡条约】 yǐndù tiáoyuē extradition treaty
【引渡罪犯】 yǐndù zuìfàn delivery of offender
【引而不发】 yǐn'érbùfā draw the bow but not discharge the arrow
【引发】 yǐnfā 〈*Chem.*〉 initiation
【引吭高歌】 yǐnháng-gāogē sing joyfully in a loud voice; sing heartily
【引航】 yǐnháng 〈*Naut.*〉 pilotage
【引航员】 yǐnyángyuán 〈*Naut.*〉 pilot
【引号】 yǐnhào quotation marks: 单～ single quotation marks (' ') / 双～ double quotation marks (" ") / 打上～ put quotation marks on
【引河】 yǐnhé **1.** (引水的河道) irrigation channel **2.** (减河) diversion canal
【引火烧身】 yǐnhuǒ-shāoshēn draw fire against oneself; make self-criticism to encourage criticism from others
【引见】 yǐnjiàn introduce sb. to; present sb. to
【引荐】 yǐnjiàn recommend
【引进】 yǐnjìn **1.** (进口) import; introduce from elsewhere: ～外国技术和设备 import foreign technology and equipment / ～外资 introduce foreign capital **2.** (引荐) recommend
【引经据典】 yǐnjīng-jùdiǎn quote the classics; copiously quote authoritative works
【引颈】 yǐnjǐng crane one's neck
【引咎】 yǐnjiù 〈*written*〉 hold oneself responsible for a serious mistake; take the blame: ～辞职 take the blame and resign / ～自责 bear the blame and reproach oneself
【引狼入室】 yǐnlángrùshì invite a wolf into the house; open the door to a dangerous foe
【引力】 yǐnlì 〈*Physics*〉 gravitation; gravitational force; attraction: 万有～ universal gravitation
【引流】 yǐnliú 〈*Med.*〉 drainage
【引路】 yǐnlù lead the way
【引起】 yǐnqǐ give rise to; lead to; set off; touch off; cause; arouse: ～并发症 lead to complications / ～注意 arouse sb's attention; attract attention / 你的错误会～严重的后果。Serious consequences may arise from your mistakes.
【引桥】 yǐnqiáo 〈*Transport*〉 bridge approach
【引擎】 yǐnqíng engine
【引缺泄余】 yǐnquē-xièyú introduce goods in shortage and make over those in surplus
【引人入胜】 yǐnrénrùshèng fascinating; enchanting: ～的小说 an engrossing novel; a gripping novel
【引人注目】 yǐnrénzhùmù noticeable; conspicuous; spectacular
【引人注意】 yǐnrénzhùyì catch the attention
【引入】 yǐnrù lead into; draw into
【引申】 yǐnshēn extend
【引申义】 yǐnshēnyì extended meaning
【引水】 yǐnshuǐ **1.** (领港) pilot a ship into harbor **2.** (引出水) draw or channel water: ～上山 draw water uphill
【引水船】 yǐnshuǐchuán 〈*Naut.*〉 pilot vessel
【引水工程】 yǐnshuǐ gōngchéng diversion works
【引题】 yǐntí eyebrow head
【引体向上】 yǐntǐ xiàngshàng 〈*Sports*〉 chin up
【引退】 yǐntuì retire from office; resign
【引文】 yǐnwén quoted passage; quotation
【引线】 yǐnxiàn **1.** (引信) detonator; fuse **2.** (媒介) go-between
【引信】 yǐnxìn detonator; fuse
【引以为戒】 yǐnyǐwéijiè learn a lesson; take warning
【引以为荣】 yǐnyǐwéiróng feel honored; count it an honor
【引用】 yǐnyòng **1.** (援引) quote; cite: ～证言 adduce evidence **2.** (任用) recommend; appoint
【引诱】 yǐnyòu lure; seduce
【引证】 yǐnzhèng use a quotation as evidence
【引种】 yǐnzhǒng 〈*Agric.*〉 introduce a fine variety
【引子】 yǐn·zi **1.** 〈*Theatre*〉 an actor's opening words **2.** 〈*Music*〉 introductory music **3.** (文字) introductory remarks; introduction **4.** (中药的) an added ingredient
【引座员】 yǐnzuòyuán usher (m.); usherette (f.)

吲 (yǐn) 〈*Chem.*〉 indole

饮 (yǐn) **1.** (喝) drink: ～水 drink water **2.** (饮品) drinks: 冷～ cold drinks **3.** (心

里存着）keep in the heart; nurse
（另见"饮"yìn）

【饮茶】 yǐnchá drink tea

【饮恨】 yǐnhèn 〈*written*〉 nurse a grievance

【饮酒】 yǐnjiǔ drink

【饮酒过度】 yǐnjiǔ guòdù insobriety

【饮料】 yǐnliào drink; beverage: 软～ soft drink

【饮片】 yǐnpiàn 〈*Chin. Med.*〉 small pieces of prepared herbal medicine

【饮泣】 yǐnqì 〈*written*〉 weep in silence

【饮泣吞声】 yǐnqì tūnshēng 〈*written*〉 choked with tears; swallow one's tears

【饮食】 yǐnshí food and drink; diet

【饮食店】 yǐnshídiàn eating house

【饮食卫生】 yǐnshí wèishēng dietetic hygiene: 注意～ pay attention to dietetic hygiene

【饮食学】 yǐnshíxué dietetics; dietetic (adj.) ‖ 饮食学家 dietitian

【饮食业】 yǐnshíyè catering trade

【饮水器】 yǐnshuǐqì drinking bowl; drinker

【饮水思源】 yǐnshuǐ-sīyuán when you drink water, think of its source; never forget where one's happiness comes from

【饮用水】 yǐnyòngshuǐ drinking water; potable water

【饮鸩止渴】 yǐnzhèn-zhǐkě drink poison to quench thirst; seek temporary relief regardless of the consequences

隐［**隱**］(yǐn) 1.（隐藏不露）hidden from view; concealed hidden 2.（潜伏的）latent; dormant; lurking

【隐蔽】 yǐnbì conceal; take cover

【隐藏】 yǐncáng hide; conceal; remain under cover

【隐恶扬善】 yǐn'è-yángshàn cover up sb's faults and publicize his merits; hide sb's wrongdoing and praise his good deeds

【隐伏】 yǐnfú lie concealed; lie low

【隐患】 yǐnhuàn snake in the grass; hidden trouble; hidden danger: 消除～ remove a hidden peril; eliminate any hidden danger

【隐讳】 yǐnhuì avoid mentioning; cover up

【隐晦】 yǐnhuì obscure; veiled

【隐疾】 yǐnjí unmentionable disease

【隐居】 yǐnjū live in seclusion; withdraw from society and live in solitude; be a hermit

【隐瞒】 yǐnmán conceal; hide; hold back: ～真相 conceal the truth

【隐秘】 yǐnmì 1.（掩盖起来）conceal; hide 2.（秘密事）secret: 揭露他人～ expose other's secret

【隐名合伙人】 yǐnmíng héhuǒrén sleeping partner

【隐匿】 yǐnnì hide; go into hiding; lie low

【隐情】 yǐnqíng facts one wishes to hide

【隐忍】 yǐnrěn bear patiently; forbear

【隐射】 yǐnshè insinuate; hint; imply

【隐士】 yǐnshì recluse; hermit

【隐私】 yǐnsī one's secrets; private matters one wants to hide

【隐私权】 yǐnsīquán right of privacy

【隐痛】 yǐntòng secret anguish

【隐退】 yǐntuì go and live in seclusion; retire from political life

【隐形飞机】 yǐnxíng fēijī stealth aircraft

【隐形轰炸机】 yǐnxíng hōngzhàjī stealth bomber

【隐形失业】 yǐnxíng shīyè hidden unemployment

【隐形收入】 yǐnxíng shōurù ghost income; invisible income

【隐形眼镜】 yǐnxíng yǎnjìng contact lens

【隐性】 yǐnxìng recessiveness; recessive (adj.)

【隐姓埋名】 yǐnxìng-máimíng conceal one's identity; keep one's identity hidden; live incognito

【隐隐】 yǐnyǐn indistinct; faint: ～约约 indistinct

【隐喻】 yǐnyù 〈*Linguistics*〉 metaphor

【隐约】 yǐnyuē indistinct; faint: ～记得 remember vaguely

【隐衷】 yǐnzhōng feelings or troubles one wishes to keep to oneself

瘾［**癮**］(yǐn) 1.（嗜好）addiction; habitual craving: 吸毒上～的人 drug addict 2.（兴趣）strong interest

印 (yìn) 1.（印章）seal; stamp; chop 2.（印迹）print; mark: 手～ fingerprint 3.（印刷）print; engrave: 付～ put sth. into print 4.（符合）tally; conform

【印第安人】 Yìndì'ānrén Indian; American

Indian

【印度大麻】 Yìndù dàmá Indian hemp; bhang

【印度教】 Yìndùjiào Hinduism ‖ 印度教徒 Hindu

【印发】 yìnfā print and distribute

【印盒】 yìnhé seal box

【印痕】 yìnhén impression

【印花】 yìnhuā 1.(税票) stamp 2.〈*Textiles*〉 print

【印花布】 yìnhuābù prints; printed calico

【印花税】 yìnhuāshuì stamp duty; stamp tax: 贴～ put on stamp duty

【印鉴】 yìnjiàn a specimen seal impression for checking when making payments

【印泥】 yìnní red ink paste used for seals

【印染】 yìnrǎn printing and dyeing

【印色盒】 yìnsèhé ink pad

【印数】 yìnshù 〈*Printing*〉 printing; impression

【印刷】 yìnshuā print

【印刷电路】 yìnshuā diànlù printed circuit

【印刷电路板】 yìnshuā diànlùbǎn printed circuit board; PCB

【印刷品】 yìnshuāpǐn printed matter

【印台】 yìntái ink pad; stamp pad

【印相】 yìnxiàng 〈*Photog.*〉 print

【印象】 yìnxiàng impression

【印象派】 yìnxiàngpài 1.(艺术流派) impressionism; impressionist school 2.(指该艺术流派的人) impressionist

【印油】 yìnyóu stamp-pad ink

【印章】 yìnzhāng seal; signet; stamp

【印章学】 yìnzhāngxué sigillography

【印证】 yìnzhèng 1.(证明) confirm; corroborate; verify 2.(用来印证的事) evidence; proof

【印子】 yìn·zi mark; trace; print

茚 (yìn) 〈*Chem.*〉 indene

饮 (yìn) give water to drink; water: ～牲口 water the cattle (另见"饮"yǐn)

荫[**廕、蔭**²] (yìn) 1. shade; shady; damp and chilly 2.〈*written*〉 shelter; protect

【荫庇】 yìnbì protect; patronize

【荫蔽】 yìnbì 1.(遮蔽) be shaded or hidden by foliage 2.(隐蔽) cover; conceal

【荫凉】 yìnliáng shady and cool

窨 (yìn) basement

【窨井】 yìnjǐng inspection shaft

ying

应[**應**] (yīng) 1.(答应) answer; respond 2.(答应做) promise; agree; accept 3.(应该) should; ought to (另见"应"yìng)

【应当】 yīngdāng should; ought to

【应得】 yīngdé deserved; due: ～的惩罚 just punishment; well-deserved punishment

【应付单据】 yīngfù dānjù notes payable

【应付债券】 yīngfù zhàiquàn bond payable

【应付账款】 yīngfù zhàngkuǎn account payable

【应该】 yīnggāi should; ought to; must

【应届】 yīngjiè this year

【应届毕业生】 yīngjiè bìyèshēng this year's graduates

【应名儿】 yīngmíngr only in name; nominally

【应收账款】 yīngshōu zhàngkuǎn account receivable

【应有】 yīngyǒu due; proper; deserved

【应有尽有】 yīngyǒu-jìnyǒu have everything that one expects to find

【应允】 yīngyǔn assent; consent

【应征税额】 yīngzhēng shuì'é rateable value; rateable value: 这家商店的～是多少? What's the rateable value of this shop?

英 (yīng) 1.(花) flower 2.(英才) hero; outstanding person: 群～会 a gathering of heroes; a conference of outstanding workers 3.(英国) Britain; Britain (adj.) 4.(英语) English

【英镑】 yīngbàng pound sterling

【英才】 yīngcái person of outstanding ability

【英尺】 yīngchǐ foot (= 0.3048 m.)

【英寸】 yīngcùn inch (= 2.54 cm.)

【英吨】 yīngdūn long ton; gross ton (=1,016 kg)

【英国】 Yīngguó Britain; England ‖ 英国人 British; Englishman (m.); Englishwoman

(f.)

【英国管】 yīngguóguǎn 〈*Music*〉 English horn

【英豪】 yīngháo heroes; outstanding figures

【英吉沙】 Yīngjíshā 〈place〉 Yengisar

【英俊】 yīngjùn 1.(指才能) eminently talented; brilliant 2.(指容貌) handsome and spirited; smart

【英里】 yīnglǐ mile (= 1.6093 km.)

【英烈】 yīngliè heroic; brave; valiant

【英灵】 yīnglíng spirit of the brave departed; spirit of a martyr

【英名】 yīngmíng illustrious name

【英明】 yīngmíng wise; brilliant

【英气】 yīngqì heroic spirit

【英文】 yīngwén English

【英文键盘】 yīngwén jiànpán 〈*Computer*〉 QWERTY keyboard

【英武】 yīngwǔ of soldierly bearing

【英雄】 yīngxióng hero; heroic (adj.)

【英雄无用武之地】 yīngxióng wú yòngwǔ zhī dì a hero with no place to display his prowess; no scope to exercise one's abilities; a fish out of water

【英勇】 yīngyǒng heroic; valiant; brave; gallant

【英语】 yīngyǔ English: 美国～ American English

【英制】 yīngzhì British system

【英姿】 yīngzī heroic bearing

莺［**鶯、鸎**］(yīng) 〈*Zool.*〉 warbler: 黄～ oriole; forest oriole

【莺歌燕舞】 yīnggē-yànwǔ warblers sing and swallows dart; the joy of spring; a scene of prosperity

婴 (yīng) baby; infant

【婴儿】 yīng'ér baby; infant

【婴儿车】 yīng'érchē perambulator; pram: 折叠式～ pushchair

【婴儿床】 yīng'érchuáng crib; cot

【婴儿猝死综合征】 yīng'ér cùsǐ zōnghézhèng SIDS; sudden infant death syndrome

缨 (yīng) 1.(穗儿) tassel 2.(带状物) ribbon

【缨子】 yīng·zi 1.(带状物) ribbon 2.(穗儿) tassel

樱 (yīng) 1.(樱桃) cherry 2.(樱花) oriental cherry

【樱花】 yīnghuā oriental cherry: 日本～ sakura; Japanese flowering cherry

【樱桃】 yīngtáo 〈*Bot.*〉 cherry

鹦 (yīng)

【鹦鹉】 yīngwǔ parrot

【鹦鹉学舌】 yīngwǔ-xuéshé the words of others like a parrot; parrot

罂［**甖**］(yīng) 〈*written*〉 small-mouthed jar

【罂粟】 yīngsù 〈*Bot.*〉 opium poppy

膺 (yīng) 1.(胸) breast: 义愤填～ be filled with righteous indignation 2.(承受) endure; receive; be awarded: 荣～勋章 be awarded a decoration

鹰 (yīng) hawk; eagle

【鹰钩鼻子】 yīnggōubí·zi aquiline nose; Roman nose

【鹰派】 yīngpài hard-line

【鹰派人物】 yīngpài rénwù hard-liner

【鹰犬】 yīngquǎn falcons and hounds; lackeys; hired thugs: ～爪牙 running dogs and attendants

迎 (yíng) 1.(迎接) go to meet; greet; welcome; receive 2.(对着) move towards; meet face to face: ～击 make a head-on attack

【迎宾馆】 yíngbīnguǎn guest house

【迎宾曲】 yíngbīnqǔ strains of welcome march

【迎春】 yíngchūn 〈*Bot.*〉 winter jasmine

【迎风】 yíngfēng 1.(顶风) facing the wind: ～航行 sail close to the wind 2.(随风) down the wind; with the wind: ～招展 flutter in the wind

【迎合】 yínghé cater to; pander to

【迎候】 yínghòu await the arrival of; greet

【迎击】 yíngjī make a head-on attack; fight against

【迎接】 yíngjiē meet; welcome; greet

【迎来送往】 yínglái-sòngwǎng welcome and speed the parting of guests

【迎面】 yíngmiàn head-on; in one's face: ～

碰撞 head-on crash

【迎刃而解】 yíngrèn'érjiě split all the way down once it's been chopped open; be readily solved

【迎头】 yíngtóu head-on; directly: ～赶上 catch up forthwith

【迎新】 yíngxīn 1.(指新年) see the new year in 2.(指新来的人) welcome new arrivals 3.(指新生) welcome new students

【迎战】 yíngzhàn meet head-on

【迎着】 yíng·zhe in face of; towards: ～困难上 press forward in face of difficulties

荧[熒](yíng)

【荧光】 yíngguāng 〈*Physics*〉 fluorescence; fluorescent light

【荧光灯】 yíngguāngdēng fluorescent lamp

【荧光屏】 yíngguāngpíng fluorescent screen; TV screen

【荧屏】 yíngpíng screen: 你看昨晚的～时装表演了吗? Did you see the fashion show on screen last night?

【荧荧】 yíngyíng twinkle; flicker

萤[螢](yíng)

〈*Zool.*〉 *firefly*; *glowworm*

【萤火虫】 yínghuǒchóng firefly; glowworm

营[營](yíng)

1.(谋求) seek: ～利 seek profits 2.(经营) operate; run; manage: 私～ privately owned; privately operated 3.〈*Mil.*〉 battalion: 炮兵～ artillery battalion 4.(军营) camp; barracks: 兵～ military camp

【营部】 yíngbù battalion headquarters

【营地】 yíngdì campsite; camping ground

【营房】 yíngfáng barracks

【营火】 yínghuǒ campfire

【营火晚会】 yínghuǒ wǎnhuì campfire party

【营建】 yíngjiàn construct; build

【营救】 yíngjiù succor; rescue

【营垒】 yínglěi 1.(指军营) barracks and the enclosing walls 2.(阵营) camp

【营利】 yínglì seek profits; make money

【营利事业所得税】 yínglì shìyè suǒdéshuì corporate profit tax

【营生】 yíngshēng earn a living

【营生】 yíng·sheng job

【营私】 yíngsī seek private gain; feather one's nest: ～舞弊 engage in malpractices for selfish ends; practice graft

【营养】 yíngyǎng 1.(指作用) nutrition; nourishment 2.(养分) nutrition: 增加～ increase nutrition

【营养不良】 yíngyǎng bùliáng be poorly nourished; malnourished (adj.)

【营业】 yíngyè do business

【营业报告】 yíngyè bàogào business report

【营业部】 yíngyèbù sales department

【营业额】 yíngyè'é turnover; volume of business: 日～超过20,000元。The day's take come to over 20,000 yuan.

【营业法】 yíngyèfǎ business law

【营业范围】 yíngyè fànwéi scope and field of business

【营业利润】 yíngyè lìrùn operating profit

【营业年度】 yíngyè niándù the business year

【营业时间】 yíngyè shíjiān business hours; opening hours

【营业收入】 yíngyè shōurù business income

【营业税】 yíngyèshuì business tax; sales taxes; transactions tax; turnover tax

【营业外收入】 yíngyèwài shōurù nonbusiness income; non-operating earning

【营业许可证】 yíngyè xǔkězhèng business permit

【营业员】 yíngyèyuán shop employees

【营业执照】 yíngyè zhízhào business licence

【营运】 yíngyùn move and do business

【营造】 yíngzào 1.〈*Archit.*〉 construct; build 2.〈*Forestry*〉 afforest

【营长】 yíngzhǎng battalion commander

【营帐】 yíngzhàng tent: 搭～ pitch a tent

萦[縈](yíng)

【萦怀】 yínghuái occupy one's mind

【萦回】 yínghuí hover; linger: ～脑际 linger in one's mind

【萦绕】 yíngrào hover; linger

潆[瀠](yíng)

【潆洄】 yínghuí swirl

盈(yíng)

1.(充满) be full of; be filled with: 丰～ plentiful; abundant 2.(多余) have a surplus of: ～千累万 in hundreds and thousands 3.(盈利) profit; gain: 转亏为～

show a turn from loss to profit

【盈亏】 yíngkuī 1.(指月亮) the waxing and waning of the moon 2.(赚钱和赔本) profit and loss：自负～ assume sole responsibility for its own profits or losses

【盈利】 yínglì profit；gain：长期的～ long-term profitability

【盈利企业】 yínglì qǐyè profit-making business；profit-making enterprise

【盈满】 yíngmǎn filled；full

【盈余】 yíngyú surplus；profit

楹 (yíng) principal columns of a hall

【楹联】 yínglián couplet written on scrolls and hung on the pillars of a hall

蝇［蠅］(yíng) fly：灭～ kill flies

【蝇卵】 yíngluǎn fly-borne

【蝇拍】 yíngpāi flyswatter；flyflap

【蝇头】 yíngtóu small as the head of a fly；tiny：～微利 petty profits

赢 (yíng) 1.(胜) win；beat：～局 win a game；score a game / 我们在比赛中～了那个队。We won our match against that team. 2.(获利) gain

【赢得】 yíngdé gain；win；obtain：～胜利 win victory / 中国运动员在奥运会上～了28块金牌。Chinese athletes won twenty-eight gold medals in the Olympics.

【赢利】 yínglì 1.(利润) profit；gain 2.(获利) get a profit；obtain a profit

【赢余】 yíngyú surplus；profit

颖 (yǐng) 1.(麦粒外壳) grain husk；glume 2.(尖端) tip；point 3.(聪明) clever；intelligent

【颖慧】 yǐnghuì clever；bright；intelligent

影 (yǐng) 1.(影子) shadow 2.(影像) reflection；image 3.(模糊形象) trace；vague impression；sign 4.(照片) photograph；picture：留～ have a photograph taken 5.(电影) motion picture；film；movie：～剧本 a film play

【影壁】 yǐngbì 1.(照壁) screen wall 2.(塑有形象的墙壁) wall with carved murals

【影碟】 yǐngdié video disk

【影集】 yǐngjí photograph album

【影剧界】 yǐngjùjiè the entertainment world；movie and drama circles

【影剧院】 yǐngjùyuàn cinema and theater

【影迷】 yǐngmí movie fan

【影片】 yǐngpiàn 1.(电影片) film；movie；picture：彩色～ color film / 电视广告～ commercial film / 广告～ spot / 由小说改编的～ film adapted from a novel 2.(胶片) film；copy

【影评】 yǐngpíng film review

【影射】 yǐngshè allude to；hint obliquely at；insinuate

【影视】 yǐngshì movie and television

【影视圈】 yǐngshìquān movie and TV circles

【影坛】 yǐngtán the movie circle；moviedom

【影响】 yǐngxiǎng 1.(起作用) influence；affect：～交通 hold up traffic / 吸烟～了他的健康。Smoking affected his health. 2.(所起的作用) effect；influence：社会～ social influence

【影像】 yǐngxiàng an image；a portrait

【影星】 yǐngxīng movie star；film star

【影印】 yǐngyìn 〈*Printing*〉 photoprint；photo-offset process

【影印本】 yǐngyìnběn 〈*Printing*〉 photo-offset copy

【影院】 yǐngyuàn cinema；movie theater

【影展】 yǐngzhǎn 1.(摄影展) photo exhibition 2.(电影展) film exhibition

【影子】 yǐng·zi 1.(影) shadow；reflection 2.(模糊形象) trace；sign；vague impression

【影子价格】 yǐng·zi jiàgé shadow price

【影子内阁】 yǐng·zi nèigé shadow cabinet

瘿 (yǐng) 1.〈*Chin. Med.*〉 goitre 2.(虫瘿) gall insect

应［應］(yìng) 1.(回答) answer；respond；echo 2.(满足要求) comply with；grant：以～急需 in order to fill an urgent need 3.(顺应;适应) suit；respond to 4.(应付) deal with；cope with
(另见“应”yīng)

【应变】 yìngbiàn 1.(应付事变) meet an emergency：随机～ adjust to changing circumstances；act according to circumstances 2.〈*Physics*〉 strain

【应承】 yìngchéng agree；promise；consent：～履约 promising to carry out an agreement

【应酬】 yìng·chou 1.(指交往) engage in social activities; have social intercourse 2.(私人宴会) private party

【应酬话】 yìng·chouhuà polite words

【应答】 yìngdá reply; answer

【应敌】 yìngdí deal with the enemy; cope with the enemy

【应对】 yìngduì reply; answer: ～如流 give quick and ready answers

【应付】 yìng·fu 1.(采取方法) meet; cope with; deal with; handle: 难于～ be difficult to deal with 2.(敷衍) do sth. perfunctorily; do sth. after a fashion: ～事儿 go through the motions 3.(将就) make do

【应急】 yìngjí meet an urgent need; meet an emergency

【应急灯】 yìngjídēng emergency light

【应急计划】 yìngjí jìhuà emergency plan

【应急供氧装置】 yìngjí gòngyǎng zhuāngzhì 〈*Aeron.*〉 emergency oxygen apparatus

【应接不暇】 yìngjiē-bùxiá have more visitors or business that one can attend to

【应景】 yìngjǐng do sth. for the occasion

【应考】 yìngkǎo take an examination

【应力】 yìnglì stress: 内～ internal stress / 预～ prestress

【应募】 yìngmù respond to a call for recruits; enlist; join up

【应诺】 yìngnuò agree; promise; undertake

【应聘】 yìngpìn accept an offer of employment

【应声】 yìngshēng at the sound of

【应声虫】 yìngshēngchóng yesman; echo

【应时】 yìngshí 1.(适合时令) seasonable; seasonal; in season: ～果品 seasonal fruits / ～商品 seasonable goods 2.(立刻) at once; immediately: ～而动 act according to circumstance

【应验】 yìngyàn come true; be confirmed; be fulfilled: ～良方 an effective prescription

【应邀】 yìngyāo at sb's invitation; on invitation

【应用】 yìngyòng 1.(使用) apply; use: 在工业上～新的技术流程 apply a new technical process to industry 2.(直接用于生活的) applied

【应用程序】 yìngyòng chéngxù application program

【应用化学】 yìngyòng huàxué applied chemistry

【应用科学】 yìngyòng kēxué applied science

【应用数学】 yìngyòng shùxué applied mathematics

【应用卫星】 yìngyòng wèixīng application satellite

【应用文】 yìngyòngwén practical writing

【应用知识】 yìngyòng zhī·shi working knowledge

【应运而生】 yìngyùn'érshēng arise at the historic moment; emerge as the times require

【应战】 yìngzhàn 1.(跟敌人作战) meet an enemy attack 2.(接受挑战) accept a challenge

【应战书】 yìngzhànshū letter accepting a challenge

【应召女郎】 yìngzhào nǚláng call girl

【应诊】 yìngzhěn see patients

【应征】 yìngzhēng 1.(响应征兵号召) be recruited; enlist 2.(泛指) answer to calls; answer to requests

映 (yìng) 1.(反映) reflect; mirror: ～入眼帘 greet the eye 2.(放电影) project a movie: 首～ first showing

【映衬】 yìngchèn set off

【映入】 yìngrù map into

【映射】 yìngshè shine upon; cast light upon

【映像】 yìngxiàng map; image

【映像记忆】 yìngxiàng jìyì iconic memory

【映照】 yìngzhào shine upon; cast light upon

硬 (yìng) 1.(坚硬) hard; stiff; tough 2.(刚强) strong; firm; tough; obstinate 3.(勉强) forcibly; arbitrarily; manage to do sth. with difficulty 4.(能力强;质量好) good; able: ～手 a good hand

【硬邦邦】 yìngbāngbāng very hard; very stiff

【硬币】 yìngbì coin; specie

【硬磁盘】 yìngcípán 〈*Computer*〉 hard disk

【硬度】 yìngdù 〈*Physics*〉 hardness

【硬腭】 yìng'è 〈*Anat.*〉 hard palate

【硬干】 yìnggàn do sth. in disregard of obstacles

【硬骨头】 yìnggǔ·tou a man with unbending will; a dauntless person

【硬汉】 yìnghàn a dauntless, unyielding man; a man of iron

【硬化】 yìnghuà 1.(变硬) harden; stiffen 2.〈*Med*.〉 sclerosis; hardening: 动脉～ hardening of the arteries; arteriosclerosis / 血管～ vascular sclerosis
【硬件】 yìngjiàn 〈*Computer*〉 hardware
【硬结】 yìngjié 1.(结成硬块) indurate; harden 2.〈*Med*.〉 scleroma
【硬拷贝】 yìngkǎobèi 〈*Computer*〉 hard copy
【硬科学】 yìngkēxué hard science
【硬朗】 yìng·lang 〈*colloq*.〉 hale and hearty
【硬路肩】 yìnglùjiān shoulder (AmE.); hard shoulder (BrE.)
【硬煤】 yìngméi hard coal; anthracite
【硬膜外】 yìngmówài 〈*Med*.〉 epidural
【硬木】 yìngmù hardwood: ～家具 hardwood furniture
【硬盘】 yìngpán 〈*Computer*〉 hard disk
【硬拼】 yìngpīn fight recklessly
【硬任务】 yìngrèn·wu hard task
【硬水】 yìngshuǐ hard water
【硬挺】 yìngtǐng endure with all one's will; hold out with all one's might
【硬通货】 yìngtōnghuò hard currency
【硬卧】 yìngwò 〈*Railway*〉 hard berth; hard sleeper
【硬席】 yìngxí 〈*Railway*〉 hard seats
【硬性】 yìngxìng rigid; stiff; inflexible
【硬性规定】 yìngxìng guīdìng rigid and inflexible rules
【硬仗】 yìngzhàng 1.(指战斗) tough battle 2.(指任务) formidable task
【硬着头皮】 yìng·zhe tóupí toughen one's scalp; brace oneself; force oneself to do sth. against one's will
【硬指标】 yìngzhǐbiāo hard quota
【硬着陆】 yìngzhuólù hard landing
【硬座】 yìngzuò 〈*Railway*〉 hard seats

yong

佣[傭] (yōng) 1.(雇用) hire 2.(帮佣) help; hired help; lady help (f.)
(另见"佣"yòng)

拥[擁] (yōng) 1.(拥抱) hold in one's arms; embrace; hug 2.(围着) gather around 3.(拥挤) crowd; throng; swarm: 一～而入 come swarming in all at once 4.(拥护) support 5.(拥有) have; possess
【拥抱】 yōngbào embrace; hug; hold in one's arms
【拥戴】 yōngdài support
【拥护】 yōnghù support; uphold; endorse
【拥护者】 yōnghùzhě adherent: 提案赢得了越来越多的～。The proposal is gaining more and more adherents.
【拥挤】 yōngjǐ crowd; push and squeeze
【拥军爱民】 yōngjūn-àimín support the army and cherish the people
【拥军优属】 yōngjūn-yōushǔ support the army and give preferential treatment to the families of the armyman and martyrs
【拥入】 yōngrù crowd into
【拥塞】 yōngsè jam; congest
【拥有】 yōngyǒu possess; have; own: ～核武器 possess nuclear weapons
【拥政爱民】 yōngzhèng-àimín support the government and cherish the people

痈[癰] (yōng) 〈*Med*.〉 carbuncle: 养～遗患 neglecting a carbuncle will cause trouble; failure to deal sternly with evil-doers will lead to serious trouble
【痈疽】 yōngjū ulcer

庸 (yōng) 1.(平庸) commonplace; mediocre: ～言～行 commonplace words and deeds 2.(不高明) inferior; second-rate: ～～碌碌 mediocre and unambitious 3.(用) need: 无～细述。There is no need to go into details.
【庸才】 yōngcái 〈*written*〉 mediocre person; mediocrity
【庸碌】 yōnglù mediocre and unambitious: ～之辈 an ordinary class of person
【庸人】 yōngrén mediocre person
【庸人自扰】 yōngrén-zìrǎo worry about troubles of one's own imagining
【庸俗】 yōngsú vulgar; philistine; low
【庸俗化】 yōngsúhuà vulgarize; debase
【庸言】 yōngyán a trite remark
【庸医】 yōngyí quack; charlatan

鳙 (yōng) 〈*Zool*.〉 *bighead*
【鳙鱼】 yōngyú bighead

雍(yōng) harmony

【雍容】 yōngróng natural, graceful and poised: ～华贵 elegant and poised; distingué

壅(yōng) 1.(堵塞) stop up; obstruct; block 2.(培土、肥) heap soil or fertilizer over and around the roots: ～肥 heap fertilizer around the roots

【壅塞】 yōngsè clogged up; jammed; congested

【壅土】 yōngtǔ hill; hilling (n.)

臃(yōng)

【臃肿】 yōngzhǒng 1.(指身体) too fat to move: 穿得太～ be cumbersomely dressed; be encumbered by too much clothing 2.(指机构) overstaffed: ～的机构 overstaffed organizations

永(yǒng) perpetually; forever; always

【永别】 yǒngbié part never to meet again; part forever; be parted by death

【永垂不朽】 yǒngchuí-bùxiǔ be immortal

【永存】 yǒngcún last forever; remain forever; eternal (adj.)

【永恒】 yǒnghéng eternal; perpetual: ～的友谊 eternal friendship

【永久】 yǒngjiǔ permanent; perpetual; everlasting: ～的和平 permanent peace; everlasting peace

【永久性】 yǒngjiǔxìng perpetual: ～条款 perpetual provision

【永诀】 yǒngjué part forever; be separated by death

【永生】 yǒngshēng 1.(哀悼语) immortal 2.〈*Religion*〉 eternal life 3.(终生) all one's life

【永世】 yǒngshì forever: ～长存 live for ever and ever

【永无宁日】 yǒngwúníngrì never will there be days of peace

【永远】 yǒngyuǎn 〈*adv.*〉 always; forever; ever; in perpetuity

【永志不忘】 yǒngzhì-bùwàng will always bear in mind; will always cherish the memory of sb. or sth.

咏[詠](yǒng) 1.(诵读) chant; intone 2.(写诗词) sing of; express in poetic form

【咏叹】 yǒngtàn intone; chant; sing

【咏叹调】 yǒngtàndiào 〈*Music*〉 aria: 她唱的《托斯卡》中的～是我最喜爱的。The aria she sang from "Tosca" was my favorite.

【咏赞】 yǒngzhàn sing the praises of; praise

泳(yǒng) swim ‖ 侧泳 sidestroke / 蝶泳 butterfly; butterfly stroke / 蛙泳 breaststroke / 仰泳 backstroke; back crawl / 自由泳 freestyle; crawl

【泳道】 yǒngdào 〈*Swimming*〉 lane; swimming lane

【泳裤】 yǒngkù swimming trunks

【泳帽】 yǒngmào swimming cap

【泳衣】 yǒngyī swimsuit; swimming suit

甬(yǒng)

【甬道】 yǒngdào 1.(甬路) paved path leading to a main hall or a tomb 2.(走廊) corridor

【甬路】 yǒnglù paved path leading to a main hall or a tomb

俑(yǒng) tomb figure; figurine; wooden or earthen human figure buried with the dead in ancient times: 陶～ pottery figure / 武士～ warrior figure; terracotta warriors

勇(yǒng) brave; valiant; courageous: ～攀高峰 be bold in scaling heights

【勇不可挡】 yǒngbùkědǎng too courageous to be met with

【勇敢】 yǒnggǎn brave; courageous

【勇冠三军】 yǒngguànsānjūn peerless or matchless in bravery or valor

【勇猛】 yǒngměng bold and powerful; full of valor and vigor

【勇气】 yǒngqì courage; nerve: 鼓起～ pluck up one's courage / 有足够的～ have plenty of grit

【勇士】 yǒngshì warrior; a brave and strong man

【勇挑重担】 yǒngtiāo-zhòngdàn be brave to take on heavy responsibilities

【勇往直前】 yǒngwǎng-zhíqián march forward courageously; advance bravely

【勇武】 yǒngwǔ valiant

【勇于】 yǒngyú be brave in; be bold in; have the courage to: ～承认错误 have the courage to admit one's mistake / ～冒险犯难 brave danger and hardship

涌(yǒng) 1.(冒出) gush; well; pour; surge 2.(从中冒出) rise; surge; emerge

【涌现】 yǒngxiàn emerge in large numbers; spring up; come to the fore

蛹(yǒng) pupa: 蚕～ silkworm chrysalis

踊[踴](yǒng) leap up; jump up

【踊跃】 yǒngyuè 1.(跳跃) leap; jump 2.(形容情绪) vying with one another; eagerly; enthusiastically: ～参加 take an active part in; eagerly join in

用(yòng) 1.(使用) use; employ; apply 2.(费用) expenses; outlay: 日～ daily expenses 3.(用处) usefulness; use: 有点儿～ of little avail / 无～ of no avail; to no avail / 物尽其～ make the best use of everything 4.(需要) need: 不～说 needless to say 5.(吃;喝) eat; drink; take

【用兵】 yòngbīng 1.(使用武力) resort to arms; use military forces: 不得已而～ have no alternative but to resort to arms 2.(指挥作战) command troops: 善于～ well versed in the art of war

【用场】 yòngchǎng use; application: 有～ be useful

【用处】 yòng·chu use; good: 没有～ be of no use

【用度】 yòngdù expenditure; expense; outlay

【用法】 yòngfǎ use; usage

【用饭】 yòngfàn have a meal; take a meal

【用非所长】 yòngfēisuǒcháng be engaged in an occupation having nothing to do with one's specialty

【用非所学】 yòngfēisuǒxué be engaged in an occupation not related to one's training

【用费】 yòngfèi expense; cost

【用功】 yònggóng hardworking; diligent; studious: 如果你在学习上～,你就会成功的。If you show application in your studies you will succeed.

【用光】 yòngguāng use up; exhaust

【用户】 yònghù consumer; user: 电话～ telephone subscriber / 最终～ end user

【用户电报】 yònghù diànbào telex

【用户界面友好】 yònghù jièmiàn yǒuhǎo 〈*Computer*〉 user-friendly

【用户手册】 yònghù shǒucè user's guide; user's manual

【用户主义】 yònghù zhǔyì consumerism

【用劲】 yòngjìn exert oneself; put forth one's strength

【用尽】 yòngjìn exhaust; use up: ～心机 exhaust one's abilities

【用具】 yòngjù utensil; apparatus; appliance: 钓鱼～ fishing tackle / 剃须～ shaving tackle

【用力】 yònglì exert oneself; put forth one's strength

【用料精选】 yòngliào jīngxuǎn carefully selected materials

【用料上乘】 yòngliào shàngchéng selected materials

【用品】 yòngpǐn appliance; articles: 生活～ articles for daily use; daily necessities / 体育～ sports goods; athletic equipment

【用钱】 yòngqián spend money

【用去】 yòngqù have spent; used

【用人】 yòngrén 1.(指选择与使用) choose a person for a job; make use of personnel: ～不当 not choose the right person for the job 2.(指需要) need hands

【用人】 yòng·ren servant

【用事】 yòngshì act: 感情～ act impetuously

【用途】 yòngtú use: ～广 be widely used / 有广泛～ have a wide application

【用武】 yòngwǔ use force; display one's abilities or talents: 在…大有～之地 there's ample scope for one's abilities inn

【用贤任能】 yòngxián rènnéng use the capable and employ the skilled

【用项】 yòngxiàng items of expenditure; expenditures

【用心】 yòngxīn 1.(用心力) diligently: ～做习题 work hard at exercises 2.(居心) motive; intention: ～良苦 have really given much thought to the matter

【用以】 yòngyǐ in order to; so as to

【用意】 yòngyì intention; purpose

【用语】 yòngyǔ 1.(措词) choice of words; wording: ～不当 inappropriate choice of words; incorrect wording 2.(专门词语)

phraseology; term: 外交～ diplomatic terms

佣(yòng)
(另见"佣"yōng)

【佣金】 yòngyīn commission; middleman's fee; brokerage

you

优[優](yōu) excellent

【优待】 yōudài give preferential treatment
【优待券】 yōudàiquàn complimentary ticket
【优等】 yōuděng high-class; first-rate; excellent
【优等生】 yōuděngshēng top student
【优点】 yōudiǎn merit; strong point; advantage
【优厚】 yōuhòu munificent; liberal; favorable
【优化】 yōuhuà optimize
【优惠】 yōuhuì 〈*Econ*.〉 preferential; favorable
【优惠办法】 yōuhuì bànfǎ preferential measure
【优惠贷款】 yōuhuì dàikuǎn loan on favorable terms
【优惠待遇】 yōuhuì dàiyù preferential treatment
【优惠关税】 yōuhuì guānshuì preferential duties
【优惠关税协定】 yōuhuì guānshuì xiédìng preferential tariff agreements
【优惠国】 yōuhuìguó favored nation
【优惠汇率】 yōuhuì huìlǜ preferential rate
【优惠价格】 yōuhuì jiàgé preferential prices
【优惠期】 yōuhuìqī days of grace
【优惠政策】 yōuhuì zhèngcè preferential policies
【优教】 yōujiào good education
【优良】 yōuliáng fine; good; excellent
【优良传统】 yōuliáng chuántǒng fine tradition
【优良品质】 yōuliáng pǐnzhì fine quality
【优良品种】 yōuliáng pǐnzhǒng good strains of seeds
【优良作风】 yōuliáng zuòfēng fine style of work
【优美】 yōuměi graceful; fine; exquisite: ～的风景 fine scenery
【优柔寡断】 yōuróu-guǎduàn be irresolute and hesitant; be indecisive
【优生】 yōushēng healthy propagation: ～优育 give a good birth and good care
【优生学】 yōushēngxué 〈*Biol*.〉 eugenics
【优胜】 yōushèng winning; superior
【优胜奖】 yōushèngjiǎng winning prize
【优胜劣败】 yōushèng-lièbài survival of the fittest
【优胜劣汰】 yōushèng-liètài the efficient one's will prosper and the inefficient one's will be eliminated
【优势】 yōushì superiority; preponderance; dominant position: 绝对～ overwhelming superiority / 空中～ air supremacy / 占～ have a clear superiority / 个子高的球队在篮球比赛中占～。The taller team has an advantage in a basketball game.
【优先】 yōuxiān have priority; take precedence
【优先股】 yōuxiāngǔ preference stock; preference shares
【优先股本】 yōuxiān gǔběn capital stock-preferred
【优先权】 yōuxiānquán priority; preference
【优先项目】 yōuxiān xiàngmù priority
【优闲】 yōuxián carefree and leisurely
【优秀】 yōuxiù outstanding; excellent; splendid; fine: ～选手 topnotch player
【优选】 yōuxuǎn optimize
【优选法】 yōuxuǎnfǎ optimization
【优雅】 yōuyǎ elegance; elegant (adj.): 步态～地下楼 walk down stairs with grace
【优养】 yōuyǎng good nurturing and training
【优异】 yōuyì excellent; outstanding
【优育】 yōuyù scientific nurture
【优裕】 yōuyù affluent; abundant
【优越】 yōuyuè superior; advantageous
【优越感】 yōuyuègǎn sense of superiority; superiority complex
【优越性】 yōuyuèxìng superiority; advantage
【优哉游哉】 yōuzāi-yóuzāi 〈*written*〉 living a life of ease and leisure; leisurely and carefree; leisurely and unhurried
【优质】 yōuzhì high quality; high grade: ～产品 products of quality

忧［憂］(yōu) 1.(忧愁) worry; be worried 2.(犯愁的事) sorrow; anxiety; concern; care: 无～无虑 carefree; free from all anxieties

【忧愁】 yōuchóu sad; worried; depressed

【忧国忧民】 yōuguó-yōumín be concerned about one's country and one's people

【忧患】 yōuhuàn suffering; misery; hardship

【忧惧】 yōujù worried and apprehensive

【忧劳成疾】 yōuláochéngjí fall sick with grievance and toil

【忧虑】 yōulǜ worried; anxious; concerned: 深感～ feel extremely anxious; be very worried

【忧闷】 yōumèn depressed; feeling low; weighed down with cares

【忧伤】 yōushāng distressed; weighed down with sorrow; laden with grief

【忧心】 yōuxīn 〈*written*〉 worry; anxiety: ～忡忡 laden with anxieties

【忧郁】 yōuyù melancholy; heavyhearted; dejected

【忧郁症】 yōuyùzhèng 〈*Med.*〉 melancholia: melancholic (adj.)

悠(yōu) 1.(久;远) long-drawn-out; remote in time or space 2.(闲适) leisurely 3.(悠荡) swing

【悠长】 yōucháng long; long-drawn-out

【悠荡】 yōudàng swing; sway

【悠久】 yōujiǔ long; long-standing; age-old: 历史～ have a long history

【悠然】 yōurán 1.(悠闲) carefree and leisurely: ～自得 be carefree and content 2.(遥远) long; distant; far away: ～神往 one's thoughts turn to things distant

【悠闲自得】 yōuxián-zìdé with abundant leisure one is contented

【悠扬】 yōuyáng rising and falling; melodious

【悠悠】 yōuyōu 1.(长久) long; remote: ～无期 at some distant time 2.(从容) leisurely; unhurried: ～自得 be carefree and content

【悠悠荡荡】 yōuyōu-dàngdàng floating about

【悠远】 yōuyuǎn 1.(时间长) a long time ago; long ago 2.(距离远) far off; remote; distant

【悠哉悠哉】 yōuzāi-yōuzāi free from restraint

幽(yōu) 1.(深远) deep and remote; secluded; dim 2.(隐蔽) secret; hidden: ～居 live in seclusion 3.(沉静) quiet; tranquil; serene 4.(囚禁) imprison 5.(阴间) of the nether world

【幽暗】 yōu'àn dim; gloomy

【幽闭】 yōubì 1.(幽禁) put under house arrest 2.(深居) confine oneself indoors

【幽愤】 yōufèn hidden resentment

【幽谷】 yōugǔ a deep and secluded valley

【幽会】 yōuhuì a secret meeting of lovers; a lovers' rendezvous; tryst

【幽魂】 yōuhún ghost

【幽禁】 yōujìn 1.(软禁) put under house arrest 2.(囚禁) imprison; keep under detention

【幽静】 yōujìng quiet and secluded; peaceful

【幽灵】 yōulíng ghost; specter; spirit

【幽门】 yōumén 〈*Anat.*〉 pylorus

【幽默】 yōumò humor (AmE.); humour (BrE.); humorous (adj.)

【幽默感】 yōumògǎn sense of humor

【幽情】 yōuqíng exquisite feelings: 发思古之～ muse over things of the remote past

【幽深】 yōushēn deep and serene; deep and quiet

【幽思】 yōusī 1.(深思) ponder; meditate 2.(内心感情) inmost thoughts; inmost feelings

【幽闲】 yōuxián 1.(安详) gentle and serene 2.(闲适) leisurely and carefree

【幽香】 yōuxiāng a delicate fragrance

【幽雅】 yōuyǎ quiet and tastefully laid out

【幽幽】 yōuyōu 1.(微弱) faint 2.(深远) faraway; distant; looming in the distance

【幽怨】 yōuyuàn hidden bitterness

尤［尢］(yóu) 1.(突出) outstanding: 无耻之～ have absolutely no sense of shame; brazen in the extreme 2.(尤其) particularly; especially 3.(过失) fault; wrongdoing: 效～ knowing follow the example of a wrongdoer 4.(怨恨) have a grudge against; blame: 怨天～人 blame god and man; blame everyone and everything but oneself

【尤里卡计划】 Yóulǐkǎ Jìhuà Eureka Program

【尤其】 yóuqí especially; particularly

犹[猶] (yóu) 1.(如同) just; as; like 2.(还;尚且) still

【犹可】 yóukě still all right

【犹如】 yóurú just as; like; as if

【犹太教】 Yóutàijiào Judaism ‖ 犹太教徒 Judaism

【犹太人】 Yóutàirén Jew (m.); Jewess (f.)

【犹言在耳】 yóuyánzài'ěr ring in one's ears

【犹疑】 yóuyí hesitate

【犹有可为】 yóuyǒukěwéi still retrievable

【犹有余悸】 yóuyǒuyújì even now one is scared

【犹豫】 yóuyù hesitate; be irresolute: ～不决 hesitate; remain undecided

疣[肬] (yóu) 〈*Med.*〉 wart

鱿 (yóu)

【鱿鱼】 yóuyú 〈*Zool.*〉 squid

由 (yóu) 1.(原由) cause; reason 2.(由于) because of; due to 3.(经由) by; through; via: 她是～海路去的。She went there by sea. 4.(顺从) follow; obey 5.〈*prep.*〉(由…做)～他负责这项工作。Leave this work to him. 6.〈*prep.*〉(表示起点) from: ～表及里 proceed from the surface to the inner essence / ～南往北 from south to north

【由不得】 yóu·bu·de 1.(不得依从) not be up to sb. to decide; be beyond the control of: 这件事～他们。It's not up to them. 2.(不由自主) cannot help

【由此】 yóucǐ from this; therefrom; thus: ～向前 go forward from here

【由此可见】 yóucǐ-kějiàn thus it can seen; this shows; that proves

【由近及远】 yóujìn-jíyuǎn from the near to the distant

【由来】 yóulái 1.(从开始到现在) since the beginning 2.(原由) origin

【由来已久】 yóulái-yǐjiǔ long-standing; time-honored: 此事～。It has lasted for a long time.

【由浅入深】 yóuqiǎn-rùshēn go from the easy to the difficult and complicated

【由小而大顺序】 yóuxiǎo érdà shùnxù ascending order

【由于】 yóuyú 〈*prep.*〉 owing to; thanks to; as a result of; due to; in virtue of: ～他在背后议论我,我再也不和他说话了。I shall never speak to him again after what he has said about me.

【由衷】 yóuzhōng from the bottom of one's heart; sincere; heartfelt: 表示～的感激 extend one's heartfelt thanks

邮[郵] (yóu) 1.(邮寄) post; mail 2.(邮务的) postal; mail: ～局 post office

【邮包】 yóubāo postal parcel; parcel

【邮包保险】 yóubāo bǎoxiǎn parcel post insurance

【邮编】 yóubiān zip code (AmE.); postcode (BrE.)

【邮车】 yóuchē postal car

【邮船】 yóuchuán ocean liner; liner; packet ship

【邮戳】 yóuchuō postmark: 纪念～ cachet

【邮袋】 yóudài mailbag; postbag; pouch

【邮递】 yóudì postal delivery

【邮递区】 yóudìqū postal delivery zone

【邮递员】 yóudìyuán postman; mailman (m.); postwoman; mailwoman (f.)

【邮电】 yóudiàn post and telecommunications

【邮电局】 yóudiànjú post and telecommunications office

【邮订】 yóudìng mail-order; mail order (n.)

【邮订广告】 yóudìng guǎnggào mail-order advertising

【邮费】 yóufèi postage

【邮购】 yóugòu mail-order; mail order (n.)

【邮购商店】 yóugòu shāngdiàn mail-order house

【邮汇】 yóuhuì remit by post; send money by post

【邮集】 yóují stamp album

【邮寄】 yóujì send by post; post: 作快件～ send by express mail

【邮简】 yóujiǎn stamped envelope: 航空～ aerogram; air letter aerogram

【邮件】 yóujiàn postal matter; post; mail: 挂号～ registered post / 航空～ air mail

【邮局】 yóujú post office

【邮路】 yóulù postal route
【邮轮】 yóulún liner
【邮票】 yóupiào stamp; postage stamp: 纪念～ commemorative stamp
【邮亭】 yóutíng postal kiosk
【邮筒】 yóutǒng pillar-box; postbox; mailbox
【邮务船】 yóuwùchuán post ship
【邮箱】 yóuxiāng postbox; mailbox
【邮运】 yóuyùn deliver by mail; mail transportation
【邮展】 yóuzhǎn stamps exhibition
【邮政】 yóuzhèng postal service
【邮政编码】 yóuzhèng biānmǎ zip code (AmE.); postcode (BrE.)
【邮政储蓄】 yóuzhèng chǔxù postal savings
【邮政特快专递】 yóuzhèng tèkuài zhuāndì EMS; Express Mail Service
【邮政信箱】 yóuzhèng xìnxiāng post office box; P. O. Box
【邮资】 yóuzī postage
【邮资费率】 yóuzī fèilǜ postage tariff
【邮资已付】 yóuzī yǐfù postpaid; postage paid
【邮资总付】 yóuzī zǒngfù freepost

油 (yóu) **1.** (油脂) oil; fat; grease **2.** (涂油) apply tung oil or paint **3.** (油污) be stained with oil or grease **4.** (油滑) oily; glib
【油爆虾】 yóubàoxiā fried shrimps
【油泵】 yóubèng oil pump
【油饼】 yóubǐng **1.** (食品) deep-fried dough cake **2.** 〈*Agric.*〉 oil cake
【油布】 yóubù oilcloth; oilskin; tarpaulin
【油彩】 yóucǎi greasepaint; paint
【油菜】 yóucài 〈*Bot.*〉 rape; bird rape
【油菜籽】 yóucàizǐ rapeseed
【油舱】 yóucāng 〈*Naut.*〉 tank
【油层】 yóucéng 〈*Petroleum*〉 oil reservoir; oil layer; oil horizon
【油茶】 yóuchá **1.** 〈*Bot.*〉 tea-oil tree; oil-tea camellia **2.** (食品) a gruel of sweetened, fried flour
【油茶面儿】 yóuchámiànr flour fried in beef fat with sugar and sesame
【油尺】 yóuchǐ 〈*Auto*〉 dipstick
【油船】 yóuchuán tanker; oil carrier
【油灯】 yóudēng oil lamp; kerosene lamp
【油坊】 yóufáng oil mill
【油橄榄】 yóugǎnlǎn 〈*Bot.*〉 olive
【油管】 yóuguǎn **1.** (输油的) oil pipe **2.** (采油的) oil tube
【油罐】 yóuguàn oil tank; storage tank
【油罐汽车】 yóuguàn qìchē oil car
【油光】 yóuguāng glossy; shiny; varnished
【油壶】 yóuhú oilcan; oiler
【油滑】 yóuhuá slippery; foxy
【油画】 yóuhuà oil painting ‖ 油画家 oil painter
【油画颜料】 yóuhuà yánliào oil paint; oil color
【油迹】 yóujì oil stains; grease spots
【油井】 yóujǐng oil well: 钻一口～ drill a well
【油库】 yóukù oil depot; tank farm
【油矿】 yóukuàng **1.** (石油矿床) oil deposit **2.** (油田) oil field
【油亮】 yóuliàng glossy; shiny
【油量表】 yóuliàngbiǎo 〈*Auto*〉 fuel indicator
【油料】 yóuliào oil yielding material
【油料作物】 yóuliào zuòwù oil-bearing crops; oil crops; oil plant
【油轮】 yóulún tanker; oil tanker
【油码头】 yóumǎ·tou oil jetty; oil wharf; tanker terminal
【油毛毡】 yóumáozhān asphalt felt
【油门】 yóumén 〈*Mech.*〉 throttle
【油门握把】 yóumén wòbǎ 〈*Motorcycle*〉 throttle twist grip
【油墨】 yóumò printing ink
【油泥】 yóuní greasy filth; grease
【油腻】 yóunì **1.** (油大的) greasy; oily **2.** (油大的食物) greasy food; oily food
【油漆】 yóuqī **1.** (涂料) paint **2.** (涂油漆) cover with paint; paint
【油腔滑调】 yóuqiāng-huádiào glib; unctuous; have a smooth, oily tongue
【油然】 yóurán **1.** (自然) spontaneously; involuntarily **2.** (形容云气) densely; profusely
【油然而生】 yóurán'érshēng arise spontaneously; be produced of itself
【油石】 yóushí whetstone; oilstone
【油水】 yóu·shui **1.** (饭菜的脂肪) grease **2.** (好处) profit: ～不大 not very profitable
【油提】 yóutí oil dipper
【油田】 yóutián oil field

【油条】 yóutiáo 1.(面食) deep-fried twisted dough sticks 2.(油滑的人) slippery person
【油桐】 yóutóng 〈*Bot*.〉 tung tree; tung oil tree
【油桶】 yóutǒng oil drum
【油头粉面】 yóutóu-fěnmiàn dressy or foppish; sleek-haired and creamy-faced
【油头滑脑】 yóutóu-huánǎo slick; flippant; oily: 一个～的家伙 a shifty-looking fellow
【油污】 yóuwū greasy dirt
【油箱】 yóuxiáng gas tank; oil box; fuel tank: 副～ auxiliary fuel tank; auxiliary tank
【油箱盖】 yóuxiánggài gas tank door
【油压表】 yóuyābiǎo 〈*Auto*〉 oil pressure gauge
【油烟】 yóuyān lampblack
【油盐酱醋】 yóuyánjiàngcù daily necessaries
【油印】 yóuyìn mimeograph
【油印机】 yóuyìnjī mimeograph
【油渣】 yóuzhā 1.(猪油的) dregs of fat 2.〈*Petroleum*〉 oil residue
【油炸】 yóuzhá fry in deep fat
【油炸土豆片】 yóuzhá tǔdòupiàn potato crisp
【油毡】 yóuzhān 〈*Archit*.〉 asphalt felt
【油脂】 yóuzhī oil; fat
【油渍】 yóuzì oil stain
【油嘴】 yóuzuǐ 1.(油滑) glib 2.(油滑的人) glib talker
【油嘴滑舌】 yóuzuǐ-huáshé with a glib tongue; be glib-tongued

柚 (yóu)
(另见"柚"yòu)
【柚木】 yóumù 〈*Bot*.〉 teak

铀 (yóu) 〈*Chem*.〉 uranium (元素符号 U): 浓缩～ enriched uranium

蚰 (yóu)
【蚰蜒】 yóu·yan 〈*Zool*.〉 common house centipede

莜 (yóu)
【莜麦】 yóumài 〈*Bot*.〉 naked oat

游[遊[2,3]] (yóu) 1.(游泳) swim 2.(旅游) rove around; wander; travel; tour: 周～世界 travel round the world 3.(不固定) roving; itinerant 4.(河段) part of a river; reach: 上～ the upper reaches / 下～ the lower reaches / 中～ the middle reaches
【游伴】 yóubàn travel companion
【游标】 yóubiāo cursor
【游标尺】 yóubiāochǐ vernier
【游船】 yóuchuán pleasure-boat
【游荡】 yóudàng 1.(闲游;闲逛) loaf about; loiter; roam 2.(飘荡) drift; float; wave
【游动】 yóudòng move about; go from place to place
【游舫】 yóufǎng pleasure-boat
【游逛】 yóuguàng go sight-seeing; stroll about
【游击】 yóujī guerrilla warfare
【游击队】 yóujīduì guerrilla forces; a guerrilla detachment
【游击队员】 yóujīduìyuán guerrilla; guerilla
【游击手】 yóujīshǒu 〈*Baseball*〉 shortstop
【游击战】 yóujīzhàn guerrilla warfare
【游记】 yóujì travel notes; travels
【游客】 yóukè tourist; visitor; excursionist
【游览】 yóulǎn tour; visit; go sight-seeing
【游览车】 yóulǎnchē tourist coach
【游览地】 yóulǎndì place for sight-seeing; excursion center
【游览图】 yóulǎntú tourist map
【游廊】 yóuláng covered corridor
【游乐场】 yóulèchǎng amusement park
【游乐园】 yóulèyuán amusement park
【游离】 yóulí 1.〈*Chem*.〉 free 2.(指人) dissociate; drift away
【游离基】 yóulíjī free radical
【游历】 yóulì travel for pleasure; travel; tour
【游轮】 yóulún belt tightening pulley; loose pulley
【游民】 yóumín vagrant; vagabond: 无业～ vagrant
【游牧】 yóumù move about in search of pasture; rove around as a nomad
【游牧部落】 yóumù bùluò nomadic tribe
【游牧民族】 yóumù mínzú nomadic people
【游禽】 yóuqín natatorial bird
【游人】 yóurén tourist; visitor; sightseer
【游山玩水】 yóushān-wánshuǐ make a sightseeing tour; tour the scenic spots
【游手好闲】 yóushǒu-hàoxián idle about; loaf

【游说】 yóushuì go canvassing; go about selling an idea; go about drumming up support for an idea

【游丝】 yóusī 1.(飘着的蛛丝) gossamer 2.(钟表的) hairspring

【游艇】 yóutǐng yacht; pleasure-boat

【游玩】 yóuwán 1.(游戏) amuse oneself; play 2.(游逛) go sight-seeing; stroll about

【游戏】 yóuxì 1.(娱乐) recreation; game: 做～ play games 2.(玩耍) play

【游行】 yóuxíng 1.(到处走) travel around; roam about 2.(群众游行) parade; march; demonstration

【游兴】 yóuxìng interest in going on an excursion

【游医】 yóuyī itinerant doctor

【游移】 yóuyí 1.(来回移动) move about; go from place to place 2.(态度摇摆) waver; vacillate; wobble: ～其辞 be hesitated in words

【游弋】 yóuyì cruise: 在海上～ cruise on the sea

【游艺】 yóuyì amusement; entertainment; recreation

【游艺场】 yóuyìchǎng amusement park

【游艺室】 yóuyìshì recreation room

【游泳】 yóuyǒng swim

【游泳比赛】 yóuyǒng bǐsài swimming contest

【游泳池】 yóuyǒngchí swimming pool: 室内～ indoor pool; swimming bath / 室外～ outdoor pool; open air pool

【游泳馆】 yóuyǒngguǎn natatorium

【游泳衣】 yóuyǒngyī swimsuit; swimming suit: 三点式～ bikini

【游泳运动员】 yóuyǒng yùndòngyuán swimmer

【游园】 yóuyuán 1.(逛公园) visit a garden; visit a park 2.(游园庆祝会) mass celebration in parks

【游园会】 yóuyuánhuì garden party

【游资】 yóuzī idle fund; idle money; floating capital: 吸收～ absorb idle funds

【游子】 yóuzǐ 〈*written*〉 man travelling or residing in a place far away from home

友 (yǒu) 1.(朋友) friend 2.(友好的) friendly

【友爱】 yǒu'ài friendly affection; fraternal love: ～之谊 the friendliness of brothers / 团结～ solidarity and fraternity

【友邦】 yǒubāng friendly nation

【友好】 yǒuhǎo 1.(好朋友) close friend; friend 2.(亲近和睦) friendly; amicable: ～往来 friendly intercourse / 两国唇齿相依，世代～相处。The two countries have lived side by side in amity for generations.

【友好代表团】 yǒuhǎo dàibiǎotuán goodwill mission

【友好访问】 yǒuhǎo fǎngwèn friendly visit

【友好合作条约】 yǒuhǎo hézuò tiáoyuē treaty of friendship and cooperation: 两位领导人签署了～。The two leaders signed a treaty of entente and cooperation.

【友好人士】 yǒuhǎo rénshì friendly personage; friend

【友好使者】 yǒuhǎo shǐzhě envoy of friendship

【友好条约】 yǒuhǎo tiáoyuē treaty of friendship

【友好协会】 yǒuhǎo xiéhuì friendship association

【友好邀请赛】 yǒuhǎo yāoqǐngsài friendship invitational tournament

【友情】 yǒuqíng friendly sentiments; friendship

【友人】 yǒurén friend: 外国～ foreign friend

【友谊】 yǒuyì friendship

【友谊赛】 yǒuyìsài friendly match

有 (yǒu) 1.(拥有) have; possess: ～空 be free / 你～笔吗? Do you have a pen? (或: Do you have any pens?) / 我～笔。I have a pen. (或: I have some pens.) 2.(存在) there is; exist: 这个看法在许多书里都～。The idea appears in many books. 3.(估量) as ... as: 他～他哥哥那么高。He is as tall as his brother. 4.(发生) 孩子们～了许多进步。The children have made much progress. 5.(表示多,大) ～经验 be experienced 6.(用于泛指) one; some: ～人告诉我 someone told me

【有碍】 yǒu'ài be a hindrance to; get in way of; obstruct: ～交通 hinder traffic

【有案可查】 yǒu'àn kěchá be a matter of record; be on record; be documented

【有板有眼】 yǒubǎn-yǒuyǎn rhythmical;

measured; orderly

【有备无患】 yǒubèi-wúhuàn where there is precaution, there is no danger; preparedness averts peril

【有背景】 yǒu bèijǐng have powerful connections

【有本领】 yǒu běnlǐng capable; talented; resourceful

【有病】 yǒubìng be ill; come down with a disease

【有产阶级】 yǒuchǎn jiējí the propertied classes

【有产者】 yǒuchǎnzhě a man of property

【有偿】 yǒucháng paid

【有偿服务】 yǒucháng fúwù paid service

【有偿新闻】 yǒucháng xīnwén paid news report

【有偿转让】 yǒucháng zhuǎnràng paid transfer

【有吃有穿】 yǒuchī-yǒuchuān have ample food and clothing; well provided with food and clothing

【有待】 yǒudài remain; await: ～改进 have much room for improvement

【有德行】 yǒu déxíng virtuous

【有的】 yǒu·de some: ～赞成,～反对。Some are in favor of it, some are against it.

【有底】 yǒudǐ know how things stand and feel confident of handling them; be fully prepared for what is coming

【有的放矢】 yǒudì-fàngshǐ shoot the arrow at the target; have a definite object in view

【有点儿】 yǒudiǎnr 1.(不多) some; a little 2.〈*adv*.〉somewhat; rather; a bit

【有毒】 yǒudú poisonous; venomous

【有方】 yǒufāng with the proper method; in the right way: 教导～ have the right way to educate and guide

【有分寸】 yǒufēncùn having a sense of propriety; knowing how far to go and when to stop

【有份儿】 yǒufènr have a share; have taken part in

【有夫之妇】 yǒufūzhīfù married woman

【有福气】 yǒu fúqì be blessed; favored by fortune

【有负众望】 yǒufù-zhòngwàng disappoint those who had confidence in a person

【有妇之夫】 yǒufùzhīfū married man

【有感而发】 yǒugǎn'érfā explode not without reason

【有功】 yǒugōng have rendered great service; have performed meritorious service

【有瓜葛】 yǒuguāgé 1.(与…有关) have relation 2.(有些复杂) have complication

【有关】 yǒuguān 1.(有关系) have sth. to do with; have a bearing on; relate to; concern: 此事与她～。She has something to do with the matter. 2.(涉及到的) concerned; related; relevant: ～部门 the departments concerned / ～当局 the authorities concerned / ～方面 the parties concerned

【有光】 yǒuguāng 1.(上光的) glazed 2.〈*Textiles*〉bright

【有光人造丝】 yǒuguāng rénzàosī bright rayon

【有轨电车】 yǒuguǐ diànchē tram; tramcar; streetcar

【有鬼】 yǒuguǐ there's something fishy: 心里～ have a guilty conscience

【有害】 yǒuhài harmful; pernicious; detrimental: 对健康～ harmful to one's health

【有行无市】 yǒuháng-wúshì have only quotation but no actual trading

【有机】 yǒujī 1.〈*Chem*.〉organic 2.(互相关连) organic; integral: ～联系 organic relations / ～组成部分 an organic part

【有机玻璃】 yǒujī bō·li plexiglass; perspex; polymethyl methacrylate

【有机化学】 yǒujī huàxué organic chemistry

【有机可乘】 yǒujī kěchéng there's an opportunity to take advantage of; there's a loophole that can be used

【有计划商品经济】 yǒu jìhuà shāngpǐn jīngjì planned commodity economy

【有价证券】 yǒujià zhèngquàn negotiable securities; securities

【有奖销售】 yǒujiǎng xiāoshòu comeback premium; premium sale promotion

【有救】 yǒujiù can be saved; can be cured

【有空】 yǒukòng be free; have time to spare; be not occupied: 你～吗? Are you occupied?

【有口皆碑】 yǒukǒu-jiēbēi win universal praise; be universally acclaimed

【有口难辩】 yǒukǒu-nánbiàn find it hard to vindicate oneself

【有口难言】 yǒukǒu-nányán cannot bring oneself to mention sth.; find it hard or embarrassing to bring up a matter

【有口无心】 yǒukǒu-wúxīn be sharp-tongued but not malicious

【有来有往】 yǒulái-yǒuwǎng reciprocal

【有赖】 yǒulài depend on; rest on

【有劳】 yǒuláo have troubled you; please do me the favor by

【有理】 yǒulǐ 1.(有道理) reasonable; justified; in the right 2.〈*Math*.〉 rational

【有理数】 yǒulǐshù 〈*Math*.〉 rational number

【有力】 yǒulì strong; powerful; forceful; energetic; vigorous: ～的打击 a forceful blow

【有利】 yǒulì advantageous; beneficial; favorable: ～健康 beneficial to health / ～因素 favorable conditions

【有利可图】 yǒulì kětú have good prospects of gain; stand to gain; be profitable

【有路子】 yǒulù·zi have friends in high places

【有眉目】 yǒu méi·mu begin to take shape; about to materialize

【有门儿】 yǒuménr 1.(得到诀窍) get the hang 2.(有希望) find the beginning of a solution; be hopeful

【有面子】 yǒumiàn·zi have one's honor preserved; have one's vanity satisfied

【有名】 yǒumíng well-known; famous; celebrated

【有名无实】 yǒumíng-wúshí in name but not in reality; merely nominal; titular

【有目共睹】 yǒumù-gòngdǔ be there for all to see; be perfectly obvious

【有男子气概】 yǒu nánzǐ qìgài virile

【有凭有据】 yǒupíng-yǒujù having proof and evidence

【有期徒刑】 yǒuqī túxíng 〈*Law*〉 set term of imprisonment

【有其父,必有其子】 yǒu qí fù, bì yǒu qí zǐ like father, like son

【有起色】 yǒuqǐsè show signs of a rise

【有气无力】 yǒuqì wúlì weakly; feeble

【有钱】 yǒuqián rich; wealthy; well of

【有前科】 yǒuqiánkē previous conviction

【有求必应】 yǒuqiú-bìyìng respond to every plea; grant whatever is requested

【有趣】 yǒuqù interesting; fascinating; amusing

【有权代理】 yǒuquán dàilǐ authorized agency

【有人】 yǒurén anybody: ～在这儿吗? Is anybody there? / ～看见我的钢笔了吗? Has anybody seen my pen?

【有人缘儿】 yǒurényuánr likable; popular

【有色】 yǒusè colored

【有色金属】 yǒusè jīnshǔ nonferrous metal

【有色人种】 yǒusè rénzhǒng colored race

【有色眼镜】 yǒusè yǎnjìng colored spectacles

【有身子】 yǒushēn·zi be pregnant; be expecting

【有神论】 yǒushénlùn theism; theist (adj.) ‖ 有神论者 theist

【有生力量】 yǒushēng lìliàng effective strength; effectives

【有生以来】 yǒushēng yǐlái ever since one's birth: ～第一次 the first time in one's life

【有生之年】 yǒushēngzhīnián for the rest of one's life

【有声动画片】 yǒushēng dònghuàpiān sound cartoon

【有声读物】 yǒushēng dúwù talking books; books with recordings

【有声片】 yǒushēngpiàn sound film; talkie; phonofilm

【有声有色】 yǒushēng-yǒusè full of sound and color; vivid and dramatic; very impressive

【有失身份】 yǒushī shēnfèn infra dig; beneath one's rank or station

【有识之士】 yǒushízhīshì a person with breadth of vision; a man of insight

【有时】 yǒushí sometimes; at times; now and then

【有史以来】 yǒushǐ-yǐlái since the beginning of history; throughout history

【有始无终】 yǒushǐ-wúzhōng start sth. but fail to carry it through

【有始有终】 yǒushǐ-yǒuzhōng carry sth. through to the end

【有事】 yǒushì 1.(有事情做) be engaged; occupied; busy 2.(有问题) when problems crop up; if sth. happens

【有恃无恐】 yǒushì-wúkǒng secure in the knowledge that one has strong backing

【有数】 yǒushù 1.(不多) not many; only a few 2.(了解) know exactly how things stand; have a definite idea of what one's doing: 心中～ know fairly well; know what's what

【有所】 yǒusuǒ to some extent; somewhat: ～追求 be after something

【有条不紊】 yǒutiáo-bùwěn in an orderly way; methodically; systematically

【有条有理】 yǒutiáo-yǒulǐ systematically; in perfect order

【有头无尾】 yǒutóu-wúwěi start sth. but fail to carry it through

【有头绪】 yǒu tóuxù be near solution or success; have found the clue

【有头有脸儿】 yǒutóu-yǒuliǎnr honored; respected; presentable

【有头有尾】 yǒutóu-yǒuwěi carry sth. through to the end

【有望】 yǒuwàng hopeful; expectant

【有为】 yǒuwéi promising: 年轻～ young and promising

【有味儿】 yǒuwèir 1.(好吃) tasty; delicious 2.(美好) delightful 3.(腐烂) stink

【有喜】 yǒuxǐ 〈*colloq.*〉 be pregnant; be expecting

【有隙可乘】 yǒuxì-kěchéng there is a crack to squeeze through; there is a loophole to exploit

【有戏剧效果】 yǒu xìjù xiàoguǒ stage wise

【有闲阶级】 yǒuxián jiējí leisure class

【有限】 yǒuxiàn limited; finite; restricted: 对高价汽车的需求极～ a restricted demand for expensive cars

【有线】 yǒuxiàn wired

【有线传真】 yǒuxiàn chuánzhēn wirephoto

【有线电话】 yǒuxiàn diànhuà telephone

【有线电视】 yǒuxiàn diànshì cable television

【有限公司】 yǒuxiàn gōngsī limited company; limited liability company

【有线广播】 yǒuxiàn guǎngbō wire broadcasting; wired broadcasting

【有效】 yǒuxiào efficacious; effective; valid: 六个月～ valid for six months / ～措施 effective measure 这张票两星期～。This ticket is good for two weeks.

【有效期】 yǒuxiàoqī term of validity

【有些】 yǒuxiē 1.(有的) some: ～人 some people 2.(有一些) somewhat; rather: ～不好意思 be somewhat embarrassed

【有心】 yǒuxīn 1.(有某种想法) have a mind to; set one's mind on: ～人 one who sets his mind on doing sth. useful 2.(存心) intentionally; deliberately; purposely

【有形】 yǒuxíng tangible; visible

【有形贸易】 yǒuxíng màoyì visible trade

【有形资产】 yǒuxíng zīchǎn tangible assets; tangibles

【有性】 yǒuxìng 〈*Biol.*〉 sexual

【有性生殖】 yǒuxìng shēngzhí zoogamy; sexual reproduction

【有性杂交】 yǒuxìng zájiāo sexual hybridization

【有血有肉】 yǒuxuè-yǒuròu true to life; vivid: 这个故事～。The story is true to life.

【有言在先】 yǒuyán-zàixiān make clear beforehand; forewarn

【有眼无珠】 yǒuyǎn-wúzhū have eyes but not see

【有一说一】 yǒuyī-shuōyī speak the whole truth; call a spade a spade

【有益】 yǒuyì profitable; beneficial; useful

【有意】 yǒuyì 1.(有心思) have a mind to; be inclined 2.(故意地) intentionally; deliberately; purposely 3.(有爱慕之心) adore; admire

【有意识】 yǒu yì·shi consciously; knowingly; wittingly

【有意思】 yǒu yì·si 1.(有意义) significant 2.(有趣味) interesting; enjoyable 3.(有爱慕之心) adore; admire

【有瘾】 yǒuyǐn be addicted to; have formed a habit

【有勇无谋】 yǒuyǒng-wúmóu have valor but lack strategy; be brave but not resourceful; be foolhardy

【有用】 yǒuyòng useful; helpful

【有余】 yǒuyú 1.(有剩余) have a surplus; have enough and to spare: 绰绰～ more than enough; enough and to spare 2.(有零) odd: 50～ fifty odd

【有缘】 yǒuyuán linked by ties of fate

【有约在先】 yǒuyuézàixiān have a previous engagement
【有孕】 yǒuyùn be pregnant; be expecting
【有则改之,无则加勉】 yǒu zhé gǎi zhī, wú zé jiā miǎn correct mistakes if you have made any and guard against them if you have not
【有朝一日】 yǒuzhāo-yīrì some day; one day
【有职有权】 yǒuzhí-yǒuquán be entrusted with the responsibility and authority inherent in one's post
【有志者事竟成】 yǒuzhìzhě shì jìng chéng where there's a will there's a way
【有志之士】 yǒuzhìzhīshì a person of noble aspirations; a person with lofty ideals
【有助于】 yǒuzhùyú contribute to; be conducive to; conduce to
【有资格】 yǒuzīgé capable; qualified: ～取得专利权的 patentable
【有罪】 yǒuzuì culpable; guilty

铕(yǒu) 〈*Chem.*〉 europium (元素符号 Eu)

莠(yǒu) 1.(狗尾草) green bristlegrass 2.(坏人) bad people: 良～ some good and some bad

黝(yǒu) black; dark

【黝黑】 yǒuhēi dark; swarthy

又(yòu) 〈adv.〉1.(重复) again 一次～一次 again and again / 他走了～走。He walked and walked. 2.(同时存在) and; at the same time; at once: 这些杂志～便宜～好。These magazines are cheap but good. 3.(再加上) and: 一～二分之一 one and a half 4.(表示转折) as well; moreover; but: 我想去,～怕没时间。I'd like to go, but I'm not sure if I can find the time
【又红又专】 yòuhóng-yòuzhuān both red and expert
【又及】 yòují postscript
【又惊又喜】 yòujīng-yòuxǐ alarmed and happy at the same time
【又哭又笑】 yòukū-yòuxiào cry and laugh at the same time

右(yòu) 1.(跟"左"相对) the right side; the right: 靠～行驶 keep to the right 2.(保守的) the Right 3.(西) west
【右岸】 yòu'àn right bank
【右臂】 yòubì the right arm
【右边】 yòubiān the right side; the right
【右边锋】 yòubiānfēng 〈*Football*〉 outside right; right wing
【右锋】 yòufēng 〈*Basketball*〉 right forward
【右钩拳】 yògōuquán 〈*Boxing*〉 right hook
【右后卫】 yòuhòuwèi 〈*Football*〉 right back
【右内锋】 yòunèifēng 〈*Football*〉 inside right
【右派】 yòupài the Right; the right wing
【右前卫】 yòuqiánwèi 〈*Football*〉 right half-back; right half
【右倾】 yòuqīng Right deviation
【右倾机会主义】 yòuqīng jīhuì zhǔyì Right opportunism
【右肾】 yòushèn 〈*Anat.*〉 right kidney
【右手】 yòushǒu right hand; right-hand (adj.)
【右首】 yòushǒu the right-hand side; the right
【右心房】 yòuxīnfáng 〈*Anat.*〉 right atrium
【右心室】 yòuxīnshì 〈*Anat.*〉 right ventricle
【右页】 yòuyè 〈*Printing*〉 recto
【右翼】 yòuyì 1.(右侧部队) right wing; right flank 2.(保守的) the Right; the right wing 3.(飞机右翼) starboard wing
【右翼分子】 yòuyì fènzǐ right-winger; member of the Right
【右转弯】 yòuzhuǎnwān turn right
【右转弯标志】 yòuzhuǎnwān biāozhì 〈*Transport*〉 lane arrow for turning right

幼(yòu) 1.(小) young; under age: ～子 the youngest son 2.(小孩儿) children; the young: 扶老携～ bringing along the old and the young
【幼虫】 yòuchóng 〈*Zool.*〉 *larva*
【幼儿】 yòu'ér child; infant
【幼儿教育】 yòu'ér jiàoyù preschool education
【幼儿园】 yòu'éryuán kindergarten; nursery school; infant school
【幼教】 yòujiào preschool education
【幼苗】 yòumiáo seedling
【幼年】 yòunián childhood; infancy
【幼小】 yòuxiǎo immature
【幼芽】 yòuyá young shoot; bud
【幼稚】 yòuzhì 1.(年龄小) young 2.(头脑简单) childish; puerile; naive: ～可笑 childish

and ridiculous
【幼稚病】 yòuzhìbìng 1.〈*Psycho.*〉infantilism 2.(政治上的) infantile disorder
【幼稚园】 yòuzhìyuán kindergarten; nursery school; infant school
【幼子】 yòuzǐ the youngest son

囿(yòu) limited; hampered
【囿于成见】 yòuyú-chéngjiàn blinded by prejudice
【囿于习俗】 yòuyú-xísú constrained by custom
【囿于一隅】 yòuyú yīyú be restricted to a narrow confine

柚(yòu) 〈*Bot.*〉shaddock; pomelo
【柚子】 yòu·zi shaddock; pomelo
(另见"柚"yóu)

釉(yòu) glaze
【釉瓷】 yòucí vitreous enamel
【釉工】 yògōng glazer
【釉料】 yòuliào frit; fritt
【釉陶】 yòutáo glazed pottery
【釉质】 yòuzhì 〈*Physiol.*〉enamel
【釉子】 yòi·zi glaze

鼬(yòu) 〈*Zool.*〉*weasel*: 白～ *stoat*; *ermine* / 黄～(黄鼠狼) *Siberian weasel* / 伶～(银鼠) *weasel*; *least weasel*

诱(yòu) 1.(诱导) guide; lead; induce 2.(诱使) lure; seduce; entice: ～人为恶 seduce others to evil
【诱捕】 yòubǔ trap; entrap
【诱导】 yòudǎo 1.(劝诱) guide; lead; induce: ～他改过自新 guide him to mend his ways 2.〈*Med.*〉revulsion; revulsive (adj.)
【诱导药】 yòudǎoyào revulsive
【诱饵】 yòu'ěr bait
【诱发】 yòufā bring out; induce; cause to happen
【诱供】 yògòng trap a person into a confession; inducement leading to confession
【诱拐】 yòuguǎi abduct; carry off by fraud; kidnap: 警察认为那个孩子已被人～了。The police think the boy has been abducted.
【诱惑】 yòuhuò 1.(引诱) tempt; temptation (n.); seduce; seduction (n.); lure: 受～ fall into temptation; be lured / 经不住～ give way to temptation 2.(吸引) attract; allure; fascinate: ～人的微笑 bewitching smiles
【诱奸】 yòujiān entice into unlawful sexual intercourse; seduce
【诱骗】 yòupiàn inveigle; cajole; trap; trick
【诱人的】 yòurén·de attractive; tempting: ～出价 a tempting offer
【诱杀】 yòushā trap and kill; lure to destruction
【诱降】 yòuxiáng lure into surrender; cajole sb. into surrender
【诱因】 yòuyīn causality

yu

迂(yū) 1.(曲折) circuitous; winding; roundabout 2.(迂腐) clinging to outworn rules and ideas; pedantic: ～夫子 pedant
【迂腐】 yūfǔ stubborn adherence to outworn rules and ideas; pedantry
【迂缓】 yūhuǎn slow in movement; dilatory
【迂回】 yūhuí 1.(回旋) roundabout; circuitous; tortuous: ～曲折 full of twists and turns; circuitous; tortuous 2.〈*Mil.*〉outflank: ～战术 outflanking tactics
【迂回生产】 yūhuí shēngchǎn roundabout production
【迂见】 yūjiàn absurd view; impractical opinion
【迂阔】 yūkuò high-sounding and impracticable: ～之论 impractical views
【迂论】 yūlùn impractical argument; unrealistic statement
【迂曲】 yūqū tortuous; circuitous
【迂直】 yūzhí impractical and artless
【迂拙】 yūzhuō impractical and foolish

纡(yū)
【纡回】 yūhuí 〈*written*〉roundabout; circuitous; tortuous
【纡徐】 yūxú 〈*written*〉unhurried; steadily

淤[瘀[3]](yū) 1.(淤积) become silted up 2.(淤泥) silt 3.(血瘀) stasis
【淤点】 yūdiǎn 〈*Med.*〉petechia
【淤灌】 yūguàn 〈*Agric.*〉warping

【淤积】 yūjī silt up; deposit
【淤浆】 yūjiāng slurry
【淤泥】 yūní silt; sludge; ooze
【淤塞】 yūsè silt up; be choked with silt: 河流～了。The river was silted up.
【淤沙】 yūshā silt
【淤血】 yūxuè extravasated blood
【淤滞】 yūzhì be retarded by silt; silt up

于[於] (yú) 〈prep.〉1.(在) in; at; on: 生～1950年 be born in 1950 2.(对于) for; to: 有益～人民 be beneficial to the people 3.(自;从) from: 出～自愿 of one's own free will; of one's own accord 4.(表示比较) than: 多～ more than
【于今】 yújīn 1.(到现在) up to the present; since 2.(如今) nowadays; today; now
【于是】 yúshì 〈conj.〉 thereupon; hence; as a result; consequently

盂 (yú) jar: 痰～ spittoon

余[餘[1-3]] (yú) 1.(剩下) surplus; spare; remaining 2.(零头) more than; odd; over 3.(后) beyond; after: 工作之～ spare time; after work 4.(我) I
【余波】 yúbō repercussions; after-effect: 地震～ the after-effects of the earthquake
【余党】 yúdǎng remnants of an overthrown clique; remaining confederates
【余地】 yúdì leeway; margin; room; latitude: 留有～ leave some leeway
【余毒】 yúdú residual poison; pernicious vestige; pernicious influence
【余额】 yú'é 1.(指名额) vacancy; vacancies yet to be filled 2.(指账目金额) remaining sum; balance: 贷方～ credit balance / 负债方～ passive balance / 借方～ balance due / 银行账上～ bank balance
【余额表】 yú'ébiǎo balance sheet
【余割】 yúgē 〈*Math.*〉 cosecant
【余辉】 yúhuī twilight at sunset; afterglow
【余悸】 yújì lingering fear: 心有～ have a lingering fear
【余烬】 yújìn 1.(燃烧后的灰) ashes; embers 2.(比喻战后残存的东西) embers: 劫后～ a devastated waste of smoldering embers
【余款】 yúkuǎn balance; remaining sum
【余力】 yúlì strength or energy to spare
【余粮】 yúliáng surplus grain; grain reserves
【余量】 yúliàng margin
【余年】 yúnián one's remaining years: ～可数 one's failing years are numbered
【余孽】 yúniè remaining evil element; leftover evil; surviving supporter of an evil cause: 封建～ dregs of feudalism
【余怒未消】 yúnù-wèixiāo feel the lingering anger
【余切】 yúqiē 〈*Math.*〉 cotangent
【余权】 yúquán remaining power
【余缺】 yú-quē surplus and deficiency
【余热】 yúrè surplus heat
【余生】 yúshēng 1.(指晚年) the remaining years of one's life; old age: ～著书 write a book in the declining years of one's life 2.(侥幸活命) survival: 劫后～ be a survivor of a disaster
【余剩】 yúshèng surplus; remainder
【余数】 yúshù remainder
【余威】 yúwēi remaining prestige or influence
【余味】 yúwèi pleasant impression; agreeable aftertaste: ～无穷 leave a lasting and pleasant impression or aftertaste
【余暇】 yúxiá spare time; leisure time; leisure
【余弦】 yúxián 〈*Math.*〉 cosine
【余兴】 yúxìng 1.(指兴致) lingering interest; a wish to prolong a pleasant diversion 2.(附带的表演等) entertainment after a meeting or a dinner party
【余音】 yúyīn lingering sound
【余荫】 yúyìn blessing left to one's children
【余震】 yúzhèn 〈*Geol.*〉 aftershock

馀 (yú) 1.(剩下) surplus; spare; remaining: ～年 sb's remaining years 2.(零头) more than; odd; over 3.(后) beyond; after: 工作之～ spare time; after work

鱼[魚] (yú) fish
【鱼白】 yúbái fish sperm; milt
【鱼鳔】 yúbiào air bladder
【鱼叉】 yúchā fish spear; fish fork
【鱼场】 yúchǎng fish farm
【鱼翅】 yúchì shark's fin

【鱼虫】 yúchóng water flea
【鱼刺】 yúcì fishbone
【鱼肚】 yúdǔ maw; fish maw
【鱼肚白】 yúdùbái the whitish color of a fish's belly; grey down
【鱼饵】 yú'ěr bait
【鱼粉】 yúfěn fish meal
【鱼竿】 yúgān fishing rod
【鱼肝油】 yúgānyóu cod-liver oil
【鱼缸】 yúgāng fish jar; fish bowl
【鱼钩】 yúgōu fishhook
【鱼骨】 yúgǔ fish-bone
【鱼骨形天线】 yúgǔxíng tiānxiàn fishbone antennas
【鱼贯】 yúguàn one following the other; in single file: ～而入 enter in single file; file in
【鱼胶】 yújiāo fish glue; isinglass
【鱼块】 yúkuài steak
【鱼雷】 yúléi 〈*Mil.*〉 torpedo
【鱼雷艇】 yúléitǐng torpedo boat
【鱼鳞】 yúlín fish scale; scale
【鱼龙混杂】 yúlóng-hùnzá dragons and fish jumbled together; good and bad people mixed up
【鱼卵】 yúluǎn roe; hard roe
【鱼米之乡】 yúmǐzhīxiāng a land of fish and rice; land of abundance
【鱼苗】 yúmiáo fry; fish fry
【鱼目混珠】 yúmù-hùnzhū pass off fish eyes as pearls; pass off the sham as the genuine
【鱼片】 yúpiàn fillet
【鱼片汤】 yúpiàntāng sliced fish soup
【鱼漂】 yúpiāo float; cork on a fishing line
【鱼群】 yúqún shoal of fish
【鱼肉】 yúròu **1.** (鱼的肉) the flesh of fish **2.** (鱼和肉) fish and meat **3.** (压榨; 宰割) oppress; victimize: ～百姓 cruelly oppress the people
【鱼市】 yúshì fish market
【鱼水】 yúshuǐ fish and water
【鱼水情深】 yúshuǐ qíngshēn be close as fish and water
【鱼松】 yúsōng dried fish floss
【鱼塘】 yútáng fish pond
【鱼网】 yúwǎng fishnet; fishing net
【鱼尾板】 yúwěibǎn 〈*Railway*〉 fishplate; joint bar
【鱼尾号】 yúwěihào boldface square brackets (〖 〗; 【 】)
【鱼鲜】 yúxiān fish and shellfish as food; seafood
【鱼腥味】 yúxīngwèi fishlike smell; fishy taste
【鱼汛】 yúxùn fishing season
【鱼眼镜头】 yúyǎnjìngtóu 〈*Photog.*〉 fish-eye lens
【鱼秧】 yúyāng fingerling
【鱼鹰】 yúyīng **1.** (鹗) osprey; fish hawk; sea eagle **2.** (鸬鹚) cormorant
【鱼跃】 yúyuè 〈*Volleyball*〉 fish dive: ～救球 diving save
【鱼跃顶球】 yúyuè dǐngqiú 〈*Football*〉 diving header
【鱼子】 yúzǐ 〈*Food*〉 roe
【鱼子酱】 yúzǐjiàng caviare

渔［漁］(yú) **1.** (捕鱼) fishing **2.** (谋取) take sth. one is not entitled to: ～利 reap unfair gains
【渔产】 yúchǎn aquatic products
【渔场】 yúchǎng fishing ground; fishery
【渔船】 yúchuán fishing vessel; fishing boat
【渔村】 yúcūn fishing village
【渔港】 yúgǎng fishing port; fishing harbor
【渔歌】 yúgē fisherman's song
【渔火】 yúhuǒ lights on fishing boats
【渔获量】 yúhuòliàng catch
【渔具】 yújù fishing tackle
【渔利】 yúlì **1.** (谋利) reap unfair gains; profit at others' expense: 从中～ take advantage of a situation to benefit oneself **2.** (指所谋之利) easy gains; spoils: 坐收～ profit from others' conflict
【渔猎】 yúliè fish and hunt
【渔轮】 yúlún fishing vessel
【渔民】 yúmín fisherman; fisherfolk
【渔业】 yúyè fishery
【渔业资源】 yúyè zīyuán fishery resources

隅 (yú) **1.** (角落) corner; nook: 城～ the corner of a city wall **2.** (靠边的地方) outlying place; border: 海～ seaboard

愚 (yú) **1.** (愚笨) foolish; stupid **2.** (愚弄) make a fool of; fool: **3.** 〈*politeness*〉 I; my: 据本人～见 in my humble opinion
【愚笨】 yúbèn foolish; stupid; clumsy

【愚不可及】 yúbùkějí a fool to the third degrees; be hopelessly stupid
【愚蠢】 yúchǔn stupid; foolish; silly: 他～到了极点。He takes the cake for stupidity.
【愚钝】 yúdùn stupid; slow-witted
【愚见所及】 yújiànsuǒjí as far as my humble opinion goes
【愚昧落后】 yúmèi luòhòu ignorant and backward
【愚昧无知】 yúmèi-wúzhī ignorant; benighted
【愚民政策】 yúmín zhèngcè policy of keeping the people in ignorance; obscurantist policy
【愚弄】 yúnòng deceive; make a fool of; dupe
【愚人】 yúrén a fool; a simpleton
【愚人节】 yúrénjié All Fools' Day
【愚妄】 yúwàng ignorant but self-important; stupid but conceited
【愚直】 yúzhí stupidly honest
【愚拙】 yúzhuō stupid and clumsy

揄(yú)

【揄扬】 yúyáng 1.(称赞) praise; commend 2.(宣扬) propagate

愉(yú) pleased; happy; joyful; cheerful

【愉快】 yúkuài happy; joyful; cheerful: 心情～ be in a happy mood; be joyful
【愉悦】 yúyuè joyful; cheerful; delighted

逾[踰[1]](yú) 1.(超过) exceed; go beyond: ～额 exceed the allowed 2.(更加) even more

【逾假不归】 yújiàbùguī absent over leave
【逾期】 yúqī exceed the time limit; be overdue
【逾越】 yúyuè exceed; go beyond: ～权限 overstep one's authority

瑜(yú) 1.(美玉) fine jade; gem 2.(优点) virtues; good points: 瑕不掩～ the defects do not obscure the virtues

【瑜伽】 yújiā yoga

榆(yú) 〈*Bot.*〉 elm

【榆木脑袋】 yúmù-nǎo·dai blockhead; foolish
【榆树】 yúshù elm

娱(yú) 1.(使快乐) give pleasure to; amuse 2.(快乐) joy; pleasure; amusement

【娱乐】 yúlè amusement; entertainment; recreation
【娱乐场所】 yúlè chǎngsuǒ public place of entertainment
【娱乐圈】 yúlèquān entertainment world

虞(yú) 1.(预料) supposition; prediction: 以备不～ be prepared for any contingency 2.(忧虑) anxiety; worry 3.(欺骗) deceive; cheat; fool: 尔～我诈 each trying to cheat the other

舆(yú) 1.(地) area; territory 2.(众人的) public; popular

【舆论】 yúlùn public opinion
【舆论工具】 yúlùn gōngjù mass media; the media
【舆论界】 yúlùnjiè the media; press circles

与[與](yǔ) 1.(给) give; offer; grant 2.〈prep.〉(跟) with; against 3.(和) and; together with: 工业～农业 industry and agriculture
(另见"与"yù)

【与此相反】 yǔcǐxiāngfǎn contrariwise: 他同意,～,她表示拒绝。He gives permission, and, contrariwise, she refuses it.
【与其…不如】 yǔqí … bùrú would rater ... than ...: ～苟且偷生,～一死 prefer to die rather than drag out an ignoble existence
【与人为善】 yǔrén-wéishàn aim at helping others; with good intentions toward others
【与日俱增】 yǔrì-jùzēng grow with each passing day; be steadily on the increase
【与世长辞】 yǔshì-chángcí depart from the world for ever; pass away
【与世隔绝】 yǔshì-géjué seclude from the world
【与世无争】 yǔshì-wúzhēng hold oneself aloof from the world; stand aloof from worldly success
【与现实不符】 yǔ xiànshí bùfú unrealistic
【与众不同】 yǔzhòng-bùtóng out of the ordinary

予(yǔ) give; grant; bestow: 不～考虑 refuse to take into consideration / 免～处分 exempt sb. from punishment

【予人口实】 yǔrén-kǒushí give sb. a handle; give cause for gossip
【予以】 yǔyǐ give; grant: ～解释 throw some

light on

宇(yǔ) 1.(房檐) eaves 2.(房屋) house 3.(宇宙;世界) space; universe; world

【宇航】 yǔháng astronavigation; space flight; astronautic (adj.)

【宇航员】 yǔhángyuán astronaut; cosmonaut

【宇内】 yǔnèi in the world: ～闻名 be reputed in the world

【宇宙】 yǔzhòu 1.(无限空间) universe; cosmos 2.(世界) world

【宇宙飞船】 yǔzhòu fēichuán spaceship; space ship; spacecraft

【宇宙飞行】 yǔzhòu fēixíng space flight

【宇宙飞行员】 yǔzhòu fēixíngyuán astronaut; spaceman; cosmonaut

【宇宙服】 yǔzhòufú gravity suit

【宇宙观】 yǔzhòuguān world view; world outlook

【宇宙航行】 yǔzhòu hángxíng astronavigation; space navigation

【宇宙火箭】 yǔzhòu huǒjiàn space rocket

【宇宙空间】 yǔzhòu kōngjiān space; cosmic space

【宇宙空间站】 yǔzhòu kōngjiānzhàn space station

羽(yǔ) feather; plume

【羽冠】 yǔguān crest

【羽毛】 yǔmáo feather; plume

【羽毛球】 yǔmáoqiú 1.〈*Badminton*〉badminton 2.(指球) shuttlecock ‖ 羽毛球运动员 badminton player

【羽毛球拍】 yǔmáoqiúpāi racket

【羽毛球赛】 yǔmáoqiúsài badminton match

【羽毛球网】 yǔmáoqiúwǎng badminton net

【羽绒】 yǔróng eider down

【羽绒被】 yǔróngbèi duvet

【羽绒服】 yǔróngfú down-filled clothing

【羽纱】 yǔshā camlet

【羽坛】 yǔtán badminton circles

【羽翼】 yǔyì 1.(鸟翅) wing 2.(辅佐的人或力量) assistant

雨(yǔ) rain: 下～ rain / 大～瓢泼而下。It was teeming with rain.

【雨布】 yǔbù waterproof cloth; waterproof

【雨层云】 yǔcéngyún 〈*Meteorol.*〉 nimbostratus

【雨点】 yǔdiǎn raindrop

【雨刮器】 yǔguāqì 〈*Auto*〉 windshield wiper (AmE.); windscreen wiper (BrE.)

【雨过天晴】 yǔguò-tiānqíng after gloom comes brightness; the sun shines again after the rain

【雨后春笋】 yǔhòu-chūnsǔn bamboo shoots after a spring rain: 近几年学校里计算机的数量如～般地增长。The number of computers in schools has mushroomed in recent years.

【雨季】 yǔjì rainy season

【雨夹雪】 yǔjiāxuě rain and snow mixed

【雨具】 yǔjù rain gear

【雨量】 yǔliàng 〈*Meteorol.*〉 rainfall

【雨林】 yǔlín rainforest

【雨露】 yǔlù 1.(雨和露) rain and dew 2.(恩惠) favor; grace; bounty

【雨帽】 yǔmào rain cap

【雨期】 yǔqī pluvial

【雨情】 yǔqíng rainfall

【雨伞】 yǔsǎn umbrella

【雨刷】 yǔshuā 〈*Auto*〉 windshield wiper (AmE.); windscreen wiper (BrE.)

【雨水】 yǔshuǐ 1.(降雨的水) rainwater; rainfall; rain: 今年夏天～太多了。We've had too much rain this summer. 2.(节气) the Rain Water (2月18-20日交节)

【雨天】 yǔtiān rainy day; wet day

【雨鞋】 yǔxié rubber boots; galoshes; rubbers

【雨靴】 yǔxuē wellington boot (AmE.); rubber boots (BrE.)

【雨雪纷纷】 yǔxuě fēnfēn confused falling of rain and snow

【雨衣】 yǔyī raincoat; waterproof

【雨意】 yǔyì signs of approaching rain

【雨云】 yǔyún nimbus

语(yǔ) 1.(语言) language; tongue; words: 外国～ foreign language 2.(说) speak; say: 低～ speak in a low voice 3.(谚语) set phrase; proverb; saying 4.(代替语) nonlinguistic means of communicating ideas; sign; signal

【语病】 yǔbìng faulty wording or formulation

【语词】 yǔcí words and phrases

【语次转变】 yǔcì zhuǎnbiàn transition

【语调】 yǔdiào 〈*Phonet*.〉 intonation
【语法】 yǔfǎ grammar; grammatical (adj.): 一本英语～书 an English grammar
【语汇】 yǔhuì vocabulary
【语句】 yǔjù sentence
【语录】 yǔlù quotations; recorded utterance
【语气】 yǔqì 1.(说话口气) tone; manner of speaking 2.〈*Phonet*.〉 mood; modal (adj.)
【语气词】 yǔqìcí modal particle
【语塞】 yǔsè tongue-tied
【语素】 yǔsù morpheme
【语速】 yǔsù speech pacing
【语态】 yǔtài 〈*Gram*.〉 voice
【语体】 yǔtǐ 〈*Gram*.〉 type of writing; style
【语文】 yǔwén 1.(中文) Chinese 2.(语言文字) language 3.(语言和文学) language and literature
【语无伦次】 yǔwúlúncì speak incoherently; talk in a confused manner
【语系】 yǔxì 〈*Gram*.〉 family of languages; language family: 拉丁～ the Latin family of languages
【语序】 yǔxù 〈*Gram*.〉 word order
【语言】 yǔyán language; linguistic (adj.): ～能力 linguistic competence
【语言学】 yǔyánxué linguistics; linguistic science; linguistic (adj.) ‖ 语言学家 linguist
【语义】 yǔyì semantic
【语义学】 yǔyìxué semantics
【语音】 yǔyīn 1.(说话声音) speech sounds 2.(发音) pronunciation; phonetic (adj.): ～课 phonetics class
【语音学】 yǔyīnxué phonetics; phonetic (adj.)
【语源】 yǔyuán history of words
【语源学】 yǔyuánxué etymology; etymological (adj.)
【语重心长】 yǔzhòng-xīncháng sincere words and earnest wishes
【语助词】 yǔzhùcí 〈*Gram*.〉 an auxiliary word that indicates

与[與] (yù) take part in; participate in
(另见"与"yǔ)
【与会】 yùhuì participate in conference
【与闻】 yùwén have a participant's knowledge of: ～此事 have a participant's knowledge of this matter

玉 (yù) 1.(玉石) jade 2.(比喻) pure; fair; handsome; beautiful: 亭亭～立 fair, slim and graceful 3.〈*politeness*〉 your: ～照 your photograph
【玉帛】 yùbó 〈*written*〉 jade objects and silk fabrics: 化干戈为～ turn hostility into friendship
【玉成其事】 yùchéng-qíshì 〈*politeness*〉 kindly help make a success of it; assistant another in accomplishing a task or attaining a goal
【玉带】 yùdài jade belt
【玉雕】 yùdiāo jade carving; jade sculpture
【玉兰】 yùlán 〈*Bot*.〉 magnolia; yulan magnolia
【玉兰片】 yùlánpiàn 〈*Food*〉 dried slices of tender bamboo shoots
【玉米】 yùmǐ 1.(玉蜀黍) maize; Indian corn; corn 2.(玉米穗) ear of maize
【玉米面】 yùmǐmiàn maize flour; corn flour
【玉米片】 yùmǐpiàn cornflake
【玉器】 yùqì jade article; jade object; jadeware
【玉色】 yùsè jade green; light bluish green
【玉石】 yùshí jade: ～雕刻品 jade sculpture
【玉石俱焚】 yùshí jùfén jade and stone burned together; destruction of good and bad alike
【玉蜀黍】 yùshǔshǔ 〈*Bot*.〉 maize; Indian corn; corn
【玉玺】 yùxǐ imperial jade seal
【玉宇】 yùyǔ 1.(天空) the sky 2.(宇宙) the universe 3.(宫殿) beautiful palace: 琼楼～ magnificent houses
【玉簪】 yùzān 1.(玉制的簪子) jade hairpin 2.〈*Bot*.〉 fragrant plantain lily

驭 (yù) drive
【驭手】 yùshǒu soldier in charge of pack animals; driver of a military pack train

芋 (yù) 1.〈*Bot*.〉 dasheen: 野～ taro 2.(泛指马铃薯等) tuber crops: 洋～ potato / 山～ sweet potato
【芋头】 yù·tou 〈*Bot*.〉 dasheen

吁[籲] (yù) appeal; call on
(另见"吁"xū)
【吁请】 yùqǐng appeal and request

浴 (yù) bath; bathe

【浴场】 yùchǎng outdoor bathing place：海滨～ bathing beach

【浴池】 yùchí 1.（澡堂内的池子）common bathing pool 2.（澡堂）public bathhouse; public baths

【浴缸】 yùgāng bathtub; bath：水流按摩～ Jacuzzi

【浴巾】 yùjīn bath towel

【浴盆】 yùpén bathtub

【浴盆帘】 yùpénlián shower curtain

【浴室】 yùshì bathroom; shower room

【浴血】 yùxuè bathed in blood; bloody：～奋战 fight a bloody battle

【浴衣】 yùyī bathrobe

【浴皂盒】 yùzhàohé soap dish

欲［慾[1]］(yù) 1.（欲望）desire; longing; wish 2.（希望）wish; want; desire：畅所～言 speak one's mind freely 3.（将要）about to; just going to; on the point of：摇摇～坠 on the verge of collapse; crumbling; tottering

【欲罢不能】 yùbà-bùnéng try to stop but cannot; be unable to stop even thought one wants to

【欲盖弥彰】 yùgài-mízhāng the more one tries to hide, the more one is exposed; try to cover up a misdeed, only to make it more conspicuous

【欲壑难填】 yùhè-nántián greed is like a valley that can never be filled; avarice knows no bounds

【欲速则不达】 yù sù zé bù dá haste brings no success; more haste, less speed

【欲言又止】 yùyányòuzhǐ wish to speak but do not to on a second thought

裕 (yù) abundant; plentiful：富～ abundant; affluent; well-to-do; well-off

【裕固族】 Yùgùzú Yugur（中国少数民族，主要分布在甘肃）

【裕国裕民】 yùguó-yùmín enrich the state and the people

【裕如】 yùrú effortlessly; with ease：应付～ handle with ease

郁［鬱[2,3]］(yù) 1.（香气浓厚）strongly fragrant 2.（茂盛）luxuriant; lush 3.（忧郁）gloomy; depressed

【郁馥】 yùfù fragrant; aromatic

【郁积】 yùjī 1.（不得发泄）smoldering; pent-up; restrained 2.〈*Med.*〉stasis

【郁结】 yùjié smoldering; pent-up; restrained

【郁金香】 yùjīnxiāng 〈*Bot.*〉tulip

【郁闷】 yùmèn gloomy; depressed：心情～ be depressed; with pent-up emotions

【郁血】 yùxuè 〈*Med.*〉stagnation of the blood; venous stasis

【郁郁不乐】 yùyù-bùlè depressed; melancholy; joyless

【郁郁葱葱】 yùyù-cōngcōng lush and green

育 (yù) 1.（生育）give birth to：节～ birth control 2.（养活）rear; raise; bring up; breed：～婴 nurse a baby 3.（教育）educate：智～ intellectual education

【育龄】 yùlíng child-bearing age

【育龄夫妇】 yùlíng fūfù couples of child-bearing age

【育龄妇女】 yùlíng fùnǚ women of child-bearing age

【育苗】 yùmiáo 〈*Agric.*〉grow seedlings

【育苗区】 yùmiáoqū 〈*Agric.*〉nursery garden

【育秧】 yùyāng raise rice seedlings

【育种】 yùzhǒng 〈*Agric.*〉breed

狱［獄］(yù) 1.（监狱）prison; jail; gaol：入～ go to prison; be imprisoned 2.（官司）lawsuit; case：冤～ an unjust charge; an unjust verdict

【狱警】 yùjǐng jailer; gaoler

预 (yù) in advance; beforehand：～约 make an appointment / ～祝成功 wish sb. success

【预报】 yùbào forecast：地震～ earthquake forecast; earthquake prediction / 天气～ weather forecast

【预备】 yùbèi 1.（做好准备）prepare; get ready 2.〈*Sports*〉'Get set!'

【预备党员】 yùbèi dǎngyuán probationary Party member

【预备会议】 yùbèi huìyì preparatory meeting

【预备期】 yùbèiqī probationary period

【预备役】 yùbèiyì 〈*Mil.*〉reserve duty

【预卜】 yùbǔ augur; foretell

【预测】 yùcè calculate; forecast

【预产期】 yùchǎnqī 〈*Med.*〉 expected date of childbirth

【预订】 yùdìng subscribe; book; place an order: ～火车票 book a train ticket

【预定】 yùdìng fix in advance; predetermine; schedule: ～时间 scheduled time

【预防】 yùfáng prevent; take precautions against; guard against: ～为主 put prevention first / ～与治疗相结合 combine treatment with prevention

【预付】 yùfù payment in advance: 老板～了我 500 元,从下月工资里扣。My boss advanced me 500 yuan against next month's salary.

【预付保证金】 yùfù bǎozhèngjīn advance money on security

【预付款】 yùfùkuǎn advance charge; advance payment

【预付租金】 yùfù zūjīn advance deposit

【预感】 yùgǎn 1.(事先感觉) have a premonition 2.(事先感觉到的) premonition; presentiment: 不祥的～ a premonition of danger

【预告】 yùgào 1.(事先通知) announce in advance; herald: ～春天的到来 herald the coming of spring 2.(事先通知的) advance notice

【预告片】 yùgàopiàn 〈*TV*〉 trailer

【预购】 yùgòu purchase in advance

【预会】 yùhuì participate in conference

【预计】 yùjì calculate in advance; estimate

【预见】 yùjiàn 1.(预先料到) foresee; predict: 在可以～到的将来 in the foreseeable future / ～到有问题 foresee trouble 2.(指见识) foresight; prevision: 科学的～ scientific prediction

【预警】 yùjǐng give an alarm in advance; give a prior-warning; early warning (n.)

【预警装置】 yùjǐng zhuāngzhì the prior-warning device

【预科】 yùkē preparatory course; prep school

【预科学生】 yùkē xué·sheng preppy

【预料】 yùliào expect; predict; anticipate

【预谋】 yùmóu premeditate; plan beforehand: ～犯罪 calculated crime / ～事件 a contrived incident

【预期】 yùqī expect; anticipate: 达到～的效果 achieve the desired results

【预期寿命】 yùqī shòumìng life expectancy

【预赛】 yùsài 〈*Sports*〉 preliminary contest; preliminary heats; preliminary; trial match

【预审】 yùshěn antecedent trial; preliminary hearing; inquiry

【预示】 yùshì indicate; presage; forebode; betoken: 黑云～暴风雨将要到来。The dark clouds announced the coming of a storm.

【预售】 yùshòu open to booking; advance booking: 保证～ provide sales / 提供～报告 present a sales account

【预算】 yùsuàn budget: 编制～ build up budget

【预算赤字】 yùsuàn chìzì budget deficit

【预算内】 yùsuànnèi budgetary: ～资金 budgetary funds

【预算年度】 yùsuàn niándù budget year

【预算收入】 yùsuàn shōurù budgetary receipts

【预算税额】 yùsuàn shuì'é estimated assessment

【预算外】 yùsuànwài extra-budgetary

【预算外资金】 yùsuànwài zījīn extra-budgetary funds

【预算项目】 yùsuàn xiàngmù budget items

【预算支出】 yùsuàn zhīchū budget of expenditure

【预习】 yùxí prepare lessons before class

【预先】 yùxiān in advance; beforehand: ～通知 notify in advance

【预想】 yùxiǎng anticipate; expect

【预选】 yùxuǎn forward selection

【预言】 yùyán 1.(预先说出) prophesy; predict; foretell 2.(所作的预言) prophecy; prediction

【预言家】 yùyánjiā prophet

【预演】 yùyǎn preview

【预应力的】 yùyìnglì·de prestressed

【预约】 yùyuē 1.(预先约定) make an appointment 2.(预订) order; subscribe

【预展】 yùzhǎn preview

【预兆】 yùzhào 1.(兆头) omen; presage; harbinger 2.(预示) sign

【预支】 yùzhī 1.(预先支取) get an advance: ～工资 get an advance of one's pay 2.(预支的钱) advance; prepay

【预制】 yùzhì prefabricate

【预制板】 yùzhìbǎn prefabricated parts

【预祝】 yùzhù congratulate beforehand

谕(yù) instruct; instruction (n.): 面～ give instructions in person

喻(yù) 1.(说明) explain; make clear; inform: ～以利害 explain the consequences of an action 2.(明白;了解) understand; know: 不言而～ it goes without saying that 3.(比方) analogy: 比～ metaphor; analogy

愈[瘉[1]](yù) 1.(痊愈) recover: 病～ recover from an illness 2.(叠用) the more ... the more; more and more: ～早～好。The sooner the better.

【愈合】 yùhé 〈*Med.*〉 heal up

【愈加】 yùjiā increasingly; even more; all the more

御[禦[3]](yù) 1.(驾御) drive 2.(皇帝的) imperial 3.(抵御) resist; keep out: ～敌 resist the enemy attack

【御笔】 yùbǐ emperor's handwriting

【御寒】 yùhán keep out the cold

【御花园】 yùhuāyuán imperial garden

【御侮】 yùwǔ resist invasion

【御用】 yùyòng 1.(帝王所用) employed by the emperor; for the use of an emperor 2.(帮凶) hired; in the pay of: ～文人 hired scribbler; hack writer

【御者】 yùzhě driver

寓[庽](yù) 1.(居住) reside; live 2.(住的地方) residence; abode 3.(寄托) imply; contain

【寓教于乐】 yùjiàoyúlè combine education with recreation

【寓居】 yùjū live; make one's home in

【寓所】 yùsuǒ residence; abode; dwelling place

【寓言】 yùyán 1.(比喻) allegory 2.(故事) fable; parable

【寓意】 yùyì implied meaning; moral; message; import: ～深刻 be pregnant with meaning

遇(yù) 1.(相逢) meet: 巧～ meet by chance 2.(对待) treat; receive: 待～ treatment 3.(机会) chance; opportunity: 机～ favorable circumstances; opportunity

【遇刺】 yùcì be attacked by an assassin

【遇到】 yùdào run into; encounter; come across

【遇害】 yùhài be murdered; be assassinated

【遇见】 yùjiàn meet; come across

【遇救】 yùjiù be rescued; be saved

【遇难】 yùnàn 1.(意外死亡) die in an accident 2.(被杀) be murdered

【遇难船只残骸】 yùnàn chuánzhī cánhái flotsam and jetsam

【遇事】 yùshì when anything crops

【遇事干涉】 yùshì gānshè have an oar in every man's boat

【遇险】 yùxiǎn meet with a mishap; be in danger; be in distress: ～船只 ship in distress

【遇险信号】 yùxiǎn xìnhào distress signal; SOS

鹬(yù) 〈*Zool.*〉 sandpiper; snipe; woodcocks: 丘～ Eurasian woodcock

【鹬蚌相争,渔人得利】 yù-bàng xiāng zhēng, yúrén dé lì when the snipe and the clam grapple, the fisherman profits; it's the third party that benefits from the tussle

誉[譽](yù) 1.(名声) reputation; fame: ～满全国 be famed all over the country 2.(称赞) praise: ～不绝口 be praised all the while

yuan

鸢(yuān) 〈*Zool.*〉 red kite

鸳(yuān)

【鸳鸯】 yuānyāng 1.〈*Zool.*〉(水禽) mandarin duck 2.(比喻夫妻) an affectionate couple

【鸳鸯楼】 yuānyānglóu mandarin duck building

冤[寃](yuān) 1.(冤枉) wrong; injustice: 不白之～ unrighted wrong; unredressed injustice 2.(冤仇) feeling of bitterness; hatred; enmity 3.(欺骗) kid; fool; pull sb's leg: 别～人。Don't kid me. 4.(吃亏) bad luck; loss; disadvantage

【冤案】 yuān'àn case of injustice; unjust

charge

【冤仇】 yuānchóu rancor; enmity

【冤家】 yuān·jia 1.（仇人）enemy; foe 2.（称情人）one's destined love; sweetheart; lover

【冤家对头】 yuānjiā-duì·tou adversary; opponent; antagonist

【冤家路窄】 yuānjiā-lùzhǎi enemies are bound to meet on a narrow road; one can't avoid one's enemy

【冤假错案】 yuān-jiǎ cuò'àn unjust; framed-up and wrong cases

【冤情】 yuānqíng grievance

【冤屈】 yuānqū 1.（冤枉）wrong; treat unjustly 2.（不公平的待遇）wrongful treatment; injustice

【冤枉】 yuān·wang 1.（不公待遇）wrong; treat unjustly 别～好人。Don't wrong an innocent person. 2.（给人加恶名）frame up; fabricate an accusation：～好人 frame up an innocent person 3.（不值得）not worthwhile; not repaying the effort：走～路 go the long way

【冤狱】 yuānyù an unjust charge or verdict; a miscarriage of justice：平反～ reverse an unjust verdict

渊［淵］（yuān） 1.（深水）deep pool：为～驱鱼 drive the fish into deep waters 2.（深）deep：～泉 a deep spring

【渊博】 yuānbó broad and profound; erudite

【渊识博学】 yuānshì-bóxué profound knowledge and extensive learning

【渊薮】 yuānsǒu a gathering place of fish or beasts; den; haunt

【渊源】 yuānyuán origin; source

元（yuán） 1.（开始的）first; primary：～月 the first month of the year 2.（为首的）chief; principal：～首 head of state 3.（主要）basic; fundamental：～音 vowel 4.（构成整体的）unit; component：单～ unit 5.（货币单位）yuan

【元宝】 yuánbǎo ingot：金～ gold ingot / 银～ silver ingot

【元旦】 yuándàn New Year's Day

【元件】 yuánjiàn element; component; cell

【元老】 yuánlǎo senior statesman; founding member

【元年】 yuánnián the first year

【元配】 yuánpèi a man's first wife

【元气】 yuánqì vitality; vigor：大伤～ undermine one's constitution; sap one's vitality / 恢复～ regain one's vigor

【元首】 yuánshǒu head of state

【元帅】 yuánshuài 1.（军衔）marshal 2.（全军主帅）supreme commander

【元素】 yuánsù 1.（要素）element 2.〈*Math.*〉element 3.〈*Chem.*〉element：放射性～ radioactive element

【元素符号】 yuánsù fúhào symbol of element

【元宵】 yuánxiāo 1.（节日）the night of the 15th of the 1st lunar month 2.（食品）sweet dumplings made of glutinous rice flour

【元宵节】 yuánxiāojié the Lantern Festival

【元凶】 yuánxiōng prime culprit; arch-criminal

【元勋】 yuánxūn a man of great merit; founding father：开国～ founders of a state

【元音】 yuányīn 〈*Phonet.*〉vowel

【元月】 yuányuè 1.（一月）January 2.（第一月）the first month of a year

芫（yuán）（另见"芫"yán）

【芫花】 yuánhuā 〈*Bot.*〉lilac daphne

园［園］（yuán） 1.（菜园、果园）garden：菜～ vegetable garden 2.（公园、花园）park; garden：动物～ zoological garden; zoo

【园地】 yuándì 1.（统称）garden plot 2.（活动范围）field; scope

【园丁】 yuándīng 1.（花工）gardener 2.（喻教师）teacher

【园林】 yuánlín gardens; park

【园林式】 yuánlínshì landscape style

【园林艺术】 yuánlín yìshù horticulture; art of gardening

【园圃】 yuánpǔ garden, ground used for growing vegetables, flowers or fruit

【园田】 yuántián vegetable garden：耕作～化 gardenstyle cultivation of farmland

【园土】 yuántǔ garden mold

【园艺】 yuányì horticulture; art of gardening ‖ 园艺家 horticulturist

【园艺学】 yuányìxué horticulture; gardening

鼋［黿］（yuán）

【鼋鱼】 yuányú soft-shelled turtle

员 (yuán) 1.(人员) a person: 演～ actor; actress / 学～ student 2.(成员) member 3.〈*classifier*〉一～大将 an able general

【员额】 yuán'é personnel quota

【员工】 yuángōng staff; staff members; personnel: 师生～ teachers, students, administrative personnel and workers

圆 (yuán) 1.(圆形的) round; circular; spherical: ～锯 circular saw / ～孔 a round hole 2.〈*Math.*〉circle (符号为 ⊙): 半～ semicircle 3.(周全) tactful; satisfactory 4.(使圆满) make plausible; justify 5.(货币单位) yuan 6.(圆形钱币) a coin of fixed value and weight: 银～ silver dollar

【圆场】 yuánchǎng mediate; help to effect a compromise: 打～ mediate a dispute; smooth things over

【圆场谎】 yuánchǎnghuǎng white lie

【圆顶】 yuándǐng dome

【圆房】 yuánfáng consummate; consummation

【圆规】 yuánguī compasses

【圆号】 yuánhào 〈*Music*〉French horn

【圆弧】 yuánhú an arc

【圆花窗】 yuánhuāchuāng rose window

【圆滑】 yuánhuá smooth and evasive; slick and sly

【圆寂】 yuánjì 〈*Buddhism*〉Parinirvana; pass away

【圆锯】 yuánjù circular saw

【圆括号】 yuánkuòhào parenthesis; curves ( )

【圆满】 yuánmǎn satisfactory; successful

【圆盘】 yuánpán disk; disc

【圆盘机徽】 yuánpán jīhuī (军用飞机的国别标志) roundel

【圆球】 yuánqiú a ball; a globe

【圆圈】 yuánquān circle; ring

【圆润】 yuánrùn mellow and full

【圆熟】 yuánshú skillful; proficient; dexterous

【圆台】 yuántái truncated cone

【圆通】 yuántōng flexible; accommodating

【圆筒】 yuántǒng a cylinder

【圆舞曲】 yuánwǔqǔ 〈*Music*〉waltz

【圆心】 yuánxīn the center of a circle

【圆心角】 yuánxīnjiǎo central angle

【圆形】 yuánxíng circle; circular; round

【圆形剧场】 yuánxíng jùchǎng amphitheater bowl

【圆周】 yuánzhōu circumference (符号为 ○)

【圆周率】 yuánzhōulǜ pi (符号为 π)

【圆珠笔】 yuánzhūbǐ ball-pen; ballpoint; ballpoint pen

【圆柱】 yuánzhù cylinder

【圆锥】 yuánzhuī cone; circular cone; taper

【圆桌】 yuánzhuō round table

【圆桌会谈】 yuánzhuō huìtán round-table discussion

【圆桌会议】 yuánzhuō huìyì round-table conference

垣 (yuán) 1.(墙) wall: 城～ city wall 2.(城) city

援 (yuán) 1.(用手拉) pull by hand; hold 2.(引用) quote; cite 3.(援助) help; aid; rescue: 求～ ask for help; appeal for aid

【援兵】 yuánbīng reinforcements; relief troops

【援救】 yuánjiù rescue; save; deliver from danger

【援军】 yuánjūn reinforcements; relief troops

【援例】 yuánlì cite a precedent

【援外】 yuánwài foreign aid: ～物资 materials in aid of a foreign country

【援引】 yuányǐn 1.(引用) quote; cite 2.(提拔，引荐) recommend or appoint one's friends or favorites

【援用】 yuányòng quote; cite; invoke: ～条约 invoke a treaty

【援助】 yuánzhù help; support; aid: 财政～ financial aid / 发展～ development aid / 国际～ international support / 技术～ technical assistance / 经济～ economic aid / 经济形式的～ assistance in grant form / 信贷～ credit aid / 利用～ utilize aid

原 (yuán) 1.(最初的) primary; original; former; at first: ～处 original place 2.(没加工的) unprocessed; raw: ～粮 unprocessed food grains / ～煤 raw coal / ～油 crude oil 3.(原谅) excuse; pardon: 情有可～ excusable; pardonable 4.(平原) level; open country; plain: 雪～ snow-clad plain

【原版】 yuánbǎn original edition

【原版片】 yuánbǎnpiàn film in the original
【原本】 yuánběn 1.（原稿）original manuscript; master copy 2.（原书）the original 3.（本来）originally; formerly
【原材料】 yuáncáiliào raw and processed materials
【原产地】 yuánchǎndì country of origin; place of origin
【原地】 yuándì original place: ～踏步 make no progress
【原订租约】 yuándìng zūyuē original tenancy
【原动力】 yuándònglì motive power; motivity
【原封】 yuánfēng with the seal unbroken; intact: ～不动 be left intact
【原稿】 yuángǎo original manuscript; master copy
【原告】 yuángào 〈*Law*〉 1.（民事的）plaintiff 2.（刑事的）prosecutor
【原国籍】 yuánguójí nationality of origin
【原籍】 yuánjí ancestral home
【原价】 yuánjià cost price
【原价转让】 yuánjià zhuǎnràng assignment: ～合同 assignment of a contract
【原件】 yuánjiàn script
【原来】 yuánlái 1.（起初）original; former 2.（表示发现实情）so; turn out to be: ～如此! So that's how it is!
【原理】 yuánlǐ principle; tenet
【原谅】 yuánliàng excuse; forgive; pardon
【原料】 yuánliào raw material: ～生产 production of material
【原料市场】 yuánliào shìchǎng raw materials market
【原料消耗】 yuánliào xiāohào material consumption
【原煤】 yuánméi raw coal
【原棉】 yuánmián 〈*Textiles*〉 raw cotton
【原木】 yuánmù log
【原判】 yuánpàn original judgement; original sentence
【原配】 yuánpèi a man's first wife
【原色】 yuánsè （红、蓝、黄）primary color
【原审】 yuánshěn 〈*Law*〉 first trial
【原声带】 yuánshēngdài original sound tape
【原始】 yuánshǐ 1.（最初的）original; firsthand: ～积累 primitive accumulation / ～记录 original record / ～凭证 original certificate / ～数据 raw data / ～资料 initial data 2.（最古老的；未开发的）primeval; primitive: ～森林 primeval forest; virgin forest / ～社会 primitive society
【原诉】 yuánsù original suit
【原委】 yuánwěi how a thing happened from beginning to end; the whole story; all the details: 说明～ tell the whole story
【原文】 yuánwén original text; the original: 忠实于～ be faithful to the original
【原物】 yuánwù original
【原先】 yuánxiān former; original
【原形】 yuánxíng original shape; the true shape under the disguise: ～毕露 be revealed for what one is; show one's true colors
【原型】 yuánxíng 〈*Mech.*〉 prototype
【原选区】 yuánxuǎnqū home constituency
【原盐】 yuányán crude salt
【原野】 yuányě open country
【原意】 yuányì meaning; original intention
【原因】 yuányīn cause; reason: 成功的～ reasons for the success
【原油】 yuányóu crude oil; crude
【原有】 yuányǒu original
【原原本本】 yuányuán-běnběn from beginning to end; the whole story
【原则】 yuánzé 1.（标准）principle 2.（大体上）in principle: ～同意 agree in principle
【原汁】 yuánzhī neat juice
【原职】 yuánzhí former post
【原址】 yuánzhǐ former address
【原主】 yuánzhǔ original owner: 物归～ return sth. to its owner
【原著】 yuánzhù original work; original
【原装】 yuánzhuāng original
【原状】 yuánzhuàng original state; previous condition; status quo: 维持～ maintain the status quo
【原子】 yuánzǐ atom; atomic (adj.)
【原子尘】 yuánzǐchén fallout
【原子弹】 yuánzǐdàn atom bomb; atomic bomb; A bomb
【原子讹诈】 yuánzǐ ézhà atomic blackmail
【原子反应堆】 yuánzǐ fǎnyìngduī atomic reactor; atomic pile
【原子核】 yuánzǐhé atomic nucleus
【原子能】 yuánzǐnéng atomic energy

【原罪】 yuánzuì 〈*RC Ch.*〉 original sin

【原作】 yuánzuò original work; original

源(yuán) 1.(源流) source; fountain-head 2.(来源) source; cause: 病～ cause of a disease / 财～ source of income / 货～ the source of supplies

【源程序】 yuánchéngxù 〈*Computer*〉 source program

【源程序库】 yuánchéngxùkù 〈*Computer*〉 source library

【源代码】 yuándàimǎ 〈*Computer*〉 source code

【源流】 yuánliú source and course; origin and development

【源泉】 yuánquán source; fountainhead: 知识～ source of knowledge

【源数据】 yuánshùjù 〈*Computer*〉 source data

【源头】 yuántóu fountainhead; source

【源源】 yuányuán in a steady stream; continuously: ～不断的供应 an unfailing supply of sth.

【源远流长】 yuányuǎn-liúcháng a distant source and a long stream; of long standing and well established

猿[猨](yuán) ape

【猿猴】 yuánhóu apes and monkeys

【猿人】 yuánrén ape-man: 北京～ Beijing man

辕(yuán) shafts of a cart or carriage

【辕马】 yuánmǎ horse in the shafts; shaft-horse

缘(yuán) 1.(缘故) reason: 无～无故 without rhyme or reason; for no reason at all 2.(边缘) edge; fringe; brink 3.(缘分) predestined relationship 4.(沿着) along 5.〈*Buddhism*〉 conditioning cause: 结～ form cause; lay the basis for future relationship

【缘分】 yuánfèn 1.(机会) lot or luck by which people are brought together 2.〈*Buddhism*〉 destiny as conditioned by one's past

【缘故】 yuángù cause; reason: 为…的～ for the cause of ...

【缘何】 yuánhé why

【缘木求鱼】 yuánmù-qiúyú climb a tree to catch fish; a fruitless approach

【缘石】 yuánshí curb (AmE.); kerb (BrE.)

【缘由】 yuányóu reason; cause

远[遠](yuǎn) far; distant; remote: 不要走得太～。Do not go too far afield.

【远程】 yuǎnchéng long-range; long-distance: ～航行 long voyage / ～火箭 long-range rocket

【远程宽体客机】 yuǎnchéng kuāntǐ kèjī wide-body long haul airliner

【远处】 yuǎnchù in the distance: 汽车的大灯灯光在很～还看得见。The car's headlights gleamed in the distance.

【远大】 yuǎndà long-range; broad; ambitious: ～的计划 a long-range plan; an ambitious plan

【远道】 yuǎndào a long way: ～而来 come a long way; come from afar

【远地点】 yuǎndìdiǎn 〈*Astron.*〉 apogee

【远东】 yuǎndōng the Far East

【远方】 yuǎnfāng distant place; remote place: ～来的朋友 friends from afar

【远房】 yuǎnfáng distantly related

【远隔重洋】 yuǎngé-chóngyáng be separated by vast oceans

【远古】 yuǎngǔ remote antiquity; remote ancient times

【远海】 yuǎnhǎi distant sea waters

【远航】 yuǎnháng long voyage

【远见】 yuǎnjiàn foresight; vision: ～卓识 foresight and sagacity

【远郊】 yuǎnjiāo outer suburbs

【远近】 yuǎnjìn 1.(近处和远处) far and near: ～闻名 be know far and wide 2.(距离长短) distance

【远景】 yuǎnjǐng 1.(远处景物) distant view 2.(将来的) long-range perspective; prospect: ～规划 a long-range plan 3.〈*Cinematog.*〉 long shot

【远距离投篮】 yuǎnjùlí tóulán 〈*Sports*〉 long shot

【远离家乡】 yuǎnlí jiāxiāng far away from one's native village

【远虑】 yuǎnlǜ foresight; long view: 深谋～ think deeply and plan carefully; be circumspect and farsighted

【远门】 yuǎnmén far away from home: 出～

go on a long journey
【远期】 yuǎnqī at a specified future date; forward: ～汇价 forward rate
【远亲】 yuǎnqīn distant relative; remote kinsfolk
【远日点】 yuǎnrìdiǎn 〈*Astron*.〉 aphelion
【远射】 yuǎnshè 〈*Football*〉 long drive
【远涉重洋】 yuǎnshè-chóngyáng travel across the high seas
【远视】 yuǎnshì 〈*Med*.〉 long sight
【远视眼】 yuǎnshìyǎn 〈*Med*.〉 hyperopia; farsightedness; farsighted (adj.)
【远视眼镜】 yuǎnshì yǎnjìng spectacles for long sight; spectacles for the farsighted
【远销】 yuǎnxiāo sale to distant places
【远行】 yuǎnxíng go on a long journey
【远洋】 yuǎnyáng ocean; oceanic
【远洋航线】 yuǎnyáng hángxiàn ocean lane; ocean route
【远洋客货班轮】 yuǎnyáng kèhuò bānlún combined cargo and passenger liner
【远游】 yuǎnyóu travel faraway
【远征】 yuǎnzhēng expedition
【远征军】 yuǎnzhēngjūn expeditionary army
【远走高飞】 yuǎnzǒu-gāofēi fly far and high; be off to distant parts
【远足】 yuǎnzú pleasure trip on foot; hike; walking tour

苑 (yuàn) **1**.(帝王花园) enclosure: 鹿～ deer park **2**.(荟萃之处) center; world: 文～ the art and literature world

怨 (yuàn) **1**.(怨恨) resentment; enmity: 抱～ complain; grumble **2**.(责怪) blame; complain: 任劳任～ bear hardships and blame
【怨不得】 yuàn·bu·de **1**.(不能抱怨) cannot blame **2**.(难怪) no wonder
【怨愤】 yuànfèn discontent and indignation
【怨恨】 yuànhèn **1**.(对人不满或仇恨) have a grudge against sb.; hate **2**.(不满或仇恨) resentment; grudge; enmity
【怨偶】 yuàn'ǒu an unhappy couple
【怨气】 yuànqì grievance; complaint; resentment
【怨声载道】 yuànshēng-zàidào complaints are heard everywhere; cries of discontent rise all round
【怨天尤人】 yuàntiān-yóurén blame god and man; blame everyone and everything but oneself
【怨言】 tuànyán complaint; grumble

院 (yuàn) **1**.(院子) courtyard; yard; compound: 居民大～ neighborhood compound **2**.(机关名称)国务～ state council / 科学～ the academy of sciences **3**.(学院) college **4**.(医院) hospital: 出～ be out of hospital; be discharged from hospital / 转～ transfer to another hospital
【院落】 yuànluò courtyard; yard; compound
【院士】 yuànshì academician
【院子】 yuàn·zi courtyard; yard

愿 [願] (yuàn) **1**.(愿望) hope; wish; desire: 平生之～ a lifelong wish **2**.(愿意) be willing; be ready: 他不～为那么一本书花 30 元。He grudges paying 30 yuan for such a book. **3**.(愿心) vow: 还～ redeem a vow
【愿望】 yuànwàng desire; wish; aspiration: 要求独立的～ the desire for independence
【愿意】 yuànyì **1**.(同意) be willing; be ready: ～作出任何牺牲 be willing to make any sacrifice / 我将很～帮助你。I'll be glad to help you. **2**.(希望) wish; like; want: 我不～打扰你。I don't want to bother you.

yue

曰 (yuē) **1**.(说) say **2**.(称作) be named as; be called

约 (yuē) **1**.(提出或商量) make an appointment; arrange: ～某人做某事 make an appointment with sb. for sth. **2**.(邀请) ask or invite in advance **3**.(约定的事) pact; agreement; appointment: 践～ keep an appointment / 立～ make a pact; come to an agreement / 私下立～卖车 sell a car by private treaty **4**.(拘束) restrict; restrain **5**.(俭省) economical; frugal: 节～ economize **6**. 〈*Math*.〉 reduction of a fraction **7**.(简要) simple; brief **8**.(大概) about; around: ～一个月 about a month
(另见"约"yāo)
【约等于】 yuēděngyú is approximately (符号为 ≈)

【约定】 yuēdìng agree on; appoint; arrange: 我~好时间去看医生。I made an appointment to see the doctor. / 他们将在~的时间和地点会面。They were to meet at a given time and place.

【约定价】 yuēdìngjià striking price

【约定俗成】 yuēdìng-súchéng established by usage; accepted through common practice

【约法】 yuēfǎ provisional constitution

【约访】 yuēfǎng invite people to come and discuss certain questions

【约分】 yuēfēn 〈*Math.*〉 reduction of a fraction

【约古宗列渠】 Yuēgǔzōnglièqú 〈place〉 Yoigilangleb Qu

【约会】 yuēhuì **1.**(约定) make an appointment **2.**(相会) appointment; engagement: 赴~ keep an appointment

【约集】 yuējí meet by appointment; gather

【约计】 yuējì count roughly; come roughly to

【约略】 yuēlüè rough; approximate: ~的估计 a rough estimate

【约莫】 yuē·mo about; roughly; or so

【约摸】 yuē·mo 同"约莫"

【约期】 yuēqī **1.**(约定日期) fix a date; appoint a time: ~会晤 fix a date for the interview **2.**(约定的日期) date fixed; appointment: 耽误了~ fail to keep an appointment **3.**(契约期限) stated period: ~已满。The contract is no longer valid.

【约请】 yuēqǐng invite; ask

【约束】 yuēshù keep within bounds; restrain; bind: ~严明 practice rigid discipline

【约束力】 yuēshùlì binding force

【约数】 yuēshù **1.**(大约的数) approximate number **2.**〈*Math.*〉 divisor: 公~ common divisor

【约言】 yuēyán promise; word; pledge: 违背~ break one's promise; go back on one's word

月 (yuè) **1.**(月球) the moon **2.**(月份) month: 本~ this month **3.**(每月的) monthly: ~报表 monthly report / ~产量 monthly output **4.**(像月亮的) round; full-moon shaped

【月白】 yuèbái bluish white; very pale blue

【月半】 yuèbàn the 15th day of a month

【月报】 yuèbào **1.**(月刊) monthly magazine; monthly **2.**(每月的汇报) monthly report

【月饼】 yuè·bing moon cake

【月初】 yuèchū the beginning of a month

【月底】 yuèdǐ the end of a month; e.o.m.

【月度】 yuèdù monthly: ~计划 a monthly plan

【月份】 yuèfèn month: 上个~ last month

【月份牌】 yuèfènpái calendar

【月光】 yuèguāng moonlight; moonbeam

【月桂树】 yuèguìshù 〈*Bot.*〉 laurel; bay tree

【月华】 yuèhuá **1.**(日光) moonlight: ~如水 watery moonbeams; a flood of translucent moonlight **2.**〈*Meteorol.*〉 lunar corona

【月季】 yuèjì 〈*Bot.*〉 rose; Chinese rose

【月经】 yuèjīng 〈*Physiol.*〉 menses; menstruation; period; menstrual (adj.)

【月经不调】 yuèjīng bùtiáo 〈*Med.*〉 irregular menstruation

【月经过多】 yuèjīng guòduō 〈*Med.*〉 menorrhagia

【月经来潮】 yuèjīng láicháo 〈*Physiol.*〉 menstruation

【月经棉条】 yuèjīng miántiáo tampon

【月刊】 yuèkān monthly magazine; monthly

【月历】 yuèlì monthly calendar

【月亮】 yuè·liang the moon

【月亮门儿】 yuè·liangménr moon gate; round gate

【月末】 yuèmò the end of a month

【月偏食】 yuèpiānshí 〈*Astron.*〉 partial lunar eclipse

【月票】 yuèpiào monthly ticket

【月琴】 yuèqín *yueqin*; 4-stringed full-moon-shaped Chinese mandolin

【月球】 yuèqiú 〈*Astron.*〉 the moon

【月全食】 yuèquánshí 〈*Astron.*〉 total lunar eclipse

【月色】 yuèsè moonlight

【月食】 yuèshí 〈*Astron.*〉 lunar eclipse

【月台】 yuètái 〈*Railway*〉 platform

【月台票】 yuètáipiào 〈*Railway*〉 platform ticket

【月尾】 yuèwěi the end of a month

【月息】 yuèxī monthly interest

【月下老】 yuèxiàlǎo matchmaker

【月薪】 yuèxīn monthly pay
【月牙】 yuèyá 〈*colloq.*〉 crescent moon
【月夜】 yuèyè moonlit night
【月晕】 yuèyùn lunar halo
【月中】 yuèzhōng the middle of a month
【月子】 yuè·zi **1.** (分娩后的第一月) month of confinement after giving birth to a child: 坐～ be in confinement **2.** (分娩时期) time of childbirth; confinement
【月子病】 yuè·zibìng puerperal fever

乐[**樂**] (yuè) music (另见"乐"lè)

【乐池】 yuèchí orchestra pit; orchestra
【乐队】 yuèduì orchestra; band: 管弦～ orchestra / 爵士～ jazz band
【乐队指挥】 yuèduì zhǐhuī conductor
【乐理】 yuèlǐ 〈*Music*〉 music theory
【乐谱】 yuèpǔ music score; music
【乐器】 yuèqì musical instrument; instrument: 键盘～ keyboard instruments / 打击～ percussion instruments / 弦～ stringed instruments / 弓弦～ bowed stringed instruments / 拨弦～ plucked instruments / 击弦～ hammered string instruments
【乐曲】 yuèqǔ musical composition; composition; music
【乐师】 yuèshī musicians
【乐坛】 yuètán music circles
【乐团】 yuètuán **1.** (交响乐团) philharmonic society **2.** (交响乐团管弦乐队) philharmonic orchestra: 交响～ symphony orchestra / 民族～ national music ensemble
【乐舞】 yuèwǔ dance accompanied by music
【乐章】 yuèzhāng 〈*Music*〉 movement

岳[**嶽**[1]] (yuè) **1.** (高山) high mountain **2.** (称妻子父母) wife's parents

【岳得尔调】 yuèdé'ěrdiào 〈*Music*〉 yodel
【岳父】 yuèfù father-in-law; wife's father
【岳母】 yuèmǔ mother-in-law; wife's mother

悦 (yuè) **1.** (高兴) happy; pleased; delighted: 和颜～色 a kindly countenance; a genial look **2.** (使愉快) please delight: 取～于人 try to please sb.

【悦耳】 yuè'ěr be pleasing to the ear; be melodious; tuneful: ～的歌声 sweet song
【悦服】 yuèfú heartily admire
【悦目】 yuèmù pleasing to the eye; good-looking

阅 (yuè) **1.** (阅读) read; go over: 请～背面。Please turn over. (P. T. O.) / 请～抄本 see copy (S. C) **2.** (检阅) review; inspect **3.** (经历) experience; pass through

【阅兵】 yuèbīng review troops
【阅兵场】 yuèbīngchǎng parade ground
【阅兵式】 yuèbīngshì military review; parade
【阅读】 yuèdú read
【阅读困难】 yuèdú kùn·nan 〈*Med.*〉 dyslexia
【阅卷】 yuèjuàn mark a paper; grade examination
【阅览】 yuèlǎn read
【阅览室】 yuèlǎnshì reading room
【阅历】 yuèlì **1.** (亲身经历) see, hear or do for oneself **2.** (由此得来的知识) experience: ～浅 having little experience; inexperienced
【阅批】 yuèpī go over and make written comments
【阅世】 yuèshì see the world: ～甚深 be deeply experienced in worldly affairs

越 (yuè) **1.** (跨过) get over; jump over: ～墙而入 enter by climbing over the wall **2.** (超出) exceed; overstep **3.** (昂扬) be at high pitch: 激～ intense; loud and strong **4.** (叠用) the more ... the more; more and more: ～多～好 the more the better / ～快～好 the faster, the better / ～早～好 the earlier, the better

【越冬】 yuèdōng live through the winter
【越发】 yuèfā all the more; even more: 天儿～热了。It's getting even hotter.
【越轨】 yuèguǐ exceed the bounds; transgress: ～行为 impermissible behavior; transgression
【越过】 yuèguò cross; surmount; negotiate: ～篱笆 get over a fence / ～障碍 surmount obstacles
【越级】 yuèjí **1.** (越过本单位领导) bypass the immediate leadership **2.** (不按一般次序) skip a grade or rank: ～提升 promote sb. more than one grade at a time
【越界】 yuèjiè overstep the boundary; cross the border
【越境】 yuèjìng cross the boundary illegally;

sneak in or out of a country

【越橘】 yuèjú 〈*Bot.*〉 cowberry

【越来越…】 yuèláiyuè… more and more：～深入人心 penetrate deeper and deeper into the hearts and minds of the people

【越权】 yuèquán exceed one's power or authority：～行为 act in excess of authority

【越位】 yuèwèi 〈*Sports*〉 offside

【越野】 yuèyě cross-country

【越野摩托车】 yuèyě mótuōchē cross-country motorcycle

【越野汽车】 yuèyě qìchē cross-country car

【越野赛】 yuèyěsài cross-country race; cross-country

【越狱】 yuèyù escape from prison; break prison

跃[躍](yuè) leap; jump：～居世界首位 leap to first place in the world

【跃进】 yuèjìn make a leap; leap forward

【跃马飞驰】 yuèmǎ-fēichí leap on a horse and ride swiftly

【跃然】 yuèrán appear vividly：～纸上 full of life

【跃跃欲试】 yuèyuè-yùshì be eager to have a try; itch to have a go

yun

晕(yūn) **1.**(头脑发昏) dizzy; giddy **2.**(昏迷) swoon; faint
(另见"晕"yùn)

【晕倒】 yūndǎo fall in a faint; pass out

【晕头转向】 yūntóu-zhuànxiàng confused and disoriented

云[雲^{2}](yún) **1.**(说) say：人～亦～ repeat what others say; parrot **2.**(云彩) cloud：乌～ dark clouds

【云豹】 yúnbào 〈*Zool.*〉 clouded leopard

【云层】 yúncéng cloud layer

【云堤】 yúndī 〈*Meteorol.*〉 cloudbank

【云海】 yúnhǎi a sea of clouds

【云集】 yúnjí come together in crowds; gather; converge：外商～广州。Many foreign merchants gathered in Guangzhou.

【云猫】 yúnmāo 〈*Zool.*〉 marbled cat

【云母】 yúnmǔ 〈*Mineral.*〉 mica

【云气】 yúnqì thin, floating clouds

【云雀】 yúnquè 〈*Zool.*〉 skylark

【云杉】 yúnshān 〈*Bot.*〉 dragon spruce; Chinese spruce：欧洲～ European spruce

【云山雾罩】 yúnshān-wùzhào extravagant and baseless talk

【云鼠】 yúnshǔ 〈*Zool.*〉 cloud rat

【云梯】 yúntī scaling ladder

【云图】 yúntú 〈*Meteorol.*〉 cloud atlas; cloud chart

【云雾】 yúnwù cloud and mist; mist

【云霞】 yúnxiá rosy clouds

【云霄】 yúnxiāo the skies：响彻～ resound to the skies

【云消雾散】 yúnxiāo-wùsàn the clouds melt and the mists disperse; vanish into thin air

【云烟】 yúnyān cloud and mist

芸[蕓](yún)

【芸豆】 yúndòu kidney bean

【芸香】 yúnxiāng 〈*Bot.*〉 rue

【芸芸】 yúnyún many; numerous

【芸芸众生】 yúnyún-zhòngshēng 〈*Buddhism*〉 all living things; all mortal beings

纭(yún)

【纭纭】 yúnyún numerous and disorderly; diverse and confused

耘(yún) weed out; hoe

匀(yún) **1.**(均匀) even; smooth：分得不～ be not evenly divided **2.**(使均匀) even up; divide evenly **3.**(分出一部分) spare：你们能～一些化肥给我们吗？Would you spare us some chemical fertilizer?

【匀称】 yún·chèn well-proportioned; well-balanced; symmetrical：身材～ of proportional build

【匀净】 yún·jing uniform; even

【匀整】 yúnzhěng neat and well spaced; even and orderly

允(yǔn) **1.**(允许) permit; allow; consent：应～ consent **2.**(公平) fair; just：公～ fair; equitable

【允诺】 yǔnnuò promise; consent; undertake：欣然～ readily consent

【允许】 yǔnxǔ permit; allow：～10%的通货

膨胀 allow 10% for inflation

陨(yǔn) fall from the sky or outer space

【陨落】 yǔnluò fall from the sky of outer space

【陨星】 yǔnxīng 〈*Astron.*〉 meteorite：石～ aerolite; stony meteorite / 铁～ siderite; iron meteorite

【陨星雨】 yǔnxīngyǔ 〈*Astron.*〉 meteorite rain

殒(yǔn) perish; die

【殒命】 yǔnmìng 〈*written*〉 meet one's death; perish

【殒身】 yǔnshēn 〈*written*〉 meet one's death; perish

孕(yùn) 1.(怀孕) be pregnant：怀～ be pregnant 2.(身孕) pregnancy

【孕妇】 yùnfù pregnant woman; expectant mother; mother-to-be

【孕期】 yùnqī 〈*Med.*〉 pregnancy; gestation

【孕酮】 yùntóng progesterone

【孕吐】 yùntù 〈*Med.*〉 vomit during pregnancy

【孕育】 yùnyù be pregnant with; breed

【孕甾酮】 yùnzāitóng progesterone

运[運](yùn) 1.(运动) motion; movement 2.(运输) carry; transport：货～ freight transport / 空～ air transport; airlift / 用卡车把货物～往山区 transport goods to the mountain regions by truck 3.(运用) use; wield; utilize 4.(运气) fortune; luck; fate：好～ good luck

【运程】 yùnchéng haul

【运筹】 yùnchóu map out a strategy

【运筹帷幄】 yùnchóu-wéiwò devise strategies within a command tent

【运筹学】 yùnchóuxué operational research; operations research

【运单】 yùndān waybill：货～ cargo waybill

【运动】 yùndòng 1.〈*Physics*〉 motion; movement 2.(体育) sports; athletics; exercise：体育～ athletic sports / 冰上～ ice sports / 冬季～ winter sports / 球类～ ball games / 室内～ indoor sports / 水上～ aquatic sports / 田径～ athletics; track and field / 夏季～ summer sports / 现代五项～ modern pentathlon 3.(活动) movement; campaign; drive：国际共产主义～ international communist movement

【运动】 yùn·dong (奔走钻营) be busy running about in order to seek personal gain

【运动包】 yùndòngbāo gym bag

【运动场】 yùndòngchǎng playing-field; sports ground

【运动服】 yùndòngfú sportswear：～上衣 sports coat; sport coat

【运动会】 yùndònghuì sports meet; games：全国～ National Games / 亚洲～ Asian Games

【运动健将】 yùndòng jiànjiàng master of sports

【运动量】 yùndòngliàng amount of exercises

【运动鞋】 yùndòngxié sport shoes; gym shoes

【运动学】 yùndòngxué 〈*Physics*〉 kinematics; kinematic (adj.)

【运动员】 yùndòngyuán sportsman (m.); sportswoman (f.)：田径～ athlete / 球类～ player

【运费】 yùnfèi transportation expenses; freight; carriage：纯～ clean freight / 降低～ discount from freight

【运河】 yùnhé canal：巴拿马～把大西洋和太平洋连接起来了。The Panama Canal connects the Atlantic and Pacific Oceans.

【运价】 yùnjià traffic fee

【运力】 yùnlì transport capacity

【运气】 yùnqì 1.(贯注气力) directing one's strength, through concentration, to a part of the body 2. yùn·qi (命运) fortune; luck 3.(幸运) lucky

【运球】 yùnqiú 〈*Sports*〉 dribble

【运输】 yùnshū transport; carriage; conveyance

【运输工具】 yùnshū gōngjù means of transport

【运输机】 yùnshūjī transport plane

【运输舰】 yùnshūjiàn transport ship

【运送】 yùnsòng transport; ship; convey

【运算】 yùnsuàn 〈*Math.*〉 operate; operation (n.)

【运算器】 yùnsuànqì 〈*Computer*〉 arithmetic unit

【运销】 yùnxiāo transportation and sale

【运销渠道】 yùnxiāo qúdào channel of distribution
【运行】 yùnxíng move; be in motion
【运行图】 yùnxíngtú 〈*Railway*〉 railroads chart; railways chart
【运营】 yùnyíng **1.**（运行和营业）run; operate; play **2.**（经营）maintenance; operation; running; service; working
【运用】 yùnyòng utilize; wield; apply; put to use: ～自如 handle very skillfully; have a perfect command of
【运载工具】 yùnzài gōngjù means of delivery
【运载火箭】 yùnzài huǒjiàn carrier rocket
【运载量】 yùnzàiliàng 〈*Transport*〉 busload
【运转】 yùnzhuǎn **1.**（沿轨道运转）revolve; turn round **2.**（指机器）work; operate: 机器～正常。The machine works well. **3.**（喻组织、机构）maintain; operate; run; work
【运作】 yùnzuò operate; run; work

酝［醞］(yùn) brew
【酝酿】 yùnniàng **1.**（图谋）brew; ferment **2.**（非正式讨论）have a preliminary informal discussion; deliberate on: ～中的方案 a scheme afoot

晕(yùn) **1.**（头昏）dizzy; giddy; faint: 头～目眩 have a dizzy spell; be afflicted with vertigo **2.**〈*Meteorol.*〉 halo: 日～ solar halo / 月～ lunar halo
（另见“晕”yūn）
【晕场】 yùnchǎng have stage fright
【晕车】 yùnchē carsickness; carsick (adj.)
【晕船】 yùnchuán seasickness; seasick (adj.)
【晕火车】 yùnhuǒchē trainsickness; trainsick (adj.)
【晕机】 yùnjī airsickness; airsick (adj.)
【晕针】 yùnzhēn 〈*Chin. Med.*〉 have a fainting spell during acupuncture treatment

愠(yùn)
【愠怒】 yùnnù be inwardly angry
【愠色】 yùnsè gloomy countenance

蕴(yùn) contain
【蕴藏】 yùncáng hold in store; contain
【蕴藏量】 yùncángliàng reserves; deposits: 煤炭～ coal deposits
【蕴涵】 yùnhán 〈*Logic*〉 implication
【蕴蓄】 yùnxù lie hidden and undeveloped; be latent

韵［韻］(yùn) **1.**（声音）musical sound; sweet tone **2.**（韵母）rhyme: 平～ rhymes in the even tone / 押～ be in rhyme / 仄～ oblique rhymes **3.**（情趣）charm: 风～ personal charm; graceful bearing
【韵脚】 yùnjiǎo the rhyming word that ends a line of verse; rhyme
【韵律】 yùnlǜ **1.**（平仄格式）meter **2.**（押韵规则）rules of rhyming; rhyme scheme
【韵律体操】 yùnlǜ tǐcāo rhythmic gymnastics
【韵事】 yùnshì **1.**（风雅的）literary or artistic pursuits; often with pretense to good taste and refinement **2.**（浪漫的）romantic affair
【韵味】 yùnwèi lingering charm; lasting appeal: 别有～ possess special charm
【韵文】 yùnwén literary composition in rhyme; verse

熨(yùn) iron; press: ～衣服 iron clothes / 快干免～ wash and wear
【熨斗】 yùndǒu flatiron; iron: 电～ electric iron

Z

za

扎［紮、紥］(zā) tie; bind: ～起头发 tie one's hair up / ～上鞋带 tie a shoelace
(另见"扎"zhā)

匝［帀］(zā) 1.(周) circle; circumference 2.(环绕) surround; encircle 3.(茂密) dense; full; thick

咂(zā) 1.(吸) sip; suck 2.(咂嘴) make clicks (of admiration, praise, etc.) 3.(辨别滋味) savor carefully; taste carefully

【咂嘴】 zāzuǐ make clicks (of admiration, praise, etc.)

杂［襍、雜、㮶］(zá) 1.(多种多样) miscellaneous; sundry; mixed: ～集 mixed bag 2.(搀杂) mix; mingle: 夹～ be mixed up with; be mingled with

【杂拌儿】 zábànr 1.(杂干果) assorted preserved fruits; mixed sweetmeats 2.(杂凑的事物) mixture; miscellany; medley

【杂草】 zácǎo weeds; rank grass: ～丛生 be overgrown with weeds

【杂凑】 zácòu knock together; odds and ends

【杂费】 záfèi 1.(零碎费用) incidental expenses; incidentals 2.(额外费用) sundry fees; extras

【杂感】 zágǎn 1.(指感想) random thoughts 2.(杂记) a type of literature recording such thoughts

【杂烩】 záhuì 1.(菜名) mixed stew; hotchpotch 2.(杂凑起来的事物) mixture; miscellany; medley; hotchpotch

【杂货】 záhuò sundry goods; groceries

【杂货店】 záhuòdiàn grocery

【杂记】 zájì 1.(笔记) jottings; notes 2.(一种文体) miscellanies

【杂技】 zájì acrobatics: ～表演 acrobatic show ‖ 杂技演员 acrobat

【杂技团】 zájìtuán acrobatic troupe

【杂家】 zájiā the Eclectics

【杂交】 zájiāo 〈*Biol.*〉 hybridize; hybridization (n.); cross

【杂交水稻】 zájiāo shuǐdào hybrid rice

【杂交玉米】 zájiāo yùmǐ hybrid maize

【杂居】 zájū live together

【杂粮】 záliáng coarse cereals; food grains other than wheat and rice

【杂乱】 záluàn mixed and disorderly; in a jumble; in a muddle

【杂乱无章】 záluàn-wúzhāng disorderly and unsystematic; disorganized

【杂念】 zániàn distracting thoughts

【杂牌】 zápái a less known and inferior brand

【杂牌货】 zápáihuò goods of an inferior brand

【杂色】 zásè variegated; parti-colored; party-colored; motley

【杂耍】 záshuǎ variety show; vaudeville ‖ 杂耍演员 acrobat

【杂税】 záshuì miscellaneous levies; sundry tax

【杂碎】 zá·sui chopped cooked entrails (of sheep or oxen)

【杂谈】 zátán chat; rambling talk; random talk

【杂文】 záwén essay

【杂务】 záwù odd jobs; sundry duties

【杂务工】 záwùgōng odd-job man

【杂项】 záxiàng sundry

【杂项费用】 záxiàng fèiyòng miscellaneous expenses

【杂项收益】 záxiàng shōuyì miscellaneous income

【杂项支出】 záxiàng zhīchū miscellaneous payments

【杂音】 záyīn 1.（非正常声音）noise 2.〈*Electr.*〉static 3.〈*Med.*〉murmur：心脏～ heart murmur

【杂志】 zázhì magazine

【杂质】 zázhì 1.（不纯成分）impurity 2.〈*Chem.*〉foreign matter

【杂质离子】 zázhì lízǐ foreign ion

【杂种】 zázhǒng 1.〈*Biol.*〉hybrid; crossbreed 2.（骂人话）bastard; son of a bitch

砸（zá） 1.（撞；打）pound; tamp 2.（打破）break; smash

【砸饭碗】 zá fànwǎn get the sack; be fired; lose one's work

【砸碎】 zásuì break into pieces; smash; shatter

咋［唓］（zǎ） how; why

zai

灾［災］（zāi） 1.（灾害）calamity; disaster 2.（不幸）personal misfortune; adversity

【灾害】 zāihài calamity; disaster：自然～ natural calamity; natural disaster

【灾患】 zāihuàn 〈*written*〉calamity; disaster

【灾荒】 zāihuāng famine; famine due to crop failures

【灾祸】 zāihuò disaster; calamity; catastrophe

【灾民】 zāimín victims of a natural calamity

【灾难】 zāinàn suffering; calamity; disaster; catastrophe

【灾情】 zāiqíng the condition of a disaster

【灾区】 zāiqū disaster area

【灾星】 zāixīng Jonah

甾（zāi） 〈*Chem.*〉steroid

【甾醇】 zāichún 〈*Chem.*〉sterol

栽（zāi） 1.（栽种）plant; grow：～花 grow flowers / ～树 plant trees 2.（插上）stick in; insert; plant 3.（硬安）frame up; force sth. on sb.; impose：把罪名～在某人身上 frame up a case against sb. 4.（跌倒）tumble; fall：～进河里 fall into a river

【栽跟头】 zāi gēn·tou 1.（跌倒）tumble; fall 2.（失败或出丑）suffer a setback; come a cropper

【栽培】 zāipéi 1.（种植）cultivate; grow：外国～的苹果 apples of foreign growth 2.（造就）foster; train; educate：～人才 cultivate and nourish talent 3.（提拔）help advance sb's career; patronize

【栽赃】 zāizāng 1.（陷害）plant stolen or banned goods on sb. 2.（硬安罪名）frame sb.; fabricate a charge against sb.

【栽植】 zāizhí plant; transplant

【栽种】 zāizhòng plant; grow; cultivate

载（zǎi） 1.（年）year：数～ several years 2.（记载）put down in writing; record：～入史册 go down in history

（另见"载"zài）

宰（zǎi） 1.（杀）slaughter; butcher：～羊 butcher sheep 2.（主管；主持）govern; rule：主～ dominate; dictate

【宰割】 zǎigē invade, oppress and exploit：任人～ subject to oppression and exploitation

【宰杀】 zǎishā slaughter; butcher

崽［仔］（zǎi） 1.（儿子）son 2.（幼小动物）young animal; whelp

【崽子】 zǎi·zi （骂人的话）whelp; bastard：兔～ brat

仔（zǎi） 1.（儿子）son 2.（幼小动物）young animal; whelp

（另见"仔"zǐ）

【仔裤】 zǎikù jeans; blue jeans

再（zài） 〈*adv.*〉 1.（又一次）another time; again; once more try again ～试一次 try again / 请～来。Come again. / 请～说一遍。Please say that again. 2.（如果继续）你～不走，就要迟到了。You'll be late if you don't start now. 3.（然后）then; before：你仔细想想之后～回答 。Think carefully before you answer. 4.（再继续）come back; return：～行任事 return to one's work

【再版】 zàibǎn 1.（第二版）second edition 2.（第二印）reprint; second impression

【再保险】 zài bǎoxiǎn reinsurance：义务～ obligatory reinsurance

【再出口】 zài chūkǒu 〈*Trade*〉 reexport：～贸易 reexport trade

【再次】 zàicì once more; a second time; once again

【再度】 zàidù once more; a second time; once again：～当选 be reelected

【再犯】 zàifàn repeat an offense

【再会】 zàihuì 〈*politeness*〉 good-bye; see you again

【再婚】 zàihūn remarry; marry again; deuterogamy; digamy

【再嫁】 zàijià remarry

【再见】 zàijiàn 〈*politeness*〉 good-bye; see you again; adieu：当我们说～时，我就没期望能再见到她。When we said adieu, I never expected to see her again.

【再接再励】 zàijiē-zàilì make persistent efforts; continue to exert oneself; work ceaselessly and unremittingly

【再进口】 zài jìnkǒu 〈*Trade*〉 reimport

【再起】 zàiqǐ recurrence; resurgence; revival

【再三】 zàisān over and over again; time and again; again and again; repeatedly：～考虑 consider over and over again

【再审】 zàishěn 1.（重新审查）examine again; review 2.〈*Law*〉 retrial; new trial; reopening of a case; rehear

【再生】 zàishēng 1.（死而复生）revive; rise again 2.〈*Biol*.〉 regeneration 3.（回收再制）regenerate; reprocess

【再生产】 zài shēngchǎn 〈*Econ*.〉 reproduction：简单～ simple reproduction / 扩大～ reproduction on an extended scale; extended reproduction

【再生性】 zàishēngxìng reproducibility

【再生之德】 zàishēngzhīdé the grace of rebirth; one's grateful acknowledgment

【再说】 zàishuō 1.（留待以后办理）put off until some time later 2.（表示进一步）what's more; besides

【再调整】 zàitiáozhěng retrim; readjustment

【再贴现】 zàitiēxiàn 〈*Econ*.〉 rediscount; retrocession

【再现】 zàixiàn reappear; be reproduced

【再则】 zàizé moreover; furthermore; besides

【再者】 zàizhě moreover; furthermore; besides

在 (zài) 1.（存在；生存）exist; be living 2.（表示位置）at：在 120 公里处 at 120 kilometers / 一辆红色的公共汽车停～了汽车站。A red bus is stopping at the bus stop. / 他不～香港。He is absent from Hong Kong. 3.（参加；属于）join or belong to an organization; be a member of an organization 4.（表示时间、地点、情形、范围等）事情发生～上周。It happened last week. 5.（表示正在进行）他～工作。He is at work. 6.（在于；决定于）rest with; depend on：事～人为。Human effort is the decisive factor.

【在编】 zàibiān be on the permanent staff; be on the regular payroll

【在编人员】 zàibiān rényuán permanent staff; those on the regular payroll

【在场】 zàichǎng be on the scene; be on the spot; be present; presence

【在行】 zàiháng be expert at sth.; know a job, trade, etc. well

【在乎】 zài·hu 1.（在意）care about; mind; take to heart 2.（在于）lie in; rest with

【在即】 zàijí near at hand; shortly; soon

【在家】 zàijiā 1.（在家里）be at home; be in 2.（与"出家"相对）remain a layman

【在建】 zàijiàn be under construction

【在教】 zàijiào 1.（信教）believe in (a religion) 2.（信伊斯兰教）believe in Islam

【在劫难逃】 zàijié-nántáo if you're doomed, you're doomed; there's no escape

【在理】 zàilǐ reasonable; sensible; right

【在世】 zàishì be living

【在所不辞】 zàisuǒbùcí will not refuse under any circumstances; will not hesitate to

【在所不惜】 zàisuǒbùxī will not grudge; will never balk at

【在所难免】 zàisuǒnánmiǎn can hardly be avoided; be unavoidable

【在逃】 zàitáo 〈*Law*〉 on the run; has escaped; be at large

【在望】 zàiwàng 1.（可以望见）be visible; be in sight; be in view 2.（即将到来）will soon materialize; be in sight; be in the offing: 成功～。Success is in sight.

【在位】 zàiwèi 1.(指君主) be on the throne; reign 2.(指领导人) be in power

【在握】 zàiwò be in one's hands; be within one's grasp; be under one's control

【在先】 zàixiān 1.(从前;早先) formerly; in the past; before 2.(预先;事先) in advance; in anticipation

【在线计算机】 zàixiàn jìsuànjī line computer

【在心】 zàixīn feel concerned; mind; be attentive

【在押】 zàiyā 〈*Law*〉 behind bars; be under detention; be in custody; be in prison

【在押犯】 zàiyāfàn criminal in custody; prisoner

【在野】 zàiyě not be in office; be out of office

【在野党】 zàiyědǎng a party not in office

【在意】 zàiyì take notice of; care about; mind; take to heart: 毫不～ not care about it at all

【在于】 zàiyú 1.(本质所在) lie in; rest with: 问题～ the problem lies in ... 2.(决定于) be determined by; depend on

【在职】 zàizhí be on the job; be at one's post

【在职干部】 zàizhí gànbù cadres at their posts

【在职教育】 zàizhí jiàoyù in service education

【在职无业者】 zàizhí wúyèzhě a job-holder without work

【在职训练】 zàizhí xùnliàn in-service training; on-the-job training

【在制品】 zàizhìpǐn goods in process; unfinished products

【在座】 zàizuò be present (at a meeting, banquet, etc.): ～的人都听到了他说的话。The whole table heard what he said.

载(zài) 1.(装载) carry; hold; be loaded with 2.(充满道路) all over the road; everywhere along the way 3.(又) and; as well as; at the same time
(另见"载"zǎi)

【载波】 zàibō signal carrier; carrier wave; carrier

【载歌载舞】 zàigē-zàiwǔ festively singing and dancing

【载荷】 zàihè load; lading

【载货】 zàihuò carry cargo

【载频】 zàipín 〈*Radio*〉 carrier frequency

【载人飞行器】 zàirén fēixíngqì manned vehicle

【载人航天飞行】 zàirén hángtiān fēixíng manned space flight

【载体】 zàitǐ 〈*Chem.*〉 carrier

【载誉归来】 zàiyù guīlái return home, enjoying tremendous popularity; come back winning high praise

【载运】 zàiyùn convey by vehicles, ships, etc,; transport; carry

【载重】 zàizhòng load; carrying capacity

【载重量】 zàizhòngliàng loading capacity; carrying capacity

【载重汽车】 zàizhòng qìchē truck (AmE.); lorry (BrE.)

zan

糌(zān)

【糌粑】 zān·ba roasted barley flour

簪(zān) 1.(簪子) hair clasp 2.(插在头上) wear in one's hair

【簪子】 zān·zi hair clasp

咱[喒、偺](zán) 1.(我们) we; our 2.(我) I; my

【咱们】 zán·men 1.(我们) we: ～走吧! Let's go. 2.(我和你) you and I

攒[儧](zǎn) accumulate; hoard; save: ～钱 save up money
(另见"攒"cuán)

暂(zàn) 1.(时间短) of short duration: 短～ of short duration; brief 2.(暂时) temporary; for the time being; for the moment: ～代 act for sb.

【暂存存储器】 zàncún cúnchǔqì 〈*Computer*〉 temporary storage

【暂定】 zàndìng arranged for the time being; tentative; provisional

【暂缓】 zànhuǎn postpone; put off; defer

【暂且】 zànqiě for the time being; for the moment

【暂缺】 zànquē (of a post) be left vacant for

the time being; (of a commodity) be out of stock at the moment

【暂时】 zànshí temporary; transient; provisional

【暂停】 zàntíng 1.(短暂停止) suspend; pause: 谈判～。Negotiations are suspended for the present. 2.〈*Sports*〉 time-out: 要求～ ask for time-out

【暂停指令】 zàntíng zhǐlìng pause instruction

【暂行】 zànxíng provisional; temporary

【暂行办法】 zànxíng bànfǎ interim procedures

【暂行法令】 zànxíng fǎlìng interim order

【暂行规定】 zànxíng guīdìng temporary provisions

【暂行条例】 zànxíng tiáolì provisional regulations

【暂行条文】 zànxíng tiáowén transitional provisions

【暂住】 zànzhù stay temporarily (at a place)

錾 (zàn) 1.(凿;刻) engrave on gold or silver; carve; chisel: ～花 carve flowers or patterns 2.(凿子) engraving tool; chisel

【錾刀】 zàndāo burin; graver

【錾子】 zàn·zi chisel

赞[賛、讚²] (zàn) 1.(帮助) support; favor; assist: ～助 support; assistance 2.(称赞) praise; commend: 盛～ highly praise

【赞不绝口】 zànbùjuékǒu be profuse in praise; be full of praise

【赞成】 zànchéng approve of; be in favor; agree with: ～一项建议 go along with a suggestion / 我们～接受这个报价。We are all for accepting the offer.

【赞成票】 zànchéngpiào affirmative vote; yes; aye: ～占多数。The ayes have it.

【赞歌】 zàngē song of praise; paean

【赞美】 zànměi praise; eulogize

【赞美诗】 zànměishī hymn; canticle; chant

【赞赏】 zànshǎng appreciate; admire

【赞颂】 zànsòng extol; eulogize; sing the praises of

【赞叹】 zàntàn gasp in admiration; highly praise

【赞叹不已】 zàntànbùyǐ praise somebody greatly; be full of praise

【赞同】 zàntóng approve of; agree with; endorse: 我～你的意见。I agree with you.

【赞许】 zànxǔ speak favorably of; praise; commend: 他用微笑表示～。He showed his approval by smiling.

【赞扬】 zànyáng speak highly of; praise; commend

【赞助】 zànzhù support; assistance: 得到政府～ receive financial assistance from the government / 免费音乐会是由歌剧院～举行的。The free concerts were offered under the auspices of the opera company.

【赞助人】 zànzhùrén patron; sponsor; promoter

zang

赃[贜、賍] (zāng) 1.(赃物) stolen goods; booty; spoils: 分～ share the booty; divide the spoils / 窝～ harbor stolen goods 2.(贿赂) bribes: 贪～ take bribes; practice graft

【赃官】 zāngguān corrupt official

【赃款】 zāngkuǎn money stolen, embezzled or received in bribes; illicit money; filthy lucre

【赃物】 zāngwù 1.(盗窃来的东西) stolen goods; booty; spoils 2.(受贿之物) bribes

【赃物窝藏人】 zāngwù wōcángrén holder of stolen goods

脏[髒] (zāng) dirty; soiled; filthy: ～水 filthy water; slops, sewage / 把衬衣弄～了 have made the shirt dirty (另见"脏"zàng)

【脏病】 zāngbìng V.D.; venereal disease

【脏话】 zānghuà filthy and obscene language; dirty words

【脏土】 zāngtǔ dust; garbage

【脏字】 zāngzì obscene word; dirty word: 请不要口带～。Please don't use such abusive language.

葬 (zàng) 1.(埋葬) bury; inter 2.(葬礼) burial; funeral

【葬礼】 zànglǐ funeral rites; burial; funeral

【葬礼进行曲】 zànglǐ jìnxíngqǔ dead march

【葬身】 zàngshēn be buried
【葬送】 zàngsòng ruin; spell an end to: ～前途 ruin one's future

脏［臟］(zàng) internal organs of the body
(另见"脏"zāng)

【脏腑】 zàngfǔ 〈*Chin. Med.*〉 internal organs; viscera
【脏器】 zàngqì viscera; internal organs of the body

藏(zàng) 1.(宝藏) storing place; depository: 宝～ precious (mineral) deposits 2.(佛教、道教经典) Buddhist or Taoist scriptures: 道～ Taoist scriptures 3.(西藏) Xizang; Tibet; Tibetan (adj.)
(另见"藏"cáng)

【藏红花】 zànghónghuā 1.〈*Bot.*〉 saffron crocus 2.〈*Chin. Pharm.*〉 saffron
【藏蓝】 zànglán purplish blue
【藏青】 zàngqīng dark blue
【藏医】 zàngyī Tibetan medicine
【藏族】 Zàngzú Zang (中国少数民族,主要分布在西藏及四川、青海、甘肃、云南等地)

zao

遭(zāo) 1.(遇到) meet with (disaster, misfortune, etc.); suffer 2.〈*classifier*〉(周) round: 走一～ make a trip 3.〈*classifier*〉(回;次) time; turn

【遭到】 zāodào suffer; meet with; encounter: ～不幸 suffer a misfortune
【遭逢】 zāoféng meet with; come across; encounter: ～不幸 suffer misfortune
【遭劫】 zāojié meet with catastrophe
【遭难】 zāonàn meet with disaster; suffer disaster
【遭受】 zāoshòu suffer; be subjected to; sustain: ～水灾 be hit by floods
【遭殃】 zāoyāng suffer disaster; suffer
【遭遇】 zāoyù 1.(碰上;遇到) meet with; encounter; run up against 2.(遇到的事情) (bitter) experience; (hard) lot
【遭灾】 zāozāi be hit by a natural calamity

糟(zāo) 1.(酒糟) distillers' grains; grains 2.(用酒、糟腌制) be pickled with grains or in wine 3.(不结实) rotten; poor 4.(坏) in a wretched state; in a mess: ～得很! It's terrible!

【糟糕】 zāogāo 〈*colloq.*〉 how terrible; what bad luck; too bad
【糟粕】 zāopò waste matter; dross; dregs
【糟蹋】 zāo·ta 1.(浪费;损坏) waste; ruin; spoil: 不要～粮食。Never waste grain. 2.(侮辱;蹂躏) insult; trample on; ravage; violate: ～妇女 violate a woman
【糟透】 zāotòu terrible; abominable: 这吃的～了。The food is terrible. / 天气～了。The weather was abominable.
【糟心】 zāoxīn vexed; annoyed; dejected

凿［鑿］(záo) 1.(凿子) chisel 2.(打孔;挖掘) cut a hole; chisel or dig: ～孔 bore a hole 3.(明确) certain; authentic; irrefutable: 确～ authentic; conclusive 4.(卯眼) mortise

【凿井】 záojǐng 1.(挖井) dig a well 2.〈*Mineral.*〉 shaft sinking; pit sinking
【凿凿】 záozáo 〈*written*〉 true; certain; verified: 言之～ say sth. with certainty
【凿子】 záo·zi chisel

早(zǎo) 1.(早晨) (early) morning 2.(很久以前) long ago; as early as; for a long time 3.(比…靠前) early; in advance; beforehand: 纽约标准时间比太平洋标准时间～3个小时。Standard time in New York is three hours ahead of Pacific Standard Time. 4.(招呼语) morning; good morning

【早安】 zǎo'ān good morning
【早班】 zǎobān morning shift
【早餐】 zǎocān breakfast
【早操】 zǎocāo morning exercises; setting-up exercises
【早茶】 zǎochá morning tea; breakfast
【早产】 zǎochǎn 〈*Med.*〉 premature birth; premature labor; premature delivery
【早产儿】 zǎochǎnr premature; premature infant
【早场】 zǎochǎng morning show
【早晨】 zǎo·chen (early) morning: maturinal (adj.)
【早春】 zǎochūn early spring
【早稻】 zǎodào early (season) rice

【早点】 zǎodiǎn (light) breakfast
【早饭】 zǎofàn breakfast：吃～ have a breakfast
【早该】 zǎogāi about time ...：你～停止撒野犯混了。It's about time you stopped being so rude.
【早慧】 zǎohuì an early bloomer; precocious
【早婚】 zǎohūn marrying too early; early marriage
【早兼午餐】 zǎojiānwǔcān brunch
【早年】 zǎonián 1.（从前）previously; in the past 2.（年轻时候）one's early years
【早期】 zǎoqī early stage; early phase
【早秋】 zǎoqiū early autumn
【早日】 zǎorì 1.（早早儿）at an early date; early; soon 2.（从前；先前）in the past
【早上】 zǎo·shang (early) morning
【早市】 zǎoshì morning market
【早熟】 zǎoshú 1.〈*Physiol*.〉precocity 2.（生长期短）early-maturing; early-ripe
【早退】 zǎotuì leave earlier than one should; leave early
【早晚】 zǎowǎn 1.（早晨和晚上）morning and evening 2.（或早或晚）sooner or later 3.（将来某个时候）some time in the future; some day
【早先】 zǎoxiān previously; in the past
【早泄】 zǎoxiè 〈*Med*.〉premature ejaculation
【早已】 zǎoyǐ long ago; for a long time

枣［棗］(zǎo) 1.〈*Bot*.〉jujube; Chinese date：酸～ spine date 2.（果实）date
【枣红】 zǎohóng purplish red; claret
【枣泥】 zǎoní jujube paste
【枣树】 zǎoshù jujube tree

蚤 (zǎo) 〈*Zool*.〉flea

澡 (zǎo) bath：洗～ bathe (AmE.); bath (BrE.)
【澡盆】 zǎopén bathtub
【澡堂】 zǎotáng public baths; bathhouse

藻 (zǎo) 1.（藻类植物）algae 2.（水生植物）aquatic plants 3.（辞藻）literary embellishment：辞～ ornate diction
【藻类植物】 zǎolèi zhíwù algae; algas

皂［皁］(zào) 1.（黑色）black 2.（肥皂）soap
【皂白】 zàobái black and white; right and wrong
【皂粉】 zàofěn detergent powder
【皂荚】 zàojiá 1.〈*Bot*.〉honey locust 2.（其荚果）honey locust bean
【皂片】 zàopiàn soap chips; soap flakes

灶［竈］(zào) 1.（炉灶）stove (AmE); cooker (BrE); kitchen range; cooking stove：煤气～ gas range 2.（厨房）kitchen; mess; canteen 3.（食堂）dining room; dining hall：学生～ students' dining room
【灶间】 zàojiān kitchen

造 (zào) 1.（制造）make; build; create：～机器 make a machine 2.（编制）draw up：～名册 draw up a list 3.（假编；捏造）invent; cook up; concoct：编～一个故事 concoct a story 4.（造就）train; educate：深～ pursue advanced studies 5.（前往；到）go to; arrive at：～访 pay a visit
【造报表】 zàobàobiǎo prepare a financial report
【造表】 zàobiǎo draw up a form or list
【造波机】 zàobōjī wave machine
【造成】 zàochéng cause; bring about; give rise to：～巨大损失 cause enormous losses
【造船】 zàochuán build a ship; shipbuilding (n.)
【造船厂】 zàochuánchǎng shipyard; dockyard
【造次】 zàocì 1.（匆忙）hurried; hasty 2.（鲁莽）rash; impetuous
【造反】 zàofǎn rise in rebellion; rebel; revolt
【造福】 zàofú bring benefit to; benefit：为子孙后代～ bring benefit to our posterity
【造化】 zàohuà 1.（自然界创造者）creator 2.（创造）create; creation (n.)
【造化】 zào·hua （福气）good fortune; good luck：我们也没有这么大的～。We have no such good fortune, are not so lucky.
【造价】 zàojià cost of building; cost of manufacture
【造就】 zàojiù 1.（培养）bring up; train 2.

(造诣；成就) achievements; attainments
【造句】 zàojù sentence-making
【造林】 zàolín afforestation; forestation; afforest (v.)
【造孽】 zàoniè 〈*Buddhism*〉 do evil; commit a sin
【造物】 zàowù the divine force that created the universe; Nature
【造物主】 zàowùzhǔ 〈*Christianity*〉 God; the Creator
【造像】 zàoxiàng 〈*Art*〉 statue
【造型】 zàoxíng **1.** (指创造) model; make mold **2.** (指创造出的形象) model; mold **3.** 〈*Mech.*〉 molding
【造型艺术】 zàoxíng yìshù plastic arts
【造血】 zàoxuè 〈*Med.*〉 hematopoiesis; hemopoiesis
【造谣】 zàoyáo start a rumor; cook up a story and spread it around: ～中伤 spread rumors to injure others' reputation
【造诣】 zàoyì (academic or artistic) attainments: 在一些领域有很深～的人 a man of great attainments in several fields
【造影】 zàoyǐng 〈*Med.*〉 radiography
【造预算】 zàoyùsuàn draw up a budget
【造纸】 zàozhǐ papermaking
【造作】 zàozuò **1.** (制造) make; manufacture **2.** (做作) affected; artificial

噪［譟²］(zào) **1.** (鸟、虫叫) chirp **2.** (大声叫嚷) a confusion of voices: 鼓～ make an uproar; clamor
【噪声】 zàoshēng noise; buzz; roar; rumble
【噪声测试】 zàoshēng cèshì noise testing
【噪声计】 zàoshēngjì psophometer
【噪声污染】 zàoshēng wūrǎn noise pollution
【噪音】 zàoyīn noise; undesired sound
【噪音污染】 zàoyīn wūrǎn noise pollution; sound pollution

燥 (zào) dry
【燥热】 zàorè hot and dry

躁 (zào) rash; impetuous; restless: 戒骄戒～ guard against arrogance and rashness
【躁动】 zàodòng move restlessly
【躁急】 zàojí restless; uneasy
【躁狂】 zàokuáng 〈*Med.*〉 mania
【躁狂症】 zàokuángzhèng 〈*Med.*〉 mania

ze

则 (zé) **1.** (规范) standard; norm; criterion: 准～ criterion; standard **2.** (规则) rule; regulation: 法～ law; rule / 总～ general rule **3.** 〈*classifier*〉 一～消息 an item of news **4.** (表示因果条件等)有～改之,无～加勉。Correct mistakes if you have made any, guard against them if you have not. **5.** (表示转折、对比等)今～不然。However, things are quite different today **6.** 〈*written*〉(用于列举) 这篇故事不合适,一～太长,二～太乏味。This story is unsuitable. For one thing it's too long, for another it's too dull.

责 (zé) **1.** (责任) duty; responsibility **2.** (标准) demand; require **3.** (责备) blame; reproach; reprove **4.** (诘问) question closely; call sb. to account
【责备】 zébèi reproach; blame; reprove; take sb. to task
【责编】 zébiān responsible editor
【责成】 zéchéng instruct (sb. to fulfill a task); charge (sb. with a task); enjoin (sb. to do sth.)
【责罚】 zéfá punish
【责怪】 zéguài blame; accuse
【责令】 zélìng order; instruct; charge
【责骂】 zémà scold; rebuke; dress down
【责难】 zénàn censure; blame
【责任】 zérèn **1.** (指工作) duty; responsibility: 负完全～ assume full responsibility / 逃避对…的～ shirk one's duty towards ... **2.** (指过失) responsibility for a fault or wrong; blame: 追究～ find out who is to blame
【责任编辑】 zérèn biānjí responsible editor
【责任感】 zérèngǎn sense of responsibility
【责任事故】 zérèn shìgù liability accident
【责任条款】 zérèn tiáokuǎn liability clause
【责任心】 zérènxīn sense of responsibility
【责任制】 zérènzhì system of job responsibility: 承包经营～ contract system of managerial responsibility / 经济～ economic responsibility system / 经营～ managerial responsibility system / 联产承包～ output-related

system of contracted responsibilities

【责问】 zéwèn call sb. to account; force sb. to give an explanation

【责无旁贷】 zéwúpángdài there is no shirking the responsibility; be duty-bound

啧(zé)

【啧啧】 zézé 1.(咂嘴声) click of the tongue: ～称羡 click the tongue in admiration 2.(说话声) 人言～。There is a good deal of unfavorable comment.

择[擇](zé) select; choose; pick: 不～手段 by hook or by crook; unscrupulously

(另见"择"zhái)

【择吉】 zéjí pick an auspicious day (for a marriage, funeral, etc.)

【择交】 zéjiāo choose friends

【择偶】 zé'ǒu choose a spouse

【择期】 zéqī select a day; select a date

【择日启程】 zérì qǐchéng fix a departure date

【择优】 zéyōu select the best

【择优录取】 zéyōu lùqǔ enroll only those who are outstanding; anyone who made a good enough score can be accepted

【择友】 zéyǒu choose friends

泽[澤](zé) 1.(水泽) pool; pond 2.(湿) damp; moist 3.(光) luster; gloss: 光～ luster; gloss; sheen / 色～ color and luster

【泽国】 zéguó 1.(多河湖地区) a land that abounds in rivers and lakes 2.(水淹地区) inundated area: 尽成～ a whole area became submerged

zei

贼(zéi) 1.(偷东西的) thief 2.(工贼,卖国贼) traitor; enemy: 卖国～ traitor 3.(邪的) crooked; wicked; evil; furtive 4.(狡猾) crafty; sly; cunning; deceitful: 这家伙真～。This fellow is really cunning. 5.〈*dial.*〉(极,非常) extremely: ～冷 terribly cold

【贼船】 zéichuán pirate ship: 上～ board the pirate ship; join a reactionary faction

【贼喊捉贼】 zéihǎn-zhuōzéi a thief crying "Stop thief!"

【贼眉鼠眼】 zéiméi-shǔyǎn shifty-eyed; thievish-looking

【贼头贼脑】 zéitóu-zéinǎo behaving stealthily like a thief; stealthy; furtive

【贼窝】 zéiwō den

【贼心】 zéixīn wicked heart; evil designs; evil intentions

【贼心不死】 zéixīn-bùsǐ refuse to give up one's evil designs

【贼赃】 zéizāng stolen goods; booty; spoils

zen

怎(zěn) 〈*dial.*〉 why; how

【怎地】 zěn·di 同"怎的"

【怎的】 zěn·di how?; in what way?; what?

【怎敢】 zěngǎn how can I dare; don't dare

【怎么】 zěn·me 1.(用于询问) ～办? What's to be done? 2.(表示泛指) 你愿意～办就～办。Do as you please. 3.(表示程度) 这个我不～熟悉。I don't know much about this.

【怎么样】 zěn·meyàng 1.(用于询问)你觉得这场演出～? How do you like the performance? 2.(委婉说法)她绘画不～。She's not much of a painter.

【怎么着】 zěn·me·zhe 1.(用于询问)我要去商店,你打算～? I'm going shopping. What about you? 2.(表现泛指)你不能想～就～。You can't do as you please.

【怎能】 zěnnéng how can; how could

【怎样】 zěnyàng 1.(用于询问)这是～做的? How is it done? 2.(表示泛指)你能～做,就～做吧。Do it how you can.

谮(zèn) slander; calumniate

【谮言】 zènyán slander; calumny; defamation

zeng

曾(zēng) great-grand-

(另见"曾"céng)

【曾孙】 zēngsūn great-grandson

【曾孙女】 zēngsūn·nǚ great-granddaughter

【曾祖】 zēngzǔ （paternal）great-grandfather

【曾祖母】 zēngzǔmǔ （paternal）great-grandmother

增 (zēng) increase; gain; add: ～兵 throw in reinforcements

【增补】 zēngbǔ augment; supplement: ～人员 augment the staff

【增补本】 zēngbǔběn enlarged edition

【增产】 zēngchǎn increase production: 农业～措施 measures for increasing agricultural output

【增产节约】 zēngchǎn jiéyuē increase production and practice economy

【增产增收】 zēngchǎn zēngshōu increase both production and income

【增订】 zēngdìng revise and enlarge (a book)

【增订本】 zēngdìngběn revised and enlarged edition

【增多】 zēngduō grow in number or quantity; increase

【增幅】 zēngfú increasing range; growing rate

【增股筹资】 zēnggǔ chóuzī equity financing

【增光】 zēngguāng add luster to; do credit to; add to the prestige of: 为国～ do credit to one's country

【增辉】 zēnghuī add luster to; do credit to; add to the prestige of

【增加】 zēngjiā increase; raise; add: ～财政收入 increase revenues / ～对农业的投入 increase investment in agriculture / ～工资 increase the wages and salaries / ～国民收入 increase national income / ～花色品种 increase varieties and designs / ～教育经费 increase the funds allocated for education / ～收入 increase income

【增进】 zēngjìn enhance; promote; further: ～友谊 promote friendship / ～相互了解 enhance mutual understanding

【增刊】 zēngkān supplement (to a newspaper or periodical); supplementary issue

【增强】 zēngqiáng strengthen; heighten; enhance: ～免疫力 develop immunity from disease/ ～信心 heighten one's confidence

【增删】 zēngshān additions and deletions; emendation

【增生】 zēngshēng 〈*Med.*〉 hyperplasia; proliferation; multiplication

【增收】 zēngshōu increase income

【增收节支】 zēngshōu jiézhī increase income and save unnecessary expenses

【增添】 zēngtiān add; increase: ～设备 get additional equipment

【增添麻烦】 zēngtiān-má·fan cause more trouble

【增销】 zēngxiāo increase of sales

【增效】 zēngxiào synergism; synergia; synergy

【增效剂】 zēngxiàojì 〈*Chem.*〉 synergist

【增选】 zēngxuǎn select a supplement

【增压】 zēngyā pressure boost

【增援】 zēngyuán 〈*Mil.*〉 reinforce

【增援部队】 zēngyuán bùduì reinforcements; reinforcing units

【增长】 zēngzhǎng increase; rise; grow: 控制人口～ control population growth

【增值】 zēngzhí 〈*Econ.*〉 rise in value; appreciation; increment: 自然～ unearned increment / 这块土地在未来的年代里将继续～。This land will continue to appreciate in the years ahead.

【增殖】 zēngzhí 1.〈*Med.*〉 proliferation 2.（繁殖）breed; reproduce; multiply; propagate

【增值税】 zēngzhíshuì value added tax; VAT

【增重食物】 zēngzhòng shíwù growth food

憎 (zēng) hate; detest; abhor: 面目可～ repulsive in appearance

【憎恨】 zēnghèn hate; detest

【憎恶】 zēngwù abhor; loathe; abominate

锃 (zèng) polished

【锃光瓦亮】 zèngguāng-wǎliàng 见"锃亮"

【锃亮】 zèngliàng shiny; polished; glistening

甑 (zèng) 〈*Chem.*〉曲颈～ retort

赠 (zèng) give as a present; present as a gift: ～书 present sb. with a book

【赠答】 zèngdá present each other with gifts, poems, etc.

【赠款】 zèngkuǎn grant

【赠款人】 zèngkuǎnrén donor

【赠品】 zèngpǐn gift; giveaway; complimentary article

【赠券】 zèngquàn gift coupon; a complimentary ticket
【赠送】 zèngsòng give as a present; present as a gift
【赠言】 zèngyán words of advice or encouragement given to a friend at parting: 临别～ parting words of advice or encouragement
【赠与】 zèngyǔ favor; gift; grant
【赠阅】 zèngyuè given free by the publisher
【赠阅本】 zèngyuèběn complimentary copy

zha

扎[紮[3]、紥] (zhā) 1.(刺) prick; run or stick (a needle, etc.) into: 我手指头上～了一个刺。I've got a prick in my finger. 2.(钻进去) plunge into; get into: ～到人群里 dash into the crowd 3.(驻扎) pitch (a tent, etc.); encamp
(另见"扎"zā)
【扎除】 zhāchú removal by ligature
【扎根】 zhāgēn take root
【扎陵湖】 Zhālínghú 〈place〉 Gyaring Hu
【扎啤】 zhāpí draft beer; draught beer; jar beer
【扎实】 zhā·shi 1.(结实) sturdy; strong 2.(实在) solid; sound; down-to-earth: 工作很～ do a solid job
【扎手】 zhāshǒu 1.(刺手) prick the hand 2.(事情难办) difficult to handle; thorny: 这事真～。This is really a hard nut to crack.
【扎眼】 zhāyǎn 1.(刺眼) dazzling; offending to the eye; loud; garish: ～的颜色 loud color; color unpleasant to the eye 2.(惹人注意) offensively conspicuous
【扎营】 zhāyín pitch a tent or camp; encamp
【扎针】 zhāzhēn 〈*Chin. Med.*〉 give an acupuncture treatment

渣 (zhā) 1.(渣滓) dregs; sediment; residue: 炉～ slag; cinder 2.(碎屑) broken bits: 面包～儿 (bread) crumbs
【渣油】 zhāyóu 〈*Petroleum*〉 residuum; residual oil
【渣油路】 zhāyóulù residual-oil road
【渣滓】 zhā·zi dregs; sediment; residue: 社会～ dregs of society

札 (zhá) 〈*written*〉 letter: 适奉大～。I have just received your esteemed letter.
【札记】 zhájì reading notes

轧 (zhá) roll (steel)
(另见"轧"yà)
【轧钢】 zhágāng 1.(轧制钢材) roll steel 2.(轧好的钢材) rolled steel
【轧钢厂】 zhágāngchǎng steel rolling mill: 大型～ heavy rolling mill
【轧钢机】 zhágāngjī rolling mill
【轧机】 zhájī 〈*Metall.*〉 rolling mill
【轧件】 zhájiàn rolled piece

闸[牐] (zhá) 1.(水闸) floodgate; sluice gate; water gate 2.(把水截住) dam up water 3.(制动器) brake: 手～ hand brake / 捏～ apply the hand brake 4.(电闸) switch: 扳～ operate a switch; switch on or off
【闸把】 zhábà brake handle
【闸刀开关】 zhádāo kāiguān chopper switch; knife-switch
【闸盒】 zháhé fuse-box
【闸门】 zhámén 1.(水闸) sluice gate; gate; water gate 2.(船闸) lock gate 3.〈*Mech.*〉 throttle valve
【闸皮】 zhápí 〈*Bicycle*〉 brake shoe
【闸线】 zháxiàn 〈*Bicycle*〉 brake cable

炸[煠] (zhá) fry in deep fat or oil; deep-fry: ～烹大虾 grilled prawns in sauce / ～土豆片 deep-fry the chips
(另见"炸"zhà)
【炸鸡】 zhájī fried chicken
【炸酱】 zhájiàng fried bean sauce
【炸鱼】 zháyú deep-fried fish

铡 (zhá) 1.(铡刀) hand hay cutter; fodder chopper 2.(用铡刀切) cut up with a hay cutter: ～草料 cut hay
【铡草机】 zhácǎojī hay cutter; chaffcutter; chaff slicer; straw breaker
【铡刀】 zhádāo hand hay cutter; fodder chopper; straw chopper

砟 (zhǎ) tiny fragments: 煤～ fragments of coal
【砟子】 zhǎ·zi tiny fragments of coat, etc.

眨 (zhǎ) blink; wink: 眼睛一～ blink (one's eyes)

【眨眼】 zhǎyǎn 1.（眨眼睛）wink; blink one's eyes 2.（时间极短）very short time; wink; twinkle: 一～就不见了 disappear in a twinkling; disappear in the twinkling of an eye

乍（zhà） 1.（起初）first; for the first time: 新来～到 be a newcomer; be a new arrival 2.（忽然）suddenly; abruptly: 天气～冷～热。The temperature changes abruptly. 3.（张开）spread; extend: ～翅 spread wings

【乍暖还寒】 zhànuǎn-háihán After suddenly getting warmer, the weather has turned cold again.

诈（zhà） 1.（欺骗）cheat; swindle: ～人钱财 cheat a man out of his money; swindle money out of a person 2.（假装）pretend; feign: ～败 feign defeat / ～死 feign death; play dead 3.（用假话试探）bluff sb. into giving information: 他是拿话～我。He was trying to draw me out.

【诈病】 zhàbìng malinger; malingering

【诈唬】 zhà·hu bluff; bluster

【诈骗】 zhàpiàn defraud; swindle: ～钱财 obtain money under false pretenses

【诈骗犯】 zhàpiànfàn swindler

【诈骗罪】 zhàpiànzuì crime of fraud

【诈降】 zhàxiáng pretend to surrender; feign surrender

炸（zhà） 1.（突然破裂）explode; burst: 一颗炸弹在离我们站的地方几米处～了。A bomb burst a few meters away from where we stood. 2.（轰炸）blow up; blast; bomb: ～毁 blow up; blast to pieces; demolish / ～沉 bomb and sink 3.（发作）fly into a rage; flare up

（另见"炸"zhá）

【炸弹】 zhàdàn bomb: 定时～ time bomb / 书信～ letter-bomb

【炸胶】 zhàjiāo gelignite

【炸雷】 zhàléi a clap of thunder

【炸碎】 zhàsuì scrap

【炸药】 zhàyào explosive (charges); dynamite: 烈性～ high explosive

【炸药包】 zhàyàobāo pack of dynamite

痄（zhà）

【痄腮】 zhà·sai 〈*Med.*〉 mumps

蚱（zhà）

【蚱蝉】 zhàchán 〈*Zool.*〉 cicada

【蚱蜢】 zhàměng 〈*Zool.*〉 grasshopper

榨［搾[1]］（zhà） 1.（压榨汁液）press; extract: ～油 extract oil 2.（器具）a press for extracting juice, oil, etc.

【榨菜】 zhàcài 1.〈*Bot.*〉 Indica mustard tsatsai 2.（副食）hot pickled mustard tuber

【榨出】 zhàchū squeeze out

【榨取】 zhàqǔ 1.（压榨）squeeze 2.（搜刮）extort: ～钱财 extort money

【榨汁】 zhàzhī liquidize

【榨汁机】 zhàzhījī juicer; liquidizer

栅［柵］（zhà） railings; paling; bars: 木～ paling; palisade

（另见"栅"shān）

【栅栏】 zhà·lan 1.（篱笆状物）railings; paling; bars: 铁～ iron railings 2.〈*Mil.*〉 boom

【栅栏网】 zhà·lanwǎng boom nets

【栅门】 zhàmén fence gate

zhai

侧（zhāi） incline; slant

（另见"侧"cè）

【侧棱】 zhāi·leng incline; slant

【侧歪】 zhāi·wai incline; slant

斋［齋］（zhāi） 1.（斋戒）fast 2.（素食）vegetarian diet adopted for religious reasons: 吃～ practice abstinence from meat; be a vegetarian for religious reasons 3.（向僧人舍饭）give alms (to a monk) 4.（屋子）room; building: 书～ study

【斋饭】 zhāifàn vegetarian food

【斋戒】 zhāijiè abstain from meat, wine, etc.; fast

【斋戒节】 zhāijièjié Ramadan; the fast of Ramadan

【斋戒日】 zhāijièrì fast day

【斋戒沐浴】 zhāijiè mùyù fast and ablution; fast and take a bath before a religious observance

【斋期】 zhāiqī fast days; fast; Lenten

【斋月】 zhāiyuè 〈*Islam*〉 Ramadan; the

month of fast

摘 (zhāi) 1.（取）pick; pluck; take off: ～苹果 pick apples 2.（选取）select; make extracts from: ～译 translation of selected passages

【摘编】 zhāibiān 1.（摘录编辑）extract and compile 2.（摘编的资料）extracts

【摘抄】 zhāichāo 1.（摘录）take passages; make extracts; extract; excerpt 2.（摘录的文章）extracts; excerpts

【摘除】 zhāichú 〈*Med.*〉 excise; remove

【摘掉】 zhāidiào take off: ～帽子 take off one's hat

【摘记】 zhāijì 1.（摘要记录）take notes 2.（摘录）extracts; excerpts

【摘录】 zhāilù 1.（摘抄）take passages; make extracts; extract; excerpt 2.（摘记的要点）extracts; excerpts: 文件～ extracts from a document

【摘棉花机】 zhāimiánhuājī cotton picker

【摘穗机】 zhāisuìjī stripper

【摘要】 zhāiyào 1.（摘录）make a summary: ～发表 publish excerpts of sth. / 请给这篇科学论文写个～。Please abstract this scientific article. 2.（摘录的要点）summary; abstract: 文章～ summary of a article

【摘引】 zhāiyǐn quote

宅 (zhái) residence; house

【宅邸】 zháidǐ residence; abode; habitation

【宅基】 zháijī 〈*Archit.*〉 ground; foundation

【宅门】 zháimén 1.（大门）gate of an old-style big house 2.（人家）rich or powerful family living in such a house

【宅院】 zháiyuàn a house with a courtyard; house

择［擇］ (zhái) select; choose; pick （另见"择"zé）

【择菜】 zháicài trim vegetables for cooking

【择席】 zháixí be unable to sleep well in a new place

窄 (zhǎi) 1.（不宽）narrow: ～胡同 a narrow lane 2.（气量小）narrow-minded; petty; narrow: 心眼儿～ petty; oversensitive 3.（不宽裕）hard up; badly off: 手头儿～ be hard up

【窄道】 zhǎidào narrow path

【窄轨铁路】 zhǎiguǐ tiělù narrowgauge railway; light railway

债 (zhài) debt: 内～ internal debt / 外～ external debt

【债户】 zhàihù debtor

【债款】 zhàikuǎn loan

【债权】 zhàiquán 〈*Law*〉 creditor's rights; obligatory right

【债权国】 zhàiquánguó creditor nation

【债权人】 zhàiquánrén creditor

【债券】 zhàiquàn bond; debenture: 大面额～ large bond

【债券持有者】 zhàiquàn chíyǒuzhě bondholder; bond holder

【债券股利】 zhàiquàn gǔlì bond dividends

【债券折价】 zhàiquàn zhéjià bond discount

【债台高筑】 zhàitái-gāozhù be heavily in debt; be up to one's ears in debt; be debt-ridden

【债务】 zhàiwù debt; liabilities; amount due: 长期～ long-term obligation / 短期～ short-term obligation

【债务国】 zhàiwùguó debtor nation

【债务纠纷】 zhàiwù jiūfēn dispute over obligation

【债务人】 zhàiwùrén debtor

【债主】 zhàizhǔ creditor

寨 (zhài) 1.（栅栏）stockade 2.（村寨）stockaded village 3.（营寨）camp: 安营扎～ pitch a camp; encamp 4.（山寨）mountain stronghold

【寨子】 zhài·zi 1.（栅栏）stockade 2.（村寨）stockaded village

zhan

占 (zhān) practice divination: ～卦问卜 consult the oracle; inquire about by divination
（另见"占"zhàn）

【占卜】 zhānbǔ practice divination; divine

【占卦】 zhānguà divination

沾［霑[1,2]］ (zhān) 1.（浸湿）moisten; wet; soak 2.（沾上）be

stained with：～水 get wet 3.（碰上；挨上）touch：滴酒不～ not touch any alcoholic drinks 4.（得到好处）get sth. out of association with sb. or sth.：利益均～ share the benefit equally；have equal shares of the benefit

【沾边】 zhānbiān 1.（有接触）touch on only lightly：这事他没～。He has nothing to do with the matter. 2.（与事实接近）be close to what it should be；be relevant：她说的一点也不～。What she said is completely irrelevant.

【沾光】 zhānguāng benefit from association with sb. or sth.

【沾花惹草】 zhānhuā-rěcǎo be promiscuous in sex relations

【沾亲带故】 zhānqīn-dàigù have ties of kinship or friendship

【沾染】 zhānrǎn be infected with；be contaminated by；be tainted with：～恶习 slide into bad habits

【沾手】 zhānshǒu 1.（接触）touch with one's hand 2.（参与）have a hand in

【沾沾自喜】 zhānzhān-zìxǐ feel complacent；be pleased with oneself

毡［氈、氊］（zhān） felt：～帽 felt hat

【毡衬】 zhānchèn blanket；feltless packing

【毡垫】 zhāndiàn felt pad

【毡房】 zhānfáng yurt

【毡头墨水笔】 zhāntóu mòshuǐbǐ felt-tipped pen；felt-tip pen

【毡子】 zhān·zi felt；felt rug；felt blanket

粘（zhān） glue；stick；paste：男孩把两块木头～在一起了。The boy glued two pieces of wood together.
（另见"粘"nián）

【粘剂】 zhānjì splice

【粘连】 zhānlián 〈*Med.*〉 adhesion：肠～ intestinal adhesion

【粘连现象】 zhānlián xiànxiàng 〈*Med.*〉 adhesion phenomenon

【粘鸟胶】 zhānniǎojiāo birdlime

【粘贴】 zhāntiē paste；stick

【粘蝇纸】 zhānyíngzhǐ flypaper

谵（zhān） be delirious

【谵妄】 zhānwàng delirium

【谵语】 zhānyǔ delirious ravings；wild talk

瞻（zhān） look up or forward

【瞻顾】 zhāngù 〈*written*〉 look ahead and behind

【瞻念】 zhānniàn look to；think of

【瞻前顾后】 zhānqián-gùhòu look ahead and behind；be over-cautious and indecisive

【瞻望】 zhānwàng look forward；look far ahead：～未来 look into the future

【瞻仰】 zhānyǎng look at with reverence：～遗容 pay respects to someone's remains

斩（zhǎn） 1.（砍）chop；cut 2.（杀头）behead；decapitate

【斩波】 zhǎnbō chopped wave

【斩草除根】 zhǎncǎo-chúgēn cut the weeds and dig up the roots；destroy root and branch；stamp out the source of trouble

【斩钉截铁】 zhǎndīng-jiétiě resolute and decisive；categorical：～地回答 give a categorical answer

【斩尽杀绝】 zhǎnjìn-shājué kill all；wipe out the whole lot

【斩首】 zhǎnshǒu behead；decapitate

崭（zhǎn） 1.（高峻）towering（over）2.（优异）fine；swell

【崭露头角】 zhǎnlù-tóujiǎo cut a striking figure；stand out conspicuously；make oneself conspicuous

【崭新】 zhǎnxīn brand-new；completely new

盏［盞］（zhǎn） 1.（小杯子）small cup：酒～ small wine cup 2.〈*classifier*〉一～电灯 an electric lamp

展（zhǎn） 1.（张开）open up；spread out；unfold；unfurl 2.（施展）put to good use；give free play to 3.（展缓）postpone；extend；prolong 4.（展览）exhibition：预～ preview

【展播】 zhǎnbō show broadcast

【展翅】 zhǎnchì spread the wings；get ready for flight

【展出】 zhǎnchū put on display；be on show；exhibit

【展开】 zhǎnkāi 1.（张开）spread out；unfold；open up：～画卷 unfold a picture scroll

2.(大规模进行) launch; unfold; develop; carry out: ～攻势 unfold an offensive

【展览】 zhǎnlǎn put on display; exhibit; show

【展览馆】 zhǎnlǎnguǎn exhibition center

【展览会】 zhǎnlǎnhuì exhibition; exposition

【展览品】 zhǎnlǎnpǐn exhibit; item on display

【展品】 zhǎnpǐn exhibit; item on display

【展期】 zhǎnqī 1.(往后推迟) extend a time limit; postpone: 交易会～举行。The fair has been postponed. 2.(展览期限) duration of an exhibition; exhibition period

【展区】 zhǎnqū exhibition area

【展示】 zhǎnshì open up before one's eyes; reveal; show; lay bare

【展厅】 zhǎntīng exhibition hall

【展望】 zhǎnwàng 1.(往远处看) look into the distance 2.(往将来看) look into the future; look ahead: ～未来 look forward to the future 3.(对前途的预测) forecast; prospect

【展现】 zhǎnxiàn unfold before one's eyes; emerge

【展销】 zhǎnxiāo exhibit and sell; display

【展销会】 zhǎnxiāohuì sales exhibition

搌 (zhǎn) wipe; dab

【搌布】 zhǎn·bu dishcloth; dish towel

辗 (zhǎn)

【辗转】 zhǎnzhuǎn 1.(身体翻来覆去) toss about (in bed): ～不能成眠 toss and turn (in bed); unable to go to sleep 2.(经过多或许多地方) pass through many hands or places: ～流传 spread from place to place; pass through many places

【辗转不安】 zhǎnzhuǎn-bù'ān 〈*Med.*〉 jactitation; jactation

【辗转反侧】 zhǎnzhuǎn-fǎncè toss about (in bed); toss and turn restlessly

【辗转相告】 zhǎnzhuǎn-xiānggào pass from mouth to mouth

占[佔] (zhàn) 1.(占据) occupy; seize; take: 强～ forcibly occupy; seize / 那桌子～的地方太大。The table takes up a lot of space. 2.(处于) constitute; hold; make up; account for: ～多数 constitute the majority 3.(占用) take (up) (另见"占"zhān)

【占机信号】 zhànjī xìnhào seizing signal

【占据】 zhànjù occupy; hold

【占领】 zhànlǐng 1.(用武力取得) capture; occupy; seize: ～一座城镇 take a town 2.(控制) dominate; command: ～市场 dominate the market; command the market

【占领军】 zhànlǐngjūn occupation army

【占领区】 zhànlǐngqū occupied area

【占便宜】 zhàn pián·yi 1.(取得额外利益) gain extra advantage by unfair means; profit at other people's expense: 占小便宜 gain petty advantages 2.(有优势) advantageous; favorable: 你个子高,打排球～。In playing volleyball you have the advantage of being tall.

【占上风】 zhàn shàngfēng gain the upper hand; have the advantage (over); come out top dog

【占先】 zhànxiān take precedence; take the lead; get ahead of

【占线】 zhànxiàn 〈*Telephone*〉 the line's busy; busy line

【占线音】 zhànxiànyīn engaged tone

【占用】 zhànyòng occupancy; occupation; occupy (v.)

【占用公款】 zhànyòng gōngkuǎn conversion of public money to one's own use

【占有】 zhànyǒu 1.(占据) own; possess; have: ～生产资料 have the means of production 2.(处在) occupy; hold: ～重要地位 occupy an important place 3.(掌握) have; own: 人均粮食的～量 the average per-capita amount of grain

【占有率】 zhànyǒulǜ share: 市场～ the market share

【占着茅坑不拉屎】 zhàn·zhe máokēng bù lāshǐ be a dog in the manger

战[戰] (zhàn) 1.(战争) war; warfare; battle; fight: 内～ civil war 2.(作战) fight 3.(发抖) shiver; tremble; shudder: 冷得打～ shiver with cold

【战败】 zhànbài 1.(打败仗) be defeated; be vanquished; lose (a battle or war) 2.(打胜)

defeat; vanquish beat: ～敌人 defeat the enemy

【战败国】 zhànbàiguó vanquished nation

【战报】 zhànbào war communiqué; battlefield report

【战备】 zhànbèi war preparedness; combat readiness

【战场】 zhànchǎng battlefield; battlefront: 开辟新～ open another front / 上～ go to the battlefield

【战车】 zhànchē (war) chariot

【战刀】 zhàndāo saber: 挥舞～ rattle the saber

【战地】 zhàndì battlefield; battleground; combat zone

【战地记者】 zhàndì jìzhě war correspondent

【战抖】 zhàndǒu tremble; shiver; shudder

【战斗】 zhàndòu 1.(武装冲突) fight; battle; combat; action 2.(斗争) militant; fighting

【战斗服】 zhàndòufú battledress

【战斗力】 zhàndòulì combat effectiveness; fighting capacity: ～强 high combat effectiveness

【战端】 zhànduān the beginning of a war: 重开～。War broke out again.

【战犯】 zhànfàn war criminal

【战俘】 zhànfú prisoner of war (P.O.W.)

【战俘营】 zhànfúyíng prisoner-of-war camp

【战歌】 zhàngē battle song; fighting song

【战功】 zhàngōng meritorious military service; outstanding military exploit: 荣立～ perform military exploits

【战鼓】 zhàngǔ war drum; battle drum

【战果】 zhànguǒ results of battle; combat success; victory: 辉煌的～ splendid victory; outstanding triumph / 扩大～ exploit the victory

【战壕】 zhànháo trench; entrenchment

【战后】 zhànhòu postwar: ～余殃 the aftermath of war

【战火】 zhànhuǒ flames of war

【战祸】 zhànhuò disaster of war

【战机】 zhànjī 1.(战斗机) fighter plane 2.(作战时机) opportunity for combat 3.(战事机密) military secrets

【战舰】 zhànjiàn warship

【战局】 zhànjú war situation

【战况】 zhànkuàng situation on the battlefield; progress of a battle

【战利品】 zhànlìpǐn spoils of war; war trophies; captured equipment

【战例】 zhànlì a specific example of a battle (in military science): 有名的～ a famous battle

【战栗】 zhànlì tremble; shiver; shudder

【战列舰】 zhànlièjiàn battleship

【战乱】 zhànluàn chaos caused by war

【战略】 zhànlüè strategy; strategic (adj.): 全球～ global strategy

【战略部署】 zhànlüè bùshǔ strategic arrangement

【战略防御计划】 zhànlüè fángyù jìhuà strategic defense initiative; SDI

【战略物资】 zhànlüè wùzī strategic materials

【战马】 zhànmǎ battle steed; war-horse

【战前】 zhànqián prewar

【战区】 zhànqū war zone; theatre of operations

【战区导弹防御系统】 zhànqū dǎodàn fángyù xìtǒng TMD

【战胜】 zhànshèng defeat; triumph over; overcome: ～敌人 defeat the enemy / ～对手 triumph over the opponent / ～困难 overcome a difficulty

【战胜国】 zhànshèngguó conqueror nation; victorious nation

【战时】 zhànshí wartime

【战士】 zhànshì 1.(士兵) soldier; man 2.(为正义而战的人) champion; warrior; fighter

【战事】 zhànshì war; hostilities

【战术】 zhànshù (military) tactics: 赢得战争靠战略,打赢战役靠～。Strategy wins wars; tactics wins battles.

【战天斗地】 zhàntiān-dòudì fight against heaven and earth; combat nature; brave the elements

【战无不胜】 zhànwúbùshèng invincible; ever-victorious; all conquering

【战线】 zhànxiàn battle line; battlefront: 缩短～ contract the front

【战役】 zhànyì campaign; battle

【战鹰】 zhànyīng fighter plane

【战友】 zhànyǒu comrade-in-arms; battle companion: ～重逢 reunion of comrade-in-arms

【战云】 zhànyún war cloud

【战战兢兢】 zhànzhàn-jīngjīng 1.(怕得发抖) trembling with fear; with fear and trepidation 2.(小心谨慎) with caution; gingerly

【战争】 zhànzhēng war; warfare：解放～ the war of liberation / 抗日～ the War of Resistance Against Japan (1937-1945)

【战争创伤】 zhànzhēng chuāngshāng the war wounds：医治～ heal the war wounds

【战争贩子】 zhànzhēng fàn·zi warmonger

【战争受难者】 zhànzhēng shòunànzhě war victim

站 (zhàn) 1.(站立) stand; be on one's feet; take a stand：请～起来。Stand up, please. 2.(停留) stop; halt 3.(车站) station; stop：公共汽车～ bus stop / 火车～ railway station 4.(业务机构) station or center for rendering certain services：保健～ health center

【站不住脚】 zhàn·buzhùjiǎo untenable; unable to stand one's ground; impossible to defend：这种理论～。This theory is no longer tenable.

【站队】 zhànduì line up; fall in; stand in line

【站岗】 zhàngǎng stand guard; be on sentry duty

【站柜台】 zhànguìtái serve as a shop assistant

【站立】 zhànlì stand

【站立摔】 zhànlìshuāi 〈*Wrestling*〉 standing wrestling

【站排】 zhànpái line up

【站票】 zhànpiào ticket without seat

【站台】 zhàntái 〈*Railway*〉 platform

【站台票】 zhàntáipiào 〈*Railway*〉 platform ticket

【站稳】 zhànwěn 1.(停稳当) come to a stop 2.(坚定) stand firm; take a firm stand

【站长】 zhànzhǎng head of a station, center, etc.

【站住】 zhànzhù 1.(停止行动) stop; halt 2.(站稳) stand firmly on one's feet; keep one's feet 3.(待下去) stand one's ground; consolidate one's position 4.(理由成立) hold water; be tenable：他的说法站不住。His opinion doesn't hold water.

【站住脚】 zhànzhùjiǎo 1.(停止行走) stop; halt 2.(待在某地) stand one's ground; consolidate one's position 3.(理由成立) hold water; be tenable：这个论点站不住脚。This argument isn't tenable.

栈[棧] (zhàn) 1.(栈房) warehouse：货～ warehouse; storehouse 2.(旅店) inn：客～ inn 3.(畜栏) shed; pen：马～ horse shed / 羊～ sheep pen

【栈道】 zhàndào a plank road built along the face of a cliff

【栈房】 zhànfáng 1.(仓库) warehouse; storehouse 2.(旅馆) inn

【栈桥】 zhànqiáo 1.(港口的) landing stage; pier 2.(火车站的) loading bridge

湛 (zhàn) 1.(深) profound; deep：精～ consummate; exquisite 2.(清澈) crystal clear

【湛蓝】 zhànlán azure blue; azure

颤 (zhàn) tremble; shiver; shudder (另见"颤"chàn)

【颤栗】 zhànlì tremble; shiver; shudder

蘸 (zhàn) dip in：～墨水 dip in ink

【蘸水钢笔】 zhànshuǐ gāngbǐ pen

zhang

张[張] (zhāng) 1.(张开) open; spread; stretch：～网 spread a net 2.(夸张) magnify; exaggerate：夸～ exaggerate; overstate 3.(张望) look：东～西望 gaze around 4.(商店开张) opening of a new shop：开～ open a business; begin doing business 5.〈*classifier*〉两～画 two pictures

【张驰】 zhāngchí relaxation

【张大】 zhāngdà magnify; exaggerate; publicize widely

【张灯结彩】 zhāngdēng-jiécǎi be decorated with lanterns and colored streamers

【张冠李戴】 zhāngguān-lǐdài put Zhang's hat on Li's head; attribute sth. to the wrong person or confuse one thing with another

【张皇】 zhānghuáng alarmed; scared; flurried; flustered

【张皇失措】 zhānghuáng-shīcuò fall into a

fluster; be all in a fluster

【张开】 zhāngkāi open; stretch; spread

【张口结舌】 zhāngkǒu-jiéshé be agape and tongue-tied; be at a loss for words

【张力】 zhānglì 1.〈*Physics*〉tension 2.(拉力) pulling force

【张力摩擦】 zhānglì mócā tenso-friction

【张罗】 zhāng·luo 1.(料理) get busy about; take care of 2.(筹划) raise (funds); get together (money): ～一笔款 raise a sum of money 3.(接待) greet and entertain; attend to: ～顾客 attend to customers

【张目】 zhāngmù 1.(睁大眼) open one's eyes wide 2.(为人助声势) 为某人～ boost sb.'s arrogance; build up another

【张三李四】 Zhāngsān-Lǐsì any Tom, Dick, and Harry; every Tom, Dick or Harry

【张贴】 zhāngtiē put up

【张望】 zhāngwàng 1.(从孔、缝里看) peep 2.(向四周看) look around: 四顾～ look around 3.(向远处看) look ahead

【张牙舞爪】 zhāngyá-wǔzhǎo bare fangs and brandish claws; make threatening gestures; engage in saber rattling

【张扬】 zhāngyáng make widely known; make public

【张着嘴看】 zhāng·zhezhuǐ kàn gape: 观众们～魔术师把女郎拦腰锯成两截。The audience gaped as the magician sawed the girl in half.

【张嘴】 zhāngzuǐ 1.(说话) open one's mouth (to say sth.) 2.(向人借贷或请求) ask for a loan; ask for a favor

章 (zhāng) 1.(歌曲、诗文的段落) chapter; section 2.(条理) order 3.(条目) point: 约法三～ agree on a three-point law 4.(章程) rules; regulations; constitution: 规～制度 rules and regulations / 违～ break the rules 5.(图章) seal; stamp: 公～ official seal 6.(标志) badge; medal: 领～ collar badge

【章程】 zhāngchéng 1.(规程或条例) rules; regulations; constitution 2.(办法) solution; way

【章动】 zhāngdòng 〈*Astron.*〉 nutation

【章法】 zhāngfǎ 1.(文章结构) presentation of ideas in a piece of writing; art of composition: (文章)有～ be well organized. 2.(办事程序、规则) orderly (办事)有～ be methodical in one's work

【章节】 zhāngjié chapters and sections

【章鱼】 zhāngyú 〈*Zool.*〉 octopus

【章子】 zhāng·zi seal; stamp

獐[麞] (zhāng) 〈*Zool.*〉 water deer

【獐子】 zhāng·zi water deer; river deer

樟 (zhāng) 〈*Bot.*〉 camphor tree

【樟木】 zhāngmù camphor wood

【樟脑】 zhāngnǎo camphor

【樟脑丸】 zhāngnǎowán camphor ball; mothball

【樟脑油】 zhāngnǎoyóu camphor oil

【樟树】 zhāngshù camphor tree

蟑 (zhāng)

【蟑螂】 zhāngláng 〈*Zool.*〉 cockroach; roach

长[長] (zhǎng) 1.(年纪较大) older; elder; senior 2.(排行最大) eldest; oldest: ～女 eldest daughter / ～兄 eldest brother 3.(领导人) chief; head: 首～ leading cadre 4.(生长) grow; develop 5.(生) come into being; begin to grow; form: ～锈 get rusty 6.(增长) acquire; enhance; increase
(另见"长"cháng)

【长辈】 zhǎngbèi elder member of a family; elder; senior

【长膘】 zhǎngbiāo get fat; put on flesh; flesh out

【长大】 zhǎngdà grow up; be brought up: ～成人 have grown up; become an adult

【长官】 zhǎngguān senior officer; senior official; commanding officer

【长机】 zhǎngjī 〈*Mil.*〉 lead craft; leader

【长见识】 zhǎngjiàn·shi increase one's knowledge; gain experience

【长进】 zhǎngjìn progress

【长老】 zhǎnglǎo 1.(年纪大的人) elder 2.(对和尚的尊称) elder of a Buddhist monastery

【长势】 zhǎngshì the way a crop is growing

【长孙】 zhǎngsūn son's eldest son; eldest grandson

【长相】 zhǎngxiàng looks; appearance：他～难看。He has an ugly looks.

【长者】 zhǎngzhě 1.（年纪辈分高者）elder; senior 2.（年高有德者）venerable elder

【长子】 zhǎngzǐ eldest son

涨［漲］（zhǎng） rise; go up：物价上～。The prices soared.
（另见"涨"zhàng）

【涨潮】 zhǎngcháo rising tide; flood tide

【涨风】 zhǎngfēng upward trend of prices

【涨幅】 zhǎngfú rate of rise

【涨价】 zhǎngjià rise in price

【涨落】 zhǎngluò rise and fall; fluctuate：价格的～ fluctuations of prices

掌（zhǎng） 1.（手掌）palm：鼓～ clap hands; applaud 2.（用手掌打）strike with the palm of the hand; slap 3.（掌握）hold in one's hand; be in charge of; control; wield 4.（某些兽的掌）the bottom of certain animals' feet; pad; sole：熊～ bear's paw 5.（鞋掌）shoe sole or heel：后～ shoe heel 6.（马蹄铁）horseshoe

【掌舵】 zhǎngduò 1.（操舵）be at the helm; operate the rudder; take the tiller; steer a boat 2.（舵手）helmsman; steersman

【掌舵人】 zhǎngduòrén helmsman; steersman

【掌骨】 zhǎnggǔ 〈*Anat.*〉 metacarpal bone: metacarpal (adj.)

【掌故】 zhǎnggù anecdotes

【掌管】 zhǎngguǎn be in charge of; administer：～财政 administer finances

【掌柜】 zhǎngguì shopkeeper; manager (of a shop)

【掌权】 zhǎngquán be in power; wield power; exercise control

【掌上明珠】 zhǎngshàng-míngzhū a pearl in the palm; a beloved daughter

【掌声】 zhǎngshēng clapping; applause：博得经久不息的～ win prolonged applause

【掌纹】 zhǎngwén palmprint

【掌握】 zhǎngwò 1.（支配）grasp; master; know well：～技术 master techniques / ～原则 have a good grasp of the principles 2.（控制）have in hand; take into one's hands; control：～进攻节奏 set the pace / ～主动权 have the initiative in one's hands

【掌心】 zhǎngxīn 1.（手掌心）the center of the palm 2.（掌握）scope of power; control：逃不出某人的～ cannot get away from sb's control

【掌子】 zhǎng·zi 〈*Mineral.*〉 work area

丈（zhàng） 1.（丈量）measure (land) 2.（称呼）a form of address for certain male relatives by marriage：岳～ wife's father; father-in-law 3.（长度单位）*zhang* (= 3.33 meters)

【丈夫】 zhàng·fu 1.（妻子的配偶）husband 2.（男子汉）man：男子汉大～ manly man

【丈量】 zhàngliáng measure (land)

【丈母娘】 zhàng·muniáng mother-in-law; wife's mother

【丈人】 zhàng·ren father-in-law; wife's father

仗（zhàng） 1.（古代兵器总称）weaponry; weapons：仪～ flags, weapons, etc. carried by a guard of honor 2.（拿着）hold (a weapon) 3.（倚仗）rely on; depend on：倚～权势 rely on one's power and position 4.（战争）battle; war：打～ go to war; be at war

【仗势欺人】 zhàngshì-qīrén take advantage of one's or sb. else's power to bully people; bully others on the strength of one's powerful connections or position

【仗义疏财】 zhàngyì-shūcái be generous in aiding needy people

杖（zhàng） 1.（手杖）cane; stick：扶～而行 walk with a cane 2.（棍棒）rod or staff used for a specific purpose：擀面～ rolling pin

帐［帳］（zhàng） 1.（帐子）curtain; canopy 2.同"账"

【帐钩】 zhànggōu bed-curtain or mosquito net hook

【帐幕】 zhàngmù tent

【帐篷】 zhàng·peng tent

【帐子】 zhàng·zi 1.（床帐）bed-curtain 2.（蚊帐）mosquito net

账［賬］（zhàng） 1.（账目）account：记～ keep accounts / 算经济～

keep economic accounts 2.（账簿）account book 3.（债）debt；credit：还～ repay a debt ‖“账”亦作“帐”

【账本】 zhàngběn account book

【账簿】 zhàngbù account book

【账册】 zhàngcè account book

【账单】 zhàngdān bill；check：付～ foot the bill

【账房】 zhàngfáng 1.（指办公室）accountant's office 2.（指人员）accountant

【账户】 zhànghù account：开～ open an account / 开银行～ open a bank account / 他把钱存在他的银行～上。He paid the money into his bank account.

【账款】 zhàngkuǎn funds on account；credit

【账面价格】 zhàngmiàn jiàgé accounting price

【账目】 zhàngmù items of an account；accounts：冲销～ counterbalance accounts / 与(某人)结清～ settle one's account with sb.

胀［脹］（zhàng） 1.（膨胀）expand；distend：热～冷缩 expand when heated and contract when cooled 2.（肿胀）swell；be bloated：肿～ swollen

【胀闸】 zhàngzhá hub brake

涨［漲］（zhàng） 1.（涨大）swell after absorbing water, etc. 2.（头部充血）be swelled by a rush of blood：头昏脑～ feel one's head swimming

（另见“涨”zhǎng）

障（zhàng） 1.（障碍）hinder；obstruct 2.（障碍物）barrier；block：路～ roadblock；barricade 3.（屏障）shield；screen；shelter

【障碍】 zhàng'ài 1.（阻碍）hinder；obstruct 2.（障碍物）obstacle；obstruction；barrier；impediment

【障碍区】 zhàng'àiqū 〈*Golf*〉rough

【障碍赛跑】 zhàng'ài sàipǎo obstacle race

【障碍物】 zhàng'àiwù obstacle；obstruction；barrier；impediment

【障蔽】 zhàngbì block；obstruct；shut out

【障眼法】 zhàngyǎnfǎ cover-up；camouflage

嶂（zhàng） a screen-like mountain peak：层峦叠～ peaks rising one higher than another

幛（zhàng） large scroll of cloth or silk：贺～ congratulatory scroll of cloth or silk

【幛子】 zhàng·zi large scroll of cloth or silk

瘴（zhàng） miasma

【瘴疠】 zhànglì infectious subtropical disease

【瘴气】 zhàngqì miasma

zhao

招（zhāo） 1.（招手）beckon；wave 2.（招收）recruit；enlist；enroll：～工 recruit workers 3.（引来）attract；incur；court 4.（招惹）provoke；tease：别～他。Don't tease him. 5.（承认罪行）confess；own up pressed 6.（计策；一步）trick；device；move

【招办】 zhāobàn admissions office

【招标】 zhāobiāo invite tenders；call for tenders：为一座新的饭店～ invite tenders for a new hotel / 采用国际竞争性～方式采购 purchase by way of international competitive bidding (ICB)

【招兵】 zhāobīng recruit soldiers；raise troops

【招兵买马】 zhāobīng-mǎimǎ recruit men and buy horses；raise or enlarge an army；recruit followers

【招待】 zhāodài receive (guests)；entertain；serve (customers)：设宴～外宾 give a dinner for foreign guests

【招待会】 zhāodàihuì reception：记者～ press conference / 冷餐～ buffet reception

【招待所】 zhāodàisuǒ hostel；guest house

【招待员】 zhāodàiyuán receptionist

【招儿】 zhāor a trick or strike in Chinese boxing

【招供】 zhāogòng confess；make a confession of one's crime

【招股】 zhāogǔ raise capital by floating shares

【招呼】 zhāo·hu 1.（呼唤）call 2.（问候）hail；greet；say hello to 3.（吩咐）notify；tell：～他赶快来。Tell him to come at once. 4.（照料）care of：～病人 take care of the patients

【招呼站】 zhāo·huzhàn request stop

【招祸】 zhāohuò court disaster

【招架】 zhāojià ward off blows; hold one's own: ～不住 not able to ward off

【招考】 zhāokǎo give public notice of entrance examination; admit (students, applicants, etc.) by examination

【招徕】 zhāolái solicit (customers or business); canvass: ～顾客 solicit customers

【招揽】 zhāolǎn solicit (customers or business); canvass: ～生意 canvass business orders; drum up trade / ～主顾 solicit customers

【招领】 zhāolǐng announce the finding of lost property: 失物～ Found / ～失物 announce the finding of lost property

【招募】 zhāomù recruit; enlist

【招女婿】 zhāo nǚ·xu take in a son-in-law to bear bride's family name

【招牌】 zhāo·pai shop sign; signboard; shingle

【招盘】 zhāopán put a business up for sale

【招聘】 zhāopìn advertise for; give public notice of a vacancy to be filled; invite applications for a job: ～工程师 advertise for engineers

【招聘广告】 zhāopìn guǎnggào want ad

【招聘考试】 zhāopìn kǎoshì recruitment examination

【招惹】 zhāo·re 1.(引起) provoke; incur; court: ～是非 bring trouble on oneself 2.(触动;逗引) tease; provoke: 这人～不得。You'd better not provoke that fellow.

【招认】 zhāorèn confess one's crime; plead guilty; shrift

【招生】 zhāoshēng enroll new students; recruit students

【招生简章】 zhāoshēng jiǎnzhāng briefings to enrollment

【招事】 zhāoshì bring trouble on oneself; invite trouble

【招收】 zhāoshōu recruit; take in

【招手】 zhāoshǒu beckon; wave: ～致意 wave one's greetings; wave back in acknowledgement

【招数】 zhāoshù 同"着数"

【招贴】 zhāotiē poster; placard; bill

【招贴画】 zhāotiēhuà pictorial poster

【招贴纸】 zhāotiēzhǐ poster paper

【招降】 zhāoxiáng summon sb. to surrender

【招摇过市】 zhāoyáo-guòshì swagger through the streets; blatantly seek publicity

【招摇撞骗】 zhāoyáo-zhuàngpiàn swindle and bluff; bluff and deceive

【招引】 zhāoyǐn attract; induce

【招怨】 zhāoyuàn incur animosity or grudge

【招灾】 zhāozāi court disaster

【招灾惹祸】 zhāozāi-rěhuò court disaster; invite trouble

【招展】 zhāozhǎn flutter; wave: 彩旗迎风～。Colored flags are fluttering in the wind.

【招致】 zhāozhì 1.(搜罗) recruit; scout about for: ～追随者 recruit followers / ～人才 scout about for talents 2.(引起) incur; bring about; lead to: ～重大损失 incur a heavy loss

【招赘】 zhāozhuì take in a son-in-law to bear bride's family name

【招租】 zhāozū let: ～房屋 let a house / "房屋～" House to Let

昭 (zhāo) clear; obvious

【昭然若揭】 zhāorán-ruòjiē abundantly clear; all too clear

【昭示】 zhāoshì make clear to all; declare publicly

【昭乌达盟】 Zhāowūdáméng 〈place〉 Ju Ud Meng

【昭信中外】 zhāoxìn-zhōngwài show good faith to the nation and abroad

【昭雪】 zhāoxuě exonerate; rehabilitate

【昭彰】 zhāozhāng clear; manifest; evident: 罪恶～ have committed flagrant crimes

【昭著】 zhāozhù clear; evident; obvious: 臭名～ notorious; of ill repute

着[招] (zhāo) 1.(下棋的) a move in chess: 高～儿 a clever move 2.(计策;手段) trick; artifice; device; move
(另见"着"zháo, zhuó)

【着数】 zhāoshù 1.(下棋的) a move in chess 2.(武术的) a movement in *wushu* 3.(计策;手段) trick; device

朝 (zhāo) 1.(早晨) early morning; morning: ～阳 morning sun 2.(日;天) day: 今

～ today; the present
(另见"朝"cháo)

【朝不保夕】 zhāobù-bǎoxī not know in the morning what may happen in the evening; be in a precarious state

【朝晖】 zhāohuī morning sunlight

【朝令夕改】 zhāolìng-xīgǎi issue an order in the morning and rescind it in the evening; make unpredictable changes in policy

【朝露】 zhāolù 〈*written*〉 morning dew; ephemeral

【朝气】 zhāoqì youthful spirit; vigor; vitality

【朝气蓬勃】 zhāoqì-péngbó full of youthful spirit; full of vigor and vitality; imbued with vitality

【朝三暮四】 zhāosān-mùsì blow hot and cold; play fast and loose; chop and change

【朝思暮想】 zhāosī-mùxiǎng yearn day and night

【朝夕】 zhāoxī 1.(时时) morning and evening; from morning to night; day and night; daily 2.(非常短的时间) a very short time

【朝霞】 zhāoxiá rosy clouds of dawn; rosy dawn

【朝阳】 zhāoyáng the rising sun; the morning sun

【朝朝暮暮】 zhāozhāo-mùmù every morning and evening; day and night

着 (zháo) 1.(接触) touch 2.(感受) feel; be affected by 3.(点着;烧着) burn; light: 消防车赶到时房子已经全～了。The house was completely ablaze when the fire trucks arrived. 4.(睡着) fall asleep
(另见"着"zhāo, zhuó)

【着慌】 zháohuāng become flustered; be thrown into a panic; get alarmed

【着火】 zháohuǒ inflammation; kindle; catch fire; be on fire

【着急】 zháojí worry; feel anxious

【着凉】 zháoliáng catch cold; catch a chill

【着陆】 zháolù land; landing (n.)

【着忙】 zháománg 1.(加快动作) be in a hurry: 不要～。Don't hurry. 2.(着急;慌张) worry; feel anxious

【着迷】 zháomí be fascinated; be captivated

【着魔】 zháomó be bewitched; be possessed

【着色】 zháosè colorate; coloration (n.)

爪 (zhǎo) claw; talon
(另见"爪"zhuǎ)

【爪牙】 zhǎoyá talons and fangs; lackeys; underlings

【爪牙鹰犬】 zhǎoyá-yīngquǎn lackeyes and hired ruffians

找 (zhǎo) 1.(寻找) look for; try to find; seek: ～矿 look for mineral deposits / ～票 ask for the tickets 2.(找人) want to see; call on; approach; ask for: 谁～我? Who asked for me? 3.(找钱) give change

【找补】 zhǎo·bu make up a deficiency

【找茬儿】 zhǎochár find fault; pick a quarrel

【找到】 zhǎodào get: 我为他～了一份工作。I got a job for him.

【找对象】 zhǎoduìxiàng look for a partner in marriage

【找麻烦】 zhǎo má·fan 1.(自找) look for trouble: 自～ ask for trouble; ask for it 2.(给他人) cause sb. trouble

【找齐】 zhǎoqí 1.(使相差不多) make uniform; even up 2.(补足) make up a deficiency

【找钱】 zhǎoqián give change

【找事】 zhǎoshì 1.(找工作) look for a job 2.(找茬儿) pick a quarrel

【找死】 zhǎosǐ court death

【找台阶】 zhǎo táijiē find an out; find a way out

【找头】 zhǎo·tou change

【找寻】 zhǎoxún look for; seek

【找辙】 zhǎozhé find an excuse; find a pretext

沼 (zhǎo) natural pond

【沼气】 zhǎoqì biogas; sludge gas; marsh gas; methane

【沼气池】 zhǎoqìchí methane-generating pit

【沼泽】 zhǎozé marsh; swamp

【沼泽地】 zhǎozédì swamp

召 (zhào) call together; convene; summon

【召唤】 zhàohuàn call; summon

【召回】 zhàohuí recall: ～大使 recall an ambassador

【召集】 zhàojí call together; convene
【召集人】 zhàojírén convener
【召见】 zhàojiàn 1.〈*Foreign Affairs*〉 summon (an envoy) to an interview 2.(约见下级) call in (a subordinate)
【召开】 zhàokāi convene; convoke: ～一次国际学术讨论会 convene an international symposium

照 (zhào) 1.(照射) shine; illuminate; light up: 阳光普～。The sun illuminates everything. 2.(照镜子) reflect; mirror: ～镜子 look in the mirror 3.(照相) take a picture; photograph; film; shoot: 我想～一张相。I want to have a picture taken. 4.(相片) photograph; picture: 彩～ color photograph 5.(执照) license; permit: 驾驶执～ a driving licence 6.(照料) take care of; look after: ～应 look after; take care of 7.(通知) notify: 关～ notify; inform 8.(比照) contrast: 对～ contrast; check against 9.(知晓) understand: 心～不宣 have a tacit understanding 10.(向着) in the direction of; towards: ～这个方向走。Go in this direction. 11.(依照) according to; in accordance with: ～我做的样子做。Do it as I do it.
【照搬】 zhàobān indiscriminately imitate; copy: ～外国模式 copy the models of other countries
【照办】 zhàobàn act accordingly; act in accordance with; act upon; comply with; follow
【照本宣科】 zhàoběn-xuānkē read item by item from the text; repeat what the book says
【照常】 zhàocháng as usual: 一切～。All as usual.
【照抄】 zhàochāo copy word for word
【照出】 zhàochū break forth; emit rays of light; give light
【照发】 zhàofā 1.(照例发给) issue as before: 女工产假期间工资～。Women workers are entitled to maternity leave with full pay. 2.(文件批语) approved for distribution
【照顾】 zhào·gu 1.(考虑到) give consideration to; show consideration for; make allowance(s) for: ～国家、集体和个人利益 take into consideration the interests of the state, the collective and the individual / ～现实情况 in consideration of the actual conditions 2.(关心;照料) look after; care for; attend to: 给予～ extend to sb. accommodation
【照管】 zhàoguǎn look after; tend; be in charge of: 你去度假时,谁来～花园? Who will tend the garden while you're on vacation?
【照护】 zhàohù look after
【照会】 zhàohuì 1.(通知) present a note to: ～日本政府 present a note to the Japanese government 2.(外交文件) note: 普通～ note verbal; verbal note / 通知～ circular note / 正式～ formal note
【照价】 zhàojià according to the set price
【照旧】 zhàojiù as before; as usual; as of old
【照看】 zhàokàn look after; attend to; keep an eye on: ～病人 attend to the patient / ～孩子 look after a child
【照理】 zhàolǐ 1.(按理) according to reason; normally 2.(照料) take care of; attend to; tend; mind
【照例】 zhàolì as a rule; as usual; usually
【照料】 zhàoliào take care of; attend to; tend; mind
【照猫画虎】 zhàomāo-huàhǔ draw a tiger with a cat as a model; copy; imitate
【照面儿】 zhàomiànr 1.(露面) put in an appearance; show up; turn up: 互不～ avoid each other 2.(不期而遇) encounter; come across
【照明】 zhàomíng illumination; lighting
【照明弹】 zhàomíngdàn flare; star shell
【照明度】 zhàomíngdù intensity of illumination
【照明技师】 zhàomíng jìshī lighting technician
【照排】 zhàopái phototypesetting; filmsetting
【照排机】 zhàopáijī phototypesetting composing machine
【照片】 zhàopiàn photograph; picture
【照射】 zhàoshè shine; illuminate; light up;

irradiate
【照实】 zhàoshí according to the facts
【照说】 zhàoshuō ordinarily; as a rule
【照相】 zhàoxiàng 1.（拍照）take a picture; take pictures; take photographs; take photos 2.（请别人给自己拍）have one's picture taken
【照相簿】 zhàoxiàngbù photo album
【照相机】 zhàoxiàngjī camera: 自动～ automatic camera
【照样】 zhàoyàng 1.（依照样式）after a pattern; after a model 2.（依然）in the same old way; all the same; as before: ～要感谢你。Thank you all the same.
【照妖镜】 zhàoyāojìng monster-revealing mirror; demon detector
【照耀】 zhàoyào shine; illuminate
【照应】 zhàoyìng （呼应）coordinate; correlate: 相互～ coordinate with each other
【照应】 zhào·ying （照料）look after; take care of
【照章办事】 zhàozhāng-bànshì act according to the rules; do everything by rule
【照直】 zhàozhí 1.（一直朝前）go straight on 2.（直截了当）direct; in plain terms

兆 (zhào) 1.（预兆）sign; omen; portent: 不祥之～ bad omen 2.（预示）portend; foretell: 瑞雪～丰年。A timely snow promises a good harvest. 3.（100万）million; millionth; mega-
【兆伏】 zhàofú megavolt
【兆赫】 zhàohè 〈*Electr.*〉 megahertz; megacycle per second
【兆头】 zhào·tou sign; omen; portent: 好～ a good omen / 坏～ a bad omen

笊 (zhào)
【笊篱】 zhào·li strainer; wicker strainer: 柳条～ wicker strainer / 铁丝～ wire strainer / 竹篾～ bamboo strainer

罩 (zhào) 1.（遮盖）cover; overspread; wrap: 烟笼雾～ be shrouded in smog 2.（罩子）cover; shade; hood; casing 3.（渔具）coop; a bamboo fish trap
【罩盖】 zhàogài shroud
【罩面】 zhàomiàn mat coat
【罩袍】 zhàopáo dust-robe; dust-gown
【罩衫】 zhàoshān overall; dustcoat
【罩袖】 zhàoxiù oversleeve; sleevelet
【罩衣】 zhàoyī dustcoat; overall
【罩子】 zhào·zi cover; shade; hood; casing

肇［肈］(zhào) 1.（开始）start; commence; initiate 2.（发生）cause (trouble, etc.)
【肇祸】 zhàohuò cause trouble; cause an accident
【肇始】 zhàoshǐ start; commence; initiate
【肇事】 zhàoshì cause trouble; create a disturbance
【肇事后逃逸】 zhàoshìhòu táoyì hit-and-run
【肇事者】 zhàoshìzhě troublemaker; fomenter

zhe

折 (zhē) 1.（翻转）roll over; turn over 2.（倒来倒去）pour back and forth between two containers: 水太热，用两个杯子～一～就凉了。The water is too hot. Cool it down by pouring it one cup to another.
（另见"折"shé，zhé）
【折腾】 zhē·teng 1.（翻来倒去）turn from side to side; toss about 2.（反复做）do sth. over and over again 3.（折磨）cause physical or mental suffering; get sb. down: 牙疼真～人。A toothache can get you down.

蜇 (zhē) sting; irritate: 马蜂～人。Wasps sting.
（另见"蜇"zhé）

遮 (zhē) 1.（挡住）hide from view; cover; screen 2.（拦住）block; obstruct; impede 3.（掩盖）cover up: ～人耳目 try to hoodwink people
【遮蔽】 zhēbì 1.（挡住）cover; screen; hide from view 2.（阻隔）obstruct; block: ～视线 obstruct the view 3.〈*Mil.*〉 defilade
【遮藏】 zhēcáng hide; conceal; cover up
【遮丑】 zhēchǒu gloss over one's blemishes; cover up one's defect; hide one's shame
【遮挡】 zhēdǎng shelter from; keep out
【遮风挡雨】 zhēfēng-dǎngyǔ keep out wind and rain

【遮幅式宽银幕】 zhēfúshì kuānyínmù 〈*Cinematog.*〉 superscope; flat wide-screen

【遮盖】 zhēgài 1.(遮住) cover; overspread 2.(隐瞒) hide; conceal; cover up: 错误总是～不住的。Mistakes can never be hidden.

【遮光】 zhēguāng shading

【遮光罩】 zhēguāngzhào 〈*Photog.*〉 lens hood

【遮拦】 zhēlán block; obstruct; impede

【遮羞】 zhēxiū hush up a scandal; cover up one's embarrassment

【遮羞布】 zhēxiūbù fig leaf; G-string

【遮掩】 zhēyǎn 1.(遮蔽) cover; overspread; envelope 2.(掩饰) cover up; hide; conceal: ～错误 cover up the mistakes

【遮阳】 zhēyáng sunshade

【遮阳卷帘】 zhēyáng juǎnlián roller blind

【遮阳篷】 zhēyángpéng awning

【遮阳伞】 zhēyángsǎn sunshade

折 (zhé) 1.(折断) break; snap: 把棍子～成两截 snap a stick in two 2.(损失) lose; suffer the loss of 3.(弯曲; 弯) bend; twist 4.(转变方向) turn back; change direction: ～向南方 turn southward 5.(折服) be convinced; be filled with admiration 6.(折合) convert into; amount to: 把华氏温度～成摄氏温度 convert Fahrenheit degrees into Celsius 7.(折扣) discount; rebate: 打九～ give 10% discount; charge 90% of the original price 8.(折叠) fold: 把地图～好 fold the map 9.(折子) booklet; folder: 存～ bankbook; deposit book
(另见"折"shé, zhē)

【折半】 zhébàn reduce (a price) by half; give 50% discount

【折边机】 zhébiānjī cramp folding machine

【折尺】 zhéchǐ folding rule

【折刀】 zhédāo clasp-knife; jack knife: 弹簧～ flick knife

【折凳】 zhédèng camp stool

【折叠】 zhédié fold

【折叠床】 zhédiéchuáng folding bed

【折叠椅】 zhédiéyǐ folding chair

【折叠桌】 zhédiézhuō flap table

【折兑】 zhéduì exchange (gold or silver) for money; convert

【折返段】 zhéfǎnduàn 〈*Railway*〉 back-turning section

【折服】 zhéfú 1.(说服) subdue; bring into submission: 强词夺理不能～人。No one can be persuaded by sophistry. 2.(信服) be convinced; be filled with admiration: 令人～ compel admiration

【折光】 zhéguāng refracted light

【折合】 zhéhé convert into; amount to: 这笔外币～成人民币是多少? How much does this sum of foreign money amount to in Renminbi?

【折痕】 zhéhén laps

【折回】 zhéhuí turn back on the road; return on the road: 半路～ turn back halfway

【折价】 zhéjià convert into money; evaluate in terms of money

【折旧】 zhéjiù 〈*Econ.*〉 depreciation

【折旧费】 zhéjiùfèi depreciation charge

【折扣】 zhé·kòu discount; rebate: 打～ offer a discount

【折扣价格】 zhé·kòu jiàgé prices at a discount

【折扣率】 zhé·kòulǜ discount rate

【折磨】 zhé·mó cause physical or mental suffering; torment; harassment

【折扇】 zhéshàn folding fan

【折射】 zhéshè 〈*Physics*〉 refraction; interception

【折实】 zhéshí 1.(折后的实数) reckon the actual amount after a discount 2.(折成实物价格) adjust payment in accordance with the price index of certain commodities

【折算】 zhésuàn convert

【折算率】 zhésuànlǜ conversion rate

【折梯】 zhétī folding stair

【折腰】 zhéyāo bow; humble oneself

【折页】 zhéyè 〈*Printing*〉 folding

【折椅】 zhéyǐ folding chair

【折账】 zhézhàng pay a debt in kind

【折纸】 zhézhǐ paper folding

【折纸手工】 zhézhǐ shǒugōng origami (Jap.)

【折中】 zhézhōng compromise: ～方案 a compromise proposal

【折衷】 zhézhōng 同"折中"

【折衷主义】 zhézhōng zhǔyì eclecticism

【折子】 zhé·zi booklet (used for keeping accounts, etc.)

【折子戏】 zhé·zixì highlights from operas

哲［喆］(zhé) **1.**（有智慧）wise; sagacious **2.**（有智慧的人）wise man; sage: 先～ the sages of old

【哲里木盟】 Zhélǐmùméng 〈place〉 Jirem Meng

【哲理】 zhélǐ philosophic theory; philosophy

【哲学】 zhéxué philosophy; philosophic (adj.) ‖ 哲学家 philosopher

蜇 (zhé) 〈*Zool.*〉 jellyfish (另见"蜇"zhē)

【蜇皮】 zhépí umbrella of jellyfish

【蜇头】 zhétóu oral arms of jellyfish

辄［輒］(zhé) always; whenever; frequently

蛰［蟄］(zhé) hibernate

【蛰伏】 zhéfú 〈*Zool.*〉 hibernate (v.); hibernation (n.); dormancy (n.)

【蛰居】 zhéjū live in seclusion

谪［謫］(zhé) **1.**（谴责）blame; criticize; reprimand **2.**（贬官）relegate a high-ranking official; lower in rank

辙 (zhé) **1.**（车辙）the track of a wheel; rut **2.**（韵）rhyme: 合～ in rhyme **3.**（主意;办法）way; idea: 没～ can find no way out; be at the end of one's rope

者 (zhě) **1.**（人）man **2.**（…的人）-er; -ist: 地质工作～ geologist / 马克思主义～ Marxist / 医务工作～ medical worker **3.**（与数字连用）二～必居其一。It must be one or the other.

锗 (zhě) 〈*Chem.*〉 germanium（元素符号 Ge）

【锗晶体管】 zhějīngtǐguǎn germanium transistor

赭 (zhě) reddish brown; burnt ocher; burnt ochre

【赭石】 zhěshí 〈*Mineral.*〉 ocher; ochre

褶［襵］(zhě) pleat; crease: 百～裙 pleated skirt; accordion pleated skirt / 这种料子容易起～ This material creases easily.

【褶皱】 zhězhòu **1.**（皮肤上的）wrinkle **2.** 〈*Geol.*〉 fold: ～山 folded mountain

【褶子】 zhě·zi **1.**（衣服的褶纹）pleat **2.**（折叠的痕迹）crease; fold; wrinkle **3.**（脸上的皱纹）wrinkle; line (on the face)

这［這］(zhè) **1.**（指示代词）this: ～地方 this place / ～人是谁? Who is this? / ～是什么? What's this? / ～些比那些好。These are better than those. / ～是北京广播电台。This is Radio Beijing. **2.**（这时候）now: 她～就走。She is leaving right now.

【这般】 zhèbān such; so; like this: ～大小 this size; this big

【这边】 zhèbiān this side; here: 请～走。Come this way please.

【这次】 zhècì this time; present; current: ～会议 the present session

【这个】 zhègè this one; this: ～比那个好。This one is better than that one.

【这会儿】 zhèhuìr now; at the moment; at present: ～电话占线。The line's busy at the moment.

【这里】 zhèlǐ here

【这么】 zhè·me so; such; this way; like this: 它竟有～长。It's about this long. / 应当～做。It should be done this way.

【这么些】 zhè·mexiē so much; so many

【这么着】 zhè·me·zhe like this; so: ～好。It's better this way.

【这儿】 zhèr **1.**（这里）here **2.**（只用在"打、从、由"后面）now; then: 从～以后,我们要好好学习。From now on we'll study hard.

【这些】 zhèxiē these

【这样】 zhèyàng so; such; like this; this way: 照～做。Do it like this.

柘 (zhè) 〈*Bot.*〉 tricuspid cudrania

【柘黄】 zhèhuáng cudrania yellow

【柘树】 zhèshù tricuspid cudrania

蔗 (zhè) 〈*Bot.*〉 sweetcane; sugarcane

【蔗农】 zhènóng sugarcane grower

【蔗糖】 zhètáng **1.** 〈*Chem.*〉 sucrose **2.**（甘蔗榨的糖）cane sugar

【蔗渣】 zhèzhā bagasse

鹧 (zhè)

【鹧鸪】 zhègū 〈*Zool.*〉 Chinese francolin; partridge

zhen

贞 (zhēn) 1.(坚定不变) loyal; faithful: 坚～ staunch and faithful 2.(贞节) chastity; virginity

【贞操】 zhēncāo 1.(贞节) chastity; virginity 2.(忠贞) loyalty; moral integrity

【贞节】 zhēnjié chastity; virginity

【贞洁】 zhēnjié chaste and undefiled

【贞烈】 zhēnliè ready to die to preserve one's chastity

侦 (zhēn) detect; scout; investigate

【侦办】 zhēnbàn investigate and handle

【侦查】 zhēnchá 〈*Law*〉 investigate (a crime)

【侦查程序】 zhēnchá chéngxù procedure of investigation

【侦查员】 zhēncháyuán investigator

【侦察】 zhēnchá 〈*Mil.*〉 reconnoiter; scout: ～敌情 gather intelligence about the enemy

【侦察兵】 zhēnchábīng scout

【侦察机】 zhēnchájī reconnaissance plane; scout

【侦察卫星】 zhēnchá wèixīng reconnaissance satellite

【侦察员】 zhēncháyuán scout

【侦缉】 zhēnjī track down and arrest

【侦破】 zhēnpò investigate and unearth

【侦探】 zhēntàn 1.(指工作) do detective work 2.(指人) detective; spy

【侦探小说】 zhēntàn xiǎoshuō detective story; detective novel

【侦听】 zhēntīng 〈*Mil.*〉 intercept (enemy radio communications); monitor

【侦听录音机】 zhēntīng-lùyīnjī dictagraph; Dictograph

【侦听员】 zhēntīngyuán monitor

帧 (zhēn) (用于字画) 一～油画 an oil painting

【帧频】 zhēnpín 〈*TV*〉 frame frequency; picture frequency

针[鍼] (zhēn) 1.(缝衣针) needle 2.(针脚) stitch: 伤口缝了六～ closed the wound with six stitches / 粗略地缝上几～ put a few tacks in 3.(针状物) anything like a needle: 分～ minute hand / 时～ hour hand 4.(针剂) injection; shot: 打～ give an injection 5.(针刺) acupuncture: 耳～ ear acupuncture

【针鼻儿】 zhēnbír eye of a needle

【针插】 zhēnchā pincushion

【针刺疗法】 zhēncì liáofǎ acupuncture treatment

【针刺麻醉】 zhēncì mázuì acupuncture anesthesia

【针刀医学】 zhēndāo yīxué acupunctural surgery

【针对】 zhēnduì 1.(对准) be directed against; be aimed at; counter: 不～任何第三国 be not directed against any third country 2.(依照) in the light of; in accordance with; in connection with: ～目前情况 in view of existing situation

【针锋相对】 zhēnfēng-xiāngduì give tit for tat; be diametrically opposed to

【针管】 zhēnguǎn syringe

【针剂】 zhēnjì 〈*Pharm.*〉 injection

【针尖】 zhēnjiān needle-point

【针脚】 zhēn·jiao stitch: 用粗～ use a tacking stitch

【针灸】 zhēnjiǔ acupuncture and moxibustion

【针式打印机】 zhēnshì dǎyìnjī needle printer; matrix printer: 24 针～ 24-pin dot matrix printer

【针头】 zhēntóu 〈*Med.*〉 syringe needle; pip; needle head

【针线】 zhēn·xian needlework

【针眼】 zhēnyǎn 1.(针鼻儿) the eye of a needle 2.(针刺的孔) pinprick

【针眼】 zhēn·yan 〈*Med.*〉 sty

【针叶】 zhēnyè acerose leaf

【针叶林】 zhēnyèlín coniferous forest

【针叶树】 zhēnyèshù coniferous tree; conifer

【针织】 zhēnzhī knitting

【针织品】 zhēnzhīpǐn knitwear; knitted and woven goods

【针状】 zhēnzhuàng acicular

珍[珎] (zhēn) 1.(宝物) treasure: 奇～异宝 rare treasures 2.(宝贵) precious; valuable; rare 3.(珍重) value highly; treasure

【珍爱】 zhēn'ài treasure; love dearly; be very fond of

【珍宝】 zhēnbǎo jewellery; treasure

【珍本】 zhēnběn rare edition; rare book

【珍藏】 zhēncáng 1.（有价值而收藏）collect (rare books, art treasures) 2.（收藏品）collection

【珍藏品】 zhēncángpǐn collector's piece; collector's item

【珍贵】 zhēnguì valuable; precious: ～的资料 valuable material

【珍品】 zhēnpǐn treasure: 艺术～ art treasure

【珍奇】 zhēnqí rare: ～的动物 rare animals

【珍禽异兽】 zhēnqín-yìshòu rare fowls and strange animals; rare animals and birds

【珍视】 zhēnshì value; prize; cherish; treasure

【珍玩】 zhēnwán rare curios

【珍闻】 zhēnwén news titbits; fillers

【珍惜】 zhēnxī treasure; value; cherish: ～时间 value one's time

【珍稀】 zhēnxī precious and rare

【珍馐】 zhēnxiū delicacies

【珍异】 zhēnyì rare

【珍重】 zhēnzhòng 1.（爱惜;珍爱）treasure; highly value; set great store 2.（保重）take good care of yourself: 多多～。Please take good care of yourself.

【珍珠】 zhēnzhū pearl

【珍珠贝】 zhēnzhūbèi pearl shell; pearl oyster

【珍珠霜】 zhēnzhūshuāng pearl cream

胗 (zhēn) gizzard: 鸡～ chicken's gizzard / 鸭～ duck's gizzard

【胗肝儿】 zhēngānr gizzard and liver

真 (zhēn) 1.（真实）true; real; genuine: 这枚戒指是～金的。This ring is genuine gold. 2.（的确）really; truly; indeed 3.（清楚）clearly; unmistakably

【真北】 zhēnběi 〈*Aeron*. & *Naut*.〉 true north

【真才实学】 zhēncái-shíxué real ability and learning; genuine talent

【真诚】 zhēnchéng sincere; genuine; true: 给青年～的引导 give young people genuine guidance

【真刀真枪】 zhēndāo-zhēnqiāng real swords and spears; the real thing

【真谛】 zhēndì true essence; true meaning

【真分数】 zhēnfēnshù 〈*Math*.〉 proper fraction

【真迹】 zhēnjì authentic work (of painting or calligraphy)

【真假】 zhēnjiǎ true and false; genuine and sham: ～莫辨 not to know the real from the false

【真金】 zhēnjīn true gold; genuine gold

【真金不怕火炼】 zhēnjīn bù pà huǒ liàn true gold fears no fire; a person of integrity can stand severe tests

【真菌】 zhēnjūn 〈*Biol*.〉 fungus

【真空】 zhēnkōng 〈*Physics*〉 vacuum

【真空包装】 zhēnkōng bāozhuāng vacuum-packed

【真空泵】 zhēnkōngbèng vacuum pump

【真空表】 zhēnkōngbiǎo vacuum meter

【真空装置】 zhēnkōng zhuāngzhì autovac

【真理】 zhēnlǐ truth: 绝对～ absolute truth / 客观～ objective truth / 相对～ relative truth

【真面目】 zhēnmiànmù true features; true colors

【真凭实据】 zhēnpíng-shíjù conclusive evidence; hard evidence

【真漆】 zhēnqī lacquer

【真枪实弹】 zhēnqiāng-shídàn real guns and bullets; live ammunition: 进行～的演习 conduct exercises with live ammunition

【真切】 zhēnqiè 1.（清楚）vivid; clear; distinct 2.（真诚）sincere; genuine; true

【真情】 zhēnqíng 1.（指情况）the real situation; the facts; the actual state of affairs; truth 2.（指心情、感情）true feelings; real sentiments

【真人】 zhēnrén real people; actual person

【真人真事】 zhēnrén-zhēnshì real people and real events; actual persons and events

【真善美】 zhēn-shàn-měi the true, the good and the beautiful

【真实】 zhēnshí true; real; authentic: ～情况 the real situation / 这本书是以～事件为基础的。This book is based on an actual case.

【真率】 zhēnshuài sincere; unaffected; straightforward

【真丝】 zhēnsī real silk

【真髓】 zhēnsuí essence

【真相】 zhēnxiàng face; naked truth; truth; the actual state of affairs: ～大白。The whole truth has come out.

【真心】 zhēnxīn wholehearted; heartfelt; sincere

【真心实意】 zhēnxīn-shíyì genuinely and sincerely; truly and wholeheartedly; wholeheartedly; sincerely

【真正】 zhēnzhèng genuine; true; real: 把经营权～交给企业 give enterprises real power of management

【真知】 zhēnzhī genuine knowledge

【真知灼见】 zhēnzhī-zhuójiàn real knowledge and deep insight; penetrating judgment; high perspicacity

【真挚】 zhēnzhì sincere; cordial: ～的友谊 sincere friendship

【真主】 zhēnzhǔ 〈*Islam*〉 Allah

【真抓实干】 zhēnzhuā-shígàn do solid work

砧［碪］(zhēn) hammering block; anvil

【砧板】 zhēnbǎn chopping block

【砧木】 zhēnmù 〈*Agric*.〉 stock

【砧子】 zhēn·zi hammering block; anvil

榛(zhēn) 〈*Bot*.〉 hazel

【榛子】 zhēn·zi 1.(榛树) hazel 2.(坚果) hazelnut

【榛子树】 zhēn·zishù hazel

臻(zhēn) 〈*written*〉 attain (a high level): 方法日～完善。The methods are being perfected.

斟(zhēn) pour: ～一杯茶 pour a cup of tea

【斟酌】 zhēnzhuó consider; deliberate: 很费～ call for much deliberation

甄(zhēn) 〈*written*〉 discriminate; distinguish; examine

【甄别】 zhēnbié 1.(审查辨别) examine and distinguish; screen; discriminate 2.(考核鉴定) reexamine a case

【甄选】 zhēnxuǎn select

诊(zhěn) examine (a patient)

【诊病】 zhěnbìng diagnose a disease

【诊察】 zhěnchá examine (a patient) examination

【诊断】 zhěnduàn diagnose; diagnostics (n.): ～为… diagnose the case as . . .

【诊断书】 zhěnduànshū medical certificate: 开～ make out a medical certificate

【诊疗】 zhěnliáo make a diagnosis and give treatment

【诊脉】 zhěnmài feel the pulse

【诊室】 zhěnshì consulting room

【诊所】 zhěnsuǒ clinic

【诊治】 zhěnzhì make a diagnosis and give treatment

疹(zhěn) rash: 荨麻～ nettle rash

【疹子】 zhěn·zi measles

枕(zhěn) 1.(枕头) pillow 2.(把头枕在…上) rest the head on 3.〈*Mech*.〉 block

【枕戈待旦】 zhěngē-dàidàn lie with one's head pillowed on a spear, waiting for day to break; be ready for battle; maintain combat readiness

【枕骨】 zhěngǔ 〈*Anat*.〉 occipital bone

【枕巾】 zhěnjīn a towel used to cover a pillow

【枕木】 zhěnmù 〈*Railway*〉 tie; sleeper

【枕套】 zhěntào pillowcase; pillowslip

【枕头】 zhěn·tou pillow

【枕席】 zhěnxí 1.(枕头上的凉席) pillow mat; a mat used to cover a pillow 2.(床榻) bed

【枕席不安】 zhěnxí-bù'ān toss about in bed; cannot sleep peacefully

【枕心】 zhěnxīn pillow (without the pillowcase)

缜［稹］(zhěn)

【缜密】 zhěnmì careful; meticulous; deliberate: ～的计划 a deliberate plan

阵(zhèn) 1.(军阵) battle array: 方～ square formation 2.(阵地) front; position: 上～ go to the front 3.(一段时间) a period of time 4.〈*classifier*〉 一～风 a gust of wind / 一～雨 a spatter of rain

【阵地】 zhèndì position; front: 坚守～ stick to a position
【阵地战】 zhèndìzhàn positional warfare
【阵发】 zhènfā paroxysm
【阵发性痉挛】 zhènfāxìng jìngluán clonic spasm; clonospasm
【阵风】 zhènfēng 〈*Meteorol.*〉 gust; puff of wind
【阵脚】 zhènjiǎo 1.(阵的最前方) front line 2.(用于比喻) position; situation; circumstances
【阵咳】 zhènké paroxysmal
【阵容】 zhènróng 1.(队伍外貌) battle array 2.(人力配备) lineup: ～强大 have a strong lineup
【阵势】 zhènshì 1.(作战布置) battle array; a disposition of combat forces 2.(情势;场面) situation; condition; circumstances
【阵痛】 zhèntòng 〈*Med.*〉 labor pains; throes
【阵亡】 zhènwáng be killed in action; fall in battle
【阵亡将士名册】 zhènwáng jiàngshì míngcè roll of honor
【阵线】 zhènxiàn front; ranks; alignment: 民族统一～ national united front
【阵营】 zhènyíng camp
【阵雨】 zhènyǔ shower

振 (zhèn) 1.(摇动) shake; flap 2.(奋起) rise with force and spirit; brace up: 食欲不～ lose one's appetite
【振臂】 zhènbì raise one's arm: ～高呼 raise one's arm and shout
【振翅高飞】 zhènchì-gāofēi flutter and soar high
【振荡】 zhèndàng 1.〈*Physics*〉 vibration 2.〈*Electr.*〉 oscillation
【振荡器】 zhèndàngqì oscillator
【振捣】 zhèndǎo jolt ramming
【振捣棒】 zhèndǎobàng 〈*Archit.*〉 vibrator
【振动】 zhèndòng 〈*Physics*〉 vibration
【振奋】 zhènfèn 1.(振作奋发) rouse oneself; rise with force and spirit; be inspired with enthusiasm: 我们要～起来。We should rouse ourselves up. 2.(使振奋) inspire; stimulate
【振奋人心】 zhènfèn-rénxīn inspire people; inspire the people with hope: ～的消息 heartening news
【振幅】 zhènfú 〈*Physics*〉 amplitude (of vibration)
【振铃声】 zhènlíngshēng ringing tone
【振兴】 zhènxīng develop vigorously; promote: ～工业 promote industry / ～经济 revitalize the economy / ～中华 rejuvenating China; achieve China's rejuvenation; make China prosperous and strong
【振振有辞】 zhènzhèn-yǒucí speak plausibly and at length
【振作】 zhènzuò bestir oneself; display vigor: ～精神 keep up one's spirit

赈 (zhèn) relieve; aid: 以工代～ provide work as a form of relief
【赈济】 zhènjì relieve; aid: ～难民 relieve the refugees
【赈灾】 zhènzāi relieve the people in stricken areas

震 (zhèn) 1.(震动) shake; shock; vibrate; quake 2.(情绪激动) greatly excited; deeply astonished; shocked 3.(地震) earthquake: 余～ aftershock of earthquake
【震波】 zhènbō 〈*Geol.*〉 seismic wave; earthquake wave
【震颤】 zhènchàn tremble; quiver
【震颤性麻痹】 zhènchànxìng mábì Parkinson's disease
【震颤性谵妄】 zhènchànxìng zhānwàng delirium tremens; DT
【震荡】 zhèndàng shake; shock; vibrate; quake; concussion
【震动】 zhèndòng shake; shock; vibrate; quake
【震耳欲聋】 zhèn'ěr-yùlóng deafening: ～的雷声 deafening thunder
【震撼】 zhènhàn shake; shock; vibrate: ～世界 shake the whole world / ～天地 shake the skies and land
【震级】 zhènjí 〈*Geol.*〉 (earthquake) magnitude: 里氏～ Richter scale
【震惊】 zhènjīng shock; amaze; astonish: 1915年,鲁西塔尼亚号被德国潜艇击沉,～了所有的美国人。The sinking of the Lusitania by a German U-boat in 1915 appalled all Americans.

【震怒】 zhènnù be enraged; be furious
【震情】 zhènqíng earthquake condition
【震区】 zhènqū earthquake region
【震慑】 zhènshè awe; frighten
【震天撼地】 zhèntiān-hàndì shake the skies and land; rock the earth
【震源】 zhènyuán 〈*Geol*.〉 focus (of an earthquake)
【震中】 zhènzhōng 〈*Geol*.〉 epicenter: epicentral (adj.)
【震中区】 zhènzhōngqū epicentral area

朕 (zhèn) **1**.(皇帝自称) I, the sovereign **2**.(朕兆) sign; omen
【朕兆】 zhènzhào sign; omen; portent

镇 (zhèn) **1**.(镇压) press down; keep down; ease: ～痛 ease pain **2**.(镇定) calm; tranquil; at ease: ～静 calm **3**.(维持安定) guard; garrison **4**.(镇守) garrison post: 军事重～ strategic post **5**.(城镇) town **6**.(使变凉) cool with cold water or ice: 冰～啤酒 iced beer
【镇尺】 zhènchǐ paperweight
【镇定】 zhèndìng calm; cool; composed; unruffled: 神色～ be calm and collected; show composure and presence of mind
【镇定自若】 zhèndìng-zìruò be perfectly calm and collected; be in possession of oneself
【镇静】 zhènjìng **1**.(不慌) calm; cool; composed; unruffled **2**.(使镇静) tranquilize; calm
【镇静剂】 zhènjìngjì sedative; tranquilizer; palliative
【镇守】 zhènshǒu guard; garrison: ～边疆 defend the frontier
【镇痛】 zhèntòng **1**.(止痛) ease pain **2**. 〈*Med*.〉 analgesia
【镇痛剂】 zhèntòngjì analgesic
【镇压】 zhènyā **1**.(强力压制) suppress; repress; put down: ～与宽大相结合的政策 policy of combining suppression with leniency **2**.(处决) execute **3**. 〈*Agric*.〉 rolling; compacting; tamping
【镇纸】 zhènzhǐ paperweight

zheng

正 (zhēng) (另见"正"zhèng)
【正月】 zhēngyuè the first month of the lunar year; the first moon: ～初一 the lunar New Year's Day

征[徵[3-7]] (zhēng) **1**.(远征) go on a long journey **2**.(出征) go on an expedition **3**.(征召) conscript; draft; recruit; levy (troops); call up: 新～的兵 new recruits **4**.(征收) levy; collect; impose: ～税 levy taxes **5**.(征求) ask for; solicit: ～稿 solicit contributions **6**.(证明) evidence; proof: 信而有～ borne out by evidence **7**.(现象) sign; portent: 特～ characteristic / 象～ symbol; emblem
【征兵】 zhēngbīng conscription; draft; call-up
【征程】 zhēngchéng journey: 踏上～ step on a long journey
【征调】 zhēngdiào requisition; call up
【征伐】 zhēngfá go on a punitive expedition
【征帆】 zhēngfān a ship on a long journey
【征服】 zhēngfú conquer; subjugate
【征稿】 zhēnggǎo solicit contributions
【征购】 zhēnggòu requisition by purchase; requisition
【征候】 zhēnghòu sign; indication
【征婚】 zhēnghūn seek a life partner
【征集】 zhēngjí **1**.(收集) collect **2**.(征募) draft; call up; recruit: ～新兵 recruitment
【征粮】 zhēngliáng requisitioning of grain
【征募】 zhēngmù enlist; recruit
【征聘】 zhēngpìn give public notice of vacancies to be filled; invite applications for jobs; advertise for (a secretary, teacher, etc.)
【征迁】 zhēngqiān move out local residents and vacant the place for the construction of new buildings
【征求】 zhēngqiú solicit; seek; ask for: ～意见 solicit opinions; ask for criticisms / ～某人的同意 request the consent of sb.
【征收】 zhēngshōu levy; collect; impose: ～进口税 impose import duties
【征税】 zhēngshuì levy taxes; taxation

【征讨】 zhēngtǎo go on a punitive expedition

【征途】 zhēngtú journey：艰险的～ a perilous journey / 踏上～ start on an expedition

【征文】 zhēngwén solicit articles or essays

【征文启事】 zhēngwén qǐshì a notice soliciting contributions for a special issue, etc.

【征象】 zhēngxiàng sign; omen; portent

【征询】 zhēngxún seek the opinion of; consult; ask advice of; probe

【征用】 zhēngyòng take over for use; commandeer; requisition：～土地 make a requisition of land

【征战】 zhēngzhàn go on an expedition

【征召】 zhēngzhào 1.（征兵）call up; enlist; draft; conscript 2.（委以官职）grant an official post; appoint to an official position

【征兆】 zhēngzhào sign; omen; portent

怔（zhēng）

【怔忪】 zhēngzhōng terrified; terror-stricken

症［癥］（zhēng）（另见"症"zhèng）

【症结】 zhēngjié crux; crucial reason：～所在 the crux of the problem; where the trouble lies

争（zhēng） 1.（力争）contend; vie; strive：～权 scramble for power / 不～一日之短长 not strive for only temporary superiority 2.（争执）argue; dispute：～得面红耳赤 flush to the roots of one's hair in the hot dispute

【争霸】 zhēngbà contend for hegemony; scramble for supremacy

【争辩】 zhēngbiàn argue; debate; contend：无可～ indisputable; irrefutable

【争吵】 zhēngchǎo quarrel; wrangle; squabble：那些孩子们总是为小事而～。Those children are always quarrelling over little things.

【争持】 zhēngchí refuse to give in; stick to one's guns

【争斗】 zhēngdòu fight; struggle; strife

【争端】 zhēngduān controversial issue; dispute; conflict：边界～ a border dispute / 国际～ an international dispute / 用和平手段解决～ solve disputes by peaceful means

【争夺】 zhēngduó fight for; enter into rivalry with sb. over sth.; vie with sb. for sth.：～冠军 compete against sb. for championship / ～市场 scramble for markets

【争购一空】 zhēnggòu-yīkōng buy up in a hurry

【争光】 zhēngguāng win honor for

【争论】 zhēnglùn argument; controversy; dispute; debate; contention

【争名夺利】 zhēngmíng-duólì strive for fame and wealth; spend one's energies in pursuit of fame and wealth

【争鸣】 zhēngmíng contend

【争气】 zhēngqì try to make a good showing; try to win credit for; try to bring credit to：为中国人～ win credit for the Chinese people

【争球】 zhēngqiú 〈*Rugby*〉scrum

【争取】 zhēngqǔ 1.（争取达到）strive for sth.; fight for; win over：～和平统一祖国 strive to reunify the motherland peacefully / ～大多数 win over the majority / ～主动 strive to take the lead 2.（争取实现）try to accomplish

【争权夺利】 zhēngquán-duólì scramble for power and profit

【争先】 zhēngxiān try to be the first to do sth.

【争先进】 zhēngxiānjìn strive to be a model worker

【争先恐后】 zhēngxiān-kǒnghòu strive to be the first and fear to lag behind; vie with each other in doing sth.

【争雄】 zhēngxióng contend for hegemony

【争议】 zhēngyì dispute; controversy：有～的条款 a contentious clause / 有～的地区 disputed areas

【争执】 zhēngzhí disagree; dispute; stick to one's position

挣（zhēng）（另见"挣"zhèng）

【挣扎】 zhēngzhá struggle

峥（zhēng）

【峥嵘】 zhēngróng 1.（山势高峻）lofty and steep; towering 2.（才华超群）outstanding; extraordinary：～岁月 eventful years

狰(zhēng)

【狰狞】 zhēngníng ferocious; savage; hideous: ～的面目 ferocious features; a vile visage

睁(zhēng) open (the eyes): ～不开眼 cannot keep one's eyes open

【睁一眼，闭一眼】 zhēng yī yǎn, bì yī yǎn turn a blind eye to sth.; wink at sth.; pretend not to see

筝(zhēng) 〈*Music*〉 *zheng*; 25-stringed Chinese zither

蒸(zhēng) 1.(蒸发) evaporate 2.(蒸熟) steam: ～饭 steam rice / 清～鱼 steamed fish

【蒸饼】 zhēngbǐng steamed cake

【蒸发】 zhēngfā evaporate; evaporation

【蒸发计】 zhēngfājì evaporimeter

【蒸干】 zhēnggān evaporation to dryness

【蒸锅】 zhēngguō steamer; a pot for steaming food

【蒸馏】 zhēngliú 〈*Physics*〉 distillation

【蒸馏水】 zhēngliúshuǐ distilled water

【蒸笼】 zhēnglóng food steamer; steam box

【蒸气】 zhēngqì vapor: 水～ water vapor; steam

【蒸汽】 zhēngqì steam; water vapor

【蒸汽机车】 zhēngqì jīchē steam locomotive; steam engine

【蒸汽浴】 zhēngqìyù sauna; vapor-bath

【蒸腾】 zhēngténg (of steam) rising: 热气～ steaming

【蒸蒸日上】 zhēngzhēng-rìshàng becoming more prosperous every day; flourishing; thriving

拯(zhěng) save; rescue; deliver

【拯救】 zhěngjiù save; rescue; deliver

整(zhěng) 1.(完整) whole; complete; full; entire: 10 点～ ten o'clock sharp / ～夜不睡 lie awake all night; lie awake the whole night 2.(整齐) orderly; in good order; neat; tidy: 衣冠不～ slovenly in one's dress; not properly dressed 3.(整顿) put in order; rectify 4.(整修) repair; mend; renovate 5.(整人) make sb. suffer; punish; fix: 挨～ be the target of criticism or attack

【整编】 zhěngbiān reorganize (troops)

【整饬】 zhěngchì 1.(整顿) rectify; consolidate; straighten out: ～纪律 strengthened discipline 2.(整齐) in good order; neat; tidy: 军容～ in fine battle array

【整除】 zhěngchú 〈*Math.*〉 be divided with no remainder; divide exactly: 四能～二十四 4 is an aliquot part of 24

【整党】 zhěngdǎng consolidate the Party organization

【整地】 zhěngdì soil preparation

【整队】 zhěngduì dress the ranks; line up

【整顿】 zhěngdùn rectify; consolidate; reorganize: ～党风 rectify the working style of the Party

【整份股票】 zhěngfèn gǔpiào round lot

【整风】 zhěngfēng rectify; rectification (n.)

【整改】 zhěnggǎi rectify and reform

【整个】 zhěnggè whole; entire

【整行】 zhěngháng whole line

【整洁】 zhěngjié clean and tidy; neat; trim

【整旧如新】 zhěngjiùrúxīn restore sth. to its original shape and appearance; repair sth. old and make it as good as new

【整理】 zhěnglǐ put in order; straighten out; arrange; sort out: ～财政 regulate finances / ～资料 sort out the data / 他把书架上的书～了一下。He arranged the books on the shelf.

【整流器】 zhěngliúqì 〈*Electr.*〉 rectifier

【整齐】 zhěngqí 1.(不乱) in good order; neat; tidy: 桌子摆得很～。The tables are in alignment. 2.(规则，差不多) even; regular: 步伐～ march in step

【整人】 zhěngrén give sb. a hard time

【整日】 zhěngrì whole day; all day long

【整容】 zhěngróng tidy up one's appearance

【整容术】 zhěngróngshù cosmetic operation; face-lifting

【整数】 zhěngshù 1.(不含分数、小数) integer; whole number 2.(没有零头) round number

【整套】 zhěngtào a complete set of: ～承包合同 turnkey contract / ～设备 a complete set of equipment

【整体】 zhěngtǐ whole; entirety: ～利益

overall interests

【整体观念】 zhěngtǐ guānniàn the concept of viewing the situation as a whole

【整天】 zhěngtiān the whole day; all day; all day long

【整形】 zhěngxíng 〈*Med.*〉 plastic

【整形手术】 zhěngxíng shǒushù plastic operation

【整形外科】 zhěngxíng wàikē plastic surgery; plastics; orthopedics

【整修】 zhěngxiū rebuild; renovate; recondition

【整枝】 zhěngzhī 〈*Agric.*〉 training; pruning

【整治】 zhěngzhì **1.**(修理;整理) renovate; repair; dredge (a river, etc.): ～航道 dredge waterways **2.**(整人) punish; fix

【整装】 zhěngzhuāng get one's things ready (for a journey, etc.): ～待命 be ready for orders

正 (zhèng) **1.**(不偏,不斜) straight; upright: ～北 due north / ～东 due east / ～南 due south / ～西 due west / 将地图挂～ put the map straight **2.**(位置居中) situated in the middle; main: ～门 main entrance / ～厅 main hall **3.**(图形各边、角都相等) regular: ～三角形 equilateral triangle **4.**(正点) punctually; sharp: 10 点～ at ten o'clock sharp **5.**(正直) honest; upright: 公～ just; fair **6.**(正当) correct; right: ～理 correct principle; valid reason; the right thing to do **7.**(纯正) pure; right: ～黄 pure yellow / 气味不～ not of the right smell **8.**(主要的) chief; principal: ～驾驶员 first pilot **9.** 〈*Physics*〉 positive; plus: ～离子 positive ion; cation **10.**〈*Math.*〉(大于零的) positive: ～号 positive sign; plus sign **11.**(使端正) set right; rectify; straighten out: ～一～帽子 set one's cap right **12.**(改正) correct; rectify: ～误 correct mistakes / ～音 correct one's pronunciation **13.**(恰好) just; right; precisely; exactly **14.**(正在) be doing (另见"正"zhēng)

【正本】 zhèngběn **1.**(指图书) reserved copy (of a library book) **2.**(指文件) original (of a document)

【正比】 zhèngbǐ 〈*Math.*〉 direct ratio: 成～ be in direct proportion to

【正比例】 zhèngbǐlì direct proportion

【正步】 zhèngbù 〈*Mil.*〉 parade step; goose step

【正步走】 zhèngbùzǒu Parade step, march!

【正常】 zhèngcháng normal; regular: ～价格 normal price / ～亏损 normal loss / ～损耗 normal loss / ～需求 normal demand

【正常化】 zhèngchánghuà normalize; normalization: 两国关系的～ normalization of relations between the two countries

【正大】 zhèngdà upright; honest; aboveboard: ～光明 open and aboveboard; just and honorable

【正当】 zhèngdāng (正处在) just when; just the time for

【正当防卫】 zhèngdāng fángwèi justifiable defense

【正当业务】 zhèngdāng yèwù legitimate business

【正当】 zhèngdàng **1.**(合理合法的) proper; rightful: ～理由 good cause / ～手段 proper means / ～要求 just demand **2.**(指人品) correct; proper; upright

【正道】 zhèngdào the right way; the correct path

【正点】 zhèngdiǎn on schedule; on time; punctually: ～运行 running on schedule

【正电】 zhèngdiàn positive electricity

【正殿】 zhèngdiàn main hall (in a palace or temple)

【正法】 zhèngfǎ execute (a criminal): 就地～ execute (a criminal) on the spot

【正反】 zhèngfǎn positive and negative: ～双方的看法 the pros and cons

【正反应】 zhèngfǎnyìng positive reaction

【正犯】 zhèngfàn principal criminal

【正方】 zhèngfāng **1.**(正四方形) square **2.**(与"反方"相对) positive side

【正方体】 zhèngfāngtǐ cube; cubic (adj.)

【正方形】 zhèngfāngxíng square

【正房】 zhèngfáng **1.**(指房子) principal rooms **2.**(指妻室) legal wife

【正负号】 zhèngfùhào plus or minus (符号为 ±)

【正该】 zhènggāi should; must; it's proper

【正赶上】 zhènggǎn·shang just in time for
【正告】 zhènggào earnestly admonish; warn sternly
【正宫】 zhènggōng empress
【正规】 zhèngguī regular; standard
【正规部队】 zhèngguī bùduì regular troops; regulars
【正规化】 zhèngguīhuà regularize; standardize; be put on a regular basis
【正规教育】 zhèngguī jiàoyù regular education; proper education
【正规军】 zhèngguījūn regular army
【正轨】 zhèngguǐ the right path: 纳入～ lead onto the correct path; put on the right track / 走上～ step onto the right track
【正好】 zhènghǎo 1.(恰好) just in time; just right; just enough: 这帽子我戴着～。This hat fits me nicely. 2.(碰巧) happen to; chance to; as it happens: ～我也在这里。It happened that I was also here.
【正号】 zhènghào plus (符号为 +)
【正极】 zhèngjí 〈*Electr.*〉 positive electrode; positive pole; anode
【正极板】 zhèngjíbǎn 〈*Electr.*〉 positive plate
【正教】 zhèngjiào 〈*Religion*〉 Orthodox: 俄罗斯～ Russian Orthodox / 希腊～ Greek Orthodox
【正教会】 zhèngjiàohuì 〈*Religion*〉 Orthodox Church
【正襟危坐】 zhèngjīn-wēizuò 〈*written*〉 straighten one's clothes and sit properly
【正经】 zhèng·jing 1.(端庄正派) decent; respectable; honest: ～人 a decent person 2.(正当) serious: ～事儿 serious affairs 3.(合乎标准) standard: ～货 standard goods
【正楷】 zhèngkǎi regular script
【正理】 zhènglǐ correct principle; valid reason
【正路】 zhènglù the right way; the correct path: 走～ follow the correct path
【正门】 zhèngmén front door; main entrance
【正面】 zhèngmiàn 1.(区别于"侧面") front; frontage; facade: ～图 front view 2.(区别于"背面") the obverse side; the right side: 硬币的～ the obverse side of a coin 3.(区别于"反面") positive: ～教育 educate by positive measures or examples; positive education 4.(直接) directly; openly: ～提意见 make a criticism directly
【正面人物】 zhèngmiàn rénwù positive character
【正拍击球】 zhèngpāi jīqiú 〈*Badminton*〉 forehand stroke
【正牌】 zhèngpái regular; standard
【正派】 zhèngpài upright; honest; decent: 作风～ be honorable in one's way
【正片】 zhèngpiàn 1.〈*Photog.*〉 positive 2.(电影拷贝) copy 3.(区别于电影加片) feature (film)
【正品】 zhèngpǐn certified products; quality products
【正气】 zhèngqì 1.(指作风) healthy atmosphere 2.(指气节) probity; integrity
【正巧】 zhèngqiǎo 1.(正好) happen to; chance to; as it happens 2.(刚巧) just in time; in the nick of time; just at the right time
【正切】 zhèngqiē 〈*Math.*〉 tangent
【正确】 zhèngquè correct; right; proper
【正人君子】 zhèngrén-jūnzǐ a man of honor; gentleman
【正如】 zhèngrú exactly as; just as: ～你知道的 as you know
【正色】 zhèngsè 1.(指颜色) pure colors 2.(指神色) with a severe countenance
【正史】 zhèngshǐ history books written in biographical style
【正视】 zhèngshì face squarely; look squarely at; face up to: ～现实 look reality in the face
【正事】 zhèngshì one's proper business
【正式】 zhèngshì formal; official; regular: 达成～协议 reach a formal agreement
【正式代表】 zhèngshì dàibiǎo regular representative
【正式访问】 zhèngshì fǎngwèn official visit
【正式签署】 zhèngshì qiānshǔ official signature
【正式声明】 zhèngshì shēngmíng official statement
【正式照会】 zhèngshì zhàohuì official communication

【正数】 zhèngshù 〈*Math.*〉 positive number

【正题】 zhèngtí 1.（主要题目）subject of a talk or essay 2.〈*Philos.*〉 thesis

【正体】 zhèngtǐ 1.（标准字形）standardized form of Chinese characters 2.（楷书）regular script 3.（印刷体）block letter

【正厅】 zhèngtīng 1.（大厅）main hall 2.（剧场正厅）stalls

【正统】 zhèngtǒng 1.（王朝的）legitimism 2.（党派、学派的）orthodox：～观念 orthodox ideas

【正统派】 zhèngtǒngpài orthodox party or school

【正文】 zhèngwén main body; text：词典～ the main body of a dictionary; the dictionary proper

【正午】 zhèngwǔ high noon

【正误】 zhèngwù correct（typographical）errors

【正误表】 zhèngwùbiǎo errata; corrigenda

【正弦】 zhèngxián 〈*Math.*〉 sine

【正相反】 zhèngxiāngfǎn contrariwise：我们从左向右写，而他～。We write from left to right, he writes contrariwise.

【正项】 zhèngxiàng regular item

【正颜厉色】 zhèngyán-lìsè look serious and severe; put on a stern countenance

【正要】 zhèngyào be about to：当你打断我的时候，我～说… As I was just about to say, when you interrupted me ...

【正业】 zhèngyè regular occupation; proper duties

【正义】 zhèngyì 1.（指道理）justice：伸张～ do justice 2.（公正的）just; righteous：～战争 just war / ～之师 an army dedicated to a just cause

【正义感】 zhèngyìgǎn sense of justice

【正音】 zhèngyīn 1.（矫正语音）correct one's pronunciation 2.（标准音）standard pronunciation

【正音法】 zhèngyīnfǎ orthoepy

【正在】 zhèngzài 〈adv.〉 in process of; in course of; be doing

【正直】 zhèngzhí honest; upright; fair-minded

【正直无私】 zhèngzhí-wúsī upright; without partiality

【正职】 zhèngzhí 1.（指职务）chief 2.（指职业）main profession; principal profession

【正中】 zhèngzhōng middle; center

【正中下怀】 zhèngzhòng-xiàhuái be just what one hopes for; fit in exactly with one's wishes

【正中要害】 zhèngzhòng-yàohài hit the nail on the head; be to the point

【正字】 zhèngzì 1.（规范字形）standardize form of Chinese characters 2.（楷书）regular script

【正字法】 zhèngzìfǎ orthography; orthographic

【正宗】 zhèngzōng 1.（正统派）orthodox school 2.（真正的）genuine

【正座】 zhèngzuò orchestra seat

证［證］（zhèng） 1.（证明）prove; demonstrate：论～ demonstration 2.（证据）evidence; proof; testimony：人～ testimony of a witness 3.（证件；证书）certificate; card：出生～ birth certificate / 逮捕～ arrest warrant / 工作～ employee's I.D. card / 拘留～ order for provisional apprehension / 身份～ identification card / 许可～ permit

【证词】 zhèngcí testimony

【证婚人】 zhènghūnrén chief witness at a wedding ceremony

【证件】 zhèngjiàn credentials; papers; certificate

【证据】 zhèngjù evidence; proof; testimony：无说服力的～ unconvincing evidence / 提供～ produce evidence

【证据不足】 zhèngjù bùzú lack of evidence; insufficiency of evidence

【证据充足】 zhèngjù chōngzú sufficient evidence

【证据分类】 zhèngjù fēnlèi classification of evidence

【证据作用】 zhèngjù zuòyòng evidential function

【证明】 zhèngmíng 1.（表明）prove; testify; bear out：～行之有效的改革措施 reform measures that have proved effective / 律师～遗嘱是真的。The lawyer authenticated the will. **2**.(证明书或信) certificate; identification; testimonial: 医生～ medical certificate

【证明人】 zhèngmíngrén authenticator

【证明书】 zhèngmíngshū certificate; testimonial: 验收～ acceptance certificate / 移交工程项目～ handing-over certificate

【证明文件】 zhèngmíng wénjiàn certificate; testimonial; papers

【证明信】 zhèngmíngxìng letter of certification

【证券】 zhèngquàn bond; security; negotiable securities: 未上市～ unlisted securities

【证券公司】 zhèngquàn gōngsī securities company

【证券化】 zhèngquànhuà form of bond

【证券交易所】 zhèngquàn jiāoyìsuǒ stock exchange; securities exchange

【证券投机】 zhèngquàn tóujī speculation in securities

【证人】 zhèngrén evidence; witness

【证人席】 zhèngrénxí witness-box; witness stand

【证实】 zhèngshí affirm; demonstrate; confirm; verify

【证书】 zhèngshū certificate; credentials: 毕业～ diploma; graduation certificate / 结婚～ marriage certificate / 索赔～ damage statement / 验收～ acceptance report / 质量～ quality certificate

【证言】 zhèngyán deposition; oral testimony; testimony; verbal evidence; witness: 证人的～是假的。The witness's testimony is false.

【证章】 zhèngzhāng badge

政 (zhèng) **1**.(政治) politics; political affairs; political (adj.): 议～ discuss political affairs **2**.(国家部门的主管业务) certain administrative aspects of government: 民～ civil affairs / 邮～ postal service **3**.(事务) affairs: 家～ household management

【政变】 zhèngbiàn coup d'état; coup

【政策】 zhèngcè policy: 对外开放的～ the policy of opening to the outside world / 外交～ diplomatic policy

【政党】 zhèngdǎng political party

【政敌】 zhèngdí political opponent

【政法】 zhèngfǎ politics and law

【政法机关】 zhèngfǎ jīguān political-legal organs

【政法界】 zhèngfǎjiè political-legal circles

【政法人员】 zhèngfǎ rényuán political-legal functionaries

【政府】 zhèngfǔ government: 唯一合法～ sole legal government

【政府部门】 zhèngfǔ bùmén government departments

【政府代表】 zhèngfǔ dàibiǎo government representative

【政府公文】 zhèngfǔ gōngwén government documents

【政府公债】 zhèngfǔ gōngzhài government bonds

【政府官员】 zhèngfǔ guānyuán government official

【政府机构】 zhèngfǔ jīgòu government apparatus

【政府机关】 zhèngfǔ jīguān government bodies

【政府人士】 zhèngfǔ rénshì government circles

【政府首脑】 zhèngfǔ shǒunǎo head of government

【政府职能】 zhèngfǔ zhínéng the function of government

【政纲】 zhènggāng political program; platform

【政工】 zhènggōng **1**.(政治工作) political work **2**.(政治工作者) political worker

【政绩】 zhèngjì achievements in one's official career

【政纪】 zhèngjì administrative discipline

【政见】 zhèngjiàn political view: 持不同～ hold different political view

【政界】 zhèngjiè political circles; government circles

【政局】 zhèngjú political situation; political scene

【政客】 zhèngkè politician

【政令】 zhènglìng government decree

【政论】 zhènglùn political comment

【政论家】 zhènglùnjiā political commentator; political writer

【政论文】 zhènglùnwén political essay

【政企不分】 zhèng-qǐ bùfēn a mixture of government administration and enterprise management

【政企分开】 zhèng-qǐ fēnkāi separation of the government from the enterprises; draw a clear distinction between the responsibilities of the government and those of enterprises

【政权】 zhèngquán state political power; regime; political power：国家～ state power

【政审】 zhèngshěn examine sb's personal histories

【政体】 zhèngtǐ system of government; form of government

【政务】 zhèngwù government affairs; government administration

【政务院】 zhèngwùyuàn state council

【政协】 zhèngxié the Chinese People's Political Consultative Conference (C.P.P.C.C.)

【政治】 zhèngzhì politics; political affairs

【政治避难】 zhèngzhì bìnàn political asylum：要求～ ask for political asylum / 提供～ grant asylum to sb.

【政治部】 zhèngzhìbù political department

【政治待遇】 zhèngzhì dàiyù political treatment

【政治犯】 zhèngzhìfàn political offender; political prisoner

【政治风波】 zhèngzhì fēngbō political disturbance

【政治纲领】 zhèngzhì gānglǐng political program; platform

【政治家】 zhèngzhìjiā statesman

【政治经济学】 zhèngzhì jīngjìxué political economy

【政治局】 zhèngzhìjú the Political Bureau

【政治局常委】 zhèngzhìjú chángwěi member of the Standing Committee of the Political Bureau

【政治局委员】 zhèngzhìjú wěiyuán member of the Political Bureau

【政治路线】 zhèngzhì lùxiàn political line

【政治面目】 zhèngzhì miànmù political affiliation or background

【政治派别】 zhèngzhì pàibié political grouping or faction

【政治权利】 zhèngzhì quánlì political rights

【政治逃犯】 zhèngzhì táofàn political fugitive

【政治舞台】 zhèngzhì wǔtái political arena

【政治性】 zhèngzhìxìng political nature

【政治学】 zhèngzhìxué politics

【政治资本】 zhèngzhì zīběn political stock-in-trade

症[證] (zhèng) disease; illness：不治之～ incurable disease

(另见"症"zhēng)

【症候】 zhèng·hòu **1.** (疾病) disease **2.** (症状) symptom

【症状】 zhèngzhuàng symptom

郑[鄭] (zhèng)

【郑重】 zhèngzhòng serious; solemn; earnest：～声明 solemnly declare / ～其事 seriously; in earnest

诤 (zhèng) 〈*written*〉 criticize sb's faults frankly; admonish; expostulate

【诤言】 zhèngyán 〈*written*〉 forthright admonition

【诤友】 zhèngyǒu 〈*written*〉 a friend who will give forthright admonition

挣 (zhèng) **1.** (挣脱) struggle to get free; try to throw off **2.** (挣钱) earn; make：～钱养家 earn money to support one's family / 你每月～多少钱？ How much do you earn every month?

(另见"挣"zhēng)

【挣大钱】 zhèngdàqián make big money; hit the big time

【挣命】 zhèngmìng struggle to save one's life

【挣钱】 zhèngqián earn money; make money

【挣脱】 zhèngtuō throw off：～枷锁 throw off the shackles

zhi

之 (zhī)

【之后】 zhīhòu later; after; afterwards：两天～ two days later

【之间】 zhījiān between; among

【之类】 zhīlèi and so on; and so forth; and the like; and what not

【之流】 zhīliú and his like：希特勒～ Hitler and his like

【之内】 zhīnèi in; within：在五天～ in five

days

【之前】 zhīqián before; prior to; ago: 在他动身～ prior to his departure

【之上】 zhīshàng over; above

【之外】 zhīwài besides; except; beyond: 除了雨天～, 她总骑自行车上班。She usually goes to work by bike except on rainy days.

【之下】 zhīxià under: 光天化日～ in broad daylight

【之一】 zhīyī one among: 她是我最欢迎的来访者～。She is among my most welcome visitors. / 你只是众多需要帮助的人～。You are only one among many who need help.

【之中】 zhīzhōng in; in the midst of; among: 他们住在群山～。They live among the mountains.

【之字形】 zhīzìxíng zigzag: ～的路线 a zigzag line

【之字路】 zhīzìlù zigzag course; S curve in a road

芝 (zhī)

【芝麻】 zhī·ma 1.〈*Bot.*〉 sesame 2.(芝麻种子) sesame seed

【芝麻官】 zhī·maguān petty official

【芝麻酱】 zhī·majiàng sesame paste

【芝麻油】 zhī·mayóu sesame-seed oil; sesame oil

支 (zhī)

1.(撑) prop up; put up: ～帐篷 put up a tent 2.(伸出; 竖起) protrude; raise 3.(支持) support; sustain; bear: 疼得～不住了 cannot bear the pain any longer 4.(指使) send away; put sb. off: 把孩子们～开 put the children off with excuses; send the children away upon some pretext 5.(支出, 支取) pay or draw money: 收～平衡。Income and expenses are balanced. 6.(分支) branch; offshoot: ～店 branch store 7.〈*classifier*〉 三～队伍 three contingents of troops 8.〈*Textiles*〉 count: 90～纱 90-count yarn

【支边】 zhībiān support the border areas

【支部】 zhībù branch: 党～ Party branch / 团～ League branch

【支部书记】 zhībù shū·ji branch secretary

【支部委员】 zhībù wěiyuán member of the branch committee

【支撑】 zhīchēng 1.(抵住压力) prop up; sustain; support: ～危局 prop up a perilous situation 2.〈*Archit.*〉 strut; brace 3.(勉强维持) support; prop up: ～门面 maintain the front

【支撑点】 zhīchēngdiǎn 〈*Mil.*〉 strong point; center of resistance

【支持】 zhīchí 1.(勉强维持) sustain; hold out; bear 2.(鼓励或赞助) support; back; stand by: 在…支持下 under the auspices of

【支出】 zhīchū 1.(支付) pay; expend; disburse 2.(支付的款项) expenses; expenditure; outlay; disbursement: 定额～ cost standards / 国防～ expenditure on national defense / 计划～ planned costs / 每日～ costs per day / 年度～ annual cost / 实际～ actual cost / 一次性～ lump sum cost / 意外～ incidental expenses / 追加～ supplementary expenditure

【支点】 zhīdiǎn 1.〈*Physics*〉 fulcrum 2.(关键) key

【支店】 zhīdiàn sub-branch

【支付】 zhīfù pay; pay money; defray

【支付日期】 zhīfù rìqī date of disbursement

【支付手段】 zhīfù shǒuduàn means of payment

【支付协定】 zhīfù xiédìng payments agreement

【支行】 zhīháng subbranch

【支架】 zhījià 1.(支撑) support; stand; trestle 2.〈*Motorcycle*〉 motorcycle stand 3.(飞机发动机的) prop stand

【支教】 zhījiào support educational undertakings

【支解】 zhījiě dismember; dismemberment (n.); dissect

【支局】 zhījú suboffice

【支离破碎】 zhīlí-pòsuì torn to pieces; broken up; fragmented

【支流】 zhīliú 1.(河的支流) tributary; affluent; streams 2.(次要事物) minor aspects; nonessentials: 分清主流和～ distinguish between the essentials and the nonessential

【支脉】 zhīmài offshoot; branch range

【支农】 zhīnóng support agriculture; supply the needs of agriculture

【支派】 zhīpài 1.（分支）branch; sect; offshoot 2.（支使）order; send; dispatch

【支配】 zhīpèi 1.（安排）arrange; allocate; budget：她善于～时间。She is good at budgeting her time. 2.（控制）control; dominate; govern：～某人 control sb.

【支票】 zhīpiào check (AmE.); cheque (BrE.)：不记名～ bearer check / 付后～ paid check / 划线～ crossed check / 记名～ order check / 空白～ blank check / 空头～ rubber check / 旅行～ traveller's check / 银行拒收～ dishonored check / 开～ write a check; draw a check

【支票簿】 zhīpiàobù checkbook

【支票票根】 zhīpiào piàogēn stub of a check; counterfoil

【支气管】 zhīqìguǎn 〈*Anat.*〉 bronchus

【支气管炎】 zhīqìguǎnyán 〈*Med.*〉 bronchitis

【支渠】 zhīqú branch canal

【支取】 zhīqǔ draw; withdraw：从银行～存款 draw one's deposit from a bank

【支使】 zhī·shi 1.（命人做事）order about：不听他的～ refuse to be ordered about by him 2.（让人到别处去）send away; put sb. off：把他们～走 send them away

【支书】 zhīshū 1.（党支部的）secretary of a Party branch 2.（团支部的）secretary of a League branch

【支吾】 zhī·wu prevaricate; equivocate; hum and haw：～其词 speak evasively; hum and haw

【支线】 zhīxiàn branch line; feeder

【支应】 zhīyìng 1.（应付）cope with; deal with 2.（守候）wait on; attend to 3.（搪塞）prevaricate; equivocate

【支援】 zhīyuán support; assist; help：～灾区 help the disaster area / 互相～ help and support each other

【支柱】 zhīzhù 1.（柱子）pillar; prop; mainstay：矿用～ pit prop 2.（主要的）main; principal：～产业 principal industry

吱（zhī） 〈*onomat.*〉 creak; squeak（另见"吱"zī）

枝（zhī） 1.（枝子）branch; twig：树～ branches 2.〈*classifier*〉 一～玫瑰花 a spray of rose 3.（杆状物）一～笔 a pen

【枝节】 zhījié 1.（次要的）minor matters：～问题 a minor problem; a side issue 2.（麻烦事）unexpected difficulty; complication：横生～ raise unexpected difficulties; deliberately complicate an issue; create side issues

【枝条】 zhītiáo branch; twig

【枝头】 zhītóu on the branch

【枝叶】 zhīyè 1.（枝和叶）branches and leaves 2.（琐碎事）nonessentials; minor details

【枝子】 zhī·zi branch; twig

肢（zhī） limb：四～ the four limbs

【肢解】 zhījiě dismember; dismemberment (n.)

【肢体】 zhītǐ 1.（四肢）limbs 2.（四肢和躯干）limbs and trunk

只［隻］（zhī） 1.（单独的）single; one only：～字不提 not say a single word 2.〈*classifier*〉两～耳朵 two ears / 一～鸡 a chicken / 一～手提箱 a suitcase（另见"只"zhǐ）

【只身】 zhīshēn alone; by oneself

【只言片语】 zhīyán-piànyǔ a word or two; a few isolated words and phrases：只听到～ catch only a word or two

织［織］（zhī） 1.（纺织）weave：～布 weave cotton cloth 2.（编织）knit：～毛袜子 knit wool into socks

【织补】 zhībǔ darning; invisible mending

【织布】 zhībù weave cotton cloth; weaving (n.)

【织机】 zhījī loom

【织锦】 zhījǐn 1.（锦缎）brocade 2.（织锦画）picture-weaving in silk：风景～ landscape woven in silk

【织锦厂】 zhījǐnchǎng brocade mill

【织锦缎】 zhījǐnduàn tapestry satin

【织女】 zhīnǚ woman weaver

【织女星】 Zhīnǚxīng 〈*Astron.*〉 Vega（织女一，天琴座 α）

【织品】 zhīpǐn fabrics; textile

【织物】 zhīwù fabric：机织～ woven fabric

【织造】 zhīzào weave; weaving (n.)

【织造厂】 zhīzàochǎng weaving mill

栀［梔］(zhī)

【栀子】 zhī·zi 〈*Bot.*〉 cape jasmine

汁 (zhī) juice：橙～ orange juice

【汁液】 zhīyè juice

知 (zhī) 1.（知道）know; realize; be aware of：为…所熟～ be known to / 无所不～ know everything; omniscient 2.（使知道）inform; notify; tell：通～ inform; notify 3.（知识）knowledge：求～ seek knowledge / 对于历史他所～不多。He has not much knowledge of history.

【知彼知己，百战不殆】 zhī bǐ zhī jǐ, bǎi zhàn bù dài know the enemy and know yourself, and you can fight a hundred battles with no danger of defeat

【知道】 zhīdào know; realize; be aware of：她～你的意思。She knows what you mean.

【知底】 zhīdǐ know the inside story; be in the know

【知法犯法】 zhīfǎ-fànfǎ knowingly violate the law; deliberately break the law

【知根知底】 zhīgēn-zhīdǐ know the inside story; be in the know

【知会】 zhī·hui notify; tell

【知己】 zhījǐ 1.（情谊深）intimate; understanding：～的朋友 bosom friend 2.（知己的人）bosom friend; intimate friend

【知近】 zhījìn intimate：～的朋友 intimate friend

【知觉】 zhījué 1.（感觉）consciousness：失去～ lose consciousness 2.〈*Psycho.*〉 perception

【知了】 zhīliǎo 〈*Zool.*〉 cicada

【知名】 zhīmíng well-known; noted; celebrated; famous

【知名度】 zhīmíngdù recognition; visibility：提高产品～ raise the recognition of products; raise the visibility of products

【知名人士】 zhīmíng rénshì well-known personage; public figure; celebrity

【知难而进】 zhīnán'érjìn press forward in the face of difficulties; advance despite difficulties

【知难而退】 zhīnán'értuì beat a retreat in the face of difficulties; shrink back from difficulties

【知情】 zhīqíng know the facts of a case or the details of an incident; be in the know：～不举 conceal what one knows of a case

【知情人】 zhīqíngrén person in the know; insider

【知趣】 zhīqù know how to behave in a delicate situation; be sensible; be tactful

【知人善任】 zhīrén-shànrèn know one's subordinates well enough to assign them jobs commensurate with their abilities

【知人知面不知心】 zhī rén zhī miàn bù zhī xīn you may know a person's face but not his heart; one may know a person for a long time without understanding his true nature

【知识】 zhī·shi 1.（认识和经验）knowledge：肤浅的～ superficial knowledge / 更新～ renew one's knowledge / ～就是力量。Knowledge is power. 2.（学术文化的）pertaining to learning or culture; intellectual

【知识产权】 zhī·shi cǎnquán intellectual property：世界～组织 World Intellectual Property Organization

【知识产业】 zhī·shi chǎnyè intellectual industry

【知识分子】 zhīshi fènzǐ intellectual; professional; the intelligentsia

【知识界】 zhī·shijiè intellectual circles; the intelligentsia

【知识经济】 zhī·shi jīngjì knowledge economy

【知悉】 zhīxī know; learn; be informed of

【知晓】 zhīxiǎo know; be aware of; understand

【知心】 zhīxīn intimate; understanding：～朋友 intimate friend

【知心话】 zhīxīnhuà intimate words; heart-to-heart talk

【知音】 zhīyīn a friend keenly appreciative of one's talents; bosom friend

【知遇】 zhīyù have found a patron or superior appreciative of one's ability

【知足】 zhīzú be content with one's lot：～常乐 happy is he who is content

蜘 (zhī)

【蜘蛛】 zhīzhū 〈*Zool.*〉 spider

【蜘蛛丝】 zhīzhūsī the thread of a spider web; cobweb

【蜘蛛网】 zhīzhūwǎng spider web; cobweb

【蜘蛛蟹】 zhīzhūxiè 〈*Zool.*〉 spider crab

脂 (zhī) 1.(油脂) fat; grease; tallow: 油～ fat; grease 2.(胭脂) rouge

【脂肪】 zhīfáng fat: 动物～ animal fat / 植物～ vegetable fat

【脂肪酸】 zhīfángsuān fatty acid

【脂粉】 zhīfěn rouge and powder; cosmetics

【脂粉气】 zhīfěnqì womanish; feminine

执［執］(zhí) 1.(拿着) hold; grasp 2.(执掌) take charge of; direct; manage: ～教 be a teacher; teach 3.(坚持) stick to; persist: ～意不肯 firmly refuse 4.(执行) carry out; observe 5.(凭单) written acknowledgement: 回～ receipt

【执笔】 zhíbǐ write; do the actual writing

【执导】 zhídǎo direct (a film, play, etc.); director

【执法】 zhífǎ enforce the law; put law into practice

【执法不公】 zhífǎ bùgōng denial of justice

【执法机关】 zhífǎ jīguān law enforcement agency

【执法人员】 zhífǎ rényuán law enforcement officials

【执法者】 zhífǎzhě law-executor

【执教】 zhíjiào teach; coach

【执迷不悟】 zhímí-bùwù obstinately stick to a wrong course; be perverse; refuse to come to one's senses

【执拗】 zhíniù stubborn; pigheaded; willful

【执勤】 zhíqín be on duty; do guard duty

【执行】 zhíxíng carry out; execute; implement: ～决议 implement a decision / ～命令 carry out orders / ～判决 enforcement of judgment

【执行机构】 zhíxíng jīgòu executive body

【执行机关】 zhíxíng jīguān executive organ

【执行委员会】 zhíxíng wěiyuánhuì executive committee

【执行主席】 zhíxíng zhǔxí executive chairman

【执意】 zhíyì insist on; be determined to; be bent on: 她～要去游泳。She insists on going to swim.

【执掌】 zhízhǎng wield; be in control of: ～兵权 wield military power / ～大权 be in control of power

【执照】 zhízhào license; permit: 申请驾驶～ apply for a driver's license

【执照税】 zhízhàoshuì fee of permit

【执政】 zhízhèng be in power; be in office; be at the helm of the state

【执政党】 zhízhèngdǎng the party in power; the ruling party

【执著】 zhízhuó persistent; persevering

【执着】 zhízhuó 同"执著"

直 (zhí) 1.(成直线的) straight 2.(垂直) vertical; perpendicular 3.(挺直) straighten 4.(公正) just; upright: 是非曲～ rights and wrongs; truth and falsehood 5.(直爽) frank; straightforward: 我对他～说。I told him straight. 6.(直接; 一直) directly; straight: 这条路～通火车站。This road leads directly to the railway station. 7.(不断地) continuously 8.(简直) just; simply

【直拨】 zhíbō direct dialing

【直拨电话】 zhíbō diànhuà direct-dial call

【直播】 zhíbō 1.〈*Agric.*〉 direct seeding 2.〈*Broadcasting & TV*〉 direct broadcast

【直播卫星】 zhíbō wèixīng DBS; direct-broadcast satellite

【直肠】 zhícháng 〈*Anat.*〉 rectum; rectal (adj.)

【直尺】 zhíchǐ straightedge

【直达】 zhídá through; nonstop: ～上海的火车 a through train to Shanghai

【直达车】 zhídáchē 1.(指火车) through train 2.(指公共汽车) through bus

【直达车票】 zhídá chēpiào through ticket

【直达快车】 zhídá kuàichē through express

【直达路线】 zhídá lùxiàn through route

【直到】 zhídào 1.(直到某时才完成) until: 她～晚上很晚才回来。She didn't come back until late in the evening. 2.(直到某时还未完成) up to: ～现在我还没收到她的信。I haven't received any letter from her up to the present.

【直道】 zhídào 〈*Sports*〉 straight

【直飞】 zhífēi direct flight; straight flight

【直观】 zhíguān audio-visual; directly perceived through the senses

【直观教具】 zhíguān jiàojù aids to object teaching; audio-visual aids
【直观教学】 zhíguān jiàoxué object teaching
【直航】 zhíháng nonstop
【直航班机】 zhíháng bānjī direct flight
【直角】 zhíjiǎo 〈*Math*.〉 right angle
【直角尺】 zhíjiǎochǐ square
【直角三角形】 zhíjiǎo sānjiǎoxíng right triangle; right-angled triangle
【直接】 zhíjiē direct; immediate: 他～前往纽约。He went straight to New York without stopping anywhere.
【直接宾语】 zhíjiē bīnyǔ direct object
【直接成本】 zhíjiē chéngběn direct cost
【直接反应】 zhíjiē fǎnyìng direct reaction
【直接后果】 zhíjiē hòuguǒ immediate consequence
【直接教学法】 zhíjiē jiàoxuéfǎ direct method
【直接起飞】 zhíjiē qǐfēi rolling takeoff; rolling start
【直接损失】 zhíjiē sǔnshī direct loss
【直接投资】 zhíjiē tóuzī direct investment
【直接选举】 zhíjiē xuǎnjǔ direct election
【直接责任】 zhíjiē zérèn direct liability
【直接照明】 zhíjiē zhàomíng direct lighting
【直接着陆】 zhíjiē zhuólù straight-in landing
【直截】 zhíjié straight; pointblank; blunt
【直截了当】 zhíjié-liǎodàng straightforward; pointblank; blunt
【直径】 zhíjìng diameter
【直觉】 zhíjué 〈*Psycho*.〉 intuition
【直快】 zhíkuài through express
【直来直去】 zhílái-zhíqù go and return without undue delay
【直立】 zhílì stand; erect
【直立茎】 zhílìjīng 〈*Bot*.〉 erect stern
【直立旋转】 zhílì xuánzhuǎn 〈*Skating*〉 upright spin
【直立植物】 zhílì zhíwù upright plant
【直流电】 zhíliúdiàn direct current (D.C.)
【直面】 zhímiàn face; look in the face
【直拳】 zhíquán 〈*Boxing*〉 straight punch
【直升机】 zhíshēngjī helicopter; copter
【直升机航空母舰】 zhíshēngjī hángkōngmǔjiàn helicopter carrier
【直升机机场】 zhíshēngjī jīchǎng heliport
【直升机驾驶员】 zhíshēngjī jiàshǐyuán helicopterist
【直视】 zhíshì look steadily at
【直抒】 zhíshū state frankly
【直抒己见】 zhíshū-jǐjiàn state one's views frankly
【直属】 zhíshǔ directly under; directly subordinate to: 国务院～机关 departments directly under the State Council
【直率】 zhíshuài frank; candid; straightforward
【直爽】 zhíshuǎng frank; candid; straightforward: 性格～ be forthright in character
【直系】 zhíxì direct line; lineal (adj.)
【直系继承人】 zhíxì jìchéngrén heir of line; heir of one's body
【直系亲属】 zhíxì qīnshǔ lineal relative
【直辖】 zhíxiá directly under the jurisdiction of
【直辖市】 zhíxiáshì municipality directly under the Central Government
【直线】 zhíxiàn 1.〈*Math*.〉 straight line 2.(急剧的) steep; sharp
【直销】 zhíxiāo direct selling
【直行】 zhíxíng 1.(照直向前) straight ahead 2.(交通标志) lane arrow for going straight
【直性子】 zhíxìng·zi 1.(直爽) straightforward; downright; forthright 2.(直爽的人) straightforward person
【直言不讳】 zhíyán-bùhuì speak without reservation; not mince words; call a spade a spade
【直译】 zhíyì literal translation; word-for-word translation
【直邮】 zhíyóu direct mail
【直至】 zhízhì till; until; up to

值 (zhí) 1.(价值) value 2.(相当) be worth: 分文不～ be not worth a farthing; be worth nothing; not worth a cent 3.(值得) be worth: 不～一提 not worth mentioning 4.(遇到) happen to: ～此危急之秋 at such a critical juncture 5.(值班) be on duty; take one's turn at sth.: ～夜 be on night duty; be on the night shift 6.〈*Math*.〉 value: 绝对～ absolute value / 求 X 之～ determine the value of X
【值班】 zhíbān be on duty

【值班员】 zhíbānyuán person on duty

【值得】 zhí·de be worth; merit; deserve: ～买 be worth buying / ～一提 to speak of; deserve to be mentioned / ～赞许 deserve commendation; be praiseworthy

【值钱】 zhíqián costly; valuable; worth a lot: 不～ valueless; worthless / 如今 XXX 不～。A XXX doesn't go far nowadays.

【值勤】 zhíqín be on duty

【值勤交通警】 zhíqín jiāotōngjǐng policeman on point duty

【值勤人员】 zhíqín rényuán personnel on duty

【值日】 zhírì be on duty for the day; be one's turn to be on duty: 轮流～ take turns to be on duty

植 (zhí) 1.(种植) plant; grow: ～树 plant trees 2.(树立) set up; establish

【植被】 zhíbèi 〈*Bot*.〉 vegetation

【植皮】 zhípí 〈*Med*.〉 graft; skin-grafting; make skin grafts

【植皮刀】 zhípídāo 〈*Med*.〉 dermatome

【植皮术】 zhípíshù 〈*Med*.〉 skin grafting

【植绒墙纸】 zhíróng qiángzhǐ flock-wallpaper; flock-paper

【植入】 zhírù embedding

【植树】 zhíshù 〈*Forestry*〉 tree planting; plant trees

【植树运动】 zhíshù yùndòng afforestation campaign

【植物】 zhíwù plant; flora; botanical (adj.): 草本～ herbaceous plants

【植物保护】 zhíwù bǎohù plant protection

【植物病害】 zhíwù bìnghài plant disease

【植物病理学】 zhíwù bìnglǐxué plant pathology

【植物检疫】 zhíwù jiǎnyì plant quarantine

【植物界】 zhíwùjiè plant kingdom

【植物人】 zhíwùrén human vegetable; vegetation state

【植物生态学】 zhíwù shēngtàixué plant ecology

【植物学】 zhíwùxué botany; botanical (adj.) ‖ 植物学家 botanist

【植物油】 zhíwùyóu vegetable oil

【植物育种】 zhíwù yùzhǒng plant breeding

【植物园】 zhíwùyuán botanical garden

殖 (zhí) breed; multiply: 繁～ multiply; propagate / 生～ breed; reproduce

【殖民】 zhímín establish a colony; colonize

【殖民当局】 zhímín dāngjú colonial authorities

【殖民地】 zhímíndì colony

【殖民地国家】 zhímíndì guójiā colonial country

【殖民国家】 zhímín guójiā colonialist power

【殖民战争】 zhímín zhànzhēng colonialist war

【殖民主义】 zhímín zhǔyì colonialism: 新～ new colonialism; neocolonialism ‖ 殖民主义者 colonialist

侄［姪］(zhí) nephew; brother's son

【侄女】 zhí·nǚ niece; brother's daughter

【侄孙】 zhísūn grandnephew; brother's grandson

【侄孙女】 zhísūn·nü grandniece; brother's granddaughter

【侄媳妇】 zhíxí·fu nephew's wife; wife of brother's son

【侄子】 zhí·zi nephew; brother's son

职［職］(zhí) 1.(职务) duty; job: 做好本～工作 do one's job well 2.(职位) post; office: 任～期间 tenure of office

【职称】 zhíchēng the title of a technical or professional post

【职称晋级】 zhíchēng jìnjí academic promotion

【职称评定】 zhíchēng píngdìng professional title appraisal

【职称评审委员会】 zhíchēng píngshěng wěiyuánhuì evaluation committee of professional titles

【职工】 zhígōng staff and workers; workers and staff members

【职工大学】 zhígōng dàxué university for workers and staff members

【职工代表大会】 zhígōng dàibiǎo dàhuì workers congress

【职工夜校】 zhígōng yèxiào evening school for workers and staff members

【职能】 zhínéng function: 着眼于转变～ focus on introducing changes in functions

【职能机构】 zhínéng jīgòu functional organization

【职权】 zhíquán powers of office; authority

of office：利用～ take advantage of one's position and power；exploit one's office / 滥用～ abuse one's powers / 行使～ exercise one's functions and powers

【职权范围】 zhíquán fànwéi limits of one's functions and powers；terms of reference

【职守】 zhíshǒu post；duty：忠于～ be faithful in the discharge of one's duties

【职位】 zhíwèi position；post：他在银行谋得一个～。He got a position in the bank.

【职务】 zhíwù post；duties；job

【职务工资】 zhíwù gōngzī salaries attached to the offices

【职务津贴】 zhíwù jīntiē duty allowance

【职衔】 zhíxián 1.（职位和军衔）post and rank 2.（官衔）official title

【职业】 zhíyè 1.（工作）occupation；profession；vocation；occupational（adj.）2.（专业的）professional：～特权 professional privilege

【职业病】 zhíyèbìng occupational disease

【职业道德】 zhíyè dàodé professional ethics：缺乏～ be unethical

【职业妇女】 zhíyè fùnǚ career woman

【职业高中】 zhíyè gāozhōng vocational senior middle school

【职业技能】 zhíyè jìnéng professional skill

【职业教育】 zhíyè jiàoyù vocational education

【职业介绍所】 zhíyè jièshàosuǒ employment office；employment exchange；labor exchange

【职业杀手】 zhíyè shāshǒu hatchet man；hit man

【职业外交官】 zhíyè wàijiāoguān career diplomat；professional diplomat

【职业学校】 zhíyè xuéxiào vocational school

【职业训练】 zhíyè xùnliàn vocational training

【职业运动员】 zhíyè yùndòngyuán professional athlete；professional

【职业中学】 zhíyè zhōngxué vocational middle school

【职员】 zhíyuán office worker；staff member；functionary：学校的教～ the teaching staff of a school

【职责】 zhízé duty；obligation；responsibility

【职责范围】 zhízé fànwéi scope of official duty

止（zhǐ） 1.（停止）stop；cease；discontinue 2.（使停止）stop；quench：～渴 quench one's thirst / ～血 stop bleeding 3.（到…为止）to；till：到目前为～ to date；till now；up to the present / 到年底为～ by the end of the year 4.（仅；只）only 不～一次 not just once；more than once

【止步】 zhǐbù halt；stop；go no further：游人～ no visitors；no admission

【止付】 zhǐfù 〈*Econ.*〉 stop payment

【止付通知书】 zhǐfù tōngzhīshū stop-payment notice

【止付支票】 zhǐfù zhīpiào stopped check；stopping payment of check

【止境】 zhǐjìng end；limit：进步无～。There is no end to progress.

【止咳】 zhǐké relieve a cough

【止咳糖浆】 zhǐké tángjiāng cough syrup；cough mixture

【止渴】 zhǐkě quench one's thirst

【止痛】 zhǐtòng relieve pain；stop pain

【止痛药】 zhǐtòngyào anodyne；analgesic；pain-killer

【止血】 zhǐxuè stop bleeding；stanch bleeding

【止血带】 zhǐxuèdài tourniquet

【止血棉】 zhǐxuèmián hemostatic cotton

【止血器】 zhǐxuèqì hemostat

【止血钳】 zhǐxuèqián hemostat

【止血散】 zhǐxuèsǎn styptic powder

【止血纱布】 zhǐxuè shābù hemostatic gauze

【止血药】 zhǐxuèyào hemostatic

【止痒】 zhǐyǎng relieve itching

【止痒药】 zhǐyǎngyào antipruritic

【止住】 zhǐzhù stop；halt；desist；bring to a stop

址［阯］（zhǐ） location；site：地～ address / 校～ school site

趾（zhǐ） 1.（脚）foot 2.（脚指）toe

【趾高气扬】 zhǐgāo-qìyáng strut about and give oneself airs；be swollen with arrogance

【趾骨】 zhǐgǔ 〈*Anat.*〉 phalanges

【趾甲】 zhǐjiǎ toenail

只［衹、秖］（zhǐ） 〈adv.〉 only；merely；just：我～能告诉你我所知道的。I can only tell you what I know. / 我～问了他的姓名。I merely asked

his name. / ～此一家。This is the only shop of its kind.
(另见"只"zhī)

【只不过】 zhǐ·buguò only; just; merely; no more than: 她～是个孩子。She is just a child.

【只得】 zhǐdé have no alternative but to; have to; be obliged to: ～如此 have no choice

【只读存储器】 zhǐdú cúnchǔqì 〈*Computer*〉 read-only memory; ROM

【只顾】 zhǐgù **1.**(专一) merely; simply; be absorbed in: 他～看书,连饭都忘了吃。He was completely absorbed in reading and forgot even to take his meal. **2.**(只考虑) only cared for: 他～个人利益。He cares only for his own interests.

【只管】 zhǐguǎn **1.**(尽管) by all means; not hesitate to: 有什么问题～问。If you have any questions, don't hesitate to ask. **2.**(只顾) merely; simply; be absorbed in

【只好】 zhǐhǎo have to; be forced to: ～另想办法 cannot but seek other means

【只怕】 zhǐpà be afraid of only one thing

【只是】 zhǐshì **1.**(仅仅是) merely; only; just: 这～托词而已。It is merely a pretense. **2.**(仅限于) simply: 这～手续问题。This is simply a question of formalities. **3.**(但是) however; but then; only: 我很想去,～忙不过来。I would very much like to go there, however my hands are full.

【只消】 zhǐxiāo have only to; need only

【只要】 zhǐyào 〈*conj.*〉 so long as; provided: ～你做完工作就可以走了。You may go, provided your work is done.

【只因】 zhǐyīn only because; for the simple reason that ...

【只有】 zhǐyǒu only; alone: ～这把钥匙能开这个门。The key alone will open the door.

【只争朝夕】 zhǐzhēng-zhāoxī seize the day, seize the hour; seize every minute; race against time

【只知其一,不知其二】 zhǐ zhī qí yī, bù zhī qí èr one cannot see the wood for the trees

枳 (zhǐ) 〈*Bot.*〉 trifoliate orange

【枳壳】 zhǐké **1.**〈*Pharm.*〉 fruit of trifoliate orange **2.**〈*Pharm.*〉 fruit of citron

【枳实】 zhǐshí **1.**〈*Pharm.*〉 immature fruit of trifoliate orange **2.**〈*Pharm.*〉 immature fruit of citron

咫 (zhǐ)

【咫尺】 zhǐchǐ 〈*written*〉 very close: 近在～ close at hand

【咫尺天涯】 zhǐchǐ-tiānyá a short distance away, and yet poles apart; see little of each other though living nearby

旨［**恉**[1]］(zhǐ) **1.**(意义;用意) purport; purpose; aim **2.**(意旨) decree: 圣～ imperial decree

【旨趣】 zhǐqù 〈*written*〉 purport; objective

【旨意】 zhǐyì decree; order

指 (zhǐ) **1.**(手指) finger: 屈～可数 can be counted on one's fingers; very few **2.**(指向) point at; point to: 向南～ point to the south **3.**(一指宽度) fingerbreadth; digit: 二～宽 two digits wide **4.**(指点) indicate; point out; refer to **5.**(指靠) depend on; count on: 大家就～着你帮忙。We're counting on your help. **6.**(影射) allude to: 很明显她～的是王先生。It was clear she was alluding to Mr. Wang.

【指板】 zhǐbǎn 〈*Music*〉 fingerboard

【指北针】 zhǐběizhēn compass

【指标】 zhǐbiāo target; quota; norm; index: 生产～ production quota

【指出】 zhǐchū point out; lay one's finger on

【指导】 zhǐdǎo guide; direct: 在…～下 under the guidance of ... / 基金将在委员会的～下开支。Funds will be spent under the committee's guidance.

【指导价】 zhǐdǎojià guiding price

【指导路线】 zhǐdǎo lùxiàn guide line

【指导思想】 zhǐdǎo sīxiǎng guiding ideology

【指导性计划】 zhǐdǎoxìng jìhuà guided planning

【指导员】 zhǐdǎoyuán 〈*Mil.*〉 political instructor

【指导作用】 zhǐdǎo zuòyòng directive function

【指点】 zhǐdiǎn **1.**(指出) give directions;

show how 2.(挑毛病) find fault; pick hole in sth.
【指定】 zhǐdìng appoint; assign: ～某人任某职 designate sb. to an office / ～下次会议的日期 assign a day for the next meeting
【指定代理人】 zhǐdìng dàilǐrén authorized agent
【指定管辖】 zhǐdìng guǎnxiá designated jurisdiction
【指定继承人】 zhǐdìng jìchéngrén designated heir
【指定监护人】 zhǐdìng jiānhùrén designated guardian
【指法】 zhǐfǎ 〈*Music*〉 fingering
【指骨】 zhǐgǔ 〈*Anat.*〉 phalange
【指挥】 zhǐhuī 1.(调度) command; direct; conduct: ～一个战役? direct a battle 2.(指挥者) commander; director 3.(乐队指挥) conductor
【指挥棒】 zhǐhuībàng 1.〈*Music*〉 baton 2.(泛指) baton
【指挥部】 zhǐhuībù command post; headquarters
【指挥车】 zhǐhuīchē command car
【指挥刀】 zhǐhuīdāo officer's sword
【指挥官】 zhǐhuīguān commanding officer; commander
【指挥所】 zhǐhuīsuǒ command post
【指挥塔台】 zhǐhuī tǎtái 〈*Aeron.*〉 control tower
【指挥系统】 zhǐhuī xìtǒng command system
【指挥员】 zhǐhuīyuán 〈*Mil.*〉 commander
【指甲】 zhǐ·jia nail: 手～ fingernail / 脚～ toenail / 剪～ clip the nails / 修～ have a manicure
【指甲锉】 zhǐ·jiacuò nail clipper
【指甲刀】 zhǐ·jiadāo nail clippers
【指甲盖儿】 zhǐ·jiagàir nail
【指甲夹】 zhǐ·jiajiā nail clipper
【指甲剪】 zhǐ·jiajiǎn nail scissors
【指甲油】 zhǐ·jiayóu nail polish
【指尖】 zhǐjiān finger tip
【指教】 zhǐjiào 1.(指点) tell how to do; give advice 2.〈*politeness*〉 advice; give advice; give comments
【指靠】 zhǐkào depend on; look to; count on
【指控】 zhǐkòng accuse; charge: ～某人犯罪 accuse sb. of a crime / 在他的陈述中,他～被告在犯罪现场。In his statement he alleged that the accused man was seen at the scene of the crime.
【指令】 zhǐlìng 1.(指示;命令) instruct; order; direct; instruction (n.) 2.〈*Computer*〉 instruction
【指令舱】 zhǐlìngcāng 〈*Aeron.*〉 command module
【指令码】 zhǐlìngmǎ instruction code
【指令系统】 zhǐlìng xìtǒng instruction repertoire; instruction set
【指令性计划】 zhǐlìngxìng jìhuà mandatory plan; mandatory planning
【指路牌】 zhǐlùpái signpost; fingerpost; guidepost
【指鹿为马】 zhǐlùwéimǎ confuse right and wrong
【指名】 zhǐmíng mention by name; name: ～漫骂 abuse sb. by mentioning his name
【指明】 zhǐmíng show clearly; demonstrate; point out: ～出路 point the way out
【指南】 zhǐnán guide; guidebook: 操作～ technical instruction / 工作～ working instruction / 旅行～ travel guide
【指南针】 zhǐnánzhēn compass
【指派】 zhǐpài appoint; name; designate: 那位记者被～负责国际新闻版。The reporter was assigned to cover international news.
【指日可待】 zhǐrì-kědài be just round the corner; can be expected soon
【指桑骂槐】 zhǐsāng-màhuái point at the mulberry and abuse the locust; point at one but abuse another; make oblique accusations
【指使】 zhǐshǐ instigate; incite; put sb. up to sth.: ～某人做坏事 instigate sb. to do evil
【指示】 zhǐshì 1.(指给人看) indicate; point out 2.(指示下级) instruct: ～某人做某事 instruct sb. to do sth. 3.(下达的指示) directive; instructions: 发出～ give instructions
【指示板】 zhǐshìbǎn indicator board
【指示代词】 zhǐshì dàicí 〈*Gram.*〉 demonstrative pronoun
【指示灯】 zhǐshìdēng pilot lamp; pilot light; indicator lamp

【指示器】 zhǐshìqì indicator

【指手划脚】 zhǐshǒu-huàjiǎo 1.(示意) make gestures; gesticulate 2.(轻率批评) make indiscreet remarks or criticisms

【指数】 zhǐshù 1.〈*Econ.*〉 index number; index: 价格～ price index / 价值～ value index / 实际工资～ index of real wages 2.〈*Math.*〉 exponent

【指头】 zhǐ·tou 1.(手指) finger 2.(脚指) toe

【指头肚儿】 zhǐ·toudùr finger pad

【指望】 zhǐ·wang 1.(盼望) look to; count on; look forward to: 不～他帮忙 not look to him to help us; not count on him for help 2.(盼头) prospect; hope: 他的病还有～。There is still hope of his recovery.

【指纹】 zhǐwén 1.(手指的纹) loops and whorls on a finger 2.(指纹痕迹) fingerprint

【指纹档案】 zhǐwén dàng'àn fingerprint file

【指纹鉴定】 zhǐwén jiàndìng fingerprint identification

【指纹学】 zhǐwénxué dactylography

【指向】 zhǐxiàng directional

【指向性增益】 zhǐxiàngxìng-zēngyì directional gain

【指引】 zhǐyǐn point (the way); guide; show

【指印】 zhǐyìn fingerprint; finger mark

【指责】 zhǐzé censure; criticize; find fault with: ～某人做某事 censure sb. for doing sth.

【指战员】 zhǐzhànyuán officers and men

【指针】 zhǐzhēn 1.(钟、表的针) indicator; pointer; needle 2.(指导) guiding principle; guide: 今后行动的～ guiding principle for future work

【指针式温度计】 zhǐzhēnshì wēndùjì dial thermometer

【指诊】 zhǐzhěn 〈*Med.*〉 touch: 肛门～ rectal touch / 阴道～ vaginal touch

【指正】 zhǐzhèng 1.(指出错误并改正) point out mistakes so that they can be corrected 2.(请人提出意见) make a comment or criticism: 请大家给予～。Please oblige me with your valuable comments.

【指指点点】 zhǐzhǐ-diǎndiǎn gesticulate; gesticulating

酯 (zhǐ) 〈*Chem.*〉 ester: 聚～ polyester

【酯化】 zhǐhuà 〈*Chem.*〉 esterification

【酯酶】 zhǐméi 〈*Chem.*〉 esterase

纸[帋] (zhǐ) 1.(纸张) paper: 包装～ wrapper / 玻璃～ cellophane / 复写～ carbon paper / 绘图～ drawing paper / 美术～ art paper / 牛皮～ kraft paper / 砂～ abrasive paper / 晒图～ blueprint paper / 双面复写～ articulating paper / 新闻～ newsprint / 账簿～ account book paper / 皱纹～ crepe paper 2.〈*classifier*〉一～空文 a mere scrap of paper

【纸板】 zhǐbǎn paperboard; cardboard

【纸版】 zhǐbǎn 〈*Printing*〉 paper mold; paper matrix

【纸包】 zhǐbāo paper parcel

【纸币】 zhǐbì paper money; paper currency; note

【纸带】 zhǐdài 〈*Computer*〉 paper-tape

【纸花】 zhǐhuā paper flower

【纸浆】 zhǐjiāng paper pulp; pulp

【纸巾】 zhǐjīn facial-tissue; tissue-paper

【纸牌】 zhǐpái playing cards

【纸片】 zhǐpiàn scraps of paper

【纸上谈兵】 zhǐshàng-tánbīng fight only on paper; be an armchair strategist; engage in idle theorizing

【纸条】 zhǐtiáo a slip of paper

【纸型】 zhǐxíng 〈*Printing*〉 paper mold; paper matrix

【纸烟】 zhǐyān cigarette

【纸样】 zhǐyàng paper sample

【纸张】 zhǐzhāng paper

【纸醉金迷】 zhǐzuì-jīnmí luxury and dissipation

至 (zhì) 1.(到) to; until; till: 由东～西 from east to west / 自春～冬 from spring till winter 2.(极;最) extremely; most: 欢迎之～。You are most welcome.

【至宝】 zhìbǎo most valuable treasure: 如获～ feel as if one had found a priceless treasure

【至诚】 zhì·cheng 1.(诚心诚意) complete sincerity 2.(诚恳) sincere; straightforward:

～的朋友 a sincere friend

【至多】 zhìduō 〈*adv*.〉 at most; no more than: ～五个 at most five

【至高频】 zhìgāopín super high frequency (SHF)

【至高无上】 zhìgāo-wúshàng paramount; supreme; most lofty

【至极】 zhìjí extremely; most

【至交】 zhìjiāo most intimate friend; best friend

【至今】 zhìjīn up to now; to this day; so far

【至理名言】 zhìlǐ-míngyán famous dictum; maxim; axiom; golden saying

【至亲】 zhìqīn very close relative; close kin

【至上】 zhìshàng supreme; the highest

【至少】 zhìshǎo at least

【至死】 zhìsǐ unto death; till death: ～不渝 will never change until death

【至意】 zhìyì the best and sincerest intention

【至于】 zhìyú **1**.(达到某种程度) go so far as to: 她不～不来上学。She wouldn't go so far as to refuse to attend school. **2**.(表示另一件事) as for; as to: ～你的能力，我表示怀疑。I have no doubts as to you ability.

桎 (zhì)

【桎梏】 zhìgù 〈*written*〉 fetters and handcuffs; shackles

致[緻[4]] (zhì)

1.(给与) send; extend; deliver: ～电 send a telegram / ～欢迎词 deliver a welcoming speech **2**.(专心于) devote: 专心～志 be wholly absorbed in; be wholeheartedly devoted to **3**.(招致) incur; result in; cause: 招～重大损失 incur a heavy loss **4**.(精致) fine; delicate: 精～ exquisite **5**.(情趣) manner or style that engages attention or arouses interest: 兴～ interest; mood for enjoyment

【致癌】 zhì'ái carcinogenic

【致癌基因】 zhì'ái jīyīn 〈*Med*.〉 oncogene

【致癌物质】 zhì'ái wùzhì carcinogen; carcinogenic substance

【致辞】 zhìcí make a speech: 请来宾向大会～ call upon a guest to address the conference

【致富】 zhìfù become rich; acquire wealth

【致函】 zhìhán send a letter to ...

【致敬】 zhìjìng salute; pay one's respects to; pay tribute to

【致敬电】 zhìjìngdiàn message of greeting

【致冷】 zhìlěng refrigerate; refrigeration (n.)

【致冷剂】 zhìlěngjì refrigerant

【致力】 zhìlì devote oneself to; work for: ～于科研工作 devote oneself to the scientific study

【致密】 zhìmì fine and close; compact: ～的布 closely-knit cloth

【致命】 zhìmìng causing death; fatal; mortal; deadly: 给予～的打击 deal a deadly blow to

【致命剂量】 zhìmìng jìliàng lethal dose

【致命伤】 zhìmìngshāng mortal wound: 受～ be mortally wounded

【致使】 zhìshǐ cause; result in

【致死】 zhìsǐ causing death; lethal; deadly: 一剂～的毒药 a lethal dose of poison

【致谢】 zhìxiè express one's thanks; extend thanks to

【致意】 zhìyì send one's greetings; give one's regards; present one's compliments: 点头～ nod a greeting

【致用】 zhìyòng attain practical use; for practical purpose

窒 (zhì)

【窒息】 zhìxī stifle; suffocate

【窒息死亡】 zhìxī sǐwáng death by suffocation

蛭 (zhì)

1.(水蛭) leech **2**.(肝蛭) liver fluke

志[誌[2-4]] (zhì)

1.(志向) will; aspiration; ideal: 人各有～。Each has his own ideal. **2**.(记) keep in mind: 永～不忘 forever bear in mind **3**.(文字记录) records; annals: 县～ annals of a county **4**.(标志) mark; sign

【志哀】 zhì'āi indicate mourning

【志大才疏】 zhìdà-cáishū have great ambition but little talent; have high aspirations but little ability

【志气】 zhìqì aspiration; ambition: 有～ have aspirations; have ambitions

【志趣】 zhìqù aspiration and interest; inclination; bent

【志士】 zhìshì person of ideals and integrity: ～仁人 people with lofty ideals / 爱国～ nobleminded patriot

【志同道合】 zhìtóng-dàohé cherish the same ideals and follow the same path; have a common goal

【志向】 zhì·xiàng aspiration; ideal; ambition

【志愿】 zhìyuàn 1.（志向和愿望）aspiration; wish; idea 2.（自愿）do sth. of one's own free will; volunteer

【志愿兵】 zhìyuànbīng volunteer

【志愿军】 zhìyuànjūn volunteers

【志愿书】 zhìyuánshū application form

痣（zhì） nevus; mole: 色～ pigmented mole / 胎～ birthmark

【痣癌】 zhì'ái nevocarcinoma

秩（zhì）

【秩序】 zhìxù order; sequence: ～大乱 in total disorder / ～井然 in perfect or apple-pie order / 工作～ sequence of work / 维持社会～ maintain public order

制［製[1]］（zhì） 1.（制造）make; manufacture: ～图 map-making; drafting 2.（制定）work out; formulate 3.（制约）restrict; control: 控～ control / 限～ restrict 4.（制度）system: 公～ the metric system

【制版】 zhìbǎn 〈*Printing*〉 plate making

【制表】 zhìbiǎo 〈*Statistics*〉 tabulation

【制裁】 zhìcái sanction; punish (v.): 经济～ economic sanctions / 依法～ punish according to the law

【制成品】 zhìchéngpǐn finished products; manufactured goods; manufactures

【制导】 zhìdǎo control and guide (a missile, etc.)

【制导系统】 zhìdǎo xìtǒng guidance system

【制导炸弹】 zhìdǎo zhàdàn guided bomb

【制订】 zhìdìng work out; formulate: ～计划 make a plan

【制定】 zhìdìng lay down; draw up; formulate; draft: ～操作规程 lay down operating rules

【制动】 zhìdòng apply the brake; brake

【制动鼓】 zhìdònggǔ 〈*Auto*〉 brake drum

【制动火箭】 zhìdòng huǒjiàn retrorocket

【制动马力】 zhìdòng mǎlì b. h. p.; brake horsepower

【制动踏板】 zhìdòng tàbǎn 〈*Auto*〉 brake pedal

【制度】 zhìdù 1.（规章）rules; regulations: 税收～ tax rules and regulations 2.（体系）system; institution: 社会～ social system

【制伏】 zhìfú check; subdue; bring under control: ～一匹马 bring a horse under control

【制服】 zhìfú 1.（制样服装）uniform: 穿～的 in uniform 2.（压服）subdue; bring under control

【制高点】 zhìgāodiǎn commanding point

【制革】 zhìgé process hides; tan

【制剂】 zhìjì 〈*Pharm.*〉 preparation: 标准～ standard preparation

【制冷】 zhìlěng refrigerate; refrigeration (n.)

【制冷机】 zhìlěngjī refrigerator

【制冷剂】 zhìlěngjì cold-producing medium

【制片人】 zhìpiànrén 〈*Cinematog.*〉 producer

【制品】 zhìpǐn products; goods: 钢铁～ iron and steel products / 塑料～ plastic goods

【制胜】 zhìshèng get the upper hand of; subdue: 出奇～ defeat one's opponent by a surprise move

【制式】 zhìshì 1.（标准）standard model; system 2.〈*TV*〉 system

【制糖】 zhìtáng refine sugar

【制糖厂】 zhìtángchǎng sugar refinery

【制图】 zhìtú 1.（制地图）charting; mapmaking 2.（制图样）drafting

【制图员】 zhìtúyuán 1.〈*Geol.*〉 cartographer 2.〈*Mech. & Archit.*〉 draftsman

【制药】 zhìyào pharmacy

【制约】 zhìyuē restrict; condition: 互相～ condition each other; interact

【制造】 zhìzào 1.（加工）make; manufacture: 保证正确～ guarantee proper manufacture 2.（造成）engineer; create; fabricate: ～紧张局势 create tension / ～谣言 fabricate rumors

【制造商】 zhìzàoshāng manufacturer

【制造业】 zhìzàoyè manufacturing industry

【制止】 zhìzhǐ check; curb; prevent; stop: ～某人做某事 stop sb. from doing sth.

【制作】 zhìzuò make; manufacture

质［質］(zhì) 1.（性质）nature; character: 实～ essence; substance 2.（质量）quality: ～变 qualitative change 3.（物质）matter; substance: 木～纤维 wood fiber 4.（朴素）simple; plain 5.（询问）question: ～疑 call in question 6.（抵押品）pledge: 人～ hostage 7.（抵押）pawn; mortgage; pledge

【质保】 zhìbǎo guarantee: 这辆新车有三年的～。The new car has a three-year guarantee.

【质变】 zhìbiàn 〈*Philos*.〉 qualitative change

【质地】 zhìdì 1.（材料性质）quality: ～考究 superior quality / ～优良 fine quality 2.（人品）character; disposition

【质量】 zhìliàng 1.〈*Physics*〉 mass 2.（优劣程度）quality: 教学～ teaching quality / ～差 of poor quality / ～高 of high quality / ～符合… the quality conforms to ...

【质量保证书】 zhìliàng bǎozhèngshū quality certificate

【质量标准】 zhìliàng biāozhǔn quality standard

【质量检查制度】 zhìliàng jiǎnchá zhìdù rules for testing quality

【质量亏损】 zhìliàng kuīsǔn mass defect

【质量要求】 zhìliàng yāoqiú quality requirement

【质朴】 zhìpǔ simple and unadorned; unaffected; plain: ～无华 simple and unadorned

【质数】 zhìshù 〈*Math*.〉 prime number

【质问】 zhìwèn interrogate; interrogation (n.); call to account; question: 提出～ bring sb. to account

【质询】 zhìxún address inquiries to; ask for an explanation

【质疑】 zhìyí call in question; query: ～问难 raise doubts and difficult questions for discussion

【质子】 zhìzǐ 〈*Physics*〉 proton

炙(zhì) 1.（烤）broil; roast 2.（烤熟的肉）roast meat

【炙手可热】 zhìshǒu-kěrè if you stretch out your hand you feel the heat; the supreme arrogance of a person with great power

治(zhì) 1.（治理）rule; govern; administer; manage: 分而～之 divide and rule 2.（安定太平）order; peace 3.（医治）treat; cure: 给某人～病 treat sb. for his illness; cure sb. of his disease 4.（控制）control; harness; wipe out: ～土改水 bring the water under control and improve the soil 5.（惩办）punish

【治安】 zhì'ān public order; public security: 维持～ keep the public order / 社会～明显好转。There has been a marked turn for the better in public order.

【治安保卫】 zhì'ān bǎowèi public security

【治安保卫人员】 zhì'ān bǎowèi rényuán guardian of the peace; security personnel

【治安机关】 zhì'ān jīguān law enforcement office

【治本】 zhìběn effect a permanent cure; get at the root; take radical measures

【治标】 zhìbiāo merely alleviate the symptoms of an illness; bring about a temporary solution; take stopgap measures

【治病救人】 zhìbìng-jiùrén cure the sickness to save the patient; help sb. mend his ways to save him

【治理】 zhìlǐ 1.（管理）administer; govern: ～国家 administer a country; run a state 2.（整修）harness; bring under control; put in order: ～黄河 bring the Huanghe River under control

【治理整顿】 zhìlǐ-zhěngdùn improve and rectify; improvement and rectification (n.)

【治疗】 zhìliáo treat; cure; treatment (n.): 病人得到及时～ receive timely treatment / 对病人及时～ give timely treatment / 医生的～使他的病痊愈了。The doctor's treatment cured him.

【治贫】 zhìpín eliminate poverty

【治丧】 zhìsāng make funeral arrangements

【治丧委员会】 zhìsāng wěiyuánhuì funeral committee

【治水】 zhìshuǐ regulate rivers and watercourses; prevent floods by water control

【治外法权】 zhìwài fǎquán extraterritoriality; extraterritorial (adj.)

【治学】 zhìxué pursue one's studies; do scholarly research
【治愚】 zhìyú eliminate ignorance and backwardness
【治愈率】 zhìyùlǜ cure rate: ～达97% a 97 percent cure rate
【治罪】 zhìzuì punish sb.; condemn sb.

栉[櫛] (zhì) 1.(梳子) comb 2.(梳头) comb hair
【栉比】 zhìbǐ 〈written〉 placed closely side by side
【栉比鳞次】 zhìbǐ-líncì row upon row of (buildings)

痔 (zhì) 〈Med.〉 hemorrhoids; piles: 内～ internal piles / 外～ external piles
【痔疮】 zhìchuāng 〈Med.〉 hemorrhoids; piles
【痔漏】 zhìlòu 〈Med.〉 anal fistula

挚[摯] (zhì) sincere; intimate
【挚爱】 zhì'ài sincere love
【挚友】 zhìyǒu intimate friend; bosom friend

掷[擲] (zhì) throw; cast: 弃～ cast aside; throw away
【掷币猜先】 zhìbì cāixiān 〈Sports〉 toss
【掷币决定胜负】 zhìbì juédìng shèngfù toss-up
【掷边线球】 zhì biānxiànqiú 〈Football〉 throw-in
【掷标枪】 zhìbiāoqiāng 〈Sports〉 javelin throw
【掷界外球】 zhì jièwàiqiú 〈Football〉 throw-in
【掷色子】 zhì shǎi·zi throw; throw dice; roll dice
【掷铁饼】 zhì tiěbǐng 〈Sports〉 discus throw

智 (zhì) wisdom; resourcefulness; wit: ～德齐备 have both wisdom and virtue
【智慧】 zhìhuì wisdom; intelligence
【智力】 zhìlì intelligence; intellect
【智力测验】 zhìlì cèyàn intelligence test
【智力开发】 zhìlì kāifā intellectual development
【智力库】 zhìlìkù storehouse of intelligence
【智力年龄】 zhìlì niánlíng intelligence age (IA)
【智力缺陷】 zhìlì quēxiàn mental deficiency
【智力投资】 zhìlì tóuzī intellectual investment
【智谋】 zhìmóu resourcefulness
【智囊】 zhìnáng brain truster
【智囊团】 zhìnángtuán think tank; brain trust
【智能】 zhìnéng intellect; intelligence
【智能卡】 zhìnéngkǎ intelligence card; IC card
【智能终端】 zhìnéng zhōngduān 〈Computer〉 intelligent terminal; smart terminal
【智取】 zhìqǔ take by strategy
【智商】 zhìshāng intelligence quotient (IQ)
【智勇双全】 zhìyǒng-shuāngquán both brave and resourceful; both intelligent and courageous
【智育】 zhìyù intellectual education; intellectual development: 使学生在德育、～、体育几方面都得到发展 enable the students to develop morally, intellectually and physically
【智源】 zhìyuán intelligence resources

滞[滯] (zhì) stagnant; sluggish
【滞后】 zhìhòu lag; be behind; be lagged
【滞后现象】 zhìhòu xiànxiàng 〈Physics〉 hysteresis
【滞留】 zhìliú be detained; be held up
【滞留成本】 zhìliú chéngběn sunk cost
【滞纳金】 zhìnàjīn fine for delaying payment; fine for paying late; overdue fine
【滞销】 zhìxiāo unsalable; unsaleable; unmarketable
【滞销货】 zhìxiāohuò a drug on the market; unsalable goods; unsaleable goods

置 (zhì) 1.(放置) place; put: 安～ find a place for; help sb. to settle down 2.(布置) set up; establish; install: 设～障碍 set up obstacles 3.(购置) buy: 购～ add to one's belongings
【置办】 zhìbàn buy; purchase: ～家具 buy furniture
【置备】 zhìbèi purchase
【置酒】 zhìjiǔ give a feast
【置若罔闻】 zhìruò-wǎngwén turn a deaf ear to; pay no heed to: 对对方的论点～ give short shrift to an opponent argument
【置身】 zhìshēn place oneself; stay: ～其间 be involved
【置信】 zhìxìng believe: 难以～ hard to believe; unbelievable; incredible

【置业费】 zhìyèfèi acquisition cost

【置疑】 zhìyí doubt：不容～ allow of no doubt；not be open to doubt

【置之不理】 zhìzhī-bùlǐ ignore；brush aside；pay no attention to

【置之度外】 zhìzhī-dùwài give no thought to；have no regard to

【置之死地而后快】 zhì zhī sǐdì érhòu kuài will be content with nothing less than sb's destruction

雉 (zhì)〈*Zool*.〉pheasant

稚［穉］(zhì) young；childish：幼～ childish

【稚气】 zhìqì childishness

zhong

中 (zhōng) 1.（中心）center；middle：华～ central China 2.（中国）China；Chinese 3.（里面）in；among；amidst：记在心～ keep in mind 4.（中间）middle；mid-：期～考试 mid-term exam 5.（中等）medium；intermediate 6.（不偏不倚）mean；halfway between two extremes：适～ moderate 7.（中人）intermediary 8.（适于）fit for；good for：～听 be pleasant to the ear / 不～用 good for nothing 9.（在…过程中）in the process of；in the course of：行军～ on the march / 在考虑～ under consideration（另见"中"zhòng）

【中巴】 zhōngbā midi bus（可乘 25 人左右）

【中班】 zhōngbān 1.（幼儿园的）the middle class in a kindergarten 2.（指工作的）middle shift

【中板】 zhōngbǎn 〈*Music*〉moderato

【中饱私囊】 zhōngbǎo-sīnáng embezzle；batten on money entrusted to one's care；line one's pockets with public funds or other people's money

【中部】 zhōngbù central section；middle part

【中餐】 zhōngcān Chinese meal；Chinese food

【中草药】 zhōngcǎoyào Chinese herbal medicine

【中层】 zhōngcéng middle-level

【中层干部】 zhōngcéng gànbù middle-level cadres

【中产阶级】 zhōngchǎn jiējí middle class；middle bourgeoisie

【中场】 zhōngchǎng 〈*Football*〉midfield

【中程】 zhōngchéng intermediate range；medium range

【中程弹道导弹】 zhōngchéng dàndào dǎodàn medium-range ballistic missile

【中程轰炸机】 zhōngchéng hōngzhàjī medium bomber

【中成药】 zhōngchéngyào prepared Chinese medicine

【中辍】 zhōngchuò stop（doing sth.）halfway；give up halfway

【中档】 zhōngdàng middle grade

【中稻】 zhōngdào semilate rice；middle-season rice

【中等】 zhōngděng 1.（高低、上下之间）secondary；intermediate；moderate：～发达国家 moderately developed country / ～教育 secondary education / ～职业学校 secondary vocational schools 2.（高矮、大小之间）medium；moderate；middling：～身材 of medium height；of middle size

【中点】 zhōngdiǎn 〈*Tennis*〉center mark

【中东】 Zhōngdōng the Middle East；Mideast：～战争 Middle East War

【中断】 zhōngduàn suspend；break off；discontinue：～外交关系 suspend diplomatic relations

【中队】 zhōngduì 1.（队伍编制）detachment 2.〈*Mil*.〉squadron：轰炸机～ bomber squadron

【中队长】 zhōngduìzhǎng detachment chief；detachment head

【中耳】 zhōng'ěr 〈*Anat*.〉auris media；middle ear

【中耳炎】 zhōng'ěryán 〈*Med*.〉otitis media

【中饭】 zhōngfàn midday meal；lunch

【中分线】 zhōngfēnxiàn 〈*Card*〉dividing line

【中锋】 zhōngfēng 1.〈*Football & Water Polo*〉center forward 2.〈*Basketball*〉center

【中耕】 zhōnggēng 〈*Agric*.〉intertill；intertillage

【中耕机】 zhōnggēngjī 〈*Agric*.〉cultivator

【中梗阻】 zhōnggēngzǔ middle-way obstruc-

tion
【中共中央】 Zhōnggòng Zhōngyāng Central Committee of CPC
【中国】 Zhōngguó China; Chinese (adj.) ‖ 中国人 Chinese
【中国长城】 Zhōngguó Chángchéng Great Wall
【中国共产党】 Zhōngguó Gòngchǎndǎng the Communist Party of China
【中国共产主义青年团】 Zhōngguó Gòngchǎnzhǔyì Qīngniántuán the Communist Youth League of China
【中国国籍】 Zhōngguó guójí Chinese nationality
【中国话】 zhōngguóhuà the Chinese language; Chinese
【中国画】 zhōngguóhuà traditional Chinese painting
【中国科学院】 Zhōngguó Kēxuéyuàng the Chinese Academy of Sciences
【中国民航】 Zhōngguó Mínháng CAAC (中国民用航空总局 Civil Aviation Administration of China 的缩写)
【中国人民解放军】 Zhōngguó Rénmín Jiěfàngjūn the Chinese People's Liberation Army
【中国人民政治协商会议】 Zhōngguó Rénmín Zhèngzhì Xiéshāng Huìyì the Chinese People's Political Consultative Conference
【中国特色】 Zhōngguó tèsè Chinese characteristic
【中果皮】 zhōngguǒpí 〈*Bot.*〉 mesocarp
【中华】 Zhōnghuá China; Chinese (adj.): 振兴～ reconstruct China
【中华猕猴桃】 zhōnghuá míhóutáo 〈*Bot.*〉 yangtao actinidia
【中华民族】 Zhōnghuá Mínzú the Chinese nation
【中华人民共和国】 Zhōnghuá Rénmín Gònghéguó the People's Republic of China
【中华人民共和国国务院】 Zhōnghuá Rénmín Gònghéguó Guówùyuàn the State Council of the People's Republic of China
【中级】 zhōngjí middle rank; intermediate
【中级人民法院】 zhōngjí rénmín fǎyuàn intermediate people's court
【中继】 zhōngjì 〈*Electr.*〉 relay
【中继线】 zhōngjìxiàn trunk line
【中坚】 zhōngjiān nucleus; hard core; backbone
【中坚人物】 zhōngjiān rénwù key personnel
【中间】 zhōngjiān 1.(里面) among; between: 隐藏在树丛～ hide among the bushes 2.(中心) center; centre; middle 3.(两者之间) middle; intermediate
【中间插页】 zhōngjiān chāyè centerfold
【中间管理制】 zhōngjiān guǎnlǐzhì intermediate management
【中间派】 zhōngjiānpài 1.(指人) intermediate element 2.(指势力) intermediate forces 3.(指派别) intermediate section
【中间商】 zhōngjiānshāng middleman; broker
【中将】 zhōngjiàng 1.(陆军) Lieutenant General 2.(空军) Air Lieutenant General 3.(海军) Vice Admiral
【中介】 zhōngjiè intermediary; medium
【中距离】 zhōngjùlí 〈*Sports*〉 middle distance
【中距离赛跑】 zhōngjùlí sàipǎo middle-distance running; middle-distance race
【中看】 zhōngkàn be pleasant to the eyes
【中考】 zhōngkǎo entrance examination for senior-level middle school
【中肯之言】 zhōngkěnzhīyán a statement that meets the exigency
【中立】 zhōnglì neutrality: 保持～ maintain neutrality
【中立地带】 zhōnglì dìdài neutral zone
【中立法】 zhōnglìfǎ law of neutrality; neutrality law
【中立港】 zhōnglìgǎng neutral port
【中立公约】 zhōnglì gōngyuē neutrality pact
【中立国】 zhōnglìguó neutral state; neutral country
【中立国船只】 zhōnglìguó chuánzhī neutral ship
【中立政策】 zhōnglì zhèngcè policy of neutrality
【中立主义】 zhōnglì zhǔyì neutralism
【中流】 zhōngliú midstream: ～砥柱 firm rock in midstream; main stay
【中略】 zhōnglüè syncope; syncopation
【中年】 zhōngnián middle age; middle-aged (adj.): ～妇女 middle-aged woman / ～知识分子 middle-aged intellectual / 人到 40

岁，已步入～。At 40 a man has reached middle age.

【中农】 zhōngnóng middle peasant

【中跑】 zhōngpǎo 〈*Sports*〉 middle-distance running; middle-distance race

【中篇小说】 zhōngpiān xiǎoshuō novelette; medium-length novel

【中频】 zhōngpín intermediate frequency

【中期】 zhōngqī mid-term; medium term: ～贷款 medium term loan

【中秋节】 Zhōngqiūjié the Midautumn Festival

【中圈】 zhōngquān 〈*Basketball & Football*〉 center circle

【中人】 zhōngrén middleman; go-between

【中山公园】 Zhōngshān Gōngyuán Zhongshan Park; Dr Sun Yat-sen Park

【中山堂】 Zhōngshāntáng Dr. Sun Yat-sen Memorial Hall

【中山装】 zhōngshānzhuāng Chinese tunic suit

【中士】 zhōngshì **1.**（陆军）Sergeant **2.**（空军）Air Sergeant **3.**（海军）Petty Officer Second Class

【中世纪】 zhōngshìjì Middle Ages

【中式】 zhōngshì Chinese style: ～服装 Chinese style clothing

【中枢】 zhōngshū center: 电讯～ telecommunications center / ～神经系统 central nervous system

【中速】 zhōngsù moderate speed: ～行驶，安全礼让。Drive at moderate speed; give another vehicle the right of way for the sake of safety

【中提琴】 zhōngtíqín 〈*Music*〉 viola

【中途】 zhōngtú halfway; midway: ～折回 return halfway

【中外】 zhōngwài China and foreign countries; at home and abroad

【中外合资经营企业】 zhōngwài hézī jīngyíng qǐyè Chinese-foreign joint venture

【中外合作经营企业】 zhōngwài hézuò jīngyíng qǐyè enterprise jointly managed by China and foreign countries

【中卫】 zhōngwèi 〈*Football*〉 center half back

【中尉】 zhōngwèi **1.**（陆军）First Lieutenant **2.**（空军）Air First Lieutenant **3.**（海军）Lieutenant Junior Class

【中文】 zhōngwén the Chinese language; Chinese

【中午】 zhōngwǔ noon; midday

【中西】 Zhōng-Xī Chinese and Western

【中西医结合】 Zhōng-Xīyī jiéhé combine traditional Chinese and Western medicine

【中线】 zhōngxiàn **1.**〈*Math.*〉 central line **2.**〈*Volleyball & Tennis*〉 center line **3.**〈*Basketball*〉 division line; center line; midcourt line **4.**〈*Football*〉 midcourt line

【中线裁判员】 zhōngxiàn cáipànyuán 〈*Tennis*〉 center line judge

【中校】 zhōngxiào **1.**（陆军）Lieutenant Colonel **2.**（空军）Air Lieutenant Colonel **3.**（海军）Commander

【中心】 zhōngxīn **1.**（指位置、地区）center (AmE.); centre (BrE.); focus; core: 贸易～ a center of trade / 商业～ business center / **2.**（主要的）central; main: ～工作 central task ～思想 central idea; gist / ～问题 central issue; crucial question **3.**（指机构等）center; centre: 购物～ shopping center / 文化～ cultural center / 信息～ information center

【中心城市】 zhōngxīn chéngshì key city

【中心快门】 zhōngxīn kuàimén 〈*Photog.*〉 between-lens shutter

【中兴】 zhōngxīng resurge; resurgence (n.)

【中型】 zhōngxíng medium-sized; middle-sized

【中性】 zhōngxìng **1.**〈*Chem.*〉 neutral **2.**〈*Gram.*〉 neuter

【中性包装】 zhōngxìng bāozhuāng neutral packing

【中学】 zhōngxué middle school; secondary school

【中学生】 zhōngxuéshēng middle school student; schoolboy (m.); schoolgirl (f.)

【中雪】 zhōngxuě middle snow

【中旬】 zhōngxún the middle ten days of a month

【中央】 zhōngyāng **1.**（中心）center; middle **2.**（最高领导机构）central authorities: 党～ the Central Committee of the Party; the

Party Central Committee

【中央处理器】 zhōngyāng chǔlǐqì 〈*Computer*〉 central processing unit (CPU)

【中央隔离带】 zhōngyāng gélídài median strip (AmE.); central reservation (BrE.)

【中央工作会议】 zhōngyāng gōngzuò huìyì the Central Working Conference

【中央环岛】 zhōngyāng huándǎo (大转盘) traffic circle (AmE.); roundabout (BrE.)

【中央集权】 zhōngyāng jíquán centralization (of authority)

【中央纪律检查委员会】 Zhōngyāng Jìlǜ Jiǎnchá Wěiyuánhuì the Central Commission for Discipline Inspection

【中央军事委员会】 Zhōngyāng Jūnshì Wěiyuánhuì Central Military Commission

【中央全会】 Zhōngyāng Quánhuì plenary session of the Central Committee

【中央银行】 zhōngyāng yínháng central bank

【中央直属机关】 zhōngyāng zhíshǔ jīguān departments under the Party Central Committee

【中药】 zhōngyào traditional Chinese medicine

【中叶】 zhōngyè middle period: 20 世纪～ mid-20th century

【中医】 zhōngyī **1.** (指医学) traditional Chinese medical science **2.** (指医生) doctor of traditional Chinese medicine; practitioner of Chinese medicine

【中医学】 zhōngyīxué traditional Chinese medicine

【中医学院】 zhōngyī xuéyuàn college of traditional Chinese medicine

【中音拾音器】 zhōngyīn shíyīnqì 〈*Music*〉 middle pick-up

【中庸之道】 zhōngyōngzhīdào the doctrine of the mean

【中用】 zhōngyòng of use; useful: 不～ of no use

【中游】 zhōngyóu **1.** (河流的) middle reaches **2.** (指状态) the state of being middling: 甘居～ be resigned to the middling state; be content to stay middling

【中正】 zhōngzhèng just

【中指】 zhōngzhǐ middle finger

【中止】 zhōngzhǐ discontinue; suspend; break off

【中止上诉】 zhōngzhǐ shàngsù discontinuance of appeal

【中止诉讼】 zhōngzhǐ sùsòng abatement of action; stop a case

【中轴曲柄】 zhōngzhóu qūbǐng 〈*Bicycle*〉 crank arm

【中专】 zhōngzhuān technical secondary school

【中转】 zhōngzhuǎn 〈*Railway*〉 change trains

【中转站】 zhōngzhuǎnzhàn transfer station

【中子弹】 zhōngzǐdàn neutron bomb

【中子星】 zhōngzǐxīng neutron star

忠 (zhōng) loyal; devoted; honest

【忠臣】 zhōngchén loyal courtier

【忠诚】 zhōngchéng loyal; faithful; staunch: ～可靠 both loyal and trustworthy

【忠告】 zhōnggào **1.** (指劝告) sincerely advise; admonish **2.** (忠告的话) sincere advice; advice: 向某人提几句～ give sb. a few words of advice / 接受某人的～ take sb's advice

【忠厚】 zhōnghòu honest and tolerant; sincere and kindly: ～待人 treat a man with honesty

【忠实】 zhōngshí **1.** (忠诚) true; faithful: ～的朋友 devoted friend / ～的信徒 faithful disciple **2.** (真的) authentic; faithful: ～记录 authentic records

【忠心】 zhōngxīn loyalty; devotion

【忠心耿耿】 zhōngxīn-gěnggěng loyal and devoted; most faithful and true

【忠言】 zhōngyán sincere advice; earnest advice: ～逆耳 good advice jars on the ear

【忠于】 zhōngyú true to; loyal to; faithful to; devoted to: ～职守 be devoted to one's duty

【忠贞】 zhōngzhēn loyal and steadfast: ～之士 a man of loyalty and chastity

盅 (zhōng) handleless cup: 酒～ winecup / 一～酒 a cup of wine

钟［鐘[1-3]、鍾[4,5]］(zhōng) **1.** (响器) bell **2.** (钟表) clock: 挂～ wall clock / 闹～ alarm clock **3.** (钟点) time as measured in hours and minutes: 6 点～ six o'clock **4.** (钟情)

concentrate one's affections **5.**（盅）handleless cup

【钟爱】 zhōng'ài dote on (a child); cherish

【钟摆】 zhōngbǎi pendulum

【钟表】 zhōngbiǎo clocks and watches; timepiece

【钟表店】 zhōngbiǎodiàn watchmaker's shop

【钟点】 zhōngdiǎn **1.**（指时间）time：～到了，我们上课吧。It's time. Let's begin our lesson. **2.**（小时）hour：三个～ three hours

【钟楼】 zhōnglóu **1.**（挂有大钟的）bell tower; belfry **2.**（安有时钟的）clock tower

【钟情】 zhōngqíng be deeply in love：一见～ fall in love at first sight

【钟乳石】 zhōngrǔshí 〈*Geol.*〉 stalactite

【钟舌】 zhōngshé clapper

【钟头】 zhōngtóu 〈*colloq.*〉 hour

衷 (zhōng) inner feelings heart：由～之言 words spoken from the bottom of one's heart

【衷肠】 zhōngcháng 〈*written*〉 words right from one's heart

【衷情】 zhōngqíng 〈*written*〉 heartfelt emotion; inner feelings

【衷心】 zhōngxīn heartfelt; wholehearted; cordial：表示～的感激 express one's heartfelt gratitude

终 (zhōng) **1.**（最终）end; finish：期～ end of semester / ～成泡影 end up in a bubble; come to nothing **2.**（指人死）death; end：临～ on one's deathbed; just before one dies **3.**（终归）eventually; after all; in the end **4.**（自始至终）whole; entire; all：～日 all day long

【终场】 zhōngchǎng end of a performance or show

【终场哨声】 zhōngchǎng shàoshēng final whistle

【终场时间】 zhōngchǎng shíjiān gun time

【终点】 zhōngdiǎn **1.**（路程结束处）terminal point; destination **2.** 〈*Sports*〉 finish

【终点裁判员】 zhōngdiǎn cáipànyuán 〈*Sports*〉 judge at the finish

【终点触线】 zhōngdiǎn chùxiàn 〈*Sports*〉 touch the finishing line

【终点带】 zhōngdiǎndài 〈*Sports*〉 finishing tape

【终点线】 zhōngdiǎnxiàn 〈*Sports*〉 finishing line; finishing tape

【终点站】 zhōngdiǎnzhàn terminus

【终端】 zhōngduān 〈*Electr.*〉 terminal

【终端机】 zhōngduānjī terminating machine

【终归】 zhōngguī eventually; in the end; after all：她～会明白的。She will understand eventually.

【终极】 zhōngjí ultimate：～目标 ultimate aim

【终结】 zhōngjié end; final stage

【终结账簿】 zhōngjié zhàngbù book of final entry

【终究】 zhōngjiū eventually; in the end; after all

【终局】 zhōngjú end; outcome

【终了】 zhōngliǎo end

【终年】 zhōngnián **1.**（全年）throughout the year; all the year round：～积雪 be permanently covered with snow; be covered with snow all the year round **2.**（去世年龄）the age at which one dies

【终曲】 zhōngqǔ 〈*Music*〉 finale

【终身】 zhōngshēn lifelong; all one's life：～伴侣 lifelong companion

【终身残废】 zhōngshēn cánfèi permanent disability

【终身监禁】 zhōngshēn jiānjìn life imprisonment

【终身人寿险】 zhōngshēn rénshòuxiǎn whole life insurance

【终身职务】 zhōngshēn zhíwù freehold of office

【终身制】 zhōngshēnzhì de facto life tenure; life-time service system

【终审】 zhōngshěn 〈*Law*〉 last instance; final judgment

【终审判决】 zhōngshěn pànjué final adjudication; final judgement

【终生】 zhōngshēng all one's life; throughout one's life

【终须】 zhōngxū have to in the end; unavoidable in the long run

【终于】 zhōngyú at last; in the end; finally：冤案～得到了昭雪。At long last the wrong has been righted.

【终止】 zhōngzhǐ 1.（结束）stop; end 2.（停止）termination; annulment; abrogation
【终止符】 zhōngzhǐfú 〈*Music*〉a full stop; a period

螽（zhōng）
【螽斯】 zhōngsī 〈*Zool.*〉longhorned grasshopper

肿［**腫**］（zhǒng）swelling; swollen
【肿大】 zhǒngdà enlargement; tumefaction; swelling: 肝～ enlargement of the liver
【肿块】 zhǒngkuài phyma; tumor; mass
【肿瘤】 zhǒngliú 〈*Med.*〉tumor: 恶性～ malignant tumor
【肿胀】 zhǒngzhàng swelling

种［**種**］（zhǒng）1.（物种）species 2.（种类）kind; sort; type: 各～树 different kinds of trees 3.（人种）race: 黄～人 the yellow race 4.（种子）seed: 选～ strain selection 5.（传代）seed; strain; breed: 纯～ pure breed / 混血～ mixed blood 6.（胆量或勇气）guts; grit: 这条汉子真有～。He is really a man with plenty of guts.
（另见"种"zhòng）
【种畜】 zhǒngchù 〈*Herd*〉breeding stock; stud stock
【种类】 zhǒnglèi kind; type; variety
【种马场】 zhǒngmǎchǎng stud-farm
【种群】 zhǒngqún stock; population
【种姓】 zhǒngxìng caste (of India)
【种姓制度】 zhǒngxìng zhìdù caste system
【种种】 zhǒngzhǒng all sorts of; a variety of: ～理由 all sorts of reasons
【种子】 zhǒng·zǐ 〈*Agric.*〉seed
【种子队】 zhǒng·zǐduì 〈*Sports*〉seed team
【种子选手】 zhǒng·zǐ xuǎnshǒu 〈*Sports*〉seeded player; seed
【种子植物】 zhǒng·zǐ zhíwù seed plant
【种族】 zhǒngzú race; racial (adj.): ～关系 race relations
【种族隔离】 zhǒngzú gélí apartheid; racial segregation
【种族灭绝】 zhǒngzú mièjué genocide
【种族偏见】 zhǒngzú piānjiàn racial prejudice
【种族歧视】 zhǒngzú qíshì racial discrimination
【种族主义】 zhǒngzú zhǔyì racism; racialism ‖ 种族主义者 racist

冢［**塚**］（zhǒng）tomb; grave; sepulcher

踵（zhǒng）1.（脚跟）heel: 接～而来 come one after another; follow hard at heel 2.（亲自登门）call in person 3.（紧跟）follow close behind

中（zhòng）1.（正对上）fit exactly; hit: ～靶 hit the target / 说～ be right about 2.（受到）be hit by; fall into; be affected by; suffer: ～圈套 fall into a trap
（另见"中"zhōng）
【中标】 zhòngbiāo be chose to be the tender; win a bid
【中弹】 zhòngdàn be struck by a bullet; get shot
【中的】 zhòngdì hit the target; make a bull's eye
【中毒】 zhòngdú poisoning; toxicosis: 煤气～ gas poisoning
【中风】 zhòngfēng 〈*Med.*〉apoplexy
【中计】 zhòngjì be trapped; walk into a trap; be victimized by scheme
【中奖】 zhòngjiǎng draw a prizewinning ticket in a lottery; get the winning number in a bond
【中肯】 zhòngkěn 1.（指言论）apropos; pertinent; to the point: ～的批评 pertinent comments 2.〈*Physics*〉critical: ～质量 critical mass
【中签】 zhòngqiān be the lucky number
【中伤】 zhòngshāng slander; malign; vilify: 恶语～ malign sb. viciously / ～某人的名誉 cast aspersions up/upon sb's honor
【中暑】 zhòngshǔ 1.（日射病）heatstroke; sunstroke 2.（得日射病）suffer heatstroke; suffer sunstroke; be affected by the heat
【中听】 zhòngtīng be pleasant to the ear; agreeable to the hearer
【中选】 zhòngxuǎn be chosen; be selected
【中意】 zhòngyì be to one's liking; catch the fancy of

仲（zhòng）1.（每季第二月）mid-; second: ～夏 the second month of summer 2.（排

行第二者）the second **3.**（地位居中）middle; intermediate

【仲裁】 zhòngcái arbitrate; arbitration: 将争端付诸～ submit a dispute to arbitration / 工会同意提请～。The labor union agreed to arbitration.

【仲裁法庭】 zhòngcái fǎtíng arbitration tribunal; court of arbitration

【仲裁费用】 zhòngcái fèiyòng expense on arbitration

【仲裁机关】 zhòngcái jīguān arbitrary body

【仲裁人】 zhòngcáirén arbitrator: 首席～ umpire

【仲裁书】 zhòngcáishū award

【仲裁委员会】 zhòngcái wěiyuánhuì board of arbitration

【仲裁协定】 zhòngcái xiédìng arbitration agreement

【仲继贸易】 zhòngjì màoyì intermediary trade

【仲介贸易】 zhòngjiè màoyì merchanting trade

种［種］（zhòng）grow; plant; cultivate: ～花 cultivate flowers / ～小麦 grow wheat
（另见"种"zhǒng）

【种地】 zhòngdì land; go in for farming

【种痘】 zhòngdòu 〈*Med.*〉 vaccinate; vaccination (n.)

【种田】 zhòngtián till the land; farm

【种植】 zhòngzhí plant; grow

【种植计划】 zhòngzhí jìhuà planting scheme

【种植季节】 zhòngzhí jìjié planting season

【种植园】 zhòngzhíyuán plantation

众［衆］（zhòng）**1.**（许多）many; numerous: 人口～多的城市 multitudinous city **2.**（许多人）crowd; multitude: 听～ audience; listeners

【众多】 zhòngduō multitudinous; numerous

【众口难调】 zhòngkǒu-nántiáo it is difficult to cater for all tastes

【众目睽睽】 zhòngmù-kuíkuí the eyes of the masses are fixed on sb. or sth.: ～之下 in the full glare of publicity; in the public eye; in the public gaze

【众叛亲离】 zhòngpàn-qīnlí the masses are in rebellion and one's friends are deserting; be opposed by the masses and deserted by one's followers; be utterly isolated

【众人】 zhòngrén everybody; everyone

【众矢之的】 zhòngshǐzhīdì target of public criticism

【众说纷纭】 zhòngshuō-fēnyún opinions vary

【众所周知】 zhòngsuǒzhōuzhī as everyone knows; as is known to all; it is common knowledge that

【众望】 zhòngwàng people's expectations; popular confidence

【众望所归】 zhòngwàng-suǒguī enjoy popular confidence

【众议院】 zhòngyìyuàn **1.**（美、澳、日等国的）House of Representatives **2.**（意、墨、智等国的）Chamber of Deputies

【众志成城】 zhòngzhì-chéngchéng unity of will is an impregnable stronghold; unity is strength

重（zhòng）**1.**（重量）weight: 过～ over weight / 你体～有多少? What is your weight? **2.**（重量大）heavy; weighty; important: 他比我～。He is heavier than me. **3.**（程度深）deep; heavy; serious: ～伤 severe wound **4.**（重要）important: 分别轻～ distinguish the trivial from the important **5.**（重视）lay stress on; attach importance to: ～信义 pay stress to faith and righteousness / ～友谊 set store by friendship; value friendship **6.**（不轻率）discreet
（另见"重"chóng）

【重兵】 zhòngbīng 〈*Mil.*〉 a large number of troops; massive forces

【重创】 zhòngchuàng inflict heavy losses on; maul heavily

【重大】 zhòngdà great; weighty; major; significant: ～案件 important case / ～突破 quantum jump

【重担】 zhòngdàn heavy burden; difficult task: 挑～ take up the heavy responsibility

【重地】 zhòngdì important place: 军事～ important military site

【重点】 zhòngdiǎn **1.**（阻力点）weight bearing point **2.**（主要的）key; emphasis; focal point: 把～放在…上 put emphasis on sth. **3.**（有重点地）center on; with an emphasis:

~讨论减少浪费问题。The discussion centered around reducing waste.

【重点大学】 zhòngdiǎn dàxué key university

【重点工程】 zhòngdiǎn gōngchéng major project; key project

【重吊杆】 zhòngdiàogān 〈*Naut*.〉heavy lift

【重读】 zhòngdú 〈*Gram*.〉stress: ~音节 stressed syllable

【重犯】 zhòngfàn major criminal

【重负】 zhòngfù heavy burden; heavy load

【重工业】 zhònggōngyè heavy industry

【重机枪】 zhòngjīqiāng heavy machine gun

【重价】 zhòngjià high price

【重奖】 zhòngjiǎng give ample rewards to

【重金】 zhòngjīn a huge sum of money

【重金属】 zhòngjīnshǔ heavy metal

【重利】 zhònglì **1.** (指利息) high interest **2.** (指利润) huge profit **3.** (看重钱财) lay stress on money

【重力】 zhònglì 〈*Physics*〉gravity; gravitational force

【重力场】 zhònglìchǎng gravitational field

【重力秤】 zhònglìchèng gravity balance

【重力加速度】 zhònglì jiāsùdù acceleration of gravity

【重力仪】 zhònglìyí gravity meter; gravimeter

【重量】 zhòngliàng weight

【重量单】 zhòngliàngdān weight list

【重量损失】 zhòngliàng sǔnshī loss in weight

【重量证明书】 zhòngliàng zhèngmíngshū weight certificate; surveyor's report on weight

【重氢】 zhòngqīng 〈*Chem*.〉deuterium; heavy hydrogen

【重任】 zhòngrèn important task; heavy responsibility

【重任在肩】 zhòngrènzàijiān a heavy load on one's shoulders

【重伤】 zhòngshāng severe injury; severe wound; grievous bodily harm (GNH)

【重赏】 zhòngshǎng handsome reward

【重视】 zhòngshì attach importance to; pay attention to; think highly of; take sth. seriously; value: ~农业现代化 attach importance to the modernization of agriculture

【重水】 zhòngshuǐ 〈*Chem*.〉heavy water

【重税】 zhòngshuì heavy taxation

【重听】 zhòngtīng hard of hearing

【重头】 zhòngtóu accent: 今年汽车展的~是跑车。At this year's Auto Show the accent is on sports cars.

【重托】 zhòngtuō great trust

【重武器】 zhòngwǔqì heavy weapons

【重心】 zhòngxīn **1.** 〈*Physics*〉center of gravity **2.** (三角形的) center (AmE.); centre (BrE.) **3.** (指事情的) heart; core; focus

【重心位置】 zhòngxīn wèizhì center-of-gravity position

【重刑】 zhòngxíng severe punishment; heavy penalty

【重型】 zhòngxíng heavy-duty; heavy

【重型卡车】 zhòngxíng kǎchē heavy-duty truck; heavy truck

【重要】 zhòngyào important; significant; major: 这是非常~的事。This is a matter of cardinal significance.

【重要性】 zhòngyàoxìng importance; significance

【重音】 zhòngyīn stress; accent

【重用】 zhòngyòng put sb. in an important position

【重元素】 zhòngyuánsù 〈*Chem*.〉heavy element

【重灾区】 zhòngzāiqū severely afflicted area

【重责】 zhòngzé **1.** (指责任) heavy responsibility **2.** (责备) severely reprimand

【重镇】 zhòngzhèn place of strategic importance

【重资】 zhòngzī a huge sum of fund

【重子】 zhòngzǐ 〈*Physics*〉baryon

【重罪】 zhòngzuì capital felony; heavy offense

zhou

舟 (zhōu) 〈*written*〉boat

【舟车】 zhōuchē **1.** (船和车) vessel and vehicle **2.** (旅途) journey: ~之苦 the hardship of a journey

州 (zhōu) **1.** (指自治州) prefecture **2.** (美、澳等国的州) state: 加~ state of California

洲 (zhōu) 1.（大陆）continent; continental (adj.) 2.（沙洲）islet in a river; sand-bar

【洲际】 zhōujì intercontinental

【洲际弹道导弹】 zhōujì dàndào dǎodàn intercontinental ballistic missile

【洲际导弹】 zhōujì dǎodàn intercontinental missile

诌［謅］(zhōu) fabricate; make up: 胡～ fabricate wild tales

周［週］(zhōu) 1.（圆周）circumference; periphery; circuit 2.（绕一圈）make a circuit; move in a circular course 3.（普遍；全）all; whole; all over; all around 4.（周到）thoughtful; attentive: 计划不～ not well planned; not planned carefully enough 5.（星期）week 6.〈*Electr.*〉cycle: 千～ kilocycle / 兆～ megacycle

【周报】 zhōubào weekly publication; weekly

【周边国家和地区】 zhōubiān guójiā hé dìqū our neighbors

【周波】 zhōubō cycle

【周长】 zhōucháng girth; circumference; perimeter

【周到】 zhōudào attentive and satisfactory; thoughtful; considerate: 服务～ offer good service

【周而复始】 zhōu'érfùshǐ go round and begin again; go round and round; move in cycles: 今天是 1 月 1 日，一年～。It's January 1st, the year has come full circle.

【周角】 zhōujiǎo circle

【周刊】 zhōukān weekly; weekly magazine

【周密】 zhōumì careful; thorough

【周末】 zhōumò weekend

【周末晚会】 zhōumò wǎnhuì weekend evening party

【周年】 zhōunián anniversary: 50～ fiftieth anniversary

【周期】 zhōuqī period; cycle: 工作～ action cycle / 生产～ production cycle

【周期表】 zhōuqībiǎo 〈*Chem.*〉 periodic table

【周期性】 zhōuqīxìng periodicity; cyclicity; cyclical (adj.): ～变动 cyclical movement / ～波动 cyclical fluctuations / ～失业 cyclical unemployment

【周全】 zhōuquán 1.（周到全面）thorough; comprehensive: ～之计 a perfect plan 2.（成全）help sb. attain his aim

【周身】 zhōushēn the whole body; all over the body: ～湿透 be drenched all over

【周岁】 zhōusuì one full year of life: 他已 23～了。He's twenty-three now.

【周围】 zhōuwéi around; round; about: 在院子的四～有一圈篱笆。There was a fence around the yard.

【周围环境】 zhōuwéi huánjìng environment; surroundings

【周详】 zhōuxiáng comprehensive; complete; careful

【周旋】 zhōuxuán 1.（盘旋）fly around; fly above 2.（打交道）mix with other people; socialize: ～其间 walk and talk to guests circuitously 3.（较量）deal with; contend with: 与敌人～到底 fight the enemy to the finish

【周游】 zhōuyóu travel round; journey round: ～各地 travel far and wide

【周折】 zhōuzhé twists and turns; setbacks: 大费～ cause a lot of trouble

【周知】 zhōuzhī generally known; public knowledge

【周转】 zhōuzhuǎn 1.〈*Econ.*〉turnover: 资金的～ capital turnover 2.（开支调度）have enough to meet the need: ～不灵 have not enough cash to meet the needs / 加速资本～ speed up capital turnover

【周转率】 zhōuzhuǎnlǜ turnover rate

【周转税】 zhōuzhuǎnshuì turnover tax

【周转资金】 zhōuzhuǎn zījīn working fund; revolving fund; circulating fund

粥 (zhōu) gruel; porridge; congee: 麦片～ oatmeal gruel / 米～ rice gruel / 小米～ millet gruel

【粥少僧多】 zhōushǎo-sēngduō the gruel is meager and the monks are many; not enough to go round

妯 (zhóu)

【妯娌】 zhóuli sisters-in-law; wives of brothers

轴 (zhóu) 1.〈*Mech.*〉axle; shaft: 车～ car axle; axle / 汽车后～ the back axle of a car **2.**（轴儿）spool; rod; roller: 画～ roller for a scroll of Chinese painting **3.**〈*classifier*〉一～线 a spool of thread

【轴承】 zhóuchéng 〈*Mech.*〉 bearing: 滚珠～ ball bearing / 滚柱～ roller bearing

【轴距】 zhóujù wheelbase

【轴线】 zhóuxiàn **1.**〈*Mech.*〉 axis **2.**（带轴儿的线）spool thread; spool cotton

肘（zhǒu）elbow

【肘窝】 zhǒuwō fossa cubitalis

【肘子】 zhǒu·zi **1.**（猪肉部位）upper part of a leg of pork **2.**（肘）elbow

绉［縐］（zhòu）crape; crepe

【绉纸】 zhòuzhǐ crepe paper

皱［皺］（zhòu）**1.**（皱纹）wrinkles; lines **2.**（起皱纹）wrinkle; crease; crumple

【皱巴巴】 zhòubābā wrinkled; creased

【皱眉头】 zhòu méitóu knit one's brows; give a dirty look

【皱纹】 zhòuwén wrinkles; lines

【皱纹纸】 zhòuwénzhǐ crepe paper

【皱褶】 zhòuzhé fold

咒［呪］（zhòu）**1.**（咒语）incantation **2.**（咒人的话）curse; damn: 诅～ curse

【咒骂】 zhòumà curse; swear; abuse; revile

【咒语】 zhòuyǔ incantation

昼［晝］（zhòu）daytime; daylight; day

【昼盲】 zhòumáng hemeralopia

【昼梦】 zhòumèng day dreaming

【昼夜】 zhòuyè day and night; round the clock: ～相随 keep each other's company day and night

骤（zhòu）**1.**（马快跑）trot **2.**（突然）sudden abrupt: 天气～变。The weather suddenly changed.

【骤然】 zhòurán suddenly; abruptly

zhu

朱［硃²］（zhū） **1.**（朱红）vermilion; bright red **2.**（朱砂）cinnabar

【朱红】 zhūhōng vermilion; bright red

【朱雀】 zhūquè 〈*Zool.*〉 rosefinch

【朱砂】 zhūshā cinnabar

侏（zhū）

【侏儒】 zhūrú dwarf; midget; pygmy

诛（zhū）**1.**（杀）put to death **2.**（谴责处罚）punish; condemn

珠（zhū）**1.**（珠子）pearl: 养～ culture pearls **2.**（小球形物）bead; drop: 泪～儿 teardrop

【珠蚌】 zhūbàng 〈*Zool.*〉 pearl mussel

【珠宝】 zhūbǎo pearls and jewels; jewelry

【珠宝店】 zhūbǎodiàn a jeweller's

【珠宝商】 zhūbǎoshāng jeweller

【珠光】 zhūguāng pearly-luster

【珠光宝气】 zhūguāng-bǎoqì be richly bejewelled

【珠玑】 zhūjī pearl; gem

【珠联璧合】 zhūlián-bìhé strings of pearls and girdles of jade; a perfect pair; a happy combination

【珠穆朗玛峰】 Zhūmùlǎngmǎfēng 〈place〉 Qomolangma Feng

【珠算】 zhūsuàn reckoning by the abacus; calculation with an abacus

株（zhū）**1.**（露出地面的树根和茎）trunk of a tree; stem of a plant **2.**（植株）individual plant; plant **3.**〈*classifier*〉两～树 two trees

【株距】 zhūjù 〈*Agric.*〉 spacing in the rows

【株连】 zhūlián involve (others) in a criminal case; implicate

铢（zhū）

【铢积寸累】 zhūjī-cùnlěi accumulate little by little; build up bit by bit

【铢锱必较】 zhūzī-bìjiào stand on weight and measure

蛛（zhū）〈*Zool.*〉 spider

【蛛丝马迹】 zhūsī-mǎjì thread of a spider and trail of a horse; clues; traces

【蛛网】 zhūwǎng spider web; cobweb

诸（zhū）all; various

【诸多】 zhūduō 〈*written*〉 a good deal; a lot of: ～不便 a lot of trouble; great inconvenience

【诸如】 zhūrú such as: ～猫、狗之类的动物 such animals as cats and dogs

【诸如此类】 zhūrúcǐlèi things like that; such; and so on and so forth

猪［豬］(zhū) pig; hog; swine: 养～ raise pigs ‖ 公猪 boar / 母猪 sow / 小猪 piglet; pigling; shoat / 统称 herd

【猪场】 zhūchǎng pig farm; piggery

【猪圈】 zhūjuàn pigsty; pigpen

【猪排】 zhūpái pork chop

【猪皮】 zhūpí pigskin; hogskin

【猪肉】 zhūròu pork

【猪肉绦虫】 zhūròu tiáochóng pork tapeworm

【猪食】 zhūshí pig feed; pigwash

【猪蹄】 zhūtí trotter

【猪瘟】 zhūwēn swine fever; hog cholera

【猪油】 zhūyóu lard

【猪鬃】 zhūzōng bristles

潴［瀦］(zhū) 1.(积水) collect; accumulate; store 2.(积水的地方) puddle; pool

【潴留】 zhūliú 〈*Med.*〉 retention: 尿～ retention of urine

竹 (zhú) bamboo

【竹板】 zhúbǎn bamboo clappers

【竹编】 zhúbiān bamboo wearing

【竹雕】 zhúdiāo bamboo carving

【竹竿】 zhúgān bamboo pole; bamboo

【竹刻】 zhúkè bamboo carving; bamboo engraving

【竹篮打水一场空】 zhúlán dǎshuǐ yīchǎngkōng draw water with a bamboo basket; all in vain

【竹林】 zhúlín bamboo groves; bamboo forest

【竹篓】 zhúlǒu bamboo crate

【竹排】 zhúpái bamboo raft

【竹批儿】 zhúpīr bamboo strips

【竹器】 zhúqì articles made of bamboo

【竹笋】 zhúsǔn bamboo shoots

【竹叶青】 zhúyèqīng 1.(毒蛇) green bamboo snake 2.(酒) bamboo-leaf-green liqueur

【竹子】 zhú·zi bamboo

逐 (zhú) 1.(追逐) pursue; chase 2.(驱逐) expel; drive out 3.(逐一) one by one: ～年 year by year / ～日 day by day

【逐步】 zhúbù step by step; progressively: ～降低成本 progressively reduce the cost

【逐出】 zhúchū eject; drive out

【逐词翻译】 zhúcí fānyì word by word translation

【逐个】 zhúgè one by one; one after another

【逐渐】 zhújiàn gradually; by degrees; little by little

【逐客令】 zhúkèlìng order for guests to leave

【逐鹿】 zhúlù fight for the throne; bid for state power: ～中原 fight among rivals for the throne

【逐年】 zhúnián year by year; year after year

【逐日】 zhúrì day by day; every day

【逐项】 zhúxiàng successive terms

【逐一】 zhúyī one by one: ～说明 explain one by one

【逐字】 zhúzì word for word; verbatim: ～逐句 word by word and sentence by sentence; word for word

烛［燭］(zhú) 1.(蜡烛) candle: 蜡～ wax candle 2.(照亮) illuminate; light up

【烛光】 zhúguāng 〈*Physics*〉 candlepower; candle

【烛剪】 zhújiǎn snuffer

【烛台】 zhútái candlestick

主 (zhǔ) 1.(主人) host 2.(所有者) owner; master: 房～ owner of a house 3.(当事人) person concerned; party concerned 4.〈*Christianity*〉 God; Lord 5.〈*Islam*〉 Allah 6.(主要的) main; primary: 预防为～ put prevention first 7.(主持) manage; direct; be in charge of 8.(主张) stand for; be in favor of; advocate: ～和 advocate peace; be for a peaceful settlement / ～战 stand for war 9.(预示) indicate; signify

【主办】 zhǔbàn direct; sponsor; organize: ～展览会 organize an exhibition / 音乐会由文化部～演出。The concert was presented under the aegis of the Ministry of Culture.

【主编】 zhǔbiān 1.（指人）chief editor 2.（指工作）edit

【主宾席】 zhǔbīnxí head table; seat for the guest of honor

【主裁判】 zhǔcáipàn 〈*Volleyball*〉 referee

【主持】 zhǔchí 1.（负责处理）take charge of; manage; direct: ～日常事务 take care of routine matters / 主任不在时，孙先生～业务。In the absence of the director Mr. Sun is in charge of business. 2.（负责掌握）preside over; chair: ～会议 preside over a meeting 3.（主张）uphold; stand for: ～正义 uphold justice

【主持人】 zhǔchírén linkman

【主次】 zhǔcì primary and secondary: 分清～ differentiate what is primary from what is secondary

【主从】 zhǔcóng principal and subordinate

【主存储器】 zhǔcúnchǔqì 〈*Computer*〉 main memory; main storage

【主导】 zhǔdǎo 1.（主要的）leading; dominant; guiding: ～思想 dominant ideas; guiding ideology 2.（主导作用）leading factor: 对你的决定起～作用的是哪些因素？What factors governed your decision?

【主动】 zhǔdòng 1.（与“被动”相对）initiative: ～作某事 do sth. on one's own initiative; do sth. of one's own accord / 争取～ gain the initiative 2.〈*Mech.*〉 driving

【主动齿轮】 zhǔdòng chǐlún driving gear

【主动脉】 zhǔdòngmài 〈*Anat.*〉 aorta

【主动脉弓】 zhǔdòngmàigōng 〈*Anat.*〉 arch of the aorta

【主动免疫】 zhǔdòng miǎnyì active immunity

【主动轴】 zhǔdòngzhóu driving shaft; driving spindle

【主队】 zhǔduì home side; home team; host team

【主发动机喷嘴】 zhǔfādòngjī pēnzuǐ 〈*Aeron.*〉 nozzle of the main engine

【主犯】 zhǔfàn 〈*Law*〉 prime culprit; principal criminal

【主峰】 zhǔfēng the highest peak in a mountain range

【主妇】 zhǔfù housewife; hostess

【主干】 zhǔgàn 1.〈*Bot.*〉 trunk 2.（主要的）main force; mainstay

【主攻】 zhǔgōng 〈*Mil.*〉 main attack

【主攻部队】 zhǔgōng bùduì main attack force

【主攻方向】 zhǔgōng fāngxiàng main direction of attack

【主攻手】 zhǔgōngshǒu 〈*Sports*〉 spiker

【主构架】 zhǔgòujià 〈*Archit.*〉 main truss

【主顾】 zhǔgù customer; client

【主观】 zhǔguān subjective

【主观能动性】 zhǔguān néngdòngxìng subjective initiative; conscious activity

【主管】 zhǔguǎn 1.（负责管理）be responsible for; be in charge of 2.（主管人员）person in charge

【主管部门】 zhǔguǎn bùmén department responsible for the work

【主管机关】 zhǔguǎn jīguān competent authorities; responsible institution

【主航道】 zhǔhángdào main channel

【主婚】 zhǔhūn preside over a wedding ceremony

【主机】 zhǔjī 1.〈*Mil.*〉 lead plane; leader 2.〈*Mech.*〉 main engine

【主见】 zhǔjiàn ideas or thoughts of one's own; one's own judgment; definite view

【主讲】 zhǔjiǎng be the speaker; give a lecture

【主将】 zhǔjiàng chief commander; commanding general

【主教】 zhǔjiào 〈*Religion*〉 bishop

【主教练】 zhǔjiàoliàn the principal coach

【主叫方】 zhǔjiàofāng 〈*Bridge*〉 calling party

【主句】 zhǔjù 〈*Gram.*〉 main clause; principal clause

【主角】 zhǔjué 1.（主要角色）leading role; lead; protagonist: 演～ play the leading role 2.（主要人物）important figure; important person

【主考】 zhǔkǎo 1.（主持考试）be in charge of an examination 2.（主持考试的人）chief examiner

【主课】 zhǔkè main subject; major course

【主控制】 zhǔkòngzhì master control; main control

【主力】 zhǔlì main force; main strength of

an army
【主力兵团】 zhǔlì bīngtuán main formations
【主力队员】 zhǔlì duìyuán 〈Sports〉 top players of a team
【主力军】 zhǔlìjūn main force
【主流】 zhǔliú 1.(江河干流) main stream; main current; mother current 2.(事物的主要方面) essential or main aspect; main trend
【主谋】 zhǔmóu 1.(主要谋划者) head a conspiracy; be the chief plotter 2.〈Law〉 chief instigator; principal conspirator
【主起落架】 zhǔqǐluòjià 〈Aeron.〉 main landing gear unit
【主权】 zhǔquán sovereign rights; sovereignty: 领土~ territorial sovereignty / 维护~完整 safeguard national independence and the integrity of sovereignty
【主权国】 zhǔquánguó sovereign state
【主权国家】 zhǔquán guójiā sovereign state
【主权平等】 zhǔquán píngděng sovereign equality
【主人】 zhǔrén 1.(所有者) owner 2.(当家者) master 3.(与"客人"相对) host: 女~ hostess
【主人公】 zhǔréngōng leading character in a novel, etc.; hero or heroine; protagonist
【主人翁】 zhǔrénwēng 1.(当家者) master 2.(中心人物) hero; heroine
【主任】 zhǔrèn director; head; chairman
【主色】 zhǔsè preponderant color: 黄色是这个房间的~。Yellow was the preponderant color in the room.
【主食】 zhǔshí staple food; principal food
【主使】 zhǔshǐ instigate; incite; abet
【主水道】 zhǔshuǐdào main channel
【主诉】 zhǔsù action in chief; main suit; principal action
【主题】 zhǔtí theme; subject; motif: 爱情是他的诗的~。Love is a major theme of his poetry.
【主题歌】 zhǔtígē 〈Cinematog.〉 theme song
【主体】 zhǔtǐ 1.(主要部分) main body; main part; principal part 2.〈Philos. & Law〉 subject: ~和客体 subject and object; the perceiver and the world
【主体工程】 zhǔtǐ gōngchéng main project; principal part of a project
【主席】 zhǔxí 1.(主持会议者) chairman 2.(最高领导) chairman; president
【主席台】 zhǔxítái rostrum; platform
【主席团】 zhǔxítuán presidium
【主席团成员】 zhǔxítuán chéngyuán members of a presidium
【主心骨】 zhǔxīngǔ 1.(可依靠的人或物) backbone; mainstay; pillar: 她是我们车间的~。She is the mainstay of our workshop. 2.(主见) definite view; one's own judgment: 她没有~。She has no definite view of her own.
【主修】 zhǔxiū specialize; major: ~科目 major subjects
【主旋律】 zhǔxuánlǜ main melody; top melody
【主演】 zhǔyǎn 1.(扮演主角) act the leading role: 由…~ with . . . in the leading role 2.(演主角者) protagonist
【主要】 zhǔyào main; chief; principal; major: ~产品 major products; staple products
【主义】 zhǔyì doctrine; -ism; -ist (adj.): 个人~ individualism / 集体~ colectivism / 社会~ socialism / 唯物~ materialism / 资本~ capitalism
【主意】 zhǔ·yi 1.(办法) idea; plan: 好~ a good idea / 这就是我给你出的~。That's my advice to you. 2.(主见) decision; definite view: 改变~ change one's mind
【主语】 zhǔyǔ 〈Gram.〉 subject
【主语补足语】 zhǔyǔ bǔzúyǔ subject complement
【主宰】 zhǔzǎi 1.(支配) dominate; dictate; decide 2.(指力量) dominant force
【主张】 zhǔzhāng 1.(持有…见解) advocate; stand for; maintain; hold: 他~多建几所学校。He advocates building more schools. 2.(见解) view; position; stand; proposition
【主旨】 zhǔzhǐ purport; substance; gist
【主治医生】 zhǔzhì yīshēng physician-in-charge; doctor in charge of a case
【主子】 zhǔ·zi master; boss

拄 (zhǔ) lean on; be supported by: ～拐杖走路 walk with a stick

煮 (zhǔ) boil; cook: ～马铃薯 boil the potatoes

【煮沸】 zhǔfèi boil

【煮干品】 zhǔgānpǐn boil dried product

【煮熟】 zhǔshú cook thoroughly

属[屬] (zhǔ) join together; combine; connect: 前后相～ (two parts) join together

(另见"属"shǔ)

【属望】 zhǔwàng expect; look forward to

【属意】 zhǔyì fix one's mind on sb.; be dedicated to sb.

嘱[囑] (zhǔ) enjoin; advise; urge

【嘱咐】 zhǔfù enjoin; tell; exhort: ～某人做某事 exhort sb. to do sth.

【嘱托】 zhǔtuō entrust: ～某人办件事 entrust sb. with a certain task

瞩[矚] (zhǔ) gaze; look steadily: 高瞻远～ stand high and see far; take a broad and long-term view; show great foresight

【瞩目】 zhǔmù 〈*written*〉 fix one's eyes upon; focus one's attention upon: 举世～ be the focus of world attention

【瞩望】 zhǔwàng 1.(期待) expect; look forward to 2.(注视) gaze at; look long and steadily upon

伫[佇、竚] (zhù) stand for a long time

【伫候】 zhùhòu stand waiting; wait for: ～光临 wait for your presence

【伫立】 zhùlì stand for a long time

苎[苧] (zhù)

【苎麻】 zhùmá 〈*Bot.*〉 ramie

贮[貯] (zhù) store; save; lay aside

【贮备】 zhùbèi store up; have in reserve; lay aside

【贮藏】 zhùcáng store up; lay in

【贮存】 zhùcún store; keep in storage

【贮水器】 zhùshuǐqì cistern

【贮蓄】 zhùxū save up

助 (zhù) help; assist; aid: ～成其事 help to finish a business

【助产士】 zhùchǎnshì 〈*Med.*〉 midwife

【助词】 zhùcí auxiliary word

【助动词】 zhùdòngcí auxiliary verb

【助攻】 zhùgōng secondary attack

【助教】 zhùjiào assistant

【助理】 zhùlǐ assistant: 部长～ assistant minister

【助理导演】 zhùlǐ dǎoyǎn 〈*Cinematog.*〉 assistant director

【助理工程师】 zhùlǐ gōngchéngshī assistant engineer

【助理摄影师】 zhùlǐ shèyǐngshī 〈*Cinematog.*〉 assistant cameraman

【助跑】 zhùpǎo 〈*Sports*〉 run-up; approach

【助燃】 zhùrán 〈*Chem.*〉 combustion-supporting

【助手】 zhùshǒu assistant; helper; aide

【助听器】 zhùtīngqì audiphone; hearing aid; deaf-aid

【助推器】 zhùtuīqì auxiliary boost; boost motor

【助威】 zhùwēi boost the morale of; cheer

【助兴】 zhùxìng liven things up; add to the fun

【助学】 zhùxué support and help the learner

【助学金】 zhùxuéjīn stipend; grant-in-aid

【助战】 zhùzhàn 1.(协助作战) assist in fighting 2.(助威) bolster sb's morale

【助长】 zhùzhǎng 〈*derog.*〉 encourage; abet; foster; foment: ～歪风邪气 encourage evil trends

住 (zhù) 1.(居住) live; reside; stay; dwell: ～一夜 stay overnight / ～在乡下 dwell in the country 2.(停止) stop; cease: 雨～了。The rain has stopped. 3.(做补语)忍不～ cannot help

【住不下】 zhùbùxià cannot accommodate

【住处】 zhùchù residence; dwelling (place); lodging; quarters: 固定～ fixed residence / 永久～ permanent residence / ～改变 change one's residence / 寻找～ look for accommodations

【住地】 zhùdì residence

【住房】 zhùfáng 1.(住宅) house 2.(居住)

housing; lodgings
【住房基金】 zhùfáng jījīn housing-fund
【住房商品化】 zhùfáng shāngpǐnhuà commercialization of housing; housing commercialization
【住户】 zhùhù household; resident
【住口】 zhùkǒu shut up; stop talking
【住手】 zhùshǒu stay one's hand; stop
【住宿】 zhùsù stay; put up; get accommodation
【住所】 zhùsuǒ swelling place; residence; domicile: 永久~ permanent dwelling place
【住院】 zhùyuàn be in hospital; be hospitalized: 收某人~ admit to hospital
【住院病人】 zhùyuàn bìngrén inpatient
【住院部】 zhùyuànbù inpatient department
【住院处】 zhùyuànchù admission office
【住院费】 zhùyuànfèi hospitalization expenses
【住院医生】 zhùyuàn yīshēng resident
【住宅】 zhùzhái residence; dwelling; dwelling house: 这对夫妇搬进了一套新的三室~。The couple moved into a new three-room apartment.
【住宅合作社】 zhùzhái hézuòshè residential co-op
【住宅建设】 zhùzhái jiànshè residential construction
【住宅区】 zhùzháiqū settlement
【住宅小区】 zhùzhái xiǎoqū housing district
【住址】 zhùzhǐ address

注[註$^{4-6}$](zhù) 1.(灌入)pour: 他汗流如~。The sweat was pouring off him. 2.(集中) concentrate on; fix: 全神贯~ concentrate on; be engrossed in; be preoccupied with 3.(赌注) stakes: 孤~一掷 stake everything on a single throw 4.(注释) annotate; explain with notes 5.(注释文字) notes: 脚~ footnote 6.(记载;登记) record; register: ~销 write off; cancel
【注册】 zhùcè register; enroll: ~新会员的名字 register the names of the new members
【注册处】 zhùcèchù registration office; registrar's office
【注册商标】 zhùcè shāngbiāo registered trademark
【注册条款】 zhùcè tiáokuǎn interpretation section
【注册证书】 zhùcè zhèngshū registration certificate
【注册资本】 zhùcè zīběn registered capital
【注定】 zhùdìng be doomed; be destined: 命中~ decreed by fate; predestined
【注脚】 zhùjiǎo footnote
【注解】 zhùjiě 1.(解释) annotate; explain with notes 2.(解释性文字) note; annotation: ~用斜体字印刷。The annotation were printed in italics.
【注明】 zhùmíng give clear indication of
【注目】 zhùmù gaze at; fix one's eyes on: ~而视 look with fixed eyes / 引人~ be the center of attention; be attractive
【注入】 zhùrù pour into; empty into
【注入式教育】 zhùrùshì jiàoyù spoon-fed education
【注射】 zhùshè 〈*Med*.〉 inject; injection (n.): 肌肉~ intramuscular injection / 静脉~ intravenous injection / 皮下~ hypodermic injection; subcutaneous injection / ~5毫升青霉素 give an injection of 5 c. c. of penicillin
【注射器】 zhùshèqì injector; syringe
【注射针头】 zhùshè zhēntóu syringe needle
【注视】 zhùshì look attentively at; gaze at
【注释】 zhùshì 1.(解释) annotate; explain with notes 2.(注释的文字) explanatory note; annotation
【注销】 zhùxiāo cancel; write off
【注意】 zhùyì pay attention; take note to: ~后果 look to the end / 引起~ attract attention / 提请~ call attention to
【注意标志】 zhùyì biāozhì care mark; caution mark
【注意到】 zhùyìdào to take note of . . .
【注意力】 zhùyìlì attention: 集中~ concentrate one's attention
【注意事项】 zhùyì shìxiàng matters needing attention; points for attention
【注油】 zhùyóu oiling; greasing; fuel-injection
【注重】 zhùzhòng lay stress on; pay attention to; attach importance to: ~调查研究 pay attention to investigation and study / ~质量 quality oriented

驻 (zhù) 1.（停留）halt; stay: ～足 make a temporary stay 2.（住在某地）be stationed: ～京记者 resident correspondent in Beijing / ～华大使 ambassador to China

【驻地】 zhùdì 1.（部队或外勤人员的）station; encampment 2.（行政机关所在地）seat

【驻防】 zhùfáng be on garrison duty; garrison

【驻军】 zhùjūn garrison; troops stationed at specific place

【驻守】 zhùshǒu garrison; defend: 士兵～过这座城市。The soldiers garrisoned the town.

【驻外机构】 zhùwài jīgòu institution functioning abroad

【驻在国】 zhùzàiguó 〈*Foreign Affairs*〉 state to which a diplomatic envoy is accredited

【驻在期限】 zhùzàiqīxiàn term of residence

【驻扎】 zhùzhā be stationed; be quartered

【驻足】 zhùzú make a temporary stay

柱 (zhù) 1.（柱子）post; upright; pillar; column 2.（柱状物）sth. shaped like a column: 水～ water column 3.〈*Math*.〉（柱面）cylinder

【柱石】 zhùshí 1.〈*Archit*.〉 pillar; stone pillar 2.（比喻）pillar; mainstay: 国家的～ mainstay of the nation

【柱式】 zhùshì 〈*Archit*.〉 order

【柱子】 zhù·zi post; pillar

蛀 (zhù) 1.（蛀虫）moth 2.（蛀虫咬坏）bore through; be moth-eaten

【蛀虫】 zhùchóng insect that eats books, clothes or wood; moth; borer

【蛀蚀】 zhùshí bore through; be moth-eaten

【蛀牙】 zhùyá decayed tooth; carious tooth

祝 (zhù) express good wishes; wish: ～你新年快乐。I wish you a happy New Year. / ～（某国）国家繁荣昌盛人民幸福 wish prosperity to a country and well-being to its people

【祝词】 zhùcí congratulatory speech; congratulations: 新年～ New Year felicitations

【祝辞】 zhùcí 同"祝词"

【祝福】 zhùfú blessing; benediction

【祝贺】 zhùhè congratulate: 致电～ send a congratulatory telegram / 致以衷心～ extend cordial greetings / 致以衷心的～和最好的愿望 express one's sincere congratulations and best wishes

【祝捷】 zhùjié celebrate a victory

【祝捷大会】 zhùjié dàhuì victory celebration

【祝酒】 zhùjiǔ drink a toast; toast: 致～辞 propose a toast

【祝寿】 zhùshòu offer birthday congratulations

【祝颂】 zhùsòng express good wishes

【祝愿】 zhùyuàn wish: ～某人快乐 wish sb. happiness

著 (zhù) 1.（显著）marked; outstanding: 卓～ outstanding; distinguished 2.（显出）show; prove: 颇～成效 prove rather effective 3.（写作）write: ～书立说 write books to expound a doctrine 4.（著作）book; work: 译～ a translation

【著称】 zhùchēng 〈*written*〉 celebrated; famous: 以风景优美～ be celebrated for its scenic beauty

【著名】 zhùmíng famous; celebrated; well-known: ～演员 famous actor

【著述】 zhùshù 1.（写作）write; compile 2.（写作的成品）book

【著者】 zhùzhě writer; author

【著作】 zhùzuò 1.（作品）work; book; writings: ～等身 an author with many works to his credit 2.（写作）write

【著作权】 zhùzuòquán copyright

【著作权诉讼】 zhùzuòquán sùsòng copyright action

【著作人】 zhùzuòrén writer; author

箸［筯］(zhù) chopsticks

铸［鑄］(zhù) cast; found: ～钟 cast a bell / ～钱 coin money

【铸币】 zhùbì coin; specie

【铸币权】 zhùbìquán mintage

【铸成大错】 zhùchéng-dàcuò make a gross error

【铸钢】 zhùgāng 〈*Metall*.〉 cast steel

【铸工】 zhùgōng 1.（铸造）foundry work 2.（铸造工人）foundry worker; founder

【铸件】 zhùjiàn 〈*Metall*.〉 cast; casting

【铸铁】 zhùtiě 1.（炼铁）iron casting 2.（生铁）cast iron: 球墨～ nodular cast iron

【铸像】 zhùxiàng status
【铸造】 zhùzào casting; founding
【铸字】 zhùzì 〈*Printing*〉 typefounding; typecasting

筑[築](zhù) build; construct: ～堤 build a dike / ～路 construct a road

zhua

抓(zhuā) 1.(拿在手中) grab; seize; clutch 2.(挠) scratch: ～痒痒 scratch an itch 3.(捕拿) arrest; catch; press-gang: ～到 200 名俘虏 take 200 prisoners / ～到一个贼 get a thief / 警察～住了小偷。The police arrested a thief. 4.(特别着重) stress; pay special attention to: ～重点 stress the essentials 5.(负责;主管) take charge of; be responsible for: 他是～农业的。He is in charge of agriculture. 6.(吸引) attract; grip: ～住观众 grip the attention of the audience
【抓差】 zhuāchāi draft sb. for a particular task; press sb. into service
【抓点带面】 zhuādiǎn dàimiàn draw experience from selected units to promote overall work
【抓斗】 zhuādǒu 〈*Mech.*〉 clamshell
【抓耳挠腮】 zhuā'ěr-náosāi tweak one's ears and scratch one's cheeks; scratch one's head
【抓获】 zhuāhuò arrest; catch
【抓紧】 zhuājǐn firmly grasp; pay close attention to: ～时机 seize the opportunity
【抓阄儿】 zhuājiūr draw lots
【抓举】 zhuājǔ 〈*Weightlifting*〉 snatch
【抓瞎】 zhuāxiā be in a muddle at the last moment
【抓住】 zhuāzhù 1.(用手抓住) grasp; grip; clutch: ～某人的手 grasp a person's hand / ～机会 grasp at an opportunity 2.(吸引注意力) grip sb's attention 3.(逮住) arrest; catch; press-gang: 警察～了小偷。The policeman tackled the thief.

爪(zhuǎ) claw; talon
(另见“爪”zhǎo)
【爪儿】 zhuǎr 1.(小动物的) paw of a small animal 2.(器物的脚) foot of a utensil
【爪子】 zhuǎ·zi claw; paw; talon: 猫～ a cat's paws

zhuai

拽(zhuāi) throw; cast; hurl: ～球 throw a ball
(另见“拽”zhuài)

拽(zhuài) drag; pull; lug: 他～了一下绳子。He gave a pull on the rope.
(另见“拽”zhuāi)

zhuan

专[耑、嵩](zhuān) 1.(专注) concentrate: ～注 concentrate one's attention on; be absorbed in 2.(独管,独占) monopolize: ～权 monopolize power 3.(专门) special; specialized: ～程 special trip 4.(专长) expert
【专案】 zhuān'àn special case for investigation; exemplary case
【专案材料】 zhuān'àn cáiliào material connected with a case; dossier
【专案法官】 zhuān'àn fǎguān ad hoc judge
【专差】 zhuānchāi special mission
【专长】 zhuāncháng specialty; special skill or knowledge
【专场】 zhuānchǎng 1.(专为某些观众的) show intended for sb. 2.(专演某类节目的) special performance
【专车】 zhuānchē 1.(专门开行的) special train; special car 2.(专用的) private car 3.(包租的) chartered car; chartered bus
【专诚】 zhuānchéng specially: ～奉复 write a reply specially
【专程】 zhuānchéng special trip: ～来访 a formal visit
【专电】 zhuāndiàn special dispatch; special telegram
【专断】 zhuānduàn make an arbitrary decision; act arbitrarily: 个人～ make all the decisions by oneself
【专访】 zhuānfǎng special interview with sb.; special coverage of sth.

【专稿】 zhuāngǎo special manuscript
【专攻】 zhuāngōng specialize in：她～计算机科学。She specializes in computer science.
【专横】 zhuānhéng despotic; imperious; domineering：～的决定 an arbitrary decision / ～跋扈 imperious and despotic
【专机】 zhuānjī 1.（专用车）private plane 2.（班机之外的）special plane 3.（包租的）chartered plane
【专家】 zhuānjiā expert; specialist：专业面较窄的～ narrow specialist
【专刊】 zhuānkān 1.（指报刊）special issue or column 2.（指著作）monograph
【专科】 zhuānkē special course
【专科学校】 zhuānkē xuéxiào training school; vocational school
【专控】 zhuānkòng specially controlled by the state
【专款】 zhuānkuǎn special fund
【专栏】 zhuānlán special column
【专栏作家】 zhuānlán zuòjiā columnist
【专利】 zhuānlì patent
【专利保证书】 zhuānlì bǎozhèngshū patent cover
【专利登记】 zhuānlì dēngjì patents registration
【专利调查】 zhuānlì diàochá patent search
【专利法】 zhuānlìfǎ patent law
【专利局】 zhuānlìjú patent office
【专利品】 zhuānlìpǐn patent; patented article
【专利权】 zhuānlìquán patent right; patent
【专利权所有人】 zhuānlìquán suǒyǒurén patentee
【专利许可证】 zhuānlì xǔkězhèng patent licence
【专列】 zhuānliè special train
【专卖】 zhuānmài monopoly
【专卖权】 zhuānmàiquán right of monopoly
【专卖商品】 zhuānmài shāngpǐn monopolized commodities
【专门】 zhuānmén 1.（特地）specially 2.（专门从事…）special; specialized：～人才 special talents; people with specialized skills 3.（强调）～与我作对 obsessed in opposing me
【专门机构】 zhuānmén jīgòu special agency; special organ
【专门人才】 zhuānmén réncái people with professional skill
【专门术语】 zhuānmén shùyǔ technical terms; nomenclature
【专门知识】 zhuānmén zhī·shi specialized knowledge; expertise; technical know-how
【专名】 zhuānmíng 〈*Gram.*〉proper noun
【专区】 zhuānqū prefecture; subprovincial administrative region
【专权】 zhuānquán monopolize power; arrogate all the powers to oneself
【专任】 zhuānrèn full-time; regular
【专属经济区】 zhuānshǔ jīngjìqū exclusive economic zone
【专署】 zhuānshǔ prefectural commissioner's office
【专题】 zhuāntí special subject; special topic
【专题报告】 zhuāntí bàogào report on a special topic
【专题调查】 zhuāntí diàocá investigation of a special subject
【专题讲座】 zhuāntí jiǎngzuò lecture on a special subject
【专题讨论】 zhuāntí tǎolùn seminar
【专题研究】 zhuāntí yánjiū monographic study
【专线】 zhuānxiàn 1.（专用铁路线）special railway line 2.（专用电话线）special telephone line; line for special use
【专项】 zhuānxiàng special
【专项资金】 zhuānxiàng zījīn a special fund
【专心】 zhuānxīn be absorbed; concentrate one's attention：～听老师讲课 listen attentively to the teacher / ～学习 study with undivided attention / 他～于工作以至忘记了时间。His absorption in the work made him forget the time.
【专修】 zhuānxiū specialize in：～化学 specialize in chemistry
【专修科】 zhuānxiūkē special course; training course
【专业】 zhuānyè 1.（学科）special field of study; specialized subject; specialty; discipline：所需求的～ required specialty 2.（部门）specialized trade or profession; special line：掌握生产～ acquire an industrial specialty 3.（职业的）professional

【专业村】 zhuānyècūn village with special occupation

【专业队伍】 zhuānyè duìwǔ professional contingent

【专业对口】 zhuānyè duìkǒu (a job) suited to one's special training

【专业户】 zhuānyèhù specialized household

【专业化】 zhuānyèhuà specialization

【专业化部门】 zhuānyèhuà bùmén narrow specialization

【专业军士】 zhuānyè jūnshì 1.(陆军) Technical Sergeant 2.(空军) Air Technical Sergeant 3.(海军) Technical Petty Officer

【专业课】 zhuānyèkè specialized course

【专业人员】 zhuānyè rényuán professional; personnel in a specific field ‖ 非专业人员 nonprofessional

【专业水平】 zhuānyè shuǐpíng professional proficiency

【专业学校】 zhuānyè xuéxiào vocational school

【专业知识】 zhuānyè zhī·shi professional knowledge

【专一】 zhuānyī single-minded; concentrated: 爱情～ be constant in love

【专用】 zhuānyòng for a special purpose: ～电话 telephone for special use

【专用标】 zhuānyòngbiāo monopoly trademark

【专用线】 zhuānyòngxiàn access road: 汽车～ motor access road / 铁路～ spur-track

【专用信箱】 zhuānyòng xìnxiāng private letter box

【专有权】 zhuānyǒuquán patent rights

【专员】 zhuānyuán 1.(地区行政长官) administrator of a prefecture; prefectural administrator 2.〈*Foreign Affairs*〉 assistant director; commissioner: 商务～ commercial attaché 3.(担任专门职务者) person assigned for a special job

【专员公署】 zhuānyuán gōngshǔ prefecture administration

【专政】 zhuānzhèng dictatorship: 人民民主～ people's democratic dictatorship

【专政工具】 zhuānzhèng gōngjù instrument of dictatorship

【专政机关】 zhuānzhèng jīguān organ of dictatorship

【专政职能】 zhuānzhèng zhínéng functions of the dictatorship

【专职】 zhuānzhí 1.(专人担任) sole duty; specific duty 2.(专门从事) full-time: ～干部 full-time cadre

【专制】 zhuānzhì 1.(独自掌权) autocratic; despotic: 君主～ autocratic monarch 2.(独断专行) autocracy; autocratic (adj.)

【专制政府】 zhuānzhì zhèngfǔ autocratic government

【专制政体】 zhuānzhì zhèngtǐ autocracy

【专制制度】 zhuānzhì zhìdù dictatorial system

【专注】 zhuānzhù concentrate one's attention on; be absorbed in; devote one's mind to

【专著】 zhuānzhù monograph; treatise

砖[磚、甎、塼] (zhuān) brick: 玻璃～ glass brick / 瓷～ ceramic tile / 方格～ checker brick / 空心～ hollow brick / 耐火～ refractory brick; firebrick

【砖茶】 zhuānchá brick tea

【砖厂】 zhuānchǎng brickfield; brickyard

【砖房】 zhuānfáng brick house

【砖木结构】 zhuānmù jiégòu 〈*Archit.*〉 post and panel structure

【砖坯】 zhuānpī unfired brick

【砖墙】 zhuānqiáng brick wall

【砖石结构】 zhuānshí jiégòu 〈*Archit.*〉 masonry structure

【砖头】 zhuān·tou 1.(碎砖) fragment of a brick 2.(砖) brick

【砖窑】 zhuānyáo brickkiln

转[轉] (zhuǎn) 1.(转向) turn; shift; change: 汽车～过街角。The car turned round the corner. 2.(转移) pass on; transfer: ～学 transfer to another school (另见"转"zhuàn)

【转氨酶】 zhuǎn'ānméi transaminase; aminopherase

【转败为胜】 zhuǎnbàiwéishèng turn defeat into victory

【转包】 zhuǎnbāo contract out to sb. else; the contracted project one has under taken

【转变】 zhuǎnbiàn change; transform: ～态度 change one's attitude
【转播】 zhuǎnbō relay; transmit: 实况～ live transmission
【转播时间】 zhuǎnbō shíjiān time; relay time
【转播台】 zhuǎnbōtái relay station
【转产】 zhuǎnchǎn change the line of production; shift in production
【转车】 zhuǎnchē change trains or buses; transfer to another train or bus
【转储】 zhuǎnchǔ 〈*Computer*〉 dump
【转船】 zhuǎnchuán change to another ship; transship
【转船装运】 zhuǎnchuán zhuāngyùn transshipment
【转达】 zhuǎndá pass on; convey; communicate: 请向她～我的谢意。Please convey my gratitude to her.
【转道】 zhuǎndào make a detour; go by way of
【转动】 zhuǎndòng turn; move; turn round
【转发】 zhuǎnfā transmit: ～文件 transmit a document
【转告】 zhuǎngào pass on; communicate; transmit
【转滚法】 zhuǎngǔnfǎ rollover
【转化】 zhuǎnhuà 1.（转变）change; transform 2.〈*Philos.*〉change into the reverse
【转换】 zhuǎnhuàn change; transform: ～职能 change the functions
【转机】 zhuǎnjī a favorable turn; a turn for the better: 事情有了～。There is a favorable turn in the matter.
【转寄地址】 zhuǎnjì dìzhǐ forwarding address
【转嫁】 zhuǎnjià shift; transfer: ～危机 shift a crisis on to others / ～罪责 shift the responsibility upon
【转交】 zhuǎnjiāo pass on; hand to; transmit
【转角】 zhuǎnjiǎo street corner; corner
【转接】 zhuǎnjiē change-over
【转口】 zhuǎnkǒu transit
【转口货物】 zhuǎnkǒu huòwù transit goods
【转口贸易】 zhuǎnkǒu màoyì transit trade
【转口税】 zhuǎnkǒushuì transit duty
【转口运输】 zhuǎnkǒu yùnshū transshipment
【转亏为盈】 zhuǎnkuīwéiyíng show a turn from loss to profit
【转脸】 zhuǎnliǎn 1.（掉过脸）turn one's face 2.（极短时间）in no time; in the twinkling of an eye: ～不认账 go back on one's word in the twinkling of an eye
【转录】 zhuǎnlù record; recording (n.)
【转卖】 zhuǎnmài resell
【转念】 zhuǎnniàn reconsider and give up an idea; think better of
【转晴】 zhuǎnqíng turn out to be a nice day: 天终于～了。It has turned out to be a nice day after all.
【转让】 zhuǎnràng make over; transfer the possession of: 有偿～ pay for new technique to sb.; royalty
【转让合同】 zhuǎnràng hé·tong agreement of transfer
【转让权利】 zhuǎnràng quánlì assignment privilege
【转让人】 zhuǎnràngrén alienator; transferor
【转让手续费】 zhuǎnràng shǒuxùfèi transfer charges
【转让证书】 zhuǎnràng zhèngshū deed of release; letter of transfer
【转入】 zhuǎnrù change over to; shift to; switch to: ～下页 carried forward / ～正常 return to normal
【转身】 zhuǎnshēn turn round; face about
【转手】 zhuǎnshǒu 1.（转卖）sell what one has bought 2.（不直接交）pass on
【转手交易】 zhuǎnshǒu jiāoyì switch operation
【转述】 zhuǎnshù report; relate sth. as told by another
【转瞬】 zhuǎnshùn in a twinkle; in a flash
【转送】 zhuǎnsòng 1.（转交）pass on; transmit 2.（转赠）make a present of sth. given to one
【转体】 zhuǎntǐ 〈*Sports*〉 turn; twist: 空中～半周 revolution of 180° in the air; half turn / 空中～一周 revolution of 360° in the air; full turn
【转体跳】 zhuǎntǐtiào 〈*Sports*〉 turning leap
【转体跳水】 zhuǎntǐ tiàoshuǐ 〈*Sports*〉 twist dive
【转弯】 zhuǎnwān turn a corner; make a

turn：右～ right-hand bend / Z 形～ Z bend; double bend Z / 左～ left-hand bend / 商店一～就到。The shop is just round the corner.

【转弯抹角】 zhuǎnwān-mòjiǎo 1.（指路）full of twists and turns 2.（指说话）beat about the bush; speak in a round about way：说话从来不～ never mince one's words

【转危为安】 zhuǎnwēiwéi'ān take a turn for the better and be out of danger; pull through

【转位】 zhuǎnwèi transposition

【转向】 zhuǎnxiàng 1.（指方向）change direction 2.（指政治立场）change one's political stand

【转学】 zhuǎnxué change school; transfer to another school

【转眼】 zhuǎnyǎn in the twinkling of an eye; in an instant; in a flash：～之间 in a trice

【转业】 zhuǎnyè be transferred to civilian work

【转业军人】 zhuǎnyè jūnrén armyman transferred to civilian work

【转移】 zhuǎnyí 1.（改换位置）shift; transfer; divert：～视线 divert sb's attention 2.（改变）change; transform：～管辖 change of venue; change the venue 3.〈*Med.*〉metastasis：癌～ the metastasis of carcinoma

【转义】 zhuǎnyì 〈*Gram.*〉transferred meaning; figurative sense

【转译】 zhuǎnyì translate; translation (n.)

【转引】 zhuǎnyǐn quote from a secondary source

【转院】 zhuǎnyuàn change hospital; transfer to another hospital

【转运】 zhuǎnyùn 1.（运输）transport; transship; transfer 2.（运气好转）have a change of luck; luck turns in one's favor

【转运港】 zhuǎnyùngǎng port of transshipment

【转运公司】 zhuǎnyùn gōngsī transport company; forwarding agency

【转运提单】 zhuǎnyùn tídān transshipment bill of lading

【转运站】 zhuǎnyùnzhàn transfer post

【转载】 zhuǎnzǎi reprint sth. that has been published elsewhere; reprint

【转赠】 zhuǎnzèng make a present of sth. given to one

【转战】 zhuǎnzhàn fight in one place after another

【转账】 zhuǎnzhàng transfer accounts

【转账支票】 zhuǎnzhàng zhīpiào transfer-account check

【转折】 zhuǎnzhé 1.（发展过程中的）a turn in the course of events 2.（文意的）transition

【转折点】 zhuǎnzhédiǎn turning point

【转正】 zhuǎnzhèng 1.（指非正式成员）become a full member 2.（指临时工）become a regular worker

【转租】 zhuǎnzū sublet; sublease

【转租人】 zhuǎnzūrén sublessor

传［傳］(zhuàn) 1.（经传）commentaries on classics 2.（传记）biography：列～ biographies in ancient Chinese history books / 外～ unauthorized biography / 自～ autobiography 3.（小说）novel：《水浒～》*Water Margin*
（另见"传"chuán）

【传记】 zhuànjì biography

【传略】 zhuànlüè brief biography; biographical sketch

转［轉］(zhuàn) 1.（旋转）turn; revolve; rotate; gyrate：月亮绕着地球～。The moon moves round the earth. / 那个花样滑冰运动员越～越快。The figure skater gyrated faster and faster. 2.〈*classifier*〉revolution：每分钟 1650～ 1650 revolutions per minute; 1650 r.p.m.
（另见"转"zhuǎn）

【转笔刀】 zhuànbǐdāo pencil sharpener

【转动】 zhuàndòng turn; revolve; rotate：在锁眼里～钥匙 turn a key in the lock

【转经筒】 zhuànjīngtǒng 〈*Buddhism*〉prayer wheel

【转矩】 zhuànjù 〈*Mech.*〉torque

【转炉】 zhuànlú 〈*Metall.*〉converter

【转轮】 zhuànlún rotor

【转轮手枪】 zhuànlún shǒuqiāng revolver

【转门】 zhuànmén 〈*Archit.*〉revolving door

【转盘】 zhuànpán 1.〈*Mech.*〉turntable 2.〈*Sports*〉giant stride 3.〈*Acrobatics*〉disc-spinning 4.〈*Petroleum*〉rotary table：～速

度 rotary speed 5.（交通环岛）traffic circle (AmE.)；roundabout (BrE.)

【转速】 zhuànsù rotational speed

【转速计】 zhuànsùjì tachometer

【转台】 zhuàntái 1.（指剧院的）revolving stage 2.（指工具的）swivel table

【转向】 zhuànxiàng lose one's bearings；get lost：晕头～ lose one's bearings

【转椅】 zhuànyǐ swivel chair；revolving chair

【转悠】 zhuàn·you 1.（转动）turn；move from side to side 2.（漫步）stroll；saunter；take a leisurely walk

【转游】 zhuàn·you 同"转悠"

【转子】 zhuànzǐ 〈*Mech.*〉rotor

赚 (zhuàn) 1.（获得利润）make a profit；gain：～钱 make money；make a profit 2.（挣钱）earn：他～很多钱。He earns a lot of money.

【赚头】 zhuàn·tou profit：没多大～ not much profit

撰 (zhuàn) write；compose：为报纸～稿 write articles for a newspaper

【撰著】 zhuànzhù write；compose

篆 (zhuàn) 1.（篆体）seal character 2.（印章）seal

【篆刻】 zhuànkè seal cutting

【篆书】 zhuànshū seal character

zhuang

庄［莊］(zhuāng) 1.（村庄）village 2.（商店）a place of business：茶～ tea shop / 钱～ private bank

【庄家】 zhuāng·jia banker

【庄稼】 zhuāng·jia crops

【庄稼地】 zhuāng·jiadì field；cropland

【庄稼活儿】 zhuāng·jiahuór farm work

【庄稼人】 zhuāng·jiarén farmer；peasant

【庄严】 zhuāngyán solemn；dignified；stately：～的誓言 solemn oath

【庄园】 zhuāngyuán manor

【庄重】 zhuāngzhòng serious；grave；solemn

桩［樁］(zhuāng) 1.（桩子）stake；pile 2.〈*classifier*〉一～买卖 a business transaction

【桩子】 zhuāng·zi stake；pile

妆［妝、粧］(zhuāng) 1.（化妆）apply makeup；make up：梳～ dress one's hair and apply makeup 2.（装饰）woman's personal adornments；stage costume

【妆奁】 zhuānglián trousseau

【妆饰】 zhuāngshì 1.（打扮）adorn；dress up；deck out 2.（打扮的样子）adornments；decorations

装［裝］(zhuāng) 1.（装扮）dress up；attire；deck；play the part of；act：～点 deck；dress；decorate 2.（服装）outfit；clothing：冬～ winter clothing / 军～ military uniform 3.（化装）stage makeup and costume 4.（假装）pretend；feign；make believe：～作不知 affect ignorance / 不懂～懂 pretend to know what one doesn't know / 她的病完全是～的。Her sickness is just an act to get sympathy. 5.（装载）load；pack；hold：～船 load a ship 6.（安装）install；fit；assemble：给屋子～上暖气设备 install heating system in the house

【装扮】 zhuāngbàn 1.（打扮）dress up；attire；deck out 2.（化装）disguise；masquerade：～成外国商人 disguise oneself as a foreign merchant

【装备】 zhuāngbèi 1.（配备）equip；fit out：～精良 be well equipped 2.（配备的东西）equipment；outfit：现代化～ modernized equipment

【装裱】 zhuāngbiǎo mount

【装病】 zhuāngbìng affect illness

【装船】 zhuāngchuán shipment

【装船标记】 zhuāngchuán biāoji shipping mark

【装船单】 zhuāngchuándān shipping order

【装船费】 zhuāngchuánfèi shipping charges

【装船货样】 zhuāngchuán huòyàng shipment sample

【装船须知】 zhuāngchuán xūzhī shipping instructions

【装点】 zhuāngdiǎn decorate；dress；deck

【装订】 zhuāngdìng bind；bookbind：把两本书～成一册 bind up two books into one volume

【装订车间】 zhuāngdìng chējiān book-

bindery; bindery
【装订工人】 zhuāngdìng gōngrén bookbinder
【装订机】 zhuāngdìngjī bookbinding machine; binding machinery
【装疯卖傻】 zhuāngfēng-màishǎ feign madness and act like an idiot; play the fool
【装罐】 zhuāngguàn pack; can
【装罐机】 zhuāngguànjī filler
【装裹】 zhuāng·guo 1.(给死人穿衣服) dress a corpse; wrap (a corpse) in a shroud 2.(死人穿的衣服) shroud; burial suit
【装糊涂】 zhuānghútú pretend not to know; act the fool
【装潢】 zhuānghuáng 1.(装饰物品) mount; decorate; dress 2.(进行装饰) decorate; decoration (n.)
【装货】 zhuānghuò load; loading (n.)
【装货单】 zhuānghuòdān shipping order
【装货费用】 zhuānghuò-fèiyòng loading charges
【装货港】 zhuānghuògǎng port of shipment; port of loading
【装货容量】 zhuānghuò róngliàng shipping capacity
【装机容量】 zhuāngjī róngliàng 〈*Electr.*〉 installed capacity
【装甲】 zhuāngjiǎ 1.(装有防弹钢板的) armored 2.(防弹钢板) plate armor
【装甲兵】 zhuāngjiǎbīng armored force
【装甲部队】 zhuāngjiǎ bùduì armored corps; armored troops
【装甲列车】 zhuāngjiǎ lièchē armored train
【装甲汽车】 zhuāngjiǎ qìchē armored automobile; armored vehicle
【装甲师】 zhuāngjiǎshī armored division
【装假】 zhuāngjiǎ pretend; feign; make believe
【装具】 zhuāngjù harness
【装殓】 zhuāngliǎn dress and lay a corpse in a coffin
【装聋作哑】 zhuānglóng-zuòyǎ pretend to be deaf and dumb; pretend to be ignorant of sth.
【装门面】 zhuāngmén·mian put up a front; maintain an outward show; keep up appearances
【装模作样】 zhuāngmó-zuòyàng be affected; attitudinize; put on an act
【装配】 zhuāngpèi assemble; fit together: ～机器 assemble a machine
【装配车间】 zhuāngpèi chējiān assembly shop; fitting shop
【装配工】 zhuāngpèigōng assembler; fitter
【装配线】 zhuāngpèixiàn assembly line
【装瓶】 zhuāngpíng bottle; bottling (n.)
【装腔】 zhuāngqiāng behave affectedly; be artificial
【装腔作势】 zhuāngqiāng-zuòshì be affected or pretentious; strike a pose
【装入】 zhuāngrù build-in
【装饰】 zhuāngshì 1.(进行装饰) decorate; deck; adorn; ornament: 大厅～得富丽堂皇。The hall was sumptuously decorated. 2.(装饰品) decorations; adornment; ornament
【装饰品】 zhuāngshìpǐn decorations; adornment; ornament
【装饰图案】 zhuāngshì tú'àn decorative pattern
【装饰者】 zhuāngshìzhě lay-out man
【装束】 zhuāngshù dress; attire: ～入时 be dressed in the latest fashion; in fashionable dress
【装箱】 zhuāngxiāng boxing; encase
【装箱单】 zhuāngxiāngdān packing list; packing slip: 放入～ enclose a packing list
【装卸】 zhuāngxiè 1.(装上或卸下) load and unload 2.(装配和拆卸) assemble and disassemble
【装卸工】 zhuāngxiègōng loader; stevedore
【装卸机】 zhuāngxièjī charging crane
【装卸码头】 zhuāngxiè mǎtóu shipping dock
【装卸时间】 zhuāngxiè shíjiān lay days
【装卸作业】 zhuāngxiè zuòyè loading and unloading operation
【装修】 zhuāngxiū 1.〈*Archit.*〉 fit up: ～门面 fit up the front of a shop 2.(安装上的设备) fixtures; installations
【装样子】 zhuāng yàng·zi act; put on an act: 他总是装出经验丰富的样子。He is always acting the experienced man. / 他不是真道歉，这全是～。He's not really sorry; it's

all just an act.

【装运】 zhuāngyùn ship; load and transport

【装载】 zhuāngzǎi carry; load

【装载量】 zhuāngzǎiliàng loading capacity

【装帧】 zhuāngzhēn binding and layout

【装置】 zhuāngzhì 1.（安装）install; fit 2.（指设备）installation; unit; device; plant: 安全～ safety device / 暖气～ heating installation

壮［壯］(zhuàng) 1.（强壮）strong; robust: 年轻力～ young and robust 2.（加强）strengthen; make better: ～声势 to lend impetus and strength; to make it appear more vigorous and impressive 3.（雄壮）magnificent; grand: ～观 magnificent sight

【壮大】 zhuàngdà 1.（使强大）strengthen: ～社会主义经济 strengthen the socialist economy 2.（变得强大）grow 3.（强壮粗大）big; strong

【壮胆】 zhuàngdǎn encourage; boost sb's courage

【壮工】 zhuànggōng unskilled laborer

【壮观】 zhuàngguān 1.（雄伟）magnificent; grand; grandiose 2.（雄伟景象）magnificent sight

【壮举】 zhuàngjǔ magnificent feat; heroic undertaking

【壮阔】 zhuàngkuò 1.（宽广）vast; grand; expansive: 波澜～ surging forward with great momentum; unfolding on a magnificent scale 2.（宏伟）grand; magnificent; majestic: 规模～ on a majestic scale

【壮丽】 zhuànglì majestic; magnificent; glorious

【壮烈】 zhuàngliè heroic; brave: ～牺牲 heroically give one's life

【壮年】 zhuàngnián the more robust years of a person's life; prime of life

【壮实】 zhuàng·shi sturdy; robust

【壮士】 zhuàngshì heroic man; hero; warrior

【壮志】 zhuàngzhì great aspiration; lofty ideal: ～凌云 with soaring aspirations

【壮族】 Zhuàngzú Zhuang（中国少数民族，主要分布在广西及云南、广东、贵州、湖南等地）

状［狀］(zhuàng) 1.（形状）form; shape; appearance 2.（状况）state; condition: 病～ condition of illness 3.（陈述）describe: 不可名～ indescribable; nondescript; beyond description 4.（诉状）written complaint; plaint: 告～ lodge a complaint; file a suit 5.（凭证）certificate: 奖～ certificate of commendation

【状况】 zhuàngkuàng condition; state; state of affairs: 家庭～ family circumstance / 健康～ state of health / 经济～ financial situation; economic situation

【状态】 zhuàngtài state; condition; state of affairs: 混乱～ state of chaos / 紧急～ state of emergency

【状语】 zhuàngyǔ 〈*Gram.*〉 adverbial modifier; adverbial

【状元】 zhuàng·yuan 1.（本行业优秀者）the very best: 行行出～。Every profession produces its own topmost master. 2.（科考称号）Number One Scholar

【状子】 zhuàng·zi 〈*colloq.*〉 written complaint; plaint

撞(zhuàng) 1.（相碰）bump against; run into; strike; collide: ～树 bump against a tree / 两车相～。Two cars collided. 2.（碰见）meet by chance; bump into; run into 3.（莽撞）rush; dash; barge: 横冲直～ barge around; dash about madly

【撞车】 zhuàngchē 1.（车辆相撞）collision 2.（相冲突）clash

【撞倒】 zhuàngdǎo knock down; knock over: 被汽车～ get knocked over by a car

【撞击】 zhuàngjī ram; dash against; strike

【撞见】 zhuàngjiàn meet or discover by chance; catch sb. in the act; run across: 他做这事时被我～了。I caught him doing it.

【撞骗】 zhuàngpiàn look about for a chance to swindle; swindle

【撞墙】 zhuàngqiáng 1.（撞到墙上）bump against a wall 2.（碰壁）be rebuffed; meet with an unexpected rebuff

【撞人】 zhuàngrén knock down; knock over; bump

【撞入】 zhuàngrù thrust into; burst into

【撞伤】 zhuàngshāng crush injury

【撞锁】 zhuàngsuǒ spring lock

zhui

椎 (zhuī) vertebra：脊～ vertebral column / 颈～ cervical vertebra / 胸～ dorsal vertebra; thoracic / 腰～ lumbar vertebra / 骶～ sacrum / ～骨 coccyx

【椎间盘】 zhuījiānpán 〈*Anat*.〉 intervertebral disc

【椎间盘突出症】 zhuījiānpán tūchūzhèng 〈*Med*.〉 slipped disc; protrusion of the intervertebral disc

锥 (zhuī) 1.（锥子）awl 2.（像锥子的东西）anything shaped like an awl：改～ screwdriver 3.（用锥子钻）bore; drill

【锥子】 zhuī·zi awl; bradawl

追 (zhuī) 1.（追赶）chase after; pursue; run after 2.（追究）trace; look into; get to the bottom of 3.（追求）seek; go after：～名逐利 seek fame and wealth 4.（回溯）recall; reminisce 5.（事后补办）retroactively; posthumously：～认 recognize retroactively

【追本溯源】 zhuīběn-sùyuán trace to its source; get at the root of the matter

【追逼】 zhuībī 1.（追赶）pursue closely 2.（追究，追索）press for; extort：～欠款 press for repayment of debts

【追捕】 zhuībǔ pursue and capture：～逃犯 pursue and capture a runaway criminal

【追不到】 zhuībùdào unable to catch up with; unable to overtake

【追查】 zhuīchá investigate; trace; find out：～责任 find out where the responsibility lies

【追悼】 zhuīdào mourn over a person's death

【追悼会】 zhuīdàohuì memorial meeting

【追肥】 zhuīféi 〈*Agric*.〉 topdress; apply additional fertilizer

【追赶】 zhuīgǎn quicken one's pace to catch up; run after; pursue

【追根】 zhuīgēn get to the bottom of sth.：～问底 raise one question after another

【追回】 zhuīhuí recover：～赃款 recover stolen money

【追悔】 zhuīhuǐ repent; regret：～往事 repent of the past

【追击】 zhuījī pursue and attack; follow up

【追击部队】 zhuījī bùduì pursuit troops

【追记】 zhuījì 1.（事后记载）postscript 2.（事后嘉奖）cite posthumously

【追加】 zhuījiā add to (the original amount)：～贷款 complementary financial facility

【追缴税款】 zhuījiǎo shuìkuǎn pursue the tax payment

【追究】 zhuījiū look into; find out; investigate：～祸源 investigate the origin of the misfortune / ～原因 find out the cause

【追求】 zhuīqiú 1.（争取）seek; pursue：～名利 seek fame and fortune 2.（求爱）woo; court; chase; run after

【追认】 zhuīrèn 1.（事后认可）subsequently confirm or endorse; recognize retroactively 2.（批准生前要求）admit posthumously; confer posthumously

【追溯】 zhuīsù trace back to; date from

【追溯效力】 zhuīsù xiàolì retroactive effect

【追诉权】 zhuīsùquán power to prosecute

【追诉时效】 zhuīsù shíxiào limitation of prosecution

【追随】 zhuīsuí follow; adhere to

【追随者】 zhuīsuízhě follower; adherent; disciple

【追索权】 zhuīsuǒquán recourse; right of recourse

【追问】 zhuīwèn question closely; make a detailed inquiry; examine minutely

【追星族】 zhuīxīngzú hero-worship group

【追叙】 zhuīxù 1.（追述）tell about the past; relate; recount 2.（写作手法）narration of earlier episodes; flashback

【追寻】 zhuīxún pursue; search; track down

【追忆】 zhuīyì recollect; recall; look back

【追赃】 zhuīzāng order the return of stolen money or goods; recover stolen money or goods; make sb. disgorge the spoils

【追赠】 zhuīzèng confer posthumously

【追逐】 zhuīzhú 1.（追赶）pursue; chase 2.（追求）seek; quest

【追踪】 zhuīzōng follow the trail of; track; trace：～嫌疑犯 trail a suspect

【追踪试验装置】 zhuīzōng shìyàn zhuāngzhì tracer test unit

坠［墜］(zhuì) 1.(落) fall; drop: ～马 fall off a horse / 这门好像有点～了。The door seems to have dropped slightly. 2.(下垂) weigh down 3.(坠儿) weight; a hanging object

【坠毁】 zhuìhuǐ fall and break; crash

【坠机】 zhuìjī aircrash

【坠落】 zhuìluò fall; drop

【坠落损害】 zhuìluò sǔnhài sling loss

【坠子】 zhuì·zi 1.(坠) weight; plummet; pendant 2.(耳坠) ear pendant

缒 (zhuì) let down with a rope

赘 (zhuì) 1.(多余的) superfluous; redundant 2.(入赘) go to live in the household of the bride's parents 3.(拖累) be burdensome; be cumbersome

【赘述】 zhuìshù give unnecessary details; say more than is needed

【赘言】 zhuìyán verbosity; redundant words

【赘疣】 zhuìyóu 1.(疣) wart 2.(无用东西) anything superfluous or useless

zhun

肫 (zhūn) gizzard: 鸡～ chicken gizzard / 鸭～ duck gizzard

谆 (zhūn)

【谆谆】 zhūnzhūn earnestly and tirelessly: ～教诲 inculcate

准［準[2-6]］(zhǔn) 1.(准许) allow; grant; permit: ～假三天 grant sb. three days' leave / 此处不～吸烟。Smoking is not allowed here. 2.(标准) standard; norm; criterion: 以此为～ take this as the standard 3.(依据) in accordance with; follow 4.(准确) accurate; exact: 我的表不～。My watch doesn't keep good time. 5.(一定) definitely; certainly: 她～会来。Definitely she will come. 6.(类似) quasi-; para-: ～契约 quasi-contract

【准保】 zhǔnbǎo 〈adv.〉 certainly; for sure

【准备】 zhǔnbèi 1.(预先安排) prepare; get ready: 做～ make preparations for / ～接待外国游客 prepare to receive foreign visitors / 新娘的家庭负责～婚礼。The bride's family is responsible for the wedding arrangements. 2.(打算) intend; plan: 她～明年出国。She is planning on going abroad next year.

【准备活动】 zhǔnbèi huódòng 〈*Sports*〉 warming-up exercise; limbering-up exercise

【准备阶段】 zhǔnbèi jiéduàn preparatory stage

【准博士】 zhǔnbóshì all but dissertation (ABD)

【准点】 zhǔndiǎn on schedule

【准儿】 zhǔnr certain; sure

【准噶尔】 Zhǔngá'ěr 〈place〉 Junggar

【准将】 zhǔnjiàng 〈*Mil.*〉 brigadier

【准考证】 zhǔnkǎozhèng examination admission ticket

【准确】 zhǔnquè accurate; exact; precise: 发音～ pronounce accurately / ～答案 an accurate answer

【准确性】 zhǔnquèxìng accuracy

【准绳】 zhǔnshéng criterion; yardstick; standard

【准时】 zhǔnshí punctual; on time; on schedule: 火车～到达。The train arrived on schedule.

【准尉】 zhǔnwèi 〈*Mil.*〉 warrant officer

【准许】 zhǔnxǔ permit; allow

【准予】 zhǔnyǔ grant; approve; permit: ～保释 grant bail

【准则】 zhǔnzé norm; standard; criterion: 行为～ code of conduct / 国际关系中最起码的～ rudimentary code of international relations

zhuo

拙 (zhuō) 1.(笨) clumsy; awkward; dull: ～于言词 be inarticulate; be clumsy in expressing oneself 2.〈*politeness*〉 my: ～笔 my poor writing / ～稿 my poor manuscript

【拙笨】 zhuōbèn clumsy; dull; unskillful

【拙见】 zhuōjiàn my humble opinion

【拙劣】 zhuōliè clumsy; inferior: ～的表演 a clumsy performance; a bad show

捉 (zhuō) 1.(握; 抓) clutch; hold; grasp 2.(捉拿) catch; capture: ～贼 arrest a thief in the act

【捉刀】 zhuōdāo ghostwrite ‖ 捉刀人 ghostwriter

【捉襟见肘】 zhuōjīn-jiànzhǒu pull down one's jacket to conceal the raggedness, only to expose one's elbows; have too many difficulties to cope with; have too many problems to tackle

【捉迷藏】 zhuōmícáng 1.(游戏) hide-and-seek; blindman's buff 2.(说话兜圈子) be tricky and evasive; play hide-and-seek

【捉摸】 zhuō·mo fathom; ascertain: 难以～ difficult to ascertain

【捉拿】 zhuōná arrest; catch: ～归案 bring sb. to justice

【捉弄】 zhuōnòng tease; make fun of; embarrass

桌 (zhuō) 1.(桌子) table; desk: 餐～ dining table / 书～ writing desk / 满～的客人 a tableful of guests 2.〈*classifier*〉一～玩牌的人 a table of card-players

【桌布】 zhuōbù tablecloth; table cover

【桌面】 zhuōmiàn top of a table; table top

【桌子】 zhuō·zi table; desk: 把盘子都放到～上。Put all the plates on the table.

灼 (zhuó) 1.(火烧) burn; scorch: ～伤 burn 2.(明亮) bright; luminous

【灼见】 zhuójiàn profound view; penetrating view: 有真知～的人 man with profound knowledge and penetrating insight

【灼热】 zhuórè scorching hot

【灼痛】 zhuótòng burning pains

【灼灼】 zhuózhuó 〈*written*〉 shining; brilliant: 目光～ with keen, sparkling eyes

酌 (zhuó) 1.(斟;饮) pour out; drink: 独～ drink alone 2.(酒饭) a meal with wine: 便～ informal dinner 3.(斟酌) consider; think over; use one's discretion

【酌办】 zhuóbàn act according to one's judgment; do as one thinks fit

【酌减】 zhuójiǎn discretionary reduction

【酌量】 zhuóliàng consider; deliberate; use one's judgment

【酌情】 zhuóqíng take into consideration the circumstances; use one's discretion: ～办理 use one's discretion in making decisions / ～减刑 reduction at judicial discretion

茁 (zhuó) grow vigorously

【茁长】 zhuózhǎng grow vigorously

【茁壮】 zhuózhuàng become sturdy; be healthy and strong: ～成长 grow sturdily

卓 (zhuó) 1.(高而直) tall and erect 2.(高明) eminent; outstanding: ～见 brilliant idea; excellent opinion

【卓绝】 zhuójüé unsurpassed; extreme; of the highest degree: 艰苦～ extreme hardships and difficulties

【卓然】 zhuórán outstanding; stately; eminent: ～而立 stand majestically

【卓识】 zhuóshí judicious judgment; sagacity: 远见～ foresight and sagacity

【卓有成效】 zhuóyǒu-chéngxiào fruitful; highly effective

【卓越】 zhuóyuè outstanding; brilliant; remarkable: ～的人才 an eminent man of ability

【卓著】 zhuózhù distinguished; outstanding; eminent: 声誉～ eminent fame

浊［濁］(zhuó) 1.(浑浊) turbid; muddy 2.(指声音) deep and thick 3.(混乱) chaotic; confused; corrupted

【浊气】 zhuóqì foul smell

【浊世】 zhuóshì 1.(指时代) the corrupted world; chaotic times 2.〈*Buddhism*〉 the mortal world

镯［鋜］(zhuó)

【鐲子】 zhuó·zi wristlet; bracelet

啄 (zhuó) peck

【啄木鳥】 zhuómùniǎo 〈*Zool.*〉 woodpecker

琢 (zhuó) chisel; carve: 精雕細～ exquisitely carved

(另見"琢"zuó)

【琢句雕詞】 zhuójù-diāocí polish sentences and to engrave phrases

【琢磨】 zhuómó 1.(雕刻打磨) carve and polish 2.(加工) improve; polish; refine

着 (zhuó) 1.(穿) wear: ～禮服 arrayed in ceremonial robes / ～節日盛裝 in holiday attire / ～軍裝 in military array / 講究穿～ be particular about one's clothing 2.(接觸) touch; come into contact with: 附～ adhere to 3.(着落) whereabouts 4.(派遣) send: ～人前去 send sb. along 5.(公文用語) immediately; at once; right away: ～即辦理。Let it be enforced immediately.

(另見"着"zhāo, zháo)

【着筆】 zhuóbǐ put pen to paper; begin to write or paint

【着力】 zhuólì put forth effort; exert oneself

【着陸】 zhuólù land; touch down: 軟～ soft landing

【着陸艙】 zhuólùcāng landing module

【着陸場】 zhuólùchǎng landing field; landing ground

【着陸架】 zhuólùjià 〈*Aeron*.〉 landing pad

【着陸接地】 zhuólù jiēdì touchdown

【着落】 zhuóluò 1.(下落) whereabouts 2.(可指望的來源) assured source: 經費無～ no funds available

【着色】 zhuósè put color on; color

【着色法】 zhuósèfǎ coloring

【着色劑】 zhuósèjì coloring agent; coloring material

【着實】 zhuóshí 1.(確實) really; indeed 2.(分量重) severely: ～責備了她一頓 lecture her severely

【着手】 zhuóshǒu put one's hand to; set about: 從技術革新～ start with technical innovation

【着想】 zhuóxiǎng consider: 為…的利益～ consider the interest of sb.

【着眼】 zhuóyǎn have sth. in mind; see from the angle of

【着眼點】 zhuóyǎndiǎn starting point; focus of attention; object in mind

【着意】 zhuóyì 1.(用心) act with care and effort; take pains: ～經營 manage with diligent care 2.(在意;留心) care about: 不～ not care about

【着重】 zhuózhòng stress; emphasize

【着重點】 zhuózhòngdiǎn focus of attention; emphasis

【着重號】 zhuózhònghào mark of emphasis

【着裝】 zhuózhuāng 1.(穿衣) wear; put on 2.(衣着) clothing

zi

孜(zī)

【孜然】 zīrán cumin

【孜孜】 zīzī diligent; industrious; hardworking

【孜孜不倦】 zīzī-bùjuàn diligently; assiduously; indefatigably

【孜孜以求】 zīzīyǐqiú seek sth. assiduously

咨(zī) consult; take counsel

【咨文】 zīwén 1.(公文) official communication 2.(美国等的国情报告) report delivered by the head of a government on affairs of state: 国情～ State of the Union Message

【咨询】 zīxún seek advice from; hold counsel with; consult

【咨询费】 zīxúnfèi consultant fee

【咨询服务】 zīxún fúwù advisory service; consulting service: 提供～ offer advisory service

【咨询机关】 zīxún jīguān advisory body

【咨询委员会】 zīxún wěiyuánhuì consultative committee

【咨询意见】 zīxún yìjiàn advisory opinion

姿(zī) 1.(容貌) looks; appearance 2.(姿势) gesture; carriage; posture; position: 跪～ kneeling position / 立～ standing position / 卧～ prone position

【姿容】 zīróng looks; appearance

【姿色】 zīsè good looks

【姿势】 zīshì posture; gesture; form: 她～优美。She had a fine action.

【姿态】 zītài 1.(姿势) posture; carriage; gesture 2.(态度) attitude; pose: 外交～ diplomatic gesture / 友好～ friendly gesture

资(zī) 1.(费用) money; expenses: 投～ put money in; invest 2.(资助) subsidize; support 3.(提供) provide; supply: 以～借鉴 that we can draw lesson from 4.(资质) endowment; natural ability: 天～ natural endowments; aptitude 5.(资格) qualifications; record of service 6.(资方) capital: 劳～关系 labor-capital relations

【资本】 zīběn 1.(本钱) capital: 固定～ fixed capital / 借贷～ loan capital / 金融～ financial capital / 流动～ current capital; floating capital / 生产～ production capital / 银行～ banking capital / 周转～ working capital 2.(牟利的凭借) what is capitalized on; sth. used to one's own advantage：政治～ political stock-in-trade

【资本过剩】 zīběn guòshèng surplus of capital

【资本积累】 zīběn jīlěi accumulation of capital

【资本家】 zīběnjiā capitalist

【资本市场】 zīběn shìchǎng capital market

【资本输出】 zīběn shūchū export of capital

【资本外流】 zīběn wàiliú capital flight

【资本增值】 zīběn zēngzhí increase in capital

【资本周转】 zīběn zhōuzhuǎn turnover of capital; capital turnover

【资本主义】 zīběn zhǔyì capitalism; capitalist (adj.)：～经济成分 capitalist sector of the economy / ～生产方式 capitalist mode of production / ～制度 capitalist system

【资本总额】 zīběn zǒng'é capital investment

【资不抵债】 zībùdǐzhài unable to pay one's debt with all his assets

【资财】 zīcái capital and goods; assets

【资产】 zīchǎn 1.（财产）property 2.（资金）capital fund; capital 3.（资金运用情况）assets：流动～ liquid assets

【资产阶级】 zīchǎn jiējí bourgeoisie; capitalist class

【资产业务】 zīchǎn yèwù assets operation

【资方】 zīfāng those representing capital; capital

【资方代理人】 zīfāng dàilǐrén agent of the owner of a private enterprise; agent of a capitalist

【资方人员】 zīfāng rényuán capitalists and their representatives

【资格】 zīgé 1.（指条件）qualification：没有～参加比赛 be disqualified from taking part in the game 2.（指身份）seniority：摆老～ flaunt one's seniority / 我是以法律顾问的～来的。I have come in the capacity of a legal adviser.

【资格审查委员会】 zīgé shěnchá wěiyuánhuì credentials committee

【资格证书】 zīgé zhèngshū credentials

【资金】 zījīn fund：财政～ financial resources / 筹措～ raise money / 国家～ public fund / 货币～ monetary resources / 流动～ current funds; circulating funds / 预算～ budgetary funds / 折旧～ amortization fund / 为国家积累～ accumulate funds for the state

【资金技术密集型产业】 zījīn jìshù mìjíxíng chǎnyè enterprises that are capital or technology intensive

【资金外流】 zījīn wàiliú capital flight

【资金总汇】 zījīn zǒnghuì pooling of resources

【资力】 zīlì financial strength：～雄厚 have a large capital; be financially powerful

【资历】 zīlì qualifications and record of service

【资料】 zīliào 1.（必需品）means：生产～ means of production; capital goods / 生活～ means of livelihood; consumer goods 2.（材料,数据）data; material：参考～ reference material

【资料处理】 zīliào chùlǐ data processing

【资料库】 zīliàokù data bank

【资料室】 zīliàoshì reference room

【资源】 zīyuán natural resources; resources：国家～ national resources / 人力～ manpower resources / 未利用的～ idle resources / 稀缺～ tight resources

【资质】 zīzhì natural endowments; intelligence：～平庸 natural disposition is ordinary

【资助】 zīzhù aid financially; subsidize

赼［趦］(zī)

【赼趄】 zījū 1.（行走困难）drag one's feet with difficulty; walk unsteadily 2.（不能向前）hesitate to move ahead

吱(zī) 〈*onomat.*〉1.（老鼠叫）squeak 2.（小鸟叫）chirp; peep

（另见"吱"zhī）

【吱声】 zīshēng 〈*dial.*〉utter sth.; make a sound

兹［茲］(zī) 1.（这个）this 2.（现在）now; at present

【兹收到】 zīshōudào This is to acknowledge ...

滋(zī) 1.（滋生）grow; multiply：～事 create trouble 2.（增添）more 3.（喷射）spurt; burst：别～水。Don't spurt water.

【滋补】 zībǔ nourishing; nutritious

【滋补药品】 zībǔ yàopǐn tonic

【滋扰闹事】 zīrǎo-nàoshì affray：警察平息了酒吧里的～。The police broke up an affray in the bar.
【滋润】 zīrùn 1.（不干燥）moist：～的皮肤 soft skin 2.（使不干燥）moisten：用唾液～喉咙 moisten one's throat with saliva
【滋生】 zīshēng 1.（繁殖）multiply；breed；propagate 2.（引起）cause；create；provoke：～事端 cause trouble；create a disturbance
【滋事】 zīshì cause trouble
【滋味】 zīwèi taste；flavor
【滋养】 zīyǎng 1.（供给养分）nourish 2.（养分）nutriment；nourishment：丰富的～ rich nutriment
【滋养品】 zīyǎngpǐn nourishing food；nutriment；nourishment
【滋长】 zīzhǎng grow；develop

孳（zī） multiply；propagate
【孳生】 zīshēng multiply；breed；propagate

龇［呲］（zī） 〈*colloq*.〉 bare；show：～着牙 bare one's teeth
【龇牙咧嘴】 zīyá-liězuǐ 1.（凶狠）show one's teeth；look fierce 2.（疼痛难忍）contort one's face in agony；grimace in pain

髭（zī） moustache

辎（zī） an ancient covered wagon
【辎重】 zīzhòng 〈*Mil*.〉 impedimenta；supplies and gear of an army；baggage

鲻（zī） 〈*Zool*.〉 mullet
【鲻鱼】 zīyú striped mullet

子（zǐ） 1.（儿子）son；child：长～ eldest son 2.（人）person：男～ man；male person / 女～ woman；female person 3.（种子）seed：葵花～儿 sunflower seeds / 花～儿 flower seed 4.（卵）egg：鸡～儿 egg 5.（幼小的）young；tender；small：～鸡 chick 6.（粒状物）sth. small and hard：枪～儿 bullet / 石头～儿 pebble；cobblestone 7.（棋子）吃～ capture / 出～ develop
【子表】 zǐbiǎo sublist
【子程序】 zǐchéngxù 〈*Computer*〉 subprogram；sub-routines
【子程序库】 zǐchéngxùkù 〈*Computer*〉 subroutine library
【子畜】 zǐchù newborn animal；young animal
【子弹】 zǐdàn bullet；cartridge
【子弟】 zǐdì sons and younger brothers；juniors；children：纨绔～ profligate sons of the rich
【子公司】 zǐgōngsī subsidiary；subcompany；daughter firm
【子宫】 zǐgōng 〈*Anat*.〉 uterus；womb
【子宫颈】 zǐgōngjǐng 〈*Anat*.〉 cervix；carvical (adj.)
【子宫颈癌】 zǐgōngjǐng'ái 〈*Med*.〉 carvical carcinoma
【子宫颈涂片检查】 zǐgōngjǐng túpiàn jiǎnchá 〈*Med*.〉 smear test
【子宫帽】 zǐgōngmào pessary
【子宫腔】 zǐgōngqiāng 〈*Anat*.〉 cavity of the uterus
【子宫切除】 zǐgōng qiēchú 〈*Med*.〉 hysterectomy；uterectomy
【子宫脱垂】 zǐgōng tuōchuí 〈*Med*.〉 prolapse of the uterus
【子鸡】 zǐjī chick
【子棉】 zǐmián unginned cotton
【子母扣】 zǐmǔkòu snap；snap-fastener
【子目录】 zǐmùlù 〈*Computer*〉 subdirectory
【子女】 zǐnǚ sons and daughters；children：～多 have many children
【子女抚养费】 zǐnǚ fúyǎngfèi child-care expense
【子实】 zǐshí seed；grain；kernel；bean
【子实产量】 zǐshí chǎnliàng yield of kernels
【子兽】 zǐshòu young animal
【子嗣】 zǐsì son；male offspring
【子孙】 zǐsūn children and grandchildren；descendants：～后代 coming generations；descendants
【子午线】 zǐwǔxiàn 〈*Geol*.〉 meridian 本初～ the prime meridian
【子午线轮胎】 zǐwǔxiàn lúntāi radial tire；radial
【子虚】 zǐxū 〈*written*〉 fictitious；unreal
【子虚乌有】 zǐxū-wūyǒu no such man and nothing like that
【子夜】 zǐyè midnight
【子鱼】 zǐyú fry；fish fry
【子侄】 zǐzhí sons and nephews

【子猪】 zǐzhū piglet; pigling
【子子孙孙】 zǐzǐ-sūnsūn generation after generation of descendants
仔（zǐ） young：～鸡 chick / ～猪 piglet; pigling
（另见"仔"zǎi）
【仔畜】 zǐchù newborn animal; young animal
【仔盖】 zǐgài round（牛肉部位）
【仔鸡】 zǐjī chick
【仔兽】 zǐshòu young animal
【仔细】 zǐxì 1.（细心）careful; attentive：～听 listen attentively; lend an attentive ear to / ～研究 make a careful study of . . . 2.（小心）be careful; look out 3.（俭省）frugal; economical
【仔鱼】 zǐyú fry; fish fry
【仔猪】 zǐzhū piglet; pigling
籽（zǐ） seed：菜～儿 vegetable seed / 棉～儿 cotton seed
【籽粒】 zǐlì 〈*Agric*.〉 seed; grain; kernel; bean：～饱满 full grains
【籽棉】 zǐmián unginned cotton
【籽实】 zǐshí seed; grain; kernel; bean
姊（zǐ） elder sister; sister
【姊妹】 zǐmèi elder and younger sisters; sisters
【姊妹篇】 zǐmèipiān companion volume
紫（zǐ） purple; violet
【紫菜】 zǐcài 〈*Bot*.〉 laver
【紫草】 zǐcǎo 〈*Bot*.〉 gromwell; redroot gromwell
【紫貂】 zǐdiāo 〈*Zool*.〉 sable
【紫丁香】 zǐdīngxiāng 〈*Bot*.〉 early lilac
【紫红】 zǐhóng purplish red
【紫堇】 zǐjǐn 〈*Bot*.〉 corydalis
【紫禁城】 Zǐjìnchéng the Forbidden City
【紫荆】 zǐjīng 〈*Bot*.〉 redbud; Chinese redbud
【紫罗兰】 zǐluólán 〈*Bot*.〉 common stock violet
【紫杉】 zǐshān 〈*Bot*.〉 yew; Chinese yew
【紫石英】 zǐshíyīng 〈*Mineral*.〉 amethyst
【紫藤】 zǐténg 〈*Bot*.〉 Chinese wisteria
【紫外线】 zǐwàixiàn 〈*Physics*〉 ultraviolet ray
【紫药水】 zǐyàoshuǐ 〈*Pharm*.〉 gentian violet
梓（zǐ） 1.〈*Bot*.〉 ovate catalpa 2.（刻版）cut blocks for printing：付～ put into print
【梓树】 zǐshù ovate catalpa
自（zì） 1.（自己）self; oneself; one's own：～成一家 have a style of one's own 2.（自然）certainly; of course：～当努力 will certainly do one's best 3.（从；由）from; since：～上而下 from above to below
【自爱】 zì'ài regard for oneself; self-respect
【自拔】 zìbá free oneself; extricate oneself：不能～ be unable to free oneself from
【自白】 zìbái make clear one's meaning or position; vindicate oneself
【自白书】 zìbáishū a written confession
【自报公议】 zìbào-gōngyì self-assessment and public discussion
【自暴自弃】 zìbào-zìqì be backward and have no urge to make progress; be resigned to one's backwardness：他～。He abandoned himself to despair.
【自卑】 zìbēi feel oneself inferior; be self-abased
【自卑感】 zìbēigǎn inferiority complex; sense of inferiority
【自备】 zìbèi provide for oneself
【自备外汇】 zìbèi wàihuì self-provided foreign exchange
【自便】 zìbiàn at one's convenience; do as one pleases
【自不待言】 zìbùdàiyán it goes without saying; be self-evident
【自不量力】 zìbùliànglì overestimate one's strength or oneself; not know one's own limitations
【自残】 zìcán self injure
【自产自销】 zìchǎn-zìxiāo produce and market products by oneself
【自称】 zìchēng 1.（称呼自己）call oneself 2.（声称）declare oneself to be; claim to be：被告～无罪。The defendant pleaded not guilty.
【自成一家】 zìchéng-yījiā have a style of one's own; be unique in one's style
【自持】 zìchí control oneself; restrain one-

self; exercise self-restraint
【自筹资金】 zìchóu zījīn funds raised by oneself
【自传】 zìchuán 〈*Bot*.〉 self-seed
【自吹自擂】 zìchuī-zìléi blow one's own trumpet; crack oneself up
【自从】 zìcóng since: ～去年冬天以来 since last winter
【自大】 zìdà self-important; arrogant
【自得】 zìdé contented; self-satisfied: 安闲～ carefree and contented
【自动】 zìdòng **1.** (主动) voluntarily; of one's own accord **2.** 〈*Mech*.〉 automatic
【自动步枪】 zìdòng bùqiāng automatic rifle
【自动承保】 zìdòng chéngbǎo automatic cover
【自动打字机】 zìdòng dǎzìjī automatic typewriter
【自动电话】 zìdòng diànhuà automatic telephone; dial service
【自动扶梯】 zìdòng fútī escalator
【自动化】 zìdònghuà automation
【自动换挡】 zìdòng huàndǎng 〈*Auto*〉 fluid drive
【自动交换机】 zìdòng jiāohuànjī automatic exchange
【自动控制】 zìdòng kòngzhì automatic control
【自动门】 zìdòngmén auto gate; barrier gate
【自动铅笔】 zìdòng qiānbǐ propelling pencil
【自动摄影机】 zìdòng shèyǐngjī photomaton; automatic camera
【自动售票机】 zìdòng shòupiàojī ticket vendor
【自动提款机】 zìdòng tíkuǎnjī automated teller machine (ATM)
【自动洗碗机】 zìdòng xǐwǎnjī an automatic dishwasher
【自动险】 zìdòngxiǎn voluntary insurance
【自动线】 zìdòngxiàn transfer machine
【自动卸货卡车】 zìdòng xièhuò kǎchē dump truck; tip truck
【自动音量控制】 zìdòng yīnliàng kòngzhì automatic volume control
【自动装配线】 zìdòng zhuāngpèixiàn automatic assembly line
【自发】 zìfā spontaneous
【自发势力】 zìfā shìlì spontaneous influence
【自发性】 zìfāxìng spontaneity
【自肥】 zìféi enrich oneself by misappropriating funds or material; fatten oneself; feather one's nest
【自费】 zìfèi at one's own expense
【自费出版】 zìfèi chūbǎn vanity publication
【自费生】 zìfèishēng self-funded student; paying student
【自焚】 zìfén self burning
【自封】 zìfēng **1.** (自命) proclaim oneself: 她～为专家。She proclaimed herself an expert. **2.** (限制自己) confine oneself; isolate oneself: 故步～ stand still and refuse to make progress; be complacent and conservative
【自负】 zìfù **1.** (负责) be responsible for one's own action **2.** (自以为对不起) think highly of oneself; be conceited
【自负盈亏】 zìfù yíng-kuī assume sole responsibility for its profits or losses
【自甘堕落】 zìgān-duòluò abandon oneself to vice; wallow in degeneration
【自高自大】 zìgāo-zìdà self-important; conceited; arrogant
【自告奋勇】 zìgào-fènyǒng offer to undertake; volunteer
【自耕农】 zìgēngnóng owner peasant; landholding peasant
【自攻螺钉】 zìgōng luódīng self-tapping screw
【自供】 zìgòng confess
【自供状】 zìgòngzhuàng confession
【自古】 zìgǔ since the ancient times: ～以来 ever since the ancient times
【自顾不暇】 zìgù-bùxiá be unable even to fend for oneself; be busy enough with one's own affairs
【自豪】 zìháo have a proper sense of pride or dignity; be proud of sth.: 母亲为儿子的成功而～。The mother gloried in her son's success.
【自画像】 zìhuàxiàng self-portrait
【自毁】 zìhuǐ self-destruct
【自毁装置】 zìhuǐ zhuāngzhì self-destruct device
【自己】 zìjǐ oneself: ～动手 use one's own

hands

【自己人】 zìjǐrén people on one's own side; one of us：我们拿他当～。We took him as one of us.

【自给】 zìjǐ self-sufficient; self-supporting：粮食～有余 be more than self-sufficient in grain

【自给自足】 zìjǐ-zìzú self-sufficiency; self-contained and self-sufficient

【自荐】 zìjiàn recommend oneself; offer one's services

【自尽】 zìjìn suicide; commit suicide

【自救】 zìjiù save oneself; provide for and help oneself：生产～ provide for and help oneself by engaging in production

【自居】 zìjū consider oneself to be; pose as：以功臣～ give oneself the airs of a hero

【自觉】 zìjué 1.（自己感觉）be aware of 2.（有觉悟）conscious

【自决】 zìjué self-determination：民族～ national self-determination

【自决权】 zìjuéquán right to self-determination

【自觉性】 zìjuéxìng consciousness

【自觉自愿】 zìjué-zìyuàn voluntarily; willingly; of one's own free will

【自控】 zìkòng automatic control

【自夸】 zìkuā sing one's own praises; crack oneself up

【自来水】 zìláishuǐ 1.（指水）running water; tap water 2.（指设施）equipment in waterworks

【自来水笔】 zìláishuǐbǐ fountain pen

【自来水笔笔尖】 zìláishuǐbǐ bǐjiān nib

【自来水厂】 zìláishuǐchǎng waterworks

【自理】 zìlǐ take care of or provide for oneself：旅费～ pay one's own travelling expenses

【自立】 zìlì stand on one's own feet; support oneself; earn one's own living

【自力更生】 zìlì-gēngshēng regeneration through one's own efforts; self-reliance

【自量】 zìliàng estimate one's own ability or strength：不知～ overrate one's abilities

【自流】 zìliú 1.（自动地流）flow automatically; flow by itself 2.（自由发展）take its natural course; do as one please

【自留地】 zìliúdì plot for family use

【自流灌溉】 zìliú guàngài 〈*Agric.*〉 gravity irrigation

【自满】 zìmǎn complacent; self-satisfied

【自鸣得意】 zìmíng-déyì show self-satisfaction; be very pleased with oneself; preen oneself

【自命】 zìmìng consider oneself; regard oneself as：～不凡 consider oneself no ordinary being; have an unduly high opinion of oneself; think no end of oneself

【自谋出路】 zìmóu-chūlù find one's own means of livelihood; seek jobs on their own

【自馁】 zìněi have no confidence in oneself

【自拍机】 zìpāijī 〈*Photog.*〉 self-timer; autotimer

【自欺欺人】 zìqī-qīrén deceive oneself as well as others

【自强不息】 zìqiáng-bùxī make unremitting efforts to improve oneself; constantly strive to become stronger

【自取灭亡】 zìqǔ-mièwáng court destruction; take the road to one's doom

【自然】 zìrán 1.（自然界）natural world; nature 2.（自由发展）naturally; in the ordinary course of events：听其～ let things take their own course 3.（理所当然）of course; naturally：她认为这是～而然的事。She took it as a matter of course. 4.（不勉强）at ease; natural; free from affectation：笑得很～ smile naturally

【自然保护区】 zìrán bǎohùqū nature preserve; nature reserve

【自然博物馆】 zìrán bówùguǎn museum of natural history

【自然而然】 zìrán'érrán naturally; automatically; of oneself

【自然规律】 zìrán guīlǜ natural law

【自然环境】 zìrán huánjìng natural environment

【自然界】 zìránjiè natural world; nature

【自然科学】 zìrán kēxué natural science

【自然趋势】 zìrán qūshì the natural trend

【自然死亡】 zìrán sǐwáng natural death

【自然损耗】 zìrán sǔnhào natural loss

【自然淘汰】 zìrán táotài survival of the fittest

【自然通风】 zìrán tōngfēng natural draft
【自然现象】 zìrán xiànxiàng natural phenomena
【自然选择】 zìrán xuǎnzé 〈*Biol*.〉natural selection
【自然灾害】 zìrán zāihài natural calamity
【自然增长率】 zìrán zēngzhǎnglǜ natural rate of growth
【自然主义】 zìrán zhǔyì naturalism
【自然资源】 zìrán zīyuán natural resources
【自燃】 zìrán spontaneous combustion
【自认晦气】 zìrèn-huìqì accept bad luck without complaint; grin and bear it
【自如】 zìrú 〈*written*〉freely; smoothly; with facility: 运用～ handle and use with skill
【自若】 zìruò self-possessed; composed; calm and at ease: 神态～ appear calm and at ease
【自杀】 zìshā commit suicide; take one's own life: 未遂～ a would-be suicide
【自伤】 zìshāng self injure
【自上而下】 zìshàng'érxià from above to below; from top to bottom
【自身】 zìshēn self; oneself
【自身免疫】 zìshēn miǎnyì autoimmunity
【自食其果】 zìshí-qíguǒ eat one's own bitter fruit; reap what one has sown
【自食其力】 zìshí-qílì support oneself by one's own labor; earn one's own living
【自始至终】 zìshǐ-zhìzhōng from start to finish; from beginning to end
【自恃】 zìshì be self-assured for having sth. or sb. to rely on; count on; capitalize on: ～有靠山 count on sb's backing
【自视】 zìshì consider oneself: ～甚高 think highly of oneself
【自是】 zìshì naturally; of course
【自首】 zìshǒu 1.(投案) voluntarily surrender oneself; confess one's crime; give oneself up: 投案～ surrender oneself to the police or judicial department 2.(投敌) make a political recantation; surrender to the enemy
【自述】 zìshù an account in one's own words
【自私】 zìsī selfish; self-centered
【自私自利】 zìsī-zìlì self-centered; egotistic
【自讨苦吃】 zìtǎokǔchī ask for trouble
【自讨没趣】 zìtǎo-méiqù invite ridicule rebuff; make oneself unwelcome
【自停装置】 zìtíng zhuāngzhì autostopper; automatic stop arrangement
【自投罗网】 zìtóuluówǎng hurl oneself willingly into the net; bite the hook
【自卫】 zìwèi defend oneself; self-defense
【自卫行动】 zìwèi xíngdòng an act in self-defense
【自卫战争】 zìwèi zhànzhēng war of self-defense
【自慰】 zìwèi console oneself: 聊以～ just to console oneself
【自问】 zìwèn 1.(问自己) ask oneself; examine oneself: 反躬～ examine one's conscience 2.(自己衡量) reach a conclusion after weighing a matter: ～没有做错事。Upon self-examination, I can flatter myself that I have done no wrong.
【自我】 zìwǒ self; oneself
【自我保护意识】 zìwǒ bǎohù yì·shí sense of self-protection
【自我辩解】 zìwǒ biànjiě self-justification
【自我表现】 zìwǒ biǎoxiàn self-expression
【自我成就需要】 zìwǒ chéngjiù xūyào need for self-actualization
【自我吹嘘】 zìwǒ chuīxū self-glorification
【自我改造】 zìwǒ gǎizào self-remolding
【自我检查】 zìwǒ jiǎnchá self-examination; introspection
【自我教育】 zìwǒ jiàoyù self-education
【自我批评】 zìwǒ pīpíng self-criticism
【自我实现】 zìwǒ shíxiàn self-actualization; self-realization
【自我完善】 zìwǒ wánshàn self-perfection
【自我牺牲】 zìwǒ xīshēng self-sacrifice
【自我欣赏】 zìwǒ xīnshǎng self-appreciation; self-admiration
【自我中心】 zìwǒ zhōngxīn self-centeredness
【自习】 zìxí study by oneself in scheduled time or free time
【自习时间】 zìxí shíjiān time for individual study
【自下而上】 zìxià'érshàng from bottom to top; from below
【自相残杀】 zìxiāng-cánshā kill each other; cause death to one another

【自相矛盾】 zìxiāng-máodùn contradict oneself; be self-contradictory

【自新】 zìxīn turn over a new leaf; make a fresh start: 改过～ correct one's errors and make a fresh start; turn over a new leaf

【自信】 zìxìn self-confident

【自信心】 zìxìnxīn self-confidence; confidence in oneself

【自行】 zìxíng 1.(自己做) by oneself: 请～解决。Please settle it by yourself. 2.(自动) of oneself; of one's own accord; voluntarily 3.〈*Astron*.〉 proper motion

【自行车】 zìxíngchē bicycle; bike ‖ 自行车运动员 cyclist; rider

【自行车赛】 zìxíngchēsài 〈*Sports*〉 cycle racing: 公路～ circuit race

【自行车赛车场】 zìxíngchē sàichēchǎng cycling track; cycle track

【自行车专用道】 zìxíngchē zhuānyòngdào bike route

【自行车追逐赛】 zìxíngchē zhuīzhúsài pursuit race; chase race

【自行火炮】 zìxíng huǒpào self-propelled gun

【自行其是】 zìxíng-qíshì act as one thinks fit; go one's own way

【自修】 zìxiū 1.(自习) study by oneself; have selfstudy 2.(自学) study on one's own; study independently

【自诩】 zìxǔ praise oneself; crack oneself up; would-be: 一个以作家～的人 a would-be writer

【自序】【自叙】 zìxù 1.(自己写的) author's preface; preface 2.(叙述自己生平的文章) autobiographic note; brief account of oneself

【自选】 zìxuǎn 〈*Sports*〉 free; optional

【自选动作】 zìxuǎn dòngzuò optional exercise

【自选商场】 zìxuǎn shāngchǎng self-service market; supermarket

【自学】 zìxué study on one's own; study independently

【自学考试】 zìxué kǎoshì examination for self-educated people

【自言自语】 zìyán-zìyǔ talk to oneself; think aloud; soliloquize

【自已】 zìyǐ self control

【自以为是】 zìyǐwéishì consider oneself in the right; regard oneself as infallible; be opinionated

【自用】 zìyòng 1.(自以为是) obstinately holding to one's own views; opinionated; self-willed: 刚愎～ obstinate; self-opinionated 2.(私人使用) for private use; personal: ～物品 personal effects; personal belongings

【自由】 zìyóu 1.(自由权) freedom; liberty 2.(不受拘束) free; unrestrained: ～散漫 slack; lax in discipline / ～择业 be free to choose jobs

【自由度】 zìyóudù degree of freedom

【自由兑换】 zìyóu duìhuàn 〈*Econ*.〉 convertibility

【自由港】 zìyóugǎng free port

【自由购买力】 zìyóu gòumǎilì discretionary purchasing power

【自由过境】 zìyóu guòjìng free transit

【自由化】 zìyóuhuà liberalization: 资产阶级～ bourgeois liberalization

【自由汇率】 zìyóu huìlǜ free exchange rate

【自由竞争】 zìyóu jìngzhēng free competition

【自由恋爱】 zìyóu liàn'ài freedom to choose one's spouse

【自由贸易】 zìyóu màoyì free trade

【自由贸易区】 zìyóu màoyìqū free trade zone

【自由市场】 zìyóu shìchǎng free market

【自由式摔跤】 zìyóushì shuāijiāo 〈*Sports*〉 free style wrestling

【自由体操】 zìyóu tǐcāo free exercise; floor exercise; free calisthenics

【自由外汇】 zìyóu wàihuì convertible foreign exchange

【自由王国】 zìyóu wángguó realm of freedom

【自由泳】 zìyóuyǒng freestyle (swimming); crawl

【自由主义】 zìyóu zhǔyì liberalism ‖ 自由主义者 liberal

【自由自在】 zìyóu-zìzài leisurely and carefree; free and unrestrained

【自有资金】 zìyǒu zījīn one's own reserves

【自圆其说】 zìyuán-qíshūo make one's statement consistent; justify oneself

【自愿】 zìyuàn voluntary; of one's own accord; of one's own free will: ～做某事 volunteer to do sth.

【自怨自艾】 zìyuàn-zìyì 1.(悔恨) repent and redress one's errors 2.(后悔) be full of remorse

【自在】 zìzài 1.(自由) free; unrestrained: 逍遥～ leisurely and carefree; free from trammels; at liberty to enjoy oneself 2.(安闲舒适) comfortable; at ease: 觉得不～ feel ill at ease

【自责】 zìzé self-accusation

【自找麻烦】 zìzhǎo má·fan be looking for trouble; ask for trouble

【自知】 zìzhī self-knowledge

【自知之明】 zìzhīzhīmíng have a thorough knowledge of oneself

【自治】 zìzhì autonomy; self-government: 民族区域～ regional national autonomy

【自制】 zìzhì 1.(制造) made by oneself 2.(克制) self-control; self-restraint: 失去～ lose self-control

【自治能力】 zìzhì nénglì capacity of self-government

【自治区】 zìzhìqū autonomous region

【自治权】 zìzhìquán autonomy: 享有高度的～ enjoy a high degree of autonomy

【自治条例】 zìzhì tiáolì regulations on the exercise of autonomy

【自治县】 zìzhìxiàn autonomous county

【自治州】 zìzhìzhōu autonomous prefecture

【自重】 zìzhòng 1.(注意自己言行) conduct oneself with dignity; be self-possessed 2.(自身重量) dead weight

【自主】 zìzhǔ act on one's own; decide for oneself; keep the initiative in one's own hands: 独立～ independently and with the initiative in one's own hands

【自主企业】 zìzhǔ qǐyè autonomous enterprise

【自主权】 zìzhǔquán decision-making power

【自助餐】 zìzhùcān buffet; buffet dinner

【自助餐馆】 zìzhù cānguǎn cafeteria

【自助食堂】 zìzhù shítáng automat

【自助洗衣房】 zìzhù xǐyīfáng laundromat

【自传】 zìzhuàn autobiography

【自转】 zìzhuàn 〈*Astron*.〉 rotation

【自走式起重机】 zìzǒushì qǐzhòngjī traveling crane

【自尊】 zìzūn self-respect; self-esteem; proper pride

【自尊心】 zìzūnxīn sense of self respect: 民族～ sense of national pride

【自作聪明】 zìzuò-cōngmíng think oneself clever

【自作多情】 zìzuò-duōqíng imagine oneself as the favorite of one of the opposite sex

【自作主张】 zìzuò-zhǔzhāng act on one's own; decide for oneself; take matter into one's own hand

【自作自受】 zìzuò-zìshòu suffer from one's own actions; as a man sows, so shall he reap; self do; self have

字 (zì) 1.(文字) word; character: 常用～ basic vocabulary; general service words / 繁体～ the original complex form of a simplified Chinese character / 简体～ simplified Chinese character / 异体～ a variant form of a Chinese character 2.(字音) pronunciation 3.(字体) form of a written or printed character; style of handwriting; printing type 4.(书法作品) scripts; writings; calligraphy 5.(字据) receipt; written pledge

【字处理】 zìchùlǐ 〈*Computer*〉 word processing

【字代码】 zìdàimǎ word code

【字典】 zìdiǎn dictionary: 查～ consult a dictionary

【字典纸】 zìdiǎnzhǐ India paper; Bible paper

【字段长度】 zìduàn chángdù 〈*Computer*〉 field length

【字符】 zìfú 〈*Computer*〉 character

【字符串】 zìfúchuàn 〈*Computer*〉 alphabetic string

【字符集】 zìfújí character sets

【字号】 zìhào the name of a shop

【字画】 zìhuà calligraphy and painting

【字迹】 zìjì handwriting; writing

【字间间隔】 zìjiān jiāngé word space

【字节】 zìjié 〈*Computer*〉 byte

【字句】 zìjù words and expressions; writing

【字据】 zìjù written pledge: 立～ give a written pledge

【字块长度】 zìkuài chángdù 〈*Computer*〉 length of block

【字块输出】 zìkuài shūchū 〈*Computer*〉

block output

【字里行间】 zìlǐ-hángjiān between the lines

【字轮】 zìlún print wheel

【字轮式打印机】 zìlúnshì dǎyìnjī wheel printer

【字码】 zìmǎ character code

【字谜】 zìmí a riddle about a character or word

【字面】 zìmiàn literal：照～翻译 translate literally

【字母】 zìmǔ letters of an alphabet；letter

【字母表】 zìmǔbiǎo alphabet

【字母顺序】 zìmǔ shùnxù alphabetical order：词典里的词汇是按～排列的。The words in a dictionary are in alphabetical order.

【字幕】 zìmù captions；subtitles

【字盘】 zìpán 〈*Printing*〉 case

【字数】 zìshù words；number of characters：每分钟～ words per minute；w. p. m.

【字体】 zìtǐ 1.（书写形式）script；typeface 2.（书法派别）style of calligraphy

【字条】 zìtiáo note；brief note

【字帖】 zìtiè copybook

【字形】 zìxíng font

【字样】 zìyàng 1.（字体规范）model of written characters 2.（字句）words；printed words；written words

【字义】 zìyì meaning of a word

【字音】 zìyīn pronunciation

【字斟句酌】 zìzhēn-jùzhuó choose one's words with great care；weigh every word

【字纸篓】 zìzhǐlǒu wastepaper basket；wastebasket

恣（zì） throw off restraint；do as one pleases

【恣情】 zìqíng act emotionally；indulge in passion

【恣意】 zìyì unscrupulous；reckless；unbridled；willful：～任性 do as one feels like it

眦［眥］（zì） canthus；corner of the eye

渍（zì） 1.（浸泡）steep；soak 2.（沾上油污等）be soiled with：～上泥 be soiled with mud / ～上油 be soiled with grease 3.（油污等）stain；sludge：油～ oil sludge

zong

宗（zōng） 1.（祖宗）ancestor：列祖列～ successive generations of ancestors 2.（宗族）clan：同～ of the same clan 3.（宗派）sect；faction；school：正～ orthodox school 4.（宗旨）principal aim；purpose 5.（效法）take as one's model；learn from 6.〈*classifier*〉大～款项 a large sum of money

【宗祠】 zōngcí ancestral temple

【宗法】 zōngfǎ patriarchal clan system

【宗法制度】 zōngfǎ zhìdù patriarch system

【宗教】 zōngjiào religion；religious（adj.）

【宗教冲突】 zōngjiào chōngtū religious clashes

【宗教会议】 zōngjiào huìyì synod

【宗教戒律】 zōngjiào jièlǜ religious taboo

【宗教界】 zōngjiàojiè religious circles

【宗教狂热】 zōngjiào kuángrè religiosity

【宗教派别】 zōngjiào pàibié religious sect

【宗教人士】 zōngjiào rénshì people in religious conscience

【宗教信仰】 zōngjiào xìnyǎng religious belief

【宗教信仰自由】 zōngjiào xìnyǎng zìyóu freedom of religious belief

【宗教仪式】 zōngjiào yíshì religious rites；ritual

【宗派】 zōngpài faction；factional（adj.）；sect；sectarian（adj.）：～活动 factional activities；sectarian activities

【宗派主义】 zōngpài zhǔyì factionalism；factionalist（adj）；sectarianism；sectarian（adj.）

【宗师】 zōngshī great scholar

【宗系】 zōngxì gens

【宗旨】 zōngzhǐ aim；purpose

【宗主国】 zōngzhǔguó suzerain；suzerain state；metropolitan state

【宗主权】 zōngzhǔquán suzerainty

【宗族】 zōngzú 1.（指家族）patriarchal clan 2.（指家族成员）clansman

【宗族观念】 zōngzú guānniàn ancestral idea

【宗族纠纷】 zōngzú jiūfēn clan dispute

综（zōng） put together；sum up：～上所述 to sum up

【综观】 zōngguān make a comprehensive survey

【综合】 zōnghé 1.（综合起来）synthesize：～有关资料 synthesize the relevant data 2.

(综合的）synthetical; comprehensive; multiple; composite: ～的研究 a synthetical study

【综合报导】 zōnghé bàodǎo comprehensive dispatch; news roundup

【综合大学】 zōnghé dàxué university; a comprehensive university

【综合管理】 zōnghé guǎnlǐ general management

【综合国力】 zōnghé guólì overall strength of the country

【综合机构】 zōnghé jīgòu complex

【综合经营】 zōnghé jīngyíng all-around development

【综合开发】 zōnghé kāifā the comprehensive exploitation

【综合考察】 zōnghé kǎochá comprehensive survey

【综合利用】 zōnghé lìyòng comprehensive utilization; multi-purpose use

【综合平衡】 zōnghé pínghéng overall balance

【综合所得税】 zōnghé suǒdéshuì consolidated income tax

【综合物价水平】 zōnghé wùjià shuǐpíng general price-level (GPL)

【综合征】 zōnghézhēng syndrome

【综合治理】 zōnghé zhìlǐ tackle a problem in a comprehensive way

【综括】 zōngkuò sum up; put together

【综览】 zōnglǎn a general or comprehensive survey; view generally

【综揽】 zōnglǎn be in overall charge

【综述】 zōngshù summarize; sum up

棕［椶］(zōng) 1.（棕榈）palm 2.（棕毛）palm fiber; coir: ～绳 coir rope

【棕编】 zōngbiān palm fiber weaving

【棕榈】 zōnglǘ palm

【棕榈油】 zōnglǘyóu palm oil

【棕毛】 zōngmáo palm fiber: ～蓑衣 palm rain cape

【棕色】 zōngsè brown

【棕熊】 zōngxióng brown bear

腙(zōng) 〈*Chem.*〉 hydrazone

踪［蹤］(zōng) footprint; track; trace: 跟～ follow the tracks of; trail

【踪迹】 zōngjì trace; track; footprints

【踪影】 zōngyǐng trace; sign: 毫无～ without any trace

鬃(zōng) hair on the neck of a pig, horse, etc.: 马～ horse's mane / 猪～ pig's bristles

【鬃刷】 zōngshuā bristle brush

总［総、總］(zǒng) 1.（总括）assemble; put together; sum up: ～起来说 to sum up 2.（全部;全面）general; overall; total: ～罢工 general strike / ～产量 total output 3.（为首的）chief; head; general: ～参谋长 chief of the general staff / ～经理 general manager 4.（一直）always; invariably 5.（总归;毕竟）anyway; after all; inevitably; sooner or later

【总部】 zǒngbù the head quarters

【总裁】 zǒngcái director general; president

【总参】 zǒngcān 见"总参谋部"

【总参谋部】 zǒngcānmóubù headquarters of the general staff

【总参谋长】 zǒngcānmóuzhǎng chief of the general staff

【总产值】 zǒngchǎnzhí gross output value

【总称】 zǒngchēng 1.（总起来叫）be called by a joint name 2.（总名称）a general designation; a general name

【总成本】 zǒngchéngběn total cost

【总代理】 zǒngdàilǐ 1.（指单位）general agency 2.（指人）general agent

【总代理人】 zǒngdàilǐrén general agent

【总得】 zǒngděi must; have to; be bound to: 无论如何,任务～完成。At any rate the task must be fulfilled.

【总督】 zǒngdū governor

【总队】 zǒngduì 1.（团级的）regiment 2.（师级的）division

【总额】 zǒng'é total; the total amount: 他的资产～达5,000万元。His total capital are 50 millions yuan.

【总而言之】 zǒng'éryánzhī in short; in a word; in brief; to make a long story short

【总方针】 zǒngfāngzhēn general policy; general principle

【总分】 zǒngfēn 〈*Sports*〉 total points; ag-

gregate score
【总干事】 zǒnggànshì secretary-general
【总纲】 zǒnggāng general program; general principles: 宪法的～ the general principles of the constitution
【总攻】 zǒnggōng general offensive
【总工程师】 zǒnggōngchéngshī chief engineer
【总工会】 zǒnggōnghuì federation of trade unions
【总公司】 zǒnggōngsī the parent company
【总共】 zǒnggòng in all; altogether; in the aggregate: 这个班～有 40 名学生。There are altogether 40 students in this class.
【总管】 zǒngguǎn manager
【总归】 zǒngguī anyhow; eventually; after
【总行】 zǒngháng head office: 中国银行～ the Head Office of the Bank of China
【总合同】 zǒnghé·tong macrocontract
【总和】 zǒnghé 1.(全部的数) sum; total; sum total 2.〈*Math*.〉 summation of (符号为 Σ)
【总后】 zǒnghòu 见"总后勤部"
【总后勤部】 zǒnghòuqínbù General Logistics Department
【总汇】 zǒnghuì 1.(指水流) come or flow together 2.(指事物) confluence; concourse; aggregate
【总机】 zǒngjī switchboard; telephone exchange
【总计】 zǒngjì 1.(总起来算) amount to; add up to; total: 观众～达 2 万人。The audience totalled 20,000. 2.〈*Math*.〉 grand total
【总监】 zǒngjiān inspector general; chief inspector
【总结】 zǒngjié 1.(做出结论) sum up; summarize: ～本课的要点 sum up the main points of the lesson 2.(结论) summary; summing up: 作～ make a summary
【总金额】 zǒngjīn'é sum: 保险～ insurance sum / 规定保险～ fix an insurance sum
【总经理】 zǒngjīnglǐ managing director; general manager
【总经销】 zǒngjīngxiāo exclusive distribution
【总开关】 zǒngkāiguān main switch
【总括】 zǒngkuò sum up
【总揽】 zǒnglǎn assume overall responsibility; take on everything: ～大权 have overall authority; assume a dominant role
【总理】 zǒnglǐ premier; prime minister: 国务院～ the Premier of the State Council / 副～ Vice-Premier
【总领事】 zǒnglǐngshì consul general
【总领事馆】 zǒnglǐngshìguǎn consulate general
【总路线】 zǒnglùxiàn the general line
【总面积】 zǒngmiànjī gross area
【总评】 zǒngpíng general comment; general review
【总谱】 zǒngpǔ 〈*Music*〉 score
【总收入】 zǒngshōurù general income
【总收益】 zǒngshōuyì total revenue
【总数】 zǒngshù total; sum total: ～为 400。The figures add up to 400.
【总司令】 zǒngsīlìng commander in chief
【总算】 zǒngsuàn 1.(终于) at long last; finally: 雨季～过去了。The rainy season has ended at last. 2.(大体上) considering everything; all things considered; on the whole: 天气～不坏。On the whole the weather is not bad.
【总体】 zǒngtǐ overall; total: ～规划 overall plan
【总统】 zǒngtǒng president: 副～ vice-president
【总务】 zǒngwù 1.(行政杂务) general affairs; general services: 他管～。He is in charge of the general affairs. 2.(负责总务的人) person in charge of general affairs
【总务处】 zǒngwùchù general affairs division
【总需求量】 zǒngxūqiúliàng aggregate demand
【总循环】 zǒngxúnhuán global cycle
【总预算】 zǒngyùsuàn general budget
【总载重量】 zǒngzǎizhòngliàng gross dead weight
【总则】 zǒngzé general rules; general principles
【总长】 zǒngzhǎng 见"总参谋长"
【总账】 zǒngzhàng ledger; general ledger
【总政】 zǒngzhèng 见"总政治部"
【总政治部】 zǒngzhèngzhìbù general political department

【总之】 zǒngzhī in a word; in short; in brief：天气不好，火车上又很挤，～这是个糟糕的旅行。The weather was bad and the trains were crowded; altogether, it was a bad journey.

【总支】 zǒngzhī general branch：党～书记 secretary of the general Party branch

【总值】 zǒngzhí total value：出口～ gross export value / 进口～ gross import value

【总指挥】 zǒngzhǐhuī 1.（军队的）commander in chief 2.（其他方面的）general director

【总装】 zǒngzhuāng general assembly

【总装备部】 zǒngzhuāngbèibù general armament department

【总装配】 zǒngzhuāngpèi general assembly

【总资产】 zǒngzīchǎn total assets

纵［縱］（zòng） 1.（指南北方向）from north to south：～贯铁路 north-south railway line 2.（竖的）vertical; longitudinal; lengthwise 3.（释放）release; set free：～囚 release a prisoner; set a prisoner free 4.（放任）indulge; let loose; let oneself go：～欲 indulge in sensual pleasures 5.（纵身）jump up; jump into the air 6.（纵然）even if; even though

【纵队】 zòngduì column; file：一路～ column of one person

【纵横】 zònghéng 1.（竖和横）in length and breadth; vertically and horizontally：～交错的铁路网 a crisscross network of railways 2.（奔放自如）with great ease; freely：～驰骋 move about freely and quickly 3.（奔驰无阻）march over unhindered

【纵横捭阖】 zònghéng-bǎihé maneuver among various political groupings

【纵火】 zònghuǒ set on fire; commit arson

【纵火犯】 zònghuǒfàn arsonist

【纵火罪】 zònghuǒzuì crime of setting on fire; offense of arson

【纵酒】 zòngjiǔ drink to excess

【纵览】 zònglǎn look far and wide; scan：～群书 read extensively

【纵目】 zòngmù look as far as one's eyes can see：～远望 gaze far into the distance

【纵情】 zòngqíng to one's heart's content; as much as one likes：～诗酒 give one's mind to poems and grant indulgence to wine

【纵然】 zòngrán even if; even though：～如此 even if it is so

【纵容】 zòngróng connive; wink at：～行为 act of connivance

【纵身】 zòngshēn jump; leap：～上马 leap onto a horse

【纵深】 zòngshēn 〈*Mil.*〉 depth：向～发展 develop in depth

【纵深防御】 zòngshēn fángyù defense in depth

【纵使】 zòngshǐ even if; even though

【纵谈】 zòngtán talk freely：～世事 talk worldly affairs freely

【纵向】 zòngxiàng vertical; from top to bottom

【纵向合并】 zòngxiàng hébìng vertical merger

【纵向联合】 zòngxiàng liánhé vertical integration

【纵向一体化】 zòngxiàng yītǐhuà vertical integration

【纵欲】 zòngyù give way to one's carnal desires; indulge in sensual pleasures：～无度 indulge in carnal pleasure without restraint

粽［糉］（zòng）

【粽子】 zòng·zi a pyramid-shaped dumpling made of glutinous rice wrapped in bamboo or reed leaves

ZOU

走（zǒu） 1.（走动）walk; go：向前～ walk straight ahead / 请这边～。Go this way, please. / 这小孩还不会～。The baby cannot walk yet. 2.（跑）run; move：奔～相告 run around spreading the news 3.（离开）leave; go away：他们7点钟来的，10点钟～了。They came at seven and went at ten. / 我得～了。I must be going now.（在别人家作客时的告辞用语）4.（探望）visit; call on：～亲戚 call on relatives 5.（通过；由）through; from 6.（改变原样）depart from the original：～样 go out of form; lose shape 7.（运转）go; run; work：你的表在～吗？Is your watch going? 8.（死）die; go：他的妻子先～了。His wife went first. 9.〈*exclamation*〉

Get moving!

【走步】 zǒubù 〈*Basketball*〉 walk; walking (n.)

【走道】 zǒudào **1.** (人走的道) pavement; sidewalk **2.** (走路) walk

【走电】 zǒudiàn short circuit

【走动】 zǒudòng **1.** (行走) walk about; stretch one's legs: 在公园里～～ stretch one's legs in the park **2.** (拜访) visit each other: 这两家过去常～。The two families used to visit each other quite often.

【走读】 zǒudú attend a day school

【走读生】 zǒudúshēng day student; nonresident student

【走访】 zǒufǎng **1.** (访问) interview; have an interview with **2.** (拜访) pay a visit to; go and see

【走风】 zǒufēng let out a secret; leak out a message

【走钢丝】 zǒugāngsī wirewalking; ropewalking ‖ 走钢丝者 wire-walker; rope-walker

【走狗】 zǒugǒu running dog; lackey; flunkey; stooge; servile follower

【走过场】 zǒu guòchǎng do sth. as a mere formality; go through the motions; do sth. perfunctorily or superficially

【走合】 zǒuhé break in; run in: 我这车还在～,所以不能开快。I'm still breaking the car in, so I won't drive fast.

【走红】 zǒuhóng be flourish; be in luck; be in favor; have good luck

【走后门】 zǒu hòumén get in by the back door; secure advantages through pull or influence

【走火】 zǒuhuǒ **1.** (枪走火) discharge; go off by accident: 枪～了。The gun went off by accident. **2.** (电线跑电) sparking **3.** (说话过头) go too far in what one says; put sth. too strongly; overstate **4.** (失火) be on fire; take fire

【走开】 zǒukāi Away with you!: 让他～! Away with him!

【走廊】 zǒuláng corridor; passage; passageway

【走漏】 zǒulòu **1.** (泄漏) leak out; divulge: ～风声 leak information **2.** (走私漏税) smuggling and tax evasion

【走露】 zǒulù leak out; divulge

【走路】 zǒulù walk; go on foot

【走马看花】 zǒumǎ-kànhuā look at flowers while riding on horseback; gain a superficial understanding through cursory observation

【走马上任】 zǒumǎ-shàngrèn go to take up office; go to one's post

【走南闯北】 zǒunán-chuǎngběi roam all over the country; travel extensively

【走俏】 zǒuqiào sell well; be in great demand

【走人】 zǒurén go away; leave

【走失】 zǒushī wander away; be lost; be missing

【走时】 zǒushí keep time: ～准 keep good time

【走兽】 zǒushòu beast; quadruped; four-footed animal

【走私】 zǒusī smuggle

【走私案件】 zǒusī ànjiàn smuggling case

【走私犯】 zǒusīfàn smuggler

【走私集团】 zǒusī jítuán smuggling ring

【走私军火】 zǒusī jūnhuǒ gun running ‖ 走私军火者 gun runner

【走私罪】 zǒusīzuì offense of smuggling

【走投无路】 zǒutóu-wúlù have no way out; be in an impasse; come to the end of one's tether

【走向】 zǒuxiàng **1.** (延伸方向) run; trend; alignment **2.** (发展) move towards; head for; be on the way to: ～光明 move towards the light **3.** 〈*Geol.*〉 strike: 矿层～ seam strike

【走形】 zǒuxíng be out of shape

【走形式】 zǒu xíngshì do sth. as a mere formality; go through the motions; do sth. perfunctorily or superficially

【走穴】 zǒuxué moonlight; moonlighting (n.)

【走样】 zǒuyàng go awry; go out of form; be different from what is expected or intended: 计划走了样。The plan have gone away.

【走运】 zǒuyùn be in luck; have good luck: 他真～。He is lucky indeed.

【走卒】 zǒuzú pawn; cat's-paw; lackey;

stooge

【走嘴】 zǒuzuǐ make a slip of the tongue; let slip an inadvertent remark

奏(zòu) 1.(演奏) play; perform; strike up: 独～ solo / 二重～ duet / ～国歌 play the national anthem 2.(取得) achieve; produce

【奏捷】 zòujié win a battle; score a success

【奏鸣曲】 zòumíngqǔ 〈*Music*〉 sonata: 小～ sonatina

【奏效】 zòuxiào prove effective; be successful; get the desired result

【奏乐】 zòuyuè play music; strike up a tune

揍(zòu) hit; strike

zu

租(zū) 1.(租用) rent; hire; charter: ～房 rent a house / ～一辆大客车 hire a bus / ～车自己驾驶 self-drive 2.(出租) rent out; let out; lease: 本市出～的房屋不多。There are not many rentals available in this city. 3.(租金) rent 4.(田赋) land tax

【租船】 zūchuán chartering

【租船代理】 zūchuán dàilǐ chartering agent

【租船合同】 zūchuán hé·tong contract of affreightment

【租船契约】 zūchuán qìyuē charter party

【租船人】 zūchuánrén charterer

【租船市场】 zūchuán shìchǎng chartering market

【租船委托书】 zūchuán wěituōshū chartering order

【租佃】 zūdiàn rent out land to tenants

【租购】 zūgòu hire purchase: ～业务 hire purchase finance

【租户】 zūhù 1.(租房的人) tenant; lessee; leaseholder 2.(租物品的人) hirer

【租界】 zūjiè concession

【租借】 zūjiè rent; hire; lease

【租借地】 zūjièdì leased territory; leasehold

【租借期限】 zūjiè qīxiàn time limit of the lease

【租借人】 zūjièrén leaseholder; lessee; tenant; hirer

【租借条件】 zūjiè tiáojiàn lease terms

【租金】 zūjīn rent; rental

【租赁】 zūlìn 1.(租用) rent; hire; charter: 2.(出租) rent out; let out; lease

【租赁合同】 zūlìn hé·tong contract of tenancy; lease contract

【租赁贸易】 zūlìn màoyì renting trade

【租赁业务】 zūlìn yèwù charter business

【租期】 zūqī lease term

【租税】 zūshuì land tax and other levies

【租用】 zūyòng rent; hire; take on lease

【租与】 zūyǔ grant

【租约】 zūyuē lease: ～的延续 continuation of tenancies / 取消～ cancel the deed of rental

足(zú) 1.(脚;腿) foot; leg: 赤～ barefoot 2.(足够) sufficient; enough; ample: 干劲十～ be full of vigor / 我们为度假带～食品。We took adequate food for the holiday. 3.(足足) full; as much as 4.(足以) enough; sufficient: 微不～道 not worth mentioning

【足本】 zúběn an unabridged version

【足不出户】 zúbùchūhù never leave one's home

【足部反射疗法】 zúbù fǎnshè liáofǎ reflexology

【足赤】 zúchì pure gold

【足够】 zúgòu enough; ample; sufficient: 有～的时间做这项工作 have enough time to do this work / 我们有～的钱去旅游。We have ample money for the journey.

【足迹】 zújì footmark; footprint; track

【足见】 zújiàn it serves to show; one can well perceive: ～这种意见是不对的。It shows that such opinion is not correct.

【足金】 zújīn pure gold; solid gold

【足龄】 zúlíng full age

【足球】 zúqiú 1.〈*Sports*〉 soccer; football; association football: 美国式～ American football / 英国式～ soccer; association football 2.(指球) football

【足球场】 zúqiúchǎng field

【足球队】 zúqiúduì football team; eleven

【足球赛】 zúqiúsài football game

【足球运动员】 zúqiú yùndòngyuán football player; footballer

【足色】 zúsè of standard purity

【足坛】 zútán football circles

【足以】 zúyǐ enough; sufficient: ～乱真 good enough to pass for genuine

【足印鉴定】 zúyìn jiàndìng footprint identification

【足月】 zúyuè mature; born after the normal period of gestation

【足智多谋】 zúzhì-duōmóu wise and full of stratagems; resourceful

卒 (zú) **1**.(兵) soldier; private **2**.(完毕) finish; end **3**.(终于) finally; at last: ～偿夙愿 have one's wishes fulfilled at last **4**.(死) die: 暴～ die all of a sudden / 病～ die of an illness **5**.(象棋子) pawn; soldier

【卒业】 zúyè graduate; finish a course of study

【卒子】 zú·zi a soldier; a private

族 (zú) **1**.(家族) clan **2**.(种族; 民族) race; nationality: 汉～ Han nationality **3**.〈*Zool*.〉 family: 猫～ the cat tribe

【族谱】 zúpǔ pedigree of a clan

【族人】 zúrén clansman

【族长】 zúzhǎng the head of a clan; the chief of a clan

诅 (zǔ)

【诅咒】 zǔzhòu curse; swear; imprecate; wish sb. evil: ～某人 swear at sb.; lay a curse upon sb.

阻 (zǔ) hinder; block; obstruct: 畅通无～ without let or hindrance; one can go through unimpeded

【阻碍】 zǔ'ài hinder; block; impede: ～生产力的发展 hinder the development of the productive forces

【阻挡】 zǔdǎng stop; stem; resist; obstruct

【阻断开关】 zǔduàn kāiguān blocking switch

【阻隔】 zǔgé separate; cut off

【阻击】 zǔjī 〈*Mil*.〉 block; check

【阻击战】 zǔjīzhàn 〈*Mil*.〉 blocking action

【阻拦】 zǔlán stop; obstruct; bar the way

【阻力】 zǔlì **1**.(阻碍发展的外力) obstruction; resistance: 冲破～ break through obstruction **2**.〈*Physics*〉 resistance; drag: 空气～ air resistance

【阻流板】 zǔliúbǎn spoiler

【阻挠】 zǔnáo obstruct; thwart; stand in the way; put a spoke in sb's wheel: 百般～ obstruct in every possible way

【阻塞】 zǔsè block; obstruct; clog: 拥挤的车辆～了道路。Heavy traffic blocked the road.

【阻止】 zǔzhǐ prevent; stop; hold back

【阻滞】 zǔzhì stoppage

【阻滞作用】 zǔzhì zuòyòng retardation

组 (zǔ) **1**.(组织) organize; form: ～阁 form a cabinet **2**.(小组) group: 学习～ a study group / 心脏专家～施行了外科手术。A team of heart specialists performed the surgery. **3**.〈*classifier*〉 set; series; battery: 一～邮票 a set of stamps

【组成】 zǔchéng form; make up; compose: 他们～了一个英语初级班。They formed a group for beginners in English.

【组成部分】 zǔchéng bù·fen component part

【组锉】 zǔcuò a set of files

【组稿】 zǔgǎo solicit contributions; commission authors to write on given topics

【组歌】 zǔgē 〈*Music*〉 suite of songs

【组阁】 zǔgé form a cabinet

【组合】 zǔhé **1**.(组织成整体) make up; compose; constitute **2**.(整体) association; combination **3**.〈*Mech*. & *Math*.〉 combination

【组合壁柜】 zǔhé bìguì wall units

【组合柜】 zǔhéguì assembled cabinet

【组合家具】 zǔhé jiājù unit furniture

【组合音响】 zǔhé yīnxiǎng music center; stereo set

【组建】 zǔjiàn form; put together

【组曲】 zǔqǔ 〈*Music*〉 suite

【组团】 zǔtuán form a delegation

【组织】 zǔzhī **1**.(组成) organize; form: ～一个歌咏队 organize a chorus **2**.(组织系统) organization; organized system: 党团～ Party and Youth League organizations **3**.(积存) accumulate: ～货源 accumulate stocks **4**.〈*Textiles*〉 weave: 平纹～ plain weave / 斜纹～ twill weave **5**.〈*Physiol*.〉 tissue: 神经～ nerve tissue

【组织法】 zǔzhīfǎ rules of organization; organic law; constituent act

【组织关系】 zǔzhī guān·xì credentials showing membership in an organization; membership credentials

【组织机构】 zǔzhī jīgòu institutional framework

【组织疗法】 zǔzhī liáofǎ tissue therapy; histotherapy

【组织生活】 zǔzhī shēnghuó regular activities of an organization

【组织条例】 zǔzhī tiáolì organic rules

【组织委员会】 zǔzhī wěiyuánhuì organizing committee

【组装】 zǔzhuāng build up; assembly

【组装生产】 zǔzhuāng shēngchǎn assembly line industries

【组装线】 zǔzhuāngxiàn assembly line

祖 (zǔ) 1.(祖父) grandfather 2.(祖宗) ancestor 3.(首创者) founder; originator

【祖辈】 zǔbèi ancestors; forefathers; ancestry

【祖产】 zǔchǎn property handed down from one's ancestors

【祖传】 zǔchuán handed down from one's ancestors: 他的～财产 his ancestral estates / ～古玩 curios handed down from forefather

【祖传秘方】 zǔchuán mìfāng a family prescription handed down from generation to generation

【祖坟】 zǔfén ancestral grave

【祖父】 zǔfù grandfather

【祖国】 zǔguó one's country; homeland; native land; motherland; fatherland

【祖籍】 zǔjí original family home; ancestral home; the land of one's ancestors

【祖母】 zǔmǔ grandmother

【祖上】 zǔshàng ancestors; forefathers; forbears

【祖师】 zǔshī 1.(学术或技术上的) the founder of a school of learning, a craft, etc. 2.(佛教、道教的) the founder of a sect of Buddhism or Taoism

【祖师爷】 zǔshīyé the founder

【祖孙】 zǔsūn grandparent and grandchild

【祖先】 zǔxiān ancestry; ancestors; forbears; forefathers

【祖宗】 zǔ·zong forefathers; ancestry; forbears

【祖祖辈辈】 zǔzǔ-bèibèi for generations; from generation to generation

zuan

钻[鑽] (zuān) 1.(钻眼) drill; bore: 在墙上～个洞 drill a hole in the wall 2.(穿过; 进入) get into; go through; make one's way into: 老鼠～进了洞。The rat got into the hole. 3.(钻研) study intensively; dig into: ～业务 dig into one's job
(另见"钻"zuàn)

【钻空子】 zuānkòng·zi find a loophole in sth.: 钻法律的空子 find a loophole in the law

【钻牛角尖】 zuān niújiǎojiān 1.(比喻) take unnecessary pains to study an insignificant or insoluble problem; split hairs 2.(行不通) get into a dead end

【钻探】 zuāntàn drilling

【钻探工】 zuāntàngōng driller

【钻探机】 zuāntànjī drilling machine

【钻探设备】 zuāntàn shèbèi drilling equipment

【钻天杨】 zuāntiānyáng 〈*Bot*.〉 lombardy poplar

【钻心】 zuānxīn unbearable; sharp

【钻研】 zuānyán study intensively; dig into: 努力～技术 endeavor to perfect one's skill

【钻营】 zuānyíng curry favor with sb. in authority for personal gain; secure personal gain

纂 (zuǎn) compile; edit: 编～词典 compile a dictionary

【纂修】 zuǎnxiū compile; edit; prepare

钻[鑽] (zuàn) 1.(打眼工具) drill; auger: 风～ pneumatic drill 2.(钻石) diamond; jewel: ～戒 diamond ring 3.(钻眼) bore; drill
(另见"钻"zuān)

【钻床】 zuànchuáng 〈*Mech*.〉 drilling machine; driller

【钻机】 zuànjī (drilling) rig; drilling machine

【钻井】 zuànjǐng well drilling

【钻井船】 zuànjǐngchuán offshore drilling rig

【钻井队】 zuànjǐngduì drilling crew; drilling team

【钻井工人】 zuànjǐng gōngrén driller

【钻井记录】 zuànjǐng jìlù drill log

【钻石】 zuànshí 1.(金刚石) diamond: 未经

琢磨的～ rough diamond 2.(宝石) jewel

【钻塔】 zuàntǎ 〈*Mineral*.〉 boring tower; derrick

【钻台】 zuàntái drilling platform

【钻头】 zuàntóu bit; drill bit

攥 (zuàn) grip

zui

嘴 (zuǐ) 1.(口) mouth: 张～ open one's mouth 2.(像嘴的东西) anything shaped or functioning like a mouth: 茶壶～ the spout of a teapot

【嘴巴】 zuǐ·ba 1.(嘴部附近) face: 打～ slap sb. in the face; box sb's ears 2.(口) mouth

【嘴笨】 zuǐbèn inarticulate; clumsy of speech

【嘴馋】 zuǐchán fond of good food

【嘴唇】 zuǐchún lip

【嘴尖】 zuǐjiān sharp-tongued

【嘴角】 zuǐjiǎo corners of the mouth; angle of the mouth

【嘴紧】 zuǐjǐn tight-lipped; close-mouthed; secretive

【嘴快】 zuǐkuài have a loose tongue

【嘴懒】 zuǐlǎn not incline to talk much; taciturn

【嘴脸】 zuǐliǎn look; features; countenance: 丑恶～ ugly features

【嘴皮子】 zuǐpí·zi 〈*colloq*.〉 lips: 耍～ talk glibly

【嘴碎】 zuǐsuì loquacious; garrulous

【嘴甜】 zuǐtián 〈*colloq*.〉 ingratiating in speech

【嘴严】 zuǐyán able to keep a secret; discreet in speech; cautious about speech

【嘴硬】 zuǐyìng stubborn and reluctant to admit mistakes or defeats: ～心软 firm in speech and soft in heart

最 (zuì) most: ～可靠的同盟者 the most reliable ally / 速度～快 the fastest

【最初】 zuìchū initial; first: ～阶段 the initial stage / ～印象 the first impression

【最大】 zuìdà maximum: ～概率 maximum probability / ～功率 maximum power / ～流量 maximum stream flow

【最低】 zuìdī lowest; minimum; rock-bottom

【最低罚款额】 zuìdī fákuǎn'é minimum fine

【最低纲领】 zuìdī gānglǐng minimum program

【最低价格】 zuìdī jiàgé the lowest price; floor price

【最低年龄】 zuìdī niánlíng minimum age

【最低限度】 zuìdī xiàndù the lowest limit; at least

【最多】 zuìduō at most; maximum

【最高】 zuìgāo highest; supreme; tallest: ～国家权力机关 the highest organ of state power

【最高法律效力】 zuìgāo fǎlǜ xiàolì supreme legal authority

【最高纲领】 zuìgāo gānglǐng maximum program

【最高国务会议】 zuìgāo guówù huìyì the Supreme State Conference

【最高级】 zuìgāojí 1.(等级最高的) highest; summit: ～会谈 top-level talks; summit talks / ～会议 summit conference 2. 〈*Gram*.〉 the superlative degree

【最高价格】 zuìgāo jiàgé ceiling price

【最高年产量】 zuìgāo niánchǎnliàng peak annual output

【最高权力】 zuìgāo quánlì supreme power

【最高速度】 zuìgāo sùdù maximum speed

【最高统帅】 zuìgāo tǒngshuài supreme commander

【最高温度】 zuìgāo wēndù maximum temperature

【最高限额】 zuìgāo xiàn'é ceiling

【最高刑罚】 zuìgāo xíngfá maximum sentence

【最高学府】 zuìgāo xuéfǔ highest seat of learning

【最好】 zuìhǎo 1.(顶好的) best; first-rate: ～的学生 the best student 2.(最好还是) had better; it would be best: 我们今天～留在家里。We'd better stay at home today.

【最后】 zuìhòu final; last; ultimate: ～，我要指出的是… Lastly, I must point out that . . .

【最后成本】 zuìhòu chéngběn final cost

【最后交货日期】 zuìhòu jiāohuò rèqī end delivery date
【最后结论】 zuìhòu jiélùn final submission
【最后条款】 zuìhòu tiáokuǎn final provisions; final articles
【最后通牒】 zuìhòu tōngdié ultimatum; a final dispatch
【最后协定】 zuìhòu xiédìng final agreement
【最后议定书】 zuìhòu yìdìngshū final protocol
【最惠国】 zuìhuìguó most-favored-nation
【最惠国待遇】 zuìhuìguó dàiyù most-favored-nation treatment：延长给中国的～ extend China's most-favored-nation status
【最惠国待遇条款】 zuìhuìguó dàiyù tiáokuǎn most-favored-nation treatment clause
【最基本收费】 zuìjīběn shōufèi cover charge
【最佳】 zuìjiā optimum：育秧的～温度 optimum temperature for seedling nursing
【最近】 zuìjìn 1.（近来）recently; lately; of late：～一期的《中国画报》the current issue of *China Pictorial* 2.（距离最近）nearest 3.（不久）in the near future; soon：她～就要出国。She'll be going abroad soon.
【最适度】 zuìshìdù optimum
【最先】 zuìxiān the first; the earliest
【最小公倍数】 zuìxiǎo gōngbèishù 〈*Math*.〉 LCM; least common multiple; lowest common multiple
【最小公分母】 zuìxiǎo gōngfēnmǔ 〈*Math*.〉 LCD; lowest common denominator; least common denominator
【最新工艺】 zuìxīn gōngyì latest technology
【最新式样】 zuìxīn shìyàng the last word：～轿车 the last word in cars
【最优惠利率】 zuìyōuhuì lìlǜ prime rate
【最终】 zuìzhōng final; ultimate
【最终裁定】 zuìzhōng cáidìng absolute decree
【最终裁决】 zuìzhōng cáijué final ruling
【最终目的地】 zuìzhōng mùdìdì final destination
【最终判决】 zuìzhōng pànjué conclusive judgement

醉（zuì） 1.（酒醉）drunk; intoxicated; tipsy：烂～如泥 be dead drunk 2.（用酒泡制）liquor-saturated; steeped in liquor：～枣 liquor-saturated date
【醉鬼】 zuìguǐ drunkard; sot; inebriate
【醉汉】 zuìhàn drunkard; drunken man
【醉生梦死】 zuìshēng-mèngsǐ live as if intoxicated or dreaming; lead a befuddled life
【醉心】 zuìxīn be bent on; be wrapped up in; be deeply interested in
【醉意】 zuìyì signs or feeling of getting drunk

罪［辠］（zuì） 1.（犯罪）crime; guilt：有～ guilty of a crime; guilty / 没犯～ be guiltless of ... / 被告之～尚有疑问。The guilt of the accused man was in doubt. 2.（归罪）fault; blame：归～于人 put the blame on others 3.（苦难）suffering; pain; hardship：受～ have a hard time; endure suffering
【罪大恶极】 zuìdà-èjí be guilty of the most heinous crimes
【罪恶】 zuì'è crime; evil：～活动 criminal activities
【罪犯】 zuìfàn criminal; offender; culprit
【罪该万死】 zuìgāiwànsǐ be guilty of a crime for which one deserves to die ten thousand deaths; be guilty of a crime for which even death cannot atone
【罪过】 zuì·guo fault; offense; sin
【罪魁】 zuìkuí chief criminal; archcriminal：～祸首 the chief offender and the ring leader
【罪名】 zuìmíng charge; accusation：莫须有的～ groundless charge
【罪孽】 zuìniè wrongdoing that brings retribution; sin
【罪人】 zuìrén guilty person; offender; sinner：千古～ person condemned by history
【罪行】 zuìxíng crime; guilt; offense
【罪有应得】 zuìyǒuyīngdé culpable of punishment; deserve the punishment
【罪责】 zuìzé responsibility for an offense
【罪证】 zuìzhèng evidence of a crime; proof of one's guilt：～确凿 proof of a crime beyond a shadow of a doubt
【罪状】 zuìzhuàng facts about a crime; charges in an indictment

zun

尊（zūn） 1.（地位或辈分高）senior; of a senior generation：～长 elders 2.（敬重）

respect; venerate; honor: 自～ self-respect 3.〈*politeness*〉～夫人 your wife

【尊称】 zūnchēng **1.**(尊敬地称呼) address sb. respectfully **2.**(尊敬的称呼) a respectful form of address; honorific title

【尊崇】 zūnchóng worship; revere; venerate

【尊贵】 zūnguì honorable; respectable; respected

【尊敬】 zūnjìng **1.**(恭敬) respect; honor; esteem: 非常～某人 hold sb. in the greatest esteem **2.**(可尊敬的) distinguished

【尊师重教】 zūnshī-zhòngjiào respect teachers and value education

【尊严】 zūnyán dignity; honor: 人格～ dignity of human personality

【尊长】 zūnzhǎng elders and betters

【尊重】 zūnzhòng **1.**(尊敬) respect; honor; esteem: 大家很～他。He was much esteemed. **2.**(严肃对待) esteem; value: ～历史 value the history / ～经济规律 respect economics laws **3.**(庄重) decent; respectable: 请放～点。Behave yourself.

遵 (zūn) abide by; obey; observe; follow: ～纪守法 observing discipline and obeying the law

【遵从】 zūncóng defer to; comply with; follow: ～法令 act in accordance with the law

【遵命】 zūnmìng 〈*politeness*〉 comply with your wish; obey your command

【遵守】 zūnshǒu observe; abide by; comply with: ～合约 observe the agreement / ～时间 be on time / ～诺言 keep one's words; stick to one's words / ～俱乐部的章程 abide by the club rules

【遵循】 zūnxún follow; abide by; adhere to

【遵照】 zūnzhào obey; conform to; comply with; act in accordance with: ～某人的劝告 act on sb's advice

鳟 (zūn) 〈*Zool.*〉 trout

【鳟鱼】 zūnyú trout

zuo

作 (zuō) workshop
(另见"作"zuò)

【作坊】 zuōfāng workshop

嘬 (zuō) suck

【嘬瘪子】 zuō biě·zi be embarrassed

昨 (zuó) yesterday: ～晚 yesterday evening; last night

【昨天】 zuótiān yesterday

琢 (zuó)
(另见"琢"zhuó)

【琢磨】 zuó·mo turn sth. over in one's mind; ponder: ～问题 turn a problem over in one's mind

左 (zuǒ) **1.**(左边) the left side; the left: 向～转 turn to the left **2.**(邪;偏) queer; unorthodox; heretical **3.**(错) wrong; incorrect **4.**(相反) different; contrary; opposite: 意见相～ hold different views **5.**(激进的) the Left: ～派 the Left; the left wing

【左岸】 zuǒ'àn left bank

【左边】 zuǒbiān the left; the left side

【左边锋】 zuǒbiānfēng 〈*Football*〉 outside left; left wing

【左道旁门】 zuǒdào-pángmén **1.**(指宗教派别) heretical sect; heterodox school **2.**(异端邪说) heresy; heterodoxy

【左顶骨】 zuǒdǐnggǔ 〈*Anat.*〉 left parietal bone

【左锋】 zuǒfēng 〈*Basketball*〉 left forward

【左顾右盼】 zuǒgù-yòupàn glance right and left

【左后卫】 zuǒhòuwèi 〈*Football*〉 left back

【左近】 zuǒjìn nearby

【左轮】 zuǒlún revolver; revolver pistol

【左面】 zuǒmiàn the left side; the left-hand side

【左内锋】 zuǒnèifēng 〈*Football*〉 inside left

【左派】 zuǒpài **1.**(指集团) the Left; the left wing **2.**(指个人) Leftist

【左撇子】 zuǒpiě·zi left-handed person; left-hander; lefty

【左前卫】 zuǒqiánwèi 〈*Football*〉 left halfback; left half

【左倾】 zuǒqīng **1.**(思想激进的) left-leaning; progressive; inclined towards the revolution **2.**(盲动的) 'Left' deviation

【左肾】 zuǒshèn 〈*Anat.*〉 left kidney

【左手】 zuǒshǒu **1.**(指手) the left hand **2.**(左边) the left; the left side

【左首】 zuǒshǒu the left side; the left-hand side

【左思右想】 zuǒsī-yòuxiǎng think from different angles; turn sth. over in one's mind

【左舷】 zuǒxián (船的) larboard

【左心房】 zuǒxīnfáng 〈*Anat*.〉 left atrium

【左心室】 zuǒxīnshì 〈*Anat*.〉 left ventricle

【左翼】 zuǒyì **1**.(指作战部队) left wing; left flank **2**.(指激进派) the left wing; the Left **3**.〈*Aeron*.〉 port wing

【左翼分子】 zuǒyì fènzǐ Leftist; Left-winger

【左右】 zuǒyòu **1**.(左右两方面) the left and right sides: ～摇摆 vacillate now to the left and now to the right **2**.(大约) about; or so; or thereabouts: 两个月～ two months or so / 十点钟左右 at 10 o'clock or thereabouts / 我们需要二百吨～。We need about 200 metric tons. **3**.(支配; 操纵) master; control; influence: 受人～ be controlled by sb. / ～局势 control the situation **4**.(随从) entourage; retinue; attendants

【左右逢源】 zuǒyòu-féngyuán **1**.(得心应手) be able to achieve success one way or another **2**.(办事圆滑) gain advantage from both sides

【左右开弓】 zuǒyòu-kāigōng shoot first with one hand, then with the other; shoot first to one side, then to the other; use first one hand and then the other in quick succession

【左右手】 zuǒyòushǒu right-hand man; valuable assistant

【左右为难】 zuǒ-yòu wéinán in a dilemma; in an awkward predicament

【左证】 zuǒzhèng evidence; proof

【左转弯标志】 zuǒzhuǎnwān biāozhì lane arrow for turning left

【左座驾驶】 zuǒzuò jiàshǐ left hand drive

佐 (zuǒ) **1**.(辅佐) assist: ～理 assist sb. with a task **2**.(辅佐别人者) assistant

【佐餐】 zuǒcān be eaten together with bread; go with bread

【佐餐酒】 zuǒcānjiǔ table wine

【佐理】 zuǒlǐ help sb. with a task

【佐证】 zuǒzhèng evidence; proof

撮 (zuǒ) 〈*classifier*〉 一～头发 lock; a strand of hair

(另见"撮"cuō)

作 (zuò) **1**.(起) rise; get up: 日出而～ get up at sunrise **2**.(写作) write; compose: ～诗 write a poem **3**.(工作) do; make **4**.(作品) work; writings **5**.(装作) pretend; affect: 故～镇静 pretend to be composed **6**.(当作) regard as; take sb. or sth. for: 把敌人看～朋友 regard an enemy as a friend; take an enemy for a friend **7**.(当) act as; be; become: ～向导 act as a guide **8**.(发作) feel; have: ～冷 feel a chill **9**.(从事) do

(另见"作"zuō)

【作案】 zuò'àn commit a crime or an offense

【作案现场】 zuò'àn xiànchǎng scene of crime

【作案凶器】 zuò'àn xiōngqì weapon of offense

【作罢】 zuòbà drop; relinquish; give up

【作伴】 zuòbàn keep company

【作保】 zuòbǎo be sb's guarantor; go bail for sb.; sponsor sb.

【作保人】 zuòbǎorén give security

【作保证人】 zuò bǎozhèngrèn guarantee

【作弊】 zuòbì practice fraud; cheat; indulge in corrupt practices: 在考试中～ cheat in an examination

【作操】 zuòcāo do gymnastics; do calisthenics; do exercises

【作词】 zuòcí write words

【作答】 zuòdá give a reply; answer

【作抵押】 zuò dǐyā on mortgage

【作对】 zuòduì set oneself against; oppose

【作恶】 zuò'è do evil: ～多端 do all kinds of evil; be steeped in iniquity

【作法】 zuòfǎ **1**.(行法术) resort to magic arts; practice magic **2**.(做法) way of doing things **3**.(文章作法) art of composition

【作废】 zuòfèi become invalid: 过期～ become invalid after a specified date / 声明～ declare sth. invalid

【作风】 zuòfēng style; style of work; way: 实事求是的～ a practical and realistic way of doing things / ～正派 act in a decent and upright way

【作梗】 zuògěng obstruct; hinder; create difficulties

【作古】 zuògǔ die; pass away

【作怪】 zuòguài do mischief; make trouble

【作家】 zuòjiā writer

【作家协会】 zuòjiā xiéhuì the Writers' Union
【作假】 zuòjiǎ 1.(故作客套) behave affectedly 2.(伪造) falsify; counterfeit 3.(耍花招) cheat; play tricks
【作价】 zuòjià fix a price for sth.; evaluate
【作奸犯科】 zuòjiān-fànkē violate the law and commit crimes; commit offenses against law and discipline
【作茧自缚】 zuòjiǎn-zìfù in a cocoon around oneself; get enmeshed in a web of one's own spinning
【作践】 zuòjiàn 1.(糟蹋) spoil; waste 2.(诽谤他人) disparage; run sb. down 3.(侮辱) humiliate; insult
【作客】 zuòkè stay with sb. as guest: ~他乡 stay away in a strange land
【作乐】 zuòlè make merry; enjoy oneself; have a good time: 寻欢~ seek pleasure and make merry
【作料】 zuòliào condiments; seasoning
【作乱】 zuòluàn stage an armed rebellion; rise in revolt
【作难】 zuònán 1.(为难) feel embarrassed; feel awkward 2.(难为人) make things difficult for sb.
【作孽】 zuònìe do evil; commit a sin
【作弄】 zuònòng tease; make a fool of; play a trick on; poke fun at
【作呕】 zuò'ǒu 1.(要呕吐) feel like vomiting; feel sick 2.(使人厌恶) disgusting; loathsome
【作陪】 zuòpéi help entertain the guest of honor; be invited along with the chief guest
【作品】 zuòpǐn works: 经典~ classic works
【作曲】 zuòqǔ write music; compose
【作曲家】 zuòqǔjiā composer
【作色】 zuòsè show signs of anger; get worked up: 愤然~ flush with indignation
【作死】 zuòsǐ seek death; take the road to ruin; look for trouble
【作速】 zuòsù hurry up; make haste
【作祟】 zuòsuì 1.(鬼神为难人) haunt 2.(捣乱) make mischief; cause trouble; exercise evil influence
【作态】 zuòtài pose; affect: 忸怩~ put on a pose of affection
【作痛】 zuòtòng have a pain
【作威作福】 zuòwēi-zuòfú tyrannically abuse one's power; ride roughshod over others; act like a tyrant
【作为】 zuòwéi 1.(行为) conduct; deed; action: 他的~是无可非议的。His conduct was blameless. 2.(作出成绩) accomplish; do sth. worthwhile: 无所~ attempt nothing and accomplish nothing 3.(可以做的事情) accomplishment; achievement: 有所~ have made some achievements 4.(当作) regard as; look on as; take for: ~知己 take sb. for a close friend 5.(就…来说) as; being
【作伪】 zuòwěi fake; make an imitation; forge
【作伪证】 zuòwěizhèng forswear; give false testimony ‖ 作伪证者 perjurer
【作文】 zuòwén 1.(写文章) write a composition 2.(文章) composition
【作物】 zuòwù crop
【作息】 zuòxī work and rest: 按时~ work and rest according to schedule
【作息制度】 zuòxī zhìdù work and rest regulations
【作训服】 zuòxùnfú battle and training wear
【作业】 zuòyè 1.(功课) school assignment; home work 2.(军事或生产的) work; task; operation; production
【作业量】 zuòyèliàng workload
【作揖】 zuòyī make a bow with hands folded in front
【作用】 zuòyòng 1.(产生影响) act on; affect 2.(指活动) action; function: 酸对金属所起的~ the action of acid on metal 3.(影响;效果) effect: 起~ take effect 4.(用意) intention; motive
【作乐】 zuòyuè play music
【作贼心虚】 zuòzéi-xīnxū uneasy lies the head of one with a guilty conscience
【作战】 zuòzhàn fight; conduct operations; do battle
【作者】 zuòzhě author; writer
【作证】 zuòzhèng testify; give evidence; bear witness: 为某人~ testify on behalf of sb. / 他出庭~。He was asked to testify at the trial.

柞 (zuò) 〈*Bot.*〉 oak

【柞蚕】 zuòcán tussah

【柞蚕丝】 zuòcánsī tussah silk

【柞树】 zuòshù oak; daimyo oak

【柞丝绸】 zuòsīchóu tussah silk; pongee

坐 (zuò) 1.(坐下) sit; take a seat: 就～ take a seat / 那车能舒舒服服地～五个人。The car will sit five people comfortably. 2.(乘;搭) travel by: ～出租汽车去 火车站 take a taxi to the railway station 3.(背对着) have its back towards: 这房子～北朝南。The house faces south. 4.(放) put: 把炒菜锅～在火上 put the frying pan on the fire 5.(下沉) sink; subside 6.(后坐) recoil; kick back

【坐标】 zuòbiāo 〈*Math*.〉 coordinate

【坐标轴】 zuòbiāozhóu coordinate axis

【坐吃山空】 zuòchī-shānkōng sit idle and eat, and in time your whole fortune will be used up

【坐待】 zuòdài 见"坐等"

【坐等】 zuòděng site back and wait

【坐地分赃】 zuòdì-fēnzāng take a share of the spoils without participating personally in the robbery

【坐垫】 zuòdiàn cushion

【坐骨】 zuògǔ 〈*Anat*.〉 ischium

【坐骨神经】 zuògǔ shénjīng 〈*Anat*.〉 sciatic nerve

【坐骨神经痛】 zuògǔ shénjīngtòng 〈*Med*.〉 sciatica; ischialgia

【坐果】 zuòguǒ 〈*Bot*.〉 setting fruit; fruit setting

【坐禁闭】 zuò jìnbì be placed in confinement

【坐井观天】 zuòjǐng-guāntiān look at the sky from the bottom of a well; have a very narrow view

【坐困】 zuòkùn be confined; be walled in; be shut up

【坐牢】 zuòláo be in jail; be imprisoned

【坐冷板凳】 zuò lěngbǎndèng 1.(受冷遇) be cold-shouldered 2.(久等) cool one's heels

【坐力】 zuòlì 〈*Physics*〉 recoil: 无～炮 recoilless gun

【坐立不安】 zuòlì-bù'ān feel uneasy whether sitting or standing; be fidgety; be on tenterhooks

【坐落】 zuòluò be situated; be located: 学校～在小河附近。The school is located near the rivulet.

【坐骑】 zuòqí horse

【坐商】 zuòshāng trademan; shopkeeper

【坐失良机】 zuòshī-liángjī let slip a golden opportunity

【坐视】 zuòshì sit back and watch

【坐视不救】 zuòshì-bùjiù sit back and watch without going to the rescue

【坐探】 zuòtàn agent provocateur

【坐臀】 zuòtún (猪肉部位) leg

【坐位】 zuòwèi 1.(指位置) a place to sit: 给老师留几个～。Reserve several seats for the teachers. 2.(椅子;凳子等) a thing to sit on; seat: 请给她搬个～来。Please get her a seat.

【坐卧不宁】 zuòwò-bùníng be unable to sit down or sleep at ease; feel restless; be on tenterhooks

【坐卧两用沙发】 zuòwò liǎngyòng shāfā sofa bed

【坐席】 zuòxí seat

【坐享其成】 zuòxiǎng-qíchéng sit idle and enjoy the fruits of others' work; reap where one has not sown

【坐药】 zuòyào 〈*Pharm*.〉 suppository

【坐以待毙】 zuòyǐ-dàibì sit still waiting for death; await one's doom; resign oneself to death

【坐以待旦】 zuòyǐdàidàn sit up and wait for daybreak; remain awake till dawn

【坐月子】 zuò yuè·zi confinement in childbirth

【坐镇】 zuòzhèn personally attend to garrison duty; assume personal command

【坐庄】 zuòzhuāng be the banker or dealer

座[坐 1] (zuò) 1.(坐位) seat; place: 入～ be seated 2.(垫东西的座子) stand; pedestal; base: 花瓶～ vase stand 3.(星座) constellation 4.〈*classifier*〉 一～水库 a reservoir

【座舱】 zuòcāng 〈*Aeron*.〉 cockpit

【座次】 zuòcì order of seats; seating arrangements

【座机】 zuòjī passenger plane

【座儿】 zuòr seat; place

【座上客】 zuòshàngkè guest of honor; hon-

ored guest
【座谈】 zuòtán have an informal discussion
【座谈会】 zuòtánhuì forum; symposium
【座位】 zuòwèi seat; place: 有…～的(汽车、飞机等) -seater
【座位垫席】 zuòwèi diànxí seat cover
【座无虚席】 zuòwúxūxí all seats are occupied; there are no empty seats
【座右铭】 zuòyòumíng motto; maxim
【座钟】 zuòzhōng desk clock
【座子】 zuò·zi 1.(垫东西的座子) stand; pedestal; base 2.〈*Bicycle*〉 saddle

做[作](zuò) 1.(制造) make; produce; manufacture 2.(写作) write; compose: ～诗 write a poem 3.(从事) do; act; engage in: ～生意 do business; carry on trade 4.(家庭庆祝) hold a family celebration: ～生日 hold a birthday party 5.(用做) be used as 6.(结成) form or contract a relationship: ～盟友 become allies 7.(担任) be; become: ～教师 be a teacher 8.(烹调) cook; prepare: ～饭 do the cooking; prepare a meal
【做爱】 zuò'ài make love; lovemaking (n.)
【做伴】 zuòbàn keep sb. company; make a companion of
【做到】 zuòdào accomplish; achieve: 说到～ be as good as one's word; abide by one's promise
【做东】 zuòdōng play the host; host sb.; act as host to sb.; one's treat: 这次我～。This is to be my treat.
【做法】 zuòfǎ way of doing or making a thing; method of work; practice
【做工】 zuògōng 1.(从事劳动) do manual work; work 2.(工作质量) workmanship: ～精细 of exquisite workmanship 3.(手工费) charge for the making of sth.
【做官】 zuòguān be an official; secure an official position
【做广告】 zuò guǎnggào advertising: ～是值得的。It pays to advertise.
【做鬼】 zuòguǐ play tricks; play an underhand game; get up to mischief
【做鬼脸】 zuò guǐliǎn make faces; pull a face
【做活儿】 zuòhuór work; do manual labor
【做假账】 zuò jiǎzhàng manipulation of account
【做绝】 zuòjué leave no room for maneuver: 坏事～ perpetrate every kind of villainy
【做客】 zuòkè be a guest
【做礼拜】 zuò lǐbài 〈*Christianity*〉 go to church; be at church
【做买卖】 zuò mǎi·mai do business
【做媒】 zuòméi be a matchmaker
【做梦】 zuòmèng 1.(睡觉做梦) have a dream; dream 2.(比喻幻想) have a pipe dream; daydream: 白日～ daydream
【做人】 zòngrén 1.(待人接物) conduct oneself; behave: 会～ get along with people quite well 2.(当正派人) be an upright person: 重新～ turn over a new leaf
【做声】 zuòshēng make a sound: 别～! Keep quiet!
【做生日】 zuò shēng·ri hold a birthday party
【做生意】 zuò shēng·yi do business
【做事】 zuòshì 1.(办事) handle affairs; do a deed; act: ～周到 do sth. up brown 2.(工作) work; have a job: 他在一家公司～。He works in a company.
【做寿】 zuòshòu hold a birthday party for the elder
【做文章】 zuò wénzhāng 1.(大发议论) make an issue of: 在枝节问题上大～ kick up a rumpus over some side issue 2.(写文章) write an essay
【做戏】 zuòxì 1.(演戏) act in a play 2.(装假) put on a show; playact
【做贼心虚】 zuòzéi-xīnxū have a guilty conscience
【做主】 zuòzhǔ 1.(作决定) decide; take the responsibility for a decision: 由你～。It's up to you to. 2.(支持) back up; support
【做作】 zuò·zuo affected; artificial: ～的方式 affected manners / 她演得太～。She overdoes her acting.

Data on China
中国资料

Provinces, Autonomous Regions, Municipalities and Special Administration Regions
中国各省、自治区、直辖市和特别行政区

Names	(名称)	Classification (区分)	Abbreviation (简称)	Capital (省会或首府)
安徽	Anhui	安徽省	皖 Wan	合肥 Hefei
北京	Beijing	北京市	京 Jing	
重庆	Chongqing	重庆市	渝 Yu	
福建	Fujian	福建省	闽 Min	福州 Fuzhou
甘肃	Gansu	甘肃省	甘、陇 Gan, Long	兰州 Lanzhou
广东	Guangdong	广东省	粤 Yue	广州 Guangzhou
广西	Guangxi	广西壮族自治区	桂 Gui	南宁 Nanning
贵州	Guizhou	贵州省	贵、黔 Gui, Qian	贵阳 Guiyang
海南	Hainan	海南省	琼 Qiong	海口 Haikou
河北	Hebei	河北省	冀 Ji	石家庄 Shijiazhuang
黑龙江	Heilongjiang	黑龙江省	黑 Hei	哈尔滨 Harbin
河南	Henan	河南省	豫 Yu	郑州 Zhengzhou
香港	Hong Kong	香港特别行政区	港 Gang	
湖北	Hubei	湖北省	鄂 E	武汉 Wuhan
湖南	Hunan	湖南省	湘 Xiang	长沙 Changsha
江西	Jiangxi	江西省	赣 Gan	南昌 Nanchang
江苏	Jiangsu	江苏省	苏 Shu	南京 Nanjing
吉林	Jilin	吉林省	吉 Ji	长春 Changchun
辽宁	Liaoning	辽宁省	辽 Liao	沈阳 Shenyang
澳门	Macao	澳门特别行政区	澳 Ao	
内蒙古	Nei Monggu	内蒙古自治区	内蒙古 Neimenggu	呼和浩特 Hohhot
宁夏	Ningxia	宁夏回族自治区	宁 Ni	银川 Yinchuan
青海	Qinghai	青海省	青 Qing	西宁 Xining
陕西	Shaanxi	陕西省	陕、秦 Shan, Qin	西安 Xi'an
山东	Shandong	山东省	鲁 Lu	济南 Jinan
上海	Shanghai	上海市	沪、申 Hu, Shen	
山西	Shanxi	山西省	晋 Jin	太原 Taiyuan
四川	Sichuan	四川省	川、蜀 Chuan, Shu	成都 Chengdu
台湾	Taiwan	台湾省	台 Tai	台北 Taibei
天津	Tianjin	天津市	津 Jin	
新疆	Xinjiang	新疆维吾尔族自治区	新 Xin	乌鲁木齐 Urumqi
西藏	Xizang	西藏自治区	藏 Zhang	拉萨 Lhasa
云南	Yunnan	云南省	云、滇 Yun, Dian	昆明 Kunming
浙江	Zhejiang	浙江省	浙 Zhe	杭州 Hangzhou

China's Nationalities
中国各民族

阿昌族	Achang	仡佬族	Gelao	满族	Man	水族	Sui
白族	Baizu	京族	Gin	毛南族	Maonan	塔吉克族	Tajik
布朗族	Blang	汉族	Han	苗族	Miao	塔塔尔族	Tatar
保安族	Bonan	哈尼族	Hani	门巴族	Monba	土族	Tu
布依族	Bouyei	赫哲族	Hezhen	蒙古族	Mongol	土家族	Tujia
朝鲜族	Chaoxian	回族	Hui	仫佬族	Mulam	维吾尔族	Uygur
傣族	Dai	景颇族	Jingpo	纳西族	Naxi	乌孜别克族	Uzbek
达斡尔族	Daur	基诺族	Jino	怒族	Nu	佤族	Va
德昂族	De'ang	哈萨克族	Kazak	鄂伦春族	Oroqen	锡伯族	Xibe
独龙族	Derung	柯尔克孜族	Kirgiz	普米族	Primi	瑶族	Yao
东乡族	Dongxiang	拉祜族	Lahu	羌族	Qiang	彝族	Yi
侗族	Dong	珞巴族	Lhoba	俄罗斯族	Russ	裕固族	Yugur
鄂温克族	Ewenki	傈僳族	Lisu	撒拉族	Salar	藏族	Zang
高山族	Gaoshan	黎族	Li	畲族	She	壮族	Zhuang

The Twenty-four Solar Terms
二十四节气表

Solar Terms **节气名(日期)**		**Equivalent Signs of the Zodiac** **相当于黄道十二宫的位置**
立春	the Beginning of Spring (Feb. 3, 4 or 5)	宝瓶宫 Aquarius
雨水	Rain Water (Feb. 18, 19 or 20)	双鱼宫 Pisces
惊蛰	the Waking of Insects (Mar. 5, 6 or 7)	双鱼宫 Pisces
春分	the Spring Equinox (Mar. 20, 21 or 22)	白羊宫 Aries
清明	Pure Brightness (Apr. 4, 5 or 6)	白羊宫 Aries
谷雨	Grain Rain (Apr. 19, 20 or 21)	金牛宫 Taurus
立夏	the Beginning of Summer (May 5, 6 or 7)	金牛宫 Taurus
小满	Grain Full (May 20, 21 or 22)	双子宫 Gemini
芒种	Grain in Ear (June 5, 6 or 7)	双子宫 Gemini
夏至	the Summer Solstice (June 21 or 22)	巨蟹宫 Cancer
小暑	Slight Heat (July 6, 7 or 8)	巨蟹宫 Cancer
大暑	Great Heat (July 22, 23 or 24)	狮子宫 Leo
立秋	the Beginning of Autumn (Aug. 7, 8 or 9)	狮子宫 Leo
处暑	the Limit of Heat (Aug. 22, 23 or 24)	室女宫 Virgo
白露	White Dew (Sep. 7, 8 or 9)	室女宫 Virgo
秋分	the Autumnal Equinox (Sep. 22, 23 or 24)	天秤宫 Libra
寒露	Cold Dew (Oct. 8 or 9)	天秤宫 Libra
霜降	Frost's Descent (Oct. 23 or 24)	天蝎宫 Scorpio
立冬	the Beginning of Winter (Nov. 7 or 8)	天蝎宫 Scorpio
小雪	Slight Snow (Nov. 22 or 23)	人马宫 Sagittarius
大雪	Great Snow (Dec. 6, 7 or 8)	人马宫 Sagittarius
冬至	the Winter Solstice (Dec. 21, 22 or 23)	摩羯宫 Capricorn
小寒	Slight Cold (Jan. 5, 6 or 7)	摩羯宫 Capricorn
大寒	Great Cold (Jan. 20 or 21)	宝瓶宫 Aquarius

Summary of Chinese Dynasties
中国朝代年表

五帝 （公元前约 26 世纪初至公元前 2070 年） The Five Rulers
夏 （公元前 2070 年至公元前 1600 年） The Xia Dynasty
商 （公元前 1600 年至公元前 1046 年） The Shang Dynasty
周 （公元前 1046 年至公元前 256 年） The Zhou Dynasty
　西周 （公元前 1046 年至公元前 771 年） The Western Zhou Dynasty
　东周 （公元前 770 年至公元前 256 年） The Eastern Zhou Dynasty
秦 （公元前 221 年至公元前 206 年） The Qin Dynasty
汉 （公元前 206 年至公元 220 年） The Han Dynasty
　西汉 （公元前 206 年至公元 23 年） The Western Han Dynasty
　东汉 （25 年至 220 年） The Eastern Han Dynasty
三国 （220 年至 280 年） The Three Kingdoms
　魏 （220 年至 265 年） The Wei Dynasty
　蜀汉 （221 年至 263 年） The Shu Han Dynasty
　吴 （222 年至 280 年） The Wu Dynasty
晋 （265 年至 420 年） The Jin Dynasty
　西晋 （265 年至 316 年） The Western Jin Dynasty
　东晋 （317 年至 420 年） The Eastern Jin Dynasty
十六国 （304 年至 439 年） The Sixteen Kingdoms
南北朝 （420 年至 589 年） Northern and Southern Dynasties
　南朝 Southern Dynasties
　　宋 （420 年至 479 年） The Song Dynasty
　　齐 （479 年至 502 年） The Qi Dynasty
　　梁 （502 年至 557 年） The Liang Dynasty
　　陈 （557 年至 589 年） The Chen Dynasty
　北朝 Northern Dynasties
　　北魏 （386 年至 534 年） The Northern Wei Dynasty
　　东魏 （534 年至 550 年） The Eastern Wei Dynasty
　　北齐 （550 年至 577 年） The Northern Qi Dynasty
　　西魏 （535 年至 556 年） The Western Wei Dynasty
　　北周 （557 年至 581 年） The Northern Zhou Dynasty
隋 （581 年至 618 年） The Sui Dynasty
唐 （618 年至 907 年） The Tang Dynasty
五代十国 （907 年至 979 年） Five Dynasties and Ten Kingdoms
　五代 （907 年至 960 年） Five Dynasties
　　后梁 （907 年至 923 年） The Posterior Liang Dynasty
　　后唐 （923 年至 936 年） The Posterior Tang Dynasty
　　后晋 （936 年至 946 年） The Posterior Jin Dynasty
　　后汉 （947 年至 950 年） The Posterior Han Dynasty
　　后周 （951 年至 960 年） The Posterior Zhou Dynasty
　十国 （902 年至 979 年） The Ten Kingdoms
宋 （960 年至 1279 年） The Song Dynasty
　北宋 （960 年至 1127 年） The Northern Song Dynasty
　南宋 （1127 年至 1279 年） The Southern Song Dynasty
辽 （907 年至 1125 年） The Liao Dynasty
西夏 （1038 年至 1227 年） The Western Xia Dynasty
金 （1115 年至 1234 年） The Jin Dynasty
元 （1279 年至 1368 年） The Yuan Dynasty
明 （1368 年至 1644 年） The Ming Dynasty
清 （1644 年至 1911 年） The Qing Dynasty

World's Countries (Regions), Peoples and Capitals 世界各国(地区)、居民和首都(首府)

AFRICA 非 洲

阿尔及利亚 Algeria
阿尔及利亚人 Algerian
阿尔及尔 Algers
安哥拉 Angola
安哥拉人 Angolan
卢安达 Luanda
贝宁 Benin
贝宁人 Beninese
波多诺伏 Port Novo
博茨瓦纳 Botswana
博茨瓦纳人 Tswana
哈博罗内 Gaborone
布基纳法索 Burkina Faso
布基纳法索人 Burkinese
瓦加杜古 Ouagadougou
布隆迪 Burundi
布隆迪人 Burundian
布琼布拉 Bujumbura
喀麦隆 Cameroon
喀麦隆人 Cameroonian
雅温得 Yaoundé
佛得角 Cape Verde
佛得角人 Cape Verdean
普拉亚 Praia
中非[1] Central Africa
中非人 Central African
班吉 Bangui
乍得 Chad
乍得人 Chadian
恩贾梅纳 Ndjamena
科摩罗 Comoros
科摩罗人 Comorian
莫罗尼 Moroni
刚果[2] Congo
刚果人 Congolese
布拉柴维尔 Brazzaville
刚果[3] Congo
刚果人 Congolese
金沙萨 Kinshasa
科特迪瓦[4] Cote d'Ivoire
科特迪瓦人 Ivorian, Ivory Coaster
亚穆苏克罗 Yamoussoukro
阿比让 Abidjan
吉布提 Djibouti
吉布提人 Djiboutian
吉布提 Djibouti
埃及 Egypt
埃及人 Egyptian
开罗 Cairo
赤道几内亚 Equatorial Guinea
赤道几内亚人 Equatorial Guinean
马拉博 Malabo
厄立特里亚 Eritrea
厄立特里亚人 Eritrean
阿斯马拉 Asmara
埃塞俄比亚 Ethiopia
埃塞俄比亚人 Ethiopian
亚的斯亚贝巴 Addis Ababa
加蓬 Gabon
加蓬人 Gabonese
利伯维尔 Libreville
冈比亚 Gambia
冈比亚人 Gambian
班珠尔 Banjul
加纳 Ghana
加纳人 Ghananian
阿克拉 Accra
几内亚 Guinea
几内亚人 Guinean
科纳克里 Conakry
几内亚比绍 Guinea-Bissau
几内亚比绍人 Guinean-Bissau
比绍 Bissau
肯尼亚 Kenya

肯尼亚人 Kenyan
内罗毕 Nairobi

莱索托 Lesotho
莱索托人 Mosotho, (pl.) Basotho
马塞卢 Maseru

利比里亚 Liberia
利比里亚人 Liberian
蒙罗维亚 Monrovia

利比亚 Libya
利比亚人 Libyan
的黎波里 Tripoli

马达加斯加 Madagascar
马达加斯加人 Madagascan
塔那那利佛 Tananarive

马拉维 Malawi
马拉维人 Malawian
利隆圭 Lilongwe

马里 Mali
马里人 Malian
巴马科 Bamako

毛里塔尼亚 Mauritania
毛里塔尼亚人 Mauritanian
努瓦克肖特 Nouakchott
乌吉亚 Ouguiya

毛里求斯 Mauritius
毛里求斯人 Mauritian
路易斯港 Port Louis

摩洛哥 Morocco
摩洛哥人 Moroccan
拉巴特 Rabat

莫桑比克 Mozambique
莫桑比克人 Mozambican
马普托 Maputo

纳米比亚 Namibia
纳米比亚人 Namibian
温得和克 Windhoek

尼日尔 Niger
尼日尔人 Nigerien
尼亚美 Niamey

尼日利亚 Nigeria
尼日利亚人 Nigerian
拉各斯 Lagos

留尼汪(法) Reunion
圣但尼 St. Denis

卢旺达 Rwanda
卢旺达人 Rwandese
基加利 Kigali

圣多美和普林西比
Sao Tomé and Principe
圣多美 Sao Tomé

塞内加尔 Senegal
塞内加尔人 Senegalese
达喀尔 Dakar

塞舌尔 Seychelles
塞舌尔人 Seychellois, Seychelloise
维多利亚 Victoria

塞拉利昂 Sierra Leone
塞拉利昂人 Sierra Leonean
弗里敦 Freetown

索马里 Somalia
索马里人 Somali
摩加迪沙 Mogadishu

南非[5] South Africa
南非人 South African
比勒陀利亚 Pretoria
开普敦 Cape Town
布隆方丹 Bloemfontein

苏丹 Sudan
苏丹人 Sudanese
喀土穆 Khartoum

斯威士兰 Swaziland
斯威士人 Swazi
姆巴巴纳 Mbabane

坦桑尼亚 Tanzania
坦桑尼亚人 Tanzanian
达累斯萨拉姆 Dar es Salaam

多哥 Togo
多哥人 Togolese
洛美 Lomé

突尼斯 Tunisia
突尼斯人 Tunisian
突尼斯 Tunis

乌干达 Uganda
乌干达人 Ugandan
坎帕拉 Kampala

赞比亚 Zambia
赞比亚人 Zambian
卢萨卡 Lusaka

津巴布韦 Zimbabwe
津巴布韦人 Zimbabwean
哈拉雷 Harare

ASIA 亚 洲

阿富汗 Afghanistan
阿富汗人 Afghan, Afgani
喀布尔 Kabul
亚美尼亚 Armenia
亚美尼亚人 Armenian
埃里温 Erivan
阿塞拜疆 Azerbaijan
阿塞拜疆人 Azerbaijani
巴库 Baku
巴林 Bahrain, Bahrein
巴林人 Bahraini, Bahreini
麦纳麦 Manama
孟加拉国 Bangladesh
孟加拉国人 Bangladeshi
达卡 Dhaka (Dacca)
不丹 Bhutan
不丹人 Bhutanese
廷布 Thimbu
文莱 Brunei
文莱人 Brunei, Bruneian
斯里巴加湾市 Bandar Seri Begawan
柬埔寨 Cambodia
柬埔寨人 Cambodian
金边 Phnom Penh
中国 China
中国人 Chinese
北京 Beijing
塞浦路斯 Cyprus
塞浦路斯人 Cypriot
尼科西亚 Nicosia
东帝汶 East Timor
帝汶人 Timorese
帝力 Dili
格鲁吉亚 Georgia
格鲁吉亚人 Georgian
第比利斯 Tbilisi
印度 India
印度人 Indian
新德里 New Dehli
印度尼西亚 Indonesia
印度尼西亚人 Indonesian
雅加达 Jakarta
伊朗 Iran
伊朗人 Iranian
德黑兰 Tehran
伊拉克 Iraq
伊拉克人 Iraqi
巴格达 Baghdad
以色列 Israel
以色列人 Israeli
特拉维夫 Tel Aviv
日本 Japan
日本人 Japanese
东京 Tokyo
约旦 Jordan
约旦人 Jordanian
安曼 Amman
哈萨克斯坦[6] Kazak(h)stan
哈萨克人 Kazak, Kazakh
阿拉木图 Alma-Ata
阿斯塔纳 Astana
吉尔吉斯斯坦 Kirgizstan
吉尔吉斯人 Kirgiz
比什凯克 Pishkek
朝鲜[7] Korea
朝鲜人 Korean
平壤 Pyongyang
韩国[8] Korea
韩国人 Korean
汉城 Seoul
科威特 Kuwait
科威特人 Kuwaiti
科威特 Kuwait
老挝 Laos
老挝人 Laotian
万象 Vientiane
黎巴嫩 Lebanon
黎巴嫩人 Lebanese
贝鲁特 Beirut
马来西亚 Malaysia
马来西亚人 Malaysian
吉隆坡 Kuala Lumpur
马尔代夫 Maldives
马尔代夫人 Maldivian
马累 Male
蒙古 Mongolia
蒙古人 Mongolian
乌兰巴托 Ulan Bator
缅甸 Myanmar (Burma)
缅甸人 Myanmese (Burmese)

仰光 Rangoon

尼泊尔 Nepal

尼泊尔人 Nepalese

加德满都 Kathmandu

阿曼 Oman

阿曼人 Omani

马斯喀特 Muscat

巴基斯坦 Pakistan

巴基斯坦人 Pakistani

伊斯兰堡 Islamabad

巴勒斯坦 Palestine

巴勒斯坦人 Palestinian

耶鲁撒冷 Jerusalem

菲律宾 Philippines

菲律宾人 Filipino

马尼拉 Manila

卡塔尔 Qatar, Katar

卡塔尔人 Qatari, Katari

多哈 Doha

沙特阿拉伯 Saudi Arabia

沙特阿拉伯人 Saudi Arabian

利雅得 Riyadh

锡金 Sikkim

锡金人 Sikkimese

甘托克 Gangtok

新加坡 Singapore

新加坡人 Singaporean

新加坡 Singapore

斯里兰卡 Sri Lanka

斯里兰卡人 Sri Lankan

科伦坡 Colombo

叙利亚 Syria

叙利亚人 Syrian

大马士革 Damascus

塔吉克斯坦 Tadzhikistan

塔吉克人 Tadzhik

杜尚别 Dushanbe

泰国 Thailand

泰国人 Thai

曼谷 Bangkok

土耳其 Turkey

土耳其人 Turk

安卡拉 Ankara

土库曼斯坦 Turkmenistan

土库曼人 Turkman

阿什克哈巴德 Ashkhabad

阿拉伯联合酋长国

United Arab Emirates

阿拉伯人 Arab

阿布扎比 Abu Dhabi

乌兹别克斯坦 Uzbekistan

乌兹别克人 Uzbek

塔什干 Tashkent

越南 Vietnam

越南人 Vietnamese

河内 Hanoi

也门 Yemen

也门人 Yemeni

萨那 San'a

EUROPE 欧洲

阿尔巴尼亚 Albania

阿尔巴尼亚人 **Albanian**

地拉那 Tirana

安道尔 Andorra

安道尔人 Andorran

安道尔 Andorra la Vella

奥地利 Austria

奥地利人 Austrian

维也纳 Vienna

比利时 Belgium

比利时人 Belgian

布鲁塞尔 Brussels

波黑[9] Bosnia and Hercegovina

波斯尼亚人 Bosnian

塞尔维亚人 Serb

萨拉热窝 Sarajevo

保加利亚 Bulgaria

保加利亚人 Bulgarian

索非亚 Sofia

白俄罗斯 Byelorussia

白俄罗斯人 Byelorussain

明斯克 Minsk

捷克 Czech

捷克人 Czech

布拉格 Prague

克罗地亚 Croatia

克罗地亚人 Croatian

萨格勒布 Zagreb

丹麦 Denmark
丹麦人 Dane
哥本哈根 Copenhagen
爱沙尼亚 Estonia
爱沙尼亚人 **Estonian**
塔林 Tallinn
法罗群岛(丹) Faeroe Is.
法罗群岛人 Faeroese, Faroese
曹斯哈恩 Thorshavn
芬兰 Finland
芬兰人 Finn
赫尔辛基 Helsinki
法国 France
法国人 Frenchman, Frenchwoman
巴黎 Paris
德国[10] Germany
德国人 German
柏林 Berlin
波恩 Bonn
希腊 Greece
希腊人 Greek
雅典 Athens
匈牙利 Hungary
匈牙利人 Hungarian
布达佩斯 Budapest
冰岛 Iceland
冰岛人 Icelandic, Icelander
雷克雅未克 Reykjavik
爱尔兰 Ireland
爱尔兰人 Irishman, Irishwoman
都柏林 Dublin
意大利 Italy
意大利人 Italian
罗马 Rome
拉脱维亚 Latvia
拉脱维亚人 Latvian
里加 Riga
列支敦士登 Liechtenstein
列支敦士登人 Liechtensteiner
瓦杜兹 Vaduz
立陶宛 Lithuania
立陶宛人 Lithuanian
维尔纽斯 Vilnius
卢森堡 Luxemburg
卢森堡人 Luxemburger
卢森堡 Luxemburg
马其顿 Macedonia
马其顿人 Macedonian
斯科普里 Skopje
马耳他 Malta
马耳他人 Maltese
瓦莱塔 Valletta
摩尔多瓦 Moldova
摩尔多瓦人 Moldavian
基什尼奥夫 Kishinev
摩纳哥 Monaco
摩纳哥人 Monacan
摩纳哥 Monaco-Ville
荷兰 Netherlands
荷兰人 Dutchman, Dutchwoman
阿姆斯特丹 Amsterdam
挪威 Norway
挪威人 Norwegian
奥斯陆 Oslo
波兰 Poland
波兰人 Pole
华沙 Warsaw
葡萄牙 Portugal
葡萄牙人 Portuguese
里斯本 Lisbon
罗马尼亚 Romania
罗马尼亚人 Romanian
布加勒斯特 Bucharest
俄罗斯 Russia
俄罗斯人 Russian
莫斯科 Moscow
圣马力诺 San Marino
圣马力诺人 San Marinese
圣马力诺 San Marino
塞尔维亚和黑山 Serbia and Montenegro
塞尔维亚人 Serb, Serbian
黑山人 Montenegrin
贝尔格莱德 Belgrade
斯洛伐克 Slovakia
斯洛伐克人 Slovak
布拉迪斯拉发 Bratislava
斯洛文尼亚 Slovenia
斯洛文尼亚人 Slovenian
卢布尔雅那 Ljubljana
西班牙 Spain
西班牙人 Spainard
马德里 Madrid
瑞典 Sweden
瑞典人 Swede

斯德哥尔摩 Stockholm

瑞士 Switzerland

瑞士人 Swiss

伯尔尼 Berne

乌克兰 Ukraine

乌克兰人 Ukrainian

基辅 Kiev

英国(联合王国) United Kingdom

英国人 Briton

伦敦 London

梵蒂冈 Vatican (State)

梵蒂冈城 Vatican City

NORTH AMERICA 北 美 洲

安圭拉(英) Anguilla

安圭拉人 Anguillan

瓦利 Valley

安提瓜和巴布达 Antigua and Barbuda

安提瓜人 Antiguan

巴布达人 Barbudan

圣约翰 St. John's

阿鲁巴(荷) Aruba

奥拉涅斯塔德 Oranjestad

巴哈马 Bahamas

巴哈马人 Bahamian

拿骚 Nassau

巴巴多斯 Barbados

巴巴多斯人 Barbadian

布里奇顿 Bridgetown

伯利兹 Belize

伯利兹人 Belizean

伯利兹 Belize

百慕大群岛(英) Bermudas Is.

百慕大人 Bermudian, Bermudan

哈密尔顿 Hamilton

加拿大 Canada

加拿大人 Canadian

渥太华 Ottawa

开曼群岛(英) Cayman Is.

开曼群岛人 Cayman Islander

乔治敦 Georgetown

哥斯达黎加 Costa Rica

哥斯达黎加人 Costa Rican

圣何塞 San José

古巴 Cuba

古巴人 Cuban

哈瓦那 Havana

多米尼克 Dominica

多米尼克人 Dominican

罗索 Rosseau

多米尼加共和国 Dominican Republic

多米尼加人 Dominican

圣多明各 Santo Domingo

萨尔瓦多 El Salvador

萨尔瓦多人 Salvadorean

圣萨尔瓦多 San Salvador

格林纳达 Grenada

格林纳达人 Grenadian

圣乔治 St. George's

格陵兰(丹) Greenland

格陵兰人 Greenlander

戈特霍布(努克) Goothab (Nuk)

瓜德罗普(法) Guadeloupe

瓜德罗普人 Guadeloupian

巴斯特尔 Basse Terre

海地 Haiti

海地人 Haitian

太子港 Port au Prince

洪都拉斯 Honduras

洪都拉斯人 Honduran

特古西加尔巴 Tegucigalpa

牙买加 Jamaica

牙买加人 Jamaican

金斯敦 Kingston

马提尼克(法) Martinique

法兰西堡 Fort de France

墨西哥 Mexico

墨西哥人 Mexican

墨西哥城 Mexico City

蒙特塞拉特(英) Montserrat

普利茅斯 Plymouth

荷属安的列斯 Netherlands Antilles

安的列斯人 Antillean

威廉斯塔德 Willemstad

尼加拉瓜 Nicaragua

尼加拉瓜人 Nicaraguan

马那瓜 Managua

巴拿马 Panama

巴拿马人 Panamanian

巴拿马城 Panama City

波多黎各(美) Puerto Rico
波多黎各人 Puerto Rican
圣胡安 San Juan
圣基茨和尼维斯 St. Kitts and Nevis
巴斯特尔 Basse Terre
圣卢西亚 St. Lucia
圣卢西亚人 St. Lucian
卡斯特里 Castries
圣皮埃尔和密克隆群岛(法)
St. Pierre and Miquelon Is.
圣皮埃尔 St Pierre
圣文森特和格林纳丁斯
St. Vicent and Grenadins
圣文森特人 Viventian
格林纳丁斯人 Grenadian
金斯敦 Kingstown
特利尼达和多巴哥 Trinidad and Tobago
特利尼达人 Trinidadian
多巴哥人 Tobagonian
西班牙港 Port of Spain
特克斯和凯科斯群岛(英) Turks and Caicos Is.
科伯恩城 Cockburn Town
美国 the United States of America
美国人 American
华盛顿 Washington
美属维尔京群岛
Virgin Islands of the United States
维尔京群岛人 Virgin Islander
夏洛特·阿马利亚 Charlotte Amalie

OCEANIA 大 洋 洲

美属萨摩亚 American Samoa
美属萨摩亚人 American Samoan
帕果帕果 Pago Pago
澳大利亚 Australia
澳大利亚人 Austrarian
堪培拉 Canberra
贝劳 Belau
科罗尔 Koror
英属维尔京群岛 British Virgin Is.
维尔京群岛人 Virgin Islander
罗德城 Road Town
库克群岛(新) Cook Is.
阿瓦鲁阿 Avarua
斐济 Fiji
斐济人 Fijian
苏瓦 Suva
法属波利尼西亚 French Polynesia
波利尼西亚人 Polunesian
帕皮提 Papeete
关岛(美) Guam
关岛人 Guamanian
阿加尼亚 Agana
基里巴斯 Kiribati
塔拉瓦 Tarawa
马绍尔群岛 Marshall Is.
马绍尔群岛人 Marshallese
马朱罗 Majuro
密克罗尼西亚[11] Micronesia
密克罗尼西亚人 Micronesian
科罗尼亚 Kolonia
瑙鲁[12] Nauru
瑙鲁人 Nauruan
亚伦区 Yaren District
新喀里多尼亚(法) New Caladonia
新喀里多尼亚人 New Caledonian
努美阿 Noumea
新西兰 New Zealand
新西兰人 New Zealander
惠灵顿 Wellington
纽埃(新) Niue
阿洛菲 Alofi
诺福克岛 Norfolk Island
金斯敦 Kingston
北马里亚纳群岛(美) Northern Mariana Is.
塞班 Saipan
巴布亚新几内亚 Papua New Guinea
巴布亚新几内亚人 Papuan
莫尔斯比港 Port Moresby
皮特开恩群岛(英) Pitcairn Is.
皮特开恩岛人 Pitcairn Islander
亚当斯敦 Adamstown
所罗门群岛 Solomon Islands
所罗门群岛人 Solomon Islander
霍尼亚拉 Honiara
托克劳(新) Tokelau
法考福 Fakaofo
汤加 Tonga
汤加人 Tongan

努库阿洛法 Nuku'alofa

图瓦鲁 Tuvalu

图瓦鲁人 Tuvaluan

富纳富提 Funafuti

瓦努阿图 Vanuatu

维拉港 Port Vila

瓦利斯群岛和富图纳群岛(法)
Wallis and Futuna

马塔乌图 Mata Utu

西萨摩亚 Western Samoa

萨摩亚人 Western Samoan

阿皮亚 Apia

SOUTH AMERICA 南 美 洲

阿根廷 Argentina

阿根廷人 Argentinian, Argentine

布宜诺斯艾利斯 Buenos Aires

玻利维亚[13] Bolivia

玻利维亚人 Bolivian

苏克雷 Sucre

拉巴斯 La Paz

巴西 Brazil

巴西人 Brazilian

巴西利亚 Brasilia

智利 Chile

智利人 Chilean

圣地亚哥 Santiago

哥伦比亚 Colombia

哥伦比亚人 Colombian

波哥大 Bogotá

厄瓜多尔 Ecuador

厄瓜多尔人 Ecuadorian

基多 Quito

法属圭亚那 French Guiana

法属圭亚那人 French Guianese

卡宴 Cayenne

危地马拉 Guatemala

危地马拉人 Guatemalan

危地马拉城 Guatemala City

圭亚那 Guyana

圭亚那人 Guyanese

乔治敦 Georgetown

巴拉圭 Paraguay

巴拉圭人 Paraguayan

阿松森 Asunció

秘鲁 Peru

秘鲁人 Peruvian

利马 Lima

苏里南 Surinam

苏里南人 Surinamese

帕拉马里博 Paramaribo

乌拉圭 Uruguay

乌拉圭人 Uruguayan

蒙得维的亚 Montevideo

委内瑞拉 Venezuela

委内瑞拉人 Venezuelan

加拉加斯 Caracas

Notes 注:

1) 中非的全称为中非共和国
The full name for Central Africa is the Central African Republic.

2) 刚果(布拉柴维尔)的全称为刚果共和国
The full name for Congo (Brazzaville) is the Republic of Congo.

3) 刚果(金沙萨)的全称为刚果民主共和国
The full name for Congo (Zaire) is the Democratic Republic of Congo.

4) 科特迪瓦首都是亚穆苏克罗,阿比让是经济首都
The capital for Cote d'Ivoire is Yamoussoukro and Abidjan is its economic capital.

5) 比勒陀利亚是南非行政首都,开普敦是立法首都,布隆方丹是司法首都
Pretoria is South Africa's administrative capital, Cape Town is where its legislative is located while Bloemfontein is the seat of the government.

6) 哈萨克斯坦的首都阿拉木图,阿斯塔纳是新都
Kazakhstan's old capital is Alma-Ata and Astana is its new capital.

7) 朝鲜的全称为朝鲜民主主义人民共和国
The full name is the Democratic People's Republic of Korea.

8) 韩国的全称为大韩民国
The full name is the Republic of Korea.

9) 波黑的全称为波斯尼亚-黑塞哥维那

The full name is Bosnia-Herzegovina.

10) 德意志联邦共和国首都是柏林,政府在波恩

The capital of the Federal Republic of Germany is Berlin although its government administration is located at Bonn.

11) 密克罗尼西亚的全称为密克罗尼西亚联邦

The full name of Micronesia is the Federal States of Micronesia.

12) 瑙鲁不设首都,其行政管理中心在亚伦区

Nauru has no capital but its seat of administration is located at the Yaren District.

13) 玻利维亚法定首都是苏克雷,议会和政府在拉巴斯

Bolivia's legal capital is Sucre but its government and legislature is located at La Paz.

The Chemical Elements
化 学 元 素

Name 元素名称		Sign 符号	Ordinal Number 序数	Atomic Weight 原子量
锕 (ā)	Actinium	Ac	89	227
铝 (lǚ)	Aluminium	Al	13	27
锑 (tī)	Antimony	Sb	51	121.8
氩 (yà)	Argon	Ar	18	39.9
砷 (shēn)	Arsenic	As	33	74.9
砹 (ài)	Astatine	At	85	210
钡 (bèi)	Barium	Ba	56	137.4
锫 (péi)) *	Berkelium	Bk	97	247
铍 (pí)	Beryllium	Be	4	9
铋 (bì)	Bismuth	Bi	83	209
硼 (péng)	Boron	B	5	10.8
溴 (xiù)	Bromine	Br	35	79.9
铯 (sè)	Caesium	Cs	55	132.9
镉 (gé)	Cadmium	Cd	48	112.4
钙 (gài)	Calcium	Ca	20	40.1
锎 (kāi) *	Californium	Cf	98	251
碳 (tàn)	Carbon	C	6	12
铈 (shì)	Cerium	Ce	58	140.1
氯 (lǜ)	Chlorine	Cl	17	35.5
钴 (gǔ)	Cobalt	Co	27	58.9
铜 (tóng)	Copper	Cu	29	63.5
铬 (gè)	Chromium	Cr	24	52
锔 (jú) *	Curium	Cm	96	247
镝 (dī)	Dysprosium	Dy	66	162.5
锿 (āi) *	Einsteinium	Es	99	254
铒 (ěr)	Erbium	Er	68	167.2
铕 (yǒu)	Europium	Eu	63	152
镄 (fèi) *	Fermium	Fm	100	257
氟 (fú)	Fluorine	F	9	39.1
钫 (fāng)	Francium	Fr	87	221
钆 (gá)	Gadolinium	Gd	64	156.9
镓 (jiā)	Gallium	Ga	31	69.7
锗 (zhě)	Germanium	Ge	32	72.6
金 (jīn)	Gold	Au	79	197.2
铪 (hā)	Hafnium	Hf	72	178.6
氦 (hài)	Helium	He	2	4
氢 (qīng)	Hydrogen	H	1	1
钬 (huǒ)	Holmium	Ho	67	164.9
铟 (yīn)	Indium	In	49	114.8
碘 (diǎn)	Iodine	I	53	126.9
铱 (yī)	Iridium	Ir	77	193.1
铁 (tiě)	Iron	Fe	26	55.8
氪 (kè)	Krypton	Kr	36	83.8
镧 (lán)	Lanthanum	La	57	138.9
铹 (láo) *	Lawrencium	Lr	103	260
铅 (qiān)	Lead	Pb	82	207.2
锂 (lǐ)	Lithium	Li	2	6.9
镥 (lǔ)	Lutetium	Lu	71	175
镁 (měi)	Magnesium	Mg	12	24.3

Name 元素名称		Sign 符号	Ordinal Number 序数	Atomic Weight 原子量
锰 (měng)	Manganese	Mn	25	54.9
钔 (mén) *	Mendelevium	Md	101	258
汞 (gǒng)	Mercury	Hg	80	200.6
钼 (mù)	Molybdenum	Mo	42	96
钕 (nǚ)	Neodymium	Nd	60	144.3
镎 (ná)	Neptunium	Np	93	237
氖 (nǎi)	Neon	Ne	10	20.2
镍 (niè)	Nickel	Ni	28	58.7
氮 (dàn)	Nitrogen	N	7	14
铌 (ní)	Niobium	Nb	41	92.9
锘 (nuò) *	Nobelium	No	102	259
锇 (é)	Osmium	Os	76	190.2
氧 (yǎng)	Oxygen	O	8	16
钯 (bǎ)	Palladium	Pd	46	106.7
磷 (lín)	Phosphorus	P	15	31
铂 (bó)	Platinum	Pt	78	195.2
钚 (bù)	Plutonium	Pu	94	244
钋 (pō)	Polonium	Po	84	210
钾 (jiǎ)	Potassium	K	19	39.1
镨 (pǔ)	Praseodymium	Pr	59	140.9
钷 (pǒ)	Promethium	Pm	61	145
镤 (pú)	Protactinium	Pa	91	238.1
镭 (léi)	Radium	Ra	88	226
氡 (dōng)	Radon	Rn	86	222
铼 (lái)	Rhenium	Re	75	186.3
铑 (lǎo)	Rhodium	Rh	45	102.9
铷 (rú)	Rubidium	Rb	37	85.5
钌 (liǎo)	Ruthenium	Ru	44	101.7
钐 (shān)	Samarium	Sm	62	150.4
钪 (kàng)	Scandium	Sc	21	45
硒 (xī)	Selenium	Se	34	79
硅 (guī)	Silicon	Si	14	28.1
银 (yín)	Silver	Ag	47	107.9
钠 (nà)	Sodium	Na	11	23
锶 (sī)	Strontium	Sr	38	87.6
硫 (liú)	Sulphur	S	16	32.1
钽 (tǎn)	Tantalum	Ta	73	180.9
锝 (dé)	Technetium	Tc	43	96
碲 (dì)	Tellurium	Te	52	127.6
铽 (tè)	Terbium	Tb	65	159.2
铊 (tā)	Thallium	Tl	81	204.4
钍 (tǔ)	Thorium	Th	90	232.1
铥 (diū)	Thulium	Tm	69	169.4
锡 (xī)	Tin	Sn	50	118.7
钛 (tài)	Titanium	Ti	22	47.9
钨 (wū)	Tungsten	W	74	183.9
铀 (yóu)	Uranium	U	92	238.1
钒 (fán)	Vanadium	V	23	51
氙 (xiān)	Xenon	Xe	54	131.3
镱 (yì)	Ytterbium	Yb	70	173
钇 (yǐ)	Yttrium	Y	39	88.9
锌 (xīn)	Zinc	Zn	30	65.4
锆 (gào)	Zirconium	Zr	40	91.2

* Man-made element 人造元素

Punctuation Marks and Related Symbols
标点和其他符号

.	句号 period
,	逗号 comma
:	冒号 colon
;	分号 semicolon
!	惊叹号 exclamation
?	问号 question mark
-	连字符 hyphen
’	省略号;所有格符号 apostrophe
—	破折号 dash
‘ ’	单引号 single quotation marks
“ ”	双引号 double quotation marks
( )	圆括号 parenthesis
[ ]	方括号 square brackets
《 》	法文引号;书名号 French quotes
. . .	省略号 ellipsis
. .	双点号 tandem colon
〃	同上 ditto
‖	双线号 parallel
/	斜线号 virgule
&	和 and, ampersand
～	代字号 swung dash
§	分节号 section; division
→	箭号;参见号 arrow
+	加号;正号 plus
−	减号;负号 minus
±	正负号 plus or minus
×	乘号 is multiplied by
÷	除号 is divided by
=	等于号 is equal to
≠	不等于号 is not equal to
≡	全等于号 is equivalent to
≌	等于或约等于号 is equal to or approximately equal to
≈	约等于号 is approximately equal to

<	小于号 is less than
>	大于号 is more than
≮	不小于号 is not less than
≯	不大于号 is not more than
≤	小于或等于号 is less than or equal to
≥	大于或等于号 is more than or equal to
%	百分之… per cent
‰	千分之… per mill
∞	无限大号 infinity
∝	与…成比例 varies as
√	平方根 (square) root
X^2	X 的平方 X squared
X^3	X 的立方 X cubed
∵	因为 since; because
∴	所以 hence
∷	等于,成比例 equals, as (proportion)
∠	角 angle
⌒	半圆 semicircle
⊙	圆 circle
○	圆周 circumference
π	圆周率 pi
△	三角形 triangle
⊥	垂直于 perpendicular to
∪	并,合集 intersection of
∩	交,通集 union of
∫	…的积分 the integral of
Σ	总和 (sigma) summation of
°	度 degree
′	分 minute
″	秒 second
#	…号 number
℃	摄氏度 Celsius system
@	单价 at

Numbers
数词

Numbers	(基数词)	Orders (序数词)	Numbers	(基数词)	Orders (序数词)
0	nought；zero		23	twenty-three	twenty-third
1	one	first	30	thirty	thirtieth
2	two	second	31	thirty-one	thirty-first
3	three	third	40	forty	fortieth
4	four	fourth	50	fifty	fiftieth
5	five	fifth	60	sixty	sixtieth
6	six	sixth	70	seventy	seventieth
7	seven	seventh	80	eighty	eightieth
8	eight	eighth	90	ninety	ninetieth
9	nine	ninth	100	a hundred	hundredth
10	ten	tenth	101	a hundred and one	hundred and first
11	eleven	eleventh	200	two hundred	two hundredth
12	twelve	twelfth	300	three hundred	three hundredth
13	thirteen	thirteenth	400	four hundred	four hundredth
14	fourteen	fourteenth	500	five hundred	five hundredth
15	fifteen	fifteenth	600	six hundred	six hundredth
16	sixteen	sixteenth	700	seven hundred	seven hundredth
17	seventeen	seventeenth	800	eight hundred	eight hundredth
18	eighteen	eighteenth	900	nine hundred	nine hundredth
19	nineteen	nineteenth	1000	a thousand	thousandth
20	twenty	twentieth	10000	ten thousand	ten thousandth
21	twenty-one	twenty-first	100000	a hundred thousand	hundred thousandth
22	twenty-two	twenty-second	1000000	a million	millionth

Roman Figures 罗马数字	Roman Figures 罗马数字	Roman Figures 罗马数字	Roman Figures 罗马数字
1 I	17 XVII	55 LV	700 DCC
2 II	18 XVIII	60 LX	800 DCCC
3 III	19 XIX	65 LXV	900 CM
4 IV	20 XX	70 LXX	1000 M
5 V	21 XXI	80 LXXX	1100 MC
6 VI	22 XXII	90 XC	1400 MCD
7 VII	25 XXV	93 XCIII	1500 MD
8 VIII	29 XXIX	95 XCV	1600 MDC
9 IX	30 XXX	98 XCVIII	1840 MDCCCXL
10 X	31 XXXI	99 IC	1899 MDCCCXCIX
11 XI	34 XXXIV	100 C	1900 MCM
12 XII	35 XXXV	200 CC	1976 MCMLXXVI
13 XIII	39 XXXIX	300 CCC	1980 MCMLXXX
14 XIV	40 XL	400 CD	1997 MCMXCVII
15 XV	50 L	500 D	1999 MCMXCIX
16 XVI	51 LI	600 DC	2000 MM

Fractions 分数

1/2 one-half; a half
1/3 one-third
3/4 three-fourths
1/5 one-fifth
2/5 two-fifths

Percentage 百分比

100% one hundred percent
0.5% point five percent

Decimals 小数

0.5 zero point five
0.34 zero point three four
0.44 zero point four four
7.005 seven point nought nought five

Fractions 分数

7/8 seven-eighths
1/10 one-tenth
1/100 one percent (%)
1/1000 one-thousandth (‰)
1/10000 one ten-thousandth

Percentage 百分比

24% twenty-four percent
0.37% point three seven percent

Decimals 小数

0.33 zero point three three
0.25 zero point two five
14.03 fourteen point nought three
45.21 forty-five point two one

Appendix: The Metric System and Anglo-American Weights and Measures
公制和英美制度量衡对照

METRIC SYSTEM (公制)

Length (长度)

毫米 millimeter (mm) = 0.001 米
厘米 centimeter (cm) = 0.01 米 = 0.3937 英寸
米 meter (m)
公里 kilometer (km) = 1000 米 = 0.6214 英里
1 米 meter (m) = 3.2808 英尺 = 1.0936 码

Land Area (地积)

公亩 are (a) = 100 平方米 = 0.0247 英亩
公顷 hectare (ha) = 100 公亩 = 2.4711 英亩

Volume (容积)

毫升 milliliter (ml) = 0.001 升
升 liter (l) = 0.2200 加仑(英) = 0.2600 加仑(美)

Weights (重量)

毫克 milligram (mg) = 0.001 克
克 gram (g)
千克(公斤) kilogram (kg) = 1000 克
吨 ton (t) = 1000 千克
1 克 = 0.0352 盎司(常衡)
1 千克 = 2.2046 磅(常衡)
1 吨 = 0.9842 长吨(英吨) = 1.1023 短吨(美吨)

ANGLO-AMERICAN SYSTEM (英美制)

Length (长度)

英寸 inch (pl. inches) = 2.5400 厘米
英尺 foot (pl. feet) = 12 英寸 = 0.3048 米
码 yard = 3 英尺 = 0.9144 米
英里 mile = 1760 码 = 1.6093 公里

Sea Distance (水程长度)

链 cable length, 1 cable's length = 185.2 米
海里 sea mile = 10 链 = 1.852 公里

Land Area (地积)

英亩 acre = 40.4686 公亩

Weights (重量)

盎司 ounce = 28.3496 克
磅 pound = 16 盎司 = 0.4539 千克
长吨(英吨) long ton = 2240 磅 = 1016.0470 千克
短吨(美吨) short ton = 2000 磅 = 907.1849 千克

Volume (liquids) (液量)

加仑 gallon = 4.546 升(英) = 3.785 升(美)